PRESENTED

TO

_____

BY

_____

ON

_____

PRESENTED

TO

_____

BY

_____

ON

_____

NIV
WOMEN'S
DEVOTIONAL BIBLE

NIV

WOMEN'S
DEVOTIONAL BIBLE

NEW INTERNATIONAL VERSION

ZONDERVAN™

GRAND RAPIDS, MICHIGAN 49530

The Holy Bible, New International Version ®
Copyright © 1973, 1978, 1984 by International Bible Society

ZONDERVAN™

Women's Devotional Bible, New International Version ®

Copyright © 1990, 1994 by The Zondervan Corporation

All rights reserved

Published by Zondervan
Grand Rapids, Michigan 49530, U.S.A.

www.zondervan.com

Library of Congress Catalog Card Number 90-081694

Printed in the United States of America

06 07 08 09 10 • 44 43 42 41 40 39 38 37

You will be pleased to know that a portion of the purchase price of your new NIV Bible has been provided to International Bible Society to help spread the gospel of Jesus Christ around the world!

CONTENTS

INTRODUCTION—NIV WOMEN'S DEVOTIONAL BIBLE

Welcome to the NIV Women's Devotional Bible! Are you ready to embark on an exciting journey through God's Word? You say you're too busy to take on any new adventures this year? The NIV Women's Devotional Bible is designed just for *you*—one of today's women who wants to step out into God's Word to discover encouragement and comfort, and yet who feels tugged in a hundred different directions.

Written for, by and about today's woman, the NIV Women's Devotional Bible will reach you right where you are. But it won't leave you there! With God's Word and the sensitive and insightful reflections of many godly women, the NIV Women's Devotional Bible will transport you step by step on a journey to Christian maturity.

Several features make the NIV Women's Devotional Bible an exceptional devotional guide:

The Bible
The NIV Women's Devotional Bible features the complete text of the Holy Bible, New International Version. This version's readability and accuracy make it the most popular modern translation available today.

The Devotions
All of the daily and weekend devotions are written by women—women who have experienced both the joys and struggles of Christian living and who are willing to share those triumphs and trials with you. Each devotion is located within the text, in close proximity to the Scripture passage on which it is based.

The Introductions
The introduction to each Bible book succinctly highlights that book's practical themes. Each introduction gives you interesting facts and helpful background information to aid your understanding as you read that particular book and the accompanying devotional meditation.

Ease of Use
If you are like most women today, your life is full—you may even say sometimes that your life is too full. There are so many things to do, so many demands on your time. So we've designed the NIV Women's Devotional Bible to give you a quick and easy Bible reading/devotional meditation plan to help you walk the road to maturity and growth.

The devotions in the NIV Women's Devotional Bible take a distinctive pattern following the days of the week: Monday, Tuesday, Wednesday, Thursday, Friday. In recognition of your need for something different on the weekend, we've developed "Weekending"—combining one provocative devotional thought with short Scripture readings for both Saturday and Sunday.

No matter what day of the week you begin your reading, you simply turn to a devotion for that day. Then for the next day, look to the bottom of the devotion for the page number on which you'll find the next day's devotion. For example, if you start on a Monday, you could turn to the first devotion in the book of Genesis, page 3. Glance at the bottom of Monday's devotion and you will see the page number where Tuesday's devotion will be found—and so on as you keep walking on through Friday.

Friday's devotion will direct you to a "Weekending," which will provide you with a reflective insight for your weekend and a Scripture reading for both Saturday and Sunday. The bottom of the "Weekending" will send you to the next Monday devotion. And you are well on your way—through a year of spending precious time in God's Word and growing closer to him.

Reading Plans

On page 1439 you'll find a plan to help you read through the entire Bible in one year. God's Word has a wonderful continuity and many treasures that you'll discover as you read it through chapter by chapter and book by book.

Author Biographies

You will most likely recognize the names of many of the women who contributed to the NIV Women's Devotional Bible. The author index, found on page 1443, gives you some interesting information about each woman, as well as a list of the pages where her devotions appear.

Subject Index

You've had a tough day as a mom; you've just started a new job; you struggle with a serious illness; you're consumed with guilt. Whatever the circumstances that confront you, the subject index will help direct you to just the right words to encourage and motivate you. Look up a wide variety of subjects in this index on page 1449, and turn to the listed page number for a devotion that fits your need.

So come on along. You're invited to open the pages of the NIV Women's Devotional Bible and start along the pathway to a growing maturity. The treasures of God's Word await you at every step along the way, and the meditations of the women who have shared a bit of themselves will give the encouragement you need to keep moving ahead. And as you go, we pray you'll become all that God intends you to be as a woman of God in today's world.

PREFACE

THE NEW INTERNATIONAL VERSION is a completely new translation of the Holy Bible made by over a hundred scholars working directly from the best available Hebrew, Aramaic and Greek texts. It had its beginning in 1965 when, after several years of exploratory study by committees from the Christian Reformed Church and the National Association of Evangelicals, a group of scholars met at Palos Heights, Illinois, and concurred in the need for a new translation of the Bible in contemporary English. This group, though not made up of official church representatives, was transdenominational. Its conclusion was endorsed by a large number of leaders from many denominations who met in Chicago in 1966.

Responsibility for the new version was delegated by the Palos Heights group to a self-governing body of fifteen, the Committee on Bible Translation, composed for the most part of biblical scholars from colleges, universities and seminaries. In 1967 the New York Bible Society (now the International Bible Society) generously undertook the financial sponsorship of the project—a sponsorship that made it possible to enlist the help of many distinguished scholars. The fact that participants from the United States, Great Britain, Canada, Australia and New Zealand worked together gave the project its international scope. That they were from many denominations—including Anglican, Assemblies of God, Baptist, Brethren, Christian Reformed, Church of Christ, Evangelical Free, Lutheran, Mennonite, Methodist, Nazarene, Presbyterian, Wesleyan and other churches—helped to safeguard the translation from sectarian bias.

How it was made helps to give the New International Version its distinctiveness. The translation of each book was assigned to a team of scholars. Next, one of the Intermediate Editorial Committees revised the initial translation, with constant reference to the Hebrew, Aramaic or Greek. Their work then went to one of the General Editorial Committees, which checked it in detail and made another thorough revision. This revision in turn was carefully reviewed by the Committee on Bible Translation, which made further changes and then released the final version for publication. In this way the entire Bible underwent three revisions, during each of which the translation was examined for its faithfulness to the original languages and for its English style.

All this involved many thousands of hours of research and discussion regarding the meaning of the texts and the precise way of putting them into English. It may well be that no other translation has been made by a more thorough process of review and revision from committee to committee than this one.

From the beginning of the project, the Committee on Bible Translation held to certain goals for the New International Version: that it would be an accurate translation and one that would have clarity and literary quality and so prove suitable for public and private reading, teaching, preaching, memorizing and liturgical use. The Committee also sought to preserve some measure of continuity with the long tradition of translating the Scriptures into English.

In working toward these goals, the translators were united in their commitment to the authority and infallibility of the Bible as God's Word in written form. They believe that it contains the divine answer to the deepest needs of humanity, that it sheds unique light on our path in a dark world, and that it sets forth the way to our eternal well-being.

The first concern of the translators has been the accuracy of the translation and its fidelity to the thought of the biblical writers. They have weighed the significance of the lexical and grammatical details of the Hebrew, Aramaic and Greek texts. At the same time, they have striven for more than a word-for-word translation. Because thought patterns and syntax differ from language to language, faithful communication of the meaning of the writers of the Bible demands frequent modifications in sentence structure and constant regard for the contextual meanings of words.

A sensitive feeling for style does not always accompany scholarship. Accordingly the Committee on Bible Translation submitted the developing version to a number of stylistic consultants. Two of them read every book of both Old and New Testaments twice—once before and once after the last major revision—and made invaluable suggestions. Samples of the translation were tested for clarity and ease of reading by various kinds of people—young and old, highly educated and less well educated, ministers and laymen.

Concern for clear and natural English—that the New International Version should be idiomatic but not idiosyncratic, contemporary but not dated—motivated the translators and consultants. At the same time, they tried to reflect the differing styles of the biblical writers. In view of the international use of English, the translators sought to avoid obvious Americanisms on the one hand and obvious Anglicisms on the other. A British edition reflects the comparatively few differences of significant idiom and of spelling.

As for the traditional pronouns "thou," "thee" and "thine" in reference to the Deity, the translators judged that to use these archaisms (along with the old verb forms such as "doest," "wouldest" and "hadst") would violate accuracy in translation. Neither Hebrew, Aramaic nor Greek uses special pronouns for the persons of the Godhead. A present-day translation is not enhanced by forms that in the time of the King James Version were used in everyday speech, whether referring to God or man.

For the Old Testament the standard Hebrew text, the Masoretic Text as published in the latest editions of *Biblia Hebraica*, was used throughout. The Dead Sea Scrolls contain material bearing on an earlier stage of the Hebrew text. They were consulted, as were the Samaritan Pentateuch and the ancient scribal traditions relating to textual changes. Sometimes a variant Hebrew reading in the margin of the Masoretic Text was followed instead of the text itself. Such instances, being variants within the Masoretic tradition, are not specified by footnotes. In rare cases, words in the consonantal text were divided differently from the way they appear in the Masoretic Text. Footnotes indicate this. The translators also consulted the more important early versions—the Septuagint; Aquila, Symmachus and Theodotion; the Vulgate; the Syriac Peshitta; the Targums; and for the Psalms the *Juxta Hebraica* of Jerome. Readings from these versions were occasionally followed where the Masoretic Text seemed doubtful and where accepted principles of textual criticism showed that one or more of these textual witnesses appeared to provide the correct reading. Such instances are footnoted. Sometimes vowel letters and vowel signs did not, in the judgment of the translators, represent the correct vowels for the original consonantal text. Accordingly some words were read with a different set of vowels. These instances are usually not indicated by footnotes.

The Greek text used in translating the New Testament was an eclectic one. No other piece of ancient literature has such an abundance of manuscript witnesses as does the New Testament. Where existing manuscripts differ, the translators made their choice of readings according to accepted principles of New Testament textual criticism. Footnotes call attention to places where there was uncertainty about what the original text was. The best current printed texts of the Greek New Testament were used.

There is a sense in which the work of translation is never wholly finished. This applies to all great literature and uniquely so to the Bible. In 1973 the New Testament in the New International Version was published. Since then, suggestions for corrections and revisions have been received from various sources. The Committee on Bible Translation carefully considered the suggestions and adopted a number of them. These were incorporated in the first printing of the entire Bible in 1978. Additional revisions were made by the Committee on Bible Translation in 1983 and appear in printings after that date.

As in other ancient documents, the precise meaning of the biblical texts is sometimes uncertain. This is more often the case with the Hebrew and Aramaic texts than with the Greek text. Although archaeological and linguistic discoveries in this century aid in understanding difficult passages, some uncertainties remain. The more significant of these have been called to the reader's attention in the footnotes.

In regard to the divine name *YHWH*, commonly referred to as the *Tetragrammaton*, the translators adopted the device used in most English versions of rendering that name as "Lord" in capital letters to distinguish it from *Adonai*, another Hebrew word rendered "Lord," for which small letters are used. Wherever the two names stand together in the Old Testament as a compound name of God, they are rendered "Sovereign Lord."

Because for most readers today the phrases "the Lord of hosts" and "God of hosts" have little meaning, this version renders them "the Lord Almighty" and "God Almighty." These renderings convey the sense of the Hebrew, namely, "he who is sovereign over all the 'hosts' (powers) in heaven and on earth, especially over the 'hosts' (armies) of Israel." For readers unacquainted with Hebrew this does not make clear the distinction between *Sabaoth* ("hosts" or "Almighty") and *Shaddai* (which can also be translated "Almighty"), but the latter occurs infrequently and is always footnoted. When *Adonai* and *YHWH Sabaoth* occur together, they are rendered "the Lord, the Lord Almighty."

As for other proper nouns, the familiar spellings of the King James Version are generally retained. Names traditionally spelled with "ch," except where it is final, are usually spelled in this translation with "k" or "c," since the biblical languages do not have the sound that "ch" frequently indicates in English—for example, in *chant*. For well-known names such as Zechariah, however, the traditional spelling has been retained. Variation in the spelling of names in the original languages has usually not been indicated. Where a person or place has two or more different names in the Hebrew, Aramaic or Greek texts, the more familiar one has generally been used, with footnotes where needed.

To achieve clarity the translators sometimes supplied words not in the original texts but required by the context. If there was uncertainty about such material, it is enclosed in brackets.

Also for the sake of clarity or style, nouns, including some proper nouns, are sometimes substituted for pronouns, and vice versa. And though the Hebrew writers often shifted back and forth between first, second and third personal pronouns without change of antecedent, this translation often makes them uniform, in accordance with English style and without the use of footnotes.

Poetical passages are printed as poetry, that is, with indentation of lines with separate stanzas. These are generally designed to reflect the structure of Hebrew poetry. This poetry is normally characterized by parallelism in balanced lines. Most of the poetry in the Bible is in the Old Testament, and scholars differ regarding the scansion of Hebrew lines. The translators determined the stanza divisions for the most part by analysis of the subject matter. The stanzas therefore serve as poetic paragraphs.

As an aid to the reader, italicized sectional headings are inserted in most of the books. They are not to be regarded as part of the NIV text, are not for oral reading, and are not intended to dictate the interpretation of the sections they head.

The footnotes in this version are of several kinds, most of which need no explanation. Those giving alternative translations begin with "Or" and generally introduce the alternative with the last word preceding it in the text, except when it is a single-word alternative; in poetry quoted in a footnote a slant mark indicates a line division. Footnotes introduced by "Or" do not have uniform significance. In some cases two possible translations were considered to have about equal validity. In other cases, though the translators were convinced that the translation in the text was correct, they judged that another interpretation was possible and of sufficient importance to be represented in a footnote.

In the New Testament, footnotes that refer to uncertainty regarding the original text are introduced by "Some manuscripts" or similar expressions. In the Old Testament, evidence for the reading chosen is given first and evidence for the alternative is added after a semicolon (for example: Septuagint; Hebrew *father*). In such notes the term "Hebrew" refers to the Masoretic Text.

It should be noted that minerals, flora and fauna, architectural details, articles of clothing and jewelry, musical instruments and other articles cannot always be identified with precision. Also measures of capacity in the biblical period are particularly uncertain (see the table of weights and measures following the text).

Like all translations of the Bible, made as they are by imperfect man, this one undoubtedly falls short of its goals. Yet we are grateful to God for the extent to which he has enabled us to realize these goals and for the strength he has given us and our colleagues to complete our task. We offer this version of the Bible to him in whose name and for whose glory it has been made. We pray that it will lead many into a better understanding of the Holy Scriptures and a fuller knowledge of Jesus Christ the incarnate Word, of whom the Scriptures so faithfully testify.

The Committee on Bible Translation

June 1978
(Revised August 1983)

Names of the translators and editors may be secured
from the International Bible Society,
translation sponsors of the New International Version,
1820 Jet Stream Drive, Colorado Springs, Colorado,
80921-3696 U.S.A.

OLD TESTAMENT

OLD TESTAMENT

*M*OSES *writes Genesis, a book of beginnings, to tell us how God creates the world, how sin comes into the world, and how God loves mankind in spite of his sin. He reports exciting stories about Adam, Noah, Abraham, Isaac, Jacob and Joseph, how God cares for them and stands beside them, no matter what they do. As you read this book, think about how God enters into a personal relationship with you, cares for you, and wants you to make serving him a priority in your life.*

GENESIS

The Beginning

1 In the beginning God created the heavens and the earth. ²Now the earth was*ᵃ* formless and empty, darkness was over the surface of the deep, and the Spirit of God was hovering over the waters.

³And God said, "Let there be light," and there was light. ⁴God saw that the light was good, and he separated the light from the darkness. ⁵God called the light "day," and the darkness he called "night." And there was eve-

ning, and there was morning—the first day.

⁶And God said, "Let there be an expanse between the waters to separate water from water." ⁷So God made the expanse and separated the water under the expanse from the water above it. And it was so. ⁸God called the expanse "sky." And there was evening, and there was morning—the second day.

⁹And God said, "Let the water under the sky be gathered to one place, and let dry ground appear." And it was so.

*ᵃ*2 Or possibly *became*

¹⁰God called the dry ground "land," and the gathered waters he called "seas." And God saw that it was good.

¹¹Then God said, "Let the land produce vegetation: seed-bearing plants and trees on the land that bear fruit with seed in it, according to their various kinds." And it was so. ¹²The land produced vegetation: plants bearing seed according to their kinds and trees bearing fruit with seed in it according to their kinds. And God saw that it was good. ¹³And there was evening, and there was morning—the third day.

¹⁴And God said, "Let there be lights in the expanse of the sky to separate the day from the night, and let them serve as signs to mark seasons and days and years, ¹⁵and let them be lights in the expanse of the sky to give light on the earth." And it was so. ¹⁶God made two great lights—the greater light to govern the day and the lesser light to govern the night. He also made the stars. ¹⁷God set them in the expanse of the sky to give light on the earth, ¹⁸to govern the day and the night, and to separate light from darkness. And God saw that it was good. ¹⁹And there was evening, and there was morning—the fourth day.

²⁰And God said, "Let the water teem with living creatures, and let birds fly above the earth across the expanse of the sky." ²¹So God created the great creatures of the sea and every living and moving thing with which the water teems, according to their kinds, and every winged bird according to its kind. And God saw that it was good. ²²God blessed them and said, "Be fruitful and increase in number and fill the water in the seas, and let the birds increase on the earth." ²³And there was evening, and there was morning—the fifth day.

²⁴And God said, "Let the land produce living creatures according to their kinds: livestock, creatures that move along the ground, and wild animals, each according to its kind." And it was so. ²⁵God made the wild animals according to their kinds, the livestock according to their kinds, and all the creatures that move along the

ground according to their kinds. And God saw that it was good.

²⁶Then God said, "Let us make man in our image, in our likeness, and let them rule over the fish of the sea and the birds of the air, over the livestock, over all the earth,ª and over all the creatures that move along the ground."

²⁷So God created man in his own image,
in the image of God he created him;
male and female he created them.

²⁸God blessed them and said to them, "Be fruitful and increase in number; fill the earth and subdue it. Rule over the fish of the sea and the birds of the air and over every living creature that moves on the ground." ²⁹Then God said, "I give you every seed-bearing plant on the face of the whole earth and every tree that has fruit with seed in it. They will be yours for food. ³⁰And to all the beasts of the earth and all the birds of the air and all the creatures that move on the ground—everything that has the breath of life in it—I give every green plant for food." And it was so.

³¹God saw all that he had made, and it was very good. And there was evening, and there was morning—the sixth day.

2 Thus the heavens and the earth were completed in all their vast array.

²By the seventh day God had finished the work he had been doing; so on the seventh day he rested ᵇ from all his work. ³And God blessed the seventh day and made it holy, because on it he rested from all the work of creating that he had done.

Adam and Eve

⁴This is the account of the heavens and the earth when they were created.

When the Lᴏʀᴅ God made the earth and the heavens— ⁵and no shrub of the field had yet appeared on the earthᶜ and no plant of the field had yet sprung up, for the Lᴏʀᴅ God had not sent rain on the earthᶜ and there was no man to work the

ª26 Hebrew; Syriac all the wild animals   ᵇ2 Or ceased; also in verse 3   ᶜ5 Or land; also in verse 6 ground, ⁶but streams^a came up from the earth and watered the whole surface of the ground— ⁷the LORD God formed the man^b from the dust of the ground and breathed into his nostrils the breath of life, and the man became a living being.

⁸Now the LORD God had planted a garden in the east, in Eden; and there he put the man he had formed. ⁹And the LORD God made all kinds of trees grow out of the ground—trees that were pleasing to the eye and good for food. In the middle of the garden were the tree of life and the tree of the knowledge of good and evil.

¹⁰A river watering the garden flowed from Eden; from there it was separated

---

^a6 Or *mist*   ^b7 The Hebrew for *man (adam)* sounds like and may be related to the Hebrew for *ground (adamah)*; it is also the name *Adam* (see Gen. 2:20).

MONDAY

VERSE FOR THE DAY:	AUTHOR:	PASSAGE FOR THE DAY:
Genesis 1:27	Ruth A. Tucker	Genesis 1:1–31

A Self-Image in the Image of God

GOD created man—male and female—in his own image. What an awesome reality that is. There *I* am in the first chapter of the Bible—a woman—distinguished from animals, distinguished from my male counterpart, and literally created in the image of God. Certainly womanhood was no afterthought with God, and it was through the creation of both male and female that God has offered his fullest self-revelation.

If somehow in our imagination we are able to recreate all the qualities of perfect man and perfect woman in one being, we have, perhaps, a faint hint of who God really is. And, as we reflect on who God is, we see a picture of the image we carry in ourselves individually.

Unfortunately, that image of God often bears virtually no resemblance to our own self-image. The reason for that, according to many Christian counselors, is because many of us suffer from a low self-image. But how can our self-image be low when we contemplate the image of God in which we were created? Personally, I find that my self-esteem is lowest when I am least reflecting the image of God. Indeed, my self-esteem has very little to do with the ego-boosting gratification that comes with awards, promotions, bonuses, and new clothes. These are the temporary "uppers" of the "me-generation," but they are not what builds a healthy self-image.

I feel best about myself, not when I read a flattering review of one of my books or when I am wearing a new outfit, but when I have selflessly reached out to someone in need and given with no thought of reward—or of self. It is only when my *self* is submerged that God's image begins to shine forth. Then I have a healthy self-image that truly reflects God's image.

Additional Scripture Readings:
Romans 12:1–2; Philippians 2:5–7

Go to page 5 for your next devotional reading.

into four headwaters. ¹¹The name of the first is the Pishon; it winds through the entire land of Havilah, where there is gold. ¹²(The gold of that land is good; aromatic resin*ᵃ* and onyx are also there.) ¹³The name of the second river is the Gihon; it winds through the entire land of Cush.*ᵇ* ¹⁴The name of the third river is the Tigris; it runs along the east side of Asshur. And the fourth river is the Euphrates.

¹⁵The Lord God took the man and put him in the Garden of Eden to work it and take care of it. ¹⁶And the Lord God commanded the man, "You are free to eat from any tree in the garden; ¹⁷but you must not eat from the tree of the knowledge of good and evil, for when you eat of it you will surely die."

¹⁸The Lord God said, "It is not good for the man to be alone. I will make a helper suitable for him."

¹⁹Now the Lord God had formed out of the ground all the beasts of the field and all the birds of the air. He brought them to the man to see what he would name them; and whatever the man called each living creature, that was its name. ²⁰So the man gave names to all the livestock, the birds of the air and all the beasts of the field.

But for Adam*ᶜ* no suitable helper was found. ²¹So the Lord God caused the man to fall into a deep sleep; and while he was sleeping, he took one of the man's ribs*ᵈ* and closed up the place with flesh. ²²Then the Lord God made a woman from the rib*ᵉ* he had taken out of the man, and he brought her to the man.

²³The man said,

"This is now bone of my bones
    and flesh of my flesh;
she shall be called 'woman,*ᶠ*'
    for she was taken out of man."

²⁴For this reason a man will leave his father and mother and be united to his wife, and they will become one flesh.

²⁵The man and his wife were both naked, and they felt no shame.

The Fall of Man

3 Now the serpent was more crafty than any of the wild animals the Lord God had made. He said to the woman, "Did God really say, 'You must not eat from any tree in the garden'?"

²The woman said to the serpent, "We may eat fruit from the trees in the garden, ³but God did say, 'You must not eat fruit from the tree that is in the middle of the garden, and you must not touch it, or you will die.' "

⁴"You will not surely die," the serpent said to the woman. ⁵"For God knows that when you eat of it your eyes will be opened, and you will be like God, knowing good and evil."

⁶When the woman saw that the fruit of the tree was good for food and pleasing to the eye, and also desirable for gaining wisdom, she took some and ate it. She also gave some to her husband, who was with her, and he ate it. ⁷Then the eyes of both of them were opened, and they realized they were naked; so they sewed fig leaves together and made coverings for themselves.

⁸Then the man and his wife heard the sound of the Lord God as he was walking in the garden in the cool of the day, and they hid from the Lord God among the trees of the garden. ⁹But the Lord God called to the man, "Where are you?"

¹⁰He answered, "I heard you in the garden, and I was afraid because I was naked; so I hid."

¹¹And he said, "Who told you that you were naked? Have you eaten from the tree that I commanded you not to eat from?"

¹²The man said, "The woman you put here with me—she gave me some fruit from the tree, and I ate it."

¹³Then the Lord God said to the woman, "What is this you have done?"

The woman said, "The serpent deceived me, and I ate."

¹⁴So the Lord God said to the serpent, "Because you have done this,

"Cursed are you above all the
        livestock
    and all the wild animals!
You will crawl on your belly
    and you will eat dust
    all the days of your life.
¹⁵And I will put enmity
    between you and the woman,
    and between your offspring*ᵍ* and
        hers;
he will crush*ʰ* your head,
    and you will strike his heel."

ᵃ12 Or good; pearls   ᵇ13 Possibly southeast Mesopotamia   ᶜ20 Or the man   ᵈ21 Or took part of the man's side   ᵉ22 Or part   ᶠ23 The Hebrew for woman sounds like the Hebrew for man.   ᵍ15 Or seed   ʰ15 Or strike

VERSE FOR THE DAY:
Genesis 3:1

AUTHOR:
Gladys M. Hunt

PASSAGE FOR THE DAY:
Genesis 3:1–6

Temptation's Strategy

SATAN is very clever. Always his strategy is to confuse reality, to make evil seem good. He knows Eve is living in all the splendor of Eden, with all of her needs met. How do you get at someone who is contented with good?

The serpent has a plan. He approaches the woman with a theological discussion about God. That is a safe subject; she likes to talk about God. The serpent queries, "Did God really say, 'You must not eat from any tree in the garden'?" The serpent makes an overstatement that he allows Eve to correct, but in doing so he makes her aware of a restriction. God is keeping something from her.

The woman corrects the serpent. "No, God isn't like that . . . ." Then she makes her own overstatement of what God has said (Genesis 3:3). Yet, instead of declaring that the garden is lavish in its provision for her need, and that one tree doesn't make all that much difference, the woman lets the serpent trick her. He focuses her attention on the one forbidden tree, suggesting that God is keeping something good from Eve. He casts doubt on the character of God. Doubting God makes it easy to "take and eat."

Eve's attention is riveted to the tree—not the garden full of goodness, not God's gracious fellowship and provision. Just the tree. It looks good; it pleases the eye; it is desirable (Genesis 3:6). The more she looks, the more appealing it becomes. It's always that way when Satan gets us to concentrate on the temptation instead of on God.

I suppose the temptation has been replayed again and again in the history of the human race, and probably in each of our lives. The specifics are different, but the strategy is often the same. How many times has the serpent tempted you to think, "A good God wouldn't keep me from this, would he?"

The serpent won his encounter with the woman. She took the fruit and gave some to her husband. It will be a long time before another One will say, "Take and eat," and this time he will provide his own body and blood as a ransom for their sins.

Additional Scripture Readings:
1 Corinthians 10:12–13; James 1:13–15

Go to page 7 for your next devotional reading.

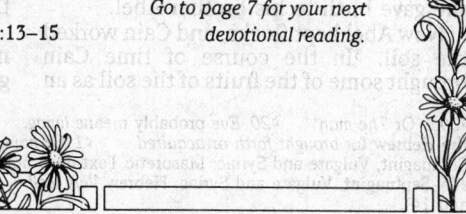

¹⁶To the woman he said,

"I will greatly increase your pains in
   childbearing;
with pain you will give birth to
   children.
Your desire will be for your husband,
   and he will rule over you."

¹⁷To Adam he said, "Because you listened to your wife and ate from the tree
about which I commanded you, 'You
must not eat of it,'

"Cursed is the ground because of you;
   through painful toil you will eat of
     it
   all the days of your life.
¹⁸It will produce thorns and thistles for
   you,
   and you will eat the plants of the
     field.
¹⁹By the sweat of your brow
   you will eat your food
until you return to the ground,
   since from it you were taken;
for dust you are
   and to dust you will return."

²⁰Adam*ᵃ* named his wife Eve,*ᵇ* because she would become the mother of
all the living.

²¹The Lᴏʀᴅ God made garments of skin
for Adam and his wife and clothed them.
²²And the Lᴏʀᴅ God said, "The man has
now become like one of us, knowing good
and evil. He must not be allowed to reach
out his hand and take also from the tree
of life and eat, and live forever." ²³So the
Lᴏʀᴅ God banished him from the Garden
of Eden to work the ground from which
he had been taken. ²⁴After he drove the
man out, he placed on the east side*ᶜ* of
the Garden of Eden cherubim and a flaming sword flashing back and forth to guard
the way to the tree of life.

Cain and Abel

4 Adam*ᵃ* lay with his wife Eve, and she
became pregnant and gave birth to
Cain.*ᵈ* She said, "With the help of the
Lᴏʀᴅ I have brought forth*ᵉ* a man." ²Later
she gave birth to his brother Abel.

Now Abel kept flocks, and Cain worked
the soil. ³In the course of time Cain
brought some of the fruits of the soil as an
offering to the Lᴏʀᴅ. ⁴But Abel brought fat
portions from some of the firstborn of his
flock. The Lᴏʀᴅ looked with favor on Abel
and his offering, ⁵but on Cain and his offering he did not look with favor. So Cain
was very angry, and his face was downcast.

⁶Then the Lᴏʀᴅ said to Cain, "Why are
you angry? Why is your face downcast? ⁷If
you do what is right, will you not be accepted? But if you do not do what is right,
sin is crouching at your door; it desires to
have you, but you must master it."

⁸Now Cain said to his brother Abel,
"Let's go out to the field."*ᶠ* And while
they were in the field, Cain attacked his
brother Abel and killed him.

⁹Then the Lᴏʀᴅ said to Cain, "Where is
your brother Abel?"

"I don't know," he replied. "Am I my
brother's keeper?"

¹⁰The Lᴏʀᴅ said, "What have you done?
Listen! Your brother's blood cries out to
me from the ground. ¹¹Now you are under
a curse and driven from the ground,
which opened its mouth to receive your
brother's blood from your hand. ¹²When
you work the ground, it will no longer
yield its crops for you. You will be a restless wanderer on the earth."

¹³Cain said to the Lᴏʀᴅ, "My punishment is more than I can bear. ¹⁴Today you
are driving me from the land, and I will be
hidden from your presence; I will be a
restless wanderer on the earth, and whoever finds me will kill me."

¹⁵But the Lᴏʀᴅ said to him, "Not so*ᵍ*; if
anyone kills Cain, he will suffer vengeance seven times over." Then the Lᴏʀᴅ
put a mark on Cain so that no one who
found him would kill him. ¹⁶So Cain went
out from the Lᴏʀᴅ's presence and lived in
the land of Nod,*ʰ* east of Eden.

¹⁷Cain lay with his wife, and she became pregnant and gave birth to Enoch.
Cain was then building a city, and he
named it after his son Enoch. ¹⁸To Enoch
was born Irad, and Irad was the father of
Mehujael, and Mehujael was the father of
Methushael, and Methushael was the father of Lamech.

¹⁹Lamech married two women, one
named Adah and the other Zillah. ²⁰Adah
gave birth to Jabal; he was the father of

ᵃ20,1 Or The man   *ᵇ20 Eve probably means living.*   *ᶜ24 Or placed in front*   *ᵈ1 Cain sounds like*
the Hebrew for *brought forth* or *acquired.*   *ᵉ1 Or have acquired*   *ᶠ8 Samaritan Pentateuch,*
Septuagint, Vulgate and Syriac; Masoretic Text does not have *"Let's go out to the field."*
ᵍ15 Septuagint, Vulgate and Syriac; Hebrew Very well   *ʰ16 Nod means wandering* (see verses 12
and 14).

those who live in tents and raise livestock. 21His brother's name was Jubal; he was the father of all who play the harp and flute. 22Zillah also had a son, Tubal-Cain, who forged all kinds of tools out of*a* bronze and iron. Tubal-Cain's sister was Naamah.

23Lamech said to his wives,

"Adah and Zillah, listen to me;
   wives of Lamech, hear my words.
I have killed*b* a man for wounding
   me,
   a young man for injuring me.
24If Cain is avenged seven times,
   then Lamech seventy-seven times."

25Adam lay with his wife again, and she gave birth to a son and named him Seth,*c* saying, "God has granted me another child in place of Abel, since Cain killed him." 26Seth also had a son, and he named him Enosh.

At that time men began to call on*d* the name of the LORD.

From Adam to Noah

5 This is the written account of Adam's line.

When God created man, he made him in the likeness of God. 2He created them male and female and blessed them. And when they were created, he called them "man.*e* "

3When Adam had lived 130 years, he had a son in his own likeness, in his own image; and he named him Seth. 4After Seth was born, Adam lived 800 years and had other sons and daughters. 5Altogether, Adam lived 930 years, and then he died.

6When Seth had lived 105 years, he became the father*f* of Enosh. 7And after he became the father of Enosh, Seth lived

---

a22 Or *who instructed all who work in*   *b23* Or *I will kill*   *c25* *Seth* probably means *granted.*
d26 Or *to proclaim*   *e2* Hebrew *adam*   *f6* *Father* may mean *ancestor;* also in verses 7-26.

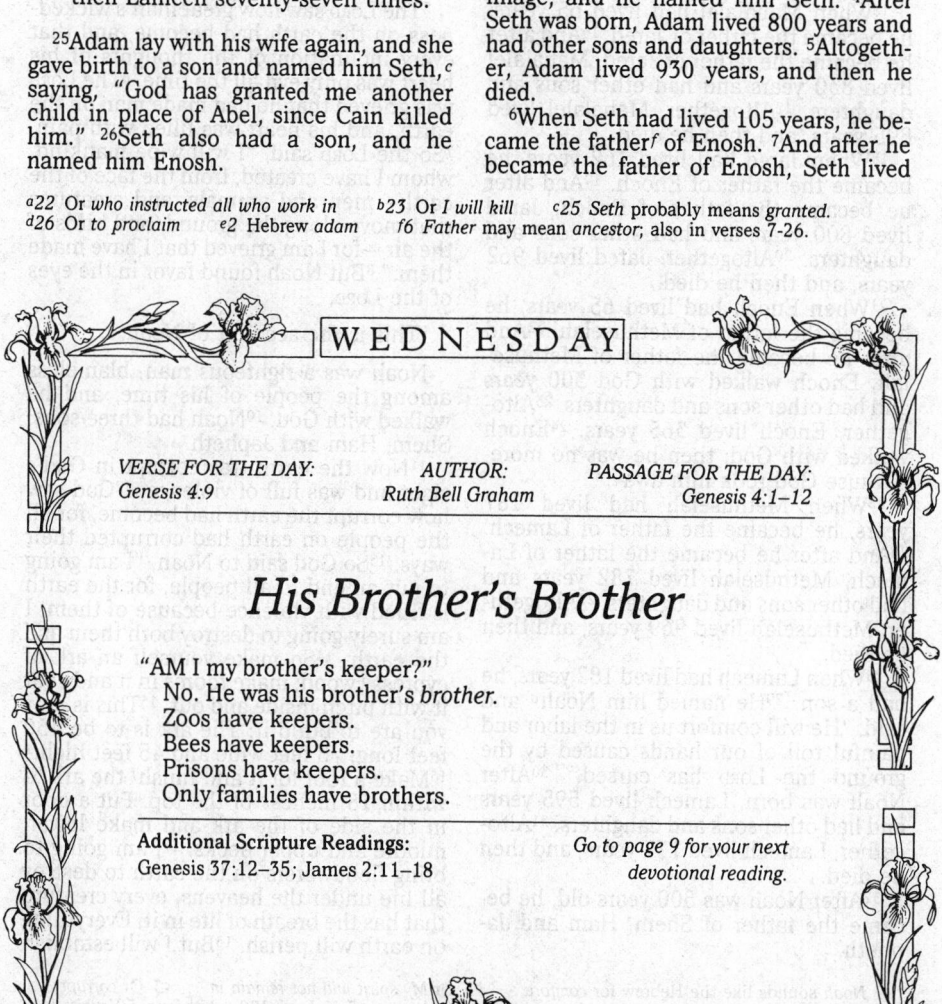

WEDNESDAY

VERSE FOR THE DAY:
Genesis 4:9

AUTHOR:
Ruth Bell Graham

PASSAGE FOR THE DAY:
Genesis 4:1–12

His Brother's Brother

"AM I my brother's keeper?"
No. He was his brother's *brother.*
Zoos have keepers.
Bees have keepers.
Prisons have keepers.
Only families have brothers.

Additional Scripture Readings:
Genesis 37:12–35; James 2:11–18

Go to page 9 for your next devotional reading.

807 years and had other sons and daughters. [8]Altogether, Seth lived 912 years, and then he died.

[9]When Enosh had lived 90 years, he became the father of Kenan. [10]And after he became the father of Kenan, Enosh lived 815 years and had other sons and daughters. [11]Altogether, Enosh lived 905 years, and then he died.

[12]When Kenan had lived 70 years, he became the father of Mahalalel. [13]And after he became the father of Mahalalel, Kenan lived 840 years and had other sons and daughters. [14]Altogether, Kenan lived 910 years, and then he died.

[15]When Mahalalel had lived 65 years, he became the father of Jared. [16]And after he became the father of Jared, Mahalalel lived 830 years and had other sons and daughters. [17]Altogether, Mahalalel lived 895 years, and then he died.

[18]When Jared had lived 162 years, he became the father of Enoch. [19]And after he became the father of Enoch, Jared lived 800 years and had other sons and daughters. [20]Altogether, Jared lived 962 years, and then he died.

[21]When Enoch had lived 65 years, he became the father of Methuselah. [22]And after he became the father of Methuselah, Enoch walked with God 300 years and had other sons and daughters. [23]Altogether, Enoch lived 365 years. [24]Enoch walked with God; then he was no more, because God took him away.

[25]When Methuselah had lived 187 years, he became the father of Lamech. [26]And after he became the father of Lamech, Methuselah lived 782 years and had other sons and daughters. [27]Altogether, Methuselah lived 969 years, and then he died.

[28]When Lamech had lived 182 years, he had a son. [29]He named him Noah[a] and said, "He will comfort us in the labor and painful toil of our hands caused by the ground the LORD has cursed." [30]After Noah was born, Lamech lived 595 years and had other sons and daughters. [31]Altogether, Lamech lived 777 years, and then he died.

[32]After Noah was 500 years old, he became the father of Shem, Ham and Japheth.

The Flood

6 When men began to increase in number on the earth and daughters were born to them, [2]the sons of God saw that the daughters of men were beautiful, and they married any of them they chose. [3]Then the LORD said, "My Spirit will not contend with[b] man forever, for he is mortal[c]; his days will be a hundred and twenty years."

[4]The Nephilim were on the earth in those days—and also afterward—when the sons of God went to the daughters of men and had children by them. They were the heroes of old, men of renown.

[5]The LORD saw how great man's wickedness on the earth had become, and that every inclination of the thoughts of his heart was only evil all the time. [6]The LORD was grieved that he had made man on the earth, and his heart was filled with pain. [7]So the LORD said, "I will wipe mankind, whom I have created, from the face of the earth—men and animals, and creatures that move along the ground, and birds of the air—for I am grieved that I have made them." [8]But Noah found favor in the eyes of the LORD.

[9]This is the account of Noah.

Noah was a righteous man, blameless among the people of his time, and he walked with God. [10]Noah had three sons: Shem, Ham and Japheth.

[11]Now the earth was corrupt in God's sight and was full of violence. [12]God saw how corrupt the earth had become, for all the people on earth had corrupted their ways. [13]So God said to Noah, "I am going to put an end to all people, for the earth is filled with violence because of them. I am surely going to destroy both them and the earth. [14]So make yourself an ark of cypress[d] wood; make rooms in it and coat it with pitch inside and out. [15]This is how you are to build it: The ark is to be 450 feet long, 75 feet wide and 45 feet high.[e] [16]Make a roof for it and finish[f] the ark to within 18 inches[g] of the top. Put a door in the side of the ark and make lower, middle and upper decks. [17]I am going to bring floodwaters on the earth to destroy all life under the heavens, every creature that has the breath of life in it. Everything on earth will perish. [18]But I will establish

---

[a]29 Noah sounds like the Hebrew for comfort.   [b]3 Or My spirit will not remain in   [c]3 Or corrupt   [d]14 The meaning of the Hebrew for this word is uncertain.   [e]15 Hebrew 300 cubits long, 50 cubits wide and 30 cubits high (about 140 meters long, 23 meters wide and 13.5 meters high)   [f]16 Or Make an opening for light by finishing   [g]16 Hebrew a cubit (about 0.5 meter)

my covenant with you, and you will enter the ark—you and your sons and your wife and your sons' wives with you. ¹⁹You are to bring into the ark two of all living creatures, male and female, to keep them alive with you. ²⁰Two of every kind of bird, of every kind of animal and of every kind of creature that moves along the ground will come to you to be kept alive. ²¹You

a2 Or seven pairs; also in verse 3

are to take every kind of food that is to be eaten and store it away as food for you and for them."

²²Noah did everything just as God commanded him.

7 The Lᴏʀᴅ then said to Noah, "Go into the ark, you and your whole family, because I have found you righteous in this generation. ²Take with you seven *a* of

THURSDAY

VERSE FOR THE DAY:
Genesis 6:9

AUTHOR:
Millie Stamm

PASSAGE FOR THE DAY:
Genesis 6:9–22

Favor in God's Eyes

NOAH lived in the midst of a wicked people. Yet he was an example of one who could live a godly life in an evil world; a life pleasing to God in his everyday environment. "But Noah found favor in the eyes of the Lᴏʀᴅ" (Genesis 6:8). His favor with the Lord was through no merit of his own but through his personal faith in God.

God could see that Noah's life was upright. He was "blameless among the people of his time" (Genesis 6:9). God recognized Noah as a perfect man, not perfect in character but in a life revealing a genuineness of faith in God.

We also read that "Noah walked with God" (Genesis 6:9). In the midst of wickedness, he was able to keep close fellowship with God. It is not the environment but the heart that determines one's walk with the Lord.

Noah was not as concerned with pleasing people as he was with pleasing God. "But Noah found favor in the eyes of the Lᴏʀᴅ.'

We may question ourselves, "Do I find favor in the eyes of the Lord?" Remembering our weaknesses and failures we realize we have no merit by which God can accept us. But God knows all about us and has provided a way by which we can be accepted by him. We find grace in God's sight through our relationship with Jesus Christ. God sees us perfect in him.

We may find ourselves in a place not conducive to Christian living, just as Noah did. Even there, God gives us grace to live victoriously. "He gives us more grace" (James 4:6).

Ponder the words, "Noah found favor in the eyes of the Lᴏʀᴅ." In the eyes of the Lord, is my life pleasing to him today? Do I find favor in his sight?

Additional Scripture Readings:
Psalm 19:14; Philippians 2:12–15

Go to page 11 for your next devotional reading.

every kind of clean animal, a male and its mate, and two of every kind of unclean animal, a male and its mate, ³and also seven of every kind of bird, male and female, to keep their various kinds alive throughout the earth. ⁴Seven days from now I will send rain on the earth for forty days and forty nights, and I will wipe from the face of the earth every living creature I have made."

⁵And Noah did all that the LORD commanded him.

⁶Noah was six hundred years old when the floodwaters came on the earth. ⁷And Noah and his sons and his wife and his sons' wives entered the ark to escape the waters of the flood. ⁸Pairs of clean and unclean animals, of birds and of all creatures that move along the ground, ⁹male and female, came to Noah and entered the ark, as God had commanded Noah. ¹⁰And after the seven days the floodwaters came on the earth.

¹¹In the six hundredth year of Noah's life, on the seventeenth day of the second month—on that day all the springs of the great deep burst forth, and the floodgates of the heavens were opened. ¹²And rain fell on the earth forty days and forty nights.

¹³On that very day Noah and his sons, Shem, Ham and Japheth, together with his wife and the wives of his three sons, entered the ark. ¹⁴They had with them every wild animal according to its kind, all livestock according to their kinds, every creature that moves along the ground according to its kind and every bird according to its kind, everything with wings. ¹⁵Pairs of all creatures that have the breath of life in them came to Noah and entered the ark. ¹⁶The animals going in were male and female of every living thing, as God had commanded Noah. Then the LORD shut him in.

¹⁷For forty days the flood kept coming on the earth, and as the waters increased they lifted the ark high above the earth. ¹⁸The waters rose and increased greatly on the earth, and the ark floated on the surface of the water. ¹⁹They rose greatly on the earth, and all the high mountains under the entire heavens were covered. ²⁰The waters rose and covered the mountains to a depth of more than twenty feet.*ᵃ, ᵇ* ²¹Every living thing that moved on the earth perished—birds, livestock,

wild animals, all the creatures that swarm over the earth, and all mankind. ²²Everything on dry land that had the breath of life in its nostrils died. ²³Every living thing on the face of the earth was wiped out; men and animals and the creatures that move along the ground and the birds of the air were wiped from the earth. Only Noah was left, and those with him in the ark.

²⁴The waters flooded the earth for a hundred and fifty days.

8 But God remembered Noah and all the wild animals and the livestock that were with him in the ark, and he sent a wind over the earth, and the waters receded. ²Now the springs of the deep and the floodgates of the heavens had been closed, and the rain had stopped falling from the sky. ³The water receded steadily from the earth. At the end of the hundred and fifty days the water had gone down, ⁴and on the seventeenth day of the seventh month the ark came to rest on the mountains of Ararat. ⁵The waters continued to recede until the tenth month, and on the first day of the tenth month the tops of the mountains became visible.

⁶After forty days Noah opened the window he had made in the ark ⁷and sent out a raven, and it kept flying back and forth until the water had dried up from the earth. ⁸Then he sent out a dove to see if the water had receded from the surface of the ground. ⁹But the dove could find no place to set its feet because there was water over all the surface of the earth; so it returned to Noah in the ark. He reached out his hand and took the dove and brought it back to himself in the ark. ¹⁰He waited seven more days and again sent out the dove from the ark. ¹¹When the dove returned to him in the evening, there in its beak was a freshly plucked olive leaf! Then Noah knew that the water had receded from the earth. ¹²He waited seven more days and sent the dove out again, but this time it did not return to him.

¹³By the first day of the first month of Noah's six hundred and first year, the water had dried up from the earth. Noah then removed the covering from the ark and saw that the surface of the ground was dry. ¹⁴By the twenty-seventh day of the second month the earth was completely dry.

ᵃ20 Hebrew *fifteen cubits* (about 6.9 meters) *were covered*   *ᵇ20* Or *rose more than twenty feet, and the mountains were covered*

¹⁵Then God said to Noah, ¹⁶"Come out of the ark, you and your wife and your sons and their wives. ¹⁷Bring out every kind of living creature that is with you — the birds, the animals, and all the creatures that move along the ground — so they can multiply on the earth and be fruitful and increase in number upon it."

¹⁸So Noah came out, together with his sons and his wife and his sons' wives. ¹⁹All the animals and all the creatures that move along the ground and all the birds — everything that moves on the earth — came out of the ark, one kind after another.

²⁰Then Noah built an altar to the LORD

ᵃ21 Or man, for

and, taking some of all the clean animals and clean birds, he sacrificed burnt offerings on it. ²¹The LORD smelled the pleasing aroma and said in his heart: "Never again will I curse the ground because of man, even though ᵃ every inclination of his heart is evil from childhood. And never again will I destroy all living creatures, as I have done.

²²"As long as the earth endures,
seedtime and harvest,
cold and heat,
summer and winter,
day and night
will never cease."

FRIDAY

VERSE FOR THE DAY: AUTHOR: PASSAGE FOR THE DAY:
Genesis 8:8–9   Gien Karssen   Genesis 8:1–12

A Place to Stand

A SINGLE lonely bird hovered over a submerged world. Below her were the results of the catastrophic flood. There was nothing to be seen but water. The world below her was desolate and seemingly without a future. Nowhere could she find a place to hold on to, to set down her tiny foot. She found no rest.

Yet the dove that fluttered around purposelessly was less lonely than she appeared to be. Noah — his name means "he who will bring rest" — had not forgotten her. He waited for her return. When the bird came, she found an outstretched hand, ready to take her into the safety of the ark. Together they were on their way to a new future. The submerged earth would be habitable again.

We can be compared with this dove. We feel lonely and forsaken. We flutter around in a world that increasingly offers less to hold on to in every way. We see little hope for humanity. Spiritually and emotionally we find no rest.

Yet there is Someone who cares about us, who watches closely for each individual: GOD! Through him we can find rest in spite of the catastrophes that harass the world. He offers us a place to stand, and hope, even in an apparently lost world. He offers a new beginning to those of us who return to him.

Additional Scripture Readings:
Isaiah 40:28–31; Ephesians 6:10–18

Go to page 14 for your next devotional reading.

God's Covenant With Noah

9 Then God blessed Noah and his sons, saying to them, "Be fruitful and increase in number and fill the earth. ²The fear and dread of you will fall upon all the beasts of the earth and all the birds of the air, upon every creature that moves along the ground, and upon all the fish of the sea; they are given into your hands. ³Everything that lives and moves will be food for you. Just as I gave you the green plants, I now give you everything.

⁴"But you must not eat meat that has its lifeblood still in it. ⁵And for your lifeblood I will surely demand an accounting. I will demand an accounting from every animal. And from each man, too, I will demand an accounting for the life of his fellow man.

⁶"Whoever sheds the blood of man,
    by man shall his blood be shed;
for in the image of God
    has God made man.

⁷As for you, be fruitful and increase in number; multiply on the earth and increase upon it."

⁸Then God said to Noah and to his sons with him: ⁹"I now establish my covenant with you and with your descendants after you ¹⁰and with every living creature that was with you—the birds, the livestock and all the wild animals, all those that came out of the ark with you—every living creature on earth. ¹¹I establish my covenant with you: Never again will all life be cut off by the waters of a flood; never again will there be a flood to destroy the earth."

¹²And God said, "This is the sign of the covenant I am making between me and you and every living creature with you, a covenant for all generations to come: ¹³I have set my rainbow in the clouds, and it will be the sign of the covenant between me and the earth. ¹⁴Whenever I bring clouds over the earth and the rainbow appears in the clouds, ¹⁵I will remember my covenant between me and you and all living creatures of every kind. Never again will the waters become a flood to destroy all life. ¹⁶Whenever the rainbow appears in the clouds, I will see it and remember the everlasting covenant between God and all living creatures of every kind on the earth."

¹⁷So God said to Noah, "This is the sign of the covenant I have established between me and all life on the earth."

The Sons of Noah

¹⁸The sons of Noah who came out of the ark were Shem, Ham and Japheth. (Ham was the father of Canaan.) ¹⁹These were the three sons of Noah, and from them came the people who were scattered over the earth.

²⁰Noah, a man of the soil, proceeded*ᵃ* to plant a vineyard. ²¹When he drank some of its wine, he became drunk and lay uncovered inside his tent. ²²Ham, the father of Canaan, saw his father's nakedness and told his two brothers outside. ²³But Shem and Japheth took a garment and laid it across their shoulders; then they walked in backward and covered their father's nakedness. Their faces were turned the other way so that they would not see their father's nakedness.

²⁴When Noah awoke from his wine and found out what his youngest son had done to him, ²⁵he said,

"Cursed be Canaan!
    The lowest of slaves
    will he be to his brothers."

²⁶He also said,

"Blessed be the Lᴏʀᴅ, the God of Shem!
    May Canaan be the slave of Shem.*ᵇ*
²⁷May God extend the territory of Japheth*ᶜ*;
    may Japheth live in the tents of Shem,
    and may Canaan be his*ᵈ* slave."

²⁸After the flood Noah lived 350 years. ²⁹Altogether, Noah lived 950 years, and then he died.

The Table of Nations

10 This is the account of Shem, Ham and Japheth, Noah's sons, who themselves had sons after the flood.

The Japhethites

²The sons*ᵉ* of Japheth:
    Gomer, Magog, Madai, Javan, Tubal, Meshech and Tiras.
³The sons of Gomer:
    Ashkenaz, Riphath and Togarmah.
⁴The sons of Javan:

ᵃ20 Or *soil, was the first*   *ᵇ26* Or *be his slave*   *ᶜ27 Japheth* sounds like the Hebrew for *extend.*
ᵈ27 Or *their*   *ᵉ2 Sons* may mean *descendants* or *successors* or *nations*; also in verses 3, 4, 6, 7, 20-23, 29 and 31.

Elishah, Tarshish, the Kittim and the Rodanim.*ª* ⁵(From these the maritime peoples spread out into their territories by their clans within their nations, each with its own language.)

The Hamites

⁶The sons of Ham:
Cush, Mizraim,*ᵇ* Put and Canaan.
⁷The sons of Cush:
Seba, Havilah, Sabtah, Raamah and Sabteca.
The sons of Raamah:
Sheba and Dedan.

⁸Cush was the father*ᶜ* of Nimrod, who grew to be a mighty warrior on the earth. ⁹He was a mighty hunter before the LORD; that is why it is said, "Like Nimrod, a mighty hunter before the LORD." ¹⁰The first centers of his kingdom were Babylon, Erech, Akkad and Calneh, in*ᵈ* Shinar.*ᵉ* ¹¹From that land he went to Assyria, where he built Nineveh, Rehoboth Ir,*ᶠ* Calah ¹²and Resen, which is between Nineveh and Calah; that is the great city.

¹³Mizraim was the father of
the Ludites, Anamites, Lehabites, Naphtuhites, ¹⁴Pathrusites, Casluhites (from whom the Philistines came) and Caphtorites.
¹⁵Canaan was the father of
Sidon his firstborn,*ᵍ* and of the Hittites, ¹⁶Jebusites, Amorites, Girgashites, ¹⁷Hivites, Arkites, Sinites, ¹⁸Arvadites, Zemarites and Hamathites.

Later the Canaanite clans scattered ¹⁹and the borders of Canaan reached from Sidon toward Gerar as far as Gaza, and then toward Sodom, Gomorrah, Admah and Zeboiim, as far as Lasha.

²⁰These are the sons of Ham by their clans and languages, in their territories and nations.

The Semites

²¹Sons were also born to Shem, whose older brother was*ʰ* Japheth; Shem was the ancestor of all the sons of Eber.

²²The sons of Shem:
Elam, Asshur, Arphaxad, Lud and Aram.
²³The sons of Aram:
Uz, Hul, Gether and Meshech.*ⁱ*
²⁴Arphaxad was the father of*ʲ* Shelah, and Shelah the father of Eber.
²⁵Two sons were born to Eber:
One was named Peleg,*ᵏ* because in his time the earth was divided; his brother was named Joktan.
²⁶Joktan was the father of
Almodad, Sheleph, Hazarmaveth, Jerah, ²⁷Hadoram, Uzal, Diklah, ²⁸Obal, Abimael, Sheba, ²⁹Ophir, Havilah and Jobab. All these were sons of Joktan.

³⁰The region where they lived stretched from Mesha toward Sephar, in the eastern hill country.

³¹These are the sons of Shem by their clans and languages, in their territories and nations.

³²These are the clans of Noah's sons, according to their lines of descent, within their nations. From these the nations spread out over the earth after the flood.

The Tower of Babel

11 Now the whole world had one language and a common speech. ²As men moved eastward,*ⁱ* they found a plain in Shinar*ᵉ* and settled there.

³They said to each other, "Come, let's make bricks and bake them thoroughly." They used brick instead of stone, and tar for mortar. ⁴Then they said, "Come, let us build ourselves a city, with a tower that reaches to the heavens, so that we may make a name for ourselves and not be scattered over the face of the whole earth."

⁵But the LORD came down to see the city and the tower that the men were building. ⁶The LORD said, "If as one people speaking the same language they have begun to do this, then nothing they plan to do will be impossible for them. ⁷Come, let us go down and confuse their language so they will not understand each other."

⁸So the LORD scattered them from there over all the earth, and they stopped building the city. ⁹That is why it was called

ª4 Some manuscripts of the Masoretic Text and Samaritan Pentateuch (see also Septuagint and 1 Chron. 1:7); most manuscripts of the Masoretic Text *Dodanim*   ᵇ6 That is, Egypt; also in verse 13   ᶜ8 *Father* may mean *ancestor* or *predecessor* or *founder*; also in verses 13, 15, 24 and 26.   ᵈ10 Or *Erech and Akkad—all of them in*   ᵉ10,2 That is, Babylonia   ᶠ11 Or *Nineveh with its city squares*   ᵍ15 Or *of the Sidonians, the foremost*   ʰ21 Or *Shem, the older brother of*   ⁱ23 See Septuagint and 1 Chron 1:17; Hebrew *Mash*   ʲ24 Hebrew; Septuagint *father of Cainan, and Cainan was the father of*   ᵏ25 *Peleg* means *division*.   ˡ2 Or *from the east*; or *in the east*

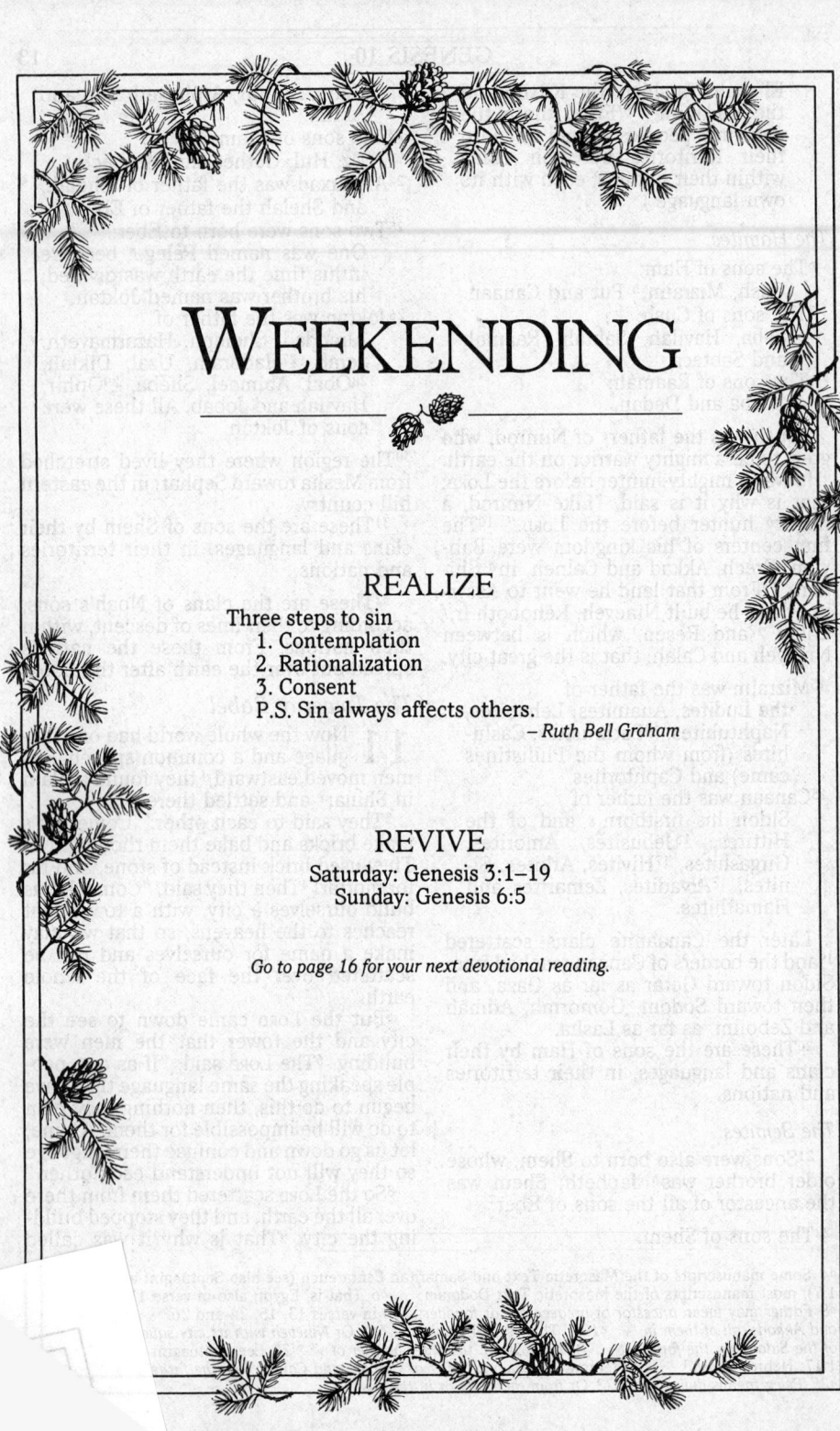

WEEKENDING

REALIZE

Three steps to sin
1. Contemplation
2. Rationalization
3. Consent
P.S. Sin always affects others.

– Ruth Bell Graham

REVIVE

Saturday: Genesis 3:1–19
Sunday: Genesis 6:5

Go to page 16 for your next devotional reading.

Babel[a]—because there the LORD confused the language of the whole world. From there the LORD scattered them over the face of the whole earth.

From Shem to Abram

[10]This is the account of Shem.

Two years after the flood, when Shem was 100 years old, he became the father[b] of Arphaxad. [11]And after he became the father of Arphaxad, Shem lived 500 years and had other sons and daughters.

[12]When Arphaxad had lived 35 years, he became the father of Shelah. [13]And after he became the father of Shelah, Arphaxad lived 403 years and had other sons and daughters.[c]

[14]When Shelah had lived 30 years, he became the father of Eber. [15]And after he became the father of Eber, Shelah lived 403 years and had other sons and daughters.

[16]When Eber had lived 34 years, he became the father of Peleg. [17]And after he became the father of Peleg, Eber lived 430 years and had other sons and daughters.

[18]When Peleg had lived 30 years, he became the father of Reu. [19]And after he became the father of Reu, Peleg lived 209 years and had other sons and daughters.

[20]When Reu had lived 32 years, he became the father of Serug. [21]And after he became the father of Serug, Reu lived 207 years and had other sons and daughters.

[22]When Serug had lived 30 years, he became the father of Nahor. [23]And after he became the father of Nahor, Serug lived 200 years and had other sons and daughters.

[24]When Nahor had lived 29 years, he became the father of Terah. [25]And after he became the father of Terah, Nahor lived 119 years and had other sons and daughters.

[26]After Terah had lived 70 years, he became the father of Abram, Nahor and Haran.

[27]This is the account of Terah.

Terah became the father of Abram, Nahor and Haran. And Haran became the father of Lot. [28]While his father Terah was still alive, Haran died in Ur of the Chaldeans, in the land of his birth. [29]Abram and Nahor both married. The name of Abram's wife was Sarai, and the name of Nahor's wife was Milcah; she was the daughter of Haran, the father of both Milcah and Iscah. [30]Now Sarai was barren; she had no children.

[31]Terah took his son Abram, his grandson Lot son of Haran, and his daughter-in-law Sarai, the wife of his son Abram, and together they set out from Ur of the Chaldeans to go to Canaan. But when they came to Haran, they settled there.

[32]Terah lived 205 years, and he died in Haran.

The Call of Abram

12 The LORD had said to Abram, "Leave your country, your people and your father's household and go to the land I will show you.

[2]"I will make you into a great nation
and I will bless you;
I will make your name great,
and you will be a blessing.
[3]I will bless those who bless you,
and whoever curses you I will curse;
and all peoples on earth
will be blessed through you."

[4]So Abram left, as the LORD had told him; and Lot went with him. Abram was seventy-five years old when he set out from Haran. [5]He took his wife Sarai, his nephew Lot, all the possessions they had accumulated and the people they had acquired in Haran, and they set out for the land of Canaan, and they arrived there.

[6]Abram traveled through the land as far as the site of the great tree of Moreh at Shechem. At that time the Canaanites were in the land. [7]The LORD appeared to Abram and said, "To your offspring[d] I will give this land." So he built an altar there to the LORD, who had appeared to him.

[8]From there he went on toward the hills east of Bethel and pitched his tent, with Bethel on the west and Ai on the east. There he built an altar to the LORD and called on the name of the LORD. [9]Then Abram set out and continued toward the Negev.

---

[a]9 That is, Babylon; *Babel* sounds like the Hebrew for *confused.*   [b]10 *Father* may mean *ancestor;* also in verses 11-25.   [c]12,13 Hebrew; Septuagint (see also Luke 3:35, 36 and note at Gen. 10:24) *35 years, he became the father of Cainan.* [13]*And after he became the father of Cainan, Arphaxad lived 430 years and had other sons and daughters, and then he died. When Cainan had lived 130 years, he became the father of Shelah. And after he became the father of Shelah, Cainan lived 330 years and had other sons and daughters*   [d]7 Or *seed*

Abram in Egypt

¹⁰Now there was a famine in the land, and Abram went down to Egypt to live there for a while because the famine was severe. ¹¹As he was about to enter Egypt, he said to his wife Sarai, "I know what a beautiful woman you are. ¹²When the Egyptians see you, they will say, 'This is his wife.' Then they will kill me but will let you live. ¹³Say you are my sister, so that I will be treated well for your sake and my life will be spared because of you."

¹⁴When Abram came to Egypt, the Egyptians saw that she was a very beautiful woman. ¹⁵And when Pharaoh's officials saw her, they praised her to Pharaoh, and she was taken into his palace. ¹⁶He treated Abram well for her sake, and Abram acquired sheep and cattle, male

MONDAY

VERSE FOR THE DAY:
Genesis 12:1,4

AUTHOR:
Patricia Beall

PASSAGE FOR THE DAY:
Genesis 12:1–9

Abram Hears God in Daily Life

WHAT was Abram doing when God spoke to him for the first time? Was he just finishing breakfast, was he talking with the shepherds about the new lambs? Was he managing the family business with Lot, was he watching Sarai organize the household servants? Was it a weekend, a change from the daily routine, or just weekday life as usual?

There was no roar of thunder, Abram wasn't suddenly surrounded by a mysterious darkness, he wasn't transported to a dimension transcending time, space or usual definition. The Scriptures just say that God spoke.

Imagine God speaking to you suddenly, as to Abram. And not just a casual word, not just a friendly greeting or some helpful advice, but a shocking directive which shatters your routine and will change your whole life. What would be the most surprising time at which God might speak? And how would you respond?

If you were amazed, would it be because God spoke, or because God spoke when everything was so normal? Just another Thursday . . . cars passing on the street as usual, or cows clumping down the lane . . . nothing different from the way things always are. But God's speaking in the midst of them: unpredictable, unexpected.

God willingly enters into our daily lives. For this is the God of the incarnation, the God of life who joins us on earth. God willingly relates to us as we wash the dishes, work in the office, travel back and forth, collect the children, work for charity, buy a lamp. For this is the God who gave Jesus to us, the God who sent the beloved Son to live with us. God willingly speaks in time and space, for this is the God who is creator: and all things, time, space, people, are the creatures of his hand.

Additional Scripture Readings:
Judges 6:11–23; Mark 1:16–20

Go to page 20 for your next
devotional reading.

and female donkeys, menservants and maidservants, and camels.

17But the LORD inflicted serious diseases on Pharaoh and his household because of Abram's wife Sarai. 18So Pharaoh summoned Abram. "What have you done to me?" he said. "Why didn't you tell me she was your wife? 19Why did you say, 'She is my sister,' so that I took her to be my wife? Now then, here is your wife. Take her and go!" 20Then Pharaoh gave orders about Abram to his men, and they sent him on his way, with his wife and everything he had.

Abram and Lot Separate

13 So Abram went up from Egypt to the Negev, with his wife and everything he had, and Lot went with him. 2Abram had become very wealthy in livestock and in silver and gold.

3From the Negev he went from place to place until he came to Bethel, to the place between Bethel and Ai where his tent had been earlier 4and where he had first built an altar. There Abram called on the name of the LORD.

5Now Lot, who was moving about with Abram, also had flocks and herds and tents. 6But the land could not support them while they stayed together, for their possessions were so great that they were not able to stay together. 7And quarreling arose between Abram's herdsmen and the herdsmen of Lot. The Canaanites and Perizzites were also living in the land at that time.

8So Abram said to Lot, "Let's not have any quarreling between you and me, or between your herdsmen and mine, for we are brothers. 9Is not the whole land before you? Let's part company. If you go to the left, I'll go to the right; if you go to the right, I'll go to the left."

10Lot looked up and saw that the whole plain of the Jordan was well watered, like the garden of the LORD, like the land of Egypt, toward Zoar. (This was before the LORD destroyed Sodom and Gomorrah.) 11So Lot chose for himself the whole plain of the Jordan and set out toward the east. The two men parted company: 12Abram lived in the land of Canaan, while Lot lived among the cities of the plain and pitched his tents near Sodom. 13Now the men of Sodom were wicked and were sinning greatly against the LORD.

14The LORD said to Abram after Lot had parted from him, "Lift up your eyes from where you are and look north and south, east and west. 15All the land that you see I will give to you and your offspring[a] forever. 16I will make your offspring like the dust of the earth, so that if anyone could count the dust, then your offspring could be counted. 17Go, walk through the length and breadth of the land, for I am giving it to you."

18So Abram moved his tents and went to live near the great trees of Mamre at Hebron, where he built an altar to the LORD.

Abram Rescues Lot

14 At this time Amraphel king of Shinar,[b] Arioch king of Ellasar, Kedorlaomer king of Elam and Tidal king of Goiim 2went to war against Bera king of Sodom, Birsha king of Gomorrah, Shinab king of Admah, Shemeber king of Zeboiim, and the king of Bela (that is, Zoar). 3All these latter kings joined forces in the Valley of Siddim (the Salt Sea[c]). 4For twelve years they had been subject to Kedorlaomer, but in the thirteenth year they rebelled.

5In the fourteenth year, Kedorlaomer and the kings allied with him went out and defeated the Rephaites in Ashteroth Karnaim, the Zuzites in Ham, the Emites in Shaveh Kiriathaim 6and the Horites in the hill country of Seir, as far as El Paran near the desert. 7Then they turned back and went to En Mishpat (that is, Kadesh), and they conquered the whole territory of the Amalekites, as well as the Amorites who were living in Hazazon Tamar.

8Then the king of Sodom, the king of Gomorrah, the king of Admah, the king of Zeboiim and the king of Bela (that is, Zoar) marched out and drew up their battle lines in the Valley of Siddim 9against Kedorlaomer king of Elam, Tidal king of Goiim, Amraphel king of Shinar and Arioch king of Ellasar—four kings against five. 10Now the Valley of Siddim was full of tar pits, and when the kings of Sodom and Gomorrah fled, some of the men fell into them and the rest fled to the hills. 11The four kings seized all the goods of Sodom and Gomorrah and all their food; then they went away. 12They also carried off Abram's nephew Lot and his possessions, since he was living in Sodom.

13One who had escaped came and reported this to Abram the Hebrew. Now

a15 Or seed; also in verse 16   b1 That is, Babylonia; also in verse 9   c3 That is, the Dead Sea

Abram was living near the great trees of Mamre the Amorite, a brother*a* of Eshcol and Aner, all of whom were allied with Abram. 14When Abram heard that his relative had been taken captive, he called out the 318 trained men born in his household and went in pursuit as far as Dan. 15During the night Abram divided his men to attack them and he routed them, pursuing them as far as Hobah, north of Damascus. 16He recovered all the goods and brought back his relative Lot and his possessions, together with the women and the other people.

17After Abram returned from defeating Kedorlaomer and the kings allied with him, the king of Sodom came out to meet him in the Valley of Shaveh (that is, the King's Valley).

18Then Melchizedek king of Salem*b* brought out bread and wine. He was priest of God Most High, 19and he blessed Abram, saying,

"Blessed be Abram by God Most
     High,
     Creator*c* of heaven and earth.
20And blessed be*d* God Most High,
     who delivered your enemies into
         your hand."

Then Abram gave him a tenth of everything.

21The king of Sodom said to Abram, "Give me the people and keep the goods for yourself."

22But Abram said to the king of Sodom, "I have raised my hand to the LORD, God Most High, Creator of heaven and earth, and have taken an oath 23that I will accept nothing belonging to you, not even a thread or the thong of a sandal, so that you will never be able to say, 'I made Abram rich.' 24I will accept nothing but what my men have eaten and the share that belongs to the men who went with me—to Aner, Eshcol and Mamre. Let them have their share."

God's Covenant With Abram

15 After this, the word of the LORD came to Abram in a vision:

"Do not be afraid, Abram.
     I am your shield,*e*
     your very great reward.*f*"

2But Abram said, "O Sovereign LORD, what can you give me since I remain childless and the one who will inherit*g* my estate is Eliezer of Damascus?" 3And Abram said, "You have given me no children; so a servant in my household will be my heir."

4Then the word of the LORD came to him: "This man will not be your heir, but a son coming from your own body will be your heir." 5He took him outside and said, "Look up at the heavens and count the stars—if indeed you can count them." Then he said to him, "So shall your offspring be."

6Abram believed the LORD, and he credited it to him as righteousness.

7He also said to him, "I am the LORD, who brought you out of Ur of the Chaldeans to give you this land to take possession of it."

8But Abram said, "O Sovereign LORD, how can I know that I will gain possession of it?"

9So the LORD said to him, "Bring me a heifer, a goat and a ram, each three years old, along with a dove and a young pigeon."

10Abram brought all these to him, cut them in two and arranged the halves opposite each other; the birds, however, he did not cut in half. 11Then birds of prey came down on the carcasses, but Abram drove them away.

12As the sun was setting, Abram fell into a deep sleep, and a thick and dreadful darkness came over him. 13Then the LORD said to him, "Know for certain that your descendants will be strangers in a country not their own, and they will be enslaved and mistreated four hundred years. 14But I will punish the nation they serve as slaves, and afterward they will come out with great possessions. 15You, however, will go to your fathers in peace and be buried at a good old age. 16In the fourth generation your descendants will come back here, for the sin of the Amorites has not yet reached its full measure."

17When the sun had set and darkness had fallen, a smoking firepot with a blazing torch appeared and passed between the pieces. 18On that day the LORD made a covenant with Abram and said, "To your descendants I give this land, from the river*h* of Egypt to the great river, the Eu-

---

a13 Or *a relative;* or *an ally*   *b18* That is, Jerusalem   *c19* Or *Possessor;* also in verse 22   *d20* Or
And praise be to   *e1* Or *sovereign*   *f1* Or *shield; / your reward will be very great*   *g2* The meaning
of the Hebrew for this phrase is uncertain.   *h18* Or *Wadi*

phrates— ¹⁹the land of the Kenites, Kenizzites, Kadmonites, ²⁰Hittites, Perizzites, Rephaites, ²¹Amorites, Canaanites, Girgashites and Jebusites."

Hagar and Ishmael

16 Now Sarai, Abram's wife, had borne him no children. But she had an Egyptian maidservant named Hagar; ²so she said to Abram, "The LORD has kept me from having children. Go, sleep with my maidservant; perhaps I can build a family through her."

Abram agreed to what Sarai said. ³So after Abram had been living in Canaan ten years, Sarai his wife took her Egyptian maidservant Hagar and gave her to her husband to be his wife. ⁴He slept with Hagar, and she conceived.

When she knew she was pregnant, she began to despise her mistress. ⁵Then Sarai said to Abram, "You are responsible for the wrong I am suffering. I put my servant in your arms, and now that she knows she is pregnant, she despises me. May the LORD judge between you and me."

⁶"Your servant is in your hands," Abram said. "Do with her whatever you think best." Then Sarai mistreated Hagar; so she fled from her.

⁷The angel of the LORD found Hagar near a spring in the desert; it was the spring that is beside the road to Shur. ⁸And he said, "Hagar, servant of Sarai, where have you come from, and where are you going?"

"I'm running away from my mistress Sarai," she answered.

⁹Then the angel of the LORD told her, "Go back to your mistress and submit to her." ¹⁰The angel added, "I will so increase your descendants that they will be too numerous to count."

¹¹The angel of the LORD also said to her:

"You are now with child
  and you will have a son.
You shall name him Ishmael,ᵃ
  for the LORD has heard of your
    misery.
¹²He will be a wild donkey of a man;
  his hand will be against everyone
  and everyone's hand against him,
  and he will live in hostility
    towardᵇ all his brothers."

¹³She gave this name to the LORD who spoke to her: "You are the God who sees me," for she said, "I have now seenᶜ the One who sees me." ¹⁴That is why the well was called Beer Lahai Roiᵈ; it is still there, between Kadesh and Bered.

¹⁵So Hagar bore Abram a son, and Abram gave the name Ishmael to the son she had borne. ¹⁶Abram was eighty-six years old when Hagar bore him Ishmael.

The Covenant of Circumcision

17 When Abram was ninety-nine years old, the LORD appeared to him and said, "I am God Almightyᵉ; walk before me and be blameless. ²I will confirm my covenant between me and you and will greatly increase your numbers."

³Abram fell facedown, and God said to him, ⁴"As for me, this is my covenant with you: You will be the father of many nations. ⁵No longer will you be called Abramᶠ; your name will be Abraham,ᵍ for I have made you a father of many nations. ⁶I will make you very fruitful; I will make nations of you, and kings will come from you. ⁷I will establish my covenant as an everlasting covenant between me and you and your descendants after you for the generations to come, to be your God and the God of your descendants after you. ⁸The whole land of Canaan, where you are now an alien, I will give as an everlasting possession to you and your descendants after you; and I will be their God."

⁹Then God said to Abraham, "As for you, you must keep my covenant, you and your descendants after you for the generations to come. ¹⁰This is my covenant with you and your descendants after you, the covenant you are to keep: Every male among you shall be circumcised. ¹¹You are to undergo circumcision, and it will be the sign of the covenant between me and you. ¹²For the generations to come every male among you who is eight days old must be circumcised, including those born in your household or bought with money from a foreigner—those who are not your offspring. ¹³Whether born in your household or bought with your money, they must be circumcised. My covenant in your flesh is to be an everlasting covenant. ¹⁴Any uncircumcised male, who has not been circumcised in the

---

ᵃ11 Ishmael means God hears.   ᵇ12 Or live to the east / of   ᶜ13 Or seen the back of   ᵈ14 Beer Lahai Roi means well of the Living One who sees me.   ᵉ1 Hebrew El-Shaddai   ᶠ5 Abram means exalted father.   ᵍ5 Abraham means father of many.

VERSE FOR THE DAY:
Genesis 18:14

AUTHOR:
Gladys M. Hunt

PASSAGE FOR THE DAY:
Genesis 16:1–16 and 18:1–15

Waiting for God

"HOPE deferred makes the heart sick," says Proverbs 13:12. Believing that God will do what he says is quite different from waiting for him to do it. Waiting is hard, but believing while waiting is harder still.

That's why people take things into their own hands. I think of a woman I knew who really believed God's instructions about Christians not being unequally yoked with unbelievers. She said she believed God would bring a man of his choice into her life. She could trust him to do this. But time went on and on and on. No man came into her life; she got tired of waiting for God. She wanted to marry and so she did. She stopped believing that God could do it; she did it herself, and the marriage had all the marks of a do-it-yourself project.

In Genesis 16 we find that Sarah got tired of waiting for God. She took matters into her own hands. I suppose, being human, we'd be slow to blame her. She really had waited a long, long time and was getting older every day. She set up a surrogate mother plan. Hagar would bear a child, and God would have the help he needed to get a son for Abraham.

Jealousy cropped up early. Sarah blamed Abraham for the bad decision. Pregnant Hagar was too much for Sarah, and Sarah mistreated Hagar until she fled to the desert. God was not unaware; he heard Hagar weeping and if Hagar learned nothing else, she found out that God knew all about her and cared.

Sarah's decision to take matters into her own hands has had far-reaching consequences. Ishmael was not the son God had promised. God had not forgotten; he had a timetable in mind. Several years later he gave Sarah a son, unquestionably a miracle. The very thought of it so embarrassed Sarah that she laughed at the Lord's announcement (Genesis 18:12).

Hearing her laughter, the Lord asked a memorable question: "Is anything too hard for the Lord?" Is anything? Can God accomplish in our lives what he knows is best?

These two women instruct us. God knows how far we've progressed in our hopes and dreams. He hears our weeping. Hagar can tell us that. And Sarah, what would she say to us? "Don't mess up your life with do-it-yourself projects when God has promised the very best for you."

Additional Scripture Readings:
1 Samuel 13:5–14; Hebrews 6:10–15

Go to page 24 for your next devotional reading.

flesh, will be cut off from his people; he has broken my covenant."

¹⁵God also said to Abraham, "As for Sarai your wife, you are no longer to call her Sarai; her name will be Sarah. ¹⁶I will bless her and will surely give you a son by her. I will bless her so that she will be the mother of nations; kings of peoples will come from her."

¹⁷Abraham fell facedown; he laughed and said to himself, "Will a son be born to a man a hundred years old? Will Sarah bear a child at the age of ninety?" ¹⁸And Abraham said to God, "If only Ishmael might live under your blessing!"

¹⁹Then God said, "Yes, but your wife Sarah will bear you a son, and you will call him Isaac.ᵃ I will establish my covenant with him as an everlasting covenant for his descendants after him. ²⁰And as for Ishmael, I have heard you: I will surely bless him; I will make him fruitful and will greatly increase his numbers. He will be the father of twelve rulers, and I will make him into a great nation. ²¹But my covenant I will establish with Isaac, whom Sarah will bear to you by this time next year." ²²When he had finished speaking with Abraham, God went up from him.

²³On that very day Abraham took his son Ishmael and all those born in his household or bought with his money, every male in his household, and circumcised them, as God told him. ²⁴Abraham was ninety-nine years old when he was circumcised, ²⁵and his son Ishmael was thirteen; ²⁶Abraham and his son Ishmael were both circumcised on that same day. ²⁷And every male in Abraham's household, including those born in his household or bought from a foreigner, was circumcised with him.

The Three Visitors

18 The LORD appeared to Abraham near the great trees of Mamre while he was sitting at the entrance to his tent in the heat of the day. ²Abraham looked up and saw three men standing nearby. When he saw them, he hurried from the entrance of his tent to meet them and bowed low to the ground.

³He said, "If I have found favor in your eyes, my lord,ᵇ do not pass your servant by. ⁴Let a little water be brought, and then you may all wash your feet and rest

under this tree. ⁵Let me get you something to eat, so you can be refreshed and then go on your way—now that you have come to your servant."

"Very well," they answered, "do as you say."

⁶So Abraham hurried into the tent to Sarah. "Quick," he said, "get three seahsᶜ of fine flour and knead it and bake some bread."

⁷Then he ran to the herd and selected a choice, tender calf and gave it to a servant, who hurried to prepare it. ⁸He then brought some curds and milk and the calf that had been prepared, and set these before them. While they ate, he stood near them under a tree.

⁹"Where is your wife Sarah?" they asked him.

"There, in the tent," he said.

¹⁰Then the LORDᵈ said, "I will surely return to you about this time next year, and Sarah your wife will have a son."

Now Sarah was listening at the entrance to the tent, which was behind him. ¹¹Abraham and Sarah were already old and well advanced in years, and Sarah was past the age of childbearing. ¹²So Sarah laughed to herself as she thought, "After I am worn out and my masterᵉ is old, will I now have this pleasure?"

¹³Then the LORD said to Abraham, "Why did Sarah laugh and say, 'Will I really have a child, now that I am old?' ¹⁴Is anything too hard for the LORD? I will return to you at the appointed time next year and Sarah will have a son."

¹⁵Sarah was afraid, so she lied and said, "I did not laugh."

But he said, "Yes, you did laugh."

Abraham Pleads for Sodom

¹⁶When the men got up to leave, they looked down toward Sodom, and Abraham walked along with them to see them on their way. ¹⁷Then the LORD said, "Shall I hide from Abraham what I am about to do? ¹⁸Abraham will surely become a great and powerful nation, and all nations on earth will be blessed through him. ¹⁹For I have chosen him, so that he will direct his children and his household after him to keep the way of the LORD by doing what is right and just, so that the LORD will bring about for Abraham what he has promised him."

²⁰Then the LORD said, "The outcry

ᵃ19 *Isaac* means *he laughs.*   ᵇ3 Or *O Lord*   ᶜ6 That is, probably about 20 quarts (about 22 liters)
ᵈ10 Hebrew *Then he*   ᵉ12 Or *husband*

against Sodom and Gomorrah is so great and their sin so grievous ²¹that I will go down and see if what they have done is as bad as the outcry that has reached me. If not, I will know."

²²The men turned away and went toward Sodom, but Abraham remained standing before the LORD.ª ²³Then Abraham approached him and said: "Will you sweep away the righteous with the wicked? ²⁴What if there are fifty righteous people in the city? Will you really sweep it away and not spareᵇ the place for the sake of the fifty righteous people in it? ²⁵Far be it from you to do such a thing—to kill the righteous with the wicked, treating the righteous and the wicked alike. Far be it from you! Will not the Judgeᶜ of all the earth do right?"

²⁶The LORD said, "If I find fifty righteous people in the city of Sodom, I will spare the whole place for their sake."

²⁷Then Abraham spoke up again: "Now that I have been so bold as to speak to the Lord, though I am nothing but dust and ashes, ²⁸what if the number of the righteous is five less than fifty? Will you destroy the whole city because of five people?"

"If I find forty-five there," he said, "I will not destroy it."

²⁹Once again he spoke to him, "What if only forty are found there?"

He said, "For the sake of forty, I will not do it."

³⁰Then he said, "May the Lord not be angry, but let me speak. What if only thirty can be found there?"

He answered, "I will not do it if I find thirty there."

³¹Abraham said, "Now that I have been so bold as to speak to the Lord, what if only twenty can be found there?"

He said, "For the sake of twenty, I will not destroy it."

³²Then he said, "May the Lord not be angry, but let me speak just once more. What if only ten can be found there?"

He answered, "For the sake of ten, I will not destroy it."

³³When the LORD had finished speaking with Abraham, he left, and Abraham returned home.

Sodom and Gomorrah Destroyed

19 The two angels arrived at Sodom in the evening, and Lot was sitting in the gateway of the city. When he saw them, he got up to meet them and bowed down with his face to the ground. ²"My lords," he said, "please turn aside to your servant's house. You can wash your feet and spend the night and then go on your way early in the morning."

"No," they answered, "we will spend the night in the square."

³But he insisted so strongly that they did go with him and entered his house. He prepared a meal for them, baking bread without yeast, and they ate. ⁴Before they had gone to bed, all the men from every part of the city of Sodom—both young and old—surrounded the house. ⁵They called to Lot, "Where are the men who came to you tonight? Bring them out to us so that we can have sex with them."

⁶Lot went outside to meet them and shut the door behind him ⁷and said, "No, my friends. Don't do this wicked thing. ⁸Look, I have two daughters who have never slept with a man. Let me bring them out to you, and you can do what you like with them. But don't do anything to these men, for they have come under the protection of my roof."

⁹"Get out of our way," they replied. And they said, "This fellow came here as an alien, and now he wants to play the judge! We'll treat you worse than them." They kept bringing pressure on Lot and moved forward to break down the door.

¹⁰But the men inside reached out and pulled Lot back into the house and shut the door. ¹¹Then they struck the men who were at the door of the house, young and old, with blindness so that they could not find the door.

¹²The two men said to Lot, "Do you have anyone else here—sons-in-law, sons or daughters, or anyone else in the city who belongs to you? Get them out of here, ¹³because we are going to destroy this place. The outcry to the LORD against its people is so great that he has sent us to destroy it."

¹⁴So Lot went out and spoke to his sons-in-law, who were pledged to marryᵈ his daughters. He said, "Hurry and get out of this place, because the LORD is about to destroy the city!" But his sons-in-law thought he was joking.

¹⁵With the coming of dawn, the angels urged Lot, saying, "Hurry! Take your wife and your two daughters who are here, or

ª22 Masoretic Text; an ancient Hebrew scribal tradition *but the LORD remained standing before Abraham*   ᵇ24 Or *forgive*; also in verse 26   ᶜ25 Or *Ruler*   ᵈ14 Or *were married to* you will be swept away when the city is punished."

¹⁶When he hesitated, the men grasped his hand and the hands of his wife and of his two daughters and led them safely out of the city, for the LORD was merciful to them. ¹⁷As soon as they had brought them out, one of them said, "Flee for your lives! Don't look back, and don't stop anywhere in the plain! Flee to the mountains or you will be swept away!"

¹⁸But Lot said to them, "No, my lords,ᵃ please! ¹⁹Yourᵇ servant has found favor in yourᵇ eyes, and youᵇ have shown great kindness to me in sparing my life. But I can't flee to the mountains; this disaster will overtake me, and I'll die. ²⁰Look, here is a town near enough to run to, and it is small. Let me flee to it—it is very small, isn't it? Then my life will be spared."

²¹He said to him, "Very well, I will grant this request too; I will not overthrow the town you speak of. ²²But flee there quickly, because I cannot do anything until you reach it." (That is why the town was called Zoar.ᶜ)

²³By the time Lot reached Zoar, the sun had risen over the land. ²⁴Then the LORD rained down burning sulfur on Sodom and Gomorrah—from the LORD out of the heavens. ²⁵Thus he overthrew those cities and the entire plain, including all those living in the cities—and also the vegetation in the land. ²⁶But Lot's wife looked back, and she became a pillar of salt.

²⁷Early the next morning Abraham got up and returned to the place where he had stood before the LORD. ²⁸He looked down toward Sodom and Gomorrah, toward all the land of the plain, and he saw dense smoke rising from the land, like smoke from a furnace.

²⁹So when God destroyed the cities of the plain, he remembered Abraham, and he brought Lot out of the catastrophe that overthrew the cities where Lot had lived.

Lot and His Daughters

³⁰Lot and his two daughters left Zoar and settled in the mountains, for he was afraid to stay in Zoar. He and his two daughters lived in a cave. ³¹One day the older daughter said to the younger, "Our father is old, and there is no man around here to lie with us, as is the custom all over the earth. ³²Let's get our father to drink wine and then lie with him and preserve our family line through our father."

³³That night they got their father to drink wine, and the older daughter went in and lay with him. He was not aware of it when she lay down or when she got up.

³⁴The next day the older daughter said to the younger, "Last night I lay with my father. Let's get him to drink wine again tonight, and you go in and lie with him so we can preserve our family line through our father." ³⁵So they got their father to drink wine that night also, and the younger daughter went and lay with him. Again he was not aware of it when she lay down or when she got up.

³⁶So both of Lot's daughters became pregnant by their father. ³⁷The older daughter had a son, and she named him Moabᵈ; he is the father of the Moabites of today. ³⁸The younger daughter also had a son, and she named him Ben-Ammiᵉ; he is the father of the Ammonites of today.

Abraham and Abimelech

20 Now Abraham moved on from there into the region of the Negev and lived between Kadesh and Shur. For a while he stayed in Gerar, ²and there Abraham said of his wife Sarah, "She is my sister." Then Abimelech king of Gerar sent for Sarah and took her.

³But God came to Abimelech in a dream one night and said to him, "You are as good as dead because of the woman you have taken; she is a married woman."

⁴Now Abimelech had not gone near her, so he said, "Lord, will you destroy an innocent nation? ⁵Did he not say to me, 'She is my sister,' and didn't she also say, 'He is my brother'? I have done this with a clear conscience and clean hands."

⁶Then God said to him in the dream, "Yes, I know you did this with a clear conscience, and so I have kept you from sinning against me. That is why I did not let you touch her. ⁷Now return the man's wife, for he is a prophet, and he will pray for you and you will live. But if you do not return her, you may be sure that you and all yours will die."

⁸Early the next morning Abimelech summoned all his officials, and when he told them all that had happened, they were very much afraid. ⁹Then Abimelech

---

ᵃ18 Or No, Lord; or No, my lord   ᵇ19 The Hebrew is singular.   ᶜ22 Zoar means small.
ᵈ37 Moab sounds like the Hebrew for from father.   ᵉ38 Ben-Ammi means son of my people.

VERSE FOR THE DAY:
Genesis 19:20

AUTHOR:
Gloria Gaither

PASSAGE FOR THE DAY:
Genesis 19:1–38

Small Minds and Spirits

"FLEE for your lives," the angel said to Lot. "Flee to the mountains or you will be swept away!" But Lot wasn't a mountain-thinker. His thoughts weren't used to soaring to the heights. He wasn't one to see the value of risking a difficult climb for the ecstasy of the summit vision. Once before Lot had chosen the fertile lowlands where he could see the plushness ready-made. He had never been a friend to struggle, even if the struggle gave birth to the promise of Canaan itself. It was typical of Lot to plead with the angel to let him trade the mountain for the small place. Zoar, they afterward called it: "small place." And *Zoar* could have been written as the ensign of Lot's life. *Think Zoar* could have been the bumper sticker on his chariot, and his name could well have been changed from *Lot* to *Less*. Zoar: small little man, small dreams, small outlook, small aspirations, small faith, and small vision.

So the angel acquiesced and let Lot go where his heart was, in Zoar. But even from Zoar, Lot's wife, who shared his smallness, did exactly what the angel asked them not to do. Instead of looking upward to the mountain, she looked back toward the garbage heap of Sodom. And she turned to salt. A block of it. Salt: In its granulated form it flavors and enhances whatever it touches. Solidified, salt becomes unyielding, unmovable, and useless for flavoring food.

How like small minds and spirits to take the very flavor God commanded that we sprinkle into the world (Matthew 5:13) from the perspective of the heights and turn it into some legalistic, unbending monument to the death of the spirit. Like Lot's wife, many religious bodies stand like tombstones of salt in the lowlands of life with the ecclesiastical epitaph *Zoar.* Small minds, small dreams, small men and women, small visions. Solidified salt in the shadow of the mountain where bushes burn and voices thunder and the finger of God carves in granite the directions to freedom.

Additional Scripture Readings:
Matthew 23:23–24; Mark 6:1–6

*Go to page 46 for your next
devotional reading.*

called Abraham in and said, "What have you done to us? How have I wronged you that you have brought such great guilt upon me and my kingdom? You have done things to me that should not be done." ¹⁰And Abimelech asked Abraham, "What was your reason for doing this?"

¹¹Abraham replied, "I said to myself, 'There is surely no fear of God in this place, and they will kill me because of my wife.' ¹²Besides, she really is my sister, the daughter of my father though not of my mother; and she became my wife. ¹³And when God had me wander from my father's household, I said to her, 'This is how you can show your love to me: Everywhere we go, say of me, "He is my brother."' "

¹⁴Then Abimelech brought sheep and cattle and male and female slaves and gave them to Abraham, and he returned Sarah his wife to him. ¹⁵And Abimelech said, "My land is before you; live wherever you like."

¹⁶To Sarah he said, "I am giving your brother a thousand shekels*ᵃ* of silver. This is to cover the offense against you before all who are with you; you are completely vindicated."

¹⁷Then Abraham prayed to God, and God healed Abimelech, his wife and his slave girls so they could have children again, ¹⁸for the LORD had closed up every womb in Abimelech's household because of Abraham's wife Sarah.

The Birth of Isaac

21 Now the LORD was gracious to Sarah as he had said, and the LORD did for Sarah what he had promised. ²Sarah became pregnant and bore a son to Abraham in his old age, at the very time God had promised him. ³Abraham gave the name Isaacᵇ to the son Sarah bore him. ⁴When his son Isaac was eight days old, Abraham circumcised him, as God commanded him. ⁵Abraham was a hundred years old when his son Isaac was born to him.

⁶Sarah said, "God has brought me laughter, and everyone who hears about this will laugh with me." ⁷And she added, "Who would have said to Abraham that Sarah would nurse children? Yet I have borne him a son in his old age."

Hagar and Ishmael Sent Away

⁸The child grew and was weaned, and on the day Isaac was weaned Abraham held a great feast. ⁹But Sarah saw that the son whom Hagar the Egyptian had borne to Abraham was mocking, ¹⁰and she said to Abraham, "Get rid of that slave woman and her son, for that slave woman's son will never share in the inheritance with my son Isaac."

¹¹The matter distressed Abraham greatly because it concerned his son. ¹²But God said to him, "Do not be so distressed about the boy and your maidservant. Listen to whatever Sarah tells you, because it is through Isaac that your offspringᶜ will be reckoned. ¹³I will make the son of the maidservant into a nation also, because he is your offspring."

¹⁴Early the next morning Abraham took some food and a skin of water and gave them to Hagar. He set them on her shoulders and then sent her off with the boy. She went on her way and wandered in the desert of Beersheba.

¹⁵When the water in the skin was gone, she put the boy under one of the bushes. ¹⁶Then she went off and sat down nearby, about a bowshot away, for she thought, "I cannot watch the boy die." And as she sat there nearby, sheᵈ began to sob.

¹⁷God heard the boy crying, and the angel of God called to Hagar from heaven and said to her, "What is the matter, Hagar? Do not be afraid; God has heard the boy crying as he lies there. ¹⁸Lift the boy up and take him by the hand, for I will make him into a great nation."

¹⁹Then God opened her eyes and she saw a well of water. So she went and filled the skin with water and gave the boy a drink.

²⁰God was with the boy as he grew up. He lived in the desert and became an archer. ²¹While he was living in the Desert of Paran, his mother got a wife for him from Egypt.

The Treaty at Beersheba

²²At that time Abimelech and Phicol the commander of his forces said to Abraham, "God is with you in everything you do. ²³Now swear to me here before God that you will not deal falsely with me or my children or my descendants. Show to me and the country where you are living

ᵃ16 That is, about 25 pounds (about 11.5 kilograms)   ᵇ3 Isaac means he laughs.   ᶜ12 Or seed
ᵈ16 Hebrew; Septuagint the child

as an alien the same kindness I have shown to you."

²⁴Abraham said, "I swear it."

²⁵Then Abraham complained to Abimelech about a well of water that Abimelech's servants had seized. ²⁶But Abimelech said, "I don't know who has done this. You did not tell me, and I heard about it only today."

²⁷So Abraham brought sheep and cattle and gave them to Abimelech, and the two men made a treaty. ²⁸Abraham set apart seven ewe lambs from the flock, ²⁹and Abimelech asked Abraham, "What is the meaning of these seven ewe lambs you have set apart by themselves?"

³⁰He replied, "Accept these seven lambs from my hand as a witness that I dug this well."

³¹So that place was called Beersheba,ᵃ because the two men swore an oath there.

³²After the treaty had been made at Beersheba, Abimelech and Phicol the commander of his forces returned to the land of the Philistines. ³³Abraham planted a tamarisk tree in Beersheba, and there he called upon the name of the LORD, the Eternal God. ³⁴And Abraham stayed in the land of the Philistines for a long time.

Abraham Tested

22 Some time later God tested Abraham. He said to him, "Abraham!"

"Here I am," he replied.

²Then God said, "Take your son, your only son, Isaac, whom you love, and go to the region of Moriah. Sacrifice him there as a burnt offering on one of the mountains I will tell you about."

³Early the next morning Abraham got up and saddled his donkey. He took with him two of his servants and his son Isaac. When he had cut enough wood for the burnt offering, he set out for the place God had told him about. ⁴On the third day Abraham looked up and saw the place in the distance. ⁵He said to his servants, "Stay here with the donkey while I and the boy go over there. We will worship and then we will come back to you."

⁶Abraham took the wood for the burnt offering and placed it on his son Isaac, and he himself carried the fire and the knife. As the two of them went on togeth-

er, ⁷Isaac spoke up and said to his father Abraham, "Father?"

"Yes, my son?" Abraham replied.

"The fire and wood are here," Isaac said, "but where is the lamb for the burnt offering?"

⁸Abraham answered, "God himself will provide the lamb for the burnt offering, my son." And the two of them went on together.

⁹When they reached the place God had told him about, Abraham built an altar there and arranged the wood on it. He bound his son Isaac and laid him on the altar, on top of the wood. ¹⁰Then he reached out his hand and took the knife to slay his son. ¹¹But the angel of the LORD called out to him from heaven, "Abraham! Abraham!"

"Here I am," he replied.

¹²"Do not lay a hand on the boy," he said. "Do not do anything to him. Now I know that you fear God, because you have not withheld from me your son, your only son."

¹³Abraham looked up and there in a thicket he saw a ramᵇ caught by its horns. He went over and took the ram and sacrificed it as a burnt offering instead of his son. ¹⁴So Abraham called that place The LORD Will Provide. And to this day it is said, "On the mountain of the LORD it will be provided."

¹⁵The angel of the LORD called to Abraham from heaven a second time ¹⁶and said, "I swear by myself, declares the LORD, that because you have done this and have not withheld your son, your only son, ¹⁷I will surely bless you and make your descendants as numerous as the stars in the sky and as the sand on the seashore. Your descendants will take possession of the cities of their enemies, ¹⁸and through your offspringᶜ all nations on earth will be blessed, because you have obeyed me."

¹⁹Then Abraham returned to his servants, and they set off together for Beersheba. And Abraham stayed in Beersheba.

Nahor's Sons

²⁰Some time later Abraham was told, "Milcah is also a mother; she has borne sons to your brother Nahor: ²¹Uz the firstborn, Buz his brother, Kemuel (the father

---

ᵃ31 Beersheba can mean well of seven or well of the oath.   ᵇ13 Many manuscripts of the Masoretic Text, Samaritan Pentateuch, Septuagint and Syriac; most manuscripts of the Masoretic Text a ram behind him,   ᶜ18 Or seed of Aram), ²²Kesed, Hazo, Pildash, Jidlaph and Bethuel." ²³Bethuel became the father of Rebekah. Milcah bore these eight sons to Abraham's brother Nahor. ²⁴His concubine, whose name was Reumah, also had sons: Tebah, Gaham, Tahash and Maacah.

The Death of Sarah

23 Sarah lived to be a hundred and twenty-seven years old. ²She died at Kiriath Arba (that is, Hebron) in the land of Canaan, and Abraham went to mourn for Sarah and to weep over her.

³Then Abraham rose from beside his dead wife and spoke to the Hittites.^a He said, ⁴"I am an alien and a stranger among you. Sell me some property for a burial site here so I can bury my dead."

⁵The Hittites replied to Abraham, ⁶"Sir, listen to us. You are a mighty prince among us. Bury your dead in the choicest of our tombs. None of us will refuse you his tomb for burying your dead."

⁷Then Abraham rose and bowed down before the people of the land, the Hittites. ⁸He said to them, "If you are willing to let me bury my dead, then listen to me and intercede with Ephron son of Zohar on my behalf ⁹so he will sell me the cave of Machpelah, which belongs to him and is at the end of his field. Ask him to sell it to me for the full price as a burial site among you."

¹⁰Ephron the Hittite was sitting among his people and he replied to Abraham in the hearing of all the Hittites who had come to the gate of his city. ¹¹"No, my lord," he said. "Listen to me; I give^b you the field, and I give^b you the cave that is in it. I give^b it to you in the presence of my people. Bury your dead."

¹²Again Abraham bowed down before the people of the land ¹³and he said to Ephron in their hearing, "Listen to me, if you will. I will pay the price of the field. Accept it from me so I can bury my dead there."

¹⁴Ephron answered Abraham, ¹⁵"Listen to me, my lord; the land is worth four hundred shekels^c of silver, but what is that between me and you? Bury your dead."

¹⁶Abraham agreed to Ephron's terms and weighed out for him the price he had named in the hearing of the Hittites: four hundred shekels of silver, according to the weight current among the merchants. ¹⁷So Ephron's field in Machpelah near Mamre—both the field and the cave in it, and all the trees within the borders of the field—was deeded ¹⁸to Abraham as his property in the presence of all the Hittites who had come to the gate of the city. ¹⁹Afterward Abraham buried his wife Sarah in the cave in the field of Machpelah near Mamre (which is at Hebron) in the land of Canaan. ²⁰So the field and the cave in it were deeded to Abraham by the Hittites as a burial site.

Isaac and Rebekah

24 Abraham was now old and well advanced in years, and the LORD had blessed him in every way. ²He said to the chief^d servant in his household, the one in charge of all that he had, "Put your hand under my thigh. ³I want you to swear by the LORD, the God of heaven and the God of earth, that you will not get a wife for my son from the daughters of the Canaanites, among whom I am living, ⁴but will go to my country and my own relatives and get a wife for my son Isaac."

⁵The servant asked him, "What if the woman is unwilling to come back with me to this land? Shall I then take your son back to the country you came from?"

⁶"Make sure that you do not take my son back there," Abraham said. ⁷"The LORD, the God of heaven, who brought me out of my father's household and my native land and who spoke to me and promised me on oath, saying, 'To your offspring^e I will give this land'—he will send his angel before you so that you can get a wife for my son from there. ⁸If the woman is unwilling to come back with you, then you will be released from this oath of mine. Only do not take my son back there." ⁹So the servant put his hand under the thigh of his master Abraham and swore an oath to him concerning this matter.

¹⁰Then the servant took ten of his master's camels and left, taking with him all kinds of good things from his master. He set out for Aram Naharaim^f and made his way to the town of Nahor. ¹¹He had the camels kneel down near the well outside the town; it was toward evening, the time the women go out to draw water.

¹²Then he prayed, "O LORD, God of my master Abraham, give me success today,

---

^a3 Or *the sons of Heth*; also in verses 5, 7, 10, 16, 18 and 20   ^b11 Or *sell*   ^c15 That is, about 10 pounds (about 4.5 kilograms)   ^d2 Or *oldest*   ^e7 Or *seed*   ^f10 That is, Northwest Mesopotamia

and show kindness to my master Abraham. ¹³See, I am standing beside this spring, and the daughters of the townspeople are coming out to draw water. ¹⁴May it be that when I say to a girl, 'Please let down your jar that I may have a drink,' and she says, 'Drink, and I'll water your camels too'—let her be the one you have chosen for your servant Isaac. By this I will know that you have shown kindness to my master."

¹⁵Before he had finished praying, Rebekah came out with her jar on her shoulder. She was the daughter of Bethuel son of Milcah, who was the wife of Abraham's brother Nahor. ¹⁶The girl was very beautiful, a virgin; no man had ever lain with her. She went down to the spring, filled her jar and came up again.

¹⁷The servant hurried to meet her and said, "Please give me a little water from your jar."

¹⁸"Drink, my lord," she said, and quickly lowered the jar to her hands and gave him a drink.

¹⁹After she had given him a drink, she said, "I'll draw water for your camels too, until they have finished drinking." ²⁰So she quickly emptied her jar into the trough, ran back to the well to draw more water, and drew enough for all his camels. ²¹Without saying a word, the man watched her closely to learn whether or not the LORD had made his journey successful.

²²When the camels had finished drinking, the man took out a gold nose ring weighing a beka*ᵃ* and two gold bracelets weighing ten shekels.*ᵇ* ²³Then he asked, "Whose daughter are you? Please tell me, is there room in your father's house for us to spend the night?"

²⁴She answered him, "I am the daughter of Bethuel, the son that Milcah bore to Nahor." ²⁵And she added, "We have plenty of straw and fodder, as well as room for you to spend the night."

²⁶Then the man bowed down and worshiped the LORD, ²⁷saying, "Praise be to the LORD, the God of my master Abraham, who has not abandoned his kindness and faithfulness to my master. As for me, the LORD has led me on the journey to the house of my master's relatives."

²⁸The girl ran and told her mother's household about these things. ²⁹Now Rebekah had a brother named Laban, and

he hurried out to the man at the spring. ³⁰As soon as he had seen the nose ring, and the bracelets on his sister's arms, and had heard Rebekah tell what the man said to her, he went out to the man and found him standing by the camels near the spring. ³¹"Come, you who are blessed by the LORD," he said. "Why are you standing out here? I have prepared the house and a place for the camels."

³²So the man went to the house, and the camels were unloaded. Straw and fodder were brought for the camels, and water for him and his men to wash their feet. ³³Then food was set before him, but he said, "I will not eat until I have told you what I have to say."

"Then tell us," Laban said.

³⁴So he said, "I am Abraham's servant. ³⁵The LORD has blessed my master abundantly, and he has become wealthy. He has given him sheep and cattle, silver and gold, menservants and maidservants, and camels and donkeys. ³⁶My master's wife Sarah has borne him a son in her*ᶜ* old age, and he has given him everything he owns. ³⁷And my master made me swear an oath, and said, 'You must not get a wife for my son from the daughters of the Canaanites, in whose land I live, ³⁸but go to my father's family and to my own clan, and get a wife for my son.'

³⁹"Then I asked my master, 'What if the woman will not come back with me?'

⁴⁰"He replied, 'The LORD, before whom I have walked, will send his angel with you and make your journey a success, so that you can get a wife for my son from my own clan and from my father's family. ⁴¹Then, when you go to my clan, you will be released from my oath even if they refuse to give her to you—you will be released from my oath.'

⁴²"When I came to the spring today, I said, 'O LORD, God of my master Abraham, if you will, please grant success to the journey on which I have come. ⁴³See, I am standing beside this spring; if a maiden comes out to draw water and I say to her, "Please let me drink a little water from your jar," ⁴⁴and if she says to me, "Drink, and I'll draw water for your camels too," let her be the one the LORD has chosen for my master's son.'

⁴⁵"Before I finished praying in my heart, Rebekah came out, with her jar on her shoulder. She went down to the

---

ᵃ22 That is, about 1/5 ounce (about 5.5 grams)   *ᵇ22* That is, about 4 ounces (about 110 grams)   *ᶜ36* Or *his* spring and drew water, and I said to her, 'Please give me a drink.'

46"She quickly lowered her jar from her shoulder and said, 'Drink, and I'll water your camels too.' So I drank, and she watered the camels also.

47"I asked her, 'Whose daughter are you?'

"She said, 'The daughter of Bethuel son of Nahor, whom Milcah bore to him.'

"Then I put the ring in her nose and the bracelets on her arms, 48and I bowed down and worshiped the LORD. I praised the LORD, the God of my master Abraham, who had led me on the right road to get the granddaughter of my master's brother for his son. 49Now if you will show kindness and faithfulness to my master, tell me; and if not, tell me, so I may know which way to turn."

50Laban and Bethuel answered, "This is from the LORD; we can say nothing to you one way or the other. 51Here is Rebekah; take her and go, and let her become the wife of your master's son, as the LORD has directed."

52When Abraham's servant heard what they said, he bowed down to the ground before the LORD. 53Then the servant brought out gold and silver jewelry and articles of clothing and gave them to Rebekah; he also gave costly gifts to her brother and to her mother. 54Then he and the men who were with him ate and drank and spent the night there.

When they got up the next morning, he said, "Send me on my way to my master."

55But her brother and her mother replied, "Let the girl remain with us ten days or so; then you*a* may go."

56But he said to them, "Do not detain me, now that the LORD has granted success to my journey. Send me on my way so I may go to my master."

57Then they said, "Let's call the girl and ask her about it." 58So they called Rebekah and asked her, "Will you go with this man?"

"I will go," she said.

59So they sent their sister Rebekah on her way, along with her nurse and Abraham's servant and his men. 60And they blessed Rebekah and said to her,

"Our sister, may you increase
    to thousands upon thousands;
may your offspring possess

the gates of their enemies."

61Then Rebekah and her maids got ready and mounted their camels and went back with the man. So the servant took Rebekah and left.

62Now Isaac had come from Beer Lahai Roi, for he was living in the Negev. 63He went out to the field one evening to meditate,*b* and as he looked up, he saw camels approaching. 64Rebekah also looked up and saw Isaac. She got down from her camel 65and asked the servant, "Who is that man in the field coming to meet us?"

"He is my master," the servant answered. So she took her veil and covered herself.

66Then the servant told Isaac all he had done. 67Isaac brought her into the tent of his mother Sarah, and he married Rebekah. So she became his wife, and he loved her; and Isaac was comforted after his mother's death.

The Death of Abraham

25 Abraham took*c* another wife, whose name was Keturah. 2She bore him Zimran, Jokshan, Medan, Midian, Ishbak and Shuah. 3Jokshan was the father of Sheba and Dedan; the descendants of Dedan were the Asshurites, the Letushites and the Leummites. 4The sons of Midian were Ephah, Epher, Hanoch, Abida and Eldaah. All these were descendants of Keturah.

5Abraham left everything he owned to Isaac. 6But while he was still living, he gave gifts to the sons of his concubines and sent them away from his son Isaac to the land of the east.

7Altogether, Abraham lived a hundred and seventy-five years. 8Then Abraham breathed his last and died at a good old age, an old man and full of years; and he was gathered to his people. 9His sons Isaac and Ishmael buried him in the cave of Machpelah near Mamre, in the field of Ephron son of Zohar the Hittite, 10the field Abraham had bought from the Hittites.*d* There Abraham was buried with his wife Sarah. 11After Abraham's death, God blessed his son Isaac, who then lived near Beer Lahai Roi.

Ishmael's Sons

12This is the account of Abraham's son

---

*a55 Or she   b63 The meaning of the Hebrew for this word is uncertain.   c1 Or had taken
d10 Or the sons of Heth

Ishmael, whom Sarah's maidservant, Hagar the Egyptian, bore to Abraham.

[13]These are the names of the sons of Ishmael, listed in the order of their birth: Nebaioth the firstborn of Ishmael, Kedar, Adbeel, Mibsam, [14]Mishma, Dumah, Massa, [15]Hadad, Tema, Jetur, Naphish and Kedemah. [16]These were the sons of Ishmael, and these are the names of the twelve tribal rulers according to their settlements and camps. [17]Altogether, Ishmael lived a hundred and thirty-seven years. He breathed his last and died, and he was gathered to his people. [18]His descendants settled in the area from Havilah to Shur, near the border of Egypt, as you go toward Asshur. And they lived in hostility toward[a] all their brothers.

Jacob and Esau

[19]This is the account of Abraham's son Isaac.

Abraham became the father of Isaac, [20]and Isaac was forty years old when he married Rebekah daughter of Bethuel the Aramean from Paddan Aram[b] and sister of Laban the Aramean.

[21]Isaac prayed to the LORD on behalf of his wife, because she was barren. The LORD answered his prayer, and his wife Rebekah became pregnant. [22]The babies jostled each other within her, and she said, "Why is this happening to me?" So she went to inquire of the LORD.

[23]The LORD said to her,

"Two nations are in your womb,
    and two peoples from within you
        will be separated;
one people will be stronger than the
        other,
    and the older will serve the
        younger."

[24]When the time came for her to give birth, there were twin boys in her womb. [25]The first to come out was red, and his whole body was like a hairy garment; so they named him Esau.[c] [26]After this, his brother came out, with his hand grasping Esau's heel; so he was named Jacob.[d] Isaac was sixty years old when Rebekah gave birth to them.

[27]The boys grew up, and Esau became a skillful hunter, a man of the open country, while Jacob was a quiet man, staying among the tents. [28]Isaac, who had a taste for wild game, loved Esau, but Rebekah loved Jacob.

[29]Once when Jacob was cooking some stew, Esau came in from the open country, famished. [30]He said to Jacob, "Quick, let me have some of that red stew! I'm famished!" (That is why he was also called Edom.[e])

[31]Jacob replied, "First sell me your birthright."

[32]"Look, I am about to die," Esau said. "What good is the birthright to me?"

[33]But Jacob said, "Swear to me first." So he swore an oath to him, selling his birthright to Jacob.

[34]Then Jacob gave Esau some bread and some lentil stew. He ate and drank, and then got up and left.

So Esau despised his birthright.

Isaac and Abimelech

26 Now there was a famine in the land—besides the earlier famine of Abraham's time—and Isaac went to Abimelech king of the Philistines in Gerar. [2]The LORD appeared to Isaac and said, "Do not go down to Egypt; live in the land where I tell you to live. [3]Stay in this land for a while, and I will be with you and will bless you. For to you and your descendants I will give all these lands and will confirm the oath I swore to your father Abraham. [4]I will make your descendants as numerous as the stars in the sky and will give them all these lands, and through your offspring[f] all nations on earth will be blessed, [5]because Abraham obeyed me and kept my requirements, my commands, my decrees and my laws." [6]So Isaac stayed in Gerar.

[7]When the men of that place asked him about his wife, he said, "She is my sister," because he was afraid to say, "She is my wife." He thought, "The men of this place might kill me on account of Rebekah, because she is beautiful."

[8]When Isaac had been there a long time, Abimelech king of the Philistines looked down from a window and saw Isaac caressing his wife Rebekah. [9]So Abimelech summoned Isaac and said, "She is really your wife! Why did you say, 'She is my sister'?"

Isaac answered him, "Because I

---

[a]18 Or *lived to the east of*   [b]20 That is, Northwest Mesopotamia   [c]25 *Esau* may mean *hairy*; he was also called Edom, which means *red*.   [d]26 *Jacob* means *he grasps the heel* (figuratively, *he deceives*).   [e]30 *Edom* means *red*.   [f]4 Or *seed*

thought I might lose my life on account of her."

¹⁰Then Abimelech said, "What is this you have done to us? One of the men might well have slept with your wife, and you would have brought guilt upon us."

¹¹So Abimelech gave orders to all the people: "Anyone who molests this man or his wife shall surely be put to death."

¹²Isaac planted crops in that land and the same year reaped a hundredfold, because the LORD blessed him. ¹³The man became rich, and his wealth continued to grow until he became very wealthy. ¹⁴He had so many flocks and herds and servants that the Philistines envied him. ¹⁵So all the wells that his father's servants had dug in the time of his father Abraham, the Philistines stopped up, filling them with earth.

¹⁶Then Abimelech said to Isaac, "Move away from us; you have become too powerful for us."

¹⁷So Isaac moved away from there and encamped in the Valley of Gerar and settled there. ¹⁸Isaac reopened the wells that had been dug in the time of his father Abraham, which the Philistines had stopped up after Abraham died, and he gave them the same names his father had given them.

¹⁹Isaac's servants dug in the valley and discovered a well of fresh water there. ²⁰But the herdsmen of Gerar quarreled with Isaac's herdsmen and said, "The water is ours!" So he named the well Esek,ᵃ because they disputed with him. ²¹Then they dug another well, but they quarreled over that one also; so he named it Sitnah.ᵇ ²²He moved on from there and dug another well, and no one quarreled over it. He named it Rehoboth,ᶜ saying, "Now the LORD has given us room and we will flourish in the land."

²³From there he went up to Beersheba. ²⁴That night the LORD appeared to him and said, "I am the God of your father Abraham. Do not be afraid, for I am with you; I will bless you and will increase the number of your descendants for the sake of my servant Abraham."

²⁵Isaac built an altar there and called on the name of the LORD. There he pitched his tent, and there his servants dug a well.

²⁶Meanwhile, Abimelech had come to him from Gerar, with Ahuzzath his personal adviser and Phicol the commander of his forces. ²⁷Isaac asked them, "Why have you come to me, since you were hostile to me and sent me away?"

²⁸They answered, "We saw clearly that the LORD was with you; so we said, 'There ought to be a sworn agreement between us'—between us and you. Let us make a treaty with you ²⁹that you will do us no harm, just as we did not molest you but always treated you well and sent you away in peace. And now you are blessed by the LORD."

³⁰Isaac then made a feast for them, and they ate and drank. ³¹Early the next morning the men swore an oath to each other. Then Isaac sent them on their way, and they left him in peace.

³²That day Isaac's servants came and told him about the well they had dug. They said, "We've found water!" ³³He called it Shibah,ᵈ and to this day the name of the town has been Beersheba.ᵉ

³⁴When Esau was forty years old, he married Judith daughter of Beeri the Hittite, and also Basemath daughter of Elon the Hittite. ³⁵They were a source of grief to Isaac and Rebekah.

Jacob Gets Isaac's Blessing

27 When Isaac was old and his eyes were so weak that he could no longer see, he called for Esau his older son and said to him, "My son."

"Here I am," he answered.

²Isaac said, "I am now an old man and don't know the day of my death. ³Now then, get your weapons—your quiver and bow—and go out to the open country to hunt some wild game for me. ⁴Prepare me the kind of tasty food I like and bring it to me to eat, so that I may give you my blessing before I die."

⁵Now Rebekah was listening as Isaac spoke to his son Esau. When Esau left for the open country to hunt game and bring it back, ⁶Rebekah said to her son Jacob, "Look, I overheard your father say to your brother Esau, ⁷'Bring me some game and prepare me some tasty food to eat, so that I may give you my blessing in the presence of the LORD before I die.' ⁸Now, my son, listen carefully and do what I tell you: ⁹Go out to the flock and bring me two choice young goats, so I can prepare some tasty food for your father, just the way he likes it. ¹⁰Then take it to your fa-

---

ᵃ20 Esek means dispute.   ᵇ21 Sitnah means opposition.   ᶜ22 Rehoboth means room.   ᵈ33 Shibah can mean oath or seven.   ᵉ33 Beersheba can mean well of the oath or well of seven.

ther to eat, so that he may give you his blessing before he dies."

¹¹Jacob said to Rebekah his mother, "But my brother Esau is a hairy man, and I'm a man with smooth skin. ¹²What if my father touches me? I would appear to be tricking him and would bring down a curse on myself rather than a blessing." ¹³His mother said to him, "My son, let the curse fall on me. Just do what I say; go and get them for me."

¹⁴So he went and got them and brought them to his mother, and she prepared some tasty food, just the way his father liked it. ¹⁵Then Rebekah took the best clothes of Esau her older son, which she had in the house, and put them on her younger son Jacob. ¹⁶She also covered his hands and the smooth part of his neck with the goatskins. ¹⁷Then she handed to her son Jacob the tasty food and the bread she had made.

¹⁸He went to his father and said, "My father."

"Yes, my son," he answered. "Who is it?"

¹⁹Jacob said to his father, "I am Esau your firstborn. I have done as you told me. Please sit up and eat some of my game so that you may give me your blessing."

²⁰Isaac asked his son, "How did you find it so quickly, my son?"

"The LORD your God gave me success," he replied.

²¹Then Isaac said to Jacob, "Come near so I can touch you, my son, to know whether you really are my son Esau or not."

²²Jacob went close to his father Isaac, who touched him and said, "The voice is the voice of Jacob, but the hands are the hands of Esau." ²³He did not recognize him, for his hands were hairy like those of his brother Esau; so he blessed him. ²⁴"Are you really my son Esau?" he asked.

"I am," he replied.

²⁵Then he said, "My son, bring me some of your game to eat, so that I may give you my blessing."

Jacob brought it to him and he ate; and he brought some wine and he drank. ²⁶Then his father Isaac said to him, "Come here, my son, and kiss me."

²⁷So he went to him and kissed him. When Isaac caught the smell of his clothes, he blessed him and said,

"Ah, the smell of my son

is like the smell of a field
    that the LORD has blessed.
²⁸May God give you of heaven's dew
    and of earth's richness—
    an abundance of grain and new
      wine.
²⁹May nations serve you
    and peoples bow down to you.
Be lord over your brothers,
    and may the sons of your mother
      bow down to you.
May those who curse you be cursed
    and those who bless you be
      blessed."

³⁰After Isaac finished blessing him and Jacob had scarcely left his father's presence, his brother Esau came in from hunting. ³¹He too prepared some tasty food and brought it to his father. Then he said to him, "My father, sit up and eat some of my game, so that you may give me your blessing."

³²His father Isaac asked him, "Who are you?"

"I am your son," he answered, "your firstborn, Esau."

³³Isaac trembled violently and said, "Who was it, then, that hunted game and brought it to me? I ate it just before you came and I blessed him—and indeed he will be blessed!"

³⁴When Esau heard his father's words, he burst out with a loud and bitter cry and said to his father, "Bless me—me too, my father!"

³⁵But he said, "Your brother came deceitfully and took your blessing."

³⁶Esau said, "Isn't he rightly named Jacob*a*? He has deceived me these two times: He took my birthright, and now he's taken my blessing!" Then he asked, "Haven't you reserved any blessing for me?"

³⁷Isaac answered Esau, "I have made him lord over you and have made all his relatives his servants, and I have sustained him with grain and new wine. So what can I possibly do for you, my son?"

³⁸Esau said to his father, "Do you have only one blessing, my father? Bless me too, my father!" Then Esau wept aloud.

³⁹His father Isaac answered him,

"Your dwelling will be
    away from the earth's richness,
    away from the dew of heaven
      above.
⁴⁰You will live by the sword

---

a36 Jacob means *he grasps the heel* (figuratively, *he deceives*).

and you will serve your brother. But when you grow restless, you will throw his yoke from off your neck."

Jacob Flees to Laban

41Esau held a grudge against Jacob because of the blessing his father had given him. He said to himself, "The days of mourning for my father are near; then I will kill my brother Jacob."

42When Rebekah was told what her older son Esau had said, she sent for her younger son Jacob and said to him, "Your brother Esau is consoling himself with the thought of killing you. 43Now then, my son, do what I say: Flee at once to my brother Laban in Haran. 44Stay with him for a while until your brother's fury subsides. 45When your brother is no longer angry with you and forgets what you did to him, I'll send word for you to come back from there. Why should I lose both of you in one day?"

46Then Rebekah said to Isaac, "I'm disgusted with living because of these Hittite women. If Jacob takes a wife from among the women of this land, from Hittite women like these, my life will not be worth living."

28 So Isaac called for Jacob and blessed[a] him and commanded him: "Do not marry a Canaanite woman. 2Go at once to Paddan Aram,[b] to the house of your mother's father Bethuel. Take a wife for yourself there, from among the daughters of Laban, your mother's brother. 3May God Almighty[c] bless you and make you fruitful and increase your numbers until you become a community of peoples. 4May he give you and your descendants the blessing given to Abraham, so that you may take possession of the land where you now live as an alien, the land God gave to Abraham." 5Then Isaac sent Jacob on his way, and he went to Paddan Aram, to Laban son of Bethuel the Aramean, the brother of Rebekah, who was the mother of Jacob and Esau.

6Now Esau learned that Isaac had blessed Jacob and had sent him to Paddan Aram to take a wife from there, and that when he blessed him he commanded him, "Do not marry a Canaanite woman," 7and that Jacob had obeyed his father and

mother and had gone to Paddan Aram. 8Esau then realized how displeasing the Canaanite women were to his father Isaac; 9so he went to Ishmael and married Mahalath, the sister of Nebaioth and daughter of Ishmael son of Abraham, in addition to the wives he already had.

Jacob's Dream at Bethel

10Jacob left Beersheba and set out for Haran. 11When he reached a certain place, he stopped for the night because the sun had set. Taking one of the stones there, he put it under his head and lay down to sleep. 12He had a dream in which he saw a stairway[d] resting on the earth, with its top reaching to heaven, and the angels of God were ascending and descending on it. 13There above it[e] stood the LORD, and he said: "I am the LORD, the God of your father Abraham and the God of Isaac. I will give you and your descendants the land on which you are lying. 14Your descendants will be like the dust of the earth, and you will spread out to the west and to the east, to the north and to the south. All peoples on earth will be blessed through you and your offspring. 15I am with you and will watch over you wherever you go, and I will bring you back to this land. I will not leave you until I have done what I have promised you."

16When Jacob awoke from his sleep, he thought, "Surely the LORD is in this place, and I was not aware of it." 17He was afraid and said, "How awesome is this place! This is none other than the house of God; this is the gate of heaven."

18Early the next morning Jacob took the stone he had placed under his head and set it up as a pillar and poured oil on top of it. 19He called that place Bethel,[f] though the city used to be called Luz. 20Then Jacob made a vow, saying, "If God will be with me and will watch over me on this journey I am taking and will give me food to eat and clothes to wear 21so that I return safely to my father's house, then the LORD[g] will be my God 22and[h] this stone that I have set up as a pillar will be God's house, and of all that you give me I will give you a tenth."

Jacob Arrives in Paddan Aram

29 Then Jacob continued on his journey and came to the land of the

---

a1 Or *greeted*   *b2* That is, Northwest Mesopotamia; also in verses 5, 6 and 7   *c3* Hebrew *El-Shaddai*
d12 Or *ladder*   *e13* Or *There beside him*   *f19* *Bethel* means *house of God.*   *g20,21* Or *Since God
... father's house, the* LORD   *h21,22* Or *house, and the* LORD *will be my God,* *22then*

eastern peoples. [2]There he saw a well in the field, with three flocks of sheep lying near it because the flocks were watered from that well. The stone over the mouth of the well was large. [3]When all the flocks were gathered there, the shepherds would roll the stone away from the well's mouth and water the sheep. Then they would return the stone to its place over the mouth of the well.

[4]Jacob asked the shepherds, "My brothers, where are you from?"

"We're from Haran," they replied.

[5]He said to them, "Do you know Laban, Nahor's grandson?"

"Yes, we know him," they answered.

[6]Then Jacob asked them, "Is he well?"

"Yes, he is," they said, "and here comes his daughter Rachel with the sheep."

[7]"Look," he said, "the sun is still high; it is not time for the flocks to be gathered. Water the sheep and take them back to pasture."

[8]"We can't," they replied, "until all the flocks are gathered and the stone has been rolled away from the mouth of the well. Then we will water the sheep."

[9]While he was still talking with them, Rachel came with her father's sheep, for she was a shepherdess. [10]When Jacob saw Rachel daughter of Laban, his mother's brother, and Laban's sheep, he went over and rolled the stone away from the mouth of the well and watered his uncle's sheep. [11]Then Jacob kissed Rachel and began to weep aloud. [12]He had told Rachel that he was a relative of her father and a son of Rebekah. So she ran and told her father.

[13]As soon as Laban heard the news about Jacob, his sister's son, he hurried to meet him. He embraced him and kissed him and brought him to his home, and there Jacob told him all these things. [14]Then Laban said to him, "You are my own flesh and blood."

Jacob Marries Leah and Rachel

After Jacob had stayed with him for a whole month, [15]Laban said to him, "Just because you are a relative of mine, should you work for me for nothing? Tell me what your wages should be."

[16]Now Laban had two daughters; the name of the older was Leah, and the name of the younger was Rachel. [17]Leah had weak[a] eyes, but Rachel was lovely in form, and beautiful. [18]Jacob was in love with Rachel and said, "I'll work for you seven years in return for your younger daughter Rachel."

[19]Laban said, "It's better that I give her to you than to some other man. Stay here with me." [20]So Jacob served seven years to get Rachel, but they seemed like only a few days to him because of his love for her.

[21]Then Jacob said to Laban, "Give me my wife. My time is completed, and I want to lie with her."

[22]So Laban brought together all the people of the place and gave a feast. [23]But when evening came, he took his daughter Leah and gave her to Jacob, and Jacob lay with her. [24]And Laban gave his servant girl Zilpah to his daughter as her maidservant.

[25]When morning came, there was Leah! So Jacob said to Laban, "What is this you have done to me? I served you for Rachel, didn't I? Why have you deceived me?"

[26]Laban replied, "It is not our custom here to give the younger daughter in marriage before the older one. [27]Finish this daughter's bridal week; then we will give you the younger one also, in return for another seven years of work."

[28]And Jacob did so. He finished the week with Leah, and then Laban gave him his daughter Rachel to be his wife. [29]Laban gave his servant girl Bilhah to his daughter Rachel as her maidservant. [30]Jacob lay with Rachel also, and he loved Rachel more than Leah. And he worked for Laban another seven years.

Jacob's Children

[31]When the LORD saw that Leah was not loved, he opened her womb, but Rachel was barren. [32]Leah became pregnant and gave birth to a son. She named him Reuben,[b] for she said, "It is because the LORD has seen my misery. Surely my husband will love me now."

[33]She conceived again, and when she gave birth to a son she said, "Because the LORD heard that I am not loved, he gave me this one too." So she named him Simeon.[c]

[34]Again she conceived, and when she gave birth to a son she said, "Now at last my husband will become attached to me,

---

[a]17 Or delicate　　[b]32 Reuben sounds like the Hebrew for he has seen my misery; the name means see, a son.　　[c]33 Simeon probably means one who hears.

because I have borne him three sons." So he was named Levi.ᵃ

³⁵She conceived again, and when she gave birth to a son she said, "This time I will praise the LORD." So she named him Judah.ᵇ Then she stopped having children.

30 When Rachel saw that she was not bearing Jacob any children, she became jealous of her sister. So she said to Jacob, "Give me children, or I'll die!"

²Jacob became angry with her and said, "Am I in the place of God, who has kept you from having children?"

³Then she said, "Here is Bilhah, my maidservant. Sleep with her so that she can bear children for me and that through her I too can build a family."

⁴So she gave him her servant Bilhah as a wife. Jacob slept with her, ⁵and she became pregnant and bore him a son. ⁶Then Rachel said, "God has vindicated me; he has listened to my plea and given me a son." Because of this she named him Dan.ᶜ

⁷Rachel's servant Bilhah conceived again and bore Jacob a second son. ⁸Then Rachel said, "I have had a great struggle with my sister, and I have won." So she named him Naphtali.ᵈ

⁹When Leah saw that she had stopped having children, she took her maidservant Zilpah and gave her to Jacob as a wife. ¹⁰Leah's servant Zilpah bore Jacob a son. ¹¹Then Leah said, "What good fortune!"ᵉ So she named him Gad.ᶠ

¹²Leah's servant Zilpah bore Jacob a second son. ¹³Then Leah said, "How happy I am! The women will call me happy." So she named him Asher.ᵍ

¹⁴During wheat harvest, Reuben went out into the fields and found some mandrake plants, which he brought to his mother Leah. Rachel said to Leah, "Please give me some of your son's mandrakes."

¹⁵But she said to her, "Wasn't it enough that you took away my husband? Will you take my son's mandrakes too?"

"Very well," Rachel said, "he can sleep with you tonight in return for your son's mandrakes."

¹⁶So when Jacob came in from the fields that evening, Leah went out to meet him. "You must sleep with me," she said. "I have hired you with my son's mandrakes." So he slept with her that night.

¹⁷God listened to Leah, and she became pregnant and bore Jacob a fifth son. ¹⁸Then Leah said, "God has rewarded me for giving my maidservant to my husband." So she named him Issachar.ʰ

¹⁹Leah conceived again and bore Jacob a sixth son. ²⁰Then Leah said, "God has presented me with a precious gift. This time my husband will treat me with honor, because I have borne him six sons." So she named him Zebulun.ⁱ

²¹Some time later she gave birth to a daughter and named her Dinah.

²²Then God remembered Rachel; he listened to her and opened her womb. ²³She became pregnant and gave birth to a son and said, "God has taken away my disgrace." ²⁴She named him Joseph,ʲ and said, "May the LORD add to me another son."

Jacob's Flocks Increase

²⁵After Rachel gave birth to Joseph, Jacob said to Laban, "Send me on my way so I can go back to my own homeland. ²⁶Give me my wives and children, for whom I have served you, and I will be on my way. You know how much work I've done for you."

²⁷But Laban said to him, "If I have found favor in your eyes, please stay. I have learned by divination thatᵏ the LORD has blessed me because of you." ²⁸He added, "Name your wages, and I will pay them."

²⁹Jacob said to him, "You know how I have worked for you and how your livestock has fared under my care. ³⁰The little you had before I came has increased greatly, and the LORD has blessed you wherever I have been. But now, when may I do something for my own household?"

³¹"What shall I give you?" he asked.

"Don't give me anything," Jacob replied. "But if you will do this one thing for me, I will go on tending your flocks and watching over them: ³²Let me go through all your flocks today and remove from them every speckled or spotted sheep, every dark-colored lamb and every spotted

---

ᵃ34 *Levi* sounds like and may be derived from the Hebrew for *attached.*   ᵇ35 *Judah* sounds like and may be derived from the Hebrew for *praise.*   ᶜ6 *Dan* here means *he has vindicated.*   ᵈ8 *Naphtali* means *my struggle.*   ᵉ11 Or *"A troop is coming!"*   ᶠ11 *Gad* can mean *good fortune* or *a troop.* ᵍ13 *Asher* means *happy.*   ʰ18 *Issachar* sounds like the Hebrew for *reward.*   ⁱ20 *Zebulun* probably means *honor.*   ʲ24 *Joseph* means *may he add.*   ᵏ27 Or possibly *have become rich and* or speckled goat. They will be my wages. ³³And my honesty will testify for me in the future, whenever you check on the wages you have paid me. Any goat in my possession that is not speckled or spotted, or any lamb that is not dark-colored, will be considered stolen."

³⁴"Agreed," said Laban. "Let it be as you have said." ³⁵That same day he removed all the male goats that were streaked or spotted, and all the speckled or spotted female goats (all that had white on them) and all the dark-colored lambs, and he placed them in the care of his sons. ³⁶Then he put a three-day journey between himself and Jacob, while Jacob continued to tend the rest of Laban's flocks.

³⁷Jacob, however, took fresh-cut branches from poplar, almond and plane trees and made white stripes on them by peeling the bark and exposing the white inner wood of the branches. ³⁸Then he placed the peeled branches in all the watering troughs, so that they would be directly in front of the flocks when they came to drink. When the flocks were in heat and came to drink, ³⁹they mated in front of the branches. And they bore young that were streaked or speckled or spotted. ⁴⁰Jacob set apart the young of the flock by themselves, but made the rest face the streaked and dark-colored animals that belonged to Laban. Thus he made separate flocks for himself and did not put them with Laban's animals. ⁴¹Whenever the stronger females were in heat, Jacob would place the branches in the troughs in front of the animals so they would mate near the branches, ⁴²but if the animals were weak, he would not place them there. So the weak animals went to Laban and the strong ones to Jacob. ⁴³In this way the man grew exceedingly prosperous and came to own large flocks, and maidservants and menservants, and camels and donkeys.

Jacob Flees From Laban

31 Jacob heard that Laban's sons were saying, "Jacob has taken everything our father owned and has gained all this wealth from what belonged to our father." ²And Jacob noticed that Laban's attitude toward him was not what it had been.

³Then the Lord said to Jacob, "Go back

to the land of your fathers and to your relatives, and I will be with you."

⁴So Jacob sent word to Rachel and Leah to come out to the fields where his flocks were. ⁵He said to them, "I see that your father's attitude toward me is not what it was before, but the God of my father has been with me. ⁶You know that I've worked for your father with all my strength, ⁷yet your father has cheated me by changing my wages ten times. However, God has not allowed him to harm me. ⁸If he said, 'The speckled ones will be your wages,' then all the flocks gave birth to speckled young; and if he said, 'The streaked ones will be your wages,' then all the flocks bore streaked young. ⁹So God has taken away your father's livestock and has given them to me.

¹⁰"In breeding season I once had a dream in which I looked up and saw that the male goats mating with the flock were streaked, speckled or spotted. ¹¹The angel of God said to me in the dream, 'Jacob.' I answered, 'Here I am.' ¹²And he said, 'Look up and see that all the male goats mating with the flock are streaked, speckled or spotted, for I have seen all that Laban has been doing to you. ¹³I am the God of Bethel, where you anointed a pillar and where you made a vow to me. Now leave this land at once and go back to your native land.' "

¹⁴Then Rachel and Leah replied, "Do we still have any share in the inheritance of our father's estate? ¹⁵Does he not regard us as foreigners? Not only has he sold us, but he has used up what was paid for us. ¹⁶Surely all the wealth that God took away from our father belongs to us and our children. So do whatever God has told you."

¹⁷Then Jacob put his children and his wives on camels, ¹⁸and he drove all his livestock ahead of him, along with all the goods he had accumulated in Paddan Aram,^a to go to his father Isaac in the land of Canaan.

¹⁹When Laban had gone to shear his sheep, Rachel stole her father's household gods. ²⁰Moreover, Jacob deceived Laban the Aramean by not telling him he was running away. ²¹So he fled with all he had, and crossing the River,^b he headed for the hill country of Gilead.

Laban Pursues Jacob

²²On the third day Laban was told that

---

^a18 That is, Northwest Mesopotamia   ^b21 That is, the Euphrates

Jacob had fled. 23Taking his relatives with him, he pursued Jacob for seven days and caught up with him in the hill country of Gilead. 24Then God came to Laban the Aramean in a dream at night and said to him, "Be careful not to say anything to Jacob, either good or bad."

25Jacob had pitched his tent in the hill country of Gilead when Laban overtook him, and Laban and his relatives camped there too. 26Then Laban said to Jacob, "What have you done? You've deceived me, and you've carried off my daughters like captives in war. 27Why did you run off secretly and deceive me? Why didn't you tell me, so I could send you away with joy and singing to the music of tambourines and harps? 28You didn't even let me kiss my grandchildren and my daughters good-by. You have done a foolish thing. 29I have the power to harm you; but last night the God of your father said to me, 'Be careful not to say anything to Jacob, either good or bad.' 30Now you have gone off because you longed to return to your father's house. But why did you steal my gods?"

31Jacob answered Laban, "I was afraid, because I thought you would take your daughters away from me by force. 32But if you find anyone who has your gods, he shall not live. In the presence of our relatives, see for yourself whether there is anything of yours here with me; and if so, take it." Now Jacob did not know that Rachel had stolen the gods.

33So Laban went into Jacob's tent and into Leah's tent and into the tent of the two maidservants, but he found nothing. After he came out of Leah's tent, he entered Rachel's tent. 34Now Rachel had taken the household gods and put them inside her camel's saddle and was sitting on them. Laban searched through everything in the tent but found nothing.

35Rachel said to her father, "Don't be angry, my lord, that I cannot stand up in your presence; I'm having my period." So he searched but could not find the household gods.

36Jacob was angry and took Laban to task. "What is my crime?" he asked Laban. "What sin have I committed that you hunt me down? 37Now that you have searched through all my goods, what have you found that belongs to your household? Put it here in front of your relatives

and mine, and let them judge between the two of us.

38"I have been with you for twenty years now. Your sheep and goats have not miscarried, nor have I eaten rams from your flocks. 39I did not bring you animals torn by wild beasts; I bore the loss myself. And you demanded payment from me for whatever was stolen by day or night. 40This was my situation: The heat consumed me in the daytime and the cold at night, and sleep fled from my eyes. 41It was like this for the twenty years I was in your household. I worked for you fourteen years for your two daughters and six years for your flocks, and you changed my wages ten times. 42If the God of my father, the God of Abraham and the Fear of Isaac, had not been with me, you would surely have sent me away empty-handed. But God has seen my hardship and the toil of my hands, and last night he rebuked you."

43Laban answered Jacob, "The women are my daughters, the children are my children, and the flocks are my flocks. All you see is mine. Yet what can I do today about these daughters of mine, or about the children they have borne? 44Come now, let's make a covenant, you and I, and let it serve as a witness between us."

45So Jacob took a stone and set it up as a pillar. 46He said to his relatives, "Gather some stones." So they took stones and piled them in a heap, and they ate there by the heap. 47Laban called it Jegar Sahadutha,a and Jacob called it Galeed.b

48Laban said, "This heap is a witness between you and me today." That is why it was called Galeed. 49It was also called Mizpah,c because he said, "May the LORD keep watch between you and me when we are away from each other. 50If you mistreat my daughters or if you take any wives besides my daughters, even though no one is with us, remember that God is a witness between you and me."

51Laban also said to Jacob, "Here is this heap, and here is this pillar I have set up between you and me. 52This heap is a witness, and this pillar is a witness, that I will not go past this heap to your side to harm you and that you will not go past this heap and pillar to my side to harm me. 53May the God of Abraham and the God of Nahor, the God of their father, judge between us."

a47 The Aramaic Jegar Sahadutha means witness heap.   b47 The Hebrew Galeed means witness heap.
c49 Mizpah means watchtower.

So Jacob took an oath in the name of the Fear of his father Isaac. 54He offered a sacrifice there in the hill country and invited his relatives to a meal. After they had eaten, they spent the night there.

55Early the next morning Laban kissed his grandchildren and his daughters and blessed them. Then he left and returned home.

Jacob Prepares to Meet Esau

32 Jacob also went on his way, and the angels of God met him. 2When Jacob saw them, he said, "This is the camp of God!" So he named that place Mahanaim.a

3Jacob sent messengers ahead of him to his brother Esau in the land of Seir, the country of Edom. 4He instructed them: "This is what you are to say to my master Esau: 'Your servant Jacob says, I have been staying with Laban and have remained there till now. 5I have cattle and donkeys, sheep and goats, menservants and maidservants. Now I am sending this message to my lord, that I may find favor in your eyes.'"

6When the messengers returned to Jacob, they said, "We went to your brother Esau, and now he is coming to meet you, and four hundred men are with him."

7In great fear and distress Jacob divided the people who were with him into two groups,b and the flocks and herds and camels as well. 8He thought, "If Esau comes and attacks one group,c the groupc that is left may escape."

9Then Jacob prayed, "O God of my father Abraham, God of my father Isaac, O LORD, who said to me, 'Go back to your country and your relatives, and I will make you prosper,' 10I am unworthy of all the kindness and faithfulness you have shown your servant. I had only my staff when I crossed this Jordan, but now I have become two groups. 11Save me, I pray, from the hand of my brother Esau, for I am afraid he will come and attack me, and also the mothers with their children. 12But you have said, 'I will surely make you prosper and will make your descendants like the sand of the sea, which cannot be counted.'"

13He spent the night there, and from what he had with him he selected a gift for his brother Esau: 14two hundred female goats and twenty male goats, two hundred ewes and twenty rams, 15thirty female camels with their young, forty cows and ten bulls, and twenty female donkeys and ten male donkeys. 16He put them in the care of his servants, each herd by itself, and said to his servants, "Go ahead of me, and keep some space between the herds."

17He instructed the one in the lead: "When my brother Esau meets you and asks, 'To whom do you belong, and where are you going, and who owns all these animals in front of you?' 18then you are to say, 'They belong to your servant Jacob. They are a gift sent to my lord Esau, and he is coming behind us.'"

19He also instructed the second, the third and all the others who followed the herds: "You are to say the same thing to Esau when you meet him. 20And be sure to say, 'Your servant Jacob is coming behind us.'" For he thought, "I will pacify him with these gifts I am sending on ahead; later, when I see him, perhaps he will receive me." 21So Jacob's gifts went on ahead of him, but he himself spent the night in the camp.

Jacob Wrestles With God

22That night Jacob got up and took his two wives, his two maidservants and his eleven sons and crossed the ford of the Jabbok. 23After he had sent them across the stream, he sent over all his possessions. 24So Jacob was left alone, and a man wrestled with him till daybreak. 25When the man saw that he could not overpower him, he touched the socket of Jacob's hip so that his hip was wrenched as he wrestled with the man. 26Then the man said, "Let me go, for it is daybreak." But Jacob replied, "I will not let you go unless you bless me."

27The man asked him, "What is your name?"

"Jacob," he answered.

28Then the man said, "Your name will no longer be Jacob, but Israel,d because you have struggled with God and with men and have overcome."

29Jacob said, "Please tell me your name."

But he replied, "Why do you ask my name?" Then he blessed him there. 30So Jacob called the place Peniel,e saying, "It is because I saw God face to face, and yet my life was spared."

a2 Mahanaim means two camps.   b7 Or camps; also in verse 10   c8 Or camp   d28 Israel means he struggles with God.   e30 Peniel means face of God.

31The sun rose above him as he passed Peniel,ᵃ and he was limping because of his hip. 32Therefore to this day the Israelites do not eat the tendon attached to the socket of the hip, because the socket of Jacob's hip was touched near the tendon.

Jacob Meets Esau

33 Jacob looked up and there was Esau, coming with his four hundred men; so he divided the children among Leah, Rachel and the two maidservants. 2He put the maidservants and their children in front, Leah and her children next, and Rachel and Joseph in the rear. 3He himself went on ahead and bowed down to the ground seven times as he approached his brother.

4But Esau ran to meet Jacob and embraced him; he threw his arms around his neck and kissed him. And they wept. 5Then Esau looked up and saw the women and children. "Who are these with you?" he asked.

Jacob answered, "They are the children God has graciously given your servant." 6Then the maidservants and their children approached and bowed down. 7Next, Leah and her children came and bowed down. Last of all came Joseph and Rachel, and they too bowed down.

8Esau asked, "What do you mean by all these droves I met?"

"To find favor in your eyes, my lord," he said.

9But Esau said, "I already have plenty, my brother. Keep what you have for yourself."

10"No, please!" said Jacob. "If I have found favor in your eyes, accept this gift from me. For to see your face is like seeing the face of God, now that you have received me favorably. 11Please accept the present that was brought to you, for God has been gracious to me and I have all I need." And because Jacob insisted, Esau accepted it.

12Then Esau said, "Let us be on our way; I'll accompany you."

13But Jacob said to him, "My lord knows that the children are tender and that I must care for the ewes and cows that are nursing their young. If they are driven hard just one day, all the animals will die. 14So let my lord go on ahead of his servant, while I move along slowly at the pace of the droves before me and that of the children, until I come to my lord in Seir."

15Esau said, "Then let me leave some of my men with you."

"But why do that?" Jacob asked. "Just let me find favor in the eyes of my lord."

16So that day Esau started on his way back to Seir. 17Jacob, however, went to Succoth, where he built a place for himself and made shelters for his livestock. That is why the place is called Succoth.ᵇ

18After Jacob came from Paddan Aram,ᶜ he arrived safely at theᵈ city of Shechem in Canaan and camped within sight of the city. 19For a hundred pieces of silver,ᵉ he bought from the sons of Hamor, the father of Shechem, the plot of ground where he pitched his tent. 20There he set up an altar and called it El Elohe Israel.ᶠ

Dinah and the Shechemites

34 Now Dinah, the daughter Leah had borne to Jacob, went out to visit the women of the land. 2When Shechem son of Hamor the Hivite, the ruler of that area, saw her, he took her and violated her. 3His heart was drawn to Dinah daughter of Jacob, and he loved the girl and spoke tenderly to her. 4And Shechem said to his father Hamor, "Get me this girl as my wife."

5When Jacob heard that his daughter Dinah had been defiled, his sons were in the fields with his livestock; so he kept quiet about it until they came home.

6Then Shechem's father Hamor went out to talk with Jacob. 7Now Jacob's sons had come in from the fields as soon as they heard what had happened. They were filled with grief and fury, because Shechem had done a disgraceful thing inᵍ Israel by lying with Jacob's daughter —a thing that should not be done.

8But Hamor said to them, "My son Shechem has his heart set on your daughter. Please give her to him as his wife. 9Intermarry with us; give us your daughters and take our daughters for yourselves. 10You can settle among us; the land is open to you. Live in it, tradeʰ in it, and acquire property in it."

11Then Shechem said to Dinah's father

ᵃ31 Hebrew Penuel, a variant of Peniel   ᵇ17 Succoth means shelters.   ᶜ18 That is, Northwest Mesopotamia   ᵈ18 Or arrived at Shalem, a   ᵉ19 Hebrew hundred kesitahs; a kesitah was a unit of money of unknown weight and value.   ᶠ20 El Elohe Israel can mean God, the God of Israel or mighty is the God of Israel.   ᵍ7 Or against   ʰ10 Or move about freely; also in verse 21 and brothers, "Let me find favor in your eyes, and I will give you whatever you ask. ¹²Make the price for the bride and the gift I am to bring as great as you like, and I'll pay whatever you ask me. Only give me the girl as my wife."

¹³Because their sister Dinah had been defiled, Jacob's sons replied deceitfully as they spoke to Shechem and his father Hamor. ¹⁴They said to them, "We can't do such a thing; we can't give our sister to a man who is not circumcised. That would be a disgrace to us. ¹⁵We will give our consent to you on one condition only: that you become like us by circumcising all your males. ¹⁶Then we will give you our daughters and take your daughters for ourselves. We'll settle among you and become one people with you. ¹⁷But if you will not agree to be circumcised, we'll take our sister *a* and go."

¹⁸Their proposal seemed good to Hamor and his son Shechem. ¹⁹The young man, who was the most honored of all his father's household, lost no time in doing what they said, because he was delighted with Jacob's daughter. ²⁰So Hamor and his son Shechem went to the gate of their city to speak to their fellow townsmen. ²¹"These men are friendly toward us," they said. "Let them live in our land and trade in it; the land has plenty of room for them. We can marry their daughters and they can marry ours. ²²But the men will consent to live with us as one people only on the condition that our males be circumcised, as they themselves are. ²³Won't their livestock, their property and all their other animals become ours? So let us give our consent to them, and they will settle among us."

²⁴All the men who went out of the city gate agreed with Hamor and his son Shechem, and every male in the city was circumcised.

²⁵Three days later, while all of them were still in pain, two of Jacob's sons, Simeon and Levi, Dinah's brothers, took their swords and attacked the unsuspecting city, killing every male. ²⁶They put Hamor and his son Shechem to the sword and took Dinah from Shechem's house and left. ²⁷The sons of Jacob came upon the dead bodies and looted the city where *b* their sister had been defiled.

²⁸They seized their flocks and herds and donkeys and everything else of theirs in the city and out in the fields. ²⁹They carried off all their wealth and all their women and children, taking as plunder everything in the houses.

³⁰Then Jacob said to Simeon and Levi, "You have brought trouble on me by making me a stench to the Canaanites and Perizzites, the people living in this land. We are few in number, and if they join forces against me and attack me, I and my household will be destroyed."

³¹But they replied, "Should he have treated our sister like a prostitute?"

Jacob Returns to Bethel

35 Then God said to Jacob, "Go up to Bethel and settle there, and build an altar there to God, who appeared to you when you were fleeing from your brother Esau."

²So Jacob said to his household and to all who were with him, "Get rid of the foreign gods you have with you, and purify yourselves and change your clothes. ³Then come, let us go up to Bethel, where I will build an altar to God, who answered me in the day of my distress and who has been with me wherever I have gone." ⁴So they gave Jacob all the foreign gods they had and the rings in their ears, and Jacob buried them under the oak at Shechem. ⁵Then they set out, and the terror of God fell upon the towns all around them so that no one pursued them.

⁶Jacob and all the people with him came to Luz (that is, Bethel) in the land of Canaan. ⁷There he built an altar, and he called the place El Bethel, *c* because it was there that God revealed himself to him when he was fleeing from his brother.

⁸Now Deborah, Rebekah's nurse, died and was buried under the oak below Bethel. So it was named Allon Bacuth. *d*

⁹After Jacob returned from Paddan Aram, *e* God appeared to him again and blessed him. ¹⁰God said to him, "Your name is Jacob, *f* but you will no longer be called Jacob; your name will be Israel. *g* " So he named him Israel.

¹¹And God said to him, "I am God Almighty *h* ; be fruitful and increase in number. A nation and a community of nations

---

*a*17 Hebrew *daughter*   *b*27 Or *because*   *c*7 *El Bethel* means *God of Bethel.*   *d*8 *Allon Bacuth* means *oak of weeping.*   *e*9 That is, Northwest Mesopotamia; also in verse 26   *f*10 *Jacob* means *he grasps the heel* (figuratively, *he deceives*).   *g*10 *Israel* means *he struggles with God.*   *h*11 Hebrew *El-Shaddai* will come from you, and kings will come from your body. [12]The land I gave to Abraham and Isaac I also give to you, and I will give this land to your descendants after you." [13]Then God went up from him at the place where he had talked with him.

[14]Jacob set up a stone pillar at the place where God had talked with him, and he poured out a drink offering on it; he also poured oil on it. [15]Jacob called the place where God had talked with him Bethel.[a]

The Deaths of Rachel and Isaac

[16]Then they moved on from Bethel. While they were still some distance from Ephrath, Rachel began to give birth and had great difficulty. [17]And as she was having great difficulty in childbirth, the midwife said to her, "Don't be afraid, for you have another son." [18]As she breathed her last—for she was dying—she named her son Ben-Oni.[b] But his father named him Benjamin.[c]

[19]So Rachel died and was buried on the way to Ephrath (that is, Bethlehem). [20]Over her tomb Jacob set up a pillar, and to this day that pillar marks Rachel's tomb.

[21]Israel moved on again and pitched his tent beyond Migdal Eder. [22]While Israel was living in that region, Reuben went in and slept with his father's concubine Bilhah, and Israel heard of it.

Jacob had twelve sons:
[23]The sons of Leah:
   Reuben the firstborn of Jacob,
   Simeon, Levi, Judah, Issachar and
   Zebulun.
[24]The sons of Rachel:
   Joseph and Benjamin.
[25]The sons of Rachel's maidservant Bilhah:
   Dan and Naphtali.
[26]The sons of Leah's maidservant Zilpah:
   Gad and Asher.
These were the sons of Jacob, who were born to him in Paddan Aram.

[27]Jacob came home to his father Isaac in Mamre, near Kiriath Arba (that is, Hebron), where Abraham and Isaac had stayed. [28]Isaac lived a hundred and eighty years. [29]Then he breathed his last and died and was gathered to his people, old and full of years. And his sons Esau and Jacob buried him.

Esau's Descendants

36 This is the account of Esau (that is, Edom).

[2]Esau took his wives from the women of Canaan: Adah daughter of Elon the Hittite, and Oholibamah daughter of Anah and granddaughter of Zibeon the Hivite— [3]also Basemath daughter of Ishmael and sister of Nebaioth.

[4]Adah bore Eliphaz to Esau, Basemath bore Reuel, [5]and Oholibamah bore Jeush, Jalam and Korah. These were the sons of Esau, who were born to him in Canaan.

[6]Esau took his wives and sons and daughters and all the members of his household, as well as his livestock and all his other animals and all the goods he had acquired in Canaan, and moved to a land some distance from his brother Jacob. [7]Their possessions were too great for them to remain together; the land where they were staying could not support them both because of their livestock. [8]So Esau (that is, Edom) settled in the hill country of Seir.

[9]This is the account of Esau the father of the Edomites in the hill country of Seir.

[10]These are the names of Esau's sons:
   Eliphaz, the son of Esau's wife
   Adah, and Reuel, the son of Esau's
   wife Basemath.
[11]The sons of Eliphaz:
   Teman, Omar, Zepho, Gatam and
   Kenaz.
[12]Esau's son Eliphaz also had a concubine named Timna, who bore him Amalek. These were grandsons of Esau's wife Adah.
[13]The sons of Reuel:
   Nahath, Zerah, Shammah and
   Mizzah. These were grandsons of
   Esau's wife Basemath.
[14]The sons of Esau's wife Oholibamah daughter of Anah and granddaughter of Zibeon, whom she bore to Esau:
   Jeush, Jalam and Korah.

[15]These were the chiefs among Esau's descendants:

---

a15 Bethel means house of God.   *b18 Ben-Oni means son of my trouble.*   *c18 Benjamin means son of my right hand.*

The sons of Eliphaz the firstborn of Esau:

Chiefs Teman, Omar, Zepho, Kenaz, [16]Korah,[a] Gatam and Amalek. These were the chiefs descended from Eliphaz in Edom; they were grandsons of Adah.

[17]The sons of Esau's son Reuel:

Chiefs Nahath, Zerah, Shammah and Mizzah. These were the chiefs descended from Reuel in Edom; they were grandsons of Esau's wife Basemath.

[18]The sons of Esau's wife Oholibamah:

Chiefs Jeush, Jalam and Korah. These were the chiefs descended from Esau's wife Oholibamah daughter of Anah.

[19]These were the sons of Esau (that is, Edom), and these were their chiefs.

[20]These were the sons of Seir the Horite, who were living in the region:

Lotan, Shobal, Zibeon, Anah, [21]Dishon, Ezer and Dishan. These sons of Seir in Edom were Horite chiefs.

[22]The sons of Lotan:

Hori and Homam.[b] Timna was Lotan's sister.

[23]The sons of Shobal:

Alvan, Manahath, Ebal, Shepho and Onam.

[24]The sons of Zibeon:

Aiah and Anah. This is the Anah who discovered the hot springs[c] in the desert while he was grazing the donkeys of his father Zibeon.

[25]The children of Anah:

Dishon and Oholibamah daughter of Anah.

[26]The sons of Dishon[d]:

Hemdan, Eshban, Ithran and Keran.

[27]The sons of Ezer:

Bilhan, Zaavan and Akan.

[28]The sons of Dishan:

Uz and Aran.

[29]These were the Horite chiefs:

Lotan, Shobal, Zibeon, Anah, [30]Dishon, Ezer and Dishan. These were the Horite chiefs, according to their divisions, in the land of Seir.

The Rulers of Edom

[31]These were the kings who reigned in Edom before any Israelite king reigned[e]:
[32]Bela son of Beor became king of Edom. His city was named Dinhabah.

[33]When Bela died, Jobab son of Zerah from Bozrah succeeded him as king.

[34]When Jobab died, Husham from the land of the Temanites succeeded him as king.

[35]When Husham died, Hadad son of Bedad, who defeated Midian in the country of Moab, succeeded him as king. His city was named Avith.

[36]When Hadad died, Samlah from Masrekah succeeded him as king.

[37]When Samlah died, Shaul from Rehoboth on the river[f] succeeded him as king.

[38]When Shaul died, Baal-Hanan son of Acbor succeeded him as king.

[39]When Baal-Hanan son of Acbor died, Hadad[g] succeeded him as king. His city was named Pau, and his wife's name was Mehetabel daughter of Matred, the daughter of Me-Zahab.

[40]These were the chiefs descended from Esau, by name, according to their clans and regions:

Timna, Alvah, Jetheth, [41]Oholibamah, Elah, Pinon, [42]Kenaz, Teman, Mibzar, [43]Magdiel and Iram. These were the chiefs of Edom, according to their settlements in the land they occupied.

This was Esau the father of the Edomites.

Joseph's Dreams

37 Jacob lived in the land where his father had stayed, the land of Canaan.

[2]This is the account of Jacob.

Joseph, a young man of seventeen, was tending the flocks with his brothers, the sons of Bilhah and the sons of Zilpah, his

---

[a]16 Masoretic Text; Samaritan Pentateuch (see also Gen. 36:11 and 1 Chron. 1:36) does not have *Korah*. [b]22 Hebrew *Hemam*, a variant of *Homam* (see 1 Chron. 1:39) [c]24 Vulgate; Syriac *discovered water*; the meaning of the Hebrew for this word is uncertain. [d]26 Hebrew *Dishan*, a variant of *Dishon* [e]31 Or *before an Israelite king reigned over them* [f]37 Possibly the Euphrates [g]39 Many manuscripts of the Masoretic Text, Samaritan Pentateuch and Syriac (see also 1 Chron. 1:50); most manuscripts of the Masoretic Text *Hadar*

father's wives, and he brought their father a bad report about them.

³Now Israel loved Joseph more than any of his other sons, because he had been born to him in his old age; and he made a richly ornamented^a robe for him. ⁴When his brothers saw that their father loved him more than any of them, they hated him and could not speak a kind word to him.

⁵Joseph had a dream, and when he told it to his brothers, they hated him all the more. ⁶He said to them, "Listen to this dream I had: ⁷We were binding sheaves of grain out in the field when suddenly my sheaf rose and stood upright, while your sheaves gathered around mine and bowed down to it."

⁸His brothers said to him, "Do you intend to reign over us? Will you actually rule us?" And they hated him all the more because of his dream and what he had said.

⁹Then he had another dream, and he told it to his brothers. "Listen," he said, "I had another dream, and this time the sun and moon and eleven stars were bowing down to me."

¹⁰When he told his father as well as his brothers, his father rebuked him and said, "What is this dream you had? Will your mother and I and your brothers actually come and bow down to the ground before you?" ¹¹His brothers were jealous of him, but his father kept the matter in mind.

Joseph Sold by His Brothers

¹²Now his brothers had gone to graze their father's flocks near Shechem, ¹³and Israel said to Joseph, "As you know, your brothers are grazing the flocks near Shechem. Come, I am going to send you to them."

"Very well," he replied.

¹⁴So he said to him, "Go and see if all is well with your brothers and with the flocks, and bring word back to me." Then he sent him off from the Valley of Hebron.

When Joseph arrived at Shechem, ¹⁵a man found him wandering around in the fields and asked him, "What are you looking for?"

¹⁶He replied, "I'm looking for my brothers. Can you tell me where they are grazing their flocks?"

¹⁷"They have moved on from here," the man answered. "I heard them say, 'Let's go to Dothan.'"

So Joseph went after his brothers and found them near Dothan. ¹⁸But they saw him in the distance, and before he reached them, they plotted to kill him.

¹⁹"Here comes that dreamer!" they said to each other. ²⁰"Come now, let's kill him and throw him into one of these cisterns and say that a ferocious animal devoured him. Then we'll see what comes of his dreams."

²¹When Reuben heard this, he tried to rescue him from their hands. "Let's not take his life," he said. ²²"Don't shed any blood. Throw him into this cistern here in the desert, but don't lay a hand on him." Reuben said this to rescue him from them and take him back to his father.

²³So when Joseph came to his brothers, they stripped him of his robe—the richly ornamented robe he was wearing— ²⁴and they took him and threw him into the cistern. Now the cistern was empty; there was no water in it.

²⁵As they sat down to eat their meal, they looked up and saw a caravan of Ishmaelites coming from Gilead. Their camels were loaded with spices, balm and myrrh, and they were on their way to take them down to Egypt.

²⁶Judah said to his brothers, "What will we gain if we kill our brother and cover up his blood? ²⁷Come, let's sell him to the Ishmaelites and not lay our hands on him; after all, he is our brother, our own flesh and blood." His brothers agreed.

²⁸So when the Midianite merchants came by, his brothers pulled Joseph up out of the cistern and sold him for twenty shekels^b of silver to the Ishmaelites, who took him to Egypt.

²⁹When Reuben returned to the cistern and saw that Joseph was not there, he tore his clothes. ³⁰He went back to his brothers and said, "The boy isn't there! Where can I turn now?"

³¹Then they got Joseph's robe, slaughtered a goat and dipped the robe in the blood. ³²They took the ornamented robe back to their father and said, "We found this. Examine it to see whether it is your son's robe."

³³He recognized it and said, "It is my son's robe! Some ferocious animal has devoured him. Joseph has surely been torn to pieces."

---

^a3 The meaning of the Hebrew for *richly ornamented* is uncertain; also in verses 23 and 32.   ^b28 That is, about 8 ounces (about 0.2 kilogram)

34Then Jacob tore his clothes, put on sackcloth and mourned for his son many days. 35All his sons and daughters came to comfort him, but he refused to be comforted. "No," he said, "in mourning will I go down to the grave*a* to my son." So his father wept for him.

36Meanwhile, the Midianites*b* sold Joseph in Egypt to Potiphar, one of Pharaoh's officials, the captain of the guard.

Judah and Tamar

38 At that time, Judah left his brothers and went down to stay with a man of Adullam named Hirah. 2There Judah met the daughter of a Canaanite man named Shua. He married her and lay with her; 3she became pregnant and gave birth to a son, who was named Er. 4She conceived again and gave birth to a son and named him Onan. 5She gave birth to still another son and named him Shelah. It was at Kezib that she gave birth to him.

6Judah got a wife for Er, his firstborn, and her name was Tamar. 7But Er, Judah's firstborn, was wicked in the LORD's sight; so the LORD put him to death.

8Then Judah said to Onan, "Lie with your brother's wife and fulfill your duty to her as a brother-in-law to produce offspring for your brother." 9But Onan knew that the offspring would not be his; so whenever he lay with his brother's wife, he spilled his semen on the ground to keep from producing offspring for his brother. 10What he did was wicked in the LORD's sight; so he put him to death also.

11Judah then said to his daughter-in-law Tamar, "Live as a widow in your father's house until my son Shelah grows up." For he thought, "He may die too, just like his brothers." So Tamar went to live in her father's house.

12After a long time Judah's wife, the daughter of Shua, died. When Judah had recovered from his grief, he went up to Timnah, to the men who were shearing his sheep, and his friend Hirah the Adullamite went with him.

13When Tamar was told, "Your father-in-law is on his way to Timnah to shear his sheep," 14she took off her widow's clothes, covered herself with a veil to disguise herself, and then sat down at the entrance to Enaim, which is on the road to Timnah. For she saw that, though She-lah had now grown up, she had not been given to him as his wife.

15When Judah saw her, he thought she was a prostitute, for she had covered her face. 16Not realizing that she was his daughter-in-law, he went over to her by the roadside and said, "Come now, let me sleep with you."

"And what will you give me to sleep with you?" she asked.

17"I'll send you a young goat from my flock," he said.

"Will you give me something as a pledge until you send it?" she asked.

18He said, "What pledge should I give you?"

"Your seal and its cord, and the staff in your hand," she answered. So he gave them to her and slept with her, and she became pregnant by him. 19After she left, she took off her veil and put on her widow's clothes again.

20Meanwhile Judah sent the young goat by his friend the Adullamite in order to get his pledge back from the woman, but he did not find her. 21He asked the men who lived there, "Where is the shrine prostitute who was beside the road at Enaim?"

"There hasn't been any shrine prostitute here," they said.

22So he went back to Judah and said, "I didn't find her. Besides, the men who lived there said, 'There hasn't been any shrine prostitute here.'"

23Then Judah said, "Let her keep what she has, or we will become a laughingstock. After all, I did send her this young goat, but you didn't find her."

24About three months later Judah was told, "Your daughter-in-law Tamar is guilty of prostitution, and as a result she is now pregnant."

Judah said, "Bring her out and have her burned to death!"

25As she was being brought out, she sent a message to her father-in-law. "I am pregnant by the man who owns these," she said. And she added, "See if you recognize whose seal and cord and staff these are."

26Judah recognized them and said, "She is more righteous than I, since I wouldn't give her to my son Shelah." And he did not sleep with her again.

27When the time came for her to give birth, there were twin boys in her womb.

a35 Hebrew *Sheol*   *b36* Samaritan Pentateuch, Septuagint, Vulgate and Syriac (see also verse 28); Masoretic Text *Medanites*

28As she was giving birth, one of them put out his hand; so the midwife took a scarlet thread and tied it on his wrist and said, "This one came out first." 29But when he drew back his hand, his brother came out, and she said, "So this is how you have broken out!" And he was named Perez.*a* 30Then his brother, who had the scarlet thread on his wrist, came out and he was given the name Zerah.*b*

Joseph and Potiphar's Wife

39 Now Joseph had been taken down to Egypt. Potiphar, an Egyptian who was one of Pharaoh's officials, the captain of the guard, bought him from the Ishmaelites who had taken him there.

2The LORD was with Joseph and he prospered, and he lived in the house of his Egyptian master. 3When his master saw that the LORD was with him and that the LORD gave him success in everything he did, 4Joseph found favor in his eyes and became his attendant. Potiphar put him in charge of his household, and he entrusted to his care everything he owned. 5From the time he put him in charge of his household and of all that he owned, the LORD blessed the household of the Egyptian because of Joseph. The blessing of the LORD was on everything Potiphar had, both in the house and in the field. 6So he left in Joseph's care everything he had; with Joseph in charge, he did not concern himself with anything except the food he ate.

Now Joseph was well-built and handsome, 7and after a while his master's wife took notice of Joseph and said, "Come to bed with me!"

8But he refused. "With me in charge," he told her, "my master does not concern himself with anything in the house; everything he owns he has entrusted to my care. 9No one is greater in this house than I am. My master has withheld nothing from me except you, because you are his wife. How then could I do such a wicked thing and sin against God?" 10And though she spoke to Joseph day after day, he refused to go to bed with her or even to be with her.

11One day he went into the house to attend to his duties, and none of the household servants was inside. 12She caught him by his cloak and said, "Come to bed with me!" But he left his cloak in her hand and ran out of the house.

13When she saw that he had left his cloak in her hand and had run out of the house, 14she called her household servants. "Look," she said to them, "this Hebrew has been brought to us to make sport of us! He came in here to sleep with me, but I screamed. 15When he heard me scream for help, he left his cloak beside me and ran out of the house."

16She kept his cloak beside her until his master came home. 17Then she told him this story: "That Hebrew slave you brought us came to me to make sport of me. 18But as soon as I screamed for help, he left his cloak beside me and ran out of the house."

19When his master heard the story his wife told him, saying, "This is how your slave treated me," he burned with anger. 20Joseph's master took him and put him in prison, the place where the king's prisoners were confined.

But while Joseph was there in the prison, 21the LORD was with him; he showed him kindness and granted him favor in the eyes of the prison warden. 22So the warden put Joseph in charge of all those held in the prison, and he was made responsible for all that was done there. 23The warden paid no attention to anything under Joseph's care, because the LORD was with Joseph and gave him success in whatever he did.

The Cupbearer and the Baker

40 Some time later, the cupbearer and the baker of the king of Egypt offended their master, the king of Egypt. 2Pharaoh was angry with his two officials, the chief cupbearer and the chief baker, 3and put them in custody in the house of the captain of the guard, in the same prison where Joseph was confined. 4The captain of the guard assigned them to Joseph, and he attended them.

After they had been in custody for some time, 5each of the two men—the cupbearer and the baker of the king of Egypt, who were being held in prison—had a dream the same night, and each dream had a meaning of its own.

6When Joseph came to them the next morning, he saw that they were dejected. 7So he asked Pharaoh's officials who were in custody with him in his master's house, "Why are your faces so sad today?"

8"We both had dreams," they an-

---

a29 Perez means breaking out.   *b30 Zerah can mean scarlet or brightness.*

VERSE FOR THE DAY:
Genesis 39:2

AUTHOR:
Millie Stamm

PASSAGE FOR THE DAY:
Genesis 39:1–23

A Prison Experience

JOSEPH attained a place of prominence in Egypt by a difficult road of loneliness and injustice. His brothers, hating him intensely, sold him into slavery, and he was taken to Egypt. Separated from family and friends, he must have been lonely and homesick. But "the LORD was with Joseph."

Through a series of events over which he had no control, he was imprisoned. Joseph's imprisonment was a training period for God's future plan for him.

He learned patience while in prison. Authority given him over the prisoners developed his leadership ability. This was preparation for him later when he directed food distribution during a severe famine.

Joseph may have questioned why his brothers mistreated him; why he was sold into slavery; why he was imprisoned on a charge of which he was innocent. Yet he didn't let his prison experience embitter him. Although he didn't understand it, nor could he see what the future held, he was aware of God's presence with him in prison.

Today you may be in a prison. Perhaps you are misunderstood by your family. Or you may be far away from home, and lonely. Whatever your prison experience, humanly speaking, there may be no way out, no immediate solution. What is your reaction? Are you rebellious? Are you questioning God?

God knows the lessons we need to learn, lessons of patience, submission and self-denial. Our faith may need strengthening. We may be so concerned that God remove us from prison that we miss the lessons he has for us in prison.

Our prison term may seem long, but the God who was with Joseph when he was taken into Egypt, and the God who was with him when he was put in prison, is the God who is with us today.

Additional Scripture Readings:
Isaiah 61:1–9; Philippians 1:12–14; 4:11–13

Go to page 57 for your next devotional reading.

swered, "but there is no one to interpret them."

Then Joseph said to them, "Do not interpretations belong to God? Tell me your dreams."

⁹So the chief cupbearer told Joseph his dream. He said to him, "In my dream I saw a vine in front of me, ¹⁰and on the vine were three branches. As soon as it budded, it blossomed, and its clusters ripened into grapes. ¹¹Pharaoh's cup was in my hand, and I took the grapes, squeezed them into Pharaoh's cup and put the cup in his hand."

¹²"This is what it means," Joseph said to him. "The three branches are three days. ¹³Within three days Pharaoh will lift up your head and restore you to your position, and you will put Pharaoh's cup in his hand, just as you used to do when you were his cupbearer. ¹⁴But when all goes well with you, remember me and show me kindness; mention me to Pharaoh and get me out of this prison. ¹⁵For I was forcibly carried off from the land of the Hebrews, and even here I have done nothing to deserve being put in a dungeon."

¹⁶When the chief baker saw that Joseph had given a favorable interpretation, he said to Joseph, "I too had a dream: On my head were three baskets of bread.ᵃ ¹⁷In the top basket were all kinds of baked goods for Pharaoh, but the birds were eating them out of the basket on my head."

¹⁸"This is what it means," Joseph said. "The three baskets are three days. ¹⁹Within three days Pharaoh will lift off your head and hang you on a tree.ᵇ And the birds will eat away your flesh."

²⁰Now the third day was Pharaoh's birthday, and he gave a feast for all his officials. He lifted up the heads of the chief cupbearer and the chief baker in the presence of his officials: ²¹He restored the chief cupbearer to his position, so that he once again put the cup into Pharaoh's hand, ²²but he hangedᶜ the chief baker, just as Joseph had said to them in his interpretation.

²³The chief cupbearer, however, did not remember Joseph; he forgot him.

Pharaoh's Dreams

41 When two full years had passed, Pharaoh had a dream: He was standing by the Nile, ²when out of the river there came up seven cows, sleek and fat, and they grazed among the reeds. ³Af-

ter them, seven other cows, ugly and gaunt, came up out of the Nile and stood beside those on the riverbank. ⁴And the cows that were ugly and gaunt ate up the seven sleek, fat cows. Then Pharaoh woke up.

⁵He fell asleep again and had a second dream: Seven heads of grain, healthy and good, were growing on a single stalk. ⁶After them, seven other heads of grain sprouted—thin and scorched by the east wind. ⁷The thin heads of grain swallowed up the seven healthy, full heads. Then Pharaoh woke up; it had been a dream.

⁸In the morning his mind was troubled, so he sent for all the magicians and wise men of Egypt. Pharaoh told them his dreams, but no one could interpret them for him.

⁹Then the chief cupbearer said to Pharaoh, "Today I am reminded of my shortcomings. ¹⁰Pharaoh was once angry with his servants, and he imprisoned me and the chief baker in the house of the captain of the guard. ¹¹Each of us had a dream the same night, and each dream had a meaning of its own. ¹²Now a young Hebrew was there with us, a servant of the captain of the guard. We told him our dreams, and he interpreted them for us, giving each man the interpretation of his dream. ¹³And things turned out exactly as he interpreted them to us: I was restored to my position, and the other man was hanged.ᶜ"

¹⁴So Pharaoh sent for Joseph, and he was quickly brought from the dungeon. When he had shaved and changed his clothes, he came before Pharaoh.

¹⁵Pharaoh said to Joseph, "I had a dream, and no one can interpret it. But I have heard it said of you that when you hear a dream you can interpret it."

¹⁶"I cannot do it," Joseph replied to Pharaoh, "but God will give Pharaoh the answer he desires."

¹⁷Then Pharaoh said to Joseph, "In my dream I was standing on the bank of the Nile, ¹⁸when out of the river there came up seven cows, fat and sleek, and they grazed among the reeds. ¹⁹After them, seven other cows came up—scrawny and very ugly and lean. I had never seen such ugly cows in all the land of Egypt. ²⁰The lean, ugly cows ate up the seven fat cows that came up first. ²¹But even after they ate them, no one could tell that they had

---

ᵃ16 Or *three wicker baskets*   ᵇ19 Or *and impale you on a pole*   ᶜ22,13 Or *impaled* done so; they looked just as ugly as before. Then I woke up.

22"In my dreams I also saw seven heads of grain, full and good, growing on a single stalk. 23After them, seven other heads sprouted—withered and thin and scorched by the east wind. 24The thin heads of grain swallowed up the seven good heads. I told this to the magicians, but none could explain it to me."

25Then Joseph said to Pharaoh, "The dreams of Pharaoh are one and the same. God has revealed to Pharaoh what he is about to do. 26The seven good cows are seven years, and the seven good heads of grain are seven years; it is one and the same dream. 27The seven lean, ugly cows that came up afterward are seven years, and so are the seven worthless heads of grain scorched by the east wind: They are seven years of famine.

28"It is just as I said to Pharaoh: God has shown Pharaoh what he is about to do. 29Seven years of great abundance are coming throughout the land of Egypt, 30but seven years of famine will follow them. Then all the abundance in Egypt will be forgotten, and the famine will ravage the land. 31The abundance in the land will not be remembered, because the famine that follows it will be so severe. 32The reason the dream was given to Pharaoh in two forms is that the matter has been firmly decided by God, and God will do it soon.

33"And now let Pharaoh look for a discerning and wise man and put him in charge of the land of Egypt. 34Let Pharaoh appoint commissioners over the land to take a fifth of the harvest of Egypt during the seven years of abundance. 35They should collect all the food of these good years that are coming and store up the grain under the authority of Pharaoh, to be kept in the cities for food. 36This food should be held in reserve for the country, to be used during the seven years of famine that will come upon Egypt, so that the country may not be ruined by the famine."

37The plan seemed good to Pharaoh and to all his officials. 38So Pharaoh asked them, "Can we find anyone like this man, one in whom is the spirit of God^a?"

39Then Pharaoh said to Joseph, "Since God has made all this known to you, there is no one so discerning and wise as you. 40You shall be in charge of my palace, and all my people are to submit to your orders. Only with respect to the throne will I be greater than you."

Joseph in Charge of Egypt

41So Pharaoh said to Joseph, "I hereby put you in charge of the whole land of Egypt." 42Then Pharaoh took his signet ring from his finger and put it on Joseph's finger. He dressed him in robes of fine linen and put a gold chain around his neck. 43He had him ride in a chariot as his second-in-command,^{b} and men shouted before him, "Make way^c!" Thus he put him in charge of the whole land of Egypt.

44Then Pharaoh said to Joseph, "I am Pharaoh, but without your word no one will lift hand or foot in all Egypt." 45Pharaoh gave Joseph the name Zaphenath-Paneah and gave him Asenath daughter of Potiphera, priest of On,^{d} to be his wife. And Joseph went throughout the land of Egypt.

46Joseph was thirty years old when he entered the service of Pharaoh king of Egypt. And Joseph went out from Pharaoh's presence and traveled throughout Egypt. 47During the seven years of abundance the land produced plentifully. 48Joseph collected all the food produced in those seven years of abundance in Egypt and stored it in the cities. In each city he put the food grown in the fields surrounding it. 49Joseph stored up huge quantities of grain, like the sand of the sea; it was so much that he stopped keeping records because it was beyond measure.

50Before the years of famine came, two sons were born to Joseph by Asenath daughter of Potiphera, priest of On. 51Joseph named his firstborn Manasseh^e and said, "It is because God has made me forget all my trouble and all my father's household." 52The second son he named Ephraim^f and said, "It is because God has made me fruitful in the land of my suffering."

53The seven years of abundance in Egypt came to an end, 54and the seven years of famine began, just as Joseph had said. There was famine in all the other lands, but in the whole land of Egypt there was food. 55When all Egypt began to

---

^{a}38 Or of the gods ^{b}43 Or in the chariot of his second-in-command; or in his second chariot ^{c}43 Or Bow down ^{d}45 That is, Heliopolis; also in verse 50 ^{e}51 Manasseh sounds like and may be derived from the Hebrew for forget. ^{f}52 Ephraim sounds like the Hebrew for twice fruitful.

feel the famine, the people cried to Pharaoh for food. Then Pharaoh told all the Egyptians, "Go to Joseph and do what he tells you."

56When the famine had spread over the whole country, Joseph opened the storehouses and sold grain to the Egyptians, for the famine was severe throughout Egypt. 57And all the countries came to Egypt to buy grain from Joseph, because the famine was severe in all the world.

Joseph's Brothers Go to Egypt

42 When Jacob learned that there was grain in Egypt, he said to his sons, "Why do you just keep looking at each other?" 2He continued, "I have heard that there is grain in Egypt. Go down there and buy some for us, so that we may live and not die."

3Then ten of Joseph's brothers went down to buy grain from Egypt. 4But Jacob did not send Benjamin, Joseph's brother, with the others, because he was afraid that harm might come to him. 5So Israel's sons were among those who went to buy grain, for the famine was in the land of Canaan also.

6Now Joseph was the governor of the land, the one who sold grain to all its people. So when Joseph's brothers arrived, they bowed down to him with their faces to the ground. 7As soon as Joseph saw his brothers, he recognized them, but he pretended to be a stranger and spoke harshly to them. "Where do you come from?" he asked.

"From the land of Canaan," they replied, "to buy food."

8Although Joseph recognized his brothers, they did not recognize him. 9Then he remembered his dreams about them and said to them, "You are spies! You have come to see where our land is unprotected."

10"No, my lord," they answered. "Your servants have come to buy food. 11We are all the sons of one man. Your servants are honest men, not spies."

12"No!" he said to them. "You have come to see where our land is unprotected."

13But they replied, "Your servants were twelve brothers, the sons of one man, who lives in the land of Canaan. The youngest is now with our father, and one is no more."

14Joseph said to them, "It is just as I told you: You are spies! 15And this is how you will be tested: As surely as Pharaoh lives, you will not leave this place unless your youngest brother comes here. 16Send one of your number to get your brother; the rest of you will be kept in prison, so that your words may be tested to see if you are telling the truth. If you are not, then as surely as Pharaoh lives, you are spies!" 17And he put them all in custody for three days.

18On the third day, Joseph said to them, "Do this and you will live, for I fear God: 19If you are honest men, let one of your brothers stay here in prison, while the rest of you go and take grain back for your starving households. 20But you must bring your youngest brother to me, so that your words may be verified and that you may not die." This they proceeded to do.

21They said to one another, "Surely we are being punished because of our brother. We saw how distressed he was when he pleaded with us for his life, but we would not listen; that's why this distress has come upon us."

22Reuben replied, "Didn't I tell you not to sin against the boy? But you wouldn't listen! Now we must give an accounting for his blood." 23They did not realize that Joseph could understand them, since he was using an interpreter.

24He turned away from them and began to weep, but then turned back and spoke to them again. He had Simeon taken from them and bound before their eyes.

25Joseph gave orders to fill their bags with grain, to put each man's silver back in his sack, and to give them provisions for their journey. After this was done for them, 26they loaded their grain on their donkeys and left.

27At the place where they stopped for the night one of them opened his sack to get feed for his donkey, and he saw his silver in the mouth of his sack. 28"My silver has been returned," he said to his brothers. "Here it is in my sack."

Their hearts sank and they turned to each other trembling and said, "What is this that God has done to us?"

29When they came to their father Jacob in the land of Canaan, they told him all that had happened to them. They said, 30"The man who is lord over the land spoke harshly to us and treated us as though we were spying on the land. 31But we said to him, 'We are honest men; we are not spies. 32We were twelve brothers, sons of one father. One is no more, and the youngest is now with our father in Canaan.'

33"Then the man who is lord over the land said to us, 'This is how I will know whether you are honest men: Leave one of your brothers here with me, and take food for your starving households and go. 34But bring your youngest brother to me so I will know that you are not spies but honest men. Then I will give your brother back to you, and you can trade*a* in the land.' "

35As they were emptying their sacks, there in each man's sack was his pouch of silver! When they and their father saw the money pouches, they were frightened. 36Their father Jacob said to them, "You have deprived me of my children. Joseph is no more and Simeon is no more, and now you want to take Benjamin. Everything is against me!"

37Then Reuben said to his father, "You may put both of my sons to death if I do not bring him back to you. Entrust him to my care, and I will bring him back."

38But Jacob said, "My son will not go down there with you; his brother is dead and he is the only one left. If harm comes to him on the journey you are taking, you will bring my gray head down to the grave*b* in sorrow."

The Second Journey to Egypt

43 Now the famine was still severe in the land. 2So when they had eaten all the grain they had brought from Egypt, their father said to them, "Go back and buy us a little more food." 3But Judah said to him, "The man warned us solemnly, 'You will not see my face again unless your brother is with you.' 4If you will send our brother along with us, we will go down and buy food for you. 5But if you will not send him, we will not go down, because the man said to us, 'You will not see my face again unless your brother is with you.' "

6Israel asked, "Why did you bring this trouble on me by telling the man you had another brother?"

7They replied, "The man questioned us closely about ourselves and our family. 'Is your father still living?' he asked us. 'Do you have another brother?' We simply answered his questions. How were we to know he would say, 'Bring your brother down here'?"

8Then Judah said to Israel his father, "Send the boy along with me and we will

go at once, so that we and you and our children may live and not die. 9I myself will guarantee his safety; you can hold me personally responsible for him. If I do not bring him back to you and set him here before you, I will bear the blame before you all my life. 10As it is, if we had not delayed, we could have gone and returned twice."

11Then their father Israel said to them, "If it must be, then do this: Put some of the best products of the land in your bags and take them down to the man as a gift —a little balm and a little honey, some spices and myrrh, some pistachio nuts and almonds. 12Take double the amount of silver with you, for you must return the silver that was put back into the mouths of your sacks. Perhaps it was a mistake. 13Take your brother also and go back to the man at once. 14And may God Almighty*c* grant you mercy before the man so that he will let your other brother and Benjamin come back with you. As for me, if I am bereaved, I am bereaved."

15So the men took the gifts and double the amount of silver, and Benjamin also. They hurried down to Egypt and presented themselves to Joseph. 16When Joseph saw Benjamin with them, he said to the steward of his house, "Take these men to my house, slaughter an animal and prepare dinner; they are to eat with me at noon."

17The man did as Joseph told him and took the men to Joseph's house. 18Now the men were frightened when they were taken to his house. They thought, "We were brought here because of the silver that was put back into our sacks the first time. He wants to attack us and overpower us and seize us as slaves and take our donkeys."

19So they went up to Joseph's steward and spoke to him at the entrance to the house. 20"Please, sir," they said, "we came down here the first time to buy food. 21But at the place where we stopped for the night we opened our sacks and each of us found his silver—the exact weight—in the mouth of his sack. So we have brought it back with us. 22We have also brought additional silver with us to buy food. We don't know who put our silver in our sacks."

23"It's all right," he said. "Don't be afraid. Your God, the God of your father, has given you treasure in your sacks; I re-

a34 Or *move about freely*   *b38* Hebrew *Sheol*   *c14* Hebrew *El-Shaddai* ceived your silver." Then he brought Simeon out to them.

²⁴The steward took the men into Joseph's house, gave them water to wash their feet and provided fodder for their donkeys. ²⁵They prepared their gifts for Joseph's arrival at noon, because they had heard that they were to eat there.

²⁶When Joseph came home, they presented to him the gifts they had brought into the house, and they bowed down before him to the ground. ²⁷He asked them how they were, and then he said, "How is your aged father you told me about? Is he still living?"

²⁸They replied, "Your servant our father is still alive and well." And they bowed low to pay him honor.

²⁹As he looked about and saw his brother Benjamin, his own mother's son, he asked, "Is this your youngest brother, the one you told me about?" And he said, "God be gracious to you, my son." ³⁰Deeply moved at the sight of his brother, Joseph hurried out and looked for a place to weep. He went into his private room and wept there.

³¹After he had washed his face, he came out and, controlling himself, said, "Serve the food."

³²They served him by himself, the brothers by themselves, and the Egyptians who ate with him by themselves, because Egyptians could not eat with Hebrews, for that is detestable to Egyptians. ³³The men had been seated before him in the order of their ages, from the firstborn to the youngest; and they looked at each other in astonishment. ³⁴When portions were served to them from Joseph's table, Benjamin's portion was five times as much as anyone else's. So they feasted and drank freely with him.

A Silver Cup in a Sack

44 Now Joseph gave these instructions to the steward of his house: "Fill the men's sacks with as much food as they can carry, and put each man's silver in the mouth of his sack. ²Then put my cup, the silver one, in the mouth of the youngest one's sack, along with the silver for his grain." And he did as Joseph said.

³As morning dawned, the men were sent on their way with their donkeys. ⁴They had not gone far from the city when Joseph said to his steward, "Go after those men at once, and when you catch up with them, say to them, 'Why have you

repaid good with evil? ⁵Isn't this the cup my master drinks from and also uses for divination? This is a wicked thing you have done.' "

⁶When he caught up with them, he repeated these words to them. ⁷But they said to him, "Why does my lord say such things? Far be it from your servants to do anything like that! ⁸We even brought back to you from the land of Canaan the silver we found inside the mouths of our sacks. So why would we steal silver or gold from your master's house? ⁹If any of your servants is found to have it, he will die; and the rest of us will become my lord's slaves."

¹⁰"Very well, then," he said, "let it be as you say. Whoever is found to have it will become my slave; the rest of you will be free from blame."

¹¹Each of them quickly lowered his sack to the ground and opened it. ¹²Then the steward proceeded to search, beginning with the oldest and ending with the youngest. And the cup was found in Benjamin's sack. ¹³At this, they tore their clothes. Then they all loaded their donkeys and returned to the city.

¹⁴Joseph was still in the house when Judah and his brothers came in, and they threw themselves to the ground before him. ¹⁵Joseph said to them, "What is this you have done? Don't you know that a man like me can find things out by divination?"

¹⁶"What can we say to my lord?" Judah replied. "What can we say? How can we prove our innocence? God has uncovered your servants' guilt. We are now my lord's slaves—we ourselves and the one who was found to have the cup."

¹⁷But Joseph said, "Far be it from me to do such a thing! Only the man who was found to have the cup will become my slave. The rest of you, go back to your father in peace."

¹⁸Then Judah went up to him and said: "Please, my lord, let your servant speak a word to my lord. Do not be angry with your servant, though you are equal to Pharaoh himself. ¹⁹My lord asked his servants, 'Do you have a father or a brother?' ²⁰And we answered, 'We have an aged father, and there is a young son born to him in his old age. His brother is dead, and he is the only one of his mother's sons left, and his father loves him.'

²¹"Then you said to your servants, 'Bring him down to me so I can see him for myself.' ²²And we said to my lord, 'The

boy cannot leave his father; if he leaves him, his father will die.' 23But you told your servants, 'Unless your youngest brother comes down with you, you will not see my face again.' 24When we went back to your servant my father, we told him what my lord had said.

25"Then our father said, 'Go back and buy a little more food.' 26But we said, 'We cannot go down. Only if our youngest brother is with us will we go. We cannot see the man's face unless our youngest brother is with us.'

27"Your servant my father said to us, 'You know that my wife bore me two sons. 28One of them went away from me, and I said, "He has surely been torn to pieces." And I have not seen him since. 29If you take this one from me too and harm comes to him, you will bring my gray head down to the grave*a* in misery.'

30"So now, if the boy is not with us when I go back to your servant my father and if my father, whose life is closely bound up with the boy's life, 31sees that the boy isn't there, he will die. Your servants will bring the gray head of our father down to the grave in sorrow. 32Your servant guaranteed the boy's safety to my father. I said, 'If I do not bring him back to you, I will bear the blame before you, my father, all my life!'

33"Now then, please let your servant remain here as my lord's slave in place of the boy, and let the boy return with his brothers. 34How can I go back to my father if the boy is not with me? No! Do not let me see the misery that would come upon my father."

Joseph Makes Himself Known

45 Then Joseph could no longer control himself before all his attendants, and he cried out, "Have everyone leave my presence!" So there was no one with Joseph when he made himself known to his brothers. 2And he wept so loudly that the Egyptians heard him, and Pharaoh's household heard about it.

3Joseph said to his brothers, "I am Joseph! Is my father still living?" But his brothers were not able to answer him, because they were terrified at his presence.

4Then Joseph said to his brothers, "Come close to me." When they had done so, he said, "I am your brother Joseph, the one you sold into Egypt! 5And now, do not be distressed and do not be angry

with yourselves for selling me here, because it was to save lives that God sent me ahead of you. 6For two years now there has been famine in the land, and for the next five years there will not be plowing and reaping. 7But God sent me ahead of you to preserve for you a remnant on earth and to save your lives by a great deliverance.*b*

8"So then, it was not you who sent me here, but God. He made me father to Pharaoh, lord of his entire household and ruler of all Egypt. 9Now hurry back to my father and say to him, 'This is what your son Joseph says: God has made me lord of all Egypt. Come down to me; don't delay. 10You shall live in the region of Goshen and be near me—you, your children and grandchildren, your flocks and herds, and all you have. 11I will provide for you there, because five years of famine are still to come. Otherwise you and your household and all who belong to you will become destitute.'

12"You can see for yourselves, and so can my brother Benjamin, that it is really I who am speaking to you. 13Tell my father about all the honor accorded me in Egypt and about everything you have seen. And bring my father down here quickly."

14Then he threw his arms around his brother Benjamin and wept, and Benjamin embraced him, weeping. 15And he kissed all his brothers and wept over them. Afterward his brothers talked with him.

16When the news reached Pharaoh's palace that Joseph's brothers had come, Pharaoh and all his officials were pleased. 17Pharaoh said to Joseph, "Tell your brothers, 'Do this: Load your animals and return to the land of Canaan, 18and bring your father and your families back to me. I will give you the best of the land of Egypt and you can enjoy the fat of the land.'

19"You are also directed to tell them, 'Do this: Take some carts from Egypt for your children and your wives, and get your father and come. 20Never mind about your belongings, because the best of all Egypt will be yours.' "

21So the sons of Israel did this. Joseph gave them carts, as Pharaoh had commanded, and he also gave them provisions for their journey. 22To each of them he gave new clothing, but to Benjamin he

*a*29 Hebrew *Sheol*; also in verse 31   *b*7 Or *save you as a great band of survivors* gave three hundred shekels*a* of silver and five sets of clothes. ²³And this is what he sent to his father: ten donkeys loaded with the best things of Egypt, and ten female donkeys loaded with grain and bread and other provisions for his journey. ²⁴Then he sent his brothers away, and as they were leaving he said to them, "Don't quarrel on the way!"

²⁵So they went up out of Egypt and came to their father Jacob in the land of Canaan. ²⁶They told him, "Joseph is still alive! In fact, he is ruler of all Egypt." Jacob was stunned; he did not believe them. ²⁷But when they told him everything Joseph had said to them, and when he saw the carts Joseph had sent to carry him back, the spirit of their father Jacob revived. ²⁸And Israel said, "I'm convinced! My son Joseph is still alive. I will go and see him before I die."

Jacob Goes to Egypt

46 So Israel set out with all that was his, and when he reached Beersheba, he offered sacrifices to the God of his father Isaac.

²And God spoke to Israel in a vision at night and said, "Jacob! Jacob!"

"Here I am," he replied.

³"I am God, the God of your father," he said. "Do not be afraid to go down to Egypt, for I will make you into a great nation there. ⁴I will go down to Egypt with you, and I will surely bring you back again. And Joseph's own hand will close your eyes."

⁵Then Jacob left Beersheba, and Israel's sons took their father Jacob and their children and their wives in the carts that Pharaoh had sent to transport him. ⁶They also took with them their livestock and the possessions they had acquired in Canaan, and Jacob and all his offspring went to Egypt. ⁷He took with him to Egypt his sons and grandsons and his daughters and granddaughters—all his offspring.

⁸These are the names of the sons of Israel (Jacob and his descendants) who went to Egypt:

Reuben the firstborn of Jacob.
⁹The sons of Reuben:

Hanoch, Pallu, Hezron and Carmi.
¹⁰The sons of Simeon:
Jemuel, Jamin, Ohad, Jakin, Zohar and Shaul the son of a Canaanite woman.
¹¹The sons of Levi:
Gershon, Kohath and Merari.
¹²The sons of Judah:
Er, Onan, Shelah, Perez and Zerah (but Er and Onan had died in the land of Canaan).
The sons of Perez:
Hezron and Hamul.
¹³The sons of Issachar:
Tola, Puah,*b* Jashub*c* and Shimron.
¹⁴The sons of Zebulun:
Sered, Elon and Jahleel.
¹⁵These were the sons Leah bore to Jacob in Paddan Aram,*d* besides his daughter Dinah. These sons and daughters of his were thirty-three in all.

¹⁶The sons of Gad:
Zephon,*e* Haggi, Shuni, Ezbon, Eri, Arodi and Areli.
¹⁷The sons of Asher:
Imnah, Ishvah, Ishvi and Beriah.
Their sister was Serah.
The sons of Beriah:
Heber and Malkiel.
¹⁸These were the children born to Jacob by Zilpah, whom Laban had given to his daughter Leah—sixteen in all.

¹⁹The sons of Jacob's wife Rachel:
Joseph and Benjamin. ²⁰In Egypt, Manasseh and Ephraim were born to Joseph by Asenath daughter of Potiphera, priest of On.*f*
²¹The sons of Benjamin:
Bela, Beker, Ashbel, Gera, Naaman, Ehi, Rosh, Muppim, Huppim and Ard.
²²These were the sons of Rachel who were born to Jacob—fourteen in all.

²³The son of Dan:
Hushim.
²⁴The sons of Naphtali:
Jahziel, Guni, Jezer and Shillem.
²⁵These were the sons born to Jacob by Bilhah, whom Laban had given to his daughter Rachel—seven in all.

²⁶All those who went to Egypt with Ja-

---

*a*22 That is, about 7 1/2 pounds (about 3.5 kilograms)   *b*13 Samaritan Pentateuch and Syriac (see also 1 Chron. 7:1); Masoretic Text *Puvah*   *c*13 Samaritan Pentateuch and some Septuagint manuscripts (see also Num. 26:24 and 1 Chron. 7:1); Masoretic Text *Iob*   *d*15 That is, Northwest Mesopotamia *e*16 Samaritan Pentateuch and Septuagint (see also Num. 26:15); Masoretic Text *Ziphion*   *f*20 That is, Heliopolis cob—those who were his direct descendants, not counting his sons' wives—numbered sixty-six persons. [27]With the two sons[a] who had been born to Joseph in Egypt, the members of Jacob's family, which went to Egypt, were seventy[b] in all.

[28]Now Jacob sent Judah ahead of him to Joseph to get directions to Goshen. When they arrived in the region of Goshen, [29]Joseph had his chariot made ready and went to Goshen to meet his father Israel. As soon as Joseph appeared before him, he threw his arms around his father[c] and wept for a long time.

[30]Israel said to Joseph, "Now I am ready to die, since I have seen for myself that you are still alive."

[31]Then Joseph said to his brothers and to his father's household, "I will go up and speak to Pharaoh and will say to him, 'My brothers and my father's household, who were living in the land of Canaan, have come to me. [32]The men are shepherds; they tend livestock, and they have brought along their flocks and herds and everything they own.' [33]When Pharaoh calls you in and asks, 'What is your occupation?' [34]you should answer, 'Your servants have tended livestock from our boyhood on, just as our fathers did.' Then you will be allowed to settle in the region of Goshen, for all shepherds are detestable to the Egyptians."

47 Joseph went and told Pharaoh, "My father and brothers, with their flocks and herds and everything they own, have come from the land of Canaan and are now in Goshen." [2]He chose five of his brothers and presented them before Pharaoh.

[3]Pharaoh asked the brothers, "What is your occupation?"

"Your servants are shepherds," they replied to Pharaoh, "just as our fathers were." [4]They also said to him, "We have come to live here awhile, because the famine is severe in Canaan and your servants' flocks have no pasture. So now, please let your servants settle in Goshen."

[5]Pharaoh said to Joseph, "Your father and your brothers have come to you, [6]and the land of Egypt is before you; settle your father and your brothers in the best part of the land. Let them live in Goshen.

And if you know of any among them with special ability, put them in charge of my own livestock."

[7]Then Joseph brought his father Jacob in and presented him before Pharaoh. After Jacob blessed[d] Pharaoh, [8]Pharaoh asked him, "How old are you?"

[9]And Jacob said to Pharaoh, "The years of my pilgrimage are a hundred and thirty. My years have been few and difficult, and they do not equal the years of the pilgrimage of my fathers." [10]Then Jacob blessed[e] Pharaoh and went out from his presence.

[11]So Joseph settled his father and his brothers in Egypt and gave them property in the best part of the land, the district of Rameses, as Pharaoh directed. [12]Joseph also provided his father and his brothers and all his father's household with food, according to the number of their children.

Joseph and the Famine

[13]There was no food, however, in the whole region because the famine was severe; both Egypt and Canaan wasted away because of the famine. [14]Joseph collected all the money that was to be found in Egypt and Canaan in payment for the grain they were buying, and he brought it to Pharaoh's palace. [15]When the money of the people of Egypt and Canaan was gone, all Egypt came to Joseph and said, "Give us food. Why should we die before your eyes? Our money is used up."

[16]"Then bring your livestock," said Joseph. "I will sell you food in exchange for your livestock, since your money is gone." [17]So they brought their livestock to Joseph, and he gave them food in exchange for their horses, their sheep and goats, their cattle and donkeys. And he brought them through that year with food in exchange for all their livestock.

[18]When that year was over, they came to him the following year and said, "We cannot hide from our lord the fact that since our money is gone and our livestock belongs to you, there is nothing left for our lord except our bodies and our land. [19]Why should we perish before your eyes —we and our land as well? Buy us and our land in exchange for food, and we with our land will be in bondage to Pharaoh. Give us seed so that we may live and

---

a27 Hebrew; Septuagint *the nine children*   b27 Hebrew (see also Exodus 1:5 and footnote); Septuagint (see also Acts 7:14) *seventy-five*   c29 Hebrew *around him*   d7 Or *greeted*   e10 Or *said farewell to* not die, and that the land may not become desolate."

20So Joseph bought all the land in Egypt for Pharaoh. The Egyptians, one and all, sold their fields, because the famine was too severe for them. The land became Pharaoh's, 21and Joseph reduced the people to servitude,a from one end of Egypt to the other. 22However, he did not buy the land of the priests, because they received a regular allotment from Pharaoh and had food enough from the allotment Pharaoh gave them. That is why they did not sell their land.

23Joseph said to the people, "Now that I have bought you and your land today for Pharaoh, here is seed for you so you can plant the ground. 24But when the crop comes in, give a fifth of it to Pharaoh. The other four-fifths you may keep as seed for the fields and as food for yourselves and your households and your children."

25"You have saved our lives," they said. "May we find favor in the eyes of our lord; we will be in bondage to Pharaoh."

26So Joseph established it as a law concerning land in Egypt—still in force today—that a fifth of the produce belongs to Pharaoh. It was only the land of the priests that did not become Pharaoh's.

27Now the Israelites settled in Egypt in the region of Goshen. They acquired property there and were fruitful and increased greatly in number.

28Jacob lived in Egypt seventeen years, and the years of his life were a hundred and forty-seven. 29When the time drew near for Israel to die, he called for his son Joseph and said to him, "If I have found favor in your eyes, put your hand under my thigh and promise that you will show me kindness and faithfulness. Do not bury me in Egypt, 30but when I rest with my fathers, carry me out of Egypt and bury me where they are buried."

"I will do as you say," he said.

31"Swear to me," he said. Then Joseph swore to him, and Israel worshiped as he leaned on the top of his staff.b

Manasseh and Ephraim

48 Some time later Joseph was told, "Your father is ill." So he took his two sons Manasseh and Ephraim along with him. 2When Jacob was told, "Your son Joseph has come to you," Israel rallied his strength and sat up on the bed.

3Jacob said to Joseph, "God Almightyc appeared to me at Luz in the land of Canaan, and there he blessed me 4and said to me, 'I am going to make you fruitful and will increase your numbers. I will make you a community of peoples, and I will give this land as an everlasting possession to your descendants after you.'

5"Now then, your two sons born to you in Egypt before I came to you here will be reckoned as mine; Ephraim and Manasseh will be mine, just as Reuben and Simeon are mine. 6Any children born to you after them will be yours; in the territory they inherit they will be reckoned under the names of their brothers. 7As I was returning from Paddan,d to my sorrow Rachel died in the land of Canaan while we were still on the way, a little distance from Ephrath. So I buried her there beside the road to Ephrath" (that is, Bethlehem).

8When Israel saw the sons of Joseph, he asked, "Who are these?"

9"They are the sons God has given me here," Joseph said to his father.

Then Israel said, "Bring them to me so I may bless them."

10Now Israel's eyes were failing because of old age, and he could hardly see. So Joseph brought his sons close to him, and his father kissed them and embraced them.

11Israel said to Joseph, "I never expected to see your face again, and now God has allowed me to see your children too."

12Then Joseph removed them from Israel's knees and bowed down with his face to the ground. 13And Joseph took both of them, Ephraim on his right toward Israel's left hand and Manasseh on his left toward Israel's right hand, and brought them close to him. 14But Israel reached out his right hand and put it on Ephraim's head, though he was the younger, and crossing his arms, he put his left hand on Manasseh's head, even though Manasseh was the firstborn.

15Then he blessed Joseph and said,

"May the God before whom my
    fathers
  Abraham and Isaac walked,
the God who has been my shepherd
  all my life to this day,

---

a21 Samaritan Pentateuch and Septuagint (see also Vulgate); Masoretic Text *and he moved the people into the cities*   b31 Or *Israel bowed down at the head of his bed*   c3 Hebrew *El-Shaddai*   d7 That is, Northwest Mesopotamia

16the Angel who has delivered me from
all harm
—may he bless these boys.
May they be called by my name
and the names of my fathers
Abraham and Isaac,
and may they increase greatly
upon the earth."

17When Joseph saw his father placing
his right hand on Ephraim's head he was
displeased; so he took hold of his father's
hand to move it from Ephraim's head to
Manasseh's head. 18Joseph said to him,
"No, my father, this one is the firstborn;
put your right hand on his head."

19But his father refused and said, "I
know, my son, I know. He too will become a people, and he too will become
great. Nevertheless, his younger brother
will be greater than he, and his descendants will become a group of nations."
20He blessed them that day and said,

"In youra name will Israel pronounce
this blessing:
'May God make you like Ephraim
and Manasseh.'"

So he put Ephraim ahead of Manasseh.

21Then Israel said to Joseph, "I am
about to die, but God will be with youb
and take youb back to the land of yourb
fathers. 22And to you, as one who is over
your brothers, I give the ridge of landc I
took from the Amorites with my sword
and my bow."

Jacob Blesses His Sons

49 Then Jacob called for his sons and
said: "Gather around so I can tell
you what will happen to you in days to
come.

2"Assemble and listen, sons of Jacob;
listen to your father Israel.

3"Reuben, you are my firstborn,
my might, the first sign of my
strength,
excelling in honor, excelling in
power.
4Turbulent as the waters, you will no
longer excel,
for you went up onto your father's
bed,
onto my couch and defiled it.

5"Simeon and Levi are brothers—
their swordsd are weapons of
violence.
6Let me not enter their council,
let me not join their assembly,
for they have killed men in their
anger
and hamstrung oxen as they
pleased.
7Cursed be their anger, so fierce,
and their fury, so cruel!
I will scatter them in Jacob
and disperse them in Israel.

8"Judah,e your brothers will praise
you;
your hand will be on the neck of
your enemies;
your father's sons will bow down to
you.
9You are a lion's cub, O Judah;
you return from the prey, my
son.
Like a lion he crouches and lies
down,
like a lioness—who dares to rouse
him?
10The scepter will not depart from
Judah,
nor the ruler's staff from between
his feet,
until he comes to whom it belongsf
and the obedience of the nations is
his.
11He will tether his donkey to a vine,
his colt to the choicest branch;
he will wash his garments in wine,
his robes in the blood of grapes.
12His eyes will be darker than wine,
his teeth whiter than milk.g

13"Zebulun will live by the seashore
and become a haven for ships;
his border will extend toward
Sidon.

14"Issachar is a rawbonedh donkey
lying down between two
saddlebags.i
15When he sees how good is his resting
place
and how pleasant is his land,
he will bend his shoulder to the
burden
and submit to forced labor.

---

a20 The Hebrew is singular.   b21 The Hebrew is plural.   c22 Or And to you I give one portion more
than to your brothers—the portion   d5 The meaning of the Hebrew for this word is uncertain.
e8 Judah sounds like and may be derived from the Hebrew for praise.   f10 Or until Shiloh comes; or
until he comes to whom tribute belongs   g12 Or will be dull from wine, / his teeth white from milk
h14 Or strong   i14 Or campfires

VERSE FOR THE DAY:
Genesis 48:15

AUTHOR:
Beth Donigan Seversen

PASSAGE FOR THE DAY:
Genesis 48:8–16

The Lord Is My Shepherd

FINAL words intrigue me. Especially those of men and women of faith. At first, I viewed Jacob's final words incredulously. He refers to God as he "who has been my shepherd all my life to this day." How could Jacob have called God his shepherd?

Wasn't it Jacob . . .

who suffered a broken relationship with his brother?

who lived as a fugitive in a foreign land for at least twenty-six years?

whose own children's treachery caused him to become a stench to the Canaanites?

who was repeatedly treated unjustly by his father-in-law?

who lost his beloved wife Rachel?

who provoked his children to such hatred that they severed him from his favored son Joseph, so that he believed the latter dead for most of his life?

who lived under famine conditions so desperate that he sent his sons to Egypt for aid?

who suffered the anguish of losing not only Joseph, but also Benjamin?

who died in Egypt, on foreign soil?

Yet, in spite of all this, Jacob still called God his shepherd. As I have wondered about Jacob's faith and declaration, I believe God has directed me to these conclusions:

First, God shepherded Jacob by rescuing him from himself. Jacob brought about his own impoverished spiritual state. But God met with Jacob at Bethel and blessed him.

Second, God restored Jacob's broken relationships with both Isaac and Esau, despite the mess Jacob had made of them through his own greed and deception.

Third, God righted the wrongs in Jacob's life. In the end, God prospered Jacob and gave him his beloved Rachel—despite Laban's injustices—and returned to him both Joseph and Benjamin.

Now I realize that Jacob had many reasons to call God his shepherd. May God, my Father, rescue me from myself, restore my broken relationships, and right the wrongs in my life. I thank him for what he did for Jacob and for what he will do in my life.

Additional Scripture Readings:
Psalm 23:1–6; Luke 15:3–7

Go to page 59 for your next devotional reading.

16"Dan*a* will provide justice for his
   people
as one of the tribes of Israel.
17Dan will be a serpent by the roadside,
   a viper along the path,
that bites the horse's heels
   so that its rider tumbles backward.

18"I look for your deliverance, O LORD.

19"Gad*b* will be attacked by a band of
   raiders,
but he will attack them at their
   heels.

20"Asher's food will be rich;
   he will provide delicacies fit for a
   king.

21"Naphtali is a doe set free
   that bears beautiful fawns.*c*

22"Joseph is a fruitful vine,
   a fruitful vine near a spring,
whose branches climb over a wall.*d*
23With bitterness archers attacked him;
   they shot at him with hostility.
24But his bow remained steady,
   his strong arms stayed*e* limber,
because of the hand of the Mighty
   One of Jacob,
because of the Shepherd, the Rock
   of Israel,
25because of your father's God, who
   helps you,
because of the Almighty,*f* who
   blesses you
with blessings of the heavens above,
   blessings of the deep that lies
   below,
blessings of the breast and womb.
26Your father's blessings are greater
   than the blessings of the ancient
   mountains,
than*g* the bounty of the age-old
   hills.
Let all these rest on the head of
   Joseph,
on the brow of the prince among*h*
   his brothers.

27"Benjamin is a ravenous wolf;
   in the morning he devours the prey,
in the evening he divides the
   plunder."

28All these are the twelve tribes of Israel, and this is what their father said to them when he blessed them, giving each the blessing appropriate to him.

The Death of Jacob

29Then he gave them these instructions: "I am about to be gathered to my people. Bury me with my fathers in the cave in the field of Ephron the Hittite, 30the cave in the field of Machpelah, near Mamre in Canaan, which Abraham bought as a burial place from Ephron the Hittite, along with the field. 31There Abraham and his wife Sarah were buried, there Isaac and his wife Rebekah were buried, and there I buried Leah. 32The field and the cave in it were bought from the Hittites.*i*"

33When Jacob had finished giving instructions to his sons, he drew his feet up into the bed, breathed his last and was gathered to his people.

50 Joseph threw himself upon his father and wept over him and kissed him. 2Then Joseph directed the physicians in his service to embalm his father Israel. So the physicians embalmed him, 3taking a full forty days, for that was the time required for embalming. And the Egyptians mourned for him seventy days.

4When the days of mourning had passed, Joseph said to Pharaoh's court, "If I have found favor in your eyes, speak to Pharaoh for me. Tell him, 5'My father made me swear an oath and said, "I am about to die; bury me in the tomb I dug for myself in the land of Canaan." Now let me go up and bury my father; then I will return.' "

6Pharaoh said, "Go up and bury your father, as he made you swear to do."

7So Joseph went up to bury his father. All Pharaoh's officials accompanied him —the dignitaries of his court and all the dignitaries of Egypt— 8besides all the members of Joseph's household and his brothers and those belonging to his father's household. Only their children and their flocks and herds were left in Goshen. 9Chariots and horsemen*j* also went up with him. It was a very large company.

10When they reached the threshing floor of Atad, near the Jordan, they lamented loudly and bitterly; and there Joseph observed a seven-day period of

---

a16 Dan here means *he provides justice.*   *b19* Gad can mean *attack* and *band of raiders.*   *c21* Or
free; / he utters beautiful words   *d22* Or *Joseph is a wild colt, / a wild colt near a spring, / a wild donkey
on a terraced hill*   *e23,24* Or *archers will attack . . . will shoot . . . will remain . . . will stay*
f25 Hebrew *Shaddai*   *g26* Or *of my progenitors, / as great as*   *h26* Or *the one separated from*
i32 Or *the sons of Heth*   *j9* Or *charioteers*

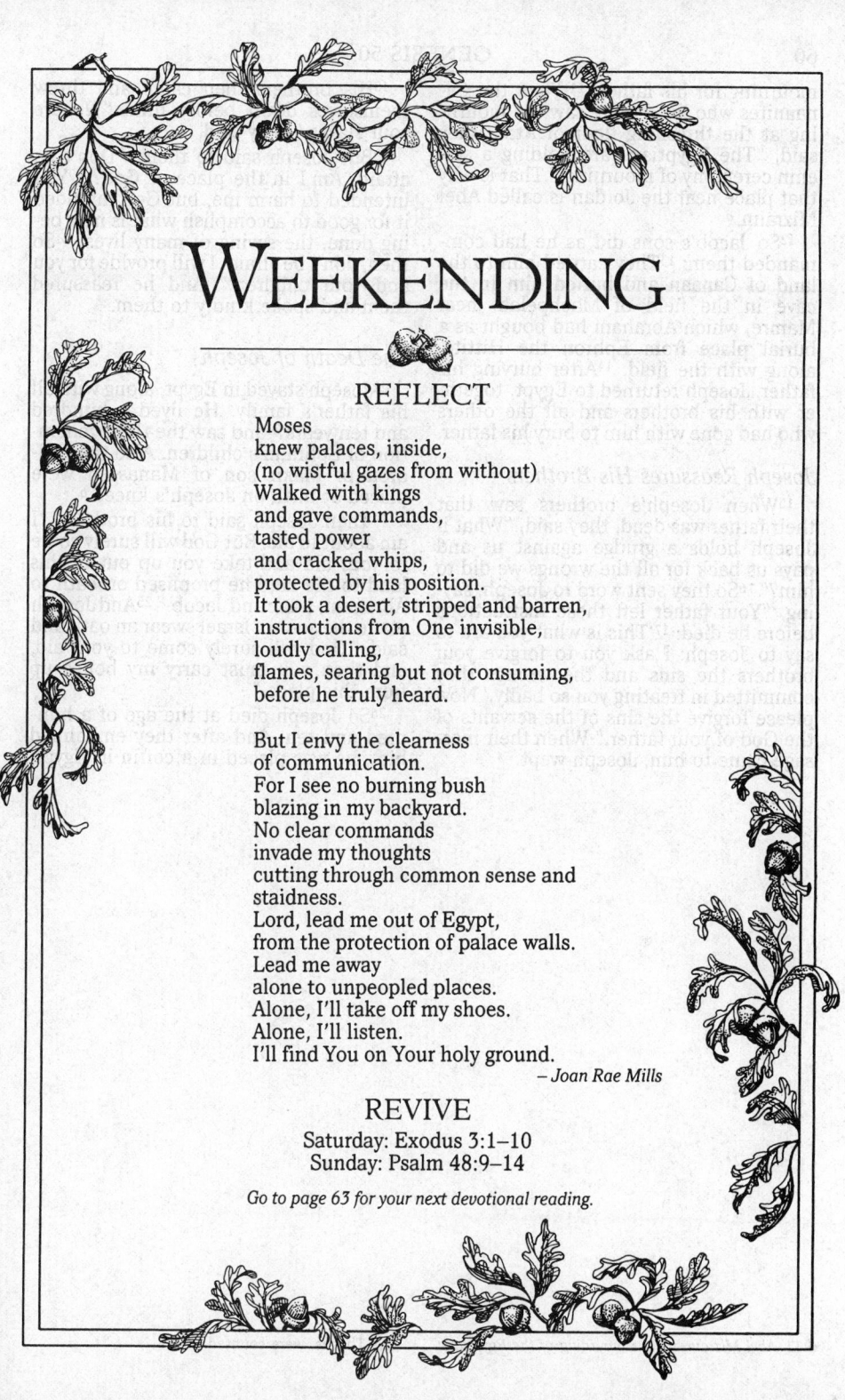

WEEKENDING

REFLECT

Moses
knew palaces, inside,
(no wistful gazes from without)
Walked with kings
and gave commands,
tasted power
and cracked whips,
protected by his position.
It took a desert, stripped and barren,
instructions from One invisible,
loudly calling,
flames, searing but not consuming,
before he truly heard.

But I envy the clearness
of communication.
For I see no burning bush
blazing in my backyard.
No clear commands
invade my thoughts
cutting through common sense and
staidness.
Lord, lead me out of Egypt,
from the protection of palace walls.
Lead me away
alone to unpeopled places.
Alone, I'll take off my shoes.
Alone, I'll listen.
I'll find You on Your holy ground.

– Joan Rae Mills

REVIVE

Saturday: Exodus 3:1–10
Sunday: Psalm 48:9–14

Go to page 63 for your next devotional reading.

mourning for his father. [11]When the Canaanites who lived there saw the mourning at the threshing floor of Atad, they said, "The Egyptians are holding a solemn ceremony of mourning." That is why that place near the Jordan is called Abel Mizraim. [a]

[12]So Jacob's sons did as he had commanded them: [13]They carried him to the land of Canaan and buried him in the cave in the field of Machpelah, near Mamre, which Abraham had bought as a burial place from Ephron the Hittite, along with the field. [14]After burying his father, Joseph returned to Egypt, together with his brothers and all the others who had gone with him to bury his father.

Joseph Reassures His Brothers

[15]When Joseph's brothers saw that their father was dead, they said, "What if Joseph holds a grudge against us and pays us back for all the wrongs we did to him?" [16]So they sent word to Joseph, saying, "Your father left these instructions before he died: [17]'This is what you are to say to Joseph: I ask you to forgive your brothers the sins and the wrongs they committed in treating you so badly.' Now please forgive the sins of the servants of the God of your father." When their message came to him, Joseph wept.

[18]His brothers then came and threw themselves down before him. "We are your slaves," they said.

[19]But Joseph said to them, "Don't be afraid. Am I in the place of God? [20]You intended to harm me, but God intended it for good to accomplish what is now being done, the saving of many lives. [21]So then, don't be afraid. I will provide for you and your children." And he reassured them and spoke kindly to them.

The Death of Joseph

[22]Joseph stayed in Egypt, along with all his father's family. He lived a hundred and ten years [23]and saw the third generation of Ephraim's children. Also the children of Makir son of Manasseh were placed at birth on Joseph's knees. [b]

[24]Then Joseph said to his brothers, "I am about to die. But God will surely come to your aid and take you up out of this land to the land he promised on oath to Abraham, Isaac and Jacob." [25]And Joseph made the sons of Israel swear an oath and said, "God will surely come to your aid, and then you must carry my bones up from this place."

[26]So Joseph died at the age of a hundred and ten. And after they embalmed him, he was placed in a coffin in Egypt.

---

[a]11 Abel Mizraim means mourning of the Egyptians.   [b]23 That is, were counted as his

*I*N the first half of this book, Moses recounts the exciting story of God delivering his people from slavery in Egypt. In the second half he tells about their stay at Mount Sinai, where they receive God's law and build the tabernacle. As you read this book, think about how God miraculously delivers you from slavery to Satan and sin through the death of his Son Jesus and how he wants you to obey his will (especially the Ten Commandments) in your daily life.

EXODUS

The Israelites Oppressed

1 These are the names of the sons of Israel who went to Egypt with Jacob, each with his family: ²Reuben, Simeon, Levi and Judah; ³Issachar, Zebulun and Benjamin; ⁴Dan and Naphtali; Gad and Asher. ⁵The descendants of Jacob numbered seventy*a* in all; Joseph was already in Egypt.

⁶Now Joseph and all his brothers and all that generation died, ⁷but the Israelites were fruitful and multiplied greatly and became exceedingly numerous, so that the land was filled with them.

⁸Then a new king, who did not know about Joseph, came to power in Egypt. ⁹"Look," he said to his people, "the Israelites have become much too numerous for us. ¹⁰Come, we must deal shrewdly with them or they will become even more numerous and, if war breaks out, will join our enemies, fight against us and leave the country."

¹¹So they put slave masters over them to oppress them with forced labor, and

---

*a*5 Masoretic Text (see also Gen. 46:27); Dead Sea Scrolls and Septuagint (see also Acts 7:14 and note at Gen. 46:27) *seventy-five* they built Pithom and Rameses as store cities for Pharaoh. ¹²But the more they were oppressed, the more they multiplied and spread; so the Egyptians came to dread the Israelites ¹³and worked them ruthlessly. ¹⁴They made their lives bitter with hard labor in brick and mortar and with all kinds of work in the fields; in all their hard labor the Egyptians used them ruthlessly.

¹⁵The king of Egypt said to the Hebrew midwives, whose names were Shiphrah and Puah, ¹⁶"When you help the Hebrew women in childbirth and observe them on the delivery stool, if it is a boy, kill him; but if it is a girl, let her live." ¹⁷The midwives, however, feared God and did not do what the king of Egypt had told them to do; they let the boys live. ¹⁸Then the king of Egypt summoned the midwives and asked them, "Why have you done this? Why have you let the boys live?"

¹⁹The midwives answered Pharaoh, "Hebrew women are not like Egyptian women; they are vigorous and give birth before the midwives arrive."

²⁰So God was kind to the midwives and the people increased and became even more numerous. ²¹And because the midwives feared God, he gave them families of their own.

²²Then Pharaoh gave this order to all his people: "Every boy that is born*a* you must throw into the Nile, but let every girl live."

The Birth of Moses

2 Now a man of the house of Levi married a Levite woman, ²and she became pregnant and gave birth to a son. When she saw that he was a fine child, she hid him for three months. ³But when she could hide him no longer, she got a papyrus basket for him and coated it with tar and pitch. Then she placed the child in it and put it among the reeds along the bank of the Nile. ⁴His sister stood at a distance to see what would happen to him.

⁵Then Pharaoh's daughter went down to the Nile to bathe, and her attendants were walking along the river bank. She saw the basket among the reeds and sent her slave girl to get it. ⁶She opened it and saw the baby. He was crying, and she felt sorry for him. "This is one of the Hebrew babies," she said.

⁷Then his sister asked Pharaoh's daughter, "Shall I go and get one of the Hebrew women to nurse the baby for you?"

⁸"Yes, go," she answered. And the girl went and got the baby's mother. ⁹Pharaoh's daughter said to her, "Take this baby and nurse him for me, and I will pay you." So the woman took the baby and nursed him. ¹⁰When the child grew older, she took him to Pharaoh's daughter and he became her son. She named him Moses,*b* saying, "I drew him out of the water."

Moses Flees to Midian

¹¹One day, after Moses had grown up, he went out to where his own people were and watched them at their hard labor. He saw an Egyptian beating a Hebrew, one of his own people. ¹²Glancing this way and that and seeing no one, he killed the Egyptian and hid him in the sand. ¹³The next day he went out and saw two Hebrews fighting. He asked the one in the wrong, "Why are you hitting your fellow Hebrew?"

¹⁴The man said, "Who made you ruler and judge over us? Are you thinking of killing me as you killed the Egyptian?" Then Moses was afraid and thought, "What I did must have become known."

¹⁵When Pharaoh heard of this, he tried to kill Moses, but Moses fled from Pharaoh and went to live in Midian, where he sat down by a well. ¹⁶Now a priest of Midian had seven daughters, and they came to draw water and fill the troughs to water their father's flock. ¹⁷Some shepherds came along and drove them away, but Moses got up and came to their rescue and watered their flock.

¹⁸When the girls returned to Reuel their father, he asked them, "Why have you returned so early today?"

¹⁹They answered, "An Egyptian rescued us from the shepherds. He even drew water for us and watered the flock."

²⁰"And where is he?" he asked his daughters. "Why did you leave him? Invite him to have something to eat."

²¹Moses agreed to stay with the man, who gave his daughter Zipporah to Moses in marriage. ²²Zipporah gave birth to a

---

a22 Masoretic Text; Samaritan Pentateuch, Septuagint and Targums *born to the Hebrews*   *b10 Moses* sounds like the Hebrew for *draw out.*

son, and Moses named him Gershom,ᵃ saying, "I have become an alien in a foreign land."

²³During that long period, the king of Egypt died. The Israelites groaned in their slavery and cried out, and their cry for help because of their slavery went up to God. ²⁴God heard their groaning and he remembered his covenant with Abraham, with Isaac and with Jacob. ²⁵So God looked on the Israelites and was concerned about them.

Moses and the Burning Bush

3 Now Moses was tending the flock of Jethro his father-in-law, the priest of Midian, and he led the flock to the far side of the desert and came to Horeb, the mountain of God. ²There the angel of the LORD appeared to him in flames of fire from within a bush. Moses saw that though the bush was on fire it did not burn up. ³So Moses thought, "I will go over and see this strange sight—why the bush does not burn up."

⁴When the LORD saw that he had gone over to look, God called to him from within the bush, "Moses! Moses!"

And Moses said, "Here I am."

⁵"Do not come any closer," God said. "Take off your sandals, for the place where you are standing is holy ground." ⁶Then he said, "I am the God of your fa-

ᵃ22 Gershom sounds like the Hebrew for an alien there.

MONDAY

VERSE FOR THE DAY:
Exodus 2:3

AUTHOR:
Jeanette Lockerbie

PASSAGE FOR THE DAY:
Exodus 2:1–10

Faith in Action

TODAY'S story tells of a mother, unknown by name to the majority of people, whose son was undoubtedly one of the greatest emancipators of all history: Moses.

His mother's name was Jochebed (Exodus 6:20).

Could she have known, that day she committed her three-month-old baby boy to the banks of the Nile (river of death for Hebrew babies, Exodus 1:22) that this was a child of destiny? To her he was "a fine child" (Exodus 2:1), but then what child is not, in his mother's eyes?

Jochebed's faith cost her something: fear of the great Pharaoh's wrath, should her deed be discovered by his executioners. Undaunted, this mother waited in expectation of deliverance for her son.

God had a plan for this boy—and his plan called for the cooperation of a mother who would dare to go against the edict of a mighty, godless ruler.

The same Lord has a plan for your son or daughter. Civil powers can make their decrees: No prayer in the schools, no Bible to be read in certain public places. Anti-God factions can spew out their atheism. God is still the "God of Jochebed." He will take note of our efforts to deliver our own children. "Nursing them" with the Word of God; "bathing them" in prayer, who knows? We may be entrusted with a "Moses"!

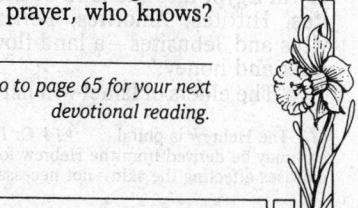

Additional Scripture Readings:
1 Samuel 1:9–28; 2 Timothy 1:5; 3:14–17

Go to page 65 for your next devotional reading.

ther, the God of Abraham, the God of Isaac and the God of Jacob." At this, Moses hid his face, because he was afraid to look at God.

7The LORD said, "I have indeed seen the misery of my people in Egypt. I have heard them crying out because of their slave drivers, and I am concerned about their suffering. 8So I have come down to rescue them from the hand of the Egyptians and to bring them up out of that land into a good and spacious land, a land flowing with milk and honey—the home of the Canaanites, Hittites, Amorites, Perizzites, Hivites and Jebusites. 9And now the cry of the Israelites has reached me, and I have seen the way the Egyptians are oppressing them. 10So now, go. I am sending you to Pharaoh to bring my people the Israelites out of Egypt."

11But Moses said to God, "Who am I, that I should go to Pharaoh and bring the Israelites out of Egypt?"

12And God said, "I will be with you. And this will be the sign to you that it is I who have sent you: When you have brought the people out of Egypt, you*a* will worship God on this mountain."

13Moses said to God, "Suppose I go to the Israelites and say to them, 'The God of your fathers has sent me to you,' and they ask me, 'What is his name?' Then what shall I tell them?"

14God said to Moses, "I AM WHO I AM.*b* This is what you are to say to the Israelites: 'I AM has sent me to you.'"

15God also said to Moses, "Say to the Israelites, 'The LORD,*c* the God of your fathers—the God of Abraham, the God of Isaac and the God of Jacob—has sent me to you.' This is my name forever, the name by which I am to be remembered from generation to generation.

16"Go, assemble the elders of Israel and say to them, 'The LORD, the God of your fathers—the God of Abraham, Isaac and Jacob—appeared to me and said: I have watched over you and have seen what has been done to you in Egypt. 17And I have promised to bring you up out of your misery in Egypt into the land of the Canaanites, Hittites, Amorites, Perizzites, Hivites and Jebusites—a land flowing with milk and honey.'

18"The elders of Israel will listen to you.

Then you and the elders are to go to the king of Egypt and say to him, 'The LORD, the God of the Hebrews, has met with us. Let us take a three-day journey into the desert to offer sacrifices to the LORD our God.' 19But I know that the king of Egypt will not let you go unless a mighty hand compels him. 20So I will stretch out my hand and strike the Egyptians with all the wonders that I will perform among them. After that, he will let you go.

21"And I will make the Egyptians favorably disposed toward this people, so that when you leave you will not go empty-handed. 22Every woman is to ask her neighbor and any woman living in her house for articles of silver and gold and for clothing, which you will put on your sons and daughters. And so you will plunder the Egyptians."

Signs for Moses

4 Moses answered, "What if they do not believe me or listen to me and say, 'The LORD did not appear to you'?"

2Then the LORD said to him, "What is that in your hand?"

"A staff," he replied.

3The LORD said, "Throw it on the ground."

Moses threw it on the ground and it became a snake, and he ran from it. 4Then the LORD said to him, "Reach out your hand and take it by the tail." So Moses reached out and took hold of the snake and it turned back into a staff in his hand. 5"This," said the LORD, "is so that they may believe that the LORD, the God of their fathers—the God of Abraham, the God of Isaac and the God of Jacob—has appeared to you."

6Then the LORD said, "Put your hand inside your cloak." So Moses put his hand into his cloak, and when he took it out, it was leprous,*d* like snow.

7"Now put it back into your cloak," he said. So Moses put his hand back into his cloak, and when he took it out, it was restored, like the rest of his flesh.

8Then the LORD said, "If they do not believe you or pay attention to the first miraculous sign, they may believe the second. 9But if they do not believe these two signs or listen to you, take some water from the Nile and pour it on the dry

---

a12 The Hebrew is plural. *b14* Or *I WILL BE WHAT I WILL BE* and may be derived from the Hebrew for *I AM* in verse 14. *c15* The Hebrew for LORD sounds like and may be derived from the Hebrew for *I AM* in verse 14. *d6* The Hebrew word was used for various diseases affecting the skin—not necessarily leprosy.

ground. The water you take from the river will become blood on the ground."

[10]Moses said to the LORD, "O Lord, I have never been eloquent, neither in the past nor since you have spoken to your servant. I am slow of speech and tongue."

[11]The LORD said to him, "Who gave man his mouth? Who makes him deaf or

TUESDAY

VERSE FOR THE DAY:
Exodus 3:5

AUTHOR:
Anne Ortlund

PASSAGE FOR THE DAY:
Exodus 3:1–5

Omnipresence

I WALKED the other day along a river
And watched the ducks and heard some
          hawklings' cries;
Then suddenly the nearness of my Saviour
Brought tears of joy and wonder to my eyes.

Oh, praise the Lord!
"This earth is crammed with heaven!"
Oh, praise the Lord!
And, Christian, look around!
For every bush you pass with fire is flaming,
And every spot you tread is holy ground.

I stopped the other day to watch a fountain
And marvelled at the magic of its grace;
Then suddenly my heart was on a mountain
And worshiping Jehovah face to face! . . .

I wept the other day—oh, Christian, hear it!
I wept the other day without control,
But suddenly the blessed Holy Spirit
Spoke peace again and calmed my needy soul.

Oh, praise the Lord!
"This earth is crammed with heaven!"
Oh, praise the Lord!
And, Christian, look around!
For every bush you pass with fire is flaming,
And every spot you tread is holy ground.

Additional Scripture Readings:
Psalm 24:1–2; 139:1–24

*Go to page 67 for your next
devotional reading.*

mute? Who gives him sight or makes him blind? Is it not I, the LORD? 12Now go; I will help you speak and will teach you what to say."

13But Moses said, "O Lord, please send someone else to do it."

14Then the LORD's anger burned against Moses and he said, "What about your brother, Aaron the Levite? I know he can speak well. He is already on his way to meet you, and his heart will be glad when he sees you. 15You shall speak to him and put words in his mouth; I will help both of you speak and will teach you what to do. 16He will speak to the people for you, and it will be as if he were your mouth and as if you were God to him. 17But take this staff in your hand so you can perform miraculous signs with it."

Moses Returns to Egypt

18Then Moses went back to Jethro his father-in-law and said to him, "Let me go back to my own people in Egypt to see if any of them are still alive."

Jethro said, "Go, and I wish you well."

19Now the LORD had said to Moses in Midian, "Go back to Egypt, for all the men who wanted to kill you are dead." 20So Moses took his wife and sons, put them on a donkey and started back to Egypt. And he took the staff of God in his hand.

21The LORD said to Moses, "When you return to Egypt, see that you perform before Pharaoh all the wonders I have given you the power to do. But I will harden his heart so that he will not let the people go. 22Then say to Pharaoh, 'This is what the LORD says: Israel is my firstborn son, 23and I told you, "Let my son go, so he may worship me." But you refused to let him go; so I will kill your firstborn son.' "

24At a lodging place on the way, the LORD met Moses,a and was about to kill him. 25But Zipporah took a flint knife, cut off her son's foreskin and touched Moses', feet with it.b "Surely you are a bridegroom of blood to me," she said. 26So the LORD let him alone. (At that time she said "bridegroom of blood," referring to circumcision.)

27The LORD said to Aaron, "Go into the desert to meet Moses." So he met Moses at the mountain of God and kissed him. 28Then Moses told Aaron everything the LORD had sent him to say, and also about all the miraculous signs he had commanded him to perform.

29Moses and Aaron brought together all the elders of the Israelites, 30and Aaron told them everything the LORD had said to Moses. He also performed the signs before the people, 31and they believed. And when they heard that the LORD was concerned about them and had seen their misery, they bowed down and worshiped.

Bricks Without Straw

5 Afterward Moses and Aaron went to Pharaoh and said, "This is what the LORD, the God of Israel, says: 'Let my people go, so that they may hold a festival to me in the desert.' "

2Pharaoh said, "Who is the LORD, that I should obey him and let Israel go? I do not know the LORD and I will not let Israel go."

3Then they said, "The God of the Hebrews has met with us. Now let us take a three-day journey into the desert to offer sacrifices to the LORD our God, or he may strike us with plagues or with the sword."

4But the king of Egypt said, "Moses and Aaron, why are you taking the people away from their labor? Get back to your work!" 5Then Pharaoh said, "Look, the people of the land are now numerous, and you are stopping them from working."

6That same day Pharaoh gave this order to the slave drivers and foremen in charge of the people: 7"You are no longer to supply the people with straw for making bricks; let them go and gather their own straw. 8But require them to make the same number of bricks as before; don't reduce the quota. They are lazy; that is why they are crying out, 'Let us go and sacrifice to our God.' 9Make the work harder for the men so that they keep working and pay no attention to lies."

10Then the slave drivers and the foremen went out and said to the people, "This is what Pharaoh says: 'I will not give you any more straw. 11Go and get your own straw wherever you can find it, but your work will not be reduced at all.' " 12So the people scattered all over Egypt to gather stubble to use for straw. 13The slave drivers kept pressing them, saying, "Complete the work required of you for each day, just as when you had straw." 14The Israelite foremen appointed by

---

a24 Or Moses' son,; Hebrew him   b25 Or and drew near Moses', feet

VERSE FOR THE DAY:
Exodus 4:11

AUTHOR:
Joni Eareckson Tada

PASSAGE FOR THE DAY:
Exodus 4:1–31

God's Sovereign Control

I RECEIVED a letter recently from a woman named Joanna. She wrote:

> Joni, thank you for your ministry to the disabled. I'm legally blind and teach at a church school. My husband and I would like to know if you have a Biblical answer to the question of whether it is right to have children when there's a possibility they might inherit a handicap. We believe children are gifts from God, but many have said it is selfish to have a child who could potentially have a handicap. We're unsure of what to do.

I searched high and low in the Bible to find a direct answer to Joanna's question. But it only says that God gives children as blessings with no reference to their abilities or disabilities. In my opinion, in the absence of a clear direction from Scripture, the decision is left up to the individual.

But there was an important verse from Exodus 4 that I was able to share with Joanna. It seems Moses was distraught about his own handicap, a kind of speech impairment. God answered him in the eleventh verse: "Who gave man his mouth? Who makes him deaf or mute? Who gives him sight or makes him blind? Is it not I, the LORD?" (Exodus 4:11).

Moses needed to hear that. But Exodus 4:11 is also a powerful statement and a wonderful assurance to an expectant mother. God controls all things, whether genetic mistakes or chromosome miscounts. Somehow, all these "accidents"—whether prenatal problems or injuries at birth—come under the sovereign control of God.

And what does God value most in any person's life, whether able-bodied or disabled? Isn't it a personal relationship with him? A life of love and kindness? A cheerful spirit and a heart that is godly? These qualities are possible for even severely disabled people to cultivate.

And Joanna and her husband? They're decorating a nursery right now.

Additional Scripture Readings:
John 9:1–3; 2 Corinthians 12:9

Go to page 77 for your next devotional reading.

Pharaoh's slave drivers were beaten and were asked, "Why didn't you meet your quota of bricks yesterday or today, as before?"

15Then the Israelite foremen went and appealed to Pharaoh: "Why have you treated your servants this way? 16Your servants are given no straw, yet we are told, 'Make bricks!' Your servants are being beaten, but the fault is with your own people."

17Pharaoh said, "Lazy, that's what you are—lazy! That is why you keep saying, 'Let us go and sacrifice to the LORD.' 18Now get to work. You will not be given any straw, yet you must produce your full quota of bricks."

19The Israelite foremen realized they were in trouble when they were told, "You are not to reduce the number of bricks required of you for each day." 20When they left Pharaoh, they found Moses and Aaron waiting to meet them, 21and they said, "May the LORD look upon you and judge you! You have made us a stench to Pharaoh and his officials and have put a sword in their hand to kill us."

God Promises Deliverance

22Moses returned to the LORD and said, "O Lord, why have you brought trouble upon this people? Is this why you sent me? 23Ever since I went to Pharaoh to speak in your name, he has brought trouble upon this people, and you have not rescued your people at all."

6 Then the LORD said to Moses, "Now you will see what I will do to Pharaoh: Because of my mighty hand he will let them go; because of my mighty hand he will drive them out of his country."

2God also said to Moses, "I am the LORD. 3I appeared to Abraham, to Isaac and to Jacob as God Almighty,a but by my name the LORDb I did not make myself known to them.c 4I also established my covenant with them to give them the land of Canaan, where they lived as aliens. 5Moreover, I have heard the groaning of the Israelites, whom the Egyptians are enslaving, and I have remembered my covenant.

6"Therefore, say to the Israelites: 'I am the LORD, and I will bring you out from under the yoke of the Egyptians. I will free you from being slaves to them, and I

will redeem you with an outstretched arm and with mighty acts of judgment. 7I will take you as my own people, and I will be your God. Then you will know that I am the LORD your God, who brought you out from under the yoke of the Egyptians. 8And I will bring you to the land I swore with uplifted hand to give to Abraham, to Isaac and to Jacob. I will give it to you as a possession. I am the LORD.' "

9Moses reported this to the Israelites, but they did not listen to him because of their discouragement and cruel bondage.

10Then the LORD said to Moses, 11"Go, tell Pharaoh king of Egypt to let the Israelites go out of his country."

12But Moses said to the LORD, "If the Israelites will not listen to me, why would Pharaoh listen to me, since I speak with faltering lipsd?"

Family Record of Moses and Aaron

13Now the LORD spoke to Moses and Aaron about the Israelites and Pharaoh king of Egypt, and he commanded them to bring the Israelites out of Egypt.

14These were the heads of their familiese:

The sons of Reuben the firstborn son of Israel were Hanoch and Pallu, Hezron and Carmi. These were the clans of Reuben.

15The sons of Simeon were Jemuel, Jamin, Ohad, Jakin, Zohar and Shaul the son of a Canaanite woman. These were the clans of Simeon.

16These were the names of the sons of Levi according to their records: Gershon, Kohath and Merari. Levi lived 137 years.

17The sons of Gershon, by clans, were Libni and Shimei.

18The sons of Kohath were Amram, Izhar, Hebron and Uzziel. Kohath lived 133 years.

19The sons of Merari were Mahli and Mushi.

These were the clans of Levi according to their records.

20Amram married his father's sister Jochebed, who bore him Aaron and Moses. Amram lived 137 years.

21The sons of Izhar were Korah, Nepheg and Zicri.

²²The sons of Uzziel were Mishael, Elzaphan and Sithri.

²³Aaron married Elisheba, daughter of Amminadab and sister of Nahshon, and she bore him Nadab and Abihu, Eleazar and Ithamar.

²⁴The sons of Korah were Assir, Elkanah and Abiasaph. These were the Korahite clans.

²⁵Eleazar son of Aaron married one of the daughters of Putiel, and she bore him Phinehas.

These were the heads of the Levite families, clan by clan.

²⁶It was this same Aaron and Moses to whom the LORD said, "Bring the Israelites out of Egypt by their divisions." ²⁷They were the ones who spoke to Pharaoh king of Egypt about bringing the Israelites out of Egypt. It was the same Moses and Aaron.

Aaron to Speak for Moses

²⁸Now when the LORD spoke to Moses in Egypt, ²⁹he said to him, "I am the LORD. Tell Pharaoh king of Egypt everything I tell you."

³⁰But Moses said to the LORD, "Since I speak with faltering lips, why would Pharaoh listen to me?"

7 Then the LORD said to Moses, "See, I have made you like God to Pharaoh, and your brother Aaron will be your prophet. ²You are to say everything I command you, and your brother Aaron is to tell Pharaoh to let the Israelites go out of his country. ³But I will harden Pharaoh's heart, and though I multiply my miraculous signs and wonders in Egypt, ⁴he will not listen to you. Then I will lay my hand on Egypt and with mighty acts of judgment I will bring out my divisions, my people the Israelites. ⁵And the Egyptians will know that I am the LORD when I stretch out my hand against Egypt and bring the Israelites out of it."

⁶Moses and Aaron did just as the LORD commanded them. ⁷Moses was eighty years old and Aaron eighty-three when they spoke to Pharaoh.

Aaron's Staff Becomes a Snake

⁸The LORD said to Moses and Aaron, ⁹"When Pharaoh says to you, 'Perform a miracle,' then say to Aaron, 'Take your staff and throw it down before Pharaoh,' and it will become a snake."

¹⁰So Moses and Aaron went to Pharaoh and did just as the LORD commanded. Aaron threw his staff down in front of Pharaoh and his officials, and it became a snake. ¹¹Pharaoh then summoned wise men and sorcerers, and the Egyptian magicians also did the same things by their secret arts: ¹²Each one threw down his staff and it became a snake. But Aaron's staff swallowed up their staffs. ¹³Yet Pharaoh's heart became hard and he would not listen to them, just as the LORD had said.

The Plague of Blood

¹⁴Then the LORD said to Moses, "Pharaoh's heart is unyielding; he refuses to let the people go. ¹⁵Go to Pharaoh in the morning as he goes out to the water. Wait on the bank of the Nile to meet him, and take in your hand the staff that was changed into a snake. ¹⁶Then say to him, 'The LORD, the God of the Hebrews, has sent me to say to you: Let my people go, so that they may worship me in the desert. But until now you have not listened. ¹⁷This is what the LORD says: By this you will know that I am the LORD: With the staff that is in my hand I will strike the water of the Nile, and it will be changed into blood. ¹⁸The fish in the Nile will die, and the river will stink; the Egyptians will not be able to drink its water.' "

¹⁹The LORD said to Moses, "Tell Aaron, 'Take your staff and stretch out your hand over the waters of Egypt—over the streams and canals, over the ponds and all the reservoirs'—and they will turn to blood. Blood will be everywhere in Egypt, even in the wooden buckets and stone jars."

²⁰Moses and Aaron did just as the LORD had commanded. He raised his staff in the presence of Pharaoh and his officials and struck the water of the Nile, and all the water was changed into blood. ²¹The fish in the Nile died, and the river smelled so bad that the Egyptians could not drink its water. Blood was everywhere in Egypt.

²²But the Egyptian magicians did the same things by their secret arts, and Pharaoh's heart became hard; he would not listen to Moses and Aaron, just as the LORD had said. ²³Instead, he turned and went into his palace, and did not take even this to heart. ²⁴And all the Egyptians dug along the Nile to get drinking water, because they could not drink the water of the river.

The Plague of Frogs

²⁵Seven days passed after the LORD

8 struck the Nile. [1]Then the LORD said to Moses, "Go to Pharaoh and say to him, 'This is what the LORD says: Let my people go, so that they may worship me. [2]If you refuse to let them go, I will plague your whole country with frogs. [3]The Nile will teem with frogs. They will come up into your palace and your bedroom and onto your bed, into the houses of your officials and on your people, and into your ovens and kneading troughs. [4]The frogs will go up on you and your people and all your officials.' "

[5]Then the LORD said to Moses, "Tell Aaron, 'Stretch out your hand with your staff over the streams and canals and ponds, and make frogs come up on the land of Egypt.' "

[6]So Aaron stretched out his hand over the waters of Egypt, and the frogs came up and covered the land. [7]But the magicians did the same things by their secret arts; they also made frogs come up on the land of Egypt.

[8]Pharaoh summoned Moses and Aaron and said, "Pray to the LORD to take the frogs away from me and my people, and I will let your people go to offer sacrifices to the LORD."

[9]Moses said to Pharaoh, "I leave to you the honor of setting the time for me to pray for you and your officials and your people that you and your houses may be rid of the frogs, except for those that remain in the Nile."

[10]"Tomorrow," Pharaoh said.

Moses replied, "It will be as you say, so that you may know there is no one like the LORD our God. [11]The frogs will leave you and your houses, your officials and your people; they will remain only in the Nile."

[12]After Moses and Aaron left Pharaoh, Moses cried out to the LORD about the frogs he had brought on Pharaoh. [13]And the LORD did what Moses asked. The frogs died in the houses, in the courtyards and in the fields. [14]They were piled into heaps, and the land reeked of them. [15]But when Pharaoh saw that there was relief, he hardened his heart and would not listen to Moses and Aaron, just as the LORD had said.

The Plague of Gnats

[16]Then the LORD said to Moses, "Tell Aaron, 'Stretch out your staff and strike the dust of the ground,' and throughout the land of Egypt the dust will become gnats." [17]They did this, and when Aaron stretched out his hand with the staff and struck the dust of the ground, gnats came upon men and animals. All the dust throughout the land of Egypt became gnats. [18]But when the magicians tried to produce gnats by their secret arts, they could not. And the gnats were on men and animals.

[19]The magicians said to Pharaoh, "This is the finger of God." But Pharaoh's heart was hard and he would not listen, just as the LORD had said.

The Plague of Flies

[20]Then the LORD said to Moses, "Get up early in the morning and confront Pharaoh as he goes to the water and say to him, 'This is what the LORD says: Let my people go, so that they may worship me. [21]If you do not let my people go, I will send swarms of flies on you and your officials, on your people and into your houses. The houses of the Egyptians will be full of flies, and even the ground where they are.

[22]" 'But on that day I will deal differently with the land of Goshen, where my people live; no swarms of flies will be there, so that you will know that I, the LORD, am in this land. [23]I will make a distinction[a] between my people and your people. This miraculous sign will occur tomorrow.' "

[24]And the LORD did this. Dense swarms of flies poured into Pharaoh's palace and into the houses of his officials, and throughout Egypt the land was ruined by the flies.

[25]Then Pharaoh summoned Moses and Aaron and said, "Go, sacrifice to your God here in the land."

[26]But Moses said, "That would not be right. The sacrifices we offer the LORD our God would be detestable to the Egyptians. And if we offer sacrifices that are detestable in their eyes, will they not stone us? [27]We must take a three-day journey into the desert to offer sacrifices to the LORD our God, as he commands us."

[28]Pharaoh said, "I will let you go to offer sacrifices to the LORD your God in the desert, but you must not go very far. Now pray for me."

[29]Moses answered, "As soon as I leave you, I will pray to the LORD, and tomorrow the flies will leave Pharaoh and his offi-

---

a23 Septuagint and Vulgate; Hebrew *will put a deliverance* cials and his people. Only be sure that Pharaoh does not act deceitfully again by not letting the people go to offer sacrifices to the LORD."

³⁰Then Moses left Pharaoh and prayed to the LORD, ³¹and the LORD did what Moses asked: The flies left Pharaoh and his officials and his people; not a fly remained. ³²But this time also Pharaoh hardened his heart and would not let the people go.

The Plague on Livestock

9 Then the LORD said to Moses, "Go to Pharaoh and say to him, 'This is what the LORD, the God of the Hebrews, says: "Let my people go, so that they may worship me." ²If you refuse to let them go and continue to hold them back, ³the hand of the LORD will bring a terrible plague on your livestock in the field—on your horses and donkeys and camels and on your cattle and sheep and goats. ⁴But the LORD will make a distinction between the livestock of Israel and that of Egypt, so that no animal belonging to the Israelites will die.' "

⁵The LORD set a time and said, "Tomorrow the LORD will do this in the land." ⁶And the next day the LORD did it: All the livestock of the Egyptians died, but not one animal belonging to the Israelites died. ⁷Pharaoh sent men to investigate and found that not even one of the animals of the Israelites had died. Yet his heart was unyielding and he would not let the people go.

The Plague of Boils

⁸Then the LORD said to Moses and Aaron, "Take handfuls of soot from a furnace and have Moses toss it into the air in the presence of Pharaoh. ⁹It will become fine dust over the whole land of Egypt, and festering boils will break out on men and animals throughout the land."

¹⁰So they took soot from a furnace and stood before Pharaoh. Moses tossed it into the air, and festering boils broke out on men and animals. ¹¹The magicians could not stand before Moses because of the boils that were on them and on all the Egyptians. ¹²But the LORD hardened Pharaoh's heart and he would not listen to Moses and Aaron, just as the LORD had said to Moses.

The Plague of Hail

¹³Then the LORD said to Moses, "Get up early in the morning, confront Pharaoh and say to him, 'This is what the LORD, the God of the Hebrews, says: Let my people go, so that they may worship me, ¹⁴or this time I will send the full force of my plagues against you and against your officials and your people, so you may know that there is no one like me in all the earth. ¹⁵For by now I could have stretched out my hand and struck you and your people with a plague that would have wiped you off the earth. ¹⁶But I have raised you up ᵃ for this very purpose, that I might show you my power and that my name might be proclaimed in all the earth. ¹⁷You still set yourself against my people and will not let them go. ¹⁸Therefore, at this time tomorrow I will send the worst hailstorm that has ever fallen on Egypt, from the day it was founded till now. ¹⁹Give an order now to bring your livestock and everything you have in the field to a place of shelter, because the hail will fall on every man and animal that has not been brought in and is still out in the field, and they will die.' "

²⁰Those officials of Pharaoh who feared the word of the LORD hurried to bring their slaves and their livestock inside. ²¹But those who ignored the word of the LORD left their slaves and livestock in the field.

²²Then the LORD said to Moses, "Stretch out your hand toward the sky so that hail will fall all over Egypt—on men and animals and on everything growing in the fields of Egypt." ²³When Moses stretched out his staff toward the sky, the LORD sent thunder and hail, and lightning flashed down to the ground. So the LORD rained hail on the land of Egypt; ²⁴hail fell and lightning flashed back and forth. It was the worst storm in all the land of Egypt since it had become a nation. ²⁵Throughout Egypt hail struck everything in the fields—both men and animals; it beat down everything growing in the fields and stripped every tree. ²⁶The only place it did not hail was the land of Goshen, where the Israelites were.

²⁷Then Pharaoh summoned Moses and Aaron. "This time I have sinned," he said to them. "The LORD is in the right, and I and my people are in the wrong. ²⁸Pray to the LORD, for we have had enough thunder

ᵃ16 Or have spared you

and hail. I will let you go; you don't have to stay any longer."

²⁹Moses replied, "When I have gone out of the city, I will spread out my hands in prayer to the LORD. The thunder will stop and there will be no more hail, so you may know that the earth is the LORD's. ³⁰But I know that you and your officials still do not fear the LORD God."

³¹(The flax and barley were destroyed, since the barley had headed and the flax was in bloom. ³²The wheat and spelt, however, were not destroyed, because they ripen later.)

³³Then Moses left Pharaoh and went out of the city. He spread out his hands toward the LORD; the thunder and hail stopped, and the rain no longer poured down on the land. ³⁴When Pharaoh saw that the rain and hail and thunder had stopped, he sinned again: He and his officials hardened their hearts. ³⁵So Pharaoh's heart was hard and he would not let the Israelites go, just as the LORD had said through Moses.

The Plague of Locusts

10 Then the LORD said to Moses, "Go to Pharaoh, for I have hardened his heart and the hearts of his officials so that I may perform these miraculous signs of mine among them ²that you may tell your children and grandchildren how I dealt harshly with the Egyptians and how I performed my signs among them, and that you may know that I am the LORD."

³So Moses and Aaron went to Pharaoh and said to him, "This is what the LORD, the God of the Hebrews, says: 'How long will you refuse to humble yourself before me? Let my people go, so that they may worship me. ⁴If you refuse to let them go, I will bring locusts into your country tomorrow. ⁵They will cover the face of the ground so that it cannot be seen. They will devour what little you have left after the hail, including every tree that is growing in your fields. ⁶They will fill your houses and those of all your officials and all the Egyptians—something neither your fathers nor your forefathers have ever seen from the day they settled in this land till now.' " Then Moses turned and left Pharaoh.

⁷Pharaoh's officials said to him, "How long will this man be a snare to us? Let the people go, so that they may worship

the LORD their God. Do you not yet realize that Egypt is ruined?"

⁸Then Moses and Aaron were brought back to Pharaoh. "Go, worship the LORD your God," he said. "But just who will be going?"

⁹Moses answered, "We will go with our young and old, with our sons and daughters, and with our flocks and herds, because we are to celebrate a festival to the LORD."

¹⁰Pharaoh said, "The LORD be with you —if I let you go, along with your women and children! Clearly you are bent on evil.ᵃ ¹¹No! Have only the men go; and worship the LORD, since that's what you have been asking for." Then Moses and Aaron were driven out of Pharaoh's presence.

¹²And the LORD said to Moses, "Stretch out your hand over Egypt so that locusts will swarm over the land and devour everything growing in the fields, everything left by the hail."

¹³So Moses stretched out his staff over Egypt, and the LORD made an east wind blow across the land all that day and all that night. By morning the wind had brought the locusts; ¹⁴they invaded all Egypt and settled down in every area of the country in great numbers. Never before had there been such a plague of locusts, nor will there ever be again. ¹⁵They covered all the ground until it was black. They devoured all that was left after the hail—everything growing in the fields and the fruit on the trees. Nothing green remained on tree or plant in all the land of Egypt.

¹⁶Pharaoh quickly summoned Moses and Aaron and said, "I have sinned against the LORD your God and against you. ¹⁷Now forgive my sin once more and pray to the LORD your God to take this deadly plague away from me."

¹⁸Moses then left Pharaoh and prayed to the LORD. ¹⁹And the LORD changed the wind to a very strong west wind, which caught up the locusts and carried them into the Red Sea.ᵇ Not a locust was left anywhere in Egypt. ²⁰But the LORD hardened Pharaoh's heart, and he would not let the Israelites go.

The Plague of Darkness

²¹Then the LORD said to Moses, "Stretch out your hand toward the sky so that darkness will spread over Egypt—

ᵃ10 Or Be careful, trouble is in store for you!　　ᵇ19 Hebrew Yam Suph; that is, Sea of Reeds darkness that can be felt." ²²So Moses stretched out his hand toward the sky, and total darkness covered all Egypt for three days. ²³No one could see anyone else or leave his place for three days. Yet all the Israelites had light in the places where they lived.

²⁴Then Pharaoh summoned Moses and said, "Go, worship the LORD. Even your women and children may go with you; only leave your flocks and herds behind."

²⁵But Moses said, "You must allow us to have sacrifices and burnt offerings to present to the LORD our God. ²⁶Our livestock too must go with us; not a hoof is to be left behind. We have to use some of them in worshiping the LORD our God, and until we get there we will not know what we are to use to worship the LORD."

²⁷But the LORD hardened Pharaoh's heart, and he was not willing to let them go. ²⁸Pharaoh said to Moses, "Get out of my sight! Make sure you do not appear before me again! The day you see my face you will die."

²⁹"Just as you say," Moses replied, "I will never appear before you again."

The Plague on the Firstborn

11 Now the LORD had said to Moses, "I will bring one more plague on Pharaoh and on Egypt. After that, he will let you go from here, and when he does, he will drive you out completely. ²Tell the people that men and women alike are to ask their neighbors for articles of silver and gold." ³(The LORD made the Egyptians favorably disposed toward the people, and Moses himself was highly regarded in Egypt by Pharaoh's officials and by the people.)

⁴So Moses said, "This is what the LORD says: 'About midnight I will go throughout Egypt. ⁵Every firstborn son in Egypt will die, from the firstborn son of Pharaoh, who sits on the throne, to the firstborn son of the slave girl, who is at her hand mill, and all the firstborn of the cattle as well. ⁶There will be loud wailing throughout Egypt—worse than there has ever been or ever will be again. ⁷But among the Israelites not a dog will bark at any man or animal.' Then you will know that the LORD makes a distinction between Egypt and Israel. ⁸All these officials of yours will come to me, bowing down before me and saying, 'Go, you and all the people who follow you!' After that

I will leave." Then Moses, hot with anger, left Pharaoh.

⁹The LORD had said to Moses, "Pharaoh will refuse to listen to you—so that my wonders may be multiplied in Egypt." ¹⁰Moses and Aaron performed all these wonders before Pharaoh, but the LORD hardened Pharaoh's heart, and he would not let the Israelites go out of his country.

The Passover

12 The LORD said to Moses and Aaron in Egypt, ²"This month is to be for you the first month, the first month of your year. ³Tell the whole community of Israel that on the tenth day of this month each man is to take a lamb*a* for his family, one for each household. ⁴If any household is too small for a whole lamb, they must share one with their nearest neighbor, having taken into account the number of people there are. You are to determine the amount of lamb needed in accordance with what each person will eat. ⁵The animals you choose must be year-old males without defect, and you may take them from the sheep or the goats. ⁶Take care of them until the fourteenth day of the month, when all the people of the community of Israel must slaughter them at twilight. ⁷Then they are to take some of the blood and put it on the sides and tops of the doorframes of the houses where they eat the lambs. ⁸That same night they are to eat the meat roasted over the fire, along with bitter herbs, and bread made without yeast. ⁹Do not eat the meat raw or cooked in water, but roast it over the fire—head, legs and inner parts. ¹⁰Do not leave any of it till morning; if some is left till morning, you must burn it. ¹¹This is how you are to eat it: with your cloak tucked into your belt, your sandals on your feet and your staff in your hand. Eat it in haste; it is the LORD's Passover.

¹²"On that same night I will pass through Egypt and strike down every firstborn—both men and animals—and I will bring judgment on all the gods of Egypt. I am the LORD. ¹³The blood will be a sign for you on the houses where you are; and when I see the blood, I will pass over you. No destructive plague will touch you when I strike Egypt.

¹⁴"This is a day you are to commemorate; for the generations to come you shall celebrate it as a festival to the LORD

a3 The Hebrew word can mean lamb or kid; also in verse 4.

—a lasting ordinance. [15]For seven days you are to eat bread made without yeast. On the first day remove the yeast from your houses, for whoever eats anything with yeast in it from the first day through the seventh must be cut off from Israel. [16]On the first day hold a sacred assembly, and another one on the seventh day. Do no work at all on these days, except to prepare food for everyone to eat—that is all you may do.

[17]"Celebrate the Feast of Unleavened Bread, because it was on this very day that I brought your divisions out of Egypt. Celebrate this day as a lasting ordinance for the generations to come. [18]In the first month you are to eat bread made without yeast, from the evening of the fourteenth day until the evening of the twenty-first day. [19]For seven days no yeast is to be found in your houses. And whoever eats anything with yeast in it must be cut off from the community of Israel, whether he is an alien or native-born. [20]Eat nothing made with yeast. Wherever you live, you must eat unleavened bread."

[21]Then Moses summoned all the elders of Israel and said to them, "Go at once and select the animals for your families and slaughter the Passover lamb. [22]Take a bunch of hyssop, dip it into the blood in the basin and put some of the blood on the top and on both sides of the doorframe. Not one of you shall go out the door of his house until morning. [23]When the LORD goes through the land to strike down the Egyptians, he will see the blood on the top and sides of the doorframe and will pass over that doorway, and he will not permit the destroyer to enter your houses and strike you down.

[24]"Obey these instructions as a lasting ordinance for you and your descendants. [25]When you enter the land that the LORD will give you as he promised, observe this ceremony. [26]And when your children ask you, 'What does this ceremony mean to you?' [27]then tell them, 'It is the Passover sacrifice to the LORD, who passed over the houses of the Israelites in Egypt and spared our homes when he struck down the Egyptians.' " Then the people bowed down and worshiped. [28]The Israelites did just what the LORD commanded Moses and Aaron.

[29]At midnight the LORD struck down all the firstborn in Egypt, from the firstborn of Pharaoh, who sat on the throne, to the firstborn of the prisoner, who was in the dungeon, and the firstborn of all the livestock as well. [30]Pharaoh and all his officials and all the Egyptians got up during the night, and there was loud wailing in Egypt, for there was not a house without someone dead.

The Exodus

[31]During the night Pharaoh summoned Moses and Aaron and said, "Up! Leave my people, you and the Israelites! Go, worship the LORD as you have requested. [32]Take your flocks and herds, as you have said, and go. And also bless me."

[33]The Egyptians urged the people to hurry and leave the country. "For otherwise," they said, "we will all die!" [34]So the people took their dough before the yeast was added, and carried it on their shoulders in kneading troughs wrapped in clothing. [35]The Israelites did as Moses instructed and asked the Egyptians for articles of silver and gold and for clothing. [36]The LORD had made the Egyptians favorably disposed toward the people, and they gave them what they asked for; so they plundered the Egyptians.

[37]The Israelites journeyed from Rameses to Succoth. There were about six hundred thousand men on foot, besides women and children. [38]Many other people went up with them, as well as large droves of livestock, both flocks and herds. [39]With the dough they had brought from Egypt, they baked cakes of unleavened bread. The dough was without yeast because they had been driven out of Egypt and did not have time to prepare food for themselves.

[40]Now the length of time the Israelite people lived in Egypt[a] was 430 years. [41]At the end of the 430 years, to the very day, all the LORD's divisions left Egypt. [42]Because the LORD kept vigil that night to bring them out of Egypt, on this night all the Israelites are to keep vigil to honor the LORD for the generations to come.

Passover Restrictions

[43]The LORD said to Moses and Aaron, "These are the regulations for the Passover:

"No foreigner is to eat of it. [44]Any slave you have bought may eat of it after you have circumcised him, [45]but a temporary resident and a hired worker may not eat of it.

---

[a]40 Masoretic Text; Samaritan Pentateuch and Septuagint *Egypt and Canaan*

46"It must be eaten inside one house; take none of the meat outside the house. Do not break any of the bones. 47The whole community of Israel must celebrate it.

48"An alien living among you who wants to celebrate the LORD's Passover must have all the males in his household circumcised; then he may take part like one born in the land. No uncircumcised male may eat of it. 49The same law applies to the native-born and to the alien living among you."

50All the Israelites did just what the LORD had commanded Moses and Aaron. 51And on that very day the LORD brought the Israelites out of Egypt by their divisions.

Consecration of the Firstborn

13 The LORD said to Moses, 2"Consecrate to me every firstborn male. The first offspring of every womb among the Israelites belongs to me, whether man or animal."

3Then Moses said to the people, "Commemorate this day, the day you came out of Egypt, out of the land of slavery, because the LORD brought you out of it with a mighty hand. Eat nothing containing yeast. 4Today, in the month of Abib, you are leaving. 5When the LORD brings you into the land of the Canaanites, Hittites, Amorites, Hivites and Jebusites—the land he swore to your forefathers to give you, a land flowing with milk and honey —you are to observe this ceremony in this month: 6For seven days eat bread made without yeast and on the seventh day hold a festival to the LORD. 7Eat unleavened bread during those seven days; nothing with yeast in it is to be seen among you, nor shall any yeast be seen anywhere within your borders. 8On that day tell your son, 'I do this because of what the LORD did for me when I came out of Egypt.' 9This observance will be for you like a sign on your hand and a reminder on your forehead that the law of the LORD is to be on your lips. For the LORD brought you out of Egypt with his mighty hand. 10You must keep this ordinance at the appointed time year after year.

11"After the LORD brings you into the land of the Canaanites and gives it to you, as he promised on oath to you and your forefathers, 12you are to give over to the LORD the first offspring of every womb. All the firstborn males of your livestock belong to the LORD. 13Redeem with a lamb every firstborn donkey, but if you do not redeem it, break its neck. Redeem every firstborn among your sons.

14"In days to come, when your son asks you, 'What does this mean?' say to him, 'With a mighty hand the LORD brought us out of Egypt, out of the land of slavery. 15When Pharaoh stubbornly refused to let us go, the LORD killed every firstborn in Egypt, both man and animal. This is why I sacrifice to the LORD the first male offspring of every womb and redeem each of my firstborn sons.' 16And it will be like a sign on your hand and a symbol on your forehead that the LORD brought us out of Egypt with his mighty hand."

Crossing the Sea

17When Pharaoh let the people go, God did not lead them on the road through the Philistine country, though that was shorter. For God said, "If they face war, they might change their minds and return to Egypt." 18So God led the people around by the desert road toward the Red Sea. a The Israelites went up out of Egypt armed for battle.

19Moses took the bones of Joseph with him because Joseph had made the sons of Israel swear an oath. He had said, "God will surely come to your aid, and then you must carry my bones up with you from this place." b

20After leaving Succoth they camped at Etham on the edge of the desert. 21By day the LORD went ahead of them in a pillar of cloud to guide them on their way and by night in a pillar of fire to give them light, so that they could travel by day or night. 22Neither the pillar of cloud by day nor the pillar of fire by night left its place in front of the people.

14 Then the LORD said to Moses, 2"Tell the Israelites to turn back and encamp near Pi Hahiroth, between Migdol and the sea. They are to encamp by the sea, directly opposite Baal Zephon. 3Pharaoh will think, 'The Israelites are wandering around the land in confusion, hemmed in by the desert.' 4And I will harden Pharaoh's heart, and he will pursue them. But I will gain glory for myself through Pharaoh and all his army, and the Egyptians will know that I am the LORD." So the Israelites did this.

a18 Hebrew Yam Suph; that is, Sea of Reeds   b19 See Gen. 50:25.

⁵When the king of Egypt was told that the people had fled, Pharaoh and his officials changed their minds about them and said, "What have we done? We have let the Israelites go and have lost their services!" ⁶So he had his chariot made ready and took his army with him. ⁷He took six hundred of the best chariots, along with all the other chariots of Egypt, with officers over all of them. ⁸The LORD hardened the heart of Pharaoh king of Egypt, so that he pursued the Israelites, who were marching out boldly. ⁹The Egyptians—all Pharaoh's horses and chariots, horsemen*a* and troops—pursued the Israelites and overtook them as they camped by the sea near Pi Hahiroth, opposite Baal Zephon.

¹⁰As Pharaoh approached, the Israelites looked up, and there were the Egyptians, marching after them. They were terrified and cried out to the LORD. ¹¹They said to Moses, "Was it because there were no graves in Egypt that you brought us to the desert to die? What have you done to us by bringing us out of Egypt? ¹²Didn't we say to you in Egypt, 'Leave us alone; let us serve the Egyptians'? It would have been better for us to serve the Egyptians than to die in the desert!"

¹³Moses answered the people, "Do not be afraid. Stand firm and you will see the deliverance the LORD will bring you today. The Egyptians you see today you will never see again. ¹⁴The LORD will fight for you; you need only to be still."

¹⁵Then the LORD said to Moses, "Why are you crying out to me? Tell the Israelites to move on. ¹⁶Raise your staff and stretch out your hand over the sea to divide the water so that the Israelites can go through the sea on dry ground. ¹⁷I will harden the hearts of the Egyptians so that they will go in after them. And I will gain glory through Pharaoh and all his army, through his chariots and his horsemen. ¹⁸The Egyptians will know that I am the LORD when I gain glory through Pharaoh, his chariots and his horsemen."

¹⁹Then the angel of God, who had been traveling in front of Israel's army, withdrew and went behind them. The pillar of cloud also moved from in front and stood behind them, ²⁰coming between the armies of Egypt and Israel. Throughout the night the cloud brought darkness to the one side and light to the other side;

so neither went near the other all night long.

²¹Then Moses stretched out his hand over the sea, and all that night the LORD drove the sea back with a strong east wind and turned it into dry land. The waters were divided, ²²and the Israelites went through the sea on dry ground, with a wall of water on their right and on their left.

²³The Egyptians pursued them, and all Pharaoh's horses and chariots and horsemen followed them into the sea. ²⁴During the last watch of the night the LORD looked down from the pillar of fire and cloud at the Egyptian army and threw it into confusion. ²⁵He made the wheels of their chariots come off*b* so that they had difficulty driving. And the Egyptians said, "Let's get away from the Israelites! The LORD is fighting for them against Egypt."

²⁶Then the LORD said to Moses, "Stretch out your hand over the sea so that the waters may flow back over the Egyptians and their chariots and horsemen." ²⁷Moses stretched out his hand over the sea, and at daybreak the sea went back to its place. The Egyptians were fleeing toward*c* it, and the LORD swept them into the sea. ²⁸The water flowed back and covered the chariots and horsemen—the entire army of Pharaoh that had followed the Israelites into the sea. Not one of them survived.

²⁹But the Israelites went through the sea on dry ground, with a wall of water on their right and on their left. ³⁰That day the LORD saved Israel from the hands of the Egyptians, and Israel saw the Egyptians lying dead on the shore. ³¹And when the Israelites saw the great power the LORD displayed against the Egyptians, the people feared the LORD and put their trust in him and in Moses his servant.

The Song of Moses and Miriam

15 Then Moses and the Israelites sang this song to the LORD:

"I will sing to the LORD,
　for he is highly exalted.
The horse and its rider
　he has hurled into the sea.
²The LORD is my strength and my song;
　he has become my salvation.
He is my God, and I will praise him,
　my father's God, and I will exalt
　him.

---

a9 Or charioteers; also in verses 17, 18, 23, 26 and 28 (see Samaritan Pentateuch, Septuagint and Syriac)　b25 Or He jammed the wheels of their chariots　c27 Or from

³The LORD is a warrior;
  the LORD is his name.
⁴Pharaoh's chariots and his army
  he has hurled into the sea.
The best of Pharaoh's officers
  are drowned in the Red Sea. ª
⁵The deep waters have covered them;
  they sank to the depths like a
  stone.

⁶"Your right hand, O LORD,
  was majestic in power.
Your right hand, O LORD,
  shattered the enemy.
⁷In the greatness of your majesty
  you threw down those who opposed
  you.
You unleashed your burning anger;
  it consumed them like stubble.

ª4 Hebrew *Yam Suph*; that is, Sea of Reeds; also in verse 22

THURSDAY

VERSE FOR THE DAY:
Exodus 14:31

AUTHOR:
Joni Eareckson Tada

PASSAGE FOR THE DAY:
Exodus 14:1—15:27

Do Not Forget

THE Israelites witnessed miracle after miracle, even as the shackles of slavery fell off their ankles. They were protected by the goodness of God from the Egyptian plagues and were led by his goodness out of Egypt.

But the most miraculous display of God's goodness was when he shored up the waves of the Red Sea to open a path for their escape. I can picture the Israelites looking up like bewildered tourists at the water, which rose like glass skyscrapers on either side. "Wow, look at that . . . God is amazing!" they must have exclaimed.

If you want to hear how thrilled they were, read Exodus 15. The people were so excited that they went on for twenty-one verses shouting hosannas to the Lord. But exactly three short verses later, in Exodus 15:24, their joy turned sour. It seems that for three days "they traveled in the desert without finding water . . . . So the people grumbled."

It was as if the miracle of the Red Sea had never happened. The excitement of the Israelites' songs and praises faded all too quickly when they ran into a little trouble. And the irony is, they grumbled about water! Didn't they recall that God could do wonderful things with water? They had just watched him hold back a whole sea of it. Yet they couldn't trust God for his goodness even for three short days. How quickly they forgot.

Yet how quickly we forget. We are slow to remember God's goodness, yet quick to complain. We doubt the protection and provision of our God. Perhaps we ought to take the advice God gave those Israelites in Deuteronomy 4:9: "Only be careful and watch yourselves closely so that you do not forget the things your eyes have seen." That's one verse we ought not to forget.

Additional Scripture Readings:
Psalm 103:1–5; Isaiah 17:9–11

Go to page 79 for your next devotional reading.

8By the blast of your nostrils
the waters piled up.
The surging waters stood firm like a
wall;
the deep waters congealed in the
heart of the sea.

9"The enemy boasted,
'I will pursue, I will overtake them.
I will divide the spoils;
I will gorge myself on them.
I will draw my sword
and my hand will destroy them.'
10But you blew with your breath,
and the sea covered them.
They sank like lead
in the mighty waters.

11"Who among the gods is like you,
O Lord?
Who is like you—
majestic in holiness,
awesome in glory,
working wonders?
12You stretched out your right hand
and the earth swallowed them.

13"In your unfailing love you will lead
the people you have redeemed.
In your strength you will guide them
to your holy dwelling.
14The nations will hear and tremble;
anguish will grip the people of
Philistia.
15The chiefs of Edom will be terrified,
the leaders of Moab will be seized
with trembling,
the people*a* of Canaan will melt
away;
16   terror and dread will fall upon
them.
By the power of your arm
they will be as still as a stone—
until your people pass by, O Lord,
until the people you bought*b* pass
by.
17You will bring them in and plant
them
on the mountain of your
inheritance—
the place, O Lord, you made for your
dwelling,
the sanctuary, O Lord, your hands
established.
18The Lord will reign
for ever and ever."

19When Pharaoh's horses, chariots and
horsemen*c* went into the sea, the Lord
brought the waters of the sea back over

them, but the Israelites walked through
the sea on dry ground. 20Then Miriam the
prophetess, Aaron's sister, took a tambourine in her hand, and all the women
followed her, with tambourines and dancing. 21Miriam sang to them:

"Sing to the Lord,
for he is highly exalted.
The horse and its rider
he has hurled into the sea."

The Waters of Marah and Elim

22Then Moses led Israel from the Red
Sea and they went into the Desert of
Shur. For three days they traveled in the
desert without finding water. 23When
they came to Marah, they could not drink
its water because it was bitter. (That is
why the place is called Marah.*d*) 24So the
people grumbled against Moses, saying,
"What are we to drink?"
25Then Moses cried out to the Lord,
and the Lord showed him a piece of
wood. He threw it into the water, and the
water became sweet.
There the Lord made a decree and a
law for them, and there he tested them.
26He said, "If you listen carefully to the
voice of the Lord your God and do what is
right in his eyes, if you pay attention to
his commands and keep all his decrees, I
will not bring on you any of the diseases
I brought on the Egyptians, for I am the
Lord, who heals you."
27Then they came to Elim, where there
were twelve springs and seventy palm
trees, and they camped there near the water.

Manna and Quail

16 The whole Israelite community set
out from Elim and came to the
Desert of Sin, which is between Elim and
Sinai, on the fifteenth day of the second
month after they had come out of Egypt.
2In the desert the whole community
grumbled against Moses and Aaron. 3The
Israelites said to them, "If only we had
died by the Lord's hand in Egypt! There
we sat around pots of meat and ate all the
food we wanted, but you have brought us
out into this desert to starve this entire
assembly to death."
4Then the Lord said to Moses, "I will
rain down bread from heaven for you. The
people are to go out each day and gather
enough for that day. In this way I will test

---

*a*15 Or *rulers*   *b*16 Or *created*   *c*19 Or *charioteers*   *d*23 *Marah* means *bitter.*

them and see whether they will follow my instructions. ⁵On the sixth day they are to prepare what they bring in, and that is to be twice as much as they gather on the other days."

⁶So Moses and Aaron said to all the Israelites, "In the evening you will know that it was the LORD who brought you out of Egypt, ⁷and in the morning you will see the glory of the LORD, because he has heard your grumbling against him. Who are we, that you should grumble against us?" ⁸Moses also said, "You will know that it was the LORD when he gives you meat to eat in the evening and all the bread you want in the morning, because he has heard your grumbling against him.

Who are we? You are not grumbling against us, but against the LORD."

⁹Then Moses told Aaron, "Say to the entire Israelite community, 'Come before the LORD, for he has heard your grumbling.'"

¹⁰While Aaron was speaking to the whole Israelite community, they looked toward the desert, and there was the glory of the LORD appearing in the cloud.

¹¹The LORD said to Moses, ¹²"I have heard the grumbling of the Israelites. Tell them, 'At twilight you will eat meat, and in the morning you will be filled with bread. Then you will know that I am the LORD your God.'"

¹³That evening quail came and covered

FRIDAY

VERSE FOR THE DAY:
Exodus 16:4

AUTHOR:
Sue Monk Kidd

PASSAGE FOR THE DAY:
Exodus 16:1–5

Day by Day

LAST summer while I was taking drawing lessons, my friend Betty learned she had cancer. The day before she went to the hospital for surgery, her spirit seemed nearly depleted. "What am I going to do?" she said, thinking about the demanding weeks ahead of her. "How will I find the strength?"

That evening I found myself doodling on my drawing board, thinking of Betty. Soon I was sketching a loaf of bread. A simple, homemade loaf. Then I put it aside and went to bed. But during the night I had the most curious dream. Betty was sitting at a table before a loaf of bread, eating a single piece.

The next morning when I came upon my drawing, an idea began to stir in my thoughts. I reached for my Bible and found the verse, "I will rain down bread from heaven" (Exodus 16:4), remembering how day by day God sent nourishment from heaven while his people wandered in the wilderness. There was always just enough for each day. They simply had to trust him for tomorrow's.

I penciled the verse beneath the sketch of bread and carried it to Betty's hospital room. It was to remind us both . . . when we walk in difficult places, God sends the strength and nourishment to face what comes our way, not all at once, but day by day.

Additional Scripture Readings:
Lamentations 3:22–24; Matthew 6:33–34

Go to page 87 for your next devotional reading.

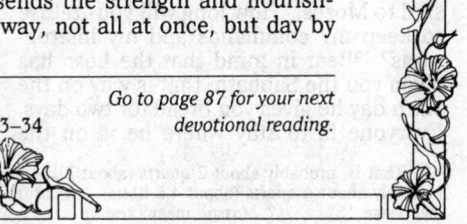

the camp, and in the morning there was a layer of dew around the camp. [14]When the dew was gone, thin flakes like frost on the ground appeared on the desert floor. [15]When the Israelites saw it, they said to each other, "What is it?" For they did not know what it was.

Moses said to them, "It is the bread the LORD has given you to eat. [16]This is what the LORD has commanded: 'Each one is to gather as much as he needs. Take an omer[a] for each person you have in your tent.' "

[17]The Israelites did as they were told; some gathered much, some little. [18]And when they measured it by the omer, he who gathered much did not have too much, and he who gathered little did not have too little. Each one gathered as much as he needed.

[19]Then Moses said to them, "No one is to keep any of it until morning."

[20]However, some of them paid no attention to Moses; they kept part of it until morning, but it was full of maggots and began to smell. So Moses was angry with them.

[21]Each morning everyone gathered as much as he needed, and when the sun grew hot, it melted away. [22]On the sixth day, they gathered twice as much—two omers[b] for each person—and the leaders of the community came and reported this to Moses. [23]He said to them, "This is what the LORD commanded: 'Tomorrow is to be a day of rest, a holy Sabbath to the LORD. So bake what you want to bake and boil what you want to boil. Save whatever is left and keep it until morning.' "

[24]So they saved it until morning, as Moses commanded, and it did not stink or get maggots in it. [25]"Eat it today," Moses said, "because today is a Sabbath to the LORD. You will not find any of it on the ground today. [26]Six days you are to gather it, but on the seventh day, the Sabbath, there will not be any."

[27]Nevertheless, some of the people went out on the seventh day to gather it, but they found none. [28]Then the LORD said to Moses, "How long will you[c] refuse to keep my commands and my instructions? [29]Bear in mind that the LORD has given you the Sabbath; that is why on the sixth day he gives you bread for two days. Everyone is to stay where he is on the seventh day; no one is to go out." [30]So the people rested on the seventh day.

[31]The people of Israel called the bread manna.[d] It was white like coriander seed and tasted like wafers made with honey. [32]Moses said, "This is what the LORD has commanded: 'Take an omer of manna and keep it for the generations to come, so they can see the bread I gave you to eat in the desert when I brought you out of Egypt.' "

[33]So Moses said to Aaron, "Take a jar and put an omer of manna in it. Then place it before the LORD to be kept for the generations to come."

[34]As the LORD commanded Moses, Aaron put the manna in front of the Testimony, that it might be kept. [35]The Israelites ate manna forty years, until they came to a land that was settled; they ate manna until they reached the border of Canaan. [36](An omer is one tenth of an ephah.)

Water From the Rock

17 The whole Israelite community set out from the Desert of Sin, traveling from place to place as the LORD commanded. They camped at Rephidim, but there was no water for the people to drink. [2]So they quarreled with Moses and said, "Give us water to drink."

Moses replied, "Why do you quarrel with me? Why do you put the LORD to the test?"

[3]But the people were thirsty for water there, and they grumbled against Moses. They said, "Why did you bring us up out of Egypt to make us and our children and livestock die of thirst?"

[4]Then Moses cried out to the LORD, "What am I to do with these people? They are almost ready to stone me."

[5]The LORD answered Moses, "Walk on ahead of the people. Take with you some of the elders of Israel and take in your hand the staff with which you struck the Nile, and go. [6]I will stand there before you by the rock at Horeb. Strike the rock, and water will come out of it for the people to drink." So Moses did this in the sight of the elders of Israel. [7]And he called the place Massah[e] and Meribah[f] because the Israelites quarreled and because they tested the LORD saying, "Is the LORD among us or not?"

---

[a]16 That is, probably about 2 quarts (about 2 liters); also in verses 18, 32, 33 and 36   [b]22 That is, probably about 4 quarts (about 4.5 liters)   [c]28 The Hebrew is plural.   [d]31 Manna means What is it? (see verse 15).   [e]7 Massah means testing.   [f]7 Meribah means quarreling.

The Amalekites Defeated

⁸The Amalekites came and attacked the Israelites at Rephidim. ⁹Moses said to Joshua, "Choose some of our men and go out to fight the Amalekites. Tomorrow I will stand on top of the hill with the staff of God in my hands."

¹⁰So Joshua fought the Amalekites as Moses had ordered, and Moses, Aaron and Hur went to the top of the hill. ¹¹As long as Moses held up his hands, the Israelites were winning, but whenever he lowered his hands, the Amalekites were winning. ¹²When Moses' hands grew tired, they took a stone and put it under him and he sat on it. Aaron and Hur held his hands up—one on one side, one on the other—so that his hands remained steady till sunset. ¹³So Joshua overcame the Amalekite army with the sword.

¹⁴Then the LORD said to Moses, "Write this on a scroll as something to be remembered and make sure that Joshua hears it, because I will completely blot out the memory of Amalek from under heaven."

¹⁵Moses built an altar and called it The LORD is my Banner. ¹⁶He said, "For hands were lifted up to the throne of the LORD. The*a* LORD will be at war against the Amalekites from generation to generation."

Jethro Visits Moses

18 Now Jethro, the priest of Midian and father-in-law of Moses, heard of everything God had done for Moses and for his people Israel, and how the LORD had brought Israel out of Egypt. ²After Moses had sent away his wife Zipporah, his father-in-law Jethro received her ³and her two sons. One son was named Gershom,*b* for Moses said, "I have become an alien in a foreign land"; ⁴and the other was named Eliezer,*c* for he said, "My father's God was my helper; he saved me from the sword of Pharaoh."

⁵Jethro, Moses' father-in-law, together with Moses' sons and wife, came to him in the desert, where he was camped near the mountain of God. ⁶Jethro had sent word to him, "I, your father-in-law Jethro, am coming to you with your wife and her two sons."

⁷So Moses went out to meet his father-in-law and bowed down and kissed him. They greeted each other and then went into the tent. ⁸Moses told his father-in-law about everything the LORD had done to Pharaoh and the Egyptians for Israel's sake and about all the hardships they had met along the way and how the LORD had saved them.

⁹Jethro was delighted to hear about all the good things the LORD had done for Israel in rescuing them from the hand of the Egyptians. ¹⁰He said, "Praise be to the LORD, who rescued you from the hand of the Egyptians and of Pharaoh, and who rescued the people from the hand of the Egyptians. ¹¹Now I know that the LORD is greater than all other gods, for he did this to those who had treated Israel arrogantly." ¹²Then Jethro, Moses' father-in-law, brought a burnt offering and other sacrifices to God, and Aaron came with all the elders of Israel to eat bread with Moses' father-in-law in the presence of God.

¹³The next day Moses took his seat to serve as judge for the people, and they stood around him from morning till evening. ¹⁴When his father-in-law saw all that Moses was doing for the people, he said, "What is this you are doing for the people? Why do you alone sit as judge, while all these people stand around you from morning till evening?"

¹⁵Moses answered him, "Because the people come to me to seek God's will. ¹⁶Whenever they have a dispute, it is brought to me, and I decide between the parties and inform them of God's decrees and laws."

¹⁷Moses' father-in-law replied, "What you are doing is not good. ¹⁸You and these people who come to you will only wear yourselves out. The work is too heavy for you; you cannot handle it alone. ¹⁹Listen now to me and I will give you some advice, and may God be with you. You must be the people's representative before God and bring their disputes to him. ²⁰Teach them the decrees and laws, and show them the way to live and the duties they are to perform. ²¹But select capable men from all the people—men who fear God, trustworthy men who hate dishonest gain—and appoint them as officials over thousands, hundreds, fifties and tens. ²²Have them serve as judges for the people at all times, but have them bring every difficult case to you; the simple cases they can decide themselves. That will

---

a16 Or "Because a hand was against the throne of the LORD, the for an alien there.　c4 Eliezer means my God is helper.　　b3 Gershom sounds like the Hebrew make your load lighter, because they will share it with you. ²³If you do this and God so commands, you will be able to stand the strain, and all these people will go home satisfied."

²⁴Moses listened to his father-in-law and did everything he said. ²⁵He chose capable men from all Israel and made them leaders of the people, officials over thousands, hundreds, fifties and tens. ²⁶They served as judges for the people at all times. The difficult cases they brought to Moses, but the simple ones they decided themselves.

²⁷Then Moses sent his father-in-law on his way, and Jethro returned to his own country.

At Mount Sinai

19 In the third month after the Israelites left Egypt—on the very day—they came to the Desert of Sinai. ²After they set out from Rephidim, they entered the Desert of Sinai, and Israel camped there in the desert in front of the mountain.

³Then Moses went up to God, and the LORD called to him from the mountain and said, "This is what you are to say to the house of Jacob and what you are to tell the people of Israel: ⁴'You yourselves have seen what I did to Egypt, and how I carried you on eagles' wings and brought you to myself. ⁵Now if you obey me fully and keep my covenant, then out of all nations you will be my treasured possession. Although the whole earth is mine, ⁶youᵃ will be for me a kingdom of priests and a holy nation.' These are the words you are to speak to the Israelites."

⁷So Moses went back and summoned the elders of the people and set before them all the words the LORD had commanded him to speak. ⁸The people all responded together, "We will do everything the LORD has said." So Moses brought their answer back to the LORD.

⁹The LORD said to Moses, "I am going to come to you in a dense cloud, so that the people will hear me speaking with you and will always put their trust in you." Then Moses told the LORD what the people had said.

¹⁰And the LORD said to Moses, "Go to the people and consecrate them today and tomorrow. Have them wash their

clothes ¹¹and be ready by the third day, because on that day the LORD will come down on Mount Sinai in the sight of all the people. ¹²Put limits for the people around the mountain and tell them, 'Be careful that you do not go up the mountain or touch the foot of it. Whoever touches the mountain shall surely be put to death. ¹³He shall surely be stoned or shot with arrows; not a hand is to be laid on him. Whether man or animal, he shall not be permitted to live.' Only when the ram's horn sounds a long blast may they go up to the mountain."

¹⁴After Moses had gone down the mountain to the people, he consecrated them, and they washed their clothes. ¹⁵Then he said to the people, "Prepare yourselves for the third day. Abstain from sexual relations."

¹⁶On the morning of the third day there was thunder and lightning, with a thick cloud over the mountain, and a very loud trumpet blast. Everyone in the camp trembled. ¹⁷Then Moses led the people out of the camp to meet with God, and they stood at the foot of the mountain. ¹⁸Mount Sinai was covered with smoke, because the LORD descended on it in fire. The smoke billowed up from it like smoke from a furnace, the whole mountainᵇ trembled violently, ¹⁹and the sound of the trumpet grew louder and louder. Then Moses spoke and the voice of God answered him.ᶜ

²⁰The LORD descended to the top of Mount Sinai and called Moses to the top of the mountain. So Moses went up ²¹and the LORD said to him, "Go down and warn the people so they do not force their way through to see the LORD and many of them perish. ²²Even the priests, who approach the LORD, must consecrate themselves, or the LORD will break out against them."

²³Moses said to the LORD, "The people cannot come up Mount Sinai, because you yourself warned us, 'Put limits around the mountain and set it apart as holy.'"

²⁴The LORD replied, "Go down and bring Aaron up with you. But the priests and the people must not force their way through to come up to the LORD, or he will break out against them."

²⁵So Moses went down to the people and told them.

ᵃ5,6 Or possession, for the whole earth is mine. ⁶You manuscripts and Septuagint all the people   ᵇ18 Most Hebrew manuscripts; a few Hebrew   ᶜ19 Or and God answered him with thunder

The Ten Commandments

20 And God spoke all these words:

²"I am the LORD your God, who brought you out of Egypt, out of the land of slavery.

³"You shall have no other gods before*a* me.

⁴"You shall not make for yourself an idol in the form of anything in heaven above or on the earth beneath or in the waters below. ⁵You shall not bow down to them or worship them; for I, the LORD your God, am a jealous God, punishing the children for the sin of the fathers to the third and fourth generation of those who hate me, ⁶but showing love to a thousand ⸤generations⸥ of those who love me and keep my commandments.

⁷"You shall not misuse the name of the LORD your God, for the LORD will not hold anyone guiltless who misuses his name.

⁸"Remember the Sabbath day by keeping it holy. ⁹Six days you shall labor and do all your work, ¹⁰but the seventh day is a Sabbath to the LORD your God. On it you shall not do any work, neither you, nor your son or daughter, nor your manservant or maidservant, nor your animals, nor the alien within your gates. ¹¹For in six days the LORD made the heavens and the earth, the sea, and all that is in them, but he rested on the seventh day. Therefore the LORD blessed the Sabbath day and made it holy.

¹²"Honor your father and your mother, so that you may live long in the land the LORD your God is giving you.

¹³"You shall not murder.

¹⁴"You shall not commit adultery.

¹⁵"You shall not steal.

¹⁶"You shall not give false testimony against your neighbor.

¹⁷"You shall not covet your neighbor's house. You shall not covet your neighbor's wife, or his manservant or maidservant, his ox or donkey, or anything that belongs to your neighbor."

¹⁸When the people saw the thunder and lightning and heard the trumpet and saw the mountain in smoke, they trembled with fear. They stayed at a distance ¹⁹and said to Moses, "Speak to us yourself and we will listen. But do not have God speak to us or we will die."

²⁰Moses said to the people, "Do not be afraid. God has come to test you, so that the fear of God will be with you to keep you from sinning."

²¹The people remained at a distance, while Moses approached the thick darkness where God was.

Idols and Altars

²²Then the LORD said to Moses, "Tell the Israelites this: 'You have seen for yourselves that I have spoken to you from heaven: ²³Do not make any gods to be alongside me; do not make for yourselves gods of silver or gods of gold.

²⁴" 'Make an altar of earth for me and sacrifice on it your burnt offerings and fellowship offerings,*b* your sheep and goats and your cattle. Wherever I cause my name to be honored, I will come to you and bless you. ²⁵If you make an altar of stones for me, do not build it with dressed stones, for you will defile it if you use a tool on it. ²⁶And do not go up to my altar on steps, lest your nakedness be exposed on it.'

21 "These are the laws you are to set before them:

Hebrew Servants

²"If you buy a Hebrew servant, he is to serve you for six years. But in the seventh year, he shall go free, without paying anything. ³If he comes alone, he is to go free alone; but if he has a wife when he comes, she is to go with him. ⁴If his master gives him a wife and she bears him sons or daughters, the woman and her children shall belong to her master, and only the man shall go free.

⁵"But if the servant declares, 'I love my master and my wife and children and do not want to go free,' ⁶then his master must take him before the judges.*c* He shall take him to the door or the doorpost and pierce his ear with an awl. Then he will be his servant for life.

⁷"If a man sells his daughter as a servant, she is not to go free as menservants do. ⁸If she does not please the master who

a3 Or *besides*   *b24* Traditionally *peace offerings*   *c6* Or *before God* has selected her for himself,[a] he must let her be redeemed. He has no right to sell her to foreigners, because he has broken faith with her. [9]If he selects her for his son, he must grant her the rights of a daughter. [10]If he marries another woman, he must not deprive the first one of her food, clothing and marital rights. [11]If he does not provide her with these three things, she is to go free, without any payment of money.

Personal Injuries

[12]"Anyone who strikes a man and kills him shall surely be put to death. [13]However, if he does not do it intentionally, but God lets it happen, he is to flee to a place I will designate. [14]But if a man schemes and kills another man deliberately, take him away from my altar and put him to death.

[15]"Anyone who attacks[b] his father or his mother must be put to death.

[16]"Anyone who kidnaps another and either sells him or still has him when he is caught must be put to death.

[17]"Anyone who curses his father or mother must be put to death.

[18]"If men quarrel and one hits the other with a stone or with his fist[c] and he does not die but is confined to bed, [19]the one who struck the blow will not be held responsible if the other gets up and walks around outside with his staff; however, he must pay the injured man for the loss of his time and see that he is completely healed.

[20]"If a man beats his male or female slave with a rod and the slave dies as a direct result, he must be punished, [21]but he is not to be punished if the slave gets up after a day or two, since the slave is his property.

[22]"If men who are fighting hit a pregnant woman and she gives birth prematurely[d] but there is no serious injury, the offender must be fined whatever the woman's husband demands and the court allows. [23]But if there is serious injury, you are to take life for life, [24]eye for eye, tooth for tooth, hand for hand, foot for foot, [25]burn for burn, wound for wound, bruise for bruise.

[26]"If a man hits a manservant or maidservant in the eye and destroys it, he must let the servant go free to compensate for the eye. [27]And if he knocks out the tooth of a manservant or maidservant, he must let the servant go free to compensate for the tooth.

[28]"If a bull gores a man or a woman to death, the bull must be stoned to death, and its meat must not be eaten. But the owner of the bull will not be held responsible. [29]If, however, the bull has had the habit of goring and the owner has been warned but has not kept it penned up and it kills a man or woman, the bull must be stoned and the owner also must be put to death. [30]However, if payment is demanded of him, he may redeem his life by paying whatever is demanded. [31]This law also applies if the bull gores a son or daughter. [32]If the bull gores a male or female slave, the owner must pay thirty shekels[e] of silver to the master of the slave, and the bull must be stoned.

[33]"If a man uncovers a pit or digs one and fails to cover it and an ox or a donkey falls into it, [34]the owner of the pit must pay for the loss; he must pay its owner, and the dead animal will be his.

[35]"If a man's bull injures the bull of another and it dies, they are to sell the live one and divide both the money and the dead animal equally. [36]However, if it was known that the bull had the habit of goring, yet the owner did not keep it penned up, the owner must pay, animal for animal, and the dead animal will be his.

Protection of Property

22 "If a man steals an ox or a sheep and slaughters it or sells it, he must pay back five head of cattle for the ox and four sheep for the sheep.

[2]"If a thief is caught breaking in and is struck so that he dies, the defender is not guilty of bloodshed; [3]but if it happens[f] after sunrise, he is guilty of bloodshed.

"A thief must certainly make restitution, but if he has nothing, he must be sold to pay for his theft.

[4]"If the stolen animal is found alive in his possession—whether ox or donkey or sheep—he must pay back double.

[5]"If a man grazes his livestock in a field or vineyard and lets them stray and they graze in another man's field, he must make restitution from the best of his own field or vineyard.

[6]"If a fire breaks out and spreads into thornbushes so that it burns shocks of grain or standing grain or the whole field,

---

[a]8 Or *master so that he does not choose her*　　[b]15 Or *kills*　　[c]18 Or *with a tool*　　[d]22 Or *she has a miscarriage*　　[e]32 That is, about 12 ounces (about 0.3 kilogram)　　[f]3 Or *if he strikes him*

the one who started the fire must make restitution.

7"If a man gives his neighbor silver or goods for safekeeping and they are stolen from the neighbor's house, the thief, if he is caught, must pay back double. 8But if the thief is not found, the owner of the house must appear before the judges[a] to determine whether he has laid his hands on the other man's property. 9In all cases of illegal possession of an ox, a donkey, a sheep, a garment, or any other lost property about which somebody says, 'This is mine,' both parties are to bring their cases before the judges. The one whom the judges declare[b] guilty must pay back double to his neighbor.

10"If a man gives a donkey, an ox, a sheep or any other animal to his neighbor for safekeeping and it dies or is injured or is taken away while no one is looking, 11the issue between them will be settled by the taking of an oath before the LORD that the neighbor did not lay hands on the other person's property. The owner is to accept this, and no restitution is required. 12But if the animal was stolen from the neighbor, he must make restitution to the owner. 13If it was torn to pieces by a wild animal, he shall bring in the remains as evidence and he will not be required to pay for the torn animal.

14"If a man borrows an animal from his neighbor and it is injured or dies while the owner is not present, he must make restitution. 15But if the owner is with the animal, the borrower will not have to pay. If the animal was hired, the money paid for the hire covers the loss.

Social Responsibility

16"If a man seduces a virgin who is not pledged to be married and sleeps with her, he must pay the bride-price, and she shall be his wife. 17If her father absolutely refuses to give her to him, he must still pay the bride-price for virgins.

18"Do not allow a sorceress to live.

19"Anyone who has sexual relations with an animal must be put to death.

20"Whoever sacrifices to any god other than the LORD must be destroyed.[c]

21"Do not mistreat an alien or oppress him, for you were aliens in Egypt.

22"Do not take advantage of a widow or an orphan. 23If you do and they cry out to me, I will certainly hear their cry. 24My anger will be aroused, and I will kill you with the sword; your wives will become widows and your children fatherless.

25"If you lend money to one of my people among you who is needy, do not be like a moneylender; charge him no interest.[d] 26If you take your neighbor's cloak as a pledge, return it to him by sunset, 27because his cloak is the only covering he has for his body. What else will he sleep in? When he cries out to me, I will hear, for I am compassionate.

28"Do not blaspheme God[e] or curse the ruler of your people.

29"Do not hold back offerings from your granaries or your vats.[f]

"You must give me the firstborn of your sons. 30Do the same with your cattle and your sheep. Let them stay with their mothers for seven days, but give them to me on the eighth day.

31"You are to be my holy people. So do not eat the meat of an animal torn by wild beasts; throw it to the dogs.

Laws of Justice and Mercy

23 "Do not spread false reports. Do not help a wicked man by being a malicious witness.

2"Do not follow the crowd in doing wrong. When you give testimony in a lawsuit, do not pervert justice by siding with the crowd, 3and do not show favoritism to a poor man in his lawsuit.

4"If you come across your enemy's ox or donkey wandering off, be sure to take it back to him. 5If you see the donkey of someone who hates you fallen down under its load, do not leave it there; be sure you help him with it.

6"Do not deny justice to your poor people in their lawsuits. 7Have nothing to do with a false charge and do not put an innocent or honest person to death, for I will not acquit the guilty.

8"Do not accept a bribe, for a bribe blinds those who see and twists the words of the righteous.

9"Do not oppress an alien; you yourselves know how it feels to be aliens, because you were aliens in Egypt.

---

a8 Or before God; also in verse 9   b9 Or whom God declares   c20 The Hebrew term refers to the irrevocable giving over of things or persons to the LORD, often by totally destroying them.   d25 Or excessive interest   e28 Or Do not revile the judges   f29 The meaning of the Hebrew for this phrase is uncertain.

Sabbath Laws

10"For six years you are to sow your fields and harvest the crops, 11but during the seventh year let the land lie unplowed and unused. Then the poor among your people may get food from it, and the wild animals may eat what they leave. Do the same with your vineyard and your olive grove.

12"Six days do your work, but on the seventh day do not work, so that your ox and your donkey may rest and the slave born in your household, and the alien as well, may be refreshed.

13"Be careful to do everything I have said to you. Do not invoke the names of other gods; do not let them be heard on your lips.

The Three Annual Festivals

14"Three times a year you are to celebrate a festival to me.

15"Celebrate the Feast of Unleavened Bread; for seven days eat bread made without yeast, as I commanded you. Do this at the appointed time in the month of Abib, for in that month you came out of Egypt.

"No one is to appear before me empty-handed.

16"Celebrate the Feast of Harvest with the firstfruits of the crops you sow in your field.

"Celebrate the Feast of Ingathering at the end of the year, when you gather in your crops from the field.

17"Three times a year all the men are to appear before the Sovereign LORD.

18"Do not offer the blood of a sacrifice to me along with anything containing yeast.

"The fat of my festival offerings must not be kept until morning.

19"Bring the best of the firstfruits of your soil to the house of the LORD your God.

"Do not cook a young goat in its mother's milk.

God's Angel to Prepare the Way

20"See, I am sending an angel ahead of you to guard you along the way and to bring you to the place I have prepared. 21Pay attention to him and listen to what he says. Do not rebel against him; he will not forgive your rebellion, since my Name is in him. 22If you listen carefully to what

he says and do all that I say, I will be an enemy to your enemies and will oppose those who oppose you. 23My angel will go ahead of you and bring you into the land of the Amorites, Hittites, Perizzites, Canaanites, Hivites and Jebusites, and I will wipe them out. 24Do not bow down before their gods or worship them or follow their practices. You must demolish them and break their sacred stones to pieces. 25Worship the LORD your God, and his blessing will be on your food and water. I will take away sickness from among you, 26and none will miscarry or be barren in your land. I will give you a full life span.

27"I will send my terror ahead of you and throw into confusion every nation you encounter. I will make all your enemies turn their backs and run. 28I will send the hornet ahead of you to drive the Hivites, Canaanites and Hittites out of your way. 29But I will not drive them out in a single year, because the land would become desolate and the wild animals too numerous for you. 30Little by little I will drive them out before you, until you have increased enough to take possession of the land.

31"I will establish your borders from the Red Sea*a* to the Sea of the Philistines,*b* and from the desert to the River.*c* I will hand over to you the people who live in the land and you will drive them out before you. 32Do not make a covenant with them or with their gods. 33Do not let them live in your land, or they will cause you to sin against me, because the worship of their gods will certainly be a snare to you."

The Covenant Confirmed

24 Then he said to Moses, "Come up to the LORD, you and Aaron, Nadab and Abihu, and seventy of the elders of Israel. You are to worship at a distance, 2but Moses alone is to approach the LORD; the others must not come near. And the people may not come up with him."

3When Moses went and told the people all the LORD's words and laws, they responded with one voice, "Everything the LORD has said we will do." 4Moses then wrote down everything the LORD had said.

He got up early the next morning and built an altar at the foot of the mountain and set up twelve stone pillars representing the twelve tribes of Israel. 5Then he

a31 Hebrew *Yam Suph*; that is, Sea of Reeds　　*b31* That is, the Mediterranean　　*c31* That is, the Euphrates

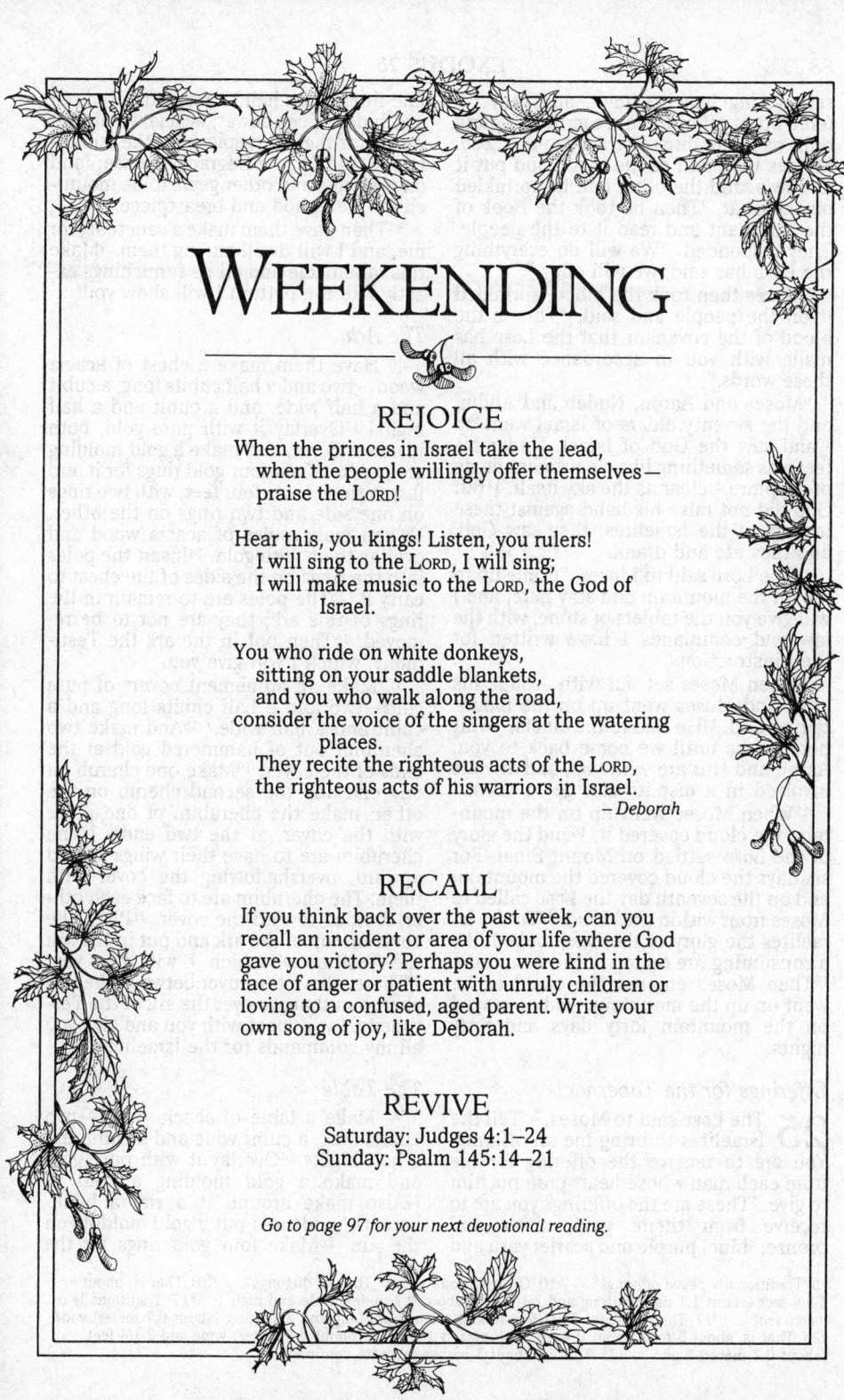

WEEKENDING

REJOICE

When the princes in Israel take the lead,
  when the people willingly offer themselves —
praise the LORD!

Hear this, you kings! Listen, you rulers!
  I will sing to the LORD, I will sing;
  I will make music to the LORD, the God of
    Israel.

You who ride on white donkeys,
  sitting on your saddle blankets,
  and you who walk along the road,
consider the voice of the singers at the watering
    places.
  They recite the righteous acts of the LORD,
  the righteous acts of his warriors in Israel.
                                        — *Deborah*

RECALL

If you think back over the past week, can you
recall an incident or area of your life where God
gave you victory? Perhaps you were kind in the
face of anger or patient with unruly children or
loving to a confused, aged parent. Write your
own song of joy, like Deborah.

REVIVE
Saturday: Judges 4:1–24
Sunday: Psalm 145:14–21

Go to page 97 for your next devotional reading.

sent young Israelite men, and they offered burnt offerings and sacrificed young bulls as fellowship offerings[a] to the Lord. [6]Moses took half of the blood and put it in bowls, and the other half he sprinkled on the altar. [7]Then he took the Book of the Covenant and read it to the people. They responded, "We will do everything the Lord has said; we will obey."

[8]Moses then took the blood, sprinkled it on the people and said, "This is the blood of the covenant that the Lord has made with you in accordance with all these words."

[9]Moses and Aaron, Nadab and Abihu, and the seventy elders of Israel went up [10]and saw the God of Israel. Under his feet was something like a pavement made of sapphire,[b] clear as the sky itself. [11]But God did not raise his hand against these leaders of the Israelites; they saw God, and they ate and drank.

[12]The Lord said to Moses, "Come up to me on the mountain and stay here, and I will give you the tablets of stone, with the law and commands I have written for their instruction."

[13]Then Moses set out with Joshua his aide, and Moses went up on the mountain of God. [14]He said to the elders, "Wait here for us until we come back to you. Aaron and Hur are with you, and anyone involved in a dispute can go to them."

[15]When Moses went up on the mountain, the cloud covered it, [16]and the glory of the Lord settled on Mount Sinai. For six days the cloud covered the mountain, and on the seventh day the Lord called to Moses from within the cloud. [17]To the Israelites the glory of the Lord looked like a consuming fire on top of the mountain. [18]Then Moses entered the cloud as he went on up the mountain. And he stayed on the mountain forty days and forty nights.

Offerings for the Tabernacle

25 The Lord said to Moses, [2]"Tell the Israelites to bring me an offering. You are to receive the offering for me from each man whose heart prompts him to give. [3]These are the offerings you are to receive from them: gold, silver and bronze; [4]blue, purple and scarlet yarn and fine linen; goat hair; [5]ram skins dyed red and hides of sea cows[c]; acacia wood; [6]olive oil for the light; spices for the anointing oil and for the fragrant incense; [7]and onyx stones and other gems to be mounted on the ephod and breastpiece.

[8]"Then have them make a sanctuary for me, and I will dwell among them. [9]Make this tabernacle and all its furnishings exactly like the pattern I will show you.

The Ark

[10]"Have them make a chest of acacia wood—two and a half cubits long, a cubit and a half wide, and a cubit and a half high.[d] [11]Overlay it with pure gold, both inside and out, and make a gold molding around it. [12]Cast four gold rings for it and fasten them to its four feet, with two rings on one side and two rings on the other. [13]Then make poles of acacia wood and overlay them with gold. [14]Insert the poles into the rings on the sides of the chest to carry it. [15]The poles are to remain in the rings of this ark; they are not to be removed. [16]Then put in the ark the Testimony, which I will give you.

[17]"Make an atonement cover[e] of pure gold—two and a half cubits long and a cubit and a half wide.[f] [18]And make two cherubim out of hammered gold at the ends of the cover. [19]Make one cherub on one end and the second cherub on the other; make the cherubim of one piece with the cover, at the two ends. [20]The cherubim are to have their wings spread upward, overshadowing the cover with them. The cherubim are to face each other, looking toward the cover. [21]Place the cover on top of the ark and put in the ark the Testimony, which I will give you. [22]There, above the cover between the two cherubim that are over the ark of the Testimony, I will meet with you and give you all my commands for the Israelites.

The Table

[23]"Make a table of acacia wood—two cubits long, a cubit wide and a cubit and a half high.[g] [24]Overlay it with pure gold and make a gold molding around it. [25]Also make around it a rim a handbreadth[h] wide and put a gold molding on the rim. [26]Make four gold rings for the

---

a5 Traditionally *peace offerings*   *b10* Or *lapis lazuli*   *c5* That is, dugongs   *d10* That is, about 3 3/4 feet (about 1.1 meters) long and 2 1/4 feet (about 0.7 meter) wide and high   *e17* Traditionally *a mercy seat*   *f17* That is, about 3 3/4 feet (about 1.1 meters) long and 2 1/4 feet (about 0.7 meter) wide   *g23* That is, about 3 feet (about 0.9 meter) long and 1 1/2 feet (about 0.5 meter) wide and 2 1/4 feet (about 0.7 meter) high   *h25* That is, about 3 inches (about 8 centimeters) table and fasten them to the four corners, where the four legs are. ²⁷The rings are to be close to the rim to hold the poles used in carrying the table. ²⁸Make the poles of acacia wood, overlay them with gold and carry the table with them. ²⁹And make its plates and dishes of pure gold, as well as its pitchers and bowls for the pouring out of offerings. ³⁰Put the bread of the Presence on this table to be before me at all times.

The Lampstand

³¹"Make a lampstand of pure gold and hammer it out, base and shaft; its flowerlike cups, buds and blossoms shall be of one piece with it. ³²Six branches are to extend from the sides of the lampstand — three on one side and three on the other. ³³Three cups shaped like almond flowers with buds and blossoms are to be on one branch, three on the next branch, and the same for all six branches extending from the lampstand. ³⁴And on the lampstand there are to be four cups shaped like almond flowers with buds and blossoms. ³⁵One bud shall be under the first pair of branches extending from the lampstand, a second bud under the second pair, and a third bud under the third pair — six branches in all. ³⁶The buds and branches shall all be of one piece with the lampstand, hammered out of pure gold.

³⁷"Then make its seven lamps and set them up on it so that they light the space in front of it. ³⁸Its wick trimmers and trays are to be of pure gold. ³⁹A talent*ᵃ* of pure gold is to be used for the lampstand and all these accessories. ⁴⁰See that you make them according to the pattern shown you on the mountain.

The Tabernacle

26 "Make the tabernacle with ten curtains of finely twisted linen and blue, purple and scarlet yarn, with cherubim worked into them by a skilled craftsman. ²All the curtains are to be the same size — twenty-eight cubits long and four cubits wide.*ᵇ* ³Join five of the curtains together, and do the same with the other five. ⁴Make loops of blue material along the edge of the end curtain in one set, and do the same with the end curtain in the

other set. ⁵Make fifty loops on one curtain and fifty loops on the end curtain of the other set, with the loops opposite each other. ⁶Then make fifty gold clasps and use them to fasten the curtains together so that the tabernacle is a unit.

⁷"Make curtains of goat hair for the tent over the tabernacle — eleven altogether. ⁸All eleven curtains are to be the same size — thirty cubits long and four cubits wide.*ᶜ* ⁹Join five of the curtains together into one set and the other six into another set. Fold the sixth curtain double at the front of the tent. ¹⁰Make fifty loops along the edge of the end curtain in one set and also along the edge of the end curtain in the other set. ¹¹Then make fifty bronze clasps and put them in the loops to fasten the tent together as a unit. ¹²As for the additional length of the tent curtains, the half curtain that is left over is to hang down at the rear of the tabernacle. ¹³The tent curtains will be a cubit*ᵈ* longer on both sides; what is left will hang over the sides of the tabernacle so as to cover it. ¹⁴Make for the tent a covering of ram skins dyed red, and over that a covering of hides of sea cows.*ᵉ*

¹⁵"Make upright frames of acacia wood for the tabernacle. ¹⁶Each frame is to be ten cubits long and a cubit and a half wide,*ᶠ* ¹⁷with two projections set parallel to each other. Make all the frames of the tabernacle in this way. ¹⁸Make twenty frames for the south side of the tabernacle ¹⁹and make forty silver bases to go under them — two bases for each frame, one under each projection. ²⁰For the other side, the north side of the tabernacle, make twenty frames ²¹and forty silver bases — two under each frame. ²²Make six frames for the far end, that is, the west end of the tabernacle, ²³and make two frames for the corners at the far end. ²⁴At these two corners they must be double from the bottom all the way to the top, and fitted into a single ring; both shall be like that. ²⁵So there will be eight frames and sixteen silver bases — two under each frame.

²⁶"Also make crossbars of acacia wood: five for the frames on one side of the tabernacle, ²⁷five for those on the other side, and five for the frames on the west, at the far end of the tabernacle. ²⁸The center

ᵃ39 That is, about 75 pounds (about 34 kilograms) and 6 feet (about 1.8 meters) wide   *ᶜ8* That is, about 45 feet (about 13.5 meters) long and 6 feet (about 1.8 meters) wide   *ᵈ13* That is, about 1 1/2 feet (about 0.5 meter)   *ᵉ14* That is, dugongs   *ᶠ16* That is, about 15 feet (about 4.5 meters) long and 2 1/4 feet (about 0.7 meter) wide   *ᵇ2* That is, about 42 feet (about 12.5 meters) long crossbar is to extend from end to end at the middle of the frames. ²⁹Overlay the frames with gold and make gold rings to hold the crossbars. Also overlay the crossbars with gold.

³⁰"Set up the tabernacle according to the plan shown you on the mountain.

³¹"Make a curtain of blue, purple and scarlet yarn and finely twisted linen, with cherubim worked into it by a skilled craftsman. ³²Hang it with gold hooks on four posts of acacia wood overlaid with gold and standing on four silver bases. ³³Hang the curtain from the clasps and place the ark of the Testimony behind the curtain. The curtain will separate the Holy Place from the Most Holy Place. ³⁴Put the atonement cover on the ark of the Testimony in the Most Holy Place. ³⁵Place the table outside the curtain on the north side of the tabernacle and put the lampstand opposite it on the south side.

³⁶"For the entrance to the tent make a curtain of blue, purple and scarlet yarn and finely twisted linen — the work of an embroiderer. ³⁷Make gold hooks for this curtain and five posts of acacia wood overlaid with gold. And cast five bronze bases for them.

The Altar of Burnt Offering

27 "Build an altar of acacia wood, three cubits^a high; it is to be square, five cubits long and five cubits wide.^b ²Make a horn at each of the four corners, so that the horns and the altar are of one piece, and overlay the altar with bronze. ³Make all its utensils of bronze — its pots to remove the ashes, and its shovels, sprinkling bowls, meat forks and firepans. ⁴Make a grating for it, a bronze network, and make a bronze ring at each of the four corners of the network. ⁵Put it under the ledge of the altar so that it is halfway up the altar. ⁶Make poles of acacia wood for the altar and overlay them with bronze. ⁷The poles are to be inserted into the rings so they will be on two sides of the altar when it is carried. ⁸Make the altar hollow, out of boards. It is to be made just as you were shown on the mountain.

The Courtyard

⁹"Make a courtyard for the tabernacle. The south side shall be a hundred cubits^c long and is to have curtains of finely twisted linen, ¹⁰with twenty posts and twenty bronze bases and with silver hooks and bands on the posts. ¹¹The north side shall also be a hundred cubits long and is to have curtains, with twenty posts and twenty bronze bases and with silver hooks and bands on the posts.

¹²"The west end of the courtyard shall be fifty cubits^d wide and have curtains, with ten posts and ten bases. ¹³On the east end, toward the sunrise, the courtyard shall also be fifty cubits wide. ¹⁴Curtains fifteen cubits^e long are to be on one side of the entrance, with three posts and three bases, ¹⁵and curtains fifteen cubits long are to be on the other side, with three posts and three bases.

¹⁶"For the entrance to the courtyard, provide a curtain twenty cubits^f long, of blue, purple and scarlet yarn and finely twisted linen — the work of an embroiderer — with four posts and four bases. ¹⁷All the posts around the courtyard are to have silver bands and hooks, and bronze bases. ¹⁸The courtyard shall be a hundred cubits long and fifty cubits wide,^g with curtains of finely twisted linen five cubits^h high, and with bronze bases. ¹⁹All the other articles used in the service of the tabernacle, whatever their function, including all the tent pegs for it and those for the courtyard, are to be of bronze.

Oil for the Lampstand

²⁰"Command the Israelites to bring you clear oil of pressed olives for the light so that the lamps may be kept burning. ²¹In the Tent of Meeting, outside the curtain that is in front of the Testimony, Aaron and his sons are to keep the lamps burning before the LORD from evening till morning. This is to be a lasting ordinance among the Israelites for the generations to come.

The Priestly Garments

28 "Have Aaron your brother brought to you from among the Israelites, along with his sons Nadab and Abihu, Eleazar and Ithamar, so they may serve me

---

^a1 That is, about 4 1/2 feet (about 1.3 meters) and wide   ^c9 That is, about 150 feet (about 46 meters); also in verse 13   ^e14 That is, about 22 1/2 feet (about 6.9 meters); also in verse 15   ^f16 That is, about 30 feet (about 9 meters)   ^g18 That is, about 150 feet (about 46 meters) long and 75 feet (about 23 meters) wide   ^h18 That is, about 7 1/2 feet (about 2.3 meters)   ^b1 That is, about 7 1/2 feet (about 2.3 meters) long   ^d12 That is, about 75 feet (about 23 meters); also in verse 13

as priests. [2]Make sacred garments for your brother Aaron, to give him dignity and honor. [3]Tell all the skilled men to whom I have given wisdom in such matters that they are to make garments for Aaron, for his consecration, so he may serve me as priest. [4]These are the garments they are to make: a breastpiece, an ephod, a robe, a woven tunic, a turban and a sash. They are to make these sacred garments for your brother Aaron and his sons, so they may serve me as priests. [5]Have them use gold, and blue, purple and scarlet yarn, and fine linen.

The Ephod

[6]"Make the ephod of gold, and of blue, purple and scarlet yarn, and of finely twisted linen—the work of a skilled craftsman. [7]It is to have two shoulder pieces attached to two of its corners, so it can be fastened. [8]Its skillfully woven waistband is to be like it—of one piece with the ephod and made with gold, and with blue, purple and scarlet yarn, and with finely twisted linen.

[9]"Take two onyx stones and engrave on them the names of the sons of Israel [10]in the order of their birth—six names on one stone and the remaining six on the other. [11]Engrave the names of the sons of Israel on the two stones the way a gem cutter engraves a seal. Then mount the stones in gold filigree settings [12]and fasten them on the shoulder pieces of the ephod as memorial stones for the sons of Israel. Aaron is to bear the names on his shoulders as a memorial before the LORD. [13]Make gold filigree settings [14]and two braided chains of pure gold, like a rope, and attach the chains to the settings.

The Breastpiece

[15]"Fashion a breastpiece for making decisions—the work of a skilled craftsman. Make it like the ephod: of gold, and of blue, purple and scarlet yarn, and of finely twisted linen. [16]It is to be square— a span[a] long and a span wide—and folded double. [17]Then mount four rows of precious stones on it. In the first row there shall be a ruby, a topaz and a beryl; [18]in the second row a turquoise, a sapphire[b] and an emerald; [19]in the third row a jacinth, an agate and an amethyst; [20]in the fourth row a chrysolite, an onyx and

a jasper.[c] Mount them in gold filigree settings. [21]There are to be twelve stones, one for each of the names of the sons of Israel, each engraved like a seal with the name of one of the twelve tribes.

[22]"For the breastpiece make braided chains of pure gold, like a rope. [23]Make two gold rings for it and fasten them to two corners of the breastpiece. [24]Fasten the two gold chains to the rings at the corners of the breastpiece, [25]and the other ends of the chains to the two settings, attaching them to the shoulder pieces of the ephod at the front. [26]Make two gold rings and attach them to the other two corners of the breastpiece on the inside edge next to the ephod. [27]Make two more gold rings and attach them to the bottom of the shoulder pieces on the front of the ephod, close to the seam just above the waistband of the ephod. [28]The rings of the breastpiece are to be tied to the rings of the ephod with blue cord, connecting it to the waistband, so that the breastpiece will not swing out from the ephod.

[29]"Whenever Aaron enters the Holy Place, he will bear the names of the sons of Israel over his heart on the breastpiece of decision as a continuing memorial before the LORD. [30]Also put the Urim and the Thummim in the breastpiece, so they may be over Aaron's heart whenever he enters the presence of the LORD. Thus Aaron will always bear the means of making decisions for the Israelites over his heart before the LORD.

Other Priestly Garments

[31]"Make the robe of the ephod entirely of blue cloth, [32]with an opening for the head in its center. There shall be a woven edge like a collar[d] around this opening, so that it will not tear. [33]Make pomegranates of blue, purple and scarlet yarn around the hem of the robe, with gold bells between them. [34]The gold bells and the pomegranates are to alternate around the hem of the robe. [35]Aaron must wear it when he ministers. The sound of the bells will be heard when he enters the Holy Place before the LORD and when he comes out, so that he will not die.

[36]"Make a plate of pure gold and engrave on it as on a seal: HOLY TO THE LORD. [37]Fasten a blue cord to it to attach it to the turban; it is to be on the front of the

---

[a]16 That is, about 9 inches (about 22 centimeters)   [b]18 Or lapis lazuli   [c]20 The precise identification of some of these precious stones is uncertain.   [d]32 The meaning of the Hebrew for this word is uncertain.

turban. 38It will be on Aaron's forehead, and he will bear the guilt involved in the sacred gifts the Israelites consecrate, whatever their gifts may be. It will be on Aaron's forehead continually so that they will be acceptable to the LORD.

39"Weave the tunic of fine linen and make the turban of fine linen. The sash is to be the work of an embroiderer. 40Make tunics, sashes and headbands for Aaron's sons, to give them dignity and honor. 41After you put these clothes on your brother Aaron and his sons, anoint and ordain them. Consecrate them so they may serve me as priests.

42"Make linen undergarments as a covering for the body, reaching from the waist to the thigh. 43Aaron and his sons must wear them whenever they enter the Tent of Meeting or approach the altar to minister in the Holy Place, so that they will not incur guilt and die.

"This is to be a lasting ordinance for Aaron and his descendants.

Consecration of the Priests

29 "This is what you are to do to consecrate them, so they may serve me as priests: Take a young bull and two rams without defect. 2And from fine wheat flour, without yeast, make bread, and cakes mixed with oil, and wafers spread with oil. 3Put them in a basket and present them in it—along with the bull and the two rams. 4Then bring Aaron and his sons to the entrance to the Tent of Meeting and wash them with water. 5Take the garments and dress Aaron with the tunic, the robe of the ephod, the ephod itself and the breastpiece. Fasten the ephod on him by its skillfully woven waistband. 6Put the turban on his head and attach the sacred diadem to the turban. 7Take the anointing oil and anoint him by pouring it on his head. 8Bring his sons and dress them in tunics 9and put headbands on them. Then tie sashes on Aaron and his sons.a The priesthood is theirs by a lasting ordinance. In this way you shall ordain Aaron and his sons.

10"Bring the bull to the front of the Tent of Meeting, and Aaron and his sons shall lay their hands on its head. 11Slaughter it in the LORD's presence at the entrance to the Tent of Meeting. 12Take some of the bull's blood and put it on the horns of the altar with your finger, and pour out the rest of it at the base of the altar. 13Then take all the fat around the inner parts, the covering of the liver, and both kidneys with the fat on them, and burn them on the altar. 14But burn the bull's flesh and its hide and its offal outside the camp. It is a sin offering.

15"Take one of the rams, and Aaron and his sons shall lay their hands on its head. 16Slaughter it and take the blood and sprinkle it against the altar on all sides. 17Cut the ram into pieces and wash the inner parts and the legs, putting them with the head and the other pieces. 18Then burn the entire ram on the altar. It is a burnt offering to the LORD, a pleasing aroma, an offering made to the LORD by fire.

19"Take the other ram, and Aaron and his sons shall lay their hands on its head. 20Slaughter it, take some of its blood and put it on the lobes of the right ears of Aaron and his sons, on the thumbs of their right hands, and on the big toes of their right feet. Then sprinkle blood against the altar on all sides. 21And take some of the blood on the altar and some of the anointing oil and sprinkle it on Aaron and his garments and on his sons and their garments. Then he and his sons and their garments will be consecrated.

22"Take from this ram the fat, the fat tail, the fat around the inner parts, the covering of the liver, both kidneys with the fat on them, and the right thigh. (This is the ram for the ordination.) 23From the basket of bread made without yeast, which is before the LORD, take a loaf, and a cake made with oil, and a wafer. 24Put all these in the hands of Aaron and his sons and wave them before the LORD as a wave offering. 25Then take them from their hands and burn them on the altar along with the burnt offering for a pleasing aroma to the LORD, an offering made to the LORD by fire. 26After you take the breast of the ram for Aaron's ordination, wave it before the LORD as a wave offering, and it will be your share.

27"Consecrate those parts of the ordination ram that belong to Aaron and his sons: the breast that was waved and the thigh that was presented. 28This is always to be the regular share from the Israelites for Aaron and his sons. It is the contribution the Israelites are to make to the LORD from their fellowship offerings.b

29"Aaron's sacred garments will belong to his descendants so that they can be

---

a9 Hebrew; Septuagint on them   b28 Traditionally peace offerings anointed and ordained in them. ³⁰The son who succeeds him as priest and comes to the Tent of Meeting to minister in the Holy Place is to wear them seven days.

³¹"Take the ram for the ordination and cook the meat in a sacred place. ³²At the entrance to the Tent of Meeting, Aaron and his sons are to eat the meat of the ram and the bread that is in the basket. ³³They are to eat these offerings by which atonement was made for their ordination and consecration. But no one else may eat them, because they are sacred. ³⁴And if any of the meat of the ordination ram or any bread is left over till morning, burn it up. It must not be eaten, because it is sacred.

³⁵"Do for Aaron and his sons everything I have commanded you, taking seven days to ordain them. ³⁶Sacrifice a bull each day as a sin offering to make atonement. Purify the altar by making atonement for it, and anoint it to consecrate it. ³⁷For seven days make atonement for the altar and consecrate it. Then the altar will be most holy, and whatever touches it will be holy.

³⁸"This is what you are to offer on the altar regularly each day: two lambs a year old. ³⁹Offer one in the morning and the other at twilight. ⁴⁰With the first lamb offer a tenth of an ephah*a* of fine flour mixed with a quarter of a hin*b* of oil from pressed olives, and a quarter of a hin of wine as a drink offering. ⁴¹Sacrifice the other lamb at twilight with the same grain offering and its drink offering as in the morning—a pleasing aroma, an offering made to the LORD by fire.

⁴²"For the generations to come this burnt offering is to be made regularly at the entrance to the Tent of Meeting before the LORD. There I will meet you and speak to you; ⁴³there also I will meet with the Israelites, and the place will be consecrated by my glory.

⁴⁴"So I will consecrate the Tent of Meeting and the altar and will consecrate Aaron and his sons to serve me as priests. ⁴⁵Then I will dwell among the Israelites and be their God. ⁴⁶They will know that I am the LORD their God, who brought them out of Egypt so that I might dwell among them. I am the LORD their God.

The Altar of Incense

30 "Make an altar of acacia wood for burning incense. ²It is to be square, a cubit long and a cubit wide, and two cubits high*c*—its horns of one piece with it. ³Overlay the top and all the sides and the horns with pure gold, and make a gold molding around it. ⁴Make two gold rings for the altar below the molding—two on opposite sides—to hold the poles used to carry it. ⁵Make the poles of acacia wood and overlay them with gold. ⁶Put the altar in front of the curtain that is before the ark of the Testimony—before the atonement cover that is over the Testimony—where I will meet with you.

⁷"Aaron must burn fragrant incense on the altar every morning when he tends the lamps. ⁸He must burn incense again when he lights the lamps at twilight so incense will burn regularly before the LORD for the generations to come. ⁹Do not offer on this altar any other incense or any burnt offering or grain offering, and do not pour a drink offering on it. ¹⁰Once a year Aaron shall make atonement on its horns. This annual atonement must be made with the blood of the atoning sin offering for the generations to come. It is most holy to the LORD."

Atonement Money

¹¹Then the LORD said to Moses, ¹²"When you take a census of the Israelites to count them, each one must pay the LORD a ransom for his life at the time he is counted. Then no plague will come on them when you number them. ¹³Each one who crosses over to those already counted is to give a half shekel,*d* according to the sanctuary shekel, which weighs twenty gerahs. This half shekel is an offering to the LORD. ¹⁴All who cross over, those twenty years old or more, are to give an offering to the LORD. ¹⁵The rich are not to give more than a half shekel and the poor are not to give less when you make the offering to the LORD to atone for your lives. ¹⁶Receive the atonement money from the Israelites and use it for the service of the Tent of Meeting. It will be a memorial for the Israelites before the LORD, making atonement for your lives."

Basin for Washing

¹⁷Then the LORD said to Moses,

---

a40 That is, probably about 2 quarts (about 2 liters)   *b40* That is, probably about 1 quart (about 1 liter)   *c2* That is, about 1 1/2 feet (about 0.5 meter) long and wide and about 3 feet (about 0.9 meter) high   *d13* That is, about 1/5 ounce (about 6 grams); also in verse 15

18"Make a bronze basin, with its bronze stand, for washing. Place it between the Tent of Meeting and the altar, and put water in it. 19Aaron and his sons are to wash their hands and feet with water from it. 20Whenever they enter the Tent of Meeting, they shall wash with water so that they will not die. Also, when they approach the altar to minister by presenting an offering made to the LORD by fire, 21they shall wash their hands and feet so that they will not die. This is to be a lasting ordinance for Aaron and his descendants for the generations to come."

Anointing Oil

22Then the LORD said to Moses, 23"Take the following fine spices: 500 shekels*a* of liquid myrrh, half as much (that is, 250 shekels) of fragrant cinnamon, 250 shekels of fragrant cane, 24500 shekels of cassia—all according to the sanctuary shekel—and a hin*b* of olive oil. 25Make these into a sacred anointing oil, a fragrant blend, the work of a perfumer. It will be the sacred anointing oil. 26Then use it to anoint the Tent of Meeting, the ark of the Testimony, 27the table and all its articles, the lampstand and its accessories, the altar of incense, 28the altar of burnt offering and all its utensils, and the basin with its stand. 29You shall consecrate them so they will be most holy, and whatever touches them will be holy.

30"Anoint Aaron and his sons and consecrate them so they may serve me as priests. 31Say to the Israelites, 'This is to be my sacred anointing oil for the generations to come. 32Do not pour it on men's bodies and do not make any oil with the same formula. It is sacred, and you are to consider it sacred. 33Whoever makes perfume like it and whoever puts it on anyone other than a priest must be cut off from his people.'"

Incense

34Then the LORD said to Moses, "Take fragrant spices—gum resin, onycha and galbanum—and pure frankincense, all in equal amounts, 35and make a fragrant blend of incense, the work of a perfumer. It is to be salted and pure and sacred. 36Grind some of it to powder and place it in front of the Testimony in the Tent of Meeting, where I will meet with you. It shall be most holy to you. 37Do not make any incense with this formula for yourselves; consider it holy to the LORD. 38Whoever makes any like it to enjoy its fragrance must be cut off from his people."

Bezalel and Oholiab

31 Then the LORD said to Moses, 2"See, I have chosen Bezalel son of Uri, the son of Hur, of the tribe of Judah, 3and I have filled him with the Spirit of God, with skill, ability and knowledge in all kinds of crafts— 4to make artistic designs for work in gold, silver and bronze, 5to cut and set stones, to work in wood, and to engage in all kinds of craftsmanship. 6Moreover, I have appointed Oholiab son of Ahisamach, of the tribe of Dan, to help him. Also I have given skill to all the craftsmen to make everything I have commanded you: 7the Tent of Meeting, the ark of the Testimony with the atonement cover on it, and all the other furnishings of the tent— 8the table and its articles, the pure gold lampstand and all its accessories, the altar of incense, 9the altar of burnt offering and all its utensils, the basin with its stand— 10and also the woven garments, both the sacred garments for Aaron the priest and the garments for his sons when they serve as priests, 11and the anointing oil and fragrant incense for the Holy Place. They are to make them just as I commanded you."

The Sabbath

12Then the LORD said to Moses, 13"Say to the Israelites, 'You must observe my Sabbaths. This will be a sign between me and you for the generations to come, so you may know that I am the LORD, who makes you holy.*c*

14" 'Observe the Sabbath, because it is holy to you. Anyone who desecrates it must be put to death; whoever does any work on that day must be cut off from his people. 15For six days, work is to be done, but the seventh day is a Sabbath of rest, holy to the LORD. Whoever does any work on the Sabbath day must be put to death. 16The Israelites are to observe the Sabbath, celebrating it for the generations to come as a lasting covenant. 17It will be a sign between me and the Israelites forever, for in six days the LORD made the heavens and the earth, and on the seventh day he abstained from work and rested.' "

---

a23 That is, about 12 1/2 pounds (about 6 kilograms)　　*b24* That is, probably about 4 quarts (about 4 liters)　　*c13* Or *who sanctifies you; or who sets you apart as holy*

18When the LORD finished speaking to Moses on Mount Sinai, he gave him the two tablets of the Testimony, the tablets of stone inscribed by the finger of God.

The Golden Calf

32 When the people saw that Moses was so long in coming down from the mountain, they gathered around Aaron and said, "Come, make us gods*a* who will go before us. As for this fellow Moses who brought us up out of Egypt, we don't know what has happened to him."

2Aaron answered them, "Take off the gold earrings that your wives, your sons and your daughters are wearing, and bring them to me." 3So all the people took off their earrings and brought them to Aaron. 4He took what they handed him and made it into an idol cast in the shape of a calf, fashioning it with a tool. Then they said, "These are your gods,*b* O Israel, who brought you up out of Egypt."

5When Aaron saw this, he built an altar in front of the calf and announced, "Tomorrow there will be a festival to the LORD." 6So the next day the people rose early and sacrificed burnt offerings and presented fellowship offerings.*c* Afterward they sat down to eat and drink and got up to indulge in revelry.

7Then the LORD said to Moses, "Go down, because your people, whom you brought up out of Egypt, have become corrupt. 8They have been quick to turn away from what I commanded them and have made themselves an idol cast in the shape of a calf. They have bowed down to it and sacrificed to it and have said, 'These are your gods, O Israel, who brought you up out of Egypt.'

9"I have seen these people," the LORD said to Moses, "and they are a stiff-necked people. 10Now leave me alone so that my anger may burn against them and that I may destroy them. Then I will make you into a great nation."

11But Moses sought the favor of the LORD his God. "O LORD," he said, "why should your anger burn against your people, whom you brought out of Egypt with great power and a mighty hand? 12Why should the Egyptians say, 'It was with evil intent that he brought them out, to kill them in the mountains and to wipe them off the face of the earth'? Turn from your fierce anger; relent and do not bring di-

saster on your people. 13Remember your servants Abraham, Isaac and Israel, to whom you swore by your own self: 'I will make your descendants as numerous as the stars in the sky and I will give your descendants all this land I promised them, and it will be their inheritance forever.'" 14Then the LORD relented and did not bring on his people the disaster he had threatened.

15Moses turned and went down the mountain with the two tablets of the Testimony in his hands. They were inscribed on both sides, front and back. 16The tablets were the work of God; the writing was the writing of God, engraved on the tablets.

17When Joshua heard the noise of the people shouting, he said to Moses, "There is the sound of war in the camp." 18Moses replied:

"It is not the sound of victory,
    it is not the sound of defeat;
it is the sound of singing that I
    hear."

19When Moses approached the camp and saw the calf and the dancing, his anger burned and he threw the tablets out of his hands, breaking them to pieces at the foot of the mountain. 20And he took the calf they had made and burned it in the fire; then he ground it to powder, scattered it on the water and made the Israelites drink it.

21He said to Aaron, "What did these people do to you, that you led them into such great sin?"

22"Do not be angry, my lord," Aaron answered. "You know how prone these people are to evil. 23They said to me, 'Make us gods who will go before us. As for this fellow Moses who brought us up out of Egypt, we don't know what has happened to him.' 24So I told them, 'Whoever has any gold jewelry, take it off.' Then they gave me the gold, and I threw it into the fire, and out came this calf!"

25Moses saw that the people were running wild and that Aaron had let them get out of control and so become a laughingstock to their enemies. 26So he stood at the entrance to the camp and said, "Whoever is for the LORD, come to me." And all the Levites rallied to him.

27Then he said to them, "This is what the LORD, the God of Israel, says: 'Each

a1 Or a god; also in verses 23 and 31   *b4 Or This is your god; also in verse 8*   *c6 Traditionally peace offerings* man strap a sword to his side. Go back and forth through the camp from one end to the other, each killing his brother and friend and neighbor.' " ²⁸The Levites did as Moses commanded, and that day about three thousand of the people died. ²⁹Then Moses said, "You have been set apart to the LORD today, for you were against your own sons and brothers, and he has blessed you this day."

³⁰The next day Moses said to the people, "You have committed a great sin. But now I will go up to the LORD; perhaps I can make atonement for your sin."

³¹So Moses went back to the LORD and said, "Oh, what a great sin these people have committed! They have made themselves gods of gold. ³²But now, please forgive their sin—but if not, then blot me out of the book you have written."

³³The LORD replied to Moses, "Whoever has sinned against me I will blot out of my book. ³⁴Now go, lead the people to the place I spoke of, and my angel will go before you. However, when the time comes for me to punish, I will punish them for their sin."

³⁵And the LORD struck the people with a plague because of what they did with the calf Aaron had made.

33 Then the LORD said to Moses, "Leave this place, you and the people you brought up out of Egypt, and go up to the land I promised on oath to Abraham, Isaac and Jacob, saying, 'I will give it to your descendants.' ²I will send an angel before you and drive out the Canaanites, Amorites, Hittites, Perizzites, Hivites and Jebusites. ³Go up to the land flowing with milk and honey. But I will not go with you, because you are a stiff-necked people and I might destroy you on the way."

⁴When the people heard these distressing words, they began to mourn and no one put on any ornaments. ⁵For the LORD had said to Moses, "Tell the Israelites, 'You are a stiff-necked people. If I were to go with you even for a moment, I might destroy you. Now take off your ornaments and I will decide what to do with you.' " ⁶So the Israelites stripped off their ornaments at Mount Horeb.

The Tent of Meeting

⁷Now Moses used to take a tent and pitch it outside the camp some distance away, calling it the "tent of meeting." Anyone inquiring of the LORD would go to the tent of meeting outside the camp.

⁸And whenever Moses went out to the tent, all the people rose and stood at the entrances to their tents, watching Moses until he entered the tent. ⁹As Moses went into the tent, the pillar of cloud would come down and stay at the entrance, while the LORD spoke with Moses. ¹⁰Whenever the people saw the pillar of cloud standing at the entrance to the tent, they all stood and worshiped, each at the entrance to his tent. ¹¹The LORD would speak to Moses face to face, as a man speaks with his friend. Then Moses would return to the camp, but his young aide Joshua son of Nun did not leave the tent.

Moses and the Glory of the LORD

¹²Moses said to the LORD, "You have been telling me, 'Lead these people,' but you have not let me know whom you will send with me. You have said, 'I know you by name and you have found favor with me.' ¹³If you are pleased with me, teach me your ways so I may know you and continue to find favor with you. Remember that this nation is your people."

¹⁴The LORD replied, "My Presence will go with you, and I will give you rest."

¹⁵Then Moses said to him, "If your Presence does not go with us, do not send us up from here. ¹⁶How will anyone know that you are pleased with me and with your people unless you go with us? What else will distinguish me and your people from all the other people on the face of the earth?"

¹⁷And the LORD said to Moses, "I will do the very thing you have asked, because I am pleased with you and I know you by name."

¹⁸Then Moses said, "Now show me your glory."

¹⁹And the LORD said, "I will cause all my goodness to pass in front of you, and I will proclaim my name, the LORD, in your presence. I will have mercy on whom I will have mercy, and I will have compassion on whom I will have compassion. ²⁰But," he said, "you cannot see my face, for no one may see me and live."

²¹Then the LORD said, "There is a place near me where you may stand on a rock. ²²When my glory passes by, I will put you in a cleft in the rock and cover you with my hand until I have passed by. ²³Then I will remove my hand and you will see my back; but my face must not be seen."

The New Stone Tablets

34 The LORD said to Moses, "Chisel out two stone tablets like the first ones, and I will write on them the words that were on the first tablets, which you broke. ²Be ready in the morning, and then come up on Mount Sinai. Present yourself to me there on top of the mountain. ³No one is to come with you or be seen anywhere on the mountain; not even the flocks and herds may graze in front of the mountain."

⁴So Moses chiseled out two stone tablets like the first ones and went up Mount Sinai early in the morning, as the LORD had commanded him; and he carried the two stone tablets in his hands. ⁵Then the LORD came down in the cloud and stood there with him and proclaimed his name,

the LORD. ⁶And he passed in front of Moses, proclaiming, "The LORD, the LORD, the compassionate and gracious God, slow to anger, abounding in love and faithfulness, ⁷maintaining love to thousands, and forgiving wickedness, rebellion and sin. Yet he does not leave the guilty unpunished; he punishes the children and their children for the sin of the fathers to the third and fourth generation."

⁸Moses bowed to the ground at once and worshiped. ⁹"O Lord, if I have found favor in your eyes," he said, "then let the Lord go with us. Although this is a stiff-necked people, forgive our wickedness and our sin, and take us as your inheritance."

¹⁰Then the LORD said: "I am making a covenant with you. Before all your people I will do wonders never before done in any

	MONDAY	
VERSE FOR THE DAY: *Exodus 33:18*	*AUTHOR:* *Anne Ortlund*	*PASSAGE FOR THE DAY:* *Exodus 33:18–23*

Vision

O LORD, I need to know that you are you!
I need to have a glorious God in view;
To see your plans, so infinite and wise,
I need a mighty God before my eyes.
  Show me your glory! Show yourself anew;
  Lord, open up my eyes of faith to you.

So often, when I face which way to go
The problems seem to multiply and grow;
I do not see you standing, waiting, there,
So full of power for me, to do, to dare!
  Show me your glory! Show yourself anew;
  Lord, open up my eyes of faith to you.

O God, I know that in my present state
I could not stand the sight of you, so great;
Yet even now, the smallest glimpse is bright
Enough to bathe my soul in dazzling light!
  Show me your glory! Show yourself anew;
  Lord, open up my eyes of faith to you.

Additional Scripture Readings:
2 Kings 6:15–17; Isaiah 6:1–8

Go to page 123 for your next devotional reading.

nation in all the world. The people you live among will see how awesome is the work that I, the LORD, will do for you. [11]Obey what I command you today. I will drive out before you the Amorites, Canaanites, Hittites, Perizzites, Hivites and Jebusites. [12]Be careful not to make a treaty with those who live in the land where you are going, or they will be a snare among you. [13]Break down their altars, smash their sacred stones and cut down their Asherah poles.[a] [14]Do not worship any other god, for the LORD, whose name is Jealous, is a jealous God.

[15]"Be careful not to make a treaty with those who live in the land; for when they prostitute themselves to their gods and sacrifice to them, they will invite you and you will eat their sacrifices. [16]And when you choose some of their daughters as wives for your sons and those daughters prostitute themselves to their gods, they will lead your sons to do the same.

[17]"Do not make cast idols.

[18]"Celebrate the Feast of Unleavened Bread. For seven days eat bread made without yeast, as I commanded you. Do this at the appointed time in the month of Abib, for in that month you came out of Egypt.

[19]"The first offspring of every womb belongs to me, including all the firstborn males of your livestock, whether from herd or flock. [20]Redeem the firstborn donkey with a lamb, but if you do not redeem it, break its neck. Redeem all your firstborn sons.

"No one is to appear before me empty-handed.

[21]"Six days you shall labor, but on the seventh day you shall rest; even during the plowing season and harvest you must rest.

[22]"Celebrate the Feast of Weeks with the firstfruits of the wheat harvest, and the Feast of Ingathering at the turn of the year.[b] [23]Three times a year all your men are to appear before the Sovereign LORD, the God of Israel. [24]I will drive out nations before you and enlarge your territory, and no one will covet your land when you go up three times each year to appear before the LORD your God.

[25]"Do not offer the blood of a sacrifice to me along with anything containing yeast, and do not let any of the sacrifice from the Passover Feast remain until morning.

[26]"Bring the best of the firstfruits of your soil to the house of the LORD your God.

"Do not cook a young goat in its mother's milk."

[27]Then the LORD said to Moses, "Write down these words, for in accordance with these words I have made a covenant with you and with Israel." [28]Moses was there with the LORD forty days and forty nights without eating bread or drinking water. And he wrote on the tablets the words of the covenant—the Ten Commandments.

The Radiant Face of Moses

[29]When Moses came down from Mount Sinai with the two tablets of the Testimony in his hands, he was not aware that his face was radiant because he had spoken with the LORD. [30]When Aaron and all the Israelites saw Moses, his face was radiant, and they were afraid to come near him. [31]But Moses called to them; so Aaron and all the leaders of the community came back to him, and he spoke to them. [32]Afterward all the Israelites came near him, and he gave them all the commands the LORD had given him on Mount Sinai.

[33]When Moses finished speaking to them, he put a veil over his face. [34]But whenever he entered the LORD's presence to speak with him, he removed the veil until he came out. And when he came out and told the Israelites what he had been commanded, [35]they saw that his face was radiant. Then Moses would put the veil back over his face until he went in to speak with the LORD.

Sabbath Regulations

35 Moses assembled the whole Israelite community and said to them, "These are the things the LORD has commanded you to do: [2]For six days, work is to be done, but the seventh day shall be your holy day, a Sabbath of rest to the LORD. Whoever does any work on it must be put to death. [3]Do not light a fire in any of your dwellings on the Sabbath day."

Materials for the Tabernacle

[4]Moses said to the whole Israelite community, "This is what the LORD has commanded: [5]From what you have, take an offering for the LORD. Everyone who is willing is to bring to the LORD an offering of gold, silver and bronze; [6]blue, purple and scarlet yarn and fine linen; goat hair;

---

[a]13 That is, symbols of the goddess Asherah   [b]22 That is, in the fall

[7]ram skins dyed red and hides of sea cows[a]; acacia wood; [8]olive oil for the light; spices for the anointing oil and for the fragrant incense; [9]and onyx stones and other gems to be mounted on the ephod and breastpiece.

[10]"All who are skilled among you are to come and make everything the LORD has commanded: [11]the tabernacle with its tent and its covering, clasps, frames, crossbars, posts and bases; [12]the ark with its poles and the atonement cover and the curtain that shields it; [13]the table with its poles and all its articles and the bread of the Presence; [14]the lampstand that is for light with its accessories, lamps and oil for the light; [15]the altar of incense with its poles, the anointing oil and the fragrant incense; the curtain for the doorway at the entrance to the tabernacle; [16]the altar of burnt offering with its bronze grating, its poles and all its utensils; the bronze basin with its stand; [17]the curtains of the courtyard with its posts and bases, and the curtain for the entrance to the courtyard; [18]the tent pegs for the tabernacle and for the courtyard, and their ropes; [19]the woven garments worn for ministering in the sanctuary—both the sacred garments for Aaron the priest and the garments for his sons when they serve as priests."

[20]Then the whole Israelite community withdrew from Moses' presence, [21]and everyone who was willing and whose heart moved him came and brought an offering to the LORD for the work on the Tent of Meeting, for all its service, and for the sacred garments. [22]All who were willing, men and women alike, came and brought gold jewelry of all kinds: brooches, earrings, rings and ornaments. They all presented their gold as a wave offering to the LORD. [23]Everyone who had blue, purple or scarlet yarn or fine linen, or goat hair, ram skins dyed red or hides of sea cows brought them. [24]Those presenting an offering of silver or bronze brought it as an offering to the LORD, and everyone who had acacia wood for any part of the work brought it. [25]Every skilled woman spun with her hands and brought what she had spun—blue, purple or scarlet yarn or fine linen. [26]And all the women who were willing and had the skill spun the goat hair. [27]The leaders brought onyx stones and other gems to be mounted on the ephod and breastpiece. [28]They also brought

spices and olive oil for the light and for the anointing oil and for the fragrant incense. [29]All the Israelite men and women who were willing brought to the LORD freewill offerings for all the work the LORD through Moses had commanded them to do.

Bezalel and Oholiab

[30]Then Moses said to the Israelites, "See, the LORD has chosen Bezalel son of Uri, the son of Hur, of the tribe of Judah, [31]and he has filled him with the Spirit of God, with skill, ability and knowledge in all kinds of crafts— [32]to make artistic designs for work in gold, silver and bronze, [33]to cut and set stones, to work in wood and to engage in all kinds of artistic craftsmanship. [34]And he has given both him and Oholiab son of Ahisamach, of the tribe of Dan, the ability to teach others. [35]He has filled them with skill to do all kinds of work as craftsmen, designers, embroiderers in blue, purple and scarlet yarn and fine linen, and weavers—all of them master craftsmen and designers.

36 [1]So Bezalel, Oholiab and every skilled person to whom the LORD has given skill and ability to know how to carry out all the work of constructing the sanctuary are to do the work just as the Lord has commanded."

[2]Then Moses summoned Bezalel and Oholiab and every skilled person to whom the LORD had given ability and who was willing to come and do the work. [3]They received from Moses all the offerings the Israelites had brought to carry out the work of constructing the sanctuary. And the people continued to bring freewill offerings morning after morning. [4]So all the skilled craftsmen who were doing all the work on the sanctuary left their work [5]and said to Moses, "The people are bringing more than enough for doing the work the LORD commanded to be done."

[6]Then Moses gave an order and they sent this word throughout the camp: "No man or woman is to make anything else as an offering for the sanctuary." And so the people were restrained from bringing more, [7]because what they already had was more than enough to do all the work.

The Tabernacle

[8]All the skilled men among the workmen made the tabernacle with ten curtains of finely twisted linen and blue, pur-

a7 That is, dugongs; also in verse 23

ple and scarlet yarn, with cherubim worked into them by a skilled craftsman. 9All the curtains were the same size— twenty-eight cubits long and four cubits wide.a 10They joined five of the curtains together and did the same with the other five. 11Then they made loops of blue material along the edge of the end curtain in one set, and the same was done with the end curtain in the other set. 12They also made fifty loops on one curtain and fifty loops on the end curtain of the other set, with the loops opposite each other. 13Then they made fifty gold clasps and used them to fasten the two sets of curtains together so that the tabernacle was a unit.

14They made curtains of goat hair for the tent over the tabernacle—eleven altogether. 15All eleven curtains were the same size—thirty cubits long and four cubits wide.b 16They joined five of the curtains into one set and the other six into another set. 17Then they made fifty loops along the edge of the end curtain in one set and also along the edge of the end curtain in the other set. 18They made fifty bronze clasps to fasten the tent together as a unit. 19Then they made for the tent a covering of ram skins dyed red, and over that a covering of hides of sea cows.c

20They made upright frames of acacia wood for the tabernacle. 21Each frame was ten cubits long and a cubit and a half wide,d 22with two projections set parallel to each other. They made all the frames of the tabernacle in this way. 23They made twenty frames for the south side of the tabernacle 24and made forty silver bases to go under them—two bases for each frame, one under each projection. 25For the other side, the north side of the tabernacle, they made twenty frames 26and forty silver bases—two under each frame. 27They made six frames for the far end, that is, the west end of the tabernacle, 28and two frames were made for the corners of the tabernacle at the far end. 29At these two corners the frames were double from the bottom all the way to the top and fitted into a single ring; both were made alike. 30So there were eight frames and sixteen silver bases—two under each frame.

31They also made crossbars of acacia wood: five for the frames on one side of the tabernacle, 32five for those on the other side, and five for the frames on the west, at the far end of the tabernacle. 33They made the center crossbar so that it extended from end to end at the middle of the frames. 34They overlaid the frames with gold and made gold rings to hold the crossbars. They also overlaid the crossbars with gold.

35They made the curtain of blue, purple and scarlet yarn and finely twisted linen, with cherubim worked into it by a skilled craftsman. 36They made four posts of acacia wood for it and overlaid them with gold. They made gold hooks for them and cast their four silver bases. 37For the entrance to the tent they made a curtain of blue, purple and scarlet yarn and finely twisted linen—the work of an embroiderer; 38and they made five posts with hooks for them. They overlaid the tops of the posts and their bands with gold and made their five bases of bronze.

The Ark

37 Bezalel made the ark of acacia wood—two and a half cubits long, a cubit and a half wide, and a cubit and a half high.e 2He overlaid it with pure gold, both inside and out, and made a gold molding around it. 3He cast four gold rings for it and fastened them to its four feet, with two rings on one side and two rings on the other. 4Then he made poles of acacia wood and overlaid them with gold. 5And he inserted the poles into the rings on the sides of the ark to carry it.

6He made the atonement cover of pure gold—two and a half cubits long and a cubit and a half wide.f 7Then he made two cherubim out of hammered gold at the ends of the cover. 8He made one cherub on one end and the second cherub on the other; at the two ends he made them of one piece with the cover. 9The cherubim had their wings spread upward, overshadowing the cover with them. The cherubim faced each other, looking toward the cover.

The Table

10Theyg made the table of acacia wood

---

a9 That is, about 42 feet (about 12.5 meters) long and 6 feet (about 1.8 meters) wide   b15 That is, about 45 feet (about 13.5 meters) long and 6 feet (about 1.8 meters) wide   c19 That is, dugongs d21 That is, about 15 feet (about 4.5 meters) long and 2 1/4 feet (about 0.7 meter) wide   e1 That is, about 3 3/4 feet (about 1.1 meters) long and 2 1/4 feet (about 0.7 meter) wide and high   f6 That is, about 3 3/4 feet (about 1.1 meters) long and 2 1/4 feet (about 0.7 meter) wide   g10 Or He; also in verses 11-29

—two cubits long, a cubit wide, and a cubit and a half high.[a] ¹¹Then they overlaid it with pure gold and made a gold molding around it. ¹²They also made around it a rim a handbreadth[b] wide and put a gold molding on the rim. ¹³They cast four gold rings for the table and fastened them to the four corners, where the four legs were. ¹⁴The rings were put close to the rim to hold the poles used in carrying the table. ¹⁵The poles for carrying the table were made of acacia wood and were overlaid with gold. ¹⁶And they made from pure gold the articles for the table—its plates and dishes and bowls and its pitchers for the pouring out of drink offerings.

The Lampstand

¹⁷They made the lampstand of pure gold and hammered it out, base and shaft; its flowerlike cups, buds and blossoms were of one piece with it. ¹⁸Six branches extended from the sides of the lampstand—three on one side and three on the other. ¹⁹Three cups shaped like almond flowers with buds and blossoms were on one branch, three on the next branch and the same for all six branches extending from the lampstand. ²⁰And on the lampstand were four cups shaped like almond flowers with buds and blossoms. ²¹One bud was under the first pair of branches extending from the lampstand, a second bud under the second pair, and a third bud under the third pair—six branches in all. ²²The buds and the branches were all of one piece with the lampstand, hammered out of pure gold. ²³They made its seven lamps, as well as its wick trimmers and trays, of pure gold. ²⁴They made the lampstand and all its accessories from one talent[c] of pure gold.

The Altar of Incense

²⁵They made the altar of incense out of acacia wood. It was square, a cubit long and a cubit wide, and two cubits high[d]— its horns of one piece with it. ²⁶They overlaid the top and all the sides and the horns with pure gold, and made a gold molding around it. ²⁷They made two gold rings below the molding—two on opposite sides—to hold the poles used to carry

it. ²⁸They made the poles of acacia wood and overlaid them with gold.

²⁹They also made the sacred anointing oil and the pure, fragrant incense—the work of a perfumer.

The Altar of Burnt Offering

38 They[e] built the altar of burnt offering of acacia wood, three cubits[f] high; it was square, five cubits long and five cubits wide.[g] ²They made a horn at each of the four corners, so that the horns and the altar were of one piece, and they overlaid the altar with bronze. ³They made all its utensils of bronze—its pots, shovels, sprinkling bowls, meat forks and firepans. ⁴They made a grating for the altar, a bronze network, to be under its ledge, halfway up the altar. ⁵They cast bronze rings to hold the poles for the four corners of the bronze grating. ⁶They made the poles of acacia wood and overlaid them with bronze. ⁷They inserted the poles into the rings so they would be on the sides of the altar for carrying it. They made it hollow, out of boards.

Basin for Washing

⁸They made the bronze basin and its bronze stand from the mirrors of the women who served at the entrance to the Tent of Meeting.

The Courtyard

⁹Next they made the courtyard. The south side was a hundred cubits[h] long and had curtains of finely twisted linen, ¹⁰with twenty posts and twenty bronze bases, and with silver hooks and bands on the posts. ¹¹The north side was also a hundred cubits long and had twenty posts and twenty bronze bases, with silver hooks and bands on the posts. ¹²The west end was fifty cubits[i] wide and had curtains, with ten posts and ten bases, with silver hooks and bands on the posts. ¹³The east end, toward the sunrise, was also fifty cubits wide. ¹⁴Curtains fifteen cubits[j] long were on one side of the entrance, with three posts and three bases, ¹⁵and curtains fifteen cubits long were on the other side of the entrance to the courtyard, with three posts and three bas-

^a10 That is, about 3 feet (about 0.9 meter) long, 1 1/2 feet (about 0.5 meter) wide, and 2 1/4 feet (about 0.7 meter) high　^b12 That is, about 3 inches (about 8 centimeters)　^c24 That is, about 75 pounds (about 34 kilograms)　^d25 That is, about 1 1/2 feet (about 0.5 meter) long and wide, and about 3 feet (about 0.9 meter) high　^e1 Or He; also in verses 2-9　^f1 That is, about 4 1/2 feet (about 1.3 meters) ^g1 That is, about 7 1/2 feet (about 2.3 meters) long and wide　^h9 That is, about 150 feet (about 46 meters)　ⁱ12 That is, about 75 feet (about 23 meters)　^j14 That is, about 22 1/2 feet (about 6.9 meters)

es. 16All the curtains around the courtyard were of finely twisted linen. 17The bases for the posts were bronze. The hooks and bands on the posts were silver, and their tops were overlaid with silver; so all the posts of the courtyard had silver bands.

18The curtain for the entrance to the courtyard was of blue, purple and scarlet yarn and finely twisted linen—the work of an embroiderer. It was twenty cubits*a* long and, like the curtains of the courtyard, five cubits*b* high, 19with four posts and four bronze bases. Their hooks and bands were silver, and their tops were overlaid with silver. 20All the tent pegs of the tabernacle and of the surrounding courtyard were bronze.

The Materials Used

21These are the amounts of the materials used for the tabernacle, the tabernacle of the Testimony, which were recorded at Moses' command by the Levites under the direction of Ithamar son of Aaron, the priest. 22(Bezalel son of Uri, the son of Hur, of the tribe of Judah, made everything the LORD commanded Moses; 23with him was Oholiab son of Ahisamach, of the tribe of Dan—a craftsman and designer, and an embroiderer in blue, purple and scarlet yarn and fine linen.) 24The total amount of the gold from the wave offering used for all the work on the sanctuary was 29 talents and 730 shekels,*c* according to the sanctuary shekel.

25The silver obtained from those of the community who were counted in the census was 100 talents and 1,775 shekels,*d* according to the sanctuary shekel— 26one beka per person, that is, half a shekel,*e* according to the sanctuary shekel, from everyone who had crossed over to those counted, twenty years old or more, a total of 603,550 men. 27The 100 talents*f* of silver were used to cast the bases for the sanctuary and for the curtain— 100 bases from the 100 talents, one talent for each base. 28They used the 1,775 shekels*g* to make the hooks for the posts, to overlay the tops of the posts, and to make their bands.

29The bronze from the wave offering was 70 talents and 2,400 shekels.*h*

30They used it to make the bases for the entrance to the Tent of Meeting, the bronze altar with its bronze grating and all its utensils, 31the bases for the surrounding courtyard and those for its entrance and all the tent pegs for the tabernacle and those for the surrounding courtyard.

The Priestly Garments

39 From the blue, purple and scarlet yarn they made woven garments for ministering in the sanctuary. They also made sacred garments for Aaron, as the LORD commanded Moses.

The Ephod

2They*i* made the ephod of gold, and of blue, purple and scarlet yarn, and of finely twisted linen. 3They hammered out thin sheets of gold and cut strands to be worked into the blue, purple and scarlet yarn and fine linen—the work of a skilled craftsman. 4They made shoulder pieces for the ephod, which were attached to two of its corners, so it could be fastened. 5Its skillfully woven waistband was like it—of one piece with the ephod and made with gold, and with blue, purple and scarlet yarn, and with finely twisted linen, as the LORD commanded Moses.

6They mounted the onyx stones in gold filigree settings and engraved them like a seal with the names of the sons of Israel. 7Then they fastened them on the shoulder pieces of the ephod as memorial stones for the sons of Israel, as the LORD commanded Moses.

The Breastpiece

8They fashioned the breastpiece—the work of a skilled craftsman. They made it like the ephod: of gold, and of blue, purple and scarlet yarn, and of finely twisted linen. 9It was square—a span*j* long and a span wide—and folded double. 10Then they mounted four rows of precious stones on it. In the first row there was a ruby, a topaz and a beryl; 11in the second row a turquoise, a sapphire*k* and an emerald; 12in the third row a jacinth, an agate and an amethyst; 13in the fourth row

---

a18 That is, about 30 feet (about 9 meters)   *b18* That is, about 7 1/2 feet (about 2.3 meters)
c24 The weight of the gold was a little over one ton (about 1 metric ton).   *d25* The weight of the silver was a little over 3 3/4 tons (about 3.4 metric tons).   *e26* That is, about 1/5 ounce (about 5.5 grams)
f27 That is, about 3 3/4 tons (about 3.4 metric tons).   *g28* That is, about 45 pounds (about 20 kilograms)   *h29* The weight of the bronze was about 2 1/2 tons (about 2.4 metric tons).   *i2* Or *He;* also in verses 7, 8 and 22   *j9* That is, about 9 inches (about 22 centimeters)   *k11* Or *lapis lazuli*

a chrysolite, an onyx and a jasper.ᵃ They were mounted in gold filigree settings. ¹⁴There were twelve stones, one for each of the names of the sons of Israel, each engraved like a seal with the name of one of the twelve tribes.

¹⁵For the breastpiece they made braided chains of pure gold, like a rope. ¹⁶They made two gold filigree settings and two gold rings, and fastened the rings to two of the corners of the breastpiece. ¹⁷They fastened the two gold chains to the rings at the corners of the breastpiece, ¹⁸and the other ends of the chains to the two settings, attaching them to the shoulder pieces of the ephod at the front. ¹⁹They made two gold rings and attached them to the other two corners of the breastpiece on the inside edge next to the ephod. ²⁰Then they made two more gold rings and attached them to the bottom of the shoulder pieces on the front of the ephod, close to the seam just above the waistband of the ephod. ²¹They tied the rings of the breastpiece to the rings of the ephod with blue cord, connecting it to the waistband so that the breastpiece would not swing out from the ephod— as the LORD commanded Moses.

Other Priestly Garments

²²They made the robe of the ephod entirely of blue cloth—the work of a weaver — ²³with an opening in the center of the robe like the opening of a collar,ᵇ and a band around this opening, so that it would not tear. ²⁴They made pomegranates of blue, purple and scarlet yarn and finely twisted linen around the hem of the robe. ²⁵And they made bells of pure gold and attached them around the hem between the pomegranates. ²⁶The bells and pomegranates alternated around the hem of the robe to be worn for ministering, as the LORD commanded Moses.

²⁷For Aaron and his sons, they made tunics of fine linen—the work of a weaver — ²⁸and the turban of fine linen, the linen headbands and the undergarments of finely twisted linen. ²⁹The sash was of finely twisted linen and blue, purple and scarlet yarn—the work of an embroiderer —as the LORD commanded Moses.

³⁰They made the plate, the sacred diadem, out of pure gold and engraved on it, like an inscription on a seal: HOLY TO THE LORD. ³¹Then they fastened a blue cord to it to attach it to the turban, as the LORD commanded Moses.

Moses Inspects the Tabernacle

³²So all the work on the tabernacle, the Tent of Meeting, was completed. The Israelites did everything just as the LORD commanded Moses. ³³Then they brought the tabernacle to Moses: the tent and all its furnishings, its clasps, frames, crossbars, posts and bases; ³⁴the covering of ram skins dyed red, the covering of hides of sea cowsᶜ and the shielding curtain; ³⁵the ark of the Testimony with its poles and the atonement cover; ³⁶the table with all its articles and the bread of the Presence; ³⁷the pure gold lampstand with its row of lamps and all its accessories, and the oil for the light; ³⁸the gold altar, the anointing oil, the fragrant incense, and the curtain for the entrance to the tent; ³⁹the bronze altar with its bronze grating, its poles and all its utensils; the basin with its stand; ⁴⁰the curtains of the courtyard with its posts and bases, and the curtain for the entrance to the courtyard; the ropes and tent pegs for the courtyard; all the furnishings for the tabernacle, the Tent of Meeting; ⁴¹and the woven garments worn for ministering in the sanctuary, both the sacred garments for Aaron the priest and the garments for his sons when serving as priests.

⁴²The Israelites had done all the work just as the LORD had commanded Moses. ⁴³Moses inspected the work and saw that they had done it just as the LORD had commanded. So Moses blessed them.

Setting Up the Tabernacle

40 Then the LORD said to Moses: ²"Set up the tabernacle, the Tent of Meeting, on the first day of the first month. ³Place the ark of the Testimony in it and shield the ark with the curtain. ⁴Bring in the table and set out what belongs on it. Then bring in the lampstand and set up its lamps. ⁵Place the gold altar of incense in front of the ark of the Testimony and put the curtain at the entrance to the tabernacle.

⁶"Place the altar of burnt offering in front of the entrance to the tabernacle, the Tent of Meeting; ⁷place the basin between the Tent of Meeting and the altar and put water in it. ⁸Set up the courtyard

---

ᵃ13 The precise identification of some of these precious stones is uncertain.   ᵇ23 The meaning of the Hebrew for this word is uncertain.   ᶜ34 That is, dugongs around it and put the curtain at the entrance to the courtyard.

9"Take the anointing oil and anoint the tabernacle and everything in it; consecrate it and all its furnishings, and it will be holy. 10Then anoint the altar of burnt offering and all its utensils; consecrate the altar, and it will be most holy. 11Anoint the basin and its stand and consecrate them.

12"Bring Aaron and his sons to the entrance to the Tent of Meeting and wash them with water. 13Then dress Aaron in the sacred garments, anoint him and consecrate him so he may serve me as priest. 14Bring his sons and dress them in tunics. 15Anoint them just as you anointed their father, so they may serve me as priests. Their anointing will be to a priesthood that will continue for all generations to come." 16Moses did everything just as the LORD commanded him.

17So the tabernacle was set up on the first day of the first month in the second year. 18When Moses set up the tabernacle, he put the bases in place, erected the frames, inserted the crossbars and set up the posts. 19Then he spread the tent over the tabernacle and put the covering over the tent, as the LORD commanded him.

20He took the Testimony and placed it in the ark, attached the poles to the ark and put the atonement cover over it. 21Then he brought the ark into the tabernacle and hung the shielding curtain and shielded the ark of the Testimony, as the LORD commanded him.

22Moses placed the table in the Tent of Meeting on the north side of the tabernacle outside the curtain 23and set out the bread on it before the LORD, as the LORD commanded him.

24He placed the lampstand in the Tent of Meeting opposite the table on the south side of the tabernacle 25and set up the lamps before the LORD, as the LORD commanded him.

26Moses placed the gold altar in the Tent of Meeting in front of the curtain 27and burned fragrant incense on it, as the LORD commanded him. 28Then he put up the curtain at the entrance to the tabernacle.

29He set the altar of burnt offering near the entrance to the tabernacle, the Tent of Meeting, and offered on it burnt offerings and grain offerings, as the LORD commanded him.

30He placed the basin between the Tent of Meeting and the altar and put water in it for washing, 31and Moses and Aaron and his sons used it to wash their hands and feet. 32They washed whenever they entered the Tent of Meeting or approached the altar, as the LORD commanded Moses.

33Then Moses set up the courtyard around the tabernacle and altar and put up the curtain at the entrance to the courtyard. And so Moses finished the work.

The Glory of the LORD

34Then the cloud covered the Tent of Meeting, and the glory of the LORD filled the tabernacle. 35Moses could not enter the Tent of Meeting because the cloud had settled upon it, and the glory of the LORD filled the tabernacle.

36In all the travels of the Israelites, whenever the cloud lifted from above the tabernacle, they would set out; 37but if the cloud did not lift, they did not set out—until the day it lifted. 38So the cloud of the LORD was over the tabernacle by day, and fire was in the cloud by night, in the sight of all the house of Israel during all their travels.

MOSES writes this book while the Israelites are in the wilderness, before they enter the promised land. In it he reports to them the numerous religious, civil and moral laws that God revealed to him on Mount Sinai. As you read this book, some of it may seem dull and boring. But think about how holy God is, how he wants you to serve him in every part of your life and in all you do.

LEVITICUS

The Burnt Offering

1 The LORD called to Moses and spoke to him from the Tent of Meeting. He said, ²"Speak to the Israelites and say to them: 'When any of you brings an offering to the LORD, bring as your offering an animal from either the herd or the flock.

³" 'If the offering is a burnt offering from the herd, he is to offer a male without defect. He must present it at the entrance to the Tent of Meeting so that it *a* will be acceptable to the LORD. ⁴He is to lay his hand on the head of the burnt offering, and it will be accepted on his behalf to make atonement for him. ⁵He is to slaughter the young bull before the LORD, and then Aaron's sons the priests shall bring the blood and sprinkle it against the altar on all sides at the entrance to the Tent of Meeting. ⁶He is to skin the burnt offering and cut it into pieces. ⁷The sons of Aaron the priest are to put fire on the altar and arrange wood on the fire. ⁸Then Aaron's sons the priests shall arrange the pieces, including the head and the fat, on the burning wood that is on the altar. ⁹He is to wash the inner parts and the legs with water, and the priest is to burn all of it on the altar. It is a burnt offering, an offering made by fire, an aroma pleasing to the LORD.

¹⁰" 'If the offering is a burnt offering from the flock, from either the sheep or the goats, he is to offer a male without

*a*3 Or *he*

defect. ¹¹He is to slaughter it at the north side of the altar before the LORD, and Aaron's sons the priests shall sprinkle its blood against the altar on all sides. ¹²He is to cut it into pieces, and the priest shall arrange them, including the head and the fat, on the burning wood that is on the altar. ¹³He is to wash the inner parts and the legs with water, and the priest is to bring all of it and burn it on the altar. It is a burnt offering, an offering made by fire, an aroma pleasing to the LORD.

¹⁴" 'If the offering to the LORD is a burnt offering of birds, he is to offer a dove or a young pigeon. ¹⁵The priest shall bring it to the altar, wring off the head and burn it on the altar; its blood shall be drained out on the side of the altar. ¹⁶He is to remove the crop with its contents[a] and throw it to the east side of the altar, where the ashes are. ¹⁷He shall tear it open by the wings, not severing it completely, and then the priest shall burn it on the wood that is on the fire on the altar. It is a burnt offering, an offering made by fire, an aroma pleasing to the LORD.

The Grain Offering

2 " 'When someone brings a grain offering to the LORD, his offering is to be of fine flour. He is to pour oil on it, put incense on it ²and take it to Aaron's sons the priests. The priest shall take a handful of the fine flour and oil, together with all the incense, and burn this as a memorial portion on the altar, an offering made by fire, an aroma pleasing to the LORD. ³The rest of the grain offering belongs to Aaron and his sons; it is a most holy part of the offerings made to the LORD by fire.

⁴" 'If you bring a grain offering baked in an oven, it is to consist of fine flour: cakes made without yeast and mixed with oil, or[b] wafers made without yeast and spread with oil. ⁵If your grain offering is prepared on a griddle, it is to be made of fine flour mixed with oil, and without yeast. ⁶Crumble it and pour oil on it; it is a grain offering. ⁷If your grain offering is cooked in a pan, it is to be made of fine flour and oil. ⁸Bring the grain offering made of these things to the LORD; present it to the priest, who shall take it to the altar. ⁹He shall take out the memorial portion from the grain offering and burn it on the altar as an offering made by fire,

an aroma pleasing to the LORD. ¹⁰The rest of the grain offering belongs to Aaron and his sons; it is a most holy part of the offerings made to the LORD by fire.

¹¹" 'Every grain offering you bring to the LORD must be made without yeast, for you are not to burn any yeast or honey in an offering made to the LORD by fire. ¹²You may bring them to the LORD as an offering of the firstfruits, but they are not to be offered on the altar as a pleasing aroma. ¹³Season all your grain offerings with salt. Do not leave the salt of the covenant of your God out of your grain offerings; add salt to all your offerings.

¹⁴" 'If you bring a grain offering of firstfruits to the LORD, offer crushed heads of new grain roasted in the fire. ¹⁵Put oil and incense on it; it is a grain offering. ¹⁶The priest shall burn the memorial portion of the crushed grain and the oil, together with all the incense, as an offering made to the LORD by fire.

The Fellowship Offering

3 " 'If someone's offering is a fellowship offering,[c] and he offers an animal from the herd, whether male or female, he is to present before the LORD an animal without defect. ²He is to lay his hand on the head of his offering and slaughter it at the entrance to the Tent of Meeting. Then Aaron's sons the priests shall sprinkle the blood against the altar on all sides. ³From the fellowship offering he is to bring a sacrifice made to the LORD by fire: all the fat that covers the inner parts or is connected to them, ⁴both kidneys with the fat on them near the loins, and the covering of the liver, which he will remove with the kidneys. ⁵Then Aaron's sons are to burn it on the altar on top of the burnt offering that is on the burning wood, as an offering made by fire, an aroma pleasing to the LORD.

⁶" 'If he offers an animal from the flock as a fellowship offering to the LORD, he is to offer a male or female without defect. ⁷If he offers a lamb, he is to present it before the LORD. ⁸He is to lay his hand on the head of his offering and slaughter it in front of the Tent of Meeting. Then Aaron's sons shall sprinkle its blood against the altar on all sides. ⁹From the fellowship offering he is to bring a sacrifice made to the LORD by fire: its fat, the entire fat tail cut off close to the backbone, all

---

[a]16 Or *crop and the feathers*; the meaning of the Hebrew for this word is uncertain.   [b]4 Or *and*
[c]1 Traditionally *peace offering*; also in verses 3, 6 and 9

the fat that covers the inner parts or is connected to them, [10]both kidneys with the fat on them near the loins, and the covering of the liver, which he will remove with the kidneys. [11]The priest shall burn them on the altar as food, an offering made to the LORD by fire.

[12]" 'If his offering is a goat, he is to present it before the LORD. [13]He is to lay his hand on its head and slaughter it in front of the Tent of Meeting. Then Aaron's sons shall sprinkle its blood against the altar on all sides. [14]From what he offers he is to make this offering to the LORD by fire: all the fat that covers the inner parts or is connected to them, [15]both kidneys with the fat on them near the loins, and the covering of the liver, which he will remove with the kidneys. [16]The priest shall burn them on the altar as food, an offering made by fire, a pleasing aroma. All the fat is the LORD's.

[17]" 'This is a lasting ordinance for the generations to come, wherever you live: You must not eat any fat or any blood.' "

The Sin Offering

4 The LORD said to Moses, [2]"Say to the Israelites: 'When anyone sins unintentionally and does what is forbidden in any of the LORD's commands—

[3]" 'If the anointed priest sins, bringing guilt on the people, he must bring to the LORD a young bull without defect as a sin offering for the sin he has committed. [4]He is to present the bull at the entrance to the Tent of Meeting before the LORD. He is to lay his hand on its head and slaughter it before the LORD. [5]Then the anointed priest shall take some of the bull's blood and carry it into the Tent of Meeting. [6]He is to dip his finger into the blood and sprinkle some of it seven times before the LORD, in front of the curtain of the sanctuary. [7]The priest shall then put some of the blood on the horns of the altar of fragrant incense that is before the LORD in the Tent of Meeting. The rest of the bull's blood he shall pour out at the base of the altar of burnt offering at the entrance to the Tent of Meeting. [8]He shall remove all the fat from the bull of the sin offering— the fat that covers the inner parts or is connected to them, [9]both kidneys with the fat on them near the loins, and the covering of the liver, which he will re-

move with the kidneys— [10]just as the fat is removed from the ox[a] sacrificed as a fellowship offering.[b] Then the priest shall burn them on the altar of burnt offering. [11]But the hide of the bull and all its flesh, as well as the head and legs, the inner parts and offal— [12]that is, all the rest of the bull—he must take outside the camp to a place ceremonially clean, where the ashes are thrown, and burn it in a wood fire on the ash heap.

[13]" 'If the whole Israelite community sins unintentionally and does what is forbidden in any of the LORD's commands, even though the community is unaware of the matter, they are guilty. [14]When they become aware of the sin they committed, the assembly must bring a young bull as a sin offering and present it before the Tent of Meeting. [15]The elders of the community are to lay their hands on the bull's head before the LORD, and the bull shall be slaughtered before the LORD. [16]Then the anointed priest is to take some of the bull's blood into the Tent of Meeting. [17]He shall dip his finger into the blood and sprinkle it before the LORD seven times in front of the curtain. [18]He is to put some of the blood on the horns of the altar that is before the LORD in the Tent of Meeting. The rest of the blood he shall pour out at the base of the altar of burnt offering at the entrance to the Tent of Meeting. [19]He shall remove all the fat from it and burn it on the altar, [20]and do with this bull just as he did with the bull for the sin offering. In this way the priest will make atonement for them, and they will be forgiven. [21]Then he shall take the bull outside the camp and burn it as he burned the first bull. This is the sin offering for the community.

[22]" 'When a leader sins unintentionally and does what is forbidden in any of the commands of the LORD his God, he is guilty. [23]When he is made aware of the sin he committed, he must bring as his offering a male goat without defect. [24]He is to lay his hand on the goat's head and slaughter it at the place where the burnt offering is slaughtered before the LORD. It is a sin offering. [25]Then the priest shall take some of the blood of the sin offering with his finger and put it on the horns of the altar of burnt offering and pour out the rest of the blood at the base of the

---

[a]10 The Hebrew word can include both male and female.   [b]10 Traditionally *peace offering*; also in verses 26, 31 and 35

altar. ²⁶He shall burn all the fat on the altar as he burned the fat of the fellowship offering. In this way the priest will make atonement for the man's sin, and he will be forgiven.

²⁷" 'If a member of the community sins unintentionally and does what is forbidden in any of the Lord's commands, he is guilty. ²⁸When he is made aware of the sin he committed, he must bring as his offering for the sin he committed a female goat without defect. ²⁹He is to lay his hand on the head of the sin offering and slaughter it at the place of the burnt offering. ³⁰Then the priest is to take some of the blood with his finger and put it on the horns of the altar of burnt offering and pour out the rest of the blood at the base of the altar. ³¹He shall remove all the fat, just as the fat is removed from the fellowship offering, and the priest shall burn it on the altar as an aroma pleasing to the Lord. In this way the priest will make atonement for him, and he will be forgiven.

³²" 'If he brings a lamb as his sin offering, he is to bring a female without defect. ³³He is to lay his hand on its head and slaughter it for a sin offering at the place where the burnt offering is slaughtered. ³⁴Then the priest shall take some of the blood of the sin offering with his finger and put it on the horns of the altar of burnt offering and pour out the rest of the blood at the base of the altar. ³⁵He shall remove all the fat, just as the fat is removed from the lamb of the fellowship offering, and the priest shall burn it on the altar on top of the offerings made to the Lord by fire. In this way the priest will make atonement for him for the sin he has committed, and he will be forgiven.

5 " 'If a person sins because he does not speak up when he hears a public charge to testify regarding something he has seen or learned about, he will be held responsible.

²" 'Or if a person touches anything ceremonially unclean—whether the carcasses of unclean wild animals or of unclean livestock or of unclean creatures that move along the ground—even though he is unaware of it, he has become unclean and is guilty.

³" 'Or if he touches human uncleanness—anything that would make him un-

clean—even though he is unaware of it, when he learns of it he will be guilty.

⁴" 'Or if a person thoughtlessly takes an oath to do anything, whether good or evil—in any matter one might carelessly swear about—even though he is unaware of it, in any case when he learns of it he will be guilty.

⁵" 'When anyone is guilty in any of these ways, he must confess in what way he has sinned ⁶and, as a penalty for the sin he has committed, he must bring to the Lord a female lamb or goat from the flock as a sin offering; and the priest shall make atonement for him for his sin.

⁷" 'If he cannot afford a lamb, he is to bring two doves or two young pigeons to the Lord as a penalty for his sin—one for a sin offering and the other for a burnt offering. ⁸He is to bring them to the priest, who shall first offer the one for the sin offering. He is to wring its head from its neck, not severing it completely, ⁹and is to sprinkle some of the blood of the sin offering against the side of the altar; the rest of the blood must be drained out at the base of the altar. It is a sin offering. ¹⁰The priest shall then offer the other as a burnt offering in the prescribed way and make atonement for him for the sin he has committed, and he will be forgiven.

¹¹" 'If, however, he cannot afford two doves or two young pigeons, he is to bring as an offering for his sin a tenth of an ephah^a of fine flour for a sin offering. He must not put oil or incense on it, because it is a sin offering. ¹²He is to bring it to the priest, who shall take a handful of it as a memorial portion and burn it on the altar on top of the offerings made to the Lord by fire. It is a sin offering. ¹³In this way the priest will make atonement for him for any of these sins he has committed, and he will be forgiven. The rest of the offering will belong to the priest, as in the case of the grain offering.' "

The Guilt Offering

¹⁴The Lord said to Moses: ¹⁵"When a person commits a violation and sins unintentionally in regard to any of the Lord's holy things, he is to bring to the Lord as a penalty a ram from the flock, one without defect and of the proper value in silver, according to the sanctuary shekel.^b It is a guilt offering. ¹⁶He must make restitution for what he has failed to do in regard to the holy things, add a fifth of the

^a11 That is, probably about 2 quarts (about 2 liters)   ^b15 That is, about 2/5 ounce (about 11.5 grams)

value to that and give it all to the priest, who will make atonement for him with the ram as a guilt offering, and he will be forgiven.

17"If a person sins and does what is forbidden in any of the LORD's commands, even though he does not know it, he is guilty and will be held responsible. 18He is to bring to the priest as a guilt offering a ram from the flock, one without defect and of the proper value. In this way the priest will make atonement for him for the wrong he has committed unintentionally, and he will be forgiven. 19It is a guilt offering; he has been guilty of^a wrongdoing against the LORD."

6 The LORD said to Moses: 2"If anyone sins and is unfaithful to the LORD by deceiving his neighbor about something entrusted to him or left in his care or stolen, or if he cheats him, 3or if he finds lost property and lies about it, or if he swears falsely, or if he commits any such sin that people may do— 4when he thus sins and becomes guilty, he must return what he has stolen or taken by extortion, or what was entrusted to him, or the lost property he found, 5or whatever it was he swore falsely about. He must make restitution in full, add a fifth of the value to it and give it all to the owner on the day he presents his guilt offering. 6And as a penalty he must bring to the priest, that is, to the LORD, his guilt offering, a ram from the flock, one without defect and of the proper value. 7In this way the priest will make atonement for him before the LORD, and he will be forgiven for any of these things he did that made him guilty."

The Burnt Offering

8The LORD said to Moses: 9"Give Aaron and his sons this command: 'These are the regulations for the burnt offering: The burnt offering is to remain on the altar hearth throughout the night, till morning, and the fire must be kept burning on the altar. 10The priest shall then put on his linen clothes, with linen undergarments next to his body, and shall remove the ashes of the burnt offering that the fire has consumed on the altar and place them beside the altar. 11Then he is to take off these clothes and put on others, and carry the ashes outside the camp to a place that is ceremonially clean. 12The

fire on the altar must be kept burning; it must not go out. Every morning the priest is to add firewood and arrange the burnt offering on the fire and burn the fat of the fellowship offerings^b on it. 13The fire must be kept burning on the altar continuously; it must not go out.

The Grain Offering

14" 'These are the regulations for the grain offering: Aaron's sons are to bring it before the LORD, in front of the altar. 15The priest is to take a handful of fine flour and oil, together with all the incense on the grain offering, and burn the memorial portion on the altar as an aroma pleasing to the LORD. 16Aaron and his sons shall eat the rest of it, but it is to be eaten without yeast in a holy place; they are to eat it in the courtyard of the Tent of Meeting. 17It must not be baked with yeast; I have given it as their share of the offerings made to me by fire. Like the sin offering and the guilt offering, it is most holy. 18Any male descendant of Aaron may eat it. It is his regular share of the offerings made to the LORD by fire for the generations to come. Whatever touches them will become holy.$^{c'}$ "

19The LORD also said to Moses, 20"This is the offering Aaron and his sons are to bring to the LORD on the day he^d is anointed: a tenth of an ephah^e of fine flour as a regular grain offering, half of it in the morning and half in the evening. 21Prepare it with oil on a griddle; bring it well-mixed and present the grain offering broken^f in pieces as an aroma pleasing to the LORD. 22The son who is to succeed him as anointed priest shall prepare it. It is the LORD's regular share and is to be burned completely. 23Every grain offering of a priest shall be burned completely; it must not be eaten."

The Sin Offering

24The LORD said to Moses, 25"Say to Aaron and his sons: 'These are the regulations for the sin offering: The sin offering is to be slaughtered before the LORD in the place the burnt offering is slaughtered; it is most holy. 26The priest who offers it shall eat it; it is to be eaten in a holy place, in the courtyard of the Tent of Meeting. 27Whatever touches any of the flesh will become holy, and if any of the

---

^{a}19 Or *has made full expiation for his* ^{b}12 Traditionally *peace offerings* ^{c}18 Or *Whoever touches them must be holy*; similarly in verse 27 ^{d}20 Or *each* ^{e}20 That is, probably about 2 quarts (about 2 liters) ^{f}21 The meaning of the Hebrew for this word is uncertain.

blood is spattered on a garment, you must wash it in a holy place. 28The clay pot the meat is cooked in must be broken; but if it is cooked in a bronze pot, the pot is to be scoured and rinsed with water. 29Any male in a priest's family may eat it; it is most holy. 30But any sin offering whose blood is brought into the Tent of Meeting to make atonement in the Holy Place must not be eaten; it must be burned.

The Guilt Offering

7 " 'These are the regulations for the guilt offering, which is most holy: 2The guilt offering is to be slaughtered in the place where the burnt offering is slaughtered, and its blood is to be sprinkled against the altar on all sides. 3All its fat shall be offered: the fat tail and the fat that covers the inner parts, 4both kidneys with the fat on them near the loins, and the covering of the liver, which is to be removed with the kidneys. 5The priest shall burn them on the altar as an offering made to the LORD by fire. It is a guilt offering. 6Any male in a priest's family may eat it, but it must be eaten in a holy place; it is most holy.

7" 'The same law applies to both the sin offering and the guilt offering: They belong to the priest who makes atonement with them. 8The priest who offers a burnt offering for anyone may keep its hide for himself. 9Every grain offering baked in an oven or cooked in a pan or on a griddle belongs to the priest who offers it, 10and every grain offering, whether mixed with oil or dry, belongs equally to all the sons of Aaron.

The Fellowship Offering

11" 'These are the regulations for the fellowship offering*a* a person may present to the LORD:

12" 'If he offers it as an expression of thankfulness, then along with this thank offering he is to offer cakes of bread made without yeast and mixed with oil, wafers made without yeast and spread with oil, and cakes of fine flour well-kneaded and mixed with oil. 13Along with his fellowship offering of thanksgiving he is to present an offering with cakes of bread made with yeast. 14He is to bring one of each kind as an offering, a contribution to the LORD; it belongs to the priest who sprinkles the blood of the fellowship offerings. 15The meat of his fellowship of-

fering of thanksgiving must be eaten on the day it is offered; he must leave none of it till morning.

16" 'If, however, his offering is the result of a vow or is a freewill offering, the sacrifice shall be eaten on the day he offers it, but anything left over may be eaten on the next day. 17Any meat of the sacrifice left over till the third day must be burned up. 18If any meat of the fellowship offering is eaten on the third day, it will not be accepted. It will not be credited to the one who offered it, for it is impure; the person who eats any of it will be held responsible.

19" 'Meat that touches anything ceremonially unclean must not be eaten; it must be burned up. As for other meat, anyone ceremonially clean may eat it. 20But if anyone who is unclean eats any meat of the fellowship offering belonging to the LORD, that person must be cut off from his people. 21If anyone touches something unclean—whether human uncleanness or an unclean animal or any unclean, detestable thing—and then eats any of the meat of the fellowship offering belonging to the LORD, that person must be cut off from his people.' "

Eating Fat and Blood Forbidden

22The LORD said to Moses, 23"Say to the Israelites: 'Do not eat any of the fat of cattle, sheep or goats. 24The fat of an animal found dead or torn by wild animals may be used for any other purpose, but you must not eat it. 25Anyone who eats the fat of an animal from which an offering by fire may be*b* made to the LORD must be cut off from his people. 26And wherever you live, you must not eat the blood of any bird or animal. 27If anyone eats blood, that person must be cut off from his people.' "

The Priests' Share

28The LORD said to Moses, 29"Say to the Israelites: 'Anyone who brings a fellowship offering to the LORD is to bring part of it as his sacrifice to the LORD. 30With his own hands he is to bring the offering made to the LORD by fire; he is to bring the fat, together with the breast, and wave the breast before the LORD as a wave offering. 31The priest shall burn the fat on the altar, but the breast belongs to Aaron and his sons. 32You are to give the right thigh of your fellowship offerings to the priest

a11 Traditionally peace offering; also in verses 13-37   *b25 Or fire is* as a contribution. ³³The son of Aaron who offers the blood and the fat of the fellowship offering shall have the right thigh as his share. ³⁴From the fellowship offerings of the Israelites, I have taken the breast that is waved and the thigh that is presented and have given them to Aaron the priest and his sons as their regular share from the Israelites.' "

³⁵This is the portion of the offerings made to the LORD by fire that were allotted to Aaron and his sons on the day they were presented to serve the LORD as priests. ³⁶On the day they were anointed, the LORD commanded that the Israelites give this to them as their regular share for the generations to come.

³⁷These, then, are the regulations for the burnt offering, the grain offering, the sin offering, the guilt offering, the ordination offering and the fellowship offering, ³⁸which the LORD gave Moses on Mount Sinai on the day he commanded the Israelites to bring their offerings to the LORD, in the Desert of Sinai.

The Ordination of Aaron and His Sons

8 The LORD said to Moses, ²"Bring Aaron and his sons, their garments, the anointing oil, the bull for the sin offering, the two rams and the basket containing bread made without yeast, ³and gather the entire assembly at the entrance to the Tent of Meeting." ⁴Moses did as the LORD commanded him, and the assembly gathered at the entrance to the Tent of Meeting.

⁵Moses said to the assembly, "This is what the LORD has commanded to be done." ⁶Then Moses brought Aaron and his sons forward and washed them with water. ⁷He put the tunic on Aaron, tied the sash around him, clothed him with the robe and put the ephod on him. He also tied the ephod to him by its skillfully woven waistband; so it was fastened to him. ⁸He placed the breastpiece on him and put the Urim and Thummim in the breastpiece. ⁹Then he placed the turban on Aaron's head and set the gold plate, the sacred diadem, on the front of it, as the LORD commanded Moses.

¹⁰Then Moses took the anointing oil and anointed the tabernacle and everything in it, and so consecrated them. ¹¹He sprinkled some of the oil on the altar seven times, anointing the altar and all its utensils and the basin with its stand, to consecrate them. ¹²He poured some of the anointing oil on Aaron's head and anointed him to consecrate him. ¹³Then he brought Aaron's sons forward, put tunics on them, tied sashes around them and put headbands on them, as the LORD commanded Moses.

¹⁴He then presented the bull for the sin offering, and Aaron and his sons laid their hands on its head. ¹⁵Moses slaughtered the bull and took some of the blood, and with his finger he put it on all the horns of the altar to purify the altar. He poured out the rest of the blood at the base of the altar. So he consecrated it to make atonement for it. ¹⁶Moses also took all the fat around the inner parts, the covering of the liver, and both kidneys and their fat, and burned it on the altar. ¹⁷But the bull with its hide and its flesh and its offal he burned up outside the camp, as the LORD commanded Moses.

¹⁸He then presented the ram for the burnt offering, and Aaron and his sons laid their hands on its head. ¹⁹Then Moses slaughtered the ram and sprinkled the blood against the altar on all sides. ²⁰He cut the ram into pieces and burned the head, the pieces and the fat. ²¹He washed the inner parts and the legs with water and burned the whole ram on the altar as a burnt offering, a pleasing aroma, an offering made to the LORD by fire, as the LORD commanded Moses.

²²He then presented the other ram, the ram for the ordination, and Aaron and his sons laid their hands on its head. ²³Moses slaughtered the ram and took some of its blood and put it on the lobe of Aaron's right ear, on the thumb of his right hand and on the big toe of his right foot. ²⁴Moses also brought Aaron's sons forward and put some of the blood on the lobes of their right ears, on the thumbs of their right hands and on the big toes of their right feet. Then he sprinkled blood against the altar on all sides. ²⁵He took the fat, the fat tail, all the fat around the inner parts, the covering of the liver, both kidneys and their fat and the right thigh. ²⁶Then from the basket of bread made without yeast, which was before the LORD, he took a cake of bread, and one made with oil, and a wafer; he put these on the fat portions and on the right thigh. ²⁷He put all these in the hands of Aaron and his sons and waved them before the LORD as a wave offering. ²⁸Then Moses took them from their hands and burned them on the altar on top of the burnt offering as

an ordination offering, a pleasing aroma, an offering made to the LORD by fire. ²⁹He also took the breast—Moses' share of the ordination ram—and waved it before the LORD as a wave offering, as the LORD commanded Moses.

³⁰Then Moses took some of the anointing oil and some of the blood from the altar and sprinkled them on Aaron and his garments and on his sons and their garments. So he consecrated Aaron and his garments and his sons and their garments.

³¹Moses then said to Aaron and his sons, "Cook the meat at the entrance to the Tent of Meeting and eat it there with the bread from the basket of ordination offerings, as I commanded, saying,ᵃ 'Aaron and his sons are to eat it.' ³²Then burn up the rest of the meat and the bread. ³³Do not leave the entrance to the Tent of Meeting for seven days, until the days of your ordination are completed, for your ordination will last seven days. ³⁴What has been done today was commanded by the LORD to make atonement for you. ³⁵You must stay at the entrance to the Tent of Meeting day and night for seven days and do what the LORD requires, so you will not die; for that is what I have been commanded." ³⁶So Aaron and his sons did everything the LORD commanded through Moses.

The Priests Begin Their Ministry

9 On the eighth day Moses summoned Aaron and his sons and the elders of Israel. ²He said to Aaron, "Take a bull calf for your sin offering and a ram for your burnt offering, both without defect, and present them before the LORD. ³Then say to the Israelites: 'Take a male goat for a sin offering, a calf and a lamb—both a year old and without defect—for a burnt offering, ⁴and an oxᵇ and a ram for a fellowship offeringᶜ to sacrifice before the LORD, together with a grain offering mixed with oil. For today the LORD will appear to you.' "

⁵They took the things Moses commanded to the front of the Tent of Meeting, and the entire assembly came near and stood before the LORD. ⁶Then Moses said, "This is what the LORD has commanded you to do, so that the glory of the LORD may appear to you."

⁷Moses said to Aaron, "Come to the al-

tar and sacrifice your sin offering and your burnt offering and make atonement for yourself and the people; sacrifice the offering that is for the people and make atonement for them, as the LORD has commanded."

⁸So Aaron came to the altar and slaughtered the calf as a sin offering for himself. ⁹His sons brought the blood to him, and he dipped his finger into the blood and put it on the horns of the altar; the rest of the blood he poured out at the base of the altar. ¹⁰On the altar he burned the fat, the kidneys and the covering of the liver from the sin offering, as the LORD commanded Moses; ¹¹the flesh and the hide he burned up outside the camp.

¹²Then he slaughtered the burnt offering. His sons handed him the blood, and he sprinkled it against the altar on all sides. ¹³They handed him the burnt offering piece by piece, including the head, and he burned them on the altar. ¹⁴He washed the inner parts and the legs and burned them on top of the burnt offering on the altar.

¹⁵Aaron then brought the offering that was for the people. He took the goat for the people's sin offering and slaughtered it and offered it for a sin offering as he did with the first one.

¹⁶He brought the burnt offering and offered it in the prescribed way. ¹⁷He also brought the grain offering, took a handful of it and burned it on the altar in addition to the morning's burnt offering.

¹⁸He slaughtered the ox and the ram as the fellowship offering for the people. His sons handed him the blood, and he sprinkled it against the altar on all sides. ¹⁹But the fat portions of the ox and the ram— the fat tail, the layer of fat, the kidneys and the covering of the liver— ²⁰these they laid on the breasts, and then Aaron burned the fat on the altar. ²¹Aaron waved the breasts and the right thigh before the LORD as a wave offering, as Moses commanded.

²²Then Aaron lifted his hands toward the people and blessed them. And having sacrificed the sin offering, the burnt offering and the fellowship offering, he stepped down.

²³Moses and Aaron then went into the Tent of Meeting. When they came out, they blessed the people; and the glory of the LORD appeared to all the people.

ᵃ31 Or I was commanded: ᵇ4 The Hebrew word can include both male and female; also in verses 18 and 19.   ᶜ4 Traditionally peace offering; also in verses 18 and 22

²⁴Fire came out from the presence of the LORD and consumed the burnt offering and the fat portions on the altar. And when all the people saw it, they shouted for joy and fell facedown.

The Death of Nadab and Abihu

10 Aaron's sons Nadab and Abihu took their censers, put fire in them and added incense; and they offered unauthorized fire before the LORD, contrary to his command. ²So fire came out from the presence of the LORD and consumed them, and they died before the LORD. ³Moses then said to Aaron, "This is what the LORD spoke of when he said:

" 'Among those who approach me
    I will show myself holy;
in the sight of all the people
    I will be honored.' "

Aaron remained silent.

⁴Moses summoned Mishael and Elzaphan, sons of Aaron's uncle Uzziel, and said to them, "Come here; carry your cousins outside the camp, away from the front of the sanctuary." ⁵So they came and carried them, still in their tunics, outside the camp, as Moses ordered.

⁶Then Moses said to Aaron and his sons Eleazar and Ithamar, "Do not let your hair become unkempt,ᵃ and do not tear your clothes, or you will die and the LORD will be angry with the whole community. But your relatives, all the house of Israel, may mourn for those the LORD has destroyed by fire. ⁷Do not leave the entrance to the Tent of Meeting or you will die, because the LORD's anointing oil is on you." So they did as Moses said.

⁸Then the LORD said to Aaron, ⁹"You and your sons are not to drink wine or other fermented drink whenever you go into the Tent of Meeting, or you will die. This is a lasting ordinance for the generations to come. ¹⁰You must distinguish between the holy and the common, between the unclean and the clean, ¹¹and you must teach the Israelites all the decrees the LORD has given them through Moses."

¹²Moses said to Aaron and his remaining sons, Eleazar and Ithamar, "Take the grain offering left over from the offerings made to the LORD by fire and eat it prepared without yeast beside the altar, for it is most holy. ¹³Eat it in a holy place, because it is your share and your sons' share

of the offerings made to the LORD by fire; for so I have been commanded. ¹⁴But you and your sons and your daughters may eat the breast that was waved and the thigh that was presented. Eat them in a ceremonially clean place; they have been given to you and your children as your share of the Israelites' fellowship offerings.ᵇ ¹⁵The thigh that was presented and the breast that was waved must be brought with the fat portions of the offerings made by fire, to be waved before the LORD as a wave offering. This will be the regular share for you and your children, as the LORD has commanded."

¹⁶When Moses inquired about the goat of the sin offering and found that it had been burned up, he was angry with Eleazar and Ithamar, Aaron's remaining sons, and asked, ¹⁷"Why didn't you eat the sin offering in the sanctuary area? It is most holy; it was given to you to take away the guilt of the community by making atonement for them before the LORD. ¹⁸Since its blood was not taken into the Holy Place, you should have eaten the goat in the sanctuary area, as I commanded."

¹⁹Aaron replied to Moses, "Today they sacrificed their sin offering and their burnt offering before the LORD, but such things as this have happened to me. Would the LORD have been pleased if I had eaten the sin offering today?" ²⁰When Moses heard this, he was satisfied.

Clean and Unclean Food

11 The LORD said to Moses and Aaron, ²"Say to the Israelites: 'Of all the animals that live on land, these are the ones you may eat: ³You may eat any animal that has a split hoof completely divided and that chews the cud.

⁴" 'There are some that only chew the cud or only have a split hoof, but you must not eat them. The camel, though it chews the cud, does not have a split hoof; it is ceremonially unclean for you. ⁵The coney,ᶜ though it chews the cud, does not have a split hoof; it is unclean for you. ⁶The rabbit, though it chews the cud, does not have a split hoof; it is unclean for you. ⁷And the pig, though it has a split hoof completely divided, does not chew the cud; it is unclean for you. ⁸You must not eat their meat or touch their carcasses; they are unclean for you.

⁹" 'Of all the creatures living in the wa-

ᵃ6 Or *Do not uncover your heads*   ᵇ14 Traditionally *peace offerings*   ᶜ5 That is, the hyrax or rock
badger

ter of the seas and the streams, you may eat any that have fins and scales. ¹⁰But all creatures in the seas or streams that do not have fins and scales—whether among all the swarming things or among all the other living creatures in the water—you are to detest. ¹¹And since you are to detest them, you must not eat their meat and you must detest their carcasses. ¹²Anything living in the water that does not have fins and scales is to be detestable to you.

¹³" 'These are the birds you are to detest and not eat because they are detestable: the eagle, the vulture, the black vulture, ¹⁴the red kite, any kind of black kite, ¹⁵any kind of raven, ¹⁶the horned owl, the screech owl, the gull, any kind of hawk, ¹⁷the little owl, the cormorant, the great owl, ¹⁸the white owl, the desert owl, the osprey, ¹⁹the stork, any kind of heron, the hoopoe and the bat.ᵃ

²⁰" 'All flying insects that walk on all fours are to be detestable to you. ²¹There are, however, some winged creatures that walk on all fours that you may eat: those that have jointed legs for hopping on the ground. ²²Of these you may eat any kind of locust, katydid, cricket or grasshopper. ²³But all other winged creatures that have four legs you are to detest.

²⁴" 'You will make yourselves unclean by these; whoever touches their carcasses will be unclean till evening. ²⁵Whoever picks up one of their carcasses must wash his clothes, and he will be unclean till evening.

²⁶" 'Every animal that has a split hoof not completely divided or that does not chew the cud is unclean for you; whoever touches ,the carcass of, any of them will be unclean. ²⁷Of all the animals that walk on all fours, those that walk on their paws are unclean for you; whoever touches their carcasses will be unclean till evening. ²⁸Anyone who picks up their carcasses must wash his clothes, and he will be unclean till evening. They are unclean for you.

²⁹" 'Of the animals that move about on the ground, these are unclean for you: the weasel, the rat, any kind of great lizard, ³⁰the gecko, the monitor lizard, the wall lizard, the skink and the chameleon. ³¹Of all those that move along the ground, these are unclean for you. Whoever touches them when they are dead will be unclean till evening. ³²When one of them

dies and falls on something, that article, whatever its use, will be unclean, whether it is made of wood, cloth, hide or sackcloth. Put it in water; it will be unclean till evening, and then it will be clean. ³³If one of them falls into a clay pot, everything in it will be unclean, and you must break the pot. ³⁴Any food that could be eaten but has water on it from such a pot is unclean, and any liquid that could be drunk from it is unclean. ³⁵Anything that one of their carcasses falls on becomes unclean; an oven or cooking pot must be broken up. They are unclean, and you are to regard them as unclean. ³⁶A spring, however, or a cistern for collecting water remains clean, but anyone who touches one of these carcasses is unclean. ³⁷If a carcass falls on any seeds that are to be planted, they remain clean. ³⁸But if water has been put on the seed and a carcass falls on it, it is unclean for you.

³⁹" 'If an animal that you are allowed to eat dies, anyone who touches the carcass will be unclean till evening. ⁴⁰Anyone who eats some of the carcass must wash his clothes, and he will be unclean till evening. Anyone who picks up the carcass must wash his clothes, and he will be unclean till evening.

⁴¹" 'Every creature that moves about on the ground is detestable; it is not to be eaten. ⁴²You are not to eat any creature that moves about on the ground, whether it moves on its belly or walks on all fours or on many feet; it is detestable. ⁴³Do not defile yourselves by any of these creatures. Do not make yourselves unclean by means of them or be made unclean by them. ⁴⁴I am the LORD your God; consecrate yourselves and be holy, because I am holy. Do not make yourselves unclean by any creature that moves about on the ground. ⁴⁵I am the LORD who brought you up out of Egypt to be your God; therefore be holy, because I am holy.

⁴⁶" 'These are the regulations concerning animals, birds, every living thing that moves in the water and every creature that moves about on the ground. ⁴⁷You must distinguish between the unclean and the clean, between living creatures that may be eaten and those that may not be eaten.' "

Purification After Childbirth

12 The LORD said to Moses, ²"Say to the Israelites: 'A woman who be-

ᵃ19 The precise identification of some of the birds, insects and animals in this chapter is uncertain.

comes pregnant and gives birth to a son will be ceremonially unclean for seven days, just as she is unclean during her monthly period. ³On the eighth day the boy is to be circumcised. ⁴Then the woman must wait thirty-three days to be purified from her bleeding. She must not touch anything sacred or go to the sanctuary until the days of her purification are over. ⁵If she gives birth to a daughter, for two weeks the woman will be unclean, as during her period. Then she must wait sixty-six days to be purified from her bleeding.

⁶" 'When the days of her purification for a son or daughter are over, she is to bring to the priest at the entrance to the Tent of Meeting a year-old lamb for a burnt offering and a young pigeon or a dove for a sin offering. ⁷He shall offer them before the LORD to make atonement for her, and then she will be ceremonially clean from her flow of blood.

" 'These are the regulations for the woman who gives birth to a boy or a girl. ⁸If she cannot afford a lamb, she is to bring two doves or two young pigeons, one for a burnt offering and the other for a sin offering. In this way the priest will make atonement for her, and she will be clean.' "

Regulations About Infectious Skin Diseases

13 The LORD said to Moses and Aaron, ²"When anyone has a swelling or a rash or a bright spot on his skin that may become an infectious skin disease,ᵃ he must be brought to Aaron the priest or to one of his sonsᵇ who is a priest. ³The priest is to examine the sore on his skin, and if the hair in the sore has turned white and the sore appears to be more than skin deep,ᶜ it is an infectious skin disease. When the priest examines him, he shall pronounce him ceremonially unclean. ⁴If the spot on his skin is white but does not appear to be more than skin deep and the hair in it has not turned white, the priest is to put the infected person in isolation for seven days. ⁵On the seventh day the priest is to examine him, and if he sees that the sore is unchanged and has not spread in the skin, he is to keep him in isolation another seven days. ⁶On the seventh day the priest is

to examine him again, and if the sore has faded and has not spread in the skin, the priest shall pronounce him clean; it is only a rash. The man must wash his clothes, and he will be clean. ⁷But if the rash does spread in his skin after he has shown himself to the priest to be pronounced clean, he must appear before the priest again. ⁸The priest is to examine him, and if the rash has spread in the skin, he shall pronounce him unclean; it is an infectious disease.

⁹"When anyone has an infectious skin disease, he must be brought to the priest. ¹⁰The priest is to examine him, and if there is a white swelling in the skin that has turned the hair white and if there is raw flesh in the swelling, ¹¹it is a chronic skin disease and the priest shall pronounce him unclean. He is not to put him in isolation, because he is already unclean.

¹²"If the disease breaks out all over his skin and, so far as the priest can see, it covers all the skin of the infected person from head to foot, ¹³the priest is to examine him, and if the disease has covered his whole body, he shall pronounce that person clean. Since it has all turned white, he is clean. ¹⁴But whenever raw flesh appears on him, he will be unclean. ¹⁵When the priest sees the raw flesh, he shall pronounce him unclean. The raw flesh is unclean; he has an infectious disease. ¹⁶Should the raw flesh change and turn white, he must go to the priest. ¹⁷The priest is to examine him, and if the sores have turned white, the priest shall pronounce the infected person clean; then he will be clean.

¹⁸"When someone has a boil on his skin and it heals, ¹⁹and in the place where the boil was, a white swelling or reddish-white spot appears, he must present himself to the priest. ²⁰The priest is to examine it, and if it appears to be more than skin deep and the hair in it has turned white, the priest shall pronounce him unclean. It is an infectious skin disease that has broken out where the boil was. ²¹But if, when the priest examines it, there is no white hair in it and it is not more than skin deep and has faded, then the priest is to put him in isolation for seven days. ²²If it is spreading in the skin, the priest shall pronounce him unclean; it is infec-

---

ᵃ2 Traditionally *leprosy*; the Hebrew word was used for various diseases affecting the skin—not necessarily leprosy; also elsewhere in this chapter.   ᵇ2 Or *descendants*   ᶜ3 Or *be lower than the rest of the skin*; also elsewhere in this chapter tious. 23But if the spot is unchanged and has not spread, it is only a scar from the boil, and the priest shall pronounce him clean.

24"When someone has a burn on his skin and a reddish-white or white spot appears in the raw flesh of the burn, 25the priest is to examine the spot, and if the hair in it has turned white, and it appears to be more than skin deep, it is an infectious disease that has broken out in the burn. The priest shall pronounce him unclean; it is an infectious skin disease. 26But if the priest examines it and there is no white hair in the spot and if it is not more than skin deep and has faded, then the priest is to put him in isolation for seven days. 27On the seventh day the priest is to examine him, and if it is spreading in the skin, the priest shall pronounce him unclean; it is an infectious skin disease. 28If, however, the spot is unchanged and has not spread in the skin but has faded, it is a swelling from the burn, and the priest shall pronounce him clean; it is only a scar from the burn.

29"If a man or woman has a sore on the head or on the chin, 30the priest is to examine the sore, and if it appears to be more than skin deep and the hair in it is yellow and thin, the priest shall pronounce that person unclean; it is an itch, an infectious disease of the head or chin. 31But if, when the priest examines this kind of sore, it does not seem to be more than skin deep and there is no black hair in it, then the priest is to put the infected person in isolation for seven days. 32On the seventh day the priest is to examine the sore, and if the itch has not spread and there is no yellow hair in it and it does not appear to be more than skin deep, 33he must be shaved except for the diseased area, and the priest is to keep him in isolation another seven days. 34On the seventh day the priest is to examine the itch, and if it has not spread in the skin and appears to be no more than skin deep, the priest shall pronounce him clean. He must wash his clothes, and he will be clean. 35But if the itch does spread in the skin after he is pronounced clean, 36the priest is to examine him, and if the itch has spread in the skin, the priest does not need to look for yellow hair; the person is unclean. 37If, however, in his judgment it is unchanged and black hair has grown in it, the itch is healed. He is

clean, and the priest shall pronounce him clean.

38"When a man or woman has white spots on the skin, 39the priest is to examine them, and if the spots are dull white, it is a harmless rash that has broken out on the skin; that person is clean.

40"When a man has lost his hair and is bald, he is clean. 41If he has lost his hair from the front of his scalp and has a bald forehead, he is clean. 42But if he has a reddish-white sore on his bald head or forehead, it is an infectious disease breaking out on his head or forehead. 43The priest is to examine him, and if the swollen sore on his head or forehead is reddish-white like an infectious skin disease, 44the man is diseased and is unclean. The priest shall pronounce him unclean because of the sore on his head.

45"The person with such an infectious disease must wear torn clothes, let his hair be unkempt,a cover the lower part of his face and cry out, 'Unclean! Unclean!' 46As long as he has the infection he remains unclean. He must live alone; he must live outside the camp.

Regulations About Mildew

47"If any clothing is contaminated with mildew—any woolen or linen clothing, 48any woven or knitted material of linen or wool, any leather or anything made of leather— 49and if the contamination in the clothing, or leather, or woven or knitted material, or any leather article, is greenish or reddish, it is a spreading mildew and must be shown to the priest. 50The priest is to examine the mildew and isolate the affected article for seven days. 51On the seventh day he is to examine it, and if the mildew has spread in the clothing, or the woven or knitted material, or the leather, whatever its use, it is a destructive mildew; the article is unclean. 52He must burn up the clothing, or the woven or knitted material of wool or linen, or any leather article that has the contamination in it, because the mildew is destructive; the article must be burned up.

53"But if, when the priest examines it, the mildew has not spread in the clothing, or the woven or knitted material, or the leather article, 54he shall order that the contaminated article be washed. Then he is to isolate it for another seven days. 55After the affected article has been

a45 Or clothes, uncover his head

LEVITICUS 14 117

washed, the priest is to examine it, and if the mildew has not changed its appearance, even though it has not spread, it is unclean. Burn it with fire, whether the mildew has affected one side or the other. 56If, when the priest examines it, the mildew has faded after the article has been washed, he is to tear the contaminated part out of the clothing, or the leather, or the woven or knitted material. 57But if it reappears in the clothing, or in the woven or knitted material, or in the leather article, it is spreading, and whatever has the mildew must be burned with fire. 58The clothing, or the woven or knitted material, or any leather article that has been washed and is rid of the mildew, must be washed again, and it will be clean."

59These are the regulations concerning contamination by mildew in woolen or linen clothing, woven or knitted material, or any leather article, for pronouncing them clean or unclean.

Cleansing From Infectious Skin Diseases

14 The LORD said to Moses, 2"These are the regulations for the diseased person at the time of his ceremonial cleansing, when he is brought to the priest: 3The priest is to go outside the camp and examine him. If the person has been healed of his infectious skin disease,a 4the priest shall order that two live clean birds and some cedar wood, scarlet yarn and hyssop be brought for the one to be cleansed. 5Then the priest shall order that one of the birds be killed over fresh water in a clay pot. 6He is then to take the live bird and dip it, together with the cedar wood, the scarlet yarn and the hyssop, into the blood of the bird that was killed over the fresh water. 7Seven times he shall sprinkle the one to be cleansed of the infectious disease and pronounce him clean. Then he is to release the live bird in the open fields.

8"The person to be cleansed must wash his clothes, shave off all his hair and bathe with water; then he will be ceremonially clean. After this he may come into the camp, but he must stay outside his tent for seven days. 9On the seventh day he must shave off all his hair; he must shave his head, his beard, his eyebrows

and the rest of his hair. He must wash his clothes and bathe himself with water, and he will be clean.

10"On the eighth day he must bring two male lambs and one ewe lamb a year old, each without defect, along with three-tenths of an ephahb of fine flour mixed with oil for a grain offering, and one logc of oil. 11The priest who pronounces him clean shall present both the one to be cleansed and his offerings before the LORD at the entrance to the Tent of Meeting.

12"Then the priest is to take one of the male lambs and offer it as a guilt offering, along with the log of oil; he shall wave them before the LORD as a wave offering. 13He is to slaughter the lamb in the holy place where the sin offering and the burnt offering are slaughtered. Like the sin offering, the guilt offering belongs to the priest; it is most holy. 14The priest is to take some of the blood of the guilt offering and put it on the lobe of the right ear of the one to be cleansed, on the thumb of his right hand and on the big toe of his right foot. 15The priest shall then take some of the log of oil, pour it in the palm of his own left hand, 16dip his right forefinger into the oil in his palm, and with his finger sprinkle some of it before the LORD seven times. 17The priest is to put some of the oil remaining in his palm on the lobe of the right ear of the one to be cleansed, on the thumb of his right hand and on the big toe of his right foot, on top of the blood of the guilt offering. 18The rest of the oil in his palm the priest shall put on the head of the one to be cleansed and make atonement for him before the LORD.

19"Then the priest is to sacrifice the sin offering and make atonement for the one to be cleansed from his uncleanness. After that, the priest shall slaughter the burnt offering 20and offer it on the altar, together with the grain offering, and make atonement for him, and he will be clean.

21"If, however, he is poor and cannot afford these, he must take one male lamb as a guilt offering to be waved to make atonement for him, together with a tenth of an ephahd of fine flour mixed with oil for a grain offering, a log of oil, 22and two doves or two young pigeons, which he can

---

a3 Traditionally *leprosy*; the Hebrew word was used for various diseases affecting the skin—not necessarily leprosy; also elsewhere in this chapter.   b10 That is, probably about 6 quarts (about 6.5 liters)   c10 That is, probably about 2/3 pint (about 0.3 liter); also in verses 12, 15, 21 and 24   d21 That is, probably about 2 quarts (about 2 liters) afford, one for a sin offering and the other for a burnt offering.

23"On the eighth day he must bring them for his cleansing to the priest at the entrance to the Tent of Meeting, before the LORD. 24The priest is to take the lamb for the guilt offering, together with the log of oil, and wave them before the LORD as a wave offering. 25He shall slaughter the lamb for the guilt offering and take some of its blood and put it on the lobe of the right ear of the one to be cleansed, on the thumb of his right hand and on the big toe of his right foot. 26The priest is to pour some of the oil into the palm of his own left hand, 27and with his right forefinger sprinkle some of the oil from his palm seven times before the LORD. 28Some of the oil in his palm he is to put on the same places he put the blood of the guilt offering—on the lobe of the right ear of the one to be cleansed, on the thumb of his right hand and on the big toe of his right foot. 29The rest of the oil in his palm the priest shall put on the head of the one to be cleansed, to make atonement for him before the LORD. 30Then he shall sacrifice the doves or the young pigeons, which the person can afford, 31one*a* as a sin offering and the other as a burnt offering, together with the grain offering. In this way the priest will make atonement before the LORD on behalf of the one to be cleansed."

32These are the regulations for anyone who has an infectious skin disease and who cannot afford the regular offerings for his cleansing.

Cleansing From Mildew

33The LORD said to Moses and Aaron, 34"When you enter the land of Canaan, which I am giving you as your possession, and I put a spreading mildew in a house in that land, 35the owner of the house must go and tell the priest, 'I have seen something that looks like mildew in my house.' 36The priest is to order the house to be emptied before he goes in to examine the mildew, so that nothing in the house will be pronounced unclean. After this the priest is to go in and inspect the house. 37He is to examine the mildew on the walls, and if it has greenish or reddish depressions that appear to be deeper than the surface of the wall, 38the priest shall go out the doorway of the house and close it up for seven days. 39On the sev-

enth day the priest shall return to inspect the house. If the mildew has spread on the walls, 40he is to order that the contaminated stones be torn out and thrown into an unclean place outside the town. 41He must have all the inside walls of the house scraped and the material that is scraped off dumped into an unclean place outside the town. 42Then they are to take other stones to replace these and take new clay and plaster the house.

43"If the mildew reappears in the house after the stones have been torn out and the house scraped and plastered, 44the priest is to go and examine it and, if the mildew has spread in the house, it is a destructive mildew; the house is unclean. 45It must be torn down—its stones, timbers and all the plaster—and taken out of the town to an unclean place.

46"Anyone who goes into the house while it is closed up will be unclean till evening. 47Anyone who sleeps or eats in the house must wash his clothes.

48"But if the priest comes to examine it and the mildew has not spread after the house has been plastered, he shall pronounce the house clean, because the mildew is gone. 49To purify the house he is to take two birds and some cedar wood, scarlet yarn and hyssop. 50He shall kill one of the birds over fresh water in a clay pot. 51Then he is to take the cedar wood, the hyssop, the scarlet yarn and the live bird, dip them into the blood of the dead bird and the fresh water, and sprinkle the house seven times. 52He shall purify the house with the bird's blood, the fresh water, the live bird, the cedar wood, the hyssop and the scarlet yarn. 53Then he is to release the live bird in the open fields outside the town. In this way he will make atonement for the house, and it will be clean."

54These are the regulations for any infectious skin disease, for an itch, 55for mildew in clothing or in a house, 56and for a swelling, a rash or a bright spot, 57to determine when something is clean or unclean.

These are the regulations for infectious skin diseases and mildew.

Discharges Causing Uncleanness

15 The LORD said to Moses and Aaron, 2"Speak to the Israelites and say to them: 'When any man has a bodily discharge, the discharge is unclean. 3Wheth-

---

a31 Septuagint and Syriac; Hebrew 31such as the person can afford, one er it continues flowing from his body or is blocked, it will make him unclean. This is how his discharge will bring about uncleanness:

4" 'Any bed the man with a discharge lies on will be unclean, and anything he sits on will be unclean. ⁵Anyone who touches his bed must wash his clothes and bathe with water, and he will be unclean till evening. ⁶Whoever sits on anything that the man with a discharge sat on must wash his clothes and bathe with water, and he will be unclean till evening.

7" 'Whoever touches the man who has a discharge must wash his clothes and bathe with water, and he will be unclean till evening.

8" 'If the man with the discharge spits on someone who is clean, that person must wash his clothes and bathe with water, and he will be unclean till evening.

9" 'Everything the man sits on when riding will be unclean, ¹⁰and whoever touches any of the things that were under him will be unclean till evening; whoever picks up those things must wash his clothes and bathe with water, and he will be unclean till evening.

11" 'Anyone the man with a discharge touches without rinsing his hands with water must wash his clothes and bathe with water, and he will be unclean till evening.

12" 'A clay pot that the man touches must be broken, and any wooden article is to be rinsed with water.

13" 'When a man is cleansed from his discharge, he is to count off seven days for his ceremonial cleansing; he must wash his clothes and bathe himself with fresh water, and he will be clean. ¹⁴On the eighth day he must take two doves or two young pigeons and come before the Lᴏʀᴅ to the entrance to the Tent of Meeting and give them to the priest. ¹⁵The priest is to sacrifice them, the one for a sin offering and the other for a burnt offering. In this way he will make atonement before the Lᴏʀᴅ for the man because of his discharge.

16" 'When a man has an emission of semen, he must bathe his whole body with water, and he will be unclean till evening. ¹⁷Any clothing or leather that has semen on it must be washed with water, and it will be unclean till evening. ¹⁸When a man lies with a woman and there is an emission of semen, both must bathe with

water, and they will be unclean till evening.

19" 'When a woman has her regular flow of blood, the impurity of her monthly period will last seven days, and anyone who touches her will be unclean till evening.

20" 'Anything she lies on during her period will be unclean, and anything she sits on will be unclean. ²¹Whoever touches her bed must wash his clothes and bathe with water, and he will be unclean till evening. ²²Whoever touches anything she sits on must wash his clothes and bathe with water, and he will be unclean till evening. ²³Whether it is the bed or anything she was sitting on, when anyone touches it, he will be unclean till evening.

24" 'If a man lies with her and her monthly flow touches him, he will be unclean for seven days; any bed he lies on will be unclean.

25" 'When a woman has a discharge of blood for many days at a time other than her monthly period or has a discharge that continues beyond her period, she will be unclean as long as she has the discharge, just as in the days of her period. ²⁶Any bed she lies on while her discharge continues will be unclean, as is her bed during her monthly period, and anything she sits on will be unclean, as during her period. ²⁷Whoever touches them will be unclean; he must wash his clothes and bathe with water, and he will be unclean till evening.

28" 'When she is cleansed from her discharge, she must count off seven days, and after that she will be ceremonially clean. ²⁹On the eighth day she must take two doves or two young pigeons and bring them to the priest at the entrance to the Tent of Meeting. ³⁰The priest is to sacrifice one for a sin offering and the other for a burnt offering. In this way he will make atonement for her before the Lᴏʀᴅ for the uncleanness of her discharge.

31" 'You must keep the Israelites separate from things that make them unclean, so they will not die in their uncleanness for defiling my dwelling place,ᵃ which is among them.' "

³²These are the regulations for a man with a discharge, for anyone made unclean by an emission of semen, ³³for a woman in her monthly period, for a man or a woman with a discharge, and for a

ᵃ31 Or *my tabernacle*

man who lies with a woman who is ceremonially unclean.

The Day of Atonement

16 The LORD spoke to Moses after the death of the two sons of Aaron who died when they approached the LORD. ²The LORD said to Moses: "Tell your brother Aaron not to come whenever he chooses into the Most Holy Place behind the curtain in front of the atonement cover on the ark, or else he will die, because I appear in the cloud over the atonement cover.

³"This is how Aaron is to enter the sanctuary area: with a young bull for a sin offering and a ram for a burnt offering. ⁴He is to put on the sacred linen tunic, with linen undergarments next to his body; he is to tie the linen sash around him and put on the linen turban. These are sacred garments; so he must bathe himself with water before he puts them on. ⁵From the Israelite community he is to take two male goats for a sin offering and a ram for a burnt offering.

⁶"Aaron is to offer the bull for his own sin offering to make atonement for himself and his household. ⁷Then he is to take the two goats and present them before the LORD at the entrance to the Tent of Meeting. ⁸He is to cast lots for the two goats—one lot for the LORD and the other for the scapegoat.ᵃ ⁹Aaron shall bring the goat whose lot falls to the LORD and sacrifice it for a sin offering. ¹⁰But the goat chosen by lot as the scapegoat shall be presented alive before the LORD to be used for making atonement by sending it into the desert as a scapegoat.

¹¹"Aaron shall bring the bull for his own sin offering to make atonement for himself and his household, and he is to slaughter the bull for his own sin offering. ¹²He is to take a censer full of burning coals from the altar before the LORD and two handfuls of finely ground fragrant incense and take them behind the curtain. ¹³He is to put the incense on the fire before the LORD, and the smoke of the incense will conceal the atonement cover above the Testimony, so that he will not die. ¹⁴He is to take some of the bull's blood and with his finger sprinkle it on the front of the atonement cover; then he shall sprinkle some of it with his finger seven times before the atonement cover.

¹⁵"He shall then slaughter the goat for the sin offering for the people and take its blood behind the curtain and do with it as he did with the bull's blood: He shall sprinkle it on the atonement cover and in front of it. ¹⁶In this way he will make atonement for the Most Holy Place because of the uncleanness and rebellion of the Israelites, whatever their sins have been. He is to do the same for the Tent of Meeting, which is among them in the midst of their uncleanness. ¹⁷No one is to be in the Tent of Meeting from the time Aaron goes in to make atonement in the Most Holy Place until he comes out, having made atonement for himself, his household and the whole community of Israel.

¹⁸"Then he shall come out to the altar that is before the LORD and make atonement for it. He shall take some of the bull's blood and some of the goat's blood and put it on all the horns of the altar. ¹⁹He shall sprinkle some of the blood on it with his finger seven times to cleanse it and to consecrate it from the uncleanness of the Israelites.

²⁰"When Aaron has finished making atonement for the Most Holy Place, the Tent of Meeting and the altar, he shall bring forward the live goat. ²¹He is to lay both hands on the head of the live goat and confess over it all the wickedness and rebellion of the Israelites—all their sins—and put them on the goat's head. He shall send the goat away into the desert in the care of a man appointed for the task. ²²The goat will carry on itself all their sins to a solitary place; and the man shall release it in the desert.

²³"Then Aaron is to go into the Tent of Meeting and take off the linen garments he put on before he entered the Most Holy Place, and he is to leave them there. ²⁴He shall bathe himself with water in a holy place and put on his regular garments. Then he shall come out and sacrifice the burnt offering for himself and the burnt offering for the people, to make atonement for himself and for the people. ²⁵He shall also burn the fat of the sin offering on the altar.

²⁶"The man who releases the goat as a scapegoat must wash his clothes and bathe himself with water; afterward he may come into the camp. ²⁷The bull and the goat for the sin offerings, whose blood was brought into the Most Holy Place to make atonement, must be taken outside

---

ᵃ8 That is, the goat of removal; Hebrew *azazel*; also in verses 10 and 26 the camp; their hides, flesh and offal are to be burned up. 28The man who burns them must wash his clothes and bathe himself with water; afterward he may come into the camp.

29"This is to be a lasting ordinance for you: On the tenth day of the seventh month you must deny yourselves*a* and not do any work—whether native-born or an alien living among you— 30because on this day atonement will be made for you, to cleanse you. Then, before the Lord, you will be clean from all your sins. 31It is a sabbath of rest, and you must deny yourselves; it is a lasting ordinance. 32The priest who is anointed and ordained to succeed his father as high priest is to make atonement. He is to put on the sacred linen garments 33and make atonement for the Most Holy Place, for the Tent of Meeting and the altar, and for the priests and all the people of the community.

34"This is to be a lasting ordinance for you: Atonement is to be made once a year for all the sins of the Israelites."

And it was done, as the Lord commanded Moses.

Eating Blood Forbidden

17 The Lord said to Moses, 2"Speak to Aaron and his sons and to all the Israelites and say to them: 'This is what the Lord has commanded: 3Any Israelite who sacrifices an ox,*b* a lamb or a goat in the camp or outside of it 4instead of bringing it to the entrance to the Tent of Meeting to present it as an offering to the Lord in front of the tabernacle of the Lord—that man shall be considered guilty of bloodshed; he has shed blood and must be cut off from his people. 5This is so the Israelites will bring to the Lord the sacrifices they are now making in the open fields. They must bring them to the priest, that is, to the Lord, at the entrance to the Tent of Meeting and sacrifice them as fellowship offerings.*c* 6The priest is to sprinkle the blood against the altar of the Lord at the entrance to the Tent of Meeting and burn the fat as an aroma pleasing to the Lord. 7They must no longer offer any of their sacrifices to the goat idols*d* to whom they prostitute themselves. This is to be a lasting ordinance for them and for the generations to come.'

8"Say to them: 'Any Israelite or any alien living among them who offers a burnt offering or sacrifice 9and does not bring it to the entrance to the Tent of Meeting to sacrifice it to the Lord—that man must be cut off from his people.

10" 'Any Israelite or any alien living among them who eats any blood—I will set my face against that person who eats blood and will cut him off from his people. 11For the life of a creature is in the blood, and I have given it to you to make atonement for yourselves on the altar; it is the blood that makes atonement for one's life. 12Therefore I say to the Israelites, "None of you may eat blood, nor may an alien living among you eat blood."

13" 'Any Israelite or any alien living among you who hunts any animal or bird that may be eaten must drain out the blood and cover it with earth, 14because the life of every creature is its blood. That is why I have said to the Israelites, "You must not eat the blood of any creature, because the life of every creature is its blood; anyone who eats it must be cut off."

15" 'Anyone, whether native-born or alien, who eats anything found dead or torn by wild animals must wash his clothes and bathe with water, and he will be ceremonially unclean till evening; then he will be clean. 16But if he does not wash his clothes and bathe himself, he will be held responsible.' "

Unlawful Sexual Relations

18 The Lord said to Moses, 2"Speak to the Israelites and say to them: 'I am the Lord your God. 3You must not do as they do in Egypt, where you used to live, and you must not do as they do in the land of Canaan, where I am bringing you. Do not follow their practices. 4You must obey my laws and be careful to follow my decrees. I am the Lord your God. 5Keep my decrees and laws, for the man who obeys them will live by them. I am the Lord.

6" 'No one is to approach any close relative to have sexual relations. I am the Lord.

7" 'Do not dishonor your father by having sexual relations with your mother. She is your mother; do not have relations with her.

8" 'Do not have sexual relations with

---

a29 Or *must fast*; also in verse 31   *b3* The Hebrew word can include both male and female.
c5 Traditionally *peace offerings*   *d7* Or *demons*

your father's wife; that would dishonor your father.

9" 'Do not have sexual relations with your sister, either your father's daughter or your mother's daughter, whether she was born in the same home or elsewhere.

10" 'Do not have sexual relations with your son's daughter or your daughter's daughter; that would dishonor you.

11" 'Do not have sexual relations with the daughter of your father's wife, born to your father; she is your sister.

12" 'Do not have sexual relations with your father's sister; she is your father's close relative.

13" 'Do not have sexual relations with your mother's sister, because she is your mother's close relative.

14" 'Do not dishonor your father's brother by approaching his wife to have sexual relations; she is your aunt.

15" 'Do not have sexual relations with your daughter-in-law. She is your son's wife; do not have relations with her.

16" 'Do not have sexual relations with your brother's wife; that would dishonor your brother.

17" 'Do not have sexual relations with both a woman and her daughter. Do not have sexual relations with either her son's daughter or her daughter's daughter; they are her close relatives. That is wickedness.

18" 'Do not take your wife's sister as a rival wife and have sexual relations with her while your wife is living.

19" 'Do not approach a woman to have sexual relations during the uncleanness of her monthly period.

20" 'Do not have sexual relations with your neighbor's wife and defile yourself with her.

21" 'Do not give any of your children to be sacrificed[a] to Molech, for you must not profane the name of your God. I am the Lord.

22" 'Do not lie with a man as one lies with a woman; that is detestable.

23" 'Do not have sexual relations with an animal and defile yourself with it. A woman must not present herself to an animal to have sexual relations with it; that is a perversion.

24" 'Do not defile yourselves in any of these ways, because this is how the nations that I am going to drive out before you became defiled. 25Even the land was defiled; so I punished it for its sin, and

the land vomited out its inhabitants. 26But you must keep my decrees and my laws. The native-born and the aliens living among you must not do any of these detestable things, 27for all these things were done by the people who lived in the land before you, and the land became defiled. 28And if you defile the land, it will vomit you out as it vomited out the nations that were before you.

29" 'Everyone who does any of these detestable things—such persons must be cut off from their people. 30Keep my requirements and do not follow any of the detestable customs that were practiced before you came and do not defile yourselves with them. I am the Lord your God.' "

Various Laws

19 The Lord said to Moses, 2"Speak to the entire assembly of Israel and say to them: 'Be holy because I, the Lord your God, am holy.

3" 'Each of you must respect his mother and father, and you must observe my Sabbaths. I am the Lord your God.

4" 'Do not turn to idols or make gods of cast metal for yourselves. I am the Lord your God.

5" 'When you sacrifice a fellowship offering[b] to the Lord, sacrifice it in such a way that it will be accepted on your behalf. 6It shall be eaten on the day you sacrifice it or on the next day; anything left over until the third day must be burned up. 7If any of it is eaten on the third day, it is impure and will not be accepted. 8Whoever eats it will be held responsible because he has desecrated what is holy to the Lord; that person must be cut off from his people.

9" 'When you reap the harvest of your land, do not reap to the very edges of your field or gather the gleanings of your harvest. 10Do not go over your vineyard a second time or pick up the grapes that have fallen. Leave them for the poor and the alien. I am the Lord your God.

11" 'Do not steal.

" 'Do not lie.

" 'Do not deceive one another.

12" 'Do not swear falsely by my name and so profane the name of your God. I am the Lord.

13" 'Do not defraud your neighbor or rob him.

---

a21 Or to be passed through the fire.   *b5 Traditionally peace offering*

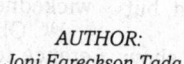

TUESDAY

VERSE FOR THE DAY:
Leviticus 19:2

AUTHOR:
Joni Eareckson Tada

PASSAGE FOR THE DAY:
Leviticus 19:1–37

"Spiritual" Activities

HAVE you noticed how some activities you do seem a lot more spiritual—more sacred—than others? Singing hymns, teaching church school, working at a soup kitchen or preparing a care basket for a sick friend—all of these seem more exalted than other activities. Even something as common as a holiday family gathering seems . . . sacred.

But what about when you drive to the Chevron station to fill your tank with gas? Or when you count out coupons to the clerk at the supermarket? Or while you're waiting for the salesperson to wrap your purchases? Those activities seem far from spiritual and anything but sacred.

We do it all the time—separate "religious" activities into one group and "regular" into another. But Levitcus 19 addresses that problem. In one verse Moses says, "Do not steal" (Leviticus 19:11). Yet the verse next to it states, "Do not go over your vineyard a second time or pick up the grapes that have fallen" (Leviticus 19:10).

Again he says in one verse, "Do not seek revenge . . . but love your neighbor as yourself" (Leviticus 19:18). And the verse following? "Do not mate different kinds of animals" (Leviticus 19:19).

Why didn't Moses simply group together all the spiritual activities and leave the rest of those nonessential, nonspiritual things for another chapter? Well, it's no mistake that God spoke all these commands in one breath, mingling "spiritual" and "nonspiritual."

God is telling his people what he expects of them in their worship. God wants his people to understand that all life is spiritual; all of life's activities come under his domain. How we plow our fields or how we shop at the market. How we mate our animals or even how we talk to a gas station attendant. Everything we do can be a way of worshiping him.

Think about that the next time you wash dishes.

Additional Scripture Readings:
Colossians 3:17; 1 Thessalonians 4:11–12

*Go to page 127 for your next
devotional reading.*

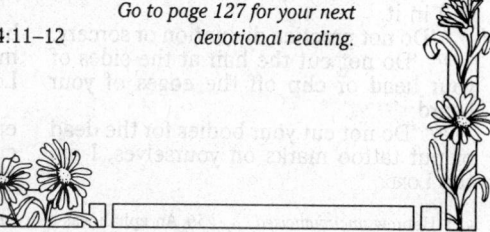

" 'Do not hold back the wages of a hired man overnight.

14" 'Do not curse the deaf or put a stumbling block in front of the blind, but fear your God. I am the LORD.

15" 'Do not pervert justice; do not show partiality to the poor or favoritism to the great, but judge your neighbor fairly.

16" 'Do not go about spreading slander among your people.

" 'Do not do anything that endangers your neighbor's life. I am the LORD.

17" 'Do not hate your brother in your heart. Rebuke your neighbor frankly so you will not share in his guilt.

18" 'Do not seek revenge or bear a grudge against one of your people, but love your neighbor as yourself. I am the LORD.

19" 'Keep my decrees.

" 'Do not mate different kinds of animals.

" 'Do not plant your field with two kinds of seed.

" 'Do not wear clothing woven of two kinds of material.

20" 'If a man sleeps with a woman who is a slave girl promised to another man but who has not been ransomed or given her freedom, there must be due punishment. Yet they are not to be put to death, because she had not been freed. 21The man, however, must bring a ram to the entrance to the Tent of Meeting for a guilt offering to the LORD. 22With the ram of the guilt offering the priest is to make atonement for him before the LORD for the sin he has committed, and his sin will be forgiven.

23" 'When you enter the land and plant any kind of fruit tree, regard its fruit as forbidden.a For three years you are to consider it forbiddena; it must not be eaten. 24In the fourth year all its fruit will be holy, an offering of praise to the LORD. 25But in the fifth year you may eat its fruit. In this way your harvest will be increased. I am the LORD your God.

26" 'Do not eat any meat with the blood still in it.

" 'Do not practice divination or sorcery.

27" 'Do not cut the hair at the sides of your head or clip off the edges of your beard.

28" 'Do not cut your bodies for the dead or put tattoo marks on yourselves. I am the LORD.

29" 'Do not degrade your daughter by making her a prostitute, or the land will turn to prostitution and be filled with wickedness.

30" 'Observe my Sabbaths and have reverence for my sanctuary. I am the LORD.

31" 'Do not turn to mediums or seek out spiritists, for you will be defiled by them. I am the LORD your God.

32" 'Rise in the presence of the aged, show respect for the elderly and revere your God. I am the LORD.

33" 'When an alien lives with you in your land, do not mistreat him. 34The alien living with you must be treated as one of your native-born. Love him as yourself, for you were aliens in Egypt. I am the LORD your God.

35" 'Do not use dishonest standards when measuring length, weight or quantity. 36Use honest scales and honest weights, an honest ephahb and an honest hin.c I am the LORD your God, who brought you out of Egypt.

37" 'Keep all my decrees and all my laws and follow them. I am the LORD.' "

Punishments for Sin

20 The LORD said to Moses, 2"Say to the Israelites: 'Any Israelite or any alien living in Israel who givesd any of his children to Molech must be put to death. The people of the community are to stone him. 3I will set my face against that man and I will cut him off from his people; for by giving his children to Molech, he has defiled my sanctuary and profaned my holy name. 4If the people of the community close their eyes when that man gives one of his children to Molech and they fail to put him to death, 5I will set my face against that man and his family and will cut off from their people both him and all who follow him in prostituting themselves to Molech.

6" 'I will set my face against the person who turns to mediums and spiritists to prostitute himself by following them, and I will cut him off from his people.

7" 'Consecrate yourselves and be holy, because I am the LORD your God. 8Keep my decrees and follow them. I am the LORD, who makes you holy.e

9" 'If anyone curses his father or mother, he must be put to death. He has cursed his father or his mother, and his blood will be on his own head.

---

a23 Hebrew uncircumcised   b36 An ephah was a dry measure.   c36 A hin was a liquid measure.
d2 Or sacrifices; also in verses 3 and 4   e8 Or who sanctifies you; or who sets you apart as holy

¹⁰" 'If a man commits adultery with another man's wife — with the wife of his neighbor — both the adulterer and the adulteress must be put to death.

¹¹" 'If a man sleeps with his father's wife, he has dishonored his father. Both the man and the woman must be put to death; their blood will be on their own heads.

¹²" 'If a man sleeps with his daughter-in-law, both of them must be put to death. What they have done is a perversion; their blood will be on their own heads.

¹³" 'If a man lies with a man as one lies with a woman, both of them have done what is detestable. They must be put to death; their blood will be on their own heads.

¹⁴" 'If a man marries both a woman and her mother, it is wicked. Both he and they must be burned in the fire, so that no wickedness will be among you.

¹⁵" 'If a man has sexual relations with an animal, he must be put to death, and you must kill the animal.

¹⁶" 'If a woman approaches an animal to have sexual relations with it, kill both the woman and the animal. They must be put to death; their blood will be on their own heads.

¹⁷" 'If a man marries his sister, the daughter of either his father or his mother, and they have sexual relations, it is a disgrace. They must be cut off before the eyes of their people. He has dishonored his sister and will be held responsible.

¹⁸" 'If a man lies with a woman during her monthly period and has sexual relations with her, he has exposed the source of her flow, and she has also uncovered it. Both of them must be cut off from their people.

¹⁹" 'Do not have sexual relations with the sister of either your mother or your father, for that would dishonor a close relative; both of you would be held responsible.

²⁰" 'If a man sleeps with his aunt, he has dishonored his uncle. They will be held responsible; they will die childless.

²¹" 'If a man marries his brother's wife, it is an act of impurity; he has dishonored his brother. They will be childless.

²²" 'Keep all my decrees and laws and follow them, so that the land where I am bringing you to live may not vomit you out. ²³You must not live according to the customs of the nations I am going to drive out before you. Because they did all these things, I abhorred them. ²⁴But I said to you, "You will possess their land; I will give it to you as an inheritance, a land flowing with milk and honey." I am the LORD your God, who has set you apart from the nations.

²⁵" 'You must therefore make a distinction between clean and unclean animals and between unclean and clean birds. Do not defile yourselves by any animal or bird or anything that moves along the ground — those which I have set apart as unclean for you. ²⁶You are to be holy to me[a] because I, the LORD, am holy, and I have set you apart from the nations to be my own.

²⁷" 'A man or woman who is a medium or spiritist among you must be put to death. You are to stone them; their blood will be on their own heads.' "

Rules for Priests

21 The LORD said to Moses, "Speak to the priests, the sons of Aaron, and say to them: 'A priest must not make himself ceremonially unclean for any of his people who die, ²except for a close relative, such as his mother or father, his son or daughter, his brother, ³or an unmarried sister who is dependent on him since she has no husband — for her he may make himself unclean. ⁴He must not make himself unclean for people related to him by marriage,[b] and so defile himself.

⁵" 'Priests must not shave their heads or shave off the edges of their beards or cut their bodies. ⁶They must be holy to their God and must not profane the name of their God. Because they present the offerings made to the LORD by fire, the food of their God, they are to be holy.

⁷" 'They must not marry women defiled by prostitution or divorced from their husbands, because priests are holy to their God. ⁸Regard them as holy, because they offer up the food of your God. Consider them holy, because I the LORD am holy — I who make you holy.[c]

⁹" 'If a priest's daughter defiles herself by becoming a prostitute, she disgraces her father; she must be burned in the fire.

¹⁰" 'The high priest, the one among his brothers who has had the anointing oil poured on his head and who has been or-

---

[a]26 Or *be my holy ones*   [b]4 Or *unclean as a leader among his people*   [c]8 Or *who sanctify you; or who set you apart as holy*

dained to wear the priestly garments, must not let his hair become unkempt[a] or tear his clothes. [11]He must not enter a place where there is a dead body. He must not make himself unclean, even for his father or mother, [12]nor leave the sanctuary of his God or desecrate it, because he has been dedicated by the anointing oil of his God. I am the LORD.

[13]" 'The woman he marries must be a virgin. [14]He must not marry a widow, a divorced woman, or a woman defiled by prostitution, but only a virgin from his own people, [15]so he will not defile his offspring among his people. I am the LORD, who makes him holy.[b]' "

[16]The LORD said to Moses, [17]"Say to Aaron: 'For the generations to come none of your descendants who has a defect may come near to offer the food of his God. [18]No man who has any defect may come near: no man who is blind or lame, disfigured or deformed; [19]no man with a crippled foot or hand, [20]or who is hunchbacked or dwarfed, or who has any eye defect, or who has festering or running sores or damaged testicles. [21]No descendant of Aaron the priest who has any defect is to come near to present the offerings made to the LORD by fire. He has a defect; he must not come near to offer the food of his God. [22]He may eat the most holy food of his God, as well as the holy food; [23]yet because of his defect, he must not go near the curtain or approach the altar, and so desecrate my sanctuary. I am the LORD, who makes them holy.[c]' "

[24]So Moses told this to Aaron and his sons and to all the Israelites.

22 The LORD said to Moses, [2]"Tell Aaron and his sons to treat with respect the sacred offerings the Israelites consecrate to me, so they will not profane my holy name. I am the LORD.

[3]"Say to them: 'For the generations to come, if any of your descendants is ceremonially unclean and yet comes near the sacred offerings that the Israelites consecrate to the LORD, that person must be cut off from my presence. I am the LORD.

[4]" 'If a descendant of Aaron has an infectious skin disease[d] or a bodily discharge, he may not eat the sacred offerings until he is cleansed. He will also be unclean if he touches something defiled by a corpse or by anyone who has an emission of semen, [5]or if he touches any crawling thing that makes him unclean, or any person who makes him unclean, whatever the uncleanness may be. [6]The one who touches any such thing will be unclean till evening. He must not eat any of the sacred offerings unless he has bathed himself with water. [7]When the sun goes down, he will be clean, and after that he may eat the sacred offerings, for they are his food. [8]He must not eat anything found dead or torn by wild animals, and so become unclean through it. I am the LORD.

[9]" 'The priests are to keep my requirements so that they do not become guilty and die for treating them with contempt. I am the LORD, who makes them holy.[e]

[10]" 'No one outside a priest's family may eat the sacred offering, nor may the guest of a priest or his hired worker eat it. [11]But if a priest buys a slave with money, or if a slave is born in his household, that slave may eat his food. [12]If a priest's daughter marries anyone other than a priest, she may not eat any of the sacred contributions. [13]But if a priest's daughter becomes a widow or is divorced, yet has no children, and she returns to live in her father's house as in her youth, she may eat of her father's food. No unauthorized person, however, may eat any of it.

[14]" 'If anyone eats a sacred offering by mistake, he must make restitution to the priest for the offering and add a fifth of the value to it. [15]The priests must not desecrate the sacred offerings the Israelites present to the LORD [16]by allowing them to eat the sacred offerings and so bring upon them guilt requiring payment. I am the LORD, who makes them holy.' "

Unacceptable Sacrifices

[17]The LORD said to Moses, [18]"Speak to Aaron and his sons and to all the Israelites and say to them: 'If any of you—either an Israelite or an alien living in Israel—presents a gift for a burnt offering to the LORD, either to fulfill a vow or as a freewill offering, [19]you must present a male without defect from the cattle, sheep or goats in order that it may be accepted on your behalf. [20]Do not bring anything with a defect, because it will not

---

[a]10 Or *not uncover his head*   [b]15 Or *who sanctifies him; or who sets him apart as holy*   [c]23 Or *who sanctifies them; or who sets them apart as holy*   [d]4 Traditionally *leprosy*; the Hebrew word was used for various diseases affecting the skin—not necessarily leprosy.   [e]9 Or *who sanctifies them; or who sets them apart as holy*; also in verse 16

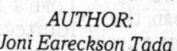

VERSE FOR THE DAY: *Leviticus 21:17*	*AUTHOR:* *Joni Eareckson Tada*	*PASSAGE FOR THE DAY:* *Leviticus 21:1–24*

Come Before God in Purity

I RECALL the good old days—or should I say the bad old days—when I was struggling to understand God's view of my disability. It didn't help matters when I stumbled across Leviticus 21:16–24. "No man who has any defect may come near [to offer sacrifices to God]: no man who is blind or lame, disfigured or deformed; no man with a crippled foot or hand."

I slammed shut my Bible. I knew it—God *did* have a problem with my handicap. It seemed my handicap offended him in the same way my wheelchair offended waiters in restaurants!

But years later I discovered the true meaning behind these verses. Leviticus 21 is a strict list of do's and don't's for men entering the priesthood of Aaron. Such a priest had to be pure, with no physical defects. Why? Because the priest was a physical symbol of a future spiritual reality—a very important type of the coming Messiah. God was looking for a physically perfect man as a priest to represent the spiritually perfect man, the Lord Jesus.

That's why Old Testament priests could not be lame, blind or handicapped in any way. A violation of the Old Testament picture would defile the New Testament fulfillment of Christ's perfection as our high priest.

This passage can speak to us today, whether we're disabled or not. As part of a "royal priesthood" (1 Peter 2:9), God welcomes us into his presence, accepting us no matter how "disfigured or deformed" we are. But when we come before him in worship, we need to make certain that we have been washed in Jesus' blood and our hearts are clean, harboring no blemish of pride or defect of impurity. We may not be tied to strict do's and don't's, but if God wanted Old Testament people to be pure when they came before him, surely he expects the same of us.

Additional Scripture Readings:
Isaiah 35:5–10; 1 Peter 1:13–22

Go to page 147 for your next
devotional reading.

be accepted on your behalf. [21]When anyone brings from the herd or flock a fellowship offering[a] to the LORD to fulfill a special vow or as a freewill offering, it must be without defect or blemish to be acceptable. [22]Do not offer to the LORD the blind, the injured or the maimed, or anything with warts or festering or running sores. Do not place any of these on the altar as an offering made to the LORD by fire. [23]You may, however, present as a freewill offering an ox[b] or a sheep that is deformed or stunted, but it will not be accepted in fulfillment of a vow. [24]You must not offer to the LORD an animal whose testicles are bruised, crushed, torn or cut. You must not do this in your own land, [25]and you must not accept such animals from the hand of a foreigner and offer them as the food of your God. They will not be accepted on your behalf, because they are deformed and have defects.' "

[26]The LORD said to Moses, [27]"When a calf, a lamb or a goat is born, it is to remain with its mother for seven days. From the eighth day on, it will be acceptable as an offering made to the LORD by fire. [28]Do not slaughter a cow or a sheep and its young on the same day.

[29]"When you sacrifice a thank offering to the LORD, sacrifice it in such a way that it will be accepted on your behalf. [30]It must be eaten that same day; leave none of it till morning. I am the LORD.

[31]"Keep my commands and follow them. I am the LORD. [32]Do not profane my holy name. I must be acknowledged as holy by the Israelites. I am the LORD, who makes[c] you holy[d] [33]and who brought you out of Egypt to be your God. I am the LORD."

23 The LORD said to Moses, [2]"Speak to the Israelites and say to them: 'These are my appointed feasts, the appointed feasts of the LORD, which you are to proclaim as sacred assemblies.

The Sabbath

[3]" 'There are six days when you may work, but the seventh day is a Sabbath of rest, a day of sacred assembly. You are not to do any work; wherever you live, it is a Sabbath to the LORD.

The Passover and Unleavened Bread

[4]" 'These are the LORD's appointed feasts, the sacred assemblies you are to proclaim at their appointed times: [5]The LORD's Passover begins at twilight on the fourteenth day of the first month. [6]On the fifteenth day of that month the LORD's Feast of Unleavened Bread begins; for seven days you must eat bread made without yeast. [7]On the first day hold a sacred assembly and do no regular work. [8]For seven days present an offering made to the LORD by fire. And on the seventh day hold a sacred assembly and do no regular work.' "

Firstfruits

[9]The LORD said to Moses, [10]"Speak to the Israelites and say to them: 'When you enter the land I am going to give you and you reap its harvest, bring to the priest a sheaf of the first grain you harvest. [11]He is to wave the sheaf before the LORD so it will be accepted on your behalf; the priest is to wave it on the day after the Sabbath. [12]On the day you wave the sheaf, you must sacrifice as a burnt offering to the LORD a lamb a year old without defect, [13]together with its grain offering of two-tenths of an ephah[e] of fine flour mixed with oil—an offering made to the LORD by fire, a pleasing aroma—and its drink offering of a quarter of a hin[f] of wine. [14]You must not eat any bread, or roasted or new grain, until the very day you bring this offering to your God. This is to be a lasting ordinance for the generations to come, wherever you live.

Feast of Weeks

[15]" 'From the day after the Sabbath, the day you brought the sheaf of the wave offering, count off seven full weeks. [16]Count off fifty days up to the day after the seventh Sabbath, and then present an offering of new grain to the LORD. [17]From wherever you live, bring two loaves made of two-tenths of an ephah of fine flour, baked with yeast, as a wave offering of firstfruits to the LORD. [18]Present with this bread seven male lambs, each a year old and without defect, one young bull and two rams. They will be a burnt offering to the LORD, together with their grain offerings and drink offerings—an offering made by fire, an aroma pleasing to the

---

[a]21 Traditionally *peace offering*   [b]23 The Hebrew word can include both male and female.   [c]32 Or *made*   [d]32 Or *who sanctifies you*; or *who sets you apart as holy*   [e]13 That is, probably about 4 quarts (about 4.5 liters); also in verse 17   [f]13 That is, probably about 1 quart (about 1 liter)

LORD. [19]Then sacrifice one male goat for a sin offering and two lambs, each a year old, for a fellowship offering.[a] [20]The priest is to wave the two lambs before the LORD as a wave offering, together with the bread of the firstfruits. They are a sacred offering to the LORD for the priest. [21]On that same day you are to proclaim a sacred assembly and do no regular work. This is to be a lasting ordinance for the generations to come, wherever you live.

[22]" 'When you reap the harvest of your land, do not reap to the very edges of your field or gather the gleanings of your harvest. Leave them for the poor and the alien. I am the LORD your God.' "

Feast of Trumpets

[23]The LORD said to Moses, [24]"Say to the Israelites: 'On the first day of the seventh month you are to have a day of rest, a sacred assembly commemorated with trumpet blasts. [25]Do no regular work, but present an offering made to the LORD by fire.' "

Day of Atonement

[26]The LORD said to Moses, [27]"The tenth day of this seventh month is the Day of Atonement. Hold a sacred assembly and deny yourselves,[b] and present an offering made to the LORD by fire. [28]Do no work on that day, because it is the Day of Atonement, when atonement is made for you before the LORD your God. [29]Anyone who does not deny himself on that day must be cut off from his people. [30]I will destroy from among his people anyone who does any work on that day. [31]You shall do no work at all. This is to be a lasting ordinance for the generations to come, wherever you live. [32]It is a sabbath of rest for you, and you must deny yourselves. From the evening of the ninth day of the month until the following evening you are to observe your sabbath."

Feast of Tabernacles

[33]The LORD said to Moses, [34]"Say to the Israelites: 'On the fifteenth day of the seventh month the LORD's Feast of Tabernacles begins, and it lasts for seven days. [35]The first day is a sacred assembly; do no regular work. [36]For seven days present offerings made to the LORD by fire, and on the eighth day hold a sacred assembly and present an offering made to the LORD by fire. It is the closing assembly; do no regular work.

[37](" 'These are the LORD's appointed feasts, which you are to proclaim as sacred assemblies for bringing offerings made to the LORD by fire—the burnt offerings and grain offerings, sacrifices and drink offerings required for each day. [38]These offerings are in addition to those for the LORD's Sabbaths and[c] in addition to your gifts and whatever you have vowed and all the freewill offerings you give to the LORD.)

[39]" 'So beginning with the fifteenth day of the seventh month, after you have gathered the crops of the land, celebrate the festival to the LORD for seven days; the first day is a day of rest, and the eighth day also is a day of rest. [40]On the first day you are to take choice fruit from the trees, and palm fronds, leafy branches and poplars, and rejoice before the LORD your God for seven days. [41]Celebrate this as a festival to the LORD for seven days each year. This is to be a lasting ordinance for the generations to come; celebrate it in the seventh month. [42]Live in booths for seven days: All native-born Israelites are to live in booths [43]so your descendants will know that I had the Israelites live in booths when I brought them out of Egypt. I am the LORD your God.' "

[44]So Moses announced to the Israelites the appointed feasts of the LORD.

Oil and Bread Set Before the LORD

24 The LORD said to Moses, [2]"Command the Israelites to bring you clear oil of pressed olives for the light so that the lamps may be kept burning continually. [3]Outside the curtain of the Testimony in the Tent of Meeting, Aaron is to tend the lamps before the LORD from evening till morning, continually. This is to be a lasting ordinance for the generations to come. [4]The lamps on the pure gold lampstand before the LORD must be tended continually.

[5]"Take fine flour and bake twelve loaves of bread, using two-tenths of an ephah[d] for each loaf. [6]Set them in two rows, six in each row, on the table of pure gold before the LORD. [7]Along each row put some pure incense as a memorial portion to represent the bread and to be an offer-

---

[a]19 Traditionally *peace offering*   [b]27 Or *and fast*; also in verses 29 and 32   [c]38 Or *These feasts are in addition to the LORD's Sabbaths, and these offerings are*   [d]5 That is, probably about 4 quarts (about 4.5 liters)

ing made to the LORD by fire. ⁸This bread is to be set out before the LORD regularly, Sabbath after Sabbath, on behalf of the Israelites, as a lasting covenant. ⁹It belongs to Aaron and his sons, who are to eat it in a holy place, because it is a most holy part of their regular share of the offerings made to the LORD by fire."

A Blasphemer Stoned

¹⁰Now the son of an Israelite mother and an Egyptian father went out among the Israelites, and a fight broke out in the camp between him and an Israelite. ¹¹The son of the Israelite woman blasphemed the Name with a curse; so they brought him to Moses. (His mother's name was Shelomith, the daughter of Dibri the Danite.) ¹²They put him in custody until the will of the LORD should be made clear to them.

¹³Then the LORD said to Moses: ¹⁴"Take the blasphemer outside the camp. All those who heard him are to lay their hands on his head, and the entire assembly is to stone him. ¹⁵Say to the Israelites: 'If anyone curses his God, he will be held responsible; ¹⁶anyone who blasphemes the name of the LORD must be put to death. The entire assembly must stone him. Whether an alien or native-born, when he blasphemes the Name, he must be put to death.

¹⁷"'If anyone takes the life of a human being, he must be put to death. ¹⁸Anyone who takes the life of someone's animal must make restitution—life for life. ¹⁹If anyone injures his neighbor, whatever he has done must be done to him: ²⁰fracture for fracture, eye for eye, tooth for tooth. As he has injured the other, so he is to be injured. ²¹Whoever kills an animal must make restitution, but whoever kills a man must be put to death. ²²You are to have the same law for the alien and the native-born. I am the LORD your God.' "

²³Then Moses spoke to the Israelites, and they took the blasphemer outside the camp and stoned him. The Israelites did as the LORD commanded Moses.

The Sabbath Year

25 The LORD said to Moses on Mount Sinai, ²"Speak to the Israelites and say to them: 'When you enter the land I am going to give you, the land itself must observe a sabbath to the LORD. ³For six years sow your fields, and for six years prune your vineyards and gather their crops. ⁴But in the seventh year the land is

to have a sabbath of rest, a sabbath to the LORD. Do not sow your fields or prune your vineyards. ⁵Do not reap what grows of itself or harvest the grapes of your untended vines. The land is to have a year of rest. ⁶Whatever the land yields during the sabbath year will be food for you—for yourself, your manservant and maidservant, and the hired worker and temporary resident who live among you, ⁷as well as for your livestock and the wild animals in your land. Whatever the land produces may be eaten.

The Year of Jubilee

⁸"'Count off seven sabbaths of years—seven times seven years—so that the seven sabbaths of years amount to a period of forty-nine years. ⁹Then have the trumpet sounded everywhere on the tenth day of the seventh month; on the Day of Atonement sound the trumpet throughout your land. ¹⁰Consecrate the fiftieth year and proclaim liberty throughout the land to all its inhabitants. It shall be a jubilee for you; each one of you is to return to his family property and each to his own clan. ¹¹The fiftieth year shall be a jubilee for you; do not sow and do not reap what grows of itself or harvest the untended vines. ¹²For it is a jubilee and is to be holy for you; eat only what is taken directly from the fields.

¹³"'In this Year of Jubilee everyone is to return to his own property.

¹⁴"'If you sell land to one of your countrymen or buy any from him, do not take advantage of each other. ¹⁵You are to buy from your countryman on the basis of the number of years since the Jubilee. And he is to sell to you on the basis of the number of years left for harvesting crops. ¹⁶When the years are many, you are to increase the price, and when the years are few, you are to decrease the price, because what he is really selling you is the number of crops. ¹⁷Do not take advantage of each other, but fear your God. I am the LORD your God.

¹⁸"'Follow my decrees and be careful to obey my laws, and you will live safely in the land. ¹⁹Then the land will yield its fruit, and you will eat your fill and live there in safety. ²⁰You may ask, "What will we eat in the seventh year if we do not plant or harvest our crops?" ²¹I will send you such a blessing in the sixth year that the land will yield enough for three years. ²²While you plant during the eighth year, you will eat from the old crop and will

continue to eat from it until the harvest of the ninth year comes in.

²³" 'The land must not be sold permanently, because the land is mine and you are but aliens and my tenants. ²⁴Throughout the country that you hold as a possession, you must provide for the redemption of the land.

²⁵" 'If one of your countrymen becomes poor and sells some of his property, his nearest relative is to come and redeem what his countryman has sold. ²⁶If, however, a man has no one to redeem it for him but he himself prospers and acquires sufficient means to redeem it, ²⁷he is to determine the value for the years since he sold it and refund the balance to the man to whom he sold it; he can then go back to his own property. ²⁸But if he does not acquire the means to repay him, what he sold will remain in the possession of the buyer until the Year of Jubilee. It will be returned in the Jubilee, and he can then go back to his property.

²⁹" 'If a man sells a house in a walled city, he retains the right of redemption a full year after its sale. During that time he may redeem it. ³⁰If it is not redeemed before a full year has passed, the house in the walled city shall belong permanently to the buyer and his descendants. It is not to be returned in the Jubilee. ³¹But houses in villages without walls around them are to be considered as open country. They can be redeemed, and they are to be returned in the Jubilee.

³²" 'The Levites always have the right to redeem their houses in the Levitical towns, which they possess. ³³So the property of the Levites is redeemable—that is, a house sold in any town they hold—and is to be returned in the Jubilee, because the houses in the towns of the Levites are their property among the Israelites. ³⁴But the pastureland belonging to their towns must not be sold; it is their permanent possession.

³⁵" 'If one of your countrymen becomes poor and is unable to support himself among you, help him as you would an alien or a temporary resident, so he can continue to live among you. ³⁶Do not take interest of any kind^a from him, but fear your God, so that your countryman may continue to live among you. ³⁷You must not lend him money at interest or sell him food at a profit. ³⁸I am the LORD your God, who brought you out of Egypt to give you the land of Canaan and to be your God.

³⁹" 'If one of your countrymen becomes poor among you and sells himself to you, do not make him work as a slave. ⁴⁰He is to be treated as a hired worker or a temporary resident among you; he is to work for you until the Year of Jubilee. ⁴¹Then he and his children are to be released, and he will go back to his own clan and to the property of his forefathers. ⁴²Because the Israelites are my servants, whom I brought out of Egypt, they must not be sold as slaves. ⁴³Do not rule over them ruthlessly, but fear your God.

⁴⁴" 'Your male and female slaves are to come from the nations around you; from them you may buy slaves. ⁴⁵You may also buy some of the temporary residents living among you and members of their clans born in your country, and they will become your property. ⁴⁶You can will them to your children as inherited property and can make them slaves for life, but you must not rule over your fellow Israelites ruthlessly.

⁴⁷" 'If an alien or a temporary resident among you becomes rich and one of your countrymen becomes poor and sells himself to the alien living among you or to a member of the alien's clan, ⁴⁸he retains the right of redemption after he has sold himself. One of his relatives may redeem him: ⁴⁹An uncle or a cousin or any blood relative in his clan may redeem him. Or if he prospers, he may redeem himself. ⁵⁰He and his buyer are to count the time from the year he sold himself up to the Year of Jubilee. The price for his release is to be based on the rate paid to a hired man for that number of years. ⁵¹If many years remain, he must pay for his redemption a larger share of the price paid for him. ⁵²If only a few years remain until the Year of Jubilee, he is to compute that and pay for his redemption accordingly. ⁵³He is to be treated as a man hired from year to year; you must see to it that his owner does not rule over him ruthlessly.

⁵⁴" 'Even if he is not redeemed in any of these ways, he and his children are to be released in the Year of Jubilee, ⁵⁵for the Israelites belong to me as servants. They are my servants, whom I brought out of Egypt. I am the LORD your God.

Reward for Obedience

26 " 'Do not make idols or set up an image or a sacred stone for your-

a36 Or *take excessive interest*; similarly in verse 37

selves, and do not place a carved stone in your land to bow down before it. I am the LORD your God.

2" 'Observe my Sabbaths and have reverence for my sanctuary. I am the LORD.

3" 'If you follow my decrees and are careful to obey my commands, 4I will send you rain in its season, and the ground will yield its crops and the trees of the field their fruit. 5Your threshing will continue until grape harvest and the grape harvest will continue until planting, and you will eat all the food you want and live in safety in your land.

6" 'I will grant peace in the land, and you will lie down and no one will make you afraid. I will remove savage beasts from the land, and the sword will not pass through your country. 7You will pursue your enemies, and they will fall by the sword before you. 8Five of you will chase a hundred, and a hundred of you will chase ten thousand, and your enemies will fall by the sword before you.

9" 'I will look on you with favor and make you fruitful and increase your numbers, and I will keep my covenant with you. 10You will still be eating last year's harvest when you will have to move it out to make room for the new. 11I will put my dwelling place[a] among you, and I will not abhor you. 12I will walk among you and be your God, and you will be my people. 13I am the LORD your God, who brought you out of Egypt so that you would no longer be slaves to the Egyptians; I broke the bars of your yoke and enabled you to walk with heads held high.

Punishment for Disobedience

14" 'But if you will not listen to me and carry out all these commands, 15and if you reject my decrees and abhor my laws and fail to carry out all my commands and so violate my covenant, 16then I will do this to you: I will bring upon you sudden terror, wasting diseases and fever that will destroy your sight and drain away your life. You will plant seed in vain, because your enemies will eat it. 17I will set my face against you so that you will be defeated by your enemies; those who hate you will rule over you, and you will flee even when no one is pursuing you.

18" 'If after all this you will not listen to me, I will punish you for your sins seven times over. 19I will break down your stubborn pride and make the sky above you

like iron and the ground beneath you like bronze. 20Your strength will be spent in vain, because your soil will not yield its crops, nor will the trees of the land yield their fruit.

21" 'If you remain hostile toward me and refuse to listen to me, I will multiply your afflictions seven times over, as your sins deserve. 22I will send wild animals against you, and they will rob you of your children, destroy your cattle and make you so few in number that your roads will be deserted.

23" 'If in spite of these things you do not accept my correction but continue to be hostile toward me, 24I myself will be hostile toward you and will afflict you for your sins seven times over. 25And I will bring the sword upon you to avenge the breaking of the covenant. When you withdraw into your cities, I will send a plague among you, and you will be given into enemy hands. 26When I cut off your supply of bread, ten women will be able to bake your bread in one oven, and they will dole out the bread by weight. You will eat, but you will not be satisfied.

27" 'If in spite of this you still do not listen to me but continue to be hostile toward me, 28then in my anger I will be hostile toward you, and I myself will punish you for your sins seven times over. 29You will eat the flesh of your sons and the flesh of your daughters. 30I will destroy your high places, cut down your incense altars and pile your dead bodies on the lifeless forms of your idols, and I will abhor you. 31I will turn your cities into ruins and lay waste your sanctuaries, and I will take no delight in the pleasing aroma of your offerings. 32I will lay waste the land, so that your enemies who live there will be appalled. 33I will scatter you among the nations and will draw out my sword and pursue you. Your land will be laid waste, and your cities will lie in ruins. 34Then the land will enjoy its sabbath years all the time that it lies desolate and you are in the country of your enemies; then the land will rest and enjoy its sabbaths. 35All the time that it lies desolate, the land will have the rest it did not have during the sabbaths you lived in it.

36" 'As for those of you who are left, I will make their hearts so fearful in the lands of their enemies that the sound of a windblown leaf will put them to flight. They will run as though fleeing from the sword, and they will fall, even though no one is pursuing them. ³⁷They will stumble over one another as though fleeing from the sword, even though no one is pursuing them. So you will not be able to stand before your enemies. ³⁸You will perish among the nations; the land of your enemies will devour you. ³⁹Those of you who are left will waste away in the lands of their enemies because of their sins; also because of their fathers' sins they will waste away.

⁴⁰"'But if they will confess their sins and the sins of their fathers—their treachery against me and their hostility toward me, ⁴¹which made me hostile toward them so that I sent them into the land of their enemies—then when their uncircumcised hearts are humbled and they pay for their sin, ⁴²I will remember my covenant with Jacob and my covenant with Isaac and my covenant with Abraham, and I will remember the land. ⁴³For the land will be deserted by them and will enjoy its sabbaths while it lies desolate without them. They will pay for their sins because they rejected my laws and abhorred my decrees. ⁴⁴Yet in spite of this, when they are in the land of their enemies, I will not reject them or abhor them so as to destroy them completely, breaking my covenant with them. I am the LORD their God. ⁴⁵But for their sake I will remember the covenant with their ancestors whom I brought out of Egypt in the sight of the nations to be their God. I am the LORD.'"

⁴⁶These are the decrees, the laws and the regulations that the LORD established on Mount Sinai between himself and the Israelites through Moses.

Redeeming What Is the LORD's

27 The LORD said to Moses, ²"Speak to the Israelites and say to them: 'If anyone makes a special vow to dedicate persons to the LORD by giving equivalent values, ³set the value of a male between the ages of twenty and sixty at fifty shekels*ᵃ* of silver, according to the sanctuary shekel*ᵇ*; ⁴and if it is a female, set her value at thirty shekels. *ᶜ* ⁵If it is a person between the ages of five and twenty,

set the value of a male at twenty shekels*ᵈ* and of a female at ten shekels. *ᵉ* ⁶If it is a person between one month and five years, set the value of a male at five shekels*ᶠ* of silver and that of a female at three shekels*ᵍ* of silver. ⁷If it is a person sixty years old or more, set the value of a male at fifteen shekels*ʰ* and of a female at ten shekels. ⁸If anyone making the vow is too poor to pay the specified amount, he is to present the person to the priest, who will set the value for him according to what the man making the vow can afford.

⁹"'If what he vowed is an animal that is acceptable as an offering to the LORD, such an animal given to the LORD becomes holy. ¹⁰He must not exchange it or substitute a good one for a bad one, or a bad one for a good one; if he should substitute one animal for another, both it and the substitute become holy. ¹¹If what he vowed is a ceremonially unclean animal—one that is not acceptable as an offering to the LORD—the animal must be presented to the priest, ¹²who will judge its quality as good or bad. Whatever value the priest then sets, that is what it will be. ¹³If the owner wishes to redeem the animal, he must add a fifth to its value.

¹⁴"'If a man dedicates his house as something holy to the LORD, the priest will judge its quality as good or bad. Whatever value the priest then sets, so it will remain. ¹⁵If the man who dedicates his house redeems it, he must add a fifth to its value, and the house will again become his.

¹⁶"'If a man dedicates to the LORD part of his family land, its value is to be set according to the amount of seed required for it—fifty shekels of silver to a homer*ⁱ* of barley seed. ¹⁷If he dedicates his field during the Year of Jubilee, the value that has been set remains. ¹⁸But if he dedicates his field after the Jubilee, the priest will determine the value according to the number of years that remain until the next Year of Jubilee, and its set value will be reduced. ¹⁹If the man who dedicates the field wishes to redeem it, he must add a fifth to its value, and the field will again become his. ²⁰If, however, he does not redeem the field, or if he has sold it to someone else, it can never be redeemed.

ᵃ3 That is, about 1 1/4 pounds (about 0.6 kilogram); also in verse 16   *ᵇ3* That is, about 2/5 ounce (about 11.5 grams); also in verse 25   *ᶜ4* That is, about 12 ounces (about 0.3 kilogram)   *ᵈ5* That is, about 8 ounces (about 0.2 kilogram)   *ᵉ5* That is, about 4 ounces (about 110 grams); also in verse 7   *ᶠ6* That is, about 2 ounces (about 55 grams)   *ᵍ6* That is, about 1 1/4 ounces (about 35 grams)   *ʰ7* That is, about 6 ounces (about 170 grams)   *ⁱ16* That is, probably about 6 bushels (about 220 liters)

²¹When the field is released in the Jubilee, it will become holy, like a field devoted to the LORD; it will become the property of the priests.ᵃ

²²"'If a man dedicates to the LORD a field he has bought, which is not part of his family land, ²³the priest will determine its value up to the Year of Jubilee, and the man must pay its value on that day as something holy to the LORD. ²⁴In the Year of Jubilee the field will revert to the person from whom he bought it, the one whose land it was. ²⁵Every value is to be set according to the sanctuary shekel, twenty gerahs to the shekel.

²⁶"'No one, however, may dedicate the firstborn of an animal, since the firstborn already belongs to the LORD; whether an oxᵇ or a sheep, it is the LORD's. ²⁷If it is one of the unclean animals, he may buy it back at its set value, adding a fifth of the value to it. If he does not redeem it, it is to be sold at its set value.

²⁸"'But nothing that a man owns and devotesᶜ to the LORD—whether man or animal or family land—may be sold or redeemed; everything so devoted is most holy to the LORD.

²⁹"'No person devoted to destructionᵈ may be ransomed; he must be put to death.

³⁰"'A tithe of everything from the land, whether grain from the soil or fruit from the trees, belongs to the LORD; it is holy to the LORD. ³¹If a man redeems any of his tithe, he must add a fifth of the value to it. ³²The entire tithe of the herd and flock—every tenth animal that passes under the shepherd's rod—will be holy to the LORD. ³³He must not pick out the good from the bad or make any substitution. If he does make a substitution, both the animal and its substitute become holy and cannot be redeemed.'"

³⁴These are the commands the LORD gave Moses on Mount Sinai for the Israelites.

ᵃ21 Or *priest*   ᵇ26 The Hebrew word can include both male and female.   ᶜ28 The Hebrew term refers to the irrevocable giving over of things or persons to the LORD.   ᵈ29 The Hebrew term refers to the irrevocable giving over of things or persons to the LORD, often by totally destroying them.

M OSES records in this book the number of the Israelites and how he organizes them around the tabernacle. To this he adds an account of what happens as they wander in the wilderness. Note especially that in spite of their numerous rebellions, God still loves them and watches over them. As you read this book, rejoice in God's love and care in your life in spite of your sins; promise God that you will do your best to trust and obey him.

NUMBERS

The Census

1 The LORD spoke to Moses in the Tent of Meeting in the Desert of Sinai on the first day of the second month of the second year after the Israelites came out of Egypt. He said: ²"Take a census of the whole Israelite community by their clans and families, listing every man by name, one by one. ³You and Aaron are to number by their divisions all the men in Israel twenty years old or more who are able to serve in the army. ⁴One man from each tribe, each the head of his family, is to help you. ⁵These are the names of the men who are to assist you:

from Reuben, Elizur son of Shedeur;

⁶from Simeon, Shelumiel son of Zuri-shaddai;
⁷from Judah, Nahshon son of Amminadab;
⁸from Issachar, Nethanel son of Zuar;
⁹from Zebulun, Eliab son of Helon;
¹⁰from the sons of Joseph:
    from Ephraim, Elishama son of Ammihud;
    from Manasseh, Gamaliel son of Pedahzur;
¹¹from Benjamin, Abidan son of Gideoni;
¹²from Dan, Ahiezer son of Ammishaddai;
¹³from Asher, Pagiel son of Ocran;
¹⁴from Gad, Eliasaph son of Deuel;

15from Naphtali, Ahira son of Enan."

16These were the men appointed from the community, the leaders of their ancestral tribes. They were the heads of the clans of Israel.

17Moses and Aaron took these men whose names had been given, 18and they called the whole community together on the first day of the second month. The people indicated their ancestry by their clans and families, and the men twenty years old or more were listed by name, one by one, 19as the LORD commanded Moses. And so he counted them in the Desert of Sinai:

20From the descendants of Reuben the firstborn son of Israel:

All the men twenty years old or more who were able to serve in the army were listed by name, one by one, according to the records of their clans and families. 21The number from the tribe of Reuben was 46,500.

22From the descendants of Simeon:

All the men twenty years old or more who were able to serve in the army were counted and listed by name, one by one, according to the records of their clans and families. 23The number from the tribe of Simeon was 59,300.

24From the descendants of Gad:

All the men twenty years old or more who were able to serve in the army were listed by name, according to the records of their clans and families. 25The number from the tribe of Gad was 45,650.

26From the descendants of Judah:

All the men twenty years old or more who were able to serve in the army were listed by name, according to the records of their clans and families. 27The number from the tribe of Judah was 74,600.

28From the descendants of Issachar:

All the men twenty years old or more who were able to serve in the army were listed by name, according to the records of their clans and families. 29The number from the tribe of Issachar was 54,400.

30From the descendants of Zebulun:

All the men twenty years old or more who were able to serve in the army were listed by name, according to the records of their clans and families. 31The number from the tribe of Zebulun was 57,400.

32From the sons of Joseph:

From the descendants of Ephraim:

All the men twenty years old or more who were able to serve in the army were listed by name, according to the records of their clans and families. 33The number from the tribe of Ephraim was 40,500.

34From the descendants of Manasseh:

All the men twenty years old or more who were able to serve in the army were listed by name, according to the records of their clans and families. 35The number from the tribe of Manasseh was 32,200.

36From the descendants of Benjamin:

All the men twenty years old or more who were able to serve in the army were listed by name, according to the records of their clans and families. 37The number from the tribe of Benjamin was 35,400.

38From the descendants of Dan:

All the men twenty years old or more who were able to serve in the army were listed by name, according to the records of their clans and families. 39The number from the tribe of Dan was 62,700.

40From the descendants of Asher:

All the men twenty years old or more who were able to serve in the army were listed by name, according to the records of their clans and families. 41The number from the tribe of Asher was 41,500.

42From the descendants of Naphtali:

All the men twenty years old or more who were able to serve in the army were listed by name, according to the records of their clans and families. 43The number from the tribe of Naphtali was 53,400.

44These were the men counted by Moses and Aaron and the twelve leaders of Israel, each one representing his family. 45All the Israelites twenty years old or more who were able to serve in Israel's army were counted according to their families. 46The total number was 603,550.

47The families of the tribe of Levi, however, were not counted along with the others. 48The LORD had said to Moses: 49"You must not count the tribe of Levi or include them in the census of the other Israelites. 50Instead, appoint the Levites to be in charge of the tabernacle of the Testimony—over all its furnishings and everything belonging to it. They are to carry the tabernacle and all its furnishings; they are to take care of it and encamp around it. 51Whenever the tabernacle is to move, the Levites are to take it down, and whenever the tabernacle is to be set up, the Levites shall do it. Anyone else who goes near it shall be put to death. 52The Israelites are to set up their tents by divisions, each man in his own camp under his own standard. 53The Levites, however, are to set up their tents around the tabernacle of the Testimony so that wrath will not fall on the Israelite community. The Levites are to be responsible for the care of the tabernacle of the Testimony."

54The Israelites did all this just as the LORD commanded Moses.

The Arrangement of the Tribal Camps

2 The LORD said to Moses and Aaron: 2"The Israelites are to camp around the Tent of Meeting some distance from it, each man under his standard with the banners of his family."

3On the east, toward the sunrise, the divisions of the camp of Judah are to encamp under their standard. The leader of the people of Judah is Nahshon son of Amminadab. 4His division numbers 74,600.

5The tribe of Issachar will camp next to them. The leader of the people of Issachar is Nethanel son of Zuar. 6His division numbers 54,400.

7The tribe of Zebulun will be next. The leader of the people of Zebulun is Eliab son of Helon. 8His division numbers 57,400.

9All the men assigned to the camp of Judah, according to their divisions, number 186,400. They will set out first.

10On the south will be the divisions of the camp of Reuben under their standard. The leader of the people of Reuben is Elizur son of Shedeur. 11His division numbers 46,500.

12The tribe of Simeon will camp next to them. The leader of the people of Simeon is Shelumiel son of Zurishaddai. 13His division numbers 59,300.

14The tribe of Gad will be next. The leader of the people of Gad is Eliasaph son of Deuel.a 15His division numbers 45,650.

16All the men assigned to the camp of Reuben, according to their divisions, number 151,450. They will set out second.

17Then the Tent of Meeting and the camp of the Levites will set out in the middle of the camps. They will set out in the same order as they encamp, each in his own place under his standard.

18On the west will be the divisions of the camp of Ephraim under their standard. The leader of the people of Ephraim is Elishama son of Ammihud. 19His division numbers 40,500.

20The tribe of Manasseh will be next to them. The leader of the people of Manasseh is Gamaliel son of Pedahzur. 21His division numbers 32,200.

22The tribe of Benjamin will be next. The leader of the people of Benjamin is Abidan son of Gideoni. 23His division numbers 35,400.

24All the men assigned to the camp of Ephraim, according to their divisions, number 108,100. They will set out third.

25On the north will be the divisions of the camp of Dan, under their standard. The leader of the people of Dan is Ahiezer son of Ammishaddai. 26His division numbers 62,700.

27The tribe of Asher will camp next to them. The leader of the people of Asher is Pagiel son of Ocran. 28His division numbers 41,500.

29The tribe of Naphtali will be next. The leader of the people of Naphtali is Ahira son of Enan. 30His division numbers 53,400.

31All the men assigned to the camp of Dan number 157,600. They will set out last, under their standards.

32These are the Israelites, counted

---

a14 Many manuscripts of the Masoretic Text, Samaritan Pentateuch and Vulgate (see also Num. 1:14); most manuscripts of the Masoretic Text *Reuel* according to their families. All those in the camps, by their divisions, number 603,550. [33]The Levites, however, were not counted along with the other Israelites, as the LORD commanded Moses.

[34]So the Israelites did everything the LORD commanded Moses; that is the way they encamped under their standards, and that is the way they set out, each with his clan and family.

The Levites

3 This is the account of the family of Aaron and Moses at the time the LORD talked with Moses on Mount Sinai.

[2]The names of the sons of Aaron were Nadab the firstborn and Abihu, Eleazar and Ithamar. [3]Those were the names of Aaron's sons, the anointed priests, who were ordained to serve as priests. [4]Nadab and Abihu, however, fell dead before the LORD when they made an offering with unauthorized fire before him in the Desert of Sinai. They had no sons; so only Eleazar and Ithamar served as priests during the lifetime of their father Aaron.

[5]The LORD said to Moses, [6]"Bring the tribe of Levi and present them to Aaron the priest to assist him. [7]They are to perform duties for him and for the whole community at the Tent of Meeting by doing the work of the tabernacle. [8]They are to take care of all the furnishings of the Tent of Meeting, fulfilling the obligations of the Israelites by doing the work of the tabernacle. [9]Give the Levites to Aaron and his sons; they are the Israelites who are to be given wholly to him.[a] [10]Appoint Aaron and his sons to serve as priests; anyone else who approaches the sanctuary must be put to death."

[11]The LORD also said to Moses, [12]"I have taken the Levites from among the Israelites in place of the first male offspring of every Israelite woman. The Levites are mine, [13]for all the firstborn are mine. When I struck down all the firstborn in Egypt, I set apart for myself every firstborn in Israel, whether man or animal. They are to be mine. I am the LORD."

[14]The LORD said to Moses in the Desert of Sinai, [15]"Count the Levites by their families and clans. Count every male a month old or more." [16]So Moses counted them, as he was commanded by the word of the LORD.

[17]These were the names of the sons of Levi:

Gershon, Kohath and Merari.

[18]These were the names of the Gershonite clans:

Libni and Shimei.

[19]The Kohathite clans:

Amram, Izhar, Hebron and Uzziel.

[20]The Merarite clans:

Mahli and Mushi.

These were the Levite clans, according to their families.

[21]To Gershon belonged the clans of the Libnites and Shimeites; these were the Gershonite clans. [22]The number of all the males a month old or more who were counted was 7,500. [23]The Gershonite clans were to camp on the west, behind the tabernacle. [24]The leader of the families of the Gershonites was Eliasaph son of Lael. [25]At the Tent of Meeting the Gershonites were responsible for the care of the tabernacle and tent, its coverings, the curtain at the entrance to the Tent of Meeting, [26]the curtains of the courtyard, the curtain at the entrance to the courtyard surrounding the tabernacle and altar, and the ropes—and everything related to their use.

[27]To Kohath belonged the clans of the Amramites, Izharites, Hebronites and Uzzielites; these were the Kohathite clans. [28]The number of all the males a month old or more was 8,600.[b] The Kohathites were responsible for the care of the sanctuary. [29]The Kohathite clans were to camp on the south side of the tabernacle. [30]The leader of the families of the Kohathite clans was Elizaphan son of Uzziel. [31]They were responsible for the care of the ark, the table, the lampstand, the altars, the articles of the sanctuary used in ministering, the curtain, and everything related to their use. [32]The chief leader of the Levites was Eleazar son of Aaron, the priest. He was appointed over those who were responsible for the care of the sanctuary.

[33]To Merari belonged the clans of the Mahlites and the Mushites; these were the Merarite clans. [34]The number of all

---

[a]9 Most manuscripts of the Masoretic Text; some manuscripts of the Masoretic Text, Samaritan Pentateuch and Septuagint (see also Num. 8:16) *to me*   [b]28 Hebrew; some Septuagint manuscripts 8,300

the males a month old or more who were counted was 6,200. 35The leader of the families of the Merarite clans was Zuriel son of Abihail; they were to camp on the north side of the tabernacle. 36The Merarites were appointed to take care of the frames of the tabernacle, its crossbars, posts, bases, all its equipment, and everything related to their use, 37as well as the posts of the surrounding courtyard with their bases, tent pegs and ropes.

38Moses and Aaron and his sons were to camp to the east of the tabernacle, toward the sunrise, in front of the Tent of Meeting. They were responsible for the care of the sanctuary on behalf of the Israelites. Anyone else who approached the sanctuary was to be put to death.

39The total number of Levites counted at the LORD's command by Moses and Aaron according to their clans, including every male a month old or more, was 22,000.

40The LORD said to Moses, "Count all the firstborn Israelite males who are a month old or more and make a list of their names. 41Take the Levites for me in place of all the firstborn of the Israelites, and the livestock of the Levites in place of all the firstborn of the livestock of the Israelites. I am the LORD."

42So Moses counted all the firstborn of the Israelites, as the LORD commanded him. 43The total number of firstborn males a month old or more, listed by name, was 22,273.

44The LORD also said to Moses, 45"Take the Levites in place of all the firstborn of Israel, and the livestock of the Levites in place of their livestock. The Levites are to be mine. I am the LORD. 46To redeem the 273 firstborn Israelites who exceed the number of the Levites, 47collect five shekels*a* for each one, according to the sanctuary shekel, which weighs twenty gerahs. 48Give the money for the redemption of the additional Israelites to Aaron and his sons."

49So Moses collected the redemption money from those who exceeded the number redeemed by the Levites. 50From the firstborn of the Israelites he collected silver weighing 1,365 shekels,*b* accord-ing to the sanctuary shekel. 51Moses gave the redemption money to Aaron and his sons, as he was commanded by the word of the LORD.

The Kohathites

4 The LORD said to Moses and Aaron: 2"Take a census of the Kohathite branch of the Levites by their clans and families. 3Count all the men from thirty to fifty years of age who come to serve in the work in the Tent of Meeting.

4"This is the work of the Kohathites in the Tent of Meeting: the care of the most holy things. 5When the camp is to move, Aaron and his sons are to go in and take down the shielding curtain and cover the ark of the Testimony with it. 6Then they are to cover this with hides of sea cows,*c* spread a cloth of solid blue over that and put the poles in place.

7"Over the table of the Presence they are to spread a blue cloth and put on it the plates, dishes and bowls, and the jars for drink offerings; the bread that is continually there is to remain on it. 8Over these they are to spread a scarlet cloth, cover that with hides of sea cows and put its poles in place.

9"They are to take a blue cloth and cover the lampstand that is for light, together with its lamps, its wick trimmers and trays, and all its jars for the oil used to supply it. 10Then they are to wrap it and all its accessories in a covering of hides of sea cows and put it on a carrying frame.

11"Over the gold altar they are to spread a blue cloth and cover that with hides of sea cows and put its poles in place.

12"They are to take all the articles used for ministering in the sanctuary, wrap them in a blue cloth, cover that with hides of sea cows and put them on a carrying frame.

13"They are to remove the ashes from the bronze altar and spread a purple cloth over it. 14Then they are to place on it all the utensils used for ministering at the altar, including the firepans, meat forks, shovels and sprinkling bowls. Over it they are to spread a covering of hides of sea cows and put its poles in place.

15"After Aaron and his sons have finished covering the holy furnishings and all the holy articles, and when the camp is ready to move, the Kohathites are to

---

a47 That is, about 2 ounces (about 55 grams)   *b50* That is, about 35 pounds (about 15.5 kilograms)
c6 That is, dugongs; also in verses 8, 10, 11, 12, 14 and 25

come to do the carrying. But they must not touch the holy things or they will die. The Kohathites are to carry those things that are in the Tent of Meeting.

16"Eleazar son of Aaron, the priest, is to have charge of the oil for the light, the fragrant incense, the regular grain offering and the anointing oil. He is to be in charge of the entire tabernacle and everything in it, including its holy furnishings and articles."

17The LORD said to Moses and Aaron, 18"See that the Kohathite tribal clans are not cut off from the Levites. 19So that they may live and not die when they come near the most holy things, do this for them: Aaron and his sons are to go into the sanctuary and assign to each man his work and what he is to carry. 20But the Kohathites must not go in to look at the holy things, even for a moment, or they will die."

The Gershonites

21The LORD said to Moses, 22"Take a census also of the Gershonites by their families and clans. 23Count all the men from thirty to fifty years of age who come to serve in the work at the Tent of Meeting.

24"This is the service of the Gershonite clans as they work and carry burdens: 25They are to carry the curtains of the tabernacle, the Tent of Meeting, its covering and the outer covering of hides of sea cows, the curtains for the entrance to the Tent of Meeting, 26the curtains of the courtyard surrounding the tabernacle and altar, the curtain for the entrance, the ropes and all the equipment used in its service. The Gershonites are to do all that needs to be done with these things. 27All their service, whether carrying or doing other work, is to be done under the direction of Aaron and his sons. You shall assign to them as their responsibility all they are to carry. 28This is the service of the Gershonite clans at the Tent of Meeting. Their duties are to be under the direction of Ithamar son of Aaron, the priest.

The Merarites

29"Count the Merarites by their clans and families. 30Count all the men from thirty to fifty years of age who come to serve in the work at the Tent of Meeting. 31This is their duty as they perform service at the Tent of Meeting: to carry the frames of the tabernacle, its crossbars, posts and bases, 32as well as the posts of the surrounding courtyard with their bases, tent pegs, ropes, all their equipment and everything related to their use. Assign to each man the specific things he is to carry. 33This is the service of the Merarite clans as they work at the Tent of Meeting under the direction of Ithamar son of Aaron, the priest."

The Numbering of the Levite Clans

34Moses, Aaron and the leaders of the community counted the Kohathites by their clans and families. 35All the men from thirty to fifty years of age who came to serve in the work in the Tent of Meeting, 36counted by clans, were 2,750. 37This was the total of all those in the Kohathite clans who served in the Tent of Meeting. Moses and Aaron counted them according to the LORD's command through Moses.

38The Gershonites were counted by their clans and families. 39All the men from thirty to fifty years of age who came to serve in the work at the Tent of Meeting, 40counted by their clans and families, were 2,630. 41This was the total of those in the Gershonite clans who served at the Tent of Meeting. Moses and Aaron counted them according to the LORD's command.

42The Merarites were counted by their clans and families. 43All the men from thirty to fifty years of age who came to serve in the work at the Tent of Meeting, 44counted by their clans, were 3,200. 45This was the total of those in the Merarite clans. Moses and Aaron counted them according to the LORD's command through Moses.

46So Moses, Aaron and the leaders of Israel counted all the Levites by their clans and families. 47All the men from thirty to fifty years of age who came to do the work of serving and carrying the Tent of Meeting 48numbered 8,580. 49At the LORD's command through Moses, each was assigned his work and told what to carry.

Thus they were counted, as the LORD commanded Moses.

The Purity of the Camp

5 The LORD said to Moses, 2"Command the Israelites to send away from the camp anyone who has an infectious skin

disease*a* or a discharge of any kind, or who is ceremonially unclean because of a dead body. ³Send away male and female alike; send them outside the camp so they will not defile their camp, where I dwell among them." ⁴The Israelites did this; they sent them outside the camp. They did just as the Lord had instructed Moses.

Restitution for Wrongs

⁵The Lord said to Moses, ⁶"Say to the Israelites: 'When a man or woman wrongs another in any way*b* and so is unfaithful to the Lord, that person is guilty ⁷and must confess the sin he has committed. He must make full restitution for his wrong, add one fifth to it and give it all to the person he has wronged. ⁸But if that person has no close relative to whom restitution can be made for the wrong, the restitution belongs to the Lord and must be given to the priest, along with the ram with which atonement is made for him. ⁹All the sacred contributions the Israelites bring to a priest will belong to him. ¹⁰Each man's sacred gifts are his own, but what he gives to the priest will belong to the priest.' "

The Test for an Unfaithful Wife

¹¹Then the Lord said to Moses, ¹²"Speak to the Israelites and say to them: 'If a man's wife goes astray and is unfaithful to him ¹³by sleeping with another man, and this is hidden from her husband and her impurity is undetected (since there is no witness against her and she has not been caught in the act), ¹⁴and if feelings of jealousy come over her husband and he suspects his wife and she is impure—or if he is jealous and suspects her even though she is not impure—¹⁵then he is to take his wife to the priest. He must also take an offering of a tenth of an ephah*c* of barley flour on her behalf. He must not pour oil on it or put incense on it, because it is a grain offering for jealousy, a reminder offering to draw attention to guilt.

¹⁶" 'The priest shall bring her and have her stand before the Lord. ¹⁷Then he shall take some holy water in a clay jar and put some dust from the tabernacle floor into the water. ¹⁸After the priest has had the woman stand before the Lord, he shall loosen her hair and place in her hands the reminder offering, the grain offering for jealousy, while he himself holds the bitter water that brings a curse. ¹⁹Then the priest shall put the woman under oath and say to her, "If no other man has slept with you and you have not gone astray and become impure while married to your husband, may this bitter water that brings a curse not harm you. ²⁰But if you have gone astray while married to your husband and you have defiled yourself by sleeping with a man other than your husband"— ²¹here the priest is to put the woman under this curse of the oath— "may the Lord cause your people to curse and denounce you when he causes your thigh to waste away and your abdomen to swell.*d* ²²May this water that brings a curse enter your body so that your abdomen swells and your thigh wastes away.*e* "

" 'Then the woman is to say, "Amen. So be it."

²³" 'The priest is to write these curses on a scroll and then wash them off into the bitter water. ²⁴He shall have the woman drink the bitter water that brings a curse, and this water will enter her and cause bitter suffering. ²⁵The priest is to take from her hands the grain offering for jealousy, wave it before the Lord and bring it to the altar. ²⁶The priest is then to take a handful of the grain offering as a memorial offering and burn it on the altar; after that, he is to have the woman drink the water. ²⁷If she has defiled herself and been unfaithful to her husband, then when she is made to drink the water that brings a curse, it will go into her and cause bitter suffering; her abdomen will swell and her thigh waste away,*f* and she will become accursed among her people. ²⁸If, however, the woman has not defiled herself and is free from impurity, she will be cleared of guilt and will be able to have children.

²⁹" 'This, then, is the law of jealousy when a woman goes astray and defiles herself while married to her husband, ³⁰or when feelings of jealousy come over a man because he suspects his wife. The

---

a2 Traditionally *leprosy*; the Hebrew word was used for various diseases affecting the skin—not necessarily leprosy.   *b6* Or *woman commits any wrong common to mankind*   *c15* That is, probably about 2 quarts (about 2 liters)   *d21* Or *causes you to have a miscarrying womb and barrenness*   *e22* Or *body and cause you to be barren and have a miscarrying womb*   *f27* Or *suffering; she will have barrenness and a miscarrying womb* priest is to have her stand before the LORD and is to apply this entire law to her. [31]The husband will be innocent of any wrongdoing, but the woman will bear the consequences of her sin.' "

The Nazirite

6 The LORD said to Moses, [2]"Speak to the Israelites and say to them: 'If a man or woman wants to make a special vow, a vow of separation to the LORD as a Nazirite, [3]he must abstain from wine and other fermented drink and must not drink vinegar made from wine or from other fermented drink. He must not drink grape juice or eat grapes or raisins. [4]As long as he is a Nazirite, he must not eat anything that comes from the grapevine, not even the seeds or skins.

[5]" 'During the entire period of his vow of separation no razor may be used on his head. He must be holy until the period of his separation to the LORD is over; he must let the hair of his head grow long. [6]Throughout the period of his separation to the LORD he must not go near a dead body. [7]Even if his own father or mother or brother or sister dies, he must not make himself ceremonially unclean on account of them, because the symbol of his separation to God is on his head. [8]Throughout the period of his separation he is consecrated to the LORD.

[9]" 'If someone dies suddenly in his presence, thus defiling the hair he has dedicated, he must shave his head on the day of his cleansing—the seventh day. [10]Then on the eighth day he must bring two doves or two young pigeons to the priest at the entrance to the Tent of Meeting. [11]The priest is to offer one as a sin offering and the other as a burnt offering to make atonement for him because he sinned by being in the presence of the dead body. That same day he is to consecrate his head. [12]He must dedicate himself to the LORD for the period of his separation and must bring a year-old male lamb as a guilt offering. The previous days do not count, because he became defiled during his separation.

[13]" 'Now this is the law for the Nazirite when the period of his separation is over. He is to be brought to the entrance to the Tent of Meeting. [14]There he is to present his offerings to the LORD: a year-old male lamb without defect for a burnt offering, a year-old ewe lamb without defect for a

sin offering, a ram without defect for a fellowship offering,[a] [15]together with their grain offerings and drink offerings, and a basket of bread made without yeast— cakes made of fine flour mixed with oil, and wafers spread with oil.

[16]" 'The priest is to present them before the LORD and make the sin offering and the burnt offering. [17]He is to present the basket of unleavened bread and is to sacrifice the ram as a fellowship offering to the LORD, together with its grain offering and drink offering.

[18]" 'Then at the entrance to the Tent of Meeting, the Nazirite must shave off the hair that he dedicated. He is to take the hair and put it in the fire that is under the sacrifice of the fellowship offering.

[19]" 'After the Nazirite has shaved off the hair of his dedication, the priest is to place in his hands a boiled shoulder of the ram, and a cake and a wafer from the basket, both made without yeast. [20]The priest shall then wave them before the LORD as a wave offering; they are holy and belong to the priest, together with the breast that was waved and the thigh that was presented. After that, the Nazirite may drink wine.

[21]" 'This is the law of the Nazirite who vows his offering to the LORD in accordance with his separation, in addition to whatever else he can afford. He must fulfill the vow he has made, according to the law of the Nazirite.' "

The Priestly Blessing

[22]The LORD said to Moses, [23]"Tell Aaron and his sons, 'This is how you are to bless the Israelites. Say to them:

[24]" ' "The LORD bless you
    and keep you;
[25]the LORD make his face shine upon
    you
    and be gracious to you;
[26]the LORD turn his face toward you
    and give you peace." '

[27]"So they will put my name on the Israelites, and I will bless them."

Offerings at the Dedication of the Tabernacle

7 When Moses finished setting up the tabernacle, he anointed it and consecrated it and all its furnishings. He also anointed and consecrated the altar and all its utensils. [2]Then the leaders of Isra-

---

[a]14 Traditionally peace offering; also in verses 17 and 18

el, the heads of families who were the tribal leaders in charge of those who were counted, made offerings. ³They brought as their gifts before the LORD six covered carts and twelve oxen—an ox from each leader and a cart from every two. These they presented before the tabernacle.

⁴The LORD said to Moses, ⁵"Accept these from them, that they may be used in the work at the Tent of Meeting. Give them to the Levites as each man's work requires."

⁶So Moses took the carts and oxen and gave them to the Levites. ⁷He gave two carts and four oxen to the Gershonites, as their work required, ⁸and he gave four carts and eight oxen to the Merarites, as their work required. They were all under the direction of Ithamar son of Aaron, the priest. ⁹But Moses did not give any to the Kohathites, because they were to carry on their shoulders the holy things, for which they were responsible.

¹⁰When the altar was anointed, the leaders brought their offerings for its dedication and presented them before the altar. ¹¹For the LORD had said to Moses, "Each day one leader is to bring his offering for the dedication of the altar."

¹²The one who brought his offering on the first day was Nahshon son of Amminadab of the tribe of Judah. ¹³His offering was one silver plate weighing a hundred and thirty shekels,ᵃ and one silver sprinkling bowl weighing seventy shekels,ᵇ both according to the sanctuary shekel, each filled with fine flour mixed with oil as a grain offering; ¹⁴one gold dish weighing ten shekels,ᶜ filled with incense; ¹⁵one young bull, one ram and one male lamb a year old, for a burnt offering; ¹⁶one male goat for a sin offering; ¹⁷and two oxen, five rams, five male goats and five male lambs a year old, to be sacrificed as a fellowship offering.ᵈ This was the offering of Nahshon son of Amminadab.

¹⁸On the second day Nethanel son of Zuar, the leader of Issachar, brought his offering. ¹⁹The offering he brought was one silver plate weighing a hundred and thirty shekels, and one silver sprin-

kling bowl weighing seventy shekels, both according to the sanctuary shekel, each filled with fine flour mixed with oil as a grain offering; ²⁰one gold dish weighing ten shekels, filled with incense; ²¹one young bull, one ram and one male lamb a year old, for a burnt offering; ²²one male goat for a sin offering; ²³and two oxen, five rams, five male goats and five male lambs a year old, to be sacrificed as a fellowship offering. This was the offering of Nethanel son of Zuar.

²⁴On the third day, Eliab son of Helon, the leader of the people of Zebulun, brought his offering. ²⁵His offering was one silver plate weighing a hundred and thirty shekels, and one silver sprinkling bowl weighing seventy shekels, both according to the sanctuary shekel, each filled with fine flour mixed with oil as a grain offering; ²⁶one gold dish weighing ten shekels, filled with incense; ²⁷one young bull, one ram and one male lamb a year old, for a burnt offering; ²⁸one male goat for a sin offering; ²⁹and two oxen, five rams, five male goats and five male lambs a year old, to be sacrificed as a fellowship offering. This was the offering of Eliab son of Helon.

³⁰On the fourth day Elizur son of Shedeur, the leader of the people of Reuben, brought his offering. ³¹His offering was one silver plate weighing a hundred and thirty shekels, and one silver sprinkling bowl weighing seventy shekels, both according to the sanctuary shekel, each filled with fine flour mixed with oil as a grain offering; ³²one gold dish weighing ten shekels, filled with incense; ³³one young bull, one ram and one male lamb a year old, for a burnt offering; ³⁴one male goat for a sin offering; ³⁵and two oxen, five rams, five male goats and five male lambs a year old, to be sacrificed as a fellowship offering. This was the offering of Elizur son of Shedeur.

³⁶On the fifth day Shelumiel son of Zuri-

ᵃ13 That is, about 3 1/4 pounds (about 1.5 kilograms); also elsewhere in this chapter   ᵇ13 That is, about 1 3/4 pounds (about 0.8 kilogram); also elsewhere in this chapter   ᶜ14 That is, about 4 ounces (about 110 grams); also elsewhere in this chapter   ᵈ17 Traditionally *peace offering*; also elsewhere in this chapter shaddai, the leader of the people of Simeon, brought his offering.

37His offering was one silver plate weighing a hundred and thirty shekels, and one silver sprinkling bowl weighing seventy shekels, both according to the sanctuary shekel, each filled with fine flour mixed with oil as a grain offering; 38one gold dish weighing ten shekels, filled with incense; 39one young bull, one ram and one male lamb a year old, for a burnt offering; 40one male goat for a sin offering; 41and two oxen, five rams, five male goats and five male lambs a year old, to be sacrificed as a fellowship offering. This was the offering of Shelumiel son of Zurishaddai.

42On the sixth day Eliasaph son of Deuel, the leader of the people of Gad, brought his offering.

43His offering was one silver plate weighing a hundred and thirty shekels, and one silver sprinkling bowl weighing seventy shekels, both according to the sanctuary shekel, each filled with fine flour mixed with oil as a grain offering; 44one gold dish weighing ten shekels, filled with incense; 45one young bull, one ram and one male lamb a year old, for a burnt offering; 46one male goat for a sin offering; 47and two oxen, five rams, five male goats and five male lambs a year old, to be sacrificed as a fellowship offering. This was the offering of Eliasaph son of Deuel.

48On the seventh day Elishama son of Ammihud, the leader of the people of Ephraim, brought his offering.

49His offering was one silver plate weighing a hundred and thirty shekels, and one silver sprinkling bowl weighing seventy shekels, both according to the sanctuary shekel, each filled with fine flour mixed with oil as a grain offering; 50one gold dish weighing ten shekels, filled with incense; 51one young bull, one ram and one male lamb a year old, for a burnt offering; 52one male goat for a sin offering; 53and two oxen, five rams, five male goats and five male lambs a year old, to be sacrificed as a fellowship offering. This was the offering of Elishama son of Ammihud.

54On the eighth day Gamaliel son of Pe-

dahzur, the leader of the people of Manasseh, brought his offering.

55His offering was one silver plate weighing a hundred and thirty shekels, and one silver sprinkling bowl weighing seventy shekels, both according to the sanctuary shekel, each filled with fine flour mixed with oil as a grain offering; 56one gold dish weighing ten shekels, filled with incense; 57one young bull, one ram and one male lamb a year old, for a burnt offering; 58one male goat for a sin offering; 59and two oxen, five rams, five male goats and five male lambs a year old, to be sacrificed as a fellowship offering. This was the offering of Gamaliel son of Pedahzur.

60On the ninth day Abidan son of Gideoni, the leader of the people of Benjamin, brought his offering.

61His offering was one silver plate weighing a hundred and thirty shekels, and one silver sprinkling bowl weighing seventy shekels, both according to the sanctuary shekel, each filled with fine flour mixed with oil as a grain offering; 62one gold dish weighing ten shekels, filled with incense; 63one young bull, one ram and one male lamb a year old, for a burnt offering; 64one male goat for a sin offering; 65and two oxen, five rams, five male goats and five male lambs a year old, to be sacrificed as a fellowship offering. This was the offering of Abidan son of Gideoni.

66On the tenth day Ahiezer son of Ammishaddai, the leader of the people of Dan, brought his offering.

67His offering was one silver plate weighing a hundred and thirty shekels, and one silver sprinkling bowl weighing seventy shekels, both according to the sanctuary shekel, each filled with fine flour mixed with oil as a grain offering; 68one gold dish weighing ten shekels, filled with incense; 69one young bull, one ram and one male lamb a year old, for a burnt offering; 70one male goat for a sin offering; 71and two oxen, five rams, five male goats and five male lambs a year old, to be sacrificed as a fellowship offering. This was the offering of Ahiezer son of Ammishaddai.

72On the eleventh day Pagiel son of Ocran, the leader of the people of Asher, brought his offering.

73His offering was one silver plate weighing a hundred and thirty shekels, and one silver sprinkling bowl weighing seventy shekels, both according to the sanctuary shekel, each filled with fine flour mixed with oil as a grain offering; 74one gold dish weighing ten shekels, filled with incense; 75one young bull, one ram and one male lamb a year old, for a burnt offering; 76one male goat for a sin offering; 77and two oxen, five rams, five male goats and five male lambs a year old, to be sacrificed as a fellowship offering. This was the offering of Pagiel son of Ocran.

78On the twelfth day Ahira son of Enan, the leader of the people of Naphtali, brought his offering.

79His offering was one silver plate weighing a hundred and thirty shekels, and one silver sprinkling bowl weighing seventy shekels, both according to the sanctuary shekel, each filled with fine flour mixed with oil as a grain offering; 80one gold dish weighing ten shekels, filled with incense; 81one young bull, one ram and one male lamb a year old, for a burnt offering; 82one male goat for a sin offering; 83and two oxen, five rams, five male goats and five male lambs a year old, to be sacrificed as a fellowship offering. This was the offering of Ahira son of Enan.

84These were the offerings of the Israelite leaders for the dedication of the altar when it was anointed: twelve silver plates, twelve silver sprinkling bowls and twelve gold dishes. 85Each silver plate weighed a hundred and thirty shekels, and each sprinkling bowl seventy shekels. Altogether, the silver dishes weighed two thousand four hundred shekels,*a* according to the sanctuary shekel. 86The twelve gold dishes filled with incense weighed ten shekels each, according to the sanctuary shekel. Altogether, the gold dishes weighed a hundred and twenty shekels.*b* 87The total number of animals for the burnt offering came to twelve young bulls, twelve rams and twelve male lambs a year old, together with their grain offering. Twelve male goats were used for the sin offering. 88The total number of ani-

mals for the sacrifice of the fellowship offering came to twenty-four oxen, sixty rams, sixty male goats and sixty male lambs a year old. These were the offerings for the dedication of the altar after it was anointed.

89When Moses entered the Tent of Meeting to speak with the LORD, he heard the voice speaking to him from between the two cherubim above the atonement cover on the ark of the Testimony. And he spoke with him.

Setting Up the Lamps

8 The LORD said to Moses, 2"Speak to Aaron and say to him, 'When you set up the seven lamps, they are to light the area in front of the lampstand.' "

3Aaron did so; he set up the lamps so that they faced forward on the lampstand, just as the LORD commanded Moses. 4This is how the lampstand was made: It was made of hammered gold—from its base to its blossoms. The lampstand was made exactly like the pattern the LORD had shown Moses.

The Setting Apart of the Levites

5The LORD said to Moses: 6"Take the Levites from among the other Israelites and make them ceremonially clean. 7To purify them, do this: Sprinkle the water of cleansing on them; then have them shave their whole bodies and wash their clothes, and so purify themselves. 8Have them take a young bull with its grain offering of fine flour mixed with oil; then you are to take a second young bull for a sin offering. 9Bring the Levites to the front of the Tent of Meeting and assemble the whole Israelite community. 10You are to bring the Levites before the LORD, and the Israelites are to lay their hands on them. 11Aaron is to present the Levites before the LORD as a wave offering from the Israelites, so that they may be ready to do the work of the LORD.

12"After the Levites lay their hands on the heads of the bulls, use the one for a sin offering to the LORD and the other for a burnt offering, to make atonement for the Levites. 13Have the Levites stand in front of Aaron and his sons and then present them as a wave offering to the LORD. 14In this way you are to set the Levites apart from the other Israelites, and the Levites will be mine.

---

a85 That is, about 60 pounds (about 28 kilograms)   *b86* That is, about 3 pounds (about 1.4 kilograms)

¹⁵"After you have purified the Levites and presented them as a wave offering, they are to come to do their work at the Tent of Meeting. ¹⁶They are the Israelites who are to be given wholly to me. I have taken them as my own in place of the firstborn, the first male offspring from every Israelite woman. ¹⁷Every firstborn male in Israel, whether man or animal, is mine. When I struck down all the firstborn in Egypt, I set them apart for myself. ¹⁸And I have taken the Levites in place of all the firstborn sons in Israel. ¹⁹Of all the Israelites, I have given the Levites as gifts to Aaron and his sons to do the work at the Tent of Meeting on behalf of the Israelites and to make atonement for them so that no plague will strike the Israelites when they go near the sanctuary."

²⁰Moses, Aaron and the whole Israelite community did with the Levites just as the LORD commanded Moses. ²¹The Levites purified themselves and washed their clothes. Then Aaron presented them as a wave offering before the LORD and made atonement for them to purify them. ²²After that, the Levites came to do their work at the Tent of Meeting under the supervision of Aaron and his sons. They did with the Levites just as the LORD commanded Moses.

²³The LORD said to Moses, ²⁴"This applies to the Levites: Men twenty-five years old or more shall come to take part in the work at the Tent of Meeting, ²⁵but at the age of fifty, they must retire from their regular service and work no longer. ²⁶They may assist their brothers in performing their duties at the Tent of Meeting, but they themselves must not do the work. This, then, is how you are to assign the responsibilities of the Levites."

The Passover

9 The LORD spoke to Moses in the Desert of Sinai in the first month of the second year after they came out of Egypt. He said, ²"Have the Israelites celebrate the Passover at the appointed time. ³Celebrate it at the appointed time, at twilight on the fourteenth day of this month, in accordance with all its rules and regulations."

⁴So Moses told the Israelites to celebrate the Passover, ⁵and they did so in the Desert of Sinai at twilight on the fourteenth day of the first month. The Israelites did everything just as the LORD commanded Moses.

⁶But some of them could not celebrate the Passover on that day because they were ceremonially unclean on account of a dead body. So they came to Moses and Aaron that same day ⁷and said to Moses, "We have become unclean because of a dead body, but why should we be kept from presenting the LORD's offering with the other Israelites at the appointed time?"

⁸Moses answered them, "Wait until I find out what the LORD commands concerning you."

⁹Then the LORD said to Moses, ¹⁰"Tell the Israelites: 'When any of you or your descendants are unclean because of a dead body or are away on a journey, they may still celebrate the LORD's Passover. ¹¹They are to celebrate it on the fourteenth day of the second month at twilight. They are to eat the lamb, together with unleavened bread and bitter herbs. ¹²They must not leave any of it till morning or break any of its bones. When they celebrate the Passover, they must follow all the regulations. ¹³But if a man who is ceremonially clean and not on a journey fails to celebrate the Passover, that person must be cut off from his people because he did not present the LORD's offering at the appointed time. That man will bear the consequences of his sin.

¹⁴" 'An alien living among you who wants to celebrate the LORD's Passover must do so in accordance with its rules and regulations. You must have the same regulations for the alien and the native-born.' "

The Cloud Above the Tabernacle

¹⁵On the day the tabernacle, the Tent of the Testimony, was set up, the cloud covered it. From evening till morning the cloud above the tabernacle looked like fire. ¹⁶That is how it continued to be; the cloud covered it, and at night it looked like fire. ¹⁷Whenever the cloud lifted from above the Tent, the Israelites set out; wherever the cloud settled, the Israelites encamped. ¹⁸At the LORD's command the Israelites set out, and at his command they encamped. As long as the cloud stayed over the tabernacle, they remained in camp. ¹⁹When the cloud remained over the tabernacle a long time, the Israelites obeyed the LORD's order and did not set out. ²⁰Sometimes the cloud was over the tabernacle only a few days; at the LORD's command they would encamp, and then at his command they would set out. ²¹Sometimes the cloud stayed only from

evening till morning, and when it lifted in the morning, they set out. Whether by day or by night, whenever the cloud lifted, they set out. ²²Whether the cloud stayed over the tabernacle for two days or a month or a year, the Israelites would remain in camp and not set out; but when it lifted, they would set out. ²³At the LORD's command they encamped, and at the LORD's command they set out. They obeyed the LORD's order, in accordance with his command through Moses.

The Silver Trumpets

10 The LORD said to Moses: ²"Make two trumpets of hammered silver, and use them for calling the community together and for having the camps set out. ³When both are sounded, the whole community is to assemble before you at the entrance to the Tent of Meeting. ⁴If only one is sounded, the leaders—the heads of the clans of Israel—are to assemble before you. ⁵When a trumpet blast is sounded, the tribes camping on

THURSDAY

VERSE FOR THE DAY:
Numbers 9:19

AUTHOR:
Millie Stamm

PASSAGE FOR THE DAY:
Numbers 9:15–23

Steps and Stops

THE children of Israel had been told to watch the cloud for guidance. But there were also times when the cloud indicated that they were to wait.

The wilderness was not the most delightful place in which to wait. The barrenness of the desert was not inviting. Waiting in itself is not easy. Regardless of their strength and eagerness to start out again, regardless of their impatience to be on the way, the Israelites did not move until God, by means of the cloud, directed them to do so. It may not have been difficult to wait a short time. But in the above verse of Scripture we read that they had to wait "a long time." This was no doubt difficult. It was the test of their obedience.

Sometimes we are kept waiting, too. We may be in the midst of heartaches, of problems, of trials, of temptations when we see the cloud stop and wait. Sometimes our waiting is for a short period. We may, on the other hand, be kept waiting for a long time. But we dare not move until he moves us.

There are times when we seem settled in a comfortable place. We are happy and contented. Suddenly the cloud begins to move. We may not want to move, yet we will have his blessing only if we willingly move with his cloud.

If the LORD delights in a man's way,
he makes his steps firm (Psalm 37:23).

Both the steps and the stops of our lives are ordered by the Lord. The important thing is for us to follow where he leads.

Additional Scripture Readings:
Exodus 14:14–15; Titus 2:11–14

Go to page 152 for your next devotional reading.

the east are to set out. 6At the sounding of a second blast, the camps on the south are to set out. The blast will be the signal for setting out. 7To gather the assembly, blow the trumpets, but not with the same signal.

8"The sons of Aaron, the priests, are to blow the trumpets. This is to be a lasting ordinance for you and the generations to come. 9When you go into battle in your own land against an enemy who is oppressing you, sound a blast on the trumpets. Then you will be remembered by the LORD your God and rescued from your enemies. 10Also at your times of rejoicing— your appointed feasts and New Moon festivals—you are to sound the trumpets over your burnt offerings and fellowship offerings,a and they will be a memorial for you before your God. I am the LORD your God."

The Israelites Leave Sinai

11On the twentieth day of the second month of the second year, the cloud lifted from above the tabernacle of the Testimony. 12Then the Israelites set out from the Desert of Sinai and traveled from place to place until the cloud came to rest in the Desert of Paran. 13They set out, this first time, at the LORD's command through Moses.

14The divisions of the camp of Judah went first, under their standard. Nahshon son of Amminadab was in command. 15Nethanel son of Zuar was over the division of the tribe of Issachar, 16and Eliab son of Helon was over the division of the tribe of Zebulun. 17Then the tabernacle was taken down, and the Gershonites and Merarites, who carried it, set out.

18The divisions of the camp of Reuben went next, under their standard. Elizur son of Shedeur was in command. 19Shelumiel son of Zurishaddai was over the division of the tribe of Simeon, 20and Eliasaph son of Deuel was over the division of the tribe of Gad. 21Then the Kohathites set out, carrying the holy things. The tabernacle was to be set up before they arrived.

22The divisions of the camp of Ephraim went next, under their standard. Elishama son of Ammihud was in command. 23Gamaliel son of Pedahzur was over the division of the tribe of Manasseh, 24and Abidan son of Gideoni was over the division of the tribe of Benjamin.

25Finally, as the rear guard for all the units, the divisions of the camp of Dan set out, under their standard. Ahiezer son of Ammishaddai was in command. 26Pagiel son of Ocran was over the division of the tribe of Asher, 27and Ahira son of Enan was over the division of the tribe of Naphtali. 28This was the order of march for the Israelite divisions as they set out.

29Now Moses said to Hobab son of Reuel the Midianite, Moses' father-in-law, "We are setting out for the place about which the LORD said, 'I will give it to you.' Come with us and we will treat you well, for the LORD has promised good things to Israel."

30He answered, "No, I will not go; I am going back to my own land and my own people."

31But Moses said, "Please do not leave us. You know where we should camp in the desert, and you can be our eyes. 32If you come with us, we will share with you whatever good things the LORD gives us."

33So they set out from the mountain of the LORD and traveled for three days. The ark of the covenant of the LORD went before them during those three days to find them a place to rest. 34The cloud of the LORD was over them by day when they set out from the camp.

35Whenever the ark set out, Moses said,

"Rise up, O LORD!
　May your enemies be scattered;
　may your foes flee before you."

36Whenever it came to rest, he said,

"Return, O LORD,
　to the countless thousands of
　　Israel."

Fire From the LORD

11 Now the people complained about their hardships in the hearing of the LORD, and when he heard them his anger was aroused. Then fire from the LORD burned among them and consumed some of the outskirts of the camp. 2When the people cried out to Moses, he prayed to the LORD and the fire died down. 3So that place was called Taberah,b because fire from the LORD had burned among them.

Quail From the LORD

4The rabble with them began to crave other food, and again the Israelites start-

---

a10 Traditionally peace offerings　　b3 Taberah means burning.

ed wailing and said, "If only we had meat to eat! ⁵We remember the fish we ate in Egypt at no cost—also the cucumbers, melons, leeks, onions and garlic. ⁶But now we have lost our appetite; we never see anything but this manna!"

⁷The manna was like coriander seed and looked like resin. ⁸The people went around gathering it, and then ground it in a handmill or crushed it in a mortar. They cooked it in a pot or made it into cakes. And it tasted like something made with olive oil. ⁹When the dew settled on the camp at night, the manna also came down.

¹⁰Moses heard the people of every family wailing, each at the entrance to his tent. The LORD became exceedingly angry, and Moses was troubled. ¹¹He asked the LORD, "Why have you brought this trouble on your servant? What have I done to displease you that you put the burden of all these people on me? ¹²Did I conceive all these people? Did I give them birth? Why do you tell me to carry them in my arms, as a nurse carries an infant, to the land you promised on oath to their forefathers? ¹³Where can I get meat for all these people? They keep wailing to me, 'Give us meat to eat!' ¹⁴I cannot carry all these people by myself; the burden is too heavy for me. ¹⁵If this is how you are going to treat me, put me to death right now—if I have found favor in your eyes—and do not let me face my own ruin."

¹⁶The LORD said to Moses: "Bring me seventy of Israel's elders who are known to you as leaders and officials among the people. Have them come to the Tent of Meeting, that they may stand there with you. ¹⁷I will come down and speak with you there, and I will take of the Spirit that is on you and put the Spirit on them. They will help you carry the burden of the people so that you will not have to carry it alone.

¹⁸"Tell the people: 'Consecrate yourselves in preparation for tomorrow, when you will eat meat. The LORD heard you when you wailed, "If only we had meat to eat! We were better off in Egypt!" Now the LORD will give you meat, and you will eat it. ¹⁹You will not eat it for just one day, or two days, or five, ten or twenty days, ²⁰but for a whole month—until it comes out of your nostrils and you loathe it—because

you have rejected the LORD, who is among you, and have wailed before him, saying, "Why did we ever leave Egypt?" ' "

²¹But Moses said, "Here I am among six hundred thousand men on foot, and you say, 'I will give them meat to eat for a whole month!' ²²Would they have enough if flocks and herds were slaughtered for them? Would they have enough if all the fish in the sea were caught for them?"

²³The LORD answered Moses, "Is the LORD's arm too short? You will now see whether or not what I say will come true for you."

²⁴So Moses went out and told the people what the LORD had said. He brought together seventy of their elders and had them stand around the Tent. ²⁵Then the LORD came down in the cloud and spoke with him, and he took of the Spirit that was on him and put the Spirit on the seventy elders. When the Spirit rested on them, they prophesied, but they did not do so again.ᵃ

²⁶However, two men, whose names were Eldad and Medad, had remained in the camp. They were listed among the elders, but did not go out to the Tent. Yet the Spirit also rested on them, and they prophesied in the camp. ²⁷A young man ran and told Moses, "Eldad and Medad are prophesying in the camp."

²⁸Joshua son of Nun, who had been Moses' aide since youth, spoke up and said, "Moses, my lord, stop them!"

²⁹But Moses replied, "Are you jealous for my sake? I wish that all the LORD's people were prophets and that the LORD would put his Spirit on them!" ³⁰Then Moses and the elders of Israel returned to the camp.

³¹Now a wind went out from the LORD and drove quail in from the sea. It brought themᵇ down all around the camp to about three feetᶜ above the ground, as far as a day's walk in any direction. ³²All that day and night and all the next day the people went out and gathered quail. No one gathered less than ten homers.ᵈ Then they spread them out all around the camp. ³³But while the meat was still between their teeth and before it could be consumed, the anger of the LORD burned against the people, and he struck them with a severe plague. ³⁴Therefore the

---

ᵃ25 Or prophesied and continued to do so   ᵇ31 Or They flew   ᶜ31 Hebrew two cubits (about 1 meter)   ᵈ32 That is, probably about 60 bushels (about 2.2 kiloliters) place was named Kibroth Hattaavah,[a] because there they buried the people who had craved other food.

[35]From Kibroth Hattaavah the people traveled to Hazeroth and stayed there.

Miriam and Aaron Oppose Moses

12 Miriam and Aaron began to talk against Moses because of his Cushite wife, for he had married a Cushite. [2]"Has the LORD spoken only through Moses?" they asked. "Hasn't he also spoken through us?" And the LORD heard this.

[3](Now Moses was a very humble man, more humble than anyone else on the face of the earth.)

[4]At once the LORD said to Moses, Aaron and Miriam, "Come out to the Tent of Meeting, all three of you." So the three of them came out. [5]Then the LORD came down in a pillar of cloud; he stood at the entrance to the Tent and summoned Aaron and Miriam. When both of them stepped forward, [6]he said, "Listen to my words:

"When a prophet of the LORD is
    among you,
  I reveal myself to him in visions,
  I speak to him in dreams.
[7]But this is not true of my servant
    Moses;
  he is faithful in all my house.
[8]With him I speak face to face,
  clearly and not in riddles;
  he sees the form of the LORD.
Why then were you not afraid
  to speak against my servant
    Moses?"

[9]The anger of the LORD burned against them, and he left them.

[10]When the cloud lifted from above the Tent, there stood Miriam—leprous,[b] like snow. Aaron turned toward her and saw that she had leprosy; [11]and he said to Moses, "Please, my lord, do not hold against us the sin we have so foolishly committed. [12]Do not let her be like a stillborn infant coming from its mother's womb with its flesh half eaten away."

[13]So Moses cried out to the LORD, "O God, please heal her!"

[14]The LORD replied to Moses, "If her father had spit in her face, would she not have been in disgrace for seven days? Confine her outside the camp for seven days; after that she can be brought back."
[15]So Miriam was confined outside the camp for seven days, and the people did not move on till she was brought back. [16]After that, the people left Hazeroth and encamped in the Desert of Paran.

Exploring Canaan

13 The LORD said to Moses, [2]"Send some men to explore the land of Canaan, which I am giving to the Israelites. From each ancestral tribe send one of its leaders."

[3]So at the LORD's command Moses sent them out from the Desert of Paran. All of them were leaders of the Israelites. [4]These are their names:

from the tribe of Reuben, Shammua
  son of Zaccur;
[5]from the tribe of Simeon, Shaphat
  son of Hori;
[6]from the tribe of Judah, Caleb son of
  Jephunneh;
[7]from the tribe of Issachar, Igal son of
  Joseph;
[8]from the tribe of Ephraim, Hoshea
  son of Nun;
[9]from the tribe of Benjamin, Palti son
  of Raphu;
[10]from the tribe of Zebulun, Gaddiel
  son of Sodi;
[11]from the tribe of Manasseh (a tribe of
  Joseph), Gaddi son of Susi;
[12]from the tribe of Dan, Ammiel son of
  Gemalli;
[13]from the tribe of Asher, Sethur son of
  Michael;
[14]from the tribe of Naphtali, Nahbi son
  of Vophsi;
[15]from the tribe of Gad, Geuel son of
  Maki.

[16]These are the names of the men Moses sent to explore the land. (Moses gave Hoshea son of Nun the name Joshua.)

[17]When Moses sent them to explore Canaan, he said, "Go up through the Negev and on into the hill country. [18]See what the land is like and whether the people who live there are strong or weak, few or many. [19]What kind of land do they live in? Is it good or bad? What kind of towns do they live in? Are they unwalled or fortified? [20]How is the soil? Is it fertile or poor? Are there trees on it or not? Do your best to bring back some of the fruit of the

---

[a]34 *Kibroth Hattaavah* means *graves of craving.*   [b]10 The Hebrew word was used for various diseases
affecting the skin—not necessarily leprosy.

land." (It was the season for the first ripe grapes.)

21So they went up and explored the land from the Desert of Zin as far as Rehob, toward Lebo*a* Hamath. 22They went up through the Negev and came to Hebron, where Ahiman, Sheshai and Talmai, the descendants of Anak, lived. (Hebron had been built seven years before Zoan in Egypt.) 23When they reached the Valley of Eshcol,*b* they cut off a branch bearing a single cluster of grapes. Two of them carried it on a pole between them, along with some pomegranates and figs. 24That place was called the Valley of Eshcol because of the cluster of grapes the Israelites cut off there. 25At the end of forty days they returned from exploring the land.

Report on the Exploration

26They came back to Moses and Aaron and the whole Israelite community at Kadesh in the Desert of Paran. There they reported to them and to the whole assembly and showed them the fruit of the land. 27They gave Moses this account: "We went into the land to which you sent us, and it does flow with milk and honey! Here is its fruit. 28But the people who live there are powerful, and the cities are fortified and very large. We even saw descendants of Anak there. 29The Amalekites live in the Negev; the Hittites, Jebusites and Amorites live in the hill country; and the Canaanites live near the sea and along the Jordan."

30Then Caleb silenced the people before Moses and said, "We should go up and take possession of the land, for we can certainly do it."

31But the men who had gone up with him said, "We can't attack those people; they are stronger than we are." 32And they spread among the Israelites a bad report about the land they had explored. They said, "The land we explored devours those living in it. All the people we saw there are of great size. 33We saw the Nephilim there (the descendants of Anak come from the Nephilim). We seemed like grasshoppers in our own eyes, and we looked the same to them."

The People Rebel

14 That night all the people of the community raised their voices and wept aloud. 2All the Israelites grumbled against Moses and Aaron, and the whole assembly said to them, "If only we had died in Egypt! Or in this desert! 3Why is the LORD bringing us to this land only to let us fall by the sword? Our wives and children will be taken as plunder. Wouldn't it be better for us to go back to Egypt?" 4And they said to each other, "We should choose a leader and go back to Egypt."

5Then Moses and Aaron fell facedown in front of the whole Israelite assembly gathered there. 6Joshua son of Nun and Caleb son of Jephunneh, who were among those who had explored the land, tore their clothes 7and said to the entire Israelite assembly, "The land we passed through and explored is exceedingly good. 8If the LORD is pleased with us, he will lead us into that land, a land flowing with milk and honey, and will give it to us. 9Only do not rebel against the LORD. And do not be afraid of the people of the land, because we will swallow them up. Their protection is gone, but the LORD is with us. Do not be afraid of them."

10But the whole assembly talked about stoning them. Then the glory of the LORD appeared at the Tent of Meeting to all the Israelites. 11The LORD said to Moses, "How long will these people treat me with contempt? How long will they refuse to believe in me, in spite of all the miraculous signs I have performed among them? 12I will strike them down with a plague and destroy them, but I will make you into a nation greater and stronger than they."

13Moses said to the LORD, "Then the Egyptians will hear about it! By your power you brought these people up from among them. 14And they will tell the inhabitants of this land about it. They have already heard that you, O LORD, are with these people and that you, O LORD, have been seen face to face, that your cloud stays over them, and that you go before them in a pillar of cloud by day and a pillar of fire by night. 15If you put these people to death all at one time, the nations who have heard this report about you will say, 16'The LORD was not able to bring these people into the land he promised them on oath; so he slaughtered them in the desert.'

17"Now may the Lord's strength be displayed, just as you have declared: 18'The LORD is slow to anger, abounding in love

---

a21 Or *toward the entrance to*   *b23* Eshcol means *cluster;* also in verse 24.

and forgiving sin and rebellion. Yet he does not leave the guilty unpunished; he punishes the children for the sin of the fathers to the third and fourth generation.' ¹⁹In accordance with your great love, forgive the sin of these people, just as you have pardoned them from the time they left Egypt until now."

²⁰The LORD replied, "I have forgiven them, as you asked. ²¹Nevertheless, as surely as I live and as surely as the glory of the LORD fills the whole earth, ²²not one of the men who saw my glory and the miraculous signs I performed in Egypt and in the desert but who disobeyed me and tested me ten times— ²³not one of them will ever see the land I promised on oath to their forefathers. No one who has treated me with contempt will ever see it. ²⁴But because my servant Caleb has a different spirit and follows me wholeheartedly, I will bring him into the land he went to, and his descendants will inherit it. ²⁵Since the Amalekites and Canaanites are living in the valleys, turn back tomorrow and set out toward the desert along the route to the Red Sea. ª"

²⁶The LORD said to Moses and Aaron:

ª25 Hebrew *Yam Suph*; that is, Sea of Reeds

FRIDAY

VERSE FOR THE DAY:
Numbers 14:31

AUTHOR:
Jeanette Lockerbie

PASSAGE FOR THE DAY:
Numbers 14:1–4,31

But My Children

REAL concern for one's children, as evidenced in verse three, is commendable. But how could these people have so soon forgotten the promises of God? How could they be so woefully lacking in trust in the almighty God?

Can we learn from their experience, that God is infinitely more concerned over our children than we can ever be? That he is abundantly able to care for them in any and every situation to which he leads us?

A Christian couple, parents of a teenage son and daughter, were convinced God was calling them to leave a lucrative position to serve him where the rewards and "security" were almost nil. They were heckled by head-wagging, would-be advisers.

"This may be all right for you, but what about your children," they would say. "Your brilliant son, your talented daughter? Do you realize you will never be able to send them to college? Their potential will never be realized because you're making this move."

Years passed and the very people who made these dire predictions witnessed the opportunities afforded the young people for whose futures they feared. Honors have been heaped on the Christian young man. His sister, like her parents, has done a phenomenal work for God in a distant land.

Our children—and we ourselves—are never safer, or more blessed, than in the place of God's appointment.

Additional Scripture Readings:
Proverbs 22:6; Isaiah 49:15–23

Go to page 158 for your next devotional reading.

²⁷"How long will this wicked community grumble against me? I have heard the complaints of these grumbling Israelites. ²⁸So tell them, 'As surely as I live, declares the LORD, I will do to you the very things I heard you say: ²⁹In this desert your bodies will fall—every one of you twenty years old or more who was counted in the census and who has grumbled against me. ³⁰Not one of you will enter the land I swore with uplifted hand to make your home, except Caleb son of Jephunneh and Joshua son of Nun. ³¹As for your children that you said would be taken as plunder, I will bring them in to enjoy the land you have rejected. ³²But you —your bodies will fall in this desert. ³³Your children will be shepherds here for forty years, suffering for your unfaithfulness, until the last of your bodies lies in the desert. ³⁴For forty years—one year for each of the forty days you explored the land—you will suffer for your sins and know what it is like to have me against you.' ³⁵I, the LORD, have spoken, and I will surely do these things to this whole wicked community, which has banded together against me. They will meet their end in this desert; here they will die."

³⁶So the men Moses had sent to explore the land, who returned and made the whole community grumble against him by spreading a bad report about it— ³⁷these men responsible for spreading the bad report about the land were struck down and died of a plague before the LORD. ³⁸Of the men who went to explore the land, only Joshua son of Nun and Caleb son of Jephunneh survived.

³⁹When Moses reported this to all the Israelites, they mourned bitterly. ⁴⁰Early the next morning they went up toward the high hill country. "We have sinned," they said. "We will go up to the place the LORD promised."

⁴¹But Moses said, "Why are you disobeying the LORD's command? This will not succeed! ⁴²Do not go up, because the LORD is not with you. You will be defeated by your enemies, ⁴³for the Amalekites and Canaanites will face you there. Because you have turned away from the LORD, he will not be with you and you will fall by the sword."

⁴⁴Nevertheless, in their presumption they went up toward the high hill country, though neither Moses nor the ark of the LORD's covenant moved from the camp. ⁴⁵Then the Amalekites and Canaanites who lived in that hill country came down and attacked them and beat them down all the way to Hormah.

Supplementary Offerings

15 The LORD said to Moses, ²"Speak to the Israelites and say to them: 'After you enter the land I am giving you as a home ³and you present to the LORD offerings made by fire, from the herd or the flock, as an aroma pleasing to the LORD—whether burnt offerings or sacrifices, for special vows or freewill offerings or festival offerings— ⁴then the one who brings his offering shall present to the LORD a grain offering of a tenth of an ephah*ᵃ* of fine flour mixed with a quarter of a hin*ᵇ* of oil. ⁵With each lamb for the burnt offering or the sacrifice, prepare a quarter of a hin of wine as a drink offering.

⁶" 'With a ram prepare a grain offering of two-tenths of an ephah*ᶜ* of fine flour mixed with a third of a hin*ᵈ* of oil, ⁷and a third of a hin of wine as a drink offering. Offer it as an aroma pleasing to the LORD.

⁸" 'When you prepare a young bull as a burnt offering or sacrifice, for a special vow or a fellowship offering*ᵉ* to the LORD, ⁹bring with the bull a grain offering of three-tenths of an ephah*ᶠ* of fine flour mixed with half a hin*ᵍ* of oil. ¹⁰Also bring half a hin of wine as a drink offering. It will be an offering made by fire, an aroma pleasing to the LORD. ¹¹Each bull or ram, each lamb or young goat, is to be prepared in this manner. ¹²Do this for each one, for as many as you prepare.

¹³" 'Everyone who is native-born must do these things in this way when he brings an offering made by fire as an aroma pleasing to the LORD. ¹⁴For the generations to come, whenever an alien or anyone else living among you presents an offering made by fire as an aroma pleasing to the LORD, he must do exactly as you do. ¹⁵The community is to have the same rules for you and for the alien living among you; this is a lasting ordinance for the generations to come. You and the alien shall be the same before the LORD:

ᵃ4 That is, probably about 2 quarts (about 2 liters) also in verse 5   *ᶜ6* That is, probably about 4 quarts (about 4.5 liters)   *ᵈ6* That is, probably about 1 1/4 quarts (about 1.2 liters); also in verse 7   *ᵇ4* That is, probably about 1 quart (about 1 liter); *ᵉ8* Traditionally *peace offering*   *ᶠ9* That is, probably about 6 quarts (about 6.5 liters)   *ᵍ9* That is, probably about 2 quarts (about 2 liters); also in verse 10

16The same laws and regulations will apply both to you and to the alien living among you.' "

17The LORD said to Moses, 18"Speak to the Israelites and say to them: 'When you enter the land to which I am taking you 19and you eat the food of the land, present a portion as an offering to the LORD. 20Present a cake from the first of your ground meal and present it as an offering from the threshing floor. 21Throughout the generations to come you are to give this offering to the LORD from the first of your ground meal.

Offerings for Unintentional Sins

22" 'Now if you unintentionally fail to keep any of these commands the LORD gave Moses— 23any of the LORD's commands to you through him, from the day the LORD gave them and continuing through the generations to come— 24and if this is done unintentionally without the community being aware of it, then the whole community is to offer a young bull for a burnt offering as an aroma pleasing to the LORD, along with its prescribed grain offering and drink offering, and a male goat for a sin offering. 25The priest is to make atonement for the whole Israelite community, and they will be forgiven, for it was not intentional and they have brought to the LORD for their wrong an offering made by fire and a sin offering. 26The whole Israelite community and the aliens living among them will be forgiven, because all the people were involved in the unintentional wrong.

27" 'But if just one person sins unintentionally, he must bring a year-old female goat for a sin offering. 28The priest is to make atonement before the LORD for the one who erred by sinning unintentionally, and when atonement has been made for him, he will be forgiven. 29One and the same law applies to everyone who sins unintentionally, whether he is a native-born Israelite or an alien.

30" 'But anyone who sins defiantly, whether native-born or alien, blasphemes the LORD, and that person must be cut off from his people. 31Because he has despised the LORD's word and broken his commands, that person must surely be cut off; his guilt remains on him.' "

The Sabbath-Breaker Put to Death

32While the Israelites were in the desert, a man was found gathering wood on the Sabbath day. 33Those who found him gathering wood brought him to Moses and Aaron and the whole assembly, 34and they kept him in custody, because it was not clear what should be done to him. 35Then the LORD said to Moses, "The man must die. The whole assembly must stone him outside the camp." 36So the assembly took him outside the camp and stoned him to death, as the LORD commanded Moses.

Tassels on Garments

37The LORD said to Moses, 38"Speak to the Israelites and say to them: 'Throughout the generations to come you are to make tassels on the corners of your garments, with a blue cord on each tassel. 39You will have these tassels to look at and so you will remember all the commands of the LORD, that you may obey them and not prostitute yourselves by going after the lusts of your own hearts and eyes. 40Then you will remember to obey all my commands and will be consecrated to your God. 41I am the LORD your God, who brought you out of Egypt to be your God. I am the LORD your God.' "

Korah, Dathan and Abiram

16 Korah son of Izhar, the son of Kohath, the son of Levi, and certain Reubenites—Dathan and Abiram, sons of Eliab, and On son of Peleth—became insolenta 2and rose up against Moses. With them were 250 Israelite men, well-known community leaders who had been appointed members of the council. 3They came as a group to oppose Moses and Aaron and said to them, "You have gone too far! The whole community is holy, every one of them, and the LORD is with them. Why then do you set yourselves above the LORD's assembly?"

4When Moses heard this, he fell facedown. 5Then he said to Korah and all his followers: "In the morning the LORD will show who belongs to him and who is holy, and he will have that person come near him. The man he chooses he will cause to come near him. 6You, Korah, and all your followers are to do this: Take censers 7and tomorrow put fire and incense in them before the LORD. The man the LORD chooses will be the one who is holy. You Levites have gone too far!"

8Moses also said to Korah, "Now listen,

a1 Or Peleth—took men,

you Levites! 9Isn't it enough for you that the God of Israel has separated you from the rest of the Israelite community and brought you near himself to do the work at the Lord's tabernacle and to stand before the community and minister to them? 10He has brought you and all your fellow Levites near himself, but now you are trying to get the priesthood too. 11It is against the Lord that you and all your followers have banded together. Who is Aaron that you should grumble against him?"

12Then Moses summoned Dathan and Abiram, the sons of Eliab. But they said, "We will not come! 13Isn't it enough that you have brought us up out of a land flowing with milk and honey to kill us in the desert? And now you also want to lord it over us? 14Moreover, you haven't brought us into a land flowing with milk and honey or given us an inheritance of fields and vineyards. Will you gouge out the eyes ofᵃ these men? No, we will not come!"

15Then Moses became very angry and said to the Lord, "Do not accept their offering. I have not taken so much as a donkey from them, nor have I wronged any of them."

16Moses said to Korah, "You and all your followers are to appear before the Lord tomorrow—you and they and Aaron. 17Each man is to take his censer and put incense in it—250 censers in all—and present it before the Lord. You and Aaron are to present your censers also." 18So each man took his censer, put fire and incense in it, and stood with Moses and Aaron at the entrance to the Tent of Meeting. 19When Korah had gathered all his followers in opposition to them at the entrance to the Tent of Meeting, the glory of the Lord appeared to the entire assembly. 20The Lord said to Moses and Aaron, 21"Separate yourselves from this assembly so I can put an end to them at once."

22But Moses and Aaron fell facedown and cried out, "O God, God of the spirits of all mankind, will you be angry with the entire assembly when only one man sins?"

23Then the Lord said to Moses, 24"Say to the assembly, 'Move away from the tents of Korah, Dathan and Abiram.' "

25Moses got up and went to Dathan and Abiram, and the elders of Israel followed him. 26He warned the assembly, "Move back from the tents of these wicked men!

Do not touch anything belonging to them, or you will be swept away because of all their sins." 27So they moved away from the tents of Korah, Dathan and Abiram. Dathan and Abiram had come out and were standing with their wives, children and little ones at the entrances to their tents.

28Then Moses said, "This is how you will know that the Lord has sent me to do all these things and that it was not my idea: 29If these men die a natural death and experience only what usually happens to men, then the Lord has not sent me. 30But if the Lord brings about something totally new, and the earth opens its mouth and swallows them, with everything that belongs to them, and they go down alive into the grave,ᵇ then you will know that these men have treated the Lord with contempt."

31As soon as he finished saying all this, the ground under them split apart 32and the earth opened its mouth and swallowed them, with their households and all Korah's men and all their possessions. 33They went down alive into the grave, with everything they owned; the earth closed over them, and they perished and were gone from the community. 34At their cries, all the Israelites around them fled, shouting, "The earth is going to swallow us too!"

35And fire came out from the Lord and consumed the 250 men who were offering the incense.

36The Lord said to Moses, 37"Tell Eleazar son of Aaron, the priest, to take the censers out of the smoldering remains and scatter the coals some distance away, for the censers are holy— 38the censers of the men who sinned at the cost of their lives. Hammer the censers into sheets to overlay the altar, for they were presented before the Lord and have become holy. Let them be a sign to the Israelites."

39So Eleazar the priest collected the bronze censers brought by those who had been burned up, and he had them hammered out to overlay the altar, 40as the Lord directed him through Moses. This was to remind the Israelites that no one except a descendant of Aaron should come to burn incense before the Lord, or he would become like Korah and his followers.

41The next day the whole Israelite community grumbled against Moses and Aar-

---

ᵃ14 Or *you make slaves of*; or *you deceive*   ᵇ30 Hebrew *Sheol*; also in verse 33 on. "You have killed the LORD's people," they said.

⁴²But when the assembly gathered in opposition to Moses and Aaron and turned toward the Tent of Meeting, suddenly the cloud covered it and the glory of the LORD appeared. ⁴³Then Moses and Aaron went to the front of the Tent of Meeting, ⁴⁴and the LORD said to Moses, ⁴⁵"Get away from this assembly so I can put an end to them at once." And they fell facedown.

⁴⁶Then Moses said to Aaron, "Take your censer and put incense in it, along with fire from the altar, and hurry to the assembly to make atonement for them. Wrath has come out from the LORD; the plague has started." ⁴⁷So Aaron did as Moses said, and ran into the midst of the assembly. The plague had already started among the people, but Aaron offered the incense and made atonement for them. ⁴⁸He stood between the living and the dead, and the plague stopped. ⁴⁹But 14,700 people died from the plague, in addition to those who had died because of Korah. ⁵⁰Then Aaron returned to Moses at the entrance to the Tent of Meeting, for the plague had stopped.

The Budding of Aaron's Staff

17 The LORD said to Moses, ²"Speak to the Israelites and get twelve staffs from them, one from the leader of each of their ancestral tribes. Write the name of each man on his staff. ³On the staff of Levi write Aaron's name, for there must be one staff for the head of each ancestral tribe. ⁴Place them in the Tent of Meeting in front of the Testimony, where I meet with you. ⁵The staff belonging to the man I choose will sprout, and I will rid myself of this constant grumbling against you by the Israelites."

⁶So Moses spoke to the Israelites, and their leaders gave him twelve staffs, one for the leader of each of their ancestral tribes, and Aaron's staff was among them. ⁷Moses placed the staffs before the LORD in the Tent of the Testimony.

⁸The next day Moses entered the Tent of the Testimony and saw that Aaron's staff, which represented the house of Levi, had not only sprouted but had budded, blossomed and produced almonds. ⁹Then Moses brought out all the staffs from the LORD's presence to all the Israelites. They looked at them, and each man took his own staff.

¹⁰The LORD said to Moses, "Put back Aaron's staff in front of the Testimony, to be kept as a sign to the rebellious. This will put an end to their grumbling against me, so that they will not die." ¹¹Moses did just as the LORD commanded him.

¹²The Israelites said to Moses, "We will die! We are lost, we are all lost! ¹³Anyone who even comes near the tabernacle of the LORD will die. Are we all going to die?"

Duties of Priests and Levites

18 The LORD said to Aaron, "You, your sons and your father's family are to bear the responsibility for offenses against the sanctuary, and you and your sons alone are to bear the responsibility for offenses against the priesthood. ²Bring your fellow Levites from your ancestral tribe to join you and assist you when you and your sons minister before the Tent of the Testimony. ³They are to be responsible to you and are to perform all the duties of the Tent, but they must not go near the furnishings of the sanctuary or the altar, or both they and you will die. ⁴They are to join you and be responsible for the care of the Tent of Meeting — all the work at the Tent — and no one else may come near where you are.

⁵"You are to be responsible for the care of the sanctuary and the altar, so that wrath will not fall on the Israelites again. ⁶I myself have selected your fellow Levites from among the Israelites as a gift to you, dedicated to the LORD to do the work at the Tent of Meeting. ⁷But only you and your sons may serve as priests in connection with everything at the altar and inside the curtain. I am giving you the service of the priesthood as a gift. Anyone else who comes near the sanctuary must be put to death."

Offerings for Priests and Levites

⁸Then the LORD said to Aaron, "I myself have put you in charge of the offerings presented to me; all the holy offerings the Israelites give me I give to you and your sons as your portion and regular share. ⁹You are to have the part of the most holy offerings that is kept from the fire. From all the gifts they bring me as most holy offerings, whether grain or sin or guilt offerings, that part belongs to you and your sons. ¹⁰Eat it as something most holy; every male shall eat it. You must regard it as holy.

¹¹"This also is yours: whatever is set aside from the gifts of all the wave offerings of the Israelites. I give this to you and

your sons and daughters as your regular share. Everyone in your household who is ceremonially clean may eat it.

¹²"I give you all the finest olive oil and all the finest new wine and grain they give the Lord as the firstfruits of their harvest. ¹³All the land's firstfruits that they bring to the Lord will be yours. Everyone in your household who is ceremonially clean may eat it.

¹⁴"Everything in Israel that is devoted*ᵃ* to the Lord is yours. ¹⁵The first offspring of every womb, both man and animal, that is offered to the Lord is yours. But you must redeem every firstborn son and every firstborn male of unclean animals. ¹⁶When they are a month old, you must redeem them at the redemption price set at five shekels*ᵇ* of silver, according to the sanctuary shekel, which weighs twenty gerahs.

¹⁷"But you must not redeem the firstborn of an ox, a sheep or a goat; they are holy. Sprinkle their blood on the altar and burn their fat as an offering made by fire, an aroma pleasing to the Lord. ¹⁸Their meat is to be yours, just as the breast of the wave offering and the right thigh are yours. ¹⁹Whatever is set aside from the holy offerings the Israelites present to the Lord I give to you and your sons and daughters as your regular share. It is an everlasting covenant of salt before the Lord for both you and your offspring."

²⁰The Lord said to Aaron, "You will have no inheritance in their land, nor will you have any share among them; I am your share and your inheritance among the Israelites.

²¹"I give to the Levites all the tithes in Israel as their inheritance in return for the work they do while serving at the Tent of Meeting. ²²From now on the Israelites must not go near the Tent of Meeting, or they will bear the consequences of their sin and will die. ²³It is the Levites who are to do the work at the Tent of Meeting and bear the responsibility for offenses against it. This is a lasting ordinance for the generations to come. They will receive no inheritance among the Israelites. ²⁴Instead, I give to the Levites as their inheritance the tithes that the Israelites present as an offering to the Lord. That is why I said concerning them: 'They will have no inheritance among the Israelites.' "

²⁵The Lord said to Moses, ²⁶"Speak to the Levites and say to them: 'When you receive from the Israelites the tithe I give you as your inheritance, you must present a tenth of that tithe as the Lord's offering. ²⁷Your offering will be reckoned to you as grain from the threshing floor or juice from the winepress. ²⁸In this way you also will present an offering to the Lord from all the tithes you receive from the Israelites. From these tithes you must give the Lord's portion to Aaron the priest. ²⁹You must present as the Lord's portion the best and holiest part of everything given to you.'

³⁰"Say to the Levites: 'When you present the best part, it will be reckoned to you as the product of the threshing floor or the winepress. ³¹You and your households may eat the rest of it anywhere, for it is your wages for your work at the Tent of Meeting. ³²By presenting the best part of it you will not be guilty in this matter; then you will not defile the holy offerings of the Israelites, and you will not die.' "

The Water of Cleansing

19 The Lord said to Moses and Aaron: ²"This is a requirement of the law that the Lord has commanded: Tell the Israelites to bring you a red heifer without defect or blemish and that has never been under a yoke. ³Give it to Eleazar the priest; it is to be taken outside the camp and slaughtered in his presence. ⁴Then Eleazar the priest is to take some of its blood on his finger and sprinkle it seven times toward the front of the Tent of Meeting. ⁵While he watches, the heifer is to be burned—its hide, flesh, blood and offal. ⁶The priest is to take some cedar wood, hyssop and scarlet wool and throw them onto the burning heifer. ⁷After that, the priest must wash his clothes and bathe himself with water. He may then come into the camp, but he will be ceremonially unclean till evening. ⁸The man who burns it must also wash his clothes and bathe with water, and he too will be unclean till evening.

⁹"A man who is clean shall gather up the ashes of the heifer and put them in a ceremonially clean place outside the camp. They shall be kept by the Israelite community for use in the water of cleansing; it is for purification from sin. ¹⁰The

ᵃ14 The Hebrew term refers to the irrevocable giving over of things or persons to the Lord.   ᵇ16 That is, about 2 ounces (about 55 grams)

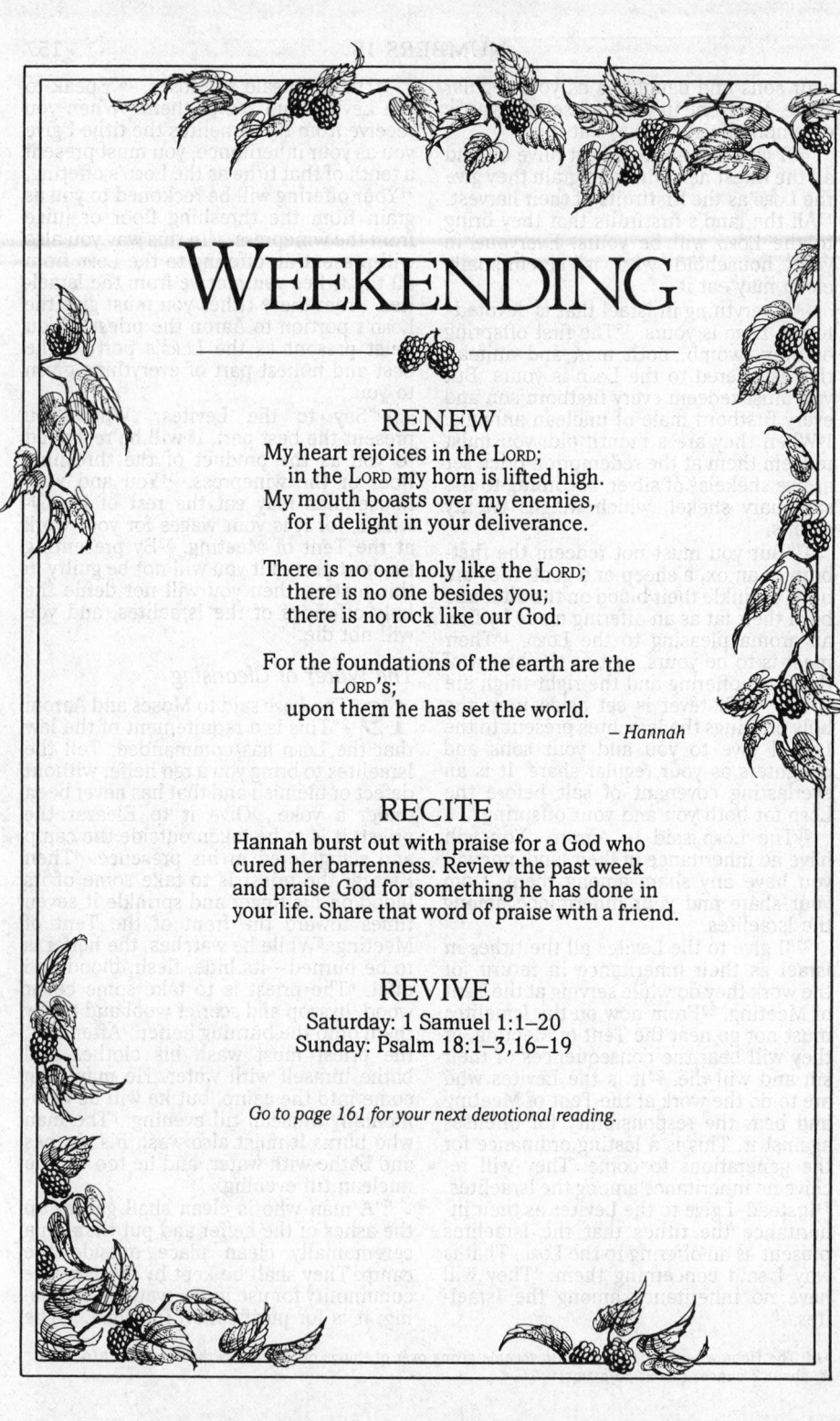

WEEKENDING

RENEW

My heart rejoices in the LORD;
    in the LORD my horn is lifted high.
My mouth boasts over my enemies,
    for I delight in your deliverance.

There is no one holy like the LORD;
    there is no one besides you;
    there is no rock like our God.

For the foundations of the earth are the
    LORD's;
    upon them he has set the world.

– Hannah

RECITE

Hannah burst out with praise for a God who
cured her barrenness. Review the past week
and praise God for something he has done in
your life. Share that word of praise with a friend.

REVIVE

Saturday: 1 Samuel 1:1–20
Sunday: Psalm 18:1–3,16–19

Go to page 161 for your next devotional reading.

man who gathers up the ashes of the heifer must also wash his clothes, and he too will be unclean till evening. This will be a lasting ordinance both for the Israelites and for the aliens living among them.

11"Whoever touches the dead body of anyone will be unclean for seven days. 12He must purify himself with the water on the third day and on the seventh day; then he will be clean. But if he does not purify himself on the third and seventh days, he will not be clean. 13Whoever touches the dead body of anyone and fails to purify himself defiles the LORD's tabernacle. That person must be cut off from Israel. Because the water of cleansing has not been sprinkled on him, he is unclean; his uncleanness remains on him.

14"This is the law that applies when a person dies in a tent: Anyone who enters the tent and anyone who is in it will be unclean for seven days, 15and every open container without a lid fastened on it will be unclean.

16"Anyone out in the open who touches someone who has been killed with a sword or someone who has died a natural death, or anyone who touches a human bone or a grave, will be unclean for seven days.

17"For the unclean person, put some ashes from the burned purification offering into a jar and pour fresh water over them. 18Then a man who is ceremonially clean is to take some hyssop, dip it in the water and sprinkle the tent and all the furnishings and the people who were there. He must also sprinkle anyone who has touched a human bone or a grave or someone who has been killed or someone who has died a natural death. 19The man who is clean is to sprinkle the unclean person on the third and seventh days, and on the seventh day he is to purify him. The person being cleansed must wash his clothes and bathe with water, and that evening he will be clean. 20But if a person who is unclean does not purify himself, he must be cut off from the community, because he has defiled the sanctuary of the LORD. The water of cleansing has not been sprinkled on him, and he is unclean. 21This is a lasting ordinance for them.

"The man who sprinkles the water of cleansing must also wash his clothes, and anyone who touches the water of cleansing will be unclean till evening. 22Anything that an unclean person touches becomes unclean, and anyone who touches it becomes unclean till evening."

Water From the Rock

20 In the first month the whole Israelite community arrived at the Desert of Zin, and they stayed at Kadesh. There Miriam died and was buried.

2Now there was no water for the community, and the people gathered in opposition to Moses and Aaron. 3They quarreled with Moses and said, "If only we had died when our brothers fell dead before the LORD! 4Why did you bring the LORD's community into this desert, that we and our livestock should die here? 5Why did you bring us up out of Egypt to this terrible place? It has no grain or figs, grapevines or pomegranates. And there is no water to drink!"

6Moses and Aaron went from the assembly to the entrance to the Tent of Meeting and fell facedown, and the glory of the LORD appeared to them. 7The LORD said to Moses, 8"Take the staff, and you and your brother Aaron gather the assembly together. Speak to that rock before their eyes and it will pour out its water. You will bring water out of the rock for the community so they and their livestock can drink."

9So Moses took the staff from the LORD's presence, just as he commanded him. 10He and Aaron gathered the assembly together in front of the rock and Moses said to them, "Listen, you rebels, must we bring you water out of this rock?" 11Then Moses raised his arm and struck the rock twice with his staff. Water gushed out, and the community and their livestock drank.

12But the LORD said to Moses and Aaron, "Because you did not trust in me enough to honor me as holy in the sight of the Israelites, you will not bring this community into the land I give them."

13These were the waters of Meribah,a where the Israelites quarreled with the LORD and where he showed himself holy among them.

Edom Denies Israel Passage

14Moses sent messengers from Kadesh to the king of Edom, saying:

"This is what your brother Israel says: You know about all the hardships that have come upon us. 15Our

---

a13 Meribah means quarreling.

forefathers went down into Egypt, and we lived there many years. The Egyptians mistreated us and our fathers, [16]but when we cried out to the Lord, he heard our cry and sent an angel and brought us out of Egypt.

"Now we are here at Kadesh, a town on the edge of your territory. [17]Please let us pass through your country. We will not go through any field or vineyard, or drink water from any well. We will travel along the king's highway and not turn to the right or to the left until we have passed through your territory."

[18]But Edom answered:

"You may not pass through here; if you try, we will march out and attack you with the sword."

[19]The Israelites replied:

"We will go along the main road, and if we or our livestock drink any of your water, we will pay for it. We only want to pass through on foot—nothing else."

[20]Again they answered:

"You may not pass through."

Then Edom came out against them with a large and powerful army. [21]Since Edom refused to let them go through their territory, Israel turned away from them.

The Death of Aaron

[22]The whole Israelite community set out from Kadesh and came to Mount Hor. [23]At Mount Hor, near the border of Edom, the Lord said to Moses and Aaron, [24]"Aaron will be gathered to his people. He will not enter the land I give the Israelites, because both of you rebelled against my command at the waters of Meribah. [25]Get Aaron and his son Eleazar and take them up Mount Hor. [26]Remove Aaron's garments and put them on his son Eleazar, for Aaron will be gathered to his people; he will die there."

[27]Moses did as the Lord commanded: They went up Mount Hor in the sight of the whole community. [28]Moses removed Aaron's garments and put them on his son Eleazar. And Aaron died there on top of the mountain. Then Moses and Eleazar

came down from the mountain, [29]and when the whole community learned that Aaron had died, the entire house of Israel mourned for him thirty days.

Arad Destroyed

21 When the Canaanite king of Arad, who lived in the Negev, heard that Israel was coming along the road to Atharim, he attacked the Israelites and captured some of them. [2]Then Israel made this vow to the Lord: "If you will deliver these people into our hands, we will totally destroy[a] their cities." [3]The Lord listened to Israel's plea and gave the Canaanites over to them. They completely destroyed them and their towns; so the place was named Hormah.[b]

The Bronze Snake

[4]They traveled from Mount Hor along the route to the Red Sea,[c] to go around Edom. But the people grew impatient on the way; [5]they spoke against God and against Moses, and said, "Why have you brought us up out of Egypt to die in the desert? There is no bread! There is no water! And we detest this miserable food!"

[6]Then the Lord sent venomous snakes among them; they bit the people and many Israelites died. [7]The people came to Moses and said, "We sinned when we spoke against the Lord and against you. Pray that the Lord will take the snakes away from us." So Moses prayed for the people.

[8]The Lord said to Moses, "Make a snake and put it up on a pole; anyone who is bitten can look at it and live." [9]So Moses made a bronze snake and put it up on a pole. Then when anyone was bitten by a snake and looked at the bronze snake, he lived.

The Journey to Moab

[10]The Israelites moved on and camped at Oboth. [11]Then they set out from Oboth and camped in Iye Abarim, in the desert that faces Moab toward the sunrise. [12]From there they moved on and camped in the Zered Valley. [13]They set out from there and camped alongside the Arnon, which is in the desert extending into Amorite territory. The Arnon is the border of Moab, between Moab and the Amorites.

---

[a]2 The Hebrew term refers to the irrevocable giving over of things or persons to the Lord, often by totally destroying them; also in verse 3.   [b]3 *Hormah* means *destruction*.   [c]4 Hebrew *Yam Suph*; that is, Sea of Reeds

¹⁴That is why the Book of the Wars of the LORD says:

"... Waheb in Suphah*a* and the ravines,
the Arnon ¹⁵and*b* the slopes of the ravines
that lead to the site of Ar
and lie along the border of Moab."

¹⁶From there they continued on to Beer,

the well where the LORD said to Moses, "Gather the people together and I will give them water."

¹⁷Then Israel sang this song:

"Spring up, O well!
Sing about it,
¹⁸about the well that the princes dug,
that the nobles of the people sank—

a14 The meaning of the Hebrew for this phrase is uncertain. *Suphah and the ravines / of the Arnon 15to*   *b14,15* Or "*I have been given from*

VERSE FOR THE DAY:	AUTHOR:	PASSAGE FOR THE DAY:
Numbers 21:4	Millie Stamm	Numbers 21:4–9

Strength for the Wilderness

THE Israelites had been traveling through the desert wilderness to the land of promise. The way was hot, sandy and rough; there was little water. But God had promised that he would guide them and provide for them. However, like many of us, they became discouraged. If only they had trusted God's promise that he who had led would continue to lead, if only they had believed that he who had supplied would continue to supply, instead of being discouraged they would have been encouraged. Discouragement turns to encouragement when we look away from our circumstances and focus our eyes on the Lord.

In 1 Samuel 30 we read about David in the midst of trouble. The Amalekites had burned Ziklag, his private property and residence. But his distress drove him to the Lord. "But David found strength in the LORD his God" (1 Samuel 30:6). Someone has said, "To look around is to be distressed; to look within is to be depressed; to look up is to be blessed."

Today our way may be through the wilderness. It may be easy to become discouraged. Discouragement is a tool of Satan. The story is told that Satan was "going out of business." All of his tools were offered for sale. They were attractively displayed on a table. What an array—hatred, envy, jealousy, deceit! One harmless-looking one, much worn, was priced higher than any of the others. "What is that tool?" someone asked. "Discouragement," was the reply. "Why is it so expensive?" Satan answered, "Because it is more useful to me than any of the others."

Will our distress drive us to despair and discouragement or to God? May we, like David, find strength in the Lord our God.

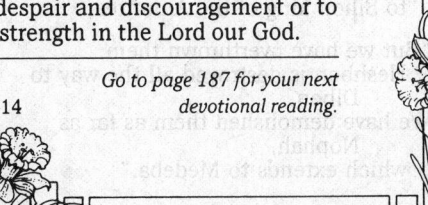

Additional Scripture Readings:
2 Chronicles 20:14–22; Psalm 27:7–14

Go to page 187 for your next devotional reading.

the nobles with scepters and staffs."

Then they went from the desert to Mattanah, 19from Mattanah to Nahaliel, from Nahaliel to Bamoth, 20and from Bamoth to the valley in Moab where the top of Pisgah overlooks the wasteland.

Defeat of Sihon and Og

21Israel sent messengers to say to Sihon king of the Amorites:

22"Let us pass through your country. We will not turn aside into any field or vineyard, or drink water from any well. We will travel along the king's highway until we have passed through your territory."

23But Sihon would not let Israel pass through his territory. He mustered his entire army and marched out into the desert against Israel. When he reached Jahaz, he fought with Israel. 24Israel, however, put him to the sword and took over his land from the Arnon to the Jabbok, but only as far as the Ammonites, because their border was fortified. 25Israel captured all the cities of the Amorites and occupied them, including Heshbon and all its surrounding settlements. 26Heshbon was the city of Sihon king of the Amorites, who had fought against the former king of Moab and had taken from him all his land as far as the Arnon.

27That is why the poets say:

"Come to Heshbon and let it be rebuilt;
let Sihon's city be restored.

28"Fire went out from Heshbon,
a blaze from the city of Sihon.
It consumed Ar of Moab,
the citizens of Arnon's heights.
29Woe to you, O Moab!
You are destroyed, O people of Chemosh!
He has given up his sons as fugitives
and his daughters as captives
to Sihon king of the Amorites.

30"But we have overthrown them;
Heshbon is destroyed all the way to Dibon.
We have demolished them as far as Nophah,
which extends to Medeba."

31So Israel settled in the land of the Amorites.

32After Moses had sent spies to Jazer, the Israelites captured its surrounding settlements and drove out the Amorites who were there. 33Then they turned and went up along the road toward Bashan, and Og king of Bashan and his whole army marched out to meet them in battle at Edrei.

34The LORD said to Moses, "Do not be afraid of him, for I have handed him over to you, with his whole army and his land. Do to him what you did to Sihon king of the Amorites, who reigned in Heshbon."

35So they struck him down, together with his sons and his whole army, leaving them no survivors. And they took possession of his land.

Balak Summons Balaam

22 Then the Israelites traveled to the plains of Moab and camped along the Jordan across from Jericho.ᵃ

2Now Balak son of Zippor saw all that Israel had done to the Amorites, 3and Moab was terrified because there were so many people. Indeed, Moab was filled with dread because of the Israelites.

4The Moabites said to the elders of Midian, "This horde is going to lick up everything around us, as an ox licks up the grass of the field."

So Balak son of Zippor, who was king of Moab at that time, 5sent messengers to summon Balaam son of Beor, who was at Pethor, near the River,ᵇ in his native land. Balak said:

"A people has come out of Egypt; they cover the face of the land and have settled next to me. 6Now come and put a curse on these people, because they are too powerful for me. Perhaps then I will be able to defeat them and drive them out of the country. For I know that those you bless are blessed, and those you curse are cursed."

7The elders of Moab and Midian left, taking with them the fee for divination. When they came to Balaam, they told him what Balak had said.

8"Spend the night here," Balaam said to them, "and I will bring you back the answer the LORD gives me." So the Moabite princes stayed with him.

ᵃ1 Hebrew *Jordan of Jericho*; possibly an ancient name for the Jordan River   ᵇ5 That is, the Euphrates

⁹God came to Balaam and asked, "Who are these men with you?"

¹⁰Balaam said to God, "Balak son of Zippor, king of Moab, sent me this message: ¹¹'A people that has come out of Egypt covers the face of the land. Now come and put a curse on them for me. Perhaps then I will be able to fight them and drive them away.'"

¹²But God said to Balaam, "Do not go with them. You must not put a curse on those people, because they are blessed."

¹³The next morning Balaam got up and said to Balak's princes, "Go back to your own country, for the LORD has refused to let me go with you."

¹⁴So the Moabite princes returned to Balak and said, "Balaam refused to come with us."

¹⁵Then Balak sent other princes, more numerous and more distinguished than the first. ¹⁶They came to Balaam and said:

"This is what Balak son of Zippor says: Do not let anything keep you from coming to me, ¹⁷because I will reward you handsomely and do whatever you say. Come and put a curse on these people for me."

¹⁸But Balaam answered them, "Even if Balak gave me his palace filled with silver and gold, I could not do anything great or small to go beyond the command of the LORD my God. ¹⁹Now stay here tonight as the others did, and I will find out what else the LORD will tell me."

²⁰That night God came to Balaam and said, "Since these men have come to summon you, go with them, but do only what I tell you."

Balaam's Donkey

²¹Balaam got up in the morning, saddled his donkey and went with the princes of Moab. ²²But God was very angry when he went, and the angel of the LORD stood in the road to oppose him. Balaam was riding on his donkey, and his two servants were with him. ²³When the donkey saw the angel of the LORD standing in the road with a drawn sword in his hand, she turned off the road into a field. Balaam beat her to get her back on the road.

²⁴Then the angel of the LORD stood in a narrow path between two vineyards, with walls on both sides. ²⁵When the donkey saw the angel of the LORD, she pressed close to the wall, crushing Balaam's foot against it. So he beat her again.

²⁶Then the angel of the LORD moved on ahead and stood in a narrow place where there was no room to turn, either to the right or to the left. ²⁷When the donkey saw the angel of the LORD, she lay down under Balaam, and he was angry and beat her with his staff. ²⁸Then the LORD opened the donkey's mouth, and she said to Balaam, "What have I done to you to make you beat me these three times?"

²⁹Balaam answered the donkey, "You have made a fool of me! If I had a sword in my hand, I would kill you right now."

³⁰The donkey said to Balaam, "Am I not your own donkey, which you have always ridden, to this day? Have I been in the habit of doing this to you?"

"No," he said.

³¹Then the LORD opened Balaam's eyes, and he saw the angel of the LORD standing in the road with his sword drawn. So he bowed low and fell facedown.

³²The angel of the LORD asked him, "Why have you beaten your donkey these three times? I have come here to oppose you because your path is a reckless one before me.ᵃ ³³The donkey saw me and turned away from me these three times. If she had not turned away, I would certainly have killed you by now, but I would have spared her."

³⁴Balaam said to the angel of the LORD, "I have sinned. I did not realize you were standing in the road to oppose me. Now if you are displeased, I will go back."

³⁵The angel of the LORD said to Balaam, "Go with the men, but speak only what I tell you." So Balaam went with the princes of Balak.

³⁶When Balak heard that Balaam was coming, he went out to meet him at the Moabite town on the Arnon border, at the edge of his territory. ³⁷Balak said to Balaam, "Did I not send you an urgent summons? Why didn't you come to me? Am I really not able to reward you?"

³⁸"Well, I have come to you now," Balaam replied. "But can I say just anything? I must speak only what God puts in my mouth."

³⁹Then Balaam went with Balak to Kiriath Huzoth. ⁴⁰Balak sacrificed cattle and sheep, and gave some to Balaam and the princes who were with him. ⁴¹The next morning Balak took Balaam up to Ba-

---

ᵃ32 The meaning of the Hebrew for this clause is uncertain.

moth Baal, and from there he saw part of the people.

Balaam's First Oracle

23 Balaam said, "Build me seven altars here, and prepare seven bulls and seven rams for me." [2]Balak did as Balaam said, and the two of them offered a bull and a ram on each altar.

[3]Then Balaam said to Balak, "Stay here beside your offering while I go aside. Perhaps the LORD will come to meet with me. Whatever he reveals to me I will tell you." Then he went off to a barren height.

[4]God met with him, and Balaam said, "I have prepared seven altars, and on each altar I have offered a bull and a ram."

[5]The LORD put a message in Balaam's mouth and said, "Go back to Balak and give him this message."

[6]So he went back to him and found him standing beside his offering, with all the princes of Moab. [7]Then Balaam uttered his oracle:

"Balak brought me from Aram,
　the king of Moab from the eastern
　　mountains.
'Come,' he said, 'curse Jacob for me;
　come, denounce Israel.'
[8]How can I curse
　those whom God has not cursed?
How can I denounce
　those whom the LORD has not
　　denounced?
[9]From the rocky peaks I see them,
　from the heights I view them.
I see a people who live apart
　and do not consider themselves one
　　of the nations.
[10]Who can count the dust of Jacob
　or number the fourth part of Israel?
Let me die the death of the righteous,
　and may my end be like theirs!"

[11]Balak said to Balaam, "What have you done to me? I brought you to curse my enemies, but you have done nothing but bless them!"

[12]He answered, "Must I not speak what the LORD puts in my mouth?"

Balaam's Second Oracle

[13]Then Balak said to him, "Come with me to another place where you can see them; you will see only a part but not all of them. And from there, curse them for me." [14]So he took him to the field of Zo-phim on the top of Pisgah, and there he built seven altars and offered a bull and a ram on each altar.

[15]Balaam said to Balak, "Stay here beside your offering while I meet with him over there."

[16]The LORD met with Balaam and put a message in his mouth and said, "Go back to Balak and give him this message."

[17]So he went to him and found him standing beside his offering, with the princes of Moab. Balak asked him, "What did the LORD say?"

[18]Then he uttered his oracle:

"Arise, Balak, and listen;
　hear me, son of Zippor.
[19]God is not a man, that he should lie,
　nor a son of man, that he should
　　change his mind.
Does he speak and then not act?
　Does he promise and not fulfill?
[20]I have received a command to bless;
　he has blessed, and I cannot
　　change it.

[21]"No misfortune is seen in Jacob,
　no misery observed in Israel. [a]
The LORD their God is with them;
　the shout of the King is among
　　them.
[22]God brought them out of Egypt;
　they have the strength of a wild ox.
[23]There is no sorcery against Jacob,
　no divination against Israel.
It will now be said of Jacob
　and of Israel, 'See what God has
　　done!'
[24]The people rise like a lioness;
　they rouse themselves like a lion
that does not rest till he devours his
　　prey
　and drinks the blood of his
　　victims."

[25]Then Balak said to Balaam, "Neither curse them at all nor bless them at all!"

[26]Balaam answered, "Did I not tell you I must do whatever the LORD says?"

Balaam's Third Oracle

[27]Then Balak said to Balaam, "Come, let me take you to another place. Perhaps it will please God to let you curse them for me from there." [28]And Balak took Balaam to the top of Peor, overlooking the wasteland.

[29]Balaam said, "Build me seven altars here, and prepare seven bulls and seven

---

a21 Or He has not looked on Jacob's offenses / or on the wrongs found in Israel.

rams for me." ³⁰Balak did as Balaam had said, and offered a bull and a ram on each altar.

24 Now when Balaam saw that it pleased the LORD to bless Israel, he did not resort to sorcery as at other times, but turned his face toward the desert. ²When Balaam looked out and saw Israel encamped tribe by tribe, the Spirit of God came upon him ³and he uttered his oracle:

"The oracle of Balaam son of Beor,
    the oracle of one whose eye sees
        clearly,
⁴the oracle of one who hears the words
        of God,
    who sees a vision from the
        Almighty,^a
    who falls prostrate, and whose eyes
        are opened:

⁵"How beautiful are your tents,
        O Jacob,
    your dwelling places, O Israel!

⁶"Like valleys they spread out,
    like gardens beside a river,
    like aloes planted by the LORD,
    like cedars beside the waters.
⁷Water will flow from their buckets;
    their seed will have abundant
        water.

"Their king will be greater than Agag;
    their kingdom will be exalted.

⁸"God brought them out of Egypt;
    they have the strength of a wild ox.
They devour hostile nations
    and break their bones in pieces;
    with their arrows they pierce them.
⁹Like a lion they crouch and lie down,
    like a lioness—who dares to rouse
        them?

"May those who bless you be blessed
    and those who curse you be
        cursed!"

¹⁰Then Balak's anger burned against Balaam. He struck his hands together and said to him, "I summoned you to curse my enemies, but you have blessed them these three times. ¹¹Now leave at once and go home! I said I would reward you handsomely, but the LORD has kept you from being rewarded."

¹²Balaam answered Balak, "Did I not tell the messengers you sent me, ¹³'Even if Balak gave me his palace filled with silver and gold, I could not do anything of my own accord, good or bad, to go beyond the command of the LORD—and I must say only what the LORD says'? ¹⁴Now I am going back to my people, but come, let me warn you of what this people will do to your people in days to come."

Balaam's Fourth Oracle

¹⁵Then he uttered his oracle:

"The oracle of Balaam son of Beor,
    the oracle of one whose eye sees
        clearly,
¹⁶the oracle of one who hears the words
        of God,
    who has knowledge from the Most
        High,
    who sees a vision from the Almighty,
    who falls prostrate, and whose eyes
        are opened:

¹⁷"I see him, but not now;
    I behold him, but not near.
A star will come out of Jacob;
    a scepter will rise out of Israel.
He will crush the foreheads of Moab,
    the skulls^b of^c all the sons of
        Sheth.^d
¹⁸Edom will be conquered;
    Seir, his enemy, will be conquered,
    but Israel will grow strong.
¹⁹A ruler will come out of Jacob
    and destroy the survivors of the
        city."

Balaam's Final Oracles

²⁰Then Balaam saw Amalek and uttered his oracle:

"Amalek was first among the nations,
    but he will come to ruin at last."

²¹Then he saw the Kenites and uttered his oracle:

"Your dwelling place is secure,
    your nest is set in a rock;
²²yet you Kenites will be destroyed
    when Asshur takes you captive."

²³Then he uttered his oracle:

"Ah, who can live when God does
    this?^e
²⁴ Ships will come from the shores of
        Kittim;

---

^a4 Hebrew *Shaddai*; also in verse 16   ^b17 Samaritan Pentateuch (see also Jer. 48:45); the meaning of the word in the Masoretic Text is uncertain.   ^c17 Or possibly *Moab, / batter*   ^d17 Or *all the noisy boasters*   ^e23 Masoretic Text; with a different word division of the Hebrew *A people will gather from the north.*

they will subdue Asshur and Eber,
  but they too will come to ruin."

25Then Balaam got up and returned
home and Balak went his own way.

Moab Seduces Israel

25 While Israel was staying in
Shittim, the men began to indulge
in sexual immorality with Moabite wom-
en, 2who invited them to the sacrifices to
their gods. The people ate and bowed
down before these gods. 3So Israel joined
in worshiping the Baal of Peor. And the
LORD's anger burned against them.

4The LORD said to Moses, "Take all the
leaders of these people, kill them and expose them in broad daylight before the
LORD, so that the LORD's fierce anger may
turn away from Israel."

5So Moses said to Israel's judges, "Each
of you must put to death those of your
men who have joined in worshiping the
Baal of Peor."

6Then an Israelite man brought to his
family a Midianite woman right before
the eyes of Moses and the whole assembly of Israel while they were weeping at
the entrance to the Tent of Meeting.
7When Phinehas son of Eleazar, the son
of Aaron, the priest, saw this, he left the
assembly, took a spear in his hand 8and
followed the Israelite into the tent. He
drove the spear through both of them—
through the Israelite and into the woman's body. Then the plague against the
Israelites was stopped; 9but those who
died in the plague numbered 24,000.

10The LORD said to Moses, 11"Phinehas
son of Eleazar, the son of Aaron, the
priest, has turned my anger away from the
Israelites; for he was as zealous as I am for
my honor among them, so that in my zeal
I did not put an end to them. 12Therefore
tell him I am making my covenant of
peace with him. 13He and his descendants will have a covenant of a lasting
priesthood, because he was zealous for
the honor of his God and made atonement for the Israelites."

14The name of the Israelite who was
killed with the Midianite woman was
Zimri son of Salu, the leader of a Simeon-
ite family. 15And the name of the Midianite woman who was put to death was Cozbi daughter of Zur, a tribal chief of a Midianite family.

16The LORD said to Moses, 17"Treat the

Midianites as enemies and kill them,
18because they treated you as enemies
when they deceived you in the affair of
Peor and their sister Cozbi, the daughter
of a Midianite leader, the woman who
was killed when the plague came as a result of Peor."

The Second Census

26 After the plague the LORD said to
Moses and Eleazar son of Aaron,
the priest, 2"Take a census of the whole
Israelite community by families—all
those twenty years old or more who are
able to serve in the army of Israel." 3So on
the plains of Moab by the Jordan across
from Jericho,ᵃ Moses and Eleazar the
priest spoke with them and said, 4"Take
a census of the men twenty years old or
more, as the LORD commanded Moses."

These were the Israelites who came out
of Egypt:

5The descendants of Reuben, the firstborn son of Israel, were:
  through Hanoch, the Hanochite
    clan;
  through Pallu, the Palluite clan;
  6through Hezron, the Hezronite clan;
  through Carmi, the Carmite clan.
7These were the clans of Reuben; those
numbered were 43,730.

8The son of Pallu was Eliab, 9and the
sons of Eliab were Nemuel, Dathan and
Abiram. The same Dathan and Abiram
were the community officials who rebelled against Moses and Aaron and were
among Korah's followers when they rebelled against the LORD. 10The earth
opened its mouth and swallowed them
along with Korah, whose followers died
when the fire devoured the 250 men. And
they served as a warning sign. 11The line
of Korah, however, did not die out.

12The descendants of Simeon by their
clans were:
  through Nemuel, the Nemuelite
    clan;
  through Jamin, the Jaminite clan;
  through Jakin, the Jakinite clan;
  13through Zerah, the Zerahite clan;
  through Shaul, the Shaulite clan.
14These were the clans of Simeon; there
were 22,200 men.

15The descendants of Gad by their clans
were:
  through Zephon, the Zephonite clan;

ᵃ3 Hebrew *Jordan of Jericho*; possibly an ancient name for the Jordan River; also in verse 63

through Haggi, the Haggite clan;
through Shuni, the Shunite clan;
16through Ozni, the Oznite clan;
through Eri, the Erite clan;
17through Arodi,ᵃ the Arodite clan;
through Areli, the Arelite clan.
18These were the clans of Gad; those numbered were 40,500.

19Er and Onan were sons of Judah, but they died in Canaan.
20The descendants of Judah by their clans were:
through Shelah, the Shelanite clan;
through Perez, the Perezite clan;
through Zerah, the Zerahite clan.
21The descendants of Perez were:
through Hezron, the Hezronite clan;
through Hamul, the Hamulite clan.
22These were the clans of Judah; those numbered were 76,500.

23The descendants of Issachar by their clans were:
through Tola, the Tolaite clan;
through Puah, the Puiteᵇ clan;
24through Jashub, the Jashubite clan;
through Shimron, the Shimronite clan.
25These were the clans of Issachar; those numbered were 64,300.

26The descendants of Zebulun by their clans were:
through Sered, the Seredite clan;
through Elon, the Elonite clan;
through Jahleel, the Jahleelite clan.
27These were the clans of Zebulun; those numbered were 60,500.

28The descendants of Joseph by their clans through Manasseh and Ephraim were:

29The descendants of Manasseh:
through Makir, the Makirite clan (Makir was the father of Gilead);
through Gilead, the Gileadite clan.
30These were the descendants of Gilead:
through Iezer, the Iezerite clan;
through Helek, the Helekite clan;
31through Asriel, the Asrielite clan;
through Shechem, the Shechemite clan;

32through Shemida, the Shemidaite clan;
through Hepher, the Hepherite clan.
33(Zelophehad son of Hepher had no sons; he had only daughters, whose names were Mahlah, Noah, Hoglah, Milcah and Tirzah.)
34These were the clans of Manasseh; those numbered were 52,700.

35These were the descendants of Ephraim by their clans:
through Shuthelah, the Shuthelahite clan;
through Beker, the Bekerite clan;
through Tahan, the Tahanite clan.
36These were the descendants of Shuthelah:
through Eran, the Eranite clan.
37These were the clans of Ephraim; those numbered were 32,500.

These were the descendants of Joseph by their clans.

38The descendants of Benjamin by their clans were:
through Bela, the Belaite clan;
through Ashbel, the Ashbelite clan;
through Ahiram, the Ahiramite clan;
39through Shupham,ᶜ the Shuphamite clan;
through Hupham, the Huphamite clan.
40The descendants of Bela through Ard and Naaman were:
through Ard,ᵈ the Ardite clan;
through Naaman, the Naamite clan.
41These were the clans of Benjamin; those numbered were 45,600.

42These were the descendants of Dan by their clans:
through Shuham, the Shuhamite clan.
These were the clans of Dan: 43All of them were Shuhamite clans; and those numbered were 64,400.

44The descendants of Asher by their clans were:
through Imnah, the Imnite clan;
through Ishvi, the Ishvite clan;
through Beriah, the Beriite clan;

ᵃ17 Samaritan Pentateuch and Syriac (see also Gen. 46:16); Masoretic Text *Arod*   ᵇ23 Samaritan Pentateuch, Septuagint, Vulgate and Syriac (see also 1 Chron. 7:1); Masoretic Text *through Puvah, the Punite*   ᶜ39 A few manuscripts of the Masoretic Text, Samaritan Pentateuch, Vulgate and Syriac (see also Septuagint); most manuscripts of the Masoretic Text *Shephupham*   ᵈ40 Samaritan Pentateuch and Vulgate (see also Septuagint); Masoretic Text does not have *through Ard*.

45and through the descendants of Beriah:

through Heber, the Heberite clan;
through Malkiel, the Malkielite clan.

46(Asher had a daughter named Serah.)

47These were the clans of Asher; those numbered were 53,400.

48The descendants of Naphtali by their clans were:

through Jahzeel, the Jahzeelite clan;
through Guni, the Gunite clan;
49through Jezer, the Jezerite clan;
through Shillem, the Shillemite clan.

50These were the clans of Naphtali; those numbered were 45,400.

51The total number of the men of Israel was 601,730.

52The LORD said to Moses, 53"The land is to be allotted to them as an inheritance based on the number of names. 54To a larger group give a larger inheritance, and to a smaller group a smaller one; each is to receive its inheritance according to the number of those listed. 55Be sure that the land is distributed by lot. What each group inherits will be according to the names for its ancestral tribe. 56Each inheritance is to be distributed by lot among the larger and smaller groups."

57These were the Levites who were counted by their clans:

through Gershon, the Gershonite clan;
through Kohath, the Kohathite clan;
through Merari, the Merarite clan.

58These also were Levite clans:

the Libnite clan,
the Hebronite clan,
the Mahlite clan,
the Mushite clan,
the Korahite clan.

(Kohath was the forefather of Amram; 59the name of Amram's wife was Jochebed, a descendant of Levi, who was born to the Levitesa in Egypt. To Amram she bore Aaron, Moses and their sister Miriam. 60Aaron was the father of Nadab and Abihu, Eleazar and Ithamar. 61But Nadab and Abihu died when they made an offering before the LORD with unauthorized fire.)

62All the male Levites a month old or more numbered 23,000. They were not counted along with the other Israelites because they received no inheritance among them.

63These are the ones counted by Moses and Eleazar the priest when they counted the Israelites on the plains of Moab by the Jordan across from Jericho. 64Not one of them was among those counted by Moses and Aaron the priest when they counted the Israelites in the Desert of Sinai. 65For the LORD had told those Israelites they would surely die in the desert, and not one of them was left except Caleb son of Jephunneh and Joshua son of Nun.

Zelophehad's Daughters

27 The daughters of Zelophehad son of Hepher, the son of Gilead, the son of Makir, the son of Manasseh, belonged to the clans of Manasseh son of Joseph. The names of the daughters were Mahlah, Noah, Hoglah, Milcah and Tirzah. They approached 2the entrance to the Tent of Meeting and stood before Moses, Eleazar the priest, the leaders and the whole assembly, and said, 3"Our father died in the desert. He was not among Korah's followers, who banded together against the LORD, but he died for his own sin and left no sons. 4Why should our father's name disappear from his clan because he had no son? Give us property among our father's relatives."

5So Moses brought their case before the LORD 6and the LORD said to him, 7"What Zelophehad's daughters are saying is right. You must certainly give them property as an inheritance among their father's relatives and turn their father's inheritance over to them.

8"Say to the Israelites, 'If a man dies and leaves no son, turn his inheritance over to his daughter. 9If he has no daughter, give his inheritance to his brothers. 10If he has no brothers, give his inheritance to his father's brothers. 11If his father had no brothers, give his inheritance to the nearest relative in his clan, that he may possess it. This is to be a legal requirement for the Israelites, as the LORD commanded Moses.' "

Joshua to Succeed Moses

12Then the LORD said to Moses, "Go up this mountain in the Abarim range and see the land I have given the Israelites.

a59 Or Jochebed, a daughter of Levi, who was born to Levi

13After you have seen it, you too will be gathered to your people, as your brother Aaron was, 14for when the community rebelled at the waters in the Desert of Zin, both of you disobeyed my command to honor me as holy before their eyes." (These were the waters of Meribah Kadesh, in the Desert of Zin.)

15Moses said to the Lord, 16"May the Lord, the God of the spirits of all mankind, appoint a man over this community 17to go out and come in before them, one who will lead them out and bring them in, so the Lord's people will not be like sheep without a shepherd."

18So the Lord said to Moses, "Take Joshua son of Nun, a man in whom is the spirit,a and lay your hand on him. 19Have him stand before Eleazar the priest and the entire assembly and commission him in their presence. 20Give him some of your authority so the whole Israelite community will obey him. 21He is to stand before Eleazar the priest, who will obtain decisions for him by inquiring of the Urim before the Lord. At his command he and the entire community of the Israelites will go out, and at his command they will come in."

22Moses did as the Lord commanded him. He took Joshua and had him stand before Eleazar the priest and the whole assembly. 23Then he laid his hands on him and commissioned him, as the Lord instructed through Moses.

Daily Offerings

28 The Lord said to Moses, 2"Give this command to the Israelites and say to them: 'See that you present to me at the appointed time the food for my offerings made by fire, as an aroma pleasing to me.' 3Say to them: 'This is the offering made by fire that you are to present to the Lord: two lambs a year old without defect, as a regular burnt offering each day. 4Prepare one lamb in the morning and the other at twilight, 5together with a grain offering of a tenth of an ephahb of fine flour mixed with a quarter of a hinc of oil from pressed olives. 6This is the regular burnt offering instituted at Mount Sinai as a pleasing aroma, an offering made to the Lord by fire. 7The accompanying

drink offering is to be a quarter of a hin of fermented drink with each lamb. Pour out the drink offering to the Lord at the sanctuary. 8Prepare the second lamb at twilight, along with the same kind of grain offering and drink offering that you prepare in the morning. This is an offering made by fire, an aroma pleasing to the Lord.

Sabbath Offerings

9" 'On the Sabbath day, make an offering of two lambs a year old without defect, together with its drink offering and a grain offering of two-tenths of an ephahd of fine flour mixed with oil. 10This is the burnt offering for every Sabbath, in addition to the regular burnt offering and its drink offering.

Monthly Offerings

11" 'On the first of every month, present to the Lord a burnt offering of two young bulls, one ram and seven male lambs a year old, all without defect. 12With each bull there is to be a grain offering of three-tenths of an ephahe of fine flour mixed with oil; with the ram, a grain offering of two-tenths of an ephah of fine flour mixed with oil; 13and with each lamb, a grain offering of a tenth of an ephah of fine flour mixed with oil. This is for a burnt offering, a pleasing aroma, an offering made to the Lord by fire. 14With each bull there is to be a drink offering of half a hinf of wine; with the ram, a third of a hing; and with each lamb, a quarter of a hin. This is the monthly burnt offering to be made at each new moon during the year. 15Besides the regular burnt offering with its drink offering, one male goat is to be presented to the Lord as a sin offering.

The Passover

16" 'On the fourteenth day of the first month the Lord's Passover is to be held. 17On the fifteenth day of this month there is to be a festival; for seven days eat bread made without yeast. 18On the first day hold a sacred assembly and do no regular work. 19Present to the Lord an offering made by fire, a burnt offering of two young bulls, one ram and seven male

---

a18 Or Spirit   b5 That is, probably about 2 quarts (about 2 liters); also in verses 13, 21 and 29
c5 That is, probably about 1 quart (about 1 liter); also in verses 7 and 14   d9 That is, probably about
4 quarts (about 4.5 liters); also in verses 12, 20 and 28   e12 That is, probably about 6 quarts (about
6.5 liters); also in verses 20 and 28   f14 That is, probably about 2 quarts (about 2 liters)   g14 That
is, probably about 1 1/4 quarts (about 1.2 liters)

lambs a year old, all without defect.
²⁰With each bull prepare a grain offering
of three-tenths of an ephah of fine flour
mixed with oil; with the ram, two-tenths;
²¹and with each of the seven lambs, one-
tenth. ²²Include one male goat as a sin
offering to make atonement for you.
²³Prepare these in addition to the regular
morning burnt offering. ²⁴In this way prepare the food for the offering made by fire
every day for seven days as an aroma
pleasing to the LORD; it is to be prepared
in addition to the regular burnt offering
and its drink offering. ²⁵On the seventh
day hold a sacred assembly and do no regular work.

Feast of Weeks

²⁶" 'On the day of firstfruits, when you
present to the LORD an offering of new
grain during the Feast of Weeks, hold a
sacred assembly and do no regular work.
²⁷Present a burnt offering of two young
bulls, one ram and seven male lambs a
year old as an aroma pleasing to the LORD.
²⁸With each bull there is to be a grain offering of three-tenths of an ephah of fine
flour mixed with oil; with the ram, two-
tenths; ²⁹and with each of the seven
lambs, one-tenth. ³⁰Include one male
goat to make atonement for you. ³¹Pre-
pare these together with their drink offerings, in addition to the regular burnt offering and its grain offering. Be sure the
animals are without defect.

Feast of Trumpets

29 " 'On the first day of the seventh
month hold a sacred assembly and
do no regular work. It is a day for you to
sound the trumpets. ²As an aroma pleasing to the LORD, prepare a burnt offering
of one young bull, one ram and seven
male lambs a year old, all without defect.
³With the bull prepare a grain offering of
three-tenths of an ephah ͣ of fine flour
mixed with oil; with the ram, two-
tenths ͣ; ⁴and with each of the seven
lambs, one-tenth. ͨ ⁵Include one male
goat as a sin offering to make atonement
for you. ⁶These are in addition to the
monthly and daily burnt offerings with
their grain offerings and drink offerings as
specified. They are offerings made to the
LORD by fire—a pleasing aroma.

Day of Atonement

⁷" 'On the tenth day of this seventh
month hold a sacred assembly. You must
deny yourselves ͩ and do no work.
⁸Present as an aroma pleasing to the LORD
a burnt offering of one young bull, one
ram and seven male lambs a year old, all
without defect. ⁹With the bull prepare a
grain offering of three-tenths of an ephah
of fine flour mixed with oil; with the ram,
two-tenths; ¹⁰and with each of the seven
lambs, one-tenth. ¹¹Include one male
goat as a sin offering, in addition to the
sin offering for atonement and the regular
burnt offering with its grain offering, and
their drink offerings.

Feast of Tabernacles

¹²" 'On the fifteenth day of the seventh
month, hold a sacred assembly and do no
regular work. Celebrate a festival to the
LORD for seven days. ¹³Present an offering
made by fire as an aroma pleasing to the
LORD, a burnt offering of thirteen young
bulls, two rams and fourteen male lambs
a year old, all without defect. ¹⁴With each
of the thirteen bulls prepare a grain offering of three-tenths of an ephah of fine
flour mixed with oil; with each of the two
rams, two-tenths; ¹⁵and with each of the
fourteen lambs, one-tenth. ¹⁶Include one
male goat as a sin offering, in addition to
the regular burnt offering with its grain
offering and drink offering.

¹⁷" 'On the second day prepare twelve
young bulls, two rams and fourteen male
lambs a year old, all without defect.
¹⁸With the bulls, rams and lambs, prepare
their grain offerings and drink offerings
according to the number specified. ¹⁹In-
clude one male goat as a sin offering, in
addition to the regular burnt offering with
its grain offering, and their drink offerings.

²⁰" 'On the third day prepare eleven
bulls, two rams and fourteen male lambs
a year old, all without defect. ²¹With the
bulls, rams and lambs, prepare their grain
offerings and drink offerings according to
the number specified. ²²Include one male
goat as a sin offering, in addition to the
regular burnt offering with its grain offering and drink offering.

²³" 'On the fourth day prepare ten
bulls, two rams and fourteen male lambs
a year old, all without defect. ²⁴With the

ͣ3 That is, probably about 6 quarts (about 6.5 liters); also in verses 9 and 14   ͣ3 That is, probably
about 4 quarts (about 4.5 liters); also in verses 9 and 14   ͨ4 That is, probably about 2 quarts (about
2 liters); also in verses 10 and 15   ͩ7 Or *must fast*

bulls, rams and lambs, prepare their grain offerings and drink offerings according to the number specified. 25Include one male goat as a sin offering, in addition to the regular burnt offering with its grain offering and drink offering.

26" 'On the fifth day prepare nine bulls, two rams and fourteen male lambs a year old, all without defect. 27With the bulls, rams and lambs, prepare their grain offerings and drink offerings according to the number specified. 28Include one male goat as a sin offering, in addition to the regular burnt offering with its grain offering and drink offering.

29" 'On the sixth day prepare eight bulls, two rams and fourteen male lambs a year old, all without defect. 30With the bulls, rams and lambs, prepare their grain offerings and drink offerings according to the number specified. 31Include one male goat as a sin offering, in addition to the regular burnt offering with its grain offering and drink offering.

32" 'On the seventh day prepare seven bulls, two rams and fourteen male lambs a year old, all without defect. 33With the bulls, rams and lambs, prepare their grain offerings and drink offerings according to the number specified. 34Include one male goat as a sin offering, in addition to the regular burnt offering with its grain offering and drink offering.

35" 'On the eighth day hold an assembly and do no regular work. 36Present an offering made by fire as an aroma pleasing to the LORD, a burnt offering of one bull, one ram and seven male lambs a year old, all without defect. 37With the bull, the ram and the lambs, prepare their grain offerings and drink offerings according to the number specified. 38Include one male goat as a sin offering, in addition to the regular burnt offering with its grain offering and drink offering.

39" 'In addition to what you vow and your freewill offerings, prepare these for the LORD at your appointed feasts: your burnt offerings, grain offerings, drink offerings and fellowship offerings.ᵃ' "

40Moses told the Israelites all that the LORD commanded him.

Vows

30 Moses said to the heads of the tribes of Israel: "This is what the LORD commands: 2When a man makes a vow to the LORD or takes an oath to obligate himself by a pledge, he must not break his word but must do everything he said.

3"When a young woman still living in her father's house makes a vow to the LORD or obligates herself by a pledge 4and her father hears about her vow or pledge but says nothing to her, then all her vows and every pledge by which she obligated herself will stand. 5But if her father forbids her when he hears about it, none of her vows or the pledges by which she obligated herself will stand; the LORD will release her because her father has forbidden her.

6"If she marries after she makes a vow or after her lips utter a rash promise by which she obligates herself 7and her husband hears about it but says nothing to her, then her vows or the pledges by which she obligated herself will stand. 8But if her husband forbids her when he hears about it, he nullifies the vow that obligates her or the rash promise by which she obligates herself, and the LORD will release her.

9"Any vow or obligation taken by a widow or divorced woman will be binding on her.

10"If a woman living with her husband makes a vow or obligates herself by a pledge under oath 11and her husband hears about it but says nothing to her and does not forbid her, then all her vows or the pledges by which she obligated herself will stand. 12But if her husband nullifies them when he hears about them, then none of the vows or pledges that came from her lips will stand. Her husband has nullified them, and the LORD will release her. 13Her husband may confirm or nullify any vow she makes or any sworn pledge to deny herself. 14But if her husband says nothing to her about it from day to day, then he confirms all her vows or the pledges binding on her. He confirms them by saying nothing to her when he hears about them. 15If, however, he nullifies them some time after he hears about them, then he is responsible for her guilt."

16These are the regulations the LORD gave Moses concerning relationships between a man and his wife, and between a father and his young daughter still living in his house.

Vengeance on the Midianites

31 The LORD said to Moses, [2]"Take vengeance on the Midianites for the Israelites. After that, you will be gathered to your people."

[3]So Moses said to the people, "Arm some of your men to go to war against the Midianites and to carry out the LORD's vengeance on them. [4]Send into battle a thousand men from each of the tribes of Israel." [5]So twelve thousand men armed for battle, a thousand from each tribe, were supplied from the clans of Israel. [6]Moses sent them into battle, a thousand from each tribe, along with Phinehas son of Eleazar, the priest, who took with him articles from the sanctuary and the trumpets for signaling.

[7]They fought against Midian, as the LORD commanded Moses, and killed every man. [8]Among their victims were Evi, Rekem, Zur, Hur and Reba—the five kings of Midian. They also killed Balaam son of Beor with the sword. [9]The Israelites captured the Midianite women and children and took all the Midianite herds, flocks and goods as plunder. [10]They burned all the towns where the Midianites had settled, as well as all their camps. [11]They took all the plunder and spoils, including the people and animals, [12]and brought the captives, spoils and plunder to Moses and Eleazar the priest and the Israelite assembly at their camp on the plains of Moab, by the Jordan across from Jericho.[a]

[13]Moses, Eleazar the priest and all the leaders of the community went to meet them outside the camp. [14]Moses was angry with the officers of the army—the commanders of thousands and commanders of hundreds—who returned from the battle.

[15]"Have you allowed all the women to live?" he asked them. [16]"They were the ones who followed Balaam's advice and were the means of turning the Israelites away from the LORD in what happened at Peor, so that a plague struck the LORD's people. [17]Now kill all the boys. And kill every woman who has slept with a man, [18]but save for yourselves every girl who has never slept with a man.

[19]"All of you who have killed anyone or touched anyone who was killed must stay outside the camp seven days. On the third and seventh days you must purify yourselves and your captives. [20]Purify every garment as well as everything made of leather, goat hair or wood."

[21]Then Eleazar the priest said to the soldiers who had gone into battle, "This is the requirement of the law that the LORD gave Moses: [22]Gold, silver, bronze, iron, tin, lead [23]and anything else that can withstand fire must be put through the fire, and then it will be clean. But it must also be purified with the water of cleansing. And whatever cannot withstand fire must be put through that water. [24]On the seventh day wash your clothes and you will be clean. Then you may come into the camp."

Dividing the Spoils

[25]The LORD said to Moses, [26]"You and Eleazar the priest and the family heads of the community are to count all the people and animals that were captured. [27]Divide the spoils between the soldiers who took part in the battle and the rest of the community. [28]From the soldiers who fought in the battle, set apart as tribute for the LORD one out of every five hundred, whether persons, cattle, donkeys, sheep or goats. [29]Take this tribute from their half share and give it to Eleazar the priest as the LORD's part. [30]From the Israelites' half, select one out of every fifty, whether persons, cattle, donkeys, sheep, goats or other animals. Give them to the Levites, who are responsible for the care of the LORD's tabernacle." [31]So Moses and Eleazar the priest did as the LORD commanded Moses.

[32]The plunder remaining from the spoils that the soldiers took was 675,000 sheep, [33]72,000 cattle, [34]61,000 donkeys [35]and 32,000 women who had never slept with a man.

[36]The half share of those who fought in the battle was:

337,500 sheep, [37]of which the tribute for the LORD was 675;
[38]36,000 cattle, of which the tribute for the LORD was 72;
[39]30,500 donkeys, of which the tribute for the LORD was 61;
[40]16,000 people, of which the tribute for the LORD was 32.

[41]Moses gave the tribute to Eleazar the priest as the LORD's part, as the LORD commanded Moses.

[42]The half belonging to the Israelites,

[a]12 Hebrew *Jordan of Jericho*; possibly an ancient name for the Jordan River

which Moses set apart from that of the fighting men— [43]the community's half— was 337,500 sheep, [44]36,000 cattle, [45]30,500 donkeys [46]and 16,000 people. [47]From the Israelites' half, Moses selected one out of every fifty persons and animals, as the LORD commanded him, and gave them to the Levites, who were responsible for the care of the LORD's tabernacle.

[48]Then the officers who were over the units of the army—the commanders of thousands and commanders of hundreds —went to Moses [49]and said to him, "Your servants have counted the soldiers under our command, and not one is missing. [50]So we have brought as an offering to the LORD the gold articles each of us acquired —armlets, bracelets, signet rings, earrings and necklaces—to make atonement for ourselves before the LORD."

[51]Moses and Eleazar the priest accepted from them the gold—all the crafted articles. [52]All the gold from the commanders of thousands and commanders of hundreds that Moses and Eleazar presented as a gift to the LORD weighed 16,750 shekels.[a] [53]Each soldier had taken plunder for himself. [54]Moses and Eleazar the priest accepted the gold from the commanders of thousands and commanders of hundreds and brought it into the Tent of Meeting as a memorial for the Israelites before the LORD.

The Transjordan Tribes

32 The Reubenites and Gadites, who had very large herds and flocks, saw that the lands of Jazer and Gilead were suitable for livestock. [2]So they came to Moses and Eleazar the priest and to the leaders of the community, and said, [3]"Ataroth, Dibon, Jazer, Nimrah, Heshbon, Elealeh, Sebam, Nebo and Beon— [4]the land the LORD subdued before the people of Israel—are suitable for livestock, and your servants have livestock. [5]If we have found favor in your eyes," they said, "let this land be given to your servants as our possession. Do not make us cross the Jordan."

[6]Moses said to the Gadites and Reubenites, "Shall your countrymen go to war while you sit here? [7]Why do you discourage the Israelites from going over into the land the LORD has given them? [8]This is what your fathers did when I sent them from Kadesh Barnea to look over the land. [9]After they went up to the Valley of Eshcol and viewed the land, they discouraged the Israelites from entering the land the LORD had given them. [10]The LORD's anger was aroused that day and he swore this oath: [11]'Because they have not followed me wholeheartedly, not one of the men twenty years old or more who came up out of Egypt will see the land I promised on oath to Abraham, Isaac and Jacob— [12]not one except Caleb son of Jephunneh the Kenizzite and Joshua son of Nun, for they followed the LORD wholeheartedly.' [13]The LORD's anger burned against Israel and he made them wander in the desert forty years, until the whole generation of those who had done evil in his sight was gone.

[14]"And here you are, a brood of sinners, standing in the place of your fathers and making the LORD even more angry with Israel. [15]If you turn away from following him, he will again leave all this people in the desert, and you will be the cause of their destruction."

[16]Then they came up to him and said, "We would like to build pens here for our livestock and cities for our women and children. [17]But we are ready to arm ourselves and go ahead of the Israelites until we have brought them to their place. Meanwhile our women and children will live in fortified cities, for protection from the inhabitants of the land. [18]We will not return to our homes until every Israelite has received his inheritance. [19]We will not receive any inheritance with them on the other side of the Jordan, because our inheritance has come to us on the east side of the Jordan."

[20]Then Moses said to them, "If you will do this—if you will arm yourselves before the LORD for battle, [21]and if all of you will go armed over the Jordan before the LORD until he has driven his enemies out before him— [22]then when the land is subdued before the LORD, you may return and be free from your obligation to the LORD and to Israel. And this land will be your possession before the LORD.

[23]"But if you fail to do this, you will be sinning against the LORD; and you may be sure that your sin will find you out. [24]Build cities for your women and children, and pens for your flocks, but do what you have promised."

[25]The Gadites and Reubenites said to Moses, "We your servants will do as our

---

[a]52 That is, about 420 pounds (about 190 kilograms)

lord commands. ²⁶Our children and wives, our flocks and herds will remain here in the cities of Gilead. ²⁷But your servants, every man armed for battle, will cross over to fight before the LORD, just as our lord says."

²⁸Then Moses gave orders about them to Eleazar the priest and Joshua son of Nun and to the family heads of the Israelite tribes. ²⁹He said to them, "If the Gadites and Reubenites, every man armed for battle, cross over the Jordan with you before the LORD, then when the land is subdued before you, give them the land of Gilead as their possession. ³⁰But if they do not cross over with you armed, they must accept their possession with you in Canaan."

³¹The Gadites and Reubenites answered, "Your servants will do what the LORD has said. ³²We will cross over before the LORD into Canaan armed, but the property we inherit will be on this side of the Jordan."

³³Then Moses gave to the Gadites, the Reubenites and the half-tribe of Manasseh son of Joseph the kingdom of Sihon king of the Amorites and the kingdom of Og king of Bashan—the whole land with its cities and the territory around them. ³⁴The Gadites built up Dibon, Ataroth, Aroer, ³⁵Atroth Shophan, Jazer, Jogbehah, ³⁶Beth Nimrah and Beth Haran as fortified cities, and built pens for their flocks. ³⁷And the Reubenites rebuilt Heshbon, Elealeh and Kiriathaim, ³⁸as well as Nebo and Baal Meon (these names were changed) and Sibmah. They gave names to the cities they rebuilt.

³⁹The descendants of Makir son of Manasseh went to Gilead, captured it and drove out the Amorites who were there. ⁴⁰So Moses gave Gilead to the Makirites, the descendants of Manasseh, and they settled there. ⁴¹Jair, a descendant of Manasseh, captured their settlements and called them Havvoth Jair.^a ⁴²And Nobah captured Kenath and its surrounding settlements and called it Nobah after himself.

Stages in Israel's Journey

33 Here are the stages in the journey of the Israelites when they came out of Egypt by divisions under the leadership of Moses and Aaron. ²At the LORD's command Moses recorded the stages in their journey. This is their journey by stages:

³The Israelites set out from Rameses on the fifteenth day of the first month, the day after the Passover. They marched out boldly in full view of all the Egyptians, ⁴who were burying all their firstborn, whom the LORD had struck down among them; for the LORD had brought judgment on their gods.

⁵The Israelites left Rameses and camped at Succoth.

⁶They left Succoth and camped at Etham, on the edge of the desert.

⁷They left Etham, turned back to Pi Hahiroth, to the east of Baal Zephon, and camped near Migdol.

⁸They left Pi Hahiroth^b and passed through the sea into the desert, and when they had traveled for three days in the Desert of Etham, they camped at Marah.

⁹They left Marah and went to Elim, where there were twelve springs and seventy palm trees, and they camped there.

¹⁰They left Elim and camped by the Red Sea.^c

¹¹They left the Red Sea and camped in the Desert of Sin.

¹²They left the Desert of Sin and camped at Dophkah.

¹³They left Dophkah and camped at Alush.

¹⁴They left Alush and camped at Rephidim, where there was no water for the people to drink.

¹⁵They left Rephidim and camped in the Desert of Sinai.

¹⁶They left the Desert of Sinai and camped at Kibroth Hattaavah.

¹⁷They left Kibroth Hattaavah and camped at Hazeroth.

¹⁸They left Hazeroth and camped at Rithmah.

¹⁹They left Rithmah and camped at Rimmon Perez.

²⁰They left Rimmon Perez and camped at Libnah.

²¹They left Libnah and camped at Rissah.

²²They left Rissah and camped at Kehelathah.

^a41 Or *them the settlements of Jair*   ^b8 Many manuscripts of the Masoretic Text, Samaritan Pentateuch and Vulgate; most manuscripts of the Masoretic Text *left from before Hahiroth*   ^c10 Hebrew *Yam Suph*; that is, Sea of Reeds; also in verse 11

²³They left Kehelathah and camped at Mount Shepher.

²⁴They left Mount Shepher and camped at Haradah.

²⁵They left Haradah and camped at Makheloth.

²⁶They left Makheloth and camped at Tahath.

²⁷They left Tahath and camped at Terah.

²⁸They left Terah and camped at Mithcah.

²⁹They left Mithcah and camped at Hashmonah.

³⁰They left Hashmonah and camped at Moseroth.

³¹They left Moseroth and camped at Bene Jaakan.

³²They left Bene Jaakan and camped at Hor Haggidgad.

³³They left Hor Haggidgad and camped at Jotbathah.

³⁴They left Jotbathah and camped at Abronah.

³⁵They left Abronah and camped at Ezion Geber.

³⁶They left Ezion Geber and camped at Kadesh, in the Desert of Zin.

³⁷They left Kadesh and camped at Mount Hor, on the border of Edom. ³⁸At the LORD's command Aaron the priest went up Mount Hor, where he died on the first day of the fifth month of the fortieth year after the Israelites came out of Egypt. ³⁹Aaron was a hundred and twenty-three years old when he died on Mount Hor.

⁴⁰The Canaanite king of Arad, who lived in the Negev of Canaan, heard that the Israelites were coming.

⁴¹They left Mount Hor and camped at Zalmonah.

⁴²They left Zalmonah and camped at Punon.

⁴³They left Punon and camped at Oboth.

⁴⁴They left Oboth and camped at Iye Abarim, on the border of Moab.

⁴⁵They left Iyim ᵃ and camped at Dibon Gad.

⁴⁶They left Dibon Gad and camped at Almon Diblathaim.

⁴⁷They left Almon Diblathaim and camped in the mountains of Abarim, near Nebo.

⁴⁸They left the mountains of Abarim and camped on the plains of Moab by the Jordan across from Jericho. ᵇ ⁴⁹There on the plains of Moab they camped along the Jordan from Beth Jeshimoth to Abel Shittim.

⁵⁰On the plains of Moab by the Jordan across from Jericho the LORD said to Moses, ⁵¹"Speak to the Israelites and say to them: 'When you cross the Jordan into Canaan, ⁵²drive out all the inhabitants of the land before you. Destroy all their carved images and their cast idols, and demolish all their high places. ⁵³Take possession of the land and settle in it, for I have given you the land to possess. ⁵⁴Distribute the land by lot, according to your clans. To a larger group give a larger inheritance, and to a smaller group a smaller one. Whatever falls to them by lot will be theirs. Distribute it according to your ancestral tribes.

⁵⁵"'But if you do not drive out the inhabitants of the land, those you allow to remain will become barbs in your eyes and thorns in your sides. They will give you trouble in the land where you will live. ⁵⁶And then I will do to you what I plan to do to them.'"

Boundaries of Canaan

34 The LORD said to Moses, ²"Command the Israelites and say to them: 'When you enter Canaan, the land that will be allotted to you as an inheritance will have these boundaries:

³"'Your southern side will include some of the Desert of Zin along the border of Edom. On the east, your southern boundary will start from the end of the Salt Sea, ᶜ ⁴cross south of Scorpion ᵈ Pass, continue on to Zin and go south of Kadesh Barnea. Then it will go to Hazar Addar and over to Azmon, ⁵where it will turn, join the Wadi of Egypt and end at the Sea. ᵉ

⁶"'Your western boundary will be the coast of the Great Sea. This will be your boundary on the west.

⁷"'For your northern boundary, run a line from the Great Sea to Mount Hor ⁸and from Mount Hor to Lebo ᶠ Hamath. Then the boundary will go to Zedad, ⁹con-

---

ᵃ45 That is, Iye Abarim   ᵇ48 Hebrew *Jordan of Jericho*; possibly an ancient name for the Jordan River; also in verse 50   ᶜ3 That is, the Dead Sea; also in verse 12   ᵈ4 Hebrew *Akrabbim*   ᵉ5 That is, the Mediterranean; also in verses 6 and 7   ᶠ8 Or *to the entrance to* tinue to Ziphron and end at Hazar Enan. This will be your boundary on the north.

¹⁰" 'For your eastern boundary, run a line from Hazar Enan to Shepham. ¹¹The boundary will go down from Shepham to Riblah on the east side of Ain and continue along the slopes east of the Sea of Kinnereth.ᵃ ¹²Then the boundary will go down along the Jordan and end at the Salt Sea.

" 'This will be your land, with its boundaries on every side.' "

¹³Moses commanded the Israelites: "Assign this land by lot as an inheritance. The LORD has ordered that it be given to the nine and a half tribes, ¹⁴because the families of the tribe of Reuben, the tribe of Gad and the half-tribe of Manasseh have received their inheritance. ¹⁵These two and a half tribes have received their inheritance on the east side of the Jordan of Jericho,ᵇ toward the sunrise."

¹⁶The LORD said to Moses, ¹⁷"These are the names of the men who are to assign the land for you as an inheritance: Eleazar the priest and Joshua son of Nun. ¹⁸And appoint one leader from each tribe to help assign the land. ¹⁹These are their names:

Caleb son of Jephunneh,
    from the tribe of Judah;
²⁰Shemuel son of Ammihud,
    from the tribe of Simeon;
²¹Elidad son of Kislon,
    from the tribe of Benjamin;
²²Bukki son of Jogli,
    the leader from the tribe of Dan;
²³Hanniel son of Ephod,
    the leader from the tribe of Manasseh son of Joseph;
²⁴Kemuel son of Shiphtan,
    the leader from the tribe of Ephraim son of Joseph;
²⁵Elizaphan son of Parnach,
    the leader from the tribe of Zebulun;
²⁶Paltiel son of Azzan,
    the leader from the tribe of Issachar;
²⁷Ahihud son of Shelomi,
    the leader from the tribe of Asher;
²⁸Pedahel son of Ammihud,
    the leader from the tribe of Naphtali."

²⁹These are the men the LORD commanded to assign the inheritance to the Israelites in the land of Canaan.

Towns for the Levites

35 On the plains of Moab by the Jordan across from Jericho,ᶜ the LORD said to Moses, ²"Command the Israelites to give the Levites towns to live in from the inheritance the Israelites will possess. And give them pasturelands around the towns. ³Then they will have towns to live in and pasturelands for their cattle, flocks and all their other livestock.

⁴"The pasturelands around the towns that you give the Levites will extend out fifteen hundred feetᵈ from the town wall. ⁵Outside the town, measure three thousand feetᵉ on the east side, three thousand on the south side, three thousand on the west and three thousand on the north, with the town in the center. They will have this area as pastureland for the towns.

Cities of Refuge

⁶"Six of the towns you give the Levites will be cities of refuge, to which a person who has killed someone may flee. In addition, give them forty-two other towns. ⁷In all you must give the Levites forty-eight towns, together with their pasturelands. ⁸The towns you give the Levites from the land the Israelites possess are to be given in proportion to the inheritance of each tribe: Take many towns from a tribe that has many, but few from one that has few."

⁹Then the LORD said to Moses: ¹⁰"Speak to the Israelites and say to them: 'When you cross the Jordan into Canaan, ¹¹select some towns to be your cities of refuge, to which a person who has killed someone accidentally may flee. ¹²They will be places of refuge from the avenger, so that a person accused of murder may not die before he stands trial before the assembly. ¹³These six towns you give will be your cities of refuge. ¹⁴Give three on this side of the Jordan and three in Canaan as cities of refuge. ¹⁵These six towns will be a place of refuge for Israelites, aliens and any other people living among them, so that anyone who has killed another accidentally can flee there.

ᵃ11 That is, Galilee   ᵇ15 Jordan of Jericho was possibly an ancient name for the Jordan River.
ᶜ1 Hebrew Jordan of Jericho; possibly an ancient name for the Jordan River   ᵈ4 Hebrew a thousand cubits (about 450 meters)   ᵉ5 Hebrew two thousand cubits (about 900 meters)

16" 'If a man strikes someone with an iron object so that he dies, he is a murderer; the murderer shall be put to death. 17Or if anyone has a stone in his hand that could kill, and he strikes someone so that he dies, he is a murderer; the murderer shall be put to death. 18Or if anyone has a wooden object in his hand that could kill, and he hits someone so that he dies, he is a murderer; the murderer shall be put to death. 19The avenger of blood shall put the murderer to death; when he meets him, he shall put him to death. 20If anyone with malice aforethought shoves another or throws something at him intentionally so that he dies 21or if in hostility he hits him with his fist so that he dies, that person shall be put to death; he is a murderer. The avenger of blood shall put the murderer to death when he meets him.

22" 'But if without hostility someone suddenly shoves another or throws something at him unintentionally 23or, without seeing him, drops a stone on him that could kill him, and he dies, then since he was not his enemy and he did not intend to harm him, 24the assembly must judge between him and the avenger of blood according to these regulations. 25The assembly must protect the one accused of murder from the avenger of blood and send him back to the city of refuge to which he fled. He must stay there until the death of the high priest, who was anointed with the holy oil.

26" 'But if the accused ever goes outside the limits of the city of refuge to which he has fled 27and the avenger of blood finds him outside the city, the avenger of blood may kill the accused without being guilty of murder. 28The accused must stay in his city of refuge until the death of the high priest; only after the death of the high priest may he return to his own property.

29" 'These are to be legal requirements for you throughout the generations to come, wherever you live.

30" 'Anyone who kills a person is to be put to death as a murderer only on the testimony of witnesses. But no one is to be put to death on the testimony of only one witness.

31" 'Do not accept a ransom for the life of a murderer, who deserves to die. He must surely be put to death.

32" 'Do not accept a ransom for anyone who has fled to a city of refuge and so allow him to go back and live on his own land before the death of the high priest. 33" 'Do not pollute the land where you are. Bloodshed pollutes the land, and atonement cannot be made for the land on which blood has been shed, except by the blood of the one who shed it. 34Do not defile the land where you live and where I dwell, for I, the LORD, dwell among the Israelites.' "

Inheritance of Zelophehad's Daughters

36 The family heads of the clan of Gilead son of Makir, the son of Manasseh, who were from the clans of the descendants of Joseph, came and spoke before Moses and the leaders, the heads of the Israelite families. 2They said, "When the LORD commanded my lord to give the land as an inheritance to the Israelites by lot, he ordered you to give the inheritance of our brother Zelophehad to his daughters. 3Now suppose they marry men from other Israelite tribes; then their inheritance will be taken from our ancestral inheritance and added to that of the tribe they marry into. And so part of the inheritance allotted to us will be taken away. 4When the Year of Jubilee for the Israelites comes, their inheritance will be added to that of the tribe into which they marry, and their property will be taken from the tribal inheritance of our forefathers."

5Then at the LORD's command Moses gave this order to the Israelites: "What the tribe of the descendants of Joseph is saying is right. 6This is what the LORD commands for Zelophehad's daughters: They may marry anyone they please as long as they marry within the tribal clan of their father. 7No inheritance in Israel is to pass from tribe to tribe, for every Israelite shall keep the tribal land inherited from his forefathers. 8Every daughter who inherits land in any Israelite tribe must marry someone in her father's tribal clan, so that every Israelite will possess the inheritance of his fathers. 9No inheritance may pass from tribe to tribe, for each Israelite tribe is to keep the land it inherits."

10So Zelophehad's daughters did as the LORD commanded Moses. 11Zelophehad's daughters—Mahlah, Tirzah, Hoglah, Milcah and Noah—married their cousins on their father's side. 12They married within the clans of the descendants of Manasseh son of Joseph, and their inheritance remained in their father's clan and tribe.

[13]These are the commands and regulations the LORD gave through Moses to the Israelites on the plains of Moab by the Jordan across from Jericho.[a]

---

[a]13 Hebrew *Jordan of Jericho*; possibly an ancient name for the Jordan River

*I*N this book Moses records his farewell address to the nation of Israel as
they wait on the bank of the Jordan
River, ready to cross over into the land
of Canaan. He reminds them of God's
care in the past and of his laws, and he
challenges them to rededicate their lives
to serving the Lord. As you read this
book, think about God's daily care in
your life and his desire that you dedicate your life to serving him.

DEUTERONOMY

The Command to Leave Horeb

1 These are the words Moses spoke to all Israel in the desert east of the Jordan—that is, in the Arabah—opposite Suph, between Paran and Tophel, Laban, Hazeroth and Dizahab. ²(It takes eleven days to go from Horeb to Kadesh Barnea by the Mount Seir road.)

³In the fortieth year, on the first day of the eleventh month, Moses proclaimed to the Israelites all that the LORD had commanded him concerning them. ⁴This was after he had defeated Sihon king of the Amorites, who reigned in Heshbon, and at Edrei had defeated Og king of Bashan, who reigned in Ashtaroth.

⁵East of the Jordan in the territory of Moab, Moses began to expound this law, saying:

⁶The LORD our God said to us at Horeb, "You have stayed long enough at this mountain. ⁷Break camp and advance into the hill country of the Amorites; go to all the neighboring peoples in the Arabah, in the mountains, in the western foothills, in the Negev and along the coast, to the land of the Canaanites and to Lebanon, as far as the great river, the Euphrates. ⁸See, I have given you this land. Go in and take possession of the land that the LORD swore he would give to your fathers—to Abraham, Isaac and Jacob—and to their descendants after them."

The Appointment of Leaders

9At that time I said to you, "You are too heavy a burden for me to carry alone. 10The LORD your God has increased your numbers so that today you are as many as the stars in the sky. 11May the LORD, the God of your fathers, increase you a thousand times and bless you as he has promised! 12But how can I bear your problems and your burdens and your disputes all by myself? 13Choose some wise, understanding and respected men from each of your tribes, and I will set them over you."

14You answered me, "What you propose to do is good."

15So I took the leading men of your tribes, wise and respected men, and appointed them to have authority over you —as commanders of thousands, of hundreds, of fifties and of tens and as tribal officials. 16And I charged your judges at that time: Hear the disputes between your brothers and judge fairly, whether the case is between brother Israelites or between one of them and an alien. 17Do not show partiality in judging; hear both small and great alike. Do not be afraid of any man, for judgment belongs to God. Bring me any case too hard for you, and I will hear it. 18And at that time I told you everything you were to do.

Spies Sent Out

19Then, as the LORD our God commanded us, we set out from Horeb and went toward the hill country of the Amorites through all that vast and dreadful desert that you have seen, and so we reached Kadesh Barnea. 20Then I said to you, "You have reached the hill country of the Amorites, which the LORD our God is giving us. 21See, the LORD your God has given you the land. Go up and take possession of it as the LORD, the God of your fathers, told you. Do not be afraid; do not be discouraged."

22Then all of you came to me and said, "Let us send men ahead to spy out the land for us and bring back a report about the route we are to take and the towns we will come to."

23The idea seemed good to me; so I selected twelve of you, one man from each tribe. 24They left and went up into the hill country, and came to the Valley of Eshcol and explored it. 25Taking with them some of the fruit of the land, they brought it down to us and reported, "It is a good land that the LORD our God is giving us."

Rebellion Against the LORD

26But you were unwilling to go up; you rebelled against the command of the LORD your God. 27You grumbled in your tents and said, "The LORD hates us; so he brought us out of Egypt to deliver us into the hands of the Amorites to destroy us. 28Where can we go? Our brothers have made us lose heart. They say, 'The people are stronger and taller than we are; the cities are large, with walls up to the sky. We even saw the Anakites there.' "

29Then I said to you, "Do not be terrified; do not be afraid of them. 30The LORD your God, who is going before you, will fight for you, as he did for you in Egypt, before your very eyes, 31and in the desert. There you saw how the LORD your God carried you, as a father carries his son, all the way you went until you reached this place."

32In spite of this, you did not trust in the LORD your God, 33who went ahead of you on your journey, in fire by night and in a cloud by day, to search out places for you to camp and to show you the way you should go.

34When the LORD heard what you said, he was angry and solemnly swore: 35"Not a man of this evil generation shall see the good land I swore to give your forefathers, 36except Caleb son of Jephunneh. He will see it, and I will give him and his descendants the land he set his feet on, because he followed the LORD wholeheartedly."

37Because of you the LORD became angry with me also and said, "You shall not enter it, either. 38But your assistant, Joshua son of Nun, will enter it. Encourage him, because he will lead Israel to inherit it. 39And the little ones that you said would be taken captive, your children who do not yet know good from bad— they will enter the land. I will give it to them and they will take possession of it. 40But as for you, turn around and set out toward the desert along the route to the Red Sea.a"

41Then you replied, "We have sinned against the LORD. We will go up and fight, as the LORD our God commanded us." So every one of you put on his weapons, thinking it easy to go up into the hill country.

42But the LORD said to me, "Tell them,

a40 Hebrew Yam Suph; that is, Sea of Reeds

'Do not go up and fight, because I will not be with you. You will be defeated by your enemies.' "

⁴³So I told you, but you would not listen. You rebelled against the LORD's command and in your arrogance you marched up into the hill country. ⁴⁴The Amorites who lived in those hills came out against you; they chased you like a swarm of bees and beat you down from Seir all the way to Hormah. ⁴⁵You came back and wept before the LORD, but he paid no attention to your weeping and turned a deaf ear to you. ⁴⁶And so you stayed in Kadesh many days — all the time you spent there.

Wanderings in the Desert

2 Then we turned back and set out toward the desert along the route to the Red Sea,ᵃ as the LORD had directed me. For a long time we made our way around the hill country of Seir.

²Then the LORD said to me, ³"You have made your way around this hill country long enough; now turn north. ⁴Give the people these orders: 'You are about to pass through the territory of your brothers the descendants of Esau, who live in Seir. They will be afraid of you, but be very careful. ⁵Do not provoke them to war, for I will not give you any of their land, not even enough to put your foot on. I have given Esau the hill country of Seir as his own. ⁶You are to pay them in silver for the food you eat and the water you drink.' "

⁷The LORD your God has blessed you in all the work of your hands. He has watched over your journey through this vast desert. These forty years the LORD your God has been with you, and you have not lacked anything.

⁸So we went on past our brothers the descendants of Esau, who live in Seir. We turned from the Arabah road, which comes up from Elath and Ezion Geber, and traveled along the desert road of Moab.

⁹Then the LORD said to me, "Do not harass the Moabites or provoke them to war, for I will not give you any part of their land. I have given Ar to the descendants of Lot as a possession."

¹⁰(The Emites used to live there — a people strong and numerous, and as tall as the Anakites. ¹¹Like the Anakites, they too were considered Rephaites, but the Moabites called them Emites. ¹²Horites used to live in Seir, but the descendants

of Esau drove them out. They destroyed the Horites from before them and settled in their place, just as Israel did in the land the LORD gave them as their possession.)

¹³And the LORD said, "Now get up and cross the Zered Valley." So we crossed the valley.

¹⁴Thirty-eight years passed from the time we left Kadesh Barnea until we crossed the Zered Valley. By then, that entire generation of fighting men had perished from the camp, as the LORD had sworn to them. ¹⁵The LORD's hand was against them until he had completely eliminated them from the camp.

¹⁶Now when the last of these fighting men among the people had died, ¹⁷the LORD said to me, ¹⁸"Today you are to pass by the region of Moab at Ar. ¹⁹When you come to the Ammonites, do not harass them or provoke them to war, for I will not give you possession of any land belonging to the Ammonites. I have given it as a possession to the descendants of Lot."

²⁰(That too was considered a land of the Rephaites, who used to live there; but the Ammonites called them Zamzummites. ²¹They were a people strong and numerous, and as tall as the Anakites. The LORD destroyed them from before the Ammonites, who drove them out and settled in their place. ²²The LORD had done the same for the descendants of Esau, who lived in Seir, when he destroyed the Horites from before them. They drove them out and have lived in their place to this day. ²³And as for the Avvites who lived in villages as far as Gaza, the Caphtorites coming out from Caphtorᵇ destroyed them and settled in their place.)

Defeat of Sihon King of Heshbon

²⁴"Set out now and cross the Arnon Gorge. See, I have given into your hand Sihon the Amorite, king of Heshbon, and his country. Begin to take possession of it and engage him in battle. ²⁵This very day I will begin to put the terror and fear of you on all the nations under heaven. They will hear reports of you and will tremble and be in anguish because of you."

²⁶From the desert of Kedemoth I sent messengers to Sihon king of Heshbon offering peace and saying, ²⁷"Let us pass through your country. We will stay on the main road; we will not turn aside to the right or to the left. ²⁸Sell us food to eat

---

ᵃ1 Hebrew *Yam Suph*; that is, Sea of Reeds   ᵇ23 That is, Crete and water to drink for their price in silver. Only let us pass through on foot— [29]as the descendants of Esau, who live in Seir, and the Moabites, who live in Ar, did for us—until we cross the Jordan into the land the LORD our God is giving us." [30]But Sihon king of Heshbon refused to let us pass through. For the LORD your God had made his spirit stubborn and his heart obstinate in order to give him into your hands, as he has now done.

[31]The LORD said to me, "See, I have begun to deliver Sihon and his country over to you. Now begin to conquer and possess his land."

[32]When Sihon and all his army came out to meet us in battle at Jahaz, [33]the LORD our God delivered him over to us and we struck him down, together with his sons and his whole army. [34]At that time we took all his towns and completely destroyed[a] them—men, women and children. We left no survivors. [35]But the livestock and the plunder from the towns we had captured we carried off for ourselves. [36]From Aroer on the rim of the Arnon Gorge, and from the town in the gorge, even as far as Gilead, not one town was too strong for us. The LORD our God gave us all of them. [37]But in accordance with the command of the LORD our God, you did not encroach on any of the land of the Ammonites, neither the land along the course of the Jabbok nor that around the towns in the hills.

Defeat of Og King of Bashan

3 Next we turned and went up along the road toward Bashan, and Og king of Bashan with his whole army marched out to meet us in battle at Edrei. [2]The LORD said to me, "Do not be afraid of him, for I have handed him over to you with his whole army and his land. Do to him what you did to Sihon king of the Amorites, who reigned in Heshbon."

[3]So the LORD our God also gave into our hands Og king of Bashan and all his army. We struck them down, leaving no survivors. [4]At that time we took all his cities. There was not one of the sixty cities that we did not take from them—the whole region of Argob, Og's kingdom in Bashan. [5]All these cities were fortified with high walls and with gates and bars, and there were also a great many unwalled villages. [6]We completely destroyed[a] them, as we had done with Sihon king of Heshbon, destroying[a] every city—men, women and children. [7]But all the livestock and the plunder from their cities we carried off for ourselves.

[8]So at that time we took from these two kings of the Amorites the territory east of the Jordan, from the Arnon Gorge as far as Mount Hermon. [9](Hermon is called Sirion by the Sidonians; the Amorites call it Senir.) [10]We took all the towns on the plateau, and all Gilead, and all Bashan as far as Salecah and Edrei, towns of Og's kingdom in Bashan. [11](Only Og king of Bashan was left of the remnant of the Rephaites. His bed[b] was made of iron and was more than thirteen feet long and six feet wide.[c] It is still in Rabbah of the Ammonites.)

Division of the Land

[12]Of the land that we took over at that time, I gave the Reubenites and the Gadites the territory north of Aroer by the Arnon Gorge, including half the hill country of Gilead, together with its towns. [13]The rest of Gilead and also all of Bashan, the kingdom of Og, I gave to the half tribe of Manasseh. (The whole region of Argob in Bashan used to be known as a land of the Rephaites. [14]Jair, a descendant of Manasseh, took the whole region of Argob as far as the border of the Geshurites and the Maacathites; it was named after him, so that to this day Bashan is called Havvoth Jair.[d]) [15]And I gave Gilead to Makir. [16]But to the Reubenites and the Gadites I gave the territory extending from Gilead down to the Arnon Gorge (the middle of the gorge being the border) and out to the Jabbok River, which is the border of the Ammonites. [17]Its western border was the Jordan in the Arabah, from Kinnereth to the Sea of the Arabah (the Salt Sea[e]), below the slopes of Pisgah.

[18]I commanded you at that time: "The LORD your God has given you this land to take possession of it. But all your able-bodied men, armed for battle, must cross over ahead of your brother Israelites. [19]However, your wives, your children and your livestock (I know you have much livestock) may stay in the towns I have

---

[a]34,6 The Hebrew term refers to the irrevocable giving over of things or persons to the LORD, often by totally destroying them.   [b]11 Or sarcophagus   [c]11 Hebrew nine cubits long and four cubits wide (about 4 meters long and 1.8 meters wide)   [d]14 Or called the settlements of Jair   [e]17 That is, the Dead Sea

given you, 20until the LORD gives rest to your brothers as he has to you, and they too have taken over the land that the LORD your God is giving them, across the Jordan. After that, each of you may go back to the possession I have given you."

Moses Forbidden to Cross the Jordan

21At that time I commanded Joshua: "You have seen with your own eyes all that the LORD your God has done to these two kings. The LORD will do the same to all the kingdoms over there where you are going. 22Do not be afraid of them; the LORD your God himself will fight for you."

23At that time I pleaded with the LORD: 24"O Sovereign LORD, you have begun to show to your servant your greatness and your strong hand. For what god is there in heaven or on earth who can do the deeds and mighty works you do? 25Let me go over and see the good land beyond the Jordan—that fine hill country and Lebanon."

26But because of you the LORD was angry with me and would not listen to me. "That is enough," the LORD said. "Do not speak to me anymore about this matter. 27Go up to the top of Pisgah and look west and north and south and east. Look at the land with your own eyes, since you are not going to cross this Jordan. 28But commission Joshua, and encourage and strengthen him, for he will lead this people across and will cause them to inherit the land that you will see." 29So we stayed in the valley near Beth Peor.

Obedience Commanded

4 Hear now, O Israel, the decrees and laws I am about to teach you. Follow them so that you may live and may go in and take possession of the land that the LORD, the God of your fathers, is giving you. 2Do not add to what I command you and do not subtract from it, but keep the commands of the LORD your God that I give you.

3You saw with your own eyes what the LORD did at Baal Peor. The LORD your God destroyed from among you everyone who followed the Baal of Peor, 4but all of you who held fast to the LORD your God are still alive today.

5See, I have taught you decrees and laws as the LORD my God commanded me, so that you may follow them in the land you are entering to take possession of it.

6Observe them carefully, for this will show your wisdom and understanding to the nations, who will hear about all these decrees and say, "Surely this great nation is a wise and understanding people." 7What other nation is so great as to have their gods near them the way the LORD our God is near us whenever we pray to him? 8And what other nation is so great as to have such righteous decrees and laws as this body of laws I am setting before you today?

9Only be careful, and watch yourselves closely so that you do not forget the things your eyes have seen or let them slip from your heart as long as you live. Teach them to your children and to their children after them. 10Remember the day you stood before the LORD your God at Horeb, when he said to me, "Assemble the people before me to hear my words so that they may learn to revere me as long as they live in the land and may teach them to their children." 11You came near and stood at the foot of the mountain while it blazed with fire to the very heavens, with black clouds and deep darkness. 12Then the LORD spoke to you out of the fire. You heard the sound of words but saw no form; there was only a voice. 13He declared to you his covenant, the Ten Commandments, which he commanded you to follow and then wrote them on two stone tablets. 14And the LORD directed me at that time to teach you the decrees and laws you are to follow in the land that you are crossing the Jordan to possess.

Idolatry Forbidden

15You saw no form of any kind the day the LORD spoke to you at Horeb out of the fire. Therefore watch yourselves very carefully, 16so that you do not become corrupt and make for yourselves an idol, an image of any shape, whether formed like a man or a woman, 17or like any animal on earth or any bird that flies in the air, 18or like any creature that moves along the ground or any fish in the waters below. 19And when you look up to the sky and see the sun, the moon and the stars—all the heavenly array—do not be enticed into bowing down to them and worshiping things the LORD your God has apportioned to all the nations under heaven. 20But as for you, the LORD took you and brought you out of the iron-smelting furnace, out of Egypt, to be the people of his inheritance, as you now are. 21The LORD was angry with me because of you, and he solemnly swore that I would not cross the Jordan and enter the good land the LORD your God is giving you as your inheritance. ²²I will die in this land; I will not cross the Jordan; but you are about to cross over and take possession of that good land. ²³Be careful not to forget the covenant of the LORD your God that he made with you; do not make for yourselves an idol in the form of anything the LORD your God has forbidden. ²⁴For the LORD your God is a consuming fire, a jealous God.

²⁵After you have had children and grandchildren and have lived in the land a long time—if you then become corrupt and make any kind of idol, doing evil in the eyes of the LORD your God and provoking him to anger, ²⁶I call heaven and earth as witnesses against you this day that you will quickly perish from the land that you are crossing the Jordan to possess. You will not live there long but will certainly be destroyed. ²⁷The LORD will scatter you among the peoples, and only a few of you will survive among the nations to which the LORD will drive you. ²⁸There you will worship man-made gods of wood and stone, which cannot see or hear or eat or smell. ²⁹But if from there you seek the LORD your God, you will find him if you look for him with all your heart and with all your soul. ³⁰When you are in distress and all these things have happened to you, then in later days you will return to the LORD your God and obey him. ³¹For the LORD your God is a merciful God; he will not abandon or destroy you or forget the covenant with your forefathers, which he confirmed to them by oath.

The LORD Is God

³²Ask now about the former days, long before your time, from the day God created man on the earth; ask from one end of the heavens to the other. Has anything so great as this ever happened, or has anything like it ever been heard of? ³³Has any other people heard the voice of God[a] speaking out of fire, as you have, and lived? ³⁴Has any god ever tried to take for himself one nation out of another nation, by testings, by miraculous signs and wonders, by war, by a mighty hand and an outstretched arm, or by great and awesome deeds, like all the things the LORD your God did for you in Egypt before your very eyes?

³⁵You were shown these things so that you might know that the LORD is God; besides him there is no other. ³⁶From heaven he made you hear his voice to discipline you. On earth he showed you his great fire, and you heard his words from out of the fire. ³⁷Because he loved your forefathers and chose their descendants after them, he brought you out of Egypt by his Presence and his great strength, ³⁸to drive out before you nations greater and stronger than you and to bring you into their land to give it to you for your inheritance, as it is today.

³⁹Acknowledge and take to heart this day that the LORD is God in heaven above and on the earth below. There is no other. ⁴⁰Keep his decrees and commands, which I am giving you today, so that it may go well with you and your children after you and that you may live long in the land the LORD your God gives you for all time.

Cities of Refuge

⁴¹Then Moses set aside three cities east of the Jordan, ⁴²to which anyone who had killed a person could flee if he had unintentionally killed his neighbor without malice aforethought. He could flee into one of these cities and save his life. ⁴³The cities were these: Bezer in the desert plateau, for the Reubenites; Ramoth in Gilead, for the Gadites; and Golan in Bashan, for the Manassites.

Introduction to the Law

⁴⁴This is the law Moses set before the Israelites. ⁴⁵These are the stipulations, decrees and laws Moses gave them when they came out of Egypt ⁴⁶and were in the valley near Beth Peor east of the Jordan, in the land of Sihon king of the Amorites, who reigned in Heshbon and was defeated by Moses and the Israelites as they came out of Egypt. ⁴⁷They took possession of his land and the land of Og king of Bashan, the two Amorite kings east of the Jordan. ⁴⁸This land extended from Aroer on the rim of the Arnon Gorge to Mount Siyon[b] (that is, Hermon), ⁴⁹and included all the Arabah east of the Jordan, as far as the Sea of the Arabah,[c] below the slopes of Pisgah.

The Ten Commandments

5 Moses summoned all Israel and said: Hear, O Israel, the decrees and laws I declare in your hearing today. Learn them

---

a33 Or *of a god*   *b48* Hebrew; Syriac (see also Deut. 3:9) *Sirion*   *c49* That is, the Dead Sea and be sure to follow them. ²The Lord our God made a covenant with us at Horeb. ³It was not with our fathers that the Lord made this covenant, but with us, with all of us who are alive here today. ⁴The Lord spoke to you face to face out of the fire on the mountain. ⁵(At that time I stood between the Lord and you to declare to you the word of the Lord, because you were afraid of the fire and did not go up the mountain.) And he said:

> ⁶"I am the Lord your God, who brought you out of Egypt, out of the land of slavery.
>
> ⁷"You shall have no other gods before[a] me.
>
> ⁸"You shall not make for yourself an idol in the form of anything in heaven above or on the earth beneath or in the waters below. ⁹You shall not bow down to them or worship them; for I, the Lord your God, am a jealous God, punishing the children for the sin of the fathers to the third and fourth generation of those who hate me, ¹⁰but showing love to a thousand ⸤generations⸥ of those who love me and keep my commandments.
>
> ¹¹"You shall not misuse the name of the Lord your God, for the Lord will not hold anyone guiltless who misuses his name.
>
> ¹²"Observe the Sabbath day by keeping it holy, as the Lord your God has commanded you. ¹³Six days you shall labor and do all your work, ¹⁴but the seventh day is a Sabbath to the Lord your God. On it you shall not do any work, neither you, nor your son or daughter, nor your manservant or maidservant, nor your ox, your donkey or any of your animals, nor the alien within your gates, so that your manservant and maidservant may rest, as you do. ¹⁵Remember that you were slaves in Egypt and that the Lord your God brought you out of there with a mighty hand and an outstretched arm. Therefore the Lord your God has commanded you to observe the Sabbath day.
>
> ¹⁶"Honor your father and your mother,

as the Lord your God has commanded you, so that you may live long and that it may go well with you in the land the Lord your God is giving you.

> ¹⁷"You shall not murder.
>
> ¹⁸"You shall not commit adultery.
>
> ¹⁹"You shall not steal.
>
> ²⁰"You shall not give false testimony against your neighbor.
>
> ²¹"You shall not covet your neighbor's wife. You shall not set your desire on your neighbor's house or land, his manservant or maidservant, his ox or donkey, or anything that belongs to your neighbor."

²²These are the commandments the Lord proclaimed in a loud voice to your whole assembly there on the mountain from out of the fire, the cloud and the deep darkness; and he added nothing more. Then he wrote them on two stone tablets and gave them to me.

²³When you heard the voice out of the darkness, while the mountain was ablaze with fire, all the leading men of your tribes and your elders came to me. ²⁴And you said, "The Lord our God has shown us his glory and his majesty, and we have heard his voice from the fire. Today we have seen that a man can live even if God speaks with him. ²⁵But now, why should we die? This great fire will consume us, and we will die if we hear the voice of the Lord our God any longer. ²⁶For what mortal man has ever heard the voice of the living God speaking out of fire, as we have, and survived? ²⁷Go near and listen to all that the Lord our God says. Then tell us whatever the Lord our God tells you. We will listen and obey."

²⁸The Lord heard you when you spoke to me and the Lord said to me, "I have heard what this people said to you. Everything they said was good. ²⁹Oh, that their hearts would be inclined to fear me and keep all my commands always, so that it might go well with them and their children forever!

³⁰"Go, tell them to return to their tents. ³¹But you stay here with me so that I may give you all the commands, decrees and laws you are to teach them to follow in the land I am giving them to possess."

³²So be careful to do what the Lord your God has commanded you; do not

---

a 7 Or besides

turn aside to the right or to the left.
³³Walk in all the way that the LORD your God has commanded you, so that you may live and prosper and prolong your days in the land that you will possess.

Love the LORD Your God

6 These are the commands, decrees and laws the LORD your God directed me to teach you to observe in the land that you are crossing the Jordan to possess, ²so that you, your children and their children after them may fear the LORD your God as long as you live by keeping all his decrees and commands that I give you, and so that you may enjoy long life. ³Hear, O Israel, and be careful to obey so that it may go well with you and that you may increase greatly in a land flowing with milk and honey, just as the LORD, the God of your fathers, promised you.

⁴Hear, O Israel: The LORD our God, the LORD is one.ᵃ ⁵Love the LORD your God with all your heart and with all your soul and with all your strength. ⁶These commandments that I give you today are to be upon your hearts. ⁷Impress them on your children. Talk about them when you sit at home and when you walk along the road, when you lie down and when you get up. ⁸Tie them as symbols on your hands and bind them on your foreheads. ⁹Write them on the doorframes of your houses and on your gates.

¹⁰When the LORD your God brings you into the land he swore to your fathers, to Abraham, Isaac and Jacob, to give you—a land with large, flourishing cities you did not build, ¹¹houses filled with all kinds of good things you did not provide, wells you did not dig, and vineyards and olive groves you did not plant—then when you eat and are satisfied, ¹²be careful that you do not forget the LORD, who brought you out of Egypt, out of the land of slavery.

¹³Fear the LORD your God, serve him only and take your oaths in his name. ¹⁴Do not follow other gods, the gods of the peoples around you; ¹⁵for the LORD your God, who is among you, is a jealous God and his anger will burn against you, and he will destroy you from the face of the land. ¹⁶Do not test the LORD your God as you did at Massah. ¹⁷Be sure to keep

the commands of the LORD your God and the stipulations and decrees he has given you. ¹⁸Do what is right and good in the LORD's sight, so that it may go well with you and you may go in and take over the good land that the LORD promised on oath to your forefathers, ¹⁹thrusting out all your enemies before you, as the LORD said.

²⁰In the future, when your son asks you, "What is the meaning of the stipulations, decrees and laws the LORD our God has commanded you?" ²¹tell him: "We were slaves of Pharaoh in Egypt, but the LORD brought us out of Egypt with a mighty hand. ²²Before our eyes the LORD sent miraculous signs and wonders—great and terrible—upon Egypt and Pharaoh and his whole household. ²³But he brought us out from there to bring us in and give us the land that he promised on oath to our forefathers. ²⁴The LORD commanded us to obey all these decrees and to fear the LORD our God, so that we might always prosper and be kept alive, as is the case today. ²⁵And if we are careful to obey all this law before the LORD our God, as he has commanded us, that will be our righteousness."

Driving Out the Nations

7 When the LORD your God brings you into the land you are entering to possess and drives out before you many nations—the Hittites, Girgashites, Amorites, Canaanites, Perizzites, Hivites and Jebusites, seven nations larger and stronger than you— ²and when the LORD your God has delivered them over to you and you have defeated them, then you must destroy them totally.ᵇ Make no treaty with them, and show them no mercy. ³Do not intermarry with them. Do not give your daughters to their sons or take their daughters for your sons, ⁴for they will turn your sons away from following me to serve other gods, and the LORD's anger will burn against you and will quickly destroy you. ⁵This is what you are to do to them: Break down their altars, smash their sacred stones, cut down their Asherah polesᶜ and burn their idols in the fire. ⁶For you are a people holy to the LORD your God. The LORD your God has chosen you out of all the peoples on the face of

---

ᵃ4 Or *The LORD our God is one LORD*; or *The LORD is our God, the LORD is one*; or *The LORD is our God, the LORD alone*   ᵇ2 The Hebrew term refers to the irrevocable giving over of things or persons to the LORD, often by totally destroying them; also in verse 26.   ᶜ5 That is, symbols of the goddess Asherah; here and elsewhere in Deuteronomy

VERSE FOR THE DAY:
Deuteronomy 6:5

AUTHOR:
Beverly LaHaye

PASSAGE FOR THE DAY:
Deuteronomy 6:5–12

Love the Lord

AS a young woman just entering college, I dedicated my life to the Lord for whatever he had for me to do. I really wanted to obey Deuteronomy 6:5: "Love the LORD your God with all your heart and with all your soul and with all your strength."

That same desire—to love the Lord totally—remained with me through college and into marriage. I fell in love with Tim and entered marriage knowing that he was called to be a minister. As his partner, I was committed to being a minister's wife and a disciple who dearly loved the Lord.

The early days of our ministry were typical—we had lots of zeal and energy for the Lord, but little money. Our early churches paid very small salaries, and we had to struggle to make ends meet.

God blessed our ministry and our marriage and gave us four wonderful children. Tim worked hard to keep up with a growing ministry and to provide sound Bible teaching. We loved the Lord with all our heart, our soul and strength.

But, practically speaking, we were hurting financially. It became increasingly difficult for us to live on the meager salary many pastors received at that time.

We decided that I would have to work outside the home for a brief period of time until the church could increase our salary. I started by teaching school as a substitute but later took a better-paying position with a company associated with the New York Stock Exchange.

This latter job was a good one that provided early hours so that I could be home when the children were out of school. After one year I was offered an excellent promotion that meant higher wages and a commitment for long-term career employment. This offer for financial security was tempting, but the truth of Deuteronomy 6:6–7 nagged at me. Who would teach this love for God to my children when they sit in my house, when they walk along the road, when they lie down and get up? I wanted that person to be me—not a substitute mom. All the money in the world could not replace that thrill.

I made my choice and my children have been my high priority. We decided to live with less financial security, and as Deuteronomy 6:12 says, we have not forgotten that the Lord brought us through those times, out of financial bondage.

Additional Scripture Readings:
Luke 12:22–34; 1 Timothy 6:6–11

Go to page 189 for your next devotional reading.

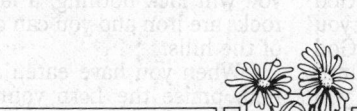

the earth to be his people, his treasured possession.

7The LORD did not set his affection on you and choose you because you were more numerous than other peoples, for you were the fewest of all peoples. 8But it was because the LORD loved you and kept the oath he swore to your forefathers that he brought you out with a mighty hand and redeemed you from the land of slavery, from the power of Pharaoh king of Egypt. 9Know therefore that the LORD your God is God; he is the faithful God, keeping his covenant of love to a thousand generations of those who love him and keep his commands. 10But

those who hate him he will repay to
    their face by destruction;
he will not be slow to repay to their
    face those who hate him.

11Therefore, take care to follow the commands, decrees and laws I give you today.

12If you pay attention to these laws and are careful to follow them, then the LORD your God will keep his covenant of love with you, as he swore to your forefathers. 13He will love you and bless you and increase your numbers. He will bless the fruit of your womb, the crops of your land —your grain, new wine and oil—the calves of your herds and the lambs of your flocks in the land that he swore to your forefathers to give you. 14You will be blessed more than any other people; none of your men or women will be childless, nor any of your livestock without young. 15The LORD will keep you free from every disease. He will not inflict on you the horrible diseases you knew in Egypt, but he will inflict them on all who hate you. 16You must destroy all the peoples the LORD your God gives over to you. Do not look on them with pity and do not serve their gods, for that will be a snare to you.

17You may say to yourselves, "These nations are stronger than we are. How can we drive them out?" 18But do not be afraid of them; remember well what the LORD your God did to Pharaoh and to all Egypt. 19You saw with your own eyes the great trials, the miraculous signs and wonders, the mighty hand and outstretched arm, with which the LORD your God brought you out. The LORD your God will do the same to all the peoples you now fear. 20Moreover, the LORD your God will send the hornet among them until even the survivors who hide from you have perished. 21Do not be terrified by them, for the LORD your God, who is among you, is a great and awesome God. 22The LORD your God will drive out those nations before you, little by little. You will not be allowed to eliminate them all at once, or the wild animals will multiply around you. 23But the LORD your God will deliver them over to you, throwing them into great confusion until they are destroyed. 24He will give their kings into your hand, and you will wipe out their names from under heaven. No one will be able to stand up against you; you will destroy them. 25The images of their gods you are to burn in the fire. Do not covet the silver and gold on them, and do not take it for yourselves, or you will be ensnared by it, for it is detestable to the LORD your God. 26Do not bring a detestable thing into your house or you, like it, will be set apart for destruction. Utterly abhor and detest it, for it is set apart for destruction.

Do Not Forget the LORD

8 Be careful to follow every command I am giving you today, so that you may live and increase and may enter and possess the land that the LORD promised on oath to your forefathers. 2Remember how the LORD your God led you all the way in the desert these forty years, to humble you and to test you in order to know what was in your heart, whether or not you would keep his commands. 3He humbled you, causing you to hunger and then feeding you with manna, which neither you nor your fathers had known, to teach you that man does not live on bread alone but on every word that comes from the mouth of the LORD. 4Your clothes did not wear out and your feet did not swell during these forty years. 5Know then in your heart that as a man disciplines his son, so the LORD your God disciplines you.

6Observe the commands of the LORD your God, walking in his ways and revering him. 7For the LORD your God is bringing you into a good land—a land with streams and pools of water, with springs flowing in the valleys and hills; 8a land with wheat and barley, vines and fig trees, pomegranates, olive oil and honey; 9a land where bread will not be scarce and you will lack nothing; a land where the rocks are iron and you can dig copper out of the hills.

10When you have eaten and are satisfied, praise the LORD your God for the good land he has given you. 11Be careful

VERSE FOR THE DAY:
Deuteronomy 7:9

AUTHOR:
Millie Stamm

PASSAGE FOR THE DAY:
Deuteronomy 7:7–11

A Faithful Friend

FRIENDS are an important part of our lives. Some are casual acquaintances; others close friends; still others more intimate, dear ones. How we appreciate those whom we characterize as "faithful friends," friends who are steadfastly loyal, friends on whom we can depend at all times and for every need.

Yet most of us have experienced the hurt that comes from friends who are unfaithful. Even members of our family may prove unfaithful.

How reassuring to know there is one who is faithful—faithful always and faithful in everything. "Know therefore that the LORD your God is God; he is the faithful God" (Deuteronomy 7:9). Because of his very nature, he could not be God and be unfaithful. We read in 2 Timothy 2:13:

> If we are faithless,
> he will remain faithful,
> for he cannot disown himself.

He never changes. He never fails. He never goes back on one of his promises. God, being who he is, cannot cease to be what he is. He cannot act out of character with himself. Because he is faithful, he will be faithful in his actions.

At times we may forget his faithfulness to us. When trials and testings come, it may seem as if God has surely forgotten us. When friends fail us and our lives are falling apart, we may feel he has forsaken us. There seem to be so few people we can trust. Many people do not keep their word. Our faith in human nature becomes shaken, and we wonder if anyone is honest.

Yet there is One, the faithful God, on whom we can depend. He will never let us down. He has promised:

> "Never will I leave you;
> never will I forsake you" (Hebrews 13:5).

Additional Scripture Readings:
Isaiah 41:9–10; 1 Corinthians 10:13

Go to page 192 for your next devotional reading.

that you do not forget the LORD your God, failing to observe his commands, his laws and his decrees that I am giving you this day. [12]Otherwise, when you eat and are satisfied, when you build fine houses and settle down, [13]and when your herds and flocks grow large and your silver and gold increase and all you have is multiplied, [14]then your heart will become proud and you will forget the LORD your God, who brought you out of Egypt, out of the land of slavery. [15]He led you through the vast and dreadful desert, that thirsty and waterless land, with its venomous snakes and scorpions. He brought you water out of hard rock. [16]He gave you manna to eat in the desert, something your fathers had never known, to humble and to test you so that in the end it might go well with you. [17]You may say to yourself, "My power and the strength of my hands have produced this wealth for me." [18]But remember the LORD your God, for it is he who gives you the ability to produce wealth, and so confirms his covenant, which he swore to your forefathers, as it is today.

[19]If you ever forget the LORD your God and follow other gods and worship and bow down to them, I testify against you today that you will surely be destroyed. [20]Like the nations the LORD destroyed before you, so you will be destroyed for not obeying the LORD your God.

Not Because of Israel's Righteousness

9 Hear, O Israel. You are now about to cross the Jordan to go in and dispossess nations greater and stronger than you, with large cities that have walls up to the sky. [2]The people are strong and tall—Anakites! You know about them and have heard it said: "Who can stand up against the Anakites?" [3]But be assured today that the LORD your God is the one who goes across ahead of you like a devouring fire. He will destroy them; he will subdue them before you. And you will drive them out and annihilate them quickly, as the LORD has promised you.

[4]After the LORD your God has driven them out before you, do not say to yourself, "The LORD has brought me here to take possession of this land because of my righteousness." No, it is on account of the wickedness of these nations that the LORD is going to drive them out before you. [5]It is not because of your righteous-

ness or your integrity that you are going in to take possession of their land; but on account of the wickedness of these nations, the LORD your God will drive them out before you, to accomplish what he swore to your fathers, to Abraham, Isaac and Jacob. [6]Understand, then, that it is not because of your righteousness that the LORD your God is giving you this good land to possess, for you are a stiff-necked people.

The Golden Calf

[7]Remember this and never forget how you provoked the LORD your God to anger in the desert. From the day you left Egypt until you arrived here, you have been rebellious against the LORD. [8]At Horeb you aroused the LORD's wrath so that he was angry enough to destroy you. [9]When I went up on the mountain to receive the tablets of stone, the tablets of the covenant that the LORD had made with you, I stayed on the mountain forty days and forty nights; I ate no bread and drank no water. [10]The LORD gave me two stone tablets inscribed by the finger of God. On them were all the commandments the LORD proclaimed to you on the mountain out of the fire, on the day of the assembly.

[11]At the end of the forty days and forty nights, the LORD gave me the two stone tablets, the tablets of the covenant. [12]Then the LORD told me, "Go down from here at once, because your people whom you brought out of Egypt have become corrupt. They have turned away quickly from what I commanded them and have made a cast idol for themselves."

[13]And the LORD said to me, "I have seen this people, and they are a stiff-necked people indeed! [14]Let me alone, so that I may destroy them and blot out their name from under heaven. And I will make you into a nation stronger and more numerous than they."

[15]So I turned and went down from the mountain while it was ablaze with fire. And the two tablets of the covenant were in my hands.[a] [16]When I looked, I saw that you had sinned against the LORD your God; you had made for yourselves an idol cast in the shape of a calf. You had turned aside quickly from the way that the LORD had commanded you. [17]So I took the two tablets and threw them out of my hands, breaking them to pieces before your eyes. [18]Then once again I fell prostrate be-

---

[a]15 Or *And I had the two tablets of the covenant with me, one in each hand*

fore the LORD for forty days and forty nights; I ate no bread and drank no water, because of all the sin you had committed, doing what was evil in the LORD's sight and so provoking him to anger. ¹⁹I feared the anger and wrath of the LORD, for he was angry enough with you to destroy you. But again the LORD listened to me. ²⁰And the LORD was angry enough with Aaron to destroy him, but at that time I prayed for Aaron too. ²¹Also I took that sinful thing of yours, the calf you had made, and burned it in the fire. Then I crushed it and ground it to powder as fine as dust and threw the dust into a stream that flowed down the mountain.

²²You also made the LORD angry at Taberah, at Massah and at Kibroth Hattaavah.

²³And when the LORD sent you out from Kadesh Barnea, he said, "Go up and take possession of the land I have given you." But you rebelled against the command of the LORD your God. You did not trust him or obey him. ²⁴You have been rebellious against the LORD ever since I have known you.

²⁵I lay prostrate before the LORD those forty days and forty nights because the LORD had said he would destroy you. ²⁶I prayed to the LORD and said, "O Sovereign LORD, do not destroy your people, your own inheritance that you redeemed by your great power and brought out of Egypt with a mighty hand. ²⁷Remember your servants Abraham, Isaac and Jacob. Overlook the stubbornness of this people, their wickedness and their sin. ²⁸Otherwise, the country from which you brought us will say, 'Because the LORD was not able to take them into the land he had promised them, and because he hated them, he brought them out to put them to death in the desert.' ²⁹But they are your people, your inheritance that you brought out by your great power and your outstretched arm."

Tablets Like the First Ones

10 At that time the LORD said to me, "Chisel out two stone tablets like the first ones and come up to me on the mountain. Also make a wooden chest.ᵃ ²I will write on the tablets the words that were on the first tablets, which you broke. Then you are to put them in the chest."

³So I made the ark out of acacia wood and chiseled out two stone tablets like the first ones, and I went up on the mountain with the two tablets in my hands. ⁴The LORD wrote on these tablets what he had written before, the Ten Commandments he had proclaimed to you on the mountain, out of the fire, on the day of the assembly. And the LORD gave them to me. ⁵Then I came back down the mountain and put the tablets in the ark I had made, as the LORD commanded me, and they are there now.

⁶(The Israelites traveled from the wells of the Jaakanites to Moserah. There Aaron died and was buried, and Eleazar his son succeeded him as priest. ⁷From there they traveled to Gudgodah and on to Jotbathah, a land with streams of water. ⁸At that time the LORD set apart the tribe of Levi to carry the ark of the covenant of the LORD, to stand before the LORD to minister and to pronounce blessings in his name, as they still do today. ⁹That is why the Levites have no share or inheritance among their brothers; the LORD is their inheritance, as the LORD your God told them.)

¹⁰Now I had stayed on the mountain forty days and nights, as I did the first time, and the LORD listened to me at this time also. It was not his will to destroy you. ¹¹"Go," the LORD said to me, "and lead the people on their way, so that they may enter and possess the land that I swore to their fathers to give them."

Fear the LORD

¹²And now, O Israel, what does the LORD your God ask of you but to fear the LORD your God, to walk in all his ways, to love him, to serve the LORD your God with all your heart and with all your soul, ¹³and to observe the LORD's commands and decrees that I am giving you today for your own good?

¹⁴To the LORD your God belong the heavens, even the highest heavens, the earth and everything in it. ¹⁵Yet the LORD set his affection on your forefathers and loved them, and he chose you, their descendants, above all the nations, as it is today. ¹⁶Circumcise your hearts, therefore, and do not be stiff-necked any longer. ¹⁷For the LORD your God is God of gods and Lord of lords, the great God, mighty and awesome, who shows no partiality and accepts no bribes. ¹⁸He defends the

---

ᵃ1 That is, an ark

cause of the fatherless and the widow, and loves the alien, giving him food and clothing. ¹⁹And you are to love those who are aliens, for you yourselves were aliens in Egypt. ²⁰Fear the LORD your God and serve him. Hold fast to him and take your oaths in his name. ²¹He is your praise; he is your God, who performed for you those great and awesome wonders you saw with your own eyes. ²²Your forefathers who went down into Egypt were seventy in all, and now the LORD your God has made you as numerous as the stars in the sky.

Love and Obey the LORD

11 Love the LORD your God and keep his requirements, his decrees, his laws and his commands always. ²Remember today that your children were not the ones who saw and experienced the discipline of the LORD your God: his majesty, his mighty hand, his outstretched arm; ³the signs he performed and the things he did in the heart of Egypt, both to Pharaoh king of Egypt and to his whole country; ⁴what he did to the Egyptian army, to its horses and chariots, how he overwhelmed

THURSDAY

VERSE FOR THE DAY:
Deuteronomy 10:16

AUTHOR:
Susan L. Lenzkes

PASSAGE FOR THE DAY:
Deuteronomy 10:12–22

Flexible Living

MANY of us are crippled from birth. The backbone of our standard for living comes fused into unyielding rules and regulations. We are rigid in our determination to control life's course and outcome.

We're sure, for example, how people ought to look, behave, and respond. Things have to be done a certain way—our way. We know, too, exactly how a godly marriage should operate; and we're quite familiar with the model of the ideal Christian family scene—which, of course, we intend to duplicate perfectly.

Then real life sneaks up and whacks us from behind, seeking to break our unbending back and our stiff neck, threatening to paralyze us.

There is a cure. We are offered opportunity to exercise the suppleness of godly grace and perspective. Each time life throws us a punch, we can do a deep-knee bend, forcing our muscles of faith, hope, and understanding to stretch.

Eventually that brittle backbone will grow strong and supple, bending with the rhythms of grace yet standing tall and firm in the face of compromise.

All of this requires considerable daily "give." Such give is not a one-time choice but a lifestyle of generosity, spontaneity, and openness to truth.

How often I have thought that if I could give just one gift to my children—besides a heart for God—it would be the golden gift of flexibility.

Additional Scripture Readings:
Matthew 23:23–24; 1 Corinthians 9:19–23

Go to page 211 for your next devotional reading.

them with the waters of the Red Sea[a] as they were pursuing you, and how the LORD brought lasting ruin on them. [5]It was not your children who saw what he did for you in the desert until you arrived at this place, [6]and what he did to Dathan and Abiram, sons of Eliab the Reubenite, when the earth opened its mouth right in the middle of all Israel and swallowed them up with their households, their tents and every living thing that belonged to them. [7]But it was your own eyes that saw all these great things the LORD has done.

[8]Observe therefore all the commands I am giving you today, so that you may have the strength to go in and take over the land that you are crossing the Jordan to possess, [9]and so that you may live long in the land that the LORD swore to your forefathers to give to them and their descendants, a land flowing with milk and honey. [10]The land you are entering to take over is not like the land of Egypt, from which you have come, where you planted your seed and irrigated it by foot as in a vegetable garden. [11]But the land you are crossing the Jordan to take possession of is a land of mountains and valleys that drinks rain from heaven. [12]It is a land the LORD your God cares for; the eyes of the LORD your God are continually on it from the beginning of the year to its end.

[13]So if you faithfully obey the commands I am giving you today—to love the LORD your God and to serve him with all your heart and with all your soul— [14]then I will send rain on your land in its season, both autumn and spring rains, so that you may gather in your grain, new wine and oil. [15]I will provide grass in the fields for your cattle, and you will eat and be satisfied.

[16]Be careful, or you will be enticed to turn away and worship other gods and bow down to them. [17]Then the LORD's anger will burn against you, and he will shut the heavens so that it will not rain and the ground will yield no produce, and you will soon perish from the good land the LORD is giving you. [18]Fix these words of mine in your hearts and minds; tie them as symbols on your hands and bind them on your foreheads. [19]Teach them to your children, talking about them when you sit at home and when you walk along the road, when you lie down and when you get up. [20]Write them on the doorframes of your houses and on your gates, [21]so that your days and the days of your children may be many in the land that the LORD swore to give your forefathers, as many as the days that the heavens are above the earth.

[22]If you carefully observe all these commands I am giving you to follow—to love the LORD your God, to walk in all his ways and to hold fast to him— [23]then the LORD will drive out all these nations before you, and you will dispossess nations larger and stronger than you. [24]Every place where you set your foot will be yours: Your territory will extend from the desert to Lebanon, and from the Euphrates River to the western sea.[b] [25]No man will be able to stand against you. The LORD your God, as he promised you, will put the terror and fear of you on the whole land, wherever you go.

[26]See, I am setting before you today a blessing and a curse— [27]the blessing if you obey the commands of the LORD your God that I am giving you today; [28]the curse if you disobey the commands of the LORD your God and turn from the way that I command you today by following other gods, which you have not known. [29]When the LORD your God has brought you into the land you are entering to possess, you are to proclaim on Mount Gerizim the blessings, and on Mount Ebal the curses. [30]As you know, these mountains are across the Jordan, west of the road,[c] toward the setting sun, near the great trees of Moreh, in the territory of those Canaanites living in the Arabah in the vicinity of Gilgal. [31]You are about to cross the Jordan to enter and take possession of the land the LORD your God is giving you. When you have taken it over and are living there, [32]be sure that you obey all the decrees and laws I am setting before you today.

The One Place of Worship

12 These are the decrees and laws you must be careful to follow in the land that the LORD, the God of your fathers, has given you to possess—as long as you live in the land. [2]Destroy completely all the places on the high mountains and on the hills and under every

a4 Hebrew Yam Suph; that is, Sea of Reeds   b24 That is, the Mediterranean   c30 Or Jordan, westward spreading tree where the nations you are dispossessing worship their gods. ³Break down their altars, smash their sacred stones and burn their Asherah poles in the fire; cut down the idols of their gods and wipe out their names from those places.

⁴You must not worship the LORD your God in their way. ⁵But you are to seek the place the LORD your God will choose from among all your tribes to put his Name there for his dwelling. To that place you must go; ⁶there bring your burnt offerings and sacrifices, your tithes and special gifts, what you have vowed to give and your freewill offerings, and the firstborn of your herds and flocks. ⁷There, in the presence of the LORD your God, you and your families shall eat and shall rejoice in everything you have put your hand to, because the LORD your God has blessed you.

⁸You are not to do as we do here today, everyone as he sees fit, ⁹since you have not yet reached the resting place and the inheritance the LORD your God is giving you. ¹⁰But you will cross the Jordan and settle in the land the LORD your God is giving you as an inheritance, and he will give you rest from all your enemies around you so that you will live in safety. ¹¹Then to the place the LORD your God will choose as a dwelling for his Name—there you are to bring everything I command you: your burnt offerings and sacrifices, your tithes and special gifts, and all the choice possessions you have vowed to the LORD. ¹²And there rejoice before the LORD your God, you, your sons and daughters, your menservants and maidservants, and the Levites from your towns, who have no allotment or inheritance of their own. ¹³Be careful not to sacrifice your burnt offerings anywhere you please. ¹⁴Offer them only at the place the LORD will choose in one of your tribes, and there observe everything I command you.

¹⁵Nevertheless, you may slaughter your animals in any of your towns and eat as much of the meat as you want, as if it were gazelle or deer, according to the blessing the LORD your God gives you. Both the ceremonially unclean and the clean may eat it. ¹⁶But you must not eat the blood; pour it out on the ground like water. ¹⁷You must not eat in your own towns the tithe of your grain and new wine and oil, or the firstborn of your herds and flocks, or whatever you have vowed to give, or your freewill offerings or special gifts. ¹⁸Instead, you are to eat them in the

presence of the LORD your God at the place the LORD your God will choose— you, your sons and daughters, your menservants and maidservants, and the Levites from your towns—and you are to rejoice before the LORD your God in everything you put your hand to. ¹⁹Be careful not to neglect the Levites as long as you live in your land.

²⁰When the LORD your God has enlarged your territory as he promised you, and you crave meat and say, "I would like some meat," then you may eat as much of it as you want. ²¹If the place where the LORD your God chooses to put his Name is too far away from you, you may slaughter animals from the herds and flocks the LORD has given you, as I have commanded you, and in your own towns you may eat as much of them as you want. ²²Eat them as you would gazelle or deer. Both the ceremonially unclean and the clean may eat. ²³But be sure you do not eat the blood, because the blood is the life, and you must not eat the life with the meat. ²⁴You must not eat the blood; pour it out on the ground like water. ²⁵Do not eat it, so that it may go well with you and your children after you, because you will be doing what is right in the eyes of the LORD.

²⁶But take your consecrated things and whatever you have vowed to give, and go to the place the LORD will choose. ²⁷Present your burnt offerings on the altar of the LORD your God, both the meat and the blood. The blood of your sacrifices must be poured beside the altar of the LORD your God, but you may eat the meat. ²⁸Be careful to obey all these regulations I am giving you, so that it may always go well with you and your children after you, because you will be doing what is good and right in the eyes of the LORD your God.

²⁹The LORD your God will cut off before you the nations you are about to invade and dispossess. But when you have driven them out and settled in their land, ³⁰and after they have been destroyed before you, be careful not to be ensnared by inquiring about their gods, saying, "How do these nations serve their gods? We will do the same." ³¹You must not worship the LORD your God in their way, because in worshiping their gods, they do all kinds of detestable things the LORD hates. They even burn their sons and daughters in the fire as sacrifices to their gods.

³²See that you do all I command you; do not add to it or take away from it.

Worshiping Other Gods

13 If a prophet, or one who foretells by dreams, appears among you and announces to you a miraculous sign or wonder, ²and if the sign or wonder of which he has spoken takes place, and he says, "Let us follow other gods" (gods you have not known) "and let us worship them," ³you must not listen to the words of that prophet or dreamer. The LORD your God is testing you to find out whether you love him with all your heart and with all your soul. ⁴It is the LORD your God you must follow, and him you must revere. Keep his commands and obey him; serve him and hold fast to him. ⁵That prophet or dreamer must be put to death, because he preached rebellion against the LORD your God, who brought you out of Egypt and redeemed you from the land of slavery; he has tried to turn you from the way the LORD your God commanded you to follow. You must purge the evil from among you.

⁶If your very own brother, or your son or daughter, or the wife you love, or your closest friend secretly entices you, saying, "Let us go and worship other gods" (gods that neither you nor your fathers have known, ⁷gods of the peoples around you, whether near or far, from one end of the land to the other), ⁸do not yield to him or listen to him. Show him no pity. Do not spare him or shield him. ⁹You must certainly put him to death. Your hand must be the first in putting him to death, and then the hands of all the people. ¹⁰Stone him to death, because he tried to turn you away from the LORD your God, who brought you out of Egypt, out of the land of slavery. ¹¹Then all Israel will hear and be afraid, and no one among you will do such an evil thing again.

¹²If you hear it said about one of the towns the LORD your God is giving you to live in ¹³that wicked men have arisen among you and have led the people of their town astray, saying, "Let us go and worship other gods" (gods you have not known), ¹⁴then you must inquire, probe and investigate it thoroughly. And if it is true and it has been proved that this detestable thing has been done among you, ¹⁵you must certainly put to the sword all who live in that town. Destroy it completely,ᵃ both its people and its livestock.

¹⁶Gather all the plunder of the town into the middle of the public square and completely burn the town and all its plunder as a whole burnt offering to the LORD your God. It is to remain a ruin forever, never to be rebuilt. ¹⁷None of those condemned thingsᵃ shall be found in your hands, so that the LORD will turn from his fierce anger; he will show you mercy, have compassion on you, and increase your numbers, as he promised on oath to your forefathers, ¹⁸because you obey the LORD your God, keeping all his commands that I am giving you today and doing what is right in his eyes.

Clean and Unclean Food

14 You are the children of the LORD your God. Do not cut yourselves or shave the front of your heads for the dead, ²for you are a people holy to the LORD your God. Out of all the peoples on the face of the earth, the LORD has chosen you to be his treasured possession.

³Do not eat any detestable thing. ⁴These are the animals you may eat: the ox, the sheep, the goat, ⁵the deer, the gazelle, the roe deer, the wild goat, the ibex, the antelope and the mountain sheep.ᵇ ⁶You may eat any animal that has a split hoof divided in two and that chews the cud. ⁷However, of those that chew the cud or that have a split hoof completely divided you may not eat the camel, the rabbit or the coney.ᶜ Although they chew the cud, they do not have a split hoof; they are ceremonially unclean for you. ⁸The pig is also unclean; although it has a split hoof, it does not chew the cud. You are not to eat their meat or touch their carcasses.

⁹Of all the creatures living in the water, you may eat any that has fins and scales. ¹⁰But anything that does not have fins and scales you may not eat; for you it is unclean.

¹¹You may eat any clean bird. ¹²But these you may not eat: the eagle, the vulture, the black vulture, ¹³the red kite, the black kite, any kind of falcon, ¹⁴any kind of raven, ¹⁵the horned owl, the screech owl, the gull, any kind of hawk, ¹⁶the little owl, the great owl, the white owl, ¹⁷the desert owl, the osprey, the cormorant, ¹⁸the stork, any kind of heron, the hoopoe and the bat.

ᵃ15,17 The Hebrew term refers to the irrevocable giving over of things or persons to the LORD, often by totally destroying them.   ᵇ5 The precise identification of some of the birds and animals in this chapter is uncertain.   ᶜ7 That is, the hyrax or rock badger

¹⁹All flying insects that swarm are unclean to you; do not eat them. ²⁰But any winged creature that is clean you may eat.

²¹Do not eat anything you find already dead. You may give it to an alien living in any of your towns, and he may eat it, or you may sell it to a foreigner. But you are a people holy to the Lord your God.

Do not cook a young goat in its mother's milk.

Tithes

²²Be sure to set aside a tenth of all that your fields produce each year. ²³Eat the tithe of your grain, new wine and oil, and the firstborn of your herds and flocks in the presence of the Lord your God at the place he will choose as a dwelling for his Name, so that you may learn to revere the Lord your God always. ²⁴But if that place is too distant and you have been blessed by the Lord your God and cannot carry your tithe (because the place where the Lord will choose to put his Name is so far away), ²⁵then exchange your tithe for silver, and take the silver with you and go to the place the Lord your God will choose. ²⁶Use the silver to buy whatever you like: cattle, sheep, wine or other fermented drink, or anything you wish. Then you and your household shall eat there in the presence of the Lord your God and rejoice. ²⁷And do not neglect the Levites living in your towns, for they have no allotment or inheritance of their own.

²⁸At the end of every three years, bring all the tithes of that year's produce and store it in your towns, ²⁹so that the Levites (who have no allotment or inheritance of their own) and the aliens, the fatherless and the widows who live in your towns may come and eat and be satisfied, and so that the Lord your God may bless you in all the work of your hands.

The Year for Canceling Debts

15 At the end of every seven years you must cancel debts. ²This is how it is to be done: Every creditor shall cancel the loan he has made to his fellow Israelite. He shall not require payment from his fellow Israelite or brother, because the Lord's time for canceling debts has been proclaimed. ³You may require payment from a foreigner, but you must cancel any debt your brother owes you. ⁴However, there should be no poor among you, for in the land the Lord your God is giving you to possess as your inheritance, he will

richly bless you, ⁵if only you fully obey the Lord your God and are careful to follow all these commands I am giving you today. ⁶For the Lord your God will bless you as he has promised, and you will lend to many nations but will borrow from none. You will rule over many nations but none will rule over you.

⁷If there is a poor man among your brothers in any of the towns of the land that the Lord your God is giving you, do not be hardhearted or tightfisted toward your poor brother. ⁸Rather be openhanded and freely lend him whatever he needs. ⁹Be careful not to harbor this wicked thought: "The seventh year, the year for canceling debts, is near," so that you do not show ill will toward your needy brother and give him nothing. He may then appeal to the Lord against you, and you will be found guilty of sin. ¹⁰Give generously to him and do so without a grudging heart; then because of this the Lord your God will bless you in all your work and in everything you put your hand to. ¹¹There will always be poor people in the land. Therefore I command you to be openhanded toward your brothers and toward the poor and needy in your land.

Freeing Servants

¹²If a fellow Hebrew, a man or a woman, sells himself to you and serves you six years, in the seventh year you must let him go free. ¹³And when you release him, do not send him away empty-handed. ¹⁴Supply him liberally from your flock, your threshing floor and your winepress. Give to him as the Lord your God has blessed you. ¹⁵Remember that you were slaves in Egypt and the Lord your God redeemed you. That is why I give you this command today.

¹⁶But if your servant says to you, "I do not want to leave you," because he loves you and your family and is well off with you, ¹⁷then take an awl and push it through his ear lobe into the door, and he will become your servant for life. Do the same for your maidservant.

¹⁸Do not consider it a hardship to set your servant free, because his service to you these six years has been worth twice as much as that of a hired hand. And the Lord your God will bless you in everything you do.

The Firstborn Animals

¹⁹Set apart for the Lord your God every firstborn male of your herds and flocks.

Do not put the firstborn of your oxen to work, and do not shear the firstborn of your sheep. [20]Each year you and your family are to eat them in the presence of the LORD your God at the place he will choose. [21]If an animal has a defect, is lame or blind, or has any serious flaw, you must not sacrifice it to the LORD your God. [22]You are to eat it in your own towns. Both the ceremonially unclean and the clean may eat it, as if it were gazelle or deer. [23]But you must not eat the blood; pour it out on the ground like water.

Passover

16 Observe the month of Abib and celebrate the Passover of the LORD your God, because in the month of Abib he brought you out of Egypt by night. [2]Sacrifice as the Passover to the LORD your God an animal from your flock or herd at the place the LORD will choose as a dwelling for his Name. [3]Do not eat it with bread made with yeast, but for seven days eat unleavened bread, the bread of affliction, because you left Egypt in haste—so that all the days of your life you may remember the time of your departure from Egypt. [4]Let no yeast be found in your possession in all your land for seven days. Do not let any of the meat you sacrifice on the evening of the first day remain until morning.

[5]You must not sacrifice the Passover in any town the LORD your God gives you [6]except in the place he will choose as a dwelling for his Name. There you must sacrifice the Passover in the evening, when the sun goes down, on the anniversary[a] of your departure from Egypt. [7]Roast it and eat it at the place the LORD your God will choose. Then in the morning return to your tents. [8]For six days eat unleavened bread and on the seventh day hold an assembly to the LORD your God and do no work.

Feast of Weeks

[9]Count off seven weeks from the time you begin to put the sickle to the standing grain. [10]Then celebrate the Feast of Weeks to the LORD your God by giving a freewill offering in proportion to the blessings the LORD your God has given you. [11]And rejoice before the LORD your God at the place he will choose as a dwelling for his Name—you, your sons and daughters, your menservants and

maidservants, the Levites in your towns, and the aliens, the fatherless and the widows living among you. [12]Remember that you were slaves in Egypt, and follow carefully these decrees.

Feast of Tabernacles

[13]Celebrate the Feast of Tabernacles for seven days after you have gathered the produce of your threshing floor and your winepress. [14]Be joyful at your Feast—you, your sons and daughters, your menservants and maidservants, and the Levites, the aliens, the fatherless and the widows who live in your towns. [15]For seven days celebrate the Feast to the LORD your God at the place the LORD will choose. For the LORD your God will bless you in all your harvest and in all the work of your hands, and your joy will be complete.

[16]Three times a year all your men must appear before the LORD your God at the place he will choose: at the Feast of Unleavened Bread, the Feast of Weeks and the Feast of Tabernacles. No man should appear before the LORD empty-handed: [17]Each of you must bring a gift in proportion to the way the LORD your God has blessed you.

Judges

[18]Appoint judges and officials for each of your tribes in every town the LORD your God is giving you, and they shall judge the people fairly. [19]Do not pervert justice or show partiality. Do not accept a bribe, for a bribe blinds the eyes of the wise and twists the words of the righteous. [20]Follow justice and justice alone, so that you may live and possess the land the LORD your God is giving you.

Worshiping Other Gods

[21]Do not set up any wooden Asherah pole[b] beside the altar you build to the LORD your God, [22]and do not erect a sacred stone, for these the LORD your God hates.

17 Do not sacrifice to the LORD your God an ox or a sheep that has any defect or flaw in it, for that would be detestable to him.

[2]If a man or woman living among you in one of the towns the LORD gives you is found doing evil in the eyes of the LORD your God in violation of his covenant, [3]and contrary to my command has wor-

---

a6 Or down, at the time of day   *b21 Or Do not plant any tree dedicated to Asherah* shiped other gods, bowing down to them or to the sun or the moon or the stars of the sky, [4]and this has been brought to your attention, then you must investigate it thoroughly. If it is true and it has been proved that this detestable thing has been done in Israel, [5]take the man or woman who has done this evil deed to your city gate and stone that person to death. [6]On the testimony of two or three witnesses a man shall be put to death, but no one shall be put to death on the testimony of only one witness. [7]The hands of the witnesses must be the first in putting him to death, and then the hands of all the people. You must purge the evil from among you.

Law Courts

[8]If cases come before your courts that are too difficult for you to judge — whether bloodshed, lawsuits or assaults — take them to the place the LORD your God will choose. [9]Go to the priests, who are Levites, and to the judge who is in office at that time. Inquire of them and they will give you the verdict. [10]You must act according to the decisions they give you at the place the LORD will choose. Be careful to do everything they direct you to do. [11]Act according to the law they teach you and the decisions they give you. Do not turn aside from what they tell you, to the right or to the left. [12]The man who shows contempt for the judge or for the priest who stands ministering there to the LORD your God must be put to death. You must purge the evil from Israel. [13]All the people will hear and be afraid, and will not be contemptuous again.

The King

[14]When you enter the land the LORD your God is giving you and have taken possession of it and settled in it, and you say, "Let us set a king over us like all the nations around us," [15]be sure to appoint over you the king the LORD your God chooses. He must be from among your own brothers. Do not place a foreigner over you, one who is not a brother Israelite. [16]The king, moreover, must not acquire great numbers of horses for himself or make the people return to Egypt to get more of them, for the LORD has told you, "You are not to go back that way again." [17]He must not take many wives, or his heart will be led astray. He must not accumulate large amounts of silver and gold.

[18]When he takes the throne of his kingdom, he is to write for himself on a scroll a copy of this law, taken from that of the priests, who are Levites. [19]It is to be with him, and he is to read it all the days of his life so that he may learn to revere the LORD his God and follow carefully all the words of this law and these decrees [20]and not consider himself better than his brothers and turn from the law to the right or to the left. Then he and his descendants will reign a long time over his kingdom in Israel.

Offerings for Priests and Levites

18 The priests, who are Levites — indeed the whole tribe of Levi — are to have no allotment or inheritance with Israel. They shall live on the offerings made to the LORD by fire, for that is their inheritance. [2]They shall have no inheritance among their brothers; the LORD is their inheritance, as he promised them.

[3]This is the share due the priests from the people who sacrifice a bull or a sheep: the shoulder, the jowls and the inner parts. [4]You are to give them the firstfruits of your grain, new wine and oil, and the first wool from the shearing of your sheep, [5]for the LORD your God has chosen them and their descendants out of all your tribes to stand and minister in the LORD's name always.

[6]If a Levite moves from one of your towns anywhere in Israel where he is living, and comes in all earnestness to the place the LORD will choose, [7]he may minister in the name of the LORD his God like all his fellow Levites who serve there in the presence of the LORD. [8]He is to share equally in their benefits, even though he has received money from the sale of family possessions.

Detestable Practices

[9]When you enter the land the LORD your God is giving you, do not learn to imitate the detestable ways of the nations there. [10]Let no one be found among you who sacrifices his son or daughter in[a] the fire, who practices divination or sorcery, interprets omens, engages in witchcraft, [11]or casts spells, or who is a medium or spiritist or who consults the dead. [12]Anyone

---

[a]10 Or *who makes his son or daughter pass through*

who does these things is detestable to the Lord, and because of these detestable practices the Lord your God will drive out those nations before you. ¹³You must be blameless before the Lord your God.

The Prophet

¹⁴The nations you will dispossess listen to those who practice sorcery or divination. But as for you, the Lord your God has not permitted you to do so. ¹⁵The Lord your God will raise up for you a prophet like me from among your own brothers. You must listen to him. ¹⁶For this is what you asked of the Lord your God at Horeb on the day of the assembly when you said, "Let us not hear the voice of the Lord our God nor see this great fire anymore, or we will die."

¹⁷The Lord said to me: "What they say is good. ¹⁸I will raise up for them a prophet like you from among their brothers; I will put my words in his mouth, and he will tell them everything I command him. ¹⁹If anyone does not listen to my words that the prophet speaks in my name, I myself will call him to account. ²⁰But a prophet who presumes to speak in my name anything I have not commanded him to say, or a prophet who speaks in the name of other gods, must be put to death."

²¹You may say to yourselves, "How can we know when a message has not been spoken by the Lord?" ²²If what a prophet proclaims in the name of the Lord does not take place or come true, that is a message the Lord has not spoken. That prophet has spoken presumptuously. Do not be afraid of him.

Cities of Refuge

19 When the Lord your God has destroyed the nations whose land he is giving you, and when you have driven them out and settled in their towns and houses, ²then set aside for yourselves three cities centrally located in the land the Lord your God is giving you to possess. ³Build roads to them and divide into three parts the land the Lord your God is giving you as an inheritance, so that anyone who kills a man may flee there.

⁴This is the rule concerning the man who kills another and flees there to save his life—one who kills his neighbor unintentionally, without malice aforethought. ⁵For instance, a man may go into the forest with his neighbor to cut wood, and as he swings his ax to fell a tree, the head may fly off and hit his neighbor and kill him. That man may flee to one of these cities and save his life. ⁶Otherwise, the avenger of blood might pursue him in a rage, overtake him if the distance is too great, and kill him even though he is not deserving of death, since he did it to his neighbor without malice aforethought. ⁷This is why I command you to set aside for yourselves three cities.

⁸If the Lord your God enlarges your territory, as he promised on oath to your forefathers, and gives you the whole land he promised them, ⁹because you carefully follow all these laws I command you today—to love the Lord your God and to walk always in his ways—then you are to set aside three more cities. ¹⁰Do this so that innocent blood will not be shed in your land, which the Lord your God is giving you as your inheritance, and so that you will not be guilty of bloodshed.

¹¹But if a man hates his neighbor and lies in wait for him, assaults and kills him, and then flees to one of these cities, ¹²the elders of his town shall send for him, bring him back from the city, and hand him over to the avenger of blood to die. ¹³Show him no pity. You must purge from Israel the guilt of shedding innocent blood, so that it may go well with you.

¹⁴Do not move your neighbor's boundary stone set up by your predecessors in the inheritance you receive in the land the Lord your God is giving you to possess.

Witnesses

¹⁵One witness is not enough to convict a man accused of any crime or offense he may have committed. A matter must be established by the testimony of two or three witnesses.

¹⁶If a malicious witness takes the stand to accuse a man of a crime, ¹⁷the two men involved in the dispute must stand in the presence of the Lord before the priests and the judges who are in office at the time. ¹⁸The judges must make a thorough investigation, and if the witness proves to be a liar, giving false testimony against his brother, ¹⁹then do to him as he intended to do to his brother. You must purge the evil from among you. ²⁰The rest of the people will hear of this and be afraid, and never again will such an evil thing be done among you. ²¹Show no pity: life for life, eye for eye, tooth for tooth, hand for hand, foot for foot.

Going to War

20 When you go to war against your enemies and see horses and chariots and an army greater than yours, do not be afraid of them, because the LORD your God, who brought you up out of Egypt, will be with you. ²When you are about to go into battle, the priest shall come forward and address the army. ³He shall say: "Hear, O Israel, today you are going into battle against your enemies. Do not be fainthearted or afraid; do not be terrified or give way to panic before them. ⁴For the LORD your God is the one who goes with you to fight for you against your enemies to give you victory."

⁵The officers shall say to the army: "Has anyone built a new house and not dedicated it? Let him go home, or he may die in battle and someone else may dedicate it. ⁶Has anyone planted a vineyard and not begun to enjoy it? Let him go home, or he may die in battle and someone else enjoy it. ⁷Has anyone become pledged to a woman and not married her? Let him go home, or he may die in battle and someone else marry her." ⁸Then the officers shall add, "Is any man afraid or fainthearted? Let him go home so that his brothers will not become disheartened too." ⁹When the officers have finished speaking to the army, they shall appoint commanders over it.

¹⁰When you march up to attack a city, make its people an offer of peace. ¹¹If they accept and open their gates, all the people in it shall be subject to forced labor and shall work for you. ¹²If they refuse to make peace and they engage you in battle, lay siege to that city. ¹³When the LORD your God delivers it into your hand, put to the sword all the men in it. ¹⁴As for the women, the children, the livestock and everything else in the city, you may take these as plunder for yourselves. And you may use the plunder the LORD your God gives you from your enemies. ¹⁵This is how you are to treat all the cities that are at a distance from you and do not belong to the nations nearby.

¹⁶However, in the cities of the nations the LORD your God is giving you as an inheritance, do not leave alive anything that breathes. ¹⁷Completely destroy*a* them—the Hittites, Amorites, Canaanites, Perizzites, Hivites and Jebusites—as the LORD your God has commanded you.

¹⁸Otherwise, they will teach you to follow all the detestable things they do in worshiping their gods, and you will sin against the LORD your God.

¹⁹When you lay siege to a city for a long time, fighting against it to capture it, do not destroy its trees by putting an ax to them, because you can eat their fruit. Do not cut them down. Are the trees of the field people, that you should besiege them?*b* ²⁰However, you may cut down trees that you know are not fruit trees and use them to build siege works until the city at war with you falls.

Atonement for an Unsolved Murder

21 If a man is found slain, lying in a field in the land the LORD your God is giving you to possess, and it is not known who killed him, ²your elders and judges shall go out and measure the distance from the body to the neighboring towns. ³Then the elders of the town nearest the body shall take a heifer that has never been worked and has never worn a yoke ⁴and lead her down to a valley that has not been plowed or planted and where there is a flowing stream. There in the valley they are to break the heifer's neck. ⁵The priests, the sons of Levi, shall step forward, for the LORD your God has chosen them to minister and to pronounce blessings in the name of the LORD and to decide all cases of dispute and assault. ⁶Then all the elders of the town nearest the body shall wash their hands over the heifer whose neck was broken in the valley, ⁷and they shall declare: "Our hands did not shed this blood, nor did our eyes see it done. ⁸Accept this atonement for your people Israel, whom you have redeemed, O LORD, and do not hold your people guilty of the blood of an innocent man." And the bloodshed will be atoned for. ⁹So you will purge from yourselves the guilt of shedding innocent blood, since you have done what is right in the eyes of the LORD.

Marrying a Captive Woman

¹⁰When you go to war against your enemies and the LORD your God delivers them into your hands and you take captives, ¹¹if you notice among the captives a beautiful woman and are attracted to her, you may take her as your wife. ¹²Bring her into your home and have her shave her head,

---

a17 The Hebrew term refers to the irrevocable giving over of things or persons to the LORD, often by totally destroying them.　　*b19* Or *down to use in the siege, for the fruit trees are for the benefit of man.*

trim her nails [13]and put aside the clothes she was wearing when captured. After she has lived in your house and mourned her father and mother for a full month, then you may go to her and be her husband and she shall be your wife. [14]If you are not pleased with her, let her go wherever she wishes. You must not sell her or treat her as a slave, since you have dishonored her.

The Right of the Firstborn

[15]If a man has two wives, and he loves one but not the other, and both bear him sons but the firstborn is the son of the wife he does not love, [16]when he wills his property to his sons, he must not give the rights of the firstborn to the son of the wife he loves in preference to his actual firstborn, the son of the wife he does not love. [17]He must acknowledge the son of his unloved wife as the firstborn by giving him a double share of all he has. That son is the first sign of his father's strength. The right of the firstborn belongs to him.

A Rebellious Son

[18]If a man has a stubborn and rebellious son who does not obey his father and mother and will not listen to them when they discipline him, [19]his father and mother shall take hold of him and bring him to the elders at the gate of his town. [20]They shall say to the elders, "This son of ours is stubborn and rebellious. He will not obey us. He is a profligate and a drunkard." [21]Then all the men of his town shall stone him to death. You must purge the evil from among you. All Israel will hear of it and be afraid.

Various Laws

[22]If a man guilty of a capital offense is put to death and his body is hung on a tree, [23]you must not leave his body on the tree overnight. Be sure to bury him that same day, because anyone who is hung on a tree is under God's curse. You must not desecrate the land the LORD your God is giving you as an inheritance.

22 If you see your brother's ox or sheep straying, do not ignore it but be sure to take it back to him. [2]If the brother does not live near you or if you do not know who he is, take it home with you and keep it until he comes looking for it. Then give it back to him. [3]Do the same if you find your brother's donkey or his cloak or anything he loses. Do not ignore it.

[4]If you see your brother's donkey or his ox fallen on the road, do not ignore it. Help him get it to its feet.

[5]A woman must not wear men's clothing, nor a man wear women's clothing, for the LORD your God detests anyone who does this.

[6]If you come across a bird's nest beside the road, either in a tree or on the ground, and the mother is sitting on the young or on the eggs, do not take the mother with the young. [7]You may take the young, but be sure to let the mother go, so that it may go well with you and you may have a long life.

[8]When you build a new house, make a parapet around your roof so that you may not bring the guilt of bloodshed on your house if someone falls from the roof.

[9]Do not plant two kinds of seed in your vineyard; if you do, not only the crops you plant but also the fruit of the vineyard will be defiled. [a]

[10]Do not plow with an ox and a donkey yoked together.

[11]Do not wear clothes of wool and linen woven together.

[12]Make tassels on the four corners of the cloak you wear.

Marriage Violations

[13]If a man takes a wife and, after lying with her, dislikes her [14]and slanders her and gives her a bad name, saying, "I married this woman, but when I approached her, I did not find proof of her virginity," [15]then the girl's father and mother shall bring proof that she was a virgin to the town elders at the gate. [16]The girl's father will say to the elders, "I gave my daughter in marriage to this man, but he dislikes her. [17]Now he has slandered her and said, 'I did not find your daughter to be a virgin.' But here is the proof of my daughter's virginity." Then her parents shall display the cloth before the elders of the town, [18]and the elders shall take the man and punish him. [19]They shall fine him a hundred shekels of silver[b] and give them to the girl's father, because this man has given an Israelite virgin a bad name. She shall continue to be his wife; he must not divorce her as long as he lives.

[20]If, however, the charge is true and no proof of the girl's virginity can be found, [21]she shall be brought to the door of her

a9 Or *be forfeited to the sanctuary*　　*b19* That is, about 2 1/2 pounds (about 1 kilogram) father's house and there the men of her town shall stone her to death. She has done a disgraceful thing in Israel by being promiscuous while still in her father's house. You must purge the evil from among you.

²²If a man is found sleeping with another man's wife, both the man who slept with her and the woman must die. You must purge the evil from Israel.

²³If a man happens to meet in a town a virgin pledged to be married and he sleeps with her, ²⁴you shall take both of them to the gate of that town and stone them to death—the girl because she was in a town and did not scream for help, and the man because he violated another man's wife. You must purge the evil from among you.

²⁵But if out in the country a man happens to meet a girl pledged to be married and rapes her, only the man who has done this shall die. ²⁶Do nothing to the girl; she has committed no sin deserving death. This case is like that of someone who attacks and murders his neighbor, ²⁷for the man found the girl out in the country, and though the betrothed girl screamed, there was no one to rescue her.

²⁸If a man happens to meet a virgin who is not pledged to be married and rapes her and they are discovered, ²⁹he shall pay the girl's father fifty shekels of silver.ᵃ He must marry the girl, for he has violated her. He can never divorce her as long as he lives.

³⁰A man is not to marry his father's wife; he must not dishonor his father's bed.

Exclusion From the Assembly

23 No one who has been emasculated by crushing or cutting may enter the assembly of the LORD.

²No one born of a forbidden marriageᵇ nor any of his descendants may enter the assembly of the LORD, even down to the tenth generation.

³No Ammonite or Moabite or any of his descendants may enter the assembly of the LORD, even down to the tenth generation. ⁴For they did not come to meet you with bread and water on your way when you came out of Egypt, and they hired Balaam son of Beor from Pethor in Aram Naharaimᶜ to pronounce a curse on you. ⁵However, the LORD your God would not

listen to Balaam but turned the curse into a blessing for you, because the LORD your God loves you. ⁶Do not seek a treaty of friendship with them as long as you live.

⁷Do not abhor an Edomite, for he is your brother. Do not abhor an Egyptian, because you lived as an alien in his country. ⁸The third generation of children born to them may enter the assembly of the LORD.

Uncleanness in the Camp

⁹When you are encamped against your enemies, keep away from everything impure. ¹⁰If one of your men is unclean because of a nocturnal emission, he is to go outside the camp and stay there. ¹¹But as evening approaches he is to wash himself, and at sunset he may return to the camp.

¹²Designate a place outside the camp where you can go to relieve yourself. ¹³As part of your equipment have something to dig with, and when you relieve yourself, dig a hole and cover up your excrement. ¹⁴For the LORD your God moves about in your camp to protect you and to deliver your enemies to you. Your camp must be holy, so that he will not see among you anything indecent and turn away from you.

Miscellaneous Laws

¹⁵If a slave has taken refuge with you, do not hand him over to his master. ¹⁶Let him live among you wherever he likes and in whatever town he chooses. Do not oppress him.

¹⁷No Israelite man or woman is to become a shrine prostitute. ¹⁸You must not bring the earnings of a female prostitute or of a male prostituteᵈ into the house of the LORD your God to pay any vow, because the LORD your God detests them both.

¹⁹Do not charge your brother interest, whether on money or food or anything else that may earn interest. ²⁰You may charge a foreigner interest, but not a brother Israelite, so that the LORD your God may bless you in everything you put your hand to in the land you are entering to possess.

²¹If you make a vow to the LORD your God, do not be slow to pay it, for the LORD your God will certainly demand it of you and you will be guilty of sin. ²²But if you refrain from making a vow, you will not be

---

ᵃ29 That is, about 1 1/4 pounds (about 0.6 kilogram)   ᵇ2 Or one of illegitimate birth   ᶜ4 That is,
Northwest Mesopotamia   ᵈ18 Hebrew of a dog

guilty. 23Whatever your lips utter you must be sure to do, because you made your vow freely to the LORD your God with your own mouth.

24If you enter your neighbor's vineyard, you may eat all the grapes you want, but do not put any in your basket. 25If you enter your neighbor's grainfield, you may pick kernels with your hands, but you must not put a sickle to his standing grain.

24 If a man marries a woman who becomes displeasing to him because he finds something indecent about her, and he writes her a certificate of divorce, gives it to her and sends her from his house, 2and if after she leaves his house she becomes the wife of another man, 3and her second husband dislikes her and writes her a certificate of divorce, gives it to her and sends her from his house, or if he dies, 4then her first husband, who divorced her, is not allowed to marry her again after she has been defiled. That would be detestable in the eyes of the LORD. Do not bring sin upon the land the LORD your God is giving you as an inheritance.

5If a man has recently married, he must not be sent to war or have any other duty laid on him. For one year he is to be free to stay at home and bring happiness to the wife he has married.

6Do not take a pair of millstones—not even the upper one—as security for a debt, because that would be taking a man's livelihood as security.

7If a man is caught kidnapping one of his brother Israelites and treats him as a slave or sells him, the kidnapper must die. You must purge the evil from among you.

8In cases of leprous*a* diseases be very careful to do exactly as the priests, who are Levites, instruct you. You must follow carefully what I have commanded them. 9Remember what the LORD your God did to Miriam along the way after you came out of Egypt.

10When you make a loan of any kind to your neighbor, do not go into his house to get what he is offering as a pledge. 11Stay outside and let the man to whom you are making the loan bring the pledge out to you. 12If the man is poor, do not go to sleep with his pledge in your possession. 13Return his cloak to him by sunset so that he may sleep in it. Then he will

thank you, and it will be regarded as a righteous act in the sight of the LORD your God.

14Do not take advantage of a hired man who is poor and needy, whether he is a brother Israelite or an alien living in one of your towns. 15Pay him his wages each day before sunset, because he is poor and is counting on it. Otherwise he may cry to the LORD against you, and you will be guilty of sin.

16Fathers shall not be put to death for their children, nor children put to death for their fathers; each is to die for his own sin.

17Do not deprive the alien or the fatherless of justice, or take the cloak of the widow as a pledge. 18Remember that you were slaves in Egypt and the LORD your God redeemed you from there. That is why I command you to do this.

19When you are harvesting in your field and you overlook a sheaf, do not go back to get it. Leave it for the alien, the fatherless and the widow, so that the LORD your God may bless you in all the work of your hands. 20When you beat the olives from your trees, do not go over the branches a second time. Leave what remains for the alien, the fatherless and the widow. 21When you harvest the grapes in your vineyard, do not go over the vines again. Leave what remains for the alien, the fatherless and the widow. 22Remember that you were slaves in Egypt. That is why I command you to do this.

25 When men have a dispute, they are to take it to court and the judges will decide the case, acquitting the innocent and condemning the guilty. 2If the guilty man deserves to be beaten, the judge shall make him lie down and have him flogged in his presence with the number of lashes his crime deserves, 3but he must not give him more than forty lashes. If he is flogged more than that, your brother will be degraded in your eyes.

4Do not muzzle an ox while it is treading out the grain.

5If brothers are living together and one of them dies without a son, his widow must not marry outside the family. Her husband's brother shall take her and marry her and fulfill the duty of a brother-in-law to her. 6The first son she bears shall carry on the name of the dead brother so

---

a8 The Hebrew word was used for various diseases affecting the skin—not necessarily leprosy.

that his name will not be blotted out from Israel.

7However, if a man does not want to marry his brother's wife, she shall go to the elders at the town gate and say, "My husband's brother refuses to carry on his brother's name in Israel. He will not fulfill the duty of a brother-in-law to me." 8Then the elders of his town shall summon him and talk to him. If he persists in saying, "I do not want to marry her," 9his brother's widow shall go up to him in the presence of the elders, take off one of his sandals, spit in his face and say, "This is what is done to the man who will not build up his brother's family line." 10That man's line shall be known in Israel as The Family of the Unsandaled.

11If two men are fighting and the wife of one of them comes to rescue her husband from his assailant, and she reaches out and seizes him by his private parts, 12you shall cut off her hand. Show her no pity.

13Do not have two differing weights in your bag—one heavy, one light. 14Do not have two differing measures in your house—one large, one small. 15You must have accurate and honest weights and measures, so that you may live long in the land the LORD your God is giving you. 16For the LORD your God detests anyone who does these things, anyone who deals dishonestly.

17Remember what the Amalekites did to you along the way when you came out of Egypt. 18When you were weary and worn out, they met you on your journey and cut off all who were lagging behind; they had no fear of God. 19When the LORD your God gives you rest from all the enemies around you in the land he is giving you to possess as an inheritance, you shall blot out the memory of Amalek from under heaven. Do not forget!

Firstfruits and Tithes

26 When you have entered the land the LORD your God is giving you as an inheritance and have taken possession of it and settled in it, 2take some of the firstfruits of all that you produce from the soil of the land the LORD your God is giving you and put them in a basket. Then go to the place the LORD your God will choose as a dwelling for his Name 3and say to the priest in office at the time, "I declare today to the LORD your God that I have come to the land the LORD swore to our forefathers to give us." 4The priest shall take the basket from your hands and set it down in front of the altar of the LORD your God. 5Then you shall declare before the LORD your God: "My father was a wandering Aramean, and he went down into Egypt with a few people and lived there and became a great nation, powerful and numerous. 6But the Egyptians mistreated us and made us suffer, putting us to hard labor. 7Then we cried out to the LORD, the God of our fathers, and the LORD heard our voice and saw our misery, toil and oppression. 8So the LORD brought us out of Egypt with a mighty hand and an outstretched arm, with great terror and with miraculous signs and wonders. 9He brought us to this place and gave us this land, a land flowing with milk and honey; 10and now I bring the firstfruits of the soil that you, O LORD, have given me." Place the basket before the LORD your God and bow down before him. 11And you and the Levites and the aliens among you shall rejoice in all the good things the LORD your God has given to you and your household.

12When you have finished setting aside a tenth of all your produce in the third year, the year of the tithe, you shall give it to the Levite, the alien, the fatherless and the widow, so that they may eat in your towns and be satisfied. 13Then say to the LORD your God: "I have removed from my house the sacred portion and have given it to the Levite, the alien, the fatherless and the widow, according to all you commanded. I have not turned aside from your commands nor have I forgotten any of them. 14I have not eaten any of the sacred portion while I was in mourning, nor have I removed any of it while I was unclean, nor have I offered any of it to the dead. I have obeyed the LORD my God; I have done everything you commanded me. 15Look down from heaven, your holy dwelling place, and bless your people Israel and the land you have given us as you promised on oath to our forefathers, a land flowing with milk and honey."

Follow the LORD's Commands

16The LORD your God commands you this day to follow these decrees and laws; carefully observe them with all your heart and with all your soul. 17You have declared this day that the LORD is your God and that you will walk in his ways, that you will keep his decrees, commands and laws, and that you will obey him. 18And the LORD has declared this day that you are his people, his treasured possession as he promised, and that you are to keep all his commands. ¹⁹He has declared that he will set you in praise, fame and honor high above all the nations he has made and that you will be a people holy to the LORD your God, as he promised.

The Altar on Mount Ebal

27 Moses and the elders of Israel commanded the people: "Keep all these commands that I give you today. ²When you have crossed the Jordan into the land the LORD your God is giving you, set up some large stones and coat them with plaster. ³Write on them all the words of this law when you have crossed over to enter the land the LORD your God is giving you, a land flowing with milk and honey, just as the LORD, the God of your fathers, promised you. ⁴And when you have crossed the Jordan, set up these stones on Mount Ebal, as I command you today, and coat them with plaster. ⁵Build there an altar to the LORD your God, an altar of stones. Do not use any iron tool upon them. ⁶Build the altar of the LORD your God with fieldstones and offer burnt offerings on it to the LORD your God. ⁷Sacrifice fellowship offerings*a* there, eating them and rejoicing in the presence of the LORD your God. ⁸And you shall write very clearly all the words of this law on these stones you have set up."

Curses From Mount Ebal

⁹Then Moses and the priests, who are Levites, said to all Israel, "Be silent, O Israel, and listen! You have now become the people of the LORD your God. ¹⁰Obey the LORD your God and follow his commands and decrees that I give you today."

¹¹On the same day Moses commanded the people:

¹²When you have crossed the Jordan, these tribes shall stand on Mount Gerizim to bless the people: Simeon, Levi, Judah, Issachar, Joseph and Benjamin. ¹³And these tribes shall stand on Mount Ebal to pronounce curses: Reuben, Gad, Asher, Zebulun, Dan and Naphtali.

¹⁴The Levites shall recite to all the people of Israel in a loud voice:

¹⁵"Cursed is the man who carves an image or casts an idol—a thing detestable to the LORD, the work of the craftsman's hands—and sets it up in secret."

Then all the people shall say, "Amen!"

¹⁶"Cursed is the man who dishonors his father or his mother."

Then all the people shall say, "Amen!"

¹⁷"Cursed is the man who moves his neighbor's boundary stone."

Then all the people shall say, "Amen!"

¹⁸"Cursed is the man who leads the blind astray on the road."

Then all the people shall say, "Amen!"

¹⁹"Cursed is the man who withholds justice from the alien, the fatherless or the widow."

Then all the people shall say, "Amen!"

²⁰"Cursed is the man who sleeps with his father's wife, for he dishonors his father's bed."

Then all the people shall say, "Amen!"

²¹"Cursed is the man who has sexual relations with any animal."

Then all the people shall say, "Amen!"

²²"Cursed is the man who sleeps with his sister, the daughter of his father or the daughter of his mother."

Then all the people shall say, "Amen!"

²³"Cursed is the man who sleeps with his mother-in-law."

Then all the people shall say, "Amen!"

²⁴"Cursed is the man who kills his neighbor secretly."

Then all the people shall say, "Amen!"

²⁵"Cursed is the man who accepts a bribe to kill an innocent person."

Then all the people shall say, "Amen!"

²⁶"Cursed is the man who does not uphold the words of this law by carrying them out."

Then all the people shall say, "Amen!"

Blessings for Obedience

28 If you fully obey the LORD your God and carefully follow all his commands I give you today, the LORD your God will set you high above all the nations on earth. ²All these blessings will

---

*a*7 Traditionally *peace offerings*

come upon you and accompany you if you obey the LORD your God:

³You will be blessed in the city and blessed in the country.

⁴The fruit of your womb will be blessed, and the crops of your land and the young of your livestock—the calves of your herds and the lambs of your flocks.

⁵Your basket and your kneading trough will be blessed.

⁶You will be blessed when you come in and blessed when you go out.

⁷The LORD will grant that the enemies who rise up against you will be defeated before you. They will come at you from one direction but flee from you in seven.

⁸The LORD will send a blessing on your barns and on everything you put your hand to. The LORD your God will bless you in the land he is giving you.

⁹The LORD will establish you as his holy people, as he promised you on oath, if you keep the commands of the LORD your God and walk in his ways. ¹⁰Then all the peoples on earth will see that you are called by the name of the LORD, and they will fear you. ¹¹The LORD will grant you abundant prosperity—in the fruit of your womb, the young of your livestock and the crops of your ground—in the land he swore to your forefathers to give you.

¹²The LORD will open the heavens, the storehouse of his bounty, to send rain on your land in season and to bless all the work of your hands. You will lend to many nations but will borrow from none. ¹³The LORD will make you the head, not the tail. If you pay attention to the commands of the LORD your God that I give you this day and carefully follow them, you will always be at the top, never at the bottom. ¹⁴Do not turn aside from any of the commands I give you today, to the right or to the left, following other gods and serving them.

Curses for Disobedience

¹⁵However, if you do not obey the LORD your God and do not carefully follow all his commands and decrees I am giving you today, all these curses will come upon you and overtake you:

¹⁶You will be cursed in the city and cursed in the country.

¹⁷Your basket and your kneading trough will be cursed.

¹⁸The fruit of your womb will be cursed, and the crops of your land, and the calves of your herds and the lambs of your flocks.

¹⁹You will be cursed when you come in and cursed when you go out.

²⁰The LORD will send on you curses, confusion and rebuke in everything you put your hand to, until you are destroyed and come to sudden ruin because of the evil you have done in forsaking him.ᵃ ²¹The LORD will plague you with diseases until he has destroyed you from the land you are entering to possess. ²²The LORD will strike you with wasting disease, with fever and inflammation, with scorching heat and drought, with blight and mildew, which will plague you until you perish. ²³The sky over your head will be bronze, the ground beneath you iron. ²⁴The LORD will turn the rain of your country into dust and powder; it will come down from the skies until you are destroyed.

²⁵The LORD will cause you to be defeated before your enemies. You will come at them from one direction but flee from them in seven, and you will become a thing of horror to all the kingdoms on earth. ²⁶Your carcasses will be food for all the birds of the air and the beasts of the earth, and there will be no one to frighten them away. ²⁷The LORD will afflict you with the boils of Egypt and with tumors, festering sores and the itch, from which you cannot be cured. ²⁸The LORD will afflict you with madness, blindness and confusion of mind. ²⁹At midday you will grope about like a blind man in the dark. You will be unsuccessful in everything you do; day after day you will be oppressed and robbed, with no one to rescue you.

³⁰You will be pledged to be married to a woman, but another will take her and ravish her. You will build a house, but you will not live in it. You will plant a vineyard, but you will not even begin to enjoy its fruit. ³¹Your ox will be slaughtered before your eyes, but you will eat none of it. Your donkey will be forcibly taken from you and will not be returned. Your sheep will be given to your enemies, and no one will rescue them. ³²Your sons and daughters will be given to another nation, and

ᵃ20 Hebrew me

you will wear out your eyes watching for them day after day, powerless to lift a hand. ³³A people that you do not know will eat what your land and labor produce, and you will have nothing but cruel oppression all your days. ³⁴The sights you see will drive you mad. ³⁵The LORD will afflict your knees and legs with painful boils that cannot be cured, spreading from the soles of your feet to the top of your head.

³⁶The LORD will drive you and the king you set over you to a nation unknown to you or your fathers. There you will worship other gods, gods of wood and stone. ³⁷You will become a thing of horror and an object of scorn and ridicule to all the nations where the LORD will drive you.

³⁸You will sow much seed in the field but you will harvest little, because locusts will devour it. ³⁹You will plant vineyards and cultivate them but you will not drink the wine or gather the grapes, because worms will eat them. ⁴⁰You will have olive trees throughout your country but you will not use the oil, because the olives will drop off. ⁴¹You will have sons and daughters but you will not keep them, because they will go into captivity. ⁴²Swarms of locusts will take over all your trees and the crops of your land.

⁴³The alien who lives among you will rise above you higher and higher, but you will sink lower and lower. ⁴⁴He will lend to you, but you will not lend to him. He will be the head, but you will be the tail.

⁴⁵All these curses will come upon you. They will pursue you and overtake you until you are destroyed, because you did not obey the LORD your God and observe the commands and decrees he gave you. ⁴⁶They will be a sign and a wonder to you and your descendants forever. ⁴⁷Because you did not serve the LORD your God joyfully and gladly in the time of prosperity, ⁴⁸therefore in hunger and thirst, in nakedness and dire poverty, you will serve the enemies the LORD sends against you. He will put an iron yoke on your neck until he has destroyed you.

⁴⁹The LORD will bring a nation against you from far away, from the ends of the earth, like an eagle swooping down, a nation whose language you will not understand, ⁵⁰a fierce-looking nation without respect for the old or pity for the young. ⁵¹They will devour the young of your livestock and the crops of your land until you are destroyed. They will leave you no grain, new wine or oil, nor any calves of your herds or lambs of your flocks until you are ruined. ⁵²They will lay siege to all the cities throughout your land until the high fortified walls in which you trust fall down. They will besiege all the cities throughout the land the LORD your God is giving you.

⁵³Because of the suffering that your enemy will inflict on you during the siege, you will eat the fruit of the womb, the flesh of the sons and daughters the LORD your God has given you. ⁵⁴Even the most gentle and sensitive man among you will have no compassion on his own brother or the wife he loves or his surviving children, ⁵⁵and he will not give to one of them any of the flesh of his children that he is eating. It will be all he has left because of the suffering your enemy will inflict on you during the siege of all your cities. ⁵⁶The most gentle and sensitive woman among you — so sensitive and gentle that she would not venture to touch the ground with the sole of her foot — will begrudge the husband she loves and her own son or daughter ⁵⁷the afterbirth from her womb and the children she bears. For she intends to eat them secretly during the siege and in the distress that your enemy will inflict on you in your cities.

⁵⁸If you do not carefully follow all the words of this law, which are written in this book, and do not revere this glorious and awesome name — the LORD your God — ⁵⁹the LORD will send fearful plagues on you and your descendants, harsh and prolonged disasters, and severe and lingering illnesses. ⁶⁰He will bring upon you all the diseases of Egypt that you dreaded, and they will cling to you. ⁶¹The LORD will also bring on you every kind of sickness and disaster not recorded in this Book of the Law, until you are destroyed. ⁶²You who were as numerous as the stars in the sky will be left but few in number, because you did not obey the LORD your God. ⁶³Just as it pleased the LORD to make you prosper and increase in number, so it will please him to ruin and destroy you. You will be uprooted from the land you are entering to possess.

⁶⁴Then the LORD will scatter you among all nations, from one end of the earth to the other. There you will worship other gods — gods of wood and stone, which neither you nor your fathers have known. ⁶⁵Among those nations you will find no repose, no resting place for the sole of your foot. There the LORD will give you an anxious mind, eyes weary with longing,

and a despairing heart. 66You will live in constant suspense, filled with dread both night and day, never sure of your life. 67In the morning you will say, "If only it were evening!" and in the evening, "If only it were morning!"—because of the terror that will fill your hearts and the sights that your eyes will see. 68The LORD will send you back in ships to Egypt on a journey I said you should never make again. There you will offer yourselves for sale to your enemies as male and female slaves, but no one will buy you.

Renewal of the Covenant

29 These are the terms of the covenant the LORD commanded Moses to make with the Israelites in Moab, in addition to the covenant he had made with them at Horeb.

2Moses summoned all the Israelites and said to them:

Your eyes have seen all that the LORD did in Egypt to Pharaoh, to all his officials and to all his land. 3With your own eyes you saw those great trials, those miraculous signs and great wonders. 4But to this day the LORD has not given you a mind that understands or eyes that see or ears that hear. 5During the forty years that I led you through the desert, your clothes did not wear out, nor did the sandals on your feet. 6You ate no bread and drank no wine or other fermented drink. I did this so that you might know that I am the LORD your God.

7When you reached this place, Sihon king of Heshbon and Og king of Bashan came out to fight against us, but we defeated them. 8We took their land and gave it as an inheritance to the Reubenites, the Gadites and the half-tribe of Manasseh.

9Carefully follow the terms of this covenant, so that you may prosper in everything you do. 10All of you are standing today in the presence of the LORD your God —your leaders and chief men, your elders and officials, and all the other men of Israel, 11together with your children and your wives, and the aliens living in your camps who chop your wood and carry your water. 12You are standing here in order to enter into a covenant with the LORD your God, a covenant the LORD is making with you this day and sealing with an oath, 13to confirm you this day as his peo-

ple, that he may be your God as he promised you and as he swore to your fathers, Abraham, Isaac and Jacob. 14I am making this covenant, with its oath, not only with you 15who are standing here with us today in the presence of the LORD our God but also with those who are not here today.

16You yourselves know how we lived in Egypt and how we passed through the countries on the way here. 17You saw among them their detestable images and idols of wood and stone, of silver and gold. 18Make sure there is no man or woman, clan or tribe among you today whose heart turns away from the LORD our God to go and worship the gods of those nations; make sure there is no root among you that produces such bitter poison.

19When such a person hears the words of this oath, he invokes a blessing on himself and therefore thinks, "I will be safe, even though I persist in going my own way." This will bring disaster on the watered land as well as the dry.ᵃ 20The LORD will never be willing to forgive him; his wrath and zeal will burn against that man. All the curses written in this book will fall upon him, and the LORD will blot out his name from under heaven. 21The LORD will single him out from all the tribes of Israel for disaster, according to all the curses of the covenant written in this Book of the Law.

22Your children who follow you in later generations and foreigners who come from distant lands will see the calamities that have fallen on the land and the diseases with which the LORD has afflicted it. 23The whole land will be a burning waste of salt and sulfur—nothing planted, nothing sprouting, no vegetation growing on it. It will be like the destruction of Sodom and Gomorrah, Admah and Zeboiim, which the LORD overthrew in fierce anger. 24All the nations will ask: "Why has the LORD done this to this land? Why this fierce, burning anger?"

25And the answer will be: "It is because this people abandoned the covenant of the LORD, the God of their fathers, the covenant he made with them when he brought them out of Egypt. 26They went off and worshiped other gods and bowed down to them, gods they did not know, gods he had not given them. 27Therefore the LORD's anger burned against this land, so that he brought on it all the curses

---

ᵃ19 Or way, in order to add drunkenness to thirst."

written in this book. 28In furious anger and in great wrath the LORD uprooted them from their land and thrust them into another land, as it is now."

29The secret things belong to the LORD our God, but the things revealed belong to us and to our children forever, that we may follow all the words of this law.

Prosperity After Turning to the LORD

30 When all these blessings and curses I have set before you come upon you and you take them to heart wherever the LORD your God disperses you among the nations, 2and when you and your children return to the LORD your God and obey him with all your heart and with all your soul according to everything I command you today, 3then the LORD your God will restore your fortunes*a* and have compassion on you and gather you again from all the nations where he scattered you. 4Even if you have been banished to the most distant land under the heavens, from there the LORD your God will gather you and bring you back. 5He will bring you to the land that belonged to your fathers, and you will take possession of it. He will make you more prosperous and numerous than your fathers. 6The LORD your God will circumcise your hearts and the hearts of your descendants, so that you may love him with all your heart and with all your soul, and live. 7The LORD your God will put all these curses on your enemies who hate and persecute you. 8You will again obey the LORD and follow all his commands I am giving you today. 9Then the LORD your God will make you most prosperous in all the work of your hands and in the fruit of your womb, the young of your livestock and the crops of your land. The LORD will again delight in you and make you prosperous, just as he delighted in your fathers, 10if you obey the LORD your God and keep his commands and decrees that are written in this Book of the Law and turn to the LORD your God with all your heart and with all your soul.

The Offer of Life or Death

11Now what I am commanding you today is not too difficult for you or beyond your reach. 12It is not up in heaven, so that you have to ask, "Who will ascend into heaven to get it and proclaim it to us so we may obey it?" 13Nor is it beyond the sea, so that you have to ask, "Who will cross the sea to get it and proclaim it to us so we may obey it?" 14No, the word is very near you; it is in your mouth and in your heart so you may obey it.

15See, I set before you today life and prosperity, death and destruction. 16For I command you today to love the LORD your God, to walk in his ways, and to keep his commands, decrees and laws; then you will live and increase, and the LORD your God will bless you in the land you are entering to possess.

17But if your heart turns away and you are not obedient, and if you are drawn away to bow down to other gods and worship them, 18I declare to you this day that you will certainly be destroyed. You will not live long in the land you are crossing the Jordan to enter and possess.

19This day I call heaven and earth as witnesses against you that I have set before you life and death, blessings and curses. Now choose life, so that you and your children may live 20and that you may love the LORD your God, listen to his voice, and hold fast to him. For the LORD is your life, and he will give you many years in the land he swore to give to your fathers, Abraham, Isaac and Jacob.

Joshua to Succeed Moses

31 Then Moses went out and spoke these words to all Israel: 2"I am now a hundred and twenty years old and I am no longer able to lead you. The LORD has said to me, 'You shall not cross the Jordan.' 3The LORD your God himself will cross over ahead of you. He will destroy these nations before you, and you will take possession of their land. Joshua also will cross over ahead of you, as the LORD said. 4And the LORD will do to them what he did to Sihon and Og, the kings of the Amorites, whom he destroyed along with their land. 5The LORD will deliver them to you, and you must do to them all that I have commanded you. 6Be strong and courageous. Do not be afraid or terrified because of them, for the LORD your God goes with you; he will never leave you nor forsake you."

7Then Moses summoned Joshua and said to him in the presence of all Israel, "Be strong and courageous, for you must go with this people into the land that the LORD swore to their forefathers to give them, and you must divide it among them

a3 Or will bring you back from captivity

as their inheritance. ⁸The Lord himself goes before you and will be with you; he will never leave you nor forsake you. Do not be afraid; do not be discouraged."

The Reading of the Law

⁹So Moses wrote down this law and gave it to the priests, the sons of Levi, who carried the ark of the covenant of the Lord, and to all the elders of Israel. ¹⁰Then Moses commanded them: "At the end of every seven years, in the year for canceling debts, during the Feast of Tabernacles, ¹¹when all Israel comes to appear before the Lord your God at the place he will choose, you shall read this law before them in their hearing. ¹²Assemble the people—men, women and children, and the aliens living in your towns—so they can listen and learn to fear the Lord your God and follow carefully all the words of this law. ¹³Their children, who do not know this law, must hear it and learn to fear the Lord your God as long as you live in the land you are crossing the Jordan to possess."

Israel's Rebellion Predicted

¹⁴The Lord said to Moses, "Now the day of your death is near. Call Joshua and present yourselves at the Tent of Meeting, where I will commission him." So Moses and Joshua came and presented themselves at the Tent of Meeting.

¹⁵Then the Lord appeared at the Tent in a pillar of cloud, and the cloud stood over the entrance to the Tent. ¹⁶And the Lord said to Moses: "You are going to rest with your fathers, and these people will soon prostitute themselves to the foreign gods of the land they are entering. They will forsake me and break the covenant I made with them. ¹⁷On that day I will become angry with them and forsake them; I will hide my face from them, and they will be destroyed. Many disasters and difficulties will come upon them, and on that day they will ask, 'Have not these disasters come upon us because our God is not with us?' ¹⁸And I will certainly hide my face on that day because of all their wickedness in turning to other gods.

¹⁹"Now write down for yourselves this song and teach it to the Israelites and have them sing it, so that it may be a witness for me against them. ²⁰When I have brought them into the land flowing with milk and honey, the land I promised on oath to their forefathers, and when they eat their fill and thrive, they will turn to other gods and worship them, rejecting me and breaking my covenant. ²¹And when many disasters and difficulties come upon them, this song will testify against them, because it will not be forgotten by their descendants. I know what they are disposed to do, even before I bring them into the land I promised them on oath." ²²So Moses wrote down this song that day and taught it to the Israelites.

²³The Lord gave this command to Joshua son of Nun: "Be strong and courageous, for you will bring the Israelites into the land I promised them on oath, and I myself will be with you."

²⁴After Moses finished writing in a book the words of this law from beginning to end, ²⁵he gave this command to the Levites who carried the ark of the covenant of the Lord: ²⁶"Take this Book of the Law and place it beside the ark of the covenant of the Lord your God. There it will remain as a witness against you. ²⁷For I know how rebellious and stiffnecked you are. If you have been rebellious against the Lord while I am still alive and with you, how much more will you rebel after I die! ²⁸Assemble before me all the elders of your tribes and all your officials, so that I can speak these words in their hearing and call heaven and earth to testify against them. ²⁹For I know that after my death you are sure to become utterly corrupt and to turn from the way I have commanded you. In days to come, disaster will fall upon you because you will do evil in the sight of the Lord and provoke him to anger by what your hands have made."

The Song of Moses

³⁰And Moses recited the words of this song from beginning to end in the hearing of the whole assembly of Israel:

32 Listen, O heavens, and I will speak;
hear, O earth, the words of my mouth.
²Let my teaching fall like rain
and my words descend like dew,
like showers on new grass,
like abundant rain on tender plants.

³I will proclaim the name of the Lord.
Oh, praise the greatness of our God!
⁴He is the Rock, his works are perfect,
and all his ways are just.
A faithful God who does no wrong,

VERSE FOR THE DAY:
Deuteronomy 32:4

AUTHOR:
Diane Head

PASSAGE FOR THE DAY:
Deuteronomy 32:1–4

His Trustworthiness

A MOTHER comes equipped with an internal anxiety meter. It's right in the middle of her heart and has each child's name engraved on it. There are certain phrases in the English language that cause it to jump and spin . . . "Mom, my teacher wants a conference with you right away!" "Mom, remember how long Susie's hair used to be? We've been playing beauty parlor and . . ." "Hello. This is the school nurse. We've been checking for head lice and . . ." "Mom, Jamie's mother is on her way over and she looks mad!" "Mom, remember the pretty flowers that used to be in front of Mr. Crabb's house? Here, these are for you . . ."

These are the standard meter spinners. We also have our family's encounters with each other, interaction with the neighbors, school friends, teachers, and others, not to mention the physical dangers our children are exposed to each day.

During the early years of their lives we nurture and prepare these little birds in the nest. Then it becomes time to let them try their wings in all kinds of new situations—social, emotional, physical, and even intellectual. As we watch these solo flights we are proud, but a little scared; hopeful, but a little apprehensive. We want to stand back and give them room to soar . . . but at the same time we want to hold their hands.

But we do release them into the world. And our anxiety meters begin to spin.

But the same God who gave us our children—these precious gifts of his love—is worthy and able to take care of them. He is worthy of our complete trust.

Trust: A conscious act of placing each child in his hands. With that act comes a beautiful awareness that through each experience—social, emotional, physical, and intellectual—he is at work in their lives. He is molding them into what he would have them become. Turning even what we perceive as hurtful into his good. Turning their failures—and ours—into footsteps . . . footsteps toward himself.

Additional Scripture Readings:
Isaiah 26:3–4,12; Romans 8:26–28

Go to page 215 for your next devotional reading.

upright and just is he.

5They have acted corruptly toward
him;
to their shame they are no longer
his children,
but a warped and crooked
generation.a
6Is this the way you repay the LORD,
O foolish and unwise people?
Is he not your Father, your Creator,b
who made you and formed you?

7Remember the days of old;
consider the generations long past.
Ask your father and he will tell you,
your elders, and they will explain to
you.
8When the Most High gave the nations
their inheritance,
when he divided all mankind,
he set up boundaries for the peoples
according to the number of the
sons of Israel.c
9For the LORD's portion is his people,
Jacob his allotted inheritance.

10In a desert land he found him,
in a barren and howling waste.
He shielded him and cared for him;
he guarded him as the apple of his
eye,
11like an eagle that stirs up its nest
and hovers over its young,
that spreads its wings to catch them
and carries them on its pinions.
12The LORD alone led him;
no foreign god was with him.

13He made him ride on the heights of
the land
and fed him with the fruit of the
fields.
He nourished him with honey from
the rock,
and with oil from the flinty crag,
14with curds and milk from herd and
flock
and with fattened lambs and goats,
with choice rams of Bashan
and the finest kernels of wheat.
You drank the foaming blood of the
grape.

15Jeshurund grew fat and kicked;
filled with food, he became heavy
and sleek.
He abandoned the God who made
him

and rejected the Rock his Savior.
16They made him jealous with their
foreign gods
and angered him with their
detestable idols.
17They sacrificed to demons, which are
not God—
gods they had not known,
gods that recently appeared,
gods your fathers did not fear.
18You deserted the Rock, who fathered
you;
you forgot the God who gave you
birth.

19The LORD saw this and rejected them
because he was angered by his sons
and daughters.
20"I will hide my face from them," he
said,
"and see what their end will be;
for they are a perverse generation,
children who are unfaithful.
21They made me jealous by what is no
god
and angered me with their
worthless idols.
I will make them envious by those
who are not a people;
I will make them angry by a nation
that has no understanding.
22For a fire has been kindled by my
wrath,
one that burns to the realm of
deathe below.
It will devour the earth and its
harvests
and set afire the foundations of the
mountains.

23"I will heap calamities upon them
and spend my arrows against them.
24I will send wasting famine against
them,
consuming pestilence and deadly
plague;
I will send against them the fangs of
wild beasts,
the venom of vipers that glide in
the dust.
25In the street the sword will make
them childless;
in their homes terror will reign.
Young men and young women will
perish,
infants and gray-haired men.
26I said I would scatter them

a5 Or Corrupt are they and not his children, / a generation warped and twisted to their shame   b6 Or
Father, who bought you   c8 Masoretic Text; Dead Sea Scrolls (see also Septuagint) sons of God
d15 Jeshurun means the upright one, that is, Israel.   e22 Hebrew to Sheol

and blot out their memory from
    mankind,
²⁷but I dreaded the taunt of the enemy,
    lest the adversary misunderstand
and say, 'Our hand has triumphed;
    the LORD has not done all this.' "

²⁸They are a nation without sense,
    there is no discernment in them.
²⁹If only they were wise and would
    understand this
    and discern what their end will be!
³⁰How could one man chase a
    thousand,
    or two put ten thousand to flight,
unless their Rock had sold them,
    unless the LORD had given them up?
³¹For their rock is not like our Rock,
    as even our enemies concede.
³²Their vine comes from the vine of
    Sodom
    and from the fields of Gomorrah.
Their grapes are filled with poison,
    and their clusters with bitterness.
³³Their wine is the venom of serpents,
    the deadly poison of cobras.

³⁴"Have I not kept this in reserve
    and sealed it in my vaults?
³⁵It is mine to avenge; I will repay.
    In due time their foot will slip;
their day of disaster is near
    and their doom rushes upon them."

³⁶The LORD will judge his people
    and have compassion on his
    servants
when he sees their strength is gone
    and no one is left, slave or free.
³⁷He will say: "Now where are their
    gods,
    the rock they took refuge in,
³⁸the gods who ate the fat of their
    sacrifices
    and drank the wine of their drink
    offerings?
Let them rise up to help you!
    Let them give you shelter!

³⁹"See now that I myself am He!
    There is no god besides me.
I put to death and I bring to life,
    I have wounded and I will heal,
    and no one can deliver out of my
    hand.
⁴⁰I lift my hand to heaven and declare:
    As surely as I live forever,
⁴¹when I sharpen my flashing sword
    and my hand grasps it in judgment,

I will take vengeance on my
    adversaries
    and repay those who hate me.
⁴²I will make my arrows drunk with
    blood,
    while my sword devours flesh:
the blood of the slain and the
    captives,
    the heads of the enemy leaders."

⁴³Rejoice, O nations, with his
    people,ᵃ, ᵇ
    for he will avenge the blood of his
    servants;
he will take vengeance on his
    enemies
    and make atonement for his land
    and people.

⁴⁴Moses came with Joshuaᶜ son of Nun
and spoke all the words of this song in the
hearing of the people. ⁴⁵When Moses finished reciting all these words to all Israel,
⁴⁶he said to them, "Take to heart all the
words I have solemnly declared to you
this day, so that you may command your
children to obey carefully all the words of
this law. ⁴⁷They are not just idle words for
you—they are your life. By them you will
live long in the land you are crossing the
Jordan to possess."

Moses to Die on Mount Nebo

⁴⁸On that same day the LORD told Moses, ⁴⁹"Go up into the Abarim Range to
Mount Nebo in Moab, across from Jericho, and view Canaan, the land I am giving the Israelites as their own possession.
⁵⁰There on the mountain that you have
climbed you will die and be gathered to
your people, just as your brother Aaron
died on Mount Hor and was gathered to
his people. ⁵¹This is because both of you
broke faith with me in the presence of the
Israelites at the waters of Meribah Kadesh in the Desert of Zin and because you
did not uphold my holiness among the
Israelites. ⁵²Therefore, you will see the
land only from a distance; you will not
enter the land I am giving to the people of
Israel."

Moses Blesses the Tribes

33 This is the blessing that Moses the
man of God pronounced on the Israelites before his death. ²He said:

"The LORD came from Sinai

ᵃ43 Or *Make his people rejoice, O nations*   ᵇ43 Masoretic Text; Dead Sea Scrolls (see also Septuagint)
people, / and let all the angels worship him /   ᶜ44 Hebrew *Hoshea,* a variant of *Joshua*

and dawned over them from Seir;
he shone forth from Mount Paran.
He came with^a myriads of holy ones
from the south, from his mountain
slopes.^b
³Surely it is you who love the people;
all the holy ones are in your hand.
At your feet they all bow down,
and from you receive instruction,
⁴the law that Moses gave us,
the possession of the assembly of
Jacob.
⁵He was king over Jeshurun^c
when the leaders of the people
assembled,
along with the tribes of Israel.

⁶"Let Reuben live and not die,
nor^d his men be few."

⁷And this he said about Judah:

"Hear, O LORD, the cry of Judah;
bring him to his people.
With his own hands he defends his
cause.
Oh, be his help against his foes!"

⁸About Levi he said:

"Your Thummim and Urim belong
to the man you favored.
You tested him at Massah;
you contended with him at the
waters of Meribah.
⁹He said of his father and mother,
'I have no regard for them.'
He did not recognize his brothers
or acknowledge his own children,
but he watched over your word
and guarded your covenant.
¹⁰He teaches your precepts to Jacob
and your law to Israel.
He offers incense before you
and whole burnt offerings on your
altar.
¹¹Bless all his skills, O LORD,
and be pleased with the work of his
hands.
Smite the loins of those who rise up
against him;
strike his foes till they rise no
more."

¹²About Benjamin he said:

"Let the beloved of the LORD rest
secure in him,
for he shields him all day long,

and the one the LORD loves rests
between his shoulders."

¹³About Joseph he said:

"May the LORD bless his land
with the precious dew from heaven
above
and with the deep waters that lie
below;
¹⁴with the best the sun brings forth
and the finest the moon can yield;
¹⁵with the choicest gifts of the ancient
mountains
and the fruitfulness of the
everlasting hills;
¹⁶with the best gifts of the earth and its
fullness
and the favor of him who dwelt in
the burning bush.
Let all these rest on the head of
Joseph,
on the brow of the prince among^e
his brothers.
¹⁷In majesty he is like a firstborn bull;
his horns are the horns of a wild
ox.
With them he will gore the nations,
even those at the ends of the earth.
Such are the ten thousands of
Ephraim;
such are the thousands of
Manasseh."

¹⁸About Zebulun he said:

"Rejoice, Zebulun, in your going out,
and you, Issachar, in your tents.
¹⁹They will summon peoples to the
mountain
and there offer sacrifices of
righteousness;
they will feast on the abundance of
the seas,
on the treasures hidden in the
sand."

²⁰About Gad he said:

"Blessed is he who enlarges Gad's
domain!
Gad lives there like a lion,
tearing at arm or head.
²¹He chose the best land for himself;
the leader's portion was kept for
him.
When the heads of the people
assembled,
he carried out the LORD's righteous
will,

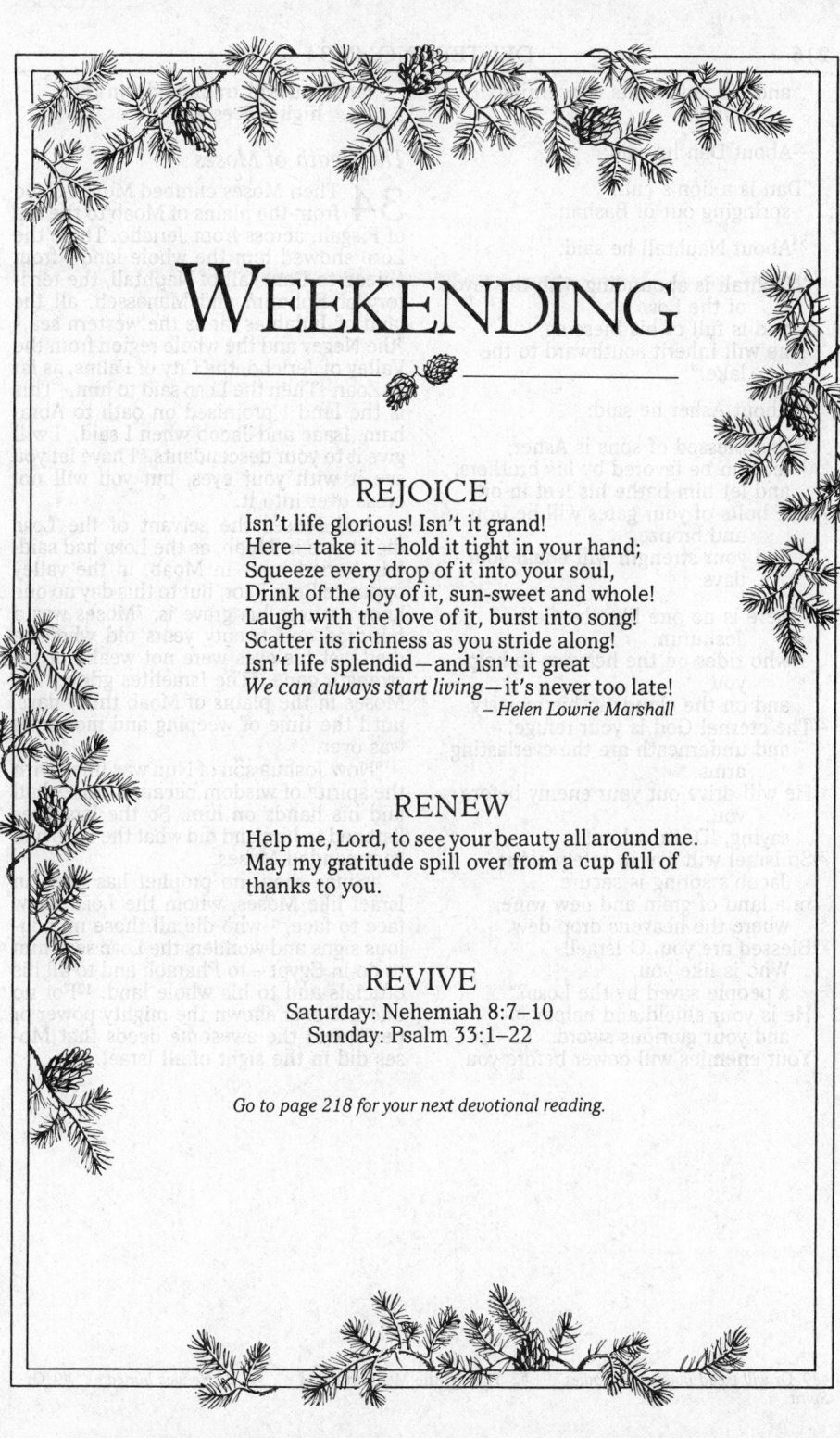

WEEKENDING

REJOICE

Isn't life glorious! Isn't it grand!
Here—take it—hold it tight in your hand;
Squeeze every drop of it into your soul,
Drink of the joy of it, sun-sweet and whole!
Laugh with the love of it, burst into song!
Scatter its richness as you stride along!
Isn't life splendid—and isn't it great
We can always start living—it's never too late!
— *Helen Lowrie Marshall*

RENEW

Help me, Lord, to see your beauty all around me.
May my gratitude spill over from a cup full of
thanks to you.

REVIVE

Saturday: Nehemiah 8:7–10
Sunday: Psalm 33:1–22

Go to page 218 for your next devotional reading.

and his judgments concerning
Israel."

22About Dan he said:

"Dan is a lion's cub,
  springing out of Bashan."

23About Naphtali he said:

"Naphtali is abounding with the favor
    of the LORD
  and is full of his blessing;
  he will inherit southward to the
    lake."

24About Asher he said:

"Most blessed of sons is Asher;
  let him be favored by his brothers,
  and let him bathe his feet in oil.
25The bolts of your gates will be iron
    and bronze,
  and your strength will equal your
    days.

26"There is no one like the God of
    Jeshurun,
  who rides on the heavens to help
    you
  and on the clouds in his majesty.
27The eternal God is your refuge,
  and underneath are the everlasting
    arms.
He will drive out your enemy before
    you,
  saying, 'Destroy him!'
28So Israel will live in safety alone;
  Jacob's spring is secure
in a land of grain and new wine,
  where the heavens drop dew.
29Blessed are you, O Israel!
  Who is like you,
  a people saved by the LORD?
He is your shield and helper
  and your glorious sword.
Your enemies will cower before you,

and you will trample down their
    high places.ᵃ"

The Death of Moses

34 Then Moses climbed Mount Nebo
from the plains of Moab to the top
of Pisgah, across from Jericho. There the
LORD showed him the whole land—from
Gilead to Dan, 2all of Naphtali, the territory of Ephraim and Manasseh, all the
land of Judah as far as the western sea,ᵇ
3the Negev and the whole region from the
Valley of Jericho, the City of Palms, as far
as Zoar. 4Then the LORD said to him, "This
is the land I promised on oath to Abraham, Isaac and Jacob when I said, 'I will
give it to your descendants.' I have let you
see it with your eyes, but you will not
cross over into it."

5And Moses the servant of the LORD
died there in Moab, as the LORD had said.
6He buried himᶜ in Moab, in the valley
opposite Beth Peor, but to this day no one
knows where his grave is. 7Moses was a
hundred and twenty years old when he
died, yet his eyes were not weak nor his
strength gone. 8The Israelites grieved for
Moses in the plains of Moab thirty days,
until the time of weeping and mourning
was over.

9Now Joshua son of Nun was filled with
the spiritᵈ of wisdom because Moses had
laid his hands on him. So the Israelites
listened to him and did what the LORD had
commanded Moses.

10Since then, no prophet has risen in
Israel like Moses, whom the LORD knew
face to face, 11who did all those miraculous signs and wonders the LORD sent him
to do in Egypt—to Pharaoh and to all his
officials and to his whole land. 12For no
one has ever shown the mighty power or
performed the awesome deeds that Moses did in the sight of all Israel.

ᵃ29 Or *will tread upon their bodies*   ᵇ2 That is, the Mediterranean   ᶜ6 Or *He was buried*   ᵈ9 Or
Spirit

*JOSHUA tells the story of how the
Israelites conquer their enemies in the
promised land and divide it up among
the twelve tribes. As long as the people
trust God and obey his will, he gives
them victory in their battles. By the end
of the book, the people choose to serve
only the Lord. As you read this book,
make your own choice to serve the
Lord, to do his will, and to depend on
him to give you victory over the evil one.*

JOSHUA

The LORD Commands Joshua

1 After the death of Moses the servant of the LORD, the LORD said to Joshua son of Nun, Moses' aide: ²"Moses my servant is dead. Now then, you and all these people, get ready to cross the Jordan River into the land I am about to give to them —to the Israelites. ³I will give you every place where you set your foot, as I promised Moses. ⁴Your territory will extend from the desert to Lebanon, and from the great river, the Euphrates—all the Hittite country—to the Great Sea*ᵃ* on the west. ⁵No one will be able to stand up against you all the days of your life. As I was with Moses, so I will be with you; I will never leave you nor forsake you.

⁶"Be strong and courageous, because you will lead these people to inherit the land I swore to their forefathers to give them. ⁷Be strong and very courageous. Be careful to obey all the law my servant Moses gave you; do not turn from it to the right or to the left, that you may be successful wherever you go. ⁸Do not let this Book of the Law depart from your mouth; meditate on it day and night, so that you may be careful to do everything written in it. Then you will be prosperous and successful. ⁹Have I not commanded you? Be strong and courageous. Do not be terrified; do not be discouraged, for the LORD your God will be with you wherever you go."

ᵃ4 That is, the Mediterranean

¹⁰So Joshua ordered the officers of the people: ¹¹"Go through the camp and tell the people, 'Get your supplies ready. Three days from now you will cross the Jordan here to go in and take possession of the land the Lord your God is giving you for your own.'"

¹²But to the Reubenites, the Gadites and the half-tribe of Manasseh, Joshua said, ¹³"Remember the command that Moses the servant of the Lord gave you: 'The Lord your God is giving you rest and has granted you this land.' ¹⁴Your wives, your children and your livestock may stay in the land that Moses gave you east of the Jordan, but all your fighting men, fully armed, must cross over ahead of your brothers. You are to help your brothers ¹⁵until the Lord gives them rest, as he has done for you, and until they too have tak-

en possession of the land that the Lord your God is giving them. After that, you may go back and occupy your own land, which Moses the servant of the Lord gave you east of the Jordan toward the sunrise."

¹⁶Then they answered Joshua, "Whatever you have commanded us we will do, and wherever you send us we will go. ¹⁷Just as we fully obeyed Moses, so we will obey you. Only may the Lord your God be with you as he was with Moses. ¹⁸Whoever rebels against your word and does not obey your words, whatever you may command them, will be put to death. Only be strong and courageous!"

Rahab and the Spies

2 Then Joshua son of Nun secretly sent two spies from Shittim. "Go, look

MONDAY

VERSE FOR THE DAY:
Joshua 1:9

AUTHOR:
Mary Jane Worden

PASSAGE FOR THE DAY:
Joshua 1:1–9

Our Why Questions

SOMETIMES when we ask God our Why questions, instead of giving us answers he gives us himself, the Comforter. From Luke 11:13: Even as fathers give good gifts to their children, so our Father gives the best gift, the Holy Spirit, the Comforter, to us as we ask. It reminded me of conversations with my daughter Jessie about why I wouldn't allow her to sleep over at a friend's house. "I can give you my reasons, but you won't like them or understand them, and you'd only argue with me. So let's just accept that this is the way it's going to be, and I'm sorry you feel sad." *Is it a little like that, Lord? Only without the impatient tone of voice . . . ?*

And from the same conversation: Often when we ask God for guidance, what we really want is a guide. My friend told me of a conversation he had with his young son shortly after they moved into their new house. "You can find your way to your new bedroom in the dark by simply turning on the lights in each room as you go." There was an uncertain pause, then, "But, Daddy, won't you please go with me?"

"Do not be terrified; do not be discouraged, for the Lord your God will be with you wherever you go" (Joshua 1:9).

Additional Scripture Readings:
Isaiah 30:19–21; John 14:26–27

Go to page 237 for your next devotional reading.

over the land," he said, "especially Jericho." So they went and entered the house of a prostitute[a] named Rahab and stayed there.

[2]The king of Jericho was told, "Look! Some of the Israelites have come here tonight to spy out the land." [3]So the king of Jericho sent this message to Rahab: "Bring out the men who came to you and entered your house, because they have come to spy out the whole land."

[4]But the woman had taken the two men and hidden them. She said, "Yes, the men came to me, but I did not know where they had come from. [5]At dusk, when it was time to close the city gate, the men left. I don't know which way they went. Go after them quickly. You may catch up with them." [6](But she had taken them up to the roof and hidden them under the stalks of flax she had laid out on the roof.) [7]So the men set out in pursuit of the spies on the road that leads to the fords of the Jordan, and as soon as the pursuers had gone out, the gate was shut.

[8]Before the spies lay down for the night, she went up on the roof [9]and said to them, "I know that the LORD has given this land to you and that a great fear of you has fallen on us, so that all who live in this country are melting in fear because of you. [10]We have heard how the LORD dried up the water of the Red Sea[b] for you when you came out of Egypt, and what you did to Sihon and Og, the two kings of the Amorites east of the Jordan, whom you completely destroyed.[c] [11]When we heard of it, our hearts melted and everyone's courage failed because of you, for the LORD your God is God in heaven above and on the earth below. [12]Now then, please swear to me by the LORD that you will show kindness to my family, because I have shown kindness to you. Give me a sure sign [13]that you will spare the lives of my father and mother, my brothers and sisters, and all who belong to them, and that you will save us from death."

[14]"Our lives for your lives!" the men assured her. "If you don't tell what we are doing, we will treat you kindly and faithfully when the LORD gives us the land."

[15]So she let them down by a rope through the window, for the house she lived in was part of the city wall. [16]Now

she had said to them, "Go to the hills so the pursuers will not find you. Hide yourselves there three days until they return, and then go on your way."

[17]The men said to her, "This oath you made us swear will not be binding on us [18]unless, when we enter the land, you have tied this scarlet cord in the window through which you let us down, and unless you have brought your father and mother, your brothers and all your family into your house. [19]If anyone goes outside your house into the street, his blood will be on his own head; we will not be responsible. As for anyone who is in the house with you, his blood will be on our head if a hand is laid on him. [20]But if you tell what we are doing, we will be released from the oath you made us swear."

[21]"Agreed," she replied. "Let it be as you say." So she sent them away and they departed. And she tied the scarlet cord in the window.

[22]When they left, they went into the hills and stayed there three days, until the pursuers had searched all along the road and returned without finding them. [23]Then the two men started back. They went down out of the hills, forded the river and came to Joshua son of Nun and told him everything that had happened to them. [24]They said to Joshua, "The LORD has surely given the whole land into our hands; all the people are melting in fear because of us."

Crossing the Jordan

3 Early in the morning Joshua and all the Israelites set out from Shittim and went to the Jordan, where they camped before crossing over. [2]After three days the officers went throughout the camp, [3]giving orders to the people: "When you see the ark of the covenant of the LORD your God, and the priests, who are Levites, carrying it, you are to move out from your positions and follow it. [4]Then you will know which way to go, since you have never been this way before. But keep a distance of about a thousand yards[d] between you and the ark; do not go near it."

[5]Joshua told the people, "Consecrate yourselves, for tomorrow the LORD will do amazing things among you."

[6]Joshua said to the priests, "Take up

---

[a]1 Or possibly *an innkeeper*   [b]10 Hebrew *Yam Suph*; that is, Sea of Reeds   [c]10 The Hebrew term refers to the irrevocable giving over of things or persons to the LORD, often by totally destroying them. [d]4 Hebrew *about two thousand cubits* (about 900 meters)

the ark of the covenant and pass on ahead of the people." So they took it up and went ahead of them.

[7]And the LORD said to Joshua, "Today I will begin to exalt you in the eyes of all Israel, so they may know that I am with you as I was with Moses. [8]Tell the priests who carry the ark of the covenant: 'When you reach the edge of the Jordan's waters, go and stand in the river.' "

[9]Joshua said to the Israelites, "Come here and listen to the words of the LORD your God. [10]This is how you will know that the living God is among you and that he will certainly drive out before you the Canaanites, Hittites, Hivites, Perizzites, Girgashites, Amorites and Jebusites. [11]See, the ark of the covenant of the Lord of all the earth will go into the Jordan ahead of you. [12]Now then, choose twelve men from the tribes of Israel, one from each tribe. [13]And as soon as the priests who carry the ark of the LORD—the Lord of all the earth—set foot in the Jordan, its waters flowing downstream will be cut off and stand up in a heap."

[14]So when the people broke camp to cross the Jordan, the priests carrying the ark of the covenant went ahead of them. [15]Now the Jordan is at flood stage all during harvest. Yet as soon as the priests who carried the ark reached the Jordan and their feet touched the water's edge, [16]the water from upstream stopped flowing. It piled up in a heap a great distance away, at a town called Adam in the vicinity of Zarethan, while the water flowing down to the Sea of the Arabah (the Salt Sea [a]) was completely cut off. So the people crossed over opposite Jericho. [17]The priests who carried the ark of the covenant of the LORD stood firm on dry ground in the middle of the Jordan, while all Israel passed by until the whole nation had completed the crossing on dry ground.

4 When the whole nation had finished crossing the Jordan, the LORD said to Joshua, [2]"Choose twelve men from among the people, one from each tribe, [3]and tell them to take up twelve stones from the middle of the Jordan from right where the priests stood and to carry them over with you and put them down at the place where you stay tonight."

[4]So Joshua called together the twelve men he had appointed from the Israelites, one from each tribe, [5]and said to them, "Go over before the ark of the LORD your God into the middle of the Jordan. Each of you is to take up a stone on his shoulder, according to the number of the tribes of the Israelites, [6]to serve as a sign among you. In the future, when your children ask you, 'What do these stones mean?' [7]tell them that the flow of the Jordan was cut off before the ark of the covenant of the LORD. When it crossed the Jordan, the waters of the Jordan were cut off. These stones are to be a memorial to the people of Israel forever."

[8]So the Israelites did as Joshua commanded them. They took twelve stones from the middle of the Jordan, according to the number of the tribes of the Israelites, as the LORD had told Joshua; and they carried them over with them to their camp, where they put them down. [9]Joshua set up the twelve stones that had been[b] in the middle of the Jordan at the spot where the priests who carried the ark of the covenant had stood. And they are there to this day.

[10]Now the priests who carried the ark remained standing in the middle of the Jordan until everything the LORD had commanded Joshua was done by the people, just as Moses had directed Joshua. The people hurried over, [11]and as soon as all of them had crossed, the ark of the LORD and the priests came to the other side while the people watched. [12]The men of Reuben, Gad and the half-tribe of Manasseh crossed over, armed, in front of the Israelites, as Moses had directed them. [13]About forty thousand armed for battle crossed over before the LORD to the plains of Jericho for war.

[14]That day the LORD exalted Joshua in the sight of all Israel; and they revered him all the days of his life, just as they had revered Moses.

[15]Then the LORD said to Joshua, [16]"Command the priests carrying the ark of the Testimony to come up out of the Jordan."

[17]So Joshua commanded the priests, "Come up out of the Jordan."

[18]And the priests came up out of the river carrying the ark of the covenant of the LORD. No sooner had they set their feet on the dry ground than the waters of the Jordan returned to their place and ran at flood stage as before.

[19]On the tenth day of the first month the people went up from the Jordan and

_____
[a]16 That is, the Dead Sea   [b]9 Or *Joshua also set up twelve stones*

camped at Gilgal on the eastern border of Jericho. ²⁰And Joshua set up at Gilgal the twelve stones they had taken out of the Jordan. ²¹He said to the Israelites, "In the future when your descendants ask their fathers, 'What do these stones mean?' ²²tell them, 'Israel crossed the Jordan on dry ground.' ²³For the LORD your God dried up the Jordan before you until you had crossed over. The LORD your God did to the Jordan just what he had done to the Red Sea^a when he dried it up before us until we had crossed over. ²⁴He did this so that all the peoples of the earth might know that the hand of the LORD is powerful and so that you might always fear the LORD your God."

Circumcision at Gilgal

5 Now when all the Amorite kings west of the Jordan and all the Canaanite kings along the coast heard how the LORD had dried up the Jordan before the Israelites until we had crossed over, their hearts melted and they no longer had the courage to face the Israelites.

²At that time the LORD said to Joshua, "Make flint knives and circumcise the Israelites again." ³So Joshua made flint knives and circumcised the Israelites at Gibeath Haaraloth.^b

⁴Now this is why he did so: All those who came out of Egypt—all the men of military age—died in the desert on the way after leaving Egypt. ⁵All the people that came out had been circumcised, but all the people born in the desert during the journey from Egypt had not. ⁶The Israelites had moved about in the desert forty years until all the men who were of military age when they left Egypt had died, since they had not obeyed the LORD. For the LORD had sworn to them that they would not see the land that he had solemnly promised their fathers to give us, a land flowing with milk and honey. ⁷So he raised up their sons in their place, and these were the ones Joshua circumcised. They were still uncircumcised because they had not been circumcised on the way. ⁸And after the whole nation had been circumcised, they remained where they were in camp until they were healed.

⁹Then the LORD said to Joshua, "Today I have rolled away the reproach of Egypt from you." So the place has been called Gilgal^c to this day.

¹⁰On the evening of the fourteenth day of the month, while camped at Gilgal on the plains of Jericho, the Israelites celebrated the Passover. ¹¹The day after the Passover, that very day, they ate some of the produce of the land: unleavened bread and roasted grain. ¹²The manna stopped the day after^d they ate this food from the land; there was no longer any manna for the Israelites, but that year they ate of the produce of Canaan.

The Fall of Jericho

¹³Now when Joshua was near Jericho, he looked up and saw a man standing in front of him with a drawn sword in his hand. Joshua went up to him and asked, "Are you for us or for our enemies?"

¹⁴"Neither," he replied, "but as commander of the army of the LORD I have now come." Then Joshua fell facedown to the ground in reverence, and asked him, "What message does my Lord^e have for his servant?"

¹⁵The commander of the LORD's army replied, "Take off your sandals, for the place where you are standing is holy." And Joshua did so.

6 Now Jericho was tightly shut up because of the Israelites. No one went out and no one came in.

²Then the LORD said to Joshua, "See, I have delivered Jericho into your hands, along with its king and its fighting men. ³March around the city once with all the armed men. Do this for six days. ⁴Have seven priests carry trumpets of rams' horns in front of the ark. On the seventh day, march around the city seven times, with the priests blowing the trumpets. ⁵When you hear them sound a long blast on the trumpets, have all the people give a loud shout; then the wall of the city will collapse and the people will go up, every man straight in."

⁶So Joshua son of Nun called the priests and said to them, "Take up the ark of the covenant of the LORD and have seven priests carry trumpets in front of it." ⁷And he ordered the people, "Advance! March around the city, with the armed guard going ahead of the ark of the LORD."

⁸When Joshua had spoken to the people, the seven priests carrying the seven trumpets before the LORD went forward, blowing their trumpets, and the ark of the LORD's covenant followed them. ⁹The

---

^a23 Hebrew *Yam Suph*; that is, Sea of Reeds ^b3 *Gibeath Haaraloth* means *hill of foreskins.*
^c9 *Gilgal* sounds like the Hebrew for *roll.* ^d12 Or *the day* ^e14 Or *lord*

armed guard marched ahead of the priests who blew the trumpets, and the rear guard followed the ark. All this time the trumpets were sounding. ¹⁰But Joshua had commanded the people, "Do not give a war cry, do not raise your voices, do not say a word until the day I tell you to shout. Then shout!" ¹¹So he had the ark of the LORD carried around the city, circling it once. Then the people returned to camp and spent the night there.

¹²Joshua got up early the next morning and the priests took up the ark of the LORD. ¹³The seven priests carrying the seven trumpets went forward, marching before the ark of the LORD and blowing the trumpets. The armed men went ahead of them and the rear guard followed the ark of the LORD, while the trumpets kept sounding. ¹⁴So on the second day they marched around the city once and returned to the camp. They did this for six days.

¹⁵On the seventh day, they got up at daybreak and marched around the city seven times in the same manner, except that on that day they circled the city seven times. ¹⁶The seventh time around, when the priests sounded the trumpet blast, Joshua commanded the people, "Shout! For the LORD has given you the city! ¹⁷The city and all that is in it are to be devoted^a to the LORD. Only Rahab the prostitute^b and all who are with her in her house shall be spared, because she hid the spies we sent. ¹⁸But keep away from the devoted things, so that you will not bring about your own destruction by taking any of them. Otherwise you will make the camp of Israel liable to destruction and bring trouble on it. ¹⁹All the silver and gold and the articles of bronze and iron are sacred to the LORD and must go into his treasury."

²⁰When the trumpets sounded, the people shouted, and at the sound of the trumpet, when the people gave a loud shout, the wall collapsed; so every man charged straight in, and they took the city. ²¹They devoted the city to the LORD and destroyed with the sword every living thing in it—men and women, young and old, cattle, sheep and donkeys.

²²Joshua said to the two men who had spied out the land, "Go into the prostitute's house and bring her out and all who belong to her, in accordance with your oath to her." ²³So the young men who had done the spying went in and brought out Rahab, her father and mother and brothers and all who belonged to her. They brought out her entire family and put them in a place outside the camp of Israel.

²⁴Then they burned the whole city and everything in it, but they put the silver and gold and the articles of bronze and iron into the treasury of the LORD's house. ²⁵But Joshua spared Rahab the prostitute, with her family and all who belonged to her, because she hid the men Joshua had sent as spies to Jericho—and she lives among the Israelites to this day.

²⁶At that time Joshua pronounced this solemn oath: "Cursed before the LORD is the man who undertakes to rebuild this city, Jericho:

"At the cost of his firstborn son
    will he lay its foundations;
at the cost of his youngest
    will he set up its gates."

²⁷So the LORD was with Joshua, and his fame spread throughout the land.

Achan's Sin

7 But the Israelites acted unfaithfully in regard to the devoted things^c; Achan son of Carmi, the son of Zimri,^d the son of Zerah, of the tribe of Judah, took some of them. So the LORD's anger burned against Israel.

²Now Joshua sent men from Jericho to Ai, which is near Beth Aven to the east of Bethel, and told them, "Go up and spy out the region." So the men went up and spied out Ai.

³When they returned to Joshua, they said, "Not all the people will have to go up against Ai. Send two or three thousand men to take it and do not weary all the people, for only a few men are there." ⁴So about three thousand men went up; but they were routed by the men of Ai, ⁵who killed about thirty-six of them. They chased the Israelites from the city gate as far as the stone quarries^e and struck them down on the slopes. At this the

---

^a17 The Hebrew term refers to the irrevocable giving over of things or persons to the LORD, often by totally destroying them; also in verses 18 and 21.   ^b17 Or possibly *innkeeper*; also in verses 22 and 25   ^c1 The Hebrew term refers to the irrevocable giving over of things or persons to the LORD, often by totally destroying them; also in verses 11, 12, 13 and 15.   ^d1 See Septuagint and 1 Chron. 2:6; Hebrew *Zabdi*; also in verses 17 and 18.   ^e5 Or *as far as Shebarim*

hearts of the people melted and became like water.

⁶Then Joshua tore his clothes and fell facedown to the ground before the ark of the Lord, remaining there till evening. The elders of Israel did the same, and sprinkled dust on their heads. ⁷And Joshua said, "Ah, Sovereign Lord, why did you ever bring this people across the Jordan to deliver us into the hands of the Amorites to destroy us? If only we had been content to stay on the other side of the Jordan! ⁸O Lord, what can I say, now that Israel has been routed by its enemies? ⁹The Canaanites and the other people of the country will hear about this and they will surround us and wipe out our name from the earth. What then will you do for your own great name?"

¹⁰The Lord said to Joshua, "Stand up! What are you doing down on your face? ¹¹Israel has sinned; they have violated my covenant, which I commanded them to keep. They have taken some of the devoted things; they have stolen, they have lied, they have put them with their own possessions. ¹²That is why the Israelites cannot stand against their enemies; they turn their backs and run because they have been made liable to destruction. I will not be with you anymore unless you destroy whatever among you is devoted to destruction.

¹³"Go, consecrate the people. Tell them, 'Consecrate yourselves in preparation for tomorrow; for this is what the Lord, the God of Israel, says: That which is devoted is among you, O Israel. You cannot stand against your enemies until you remove it.

¹⁴"'In the morning, present yourselves tribe by tribe. The tribe that the Lord takes shall come forward clan by clan; the clan that the Lord takes shall come forward family by family; and the family that the Lord takes shall come forward man by man. ¹⁵He who is caught with the devoted things shall be destroyed by fire, along with all that belongs to him. He has violated the covenant of the Lord and has done a disgraceful thing in Israel!' "

¹⁶Early the next morning Joshua had Israel come forward by tribes, and Judah was taken. ¹⁷The clans of Judah came forward, and he took the Zerahites. He had the clan of the Zerahites come forward by

families, and Zimri was taken. ¹⁸Joshua had his family come forward man by man, and Achan son of Carmi, the son of Zimri, the son of Zerah, of the tribe of Judah, was taken.

¹⁹Then Joshua said to Achan, "My son, give glory to the Lord,ᵃ the God of Israel, and give him the praise.ᵇ Tell me what you have done; do not hide it from me."

²⁰Achan replied, "It is true! I have sinned against the Lord, the God of Israel. This is what I have done: ²¹When I saw in the plunder a beautiful robe from Babylonia,ᶜ two hundred shekelsᵈ of silver and a wedge of gold weighing fifty shekels,ᵉ I coveted them and took them. They are hidden in the ground inside my tent, with the silver underneath."

²²So Joshua sent messengers, and they ran to the tent, and there it was, hidden in his tent, with the silver underneath. ²³They took the things from the tent, brought them to Joshua and all the Israelites and spread them out before the Lord.

²⁴Then Joshua, together with all Israel, took Achan son of Zerah, the silver, the robe, the gold wedge, his sons and daughters, his cattle, donkeys and sheep, his tent and all that he had, to the Valley of Achor. ²⁵Joshua said, "Why have you brought this trouble on us? The Lord will bring trouble on you today."

Then all Israel stoned him, and after they had stoned the rest, they burned them. ²⁶Over Achan they heaped up a large pile of rocks, which remains to this day. Then the Lord turned from his fierce anger. Therefore that place has been called the Valley of Achorᶠ ever since.

Ai Destroyed

8 Then the Lord said to Joshua, "Do not be afraid; do not be discouraged. Take the whole army with you, and go up and attack Ai. For I have delivered into your hands the king of Ai, his people, his city and his land. ²You shall do to Ai and its king as you did to Jericho and its king, except that you may carry off their plunder and livestock for yourselves. Set an ambush behind the city."

³So Joshua and the whole army moved out to attack Ai. He chose thirty thousand of his best fighting men and sent them out at night ⁴with these orders: "Listen carefully. You are to set an ambush be-

---

ᵃ19 A solemn charge to tell the truth   ᵇ19 Or *and confess to him*   ᶜ21 Hebrew *Shinar*   ᵈ21 That is, about 5 pounds (about 2.3 kilograms)   ᵉ21 That is, about 1 1/4 pounds (about 0.6 kilogram)   ᶠ26 *Achor* means *trouble*.

hind the city. Don't go very far from it. All of you be on the alert. ⁵I and all those with me will advance on the city, and when the men come out against us, as they did before, we will flee from them. ⁶They will pursue us until we have lured them away from the city, for they will say, 'They are running away from us as they did before.' So when we flee from them, ⁷you are to rise up from ambush and take the city. The LORD your God will give it into your hand. ⁸When you have taken the city, set it on fire. Do what the LORD has commanded. See to it; you have my orders."

⁹Then Joshua sent them off, and they went to the place of ambush and lay in wait between Bethel and Ai, to the west of Ai—but Joshua spent that night with the people.

¹⁰Early the next morning Joshua mustered his men, and he and the leaders of Israel marched before them to Ai. ¹¹The entire force that was with him marched up and approached the city and arrived in front of it. They set up camp north of Ai, with the valley between them and the city. ¹²Joshua had taken about five thousand men and set them in ambush between Bethel and Ai, to the west of the city. ¹³They had the soldiers take up their positions—all those in the camp to the north of the city and the ambush to the west of it. That night Joshua went into the valley.

¹⁴When the king of Ai saw this, he and all the men of the city hurried out early in the morning to meet Israel in battle at a certain place overlooking the Arabah. But he did not know that an ambush had been set against him behind the city. ¹⁵Joshua and all Israel let themselves be driven back before them, and they fled toward the desert. ¹⁶All the men of Ai were called to pursue them, and they pursued Joshua and were lured away from the city. ¹⁷Not a man remained in Ai or Bethel who did not go after Israel. They left the city open and went in pursuit of Israel.

¹⁸Then the LORD said to Joshua, "Hold out toward Ai the javelin that is in your hand, for into your hand I will deliver the city." So Joshua held out his javelin toward Ai. ¹⁹As soon as he did this, the men in the ambush rose quickly from their position and rushed forward. They entered the city and captured it and quickly set it on fire.

²⁰The men of Ai looked back and saw the smoke of the city rising against the sky, but they had no chance to escape in any direction, for the Israelites who had been fleeing toward the desert had turned back against their pursuers. ²¹For when Joshua and all Israel saw that the ambush had taken the city and that smoke was going up from the city, they turned around and attacked the men of Ai. ²²The men of the ambush also came out of the city against them, so that they were caught in the middle, with Israelites on both sides. Israel cut them down, leaving them neither survivors nor fugitives. ²³But they took the king of Ai alive and brought him to Joshua.

²⁴When Israel had finished killing all the men of Ai in the fields and in the desert where they had chased them, and when every one of them had been put to the sword, all the Israelites returned to Ai and killed those who were in it. ²⁵Twelve thousand men and women fell that day— all the people of Ai. ²⁶For Joshua did not draw back the hand that held out his javelin until he had destroyed[a] all who lived in Ai. ²⁷But Israel did carry off for themselves the livestock and plunder of this city, as the LORD had instructed Joshua.

²⁸So Joshua burned Ai and made it a permanent heap of ruins, a desolate place to this day. ²⁹He hung the king of Ai on a tree and left him there until evening. At sunset, Joshua ordered them to take his body from the tree and throw it down at the entrance of the city gate. And they raised a large pile of rocks over it, which remains to this day.

The Covenant Renewed at Mount Ebal

³⁰Then Joshua built on Mount Ebal an altar to the LORD, the God of Israel, ³¹as Moses the servant of the LORD had commanded the Israelites. He built it according to what is written in the Book of the Law of Moses—an altar of uncut stones, on which no iron tool had been used. On it they offered to the LORD burnt offerings and sacrificed fellowship offerings.[b] ³²There, in the presence of the Israelites, Joshua copied on stones the law of Moses, which he had written. ³³All Israel, aliens and citizens alike, with their el-

---

a26 The Hebrew term refers to the irrevocable giving over of things or persons to the LORD, often by totally destroying them.   b31 Traditionally peace offerings ders, officials and judges, were standing on both sides of the ark of the covenant of the Lord, facing those who carried it—the priests, who were Levites. Half of the people stood in front of Mount Gerizim and half of them in front of Mount Ebal, as Moses the servant of the Lord had formerly commanded when he gave instructions to bless the people of Israel.

34Afterward, Joshua read all the words of the law—the blessings and the curses—just as it is written in the Book of the Law. 35There was not a word of all that Moses had commanded that Joshua did not read to the whole assembly of Israel, including the women and children, and the aliens who lived among them.

The Gibeonite Deception

9 Now when all the kings west of the Jordan heard about these things—those in the hill country, in the western foothills, and along the entire coast of the Great Sea*a* as far as Lebanon (the kings of the Hittites, Amorites, Canaanites, Perizzites, Hivites and Jebusites)— 2they came together to make war against Joshua and Israel.

3However, when the people of Gibeon heard what Joshua had done to Jericho and Ai, 4they resorted to a ruse: They went as a delegation whose donkeys were loaded*b* with worn-out sacks and old wineskins, cracked and mended. 5The men put worn and patched sandals on their feet and wore old clothes. All the bread of their food supply was dry and moldy. 6Then they went to Joshua in the camp at Gilgal and said to him and the men of Israel, "We have come from a distant country; make a treaty with us."

7The men of Israel said to the Hivites, "But perhaps you live near us. How then can we make a treaty with you?"

8"We are your servants," they said to Joshua.

But Joshua asked, "Who are you and where do you come from?"

9They answered: "Your servants have come from a very distant country because of the fame of the Lord your God. For we have heard reports of him: all that he did in Egypt, 10and all that he did to the two kings of the Amorites east of the Jordan—Sihon king of Heshbon, and Og king of Bashan, who reigned in Ashtaroth. 11And our elders and all those living in our

country said to us, 'Take provisions for your journey; go and meet them and say to them, "We are your servants; make a treaty with us."' 12This bread of ours was warm when we packed it at home on the day we left to come to you. But now see how dry and moldy it is. 13And these wineskins that we filled were new, but see how cracked they are. And our clothes and sandals are worn out by the very long journey."

14The men of Israel sampled their provisions but did not inquire of the Lord. 15Then Joshua made a treaty of peace with them to let them live, and the leaders of the assembly ratified it by oath.

16Three days after they made the treaty with the Gibeonites, the Israelites heard that they were neighbors, living near them. 17So the Israelites set out and on the third day came to their cities: Gibeon, Kephirah, Beeroth and Kiriath Jearim. 18But the Israelites did not attack them, because the leaders of the assembly had sworn an oath to them by the Lord, the God of Israel.

The whole assembly grumbled against the leaders, 19but all the leaders answered, "We have given them our oath by the Lord, the God of Israel, and we cannot touch them now. 20This is what we will do to them: We will let them live, so that wrath will not fall on us for breaking the oath we swore to them." 21They continued, "Let them live, but let them be woodcutters and water carriers for the entire community." So the leaders' promise to them was kept.

22Then Joshua summoned the Gibeonites and said, "Why did you deceive us by saying, 'We live a long way from you,' while actually you live near us? 23You are now under a curse: You will never cease to serve as woodcutters and water carriers for the house of my God."

24They answered Joshua, "Your servants were clearly told how the Lord your God had commanded his servant Moses to give you the whole land and to wipe out all its inhabitants from before you. So we feared for our lives because of you, and that is why we did this. 25We are now in your hands. Do to us whatever seems good and right to you."

26So Joshua saved them from the Israelites, and they did not kill them. 27That day he made the Gibeonites woodcutters

---

a1 That is, the Mediterranean   *b4* Most Hebrew manuscripts; some Hebrew manuscripts, Vulgate and Syriac (see also Septuagint) *They prepared provisions and loaded their donkeys* and water carriers for the community and for the altar of the LORD at the place the LORD would choose. And that is what they are to this day.

The Sun Stands Still

10 Now Adoni-Zedek king of Jerusalem heard that Joshua had taken Ai and totally destroyed^a it, doing to Ai and its king as he had done to Jericho and its king, and that the people of Gibeon had made a treaty of peace with Israel and were living near them. ²He and his people were very much alarmed at this, because Gibeon was an important city, like one of the royal cities; it was larger than Ai, and all its men were good fighters. ³So Adoni-Zedek king of Jerusalem appealed to Hoham king of Hebron, Piram king of Jarmuth, Japhia king of Lachish and Debir king of Eglon. ⁴"Come up and help me attack Gibeon," he said, "because it has made peace with Joshua and the Israelites."

⁵Then the five kings of the Amorites—the kings of Jerusalem, Hebron, Jarmuth, Lachish and Eglon—joined forces. They moved up with all their troops and took up positions against Gibeon and attacked it.

⁶The Gibeonites then sent word to Joshua in the camp at Gilgal: "Do not abandon your servants. Come up to us quickly and save us! Help us, because all the Amorite kings from the hill country have joined forces against us."

⁷So Joshua marched up from Gilgal with his entire army, including all the best fighting men. ⁸The LORD said to Joshua, "Do not be afraid of them; I have given them into your hand. Not one of them will be able to withstand you."

⁹After an all-night march from Gilgal, Joshua took them by surprise. ¹⁰The LORD threw them into confusion before Israel, who defeated them in a great victory at Gibeon. Israel pursued them along the road going up to Beth Horon and cut them down all the way to Azekah and Makkedah. ¹¹As they fled before Israel on the road down from Beth Horon to Azekah, the LORD hurled large hailstones down on them from the sky, and more of them died from the hailstones than were killed by the swords of the Israelites.

¹²On the day the LORD gave the Amorites over to Israel, Joshua said to the LORD in the presence of Israel:

"O sun, stand still over Gibeon,
    O moon, over the Valley of
        Aijalon."
¹³So the sun stood still,
    and the moon stopped,
    till the nation avenged itself on^b its
        enemies,

as it is written in the Book of Jashar.

The sun stopped in the middle of the sky and delayed going down about a full day. ¹⁴There has never been a day like it before or since, a day when the LORD listened to a man. Surely the LORD was fighting for Israel!

¹⁵Then Joshua returned with all Israel to the camp at Gilgal.

Five Amorite Kings Killed

¹⁶Now the five kings had fled and hidden in the cave at Makkedah. ¹⁷When Joshua was told that the five kings had been found hiding in the cave at Makkedah, ¹⁸he said, "Roll large rocks up to the mouth of the cave, and post some men there to guard it. ¹⁹But don't stop! Pursue your enemies, attack them from the rear and don't let them reach their cities, for the LORD your God has given them into your hand."

²⁰So Joshua and the Israelites destroyed them completely—almost to a man—but the few who were left reached their fortified cities. ²¹The whole army then returned safely to Joshua in the camp at Makkedah, and no one uttered a word against the Israelites.

²²Joshua said, "Open the mouth of the cave and bring those five kings out to me." ²³So they brought the five kings out of the cave—the kings of Jerusalem, Hebron, Jarmuth, Lachish and Eglon. ²⁴When they had brought these kings to Joshua, he summoned all the men of Israel and said to the army commanders who had come with him, "Come here and put your feet on the necks of these kings." So they came forward and placed their feet on their necks.

²⁵Joshua said to them, "Do not be afraid; do not be discouraged. Be strong and courageous. This is what the LORD will do to all the enemies you are going to fight." ²⁶Then Joshua struck and killed the kings and hung them on five trees,

---

^a1 The Hebrew term refers to the irrevocable giving over of things or persons to the LORD, often by totally destroying them; also in verses 28, 35, 37, 39 and 40.   ^b13 Or *nation triumphed over*

and they were left hanging on the trees until evening.

²⁷At sunset Joshua gave the order and they took them down from the trees and threw them into the cave where they had been hiding. At the mouth of the cave they placed large rocks, which are there to this day.

²⁸That day Joshua took Makkedah. He put the city and its king to the sword and totally destroyed everyone in it. He left no survivors. And he did to the king of Makkedah as he had done to the king of Jericho.

Southern Cities Conquered

²⁹Then Joshua and all Israel with him moved on from Makkedah to Libnah and attacked it. ³⁰The Lord also gave that city and its king into Israel's hand. The city and everyone in it Joshua put to the sword. He left no survivors there. And he did to its king as he had done to the king of Jericho.

³¹Then Joshua and all Israel with him moved on from Libnah to Lachish; he took up positions against it and attacked it. ³²The Lord handed Lachish over to Israel, and Joshua took it on the second day. The city and everyone in it he put to the sword, just as he had done to Libnah. ³³Meanwhile, Horam king of Gezer had come up to help Lachish, but Joshua defeated him and his army—until no survivors were left.

³⁴Then Joshua and all Israel with him moved on from Lachish to Eglon; they took up positions against it and attacked it. ³⁵They captured it that same day and put it to the sword and totally destroyed everyone in it, just as they had done to Lachish.

³⁶Then Joshua and all Israel with him went up from Eglon to Hebron and attacked it. ³⁷They took the city and put it to the sword, together with its king, its villages and everyone in it. They left no survivors. Just as at Eglon, they totally destroyed it and everyone in it.

³⁸Then Joshua and all Israel with him turned around and attacked Debir. ³⁹They took the city, its king and its villages, and put them to the sword. Everyone in it they totally destroyed. They left no survivors. They did to Debir and its king as they had done to Libnah and its king and to Hebron.

⁴⁰So Joshua subdued the whole region, including the hill country, the Negev, the western foothills and the mountain slopes, together with all their kings. He left no survivors. He totally destroyed all who breathed, just as the Lord, the God of Israel, had commanded. ⁴¹Joshua subdued them from Kadesh Barnea to Gaza and from the whole region of Goshen to Gibeon. ⁴²All these kings and their lands Joshua conquered in one campaign, because the Lord, the God of Israel, fought for Israel.

⁴³Then Joshua returned with all Israel to the camp at Gilgal.

Northern Kings Defeated

11 When Jabin king of Hazor heard of this, he sent word to Jobab king of Madon, to the kings of Shimron and Acshaph, ²and to the northern kings who were in the mountains, in the Arabah south of Kinnereth, in the western foothills and in Naphoth Dor*ᵃ* on the west; ³to the Canaanites in the east and west; to the Amorites, Hittites, Perizzites and Jebusites in the hill country; and to the Hivites below Hermon in the region of Mizpah. ⁴They came out with all their troops and a large number of horses and chariots—a huge army, as numerous as the sand on the seashore. ⁵All these kings joined forces and made camp together at the Waters of Merom, to fight against Israel.

⁶The Lord said to Joshua, "Do not be afraid of them, because by this time tomorrow I will hand all of them over to Israel, slain. You are to hamstring their horses and burn their chariots."

⁷So Joshua and his whole army came against them suddenly at the Waters of Merom and attacked them, ⁸and the Lord gave them into the hand of Israel. They defeated them and pursued them all the way to Greater Sidon, to Misrephoth Maim, and to the Valley of Mizpah on the east, until no survivors were left. ⁹Joshua did to them as the Lord had directed: He hamstrung their horses and burned their chariots.

¹⁰At that time Joshua turned back and captured Hazor and put its king to the sword. (Hazor had been the head of all these kingdoms.) ¹¹Everyone in it they put to the sword. They totally destroyed*ᵇ*

---

*ᵃ*2 Or *in the heights of Dor*   *ᵇ*11 The Hebrew term refers to the irrevocable giving over of things or persons to the Lord, often by totally destroying them; also in verses 12, 20 and 21.

them, not sparing anything that breathed, and he burned up Hazor itself.

¹²Joshua took all these royal cities and their kings and put them to the sword. He totally destroyed them, as Moses the servant of the LORD had commanded. ¹³Yet Israel did not burn any of the cities built on their mounds—except Hazor, which Joshua burned. ¹⁴The Israelites carried off for themselves all the plunder and livestock of these cities, but all the people they put to the sword until they completely destroyed them, not sparing anyone that breathed. ¹⁵As the LORD commanded his servant Moses, so Moses commanded Joshua, and Joshua did it; he left nothing undone of all that the LORD commanded Moses.

¹⁶So Joshua took this entire land: the hill country, all the Negev, the whole region of Goshen, the western foothills, the Arabah and the mountains of Israel with their foothills, ¹⁷from Mount Halak, which rises toward Seir, to Baal Gad in the Valley of Lebanon below Mount Hermon. He captured all their kings and struck them down, putting them to death. ¹⁸Joshua waged war against all these kings for a long time. ¹⁹Except for the Hivites living in Gibeon, not one city made a treaty of peace with the Israelites, who took them all in battle. ²⁰For it was the LORD himself who hardened their hearts to wage war against Israel, so that he might destroy them totally, exterminating them without mercy, as the LORD had commanded Moses.

²¹At that time Joshua went and destroyed the Anakites from the hill country: from Hebron, Debir and Anab, from all the hill country of Judah, and from all the hill country of Israel. Joshua totally destroyed them and their towns. ²²No Anakites were left in Israelite territory; only in Gaza, Gath and Ashdod did any survive. ²³So Joshua took the entire land, just as the LORD had directed Moses, and he gave it as an inheritance to Israel according to their tribal divisions.

Then the land had rest from war.

List of Defeated Kings

12 These are the kings of the land whom the Israelites had defeated and whose territory they took over east of the Jordan, from the Arnon Gorge to Mount Hermon, including all the eastern side of the Arabah:

²Sihon king of the Amorites,
who reigned in Heshbon. He ruled from Aroer on the rim of the Arnon Gorge—from the middle of the gorge—to the Jabbok River, which is the border of the Ammonites. This included half of Gilead. ³He also ruled over the eastern Arabah from the Sea of Kinnereth[a] to the Sea of the Arabah (the Salt Sea[b]), to Beth Jeshimoth, and then southward below the slopes of Pisgah.

⁴And the territory of Og king of Bashan, one of the last of the Rephaites, who reigned in Ashtaroth and Edrei. ⁵He ruled over Mount Hermon, Salecah, all of Bashan to the border of the people of Geshur and Maacah, and half of Gilead to the border of Sihon king of Heshbon.

⁶Moses, the servant of the LORD, and the Israelites conquered them. And Moses the servant of the LORD gave their land to the Reubenites, the Gadites and the half-tribe of Manasseh to be their possession.

⁷These are the kings of the land that Joshua and the Israelites conquered on the west side of the Jordan, from Baal Gad in the Valley of Lebanon to Mount Halak, which rises toward Seir (their lands Joshua gave as an inheritance to the tribes of Israel according to their tribal divisions—⁸the hill country, the western foothills, the Arabah, the mountain slopes, the desert and the Negev—the lands of the Hittites, Amorites, Canaanites, Perizzites, Hivites and Jebusites):

⁹the king of Jericho	one
the king of Ai (near Bethel)	one
¹⁰the king of Jerusalem	one
the king of Hebron	one
¹¹the king of Jarmuth	one
the king of Lachish	one
¹²the king of Eglon	one
the king of Gezer	one
¹³the king of Debir	one
the king of Geder	one
¹⁴the king of Hormah	one
the king of Arad	one
¹⁵the king of Libnah	one
the king of Adullam	one
¹⁶the king of Makkedah	one
the king of Bethel	one
¹⁷the king of Tappuah	one
the king of Hepher	one

a3 That is, Galilee   b3 That is, the Dead Sea

[18]the king of Aphek   one
  the king of Lasharon   one
[19]the king of Madon   one
  the king of Hazor   one
[20]the king of Shimron Meron   one
  the king of Acshaph   one
[21]the king of Taanach   one
  the king of Megiddo   one
[22]the king of Kedesh   one
  the king of Jokneam in
    Carmel   one
[23]the king of Dor (in Naphoth
    Dor[a])   one
  the king of Goyim in Gilgal   one
[24]the king of Tirzah   one
thirty-one kings in all.

Land Still to Be Taken

13 When Joshua was old and well advanced in years, the LORD said to him, "You are very old, and there are still very large areas of land to be taken over.

[2]"This is the land that remains: all the regions of the Philistines and Geshurites: [3]from the Shihor River on the east of Egypt to the territory of Ekron on the north, all of it counted as Canaanite (the territory of the five Philistine rulers in Gaza, Ashdod, Ashkelon, Gath and Ekron—that of the Avvites); [4]from the south, all the land of the Canaanites, from Arah of the Sidonians as far as Aphek, the region of the Amorites, [5]the area of the Gebalites[b]; and all Lebanon to the east, from Baal Gad below Mount Hermon to Lebo[c] Hamath.

[6]"As for all the inhabitants of the mountain regions from Lebanon to Misrephoth Maim, that is, all the Sidonians, I myself will drive them out before the Israelites. Be sure to allocate this land to Israel for an inheritance, as I have instructed you, [7]and divide it as an inheritance among the nine tribes and half of the tribe of Manasseh."

Division of the Land East of the Jordan

[8]The other half of Manasseh,[d] the Reubenites and the Gadites had received the inheritance that Moses had given them east of the Jordan, as he, the servant of the LORD, had assigned it to them.

[9]It extended from Aroer on the rim of the Arnon Gorge, and from the town in the middle of the gorge, and included the whole plateau of Medeba as far as Dibon, [10]and all the towns of Sihon king of the Amorites, who ruled in Heshbon, out to the border of the Ammonites. [11]It also included Gilead, the territory of the people of Geshur and Maacah, all of Mount Hermon and all Bashan as far as Salecah— [12]that is, the whole kingdom of Og in Bashan, who had reigned in Ashtaroth and Edrei and had survived as one of the last of the Rephaites. Moses had defeated them and taken over their land. [13]But the Israelites did not drive out the people of Geshur and Maacah, so they continue to live among the Israelites to this day.

[14]But to the tribe of Levi he gave no inheritance, since the offerings made by fire to the LORD, the God of Israel, are their inheritance, as he promised them.

[15]This is what Moses had given to the tribe of Reuben, clan by clan:

[16]The territory from Aroer on the rim of the Arnon Gorge, and from the town in the middle of the gorge, and the whole plateau past Medeba [17]to Heshbon and all its towns on the plateau, including Dibon, Bamoth Baal, Beth Baal Meon, [18]Jahaz, Kedemoth, Mephaath, [19]Kiriathaim, Sibmah, Zereth Shahar on the hill in the valley, [20]Beth Peor, the slopes of Pisgah, and Beth Jeshimoth [21]—all the towns on the plateau and the entire realm of Sihon king of the Amorites, who ruled at Heshbon. Moses had defeated him and the Midianite chiefs, Evi, Rekem, Zur, Hur and Reba—princes allied with Sihon—who lived in that country. [22]In addition to those slain in battle, the Israelites had put to the sword Balaam son of Beor, who practiced divination. [23]The boundary of the Reubenites was the bank of the Jordan. These towns and their villages were the inheritance of the Reubenites, clan by clan.

[24]This is what Moses had given to the tribe of Gad, clan by clan:

---

[a]23 Or *in the heights of Dor*   [b]5 That is, the area of Byblos   [c]5 Or *to the entrance to*   [d]8 Hebrew *With it* (that is, with the other half of Manasseh)

25The territory of Jazer, all the towns of Gilead and half the Ammonite country as far as Aroer, near Rabbah; 26and from Heshbon to Ramath Mizpah and Betonim, and from Mahanaim to the territory of Debir; 27and in the valley, Beth Haram, Beth Nimrah, Succoth and Zaphon with the rest of the realm of Sihon king of Heshbon (the east side of the Jordan, the territory up to the end of the Sea of Kinnereth*a*). 28These towns and their villages were the inheritance of the Gadites, clan by clan.

29This is what Moses had given to the half-tribe of Manasseh, that is, to half the family of the descendants of Manasseh, clan by clan:

30The territory extending from Mahanaim and including all of Bashan, the entire realm of Og king of Bashan—all the settlements of Jair in Bashan, sixty towns, 31half of Gilead, and Ashtaroth and Edrei (the royal cities of Og in Bashan). This was for the descendants of Makir son of Manasseh—for half of the sons of Makir, clan by clan.

32This is the inheritance Moses had given when he was in the plains of Moab across the Jordan east of Jericho. 33But to the tribe of Levi, Moses had given no inheritance; the Lord, the God of Israel, is their inheritance, as he promised them.

Division of the Land West of the Jordan

14 Now these are the areas the Israelites received as an inheritance in the land of Canaan, which Eleazar the priest, Joshua son of Nun and the heads of the tribal clans of Israel allotted to them. 2Their inheritances were assigned by lot to the nine-and-a-half tribes, as the Lord had commanded through Moses. 3Moses had granted the two-and-a-half tribes their inheritance east of the Jordan but had not granted the Levites an inheritance among the rest, 4for the sons of Joseph had become two tribes—Manasseh and Ephraim. The Levites received no share of the land but only towns to live in, with pasturelands for their flocks and herds. 5So the Israelites divided the land, just as the Lord had commanded Moses.

Hebron Given to Caleb

6Now the men of Judah approached Joshua at Gilgal, and Caleb son of Jephunneh the Kenizzite said to him, "You know what the Lord said to Moses the man of God at Kadesh Barnea about you and me. 7I was forty years old when Moses the servant of the Lord sent me from Kadesh Barnea to explore the land. And I brought him back a report according to my convictions, 8but my brothers who went up with me made the hearts of the people melt with fear. I, however, followed the Lord my God wholeheartedly. 9So on that day Moses swore to me, 'The land on which your feet have walked will be your inheritance and that of your children forever, because you have followed the Lord my God wholeheartedly.'*b*

10"Now then, just as the Lord promised, he has kept me alive for forty-five years since the time he said this to Moses, while Israel moved about in the desert. So here I am today, eighty-five years old! 11I am still as strong today as the day Moses sent me out; I'm just as vigorous to go out to battle now as I was then. 12Now give me this hill country that the Lord promised me that day. You yourself heard then that the Anakites were there and their cities were large and fortified, but, the Lord helping me, I will drive them out just as he said."

13Then Joshua blessed Caleb son of Jephunneh and gave him Hebron as his inheritance. 14So Hebron has belonged to Caleb son of Jephunneh the Kenizzite ever since, because he followed the Lord, the God of Israel, wholeheartedly. 15(Hebron used to be called Kiriath Arba after Arba, who was the greatest man among the Anakites.)

Then the land had rest from war.

Allotment for Judah

15 The allotment for the tribe of Judah, clan by clan, extended down to the territory of Edom, to the Desert of Zin in the extreme south. 2Their southern boundary started from the bay at the southern end of the Salt Sea,*c* 3crossed south of Scorpion*d* Pass, continued on to Zin and went over to the south of Kadesh Barnea. Then it ran past Hezron up to Addar and curved around to Karka. 4It then passed along to Azmon

*a*27 That is, Galilee   *b*9 Deut. 1:36   *c*2 That is, the Dead Sea; also in verse 5   *d*3 Hebrew Akrabbim and joined the Wadi of Egypt, ending at the sea. This is their[a] southern boundary.

⁵The eastern boundary is the Salt Sea as far as the mouth of the Jordan.

The northern boundary started from the bay of the sea at the mouth of the Jordan, ⁶went up to Beth Hoglah and continued north of Beth Arabah to the Stone of Bohan son of Reuben. ⁷The boundary then went up to Debir from the Valley of Achor and turned north to Gilgal, which faces the Pass of Adummim south of the gorge. It continued along to the waters of En Shemesh and came out at En Rogel. ⁸Then it ran up the Valley of Ben Hinnom along the southern slope of the Jebusite city (that is, Jerusalem). From there it climbed to the top of the hill west of the Hinnom Valley at the northern end of the Valley of Rephaim. ⁹From the hilltop the boundary headed toward the spring of the waters of Nephtoah, came out at the towns of Mount Ephron and went down toward Baalah (that is, Kiriath Jearim). ¹⁰Then it curved westward from Baalah to Mount Seir, ran along the northern slope of Mount Jearim (that is, Kesalon), continued down to Beth Shemesh and crossed to Timnah. ¹¹It went to the northern slope of Ekron, turned toward Shikkeron, passed along to Mount Baalah and reached Jabneel. The boundary ended at the sea.

¹²The western boundary is the coastline of the Great Sea.[b]

These are the boundaries around the people of Judah by their clans.

¹³In accordance with the LORD's command to him, Joshua gave to Caleb son of Jephunneh a portion in Judah—Kiriath Arba, that is, Hebron. (Arba was the forefather of Anak.) ¹⁴From Hebron Caleb drove out the three Anakites—Sheshai, Ahiman and Talmai—descendants of Anak. ¹⁵From there he marched against the people living in Debir (formerly called Kiriath Sepher). ¹⁶And Caleb said, "I will give my daughter Acsah in marriage to the man who attacks and captures Kiriath Sepher." ¹⁷Othniel son of Kenaz, Caleb's

brother, took it; so Caleb gave his daughter Acsah to him in marriage.

¹⁸One day when she came to Othniel, she urged him[c] to ask her father for a field. When she got off her donkey, Caleb asked her, "What can I do for you?"

¹⁹She replied, "Do me a special favor. Since you have given me land in the Negev, give me also springs of water." So Caleb gave her the upper and lower springs.

²⁰This is the inheritance of the tribe of Judah, clan by clan:

²¹The southernmost towns of the tribe of Judah in the Negev toward the boundary of Edom were:

Kabzeel, Eder, Jagur, ²²Kinah, Dimonah, Adadah, ²³Kedesh, Hazor, Ithnan, ²⁴Ziph, Telem, Bealoth, ²⁵Hazor Hadattah, Kerioth Hezron (that is, Hazor), ²⁶Amam, Shema, Moladah, ²⁷Hazar Gaddah, Heshmon, Beth Pelet, ²⁸Hazar Shual, Beersheba, Biziothiah, ²⁹Baalah, Iim, Ezem, ³⁰Eltolad, Kesil, Hormah, ³¹Ziklag, Madmannah, Sansannah, ³²Lebaoth, Shilhim, Ain and Rimmon—a total of twenty-nine towns and their villages.

³³In the western foothills:

Eshtaol, Zorah, Ashnah, ³⁴Zanoah, En Gannim, Tappuah, Enam, ³⁵Jarmuth, Adullam, Socoh, Azekah, ³⁶Shaaraim, Adithaim and Gederah (or Gederothaim)[d]—fourteen towns and their villages.

³⁷Zenan, Hadashah, Migdal Gad, ³⁸Dilean, Mizpah, Joktheel, ³⁹Lachish, Bozkath, Eglon, ⁴⁰Cabbon, Lahmas, Kitlish, ⁴¹Gederoth, Beth Dagon, Naamah and Makkedah—sixteen towns and their villages.

⁴²Libnah, Ether, Ashan, ⁴³Iphtah, Ashnah, Nezib, ⁴⁴Keilah, Aczib and Mareshah—nine towns and their villages.

⁴⁵Ekron, with its surrounding settlements and villages; ⁴⁶west of Ekron, all that were in the vicinity of Ashdod, together with their villages; ⁴⁷Ashdod, its surrounding settlements and villages; and Gaza, its settlements and villages, as far as the Wadi of Egypt and the coastline of the Great Sea.

---

a4 Hebrew your   b12 That is, the Mediterranean; also in verse 47   c18 Hebrew and some Septuagint manuscripts; other Septuagint manuscripts (see also note at Judges 1:14) Othniel, he urged her   d36 Or Gederah and Gederothaim

48In the hill country:

Shamir, Jattir, Socoh, 49Dannah, Kiriath Sannah (that is, Debir), 50Anab, Eshtemoh, Anim, 51Goshen, Holon and Giloh—eleven towns and their villages.

52Arab, Dumah, Eshan, 53Janim, Beth Tappuah, Aphekah, 54Humtah, Kiriath Arba (that is, Hebron) and Zior—nine towns and their villages.

55Maon, Carmel, Ziph, Juttah, 56Jezreel, Jokdeam, Zanoah, 57Kain, Gibeah and Timnah—ten towns and their villages.

58Halhul, Beth Zur, Gedor, 59Maarath, Beth Anoth and Eltekon—six towns and their villages.

60Kiriath Baal (that is, Kiriath Jearim) and Rabbah—two towns and their villages.

61In the desert:

Beth Arabah, Middin, Secacah, 62Nibshan, the City of Salt and En Gedi—six towns and their villages.

63Judah could not dislodge the Jebusites, who were living in Jerusalem; to this day the Jebusites live there with the people of Judah.

Allotment for Ephraim and Manasseh

16 The allotment for Joseph began at the Jordan of Jericho,*a* east of the waters of Jericho, and went up from there through the desert into the hill country of Bethel. 2It went on from Bethel (that is, Luz),*b* crossed over to the territory of the Arkites in Ataroth, 3descended westward to the territory of the Japhletites as far as the region of Lower Beth Horon and on to Gezer, ending at the sea.

4So Manasseh and Ephraim, the descendants of Joseph, received their inheritance.

5This was the territory of Ephraim, clan by clan:

The boundary of their inheritance went from Ataroth Addar in the east to Upper Beth Horon 6and continued to the sea. From Micmethath on the north it curved eastward to Taanath Shiloh, passing by it to Janoah on the east. 7Then it went down from Janoah to Ataroth and Naarah, touched Jericho and came out at the Jordan. 8From Tappuah the border went west to the Kanah Ravine and ended at the sea. This was the inheritance of the tribe of the Ephraimites, clan by clan. 9It also included all the towns and their villages that were set aside for the Ephraimites within the inheritance of the Manassites.

10They did not dislodge the Canaanites living in Gezer; to this day the Canaanites live among the people of Ephraim but are required to do forced labor.

17 This was the allotment for the tribe of Manasseh as Joseph's firstborn, that is, for Makir, Manasseh's firstborn. Makir was the ancestor of the Gileadites, who had received Gilead and Bashan because the Makirites were great soldiers. 2So this allotment was for the rest of the people of Manasseh—the clans of Abiezer, Helek, Asriel, Shechem, Hepher and Shemida. These are the other male descendants of Manasseh son of Joseph by their clans.

3Now Zelophehad son of Hepher, the son of Gilead, the son of Makir, the son of Manasseh, had no sons but only daughters, whose names were Mahlah, Noah, Hoglah, Milcah and Tirzah. 4They went to Eleazar the priest, Joshua son of Nun, and the leaders and said, "The LORD commanded Moses to give us an inheritance among our brothers." So Joshua gave them an inheritance along with the brothers of their father, according to the LORD's command. 5Manasseh's share consisted of ten tracts of land besides Gilead and Bashan east of the Jordan, 6because the daughters of the tribe of Manasseh received an inheritance among the sons. The land of Gilead belonged to the rest of the descendants of Manasseh.

7The territory of Manasseh extended from Asher to Micmethath east of Shechem. The boundary ran southward from there to include the people living at En Tappuah. 8(Manasseh had the land of Tappuah, but Tappuah itself, on the boundary of Manasseh, belonged to the Ephraimites.) 9Then the boundary continued south to the Kanah Ravine. There were towns belonging to Ephraim lying among the towns of Manasseh, but the boundary of Manasseh was the northern side of the ravine and

---

a1 Jordan of Jericho was possibly an ancient name for the Jordan River.   *b2* Septuagint; Hebrew *Bethel to Luz* ended at the sea. ¹⁰On the south the land belonged to Ephraim, on the north to Manasseh. The territory of Manasseh reached the sea and bordered Asher on the north and Issachar on the east.

¹¹Within Issachar and Asher, Manasseh also had Beth Shan, Ibleam and the people of Dor, Endor, Taanach and Megiddo, together with their surrounding settlements (the third in the list is Naphoth*ᵃ*).

¹²Yet the Manassites were not able to occupy these towns, for the Canaanites were determined to live in that region. ¹³However, when the Israelites grew stronger, they subjected the Canaanites to forced labor but did not drive them out completely.

¹⁴The people of Joseph said to Joshua, "Why have you given us only one allotment and one portion for an inheritance? We are a numerous people and the LORD has blessed us abundantly."

¹⁵"If you are so numerous," Joshua answered, "and if the hill country of Ephraim is too small for you, go up into the forest and clear land for yourselves there in the land of the Perizzites and Rephaites."

¹⁶The people of Joseph replied, "The hill country is not enough for us, and all the Canaanites who live in the plain have iron chariots, both those in Beth Shan and its settlements and those in the Valley of Jezreel."

¹⁷But Joshua said to the house of Joseph—to Ephraim and Manasseh—"You are numerous and very powerful. You will have not only one allotment ¹⁸but the forested hill country as well. Clear it, and its farthest limits will be yours; though the Canaanites have iron chariots and though they are strong, you can drive them out."

Division of the Rest of the Land

18 The whole assembly of the Israelites gathered at Shiloh and set up the Tent of Meeting there. The country was brought under their control, ²but there were still seven Israelite tribes who had not yet received their inheritance.

³So Joshua said to the Israelites: "How long will you wait before you begin to take possession of the land that the LORD, the God of your fathers, has given you? ⁴Appoint three men from each tribe. I will send them out to make a survey of the land and to write a description of it, according to the inheritance of each. Then they will return to me. ⁵You are to divide the land into seven parts. Judah is to remain in its territory on the south and the house of Joseph in its territory on the north. ⁶After you have written descriptions of the seven parts of the land, bring them here to me and I will cast lots for you in the presence of the LORD our God. ⁷The Levites, however, do not get a portion among you, because the priestly service of the LORD is their inheritance. And Gad, Reuben and the half-tribe of Manasseh have already received their inheritance on the east side of the Jordan. Moses the servant of the LORD gave it to them."

⁸As the men started on their way to map out the land, Joshua instructed them, "Go and make a survey of the land and write a description of it. Then return to me, and I will cast lots for you here at Shiloh in the presence of the LORD." ⁹So the men left and went through the land. They wrote its description on a scroll, town by town, in seven parts, and returned to Joshua in the camp at Shiloh. ¹⁰Joshua then cast lots for them in Shiloh in the presence of the LORD, and there he distributed the land to the Israelites according to their tribal divisions.

Allotment for Benjamin

¹¹The lot came up for the tribe of Benjamin, clan by clan. Their allotted territory lay between the tribes of Judah and Joseph:

¹²On the north side their boundary began at the Jordan, passed the northern slope of Jericho and headed west into the hill country, coming out at the desert of Beth Aven. ¹³From there it crossed to the south slope of Luz (that is, Bethel) and went down to Ataroth Addar on the hill south of Lower Beth Horon.

¹⁴From the hill facing Beth Horon on the south the boundary turned south along the western side and came out at Kiriath Baal (that is, Kiriath Jearim), a town of the people of Judah. This was the western side.

¹⁵The southern side began at the outskirts of Kiriath Jearim on the west, and the boundary came out at the spring of the waters of Nephtoah. ¹⁶The boundary went down to the

foot of the hill facing the Valley of Ben Hinnom, north of the Valley of Rephaim. It continued down the Hinnom Valley along the southern slope of the Jebusite city and so to En Rogel. ¹⁷It then curved north, went to En Shemesh, continued to Geliloth, which faces the Pass of Adummim, and ran down to the Stone of Bohan son of Reuben. ¹⁸It continued to the northern slope of Beth Arabah[a] and on down into the Arabah. ¹⁹It then went to the northern slope of Beth Hoglah and came out at the northern bay of the Salt Sea,[b] at the mouth of the Jordan in the south. This was the southern boundary.

²⁰The Jordan formed the boundary on the eastern side.

These were the boundaries that marked out the inheritance of the clans of Benjamin on all sides.

²¹The tribe of Benjamin, clan by clan, had the following cities:

Jericho, Beth Hoglah, Emek Keziz, ²²Beth Arabah, Zemaraim, Bethel, ²³Avvim, Parah, Ophrah, ²⁴Kephar Ammoni, Ophni and Geba—twelve towns and their villages.

²⁵Gibeon, Ramah, Beeroth, ²⁶Mizpah, Kephirah, Mozah, ²⁷Rekem, Irpeel, Taralah, ²⁸Zelah, Haeleph, the Jebusite city (that is, Jerusalem), Gibeah and Kiriath—fourteen towns and their villages.

This was the inheritance of Benjamin for its clans.

Allotment for Simeon

19 The second lot came out for the tribe of Simeon, clan by clan. Their inheritance lay within the territory of Judah. ²It included:

Beersheba (or Sheba),[c] Moladah, ³Hazar Shual, Balah, Ezem, ⁴Eltolad, Bethul, Hormah, ⁵Ziklag, Beth Marcaboth, Hazar Susah, ⁶Beth Lebaoth and Sharuhen—thirteen towns and their villages;

⁷Ain, Rimmon, Ether and Ashan—four towns and their villages—⁸and all the villages around these towns as far as Baalath Beer (Ramah in the Negev).

This was the inheritance of the tribe of

the Simeonites, clan by clan. ⁹The inheritance of the Simeonites was taken from the share of Judah, because Judah's portion was more than they needed. So the Simeonites received their inheritance within the territory of Judah.

Allotment for Zebulun

¹⁰The third lot came up for Zebulun, clan by clan:

The boundary of their inheritance went as far as Sarid. ¹¹Going west it ran to Maralah, touched Dabbesheth, and extended to the ravine near Jokneam. ¹²It turned east from Sarid toward the sunrise to the territory of Kisloth Tabor and went on to Daberath and up to Japhia. ¹³Then it continued eastward to Gath Hepher and Eth Kazin; it came out at Rimmon and turned toward Neah. ¹⁴There the boundary went around on the north to Hannathon and ended at the Valley of Iphtah El. ¹⁵Included were Kattath, Nahalal, Shimron, Idalah and Bethlehem. There were twelve towns and their villages.

¹⁶These towns and their villages were the inheritance of Zebulun, clan by clan.

Allotment for Issachar

¹⁷The fourth lot came out for Issachar, clan by clan. ¹⁸Their territory included:

Jezreel, Kesulloth, Shunem, ¹⁹Hapharaim, Shion, Anaharath, ²⁰Rabbith, Kishion, Ebez, ²¹Remeth, En Gannim, En Haddah and Beth Pazzez. ²²The boundary touched Tabor, Shahazumah and Beth Shemesh, and ended at the Jordan. There were sixteen towns and their villages.

²³These towns and their villages were the inheritance of the tribe of Issachar, clan by clan.

Allotment for Asher

²⁴The fifth lot came out for the tribe of Asher, clan by clan. ²⁵Their territory included:

Helkath, Hali, Beten, Acshaph, ²⁶Allammelech, Amad and Mishal. On the west the boundary touched Carmel and Shihor Libnath. ²⁷It then turned east toward Beth Dagon, touched Zebulun and the Valley of Iphtah El, and went north to Beth

---

a18 Septuagint; Hebrew *slope facing the Arabah Sheba;* 1 Chron. 4:28 does not have *Sheba.*   *b19* That is, the Dead Sea   *c2* Or *Beersheba,*

Emek and Neiel, passing Cabul on the left. [28]It went to Abdon,[a] Rehob, Hammon and Kanah, as far as Greater Sidon. [29]The boundary then turned back toward Ramah and went to the fortified city of Tyre, turned toward Hosah and came out at the sea in the region of Aczib, [30]Ummah, Aphek and Rehob. There were twenty-two towns and their villages.

[31]These towns and their villages were the inheritance of the tribe of Asher, clan by clan.

Allotment for Naphtali

[32]The sixth lot came out for Naphtali, clan by clan:

[33]Their boundary went from Heleph and the large tree in Zaanannim, passing Adami Nekeb and Jabneel to Lakkum and ending at the Jordan. [34]The boundary ran west through Aznoth Tabor and came out at Hukkok. It touched Zebulun on the south, Asher on the west and the Jordan[b] on the east. [35]The fortified cities were Ziddim, Zer, Hammath, Rakkath, Kinnereth, [36]Adamah, Ramah, Hazor, [37]Kedesh, Edrei, En Hazor, [38]Iron, Migdal El, Horem, Beth Anath and Beth Shemesh. There were nineteen towns and their villages.

[39]These towns and their villages were the inheritance of the tribe of Naphtali, clan by clan.

Allotment for Dan

[40]The seventh lot came out for the tribe of Dan, clan by clan. [41]The territory of their inheritance included:

Zorah, Eshtaol, Ir Shemesh, [42]Shaalabbin, Aijalon, Ithlah, [43]Elon, Timnah, Ekron, [44]Eltekeh, Gibbethon, Baalath, [45]Jehud, Bene Berak, Gath Rimmon, [46]Me Jarkon and Rakkon, with the area facing Joppa.

[47](But the Danites had difficulty taking possession of their territory, so they went up and attacked Leshem, took it, put it to the sword and occupied it. They settled in Leshem and named it Dan after their forefather.) [48]These towns and their villages were the inheritance of the tribe of Dan, clan by clan.

Allotment for Joshua

[49]When they had finished dividing the land into its allotted portions, the Israelites gave Joshua son of Nun an inheritance among them, [50]as the LORD had commanded. They gave him the town he asked for—Timnath Serah[c] in the hill country of Ephraim. And he built up the town and settled there.

[51]These are the territories that Eleazar the priest, Joshua son of Nun and the heads of the tribal clans of Israel assigned by lot at Shiloh in the presence of the LORD at the entrance to the Tent of Meeting. And so they finished dividing the land.

Cities of Refuge

20 Then the LORD said to Joshua: [2]"Tell the Israelites to designate the cities of refuge, as I instructed you through Moses, [3]so that anyone who kills a person accidentally and unintentionally may flee there and find protection from the avenger of blood.

[4]"When he flees to one of these cities, he is to stand in the entrance of the city gate and state his case before the elders of that city. Then they are to admit him into their city and give him a place to live with them. [5]If the avenger of blood pursues him, they must not surrender the one accused, because he killed his neighbor unintentionally and without malice aforethought. [6]He is to stay in that city until he has stood trial before the assembly and until the death of the high priest who is serving at that time. Then he may go back to his own home in the town from which he fled."

[7]So they set apart Kedesh in Galilee in the hill country of Naphtali, Shechem in the hill country of Ephraim, and Kiriath Arba (that is, Hebron) in the hill country of Judah. [8]On the east side of the Jordan of Jericho[d] they designated Bezer in the desert on the plateau in the tribe of Reuben, Ramoth in Gilead in the tribe of Gad, and Golan in Bashan in the tribe of Manasseh. [9]Any of the Israelites or any alien living among them who killed someone accidentally could flee to these designated cities and not be killed by the avenger of blood prior to standing trial before the assembly.

---

[a]28 Some Hebrew manuscripts (see also Joshua 21:30); most Hebrew manuscripts *Ebron*
[b]34 Septuagint; Hebrew *west, and Judah, the Jordan,*   [c]50 Also known as *Timnath Heres* (see Judges 2:9)   [d]8 *Jordan of Jericho* was possibly an ancient name for the Jordan River.

Towns for the Levites

21 Now the family heads of the Levites approached Eleazar the priest, Joshua son of Nun, and the heads of the other tribal families of Israel ²at Shiloh in Canaan and said to them, "The LORD commanded through Moses that you give us towns to live in, with pasturelands for our livestock." ³So, as the LORD had commanded, the Israelites gave the Levites the following towns and pasturelands out of their own inheritance:

⁴The first lot came out for the Kohathites, clan by clan. The Levites who were descendants of Aaron the priest were allotted thirteen towns from the tribes of Judah, Simeon and Benjamin. ⁵The rest of Kohath's descendants were allotted ten towns from the clans of the tribes of Ephraim, Dan and half of Manasseh.

⁶The descendants of Gershon were allotted thirteen towns from the clans of the tribes of Issachar, Asher, Naphtali and the half-tribe of Manasseh in Bashan.

⁷The descendants of Merari, clan by clan, received twelve towns from the tribes of Reuben, Gad and Zebulun.

⁸So the Israelites allotted to the Levites these towns and their pasturelands, as the LORD had commanded through Moses.

⁹From the tribes of Judah and Simeon they allotted the following towns by name ¹⁰(these towns were assigned to the descendants of Aaron who were from the Kohathite clans of the Levites, because the first lot fell to them):

¹¹They gave them Kiriath Arba (that is, Hebron), with its surrounding pastureland, in the hill country of Judah. (Arba was the forefather of Anak.) ¹²But the fields and villages around the city they had given to Caleb son of Jephunneh as his possession.

¹³So to the descendants of Aaron the priest they gave Hebron (a city of refuge for one accused of murder), Libnah, ¹⁴Jattir, Eshtemoa, ¹⁵Holon, Debir, ¹⁶Ain, Juttah and Beth Shemesh, together with their pasturelands—nine towns from these two tribes.

¹⁷And from the tribe of Benjamin they gave them Gibeon, Geba, ¹⁸Anathoth and Almon, together with their pasturelands—four towns.

¹⁹All the towns for the priests, the descendants of Aaron, were thirteen, together with their pasturelands.

²⁰The rest of the Kohathite clans of the Levites were allotted towns from the tribe of Ephraim:

²¹In the hill country of Ephraim they were given Shechem (a city of refuge for one accused of murder) and Gezer, ²²Kibzaim and Beth Horon, together with their pasturelands—four towns.

²³Also from the tribe of Dan they received Eltekeh, Gibbethon, ²⁴Aijalon and Gath Rimmon, together with their pasturelands—four towns.

²⁵From half the tribe of Manasseh they received Taanach and Gath Rimmon, together with their pasturelands—two towns.

²⁶All these ten towns and their pasturelands were given to the rest of the Kohathite clans.

²⁷The Levite clans of the Gershonites were given:

from the half-tribe of Manasseh,
Golan in Bashan (a city of refuge for one accused of murder) and Be Eshtarah, together with their pasturelands—two towns;

²⁸from the tribe of Issachar,
Kishion, Daberath, ²⁹Jarmuth and En Gannim, together with their pasturelands—four towns;

³⁰from the tribe of Asher,
Mishal, Abdon, ³¹Helkath and Rehob, together with their pasturelands—four towns;

³²from the tribe of Naphtali,
Kedesh in Galilee (a city of refuge for one accused of murder), Hammoth Dor and Kartan, together with their pasturelands—three towns.

³³All the towns of the Gershonite clans were thirteen, together with their pasturelands.

³⁴The Merarite clans (the rest of the Levites) were given:

from the tribe of Zebulun,
Jokneam, Kartah, ³⁵Dimnah and Nahalal, together with their pasturelands—four towns;

³⁶from the tribe of Reuben,
Bezer, Jahaz, ³⁷Kedemoth and Mephaath, together with their pasturelands—four towns;

³⁸from the tribe of Gad,

Ramoth in Gilead (a city of refuge for one accused of murder), Mahanaim, ³⁹Heshbon and Jazer, together with their pasturelands—four towns in all.

⁴⁰All the towns allotted to the Merarite clans, who were the rest of the Levites, were twelve.

⁴¹The towns of the Levites in the territory held by the Israelites were forty-eight in all, together with their pasturelands. ⁴²Each of these towns had pasturelands surrounding it; this was true for all these towns.

⁴³So the Lord gave Israel all the land he had sworn to give their forefathers, and

they took possession of it and settled there. ⁴⁴The Lord gave them rest on every side, just as he had sworn to their forefathers. Not one of their enemies withstood them; the Lord handed all their enemies over to them. ⁴⁵Not one of all the Lord's good promises to the house of Israel failed; every one was fulfilled.

Eastern Tribes Return Home

22 Then Joshua summoned the Reubenites, the Gadites and the half-tribe of Manasseh ²and said to them, "You have done all that Moses the servant of the Lord commanded, and you have obeyed me in everything I commanded. ³For a long time now—to this very day—

TUESDAY

VERSE FOR THE DAY:
Joshua 21:45

AUTHOR:
Hannah Whitall Smith

PASSAGE FOR THE DAY:
Joshua 21:43–45

God Is Enough

THE greatest lesson a soul has to learn is that God, and God alone, is enough for all its needs. This is the lesson that all God's dealings with us are meant to teach, and this is the crowning discovery of our entire Christian life. GOD IS ENOUGH!

No soul can really be at rest until it has given up dependence on everything else and has been forced to depend on the Lord alone. As long as our expectation is from other things, nothing but disappointment awaits us. Feelings may change, doctrines and dogmas may be upset, the Christian work may come to nought, prayers may seem to lose their fervency, promises may seem to fail, everything that we have believed in or depended on may seem to be swept away, and only God is left—just God, the bare God if I may be allowed the expression, simply and only God.

If God is what he would seem to be from his revealings; if he is indeed the "God of all comfort" (2 Corinthians 1:3); if he is our shepherd; if he is really and truly our Father; if, in short, all the many aspects he has told us of his character and his ways are actually true, then we must come to the positive conviction that he is, in himself alone, enough for all our needs and that we may safely rest in him absolutely and forever.

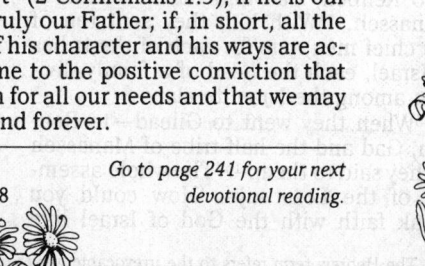

Additional Scripture Readings:
Psalm 73:23–26; 2 Timothy 4:16–18

Go to page 241 for your next devotional reading.

you have not deserted your brothers but have carried out the mission the LORD your God gave you. 4Now that the LORD your God has given your brothers rest as he promised, return to your homes in the land that Moses the servant of the LORD gave you on the other side of the Jordan. 5But be very careful to keep the commandment and the law that Moses the servant of the LORD gave you: to love the LORD your God, to walk in all his ways, to obey his commands, to hold fast to him and to serve him with all your heart and all your soul."

6Then Joshua blessed them and sent them away, and they went to their homes. 7(To the half-tribe of Manasseh Moses had given land in Bashan, and to the other half of the tribe Joshua gave land on the west side of the Jordan with their brothers.) When Joshua sent them home, he blessed them, 8saying, "Return to your homes with your great wealth—with large herds of livestock, with silver, gold, bronze and iron, and a great quantity of clothing—and divide with your brothers the plunder from your enemies."

9So the Reubenites, the Gadites and the half-tribe of Manasseh left the Israelites at Shiloh in Canaan to return to Gilead, their own land, which they had acquired in accordance with the command of the LORD through Moses.

10When they came to Geliloth near the Jordan in the land of Canaan, the Reubenites, the Gadites and the half-tribe of Manasseh built an imposing altar there by the Jordan. 11And when the Israelites heard that they had built the altar on the border of Canaan at Geliloth near the Jordan on the Israelite side, 12the whole assembly of Israel gathered at Shiloh to go to war against them.

13So the Israelites sent Phinehas son of Eleazar, the priest, to the land of Gilead —to Reuben, Gad and the half-tribe of Manasseh. 14With him they sent ten of the chief men, one for each of the tribes of Israel, each the head of a family division among the Israelite clans.

15When they went to Gilead—to Reuben, Gad and the half-tribe of Manasseh —they said to them: 16"The whole assembly of the LORD says: 'How could you break faith with the God of Israel like

this? How could you turn away from the LORD and build yourselves an altar in rebellion against him now? 17Was not the sin of Peor enough for us? Up to this very day we have not cleansed ourselves from that sin, even though a plague fell on the community of the LORD! 18And are you now turning away from the LORD?

" 'If you rebel against the LORD today, tomorrow he will be angry with the whole community of Israel. 19If the land you possess is defiled, come over to the LORD's land, where the LORD's tabernacle stands, and share the land with us. But do not rebel against the LORD or against us by building an altar for yourselves, other than the altar of the LORD our God. 20When Achan son of Zerah acted unfaithfully regarding the devoted things,a did not wrath come upon the whole community of Israel? He was not the only one who died for his sin.' "

21Then Reuben, Gad and the half-tribe of Manasseh replied to the heads of the clans of Israel: 22"The Mighty One, God, the LORD! The Mighty One, God, the LORD! He knows! And let Israel know! If this has been in rebellion or disobedience to the LORD, do not spare us this day. 23If we have built our own altar to turn away from the LORD and to offer burnt offerings and grain offerings, or to sacrifice fellowship offeringsb on it, may the LORD himself call us to account.

24"No! We did it for fear that some day your descendants might say to ours, 'What do you have to do with the LORD, the God of Israel? 25The LORD has made the Jordan a boundary between us and you—you Reubenites and Gadites! You have no share in the LORD.' So your descendants might cause ours to stop fearing the LORD.

26"That is why we said, 'Let us get ready and build an altar—but not for burnt offerings or sacrifices.' 27On the contrary, it is to be a witness between us and you and the generations that follow, that we will worship the LORD at his sanctuary with our burnt offerings, sacrifices and fellowship offerings. Then in the future your descendants will not be able to say to ours, 'You have no share in the LORD.'

28"And we said, 'If they ever say this to

---

a20 The Hebrew term refers to the irrevocable giving over of things or persons to the LORD, often by totally destroying them.   b23 Traditionally peace offerings; also in verse 27 us, or to our descendants, we will answer: Look at the replica of the LORD's altar, which our fathers built, not for burnt offerings and sacrifices, but as a witness between us and you.'

²⁹"Far be it from us to rebel against the LORD and turn away from him today by building an altar for burnt offerings, grain offerings and sacrifices, other than the altar of the LORD our God that stands before his tabernacle."

³⁰When Phinehas the priest and the leaders of the community—the heads of the clans of the Israelites—heard what Reuben, Gad and Manasseh had to say, they were pleased. ³¹And Phinehas son of Eleazar, the priest, said to Reuben, Gad and Manasseh, "Today we know that the LORD is with us, because you have not acted unfaithfully toward the LORD in this matter. Now you have rescued the Israelites from the LORD's hand."

³²Then Phinehas son of Eleazar, the priest, and the leaders returned to Canaan from their meeting with the Reubenites and Gadites in Gilead and reported to the Israelites. ³³They were glad to hear the report and praised God. And they talked no more about going to war against them to devastate the country where the Reubenites and the Gadites lived.

³⁴And the Reubenites and the Gadites gave the altar this name: A Witness Between Us that the LORD is God.

Joshua's Farewell to the Leaders

23 After a long time had passed and the LORD had given Israel rest from all their enemies around them, Joshua, by then old and well advanced in years, ²summoned all Israel—their elders, leaders, judges and officials—and said to them: "I am old and well advanced in years. ³You yourselves have seen everything the LORD your God has done to all these nations for your sake; it was the LORD your God who fought for you. ⁴Remember how I have allotted as an inheritance for your tribes all the land of the nations that remain—the nations I conquered—between the Jordan and the Great Sea*ᵃ* in the west. ⁵The LORD your God himself will drive them out of your way. He will push them out before you, and you will take possession of their land, as the LORD your God promised you.

⁶"Be very strong; be careful to obey all that is written in the Book of the Law of Moses, without turning aside to the right or to the left. ⁷Do not associate with these nations that remain among you; do not invoke the names of their gods or swear by them. You must not serve them or bow down to them. ⁸But you are to hold fast to the LORD your God, as you have until now.

⁹"The LORD has driven out before you great and powerful nations; to this day no one has been able to withstand you. ¹⁰One of you routs a thousand, because the LORD your God fights for you, just as he promised. ¹¹So be very careful to love the LORD your God.

¹²"But if you turn away and ally yourselves with the survivors of these nations that remain among you and if you intermarry with them and associate with them, ¹³then you may be sure that the LORD your God will no longer drive out these nations before you. Instead, they will become snares and traps for you, whips on your backs and thorns in your eyes, until you perish from this good land, which the LORD your God has given you.

¹⁴"Now I am about to go the way of all the earth. You know with all your heart and soul that not one of all the good promises the LORD your God gave you has failed. Every promise has been fulfilled; not one has failed. ¹⁵But just as every good promise of the LORD your God has come true, so the LORD will bring on you all the evil he has threatened, until he has destroyed you from this good land he has given you. ¹⁶If you violate the covenant of the LORD your God, which he commanded you, and go and serve other gods and bow down to them, the LORD's anger will burn against you, and you will quickly perish from the good land he has given you."

The Covenant Renewed at Shechem

24 Then Joshua assembled all the tribes of Israel at Shechem. He summoned the elders, leaders, judges and officials of Israel, and they presented themselves before God.

²Joshua said to all the people, "This is what the LORD, the God of Israel, says: 'Long ago your forefathers, including Terah the father of Abraham and Nahor,

---

ᵃ4 That is, the Mediterranean

lived beyond the River[a] and worshiped other gods. [3]But I took your father Abraham from the land beyond the River and led him throughout Canaan and gave him many descendants. I gave him Isaac, [4]and to Isaac I gave Jacob and Esau. I assigned the hill country of Seir to Esau, but Jacob and his sons went down to Egypt.

[5]" 'Then I sent Moses and Aaron, and I afflicted the Egyptians by what I did there, and I brought you out. [6]When I brought your fathers out of Egypt, you came to the sea, and the Egyptians pursued them with chariots and horsemen[b] as far as the Red Sea.[c] [7]But they cried to the LORD for help, and he put darkness between you and the Egyptians; he brought the sea over them and covered them. You saw with your own eyes what I did to the Egyptians. Then you lived in the desert for a long time.

[8]" 'I brought you to the land of the Amorites who lived east of the Jordan. They fought against you, but I gave them into your hands. I destroyed them from before you, and you took possession of their land. [9]When Balak son of Zippor, the king of Moab, prepared to fight against Israel, he sent for Balaam son of Beor to put a curse on you. [10]But I would not listen to Balaam, so he blessed you again and again, and I delivered you out of his hand.

[11]" 'Then you crossed the Jordan and came to Jericho. The citizens of Jericho fought against you, as did also the Amorites, Perizzites, Canaanites, Hittites, Girgashites, Hivites and Jebusites, but I gave them into your hands. [12]I sent the hornet ahead of you, which drove them out before you—also the two Amorite kings. You did not do it with your own sword and bow. [13]So I gave you a land on which you did not toil and cities you did not build; and you live in them and eat from vineyards and olive groves that you did not plant.'

[14]"Now fear the LORD and serve him with all faithfulness. Throw away the gods your forefathers worshiped beyond the River and in Egypt, and serve the LORD. [15]But if serving the LORD seems undesirable to you, then choose for yourselves this day whom you will serve, whether the gods your forefathers served beyond the River, or the gods of the Amorites, in whose land you are living. But as for me and my household, we will serve the LORD."

[16]Then the people answered, "Far be it from us to forsake the LORD to serve other gods! [17]It was the LORD our God himself who brought us and our fathers up out of Egypt, from that land of slavery, and performed those great signs before our eyes. He protected us on our entire journey and among all the nations through which we traveled. [18]And the LORD drove out before us all the nations, including the Amorites, who lived in the land. We too will serve the LORD, because he is our God."

[19]Joshua said to the people, "You are not able to serve the LORD. He is a holy God; he is a jealous God. He will not forgive your rebellion and your sins. [20]If you forsake the LORD and serve foreign gods, he will turn and bring disaster on you and make an end of you, after he has been good to you."

[21]But the people said to Joshua, "No! We will serve the LORD."

[22]Then Joshua said, "You are witnesses against yourselves that you have chosen to serve the LORD."

"Yes, we are witnesses," they replied.

[23]"Now then," said Joshua, "throw away the foreign gods that are among you and yield your hearts to the LORD, the God of Israel."

[24]And the people said to Joshua, "We will serve the LORD our God and obey him."

[25]On that day Joshua made a covenant for the people, and there at Shechem he drew up for them decrees and laws. [26]And Joshua recorded these things in the Book of the Law of God. Then he took a large stone and set it up there under the oak near the holy place of the LORD.

[27]"See!" he said to all the people. "This stone will be a witness against us. It has heard all the words the LORD has said to us. It will be a witness against you if you are untrue to your God."

Buried in the Promised Land

[28]Then Joshua sent the people away, each to his own inheritance.

[29]After these things, Joshua son of Nun, the servant of the LORD, died at the age of a hundred and ten. [30]And they bur-

---

[a]2 That is, the Euphrates; also in verses 3, 14 and 15 that is, Sea of Reeds   [b]6 Or charioteers   [c]6 Hebrew Yam Suph;

ied him in the land of his inheritance, at Timnath Serah*a* in the hill country of Ephraim, north of Mount Gaash.

³¹Israel served the LORD throughout the lifetime of Joshua and of the elders who outlived him and who had experienced everything the LORD had done for Israel. ³²And Joseph's bones, which the Israelites had brought up from Egypt, were buried at Shechem in the tract of land that

a30 Also known as Timnath Heres (see Judges 2:9)

WEDNESDAY

VERSE FOR THE DAY:	AUTHOR:	PASSAGE FOR THE DAY:
Joshua 24:15	Jean E. Syswerda	Joshua 24:1–27

Housebuilding

WE were facing yet another problem in our housebuilding project. Our patience and our purses were beginning to wear thin.

We hadn't decided to move to a new community and build a new home (by ourselves, no hired carpenters involved) on a whim. Only after much prayer and talk and seeking God's will did we make the move.

But now, one water-filled basement, two broken ribs, several lost cupboards, and many tears later, we were beginning to wonder. Had we missed a cue somewhere? Was there a direction from the Lord that we had missed? Or, worse, ignored?

We soon realized that worrying and fretting about whether we had made a wrong or a right decision accomplished nothing. We had consciously included the Lord in our decision-making. We couldn't go back. We could only plug away, night after night, Saturday after Saturday, and finish this do-it-yourself project.

And in the work, in the middle of problems, usually unexpectedly, would come peace. A sense of well-being. A sure knowledge that God was with our family in this new community, in this new and problem-filled house. We hadn't abandoned him, and he wouldn't abandon us.

That's why, as a finishing touch, we had a friend's father cut out of wood those words of Joshua. Today they stretch across the front of our fireplace mantel—a testimony to our friends and a reminder to us:

> As for me and my household, we will serve the LORD.

Additional Scripture Readings:
Psalm 1:1–3; Philippians 4:4–7

Go to page 247 for your next devotional reading.

Jacob bought for a hundred pieces of silver[a] from the sons of Hamor, the father of Shechem. This became the inheritance of Joseph's descendants.

[33]And Eleazar son of Aaron died and was buried at Gibeah, which had been allotted to his son Phinehas in the hill country of Ephraim.

---

*J*UDGES *recounts a regular pattern that develops for God's people in their new land: the people serve idols, God punishes them by an enemy invasion, they cry to the Lord, and he sends a judge (such as Deborah, Gideon, Jephthah or Samson) to save them. As you read this book, remember that only God can give you victory over sin and evil and that you will receive his help only when you serve him alone.*

JUDGES

Israel Fights the Remaining Canaanites

1 After the death of Joshua, the Israelites asked the LORD, "Who will be the first to go up and fight for us against the Canaanites?"

²The LORD answered, "Judah is to go; I have given the land into their hands."

³Then the men of Judah said to the Simeonites their brothers, "Come up with us into the territory allotted to us, to fight against the Canaanites. We in turn will go with you into yours." So the Simeonites went with them.

⁴When Judah attacked, the LORD gave the Canaanites and Perizzites into their hands and they struck down ten thousand men at Bezek. ⁵It was there that they found Adoni-Bezek and fought against him, putting to rout the Canaanites and Perizzites. ⁶Adoni-Bezek fled, but they chased him and caught him, and cut off his thumbs and big toes.

⁷Then Adoni-Bezek said, "Seventy kings with their thumbs and big toes cut off have picked up scraps under my table. Now God has paid me back for what I did to them." They brought him to Jerusalem, and he died there.

⁸The men of Judah attacked Jerusalem also and took it. They put the city to the sword and set it on fire.

⁹After that, the men of Judah went down to fight against the Canaanites living in the hill country, the Negev and the western foothills. ¹⁰They advanced against the Canaanites living in Hebron

(formerly called Kiriath Arba) and defeated Sheshai, Ahiman and Talmai.

[11]From there they advanced against the people living in Debir (formerly called Kiriath Sepher). [12]And Caleb said, "I will give my daughter Acsah in marriage to the man who attacks and captures Kiriath Sepher." [13]Othniel son of Kenaz, Caleb's younger brother, took it; so Caleb gave his daughter Acsah to him in marriage.

[14]One day when she came to Othniel, she urged him[a] to ask her father for a field. When she got off her donkey, Caleb asked her, "What can I do for you?"

[15]She replied, "Do me a special favor. Since you have given me land in the Negev, give me also springs of water." Then Caleb gave her the upper and lower springs.

[16]The descendants of Moses' father-in-law, the Kenite, went up from the City of Palms[b] with the men of Judah to live among the people of the Desert of Judah in the Negev near Arad.

[17]Then the men of Judah went with the Simeonites their brothers and attacked the Canaanites living in Zephath, and they totally destroyed[c] the city. Therefore it was called Hormah.[d] [18]The men of Judah also took[e] Gaza, Ashkelon and Ekron—each city with its territory.

[19]The LORD was with the men of Judah. They took possession of the hill country, but they were unable to drive the people from the plains, because they had iron chariots. [20]As Moses had promised, Hebron was given to Caleb, who drove from it the three sons of Anak. [21]The Benjamites, however, failed to dislodge the Jebusites, who were living in Jerusalem; to this day the Jebusites live there with the Benjamites.

[22]Now the house of Joseph attacked Bethel, and the LORD was with them. [23]When they sent men to spy out Bethel (formerly called Luz), [24]the spies saw a man coming out of the city and they said to him, "Show us how to get into the city and we will see that you are treated well." [25]So he showed them, and they put the city to the sword but spared the man and his whole family. [26]He then went to the land of the Hittites, where he built a city and called it Luz, which is its name to this day.

[27]But Manasseh did not drive out the people of Beth Shan or Taanach or Dor or Ibleam or Megiddo and their surrounding settlements, for the Canaanites were determined to live in that land. [28]When Israel became strong, they pressed the Canaanites into forced labor but never drove them out completely. [29]Nor did Ephraim drive out the Canaanites living in Gezer, but the Canaanites continued to live there among them. [30]Neither did Zebulun drive out the Canaanites living in Kitron or Nahalol, who remained among them; but they did subject them to forced labor. [31]Nor did Asher drive out those living in Acco or Sidon or Ahlab or Aczib or Helbah or Aphek or Rehob, [32]and because of this the people of Asher lived among the Canaanite inhabitants of the land. [33]Neither did Naphtali drive out those living in Beth Shemesh or Beth Anath; but the Naphtalites too lived among the Canaanite inhabitants of the land, and those living in Beth Shemesh and Beth Anath became forced laborers for them. [34]The Amorites confined the Danites to the hill country, not allowing them to come down into the plain. [35]And the Amorites were determined also to hold out in Mount Heres, Aijalon and Shaalbim, but when the power of the house of Joseph increased, they too were pressed into forced labor. [36]The boundary of the Amorites was from Scorpion[f] Pass to Sela and beyond.

The Angel of the LORD at Bokim

2 The angel of the LORD went up from Gilgal to Bokim and said, "I brought you up out of Egypt and led you into the land that I swore to give to your forefathers. I said, 'I will never break my covenant with you, [2]and you shall not make a covenant with the people of this land, but you shall break down their altars.' Yet you have disobeyed me. Why have you done this? [3]Now therefore I tell you that I will not drive them out before you; they will be thorns in your sides and their gods will be a snare to you."

[4]When the angel of the LORD had spoken these things to all the Israelites, the people wept aloud, [5]and they called that place Bokim.[g] There they offered sacrifices to the LORD.

---

[a]14 Hebrew; Septuagint and Vulgate *Othniel, he urged her*   [b]16 That is, Jericho   [c]17 The Hebrew term refers to the irrevocable giving over of things or persons to the LORD, often by totally destroying them.   [d]17 *Hormah* means destruction.   [e]18 Hebrew; Septuagint *Judah did not take*   [f]36 Hebrew *Akrabbim*   [g]5 *Bokim* means *weepers*.

Disobedience and Defeat

[6]After Joshua had dismissed the Israelites, they went to take possession of the land, each to his own inheritance. [7]The people served the LORD throughout the lifetime of Joshua and of the elders who outlived him and who had seen all the great things the LORD had done for Israel. [8]Joshua son of Nun, the servant of the LORD, died at the age of a hundred and ten. [9]And they buried him in the land of his inheritance, at Timnath Heres[a] in the hill country of Ephraim, north of Mount Gaash.

[10]After that whole generation had been gathered to their fathers, another generation grew up, who knew neither the LORD nor what he had done for Israel. [11]Then the Israelites did evil in the eyes of the LORD and served the Baals. [12]They forsook the LORD, the God of their fathers, who had brought them out of Egypt. They followed and worshiped various gods of the peoples around them. They provoked the LORD to anger [13]because they forsook him and served Baal and the Ashtoreths. [14]In his anger against Israel the LORD handed them over to raiders who plundered them. He sold them to their enemies all around, whom they were no longer able to resist. [15]Whenever Israel went out to fight, the hand of the LORD was against them to defeat them, just as he had sworn to them. They were in great distress.

[16]Then the LORD raised up judges,[b] who saved them out of the hands of these raiders. [17]Yet they would not listen to their judges but prostituted themselves to other gods and worshiped them. Unlike their fathers, they quickly turned from the way in which their fathers had walked, the way of obedience to the LORD's commands. [18]Whenever the LORD raised up a judge for them, he was with the judge and saved them out of the hands of their enemies as long as the judge lived; for the LORD had compassion on them as they groaned under those who oppressed and afflicted them. [19]But when the judge died, the people returned to ways even more corrupt than those of their fathers, following other gods and serving and worshiping them. They refused to give up their evil practices and stubborn ways.

[20]Therefore the LORD was very angry with Israel and said, "Because this nation has violated the covenant that I laid down for their forefathers and has not listened to me, [21]I will no longer drive out before them any of the nations Joshua left when he died. [22]I will use them to test Israel and see whether they will keep the way of the LORD and walk in it as their forefathers did." [23]The LORD had allowed those nations to remain; he did not drive them out at once by giving them into the hands of Joshua.

3 These are the nations the LORD left to test all those Israelites who had not experienced any of the wars in Canaan [2](he did this only to teach warfare to the descendants of the Israelites who had not had previous battle experience): [3]the five rulers of the Philistines, all the Canaanites, the Sidonians, and the Hivites living in the Lebanon mountains from Mount Baal Hermon to Lebo[c] Hamath. [4]They were left to test the Israelites to see whether they would obey the LORD's commands, which he had given their forefathers through Moses.

[5]The Israelites lived among the Canaanites, Hittites, Amorites, Perizzites, Hivites and Jebusites. [6]They took their daughters in marriage and gave their own daughters to their sons, and served their gods.

Othniel

[7]The Israelites did evil in the eyes of the LORD; they forgot the LORD their God and served the Baals and the Asherahs. [8]The anger of the LORD burned against Israel so that he sold them into the hands of Cushan-Rishathaim king of Aram Naharaim,[d] to whom the Israelites were subject for eight years. [9]But when they cried out to the LORD, he raised up for them a deliverer, Othniel son of Kenaz, Caleb's younger brother, who saved them. [10]The Spirit of the LORD came upon him, so that he became Israel's judge[e] and went to war. The LORD gave Cushan-Rishathaim king of Aram into the hands of Othniel, who overpowered him. [11]So the land had peace for forty years, until Othniel son of Kenaz died.

Ehud

[12]Once again the Israelites did evil in the eyes of the LORD, and because they did this evil the LORD gave Eglon king of Moab power over Israel. [13]Getting the Ammonites and Amalekites to join him, Eglon

---

[a]9 Also known as *Timnath Serah* (see Joshua 19:50 and 24:30)   [b]16 Or *leaders;* similarly in verses 17-19   [c]3 Or *to the entrance to*   [d]8 That is, Northwest Mesopotamia   [e]10 Or *leader*

came and attacked Israel, and they took possession of the City of Palms.*a* ¹⁴The Israelites were subject to Eglon king of Moab for eighteen years.

¹⁵Again the Israelites cried out to the LORD, and he gave them a deliverer— Ehud, a left-handed man, the son of Gera the Benjamite. The Israelites sent him with tribute to Eglon king of Moab. ¹⁶Now Ehud had made a double-edged sword about a foot and a half*b* long, which he strapped to his right thigh under his clothing. ¹⁷He presented the tribute to Eglon king of Moab, who was a very fat man. ¹⁸After Ehud had presented the tribute, he sent on their way the men who had carried it. ¹⁹At the idols*c* near Gilgal he himself turned back and said, "I have a secret message for you, O king."

The king said, "Quiet!" And all his attendants left him.

²⁰Ehud then approached him while he was sitting alone in the upper room of his summer palace*d* and said, "I have a message from God for you." As the king rose from his seat, ²¹Ehud reached with his left hand, drew the sword from his right thigh and plunged it into the king's belly. ²²Even the handle sank in after the blade, which came out his back. Ehud did not pull the sword out, and the fat closed in over it. ²³Then Ehud went out to the porch*e*; he shut the doors of the upper room behind him and locked them.

²⁴After he had gone, the servants came and found the doors of the upper room locked. They said, "He must be relieving himself in the inner room of the house." ²⁵They waited to the point of embarrassment, but when he did not open the doors of the room, they took a key and unlocked them. There they saw their lord fallen to the floor, dead.

²⁶While they waited, Ehud got away. He passed by the idols and escaped to Seirah. ²⁷When he arrived there, he blew a trumpet in the hill country of Ephraim, and the Israelites went down with him from the hills, with him leading them.

²⁸"Follow me," he ordered, "for the LORD has given Moab, your enemy, into your hands." So they followed him down and, taking possession of the fords of the Jordan that led to Moab, they allowed no one to cross over. ²⁹At that time they struck down about ten thousand Moabites, all vigorous and strong; not a man escaped. ³⁰That day Moab was made subject to Israel, and the land had peace for eighty years.

Shamgar

³¹After Ehud came Shamgar son of Anath, who struck down six hundred Philistines with an oxgoad. He too saved Israel.

Deborah

4 After Ehud died, the Israelites once again did evil in the eyes of the LORD. ²So the LORD sold them into the hands of Jabin, a king of Canaan, who reigned in Hazor. The commander of his army was Sisera, who lived in Harosheth Haggoyim. ³Because he had nine hundred iron chariots and had cruelly oppressed the Israelites for twenty years, they cried to the LORD for help.

⁴Deborah, a prophetess, the wife of Lappidoth, was leading*f* Israel at that time. ⁵She held court under the Palm of Deborah between Ramah and Bethel in the hill country of Ephraim, and the Israelites came to her to have their disputes decided. ⁶She sent for Barak son of Abinoam from Kedesh in Naphtali and said to him, "The LORD, the God of Israel, commands you: 'Go, take with you ten thousand men of Naphtali and Zebulun and lead the way to Mount Tabor. ⁷I will lure Sisera, the commander of Jabin's army, with his chariots and his troops to the Kishon River and give him into your hands.' "

⁸Barak said to her, "If you go with me, I will go; but if you don't go with me, I won't go."

⁹"Very well," Deborah said, "I will go with you. But because of the way you are going about this,*g* the honor will not be yours, for the LORD will hand Sisera over to a woman." So Deborah went with Barak to Kedesh, ¹⁰where he summoned Zebulun and Naphtali. Ten thousand men followed him, and Deborah also went with him.

¹¹Now Heber the Kenite had left the other Kenites, the descendants of Hobab, Moses' brother-in-law,*h* and pitched his

---

a13 That is, Jericho   *b16* Hebrew *a cubit* (about 0.5 meter)   *c19* Or *the stone quarries;* also in verse 26   *d20* The meaning of the Hebrew for this phrase is uncertain.   *e23* The meaning of the Hebrew for this word is uncertain.   *f4* Traditionally *judging*   *g9* Or *But on the expedition you are undertaking* *h11* Or *father-in-law*

VERSE FOR THE DAY:
Judges 4:4

AUTHOR:
June Gunden

PASSAGE FOR THE DAY:
Judges 4:4 — 5:31

Usefulness to God

DEBORAH—the only woman in Israel to become a judge. Who was she? What made her so outstanding that she was given the job? We know that she was a wife (Judges 4:4) and mother (Judges 5:7). How did she juggle her job with her family responsibilities?

The fact that we aren't told these things may be significant. It may be because to her and to the writer of the book of Judges, Deborah herself wasn't the emphasis. Her usefulness to God and to the nation of Israel was what mattered. The fact that she could keep that perspective, rather than thinking about her position, is probably a reason she was uniquely used. Even after the victory over Sisera, when it would have been tempting to take some personal credit, Deborah sang a song in praise of the Lord.

Have you ever experienced a unique time of usefulness to God, then found that in a very short time you had gotten quite far from him? Perhaps it was because you became overwhelmed with your service to God rather than with God himself. The devil has many subtle ways to turn your eyes from God. He knows that if you are all caught up in your own service, regardless of how many people you may be helping, you will eventually burn out or become ineffective because your work is simply revolving around you.

Service for the kingdom does not consist of what you do or what you give; it depends on who you are. When you give God control, he will give you ways to serve. You will not need to drum up any areas to be of use to God. He will give you a zestful, fruitful life purely as his gift to you because you gave your life to him.

And then, when he is using you, be careful to keep your eyes on him. To begin to look anywhere else, as Peter discovered when he tried to walk on the water (Matthew 14:30), spells failure.

Additional Scripture Readings:
Judges 8:22–27; Romans 12:1–8

Go to page 250 for your next devotional reading.

tent by the great tree in Zaanannim near Kedesh.

¹²When they told Sisera that Barak son of Abinoam had gone up to Mount Tabor, ¹³Sisera gathered together his nine hundred iron chariots and all the men with him, from Harosheth Haggoyim to the Kishon River.

¹⁴Then Deborah said to Barak, "Go! This is the day the LORD has given Sisera into your hands. Has not the LORD gone ahead of you?" So Barak went down Mount Tabor, followed by ten thousand men. ¹⁵At Barak's advance, the LORD routed Sisera and all his chariots and army by the sword, and Sisera abandoned his chariot and fled on foot. ¹⁶But Barak pursued the chariots and army as far as Harosheth Haggoyim. All the troops of Sisera fell by the sword; not a man was left.

¹⁷Sisera, however, fled on foot to the tent of Jael, the wife of Heber the Kenite, because there were friendly relations between Jabin king of Hazor and the clan of Heber the Kenite.

¹⁸Jael went out to meet Sisera and said to him, "Come, my lord, come right in. Don't be afraid." So he entered her tent, and she put a covering over him.

¹⁹"I'm thirsty," he said. "Please give me some water." She opened a skin of milk, gave him a drink, and covered him up.

²⁰"Stand in the doorway of the tent," he told her. "If someone comes by and asks you, 'Is anyone here?' say 'No.' "

²¹But Jael, Heber's wife, picked up a tent peg and a hammer and went quietly to him while he lay fast asleep, exhausted. She drove the peg through his temple into the ground, and he died.

²²Barak came by in pursuit of Sisera, and Jael went out to meet him. "Come," she said, "I will show you the man you're looking for." So he went in with her, and there lay Sisera with the tent peg through his temple—dead.

²³On that day God subdued Jabin, the Canaanite king, before the Israelites. ²⁴And the hand of the Israelites grew stronger and stronger against Jabin, the Canaanite king, until they destroyed him.

The Song of Deborah

5 On that day Deborah and Barak son of Abinoam sang this song:

²"When the princes in Israel take the lead,
  when the people willingly offer themselves—
  praise the LORD!

³"Hear this, you kings! Listen, you rulers!
  I will sing to*ᵃ* the LORD, I will sing;
  I will make music to*ᵇ* the LORD, the God of Israel.

⁴"O LORD, when you went out from Seir,
  when you marched from the land of Edom,
  the earth shook, the heavens poured,
  the clouds poured down water.
⁵The mountains quaked before the LORD, the One of Sinai,
  before the LORD, the God of Israel.

⁶"In the days of Shamgar son of Anath,
  in the days of Jael, the roads were abandoned;
  travelers took to winding paths.
⁷Village life*ᶜ* in Israel ceased,
  ceased until I,*ᵈ* Deborah, arose,
  arose a mother in Israel.
⁸When they chose new gods,
  war came to the city gates,
  and not a shield or spear was seen
  among forty thousand in Israel.
⁹My heart is with Israel's princes,
  with the willing volunteers among the people.
  Praise the LORD!

¹⁰"You who ride on white donkeys,
  sitting on your saddle blankets,
  and you who walk along the road,
  consider ¹¹the voice of the singers*ᵉ* at the watering places.
  They recite the righteous acts of the LORD,
  the righteous acts of his warriors*ᶠ* in Israel.

"Then the people of the LORD
  went down to the city gates.
¹²'Wake up, wake up, Deborah!
  Wake up, wake up, break out in song!
Arise, O Barak!
  Take captive your captives, O son of Abinoam.'

¹³"Then the men who were left
  came down to the nobles;

ᵃ3 Or of   *ᵇ3* Or / with song I will praise   *ᶜ7* Or Warriors   *ᵈ7* Or you   *ᵉ11* Or archers; the meaning of the Hebrew for this word is uncertain.   *ᶠ11* Or villagers

the people of the Lord
came to me with the mighty.
¹⁴Some came from Ephraim, whose
roots were in Amalek;
Benjamin was with the people who
followed you.
From Makir captains came down,
from Zebulun those who bear a
commander's staff.
¹⁵The princes of Issachar were with
Deborah;
yes, Issachar was with Barak,
rushing after him into the valley.
In the districts of Reuben
there was much searching of heart.
¹⁶Why did you stay among the
campfires[a]
to hear the whistling for the flocks?
In the districts of Reuben
there was much searching of heart.
¹⁷Gilead stayed beyond the Jordan.
And Dan, why did he linger by the
ships?
Asher remained on the coast
and stayed in his coves.
¹⁸The people of Zebulun risked their
very lives;
so did Naphtali on the heights of
the field.

¹⁹"Kings came, they fought;
the kings of Canaan fought
at Taanach by the waters of Megiddo,
but they carried off no silver, no
plunder.
²⁰From the heavens the stars fought,
from their courses they fought
against Sisera.
²¹The river Kishon swept them away,
the age-old river, the river Kishon.
March on, my soul; be strong!
²²Then thundered the horses' hoofs—
galloping, galloping go his mighty
steeds.
²³'Curse Meroz,' said the angel of the
Lord.
'Curse its people bitterly,
because they did not come to help
the Lord,
to help the Lord against the
mighty.'

²⁴"Most blessed of women be Jael,
the wife of Heber the Kenite,
most blessed of tent-dwelling
women.
²⁵He asked for water, and she gave him
milk;

in a bowl fit for nobles she brought
him curdled milk.
²⁶Her hand reached for the tent peg,
her right hand for the workman's
hammer.
She struck Sisera, she crushed his
head,
she shattered and pierced his
temple.
²⁷At her feet he sank,
he fell; there he lay.
At her feet he sank, he fell;
where he sank, there he fell—dead.

²⁸"Through the window peered Sisera's
mother;
behind the lattice she cried out,
'Why is his chariot so long in coming?
Why is the clatter of his chariots
delayed?'
²⁹The wisest of her ladies answer her;
indeed, she keeps saying to herself,
³⁰'Are they not finding and dividing the
spoils:
a girl or two for each man,
colorful garments as plunder for
Sisera,
colorful garments embroidered,
highly embroidered garments for my
neck—
all this as plunder?'

³¹"So may all your enemies perish,
O Lord!
But may they who love you be like
the sun
when it rises in its strength."

Then the land had peace forty years.

Gideon

6 Again the Israelites did evil in the eyes of the Lord, and for seven years he gave them into the hands of the Midianites. ²Because the power of Midian was so oppressive, the Israelites prepared shelters for themselves in mountain clefts, caves and strongholds. ³Whenever the Israelites planted their crops, the Midianites, Amalekites and other eastern peoples invaded the country. ⁴They camped on the land and ruined the crops all the way to Gaza and did not spare a living thing for Israel, neither sheep nor cattle nor donkeys. ⁵They came up with their livestock and their tents like swarms of locusts. It was impossible to count the men and their camels; they invaded the land to ravage it. ⁶Midian so impover-

---

[a]16 Or *saddlebags*

ished the Israelites that they cried out to the LORD for help.

⁷When the Israelites cried to the LORD because of Midian, ⁸he sent them a prophet, who said, "This is what the LORD, the God of Israel, says: I brought you up out of Egypt, out of the land of slavery. ⁹I snatched you from the power of Egypt and from the hand of all your oppressors. I drove them from before you and gave you their land. ¹⁰I said to you, 'I am the LORD your God; do not worship the gods of the Amorites, in whose land you live.' But you have not listened to me."

¹¹The angel of the LORD came and sat down under the oak in Ophrah that belonged to Joash the Abiezrite, where his son Gideon was threshing wheat in a winepress to keep it from the Midianites. ¹²When the angel of the LORD appeared to Gideon, he said, "The LORD is with you, mighty warrior."

¹³"But sir," Gideon replied, "if the LORD is with us, why has all this happened to us? Where are all his wonders that our fathers told us about when they said, 'Did not the LORD bring us up out of Egypt?' But now the LORD has abandoned us and put us into the hand of Midian."

¹⁴The LORD turned to him and said, "Go in the strength you have and save Israel out of Midian's hand. Am I not sending you?"

¹⁵"But Lord,ᵃ" Gideon asked, "how can I save Israel? My clan is the weakest in Manasseh, and I am the least in my family."

¹⁶The LORD answered, "I will be with you, and you will strike down all the Midianites together."

¹⁷Gideon replied, "If now I have found favor in your eyes, give me a sign that it is really you talking to me. ¹⁸Please do not

ᵃ15 Or sir

FRIDAY

VERSE FOR THE DAY:
Judges 6:15

AUTHOR:
Florence Littauer

PASSAGE FOR THE DAY:
Judges 6:1–16

Wealth

SOME of us feel that it is a lack of money that holds us down. Gideon replied to God's request, "But Lord . . . how can I save Israel? My clan is the weakest in Manasseh, and I am the least of my family" (Judges 6:15). With no finances behind him at all, Gideon was turned into a wise prophet by God's commanding power. Many times I have had sweet Christians tell me they cannot have friends in for fellowship because they do not have good china or matching napkins, because their house is too small, or because their talent is too slight. But these are only excuses for our unwillingness to do as God has asked us. "Offer hospitality to one another without grumbling" (1 Peter 4:9). I would enjoy a peanut butter sandwich if someone else prepared it and handed it to me.

The world tells us that we need money to be happy, but as God told Gideon, "I will be with you" (Judges 6:16). Should not his presence be assurance enough?

Additional Scripture Readings:
2 Corinthians 8:1–7; James 2:1–5

Go to page 256 for your next devotional reading.

go away until I come back and bring my offering and set it before you."

And the Lord said, "I will wait until you return."

¹⁹Gideon went in, prepared a young goat, and from an ephah* of flour he made bread without yeast. Putting the meat in a basket and its broth in a pot, he brought them out and offered them to him under the oak.

²⁰The angel of God said to him, "Take the meat and the unleavened bread, place them on this rock, and pour out the broth." And Gideon did so. ²¹With the tip of the staff that was in his hand, the angel of the Lord touched the meat and the unleavened bread. Fire flared from the rock, consuming the meat and the bread. And the angel of the Lord disappeared. ²²When Gideon realized that it was the angel of the Lord, he exclaimed, "Ah, Sovereign Lord! I have seen the angel of the Lord face to face!"

²³But the Lord said to him, "Peace! Do not be afraid. You are not going to die."

²⁴So Gideon built an altar to the Lord there and called it The Lord is Peace. To this day it stands in Ophrah of the Abiezrites.

²⁵That same night the Lord said to him, "Take the second bull from your father's herd, the one seven years old.ᵇ Tear down your father's altar to Baal and cut down the Asherah poleᶜ beside it. ²⁶Then build a proper kind ofᵈ altar to the Lord your God on the top of this height. Using the wood of the Asherah pole that you cut down, offer the secondᵉ bull as a burnt offering."

²⁷So Gideon took ten of his servants and did as the Lord told him. But because he was afraid of his family and the men of the town, he did it at night rather than in the daytime.

²⁸In the morning when the men of the town got up, there was Baal's altar, demolished, with the Asherah pole beside it cut down and the second bull sacrificed on the newly built altar!

²⁹They asked each other, "Who did this?"

When they carefully investigated, they were told, "Gideon son of Joash did it."

³⁰The men of the town demanded of Joash, "Bring out your son. He must die, because he has broken down Baal's altar and cut down the Asherah pole beside it."

³¹But Joash replied to the hostile crowd around him, "Are you going to plead Baal's cause? Are you trying to save him? Whoever fights for him shall be put to death by morning! If Baal really is a god, he can defend himself when someone breaks down his altar." ³²So that day they called Gideon "Jerub-Baal,ᶠ" saying, "Let Baal contend with him," because he broke down Baal's altar.

³³Now all the Midianites, Amalekites and other eastern peoples joined forces and crossed over the Jordan and camped in the Valley of Jezreel. ³⁴Then the Spirit of the Lord came upon Gideon, and he blew a trumpet, summoning the Abiezrites to follow him. ³⁵He sent messengers throughout Manasseh, calling them to arms, and also into Asher, Zebulun and Naphtali, so that they too went up to meet them.

³⁶Gideon said to God, "If you will save Israel by my hand as you have promised— ³⁷look, I will place a wool fleece on the threshing floor. If there is dew only on the fleece and all the ground is dry, then I will know that you will save Israel by my hand, as you said." ³⁸And that is what happened. Gideon rose early the next day; he squeezed the fleece and wrung out the dew—a bowlful of water.

³⁹Then Gideon said to God, "Do not be angry with me. Let me make just one more request. Allow me one more test with the fleece. This time make the fleece dry and the ground covered with dew." ⁴⁰That night God did so. Only the fleece was dry; all the ground was covered with dew.

Gideon Defeats the Midianites

7 Early in the morning, Jerub-Baal (that is, Gideon) and all his men camped at the spring of Harod. The camp of Midian was north of them in the valley near the hill of Moreh. ²The Lord said to Gideon, "You have too many men for me to deliver Midian into their hands. In order that Israel may not boast against me that her own strength has saved her, ³announce now to the people, 'Anyone who trembles with fear may turn back and leave Mount Gilead.'" So twenty-two

---

ᵃ19 That is, probably about 3/5 bushel (about 22 liters)   ᵇ25 Or Take a full-grown, mature bull from your father's herd   ᶜ25 That is, a symbol of the goddess Asherah; here and elsewhere in Judges   ᵈ26 Or build with layers of stone an   ᵉ26 Or full-grown; also in verse 28   ᶠ32 Jerub-Baal means let Baal contend.

thousand men left, while ten thousand remained.

4But the LORD said to Gideon, "There are still too many men. Take them down to the water, and I will sift them for you there. If I say, 'This one shall go with you,' he shall go; but if I say, 'This one shall not go with you,' he shall not go."

5So Gideon took the men down to the water. There the LORD told him, "Separate those who lap the water with their tongues like a dog from those who kneel down to drink." 6Three hundred men lapped with their hands to their mouths. All the rest got down on their knees to drink.

7The LORD said to Gideon, "With the three hundred men that lapped I will save you and give the Midianites into your hands. Let all the other men go, each to his own place." 8So Gideon sent the rest of the Israelites to their tents but kept the three hundred, who took over the provisions and trumpets of the others.

Now the camp of Midian lay below him in the valley. 9During that night the LORD said to Gideon, "Get up, go down against the camp, because I am going to give it into your hands. 10If you are afraid to attack, go down to the camp with your servant Purah 11and listen to what they are saying. Afterward, you will be encouraged to attack the camp." So he and Purah his servant went down to the outposts of the camp. 12The Midianites, the Amalekites and all the other eastern peoples had settled in the valley, thick as locusts. Their camels could no more be counted than the sand on the seashore.

13Gideon arrived just as a man was telling a friend his dream. "I had a dream," he was saying. "A round loaf of barley bread came tumbling into the Midianite camp. It struck the tent with such force that the tent overturned and collapsed."

14His friend responded, "This can be nothing other than the sword of Gideon son of Joash, the Israelite. God has given the Midianites and the whole camp into his hands."

15When Gideon heard the dream and its interpretation, he worshiped God. He returned to the camp of Israel and called out, "Get up! The LORD has given the Midianite camp into your hands." 16Dividing the three hundred men into three companies, he placed trumpets and empty jars in the hands of all of them, with torches inside.

17"Watch me," he told them. "Follow my lead. When I get to the edge of the camp, do exactly as I do. 18When I and all who are with me blow our trumpets, then from all around the camp blow yours and shout, 'For the LORD and for Gideon.' "

19Gideon and the hundred men with him reached the edge of the camp at the beginning of the middle watch, just after they had changed the guard. They blew their trumpets and broke the jars that were in their hands. 20The three companies blew the trumpets and smashed the jars. Grasping the torches in their left hands and holding in their right hands the trumpets they were to blow, they shouted, "A sword for the LORD and for Gideon!" 21While each man held his position around the camp, all the Midianites ran, crying out as they fled.

22When the three hundred trumpets sounded, the LORD caused the men throughout the camp to turn on each other with their swords. The army fled to Beth Shittah toward Zererah as far as the border of Abel Meholah near Tabbath. 23Israelites from Naphtali, Asher and all Manasseh were called out, and they pursued the Midianites. 24Gideon sent messengers throughout the hill country of Ephraim, saying, "Come down against the Midianites and seize the waters of the Jordan ahead of them as far as Beth Barah."

So all the men of Ephraim were called out and they took the waters of the Jordan as far as Beth Barah. 25They also captured two of the Midianite leaders, Oreb and Zeeb. They killed Oreb at the rock of Oreb, and Zeeb at the winepress of Zeeb. They pursued the Midianites and brought the heads of Oreb and Zeeb to Gideon, who was by the Jordan.

Zebah and Zalmunna

8 Now the Ephraimites asked Gideon, "Why have you treated us like this? Why didn't you call us when you went to fight Midian?" And they criticized him sharply.

2But he answered them, "What have I accomplished compared to you? Aren't the gleanings of Ephraim's grapes better than the full grape harvest of Abiezer? 3God gave Oreb and Zeeb, the Midianite leaders, into your hands. What was I able to do compared to you?" At this, their resentment against him subsided.

4Gideon and his three hundred men, exhausted yet keeping up the pursuit, came to the Jordan and crossed it. 5He said to the men of Succoth, "Give my troops some bread; they are worn out, and I am still pursuing Zebah and Zalmunna, the kings of Midian."

6But the officials of Succoth said, "Do you already have the hands of Zebah and Zalmunna in your possession? Why should we give bread to your troops?"

7Then Gideon replied, "Just for that, when the LORD has given Zebah and Zalmunna into my hand, I will tear your flesh with desert thorns and briers."

8From there he went up to Peniel*a* and made the same request of them, but they answered as the men of Succoth had. 9So he said to the men of Peniel, "When I return in triumph, I will tear down this tower."

10Now Zebah and Zalmunna were in Karkor with a force of about fifteen thousand men, all that were left of the armies of the eastern peoples; a hundred and twenty thousand swordsmen had fallen. 11Gideon went up by the route of the nomads east of Nobah and Jogbehah and fell upon the unsuspecting army. 12Zebah and Zalmunna, the two kings of Midian, fled, but he pursued them and captured them, routing their entire army.

13Gideon son of Joash then returned from the battle by the Pass of Heres. 14He caught a young man of Succoth and questioned him, and the young man wrote down for him the names of the seventy-seven officials of Succoth, the elders of the town. 15Then Gideon came and said to the men of Succoth, "Here are Zebah and Zalmunna, about whom you taunted me by saying, 'Do you already have the hands of Zebah and Zalmunna in your possession? Why should we give bread to your exhausted men?' " 16He took the elders of the town and taught the men of Succoth a lesson by punishing them with desert thorns and briers. 17He also pulled down the tower of Peniel and killed the men of the town.

18Then he asked Zebah and Zalmunna, "What kind of men did you kill at Tabor?"

"Men like you," they answered, "each one with the bearing of a prince."

19Gideon replied, "Those were my brothers, the sons of my own mother. As surely as the LORD lives, if you had spared their lives, I would not kill you." 20Turning to Jether, his oldest son, he said, "Kill them!" But Jether did not draw his sword,

because he was only a boy and was afraid.

21Zebah and Zalmunna said, "Come, do it yourself. 'As is the man, so is his strength.' " So Gideon stepped forward and killed them, and took the ornaments off their camels' necks.

Gideon's Ephod

22The Israelites said to Gideon, "Rule over us—you, your son and your grandson—because you have saved us out of the hand of Midian."

23But Gideon told them, "I will not rule over you, nor will my son rule over you. The LORD will rule over you." 24And he said, "I do have one request, that each of you give me an earring from your share of the plunder." (It was the custom of the Ishmaelites to wear gold earrings.)

25They answered, "We'll be glad to give them." So they spread out a garment, and each man threw a ring from his plunder onto it. 26The weight of the gold rings he asked for came to seventeen hundred shekels,*b* not counting the ornaments, the pendants and the purple garments worn by the kings of Midian or the chains that were on their camels' necks. 27Gideon made the gold into an ephod, which he placed in Ophrah, his town. All Israel prostituted themselves by worshiping it there, and it became a snare to Gideon and his family.

Gideon's Death

28Thus Midian was subdued before the Israelites and did not raise its head again. During Gideon's lifetime, the land enjoyed peace forty years.

29Jerub-Baal son of Joash went back home to live. 30He had seventy sons of his own, for he had many wives. 31His concubine, who lived in Shechem, also bore him a son, whom he named Abimelech. 32Gideon son of Joash died at a good old age and was buried in the tomb of his father Joash in Ophrah of the Abiezrites.

33No sooner had Gideon died than the Israelites again prostituted themselves to the Baals. They set up Baal-Berith as their god and 34did not remember the LORD their God, who had rescued them from the hands of all their enemies on every side. 35They also failed to show kindness to the family of Jerub-Baal (that is, Gideon) for all the good things he had done for them.

a8 Hebrew *Penuel*, a variant of *Peniel*; also in verses 9 and 17   *b26* That is, about 43 pounds (about 19.5 kilograms)

Abimelech

9 Abimelech son of Jerub-Baal went to his mother's brothers in Shechem and said to them and to all his mother's clan, 2"Ask all the citizens of Shechem, 'Which is better for you: to have all seventy of Jerub-Baal's sons rule over you, or just one man?' Remember, I am your flesh and blood."

3When the brothers repeated all this to the citizens of Shechem, they were inclined to follow Abimelech, for they said, "He is our brother." 4They gave him seventy shekels[a] of silver from the temple of Baal-Berith, and Abimelech used it to hire reckless adventurers, who became his followers. 5He went to his father's home in Ophrah and on one stone murdered his seventy brothers, the sons of Jerub-Baal. But Jotham, the youngest son of Jerub-Baal, escaped by hiding. 6Then all the citizens of Shechem and Beth Millo gathered beside the great tree at the pillar in Shechem to crown Abimelech king.

7When Jotham was told about this, he climbed up on the top of Mount Gerizim and shouted to them, "Listen to me, citizens of Shechem, so that God may listen to you. 8One day the trees went out to anoint a king for themselves. They said to the olive tree, 'Be our king.'

9"But the olive tree answered, 'Should I give up my oil, by which both gods and men are honored, to hold sway over the trees?'

10"Next, the trees said to the fig tree, 'Come and be our king.'

11"But the fig tree replied, 'Should I give up my fruit, so good and sweet, to hold sway over the trees?'

12"Then the trees said to the vine, 'Come and be our king.'

13"But the vine answered, 'Should I give up my wine, which cheers both gods and men, to hold sway over the trees?'

14"Finally all the trees said to the thornbush, 'Come and be our king.'

15"The thornbush said to the trees, 'If you really want to anoint me king over you, come and take refuge in my shade; but if not, then let fire come out of the thornbush and consume the cedars of Lebanon!'

16"Now if you have acted honorably and in good faith when you made Abimelech king, and if you have been fair to Jerub-Baal and his family, and if you have treated him as he deserves— 17and to think that my father fought for you, risked his life to rescue you from the hand of Midian 18(but today you have revolted against my father's family, murdered his seventy sons on a single stone, and made Abimelech, the son of his slave girl, king over the citizens of Shechem because he is your brother)— 19if then you have acted honorably and in good faith toward Jerub-Baal and his family today, may Abimelech be your joy, and may you be his, too! 20But if you have not, let fire come out from Abimelech and consume you, citizens of Shechem and Beth Millo, and let fire come out from you, citizens of Shechem and Beth Millo, and consume Abimelech!"

21Then Jotham fled, escaping to Beer, and he lived there because he was afraid of his brother Abimelech.

22After Abimelech had governed Israel three years, 23God sent an evil spirit between Abimelech and the citizens of Shechem, who acted treacherously against Abimelech. 24God did this in order that the crime against Jerub-Baal's seventy sons, the shedding of their blood, might be avenged on their brother Abimelech and on the citizens of Shechem, who helped him murder his brothers. 25In opposition to him these citizens of Shechem set men on the hilltops to ambush and rob everyone who passed by, and this was reported to Abimelech.

26Now Gaal son of Ebed moved with his brothers into Shechem, and its citizens put their confidence in him. 27After they had gone out into the fields and gathered the grapes and trodden them, they held a festival in the temple of their god. While they were eating and drinking, they cursed Abimelech. 28Then Gaal son of Ebed said, "Who is Abimelech, and who is Shechem, that we should be subject to him? Isn't he Jerub-Baal's son, and isn't Zebul his deputy? Serve the men of Hamor, Shechem's father! Why should we serve Abimelech? 29If only this people were under my command! Then I would get rid of him. I would say to Abimelech, 'Call out your whole army!' "[b]

30When Zebul the governor of the city heard what Gaal son of Ebed said, he was very angry. 31Under cover he sent messengers to Abimelech, saying, "Gaal son of

---

[a]4 That is, about 1 3/4 pounds (about 0.8 kilogram)
[b]29 Septuagint; Hebrew him." Then he said to Abimelech, "Call out your whole army!"

Ebed and his brothers have come to Shechem and are stirring up the city against you. ³²Now then, during the night you and your men should come and lie in wait in the fields. ³³In the morning at sunrise, advance against the city. When Gaal and his men come out against you, do whatever your hand finds to do."

³⁴So Abimelech and all his troops set out by night and took up concealed positions near Shechem in four companies. ³⁵Now Gaal son of Ebed had gone out and was standing at the entrance to the city gate just as Abimelech and his soldiers came out from their hiding place.

³⁶When Gaal saw them, he said to Zebul, "Look, people are coming down from the tops of the mountains!"

Zebul replied, "You mistake the shadows of the mountains for men."

³⁷But Gaal spoke up again: "Look, people are coming down from the center of the land, and a company is coming from the direction of the soothsayers' tree."

³⁸Then Zebul said to him, "Where is your big talk now, you who said, 'Who is Abimelech that we should be subject to him?' Aren't these the men you ridiculed? Go out and fight them!"

³⁹So Gaal led out ᵃ the citizens of Shechem and fought Abimelech. ⁴⁰Abimelech chased him, and many fell wounded in the flight — all the way to the entrance to the gate. ⁴¹Abimelech stayed in Arumah, and Zebul drove Gaal and his brothers out of Shechem.

⁴²The next day the people of Shechem went out to the fields, and this was reported to Abimelech. ⁴³So he took his men, divided them into three companies and set an ambush in the fields. When he saw the people coming out of the city, he rose to attack them. ⁴⁴Abimelech and the companies with him rushed forward to a position at the entrance to the city gate. Then two companies rushed upon those in the fields and struck them down. ⁴⁵All that day Abimelech pressed his attack against the city until he had captured it and killed its people. Then he destroyed the city and scattered salt over it.

⁴⁶On hearing this, the citizens in the tower of Shechem went into the stronghold of the temple of El-Berith. ⁴⁷When Abimelech heard that they had assembled there, ⁴⁸he and all his men went up Mount Zalmon. He took an ax and cut off

some branches, which he lifted to his shoulders. He ordered the men with him, "Quick! Do what you have seen me do!" ⁴⁹So all the men cut branches and followed Abimelech. They piled them against the stronghold and set it on fire over the people inside. So all the people in the tower of Shechem, about a thousand men and women, also died.

⁵⁰Next Abimelech went to Thebez and besieged it and captured it. ⁵¹Inside the city, however, was a strong tower, to which all the men and women — all the people of the city — fled. They locked themselves in and climbed up on the tower roof. ⁵²Abimelech went to the tower and stormed it. But as he approached the entrance to the tower to set it on fire, ⁵³a woman dropped an upper millstone on his head and cracked his skull.

⁵⁴Hurriedly he called to his armor-bearer, "Draw your sword and kill me, so that they can't say, 'A woman killed him.' " So his servant ran him through, and he died. ⁵⁵When the Israelites saw that Abimelech was dead, they went home.

⁵⁶Thus God repaid the wickedness that Abimelech had done to his father by murdering his seventy brothers. ⁵⁷God also made the men of Shechem pay for all their wickedness. The curse of Jotham son of Jerub-Baal came on them.

Tola

10 After the time of Abimelech a man of Issachar, Tola son of Puah, the son of Dodo, rose to save Israel. He lived in Shamir, in the hill country of Ephraim. ²He led ᵇ Israel twenty-three years; then he died, and was buried in Shamir.

Jair

³He was followed by Jair of Gilead, who led Israel twenty-two years. ⁴He had thirty sons, who rode thirty donkeys. They controlled thirty towns in Gilead, which to this day are called Havvoth Jair. ᶜ ⁵When Jair died, he was buried in Kamon.

Jephthah

⁶Again the Israelites did evil in the eyes of the Lord. They served the Baals and the Ashtoreths, and the gods of Aram, the gods of Sidon, the gods of Moab, the gods of the Ammonites and the gods of the Philistines. And because the Israelites

---

ᵃ39 Or Gaal went out in the sight of   ᵇ2 Traditionally judged; also in verse 3   ᶜ4 Or called the
settlements of Jair

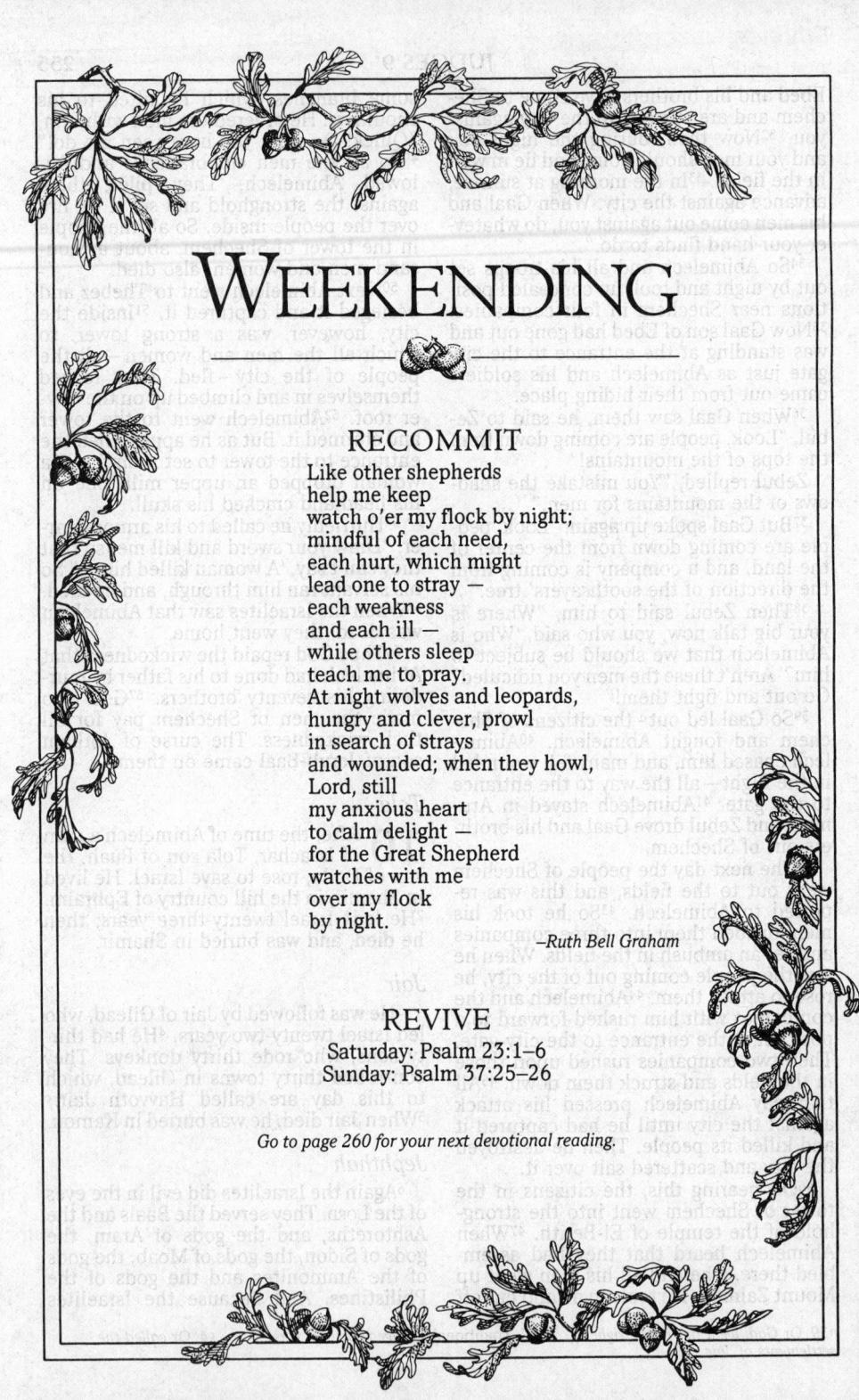

WEEKENDING

RECOMMIT

Like other shepherds
help me keep
watch o'er my flock by night;
mindful of each need,
each hurt, which might
lead one to stray —
each weakness
and each ill —
while others sleep
teach me to pray.
At night wolves and leopards,
hungry and clever, prowl
in search of strays
and wounded; when they howl,
Lord, still
my anxious heart
to calm delight —
for the Great Shepherd
watches with me
over my flock
by night.

—Ruth Bell Graham

REVIVE

Saturday: Psalm 23:1–6
Sunday: Psalm 37:25–26

Go to page 260 for your next devotional reading.

forsook the LORD and no longer served him, [7]he became angry with them. He sold them into the hands of the Philistines and the Ammonites, [8]who that year shattered and crushed them. For eighteen years they oppressed all the Israelites on the east side of the Jordan in Gilead, the land of the Amorites. [9]The Ammonites also crossed the Jordan to fight against Judah, Benjamin and the house of Ephraim; and Israel was in great distress. [10]Then the Israelites cried out to the LORD, "We have sinned against you, forsaking our God and serving the Baals."

[11]The LORD replied, "When the Egyptians, the Amorites, the Ammonites, the Philistines, [12]the Sidonians, the Amalekites and the Maonites[a] oppressed you and you cried to me for help, did I not save you from their hands? [13]But you have forsaken me and served other gods, so I will no longer save you. [14]Go and cry out to the gods you have chosen. Let them save you when you are in trouble!"

[15]But the Israelites said to the LORD, "We have sinned. Do with us whatever you think best, but please rescue us now." [16]Then they got rid of the foreign gods among them and served the LORD. And he could bear Israel's misery no longer.

[17]When the Ammonites were called to arms and camped in Gilead, the Israelites assembled and camped at Mizpah. [18]The leaders of the people of Gilead said to each other, "Whoever will launch the attack against the Ammonites will be the head of all those living in Gilead."

11 Jephthah the Gileadite was a mighty warrior. His father was Gilead; his mother was a prostitute. [2]Gilead's wife also bore him sons, and when they were grown up, they drove Jephthah away. "You are not going to get any inheritance in our family," they said, "because you are the son of another woman." [3]So Jephthah fled from his brothers and settled in the land of Tob, where a group of adventurers gathered around him and followed him.

[4]Some time later, when the Ammonites made war on Israel, [5]the elders of Gilead went to get Jephthah from the land of Tob. [6]"Come," they said, "be our commander, so we can fight the Ammonites."

[7]Jephthah said to them, "Didn't you hate me and drive me from my father's

house? Why do you come to me now, when you're in trouble?"

[8]The elders of Gilead said to him, "Nevertheless, we are turning to you now; come with us to fight the Ammonites, and you will be our head over all who live in Gilead."

[9]Jephthah answered, "Suppose you take me back to fight the Ammonites and the LORD gives them to me—will I really be your head?"

[10]The elders of Gilead replied, "The LORD is our witness; we will certainly do as you say." [11]So Jephthah went with the elders of Gilead, and the people made him head and commander over them. And he repeated all his words before the LORD in Mizpah.

[12]Then Jephthah sent messengers to the Ammonite king with the question: "What do you have against us that you have attacked our country?"

[13]The king of the Ammonites answered Jephthah's messengers, "When Israel came up out of Egypt, they took away my land from the Arnon to the Jabbok, all the way to the Jordan. Now give it back peaceably."

[14]Jephthah sent back messengers to the Ammonite king, [15]saying:

"This is what Jephthah says: Israel did not take the land of Moab or the land of the Ammonites. [16]But when they came up out of Egypt, Israel went through the desert to the Red Sea[b] and on to Kadesh. [17]Then Israel sent messengers to the king of Edom, saying, 'Give us permission to go through your country,' but the king of Edom would not listen. They sent also to the king of Moab, and he refused. So Israel stayed at Kadesh.

[18]"Next they traveled through the desert, skirted the lands of Edom and Moab, passed along the eastern side of the country of Moab, and camped on the other side of the Arnon. They did not enter the territory of Moab, for the Arnon was its border.

[19]"Then Israel sent messengers to Sihon king of the Amorites, who ruled in Heshbon, and said to him, 'Let us pass through your country to our own place.' [20]Sihon, however, did not trust Israel[c] to pass through

---

a12 Hebrew; some Septuagint manuscripts *Midianites*   *b16* Hebrew *Yam Suph*; that is, Sea of Reeds
c20 Or *however, would not make an agreement for Israel*

his territory. He mustered all his men and encamped at Jahaz and fought with Israel.

21"Then the LORD, the God of Israel, gave Sihon and all his men into Israel's hands, and they defeated them. Israel took over all the land of the Amorites who lived in that country, 22capturing all of it from the Arnon to the Jabbok and from the desert to the Jordan.

23"Now since the LORD, the God of Israel, has driven the Amorites out before his people Israel, what right have you to take it over? 24Will you not take what your god Chemosh gives you? Likewise, whatever the LORD our God has given us, we will possess. 25Are you better than Balak son of Zippor, king of Moab? Did he ever quarrel with Israel or fight with them? 26For three hundred years Israel occupied Heshbon, Aroer, the surrounding settlements and all the towns along the Arnon. Why didn't you retake them during that time? 27I have not wronged you, but you are doing me wrong by waging war against me. Let the LORD, the Judge,ᵃ decide the dispute this day between the Israelites and the Ammonites."

28The king of Ammon, however, paid no attention to the message Jephthah sent him.

29Then the Spirit of the LORD came upon Jephthah. He crossed Gilead and Manasseh, passed through Mizpah of Gilead, and from there he advanced against the Ammonites. 30And Jephthah made a vow to the LORD: "If you give the Ammonites into my hands, 31whatever comes out of the door of my house to meet me when I return in triumph from the Ammonites will be the LORD's, and I will sacrifice it as a burnt offering."

32Then Jephthah went over to fight the Ammonites, and the LORD gave them into his hands. 33He devastated twenty towns from Aroer to the vicinity of Minnith, as far as Abel Keramim. Thus Israel subdued Ammon.

34When Jephthah returned to his home in Mizpah, who should come out to meet him but his daughter, dancing to the sound of tambourines! She was an only child. Except for her he had neither son nor daughter. 35When he saw her, he tore his clothes and cried, "Oh! My daughter! You have made me miserable and wretched, because I have made a vow to the LORD that I cannot break."

36"My father," she replied, "you have given your word to the LORD. Do to me just as you promised, now that the LORD has avenged you of your enemies, the Ammonites. 37But grant me this one request," she said. "Give me two months to roam the hills and weep with my friends, because I will never marry."

38"You may go," he said. And he let her go for two months. She and the girls went into the hills and wept because she would never marry. 39After the two months, she returned to her father and he did to her as he had vowed. And she was a virgin.

From this comes the Israelite custom 40that each year the young women of Israel go out for four days to commemorate the daughter of Jephthah the Gileadite.

Jephthah and Ephraim

12 The men of Ephraim called out their forces, crossed over to Zaphon and said to Jephthah, "Why did you go to fight the Ammonites without calling us to go with you? We're going to burn down your house over your head."

2Jephthah answered, "I and my people were engaged in a great struggle with the Ammonites, and although I called, you didn't save me out of their hands. 3When I saw that you wouldn't help, I took my life in my hands and crossed over to fight the Ammonites, and the LORD gave me the victory over them. Now why have you come up today to fight me?"

4Jephthah then called together the men of Gilead and fought against Ephraim. The Gileadites struck them down because the Ephraimites had said, "You Gileadites are renegades from Ephraim and Manasseh." 5The Gileadites captured the fords of the Jordan leading to Ephraim, and whenever a survivor of Ephraim said, "Let me cross over," the men of Gilead asked him, "Are you an Ephraimite?" If he replied, "No," 6they said, "All right, say 'Shibboleth.' " If he said, "Sibboleth," because he could not pronounce the word correctly, they seized him and killed him at the fords of the Jordan. Forty-two thousand Ephraimites were killed at that time.

7Jephthah ledᵇ Israel six years. Then

ᵃ27 Or Ruler　　ᵇ7 Traditionally judged; also in verses 8-14

Jephthah the Gileadite died, and was buried in a town in Gilead.

Ibzan, Elon and Abdon

8After him, Ibzan of Bethlehem led Israel. 9He had thirty sons and thirty daughters. He gave his daughters away in marriage to those outside his clan, and for his sons he brought in thirty young women as wives from outside his clan. Ibzan led Israel seven years. 10Then Ibzan died, and was buried in Bethlehem.

11After him, Elon the Zebulunite led Israel ten years. 12Then Elon died, and was buried in Aijalon in the land of Zebulun.

13After him, Abdon son of Hillel, from Pirathon, led Israel. 14He had forty sons and thirty grandsons, who rode on seventy donkeys. He led Israel eight years. 15Then Abdon son of Hillel died, and was buried at Pirathon in Ephraim, in the hill country of the Amalekites.

The Birth of Samson

13 Again the Israelites did evil in the eyes of the LORD, so the LORD delivered them into the hands of the Philistines for forty years.

2A certain man of Zorah, named Manoah, from the clan of the Danites, had a wife who was sterile and remained childless. 3The angel of the LORD appeared to her and said, "You are sterile and childless, but you are going to conceive and have a son. 4Now see to it that you drink no wine or other fermented drink and that you do not eat anything unclean, 5because you will conceive and give birth to a son. No razor may be used on his head, because the boy is to be a Nazirite, set apart to God from birth, and he will begin the deliverance of Israel from the hands of the Philistines."

6Then the woman went to her husband and told him, "A man of God came to me. He looked like an angel of God, very awesome. I didn't ask him where he came from, and he didn't tell me his name. 7But he said to me, 'You will conceive and give birth to a son. Now then, drink no wine or other fermented drink and do not eat anything unclean, because the boy will be a Nazirite of God from birth until the day of his death.' "

8Then Manoah prayed to the LORD: "O Lord, I beg you, let the man of God you sent to us come again to teach us how to bring up the boy who is to be born."

9God heard Manoah, and the angel of God came again to the woman while she was out in the field; but her husband Manoah was not with her. 10The woman hurried to tell her husband, "He's here! The man who appeared to me the other day!"

11Manoah got up and followed his wife. When he came to the man, he said, "Are you the one who talked to my wife?"

"I am," he said.

12So Manoah asked him, "When your words are fulfilled, what is to be the rule for the boy's life and work?"

13The angel of the LORD answered, "Your wife must do all that I have told her. 14She must not eat anything that comes from the grapevine, nor drink any wine or other fermented drink nor eat anything unclean. She must do everything I have commanded her."

15Manoah said to the angel of the LORD, "We would like you to stay until we prepare a young goat for you."

16The angel of the LORD replied, "Even though you detain me, I will not eat any of your food. But if you prepare a burnt offering, offer it to the LORD." (Manoah did not realize that it was the angel of the LORD.)

17Then Manoah inquired of the angel of the LORD, "What is your name, so that we may honor you when your word comes true?"

18He replied, "Why do you ask my name? It is beyond understanding.[a]"

19Then Manoah took a young goat, together with the grain offering, and sacrificed it on a rock to the LORD. And the LORD did an amazing thing while Manoah and his wife watched: 20As the flame blazed up from the altar toward heaven, the angel of the LORD ascended in the flame. Seeing this, Manoah and his wife fell with their faces to the ground. 21When the angel of the LORD did not show himself again to Manoah and his wife, Manoah realized that it was the angel of the LORD.

22"We are doomed to die!" he said to his wife. "We have seen God!"

23But his wife answered, "If the LORD had meant to kill us, he would not have accepted a burnt offering and grain offering from our hands, nor shown us all these things or now told us this."

24The woman gave birth to a boy and named him Samson. He grew and the LORD blessed him, 25and the Spirit of the

---

a18 Or is wonderful

VERSE FOR THE DAY:
Judges 13:8

AUTHOR:
Jean E. Syswerda

PASSAGE FOR THE DAY:
Judges 13:1–14

Help for Parents

IT was early evening, and my eight-year-old son was out on the driveway practicing basketball. Over and over he grabbed the basketball and shot at the hoop high over his head. I watched this familiar little stranger, with his cut-off sweat pants (like his basketball-playing uncles) and his dimples (like his dad) and his close-shaved haircut (like no one but himself), and I couldn't believe how stubbornly he kept trying to put the ball through the hoop.

Then again, I could believe it. Stubbornness is one of his major traits.

As I stood on our front porch watching him, I felt overwhelmed . . . overwhelmed by the strength of my love for him and overwhelmed by my part in the task of building a Christian adult out of him.

And that's where Manoah comes in.

He felt the same way I do sometimes. And he knew where to go for help.

> "O Lord, I beg you, let the man of God [an angel]
> you sent to us come again to teach us how to bring
> up the boy who is to be born" (Judges 13:8).

Then verse nine is the clincher: "God heard Manoah, and the angel of God came again."

Now I can't say as I've asked lately for an angelic visit for help in raising my family, but I've certainly called on, even cried out to, God for help.

And his "angels" have come to my aid in the most unexpected ways: An elderly neighbor woman who tells me (I needed the reminder) what wonderful kids I've got. My mom who calls and encourages me. My husband who comes home from work and pitches in to help. A friend who calls and affirms a decision I made regarding my teenager.

Maybe they don't wear wings, but they were certainly God's "angels" in answer to my call for help.

Additional Scripture Readings:
Philippians 2:1–4; Hebrews 10:22–25

*Go to page 272 for your next
devotional reading.*

LORD began to stir him while he was in Mahaneh Dan, between Zorah and Eshtaol.

Samson's Marriage

14 Samson went down to Timnah and saw there a young Philistine woman. ²When he returned, he said to his father and mother, "I have seen a Philistine woman in Timnah; now get her for me as my wife."

³His father and mother replied, "Isn't there an acceptable woman among your relatives or among all our people? Must you go to the uncircumcised Philistines to get a wife?"

But Samson said to his father, "Get her for me. She's the right one for me." ⁴(His parents did not know that this was from the LORD, who was seeking an occasion to confront the Philistines; for at that time they were ruling over Israel.) ⁵Samson went down to Timnah together with his father and mother. As they approached the vineyards of Timnah, suddenly a young lion came roaring toward him. ⁶The Spirit of the LORD came upon him in power so that he tore the lion apart with his bare hands as he might have torn a young goat. But he told neither his father nor his mother what he had done. ⁷Then he went down and talked with the woman, and he liked her.

⁸Some time later, when he went back to marry her, he turned aside to look at the lion's carcass. In it was a swarm of bees and some honey, ⁹which he scooped out with his hands and ate as he went along. When he rejoined his parents, he gave them some, and they too ate it. But he did not tell them that he had taken the honey from the lion's carcass.

¹⁰Now his father went down to see the woman. And Samson made a feast there, as was customary for bridegrooms. ¹¹When he appeared, he was given thirty companions.

¹²"Let me tell you a riddle," Samson said to them. "If you can give me the answer within the seven days of the feast, I will give you thirty linen garments and thirty sets of clothes. ¹³If you can't tell me the answer, you must give me thirty linen garments and thirty sets of clothes."

"Tell us your riddle," they said. "Let's hear it."

¹⁴He replied,

"Out of the eater, something to eat;
    out of the strong, something
    sweet."

For three days they could not give the answer.

¹⁵On the fourth ᵃ day, they said to Samson's wife, "Coax your husband into explaining the riddle for us, or we will burn you and your father's household to death. Did you invite us here to rob us?"

¹⁶Then Samson's wife threw herself on him, sobbing, "You hate me! You don't really love me. You've given my people a riddle, but you haven't told me the answer."

"I haven't even explained it to my father or mother," he replied, "so why should I explain it to you?" ¹⁷She cried the whole seven days of the feast. So on the seventh day he finally told her, because she continued to press him. She in turn explained the riddle to her people.

¹⁸Before sunset on the seventh day the men of the town said to him,

"What is sweeter than honey?
    What is stronger than a lion?"

Samson said to them,

"If you had not plowed with my
    heifer,
    you would not have solved my
    riddle."

¹⁹Then the Spirit of the LORD came upon him in power. He went down to Ashkelon, struck down thirty of their men, stripped them of their belongings and gave their clothes to those who had explained the riddle. Burning with anger, he went up to his father's house. ²⁰And Samson's wife was given to the friend who had attended him at his wedding.

Samson's Vengeance on the Philistines

15 Later on, at the time of wheat harvest, Samson took a young goat and went to visit his wife. He said, "I'm going to my wife's room." But her father would not let him go in.

²"I was so sure you thoroughly hated her," he said, "that I gave her to your friend. Isn't her younger sister more attractive? Take her instead."

³Samson said to them, "This time I have a right to get even with the Philistines; I will really harm them." ⁴So he

---

ᵃ15 Some Septuagint manuscripts and Syriac; Hebrew *seventh* went out and caught three hundred foxes and tied them tail to tail in pairs. He then fastened a torch to every pair of tails, 5lit the torches and let the foxes loose in the standing grain of the Philistines. He burned up the shocks and standing grain, together with the vineyards and olive groves.

6When the Philistines asked, "Who did this?" they were told, "Samson, the Timnite's son-in-law, because his wife was given to his friend."

So the Philistines went up and burned her and her father to death. 7Samson said to them, "Since you've acted like this, I won't stop until I get my revenge on you." 8He attacked them viciously and slaughtered many of them. Then he went down and stayed in a cave in the rock of Etam.

9The Philistines went up and camped in Judah, spreading out near Lehi. 10The men of Judah asked, "Why have you come to fight us?"

"We have come to take Samson prisoner," they answered, "to do to him as he did to us."

11Then three thousand men from Judah went down to the cave in the rock of Etam and said to Samson, "Don't you realize that the Philistines are rulers over us? What have you done to us?"

He answered, "I merely did to them what they did to me."

12They said to him, "We've come to tie you up and hand you over to the Philistines."

Samson said, "Swear to me that you won't kill me yourselves."

13"Agreed," they answered. "We will only tie you up and hand you over to them. We will not kill you." So they bound him with two new ropes and led him up from the rock. 14As he approached Lehi, the Philistines came toward him shouting. The Spirit of the Lord came upon him in power. The ropes on his arms became like charred flax, and the bindings dropped from his hands. 15Finding a fresh jawbone of a donkey, he grabbed it and struck down a thousand men.

16Then Samson said,

"With a donkey's jawbone
  I have made donkeys of them.a
With a donkey's jawbone
  I have killed a thousand men."

17When he finished speaking, he threw away the jawbone; and the place was called Ramath Lehi.b

18Because he was very thirsty, he cried out to the Lord, "You have given your servant this great victory. Must I now die of thirst and fall into the hands of the uncircumcised?" 19Then God opened up the hollow place in Lehi, and water came out of it. When Samson drank, his strength returned and he revived. So the spring was called En Hakkore,c and it is still there in Lehi.

20Samson ledd Israel for twenty years in the days of the Philistines.

Samson and Delilah

16 One day Samson went to Gaza, where he saw a prostitute. He went in to spend the night with her. 2The people of Gaza were told, "Samson is here!" So they surrounded the place and lay in wait for him all night at the city gate. They made no move during the night, saying, "At dawn we'll kill him."

3But Samson lay there only until the middle of the night. Then he got up and took hold of the doors of the city gate, together with the two posts, and tore them loose, bar and all. He lifted them to his shoulders and carried them to the top of the hill that faces Hebron.

4Some time later, he fell in love with a woman in the Valley of Sorek whose name was Delilah. 5The rulers of the Philistines went to her and said, "See if you can lure him into showing you the secret of his great strength and how we can overpower him so we may tie him up and subdue him. Each one of us will give you eleven hundred shekelse of silver."

6So Delilah said to Samson, "Tell me the secret of your great strength and how you can be tied up and subdued."

7Samson answered her, "If anyone ties me with seven fresh thongsf that have not been dried, I'll become as weak as any other man."

8Then the rulers of the Philistines brought her seven fresh thongs that had not been dried, and she tied him with them. 9With men hidden in the room, she called to him, "Samson, the Philistines are upon you!" But he snapped the thongs as easily as a piece of string snaps when it comes close to a flame. So the

---

a16 Or made a heap or two; the Hebrew for donkey sounds like the Hebrew for heap.   b17 Ramath Lehi means jawbone hill.   c19 En Hakkore means caller's spring.   d20 Traditionally judged   e5 That is, about 28 pounds (about 13 kilograms)   f7 Or bowstrings; also in verses 8 and 9 secret of his strength was not discovered.

[10]Then Delilah said to Samson, "You have made a fool of me; you lied to me. Come now, tell me how you can be tied."

[11]He said, "If anyone ties me securely with new ropes that have never been used, I'll become as weak as any other man."

[12]So Delilah took new ropes and tied him with them. Then, with men hidden in the room, she called to him, "Samson, the Philistines are upon you!" But he snapped the ropes off his arms as if they were threads.

[13]Delilah then said to Samson, "Until now, you have been making a fool of me and lying to me. Tell me how you can be tied."

He replied, "If you weave the seven braids of my head into the fabric on the loom, and tighten it with the pin, I'll become as weak as any other man." So while he was sleeping, Delilah took the seven braids of his head, wove them into the fabric [14]and[a] tightened it with the pin.

Again she called to him, "Samson, the Philistines are upon you!" He awoke from his sleep and pulled up the pin and the loom, with the fabric.

[15]Then she said to him, "How can you say, 'I love you,' when you won't confide in me? This is the third time you have made a fool of me and haven't told me the secret of your great strength." [16]With such nagging she prodded him day after day until he was tired to death.

[17]So he told her everything. "No razor has ever been used on my head," he said, "because I have been a Nazirite set apart to God since birth. If my head were shaved, my strength would leave me, and I would become as weak as any other man."

[18]When Delilah saw that he had told her everything, she sent word to the rulers of the Philistines, "Come back once more; he has told me everything." So the rulers of the Philistines returned with the silver in their hands. [19]Having put him to sleep on her lap, she called a man to shave off the seven braids of his hair, and so began to subdue him.[b] And his strength left him.

[20]Then she called, "Samson, the Philistines are upon you!"

He awoke from his sleep and thought,

"I'll go out as before and shake myself free." But he did not know that the LORD had left him.

[21]Then the Philistines seized him, gouged out his eyes and took him down to Gaza. Binding him with bronze shackles, they set him to grinding in the prison. [22]But the hair on his head began to grow again after it had been shaved.

The Death of Samson

[23]Now the rulers of the Philistines assembled to offer a great sacrifice to Dagon their god and to celebrate, saying, "Our god has delivered Samson, our enemy, into our hands."

[24]When the people saw him, they praised their god, saying,

"Our god has delivered our enemy
  into our hands,
the one who laid waste our land
  and multiplied our slain."

[25]While they were in high spirits, they shouted, "Bring out Samson to entertain us." So they called Samson out of the prison, and he performed for them.

When they stood him among the pillars, [26]Samson said to the servant who held his hand, "Put me where I can feel the pillars that support the temple, so that I may lean against them." [27]Now the temple was crowded with men and women; all the rulers of the Philistines were there, and on the roof were about three thousand men and women watching Samson perform. [28]Then Samson prayed to the LORD, "O Sovereign LORD, remember me. O God, please strengthen me just once more, and let me with one blow get revenge on the Philistines for my two eyes." [29]Then Samson reached toward the two central pillars on which the temple stood. Bracing himself against them, his right hand on the one and his left hand on the other, [30]Samson said, "Let me die with the Philistines!" Then he pushed with all his might, and down came the temple on the rulers and all the people in it. Thus he killed many more when he died than while he lived.

[31]Then his brothers and his father's whole family went down to get him. They brought him back and buried him between Zorah and Eshtaol in the tomb of

---

[a]13,14 Some Septuagint manuscripts; Hebrew "I can, if you weave the seven braids of my head into the fabric on the loom." 14So she   [b]19 Hebrew; some Septuagint manuscripts and he began to weaken

Manoah his father. He had led[a] Israel twenty years.

Micah's Idols

17 Now a man named Micah from the hill country of Ephraim [2]said to his mother, "The eleven hundred shekels[b] of silver that were taken from you and about which I heard you utter a curse—I have that silver with me; I took it."

Then his mother said, "The LORD bless you, my son!"

[3]When he returned the eleven hundred shekels of silver to his mother, she said, "I solemnly consecrate my silver to the LORD for my son to make a carved image and a cast idol. I will give it back to you."

[4]So he returned the silver to his mother, and she took two hundred shekels[c] of silver and gave them to a silversmith, who made them into the image and the idol. And they were put in Micah's house.

[5]Now this man Micah had a shrine, and he made an ephod and some idols and installed one of his sons as his priest. [6]In those days Israel had no king; everyone did as he saw fit.

[7]A young Levite from Bethlehem in Judah, who had been living within the clan of Judah, [8]left that town in search of some other place to stay. On his way[d] he came to Micah's house in the hill country of Ephraim.

[9]Micah asked him, "Where are you from?"

"I'm a Levite from Bethlehem in Judah," he said, "and I'm looking for a place to stay."

[10]Then Micah said to him, "Live with me and be my father and priest, and I'll give you ten shekels[e] of silver a year, your clothes and your food." [11]So the Levite agreed to live with him, and the young man was to him like one of his sons. [12]Then Micah installed the Levite, and the young man became his priest and lived in his house. [13]And Micah said, "Now I know that the LORD will be good to me, since this Levite has become my priest."

Danites Settle in Laish

18 In those days Israel had no king. And in those days the tribe of the Danites was seeking a place of their own where they might settle, because they had not yet come into an inheritance among the tribes of Israel. [2]So the Danites sent five warriors from Zorah and Eshtaol to spy out the land and explore it. These men represented all their clans. They told them, "Go, explore the land."

The men entered the hill country of Ephraim and came to the house of Micah, where they spent the night. [3]When they were near Micah's house, they recognized the voice of the young Levite; so they turned in there and asked him, "Who brought you here? What are you doing in this place? Why are you here?"

[4]He told them what Micah had done for him, and said, "He has hired me and I am his priest."

[5]Then they said to him, "Please inquire of God to learn whether our journey will be successful."

[6]The priest answered them, "Go in peace. Your journey has the LORD's approval."

[7]So the five men left and came to Laish, where they saw that the people were living in safety, like the Sidonians, unsuspecting and secure. And since their land lacked nothing, they were prosperous.[f] Also, they lived a long way from the Sidonians and had no relationship with anyone else.[g]

[8]When they returned to Zorah and Eshtaol, their brothers asked them, "How did you find things?"

[9]They answered, "Come on, let's attack them! We have seen that the land is very good. Aren't you going to do something? Don't hesitate to go there and take it over. [10]When you get there, you will find an unsuspecting people and a spacious land that God has put into your hands, a land that lacks nothing whatever."

[11]Then six hundred men from the clan of the Danites, armed for battle, set out from Zorah and Eshtaol. [12]On their way they set up camp near Kiriath Jearim in Judah. This is why the place west of Kiriath Jearim is called Mahaneh Dan[h] to this day. [13]From there they went on to the hill country of Ephraim and came to Micah's house.

[14]Then the five men who had spied out the land of Laish said to their brothers, "Do you know that one of these houses

---

a31 Traditionally *judged*   b2 That is, about 28 pounds (about 13 kilograms)   c4 That is, about 5 pounds (about 2.3 kilograms)   d8 Or *To carry on his profession*   e10 That is, about 4 ounces (about 110 grams)   f7 The meaning of the Hebrew for this clause is uncertain.   g7 Hebrew; some Septuagint manuscripts *with the Arameans*   h12 *Mahaneh Dan* means *Dan's camp.*

has an ephod, other household gods, a carved image and a cast idol? Now you know what to do." 15So they turned in there and went to the house of the young Levite at Micah's place and greeted him. 16The six hundred Danites, armed for battle, stood at the entrance to the gate. 17The five men who had spied out the land went inside and took the carved image, the ephod, the other household gods and the cast idol while the priest and the six hundred armed men stood at the entrance to the gate.

18When these men went into Micah's house and took the carved image, the ephod, the other household gods and the cast idol, the priest said to them, "What are you doing?"

19They answered him, "Be quiet! Don't say a word. Come with us, and be our father and priest. Isn't it better that you serve a tribe and clan in Israel as priest rather than just one man's household?" 20Then the priest was glad. He took the ephod, the other household gods and the carved image and went along with the people. 21Putting their little children, their livestock and their possessions in front of them, they turned away and left.

22When they had gone some distance from Micah's house, the men who lived near Micah were called together and overtook the Danites. 23As they shouted after them, the Danites turned and said to Micah, "What's the matter with you that you called out your men to fight?"

24He replied, "You took the gods I made, and my priest, and went away. What else do I have? How can you ask, 'What's the matter with you?' "

25The Danites answered, "Don't argue with us, or some hot-tempered men will attack you, and you and your family will lose your lives." 26So the Danites went their way, and Micah, seeing that they were too strong for him, turned around and went back home.

27Then they took what Micah had made, and his priest, and went on to Laish, against a peaceful and unsuspecting people. They attacked them with the sword and burned down their city. 28There was no one to rescue them because they lived a long way from Sidon and had no relationship with anyone else. The city was in a valley near Beth Rehob.

The Danites rebuilt the city and settled there. 29They named it Dan after their forefather Dan, who was born to Israel— though the city used to be called Laish. 30There the Danites set up for themselves the idols, and Jonathan son of Gershom, the son of Moses,ᵃ and his sons were priests for the tribe of Dan until the time of the captivity of the land. 31They continued to use the idols Micah had made, all the time the house of God was in Shiloh.

A Levite and His Concubine

19 In those days Israel had no king.
Now a Levite who lived in a remote area in the hill country of Ephraim took a concubine from Bethlehem in Judah. 2But she was unfaithful to him. She left him and went back to her father's house in Bethlehem, Judah. After she had been there four months, 3her husband went to her to persuade her to return. He had with him his servant and two donkeys. She took him into her father's house, and when her father saw him, he gladly welcomed him. 4His father-in-law, the girl's father, prevailed upon him to stay; so he remained with him three days, eating and drinking, and sleeping there.

5On the fourth day they got up early and he prepared to leave, but the girl's father said to his son-in-law, "Refresh yourself with something to eat; then you can go." 6So the two of them sat down to eat and drink together. Afterward the girl's father said, "Please stay tonight and enjoy yourself." 7And when the man got up to go, his father-in-law persuaded him, so he stayed there that night. 8On the morning of the fifth day, when he rose to go, the girl's father said, "Refresh yourself. Wait till afternoon!" So the two of them ate together.

9Then when the man, with his concubine and his servant, got up to leave, his father-in-law, the girl's father, said, "Now look, it's almost evening. Spend the night here; the day is nearly over. Stay and enjoy yourself. Early tomorrow morning you can get up and be on your way home." 10But, unwilling to stay another night, the man left and went toward Jebus (that is, Jerusalem), with his two saddled donkeys and his concubine.

11When they were near Jebus and the day was almost gone, the servant said to his master, "Come, let's stop at this city of the Jebusites and spend the night."

ᵃ30 An ancient Hebrew scribal tradition, some Septuagint manuscripts and Vulgate; Masoretic Text *Manasseh*

¹²His master replied, "No. We won't go into an alien city, whose people are not Israelites. We will go on to Gibeah." ¹³He added, "Come, let's try to reach Gibeah or Ramah and spend the night in one of those places." ¹⁴So they went on, and the sun set as they neared Gibeah in Benjamin. ¹⁵There they stopped to spend the night. They went and sat in the city square, but no one took them into his home for the night.

¹⁶That evening an old man from the hill country of Ephraim, who was living in Gibeah (the men of the place were Benjamites), came in from his work in the fields. ¹⁷When he looked and saw the traveler in the city square, the old man asked, "Where are you going? Where did you come from?"

¹⁸He answered, "We are on our way from Bethlehem in Judah to a remote area in the hill country of Ephraim where I live. I have been to Bethlehem in Judah and now I am going to the house of the LORD. No one has taken me into his house. ¹⁹We have both straw and fodder for our donkeys and bread and wine for ourselves your servants—me, your maidservant, and the young man with us. We don't need anything."

²⁰"You are welcome at my house," the old man said. "Let me supply whatever you need. Only don't spend the night in the square." ²¹So he took him into his house and fed his donkeys. After they had washed their feet, they had something to eat and drink.

²²While they were enjoying themselves, some of the wicked men of the city surrounded the house. Pounding on the door, they shouted to the old man who owned the house, "Bring out the man who came to your house so we can have sex with him."

²³The owner of the house went outside and said to them, "No, my friends, don't be so vile. Since this man is my guest, don't do this disgraceful thing. ²⁴Look, here is my virgin daughter, and his concubine. I will bring them out to you now, and you can use them and do to them whatever you wish. But to this man, don't do such a disgraceful thing."

²⁵But the men would not listen to him. So the man took his concubine and sent her outside to them, and they raped her and abused her throughout the night, and at dawn they let her go. ²⁶At daybreak the woman went back to the house where her master was staying, fell down at the door and lay there until daylight.

²⁷When her master got up in the morning and opened the door of the house and stepped out to continue on his way, there lay his concubine, fallen in the doorway of the house, with her hands on the threshold. ²⁸He said to her, "Get up; let's go." But there was no answer. Then the man put her on his donkey and set out for home.

²⁹When he reached home, he took a knife and cut up his concubine, limb by limb, into twelve parts and sent them into all the areas of Israel. ³⁰Everyone who saw it said, "Such a thing has never been seen or done, not since the day the Israelites came up out of Egypt. Think about it! Consider it! Tell us what to do!"

Israelites Fight the Benjamites

20 Then all the Israelites from Dan to Beersheba and from the land of Gilead came out as one man and assembled before the LORD in Mizpah. ²The leaders of all the people of the tribes of Israel took their places in the assembly of the people of God, four hundred thousand soldiers armed with swords. ³(The Benjamites heard that the Israelites had gone up to Mizpah.) Then the Israelites said, "Tell us how this awful thing happened."

⁴So the Levite, the husband of the murdered woman, said, "I and my concubine came to Gibeah in Benjamin to spend the night. ⁵During the night the men of Gibeah came after me and surrounded the house, intending to kill me. They raped my concubine, and she died. ⁶I took my concubine, cut her into pieces and sent one piece to each region of Israel's inheritance, because they committed this lewd and disgraceful act in Israel. ⁷Now, all you Israelites, speak up and give your verdict."

⁸All the people rose as one man, saying, "None of us will go home. No, not one of us will return to his house. ⁹But now this is what we'll do to Gibeah: We'll go up against it as the lot directs. ¹⁰We'll take ten men out of every hundred from all the tribes of Israel, and a hundred from a thousand, and a thousand from ten thousand, to get provisions for the army. Then, when the army arrives at Gibeah*ᵃ* in Benjamin, it can give them what they

---

ᵃ10 One Hebrew manuscript; most Hebrew manuscripts Geba, a variant of Gibeah deserve for all this vileness done in Israel." ¹¹So all the men of Israel got together and united as one man against the city.

¹²The tribes of Israel sent men throughout the tribe of Benjamin, saying, "What about this awful crime that was committed among you? ¹³Now surrender those wicked men of Gibeah so that we may put them to death and purge the evil from Israel."

But the Benjamites would not listen to their fellow Israelites. ¹⁴From their towns they came together at Gibeah to fight against the Israelites. ¹⁵At once the Benjamites mobilized twenty-six thousand swordsmen from their towns, in addition to seven hundred chosen men from those living in Gibeah. ¹⁶Among all these soldiers there were seven hundred chosen men who were left-handed, each of whom could sling a stone at a hair and not miss.

¹⁷Israel, apart from Benjamin, mustered four hundred thousand swordsmen, all of them fighting men.

¹⁸The Israelites went up to Bethel*ᵃ* and inquired of God. They said, "Who of us shall go first to fight against the Benjamites?"

The LORD replied, "Judah shall go first."

¹⁹The next morning the Israelites got up and pitched camp near Gibeah. ²⁰The men of Israel went out to fight the Benjamites and took up battle positions against them at Gibeah. ²¹The Benjamites came out of Gibeah and cut down twenty-two thousand Israelites on the battlefield that day. ²²But the men of Israel encouraged one another and again took up their positions where they had stationed themselves the first day. ²³The Israelites went up and wept before the LORD until evening, and they inquired of the LORD. They said, "Shall we go up again to battle against the Benjamites, our brothers?"

The LORD answered, "Go up against them."

²⁴Then the Israelites drew near to Benjamin the second day. ²⁵This time, when the Benjamites came out from Gibeah to oppose them, they cut down another eighteen thousand Israelites, all of them armed with swords.

²⁶Then the Israelites, all the people, went up to Bethel, and there they sat weeping before the LORD. They fasted that day until evening and presented burnt offerings and fellowship offeringsᵇ to the LORD. ²⁷And the Israelites inquired of the LORD. (In those days the ark of the covenant of God was there, ²⁸with Phinehas son of Eleazar, the son of Aaron, ministering before it.) They asked, "Shall we go up again to battle with Benjamin our brother, or not?"

The LORD responded, "Go, for tomorrow I will give them into your hands."

²⁹Then Israel set an ambush around Gibeah. ³⁰They went up against the Benjamites on the third day and took up positions against Gibeah as they had done before. ³¹The Benjamites came out to meet them and were drawn away from the city. They began to inflict casualties on the Israelites as before, so that about thirty men fell in the open field and on the roads—the one leading to Bethel and the other to Gibeah.

³²While the Benjamites were saying, "We are defeating them as before," the Israelites were saying, "Let's retreat and draw them away from the city to the roads."

³³All the men of Israel moved from their places and took up positions at Baal Tamar, and the Israelite ambush charged out of its place on the westᶜ of Gibeah.ᵈ ³⁴Then ten thousand of Israel's finest men made a frontal attack on Gibeah. The fighting was so heavy that the Benjamites did not realize how near disaster was. ³⁵The LORD defeated Benjamin before Israel, and on that day the Israelites struck down 25,100 Benjamites, all armed with swords. ³⁶Then the Benjamites saw that they were beaten.

Now the men of Israel had given way before Benjamin, because they relied on the ambush they had set near Gibeah. ³⁷The men who had been in ambush made a sudden dash into Gibeah, spread out and put the whole city to the sword. ³⁸The men of Israel had arranged with the ambush that they should send up a great cloud of smoke from the city, ³⁹and then the men of Israel would turn in the battle.

The Benjamites had begun to inflict casualties on the men of Israel (about thirty), and they said, "We are defeating them as in the first battle." ⁴⁰But when the column of smoke began to rise from the city, the Benjamites turned and saw the

ᵃ18 Or *to the house of God*; also in verse 26   ᵇ26 Traditionally *peace offerings*   ᶜ33 Some Septuagint manuscripts and Vulgate; the meaning of the Hebrew for this word is uncertain.   ᵈ33 Hebrew *Geba*, a variant of *Gibeah* smoke of the whole city going up into the sky. ⁴¹Then the men of Israel turned on them, and the men of Benjamin were terrified, because they realized that disaster had come upon them. ⁴²So they fled before the Israelites in the direction of the desert, but they could not escape the battle. And the men of Israel who came out of the towns cut them down there. ⁴³They surrounded the Benjamites, chased them and easilyᵃ overran them in the vicinity of Gibeah on the east. ⁴⁴Eighteen thousand Benjamites fell, all of them valiant fighters. ⁴⁵As they turned and fled toward the desert to the rock of Rimmon, the Israelites cut down five thousand men along the roads. They kept pressing after the Benjamites as far as Gidom and struck down two thousand more.

⁴⁶On that day twenty-five thousand Benjamite swordsmen fell, all of them valiant fighters. ⁴⁷But six hundred men turned and fled into the desert to the rock of Rimmon, where they stayed four months. ⁴⁸The men of Israel went back to Benjamin and put all the towns to the sword, including the animals and everything else they found. All the towns they came across they set on fire.

Wives for the Benjamites

21 The men of Israel had taken an oath at Mizpah: "Not one of us will give his daughter in marriage to a Benjamite."

²The people went to Bethel,ᵇ where they sat before God until evening, raising their voices and weeping bitterly. ³"O LORD, the God of Israel," they cried, "why has this happened to Israel? Why should one tribe be missing from Israel today?"

⁴Early the next day the people built an altar and presented burnt offerings and fellowship offerings.ᶜ

⁵Then the Israelites asked, "Who from all the tribes of Israel has failed to assemble before the LORD?" For they had taken a solemn oath that anyone who failed to assemble before the LORD at Mizpah should certainly be put to death.

⁶Now the Israelites grieved for their brothers, the Benjamites. "Today one tribe is cut off from Israel," they said. ⁷"How can we provide wives for those who are left, since we have taken an oath by the LORD not to give them any of our daughters in marriage?" ⁸Then they

asked, "Which one of the tribes of Israel failed to assemble before the LORD at Mizpah?" They discovered that no one from Jabesh Gilead had come to the camp for the assembly. ⁹For when they counted the people, they found that none of the people of Jabesh Gilead were there.

¹⁰So the assembly sent twelve thousand fighting men with instructions to go to Jabesh Gilead and put to the sword those living there, including the women and children. ¹¹"This is what you are to do," they said. "Kill every male and every woman who is not a virgin." ¹²They found among the people living in Jabesh Gilead four hundred young women who had never slept with a man, and they took them to the camp at Shiloh in Canaan.

¹³Then the whole assembly sent an offer of peace to the Benjamites at the rock of Rimmon. ¹⁴So the Benjamites returned at that time and were given the women of Jabesh Gilead who had been spared. But there were not enough for all of them.

¹⁵The people grieved for Benjamin, because the LORD had made a gap in the tribes of Israel. ¹⁶And the elders of the assembly said, "With the women of Benjamin destroyed, how shall we provide wives for the men who are left? ¹⁷The Benjamite survivors must have heirs," they said, "so that a tribe of Israel will not be wiped out. ¹⁸We can't give them our daughters as wives, since we Israelites have taken this oath: 'Cursed be anyone who gives a wife to a Benjamite.' ¹⁹But look, there is the annual festival of the LORD in Shiloh, to the north of Bethel, and east of the road that goes from Bethel to Shechem, and to the south of Lebonah."

²⁰So they instructed the Benjamites, saying, "Go and hide in the vineyards ²¹and watch. When the girls of Shiloh come out to join in the dancing, then rush from the vineyards and each of you seize a wife from the girls of Shiloh and go to the land of Benjamin. ²²When their fathers or brothers complain to us, we will say to them, 'Do us a kindness by helping them, because we did not get wives for them during the war, and you are innocent, since you did not give your daughters to them.' "

²³So that is what the Benjamites did. While the girls were dancing, each man caught one and carried her off to be his

---

ᵃ43 The meaning of the Hebrew for this word is uncertain.   ᵇ2 Or *to the house of God*
ᶜ4 Traditionally *peace offerings*

wife. Then they returned to their inheritance and rebuilt the towns and settled in them.

²⁴At that time the Israelites left that place and went home to their tribes and clans, each to his own inheritance.

²⁵In those days Israel had no king; everyone did as he saw fit.

*R*UTH'S *story, occurring during the time of the judges, recalls the tragedy of Elimelech's family. They desert God's land during a famine, but God still cares about them. When Naomi returns to Judah, her daughter-in-law Ruth marries Boaz to carry on the family name and becomes an ancestor of David and Jesus. As you read this book, think about how God cares about you even when you sin and how wonderful it is that he sent Jesus, son of David, into the world.*

RUTH

Naomi and Ruth

1 In the days when the judges ruled,*a* there was a famine in the land, and a man from Bethlehem in Judah, together with his wife and two sons, went to live for a while in the country of Moab. ²The man's name was Elimelech, his wife's name Naomi, and the names of his two sons were Mahlon and Kilion. They were Ephrathites from Bethlehem, Judah. And they went to Moab and lived there.

³Now Elimelech, Naomi's husband, died, and she was left with her two sons. ⁴They married Moabite women, one named Orpah and the other Ruth. After they had lived there about ten years, ⁵both Mahlon and Kilion also died, and Naomi was left without her two sons and her husband.

⁶When she heard in Moab that the LORD had come to the aid of his people by providing food for them, Naomi and her daughters-in-law prepared to return home from there. ⁷With her two daughters-in-law she left the place where she had been living and set out on the road that would take them back to the land of Judah.

a1 Traditionally judged

⁸Then Naomi said to her two daughters-in-law, "Go back, each of you, to your mother's home. May the LORD show kindness to you, as you have shown to your dead and to me. ⁹May the LORD grant that each of you will find rest in the home of another husband."

Then she kissed them and they wept aloud ¹⁰and said to her, "We will go back with you to your people."

¹¹But Naomi said, "Return home, my daughters. Why would you come with me? Am I going to have any more sons, who could become your husbands? ¹²Return home, my daughters; I am too old to have another husband. Even if I thought there was still hope for me—even if I had a husband tonight and then gave birth to sons— ¹³would you wait until they grew up? Would you remain unmarried for them? No, my daughters. It is more bitter for me than for you, because the LORD's hand has gone out against me!"

¹⁴At this they wept again. Then Orpah kissed her mother-in-law good-by, but Ruth clung to her.

¹⁵"Look," said Naomi, "your sister-in-law is going back to her people and her gods. Go back with her."

¹⁶But Ruth replied, "Don't urge me to leave you or to turn back from you. Where you go I will go, and where you stay I will stay. Your people will be my people and your God my God. ¹⁷Where you die I will die, and there I will be buried. May the LORD deal with me, be it ever so severely, if anything but death separates you and me." ¹⁸When Naomi realized that Ruth was determined to go with her, she stopped urging her.

¹⁹So the two women went on until they came to Bethlehem. When they arrived in Bethlehem, the whole town was stirred because of them, and the women exclaimed, "Can this be Naomi?"

²⁰"Don't call me Naomi,ᵃ" she told them. "Call me Mara,ᵇ because the Almightyᶜ has made my life very bitter. ²¹I went away full, but the LORD has brought me back empty. Why call me Naomi? The LORD has afflictedᵈ me; the Almighty has brought misfortune upon me."

²²So Naomi returned from Moab accompanied by Ruth the Moabitess, her daughter-in-law, arriving in Bethlehem as the barley harvest was beginning.

Ruth Meets Boaz

2 Now Naomi had a relative on her husband's side, from the clan of Elimelech, a man of standing, whose name was Boaz.

²And Ruth the Moabitess said to Naomi, "Let me go to the fields and pick up the leftover grain behind anyone in whose eyes I find favor."

Naomi said to her, "Go ahead, my daughter." ³So she went out and began to glean in the fields behind the harvesters. As it turned out, she found herself working in a field belonging to Boaz, who was from the clan of Elimelech.

⁴Just then Boaz arrived from Bethlehem and greeted the harvesters, "The LORD be with you!"

"The LORD bless you!" they called back.

⁵Boaz asked the foreman of his harvesters, "Whose young woman is that?"

⁶The foreman replied, "She is the Moabitess who came back from Moab with Naomi. ⁷She said, 'Please let me glean and gather among the sheaves behind the harvesters.' She went into the field and has worked steadily from morning till now, except for a short rest in the shelter."

⁸So Boaz said to Ruth, "My daughter, listen to me. Don't go and glean in another field and don't go away from here. Stay here with my servant girls. ⁹Watch the field where the men are harvesting, and follow along after the girls. I have told the men not to touch you. And whenever you are thirsty, go and get a drink from the water jars the men have filled."

¹⁰At this, she bowed down with her face to the ground. She exclaimed, "Why have I found such favor in your eyes that you notice me—a foreigner?"

¹¹Boaz replied, "I've been told all about what you have done for your mother-in-law since the death of your husband—how you left your father and mother and your homeland and came to live with a people you did not know before. ¹²May the LORD repay you for what you have done. May you be richly rewarded by the LORD, the God of Israel, under whose wings you have come to take refuge."

¹³"May I continue to find favor in your eyes, my lord," she said. "You have given me comfort and have spoken kindly to your servant—though I do not have the standing of one of your servant girls."

ᵃ20 Naomi means pleasant; also in verse 21.   ᵇ20 Mara means bitter.   ᶜ20 Hebrew Shaddai; also in verse 21   ᵈ21 Or has testified against

VERSE FOR THE DAY:
Ruth 1:16–17

AUTHOR:
Dorothy Patterson

PASSAGE FOR THE DAY:
Ruth 1:1–22

Commitment in Adversity

WHEN I made a commitment to marry a preacher, it was with joy, excitement and the dream of serving God with all my heart. Up to that point, I had experienced good health, success, achievement, praise and gratitude. I had every reason to expect that a life of ministry would mean more of the same—plus greater joy and usefulness. I was not prepared for serious and debilitating illness, the miscarriage of a baby, the trauma of a financially troubled church and personal attacks from the family of faith.

Within one of my husband's sermons, I found a nugget of hope: "Our adversities are God's universities." The adversities drove me to God, and God had what I needed to endure and fulfill the commitment I had made.

In Ruth 1:16–17 the innocent young widow Ruth expressed her passionate and devoted love for her old and bitter mother-in-law. It was not Naomi's beauty, wealth or even joyfulness that drew Ruth to her, for all of these had long since fallen away. Rather it was Naomi's faith in the living God, her spiritual wisdom and her consistent piety that bound the young pagan widow to her. Ruth made a commitment to travel, live and pursue life with Naomi, to accept her God and even to die and be buried in Naomi's homeland. Her commitment was not just with loving words and well-meaning feelings, as her sister-in-law Orpah (Ruth 1:14), but with purposeful love and devoted deeds.

Commitment must be fueled not merely by head knowledge but also by heart determination. Ruth had nothing to offer to Naomi or to God but herself, and that she gave willingly and eagerly. Every woman, whatever her circumstances or position, has at least that to give the Savior, and it is enough!

Additional Scripture Readings:
Esther 4:6–17; Hebrews 12:1–3

Go to page 277 for your next devotional reading.

¹⁴At mealtime Boaz said to her, "Come over here. Have some bread and dip it in the wine vinegar."

When she sat down with the harvesters, he offered her some roasted grain. She ate all she wanted and had some left over. ¹⁵As she got up to glean, Boaz gave orders to his men, "Even if she gathers among the sheaves, don't embarrass her. ¹⁶Rather, pull out some stalks for her from the bundles and leave them for her to pick up, and don't rebuke her."

¹⁷So Ruth gleaned in the field until evening. Then she threshed the barley she had gathered, and it amounted to about an ephah.ᵃ ¹⁸She carried it back to town, and her mother-in-law saw how much she had gathered. Ruth also brought out and gave her what she had left over after she had eaten enough.

¹⁹Her mother-in-law asked her, "Where did you glean today? Where did you work? Blessed be the man who took notice of you!"

Then Ruth told her mother-in-law about the one at whose place she had been working. "The name of the man I worked with today is Boaz," she said.

²⁰"The LORD bless him!" Naomi said to her daughter-in-law. "He has not stopped showing his kindness to the living and the dead." She added, "That man is our close relative; he is one of our kinsman-redeemers."

²¹Then Ruth the Moabitess said, "He even said to me, 'Stay with my workers until they finish harvesting all my grain.' "

²²Naomi said to Ruth her daughter-in-law, "It will be good for you, my daughter, to go with his girls, because in someone else's field you might be harmed."

²³So Ruth stayed close to the servant girls of Boaz to glean until the barley and wheat harvests were finished. And she lived with her mother-in-law.

Ruth and Boaz at the Threshing Floor

3 One day Naomi her mother-in-law said to her, "My daughter, should I not try to find a homeᵇ for you, where you will be well provided for? ²Is not Boaz, with whose servant girls you have been, a kinsman of ours? Tonight he will be winnowing barley on the threshing floor. ³Wash and perfume yourself, and put on your best clothes. Then go down to the threshing floor, but don't let him know you are there until he has finished eating and drinking. ⁴When he lies down, note the place where he is lying. Then go and uncover his feet and lie down. He will tell you what to do."

⁵"I will do whatever you say," Ruth answered. ⁶So she went down to the threshing floor and did everything her mother-in-law told her to do.

⁷When Boaz had finished eating and drinking and was in good spirits, he went over to lie down at the far end of the grain pile. Ruth approached quietly, uncovered his feet and lay down. ⁸In the middle of the night something startled the man, and he turned and discovered a woman lying at his feet.

⁹"Who are you?" he asked.

"I am your servant Ruth," she said. "Spread the corner of your garment over me, since you are a kinsman-redeemer."

¹⁰"The LORD bless you, my daughter," he replied. "This kindness is greater than that which you showed earlier: You have not run after the younger men, whether rich or poor. ¹¹And now, my daughter, don't be afraid. I will do for you all you ask. All my fellow townsmen know that you are a woman of noble character. ¹²Although it is true that I am near of kin, there is a kinsman-redeemer nearer than I. ¹³Stay here for the night, and in the morning if he wants to redeem, good; let him redeem. But if he is not willing, as surely as the LORD lives I will do it. Lie here until morning."

¹⁴So she lay at his feet until morning, but got up before anyone could be recognized; and he said, "Don't let it be known that a woman came to the threshing floor."

¹⁵He also said, "Bring me the shawl you are wearing and hold it out." When she did so, he poured into it six measures of barley and put it on her. Then heᶜ went back to town.

¹⁶When Ruth came to her mother-in-law, Naomi asked, "How did it go, my daughter?"

Then she told her everything Boaz had done for her ¹⁷and added, "He gave me these six measures of barley, saying, 'Don't go back to your mother-in-law empty-handed.' "

¹⁸Then Naomi said, "Wait, my daugh-

ter, until you find out what happens. For the man will not rest until the matter is settled today."

Boaz Marries Ruth

4 Meanwhile Boaz went up to the town gate and sat there. When the kinsman-redeemer he had mentioned came along, Boaz said, "Come over here, my friend, and sit down." So he went over and sat down.

[2]Boaz took ten of the elders of the town and said, "Sit here," and they did so. [3]Then he said to the kinsman-redeemer, "Naomi, who has come back from Moab, is selling the piece of land that belonged to our brother Elimelech. [4]I thought I should bring the matter to your attention and suggest that you buy it in the presence of these seated here and in the presence of the elders of my people. If you will redeem it, do so. But if you[a] will not, tell me, so I will know. For no one has the right to do it except you, and I am next in line."

"I will redeem it," he said.

[5]Then Boaz said, "On the day you buy the land from Naomi and from Ruth the Moabitess, you acquire[b] the dead man's widow, in order to maintain the name of the dead with his property."

[6]At this, the kinsman-redeemer said, "Then I cannot redeem it because I might endanger my own estate. You redeem it yourself. I cannot do it."

[7](Now in earlier times in Israel, for the redemption and transfer of property to become final, one party took off his sandal and gave it to the other. This was the method of legalizing transactions in Israel.)

[8]So the kinsman-redeemer said to Boaz, "Buy it yourself." And he removed his sandal.

[9]Then Boaz announced to the elders and all the people, "Today you are witnesses that I have bought from Naomi all the property of Elimelech, Kilion and Mahlon. [10]I have also acquired Ruth the Moabitess, Mahlon's widow, as my wife, in order to maintain the name of the dead with his property, so that his name will not disappear from among his family or from the town records. Today you are witnesses!"

[11]Then the elders and all those at the gate said, "We are witnesses. May the LORD make the woman who is coming into your home like Rachel and Leah, who together built up the house of Israel. May you have standing in Ephrathah and be famous in Bethlehem. [12]Through the offspring the LORD gives you by this young woman, may your family be like that of Perez, whom Tamar bore to Judah."

The Genealogy of David

[13]So Boaz took Ruth and she became his wife. Then he went to her, and the LORD enabled her to conceive, and she gave birth to a son. [14]The women said to Naomi: "Praise be to the LORD, who this day has not left you without a kinsman-redeemer. May he become famous throughout Israel! [15]He will renew your life and sustain you in your old age. For your daughter-in-law, who loves you and who is better to you than seven sons, has given him birth."

[16]Then Naomi took the child, laid him in her lap and cared for him. [17]The women living there said, "Naomi has a son." And they named him Obed. He was the father of Jesse, the father of David.

[18]This, then, is the family line of Perez:

Perez was the father of Hezron,
[19]Hezron the father of Ram,
    Ram the father of Amminadab,
[20]Amminadab the father of Nahshon,
    Nahshon the father of Salmon,[c]
[21]Salmon the father of Boaz,
    Boaz the father of Obed,
[22]Obed the father of Jesse,
    and Jesse the father of David.

---

[a]4 Many Hebrew manuscripts, Septuagint, Vulgate and Syriac; most Hebrew manuscripts *he*   [b]5 Hebrew; Vulgate and Syriac *Naomi, you acquire Ruth the Moabitess,*   [c]20 A few Hebrew manuscripts, some Septuagint manuscripts and Vulgate (see also verse 21 and Septuagint of 1 Chron. 2:11); most Hebrew manuscripts *Salma*

*T*HIS book tells the story of Samuel, the last judge, and of Saul, Israel's first king. Saul's sin and disobedience lead God to reject him and anoint David as Israel's second king. In spite of numerous threats to David's life from both the Philistines and from Saul, God keeps him safe. As you read this book, think how God will protect and bless you if you trust in him; be warned that if you disobey God, you may face many difficulties.

1 SAMUEL

The Birth of Samuel

1 There was a certain man from Ramathaim, a Zuphite*a* from the hill country of Ephraim, whose name was Elkanah son of Jeroham, the son of Elihu, the son of Tohu, the son of Zuph, an Ephraimite. [2] He had two wives; one was called Hannah and the other Peninnah. Peninnah had children, but Hannah had none.

[3] Year after year this man went up from his town to worship and sacrifice to the LORD Almighty at Shiloh, where Hophni and Phinehas, the two sons of Eli, were priests of the LORD. [4] Whenever the day came for Elkanah to sacrifice, he would give portions of the meat to his wife Peninnah and to all her sons and daughters. [5] But to Hannah he gave a double portion because he loved her, and the LORD had closed her womb. [6] And because the LORD had closed her womb, her rival kept provoking her in order to irritate her. [7] This went on year after year. Whenever Hannah went up to the house of the LORD, her rival provoked her till she wept and would not eat. [8] Elkanah her husband would say to her, "Hannah, why are you weeping? Why don't you eat? Why are you downhearted? Don't I mean more to you than ten sons?"

a1 Or from Ramathaim Zuphim

⁹Once when they had finished eating and drinking in Shiloh, Hannah stood up. Now Eli the priest was sitting on a chair by the doorpost of the LORD's temple.ᵃ ¹⁰In bitterness of soul Hannah wept much and prayed to the LORD. ¹¹And she made a vow, saying, "O LORD Almighty, if you will only look upon your servant's misery and remember me, and not forget your servant but give her a son, then I will give him to the LORD for all the days of his life, and no razor will ever be used on his head."

¹²As she kept on praying to the LORD, Eli observed her mouth. ¹³Hannah was praying in her heart, and her lips were moving but her voice was not heard. Eli thought she was drunk ¹⁴and said to her, "How long will you keep on getting drunk? Get rid of your wine."

¹⁵"Not so, my lord," Hannah replied, "I am a woman who is deeply troubled. I have not been drinking wine or beer; I was pouring out my soul to the LORD. ¹⁶Do not take your servant for a wicked woman; I have been praying here out of my great anguish and grief."

¹⁷Eli answered, "Go in peace, and may the God of Israel grant you what you have asked of him."

¹⁸She said, "May your servant find favor in your eyes." Then she went her way and ate something, and her face was no longer downcast.

¹⁹Early the next morning they arose and worshiped before the LORD and then went back to their home at Ramah. Elkanah lay with Hannah his wife, and the LORD remembered her. ²⁰So in the course of time Hannah conceived and gave birth to a son. She named him Samuel,ᵇ saying, "Because I asked the LORD for him."

Hannah Dedicates Samuel

²¹When the man Elkanah went up with all his family to offer the annual sacrifice to the LORD and to fulfill his vow, ²²Hannah did not go. She said to her husband, "After the boy is weaned, I will take him and present him before the LORD, and he will live there always."

²³"Do what seems best to you," Elkanah her husband told her. "Stay here until you have weaned him; only may the LORD make good hisᶜ word." So the woman stayed at home and nursed her son until she had weaned him.

²⁴After he was weaned, she took the boy with her, young as he was, along with a three-year-old bull,ᵈ an ephahᵉ of flour and a skin of wine, and brought him to the house of the LORD at Shiloh. ²⁵When they had slaughtered the bull, they brought the boy to Eli, ²⁶and she said to him, "As surely as you live, my lord, I am the woman who stood here beside you praying to the LORD. ²⁷I prayed for this child, and the LORD has granted me what I asked of him. ²⁸So now I give him to the LORD. For his whole life he will be given over to the LORD." And he worshiped the LORD there.

Hannah's Prayer

2 Then Hannah prayed and said:

"My heart rejoices in the LORD;
　in the LORD my hornᶠ is lifted high.
My mouth boasts over my enemies,
　for I delight in your deliverance.

²"There is no one holyᵍ like the LORD;
　there is no one besides you;
　there is no Rock like our God.

³"Do not keep talking so proudly
　or let your mouth speak such
　　arrogance,
for the LORD is a God who knows,
　and by him deeds are weighed.

⁴"The bows of the warriors are broken,
　but those who stumbled are armed
　　with strength.
⁵Those who were full hire themselves
　　out for food,
　but those who were hungry hunger
　　no more.
She who was barren has borne seven
　　children,
　but she who has had many sons
　　pines away.

⁶"The LORD brings death and makes
　　alive;
　he brings down to the graveʰ and
　　raises up.
⁷The LORD sends poverty and wealth;
　he humbles and he exalts.
⁸He raises the poor from the dust
　and lifts the needy from the ash
　　heap;
　he seats them with princes

ᵃ9 That is, tabernacle ᵇ20 Samuel sounds like the Hebrew for heard of God. ᶜ23 Masoretic Text; Dead Sea Scrolls, Septuagint and Syriac your ᵈ24 Dead Sea Scrolls, Septuagint and Syriac; Masoretic Text with three bulls ᵉ24 That is, probably about 3/5 bushel (about 22 liters) ᶠ1 Horn here symbolizes strength; also in verse 10. ᵍ2 Or no Holy One ʰ6 Hebrew Sheol

VERSE FOR THE DAY:
1 Samuel 1:10

AUTHOR:
Gladys M. Hunt

PASSAGE FOR THE DAY:
1 Samuel 1:1 — 2:11

Hannah's Prayers

WAITING is one of the hardest things we do, especially when the years go by and we see no fulfillment of our dreams and hopes. It's a good thing to learn to wait; we spend a large amount of our lives waiting.

Hannah knew the misery of waiting for dreams that did not come true. She was childless. It didn't help that the second wife her husband had taken (did he take her because Hannah was barren?) mocked Hannah by gloating over her many children. Even her husband Elkanah didn't seem to understand her acute distress.

When Hannah poured out her agony before God, Eli the priest didn't understand either. He thought she was drunk. Yet something about going before God and spelling out her trouble reminded Hannah who God was. She expected him to *look* on her, to *remember,* and to *give* her a son. She went away contented (1 Samuel 1:18). God understood; he would remember her.

Hannah's prayers were answered. She conceived and had a son. When he was old enough, she took him, as she had promised, to the house of the Lord and gave him back to God.

Hannah's second prayer (1 Samuel 2:1–11) is far different from the pain of her first prayer in 1 Samuel 1:11. It's an amazing song of praise to the God whom she sees as sovereign over all of life. Reread it and notice all that Hannah believes about God. Can we say we believe these things?

Hannah makes no mention in this second prayer of the son for whom she prayed so fervently. The subject is not her need or her son. The subject of this prayer is God!

Could it be that Hannah learned what we need to learn—that it is God who makes life complete? Oh, we yearn for this and ache for that. We concentrate on our need instead of on God. It is God who is enough. "The LORD" Hannah says, "is a God who knows" (1 Samuel 2:3). No wonder the Scripture says over and over: Wait for the Lord! Not for the thing you want, but for the Lord!

Additional Scripture Readings:
Psalm 40:1–3; Luke 2:25–35

Go to page 283 for your next devotional reading.

and has them inherit a throne of honor.

"For the foundations of the earth are
the LORD's;
    upon them he has set the world.
⁹He will guard the feet of his saints,
    but the wicked will be silenced in
    darkness.

"It is not by strength that one
    prevails;
¹⁰ those who oppose the LORD will be
    shattered.
He will thunder against them from
    heaven;
    the LORD will judge the ends of the
    earth.

"He will give strength to his king
    and exalt the horn of his anointed."

¹¹Then Elkanah went home to Ramah,
but the boy ministered before the LORD
under Eli the priest.

Eli's Wicked Sons

¹²Eli's sons were wicked men; they had
no regard for the LORD. ¹³Now it was the
practice of the priests with the people
that whenever anyone offered a sacrifice
and while the meat was being boiled, the
servant of the priest would come with a
three-pronged fork in his hand. ¹⁴He
would plunge it into the pan or kettle or
caldron or pot, and the priest would take
for himself whatever the fork brought up.
This is how they treated all the Israelites
who came to Shiloh. ¹⁵But even before
the fat was burned, the servant of the
priest would come and say to the man
who was sacrificing, "Give the priest
some meat to roast; he won't accept
boiled meat from you, but only raw."

¹⁶If the man said to him, "Let the fat be
burned up first, and then take whatever
you want," the servant would then answer, "No, hand it over now; if you don't,
I'll take it by force."

¹⁷This sin of the young men was very
great in the LORD's sight, for theyᵃ were
treating the LORD's offering with contempt.

¹⁸But Samuel was ministering before
the LORD—a boy wearing a linen ephod.
¹⁹Each year his mother made him a little
robe and took it to him when she went up
with her husband to offer the annual sacrifice. ²⁰Eli would bless Elkanah and his
wife, saying, "May the LORD give you children by this woman to take the place of
the one she prayed for and gave to the
LORD." Then they would go home. ²¹And
the LORD was gracious to Hannah; she
conceived and gave birth to three sons
and two daughters. Meanwhile, the boy
Samuel grew up in the presence of the
LORD.

²²Now Eli, who was very old, heard
about everything his sons were doing to
all Israel and how they slept with the
women who served at the entrance to the
Tent of Meeting. ²³So he said to them,
"Why do you do such things? I hear from
all the people about these wicked deeds
of yours. ²⁴No, my sons; it is not a good
report that I hear spreading among the
LORD's people. ²⁵If a man sins against another man, Godᵇ may mediate for him;
but if a man sins against the LORD, who
will intercede for him?" His sons, however, did not listen to their father's rebuke,
for it was the LORD's will to put them to
death.

²⁶And the boy Samuel continued to
grow in stature and in favor with the LORD
and with men.

Prophecy Against the House of Eli

²⁷Now a man of God came to Eli and
said to him, "This is what the LORD says:
'Did I not clearly reveal myself to your
father's house when they were in Egypt
under Pharaoh? ²⁸I chose your father out
of all the tribes of Israel to be my priest,
to go up to my altar, to burn incense, and
to wear an ephod in my presence. I also
gave your father's house all the offerings
made with fire by the Israelites. ²⁹Why do
youᶜ scorn my sacrifice and offering that
I prescribed for my dwelling? Why do you
honor your sons more than me by fatten-
ing yourselves on the choice parts of every
offering made by my people Israel?'

³⁰"Therefore the LORD, the God of Israel, declares: 'I promised that your house
and your father's house would minister
before me forever.' But now the LORD declares: 'Far be it from me! Those who
honor me I will honor, but those who despise me will be disdained. ³¹The time is
coming when I will cut short your
strength and the strength of your father's
house, so that there will not be an old
man in your family line ³²and you will see
distress in my dwelling. Although good
will be done to Israel, in your family line
there will never be an old man. ³³Every

ᵃ17 Or men   ᵇ25 Or the judges   ᶜ29 The Hebrew is plural.

one of you that I do not cut off from my altar will be spared only to blind your eyes with tears and to grieve your heart, and all your descendants will die in the prime of life.

34"'And what happens to your two sons, Hophni and Phinehas, will be a sign to you—they will both die on the same day. 35I will raise up for myself a faithful priest, who will do according to what is in my heart and mind. I will firmly establish his house, and he will minister before my anointed one always. 36Then everyone left in your family line will come and bow down before him for a piece of silver and a crust of bread and plead, "Appoint me to some priestly office so I can have food to eat." ' "

The Lord Calls Samuel

3 The boy Samuel ministered before the Lord under Eli. In those days the word of the Lord was rare; there were not many visions.

2One night Eli, whose eyes were becoming so weak that he could barely see, was lying down in his usual place. 3The lamp of God had not yet gone out, and Samuel was lying down in the temple[a] of the Lord, where the ark of God was. 4Then the Lord called Samuel.

Samuel answered, "Here I am." 5And he ran to Eli and said, "Here I am; you called me."

But Eli said, "I did not call; go back and lie down." So he went and lay down.

6Again the Lord called, "Samuel!" And Samuel got up and went to Eli and said, "Here I am; you called me."

"My son," Eli said, "I did not call; go back and lie down."

7Now Samuel did not yet know the Lord: The word of the Lord had not yet been revealed to him.

8The Lord called Samuel a third time, and Samuel got up and went to Eli and said, "Here I am; you called me."

Then Eli realized that the Lord was calling the boy. 9So Eli told Samuel, "Go and lie down, and if he calls you, say, 'Speak, Lord, for your servant is listening.' " So Samuel went and lay down in his place.

10The Lord came and stood there, calling as at the other times, "Samuel! Samuel!"

Then Samuel said, "Speak, for your servant is listening."

11And the Lord said to Samuel: "See, I am about to do something in Israel that will make the ears of everyone who hears of it tingle. 12At that time I will carry out against Eli everything I spoke against his family—from beginning to end. 13For I told him that I would judge his family forever because of the sin he knew about; his sons made themselves contemptible,[b] and he failed to restrain them. 14Therefore, I swore to the house of Eli, 'The guilt of Eli's house will never be atoned for by sacrifice or offering.' "

15Samuel lay down until morning and then opened the doors of the house of the Lord. He was afraid to tell Eli the vision, 16but Eli called him and said, "Samuel, my son."

Samuel answered, "Here I am."

17"What was it he said to you?" Eli asked. "Do not hide it from me. May God deal with you, be it ever so severely, if you hide from me anything he told you." 18So Samuel told him everything, hiding nothing from him. Then Eli said, "He is the Lord; let him do what is good in his eyes."

19The Lord was with Samuel as he grew up, and he let none of his words fall to the ground. 20And all Israel from Dan to Beersheba recognized that Samuel was attested as a prophet of the Lord. 21The Lord continued to appear at Shiloh, and there he revealed himself to Samuel through his word.

4 And Samuel's word came to all Israel.

The Philistines Capture the Ark

Now the Israelites went out to fight against the Philistines. The Israelites camped at Ebenezer, and the Philistines at Aphek. 2The Philistines deployed their forces to meet Israel, and as the battle spread, Israel was defeated by the Philistines, who killed about four thousand of them on the battlefield. 3When the soldiers returned to camp, the elders of Israel asked, "Why did the Lord bring defeat upon us today before the Philistines? Let us bring the ark of the Lord's covenant from Shiloh, so that it[c] may go with us and save us from the hand of our enemies."

4So the people sent men to Shiloh, and they brought back the ark of the covenant of the Lord Almighty, who is enthroned

a3 That is, tabernacle   b13 Masoretic Text; an ancient Hebrew scribal tradition and Septuagint *sons blasphemed God*   c3 Or *he* between the cherubim. And Eli's two sons, Hophni and Phinehas, were there with the ark of the covenant of God.

⁵When the ark of the LORD's covenant came into the camp, all Israel raised such a great shout that the ground shook. ⁶Hearing the uproar, the Philistines asked, "What's all this shouting in the Hebrew camp?"

When they learned that the ark of the LORD had come into the camp, ⁷the Philistines were afraid. "A god has come into the camp," they said. "We're in trouble! Nothing like this has happened before. ⁸Woe to us! Who will deliver us from the hand of these mighty gods? They are the gods who struck the Egyptians with all kinds of plagues in the desert. ⁹Be strong, Philistines! Be men, or you will be subject to the Hebrews, as they have been to you. Be men, and fight!"

¹⁰So the Philistines fought, and the Israelites were defeated and every man fled to his tent. The slaughter was very great; Israel lost thirty thousand foot soldiers; ¹¹The ark of God was captured, and Eli's two sons, Hophni and Phinehas, died.

Death of Eli

¹²That same day a Benjamite ran from the battle line and went to Shiloh, his clothes torn and dust on his head. ¹³When he arrived, there was Eli sitting on his chair by the side of the road, watching, because his heart feared for the ark of God. When the man entered the town and told what had happened, the whole town sent up a cry.

¹⁴Eli heard the outcry and asked, "What is the meaning of this uproar?"

The man hurried over to Eli, ¹⁵who was ninety-eight years old and whose eyes were set so that he could not see. ¹⁶He told Eli, "I have just come from the battle line; I fled from it this very day."

Eli asked, "What happened, my son?"

¹⁷The man who brought the news replied, "Israel fled before the Philistines, and the army has suffered heavy losses. Also your two sons, Hophni and Phinehas, are dead, and the ark of God has been captured."

¹⁸When he mentioned the ark of God, Eli fell backward off his chair by the side of the gate. His neck was broken and he died, for he was an old man and heavy. He had led*a* Israel forty years.

¹⁹His daughter-in-law, the wife of Phinehas, was pregnant and near the time of delivery. When she heard the news that the ark of God had been captured and that her father-in-law and her husband were dead, she went into labor and gave birth, but was overcome by her labor pains. ²⁰As she was dying, the women attending her said, "Don't despair; you have given birth to a son." But she did not respond or pay any attention.

²¹She named the boy Ichabod,*b* saying, "The glory has departed from Israel"— because of the capture of the ark of God and the deaths of her father-in-law and her husband. ²²She said, "The glory has departed from Israel, for the ark of God has been captured."

The Ark in Ashdod and Ekron

5 After the Philistines had captured the ark of God, they took it from Ebenezer to Ashdod. ²Then they carried the ark into Dagon's temple and set it beside Dagon. ³When the people of Ashdod rose early the next day, there was Dagon, fallen on his face on the ground before the ark of the LORD! They took Dagon and put him back in his place. ⁴But the following morning when they rose, there was Dagon, fallen on his face on the ground before the ark of the LORD! His head and hands had been broken off and were lying on the threshold; only his body remained. ⁵That is why to this day neither the priests of Dagon nor any others who enter Dagon's temple at Ashdod step on the threshold.

⁶The LORD's hand was heavy upon the people of Ashdod and its vicinity; he brought devastation upon them and afflicted them with tumors.*c* ⁷When the men of Ashdod saw what was happening, they said, "The ark of the god of Israel must not stay here with us, because his hand is heavy upon us and upon Dagon our god." ⁸So they called together all the rulers of the Philistines and asked them, "What shall we do with the ark of the god of Israel?"

They answered, "Have the ark of the god of Israel moved to Gath." So they moved the ark of the God of Israel.

⁹But after they had moved it, the LORD's hand was against that city, throwing it into a great panic. He afflicted the people of the city, both young and old, with an

---

a18 Traditionally judged   b21 Ichabod means no glory.   c6 Hebrew; Septuagint and Vulgate tumors. And rats appeared in their land, and death and destruction were throughout the city outbreak of tumors.[a] [10]So they sent the ark of God to Ekron.

As the ark of God was entering Ekron, the people of Ekron cried out, "They have brought the ark of the god of Israel around to us to kill us and our people." [11]So they called together all the rulers of the Philistines and said, "Send the ark of the god of Israel away; let it go back to its own place, or it[b] will kill us and our people." For death had filled the city with panic; God's hand was very heavy upon it. [12]Those who did not die were afflicted with tumors, and the outcry of the city went up to heaven.

The Ark Returned to Israel

6 When the ark of the Lord had been in Philistine territory seven months, [2]the Philistines called for the priests and the diviners and said, "What shall we do with the ark of the Lord? Tell us how we should send it back to its place."

[3]They answered, "If you return the ark of the god of Israel, do not send it away empty, but by all means send a guilt offering to him. Then you will be healed, and you will know why his hand has not been lifted from you."

[4]The Philistines asked, "What guilt offering should we send to him?"

They replied, "Five gold tumors and five gold rats, according to the number of the Philistine rulers, because the same plague has struck both you and your rulers. [5]Make models of the tumors and of the rats that are destroying the country, and pay honor to Israel's god. Perhaps he will lift his hand from you and your gods and your land. [6]Why do you harden your hearts as the Egyptians and Pharaoh did? When he[c] treated them harshly, did they not send the Israelites out so they could go on their way?

[7]"Now then, get a new cart ready, with two cows that have calved and have never been yoked. Hitch the cows to the cart, but take their calves away and pen them up. [8]Take the ark of the Lord and put it on the cart, and in a chest beside it put the gold objects you are sending back to him as a guilt offering. Send it on its way, [9]but keep watching it. If it goes up to its own territory, toward Beth Shemesh, then the Lord has brought this great disaster on

us. But if it does not, then we will know that it was not his hand that struck us and that it happened to us by chance."

[10]So they did this. They took two such cows and hitched them to the cart and penned up their calves. [11]They placed the ark of the Lord on the cart and along with it the chest containing the gold rats and the models of the tumors. [12]Then the cows went straight up toward Beth Shemesh, keeping on the road and lowing all the way; they did not turn to the right or to the left. The rulers of the Philistines followed them as far as the border of Beth Shemesh.

[13]Now the people of Beth Shemesh were harvesting their wheat in the valley, and when they looked up and saw the ark, they rejoiced at the sight. [14]The cart came to the field of Joshua of Beth Shemesh, and there it stopped beside a large rock. The people chopped up the wood of the cart and sacrificed the cows as a burnt offering to the Lord. [15]The Levites took down the ark of the Lord, together with the chest containing the gold objects, and placed them on the large rock. On that day the people of Beth Shemesh offered burnt offerings and made sacrifices to the Lord. [16]The five rulers of the Philistines saw all this and then returned that same day to Ekron.

[17]These are the gold tumors the Philistines sent as a guilt offering to the Lord— one each for Ashdod, Gaza, Ashkelon, Gath and Ekron. [18]And the number of the gold rats was according to the number of Philistine towns belonging to the five rulers—the fortified towns with their country villages. The large rock, on which[d] they set the ark of the Lord, is a witness to this day in the field of Joshua of Beth Shemesh.

[19]But God struck down some of the men of Beth Shemesh, putting seventy[e] of them to death because they had looked into the ark of the Lord. The people mourned because of the heavy blow the Lord had dealt them, [20]and the men of Beth Shemesh asked, "Who can stand in the presence of the Lord, this holy God? To whom will the ark go up from here?"

[21]Then they sent messengers to the people of Kiriath Jearim, saying, "The Philistines have returned the ark of the Lord. Come down and take it up to your

---

a9 Or with tumors in the groin (see Septuagint)   b11 Or he   c6 That is, God   d18 A few Hebrew manuscripts (see also Septuagint); most Hebrew manuscripts villages as far as Greater Abel, where   e19 A few Hebrew manuscripts; most Hebrew manuscripts and Septuagint 50,070

7 place." ¹So the men of Kiriath Jearim came and took up the ark of the LORD. They took it to Abinadab's house on the hill and consecrated Eleazar his son to guard the ark of the LORD.

Samuel Subdues the Philistines at Mizpah

²It was a long time, twenty years in all, that the ark remained at Kiriath Jearim, and all the people of Israel mourned and sought after the LORD. ³And Samuel said to the whole house of Israel, "If you are returning to the LORD with all your hearts, then rid yourselves of the foreign gods and the Ashtoreths and commit yourselves to the LORD and serve him only, and he will deliver you out of the hand of the Philistines." ⁴So the Israelites put away their Baals and Ashtoreths, and served the LORD only.

⁵Then Samuel said, "Assemble all Israel at Mizpah and I will intercede with the LORD for you." ⁶When they had assembled at Mizpah, they drew water and poured it out before the LORD. On that day they fasted and there they confessed, "We have sinned against the LORD." And Samuel was leader*ª* of Israel at Mizpah.

⁷When the Philistines heard that Israel had assembled at Mizpah, the rulers of the Philistines came up to attack them. And when the Israelites heard of it, they were afraid because of the Philistines. ⁸They said to Samuel, "Do not stop crying out to the LORD our God for us, that he may rescue us from the hand of the Philistines." ⁹Then Samuel took a suckling lamb and offered it up as a whole burnt offering to the LORD. He cried out to the LORD on Israel's behalf, and the LORD answered him.

¹⁰While Samuel was sacrificing the burnt offering, the Philistines drew near to engage Israel in battle. But that day the LORD thundered with loud thunder against the Philistines and threw them into such a panic that they were routed before the Israelites. ¹¹The men of Israel rushed out of Mizpah and pursued the Philistines, slaughtering them along the way to a point below Beth Car.

¹²Then Samuel took a stone and set it up between Mizpah and Shen. He named it Ebenezer,*ᵇ* saying, "Thus far has the LORD helped us." ¹³So the Philistines were subdued and did not invade Israelite territory again.

Throughout Samuel's lifetime, the hand of the LORD was against the Philistines. ¹⁴The towns from Ekron to Gath that the Philistines had captured from Israel were restored to her, and Israel delivered the neighboring territory from the power of the Philistines. And there was peace between Israel and the Amorites.

¹⁵Samuel continued as judge over Israel all the days of his life. ¹⁶From year to year he went on a circuit from Bethel to Gilgal to Mizpah, judging Israel in all those places. ¹⁷But he always went back to Ramah, where his home was, and there he also judged Israel. And he built an altar there to the LORD.

Israel Asks for a King

8 When Samuel grew old, he appointed his sons as judges for Israel. ²The name of his firstborn was Joel and the name of his second was Abijah, and they served at Beersheba. ³But his sons did not walk in his ways. They turned aside after dishonest gain and accepted bribes and perverted justice.

⁴So all the elders of Israel gathered together and came to Samuel at Ramah. ⁵They said to him, "You are old, and your sons do not walk in your ways; now appoint a king to lead*ᶜ* us, such as all the other nations have."

⁶But when they said, "Give us a king to lead us," this displeased Samuel; so he prayed to the LORD. ⁷And the LORD told him: "Listen to all that the people are saying to you; it is not you they have rejected, but they have rejected me as their king. ⁸As they have done from the day I brought them up out of Egypt until this day, forsaking me and serving other gods, so they are doing to you. ⁹Now listen to them; but warn them solemnly and let them know what the king who will reign over them will do."

¹⁰Samuel told all the words of the LORD to the people who were asking him for a king. ¹¹He said, "This is what the king who will reign over you will do: He will take your sons and make them serve with his chariots and horses, and they will run in front of his chariots. ¹²Some he will assign to be commanders of thousands and commanders of fifties, and others to plow his ground and reap his harvest, and

---

ª6 Traditionally judge; and 20   *ᵇ12 Ebenezer means stone of help.*   *ᶜ5 Traditionally judge; also in verses 6*

VERSE FOR THE DAY:	AUTHOR:	PASSAGE FOR THE DAY:
1 Samuel 7:12	Millie Stamm	1 Samuel 7:2–13

A Stone Called Ebenezer

AN old hymn of the church reads:

> O God, our help in ages past;
> our hope for years to come;
> our shelter from the stormy blast;
> and our eternal home.

It has been said that God is the God of every tense—past, present and future. He is the help of our past, the hope of our future, and the great "I am" of today.

After the Israelites had defeated the Philistines, they planted a stone and called it Ebenezer, saying, "Thus far has the LORD helped us." We, too, need to be reminded occasionally how the Lord has led in the past. If we placed a stone each time the Lord helped us, what a wall we would have. God has been our help in the past.

As we look into the unknown future, with no clear path before us, we may become fearful. But God has provided for our future. Paul wrote, "And my God will meet all your needs according to his glorious riches in Christ Jesus" (Philippians 4:19). It does not say "perhaps he will provide," or "he is able to," but he "will" provide. God is our hope for the future.

We can thank him for the past and have confidence in him for the future. Yet sometimes we find it difficult to trust him for the needs of today. But we must remember he is willing to do the same for us today as he did in the past and will do in the future. He is the great "I am" of today, the all-sufficient One for this very moment. "The Lord is my helper" (Hebrews 13:6).

Sometimes he takes us out of situations, problems or needs; other times he takes us through them. Regardless of the way he works in our lives, we can trust him as our ever-present guide for today.

Additional Scripture Readings:
Genesis 28:10–22; Psalm 90:1–2

*Go to page 293 for your next
devotional reading.*

still others to make weapons of war and equipment for his chariots. ¹³He will take your daughters to be perfumers and cooks and bakers. ¹⁴He will take the best of your fields and vineyards and olive groves and give them to his attendants. ¹⁵He will take a tenth of your grain and of your vintage and give it to his officials and attendants. ¹⁶Your menservants and maidservants and the best of your cattle*a* and donkeys he will take for his own use. ¹⁷He will take a tenth of your flocks, and you yourselves will become his slaves. ¹⁸When that day comes, you will cry out for relief from the king you have chosen, and the LORD will not answer you in that day."

¹⁹But the people refused to listen to Samuel. "No!" they said. "We want a king over us. ²⁰Then we will be like all the other nations, with a king to lead us and to go out before us and fight our battles."

²¹When Samuel heard all that the people said, he repeated it before the LORD. ²²The LORD answered, "Listen to them and give them a king."

Then Samuel said to the men of Israel, "Everyone go back to his town."

Samuel Anoints Saul

9 There was a Benjamite, a man of standing, whose name was Kish son of Abiel, the son of Zeror, the son of Becorath, the son of Aphiah of Benjamin. ²He had a son named Saul, an impressive young man without equal among the Israelites—a head taller than any of the others.

³Now the donkeys belonging to Saul's father Kish were lost, and Kish said to his son Saul, "Take one of the servants with you and go and look for the donkeys." ⁴So he passed through the hill country of Ephraim and through the area around Shalisha, but they did not find them. They went on into the district of Shaalim, but the donkeys were not there. Then he passed through the territory of Benjamin, but they did not find them.

⁵When they reached the district of Zuph, Saul said to the servant who was with him, "Come, let's go back, or my father will stop thinking about the donkeys and start worrying about us."

⁶But the servant replied, "Look, in this town there is a man of God; he is highly respected, and everything he says comes true. Let's go there now. Perhaps he will tell us what way to take."

⁷Saul said to his servant, "If we go, what can we give the man? The food in our sacks is gone. We have no gift to take to the man of God. What do we have?"

⁸The servant answered him again. "Look," he said, "I have a quarter of a shekel*b* of silver. I will give it to the man of God so that he will tell us what way to take." ⁹(Formerly in Israel, if a man went to inquire of God, he would say, "Come, let us go to the seer," because the prophet of today used to be called a seer.)

¹⁰"Good," Saul said to his servant. "Come, let's go." So they set out for the town where the man of God was.

¹¹As they were going up the hill to the town, they met some girls coming out to draw water, and they asked them, "Is the seer here?"

¹²"He is," they answered. "He's ahead of you. Hurry now; he has just come to our town today, for the people have a sacrifice at the high place. ¹³As soon as you enter the town, you will find him before he goes up to the high place to eat. The people will not begin eating until he comes, because he must bless the sacrifice; afterward, those who are invited will eat. Go up now; you should find him about this time."

¹⁴They went up to the town, and as they were entering it, there was Samuel, coming toward them on his way up to the high place.

¹⁵Now the day before Saul came, the LORD had revealed this to Samuel: ¹⁶"About this time tomorrow I will send you a man from the land of Benjamin. Anoint him leader over my people Israel; he will deliver my people from the hand of the Philistines. I have looked upon my people, for their cry has reached me."

¹⁷When Samuel caught sight of Saul, the LORD said to him, "This is the man I spoke to you about; he will govern my people."

¹⁸Saul approached Samuel in the gateway and asked, "Would you please tell me where the seer's house is?"

¹⁹"I am the seer," Samuel replied. "Go up ahead of me to the high place, for today you are to eat with me, and in the morning I will let you go and will tell you all that is in your heart. ²⁰As for the donkeys you lost three days ago, do not worry about them; they have been found. And to whom is all the desire of Israel turned, if not to you and all your father's family?"

---

a16 Septuagint; Hebrew *young men*   *b8* That is, about 1/10 ounce (about 3 grams)

²¹Saul answered, "But am I not a Benjamite, from the smallest tribe of Israel, and is not my clan the least of all the clans of the tribe of Benjamin? Why do you say such a thing to me?"

²²Then Samuel brought Saul and his servant into the hall and seated them at the head of those who were invited—about thirty in number. ²³Samuel said to the cook, "Bring the piece of meat I gave you, the one I told you to lay aside."

²⁴So the cook took up the leg with what was on it and set it in front of Saul. Samuel said, "Here is what has been kept for you. Eat, because it was set aside for you for this occasion, from the time I said, 'I have invited guests.'" And Saul dined with Samuel that day.

²⁵After they came down from the high place to the town, Samuel talked with Saul on the roof of his house. ²⁶They rose about daybreak and Samuel called to Saul on the roof, "Get ready, and I will send you on your way." When Saul got ready, he and Samuel went outside together. ²⁷As they were going down to the edge of the town, Samuel said to Saul, "Tell the servant to go on ahead of us"—and the servant did so—"but you stay here awhile, so that I may give you a message from God."

10 Then Samuel took a flask of oil and poured it on Saul's head and kissed him, saying, "Has not the LORD anointed you leader over his inheritance?ª ²When you leave me today, you will meet two men near Rachel's tomb, at Zelzah on the border of Benjamin. They will say to you, 'The donkeys you set out to look for have been found. And now your father has stopped thinking about them and is worried about you. He is asking, "What shall I do about my son?"'

³"Then you will go on from there until you reach the great tree of Tabor. Three men going up to God at Bethel will meet you there. One will be carrying three young goats, another three loaves of bread, and another a skin of wine. ⁴They will greet you and offer you two loaves of bread, which you will accept from them.

⁵"After that you will go to Gibeah of God, where there is a Philistine outpost. As you approach the town, you will meet a procession of prophets coming down from the high place with lyres, tambourines, flutes and harps being played before them, and they will be prophesying. ⁶The Spirit of the LORD will come upon you in power, and you will prophesy with them; and you will be changed into a different person. ⁷Once these signs are fulfilled, do whatever your hand finds to do, for God is with you.

⁸"Go down ahead of me to Gilgal. I will surely come down to you to sacrifice burnt offerings and fellowship offerings,ᵇ but you must wait seven days until I come to you and tell you what you are to do."

Saul Made King

⁹As Saul turned to leave Samuel, God changed Saul's heart, and all these signs were fulfilled that day. ¹⁰When they arrived at Gibeah, a procession of prophets met him; the Spirit of God came upon him in power, and he joined in their prophesying. ¹¹When all those who had formerly known him saw him prophesying with the prophets, they asked each other, "What is this that has happened to the son of Kish? Is Saul also among the prophets?"

¹²A man who lived there answered, "And who is their father?" So it became a saying: "Is Saul also among the prophets?" ¹³After Saul stopped prophesying, he went to the high place.

¹⁴Now Saul's uncle asked him and his servant, "Where have you been?"

"Looking for the donkeys," he said. "But when we saw they were not to be found, we went to Samuel."

¹⁵Saul's uncle said, "Tell me what Samuel said to you."

¹⁶Saul replied, "He assured us that the donkeys had been found." But he did not tell his uncle what Samuel had said about the kingship.

¹⁷Samuel summoned the people of Israel to the LORD at Mizpah ¹⁸and said to them, "This is what the LORD, the God of Israel, says: 'I brought Israel up out of Egypt, and I delivered you from the power of Egypt and all the kingdoms that oppressed you.' ¹⁹But you have now rejected your God, who saves you out of all your calamities and distresses. And you have said, 'No, set a king over us.' So now present yourselves before the LORD by your tribes and clans."

²⁰When Samuel brought all the tribes

ª1 Hebrew; Septuagint and Vulgate *over his people Israel? You will reign over the LORD's people and save them from the power of their enemies round about. And this will be a sign to you that the LORD has anointed you leader over his inheritance:*   ᵇ8 Traditionally *peace offerings* of Israel near, the tribe of Benjamin was chosen. ²¹Then he brought forward the tribe of Benjamin, clan by clan, and Matri's clan was chosen. Finally Saul son of Kish was chosen. But when they looked for him, he was not to be found. ²²So they inquired further of the LORD, "Has the man come here yet?"

And the LORD said, "Yes, he has hidden himself among the baggage."

²³They ran and brought him out, and as he stood among the people he was a head taller than any of the others. ²⁴Samuel said to all the people, "Do you see the man the LORD has chosen? There is no one like him among all the people."

Then the people shouted, "Long live the king!"

²⁵Samuel explained to the people the regulations of the kingship. He wrote them down on a scroll and deposited it before the LORD. Then Samuel dismissed the people, each to his own home.

²⁶Saul also went to his home in Gibeah, accompanied by valiant men whose hearts God had touched. ²⁷But some troublemakers said, "How can this fellow save us?" They despised him and brought him no gifts. But Saul kept silent.

Saul Rescues the City of Jabesh

11 Nahash the Ammonite went up and besieged Jabesh Gilead. And all the men of Jabesh said to him, "Make a treaty with us, and we will be subject to you."

²But Nahash the Ammonite replied, "I will make a treaty with you only on the condition that I gouge out the right eye of every one of you and so bring disgrace on all Israel."

³The elders of Jabesh said to him, "Give us seven days so we can send messengers throughout Israel; if no one comes to rescue us, we will surrender to you."

⁴When the messengers came to Gibeah of Saul and reported these terms to the people, they all wept aloud. ⁵Just then Saul was returning from the fields, behind his oxen, and he asked, "What is wrong with the people? Why are they weeping?" Then they repeated to him what the men of Jabesh had said.

⁶When Saul heard their words, the Spirit of God came upon him in power, and he burned with anger. ⁷He took a pair of oxen, cut them into pieces, and sent the

pieces by messengers throughout Israel, proclaiming, "This is what will be done to the oxen of anyone who does not follow Saul and Samuel." Then the terror of the LORD fell on the people, and they turned out as one man. ⁸When Saul mustered them at Bezek, the men of Israel numbered three hundred thousand and the men of Judah thirty thousand.

⁹They told the messengers who had come, "Say to the men of Jabesh Gilead, 'By the time the sun is hot tomorrow, you will be delivered.' " When the messengers went and reported this to the men of Jabesh, they were elated. ¹⁰They said to the Ammonites, "Tomorrow we will surrender to you, and you can do to us whatever seems good to you."

¹¹The next day Saul separated his men into three divisions; during the last watch of the night they broke into the camp of the Ammonites and slaughtered them until the heat of the day. Those who survived were scattered, so that no two of them were left together.

Saul Confirmed as King

¹²The people then said to Samuel, "Who was it that asked, 'Shall Saul reign over us?' Bring these men to us and we will put them to death."

¹³But Saul said, "No one shall be put to death today, for this day the LORD has rescued Israel."

¹⁴Then Samuel said to the people, "Come, let us go to Gilgal and there reaffirm the kingship." ¹⁵So all the people went to Gilgal and confirmed Saul as king in the presence of the LORD. There they sacrificed fellowship offerings*a* before the LORD, and Saul and all the Israelites held a great celebration.

Samuel's Farewell Speech

12 Samuel said to all Israel, "I have listened to everything you said to me and have set a king over you. ²Now you have a king as your leader. As for me, I am old and gray, and my sons are here with you. I have been your leader from my youth until this day. ³Here I stand. Testify against me in the presence of the LORD and his anointed. Whose ox have I taken? Whose donkey have I taken? Whom have I cheated? Whom have I oppressed? From whose hand have I accepted a bribe to make me shut my eyes? If I have done any of these, I will make it right."

a15 Traditionally *peace offerings*

4"You have not cheated or oppressed us," they replied. "You have not taken anything from anyone's hand."

5Samuel said to them, "The LORD is witness against you, and also his anointed is witness this day, that you have not found anything in my hand."

"He is witness," they said.

6Then Samuel said to the people, "It is the LORD who appointed Moses and Aaron and brought your forefathers up out of Egypt. 7Now then, stand here, because I am going to confront you with evidence before the LORD as to all the righteous acts performed by the LORD for you and your fathers.

8"After Jacob entered Egypt, they cried to the LORD for help, and the LORD sent Moses and Aaron, who brought your forefathers out of Egypt and settled them in this place.

9"But they forgot the LORD their God; so he sold them into the hand of Sisera, the commander of the army of Hazor, and into the hands of the Philistines and the king of Moab, who fought against them. 10They cried out to the LORD and said, 'We have sinned; we have forsaken the LORD and served the Baals and the Ashtoreths. But now deliver us from the hands of our enemies, and we will serve you.' 11Then the LORD sent Jerub-Baal,a Barak,b Jephthah and Samuel,c and he delivered you from the hands of your enemies on every side, so that you lived securely.

12"But when you saw that Nahash king of the Ammonites was moving against you, you said to me, 'No, we want a king to rule over us'—even though the LORD your God was your king. 13Now here is the king you have chosen, the one you asked for; see, the LORD has set a king over you. 14If you fear the LORD and serve and obey him and do not rebel against his commands, and if both you and the king who reigns over you follow the LORD your God —good! 15But if you do not obey the LORD, and if you rebel against his commands, his hand will be against you, as it was against your fathers.

16"Now then, stand still and see this great thing the LORD is about to do before your eyes! 17Is it not wheat harvest now? I will call upon the LORD to send thunder and rain. And you will realize what an evil thing you did in the eyes of the LORD when you asked for a king."

18Then Samuel called upon the LORD, and that same day the LORD sent thunder and rain. So all the people stood in awe of the LORD and of Samuel.

19The people all said to Samuel, "Pray to the LORD your God for your servants so that we will not die, for we have added to all our other sins the evil of asking for a king."

20"Do not be afraid," Samuel replied. "You have done all this evil; yet do not turn away from the LORD, but serve the LORD with all your heart. 21Do not turn away after useless idols. They can do you no good, nor can they rescue you, because they are useless. 22For the sake of his great name the LORD will not reject his people, because the LORD was pleased to make you his own. 23As for me, far be it from me that I should sin against the LORD by failing to pray for you. And I will teach you the way that is good and right. 24But be sure to fear the LORD and serve him faithfully with all your heart; consider what great things he has done for you. 25Yet if you persist in doing evil, both you and your king will be swept away."

Samuel Rebukes Saul

13 Saul was ‚thirty‚d years old when he became king, and he reigned over Israel ‚forty-‚e two years.

2Saulf chose three thousand men from Israel; two thousand were with him at Micmash and in the hill country of Bethel, and a thousand were with Jonathan at Gibeah in Benjamin. The rest of the men he sent back to their homes.

3Jonathan attacked the Philistine outpost at Geba, and the Philistines heard about it. Then Saul had the trumpet blown throughout the land and said, "Let the Hebrews hear!" 4So all Israel heard the news: "Saul has attacked the Philistine outpost, and now Israel has become a stench to the Philistines." And the people were summoned to join Saul at Gilgal.

5The Philistines assembled to fight Israel, with three thousandg chariots, six thousand charioteers, and soldiers as numerous as the sand on the seashore. They

---

a11 Also called Gideon   b11 Some Septuagint manuscripts and Syriac; Hebrew Bedan   c11 Hebrew; some Septuagint manuscripts and Syriac Samson   d1 A few late manuscripts of the Septuagint; Hebrew does not have thirty.   e1 See the round number in Acts 13:21; Hebrew does not have forty-.   f1,2 Or and when he had reigned over Israel two years, 2he   g5 Some Septuagint manuscripts and Syriac; Hebrew thirty thousand went up and camped at Micmash, east of Beth Aven. [6]When the men of Israel saw that their situation was critical and that their army was hard pressed, they hid in caves and thickets, among the rocks, and in pits and cisterns. [7]Some Hebrews even crossed the Jordan to the land of Gad and Gilead.

Saul remained at Gilgal, and all the troops with him were quaking with fear. [8]He waited seven days, the time set by Samuel; but Samuel did not come to Gilgal, and Saul's men began to scatter. [9]So he said, "Bring me the burnt offering and the fellowship offerings.[a]" And Saul offered up the burnt offering. [10]Just as he finished making the offering, Samuel arrived, and Saul went out to greet him.

[11]"What have you done?" asked Samuel.

Saul replied, "When I saw that the men were scattering, and that you did not come at the set time, and that the Philistines were assembling at Micmash, [12]I thought, 'Now the Philistines will come down against me at Gilgal, and I have not sought the LORD's favor.' So I felt compelled to offer the burnt offering."

[13]"You acted foolishly," Samuel said. "You have not kept the command the LORD your God gave you; if you had, he would have established your kingdom over Israel for all time. [14]But now your kingdom will not endure; the LORD has sought out a man after his own heart and appointed him leader of his people, because you have not kept the LORD's command."

[15]Then Samuel left Gilgal[b] and went up to Gibeah in Benjamin, and Saul counted the men who were with him. They numbered about six hundred.

Israel Without Weapons

[16]Saul and his son Jonathan and the men with them were staying in Gibeah[c] in Benjamin, while the Philistines camped at Micmash. [17]Raiding parties went out from the Philistine camp in three detachments. One turned toward Ophrah in the vicinity of Shual, [18]another toward Beth Horon, and the third toward the borderland overlooking the Valley of Zeboim facing the desert.

[19]Not a blacksmith could be found in the whole land of Israel, because the Philistines had said, "Otherwise the Hebrews will make swords or spears!" [20]So all Israel went down to the Philistines to have their plowshares, mattocks, axes and sickles[d] sharpened. [21]The price was two thirds of a shekel[e] for sharpening plowshares and mattocks, and a third of a shekel[f] for sharpening forks and axes and for repointing goads.

[22]So on the day of the battle not a soldier with Saul and Jonathan had a sword or spear in his hand; only Saul and his son Jonathan had them.

Jonathan Attacks the Philistines

[23]Now a detachment of Philistines had gone out to the pass at Micmash.

14 [1]One day Jonathan son of Saul said to the young man bearing his armor, "Come, let's go over to the Philistine outpost on the other side." But he did not tell his father.

[2]Saul was staying on the outskirts of Gibeah under a pomegranate tree in Migron. With him were about six hundred men, [3]among whom was Ahijah, who was wearing an ephod. He was a son of Ichabod's brother Ahitub son of Phinehas, the son of Eli, the LORD's priest in Shiloh. No one was aware that Jonathan had left.

[4]On each side of the pass that Jonathan intended to cross to reach the Philistine outpost was a cliff; one was called Bozez, and the other Seneh. [5]One cliff stood to the north toward Micmash, the other to the south toward Geba.

[6]Jonathan said to his young armor-bearer, "Come, let's go over to the outpost of those uncircumcised fellows. Perhaps the LORD will act in our behalf. Nothing can hinder the LORD from saving, whether by many or by few."

[7]"Do all that you have in mind," his armor-bearer said. "Go ahead; I am with you heart and soul."

[8]Jonathan said, "Come, then; we will cross over toward the men and let them see us. [9]If they say to us, 'Wait there until we come to you,' we will stay where we are and not go up to them. [10]But if they say, 'Come up to us,' we will climb up, because that will be our sign that the LORD has given them into our hands."

[11]So both of them showed themselves

---

[a]9 Traditionally *peace offerings*   [b]15 Hebrew; Septuagint *Gilgal and went his way; the rest of the people went after Saul to meet the army, and they went out of Gilgal*   [c]16 Two Hebrew manuscripts; most Hebrew manuscripts *Geba*, a variant of *Gibeah*   [d]20 Septuagint; Hebrew *plowshares*   [e]21 Hebrew *pim*; that is, about 1/4 ounce (about 8 grams)   [f]21 That is, about 1/8 ounce (about 4 grams)

to the Philistine outpost. "Look!" said the Philistines. "The Hebrews are crawling out of the holes they were hiding in." [12]The men of the outpost shouted to Jonathan and his armor-bearer, "Come up to us and we'll teach you a lesson."

So Jonathan said to his armor-bearer, "Climb up after me; the LORD has given them into the hand of Israel."

[13]Jonathan climbed up, using his hands and feet, with his armor-bearer right behind him. The Philistines fell before Jonathan, and his armor-bearer followed and killed behind him. [14]In that first attack Jonathan and his armor-bearer killed some twenty men in an area of about half an acre. [a]

Israel Routs the Philistines

[15]Then panic struck the whole army— those in the camp and field, and those in the outposts and raiding parties—and the ground shook. It was a panic sent by God. [b]

[16]Saul's lookouts at Gibeah in Benjamin saw the army melting away in all directions. [17]Then Saul said to the men who were with him, "Muster the forces and see who has left us." When they did, it was Jonathan and his armor-bearer who were not there.

[18]Saul said to Ahijah, "Bring the ark of God." (At that time it was with the Israelites.) [c] [19]While Saul was talking to the priest, the tumult in the Philistine camp increased more and more. So Saul said to the priest, "Withdraw your hand."

[20]Then Saul and all his men assembled and went to the battle. They found the Philistines in total confusion, striking each other with their swords. [21]Those Hebrews who had previously been with the Philistines and had gone up with them to their camp went over to the Israelites who were with Saul and Jonathan. [22]When all the Israelites who had hidden in the hill country of Ephraim heard that the Philistines were on the run, they joined the battle in hot pursuit. [23]So the LORD rescued Israel that day, and the battle moved on beyond Beth Aven.

Jonathan Eats Honey

[24]Now the men of Israel were in distress that day, because Saul had bound the people under an oath, saying, "Cursed be any man who eats food before evening comes, before I have avenged myself on my enemies!" So none of the troops tasted food.

[25]The entire army [d] entered the woods, and there was honey on the ground. [26]When they went into the woods, they saw the honey oozing out, yet no one put his hand to his mouth, because they feared the oath. [27]But Jonathan had not heard that his father had bound the people with the oath, so he reached out the end of the staff that was in his hand and dipped it into the honeycomb. He raised his hand to his mouth, and his eyes brightened. [e] [28]Then one of the soldiers told him, "Your father bound the army under a strict oath, saying, 'Cursed be any man who eats food today!' That is why the men are faint."

[29]Jonathan said, "My father has made trouble for the country. See how my eyes brightened [f] when I tasted a little of this honey. [30]How much better it would have been if the men had eaten today some of the plunder they took from their enemies. Would not the slaughter of the Philistines have been even greater?"

[31]That day, after the Israelites had struck down the Philistines from Micmash to Aijalon, they were exhausted. [32]They pounced on the plunder and, taking sheep, cattle and calves, they butchered them on the ground and ate them, together with the blood. [33]Then someone said to Saul, "Look, the men are sinning against the LORD by eating meat that has blood in it."

"You have broken faith," he said. "Roll a large stone over here at once." [34]Then he said, "Go out among the men and tell them, 'Each of you bring me your cattle and sheep, and slaughter them here and eat them. Do not sin against the LORD by eating meat with blood still in it.'"

So everyone brought his ox that night and slaughtered it there. [35]Then Saul built an altar to the LORD; it was the first time he had done this.

[36]Saul said, "Let us go down after the Philistines by night and plunder them till dawn, and let us not leave one of them alive."

---

[a]14 Hebrew *half a yoke;* a "yoke" was the land plowed by a yoke of oxen in one day.   [b]15 Or *a terrible panic*   [c]18 Hebrew; Septuagint *"Bring the ephod." (At that time he wore the ephod before the Israelites.)*   [d]25 Or *Now all the people of the land*   [e]27 Or *his strength was renewed*   [f]29 Or *my strength was renewed*

"Do whatever seems best to you," they replied.

But the priest said, "Let us inquire of God here."

37So Saul asked God, "Shall I go down after the Philistines? Will you give them into Israel's hand?" But God did not answer him that day.

38Saul therefore said, "Come here, all you who are leaders of the army, and let us find out what sin has been committed today. 39As surely as the LORD who rescues Israel lives, even if it lies with my son Jonathan, he must die." But not one of the men said a word.

40Saul then said to all the Israelites, "You stand over there; I and Jonathan my son will stand over here."

"Do what seems best to you," the men replied.

41Then Saul prayed to the LORD, the God of Israel, "Give me the right answer."*a* And Jonathan and Saul were taken by lot, and the men were cleared. 42Saul said, "Cast the lot between me and Jonathan my son." And Jonathan was taken.

43Then Saul said to Jonathan, "Tell me what you have done."

So Jonathan told him, "I merely tasted a little honey with the end of my staff. And now must I die?"

44Saul said, "May God deal with me, be it ever so severely, if you do not die, Jonathan."

45But the men said to Saul, "Should Jonathan die—he who has brought about this great deliverance in Israel? Never! As surely as the LORD lives, not a hair of his head will fall to the ground, for he did this today with God's help." So the men rescued Jonathan, and he was not put to death.

46Then Saul stopped pursuing the Philistines, and they withdrew to their own land.

47After Saul had assumed rule over Israel, he fought against their enemies on every side: Moab, the Ammonites, Edom, the kings*b* of Zobah, and the Philistines. Wherever he turned, he inflicted punishment on them.*c* 48He fought valiantly and defeated the Amalekites, delivering Israel

from the hands of those who had plundered them.

Saul's Family

49Saul's sons were Jonathan, Ishvi and Malki-Shua. The name of his older daughter was Merab, and that of the younger was Michal. 50His wife's name was Ahinoam daughter of Ahimaaz. The name of the commander of Saul's army was Abner son of Ner, and Ner was Saul's uncle. 51Saul's father Kish and Abner's father Ner were sons of Abiel.

52All the days of Saul there was bitter war with the Philistines, and whenever Saul saw a mighty or brave man, he took him into his service.

The LORD Rejects Saul as King

15 Samuel said to Saul, "I am the one the LORD sent to anoint you king over his people Israel; so listen now to the message from the LORD. 2This is what the LORD Almighty says: 'I will punish the Amalekites for what they did to Israel when they waylaid them as they came up from Egypt. 3Now go, attack the Amalekites and totally destroy*d* everything that belongs to them. Do not spare them; put to death men and women, children and infants, cattle and sheep, camels and donkeys.' "

4So Saul summoned the men and mustered them at Telaim—two hundred thousand foot soldiers and ten thousand men from Judah. 5Saul went to the city of Amalek and set an ambush in the ravine. 6Then he said to the Kenites, "Go away, leave the Amalekites so that I do not destroy you along with them; for you showed kindness to all the Israelites when they came up out of Egypt." So the Kenites moved away from the Amalekites.

7Then Saul attacked the Amalekites all the way from Havilah to Shur, to the east of Egypt. 8He took Agag king of the Amalekites alive, and all his people he totally destroyed with the sword. 9But Saul and the army spared Agag and the best of the sheep and cattle, the fat calves*e* and lambs—everything that was good. These they were unwilling to destroy complete-

---

a41 Hebrew; Septuagint *"Why have you not answered your servant today? If the fault is in me or my son Jonathan, respond with Urim, but if the men of Israel are at fault, respond with Thummim."*
b47 Masoretic Text; Dead Sea Scrolls and Septuagint *king*   *c47* Hebrew; Septuagint *he was victorious*
d3 The Hebrew term refers to the irrevocable giving over of things or persons to the LORD, often by totally destroying them; also in verses 8, 9, 15, 18, 20 and 21.   *e9* Or *the grown bulls*; the meaning of the Hebrew for this phrase is uncertain.

ly, but everything that was despised and weak they totally destroyed.

¹⁰Then the word of the LORD came to Samuel: ¹¹"I am grieved that I have made Saul king, because he has turned away from me and has not carried out my instructions." Samuel was troubled, and he cried out to the LORD all that night.

¹²Early in the morning Samuel got up and went to meet Saul, but he was told, "Saul has gone to Carmel. There he has set up a monument in his own honor and has turned and gone on down to Gilgal."

¹³When Samuel reached him, Saul said, "The LORD bless you! I have carried out the LORD's instructions."

¹⁴But Samuel said, "What then is this bleating of sheep in my ears? What is this lowing of cattle that I hear?"

¹⁵Saul answered, "The soldiers brought them from the Amalekites; they spared the best of the sheep and cattle to sacrifice to the LORD your God, but we totally destroyed the rest."

¹⁶"Stop!" Samuel said to Saul. "Let me tell you what the LORD said to me last night."

"Tell me," Saul replied.

¹⁷Samuel said, "Although you were once small in your own eyes, did you not become the head of the tribes of Israel? The LORD anointed you king over Israel. ¹⁸And he sent you on a mission, saying, 'Go and completely destroy those wicked people, the Amalekites; make war on them until you have wiped them out.' ¹⁹Why did you not obey the LORD? Why did you pounce on the plunder and do evil in the eyes of the LORD?"

²⁰"But I did obey the LORD," Saul said. "I went on the mission the LORD assigned me. I completely destroyed the Amalekites and brought back Agag their king. ²¹The soldiers took sheep and cattle from the plunder, the best of what was devoted to God, in order to sacrifice them to the LORD your God at Gilgal."

²²But Samuel replied:

"Does the LORD delight in burnt
    offerings and sacrifices
as much as in obeying the voice of
    the LORD?
To obey is better than sacrifice,
    and to heed is better than the fat
        of rams.
²³For rebellion is like the sin of
    divination,

and arrogance like the evil of
    idolatry.
Because you have rejected the word
    of the LORD,
he has rejected you as king."

²⁴Then Saul said to Samuel, "I have sinned. I violated the LORD's command and your instructions. I was afraid of the people and so I gave in to them. ²⁵Now I beg you, forgive my sin and come back with me, so that I may worship the LORD."

²⁶But Samuel said to him, "I will not go back with you. You have rejected the word of the LORD, and the LORD has rejected you as king over Israel!"

²⁷As Samuel turned to leave, Saul caught hold of the hem of his robe, and it tore. ²⁸Samuel said to him, "The LORD has torn the kingdom of Israel from you today and has given it to one of your neighbors —to one better than you. ²⁹He who is the Glory of Israel does not lie or change his mind; for he is not a man, that he should change his mind."

³⁰Saul replied, "I have sinned. But please honor me before the elders of my people and before Israel; come back with me, so that I may worship the LORD your God." ³¹So Samuel went back with Saul, and Saul worshiped the LORD.

³²Then Samuel said, "Bring me Agag king of the Amalekites."

Agag came to him confidently,ᵃ thinking, "Surely the bitterness of death is past."

³³But Samuel said,

"As your sword has made women
    childless,
so will your mother be childless
    among women."

And Samuel put Agag to death before the LORD at Gilgal.

³⁴Then Samuel left for Ramah, but Saul went up to his home in Gibeah of Saul. ³⁵Until the day Samuel died, he did not go to see Saul again, though Samuel mourned for him. And the LORD was grieved that he had made Saul king over Israel.

Samuel Anoints David

16 The LORD said to Samuel, "How long will you mourn for Saul, since I have rejected him as king over Israel? Fill your horn with oil and be on your way; I am sending you to Jesse of Bethle-

---

ᵃ32 Or *him trembling, yet*

hem. I have chosen one of his sons to be king."

²But Samuel said, "How can I go? Saul will hear about it and kill me."

The LORD said, "Take a heifer with you and say, 'I have come to sacrifice to the LORD.' ³Invite Jesse to the sacrifice, and I will show you what to do. You are to anoint for me the one I indicate."

⁴Samuel did what the LORD said. When he arrived at Bethlehem, the elders of the town trembled when they met him. They asked, "Do you come in peace?"

⁵Samuel replied, "Yes, in peace; I have come to sacrifice to the LORD. Consecrate yourselves and come to the sacrifice with me." Then he consecrated Jesse and his sons and invited them to the sacrifice.

⁶When they arrived, Samuel saw Eliab and thought, "Surely the LORD's anointed stands here before the LORD."

⁷But the LORD said to Samuel, "Do not consider his appearance or his height, for I have rejected him. The LORD does not look at the things man looks at. Man looks at the outward appearance, but the LORD looks at the heart."

⁸Then Jesse called Abinadab and had him pass in front of Samuel. But Samuel said, "The LORD has not chosen this one either." ⁹Jesse then had Shammah pass by, but Samuel said, "Nor has the LORD chosen this one." ¹⁰Jesse had seven of his sons pass before Samuel, but Samuel said to him, "The LORD has not chosen these." ¹¹So he asked Jesse, "Are these all the sons you have?"

"There is still the youngest," Jesse answered, "but he is tending the sheep."

Samuel said, "Send for him; we will not sit down*a* until he arrives."

¹²So he sent and had him brought in. He was ruddy, with a fine appearance and handsome features.

Then the LORD said, "Rise and anoint him; he is the one."

¹³So Samuel took the horn of oil and anointed him in the presence of his brothers, and from that day on the Spirit of the LORD came upon David in power. Samuel then went to Ramah.

David in Saul's Service

¹⁴Now the Spirit of the LORD had departed from Saul, and an evil*b* spirit from the LORD tormented him.

¹⁵Saul's attendants said to him, "See, an evil spirit from God is tormenting you. ¹⁶Let our lord command his servants here to search for someone who can play the harp. He will play when the evil spirit from God comes upon you, and you will feel better."

¹⁷So Saul said to his attendants, "Find someone who plays well and bring him to me."

¹⁸One of the servants answered, "I have seen a son of Jesse of Bethlehem who knows how to play the harp. He is a brave man and a warrior. He speaks well and is a fine-looking man. And the LORD is with him."

¹⁹Then Saul sent messengers to Jesse and said, "Send me your son David, who is with the sheep." ²⁰So Jesse took a donkey loaded with bread, a skin of wine and a young goat and sent them with his son David to Saul.

²¹David came to Saul and entered his service. Saul liked him very much, and David became one of his armor-bearers. ²²Then Saul sent word to Jesse, saying, "Allow David to remain in my service, for I am pleased with him."

²³Whenever the spirit from God came upon Saul, David would take his harp and play. Then relief would come to Saul; he would feel better, and the evil spirit would leave him.

David and Goliath

17 Now the Philistines gathered their forces for war and assembled at Socoh in Judah. They pitched camp at Ephes Dammim, between Socoh and Azekah. ²Saul and the Israelites assembled and camped in the Valley of Elah and drew up their battle line to meet the Philistines. ³The Philistines occupied one hill and the Israelites another, with the valley between them.

⁴A champion named Goliath, who was from Gath, came out of the Philistine camp. He was over nine feet*c* tall. ⁵He had a bronze helmet on his head and wore a coat of scale armor of bronze weighing five thousand shekels*d*; ⁶on his legs he wore bronze greaves, and a bronze javelin was slung on his back. ⁷His spear shaft was like a weaver's rod, and its iron point weighed six hundred shekels.*e* His shield bearer went ahead of him.

---

a11 Some Septuagint manuscripts; Hebrew *not gather around* and 23   *c4* Hebrew *was six cubits and a span* (about 3 meters) (about 57 kilograms)   *e7* That is, about 15 pounds (about 7 kilograms)   *b14* Or *injurious*; also in verses 15, 16   *d5* That is, about 125 pounds

VERSE FOR THE DAY:
1 Samuel 16:7

AUTHOR:
Mab Graff Hoover

PASSAGE FOR THE DAY:
1 Samuel 16:1–13

Clamor Girl

OH, to be chic and glamorous! I have this dream where I swoop into a room, head held high, stomach in, flawlessly attired, and not a hair out of place. Women seethe with envy, gentlemen leap to their feet and offer a chair, and I, like Princess Grace, smile regally, then sit down with knees together and slender feet crossed at the ankles. My gown is the latest fashion, spotless and wrinkle-free. When I speak, my voice is soft but sure, and I do not stammer or hesitate.

I try to make this dream a reality. And while I probably could never be considered glamorous, at least I try to have my hair fixed and have on clean clothes when I go out. But somehow, I always manage to arrive looking like a pup who has been playing in the rain.

Last night we went to the business meeting at church, and it began to rain. By the time we got there, all the good parking places were taken and we had to walk quite a way. I had on my best white slacks, too. It would be understandable to get a few little mud spots on the bottoms, but when we entered the brightly lit room I discovered I had a big muddy smear on my stomach.

"Let it dry," my husband advised. "Then you can brush it off."

I had to give my report before it dried. I knew everyone was looking at the mud, so I kept trying to hold pages over it, and I dropped some. When I bent down to pick them up, I bumped heads with the moderator who had bent down to help me.

"Does my girl feel grumpy?" my husband asked at breakfast the next day.

I groaned.

How can you love anybody who is so sloppy—so—overweight—so—*klutzy*?" I stormed.

"It's hard." He nodded with a grin.

When I began to cry he hugged me.

"If I was all rolled up in bandages," he said, "And you couldn't see me, would you still love me?"

"Of course," I snapped. "It would still be you inside."

"Guess that answers your question." He kissed me. "I love the you *inside*."

Additional Scripture Readings:
Ecclesiastes 3:11–14; 1 Peter 3:3–4

Go to page 300 for your next devotional reading.

8Goliath stood and shouted to the ranks of Israel, "Why do you come out and line up for battle? Am I not a Philistine, and are you not the servants of Saul? Choose a man and have him come down to me. 9If he is able to fight and kill me, we will become your subjects; but if I overcome him and kill him, you will become our subjects and serve us." 10Then the Philistine said, "This day I defy the ranks of Israel! Give me a man and let us fight each other." 11On hearing the Philistine's words, Saul and all the Israelites were dismayed and terrified.

12Now David was the son of an Ephrathite named Jesse, who was from Bethlehem in Judah. Jesse had eight sons, and in Saul's time he was old and well advanced in years. 13Jesse's three oldest sons had followed Saul to the war: The firstborn was Eliab; the second, Abinadab; and the third, Shammah. 14David was the youngest. The three oldest followed Saul, 15but David went back and forth from Saul to tend his father's sheep at Bethlehem.

16For forty days the Philistine came forward every morning and evening and took his stand.

17Now Jesse said to his son David, "Take this ephah*a* of roasted grain and these ten loaves of bread for your brothers and hurry to their camp. 18Take along these ten cheeses to the commander of their unit.*b* See how your brothers are and bring back some assurance*c* from them. 19They are with Saul and all the men of Israel in the Valley of Elah, fighting against the Philistines."

20Early in the morning David left the flock with a shepherd, loaded up and set out, as Jesse had directed. He reached the camp as the army was going out to its battle positions, shouting the war cry. 21Israel and the Philistines were drawing up their lines facing each other. 22David left his things with the keeper of supplies, ran to the battle lines and greeted his brothers. 23As he was talking with them, Goliath, the Philistine champion from Gath, stepped out from his lines and shouted his usual defiance, and David heard it. 24When the Israelites saw the man, they all ran from him in great fear.

25Now the Israelites had been saying, "Do you see how this man keeps coming out? He comes out to defy Israel. The king will give great wealth to the man who kills him. He will also give him his daughter in marriage and will exempt his father's family from taxes in Israel."

26David asked the men standing near him, "What will be done for the man who kills this Philistine and removes this disgrace from Israel? Who is this uncircumcised Philistine that he should defy the armies of the living God?"

27They repeated to him what they had been saying and told him, "This is what will be done for the man who kills him."

28When Eliab, David's oldest brother, heard him speaking with the men, he burned with anger at him and asked, "Why have you come down here? And with whom did you leave those few sheep in the desert? I know how conceited you are and how wicked your heart is; you came down only to watch the battle."

29"Now what have I done?" said David. "Can't I even speak?" 30He then turned away to someone else and brought up the same matter, and the men answered him as before. 31What David said was overheard and reported to Saul, and Saul sent for him.

32David said to Saul, "Let no one lose heart on account of this Philistine; your servant will go and fight him."

33Saul replied, "You are not able to go out against this Philistine and fight him; you are only a boy, and he has been a fighting man from his youth."

34But David said to Saul, "Your servant has been keeping his father's sheep. When a lion or a bear came and carried off a sheep from the flock, 35I went after it, struck it and rescued the sheep from its mouth. When it turned on me, I seized it by its hair, struck it and killed it. 36Your servant has killed both the lion and the bear; this uncircumcised Philistine will be like one of them, because he has defied the armies of the living God. 37The Lord who delivered me from the paw of the lion and the paw of the bear will deliver me from the hand of this Philistine."

Saul said to David, "Go, and the Lord be with you."

38Then Saul dressed David in his own tunic. He put a coat of armor on him and a bronze helmet on his head. 39David fastened on his sword over the tunic and tried walking around, because he was not used to them.

a17 That is, probably about 3/5 bushel (about 22 liters) or *some pledge of spoils*　　*b18* Hebrew *thousand*　　*c18* Or *some token;*

"I cannot go in these," he said to Saul, "because I am not used to them." So he took them off. ⁴⁰Then he took his staff in his hand, chose five smooth stones from the stream, put them in the pouch of his shepherd's bag and, with his sling in his hand, approached the Philistine.

⁴¹Meanwhile, the Philistine, with his shield bearer in front of him, kept coming closer to David. ⁴²He looked David over and saw that he was only a boy, ruddy and handsome, and he despised him. ⁴³He said to David, "Am I a dog, that you come at me with sticks?" And the Philistine cursed David by his gods. ⁴⁴"Come here," he said, "and I'll give your flesh to the birds of the air and the beasts of the field!"

⁴⁵David said to the Philistine, "You come against me with sword and spear and javelin, but I come against you in the name of the LORD Almighty, the God of the armies of Israel, whom you have defied. ⁴⁶This day the LORD will hand you over to me, and I'll strike you down and cut off your head. Today I will give the carcasses of the Philistine army to the birds of the air and the beasts of the earth, and the whole world will know that there is a God in Israel. ⁴⁷All those gathered here will know that it is not by sword or spear that the LORD saves; for the battle is the LORD's, and he will give all of you into our hands."

⁴⁸As the Philistine moved closer to attack him, David ran quickly toward the battle line to meet him. ⁴⁹Reaching into his bag and taking out a stone, he slung it and struck the Philistine on the forehead. The stone sank into his forehead, and he fell facedown on the ground.

⁵⁰So David triumphed over the Philistine with a sling and a stone; without a sword in his hand he struck down the Philistine and killed him.

⁵¹David ran and stood over him. He took hold of the Philistine's sword and drew it from the scabbard. After he killed him, he cut off his head with the sword.

When the Philistines saw that their hero was dead, they turned and ran. ⁵²Then the men of Israel and Judah surged forward with a shout and pursued the Philistines to the entrance of Gath[a] and to the gates of Ekron. Their dead were strewn along the Shaaraim road to Gath and Ekron. ⁵³When the Israelites returned from chasing the Philistines, they plundered their camp. ⁵⁴David took the Philistine's head and brought it to Jerusalem, and he put the Philistine's weapons in his own tent.

⁵⁵As Saul watched David going out to meet the Philistine, he said to Abner, commander of the army, "Abner, whose son is that young man?"

Abner replied, "As surely as you live, O king, I don't know."

⁵⁶The king said, "Find out whose son this young man is."

⁵⁷As soon as David returned from killing the Philistine, Abner took him and brought him before Saul, with David still holding the Philistine's head.

⁵⁸"Whose son are you, young man?" Saul asked him.

David said, "I am the son of your servant Jesse of Bethlehem."

Saul's Jealousy of David

18 After David had finished talking with Saul, Jonathan became one in spirit with David, and he loved him as himself. ²From that day Saul kept David with him and did not let him return to his father's house. ³And Jonathan made a covenant with David because he loved him as himself. ⁴Jonathan took off the robe he was wearing and gave it to David, along with his tunic, and even his sword, his bow and his belt.

⁵Whatever Saul sent him to do, David did it so successfully[b] that Saul gave him a high rank in the army. This pleased all the people, and Saul's officers as well.

⁶When the men were returning home after David had killed the Philistine, the women came out from all the towns of Israel to meet King Saul with singing and dancing, with joyful songs and with tambourines and lutes. ⁷As they danced, they sang:

"Saul has slain his thousands,
and David his tens of thousands."

⁸Saul was very angry; this refrain galled him. "They have credited David with tens of thousands," he thought, "but me with only thousands. What more can he get but the kingdom?" ⁹And from that time on Saul kept a jealous eye on David.

¹⁰The next day an evil[c] spirit from God came forcefully upon Saul. He was prophesying in his house, while David was playing the harp, as he usually did. Saul had a spear in his hand ¹¹and he hurled it,

---

a52 Some Septuagint manuscripts; Hebrew *a valley*   *b5* Or *wisely*   *c10* Or *injurious* saying to himself, "I'll pin David to the wall." But David eluded him twice.

[12]Saul was afraid of David, because the LORD was with David but had left Saul. [13]So he sent David away from him and gave him command over a thousand men, and David led the troops in their campaigns. [14]In everything he did he had great success,[a] because the LORD was with him. [15]When Saul saw how successful[b] he was, he was afraid of him. [16]But all Israel and Judah loved David, because he led them in their campaigns.

[17]Saul said to David, "Here is my older daughter Merab. I will give her to you in marriage; only serve me bravely and fight the battles of the LORD." For Saul said to himself, "I will not raise a hand against him. Let the Philistines do that!"

[18]But David said to Saul, "Who am I, and what is my family or my father's clan in Israel, that I should become the king's son-in-law?" [19]So[c] when the time came for Merab, Saul's daughter, to be given to David, she was given in marriage to Adriel of Meholah.

[20]Now Saul's daughter Michal was in love with David, and when they told Saul about it, he was pleased. [21]"I will give her to him," he thought, "so that she may be a snare to him and so that the hand of the Philistines may be against him." So Saul said to David, "Now you have a second opportunity to become my son-in-law."

[22]Then Saul ordered his attendants: "Speak to David privately and say, 'Look, the king is pleased with you, and his attendants all like you; now become his son-in-law.' "

[23]They repeated these words to David. But David said, "Do you think it is a small matter to become the king's son-in-law? I'm only a poor man and little known."

[24]When Saul's servants told him what David had said, [25]Saul replied, "Say to David, 'The king wants no other price for the bride than a hundred Philistine foreskins, to take revenge on his enemies.' " Saul's plan was to have David fall by the hands of the Philistines.

[26]When the attendants told David these things, he was pleased to become the king's son-in-law. So before the allotted time elapsed, [27]David and his men went out and killed two hundred Philistines. He brought their foreskins and presented the full number to the king so that he

might become the king's son-in-law. Then Saul gave him his daughter Michal in marriage.

[28]When Saul realized that the LORD was with David and that his daughter Michal loved David, [29]Saul became still more afraid of him, and he remained his enemy the rest of his days.

[30]The Philistine commanders continued to go out to battle, and as often as they did, David met with more success[d] than the rest of Saul's officers, and his name became well known.

Saul Tries to Kill David

19 Saul told his son Jonathan and all the attendants to kill David. But Jonathan was very fond of David [2]and warned him, "My father Saul is looking for a chance to kill you. Be on your guard tomorrow morning; go into hiding and stay there. [3]I will go out and stand with my father in the field where you are. I'll speak to him about you and will tell you what I find out."

[4]Jonathan spoke well of David to Saul his father and said to him, "Let not the king do wrong to his servant David; he has not wronged you, and what he has done has benefited you greatly. [5]He took his life in his hands when he killed the Philistine. The LORD won a great victory for all Israel, and you saw it and were glad. Why then would you do wrong to an innocent man like David by killing him for no reason?"

[6]Saul listened to Jonathan and took this oath: "As surely as the LORD lives, David will not be put to death."

[7]So Jonathan called David and told him the whole conversation. He brought him to Saul, and David was with Saul as before.

[8]Once more war broke out, and David went out and fought the Philistines. He struck them with such force that they fled before him.

[9]But an evil[e] spirit from the LORD came upon Saul as he was sitting in his house with his spear in his hand. While David was playing the harp, [10]Saul tried to pin him to the wall with his spear, but David eluded him as Saul drove the spear into the wall. That night David made good his escape.

[11]Saul sent men to David's house to watch it and to kill him in the morning.

---

[a]14 Or *he was very wise*　　[b]15 Or *wise*　　[c]19 Or *However,*　　[d]30 Or *David acted more wisely*
[e]9 Or *injurious*

But Michal, David's wife, warned him, "If you don't run for your life tonight, tomorrow you'll be killed." ¹²So Michal let David down through a window, and he fled and escaped. ¹³Then Michal took an idol*ᵃ* and laid it on the bed, covering it with a garment and putting some goats' hair at the head.

¹⁴When Saul sent the men to capture David, Michal said, "He is ill."

¹⁵Then Saul sent the men back to see David and told them, "Bring him up to me in his bed so that I may kill him." ¹⁶But when the men entered, there was the idol in the bed, and at the head was some goats' hair.

¹⁷Saul said to Michal, "Why did you deceive me like this and send my enemy away so that he escaped?"

Michal told him, "He said to me, 'Let me get away. Why should I kill you?'"

¹⁸When David had fled and made his escape, he went to Samuel at Ramah and told him all that Saul had done to him. Then he and Samuel went to Naioth and stayed there. ¹⁹Word came to Saul: "David is in Naioth at Ramah"; ²⁰so he sent men to capture him. But when they saw a group of prophets prophesying, with Samuel standing there as their leader, the Spirit of God came upon Saul's men and they also prophesied. ²¹Saul was told about it, and he sent more men, and they prophesied too. Saul sent men a third time, and they also prophesied. ²²Finally, he himself left for Ramah and went to the great cistern at Secu. And he asked, "Where are Samuel and David?"

"Over in Naioth at Ramah," they said.

²³So Saul went to Naioth at Ramah. But the Spirit of God came even upon him, and he walked along prophesying until he came to Naioth. ²⁴He stripped off his robes and also prophesied in Samuel's presence. He lay that way all that day and night. This is why people say, "Is Saul also among the prophets?"

David and Jonathan

20 Then David fled from Naioth at Ramah and went to Jonathan and asked, "What have I done? What is my crime? How have I wronged your father, that he is trying to take my life?"

²"Never!" Jonathan replied. "You are not going to die! Look, my father doesn't do anything, great or small, without confiding in me. Why would he hide this from me? It's not so!"

³But David took an oath and said, "Your father knows very well that I have found favor in your eyes, and he has said to himself, 'Jonathan must not know this or he will be grieved.' Yet as surely as the LORD lives and as you live, there is only a step between me and death."

⁴Jonathan said to David, "Whatever you want me to do, I'll do for you."

⁵So David said, "Look, tomorrow is the New Moon festival, and I am supposed to dine with the king; but let me go and hide in the field until the evening of the day after tomorrow. ⁶If your father misses me at all, tell him, 'David earnestly asked my permission to hurry to Bethlehem, his hometown, because an annual sacrifice is being made there for his whole clan.' ⁷If he says, 'Very well,' then your servant is safe. But if he loses his temper, you can be sure that he is determined to harm me. ⁸As for you, show kindness to your servant, for you have brought him into a covenant with you before the LORD. If I am guilty, then kill me yourself! Why hand me over to your father?"

⁹"Never!" Jonathan said. "If I had the least inkling that my father was determined to harm you, wouldn't I tell you?"

¹⁰David asked, "Who will tell me if your father answers you harshly?"

¹¹"Come," Jonathan said, "let's go out into the field." So they went there together.

¹²Then Jonathan said to David: "By the LORD, the God of Israel, I will surely sound out my father by this time the day after tomorrow! If he is favorably disposed toward you, will I not send you word and let you know? ¹³But if my father is inclined to harm you, may the LORD deal with me, be it ever so severely, if I do not let you know and send you away safely. May the LORD be with you as he has been with my father. ¹⁴But show me unfailing kindness like that of the LORD as long as I live, so that I may not be killed, ¹⁵and do not ever cut off your kindness from my family—not even when the LORD has cut off every one of David's enemies from the face of the earth."

¹⁶So Jonathan made a covenant with the house of David, saying, "May the LORD call David's enemies to account." ¹⁷And Jonathan had David reaffirm his oath out

---

ᵃ13 Hebrew *teraphim*; also in verse 16

of love for him, because he loved him as he loved himself.

18Then Jonathan said to David: "Tomorrow is the New Moon festival. You will be missed, because your seat will be empty. 19The day after tomorrow, toward evening, go to the place where you hid when this trouble began, and wait by the stone Ezel. 20I will shoot three arrows to the side of it, as though I were shooting at a target. 21Then I will send a boy and say, 'Go, find the arrows.' If I say to him, 'Look, the arrows are on this side of you; bring them here,' then come, because, as surely as the LORD lives, you are safe; there is no danger. 22But if I say to the boy, 'Look, the arrows are beyond you,' then you must go, because the LORD has sent you away. 23And about the matter you and I discussed—remember, the LORD is witness between you and me forever."

24So David hid in the field, and when the New Moon festival came, the king sat down to eat. 25He sat in his customary place by the wall, opposite Jonathan,*a* and Abner sat next to Saul, but David's place was empty. 26Saul said nothing that day, for he thought, "Something must have happened to David to make him ceremonially unclean—surely he is unclean." 27But the next day, the second day of the month, David's place was empty again. Then Saul said to his son Jonathan, "Why hasn't the son of Jesse come to the meal, either yesterday or today?"

28Jonathan answered, "David earnestly asked me for permission to go to Bethlehem. 29He said, 'Let me go, because our family is observing a sacrifice in the town and my brother has ordered me to be there. If I have found favor in your eyes, let me get away to see my brothers.' That is why he has not come to the king's table."

30Saul's anger flared up at Jonathan and he said to him, "You son of a perverse and rebellious woman! Don't I know that you have sided with the son of Jesse to your own shame and to the shame of the mother who bore you? 31As long as the son of Jesse lives on this earth, neither you nor your kingdom will be established. Now send and bring him to me, for he must die!"

32"Why should he be put to death? What has he done?" Jonathan asked his father. 33But Saul hurled his spear at him to kill him. Then Jonathan knew that his father intended to kill David.

34Jonathan got up from the table in fierce anger; on that second day of the month he did not eat, because he was grieved at his father's shameful treatment of David.

35In the morning Jonathan went out to the field for his meeting with David. He had a small boy with him, 36and he said to the boy, "Run and find the arrows I shoot." As the boy ran, he shot an arrow beyond him. 37When the boy came to the place where Jonathan's arrow had fallen, Jonathan called out after him, "Isn't the arrow beyond you?" 38Then he shouted, "Hurry! Go quickly! Don't stop!" The boy picked up the arrow and returned to his master. 39(The boy knew nothing of all this; only Jonathan and David knew.) 40Then Jonathan gave his weapons to the boy and said, "Go, carry them back to town."

41After the boy had gone, David got up from the south side ,of the stone, and bowed down before Jonathan three times, with his face to the ground. Then they kissed each other and wept together —but David wept the most.

42Jonathan said to David, "Go in peace, for we have sworn friendship with each other in the name of the LORD, saying, 'The LORD is witness between you and me, and between your descendants and my descendants forever.' " Then David left, and Jonathan went back to the town.

David at Nob

21 David went to Nob, to Ahimelech the priest. Ahimelech trembled when he met him, and asked, "Why are you alone? Why is no one with you?"

2David answered Ahimelech the priest, "The king charged me with a certain matter and said to me, 'No one is to know anything about your mission and your instructions.' As for my men, I have told them to meet me at a certain place. 3Now then, what do you have on hand? Give me five loaves of bread, or whatever you can find."

4But the priest answered David, "I don't have any ordinary bread on hand; however, there is some consecrated bread here—provided the men have kept themselves from women."

5David replied, "Indeed women have been kept from us, as usual whenever*b* I

---

*a*25 Septuagint; Hebrew *wall. Jonathan arose*   *b*5 Or *from us in the past few days since* set out. The men's things*a* are holy even on missions that are not holy. How much more so today!" 6So the priest gave him the consecrated bread, since there was no bread there except the bread of the Presence that had been removed from before the LORD and replaced by hot bread on the day it was taken away.

7Now one of Saul's servants was there that day, detained before the LORD; he was Doeg the Edomite, Saul's head shepherd.

8David asked Ahimelech, "Don't you have a spear or a sword here? I haven't brought my sword or any other weapon, because the king's business was urgent."

9The priest replied, "The sword of Goliath the Philistine, whom you killed in the Valley of Elah, is here; it is wrapped in a cloth behind the ephod. If you want it, take it; there is no sword here but that one."

David said, "There is none like it; give it to me."

David at Gath

10That day David fled from Saul and went to Achish king of Gath. 11But the servants of Achish said to him, "Isn't this David, the king of the land? Isn't he the one they sing about in their dances:

" 'Saul has slain his thousands,
    and David his tens of thousands'?"

12David took these words to heart and was very much afraid of Achish king of Gath. 13So he pretended to be insane in their presence; and while he was in their hands he acted like a madman, making marks on the doors of the gate and letting saliva run down his beard.

14Achish said to his servants, "Look at the man! He is insane! Why bring him to me? 15Am I so short of madmen that you have to bring this fellow here to carry on like this in front of me? Must this man come into my house?"

David at Adullam and Mizpah

22 David left Gath and escaped to the cave of Adullam. When his brothers and his father's household heard about it, they went down to him there. 2All those who were in distress or in debt or discontented gathered around him, and he became their leader. About four hundred men were with him.

3From there David went to Mizpah in Moab and said to the king of Moab, "Would you let my father and mother come and stay with you until I learn what God will do for me?" 4So he left them with the king of Moab, and they stayed with him as long as David was in the stronghold.

5But the prophet Gad said to David, "Do not stay in the stronghold. Go into the land of Judah." So David left and went to the forest of Hereth.

Saul Kills the Priests of Nob

6Now Saul heard that David and his men had been discovered. And Saul, spear in hand, was seated under the tamarisk tree on the hill at Gibeah, with all his officials standing around him. 7Saul said to them, "Listen, men of Benjamin! Will the son of Jesse give all of you fields and vineyards? Will he make all of you commanders of thousands and commanders of hundreds? 8Is that why you have all conspired against me? No one tells me when my son makes a covenant with the son of Jesse. None of you is concerned about me or tells me that my son has incited my servant to lie in wait for me, as he does today."

9But Doeg the Edomite, who was standing with Saul's officials, said, "I saw the son of Jesse come to Ahimelech son of Ahitub at Nob. 10Ahimelech inquired of the LORD for him; he also gave him provisions and the sword of Goliath the Philistine."

11Then the king sent for the priest Ahimelech son of Ahitub and his father's whole family, who were the priests at Nob, and they all came to the king. 12Saul said, "Listen now, son of Ahitub."

"Yes, my lord," he answered.

13Saul said to him, "Why have you conspired against me, you and the son of Jesse, giving him bread and a sword and inquiring of God for him, so that he has rebelled against me and lies in wait for me, as he does today?"

14Ahimelech answered the king, "Who of all your servants is as loyal as David, the king's son-in-law, captain of your bodyguard and highly respected in your household? 15Was that day the first time I inquired of God for him? Of course not! Let not the king accuse your servant or any of his father's family, for your servant knows nothing at all about this whole affair."

a5 Or bodies

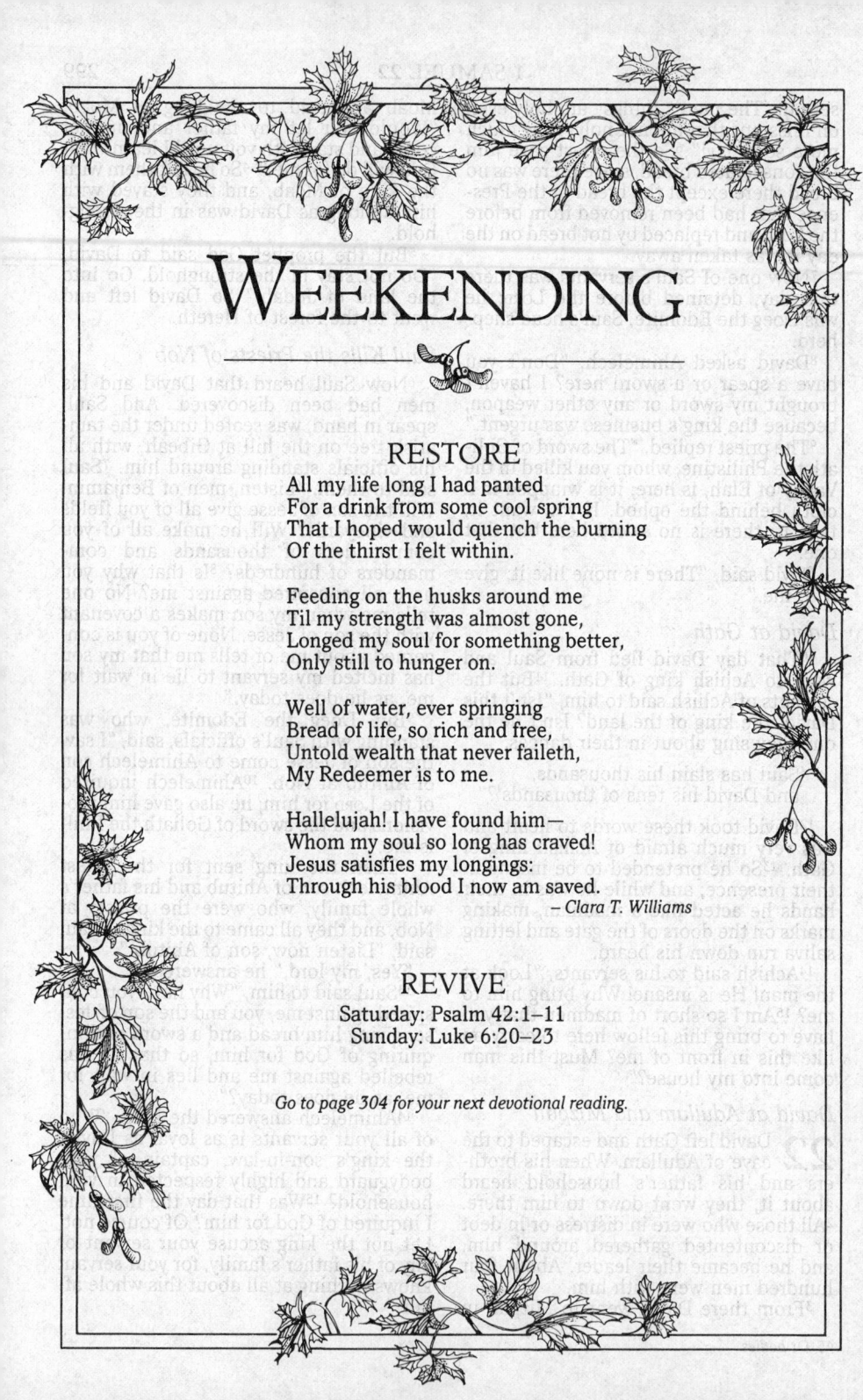

WEEKENDING

RESTORE

All my life long I had panted
For a drink from some cool spring
That I hoped would quench the burning
Of the thirst I felt within.

Feeding on the husks around me
Til my strength was almost gone,
Longed my soul for something better,
Only still to hunger on.

Well of water, ever springing
Bread of life, so rich and free,
Untold wealth that never faileth,
My Redeemer is to me.

Hallelujah! I have found him—
Whom my soul so long has craved!
Jesus satisfies my longings:
Through his blood I now am saved.
— *Clara T. Williams*

REVIVE

Saturday: Psalm 42:1–11
Sunday: Luke 6:20–23

Go to page 304 for your next devotional reading.

¹⁶But the king said, "You will surely die, Ahimelech, you and your father's whole family."

¹⁷Then the king ordered the guards at his side: "Turn and kill the priests of the LORD, because they too have sided with David. They knew he was fleeing, yet they did not tell me."

But the king's officials were not willing to raise a hand to strike the priests of the LORD.

¹⁸The king then ordered Doeg, "You turn and strike down the priests." So Doeg the Edomite turned and struck them down. That day he killed eighty-five men who wore the linen ephod. ¹⁹He also put to the sword Nob, the town of the priests, with its men and women, its children and infants, and its cattle, donkeys and sheep.

²⁰But Abiathar, a son of Ahimelech son of Ahitub, escaped and fled to join David. ²¹He told David that Saul had killed the priests of the LORD. ²²Then David said to Abiathar: "That day, when Doeg the Edomite was there, I knew he would be sure to tell Saul. I am responsible for the death of your father's whole family. ²³Stay with me; don't be afraid; the man who is seeking your life is seeking mine also. You will be safe with me."

David Saves Keilah

23 When David was told, "Look, the Philistines are fighting against Keilah and are looting the threshing floors," ²he inquired of the LORD, saying, "Shall I go and attack these Philistines?"

The LORD answered him, "Go, attack the Philistines and save Keilah."

³But David's men said to him, "Here in Judah we are afraid. How much more, then, if we go to Keilah against the Philistine forces!"

⁴Once again David inquired of the LORD, and the LORD answered him, "Go down to Keilah, for I am going to give the Philistines into your hand." ⁵So David and his men went to Keilah, fought the Philistines and carried off their livestock. He inflicted heavy losses on the Philistines and saved the people of Keilah. ⁶(Now Abiathar son of Ahimelech had brought the ephod down with him when he fled to David at Keilah.)

Saul Pursues David

⁷Saul was told that David had gone to Keilah, and he said, "God has handed him over to me, for David has imprisoned himself by entering a town with gates and bars." ⁸And Saul called up all his forces for battle, to go down to Keilah to besiege David and his men.

⁹When David learned that Saul was plotting against him, he said to Abiathar the priest, "Bring the ephod." ¹⁰David said, "O LORD, God of Israel, your servant has heard definitely that Saul plans to come to Keilah and destroy the town on account of me. ¹¹Will the citizens of Keilah surrender me to him? Will Saul come down, as your servant has heard? O LORD, God of Israel, tell your servant."

And the LORD said, "He will."

¹²Again David asked, "Will the citizens of Keilah surrender me and my men to Saul?"

And the LORD said, "They will."

¹³So David and his men, about six hundred in number, left Keilah and kept moving from place to place. When Saul was told that David had escaped from Keilah, he did not go there.

¹⁴David stayed in the desert strongholds and in the hills of the Desert of Ziph. Day after day Saul searched for him, but God did not give David into his hands.

¹⁵While David was at Horesh in the Desert of Ziph, he learned that Saul had come out to take his life. ¹⁶And Saul's son Jonathan went to David at Horesh and helped him find strength in God. ¹⁷"Don't be afraid," he said. "My father Saul will not lay a hand on you. You will be king over Israel, and I will be second to you. Even my father Saul knows this." ¹⁸The two of them made a covenant before the LORD. Then Jonathan went home, but David remained at Horesh.

¹⁹The Ziphites went up to Saul at Gibeah and said, "Is not David hiding among us in the strongholds at Horesh, on the hill of Hakilah, south of Jeshimon? ²⁰Now, O king, come down whenever it pleases you to do so, and we will be responsible for handing him over to the king."

²¹Saul replied, "The LORD bless you for your concern for me. ²²Go and make further preparation. Find out where David usually goes and who has seen him there. They tell me he is very crafty. ²³Find out about all the hiding places he uses and come back to me with definite information.ᵃ Then I will go with you; if he is in

ᵃ23 Or me at Nacon

the area, I will track him down among all the clans of Judah."

²⁴So they set out and went to Ziph ahead of Saul. Now David and his men were in the Desert of Maon, in the Arabah south of Jeshimon. ²⁵Saul and his men began the search, and when David was told about it, he went down to the rock and stayed in the Desert of Maon. When Saul heard this, he went into the Desert of Maon in pursuit of David.

²⁶Saul was going along one side of the mountain, and David and his men were on the other side, hurrying to get away from Saul. As Saul and his forces were closing in on David and his men to capture them, ²⁷a messenger came to Saul, saying, "Come quickly! The Philistines are raiding the land." ²⁸Then Saul broke off his pursuit of David and went to meet the Philistines. That is why they call this place Sela Hammahlekoth.ᵃ ²⁹And David went up from there and lived in the strongholds of En Gedi.

David Spares Saul's Life

24 After Saul returned from pursuing the Philistines, he was told, "David is in the Desert of En Gedi." ²So Saul took three thousand chosen men from all Israel and set out to look for David and his men near the Crags of the Wild Goats.

³He came to the sheep pens along the way; a cave was there, and Saul went in to relieve himself. David and his men were far back in the cave. ⁴The men said, "This is the day the LORD spoke of when he saidᵇ to you, 'I will give your enemy into your hands for you to deal with as you wish.'" Then David crept up unnoticed and cut off a corner of Saul's robe.

⁵Afterward, David was conscience-stricken for having cut off a corner of his robe. ⁶He said to his men, "The LORD forbid that I should do such a thing to my master, the LORD's anointed, or lift my hand against him; for he is the anointed of the LORD." ⁷With these words David rebuked his men and did not allow them to attack Saul. And Saul left the cave and went his way.

⁸Then David went out of the cave and called out to Saul, "My lord the king!" When Saul looked behind him, David bowed down and prostrated himself with his face to the ground. ⁹He said to Saul, "Why do you listen when men say, 'David

is bent on harming you'? ¹⁰This day you have seen with your own eyes how the LORD delivered you into my hands in the cave. Some urged me to kill you, but I spared you; I said, 'I will not lift my hand against my master, because he is the LORD's anointed.' ¹¹See, my father, look at this piece of your robe in my hand! I cut off the corner of your robe but did not kill you. Now understand and recognize that I am not guilty of wrongdoing or rebellion. I have not wronged you, but you are hunting me down to take my life. ¹²May the LORD judge between you and me. And may the LORD avenge the wrongs you have done to me, but my hand will not touch you. ¹³As the old saying goes, 'From evildoers come evil deeds,' so my hand will not touch you.

¹⁴"Against whom has the king of Israel come out? Whom are you pursuing? A dead dog? A flea? ¹⁵May the LORD be our judge and decide between us. May he consider my cause and uphold it; may he vindicate me by delivering me from your hand."

¹⁶When David finished saying this, Saul asked, "Is that your voice, David my son?" And he wept aloud. ¹⁷"You are more righteous than I," he said. "You have treated me well, but I have treated you badly. ¹⁸You have just now told me of the good you did to me; the LORD delivered me into your hands, but you did not kill me. ¹⁹When a man finds his enemy, does he let him get away unharmed? May the LORD reward you well for the way you treated me today. ²⁰I know that you will surely be king and that the kingdom of Israel will be established in your hands. ²¹Now swear to me by the LORD that you will not cut off my descendants or wipe out my name from my father's family."

²²So David gave his oath to Saul. Then Saul returned home, but David and his men went up to the stronghold.

David, Nabal and Abigail

25 Now Samuel died, and all Israel assembled and mourned for him; and they buried him at his home in Ramah.

Then David moved down into the Desert of Maon.ᶜ ²A certain man in Maon, who had property there at Carmel, was very wealthy. He had a thousand goats and three thousand sheep, which

---

ᵃ28 Sela Hammahlekoth means rock of parting.   ᵇ4 Or "Today the LORD is saying   ᶜ1 Some
Septuagint manuscripts; Hebrew Paran

he was shearing in Carmel. [3]His name was Nabal and his wife's name was Abigail. She was an intelligent and beautiful woman, but her husband, a Calebite, was surly and mean in his dealings.

[4]While David was in the desert, he heard that Nabal was shearing sheep. [5]So he sent ten young men and said to them, "Go up to Nabal at Carmel and greet him in my name. [6]Say to him: 'Long life to you! Good health to you and your household! And good health to all that is yours!

[7]"'Now I hear that it is sheep-shearing time. When your shepherds were with us, we did not mistreat them, and the whole time they were at Carmel nothing of theirs was missing. [8]Ask your own servants and they will tell you. Therefore be favorable toward my young men, since we come at a festive time. Please give your servants and your son David whatever you can find for them.'"

[9]When David's men arrived, they gave Nabal this message in David's name. Then they waited.

[10]Nabal answered David's servants, "Who is this David? Who is this son of Jesse? Many servants are breaking away from their masters these days. [11]Why should I take my bread and water, and the meat I have slaughtered for my shearers, and give it to men coming from who knows where?"

[12]David's men turned around and went back. When they arrived, they reported every word. [13]David said to his men, "Put on your swords!" So they put on their swords, and David put on his. About four hundred men went up with David, while two hundred stayed with the supplies.

[14]One of the servants told Nabal's wife Abigail: "David sent messengers from the desert to give our master his greetings, but he hurled insults at them. [15]Yet these men were very good to us. They did not mistreat us, and the whole time we were out in the fields near them nothing was missing. [16]Night and day they were a wall around us all the time we were herding our sheep near them. [17]Now think it over and see what you can do, because disaster is hanging over our master and his whole household. He is such a wicked man that no one can talk to him."

[18]Abigail lost no time. She took two hundred loaves of bread, two skins of wine, five dressed sheep, five seahs[a] of roasted grain, a hundred cakes of raisins and two hundred cakes of pressed figs, and loaded them on donkeys. [19]Then she told her servants, "Go on ahead; I'll follow you." But she did not tell her husband Nabal.

[20]As she came riding her donkey into a mountain ravine, there were David and his men descending toward her, and she met them. [21]David had just said, "It's been useless—all my watching over this fellow's property in the desert so that nothing of his was missing. He has paid me back evil for good. [22]May God deal with David,[b] be it ever so severely, if by morning I leave alive one male of all who belong to him!"

[23]When Abigail saw David, she quickly got off her donkey and bowed down before David with her face to the ground. [24]She fell at his feet and said: "My lord, let the blame be on me alone. Please let your servant speak to you; hear what your servant has to say. [25]May my lord pay no attention to that wicked man Nabal. He is just like his name—his name is Fool, and folly goes with him. But as for me, your servant, I did not see the men my master sent.

[26]"Now since the LORD has kept you, my master, from bloodshed and from avenging yourself with your own hands, as surely as the LORD lives and as you live, may your enemies and all who intend to harm my master be like Nabal. [27]And let this gift, which your servant has brought to my master, be given to the men who follow you. [28]Please forgive your servant's offense, for the LORD will certainly make a lasting dynasty for my master, because he fights the LORD's battles. Let no wrongdoing be found in you as long as you live. [29]Even though someone is pursuing you to take your life, the life of my master will be bound securely in the bundle of the living by the LORD your God. But the lives of your enemies he will hurl away as from the pocket of a sling. [30]When the LORD has done for my master every good thing he promised concerning him and has appointed him leader over Israel, [31]my master will not have on his conscience the staggering burden of needless bloodshed or of having avenged himself. And when the LORD has brought my master success, remember your servant."

[32]David said to Abigail, "Praise be to

a18 That is, probably about a bushel (about 37 liters) David's enemies

b22 Some Septuagint manuscripts; Hebrew with

the LORD, the God of Israel, who has sent you today to meet me. ³³May you be blessed for your good judgment and for keeping me from bloodshed this day and from avenging myself with my own hands. ³⁴Otherwise, as surely as the LORD, the God of Israel, lives, who has kept me from harming you, if you had not come quickly to meet me, not one male belonging to Nabal would have been left alive by daybreak."

³⁵Then David accepted from her hand what she had brought him and said, "Go home in peace. I have heard your words and granted your request."

³⁶When Abigail went to Nabal, he was in the house holding a banquet like that of a king. He was in high spirits and very drunk. So she told him nothing until daybreak. ³⁷Then in the morning, when Nabal was sober, his wife told him all these things, and his heart failed him and he became like a stone. ³⁸About ten days later, the LORD struck Nabal and he died.

MONDAY

VERSE FOR THE DAY:
1 Samuel 25:35

AUTHOR:
Gien Karssen

PASSAGE FOR THE DAY:
1 Samuel 25:4–35

A Peaceful Conscience

THERE are days when evil powers suddenly strike, wanting to harm us permanently. David experienced such a day. He had recently offered help and protection to Nabal, a wealthy herdsman. Instead of being rewarded, David was rudely rejected. He decided to get revenge. Nabal and all his colaborers would be slaughtered.

David overlooked the importance and responsibilities of his coming position. He was the anointed future king of Israel. This premeditated reckless deed would give him a bad name with his future subjects. It would deprive him of peace of conscience and peace with God.

Nabal's wife, Abigail, understood the danger. Tactfully she gave David both things that her husband denied him: recognition that was due him and food.

"Please, listen to me," she said. "When in the past people tried to kill you, God kept you from taking revenge. Leave it, therefore, to him to judge Nabal's rude behavior. When God makes you king, your conscience should not be burdened with murder."

Abigail's words restored David to sound thinking. They opened his eyes to the error of his ways. He praised the Lord for Abigail's intelligent judgment.

When the day of evil comes upon us, when we, confused by negative thinking, are in danger of making a wrong decision, may we also meet someone who warns us, who shows us the right way, who has our good conscience at heart. That is a gift of peace from God.

Additional Scripture Readings:
2 Kings 5:8–14; James 5:19–20

Go to page 318 for your next devotional reading.

³⁹When David heard that Nabal was dead, he said, "Praise be to the LORD, who has upheld my cause against Nabal for treating me with contempt. He has kept his servant from doing wrong and has brought Nabal's wrongdoing down on his own head."

Then David sent word to Abigail, asking her to become his wife. ⁴⁰His servants went to Carmel and said to Abigail, "David has sent us to you to take you to become his wife."

⁴¹She bowed down with her face to the ground and said, "Here is your maidservant, ready to serve you and wash the feet of my master's servants." ⁴²Abigail quickly got on a donkey and, attended by her five maids, went with David's messengers and became his wife. ⁴³David had also married Ahinoam of Jezreel, and they both were his wives. ⁴⁴But Saul had given his daughter Michal, David's wife, to Paltielᵃ son of Laish, who was from Gallim.

David Again Spares Saul's Life

26 The Ziphites went to Saul at Gibeah and said, "Is not David hiding on the hill of Hakilah, which faces Jeshimon?"

²So Saul went down to the Desert of Ziph, with his three thousand chosen men of Israel, to search there for David. ³Saul made his camp beside the road on the hill of Hakilah facing Jeshimon, but David stayed in the desert. When he saw that Saul had followed him there, ⁴he sent out scouts and learned that Saul had definitely arrived.ᵇ

⁵Then David set out and went to the place where Saul had camped. He saw where Saul and Abner son of Ner, the commander of the army, had lain down. Saul was lying inside the camp, with the army encamped around him.

⁶David then asked Ahimelech the Hittite and Abishai son of Zeruiah, Joab's brother, "Who will go down into the camp with me to Saul?"

"I'll go with you," said Abishai.

⁷So David and Abishai went to the army by night, and there was Saul, lying asleep inside the camp with his spear stuck in the ground near his head. Abner and the soldiers were lying around him.

⁸Abishai said to David, "Today God has delivered your enemy into your hands.

Now let me pin him to the ground with one thrust of my spear; I won't strike him twice."

⁹But David said to Abishai, "Don't destroy him! Who can lay a hand on the LORD's anointed and be guiltless? ¹⁰As surely as the LORD lives," he said, "the LORD himself will strike him; either his time will come and he will die, or he will go into battle and perish. ¹¹But the LORD forbid that I should lay a hand on the LORD's anointed. Now get the spear and water jug that are near his head, and let's go."

¹²So David took the spear and water jug near Saul's head, and they left. No one saw or knew about it, nor did anyone wake up. They were all sleeping, because the LORD had put them into a deep sleep.

¹³Then David crossed over to the other side and stood on top of the hill some distance away; there was a wide space between them. ¹⁴He called out to the army and to Abner son of Ner, "Aren't you going to answer me, Abner?"

Abner replied, "Who are you who calls to the king?"

¹⁵David said, "You're a man, aren't you? And who is like you in Israel? Why didn't you guard your lord the king? Someone came to destroy your lord the king. ¹⁶What you have done is not good. As surely as the LORD lives, you and your men deserve to die, because you did not guard your master, the LORD's anointed. Look around you. Where are the king's spear and water jug that were near his head?"

¹⁷Saul recognized David's voice and said, "Is that your voice, David my son?"

David replied, "Yes it is, my lord the king." ¹⁸And he added, "Why is my lord pursuing his servant? What have I done, and what wrong am I guilty of? ¹⁹Now let my lord the king listen to his servant's words. If the LORD has incited you against me, then may he accept an offering. If, however, men have done it, may they be cursed before the LORD! They have now driven me from my share in the LORD's inheritance and have said, 'Go, serve other gods.' ²⁰Now do not let my blood fall to the ground far from the presence of the LORD. The king of Israel has come out to look for a flea—as one hunts a partridge in the mountains."

²¹Then Saul said, "I have sinned. Come

ᵃ44 Hebrew *Palti*, a variant of *Paltiel*   ᵇ4 Or *had come to Nacon* back, David my son. Because you considered my life precious today, I will not try to harm you again. Surely I have acted like a fool and have erred greatly."

²²"Here is the king's spear," David answered. "Let one of your young men come over and get it. ²³The LORD rewards every man for his righteousness and faithfulness. The LORD delivered you into my hands today, but I would not lay a hand on the LORD's anointed. ²⁴As surely as I valued your life today, so may the LORD value my life and deliver me from all trouble."

²⁵Then Saul said to David, "May you be blessed, my son David; you will do great things and surely triumph."

So David went on his way, and Saul returned home.

David Among the Philistines

27 But David thought to himself, "One of these days I will be destroyed by the hand of Saul. The best thing I can do is to escape to the land of the Philistines. Then Saul will give up searching for me anywhere in Israel, and I will slip out of his hand."

²So David and the six hundred men with him left and went over to Achish son of Maoch king of Gath. ³David and his men settled in Gath with Achish. Each man had his family with him, and David had his two wives: Ahinoam of Jezreel and Abigail of Carmel, the widow of Nabal. ⁴When Saul was told that David had fled to Gath, he no longer searched for him.

⁵Then David said to Achish, "If I have found favor in your eyes, let a place be assigned to me in one of the country towns, that I may live there. Why should your servant live in the royal city with you?"

⁶So on that day Achish gave him Ziklag, and it has belonged to the kings of Judah ever since. ⁷David lived in Philistine territory a year and four months.

⁸Now David and his men went up and raided the Geshurites, the Girzites and the Amalekites. (From ancient times these peoples had lived in the land extending to Shur and Egypt.) ⁹Whenever David attacked an area, he did not leave a man or woman alive, but took sheep and cattle, donkeys and camels, and clothes. Then he returned to Achish.

¹⁰When Achish asked, "Where did you go raiding today?" David would say, "Against the Negev of Judah" or "Against the Negev of Jerahmeel" or "Against the Negev of the Kenites." ¹¹He did not leave a man or woman alive to be brought to Gath, for he thought, "They might inform on us and say, 'This is what David did.' " And such was his practice as long as he lived in Philistine territory. ¹²Achish trusted David and said to himself, "He has become so odious to his people, the Israelites, that he will be my servant forever."

Saul and the Witch of Endor

28 In those days the Philistines gathered their forces to fight against Israel. Achish said to David, "You must understand that you and your men will accompany me in the army."

²David said, "Then you will see for yourself what your servant can do."

Achish replied, "Very well, I will make you my bodyguard for life."

³Now Samuel was dead, and all Israel had mourned for him and buried him in his own town of Ramah. Saul had expelled the mediums and spiritists from the land.

⁴The Philistines assembled and came and set up camp at Shunem, while Saul gathered all the Israelites and set up camp at Gilboa. ⁵When Saul saw the Philistine army, he was afraid; terror filled his heart. ⁶He inquired of the LORD, but the LORD did not answer him by dreams or Urim or prophets. ⁷Saul then said to his attendants, "Find me a woman who is a medium, so I may go and inquire of her."

"There is one in Endor," they said.

⁸So Saul disguised himself, putting on other clothes, and at night he and two men went to the woman. "Consult a spirit for me," he said, "and bring up for me the one I name."

⁹But the woman said to him, "Surely you know what Saul has done. He has cut off the mediums and spiritists from the land. Why have you set a trap for my life to bring about my death?"

¹⁰Saul swore to her by the LORD, "As surely as the LORD lives, you will not be punished for this."

¹¹Then the woman asked, "Whom shall I bring up for you?"

"Bring up Samuel," he said.

¹²When the woman saw Samuel, she cried out at the top of her voice and said to Saul, "Why have you deceived me? You are Saul!"

¹³The king said to her, "Don't be afraid. What do you see?"

The woman said, "I see a spirit^a coming up out of the ground."

¹⁴"What does he look like?" he asked.

"An old man wearing a robe is coming up," she said.

Then Saul knew it was Samuel, and he bowed down and prostrated himself with his face to the ground.

¹⁵Samuel said to Saul, "Why have you disturbed me by bringing me up?"

"I am in great distress," Saul said. "The Philistines are fighting against me, and God has turned away from me. He no longer answers me, either by prophets or by dreams. So I have called on you to tell me what to do."

¹⁶Samuel said, "Why do you consult me, now that the LORD has turned away from you and become your enemy? ¹⁷The LORD has done what he predicted through me. The LORD has torn the kingdom out of your hands and given it to one of your neighbors—to David. ¹⁸Because you did not obey the LORD or carry out his fierce wrath against the Amalekites, the LORD has done this to you today. ¹⁹The LORD will hand over both Israel and you to the Philistines, and tomorrow you and your sons will be with me. The LORD will also hand over the army of Israel to the Philistines."

²⁰Immediately Saul fell full length on the ground, filled with fear because of Samuel's words. His strength was gone, for he had eaten nothing all that day and night.

²¹When the woman came to Saul and saw that he was greatly shaken, she said, "Look, your maidservant has obeyed you. I took my life in my hands and did what you told me to do. ²²Now please listen to your servant and let me give you some food so you may eat and have the strength to go on your way."

²³He refused and said, "I will not eat."

But his men joined the woman in urging him, and he listened to them. He got up from the ground and sat on the couch.

²⁴The woman had a fattened calf at the house, which she butchered at once. She took some flour, kneaded it and baked bread without yeast. ²⁵Then she set it before Saul and his men, and they ate. That same night they got up and left.

Achish Sends David Back to Ziklag

29 The Philistines gathered all their forces at Aphek, and Israel camped by the spring in Jezreel. ²As the Philistine rulers marched with their units of hundreds and thousands, David and his men were marching at the rear with Achish. ³The commanders of the Philistines asked, "What about these Hebrews?"

Achish replied, "Is this not David, who was an officer of Saul king of Israel? He has already been with me for over a year, and from the day he left Saul until now, I have found no fault in him."

⁴But the Philistine commanders were angry with him and said, "Send the man back, that he may return to the place you assigned him. He must not go with us into battle, or he will turn against us during the fighting. How better could he regain his master's favor than by taking the heads of our own men? ⁵Isn't this the David they sang about in their dances:

" 'Saul has slain his thousands,
    and David his tens of thousands'?"

⁶So Achish called David and said to him, "As surely as the LORD lives, you have been reliable, and I would be pleased to have you serve with me in the army. From the day you came to me until now, I have found no fault in you, but the rulers don't approve of you. ⁷Turn back and go in peace; do nothing to displease the Philistine rulers."

⁸"But what have I done?" asked David. "What have you found against your servant from the day I came to you until now? Why can't I go and fight against the enemies of my lord the king?"

⁹Achish answered, "I know that you have been as pleasing in my eyes as an angel of God; nevertheless, the Philistine commanders have said, 'He must not go up with us into battle.' ¹⁰Now get up early, along with your master's servants who have come with you, and leave in the morning as soon as it is light."

¹¹So David and his men got up early in the morning to go back to the land of the Philistines, and the Philistines went up to Jezreel.

David Destroys the Amalekites

30 David and his men reached Ziklag on the third day. Now the Amalek-

^a13 Or see spirits; or see gods

ites had raided the Negev and Ziklag. They had attacked Ziklag and burned it, 2and had taken captive the women and all who were in it, both young and old. They killed none of them, but carried them off as they went on their way.

3When David and his men came to Ziklag, they found it destroyed by fire and their wives and sons and daughters taken captive. 4So David and his men wept aloud until they had no strength left to weep. 5David's two wives had been captured—Ahinoam of Jezreel and Abigail, the widow of Nabal of Carmel. 6David was greatly distressed because the men were talking of stoning him; each one was bitter in spirit because of his sons and daughters. But David found strength in the LORD his God.

7Then David said to Abiathar the priest, the son of Ahimelech, "Bring me the ephod." Abiathar brought it to him, 8and David inquired of the LORD, "Shall I pursue this raiding party? Will I overtake them?"

"Pursue them," he answered. "You will certainly overtake them and succeed in the rescue."

9David and the six hundred men with him came to the Besor Ravine, where some stayed behind, 10for two hundred men were too exhausted to cross the ravine. But David and four hundred men continued the pursuit.

11They found an Egyptian in a field and brought him to David. They gave him water to drink and food to eat— 12part of a cake of pressed figs and two cakes of raisins. He ate and was revived, for he had not eaten any food or drunk any water for three days and three nights.

13David asked him, "To whom do you belong, and where do you come from?"

He said, "I am an Egyptian, the slave of an Amalekite. My master abandoned me when I became ill three days ago. 14We raided the Negev of the Kerethites and the territory belonging to Judah and the Negev of Caleb. And we burned Ziklag."

15David asked him, "Can you lead me down to this raiding party?"

He answered, "Swear to me before God that you will not kill me or hand me over to my master, and I will take you down to them."

16He led David down, and there they were, scattered over the countryside, eating, drinking and reveling because of the great amount of plunder they had taken from the land of the Philistines and from

Judah. 17David fought them from dusk until the evening of the next day, and none of them got away, except four hundred young men who rode off on camels and fled. 18David recovered everything the Amalekites had taken, including his two wives. 19Nothing was missing: young or old, boy or girl, plunder or anything else they had taken. David brought everything back. 20He took all the flocks and herds, and his men drove them ahead of the other livestock, saying, "This is David's plunder."

21Then David came to the two hundred men who had been too exhausted to follow him and who were left behind at the Besor Ravine. They came out to meet David and the people with him. As David and his men approached, he greeted them. 22But all the evil men and troublemakers among David's followers said, "Because they did not go out with us, we will not share with them the plunder we recovered. However, each man may take his wife and children and go."

23David replied, "No, my brothers, you must not do that with what the LORD has given us. He has protected us and handed over to us the forces that came against us. 24Who will listen to what you say? The share of the man who stayed with the supplies is to be the same as that of him who went down to the battle. All will share alike." 25David made this a statute and ordinance for Israel from that day to this.

26When David arrived in Ziklag, he sent some of the plunder to the elders of Judah, who were his friends, saying, "Here is a present for you from the plunder of the LORD's enemies."

27He sent it to those who were in Bethel, Ramoth Negev and Jattir; 28to those in Aroer, Siphmoth, Eshtemoa 29and Racal; to those in the towns of the Jerahmeelites and the Kenites; 30to those in Hormah, Bor Ashan, Athach 31and Hebron; and to those in all the other places where David and his men had roamed.

Saul Takes His Life

31 Now the Philistines fought against Israel; the Israelites fled before them, and many fell slain on Mount Gilboa. 2The Philistines pressed hard after Saul and his sons, and they killed his sons Jonathan, Abinadab and Malki-Shua. 3The fighting grew fierce around Saul, and when the archers overtook him, they wounded him critically.

[4]Saul said to his armor-bearer, "Draw your sword and run me through, or these uncircumcised fellows will come and run me through and abuse me."

But his armor-bearer was terrified and would not do it; so Saul took his own sword and fell on it. [5]When the armor-bearer saw that Saul was dead, he too fell on his sword and died with him. [6]So Saul and his three sons and his armor-bearer and all his men died together that same day.

[7]When the Israelites along the valley and those across the Jordan saw that the Israelite army had fled and that Saul and his sons had died, they abandoned their towns and fled. And the Philistines came and occupied them.

[8]The next day, when the Philistines came to strip the dead, they found Saul and his three sons fallen on Mount Gilboa. [9]They cut off his head and stripped off his armor, and they sent messengers throughout the land of the Philistines to proclaim the news in the temple of their idols and among their people. [10]They put his armor in the temple of the Ashtoreths and fastened his body to the wall of Beth Shan.

[11]When the people of Jabesh Gilead heard of what the Philistines had done to Saul, [12]all their valiant men journeyed through the night to Beth Shan. They took down the bodies of Saul and his sons from the wall of Beth Shan and went to Jabesh, where they burned them. [13]Then they took their bones and buried them under a tamarisk tree at Jabesh, and they fasted seven days.

*T*HIS book tells the story of David's kingship over Israel, noting both his many victories and God's promise that his descendants will be on the throne forever. After David's shameful sin with Bathsheba, severe family problems threaten his kingdom. As you read this book, consider how terrible the consequences of sin can be, but also remember the faithfulness of God, who fulfills his promise by sending his Son to reign forever as David's true son.

2 SAMUEL

David Hears of Saul's Death

1 After the death of Saul, David returned from defeating the Amalekites and stayed in Ziklag two days. ²On the third day a man arrived from Saul's camp, with his clothes torn and with dust on his head. When he came to David, he fell to the ground to pay him honor.

³"Where have you come from?" David asked him.

He answered, "I have escaped from the Israelite camp."

⁴"What happened?" David asked. "Tell me."

He said, "The men fled from the battle. Many of them fell and died. And Saul and his son Jonathan are dead."

⁵Then David said to the young man who brought him the report, "How do you know that Saul and his son Jonathan are dead?"

⁶"I happened to be on Mount Gilboa," the young man said, "and there was Saul, leaning on his spear, with the chariots and riders almost upon him. ⁷When he turned around and saw me, he called out to me, and I said, 'What can I do?'

⁸"He asked me, 'Who are you?'

" 'An Amalekite,' I answered.

⁹"Then he said to me, 'Stand over me and kill me! I am in the throes of death, but I'm still alive.'

¹⁰"So I stood over him and killed him, because I knew that after he had fallen he

could not survive. And I took the crown that was on his head and the band on his arm and have brought them here to my lord."

¹¹Then David and all the men with him took hold of their clothes and tore them. ¹²They mourned and wept and fasted till evening for Saul and his son Jonathan, and for the army of the LORD and the house of Israel, because they had fallen by the sword.

¹³David said to the young man who brought him the report, "Where are you from?"

"I am the son of an alien, an Amalekite," he answered.

¹⁴David asked him, "Why were you not afraid to lift your hand to destroy the LORD's anointed?"

¹⁵Then David called one of his men and said, "Go, strike him down!" So he struck him down, and he died. ¹⁶For David had said to him, "Your blood be on your own head. Your own mouth testified against you when you said, 'I killed the LORD's anointed.'"

David's Lament for Saul and Jonathan

¹⁷David took up this lament concerning Saul and his son Jonathan, ¹⁸and ordered that the men of Judah be taught this lament of the bow (it is written in the Book of Jashar):

¹⁹"Your glory, O Israel, lies slain on
    your heights.
How the mighty have fallen!

²⁰"Tell it not in Gath,
    proclaim it not in the streets of
       Ashkelon,
lest the daughters of the Philistines
       be glad,
    lest the daughters of the
       uncircumcised rejoice.

²¹"O mountains of Gilboa,
    may you have neither dew nor rain,
    nor fields that yield offerings ,of
       grain.
For there the shield of the mighty
       was defiled,
    the shield of Saul—no longer
       rubbed with oil.
²²From the blood of the slain,
    from the flesh of the mighty,
the bow of Jonathan did not turn
       back,
    the sword of Saul did not return
       unsatisfied.

²³"Saul and Jonathan—
    in life they were loved and gracious,
    and in death they were not parted.
They were swifter than eagles,
    they were stronger than lions.

²⁴"O daughters of Israel,
    weep for Saul,
who clothed you in scarlet and finery,
    who adorned your garments with
       ornaments of gold.

²⁵"How the mighty have fallen in battle!
    Jonathan lies slain on your heights.
²⁶I grieve for you, Jonathan my brother;
    you were very dear to me.
Your love for me was wonderful,
    more wonderful than that of
       women.

²⁷"How the mighty have fallen!
    The weapons of war have perished!"

David Anointed King Over Judah

2 In the course of time, David inquired of the LORD. "Shall I go up to one of the towns of Judah?" he asked.

The LORD said, "Go up."

David asked, "Where shall I go?"

"To Hebron," the LORD answered.

²So David went up there with his two wives, Ahinoam of Jezreel and Abigail, the widow of Nabal of Carmel. ³David also took the men who were with him, each with his family, and they settled in Hebron and its towns. ⁴Then the men of Judah came to Hebron and there they anointed David king over the house of Judah.

When David was told that it was the men of Jabesh Gilead who had buried Saul, ⁵he sent messengers to the men of Jabesh Gilead to say to them, "The LORD bless you for showing this kindness to Saul your master by burying him. ⁶May the LORD now show you kindness and faithfulness, and I too will show you the same favor because you have done this. ⁷Now then, be strong and brave, for Saul your master is dead, and the house of Judah has anointed me king over them."

War Between the Houses of David and Saul

⁸Meanwhile, Abner son of Ner, the commander of Saul's army, had taken Ish-Bosheth son of Saul and brought him over to Mahanaim. ⁹He made him king

over Gilead, Ashuri[a] and Jezreel, and also over Ephraim, Benjamin and all Israel.

[10]Ish-Bosheth son of Saul was forty years old when he became king over Israel, and he reigned two years. The house of Judah, however, followed David. [11]The length of time David was king in Hebron over the house of Judah was seven years and six months.

[12]Abner son of Ner, together with the men of Ish-Bosheth son of Saul, left Mahanaim and went to Gibeon. [13]Joab son of Zeruiah and David's men went out and met them at the pool of Gibeon. One group sat down on one side of the pool and one group on the other side.

[14]Then Abner said to Joab, "Let's have some of the young men get up and fight hand to hand in front of us."

"All right, let them do it," Joab said.

[15]So they stood up and were counted off—twelve men for Benjamin and Ish-Bosheth son of Saul, and twelve for David. [16]Then each man grabbed his opponent by the head and thrust his dagger into his opponent's side, and they fell down together. So that place in Gibeon was called Helkath Hazzurim.[b]

[17]The battle that day was very fierce, and Abner and the men of Israel were defeated by David's men.

[18]The three sons of Zeruiah were there: Joab, Abishai and Asahel. Now Asahel was as fleet-footed as a wild gazelle. [19]He chased Abner, turning neither to the right nor to the left as he pursued him. [20]Abner looked behind him and asked, "Is that you, Asahel?"

"It is," he answered.

[21]Then Abner said to him, "Turn aside to the right or to the left; take on one of the young men and strip him of his weapons." But Asahel would not stop chasing him.

[22]Again Abner warned Asahel, "Stop chasing me! Why should I strike you down? How could I look your brother Joab in the face?"

[23]But Asahel refused to give up the pursuit; so Abner thrust the butt of his spear into Asahel's stomach, and the spear came out through his back. He fell there and died on the spot. And every man

stopped when he came to the place where Asahel had fallen and died.

[24]But Joab and Abishai pursued Abner, and as the sun was setting, they came to the hill of Ammah, near Giah on the way to the wasteland of Gibeon. [25]Then the men of Benjamin rallied behind Abner. They formed themselves into a group and took their stand on top of a hill.

[26]Abner called out to Joab, "Must the sword devour forever? Don't you realize that this will end in bitterness? How long before you order your men to stop pursuing their brothers?"

[27]Joab answered, "As surely as God lives, if you had not spoken, the men would have continued the pursuit of their brothers until morning.[c]"

[28]So Joab blew the trumpet, and all the men came to a halt; they no longer pursued Israel, nor did they fight anymore.

[29]All that night Abner and his men marched through the Arabah. They crossed the Jordan, continued through the whole Bithron[d] and came to Mahanaim.

[30]Then Joab returned from pursuing Abner and assembled all his men. Besides Asahel, nineteen of David's men were found missing. [31]But David's men had killed three hundred and sixty Benjamites who were with Abner. [32]They took Asahel and buried him in his father's tomb at Bethlehem. Then Joab and his men marched all night and arrived at Hebron by daybreak.

3 The war between the house of Saul and the house of David lasted a long time. David grew stronger and stronger, while the house of Saul grew weaker and weaker.

[2]Sons were born to David in Hebron:

His firstborn was Amnon the son of Ahinoam of Jezreel;

[3]his second, Kileab the son of Abigail the widow of Nabal of Carmel;

the third, Absalom the son of Maacah daughter of Talmai king of Geshur;

[4]the fourth, Adonijah the son of Haggith;

the fifth, Shephatiah the son of Abital;

[5]and the sixth, Ithream the son of David's wife Eglah.

---

[a]9 Or *Asher*   [b]16 *Helkath Hazzurim* means *field of daggers* or *field of hostilities.*   [c]27 Or *spoken this morning, the men would not have taken up the pursuit of their brothers*; or *spoken, the men would have given up the pursuit of their brothers by morning*   [d]29 Or *morning*; or *ravine*; the meaning of the Hebrew for this word is uncertain.

These were born to David in Hebron.

Abner Goes Over to David

6During the war between the house of Saul and the house of David, Abner had been strengthening his own position in the house of Saul. 7Now Saul had had a concubine named Rizpah daughter of Aiah. And Ish-Bosheth said to Abner, "Why did you sleep with my father's concubine?"

8Abner was very angry because of what Ish-Bosheth said and he answered, "Am I a dog's head—on Judah's side? This very day I am loyal to the house of your father Saul and to his family and friends. I haven't handed you over to David. Yet now you accuse me of an offense involving this woman! 9May God deal with Abner, be it ever so severely, if I do not do for David what the LORD promised him on oath 10and transfer the kingdom from the house of Saul and establish David's throne over Israel and Judah from Dan to Beersheba." 11Ish-Bosheth did not dare to say another word to Abner, because he was afraid of him.

12Then Abner sent messengers on his behalf to say to David, "Whose land is it? Make an agreement with me, and I will help you bring all Israel over to you."

13"Good," said David. "I will make an agreement with you. But I demand one thing of you: Do not come into my presence unless you bring Michal daughter of Saul when you come to see me." 14Then David sent messengers to Ish-Bosheth son of Saul, demanding, "Give me my wife Michal, whom I betrothed to myself for the price of a hundred Philistine foreskins."

15So Ish-Bosheth gave orders and had her taken away from her husband Paltiel son of Laish. 16Her husband, however, went with her, weeping behind her all the way to Bahurim. Then Abner said to him, "Go back home!" So he went back.

17Abner conferred with the elders of Israel and said, "For some time you have wanted to make David your king. 18Now do it! For the LORD promised David, 'By my servant David I will rescue my people Israel from the hand of the Philistines and from the hand of all their enemies.'"

19Abner also spoke to the Benjamites in person. Then he went to Hebron to tell David everything that Israel and the whole house of Benjamin wanted to do. 20When Abner, who had twenty men with him, came to David at Hebron, David prepared a feast for him and his men. 21Then Abner said to David, "Let me go at once and assemble all Israel for my lord the king, so that they may make a compact with you, and that you may rule over all that your heart desires." So David sent Abner away, and he went in peace.

Joab Murders Abner

22Just then David's men and Joab returned from a raid and brought with them a great deal of plunder. But Abner was no longer with David in Hebron, because David had sent him away, and he had gone in peace. 23When Joab and all the soldiers with him arrived, he was told that Abner son of Ner had come to the king and that the king had sent him away and that he had gone in peace.

24So Joab went to the king and said, "What have you done? Look, Abner came to you. Why did you let him go? Now he is gone! 25You know Abner son of Ner; he came to deceive you and observe your movements and find out everything you are doing."

26Joab then left David and sent messengers after Abner, and they brought him back from the well of Sirah. But David did not know it. 27Now when Abner returned to Hebron, Joab took him aside into the gateway, as though to speak with him privately. And there, to avenge the blood of his brother Asahel, Joab stabbed him in the stomach, and he died.

28Later, when David heard about this, he said, "I and my kingdom are forever innocent before the LORD concerning the blood of Abner son of Ner. 29May his blood fall upon the head of Joab and upon all his father's house! May Joab's house never be without someone who has a running sore or leprosy*a* or who leans on a crutch or who falls by the sword or who lacks food."

30(Joab and his brother Abishai murdered Abner because he had killed their brother Asahel in the battle at Gibeon.)

31Then David said to Joab and all the people with him, "Tear your clothes and put on sackcloth and walk in mourning in front of Abner." King David himself walked behind the bier. 32They buried Abner in Hebron, and the king wept aloud at Abner's tomb. All the people wept also.

a29 The Hebrew word was used for various diseases affecting the skin—not necessarily leprosy.

³³The king sang this lament for Abner:

"Should Abner have died as the
    lawless die?
³⁴ Your hands were not bound,
    your feet were not fettered.
You fell as one falls before wicked
    men."

And all the people wept over him again.
³⁵Then they all came and urged David to eat something while it was still day; but David took an oath, saying, "May God deal with me, be it ever so severely, if I taste bread or anything else before the sun sets!" ³⁶All the people took note and were pleased; indeed, everything the king did pleased them. ³⁷So on that day all the people and all Israel knew that the king had no part in the murder of Abner son of Ner.

³⁸Then the king said to his men, "Do you not realize that a prince and a great man has fallen in Israel this day? ³⁹And today, though I am the anointed king, I am weak, and these sons of Zeruiah are too strong for me. May the LORD repay the evildoer according to his evil deeds!"

Ish-Bosheth Murdered

4 When Ish-Bosheth son of Saul heard that Abner had died in Hebron, he lost courage, and all Israel became alarmed. ²Now Saul's son had two men who were leaders of raiding bands. One was named Baanah and the other Recab; they were sons of Rimmon the Beerothite from the tribe of Benjamin—Beeroth is considered part of Benjamin, ³because the people of Beeroth fled to Gittaim and have lived there as aliens to this day.

⁴(Jonathan son of Saul had a son who was lame in both feet. He was five years old when the news about Saul and Jonathan came from Jezreel. His nurse picked him up and fled, but as she hurried to leave, he fell and became crippled. His name was Mephibosheth.)

⁵Now Recab and Baanah, the sons of Rimmon the Beerothite, set out for the house of Ish-Bosheth, and they arrived there in the heat of the day while he was taking his noonday rest. ⁶They went into the inner part of the house as if to get some wheat, and they stabbed him in the stomach. Then Recab and his brother Baanah slipped away.

⁷They had gone into the house while he was lying on the bed in his bedroom. After they stabbed and killed him, they cut off his head. Taking it with them, they traveled all night by way of the Arabah. ⁸They brought the head of Ish-Bosheth to David at Hebron and said to the king, "Here is the head of Ish-Bosheth son of Saul, your enemy, who tried to take your life. This day the LORD has avenged my lord the king against Saul and his offspring."

⁹David answered Recab and his brother Baanah, the sons of Rimmon the Beerothite, "As surely as the LORD lives, who has delivered me out of all trouble, ¹⁰when a man told me, 'Saul is dead,' and thought he was bringing good news, I seized him and put him to death in Ziklag. That was the reward I gave him for his news! ¹¹How much more—when wicked men have killed an innocent man in his own house and on his own bed—should I not now demand his blood from your hand and rid the earth of you!"

¹²So David gave an order to his men, and they killed them. They cut off their hands and feet and hung the bodies by the pool in Hebron. But they took the head of Ish-Bosheth and buried it in Abner's tomb at Hebron.

David Becomes King Over Israel

5 All the tribes of Israel came to David at Hebron and said, "We are your own flesh and blood. ²In the past, while Saul was king over us, you were the one who led Israel on their military campaigns. And the LORD said to you, 'You will shepherd my people Israel, and you will become their ruler.'"

³When all the elders of Israel had come to King David at Hebron, the king made a compact with them at Hebron before the LORD, and they anointed David king over Israel.

⁴David was thirty years old when he became king, and he reigned forty years. ⁵In Hebron he reigned over Judah seven years and six months, and in Jerusalem he reigned over all Israel and Judah thirty-three years.

David Conquers Jerusalem

⁶The king and his men marched to Jerusalem to attack the Jebusites, who lived there. The Jebusites said to David, "You will not get in here; even the blind and the lame can ward you off." They thought, "David cannot get in here." ⁷Nevertheless, David captured the fortress of Zion, the City of David.

⁸On that day, David said, "Anyone who

conquers the Jebusites will have to use the water shaft*a* to reach those 'lame and blind' who are David's enemies.*b*" That is why they say, "The 'blind and lame' will not enter the palace."

⁹David then took up residence in the fortress and called it the City of David. He built up the area around it, from the supporting terraces*c* inward. ¹⁰And he became more and more powerful, because the LORD God Almighty was with him.

¹¹Now Hiram king of Tyre sent messengers to David, along with cedar logs and carpenters and stonemasons, and they built a palace for David. ¹²And David knew that the LORD had established him as king over Israel and had exalted his kingdom for the sake of his people Israel.

¹³After he left Hebron, David took more concubines and wives in Jerusalem, and more sons and daughters were born to him. ¹⁴These are the names of the children born to him there: Shammua, Shobab, Nathan, Solomon, ¹⁵Ibhar, Elishua, Nepheg, Japhia, ¹⁶Elishama, Eliada and Eliphelet.

David Defeats the Philistines

¹⁷When the Philistines heard that David had been anointed king over Israel, they went up in full force to search for him, but David heard about it and went down to the stronghold. ¹⁸Now the Philistines had come and spread out in the Valley of Rephaim; ¹⁹so David inquired of the LORD, "Shall I go and attack the Philistines? Will you hand them over to me?"

The LORD answered him, "Go, for I will surely hand the Philistines over to you."

²⁰So David went to Baal Perazim, and there he defeated them. He said, "As waters break out, the LORD has broken out against my enemies before me." So that place was called Baal Perazim.*d* ²¹The Philistines abandoned their idols there, and David and his men carried them off.

²²Once more the Philistines came up and spread out in the Valley of Rephaim; ²³so David inquired of the LORD, and he answered, "Do not go straight up, but circle around behind them and attack them in front of the balsam trees. ²⁴As soon as you hear the sound of marching in the tops of the balsam trees, move quickly, because that will mean the LORD has gone out in front of you to strike the Philistine army." ²⁵So David did as the LORD commanded him, and he struck down the Philistines all the way from Gibeon*e* to Gezer.

The Ark Brought to Jerusalem

6 David again brought together out of Israel chosen men, thirty thousand in all. ²He and all his men set out from Baalah of Judah*f* to bring up from there the ark of God, which is called by the Name,*g* the name of the LORD Almighty, who is enthroned between the cherubim that are on the ark. ³They set the ark of God on a new cart and brought it from the house of Abinadab, which was on the hill. Uzzah and Ahio, sons of Abinadab, were guiding the new cart ⁴with the ark of God on it,*h* and Ahio was walking in front of it. ⁵David and the whole house of Israel were celebrating with all their might before the LORD, with songs*i* and with harps, lyres, tambourines, sistrums and cymbals.

⁶When they came to the threshing floor of Nacon, Uzzah reached out and took hold of the ark of God, because the oxen stumbled. ⁷The LORD's anger burned against Uzzah because of his irreverent act; therefore God struck him down and he died there beside the ark of God.

⁸Then David was angry because the LORD's wrath had broken out against Uzzah, and to this day that place is called Perez Uzzah.*j*

⁹David was afraid of the LORD that day and said, "How can the ark of the LORD ever come to me?" ¹⁰He was not willing to take the ark of the LORD to be with him in the City of David. Instead, he took it aside to the house of Obed-Edom the Gittite. ¹¹The ark of the LORD remained in the house of Obed-Edom the Gittite for three months, and the LORD blessed him and his entire household.

¹²Now King David was told, "The LORD has blessed the household of Obed-Edom and everything he has, because of the ark of God." So David went down and brought up the ark of God from the house of Obed-Edom to the City of David with re-

---

*a*8 Or *use scaling hooks*   *b*8 Or *are hated by David* lord who breaks out.   *e*25 Septuagint (see also 1 Chron. 14:16); Hebrew *Geba*   *c*9 Or *the Millo*   *d*20 *Baal Perazim* means *the* Jearim; Hebrew *Baale Judah*, a variant of *Baalah of Judah*   *f*2 That is, Kiriath have the Name.   *h*3,4 Dead Sea Scrolls and some Septuagint manuscripts; Masoretic Text *cart* ⁴*and* they brought it with the ark of God from the house of Abinadab, which was on the hill   *i*5 See Dead Sea Scrolls, Septuagint and 1 Chronicles 13:8; Masoretic Text *celebrating before the LORD with all kinds of* instruments made of pine.   *j*8 *Perez Uzzah* means *outbreak against Uzzah*.

joicing. ¹³When those who were carrying the ark of the LORD had taken six steps, he sacrificed a bull and a fattened calf. ¹⁴David, wearing a linen ephod, danced before the LORD with all his might, ¹⁵while he and the entire house of Israel brought up the ark of the LORD with shouts and the sound of trumpets.

¹⁶As the ark of the LORD was entering the City of David, Michal daughter of Saul watched from a window. And when she saw King David leaping and dancing before the LORD, she despised him in her heart.

¹⁷They brought the ark of the LORD and set it in its place inside the tent that David had pitched for it, and David sacrificed burnt offerings and fellowship offerings[a] before the LORD. ¹⁸After he had finished sacrificing the burnt offerings and fellowship offerings, he blessed the people in the name of the LORD Almighty. ¹⁹Then he gave a loaf of bread, a cake of dates and a cake of raisins to each person in the whole crowd of Israelites, both men and women. And all the people went to their homes.

²⁰When David returned home to bless his household, Michal daughter of Saul came out to meet him and said, "How the king of Israel has distinguished himself today, disrobing in the sight of the slave girls of his servants as any vulgar fellow would!"

²¹David said to Michal, "It was before the LORD, who chose me rather than your father or anyone from his house when he appointed me ruler over the LORD's people Israel—I will celebrate before the LORD. ²²I will become even more undignified than this, and I will be humiliated in my own eyes. But by these slave girls you spoke of, I will be held in honor."

²³And Michal daughter of Saul had no children to the day of her death.

God's Promise to David

7 After the king was settled in his palace and the LORD had given him rest from all his enemies around him, ²he said to Nathan the prophet, "Here I am, living in a palace of cedar, while the ark of God remains in a tent."

³Nathan replied to the king, "Whatever you have in mind, go ahead and do it, for the LORD is with you."

⁴That night the word of the LORD came to Nathan, saying:

⁵"Go and tell my servant David, 'This is what the LORD says: Are you the one to build me a house to dwell in? ⁶I have not dwelt in a house from the day I brought the Israelites up out of Egypt to this day. I have been moving from place to place with a tent as my dwelling. ⁷Wherever I have moved with all the Israelites, did I ever say to any of their rulers whom I commanded to shepherd my people Israel, "Why have you not built me a house of cedar?"'

⁸"Now then, tell my servant David, 'This is what the LORD Almighty says: I took you from the pasture and from following the flock to be ruler over my people Israel. ⁹I have been with you wherever you have gone, and I have cut off all your enemies from before you. Now I will make your name great, like the names of the greatest men of the earth. ¹⁰And I will provide a place for my people Israel and will plant them so that they can have a home of their own and no longer be disturbed. Wicked people will not oppress them anymore, as they did at the beginning ¹¹and have done ever since the time I appointed leaders[b] over my people Israel. I will also give you rest from all your enemies.

" 'The LORD declares to you that the LORD himself will establish a house for you: ¹²When your days are over and you rest with your fathers, I will raise up your offspring to succeed you, who will come from your own body, and I will establish his kingdom. ¹³He is the one who will build a house for my Name, and I will establish the throne of his kingdom forever. ¹⁴I will be his father, and he will be my son. When he does wrong, I will punish him with the rod of men, with floggings inflicted by men. ¹⁵But my love will never be taken away from him, as I took it away from Saul, whom I removed from before you. ¹⁶Your house and your kingdom will endure forever before me[c]; your throne will be established forever.' "

---

a17 Traditionally *peace offerings*; also in verse 18   b11 Traditionally *judges*   c16 Some Hebrew manuscripts and Septuagint; most Hebrew manuscripts *you*

¹⁷Nathan reported to David all the words of this entire revelation.

David's Prayer

¹⁸Then King David went in and sat before the LORD, and he said:

"Who am I, O Sovereign LORD, and what is my family, that you have brought me this far? ¹⁹And as if this were not enough in your sight, O Sovereign LORD, you have also spoken about the future of the house of your servant. Is this your usual way of dealing with man, O Sovereign LORD?

²⁰"What more can David say to you? For you know your servant, O Sovereign LORD. ²¹For the sake of your word and according to your will, you have done this great thing and made it known to your servant.

²²"How great you are, O Sovereign LORD! There is no one like you, and there is no God but you, as we have heard with our own ears. ²³And who is like your people Israel—the one nation on earth that God went out to redeem as a people for himself, and to make a name for himself, and to perform great and awesome wonders by driving out nations and their gods from before your people, whom you redeemed from Egypt?ᵃ ²⁴You have established your people Israel as your very own forever, and you, O LORD, have become their God.

²⁵"And now, LORD God, keep forever the promise you have made concerning your servant and his house. Do as you promised, ²⁶so that your name will be great forever. Then men will say, 'The LORD Almighty is God over Israel!' And the house of your servant David will be established before you.

²⁷"O LORD Almighty, God of Israel, you have revealed this to your servant, saying, 'I will build a house for you.' So your servant has found courage to offer you this prayer. ²⁸O Sovereign LORD, you are God! Your words are trustworthy, and you have promised these good things to your servant. ²⁹Now be pleased to bless the house of your servant, that it may continue forever in your sight; for you, O Sovereign LORD, have spoken, and with your blessing the house of your servant will be blessed forever."

David's Victories

8 In the course of time, David defeated the Philistines and subdued them, and he took Metheg Ammah from the control of the Philistines.

²David also defeated the Moabites. He made them lie down on the ground and measured them off with a length of cord. Every two lengths of them were put to death, and the third length was allowed to live. So the Moabites became subject to David and brought tribute.

³Moreover, David fought Hadadezer son of Rehob, king of Zobah, when he went to restore his control along the Euphrates River. ⁴David captured a thousand of his chariots, seven thousand charioteersᵇ and twenty thousand foot soldiers. He hamstrung all but a hundred of the chariot horses.

⁵When the Arameans of Damascus came to help Hadadezer king of Zobah, David struck down twenty-two thousand of them. ⁶He put garrisons in the Aramean kingdom of Damascus, and the Arameans became subject to him and brought tribute. The LORD gave David victory wherever he went.

⁷David took the gold shields that belonged to the officers of Hadadezer and brought them to Jerusalem. ⁸From Tebahᶜ and Berothai, towns that belonged to Hadadezer, King David took a great quantity of bronze.

⁹When Touᵈ king of Hamath heard that David had defeated the entire army of Hadadezer, ¹⁰he sent his son Joramᵉ to King David to greet him and congratulate him on his victory in battle over Hadadezer, who had been at war with Tou. Joram brought with him articles of silver and gold and bronze.

¹¹King David dedicated these articles to the LORD, as he had done with the silver and gold from all the nations he had subdued: ¹²Edomᶠ and Moab, the Ammonites and the Philistines, and Amalek. He also dedicated the plunder taken from

ᵃ23 See Septuagint and 1 Chron. 17:21; Hebrew *wonders for your land and before your people, whom you redeemed from Egypt, from the nations and their gods.*   ᵇ4 Septuagint (see also Dead Sea Scrolls and 1 Chron. 18:4); Masoretic Text *captured seventeen hundred of his charioteers*   ᶜ8 See some Septuagint manuscripts (see also 1 Chron. 18:8); Hebrew *Betah.*   ᵈ9 Hebrew *Toi,* a variant of *Tou;* also in verse 10   ᵉ10 A variant of *Hadoram*   ᶠ12 Some Hebrew manuscripts, Septuagint and Syriac (see also 1 Chron. 18:11); most Hebrew manuscripts *Aram*

VERSE FOR THE DAY:
2 Samuel 7:21

AUTHOR:
Marlene Obie

PASSAGE FOR THE DAY:
2 Samuel 7:18–29

Work Outside the Home?

WHAT'S the answer, Lord? Should we or shouldn't we?

For many years the model Christian woman was pictured as a housewife. I don't remember blatant scorn of the woman who held an outside job, although it was hinted that unless she faced real financial need, a woman should concentrate her energies on her family. It was an accepted theory that some women had jobs because they thought they had to, not because their need was genuine. Lower standards of living were suggested in order to avoid working.

This was hard for me to understand since I was raised by working women. I never doubted that the women closest to me had to have jobs. While there were times I wished they were more like the storybook moms, I admit I didn't suffer for lack of attention. Yet because I wanted so much to have that picture-book family, I fought against getting a job for many years. It wasn't that my work was distasteful or that I was enamored with housework. I was plagued by tremendous guilt for not living up to my dream. I feared that I couldn't work outside the home and be a good mother.

Forgive me, Lord, for making everyone in my family miserable. I felt so sorry for myself. Forgive me for my constant complaints.

You've changed me, Lord. Although I have to work outside my home, you've shown me that I can enjoy it and take pride in doing my job well.

Lord, I'm glad it is not my responsibility to decide whether or not Christian women should have jobs outside their homes. You've made each of us unique. We have individual abilities, interests and financial circumstances. Thank you that you promise to guide us in making decisions about working. Show us where you want to use us, and stand beside us, Lord.

Additional Scripture Readings:
Judges 6:33–40; Proverbs 31:10–31

Go to page 321 for your next devotional reading.

Hadadezer son of Rehob, king of Zobah.

¹³And David became famous after he returned from striking down eighteen thousand Edomites*a* in the Valley of Salt.

¹⁴He put garrisons throughout Edom, and all the Edomites became subject to David. The LORD gave David victory wherever he went.

David's Officials

¹⁵David reigned over all Israel, doing what was just and right for all his people. ¹⁶Joab son of Zeruiah was over the army; Jehoshaphat son of Ahilud was recorder; ¹⁷Zadok son of Ahitub and Ahimelech son of Abiathar were priests; Seraiah was secretary; ¹⁸Benaiah son of Jehoiada was over the Kerethites and Pelethites; and David's sons were royal advisers.*b*

David and Mephibosheth

9 David asked, "Is there anyone still left of the house of Saul to whom I can show kindness for Jonathan's sake?"

²Now there was a servant of Saul's household named Ziba. They called him to appear before David, and the king said to him, "Are you Ziba?"

"Your servant," he replied.

³The king asked, "Is there no one still left of the house of Saul to whom I can show God's kindness?"

Ziba answered the king, "There is still a son of Jonathan; he is crippled in both feet."

⁴"Where is he?" the king asked.

Ziba answered, "He is at the house of Makir son of Ammiel in Lo Debar."

⁵So King David had him brought from Lo Debar, from the house of Makir son of Ammiel.

⁶When Mephibosheth son of Jonathan, the son of Saul, came to David, he bowed down to pay him honor.

David said, "Mephibosheth!"

"Your servant," he replied.

⁷"Don't be afraid," David said to him, "for I will surely show you kindness for the sake of your father Jonathan. I will restore to you all the land that belonged to your grandfather Saul, and you will always eat at my table."

⁸Mephibosheth bowed down and said, "What is your servant, that you should notice a dead dog like me?"

⁹Then the king summoned Ziba, Saul's servant, and said to him, "I have given

your master's grandson everything that belonged to Saul and his family. ¹⁰You and your sons and your servants are to farm the land for him and bring in the crops, so that your master's grandson may be provided for. And Mephibosheth, grandson of your master, will always eat at my table." (Now Ziba had fifteen sons and twenty servants.)

¹¹Then Ziba said to the king, "Your servant will do whatever my lord the king commands his servant to do." So Mephibosheth ate at David's*c* table like one of the king's sons.

¹²Mephibosheth had a young son named Mica, and all the members of Ziba's household were servants of Mephibosheth. ¹³And Mephibosheth lived in Jerusalem, because he always ate at the king's table, and he was crippled in both feet.

David Defeats the Ammonites

10 In the course of time, the king of the Ammonites died, and his son Hanun succeeded him as king. ²David thought, "I will show kindness to Hanun son of Nahash, just as his father showed kindness to me." So David sent a delegation to express his sympathy to Hanun concerning his father.

When David's men came to the land of the Ammonites, ³the Ammonite nobles said to Hanun their lord, "Do you think David is honoring your father by sending men to you to express sympathy? Hasn't David sent them to you to explore the city and spy it out and overthrow it?" ⁴So Hanun seized David's men, shaved off half of each man's beard, cut off their garments in the middle at the buttocks, and sent them away.

⁵When David was told about this, he sent messengers to meet the men, for they were greatly humiliated. The king said, "Stay at Jericho till your beards have grown, and then come back."

⁶When the Ammonites realized that they had become a stench in David's nostrils, they hired twenty thousand Aramean foot soldiers from Beth Rehob and Zobah, as well as the king of Maacah with a thousand men, and also twelve thousand men from Tob.

⁷On hearing this, David sent Joab out with the entire army of fighting men. ⁸The Ammonites came out and drew up in bat-

---

a13 A few Hebrew manuscripts, Septuagint and Syriac (see also 1 Chron. 18:12); most Hebrew manuscripts *Aram* (that is, Arameans)   *b18* Or *were priests*   *c11* Septuagint; Hebrew *my* tle formation at the entrance to their city gate, while the Arameans of Zobah and Rehob and the men of Tob and Maacah were by themselves in the open country. ⁹Joab saw that there were battle lines in front of him and behind him; so he selected some of the best troops in Israel and deployed them against the Arameans. ¹⁰He put the rest of the men under the command of Abishai his brother and deployed them against the Ammonites. ¹¹Joab said, "If the Arameans are too strong for me, then you are to come to my rescue; but if the Ammonites are too strong for you, then I will come to rescue you. ¹²Be strong and let us fight bravely for our people and the cities of our God. The Lord will do what is good in his sight."

¹³Then Joab and the troops with him advanced to fight the Arameans, and they fled before him. ¹⁴When the Ammonites saw that the Arameans were fleeing, they fled before Abishai and went inside the city. So Joab returned from fighting the Ammonites and came to Jerusalem.

¹⁵After the Arameans saw that they had been routed by Israel, they regrouped. ¹⁶Hadadezer had Arameans brought from beyond the River*ᵃ*; they went to Helam, with Shobach the commander of Hadadezer's army leading them.

¹⁷When David was told of this, he gathered all Israel, crossed the Jordan and went to Helam. The Arameans formed their battle lines to meet David and fought against him. ¹⁸But they fled before Israel, and David killed seven hundred of their charioteers and forty thousand of their foot soldiers.*ᵇ* He also struck down Shobach the commander of their army, and he died there. ¹⁹When all the kings who were vassals of Hadadezer saw that they had been defeated by Israel, they made peace with the Israelites and became subject to them.

So the Arameans were afraid to help the Ammonites anymore.

David and Bathsheba

11 In the spring, at the time when kings go off to war, David sent Joab out with the king's men and the whole Israelite army. They destroyed the Ammonites and besieged Rabbah. But David remained in Jerusalem.

²One evening David got up from his bed and walked around on the roof of the palace. From the roof he saw a woman bathing. The woman was very beautiful, ³and David sent someone to find out about her. The man said, "Isn't this Bathsheba, the daughter of Eliam and the wife of Uriah the Hittite?" ⁴Then David sent messengers to get her. She came to him, and he slept with her. (She had purified herself from her uncleanness.) Then*ᶜ* she went back home. ⁵The woman conceived and sent word to David, saying, "I am pregnant."

⁶So David sent this word to Joab: "Send me Uriah the Hittite." And Joab sent him to David. ⁷When Uriah came to him, David asked him how Joab was, how the soldiers were and how the war was going. ⁸Then David said to Uriah, "Go down to your house and wash your feet." So Uriah left the palace, and a gift from the king was sent after him. ⁹But Uriah slept at the entrance to the palace with all his master's servants and did not go down to his house.

¹⁰When David was told, "Uriah did not go home," he asked him, "Haven't you just come from a distance? Why didn't you go home?"

¹¹Uriah said to David, "The ark and Israel and Judah are staying in tents, and my master Joab and my lord's men are camped in the open fields. How could I go to my house to eat and drink and lie with my wife? As surely as you live, I will not do such a thing!"

¹²Then David said to him, "Stay here one more day, and tomorrow I will send you back." So Uriah remained in Jerusalem that day and the next. ¹³At David's invitation, he ate and drank with him, and David made him drunk. But in the evening Uriah went out to sleep on his mat among his master's servants; he did not go home.

¹⁴In the morning David wrote a letter to Joab and sent it with Uriah. ¹⁵In it he wrote, "Put Uriah in the front line where the fighting is fiercest. Then withdraw from him so he will be struck down and die."

¹⁶So while Joab had the city under siege, he put Uriah at a place where he knew the strongest defenders were. ¹⁷When the men of the city came out and fought against Joab, some of the men in

---

ᵃ16 That is, the Euphrates   *ᵇ18* Some Septuagint manuscripts (see also 1 Chron. 19:18); Hebrew *horsemen*   *ᶜ4* Or *with her. When she purified herself from her uncleanness,*

VERSE FOR THE DAY:
2 Samuel 11:27

AUTHOR:
Barbara Bush

PASSAGE FOR THE DAY:
2 Samuel 11:1–27

Heart Trouble

DAVID, despite his unique knowledge and experience of God, apparently did not foresee any grave complications when he committed adultery with Bathsheba. As king he was accustomed to getting what he wanted, and he wanted Bathsheba. But to keep his disobedience to God from being revealed, David finally ordered the death of Uriah, Bathsheba's husband.

The lie we tell may seem an isolated instance. But often we end up having to deny we lied, digging ourselves deeper into a hole. We can even begin implicating others, asking them to lie for us.

If people will steal, they will not balk at lying; it is foolish to look for honor among thieves. A woman who cheats on her husband will not be a trustworthy friend either. We do, indeed, weave "a tangled web" when we first decide to deceive.

King David stands as a prime example not only of sin but also of the reality of forgiveness. The betrayals of godly character seem too numerous to count; the sordid story would seem surely to constitute the end of David's glory.

But what is God's final opinion of David? Years after David's death, God said of him, his heart was "fully devoted to the LORD his God" (1 Kings 11:4). What an epitaph! How could this be after all of David's sins?

The answer lies in Psalm 51, David's prayer of repentance.

David's story proves that our sins, no matter how repugnant, need not separate us permanently from God and his plan for us. The path back to him lies in the complete repentance mirrored in Psalm 51. The restoration to fellowship with God results not from a halfhearted "forgive me," but a broken spirit.

God specializes in miracle cures, and we, as well as David, can be known as those fully devoted to the Lord our God, no matter how serious our character lapses, or sins, may be. God knows how to make clean hearts out of dirty ones. Praise him!

Additional Scripture Readings:
Psalm 51:10–17; Acts 5:1–11

Go to page 323 for your next devotional reading.

David's army fell; moreover, Uriah the Hittite died.

18Joab sent David a full account of the battle. 19He instructed the messenger: "When you have finished giving the king this account of the battle, 20the king's anger may flare up, and he may ask you, 'Why did you get so close to the city to fight? Didn't you know they would shoot arrows from the wall? 21Who killed Abimelech son of Jerub-Besheth*? Didn't a woman throw an upper millstone on him from the wall, so that he died in Thebez? Why did you get so close to the wall?' If he asks you this, then say to him, 'Also, your servant Uriah the Hittite is dead.'"

22The messenger set out, and when he arrived he told David everything Joab had sent him to say. 23The messenger said to David, "The men overpowered us and came out against us in the open, but we drove them back to the entrance to the city gate. 24Then the archers shot arrows at your servants from the wall, and some of the king's men died. Moreover, your servant Uriah the Hittite is dead."

25David told the messenger, "Say this to Joab: 'Don't let this upset you; the sword devours one as well as another. Press the attack against the city and destroy it.' Say this to encourage Joab."

26When Uriah's wife heard that her husband was dead, she mourned for him. 27After the time of mourning was over, David had her brought to his house, and she became his wife and bore him a son. But the thing David had done displeased the LORD.

Nathan Rebukes David

12 The LORD sent Nathan to David. When he came to him, he said, "There were two men in a certain town, one rich and the other poor. 2The rich man had a very large number of sheep and cattle, 3but the poor man had nothing except one little ewe lamb he had bought. He raised it, and it grew up with him and his children. It shared his food, drank from his cup and even slept in his arms. It was like a daughter to him.

4"Now a traveler came to the rich man, but the rich man refrained from taking one of his own sheep or cattle to prepare a meal for the traveler who had come to him. Instead, he took the ewe lamb that belonged to the poor man and prepared it for the one who had come to him."

5David burned with anger against the man and said to Nathan, "As surely as the LORD lives, the man who did this deserves to die! 6He must pay for that lamb four times over, because he did such a thing and had no pity."

7Then Nathan said to David, "You are the man! This is what the LORD, the God of Israel, says: 'I anointed you king over Israel, and I delivered you from the hand of Saul. 8I gave your master's house to you, and your master's wives into your arms. I gave you the house of Israel and Judah. And if all this had been too little, I would have given you even more. 9Why did you despise the word of the LORD by doing what is evil in his eyes? You struck down Uriah the Hittite with the sword and took his wife to be your own. You killed him with the sword of the Ammonites. 10Now, therefore, the sword will never depart from your house, because you despised me and took the wife of Uriah the Hittite to be your own.'

11"This is what the LORD says: 'Out of your own household I am going to bring calamity upon you. Before your very eyes I will take your wives and give them to one who is close to you, and he will lie with your wives in broad daylight. 12You did it in secret, but I will do this thing in broad daylight before all Israel.'"

13Then David said to Nathan, "I have sinned against the LORD."

Nathan replied, "The LORD has taken away your sin. You are not going to die. 14But because by doing this you have made the enemies of the LORD show utter contempt,b the son born to you will die."

15After Nathan had gone home, the LORD struck the child that Uriah's wife had borne to David, and he became ill. 16David pleaded with God for the child. He fasted and went into his house and spent the nights lying on the ground. 17The elders of his household stood beside him to get him up from the ground, but he refused, and he would not eat any food with them.

18On the seventh day the child died. David's servants were afraid to tell him that the child was dead, for they thought, "While the child was still living, we spoke to David but he would not listen to us.

a21 Also known as *Jerub-Baal* (that is, Gideon)   b14 Masoretic Text; an ancient Hebrew scribal tradition *this you have shown utter contempt for the LORD*

How can we tell him the child is dead? He may do something desperate."

¹⁹David noticed that his servants were whispering among themselves and he realized the child was dead. "Is the child dead?" he asked.

"Yes," they replied, "he is dead."

²⁰Then David got up from the ground. After he had washed, put on lotions and changed his clothes, he went into the house of the LORD and worshiped. Then he went to his own house, and at his request they served him food, and he ate.

²¹His servants asked him, "Why are you acting this way? While the child was alive, you fasted and wept, but now that the child is dead, you get up and eat!"

²²He answered, "While the child was still alive, I fasted and wept. I thought, 'Who knows? The LORD may be gracious

THURSDAY

VERSE FOR THE DAY:	AUTHOR:	PASSAGE FOR THE DAY:
2 Samuel 12:13	Myrna Alexander	2 Samuel 12:1–31

The Turning Point

KING David is a powerful and important king. Israel's enemies have been conquered, one by one, as David experienced an unbroken series of military successes. In 2 Samuel 10 we see the Israelites take their final stand against the enemy—the Ammonites. The military expedition against the Ammonite capital of Rabbah was so important that the Israelite army took the ark of God with them into battle. It appears, however, that David did not feel it was important for him to lead his army into this battle. He sent Joab in his place. This decision to compromise was significant, for it led to the dramatic turning point in David's career.

Chapter 11 marks the pivotal point in 2 Samuel. Chapters 1-10 set forth David's victories, but chapters 12-24 emphasize King David's troubles. David had come close to the heart of God and through the Psalms had declared with great affection what God was like. David tramples underfoot the intimacy he had known, and he sins against the Lord. Now we see him fall.

Unconsciously we cry out, "Oh, no, David, not you!" How hard it is to watch this hero fall. Yet as Saint Augustine has said, "David's fall should put upon their guard all who have not fallen, and save from despair all those who have fallen."

May the earnest prayer from David's confession be answered in our lives:

> Restore to me the joy of your salvation
> and grant me a willing spirit, to sustain me.
> Then I will teach transgressors your ways,
> and sinners will turn back to you
> (Psalm 51:12–13).

Additional Scripture Readings:
Isaiah 1:16–19; Luke 22:31–34,54–62

Go to page 329 for your next devotional reading.

to me and let the child live.' ²³But now that he is dead, why should I fast? Can I bring him back again? I will go to him, but he will not return to me."

²⁴Then David comforted his wife Bathsheba, and he went to her and lay with her. She gave birth to a son, and they named him Solomon. The LORD loved him; ²⁵and because the LORD loved him, he sent word through Nathan the prophet to name him Jedidiah.ᵃ

²⁶Meanwhile Joab fought against Rabbah of the Ammonites and captured the royal citadel. ²⁷Joab then sent messengers to David, saying, "I have fought against Rabbah and taken its water supply. ²⁸Now muster the rest of the troops and besiege the city and capture it. Otherwise I will take the city, and it will be named after me."

²⁹So David mustered the entire army and went to Rabbah, and attacked and captured it. ³⁰He took the crown from the head of their kingᵇ—its weight was a talentᶜ of gold, and it was set with precious stones—and it was placed on David's head. He took a great quantity of plunder from the city ³¹and brought out the people who were there, consigning them to labor with saws and with iron picks and axes, and he made them work at brickmaking.ᵈ He did this to all the Ammonite towns. Then David and his entire army returned to Jerusalem.

Amnon and Tamar

13 In the course of time, Amnon son of David fell in love with Tamar, the beautiful sister of Absalom son of David.

²Amnon became frustrated to the point of illness on account of his sister Tamar, for she was a virgin, and it seemed impossible for him to do anything to her.

³Now Amnon had a friend named Jonadab son of Shimeah, David's brother. Jonadab was a very shrewd man. ⁴He asked Amnon, "Why do you, the king's son, look so haggard morning after morning? Won't you tell me?"

Amnon said to him, "I'm in love with Tamar, my brother Absalom's sister."

⁵"Go to bed and pretend to be ill," Jonadab said. "When your father comes to see you, say to him, 'I would like my sister Tamar to come and give me something to eat. Let her prepare the food in my sight so I may watch her and then eat it from her hand.' "

⁶So Amnon lay down and pretended to be ill. When the king came to see him, Amnon said to him, "I would like my sister Tamar to come and make some special bread in my sight, so I may eat from her hand."

⁷David sent word to Tamar at the palace: "Go to the house of your brother Amnon and prepare some food for him." ⁸So Tamar went to the house of her brother Amnon, who was lying down. She took some dough, kneaded it, made the bread in his sight and baked it. ⁹Then she took the pan and served him the bread, but he refused to eat.

"Send everyone out of here," Amnon said. So everyone left him. ¹⁰Then Amnon said to Tamar, "Bring the food here into my bedroom so I may eat from your hand." And Tamar took the bread she had prepared and brought it to her brother Amnon in his bedroom. ¹¹But when she took it to him to eat, he grabbed her and said, "Come to bed with me, my sister."

¹²"Don't, my brother!" she said to him. "Don't force me. Such a thing should not be done in Israel! Don't do this wicked thing. ¹³What about me? Where could I get rid of my disgrace? And what about you? You would be like one of the wicked fools in Israel. Please speak to the king; he will not keep me from being married to you." ¹⁴But he refused to listen to her, and since he was stronger than she, he raped her.

¹⁵Then Amnon hated her with intense hatred. In fact, he hated her more than he had loved her. Amnon said to her, "Get up and get out!"

¹⁶"No!" she said to him. "Sending me away would be a greater wrong than what you have already done to me."

But he refused to listen to her. ¹⁷He called his personal servant and said, "Get this woman out of here and bolt the door after her." ¹⁸So his servant put her out and bolted the door after her. She was wearing a richly ornamentedᵉ robe, for this was the kind of garment the virgin daughters of the king wore. ¹⁹Tamar put ashes on her head and tore the ornament-

---

ed[a] robe she was wearing. She put her hand on her head and went away, weeping aloud as she went.

²⁰Her brother Absalom said to her, "Has that Amnon, your brother, been with you? Be quiet now, my sister; he is your brother. Don't take this thing to heart." And Tamar lived in her brother Absalom's house, a desolate woman.

²¹When King David heard all this, he was furious. ²²Absalom never said a word to Amnon, either good or bad; he hated Amnon because he had disgraced his sister Tamar.

Absalom Kills Amnon

²³Two years later, when Absalom's sheepshearers were at Baal Hazor near the border of Ephraim, he invited all the king's sons to come there. ²⁴Absalom went to the king and said, "Your servant has had shearers come. Will the king and his officials please join me?"

²⁵"No, my son," the king replied. "All of us should not go; we would only be a burden to you." Although Absalom urged him, he still refused to go, but gave him his blessing.

²⁶Then Absalom said, "If not, please let my brother Amnon come with us."

The king asked him, "Why should he go with you?" ²⁷But Absalom urged him, so he sent with him Amnon and the rest of the king's sons.

²⁸Absalom ordered his men, "Listen! When Amnon is in high spirits from drinking wine and I say to you, 'Strike Amnon down,' then kill him. Don't be afraid. Have not I given you this order? Be strong and brave." ²⁹So Absalom's men did to Amnon what Absalom had ordered. Then all the king's sons got up, mounted their mules and fled.

³⁰While they were on their way, the report came to David: "Absalom has struck down all the king's sons; not one of them is left." ³¹The king stood up, tore his clothes and lay down on the ground; and all his servants stood by with their clothes torn.

³²But Jonadab son of Shimeah, David's brother, said, "My lord should not think that they killed all the princes; only Amnon is dead. This has been Absalom's expressed intention ever since the day Am-

non raped his sister Tamar. ³³My lord the king should not be concerned about the report that all the king's sons are dead. Only Amnon is dead."

³⁴Meanwhile, Absalom had fled.

Now the man standing watch looked up and saw many people on the road west of him, coming down the side of the hill. The watchman went and told the king, "I see men in the direction of Horonaim, on the side of the hill."[b]

³⁵Jonadab said to the king, "See, the king's sons are here; it has happened just as your servant said."

³⁶As he finished speaking, the king's sons came in, wailing loudly. The king, too, and all his servants wept very bitterly.

³⁷Absalom fled and went to Talmai son of Ammihud, the king of Geshur. But King David mourned for his son every day.

³⁸After Absalom fled and went to Geshur, he stayed there three years. ³⁹And the spirit of the king[c] longed to go to Absalom, for he was consoled concerning Amnon's death.

Absalom Returns to Jerusalem

14 Joab son of Zeruiah knew that the king's heart longed for Absalom. ²So Joab sent someone to Tekoa and had a wise woman brought from there. He said to her, "Pretend you are in mourning. Dress in mourning clothes, and don't use any cosmetic lotions. Act like a woman who has spent many days grieving for the dead. ³Then go to the king and speak these words to him." And Joab put the words in her mouth.

⁴When the woman from Tekoa went[d] to the king, she fell with her face to the ground to pay him honor, and she said, "Help me, O king!"

⁵The king asked her, "What is troubling you?"

She said, "I am indeed a widow; my husband is dead. ⁶I your servant had two sons. They got into a fight with each other in the field, and no one was there to separate them. One struck the other and killed him. ⁷Now the whole clan has risen up against your servant; they say, 'Hand over the one who struck his brother down, so that we may put him to death for the

---

[a]19 The meaning of the Hebrew for this word is uncertain.   [b]34 Septuagint; Hebrew does not have this sentence.   [c]39 Dead Sea Scrolls and some Septuagint manuscripts; Masoretic Text But the spirit of, David the king   [d]4 Many Hebrew manuscripts, Septuagint, Vulgate and Syriac; most Hebrew manuscripts spoke

life of his brother whom he killed; then we will get rid of the heir as well.' They would put out the only burning coal I have left, leaving my husband neither name nor descendant on the face of the earth."

8The king said to the woman, "Go home, and I will issue an order in your behalf."

9But the woman from Tekoa said to him, "My lord the king, let the blame rest on me and on my father's family, and let the king and his throne be without guilt."

10The king replied, "If anyone says anything to you, bring him to me, and he will not bother you again."

11She said, "Then let the king invoke the LORD his God to prevent the avenger of blood from adding to the destruction, so that my son will not be destroyed."

"As surely as the LORD lives," he said, "not one hair of your son's head will fall to the ground."

12Then the woman said, "Let your servant speak a word to my lord the king."

"Speak," he replied.

13The woman said, "Why then have you devised a thing like this against the people of God? When the king says this, does he not convict himself, for the king has not brought back his banished son? 14Like water spilled on the ground, which cannot be recovered, so we must die. But God does not take away life; instead, he devises ways so that a banished person may not remain estranged from him.

15"And now I have come to say this to my lord the king because the people have made me afraid. Your servant thought, 'I will speak to the king; perhaps he will do what his servant asks. 16Perhaps the king will agree to deliver his servant from the hand of the man who is trying to cut off both me and my son from the inheritance God gave us.'

17"And now your servant says, 'May the word of my lord the king bring me rest, for my lord the king is like an angel of God in discerning good and evil. May the LORD your God be with you.' "

18Then the king said to the woman, "Do not keep from me the answer to what I am going to ask you."

"Let my lord the king speak," the woman said.

19The king asked, "Isn't the hand of Joab with you in all this?"

The woman answered, "As surely as you live, my lord the king, no one can turn to the right or to the left from anything my lord the king says. Yes, it was your servant Joab who instructed me to do this and who put all these words into the mouth of your servant. 20Your servant Joab did this to change the present situation. My lord has wisdom like that of an angel of God—he knows everything that happens in the land."

21The king said to Joab, "Very well, I will do it. Go, bring back the young man Absalom."

22Joab fell with his face to the ground to pay him honor, and he blessed the king. Joab said, "Today your servant knows that he has found favor in your eyes, my lord the king, because the king has granted his servant's request."

23Then Joab went to Geshur and brought Absalom back to Jerusalem. 24But the king said, "He must go to his own house; he must not see my face." So Absalom went to his own house and did not see the face of the king.

25In all Israel there was not a man so highly praised for his handsome appearance as Absalom. From the top of his head to the sole of his foot there was no blemish in him. 26Whenever he cut the hair of his head—he used to cut his hair from time to time when it became too heavy for him—he would weigh it, and its weight was two hundred shekels*a* by the royal standard.

27Three sons and a daughter were born to Absalom. The daughter's name was Tamar, and she became a beautiful woman.

28Absalom lived two years in Jerusalem without seeing the king's face. 29Then Absalom sent for Joab in order to send him to the king, but Joab refused to come to him. So he sent a second time, but he refused to come. 30Then he said to his servants, "Look, Joab's field is next to mine, and he has barley there. Go and set it on fire." So Absalom's servants set the field on fire.

31Then Joab did go to Absalom's house and he said to him, "Why have your servants set my field on fire?"

32Absalom said to Joab, "Look, I sent word to you and said, 'Come here so I can send you to the king to ask, "Why have I come from Geshur? It would be better for me if I were still there!" ' Now then, I want to see the king's face, and if I am

a26 That is, about 5 pounds (about 2.3 kilograms)

guilty of anything, let him put me to death."

³³So Joab went to the king and told him this. Then the king summoned Absalom, and he came in and bowed down with his face to the ground before the king. And the king kissed Absalom.

Absalom's Conspiracy

15 In the course of time, Absalom provided himself with a chariot and horses and with fifty men to run ahead of him. ²He would get up early and stand by the side of the road leading to the city gate. Whenever anyone came with a complaint to be placed before the king for a decision, Absalom would call out to him, "What town are you from?" He would answer, "Your servant is from one of the tribes of Israel." ³Then Absalom would say to him, "Look, your claims are valid and proper, but there is no representative of the king to hear you." ⁴And Absalom would add, "If only I were appointed judge in the land! Then everyone who has a complaint or case could come to me and I would see that he gets justice."

⁵Also, whenever anyone approached him to bow down before him, Absalom would reach out his hand, take hold of him and kiss him. ⁶Absalom behaved in this way toward all the Israelites who came to the king asking for justice, and so he stole the hearts of the men of Israel.

⁷At the end of four[a] years, Absalom said to the king, "Let me go to Hebron and fulfill a vow I made to the LORD. ⁸While your servant was living at Geshur in Aram, I made this vow: 'If the LORD takes me back to Jerusalem, I will worship the LORD in Hebron.[b]'"

⁹The king said to him, "Go in peace." So he went to Hebron.

¹⁰Then Absalom sent secret messengers throughout the tribes of Israel to say, "As soon as you hear the sound of the trumpets, then say, 'Absalom is king in Hebron.'" ¹¹Two hundred men from Jerusalem had accompanied Absalom. They had been invited as guests and went quite innocently, knowing nothing about the matter. ¹²While Absalom was offering sacrifices, he also sent for Ahithophel the Gilonite, David's counselor, to come from Giloh, his hometown. And so the conspiracy gained strength, and Absalom's following kept on increasing.

David Flees

¹³A messenger came and told David, "The hearts of the men of Israel are with Absalom."

¹⁴Then David said to all his officials who were with him in Jerusalem, "Come! We must flee, or none of us will escape from Absalom. We must leave immediately, or he will move quickly to overtake us and bring ruin upon us and put the city to the sword."

¹⁵The king's officials answered him, "Your servants are ready to do whatever our lord the king chooses."

¹⁶The king set out, with his entire household following him; but he left ten concubines to take care of the palace. ¹⁷So the king set out, with all the people following him, and they halted at a place some distance away. ¹⁸All his men marched past him, along with all the Kerethites and Pelethites; and all the six hundred Gittites who had accompanied him from Gath marched before the king.

¹⁹The king said to Ittai the Gittite, "Why should you come along with us? Go back and stay with King Absalom. You are a foreigner, an exile from your homeland. ²⁰You came only yesterday. And today shall I make you wander about with us, when I do not know where I am going? Go back, and take your countrymen. May kindness and faithfulness be with you."

²¹But Ittai replied to the king, "As surely as the LORD lives, and as my lord the king lives, wherever my lord the king may be, whether it means life or death, there will your servant be."

²²David said to Ittai, "Go ahead, march on." So Ittai the Gittite marched on with all his men and the families that were with him.

²³The whole countryside wept aloud as all the people passed by. The king also crossed the Kidron Valley, and all the people moved on toward the desert.

²⁴Zadok was there, too, and all the Levites who were with him were carrying the ark of the covenant of God. They set down the ark of God, and Abiathar offered sacrifices[c] until all the people had finished leaving the city.

²⁵Then the king said to Zadok, "Take the ark of God back into the city. If I find

---

[a]7 Some Septuagint manuscripts, Syriac and Josephus; Hebrew *forty*   [b]8 Some Septuagint manuscripts;
Hebrew does not have *in Hebron.*   [c]24 Or *Abiathar went up*

favor in the LORD's eyes, he will bring me back and let me see it and his dwelling place again. ²⁶But if he says, 'I am not pleased with you,' then I am ready; let him do to me whatever seems good to him."

²⁷The king also said to Zadok the priest, "Aren't you a seer? Go back to the city in peace, with your son Ahimaaz and Jonathan son of Abiathar. You and Abiathar take your two sons with you. ²⁸I will wait at the fords in the desert until word comes from you to inform me." ²⁹So Zadok and Abiathar took the ark of God back to Jerusalem and stayed there.

³⁰But David continued up the Mount of Olives, weeping as he went; his head was covered and he was barefoot. All the people with him covered their heads too and were weeping as they went up. ³¹Now David had been told, "Ahithophel is among the conspirators with Absalom." So David prayed, "O LORD, turn Ahithophel's counsel into foolishness."

³²When David arrived at the summit, where people used to worship God, Hushai the Arkite was there to meet him, his robe torn and dust on his head. ³³David said to him, "If you go with me, you will be a burden to me. ³⁴But if you return to the city and say to Absalom, 'I will be your servant, O king; I was your father's servant in the past, but now I will be your servant,' then you can help me by frustrating Ahithophel's advice. ³⁵Won't the priests Zadok and Abiathar be there with you? Tell them anything you hear in the king's palace. ³⁶Their two sons, Ahimaaz son of Zadok and Jonathan son of Abiathar, are there with them. Send them to me with anything you hear."

³⁷So David's friend Hushai arrived at Jerusalem as Absalom was entering the city.

David and Ziba

16 When David had gone a short distance beyond the summit, there was Ziba, the steward of Mephibosheth, waiting to meet him. He had a string of donkeys saddled and loaded with two hundred loaves of bread, a hundred cakes of raisins, a hundred cakes of figs and a skin of wine.

²The king asked Ziba, "Why have you brought these?"

Ziba answered, "The donkeys are for the king's household to ride on, the bread and fruit are for the men to eat, and the wine is to refresh those who become exhausted in the desert."

³The king then asked, "Where is your master's grandson?"

Ziba said to him, "He is staying in Jerusalem, because he thinks, 'Today the house of Israel will give me back my grandfather's kingdom.'"

⁴Then the king said to Ziba, "All that belonged to Mephibosheth is now yours."

"I humbly bow," Ziba said. "May I find favor in your eyes, my lord the king."

Shimei Curses David

⁵As King David approached Bahurim, a man from the same clan as Saul's family came out from there. His name was Shimei son of Gera, and he cursed as he came out. ⁶He pelted David and all the king's officials with stones, though all the troops and the special guard were on David's right and left. ⁷As he cursed, Shimei said, "Get out, get out, you man of blood, you scoundrel! ⁸The LORD has repaid you for all the blood you shed in the household of Saul, in whose place you have reigned. The LORD has handed the kingdom over to your son Absalom. You have come to ruin because you are a man of blood!"

⁹Then Abishai son of Zeruiah said to the king, "Why should this dead dog curse my lord the king? Let me go over and cut off his head."

¹⁰But the king said, "What do you and I have in common, you sons of Zeruiah? If he is cursing because the LORD said to him, 'Curse David,' who can ask, 'Why do you do this?'"

¹¹David then said to Abishai and all his officials, "My son, who is of my own flesh, is trying to take my life. How much more, then, this Benjamite! Leave him alone; let him curse, for the LORD has told him to. ¹²It may be that the LORD will see my distress and repay me with good for the cursing I am receiving today."

¹³So David and his men continued along the road while Shimei was going along the hillside opposite him, cursing as he went and throwing stones at him and showering him with dirt. ¹⁴The king and all the people with him arrived at their destination exhausted. And there he refreshed himself.

The Advice of Hushai and Ahithophel

¹⁵Meanwhile, Absalom and all the men

VERSE FOR THE DAY:	AUTHOR:	PASSAGE FOR THE DAY:
2 Samuel 15:19–20	Myrna Alexander	2 Samuel 15:13–37

How to Stand

THERE are times in life when we are shattered, times when we feel helpless and don't know what to do next. As David left his beloved Jerusalem, he expressed such feelings to a group of supporters who sought to join him.

"Why should you come along with us? Go back and stay with King Absalom . . . . You came only yesterday. And today shall I make you wander about with us, when I do not know where I am going?" (2 Samuel 15:19–20).

Today you may feel like a failure—as a friend, as a mother, as a wife. Perhaps your husband has chosen another woman over you, or maybe little is left of a ministry to which you have poured out your heart. Lurking in the corners of your mind may be a what's-the-use-anyway attitude that ends in hopelessness. What do you do about this attitude? How do you get up and stand once more when you're flat on the ground?

David was humiliated, weakened and mocked. Yet in this passage we see the result of David's decision to look away from the terrible circumstances in his life and shift his attention to God.

During this time, David used even the wakeful hours of the night to remind himself of what his God was like:

On my bed I remember you;
I think of you through the watches of the
night.
Because you are my help,
I sing in the shadow of your wings
(Psalm 63:6–7).

But you are a shield around me, O LORD;
you bestow glory on me and lift up my
head. . . .
the LORD sustains me.
I will not fear the tens of thousands
(Psalm 3:3,5–6).

Because of this perspective, with David we are able to declare by faith:

But the king will rejoice in God;
all who swear by God's name will praise him
(Psalm 63:11).

Additional Scripture Readings:
Numbers 14:1–19; 2 Corinthians 1:8–11

Go to page 337 for your next devotional reading.

of Israel came to Jerusalem, and Ahithophel was with him. [16]Then Hushai the Arkite, David's friend, went to Absalom and said to him, "Long live the king! Long live the king!"

[17]Absalom asked Hushai, "Is this the love you show your friend? Why didn't you go with your friend?"

[18]Hushai said to Absalom, "No, the one chosen by the LORD, by these people, and by all the men of Israel—his I will be, and I will remain with him. [19]Furthermore, whom should I serve? Should I not serve the son? Just as I served your father, so I will serve you."

[20]Absalom said to Ahithophel, "Give us your advice. What should we do?"

[21]Ahithophel answered, "Lie with your father's concubines whom he left to take care of the palace. Then all Israel will hear that you have made yourself a stench in your father's nostrils, and the hands of everyone with you will be strengthened." [22]So they pitched a tent for Absalom on the roof, and he lay with his father's concubines in the sight of all Israel.

[23]Now in those days the advice Ahithophel gave was like that of one who inquires of God. That was how both David and Absalom regarded all of Ahithophel's advice.

17 Ahithophel said to Absalom, "I would[a] choose twelve thousand men and set out tonight in pursuit of David. [2]I would[b] attack him while he is weary and weak. I would[b] strike him with terror, and then all the people with him will flee. I would[b] strike down only the king [3]and bring all the people back to you. The death of the man you seek will mean the return of all; all the people will be unharmed." [4]This plan seemed good to Absalom and to all the elders of Israel.

[5]But Absalom said, "Summon also Hushai the Arkite, so we can hear what he has to say." [6]When Hushai came to him, Absalom said, "Ahithophel has given this advice. Should we do what he says? If not, give us your opinion."

[7]Hushai replied to Absalom, "The advice Ahithophel has given is not good this time. [8]You know your father and his men; they are fighters, and as fierce as a wild bear robbed of her cubs. Besides, your father is an experienced fighter; he will not spend the night with the troops. [9]Even now, he is hidden in a cave or some other

place. If he should attack your troops first,[c] whoever hears about it will say, 'There has been a slaughter among the troops who follow Absalom.' [10]Then even the bravest soldier, whose heart is like the heart of a lion, will melt with fear, for all Israel knows that your father is a fighter and that those with him are brave.

[11]"So I advise you: Let all Israel, from Dan to Beersheba—as numerous as the sand on the seashore—be gathered to you, with you yourself leading them into battle. [12]Then we will attack him wherever he may be found, and we will fall on him as dew settles on the ground. Neither he nor any of his men will be left alive. [13]If he withdraws into a city, then all Israel will bring ropes to that city, and we will drag it down to the valley until not even a piece of it can be found."

[14]Absalom and all the men of Israel said, "The advice of Hushai the Arkite is better than that of Ahithophel." For the LORD had determined to frustrate the good advice of Ahithophel in order to bring disaster on Absalom.

[15]Hushai told Zadok and Abiathar, the priests, "Ahithophel has advised Absalom and the elders of Israel to do such and such, but I have advised them to do so and so. [16]Now send a message immediately and tell David, 'Do not spend the night at the fords in the desert; cross over without fail, or the king and all the people with him will be swallowed up.' "

[17]Jonathan and Ahimaaz were staying at En Rogel. A servant girl was to go and inform them, and they were to go and tell King David, for they could not risk being seen entering the city. [18]But a young man saw them and told Absalom. So the two of them left quickly and went to the house of a man in Bahurim. He had a well in his courtyard, and they climbed down into it. [19]His wife took a covering and spread it out over the opening of the well and scattered grain over it. No one knew anything about it.

[20]When Absalom's men came to the woman at the house, they asked, "Where are Ahimaaz and Jonathan?"

The woman answered them, "They crossed over the brook."[d] The men searched but found no one, so they returned to Jerusalem.

[21]After the men had gone, the two climbed out of the well and went to in-

---

a1 Or Let me   b2 Or will   c9 Or When some of the men fall at the first attack   d20 Or "They passed by the sheep pen toward the water."

form King David. They said to him, "Set out and cross the river at once; Ahithophel has advised such and such against you." [22]So David and all the people with him set out and crossed the Jordan. By daybreak, no one was left who had not crossed the Jordan.

[23]When Ahithophel saw that his advice had not been followed, he saddled his donkey and set out for his house in his hometown. He put his house in order and then hanged himself. So he died and was buried in his father's tomb.

[24]David went to Mahanaim, and Absalom crossed the Jordan with all the men of Israel. [25]Absalom had appointed Amasa over the army in place of Joab. Amasa was the son of a man named Jether,[a] an Israelite[b] who had married Abigail,[c] the daughter of Nahash and sister of Zeruiah the mother of Joab. [26]The Israelites and Absalom camped in the land of Gilead.

[27]When David came to Mahanaim, Shobi son of Nahash from Rabbah of the Ammonites, and Makir son of Ammiel from Lo Debar, and Barzillai the Gileadite from Rogelim [28]brought bedding and bowls and articles of pottery. They also brought wheat and barley, flour and roasted grain, beans and lentils,[d] [29]honey and curds, sheep, and cheese from cows' milk for David and his people to eat. For they said, "The people have become hungry and tired and thirsty in the desert."

Absalom's Death

18 David mustered the men who were with him and appointed over them commanders of thousands and commanders of hundreds. [2]David sent the troops out—a third under the command of Joab, a third under Joab's brother Abishai son of Zeruiah, and a third under Ittai the Gittite. The king told the troops, "I myself will surely march out with you."

[3]But the men said, "You must not go out; if we are forced to flee, they won't care about us. Even if half of us die, they won't care; but you are worth ten thousand of us.[e] It would be better now for you to give us support from the city."

[4]The king answered, "I will do whatever seems best to you."

So the king stood beside the gate while all the men marched out in units of hundreds and of thousands. [5]The king commanded Joab, Abishai and Ittai, "Be gentle with the young man Absalom for my sake." And all the troops heard the king giving orders concerning Absalom to each of the commanders.

[6]The army marched into the field to fight Israel, and the battle took place in the forest of Ephraim. [7]There the army of Israel was defeated by David's men, and the casualties that day were great—twenty thousand men. [8]The battle spread out over the whole countryside, and the forest claimed more lives that day than the sword.

[9]Now Absalom happened to meet David's men. He was riding his mule, and as the mule went under the thick branches of a large oak, Absalom's head got caught in the tree. He was left hanging in midair, while the mule he was riding kept on going.

[10]When one of the men saw this, he told Joab, "I just saw Absalom hanging in an oak tree."

[11]Joab said to the man who had told him this, "What! You saw him? Why didn't you strike him to the ground right there? Then I would have had to give you ten shekels[f] of silver and a warrior's belt."

[12]But the man replied, "Even if a thousand shekels[g] were weighed out into my hands, I would not lift my hand against the king's son. In our hearing the king commanded you and Abishai and Ittai, 'Protect the young man Absalom for my sake.'[h] [13]And if I had put my life in jeopardy[i]—and nothing is hidden from the king—you would have kept your distance from me."

[14]Joab said, "I'm not going to wait like this for you." So he took three javelins in his hand and plunged them into Absalom's heart while Absalom was still alive in the oak tree. [15]And ten of Joab's armorbearers surrounded Absalom, struck him and killed him.

---

[a]25 Hebrew *Ithra*, a variant of *Jether*   [b]25 Hebrew and some Septuagint manuscripts; other Septuagint manuscripts (see also 1 Chron. 2:17) *Ishmaelite* or *Jezreelite*   [c]25 Hebrew *Abigal*, a variant of *Abigail*   [d]28 Most Septuagint manuscripts and Syriac; Hebrew *lentils, and roasted grain*   [e]3 Two Hebrew manuscripts, some Septuagint manuscripts and Vulgate; most Hebrew manuscripts *care; for now there are ten thousand like us*   [f]11 That is, about 4 ounces (about 115 grams)   [g]12 That is, about 25 pounds (about 11 kilograms)   [h]12 A few Hebrew manuscripts, Septuagint, Vulgate and Syriac; most Hebrew manuscripts may be translated *Absalom, whoever you may be.*   [i]13 Or *Otherwise, if I had acted treacherously toward him*

16Then Joab sounded the trumpet, and the troops stopped pursuing Israel, for Joab halted them. 17They took Absalom, threw him into a big pit in the forest and piled up a large heap of rocks over him. Meanwhile, all the Israelites fled to their homes.

18During his lifetime Absalom had taken a pillar and erected it in the King's Valley as a monument to himself, for he thought, "I have no son to carry on the memory of my name." He named the pillar after himself, and it is called Absalom's Monument to this day.

David Mourns

19Now Ahimaaz son of Zadok said, "Let me run and take the news to the king that the LORD has delivered him from the hand of his enemies."

20"You are not the one to take the news today," Joab told him. "You may take the news another time, but you must not do so today, because the king's son is dead."

21Then Joab said to a Cushite, "Go, tell the king what you have seen." The Cushite bowed down before Joab and ran off.

22Ahimaaz son of Zadok again said to Joab, "Come what may, please let me run behind the Cushite."

But Joab replied, "My son, why do you want to go? You don't have any news that will bring you a reward."

23He said, "Come what may, I want to run."

So Joab said, "Run!" Then Ahimaaz ran by way of the plain*a* and outran the Cushite.

24While David was sitting between the inner and outer gates, the watchman went up to the roof of the gateway by the wall. As he looked out, he saw a man running alone. 25The watchman called out to the king and reported it.

The king said, "If he is alone, he must have good news." And the man came closer and closer.

26Then the watchman saw another man running, and he called down to the gatekeeper, "Look, another man running alone!"

The king said, "He must be bringing good news, too."

27The watchman said, "It seems to me that the first one runs like Ahimaaz son of Zadok."

"He's a good man," the king said. "He comes with good news."

28Then Ahimaaz called out to the king, "All is well!" He bowed down before the king with his face to the ground and said, "Praise be to the LORD your God! He has delivered up the men who lifted their hands against my lord the king."

29The king asked, "Is the young man Absalom safe?"

Ahimaaz answered, "I saw great confusion just as Joab was about to send the king's servant and me, your servant, but I don't know what it was."

30The king said, "Stand aside and wait here." So he stepped aside and stood there.

31Then the Cushite arrived and said, "My lord the king, hear the good news! The LORD has delivered you today from all who rose up against you."

32The king asked the Cushite, "Is the young man Absalom safe?"

The Cushite replied, "May the enemies of my lord the king and all who rise up to harm you be like that young man."

33The king was shaken. He went up to the room over the gateway and wept. As he went, he said: "O my son Absalom! My son, my son Absalom! If only I had died instead of you—O Absalom, my son, my son!"

19

Joab was told, "The king is weeping and mourning for Absalom." 2And for the whole army the victory that day was turned into mourning, because on that day the troops heard it said, "The king is grieving for his son." 3The men stole into the city that day as men steal in who are ashamed when they flee from battle. 4The king covered his face and cried aloud, "O my son Absalom! O Absalom, my son, my son!"

5Then Joab went into the house to the king and said, "Today you have humiliated all your men, who have just saved your life and the lives of your sons and daughters and the lives of your wives and concubines. 6You love those who hate you and hate those who love you. You have made it clear today that the commanders and their men mean nothing to you. I see that you would be pleased if Absalom were alive today and all of us were dead. 7Now go out and encourage your men. I swear by the LORD that if you don't go out, not a man will be left with you by nightfall. This will be worse for you than all the calamities that have come upon you from your youth till now."

a23 That is, the plain of the Jordan

⁸So the king got up and took his seat in the gateway. When the men were told, "The king is sitting in the gateway," they all came before him.

David Returns to Jerusalem

Meanwhile, the Israelites had fled to their homes. ⁹Throughout the tribes of Israel, the people were all arguing with each other, saying, "The king delivered us from the hand of our enemies; he is the one who rescued us from the hand of the Philistines. But now he has fled the country because of Absalom; ¹⁰and Absalom, whom we anointed to rule over us, has died in battle. So why do you say nothing about bringing the king back?"

¹¹King David sent this message to Zadok and Abiathar, the priests: "Ask the elders of Judah, 'Why should you be the last to bring the king back to his palace, since what is being said throughout Israel has reached the king at his quarters? ¹²You are my brothers, my own flesh and blood. So why should you be the last to bring back the king?' ¹³And say to Amasa, 'Are you not my own flesh and blood? May God deal with me, be it ever so severely, if from now on you are not the commander of my army in place of Joab.'"

¹⁴He won over the hearts of all the men of Judah as though they were one man. They sent word to the king, "Return, you and all your men." ¹⁵Then the king returned and went as far as the Jordan.

Now the men of Judah had come to Gilgal to go out and meet the king and bring him across the Jordan. ¹⁶Shimei son of Gera, the Benjamite from Bahurim, hurried down with the men of Judah to meet King David. ¹⁷With him were a thousand Benjamites, along with Ziba, the steward of Saul's household, and his fifteen sons and twenty servants. They rushed to the Jordan, where the king was. ¹⁸They crossed at the ford to take the king's household over and to do whatever he wished.

When Shimei son of Gera crossed the Jordan, he fell prostrate before the king ¹⁹and said to him, "May my lord not hold me guilty. Do not remember how your servant did wrong on the day my lord the king left Jerusalem. May the king put it out of his mind. ²⁰For I your servant know that I have sinned, but today I have come here as the first of the whole house of Joseph to come down and meet my lord the king."

²¹Then Abishai son of Zeruiah said, "Shouldn't Shimei be put to death for this? He cursed the Lord's anointed."

²²David replied, "What do you and I have in common, you sons of Zeruiah? This day you have become my adversaries! Should anyone be put to death in Israel today? Do I not know that today I am king over Israel?" ²³So the king said to Shimei, "You shall not die." And the king promised him on oath.

²⁴Mephibosheth, Saul's grandson, also went down to meet the king. He had not taken care of his feet or trimmed his mustache or washed his clothes from the day the king left until the day he returned safely. ²⁵When he came from Jerusalem to meet the king, the king asked him, "Why didn't you go with me, Mephibosheth?"

²⁶He said, "My lord the king, since I your servant am lame, I said, 'I will have my donkey saddled and will ride on it, so I can go with the king.' But Ziba my servant betrayed me. ²⁷And he has slandered your servant to my lord the king. My lord the king is like an angel of God; so do whatever pleases you. ²⁸All my grandfather's descendants deserved nothing but death from my lord the king, but you gave your servant a place among those who eat at your table. So what right do I have to make any more appeals to the king?"

²⁹The king said to him, "Why say more? I order you and Ziba to divide the fields."

³⁰Mephibosheth said to the king, "Let him take everything, now that my lord the king has arrived home safely."

³¹Barzillai the Gileadite also came down from Rogelim to cross the Jordan with the king and to send him on his way from there. ³²Now Barzillai was a very old man, eighty years of age. He had provided for the king during his stay in Mahanaim, for he was a very wealthy man. ³³The king said to Barzillai, "Cross over with me and stay with me in Jerusalem, and I will provide for you."

³⁴But Barzillai answered the king, "How many more years will I live, that I should go up to Jerusalem with the king? ³⁵I am now eighty years old. Can I tell the difference between what is good and what is not? Can your servant taste what he eats and drinks? Can I still hear the voices of men and women singers? Why should your servant be an added burden to my lord the king? ³⁶Your servant will cross over the Jordan with the king for a short distance, but why should the king

reward me in this way? 37Let your servant return, that I may die in my own town near the tomb of my father and mother. But here is your servant Kimham. Let him cross over with my lord the king. Do for him whatever pleases you."

38The king said, "Kimham shall cross over with me, and I will do for him whatever pleases you. And anything you desire from me I will do for you."

39So all the people crossed the Jordan, and then the king crossed over. The king kissed Barzillai and gave him his blessing, and Barzillai returned to his home.

40When the king crossed over to Gilgal, Kimham crossed with him. All the troops of Judah and half the troops of Israel had taken the king over.

41Soon all the men of Israel were coming to the king and saying to him, "Why did our brothers, the men of Judah, steal the king away and bring him and his household across the Jordan, together with all his men?"

42All the men of Judah answered the men of Israel, "We did this because the king is closely related to us. Why are you angry about it? Have we eaten any of the king's provisions? Have we taken anything for ourselves?"

43Then the men of Israel answered the men of Judah, "We have ten shares in the king; and besides, we have a greater claim on David than you have. So why do you treat us with contempt? Were we not the first to speak of bringing back our king?"

But the men of Judah responded even more harshly than the men of Israel.

Sheba Rebels Against David

20 Now a troublemaker named Sheba son of Bicri, a Benjamite, happened to be there. He sounded the trumpet and shouted,

"We have no share in David,
    no part in Jesse's son!
Every man to his tent, O Israel!"

2So all the men of Israel deserted David to follow Sheba son of Bicri. But the men of Judah stayed by their king all the way from the Jordan to Jerusalem.

3When David returned to his palace in Jerusalem, he took the ten concubines he had left to take care of the palace and put them in a house under guard. He provided for them, but did not lie with them.

They were kept in confinement till the day of their death, living as widows.

4Then the king said to Amasa, "Summon the men of Judah to come to me within three days, and be here yourself." 5But when Amasa went to summon Judah, he took longer than the time the king had set for him.

6David said to Abishai, "Now Sheba son of Bicri will do us more harm than Absalom did. Take your master's men and pursue him, or he will find fortified cities and escape from us." 7So Joab's men and the Kerethites and Pelethites and all the mighty warriors went out under the command of Abishai. They marched out from Jerusalem to pursue Sheba son of Bicri.

8While they were at the great rock in Gibeon, Amasa came to meet them. Joab was wearing his military tunic, and strapped over it at his waist was a belt with a dagger in its sheath. As he stepped forward, it dropped out of its sheath.

9Joab said to Amasa, "How are you, my brother?" Then Joab took Amasa by the beard with his right hand to kiss him. 10Amasa was not on his guard against the dagger in Joab's hand, and Joab plunged it into his belly, and his intestines spilled out on the ground. Without being stabbed again, Amasa died. Then Joab and his brother Abishai pursued Sheba son of Bicri.

11One of Joab's men stood beside Amasa and said, "Whoever favors Joab, and whoever is for David, let him follow Joab!" 12Amasa lay wallowing in his blood in the middle of the road, and the man saw that all the troops came to a halt there. When he realized that everyone who came up to Amasa stopped, he dragged him from the road into a field and threw a garment over him. 13After Amasa had been removed from the road, all the men went on with Joab to pursue Sheba son of Bicri.

14Sheba passed through all the tribes of Israel to Abel Beth Maacah[a] and through the entire region of the Berites, who gathered together and followed him. 15All the troops with Joab came and besieged Sheba in Abel Beth Maacah. They built a siege ramp up to the city, and it stood against the outer fortifications. While they were battering the wall to bring it down, 16a wise woman called from the city, "Listen! Listen! Tell Joab to come

a14 Or Abel, even Beth Maacah; also in verse 15

here so I can speak to him." ¹⁷He went toward her, and she asked, "Are you Joab?"

"I am," he answered.

She said, "Listen to what your servant has to say."

"I'm listening," he said.

¹⁸She continued, "Long ago they used to say, 'Get your answer at Abel,' and that settled it. ¹⁹We are the peaceful and faithful in Israel. You are trying to destroy a city that is a mother in Israel. Why do you want to swallow up the LORD's inheritance?"

²⁰"Far be it from me!" Joab replied, "Far be it from me to swallow up or destroy! ²¹That is not the case. A man named Sheba son of Bicri, from the hill country of Ephraim, has lifted up his hand against the king, against David. Hand over this one man, and I'll withdraw from the city."

The woman said to Joab, "His head will be thrown to you from the wall."

²²Then the woman went to all the people with her wise advice, and they cut off the head of Sheba son of Bicri and threw it to Joab. So he sounded the trumpet, and his men dispersed from the city, each returning to his home. And Joab went back to the king in Jerusalem.

²³Joab was over Israel's entire army; Benaiah son of Jehoiada was over the Kerethites and Pelethites; ²⁴Adoniram*ᵃ* was in charge of forced labor; Jehoshaphat son of Ahilud was recorder; ²⁵Sheva was secretary; Zadok and Abiathar were priests; ²⁶and Ira the Jairite was David's priest.

The Gibeonites Avenged

21 During the reign of David, there was a famine for three successive years; so David sought the face of the LORD. The LORD said, "It is on account of Saul and his blood-stained house; it is because he put the Gibeonites to death."

²The king summoned the Gibeonites and spoke to them. (Now the Gibeonites were not a part of Israel but were survivors of the Amorites; the Israelites had sworn to spare them, but Saul in his zeal for Israel and Judah had tried to annihilate them.) ³David asked the Gibeonites, "What shall I do for you? How shall I

make amends so that you will bless the LORD's inheritance?"

⁴The Gibeonites answered him, "We have no right to demand silver or gold from Saul or his family, nor do we have the right to put anyone in Israel to death."

"What do you want me to do for you?" David asked.

⁵They answered the king, "As for the man who destroyed us and plotted against us so that we have been decimated and have no place anywhere in Israel, ⁶let seven of his male descendants be given to us to be killed and exposed before the LORD at Gibeah of Saul—the LORD's chosen one."

So the king said, "I will give them to you."

⁷The king spared Mephibosheth son of Jonathan, the son of Saul, because of the oath before the LORD between David and Jonathan son of Saul. ⁸But the king took Armoni and Mephibosheth, the two sons of Aiah's daughter Rizpah, whom she had borne to Saul, together with the five sons of Saul's daughter Merab,ᵇ whom she had borne to Adriel son of Barzillai the Meholathite. ⁹He handed them over to the Gibeonites, who killed and exposed them on a hill before the LORD. All seven of them fell together; they were put to death during the first days of the harvest, just as the barley harvest was beginning.

¹⁰Rizpah daughter of Aiah took sackcloth and spread it out for herself on a rock. From the beginning of the harvest till the rain poured down from the heavens on the bodies, she did not let the birds of the air touch them by day or the wild animals by night. ¹¹When David was told what Aiah's daughter Rizpah, Saul's concubine, had done, ¹²he went and took the bones of Saul and his son Jonathan from the citizens of Jabesh Gilead. (They had taken them secretly from the public square at Beth Shan, where the Philistines had hung them after they struck Saul down on Gilboa.) ¹³David brought the bones of Saul and his son Jonathan from there, and the bones of those who had been killed and exposed were gathered up.

¹⁴They buried the bones of Saul and his son Jonathan in the tomb of Saul's father Kish, at Zela in Benjamin, and did every-

thing the king commanded. After that, God answered prayer in behalf of the land.

Wars Against the Philistines

15Once again there was a battle between the Philistines and Israel. David went down with his men to fight against the Philistines, and he became exhausted. 16And Ishbi-Benob, one of the descendants of Rapha, whose bronze spearhead weighed three hundred shekels*a* and who was armed with a new ,sword,, said he would kill David. 17But Abishai son of Zeruiah came to David's rescue; he struck the Philistine down and killed him. Then David's men swore to him, saying, "Never again will you go out with us to battle, so that the lamp of Israel will not be extinguished."

18In the course of time, there was another battle with the Philistines, at Gob. At that time Sibbecai the Hushathite killed Saph, one of the descendants of Rapha.

19In another battle with the Philistines at Gob, Elhanan son of Jaare-Oregim*b* the Bethlehemite killed Goliath*c* the Gittite, who had a spear with a shaft like a weaver's rod.

20In still another battle, which took place at Gath, there was a huge man with six fingers on each hand and six toes on each foot—twenty-four in all. He also was descended from Rapha. 21When he taunted Israel, Jonathan son of Shimeah, David's brother, killed him.

22These four were descendants of Rapha in Gath, and they fell at the hands of David and his men.

David's Song of Praise

22 David sang to the LORD the words of this song when the LORD delivered him from the hand of all his enemies and from the hand of Saul. 2He said:

"The LORD is my rock, my fortress and
    my deliverer;
3   my God is my rock, in whom I take
    refuge,
    my shield and the horn*d* of my
    salvation.
He is my stronghold, my refuge and
    my savior—

from violent men you save me.
4I call to the LORD, who is worthy of
    praise,
    and I am saved from my enemies.

5"The waves of death swirled about
    me;
    the torrents of destruction
    overwhelmed me.
6The cords of the grave*e* coiled around
    me;
    the snares of death confronted me.
7In my distress I called to the LORD;
    I called out to my God.
From his temple he heard my voice;
    my cry came to his ears.

8"The earth trembled and quaked,
    the foundations of the heavens*f*
    shook;
    they trembled because he was
    angry.
9Smoke rose from his nostrils;
    consuming fire came from his
    mouth,
    burning coals blazed out of it.
10He parted the heavens and came
    down;
    dark clouds were under his feet.
11He mounted the cherubim and flew;
    he soared*g* on the wings of the
    wind.
12He made darkness his canopy around
    him—
    the dark*h* rain clouds of the sky.
13Out of the brightness of his presence
    bolts of lightning blazed forth.
14The LORD thundered from heaven;
    the voice of the Most High
    resounded.
15He shot arrows and scattered ,the
    enemies,,
    bolts of lightning and routed them.
16The valleys of the sea were exposed
    and the foundations of the earth
    laid bare
at the rebuke of the LORD,
    at the blast of breath from his
    nostrils.

17"He reached down from on high and
    took hold of me;
    he drew me out of deep waters.
18He rescued me from my powerful
    enemy,

---

a16 That is, about 7 1/2 pounds (about 3.5 kilograms)   *b19* Or *son of Jair the weaver*   *c19* Hebrew and Septuagint; 1 Chron. 20:5 *son of Jair killed Lahmi the brother of Goliath*   *d3* Horn here symbolizes strength.   *e6* Hebrew *Sheol*   *f8* Hebrew; Vulgate and Syriac (see also Psalm 18:7) *mountains* *g11* Many Hebrew manuscripts (see also Psalm 18:10); most Hebrew manuscripts *appeared* *h12* Septuagint and Vulgate (see also Psalm 18:11); Hebrew *massed*

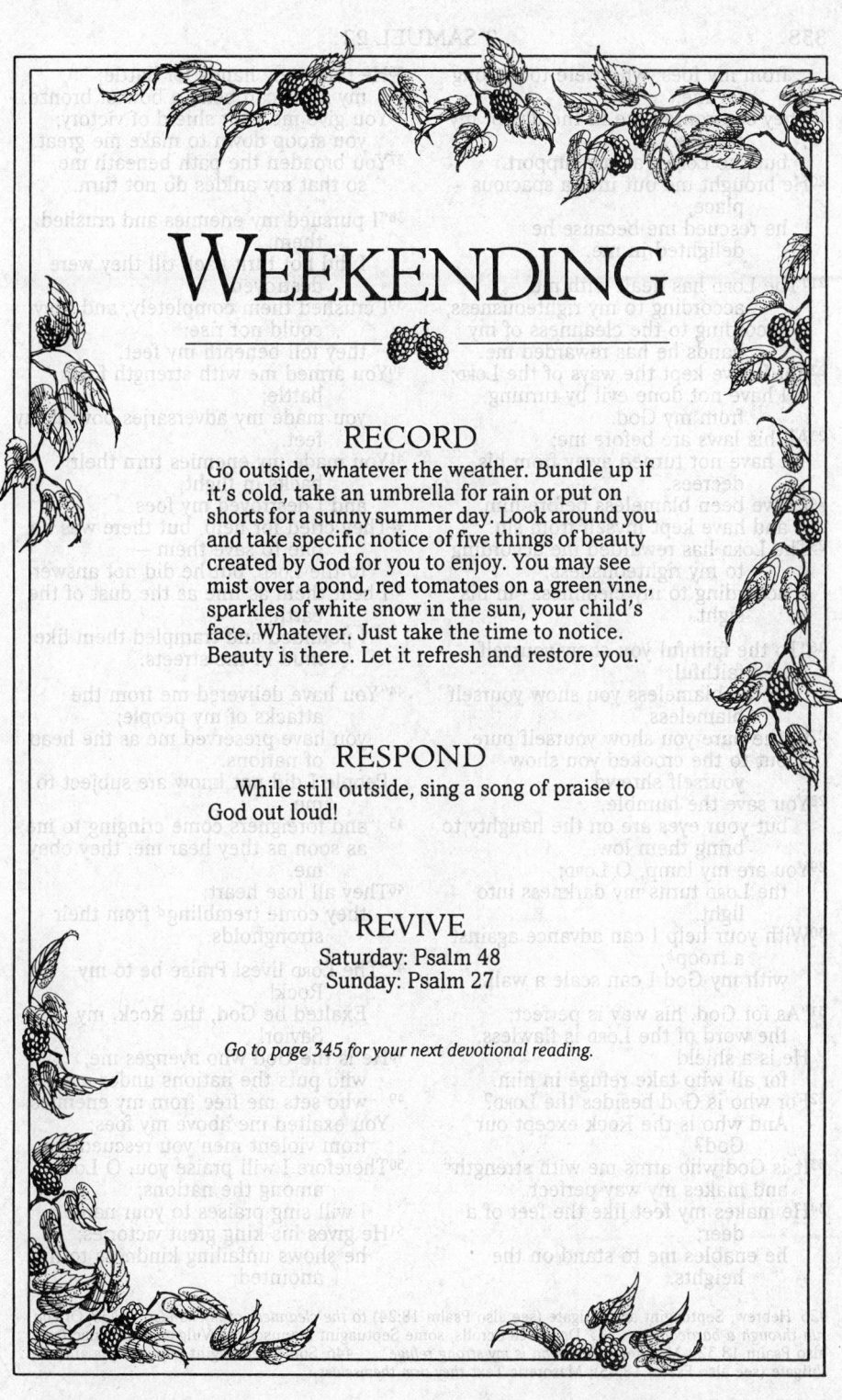

WEEKENDING

RECORD

Go outside, whatever the weather. Bundle up if it's cold, take an umbrella for rain or put on shorts for a sunny summer day. Look around you and take specific notice of five things of beauty created by God for you to enjoy. You may see mist over a pond, red tomatoes on a green vine, sparkles of white snow in the sun, your child's face. Whatever. Just take the time to notice. Beauty is there. Let it refresh and restore you.

RESPOND

While still outside, sing a song of praise to God out loud!

REVIVE

Saturday: Psalm 48
Sunday: Psalm 27

Go to page 345 for your next devotional reading.

from my foes, who were too strong
for me.
¹⁹They confronted me in the day of my
disaster,
but the LORD was my support.
²⁰He brought me out into a spacious
place;
he rescued me because he
delighted in me.

²¹"The LORD has dealt with me
according to my righteousness;
according to the cleanness of my
hands he has rewarded me.
²²For I have kept the ways of the LORD;
I have not done evil by turning
from my God.
²³All his laws are before me;
I have not turned away from his
decrees.
²⁴I have been blameless before him
and have kept myself from sin.
²⁵The LORD has rewarded me according
to my righteousness,
according to my cleanness*a* in his
sight.

²⁶"To the faithful you show yourself
faithful,
to the blameless you show yourself
blameless,
²⁷to the pure you show yourself pure,
but to the crooked you show
yourself shrewd.
²⁸You save the humble,
but your eyes are on the haughty to
bring them low.
²⁹You are my lamp, O LORD;
the LORD turns my darkness into
light.
³⁰With your help I can advance against
a troop*b*;
with my God I can scale a wall.

³¹"As for God, his way is perfect;
the word of the LORD is flawless.
He is a shield
for all who take refuge in him.
³²For who is God besides the LORD?
And who is the Rock except our
God?
³³It is God who arms me with strength*c*
and makes my way perfect.
³⁴He makes my feet like the feet of a
deer;
he enables me to stand on the
heights.

³⁵He trains my hands for battle;
my arms can bend a bow of bronze.
³⁶You give me your shield of victory;
you stoop down to make me great.
³⁷You broaden the path beneath me,
so that my ankles do not turn.

³⁸"I pursued my enemies and crushed
them;
I did not turn back till they were
destroyed.
³⁹I crushed them completely, and they
could not rise;
they fell beneath my feet.
⁴⁰You armed me with strength for
battle;
you made my adversaries bow at my
feet.
⁴¹You made my enemies turn their
backs in flight,
and I destroyed my foes.
⁴²They cried for help, but there was no
one to save them—
to the LORD, but he did not answer.
⁴³I beat them as fine as the dust of the
earth;
I pounded and trampled them like
mud in the streets.

⁴⁴"You have delivered me from the
attacks of my people;
you have preserved me as the head
of nations.
People I did not know are subject to
me,
⁴⁵   and foreigners come cringing to me;
as soon as they hear me, they obey
me.
⁴⁶They all lose heart;
they come trembling*d* from their
strongholds.

⁴⁷"The LORD lives! Praise be to my
Rock!
Exalted be God, the Rock, my
Savior!
⁴⁸He is the God who avenges me,
who puts the nations under me,
⁴⁹   who sets me free from my enemies.
You exalted me above my foes;
from violent men you rescued me.
⁵⁰Therefore I will praise you, O LORD,
among the nations;
I will sing praises to your name.
⁵¹He gives his king great victories;
he shows unfailing kindness to his
anointed,

a25 Hebrew; Septuagint and Vulgate (see also Psalm 18:24) *to the cleanness of my hands*   *b30* Or *can
run through a barricade*   *c33* Dead Sea Scrolls, some Septuagint manuscripts, Vulgate and Syriac (see
also Psalm 18:32); Masoretic Text *who is my strong refuge*   *d46* Some Septuagint manuscripts and
Vulgate (see also Psalm 18:45); Masoretic Text *they arm themselves.*

to David and his descendants forever."

The Last Words of David

23 These are the last words of David:

"The oracle of David son of Jesse,
the oracle of the man exalted by the Most High,
the man anointed by the God of Jacob,
Israel's singer of songs*a*:

2"The Spirit of the LORD spoke through me;
his word was on my tongue.
3The God of Israel spoke,
the Rock of Israel said to me:
'When one rules over men in righteousness,
when he rules in the fear of God,
4he is like the light of morning at sunrise
on a cloudless morning,
like the brightness after rain
that brings the grass from the earth.'

5"Is not my house right with God?
Has he not made with me an everlasting covenant,
arranged and secured in every part?
Will he not bring to fruition my salvation
and grant me my every desire?
6But evil men are all to be cast aside like thorns,
which are not gathered with the hand.
7Whoever touches thorns
uses a tool of iron or the shaft of a spear;
they are burned up where they lie."

David's Mighty Men

8These are the names of David's mighty men:

Josheb-Basshebeth,*b* a Tahkemonite,*c* was chief of the Three; he raised his spear against eight hundred men, whom he killed*d* in one encounter.
9Next to him was Eleazar son of Dodai the Ahohite. As one of the three mighty men, he was with David when they taunt-

ed the Philistines gathered ₁at Pas Dammim,*e* for battle. Then the men of Israel retreated, 10but he stood his ground and struck down the Philistines till his hand grew tired and froze to the sword. The LORD brought about a great victory that day. The troops returned to Eleazar, but only to strip the dead.
11Next to him was Shammah son of Agee the Hararite. When the Philistines banded together at a place where there was a field full of lentils, Israel's troops fled from them. 12But Shammah took his stand in the middle of the field. He defended it and struck the Philistines down, and the LORD brought about a great victory.

13During harvest time, three of the thirty chief men came down to David at the cave of Adullam, while a band of Philistines was encamped in the Valley of Rephaim. 14At that time David was in the stronghold, and the Philistine garrison was at Bethlehem. 15David longed for water and said, "Oh, that someone would get me a drink of water from the well near the gate of Bethlehem!" 16So the three mighty men broke through the Philistine lines, drew water from the well near the gate of Bethlehem and carried it back to David. But he refused to drink it; instead, he poured it out before the LORD. 17"Far be it from me, O LORD, to do this!" he said. "Is it not the blood of men who went at the risk of their lives?" And David would not drink it.

Such were the exploits of the three mighty men.

18Abishai the brother of Joab son of Zeruiah was chief of the Three.*f* He raised his spear against three hundred men, whom he killed, and so he became as famous as the Three. 19Was he not held in greater honor than the Three? He became their commander, even though he was not included among them.

20Benaiah son of Jehoiada was a valiant fighter from Kabzeel, who performed great exploits. He struck down two of Moab's best men. He also went down into a pit on a snowy day and killed a lion. 21And he struck down a huge Egyptian. Although the Egyptian had a spear in his hand, Benaiah went against him with a

---

a1 Or *Israel's beloved singer*   *b8* Hebrew; some Septuagint manuscripts suggest *Ish-Bosheth,* that is, *Esh-Baal* (see also 1 Chron. 11:11 *Jashobeam*).   *c8* Probably a variant of *Hacmonite* (see 1 Chron. 11:11)   *d8* Some Septuagint manuscripts (see also 1 Chron. 11:11); Hebrew and other Septuagint manuscripts *Three; it was Adino the Eznite who killed eight hundred men*   *e9* See 1 Chron. 11:13; Hebrew *gathered there.*   *f18* Most Hebrew manuscripts (see also 1 Chron. 11:20); two Hebrew manuscripts and Syriac *Thirty* club. He snatched the spear from the Egyptian's hand and killed him with his own spear. 22Such were the exploits of Benaiah son of Jehoiada; he too was as famous as the three mighty men. 23He was held in greater honor than any of the Thirty, but he was not included among the Three. And David put him in charge of his bodyguard.

24Among the Thirty were:

Asahel the brother of Joab,
Elhanan son of Dodo from Bethlehem,
25Shammah the Harodite,
Elika the Harodite,
26Helez the Paltite,
Ira son of Ikkesh from Tekoa,
27Abiezer from Anathoth,
Mebunnai*a* the Hushathite,
28Zalmon the Ahohite,
Maharai the Netophathite,
29Heled*b* son of Baanah the Netophathite,
Ithai son of Ribai from Gibeah in Benjamin,
30Benaiah the Pirathonite,
Hiddai*c* from the ravines of Gaash,
31Abi-Albon the Arbathite,
Azmaveth the Barhumite,
32Eliahba the Shaalbonite,
the sons of Jashen,
Jonathan 33son of*d* Shammah the Hararite,
Ahiam son of Sharar*e* the Hararite,
34Eliphelet son of Ahasbai the Maacathite,
Eliam son of Ahithophel the Gilonite,
35Hezro the Carmelite,
Paarai the Arbite,
36Igal son of Nathan from Zobah,
the son of Hagri,*f*
37Zelek the Ammonite,
Naharai the Beerothite, the armorbearer of Joab son of Zeruiah,
38Ira the Ithrite,
Gareb the Ithrite
39and Uriah the Hittite.
There were thirty-seven in all.

David Counts the Fighting Men

24 Again the anger of the Lord burned against Israel, and he incited David against them, saying, "Go and take a census of Israel and Judah."

2So the king said to Joab and the army commanders*g* with him, "Go throughout the tribes of Israel from Dan to Beersheba and enroll the fighting men, so that I may know how many there are."

3But Joab replied to the king, "May the Lord your God multiply the troops a hundred times over, and may the eyes of my lord the king see it. But why does my lord the king want to do such a thing?"

4The king's word, however, overruled Joab and the army commanders; so they left the presence of the king to enroll the fighting men of Israel.

5After crossing the Jordan, they camped near Aroer, south of the town in the gorge, and then went through Gad and on to Jazer. 6They went to Gilead and the region of Tahtim Hodshi, and on to Dan Jaan and around toward Sidon. 7Then they went toward the fortress of Tyre and all the towns of the Hivites and Canaanites. Finally, they went on to Beersheba in the Negev of Judah.

8After they had gone through the entire land, they came back to Jerusalem at the end of nine months and twenty days.

9Joab reported the number of the fighting men to the king: In Israel there were eight hundred thousand able-bodied men who could handle a sword, and in Judah five hundred thousand.

10David was conscience-stricken after he had counted the fighting men, and he said to the Lord, "I have sinned greatly in what I have done. Now, O Lord, I beg you, take away the guilt of your servant. I have done a very foolish thing."

11Before David got up the next morning, the word of the Lord had come to Gad the prophet, David's seer: 12"Go and tell David, 'This is what the Lord says: I am giving you three options. Choose one of them for me to carry out against you.'"

13So Gad went to David and said to him, "Shall there come upon you three*h* years of famine in your land? Or three

---

a27 Hebrew; some Septuagint manuscripts (see also 1 Chron. 11:29) *Sibbecai*   *b29* Some Hebrew manuscripts and Vulgate (see also 1 Chron. 11:30); most Hebrew manuscripts *Heleb*   *c30* Hebrew; some Septuagint manuscripts (see also 1 Chron. 11:32) *Hurai*   *d33* Some Septuagint manuscripts (see also 1 Chron. 11:34); Hebrew does not have *son of.*   *e33* Hebrew; some Septuagint manuscripts (see also 1 Chron. 11:35) *Sacar*   *f36* Some Septuagint manuscripts (see also 1 Chron. 11:38); Hebrew *Haggadi*   *g2* Septuagint (see also verse 4 and 1 Chron. 21:2); Hebrew *Joab the army commander*   *h13* Septuagint (see also 1 Chron. 21:12); Hebrew *seven* months of fleeing from your enemies while they pursue you? Or three days of plague in your land? Now then, think it over and decide how I should answer the one who sent me."

14David said to Gad, "I am in deep distress. Let us fall into the hands of the LORD, for his mercy is great; but do not let me fall into the hands of men."

15So the LORD sent a plague on Israel from that morning until the end of the time designated, and seventy thousand of the people from Dan to Beersheba died. 16When the angel stretched out his hand to destroy Jerusalem, the LORD was grieved because of the calamity and said to the angel who was afflicting the people, "Enough! Withdraw your hand." The angel of the LORD was then at the threshing floor of Araunah the Jebusite.

17When David saw the angel who was striking down the people, he said to the LORD, "I am the one who has sinned and done wrong. These are but sheep. What have they done? Let your hand fall upon me and my family."

David Builds an Altar

18On that day Gad went to David and said to him, "Go up and build an altar to the LORD on the threshing floor of Arau-nah the Jebusite." 19So David went up, as the LORD had commanded through Gad. 20When Araunah looked and saw the king and his men coming toward him, he went out and bowed down before the king with his face to the ground.

21Araunah said, "Why has my lord the king come to his servant?"

"To buy your threshing floor," David answered, "so I can build an altar to the LORD, that the plague on the people may be stopped."

22Araunah said to David, "Let my lord the king take whatever pleases him and offer it up. Here are oxen for the burnt offering, and here are threshing sledges and ox yokes for the wood. 23O king, Araunah gives all this to the king." Araunah also said to him, "May the LORD your God accept you."

24But the king replied to Araunah, "No, I insist on paying you for it. I will not sacrifice to the LORD my God burnt offerings that cost me nothing."

So David bought the threshing floor and the oxen and paid fifty shekels[a] of silver for them. 25David built an altar to the LORD there and sacrificed burnt offerings and fellowship offerings.[b] Then the LORD answered prayer in behalf of the land, and the plague on Israel was stopped.

---

a24 That is, about 1 1/4 pounds (about 0.6 kilogram)   b25 Traditionally peace offerings

*T*HIS book begins by covering the excitement of Solomon's building of the temple, but it then goes on to describe the sad events that take place after Solomon begins serving other gods. The kingdom is divided into two nations, Israel and Judah. All of Israel's kings are wicked, half of Judah's are. God sends prophets (like Elijah) to preach God's word and to warn the rulers against idolatry. As you read this book, realize how severe it is to disobey God's word. Like the Israelites on Mount Carmel, confess, "The LORD—he is God" (1 Kings 18:39).

1 KINGS

Adonijah Sets Himself Up as King

1 When King David was old and well advanced in years, he could not keep warm even when they put covers over him. ²So his servants said to him, "Let us look for a young virgin to attend the king and take care of him. She can lie beside him so that our lord the king may keep warm."

³Then they searched throughout Israel for a beautiful girl and found Abishag, a Shunammite, and brought her to the king. ⁴The girl was very beautiful; she took care of the king and waited on him, but the king had no intimate relations with her.

⁵Now Adonijah, whose mother was Haggith, put himself forward and said, "I will be king." So he got chariots and horses*ᵃ* ready, with fifty men to run ahead of him. ⁶(His father had never interfered with him by asking, "Why do you

ᵃ5 Or charioteers

behave as you do?" He was also very handsome and was born next after Absalom.)

7Adonijah conferred with Joab son of Zeruiah and with Abiathar the priest, and they gave him their support. 8But Zadok the priest, Benaiah son of Jehoiada, Nathan the prophet, Shimei and Rei*a* and David's special guard did not join Adonijah.

9Adonijah then sacrificed sheep, cattle and fattened calves at the Stone of Zoheleth near En Rogel. He invited all his brothers, the king's sons, and all the men of Judah who were royal officials, 10but he did not invite Nathan the prophet or Benaiah or the special guard or his brother Solomon.

11Then Nathan asked Bathsheba, Solomon's mother, "Have you not heard that Adonijah, the son of Haggith, has become king without our lord David's knowing it? 12Now then, let me advise you how you can save your own life and the life of your son Solomon. 13Go in to King David and say to him, 'My lord the king, did you not swear to me your servant: "Surely Solomon your son shall be king after me, and he will sit on my throne"? Why then has Adonijah become king?' 14While you are still there talking to the king, I will come in and confirm what you have said."

15So Bathsheba went to see the aged king in his room, where Abishag the Shunammite was attending him. 16Bathsheba bowed low and knelt before the king.

"What is it you want?" the king asked.

17She said to him, "My lord, you yourself swore to me your servant by the LORD your God: 'Solomon your son shall be king after me, and he will sit on my throne.' 18But now Adonijah has become king, and you, my lord the king, do not know about it. 19He has sacrificed great numbers of cattle, fattened calves, and sheep, and has invited all the king's sons, Abiathar the priest and Joab the commander of the army, but he has not invited Solomon your servant. 20My lord the king, the eyes of all Israel are on you, to learn from you who will sit on the throne of my lord the king after him. 21Otherwise, as soon as my lord the king is laid to rest with his fathers, I and my son Solomon will be treated as criminals."

22While she was still speaking with the king, Nathan the prophet arrived. 23And they told the king, "Nathan the prophet is here." So he went before the king and bowed with his face to the ground.

24Nathan said, "Have you, my lord the king, declared that Adonijah shall be king after you, and that he will sit on your throne? 25Today he has gone down and sacrificed great numbers of cattle, fattened calves, and sheep. He has invited all the king's sons, the commanders of the army and Abiathar the priest. Right now they are eating and drinking with him and saying, 'Long live King Adonijah!' 26But me your servant, and Zadok the priest, and Benaiah son of Jehoiada, and your servant Solomon he did not invite. 27Is this something my lord the king has done without letting his servants know who should sit on the throne of my lord the king after him?"

David Makes Solomon King

28Then King David said, "Call in Bathsheba." So she came into the king's presence and stood before him.

29The king then took an oath: "As surely as the LORD lives, who has delivered me out of every trouble, 30I will surely carry out today what I swore to you by the LORD, the God of Israel: Solomon your son shall be king after me, and he will sit on my throne in my place."

31Then Bathsheba bowed low with her face to the ground and, kneeling before the king, said, "May my lord King David live forever!"

32King David said, "Call in Zadok the priest, Nathan the prophet and Benaiah son of Jehoiada." When they came before the king, 33he said to them: "Take your lord's servants with you and set Solomon my son on my own mule and take him down to Gihon. 34There have Zadok the priest and Nathan the prophet anoint him king over Israel. Blow the trumpet and shout, 'Long live King Solomon!' 35Then you are to go up with him, and he is to come and sit on my throne and reign in my place. I have appointed him ruler over Israel and Judah."

36Benaiah son of Jehoiada answered the king, "Amen! May the LORD, the God of my lord the king, so declare it. 37As the LORD was with my lord the king, so may he be with Solomon to make his throne even greater than the throne of my lord King David!"

38So Zadok the priest, Nathan the

a8 Or *and his friends*

prophet, Benaiah son of Jehoiada, the Kerethites and the Pelethites went down and put Solomon on King David's mule and escorted him to Gihon. ³⁹Zadok the priest took the horn of oil from the sacred tent and anointed Solomon. Then they sounded the trumpet and all the people shouted, "Long live King Solomon!" ⁴⁰And all the people went up after him, playing flutes and rejoicing greatly, so that the ground shook with the sound.

⁴¹Adonijah and all the guests who were with him heard it as they were finishing their feast. On hearing the sound of the trumpet, Joab asked, "What's the meaning of all the noise in the city?"

⁴²Even as he was speaking, Jonathan son of Abiathar the priest arrived. Adonijah said, "Come in. A worthy man like you must be bringing good news."

⁴³"Not at all!" Jonathan answered. "Our lord King David has made Solomon king. ⁴⁴The king has sent with him Zadok the priest, Nathan the prophet, Benaiah son of Jehoiada, the Kerethites and the Pelethites, and they have put him on the king's mule, ⁴⁵and Zadok the priest and Nathan the prophet have anointed him king at Gihon. From there they have gone up cheering, and the city resounds with it. That's the noise you hear. ⁴⁶Moreover, Solomon has taken his seat on the royal throne. ⁴⁷Also, the royal officials have come to congratulate our lord King David, saying, 'May your God make Solomon's name more famous than yours and his throne greater than yours!' And the king bowed in worship on his bed ⁴⁸and said, 'Praise be to the LORD, the God of Israel, who has allowed my eyes to see a successor on my throne today.'"

⁴⁹At this, all Adonijah's guests rose in alarm and dispersed. ⁵⁰But Adonijah, in fear of Solomon, went and took hold of the horns of the altar. ⁵¹Then Solomon was told, "Adonijah is afraid of King Solomon and is clinging to the horns of the altar. He says, 'Let King Solomon swear to me today that he will not put his servant to death with the sword.'"

⁵²Solomon replied, "If he shows himself to be a worthy man, not a hair of his head will fall to the ground; but if evil is found in him, he will die." ⁵³Then King Solomon sent men, and they brought him down from the altar. And Adonijah came and bowed down to King Solomon, and Solomon said, "Go to your home."

David's Charge to Solomon

2 When the time drew near for David to die, he gave a charge to Solomon his son.

²"I am about to go the way of all the earth," he said. "So be strong, show yourself a man, ³and observe what the LORD your God requires: Walk in his ways, and keep his decrees and commands, his laws and requirements, as written in the Law of Moses, so that you may prosper in all you do and wherever you go, ⁴and that the LORD may keep his promise to me: 'If your descendants watch how they live, and if they walk faithfully before me with all their heart and soul, you will never fail to have a man on the throne of Israel.'

⁵"Now you yourself know what Joab son of Zeruiah did to me—what he did to the two commanders of Israel's armies, Abner son of Ner and Amasa son of Jether. He killed them, shedding their blood in peacetime as if in battle, and with that blood stained the belt around his waist and the sandals on his feet. ⁶Deal with him according to your wisdom, but do not let his gray head go down to the grave*a* in peace.

⁷"But show kindness to the sons of Barzillai of Gilead and let them be among those who eat at your table. They stood by me when I fled from your brother Absalom.

⁸"And remember, you have with you Shimei son of Gera, the Benjamite from Bahurim, who called down bitter curses on me the day I went to Mahanaim. When he came down to meet me at the Jordan, I swore to him by the LORD: 'I will not put you to death by the sword.' ⁹But now, do not consider him innocent. You are a man of wisdom; you will know what to do to him. Bring his gray head down to the grave in blood."

¹⁰Then David rested with his fathers and was buried in the City of David. ¹¹He had reigned forty years over Israel—seven years in Hebron and thirty-three in Jerusalem. ¹²So Solomon sat on the throne of his father David, and his rule was firmly established.

Solomon's Throne Established

¹³Now Adonijah, the son of Haggith, went to Bathsheba, Solomon's mother.

---

a6 Hebrew Sheol; also in verse 9

Bathsheba asked him, "Do you come peacefully?"

He answered, "Yes, peacefully." [14]Then he added, "I have something to say to you."

"You may say it," she replied.

[15]"As you know," he said, "the kingdom was mine. All Israel looked to me as their king. But things changed, and the kingdom has gone to my brother; for it has come to him from the LORD. [16]Now I have one request to make of you. Do not refuse me."

"You may make it," she said.

[17]So he continued, "Please ask King Solomon—he will not refuse you—to give me Abishag the Shunammite as my wife."

[18]"Very well," Bathsheba replied, "I will speak to the king for you."

[19]When Bathsheba went to King Solomon to speak to him for Adonijah, the

MONDAY

VERSE FOR THE DAY:
1 Kings 2:3

AUTHOR:
Myrna Alexander

PASSAGE FOR THE DAY:
1 Kings 2:1–12

The Charge

THE Scripture declares, "The eyes of the LORD range throughout the earth to strengthen those whose hearts are fully committed to him" (2 Chronicles 16:9). We want his eyes to see that our children's hearts are his. We want them to know his strong support in their lives.

Therefore, communicating the priority of knowing God and following in his ways is the most important thing we can do for them. And when this priority becomes their hearts' desire, then they will be after his heart.

My husband and I are not perfect at this job. We have had many good intentions that have seemed to fail, and there have been times our own sin has gotten in the way of accurately communicating what knowing God and following in his ways involve.

But God is powerful. Through the strength and wisdom of his Spirit we have had opportunity to demonstrate to our children in many practical ways the same important reality of David's charge to his son: "Observe what the LORD your God requires: Walk in his ways, and keep his decrees and commands, his laws and requirements, as written in the Law of Moses, so that you may prosper in all you do and wherever you go" (1 Kings 2:3). David wanted Solomon to succeed, and he knew that the only route was to follow God's ways. Before Solomon could follow God's ways, he had to know them. David, therefore, stressed the priority of God's word to his son.

David teaches us a practical lesson through his challenge to Solomon. When we respond to David's message, our children witness the good effect of God's truth in our lives. In turn they will be encouraged to live life God's way.

Additional Scripture Readings:
Psalm 119:9–11; Hebrews 12:10–11

Go to page 348 for your next devotional reading.

king stood up to meet her, bowed down to her and sat down on his throne. He had a throne brought for the king's mother, and she sat down at his right hand.

²⁰"I have one small request to make of you," she said. "Do not refuse me."

The king replied, "Make it, my mother; I will not refuse you."

²¹So she said, "Let Abishag the Shunammite be given in marriage to your brother Adonijah."

²²King Solomon answered his mother, "Why do you request Abishag the Shunammite for Adonijah? You might as well request the kingdom for him—after all, he is my older brother—yes, for him and for Abiathar the priest and Joab son of Zeruiah!"

²³Then King Solomon swore by the LORD: "May God deal with me, be it ever so severely, if Adonijah does not pay with his life for this request! ²⁴And now, as surely as the LORD lives—he who has established me securely on the throne of my father David and has founded a dynasty for me as he promised—Adonijah shall be put to death today!" ²⁵So King Solomon gave orders to Benaiah son of Jehoiada, and he struck down Adonijah and he died.

²⁶To Abiathar the priest the king said, "Go back to your fields in Anathoth. You deserve to die, but I will not put you to death now, because you carried the ark of the Sovereign LORD before my father David and shared all my father's hardships." ²⁷So Solomon removed Abiathar from the priesthood of the LORD, fulfilling the word the LORD had spoken at Shiloh about the house of Eli.

²⁸When the news reached Joab, who had conspired with Adonijah though not with Absalom, he fled to the tent of the LORD and took hold of the horns of the altar. ²⁹King Solomon was told that Joab had fled to the tent of the LORD and was beside the altar. Then Solomon ordered Benaiah son of Jehoiada, "Go, strike him down!"

³⁰So Benaiah entered the tent of the LORD and said to Joab, "The king says, 'Come out!'"

But he answered, "No, I will die here."

Benaiah reported to the king, "This is how Joab answered me."

³¹Then the king commanded Benaiah, "Do as he says. Strike him down and bury him, and so clear me and my father's house of the guilt of the innocent blood that Joab shed. ³²The LORD will repay him for the blood he shed, because without the knowledge of my father David he attacked two men and killed them with the sword. Both of them—Abner son of Ner, commander of Israel's army, and Amasa son of Jether, commander of Judah's army—were better men and more upright than he. ³³May the guilt of their blood rest on the head of Joab and his descendants forever. But on David and his descendants, his house and his throne, may there be the LORD's peace forever."

³⁴So Benaiah son of Jehoiada went up and struck down Joab and killed him, and he was buried on his own land*ᵃ* in the desert. ³⁵The king put Benaiah son of Jehoiada over the army in Joab's position and replaced Abiathar with Zadok the priest.

³⁶Then the king sent for Shimei and said to him, "Build yourself a house in Jerusalem and live there, but do not go anywhere else. ³⁷The day you leave and cross the Kidron Valley, you can be sure you will die; your blood will be on your own head."

³⁸Shimei answered the king, "What you say is good. Your servant will do as my lord the king has said." And Shimei stayed in Jerusalem for a long time.

³⁹But three years later, two of Shimei's slaves ran off to Achish son of Maacah, king of Gath, and Shimei was told, "Your slaves are in Gath." ⁴⁰At this, he saddled his donkey and went to Achish at Gath in search of his slaves. So Shimei went away and brought the slaves back from Gath.

⁴¹When Solomon was told that Shimei had gone from Jerusalem to Gath and had returned, ⁴²the king summoned Shimei and said to him, "Did I not make you swear by the LORD and warn you, 'On the day you leave to go anywhere else, you can be sure you will die'? At that time you said to me, 'What you say is good. I will obey.' ⁴³Why then did you not keep your oath to the LORD and obey the command I gave you?"

⁴⁴The king also said to Shimei, "You know in your heart all the wrong you did to my father David. Now the LORD will repay you for your wrongdoing. ⁴⁵But King Solomon will be blessed, and David's throne will remain secure before the LORD forever."

⁴⁶Then the king gave the order to Bena-

ᵃ34 Or *buried in his tomb*

iah son of Jehoiada, and he went out and struck Shimei down and killed him.

The kingdom was now firmly established in Solomon's hands.

Solomon Asks for Wisdom

3 Solomon made an alliance with Pharaoh king of Egypt and married his daughter. He brought her to the City of David until he finished building his palace and the temple of the LORD, and the wall around Jerusalem. ²The people, however, were still sacrificing at the high places, because a temple had not yet been built for the Name of the LORD. ³Solomon showed his love for the LORD by walking according to the statutes of his father David, except that he offered sacrifices and burned incense on the high places.

⁴The king went to Gibeon to offer sacrifices, for that was the most important high place, and Solomon offered a thousand burnt offerings on that altar. ⁵At Gibeon the LORD appeared to Solomon during the night in a dream, and God said, "Ask for whatever you want me to give you."

⁶Solomon answered, "You have shown great kindness to your servant, my father David, because he was faithful to you and righteous and upright in heart. You have continued this great kindness to him and have given him a son to sit on his throne this very day.

⁷"Now, O LORD my God, you have made your servant king in place of my father David. But I am only a little child and do not know how to carry out my duties. ⁸Your servant is here among the people you have chosen, a great people, too numerous to count or number. ⁹So give your servant a discerning heart to govern your people and to distinguish between right and wrong. For who is able to govern this great people of yours?"

¹⁰The Lord was pleased that Solomon had asked for this. ¹¹So God said to him, "Since you have asked for this and not for long life or wealth for yourself, nor have asked for the death of your enemies but for discernment in administering justice, ¹²I will do what you have asked. I will give you a wise and discerning heart, so that there will never have been anyone like you, nor will there ever be. ¹³Moreover, I will give you what you have not asked for — both riches and honor — so that in your

lifetime you will have no equal among kings. ¹⁴And if you walk in my ways and obey my statutes and commands as David your father did, I will give you a long life." ¹⁵Then Solomon awoke — and he realized it had been a dream.

He returned to Jerusalem, stood before the ark of the Lord's covenant and sacrificed burnt offerings and fellowship offerings.ᵃ Then he gave a feast for all his court.

A Wise Ruling

¹⁶Now two prostitutes came to the king and stood before him. ¹⁷One of them said, "My lord, this woman and I live in the same house. I had a baby while she was there with me. ¹⁸The third day after my child was born, this woman also had a baby. We were alone; there was no one in the house but the two of us.

¹⁹"During the night this woman's son died because she lay on him. ²⁰So she got up in the middle of the night and took my son from my side while I your servant was asleep. She put him by her breast and put her dead son by my breast. ²¹The next morning, I got up to nurse my son — and he was dead! But when I looked at him closely in the morning light, I saw that it wasn't the son I had borne."

²²The other woman said, "No! The living one is my son; the dead one is yours." But the first one insisted, "No! The dead one is yours; the living one is mine." And so they argued before the king.

²³The king said, "This one says, 'My son is alive and your son is dead,' while that one says, 'No! Your son is dead and mine is alive.'"

²⁴Then the king said, "Bring me a sword." So they brought a sword for the king. ²⁵He then gave an order: "Cut the living child in two and give half to one and half to the other."

²⁶The woman whose son was alive was filled with compassion for her son and said to the king, "Please, my lord, give her the living baby! Don't kill him!"

But the other said, "Neither I nor you shall have him. Cut him in two!"

²⁷Then the king gave his ruling: "Give the living baby to the first woman. Do not kill him; she is his mother."

²⁸When all Israel heard the verdict the king had given, they held the king in awe, because they saw that he had wisdom from God to administer justice.

ᵃ15 Traditionally peace offerings

Solomon's Officials and Governors

4 So King Solomon ruled over all Israel. ²And these were his chief officials:

Azariah son of Zadok—the priest;
³Elihoreph and Ahijah, sons of Shisha
—secretaries;
Jehoshaphat son of Ahilud—recorder;
⁴Benaiah son of Jehoiada—commander in chief;
Zadok and Abiathar—priests;
⁵Azariah son of Nathan—in charge of the district officers;
Zabud son of Nathan—a priest and personal adviser to the king;

⁶Ahishar—in charge of the palace;
Adoniram son of Abda—in charge of forced labor.

⁷Solomon also had twelve district governors over all Israel, who supplied provisions for the king and the royal household. Each one had to provide supplies for one month in the year. ⁸These are their names:

Ben-Hur—in the hill country of Ephraim;
⁹Ben-Deker—in Makaz, Shaalbim, Beth Shemesh and Elon Bethhanan;
¹⁰Ben-Hesed—in Arubboth (Socoh

TUESDAY

VERSE FOR THE DAY:
1 Kings 3:9

AUTHOR:
Carol Kuykendall

PASSAGE FOR THE DAY:
1 Kings 3:1–9

An Understanding Heart

I HUG my friend Lois when she opens her front door: "How are you today?" I ask, realizing how powerful her honest answer could be. Lois has inoperable lung cancer.

"I'm okay," she smiles, but her shoulders feel thin to me. I visit her often these days, to bring a basket of fresh peaches, a bunch of helium balloons or a new prescription of pills. Today I've come to help plan her forty-third birthday party. Though she doesn't like big-deal celebrations, she's agreed to a small gathering of family and friends. But as we sit together at her kitchen table, pencil and paper in hand, our conversation wanders away from party planning and cake flavors. We talk about planning the future.

"I don't know how to plan an uncertain future . . . ," she confesses, and then she is crying. My heart aches. Ever since I learned of her cancer, I have prayed not only for her miraculous healing, but that we, her friends, would be able to meet her needs. Sometimes, like right now, I feel so helpless and inadequate. What can I do or say to ease her hurt?

"Lois," I almost plead, "if our roles were reversed—if you were me—what would you say right now?"

"Nothing," she answers quietly. "I'd just listen."

And there in her simple response is my answer. As a friend, I can't heal or change this painful situation. But I can listen . . . with ears that open into my heart.

Additional Scripture Readings:
Proverbs 18:13–15; James 1:19

Go to page 358 for your next devotional reading.

and all the land of Hepher were his);

11Ben-Abinadab—in Naphoth Dor*a* (he was married to Taphath daughter of Solomon);

12Baana son of Ahilud—in Taanach and Megiddo, and in all of Beth Shan next to Zarethan below Jezreel, from Beth Shan to Abel Meholah across to Jokmeam;

13Ben-Geber—in Ramoth Gilead (the settlements of Jair son of Manasseh in Gilead were his, as well as the district of Argob in Bashan and its sixty large walled cities with bronze gate bars);

14Ahinadab son of Iddo—in Mahanaim;

15Ahimaaz—in Naphtali (he had married Basemath daughter of Solomon);

16Baana son of Hushai—in Asher and in Aloth;

17Jehoshaphat son of Paruah—in Issachar;

18Shimei son of Ela—in Benjamin;

19Geber son of Uri—in Gilead (the country of Sihon king of the Amorites and the country of Og king of Bashan). He was the only governor over the district.

Solomon's Daily Provisions

20The people of Judah and Israel were as numerous as the sand on the seashore; they ate, they drank and they were happy. 21And Solomon ruled over all the kingdoms from the River*b* to the land of the Philistines, as far as the border of Egypt. These countries brought tribute and were Solomon's subjects all his life.

22Solomon's daily provisions were thirty cors*c* of fine flour and sixty cors*d* of meal, 23ten head of stall-fed cattle, twenty of pasture-fed cattle and a hundred sheep and goats, as well as deer, gazelles, roebucks and choice fowl. 24For he ruled over all the kingdoms west of the River, from Tiphsah to Gaza, and had peace on all sides. 25During Solomon's lifetime Judah and Israel, from Dan to Beersheba, lived in safety, each man under his own vine and fig tree.

26Solomon had four*e* thousand stalls for chariot horses, and twelve thousand horses.*f*

27The district officers, each in his month, supplied provisions for King Solomon and all who came to the king's table. They saw to it that nothing was lacking. 28They also brought to the proper place their quotas of barley and straw for the chariot horses and the other horses.

Solomon's Wisdom

29God gave Solomon wisdom and very great insight, and a breadth of understanding as measureless as the sand on the seashore. 30Solomon's wisdom was greater than the wisdom of all the men of the East, and greater than all the wisdom of Egypt. 31He was wiser than any other man, including Ethan the Ezrahite—wiser than Heman, Calcol and Darda, the sons of Mahol. And his fame spread to all the surrounding nations. 32He spoke three thousand proverbs and his songs numbered a thousand and five. 33He described plant life, from the cedar of Lebanon to the hyssop that grows out of walls. He also taught about animals and birds, reptiles and fish. 34Men of all nations came to listen to Solomon's wisdom, sent by all the kings of the world, who had heard of his wisdom.

Preparations for Building the Temple

5 When Hiram king of Tyre heard that Solomon had been anointed king to succeed his father David, he sent his envoys to Solomon, because he had always been on friendly terms with David. 2Solomon sent back this message to Hiram:

3"You know that because of the wars waged against my father David from all sides, he could not build a temple for the Name of the Lord his God until the Lord put his enemies under his feet. 4But now the Lord my God has given me rest on every side, and there is no adversary or disaster. 5I intend, therefore, to build a temple for the Name of the Lord my God, as the Lord told my father David, when he said, 'Your son whom I will put on the throne in your place will build the temple for my Name.'

6"So give orders that cedars of Lebanon be cut for me. My men will

---

a11 Or *in the heights of Dor*   *b21* That is, the Euphrates; also in verse 24   *c22* That is, probably about 185 bushels (about 6.6 kiloliters)   *d22* That is, probably about 375 bushels (about 13.2 kiloliters)   *e26* Some Septuagint manuscripts (see also 2 Chron. 9:25); Hebrew *forty*   *f26* Or *charioteers* work with yours, and I will pay you for your men whatever wages you set. You know that we have no one so skilled in felling timber as the Sidonians."

[7]When Hiram heard Solomon's message, he was greatly pleased and said, "Praise be to the LORD today, for he has given David a wise son to rule over this great nation."

[8]So Hiram sent word to Solomon:

"I have received the message you sent me and will do all you want in providing the cedar and pine logs. [9]My men will haul them down from Lebanon to the sea, and I will float them in rafts by sea to the place you specify. There I will separate them and you can take them away. And you are to grant my wish by providing food for my royal household."

[10]In this way Hiram kept Solomon supplied with all the cedar and pine logs he wanted, [11]and Solomon gave Hiram twenty thousand cors[a] of wheat as food for his household, in addition to twenty thousand baths[b,c] of pressed olive oil. Solomon continued to do this for Hiram year after year. [12]The LORD gave Solomon wisdom, just as he had promised him. There were peaceful relations between Hiram and Solomon, and the two of them made a treaty.

[13]King Solomon conscripted laborers from all Israel—thirty thousand men. [14]He sent them off to Lebanon in shifts of ten thousand a month, so that they spent one month in Lebanon and two months at home. Adoniram was in charge of the forced labor. [15]Solomon had seventy thousand carriers and eighty thousand stonecutters in the hills, [16]as well as thirty-three hundred[d] foremen who supervised the project and directed the workmen. [17]At the king's command they removed from the quarry large blocks of quality stone to provide a foundation of dressed stone for the temple. [18]The craftsmen of Solomon and Hiram and the men of Gebal[e] cut and prepared the timber and stone for the building of the temple.

Solomon Builds the Temple

6 In the four hundred and eightieth[f] year after the Israelites had come out of Egypt, in the fourth year of Solomon's reign over Israel, in the month of Ziv, the second month, he began to build the temple of the LORD.

[2]The temple that King Solomon built for the LORD was sixty cubits long, twenty wide and thirty high.[g] [3]The portico at the front of the main hall of the temple extended the width of the temple, that is twenty cubits,[h] and projected ten cubits[i] from the front of the temple. [4]He made narrow clerestory windows in the temple. [5]Against the walls of the main hall and inner sanctuary he built a structure around the building, in which there were side rooms. [6]The lowest floor was five cubits[j] wide, the middle floor six cubits[k] and the third floor seven.[l] He made offset ledges around the outside of the temple so that nothing would be inserted into the temple walls.

[7]In building the temple, only blocks dressed at the quarry were used, and no hammer, chisel or any other iron tool was heard at the temple site while it was being built.

[8]The entrance to the lowest[m] floor was on the south side of the temple; a stairway led up to the middle level and from there to the third. [9]So he built the temple and completed it, roofing it with beams and cedar planks. [10]And he built the side rooms all along the temple. The height of each was five cubits, and they were attached to the temple by beams of cedar.

[11]The word of the LORD came to Solomon: [12]"As for this temple you are building, if you follow my decrees, carry out my regulations and keep all my commands and obey them, I will fulfill through you the promise I gave to David your father. [13]And I will live among the Israelites and will not abandon my people Israel."

[14]So Solomon built the temple and completed it. [15]He lined its interior walls with cedar boards, paneling them from

---

[a]11 That is, probably about 125,000 bushels (about 4,400 kiloliters)   [b]11 Septuagint (see also 2 Chron. 2:10); Hebrew *twenty cors*   [c]11 That is, about 115,000 gallons (about 440 kiloliters)   [d]16 Hebrew; some Septuagint manuscripts (see also 2 Chron. 2:2, 18) *thirty-six hundred*   [e]18 That is, Byblos   [f]1 Hebrew; Septuagint *four hundred and fortieth*   [g]2 That is, about 90 feet (about 27 meters) long and 30 feet (about 9 meters) wide and 45 feet (about 13.5 meters) high   [h]3 That is, about 30 feet (about 9 meters)   [i]3 That is, about 15 feet (about 4.5 meters)   [j]6 That is, about 7 1/2 feet (about 2.3 meters); also in verses 10 and 24   [k]6 That is, about 9 feet (about 2.7 meters)   [l]6 That is, about 10 1/2 feet (about 3.1 meters)   [m]8 Septuagint; Hebrew *middle*

the floor of the temple to the ceiling, and covered the floor of the temple with planks of pine. [16]He partitioned off twenty cubits[a] at the rear of the temple with cedar boards from floor to ceiling to form within the temple an inner sanctuary, the Most Holy Place. [17]The main hall in front of this room was forty cubits[b] long. [18]The inside of the temple was cedar, carved with gourds and open flowers. Everything was cedar; no stone was to be seen.

[19]He prepared the inner sanctuary within the temple to set the ark of the covenant of the LORD there. [20]The inner sanctuary was twenty cubits long, twenty wide and twenty high.[c] He overlaid the inside with pure gold, and he also overlaid the altar of cedar. [21]Solomon covered the inside of the temple with pure gold, and he extended gold chains across the front of the inner sanctuary, which was overlaid with gold. [22]So he overlaid the whole interior with gold. He also overlaid with gold the altar that belonged to the inner sanctuary.

[23]In the inner sanctuary he made a pair of cherubim of olive wood, each ten cubits[d] high. [24]One wing of the first cherub was five cubits long, and the other wing five cubits—ten cubits from wing tip to wing tip. [25]The second cherub also measured ten cubits, for the two cherubim were identical in size and shape. [26]The height of each cherub was ten cubits. [27]He placed the cherubim inside the innermost room of the temple, with their wings spread out. The wing of one cherub touched one wall, while the wing of the other touched the other wall, and their wings touched each other in the middle of the room. [28]He overlaid the cherubim with gold.

[29]On the walls all around the temple, in both the inner and outer rooms, he carved cherubim, palm trees and open flowers. [30]He also covered the floors of both the inner and outer rooms of the temple with gold.

[31]For the entrance of the inner sanctuary he made doors of olive wood with five-sided jambs. [32]And on the two olive wood doors he carved cherubim, palm trees and open flowers, and overlaid the cherubim and palm trees with beaten gold. [33]In the

same way he made four-sided jambs of olive wood for the entrance to the main hall. [34]He also made two pine doors, each having two leaves that turned in sockets. [35]He carved cherubim, palm trees and open flowers on them and overlaid them with gold hammered evenly over the carvings.

[36]And he built the inner courtyard of three courses of dressed stone and one course of trimmed cedar beams.

[37]The foundation of the temple of the LORD was laid in the fourth year, in the month of Ziv. [38]In the eleventh year in the month of Bul, the eighth month, the temple was finished in all its details according to its specifications. He had spent seven years building it.

Solomon Builds His Palace

7 It took Solomon thirteen years, however, to complete the construction of his palace. [2]He built the Palace of the Forest of Lebanon a hundred cubits long, fifty wide and thirty high,[e] with four rows of cedar columns supporting trimmed cedar beams. [3]It was roofed with cedar above the beams that rested on the columns—forty-five beams, fifteen to a row. [4]Its windows were placed high in sets of three, facing each other. [5]All the doorways had rectangular frames; they were in the front part in sets of three, facing each other.[f]

[6]He made a colonnade fifty cubits long and thirty wide.[g] In front of it was a portico, and in front of that were pillars and an overhanging roof.

[7]He built the throne hall, the Hall of Justice, where he was to judge, and he covered it with cedar from floor to ceiling.[h] [8]And the palace in which he was to live, set farther back, was similar in design. Solomon also made a palace like this hall for Pharaoh's daughter, whom he had married.

[9]All these structures, from the outside to the great courtyard and from foundation to eaves, were made of blocks of high-grade stone cut to size and trimmed with a saw on their inner and outer faces. [10]The foundations were laid with large stones of good quality, some measuring ten cubits[d] and some eight.[i] [11]Above

---

[a]16 That is, about 30 feet (about 9 meters)   [b]17 That is, about 60 feet (about 18 meters) [c]20 That is, about 30 feet (about 9 meters) long, wide and high   [d]23,10 That is, about 15 feet (about 4.5 meters)   [e]2 That is, about 150 feet (about 46 meters) long, 75 feet (about 23 meters) wide and 45 feet (about 13.5 meters) high   [f]5 The meaning of the Hebrew for this verse is uncertain.   [g]6 That is, about 75 feet (about 23 meters) long and 45 feet (about 13.5 meters) wide   [h]7 Vulgate and Syriac; Hebrew floor   [i]10 That is, about 12 feet (about 3.6 meters)

were high-grade stones, cut to size, and cedar beams. [12]The great courtyard was surrounded by a wall of three courses of dressed stone and one course of trimmed cedar beams, as was the inner courtyard of the temple of the Lord with its portico.

The Temple's Furnishings

[13]King Solomon sent to Tyre and brought Huram,[a] [14]whose mother was a widow from the tribe of Naphtali and whose father was a man of Tyre and a craftsman in bronze. Huram was highly skilled and experienced in all kinds of bronze work. He came to King Solomon and did all the work assigned to him.

[15]He cast two bronze pillars, each eighteen cubits high and twelve cubits around,[b] by line. [16]He also made two capitals of cast bronze to set on the tops of the pillars; each capital was five cubits[c] high. [17]A network of interwoven chains festooned the capitals on top of the pillars, seven for each capital. [18]He made pomegranates in two rows[d] encircling each network to decorate the capitals on top of the pillars.[e] He did the same for each capital. [19]The capitals on top of the pillars in the portico were in the shape of lilies, four cubits[f] high. [20]On the capitals of both pillars, above the bowl-shaped part next to the network, were the two hundred pomegranates in rows all around. [21]He erected the pillars at the portico of the temple. The pillar to the south he named Jakin[g] and the one to the north Boaz.[h] [22]The capitals on top were in the shape of lilies. And so the work on the pillars was completed.

[23]He made the Sea of cast metal, circular in shape, measuring ten cubits[i] from rim to rim and five cubits high. It took a line of thirty cubits[j] to measure around it. [24]Below the rim, gourds encircled it — ten to a cubit. The gourds were cast in two rows in one piece with the Sea.

[25]The Sea stood on twelve bulls, three facing north, three facing west, three facing south and three facing east. The Sea rested on top of them, and their hindquarters were toward the center. [26]It was a handbreadth[k] in thickness, and its rim was like the rim of a cup, like a lily blossom. It held two thousand baths.[l]

[27]He also made ten movable stands of bronze; each was four cubits long, four wide and three high.[m] [28]This is how the stands were made: They had side panels attached to uprights. [29]On the panels between the uprights were lions, bulls and cherubim — and on the uprights as well. Above and below the lions and bulls were wreaths of hammered work. [30]Each stand had four bronze wheels with bronze axles, and each had a basin resting on four supports, cast with wreaths on each side. [31]On the inside of the stand there was an opening that had a circular frame one cubit[n] deep. This opening was round, and with its basework it measured a cubit and a half.[o] Around its opening there was engraving. The panels of the stands were square, not round. [32]The four wheels were under the panels, and the axles of the wheels were attached to the stand. The diameter of each wheel was a cubit and a half. [33]The wheels were made like chariot wheels; the axles, rims, spokes and hubs were all of cast metal.

[34]Each stand had four handles, one on each corner, projecting from the stand. [35]At the top of the stand there was a circular band half a cubit[p] deep. The supports and panels were attached to the top of the stand. [36]He engraved cherubim, lions and palm trees on the surfaces of the supports and on the panels, in every available space, with wreaths all around. [37]This is the way he made the ten stands. They were all cast in the same molds and were identical in size and shape.

[38]He then made ten bronze basins, each holding forty baths[q] and measuring four cubits across, one basin to go on each of the ten stands. [39]He placed five of the stands on the south side of the temple and five on the north. He placed the Sea on the south side, at the southeast corner

---

a13 Hebrew *Hiram,* a variant of *Huram;* also in verses 40 and 45   *b15* That is, about 27 feet (about 8.1 meters) high and 18 feet (about 5.4 meters) around   *c16* That is, about 7 1/2 feet (about 2.3 meters); also in verse 23   *d18* Two Hebrew manuscripts and Septuagint; most Hebrew manuscripts *made the pillars, and there were two rows*   *e18* Many Hebrew manuscripts and Syriac; most Hebrew manuscripts *pomegranates*   *f19* That is, about 6 feet (about 1.8 meters); also in verse 38   *g21* *Jakin* probably means *he establishes.*   *h21* *Boaz* probably means *in him is strength.*   *i23* That is, about 15 feet (about 4.5 meters)   *j23* That is, about 45 feet (about 13.5 meters)   *k26* That is, about 3 inches (about 8 centimeters)   *l26* That is, probably about 11,500 gallons (about 44 kiloliters); the Septuagint does not have this sentence.   *m27* That is, about 6 feet (about 1.8 meters) long and wide and about 4 1/2 feet (about 1.3 meters) high   *n31* That is, about 1 1/2 feet (about 0.5 meter)   *o31* That is, about 2 1/4 feet (about 0.7 meter); also in verse 32   *p35* That is, about 3/4 foot (about 0.2 meter)   *q38* That is, about 230 gallons (about 880 liters) of the temple. ⁴⁰He also made the basins and shovels and sprinkling bowls.

So Huram finished all the work he had undertaken for King Solomon in the temple of the LORD:

⁴¹the two pillars;
the two bowl-shaped capitals on top of the pillars;
the two sets of network decorating the two bowl-shaped capitals on top of the pillars;
⁴²the four hundred pomegranates for the two sets of network (two rows of pomegranates for each network, decorating the bowl-shaped capitals on top of the pillars);
⁴³the ten stands with their ten basins;
⁴⁴the Sea and the twelve bulls under it;
⁴⁵the pots, shovels and sprinkling bowls.

All these objects that Huram made for King Solomon for the temple of the LORD were of burnished bronze. ⁴⁶The king had them cast in clay molds in the plain of the Jordan between Succoth and Zarethan. ⁴⁷Solomon left all these things unweighed, because there were so many; the weight of the bronze was not determined.

⁴⁸Solomon also made all the furnishings that were in the LORD's temple:

the golden altar;
the golden table on which was the bread of the Presence;
⁴⁹the lampstands of pure gold (five on the right and five on the left, in front of the inner sanctuary);
the gold floral work and lamps and tongs;
⁵⁰the pure gold basins, wick trimmers, sprinkling bowls, dishes and censers;
and the gold sockets for the doors of the innermost room, the Most Holy Place, and also for the doors of the main hall of the temple.

⁵¹When all the work King Solomon had done for the temple of the LORD was finished, he brought in the things his father David had dedicated—the silver and gold and the furnishings—and he placed them in the treasuries of the LORD's temple.

The Ark Brought to the Temple

8 Then King Solomon summoned into his presence at Jerusalem the elders of Israel, all the heads of the tribes and the chiefs of the Israelite families, to bring up the ark of the LORD's covenant from Zion, the City of David. ²All the men of Israel came together to King Solomon at the time of the festival in the month of Ethanim, the seventh month.

³When all the elders of Israel had arrived, the priests took up the ark, ⁴and they brought up the ark of the LORD and the Tent of Meeting and all the sacred furnishings in it. The priests and Levites carried them up, ⁵and King Solomon and the entire assembly of Israel that had gathered about him were before the ark, sacrificing so many sheep and cattle that they could not be recorded or counted.

⁶The priests then brought the ark of the LORD's covenant to its place in the inner sanctuary of the temple, the Most Holy Place, and put it beneath the wings of the cherubim. ⁷The cherubim spread their wings over the place of the ark and overshadowed the ark and its carrying poles. ⁸These poles were so long that their ends could be seen from the Holy Place in front of the inner sanctuary, but not from outside the Holy Place; and they are still there today. ⁹There was nothing in the ark except the two stone tablets that Moses had placed in it at Horeb, where the LORD made a covenant with the Israelites after they came out of Egypt.

¹⁰When the priests withdrew from the Holy Place, the cloud filled the temple of the LORD. ¹¹And the priests could not perform their service because of the cloud, for the glory of the LORD filled his temple.

¹²Then Solomon said, "The LORD has said that he would dwell in a dark cloud; ¹³I have indeed built a magnificent temple for you, a place for you to dwell forever."

¹⁴While the whole assembly of Israel was standing there, the king turned around and blessed them. ¹⁵Then he said:

"Praise be to the LORD, the God of Israel, who with his own hand has fulfilled what he promised with his own mouth to my father David. For he said, ¹⁶'Since the day I brought my people Israel out of Egypt, I have not chosen a city in any tribe of Israel to have a temple built for my Name to be there, but I have chosen David to rule my people Israel.'

¹⁷"My father David had it in his heart to build a temple for the Name of the LORD, the God of Israel. ¹⁸But the LORD said to my father David, 'Because it was in your heart to build

a temple for my Name, you did well to have this in your heart. [19]Nevertheless, you are not the one to build the temple, but your son, who is your own flesh and blood—he is the one who will build the temple for my Name.'

[20]"The LORD has kept the promise he made: I have succeeded David my father and now I sit on the throne of Israel, just as the LORD promised, and I have built the temple for the Name of the LORD, the God of Israel. [21]I have provided a place there for the ark, in which is the covenant of the LORD that he made with our fathers when he brought them out of Egypt."

Solomon's Prayer of Dedication

[22]Then Solomon stood before the altar of the LORD in front of the whole assembly of Israel, spread out his hands toward heaven [23]and said:

"O LORD, God of Israel, there is no God like you in heaven above or on earth below—you who keep your covenant of love with your servants who continue wholeheartedly in your way. [24]You have kept your promise to your servant David my father; with your mouth you have promised and with your hand you have fulfilled it—as it is today.

[25]"Now LORD, God of Israel, keep for your servant David my father the promises you made to him when you said, 'You shall never fail to have a man to sit before me on the throne of Israel, if only your sons are careful in all they do to walk before me as you have done.' [26]And now, O God of Israel, let your word that you promised your servant David my father come true.

[27]"But will God really dwell on earth? The heavens, even the highest heaven, cannot contain you. How much less this temple I have built! [28]Yet give attention to your servant's prayer and his plea for mercy, O LORD my God. Hear the cry and the prayer that your servant is praying in your presence this day. [29]May your eyes be open toward this temple night and day, this place of which you said, 'My Name shall be there,' so that you will hear the prayer your servant prays toward this place. [30]Hear the supplication of your servant and of your people Israel when they pray toward this place. Hear from heaven, your dwelling place, and when you hear, forgive.

[31]"When a man wrongs his neighbor and is required to take an oath and he comes and swears the oath before your altar in this temple, [32]then hear from heaven and act. Judge between your servants, condemning the guilty and bringing down on his own head what he has done. Declare the innocent not guilty, and so establish his innocence.

[33]"When your people Israel have been defeated by an enemy because they have sinned against you, and when they turn back to you and confess your name, praying and making supplication to you in this temple, [34]then hear from heaven and forgive the sin of your people Israel and bring them back to the land you gave to their fathers.

[35]"When the heavens are shut up and there is no rain because your people have sinned against you, and when they pray toward this place and confess your name and turn from their sin because you have afflicted them, [36]then hear from heaven and forgive the sin of your servants, your people Israel. Teach them the right way to live, and send rain on the land you gave your people for an inheritance.

[37]"When famine or plague comes to the land, or blight or mildew, locusts or grasshoppers, or when an enemy besieges them in any of their cities, whatever disaster or disease may come, [38]and when a prayer or plea is made by any of your people Israel—each one aware of the afflictions of his own heart, and spreading out his hands toward this temple—[39]then hear from heaven, your dwelling place. Forgive and act; deal with each man according to all he does, since you know his heart (for you alone know the hearts of all men), [40]so that they will fear you all the time they live in the land you gave our fathers.

[41]"As for the foreigner who does not belong to your people Israel but has come from a distant land because of your name — [42]for men will

hear of your great name and your mighty hand and your outstretched arm—when he comes and prays toward this temple, ⁴³then hear from heaven, your dwelling place, and do whatever the foreigner asks of you, so that all the peoples of the earth may know your name and fear you, as do your own people Israel, and may know that this house I have built bears your Name.

⁴⁴"When your people go to war against their enemies, wherever you send them, and when they pray to the LORD toward the city you have chosen and the temple I have built for your Name, ⁴⁵then hear from heaven their prayer and their plea, and uphold their cause.

⁴⁶"When they sin against you—for there is no one who does not sin—and you become angry with them and give them over to the enemy, who takes them captive to his own land, far away or near; ⁴⁷and if they have a change of heart in the land where they are held captive, and repent and plead with you in the land of their conquerors and say, 'We have sinned, we have done wrong, we have acted wickedly'; ⁴⁸and if they turn back to you with all their heart and soul in the land of their enemies who took them captive, and pray to you toward the land you gave their fathers, toward the city you have chosen and the temple I have built for your Name; ⁴⁹then from heaven, your dwelling place, hear their prayer and their plea, and uphold their cause. ⁵⁰And forgive your people, who have sinned against you; forgive all the offenses they have committed against you, and cause their conquerors to show them mercy; ⁵¹for they are your people and your inheritance, whom you brought out of Egypt, out of that iron-smelting furnace.

⁵²"May your eyes be open to your servant's plea and to the plea of your people Israel, and may you listen to them whenever they cry out to you. ⁵³For you singled them out from all the nations of the world to be your own inheritance, just as you declared through your servant Moses when you, O Sovereign LORD, brought our fathers out of Egypt."

⁵⁴When Solomon had finished all these prayers and supplications to the LORD, he rose from before the altar of the LORD, where he had been kneeling with his hands spread out toward heaven. ⁵⁵He stood and blessed the whole assembly of Israel in a loud voice, saying:

⁵⁶"Praise be to the LORD, who has given rest to his people Israel just as he promised. Not one word has failed of all the good promises he gave through his servant Moses. ⁵⁷May the LORD our God be with us as he was with our fathers; may he never leave us nor forsake us. ⁵⁸May he turn our hearts to him, to walk in all his ways and to keep the commands, decrees and regulations he gave our fathers. ⁵⁹And may these words of mine, which I have prayed before the LORD, be near to the LORD our God day and night, that he may uphold the cause of his servant and the cause of his people Israel according to each day's need, ⁶⁰so that all the peoples of the earth may know that the LORD is God and that there is no other. ⁶¹But your hearts must be fully committed to the LORD our God, to live by his decrees and obey his commands, as at this time."

The Dedication of the Temple

⁶²Then the king and all Israel with him offered sacrifices before the LORD. ⁶³Solomon offered a sacrifice of fellowship offeringsᵃ to the LORD: twenty-two thousand cattle and a hundred and twenty thousand sheep and goats. So the king and all the Israelites dedicated the temple of the LORD.

⁶⁴On that same day the king consecrated the middle part of the courtyard in front of the temple of the LORD, and there he offered burnt offerings, grain offerings and the fat of the fellowship offerings, because the bronze altar before the LORD was too small to hold the burnt offerings, the grain offerings and the fat of the fellowship offerings.

⁶⁵So Solomon observed the festival at that time, and all Israel with him—a vast assembly, people from Leboᵇ Hamath to the Wadi of Egypt. They celebrated it before the LORD our God for seven days and seven days more, fourteen days in all. ⁶⁶On the following day he sent the people

ᵃ63 Traditionally *peace offerings*; also in verse 64   ᵇ65 Or *from the entrance to* away. They blessed the king and then went home, joyful and glad in heart for all the good things the Lord had done for his servant David and his people Israel.

The Lord Appears to Solomon

9 When Solomon had finished building the temple of the Lord and the royal palace, and had achieved all he had desired to do, ²the Lord appeared to him a second time, as he had appeared to him at Gibeon. ³The Lord said to him:

"I have heard the prayer and plea you have made before me; I have consecrated this temple, which you have built, by putting my Name there forever. My eyes and my heart will always be there.

⁴"As for you, if you walk before me in integrity of heart and uprightness, as David your father did, and do all I command and observe my decrees and laws, ⁵I will establish your royal throne over Israel forever, as I promised David your father when I said, 'You shall never fail to have a man on the throne of Israel.'

⁶"But if you^a or your sons turn away from me and do not observe the commands and decrees I have given you^a and go off to serve other gods and worship them, ⁷then I will cut off Israel from the land I have given them and will reject this temple I have consecrated for my Name. Israel will then become a byword and an object of ridicule among all peoples. ⁸And though this temple is now imposing, all who pass by will be appalled and will scoff and say, 'Why has the Lord done such a thing to this land and to this temple?' ⁹People will answer, 'Because they have forsaken the Lord their God, who brought their fathers out of Egypt, and have embraced other gods, worshiping and serving them—that is why the Lord brought all this disaster on them.' "

Solomon's Other Activities

¹⁰At the end of twenty years, during which Solomon built these two buildings —the temple of the Lord and the royal palace— ¹¹King Solomon gave twenty towns in Galilee to Hiram king of Tyre, because Hiram had supplied him with all the cedar and pine and gold he wanted. ¹²But when Hiram went from Tyre to see the towns that Solomon had given him, he was not pleased with them. ¹³"What kind of towns are these you have given me, my brother?" he asked. And he called them the Land of Cabul,^b a name they have to this day. ¹⁴Now Hiram had sent to the king 120 talents^c of gold.

¹⁵Here is the account of the forced labor King Solomon conscripted to build the Lord's temple, his own palace, the supporting terraces,^d the wall of Jerusalem, and Hazor, Megiddo and Gezer. ¹⁶(Pharaoh king of Egypt had attacked and captured Gezer. He had set it on fire. He killed its Canaanite inhabitants and then gave it as a wedding gift to his daughter, Solomon's wife. ¹⁷And Solomon rebuilt Gezer.) He built up Lower Beth Horon, ¹⁸Baalath, and Tadmor^e in the desert, within his land, ¹⁹as well as all his store cities and the towns for his chariots and for his horses^f—whatever he desired to build in Jerusalem, in Lebanon and throughout all the territory he ruled.

²⁰All the people left from the Amorites, Hittites, Perizzites, Hivites and Jebusites (these peoples were not Israelites), ²¹that is, their descendants remaining in the land, whom the Israelites could not exterminate^g—these Solomon conscripted for his slave labor force, as it is to this day. ²²But Solomon did not make slaves of any of the Israelites; they were his fighting men, his government officials, his officers, his captains, and the commanders of his chariots and charioteers. ²³They were also the chief officials in charge of Solomon's projects—550 officials supervising the men who did the work.

²⁴After Pharaoh's daughter had come up from the City of David to the palace Solomon had built for her, he constructed the supporting terraces.

²⁵Three times a year Solomon sacrificed burnt offerings and fellowship offerings^h on the altar he had built for the Lord, burning incense before the Lord along with them, and so fulfilled the temple obligations.

²⁶King Solomon also built ships at Ezion Geber, which is near Elath in Edom,

---

^a6 The Hebrew is plural.   ^b13 Cabul sounds like the Hebrew for good-for-nothing.   ^c14 That is, about 4 1/2 tons (about 4 metric tons)   ^d15 Or the Millo; also in verse 24   ^e18 The Hebrew may also be read Tamar.   ^f19 Or charioteers   ^g21 The Hebrew term refers to the irrevocable giving over of things or persons to the Lord, often by totally destroying them.   ^h25 Traditionally peace offerings on the shore of the Red Sea.ᵃ ²⁷And Hiram sent his men—sailors who knew the sea—to serve in the fleet with Solomon's men. ²⁸They sailed to Ophir and brought back 420 talentsᵇ of gold, which they delivered to King Solomon.

The Queen of Sheba Visits Solomon

10 When the queen of Sheba heard about the fame of Solomon and his relation to the name of the LORD, she came to test him with hard questions. ²Arriving at Jerusalem with a very great caravan—with camels carrying spices, large quantities of gold, and precious stones—she came to Solomon and talked with him about all that she had on her mind. ³Solomon answered all her questions; nothing was too hard for the king to explain to her. ⁴When the queen of Sheba saw all the wisdom of Solomon and the palace he had built, ⁵the food on his table, the seating of his officials, the attending servants in their robes, his cupbearers, and the burnt offerings he made atᶜ the temple of the LORD, she was overwhelmed.

⁶She said to the king, "The report I heard in my own country about your achievements and your wisdom is true. ⁷But I did not believe these things until I came and saw with my own eyes. Indeed, not even half was told me; in wisdom and wealth you have far exceeded the report I heard. ⁸How happy your men must be! How happy your officials, who continually stand before you and hear your wisdom! ⁹Praise be to the LORD your God, who has delighted in you and placed you on the throne of Israel. Because of the LORD's eternal love for Israel, he has made you king, to maintain justice and righteousness."

¹⁰And she gave the king 120 talentsᵈ of gold, large quantities of spices, and precious stones. Never again were so many spices brought in as those the queen of Sheba gave to King Solomon.

¹¹(Hiram's ships brought gold from Ophir; and from there they brought great cargoes of almugwoodᵉ and precious stones. ¹²The king used the almugwood to make supports for the temple of the LORD and for the royal palace, and to make harps and lyres for the musicians. So much almugwood has never been imported or seen since that day.)

¹³King Solomon gave the queen of Sheba all she desired and asked for, besides what he had given her out of his royal bounty. Then she left and returned with her retinue to her own country.

Solomon's Splendor

¹⁴The weight of the gold that Solomon received yearly was 666 talents,ᶠ ¹⁵not including the revenues from merchants and traders and from all the Arabian kings and the governors of the land.

¹⁶King Solomon made two hundred large shields of hammered gold; six hundred bekasᵍ of gold went into each shield. ¹⁷He also made three hundred small shields of hammered gold, with three minasʰ of gold in each shield. The king put them in the Palace of the Forest of Lebanon.

¹⁸Then the king made a great throne inlaid with ivory and overlaid with fine gold. ¹⁹The throne had six steps, and its back had a rounded top. On both sides of the seat were armrests, with a lion standing beside each of them. ²⁰Twelve lions stood on the six steps, one at either end of each step. Nothing like it had ever been made for any other kingdom. ²¹All King Solomon's goblets were gold, and all the household articles in the Palace of the Forest of Lebanon were pure gold. Nothing was made of silver, because silver was considered of little value in Solomon's days. ²²The king had a fleet of trading shipsⁱ at sea along with the ships of Hiram. Once every three years it returned, carrying gold, silver and ivory, and apes and baboons.

²³King Solomon was greater in riches and wisdom than all the other kings of the earth. ²⁴The whole world sought audience with Solomon to hear the wisdom God had put in his heart. ²⁵Year after year, everyone who came brought a gift—articles of silver and gold, robes, weapons and spices, and horses and mules.

²⁶Solomon accumulated chariots and horses; he had fourteen hundred chariots and twelve thousand horses,ʲ which he kept in the chariot cities and also with

---

ᵃ26 Hebrew *Yam Suph*; that is, Sea of Reeds   ᵇ28 That is, about 16 tons (about 14.5 metric tons)
ᶜ5 Or *the ascent by which he went up to*   ᵈ10 That is, about 4 1/2 tons (about 4 metric tons)
ᵉ11 Probably a variant of *algumwood*; also in verse 12   ᶠ14 That is, about 25 tons (about 23 metric tons)   ᵍ16 That is, about 7 1/2 pounds (about 3.5 kilograms)   ʰ17 That is, about 3 3/4 pounds (about 1.7 kilograms)   ⁱ22 Hebrew *of ships of Tarshish*   ʲ26 Or *charioteers*

him in Jerusalem. ²⁷The king made silver as common in Jerusalem as stones, and cedar as plentiful as sycamore-fig trees in the foothills. ²⁸Solomon's horses were imported from Egypt*a* and from Kue*b*— the royal merchants purchased them from Kue. ²⁹They imported a chariot from Egypt for six hundred shekels*c* of silver, and a horse for a hundred and fifty.*d* They also exported them to all the kings of the Hittites and of the Arameans.

Solomon's Wives

11 King Solomon, however, loved many foreign women besides Pharaoh's daughter—Moabites, Ammonites, Edomites, Sidonians and Hittites. ²They were from nations about which the Lord had told the Israelites, "You must

not intermarry with them, because they will surely turn your hearts after their gods." Nevertheless, Solomon held fast to them in love. ³He had seven hundred wives of royal birth and three hundred concubines, and his wives led him astray. ⁴As Solomon grew old, his wives turned his heart after other gods, and his heart was not fully devoted to the Lord his God, as the heart of David his father had been. ⁵He followed Ashtoreth the goddess of the Sidonians, and Molech*e* the detestable god of the Ammonites. ⁶So Solomon did evil in the eyes of the Lord; he did not follow the Lord completely, as David his father had done.

⁷On a hill east of Jerusalem, Solomon built a high place for Chemosh the detestable god of Moab, and for Molech the

a28 Or possibly *Muzur*, a region in Cilicia; also in verse 29   *b28* Probably *Cilicia*   *c29* That is, about 15 pounds (about 7 kilograms)   *d29* That is, about 3 3/4 pounds (about 1.7 kilograms)   *e5* Hebrew *Milcom*; also in verse 33

WEDNESDAY

VERSE FOR THE DAY:
1 Kings 10:9

AUTHOR:
Samantha McGarrity

PASSAGE FOR THE DAY:
1 Kings 10:1–13

A Role Model

NOT too long ago, I read a piece in the newspaper stating that there was evidence from a current archeological dig that the Queen of Sheba really did exist. A few days later during my morning Bible reading, I randomly flipped to a passage and came upon the story of the queen's visit to King Solomon. She sounded like a very independent woman with a healthy curiosity. A woman of means, she didn't mind hitting the road occasionally to seek out answers. And she was honest, straightforward, in telling King Solomon just what she thought of him, after she'd tested his knowledge.

She was also a woman who gave credit where credit was due—something I often forget to do myself. She praised Solomon's God for the splendor of his kingdom. That may have been the reason why, after all these centuries, the Queen of Sheba is still remembered.

I'd like to take her as a role model. Honesty, giving credit, praising God—all traits that will help me daily, and, I like to think, keep me a nice memory in the minds of others.

Additional Scripture Readings:
Luke 23:47; 1 Thessalonians 1:6–10

Go to page 369 for your next devotional reading.

detestable god of the Ammonites. ⁸He did the same for all his foreign wives, who burned incense and offered sacrifices to their gods.

⁹The LORD became angry with Solomon because his heart had turned away from the LORD, the God of Israel, who had appeared to him twice. ¹⁰Although he had forbidden Solomon to follow other gods, Solomon did not keep the LORD's command. ¹¹So the LORD said to Solomon, "Since this is your attitude and you have not kept my covenant and my decrees, which I commanded you, I will most certainly tear the kingdom away from you and give it to one of your subordinates. ¹²Nevertheless, for the sake of David your father, I will not do it during your lifetime. I will tear it out of the hand of your son. ¹³Yet I will not tear the whole kingdom from him, but will give him one tribe for the sake of David my servant and for the sake of Jerusalem, which I have chosen."

Solomon's Adversaries

¹⁴Then the LORD raised up against Solomon an adversary, Hadad the Edomite, from the royal line of Edom. ¹⁵Earlier when David was fighting with Edom, Joab the commander of the army, who had gone up to bury the dead, had struck down all the men in Edom. ¹⁶Joab and all the Israelites stayed there for six months, until they had destroyed all the men in Edom. ¹⁷But Hadad, still only a boy, fled to Egypt with some Edomite officials who had served his father. ¹⁸They set out from Midian and went to Paran. Then taking men from Paran with them, they went to Egypt, to Pharaoh king of Egypt, who gave Hadad a house and land and provided him with food.

¹⁹Pharaoh was so pleased with Hadad that he gave him a sister of his own wife, Queen Tahpenes, in marriage. ²⁰The sister of Tahpenes bore him a son named Genubath, whom Tahpenes brought up in the royal palace. There Genubath lived with Pharaoh's own children.

²¹While he was in Egypt, Hadad heard that David rested with his fathers and that Joab the commander of the army was also dead. Then Hadad said to Pharaoh, "Let me go, that I may return to my own country."

²²"What have you lacked here that you want to go back to your own country?" Pharaoh asked.

"Nothing," Hadad replied, "but do let me go!"

²³And God raised up against Solomon another adversary, Rezon son of Eliada, who had fled from his master, Hadadezer king of Zobah. ²⁴He gathered men around him and became the leader of a band of rebels when David destroyed the forces[a] of Zobah,; the rebels went to Damascus, where they settled and took control. ²⁵Rezon was Israel's adversary as long as Solomon lived, adding to the trouble caused by Hadad. So Rezon ruled in Aram and was hostile toward Israel.

Jeroboam Rebels Against Solomon

²⁶Also, Jeroboam son of Nebat rebelled against the king. He was one of Solomon's officials, an Ephraimite from Zeredah, and his mother was a widow named Zeruah.

²⁷Here is the account of how he rebelled against the king: Solomon had built the supporting terraces[b] and had filled in the gap in the wall of the city of David his father. ²⁸Now Jeroboam was a man of standing, and when Solomon saw how well the young man did his work, he put him in charge of the whole labor force of the house of Joseph.

²⁹About that time Jeroboam was going out of Jerusalem, and Ahijah the prophet of Shiloh met him on the way, wearing a new cloak. The two of them were alone out in the country, ³⁰and Ahijah took hold of the new cloak he was wearing and tore it into twelve pieces. ³¹Then he said to Jeroboam, "Take ten pieces for yourself, for this is what the LORD, the God of Israel, says: 'See, I am going to tear the kingdom out of Solomon's hand and give you ten tribes. ³²But for the sake of my servant David and the city of Jerusalem, which I have chosen out of all the tribes of Israel, he will have one tribe. ³³I will do this because they have[c] forsaken me and worshiped Ashtoreth the goddess of the Sidonians, Chemosh the god of the Moabites, and Molech the god of the Ammonites, and have not walked in my ways, nor done what is right in my eyes, nor kept my statutes and laws as David, Solomon's father, did.

³⁴" 'But I will not take the whole kingdom out of Solomon's hand; I have made

---

a24 Hebrew *destroyed them*   b27 Or *the Millo*   c33 Hebrew; Septuagint, Vulgate and Syriac *because he has* him ruler all the days of his life for the sake of David my servant, whom I chose and who observed my commands and statutes. 35I will take the kingdom from his son's hands and give you ten tribes. 36I will give one tribe to his son so that David my servant may always have a lamp before me in Jerusalem, the city where I chose to put my Name. 37However, as for you, I will take you, and you will rule over all that your heart desires; you will be king over Israel. 38If you do whatever I command you and walk in my ways and do what is right in my eyes by keeping my statutes and commands, as David my servant did, I will be with you. I will build you a dynasty as enduring as the one I built for David and will give Israel to you. 39I will humble David's descendants because of this, but not forever.' "

40Solomon tried to kill Jeroboam, but Jeroboam fled to Egypt, to Shishak the king, and stayed there until Solomon's death.

Solomon's Death

41As for the other events of Solomon's reign—all he did and the wisdom he displayed—are they not written in the book of the annals of Solomon? 42Solomon reigned in Jerusalem over all Israel forty years. 43Then he rested with his fathers and was buried in the city of David his father. And Rehoboam his son succeeded him as king.

Israel Rebels Against Rehoboam

12 Rehoboam went to Shechem, for all the Israelites had gone there to make him king. 2When Jeroboam son of Nebat heard this (he was still in Egypt, where he had fled from King Solomon), he returned from*a* Egypt. 3So they sent for Jeroboam, and he and the whole assembly of Israel went to Rehoboam and said to him: 4"Your father put a heavy yoke on us, but now lighten the harsh labor and the heavy yoke he put on us, and we will serve you."

5Rehoboam answered, "Go away for three days and then come back to me." So the people went away.

6Then King Rehoboam consulted the elders who had served his father Solomon during his lifetime. "How would you advise me to answer these people?" he asked.

7They replied, "If today you will be a servant to these people and serve them and give them a favorable answer, they will always be your servants."

8But Rehoboam rejected the advice the elders gave him and consulted the young men who had grown up with him and were serving him. 9He asked them, "What is your advice? How should we answer these people who say to me, 'Lighten the yoke your father put on us'?"

10The young men who had grown up with him replied, "Tell these people who have said to you, 'Your father put a heavy yoke on us, but make our yoke lighter'—tell them, 'My little finger is thicker than my father's waist. 11My father laid on you a heavy yoke; I will make it even heavier. My father scourged you with whips; I will scourge you with scorpions.' "

12Three days later Jeroboam and all the people returned to Rehoboam, as the king had said, "Come back to me in three days." 13The king answered the people harshly. Rejecting the advice given him by the elders, 14he followed the advice of the young men and said, "My father made your yoke heavy; I will make it even heavier. My father scourged you with whips; I will scourge you with scorpions." 15So the king did not listen to the people, for this turn of events was from the LORD, to fulfill the word the LORD had spoken to Jeroboam son of Nebat through Ahijah the Shilonite.

16When all Israel saw that the king refused to listen to them, they answered the king:

"What share do we have in David,
    what part in Jesse's son?
To your tents, O Israel!
    Look after your own house,
        O David!"

So the Israelites went home. 17But as for the Israelites who were living in the towns of Judah, Rehoboam still ruled over them.

18King Rehoboam sent out Adoniram,*b* who was in charge of forced labor, but all Israel stoned him to death. King Rehoboam, however, managed to get into his chariot and escape to Jerusalem. 19So Israel has been in rebellion against the house of David to this day.

20When all the Israelites heard that Jeroboam had returned, they sent and called

a2 Or *he remained in*   *b18* Some Septuagint manuscripts and Syriac (see also 1 Kings 4:6 and 5:14); Hebrew *Adoram* him to the assembly and made him king over all Israel. Only the tribe of Judah remained loyal to the house of David.

²¹When Rehoboam arrived in Jerusalem, he mustered the whole house of Judah and the tribe of Benjamin—a hundred and eighty thousand fighting men—to make war against the house of Israel and to regain the kingdom for Rehoboam son of Solomon.

²²But this word of God came to Shemaiah the man of God: ²³"Say to Rehoboam son of Solomon king of Judah, to the whole house of Judah and Benjamin, and to the rest of the people, ²⁴'This is what the Lord says: Do not go up to fight against your brothers, the Israelites. Go home, every one of you, for this is my doing.'" So they obeyed the word of the Lord and went home again, as the Lord had ordered.

Golden Calves at Bethel and Dan

²⁵Then Jeroboam fortified Shechem in the hill country of Ephraim and lived there. From there he went out and built up Peniel.ᵃ

²⁶Jeroboam thought to himself, "The kingdom will now likely revert to the house of David. ²⁷If these people go up to offer sacrifices at the temple of the Lord in Jerusalem, they will again give their allegiance to their lord, Rehoboam king of Judah. They will kill me and return to King Rehoboam."

²⁸After seeking advice, the king made two golden calves. He said to the people, "It is too much for you to go up to Jerusalem. Here are your gods, O Israel, who brought you up out of Egypt." ²⁹One he set up in Bethel, and the other in Dan. ³⁰And this thing became a sin; the people went even as far as Dan to worship the one there.

³¹Jeroboam built shrines on high places and appointed priests from all sorts of people, even though they were not Levites. ³²He instituted a festival on the fifteenth day of the eighth month, like the festival held in Judah, and offered sacrifices on the altar. This he did in Bethel, sacrificing to the calves he had made. And at Bethel he also installed priests at the high places he had made. ³³On the fifteenth day of the eighth month, a month of his own choosing, he offered sacrifices on the altar he had built at Bethel. So he instituted the festival for

the Israelites and went up to the altar to make offerings.

The Man of God From Judah

13 By the word of the Lord a man of God came from Judah to Bethel, as Jeroboam was standing by the altar to make an offering. ²He cried out against the altar by the word of the Lord: "O altar, altar! This is what the Lord says: 'A son named Josiah will be born to the house of David. On you he will sacrifice the priests of the high places who now make offerings here, and human bones will be burned on you.'" ³That same day the man of God gave a sign: "This is the sign the Lord has declared: The altar will be split apart and the ashes on it will be poured out."

⁴When King Jeroboam heard what the man of God cried out against the altar at Bethel, he stretched out his hand from the altar and said, "Seize him!" But the hand he stretched out toward the man shriveled up, so that he could not pull it back. ⁵Also, the altar was split apart and its ashes poured out according to the sign given by the man of God by the word of the Lord.

⁶Then the king said to the man of God, "Intercede with the Lord your God and pray for me that my hand may be restored." So the man of God interceded with the Lord, and the king's hand was restored and became as it was before.

⁷The king said to the man of God, "Come home with me and have something to eat, and I will give you a gift."

⁸But the man of God answered the king, "Even if you were to give me half your possessions, I would not go with you, nor would I eat bread or drink water here. ⁹For I was commanded by the word of the Lord: 'You must not eat bread or drink water or return by the way you came.'" ¹⁰So he took another road and did not return by the way he had come to Bethel.

¹¹Now there was a certain old prophet living in Bethel, whose sons came and told him all that the man of God had done there that day. They also told their father what he had said to the king. ¹²Their father asked them, "Which way did he go?" And his sons showed him which road the man of God from Judah had taken. ¹³So he said to his sons, "Saddle the donkey for me." And when they had saddled the

---

ᵃ25 Hebrew *Penuel*, a variant of *Peniel*

donkey for him, he mounted it [14]and rode after the man of God. He found him sitting under an oak tree and asked, "Are you the man of God who came from Judah?"

"I am," he replied.

[15]So the prophet said to him, "Come home with me and eat."

[16]The man of God said, "I cannot turn back and go with you, nor can I eat bread or drink water with you in this place. [17]I have been told by the word of the LORD: 'You must not eat bread or drink water there or return by the way you came.' "

[18]The old prophet answered, "I too am a prophet, as you are. And an angel said to me by the word of the LORD: 'Bring him back with you to your house so that he may eat bread and drink water.' " (But he was lying to him.) [19]So the man of God returned with him and ate and drank in his house.

[20]While they were sitting at the table, the word of the LORD came to the old prophet who had brought him back. [21]He cried out to the man of God who had come from Judah, "This is what the LORD says: 'You have defied the word of the LORD and have not kept the command the LORD your God gave you. [22]You came back and ate bread and drank water in the place where he told you not to eat or drink. Therefore your body will not be buried in the tomb of your fathers.' "

[23]When the man of God had finished eating and drinking, the prophet who had brought him back saddled his donkey for him. [24]As he went on his way, a lion met him on the road and killed him, and his body was thrown down on the road, with both the donkey and the lion standing beside it. [25]Some people who passed by saw the body thrown down there, with the lion standing beside the body, and they went and reported it in the city where the old prophet lived.

[26]When the prophet who had brought him back from his journey heard of it, he said, "It is the man of God who defied the word of the LORD. The LORD has given him over to the lion, which has mauled him and killed him, as the word of the LORD had warned him."

[27]The prophet said to his sons, "Saddle the donkey for me," and they did so. [28]Then he went out and found the body thrown down on the road, with the donkey and the lion standing beside it. The lion had neither eaten the body nor mauled the donkey. [29]So the prophet picked up the body of the man of God, laid it on the donkey, and brought it back to his own city to mourn for him and bury him. [30]Then he laid the body in his own tomb, and they mourned over him and said, "Oh, my brother!"

[31]After burying him, he said to his sons, "When I die, bury me in the grave where the man of God is buried; lay my bones beside his bones. [32]For the message he declared by the word of the LORD against the altar in Bethel and against all the shrines on the high places in the towns of Samaria will certainly come true."

[33]Even after this, Jeroboam did not change his evil ways, but once more appointed priests for the high places from all sorts of people. Anyone who wanted to become a priest he consecrated for the high places. [34]This was the sin of the house of Jeroboam that led to its downfall and to its destruction from the face of the earth.

Ahijah's Prophecy Against Jeroboam

14 At that time Abijah son of Jeroboam became ill, [2]and Jeroboam said to his wife, "Go, disguise yourself, so you won't be recognized as the wife of Jeroboam. Then go to Shiloh. Ahijah the prophet is there—the one who told me I would be king over this people. [3]Take ten loaves of bread with you, some cakes and a jar of honey, and go to him. He will tell you what will happen to the boy." [4]So Jeroboam's wife did what he said and went to Ahijah's house in Shiloh.

Now Ahijah could not see; his sight was gone because of his age. [5]But the LORD had told Ahijah, "Jeroboam's wife is coming to ask you about her son, for he is ill, and you are to give her such and such an answer. When she arrives, she will pretend to be someone else."

[6]So when Ahijah heard the sound of her footsteps at the door, he said, "Come in, wife of Jeroboam. Why this pretense? I have been sent to you with bad news. [7]Go, tell Jeroboam that this is what the LORD, the God of Israel, says: 'I raised you up from among the people and made you a leader over my people Israel. [8]I tore the kingdom away from the house of David and gave it to you, but you have not been like my servant David, who kept my commands and followed me with all his heart, doing only what was right in my eyes. [9]You have done more evil than all who lived before you. You have made for yourself other gods, idols made of metal; you

have provoked me to anger and thrust me behind your back.

10"'Because of this, I am going to bring disaster on the house of Jeroboam. I will cut off from Jeroboam every last male in Israel—slave or free. I will burn up the house of Jeroboam as one burns dung, until it is all gone. 11Dogs will eat those belonging to Jeroboam who die in the city, and the birds of the air will feed on those who die in the country. The LORD has spoken!'

12"As for you, go back home. When you set foot in your city, the boy will die. 13All Israel will mourn for him and bury him. He is the only one belonging to Jeroboam who will be buried, because he is the only one in the house of Jeroboam in whom the LORD, the God of Israel, has found anything good.

14"The LORD will raise up for himself a king over Israel who will cut off the family of Jeroboam. This is the day! What? Yes, even now.a 15And the LORD will strike Israel, so that it will be like a reed swaying in the water. He will uproot Israel from this good land that he gave to their forefathers and scatter them beyond the River,b because they provoked the LORD to anger by making Asherah poles.c 16And he will give Israel up because of the sins Jeroboam has committed and has caused Israel to commit."

17Then Jeroboam's wife got up and left and went to Tirzah. As soon as she stepped over the threshold of the house, the boy died. 18They buried him, and all Israel mourned for him, as the LORD had said through his servant the prophet Ahijah.

19The other events of Jeroboam's reign, his wars and how he ruled, are written in the book of the annals of the kings of Israel. 20He reigned for twenty-two years and then rested with his fathers. And Nadab his son succeeded him as king.

Rehoboam King of Judah

21Rehoboam son of Solomon was king in Judah. He was forty-one years old when he became king, and he reigned seventeen years in Jerusalem, the city the LORD had chosen out of all the tribes of Israel in which to put his Name. His mother's name was Naamah; she was an Ammonite.

22Judah did evil in the eyes of the LORD. By the sins they committed they stirred up his jealous anger more than their fathers had done. 23They also set up for themselves high places, sacred stones and Asherah poles on every high hill and under every spreading tree. 24There were even male shrine prostitutes in the land; the people engaged in all the detestable practices of the nations the LORD had driven out before the Israelites.

25In the fifth year of King Rehoboam, Shishak king of Egypt attacked Jerusalem. 26He carried off the treasures of the temple of the LORD and the treasures of the royal palace. He took everything, including all the gold shields Solomon had made. 27So King Rehoboam made bronze shields to replace them and assigned these to the commanders of the guard on duty at the entrance to the royal palace. 28Whenever the king went to the LORD's temple, the guards bore the shields, and afterward they returned them to the guardroom.

29As for the other events of Rehoboam's reign, and all he did, are they not written in the book of the annals of the kings of Judah? 30There was continual warfare between Rehoboam and Jeroboam. 31And Rehoboam rested with his fathers and was buried with them in the City of David. His mother's name was Naamah; she was an Ammonite. And Abijahd his son succeeded him as king.

Abijah King of Judah

15 In the eighteenth year of the reign of Jeroboam son of Nebat, Abijahe became king of Judah, 2and he reigned in Jerusalem three years. His mother's name was Maacah daughter of Abishalom.f

3He committed all the sins his father had done before him; his heart was not fully devoted to the LORD his God, as the heart of David his forefather had been. 4Nevertheless, for David's sake the LORD his God gave him a lamp in Jerusalem by raising up a son to succeed him and by making Jerusalem strong. 5For David had done what was right in the eyes of the

---

a14 The meaning of the Hebrew for this sentence is uncertain.   b15 That is, the Euphrates   c15 That is, symbols of the goddess Asherah; here and elsewhere in 1 Kings   d31 Some Hebrew manuscripts and Septuagint (see also 2 Chron. 12:16); most Hebrew manuscripts Abijam   e1 Some Hebrew manuscripts and Septuagint (see also 2 Chron. 12:16); most Hebrew manuscripts Abijam; also in verses 7 and 8   f2 A variant of Absalom; also in verse 10

LORD and had not failed to keep any of the LORD's commands all the days of his life — except in the case of Uriah the Hittite. [6]There was war between Rehoboam[a] and Jeroboam throughout Abijah's lifetime. [7]As for the other events of Abijah's reign, and all he did, are they not written in the book of the annals of the kings of Judah? There was war between Abijah and Jeroboam. [8]And Abijah rested with his fathers and was buried in the City of David. And Asa his son succeeded him as king.

Asa King of Judah

[9]In the twentieth year of Jeroboam king of Israel, Asa became king of Judah, [10]and he reigned in Jerusalem forty-one years. His grandmother's name was Maacah daughter of Abishalom.

[11]Asa did what was right in the eyes of the LORD, as his father David had done. [12]He expelled the male shrine prostitutes from the land and got rid of all the idols his fathers had made. [13]He even deposed his grandmother Maacah from her position as queen mother, because she had made a repulsive Asherah pole. Asa cut the pole down and burned it in the Kidron Valley. [14]Although he did not remove the high places, Asa's heart was fully committed to the LORD all his life. [15]He brought into the temple of the LORD the silver and gold and the articles that he and his father had dedicated.

[16]There was war between Asa and Baasha king of Israel throughout their reigns. [17]Baasha king of Israel went up against Judah and fortified Ramah to prevent anyone from leaving or entering the territory of Asa king of Judah.

[18]Asa then took all the silver and gold that was left in the treasuries of the LORD's temple and of his own palace. He entrusted it to his officials and sent them to Ben-Hadad son of Tabrimmon, the son of Hezion, the king of Aram, who was ruling in Damascus. [19]"Let there be a treaty between me and you," he said, "as there was between my father and your father. See, I am sending you a gift of silver and gold. Now break your treaty with Baasha king of Israel so he will withdraw from me."

[20]Ben-Hadad agreed with King Asa and sent the commanders of his forces against the towns of Israel. He conquered Ijon, Dan, Abel Beth Maacah and all Kin-

nereth in addition to Naphtali. [21]When Baasha heard this, he stopped building Ramah and withdrew to Tirzah. [22]Then King Asa issued an order to all Judah — no one was exempt — and they carried away from Ramah the stones and timber Baasha had been using there. With them King Asa built up Geba in Benjamin, and also Mizpah.

[23]As for all the other events of Asa's reign, all his achievements, all he did and the cities he built, are they not written in the book of the annals of the kings of Judah? In his old age, however, his feet became diseased. [24]Then Asa rested with his fathers and was buried with them in the city of his father David. And Jehoshaphat his son succeeded him as king.

Nadab King of Israel

[25]Nadab son of Jeroboam became king of Israel in the second year of Asa king of Judah, and he reigned over Israel two years. [26]He did evil in the eyes of the LORD, walking in the ways of his father and in his sin, which he had caused Israel to commit.

[27]Baasha son of Ahijah of the house of Issachar plotted against him, and he struck him down at Gibbethon, a Philistine town, while Nadab and all Israel were besieging it. [28]Baasha killed Nadab in the third year of Asa king of Judah and succeeded him as king.

[29]As soon as he began to reign, he killed Jeroboam's whole family. He did not leave Jeroboam anyone that breathed, but destroyed them all, according to the word of the LORD given through his servant Ahijah the Shilonite — [30]because of the sins Jeroboam had committed and had caused Israel to commit, and because he provoked the LORD, the God of Israel, to anger.

[31]As for the other events of Nadab's reign, and all he did, are they not written in the book of the annals of the kings of Israel? [32]There was war between Asa and Baasha king of Israel throughout their reigns.

Baasha King of Israel

[33]In the third year of Asa king of Judah, Baasha son of Ahijah became king of all Israel in Tirzah, and he reigned twenty-four years. [34]He did evil in the eyes of the LORD, walking in the ways of Jeroboam

---

[a]6 Most Hebrew manuscripts; some Hebrew manuscripts and Syriac *Abijam* (that is, Abijah)

and in his sin, which he had caused Israel to commit.

16 Then the word of the LORD came to Jehu son of Hanani against Baasha: ²"I lifted you up from the dust and made you leader of my people Israel, but you walked in the ways of Jeroboam and caused my people Israel to sin and to provoke me to anger by their sins. ³So I am about to consume Baasha and his house, and I will make your house like that of Jeroboam son of Nebat. ⁴Dogs will eat those belonging to Baasha who die in the city, and the birds of the air will feed on those who die in the country."

⁵As for the other events of Baasha's reign, what he did and his achievements, are they not written in the book of the annals of the kings of Israel? ⁶Baasha rested with his fathers and was buried in Tirzah. And Elah his son succeeded him as king.

⁷Moreover, the word of the LORD came through the prophet Jehu son of Hanani to Baasha and his house, because of all the evil he had done in the eyes of the LORD, provoking him to anger by the things he did, and becoming like the house of Jeroboam—and also because he destroyed it.

Elah King of Israel

⁸In the twenty-sixth year of Asa king of Judah, Elah son of Baasha became king of Israel, and he reigned in Tirzah two years.

⁹Zimri, one of his officials, who had command of half his chariots, plotted against him. Elah was in Tirzah at the time, getting drunk in the home of Arza, the man in charge of the palace at Tirzah. ¹⁰Zimri came in, struck him down and killed him in the twenty-seventh year of Asa king of Judah. Then he succeeded him as king.

¹¹As soon as he began to reign and was seated on the throne, he killed off Baasha's whole family. He did not spare a single male, whether relative or friend. ¹²So Zimri destroyed the whole family of Baasha, in accordance with the word of the LORD spoken against Baasha through the prophet Jehu— ¹³because of all the sins Baasha and his son Elah had committed and had caused Israel to commit, so that they provoked the LORD, the God of Israel, to anger by their worthless idols. ¹⁴As for the other events of Elah's

reign, and all he did, are they not written in the book of the annals of the kings of Israel?

Zimri King of Israel

¹⁵In the twenty-seventh year of Asa king of Judah, Zimri reigned in Tirzah seven days. The army was encamped near Gibbethon, a Philistine town. ¹⁶When the Israelites in the camp heard that Zimri had plotted against the king and murdered him, they proclaimed Omri, the commander of the army, king over Israel that very day there in the camp. ¹⁷Then Omri and all the Israelites with him withdrew from Gibbethon and laid siege to Tirzah. ¹⁸When Zimri saw that the city was taken, he went into the citadel of the royal palace and set the palace on fire around him. So he died, ¹⁹because of the sins he had committed, doing evil in the eyes of the LORD and walking in the ways of Jeroboam and in the sin he had committed and had caused Israel to commit.

²⁰As for the other events of Zimri's reign, and the rebellion he carried out, are they not written in the book of the annals of the kings of Israel?

Omri King of Israel

²¹Then the people of Israel were split into two factions; half supported Tibni son of Ginath for king, and the other half supported Omri. ²²But Omri's followers proved stronger than those of Tibni son of Ginath. So Tibni died and Omri became king.

²³In the thirty-first year of Asa king of Judah, Omri became king of Israel, and he reigned twelve years, six of them in Tirzah. ²⁴He bought the hill of Samaria from Shemer for two talents*a* of silver and built a city on the hill, calling it Samaria, after Shemer, the name of the former owner of the hill.

²⁵But Omri did evil in the eyes of the LORD and sinned more than all those before him. ²⁶He walked in all the ways of Jeroboam son of Nebat and in his sin, which he had caused Israel to commit, so that they provoked the LORD, the God of Israel, to anger by their worthless idols.

²⁷As for the other events of Omri's reign, what he did and the things he achieved, are they not written in the book of the annals of the kings of Israel? ²⁸Omri rested with his fathers and was

a24 That is, about 150 pounds (about 70 kilograms)

buried in Samaria. And Ahab his son succeeded him as king.

Ahab Becomes King of Israel

29In the thirty-eighth year of Asa king of Judah, Ahab son of Omri became king of Israel, and he reigned in Samaria over Israel twenty-two years. 30Ahab son of Omri did more evil in the eyes of the LORD than any of those before him. 31He not only considered it trivial to commit the sins of Jeroboam son of Nebat, but he also married Jezebel daughter of Ethbaal king of the Sidonians, and began to serve Baal and worship him. 32He set up an altar for Baal in the temple of Baal that he built in Samaria. 33Ahab also made an Asherah pole and did more to provoke the LORD, the God of Israel, to anger than did all the kings of Israel before him.

34In Ahab's time, Hiel of Bethel rebuilt Jericho. He laid its foundations at the cost of his firstborn son Abiram, and he set up its gates at the cost of his youngest son Segub, in accordance with the word of the LORD spoken by Joshua son of Nun.

Elijah Fed by Ravens

17 Now Elijah the Tishbite, from Tishbe*a* in Gilead, said to Ahab, "As the LORD, the God of Israel, lives, whom I serve, there will be neither dew nor rain in the next few years except at my word."

2Then the word of the LORD came to Elijah: 3"Leave here, turn eastward and hide in the Kerith Ravine, east of the Jordan. 4You will drink from the brook, and I have ordered the ravens to feed you there."

5So he did what the LORD had told him. He went to the Kerith Ravine, east of the Jordan, and stayed there. 6The ravens brought him bread and meat in the morning and bread and meat in the evening, and he drank from the brook.

The Widow at Zarephath

7Some time later the brook dried up because there had been no rain in the land. 8Then the word of the LORD came to him: 9"Go at once to Zarephath of Sidon and stay there. I have commanded a widow in that place to supply you with food." 10So he went to Zarephath. When he came to the town gate, a widow was there gathering sticks. He called to her and asked, "Would you bring me a little water in a jar so I may have a drink?" 11As she was going

to get it, he called, "And bring me, please, a piece of bread."

12"As surely as the LORD your God lives," she replied, "I don't have any bread—only a handful of flour in a jar and a little oil in a jug. I am gathering a few sticks to take home and make a meal for myself and my son, that we may eat it—and die."

13Elijah said to her, "Don't be afraid. Go home and do as you have said. But first make a small cake of bread for me from what you have and bring it to me, and then make something for yourself and your son. 14For this is what the LORD, the God of Israel, says: 'The jar of flour will not be used up and the jug of oil will not run dry until the day the LORD gives rain on the land.'"

15She went away and did as Elijah had told her. So there was food every day for Elijah and for the woman and her family. 16For the jar of flour was not used up and the jug of oil did not run dry, in keeping with the word of the LORD spoken by Elijah.

17Some time later the son of the woman who owned the house became ill. He grew worse and worse, and finally stopped breathing. 18She said to Elijah, "What do you have against me, man of God? Did you come to remind me of my sin and kill my son?"

19"Give me your son," Elijah replied. He took him from her arms, carried him to the upper room where he was staying, and laid him on his bed. 20Then he cried out to the LORD, "O LORD my God, have you brought tragedy also upon this widow I am staying with, by causing her son to die?" 21Then he stretched himself out on the boy three times and cried to the LORD, "O LORD my God, let this boy's life return to him!"

22The LORD heard Elijah's cry, and the boy's life returned to him, and he lived. 23Elijah picked up the child and carried him down from the room into the house. He gave him to his mother and said, "Look, your son is alive!"

24Then the woman said to Elijah, "Now I know that you are a man of God and that the word of the LORD from your mouth is the truth."

Elijah and Obadiah

18 After a long time, in the third year, the word of the LORD came to Eli-

*a*1 Or *Tishbite, of the settlers*

jah: "Go and present yourself to Ahab, and I will send rain on the land." ²So Elijah went to present himself to Ahab.

Now the famine was severe in Samaria, ³and Ahab had summoned Obadiah, who was in charge of his palace. (Obadiah was a devout believer in the LORD. ⁴While Jezebel was killing off the LORD's prophets, Obadiah had taken a hundred prophets and hidden them in two caves, fifty in each, and had supplied them with food and water.) ⁵Ahab had said to Obadiah, "Go through the land to all the springs and valleys. Maybe we can find some grass to keep the horses and mules alive so we will not have to kill any of our animals." ⁶So they divided the land they were to cover, Ahab going in one direction and Obadiah in another.

⁷As Obadiah was walking along, Elijah met him. Obadiah recognized him, bowed down to the ground, and said, "Is it really you, my lord Elijah?"

⁸"Yes," he replied. "Go tell your master, 'Elijah is here.' "

⁹"What have I done wrong," asked Obadiah, "that you are handing your servant over to Ahab to be put to death? ¹⁰As surely as the LORD your God lives, there is not a nation or kingdom where my master has not sent someone to look for you. And whenever a nation or kingdom claimed you were not there, he made them swear they could not find you. ¹¹But now you tell me to go to my master and say, 'Elijah is here.' ¹²I don't know where the Spirit of the LORD may carry you when I leave you. If I go and tell Ahab and he doesn't find you, he will kill me. Yet I your servant have worshiped the LORD since my youth. ¹³Haven't you heard, my lord, what I did while Jezebel was killing the prophets of the LORD? I hid a hundred of the LORD's prophets in two caves, fifty in each, and supplied them with food and water. ¹⁴And now you tell me to go to my master and say, 'Elijah is here.' He will kill me!"

¹⁵Elijah said, "As the LORD Almighty lives, whom I serve, I will surely present myself to Ahab today."

Elijah on Mount Carmel

¹⁶So Obadiah went to meet Ahab and told him, and Ahab went to meet Elijah. ¹⁷When he saw Elijah, he said to him, "Is that you, you troubler of Israel?"

¹⁸"I have not made trouble for Israel," Elijah replied. "But you and your father's family have. You have abandoned the LORD's commands and have followed the Baals. ¹⁹Now summon the people from all over Israel to meet me on Mount Carmel. And bring the four hundred and fifty prophets of Baal and the four hundred prophets of Asherah, who eat at Jezebel's table."

²⁰So Ahab sent word throughout all Israel and assembled the prophets on Mount Carmel. ²¹Elijah went before the people and said, "How long will you waver between two opinions? If the LORD is God, follow him; but if Baal is God, follow him."

But the people said nothing.

²²Then Elijah said to them, "I am the only one of the LORD's prophets left, but Baal has four hundred and fifty prophets. ²³Get two bulls for us. Let them choose one for themselves, and let them cut it into pieces and put it on the wood but not set fire to it. I will prepare the other bull and put it on the wood but not set fire to it. ²⁴Then you call on the name of your god, and I will call on the name of the LORD. The god who answers by fire — he is God."

Then all the people said, "What you say is good."

²⁵Elijah said to the prophets of Baal, "Choose one of the bulls and prepare it first, since there are so many of you. Call on the name of your god, but do not light the fire." ²⁶So they took the bull given them and prepared it.

Then they called on the name of Baal from morning till noon. "O Baal, answer us!" they shouted. But there was no response; no one answered. And they danced around the altar they had made.

²⁷At noon Elijah began to taunt them. "Shout louder!" he said. "Surely he is a god! Perhaps he is deep in thought, or busy, or traveling. Maybe he is sleeping and must be awakened." ²⁸So they shouted louder and slashed themselves with swords and spears, as was their custom, until their blood flowed. ²⁹Midday passed, and they continued their frantic prophesying until the time for the evening sacrifice. But there was no response, no one answered, no one paid attention.

³⁰Then Elijah said to all the people, "Come here to me." They came to him, and he repaired the altar of the LORD, which was in ruins. ³¹Elijah took twelve stones, one for each of the tribes descended from Jacob, to whom the word of the LORD had come, saying, "Your name shall be Israel." ³²With the stones he built an altar in the name of the LORD, and he

dug a trench around it large enough to hold two seahs*a* of seed. 33He arranged the wood, cut the bull into pieces and laid it on the wood. Then he said to them, "Fill four large jars with water and pour it on the offering and on the wood."

34"Do it again," he said, and they did it again.

"Do it a third time," he ordered, and they did it the third time. 35The water ran down around the altar and even filled the trench.

36At the time of sacrifice, the prophet Elijah stepped forward and prayed: "O LORD, God of Abraham, Isaac and Israel, let it be known today that you are God in Israel and that I am your servant and have done all these things at your command. 37Answer me, O LORD, answer me, so these people will know that you, O LORD, are God, and that you are turning their hearts back again."

38Then the fire of the LORD fell and burned up the sacrifice, the wood, the stones and the soil, and also licked up the water in the trench.

39When all the people saw this, they fell prostrate and cried, "The LORD—he is God! The LORD—he is God!"

40Then Elijah commanded them, "Seize the prophets of Baal. Don't let anyone get away!" They seized them, and Elijah had them brought down to the Kishon Valley and slaughtered there.

41And Elijah said to Ahab, "Go, eat and drink, for there is the sound of a heavy rain." 42So Ahab went off to eat and drink, but Elijah climbed to the top of Carmel, bent down to the ground and put his face between his knees.

43"Go and look toward the sea," he told his servant. And he went up and looked.

"There is nothing there," he said.

Seven times Elijah said, "Go back."

44The seventh time the servant reported, "A cloud as small as a man's hand is rising from the sea."

So Elijah said, "Go and tell Ahab, 'Hitch up your chariot and go down before the rain stops you.' "

45Meanwhile, the sky grew black with clouds, the wind rose, a heavy rain came on and Ahab rode off to Jezreel. 46The power of the LORD came upon Elijah and, tucking his cloak into his belt, he ran ahead of Ahab all the way to Jezreel.

Elijah Flees to Horeb

19 Now Ahab told Jezebel everything Elijah had done and how he had killed all the prophets with the sword. 2So Jezebel sent a messenger to Elijah to say, "May the gods deal with me, be it ever so severely, if by this time tomorrow I do not make your life like that of one of them."

3Elijah was afraid*b* and ran for his life. When he came to Beersheba in Judah, he left his servant there, 4while he himself went a day's journey into the desert. He came to a broom tree, sat down under it and prayed that he might die. "I have had enough, LORD," he said. "Take my life; I am no better than my ancestors." 5Then he lay down under the tree and fell asleep.

All at once an angel touched him and said, "Get up and eat." 6He looked around, and there by his head was a cake of bread baked over hot coals, and a jar of water. He ate and drank and then lay down again.

7The angel of the LORD came back a second time and touched him and said, "Get up and eat, for the journey is too much for you." 8So he got up and ate and drank. Strengthened by that food, he traveled forty days and forty nights until he reached Horeb, the mountain of God. 9There he went into a cave and spent the night.

The LORD Appears to Elijah

And the word of the LORD came to him: "What are you doing here, Elijah?"

10He replied, "I have been very zealous for the LORD God Almighty. The Israelites have rejected your covenant, broken down your altars, and put your prophets to death with the sword. I am the only one left, and now they are trying to kill me too."

11The LORD said, "Go out and stand on the mountain in the presence of the LORD, for the LORD is about to pass by."

Then a great and powerful wind tore the mountains apart and shattered the rocks before the LORD, but the LORD was not in the wind. After the wind there was an earthquake, but the LORD was not in the earthquake. 12After the earthquake came a fire, but the LORD was not in the fire. And after the fire came a gentle whisper. 13When Elijah heard it, he pulled his

---

a32 That is, probably about 13 quarts (about 15 liters)　　*b3* Or *Elijah saw*

VERSE FOR THE DAY:	**AUTHOR:**	**PASSAGE FOR THE DAY:**
1 Kings 19:4	Jean E. Syswerda	1 Kings 18:16—19:18

Prescription for Discouragement

I'VE never, all alone, faced 450 leaders of an opposing religion (1 Kings 18:22).

I've never called down fire from heaven (1 Kings 18:37).

I've never prayed for rain until I saw storm clouds gather (1 Kings 18:42).

I've never run twenty-five miles . . . I've never run five miles! (1 Kings 18:46).

I've never had a queen threaten my life (1 Kings 19:2).

But I have felt discouraged like Elijah and said, "I've had enough, Lord!" (1 Kings 19:4).

After a day of dealing with a cranky baby or a hostile teenager or a demanding boss or an unsatisfied husband . . . after a day of cereal crumbs (always on the floor, never in the cereal box) and dirty socks (always smelly and always inside out) and a car that won't start when I'm already late . . . after a day of discouragement and disappointment (in myself more than anyone or anything else) . . . I can say—no shout—with Elijah, "I've had enough, Lord!"

If I'll just follow the Lord's prescription for discouragement, given here to Elijah, I should be able to regain control of myself and my emotions:

1) Get enough rest (1 Kings 19:5). Ever notice how a short temper is directly related to a short night's sleep? Sometimes short nights cannot be helped (infants must be fed), but as much as possible get a good night's rest.

2) Eat healthy foods on a regular basis (1 Kings 19:6). Five fingerlicks of raw cookie dough do not a healthy lunch make. Foods high in protein and low in sugar will give you the strength you need for the strains of your day.

3) Spend some quiet time with yourself and the Lord (1 Kings 19:12). There's just no getting around it. No matter how busy you are, time alone with yourself and with your Lord will provide the stability to catch and handle whatever life throws your way.

4) Now go (1 Kings 19:15). There's much to be done. If you can make rules one through three your high priorities, number four will usually take care of itself.

Additional Scripture Readings:
Psalm 127:2; Luke 6:12–13

Go to page 379 for your next devotional reading.

cloak over his face and went out and stood at the mouth of the cave.

Then a voice said to him, "What are you doing here, Elijah?"

14He replied, "I have been very zealous for the LORD God Almighty. The Israelites have rejected your covenant, broken down your altars, and put your prophets to death with the sword. I am the only one left, and now they are trying to kill me too."

15The LORD said to him, "Go back the way you came, and go to the Desert of Damascus. When you get there, anoint Hazael king over Aram. 16Also, anoint Jehu son of Nimshi king over Israel, and anoint Elisha son of Shaphat from Abel Meholah to succeed you as prophet. 17Jehu will put to death any who escape the sword of Hazael, and Elisha will put to death any who escape the sword of Jehu. 18Yet I reserve seven thousand in Israel—all whose knees have not bowed down to Baal and all whose mouths have not kissed him."

The Call of Elisha

19So Elijah went from there and found Elisha son of Shaphat. He was plowing with twelve yoke of oxen, and he himself was driving the twelfth pair. Elijah went up to him and threw his cloak around him. 20Elisha then left his oxen and ran after Elijah. "Let me kiss my father and mother good-by," he said, "and then I will come with you."

"Go back," Elijah replied. "What have I done to you?"

21So Elisha left him and went back. He took his yoke of oxen and slaughtered them. He burned the plowing equipment to cook the meat and gave it to the people, and they ate. Then he set out to follow Elijah and became his attendant.

Ben-Hadad Attacks Samaria

20 Now Ben-Hadad king of Aram mustered his entire army. Accompanied by thirty-two kings with their horses and chariots, he went up and besieged Samaria and attacked it. 2He sent messengers into the city to Ahab king of Israel, saying, "This is what Ben-Hadad says: 3'Your silver and gold are mine, and the best of your wives and children are mine.' "

4The king of Israel answered, "Just as you say, my lord the king. I and all I have are yours."

5The messengers came again and said, "This is what Ben-Hadad says: 'I sent to demand your silver and gold, your wives and your children. 6But about this time tomorrow I am going to send my officials to search your palace and the houses of your officials. They will seize everything you value and carry it away.' "

7The king of Israel summoned all the elders of the land and said to them, "See how this man is looking for trouble! When he sent for my wives and my children, my silver and my gold, I did not refuse him."

8The elders and the people all answered, "Don't listen to him or agree to his demands."

9So he replied to Ben-Hadad's messengers, "Tell my lord the king, 'Your servant will do all you demanded the first time, but this demand I cannot meet.' " They left and took the answer back to Ben-Hadad.

10Then Ben-Hadad sent another message to Ahab: "May the gods deal with me, be it ever so severely, if enough dust remains in Samaria to give each of my men a handful."

11The king of Israel answered, "Tell him: 'One who puts on his armor should not boast like one who takes it off.' "

12Ben-Hadad heard this message while he and the kings were drinking in their tents,*a* and he ordered his men: "Prepare to attack." So they prepared to attack the city.

Ahab Defeats Ben-Hadad

13Meanwhile a prophet came to Ahab king of Israel and announced, "This is what the LORD says: 'Do you see this vast army? I will give it into your hand today, and then you will know that I am the LORD.' "

14"But who will do this?" asked Ahab.

The prophet replied, "This is what the LORD says: 'The young officers of the provincial commanders will do it.' "

"And who will start the battle?" he asked.

The prophet answered, "You will."

15So Ahab summoned the young officers of the provincial commanders, 232 men. Then he assembled the rest of the Israelites, 7,000 in all. 16They set out at noon while Ben-Hadad and the 32 kings allied with him were in their tents getting drunk. [17]The young officers of the provincial commanders went out first.

Now Ben-Hadad had dispatched scouts, who reported, "Men are advancing from Samaria."

[18]He said, "If they have come out for peace, take them alive; if they have come out for war, take them alive."

[19]The young officers of the provincial commanders marched out of the city with the army behind them [20]and each one struck down his opponent. At that, the Arameans fled, with the Israelites in pursuit. But Ben-Hadad king of Aram escaped on horseback with some of his horsemen. [21]The king of Israel advanced and overpowered the horses and chariots and inflicted heavy losses on the Arameans.

[22]Afterward, the prophet came to the king of Israel and said, "Strengthen your position and see what must be done, because next spring the king of Aram will attack you again."

[23]Meanwhile, the officials of the king of Aram advised him, "Their gods are gods of the hills. That is why they were too strong for us. But if we fight them on the plains, surely we will be stronger than they. [24]Do this: Remove all the kings from their commands and replace them with other officers. [25]You must also raise an army like the one you lost—horse for horse and chariot for chariot—so we can fight Israel on the plains. Then surely we will be stronger than they." He agreed with them and acted accordingly.

[26]The next spring Ben-Hadad mustered the Arameans and went up to Aphek to fight against Israel. [27]When the Israelites were also mustered and given provisions, they marched out to meet them. The Israelites camped opposite them like two small flocks of goats, while the Arameans covered the countryside.

[28]The man of God came up and told the king of Israel, "This is what the LORD says: 'Because the Arameans think the LORD is a god of the hills and not a god of the valleys, I will deliver this vast army into your hands, and you will know that I am the LORD.'"

[29]For seven days they camped opposite each other, and on the seventh day the battle was joined. The Israelites inflicted a hundred thousand casualties on the Aramean foot soldiers in one day. [30]The rest of them escaped to the city of Aphek, where the wall collapsed on twenty-seven thousand of them. And Ben-Hadad fled to the city and hid in an inner room.

[31]His officials said to him, "Look, we have heard that the kings of the house of Israel are merciful. Let us go to the king of Israel with sackcloth around our waists and ropes around our heads. Perhaps he will spare your life."

[32]Wearing sackcloth around their waists and ropes around their heads, they went to the king of Israel and said, "Your servant Ben-Hadad says: 'Please let me live.'"

The king answered, "Is he still alive? He is my brother."

[33]The men took this as a good sign and were quick to pick up his word. "Yes, your brother Ben-Hadad!" they said.

"Go and get him," the king said. When Ben-Hadad came out, Ahab had him come up into his chariot.

[34]"I will return the cities my father took from your father," Ben-Hadad offered. "You may set up your own market areas in Damascus, as my father did in Samaria."

Ahab said, "On the basis of a treaty I will set you free." So he made a treaty with him, and let him go.

A Prophet Condemns Ahab

[35]By the word of the LORD one of the sons of the prophets said to his companion, "Strike me with your weapon," but the man refused.

[36]So the prophet said, "Because you have not obeyed the LORD, as soon as you leave me a lion will kill you." And after the man went away, a lion found him and killed him.

[37]The prophet found another man and said, "Strike me, please." So the man struck him and wounded him. [38]Then the prophet went and stood by the road waiting for the king. He disguised himself with his headband down over his eyes. [39]As the king passed by, the prophet called out to him, "Your servant went into the thick of the battle, and someone came to me with a captive and said, 'Guard this man. If he is missing, it will be your life for his life, or you must pay a talent[a] of silver.' [40]While your servant was busy here and there, the man disappeared."

"That is your sentence," the king of Israel said. "You have pronounced it yourself."

a39 That is, about 75 pounds (about 34 kilograms)

⁴¹Then the prophet quickly removed the headband from his eyes, and the king of Israel recognized him as one of the prophets. ⁴²He said to the king, "This is what the LORD says: 'You have set free a man I had determined should die.ᵃ Therefore it is your life for his life, your people for his people.' " ⁴³Sullen and angry, the king of Israel went to his palace in Samaria.

Naboth's Vineyard

21 Some time later there was an incident involving a vineyard belonging to Naboth the Jezreelite. The vineyard was in Jezreel, close to the palace of Ahab king of Samaria. ²Ahab said to Naboth, "Let me have your vineyard to use for a vegetable garden, since it is close to my palace. In exchange I will give you a better vineyard or, if you prefer, I will pay you whatever it is worth."

³But Naboth replied, "The LORD forbid that I should give you the inheritance of my fathers."

⁴So Ahab went home, sullen and angry because Naboth the Jezreelite had said, "I will not give you the inheritance of my fathers." He lay on his bed sulking and refused to eat.

⁵His wife Jezebel came in and asked him, "Why are you so sullen? Why won't you eat?"

⁶He answered her, "Because I said to Naboth the Jezreelite, 'Sell me your vineyard; or if you prefer, I will give you another vineyard in its place.' But he said, 'I will not give you my vineyard.' "

⁷Jezebel his wife said, "Is this how you act as king over Israel? Get up and eat! Cheer up. I'll get you the vineyard of Naboth the Jezreelite."

⁸So she wrote letters in Ahab's name, placed his seal on them, and sent them to the elders and nobles who lived in Naboth's city with him. ⁹In those letters she wrote:

"Proclaim a day of fasting and seat Naboth in a prominent place among the people. ¹⁰But seat two scoundrels opposite him and have them testify that he has cursed both God and the king. Then take him out and stone him to death."

¹¹So the elders and nobles who lived in Naboth's city did as Jezebel directed in the letters she had written to them. ¹²They proclaimed a fast and seated Naboth in a prominent place among the people. ¹³Then two scoundrels came and sat opposite him and brought charges against Naboth before the people, saying, "Naboth has cursed both God and the king." So they took him outside the city and stoned him to death. ¹⁴Then they sent word to Jezebel: "Naboth has been stoned and is dead."

¹⁵As soon as Jezebel heard that Naboth had been stoned to death, she said to Ahab, "Get up and take possession of the vineyard of Naboth the Jezreelite that he refused to sell you. He is no longer alive, but dead." ¹⁶When Ahab heard that Naboth was dead, he got up and went down to take possession of Naboth's vineyard.

¹⁷Then the word of the LORD came to Elijah the Tishbite: ¹⁸"Go down to meet Ahab king of Israel, who rules in Samaria. He is now in Naboth's vineyard, where he has gone to take possession of it. ¹⁹Say to him, 'This is what the LORD says: Have you not murdered a man and seized his property?' Then say to him, 'This is what the LORD says: In the place where dogs licked up Naboth's blood, dogs will lick up your blood—yes, yours!' "

²⁰Ahab said to Elijah, "So you have found me, my enemy!"

"I have found you," he answered, "because you have sold yourself to do evil in the eyes of the LORD. ²¹'I am going to bring disaster on you. I will consume your descendants and cut off from Ahab every last male in Israel—slave or free. ²²I will make your house like that of Jeroboam son of Nebat and that of Baasha son of Ahijah, because you have provoked me to anger and have caused Israel to sin.'

²³"And also concerning Jezebel the LORD says: 'Dogs will devour Jezebel by the wall ofᵇ Jezreel.'

²⁴"Dogs will eat those belonging to Ahab who die in the city, and the birds of the air will feed on those who die in the country."

²⁵(There was never a man like Ahab, who sold himself to do evil in the eyes of the LORD, urged on by Jezebel his wife. ²⁶He behaved in the vilest manner by going after idols, like the Amorites the LORD drove out before Israel.)

ᵃ42 The Hebrew term refers to the irrevocable giving over of things or persons to the LORD, often by totally destroying them.　　*ᵇ23* Most Hebrew manuscripts; a few Hebrew manuscripts, Vulgate and Syriac (see also 2 Kings 9:26) *the plot of ground at*

²⁷When Ahab heard these words, he tore his clothes, put on sackcloth and fasted. He lay in sackcloth and went around meekly.

²⁸Then the word of the LORD came to Elijah the Tishbite: ²⁹"Have you noticed how Ahab has humbled himself before me? Because he has humbled himself, I will not bring this disaster in his day, but I will bring it on his house in the days of his son."

Micaiah Prophesies Against Ahab

22 For three years there was no war between Aram and Israel. ²But in the third year Jehoshaphat king of Judah went down to see the king of Israel. ³The king of Israel had said to his officials, "Don't you know that Ramoth Gilead belongs to us and yet we are doing nothing to retake it from the king of Aram?"

⁴So he asked Jehoshaphat, "Will you go with me to fight against Ramoth Gilead?"

Jehoshaphat replied to the king of Israel, "I am as you are, my people as your people, my horses as your horses." ⁵But Jehoshaphat also said to the king of Israel, "First seek the counsel of the LORD."

⁶So the king of Israel brought together the prophets—about four hundred men —and asked them, "Shall I go to war against Ramoth Gilead, or shall I refrain?"

"Go," they answered, "for the Lord will give it into the king's hand."

⁷But Jehoshaphat asked, "Is there not a prophet of the LORD here whom we can inquire of?"

⁸The king of Israel answered Jehoshaphat, "There is still one man through whom we can inquire of the LORD, but I hate him because he never prophesies anything good about me, but always bad. He is Micaiah son of Imlah."

"The king should not say that," Jehoshaphat replied.

⁹So the king of Israel called one of his officials and said, "Bring Micaiah son of Imlah at once."

¹⁰Dressed in their royal robes, the king of Israel and Jehoshaphat king of Judah were sitting on their thrones at the threshing floor by the entrance of the gate of Samaria, with all the prophets prophesying before them. ¹¹Now Zedekiah son of Kenaanah had made iron horns and he declared, "This is what the LORD says:

'With these you will gore the Arameans until they are destroyed.' "

¹²All the other prophets were prophesying the same thing. "Attack Ramoth Gilead and be victorious," they said, "for the LORD will give it into the king's hand."

¹³The messenger who had gone to summon Micaiah said to him, "Look, as one man the other prophets are predicting success for the king. Let your word agree with theirs, and speak favorably."

¹⁴But Micaiah said, "As surely as the LORD lives, I can tell him only what the LORD tells me."

¹⁵When he arrived, the king asked him, "Micaiah, shall we go to war against Ramoth Gilead, or shall I refrain?"

"Attack and be victorious," he answered, "for the LORD will give it into the king's hand."

¹⁶The king said to him, "How many times must I make you swear to tell me nothing but the truth in the name of the LORD?"

¹⁷Then Micaiah answered, "I saw all Israel scattered on the hills like sheep without a shepherd, and the LORD said, 'These people have no master. Let each one go home in peace.' "

¹⁸The king of Israel said to Jehoshaphat, "Didn't I tell you that he never prophesies anything good about me, but only bad?"

¹⁹Micaiah continued, "Therefore hear the word of the LORD: I saw the LORD sitting on his throne with all the host of heaven standing around him on his right and on his left. ²⁰And the LORD said, 'Who will entice Ahab into attacking Ramoth Gilead and going to his death there?'

"One suggested this, and another that. ²¹Finally, a spirit came forward, stood before the LORD and said, 'I will entice him.'

²²" 'By what means?' the LORD asked.

" 'I will go out and be a lying spirit in the mouths of all his prophets,' he said.

" 'You will succeed in enticing him,' said the LORD. 'Go and do it.'

²³"So now the LORD has put a lying spirit in the mouths of all these prophets of yours. The LORD has decreed disaster for you."

²⁴Then Zedekiah son of Kenaanah went up and slapped Micaiah in the face. "Which way did the spirit from ᵃ the LORD go when he went from me to speak to you?" he asked.

²⁵Micaiah replied, "You will find out on

ᵃ24 Or Spirit of

the day you go to hide in an inner room."

26The king of Israel then ordered, "Take Micaiah and send him back to Amon the ruler of the city and to Joash the king's son 27and say, 'This is what the king says: Put this fellow in prison and give him nothing but bread and water until I return safely.'"

28Micaiah declared, "If you ever return safely, the Lord has not spoken through me." Then he added, "Mark my words, all you people!"

Ahab Killed at Ramoth Gilead

29So the king of Israel and Jehoshaphat king of Judah went up to Ramoth Gilead. 30The king of Israel said to Jehoshaphat, "I will enter the battle in disguise, but you wear your royal robes." So the king of Israel disguised himself and went into battle.

31Now the king of Aram had ordered his thirty-two chariot commanders, "Do not fight with anyone, small or great, except the king of Israel." 32When the chariot commanders saw Jehoshaphat, they thought, "Surely this is the king of Israel." So they turned to attack him, but when Jehoshaphat cried out, 33the chariot commanders saw that he was not the king of Israel and stopped pursuing him.

34But someone drew his bow at random and hit the king of Israel between the sections of his armor. The king told his chariot driver, "Wheel around and get me out of the fighting. I've been wounded." 35All day long the battle raged, and the king was propped up in his chariot facing the Arameans. The blood from his wound ran onto the floor of the chariot, and that evening he died. 36As the sun was setting, a cry spread through the army: "Every man to his town; everyone to his land!"

37So the king died and was brought to Samaria, and they buried him there. 38They washed the chariot at a pool in Samaria (where the prostitutes bathed),a and the dogs licked up his blood, as the word of the Lord had declared.

39As for the other events of Ahab's reign, including all he did, the palace he built and inlaid with ivory, and the cities he fortified, are they not written in the book of the annals of the kings of Israel? 40Ahab rested with his fathers. And Ahaziah his son succeeded him as king.

Jehoshaphat King of Judah

41Jehoshaphat son of Asa became king of Judah in the fourth year of Ahab king of Israel. 42Jehoshaphat was thirty-five years old when he became king, and he reigned in Jerusalem twenty-five years. His mother's name was Azubah daughter of Shilhi. 43In everything he walked in the ways of his father Asa and did not stray from them; he did what was right in the eyes of the Lord. The high places, however, were not removed, and the people continued to offer sacrifices and burn incense there. 44Jehoshaphat was also at peace with the king of Israel.

45As for the other events of Jehoshaphat's reign, the things he achieved and his military exploits, are they not written in the book of the annals of the kings of Judah? 46He rid the land of the rest of the male shrine prostitutes who remained there even after the reign of his father Asa. 47There was then no king in Edom; a deputy ruled.

48Now Jehoshaphat built a fleet of trading shipsb to go to Ophir for gold, but they never set sail—they were wrecked at Ezion Geber. 49At that time Ahaziah son of Ahab said to Jehoshaphat, "Let my men sail with your men," but Jehoshaphat refused.

50Then Jehoshaphat rested with his fathers and was buried with them in the city of David his father. And Jehoram his son succeeded him.

Ahaziah King of Israel

51Ahaziah son of Ahab became king of Israel in Samaria in the seventeenth year of Jehoshaphat king of Judah, and he reigned over Israel two years. 52He did evil in the eyes of the Lord, because he walked in the ways of his father and mother and in the ways of Jeroboam son of Nebat, who caused Israel to sin. 53He served and worshiped Baal and provoked the Lord, the God of Israel, to anger, just as his father had done.

---

a38 Or Samaria and cleaned the weapons   b48 Hebrew of ships of Tarshish

THIS book continues the history of Israel and Judah begun in 1 Kings. When good kings reign, the people prosper; but after persistent idolatry, God finally allows the Assyrians to destroy the nation of Israel and the Babylonians to carry the nation of Judah into captivity. Yet God preserves the royal line because of the promise he made David (see 2 Kings 8:19). As you read this book, praise God for his faithful love to you in spite of your sins. But remember that God does eventually punish those who disobey.

2 KINGS

The LORD's Judgment on Ahaziah

1 After Ahab's death, Moab rebelled against Israel. ²Now Ahaziah had fallen through the lattice of his upper room in Samaria and injured himself. So he sent messengers, saying to them, "Go and consult Baal-Zebub, the god of Ekron, to see if I will recover from this injury."

³But the angel of the LORD said to Elijah the Tishbite, "Go up and meet the messengers of the king of Samaria and ask them, 'Is it because there is no God in Israel that you are going off to consult Baal-Zebub, the god of Ekron?' ⁴There-

fore this is what the LORD says: 'You will not leave the bed you are lying on. You will certainly die!'" So Elijah went.

⁵When the messengers returned to the king, he asked them, "Why have you come back?"

⁶"A man came to meet us," they replied. "And he said to us, 'Go back to the king who sent you and tell him, "This is what the LORD says: Is it because there is no God in Israel that you are sending men to consult Baal-Zebub, the god of Ekron? Therefore you will not leave the bed you are lying on. You will certainly die!"'"

7The king asked them, "What kind of man was it who came to meet you and told you this?"

8They replied, "He was a man with a garment of hair and with a leather belt around his waist."

The king said, "That was Elijah the Tishbite."

9Then he sent to Elijah a captain with his company of fifty men. The captain went up to Elijah, who was sitting on the top of a hill, and said to him, "Man of God, the king says, 'Come down!'"

10Elijah answered the captain, "If I am a man of God, may fire come down from heaven and consume you and your fifty men!" Then fire fell from heaven and consumed the captain and his men.

11At this the king sent to Elijah another captain with his fifty men. The captain said to him, "Man of God, this is what the king says, 'Come down at once!'"

12"If I am a man of God," Elijah replied, "may fire come down from heaven and consume you and your fifty men!" Then the fire of God fell from heaven and consumed him and his fifty men.

13So the king sent a third captain with his fifty men. This third captain went up and fell on his knees before Elijah. "Man of God," he begged, "please have respect for my life and the lives of these fifty men, your servants! 14See, fire has fallen from heaven and consumed the first two captains and all their men. But now have respect for my life!"

15The angel of the LORD said to Elijah, "Go down with him; do not be afraid of him." So Elijah got up and went down with him to the king.

16He told the king, "This is what the LORD says: Is it because there is no God in Israel for you to consult that you have sent messengers to consult Baal-Zebub, the god of Ekron? Because you have done this, you will never leave the bed you are lying on. You will certainly die!" 17So he died, according to the word of the LORD that Elijah had spoken.

Because Ahaziah had no son, Joram*a* succeeded him as king in the second year of Jehoram son of Jehoshaphat king of Judah. 18As for all the other events of Ahaziah's reign, and what he did, are they not written in the book of the annals of the kings of Israel?

Elijah Taken Up to Heaven

2 When the LORD was about to take Elijah up to heaven in a whirlwind, Elijah and Elisha were on their way from Gilgal. 2Elijah said to Elisha, "Stay here; the LORD has sent me to Bethel."

But Elisha said, "As surely as the LORD lives and as you live, I will not leave you." So they went down to Bethel.

3The company of the prophets at Bethel came out to Elisha and asked, "Do you know that the LORD is going to take your master from you today?"

"Yes, I know," Elisha replied, "but do not speak of it."

4Then Elijah said to him, "Stay here, Elisha; the LORD has sent me to Jericho."

And he replied, "As surely as the LORD lives and as you live, I will not leave you." So they went to Jericho.

5The company of the prophets at Jericho went up to Elisha and asked him, "Do you know that the LORD is going to take your master from you today?"

"Yes, I know," he replied, "but do not speak of it."

6Then Elijah said to him, "Stay here; the LORD has sent me to the Jordan."

And he replied, "As surely as the LORD lives and as you live, I will not leave you." So the two of them walked on.

7Fifty men of the company of the prophets went and stood at a distance, facing the place where Elijah and Elisha had stopped at the Jordan. 8Elijah took his cloak, rolled it up and struck the water with it. The water divided to the right and to the left, and the two of them crossed over on dry ground.

9When they had crossed, Elijah said to Elisha, "Tell me, what can I do for you before I am taken from you?"

"Let me inherit a double portion of your spirit," Elisha replied.

10"You have asked a difficult thing," Elijah said, "yet if you see me when I am taken from you, it will be yours—otherwise not."

11As they were walking along and talking together, suddenly a chariot of fire and horses of fire appeared and separated the two of them, and Elijah went up to heaven in a whirlwind. 12Elisha saw this and cried out, "My father! My father! The chariots and horsemen of Israel!" And

a17 Hebrew Jehoram, a variant of Joram

Elisha saw him no more. Then he took hold of his own clothes and tore them apart.

13He picked up the cloak that had fallen from Elijah and went back and stood on the bank of the Jordan. 14Then he took the cloak that had fallen from him and struck the water with it. "Where now is the LORD, the God of Elijah?" he asked. When he struck the water, it divided to the right and to the left, and he crossed over.

15The company of the prophets from Jericho, who were watching, said, "The spirit of Elijah is resting on Elisha." And they went to meet him and bowed to the ground before him. 16"Look," they said, "we your servants have fifty able men. Let them go and look for your master. Perhaps the Spirit of the LORD has picked him up and set him down on some mountain or in some valley."

"No," Elisha replied, "do not send them."

17But they persisted until he was too ashamed to refuse. So he said, "Send them." And they sent fifty men, who searched for three days but did not find him. 18When they returned to Elisha, who was staying in Jericho, he said to them, "Didn't I tell you not to go?"

Healing of the Water

19The men of the city said to Elisha, "Look, our lord, this town is well situated, as you can see, but the water is bad and the land is unproductive."

20"Bring me a new bowl," he said, "and put salt in it." So they brought it to him.

21Then he went out to the spring and threw the salt into it, saying, "This is what the LORD says: 'I have healed this water. Never again will it cause death or make the land unproductive.' " 22And the water has remained wholesome to this day, according to the word Elisha had spoken.

Elisha Is Jeered

23From there Elisha went up to Bethel. As he was walking along the road, some youths came out of the town and jeered at him. "Go on up, you baldhead!" they said. "Go on up, you baldhead!" 24He turned around, looked at them and called down a curse on them in the name of the LORD. Then two bears came out of the woods

and mauled forty-two of the youths. 25And he went on to Mount Carmel and from there returned to Samaria.

Moab Revolts

3 Joram[a] son of Ahab became king of Israel in Samaria in the eighteenth year of Jehoshaphat king of Judah, and he reigned twelve years. 2He did evil in the eyes of the LORD, but not as his father and mother had done. He got rid of the sacred stone of Baal that his father had made. 3Nevertheless he clung to the sins of Jeroboam son of Nebat, which he had caused Israel to commit; he did not turn away from them.

4Now Mesha king of Moab raised sheep, and he had to supply the king of Israel with a hundred thousand lambs and with the wool of a hundred thousand rams. 5But after Ahab died, the king of Moab rebelled against the king of Israel. 6So at that time King Joram set out from Samaria and mobilized all Israel. 7He also sent this message to Jehoshaphat king of Judah: "The king of Moab has rebelled against me. Will you go with me to fight against Moab?"

"I will go with you," he replied. "I am as you are, my people as your people, my horses as your horses."

8"By what route shall we attack?" he asked.

"Through the Desert of Edom," he answered.

9So the king of Israel set out with the king of Judah and the king of Edom. After a roundabout march of seven days, the army had no more water for themselves or for the animals with them.

10"What!" exclaimed the king of Israel. "Has the LORD called us three kings together only to hand us over to Moab?"

11But Jehoshaphat asked, "Is there no prophet of the LORD here, that we may inquire of the LORD through him?"

An officer of the king of Israel answered, "Elisha son of Shaphat is here. He used to pour water on the hands of Elijah.[b]"

12Jehoshaphat said, "The word of the LORD is with him." So the king of Israel and Jehoshaphat and the king of Edom went down to him.

13Elisha said to the king of Israel, "What do we have to do with each other? Go to the prophets of your father and the prophets of your mother."

---

a1 Hebrew *Jehoram*, a variant of *Joram*; also in verse 6   b11 That is, he was Elijah's personal servant.

"No," the king of Israel answered, "because it was the LORD who called us three kings together to hand us over to Moab."

¹⁴Elisha said, "As surely as the LORD Almighty lives, whom I serve, if I did not have respect for the presence of Jehoshaphat king of Judah, I would not look at you or even notice you. ¹⁵But now bring me a harpist."

While the harpist was playing, the hand of the LORD came upon Elisha ¹⁶and he said, "This is what the LORD says: Make this valley full of ditches. ¹⁷For this is what the LORD says: You will see neither wind nor rain, yet this valley will be filled with water, and you, your cattle and your other animals will drink. ¹⁸This is an easy thing in the eyes of the LORD; he will also hand Moab over to you. ¹⁹You will overthrow every fortified city and every major town. You will cut down every good tree, stop up all the springs, and ruin every good field with stones."

²⁰The next morning, about the time for offering the sacrifice, there it was—water flowing from the direction of Edom! And the land was filled with water.

²¹Now all the Moabites had heard that the kings had come to fight against them; so every man, young and old, who could bear arms was called up and stationed on the border. ²²When they got up early in the morning, the sun was shining on the water. To the Moabites across the way, the water looked red—like blood. ²³"That's blood!" they said. "Those kings must have fought and slaughtered each other. Now to the plunder, Moab!"

²⁴But when the Moabites came to the camp of Israel, the Israelites rose up and fought them until they fled. And the Israelites invaded the land and slaughtered the Moabites. ²⁵They destroyed the towns, and each man threw a stone on every good field until it was covered. They stopped up all the springs and cut down every good tree. Only Kir Hareseth was left with its stones in place, but men armed with slings surrounded it and attacked it as well.

²⁶When the king of Moab saw that the battle had gone against him, he took with him seven hundred swordsmen to break through to the king of Edom, but they failed. ²⁷Then he took his firstborn son, who was to succeed him as king, and offered him as a sacrifice on the city wall. The fury against Israel was great; they withdrew and returned to their own land.

The Widow's Oil

4 The wife of a man from the company of the prophets cried out to Elisha, "Your servant my husband is dead, and you know that he revered the LORD. But now his creditor is coming to take my two boys as his slaves."

²Elisha replied to her, "How can I help you? Tell me, what do you have in your house?"

"Your servant has nothing there at all," she said, "except a little oil."

³Elisha said, "Go around and ask all your neighbors for empty jars. Don't ask for just a few. ⁴Then go inside and shut the door behind you and your sons. Pour oil into all the jars, and as each is filled, put it to one side."

⁵She left him and afterward shut the door behind her and her sons. They brought the jars to her and she kept pouring. ⁶When all the jars were full, she said to her son, "Bring me another one."

But he replied, "There is not a jar left." Then the oil stopped flowing.

⁷She went and told the man of God, and he said, "Go, sell the oil and pay your debts. You and your sons can live on what is left."

The Shunammite's Son Restored to Life

⁸One day Elisha went to Shunem. And a well-to-do woman was there, who urged him to stay for a meal. So whenever he came by, he stopped there to eat. ⁹She said to her husband, "I know that this man who often comes our way is a holy man of God. ¹⁰Let's make a small room on the roof and put in it a bed and a table, a chair and a lamp for him. Then he can stay there whenever he comes to us."

¹¹One day when Elisha came, he went up to his room and lay down there. ¹²He said to his servant Gehazi, "Call the Shunammite." So he called her, and she stood before him. ¹³Elisha said to him, "Tell her, 'You have gone to all this trouble for us. Now what can be done for you? Can we speak on your behalf to the king or the commander of the army?' "

She replied, "I have a home among my own people."

¹⁴"What can be done for her?" Elisha asked.

Gehazi said, "Well, she has no son and her husband is old."

¹⁵Then Elisha said, "Call her." So he called her, and she stood in the door-

way. [16]"About this time next year," Elisha said, "you will hold a son in your arms."

"No, my lord," she objected. "Don't mislead your servant, O man of God!"

[17]But the woman became pregnant, and the next year about that same time she gave birth to a son, just as Elisha had told her.

[18]The child grew, and one day he went out to his father, who was with the reapers. [19]"My head! My head!" he said to his father.

His father told a servant, "Carry him to his mother." [20]After the servant had lifted him up and carried him to his mother, the boy sat on her lap until noon, and then he died. [21]She went up and laid him on the bed of the man of God, then shut the door and went out.

[22]She called her husband and said, "Please send me one of the servants and a donkey so I can go to the man of God quickly and return."

[23]"Why go to him today?" he asked. "It's not the New Moon or the Sabbath."

"It's all right," she said.

[24]She saddled the donkey and said to her servant, "Lead on; don't slow down for me unless I tell you." [25]So she set out

---

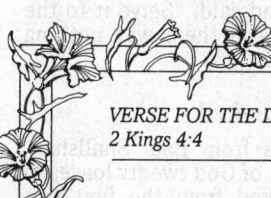

FRIDAY

VERSE FOR THE DAY:
2 Kings 4:4

AUTHOR:
Jeanette Lockerbie

PASSAGE FOR THE DAY:
2 Kings 4:1–7

Shut the Door

HOW often in the course of a day, especially in summer, does the command "Shut the door!" ring out. We shut the door against the inroads of insects, pets, heat (in winter, cold). Springs insure that doors will swing shut even when manipulated by careless or too-tiny hands.

The woman in our reading today had a two-fold need to shut her door. A creditor had come to take her two sons as slaves. She shut *in* her two boys. She shut *out* the world around them. A crisis called for nothing less than intervention from on high, and she had no intention of letting outside interests rob her of the answer to her fervent prayer. In her extreme need she gladly heeded the voice of Elisha, the man of God. The abundance of oil that God supplied met her need of paying debts.

We might well wonder what would have happened had she done everything else God commanded, but had left the door open. Distraction and possibly derision might have moved her to abandon the instructions given by the prophet. We can only speculate, but we do know that unless we deliberately shut out the world's noise there will be little chance to hear the voice of God.

Lord, I have shut the door,
Speak now the word
Which in the din and throng
Could not be heard (William M. Runyan).

Additional Scripture Readings:
2 Kings 4:31–35; Mark 5:37–43

*Go to page 381 for your next
devotional reading.*

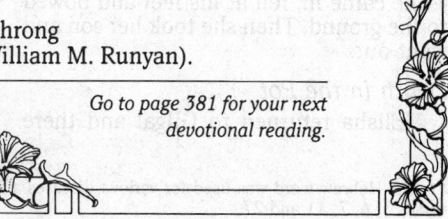

and came to the man of God at Mount Carmel.

When he saw her in the distance, the man of God said to his servant Gehazi, "Look! There's the Shunammite! 26Run to meet her and ask her, 'Are you all right? Is your husband all right? Is your child all right?' "

"Everything is all right," she said.

27When she reached the man of God at the mountain, she took hold of his feet. Gehazi came over to push her away, but the man of God said, "Leave her alone! She is in bitter distress, but the LORD has hidden it from me and has not told me why."

28"Did I ask you for a son, my lord?" she said. "Didn't I tell you, 'Don't raise my hopes'?"

29Elisha said to Gehazi, "Tuck your cloak into your belt, take my staff in your hand and run. If you meet anyone, do not greet him, and if anyone greets you, do not answer. Lay my staff on the boy's face."

30But the child's mother said, "As surely as the LORD lives and as you live, I will not leave you." So he got up and followed her.

31Gehazi went on ahead and laid the staff on the boy's face, but there was no sound or response. So Gehazi went back to meet Elisha and told him, "The boy has not awakened."

32When Elisha reached the house, there was the boy lying dead on his couch. 33He went in, shut the door on the two of them and prayed to the LORD. 34Then he got on the bed and lay upon the boy, mouth to mouth, eyes to eyes, hands to hands. As he stretched himself out upon him, the boy's body grew warm. 35Elisha turned away and walked back and forth in the room and then got on the bed and stretched out upon him once more. The boy sneezed seven times and opened his eyes.

36Elisha summoned Gehazi and said, "Call the Shunammite." And he did. When she came, he said, "Take your son." 37She came in, fell at his feet and bowed to the ground. Then she took her son and went out.

Death in the Pot

38Elisha returned to Gilgal and there was a famine in that region. While the company of the prophets was meeting with him, he said to his servant, "Put on the large pot and cook some stew for these men."

39One of them went out into the fields to gather herbs and found a wild vine. He gathered some of its gourds and filled the fold of his cloak. When he returned, he cut them up into the pot of stew, though no one knew what they were. 40The stew was poured out for the men, but as they began to eat it, they cried out, "O man of God, there is death in the pot!" And they could not eat it.

41Elisha said, "Get some flour." He put it into the pot and said, "Serve it to the people to eat." And there was nothing harmful in the pot.

Feeding of a Hundred

42A man came from Baal Shalishah, bringing the man of God twenty loaves of barley bread baked from the first ripe grain, along with some heads of new grain. "Give it to the people to eat," Elisha said.

43"How can I set this before a hundred men?" his servant asked.

But Elisha answered, "Give it to the people to eat. For this is what the LORD says: 'They will eat and have some left over.' " 44Then he set it before them, and they ate and had some left over, according to the word of the LORD.

Naaman Healed of Leprosy

5 Now Naaman was commander of the army of the king of Aram. He was a great man in the sight of his master and highly regarded, because through him the LORD had given victory to Aram. He was a valiant soldier, but he had leprosy.[a]

2Now bands from Aram had gone out and had taken captive a young girl from Israel, and she served Naaman's wife. 3She said to her mistress, "If only my master would see the prophet who is in Samaria! He would cure him of his leprosy." 4Naaman went to his master and told him what the girl from Israel had said. 5"By all means, go," the king of Aram replied. "I will send a letter to the king of

---

a1 The Hebrew word was used for various diseases affecting the skin—not necessarily leprosy; also in verses 3, 6, 7, 11 and 27.

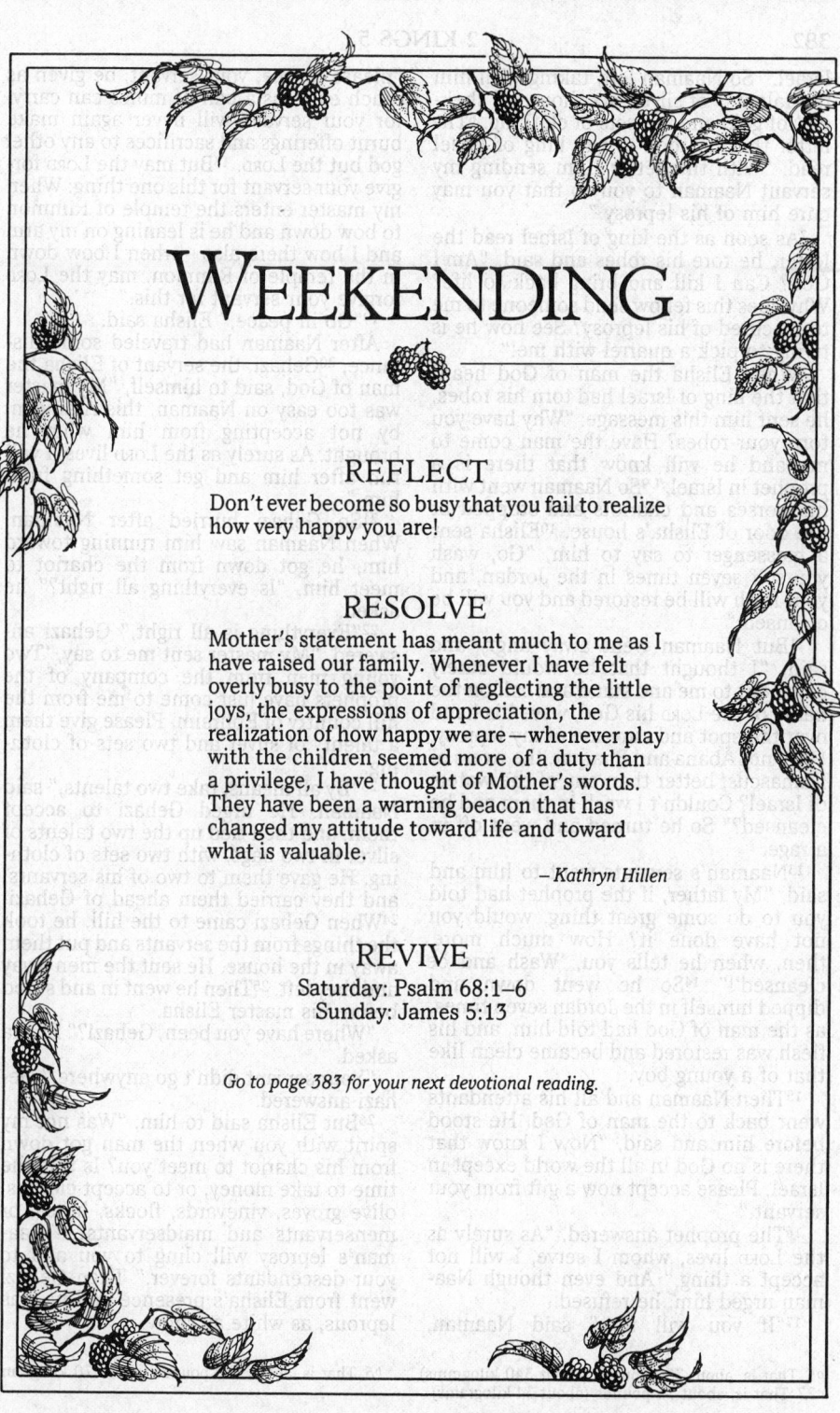

WEEKENDING

REFLECT

Don't ever become so busy that you fail to realize
how very happy you are!

RESOLVE

Mother's statement has meant much to me as I
have raised our family. Whenever I have felt
overly busy to the point of neglecting the little
joys, the expressions of appreciation, the
realization of how happy we are—whenever play
with the children seemed more of a duty than
a privilege, I have thought of Mother's words.
They have been a warning beacon that has
changed my attitude toward life and toward
what is valuable.

— *Kathryn Hillen*

REVIVE

Saturday: Psalm 68:1–6
Sunday: James 5:13

Go to page 383 for your next devotional reading.

Israel." So Naaman left, taking with him ten talents[a] of silver, six thousand shekels[b] of gold and ten sets of clothing. [6]The letter that he took to the king of Israel read: "With this letter I am sending my servant Naaman to you so that you may cure him of his leprosy."

[7]As soon as the king of Israel read the letter, he tore his robes and said, "Am I God? Can I kill and bring back to life? Why does this fellow send someone to me to be cured of his leprosy? See how he is trying to pick a quarrel with me!"

[8]When Elisha the man of God heard that the king of Israel had torn his robes, he sent him this message: "Why have you torn your robes? Have the man come to me and he will know that there is a prophet in Israel." [9]So Naaman went with his horses and chariots and stopped at the door of Elisha's house. [10]Elisha sent a messenger to say to him, "Go, wash yourself seven times in the Jordan, and your flesh will be restored and you will be cleansed."

[11]But Naaman went away angry and said, "I thought that he would surely come out to me and stand and call on the name of the LORD his God, wave his hand over the spot and cure me of my leprosy. [12]Are not Abana and Pharpar, the rivers of Damascus, better than any of the waters of Israel? Couldn't I wash in them and be cleansed?" So he turned and went off in a rage.

[13]Naaman's servants went to him and said, "My father, if the prophet had told you to do some great thing, would you not have done it? How much more, then, when he tells you, 'Wash and be cleansed'!" [14]So he went down and dipped himself in the Jordan seven times, as the man of God had told him, and his flesh was restored and became clean like that of a young boy.

[15]Then Naaman and all his attendants went back to the man of God. He stood before him and said, "Now I know that there is no God in all the world except in Israel. Please accept now a gift from your servant."

[16]The prophet answered, "As surely as the LORD lives, whom I serve, I will not accept a thing." And even though Naaman urged him, he refused.

[17]"If you will not," said Naaman, "please let me, your servant, be given as much earth as a pair of mules can carry, for your servant will never again make burnt offerings and sacrifices to any other god but the LORD. [18]But may the LORD forgive your servant for this one thing: When my master enters the temple of Rimmon to bow down and he is leaning on my arm and I bow there also—when I bow down in the temple of Rimmon, may the LORD forgive your servant for this."

[19]"Go in peace," Elisha said.

After Naaman had traveled some distance, [20]Gehazi, the servant of Elisha the man of God, said to himself, "My master was too easy on Naaman, this Aramean, by not accepting from him what he brought. As surely as the LORD lives, I will run after him and get something from him."

[21]So Gehazi hurried after Naaman. When Naaman saw him running toward him, he got down from the chariot to meet him. "Is everything all right?" he asked.

[22]"Everything is all right," Gehazi answered. "My master sent me to say, 'Two young men from the company of the prophets have just come to me from the hill country of Ephraim. Please give them a talent[c] of silver and two sets of clothing.' "

[23]"By all means, take two talents," said Naaman. He urged Gehazi to accept them, and then tied up the two talents of silver in two bags, with two sets of clothing. He gave them to two of his servants, and they carried them ahead of Gehazi. [24]When Gehazi came to the hill, he took the things from the servants and put them away in the house. He sent the men away and they left. [25]Then he went in and stood before his master Elisha.

"Where have you been, Gehazi?" Elisha asked.

"Your servant didn't go anywhere," Gehazi answered.

[26]But Elisha said to him, "Was not my spirit with you when the man got down from his chariot to meet you? Is this the time to take money, or to accept clothes, olive groves, vineyards, flocks, herds, or menservants and maidservants? [27]Naaman's leprosy will cling to you and to your descendants forever." Then Gehazi went from Elisha's presence and he was leprous, as white as snow.

VERSE FOR THE DAY:
2 Kings 5:3

AUTHOR:
June Gunden

PASSAGE FOR THE DAY:
2 Kings 5:1–15

"Insignificant" Service

HOW much can a young servant girl in a foreign land do for the kingdom of God? Very little, she probably thought. Yet, as a result of her selfless suggestion, the commander of the army of that country was led to confess, "Now I know that there is no God in all the world except in Israel" (2 Kings 5:15).

Do I want to do some great thing for God? Perhaps I feel a touch of envy for missionaries or pastors or great leaders and speakers. Perhaps I feel that because what I am doing does not seem as significant, I am not as pleasing to God.

But service for God cannot be evaluated by comparison to other people. The important thing to God is not how I measure up with others, but how I am doing with what he has given me. In the parable of the talents (Matthew 25:14–30), each person was given an amount of money "according to his ability." The man who was given five talents earned five more; the one who received two talents earned two more; but the man who received one talent buried it, refusing to make use of it in any way. The master condemned this man, not because he did not measure up to the others, but because he did not use what he had been given.

God does not see things as we do. He knows what our capabilities are and how he can best use us. If he asks me to be a caring servant to someone and I obey, that is just the same to him as if he had called me to have a worldwide ministry and I obeyed.

I must not wait for some great opportunity in the future to serve him. Whatever he has given me now I must be willing to use, however insignificant it may appear. The devil loves lethargic dreamers who say, "I could give very little right now. I'll just wait till I am prepared to do something significant." If he can keep you thinking that way, he knows your talent is just as good as buried.

The Master will never give us "big" things to do if we have been unwilling to do "small" things.

Additional Scripture Readings:
Luke 21:1–4; John 6:5–13

*Go to page 403 for your next
devotional reading.*

An Axhead Floats

6 The company of the prophets said to Elisha, "Look, the place where we meet with you is too small for us. ²Let us go to the Jordan, where each of us can get a pole; and let us build a place there for us to live."

And he said, "Go."

³Then one of them said, "Won't you please come with your servants?"

"I will," Elisha replied. ⁴And he went with them.

They went to the Jordan and began to cut down trees. ⁵As one of them was cutting down a tree, the iron axhead fell into the water. "Oh, my lord," he cried out, "it was borrowed!"

⁶The man of God asked, "Where did it fall?" When he showed him the place, Elisha cut a stick and threw it there, and made the iron float. ⁷"Lift it out," he said. Then the man reached out his hand and took it.

Elisha Traps Blinded Arameans

⁸Now the king of Aram was at war with Israel. After conferring with his officers, he said, "I will set up my camp in such and such a place."

⁹The man of God sent word to the king of Israel: "Beware of passing that place, because the Arameans are going down there." ¹⁰So the king of Israel checked on the place indicated by the man of God. Time and again Elisha warned the king, so that he was on his guard in such places.

¹¹This enraged the king of Aram. He summoned his officers and demanded of them, "Will you not tell me which of us is on the side of the king of Israel?"

¹²"None of us, my lord the king," said one of his officers, "but Elisha, the prophet who is in Israel, tells the king of Israel the very words you speak in your bedroom."

¹³"Go, find out where he is," the king ordered, "so I can send men and capture him." The report came back: "He is in Dothan." ¹⁴Then he sent horses and chariots and a strong force there. They went by night and surrounded the city.

¹⁵When the servant of the man of God got up and went out early the next morning, an army with horses and chariots had surrounded the city. "Oh, my lord, what shall we do?" the servant asked.

¹⁶"Don't be afraid," the prophet answered. "Those who are with us are more than those who are with them."

¹⁷And Elisha prayed, "O Lord, open his eyes so he may see." Then the Lord opened the servant's eyes, and he looked and saw the hills full of horses and chariots of fire all around Elisha.

¹⁸As the enemy came down toward him, Elisha prayed to the Lord, "Strike these people with blindness." So he struck them with blindness, as Elisha had asked.

¹⁹Elisha told them, "This is not the road and this is not the city. Follow me, and I will lead you to the man you are looking for." And he led them to Samaria.

²⁰After they entered the city, Elisha said, "Lord, open the eyes of these men so they can see." Then the Lord opened their eyes and they looked, and there they were, inside Samaria.

²¹When the king of Israel saw them, he asked Elisha, "Shall I kill them, my father? Shall I kill them?"

²²"Do not kill them," he answered. "Would you kill men you have captured with your own sword or bow? Set food and water before them so that they may eat and drink and then go back to their master." ²³So he prepared a great feast for them, and after they had finished eating and drinking, he sent them away, and they returned to their master. So the bands from Aram stopped raiding Israel's territory.

Famine in Besieged Samaria

²⁴Some time later, Ben-Hadad king of Aram mobilized his entire army and marched up and laid siege to Samaria. ²⁵There was a great famine in the city; the siege lasted so long that a donkey's head sold for eighty shekels*ᵃ* of silver, and a quarter of a cab*ᵇ* of seed pods*ᶜ* for five shekels.*ᵈ*

²⁶As the king of Israel was passing by on the wall, a woman cried to him, "Help me, my lord the king!"

²⁷The king replied, "If the Lord does not help you, where can I get help for you? From the threshing floor? From the winepress?" ²⁸Then he asked her, "What's the matter?"

She answered, "This woman said to me, 'Give up your son so we may eat him today, and tomorrow we'll eat my son.'

ᵃ25 That is, about 2 pounds (about 1 kilogram)　　*ᵇ25* That is, probably about 1/2 pint (about 0.3 liter)　*ᶜ25* Or *of doves' dung*　　*ᵈ25* That is, about 2 ounces (about 55 grams)

²⁹So we cooked my son and ate him. The next day I said to her, 'Give up your son so we may eat him,' but she had hidden him."

³⁰When the king heard the woman's words, he tore his robes. As he went along the wall, the people looked, and there, underneath, he had sackcloth on his body. ³¹He said, "May God deal with me, be it ever so severely, if the head of Elisha son of Shaphat remains on his shoulders today!"

³²Now Elisha was sitting in his house, and the elders were sitting with him. The king sent a messenger ahead, but before he arrived, Elisha said to the elders, "Don't you see how this murderer is sending someone to cut off my head? Look, when the messenger comes, shut the door and hold it shut against him. Is not the sound of his master's footsteps behind him?" ³³While he was still talking to them, the messenger came down to him. And the king said, "This disaster is from the LORD. Why should I wait for the LORD any longer?"

7 Elisha said, "Hear the word of the LORD. This is what the LORD says: About this time tomorrow, a seah*ᵃ* of flour will sell for a shekel*ᵇ* and two seahs*ᶜ* of barley for a shekel at the gate of Samaria."

²The officer on whose arm the king was leaning said to the man of God, "Look, even if the LORD should open the floodgates of the heavens, could this happen?"

"You will see it with your own eyes," answered Elisha, "but you will not eat any of it!"

The Siege Lifted

³Now there were four men with leprosy*ᵈ* at the entrance of the city gate. They said to each other, "Why stay here until we die? ⁴If we say, 'We'll go into the city'—the famine is there, and we will die. And if we stay here, we will die. So let's go over to the camp of the Arameans and surrender. If they spare us, we live; if they kill us, then we die."

⁵At dusk they got up and went to the camp of the Arameans. When they reached the edge of the camp, not a man was there, ⁶for the Lord had caused the Arameans to hear the sound of chariots and horses and a great army, so that they said to one another, "Look, the king of Israel has hired the Hittite and Egyptian kings to attack us!" ⁷So they got up and fled in the dusk and abandoned their tents and their horses and donkeys. They left the camp as it was and ran for their lives.

⁸The men who had leprosy reached the edge of the camp and entered one of the tents. They ate and drank, and carried away silver, gold and clothes, and went off and hid them. They returned and entered another tent and took some things from it and hid them also.

⁹Then they said to each other, "We're not doing right. This is a day of good news and we are keeping it to ourselves. If we wait until daylight, punishment will overtake us. Let's go at once and report this to the royal palace."

¹⁰So they went and called out to the city gatekeepers and told them, "We went into the Aramean camp and not a man was there—not a sound of anyone—only tethered horses and donkeys, and the tents left just as they were." ¹¹The gatekeepers shouted the news, and it was reported within the palace.

¹²The king got up in the night and said to his officers, "I will tell you what the Arameans have done to us. They know we are starving; so they have left the camp to hide in the countryside, thinking, 'They will surely come out, and then we will take them alive and get into the city.' "

¹³One of his officers answered, "Have some men take five of the horses that are left in the city. Their plight will be like that of all the Israelites left here—yes, they will only be like all these Israelites who are doomed. So let us send them to find out what happened."

¹⁴So they selected two chariots with their horses, and the king sent them after the Aramean army. He commanded the drivers, "Go and find out what has happened." ¹⁵They followed them as far as the Jordan, and they found the whole road strewn with the clothing and equipment the Arameans had thrown away in their headlong flight. So the messengers returned and reported to the king. ¹⁶Then the people went out and plundered the

---

ᵃ1 That is, probably about 7 quarts (about 7.3 liters); also in verses 16 and 18   *ᵇ1* That is, about 2/5 ounce (about 11 grams); also in verses 16 and 18   *ᶜ1* That is, probably about 13 quarts (about 15 liters); also in verses 16 and 18   *ᵈ3* The Hebrew word is used for various diseases affecting the skin—not necessarily leprosy; also in verse 8.

camp of the Arameans. So a seah of flour sold for a shekel, and two seahs of barley sold for a shekel, as the LORD had said.

¹⁷Now the king had put the officer on whose arm he leaned in charge of the gate, and the people trampled him in the gateway, and he died, just as the man of God had foretold when the king came down to his house. ¹⁸It happened as the man of God had said to the king: "About this time tomorrow, a seah of flour will sell for a shekel and two seahs of barley for a shekel at the gate of Samaria."

¹⁹The officer had said to the man of God, "Look, even if the LORD should open the floodgates of the heavens, could this happen?" The man of God had replied, "You will see it with your own eyes, but you will not eat any of it!" ²⁰And that is exactly what happened to him, for the people trampled him in the gateway, and he died.

The Shunammite's Land Restored

8 Now Elisha had said to the woman whose son he had restored to life, "Go away with your family and stay for a while wherever you can, because the LORD has decreed a famine in the land that will last seven years." ²The woman proceeded to do as the man of God said. She and her family went away and stayed in the land of the Philistines seven years.

³At the end of the seven years she came back from the land of the Philistines and went to the king to beg for her house and land. ⁴The king was talking to Gehazi, the servant of the man of God, and had said, "Tell me about all the great things Elisha has done." ⁵Just as Gehazi was telling the king how Elisha had restored the dead to life, the woman whose son Elisha had brought back to life came to beg the king for her house and land.

Gehazi said, "This is the woman, my lord the king, and this is her son whom Elisha restored to life." ⁶The king asked the woman about it, and she told him.

Then he assigned an official to her case and said to him, "Give back everything that belonged to her, including all the income from her land from the day she left the country until now."

Hazael Murders Ben-Hadad

⁷Elisha went to Damascus, and Ben-Hadad king of Aram was ill. When the king was told, "The man of God has come

all the way up here," ⁸he said to Hazael, "Take a gift with you and go to meet the man of God. Consult the LORD through him; ask him, 'Will I recover from this illness?' "

⁹Hazael went to meet Elisha, taking with him as a gift forty camel-loads of all the finest wares of Damascus. He went in and stood before him, and said, "Your son Ben-Hadad king of Aram has sent me to ask, 'Will I recover from this illness?' "

¹⁰Elisha answered, "Go and say to him, 'You will certainly recover'; but^a the LORD has revealed to me that he will in fact die." ¹¹He stared at him with a fixed gaze until Hazael felt ashamed. Then the man of God began to weep.

¹²"Why is my lord weeping?" asked Hazael.

"Because I know the harm you will do to the Israelites," he answered. "You will set fire to their fortified places, kill their young men with the sword, dash their little children to the ground, and rip open their pregnant women."

¹³Hazael said, "How could your servant, a mere dog, accomplish such a feat?"

"The LORD has shown me that you will become king of Aram," answered Elisha.

¹⁴Then Hazael left Elisha and returned to his master. When Ben-Hadad asked, "What did Elisha say to you?" Hazael replied, "He told me that you would certainly recover." ¹⁵But the next day he took a thick cloth, soaked it in water and spread it over the king's face, so that he died. Then Hazael succeeded him as king.

Jehoram King of Judah

¹⁶In the fifth year of Joram son of Ahab king of Israel, when Jehoshaphat was king of Judah, Jehoram son of Jehoshaphat began his reign as king of Judah. ¹⁷He was thirty-two years old when he became king, and he reigned in Jerusalem eight years. ¹⁸He walked in the ways of the kings of Israel, as the house of Ahab had done, for he married a daughter of Ahab. He did evil in the eyes of the LORD. ¹⁹Nevertheless, for the sake of his servant David, the LORD was not willing to destroy Judah. He had promised to maintain a lamp for David and his descendants forever.

²⁰In the time of Jehoram, Edom rebelled against Judah and set up its own

---

^a10 The Hebrew may also be read *Go and say, 'You will certainly not recover,' for.*

king. [21]So Jehoram[a] went to Zair with all his chariots. The Edomites surrounded him and his chariot commanders, but he rose up and broke through by night; his army, however, fled back home. [22]To this day Edom has been in rebellion against Judah. Libnah revolted at the same time.

[23]As for the other events of Jehoram's reign, and all he did, are they not written in the book of the annals of the kings of Judah? [24]Jehoram rested with his fathers and was buried with them in the City of David. And Ahaziah his son succeeded him as king.

Ahaziah King of Judah

[25]In the twelfth year of Joram son of Ahab king of Israel, Ahaziah son of Jehoram king of Judah began to reign. [26]Ahaziah was twenty-two years old when he became king, and he reigned in Jerusalem one year. His mother's name was Athaliah, a granddaughter of Omri king of Israel. [27]He walked in the ways of the house of Ahab and did evil in the eyes of the LORD, as the house of Ahab had done, for he was related by marriage to Ahab's family.

[28]Ahaziah went with Joram son of Ahab to war against Hazael king of Aram at Ramoth Gilead. The Arameans wounded Joram; [29]so King Joram returned to Jezreel to recover from the wounds the Arameans had inflicted on him at Ramoth[b] in his battle with Hazael king of Aram.

Then Ahaziah son of Jehoram king of Judah went down to Jezreel to see Joram son of Ahab, because he had been wounded.

Jehu Anointed King of Israel

9 The prophet Elisha summoned a man from the company of the prophets and said to him, "Tuck your cloak into your belt, take this flask of oil with you and go to Ramoth Gilead. [2]When you get there, look for Jehu son of Jehoshaphat, the son of Nimshi. Go to him, get him away from his companions and take him into an inner room. [3]Then take the flask and pour the oil on his head and declare, 'This is what the LORD says: I anoint you king over Israel.' Then open the door and run; don't delay!"

[4]So the young man, the prophet, went to Ramoth Gilead. [5]When he arrived, he found the army officers sitting together. "I have a message for you, commander," he said.

"For which of us?" asked Jehu.

"For you, commander," he replied.

[6]Jehu got up and went into the house. Then the prophet poured the oil on Jehu's head and declared, "This is what the LORD, the God of Israel, says: 'I anoint you king over the LORD's people Israel. [7]You are to destroy the house of Ahab your master, and I will avenge the blood of my servants the prophets and the blood of all the LORD's servants shed by Jezebel. [8]The whole house of Ahab will perish. I will cut off from Ahab every last male in Israel—slave or free. [9]I will make the house of Ahab like the house of Jeroboam son of Nebat and like the house of Baasha son of Ahijah. [10]As for Jezebel, dogs will devour her on the plot of ground at Jezreel, and no one will bury her.' " Then he opened the door and ran.

[11]When Jehu went out to his fellow officers, one of them asked him, "Is everything all right? Why did this madman come to you?"

"You know the man and the sort of things he says," Jehu replied.

[12]"That's not true!" they said. "Tell us."

Jehu said, "Here is what he told me: 'This is what the LORD says: I anoint you king over Israel.' "

[13]They hurried and took their cloaks and spread them under him on the bare steps. Then they blew the trumpet and shouted, "Jehu is king!"

Jehu Kills Joram and Ahaziah

[14]So Jehu son of Jehoshaphat, the son of Nimshi, conspired against Joram. (Now Joram and all Israel had been defending Ramoth Gilead against Hazael king of Aram, [15]but King Joram[c] had returned to Jezreel to recover from the wounds the Arameans had inflicted on him in the battle with Hazael king of Aram.) Jehu said, "If this is the way you feel, don't let anyone slip out of the city to go and tell the news in Jezreel." [16]Then he got into his chariot and rode to Jezreel, because Joram was resting there and Ahaziah king of Judah had gone down to see him.

[17]When the lookout standing on the tower in Jezreel saw Jehu's troops approaching, he called out, "I see some troops coming."

---

[a]21 Hebrew *Joram*, a variant of *Jehoram*; also in verses 23 and 24   [b]29 Hebrew *Ramah*, a variant of *Ramoth*   [c]15 Hebrew *Jehoram*, a variant of *Joram*; also in verses 17 and 21-24

"Get a horseman," Joram ordered. "Send him to meet them and ask, 'Do you come in peace?' "

[18]The horseman rode off to meet Jehu and said, "This is what the king says: 'Do you come in peace?' "

"What do you have to do with peace?" Jehu replied. "Fall in behind me."

The lookout reported, "The messenger has reached them, but he isn't coming back."

[19]So the king sent out a second horseman. When he came to them he said, "This is what the king says: 'Do you come in peace?' "

Jehu replied, "What do you have to do with peace? Fall in behind me."

[20]The lookout reported, "He has reached them, but he isn't coming back either. The driving is like that of Jehu son of Nimshi—he drives like a madman."

[21]"Hitch up my chariot," Joram ordered. And when it was hitched up, Joram king of Israel and Ahaziah king of Judah rode out, each in his own chariot, to meet Jehu. They met him at the plot of ground that had belonged to Naboth the Jezreelite. [22]When Joram saw Jehu he asked, "Have you come in peace, Jehu?"

"How can there be peace," Jehu replied, "as long as all the idolatry and witchcraft of your mother Jezebel abound?"

[23]Joram turned about and fled, calling out to Ahaziah, "Treachery, Ahaziah!"

[24]Then Jehu drew his bow and shot Joram between the shoulders. The arrow pierced his heart and he slumped down in his chariot. [25]Jehu said to Bidkar, his chariot officer, "Pick him up and throw him on the field that belonged to Naboth the Jezreelite. Remember how you and I were riding together in chariots behind Ahab his father when the LORD made this prophecy about him: [26]'Yesterday I saw the blood of Naboth and the blood of his sons, declares the LORD, and I will surely make you pay for it on this plot of ground, declares the LORD.'[a] Now then, pick him up and throw him on that plot, in accordance with the word of the LORD."

[27]When Ahaziah king of Judah saw what had happened, he fled up the road to Beth Haggan.[b] Jehu chased him, shouting, "Kill him too!" They wounded him in his chariot on the way up to Gur

near Ibleam, but he escaped to Megiddo and died there. [28]His servants took him by chariot to Jerusalem and buried him with his fathers in his tomb in the City of David. [29](In the eleventh year of Joram son of Ahab, Ahaziah had become king of Judah.)

Jezebel Killed

[30]Then Jehu went to Jezreel. When Jezebel heard about it, she painted her eyes, arranged her hair and looked out of a window. [31]As Jehu entered the gate, she asked, "Have you come in peace, Zimri, you murderer of your master?"[c]

[32]He looked up at the window and called out, "Who is on my side? Who?" Two or three eunuchs looked down at him. [33]"Throw her down!" Jehu said. So they threw her down, and some of her blood spattered the wall and the horses as they trampled her underfoot.

[34]Jehu went in and ate and drank. "Take care of that cursed woman," he said, "and bury her, for she was a king's daughter." [35]But when they went out to bury her, they found nothing except her skull, her feet and her hands. [36]They went back and told Jehu, who said, "This is the word of the LORD that he spoke through his servant Elijah the Tishbite: On the plot of ground at Jezreel dogs will devour Jezebel's flesh.[d] [37]Jezebel's body will be like refuse on the ground in the plot at Jezreel, so that no one will be able to say, 'This is Jezebel.' "

Ahab's Family Killed

10 Now there were in Samaria seventy sons of the house of Ahab. So Jehu wrote letters and sent them to Samaria: to the officials of Jezreel,[e] to the elders and to the guardians of Ahab's children. He said, [2]"As soon as this letter reaches you, since your master's sons are with you and you have chariots and horses, a fortified city and weapons, [3]choose the best and most worthy of your master's sons and set him on his father's throne. Then fight for your master's house."

[4]But they were terrified and said, "If two kings could not resist him, how can we?"

[5]So the palace administrator, the city governor, the elders and the guardians

sent this message to Jehu: "We are your servants and we will do anything you say. We will not appoint anyone as king; you do whatever you think best."

⁶Then Jehu wrote them a second letter, saying, "If you are on my side and will obey me, take the heads of your master's sons and come to me in Jezreel by this time tomorrow."

Now the royal princes, seventy of them, were with the leading men of the city, who were rearing them. ⁷When the letter arrived, these men took the princes and slaughtered all seventy of them. They put their heads in baskets and sent them to Jehu in Jezreel. ⁸When the messenger arrived, he told Jehu, "They have brought the heads of the princes."

Then Jehu ordered, "Put them in two piles at the entrance of the city gate until morning."

⁹The next morning Jehu went out. He stood before all the people and said, "You are innocent. It was I who conspired against my master and killed him, but who killed all these? ¹⁰Know then, that not a word the LORD has spoken against the house of Ahab will fail. The LORD has done what he promised through his servant Elijah." ¹¹So Jehu killed everyone in Jezreel who remained of the house of Ahab, as well as all his chief men, his close friends and his priests, leaving him no survivor.

¹²Jehu then set out and went toward Samaria. At Beth Eked of the Shepherds, ¹³he met some relatives of Ahaziah king of Judah and asked, "Who are you?"

They said, "We are relatives of Ahaziah, and we have come down to greet the families of the king and of the queen mother."

¹⁴"Take them alive!" he ordered. So they took them alive and slaughtered them by the well of Beth Eked—forty-two men. He left no survivor.

¹⁵After he left there, he came upon Jehonadab son of Recab, who was on his way to meet him. Jehu greeted him and said, "Are you in accord with me, as I am with you?"

"I am," Jehonadab answered.

"If so," said Jehu, "give me your hand." So he did, and Jehu helped him up into the chariot. ¹⁶Jehu said, "Come with me and see my zeal for the LORD." Then he had him ride along in his chariot.

¹⁷When Jehu came to Samaria, he killed all who were left there of Ahab's family; he destroyed them, according to the word of the LORD spoken to Elijah.

Ministers of Baal Killed

¹⁸Then Jehu brought all the people together and said to them, "Ahab served Baal a little; Jehu will serve him much. ¹⁹Now summon all the prophets of Baal, all his ministers and all his priests. See that no one is missing, because I am going to hold a great sacrifice for Baal. Anyone who fails to come will no longer live." But Jehu was acting deceptively in order to destroy the ministers of Baal.

²⁰Jehu said, "Call an assembly in honor of Baal." So they proclaimed it. ²¹Then he sent word throughout Israel, and all the ministers of Baal came; not one stayed away. They crowded into the temple of Baal until it was full from one end to the other. ²²And Jehu said to the keeper of the wardrobe, "Bring robes for all the ministers of Baal." So he brought out robes for them.

²³Then Jehu and Jehonadab son of Recab went into the temple of Baal. Jehu said to the ministers of Baal, "Look around and see that no servants of the LORD are here with you—only ministers of Baal." ²⁴So they went in to make sacrifices and burnt offerings. Now Jehu had posted eighty men outside with this warning: "If one of you lets any of the men I am placing in your hands escape, it will be your life for his life."

²⁵As soon as Jehu had finished making the burnt offering, he ordered the guards and officers: "Go in and kill them; let no one escape." So they cut them down with the sword. The guards and officers threw the bodies out and then entered the inner shrine of the temple of Baal. ²⁶They brought the sacred stone out of the temple of Baal and burned it. ²⁷They demolished the sacred stone of Baal and tore down the temple of Baal, and people have used it for a latrine to this day.

²⁸So Jehu destroyed Baal worship in Israel. ²⁹However, he did not turn away from the sins of Jeroboam son of Nebat, which he had caused Israel to commit—the worship of the golden calves at Bethel and Dan.

³⁰The LORD said to Jehu, "Because you have done well in accomplishing what is right in my eyes and have done to the house of Ahab all I had in mind to do, your descendants will sit on the throne of Israel to the fourth generation." ³¹Yet Jehu was not careful to keep the law of the LORD, the God of Israel, with all his

heart. He did not turn away from the sins of Jeroboam, which he had caused Israel to commit.

32In those days the LORD began to reduce the size of Israel. Hazael overpowered the Israelites throughout their territory 33east of the Jordan in all the land of Gilead (the region of Gad, Reuben and Manasseh), from Aroer by the Arnon Gorge through Gilead to Bashan.

34As for the other events of Jehu's reign, all he did, and all his achievements, are they not written in the book of the annals of the kings of Israel?

35Jehu rested with his fathers and was buried in Samaria. And Jehoahaz his son succeeded him as king. 36The time that Jehu reigned over Israel in Samaria was twenty-eight years.

Athaliah and Joash

11 When Athaliah the mother of Ahaziah saw that her son was dead, she proceeded to destroy the whole royal family. 2But Jehosheba, the daughter of King Jehoram[a] and sister of Ahaziah, took Joash son of Ahaziah and stole him away from among the royal princes, who were about to be murdered. She put him and his nurse in a bedroom to hide him from Athaliah; so he was not killed. 3He remained hidden with his nurse at the temple of the LORD for six years while Athaliah ruled the land.

4In the seventh year Jehoiada sent for the commanders of units of a hundred, the Carites and the guards and had them brought to him at the temple of the LORD. He made a covenant with them and put them under oath at the temple of the LORD. Then he showed them the king's son. 5He commanded them, saying, "This is what you are to do: You who are in the three companies that are going on duty on the Sabbath—a third of you guarding the royal palace, 6a third at the Sur Gate, and a third at the gate behind the guard, who take turns guarding the temple—7and you who are in the other two companies that normally go off Sabbath duty are all to guard the temple for the king. 8Station yourselves around the king, each man with his weapon in his hand. Anyone who approaches your ranks[b] must be put to death. Stay close to the king wherever he goes."

9The commanders of units of a hun-

dred did just as Jehoiada the priest ordered. Each one took his men—those who were going on duty on the Sabbath and those who were going off duty—and came to Jehoiada the priest. 10Then he gave the commanders the spears and shields that had belonged to King David and that were in the temple of the LORD. 11The guards, each with his weapon in his hand, stationed themselves around the king—near the altar and the temple, from the south side to the north side of the temple.

12Jehoiada brought out the king's son and put the crown on him; he presented him with a copy of the covenant and proclaimed him king. They anointed him, and the people clapped their hands and shouted, "Long live the king!"

13When Athaliah heard the noise made by the guards and the people, she went to the people at the temple of the LORD. 14She looked and there was the king, standing by the pillar, as the custom was. The officers and the trumpeters were beside the king, and all the people of the land were rejoicing and blowing trumpets. Then Athaliah tore her robes and called out, "Treason! Treason!"

15Jehoiada the priest ordered the commanders of units of a hundred, who were in charge of the troops: "Bring her out between the ranks[c] and put to the sword anyone who follows her." For the priest had said, "She must not be put to death in the temple of the LORD." 16So they seized her as she reached the place where the horses enter the palace grounds, and there she was put to death.

17Jehoiada then made a covenant between the LORD and the king and people that they would be the LORD's people. He also made a covenant between the king and the people. 18All the people of the land went to the temple of Baal and tore it down. They smashed the altars and idols to pieces and killed Mattan the priest of Baal in front of the altars.

Then Jehoiada the priest posted guards at the temple of the LORD. 19He took with him the commanders of hundreds, the Carites, the guards and all the people of the land, and together they brought the king down from the temple of the LORD and went into the palace, entering by way of the gate of the guards. The king then took his place on the royal throne, 20and

---

a2 Hebrew *Joram*, a variant of *Jehoram*   b8 Or *approaches the precincts*   c15 Or *out from the precincts* all the people of the land rejoiced. And the city was quiet, because Athaliah had been slain with the sword at the palace.

²¹Joash*a* was seven years old when he began to reign.

Joash Repairs the Temple

12 In the seventh year of Jehu, Joash*b* became king, and he reigned in Jerusalem forty years. His mother's name was Zibiah; she was from Beersheba. ²Joash did what was right in the eyes of the Lord all the years Jehoiada the priest instructed him. ³The high places, however, were not removed; the people continued to offer sacrifices and burn incense there.

⁴Joash said to the priests, "Collect all the money that is brought as sacred offerings to the temple of the Lord—the money collected in the census, the money received from personal vows and the money brought voluntarily to the temple. ⁵Let every priest receive the money from one of the treasurers, and let it be used to repair whatever damage is found in the temple."

⁶But by the twenty-third year of King Joash the priests still had not repaired the temple. ⁷Therefore King Joash summoned Jehoiada the priest and the other priests and asked them, "Why aren't you repairing the damage done to the temple? Take no more money from your treasurers, but hand it over for repairing the temple." ⁸The priests agreed that they would not collect any more money from the people and that they would not repair the temple themselves.

⁹Jehoiada the priest took a chest and bored a hole in its lid. He placed it beside the altar, on the right side as one enters the temple of the Lord. The priests who guarded the entrance put into the chest all the money that was brought to the temple of the Lord. ¹⁰Whenever they saw that there was a large amount of money in the chest, the royal secretary and the high priest came, counted the money that had been brought into the temple of the Lord and put it into bags. ¹¹When the amount had been determined, they gave the money to the men appointed to supervise the work on the temple. With it they paid those who worked on the temple of the Lord—the carpenters and builders, ¹²the masons and stonecutters. They pur-

chased timber and dressed stone for the repair of the temple of the Lord, and met all the other expenses of restoring the temple.

¹³The money brought into the temple was not spent for making silver basins, wick trimmers, sprinkling bowls, trumpets or any other articles of gold or silver for the temple of the Lord; ¹⁴it was paid to the workmen, who used it to repair the temple. ¹⁵They did not require an accounting from those to whom they gave the money to pay the workers, because they acted with complete honesty. ¹⁶The money from the guilt offerings and sin offerings was not brought into the temple of the Lord; it belonged to the priests.

¹⁷About this time Hazael king of Aram went up and attacked Gath and captured it. Then he turned to attack Jerusalem. ¹⁸But Joash king of Judah took all the sacred objects dedicated by his fathers—Jehoshaphat, Jehoram and Ahaziah, the kings of Judah—and the gifts he himself had dedicated and all the gold found in the treasuries of the temple of the Lord and of the royal palace, and he sent them to Hazael king of Aram, who then withdrew from Jerusalem.

¹⁹As for the other events of the reign of Joash, and all he did, are they not written in the book of the annals of the kings of Judah? ²⁰His officials conspired against him and assassinated him at Beth Millo, on the road down to Silla. ²¹The officials who murdered him were Jozabad son of Shimeath and Jehozabad son of Shomer. He died and was buried with his fathers in the City of David. And Amaziah his son succeeded him as king.

Jehoahaz King of Israel

13 In the twenty-third year of Joash son of Ahaziah king of Judah, Jehoahaz son of Jehu became king of Israel in Samaria, and he reigned seventeen years. ²He did evil in the eyes of the Lord by following the sins of Jeroboam son of Nebat, which he had caused Israel to commit, and he did not turn away from them. ³So the Lord's anger burned against Israel, and for a long time he kept them under the power of Hazael king of Aram and Ben-Hadad his son.

⁴Then Jehoahaz sought the Lord's favor, and the Lord listened to him, for he saw how severely the king of Aram was

---

a21 Hebrew *Jehoash*, a variant of *Joash*   *b1* Hebrew *Jehoash*, a variant of *Joash*; also in verses 2, 4, 6, 7 and 18 oppressing Israel. ⁵The LORD provided a deliverer for Israel, and they escaped from the power of Aram. So the Israelites lived in their own homes as they had before. ⁶But they did not turn away from the sins of the house of Jeroboam, which he had caused Israel to commit; they continued in them. Also, the Asherah pole*ᵃ* remained standing in Samaria.

⁷Nothing had been left of the army of Jehoahaz except fifty horsemen, ten chariots and ten thousand foot soldiers, for the king of Aram had destroyed the rest and made them like the dust at threshing time.

⁸As for the other events of the reign of Jehoahaz, all he did and his achievements, are they not written in the book of the annals of the kings of Israel? ⁹Jehoahaz rested with his fathers and was buried in Samaria. And Jehoash*ᵇ* his son succeeded him as king.

Jehoash King of Israel

¹⁰In the thirty-seventh year of Joash king of Judah, Jehoash son of Jehoahaz became king of Israel in Samaria, and he reigned sixteen years. ¹¹He did evil in the eyes of the LORD and did not turn away from any of the sins of Jeroboam son of Nebat, which he had caused Israel to commit; he continued in them.

¹²As for the other events of the reign of Jehoash, all he did and his achievements, including his war against Amaziah king of Judah, are they not written in the book of the annals of the kings of Israel? ¹³Jehoash rested with his fathers, and Jeroboam succeeded him on the throne. Jehoash was buried in Samaria with the kings of Israel.

¹⁴Now Elisha was suffering from the illness from which he died. Jehoash king of Israel went down to see him and wept over him. "My father! My father!" he cried. "The chariots and horsemen of Israel!"

¹⁵Elisha said, "Get a bow and some arrows," and he did so. ¹⁶"Take the bow in your hands," he said to the king of Israel. When he had taken it, Elisha put his hands on the king's hands.

¹⁷"Open the east window," he said, and he opened it. "Shoot!" Elisha said, and he shot. "The LORD's arrow of victory, the arrow of victory over Aram!" Elisha declared. "You will completely destroy the Arameans at Aphek."

¹⁸Then he said, "Take the arrows," and the king took them. Elisha told him, "Strike the ground." He struck it three times and stopped. ¹⁹The man of God was angry with him and said, "You should have struck the ground five or six times; then you would have defeated Aram and completely destroyed it. But now you will defeat it only three times."

²⁰Elisha died and was buried.

Now Moabite raiders used to enter the country every spring. ²¹Once while some Israelites were burying a man, suddenly they saw a band of raiders; so they threw the man's body into Elisha's tomb. When the body touched Elisha's bones, the man came to life and stood up on his feet.

²²Hazael king of Aram oppressed Israel throughout the reign of Jehoahaz. ²³But the LORD was gracious to them and had compassion and showed concern for them because of his covenant with Abraham, Isaac and Jacob. To this day he has been unwilling to destroy them or banish them from his presence.

²⁴Hazael king of Aram died, and Ben-Hadad his son succeeded him as king. ²⁵Then Jehoash son of Jehoahaz recaptured from Ben-Hadad son of Hazael the towns he had taken in battle from his father Jehoahaz. Three times Jehoash defeated him, and so he recovered the Israelite towns.

Amaziah King of Judah

14 In the second year of Jehoash*ᶜ* son of Jehoahaz king of Israel, Amaziah son of Joash king of Judah began to reign. ²He was twenty-five years old when he became king, and he reigned in Jerusalem twenty-nine years. His mother's name was Jehoaddin; she was from Jerusalem. ³He did what was right in the eyes of the LORD, but not as his father David had done. In everything he followed the example of his father Joash. ⁴The high places, however, were not removed; the people continued to offer sacrifices and burn incense there.

⁵After the kingdom was firmly in his grasp, he executed the officials who had murdered his father the king. ⁶Yet he did not put the sons of the assassins to death, in accordance with what is written in the

---

ᵃ6 That is, a symbol of the goddess Asherah; here and elsewhere in 2 Kings   *ᵇ9* Hebrew *Joash,* a variant of *Jehoash*; also in verses 12-14 and 25   *ᶜ1* Hebrew *Joash,* a variant of *Jehoash*; also in verses 13, 23 and 27

Book of the Law of Moses where the LORD commanded: "Fathers shall not be put to death for their children, nor children put to death for their fathers; each is to die for his own sins." *a*

7He was the one who defeated ten thousand Edomites in the Valley of Salt and captured Sela in battle, calling it Joktheel, the name it has to this day.

8Then Amaziah sent messengers to Jehoash son of Jehoahaz, the son of Jehu, king of Israel, with the challenge: "Come, meet me face to face."

9But Jehoash king of Israel replied to Amaziah king of Judah: "A thistle in Lebanon sent a message to a cedar in Lebanon, 'Give your daughter to my son in marriage.' Then a wild beast in Lebanon came along and trampled the thistle underfoot. 10You have indeed defeated Edom and now you are arrogant. Glory in your victory, but stay at home! Why ask for trouble and cause your own downfall and that of Judah also?"

11Amaziah, however, would not listen, so Jehoash king of Israel attacked. He and Amaziah king of Judah faced each other at Beth Shemesh in Judah. 12Judah was routed by Israel, and every man fled to his home. 13Jehoash king of Israel captured Amaziah king of Judah, the son of Joash, the son of Ahaziah, at Beth Shemesh. Then Jehoash went to Jerusalem and broke down the wall of Jerusalem from the Ephraim Gate to the Corner Gate—a section about six hundred feet long.*b* 14He took all the gold and silver and all the articles found in the temple of the LORD and in the treasuries of the royal palace. He also took hostages and returned to Samaria.

15As for the other events of the reign of Jehoash, what he did and his achievements, including his war against Amaziah king of Judah, are they not written in the book of the annals of the kings of Israel? 16Jehoash rested with his fathers and was buried in Samaria with the kings of Israel. And Jeroboam his son succeeded him as king.

17Amaziah son of Joash king of Judah lived for fifteen years after the death of Jehoash son of Jehoahaz king of Israel. 18As for the other events of Amaziah's reign, are they not written in the book of the annals of the kings of Judah?

19They conspired against him in Jeru-

salem, and he fled to Lachish, but they sent men after him to Lachish and killed him there. 20He was brought back by horse and was buried in Jerusalem with his fathers, in the City of David.

21Then all the people of Judah took Azariah,*c* who was sixteen years old, and made him king in place of his father Amaziah. 22He was the one who rebuilt Elath and restored it to Judah after Amaziah rested with his fathers.

Jeroboam II King of Israel

23In the fifteenth year of Amaziah son of Joash king of Judah, Jeroboam son of Jehoash king of Israel became king in Samaria, and he reigned forty-one years. 24He did evil in the eyes of the LORD and did not turn away from any of the sins of Jeroboam son of Nebat, which he had caused Israel to commit. 25He was the one who restored the boundaries of Israel from Lebo*d* Hamath to the Sea of the Arabah,*e* in accordance with the word of the LORD, the God of Israel, spoken through his servant Jonah son of Amittai, the prophet from Gath Hepher.

26The LORD had seen how bitterly everyone in Israel, whether slave or free, was suffering; there was no one to help them. 27And since the LORD had not said he would blot out the name of Israel from under heaven, he saved them by the hand of Jeroboam son of Jehoash.

28As for the other events of Jeroboam's reign, all he did, and his military achievements, including how he recovered for Israel both Damascus and Hamath, which had belonged to Yaudi,*f* are they not written in the book of the annals of the kings of Israel? 29Jeroboam rested with his fathers, the kings of Israel. And Zechariah his son succeeded him as king.

Azariah King of Judah

15 In the twenty-seventh year of Jeroboam king of Israel, Azariah son of Amaziah king of Judah began to reign. 2He was sixteen years old when he became king, and he reigned in Jerusalem fifty-two years. His mother's name was Jecoliah; she was from Jerusalem. 3He did what was right in the eyes of the LORD, just as his father Amaziah had done. 4The high places, however, were not removed; the people continued to offer sacrifices and burn incense there.

a6 Deut. 24:16   b13 Hebrew four hundred cubits (about 180 meters)   c21 Also called Uzziah
d25 Or from the entrance to   e25 That is, the Dead Sea   f28 Or Judah

⁵The LORD afflicted the king with leprosy[a] until the day he died, and he lived in a separate house.[b] Jotham the king's son had charge of the palace and governed the people of the land.

⁶As for the other events of Azariah's reign, and all he did, are they not written in the book of the annals of the kings of Judah? ⁷Azariah rested with his fathers and was buried near them in the City of David. And Jotham his son succeeded him as king.

Zechariah King of Israel

⁸In the thirty-eighth year of Azariah king of Judah, Zechariah son of Jeroboam became king of Israel in Samaria, and he reigned six months. ⁹He did evil in the eyes of the LORD, as his fathers had done. He did not turn away from the sins of Jeroboam son of Nebat, which he had caused Israel to commit.

¹⁰Shallum son of Jabesh conspired against Zechariah. He attacked him in front of the people,[c] assassinated him and succeeded him as king. ¹¹The other events of Zechariah's reign are written in the book of the annals of the kings of Israel. ¹²So the word of the LORD spoken to Jehu was fulfilled: "Your descendants will sit on the throne of Israel to the fourth generation."[d]

Shallum King of Israel

¹³Shallum son of Jabesh became king in the thirty-ninth year of Uzziah king of Judah, and he reigned in Samaria one month. ¹⁴Then Menahem son of Gadi went from Tirzah up to Samaria. He attacked Shallum son of Jabesh in Samaria, assassinated him and succeeded him as king.

¹⁵The other events of Shallum's reign, and the conspiracy he led, are written in the book of the annals of the kings of Israel.

¹⁶At that time Menahem, starting out from Tirzah, attacked Tiphsah and everyone in the city and its vicinity, because they refused to open their gates. He sacked Tiphsah and ripped open all the pregnant women.

Menahem King of Israel

¹⁷In the thirty-ninth year of Azariah king of Judah, Menahem son of Gadi became king of Israel, and he reigned in Samaria ten years. ¹⁸He did evil in the eyes of the LORD. During his entire reign he did not turn away from the sins of Jeroboam son of Nebat, which he had caused Israel to commit.

¹⁹Then Pul[e] king of Assyria invaded the land, and Menahem gave him a thousand talents[f] of silver to gain his support and strengthen his own hold on the kingdom. ²⁰Menahem exacted this money from Israel. Every wealthy man had to contribute fifty shekels[g] of silver to be given to the king of Assyria. So the king of Assyria withdrew and stayed in the land no longer.

²¹As for the other events of Menahem's reign, and all he did, are they not written in the book of the annals of the kings of Israel? ²²Menahem rested with his fathers. And Pekahiah his son succeeded him as king.

Pekahiah King of Israel

²³In the fiftieth year of Azariah king of Judah, Pekahiah son of Menahem became king of Israel in Samaria, and he reigned two years. ²⁴Pekahiah did evil in the eyes of the LORD. He did not turn away from the sins of Jeroboam son of Nebat, which he had caused Israel to commit. ²⁵One of his chief officers, Pekah son of Remaliah, conspired against him. Taking fifty men of Gilead with him, he assassinated Pekahiah, along with Argob and Arieh, in the citadel of the royal palace at Samaria. So Pekah killed Pekahiah and succeeded him as king.

²⁶The other events of Pekahiah's reign, and all he did, are written in the book of the annals of the kings of Israel.

Pekah King of Israel

²⁷In the fifty-second year of Azariah king of Judah, Pekah son of Remaliah became king of Israel in Samaria, and he reigned twenty years. ²⁸He did evil in the eyes of the LORD. He did not turn away from the sins of Jeroboam son of Nebat, which he had caused Israel to commit.

²⁹In the time of Pekah king of Israel, Tiglath-Pileser king of Assyria came and took Ijon, Abel Beth Maacah, Janoah, Kedesh and Hazor. He took Gilead and Gali-

---

a5 The Hebrew word was used for various diseases affecting the skin—not necessarily leprosy.   b5 Or in a house where he was relieved of responsibility   c10 Hebrew; some Septuagint manuscripts in Ibleam   d12 2 Kings 10:30   e19 Also called Tiglath-Pileser   f19 That is, about 37 tons (about 34 metric tons)   g20 That is, about 1 1/4 pounds (about 0.6 kilogram) lee, including all the land of Naphtali, and deported the people to Assyria. ³⁰Then Hoshea son of Elah conspired against Pekah son of Remaliah. He attacked and assassinated him, and then succeeded him as king in the twentieth year of Jotham son of Uzziah.

³¹As for the other events of Pekah's reign, and all he did, are they not written in the book of the annals of the kings of Israel?

Jotham King of Judah

³²In the second year of Pekah son of Remaliah king of Israel, Jotham son of Uzziah king of Judah began to reign. ³³He was twenty-five years old when he became king, and he reigned in Jerusalem sixteen years. His mother's name was Jerusha daughter of Zadok. ³⁴He did what was right in the eyes of the LORD, just as his father Uzziah had done. ³⁵The high places, however, were not removed; the people continued to offer sacrifices and burn incense there. Jotham rebuilt the Upper Gate of the temple of the LORD.

³⁶As for the other events of Jotham's reign, and what he did, are they not written in the book of the annals of the kings of Judah? ³⁷(In those days the LORD began to send Rezin king of Aram and Pekah son of Remaliah against Judah.) ³⁸Jotham rested with his fathers and was buried with them in the City of David, the city of his father. And Ahaz his son succeeded him as king.

Ahaz King of Judah

16 In the seventeenth year of Pekah son of Remaliah, Ahaz son of Jotham king of Judah began to reign. ²Ahaz was twenty years old when he became king, and he reigned in Jerusalem sixteen years. Unlike David his father, he did not do what was right in the eyes of the LORD his God. ³He walked in the ways of the kings of Israel and even sacrificed his son in*ᵃ* the fire, following the detestable ways of the nations the LORD had driven out before the Israelites. ⁴He offered sacrifices and burned incense at the high places, on the hilltops and under every spreading tree.

⁵Then Rezin king of Aram and Pekah son of Remaliah king of Israel marched up to fight against Jerusalem and besieged Ahaz, but they could not overpower him. ⁶At that time, Rezin king of Aram recovered Elath for Aram by driving out the men of Judah. Edomites then moved into Elath and have lived there to this day.

⁷Ahaz sent messengers to say to Tiglath-Pileser king of Assyria, "I am your servant and vassal. Come up and save me out of the hand of the king of Aram and of the king of Israel, who are attacking me." ⁸And Ahaz took the silver and gold found in the temple of the LORD and in the treasuries of the royal palace and sent it as a gift to the king of Assyria. ⁹The king of Assyria complied by attacking Damascus and capturing it. He deported its inhabitants to Kir and put Rezin to death.

¹⁰Then King Ahaz went to Damascus to meet Tiglath-Pileser king of Assyria. He saw an altar in Damascus and sent to Uriah the priest a sketch of the altar, with detailed plans for its construction. ¹¹So Uriah the priest built an altar in accordance with all the plans that King Ahaz had sent from Damascus and finished it before King Ahaz returned. ¹²When the king came back from Damascus and saw the altar, he approached it and presented offerings*ᵇ* on it. ¹³He offered up his burnt offering and grain offering, poured out his drink offering, and sprinkled the blood of his fellowship offerings*ᶜ* on the altar. ¹⁴The bronze altar that stood before the LORD he brought from the front of the temple—from between the new altar and the temple of the LORD—and put it on the north side of the new altar.

¹⁵King Ahaz then gave these orders to Uriah the priest: "On the large new altar, offer the morning burnt offering and the evening grain offering, the king's burnt offering and his grain offering, and the burnt offering of all the people of the land, and their grain offering and their drink offering. Sprinkle on the altar all the blood of the burnt offerings and sacrifices. But I will use the bronze altar for seeking guidance." ¹⁶And Uriah the priest did just as King Ahaz had ordered.

¹⁷King Ahaz took away the side panels and removed the basins from the movable stands. He removed the Sea from the bronze bulls that supported it and set it on a stone base. ¹⁸He took away the Sabbath canopy*ᵈ* that had been built at the temple and removed the royal entryway

---

ᵃ3 Or *even made his son pass through*   *ᵇ12* Or *and went up*   *ᶜ13* Traditionally *peace offerings*
ᵈ18 Or *the dais of his throne* (see Septuagint)

outside the temple of the Lord, in deference to the king of Assyria.

19As for the other events of the reign of Ahaz, and what he did, are they not written in the book of the annals of the kings of Judah? 20Ahaz rested with his fathers and was buried with them in the City of David. And Hezekiah his son succeeded him as king.

Hoshea Last King of Israel

17 In the twelfth year of Ahaz king of Judah, Hoshea son of Elah became king of Israel in Samaria, and he reigned nine years. 2He did evil in the eyes of the Lord, but not like the kings of Israel who preceded him.

3Shalmaneser king of Assyria came up to attack Hoshea, who had been Shalmaneser's vassal and had paid him tribute. 4But the king of Assyria discovered that Hoshea was a traitor, for he had sent envoys to So*a* king of Egypt, and he no longer paid tribute to the king of Assyria, as he had done year by year. Therefore Shalmaneser seized him and put him in prison. 5The king of Assyria invaded the entire land, marched against Samaria and laid siege to it for three years. 6In the ninth year of Hoshea, the king of Assyria captured Samaria and deported the Israelites to Assyria. He settled them in Halah, in Gozan on the Habor River and in the towns of the Medes.

Israel Exiled Because of Sin

7All this took place because the Israelites had sinned against the Lord their God, who had brought them up out of Egypt from under the power of Pharaoh king of Egypt. They worshiped other gods 8and followed the practices of the nations the Lord had driven out before them, as well as the practices that the kings of Israel had introduced. 9The Israelites secretly did things against the Lord their God that were not right. From watchtower to fortified city they built themselves high places in all their towns. 10They set up sacred stones and Asherah poles on every high hill and under every spreading tree. 11At every high place they burned incense, as the nations whom the Lord had driven out before them had done. They did wicked things that provoked the Lord to anger. 12They worshiped idols, though the Lord had said, "You shall not

do this."*b* 13The Lord warned Israel and Judah through all his prophets and seers: "Turn from your evil ways. Observe my commands and decrees, in accordance with the entire Law that I commanded your fathers to obey and that I delivered to you through my servants the prophets."

14But they would not listen and were as stiff-necked as their fathers, who did not trust in the Lord their God. 15They rejected his decrees and the covenant he had made with their fathers and the warnings he had given them. They followed worthless idols and themselves became worthless. They imitated the nations around them although the Lord had ordered them, "Do not do as they do," and they did the things the Lord had forbidden them to do.

16They forsook all the commands of the Lord their God and made for themselves two idols cast in the shape of calves, and an Asherah pole. They bowed down to all the starry hosts, and they worshiped Baal. 17They sacrificed their sons and daughters in*c* the fire. They practiced divination and sorcery and sold themselves to do evil in the eyes of the Lord, provoking him to anger.

18So the Lord was very angry with Israel and removed them from his presence. Only the tribe of Judah was left, 19and even Judah did not keep the commands of the Lord their God. They followed the practices Israel had introduced. 20Therefore the Lord rejected all the people of Israel; he afflicted them and gave them into the hands of plunderers, until he thrust them from his presence.

21When he tore Israel away from the house of David, they made Jeroboam son of Nebat their king. Jeroboam enticed Israel away from following the Lord and caused them to commit a great sin. 22The Israelites persisted in all the sins of Jeroboam and did not turn away from them 23until the Lord removed them from his presence, as he had warned through all his servants the prophets. So the people of Israel were taken from their homeland into exile in Assyria, and they are still there.

Samaria Resettled

24The king of Assyria brought people from Babylon, Cuthah, Avva, Hamath and

---

*a*4 Or to Sais, to the; So is possibly an abbreviation for Osorkon.　　*b*12 Exodus 20:4, 5　　*c*17 Or They made their sons and daughters pass through

Sepharvaim and settled them in the towns of Samaria to replace the Israelites. They took over Samaria and lived in its towns. 25When they first lived there, they did not worship the LORD; so he sent lions among them and they killed some of the people. 26It was reported to the king of Assyria: "The people you deported and resettled in the towns of Samaria do not know what the god of that country requires. He has sent lions among them, which are killing them off, because the people do not know what he requires."

27Then the king of Assyria gave this order: "Have one of the priests you took captive from Samaria go back to live there and teach the people what the god of the land requires." 28So one of the priests who had been exiled from Samaria came to live in Bethel and taught them how to worship the LORD.

29Nevertheless, each national group made its own gods in the several towns where they settled, and set them up in the shrines the people of Samaria had made at the high places. 30The men from Babylon made Succoth Benoth, the men from Cuthah made Nergal, and the men from Hamath made Ashima; 31the Avvites made Nibhaz and Tartak, and the Sepharvites burned their children in the fire as sacrifices to Adrammelech and Anammelech, the gods of Sepharvaim. 32They worshiped the LORD, but they also appointed all sorts of their own people to officiate for them as priests in the shrines at the high places. 33They worshiped the LORD, but they also served their own gods in accordance with the customs of the nations from which they had been brought.

34To this day they persist in their former practices. They neither worship the LORD nor adhere to the decrees and ordinances, the laws and commands that the LORD gave the descendants of Jacob, whom he named Israel. 35When the LORD made a covenant with the Israelites, he commanded them: "Do not worship any other gods or bow down to them, serve them or sacrifice to them. 36But the LORD, who brought you up out of Egypt with mighty power and outstretched arm, is the one you must worship. To him you shall bow down and to him offer sacrifices. 37You must always be careful to keep the decrees and ordinances, the laws and commands he wrote for you. Do

not worship other gods. 38Do not forget the covenant I have made with you, and do not worship other gods. 39Rather, worship the LORD your God; it is he who will deliver you from the hand of all your enemies."

40They would not listen, however, but persisted in their former practices. 41Even while these people were worshiping the LORD, they were serving their idols. To this day their children and grandchildren continue to do as their fathers did.

Hezekiah King of Judah

18 In the third year of Hoshea son of Elah king of Israel, Hezekiah son of Ahaz king of Judah began to reign. 2He was twenty-five years old when he became king, and he reigned in Jerusalem twenty-nine years. His mother's name was Abijah[a] daughter of Zechariah. 3He did what was right in the eyes of the LORD, just as his father David had done. 4He removed the high places, smashed the sacred stones and cut down the Asherah poles. He broke into pieces the bronze snake Moses had made, for up to that time the Israelites had been burning incense to it. (It was called[b] Nehushtan.[c])

5Hezekiah trusted in the LORD, the God of Israel. There was no one like him among all the kings of Judah, either before him or after him. 6He held fast to the LORD and did not cease to follow him; he kept the commands the LORD had given Moses. 7And the LORD was with him; he was successful in whatever he undertook. He rebelled against the king of Assyria and did not serve him. 8From watchtower to fortified city, he defeated the Philistines, as far as Gaza and its territory.

9In King Hezekiah's fourth year, which was the seventh year of Hoshea son of Elah king of Israel, Shalmaneser king of Assyria marched against Samaria and laid siege to it. 10At the end of three years the Assyrians took it. So Samaria was captured in Hezekiah's sixth year, which was the ninth year of Hoshea king of Israel. 11The king of Assyria deported Israel to Assyria and settled them in Halah, in Gozan on the Habor River and in towns of the Medes. 12This happened because they had not obeyed the LORD their God, but had violated his covenant—all that Moses the servant of the LORD commanded.

---

a2 Hebrew *Abi*, a variant of *Abijah*   b4 Or *He called it*   c4 *Nehushtan* sounds like the Hebrew for *bronze* and *snake* and *unclean thing*.

They neither listened to the commands nor carried them out.

[13]In the fourteenth year of King Hezekiah's reign, Sennacherib king of Assyria attacked all the fortified cities of Judah and captured them. [14]So Hezekiah king of Judah sent this message to the king of Assyria at Lachish: "I have done wrong. Withdraw from me, and I will pay whatever you demand of me." The king of Assyria exacted from Hezekiah king of Judah three hundred talents[a] of silver and thirty talents[b] of gold. [15]So Hezekiah gave him all the silver that was found in the temple of the LORD and in the treasuries of the royal palace.

[16]At this time Hezekiah king of Judah stripped off the gold with which he had covered the doors and doorposts of the temple of the LORD, and gave it to the king of Assyria.

Sennacherib Threatens Jerusalem

[17]The king of Assyria sent his supreme commander, his chief officer and his field commander with a large army, from Lachish to King Hezekiah at Jerusalem. They came up to Jerusalem and stopped at the aqueduct of the Upper Pool, on the road to the Washerman's Field. [18]They called for the king; and Eliakim son of Hilkiah the palace administrator, Shebna the secretary, and Joah son of Asaph the recorder went out to them.

[19]The field commander said to them, "Tell Hezekiah:

" 'This is what the great king, the king of Assyria, says: On what are you basing this confidence of yours? [20]You say you have strategy and military strength—but you speak only empty words. On whom are you depending, that you rebel against me? [21]Look now, you are depending on Egypt, that splintered reed of a staff, which pierces a man's hand and wounds him if he leans on it! Such is Pharaoh king of Egypt to all who depend on him. [22]And if you say to me, "We are depending on the LORD our God"—isn't he the one whose high places and altars Hezekiah removed, saying to Judah and Jerusalem, "You must worship before this altar in Jerusalem"?

[23]" 'Come now, make a bargain with my master, the king of Assyria: I will give you two thousand horses— if you can put riders on them! [24]How can you repulse one officer of the least of my master's officials, even though you are depending on Egypt for chariots and horsemen[c]? [25]Furthermore, have I come to attack and destroy this place without word from the LORD? The LORD himself told me to march against this country and destroy it.' "

[26]Then Eliakim son of Hilkiah, and Shebna and Joah said to the field commander, "Please speak to your servants in Aramaic, since we understand it. Don't speak to us in Hebrew in the hearing of the people on the wall."

[27]But the commander replied, "Was it only to your master and you that my master sent me to say these things, and not to the men sitting on the wall—who, like you, will have to eat their own filth and drink their own urine?"

[28]Then the commander stood and called out in Hebrew: "Hear the word of the great king, the king of Assyria! [29]This is what the king says: Do not let Hezekiah deceive you. He cannot deliver you from my hand. [30]Do not let Hezekiah persuade you to trust in the LORD when he says, 'The LORD will surely deliver us; this city will not be given into the hand of the king of Assyria.'

[31]"Do not listen to Hezekiah. This is what the king of Assyria says: Make peace with me and come out to me. Then every one of you will eat from his own vine and fig tree and drink water from his own cistern, [32]until I come and take you to a land like your own, a land of grain and new wine, a land of bread and vineyards, a land of olive trees and honey. Choose life and not death!

"Do not listen to Hezekiah, for he is misleading you when he says, 'The LORD will deliver us.' [33]Has the god of any nation ever delivered his land from the hand of the king of Assyria? [34]Where are the gods of Hamath and Arpad? Where are the gods of Sepharvaim, Hena and Ivvah? Have they rescued Samaria from my hand? [35]Who of all the gods of these countries has been able to save his land from me? How then can the LORD deliver Jerusalem from my hand?"

a14 That is, about 11 tons (about 10 metric tons)   b14 That is, about 1 ton (about 1 metric ton)
c24 Or charioteers

36But the people remained silent and said nothing in reply, because the king had commanded, "Do not answer him."

37Then Eliakim son of Hilkiah the palace administrator, Shebna the secretary and Joah son of Asaph the recorder went to Hezekiah, with their clothes torn, and told him what the field commander had said.

Jerusalem's Deliverance Foretold

19 When King Hezekiah heard this, he tore his clothes and put on sackcloth and went into the temple of the LORD. 2He sent Eliakim the palace administrator, Shebna the secretary and the leading priests, all wearing sackcloth, to the prophet Isaiah son of Amoz. 3They told him, "This is what Hezekiah says: This day is a day of distress and rebuke and disgrace, as when children come to the point of birth and there is no strength to deliver them. 4It may be that the LORD your God will hear all the words of the field commander, whom his master, the king of Assyria, has sent to ridicule the living God, and that he will rebuke him for the words the LORD your God has heard. Therefore pray for the remnant that still survives."

5When King Hezekiah's officials came to Isaiah, 6Isaiah said to them, "Tell your master, 'This is what the LORD says: Do not be afraid of what you have heard—those words with which the underlings of the king of Assyria have blasphemed me. 7Listen! I am going to put such a spirit in him that when he hears a certain report, he will return to his own country, and there I will have him cut down with the sword.'"

8When the field commander heard that the king of Assyria had left Lachish, he withdrew and found the king fighting against Libnah.

9Now Sennacherib received a report that Tirhakah, the Cushite*a* king of Egypt, was marching out to fight against him. So he again sent messengers to Hezekiah with this word: 10"Say to Hezekiah king of Judah: Do not let the god you depend on deceive you when he says, 'Jerusalem will not be handed over to the king of Assyria.' 11Surely you have heard what the kings of Assyria have done to all the countries, destroying them completely. And will you be delivered? 12Did the gods of the nations that were destroyed by my forefathers deliver them: the gods of Gozan, Haran, Rezeph and the people of Eden who were in Tel Assar? 13Where is the king of Hamath, the king of Arpad, the king of the city of Sepharvaim, or of Hena or Ivvah?"

Hezekiah's Prayer

14Hezekiah received the letter from the messengers and read it. Then he went up to the temple of the LORD and spread it out before the LORD. 15And Hezekiah prayed to the LORD: "O LORD, God of Israel, enthroned between the cherubim, you alone are God over all the kingdoms of the earth. You have made heaven and earth. 16Give ear, O LORD, and hear; open your eyes, O LORD, and see; listen to the words Sennacherib has sent to insult the living God.

17"It is true, O LORD, that the Assyrian kings have laid waste these nations and their lands. 18They have thrown their gods into the fire and destroyed them, for they were not gods but only wood and stone, fashioned by men's hands. 19Now, O LORD our God, deliver us from his hand, so that all kingdoms on earth may know that you alone, O LORD, are God."

Isaiah Prophesies Sennacherib's Fall

20Then Isaiah son of Amoz sent a message to Hezekiah: "This is what the LORD, the God of Israel, says: I have heard your prayer concerning Sennacherib king of Assyria. 21This is the word that the LORD has spoken against him:

" 'The Virgin Daughter of Zion
    despises you and mocks you.
The Daughter of Jerusalem
    tosses her head as you flee.
22Who is it you have insulted and
        blasphemed?
    Against whom have you raised your
        voice
and lifted your eyes in pride?
    Against the Holy One of Israel!
23By your messengers
    you have heaped insults on the
        Lord.
And you have said,
    "With my many chariots
I have ascended the heights of the
        mountains,
    the utmost heights of Lebanon.
I have cut down its tallest cedars,
    the choicest of its pines.

a9 That is, from the upper Nile region

I have reached its remotest parts,
the finest of its forests.
²⁴I have dug wells in foreign lands
and drunk the water there.
With the soles of my feet
I have dried up all the streams of
Egypt."

²⁵" 'Have you not heard?
Long ago I ordained it.
In days of old I planned it;
now I have brought it to pass,
that you have turned fortified cities
into piles of stone.
²⁶Their people, drained of power,
are dismayed and put to shame.
They are like plants in the field,
like tender green shoots,
like grass sprouting on the roof,
scorched before it grows up.

²⁷" 'But I know where you stay
and when you come and go
and how you rage against me.
²⁸Because you rage against me
and your insolence has reached my
ears,
I will put my hook in your nose
and my bit in your mouth,
and I will make you return
by the way you came.'

²⁹"This will be the sign for you,
O Hezekiah:

"This year you will eat what grows by
itself,
and the second year what springs
from that.
But in the third year sow and reap,
plant vineyards and eat their fruit.
³⁰Once more a remnant of the house of
Judah
will take root below and bear fruit
above.
³¹For out of Jerusalem will come a
remnant,
and out of Mount Zion a band of
survivors.

The zeal of the LORD Almighty will accomplish this.

³²"Therefore this is what the LORD says
concerning the king of Assyria:

"He will not enter this city
or shoot an arrow here.
He will not come before it with shield
or build a siege ramp against it.
³³By the way that he came he will
return;

he will not enter this city,
declares the LORD.
³⁴I will defend this city and save it,
for my sake and for the sake of
David my servant."

³⁵That night the angel of the LORD went
out and put to death a hundred and
eighty-five thousand men in the Assyrian
camp. When the people got up the next
morning—there were all the dead bodies!
³⁶So Sennacherib king of Assyria broke
camp and withdrew. He returned to Nineveh and stayed there.
³⁷One day, while he was worshiping in
the temple of his god Nisroch, his sons
Adrammelech and Sharezer cut him
down with the sword, and they escaped to
the land of Ararat. And Esarhaddon his
son succeeded him as king.

Hezekiah's Illness

20 In those days Hezekiah became ill
and was at the point of death. The
prophet Isaiah son of Amoz went to him
and said, "This is what the LORD says: Put
your house in order, because you are going to die; you will not recover."
²Hezekiah turned his face to the wall
and prayed to the LORD, ³"Remember, O
LORD, how I have walked before you faithfully and with wholehearted devotion and
have done what is good in your eyes." And
Hezekiah wept bitterly.
⁴Before Isaiah had left the middle
court, the word of the LORD came to him:
⁵"Go back and tell Hezekiah, the leader
of my people, 'This is what the LORD, the
God of your father David, says: I have
heard your prayer and seen your tears; I
will heal you. On the third day from now
you will go up to the temple of the LORD.
⁶I will add fifteen years to your life. And
I will deliver you and this city from the
hand of the king of Assyria. I will defend
this city for my sake and for the sake of
my servant David.' "
⁷Then Isaiah said, "Prepare a poultice
of figs." They did so and applied it to the
boil, and he recovered.
⁸Hezekiah had asked Isaiah, "What will
be the sign that the LORD will heal me and
that I will go up to the temple of the LORD
on the third day from now?"
⁹Isaiah answered, "This is the LORD's
sign to you that the LORD will do what he
has promised: Shall the shadow go forward ten steps, or shall it go back ten
steps?"
¹⁰"It is a simple matter for the shadow

to go forward ten steps," said Hezekiah. "Rather, have it go back ten steps."

11Then the prophet Isaiah called upon the Lord, and the Lord made the shadow go back the ten steps it had gone down on the stairway of Ahaz.

Envoys From Babylon

12At that time Merodach-Baladan son of Baladan king of Babylon sent Hezekiah letters and a gift, because he had heard of Hezekiah's illness. 13Hezekiah received the messengers and showed them all that was in his storehouses—the silver, the gold, the spices and the fine oil—his armory and everything found among his treasures. There was nothing in his palace or in all his kingdom that Hezekiah did not show them.

14Then Isaiah the prophet went to King Hezekiah and asked, "What did those men say, and where did they come from?"

"From a distant land," Hezekiah replied. "They came from Babylon."

15The prophet asked, "What did they see in your palace?"

"They saw everything in my palace," Hezekiah said. "There is nothing among my treasures that I did not show them."

16Then Isaiah said to Hezekiah, "Hear the word of the Lord: 17The time will surely come when everything in your palace, and all that your fathers have stored up until this day, will be carried off to Babylon. Nothing will be left, says the Lord. 18And some of your descendants, your own flesh and blood, that will be born to you, will be taken away, and they will become eunuchs in the palace of the king of Babylon."

19"The word of the Lord you have spoken is good," Hezekiah replied. For he thought, "Will there not be peace and security in my lifetime?"

20As for the other events of Hezekiah's reign, all his achievements and how he made the pool and the tunnel by which he brought water into the city, are they not written in the book of the annals of the kings of Judah? 21Hezekiah rested with his fathers. And Manasseh his son succeeded him as king.

Manasseh King of Judah

21 Manasseh was twelve years old when he became king, and he reigned in Jerusalem fifty-five years. His mother's name was Hephzibah. 2He did

evil in the eyes of the Lord, following the detestable practices of the nations the Lord had driven out before the Israelites. 3He rebuilt the high places his father Hezekiah had destroyed; he also erected altars to Baal and made an Asherah pole, as Ahab king of Israel had done. He bowed down to all the starry hosts and worshiped them. 4He built altars in the temple of the Lord, of which the Lord had said, "In Jerusalem I will put my Name." 5In both courts of the temple of the Lord, he built altars to all the starry hosts. 6He sacrificed his own son in[a] the fire, practiced sorcery and divination, and consulted mediums and spiritists. He did much evil in the eyes of the Lord, provoking him to anger.

7He took the carved Asherah pole he had made and put it in the temple, of which the Lord had said to David and to his son Solomon, "In this temple and in Jerusalem, which I have chosen out of all the tribes of Israel, I will put my Name forever. 8I will not again make the feet of the Israelites wander from the land I gave their forefathers, if only they will be careful to do everything I commanded them and will keep the whole Law that my servant Moses gave them." 9But the people did not listen. Manasseh led them astray, so that they did more evil than the nations the Lord had destroyed before the Israelites.

10The Lord said through his servants the prophets: 11"Manasseh king of Judah has committed these detestable sins. He has done more evil than the Amorites who preceded him and has led Judah into sin with his idols. 12Therefore this is what the Lord, the God of Israel, says: I am going to bring such disaster on Jerusalem and Judah that the ears of everyone who hears of it will tingle. 13I will stretch out over Jerusalem the measuring line used against Samaria and the plumb line used against the house of Ahab. I will wipe out Jerusalem as one wipes a dish, wiping it and turning it upside down. 14I will forsake the remnant of my inheritance and hand them over to their enemies. They will be looted and plundered by all their foes, 15because they have done evil in my eyes and have provoked me to anger from the day their forefathers came out of Egypt until this day."

16Moreover, Manasseh also shed so much innocent blood that he filled Jeru-

---

a6 Or *He made his own son pass through*

salem from end to end—besides the sin that he had caused Judah to commit, so that they did evil in the eyes of the LORD.

[17]As for the other events of Manasseh's reign, and all he did, including the sin he committed, are they not written in the book of the annals of the kings of Judah? [18]Manasseh rested with his fathers and was buried in his palace garden, the garden of Uzza. And Amon his son succeeded him as king.

Amon King of Judah

[19]Amon was twenty-two years old when he became king, and he reigned in Jerusalem two years. His mother's name was Meshullemeth daughter of Haruz; she was from Jotbah. [20]He did evil in the eyes of the LORD, as his father Manasseh had done. [21]He walked in all the ways of his father; he worshiped the idols his father had worshiped, and bowed down to them. [22]He forsook the LORD, the God of his fathers, and did not walk in the way of the LORD.

[23]Amon's officials conspired against him and assassinated the king in his palace. [24]Then the people of the land killed all who had plotted against King Amon, and they made Josiah his son king in his place.

[25]As for the other events of Amon's reign, and what he did, are they not written in the book of the annals of the kings of Judah? [26]He was buried in his grave in the garden of Uzza. And Josiah his son succeeded him as king.

The Book of the Law Found

22 Josiah was eight years old when he became king, and he reigned in Jerusalem thirty-one years. His mother's name was Jedidah daughter of Adaiah; she was from Bozkath. [2]He did what was right in the eyes of the LORD and walked in all the ways of his father David, not turning aside to the right or to the left.

[3]In the eighteenth year of his reign, King Josiah sent the secretary, Shaphan son of Azaliah, the son of Meshullam, to the temple of the LORD. He said: [4]"Go up to Hilkiah the high priest and have him get ready the money that has been brought into the temple of the LORD, which the doorkeepers have collected from the people. [5]Have them entrust it to the men appointed to supervise the work on the temple. And have these men pay

the workers who repair the temple of the LORD— [6]the carpenters, the builders and the masons. Also have them purchase timber and dressed stone to repair the temple. [7]But they need not account for the money entrusted to them, because they are acting faithfully."

[8]Hilkiah the high priest said to Shaphan the secretary, "I have found the Book of the Law in the temple of the LORD." He gave it to Shaphan, who read it. [9]Then Shaphan the secretary went to the king and reported to him: "Your officials have paid out the money that was in the temple of the LORD and have entrusted it to the workers and supervisors at the temple." [10]Then Shaphan the secretary informed the king, "Hilkiah the priest has given me a book." And Shaphan read from it in the presence of the king.

[11]When the king heard the words of the Book of the Law, he tore his robes. [12]He gave these orders to Hilkiah the priest, Ahikam son of Shaphan, Acbor son of Micaiah, Shaphan the secretary and Asaiah the king's attendant: [13]"Go and inquire of the LORD for me and for the people and for all Judah about what is written in this book that has been found. Great is the LORD's anger that burns against us because our fathers have not obeyed the words of this book; they have not acted in accordance with all that is written there concerning us."

[14]Hilkiah the priest, Ahikam, Acbor, Shaphan and Asaiah went to speak to the prophetess Huldah, who was the wife of Shallum son of Tikvah, the son of Harhas, keeper of the wardrobe. She lived in Jerusalem, in the Second District.

[15]She said to them, "This is what the LORD, the God of Israel, says: Tell the man who sent you to me, [16]'This is what the LORD says: I am going to bring disaster on this place and its people, according to everything written in the book the king of Judah has read. [17]Because they have forsaken me and burned incense to other gods and provoked me to anger by all the idols their hands have made,[a] my anger will burn against this place and will not be quenched.' [18]Tell the king of Judah, who sent you to inquire of the LORD, 'This is what the LORD, the God of Israel, says concerning the words you heard: [19]Because your heart was responsive and you humbled yourself before the LORD when you heard what I have spoken against this

---

[a]17 Or *by everything they have done*

VERSE FOR THE DAY:
2 Kings 22:11; 23:3

AUTHOR:
June Gunden

PASSAGE FOR THE DAY:
2 Kings 22:1—23:3

God's Instruction Manual

SUPPOSE for a moment that through a wealthy benefactor you inherit a private airplane. Not knowing how to fly, but knowing it can be done, you climb into the cockpit and begin to push buttons, determined to lift off. How ridiculous, you say. I'd crash the plane and probably kill myself. The people who made that airplane have provided instructions about how to fly it. I would certainly take some lessons from them.

Yet it is difficult for us to admit that we need "living" instructions from the One who created us. He knows how life has been designed to work. He knows, for example, that if we mistreat other people by cheating or stealing, the natural result will be suffering and pain for all involved. He cared enough about us to give us a book that would fill us in on the rules and regulations beforehand.

Moses had explained to the people of Israel the *truth* and the *consequences*: If you obey God's instructions, you will live; if you disobey, you will die (Deuteronomy 28). King Josiah believed this. When he heard what the Book of the Law said, "He tore his robes" (2 Kings 22:11), an expression of great emotion and repentance. He knew that his nation had disobeyed God's covenant, and he realized the terrible price they would have to pay as a result.

Today, when we read the same words Josiah read, do we really believe them? Or are we more like Josiah's son King Jehoiakim and his attendants, who, when they heard God's direction through the prophet Jeremiah, "showed no fear, nor did they tear their clothes" (Jeremiah 36:24)? To many people God's law is "interesting" or "inspiring," but not heartrending and life-changing.

May God help us to study his "instruction manual" every day, to believe its message, and to treasure its wisdom. With the psalmist, may we cry:

> Oh, how I love your law!
> I meditate on it all day long (Psalm 119:97).

Additional Scripture Readings:
Psalm 119:33–40; Isaiah 29:15–16

Go to page 415 for your next devotional reading.

place and its people, that they would become accursed and laid waste, and because you tore your robes and wept in my presence, I have heard you, declares the LORD. 20Therefore I will gather you to your fathers, and you will be buried in peace. Your eyes will not see all the disaster I am going to bring on this place.' "

So they took her answer back to the king.

Josiah Renews the Covenant

23 Then the king called together all the elders of Judah and Jerusalem. 2He went up to the temple of the LORD with the men of Judah, the people of Jerusalem, the priests and the prophets— all the people from the least to the greatest. He read in their hearing all the words of the Book of the Covenant, which had been found in the temple of the LORD. 3The king stood by the pillar and renewed the covenant in the presence of the LORD —to follow the LORD and keep his commands, regulations and decrees with all his heart and all his soul, thus confirming the words of the covenant written in this book. Then all the people pledged themselves to the covenant.

4The king ordered Hilkiah the high priest, the priests next in rank and the doorkeepers to remove from the temple of the LORD all the articles made for Baal and Asherah and all the starry hosts. He burned them outside Jerusalem in the fields of the Kidron Valley and took the ashes to Bethel. 5He did away with the pagan priests appointed by the kings of Judah to burn incense on the high places of the towns of Judah and on those around Jerusalem—those who burned incense to Baal, to the sun and moon, to the constellations and to all the starry hosts. 6He took the Asherah pole from the temple of the LORD to the Kidron Valley outside Jerusalem and burned it there. He ground it to powder and scattered the dust over the graves of the common people. 7He also tore down the quarters of the male shrine prostitutes, which were in the temple of the LORD and where women did weaving for Asherah.

8Josiah brought all the priests from the towns of Judah and desecrated the high places, from Geba to Beersheba, where the priests had burned incense. He broke down the shrines*a* at the gates—at the entrance to the Gate of Joshua, the city governor, which is on the left of the city gate. 9Although the priests of the high places did not serve at the altar of the LORD in Jerusalem, they ate unleavened bread with their fellow priests.

10He desecrated Topheth, which was in the Valley of Ben Hinnom, so no one could use it to sacrifice his son or daughter in*b* the fire to Molech. 11He removed from the entrance to the temple of the LORD the horses that the kings of Judah had dedicated to the sun. They were in the court near the room of an official named Nathan-Melech. Josiah then burned the chariots dedicated to the sun.

12He pulled down the altars the kings of Judah had erected on the roof near the upper room of Ahaz, and the altars Manasseh had built in the two courts of the temple of the LORD. He removed them from there, smashed them to pieces and threw the rubble into the Kidron Valley. 13The king also desecrated the high places that were east of Jerusalem on the south of the Hill of Corruption—the ones Solomon king of Israel had built for Ashtoreth the vile goddess of the Sidonians, for Chemosh the vile god of Moab, and for Molech*c* the detestable god of the people of Ammon. 14Josiah smashed the sacred stones and cut down the Asherah poles and covered the sites with human bones.

15Even the altar at Bethel, the high place made by Jeroboam son of Nebat, who had caused Israel to sin—even that altar and high place he demolished. He burned the high place and ground it to powder, and burned the Asherah pole also. 16Then Josiah looked around, and when he saw the tombs that were there on the hillside, he had the bones removed from them and burned on the altar to defile it, in accordance with the word of the LORD proclaimed by the man of God who foretold these things.

17The king asked, "What is that tombstone I see?"

The men of the city said, "It marks the tomb of the man of God who came from Judah and pronounced against the altar of Bethel the very things you have done to it."

18"Leave it alone," he said. "Don't let anyone disturb his bones." So they spared his bones and those of the prophet who had come from Samaria.

19Just as he had done at Bethel, Josiah removed and defiled all the shrines at the

---

a8 Or *high places*   *b10* Or *to make his son or daughter pass through*   *c13* Hebrew *Milcom* high places that the kings of Israel had built in the towns of Samaria that had provoked the LORD to anger. ²⁰Josiah slaughtered all the priests of those high places on the altars and burned human bones on them. Then he went back to Jerusalem.

²¹The king gave this order to all the people: "Celebrate the Passover to the LORD your God, as it is written in this Book of the Covenant." ²²Not since the days of the judges who led Israel, nor throughout the days of the kings of Israel and the kings of Judah, had any such Passover been observed. ²³But in the eighteenth year of King Josiah, this Passover was celebrated to the LORD in Jerusalem.

²⁴Furthermore, Josiah got rid of the mediums and spiritists, the household gods, the idols and all the other detestable things seen in Judah and Jerusalem. This he did to fulfill the requirements of the law written in the book that Hilkiah the priest had discovered in the temple of the LORD. ²⁵Neither before nor after Josiah was there a king like him who turned to the LORD as he did—with all his heart and with all his soul and with all his strength, in accordance with all the Law of Moses.

²⁶Nevertheless, the LORD did not turn away from the heat of his fierce anger, which burned against Judah because of all that Manasseh had done to provoke him to anger. ²⁷So the LORD said, "I will remove Judah also from my presence as I removed Israel, and I will reject Jerusalem, the city I chose, and this temple, about which I said, 'There shall my Name be.'ᵃ"

²⁸As for the other events of Josiah's reign, and all he did, are they not written in the book of the annals of the kings of Judah?

²⁹While Josiah was king, Pharaoh Neco king of Egypt went up to the Euphrates River to help the king of Assyria. King Josiah marched out to meet him in battle, but Neco faced him and killed him at Megiddo. ³⁰Josiah's servants brought his body in a chariot from Megiddo to Jerusalem and buried him in his own tomb. And the people of the land took Jehoahaz son of Josiah and anointed him and made him king in place of his father.

Jehoahaz King of Judah

³¹Jehoahaz was twenty-three years old when he became king, and he reigned in Jerusalem three months. His mother's name was Hamutal daughter of Jeremiah; she was from Libnah. ³²He did evil in the eyes of the LORD, just as his fathers had done. ³³Pharaoh Neco put him in chains at Riblah in the land of Hamathᵇ so that he might not reign in Jerusalem, and he imposed on Judah a levy of a hundred talentsᶜ of silver and a talentᵈ of gold. ³⁴Pharaoh Neco made Eliakim son of Josiah king in place of his father Josiah and changed Eliakim's name to Jehoiakim. But he took Jehoahaz and carried him off to Egypt, and there he died. ³⁵Jehoiakim paid Pharaoh Neco the silver and gold he demanded. In order to do so, he taxed the land and exacted the silver and gold from the people of the land according to their assessments.

Jehoiakim King of Judah

³⁶Jehoiakim was twenty-five years old when he became king, and he reigned in Jerusalem eleven years. His mother's name was Zebidah daughter of Pedaiah; she was from Rumah. ³⁷And he did evil in the eyes of the LORD, just as his fathers had done.

24 During Jehoiakim's reign, Nebuchadnezzar king of Babylon invaded the land, and Jehoiakim became his vassal for three years. But then he changed his mind and rebelled against Nebuchadnezzar. ²The LORD sent Babylonian,ᵉ Aramean, Moabite and Ammonite raiders against him. He sent them to destroy Judah, in accordance with the word of the LORD proclaimed by his servants the prophets. ³Surely these things happened to Judah according to the LORD's command, in order to remove them from his presence because of the sins of Manasseh and all he had done, ⁴including the shedding of innocent blood. For he had filled Jerusalem with innocent blood, and the LORD was not willing to forgive.

⁵As for the other events of Jehoiakim's reign, and all he did, are they not written in the book of the annals of the kings of Judah? ⁶Jehoiakim rested with his fathers. And Jehoiachin his son succeeded him as king.

⁷The king of Egypt did not march out

ᵃ27 1 Kings 8:29   ᵇ33 Hebrew; Septuagint (see also 2 Chron. 36:3) *Neco at Riblah in Hamath removed him*   ᶜ33 That is, about 3 3/4 tons (about 3.4 metric tons)   ᵈ33 That is, about 75 pounds (about 34 kilograms)   ᵉ2 Or *Chaldean* from his own country again, because the king of Babylon had taken all his territory, from the Wadi of Egypt to the Euphrates River.

Jehoiachin King of Judah

8Jehoiachin was eighteen years old when he became king, and he reigned in Jerusalem three months. His mother's name was Nehushta daughter of Elnathan; she was from Jerusalem. 9He did evil in the eyes of the LORD, just as his father had done.

10At that time the officers of Nebuchadnezzar king of Babylon advanced on Jerusalem and laid siege to it, 11and Nebuchadnezzar himself came up to the city while his officers were besieging it. 12Jehoiachin king of Judah, his mother, his attendants, his nobles and his officials all surrendered to him.

In the eighth year of the reign of the king of Babylon, he took Jehoiachin prisoner. 13As the LORD had declared, Nebuchadnezzar removed all the treasures from the temple of the LORD and from the royal palace, and took away all the gold articles that Solomon king of Israel had made for the temple of the LORD. 14He carried into exile all Jerusalem: all the officers and fighting men, and all the craftsmen and artisans—a total of ten thousand. Only the poorest people of the land were left.

15Nebuchadnezzar took Jehoiachin captive to Babylon. He also took from Jerusalem to Babylon the king's mother, his wives, his officials and the leading men of the land. 16The king of Babylon also deported to Babylon the entire force of seven thousand fighting men, strong and fit for war, and a thousand craftsmen and artisans. 17He made Mattaniah, Jehoiachin's uncle, king in his place and changed his name to Zedekiah.

Zedekiah King of Judah

18Zedekiah was twenty-one years old when he became king, and he reigned in Jerusalem eleven years. His mother's name was Hamutal daughter of Jeremiah; she was from Libnah. 19He did evil in the eyes of the LORD, just as Jehoiakim had done. 20It was because of the LORD's anger that all this happened to Jerusalem and Judah, and in the end he thrust them from his presence.

The Fall of Jerusalem

Now Zedekiah rebelled against the king of Babylon.

25 So in the ninth year of Zedekiah's reign, on the tenth day of the tenth month, Nebuchadnezzar king of Babylon marched against Jerusalem with his whole army. He encamped outside the city and built siege works all around it. 2The city was kept under siege until the eleventh year of King Zedekiah. 3By the ninth day of the .fourth,a month the famine in the city had become so severe that there was no food for the people to eat. 4Then the city wall was broken through, and the whole army fled at night through the gate between the two walls near the king's garden, though the Babyloniansb were surrounding the city. They fled toward the Arabah,c 5but the Babyloniand army pursued the king and overtook him in the plains of Jericho. All his soldiers were separated from him and scattered, 6and he was captured. He was taken to the king of Babylon at Riblah, where sentence was pronounced on him. 7They killed the sons of Zedekiah before his eyes. Then they put out his eyes, bound him with bronze shackles and took him to Babylon.

8On the seventh day of the fifth month, in the nineteenth year of Nebuchadnezzar king of Babylon, Nebuzaradan commander of the imperial guard, an official of the king of Babylon, came to Jerusalem. 9He set fire to the temple of the LORD, the royal palace and all the houses of Jerusalem. Every important building he burned down. 10The whole Babylonian army, under the commander of the imperial guard, broke down the walls around Jerusalem. 11Nebuzaradan the commander of the guard carried into exile the people who remained in the city, along with the rest of the populace and those who had gone over to the king of Babylon. 12But the commander left behind some of the poorest people of the land to work the vineyards and fields.

13The Babylonians broke up the bronze pillars, the movable stands and the bronze Sea that were at the temple of the LORD and they carried the bronze to Babylon. 14They also took away the pots, shovels, wick trimmers, dishes and all the bronze articles used in the temple service. 15The commander of the imperial

---

a3 See Jer. 52:6.   b4 Or Chaldeans; also in verses 13, 25 and 26   c4 Or the Jordan Valley   d5 Or Chaldean; also in verses 10 and 24 guard took away the censers and sprinkling bowls—all that were made of pure gold or silver.

16The bronze from the two pillars, the Sea and the movable stands, which Solomon had made for the temple of the LORD, was more than could be weighed. 17Each pillar was twenty-seven feet*a* high. The bronze capital on top of one pillar was four and a half feet*b* high and was decorated with a network and pomegranates of bronze all around. The other pillar, with its network, was similar.

18The commander of the guard took as prisoners Seraiah the chief priest, Zephaniah the priest next in rank and the three doorkeepers. 19Of those still in the city, he took the officer in charge of the fighting men and five royal advisers. He also took the secretary who was chief officer in charge of conscripting the people of the land and sixty of his men who were found in the city. 20Nebuzaradan the commander took them all and brought them to the king of Babylon at Riblah. 21There at Riblah, in the land of Hamath, the king had them executed.

So Judah went into captivity, away from her land.

22Nebuchadnezzar king of Babylon appointed Gedaliah son of Ahikam, the son of Shaphan, to be over the people he had left behind in Judah. 23When all the army officers and their men heard that the king of Babylon had appointed Gedaliah as governor, they came to Gedaliah at Mizpah—Ishmael son of Nethaniah, Johanan son of Kareah, Seraiah son of Tanhumeth the Netophathite, Jaazaniah the son of the Maacathite, and their men. 24Gedaliah took an oath to reassure them and their men. "Do not be afraid of the Babylonian officials," he said. "Settle down in the land and serve the king of Babylon, and it will go well with you."

25In the seventh month, however, Ishmael son of Nethaniah, the son of Elishama, who was of royal blood, came with ten men and assassinated Gedaliah and also the men of Judah and the Babylonians who were with him at Mizpah. 26At this, all the people from the least to the greatest, together with the army officers, fled to Egypt for fear of the Babylonians.

Jehoiachin Released

27In the thirty-seventh year of the exile of Jehoiachin king of Judah, in the year Evil-Merodach*c* became king of Babylon, he released Jehoiachin from prison on the twenty-seventh day of the twelfth month. 28He spoke kindly to him and gave him a seat of honor higher than those of the other kings who were with him in Babylon. 29So Jehoiachin put aside his prison clothes and for the rest of his life ate regularly at the king's table. 30Day by day the king gave Jehoiachin a regular allowance as long as he lived.

---

a17 Hebrew *eighteen cubits* (about 8.1 meters)　　*b17* Hebrew *three cubits* (about 1.3 meters)
c27 Also called *Amel-Marduk*

*T*HIS book, after listing the genealogies of God's people from Adam to David, describes in great detail how David conducts his administrative, military and religious affairs. Note David's desire for the true worship of God, shown by organizing the priests and Levites and by making extensive plans for building the temple. As you read this book, think about the importance of worshiping the Lord and the priority in your life that such worship deserves.

1 CHRONICLES

Historical Records From Adam to Abraham

To Noah's Sons

1 Adam, Seth, Enosh, ²Kenan, Mahalalel, Jared, ³Enoch, Methuselah, Lamech, Noah.

⁴The sons of Noah:ª
Shem, Ham and Japheth.

The Japhethites

⁵The sons*b* of Japheth:
Gomer, Magog, Madai, Javan, Tubal, Meshech and Tiras.
⁶The sons of Gomer:
Ashkenaz, Riphath*c* and Togarmah.
⁷The sons of Javan:
Elishah, Tarshish, the Kittim and the Rodanim.

The Hamites

⁸The sons of Ham:
Cush, Mizraim,*d* Put and Canaan.
⁹The sons of Cush:

ª4 Septuagint; Hebrew does not have *The sons of Noah:*   *b*5 *Sons* may mean *descendants* or *successors* or *nations*; also in verses 6-10, 17 and 20.   *c*6 Many Hebrew manuscripts and Vulgate (see also Septuagint and Gen. 10:3); most Hebrew manuscripts *Diphath*   *d*8 That is, Egypt; also in verse 11

Seba, Havilah, Sabta, Raamah and Sabteca.

The sons of Raamah:
Sheba and Dedan.

¹⁰Cush was the father*a* of Nimrod, who grew to be a mighty warrior on earth.

¹¹Mizraim was the father of the Ludites, Anamites, Lehabites, Naphtuhites, ¹²Pathrusites, Casluhites (from whom the Philistines came) and Caphtorites.

¹³Canaan was the father of Sidon his firstborn,*b* and of the Hittites, ¹⁴Jebusites, Amorites, Girgashites, ¹⁵Hivites, Arkites, Sinites, ¹⁶Arvadites, Zemarites and Hamathites.

The Semites

¹⁷The sons of Shem:
Elam, Asshur, Arphaxad, Lud and Aram.

The sons of Aram*c*:
Uz, Hul, Gether and Meshech.

¹⁸Arphaxad was the father of Shelah, and Shelah the father of Eber.

¹⁹Two sons were born to Eber:
One was named Peleg,*d* because in his time the earth was divided; his brother was named Joktan.

²⁰Joktan was the father of Almodad, Sheleph, Hazarmaveth, Jerah, ²¹Hadoram, Uzal, Diklah, ²²Obal,*e* Abimael, Sheba, ²³Ophir, Havilah and Jobab. All these were sons of Joktan.

²⁴Shem, Arphaxad,*f* Shelah,
²⁵Eber, Peleg, Reu,
²⁶Serug, Nahor, Terah
²⁷and Abram (that is, Abraham).

The Family of Abraham

²⁸The sons of Abraham:
Isaac and Ishmael.

Descendants of Hagar

²⁹These were their descendants:
Nebaioth the firstborn of Ishmael, Kedar, Adbeel, Mibsam, ³⁰Mishma, Dumah, Massa, Hadad, Tema,

³¹Jetur, Naphish and Kedemah. These were the sons of Ishmael.

Descendants of Keturah

³²The sons born to Keturah, Abraham's concubine:
Zimran, Jokshan, Medan, Midian, Ishbak and Shuah.

The sons of Jokshan:
Sheba and Dedan.

³³The sons of Midian:
Ephah, Epher, Hanoch, Abida and Eldaah.

All these were descendants of Keturah.

Descendants of Sarah

³⁴Abraham was the father of Isaac.
The sons of Isaac:
Esau and Israel.

Esau's Sons

³⁵The sons of Esau:
Eliphaz, Reuel, Jeush, Jalam and Korah.

³⁶The sons of Eliphaz:
Teman, Omar, Zepho,*g* Gatam and Kenaz;
by Timna: Amalek.*h*

³⁷The sons of Reuel:
Nahath, Zerah, Shammah and Mizzah.

The People of Seir in Edom

³⁸The sons of Seir:
Lotan, Shobal, Zibeon, Anah, Dishon, Ezer and Dishan.

³⁹The sons of Lotan:
Hori and Homam. Timna was Lotan's sister.

⁴⁰The sons of Shobal:
Alvan,*i* Manahath, Ebal, Shepho and Onam.

The sons of Zibeon:
Aiah and Anah.

⁴¹The son of Anah:
Dishon.

The sons of Dishon:

---

a10 Father may mean *ancestor* or *predecessor* or *founder*; also in verses 11, 13, 18 and 20.   *b13* Or *of the Sidonians, the foremost*   *c17* One Hebrew manuscript and some Septuagint manuscripts (see also Gen. 10:23); most Hebrew manuscripts do not have this line.   *d19 Peleg* means *division.*   *e22* Some Hebrew manuscripts and Syriac (see also Gen. 10:28); most Hebrew manuscripts *Ebal*   *f24* Hebrew; some Septuagint manuscripts *Arphaxad, Cainan* (see also note at Gen. 11:10)   *g36* Many Hebrew manuscripts, some Septuagint manuscripts and Syriac (see also Gen. 36:11); most Hebrew manuscripts *Zephi*   *h36* Some Septuagint manuscripts (see also Gen. 36:12); Hebrew *Gatam, Kenaz, Timna and Amalek*   *i40* Many Hebrew manuscripts and some Septuagint manuscripts (see also Gen. 36:23); most Hebrew manuscripts *Alian*

Hemdan,[a] Eshban, Ithran and Keran.

42The sons of Ezer:
Bilhan, Zaavan and Akan.[b]
The sons of Dishan[c]:
Uz and Aran.

The Rulers of Edom

43These were the kings who reigned in Edom before any Israelite king reigned[d]:
Bela son of Beor, whose city was named Dinhabah.

44When Bela died, Jobab son of Zerah from Bozrah succeeded him as king.

45When Jobab died, Husham from the land of the Temanites succeeded him as king.

46When Husham died, Hadad son of Bedad, who defeated Midian in the country of Moab, succeeded him as king. His city was named Avith.

47When Hadad died, Samlah from Masrekah succeeded him as king.

48When Samlah died, Shaul from Rehoboth on the river[e] succeeded him as king.

49When Shaul died, Baal-Hanan son of Acbor succeeded him as king.

50When Baal-Hanan died, Hadad succeeded him as king. His city was named Pau,[f] and his wife's name was Mehetabel daughter of Matred, the daughter of Me-Zahab. 51Hadad also died.

The chiefs of Edom were:
Timna, Alvah, Jetheth, 52Oholibamah, Elah, Pinon, 53Kenaz, Teman, Mibzar, 54Magdiel and Iram. These were the chiefs of Edom.

Israel's Sons

2 These were the sons of Israel:
Reuben, Simeon, Levi, Judah, Issachar, Zebulun, 2Dan, Joseph, Benjamin, Naphtali, Gad and Asher.

Judah

To Hezron's Sons

3The sons of Judah:
Er, Onan and Shelah. These three were born to him by a Canaanite woman, the daughter of Shua. Er, Judah's firstborn, was wicked in the LORD's sight; so the LORD put him to death. 4Tamar, Judah's daughter-in-law, bore him Perez and Zerah. Judah had five sons in all.

5The sons of Perez:
Hezron and Hamul.

6The sons of Zerah:
Zimri, Ethan, Heman, Calcol and Darda[g]—five in all.

7The son of Carmi:
Achar,[h] who brought trouble on Israel by violating the ban on taking devoted things.[i]

8The son of Ethan:
Azariah.

9The sons born to Hezron were:
Jerahmeel, Ram and Caleb.[j]

From Ram Son of Hezron

10Ram was the father of Amminadab, and Amminadab the father of Nahshon, the leader of the people of Judah. 11Nahshon was the father of Salmon,[k] Salmon the father of Boaz, 12Boaz the father of Obed and Obed the father of Jesse.

13Jesse was the father of
Eliab his firstborn; the second son was Abinadab, the third Shimea, 14the fourth Nethanel, the fifth Raddai, 15the sixth Ozem and the seventh David. 16Their sisters were Zeruiah and Abigail. Zeruiah's three sons were Abishai, Joab and Asahel. 17Abigail was the mother of Amasa, whose father was Jether the Ishmaelite.

Caleb Son of Hezron

18Caleb son of Hezron had children by

---

a41 Many Hebrew manuscripts and some Septuagint manuscripts (see also Gen. 36:26); most Hebrew manuscripts *Hamran*   b42 Many Hebrew and Septuagint manuscripts (see also Gen. 36:27); most Hebrew manuscripts *Zaavan, Jaakan*   c42 Hebrew *Dishon*, a variant of *Dishan*   d43 Or *before an Israelite king reigned over them*   e48 Possibly the Euphrates   f50 Many Hebrew manuscripts, some Septuagint manuscripts, Vulgate and Syriac (see also Gen. 36:39); most Hebrew manuscripts *Pai*   g6 Many Hebrew manuscripts, some Septuagint manuscripts and Syriac (see also 1 Kings 4:31); most Hebrew manuscripts *Dara*   h7 *Achar* means *trouble*; *Achar* is called *Achan* in Joshua.   i7 The Hebrew term refers to the irrevocable giving over of things or persons to the LORD, often by totally destroying them.   j9 Hebrew *Kelubai*, a variant of *Caleb*   k11 Septuagint (see also Ruth 4:21); Hebrew *Salma* his wife Azubah (and by Jerioth). These were her sons: Jesher, Shobab and Ardon. ¹⁹When Azubah died, Caleb married Ephrath, who bore him Hur. ²⁰Hur was the father of Uri, and Uri the father of Bezalel.

²¹Later, Hezron lay with the daughter of Makir the father of Gilead (he had married her when he was sixty years old), and she bore him Segub. ²²Segub was the father of Jair, who controlled twenty-three towns in Gilead. ²³(But Geshur and Aram captured Havvoth Jair,ᵃ as well as Kenath with its surrounding settlements—sixty towns.) All these were descendants of Makir the father of Gilead.

²⁴After Hezron died in Caleb Ephrathah, Abijah the wife of Hezron bore him Ashhur the fatherᵇ of Tekoa.

Jerahmeel Son of Hezron

²⁵The sons of Jerahmeel the firstborn of Hezron:
Ram his firstborn, Bunah, Oren, Ozem andᶜ Ahijah. ²⁶Jerahmeel had another wife, whose name was Atarah; she was the mother of Onam.

²⁷The sons of Ram the firstborn of Jerahmeel:
Maaz, Jamin and Eker.

²⁸The sons of Onam:
Shammai and Jada.
The sons of Shammai:
Nadab and Abishur.

²⁹Abishur's wife was named Abihail, who bore him Ahban and Molid.

³⁰The sons of Nadab:
Seled and Appaim. Seled died without children.

³¹The son of Appaim:
Ishi, who was the father of Sheshan.
Sheshan was the father of Ahlai.

³²The sons of Jada, Shammai's brother:
Jether and Jonathan. Jether died without children.

³³The sons of Jonathan:
Peleth and Zaza.

These were the descendants of Jerahmeel.

³⁴Sheshan had no sons—only daughters.
He had an Egyptian servant named Jarha. ³⁵Sheshan gave his daughter in marriage to his servant Jarha, and she bore him Attai.

³⁶Attai was the father of Nathan,
Nathan the father of Zabad,
³⁷Zabad the father of Ephlal,
Ephlal the father of Obed,
³⁸Obed the father of Jehu,
Jehu the father of Azariah,
³⁹Azariah the father of Helez,
Helez the father of Eleasah,
⁴⁰Eleasah the father of Sismai,
Sismai the father of Shallum,
⁴¹Shallum the father of Jekamiah,
and Jekamiah the father of Elishama

The Clans of Caleb

⁴²The sons of Caleb the brother of Jerahmeel:
Mesha his firstborn, who was the father of Ziph, and his son Mareshah,ᵈ who was the father of Hebron.

⁴³The sons of Hebron:
Korah, Tappuah, Rekem and Shema. ⁴⁴Shema was the father of Raham, and Raham the father of Jorkeam. Rekem was the father of Shammai. ⁴⁵The son of Shammai was Maon, and Maon was the father of Beth Zur.

⁴⁶Caleb's concubine Ephah was the mother of Haran, Moza and Gazez. Haran was the father of Gazez.

⁴⁷The sons of Jahdai:
Regem, Jotham, Geshan, Pelet, Ephah and Shaaph.

⁴⁸Caleb's concubine Maacah was the mother of Sheber and Tirhanah. ⁴⁹She also gave birth to Shaaph the father of Madmannah and to Sheva the father of Macbenah and Gibea. Caleb's daughter was Acsah. ⁵⁰These were the descendants of Caleb.

The sons of Hur the firstborn of Ephrathah:
Shobal the father of Kiriath Jearim, ⁵¹Salma the father of Bethle-

---

ᵃ23 Or captured the settlements of Jair   ᵇ24 Father may mean civic leader or military leader; also in verses 42, 45, 49-52 and possibly elsewhere.   ᶜ25 Or Oren and Ozem, by   ᵈ42 The meaning of the Hebrew for this phrase is uncertain.

hem, and Hareph the father of Beth Gader.

⁵²The descendants of Shobal the father of Kiriath Jearim were:

Haroeh, half the Manahathites, ⁵³and the clans of Kiriath Jearim: the Ithrites, Puthites, Shumathites and Mishraites. From these descended the Zorathites and Eshtaolites.

⁵⁴The descendants of Salma:

Bethlehem, the Netophathites, Atroth Beth Joab, half the Manahathites, the Zorites, ⁵⁵and the clans of scribes*a* who lived at Jabez: the Tirathites, Shimeathites and Sucathites. These are the Kenites who came from Hammath, the father of the house of Recab.*b*

The Sons of David

3 These were the sons of David born to him in Hebron:

The firstborn was Amnon the son of Ahinoam of Jezreel;

the second, Daniel the son of Abigail of Carmel;

²the third, Absalom the son of Maacah daughter of Talmai king of Geshur;

the fourth, Adonijah the son of Haggith;

³the fifth, Shephatiah the son of Abital;

and the sixth, Ithream, by his wife Eglah.

⁴These six were born to David in Hebron, where he reigned seven years and six months.

David reigned in Jerusalem thirty-three years, ⁵and these were the children born to him there:

Shammua,*c* Shobab, Nathan and Solomon. These four were by Bathsheba*d* daughter of Ammiel. ⁶There were also Ibhar, Elishua,*e* Eliphelet, ⁷Nogah, Nepheg, Japhia, ⁸Elishama, Eliada and Eliphelet—nine in all. ⁹All these were the sons of David, besides his sons by his concubines. And Tamar was their sister.

The Kings of Judah

¹⁰Solomon's son was Rehoboam,
Abijah his son,
Asa his son,
Jehoshaphat his son,
¹¹Jehoram*f* his son,
Ahaziah his son,
Joash his son,
¹²Amaziah his son,
Azariah his son,
Jotham his son,
¹³Ahaz his son,
Hezekiah his son,
Manasseh his son,
¹⁴Amon his son,
Josiah his son.
¹⁵The sons of Josiah:
Johanan the firstborn,
Jehoiakim the second son,
Zedekiah the third,
Shallum the fourth.
¹⁶The successors of Jehoiakim:
Jehoiachin*g* his son,
and Zedekiah.

The Royal Line After the Exile

¹⁷The descendants of Jehoiachin the captive:
Shealtiel his son, ¹⁸Malkiram, Pedaiah, Shenazzar, Jekamiah, Hoshama and Nedabiah.
¹⁹The sons of Pedaiah:
Zerubbabel and Shimei.
The sons of Zerubbabel:
Meshullam and Hananiah.
Shelomith was their sister.
²⁰There were also five others:
Hashubah, Ohel, Berekiah, Hasadiah and Jushab-Hesed.
²¹The descendants of Hananiah:
Pelatiah and Jeshaiah, and the sons of Rephaiah, of Arnan, of Obadiah and of Shecaniah.
²²The descendants of Shecaniah:
Shemaiah and his sons:
Hattush, Igal, Bariah, Neariah and Shaphat—six in all.
²³The sons of Neariah:
Elioenai, Hizkiah and Azrikam—three in all.
²⁴The sons of Elioenai:
Hodaviah, Eliashib, Pelaiah, Akkub, Johanan, Delaiah and Anani—seven in all.

---

a55 Or *of the Sopherites*   *b55* Or *father of Beth Recab*   *c5* Hebrew *Shimea,* a variant of *Shammua*
d5 One Hebrew manuscript and Vulgate (see also Septuagint and 2 Samuel 11:3); most Hebrew manuscripts *Bathshua*   *e6* Two Hebrew manuscripts (see also 2 Samuel 5:15 and 1 Chron. 14:5); most Hebrew manuscripts *Elishama*   *f11* Hebrew *Joram,* a variant of *Jehoram*   *g16* Hebrew *Jeconiah,* a variant of *Jehoiachin*; also in verse 17

Other Clans of Judah

4 The descendants of Judah:
Perez, Hezron, Carmi, Hur and Shobal.

²Reaiah son of Shobal was the father of Jahath, and Jahath the father of Ahumai and Lahad. These were the clans of the Zorathites.

³These were the sons[a] of Etam:
Jezreel, Ishma and Idbash. Their sister was named Hazzelelponi. ⁴Penuel was the father of Gedor, and Ezer the father of Hushah.

These were the descendants of Hur, the firstborn of Ephrathah and father[b] of Bethlehem.

⁵Ashhur the father of Tekoa had two wives, Helah and Naarah.

⁶Naarah bore him Ahuzzam, Hepher, Temeni and Haahashtari. These were the descendants of Naarah.

⁷The sons of Helah:
Zereth, Zohar, Ethnan, ⁸and Koz, who was the father of Anub and Hazzobebah and of the clans of Aharhel son of Harum.

⁹Jabez was more honorable than his brothers. His mother had named him Jabez,[c] saying, "I gave birth to him in pain." ¹⁰Jabez cried out to the God of Israel, "Oh, that you would bless me and enlarge my territory! Let your hand be with me, and keep me from harm so that I will be free from pain." And God granted his request.

¹¹Kelub, Shuhah's brother, was the father of Mehir, who was the father of Eshton. ¹²Eshton was the father of Beth Rapha, Paseah and Tehinnah the father of Ir Nahash.[d] These were the men of Recah.

¹³The sons of Kenaz:
Othniel and Seraiah.

The sons of Othniel:
Hathath and Meonothai.[e] ¹⁴Meonothai was the father of Ophrah.

Seraiah was the father of Joab, the father of Ge Harashim.[f] It was called this because its people were craftsmen.

¹⁵The sons of Caleb son of Jephunneh:
Iru, Elah and Naam.

The son of Elah:
Kenaz.

¹⁶The sons of Jehallelel:
Ziph, Ziphah, Tiria and Asarel.

¹⁷The sons of Ezrah:
Jether, Mered, Epher and Jalon.
One of Mered's wives gave birth to Miriam, Shammai and Ishbah the father of Eshtemoa. ¹⁸(His Judean wife gave birth to Jered the father of Gedor, Heber the father of Soco, and Jekuthiel the father of Zanoah.) These were the children of Pharaoh's daughter Bithiah, whom Mered had married.

¹⁹The sons of Hodiah's wife, the sister of Naham:
the father of Keilah the Garmite, and Eshtemoa the Maacathite.

²⁰The sons of Shimon:
Amnon, Rinnah, Ben-Hanan and Tilon.

The descendants of Ishi:
Zoheth and Ben-Zoheth.

²¹The sons of Shelah son of Judah:
Er the father of Lecah, Laadah the father of Mareshah and the clans of the linen workers at Beth Ashbea, ²²Jokim, the men of Cozeba, and Joash and Saraph, who ruled in Moab and Jashubi Lehem. (These records are from ancient times.) ²³They were the potters who lived at Netaim and Gederah; they stayed there and worked for the king.

Simeon

²⁴The descendants of Simeon:
Nemuel, Jamin, Jarib, Zerah and Shaul;

²⁵Shallum was Shaul's son, Mibsam his son and Mishma his son.

²⁶The descendants of Mishma:
Hammuel his son, Zaccur his son and Shimei his son.

²⁷Shimei had sixteen sons and six daughters, but his brothers did not have many children; so their entire clan did not become as numerous as the people of Judah. ²⁸They lived in Beersheba, Moladah, Hazar Shual, ²⁹Bilhah, Ezem, Tolad, ³⁰Bethuel, Hormah, Ziklag, ³¹Beth Marcaboth, Hazar Susim, Beth Biri and Shaaraim. These were their towns until the reign of David. ³²Their surrounding villages

---

a3 Some Septuagint manuscripts (see also Vulgate); Hebrew *father*   *b4* *Father* may mean *civic leader* or *military leader*; also in verses 12, 14, 17, 18 and possibly elsewhere.   *c9* *Jabez* sounds like the Hebrew for *pain*.   *d12* Or *of the city of Nahash*   *e13* Some Septuagint manuscripts and Vulgate; Hebrew does not have *and Meonothai*.   *f14* *Ge Harashim* means *valley of craftsmen*.

were Etam, Ain, Rimmon, Token and Ashan—five towns— ³³and all the villages around these towns as far as Baalath.ª These were their settlements. And they kept a genealogical record.

³⁴Meshobab, Jamlech, Joshah son of Amaziah, ³⁵Joel, Jehu son of Joshibiah, the son of Seraiah, the son of Asiel, ³⁶also Elioenai, Jaakobah, Jeshohaiah, Asaiah, Adiel, Jesimiel, Benaiah, ³⁷and Ziza son of Shiphi, the son of Allon, the son of Jedaiah, the son of Shimri, the son of Shemaiah.

³⁸The men listed above by name were leaders of their clans. Their families increased greatly, ³⁹and they went to the outskirts of Gedor to the east of the valley in search of pasture for their flocks. ⁴⁰They found rich, good pasture, and the land was spacious, peaceful and quiet. Some Hamites had lived there formerly. ⁴¹The men whose names were listed came in the days of Hezekiah king of Judah. They attacked the Hamites in their dwellings and also the Meunites who were there and completely destroyed[b] them, as is evident to this day. Then they settled in their place, because there was pasture for their flocks. ⁴²And five hundred of these Simeonites, led by Pelatiah, Neariah, Rephaiah and Uzziel, the sons of Ishi, invaded the hill country of Seir. ⁴³They killed the remaining Amalekites who had escaped, and they have lived there to this day.

Reuben

5 The sons of Reuben the firstborn of Israel (he was the firstborn, but when he defiled his father's marriage bed, his rights as firstborn were given to the sons of Joseph son of Israel; so he could not be listed in the genealogical record in accordance with his birthright, ²and though Judah was the strongest of his brothers and a ruler came from him, the rights of the firstborn belonged to Joseph)— ³the sons of Reuben the firstborn of Israel:

Hanoch, Pallu, Hezron and Carmi.
⁴The descendants of Joel:
Shemaiah his son, Gog his son, Shimei his son, ⁵Micah his son, Reaiah his son, Baal his son, ⁶and Beerah his son, whom Tiglath-Pileser[c] king of Assyria took into

exile. Beerah was a leader of the Reubenites.
⁷Their relatives by clans, listed according to their genealogical records:
Jeiel the chief, Zechariah, ⁸and Bela son of Azaz, the son of Shema, the son of Joel. They settled in the area from Aroer to Nebo and Baal Meon. ⁹To the east they occupied the land up to the edge of the desert that extends to the Euphrates River, because their livestock had increased in Gilead.
¹⁰During Saul's reign they waged war against the Hagrites, who were defeated at their hands; they occupied the dwellings of the Hagrites throughout the entire region east of Gilead.

Gad

¹¹The Gadites lived next to them in Bashan, as far as Salecah:
¹²Joel was the chief, Shapham the second, then Janai and Shaphat, in Bashan.
¹³Their relatives, by families, were:
Michael, Meshullam, Sheba, Jorai, Jacan, Zia and Eber—seven in all.
¹⁴These were the sons of Abihail son of Huri, the son of Jaroah, the son of Gilead, the son of Michael, the son of Jeshishai, the son of Jahdo, the son of Buz.
¹⁵Ahi son of Abdiel, the son of Guni, was head of their family.
¹⁶The Gadites lived in Gilead, in Bashan and its outlying villages, and on all the pasturelands of Sharon as far as they extended.
¹⁷All these were entered in the genealogical records during the reigns of Jotham king of Judah and Jeroboam king of Israel.

¹⁸The Reubenites, the Gadites and the half-tribe of Manasseh had 44,760 men ready for military service—able-bodied men who could handle shield and sword, who could use a bow, and who were trained for battle. ¹⁹They waged war against the Hagrites, Jetur, Naphish and Nodab. ²⁰They were helped in fighting them, and God handed the Hagrites and all their allies over to them, because they cried out to him during the battle. He answered their prayers, because they trust-

---

ª33 Some Septuagint manuscripts (see also Joshua 19:8); Hebrew *Baal*   b41 The Hebrew term refers to the irrevocable giving over of things or persons to the LORD, often by totally destroying them.   c6 Hebrew *Tilgath-Pilneser*, a variant of *Tiglath-Pileser*; also in verse 26

VERSE FOR THE DAY:	AUTHOR:	PASSAGE FOR THE DAY:
1 Chronicles 4:40	Alma Barkman	1 Chronicles 4:24–40

Budget Blues

I PICKED up a newspaper the other day and saw that, according to the latest statistics, our family has just pulled out of the poverty level. I had never realized our financial state of affairs was so poor.

True, the kids are wearing jeans with holes in the knees, but that's by choice, not necessity. Contrary to popular opinion, I do own two pairs of shoes, but these bedraggled, old bedroom slippers are simply the ultimate in comfort. And that old hat my husband wears is just an excuse. He claims the new styles don't do him justice.

In spite of what statistics say, we aren't forced to do without clothes, we enjoy three square meals a day, and the roof over our head is paid for, even if we shingled it ourselves. After starting with less than forty dollars between us, we thought we were sitting very comfortably. Now, twenty years of marriage, four kids, three cats, two houses, and five cars later, the experts tell me we have only been subsisting. I wonder what *real* living is like?

I realize that for some people in this world, poverty is a stark reality. For others, it's just a state of mind.

How disturbed should we be if our income falls below the national average, or even below the neighbor's? There is always the possibility that I am poor because I feel poor, not because I lack necessities.

Rather than striving to obtain a better standard of living by simply making more money, perhaps I need to adjust my attitude toward spending. If we are sincerely willing to try to stay within the amounts God has allotted us, I believe he will honor our efficiency.

Now and then it is wise to go over the budget systematically, bearing in mind Solomon's wise advice:

> Give me neither poverty nor riches,
> but give me only my daily bread
> (Proverbs 30:8).

Additional Scripture Readings:
Psalm 37:16–17; 1 Timothy 6:6–10

*Go to page 428 for your next
devotional reading.*

ed in him. ²¹They seized the livestock of the Hagrites—fifty thousand camels, two hundred fifty thousand sheep and two thousand donkeys. They also took one hundred thousand people captive, ²²and many others fell slain, because the battle was God's. And they occupied the land until the exile.

The Half-Tribe of Manasseh

²³The people of the half-tribe of Manasseh were numerous; they settled in the land from Bashan to Baal Hermon, that is, to Senir (Mount Hermon).

²⁴These were the heads of their families: Epher, Ishi, Eliel, Azriel, Jeremiah, Hodaviah and Jahdiel. They were brave warriors, famous men, and heads of their families. ²⁵But they were unfaithful to the God of their fathers and prostituted themselves to the gods of the peoples of the land, whom God had destroyed before them. ²⁶So the God of Israel stirred up the spirit of Pul king of Assyria (that is, Tiglath-Pileser king of Assyria), who took the Reubenites, the Gadites and the half-tribe of Manasseh into exile. He took them to Halah, Habor, Hara and the river of Gozan, where they are to this day.

Levi

6 The sons of Levi:
Gershon, Kohath and Merari.
²The sons of Kohath:
Amram, Izhar, Hebron and Uzziel.
³The children of Amram:
Aaron, Moses and Miriam.
The sons of Aaron:
Nadab, Abihu, Eleazar and Ithamar.
⁴Eleazar was the father of Phinehas,
Phinehas the father of Abishua,
⁵Abishua the father of Bukki,
Bukki the father of Uzzi,
⁶Uzzi the father of Zerahiah,
Zerahiah the father of Meraioth,
⁷Meraioth the father of Amariah,
Amariah the father of Ahitub,
⁸Ahitub the father of Zadok,
Zadok the father of Ahimaaz,
⁹Ahimaaz the father of Azariah,
Azariah the father of Johanan,
¹⁰Johanan the father of Azariah (it

was he who served as priest in the temple Solomon built in Jerusalem),
¹¹Azariah the father of Amariah,
Amariah the father of Ahitub,
¹²Ahitub the father of Zadok,
Zadok the father of Shallum,
¹³Shallum the father of Hilkiah,
Hilkiah the father of Azariah,
¹⁴Azariah the father of Seraiah,
and Seraiah the father of Jehozadak.
¹⁵Jehozadak was deported when the LORD sent Judah and Jerusalem into exile by the hand of Nebuchadnezzar.

¹⁶The sons of Levi:
Gershon,[a] Kohath and Merari.
¹⁷These are the names of the sons of Gershon:
Libni and Shimei.
¹⁸The sons of Kohath:
Amram, Izhar, Hebron and Uzziel.
¹⁹The sons of Merari:
Mahli and Mushi.
These are the clans of the Levites listed according to their fathers:
²⁰Of Gershon:
Libni his son, Jehath his son,
Zimmah his son, ²¹Joah his son,
Iddo his son, Zerah his son
and Jeatherai his son.
²²The descendants of Kohath:
Amminadab his son, Korah his son,
Assir his son, ²³Elkanah his son,
Ebiasaph his son, Assir his son,
²⁴Tahath his son, Uriel his son,
Uzziah his son and Shaul his son.
²⁵The descendants of Elkanah:
Amasai, Ahimoth,
²⁶Elkanah his son,[b] Zophai his son,
Nahath his son, ²⁷Eliab his son,
Jeroham his son, Elkanah his son
and Samuel his son.[c]
²⁸The sons of Samuel:
Joel[d] the firstborn
and Abijah the second son.
²⁹The descendants of Merari:
Mahli, Libni his son,
Shimei his son, Uzzah his son,
³⁰Shimea his son, Haggiah his son
and Asaiah his son.

---

^a16 Hebrew *Gershom*, a variant of *Gershon*; also in verses 17, 20, 43, 62 and 71   ^b26 Some Hebrew manuscripts, Septuagint and Syriac; most Hebrew manuscripts *Ahimoth 26and Elkanah. The sons of Elkanah:*   ^c27 Some Septuagint manuscripts (see also 1 Samuel 1:19,20 and 1 Chron. 6:33,34); Hebrew does not have *and Samuel his son.*   ^d28 Some Septuagint manuscripts and Syriac (see also 1 Samuel 8:2 and 1 Chron. 6:33); Hebrew does not have *Joel.*

The Temple Musicians

³¹These are the men David put in charge of the music in the house of the LORD after the ark came to rest there. ³²They ministered with music before the tabernacle, the Tent of Meeting, until Solomon built the temple of the LORD in Jerusalem. They performed their duties according to the regulations laid down for them.

³³Here are the men who served, together with their sons:

From the Kohathites:
Heman, the musician,
the son of Joel, the son of Samuel,
³⁴the son of Elkanah, the son of Jeroham,
the son of Eliel, the son of Toah,
³⁵the son of Zuph, the son of Elkanah,
the son of Mahath, the son of Amasai,
³⁶the son of Elkanah, the son of Joel,
the son of Azariah, the son of Zephaniah,
³⁷the son of Tahath, the son of Assir,
the son of Ebiasaph, the son of Korah,
³⁸the son of Izhar, the son of Kohath,
the son of Levi, the son of Israel;
³⁹and Heman's associate Asaph, who served at his right hand:
Asaph son of Berekiah, the son of Shimea,
⁴⁰the son of Michael, the son of Baaseiah,ᵃ
the son of Malkijah, ⁴¹the son of Ethni,
the son of Zerah, the son of Adaiah,
⁴²the son of Ethan, the son of Zimmah,
the son of Shimei, ⁴³the son of Jahath,
the son of Gershon, the son of Levi;
⁴⁴and from their associates, the Merarites, at his left hand:
Ethan son of Kishi, the son of Abdi,
the son of Malluch, ⁴⁵the son of Hashabiah,

the son of Amaziah, the son of Hilkiah,
⁴⁶the son of Amzi, the son of Bani, the son of Shemer, ⁴⁷the son of Mahli,
the son of Mushi, the son of Merari,
the son of Levi.

⁴⁸Their fellow Levites were assigned to all the other duties of the tabernacle, the house of God. ⁴⁹But Aaron and his descendants were the ones who presented offerings on the altar of burnt offering and on the altar of incense in connection with all that was done in the Most Holy Place, making atonement for Israel, in accordance with all that Moses the servant of God had commanded.

⁵⁰These were the descendants of Aaron:
Eleazar his son, Phinehas his son, Abishua his son, ⁵¹Bukki his son, Uzzi his son, Zerahiah his son, ⁵²Meraioth his son, Amariah his son, Ahitub his son, ⁵³Zadok his son and Ahimaaz his son.

⁵⁴These were the locations of their settlements allotted as their territory (they were assigned to the descendants of Aaron who were from the Kohathite clan, because the first lot was for them):

⁵⁵They were given Hebron in Judah with its surrounding pasturelands. ⁵⁶But the fields and villages around the city were given to Caleb son of Jephunneh.

⁵⁷So the descendants of Aaron were given Hebron (a city of refuge), and Libnah,ᵇ Jattir, Eshtemoa, ⁵⁸Hilen, Debir, ⁵⁹Ashan, Juttahᶜ and Beth Shemesh, together with their pasturelands. ⁶⁰And from the tribe of Benjamin they were given Gibeon,ᵈ Geba, Alemeth and Anathoth, together with their pasturelands.

These towns, which were distributed among the Kohathite clans, were thirteen in all.

⁶¹The rest of Kohath's descendants were allotted ten towns from the clans of half the tribe of Manasseh.

⁶²The descendants of Gershon, clan by clan, were allotted thirteen towns from the tribes of Issachar, Asher and Naphta-

---

ᵃ40 Most Hebrew manuscripts; some Hebrew manuscripts, one Septuagint manuscript and Syriac *Maaseiah* ᵇ57 See Joshua 21:13; Hebrew *given the cities of refuge: Hebron, Libnah.* ᶜ59 Syriac (see also Septuagint and Joshua 21:16); Hebrew does not have *Juttah.* ᵈ60 See Joshua 21:17; Hebrew does not have *Gibeon.*

li, and from the part of the tribe of Manasseh that is in Bashan.

⁶³The descendants of Merari, clan by clan, were allotted twelve towns from the tribes of Reuben, Gad and Zebulun.

⁶⁴So the Israelites gave the Levites these towns and their pasturelands. ⁶⁵From the tribes of Judah, Simeon and Benjamin they allotted the previously named towns.

⁶⁶Some of the Kohathite clans were given as their territory towns from the tribe of Ephraim.

⁶⁷In the hill country of Ephraim they were given Shechem (a city of refuge), and Gezer,ᵃ ⁶⁸Jokmeam, Beth Horon, ⁶⁹Aijalon and Gath Rimmon, together with their pasturelands.

⁷⁰And from half the tribe of Manasseh the Israelites gave Aner and Bileam, together with their pasturelands, to the rest of the Kohathite clans.

⁷¹The Gershonites received the following:

From the clan of the half-tribe of Manasseh

they received Golan in Bashan and also Ashtaroth, together with their pasturelands;

⁷²from the tribe of Issachar

they received Kedesh, Daberath, ⁷³Ramoth and Anem, together with their pasturelands;

⁷⁴from the tribe of Asher

they received Mashal, Abdon, ⁷⁵Hukok and Rehob, together with their pasturelands;

⁷⁶and from the tribe of Naphtali

they received Kedesh in Galilee, Hammon and Kiriathaim, together with their pasturelands.

⁷⁷The Merarites (the rest of the Levites) received the following:

From the tribe of Zebulun

they received Jokneam, Kartah,ᵇ Rimmono and Tabor, together with their pasturelands;

⁷⁸from the tribe of Reuben across the Jordan east of Jericho

they received Bezer in the desert, Jahzah, ⁷⁹Kedemoth and Mephaath, together with their pasturelands;

⁸⁰and from the tribe of Gad

they received Ramoth in Gilead, Mahanaim, ⁸¹Heshbon and Jazer, together with their pasturelands.

Issachar

7 The sons of Issachar:

Tola, Puah, Jashub and Shimron —four in all.

²The sons of Tola:

Uzzi, Rephaiah, Jeriel, Jahmai, Ibsam and Samuel—heads of their families. During the reign of David, the descendants of Tola listed as fighting men in their genealogy numbered 22,600.

³The son of Uzzi:

Izrahiah.

The sons of Izrahiah:

Michael, Obadiah, Joel and Isshiah. All five of them were chiefs. ⁴According to their family genealogy, they had 36,000 men ready for battle, for they had many wives and children.

⁵The relatives who were fighting men belonging to all the clans of Issachar, as listed in their genealogy, were 87,000 in all.

Benjamin

⁶Three sons of Benjamin:

Bela, Beker and Jediael.

⁷The sons of Bela:

Ezbon, Uzzi, Uzziel, Jerimoth and Iri, heads of families—five in all. Their genealogical record listed 22,034 fighting men.

⁸The sons of Beker:

Zemirah, Joash, Eliezer, Elioenai, Omri, Jeremoth, Abijah, Anathoth and Alemeth. All these were the sons of Beker. ⁹Their genealogical record listed the heads of families and 20,200 fighting men.

¹⁰The son of Jediael:

Bilhan.

The sons of Bilhan:

Jeush, Benjamin, Ehud, Kenaanah, Zethan, Tarshish and Ahishahar. ¹¹All these sons of Jediael were heads of families. There were 17,200 fighting men ready to go out to war.

¹²The Shuppites and Huppites were the descendants of Ir, and the Hushites the descendants of Aher.

ᵃ67 See Joshua 21:21; Hebrew given the cities of refuge: Shechem, Gezer.   ᵇ77 See Septuagint and Joshua 21:34; Hebrew does not have Jokneam, Kartah.

Naphtali

13The sons of Naphtali:
Jahziel, Guni, Jezer and Shillem*a*
—the descendants of Bilhah.

Manasseh

14The descendants of Manasseh:
Asriel was his descendant through his Aramean concubine. She gave birth to Makir the father of Gilead. 15Makir took a wife from among the Huppites and Shuppites. His sister's name was Maacah.

Another descendant was named Zelophehad, who had only daughters.

16Makir's wife Maacah gave birth to a son and named him Peresh. His brother was named Sheresh, and his sons were Ulam and Rakem.

17The son of Ulam:
Bedan.

These were the sons of Gilead son of Makir, the son of Manasseh. 18His sister Hammoleketh gave birth to Ishhod, Abiezer and Mahlah.

19The sons of Shemida were:
Ahian, Shechem, Likhi and Aniam.

Ephraim

20The descendants of Ephraim:
Shuthelah, Bered his son,
Tahath his son, Eleadah his son,
Tahath his son, 21Zabad his son
and Shuthelah his son.

Ezer and Elead were killed by the native-born men of Gath, when they went down to seize their livestock. 22Their father Ephraim mourned for them many days, and his relatives came to comfort him. 23Then he lay with his wife again, and she became pregnant and gave birth to a son. He named him Beriah,*b* because there had been misfortune in his family. 24His daughter was Sheerah, who built Lower and Upper Beth Horon as well as Uzzen Sheerah.

25Rephah was his son, Resheph his son,*c*
Telah his son, Tahan his son,
26Ladan his son, Ammihud his son,
Elishama his son, 27Nun his son
and Joshua his son.

28Their lands and settlements included Bethel and its surrounding villages, Naaran to the east, Gezer and its villages to the west, and Shechem and its villages all the way to Ayyah and its villages. 29Along the borders of Manasseh were Beth Shan, Taanach, Megiddo and Dor, together with their villages. The descendants of Joseph son of Israel lived in these towns.

Asher

30The sons of Asher:
Imnah, Ishvah, Ishvi and Beriah.
Their sister was Serah.

31The sons of Beriah:
Heber and Malkiel, who was the father of Birzaith.

32Heber was the father of Japhlet, Shomer and Hotham and of their sister Shua.

33The sons of Japhlet:
Pasach, Bimhal and Ashvath.
These were Japhlet's sons.

34The sons of Shomer:
Ahi, Rohgah,*d* Hubbah and Aram.

35The sons of his brother Helem:
Zophah, Imna, Shelesh and Amal.

36The sons of Zophah:
Suah, Harnepher, Shual, Beri, Imrah, 37Bezer, Hod, Shamma, Shilshah, Ithran*e* and Beera.

38The sons of Jether:
Jephunneh, Pispah and Ara.

39The sons of Ulla:
Arah, Hanniel and Rizia.

40All these were descendants of Asher—heads of families, choice men, brave warriors and outstanding leaders. The number of men ready for battle, as listed in their genealogy, was 26,000.

The Genealogy of Saul the Benjamite

8 Benjamin was the father of Bela his firstborn,
Ashbel the second son, Aharah the third,
2Nohah the fourth and Rapha the fifth.

3The sons of Bela were:
Addar, Gera, Abihud,*f* 4Abishua, Naaman, Ahoah, 5Gera, Shephuphan and Huram.

6These were the descendants of Ehud, who were heads of families

---

a13 Some Hebrew and Septuagint manuscripts (see also Gen. 46:24 and Num. 26:49); most Hebrew manuscripts *Shallum*   *b23 Beriah* sounds like the Hebrew for *misfortune.*   *c25* Some Septuagint manuscripts; Hebrew does not have *his son.*   *d34* Or *of his brother Shomer: Rohgah*   *e37* Possibly a variant of *Jether*   *f3* Or *Gera the father of Ehud* of those living in Geba and were deported to Manahath: [7]Naaman, Ahijah, and Gera, who deported them and who was the father of Uzza and Ahihud.

[8]Sons were born to Shaharaim in Moab after he had divorced his wives Hushim and Baara. [9]By his wife Hodesh he had Jobab, Zibia, Mesha, Malcam, [10]Jeuz, Sakia and Mirmah. These were his sons, heads of families. [11]By Hushim he had Abitub and Elpaal.

[12]The sons of Elpaal:
Eber, Misham, Shemed (who built Ono and Lod with its surrounding villages), [13]and Beriah and Shema, who were heads of families of those living in Aijalon and who drove out the inhabitants of Gath.

[14]Ahio, Shashak, Jeremoth, [15]Zebadiah, Arad, Eder, [16]Michael, Ishpah and Joha were the sons of Beriah.

[17]Zebadiah, Meshullam, Hizki, Heber, [18]Ishmerai, Izliah and Jobab were the sons of Elpaal.

[19]Jakim, Zicri, Zabdi, [20]Elienai, Zillethai, Eliel, [21]Adaiah, Beraiah and Shimrath were the sons of Shimei.

[22]Ishpan, Eber, Eliel, [23]Abdon, Zicri, Hanan, [24]Hananiah, Elam, Anthothijah, [25]Iphdeiah and Penuel were the sons of Shashak.

[26]Shamsherai, Shehariah, Athaliah, [27]Jaareshiah, Elijah and Zicri were the sons of Jeroham.

[28]All these were heads of families, chiefs as listed in their genealogy, and they lived in Jerusalem.

[29]Jeiel[a] the father[b] of Gibeon lived in Gibeon.
His wife's name was Maacah, [30]and his firstborn son was Abdon, followed by Zur, Kish, Baal, Ner,[c] Nadab, [31]Gedor, Ahio, Zeker [32]and Mikloth, who was the father of Shimeah. They too lived near their relatives in Jerusalem.

[33]Ner was the father of Kish, Kish the father of Saul, and Saul the father of Jonathan, Malki-Shua, Abinadab and Esh-Baal.[d]

[34]The son of Jonathan:
Merib-Baal,[e] who was the father of Micah.

[35]The sons of Micah:
Pithon, Melech, Tarea and Ahaz. [36]Ahaz was the father of Jehoaddah, Jehoaddah was the father of Alemeth, Azmaveth and Zimri, and Zimri was the father of Moza. [37]Moza was the father of Binea; Raphah was his son, Eleasah his son and Azel his son.

[38]Azel had six sons, and these were their names:
Azrikam, Bokeru, Ishmael, Sheariah, Obadiah and Hanan. All these were the sons of Azel.

[39]The sons of his brother Eshek:
Ulam his firstborn, Jeush the second son and Eliphelet the third. [40]The sons of Ulam were brave warriors who could handle the bow. They had many sons and grandsons—150 in all.

All these were the descendants of Benjamin.

9 All Israel was listed in the genealogies recorded in the book of the kings of Israel.

The People in Jerusalem

The people of Judah were taken captive to Babylon because of their unfaithfulness. [2]Now the first to resettle on their own property in their own towns were some Israelites, priests, Levites and temple servants.

[3]Those from Judah, from Benjamin, and from Ephraim and Manasseh who lived in Jerusalem were:

[4]Uthai son of Ammihud, the son of Omri, the son of Imri, the son of Bani, a descendant of Perez son of Judah.

[5]Of the Shilonites:
Asaiah the firstborn and his sons.

[6]Of the Zerahites:
Jeuel.
The people from Judah numbered 690.

[7]Of the Benjamites:
Sallu son of Meshullam, the son of Hodaviah, the son of Hassenuah; [8]Ibneiah son of Jeroham; Elah son of Uzzi, the son of Micri; and Meshullam son of Shephatiah, the son of Reuel, the son of Ibnijah. [9]The people from Benjamin, as listed in their genealogy, numbered

[a]29 Some Septuagint manuscripts (see also 1 Chron. 9:35); Hebrew does not have Jeiel. [b]29 Father may mean civic leader or military leader. [c]30 Some Septuagint manuscripts (see also 1 Chron. 9:36); Hebrew does not have Ner. [d]33 Also known as Ish-Bosheth [e]34 Also known as Mephibosheth

9⁵⁶. All these men were heads of their families.

10Of the priests:

Jedaiah; Jehoiarib; Jakin;

11Azariah son of Hilkiah, the son of Meshullam, the son of Zadok, the son of Meraioth, the son of Ahitub, the official in charge of the house of God;

12Adaiah son of Jeroham, the son of Pashhur, the son of Malkijah; and Maasai son of Adiel, the son of Jahzerah, the son of Meshullam, the son of Meshillemith, the son of Immer.

13The priests, who were heads of families, numbered 1,760. They were able men, responsible for ministering in the house of God.

14Of the Levites:

Shemaiah son of Hasshub, the son of Azrikam, the son of Hashabiah, a Merarite; 15Bakbakkar, Heresh, Galal and Mattaniah son of Mica, the son of Zicri, the son of Asaph; 16Obadiah son of Shemaiah, the son of Galal, the son of Jeduthun; and Berekiah son of Asa, the son of Elkanah, who lived in the villages of the Netophathites.

17The gatekeepers:

Shallum, Akkub, Talmon, Ahiman and their brothers, Shallum their chief 18being stationed at the King's Gate on the east, up to the present time. These were the gatekeepers belonging to the camp of the Levites. 19Shallum son of Kore, the son of Ebiasaph, the son of Korah, and his fellow gatekeepers from his family (the Korahites) were responsible for guarding the thresholds of the Tentᵃ just as their fathers had been responsible for guarding the entrance to the dwelling of the LORD. 20In earlier times Phinehas son of Eleazar was in charge of the gatekeepers, and the LORD was with him. 21Zechariah son of Meshelemiah was the gatekeeper at the entrance to the Tent of Meeting.

22Altogether, those chosen to be gatekeepers at the thresholds numbered 212. They were registered by genealogy in their villages. The gatekeepers had been assigned to their positions of trust by Da-

vid and Samuel the seer. 23They and their descendants were in charge of guarding the gates of the house of the LORD—the house called the Tent. 24The gatekeepers were on the four sides: east, west, north and south. 25Their brothers in their villages had to come from time to time and share their duties for seven-day periods. 26But the four principal gatekeepers, who were Levites, were entrusted with the responsibility for the rooms and treasuries in the house of God. 27They would spend the night stationed around the house of God, because they had to guard it; and they had charge of the key for opening it each morning.

28Some of them were in charge of the articles used in the temple service; they counted them when they were brought in and when they were taken out. 29Others were assigned to take care of the furnishings and all the other articles of the sanctuary, as well as the flour and wine, and the oil, incense and spices. 30But some of the priests took care of mixing the spices. 31A Levite named Mattithiah, the firstborn son of Shallum the Korahite, was entrusted with the responsibility for baking the offering bread. 32Some of their Kohathite brothers were in charge of preparing for every Sabbath the bread set out on the table.

33Those who were musicians, heads of Levite families, stayed in the rooms of the temple and were exempt from other duties because they were responsible for the work day and night.

34All these were heads of Levite families, chiefs as listed in their genealogy, and they lived in Jerusalem.

The Genealogy of Saul

35Jeiel the fatherᵇ of Gibeon lived in Gibeon.

His wife's name was Maacah, 36and his firstborn son was Abdon, followed by Zur, Kish, Baal, Ner, Nadab, 37Gedor, Ahio, Zechariah and Mikloth. 38Mikloth was the father of Shimeam. They too lived near their relatives in Jerusalem.

39Ner was the father of Kish, Kish the father of Saul, and Saul the father of Jonathan, Malki-Shua, Abinadab and Esh-Baal.ᶜ

40The son of Jonathan:

ᵃ19 That is, the temple; also in verses 21 and 23　ᵇ35 Father may mean civic leader or military leader.
ᶜ39 Also known as Ish-Bosheth

Merib-Baal,[a] who was the father of Micah.

⁴¹The sons of Micah:

Pithon, Melech, Tahrea and Ahaz.[b]

⁴²Ahaz was the father of Jadah, Jadah[c] was the father of Alemeth, Azmaveth and Zimri, and Zimri was the father of Moza. ⁴³Moza was the father of Binea; Rephaiah was his son, Eleasah his son and Azel his son.

⁴⁴Azel had six sons, and these were their names:

Azrikam, Bokeru, Ishmael, Sheariah, Obadiah and Hanan. These were the sons of Azel.

Saul Takes His Life

10 Now the Philistines fought against Israel; the Israelites fled before them, and many fell slain on Mount Gilboa. ²The Philistines pressed hard after Saul and his sons, and they killed his sons Jonathan, Abinadab and Malki-Shua. ³The fighting grew fierce around Saul, and when the archers overtook him, they wounded him.

⁴Saul said to his armor-bearer, "Draw your sword and run me through, or these uncircumcised fellows will come and abuse me."

But his armor-bearer was terrified and would not do it; so Saul took his own sword and fell on it. ⁵When the armor-bearer saw that Saul was dead, he too fell on his sword and died. ⁶So Saul and his three sons died, and all his house died together.

⁷When all the Israelites in the valley saw that the army had fled and that Saul and his sons had died, they abandoned their towns and fled. And the Philistines came and occupied them.

⁸The next day, when the Philistines came to strip the dead, they found Saul and his sons fallen on Mount Gilboa. ⁹They stripped him and took his head and his armor, and sent messengers throughout the land of the Philistines to proclaim the news among their idols and their people. ¹⁰They put his armor in the temple of their gods and hung up his head in the temple of Dagon.

¹¹When all the inhabitants of Jabesh Gilead heard of everything the Philistines had done to Saul, ¹²all their valiant men went and took the bodies of Saul and his sons and brought them to Jabesh. Then they buried their bones under the great tree in Jabesh, and they fasted seven days.

¹³Saul died because he was unfaithful to the Lord; he did not keep the word of the Lord and even consulted a medium for guidance, ¹⁴and did not inquire of the Lord. So the Lord put him to death and turned the kingdom over to David son of Jesse.

David Becomes King Over Israel

11 All Israel came together to David at Hebron and said, "We are your own flesh and blood. ²In the past, even while Saul was king, you were the one who led Israel on their military campaigns. And the Lord your God said to you, 'You will shepherd my people Israel, and you will become their ruler.' "

³When all the elders of Israel had come to King David at Hebron, he made a compact with them at Hebron before the Lord, and they anointed David king over Israel, as the Lord had promised through Samuel.

David Conquers Jerusalem

⁴David and all the Israelites marched to Jerusalem (that is, Jebus). The Jebusites who lived there ⁵said to David, "You will not get in here." Nevertheless, David captured the fortress of Zion, the City of David.

⁶David had said, "Whoever leads the attack on the Jebusites will become commander-in-chief." Joab son of Zeruiah went up first, and so he received the command.

⁷David then took up residence in the fortress, and so it was called the City of David. ⁸He built up the city around it, from the supporting terraces[d] to the surrounding wall, while Joab restored the rest of the city. ⁹And David became more and more powerful, because the Lord Almighty was with him.

David's Mighty Men

¹⁰These were the chiefs of David's mighty men—they, together with all Israel, gave his kingship strong support to extend it over the whole land, as the Lord

---

a40 Also known as *Mephibosheth*   *b41* Vulgate and Syriac (see also Septuagint and 1 Chron. 8:35); Hebrew does not have *and Ahaz.*   *c42* Some Hebrew manuscripts and Septuagint (see also 1 Chron. 8:36); most Hebrew manuscripts *Jarah, Jarah*   *d8* Or *the Millo* had promised— [11]this is the list of David's mighty men:

Jashobeam,[a] a Hacmonite, was chief of the officers[b]; he raised his spear against three hundred men, whom he killed in one encounter.

[12]Next to him was Eleazar son of Dodai the Ahohite, one of the three mighty men. [13]He was with David at Pas Dammim when the Philistines gathered there for battle. At a place where there was a field full of barley, the troops fled from the Philistines. [14]But they took their stand in the middle of the field. They defended it and struck the Philistines down, and the LORD brought about a great victory.

[15]Three of the thirty chiefs came down to David to the rock at the cave of Adullam, while a band of Philistines was encamped in the Valley of Rephaim. [16]At that time David was in the stronghold, and the Philistine garrison was at Bethlehem. [17]David longed for water and said, "Oh, that someone would get me a drink of water from the well near the gate of Bethlehem!" [18]So the Three broke through the Philistine lines, drew water from the well near the gate of Bethlehem and carried it back to David. But he refused to drink it; instead, he poured it out before the LORD. [19]"God forbid that I should do this!" he said. "Should I drink the blood of these men who went at the risk of their lives?" Because they risked their lives to bring it back, David would not drink it.

Such were the exploits of the three mighty men.

[20]Abishai the brother of Joab was chief of the Three. He raised his spear against three hundred men, whom he killed, and so he became as famous as the Three. [21]He was doubly honored above the Three and became their commander, even though he was not included among them.

[22]Benaiah son of Jehoiada was a valiant fighter from Kabzeel, who performed great exploits. He struck down two of Moab's best men. He also went down into a pit on a snowy day and killed a lion. [23]And he struck down an Egyptian who was seven and a half feet[c] tall. Although the Egyptian had a spear like a weaver's rod in his hand, Benaiah went against him with a club. He snatched the spear from the Egyptian's hand and killed him with his own spear. [24]Such were the exploits of Benaiah son of Jehoiada; he too was as famous as the three mighty men. [25]He was held in greater honor than any of the Thirty, but he was not included among the Three. And David put him in charge of his bodyguard.

[26]The mighty men were:

Asahel the brother of Joab,
Elhanan son of Dodo from Bethlehem,
[27]Shammoth the Harorite,
Helez the Pelonite,
[28]Ira son of Ikkesh from Tekoa,
Abiezer from Anathoth,
[29]Sibbecai the Hushathite,
Ilai the Ahohite,
[30]Maharai the Netophathite,
Heled son of Baanah the Netophathite,
[31]Ithai son of Ribai from Gibeah in Benjamin,
Benaiah the Pirathonite,
[32]Hurai from the ravines of Gaash,
Abiel the Arbathite,
[33]Azmaveth the Baharumite,
Eliahba the Shaalbonite,
[34]the sons of Hashem the Gizonite,
Jonathan son of Shagee the Hararite,
[35]Ahiam son of Sacar the Hararite,
Eliphal son of Ur,
[36]Hepher the Mekerathite,
Ahijah the Pelonite,
[37]Hezro the Carmelite,
Naarai son of Ezbai,
[38]Joel the brother of Nathan,
Mibhar son of Hagri,
[39]Zelek the Ammonite,
Naharai the Berothite, the armor-bearer of Joab son of Zeruiah,
[40]Ira the Ithrite,
Gareb the Ithrite,
[41]Uriah the Hittite,
Zabad son of Ahlai,
[42]Adina son of Shiza the Reubenite, who was chief of the Reubenites, and the thirty with him,
[43]Hanan son of Maacah,
Joshaphat the Mithnite,
[44]Uzzia the Ashterathite,
Shama and Jeiel the sons of Hotham the Aroerite,
[45]Jediael son of Shimri,
his brother Joha the Tizite,
[46]Eliel the Mahavite,

---

[a]11 Possibly a variant of Jashob-Baal   [b]11 Or Thirty; some Septuagint manuscripts Three (see also 2 Samuel 23:8)   [c]23 Hebrew five cubits (about 2.3 meters)

Jeribai and Joshaviah the sons of Elnaam,
Ithmah the Moabite,
⁴⁷Eliel, Obed and Jaasiel the Mezobaite.

Warriors Join David

12 These were the men who came to David at Ziklag, while he was banished from the presence of Saul son of Kish (they were among the warriors who helped him in battle; ²they were armed with bows and were able to shoot arrows or to sling stones right-handed or left-handed; they were kinsmen of Saul from the tribe of Benjamin):

³Ahiezer their chief and Joash the sons of Shemaah the Gibeathite; Jeziel and Pelet the sons of Azmaveth; Beracah, Jehu the Anathothite, ⁴and Ishmaiah the Gibeonite, a mighty man among the Thirty, who was a leader of the Thirty; Jeremiah, Jahaziel, Johanan, Jozabad the Gederathite, ⁵Eluzai, Jerimoth, Bealiah, Shemariah and Shephatiah the Haruphite; ⁶Elkanah, Isshiah, Azarel, Joezer and Jashobeam the Korahites; ⁷and Joelah and Zebadiah the sons of Jeroham from Gedor.

⁸Some Gadites defected to David at his stronghold in the desert. They were brave warriors, ready for battle and able to handle the shield and spear. Their faces were the faces of lions, and they were as swift as gazelles in the mountains.

⁹Ezer was the chief,
Obadiah the second in command,
Eliab the third,
¹⁰Mishmannah the fourth, Jeremiah the fifth,
¹¹Attai the sixth, Eliel the seventh,
¹²Johanan the eighth, Elzabad the ninth,
¹³Jeremiah the tenth and Macbannai the eleventh.

¹⁴These Gadites were army commanders; the least was a match for a hundred, and the greatest for a thousand. ¹⁵It was they who crossed the Jordan in the first month when it was overflowing all its banks, and they put to flight everyone living in the valleys, to the east and to the west.

¹⁶Other Benjamites and some men from Judah also came to David in his stronghold. ¹⁷David went out to meet them and said to them, "If you have come to me in peace, to help me, I am ready to have you unite with me. But if you have come to betray me to my enemies when my hands are free from violence, may the God of our fathers see it and judge you."

¹⁸Then the Spirit came upon Amasai, chief of the Thirty, and he said:

"We are yours, O David!
We are with you, O son of Jesse!
Success, success to you,
and success to those who help you,
for your God will help you."

So David received them and made them leaders of his raiding bands.

¹⁹Some of the men of Manasseh defected to David when he went with the Philistines to fight against Saul. (He and his men did not help the Philistines because, after consultation, their rulers sent him away. They said, "It will cost us our heads if he deserts to his master Saul.") ²⁰When David went to Ziklag, these were the men of Manasseh who defected to him: Adnah, Jozabad, Jediael, Michael, Jozabad, Elihu and Zillethai, leaders of units of a thousand in Manasseh. ²¹They helped David against raiding bands, for all of them were brave warriors, and they were commanders in his army. ²²Day after day men came to help David, until he had a great army, like the army of God.ᵃ

Others Join David at Hebron

²³These are the numbers of the men armed for battle who came to David at Hebron to turn Saul's kingdom over to him, as the LORD had said:
²⁴men of Judah, carrying shield and spear— 6,800 armed for battle;
²⁵men of Simeon, warriors ready for battle— 7,100;
²⁶men of Levi— 4,600, ²⁷including Jehoiada, leader of the family of Aaron, with 3,700 men, ²⁸and Zadok, a brave young warrior, with 22 officers from his family;
²⁹men of Benjamin, Saul's kinsmen— 3,000, most of whom had remained loyal to Saul's house until then;
³⁰men of Ephraim, brave warriors, famous in their own clans—20,800;
³¹men of half the tribe of Manasseh, designated by name to come and make David king—18,000;
³²men of Issachar, who understood the

ᵃ22 Or a great and mighty army

times and knew what Israel should do—200 chiefs, with all their relatives under their command;

³³men of Zebulun, experienced soldiers prepared for battle with every type of weapon, to help David with undivided loyalty—50,000;

³⁴men of Naphtali—1,000 officers, together with 37,000 men carrying shields and spears;

³⁵men of Dan, ready for battle—28,600;

³⁶men of Asher, experienced soldiers prepared for battle—40,000;

³⁷and from east of the Jordan, men of Reuben, Gad and the half-tribe of Manasseh, armed with every type of weapon—120,000.

³⁸All these were fighting men who volunteered to serve in the ranks. They came to Hebron fully determined to make David king over all Israel. All the rest of the Israelites were also of one mind to make David king. ³⁹The men spent three days there with David, eating and drinking, for their families had supplied provisions for them. ⁴⁰Also, their neighbors from as far away as Issachar, Zebulun and Naphtali came bringing food on donkeys, camels, mules and oxen. There were plentiful supplies of flour, fig cakes, raisin cakes, wine, oil, cattle and sheep, for there was joy in Israel.

Bringing Back the Ark

13 David conferred with each of his officers, the commanders of thousands and commanders of hundreds. ²He then said to the whole assembly of Israel, "If it seems good to you and if it is the will of the LORD our God, let us send word far and wide to the rest of our brothers throughout the territories of Israel, and also to the priests and Levites who are with them in their towns and pasturelands, to come and join us. ³Let us bring the ark of our God back to us, for we did not inquire of ᵃ it ᵇ during the reign of Saul." ⁴The whole assembly agreed to do this, because it seemed right to all the people.

⁵So David assembled all the Israelites, from the Shihor River in Egypt to Leboᶜ Hamath, to bring the ark of God from Kiriath Jearim. ⁶David and all the Israelites with him went to Baalah of Judah (Kiri-

ath Jearim) to bring up from there the ark of God the LORD, who is enthroned between the cherubim—the ark that is called by the Name.

⁷They moved the ark of God from Abinadab's house on a new cart, with Uzzah and Ahio guiding it. ⁸David and all the Israelites were celebrating with all their might before God, with songs and with harps, lyres, tambourines, cymbals and trumpets.

⁹When they came to the threshing floor of Kidon, Uzzah reached out his hand to steady the ark, because the oxen stumbled. ¹⁰The LORD's anger burned against Uzzah, and he struck him down because he had put his hand on the ark. So he died there before God.

¹¹Then David was angry because the LORD's wrath had broken out against Uzzah, and to this day that place is called Perez Uzzah.ᵈ

¹²David was afraid of God that day and asked, "How can I ever bring the ark of God to me?" ¹³He did not take the ark to be with him in the City of David. Instead, he took it aside to the house of Obed-Edom the Gittite. ¹⁴The ark of God remained with the family of Obed-Edom in his house for three months, and the LORD blessed his household and everything he had.

David's House and Family

14 Now Hiram king of Tyre sent messengers to David, along with cedar logs, stonemasons and carpenters to build a palace for him. ²And David knew that the LORD had established him as king over Israel and that his kingdom had been highly exalted for the sake of his people Israel.

³In Jerusalem David took more wives and became the father of more sons and daughters. ⁴These are the names of the children born to him there: Shammua, Shobab, Nathan, Solomon, ⁵Ibhar, Elishua, Elpelet, ⁶Nogah, Nepheg, Japhia, ⁷Elishama, Beeliadaᵉ and Eliphelet.

David Defeats the Philistines

⁸When the Philistines heard that David had been anointed king over all Israel, they went up in full force to search for him, but David heard about it and went out to meet them. ⁹Now the Philistines

---

ᵃ3 Or we neglected   ᵇ3 Or him   ᶜ5 Or to the entrance to   ᵈ11 Perez Uzzah means outbreak against Uzzah.   ᵉ7 A variant of Eliada had come and raided the Valley of Rephaim; ¹⁰so David inquired of God: "Shall I go and attack the Philistines? Will you hand them over to me?"

The LORD answered him, "Go, I will hand them over to you."

¹¹So David and his men went up to Baal Perazim, and there he defeated them. He said, "As waters break out, God has broken out against my enemies by my hand." So that place was called Baal Perazim. *a* ¹²The Philistines had abandoned their gods there, and David gave orders to burn them in the fire.

¹³Once more the Philistines raided the valley; ¹⁴so David inquired of God again, and God answered him, "Do not go straight up, but circle around them and attack them in front of the balsam trees. ¹⁵As soon as you hear the sound of marching in the tops of the balsam trees, move out to battle, because that will mean God has gone out in front of you to strike the Philistine army." ¹⁶So David did as God commanded him, and they struck down the Philistine army, all the way from Gibeon to Gezer.

¹⁷So David's fame spread throughout every land, and the LORD made all the nations fear him.

The Ark Brought to Jerusalem

15 After David had constructed buildings for himself in the City of David, he prepared a place for the ark of God and pitched a tent for it. ²Then David said, "No one but the Levites may carry the ark of God, because the LORD chose them to carry the ark of the LORD and to minister before him forever."

³David assembled all Israel in Jerusalem to bring up the ark of the LORD to the place he had prepared for it. ⁴He called together the descendants of Aaron and the Levites:

⁵From the descendants of Kohath,
　Uriel the leader and 120 relatives;
⁶from the descendants of Merari,
　Asaiah the leader and 220 rela
　tives;
⁷from the descendants of Gershon, *b*
　Joel the leader and 130 relatives;
⁸from the descendants of Elizaphan,
　Shemaiah the leader and 200 rela
　tives;

⁹from the descendants of Hebron,
　Eliel the leader and 80 relatives;
¹⁰from the descendants of Uzziel,
　Amminadab the leader and 112
　relatives.

¹¹Then David summoned Zadok and Abiathar the priests, and Uriel, Asaiah, Joel, Shemaiah, Eliel and Amminadab the Levites. ¹²He said to them, "You are the heads of the Levitical families; you and your fellow Levites are to consecrate yourselves and bring up the ark of the LORD, the God of Israel, to the place I have prepared for it. ¹³It was because you, the Levites, did not bring it up the first time that the LORD our God broke out in anger against us. We did not inquire of him about how to do it in the prescribed way." ¹⁴So the priests and Levites consecrated themselves in order to bring up the ark of the LORD, the God of Israel. ¹⁵And the Levites carried the ark of God with the poles on their shoulders, as Moses had commanded in accordance with the word of the LORD.

¹⁶David told the leaders of the Levites to appoint their brothers as singers to sing joyful songs, accompanied by musical instruments: lyres, harps and cymbals.

¹⁷So the Levites appointed Heman son of Joel; from his brothers, Asaph son of Berekiah; and from their brothers the Merarites, Ethan son of Kushaiah; ¹⁸and with them their brothers next in rank: Zechariah, *c* Jaaziel, Shemiramoth, Jehiel, Unni, Eliab, Benaiah, Maaseiah, Mattithiah, Eliphelehu, Mikneiah, Obed-Edom and Jeiel, *d* the gatekeepers. ¹⁹The musicians Heman, Asaph and Ethan were to sound the bronze cymbals; ²⁰Zechariah, Aziel, Shemiramoth, Jehiel, Unni, Eliab, Maaseiah and Benaiah were to play the lyres according to *alamoth,* *e* ²¹and Mattithiah, Eliphelehu, Mikneiah, Obed-Edom, Jeiel and Azaziah were to play the harps, directing according to *sheminith.* *e* ²²Kenaniah the head Levite was in charge of the singing; that was his responsibility because he was skillful at it.

²³Berekiah and Elkanah were to be doorkeepers for the ark. ²⁴Shebaniah, Joshaphat, Nethanel, Amasai, Zechariah, Benaiah and Eliezer the priests were to blow trumpets before the ark of God.

---

a11 Baal Perazim means *the lord who breaks out.*　　*b7* Hebrew *Gershom,* a variant of *Gershon*
c18 Three Hebrew manuscripts and most Septuagint manuscripts (see also verse 20 and 1 Chron. 16:5); most Hebrew manuscripts *Zechariah son and* or *Zechariah, Ben and*　　*d18* Hebrew; Septuagint (see also verse 21) *Jeiel and Azaziah*　　*e20,21* Probably a musical term

Obed-Edom and Jehiah were also to be doorkeepers for the ark.

²⁵So David and the elders of Israel and the commanders of units of a thousand went to bring up the ark of the covenant of the LORD from the house of Obed-Edom, with rejoicing. ²⁶Because God had helped the Levites who were carrying the ark of the covenant of the LORD, seven bulls and seven rams were sacrificed. ²⁷Now David was clothed in a robe of fine linen, as were all the Levites who were carrying the ark, and as were the singers, and Kenaniah, who was in charge of the singing of the choirs. David also wore a linen ephod. ²⁸So all Israel brought up the ark of the covenant of the LORD with shouts, with the sounding of rams' horns and trumpets, and of cymbals, and the playing of lyres and harps.

²⁹As the ark of the covenant of the LORD was entering the City of David, Michal daughter of Saul watched from a window. And when she saw King David dancing and celebrating, she despised him in her heart.

16 They brought the ark of God and set it inside the tent that David had pitched for it, and they presented burnt offerings and fellowship offerings*a* before God. ²After David had finished sacrificing the burnt offerings and fellowship offerings, he blessed the people in the name of the LORD. ³Then he gave a loaf of bread, a cake of dates and a cake of raisins to each Israelite man and woman.

⁴He appointed some of the Levites to minister before the ark of the LORD, to make petition, to give thanks, and to praise the LORD, the God of Israel: ⁵Asaph was the chief, Zechariah second, then Jeiel, Shemiramoth, Jehiel, Mattithiah, Eliab, Benaiah, Obed-Edom and Jeiel. They were to play the lyres and harps, Asaph was to sound the cymbals, ⁶and Benaiah and Jahaziel the priests were to blow the trumpets regularly before the ark of the covenant of God.

David's Psalm of Thanks

⁷That day David first committed to Asaph and his associates this psalm of thanks to the LORD:

⁸Give thanks to the LORD, call on his
    name;
  make known among the nations
    what he has done.
⁹Sing to him, sing praise to him;
  tell of all his wonderful acts.
¹⁰Glory in his holy name;
  let the hearts of those who seek the
    LORD rejoice.
¹¹Look to the LORD and his strength;
  seek his face always.
¹²Remember the wonders he has done,
  his miracles, and the judgments he
    pronounced,
¹³O descendants of Israel his servant,
  O sons of Jacob, his chosen ones.

¹⁴He is the LORD our God;
  his judgments are in all the earth.
¹⁵He remembers*b* his covenant forever,
  the word he commanded, for a
    thousand generations,
¹⁶the covenant he made with Abraham,
  the oath he swore to Isaac.
¹⁷He confirmed it to Jacob as a decree,
  to Israel as an everlasting covenant:
¹⁸"To you I will give the land of Canaan
  as the portion you will inherit."

¹⁹When they were but few in number,
  few indeed, and strangers in it,
²⁰they*c* wandered from nation to
    nation,
  from one kingdom to another.
²¹He allowed no man to oppress them;
  for their sake he rebuked kings:
²²"Do not touch my anointed ones;
  do my prophets no harm."

²³Sing to the LORD, all the earth;
  proclaim his salvation day after day.
²⁴Declare his glory among the nations,
  his marvelous deeds among all
    peoples.
²⁵For great is the LORD and most worthy
    of praise;
  he is to be feared above all gods.
²⁶For all the gods of the nations are
    idols,
  but the LORD made the heavens.
²⁷Splendor and majesty are before him;
  strength and joy in his dwelling
    place.
²⁸Ascribe to the LORD, O families of
    nations,
  ascribe to the LORD glory and
    strength,

---

a1 Traditionally *peace offerings*; also in verse 2 (see also Psalm 105:8); Hebrew *Remember*   *b15* Some Septuagint manuscripts (see also Psalm 105:8); Hebrew *Remember*   *c18-20* One Hebrew manuscript, Septuagint and Vulgate (see also Psalm 105:12); most Hebrew manuscripts *inherit,* / *19though you are but few in number,* / *few indeed, and strangers in it."* / *20They*

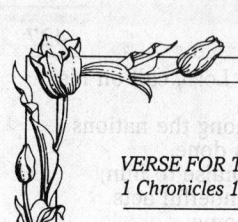

VERSE FOR THE DAY:
1 Chronicles 16:25

AUTHOR:
June Gunden

PASSAGE FOR THE DAY:
1 Chronicles 16:8–36

He Is to Be Feared

MANY times throughout the Bible we are commanded to "fear God." We know from our Bible study classes that this means much more than being "afraid" in the normal sense, but it implies a deep, reverent respect for God and an overwhelming awe in his presence. Then we go on to the next subject. But, wait a minute! Have I really learned to "fear God"? It's much easier to talk about than to do.

First, it takes time—time when I will conscientiously look away from myself and focus on God. The devil will just as conscientiously try to keep me from it. He will try to convince me that I should worship God *later,* after I've read the mail or done the dishes. That way I won't realize that he is keeping me from worshiping God, because I *intend* to worship him.

Second, to reverence God requires honesty. I must face up to the fact that the world doesn't revolve around me, but that my life is in God's hands. This comes hard since my natural self wants to be the center of my efforts. My talents? No, they're his. My money? No, it's his.

Third, to reverence God requires a certain courage, because honestly facing up to who God is makes me face up to who I am. The more I see of God's holiness, the more I see my lack of it. The more I see his power, the more I realize my weakness. The more I comprehend the depth of his love, the more I realize the shallowness of my own. Some call this "humility," but by whatever name it is simply facing up to the facts about who God is and, in that light, who I am.

"Be still," God says (stop talking and doing and going for a moment), "and know" (focus your mind on him) "that I am God" (recognize that no matter how hard you try, you can never come close to being as great as he is) (Psalm 46:10).

Additional Scripture Readings:
Exodus 20:18–20; Job 42:1–6

Go to page 440 for your next devotional reading.

²⁹ ascribe to the LORD the glory due
   his name.
Bring an offering and come before
   him;
   worship the LORD in the splendor of
     his^a holiness.
³⁰Tremble before him, all the earth!
   The world is firmly established; it
     cannot be moved.
³¹Let the heavens rejoice, let the earth
     be glad;
   let them say among the nations,
     "The LORD reigns!"
³²Let the sea resound, and all that is in
     it;
   let the fields be jubilant, and
     everything in them!
³³Then the trees of the forest will sing,
   they will sing for joy before the
     LORD,
   for he comes to judge the earth.

³⁴Give thanks to the LORD, for he is
     good;
   his love endures forever.
³⁵Cry out, "Save us, O God our Savior;
   gather us and deliver us from the
     nations,
   that we may give thanks to your holy
     name,
   that we may glory in your praise."
³⁶Praise be to the LORD, the God of
     Israel,
   from everlasting to everlasting.

Then all the people said "Amen" and
"Praise the LORD."

³⁷David left Asaph and his associates
before the ark of the covenant of the LORD
to minister there regularly, according to
each day's requirements. ³⁸He also left
Obed-Edom and his sixty-eight associates to minister with them. Obed-Edom
son of Jeduthun, and also Hosah, were
gatekeepers.

³⁹David left Zadok the priest and his
fellow priests before the tabernacle of the
LORD at the high place in Gibeon ⁴⁰to
present burnt offerings to the LORD on the
altar of burnt offering regularly, morning
and evening, in accordance with everything written in the Law of the LORD,
which he had given Israel. ⁴¹With them
were Heman and Jeduthun and the rest of
those chosen and designated by name to
give thanks to the LORD, "for his love endures forever." ⁴²Heman and Jeduthun
were responsible for the sounding of the

trumpets and cymbals and for the playing
of the other instruments for sacred song.
The sons of Jeduthun were stationed at
the gate.

⁴³Then all the people left, each for his
own home, and David returned home to
bless his family.

God's Promise to David

17 After David was settled in his palace, he said to Nathan the proph-
et, "Here I am, living in a palace of cedar,
while the ark of the covenant of the LORD
is under a tent."

²Nathan replied to David, "Whatever
you have in mind, do it, for God is with
you."

³That night the word of God came to
Nathan, saying:

⁴"Go and tell my servant David,
'This is what the LORD says: You are
not the one to build me a house to
dwell in. ⁵I have not dwelt in a house
from the day I brought Israel up out
of Egypt to this day. I have moved
from one tent site to another, from
one dwelling place to another.
⁶Wherever I have moved with all the
Israelites, did I ever say to any of
their leaders^b whom I commanded
to shepherd my people, "Why have
you not built me a house of cedar?" '

⁷"Now then, tell my servant David,
'This is what the LORD Almighty says:
I took you from the pasture and from
following the flock, to be ruler over
my people Israel. ⁸I have been with
you wherever you have gone, and I
have cut off all your enemies from
before you. Now I will make your
name like the names of the greatest
men of the earth. ⁹And I will provide
a place for my people Israel and will
plant them so that they can have a
home of their own and no longer be
disturbed. Wicked people will not
oppress them anymore, as they did at
the beginning ¹⁰and have done ever
since the time I appointed leaders
over my people Israel. I will also subdue all your enemies.

" 'I declare to you that the LORD
will build a house for you: ¹¹When
your days are over and you go to be
with your fathers, I will raise up your
offspring to succeed you, one of your
own sons, and I will establish his

---

^a29 Or LORD with the splendor of   ^b6 Traditionally judges; also in verse 10

kingdom. [12]He is the one who will build a house for me, and I will establish his throne forever. [13]I will be his father, and he will be my son. I will never take my love away from him, as I took it away from your predecessor. [14]I will set him over my house and my kingdom forever; his throne will be established forever.' "

[15]Nathan reported to David all the words of this entire revelation.

David's Prayer

[16]Then King David went in and sat before the LORD, and he said:

"Who am I, O LORD God, and what is my family, that you have brought me this far? [17]And as if this were not enough in your sight, O God, you have spoken about the future of the house of your servant. You have looked on me as though I were the most exalted of men, O LORD God.

[18]"What more can David say to you for honoring your servant? For you know your servant, [19]O LORD. For the sake of your servant and according to your will, you have done this great thing and made known all these great promises.

[20]"There is no one like you, O LORD, and there is no God but you, as we have heard with our own ears. [21]And who is like your people Israel—the one nation on earth whose God went out to redeem a people for himself, and to make a name for yourself, and to perform great and awesome wonders by driving out nations from before your people, whom you redeemed from Egypt? [22]You made your people Israel your very own forever, and you, O LORD, have become their God.

[23]"And now, LORD, let the promise you have made concerning your servant and his house be established forever. Do as you promised, [24]so that it will be established and that your name will be great forever. Then men will say, 'The LORD Almighty, the God over Israel, is Israel's God!' And the house of your servant David will be established before you.

[25]"You, my God, have revealed to your servant that you will build a house for him. So your servant has found courage to pray to you. [26]O LORD, you are God! You have promised these good things to your servant. [27]Now you have been pleased to bless the house of your servant, that it may continue forever in your sight; for you, O LORD, have blessed it, and it will be blessed forever."

David's Victories

18 In the course of time, David defeated the Philistines and subdued them, and he took Gath and its surrounding villages from the control of the Philistines.

[2]David also defeated the Moabites, and they became subject to him and brought tribute.

[3]Moreover, David fought Hadadezer king of Zobah, as far as Hamath, when he went to establish his control along the Euphrates River. [4]David captured a thousand of his chariots, seven thousand charioteers and twenty thousand foot soldiers. He hamstrung all but a hundred of the chariot horses.

[5]When the Arameans of Damascus came to help Hadadezer king of Zobah, David struck down twenty-two thousand of them. [6]He put garrisons in the Aramean kingdom of Damascus, and the Arameans became subject to him and brought tribute. The LORD gave David victory everywhere he went.

[7]David took the gold shields carried by the officers of Hadadezer and brought them to Jerusalem. [8]From Tebah[a] and Cun, towns that belonged to Hadadezer, David took a great quantity of bronze, which Solomon used to make the bronze Sea, the pillars and various bronze articles.

[9]When Tou king of Hamath heard that David had defeated the entire army of Hadadezer king of Zobah, [10]he sent his son Hadoram to King David to greet him and congratulate him on his victory in battle over Hadadezer, who had been at war with Tou. Hadoram brought all kinds of articles of gold and silver and bronze.

[11]King David dedicated these articles to the LORD, as he had done with the silver and gold he had taken from all these nations: Edom and Moab, the Ammonites and the Philistines, and Amalek.

[12]Abishai son of Zeruiah struck down eighteen thousand Edomites in the Valley of Salt. [13]He put garrisons in Edom, and

a8 Hebrew *Tibhath*, a variant of *Tebah*

all the Edomites became subject to David. The LORD gave David victory everywhere he went.

David's Officials

14David reigned over all Israel, doing what was just and right for all his people. 15Joab son of Zeruiah was over the army; Jehoshaphat son of Ahilud was recorder; 16Zadok son of Ahitub and Ahimelech*a* son of Abiathar were priests; Shavsha was secretary; 17Benaiah son of Jehoiada was over the Kerethites and Pelethites; and David's sons were chief officials at the king's side.

The Battle Against the Ammonites

19 In the course of time, Nahash king of the Ammonites died, and his son succeeded him as king. 2David thought, "I will show kindness to Hanun son of Nahash, because his father showed kindness to me." So David sent a delegation to express his sympathy to Hanun concerning his father.

When David's men came to Hanun in the land of the Ammonites to express sympathy to him, 3the Ammonite nobles said to Hanun, "Do you think David is honoring your father by sending men to you to express sympathy? Haven't his men come to you to explore and spy out the country and overthrow it?" 4So Hanun seized David's men, shaved them, cut off their garments in the middle at the buttocks, and sent them away.

5When someone came and told David about the men, he sent messengers to meet them, for they were greatly humiliated. The king said, "Stay at Jericho till your beards have grown, and then come back."

6When the Ammonites realized that they had become a stench in David's nostrils, Hanun and the Ammonites sent a thousand talents*b* of silver to hire chariots and charioteers from Aram Naharaim,*c* Aram Maacah and Zobah. 7They hired thirty-two thousand chariots and charioteers, as well as the king of Maacah with his troops, who came and camped near Medeba, while the Ammonites were mustered from their towns and moved out for battle.

8On hearing this, David sent Joab out with the entire army of fighting men. 9The Ammonites came out and drew up in battle formation at the entrance to their city, while the kings who had come were by themselves in the open country.

10Joab saw that there were battle lines in front of him and behind him; so he selected some of the best troops in Israel and deployed them against the Arameans. 11He put the rest of the men under the command of Abishai his brother, and they were deployed against the Ammonites. 12Joab said, "If the Arameans are too strong for me, then you are to rescue me; but if the Ammonites are too strong for you, then I will rescue you. 13Be strong and let us fight bravely for our people and the cities of our God. The LORD will do what is good in his sight."

14Then Joab and the troops with him advanced to fight the Arameans, and they fled before him. 15When the Ammonites saw that the Arameans were fleeing, they too fled before his brother Abishai and went inside the city. So Joab went back to Jerusalem.

16After the Arameans saw that they had been routed by Israel, they sent messengers and had Arameans brought from beyond the River,*d* with Shophach the commander of Hadadezer's army leading them.

17When David was told of this, he gathered all Israel and crossed the Jordan; he advanced against them and formed his battle lines opposite them. David formed his lines to meet the Arameans in battle, and they fought against him. 18But they fled before Israel, and David killed seven thousand of their charioteers and forty thousand of their foot soldiers. He also killed Shophach the commander of their army.

19When the vassals of Hadadezer saw that they had been defeated by Israel, they made peace with David and became subject to him.

So the Arameans were not willing to help the Ammonites anymore.

The Capture of Rabbah

20 In the spring, at the time when kings go off to war, Joab led out the armed forces. He laid waste the land of the Ammonites and went to Rabbah and besieged it, but David remained in Jerusalem. Joab attacked Rabbah and

---

a16 Some Hebrew manuscripts, Vulgate and Syriac (see also 2 Samuel 8:17); most Hebrew manuscripts *Abimelech*   *b6* That is, about 37 tons (about 34 metric tons)   *c6* That is, Northwest Mesopotamia
d16 That is, the Euphrates

left it in ruins. ²David took the crown from the head of their king*a*—its weight was found to be a talent*b* of gold, and it was set with precious stones—and it was placed on David's head. He took a great quantity of plunder from the city ³and brought out the people who were there, consigning them to labor with saws and with iron picks and axes. David did this to all the Ammonite towns. Then David and his entire army returned to Jerusalem.

War With the Philistines

⁴In the course of time, war broke out with the Philistines, at Gezer. At that time Sibbecai the Hushathite killed Sippai, one of the descendants of the Rephaites, and the Philistines were subjugated.

⁵In another battle with the Philistines, Elhanan son of Jair killed Lahmi the brother of Goliath the Gittite, who had a spear with a shaft like a weaver's rod.

⁶In still another battle, which took place at Gath, there was a huge man with six fingers on each hand and six toes on each foot—twenty-four in all. He also was descended from Rapha. ⁷When he taunted Israel, Jonathan son of Shimea, David's brother, killed him.

⁸These were descendants of Rapha in Gath, and they fell at the hands of David and his men.

David Numbers the Fighting Men

21 Satan rose up against Israel and incited David to take a census of Israel. ²So David said to Joab and the commanders of the troops, "Go and count the Israelites from Beersheba to Dan. Then report back to me so that I may know how many there are."

³But Joab replied, "May the LORD multiply his troops a hundred times over. My lord the king, are they not all my lord's subjects? Why does my lord want to do this? Why should he bring guilt on Israel?"

⁴The king's word, however, overruled Joab; so Joab left and went throughout Israel and then came back to Jerusalem. ⁵Joab reported the number of the fighting men to David: In all Israel there were one million one hundred thousand men who could handle a sword, including four hundred and seventy thousand in Judah.

⁶But Joab did not include Levi and Benjamin in the numbering, because the king's command was repulsive to him. ⁷This command was also evil in the sight of God; so he punished Israel.

⁸Then David said to God, "I have sinned greatly by doing this. Now, I beg you, take away the guilt of your servant. I have done a very foolish thing."

⁹The LORD said to Gad, David's seer, ¹⁰"Go and tell David, 'This is what the LORD says: I am giving you three options. Choose one of them for me to carry out against you.' "

¹¹So Gad went to David and said to him, "This is what the LORD says: 'Take your choice: ¹²three years of famine, three months of being swept away*c* before your enemies, with their swords overtaking you, or three days of the sword of the LORD—days of plague in the land, with the angel of the LORD ravaging every part of Israel.' Now then, decide how I should answer the one who sent me."

¹³David said to Gad, "I am in deep distress. Let me fall into the hands of the LORD, for his mercy is very great; but do not let me fall into the hands of men."

¹⁴So the LORD sent a plague on Israel, and seventy thousand men of Israel fell dead. ¹⁵And God sent an angel to destroy Jerusalem. But as the angel was doing so, the LORD saw it and was grieved because of the calamity and said to the angel who was destroying the people, "Enough! Withdraw your hand." The angel of the LORD was then standing at the threshing floor of Araunah*d* the Jebusite.

¹⁶David looked up and saw the angel of the LORD standing between heaven and earth, with a drawn sword in his hand extended over Jerusalem. Then David and the elders, clothed in sackcloth, fell facedown.

¹⁷David said to God, "Was it not I who ordered the fighting men to be counted? I am the one who has sinned and done wrong. These are but sheep. What have they done? O LORD my God, let your hand fall upon me and my family, but do not let this plague remain on your people."

¹⁸Then the angel of the LORD ordered Gad to tell David to go up and build an altar to the LORD on the threshing floor of Araunah the Jebusite. ¹⁹So David went up

---

a2 Or *of Milcom,* that is, Molech   *b2* That is, about 75 pounds (about 34 kilograms)   *c12* Hebrew; Septuagint and Vulgate (see also 2 Samuel 24:13) *of fleeing*   *d15* Hebrew *Ornan,* a variant of *Araunah;* also in verses 18-28 in obedience to the word that Gad had spoken in the name of the LORD.

²⁰While Araunah was threshing wheat, he turned and saw the angel; his four sons who were with him hid themselves. ²¹Then David approached, and when Araunah looked and saw him, he left the threshing floor and bowed down before David with his face to the ground.

²²David said to him, "Let me have the site of your threshing floor so I can build an altar to the LORD, that the plague on the people may be stopped. Sell it to me at the full price."

²³Araunah said to David, "Take it! Let my lord the king do whatever pleases him. Look, I will give the oxen for the burnt offerings, the threshing sledges for the wood, and the wheat for the grain offering. I will give all this."

²⁴But King David replied to Araunah, "No, I insist on paying the full price. I will not take for the LORD what is yours, or sacrifice a burnt offering that costs me nothing."

²⁵So David paid Araunah six hundred shekels*a* of gold for the site. ²⁶David built an altar to the LORD there and sacrificed burnt offerings and fellowship offerings.*b* He called on the LORD, and the LORD answered him with fire from heaven on the altar of burnt offering.

²⁷Then the LORD spoke to the angel, and he put his sword back into its sheath. ²⁸At that time, when David saw that the LORD had answered him on the threshing floor of Araunah the Jebusite, he offered sacrifices there. ²⁹The tabernacle of the LORD, which Moses had made in the desert, and the altar of burnt offering were at that time on the high place at Gibeon. ³⁰But David could not go before it to inquire of God, because he was afraid of the sword of the angel of the LORD.

22 Then David said, "The house of the LORD God is to be here, and also the altar of burnt offering for Israel."

Preparations for the Temple

²So David gave orders to assemble the aliens living in Israel, and from among them he appointed stonecutters to prepare dressed stone for building the house of God. ³He provided a large amount of iron to make nails for the doors of the gateways and for the fittings, and more bronze than could be weighed. ⁴He also provided more cedar logs than could be counted, for the Sidonians and Tyrians had brought large numbers of them to David.

⁵David said, "My son Solomon is young and inexperienced, and the house to be built for the LORD should be of great magnificence and fame and splendor in the sight of all the nations. Therefore I will make preparations for it." So David made extensive preparations before his death.

⁶Then he called for his son Solomon and charged him to build a house for the LORD, the God of Israel. ⁷David said to Solomon: "My son, I had it in my heart to build a house for the Name of the LORD my God. ⁸But this word of the LORD came to me: 'You have shed much blood and have fought many wars. You are not to build a house for my Name, because you have shed much blood on the earth in my sight. ⁹But you will have a son who will be a man of peace and rest, and I will give him rest from all his enemies on every side. His name will be Solomon,*c* and I will grant Israel peace and quiet during his reign. ¹⁰He is the one who will build a house for my Name. He will be my son, and I will be his father. And I will establish the throne of his kingdom over Israel forever.'

¹¹"Now, my son, the LORD be with you, and may you have success and build the house of the LORD your God, as he said you would. ¹²May the LORD give you discretion and understanding when he puts you in command over Israel, so that you may keep the law of the LORD your God. ¹³Then you will have success if you are careful to observe the decrees and laws that the LORD gave Moses for Israel. Be strong and courageous. Do not be afraid or discouraged.

¹⁴"I have taken great pains to provide for the temple of the LORD a hundred thousand talents*d* of gold, a million talents*e* of silver, quantities of bronze and iron too great to be weighed, and wood and stone. And you may add to them. ¹⁵You have many workmen: stonecutters, masons and carpenters, as well as men skilled in every kind of work ¹⁶in gold and silver, bronze and iron—craftsmen be-

---

a25 That is, about 15 pounds (about 7 kilograms)   *b26* Traditionally *peace offerings*   *c9 Solomon* sounds like and may be derived from the Hebrew for *peace.*   *d14* That is, about 3,750 tons (about 3,450 metric tons)   *e14* That is, about 37,500 tons (about 34,500 metric tons) yond number. Now begin the work, and the LORD be with you."

¹⁷Then David ordered all the leaders of Israel to help his son Solomon. ¹⁸He said to them, "Is not the LORD your God with you? And has he not granted you rest on every side? For he has handed the inhabitants of the land over to me, and the land is subject to the LORD and to his people. ¹⁹Now devote your heart and soul to seeking the LORD your God. Begin to build the sanctuary of the LORD God, so that you may bring the ark of the covenant of the LORD and the sacred articles belonging to God into the temple that will be built for the Name of the LORD."

The Levites

23 When David was old and full of years, he made his son Solomon king over Israel.

²He also gathered together all the leaders of Israel, as well as the priests and Levites. ³The Levites thirty years old or more were counted, and the total number of men was thirty-eight thousand. ⁴David said, "Of these, twenty-four thousand are to supervise the work of the temple of the LORD and six thousand are to be officials and judges. ⁵Four thousand are to be gatekeepers and four thousand are to praise the LORD with the musical instruments I have provided for that purpose."

⁶David divided the Levites into groups corresponding to the sons of Levi: Gershon, Kohath and Merari.

Gershonites

⁷Belonging to the Gershonites:
Ladan and Shimei.
⁸The sons of Ladan:
Jehiel the first, Zetham and Joel—three in all.
⁹The sons of Shimei:
Shelomoth, Haziel and Haran—three in all.
These were the heads of the families of Ladan.
¹⁰And the sons of Shimei:
Jahath, Ziza,ᵃ Jeush and Beriah.
These were the sons of Shimei—four in all.
¹¹Jahath was the first and Ziza the second, but Jeush and Beriah did not have many sons; so they were counted as one family with one assignment.

Kohathites

¹²The sons of Kohath:
Amram, Izhar, Hebron and Uzziel—four in all.
¹³The sons of Amram:
Aaron and Moses.
Aaron was set apart, he and his descendants forever, to consecrate the most holy things, to offer sacrifices before the LORD, to minister before him and to pronounce blessings in his name forever. ¹⁴The sons of Moses the man of God were counted as part of the tribe of Levi.
¹⁵The sons of Moses:
Gershom and Eliezer.
¹⁶The descendants of Gershom:
Shubael was the first.
¹⁷The descendants of Eliezer:
Rehabiah was the first.
Eliezer had no other sons, but the sons of Rehabiah were very numerous.
¹⁸The sons of Izhar:
Shelomith was the first.
¹⁹The sons of Hebron:
Jeriah the first, Amariah the second, Jahaziel the third and Jekameam the fourth.
²⁰The sons of Uzziel:
Micah the first and Isshiah the second.

Merarites

²¹The sons of Merari:
Mahli and Mushi.
The sons of Mahli:
Eleazar and Kish.
²²Eleazar died without having sons: he had only daughters. Their cousins, the sons of Kish, married them.
²³The sons of Mushi:
Mahli, Eder and Jerimoth—three in all.

²⁴These were the descendants of Levi by their families—the heads of families as they were registered under their names and counted individually, that is, the workers twenty years old or more who served in the temple of the LORD. ²⁵For David had said, "Since the LORD, the God of Israel, has granted rest to his people and has come to dwell in Jerusalem forever, ²⁶the Levites no longer need to carry the tabernacle or any of the articles used

---

ᵃ10 One Hebrew manuscript, Septuagint and Vulgate (see also verse 11); most Hebrew manuscripts *Zina*

in its service." ²⁷According to the last instructions of David, the Levites were
counted from those twenty years old or
more.

²⁸The duty of the Levites was to help
Aaron's descendants in the service of the
temple of the Lord: to be in charge of the
courtyards, the side rooms, the purification of all sacred things and the perfor-
mance of other duties at the house of
God. ²⁹They were in charge of the bread
set out on the table, the flour for the grain
offerings, the unleavened wafers, the baking and the mixing, and all measurements of quantity and size. ³⁰They were
also to stand every morning to thank and
praise the Lord. They were to do the same
in the evening ³¹and whenever burnt offerings were presented to the Lord on
Sabbaths and at New Moon festivals and
at appointed feasts. They were to serve
before the Lord regularly in the proper
number and in the way prescribed for
them.

³²And so the Levites carried out their
responsibilities for the Tent of Meeting,
for the Holy Place and, under their brothers the descendants of Aaron, for the service of the temple of the Lord.

The Divisions of Priests

24 These were the divisions of the
sons of Aaron:

The sons of Aaron were Nadab, Abihu,
Eleazar and Ithamar. ²But Nadab and
Abihu died before their father did, and
they had no sons; so Eleazar and Ithamar
served as the priests. ³With the help of
Zadok a descendant of Eleazar and Ahimelech a descendant of Ithamar, David
separated them into divisions for their
appointed order of ministering. ⁴A larger
number of leaders were found among Eleazar's descendants than among Ithamar's, and they were divided accordingly:
sixteen heads of families from Eleazar's
descendants and eight heads of families
from Ithamar's descendants. ⁵They divided them impartially by drawing lots, for
there were officials of the sanctuary and
officials of God among the descendants
of both Eleazar and Ithamar.

⁶The scribe Shemaiah son of Nethanel,
a Levite, recorded their names in the
presence of the king and of the officials:
Zadok the priest, Ahimelech son of Abiathar and the heads of families of the

priests and of the Levites—one family being taken from Eleazar and then one from
Ithamar.

⁷The first lot fell to Jehoiarib,
  the second to Jedaiah,
⁸the third to Harim,
  the fourth to Seorim,
⁹the fifth to Malkijah,
  the sixth to Mijamin,
¹⁰the seventh to Hakkoz,
  the eighth to Abijah,
¹¹the ninth to Jeshua,
  the tenth to Shecaniah,
¹²the eleventh to Eliashib,
  the twelfth to Jakim,
¹³the thirteenth to Huppah,
  the fourteenth to Jeshebeab,
¹⁴the fifteenth to Bilgah,
  the sixteenth to Immer,
¹⁵the seventeenth to Hezir,
  the eighteenth to Happizzez,
¹⁶the nineteenth to Pethahiah,
  the twentieth to Jehezkel,
¹⁷the twenty-first to Jakin,
  the twenty-second to Gamul,
¹⁸the twenty-third to Delaiah
  and the twenty-fourth to Maaziah.

¹⁹This was their appointed order of
ministering when they entered the temple of the Lord, according to the regulations prescribed for them by their forefather Aaron, as the Lord, the God of Israel,
had commanded him.

The Rest of the Levites
²⁰As for the rest of the descendants of
Levi:
  from the sons of Amram: Shubael;
  from the sons of Shubael: Jehde-
    iah.
²¹As for Rehabiah, from his sons:
  Isshiah was the first.
²²From the Izharites: Shelomoth;
  from the sons of Shelomoth: Ja-
    hath.
²³The sons of Hebron: Jeriah the
  first,^a Amariah the second, Jahaziel the third and Jekameam the
  fourth.
²⁴The son of Uzziel: Micah;
  from the sons of Micah: Shamir.
²⁵The brother of Micah: Isshiah;
  from the sons of Isshiah: Zecha-
    riah.
²⁶The sons of Merari: Mahli and Mu-
  shi.

^a23 Two Hebrew manuscripts and some Septuagint manuscripts (see also 1 Chron. 23:19); most Hebrew
manuscripts *The sons of Jeriah:*

The son of Jaaziah: Beno.

²⁷The sons of Merari:

from Jaaziah: Beno, Shoham, Zaccur and Ibri.

²⁸From Mahli: Eleazar, who had no sons.

²⁹From Kish: the son of Kish:
Jerahmeel.

³⁰And the sons of Mushi: Mahli, Eder and Jerimoth.

These were the Levites, according to their families. ³¹They also cast lots, just as their brothers the descendants of Aaron did, in the presence of King David and of Zadok, Ahimelech, and the heads of families of the priests and of the Levites. The families of the oldest brother were treated the same as those of the youngest.

The Singers

25 David, together with the commanders of the army, set apart some of the sons of Asaph, Heman and Jeduthun for the ministry of prophesying, accompanied by harps, lyres and cymbals. Here is the list of the men who performed this service:

²From the sons of Asaph:

Zaccur, Joseph, Nethaniah and Asarelah. The sons of Asaph were under the supervision of Asaph, who prophesied under the king's supervision.

³As for Jeduthun, from his sons:

Gedaliah, Zeri, Jeshaiah, Shimei,ᵃ Hashabiah and Mattithiah, six in all, under the supervision of their father Jeduthun, who prophesied, using the harp in thanking and praising the LORD.

⁴As for Heman, from his sons:

Bukkiah, Mattaniah, Uzziel, Shubael and Jerimoth; Hananiah, Hanani, Eliathah, Giddalti and Romamti-Ezer; Joshbekashah, Mallothi, Hothir and Mahazioth. ⁵All these were sons of Heman the king's seer. They were given him through the promises of God to exalt him.ᵇ God gave Heman fourteen sons and three daughters.

⁶All these men were under the supervision of their fathers for the music of the temple of the LORD, with cymbals, lyres and harps, for the ministry at the house of God. Asaph, Jeduthun and Heman were under the supervision of the king. ⁷Along with their relatives—all of them trained and skilled in music for the LORD—they numbered 288. ⁸Young and old alike, teacher as well as student, cast lots for their duties.

⁹The first lot, which was for Asaph,
fell to Joseph,
his sons and relatives,ᶜ   12ᵈ
the second to Gedaliah,
he and his relatives and
sons,   12
¹⁰the third to Zaccur,
his sons and relatives,   12
¹¹the fourth to Izri,ᵉ
his sons and relatives,   12
¹²the fifth to Nethaniah,
his sons and relatives,   12
¹³the sixth to Bukkiah,
his sons and relatives,   12
¹⁴the seventh to Jesarelah,ᶠ
his sons and relatives,   12
¹⁵the eighth to Jeshaiah,
his sons and relatives,   12
¹⁶the ninth to Mattaniah,
his sons and relatives,   12
¹⁷the tenth to Shimei,
his sons and relatives,   12
¹⁸the eleventh to Azarel,ᵍ
his sons and relatives,   12
¹⁹the twelfth to Hashabiah,
his sons and relatives,   12
²⁰the thirteenth to Shubael,
his sons and relatives,   12
²¹the fourteenth to Mattithiah,
his sons and relatives,   12
²²the fifteenth to Jerimoth,
his sons and relatives,   12
²³the sixteenth to Hananiah,
his sons and relatives,   12
²⁴the seventeenth to Joshbekashah,
his sons and relatives,   12
²⁵the eighteenth to Hanani,
his sons and relatives,   12
²⁶the nineteenth to Mallothi,
his sons and relatives,   12
²⁷the twentieth to Eliathah,
his sons and relatives,   12
²⁸the twenty-first to Hothir,
his sons and relatives,   12
²⁹the twenty-second to Giddalti,
his sons and relatives,   12
³⁰the twenty-third to Mahazioth,

ᵃ3 One Hebrew manuscript and some Septuagint manuscripts (see also verse 17); most Hebrew manuscripts do not have *Shimei.*   ᵇ5 Hebrew *exalt the horn*   ᶜ9 See Septuagint; Hebrew does not have *his sons and relatives.*   ᵈ9 See the total in verse 7; Hebrew does not have *twelve.*   ᵉ11 A variant of *Zeri*   ᶠ14 A variant of *Asarelah*   ᵍ18 A variant of *Uzziel*

his sons and relatives,   12
31the twenty-fourth to
Romamti-Ezer,
his sons and relatives,   12

The Gatekeepers

26 The divisions of the gatekeepers:
From the Korahites: Meshele-
miah son of Kore, one of the sons
of Asaph.

2Meshelemiah had sons:
Zechariah the firstborn,
Jediael the second,
Zebadiah the third,
Jathniel the fourth,
3Elam the fifth,
Jehohanan the sixth
and Eliehoenai the seventh.
4Obed-Edom also had sons:
Shemaiah the firstborn,
Jehozabad the second,
Joah the third,
Sacar the fourth,
Nethanel the fifth,
5Ammiel the sixth,
Issachar the seventh
and Peullethai the eighth.
(For God had blessed Obed-
Edom.)

6His son Shemaiah also had sons,
who were leaders in their father's
family because they were very capable men. 7The sons of Shemaiah: Othni, Rephael, Obed and Elzabad; his relatives Elihu and
Semakiah were also able men. 8All
these were descendants of Obed-
Edom; they and their sons and
their relatives were capable men
with the strength to do the work —
descendants of Obed-Edom, 62 in
all.

9Meshelemiah had sons and relatives,
who were able men — 18 in all.

10Hosah the Merarite had sons: Shimri
the first (although he was not the
firstborn, his father had appointed
him the first), 11Hilkiah the second, Tabaliah the third and Zechariah the fourth. The sons and relatives of Hosah were 13 in all.

12These divisions of the gatekeepers,
through their chief men, had duties for
ministering in the temple of the LORD, just
as their relatives had. 13Lots were cast for
each gate, according to their families,
young and old alike.

14The lot for the East Gate fell to Shelemiah.*a* Then lots were cast for his son
Zechariah, a wise counselor, and the lot
for the North Gate fell to him. 15The lot
for the South Gate fell to Obed-Edom,
and the lot for the storehouse fell to his
sons. 16The lots for the West Gate and the
Shalleketh Gate on the upper road fell to
Shuppim and Hosah.

Guard was alongside of guard: 17There
were six Levites a day on the east, four a
day on the north, four a day on the south
and two at a time at the storehouse. 18As
for the court to the west, there were four
at the road and two at the court itself.

19These were the divisions of the gatekeepers who were descendants of Korah
and Merari.

The Treasurers and Other Officials

20Their fellow Levites were*b* in charge
of the treasuries of the house of God and
the treasuries for the dedicated things.

21The descendants of Ladan, who were
Gershonites through Ladan and who were
heads of families belonging to Ladan the
Gershonite, were Jehieli, 22the sons of Jehieli, Zetham and his brother Joel. They
were in charge of the treasuries of the
temple of the LORD.

23From the Amramites, the Izharites,
the Hebronites and the Uzzielites:

24Shubael, a descendant of Gershom
son of Moses, was the officer in
charge of the treasuries. 25His relatives through Eliezer: Rehabiah
his son, Jeshaiah his son, Joram
his son, Zicri his son and Shelomith his son. 26Shelomith and his
relatives were in charge of all the
treasuries for the things dedicated
by King David, by the heads of
families who were the commanders of thousands and commanders
of hundreds, and by the other
army commanders. 27Some of the
plunder taken in battle they dedicated for the repair of the temple
of the LORD. 28And everything dedicated by Samuel the seer and by
Saul son of Kish, Abner son of Ner
and Joab son of Zeruiah, and all
the other dedicated things were in
the care of Shelomith and his relatives.

a14 A variant of *Meshelemiah*   *b20* Septuagint; Hebrew *As for the Levites, Ahijah was*

29From the Izharites: Kenaniah and his sons were assigned duties away from the temple, as officials and judges over Israel.

30From the Hebronites: Hashabiah and his relatives—seventeen hundred able men—were responsible in Israel west of the Jordan for all the work of the LORD and for the king's service. 31As for the Hebronites, Jeriah was their chief according to the genealogical records of their families. In the fortieth year of David's reign a search was made in the records, and capable men among the Hebronites were found at Jazer in Gilead. 32Jeriah had twenty-seven hundred relatives, who were able men and heads of families, and King David put them in charge of the Reubenites, the Gadites and the half-tribe of Manasseh for every matter pertaining to God and for the affairs of the king.

Army Divisions

27 This is the list of the Israelites— heads of families, commanders of thousands and commanders of hundreds, and their officers, who served the king in all that concerned the army divisions that were on duty month by month throughout the year. Each division consisted of 24,000 men.

2In charge of the first division, for the first month, was Jashobeam son of Zabdiel. There were 24,000 men in his division. 3He was a descendant of Perez and chief of all the army officers for the first month.

4In charge of the division for the second month was Dodai the Ahohite; Mikloth was the leader of his division. There were 24,000 men in his division.

5The third army commander, for the third month, was Benaiah son of Jehoiada the priest. He was chief and there were 24,000 men in his division. 6This was the Benaiah who was a mighty man among the Thirty and was over the Thirty. His son Ammizabad was in charge of his division.

7The fourth, for the fourth month, was Asahel the brother of Joab; his son Zebadiah was his successor. There were 24,000 men in his division.

8The fifth, for the fifth month, was the commander Shamhuth the Izrahite. There were 24,000 men in his division.

9The sixth, for the sixth month, was Ira the son of Ikkesh the Tekoite. There were 24,000 men in his division.

10The seventh, for the seventh month, was Helez the Pelonite, an Ephraimite. There were 24,000 men in his division.

11The eighth, for the eighth month, was Sibbecai the Hushathite, a Zerahite. There were 24,000 men in his division.

12The ninth, for the ninth month, was Abiezer the Anathothite, a Benjamite. There were 24,000 men in his division.

13The tenth, for the tenth month, was Maharai the Netophathite, a Zerahite. There were 24,000 men in his division.

14The eleventh, for the eleventh month, was Benaiah the Pirathonite, an Ephraimite. There were 24,000 men in his division.

15The twelfth, for the twelfth month, was Heldai the Netophathite, from the family of Othniel. There were 24,000 men in his division.

Officers of the Tribes

16The officers over the tribes of Israel:

over the Reubenites: Eliezer son of Zicri;
over the Simeonites: Shephatiah son of Maacah;
17over Levi: Hashabiah son of Kemuel;
over Aaron: Zadok;
18over Judah: Elihu, a brother of David;
over Issachar: Omri son of Michael;
19over Zebulun: Ishmaiah son of Obadiah;
over Naphtali: Jerimoth son of Azriel;
20over the Ephraimites: Hoshea son of Azaziah;
over half the tribe of Manasseh: Joel son of Pedaiah;
21over the half-tribe of Manasseh in Gilead: Iddo son of Zechariah;
over Benjamin: Jaasiel son of Abner;
22over Dan: Azarel son of Jeroham.

These were the officers over the tribes of Israel.

23David did not take the number of the men twenty years old or less, because the LORD had promised to make Israel as numerous as the stars in the sky. ²⁴Joab son of Zeruiah began to count the men but did not finish. Wrath came on Israel on account of this numbering, and the number was not entered in the bookᵃ of the annals of King David.

The King's Overseers

²⁵Azmaveth son of Adiel was in charge of the royal storehouses.

Jonathan son of Uzziah was in charge of the storehouses in the outlying districts, in the towns, the villages and the watchtowers.

²⁶Ezri son of Kelub was in charge of the field workers who farmed the land.

²⁷Shimei the Ramathite was in charge of the vineyards.

Zabdi the Shiphmite was in charge of the produce of the vineyards for the wine vats.

²⁸Baal-Hanan the Gederite was in charge of the olive and sycamore-fig trees in the western foothills.

Joash was in charge of the supplies of olive oil.

²⁹Shitrai the Sharonite was in charge of the herds grazing in Sharon.

Shaphat son of Adlai was in charge of the herds in the valleys.

³⁰Obil the Ishmaelite was in charge of the camels.

Jehdeiah the Meronothite was in charge of the donkeys.

³¹Jaziz the Hagrite was in charge of the flocks.

All these were the officials in charge of King David's property.

³²Jonathan, David's uncle, was a counselor, a man of insight and a scribe. Jehiel son of Hacmoni took care of the king's sons.

³³Ahithophel was the king's counselor. Hushai the Arkite was the king's friend. ³⁴Ahithophel was succeeded by Jehoiada son of Benaiah and by Abiathar.

Joab was the commander of the royal army.

David's Plans for the Temple

28 David summoned all the officials of Israel to assemble at Jerusalem: the officers over the tribes, the commanders of the divisions in the service of the king, the commanders of thousands and commanders of hundreds, and the officials in charge of all the property and live-stock belonging to the king and his sons, together with the palace officials, the mighty men and all the brave warriors.

²King David rose to his feet and said: "Listen to me, my brothers and my people. I had it in my heart to build a house as a place of rest for the ark of the covenant of the LORD, for the footstool of our God, and I made plans to build it. ³But God said to me, 'You are not to build a house for my Name, because you are a warrior and have shed blood.'

⁴"Yet the LORD, the God of Israel, chose me from my whole family to be king over Israel forever. He chose Judah as leader, and from the house of Judah he chose my family, and from my father's sons he was pleased to make me king over all Israel. ⁵Of all my sons—and the LORD has given me many—he has chosen my son Solomon to sit on the throne of the kingdom of the LORD over Israel. ⁶He said to me: 'Solomon your son is the one who will build my house and my courts, for I have chosen him to be my son, and I will be his father. ⁷I will establish his kingdom forever if he is unswerving in carrying out my commands and laws, as is being done at this time.'

⁸"So now I charge you in the sight of all Israel and of the assembly of the LORD, and in the hearing of our God: Be careful to follow all the commands of the LORD your God, that you may possess this good land and pass it on as an inheritance to your descendants forever.

⁹"And you, my son Solomon, acknowledge the God of your father, and serve him with wholehearted devotion and with a willing mind, for the LORD searches every heart and understands every motive behind the thoughts. If you seek him, he will be found by you; but if you forsake him, he will reject you forever. ¹⁰Consider now, for the LORD has chosen you to build a temple as a sanctuary. Be strong and do the work."

¹¹Then David gave his son Solomon the plans for the portico of the temple, its buildings, its storerooms, its upper parts, its inner rooms and the place of atonement. ¹²He gave him the plans of all that the Spirit had put in his mind for the courts of the temple of the LORD and all the surrounding rooms, for the treasuries of the temple of God and for the treasuries for the dedicated things. ¹³He gave him instructions for the divisions of the

ᵃ24 Septuagint; Hebrew number

priests and Levites, and for all the work of serving in the temple of the Lord, as well as for all the articles to be used in its service. ¹⁴He designated the weight of gold for all the gold articles to be used in various kinds of service, and the weight of silver for all the silver articles to be used in various kinds of service: ¹⁵the weight of gold for the gold lampstands and their lamps, with the weight for each lampstand and its lamps; and the weight of silver for each silver lampstand and its lamps, according to the use of each lampstand; ¹⁶the weight of gold for each table for consecrated bread; the weight of silver for the silver tables; ¹⁷the weight of pure gold for the forks, sprinkling bowls and pitchers; the weight of gold for each gold dish; the weight of silver for each silver dish; ¹⁸and the weight of the refined gold for the altar of incense. He also gave him the plan for the chariot, that is, the cherubim of gold that spread their wings and shelter the ark of the covenant of the Lord.

¹⁹"All this," David said, "I have in writing from the hand of the Lord upon me, and he gave me understanding in all the details of the plan."

²⁰David also said to Solomon his son, "Be strong and courageous, and do the work. Do not be afraid or discouraged, for the Lord God, my God, is with you. He will not fail you or forsake you until all the work for the service of the temple of the Lord is finished. ²¹The divisions of the priests and Levites are ready for all the work on the temple of God, and every

---

FRIDAY

VERSE FOR THE DAY:
1 Chronicles 28:9

AUTHOR:
Barbara Bush

PASSAGE FOR THE DAY:
1 Chronicles 28:1–10

Pure Heart, Holy Life

IF our hearts are pure, the rest of our lives will be pure also. We will be humble not only in our actions but also in our thoughts. Our contentment will be exhibited in our speech as well as felt in our inner desires. Our compassion will not only be godly in the deeds themselves but also in the motives behind the acts. Our diligence in detail will be mirrored by the care we take of the hidden places of our hearts. The wisdom that we offer others will be lived out in our relationships with the members of our own families.

The world is filled with troubled people—people with so much hurt, turmoil, and sin beneath the thin veneer of their lives that they spread chaos and pain wherever they go. The woman of godly character stands in contrast, a balm to the wounds of the world and a source of strength and encouragement to all who come her way.

She knows that "the Lord searches every heart and understands every motive behind the thought" (1 Chronicles 28:9), but she is not afraid. For she trusts, not in her own holiness, but in the Lord, "being confident of this, that he who began a good work in you will carry it on to completion until the day of Christ Jesus" (Philippians 1:6).

Additional Scripture Readings:
Psalm 51:6–12; 2 Timothy 2:22

Go to page 446 for your next devotional reading.

willing man skilled in any craft will help you in all the work. The officials and all the people will obey your every command."

Gifts for Building the Temple

29 Then King David said to the whole assembly: "My son Solomon, the one whom God has chosen, is young and inexperienced. The task is great, because this palatial structure is not for man but for the LORD God. ²With all my resources I have provided for the temple of my God —gold for the gold work, silver for the silver, bronze for the bronze, iron for the iron and wood for the wood, as well as onyx for the settings, turquoise,ᵃ stones of various colors, and all kinds of fine stone and marble—all of these in large quantities. ³Besides, in my devotion to the temple of my God I now give my personal treasures of gold and silver for the temple of my God, over and above everything I have provided for this holy temple: ⁴three thousand talentsᵇ of gold (gold of Ophir) and seven thousand talentsᶜ of refined silver, for the overlaying of the walls of the buildings, ⁵for the gold work and the silver work, and for all the work to be done by the craftsmen. Now, who is willing to consecrate himself today to the LORD?"

⁶Then the leaders of families, the officers of the tribes of Israel, the commanders of thousands and commanders of hundreds, and the officials in charge of the king's work gave willingly. ⁷They gave toward the work on the temple of God five thousand talentsᵈ and ten thousand daricsᵉ of gold, ten thousand talentsᶠ of silver, eighteen thousand talentsᵍ of bronze and a hundred thousand talentsʰ of iron. ⁸Any who had precious stones gave them to the treasury of the temple of the LORD in the custody of Jehiel the Gershonite. ⁹The people rejoiced at the willing response of their leaders, for they had given freely and wholeheartedly to the LORD. David the king also rejoiced greatly.

David's Prayer

¹⁰David praised the LORD in the presence of the whole assembly, saying,

"Praise be to you, O LORD,

God of our father Israel,
from everlasting to everlasting.
¹¹Yours, O LORD, is the greatness and
the power
and the glory and the majesty and
the splendor,
for everything in heaven and earth
is yours.
Yours, O LORD, is the kingdom;
you are exalted as head over all.
¹²Wealth and honor come from you;
you are the ruler of all things.
In your hands are strength and power
to exalt and give strength to all.
¹³Now, our God, we give you thanks,
and praise your glorious name.

¹⁴"But who am I, and who are my people, that we should be able to give as generously as this? Everything comes from you, and we have given you only what comes from your hand. ¹⁵We are aliens and strangers in your sight, as were all our forefathers. Our days on earth are like a shadow, without hope. ¹⁶O LORD our God, as for all this abundance that we have provided for building you a temple for your Holy Name, it comes from your hand, and all of it belongs to you. ¹⁷I know, my God, that you test the heart and are pleased with integrity. All these things have I given willingly and with honest intent. And now I have seen with joy how willingly your people who are here have given to you. ¹⁸O LORD, God of our fathers Abraham, Isaac and Israel, keep this desire in the hearts of your people forever, and keep their hearts loyal to you. ¹⁹And give my son Solomon the wholehearted devotion to keep your commands, requirements and decrees and to do everything to build the palatial structure for which I have provided."

²⁰Then David said to the whole assembly, "Praise the LORD your God." So they all praised the LORD, the God of their fathers; they bowed low and fell prostrate before the LORD and the king.

Solomon Acknowledged as King

²¹The next day they made sacrifices to the LORD and presented burnt offerings to him: a thousand bulls, a thousand rams and a thousand male lambs, together with their drink offerings, and other sacri-

---

ᵃ2 The meaning of the Hebrew for this word is uncertain.   ᵇ4 That is, about 110 tons (about 100 metric tons)   ᶜ4 That is, about 260 tons (about 240 metric tons)   ᵈ7 That is, about 190 tons (about 170 metric tons)   ᵉ7 That is, about 185 pounds (about 84 kilograms)   ᶠ7 That is, about 375 tons (about 345 metric tons)   ᵍ7 That is, about 675 tons (about 610 metric tons)   ʰ7 That is, about 3,750 tons (about 3,450 metric tons)

fices in abundance for all Israel. 22They
ate and drank with great joy in the presence of the LORD that day.

Then they acknowledged Solomon son
of David as king a second time, anointing
him before the LORD to be ruler and Zadok
to be priest. 23So Solomon sat on the
throne of the LORD as king in place of his
father David. He prospered and all Israel
obeyed him. 24All the officers and mighty
men, as well as all of King David's sons,
pledged their submission to King Solomon.

25The LORD highly exalted Solomon in
the sight of all Israel and bestowed on
him royal splendor such as no king over
Israel ever had before.

The Death of David

26David son of Jesse was king over all
Israel. 27He ruled over Israel forty years —
seven in Hebron and thirty-three in Jerusalem. 28He died at a good old age, having
enjoyed long life, wealth and honor. His
son Solomon succeeded him as king.

29As for the events of King David's
reign, from beginning to end, they are
written in the records of Samuel the seer,
the records of Nathan the prophet and
the records of Gad the seer, 30together
with the details of his reign and power,
and the circumstances that surrounded
him and Israel and the kingdoms of all
the other lands.

THIS book continues the history of God's people begun in 1 Chronicles, concentrating exclusively on the nation of Judah. It stresses God's powerful presence in the lives of those kings who believe the word of the Lord and obey his laws. Even though the people are eventually carried away to Babylon, the book ends with a reminder of God's faithfulness in bringing them back. As you read this book, think about how God keeps his promise to surround you with his love in spite of your sin.

2 CHRONICLES

Solomon Asks for Wisdom

1 Solomon son of David established himself firmly over his kingdom, for the LORD his God was with him and made him exceedingly great.

²Then Solomon spoke to all Israel—to the commanders of thousands and commanders of hundreds, to the judges and to all the leaders in Israel, the heads of families— ³and Solomon and the whole assembly went to the high place at Gibeon, for God's Tent of Meeting was there, which Moses the LORD's servant had made in the desert. ⁴Now David had brought up the ark of God from Kiriath Jearim to the place he had prepared for it, because he had pitched a tent for it in Jerusalem. ⁵But the bronze altar that Bezalel son of Uri, the son of Hur, had made was in Gibeon in front of the tabernacle of the LORD; so Solomon and the assembly inquired of him there. ⁶Solomon went up to the bronze altar before the LORD in the Tent of Meeting and offered a thousand burnt offerings on it.

⁷That night God appeared to Solomon and said to him, "Ask for whatever you want me to give you."

⁸Solomon answered God, "You have shown great kindness to David my father and have made me king in his place. ⁹Now, LORD God, let your promise to my

father David be confirmed, for you have made me king over a people who are as numerous as the dust of the earth. ¹⁰Give me wisdom and knowledge, that I may lead this people, for who is able to govern this great people of yours?"

¹¹God said to Solomon, "Since this is your heart's desire and you have not asked for wealth, riches or honor, nor for the death of your enemies, and since you have not asked for a long life but for wisdom and knowledge to govern my people over whom I have made you king, ¹²therefore wisdom and knowledge will be given you. And I will also give you wealth, riches and honor, such as no king who was before you ever had and none after you will have."

¹³Then Solomon went to Jerusalem from the high place at Gibeon, from before the Tent of Meeting. And he reigned over Israel.

¹⁴Solomon accumulated chariots and horses; he had fourteen hundred chariots and twelve thousand horses,ᵃ which he kept in the chariot cities and also with him in Jerusalem. ¹⁵The king made silver and gold as common in Jerusalem as stones, and cedar as plentiful as sycamore-fig trees in the foothills. ¹⁶Solomon's horses were imported from Egyptᵇ and from Kueᶜ—the royal merchants purchased them from Kue. ¹⁷They imported a chariot from Egypt for six hundred shekelsᵈ of silver, and a horse for a hundred and fifty.ᵉ They also exported them to all the kings of the Hittites and of the Arameans.

Preparations for Building the Temple

2 Solomon gave orders to build a temple for the Name of the LORD and a royal palace for himself. ²He conscripted seventy thousand men as carriers and eighty thousand as stonecutters in the hills and thirty-six hundred as foremen over them.

³Solomon sent this message to Hiramᶠ king of Tyre:

"Send me cedar logs as you did for my father David when you sent him cedar to build a palace to live in. ⁴Now I am about to build a temple for the Name of the LORD my God and

to dedicate it to him for burning fragrant incense before him, for setting out the consecrated bread regularly, and for making burnt offerings every morning and evening and on Sabbaths and New Moons and at the appointed feasts of the LORD our God. This is a lasting ordinance for Israel.

⁵"The temple I am going to build will be great, because our God is greater than all other gods. ⁶But who is able to build a temple for him, since the heavens, even the highest heavens, cannot contain him? Who then am I to build a temple for him, except as a place to burn sacrifices before him?

⁷"Send me, therefore, a man skilled to work in gold and silver, bronze and iron, and in purple, crimson and blue yarn, and experienced in the art of engraving, to work in Judah and Jerusalem with my skilled craftsmen, whom my father David provided.

⁸"Send me also cedar, pine and algumᵍ logs from Lebanon, for I know that your men are skilled in cutting timber there. My men will work with yours ⁹to provide me with plenty of lumber, because the temple I build must be large and magnificent. ¹⁰I will give your servants, the woodsmen who cut the timber, twenty thousand corsʰ of ground wheat, twenty thousand cors of barley, twenty thousand bathsⁱ of wine and twenty thousand baths of olive oil."

¹¹Hiram king of Tyre replied by letter to Solomon:

"Because the LORD loves his people, he has made you their king."

¹²And Hiram added:

"Praise be to the LORD, the God of Israel, who made heaven and earth! He has given King David a wise son, endowed with intelligence and discernment, who will build a temple for the LORD and a palace for himself.

¹³"I am sending you Huram-Abi, a man of great skill, ¹⁴whose mother

---

ᵃ14 Or charioteers   ᵇ16 Or possibly Muzur, a region in Cilicia; also in verse 17   ᶜ16 Probably Cilicia
ᵈ17 That is, about 15 pounds (about 7 kilograms)   ᵉ17 That is, about 3 3/4 pounds (about 1.7
kilograms)   ᶠ3 Hebrew Huram, a variant of Hiram; also in verses 11 and 12   ᵍ8 Probably a variant of
almug; possibly juniper   ʰ10 That is, probably about 125,000 bushels (about 4,400 kiloliters)
ⁱ10 That is, probably about 115,000 gallons (about 440 kiloliters)

was from Dan and whose father was from Tyre. He is trained to work in gold and silver, bronze and iron, stone and wood, and with purple and blue and crimson yarn and fine linen. He is experienced in all kinds of engraving and can execute any design given to him. He will work with your craftsmen and with those of my lord, David your father.

15"Now let my lord send his servants the wheat and barley and the olive oil and wine he promised, 16and we will cut all the logs from Lebanon that you need and will float them in rafts by sea down to Joppa. You can then take them up to Jerusalem."

17Solomon took a census of all the aliens who were in Israel, after the census his father David had taken; and they were found to be 153,600. 18He assigned 70,000 of them to be carriers and 80,000 to be stonecutters in the hills, with 3,600 foremen over them to keep the people working.

Solomon Builds the Temple

3 Then Solomon began to build the temple of the LORD in Jerusalem on Mount Moriah, where the LORD had appeared to his father David. It was on the threshing floor of Araunah*a* the Jebusite, the place provided by David. 2He began building on the second day of the second month in the fourth year of his reign.

3The foundation Solomon laid for building the temple of God was sixty cubits long and twenty cubits wide*b* (using the cubit of the old standard). 4The portico at the front of the temple was twenty cubits*c* long across the width of the building and twenty cubits*d* high.

He overlaid the inside with pure gold. 5He paneled the main hall with pine and covered it with fine gold and decorated it with palm tree and chain designs. 6He adorned the temple with precious stones. And the gold he used was gold of Parvaim. 7He overlaid the ceiling beams, doorframes, walls and doors of the temple with gold, and he carved cherubim on the walls.

8He built the Most Holy Place, its length corresponding to the width of the temple—twenty cubits long and twenty cubits wide. He overlaid the inside with six hundred talents*e* of fine gold. 9The gold nails weighed fifty shekels.*f* He also overlaid the upper parts with gold.

10In the Most Holy Place he made a pair of sculptured cherubim and overlaid them with gold. 11The total wingspan of the cherubim was twenty cubits. One wing of the first cherub was five cubits*g* long and touched the temple wall, while its other wing, also five cubits long, touched the wing of the other cherub. 12Similarly one wing of the second cherub was five cubits long and touched the other temple wall, and its other wing, also five cubits long, touched the wing of the first cherub. 13The wings of these cherubim extended twenty cubits. They stood on their feet, facing the main hall.*h*

14He made the curtain of blue, purple and crimson yarn and fine linen, with cherubim worked into it.

15In the front of the temple he made two pillars, which together, were thirty-five cubits*i* long, each with a capital on top measuring five cubits. 16He made interwoven chains*j* and put them on top of the pillars. He also made a hundred pomegranates and attached them to the chains. 17He erected the pillars in the front of the temple, one to the south and one to the north. The one to the south he named Jakin*k* and the one to the north Boaz.*l*

The Temple's Furnishings

4 He made a bronze altar twenty cubits long, twenty cubits wide and ten cubits high.*m* 2He made the Sea of cast metal, circular in shape, measuring ten cubits from rim to rim and five cubits*n* high. It took a line of thirty cubits*o* to measure around it. 3Below the rim, figures of bulls encircled it—ten to a cubit.*p* The bulls

---

a1 Hebrew *Ornan*, a variant of *Araunah* *b3* That is, about 90 feet (about 27 meters) long and 30 feet (about 9 meters) wide *c4* That is, about 30 feet (about 9 meters); also in verses 8, 11 and 13 *d4* Some Septuagint and Syriac manuscripts; Hebrew *and a hundred and twenty* *e8* That is, about 23 tons (about 21 metric tons) *f9* That is, about 1 1/4 pounds (about 0.6 kilogram) *g11* That is, about 7 1/2 feet (about 2.3 meters); also in verse 15 *h13* Or *facing inward* *i15* That is, about 52 feet (about 16 meters) *j16* Or possibly *made chains in the inner sanctuary*; the meaning of the Hebrew for this phrase is uncertain. *k17* *Jakin* probably means *he establishes.* *l17* *Boaz* probably means *in him is strength.* *m1* That is, about 30 feet (about 9 meters) long and wide, and about 15 feet (about 4.5 meters) high *n2* That is, about 7 1/2 feet (about 2.3 meters) *o2* That is, about 45 feet (about 13.5 meters) *p3* That is, about 1 1/2 feet (about 0.5 meter)

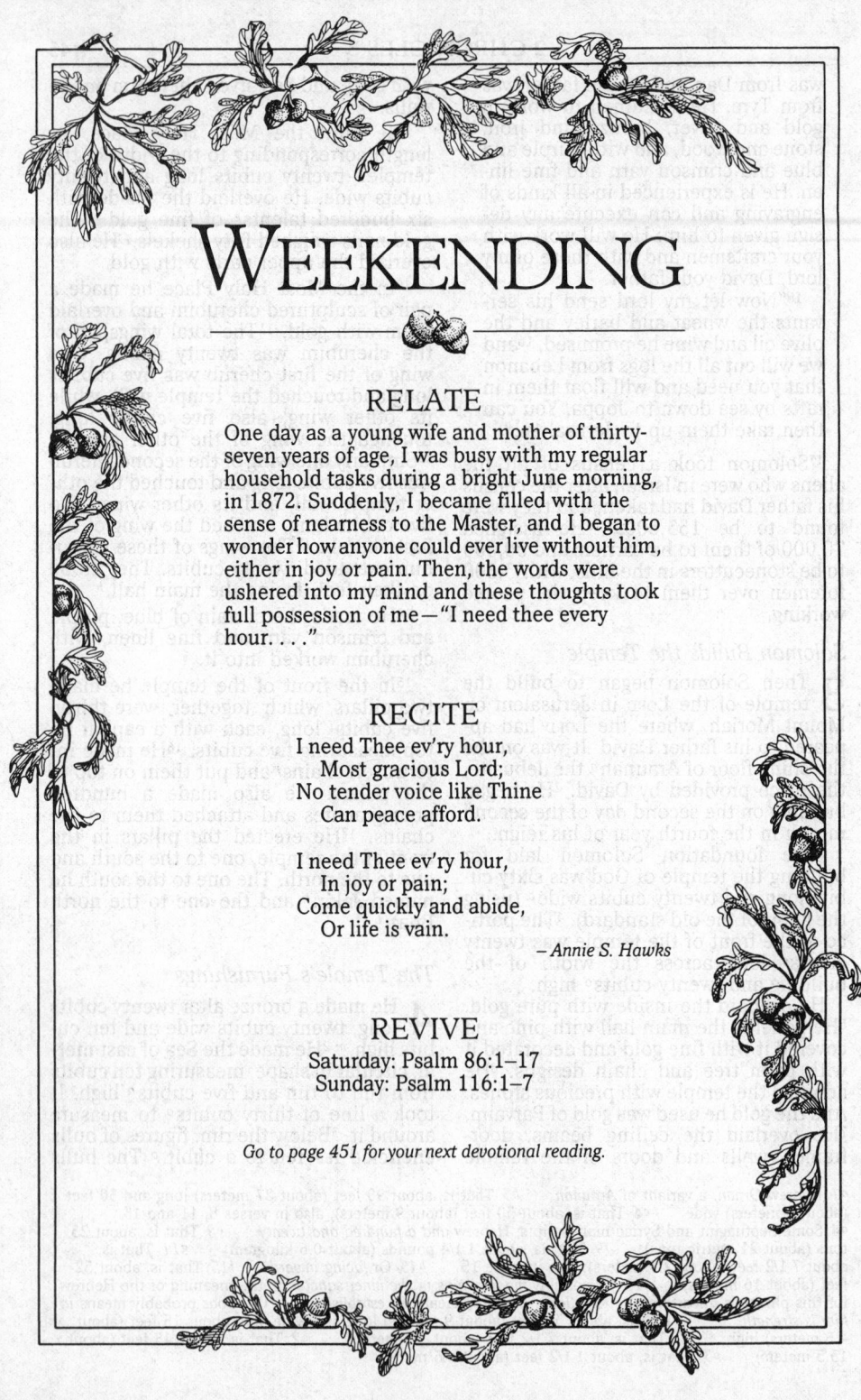

WEEKENDING

RELATE

One day as a young wife and mother of thirty-seven years of age, I was busy with my regular household tasks during a bright June morning, in 1872. Suddenly, I became filled with the sense of nearness to the Master, and I began to wonder how anyone could ever live without him, either in joy or pain. Then, the words were ushered into my mind and these thoughts took full possession of me—"I need thee every hour. . . ."

RECITE

I need Thee ev'ry hour,
    Most gracious Lord;
No tender voice like Thine
    Can peace afford.

I need Thee ev'ry hour,
    In joy or pain;
Come quickly and abide,
    Or life is vain.

— Annie S. Hawks

REVIVE

Saturday: Psalm 86:1–17
Sunday: Psalm 116:1–7

Go to page 451 for your next devotional reading.

were cast in two rows in one piece with the Sea.

⁴The Sea stood on twelve bulls, three facing north, three facing west, three facing south and three facing east. The Sea rested on top of them, and their hindquarters were toward the center. ⁵It was a handbreadth*ᵃ* in thickness, and its rim was like the rim of a cup, like a lily blossom. It held three thousand baths.*ᵇ*

⁶He then made ten basins for washing and placed five on the south side and five on the north. In them the things to be used for the burnt offerings were rinsed, but the Sea was to be used by the priests for washing.

⁷He made ten gold lampstands according to the specifications for them and placed them in the temple, five on the south side and five on the north.

⁸He made ten tables and placed them in the temple, five on the south side and five on the north. He also made a hundred gold sprinkling bowls.

⁹He made the courtyard of the priests, and the large court and the doors for the court, and overlaid the doors with bronze. ¹⁰He placed the Sea on the south side, at the southeast corner.

¹¹He also made the pots and shovels and sprinkling bowls.

So Huram finished the work he had undertaken for King Solomon in the temple of God:

¹²the two pillars;
    the two bowl-shaped capitals on top of the pillars;
    the two sets of network decorating the two bowl-shaped capitals on top of the pillars;
¹³the four hundred pomegranates for the two sets of network (two rows of pomegranates for each network, decorating the bowl-shaped capitals on top of the pillars);
¹⁴the stands with their basins;
¹⁵the Sea and the twelve bulls under it;
¹⁶the pots, shovels, meat forks and all related articles.

All the objects that Huram-Abi made for King Solomon for the temple of the LORD were of polished bronze. ¹⁷The king had them cast in clay molds in the plain of the Jordan between Succoth and Zarethan.*ᶜ* ¹⁸All these things that Solomon made amounted to so much that the

weight of the bronze was not determined.

¹⁹Solomon also made all the furnishings that were in God's temple:

    the golden altar;
    the tables on which was the bread of the Presence;
²⁰the lampstands of pure gold with their lamps, to burn in front of the inner sanctuary as prescribed;
²¹the gold floral work and lamps and tongs (they were solid gold);
²²the pure gold wick trimmers, sprinkling bowls, dishes and censers;
    and the gold doors of the temple: the inner doors to the Most Holy Place and the doors of the main hall.

5 When all the work Solomon had done for the temple of the LORD was finished, he brought in the things his father David had dedicated—the silver and gold and all the furnishings—and he placed them in the treasuries of God's temple.

The Ark Brought to the Temple

²Then Solomon summoned to Jerusalem the elders of Israel, all the heads of the tribes and the chiefs of the Israelite families, to bring up the ark of the LORD's covenant from Zion, the City of David. ³And all the men of Israel came together to the king at the time of the festival in the seventh month.

⁴When all the elders of Israel had arrived, the Levites took up the ark, ⁵and they brought up the ark and the Tent of Meeting and all the sacred furnishings in it. The priests, who were Levites, carried them up; ⁶and King Solomon and the entire assembly of Israel that had gathered about him were before the ark, sacrificing so many sheep and cattle that they could not be recorded or counted.

⁷The priests then brought the ark of the LORD's covenant to its place in the inner sanctuary of the temple, the Most Holy Place, and put it beneath the wings of the cherubim. ⁸The cherubim spread their wings over the place of the ark and covered the ark and its carrying poles. ⁹These poles were so long that their ends, extending from the ark, could be seen from in front of the inner sanctuary, but not from outside the Holy Place; and they are still there today. ¹⁰There was nothing in the ark except the two tablets that Moses

---

ᵃ5 That is, about 3 inches (about 8 centimeters)   *ᵇ5* That is, about 17,500 gallons (about 66 kiloliters)
ᶜ17 Hebrew *Zeredatha*, a variant of *Zarethan*

had placed in it at Horeb, where the Lord made a covenant with the Israelites after they came out of Egypt.

¹¹The priests then withdrew from the Holy Place. All the priests who were there had consecrated themselves, regardless of their divisions. ¹²All the Levites who were musicians—Asaph, Heman, Jeduthun and their sons and relatives—stood on the east side of the altar, dressed in fine linen and playing cymbals, harps and lyres. They were accompanied by 120 priests sounding trumpets. ¹³The trumpeters and singers joined in unison, as with one voice, to give praise and thanks to the Lord. Accompanied by trumpets, cymbals and other instruments, they raised their voices in praise to the Lord and sang:

"He is good;
    his love endures forever."

Then the temple of the Lord was filled with a cloud, ¹⁴and the priests could not perform their service because of the cloud, for the glory of the Lord filled the temple of God.

6 Then Solomon said, "The Lord has said that he would dwell in a dark cloud; ²I have built a magnificent temple for you, a place for you to dwell forever."

³While the whole assembly of Israel was standing there, the king turned around and blessed them. ⁴Then he said:

"Praise be to the Lord, the God of Israel, who with his hands has fulfilled what he promised with his mouth to my father David. For he said, ⁵'Since the day I brought my people out of Egypt, I have not chosen a city in any tribe of Israel to have a temple built for my Name to be there, nor have I chosen anyone to be the leader over my people Israel. ⁶But now I have chosen Jerusalem for my Name to be there, and I have chosen David to rule my people Israel.'

⁷"My father David had it in his heart to build a temple for the Name of the Lord, the God of Israel. ⁸But the Lord said to my father David, 'Because it was in your heart to build a temple for my Name, you did well to have this in your heart. ⁹Nevertheless, you are not the one to build the temple, but your son, who is your

own flesh and blood—he is the one who will build the temple for my Name.'

¹⁰"The Lord has kept the promise he made. I have succeeded David my father and now I sit on the throne of Israel, just as the Lord promised, and I have built the temple for the Name of the Lord, the God of Israel. ¹¹There I have placed the ark, in which is the covenant of the Lord that he made with the people of Israel."

Solomon's Prayer of Dedication

¹²Then Solomon stood before the altar of the Lord in front of the whole assembly of Israel and spread out his hands. ¹³Now he had made a bronze platform, five cubits ᵃ long, five cubits wide and three cubits ᵇ high, and had placed it in the center of the outer court. He stood on the platform and then knelt down before the whole assembly of Israel and spread out his hands toward heaven. ¹⁴He said:

"O Lord, God of Israel, there is no God like you in heaven or on earth—you who keep your covenant of love with your servants who continue wholeheartedly in your way. ¹⁵You have kept your promise to your servant David my father; with your mouth you have promised and with your hand you have fulfilled it—as it is today.

¹⁶"Now Lord, God of Israel, keep for your servant David my father the promises you made to him when you said, 'You shall never fail to have a man to sit before me on the throne of Israel, if only your sons are careful in all they do to walk before me according to my law, as you have done.' ¹⁷And now, O Lord, God of Israel, let your word that you promised your servant David come true.

¹⁸"But will God really dwell on earth with men? The heavens, even the highest heavens, cannot contain you. How much less this temple I have built! ¹⁹Yet give attention to your servant's prayer and his plea for mercy, O Lord my God. Hear the cry and the prayer that your servant is praying in your presence. ²⁰May your eyes be open toward this temple day

---

ᵃ13 That is, about 7 1/2 feet (about 2.3 meters)   ᵇ13 That is, about 4 1/2 feet (about 1.3 meters) and night, this place of which you said you would put your Name there. May you hear the prayer your servant prays toward this place. 21Hear the supplications of your servant and of your people Israel when they pray toward this place. Hear from heaven, your dwelling place; and when you hear, forgive.

22"When a man wrongs his neighbor and is required to take an oath and he comes and swears the oath before your altar in this temple, 23then hear from heaven and act. Judge between your servants, repaying the guilty by bringing down on his own head what he has done. Declare the innocent not guilty and so establish his innocence.

24"When your people Israel have been defeated by an enemy because they have sinned against you and when they turn back and confess your name, praying and making supplication before you in this temple, 25then hear from heaven and forgive the sin of your people Israel and bring them back to the land you gave to them and their fathers.

26"When the heavens are shut up and there is no rain because your people have sinned against you, and when they pray toward this place and confess your name and turn from their sin because you have afflicted them, 27then hear from heaven and forgive the sin of your servants, your people Israel. Teach them the right way to live, and send rain on the land you gave your people for an inheritance.

28"When famine or plague comes to the land, or blight or mildew, locusts or grasshoppers, or when enemies besiege them in any of their cities, whatever disaster or disease may come, 29and when a prayer or plea is made by any of your people Israel— each one aware of his afflictions and pains, and spreading out his hands toward this temple— 30then hear from heaven, your dwelling place. Forgive, and deal with each man according to all he does, since you know his heart (for you alone know the hearts of men), 31so that they will fear you and walk in your ways all the time they live in the land you gave our fathers.

32"As for the foreigner who does not belong to your people Israel but has come from a distant land because of your great name and your mighty hand and your outstretched arm—when he comes and prays toward this temple, 33then hear from heaven, your dwelling place, and do whatever the foreigner asks of you, so that all the peoples of the earth may know your name and fear you, as do your own people Israel, and may know that this house I have built bears your Name.

34"When your people go to war against their enemies, wherever you send them, and when they pray to you toward this city you have chosen and the temple I have built for your Name, 35then hear from heaven their prayer and their plea, and uphold their cause.

36"When they sin against you—for there is no one who does not sin— and you become angry with them and give them over to the enemy, who takes them captive to a land far away or near; 37and if they have a change of heart in the land where they are held captive, and repent and plead with you in the land of their captivity and say, 'We have sinned, we have done wrong and acted wickedly'; 38and if they turn back to you with all their heart and soul in the land of their captivity where they were taken, and pray toward the land you gave their fathers, toward the city you have chosen and toward the temple I have built for your Name; 39then from heaven, your dwelling place, hear their prayer and their pleas, and uphold their cause. And forgive your people, who have sinned against you.

40"Now, my God, may your eyes be open and your ears attentive to the prayers offered in this place.

41"Now arise, O LORD God, and
come to your resting place,
you and the ark of your might.
May your priests, O LORD God, be
clothed with salvation,
may your saints rejoice in your
goodness.
42O LORD God, do not reject your
anointed one.
Remember the great love
promised to David your
servant."

The Dedication of the Temple

7 When Solomon finished praying, fire came down from heaven and consumed the burnt offering and the sacrifices, and the glory of the LORD filled the temple. ²The priests could not enter the temple of the LORD because the glory of the LORD filled it. ³When all the Israelites saw the fire coming down and the glory of the LORD above the temple, they knelt on the pavement with their faces to the ground, and they worshiped and gave thanks to the LORD, saying,

"He is good;
his love endures forever."

⁴Then the king and all the people offered sacrifices before the LORD. ⁵And King Solomon offered a sacrifice of twenty-two thousand head of cattle and a hundred and twenty thousand sheep and goats. So the king and all the people dedicated the temple of God. ⁶The priests took their positions, as did the Levites with the LORD's musical instruments, which King David had made for praising the LORD and which were used when he gave thanks, saying, "His love endures forever." Opposite the Levites, the priests blew their trumpets, and all the Israelites were standing.

⁷Solomon consecrated the middle part of the courtyard in front of the temple of the LORD, and there he offered burnt offerings and the fat of the fellowship offerings,ᵃ because the bronze altar he had made could not hold the burnt offerings, the grain offerings and the fat portions.

⁸So Solomon observed the festival at that time for seven days, and all Israel with him—a vast assembly, people from Leboᵇ Hamath to the Wadi of Egypt. ⁹On the eighth day they held an assembly, for they had celebrated the dedication of the altar for seven days and the festival for seven days more. ¹⁰On the twenty-third day of the seventh month he sent the people to their homes, joyful and glad in heart for the good things the LORD had done for David and Solomon and for his people Israel.

The LORD Appears to Solomon

¹¹When Solomon had finished the temple of the LORD and the royal palace, and had succeeded in carrying out all he had in mind to do in the temple of the LORD and in his own palace, ¹²the LORD appeared to him at night and said:

"I have heard your prayer and have chosen this place for myself as a temple for sacrifices.

¹³"When I shut up the heavens so that there is no rain, or command locusts to devour the land or send a plague among my people, ¹⁴if my people, who are called by my name, will humble themselves and pray and seek my face and turn from their wicked ways, then will I hear from heaven and will forgive their sin and will heal their land. ¹⁵Now my eyes will be open and my ears attentive to the prayers offered in this place. ¹⁶I have chosen and consecrated this temple so that my Name may be there forever. My eyes and my heart will always be there.

¹⁷"As for you, if you walk before me as David your father did, and do all I command, and observe my decrees and laws, ¹⁸I will establish your royal throne, as I covenanted with David your father when I said, 'You shall never fail to have a man to rule over Israel.'

¹⁹"But if youᶜ turn away and forsake the decrees and commands I have given youᶜ and go off to serve other gods and worship them, ²⁰then I will uproot Israel from my land, which I have given them, and will reject this temple I have consecrated for my Name. I will make it a byword and an object of ridicule among all peoples. ²¹And though this temple is now so imposing, all who pass by will be appalled and say, 'Why has the LORD done such a thing to this land and to this temple?' ²²People will answer, 'Because they have forsaken the LORD, the God of their fathers, who brought them out of Egypt, and have embraced other gods, worshiping and serving them—that is why he brought all this disaster on them.' "

Solomon's Other Activities

8 At the end of twenty years, during which Solomon built the temple of the LORD and his own palace, ²Solomon rebuilt the villages that Hiramᵈ had given him, and settled Israelites in them. ³Solo-

---

ᵃ7 Traditionally peace offerings   ᵇ8 Or from the entrance to   ᶜ19 The Hebrew is plural.
ᵈ2 Hebrew Huram, a variant of Hiram; also in verse 18

mon then went to Hamath Zobah and captured it. ⁴He also built up Tadmor in the desert and all the store cities he had built in Hamath. ⁵He rebuilt Upper Beth Horon and Lower Beth Horon as fortified cities, with walls and with gates and bars, ⁶as well as Baalath and all his store cities, and all the cities for his chariots and for his horses *ᵃ*—whatever he desired to build in Jerusalem, in Lebanon and throughout all the territory he ruled.

⁷All the people left from the Hittites, Amorites, Perizzites, Hivites and Jebusites (these peoples were not Israelites), ⁸that is, their descendants remaining in the land, whom the Israelites had not destroyed—these Solomon conscripted for his slave labor force, as it is to this day. ⁹But Solomon did not make slaves of the Israelites for his work; they were his fighting men, commanders of his captains, and commanders of his chariots and

ᵃ6 Or charioteers

MONDAY

VERSE FOR THE DAY:
2 Chronicles 7:1

AUTHOR:
Hannah Whitall Smith

PASSAGE FOR THE DAY:
2 Chronicles 7:1–10

Receiving His Blessing

TO some the promise of the Father comes as a mighty and overwhelming power; to others he comes as the tender and gentle presence of love. But either way, he always makes his presence manifest; and at that day, whenever it comes, the words of our Lord, which he spoke to his disciples concerning this wondrous gift, are invariably fulfilled: "On that day you will realize that I am in my Father, and you are in me, and I am in you" (John 14:20). We may have believed it before because God says it is so in the Scriptures, but from the moment we receive it we know it by the testimony of an inward consciousness that is unassailable by any form of questioning or doubt.

The Israelites had believed the Lord was in their midst all along in their wanderings and in their years of bondage. But when the temple was built, when they all saw how "fire came down from heaven . . . and the glory of the LORD filled the temple" (2 Chronicles 7:1), they *knew* it. We cannot wonder that at once, without the need of any command from Solomon, they bowed themselves with their faces to the ground and worshiped and praised the Lord.

Words fail in seeking to tell of the blessedness of this inner life of divine union, and the spirit stands amazed before such glorious possibilities of experience! With Solomon we exclaim, "But will God really dwell on earth with men? The heavens, even the highest heavens, cannot contain you. How much less this temple I have built!" (2 Chronicles 6:18). And the Lord answers, as he did to Solomon, "I have heard your prayer and have chosen this place for myself" (2 Chronicles 7:12).

Additional Scripture Readings:
Genesis 28:10–17; Acts 26:12–23

Go to page 470 for your next
devotional reading.

charioteers. [10]They were also King Solomon's chief officials—two hundred and fifty officials supervising the men.

[11]Solomon brought Pharaoh's daughter up from the City of David to the palace he had built for her, for he said, "My wife must not live in the palace of David king of Israel, because the places the ark of the LORD has entered are holy."

[12]On the altar of the LORD that he had built in front of the portico, Solomon sacrificed burnt offerings to the LORD, [13]according to the daily requirement for offerings commanded by Moses for Sabbaths, New Moons and the three annual feasts —the Feast of Unleavened Bread, the Feast of Weeks and the Feast of Tabernacles. [14]In keeping with the ordinance of his father David, he appointed the divisions of the priests for their duties, and the Levites to lead the praise and to assist the priests according to each day's requirement. He also appointed the gatekeepers by divisions for the various gates, because this was what David the man of God had ordered. [15]They did not deviate from the king's commands to the priests or to the Levites in any matter, including that of the treasuries.

[16]All Solomon's work was carried out, from the day the foundation of the temple of the LORD was laid until its completion. So the temple of the LORD was finished.

[17]Then Solomon went to Ezion Geber and Elath on the coast of Edom. [18]And Hiram sent him ships commanded by his own officers, men who knew the sea. These, with Solomon's men, sailed to Ophir and brought back four hundred and fifty talents[a] of gold, which they delivered to King Solomon.

The Queen of Sheba Visits Solomon

9 When the queen of Sheba heard of Solomon's fame, she came to Jerusalem to test him with hard questions. Arriving with a very great caravan—with camels carrying spices, large quantities of gold, and precious stones—she came to Solomon and talked with him about all she had on her mind. [2]Solomon answered all her questions; nothing was too hard for him to explain to her. [3]When the queen of Sheba saw the wisdom of Solomon, as well as the palace he had built,

[4]the food on his table, the seating of his officials, the attending servants in their robes, the cupbearers in their robes and the burnt offerings he made at[b] the temple of the LORD, she was overwhelmed.

[5]She said to the king, "The report I heard in my own country about your achievements and your wisdom is true. [6]But I did not believe what they said until I came and saw with my own eyes. Indeed, not even half the greatness of your wisdom was told me; you have far exceeded the report I heard. [7]How happy your men must be! How happy your officials, who continually stand before you and hear your wisdom! [8]Praise be to the LORD your God, who has delighted in you and placed you on his throne as king to rule for the LORD your God. Because of the love of your God for Israel and his desire to uphold them forever, he has made you king over them, to maintain justice and righteousness."

[9]Then she gave the king 120 talents[c] of gold, large quantities of spices, and precious stones. There had never been such spices as those the queen of Sheba gave to King Solomon.

[10](The men of Hiram and the men of Solomon brought gold from Ophir; they also brought algumwood[d] and precious stones. [11]The king used the algumwood to make steps for the temple of the LORD and for the royal palace, and to make harps and lyres for the musicians. Nothing like them had ever been seen in Judah.)

[12]King Solomon gave the queen of Sheba all she desired and asked for; he gave her more than she had brought to him. Then she left and returned with her retinue to her own country.

Solomon's Splendor

[13]The weight of the gold that Solomon received yearly was 666 talents,[e] [14]not including the revenues brought in by merchants and traders. Also all the kings of Arabia and the governors of the land brought gold and silver to Solomon.

[15]King Solomon made two hundred large shields of hammered gold; six hundred bekas[f] of hammered gold went into each shield. [16]He also made three hundred small shields of hammered gold,

---

*a*18 That is, about 17 tons (about 16 metric tons)   *b*4 Or *the ascent by which he went up to*
*c*9 That is, about 4 1/2 tons (about 4 metric tons)   *d*10 Probably a variant of *almugwood*   *e*13 That
is, about 25 tons (about 23 metric tons)   *f*15 That is, about 7 1/2 pounds (about 3.5 kilograms)

with three hundred bekas[a] of gold in each shield. The king put them in the Palace of the Forest of Lebanon.

[17]Then the king made a great throne inlaid with ivory and overlaid with pure gold. [18]The throne had six steps, and a footstool of gold was attached to it. On both sides of the seat were armrests, with a lion standing beside each of them. [19]Twelve lions stood on the six steps, one at either end of each step. Nothing like it had ever been made for any other kingdom. [20]All King Solomon's goblets were gold, and all the household articles in the Palace of the Forest of Lebanon were pure gold. Nothing was made of silver, because silver was considered of little value in Solomon's day. [21]The king had a fleet of trading ships[b] manned by Hiram's[c] men. Once every three years it returned, carrying gold, silver and ivory, and apes and baboons.

[22]King Solomon was greater in riches and wisdom than all the other kings of the earth. [23]All the kings of the earth sought audience with Solomon to hear the wisdom God had put in his heart. [24]Year after year, everyone who came brought a gift—articles of silver and gold, and robes, weapons and spices, and horses and mules.

[25]Solomon had four thousand stalls for horses and chariots, and twelve thousand horses,[d] which he kept in the chariot cities and also with him in Jerusalem. [26]He ruled over all the kings from the River[e] to the land of the Philistines, as far as the border of Egypt. [27]The king made silver as common in Jerusalem as stones, and cedar as plentiful as sycamore-fig trees in the foothills. [28]Solomon's horses were imported from Egypt[f] and from all other countries.

Solomon's Death

[29]As for the other events of Solomon's reign, from beginning to end, are they not written in the records of Nathan the prophet, in the prophecy of Ahijah the Shilonite and in the visions of Iddo the seer concerning Jeroboam son of Nebat? [30]Solomon reigned in Jerusalem over all Israel forty years. [31]Then he rested with his fathers and was buried in the city of David his father. And Rehoboam his son succeeded him as king.

Israel Rebels Against Rehoboam

10 Rehoboam went to Shechem, for all the Israelites had gone there to make him king. [2]When Jeroboam son of Nebat heard this (he was in Egypt, where he had fled from King Solomon), he returned from Egypt. [3]So they sent for Jeroboam, and he and all Israel went to Rehoboam and said to him: [4]"Your father put a heavy yoke on us, but now lighten the harsh labor and the heavy yoke he put on us, and we will serve you."

[5]Rehoboam answered, "Come back to me in three days." So the people went away.

[6]Then King Rehoboam consulted the elders who had served his father Solomon during his lifetime. "How would you advise me to answer these people?" he asked.

[7]They replied, "If you will be kind to these people and please them and give them a favorable answer, they will always be your servants."

[8]But Rehoboam rejected the advice the elders gave him and consulted the young men who had grown up with him and were serving him. [9]He asked them, "What is your advice? How should we answer these people who say to me, 'Lighten the yoke your father put on us'?"

[10]The young men who had grown up with him replied, "Tell the people who have said to you, 'Your father put a heavy yoke on us, but make our yoke lighter'—tell them, 'My little finger is thicker than my father's waist. [11]My father laid on you a heavy yoke; I will make it even heavier. My father scourged you with whips; I will scourge you with scorpions.'"

[12]Three days later Jeroboam and all the people returned to Rehoboam, as the king had said, "Come back to me in three days." [13]The king answered them harshly. Rejecting the advice of the elders, [14]he followed the advice of the young men and said, "My father made your yoke heavy; I will make it even heavier. My father scourged you with whips; I will scourge you with scorpions." [15]So the king did not listen to the people, for this turn of events was from God, to fulfill the word the LORD had spoken to Jeroboam son of Nebat through Ahijah the Shilonite.

[16]When all Israel saw that the king re-

---

[a]16 That is, about 3 3/4 pounds (about 1.7 kilograms)   [b]21 Hebrew *of ships that could go to Tarshish*   [c]21 Hebrew *Huram*, a variant of *Hiram*   [d]25 Or *charioteers*   [e]26 That is, the Euphrates   [f]28 Or possibly *Muzur*, a region in Cilicia

fused to listen to them, they answered the king:

"What share do we have in David,
    what part in Jesse's son?
To your tents, O Israel!
Look after your own house,
    O David!"

So all the Israelites went home. 17But as for the Israelites who were living in the towns of Judah, Rehoboam still ruled over them.

18King Rehoboam sent out Adoniram,ᵃ who was in charge of forced labor, but the Israelites stoned him to death. King Rehoboam, however, managed to get into his chariot and escape to Jerusalem. 19So Israel has been in rebellion against the house of David to this day.

11 When Rehoboam arrived in Jerusalem, he mustered the house of Judah and Benjamin—a hundred and eighty thousand fighting men—to make war against Israel and to regain the kingdom for Rehoboam.

2But this word of the LORD came to Shemaiah the man of God: 3"Say to Rehoboam son of Solomon king of Judah and to all the Israelites in Judah and Benjamin, 4'This is what the LORD says: Do not go up to fight against your brothers. Go home, every one of you, for this is my doing.'" So they obeyed the words of the LORD and turned back from marching against Jeroboam.

Rehoboam Fortifies Judah

5Rehoboam lived in Jerusalem and built up towns for defense in Judah: 6Bethlehem, Etam, Tekoa, 7Beth Zur, Soco, Adullam, 8Gath, Mareshah, Ziph, 9Adoraim, Lachish, Azekah, 10Zorah, Aijalon and Hebron. These were fortified cities in Judah and Benjamin. 11He strengthened their defenses and put commanders in them, with supplies of food, olive oil and wine. 12He put shields and spears in all the cities, and made them very strong. So Judah and Benjamin were his.

13The priests and Levites from all their districts throughout Israel sided with him. 14The Levites even abandoned their pasturelands and property, and came to Judah and Jerusalem because Jeroboam and his sons had rejected them as priests of the LORD. 15And he appointed his own priests for the high places and for the goat and calf idols he had made. 16Those from every tribe of Israel who set their hearts on seeking the LORD, the God of Israel, followed the Levites to Jerusalem to offer sacrifices to the LORD, the God of their fathers. 17They strengthened the kingdom of Judah and supported Rehoboam son of Solomon three years, walking in the ways of David and Solomon during this time.

Rehoboam's Family

18Rehoboam married Mahalath, who was the daughter of David's son Jerimoth and of Abihail, the daughter of Jesse's son Eliab. 19She bore him sons: Jeush, Shemariah and Zaham. 20Then he married Maacah daughter of Absalom, who bore him Abijah, Attai, Ziza and Shelomith. 21Rehoboam loved Maacah daughter of Absalom more than any of his other wives and concubines. In all, he had eighteen wives and sixty concubines, twenty-eight sons and sixty daughters.

22Rehoboam appointed Abijah son of Maacah to be the chief prince among his brothers, in order to make him king. 23He acted wisely, dispersing some of his sons throughout the districts of Judah and Benjamin, and to all the fortified cities. He gave them abundant provisions and took many wives for them.

Shishak Attacks Jerusalem

12 After Rehoboam's position as king was established and he had become strong, he and all Israelᵇ with him abandoned the law of the LORD. 2Because they had been unfaithful to the LORD, Shishak king of Egypt attacked Jerusalem in the fifth year of King Rehoboam. 3With twelve hundred chariots and sixty thousand horsemen and the innumerable troops of Libyans, Sukkites and Cushitesᶜ that came with him from Egypt, 4he captured the fortified cities of Judah and came as far as Jerusalem.

5Then the prophet Shemaiah came to Rehoboam and to the leaders of Judah who had assembled in Jerusalem for fear of Shishak, and he said to them, "This is what the LORD says, 'You have abandoned me; therefore, I now abandon you to Shishak.'"

6The leaders of Israel and the king humbled themselves and said, "The LORD is just."

ᵃ18 Hebrew *Hadoram,* a variant of *Adoniram*   ᵇ1 That is, Judah, as frequently in 2 Chronicles
ᶜ3 That is, people from the upper Nile region

[7]When the LORD saw that they humbled themselves, this word of the LORD came to Shemaiah: "Since they have humbled themselves, I will not destroy them but will soon give them deliverance. My wrath will not be poured out on Jerusalem through Shishak. [8]They will, however, become subject to him, so that they may learn the difference between serving me and serving the kings of other lands."

[9]When Shishak king of Egypt attacked Jerusalem, he carried off the treasures of the temple of the LORD and the treasures of the royal palace. He took everything, including the gold shields Solomon had made. [10]So King Rehoboam made bronze shields to replace them and assigned these to the commanders of the guard on duty at the entrance to the royal palace. [11]Whenever the king went to the LORD's temple, the guards went with him, bearing the shields, and afterward they returned them to the guardroom.

[12]Because Rehoboam humbled himself, the LORD's anger turned from him, and he was not totally destroyed. Indeed, there was some good in Judah.

[13]King Rehoboam established himself firmly in Jerusalem and continued as king. He was forty-one years old when he became king, and he reigned seventeen years in Jerusalem, the city the LORD had chosen out of all the tribes of Israel in which to put his Name. His mother's name was Naamah; she was an Ammonite. [14]He did evil because he had not set his heart on seeking the LORD.

[15]As for the events of Rehoboam's reign, from beginning to end, are they not written in the records of Shemaiah the prophet and of Iddo the seer that deal with genealogies? There was continual warfare between Rehoboam and Jeroboam. [16]Rehoboam rested with his fathers and was buried in the City of David. And Abijah his son succeeded him as king.

Abijah King of Judah

13 In the eighteenth year of the reign of Jeroboam, Abijah became king of Judah, [2]and he reigned in Jerusalem three years. His mother's name was Maacah,[a] a daughter[b] of Uriel of Gibeah.

There was war between Abijah and Jeroboam. [3]Abijah went into battle with a force of four hundred thousand able fighting men, and Jeroboam drew up a battle line against him with eight hundred thousand able troops.

[4]Abijah stood on Mount Zemaraim, in the hill country of Ephraim, and said, "Jeroboam and all Israel, listen to me! [5]Don't you know that the LORD, the God of Israel, has given the kingship of Israel to David and his descendants forever by a covenant of salt? [6]Yet Jeroboam son of Nebat, an official of Solomon son of David, rebelled against his master. [7]Some worthless scoundrels gathered around him and opposed Rehoboam son of Solomon when he was young and indecisive and not strong enough to resist them.

[8]"And now you plan to resist the kingdom of the LORD, which is in the hands of David's descendants. You are indeed a vast army and have with you the golden calves that Jeroboam made to be your gods. [9]But didn't you drive out the priests of the LORD, the sons of Aaron, and the Levites, and make priests of your own as the peoples of other lands do? Whoever comes to consecrate himself with a young bull and seven rams may become a priest of what are not gods.

[10]"As for us, the LORD is our God, and we have not forsaken him. The priests who serve the LORD are sons of Aaron, and the Levites assist them. [11]Every morning and evening they present burnt offerings and fragrant incense to the LORD. They set out the bread on the ceremonially clean table and light the lamps on the gold lampstand every evening. We are observing the requirements of the LORD our God. But you have forsaken him. [12]God is with us; he is our leader. His priests with their trumpets will sound the battle cry against you. Men of Israel, do not fight against the LORD, the God of your fathers, for you will not succeed."

[13]Now Jeroboam had sent troops around to the rear, so that while he was in front of Judah the ambush was behind them. [14]Judah turned and saw that they were being attacked at both front and rear. Then they cried out to the LORD. The priests blew their trumpets [15]and the men of Judah raised the battle cry. At the sound of their battle cry, God routed Jeroboam and all Israel before Abijah and Judah. [16]The Israelites fled before Judah, and God delivered them into their hands. [17]Abijah and his men inflicted heavy losses on them, so that there were five

---

a2 Most Septuagint manuscripts and Syriac (see also 2 Chron. 11:20 and 1 Kings 15:2); Hebrew *Micaiah*
b2 Or *granddaughter*

hundred thousand casualties among Israel's able men. [18]The men of Israel were subdued on that occasion, and the men of Judah were victorious because they relied on the LORD, the God of their fathers.

[19]Abijah pursued Jeroboam and took from him the towns of Bethel, Jeshanah and Ephron, with their surrounding villages. [20]Jeroboam did not regain power during the time of Abijah. And the LORD struck him down and he died.

[21]But Abijah grew in strength. He married fourteen wives and had twenty-two sons and sixteen daughters.

[22]The other events of Abijah's reign, what he did and what he said, are written in the annotations of the prophet Iddo.

14 And Abijah rested with his fathers and was buried in the City of David. Asa his son succeeded him as king, and in his days the country was at peace for ten years.

Asa King of Judah

[2]Asa did what was good and right in the eyes of the LORD his God. [3]He removed the foreign altars and the high places, smashed the sacred stones and cut down the Asherah poles.[a] [4]He commanded Judah to seek the LORD, the God of their fathers, and to obey his laws and commands. [5]He removed the high places and incense altars in every town in Judah, and the kingdom was at peace under him. [6]He built up the fortified cities of Judah, since the land was at peace. No one was at war with him during those years, for the LORD gave him rest.

[7]"Let us build up these towns," he said to Judah, "and put walls around them, with towers, gates and bars. The land is still ours, because we have sought the LORD our God; we sought him and he has given us rest on every side." So they built and prospered.

[8]Asa had an army of three hundred thousand men from Judah, equipped with large shields and with spears, and two hundred and eighty thousand from Benjamin, armed with small shields and with bows. All these were brave fighting men.

[9]Zerah the Cushite marched out against them with a vast army[b] and three hundred chariots, and came as far as Mareshah. [10]Asa went out to meet him, and they took up battle positions in the Valley of Zephathah near Mareshah.

[11]Then Asa called to the LORD his God and said, "LORD, there is no one like you to help the powerless against the mighty. Help us, O LORD our God, for we rely on you, and in your name we have come against this vast army. O LORD, you are our God; do not let man prevail against you."

[12]The LORD struck down the Cushites before Asa and Judah. The Cushites fled, [13]and Asa and his army pursued them as far as Gerar. Such a great number of Cushites fell that they could not recover; they were crushed before the LORD and his forces. The men of Judah carried off a large amount of plunder. [14]They destroyed all the villages around Gerar, for the terror of the LORD had fallen upon them. They plundered all these villages, since there was much booty there. [15]They also attacked the camps of the herdsmen and carried off droves of sheep and goats and camels. Then they returned to Jerusalem.

Asa's Reform

15 The Spirit of God came upon Azariah son of Oded. [2]He went out to meet Asa and said to him, "Listen to me, Asa and all Judah and Benjamin. The LORD is with you when you are with him. If you seek him, he will be found by you, but if you forsake him, he will forsake you. [3]For a long time Israel was without the true God, without a priest to teach and without the law. [4]But in their distress they turned to the LORD, the God of Israel, and sought him, and he was found by them. [5]In those days it was not safe to travel about, for all the inhabitants of the lands were in great turmoil. [6]One nation was being crushed by another and one city by another, because God was troubling them with every kind of distress. [7]But as for you, be strong and do not give up, for your work will be rewarded."

[8]When Asa heard these words and the prophecy of Azariah son of[c] Oded the prophet, he took courage. He removed the detestable idols from the whole land of Judah and Benjamin and from the towns he had captured in the hills of Ephraim. He repaired the altar of the

---

[a]3 That is, symbols of the goddess Asherah; here and elsewhere in 2 Chronicles   [b]9 Hebrew *with an army of a thousand thousands* or *with an army of thousands upon thousands*   [c]8 Vulgate and Syriac (see also Septuagint and verse 1); Hebrew does not have *Azariah son of.*

Lord that was in front of the portico of the Lord's temple.

⁹Then he assembled all Judah and Benjamin and the people from Ephraim, Manasseh and Simeon who had settled among them, for large numbers had come over to him from Israel when they saw that the Lord his God was with him. ¹⁰They assembled at Jerusalem in the third month of the fifteenth year of Asa's reign. ¹¹At that time they sacrificed to the Lord seven hundred head of cattle and seven thousand sheep and goats from the plunder they had brought back. ¹²They entered into a covenant to seek the Lord, the God of their fathers, with all their heart and soul. ¹³All who would not seek the Lord, the God of Israel, were to be put to death, whether small or great, man or woman. ¹⁴They took an oath to the Lord with loud acclamation, with shouting and with trumpets and horns. ¹⁵All Judah rejoiced about the oath because they had sworn it wholeheartedly. They sought God eagerly, and he was found by them. So the Lord gave them rest on every side.

¹⁶King Asa also deposed his grandmother Maacah from her position as queen mother, because she had made a repulsive Asherah pole. Asa cut the pole down, broke it up and burned it in the Kidron Valley. ¹⁷Although he did not remove the high places from Israel, Asa's heart was fully committed to the Lord all his life. ¹⁸He brought into the temple of God the silver and gold and the articles that he and his father had dedicated.

¹⁹There was no more war until the thirty-fifth year of Asa's reign.

Asa's Last Years

16 In the thirty-sixth year of Asa's reign Baasha king of Israel went up against Judah and fortified Ramah to prevent anyone from leaving or entering the territory of Asa king of Judah.

²Asa then took the silver and gold out of the treasuries of the Lord's temple and of his own palace and sent it to Ben-Hadad king of Aram, who was ruling in Damascus. ³"Let there be a treaty between me and you," he said, "as there was between my father and your father. See, I am sending you silver and gold. Now break your treaty with Baasha king of Israel so he will withdraw from me."

⁴Ben-Hadad agreed with King Asa and sent the commanders of his forces against the towns of Israel. They conquered Ijon, Dan, Abel Maim ᵃ and all the store cities of Naphtali. ⁵When Baasha heard this, he stopped building Ramah and abandoned his work. ⁶Then King Asa brought all the men of Judah, and they carried away from Ramah the stones and timber Baasha had been using. With them he built up Geba and Mizpah.

⁷At that time Hanani the seer came to Asa king of Judah and said to him: "Because you relied on the king of Aram and not on the Lord your God, the army of the king of Aram has escaped from your hand. ⁸Were not the Cushites ᵇ and Libyans a mighty army with great numbers of chariots and horsemen ᶜ? Yet when you relied on the Lord, he delivered them into your hand. ⁹For the eyes of the Lord range throughout the earth to strengthen those whose hearts are fully committed to him. You have done a foolish thing, and from now on you will be at war."

¹⁰Asa was angry with the seer because of this; he was so enraged that he put him in prison. At the same time Asa brutally oppressed some of the people.

¹¹The events of Asa's reign, from beginning to end, are written in the book of the kings of Judah and Israel. ¹²In the thirty-ninth year of his reign Asa was afflicted with a disease in his feet. Though his disease was severe, even in his illness he did not seek help from the Lord, but only from the physicians. ¹³Then in the forty-first year of his reign Asa died and rested with his fathers. ¹⁴They buried him in the tomb that he had cut out for himself in the City of David. They laid him on a bier covered with spices and various blended perfumes, and they made a huge fire in his honor.

Jehoshaphat King of Judah

17 Jehoshaphat his son succeeded him as king and strengthened himself against Israel. ²He stationed troops in all the fortified cities of Judah and put garrisons in Judah and in the towns of Ephraim that his father Asa had captured.

³The Lord was with Jehoshaphat because in his early years he walked in the ways his father David had followed. He did not consult the Baals ⁴but sought the God of his father and followed his com-

---

ᵃ4 Also known as *Abel Beth Maacah*   ᵇ8 That is, people from the upper Nile region   ᶜ8 Or *charioteers* mands rather than the practices of Israel. ⁵The LORD established the kingdom under his control; and all Judah brought gifts to Jehoshaphat, so that he had great wealth and honor. ⁶His heart was devoted to the ways of the LORD; furthermore, he removed the high places and the Asherah poles from Judah.

⁷In the third year of his reign he sent his officials Ben-Hail, Obadiah, Zechariah, Nethanel and Micaiah to teach in the towns of Judah. ⁸With them were certain Levites—Shemaiah, Nethaniah, Zebadiah, Asahel, Shemiramoth, Jehonathan, Adonijah, Tobijah and Tob-Adonijah—and the priests Elishama and Jehoram. ⁹They taught throughout Judah, taking with them the Book of the Law of the LORD; they went around to all the towns of Judah and taught the people.

¹⁰The fear of the LORD fell on all the kingdoms of the lands surrounding Judah, so that they did not make war with Jehoshaphat. ¹¹Some Philistines brought Jehoshaphat gifts and silver as tribute, and the Arabs brought him flocks: seven thousand seven hundred rams and seven thousand seven hundred goats.

¹²Jehoshaphat became more and more powerful; he built forts and store cities in Judah ¹³and had large supplies in the towns of Judah. He also kept experienced fighting men in Jerusalem. ¹⁴Their enrollment by families was as follows:

From Judah, commanders of units of 1,000:
Adnah the commander, with 300,000 fighting men;
¹⁵next, Jehohanan the commander, with 280,000;
¹⁶next, Amasiah son of Zicri, who volunteered himself for the service of the LORD, with 200,000.
¹⁷From Benjamin:
Eliada, a valiant soldier, with 200,000 men armed with bows and shields;
¹⁸next, Jehozabad, with 180,000 men armed for battle.

¹⁹These were the men who served the king, besides those he stationed in the fortified cities throughout Judah.

Micaiah Prophesies Against Ahab

18 Now Jehoshaphat had great wealth and honor, and he allied himself with Ahab by marriage. ²Some years later he went down to visit Ahab in Samaria. Ahab slaughtered many sheep and cattle for him and the people with him and urged him to attack Ramoth Gilead. ³Ahab king of Israel asked Jehoshaphat king of Judah, "Will you go with me against Ramoth Gilead?"

Jehoshaphat replied, "I am as you are, and my people as your people; we will join you in the war." ⁴But Jehoshaphat also said to the king of Israel, "First seek the counsel of the LORD."

⁵So the king of Israel brought together the prophets—four hundred men—and asked them, "Shall we go to war against Ramoth Gilead, or shall I refrain?"

"Go," they answered, "for God will give it into the king's hand."

⁶But Jehoshaphat asked, "Is there not a prophet of the LORD here whom we can inquire of?"

⁷The king of Israel answered Jehoshaphat, "There is still one man through whom we can inquire of the LORD, but I hate him because he never prophesies anything good about me, but always bad. He is Micaiah son of Imlah."

"The king should not say that," Jehoshaphat replied.

⁸So the king of Israel called one of his officials and said, "Bring Micaiah son of Imlah at once."

⁹Dressed in their royal robes, the king of Israel and Jehoshaphat king of Judah were sitting on their thrones at the threshing floor by the entrance to the gate of Samaria, with all the prophets prophesying before them. ¹⁰Now Zedekiah son of Kenaanah had made iron horns, and he declared, "This is what the LORD says: 'With these you will gore the Arameans until they are destroyed.'"

¹¹All the other prophets were prophesying the same thing. "Attack Ramoth Gilead and be victorious," they said, "for the LORD will give it into the king's hand."

¹²The messenger who had gone to summon Micaiah said to him, "Look, as one man the other prophets are predicting success for the king. Let your word agree with theirs, and speak favorably."

¹³But Micaiah said, "As surely as the LORD lives, I can tell him only what my God says."

¹⁴When he arrived, the king asked him, "Micaiah, shall we go to war against Ramoth Gilead, or shall I refrain?"

"Attack and be victorious," he answered, "for they will be given into your hand."

¹⁵The king said to him, "How many times must I make you swear to tell me

nothing but the truth in the name of the Lord?"

[16]Then Micaiah answered, "I saw all Israel scattered on the hills like sheep without a shepherd, and the Lord said, 'These people have no master. Let each one go home in peace.' "

[17]The king of Israel said to Jehoshaphat, "Didn't I tell you that he never prophesies anything good about me, but only bad?"

[18]Micaiah continued, "Therefore hear the word of the Lord: I saw the Lord sitting on his throne with all the host of heaven standing on his right and on his left. [19]And the Lord said, 'Who will entice Ahab king of Israel into attacking Ramoth Gilead and going to his death there?'

"One suggested this, and another that. [20]Finally, a spirit came forward, stood before the Lord and said, 'I will entice him.'

" 'By what means?' the Lord asked.

[21]" 'I will go and be a lying spirit in the mouths of all his prophets,' he said.

" 'You will succeed in enticing him,' said the Lord. 'Go and do it.'

[22]"So now the Lord has put a lying spirit in the mouths of these prophets of yours. The Lord has decreed disaster for you."

[23]Then Zedekiah son of Kenaanah went up and slapped Micaiah in the face. "Which way did the spirit from[a] the Lord go when he went from me to speak to you?" he asked.

[24]Micaiah replied, "You will find out on the day you go to hide in an inner room."

[25]The king of Israel then ordered, "Take Micaiah and send him back to Amon the ruler of the city and to Joash the king's son, [26]and say, 'This is what the king says: Put this fellow in prison and give him nothing but bread and water until I return safely.' "

[27]Micaiah declared, "If you ever return safely, the Lord has not spoken through me." Then he added, "Mark my words, all you people!"

Ahab Killed at Ramoth Gilead

[28]So the king of Israel and Jehoshaphat king of Judah went up to Ramoth Gilead. [29]The king of Israel said to Jehoshaphat, "I will enter the battle in disguise, but you wear your royal robes." So the king of Israel disguised himself and went into battle.

[30]Now the king of Aram had ordered his chariot commanders, "Do not fight with anyone, small or great, except the king of Israel." [31]When the chariot commanders saw Jehoshaphat, they thought, "This is the king of Israel." So they turned to attack him, but Jehoshaphat cried out, and the Lord helped him. God drew them away from him, [32]for when the chariot commanders saw that he was not the king of Israel, they stopped pursuing him.

[33]But someone drew his bow at random and hit the king of Israel between the sections of his armor. The king told the chariot driver, "Wheel around and get me out of the fighting. I've been wounded." [34]All day long the battle raged, and the king of Israel propped himself up in his chariot facing the Arameans until evening. Then at sunset he died.

19 When Jehoshaphat king of Judah returned safely to his palace in Jerusalem, [2]Jehu the seer, the son of Hanani, went out to meet him and said to the king, "Should you help the wicked and love[b] those who hate the Lord? Because of this, the wrath of the Lord is upon you. [3]There is, however, some good in you, for you have rid the land of the Asherah poles and have set your heart on seeking God."

Jehoshaphat Appoints Judges

[4]Jehoshaphat lived in Jerusalem, and he went out again among the people from Beersheba to the hill country of Ephraim and turned them back to the Lord, the God of their fathers. [5]He appointed judges in the land, in each of the fortified cities of Judah. [6]He told them, "Consider carefully what you do, because you are not judging for man but for the Lord, who is with you whenever you give a verdict. [7]Now let the fear of the Lord be upon you. Judge carefully, for with the Lord our God there is no injustice or partiality or bribery."

[8]In Jerusalem also, Jehoshaphat appointed some of the Levites, priests and heads of Israelite families to administer the law of the Lord and to settle disputes. And they lived in Jerusalem. [9]He gave them these orders: "You must serve faithfully and wholeheartedly in the fear of the Lord. [10]In every case that comes before you from your fellow countrymen who live in the cities—whether bloodshed or other concerns of the law, commands, decrees or ordinances—you are to warn them not to sin against the Lord; other-

---

[a]23 Or *Spirit of*   [b]2 Or *and make alliances with*

wise his wrath will come on you and your brothers. Do this, and you will not sin.

¹¹"Amariah the chief priest will be over you in any matter concerning the LORD, and Zebadiah son of Ishmael, the leader of the tribe of Judah, will be over you in any matter concerning the king, and the Levites will serve as officials before you. Act with courage, and may the LORD be with those who do well."

Jehoshaphat Defeats Moab and Ammon

20 After this, the Moabites and Ammonites with some of the Meunites*a* came to make war on Jehoshaphat.

²Some men came and told Jehoshaphat, "A vast army is coming against you from Edom,*b* from the other side of the Sea.*c* It is already in Hazazon Tamar" (that is, En Gedi). ³Alarmed, Jehoshaphat resolved to inquire of the LORD, and he proclaimed a fast for all Judah. ⁴The people of Judah came together to seek help from the LORD; indeed, they came from every town in Judah to seek him.

⁵Then Jehoshaphat stood up in the assembly of Judah and Jerusalem at the temple of the LORD in the front of the new courtyard ⁶and said:

"O LORD, God of our fathers, are you not the God who is in heaven? You rule over all the kingdoms of the nations. Power and might are in your hand, and no one can withstand you. ⁷O our God, did you not drive out the inhabitants of this land before your people Israel and give it forever to the descendants of Abraham your friend? ⁸They have lived in it and have built in it a sanctuary for your Name, saying, ⁹'If calamity comes upon us, whether the sword of judgment, or plague or famine, we will stand in your presence before this temple that bears your Name and will cry out to you in our distress, and you will hear us and save us.'

¹⁰"But now here are men from Ammon, Moab and Mount Seir, whose territory you would not allow Israel to invade when they came from Egypt; so they turned away from them and did not destroy them.

¹¹See how they are repaying us by coming to drive us out of the possession you gave us as an inheritance. ¹²O our God, will you not judge them? For we have no power to face this vast army that is attacking us. We do not know what to do, but our eyes are upon you."

¹³All the men of Judah, with their wives and children and little ones, stood there before the LORD.

¹⁴Then the Spirit of the LORD came upon Jahaziel son of Zechariah, the son of Benaiah, the son of Jeiel, the son of Mattaniah, a Levite and descendant of Asaph, as he stood in the assembly.

¹⁵He said: "Listen, King Jehoshaphat and all who live in Judah and Jerusalem! This is what the LORD says to you: 'Do not be afraid or discouraged because of this vast army. For the battle is not yours, but God's. ¹⁶Tomorrow march down against them. They will be climbing up by the Pass of Ziz, and you will find them at the end of the gorge in the Desert of Jeruel. ¹⁷You will not have to fight this battle. Take up your positions; stand firm and see the deliverance the LORD will give you, O Judah and Jerusalem. Do not be afraid; do not be discouraged. Go out to face them tomorrow, and the LORD will be with you.' "

¹⁸Jehoshaphat bowed with his face to the ground, and all the people of Judah and Jerusalem fell down in worship before the LORD. ¹⁹Then some Levites from the Kohathites and Korahites stood up and praised the LORD, the God of Israel, with very loud voice.

²⁰Early in the morning they left for the Desert of Tekoa. As they set out, Jehoshaphat stood and said, "Listen to me, Judah and people of Jerusalem! Have faith in the LORD your God and you will be upheld; have faith in his prophets and you will be successful." ²¹After consulting the people, Jehoshaphat appointed men to sing to the LORD and to praise him for the splendor of his*d* holiness as they went out at the head of the army, saying:

"Give thanks to the LORD,
    for his love endures forever."

²²As they began to sing and praise, the LORD set ambushes against the men of Ammon and Moab and Mount Seir who

a1 Some Septuagint manuscripts; Hebrew *Ammonites*   *b2* One Hebrew manuscript; most Hebrew manuscripts, Septuagint and Vulgate *Aram*   *c2* That is, the Dead Sea   *d21* Or *him with the splendor of* were invading Judah, and they were defeated. ²³The men of Ammon and Moab rose up against the men from Mount Seir to destroy and annihilate them. After they finished slaughtering the men from Seir, they helped to destroy one another.

²⁴When the men of Judah came to the place that overlooks the desert and looked toward the vast army, they saw only dead bodies lying on the ground; no one had escaped. ²⁵So Jehoshaphat and his men went to carry off their plunder, and they found among them a great amount of equipment and clothing*a* and also articles of value—more than they could take away. There was so much plunder that it took three days to collect it. ²⁶On the fourth day they assembled in the Valley of Beracah, where they praised the LORD. This is why it is called the Valley of Beracah*b* to this day.

²⁷Then, led by Jehoshaphat, all the men of Judah and Jerusalem returned joyfully to Jerusalem, for the LORD had given them cause to rejoice over their enemies. ²⁸They entered Jerusalem and went to the temple of the LORD with harps and lutes and trumpets.

²⁹The fear of God came upon all the kingdoms of the countries when they heard how the LORD had fought against the enemies of Israel. ³⁰And the kingdom of Jehoshaphat was at peace, for his God had given him rest on every side.

The End of Jehoshaphat's Reign

³¹So Jehoshaphat reigned over Judah. He was thirty-five years old when he became king of Judah, and he reigned in Jerusalem twenty-five years. His mother's name was Azubah daughter of Shilhi. ³²He walked in the ways of his father Asa and did not stray from them; he did what was right in the eyes of the LORD. ³³The high places, however, were not removed, and the people still had not set their hearts on the God of their fathers.

³⁴The other events of Jehoshaphat's reign, from beginning to end, are written in the annals of Jehu son of Hanani, which are recorded in the book of the kings of Israel.

³⁵Later, Jehoshaphat king of Judah made an alliance with Ahaziah king of Israel, who was guilty of wickedness. ³⁶He agreed with him to construct a fleet of trading ships.*c* After these were built at Ezion Geber, ³⁷Eliezer son of Dodavahu of Mareshah prophesied against Jehoshaphat, saying, "Because you have made an alliance with Ahaziah, the LORD will destroy what you have made." The ships were wrecked and were not able to set sail to trade.*d*

21 Then Jehoshaphat rested with his fathers and was buried with them in the City of David. And Jehoram his son succeeded him as king. ²Jehoram's brothers, the sons of Jehoshaphat, were Azariah, Jehiel, Zechariah, Azariahu, Michael and Shephatiah. All these were sons of Jehoshaphat king of Israel.*e* ³Their father had given them many gifts of silver and gold and articles of value, as well as fortified cities in Judah, but he had given the kingdom to Jehoram because he was his firstborn son.

Jehoram King of Judah

⁴When Jehoram established himself firmly over his father's kingdom, he put all his brothers to the sword along with some of the princes of Israel. ⁵Jehoram was thirty-two years old when he became king, and he reigned in Jerusalem eight years. ⁶He walked in the ways of the kings of Israel, as the house of Ahab had done, for he married a daughter of Ahab. He did evil in the eyes of the LORD. ⁷Nevertheless, because of the covenant the LORD had made with David, the LORD was not willing to destroy the house of David. He had promised to maintain a lamp for him and his descendants forever.

⁸In the time of Jehoram, Edom rebelled against Judah and set up its own king. ⁹So Jehoram went there with his officers and all his chariots. The Edomites surrounded him and his chariot commanders, but he rose up and broke through by night. ¹⁰To this day Edom has been in rebellion against Judah.

Libnah revolted at the same time, because Jehoram had forsaken the LORD, the God of his fathers. ¹¹He had also built high places on the hills of Judah and had caused the people of Jerusalem to prostitute themselves and had led Judah astray.

¹²Jehoram received a letter from Elijah the prophet, which said:

"This is what the LORD, the God of

---

a25 Some Hebrew manuscripts and Vulgate; most Hebrew manuscripts *corpses*　　*b26 Beracah* means *praise.*　　*c36* Hebrew *of ships that could go to Tarshish*　　*d37* Hebrew *sail for Tarshish*　　*e2* That is, Judah, as frequently in 2 Chronicles your father David, says: 'You have not walked in the ways of your father Jehoshaphat or of Asa king of Judah. [13]But you have walked in the ways of the kings of Israel, and you have led Judah and the people of Jerusalem to prostitute themselves, just as the house of Ahab did. You have also murdered your own brothers, members of your father's house, men who were better than you. [14]So now the LORD is about to strike your people, your sons, your wives and everything that is yours, with a heavy blow. [15]You yourself will be very ill with a lingering disease of the bowels, until the disease causes your bowels to come out.' "

[16]The LORD aroused against Jehoram the hostility of the Philistines and of the Arabs who lived near the Cushites. [17]They attacked Judah, invaded it and carried off all the goods found in the king's palace, together with his sons and wives. Not a son was left to him except Ahaziah,[a] the youngest.

[18]After all this, the LORD afflicted Jehoram with an incurable disease of the bowels. [19]In the course of time, at the end of the second year, his bowels came out because of the disease, and he died in great pain. His people made no fire in his honor, as they had for his fathers.

[20]Jehoram was thirty-two years old when he became king, and he reigned in Jerusalem eight years. He passed away, to no one's regret, and was buried in the City of David, but not in the tombs of the kings.

Ahaziah King of Judah

22 The people of Jerusalem made Ahaziah, Jehoram's youngest son, king in his place, since the raiders, who came with the Arabs into the camp, had killed all the older sons. So Ahaziah son of Jehoram king of Judah began to reign.

[2]Ahaziah was twenty-two[b] years old when he became king, and he reigned in Jerusalem one year. His mother's name was Athaliah, a granddaughter of Omri.

[3]He too walked in the ways of the house of Ahab, for his mother encouraged him in doing wrong. [4]He did evil in the eyes of the LORD, as the house of Ahab had done, for after his father's death they became his advisers, to his undoing. [5]He also followed their counsel when he went with Joram[c] son of Ahab king of Israel to war against Hazael king of Aram at Ramoth Gilead. The Arameans wounded Joram; [6]so he returned to Jezreel to recover from the wounds they had inflicted on him at Ramoth[d] in his battle with Hazael king of Aram.

Then Ahaziah[e] son of Jehoram king of Judah went down to Jezreel to see Joram son of Ahab because he had been wounded.

[7]Through Ahaziah's visit to Joram, God brought about Ahaziah's downfall. When Ahaziah arrived, he went out with Joram to meet Jehu son of Nimshi, whom the LORD had anointed to destroy the house of Ahab. [8]While Jehu was executing judgment on the house of Ahab, he found the princes of Judah and the sons of Ahaziah's relatives, who had been attending Ahaziah, and he killed them. [9]He then went in search of Ahaziah, and his men captured him while he was hiding in Samaria. He was brought to Jehu and put to death. They buried him, for they said, "He was a son of Jehoshaphat, who sought the LORD with all his heart." So there was no one in the house of Ahaziah powerful enough to retain the kingdom.

Athaliah and Joash

[10]When Athaliah the mother of Ahaziah saw that her son was dead, she proceeded to destroy the whole royal family of the house of Judah. [11]But Jehosheba,[f] the daughter of King Jehoram, took Joash son of Ahaziah and stole him away from among the royal princes who were about to be murdered and put him and his nurse in a bedroom. Because Jehosheba,[f] the daughter of King Jehoram and wife of the priest Jehoiada, was Ahaziah's sister, she hid the child from Athaliah so she could not kill him. [12]He remained hidden with them at the temple of God for six years while Athaliah ruled the land.

23 In the seventh year Jehoiada showed his strength. He made a covenant with the commanders of units of a hundred: Azariah son of Jeroham,

---

a17 Hebrew *Jehoahaz*, a variant of *Ahaziah*   b2 Some Septuagint manuscripts and Syriac (see also 2 Kings 8:26); Hebrew *forty-two*   c5 Hebrew *Jehoram*, a variant of *Joram*; also in verses 6 and 7   d6 Hebrew *Ramah*, a variant of *Ramoth*   e6 Some Hebrew manuscripts, Septuagint, Vulgate and Syriac (see also 2 Kings 8:29); most Hebrew manuscripts *Azariah*   f11 Hebrew *Jehoshabeath*, a variant of *Jehosheba*

Ishmael son of Jehohanan, Azariah son of Obed, Maaseiah son of Adaiah, and Elishaphat son of Zicri. ²They went throughout Judah and gathered the Levites and the heads of Israelite families from all the towns. When they came to Jerusalem, ³the whole assembly made a covenant with the king at the temple of God.

Jehoiada said to them, "The king's son shall reign, as the LORD promised concerning the descendants of David. ⁴Now this is what you are to do: A third of you priests and Levites who are going on duty on the Sabbath are to keep watch at the doors, ⁵a third of you at the royal palace and a third at the Foundation Gate, and all the other men are to be in the courtyards of the temple of the LORD. ⁶No one is to enter the temple of the LORD except the priests and Levites on duty; they may enter because they are consecrated, but all the other men are to guard what the LORD has assigned to them.ᵃ ⁷The Levites are to station themselves around the king, each man with his weapons in his hand. Anyone who enters the temple must be put to death. Stay close to the king wherever he goes."

⁸The Levites and all the men of Judah did just as Jehoiada the priest ordered. Each one took his men—those who were going on duty on the Sabbath and those who were going off duty—for Jehoiada the priest had not released any of the divisions. ⁹Then he gave the commanders of units of a hundred the spears and the large and small shields that had belonged to King David and that were in the temple of God. ¹⁰He stationed all the men, each with his weapon in his hand, around the king—near the altar and the temple, from the south side to the north side of the temple.

¹¹Jehoiada and his sons brought out the king's son and put the crown on him; they presented him with a copy of the covenant and proclaimed him king. They anointed him and shouted, "Long live the king!"

¹²When Athaliah heard the noise of the people running and cheering the king, she went to them at the temple of the LORD. ¹³She looked, and there was the king, standing by his pillar at the entrance. The officers and the trumpeters were beside the king, and all the people of the land were rejoicing and blowing trumpets, and singers with musical instruments were leading the praises. Then Athaliah tore her robes and shouted, "Treason! Treason!"

¹⁴Jehoiada the priest sent out the commanders of units of a hundred, who were in charge of the troops, and said to them: "Bring her out between the ranksᵇ and put to the sword anyone who follows her." For the priest had said, "Do not put her to death at the temple of the LORD." ¹⁵So they seized her as she reached the entrance of the Horse Gate on the palace grounds, and there they put her to death.

¹⁶Jehoiada then made a covenant that he and the people and the kingᶜ would be the LORD's people. ¹⁷All the people went to the temple of Baal and tore it down. They smashed the altars and idols and killed Mattan the priest of Baal in front of the altars.

¹⁸Then Jehoiada placed the oversight of the temple of the LORD in the hands of the priests, who were Levites, to whom David had made assignments in the temple, to present the burnt offerings of the LORD as written in the Law of Moses, with rejoicing and singing, as David had ordered. ¹⁹He also stationed doorkeepers at the gates of the LORD's temple so that no one who was in any way unclean might enter.

²⁰He took with him the commanders of hundreds, the nobles, the rulers of the people and all the people of the land and brought the king down from the temple of the LORD. They went into the palace through the Upper Gate and seated the king on the royal throne, ²¹and all the people of the land rejoiced. And the city was quiet, because Athaliah had been slain with the sword.

Joash Repairs the Temple

24 Joash was seven years old when he became king, and he reigned in Jerusalem forty years. His mother's name was Zibiah; she was from Beersheba. ²Joash did what was right in the eyes of the LORD all the years of Jehoiada the priest. ³Jehoiada chose two wives for him, and he had sons and daughters.

⁴Some time later Joash decided to restore the temple of the LORD. ⁵He called together the priests and Levites and said to them, "Go to the towns of Judah and collect the money due annually from all

---

ᵃ6 Or to observe the LORD's command ,not to enter, between ,the LORD, and the people and the king that they   ᵇ14 Or out from the precincts   ᶜ16 Or covenant (see 2 Kings 11:17)

Israel, to repair the temple of your God. Do it now." But the Levites did not act at once.

⁶Therefore the king summoned Jehoiada the chief priest and said to him, "Why haven't you required the Levites to bring in from Judah and Jerusalem the tax imposed by Moses the servant of the LORD and by the assembly of Israel for the Tent of the Testimony?"

⁷Now the sons of that wicked woman Athaliah had broken into the temple of God and had used even its sacred objects for the Baals.

⁸At the king's command, a chest was made and placed outside, at the gate of the temple of the LORD. ⁹A proclamation was then issued in Judah and Jerusalem that they should bring to the LORD the tax that Moses the servant of God had required of Israel in the desert. ¹⁰All the officials and all the people brought their contributions gladly, dropping them into the chest until it was full. ¹¹Whenever the chest was brought in by the Levites to the king's officials and they saw that there was a large amount of money, the royal secretary and the officer of the chief priest would come and empty the chest and carry it back to its place. They did this regularly and collected a great amount of money. ¹²The king and Jehoiada gave it to the men who carried out the work required for the temple of the LORD. They hired masons and carpenters to restore the LORD's temple, and also workers in iron and bronze to repair the temple.

¹³The men in charge of the work were diligent, and the repairs progressed under them. They rebuilt the temple of God according to its original design and reinforced it. ¹⁴When they had finished, they brought the rest of the money to the king and Jehoiada, and with it were made articles for the LORD's temple: articles for the service and for the burnt offerings, and also dishes and other objects of gold and silver. As long as Jehoiada lived, burnt offerings were presented continually in the temple of the LORD.

¹⁵Now Jehoiada was old and full of years, and he died at the age of a hundred and thirty. ¹⁶He was buried with the kings in the City of David, because of the good he had done in Israel for God and his temple.

The Wickedness of Joash

¹⁷After the death of Jehoiada, the officials of Judah came and paid homage to the king, and he listened to them. ¹⁸They abandoned the temple of the LORD, the God of their fathers, and worshiped Asherah poles and idols. Because of their guilt, God's anger came upon Judah and Jerusalem. ¹⁹Although the LORD sent prophets to the people to bring them back to him, and though they testified against them, they would not listen.

²⁰Then the Spirit of God came upon Zechariah son of Jehoiada the priest. He stood before the people and said, "This is what God says: 'Why do you disobey the LORD's commands? You will not prosper. Because you have forsaken the LORD, he has forsaken you.' "

²¹But they plotted against him, and by order of the king they stoned him to death in the courtyard of the LORD's temple. ²²King Joash did not remember the kindness Zechariah's father Jehoiada had shown him but killed his son, who said as he lay dying, "May the LORD see this and call you to account."

²³At the turn of the year,ᵃ the army of Aram marched against Joash; it invaded Judah and Jerusalem and killed all the leaders of the people. They sent all the plunder to their king in Damascus. ²⁴Although the Aramean army had come with only a few men, the LORD delivered into their hands a much larger army. Because Judah had forsaken the LORD, the God of their fathers, judgment was executed on Joash. ²⁵When the Arameans withdrew, they left Joash severely wounded. His officials conspired against him for murdering the son of Jehoiada the priest, and they killed him in his bed. So he died and was buried in the City of David, but not in the tombs of the kings.

²⁶Those who conspired against him were Zabad,ᵇ son of Shimeath an Ammonite woman, and Jehozabad, son of Shimrithᶜ a Moabite woman. ²⁷The account of his sons, the many prophecies about him, and the record of the restoration of the temple of God are written in the annotations on the book of the kings. And Amaziah his son succeeded him as king.

ᵃ23 Probably in the spring   ᵇ26 A variant of Jozabad   ᶜ26 A variant of Shomer

Amaziah King of Judah

25 Amaziah was twenty-five years old when he became king, and he reigned in Jerusalem twenty-nine years. His mother's name was Jehoaddin*ᵃ*; she was from Jerusalem. ²He did what was right in the eyes of the LORD, but not wholeheartedly. ³After the kingdom was firmly in his control, he executed the officials who had murdered his father the king. ⁴Yet he did not put their sons to death, but acted in accordance with what is written in the Law, in the Book of Moses, where the LORD commanded: "Fathers shall not be put to death for their children, nor children put to death for their fathers; each is to die for his own sins."*ᵇ*

⁵Amaziah called the people of Judah together and assigned them according to their families to commanders of thousands and commanders of hundreds for all Judah and Benjamin. He then mustered those twenty years old or more and found that there were three hundred thousand men ready for military service, able to handle the spear and shield. ⁶He also hired a hundred thousand fighting men from Israel for a hundred talents*ᶜ* of silver.

⁷But a man of God came to him and said, "O king, these troops from Israel must not march with you, for the LORD is not with Israel—not with any of the people of Ephraim. ⁸Even if you go and fight courageously in battle, God will overthrow you before the enemy, for God has the power to help or to overthrow."

⁹Amaziah asked the man of God, "But what about the hundred talents I paid for these Israelite troops?"

The man of God replied, "The LORD can give you much more than that."

¹⁰So Amaziah dismissed the troops who had come to him from Ephraim and sent them home. They were furious with Judah and left for home in a great rage.

¹¹Amaziah then marshaled his strength and led his army to the Valley of Salt, where he killed ten thousand men of Seir. ¹²The army of Judah also captured ten thousand men alive, took them to the top of a cliff and threw them down so that all were dashed to pieces.

¹³Meanwhile the troops that Amaziah had sent back and had not allowed to take part in the war raided Judean towns from Samaria to Beth Horon. They killed three thousand people and carried off great quantities of plunder.

¹⁴When Amaziah returned from slaughtering the Edomites, he brought back the gods of the people of Seir. He set them up as his own gods, bowed down to them and burned sacrifices to them. ¹⁵The anger of the LORD burned against Amaziah, and he sent a prophet to him, who said, "Why do you consult this people's gods, which could not save their own people from your hand?"

¹⁶While he was still speaking, the king said to him, "Have we appointed you an adviser to the king? Stop! Why be struck down?"

So the prophet stopped but said, "I know that God has determined to destroy you, because you have done this and have not listened to my counsel."

¹⁷After Amaziah king of Judah consulted his advisers, he sent this challenge to Jehoash*ᵈ* son of Jehoahaz, the son of Jehu, king of Israel: "Come, meet me face to face."

¹⁸But Jehoash king of Israel replied to Amaziah king of Judah: "A thistle in Lebanon sent a message to a cedar in Lebanon, 'Give your daughter to my son in marriage.' Then a wild beast in Lebanon came along and trampled the thistle underfoot. ¹⁹You say to yourself that you have defeated Edom, and now you are arrogant and proud. But stay at home! Why ask for trouble and cause your own downfall and that of Judah also?"

²⁰Amaziah, however, would not listen, for God so worked that he might hand them over to ˎJehoashˎˎ, because they sought the gods of Edom. ²¹So Jehoash king of Israel attacked. He and Amaziah king of Judah faced each other at Beth Shemesh in Judah. ²²Judah was routed by Israel, and every man fled to his home. ²³Jehoash king of Israel captured Amaziah king of Judah, the son of Joash, the son of Ahaziah,*ᵉ* at Beth Shemesh. Then Jehoash brought him to Jerusalem and broke down the wall of Jerusalem from the Ephraim Gate to the Corner Gate—a section about six hundred feet*ᶠ* long. ²⁴He took all the gold and silver and all the articles found in the temple of God that had been in the care of Obed-Edom,

---

together with the palace treasures and the hostages, and returned to Samaria.

25Amaziah son of Joash king of Judah lived for fifteen years after the death of Jehoash son of Jehoahaz king of Israel. 26As for the other events of Amaziah's reign, from beginning to end, are they not written in the book of the kings of Judah and Israel? 27From the time that Amaziah turned away from following the LORD, they conspired against him in Jerusalem and he fled to Lachish, but they sent men after him to Lachish and killed him there. 28He was brought back by horse and was buried with his fathers in the City of Judah.

Uzziah King of Judah

26 Then all the people of Judah took Uzziah,*a* who was sixteen years old, and made him king in place of his father Amaziah. 2He was the one who rebuilt Elath and restored it to Judah after Amaziah rested with his fathers.

3Uzziah was sixteen years old when he became king, and he reigned in Jerusalem fifty-two years. His mother's name was Jecoliah; she was from Jerusalem. 4He did what was right in the eyes of the LORD, just as his father Amaziah had done. 5He sought God during the days of Zechariah, who instructed him in the fear*b* of God. As long as he sought the LORD, God gave him success.

6He went to war against the Philistines and broke down the walls of Gath, Jabneh and Ashdod. He then rebuilt towns near Ashdod and elsewhere among the Philistines. 7God helped him against the Philistines and against the Arabs who lived in Gur Baal and against the Meunites. 8The Ammonites brought tribute to Uzziah, and his fame spread as far as the border of Egypt, because he had become very powerful.

9Uzziah built towers in Jerusalem at the Corner Gate, at the Valley Gate and at the angle of the wall, and he fortified them. 10He also built towers in the desert and dug many cisterns, because he had much livestock in the foothills and in the plain. He had people working his fields and vineyards in the hills and in the fertile lands, for he loved the soil.

11Uzziah had a well-trained army, ready to go out by divisions according to their numbers as mustered by Jeiel the secretary and Maaseiah the officer under the direction of Hananiah, one of the royal officials. 12The total number of family leaders over the fighting men was 2,600. 13Under their command was an army of 307,500 men trained for war, a powerful force to support the king against his enemies. 14Uzziah provided shields, spears, helmets, coats of armor, bows and slingstones for the entire army. 15In Jerusalem he made machines designed by skillful men for use on the towers and on the corner defenses to shoot arrows and hurl large stones. His fame spread far and wide, for he was greatly helped until he became powerful.

16But after Uzziah became powerful, his pride led to his downfall. He was unfaithful to the LORD his God, and entered the temple of the LORD to burn incense on the altar of incense. 17Azariah the priest with eighty other courageous priests of the LORD followed him in. 18They confronted him and said, "It is not right for you, Uzziah, to burn incense to the LORD. That is for the priests, the descendants of Aaron, who have been consecrated to burn incense. Leave the sanctuary, for you have been unfaithful; and you will not be honored by the LORD God."

19Uzziah, who had a censer in his hand ready to burn incense, became angry. While he was raging at the priests in their presence before the incense altar in the LORD's temple, leprosy*c* broke out on his forehead. 20When Azariah the chief priest and all the other priests looked at him, they saw that he had leprosy on his forehead, so they hurried him out. Indeed, he himself was eager to leave, because the LORD had afflicted him.

21King Uzziah had leprosy until the day he died. He lived in a separate house*d* —leprous, and excluded from the temple of the LORD. Jotham his son had charge of the palace and governed the people of the land.

22The other events of Uzziah's reign, from beginning to end, are recorded by the prophet Isaiah son of Amoz. 23Uzziah rested with his fathers and was buried near them in a field for burial that belonged to the kings, for people said, "He

---

a1 Also called *Azariah*   *b5* Many Hebrew manuscripts, Septuagint and Syriac; other Hebrew manuscripts *vision*   *c19* The Hebrew word was used for various diseases affecting the skin—not necessarily leprosy; also in verses 20, 21 and 23.   *d21* Or *in a house where he was relieved of responsibilities* had leprosy." And Jotham his son succeeded him as king.

Jotham King of Judah

27 Jotham was twenty-five years old when he became king, and he reigned in Jerusalem sixteen years. His mother's name was Jerusha daughter of Zadok. ²He did what was right in the eyes of the LORD, just as his father Uzziah had done, but unlike him he did not enter the temple of the LORD. The people, however, continued their corrupt practices. ³Jotham rebuilt the Upper Gate of the temple of the LORD and did extensive work on the wall at the hill of Ophel. ⁴He built towns in the Judean hills and forts and towers in the wooded areas.

⁵Jotham made war on the king of the Ammonites and conquered them. That year the Ammonites paid him a hundred talents*ᵃ* of silver, ten thousand cors*ᵇ* of wheat and ten thousand cors of barley. The Ammonites brought him the same amount also in the second and third years.

⁶Jotham grew powerful because he walked steadfastly before the LORD his God.

⁷The other events in Jotham's reign, including all his wars and the other things he did, are written in the book of the kings of Israel and Judah. ⁸He was twenty-five years old when he became king, and he reigned in Jerusalem sixteen years. ⁹Jotham rested with his fathers and was buried in the City of David. And Ahaz his son succeeded him as king.

Ahaz King of Judah

28 Ahaz was twenty years old when he became king, and he reigned in Jerusalem sixteen years. Unlike David his father, he did not do what was right in the eyes of the LORD. ²He walked in the ways of the kings of Israel and also made cast idols for worshiping the Baals. ³He burned sacrifices in the Valley of Ben Hinnom and sacrificed his sons in the fire, following the detestable ways of the nations the LORD had driven out before the Israelites. ⁴He offered sacrifices and burned incense at the high places, on the hilltops and under every spreading tree.

⁵Therefore the LORD his God handed him over to the king of Aram. The Arameans defeated him and took many of his people as prisoners and brought them to Damascus.

He was also given into the hands of the king of Israel, who inflicted heavy casualties on him. ⁶In one day Pekah son of Remaliah killed a hundred and twenty thousand soldiers in Judah—because Judah had forsaken the LORD, the God of their fathers. ⁷Zicri, an Ephraimite warrior, killed Maaseiah the king's son, Azrikam the officer in charge of the palace, and Elkanah, second to the king. ⁸The Israelites took captive from their kinsmen two hundred thousand wives, sons and daughters. They also took a great deal of plunder, which they carried back to Samaria.

⁹But a prophet of the LORD named Oded was there, and he went out to meet the army when it returned to Samaria. He said to them, "Because the LORD, the God of your fathers, was angry with Judah, he gave them into your hand. But you have slaughtered them in a rage that reaches to heaven. ¹⁰And now you intend to make the men and women of Judah and Jerusalem your slaves. But aren't you also guilty of sins against the LORD your God? ¹¹Now listen to me! Send back your fellow countrymen you have taken as prisoners, for the LORD's fierce anger rests on you."

¹²Then some of the leaders in Ephraim—Azariah son of Jehohanan, Berekiah son of Meshillemoth, Jehizkiah son of Shallum, and Amasa son of Hadlai—confronted those who were arriving from the war. ¹³"You must not bring those prisoners here," they said, "or we will be guilty before the LORD. Do you intend to add to our sin and guilt? For our guilt is already great, and his fierce anger rests on Israel."

¹⁴So the soldiers gave up the prisoners and plunder in the presence of the officials and all the assembly. ¹⁵The men designated by name took the prisoners, and from the plunder they clothed all who were naked. They provided them with clothes and sandals, food and drink, and healing balm. All those who were weak they put on donkeys. So they took them back to their fellow countrymen at Jericho, the City of Palms, and returned to Samaria.

¹⁶At that time King Ahaz sent to the king*ᶜ* of Assyria for help. ¹⁷The Edomites

ᵃ5 That is, about 3 3/4 tons (about 3.4 metric tons)   *ᵇ5* That is, probably about 62,000 bushels (about 2,200 kiloliters)   *ᶜ16* One Hebrew manuscript, Septuagint and Vulgate (see also 2 Kings 16:7); most Hebrew manuscripts *kings* had again come and attacked Judah and carried away prisoners, 18while the Philistines had raided towns in the foothills and in the Negev of Judah. They captured and occupied Beth Shemesh, Aijalon and Gederoth, as well as Soco, Timnah and Gimzo, with their surrounding villages. 19The Lord had humbled Judah because of Ahaz king of Israel,ᵃ for he had promoted wickedness in Judah and had been most unfaithful to the Lord. 20Tiglath-Pileserᵇ king of Assyria came to him, but he gave him trouble instead of help. 21Ahaz took some of the things from the temple of the Lord and from the royal palace and from the princes and presented them to the king of Assyria, but that did not help him.

22In his time of trouble King Ahaz became even more unfaithful to the Lord. 23He offered sacrifices to the gods of Damascus, who had defeated him; for he thought, "Since the gods of the kings of Aram have helped them, I will sacrifice to them so they will help me." But they were his downfall and the downfall of all Israel.

24Ahaz gathered together the furnishings from the temple of God and took them away.ᶜ He shut the doors of the Lord's temple and set up altars at every street corner in Jerusalem. 25In every town in Judah he built high places to burn sacrifices to other gods and provoked the Lord, the God of his fathers, to anger.

26The other events of his reign and all his ways, from beginning to end, are written in the book of the kings of Judah and Israel. 27Ahaz rested with his fathers and was buried in the city of Jerusalem, but he was not placed in the tombs of the kings of Israel. And Hezekiah his son succeeded him as king.

Hezekiah Purifies the Temple

29 Hezekiah was twenty-five years old when he became king, and he reigned in Jerusalem twenty-nine years. His mother's name was Abijah daughter of Zechariah. 2He did what was right in the eyes of the Lord, just as his father David had done.

3In the first month of the first year of his reign, he opened the doors of the temple of the Lord and repaired them. 4He brought in the priests and the Levites, assembled them in the square on the east

side 5and said: "Listen to me, Levites! Consecrate yourselves now and consecrate the temple of the Lord, the God of your fathers. Remove all defilement from the sanctuary. 6Our fathers were unfaithful; they did evil in the eyes of the Lord our God and forsook him. They turned their faces away from the Lord's dwelling place and turned their backs on him. 7They also shut the doors of the portico and put out the lamps. They did not burn incense or present any burnt offerings at the sanctuary to the God of Israel. 8Therefore, the anger of the Lord has fallen on Judah and Jerusalem; he has made them an object of dread and horror and scorn, as you can see with your own eyes. 9This is why our fathers have fallen by the sword and why our sons and daughters and our wives are in captivity. 10Now I intend to make a covenant with the Lord, the God of Israel, so that his fierce anger will turn away from us. 11My sons, do not be negligent now, for the Lord has chosen you to stand before him and serve him, to minister before him and to burn incense."

12Then these Levites set to work:
from the Kohathites,
	Mahath son of Amasai and Joel son of Azariah;
from the Merarites,
	Kish son of Abdi and Azariah son of Jehallelel;
from the Gershonites,
	Joah son of Zimmah and Eden son of Joah;
13from the descendants of Elizaphan,
	Shimri and Jeiel;
from the descendants of Asaph,
	Zechariah and Mattaniah;
14from the descendants of Heman,
	Jehiel and Shimei;
from the descendants of Jeduthun,
	Shemaiah and Uzziel.

15When they had assembled their brothers and consecrated themselves, they went in to purify the temple of the Lord, as the king had ordered, following the word of the Lord. 16The priests went into the sanctuary of the Lord to purify it. They brought out to the courtyard of the Lord's temple everything unclean that they found in the temple of the Lord. The Levites took it and carried it out to the Kidron Valley. 17They began the consecration on the first day of the first month, and by the eighth day of the month they reached the portico of the LORD. For eight more days they consecrated the temple of the LORD itself, finishing on the sixteenth day of the first month.

18Then they went in to King Hezekiah and reported: "We have purified the entire temple of the LORD, the altar of burnt offering with all its utensils, and the table for setting out the consecrated bread, with all its articles. 19We have prepared and consecrated all the articles that King Ahaz removed in his unfaithfulness while he was king. They are now in front of the LORD's altar."

20Early the next morning King Hezekiah gathered the city officials together and went up to the temple of the LORD. 21They brought seven bulls, seven rams, seven male lambs and seven male goats as a sin offering for the kingdom, for the sanctuary and for Judah. The king commanded the priests, the descendants of Aaron, to offer these on the altar of the LORD. 22So they slaughtered the bulls, and the priests took the blood and sprinkled it on the altar; next they slaughtered the rams and sprinkled their blood on the altar; then they slaughtered the lambs and sprinkled their blood on the altar. 23The goats for the sin offering were brought before the king and the assembly, and they laid their hands on them. 24The priests then slaughtered the goats and presented their blood on the altar for a sin offering to atone for all Israel, because the king had ordered the burnt offering and the sin offering for all Israel.

25He stationed the Levites in the temple of the LORD with cymbals, harps and lyres in the way prescribed by David and Gad the king's seer and Nathan the prophet; this was commanded by the LORD through his prophets. 26So the Levites stood ready with David's instruments, and the priests with their trumpets.

27Hezekiah gave the order to sacrifice the burnt offering on the altar. As the offering began, singing to the LORD began also, accompanied by trumpets and the instruments of David king of Israel. 28The whole assembly bowed in worship, while the singers sang and the trumpeters played. All this continued until the sacrifice of the burnt offering was completed.

29When the offerings were finished, the king and everyone present with him knelt down and worshiped. 30King Hezekiah and his officials ordered the Levites to praise the LORD with the words of David and of Asaph the seer. So they sang praises with gladness and bowed their heads and worshiped.

31Then Hezekiah said, "You have now dedicated yourselves to the LORD. Come and bring sacrifices and thank offerings to the temple of the LORD." So the assembly brought sacrifices and thank offerings, and all whose hearts were willing brought burnt offerings.

32The number of burnt offerings the assembly brought was seventy bulls, a hundred rams and two hundred male lambs—all of them for burnt offerings to the LORD. 33The animals consecrated as sacrifices amounted to six hundred bulls and three thousand sheep and goats. 34The priests, however, were too few to skin all the burnt offerings; so their kinsmen the Levites helped them until the task was finished and until other priests had been consecrated, for the Levites had been more conscientious in consecrating themselves than the priests had been. 35There were burnt offerings in abundance, together with the fat of the fellowship offerings[a] and the drink offerings that accompanied the burnt offerings.

So the service of the temple of the LORD was reestablished. 36Hezekiah and all the people rejoiced at what God had brought about for his people, because it was done so quickly.

Hezekiah Celebrates the Passover

30 Hezekiah sent word to all Israel and Judah and also wrote letters to Ephraim and Manasseh, inviting them to come to the temple of the LORD in Jerusalem and celebrate the Passover to the LORD, the God of Israel. 2The king and his officials and the whole assembly in Jerusalem decided to celebrate the Passover in the second month. 3They had not been able to celebrate it at the regular time because not enough priests had consecrated themselves and the people had not assembled in Jerusalem. 4The plan seemed right both to the king and to the whole assembly. 5They decided to send a proclamation throughout Israel, from Beersheba to Dan, calling the people to come to Jerusalem and celebrate the Passover to the LORD, the God of Israel. It

a35 Traditionally peace offerings

had not been celebrated in large numbers according to what was written.

⁶At the king's command, couriers went throughout Israel and Judah with letters from the king and from his officials, which read:

"People of Israel, return to the LORD, the God of Abraham, Isaac and Israel, that he may return to you who are left, who have escaped from the hand of the kings of Assyria. ⁷Do not be like your fathers and brothers,

who were unfaithful to the LORD, the God of their fathers, so that he made them an object of horror, as you see. ⁸Do not be stiff-necked, as your fathers were; submit to the LORD. Come to the sanctuary, which he has consecrated forever. Serve the LORD your God, so that his fierce anger will turn away from you. ⁹If you return to the LORD, then your brothers and your children will be shown compassion by their captors and will come back to this land, for the LORD your God is

TUESDAY

VERSE FOR THE DAY:
2 Chronicles 30:9

AUTHOR:
Kathryn Hillen

PASSAGE FOR THE DAY:
2 Chronicles 30:6–9

Running Away

"I'M running away from home!" Our seven-year-old Linda had her little suitcase in her hand as she flounced out the back door. It obviously surprised her that I didn't try to talk her out of it. I simply said good-by, assured her that we loved her, and reminded her that she was always welcome to return.

I no longer remember her reasons for leaving. I'm sure she thought they were valid. At any rate, I watched as she walked down the road, her head held high. Guessing her probable destination, I called our friends and asked them to be on the lookout for her and to call if she didn't arrive shortly. Later in the afternoon, I called again with a message for our runaway, telling her that we all missed her and hoped she'd be home in time for dinner.

She came home, running and crying, and I held her close. In a few minutes she regained her composure and in a burst of pseudosophistication quipped, "That's a nice place to visit, but I wouldn't want to live there!" And she never ran away from home again.

We all know spiritual runaways, people who have turned their backs on God. Many, like the prodigal son, have gone to the far country only to discover that it wasn't even a nice place to visit, much less a place to live permanently. Others have simply made short side trips in their deviation from the pathway God intends for them to take. In every case, the Lord is waiting to receive them. Because he loves them, he is always waiting to welcome them back and restore them. What a wonderfully loving, patient Father is our God.

Additional Scripture Readings:
Ruth 1:3–7; 4:14–17; Luke 15:11–24

Go to page 473 for your next devotional reading.

gracious and compassionate. He will not turn his face from you if you return to him."

[10]The couriers went from town to town in Ephraim and Manasseh, as far as Zebulun, but the people scorned and ridiculed them. [11]Nevertheless, some men of Asher, Manasseh and Zebulun humbled themselves and went to Jerusalem. [12]Also in Judah the hand of God was on the people to give them unity of mind to carry out what the king and his officials had ordered, following the word of the LORD.

[13]A very large crowd of people assembled in Jerusalem to celebrate the Feast of Unleavened Bread in the second month. [14]They removed the altars in Jerusalem and cleared away the incense altars and threw them into the Kidron Valley.

[15]They slaughtered the Passover lamb on the fourteenth day of the second month. The priests and the Levites were ashamed and consecrated themselves and brought burnt offerings to the temple of the LORD. [16]Then they took up their regular positions as prescribed in the Law of Moses the man of God. The priests sprinkled the blood handed to them by the Levites. [17]Since many in the crowd had not consecrated themselves, the Levites had to kill the Passover lambs for all those who were not ceremonially clean and could not consecrate their lambs, to the LORD. [18]Although most of the many people who came from Ephraim, Manasseh, Issachar and Zebulun had not purified themselves, yet they ate the Passover, contrary to what was written. But Hezekiah prayed for them, saying, "May the LORD, who is good, pardon everyone [19]who sets his heart on seeking God—the LORD, the God of his fathers—even if he is not clean according to the rules of the sanctuary." [20]And the LORD heard Hezekiah and healed the people.

[21]The Israelites who were present in Jerusalem celebrated the Feast of Unleavened Bread for seven days with great rejoicing, while the Levites and priests sang to the LORD every day, accompanied by the LORD's instruments of praise.[a]

[22]Hezekiah spoke encouragingly to all the Levites, who showed good understanding of the service of the LORD. For the seven days they ate their assigned portion and offered fellowship offerings[b] and praised the LORD, the God of their fathers.

[23]The whole assembly then agreed to celebrate the festival seven more days; so for another seven days they celebrated joyfully. [24]Hezekiah king of Judah provided a thousand bulls and seven thousand sheep and goats for the assembly, and the officials provided them with a thousand bulls and ten thousand sheep and goats. A great number of priests consecrated themselves. [25]The entire assembly of Judah rejoiced, along with the priests and Levites and all who had assembled from Israel, including the aliens who had come from Israel and those who lived in Judah. [26]There was great joy in Jerusalem, for since the days of Solomon son of David king of Israel there had been nothing like this in Jerusalem. [27]The priests and the Levites stood to bless the people, and God heard them, for their prayer reached heaven, his holy dwelling place.

31 When all this had ended, the Israelites who were there went out to the towns of Judah, smashed the sacred stones and cut down the Asherah poles. They destroyed the high places and the altars throughout Judah and Benjamin and in Ephraim and Manasseh. After they had destroyed all of them, the Israelites returned to their own towns and to their own property.

Contributions for Worship

[2]Hezekiah assigned the priests and Levites to divisions—each of them according to their duties as priests or Levites—to offer burnt offerings and fellowship offerings,[b] to minister, to give thanks and to sing praises at the gates of the LORD's dwelling. [3]The king contributed from his own possessions for the morning and evening burnt offerings and for the burnt offerings on the Sabbaths, New Moons and appointed feasts as written in the Law of the LORD. [4]He ordered the people living in Jerusalem to give the portion due the priests and Levites so they could devote themselves to the Law of the LORD. [5]As soon as the order went out, the Israelites generously gave the firstfruits of their grain, new wine, oil and honey and all that the fields produced. They brought a great amount, a tithe of everything. [6]The men of Israel and Judah who lived in the

---

[a]21 Or priests praised the LORD every day with resounding instruments belonging to the LORD
[b]22,2 Traditionally peace offerings

towns of Judah also brought a tithe of their herds and flocks and a tithe of the holy things dedicated to the LORD their God, and they piled them in heaps. ⁷They began doing this in the third month and finished in the seventh month. ⁸When Hezekiah and his officials came and saw the heaps, they praised the LORD and blessed his people Israel.

⁹Hezekiah asked the priests and Levites about the heaps; ¹⁰and Azariah the chief priest, from the family of Zadok, answered, "Since the people began to bring their contributions to the temple of the LORD, we have had enough to eat and plenty to spare, because the LORD has blessed his people, and this great amount is left over."

¹¹Hezekiah gave orders to prepare storerooms in the temple of the LORD, and this was done. ¹²Then they faithfully brought in the contributions, tithes and dedicated gifts. Conaniah, a Levite, was in charge of these things, and his brother Shimei was next in rank. ¹³Jehiel, Azaziah, Nahath, Asahel, Jerimoth, Jozabad, Eliel, Ismakiah, Mahath and Benaiah were supervisors under Conaniah and Shimei his brother, by appointment of King Hezekiah and Azariah the official in charge of the temple of God.

¹⁴Kore son of Imnah the Levite, keeper of the East Gate, was in charge of the freewill offerings given to God, distributing the contributions made to the LORD and also the consecrated gifts. ¹⁵Eden, Miniamin, Jeshua, Shemaiah, Amariah and Shecaniah assisted him faithfully in the towns of the priests, distributing to their fellow priests according to their divisions, old and young alike.

¹⁶In addition, they distributed to the males three years old or more whose names were in the genealogical records— all who would enter the temple of the LORD to perform the daily duties of their various tasks, according to their responsibilities and their divisions. ¹⁷And they distributed to the priests enrolled by their families in the genealogical records and likewise to the Levites twenty years old or more, according to their responsibilities and their divisions. ¹⁸They included all the little ones, the wives, and the sons and daughters of the whole community listed in these genealogical records. For they were faithful in consecrating themselves.

¹⁹As for the priests, the descendants of Aaron, who lived on the farm lands around their towns or in any other towns, men were designated by name to distribute portions to every male among them and to all who were recorded in the genealogies of the Levites.

²⁰This is what Hezekiah did throughout Judah, doing what was good and right and faithful before the LORD his God. ²¹In everything that he undertook in the service of God's temple and in obedience to the law and the commands, he sought his God and worked wholeheartedly. And so he prospered.

Sennacherib Threatens Jerusalem

32 After all that Hezekiah had so faithfully done, Sennacherib king of Assyria came and invaded Judah. He laid siege to the fortified cities, thinking to conquer them for himself. ²When Hezekiah saw that Sennacherib had come and that he intended to make war on Jerusalem, ³he consulted with his officials and military staff about blocking off the water from the springs outside the city, and they helped him. ⁴A large force of men assembled, and they blocked all the springs and the stream that flowed through the land. "Why should the kings ᵃ of Assyria come and find plenty of water?" they said. ⁵Then he worked hard repairing all the broken sections of the wall and building towers on it. He built another wall outside that one and reinforced the supporting terraces ᵇ of the City of David. He also made large numbers of weapons and shields.

⁶He appointed military officers over the people and assembled them before him in the square at the city gate and encouraged them with these words: ⁷"Be strong and courageous. Do not be afraid or discouraged because of the king of Assyria and the vast army with him, for there is a greater power with us than with him. ⁸With him is only the arm of flesh, but with us is the LORD our God to help us and to fight our battles." And the people gained confidence from what Hezekiah the king of Judah said.

⁹Later, when Sennacherib king of Assyria and all his forces were laying siege to Lachish, he sent his officers to Jerusalem with this message for Hezekiah king of Judah and for all the people of Judah who were there:

ᵃ4 Hebrew; Septuagint and Syriac *king*   ᵇ5 Or *the Millo*

VERSE FOR THE DAY:
2 Chronicles 31:20–21

AUTHOR:
Rita Schweitz

PASSAGE FOR THE DAY:
2 Chronicles 31:11–21

The Mary and Martha in Me

I WALKED out of the pantry holding a wooden puzzle in each hand. "Which one do you want?" I asked our two-year-old, holding out both for him to see. "Those two!" he exclaimed as he snatched both puzzles.

Cale dumped all the pieces of his two puzzles in a big pile and began to work on first one, then the other. It amused me to watch him sorting pieces, trying to match Big Bird and Mickey Mouse alternately.

As I watched his actions, it seemed like God was saying, "This is what you're doing." I was moving back and forth between Mary and Martha activities, trying to sort out the two. I couldn't decide which should come first—prayer or practical attempts to complete my work—so I attempted both together. The result? Interrupted prayer. Distracted activity.

I was struggling with the delicate balance of being and doing. I wanted to sit at the feet of Jesus and learn to be the person I was created to be. And I wanted dinner to be ready on time!

As I watched my son patiently work on his two puzzles, inspecting each piece with interest, my own impatience seemed in sharp contrast. Wasn't it God who had given me both puzzles to work on?

As I thought about it, it dawned on me that the separation between "spiritual" activities and "worldly" activities was an artificial division. The contemplation of what God required, and the completion of the tasks he assigned, were interlocking pieces of the same abundant life he pictured for me. Meeting Christ, like Mary, and meeting the practical needs of those around me, like Martha, were both acceptable in God's sight. And God could speak wherever he chose—in my prayer closet or in my daily experiences. Seeking God and working wholeheartedly both have their place. The Mary and the Martha in me can live comfortably together!

Additional Scripture Readings:
Luke 10:38–42; James 2:14–17

Go to page 482 for your next devotional reading.

10"This is what Sennacherib king of Assyria says: On what are you basing your confidence, that you remain in Jerusalem under siege? 11When Hezekiah says, 'The LORD our God will save us from the hand of the king of Assyria,' he is misleading you, to let you die of hunger and thirst. 12Did not Hezekiah himself remove this god's high places and altars, saying to Judah and Jerusalem, 'You must worship before one altar and burn sacrifices on it'?

13"Do you not know what I and my fathers have done to all the peoples of the other lands? Were the gods of those nations ever able to deliver their land from my hand? 14Who of all the gods of these nations that my fathers destroyed has been able to save his people from me? How then can your god deliver you from my hand? 15Now do not let Hezekiah deceive you and mislead you like this. Do not believe him, for no god of any nation or kingdom has been able to deliver his people from my hand or the hand of my fathers. How much less will your god deliver you from my hand!"

16Sennacherib's officers spoke further against the LORD God and against his servant Hezekiah. 17The king also wrote letters insulting the LORD, the God of Israel, and saying this against him: "Just as the gods of the peoples of the other lands did not rescue their people from my hand, so the god of Hezekiah will not rescue his people from my hand." 18Then they called out in Hebrew to the people of Jerusalem who were on the wall, to terrify them and make them afraid in order to capture the city. 19They spoke about the God of Jerusalem as they did about the gods of the other peoples of the world—the work of men's hands.

20King Hezekiah and the prophet Isaiah son of Amoz cried out in prayer to heaven about this. 21And the LORD sent an angel, who annihilated all the fighting men and the leaders and officers in the camp of the Assyrian king. So he withdrew to his own land in disgrace. And when he went into the temple of his god, some of his sons cut him down with the sword.

22So the LORD saved Hezekiah and the people of Jerusalem from the hand of Sennacherib king of Assyria and from the hand of all others. He took care of them*a* on every side. 23Many brought offerings to Jerusalem for the LORD and valuable gifts for Hezekiah king of Judah. From then on he was highly regarded by all the nations.

Hezekiah's Pride, Success and Death

24In those days Hezekiah became ill and was at the point of death. He prayed to the LORD, who answered him and gave him a miraculous sign. 25But Hezekiah's heart was proud and he did not respond to the kindness shown him; therefore the LORD's wrath was on him and on Judah and Jerusalem. 26Then Hezekiah repented of the pride of his heart, as did the people of Jerusalem; therefore the LORD's wrath did not come upon them during the days of Hezekiah.

27Hezekiah had very great riches and honor, and he made treasuries for his silver and gold and for his precious stones, spices, shields and all kinds of valuables. 28He also made buildings to store the harvest of grain, new wine and oil; and he made stalls for various kinds of cattle, and pens for the flocks. 29He built villages and acquired great numbers of flocks and herds, for God had given him very great riches.

30It was Hezekiah who blocked the upper outlet of the Gihon spring and channeled the water down to the west side of the City of David. He succeeded in everything he undertook. 31But when envoys were sent by the rulers of Babylon to ask him about the miraculous sign that had occurred in the land, God left him to test him and to know everything that was in his heart.

32The other events of Hezekiah's reign and his acts of devotion are written in the vision of the prophet Isaiah son of Amoz in the book of the kings of Judah and Israel. 33Hezekiah rested with his fathers and was buried on the hill where the tombs of David's descendants are. All Judah and the people of Jerusalem honored him when he died. And Manasseh his son succeeded him as king.

Manasseh King of Judah

33 Manasseh was twelve years old when he became king, and he reigned in Jerusalem fifty-five years. 2He did evil in the eyes of the LORD, following

a22 Hebrew; Septuagint and Vulgate He gave them rest

the detestable practices of the nations the LORD had driven out before the Israelites. ³He rebuilt the high places his father Hezekiah had demolished; he also erected altars to the Baals and made Asherah poles. He bowed down to all the starry hosts and worshiped them. ⁴He built altars in the temple of the LORD, of which the LORD had said, "My Name will remain in Jerusalem forever." ⁵In both courts of the temple of the LORD, he built altars to all the starry hosts. ⁶He sacrificed his sons in*a* the fire in the Valley of Ben Hinnom, practiced sorcery, divination and witchcraft, and consulted mediums and spiritists. He did much evil in the eyes of the LORD, provoking him to anger.

⁷He took the carved image he had made and put it in God's temple, of which God had said to David and to his son Solomon, "In this temple and in Jerusalem, which I have chosen out of all the tribes of Israel, I will put my Name forever. ⁸I will not again make the feet of the Israelites leave the land I assigned to your forefathers, if only they will be careful to do everything I commanded them concerning all the laws, decrees and ordinances given through Moses." ⁹But Manasseh led Judah and the people of Jerusalem astray, so that they did more evil than the nations the LORD had destroyed before the Israelites.

¹⁰The LORD spoke to Manasseh and his people, but they paid no attention. ¹¹So the LORD brought against them the army commanders of the king of Assyria, who took Manasseh prisoner, put a hook in his nose, bound him with bronze shackles and took him to Babylon. ¹²In his distress he sought the favor of the LORD his God and humbled himself greatly before the God of his fathers. ¹³And when he prayed to him, the LORD was moved by his entreaty and listened to his plea; so he brought him back to Jerusalem and to his kingdom. Then Manasseh knew that the LORD is God.

¹⁴Afterward he rebuilt the outer wall of the City of David, west of the Gihon spring in the valley, as far as the entrance of the Fish Gate and encircling the hill of Ophel; he also made it much higher. He stationed military commanders in all the fortified cities in Judah.

¹⁵He got rid of the foreign gods and re-

moved the image from the temple of the LORD, as well as all the altars he had built on the temple hill and in Jerusalem; and he threw them out of the city. ¹⁶Then he restored the altar of the LORD and sacrificed fellowship offerings*b* and thank offerings on it, and told Judah to serve the LORD, the God of Israel. ¹⁷The people, however, continued to sacrifice at the high places, but only to the LORD their God.

¹⁸The other events of Manasseh's reign, including his prayer to his God and the words the seers spoke to him in the name of the LORD, the God of Israel, are written in the annals of the kings of Israel.*c* ¹⁹His prayer and how God was moved by his entreaty, as well as all his sins and unfaithfulness, and the sites where he built high places and set up Asherah poles and idols before he humbled himself—all are written in the records of the seers.*d* ²⁰Manasseh rested with his fathers and was buried in his palace. And Amon his son succeeded him as king.

Amon King of Judah

²¹Amon was twenty-two years old when he became king, and he reigned in Jerusalem two years. ²²He did evil in the eyes of the LORD, as his father Manasseh had done. Amon worshiped and offered sacrifices to all the idols Manasseh had made. ²³But unlike his father Manasseh, he did not humble himself before the LORD; Amon increased his guilt.

²⁴Amon's officials conspired against him and assassinated him in his palace. ²⁵Then the people of the land killed all who had plotted against King Amon, and they made Josiah his son king in his place.

Josiah's Reforms

34 Josiah was eight years old when he became king, and he reigned in Jerusalem thirty-one years. ²He did what was right in the eyes of the LORD and walked in the ways of his father David, not turning aside to the right or to the left.

³In the eighth year of his reign, while he was still young, he began to seek the God of his father David. In his twelfth year he began to purge Judah and Jerusalem of high places, Asherah poles, carved idols

---

*a*6 Or *He made his sons pass through*   *b*16 Traditionally *peace offerings*   *c*18 That is, Judah, as frequently in 2 Chronicles   *d*19 One Hebrew manuscript and Septuagint; most Hebrew manuscripts *of Hozai* and cast images. [4]Under his direction the altars of the Baals were torn down; he cut to pieces the incense altars that were above them, and smashed the Asherah poles, the idols and the images. These he broke to pieces and scattered over the graves of those who had sacrificed to them. [5]He burned the bones of the priests on their altars, and so he purged Judah and Jerusalem. [6]In the towns of Manasseh, Ephraim and Simeon, as far as Naphtali, and in the ruins around them, [7]he tore down the altars and the Asherah poles and crushed the idols to powder and cut to pieces all the incense altars throughout Israel. Then he went back to Jerusalem.

[8]In the eighteenth year of Josiah's reign, to purify the land and the temple, he sent Shaphan son of Azaliah and Maaseiah the ruler of the city, with Joah son of Joahaz, the recorder, to repair the temple of the LORD his God.

[9]They went to Hilkiah the high priest and gave him the money that had been brought into the temple of God, which the Levites who were the doorkeepers had collected from the people of Manasseh, Ephraim and the entire remnant of Israel and from all the people of Judah and Benjamin and the inhabitants of Jerusalem. [10]Then they entrusted it to the men appointed to supervise the work on the LORD's temple. These men paid the workers who repaired and restored the temple. [11]They also gave money to the carpenters and builders to purchase dressed stone, and timber for joists and beams for the buildings that the kings of Judah had allowed to fall into ruin.

[12]The men did the work faithfully. Over them to direct them were Jahath and Obadiah, Levites descended from Merari, and Zechariah and Meshullam, descended from Kohath. The Levites—all who were skilled in playing musical instruments— [13]had charge of the laborers and supervised all the workers from job to job. Some of the Levites were secretaries, scribes and doorkeepers.

The Book of the Law Found

[14]While they were bringing out the money that had been taken into the temple of the LORD, Hilkiah the priest found the Book of the Law of the LORD that had

been given through Moses. [15]Hilkiah said to Shaphan the secretary, "I have found the Book of the Law in the temple of the LORD." He gave it to Shaphan.

[16]Then Shaphan took the book to the king and reported to him: "Your officials are doing everything that has been committed to them. [17]They have paid out the money that was in the temple of the LORD and have entrusted it to the supervisors and workers." [18]Then Shaphan the secretary informed the king, "Hilkiah the priest has given me a book." And Shaphan read from it in the presence of the king.

[19]When the king heard the words of the Law, he tore his robes. [20]He gave these orders to Hilkiah, Ahikam son of Shaphan, Abdon son of Micah,[a] Shaphan the secretary and Asaiah the king's attendant: [21]"Go and inquire of the LORD for me and for the remnant in Israel and Judah about what is written in this book that has been found. Great is the LORD's anger that is poured out on us because our fathers have not kept the word of the LORD; they have not acted in accordance with all that is written in this book."

[22]Hilkiah and those the king had sent with him[b] went to speak to the prophetess Huldah, who was the wife of Shallum son of Tokhath,[c] the son of Hasrah,[d] keeper of the wardrobe. She lived in Jerusalem, in the Second District.

[23]She said to them, "This is what the LORD, the God of Israel, says: Tell the man who sent you to me, [24]'This is what the LORD says: I am going to bring disaster on this place and its people—all the curses written in the book that has been read in the presence of the king of Judah. [25]Because they have forsaken me and burned incense to other gods and provoked me to anger by all that their hands have made,[e] my anger will be poured out on this place and will not be quenched.' [26]Tell the king of Judah, who sent you to inquire of the LORD, 'This is what the LORD, the God of Israel, says concerning the words you heard: [27]Because your heart was responsive and you humbled yourself before God when you heard what he spoke against this place and its people, and because you humbled yourself before me and tore your robes and wept in my presence, I have heard you, declares the LORD.

²⁸Now I will gather you to your fathers, and you will be buried in peace. Your eyes will not see all the disaster I am going to bring on this place and on those who live here.' "

So they took her answer back to the king.

²⁹Then the king called together all the elders of Judah and Jerusalem. ³⁰He went up to the temple of the LORD with the men of Judah, the people of Jerusalem, the priests and the Levites—all the people from the least to the greatest. He read in their hearing all the words of the Book of the Covenant, which had been found in the temple of the LORD. ³¹The king stood by his pillar and renewed the covenant in the presence of the LORD—to follow the LORD and keep his commands, regulations and decrees with all his heart and all his soul, and to obey the words of the covenant written in this book.

³²Then he had everyone in Jerusalem and Benjamin pledge themselves to it; the people of Jerusalem did this in accordance with the covenant of God, the God of their fathers.

³³Josiah removed all the detestable idols from all the territory belonging to the Israelites, and he had all who were present in Israel serve the LORD their God. As long as he lived, they did not fail to follow the LORD, the God of their fathers.

Josiah Celebrates the Passover

35 Josiah celebrated the Passover to the LORD in Jerusalem, and the Passover lamb was slaughtered on the fourteenth day of the first month. ²He appointed the priests to their duties and encouraged them in the service of the LORD's temple. ³He said to the Levites, who instructed all Israel and who had been consecrated to the LORD: "Put the sacred ark in the temple that Solomon son of David king of Israel built. It is not to be carried about on your shoulders. Now serve the LORD your God and his people Israel. ⁴Prepare yourselves by families in your divisions, according to the directions written by David king of Israel and by his son Solomon.

⁵"Stand in the holy place with a group of Levites for each subdivision of the families of your fellow countrymen, the lay people. ⁶Slaughter the Passover lambs, consecrate yourselves and prepare the lambs, for your fellow countrymen, doing what the LORD commanded through Moses."

⁷Josiah provided for all the lay people who were there a total of thirty thousand sheep and goats for the Passover offerings, and also three thousand cattle—all from the king's own possessions.

⁸His officials also contributed voluntarily to the people and the priests and Levites. Hilkiah, Zechariah and Jehiel, the administrators of God's temple, gave the priests twenty-six hundred Passover offerings and three hundred cattle. ⁹Also Conaniah along with Shemaiah and Nethanel, his brothers, and Hashabiah, Jeiel and Jozabad, the leaders of the Levites, provided five thousand Passover offerings and five hundred head of cattle for the Levites.

¹⁰The service was arranged and the priests stood in their places with the Levites in their divisions as the king had ordered. ¹¹The Passover lambs were slaughtered, and the priests sprinkled the blood handed to them, while the Levites skinned the animals. ¹²They set aside the burnt offerings to give them to the subdivisions of the families of the people to offer to the LORD, as is written in the Book of Moses. They did the same with the cattle. ¹³They roasted the Passover animals over the fire as prescribed, and boiled the holy offerings in pots, caldrons and pans and served them quickly to all the people. ¹⁴After this, they made preparations for themselves and for the priests, because the priests, the descendants of Aaron, were sacrificing the burnt offerings and the fat portions until nightfall. So the Levites made preparations for themselves and for the Aaronic priests.

¹⁵The musicians, the descendants of Asaph, were in the places prescribed by David, Asaph, Heman and Jeduthun the king's seer. The gatekeepers at each gate did not need to leave their posts, because their fellow Levites made the preparations for them.

¹⁶So at that time the entire service of the LORD was carried out for the celebration of the Passover and the offering of burnt offerings on the altar of the LORD, as King Josiah had ordered. ¹⁷The Israelites who were present celebrated the Passover at that time and observed the Feast of Unleavened Bread for seven days. ¹⁸The Passover had not been observed like this in Israel since the days of the prophet Samuel; and none of the kings of Israel had ever celebrated such a Passover as did Josiah, with the priests, the Levites and all Judah and Israel who were there

with the people of Jerusalem. ¹⁹This Passover was celebrated in the eighteenth year of Josiah's reign.

The Death of Josiah

²⁰After all this, when Josiah had set the temple in order, Neco king of Egypt went up to fight at Carchemish on the Euphrates, and Josiah marched out to meet him in battle. ²¹But Neco sent messengers to him, saying, "What quarrel is there between you and me, O king of Judah? It is not you I am attacking at this time, but the house with which I am at war. God has told me to hurry; so stop opposing God, who is with me, or he will destroy you."

²²Josiah, however, would not turn away from him, but disguised himself to engage him in battle. He would not listen to what Neco had said at God's command but went to fight him on the plain of Megiddo.

²³Archers shot King Josiah, and he told his officers, "Take me away; I am badly wounded." ²⁴So they took him out of his chariot, put him in the other chariot he had and brought him to Jerusalem, where he died. He was buried in the tombs of his fathers, and all Judah and Jerusalem mourned for him.

²⁵Jeremiah composed laments for Josiah, and to this day all the men and women singers commemorate Josiah in the laments. These became a tradition in Israel and are written in the Laments.

²⁶The other events of Josiah's reign and his acts of devotion, according to what is written in the Law of the LORD — ²⁷all the events, from beginning to end, are written in the book of the kings of Israel and Judah. ¹And the people of the land took Jehoahaz son of Josiah and made him king in Jerusalem in place of his father.

Jehoahaz King of Judah

²Jehoahaz^a was twenty-three years old when he became king, and he reigned in Jerusalem three months. ³The king of Egypt dethroned him in Jerusalem and imposed on Judah a levy of a hundred talents^b of silver and a talent^c of gold. ⁴The king of Egypt made Eliakim, a brother of Jehoahaz, king over Judah and Jerusalem

and changed Eliakim's name to Jehoiakim. But Neco took Eliakim's brother Jehoahaz and carried him off to Egypt.

Jehoiakim King of Judah

⁵Jehoiakim was twenty-five years old when he became king, and he reigned in Jerusalem eleven years. He did evil in the eyes of the LORD his God. ⁶Nebuchadnezzar king of Babylon attacked him and bound him with bronze shackles to take him to Babylon. ⁷Nebuchadnezzar also took to Babylon articles from the temple of the LORD and put them in his temple^d there.

⁸The other events of Jehoiakim's reign, the detestable things he did and all that was found against him, are written in the book of the kings of Israel and Judah. And Jehoiachin his son succeeded him as king.

Jehoiachin King of Judah

⁹Jehoiachin was eighteen^e years old when he became king, and he reigned in Jerusalem three months and ten days. He did evil in the eyes of the LORD. ¹⁰In the spring, King Nebuchadnezzar sent for him and brought him to Babylon, together with articles of value from the temple of the LORD, and he made Jehoiachin's uncle,^{f} Zedekiah, king over Judah and Jerusalem.

Zedekiah King of Judah

¹¹Zedekiah was twenty-one years old when he became king, and he reigned in Jerusalem eleven years. ¹²He did evil in the eyes of the LORD his God and did not humble himself before Jeremiah the prophet, who spoke the word of the LORD. ¹³He also rebelled against King Nebuchadnezzar, who had made him take an oath in God's name. He became stiffnecked and hardened his heart and would not turn to the LORD, the God of Israel. ¹⁴Furthermore, all the leaders of the priests and the people became more and more unfaithful, following all the detestable practices of the nations and defiling the temple of the LORD, which he had consecrated in Jerusalem.

The Fall of Jerusalem

¹⁵The LORD, the God of their fathers,

---

^{a}2 Hebrew *Joahaz*, a variant of *Jehoahaz*; also in verse 4 ^{b}3 That is, about 3 3/4 tons (about 3.4 metric tons) ^{c}3 That is, about 75 pounds (about 34 kilograms) ^{d}7 Or *palace* ^{e}9 One Hebrew manuscript, some Septuagint manuscripts and Syriac (see also 2 Kings 24:8); most Hebrew manuscripts *eight* ^{f}10 Hebrew *brother*, that is, relative (see 2 Kings 24:17) sent word to them through his messengers again and again, because he had pity on his people and on his dwelling place. ¹⁶But they mocked God's messengers, despised his words and scoffed at his prophets until the wrath of the LORD was aroused against his people and there was no remedy. ¹⁷He brought up against them the king of the Babylonians,ᵃ who killed their young men with the sword in the sanctuary, and spared neither young man nor young woman, old man or aged. God handed all of them over to Nebuchadnezzar. ¹⁸He carried to Babylon all the articles from the temple of God, both large and small, and the treasures of the LORD's temple and the treasures of the king and his officials. ¹⁹They set fire to God's temple and broke down the wall of Jerusalem; they burned all the palaces and destroyed everything of value there.

²⁰He carried into exile to Babylon the remnant, who escaped from the sword, and they became servants to him and his sons until the kingdom of Persia came to power. ²¹The land enjoyed its sabbath rests; all the time of its desolation it rested, until the seventy years were completed in fulfillment of the word of the LORD spoken by Jeremiah.

²²In the first year of Cyrus king of Persia, in order to fulfill the word of the LORD spoken by Jeremiah, the LORD moved the heart of Cyrus king of Persia to make a proclamation throughout his realm and to put it in writing:

²³"This is what Cyrus king of Persia says:

" 'The LORD, the God of heaven, has given me all the kingdoms of the earth and he has appointed me to build a temple for him at Jerusalem in Judah. Anyone of his people among you—may the LORD his God be with him, and let him go up.' "

ᵃ17 Or Chaldeans

*E*ZRA tells how God helps two groups return from Babylon to the promised land, the second group led by Ezra himself. The temple of the Lord is rebuilt despite opposition, the worship of the Lord resumes, and the people realize they must not sin through mixed marriages as their ancestors did. As you read this book, rejoice that God always gives you a second chance to serve him; promise to do your best to remain faithful to his Word.

EZRA

Cyrus Helps the Exiles to Return

1 In the first year of Cyrus king of Persia, in order to fulfill the word of the LORD spoken by Jeremiah, the LORD moved the heart of Cyrus king of Persia to make a proclamation throughout his realm and to put it in writing:

2"This is what Cyrus king of Persia says:

" 'The LORD, the God of heaven, has given me all the kingdoms of the earth and he has appointed me to build a temple for him at Jerusalem in Judah. 3Anyone of his people among you—may his God be with him, and let him go up to Jerusalem in Judah and build the temple of the LORD, the God of Israel, the God who is in Jerusalem. 4And the people of any place where survivors may now be living are to provide him with silver and gold, with goods and livestock, and with freewill offerings for the temple of God in Jerusalem.' "

5Then the family heads of Judah and Benjamin, and the priests and Levites—everyone whose heart God had moved—prepared to go up and build the house of the LORD in Jerusalem. 6All their neighbors assisted them with articles of silver and gold, with goods and livestock, and with valuable gifts, in addition to all the freewill offerings. 7Moreover, King Cyrus brought out the articles belonging to the temple of the LORD, which Nebuchadnezzar had carried away from Jerusalem and had placed in the temple of his god. *a* 8Cyrus king of Persia had them brought by Mithredath the treasurer, who counted them out to Sheshbazzar the prince of Judah.

9This was the inventory:

gold dishes	30
silver dishes	1,000
silver pans*b*	29
10gold bowls	30
matching silver bowls	410
other articles	1,000

11In all, there were 5,400 articles of gold and of silver. Sheshbazzar brought all these along when the exiles came up from Babylon to Jerusalem.

The List of the Exiles Who Returned

2 Now these are the people of the province who came up from the captivity of the exiles, whom Nebuchadnezzar king of Babylon had taken captive to Babylon (they returned to Jerusalem and Judah, each to his own town, 2in company with Zerubbabel, Jeshua, Nehemiah, Seraiah, Reelaiah, Mordecai, Bilshan, Mispar, Bigvai, Rehum and Baanah):

The list of the men of the people of Israel:

3the descendants of Parosh	2,172
4of Shephatiah	372
5of Arah	775
6of Pahath-Moab (through the line of Jeshua and Joab)	2,812
7of Elam	1,254
8of Zattu	945
9of Zaccai	760
10of Bani	642
11of Bebai	623
12of Azgad	1,222
13of Adonikam	666
14of Bigvai	2,056
15of Adin	454
16of Ater (through Hezekiah)	98
17of Bezai	323
18of Jorah	112
19of Hashum	223
20of Gibbar	95
21the men of Bethlehem	123
22of Netophah	56
23of Anathoth	128
24of Azmaveth	42
25of Kiriath Jearim,*c* Kephirah and Beeroth	743
26of Ramah and Geba	621
27of Micmash	122
28of Bethel and Ai	223
29of Nebo	52
30of Magbish	156
31of the other Elam	1,254
32of Harim	320
33of Lod, Hadid and Ono	725
34of Jericho	345
35of Senaah	3,630

36The priests:

the descendants of Jedaiah (through the family of Jeshua)	973
37of Immer	1,052
38of Pashhur	1,247
39of Harim	1,017

40The Levites:

the descendants of Jeshua and Kadmiel (through the line of Hodaviah)	74

41The singers:

the descendants of Asaph	128

42The gatekeepers of the temple:

the descendants of Shallum, Ater, Talmon, Akkub, Hatita and Shobai	139

43The temple servants:

the descendants of
Ziha, Hasupha, Tabbaoth,
44Keros, Siaha, Padon,
45Lebanah, Hagabah, Akkub,
46Hagab, Shalmai, Hanan,
47Giddel, Gahar, Reaiah,
48Rezin, Nekoda, Gazzam,
49Uzza, Paseah, Besai,
50Asnah, Meunim, Nephussim,
51Bakbuk, Hakupha, Harhur,
52Bazluth, Mehida, Harsha,
53Barkos, Sisera, Temah,
54Neziah and Hatipha

55The descendants of the servants of Solomon:

the descendants of
Sotai, Hassophereth, Peruda,
56Jaala, Darkon, Giddel,
57Shephatiah, Hattil,
Pokereth-Hazzebaim and Ami

---

a7 Or *gods*   *b9* The meaning of the Hebrew for this word is uncertain.   *c25* See Septuagint (see also Neh. 7:29); Hebrew *Kiriath Arim.*

VERSE FOR THE DAY:
Ezra 1:5

AUTHOR:
Doris Rikkers

PASSAGE FOR THE DAY:
Ezra 1:1–11

Talk About Moving

THE day was blustery and cold, with a windchill factor below zero. It was a typical February day in Michigan when my new neighbors moved from West Virginia. As I watched from the warmth of my living room, the movers tracked through the snow and the wind, carrying each wrapped piece of furniture into the house.

My husband and I had done as much as we could before their arrival—we had shoveled the snow from the porch and driveway. We knew a little about our new neighbors—that they were born in Kentucky and had a four-month-old baby boy and a cat. So when we visited with warm dishes and warm hellos we didn't need to spend time on basics. By the time we said good-by, I knew they felt welcomed to the neighborhood.

The move "back home" for the Jews in exile was very different. No welcoming neighbors, no casserole dishes or hot muffins. They knew only of destruction, stories of what their homeland had been like before the captivity. They had been in exile for seventy years—what ties, what motivation was there to go back to the land of their ancestors, the land they had never known? Under ordinary circumstances there would have been no desire to leave their new land (after seventy years they had settled in and established themselves comfortably, I'm sure).

But these were no ordinary people—these were God's chosen people. And this was no ordinary land—this was the promised land. And this was no ordinary desire to move back home—this was a calling from God: "Everyone whose heart God had moved—prepared to go up and build the house of the LORD in Jerusalem" (Ezra 1:5).

Our moves today are stressful at best and traumatic at worst, whether they be across town or across the continent. But none of them are quite as traumatic as the move of the exiles back to the land God had given to Abraham.

If the Israelites could go home in faith where God led them, with no moving vans, no travel brochures, no friendly neighbors to greet them, we too, when God moves our hearts, should be able to go wherever he calls us. So the next time your spouse says, "I've been transferred," remember the Israelites and pack your boxes, knowing that no matter what the distance, God will move with you.

Additional Scripture Readings:
Genesis 12:1–5; Exodus 4:10–15

Go to page 499 for your next devotional reading.

⁵⁸The temple servants and the
descendants of the servants of
Solomon   392

⁵⁹The following came up from the
towns of Tel Melah, Tel Harsha, Ke-
rub, Addon and Immer, but they
could not show that their families
were descended from Israel:

⁶⁰The descendants of
Delaiah, Tobiah and Nekoda
                                              652

⁶¹And from among the priests:

The descendants of
Hobaiah, Hakkoz and Barzillai
(a man who had married a
daughter of Barzillai the
Gileadite and was called by that
name).

⁶²These searched for their family
records, but they could not find them
and so were excluded from the
priesthood as unclean. ⁶³The governor ordered them not to eat any of
the most sacred food until there was
a priest ministering with the Urim
and Thummim.

⁶⁴The whole company numbered
42,360, ⁶⁵besides their 7,337 menservants and maidservants; and they
also had 200 men and women singers. ⁶⁶They had 736 horses, 245
mules, ⁶⁷435 camels and 6,720 donkeys.

⁶⁸When they arrived at the house of the
LORD in Jerusalem, some of the heads of
the families gave freewill offerings toward
the rebuilding of the house of God on its
site. ⁶⁹According to their ability they gave
to the treasury for this work 61,000
drachmas*a* of gold, 5,000 minas*b* of silver and 100 priestly garments.

⁷⁰The priests, the Levites, the singers,
the gatekeepers and the temple servants
settled in their own towns, along with
some of the other people, and the rest of
the Israelites settled in their towns.

Rebuilding the Altar

3 When the seventh month came and
the Israelites had settled in their
towns, the people assembled as one man
in Jerusalem. ²Then Jeshua son of Jozadak and his fellow priests and Zerubbabel
son of Shealtiel and his associates began

to build the altar of the God of Israel to
sacrifice burnt offerings on it, in accordance with what is written in the Law of
Moses the man of God. ³Despite their fear
of the peoples around them, they built
the altar on its foundation and sacrificed
burnt offerings on it to the LORD, both the
morning and evening sacrifices. ⁴Then in
accordance with what is written, they celebrated the Feast of Tabernacles with the
required number of burnt offerings prescribed for each day. ⁵After that, they presented the regular burnt offerings, the
New Moon sacrifices and the sacrifices
for all the appointed sacred feasts of the
LORD, as well as those brought as freewill
offerings to the LORD. ⁶On the first day of
the seventh month they began to offer
burnt offerings to the LORD, though the
foundation of the LORD's temple had not
yet been laid.

Rebuilding the Temple

⁷Then they gave money to the masons
and carpenters, and gave food and drink
and oil to the people of Sidon and Tyre,
so that they would bring cedar logs by sea
from Lebanon to Joppa, as authorized by
Cyrus king of Persia.

⁸In the second month of the second
year after their arrival at the house of God
in Jerusalem, Zerubbabel son of Shealtiel, Jeshua son of Jozadak and the rest of
their brothers (the priests and the Levites
and all who had returned from the captivity to Jerusalem) began the work, appointing Levites twenty years of age and
older to supervise the building of the
house of the LORD. ⁹Jeshua and his sons
and brothers and Kadmiel and his sons
(descendants of Hodaviah*c*) and the sons
of Henadad and their sons and brothers—
all Levites—joined together in supervising those working on the house of God.

¹⁰When the builders laid the foundation of the temple of the LORD, the priests
in their vestments and with trumpets,
and the Levites (the sons of Asaph) with
cymbals, took their places to praise the
LORD, as prescribed by David king of Israel. ¹¹With praise and thanksgiving they
sang to the LORD:

"He is good;
his love to Israel endures forever."

And all the people gave a great shout of
praise to the LORD, because the founda-

---

a69 That is, about 1,100 pounds (about 500 kilograms)   *b69* That is, about 3 tons (about 2.9 metric
tons)   *c9* Hebrew *Yehudah*, probably a variant of *Hodaviah*

tion of the house of the LORD was laid. [12]But many of the older priests and Levites and family heads, who had seen the former temple, wept aloud when they saw the foundation of this temple being laid, while many others shouted for joy. [13]No one could distinguish the sound of the shouts of joy from the sound of weeping, because the people made so much noise. And the sound was heard far away.

Opposition to the Rebuilding

4 When the enemies of Judah and Benjamin heard that the exiles were building a temple for the LORD, the God of Israel, [2]they came to Zerubbabel and to the heads of the families and said, "Let us help you build because, like you, we seek your God and have been sacrificing to him since the time of Esarhaddon king of Assyria, who brought us here."

[3]But Zerubbabel, Jeshua and the rest of the heads of the families of Israel answered, "You have no part with us in building a temple to our God. We alone will build it for the LORD, the God of Israel, as King Cyrus, the king of Persia, commanded us."

[4]Then the peoples around them set out to discourage the people of Judah and make them afraid to go on building.[a] [5]They hired counselors to work against them and frustrate their plans during the entire reign of Cyrus king of Persia and down to the reign of Darius king of Persia.

Later Opposition Under Xerxes and Artaxerxes

[6]At the beginning of the reign of Xerxes,[b] they lodged an accusation against the people of Judah and Jerusalem.

[7]And in the days of Artaxerxes king of Persia, Bishlam, Mithredath, Tabeel and the rest of his associates wrote a letter to Artaxerxes. The letter was written in Aramaic script and in the Aramaic language.[c, d]

[8]Rehum the commanding officer and Shimshai the secretary wrote a letter against Jerusalem to Artaxerxes the king as follows:

[9]Rehum the commanding officer and Shimshai the secretary, together with the rest of their associates—the judges and officials over the men

from Tripolis, Persia,[e] Erech and Babylon, the Elamites of Susa, [10]and the other people whom the great and honorable Ashurbanipal[f] deported and settled in the city of Samaria and elsewhere in Trans-Euphrates.

[11](This is a copy of the letter they sent him.)

To King Artaxerxes,

From your servants, the men of Trans-Euphrates:

[12]The king should know that the Jews who came up to us from you have gone to Jerusalem and are rebuilding that rebellious and wicked city. They are restoring the walls and repairing the foundations.

[13]Furthermore, the king should know that if this city is built and its walls are restored, no more taxes, tribute or duty will be paid, and the royal revenues will suffer. [14]Now since we are under obligation to the palace and it is not proper for us to see the king dishonored, we are sending this message to inform the king, [15]so that a search may be made in the archives of your predecessors. In these records you will find that this city is a rebellious city, troublesome to kings and provinces, a place of rebellion from ancient times. That is why this city was destroyed. [16]We inform the king that if this city is built and its walls are restored, you will be left with nothing in Trans-Euphrates.

[17]The king sent this reply:

To Rehum the commanding officer, Shimshai the secretary and the rest of their associates living in Samaria and elsewhere in Trans-Euphrates:

Greetings.

[18]The letter you sent us has been read and translated in my presence. [19]I issued an order and a search was made, and it was found that this city has a long history of revolt against kings and has been a place of rebellion and sedition. [20]Jerusalem has had powerful kings ruling over the whole of Trans-Euphrates, and

---

a4 Or and troubled them as they built   b6 Hebrew Ahasuerus, a variant of Xerxes' Persian name
c7 Or written in Aramaic and translated   d7 The text of Ezra 4:8—6:18 is in Aramaic.   e9 Or
officials, magistrates and governors over the men from   f10 Aramaic Osnappar, a variant of Ashurbanipal

taxes, tribute and duty were paid to them. 21Now issue an order to these men to stop work, so that this city will not be rebuilt until I so order. 22Be careful not to neglect this matter. Why let this threat grow, to the detriment of the royal interests?

23As soon as the copy of the letter of King Artaxerxes was read to Rehum and Shimshai the secretary and their associates, they went immediately to the Jews in Jerusalem and compelled them by force to stop.

24Thus the work on the house of God in Jerusalem came to a standstill until the second year of the reign of Darius king of Persia.

Tattenai's Letter to Darius

5 Now Haggai the prophet and Zechariah the prophet, a descendant of Iddo, prophesied to the Jews in Judah and Jerusalem in the name of the God of Israel, who was over them. 2Then Zerubbabel son of Shealtiel and Jeshua son of Jozadak set to work to rebuild the house of God in Jerusalem. And the prophets of God were with them, helping them.

3At that time Tattenai, governor of Trans-Euphrates, and Shethar-Bozenai and their associates went to them and asked, "Who authorized you to rebuild this temple and restore this structure?" 4They also asked, "What are the names of the men constructing this building?"a 5But the eye of their God was watching over the elders of the Jews, and they were not stopped until a report could go to Darius and his written reply be received.

6This is a copy of the letter that Tattenai, governor of Trans-Euphrates, and Shethar-Bozenai and their associates, the officials of Trans-Euphrates, sent to King Darius. 7The report they sent him read as follows:

To King Darius:

Cordial greetings.

8The king should know that we went to the district of Judah, to the temple of the great God. The people are building it with large stones and placing the timbers in the walls. The work is being carried on with dili-

gence and is making rapid progress under their direction.

9We questioned the elders and asked them, "Who authorized you to rebuild this temple and restore this structure?" 10We also asked them their names, so that we could write down the names of their leaders for your information.

11This is the answer they gave us:

"We are the servants of the God of heaven and earth, and we are rebuilding the temple that was built many years ago, one that a great king of Israel built and finished. 12But because our fathers angered the God of heaven, he handed them over to Nebuchadnezzar the Chaldean, king of Babylon, who destroyed this temple and deported the people to Babylon.

13"However, in the first year of Cyrus king of Babylon, King Cyrus issued a decree to rebuild this house of God. 14He even removed from the templeb of Babylon the gold and silver articles of the house of God, which Nebuchadnezzar had taken from the temple in Jerusalem and brought to the templeb in Babylon.

"Then King Cyrus gave them to a man named Sheshbazzar, whom he had appointed governor, 15and he told him, 'Take these articles and go and deposit them in the temple in Jerusalem. And rebuild the house of God on its site.' 16So this Sheshbazzar came and laid the foundations of the house of God in Jerusalem. From that day to the present it has been under construction but is not yet finished."

17Now if it pleases the king, let a search be made in the royal archives of Babylon to see if King Cyrus did in fact issue a decree to rebuild this house of God in Jerusalem. Then let the king send us his decision in this matter.

The Decree of Darius

6 King Darius then issued an order, and they searched in the archives stored in the treasury at Babylon. 2A scroll was found in the citadel of Ecbatana in the

a4 See Septuagint; Aramaic 4We told them the names of the men constructing this building.   b14 Or palace province of Media, and this was written on it:

Memorandum:

[3]In the first year of King Cyrus, the king issued a decree concerning the temple of God in Jerusalem:

Let the temple be rebuilt as a place to present sacrifices, and let its foundations be laid. It is to be ninety feet[a] high and ninety feet wide, [4]with three courses of large stones and one of timbers. The costs are to be paid by the royal treasury. [5]Also, the gold and silver articles of the house of God, which Nebuchadnezzar took from the temple in Jerusalem and brought to Babylon, are to be returned to their places in the temple in Jerusalem; they are to be deposited in the house of God.

[6]Now then, Tattenai, governor of Trans-Euphrates, and Shethar-Bozenai and you, their fellow officials of that province, stay away from there. [7]Do not interfere with the work on this temple of God. Let the governor of the Jews and the Jewish elders rebuild this house of God on its site.

[8]Moreover, I hereby decree what you are to do for these elders of the Jews in the construction of this house of God:
The expenses of these men are to be fully paid out of the royal treasury, from the revenues of Trans-Euphrates, so that the work will not stop. [9]Whatever is needed—young bulls, rams, male lambs for burnt offerings to the God of heaven, and wheat, salt, wine and oil, as requested by the priests in Jerusalem—must be given them daily without fail, [10]so that they may offer sacrifices pleasing to the God of heaven and pray for the well-being of the king and his sons.
[11]Furthermore, I decree that if anyone changes this edict, a beam is to be pulled from his house and he is to be lifted up and impaled on it. And for this crime his house is to be made a pile of rubble. [12]May God, who has caused his Name to dwell there, overthrow any king or people

who lifts a hand to change this decree or to destroy this temple in Jerusalem.

I Darius have decreed it. Let it be carried out with diligence.

Completion and Dedication of the Temple

[13]Then, because of the decree King Darius had sent, Tattenai, governor of Trans-Euphrates, and Shethar-Bozenai and their associates carried it out with diligence. [14]So the elders of the Jews continued to build and prosper under the preaching of Haggai the prophet and Zechariah, a descendant of Iddo. They finished building the temple according to the command of the God of Israel and the decrees of Cyrus, Darius and Artaxerxes, kings of Persia. [15]The temple was completed on the third day of the month Adar, in the sixth year of the reign of King Darius.

[16]Then the people of Israel—the priests, the Levites and the rest of the exiles—celebrated the dedication of the house of God with joy. [17]For the dedication of this house of God they offered a hundred bulls, two hundred rams, four hundred male lambs and, as a sin offering for all Israel, twelve male goats, one for each of the tribes of Israel. [18]And they installed the priests in their divisions and the Levites in their groups for the service of God at Jerusalem, according to what is written in the Book of Moses.

The Passover

[19]On the fourteenth day of the first month, the exiles celebrated the Passover. [20]The priests and Levites had purified themselves and were all ceremonially clean. The Levites slaughtered the Passover lamb for all the exiles, for their brothers the priests and for themselves. [21]So the Israelites who had returned from the exile ate it, together with all who had separated themselves from the unclean practices of their Gentile neighbors in order to seek the LORD, the God of Israel. [22]For seven days they celebrated with joy the Feast of Unleavened Bread, because the LORD had filled them with joy by changing the attitude of the king of Assyria, so that he assisted them in the work on the house of God, the God of Israel.

---

[a]3 Aramaic sixty cubits (about 27 meters)

Ezra Comes to Jerusalem

7 After these things, during the reign of Artaxerxes king of Persia, Ezra son of Seraiah, the son of Azariah, the son of Hilkiah, ²the son of Shallum, the son of Zadok, the son of Ahitub, ³the son of Amariah, the son of Azariah, the son of Meraioth, ⁴the son of Zerahiah, the son of Uzzi, the son of Bukki, ⁵the son of Abishua, the son of Phinehas, the son of Eleazar, the son of Aaron the chief priest— ⁶this Ezra came up from Babylon. He was a teacher well versed in the Law of Moses, which the Lord, the God of Israel, had given. The king had granted him everything he asked, for the hand of the Lord his God was on him. ⁷Some of the Israelites, including priests, Levites, singers, gatekeepers and temple servants, also came up to Jerusalem in the seventh year of King Artaxerxes.

⁸Ezra arrived in Jerusalem in the fifth month of the seventh year of the king. ⁹He had begun his journey from Babylon on the first day of the first month, and he arrived in Jerusalem on the first day of the fifth month, for the gracious hand of his God was on him. ¹⁰For Ezra had devoted himself to the study and observance of the Law of the Lord, and to teaching its decrees and laws in Israel.

King Artaxerxes' Letter to Ezra

¹¹This is a copy of the letter King Artaxerxes had given to Ezra the priest and teacher, a man learned in matters concerning the commands and decrees of the Lord for Israel:

¹²ªArtaxerxes, king of kings,

To Ezra the priest, a teacher of the Law of the God of heaven:

Greetings.

¹³Now I decree that any of the Israelites in my kingdom, including priests and Levites, who wish to go to Jerusalem with you, may go. ¹⁴You are sent by the king and his seven advisers to inquire about Judah and Jerusalem with regard to the Law of your God, which is in your hand. ¹⁵Moreover, you are to take with you the silver and gold that the king and his advisers have freely given to the God of Israel, whose dwelling is in

Jerusalem, ¹⁶together with all the silver and gold you may obtain from the province of Babylon, as well as the freewill offerings of the people and priests for the temple of their God in Jerusalem. ¹⁷With this money be sure to buy bulls, rams and male lambs, together with their grain offerings and drink offerings, and sacrifice them on the altar of the temple of your God in Jerusalem.

¹⁸You and your brother Jews may then do whatever seems best with the rest of the silver and gold, in accordance with the will of your God. ¹⁹Deliver to the God of Jerusalem all the articles entrusted to you for worship in the temple of your God. ²⁰And anything else needed for the temple of your God that you may have occasion to supply, you may provide from the royal treasury.

²¹Now I, King Artaxerxes, order all the treasurers of Trans-Euphrates to provide with diligence whatever Ezra the priest, a teacher of the Law of the God of heaven, may ask of you— ²²up to a hundred talents*b* of silver, a hundred cors*c* of wheat, a hundred baths*d* of wine, a hundred baths*d* of olive oil, and salt without limit. ²³Whatever the God of heaven has prescribed, let it be done with diligence for the temple of the God of heaven. Why should there be wrath against the realm of the king and of his sons? ²⁴You are also to know that you have no authority to impose taxes, tribute or duty on any of the priests, Levites, singers, gatekeepers, temple servants or other workers at this house of God.

²⁵And you, Ezra, in accordance with the wisdom of your God, which you possess, appoint magistrates and judges to administer justice to all the people of Trans-Euphrates—all who know the laws of your God. And you are to teach any who do not know them. ²⁶Whoever does not obey the law of your God and the law of the king must surely be punished by death, banishment, confiscation of property, or imprisonment.

²⁷Praise be to the Lord, the God of our fathers, who has put it into the king's

---

a12 The text of Ezra 7:12-26 is in Aramaic.   *b22* That is, about 3 3/4 tons (about 3.4 metric tons)
c22 That is, probably about 600 bushels (about 22 kiloliters)   *d22* That is, probably about 600 gallons (about 2.2 kiloliters)

heart to bring honor to the house of the LORD in Jerusalem in this way [28]and who has extended his good favor to me before the king and his advisers and all the king's powerful officials. Because the hand of the LORD my God was on me, I took courage and gathered leading men from Israel to go up with me.

List of the Family Heads Returning With Ezra

8 These are the family heads and those registered with them who came up with me from Babylon during the reign of King Artaxerxes:

[2]of the descendants of Phinehas, Gershom;

of the descendants of Ithamar, Daniel;

of the descendants of David, Hattush [3]of the descendants of Shecaniah;

of the descendants of Parosh, Zechariah, and with him were registered 150 men;

[4]of the descendants of Pahath-Moab, Eliehoenai son of Zerahiah, and with him 200 men;

[5]of the descendants of Zattu, [a] Shecaniah son of Jahaziel, and with him 300 men;

[6]of the descendants of Adin, Ebed son of Jonathan, and with him 50 men;

[7]of the descendants of Elam, Jeshaiah son of Athaliah, and with him 70 men;

[8]of the descendants of Shephatiah, Zebadiah son of Michael, and with him 80 men;

[9]of the descendants of Joab, Obadiah son of Jehiel, and with him 218 men;

[10]of the descendants of Bani, [b] Shelomith son of Josiphiah, and with him 160 men;

[11]of the descendants of Bebai, Zechariah son of Bebai, and with him 28 men;

[12]of the descendants of Azgad, Johanan son of Hakkatan, and with him 110 men;

[13]of the descendants of Adonikam, the last ones, whose names were Eliphelet, Jeuel and Shemaiah, and with them 60 men;

[14]of the descendants of Bigvai, Uthai and Zaccur, and with them 70 men.

The Return to Jerusalem

[15]I assembled them at the canal that flows toward Ahava, and we camped there three days. When I checked among the people and the priests, I found no Levites there. [16]So I summoned Eliezer, Ariel, Shemaiah, Elnathan, Jarib, Elnathan, Nathan, Zechariah and Meshullam, who were leaders, and Joiarib and Elnathan, who were men of learning, [17]and I sent them to Iddo, the leader in Casiphia. I told them what to say to Iddo and his kinsmen, the temple servants in Casiphia, so that they might bring attendants to us for the house of our God. [18]Because the gracious hand of our God was on us, they brought us Sherebiah, a capable man, from the descendants of Mahli son of Levi, the son of Israel, and Sherebiah's sons and brothers, 18 men; [19]and Hashabiah, together with Jeshaiah from the descendants of Merari, and his brothers and nephews, 20 men. [20]They also brought 220 of the temple servants — a body that David and the officials had established to assist the Levites. All were registered by name.

[21]There, by the Ahava Canal, I proclaimed a fast, so that we might humble ourselves before our God and ask him for a safe journey for us and our children, with all our possessions. [22]I was ashamed to ask the king for soldiers and horsemen to protect us from enemies on the road, because we had told the king, "The gracious hand of our God is on everyone who looks to him, but his great anger is against all who forsake him." [23]So we fasted and petitioned our God about this, and he answered our prayer.

[24]Then I set apart twelve of the leading priests, together with Sherebiah, Hashabiah and ten of their brothers, [25]and I weighed out to them the offering of silver and gold and the articles that the king, his advisers, his officials and all Israel present there had donated for the house of our God. [26]I weighed out to them 650 talents[c] of silver, silver articles weighing 100 talents,[d] 100 talents[d] of gold, [27]20

---

[a]5 Some Septuagint manuscripts (also 1 Esdras 8:32); Hebrew does not have Zattu.   [b]10 Some Septuagint manuscripts (also 1 Esdras 8:36); Hebrew does not have Bani.   [c]26 That is, about 25 tons (about 22 metric tons)   [d]26 That is, about 3 3/4 tons (about 3.4 metric tons)

bowls of gold valued at 1,000 darics,[a] and two fine articles of polished bronze, as precious as gold.

28I said to them, "You as well as these articles are consecrated to the LORD. The silver and gold are a freewill offering to the LORD, the God of your fathers. 29Guard them carefully until you weigh them out in the chambers of the house of the LORD in Jerusalem before the leading priests and the Levites and the family heads of Israel." 30Then the priests and Levites received the silver and gold and sacred articles that had been weighed out to be taken to the house of our God in Jerusalem.

31On the twelfth day of the first month we set out from the Ahava Canal to go to Jerusalem. The hand of our God was on us, and he protected us from enemies and bandits along the way. 32So we arrived in Jerusalem, where we rested three days.

33On the fourth day, in the house of our God, we weighed out the silver and gold and the sacred articles into the hands of Meremoth son of Uriah, the priest. Eleazar son of Phinehas was with him, and so were the Levites Jozabad son of Jeshua and Noadiah son of Binnui. 34Everything was accounted for by number and weight, and the entire weight was recorded at that time.

35Then the exiles who had returned from captivity sacrificed burnt offerings to the God of Israel: twelve bulls for all Israel, ninety-six rams, seventy-seven male lambs and, as a sin offering, twelve male goats. All this was a burnt offering to the LORD. 36They also delivered the king's orders to the royal satraps and to the governors of Trans-Euphrates, who then gave assistance to the people and to the house of God.

Ezra's Prayer About Intermarriage

9 After these things had been done, the leaders came to me and said, "The people of Israel, including the priests and the Levites, have not kept themselves separate from the neighboring peoples with their detestable practices, like those of the Canaanites, Hittites, Perizzites, Jebusites, Ammonites, Moabites, Egyptians and Amorites. 2They have taken some of their daughters as wives for themselves and their sons, and have mingled the holy race with the peoples around them. And the leaders and officials have led the way in this unfaithfulness."

3When I heard this, I tore my tunic and cloak, pulled hair from my head and beard and sat down appalled. 4Then everyone who trembled at the words of the God of Israel gathered around me because of this unfaithfulness of the exiles. And I sat there appalled until the evening sacrifice.

5Then, at the evening sacrifice, I rose from my self-abasement, with my tunic and cloak torn, and fell on my knees with my hands spread out to the LORD my God 6and prayed:

"O my God, I am too ashamed and disgraced to lift up my face to you, my God, because our sins are higher than our heads and our guilt has reached to the heavens. 7From the days of our forefathers until now, our guilt has been great. Because of our sins, we and our kings and our priests have been subjected to the sword and captivity, to pillage and humiliation at the hand of foreign kings, as it is today.

8"But now, for a brief moment, the LORD our God has been gracious in leaving us a remnant and giving us a firm place in his sanctuary, and so our God gives light to our eyes and a little relief in our bondage. 9Though we are slaves, our God has not deserted us in our bondage. He has shown us kindness in the sight of the kings of Persia: He has granted us new life to rebuild the house of our God and repair its ruins, and he has given us a wall of protection in Judah and Jerusalem.

10"But now, O our God, what can we say after this? For we have disregarded the commands 11you gave through your servants the prophets when you said: 'The land you are entering to possess is a land polluted by the corruption of its peoples. By their detestable practices they have filled it with their impurity from one end to the other. 12Therefore, do not give your daughters in marriage to their sons or take their daughters for your sons. Do not seek a treaty of friendship with them at any time, that you may be strong and eat the good things of the land and leave it

---

a27 That is, about 19 pounds (about 8.5 kilograms)

to your children as an everlasting inheritance.'

13"What has happened to us is a result of our evil deeds and our great guilt, and yet, our God, you have punished us less than our sins have deserved and have given us a remnant like this. 14Shall we again break your commands and intermarry with the peoples who commit such detestable practices? Would you not be angry enough with us to destroy us, leaving us no remnant or survivor? 15O LORD, God of Israel, you are righteous! We are left this day as a remnant. Here we are before you in our guilt, though because of it not one of us can stand in your presence."

The People's Confession of Sin

10 While Ezra was praying and confessing, weeping and throwing himself down before the house of God, a large crowd of Israelites—men, women and children—gathered around him. They too wept bitterly. 2Then Shecaniah son of Jehiel, one of the descendants of Elam, said to Ezra, "We have been unfaithful to our God by marrying foreign women from the peoples around us. But in spite of this, there is still hope for Israel. 3Now let us make a covenant before our God to send away all these women and their children, in accordance with the counsel of my lord and of those who fear the commands of our God. Let it be done according to the Law. 4Rise up; this matter is in your hands. We will support you, so take courage and do it."

5So Ezra rose up and put the leading priests and Levites and all Israel under oath to do what had been suggested. And they took the oath. 6Then Ezra withdrew from before the house of God and went to the room of Jehohanan son of Eliashib. While he was there, he ate no food and drank no water, because he continued to mourn over the unfaithfulness of the exiles.

7A proclamation was then issued throughout Judah and Jerusalem for all the exiles to assemble in Jerusalem. 8Anyone who failed to appear within three days would forfeit all his property, in accordance with the decision of the officials and elders, and would himself be expelled from the assembly of the exiles.

9Within the three days, all the men of Judah and Benjamin had gathered in Jerusalem. And on the twentieth day of the ninth month, all the people were sitting in the square before the house of God, greatly distressed by the occasion and because of the rain. 10Then Ezra the priest stood up and said to them, "You have been unfaithful; you have married foreign women, adding to Israel's guilt. 11Now make confession to the LORD, the God of your fathers, and do his will. Separate yourselves from the peoples around you and from your foreign wives."

12The whole assembly responded with a loud voice: "You are right! We must do as you say. 13But there are many people here and it is the rainy season; so we cannot stand outside. Besides, this matter cannot be taken care of in a day or two, because we have sinned greatly in this thing. 14Let our officials act for the whole assembly. Then let everyone in our towns who has married a foreign woman come at a set time, along with the elders and judges of each town, until the fierce anger of our God in this matter is turned away from us." 15Only Jonathan son of Asahel and Jahzeiah son of Tikvah, supported by Meshullam and Shabbethai the Levite, opposed this.

16So the exiles did as was proposed. Ezra the priest selected men who were family heads, one from each family division, and all of them designated by name. On the first day of the tenth month they sat down to investigate the cases, 17and by the first day of the first month they finished dealing with all the men who had married foreign women.

Those Guilty of Intermarriage

18Among the descendants of the priests, the following had married foreign women:

From the descendants of Jeshua son of Jozadak, and his brothers: Maaseiah, Eliezer, Jarib and Gedaliah. 19(They all gave their hands in pledge to put away their wives, and for their guilt they each presented a ram from the flock as a guilt offering.)

20From the descendants of Immer: Hanani and Zebadiah.

21From the descendants of Harim: Maaseiah, Elijah, Shemaiah, Jehiel and Uzziah.

22From the descendants of Pashhur: Elioenai, Maaseiah, Ishmael, Nethanel, Jozabad and Elasah.

23Among the Levites:

Jozabad, Shimei, Kelaiah (that is, Kelita), Pethahiah, Judah and Eliezer.

24From the singers:
Eliashib.

From the gatekeepers:
Shallum, Telem and Uri.

25And among the other Israelites:

From the descendants of Parosh:
Ramiah, Izziah, Malkijah, Mijamin, Eleazar, Malkijah and Benaiah.

26From the descendants of Elam:
Mattaniah, Zechariah, Jehiel, Abdi, Jeremoth and Elijah.

27From the descendants of Zattu:
Elioenai, Eliashib, Mattaniah, Jeremoth, Zabad and Aziza.

28From the descendants of Bebai:
Jehohanan, Hananiah, Zabbai and Athlai.

29From the descendants of Bani:
Meshullam, Malluch, Adaiah, Jashub, Sheal and Jeremoth.

30From the descendants of Pahath-Moab:

Adna, Kelal, Benaiah, Maaseiah, Mattaniah, Bezalel, Binnui and Manasseh.

31From the descendants of Harim:
Eliezer, Ishijah, Malkijah, Shemaiah, Shimeon, 32Benjamin, Malluch and Shemariah.

33From the descendants of Hashum:
Mattenai, Mattattah, Zabad, Eliphelet, Jeremai, Manasseh and Shimei.

34From the descendants of Bani:
Maadai, Amram, Uel, 35Benaiah, Bedeiah, Keluhi, 36Vaniah, Meremoth, Eliashib, 37Mattaniah, Mattenai and Jaasu.

38From the descendants of Binnui:a
Shimei, 39Shelemiah, Nathan, Adaiah, 40Macnadebai, Shashai, Sharai, 41Azarel, Shelemiah, Shemariah, 42Shallum, Amariah and Joseph.

43From the descendants of Nebo:
Jeiel, Mattithiah, Zabad, Zebina, Jaddai, Joel and Benaiah.

44All these had married foreign women, and some of them had children by these wives.b

---

a37,38 See Septuagint (also 1 Esdras 9:34); Hebrew *Jaasu* 38*and Bani and Binnui,*   b44 Or *and they sent them away with their children*

*T*HE book of Nehemiah recounts Nehemiah's time as governor of Canaan when God's people were returning from Babylon. He rebuilds the walls of Jerusalem, along with Ezra he leads God's people in worship, and he administers their affairs. Important to his daily work is prayer, through which he expresses his dependence on God. As you read this book, ask yourself how God wants you to serve his people; be sure that everything you do is accompanied by prayer.

NEHEMIAH

Nehemiah's Prayer

1 The words of Nehemiah son of Hacaliah:

In the month of Kislev in the twentieth year, while I was in the citadel of Susa, ²Hanani, one of my brothers, came from Judah with some other men, and I questioned them about the Jewish remnant that survived the exile, and also about Jerusalem.

³They said to me, "Those who survived the exile and are back in the province are in great trouble and disgrace. The wall of Jerusalem is broken down, and its gates have been burned with fire."

⁴When I heard these things, I sat down and wept. For some days I mourned and fasted and prayed before the God of heaven. ⁵Then I said:

"O LORD, God of heaven, the great and awesome God, who keeps his covenant of love with those who love him and obey his commands, ⁶let your ear be attentive and your eyes open to hear the prayer your servant is praying before you day and night for your servants, the people of Israel. I confess the sins we Israelites, including myself and my father's house, have committed against you.

7We have acted very wickedly toward you. We have not obeyed the commands, decrees and laws you gave your servant Moses.

8"Remember the instruction you gave your servant Moses, saying, 'If you are unfaithful, I will scatter you among the nations, 9but if you return to me and obey my commands, then even if your exiled people are at the farthest horizon, I will gather them from there and bring them to the place I have chosen as a dwelling for my Name.'

10"They are your servants and your people, whom you redeemed by your great strength and your mighty hand. 11O Lord, let your ear be attentive to the prayer of this your servant and to the prayer of your servants who delight in revering your name. Give your servant success today by granting him favor in the presence of this man."

I was cupbearer to the king.

Artaxerxes Sends Nehemiah to Jerusalem

2 In the month of Nisan in the twentieth year of King Artaxerxes, when wine was brought for him, I took the wine and gave it to the king. I had not been sad in his presence before; 2so the king asked me, "Why does your face look so sad when you are not ill? This can be nothing but sadness of heart."

I was very much afraid, 3but I said to the king, "May the king live forever! Why should my face not look sad when the city where my fathers are buried lies in ruins, and its gates have been destroyed by fire?"

4The king said to me, "What is it you want?"

Then I prayed to the God of heaven, 5and I answered the king, "If it pleases the king and if your servant has found favor in his sight, let him send me to the city in Judah where my fathers are buried so that I can rebuild it."

6Then the king, with the queen sitting beside him, asked me, "How long will your journey take, and when will you get back?" It pleased the king to send me; so I set a time.

7I also said to him, "If it pleases the king, may I have letters to the governors of Trans-Euphrates, so that they will provide me safe-conduct until I arrive in Judah? 8And may I have a letter to Asaph, keeper of the king's forest, so he will give me timber to make beams for the gates of the citadel by the temple and for the city wall and for the residence I will occupy?" And because the gracious hand of my God was upon me, the king granted my requests. 9So I went to the governors of Trans-Euphrates and gave them the king's letters. The king had also sent army officers and cavalry with me.

10When Sanballat the Horonite and Tobiah the Ammonite official heard about this, they were very much disturbed that someone had come to promote the welfare of the Israelites.

Nehemiah Inspects Jerusalem's Walls

11I went to Jerusalem, and after staying there three days 12I set out during the night with a few men. I had not told anyone what my God had put in my heart to do for Jerusalem. There were no mounts with me except the one I was riding on. 13By night I went out through the Valley Gate toward the Jackala Well and the Dung Gate, examining the walls of Jerusalem, which had been broken down, and its gates, which had been destroyed by fire. 14Then I moved on toward the Fountain Gate and the King's Pool, but there was not enough room for my mount to get through; 15so I went up the valley by night, examining the wall. Finally, I turned back and reentered through the Valley Gate. 16The officials did not know where I had gone or what I was doing, because as yet I had said nothing to the Jews or the priests or nobles or officials or any others who would be doing the work. 17Then I said to them, "You see the trouble we are in: Jerusalem lies in ruins, and its gates have been burned with fire. Come, let us rebuild the wall of Jerusalem, and we will no longer be in disgrace." 18I also told them about the gracious hand of my God upon me and what the king had said to me.

They replied, "Let us start rebuilding." So they began this good work.

19But when Sanballat the Horonite, Tobiah the Ammonite official and Geshem the Arab heard about it, they mocked and ridiculed us. "What is this you are do-

a13 Or Serpent or Fig

ing?" they asked. "Are you rebelling against the king?"

20I answered them by saying, "The God of heaven will give us success. We his servants will start rebuilding, but as for you, you have no share in Jerusalem or any claim or historic right to it."

Builders of the Wall

3 Eliashib the high priest and his fellow priests went to work and rebuilt the Sheep Gate. They dedicated it and set its doors in place, building as far as the Tower of the Hundred, which they dedicated, and as far as the Tower of Hananel. 2The men of Jericho built the adjoining section, and Zaccur son of Imri built next to them.

3The Fish Gate was rebuilt by the sons of Hassenaah. They laid its beams and put its doors and bolts and bars in place. 4Meremoth son of Uriah, the son of Hakkoz, repaired the next section. Next to him Meshullam son of Berekiah, the son of Meshezabel, made repairs, and next to him Zadok son of Baana also made repairs. 5The next section was repaired by the men of Tekoa, but their nobles would not put their shoulders to the work under their supervisors.a

6The Jeshanahb Gate was repaired by Joiada son of Paseah and Meshullam son of Besodeiah. They laid its beams and put its doors and bolts and bars in place. 7Next to them, repairs were made by men from Gibeon and Mizpah—Melatiah of Gibeon and Jadon of Meronoth—places under the authority of the governor of Trans-Euphrates. 8Uzziel son of Harhaiah, one of the goldsmiths, repaired the next section; and Hananiah, one of the perfume-makers, made repairs next to that. They restoredc Jerusalem as far as the Broad Wall. 9Rephaiah son of Hur, ruler of a half-district of Jerusalem, repaired the next section. 10Adjoining this, Jedaiah son of Harumaph made repairs opposite his house, and Hattush son of Hashabneiah made repairs next to him. 11Malkijah son of Harim and Hasshub son of Pahath-Moab repaired another section and the Tower of the Ovens. 12Shallum son of Hallohesh, ruler of a half-district of

Jerusalem, repaired the next section with the help of his daughters.

13The Valley Gate was repaired by Hanun and the residents of Zanoah. They rebuilt it and put its doors and bolts and bars in place. They also repaired five hundred yardsd of the wall as far as the Dung Gate.

14The Dung Gate was repaired by Malkijah son of Recab, ruler of the district of Beth Hakkerem. He rebuilt it and put its doors and bolts and bars in place.

15The Fountain Gate was repaired by Shallun son of Col-Hozeh, ruler of the district of Mizpah. He rebuilt it, roofing it over and putting its doors and bolts and bars in place. He also repaired the wall of the Pool of Siloam,e by the King's Garden, as far as the steps going down from the City of David. 16Beyond him, Nehemiah son of Azbuk, ruler of a half-district of Beth Zur, made repairs up to a point opposite the tombsf of David, as far as the artificial pool and the House of the Heroes.

17Next to him, the repairs were made by the Levites under Rehum son of Bani. Beside him, Hashabiah, ruler of half the district of Keilah, carried out repairs for his district. 18Next to him, the repairs were made by their countrymen under Binnuig son of Henadad, ruler of the other half-district of Keilah. 19Next to him, Ezer son of Jeshua, ruler of Mizpah, repaired another section, from a point facing the ascent to the armory as far as the angle. 20Next to him, Baruch son of Zabbai zealously repaired another section, from the angle to the entrance of the house of Eliashib the high priest. 21Next to him, Meremoth son of Uriah, the son of Hakkoz, repaired another section, from the entrance of Eliashib's house to the end of it.

22The repairs next to him were made by the priests from the surrounding region. 23Beyond them, Benjamin and Hasshub made repairs in front of their house; and next to them, Azariah son of Maaseiah, the son of Ananiah, made repairs beside his house. 24Next to him, Binnui son of Henadad repaired another section, from Azariah's house to the angle and the corner, 25and Palal son of Uzai worked oppo-

a5 Or their Lord or the governor   b6 Or Old   c8 Or They left out part of   d13 Hebrew a thousand cubits (about 450 meters)   e15 Hebrew Shelah, a variant of Shiloah, that is, Siloam   f16 Hebrew; Septuagint, some Vulgate manuscripts and Syriac tomb   g18 Two Hebrew manuscripts and Syriac (see also Septuagint and verse 24); most Hebrew manuscripts Bavvai site the angle and the tower projecting from the upper palace near the court of the guard. Next to him, Pedaiah son of Parosh 26and the temple servants living on the hill of Ophel made repairs up to a point opposite the Water Gate toward the east and the projecting tower. 27Next to them, the men of Tekoa repaired another section, from the great projecting tower to the wall of Ophel.

28Above the Horse Gate, the priests made repairs, each in front of his own house. 29Next to them, Zadok son of Immer made repairs opposite his house. Next to him, Shemaiah son of Shecaniah, the guard at the East Gate, made repairs. 30Next to him, Hananiah son of Shelemiah, and Hanun, the sixth son of Zalaph, repaired another section. Next to them, Meshullam son of Berekiah made repairs opposite his living quarters. 31Next to him, Malkijah, one of the goldsmiths, made repairs as far as the house of the temple servants and the merchants, opposite the Inspection Gate, and as far as the room above the corner; 32and between the room above the corner and the Sheep Gate the goldsmiths and merchants made repairs.

Opposition to the Rebuilding

4 When Sanballat heard that we were rebuilding the wall, he became angry and was greatly incensed. He ridiculed the Jews, 2and in the presence of his associates and the army of Samaria, he said, "What are those feeble Jews doing? Will they restore their wall? Will they offer sacrifices? Will they finish in a day? Can they bring the stones back to life from those heaps of rubble—burned as they are?"

3Tobiah the Ammonite, who was at his side, said, "What they are building—if even a fox climbed up on it, he would break down their wall of stones!"

4Hear us, O our God, for we are despised. Turn their insults back on their own heads. Give them over as plunder in a land of captivity. 5Do not cover up their guilt or blot out their sins from your sight, for they have thrown insults in the face of[a] the builders.

6So we rebuilt the wall till all of it reached half its height, for the people worked with all their heart.

7But when Sanballat, Tobiah, the Arabs, the Ammonites and the men of Ashdod heard that the repairs to Jerusalem's walls had gone ahead and that the gaps were being closed, they were very angry. 8They all plotted together to come and fight against Jerusalem and stir up trouble against it. 9But we prayed to our God and posted a guard day and night to meet this threat.

10Meanwhile, the people in Judah said, "The strength of the laborers is giving out, and there is so much rubble that we cannot rebuild the wall."

11Also our enemies said, "Before they know it or see us, we will be right there among them and will kill them and put an end to the work."

12Then the Jews who lived near them came and told us ten times over, "Wherever you turn, they will attack us."

13Therefore I stationed some of the people behind the lowest points of the wall at the exposed places, posting them by families, with their swords, spears and bows. 14After I looked things over, I stood up and said to the nobles, the officials and the rest of the people, "Don't be afraid of them. Remember the Lord, who is great and awesome, and fight for your brothers, your sons and your daughters, your wives and your homes."

15When our enemies heard that we were aware of their plot and that God had frustrated it, we all returned to the wall, each to his own work.

16From that day on, half of my men did the work, while the other half were equipped with spears, shields, bows and armor. The officers posted themselves behind all the people of Judah 17who were building the wall. Those who carried materials did their work with one hand and held a weapon in the other, 18and each of the builders wore his sword at his side as he worked. But the man who sounded the trumpet stayed with me.

19Then I said to the nobles, the officials and the rest of the people, "The work is extensive and spread out, and we are widely separated from each other along the wall. 20Wherever you hear the sound of the trumpet, join us there. Our God will fight for us!"

21So we continued the work with half the men holding spears, from the first light of dawn till the stars came out. 22At that time I also said to the people, "Have every man and his helper stay inside Jerusalem at night, so they can serve us as guards by night and workmen by day." [23]Neither I nor my brothers nor my men nor the guards with me took off our clothes; each had his weapon, even when he went for water.[a]

Nehemiah Helps the Poor

5 Now the men and their wives raised a great outcry against their Jewish brothers. [2]Some were saying, "We and our sons and daughters are numerous; in order for us to eat and stay alive, we must get grain."

[3]Others were saying, "We are mortgaging our fields, our vineyards and our homes to get grain during the famine."

[4]Still others were saying, "We have had to borrow money to pay the king's tax on our fields and vineyards. [5]Although we are of the same flesh and blood as our countrymen and though our sons are as good as theirs, yet we have to subject our sons and daughters to slavery. Some of our daughters have already been enslaved, but we are powerless, because our fields and our vineyards belong to others."

[6]When I heard their outcry and these charges, I was very angry. [7]I pondered them in my mind and then accused the nobles and officials. I told them, "You are exacting usury from your own countrymen!" So I called together a large meeting to deal with them [8]and said: "As far as possible, we have bought back our Jewish brothers who were sold to the Gentiles. Now you are selling your brothers, only for them to be sold back to us!" They kept quiet, because they could find nothing to say.

[9]So I continued, "What you are doing is not right. Shouldn't you walk in the fear of our God to avoid the reproach of our Gentile enemies? [10]I and my brothers and my men are also lending the people money and grain. But let the exacting of usury stop! [11]Give back to them immediately their fields, vineyards, olive groves and houses, and also the usury you are charging them—the hundredth part of the money, grain, new wine and oil."

[12]"We will give it back," they said. "And we will not demand anything more from them. We will do as you say."

Then I summoned the priests and made the nobles and officials take an oath to do what they had promised. [13]I also shook out the folds of my robe and said, "In this way may God shake out of his house and possessions every man who does not keep this promise. So may such a man be shaken out and emptied!"

At this the whole assembly said, "Amen," and praised the LORD. And the people did as they had promised.

[14]Moreover, from the twentieth year of King Artaxerxes, when I was appointed to be their governor in the land of Judah, until his thirty-second year—twelve years —neither I nor my brothers ate the food allotted to the governor. [15]But the earlier governors—those preceding me—placed a heavy burden on the people and took forty shekels[b] of silver from them in addition to food and wine. Their assistants also lorded it over the people. But out of reverence for God I did not act like that. [16]Instead, I devoted myself to the work on this wall. All my men were assembled there for the work; we[c] did not acquire any land.

[17]Furthermore, a hundred and fifty Jews and officials ate at my table, as well as those who came to us from the surrounding nations. [18]Each day one ox, six choice sheep and some poultry were prepared for me, and every ten days an abundant supply of wine of all kinds. In spite of all this, I never demanded the food allotted to the governor, because the demands were heavy on these people.

[19]Remember me with favor, O my God, for all I have done for these people.

Further Opposition to the Rebuilding

6 When word came to Sanballat, Tobiah, Geshem the Arab and the rest of our enemies that I had rebuilt the wall and not a gap was left in it—though up to that time I had not set the doors in the gates— [2]Sanballat and Geshem sent me this message: "Come, let us meet together in one of the villages[d] on the plain of Ono."

But they were scheming to harm me; [3]so I sent messengers to them with this reply: "I am carrying on a great project and cannot go down. Why should the work stop while I leave it and go down to you?" [4]Four times they sent me the same

---

[a]23 The meaning of the Hebrew for this clause is uncertain.   [b]15 That is, about 1 pound (about 0.5 kilogram)   [c]16 Most Hebrew manuscripts; some Hebrew manuscripts, Septuagint, Vulgate and Syriac I   [d]2 Or in Kephirim

message, and each time I gave them the same answer.

⁵Then, the fifth time, Sanballat sent his aide to me with the same message, and in his hand was an unsealed letter ⁶in which was written:

"It is reported among the nations —and Geshem*ᵃ* says it is true—that you and the Jews are plotting to revolt, and therefore you are building the wall. Moreover, according to these reports you are about to become their king ⁷and have even appointed prophets to make this proclamation about you in Jerusalem: 'There is a king in Judah!' Now this report will get back to the king; so come, let us confer together."

⁸I sent him this reply: "Nothing like what you are saying is happening; you are just making it up out of your head."

⁹They were all trying to frighten us, thinking, "Their hands will get too weak for the work, and it will not be completed."

But I prayed, "Now strengthen my hands."

¹⁰One day I went to the house of Shemaiah son of Delaiah, the son of Mehetabel, who was shut in at his home. He said, "Let us meet in the house of God, inside the temple, and let us close the temple doors, because men are coming to kill you—by night they are coming to kill you."

¹¹But I said, "Should a man like me run away? Or should one like me go into the temple to save his life? I will not go!" ¹²I realized that God had not sent him, but that he had prophesied against me because Tobiah and Sanballat had hired him. ¹³He had been hired to intimidate me so that I would commit a sin by doing this, and then they would give me a bad name to discredit me.

¹⁴Remember Tobiah and Sanballat, O my God, because of what they have done; remember also the prophetess Noadiah and the rest of the prophets who have been trying to intimidate me.

The Completion of the Wall

¹⁵So the wall was completed on the twenty-fifth of Elul, in fifty-two days. ¹⁶When all our enemies heard about this, all the surrounding nations were afraid and lost their self-confidence, because they realized that this work had been done with the help of our God.

¹⁷Also, in those days the nobles of Judah were sending many letters to Tobiah, and replies from Tobiah kept coming to them. ¹⁸For many in Judah were under oath to him, since he was son-in-law to Shecaniah son of Arah, and his son Jehohanan had married the daughter of Meshullam son of Berekiah. ¹⁹Moreover, they kept reporting to me his good deeds and then telling him what I said. And Tobiah sent letters to intimidate me.

7 After the wall had been rebuilt and I had set the doors in place, the gatekeepers and the singers and the Levites were appointed. ²I put in charge of Jerusalem my brother Hanani, along with*ᵇ* Hananiah the commander of the citadel, because he was a man of integrity and feared God more than most men do. ³I said to them, "The gates of Jerusalem are not to be opened until the sun is hot. While the gatekeepers are still on duty, have them shut the doors and bar them. Also appoint residents of Jerusalem as guards, some at their posts and some near their own houses."

The List of the Exiles Who Returned

⁴Now the city was large and spacious, but there were few people in it, and the houses had not yet been rebuilt. ⁵So my God put it into my heart to assemble the nobles, the officials and the common people for registration by families. I found the genealogical record of those who had been the first to return. This is what I found written there:

⁶These are the people of the province who came up from the captivity of the exiles whom Nebuchadnezzar king of Babylon had taken captive (they returned to Jerusalem and Judah, each to his own town, ⁷in company with Zerubbabel, Jeshua, Nehemiah, Azariah, Raamiah, Nahamani, Mordecai, Bilshan, Mispereth, Bigvai, Nehum and Baanah):

The list of the men of Israel:

⁸the descendants of Parosh	2,172
⁹of Shephatiah	372
¹⁰of Arah	652
¹¹of Pahath-Moab (through the line of Jeshua and Joab)	2,818

ᵃ6 Hebrew *Gashmu,* a variant of *Geshem*   *ᵇ2* Or *Hanani, that is,*

[12]of Elam   1,254
[13]of Zattu   845
[14]of Zaccai   760
[15]of Binnui   648
[16]of Bebai   628
[17]of Azgad   2,322
[18]of Adonikam   667
[19]of Bigvai   2,067
[20]of Adin   655
[21]of Ater (through Hezekiah)   98
[22]of Hashum   328
[23]of Bezai   324
[24]of Hariph   112
[25]of Gibeon   95

[26]the men of Bethlehem and
    Netophah   188
[27]of Anathoth   128
[28]of Beth Azmaveth   42
[29]of Kiriath Jearim, Kephirah
    and Beeroth   743
[30]of Ramah and Geba   621
[31]of Micmash   122
[32]of Bethel and Ai   123
[33]of the other Nebo   52
[34]of the other Elam   1,254
[35]of Harim   320
[36]of Jericho   345
[37]of Lod, Hadid and Ono   721
[38]of Senaah   3,930

[39]The priests:

the descendants of Jedaiah
    (through the family of Jeshua)
                                                 973
[40]of Immer   1,052
[41]of Pashhur   1,247
[42]of Harim   1,017

[43]The Levites:

the descendants of Jeshua
    (through Kadmiel through
    the line of Hodaviah)   74

[44]The singers:

the descendants of Asaph   148

[45]The gatekeepers:

the descendants of
    Shallum, Ater, Talmon,
    Akkub, Hatita and Shobai   138

[46]The temple servants:

the descendants of
    Ziha, Hasupha, Tabbaoth,
[47]Keros, Sia, Padon,
[48]Lebana, Hagaba, Shalmai,

[49]Hanan, Giddel, Gahar,
[50]Reaiah, Rezin, Nekoda,
[51]Gazzam, Uzza, Paseah,
[52]Besai, Meunim, Nephussim,
[53]Bakbuk, Hakupha, Harhur,
[54]Bazluth, Mehida, Harsha,
[55]Barkos, Sisera, Temah,
[56]Neziah and Hatipha

[57]The descendants of the servants of
Solomon:

the descendants of
    Sotai, Sophereth, Perida,
[58]Jaala, Darkon, Giddel,
[59]Shephatiah, Hattil,
    Pokereth-Hazzebaim and Amon

[60]The temple servants and the
    descendants of the servants
    of Solomon   392

[61]The following came up from the
towns of Tel Melah, Tel Harsha, Ke-
rub, Addon and Immer, but they
could not show that their families
were descended from Israel:

[62]the descendants of
    Delaiah, Tobiah and
    Nekoda   642

[63]And from among the priests:

the descendants of
    Hobaiah, Hakkoz and Barzillai
    (a man who had married a
    daughter of Barzillai the
    Gileadite and was called by that
    name).
[64]These searched for their family
records, but they could not find them
and so were excluded from the
priesthood as unclean. [65]The governor, therefore, ordered them not to
eat any of the most sacred food until
there should be a priest ministering
with the Urim and Thummim.

[66]The whole company numbered
42,360, [67]besides their 7,337 menservants and maidservants; and they
also had 245 men and women singers. [68]There were 736 horses, 245
mules,[a] [69]435 camels and 6,720
donkeys.

[70]Some of the heads of the families
contributed to the work. The governor gave to the treasury 1,000 drachmas[b] of gold, 50 bowls and 530 gar-

---

[a]68 Some Hebrew manuscripts (see also Ezra 2:66); most Hebrew manuscripts do not have this verse.
[b]70 That is, about 19 pounds (about 8.5 kilograms)

ments for priests. ⁷¹Some of the heads of the families gave to the treasury for the work 20,000 drachmas*a* of gold and 2,200 minas*b* of silver. ⁷²The total given by the rest of the people was 20,000 drachmas of gold, 2,000 minas*c* of silver and 67 garments for priests.

⁷³The priests, the Levites, the gatekeepers, the singers and the temple servants, along with certain of the people and the rest of the Israelites, settled in their own towns.

Ezra Reads the Law

When the seventh month came and the

---

a71 That is, about 375 pounds (about 170 kilograms); also in verse 72   *b71* That is, about 1 1/3 tons (about 1.2 metric tons)   *c72* That is, about 1 1/4 tons (about 1.1 metric tons)

FRIDAY

| VERSE FOR THE DAY: | AUTHOR: | PASSAGE FOR THE DAY: |
| Nehemiah 8:9–10 | Marjorie Holmes | Nehemiah 8:1–10 |

For Tears and Laughter

I AM grateful, God, for tears. For the ability to cry.

How marvelously you made us that we are equipped with this way to express our emotions.

Quick tears to relieve the sudden hurt. Or for the times when we are touched, too moved to speak.

Or when deeper sorrows come, that we have this fierce and wonderful cleansing. This release that helps to wash away the very grief our crying demonstrates.

How you must love us that you thus provided for us. No other being has it, no insect, bird or beast. Only man and woman made in your likeness.

We are the only creatures who can cry.

Jesus wept, as we weep. Our very tears are testimony to your fatherhood. We too are your sons and daughters.

Thank you for this proof, and for this healing outlet, the ability to cry.

And thank you, Lord, for laughter.

And for all the people who can bring it about, make us see the funny side of things.

The world is so full of anguish; life itself sometimes seems so grim. Thank you that in your vast understanding you gave us laughter to make us forget, to restore our wounded spirits, brighten the journey, lighten the load.

Just as you saved tears for human beings, you blessed us alone with laughter.

And surely this too is a clue to your very nature. A nature akin to our own.

Thank you for this blessing, Lord. This shining gift of laughter.

Additional Scripture Readings:
Psalm 126:1–6; John 20:10–18

Go to page 501 for your next devotional reading.

8 Israelites had settled in their towns, [1]all the people assembled as one man in the square before the Water Gate. They told Ezra the scribe to bring out the Book of the Law of Moses, which the LORD had commanded for Israel.

[2]So on the first day of the seventh month Ezra the priest brought the Law before the assembly, which was made up of men and women and all who were able to understand. [3]He read it aloud from daybreak till noon as he faced the square before the Water Gate in the presence of the men, women and others who could understand. And all the people listened attentively to the Book of the Law.

[4]Ezra the scribe stood on a high wooden platform built for the occasion. Beside him on his right stood Mattithiah, Shema, Anaiah, Uriah, Hilkiah and Maaseiah; and on his left were Pedaiah, Mishael, Malkijah, Hashum, Hashbaddanah, Zechariah and Meshullam.

[5]Ezra opened the book. All the people could see him because he was standing above them; and as he opened it, the people all stood up. [6]Ezra praised the LORD, the great God; and all the people lifted their hands and responded, "Amen! Amen!" Then they bowed down and worshiped the LORD with their faces to the ground.

[7]The Levites—Jeshua, Bani, Sherebiah, Jamin, Akkub, Shabbethai, Hodiah, Maaseiah, Kelita, Azariah, Jozabad, Hanan and Pelaiah—instructed the people in the Law while the people were standing there. [8]They read from the Book of the Law of God, making it clear[a] and giving the meaning so that the people could understand what was being read.

[9]Then Nehemiah the governor, Ezra the priest and scribe, and the Levites who were instructing the people said to them all, "This day is sacred to the LORD your God. Do not mourn or weep." For all the people had been weeping as they listened to the words of the Law.

[10]Nehemiah said, "Go and enjoy choice food and sweet drinks, and send some to those who have nothing prepared. This day is sacred to our Lord. Do not grieve, for the joy of the LORD is your strength."

[11]The Levites calmed all the people, saying, "Be still, for this is a sacred day. Do not grieve."

[12]Then all the people went away to eat and drink, to send portions of food and to celebrate with great joy, because they now understood the words that had been made known to them.

[13]On the second day of the month, the heads of all the families, along with the priests and the Levites, gathered around Ezra the scribe to give attention to the words of the Law. [14]They found written in the Law, which the LORD had commanded through Moses, that the Israelites were to live in booths during the feast of the seventh month [15]and that they should proclaim this word and spread it throughout their towns and in Jerusalem: "Go out into the hill country and bring back branches from olive and wild olive trees, and from myrtles, palms and shade trees, to make booths"—as it is written.[b]

[16]So the people went out and brought back branches and built themselves booths on their own roofs, in their courtyards, in the courts of the house of God and in the square by the Water Gate and the one by the Gate of Ephraim. [17]The whole company that had returned from exile built booths and lived in them. From the days of Joshua son of Nun until that day, the Israelites had not celebrated it like this. And their joy was very great.

[18]Day after day, from the first day to the last, Ezra read from the Book of the Law of God. They celebrated the feast for seven days, and on the eighth day, in accordance with the regulation, there was an assembly.

The Israelites Confess Their Sins

9 On the twenty-fourth day of the same month, the Israelites gathered together, fasting and wearing sackcloth and having dust on their heads. [2]Those of Israelite descent had separated themselves from all foreigners. They stood in their places and confessed their sins and the wickedness of their fathers. [3]They stood where they were and read from the Book of the Law of the LORD their God for a quarter of the day, and spent another quarter in confession and in worshiping the LORD their God. [4]Standing on the stairs were the Levites—Jeshua, Bani, Kadmiel, Shebaniah, Bunni, Sherebiah, Bani and Kenani—who called with loud voices to the LORD their God. [5]And the Levites—Jeshua, Kadmiel, Bani, Hashabneiah, Sherebiah, Hodiah, Shebaniah and Pethahiah—said: "Stand up and

---

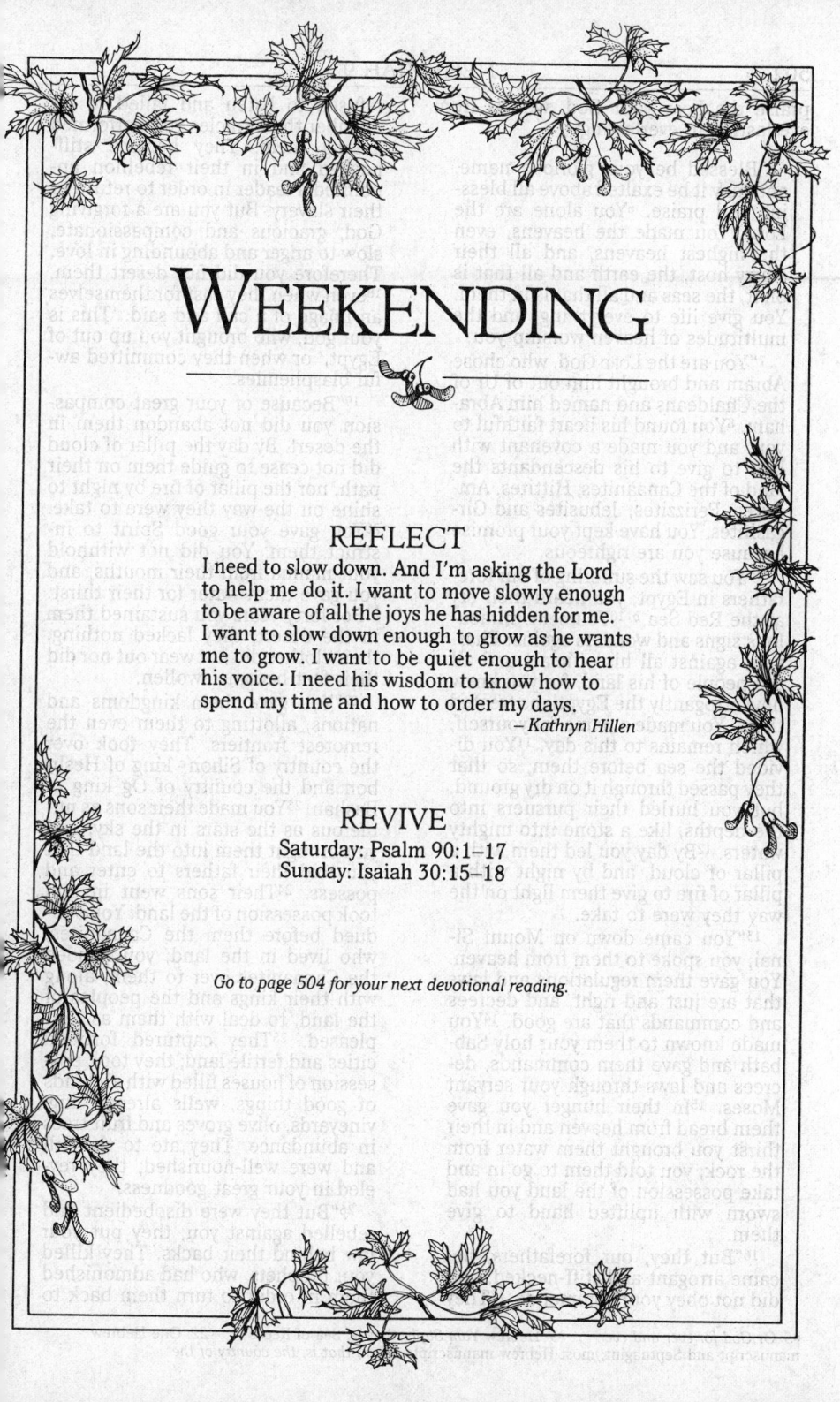

WEEKENDING

REFLECT

I need to slow down. And I'm asking the Lord
to help me do it. I want to move slowly enough
to be aware of all the joys he has hidden for me.
I want to slow down enough to grow as he wants
me to grow. I want to be quiet enough to hear
his voice. I need his wisdom to know how to
spend my time and how to order my days.

— *Kathryn Hillen*

REVIVE

Saturday: Psalm 90:1–17
Sunday: Isaiah 30:15–18

Go to page 504 for your next devotional reading.

praise the LORD your God, who is from everlasting to everlasting.*a*"

"Blessed be your glorious name, and may it be exalted above all blessing and praise. 6You alone are the LORD. You made the heavens, even the highest heavens, and all their starry host, the earth and all that is on it, the seas and all that is in them. You give life to everything, and the multitudes of heaven worship you.

7"You are the LORD God, who chose Abram and brought him out of Ur of the Chaldeans and named him Abraham. 8You found his heart faithful to you, and you made a covenant with him to give to his descendants the land of the Canaanites, Hittites, Amorites, Perizzites, Jebusites and Girgashites. You have kept your promise because you are righteous.

9"You saw the suffering of our forefathers in Egypt; you heard their cry at the Red Sea.*b* 10You sent miraculous signs and wonders against Pharaoh, against all his officials and all the people of his land, for you knew how arrogantly the Egyptians treated them. You made a name for yourself, which remains to this day. 11You divided the sea before them, so that they passed through it on dry ground, but you hurled their pursuers into the depths, like a stone into mighty waters. 12By day you led them with a pillar of cloud, and by night with a pillar of fire to give them light on the way they were to take.

13"You came down on Mount Sinai; you spoke to them from heaven. You gave them regulations and laws that are just and right, and decrees and commands that are good. 14You made known to them your holy Sabbath and gave them commands, decrees and laws through your servant Moses. 15In their hunger you gave them bread from heaven and in their thirst you brought them water from the rock; you told them to go in and take possession of the land you had sworn with uplifted hand to give them.

16"But they, our forefathers, became arrogant and stiff-necked, and did not obey your commands. 17They refused to listen and failed to remember the miracles you performed among them. They became stiff-necked and in their rebellion appointed a leader in order to return to their slavery. But you are a forgiving God, gracious and compassionate, slow to anger and abounding in love. Therefore you did not desert them, 18even when they cast for themselves an image of a calf and said, 'This is your god, who brought you up out of Egypt,' or when they committed awful blasphemies.

19"Because of your great compassion you did not abandon them in the desert. By day the pillar of cloud did not cease to guide them on their path, nor the pillar of fire by night to shine on the way they were to take. 20You gave your good Spirit to instruct them. You did not withhold your manna from their mouths, and you gave them water for their thirst. 21For forty years you sustained them in the desert; they lacked nothing, their clothes did not wear out nor did their feet become swollen.

22"You gave them kingdoms and nations, allotting to them even the remotest frontiers. They took over the country of Sihon*c* king of Heshbon and the country of Og king of Bashan. 23You made their sons as numerous as the stars in the sky, and you brought them into the land that you told their fathers to enter and possess. 24Their sons went in and took possession of the land. You subdued before them the Canaanites, who lived in the land; you handed the Canaanites over to them, along with their kings and the peoples of the land, to deal with them as they pleased. 25They captured fortified cities and fertile land; they took possession of houses filled with all kinds of good things, wells already dug, vineyards, olive groves and fruit trees in abundance. They ate to the full and were well-nourished; they reveled in your great goodness.

26"But they were disobedient and rebelled against you; they put your law behind their backs. They killed your prophets, who had admonished them in order to turn them back to

---

*a*5 Or *God for ever and ever*   *b*9 Hebrew *Yam Suph*; that is, Sea of Reeds   *c*22 One Hebrew manuscript and Septuagint; most Hebrew manuscripts *Sihon, that is, the country of the* you; they committed awful blasphemies. 27So you handed them over to their enemies, who oppressed them. But when they were oppressed they cried out to you. From heaven you heard them, and in your great compassion you gave them deliverers, who rescued them from the hand of their enemies.

28"But as soon as they were at rest, they again did what was evil in your sight. Then you abandoned them to the hand of their enemies so that they ruled over them. And when they cried out to you again, you heard from heaven, and in your compassion you delivered them time after time.

29"You warned them to return to your law, but they became arrogant and disobeyed your commands. They sinned against your ordinances, by which a man will live if he obeys them. Stubbornly they turned their backs on you, became stiff-necked and refused to listen. 30For many years you were patient with them. By your Spirit you admonished them through your prophets. Yet they paid no attention, so you handed them over to the neighboring peoples. 31But in your great mercy you did not put an end to them or abandon them, for you are a gracious and merciful God.

32"Now therefore, O our God, the great, mighty and awesome God, who keeps his covenant of love, do not let all this hardship seem trifling in your eyes—the hardship that has come upon us, upon our kings and leaders, upon our priests and prophets, upon our fathers and all your people, from the days of the kings of Assyria until today. 33In all that has happened to us, you have been just; you have acted faithfully, while we did wrong. 34Our kings, our leaders, our priests and our fathers did not follow your law; they did not pay attention to your commands or the warnings you gave them. 35Even while they were in their kingdom, enjoying your great goodness to them in the spacious and fertile land you gave them, they did not serve you or turn from their evil ways.

36"But see, we are slaves today, slaves in the land you gave our forefathers so they could eat its fruit and the other good things it produces. 37Because of our sins, its abundant harvest goes to the kings you have placed over us. They rule over our bodies and our cattle as they please. We are in great distress.

The Agreement of the People

38"In view of all this, we are making a binding agreement, putting it in writing, and our leaders, our Levites and our priests are affixing their seals to it."

10 Those who sealed it were:

Nehemiah the governor, the son of Hacaliah.

Zedekiah, 2Seraiah, Azariah, Jeremiah,
3Pashhur, Amariah, Malkijah,
4Hattush, Shebaniah, Malluch,
5Harim, Meremoth, Obadiah,
6Daniel, Ginnethon, Baruch,
7Meshullam, Abijah, Mijamin,
8Maaziah, Bilgai and Shemaiah.
These were the priests.

9The Levites:

Jeshua son of Azaniah, Binnui of the sons of Henadad, Kadmiel,
10and their associates: Shebaniah, Hodiah, Kelita, Pelaiah, Hanan,
11Mica, Rehob, Hashabiah,
12Zaccur, Sherebiah, Shebaniah,
13Hodiah, Bani and Beninu.

14The leaders of the people:

Parosh, Pahath-Moab, Elam, Zattu, Bani,
15Bunni, Azgad, Bebai,
16Adonijah, Bigvai, Adin,
17Ater, Hezekiah, Azzur,
18Hodiah, Hashum, Bezai,
19Hariph, Anathoth, Nebai,
20Magpiash, Meshullam, Hezir,
21Meshezabel, Zadok, Jaddua,
22Pelatiah, Hanan, Anaiah,
23Hoshea, Hananiah, Hasshub,
24Hallohesh, Pilha, Shobek,
25Rehum, Hashabnah, Maaseiah,
26Ahiah, Hanan, Anan,
27Malluch, Harim and Baanah.

28"The rest of the people—priests, Levites, gatekeepers, singers, temple servants and all who separated themselves from the neighboring peoples for the sake of the Law of God, together with their wives and all their sons and daughters who are able to understand— [29]all these now join their brothers the nobles, and bind themselves with a curse and an oath to follow the Law of God given through Moses the servant of God and to obey carefully all the commands, regulations and decrees of the LORD our Lord.

[30]"We promise not to give our daughters in marriage to the peoples around us or take their daughters for our sons.

[31]"When the neighboring peoples bring merchandise or grain to sell on the Sabbath, we will not buy from them on the Sabbath or on any holy day. Every seventh year we will forgo working the land and will cancel all debts.

[32]"We assume the responsibility for carrying out the commands to give a third of a shekel[a] each year for the service of the house of our God: [33]for the bread set out on the table; for the regular grain offerings and burnt offerings; for the offerings on the Sabbaths, New Moon festivals and appointed feasts; for the holy offerings; for sin offerings to make

a32 That is, about 1/8 ounce (about 4 grams)

MONDAY

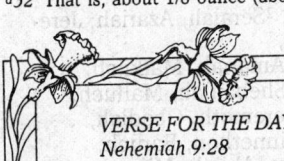

VERSE FOR THE DAY:
Nehemiah 9:28

AUTHOR:
Gien Karssen

PASSAGE FOR THE DAY:
Nehemiah 9:28–37

Wise Use of Rest

IT often proves to be less difficult to win a war than to live with peace afterward. Every person who lived through World War II and nursed high expectations about the enjoyment of peace will agree.

When the unrest of war, tension, or sorrow is replaced by a time of rest, much has to be done to spend it beneficially. A time of rest can be detrimental for a country and its people by weakening spiritual and moral values. To handle rest badly can lead to crime and drug addiction.

Rest can have a paralyzing influence. Our muscles weaken through lack of exercise. Too much rest keeps our spirits less alert. Our minds need constant stimulation for their development.

A person needs three attitudes to use a time of rest profitably: gratitude for previous blessings, a desire to correct past mistakes and prevent them in the future, and a willingness to occupy himself constructively. The best way to prevent evil is by doing good. Good intentions by themselves are not sufficient to guarantee beneficial rest.

When our rest changes to unrest, we must return to God and appeal to his forgiveness and compassion. This is corrective living. Preventive living is obeying God's Word—the Bible—in order that we take the right road from the very beginning.

Additional Scripture Readings:
Matthew 11:28–30; 2 Thessalonians 3:6–13

Go to page 514 for your next devotional reading.

atonement for Israel; and for all the duties of the house of our God.

³⁴"We—the priests, the Levites and the people—have cast lots to determine when each of our families is to bring to the house of our God at set times each year a contribution of wood to burn on the altar of the Lord our God, as it is written in the Law.

³⁵"We also assume responsibility for bringing to the house of our God each year the firstfruits of our crops and of every fruit tree.

³⁶"As it is also written in the Law, we will bring the firstborn of our sons and of our cattle, of our herds and of our flocks to the house of our God, to the priests ministering there.

³⁷"Moreover, we will bring to the storerooms of the house of our God, to the priests, the first of our ground meal, of our grain, offerings, of the fruit of all our trees and of our new wine and oil. And we will bring a tithe of our crops to the Levites, for it is the Levites who collect the tithes in all the towns where we work. ³⁸A priest descended from Aaron is to accompany the Levites when they receive the tithes, and the Levites are to bring a tenth of the tithes up to the house of our God, to the storerooms of the treasury. ³⁹The people of Israel, including the Levites, are to bring their contributions of grain, new wine and oil to the storerooms where the articles for the sanctuary are kept and where the ministering priests, the gatekeepers and the singers stay.

"We will not neglect the house of our God."

The New Residents of Jerusalem

11 Now the leaders of the people settled in Jerusalem, and the rest of the people cast lots to bring one out of every ten to live in Jerusalem, the holy city, while the remaining nine were to stay in their own towns. ²The people commended all the men who volunteered to live in Jerusalem.

³These are the provincial leaders who settled in Jerusalem (now some Israelites, priests, Levites, temple servants and descendants of Solomon's servants lived in the towns of Judah, each on his own property in the various towns, ⁴while oth-

er people from both Judah and Benjamin lived in Jerusalem):

From the descendants of Judah:

Athaiah son of Uzziah, the son of Zechariah, the son of Amariah, the son of Shephatiah, the son of Mahalalel, a descendant of Perez; ⁵and Maaseiah son of Baruch, the son of Col-Hozeh, the son of Hazaiah, the son of Adaiah, the son of Joiarib, the son of Zechariah, a descendant of Shelah. ⁶The descendants of Perez who lived in Jerusalem totaled 468 able men.

⁷From the descendants of Benjamin:

Sallu son of Meshullam, the son of Joed, the son of Pedaiah, the son of Kolaiah, the son of Maaseiah, the son of Ithiel, the son of Jeshaiah, ⁸and his followers, Gabbai and Sallai —928 men. ⁹Joel son of Zicri was their chief officer, and Judah son of Hassenuah was over the Second District of the city.

¹⁰From the priests:

Jedaiah; the son of Joiarib; Jakin; ¹¹Seraiah son of Hilkiah, the son of Meshullam, the son of Zadok, the son of Meraioth, the son of Ahitub, supervisor in the house of God, ¹²and their associates, who carried on work for the temple—822 men; Adaiah son of Jeroham, the son of Pelaliah, the son of Amzi, the son of Zechariah, the son of Pashhur, the son of Malkijah, ¹³and his associates, who were heads of families—242 men; Amashsai son of Azarel, the son of Ahzai, the son of Meshillemoth, the son of Immer, ¹⁴and hisᵃ associates, who were able men—128. Their chief officer was Zabdiel son of Haggedolim.

¹⁵From the Levites:

Shemaiah son of Hasshub, the son of Azrikam, the son of Hashabiah, the son of Bunni; ¹⁶Shabbethai and Jozabad, two of the heads of the Levites, who had charge of the outside work of the house of God; ¹⁷Mattaniah son of Mica, the son of Zabdi, the son of Asaph, the director who led in thanksgiving and prayer; Bakbukiah, second among his associates; and

ᵃ14 Most Septuagint manuscripts; Hebrew *their*

Abda son of Shammua, the son of Galal, the son of Jeduthun. [18]The Levites in the holy city totaled 284.

[19]The gatekeepers:

Akkub, Talmon and their associates, who kept watch at the gates — 172 men.

[20]The rest of the Israelites, with the priests and Levites, were in all the towns of Judah, each on his ancestral property. [21]The temple servants lived on the hill of Ophel, and Ziha and Gishpa were in charge of them.

[22]The chief officer of the Levites in Jerusalem was Uzzi son of Bani, the son of Hashabiah, the son of Mattaniah, the son of Mica. Uzzi was one of Asaph's descendants, who were the singers responsible for the service of the house of God. [23]The singers were under the king's orders, which regulated their daily activity.

[24]Pethahiah son of Meshezabel, one of the descendants of Zerah son of Judah, was the king's agent in all affairs relating to the people.

[25]As for the villages with their fields, some of the people of Judah lived in Kiriath Arba and its surrounding settlements, in Dibon and its settlements, in Jekabzeel and its villages, [26]in Jeshua, in Moladah, in Beth Pelet, [27]in Hazar Shual, in Beersheba and its settlements, [28]in Ziklag, in Meconah and its settlements, [29]in En Rimmon, in Zorah, in Jarmuth, [30]Zanoah, Adullam and their villages, in Lachish and its fields, and in Azekah and its settlements. So they were living all the way from Beersheba to the Valley of Hinnom.

[31]The descendants of the Benjamites from Geba lived in Micmash, Aija, Bethel and its settlements, [32]in Anathoth, Nob and Ananiah, [33]in Hazor, Ramah and Gittaim, [34]in Hadid, Zeboim and Neballat, [35]in Lod and Ono, and in the Valley of the Craftsmen.

[36]Some of the divisions of the Levites of Judah settled in Benjamin.

Priests and Levites

12 These were the priests and Levites who returned with Zerubbabel son of Shealtiel and with Jeshua:

Seraiah, Jeremiah, Ezra,
[2]Amariah, Malluch, Hattush,
[3]Shecaniah, Rehum, Meremoth,
[4]Iddo, Ginnethon,[a] Abijah,
[5]Mijamin,[b] Moadiah, Bilgah,
[6]Shemaiah, Joiarib, Jedaiah,
[7]Sallu, Amok, Hilkiah and Jedaiah.

These were the leaders of the priests and their associates in the days of Jeshua. [8]The Levites were Jeshua, Binnui, Kadmiel, Sherebiah, Judah, and also Mattaniah, who, together with his associates, was in charge of the songs of thanksgiving. [9]Bakbukiah and Unni, their associates, stood opposite them in the services.

[10]Jeshua was the father of Joiakim, Joiakim the father of Eliashib, Eliashib the father of Joiada, [11]Joiada the father of Jonathan, and Jonathan the father of Jaddua.

[12]In the days of Joiakim, these were the heads of the priestly families:

of Seraiah's family, Meraiah;
of Jeremiah's, Hananiah;
[13]of Ezra's, Meshullam;
of Amariah's, Jehohanan;
[14]of Malluch's, Jonathan;
of Shecaniah's,[c] Joseph;
[15]of Harim's, Adna;
of Meremoth's,[d] Helkai;
[16]of Iddo's, Zechariah;
of Ginnethon's, Meshullam;
[17]of Abijah's, Zicri;
of Miniamin's and of Moadiah's, Piltai;
[18]of Bilgah's, Shammua;
of Shemaiah's, Jehonathan;
[19]of Joiarib's, Mattenai;
of Jedaiah's, Uzzi;
[20]of Sallu's, Kallai;
of Amok's, Eber;
[21]of Hilkiah's, Hashabiah;
of Jedaiah's, Nethanel.

[22]The family heads of the Levites in the days of Eliashib, Joiada, Johanan and Jaddua, as well as those of the priests, were recorded in the reign of Darius the Persian. [23]The family heads among the descendants of Levi up to the time of Johanan son of Eliashib were recorded in the book of the annals. [24]And the leaders of the Levites were Hashabiah, Sherebiah, Jeshua son of Kadmiel, and their as-

---

a4 Many Hebrew manuscripts and Vulgate (see also Neh. 12:16); most Hebrew manuscripts *Ginnethoi*
b5 A variant of *Miniamin*   *c14* Very many Hebrew manuscripts, some Septuagint manuscripts and Syriac (see also Neh. 12:3); most Hebrew manuscripts *Shebaniah's*   *d15* Some Septuagint manuscripts (see also Neh. 12:3); Hebrew *Meraioth's*

sociates, who stood opposite them to give praise and thanksgiving, one section responding to the other, as prescribed by David the man of God.

²⁵Mattaniah, Bakbukiah, Obadiah, Meshullam, Talmon and Akkub were gatekeepers who guarded the storerooms at the gates. ²⁶They served in the days of Joiakim son of Jeshua, the son of Jozadak, and in the days of Nehemiah the governor and of Ezra the priest and scribe.

Dedication of the Wall of Jerusalem

²⁷At the dedication of the wall of Jerusalem, the Levites were sought out from where they lived and were brought to Jerusalem to celebrate joyfully the dedication with songs of thanksgiving and with the music of cymbals, harps and lyres. ²⁸The singers also were brought together from the region around Jerusalem—from the villages of the Netophathites, ²⁹from Beth Gilgal, and from the area of Geba and Azmaveth, for the singers had built villages for themselves around Jerusalem. ³⁰When the priests and Levites had purified themselves ceremonially, they purified the people, the gates and the wall.

³¹I had the leaders of Judah go up on top^a of the wall. I also assigned two large choirs to give thanks. One was to proceed on top^b of the wall to the right, toward the Dung Gate. ³²Hoshaiah and half the leaders of Judah followed them, ³³along with Azariah, Ezra, Meshullam, ³⁴Judah, Benjamin, Shemaiah, Jeremiah, ³⁵as well as some priests with trumpets, and also Zechariah son of Jonathan, the son of Shemaiah, the son of Mattaniah, the son of Micaiah, the son of Zaccur, the son of Asaph, ³⁶and his associates—Shemaiah, Azarel, Milalai, Gilalai, Maai, Nethanel, Judah and Hanani—with musical instruments ⌐prescribed by⌐ David the man of God. Ezra the scribe led the procession. ³⁷At the Fountain Gate they continued directly up the steps of the City of David on the ascent to the wall and passed above the house of David to the Water Gate on the east.

³⁸The second choir proceeded in the opposite direction. I followed them on top^c of the wall, together with half the people—past the Tower of the Ovens to the Broad Wall, ³⁹over the Gate of Ephraim, the Jeshanah^d Gate, the Fish Gate, the Tower of Hananel and the Tower of the Hundred, as far as the Sheep Gate. At the Gate of the Guard they stopped.

⁴⁰The two choirs that gave thanks then took their places in the house of God; so did I, together with half the officials, ⁴¹as well as the priests—Eliakim, Maaseiah, Miniamin, Micaiah, Elioenai, Zechariah and Hananiah with their trumpets—⁴²and also Maaseiah, Shemaiah, Eleazar, Uzzi, Jehohanan, Malkijah, Elam and Ezer. The choirs sang under the direction of Jezrahiah. ⁴³And on that day they offered great sacrifices, rejoicing because God had given them great joy. The women and children also rejoiced. The sound of rejoicing in Jerusalem could be heard far away.

⁴⁴At that time men were appointed to be in charge of the storerooms for the contributions, firstfruits and tithes. From the fields around the towns they were to bring into the storerooms the portions required by the Law for the priests and the Levites, for Judah was pleased with the ministering priests and Levites. ⁴⁵They performed the service of their God and the service of purification, as did also the singers and gatekeepers, according to the commands of David and his son Solomon. ⁴⁶For long ago, in the days of David and Asaph, there had been directors for the singers and for the songs of praise and thanksgiving to God. ⁴⁷So in the days of Zerubbabel and of Nehemiah, all Israel contributed the daily portions for the singers and gatekeepers. They also set aside the portion for the other Levites, and the Levites set aside the portion for the descendants of Aaron.

Nehemiah's Final Reforms

13 On that day the Book of Moses was read aloud in the hearing of the people and there it was found written that no Ammonite or Moabite should ever be admitted into the assembly of God, ²because they had not met the Israelites with food and water but had hired Balaam to call a curse down on them. (Our God, however, turned the curse into a blessing.) ³When the people heard this law, they excluded from Israel all who were of foreign descent.

⁴Before this, Eliashib the priest had been put in charge of the storerooms of the house of our God. He was closely associated with Tobiah, ⁵and he had provid-

---

^a31 Or go alongside   ^b31 Or proceed alongside   ^c38 Or them alongside   ^d39 Or Old

ed him with a large room formerly used to store the grain offerings and incense and temple articles, and also the tithes of grain, new wine and oil prescribed for the Levites, singers and gatekeepers, as well as the contributions for the priests.

6But while all this was going on, I was not in Jerusalem, for in the thirty-second year of Artaxerxes king of Babylon I had returned to the king. Some time later I asked his permission 7and came back to Jerusalem. Here I learned about the evil thing Eliashib had done in providing Tobiah a room in the courts of the house of God. 8I was greatly displeased and threw all Tobiah's household goods out of the room. 9I gave orders to purify the rooms, and then I put back into them the equipment of the house of God, with the grain offerings and the incense.

10I also learned that the portions assigned to the Levites had not been given to them, and that all the Levites and singers responsible for the service had gone back to their own fields. 11So I rebuked the officials and asked them, "Why is the house of God neglected?" Then I called them together and stationed them at their posts.

12All Judah brought the tithes of grain, new wine and oil into the storerooms. 13I put Shelemiah the priest, Zadok the scribe, and a Levite named Pedaiah in charge of the storerooms and made Hanan son of Zaccur, the son of Mattaniah, their assistant, because these men were considered trustworthy. They were made responsible for distributing the supplies to their brothers.

14Remember me for this, O my God, and do not blot out what I have so faithfully done for the house of my God and its services.

15In those days I saw men in Judah treading winepresses on the Sabbath and bringing in grain and loading it on donkeys, together with wine, grapes, figs and all other kinds of loads. And they were bringing all this into Jerusalem on the Sabbath. Therefore I warned them against selling food on that day. 16Men from Tyre who lived in Jerusalem were bringing in fish and all kinds of merchandise and selling them in Jerusalem on the Sabbath to the people of Judah. 17I rebuked the nobles of Judah and said to them, "What is this wicked thing you are doing—desecrating the Sabbath day?

18Didn't your forefathers do the same things, so that our God brought all this calamity upon us and upon this city? Now you are stirring up more wrath against Israel by desecrating the Sabbath."

19When evening shadows fell on the gates of Jerusalem before the Sabbath, I ordered the doors to be shut and not opened until the Sabbath was over. I stationed some of my own men at the gates so that no load could be brought in on the Sabbath day. 20Once or twice the merchants and sellers of all kinds of goods spent the night outside Jerusalem. 21But I warned them and said, "Why do you spend the night by the wall? If you do this again, I will lay hands on you." From that time on they no longer came on the Sabbath. 22Then I commanded the Levites to purify themselves and go and guard the gates in order to keep the Sabbath day holy.

Remember me for this also, O my God, and show mercy to me according to your great love.

23Moreover, in those days I saw men of Judah who had married women from Ashdod, Ammon and Moab. 24Half of their children spoke the language of Ashdod or the language of one of the other peoples, and did not know how to speak the language of Judah. 25I rebuked them and called curses down on them. I beat some of the men and pulled out their hair. I made them take an oath in God's name and said: "You are not to give your daughters in marriage to their sons, nor are you to take their daughters in marriage for your sons or for yourselves. 26Was it not because of marriages like these that Solomon king of Israel sinned? Among the many nations there was no king like him. He was loved by his God, and God made him king over all Israel, but even he was led into sin by foreign women. 27Must we hear now that you too are doing all this terrible wickedness and are being unfaithful to our God by marrying foreign women?"

28One of the sons of Joiada son of Eliashib the high priest was son-in-law to Sanballat the Horonite. And I drove him away from me.

29Remember them, O my God, because they defiled the priestly office and the covenant of the priesthood and of the Levites.

30So I purified the priests and the Levites of everything foreign, and assigned them duties, each to his own task. 31I also made provision for contributions of wood at designated times, and for the firstfruits.

Remember me with favor, O my God.

*ESTHER records God's remark-
able, providential care of his exiled
people when their enemies threaten to
destroy them completely. Though his
name is not actually mentioned in the
book, God is in control, using Esther's
position as queen to reverse the plan of
wicked Haman. As you read this book,
think how God takes care of you in
your everyday life, even making good
come out of evil.*

ESTHER

Queen Vashti Deposed

1 This is what happened during the time of Xerxes,[a] the Xerxes who ruled over 127 provinces stretching from India to Cush[b]: [2]At that time King Xerxes reigned from his royal throne in the citadel of Susa, [3]and in the third year of his reign he gave a banquet for all his nobles and officials. The military leaders of Persia and Media, the princes, and the nobles of the provinces were present.

[4]For a full 180 days he displayed the vast wealth of his kingdom and the splendor and glory of his majesty. [5]When these days were over, the king gave a banquet, lasting seven days, in the enclosed garden of the king's palace, for all the people from the least to the greatest, who were in the citadel of Susa. [6]The garden had hangings of white and blue linen, fastened with cords of white linen and purple material to silver rings on marble pillars. There were couches of gold and silver on a mosaic pavement of porphyry, marble, mother-of-pearl and other costly stones. [7]Wine was served in goblets of gold, each one different from the other, and the royal wine was abundant, in keeping with the king's liberality. [8]By the king's command each guest was allowed to drink in his own way, for the king in-

---

a1 Hebrew *Ahasuerus,* a variant of Xerxes' Persian name; here and throughout Esther   *b1* That is, the upper Nile region structed all the wine stewards to serve each man what he wished.

⁹Queen Vashti also gave a banquet for the women in the royal palace of King Xerxes.

¹⁰On the seventh day, when King Xerxes was in high spirits from wine, he commanded the seven eunuchs who served him — Mehuman, Biztha, Harbona, Bigtha, Abagtha, Zethar and Carcas — ¹¹to bring before him Queen Vashti, wearing her royal crown, in order to display her beauty to the people and nobles, for she was lovely to look at. ¹²But when the attendants delivered the king's command, Queen Vashti refused to come. Then the king became furious and burned with anger.

¹³Since it was customary for the king to consult experts in matters of law and justice, he spoke with the wise men who understood the times ¹⁴and were closest to the king — Carshena, Shethar, Admatha, Tarshish, Meres, Marsena and Memucan, the seven nobles of Persia and Media who had special access to the king and were highest in the kingdom.

¹⁵"According to law, what must be done to Queen Vashti?" he asked. "She has not obeyed the command of King Xerxes that the eunuchs have taken to her."

¹⁶Then Memucan replied in the presence of the king and the nobles, "Queen Vashti has done wrong, not only against the king but also against all the nobles and the peoples of all the provinces of King Xerxes. ¹⁷For the queen's conduct will become known to all the women, and so they will despise their husbands and say, 'King Xerxes commanded Queen Vashti to be brought before him, but she would not come.' ¹⁸This very day the Persian and Median women of the nobility who have heard about the queen's conduct will respond to all the king's nobles in the same way. There will be no end of disrespect and discord.

¹⁹"Therefore, if it pleases the king, let him issue a royal decree and let it be written in the laws of Persia and Media, which cannot be repealed, that Vashti is never again to enter the presence of King Xerxes. Also let the king give her royal position to someone else who is better than she. ²⁰Then when the king's edict is proclaimed throughout all his vast realm, all the women will respect their husbands, from the least to the greatest."

²¹The king and his nobles were pleased with this advice, so the king did as Memucan proposed. ²²He sent dispatches to all parts of the kingdom, to each province in its own script and to each people in its own language, proclaiming in each people's tongue that every man should be ruler over his own household.

Esther Made Queen

2 Later when the anger of King Xerxes had subsided, he remembered Vashti and what she had done and what he had decreed about her. ²Then the king's personal attendants proposed, "Let a search be made for beautiful young virgins for the king. ³Let the king appoint commissioners in every province of his realm to bring all these beautiful girls into the harem at the citadel of Susa. Let them be placed under the care of Hegai, the king's eunuch, who is in charge of the women; and let beauty treatments be given to them. ⁴Then let the girl who pleases the king be queen instead of Vashti." This advice appealed to the king, and he followed it.

⁵Now there was in the citadel of Susa a Jew of the tribe of Benjamin, named Mordecai son of Jair, the son of Shimei, the son of Kish, ⁶who had been carried into exile from Jerusalem by Nebuchadnezzar king of Babylon, among those taken captive with Jehoiachin*a* king of Judah. ⁷Mordecai had a cousin named Hadassah, whom he had brought up because she had neither father nor mother. This girl, who was also known as Esther, was lovely in form and features, and Mordecai had taken her as his own daughter when her father and mother died.

⁸When the king's order and edict had been proclaimed, many girls were brought to the citadel of Susa and put under the care of Hegai. Esther also was taken to the king's palace and entrusted to Hegai, who had charge of the harem. ⁹The girl pleased him and won his favor. Immediately he provided her with her beauty treatments and special food. He assigned to her seven maids selected from the king's palace and moved her and her maids into the best place in the harem.

¹⁰Esther had not revealed her nationality and family background, because Mordecai had forbidden her to do so. ¹¹Every day he walked back and forth near the courtyard of the harem to find out how

---

*a*6 Hebrew *Jeconiah*, a variant of *Jehoiachin*

Esther was and what was happening to her.

12Before a girl's turn came to go in to King Xerxes, she had to complete twelve months of beauty treatments prescribed for the women, six months with oil of myrrh and six with perfumes and cosmetics. 13And this is how she would go to the king: Anything she wanted was given her to take with her from the harem to the king's palace. 14In the evening she would go there and in the morning return to another part of the harem to the care of Shaashgaz, the king's eunuch who was in charge of the concubines. She would not return to the king unless he was pleased with her and summoned her by name.

15When the turn came for Esther (the girl Mordecai had adopted, the daughter of his uncle Abihail) to go to the king, she asked for nothing other than what Hegai, the king's eunuch who was in charge of the harem, suggested. And Esther won the favor of everyone who saw her. 16She was taken to King Xerxes in the royal residence in the tenth month, the month of Tebeth, in the seventh year of his reign.

17Now the king was attracted to Esther more than to any of the other women, and she won his favor and approval more than any of the other virgins. So he set a royal crown on her head and made her queen instead of Vashti. 18And the king gave a great banquet, Esther's banquet, for all his nobles and officials. He proclaimed a holiday throughout the provinces and distributed gifts with royal liberality.

Mordecai Uncovers a Conspiracy

19When the virgins were assembled a second time, Mordecai was sitting at the king's gate. 20But Esther had kept secret her family background and nationality just as Mordecai had told her to do, for she continued to follow Mordecai's instructions as she had done when he was bringing her up.

21During the time Mordecai was sitting at the king's gate, Bigthana[a] and Teresh, two of the king's officers who guarded the doorway, became angry and conspired to assassinate King Xerxes. 22But Mordecai found out about the plot and told Queen Esther, who in turn reported it to the king, giving credit to Mordecai. 23And when the report was investigated and

found to be true, the two officials were hanged on a gallows.[b] All this was recorded in the book of the annals in the presence of the king.

Haman's Plot to Destroy the Jews

3 After these events, King Xerxes honored Haman son of Hammedatha, the Agagite, elevating him and giving him a seat of honor higher than that of all the other nobles. 2All the royal officials at the king's gate knelt down and paid honor to Haman, for the king had commanded this concerning him. But Mordecai would not kneel down or pay him honor.

3Then the royal officials at the king's gate asked Mordecai, "Why do you disobey the king's command?" 4Day after day they spoke to him but he refused to comply. Therefore they told Haman about it to see whether Mordecai's behavior would be tolerated, for he had told them he was a Jew.

5When Haman saw that Mordecai would not kneel down or pay him honor, he was enraged. 6Yet having learned who Mordecai's people were, he scorned the idea of killing only Mordecai. Instead Haman looked for a way to destroy all Mordecai's people, the Jews, throughout the whole kingdom of Xerxes.

7In the twelfth year of King Xerxes, in the first month, the month of Nisan, they cast the pur (that is, the lot) in the presence of Haman to select a day and month. And the lot fell on[c] the twelfth month, the month of Adar.

8Then Haman said to King Xerxes, "There is a certain people dispersed and scattered among the peoples in all the provinces of your kingdom whose customs are different from those of all other people and who do not obey the king's laws; it is not in the king's best interest to tolerate them. 9If it pleases the king, let a decree be issued to destroy them, and I will put ten thousand talents[d] of silver into the royal treasury for the men who carry out this business."

10So the king took his signet ring from his finger and gave it to Haman son of Hammedatha, the Agagite, the enemy of the Jews. 11"Keep the money," the king said to Haman, "and do with the people as you please."

12Then on the thirteenth day of the first

---

a21 Hebrew *Bigthan*, a variant of *Bigthana*   b23 Or *were hung* (or *impaled*) *on poles*; similarly elsewhere in Esther   c7 Septuagint; Hebrew does not have *And the lot fell on*.   d9 That is, about 375 tons (about 345 metric tons) month the royal secretaries were summoned. They wrote out in the script of each province and in the language of each people all Haman's orders to the king's satraps, the governors of the various provinces and the nobles of the various peoples. These were written in the name of King Xerxes himself and sealed with his own ring. [13]Dispatches were sent by couriers to all the king's provinces with the order to destroy, kill and annihilate all the Jews—young and old, women and little children—on a single day, the thirteenth day of the twelfth month, the month of Adar, and to plunder their goods. [14]A copy of the text of the edict was to be issued as law in every province and made known to the people of every nationality so they would be ready for that day.

[15]Spurred on by the king's command, the couriers went out, and the edict was issued in the citadel of Susa. The king and Haman sat down to drink, but the city of Susa was bewildered.

Mordecai Persuades Esther to Help

4 When Mordecai learned of all that had been done, he tore his clothes, put on sackcloth and ashes, and went out into the city, wailing loudly and bitterly. [2]But he went only as far as the king's gate, because no one clothed in sackcloth was allowed to enter it. [3]In every province to which the edict and order of the king came, there was great mourning among the Jews, with fasting, weeping and wailing. Many lay in sackcloth and ashes.

[4]When Esther's maids and eunuchs came and told her about Mordecai, she was in great distress. She sent clothes for him to put on instead of his sackcloth, but he would not accept them. [5]Then Esther summoned Hathach, one of the king's eunuchs assigned to attend her, and ordered him to find out what was troubling Mordecai and why.

[6]So Hathach went out to Mordecai in the open square of the city in front of the king's gate. [7]Mordecai told him everything that had happened to him, including the exact amount of money Haman had promised to pay into the royal treasury for the destruction of the Jews. [8]He also gave him a copy of the text of the edict for their annihilation, which had been published in Susa, to show to Esther and explain it to her, and he told him to urge her to go into the king's presence to

beg for mercy and plead with him for her people.

[9]Hathach went back and reported to Esther what Mordecai had said. [10]Then she instructed him to say to Mordecai, [11]"All the king's officials and the people of the royal provinces know that for any man or woman who approaches the king in the inner court without being summoned the king has but one law: that he be put to death. The only exception to this is for the king to extend the gold scepter to him and spare his life. But thirty days have passed since I was called to go to the king."

[12]When Esther's words were reported to Mordecai, [13]he sent back this answer: "Do not think that because you are in the king's house you alone of all the Jews will escape. [14]For if you remain silent at this time, relief and deliverance for the Jews will arise from another place, but you and your father's family will perish. And who knows but that you have come to royal position for such a time as this?"

[15]Then Esther sent this reply to Mordecai: [16]"Go, gather together all the Jews who are in Susa, and fast for me. Do not eat or drink for three days, night or day. I and my maids will fast as you do. When this is done, I will go to the king, even though it is against the law. And if I perish, I perish."

[17]So Mordecai went away and carried out all of Esther's instructions.

Esther's Request to the King

5 On the third day Esther put on her royal robes and stood in the inner court of the palace, in front of the king's hall. The king was sitting on his royal throne in the hall, facing the entrance. [2]When he saw Queen Esther standing in the court, he was pleased with her and held out to her the gold scepter that was in his hand. So Esther approached and touched the tip of the scepter.

[3]Then the king asked, "What is it, Queen Esther? What is your request? Even up to half the kingdom, it will be given you."

[4]"If it pleases the king," replied Esther, "let the king, together with Haman, come today to a banquet I have prepared for him."

[5]"Bring Haman at once," the king said, "so that we may do what Esther asks."

So the king and Haman went to the banquet Esther had prepared. [6]As they were drinking wine, the king again asked

VERSE FOR THE DAY:
Esther 4:14

AUTHOR:
Dorothy Patterson

PASSAGE FOR THE DAY:
Esther 3:13 — 4:17

Service Through Providence

EFFECTIVE service almost always comes by assignment rather than choice. When my husband and I accompanied our college mission team to East Africa, we suspected that many of our tasks would be lowly, but we assumed that our ministry would be primarily spiritual. Once there, I was needed to prepare meals for the students, and my husband was enlisted to assist the medical team in dispensing medications to patients in bush clinics. Neither of us used our theological training, but we both were called to serve, and in that serving we were able to share Christ with countless people.

A member of a hated minority race, bereft of parents, without any material legacy, living in exile in a foreign land, untutored by formal education, Esther had been reared and trained by her older cousin Mordecai. In God's providence, this teenage orphan was thrust into the royal court of Persia.

Though perhaps not as far-reaching in influence as Esther, we are each what God has made us with our own respective circle of opportunities. In opportunity lies the real test of character. Though we usually think of affliction as the major test of character, in Esther's case, prosperity and fame were the testing ground.

Mordecai believed that Esther was placed in the king's household by divine appointment to do God's timely work. He passionately pleaded with Esther to put her life on the line because he believed the promises of God. He had watched the power and faithfulness of God unfold over the years. Mordecai understood that it is not failure that brings despair, but unfaithfulness and idleness.

Esther had her opportunity; we have ours. A difficult and dangerous human task is no excuse for failing to perform divinely assigned duty. God chooses where we are called to serve; we choose, as did Esther, whether or not to respond in obedience to that call.

Additional Scripture Readings:
Acts 16:6–10; Philemon 10–16

Go to page 521 for your next devotional reading.

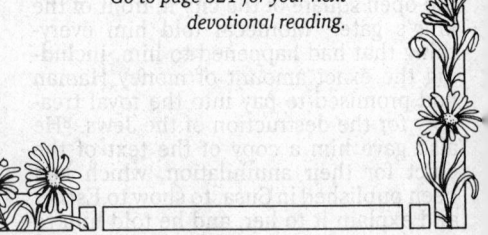

Esther, "Now what is your petition? It will be given you. And what is your request? Even up to half the kingdom, it will be granted."

[7]Esther replied, "My petition and my request is this: [8]If the king regards me with favor and if it pleases the king to grant my petition and fulfill my request, let the king and Haman come tomorrow to the banquet I will prepare for them. Then I will answer the king's question."

Haman's Rage Against Mordecai

[9]Haman went out that day happy and in high spirits. But when he saw Mordecai at the king's gate and observed that he neither rose nor showed fear in his presence, he was filled with rage against Mordecai. [10]Nevertheless, Haman restrained himself and went home.

Calling together his friends and Zeresh, his wife, [11]Haman boasted to them about his vast wealth, his many sons, and all the ways the king had honored him and how he had elevated him above the other nobles and officials. [12]"And that's not all," Haman added. "I'm the only person Queen Esther invited to accompany the king to the banquet she gave. And she has invited me along with the king tomorrow. [13]But all this gives me no satisfaction as long as I see that Jew Mordecai sitting at the king's gate."

[14]His wife Zeresh and all his friends said to him, "Have a gallows built, seventy-five feet[a] high, and ask the king in the morning to have Mordecai hanged on it. Then go with the king to the dinner and be happy." This suggestion delighted Haman, and he had the gallows built.

Mordecai Honored

6 That night the king could not sleep; so he ordered the book of the chronicles, the record of his reign, to be brought in and read to him. [2]It was found recorded there that Mordecai had exposed Bigthana and Teresh, two of the king's officers who guarded the doorway, who had conspired to assassinate King Xerxes.

[3]"What honor and recognition has Mordecai received for this?" the king asked.

"Nothing has been done for him," his attendants answered.

[4]The king said, "Who is in the court?" Now Haman had just entered the outer court of the palace to speak to the king about hanging Mordecai on the gallows he had erected for him.

[5]His attendants answered, "Haman is standing in the court."

"Bring him in," the king ordered.

[6]When Haman entered, the king asked him, "What should be done for the man the king delights to honor?"

Now Haman thought to himself, "Who is there that the king would rather honor than me?" [7]So he answered the king, "For the man the king delights to honor, [8]have them bring a royal robe the king has worn and a horse the king has ridden, one with a royal crest placed on its head. [9]Then let the robe and horse be entrusted to one of the king's most noble princes. Let them robe the man the king delights to honor, and lead him on the horse through the city streets, proclaiming before him, 'This is what is done for the man the king delights to honor!' "

[10]"Go at once," the king commanded Haman. "Get the robe and the horse and do just as you have suggested for Mordecai the Jew, who sits at the king's gate. Do not neglect anything you have recommended."

[11]So Haman got the robe and the horse. He robed Mordecai, and led him on horseback through the city streets, proclaiming before him, "This is what is done for the man the king delights to honor!"

[12]Afterward Mordecai returned to the king's gate. But Haman rushed home, with his head covered in grief, [13]and told Zeresh his wife and all his friends everything that had happened to him.

His advisers and his wife Zeresh said to him, "Since Mordecai, before whom your downfall has started, is of Jewish origin, you cannot stand against him—you will surely come to ruin!" [14]While they were still talking with him, the king's eunuchs arrived and hurried Haman away to the banquet Esther had prepared.

Haman Hanged

7 So the king and Haman went to dine with Queen Esther, [2]and as they were drinking wine on that second day, the king again asked, "Queen Esther, what is your petition? It will be given you. What is your request? Even up to half the kingdom, it will be granted."

[3]Then Queen Esther answered, "If I have found favor with you, O king, and if

---

[a]14 Hebrew *fifty cubits* (about 23 meters)

it pleases your majesty, grant me my life —this is my petition. And spare my people—this is my request. ⁴For I and my people have been sold for destruction and slaughter and annihilation. If we had merely been sold as male and female slaves, I would have kept quiet, because no such distress would justify disturbing the king.ᵃ"

⁵King Xerxes asked Queen Esther, "Who is he? Where is the man who has dared to do such a thing?"

⁶Esther said, "The adversary and enemy is this vile Haman."

Then Haman was terrified before the king and queen. ⁷The king got up in a rage, left his wine and went out into the palace garden. But Haman, realizing that the king had already decided his fate, stayed behind to beg Queen Esther for his life.

⁸Just as the king returned from the palace garden to the banquet hall, Haman was falling on the couch where Esther was reclining.

The king exclaimed, "Will he even molest the queen while she is with me in the house?"

As soon as the word left the king's mouth, they covered Haman's face. ⁹Then Harbona, one of the eunuchs attending the king, said, "A gallows seventy-five feetᵇ high stands by Haman's house. He had it made for Mordecai, who spoke up to help the king."

The king said, "Hang him on it!" ¹⁰So they hanged Haman on the gallows he had prepared for Mordecai. Then the king's fury subsided.

The King's Edict in Behalf of the Jews

8 That same day King Xerxes gave Queen Esther the estate of Haman, the enemy of the Jews. And Mordecai came into the presence of the king, for Esther had told how he was related to her. ²The king took off his signet ring, which he had reclaimed from Haman, and presented it to Mordecai. And Esther appointed him over Haman's estate.

³Esther again pleaded with the king, falling at his feet and weeping. She begged him to put an end to the evil plan of Haman the Agagite, which he had devised against the Jews. ⁴Then the king extended the gold scepter to Esther and she arose and stood before him.

⁵"If it pleases the king," she said, "and if he regards me with favor and thinks it the right thing to do, and if he is pleased with me, let an order be written overruling the dispatches that Haman son of Hammedatha, the Agagite, devised and wrote to destroy the Jews in all the king's provinces. ⁶For how can I bear to see disaster fall on my people? How can I bear to see the destruction of my family?"

⁷King Xerxes replied to Queen Esther and to Mordecai the Jew, "Because Haman attacked the Jews, I have given his estate to Esther, and they have hanged him on the gallows. ⁸Now write another decree in the king's name in behalf of the Jews as seems best to you, and seal it with the king's signet ring—for no document written in the king's name and sealed with his ring can be revoked."

⁹At once the royal secretaries were summoned—on the twenty-third day of the third month, the month of Sivan. They wrote out all Mordecai's orders to the Jews, and to the satraps, governors and nobles of the 127 provinces stretching from India to Cush.ᶜ These orders were written in the script of each province and the language of each people and also to the Jews in their own script and language. ¹⁰Mordecai wrote in the name of King Xerxes, sealed the dispatches with the king's signet ring, and sent them by mounted couriers, who rode fast horses especially bred for the king.

¹¹The king's edict granted the Jews in every city the right to assemble and protect themselves; to destroy, kill and annihilate any armed force of any nationality or province that might attack them and their women and children; and to plunder the property of their enemies. ¹²The day appointed for the Jews to do this in all the provinces of King Xerxes was the thirteenth day of the twelfth month, the month of Adar. ¹³A copy of the text of the edict was to be issued as law in every province and made known to the people of every nationality so that the Jews would be ready on that day to avenge themselves on their enemies.

¹⁴The couriers, riding the royal horses, raced out, spurred on by the king's command. And the edict was also issued in the citadel of Susa.

ᵃ4 Or *quiet, but the compensation our adversary offers cannot be compared with the loss the king would suffer*   ᵇ9 Hebrew *fifty cubits* (about 23 meters)   ᶜ9 That is, the upper Nile region

¹⁵Mordecai left the king's presence wearing royal garments of blue and white, a large crown of gold and a purple robe of fine linen. And the city of Susa held a joyous celebration. ¹⁶For the Jews it was a time of happiness and joy, gladness and honor. ¹⁷In every province and in every city, wherever the edict of the king went, there was joy and gladness among the Jews, with feasting and celebrating. And many people of other nationalities became Jews because fear of the Jews had seized them.

Triumph of the Jews

9 On the thirteenth day of the twelfth month, the month of Adar, the edict commanded by the king was to be carried out. On this day the enemies of the Jews had hoped to overpower them, but now the tables were turned and the Jews got the upper hand over those who hated them. ²The Jews assembled in their cities in all the provinces of King Xerxes to attack those seeking their destruction. No one could stand against them, because the people of all the other nationalities were afraid of them. ³And all the nobles of the provinces, the satraps, the governors and the king's administrators helped the Jews, because fear of Mordecai had seized them. ⁴Mordecai was prominent in the palace; his reputation spread throughout the provinces, and he became more and more powerful.

⁵The Jews struck down all their enemies with the sword, killing and destroying them, and they did what they pleased to those who hated them. ⁶In the citadel of Susa, the Jews killed and destroyed five hundred men. ⁷They also killed Parshandatha, Dalphon, Aspatha, ⁸Poratha, Adalia, Aridatha, ⁹Parmashta, Arisai, Aridai and Vaizatha, ¹⁰the ten sons of Haman son of Hammedatha, the enemy of the Jews. But they did not lay their hands on the plunder.

¹¹The number of those slain in the citadel of Susa was reported to the king that same day. ¹²The king said to Queen Esther, "The Jews have killed and destroyed five hundred men and the ten sons of Haman in the citadel of Susa. What have they done in the rest of the king's provinces? Now what is your petition? It will be given you. What is your request? It will also be granted."

¹³"If it pleases the king," Esther answered, "give the Jews in Susa permission to carry out this day's edict tomorrow also, and let Haman's ten sons be hanged on gallows."

¹⁴So the king commanded that this be done. An edict was issued in Susa, and they hanged the ten sons of Haman. ¹⁵The Jews in Susa came together on the fourteenth day of the month of Adar, and they put to death in Susa three hundred men, but they did not lay their hands on the plunder.

¹⁶Meanwhile, the remainder of the Jews who were in the king's provinces also assembled to protect themselves and get relief from their enemies. They killed seventy-five thousand of them but did not lay their hands on the plunder. ¹⁷This happened on the thirteenth day of the month of Adar, and on the fourteenth they rested and made it a day of feasting and joy.

Purim Celebrated

¹⁸The Jews in Susa, however, had assembled on the thirteenth and fourteenth, and then on the fifteenth they rested and made it a day of feasting and joy.

¹⁹That is why rural Jews—those living in villages—observe the fourteenth of the month of Adar as a day of joy and feasting, a day for giving presents to each other.

²⁰Mordecai recorded these events, and he sent letters to all the Jews throughout the provinces of King Xerxes, near and far, ²¹to have them celebrate annually the fourteenth and fifteenth days of the month of Adar ²²as the time when the Jews got relief from their enemies, and as the month when their sorrow was turned into joy and their mourning into a day of celebration. He wrote them to observe the days as days of feasting and joy and giving presents of food to one another and gifts to the poor.

²³So the Jews agreed to continue the celebration they had begun, doing what Mordecai had written to them. ²⁴For Haman son of Hammedatha, the Agagite, the enemy of all the Jews, had plotted against the Jews to destroy them and had cast the *pur* (that is, the lot) for their ruin and destruction. ²⁵But when the plot came to the king's attention,ᵃ he issued written orders that the evil scheme Haman had devised against the Jews should

---

ᵃ25 Or *when Esther came before the king*

come back onto his own head, and that he and his sons should be hanged on the gallows. 26(Therefore these days were called Purim, from the word *pur*.) Because of everything written in this letter and because of what they had seen and what had happened to them, 27the Jews took it upon themselves to establish the custom that they and their descendants and all who join them should without fail observe these two days every year, in the way prescribed and at the time appointed. 28These days should be remembered and observed in every generation by every family, and in every province and in every city. And these days of Purim should never cease to be celebrated by the Jews, nor should the memory of them die out among their descendants.

29So Queen Esther, daughter of Abihail, along with Mordecai the Jew, wrote with full authority to confirm this second letter concerning Purim. 30And Mordecai sent letters to all the Jews in the 127 provinces of the kingdom of Xerxes—

words of goodwill and assurance— 31to establish these days of Purim at their designated times, as Mordecai the Jew and Queen Esther had decreed for them, and as they had established for themselves and their descendants in regard to their times of fasting and lamentation. 32Esther's decree confirmed these regulations about Purim, and it was written down in the records.

The Greatness of Mordecai

10 King Xerxes imposed tribute throughout the empire, to its distant shores. 2And all his acts of power and might, together with a full account of the greatness of Mordecai to which the king had raised him, are they not written in the book of the annals of the kings of Media and Persia? 3Mordecai the Jew was second in rank to King Xerxes, preeminent among the Jews, and held in high esteem by his many fellow Jews, because he worked for the good of his people and spoke up for the welfare of all the Jews.

*J*OB presents a striking example of the news behind the news—of God at work behind the scenes of human suffering. After numerous attempts by Job and his friends to uncover the reasons for his suffering, God himself enters the dialogue with a majestic description of his power and love. As you read this book, realize that God may not answer all your questions about life's suffering; realize too that God does control Satan, who can go no farther than the Lord allows.

JOB

Prologue

1 In the land of Uz there lived a man whose name was Job. This man was blameless and upright; he feared God and shunned evil. ²He had seven sons and three daughters, ³and he owned seven thousand sheep, three thousand camels, five hundred yoke of oxen and five hundred donkeys, and had a large number of servants. He was the greatest man among all the people of the East.

⁴His sons used to take turns holding feasts in their homes, and they would invite their three sisters to eat and drink

with them. ⁵When a period of feasting had run its course, Job would send and have them purified. Early in the morning he would sacrifice a burnt offering for each of them, thinking, "Perhaps my children have sinned and cursed God in their hearts." This was Job's regular custom.

Job's First Test

⁶One day the angels *a* came to present themselves before the LORD, and Satan *b* also came with them. ⁷The LORD said to Satan, "Where have you come from?"

a6 Hebrew the sons of God   *b6 Satan means accuser.*

Satan answered the LORD, "From roaming through the earth and going back and forth in it."

⁸Then the LORD said to Satan, "Have you considered my servant Job? There is no one on earth like him; he is blameless and upright, a man who fears God and shuns evil."

⁹"Does Job fear God for nothing?" Satan replied. ¹⁰"Have you not put a hedge around him and his household and everything he has? You have blessed the work of his hands, so that his flocks and herds are spread throughout the land. ¹¹But stretch out your hand and strike everything he has, and he will surely curse you to your face."

¹²The LORD said to Satan, "Very well, then, everything he has is in your hands, but on the man himself do not lay a finger."

Then Satan went out from the presence of the LORD.

¹³One day when Job's sons and daughters were feasting and drinking wine at the oldest brother's house, ¹⁴a messenger came to Job and said, "The oxen were plowing and the donkeys were grazing nearby, ¹⁵and the Sabeans attacked and carried them off. They put the servants to the sword, and I am the only one who has escaped to tell you!"

¹⁶While he was still speaking, another messenger came and said, "The fire of God fell from the sky and burned up the sheep and the servants, and I am the only one who has escaped to tell you!"

¹⁷While he was still speaking, another messenger came and said, "The Chaldeans formed three raiding parties and swept down on your camels and carried them off. They put the servants to the sword, and I am the only one who has escaped to tell you!"

¹⁸While he was still speaking, yet another messenger came and said, "Your sons and daughters were feasting and drinking wine at the oldest brother's house, ¹⁹when suddenly a mighty wind swept in from the desert and struck the four corners of the house. It collapsed on them and they are dead, and I am the only one who has escaped to tell you!"

²⁰At this, Job got up and tore his robe and shaved his head. Then he fell to the ground in worship ²¹and said:
"Naked I came from my mother's
    womb,
    and naked I will depart.ᵃ
The LORD gave and the LORD has taken
    away;
    may the name of the LORD be
    praised."

²²In all this, Job did not sin by charging God with wrongdoing.

Job's Second Test

2 On another day the angelsᵇ came to present themselves before the LORD, and Satan also came with them to present himself before him. ²And the LORD said to Satan, "Where have you come from?"

Satan answered the LORD, "From roaming through the earth and going back and forth in it."

³Then the LORD said to Satan, "Have you considered my servant Job? There is no one on earth like him; he is blameless and upright, a man who fears God and shuns evil. And he still maintains his integrity, though you incited me against him to ruin him without any reason."

⁴"Skin for skin!" Satan replied. "A man will give all he has for his own life. ⁵But stretch out your hand and strike his flesh and bones, and he will surely curse you to your face."

⁶The LORD said to Satan, "Very well, then, he is in your hands; but you must spare his life."

⁷So Satan went out from the presence of the LORD and afflicted Job with painful sores from the soles of his feet to the top of his head. ⁸Then Job took a piece of broken pottery and scraped himself with it as he sat among the ashes.

⁹His wife said to him, "Are you still holding on to your integrity? Curse God and die!"

¹⁰He replied, "You are talking like a foolishᶜ woman. Shall we accept good from God, and not trouble?"

In all this, Job did not sin in what he said.

Job's Three Friends

¹¹When Job's three friends, Eliphaz the Temanite, Bildad the Shuhite and Zophar the Naamathite, heard about all the troubles that had come upon him, they set out from their homes and met together by agreement to go and sympathize with him

---

ᵃ21 Or *will return there* ᵇ1 Hebrew *the sons of God* ᶜ10 The Hebrew word rendered *foolish* denotes moral deficiency.

VERSE FOR THE DAY:	AUTHOR:	PASSAGE FOR THE DAY:
Job 2:7	Beth Donigan Seversen	Job 2:1–10

There's a Mole in My Camp

I LOVE a good espionage novel, although I often must go on a treasure hunt to find a wholesome story of intrigue. Espionage plots usually weave around a mole who has infiltrated the Pentagon, CIA, or a branch of government. A mole is a spy who works for an enemy and leaks "information" to the "bad" guys in order to hurt, tarnish the reputation of, or destroy the "good" guys. Moles live undercover like the burrowing little creatures who live underground.

Lately, I have been trying to flush out the enemy's mole in my life. It seems every time I get a specific area of my life submitted to Christ's lordship, the mole leaks that highly sensitive information. For, invariably, it is that area that is attacked by all kinds of temptations or accusations.

For example, recently a friend asked me to join her and eight other moms in daily prayer for our children. It was a struggle to say yes because I was afraid I might be defeated and let down the Lord.

Then God gave me an idea. Why not use my daughter's 4:00 A.M. feeding time to pray? So I made a commitment to daily prayer and saw an incredible breakthrough in my prayer life. I began to spend at least forty-five minutes in prayer each day—and often more when I prayed during other nursing times as well.

That's when the leak was sprung. There just had to be a mole letting Satan in on my secret. Within weeks the pediatrician suggested I stop nursing Kate because her lab results showed an intolerance to the lactose in breast milk. Next, several friends encouraged me to stop for other reasons. Deciding to no longer nurse made sense to all of them, but I recognized my defense strategy was in jeopardy. A mole must have leaked my secret.

I am still fighting back through prayer. By adhering to a non-dairy diet, I may yet be able to continue to nurse Kate and use these times for prayer. Through this experience I am learning to expect the leaks, suspect the moles, and recognize Satan's afflictions.

Additional Scripture Readings:
Ephesians 6:10–18; 1 Peter 5:8–10

Go to page 524 for your next devotional reading.

and comfort him. ¹²When they saw him from a distance, they could hardly recognize him; they began to weep aloud, and they tore their robes and sprinkled dust on their heads. ¹³Then they sat on the ground with him for seven days and seven nights. No one said a word to him, because they saw how great his suffering was.

Job Speaks

3 After this, Job opened his mouth and cursed the day of his birth. ²He said:

³"May the day of my birth perish,
    and the night it was said, 'A boy is born!'
⁴That day—may it turn to darkness;
    may God above not care about it;
    may no light shine upon it.
⁵May darkness and deep shadow*a*
    claim it once more;
    may a cloud settle over it;
    may blackness overwhelm its light.
⁶That night—may thick darkness seize it;
    may it not be included among the days of the year
    nor be entered in any of the months.
⁷May that night be barren;
    may no shout of joy be heard in it.
⁸May those who curse days*b* curse that day,
    those who are ready to rouse Leviathan.
⁹May its morning stars become dark;
    may it wait for daylight in vain
    and not see the first rays of dawn,
¹⁰for it did not shut the doors of the womb on me
    to hide trouble from my eyes.

¹¹"Why did I not perish at birth,
    and die as I came from the womb?
¹²Why were there knees to receive me
    and breasts that I might be nursed?
¹³For now I would be lying down in peace;
    I would be asleep and at rest
¹⁴with kings and counselors of the earth,
    who built for themselves places now lying in ruins,
¹⁵with rulers who had gold,
    who filled their houses with silver.
¹⁶Or why was I not hidden in the ground like a stillborn child,
    like an infant who never saw the light of day?
¹⁷There the wicked cease from turmoil,
    and there the weary are at rest.
¹⁸Captives also enjoy their ease;
    they no longer hear the slave driver's shout.
¹⁹The small and the great are there,
    and the slave is freed from his master.

²⁰"Why is light given to those in misery,
    and life to the bitter of soul,
²¹to those who long for death that does not come,
    who search for it more than for hidden treasure,
²²who are filled with gladness
    and rejoice when they reach the grave?
²³Why is life given to a man
    whose way is hidden,
    whom God has hedged in?
²⁴For sighing comes to me instead of food;
    my groans pour out like water.
²⁵What I feared has come upon me;
    what I dreaded has happened to me.
²⁶I have no peace, no quietness;
    I have no rest, but only turmoil."

Eliphaz

4 Then Eliphaz the Temanite replied:

²"If someone ventures a word with you, will you be impatient?
    But who can keep from speaking?
³Think how you have instructed many,
    how you have strengthened feeble hands.
⁴Your words have supported those who stumbled;
    you have strengthened faltering knees.
⁵But now trouble comes to you, and you are discouraged;
    it strikes you, and you are dismayed.
⁶Should not your piety be your confidence
    and your blameless ways your hope?

⁷"Consider now: Who, being innocent, has ever perished?
    Where were the upright ever destroyed?

---

a5 Or *and the shadow of death*   *b8* Or *the sea*

⁸As I have observed, those who plow
      evil
   and those who sow trouble reap it.
⁹At the breath of God they are
      destroyed;
   at the blast of his anger they
      perish.
¹⁰The lions may roar and growl,
   yet the teeth of the great lions are
      broken.
¹¹The lion perishes for lack of prey,
   and the cubs of the lioness are
      scattered.

¹²"A word was secretly brought to me,
   my ears caught a whisper of it.
¹³Amid disquieting dreams in the night,
   when deep sleep falls on men,
¹⁴fear and trembling seized me
   and made all my bones shake.
¹⁵A spirit glided past my face,
   and the hair on my body stood on
      end.
¹⁶It stopped,
   but I could not tell what it was.
 A form stood before my eyes,
   and I heard a hushed voice:
¹⁷'Can a mortal be more righteous than
      God?
   Can a man be more pure than his
      Maker?
¹⁸If God places no trust in his servants,
   if he charges his angels with error,
¹⁹how much more those who live in
      houses of clay,
   whose foundations are in the dust,
   who are crushed more readily than
      a moth!
²⁰Between dawn and dusk they are
      broken to pieces;
   unnoticed, they perish forever.
²¹Are not the cords of their tent pulled
      up,
   so that they die without wisdom?'ᵃ

5 "Call if you will, but who will
      answer you?
   To which of the holy ones will you
      turn?
²Resentment kills a fool,
   and envy slays the simple.
³I myself have seen a fool taking root,
   but suddenly his house was cursed.
⁴His children are far from safety,
   crushed in court without a
      defender.
⁵The hungry consume his harvest,

taking it even from among thorns,
   and the thirsty pant after his
      wealth.
⁶For hardship does not spring from the
      soil,
   nor does trouble sprout from the
      ground.
⁷Yet man is born to trouble
   as surely as sparks fly upward.

⁸"But if it were I, I would appeal to
      God;
   I would lay my cause before him.
⁹He performs wonders that cannot be
      fathomed,
   miracles that cannot be counted.
¹⁰He bestows rain on the earth;
   he sends water upon the
      countryside.
¹¹The lowly he sets on high,
   and those who mourn are lifted to
      safety.
¹²He thwarts the plans of the crafty,
   so that their hands achieve no
      success.
¹³He catches the wise in their
      craftiness,
   and the schemes of the wily are
      swept away.
¹⁴Darkness comes upon them in the
      daytime;
   at noon they grope as in the night.
¹⁵He saves the needy from the sword in
      their mouth;
   he saves them from the clutches of
      the powerful.
¹⁶So the poor have hope,
   and injustice shuts its mouth.

¹⁷"Blessed is the man whom God
      corrects;
   so do not despise the discipline of
      the Almighty.ᵇ
¹⁸For he wounds, but he also binds up;
   he injures, but his hands also heal.
¹⁹From six calamities he will rescue
      you;
   in seven no harm will befall you.
²⁰In famine he will ransom you from
      death,
   and in battle from the stroke of the
      sword.
²¹You will be protected from the lash of
      the tongue,
   and need not fear when destruction
      comes.
²²You will laugh at destruction and
      famine,

ᵃ21 Some interpreters end the quotation after verse 17.   ᵇ17 Hebrew Shaddai; here and throughout
Job

and need not fear the beasts of the earth.

²³For you will have a covenant with the stones of the field,
and the wild animals will be at peace with you.

²⁴You will know that your tent is secure;
you will take stock of your property and find nothing missing.

²⁵You will know that your children will be many,
and your descendants like the grass of the earth.

²⁶You will come to the grave in full vigor,
like sheaves gathered in season.

²⁷"We have examined this, and it is true.
So hear it and apply it to yourself."

THURSDAY

VERSE FOR THE DAY:
Job 5:7

AUTHOR:
Jeanette Lockerbie

PASSAGE FOR THE DAY:
Job 5:1–9

Why All the Trouble?

SINCE, obviously, a certain measure of trouble comes to each of us, we might think seriously about these words of Socrates (especially if we have ever wished we might trade our troubles):

> If all our misfortunes were laid in one common heap whence everyone must take an equal portion, most people would be content to take their own and depart.

God has a purpose in sending trials our way.

Oliver Wendell Holmes must have understood this truth when he wrote, "If I had a formula for ridding mankind of trouble, I think I would not reveal it, for in doing so, I would do him a disservice."

That trouble, trials, tribulation, difficulty and sorrow have enriched lives is amply borne out even in the hymns we so frequently sing. The blind Fanny Crosby, some of whose hymns bless almost every church service we attend; Horatio Spafford, who, after the horror of the devastating Chicago fire, followed by the loss of four daughters in an Atlantic shipwreck, was somehow enabled to write "It Is Well With My Soul." George Matheson, likewise, threatened by certain blindness and forsaken by a beloved fiancée, gave to us the beautiful "O Love That Will Not Let Me Go."

Although not hymn writers, we can be hymn singers, as we recognize God's plan—even when it is spelled t-r-o-u-b-l-e.

Additional Scripture Readings:
Romans 5:1–5; 1 Peter 1:6–9

Go to page 538 for your next devotional reading.

Job

6

Then Job replied:

2"If only my anguish could be
weighed
and all my misery be placed on the
scales!
3It would surely outweigh the sand of
the seas—
no wonder my words have been
impetuous.
4The arrows of the Almighty are in me,
my spirit drinks in their poison;
God's terrors are marshaled against
me.
5Does a wild donkey bray when it has
grass,
or an ox bellow when it has fodder?
6Is tasteless food eaten without salt,
or is there flavor in the white of an
egg*a*?
7I refuse to touch it;
such food makes me ill.

8"Oh, that I might have my request,
that God would grant what I hope
for,
9that God would be willing to crush
me,
to let loose his hand and cut me
off!
10Then I would still have this
consolation—
my joy in unrelenting pain—
that I had not denied the words of
the Holy One.

11"What strength do I have, that I
should still hope?
What prospects, that I should be
patient?
12Do I have the strength of stone?
Is my flesh bronze?
13Do I have any power to help myself,
now that success has been driven
from me?

14"A despairing man should have the
devotion of his friends,
even though he forsakes the fear of
the Almighty.
15But my brothers are as undependable
as intermittent streams,
as the streams that overflow
16when darkened by thawing ice
and swollen with melting snow,
17but that cease to flow in the dry
season,

and in the heat vanish from their
channels.
18Caravans turn aside from their routes;
they go up into the wasteland and
perish.
19The caravans of Tema look for water,
the traveling merchants of Sheba
look in hope.
20They are distressed, because they had
been confident;
they arrive there, only to be
disappointed.
21Now you too have proved to be of no
help;
you see something dreadful and are
afraid.
22Have I ever said, 'Give something on
my behalf,
pay a ransom for me from your
wealth,
23deliver me from the hand of the
enemy,
ransom me from the clutches of the
ruthless'?

24"Teach me, and I will be quiet;
show me where I have been wrong.
25How painful are honest words!
But what do your arguments prove?
26Do you mean to correct what I say,
and treat the words of a despairing
man as wind?
27You would even cast lots for the
fatherless
and barter away your friend.

28"But now be so kind as to look at me.
Would I lie to your face?
29Relent, do not be unjust;
reconsider, for my integrity is at
stake.*b*
30Is there any wickedness on my lips?
Can my mouth not discern malice?

7

"Does not man have hard service on
earth?
Are not his days like those of a
hired man?
2Like a slave longing for the evening
shadows,
or a hired man waiting eagerly for
his wages,
3so I have been allotted months of
futility,
and nights of misery have been
assigned to me.
4When I lie down I think, 'How long
before I get up?'

---

*a*6 The meaning of the Hebrew for this phrase is uncertain.   *b*29 Or *my righteousness still stands*

The night drags on, and I toss till
  dawn.
⁵My body is clothed with worms and
  scabs,
  my skin is broken and festering.

⁶"My days are swifter than a weaver's
  shuttle,
  and they come to an end without
  hope.
⁷Remember, O God, that my life is but
  a breath;
  my eyes will never see happiness
  again.
⁸The eye that now sees me will see me
  no longer;
  you will look for me, but I will be
  no more.
⁹As a cloud vanishes and is gone,
  so he who goes down to the grave*a*
  does not return.
¹⁰He will never come to his house
  again;
  his place will know him no more.

¹¹"Therefore I will not keep silent;
  I will speak out in the anguish of
  my spirit,
  I will complain in the bitterness of
  my soul.
¹²Am I the sea, or the monster of the
  deep,
  that you put me under guard?
¹³When I think my bed will comfort me
  and my couch will ease my
  complaint,
¹⁴even then you frighten me with
  dreams
  and terrify me with visions,
¹⁵so that I prefer strangling and death,
  rather than this body of mine.
¹⁶I despise my life; I would not live
  forever.
  Let me alone; my days have no
  meaning.

¹⁷"What is man that you make so much
  of him,
  that you give him so much
  attention,
¹⁸that you examine him every morning
  and test him every moment?
¹⁹Will you never look away from me,
  or let me alone even for an instant?
²⁰If I have sinned, what have I done to
  you,
  O watcher of men?
  Why have you made me your target?

Have I become a burden to you?*b*
²¹Why do you not pardon my offenses
  and forgive my sins?
For I will soon lie down in the dust;
  you will search for me, but I will be
  no more."

Bildad

8 Then Bildad the Shuhite replied:

²"How long will you say such
  things?
  Your words are a blustering wind.
³Does God pervert justice?
  Does the Almighty pervert what is
  right?
⁴When your children sinned against
  him,
  he gave them over to the penalty of
  their sin.
⁵But if you will look to God
  and plead with the Almighty,
⁶if you are pure and upright,
  even now he will rouse himself on
  your behalf
  and restore you to your rightful
  place.
⁷Your beginnings will seem humble,
  so prosperous will your future be.

⁸"Ask the former generations
  and find out what their fathers
  learned,
⁹for we were born only yesterday and
  know nothing,
  and our days on earth are but a
  shadow.
¹⁰Will they not instruct you and tell
  you?
  Will they not bring forth words
  from their understanding?
¹¹Can papyrus grow tall where there is
  no marsh?
  Can reeds thrive without water?
¹²While still growing and uncut,
  they wither more quickly than
  grass.
¹³Such is the destiny of all who forget
  God;
  so perishes the hope of the godless.
¹⁴What he trusts in is fragile*c*;
  what he relies on is a spider's web.
¹⁵He leans on his web, but it gives way;
  he clings to it, but it does not hold.
¹⁶He is like a well-watered plant in the
  sunshine,

---

a9 Hebrew *Sheol*   *b20* A few manuscripts of the Masoretic Text, an ancient Hebrew scribal tradition
and Septuagint; most manuscripts of the Masoretic Text *I have become a burden to myself.*   *c14* The
meaning of the Hebrew for this word is uncertain.

spreading its shoots over the
  garden;
¹⁷it entwines its roots around a pile of
  rocks
  and looks for a place among the
  stones.
¹⁸But when it is torn from its spot,
  that place disowns it and says, 'I
  never saw you.'
¹⁹Surely its life withers away,
  andᵃ from the soil other plants
  grow.

²⁰"Surely God does not reject a
  blameless man
  or strengthen the hands of
  evildoers.
²¹He will yet fill your mouth with
  laughter
  and your lips with shouts of joy.
²²Your enemies will be clothed in
  shame,
  and the tents of the wicked will be
  no more."

Job

9 Then Job replied:

²"Indeed, I know that this is true.
  But how can a mortal be righteous
  before God?
³Though one wished to dispute with
  him,
  he could not answer him one time
  out of a thousand.
⁴His wisdom is profound, his power is
  vast.
  Who has resisted him and come out
  unscathed?
⁵He moves mountains without their
  knowing it
  and overturns them in his anger.
⁶He shakes the earth from its place
  and makes its pillars tremble.
⁷He speaks to the sun and it does not
  shine;
  he seals off the light of the stars.
⁸He alone stretches out the heavens
  and treads on the waves of the sea.
⁹He is the Maker of the Bear and
  Orion,
  the Pleiades and the constellations
  of the south.
¹⁰He performs wonders that cannot be
  fathomed,
  miracles that cannot be counted.
¹¹When he passes me, I cannot see
  him;

when he goes by, I cannot perceive
  him.
¹²If he snatches away, who can stop
  him?
  Who can say to him, 'What are you
  doing?'
¹³God does not restrain his anger;
  even the cohorts of Rahab cowered
  at his feet.

¹⁴"How then can I dispute with him?
  How can I find words to argue with
  him?
¹⁵Though I were innocent, I could not
  answer him;
  I could only plead with my Judge
  for mercy.
¹⁶Even if I summoned him and he
  responded,
  I do not believe he would give me a
  hearing.
¹⁷He would crush me with a storm
  and multiply my wounds for no
  reason.
¹⁸He would not let me regain my breath
  but would overwhelm me with
  misery.
¹⁹If it is a matter of strength, he is
  mighty!
  And if it is a matter of justice, who
  will summon himᵇ?
²⁰Even if I were innocent, my mouth
  would condemn me;
  if I were blameless, it would
  pronounce me guilty.

²¹"Although I am blameless,
  I have no concern for myself;
  I despise my own life.
²²It is all the same; that is why I say,
  'He destroys both the blameless
  and the wicked.'
²³When a scourge brings sudden death,
  he mocks the despair of the
  innocent.
²⁴When a land falls into the hands of
  the wicked,
  he blindfolds its judges.
  If it is not he, then who is it?

²⁵"My days are swifter than a runner;
  they fly away without a glimpse of
  joy.
²⁶They skim past like boats of papyrus,
  like eagles swooping down on their
  prey.
²⁷If I say, 'I will forget my complaint,
  I will change my expression, and
  smile,'

ᵃ19 Or *Surely all the joy it has / is that*   ᵇ19 See Septuagint; Hebrew *me.*

²⁸I still dread all my sufferings,
  for I know you will not hold me
    innocent.
²⁹Since I am already found guilty,
  why should I struggle in vain?
³⁰Even if I washed myself with soap*ᵃ*
  and my hands with washing soda,
³¹you would plunge me into a slime pit
  so that even my clothes would
    detest me.

³²"He is not a man like me that I might
    answer him,
  that we might confront each other
    in court.
³³If only there were someone to
    arbitrate between us,
  to lay his hand upon us both,
³⁴someone to remove God's rod from
    me,
  so that his terror would frighten me
    no more.
³⁵Then I would speak up without fear
    of him,
  but as it now stands with me, I
    cannot.

10 "I loathe my very life;
    therefore I will give free rein to
      my complaint
  and speak out in the bitterness of
    my soul.
²I will say to God: Do not condemn
    me,
  but tell me what charges you have
    against me.
³Does it please you to oppress me,
  to spurn the work of your hands,
  while you smile on the schemes of
    the wicked?
⁴Do you have eyes of flesh?
  Do you see as a mortal sees?
⁵Are your days like those of a mortal
  or your years like those of a man,
⁶that you must search out my faults
  and probe after my sin—
⁷though you know that I am not guilty
  and that no one can rescue me
    from your hand?

⁸"Your hands shaped me and made
    me.
  Will you now turn and destroy me?
⁹Remember that you molded me like
    clay.
  Will you now turn me to dust
    again?
¹⁰Did you not pour me out like milk
  and curdle me like cheese,

¹¹clothe me with skin and flesh
  and knit me together with bones
    and sinews?
¹²You gave me life and showed me
    kindness,
  and in your providence watched
    over my spirit.

¹³"But this is what you concealed in
    your heart,
  and I know that this was in your
    mind:
¹⁴If I sinned, you would be watching
    me
  and would not let my offense go
    unpunished.
¹⁵If I am guilty—woe to me!
  Even if I am innocent, I cannot lift
    my head,
  for I am full of shame
  and drowned in*ᵇ* my affliction.
¹⁶If I hold my head high, you stalk me
    like a lion
  and again display your awesome
    power against me.
¹⁷You bring new witnesses against me
  and increase your anger toward me;
  your forces come against me wave
    upon wave.

¹⁸"Why then did you bring me out of
    the womb?
  I wish I had died before any eye
    saw me.
¹⁹If only I had never come into being,
  or had been carried straight from
    the womb to the grave!
²⁰Are not my few days almost over?
  Turn away from me so I can have a
    moment's joy
²¹before I go to the place of no return,
  to the land of gloom and deep
    shadow,*ᶜ*
²²to the land of deepest night,
  of deep shadow and disorder,
  where even the light is like
    darkness."

Zophar

11 Then Zophar the Naamathite re-
    plied:

²"Are all these words to go
    unanswered?
  Is this talker to be vindicated?
³Will your idle talk reduce men to
    silence?
  Will no one rebuke you when you
    mock?

ᵃ30 Or *snow*   *ᵇ15* Or *and aware of*   *ᶜ21* Or *and the shadow of death*; also in verse 22

⁴You say to God, 'My beliefs are
    flawless
  and I am pure in your sight.'
⁵Oh, how I wish that God would
    speak,
  that he would open his lips against
    you
⁶and disclose to you the secrets of
    wisdom,
  for true wisdom has two sides.
  Know this: God has even forgotten
    some of your sin.

⁷"Can you fathom the mysteries of
    God?
  Can you probe the limits of the
    Almighty?
⁸They are higher than the
    heavens—what can you do?
  They are deeper than the depths of
    the grave*ᵃ*—what can you
    know?
⁹Their measure is longer than the
    earth
  and wider than the sea.

¹⁰"If he comes along and confines you
    in prison
  and convenes a court, who can
    oppose him?
¹¹Surely he recognizes deceitful men;
  and when he sees evil, does he not
    take note?
¹²But a witless man can no more
    become wise
  than a wild donkey's colt can be
    born a man.*ᵇ*

¹³"Yet if you devote your heart to him
  and stretch out your hands to him,
¹⁴if you put away the sin that is in your
    hand
  and allow no evil to dwell in your
    tent,
¹⁵then you will lift up your face without
    shame;
  you will stand firm and without
    fear.
¹⁶You will surely forget your trouble,
  recalling it only as waters gone by.
¹⁷Life will be brighter than noonday,
  and darkness will become like
    morning.
¹⁸You will be secure, because there is
    hope;
  you will look about you and take
    your rest in safety.

¹⁹You will lie down, with no one to
    make you afraid,
  and many will court your favor.
²⁰But the eyes of the wicked will fail,
  and escape will elude them;
  their hope will become a dying
    gasp."

Job

12 Then Job replied:

²"Doubtless you are the people,
  and wisdom will die with you!
³But I have a mind as well as you;
  I am not inferior to you.
  Who does not know all these
    things?

⁴"I have become a laughingstock to my
    friends,
  though I called upon God and he
    answered—
  a mere laughingstock, though
    righteous and blameless!
⁵Men at ease have contempt for
    misfortune
  as the fate of those whose feet are
    slipping.
⁶The tents of marauders are
    undisturbed,
  and those who provoke God are
    secure—
  those who carry their god in their
    hands.*ᶜ*

⁷"But ask the animals, and they will
    teach you,
  or the birds of the air, and they will
    tell you;
⁸or speak to the earth, and it will
    teach you,
  or let the fish of the sea inform
    you.
⁹Which of all these does not know
  that the hand of the LORD has done
    this?
¹⁰In his hand is the life of every
    creature
  and the breath of all mankind.
¹¹Does not the ear test words
  as the tongue tastes food?
¹²Is not wisdom found among the aged?
  Does not long life bring
    understanding?

¹³"To God belong wisdom and power;
  counsel and understanding are his.
¹⁴What he tears down cannot be
    rebuilt;

ᵃ8 Hebrew *than Sheol*   *ᵇ12* Or *wild donkey can be born tame*   *ᶜ6* Or *secure / in what God's hand
brings them*

the man he imprisons cannot be
　　released.
15If he holds back the waters, there is
　　drought;
　　if he lets them loose, they
　　devastate the land.
16To him belong strength and victory;
　　both deceived and deceiver are
　　his.
17He leads counselors away stripped
　　and makes fools of judges.
18He takes off the shackles put on by
　　kings
　　and ties a loincloth*a* around their
　　waist.
19He leads priests away stripped
　　and overthrows men long
　　established.
20He silences the lips of trusted
　　advisers
　　and takes away the discernment of
　　elders.
21He pours contempt on nobles
　　and disarms the mighty.
22He reveals the deep things of
　　darkness
　　and brings deep shadows into the
　　light.
23He makes nations great, and destroys
　　them;
　　he enlarges nations, and disperses
　　them.
24He deprives the leaders of the earth
　　of their reason;
　　he sends them wandering through a
　　trackless waste.
25They grope in darkness with no light;
　　he makes them stagger like
　　drunkards.

13 "My eyes have seen all this,
　　my ears have heard and
　　understood it.
2What you know, I also know;
　　I am not inferior to you.
3But I desire to speak to the Almighty
　　and to argue my case with God.
4You, however, smear me with lies;
　　you are worthless physicians, all of
　　you!
5If only you would be altogether silent!
　　For you, that would be wisdom.
6Hear now my argument;
　　listen to the plea of my lips.
7Will you speak wickedly on God's
　　behalf?
　　Will you speak deceitfully for him?
8Will you show him partiality?
　　Will you argue the case for God?

9Would it turn out well if he examined
　　you?
　　Could you deceive him as you
　　might deceive men?
10He would surely rebuke you
　　if you secretly showed partiality.
11Would not his splendor terrify you?
　　Would not the dread of him fall on
　　you?
12Your maxims are proverbs of ashes;
　　your defenses are defenses of clay.

13"Keep silent and let me speak;
　　then let come to me what may.
14Why do I put myself in jeopardy
　　and take my life in my hands?
15Though he slay me, yet will I hope in
　　him;
　　I will surely*b* defend my ways to his
　　face.
16Indeed, this will turn out for my
　　deliverance,
　　for no godless man would dare
　　come before him!
17Listen carefully to my words;
　　let your ears take in what I say.
18Now that I have prepared my case,
　　I know I will be vindicated.
19Can anyone bring charges against me?
　　If so, I will be silent and die.

20"Only grant me these two things,
　　O God,
　　and then I will not hide from you:
21Withdraw your hand far from me,
　　and stop frightening me with your
　　terrors.
22Then summon me and I will answer,
　　or let me speak, and you reply.
23How many wrongs and sins have I
　　committed?
　　Show me my offense and my sin.
24Why do you hide your face
　　and consider me your enemy?
25Will you torment a windblown leaf?
　　Will you chase after dry chaff?
26For you write down bitter things
　　against me
　　and make me inherit the sins of my
　　youth.
27You fasten my feet in shackles;
　　you keep close watch on all my
　　paths
　　by putting marks on the soles of my
　　feet.

28"So man wastes away like something
　　rotten,
　　like a garment eaten by moths.

---

a18 Or *shackles of kings / and ties a belt*　　　*b15* Or *He will surely slay me; I have no hope — / yet I will*

14 "Man born of woman
is of few days and full of trouble.
²He springs up like a flower and
withers away;
like a fleeting shadow, he does not
endure.
³Do you fix your eye on such a one?
Will you bring him[a] before you for
judgment?
⁴Who can bring what is pure from the
impure?
No one!
⁵Man's days are determined;
you have decreed the number of his
months
and have set limits he cannot
exceed.
⁶So look away from him and let him
alone,
till he has put in his time like a
hired man.

⁷"At least there is hope for a tree:
If it is cut down, it will sprout
again,
and its new shoots will not fail.
⁸Its roots may grow old in the ground
and its stump die in the soil,
⁹yet at the scent of water it will bud
and put forth shoots like a plant.
¹⁰But man dies and is laid low;
he breathes his last and is no more.
¹¹As water disappears from the sea
or a riverbed becomes parched and
dry,
¹²so man lies down and does not rise;
till the heavens are no more, men
will not awake
or be roused from their sleep.

¹³"If only you would hide me in the
grave[b]
and conceal me till your anger has
passed!
If only you would set me a time
and then remember me!
¹⁴If a man dies, will he live again?
All the days of my hard service
I will wait for my renewal[c] to
come.
¹⁵You will call and I will answer you;
you will long for the creature your
hands have made.
¹⁶Surely then you will count my steps
but not keep track of my sin.
¹⁷My offenses will be sealed up in a
bag;
you will cover over my sin.

¹⁸"But as a mountain erodes and
crumbles
and as a rock is moved from its
place,
¹⁹as water wears away stones
and torrents wash away the soil,
so you destroy man's hope.
²⁰You overpower him once for all, and
he is gone;
you change his countenance and
send him away.
²¹If his sons are honored, he does not
know it;
if they are brought low, he does not
see it.
²²He feels but the pain of his own body
and mourns only for himself."

Eliphaz

15 Then Eliphaz the Temanite replied:

²"Would a wise man answer with
empty notions
or fill his belly with the hot east
wind?
³Would he argue with useless words,
with speeches that have no value?
⁴But you even undermine piety
and hinder devotion to God.
⁵Your sin prompts your mouth;
you adopt the tongue of the crafty.
⁶Your own mouth condemns you, not
mine;
your own lips testify against you.

⁷"Are you the first man ever born?
Were you brought forth before the
hills?
⁸Do you listen in on God's council?
Do you limit wisdom to yourself?
⁹What do you know that we do not
know?
What insights do you have that we
do not have?
¹⁰The gray-haired and the aged are on
our side,
men even older than your father.
¹¹Are God's consolations not enough for
you,
words spoken gently to you?
¹²Why has your heart carried you away,
and why do your eyes flash,
¹³so that you vent your rage against
God
and pour out such words from your
mouth?
¹⁴"What is man, that he could be pure,

---

a3 Septuagint, Vulgate and Syriac; Hebrew *me*   *b13* Hebrew *Sheol*   *c14* Or *release*

or one born of woman, that he
    could be righteous?
15If God places no trust in his holy
    ones,
    if even the heavens are not pure in
        his eyes,
16how much less man, who is vile and
    corrupt,
    who drinks up evil like water!

17"Listen to me and I will explain to
    you;
    let me tell you what I have seen,
18what wise men have declared,
    hiding nothing received from their
        fathers
19(to whom alone the land was given
    when no alien passed among them):
20All his days the wicked man suffers
    torment,
    the ruthless through all the years
        stored up for him.
21Terrifying sounds fill his ears;
    when all seems well, marauders
        attack him.
22He despairs of escaping the darkness;
    he is marked for the sword.
23He wanders about—food for
        vultures*a*;
    he knows the day of darkness is at
        hand.
24Distress and anguish fill him with
        terror;
    they overwhelm him, like a king
        poised to attack,
25because he shakes his fist at God
    and vaunts himself against the
        Almighty,
26defiantly charging against him
    with a thick, strong shield.

27"Though his face is covered with fat
    and his waist bulges with flesh,
28he will inhabit ruined towns
    and houses where no one lives,
    houses crumbling to rubble.
29He will no longer be rich and his
        wealth will not endure,
    nor will his possessions spread over
        the land.
30He will not escape the darkness;
    a flame will wither his shoots,
    and the breath of God's mouth will
        carry him away.
31Let him not deceive himself by
        trusting what is worthless,
    for he will get nothing in return.
32Before his time he will be paid in full,
    and his branches will not flourish.

33He will be like a vine stripped of its
    unripe grapes,
    like an olive tree shedding its
        blossoms.
34For the company of the godless will
    be barren,
    and fire will consume the tents of
        those who love bribes.
35They conceive trouble and give birth
    to evil;
    their womb fashions deceit."

Job

16

Then Job replied:
2"I have heard many things like
    these;
    miserable comforters are you all!
3Will your long-winded speeches never
        end?
    What ails you that you keep on
        arguing?
4I also could speak like you,
    if you were in my place;
    I could make fine speeches against
        you
    and shake my head at you.
5But my mouth would encourage you;
    comfort from my lips would bring
        you relief.

6"Yet if I speak, my pain is not
        relieved;
    and if I refrain, it does not go away.
7Surely, O God, you have worn me out;
    you have devastated my entire
        household.
8You have bound me—and it has
        become a witness;
    my gauntness rises up and testifies
        against me.
9God assails me and tears me in his
        anger
    and gnashes his teeth at me;
    my opponent fastens on me his
        piercing eyes.
10Men open their mouths to jeer at me;
    they strike my cheek in scorn
    and unite together against me.
11God has turned me over to evil men
    and thrown me into the clutches of
        the wicked.
12All was well with me, but he
        shattered me;
    he seized me by the neck and
        crushed me.
    He has made me his target;
13 his archers surround me.
    Without pity, he pierces my kidneys

---

*a*23 Or *about, looking for food*

and spills my gall on the ground.
[14]Again and again he bursts upon me;
he rushes at me like a warrior.

[15]"I have sewed sackcloth over my skin
and buried my brow in the dust.
[16]My face is red with weeping,
deep shadows ring my eyes;
[17]yet my hands have been free of
violence
and my prayer is pure.

[18]"O earth, do not cover my blood;
may my cry never be laid to rest!
[19]Even now my witness is in heaven;
my advocate is on high.
[20]My intercessor is my friend[a]
as my eyes pour out tears to God;
[21]on behalf of a man he pleads with
God
as a man pleads for his friend.

[22]"Only a few years will pass
before I go on the journey of no
return.

17 [1]My spirit is broken,
my days are cut short,
the grave awaits me.
[2]Surely mockers surround me;
my eyes must dwell on their
hostility.

[3]"Give me, O God, the pledge you
demand.
Who else will put up security for
me?
[4]You have closed their minds to
understanding;
therefore you will not let them
triumph.
[5]If a man denounces his friends for
reward,
the eyes of his children will fail.

[6]"God has made me a byword to
everyone,
a man in whose face people spit.
[7]My eyes have grown dim with grief;
my whole frame is but a shadow.
[8]Upright men are appalled at this;
the innocent are aroused against
the ungodly.
[9]Nevertheless, the righteous will hold
to their ways,
and those with clean hands will
grow stronger.

[10]"But come on, all of you, try again!
I will not find a wise man among
you.

[11]My days have passed, my plans are
shattered,
and so are the desires of my heart.
[12]These men turn night into day;
in the face of darkness they say,
'Light is near.'
[13]If the only home I hope for is the
grave,[b]
if I spread out my bed in darkness,
[14]if I say to corruption, 'You are my
father,'
and to the worm, 'My mother' or
'My sister,'
[15]where then is my hope?
Who can see any hope for me?
[16]Will it go down to the gates of
death[b]?
Will we descend together into the
dust?"

Bildad

18 Then Bildad the Shuhite replied:
[2]"When will you end these
speeches?
Be sensible, and then we can talk.
[3]Why are we regarded as cattle
and considered stupid in your
sight?
[4]You who tear yourself to pieces in
your anger,
is the earth to be abandoned for
your sake?
Or must the rocks be moved from
their place?

[5]"The lamp of the wicked is snuffed
out;
the flame of his fire stops burning.
[6]The light in his tent becomes dark;
the lamp beside him goes out.
[7]The vigor of his step is weakened;
his own schemes throw him down.
[8]His feet thrust him into a net
and he wanders into its mesh.
[9]A trap seizes him by the heel;
a snare holds him fast.
[10]A noose is hidden for him on the
ground;
a trap lies in his path.
[11]Terrors startle him on every side
and dog his every step.
[12]Calamity is hungry for him;
disaster is ready for him when he
falls.
[13]It eats away parts of his skin;
death's firstborn devours his limbs.
[14]He is torn from the security of his
tent

[a]20 Or *My friends treat me with scorn*   [b]13,16 Hebrew *Sheol*

and marched off to the king of
terrors.
¹⁵Fire resides^a in his tent;
  burning sulfur is scattered over his
dwelling.
¹⁶His roots dry up below
  and his branches wither above.
¹⁷The memory of him perishes from the
earth;
  he has no name in the land.
¹⁸He is driven from light into darkness
  and is banished from the world.
¹⁹He has no offspring or descendants
among his people,
  no survivor where once he lived.
²⁰Men of the west are appalled at his
fate;
  men of the east are seized with
horror.
²¹Surely such is the dwelling of an evil
man;
  such is the place of one who knows
not God."

Job

19 Then Job replied:

²"How long will you torment me
  and crush me with words?
³Ten times now you have reproached
me;
  shamelessly you attack me.
⁴If it is true that I have gone astray,
  my error remains my concern alone.
⁵If indeed you would exalt yourselves
above me
  and use my humiliation against me,
⁶then know that God has wronged me
  and drawn his net around me.

⁷"Though I cry, 'I've been wronged!' I
get no response;
  though I call for help, there is no
justice.
⁸He has blocked my way so I cannot
pass;
  he has shrouded my paths in
darkness.
⁹He has stripped me of my honor
  and removed the crown from my
head.
¹⁰He tears me down on every side till I
am gone;
  he uproots my hope like a tree.
¹¹His anger burns against me;
  he counts me among his enemies.
¹²His troops advance in force;

  they build a siege ramp against me
  and encamp around my tent.

¹³"He has alienated my brothers from
me;
  my acquaintances are completely
estranged from me.
¹⁴My kinsmen have gone away;
  my friends have forgotten me.
¹⁵My guests and my maidservants count
me a stranger;
  they look upon me as an alien.
¹⁶I summon my servant, but he does
not answer,
  though I beg him with my own
mouth.
¹⁷My breath is offensive to my wife;
  I am loathsome to my own
brothers.
¹⁸Even the little boys scorn me;
  when I appear, they ridicule me.
¹⁹All my intimate friends detest me;
  those I love have turned against
me.
²⁰I am nothing but skin and bones;
  I have escaped with only the skin
of my teeth.^b

²¹"Have pity on me, my friends, have
pity,
  for the hand of God has struck me.
²²Why do you pursue me as God does?
  Will you never get enough of my
flesh?

²³"Oh, that my words were recorded,
  that they were written on a scroll,
²⁴that they were inscribed with an iron
tool on^c lead,
  or engraved in rock forever!
²⁵I know that my Redeemer^d lives,
  and that in the end he will stand
upon the earth.^e
²⁶And after my skin has been destroyed,
yet^f in^g my flesh I will see God;
²⁷I myself will see him
  with my own eyes—I, and not
another.
  How my heart yearns within me!

²⁸"If you say, 'How we will hound him,
  since the root of the trouble lies in
him,^h'
²⁹you should fear the sword yourselves;
  for wrath will bring punishment by
the sword,

---

^a15 Or *Nothing he had remains*   ^b20 Or *only my gums*   ^c24 Or *and*   ^d25 Or *defender*   ^e25 Or
upon my grave   ^f26 Or *And after I awake, / though this ,body, has been destroyed, / then*   ^g26 Or /
apart from   ^h28 Many Hebrew manuscripts, Septuagint and Vulgate; most Hebrew manuscripts *me*

and then you will know that there
is judgment. *a* "

Zophar

20 Then Zophar the Naamathite replied:

²"My troubled thoughts prompt me to
answer
because I am greatly disturbed.
³I hear a rebuke that dishonors me,
and my understanding inspires me
to reply.

⁴"Surely you know how it has been
from of old,
ever since man *b* was placed on the
earth,
⁵that the mirth of the wicked is brief,
the joy of the godless lasts but a
moment.
⁶Though his pride reaches to the
heavens
and his head touches the clouds,
⁷he will perish forever, like his own
dung;
those who have seen him will say,
'Where is he?'
⁸Like a dream he flies away, no more
to be found,
banished like a vision of the night.
⁹The eye that saw him will not see
him again;
his place will look on him no more.
¹⁰His children must make amends to
the poor;
his own hands must give back his
wealth.
¹¹The youthful vigor that fills his bones
will lie with him in the dust.

¹²"Though evil is sweet in his mouth
and he hides it under his tongue,
¹³though he cannot bear to let it go
and keeps it in his mouth,
¹⁴yet his food will turn sour in his
stomach;
it will become the venom of
serpents within him.
¹⁵He will spit out the riches he
swallowed;
God will make his stomach vomit
them up.
¹⁶He will suck the poison of serpents;
the fangs of an adder will kill him.
¹⁷He will not enjoy the streams,
the rivers flowing with honey and
cream.

¹⁸What he toiled for he must give back
uneaten;
he will not enjoy the profit from his
trading.
¹⁹For he has oppressed the poor and
left them destitute;
he has seized houses he did not
build.

²⁰"Surely he will have no respite from
his craving;
he cannot save himself by his
treasure.
²¹Nothing is left for him to devour;
his prosperity will not endure.
²²In the midst of his plenty, distress
will overtake him;
the full force of misery will come
upon him.
²³When he has filled his belly,
God will vent his burning anger
against him
and rain down his blows upon him.
²⁴Though he flees from an iron weapon,
a bronze-tipped arrow pierces him.
²⁵He pulls it out of his back,
the gleaming point out of his liver.
Terrors will come over him;
²⁶ total darkness lies in wait for his
treasures.
A fire unfanned will consume him
and devour what is left in his tent.
²⁷The heavens will expose his guilt;
the earth will rise up against him.
²⁸A flood will carry off his house,
rushing waters *c* on the day of
God's wrath.
²⁹Such is the fate God allots the
wicked,
the heritage appointed for them by
God."

Job

21 Then Job replied:

²"Listen carefully to my words;
let this be the consolation you give
me.
³Bear with me while I speak,
and after I have spoken, mock on.

⁴"Is my complaint directed to man?
Why should I not be impatient?
⁵Look at me and be astonished;
clap your hand over your mouth.
⁶When I think about this, I am
terrified;
trembling seizes my body.

*a29 Or / that you may come to know the Almighty
will be carried off, / washed away*   *b4 Or Adam*   *c28 Or The possessions in his house*

⁷Why do the wicked live on,
    growing old and increasing in
       power?
⁸They see their children established
    around them,
    their offspring before their eyes.
⁹Their homes are safe and free from
    fear;
    the rod of God is not upon them.
¹⁰Their bulls never fail to breed;
    their cows calve and do not
       miscarry.
¹¹They send forth their children as a
    flock;
    their little ones dance about.
¹²They sing to the music of tambourine
    and harp;
    they make merry to the sound of
       the flute.
¹³They spend their years in prosperity
    and go down to the grave^a in
       peace.^b
¹⁴Yet they say to God, 'Leave us alone!
    We have no desire to know your
       ways.
¹⁵Who is the Almighty, that we should
    serve him?
    What would we gain by praying to
       him?'
¹⁶But their prosperity is not in their
    own hands,
    so I stand aloof from the counsel of
       the wicked.

¹⁷"Yet how often is the lamp of the
    wicked snuffed out?
    How often does calamity come
       upon them,
    the fate God allots in his anger?
¹⁸How often are they like straw before
    the wind,
    like chaff swept away by a gale?
¹⁹It is said, 'God stores up a man's
    punishment for his sons.'
    Let him repay the man himself, so
       that he will know it!
²⁰Let his own eyes see his destruction;
    let him drink of the wrath of the
       Almighty.^c
²¹For what does he care about the
    family he leaves behind
    when his allotted months come to
       an end?

²²"Can anyone teach knowledge to God,
    since he judges even the highest?
²³One man dies in full vigor,

completely secure and at ease,
²⁴his body^d well nourished,
    his bones rich with marrow.
²⁵Another man dies in bitterness of
    soul,
    never having enjoyed anything
       good.
²⁶Side by side they lie in the dust,
    and worms cover them both.

²⁷"I know full well what you are
    thinking,
    the schemes by which you would
       wrong me.
²⁸You say, 'Where now is the great
    man's house,
    the tents where wicked men lived?'
²⁹Have you never questioned those who
    travel?
    Have you paid no regard to their
       accounts—
³⁰that the evil man is spared from the
    day of calamity,
    that he is delivered from^e the day
       of wrath?
³¹Who denounces his conduct to his
    face?
    Who repays him for what he has
       done?
³²He is carried to the grave,
    and watch is kept over his tomb.
³³The soil in the valley is sweet to him;
    all men follow after him,
    and a countless throng goes^f
       before him.

³⁴"So how can you console me with
    your nonsense?
    Nothing is left of your answers but
       falsehood!"

Eliphaz

22 Then Eliphaz the Temanite replied:

²"Can a man be of benefit to God?
    Can even a wise man benefit him?
³What pleasure would it give the
    Almighty if you were righteous?
    What would he gain if your ways
       were blameless?

⁴"Is it for your piety that he rebukes
    you
    and brings charges against you?
⁵Is not your wickedness great?
    Are not your sins endless?

---

^a13 Hebrew *Sheol*   ^b13 Or *in an instant*   ^c17-20 Verses 17 and 18 may be taken as exclamations
and 19 and 20 as declarations.   ^d24 The meaning of the Hebrew for this word is uncertain.   ^e30 Or
man is reserved for the day of calamity, / that he is brought forth to   ^f33 Or / *as a countless throng went*

⁶You demanded security from your
    brothers for no reason;
you stripped men of their clothing,
    leaving them naked.
⁷You gave no water to the weary
    and you withheld food from the
      hungry,
⁸though you were a powerful man,
    owning land—
an honored man, living on it.
⁹And you sent widows away
    empty-handed
and broke the strength of the
    fatherless.
¹⁰That is why snares are all around you,
    why sudden peril terrifies you,
¹¹why it is so dark you cannot see,
    and why a flood of water covers
    you.

¹²"Is not God in the heights of heaven?
    And see how lofty are the highest
      stars!
¹³Yet you say, 'What does God know?
    Does he judge through such
      darkness?
¹⁴Thick clouds veil him, so he does not
    see us
as he goes about in the vaulted
    heavens.'
¹⁵Will you keep to the old path
    that evil men have trod?
¹⁶They were carried off before their
    time,
their foundations washed away by a
    flood.
¹⁷They said to God, 'Leave us alone!
    What can the Almighty do to us?'
¹⁸Yet it was he who filled their houses
    with good things,
so I stand aloof from the counsel of
    the wicked.

¹⁹"The righteous see their ruin and
    rejoice;
the innocent mock them, saying,
²⁰'Surely our foes are destroyed,
    and fire devours their wealth.'

²¹"Submit to God and be at peace with
    him;
in this way prosperity will come to
    you.
²²Accept instruction from his mouth
    and lay up his words in your heart.
²³If you return to the Almighty, you will
    be restored:
If you remove wickedness far from
    your tent

²⁴and assign your nuggets to the dust,
    your gold of Ophir to the rocks in
    the ravines,
²⁵then the Almighty will be your gold,
    the choicest silver for you.
²⁶Surely then you will find delight in
    the Almighty
and will lift up your face to God.
²⁷You will pray to him, and he will hear
    you,
and you will fulfill your vows.
²⁸What you decide on will be done,
    and light will shine on your ways.
²⁹When men are brought low and you
    say, 'Lift them up!'
then he will save the downcast.
³⁰He will deliver even one who is not
    innocent,
who will be delivered through the
    cleanness of your hands."

Job

23 Then Job replied:

²"Even today my complaint is
    bitter;
his hand*ᵃ* is heavy in spite of*ᵇ* my
    groaning.
³If only I knew where to find him;
    if only I could go to his dwelling!
⁴I would state my case before him
    and fill my mouth with arguments.
⁵I would find out what he would
    answer me,
and consider what he would say.
⁶Would he oppose me with great
    power?
No, he would not press charges
    against me.
⁷There an upright man could present
    his case before him,
and I would be delivered forever
    from my judge.

⁸"But if I go to the east, he is not
    there;
if I go to the west, I do not find
    him.
⁹When he is at work in the north, I do
    not see him;
when he turns to the south, I catch
    no glimpse of him.
¹⁰But he knows the way that I take;
    when he has tested me, I will come
    forth as gold.
¹¹My feet have closely followed his
    steps;
I have kept to his way without
    turning aside.

ᵃ2 Septuagint and Syriac; Hebrew / the hand on me   *ᵇ2 Or heavy on me in*

¹²I have not departed from the
commands of his lips;
I have treasured the words of his
mouth more than my daily
bread.

¹³"But he stands alone, and who can
oppose him?
He does whatever he pleases.
¹⁴He carries out his decree against me,
and many such plans he still has in
store.
¹⁵That is why I am terrified before him;
when I think of all this, I fear him.

¹⁶God has made my heart faint;
the Almighty has terrified me.
¹⁷Yet I am not silenced by the
darkness,
by the thick darkness that covers
my face.

24 "Why does the Almighty not set
times for judgment?
Why must those who know him
look in vain for such days?
²Men move boundary stones;
they pasture flocks they have
stolen.

FRIDAY

VERSE FOR THE DAY:
Job 23:10

AUTHOR:
Hannah Whitall Smith

PASSAGE FOR THE DAY:
Job 23:1–12

Hurting but Healing

THE story of Job is enacted over and over. The righteous suffer, and we do not know why. Mysterious providences darken and attempt to ruin the lives of those who have seemed too good to need such discipline. Even to ourselves come afflictions that we cannot understand, and Satan seems so busy in the matter that it is hard to trace the hand of the Lord in it at all. But his hand is in it nevertheless, and he overrules everything. No trial comes except by his permission and for some wise and loving purpose which perhaps only eternity will disclose.

Earthly parents deal this way continually with their children. Their watchful eyes discover incipient diseases long before their children feel any uncomfortable symptoms themselves, and they administer the needed medicines, often when it seems very mysterious and unreasonable to their children. Yet a parent's closet may be full of medicines that remain untouched for months if no need is discovered. A parent's love is too tender to inflict unnecessary doses and too strong to spare the dose that is needed.

Here lies the secret of all that seems so mysterious in the discipline of our lives. Our loving and wise Physician has discovered in us some incipient disease that he knows will ruin us if it remains unchecked, and he is applying the remedy. Would we stay his hand even if we could? Surely not. For more than anything else, we want sound health; and any remedy that will bring it to us is more than welcome.

Additional Scripture Readings:
Psalm 66:10–20; 2 Corinthians 4:7–9

*Go to page 546 for your next
devotional reading.*

³They drive away the orphan's donkey
and take the widow's ox in pledge.
⁴They thrust the needy from the path
and force all the poor of the land
into hiding.
⁵Like wild donkeys in the desert,
the poor go about their labor of
foraging food;
the wasteland provides food for
their children.
⁶They gather fodder in the fields
and glean in the vineyards of the
wicked.
⁷Lacking clothes, they spend the night
naked;
they have nothing to cover
themselves in the cold.
⁸They are drenched by mountain rains
and hug the rocks for lack of
shelter.
⁹The fatherless child is snatched from
the breast;
the infant of the poor is seized for
a debt.
¹⁰Lacking clothes, they go about naked;
they carry the sheaves, but still go
hungry.
¹¹They crush olives among the
terraces ᵃ;
they tread the winepresses, yet
suffer thirst.
¹²The groans of the dying rise from the
city,
and the souls of the wounded cry
out for help.
But God charges no one with
wrongdoing.

¹³"There are those who rebel against
the light,
who do not know its ways
or stay in its paths.
¹⁴When daylight is gone, the murderer
rises up
and kills the poor and needy;
in the night he steals forth like a
thief.
¹⁵The eye of the adulterer watches for
dusk;
he thinks, 'No eye will see me,'
and he keeps his face concealed.
¹⁶In the dark, men break into houses,
but by day they shut themselves in;
they want nothing to do with the
light.
¹⁷For all of them, deep darkness is
their morning ᵇ;

they make friends with the terrors
of darkness. ᶜ
¹⁸"Yet they are foam on the surface of
the water;
their portion of the land is cursed,
so that no one goes to the
vineyards.
¹⁹As heat and drought snatch away the
melted snow,
so the grave ᵈ snatches away those
who have sinned.
²⁰The womb forgets them,
the worm feasts on them;
evil men are no longer remembered
but are broken like a tree.
²¹They prey on the barren and childless
woman,
and to the widow show no
kindness.
²²But God drags away the mighty by his
power;
though they become established,
they have no assurance of
life.
²³He may let them rest in a feeling of
security,
but his eyes are on their ways.
²⁴For a little while they are exalted,
and then they are gone;
they are brought low and gathered
up like all others;
they are cut off like heads of grain.

²⁵"If this is not so, who can prove me
false
and reduce my words to nothing?"

Bildad

25 Then Bildad the Shuhite replied:

²"Dominion and awe belong to
God;
he establishes order in the heights
of heaven.
³Can his forces be numbered?
Upon whom does his light not rise?
⁴How then can a man be righteous
before God?
How can one born of woman be
pure?
⁵If even the moon is not bright
and the stars are not pure in his
eyes,
⁶how much less man, who is but a
maggot—
a son of man, who is only a
worm!"

ᵃ11 Or *olives between the millstones*; the meaning of the Hebrew for this word is uncertain.   ᵇ17 Or
them, their morning is like the shadow of death   ᶜ17 Or *of the shadow of death*   ᵈ19 Hebrew *Sheol*

Job

26 Then Job replied:

²"How you have helped the
powerless!
How you have saved the arm that is
feeble!
³What advice you have offered to one
without wisdom!
And what great insight you have
displayed!
⁴Who has helped you utter these
words?
And whose spirit spoke from your
mouth?

⁵"The dead are in deep anguish,
those beneath the waters and all
that live in them.
⁶Death*a* is naked before God;
Destruction*b* lies uncovered.
⁷He spreads out the northern skies
over empty space;
he suspends the earth over nothing.
⁸He wraps up the waters in his clouds,
yet the clouds do not burst under
their weight.
⁹He covers the face of the full moon,
spreading his clouds over it.
¹⁰He marks out the horizon on the face
of the waters
for a boundary between light and
darkness.
¹¹The pillars of the heavens quake,
aghast at his rebuke.
¹²By his power he churned up the sea;
by his wisdom he cut Rahab to
pieces.
¹³By his breath the skies became fair;
his hand pierced the gliding
serpent.
¹⁴And these are but the outer fringe of
his works;
how faint the whisper we hear of
him!
Who then can understand the
thunder of his power?"

27 And Job continued his discourse:

²"As surely as God lives, who has
denied me justice,
the Almighty, who has made me
taste bitterness of soul,
³as long as I have life within me,
the breath of God in my nostrils,
⁴my lips will not speak wickedness,
and my tongue will utter no deceit.
⁵I will never admit you are in the right;

till I die, I will not deny my
integrity.
⁶I will maintain my righteousness and
never let go of it;
my conscience will not reproach me
as long as I live.

⁷"May my enemies be like the wicked,
my adversaries like the unjust!
⁸For what hope has the godless when
he is cut off,
when God takes away his life?
⁹Does God listen to his cry
when distress comes upon him?
¹⁰Will he find delight in the Almighty?
Will he call upon God at all times?

¹¹"I will teach you about the power of
God;
the ways of the Almighty I will not
conceal.
¹²You have all seen this yourselves.
Why then this meaningless talk?

¹³"Here is the fate God allots to the
wicked,
the heritage a ruthless man receives
from the Almighty:
¹⁴However many his children, their fate
is the sword;
his offspring will never have enough
to eat.
¹⁵The plague will bury those who
survive him,
and their widows will not weep for
them.
¹⁶Though he heaps up silver like dust
and clothes like piles of clay,
¹⁷what he lays up the righteous will
wear,
and the innocent will divide his
silver.
¹⁸The house he builds is like a moth's
cocoon,
like a hut made by a watchman.
¹⁹He lies down wealthy, but will do so
no more;
when he opens his eyes, all is gone.
²⁰Terrors overtake him like a flood;
a tempest snatches him away in the
night.
²¹The east wind carries him off, and he
is gone;
it sweeps him out of his place.
²²It hurls itself against him without
mercy
as he flees headlong from its power.
²³It claps its hands in derision
and hisses him out of his place.

---

*a*6 Hebrew *Sheol*　　*b*6 Hebrew *Abaddon*

28 "There is a mine for silver
    and a place where gold is
    refined.
²Iron is taken from the earth,
    and copper is smelted from ore.
³Man puts an end to the darkness;
    he searches the farthest recesses
    for ore in the blackest darkness.
⁴Far from where people dwell he cuts
        a shaft,
    in places forgotten by the foot of
        man;
    far from men he dangles and sways.
⁵The earth, from which food comes,
    is transformed below as by fire;
⁶sapphires*a* come from its rocks,
    and its dust contains nuggets of
        gold.
⁷No bird of prey knows that hidden
        path,
    no falcon's eye has seen it.
⁸Proud beasts do not set foot on it,
    and no lion prowls there.
⁹Man's hand assaults the flinty rock
    and lays bare the roots of the
        mountains.
¹⁰He tunnels through the rock;
    his eyes see all its treasures.
¹¹He searches*b* the sources of the rivers
    and brings hidden things to light.

¹²"But where can wisdom be found?
    Where does understanding dwell?
¹³Man does not comprehend its worth;
    it cannot be found in the land of
        the living.
¹⁴The deep says, 'It is not in me';
    the sea says, 'It is not with me.'
¹⁵It cannot be bought with the finest
        gold,
    nor can its price be weighed in
        silver.
¹⁶It cannot be bought with the gold of
        Ophir,
    with precious onyx or sapphires.
¹⁷Neither gold nor crystal can compare
        with it,
    nor can it be had for jewels of gold.
¹⁸Coral and jasper are not worthy of
        mention;
    the price of wisdom is beyond
        rubies.
¹⁹The topaz of Cush cannot compare
        with it;
    it cannot be bought with pure gold.

²⁰"Where then does wisdom come
        from?

Where does understanding dwell?
²¹It is hidden from the eyes of every
        living thing,
    concealed even from the birds of
        the air.
²²Destruction*c* and Death say,
    'Only a rumor of it has reached our
        ears.'
²³God understands the way to it
    and he alone knows where it
        dwells,
²⁴for he views the ends of the earth
    and sees everything under the
        heavens.
²⁵When he established the force of the
        wind
    and measured out the waters,
²⁶when he made a decree for the rain
    and a path for the thunderstorm,
²⁷then he looked at wisdom and
        appraised it;
    he confirmed it and tested it.
²⁸And he said to man,
    'The fear of the Lord—that is
        wisdom,
    and to shun evil is
        understanding.' "

29 Job continued his discourse:
    ²"How I long for the months
        gone by,
    for the days when God watched
        over me,
³when his lamp shone upon my head
    and by his light I walked through
        darkness!
⁴Oh, for the days when I was in my
        prime,
    when God's intimate friendship
        blessed my house,
⁵when the Almighty was still with me
    and my children were around me,
⁶when my path was drenched with
        cream
    and the rock poured out for me
        streams of olive oil.

⁷"When I went to the gate of the city
    and took my seat in the public
        square,
⁸the young men saw me and stepped
        aside
    and the old men rose to their feet;
⁹the chief men refrained from speaking
    and covered their mouths with their
        hands;
¹⁰the voices of the nobles were hushed,

---

a6 Or *lapis lazuli*; also in verse 16   *b11* Septuagint, Aquila and Vulgate; Hebrew *He dams up*
c22 Hebrew *Abaddon*

and their tongues stuck to the roof
    of their mouths.
¹¹Whoever heard me spoke well of me,
    and those who saw me commended
    me,
¹²because I rescued the poor who cried
    for help,
    and the fatherless who had none to
    assist him.
¹³The man who was dying blessed me;
    I made the widow's heart sing.
¹⁴I put on righteousness as my clothing;
    justice was my robe and my turban.
¹⁵I was eyes to the blind
    and feet to the lame.
¹⁶I was a father to the needy;
    I took up the case of the stranger.
¹⁷I broke the fangs of the wicked
    and snatched the victims from their
    teeth.

¹⁸"I thought, 'I will die in my own
    house,
    my days as numerous as the grains
    of sand.
¹⁹My roots will reach to the water,
    and the dew will lie all night on my
    branches.
²⁰My glory will remain fresh in me,
    the bow ever new in my hand.'

²¹"Men listened to me expectantly,
    waiting in silence for my counsel.
²²After I had spoken, they spoke no
    more;
    my words fell gently on their ears.
²³They waited for me as for showers
    and drank in my words as the
    spring rain.
²⁴When I smiled at them, they scarcely
    believed it;
    the light of my face was precious to
    them. ^a
²⁵I chose the way for them and sat as
    their chief;
    I dwelt as a king among his troops;
    I was like one who comforts
    mourners.

30
"But now they mock me,
men younger than I,
whose fathers I would have disdained
    to put with my sheep dogs.
²Of what use was the strength of their
    hands to me,
    since their vigor had gone from
    them?
³Haggard from want and hunger,

they roamed^b the parched land
    in desolate wastelands at night.
⁴In the brush they gathered salt herbs,
    and their food^c was the root of the
    broom tree.
⁵They were banished from their fellow
    men,
    shouted at as if they were thieves.
⁶They were forced to live in the dry
    stream beds,
    among the rocks and in holes in
    the ground.
⁷They brayed among the bushes
    and huddled in the undergrowth.
⁸A base and nameless brood,
    they were driven out of the land.

⁹"And now their sons mock me in
    song;
    I have become a byword among
    them.
¹⁰They detest me and keep their
    distance;
    they do not hesitate to spit in my
    face.
¹¹Now that God has unstrung my bow
    and afflicted me,
    they throw off restraint in my
    presence.
¹²On my right the tribe^d attacks;
    they lay snares for my feet,
    they build their siege ramps against
    me.
¹³They break up my road;
    they succeed in destroying me—
    without anyone's helping them. ^e
¹⁴They advance as through a gaping
    breach;
    amid the ruins they come rolling in.
¹⁵Terrors overwhelm me;
    my dignity is driven away as by the
    wind,
    my safety vanishes like a cloud.

¹⁶"And now my life ebbs away;
    days of suffering grip me.
¹⁷Night pierces my bones;
    my gnawing pains never rest.
¹⁸In his great power ˌGodˌ becomes like
    clothing to me^f;
    he binds me like the neck of my
    garment.
¹⁹He throws me into the mud,
    and I am reduced to dust and
    ashes.

²⁰"I cry out to you, O God, but you do
    not answer;

---

^a24 The meaning of the Hebrew for this clause is uncertain.   ^b3 Or gnawed   ^c4 Or fuel
^d12 The meaning of the Hebrew for this word is uncertain.   ^e13 Or me. / 'No one can help him,' ˌthey
say,.   ^f18 Hebrew; Septuagint ˌGod, grasps my clothing

I stand up, but you merely look at
me.
²¹You turn on me ruthlessly;
with the might of your hand you
attack me.
²²You snatch me up and drive me
before the wind;
you toss me about in the storm.
²³I know you will bring me down to
death,
to the place appointed for all the
living.

²⁴"Surely no one lays a hand on a
broken man
when he cries for help in his
distress.
²⁵Have I not wept for those in trouble?
Has not my soul grieved for the
poor?
²⁶Yet when I hoped for good, evil came;
when I looked for light, then came
darkness.
²⁷The churning inside me never stops;
days of suffering confront me.
²⁸I go about blackened, but not by the
sun;
I stand up in the assembly and cry
for help.
²⁹I have become a brother of jackals,
a companion of owls.
³⁰My skin grows black and peels;
my body burns with fever.
³¹My harp is tuned to mourning,
and my flute to the sound of
wailing.

31 "I made a covenant with my eyes
not to look lustfully at a girl.
²For what is man's lot from God
above,
his heritage from the Almighty on
high?
³Is it not ruin for the wicked,
disaster for those who do wrong?
⁴Does he not see my ways
and count my every step?

⁵"If I have walked in falsehood
or my foot has hurried after
deceit—
⁶let God weigh me in honest scales
and he will know that I am
blameless—
⁷if my steps have turned from the
path,
if my heart has been led by my
eyes,
or if my hands have been defiled,

⁸then may others eat what I have
sown,
and may my crops be uprooted.

⁹"If my heart has been enticed by a
woman,
or if I have lurked at my neighbor's
door,
¹⁰then may my wife grind another
man's grain,
and may other men sleep with her.
¹¹For that would have been shameful,
a sin to be judged.
¹²It is a fire that burns to Destruction^a;
it would have uprooted my harvest.

¹³"If I have denied justice to my
menservants and maidservants
when they had a grievance against
me,
¹⁴what will I do when God confronts
me?
What will I answer when called to
account?
¹⁵Did not he who made me in the
womb make them?
Did not the same one form us both
within our mothers?

¹⁶"If I have denied the desires of the
poor
or let the eyes of the widow grow
weary,
¹⁷if I have kept my bread to myself,
not sharing it with the fatherless—
¹⁸but from my youth I reared him as
would a father,
and from my birth I guided the
widow—
¹⁹if I have seen anyone perishing for
lack of clothing,
or a needy man without a garment,
²⁰and his heart did not bless me
for warming him with the fleece
from my sheep,
²¹if I have raised my hand against the
fatherless,
knowing that I had influence in
court,
²²then let my arm fall from the
shoulder,
let it be broken off at the joint.
²³For I dreaded destruction from God,
and for fear of his splendor I could
not do such things.

²⁴"If I have put my trust in gold
or said to pure gold, 'You are my
security,'

25if I have rejoiced over my great
wealth,
the fortune my hands had gained,
26if I have regarded the sun in its
radiance
or the moon moving in splendor,
27so that my heart was secretly enticed
and my hand offered them a kiss of
homage,
28then these also would be sins to be
judged,
for I would have been unfaithful to
God on high.

29"If I have rejoiced at my enemy's
misfortune
or gloated over the trouble that
came to him—
30I have not allowed my mouth to sin
by invoking a curse against his
life—
31if the men of my household have
never said,
'Who has not had his fill of Job's
meat?'—
32but no stranger had to spend the
night in the street,
for my door was always open to the
traveler—
33if I have concealed my sin as men
do,a
by hiding my guilt in my heart
34because I so feared the crowd
and so dreaded the contempt of the
clans
that I kept silent and would not go
outside

35("Oh, that I had someone to hear me!
I sign now my defense—let the
Almighty answer me;
let my accuser put his indictment
in writing.
36Surely I would wear it on my
shoulder,
I would put it on like a crown.
37I would give him an account of my
every step;
like a prince I would approach
him.)—

38"if my land cries out against me
and all its furrows are wet with
tears,
39if I have devoured its yield without
payment
or broken the spirit of its tenants,

40then let briers come up instead of
wheat
and weeds instead of barley."

The words of Job are ended.

Elihu

32 So these three men stopped answering Job, because he was righteous in his own eyes. 2But Elihu son of
Barakel the Buzite, of the family of Ram,
became very angry with Job for justifying
himself rather than God. 3He was also angry with the three friends, because they
had found no way to refute Job, and yet
had condemned him.b 4Now Elihu had
waited before speaking to Job because
they were older than he. 5But when he
saw that the three men had nothing more
to say, his anger was aroused.

6So Elihu son of Barakel the Buzite
said:

"I am young in years,
and you are old;
that is why I was fearful,
not daring to tell you what I know.
7I thought, 'Age should speak;
advanced years should teach
wisdom.'
8But it is the spiritc in a man,
the breath of the Almighty, that
gives him understanding.
9It is not only the oldd who are wise,
not only the aged who understand
what is right.

10"Therefore I say: Listen to me;
I too will tell you what I know.
11I waited while you spoke,
I listened to your reasoning;
while you were searching for words,
12 I gave you my full attention.
But not one of you has proved Job
wrong;
none of you has answered his
arguments.
13Do not say, 'We have found wisdom;
let God refute him, not man.'
14But Job has not marshaled his words
against me,
and I will not answer him with your
arguments.

15"They are dismayed and have no more
to say;
words have failed them.
16Must I wait, now that they are silent,

---

a33 Or *as Adam did*   b3 Masoretic Text; an ancient Hebrew scribal tradition *Job, and so had condemned God*   c8 Or *Spirit*; also in verse 18   d9 Or *many*; or *great*

now that they stand there with no
  reply?
¹⁷I too will have my say;
  I too will tell what I know.
¹⁸For I am full of words,
  and the spirit within me compels
    me;
¹⁹inside I am like bottled-up wine,
  like new wineskins ready to burst.
²⁰I must speak and find relief;
  I must open my lips and reply.
²¹I will show partiality to no one,
  nor will I flatter any man;
²²for if I were skilled in flattery,
  my Maker would soon take me
    away.

33 "But now, Job, listen to my
  words;
  pay attention to everything I say.
²I am about to open my mouth;
  my words are on the tip of my
    tongue.
³My words come from an upright
    heart;
  my lips sincerely speak what I
    know.
⁴The Spirit of God has made me;
  the breath of the Almighty gives me
    life.
⁵Answer me then, if you can;
  prepare yourself and confront me.
⁶I am just like you before God;
  I too have been taken from clay.
⁷No fear of me should alarm you,
  nor should my hand be heavy upon
    you.

⁸"But you have said in my hearing—
  I heard the very words—
⁹'I am pure and without sin;
  I am clean and free from guilt.
¹⁰Yet God has found fault with me;
  he considers me his enemy.
¹¹He fastens my feet in shackles;
  he keeps close watch on all my
    paths.'

¹²"But I tell you, in this you are not
    right,
  for God is greater than man.
¹³Why do you complain to him
  that he answers none of man's
    words[a]?
¹⁴For God does speak—now one way,
    now another—
  though man may not perceive it.
¹⁵In a dream, in a vision of the night,

when deep sleep falls on men
  as they slumber in their beds,
¹⁶he may speak in their ears
  and terrify them with warnings,
¹⁷to turn man from wrongdoing
  and keep him from pride,
¹⁸to preserve his soul from the pit,[b]
  his life from perishing by the
    sword.[c]
¹⁹Or a man may be chastened on a bed
    of pain
  with constant distress in his bones,
²⁰so that his very being finds food
    repulsive
  and his soul loathes the choicest
    meal.
²¹His flesh wastes away to nothing,
  and his bones, once hidden, now
    stick out.
²²His soul draws near to the pit,[d]
  and his life to the messengers of
    death.[e]

²³"Yet if there is an angel on his side
  as a mediator, one out of a
    thousand,
  to tell a man what is right for him,
²⁴to be gracious to him and say,
  'Spare him from going down to the
    pit[f];
  I have found a ransom for him'—
²⁵then his flesh is renewed like a
    child's;
  it is restored as in the days of his
    youth.
²⁶He prays to God and finds favor with
    him,
  he sees God's face and shouts for
    joy;
  he is restored by God to his
    righteous state.
²⁷Then he comes to men and says,
  'I sinned, and perverted what was
    right,
  but I did not get what I deserved.
²⁸He redeemed my soul from going
    down to the pit,[g]
  and I will live to enjoy the light.'

²⁹"God does all these things to a
    man—
  twice, even three times—
³⁰to turn back his soul from the pit,[h]
  that the light of life may shine on
    him.

³¹"Pay attention, Job, and listen to me;
  be silent, and I will speak.

---

[a]13 Or *that he does not answer for any of his actions* [b]18 Or *preserve him from the grave* [c]18 Or
from crossing the River [d]22 Or *He draws near to the grave* [e]22 Or *to the dead* [f]24 Or *grave*
[g]28 Or *redeemed me from going down to the grave* [h]30 Or *turn him back from the grave*

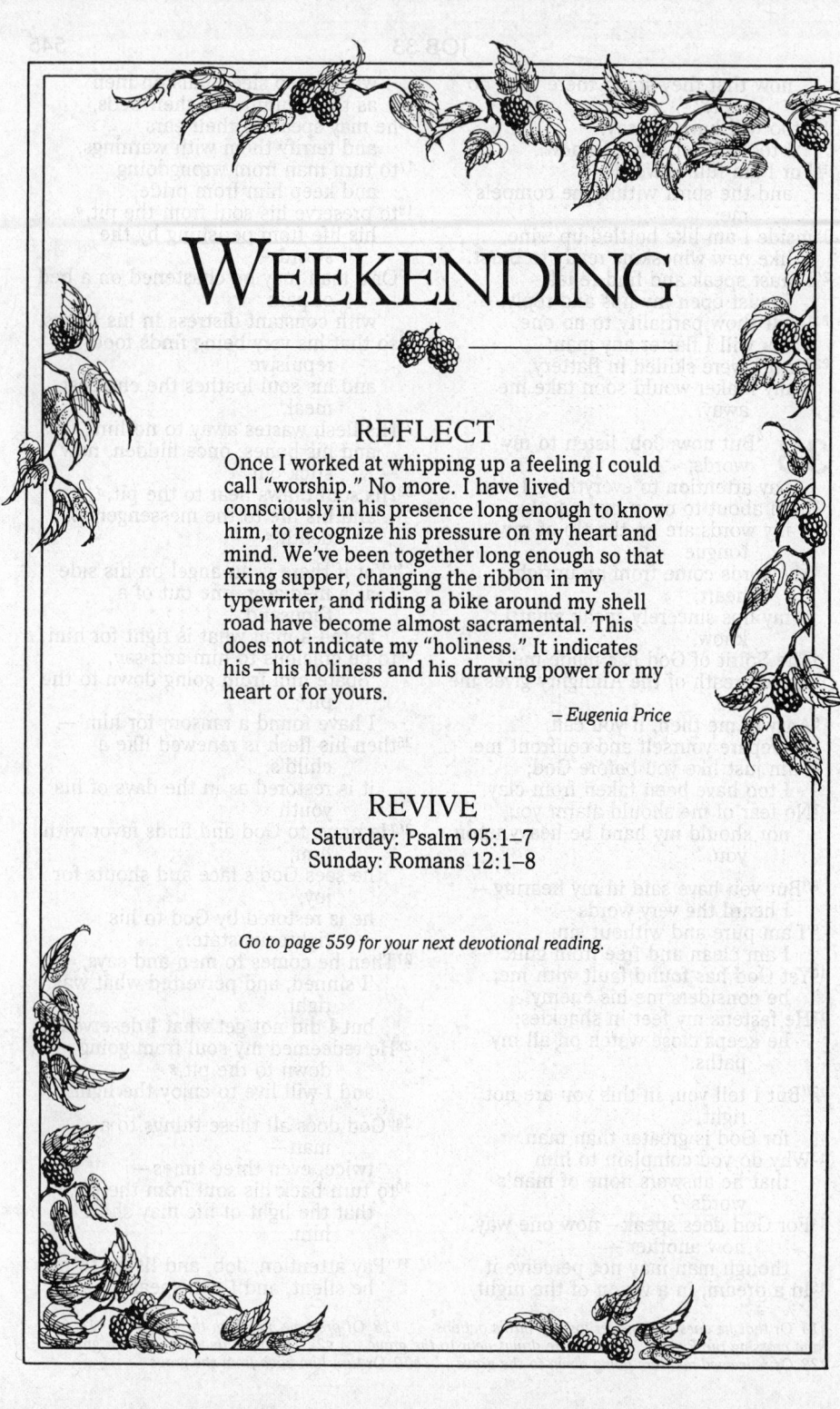

WEEKENDING

REFLECT

Once I worked at whipping up a feeling I could call "worship." No more. I have lived consciously in his presence long enough to know him, to recognize his pressure on my heart and mind. We've been together long enough so that fixing supper, changing the ribbon in my typewriter, and riding a bike around my shell road have become almost sacramental. This does not indicate my "holiness." It indicates his—his holiness and his drawing power for my heart or for yours.

— *Eugenia Price*

REVIVE

Saturday: Psalm 95:1–7
Sunday: Romans 12:1–8

Go to page 559 for your next devotional reading.

³²If you have anything to say, answer
me;
  speak up, for I want you to be
  cleared.
³³But if not, then listen to me;
  be silent, and I will teach you
  wisdom."

34

Then Elihu said:
²"Hear my words, you wise men;
  listen to me, you men of learning.
³For the ear tests words
  as the tongue tastes food.
⁴Let us discern for ourselves what is
  right;
  let us learn together what is good.

⁵"Job says, 'I am innocent,
  but God denies me justice.
⁶Although I am right,
  I am considered a liar;
  although I am guiltless,
  his arrow inflicts an incurable
  wound.'
⁷What man is like Job,
  who drinks scorn like water?
⁸He keeps company with evildoers;
  he associates with wicked men.
⁹For he says, 'It profits a man nothing
  when he tries to please God.'

¹⁰"So listen to me, you men of
  understanding.
  Far be it from God to do evil,
  from the Almighty to do wrong.
¹¹He repays a man for what he has
  done;
  he brings upon him what his
  conduct deserves.
¹²It is unthinkable that God would do
  wrong,
  that the Almighty would pervert
  justice.
¹³Who appointed him over the earth?
  Who put him in charge of the
  whole world?
¹⁴If it were his intention
  and he withdrew his spirit^a and
  breath,
¹⁵all mankind would perish together
  and man would return to the dust.

¹⁶"If you have understanding, hear this;
  listen to what I say.
¹⁷Can he who hates justice govern?
  Will you condemn the just and
  mighty One?
¹⁸Is he not the One who says to kings,
  'You are worthless,'

and to nobles, 'You are wicked,'
¹⁹who shows no partiality to princes
  and does not favor the rich over the
  poor,
  for they are all the work of his
  hands?
²⁰They die in an instant, in the middle
  of the night;
  the people are shaken and they
  pass away;
  the mighty are removed without
  human hand.

²¹"His eyes are on the ways of men;
  he sees their every step.
²²There is no dark place, no deep
  shadow,
  where evildoers can hide.
²³God has no need to examine men
  further,
  that they should come before him
  for judgment.
²⁴Without inquiry he shatters the
  mighty
  and sets up others in their place.
²⁵Because he takes note of their deeds,
  he overthrows them in the night
  and they are crushed.
²⁶He punishes them for their
  wickedness
  where everyone can see them,
²⁷because they turned from following
  him
  and had no regard for any of his
  ways.
²⁸They caused the cry of the poor to
  come before him,
  so that he heard the cry of the
  needy.
²⁹But if he remains silent, who can
  condemn him?
  If he hides his face, who can see
  him?
  Yet he is over man and nation alike,
³⁰ to keep a godless man from ruling,
  from laying snares for the people.

³¹"Suppose a man says to God,
  'I am guilty but will offend no
  more.
³²Teach me what I cannot see;
  if I have done wrong, I will not do
  so again.'
³³Should God then reward you on your
  terms,
  when you refuse to repent?
  You must decide, not I;
  so tell me what you know.

^a14 Or *Spirit*

34"Men of understanding declare,
　wise men who hear me say to me,
35'Job speaks without knowledge;
　his words lack insight.'
36Oh, that Job might be tested to the
　　utmost
　for answering like a wicked man!
37To his sin he adds rebellion;
　scornfully he claps his hands
　　among us
　and multiplies his words against
　　God."

35

Then Elihu said:

2"Do you think this is just?
You say, 'I will be cleared by
　God.ᵃ'
3Yet you ask him, 'What profit is it to
　me,ᵇ
and what do I gain by not sinning?'

4"I would like to reply to you
　and to your friends with you.
5Look up at the heavens and see;
　gaze at the clouds so high above
　　you.
6If you sin, how does that affect him?
　If your sins are many, what does
　　that do to him?
7If you are righteous, what do you give
　　to him,
　or what does he receive from your
　　hand?
8Your wickedness affects only a man
　　like yourself,
　and your righteousness only the
　　sons of men.

9"Men cry out under a load of
　　oppression;
　they plead for relief from the arm
　　of the powerful.
10But no one says, 'Where is God my
　　Maker,
　who gives songs in the night,
11who teaches more to us than toᶜ the
　　beasts of the earth
　and makes us wiser thanᵈ the birds
　　of the air?'
12He does not answer when men cry
　　out
　because of the arrogance of the
　　wicked.
13Indeed, God does not listen to their
　　empty plea;
　the Almighty pays no attention
　　to it.

14How much less, then, will he listen
　when you say that you do not see
　　him,
　that your case is before him
　and you must wait for him,
15and further, that his anger never
　　punishes
　and he does not take the least
　　notice of wickedness.ᵉ
16So Job opens his mouth with empty
　　talk;
　without knowledge he multiplies
　　words."

36

Elihu continued:

2"Bear with me a little longer
　and I will show you
that there is more to be said in
　God's behalf.
3I get my knowledge from afar;
　I will ascribe justice to my Maker.
4Be assured that my words are not
　　false;
　one perfect in knowledge is with
　　you.

5"God is mighty, but does not despise
　　men;
　he is mighty, and firm in his
　　purpose.
6He does not keep the wicked alive
　but gives the afflicted their rights.
7He does not take his eyes off the
　　righteous;
　he enthrones them with kings
　and exalts them forever.
8But if men are bound in chains,
　held fast by cords of affliction,
9he tells them what they have done—
　that they have sinned arrogantly.
10He makes them listen to correction
　and commands them to repent of
　　their evil.
11If they obey and serve him,
　they will spend the rest of their
　　days in prosperity
　and their years in contentment.
12But if they do not listen,
　they will perish by the swordᶠ
　and die without knowledge.

13"The godless in heart harbor
　　resentment;
　even when he fetters them, they do
　　not cry for help.
14They die in their youth,

ᵃ2 Or *My righteousness is more than God's*　　ᵇ3 Or *you*　　ᶜ11 Or *teaches us by*　　ᵈ11 Or *us wise by*
ᵉ15 Symmachus, Theodotion and Vulgate; the meaning of the Hebrew for this word is uncertain.
ᶠ12 Or *will cross the River*

among male prostitutes of the
shrines.
15But those who suffer he delivers in
their suffering;
he speaks to them in their
affliction.

16"He is wooing you from the jaws of
distress
to a spacious place free from
restriction,
to the comfort of your table laden
with choice food.
17But now you are laden with the
judgment due the wicked;
judgment and justice have taken
hold of you.
18Be careful that no one entices you by
riches;
do not let a large bribe turn you
aside.
19Would your wealth
or even all your mighty efforts
sustain you so you would not be in
distress?
20Do not long for the night,
to drag people away from their
homes. a
21Beware of turning to evil,
which you seem to prefer to
affliction.

22"God is exalted in his power.
Who is a teacher like him?
23Who has prescribed his ways for him,
or said to him, 'You have done
wrong'?
24Remember to extol his work,
which men have praised in song.
25All mankind has seen it;
men gaze on it from afar.
26How great is God—beyond our
understanding!
The number of his years is past
finding out.

27"He draws up the drops of water,
which distill as rain to the
streams b;
28the clouds pour down their moisture
and abundant showers fall on
mankind.
29Who can understand how he spreads
out the clouds,
how he thunders from his pavilion?
30See how he scatters his lightning
about him,
bathing the depths of the sea.

31This is the way he governs c the
nations
and provides food in abundance.
32He fills his hands with lightning
and commands it to strike its mark.
33His thunder announces the coming
storm;
even the cattle make known its
approach. d

37 "At this my heart pounds
and leaps from its place.
2Listen! Listen to the roar of his voice,
to the rumbling that comes from
his mouth.
3He unleashes his lightning beneath
the whole heaven
and sends it to the ends of the
earth.
4After that comes the sound of his
roar;
he thunders with his majestic voice.
When his voice resounds,
he holds nothing back.
5God's voice thunders in marvelous
ways;
he does great things beyond our
understanding.
6He says to the snow, 'Fall on the
earth,'
and to the rain shower, 'Be a
mighty downpour.'
7So that all men he has made may
know his work,
he stops every man from his labor. e
8The animals take cover;
they remain in their dens.
9The tempest comes out from its
chamber,
the cold from the driving winds.
10The breath of God produces ice,
and the broad waters become
frozen.
11He loads the clouds with moisture;
he scatters his lightning through
them.
12At his direction they swirl around
over the face of the whole earth
to do whatever he commands them.
13He brings the clouds to punish men,
or to water his earth f and show his
love.

14"Listen to this, Job;
stop and consider God's wonders.
15Do you know how God controls the
clouds

---

a20 The meaning of the Hebrew for verses 18-20 is uncertain.   b27 Or distill from the mist as rain
c31 Or nourishes   d33 Or announces his coming— / the One zealous against evil   e7 Or / he fills all
men with fear by his power   f13 Or to favor them

and makes his lightning flash?
¹⁶Do you know how the clouds hang
   poised,
   those wonders of him who is
      perfect in knowledge?
¹⁷You who swelter in your clothes
   when the land lies hushed under
      the south wind,
¹⁸can you join him in spreading out the
   skies,
   hard as a mirror of cast bronze?

¹⁹"Tell us what we should say to him;
   we cannot draw up our case
      because of our darkness.
²⁰Should he be told that I want to
   speak?
   Would any man ask to be
      swallowed up?
²¹Now no one can look at the sun,
   bright as it is in the skies
   after the wind has swept them
      clean.
²²Out of the north he comes in golden
   splendor;
   God comes in awesome majesty.
²³The Almighty is beyond our reach and
   exalted in power;
   in his justice and great
      righteousness, he does not
      oppress.
²⁴Therefore, men revere him,
   for does he not have regard for all
      the wise in heart?ᵃ"

The Lord Speaks

38 Then the Lord answered Job out of
the storm. He said:

²"Who is this that darkens my counsel
   with words without knowledge?
³Brace yourself like a man;
   I will question you,
   and you shall answer me.

⁴"Where were you when I laid the
   earth's foundation?
   Tell me, if you understand.
⁵Who marked off its dimensions?
   Surely you know!
   Who stretched a measuring line
      across it?
⁶On what were its footings set,
   or who laid its cornerstone—
⁷while the morning stars sang together
   and all the angelsᵇ shouted for joy?

⁸"Who shut up the sea behind doors
   when it burst forth from the womb,

⁹when I made the clouds its garment
   and wrapped it in thick darkness,
¹⁰when I fixed limits for it
   and set its doors and bars in place,
¹¹when I said, 'This far you may come
   and no farther;
   here is where your proud waves
      halt'?

¹²"Have you ever given orders to the
   morning,
   or shown the dawn its place,
¹³that it might take the earth by the
   edges
   and shake the wicked out of it?
¹⁴The earth takes shape like clay under
   a seal;
   its features stand out like those of
      a garment.
¹⁵The wicked are denied their light,
   and their upraised arm is broken.

¹⁶"Have you journeyed to the springs of
   the sea
   or walked in the recesses of the
      deep?
¹⁷Have the gates of death been shown
   to you?
   Have you seen the gates of the
      shadow of deathᶜ?
¹⁸Have you comprehended the vast
   expanses of the earth?
   Tell me, if you know all this.

¹⁹"What is the way to the abode of
   light?
   And where does darkness reside?
²⁰Can you take them to their places?
   Do you know the paths to their
      dwellings?
²¹Surely you know, for you were already
   born!
   You have lived so many years!

²²"Have you entered the storehouses of
   the snow
   or seen the storehouses of the hail,
²³which I reserve for times of trouble,
   for days of war and battle?
²⁴What is the way to the place where
   the lightning is dispersed,
   or the place where the east winds
      are scattered over the earth?
²⁵Who cuts a channel for the torrents of
   rain,
   and a path for the thunderstorm,
²⁶to water a land where no man lives,
   a desert with no one in it,
²⁷to satisfy a desolate wasteland

ᵃ24 Or *for he does not have regard for any who think they are wise.*   ᵇ7 Hebrew *the sons of God*
ᶜ17 Or *gates of deep shadows*

and make it sprout with grass?
28Does the rain have a father?
Who fathers the drops of dew?
29From whose womb comes the ice?
Who gives birth to the frost from
the heavens
30when the waters become hard as
stone,
when the surface of the deep is
frozen?

31"Can you bind the beautiful*a*
Pleiades?
Can you loose the cords of Orion?
32Can you bring forth the constellations
in their seasons*b*
or lead out the Bear*c* with its cubs?
33Do you know the laws of the
heavens?
Can you set up God's*d* dominion
over the earth?

34"Can you raise your voice to the
clouds
and cover yourself with a flood of
water?
35Do you send the lightning bolts on
their way?
Do they report to you, 'Here we
are'?
36Who endowed the heart*e* with
wisdom
or gave understanding to the
mind*e*?
37Who has the wisdom to count the
clouds?
Who can tip over the water jars of
the heavens
38when the dust becomes hard
and the clods of earth stick
together?

39"Do you hunt the prey for the lioness
and satisfy the hunger of the lions
40when they crouch in their dens
or lie in wait in a thicket?
41Who provides food for the raven
when its young cry out to God
and wander about for lack of food?

39

"Do you know when the
mountain goats give birth?
Do you watch when the doe bears
her fawn?
2Do you count the months till they
bear?
Do you know the time they give
birth?

3They crouch down and bring forth
their young;
their labor pains are ended.
4Their young thrive and grow strong in
the wilds;
they leave and do not return.

5"Who let the wild donkey go free?
Who untied his ropes?
6I gave him the wasteland as his
home,
the salt flats as his habitat.
7He laughs at the commotion in the
town;
he does not hear a driver's shout.
8He ranges the hills for his pasture
and searches for any green thing.

9"Will the wild ox consent to serve
you?
Will he stay by your manger at
night?
10Can you hold him to the furrow with
a harness?
Will he till the valleys behind you?
11Will you rely on him for his great
strength?
Will you leave your heavy work to
him?
12Can you trust him to bring in your
grain
and gather it to your threshing
floor?

13"The wings of the ostrich flap joyfully,
but they cannot compare with the
pinions and feathers of the
stork.
14She lays her eggs on the ground
and lets them warm in the sand,
15unmindful that a foot may crush
them,
that some wild animal may trample
them.
16She treats her young harshly, as if
they were not hers;
she cares not that her labor was in
vain,
17for God did not endow her with
wisdom
or give her a share of good sense.
18Yet when she spreads her feathers to
run,
she laughs at horse and rider.

19"Do you give the horse his strength
or clothe his neck with a flowing
mane?
20Do you make him leap like a locust,

---

a31 Or *the twinkling*; or *the chains of the*   *b32* Or *the morning star in its season*   *c32* Or *out Leo*
d33 Or *his*; or *their*   *e36* The meaning of the Hebrew for this word is uncertain.

striking terror with his proud
snorting?
²¹He paws fiercely, rejoicing in his
strength,
and charges into the fray.
²²He laughs at fear, afraid of nothing;
he does not shy away from the
sword.
²³The quiver rattles against his side,
along with the flashing spear and
lance.
²⁴In frenzied excitement he eats up the
ground;
he cannot stand still when the
trumpet sounds.
²⁵At the blast of the trumpet he snorts,
'Aha!'
He catches the scent of battle from
afar,
the shout of commanders and the
battle cry.

²⁶"Does the hawk take flight by your
wisdom
and spread his wings toward the
south?
²⁷Does the eagle soar at your command
and build his nest on high?
²⁸He dwells on a cliff and stays there at
night;
a rocky crag is his stronghold.
²⁹From there he seeks out his food;
his eyes detect it from afar.
³⁰His young ones feast on blood,
and where the slain are, there is
he."

40 The LORD said to Job:

²"Will the one who contends
with the Almighty correct him?
Let him who accuses God answer
him!"

³Then Job answered the LORD:

⁴"I am unworthy—how can I reply to
you?
I put my hand over my mouth.
⁵I spoke once, but I have no answer—
twice, but I will say no more."

⁶Then the LORD spoke to Job out of the
storm:

⁷"Brace yourself like a man;
I will question you,
and you shall answer me.

⁸"Would you discredit my justice?

Would you condemn me to justify
yourself?
⁹Do you have an arm like God's,
and can your voice thunder like
his?
¹⁰Then adorn yourself with glory and
splendor,
and clothe yourself in honor and
majesty.
¹¹Unleash the fury of your wrath,
look at every proud man and bring
him low,
¹²look at every proud man and humble
him,
crush the wicked where they stand.
¹³Bury them all in the dust together;
shroud their faces in the grave.
¹⁴Then I myself will admit to you
that your own right hand can save
you.

¹⁵"Look at the behemoth,ᵃ
which I made along with you
and which feeds on grass like an
ox.
¹⁶What strength he has in his loins,
what power in the muscles of his
belly!
¹⁷His tailᵇ sways like a cedar;
the sinews of his thighs are
close-knit.
¹⁸His bones are tubes of bronze,
his limbs like rods of iron.
¹⁹He ranks first among the works of
God,
yet his Maker can approach him
with his sword.
²⁰The hills bring him their produce,
and all the wild animals play
nearby.
²¹Under the lotus plants he lies,
hidden among the reeds in the
marsh.
²²The lotuses conceal him in their
shadow;
the poplars by the stream surround
him.
²³When the river rages, he is not
alarmed;
he is secure, though the Jordan
should surge against his
mouth.
²⁴Can anyone capture him by the
eyes,ᶜ
or trap him and pierce his nose?

41 "Can you pull in the leviathanᵈ
with a fishhook

ᵃ15 Possibly the hippopotamus or the elephant   ᵇ17 Possibly trunk   ᶜ24 Or by a water hole
ᵈ1 Possibly the crocodile

or tie down his tongue with a rope?
²Can you put a cord through his nose
  or pierce his jaw with a hook?
³Will he keep begging you for mercy?
  Will he speak to you with gentle
    words?
⁴Will he make an agreement with you
  for you to take him as your slave
    for life?
⁵Can you make a pet of him like a bird
  or put him on a leash for your
    girls?
⁶Will traders barter for him?
  Will they divide him up among the
    merchants?
⁷Can you fill his hide with harpoons
  or his head with fishing spears?
⁸If you lay a hand on him,
  you will remember the struggle and
    never do it again!
⁹Any hope of subduing him is false;
  the mere sight of him is
    overpowering.
¹⁰No one is fierce enough to rouse him.
  Who then is able to stand against
    me?
¹¹Who has a claim against me that I
    must pay?
  Everything under heaven belongs to
    me.
¹²"I will not fail to speak of his limbs,
  his strength and his graceful form.
¹³Who can strip off his outer coat?
  Who would approach him with a
    bridle?
¹⁴Who dares open the doors of his
    mouth,
  ringed about with his fearsome
    teeth?
¹⁵His back hasᵃ rows of shields
  tightly sealed together;
¹⁶each is so close to the next
  that no air can pass between.
¹⁷They are joined fast to one another;
  they cling together and cannot be
    parted.
¹⁸His snorting throws out flashes of
    light;
  his eyes are like the rays of dawn.
¹⁹Firebrands stream from his mouth;
  sparks of fire shoot out.
²⁰Smoke pours from his nostrils
  as from a boiling pot over a fire of
    reeds.
²¹His breath sets coals ablaze,
  and flames dart from his mouth.
²²Strength resides in his neck;

dismay goes before him.
²³The folds of his flesh are tightly
    joined;
  they are firm and immovable.
²⁴His chest is hard as rock,
  hard as a lower millstone.
²⁵When he rises up, the mighty are
    terrified;
  they retreat before his thrashing.
²⁶The sword that reaches him has no
    effect,
  nor does the spear or the dart or
    the javelin.
²⁷Iron he treats like straw
  and bronze like rotten wood.
²⁸Arrows do not make him flee;
  slingstones are like chaff to him.
²⁹A club seems to him but a piece of
    straw;
  he laughs at the rattling of the
    lance.
³⁰His undersides are jagged potsherds,
  leaving a trail in the mud like a
    threshing sledge.
³¹He makes the depths churn like a
    boiling caldron
  and stirs up the sea like a pot of
    ointment.
³²Behind him he leaves a glistening
    wake;
  one would think the deep had
    white hair.
³³Nothing on earth is his equal—
  a creature without fear.
³⁴He looks down on all that are
    haughty;
  he is king over all that are proud."

Job

42 Then Job replied to the Lord:
²"I know that you can do all
    things;
  no plan of yours can be thwarted.
³ You asked, 'Who is this that obscures
    my counsel without
    knowledge?'
  Surely I spoke of things I did not
    understand,
  things too wonderful for me to
    know.
⁴ "You said, 'Listen now, and I will
    speak;
  I will question you,
  and you shall answer me.'
⁵My ears had heard of you
  but now my eyes have seen you.

ᵃ15 Or His pride is his

⁶Therefore I despise myself
and repent in dust and ashes."

Epilogue

⁷After the Lᴏʀᴅ had said these things to Job, he said to Eliphaz the Temanite, "I am angry with you and your two friends, because you have not spoken of me what is right, as my servant Job has. ⁸So now take seven bulls and seven rams and go to my servant Job and sacrifice a burnt offering for yourselves. My servant Job will pray for you, and I will accept his prayer and not deal with you according to your folly. You have not spoken of me what is right, as my servant Job has." ⁹So Eliphaz the Temanite, Bildad the Shuhite and Zophar the Naamathite did what the Lᴏʀᴅ told them; and the Lᴏʀᴅ accepted Job's prayer.

¹⁰After Job had prayed for his friends, the Lᴏʀᴅ made him prosperous again and gave him twice as much as he had before.

¹¹All his brothers and sisters and everyone who had known him before came and ate with him in his house. They comforted and consoled him over all the trouble the Lᴏʀᴅ had brought upon him, and each one gave him a piece of silverᵃ and a gold ring.

¹²The Lᴏʀᴅ blessed the latter part of Job's life more than the first. He had fourteen thousand sheep, six thousand camels, a thousand yoke of oxen and a thousand donkeys. ¹³And he also had seven sons and three daughters. ¹⁴The first daughter he named Jemimah, the second Keziah and the third Keren-Happuch. ¹⁵Nowhere in all the land were there found women as beautiful as Job's daughters, and their father granted them an inheritance along with their brothers.

¹⁶After this, Job lived a hundred and forty years; he saw his children and their children to the fourth generation. ¹⁷And so he died, old and full of years.

ᵃ11 Hebrew *him a kesitah*; a kesitah was a unit of money of unknown weight and value.

*D*AVID, the shepherd boy and Israel's greatest king, writes most of the psalms. Together these 150 songs form the greatest collection of prayers ever written. A wide range of human emotion is expressed—joy, excitement, compassion, love, anger, grief, depression. As you read this book, remember that no matter what you are feeling, God wants to hear about it in your prayers to him. He promises to listen to all your concerns and to answer them for Jesus' sake.

PSALMS

BOOK I

Psalms 1–41

Psalm 1

¹Blessed is the man
  who does not walk in the counsel
    of the wicked
or stand in the way of sinners
  or sit in the seat of mockers.
²But his delight is in the law of the
    LORD,
  and on his law he meditates day
    and night.

³He is like a tree planted by streams
    of water,
  which yields its fruit in season
and whose leaf does not wither.
  Whatever he does prospers.

⁴Not so the wicked!
  They are like chaff
  that the wind blows away.
⁵Therefore the wicked will not stand in
    the judgment,
  nor sinners in the assembly of the
    righteous.

⁶For the LORD watches over the way of
    the righteous,

but the way of the wicked will
perish.

Psalm 2

[1]Why do the nations conspire[a]
and the peoples plot in vain?
[2]The kings of the earth take their
stand
and the rulers gather together
against the LORD
and against his Anointed One.[b]
[3]"Let us break their chains," they say,
"and throw off their fetters."

[4]The One enthroned in heaven laughs;
the Lord scoffs at them.
[5]Then he rebukes them in his anger
and terrifies them in his wrath,
saying,
[6]"I have installed my King[c]
on Zion, my holy hill."

[7]I will proclaim the decree of the LORD:

He said to me, "You are my Son[d];
today I have become your Father.[e]
[8]Ask of me,
and I will make the nations your
inheritance,
the ends of the earth your
possession.
[9]You will rule them with an iron
scepter[f];
you will dash them to pieces like
pottery."

[10]Therefore, you kings, be wise;
be warned, you rulers of the earth.
[11]Serve the LORD with fear
and rejoice with trembling.
[12]Kiss the Son, lest he be angry
and you be destroyed in your way,
for his wrath can flare up in a
moment.
Blessed are all who take refuge in
him.

Psalm 3

A psalm of David. When he fled from
his son Absalom.

[1]O LORD, how many are my foes!
How many rise up against me!
[2]Many are saying of me,
"God will not deliver him." Selah[g]

[3]But you are a shield around me,
O LORD;
you bestow glory on me and lift[h]
up my head.
[4]To the LORD I cry aloud,
and he answers me from his holy
hill. Selah

[5]I lie down and sleep;
I wake again, because the LORD
sustains me.
[6]I will not fear the tens of thousands
drawn up against me on every side.

[7]Arise, O LORD!
Deliver me, O my God!
Strike all my enemies on the jaw;
break the teeth of the wicked.

[8]From the LORD comes deliverance.
May your blessing be on your
people. Selah

Psalm 4

For the director of music. With stringed
instruments. A psalm of David.

[1]Answer me when I call to you,
O my righteous God.
Give me relief from my distress;
be merciful to me and hear my
prayer.

[2]How long, O men, will you turn my
glory into shame[i]?
How long will you love delusions
and seek false gods[j]? Selah
[3]Know that the LORD has set apart the
godly for himself;
the LORD will hear when I call to
him.

[4]In your anger do not sin;
when you are on your beds,
search your hearts and be silent.
Selah
[5]Offer right sacrifices
and trust in the LORD.

[6]Many are asking, "Who can show us
any good?"
Let the light of your face shine
upon us, O LORD.
[7]You have filled my heart with greater
joy
than when their grain and new wine
abound.
[8]I will lie down and sleep in peace,

---

[a]1 Hebrew; Septuagint rage　　[b]2 Or anointed one　　[c]6 Or king　　[d]7 Or son; also in verse 12
[e]7 Or have begotten you　　[f]9 Or will break them with a rod of iron　　[g]2 A word of uncertain meaning,
occurring frequently in the Psalms; possibly a musical term　　[h]3 Or LORD, / my Glorious One, who lifts
[i]2 Or you dishonor my Glorious One　　[j]2 Or seek lies

for you alone, O Lord,
make me dwell in safety.

Psalm 5

For the director of music. For flutes.
A psalm of David.

[1] Give ear to my words, O Lord,
consider my sighing.
[2] Listen to my cry for help,
my King and my God,
for to you I pray.
[3] In the morning, O Lord, you hear my
voice;
in the morning I lay my requests
before you
and wait in expectation.

[4] You are not a God who takes pleasure
in evil;
with you the wicked cannot dwell.
[5] The arrogant cannot stand in your
presence;
you hate all who do wrong.
[6] You destroy those who tell lies;
bloodthirsty and deceitful men
the Lord abhors.

[7] But I, by your great mercy,
will come into your house;
in reverence will I bow down
toward your holy temple.
[8] Lead me, O Lord, in your
righteousness
because of my enemies—
make straight your way before me.

[9] Not a word from their mouth can be
trusted;
their heart is filled with
destruction.
Their throat is an open grave;
with their tongue they speak deceit.
[10] Declare them guilty, O God!
Let their intrigues be their
downfall.
Banish them for their many sins,
for they have rebelled against you.

[11] But let all who take refuge in you be
glad;
let them ever sing for joy.
Spread your protection over them,
that those who love your name may
rejoice in you.
[12] For surely, O Lord, you bless the
righteous;
you surround them with your favor
as with a shield.

Psalm 6

For the director of music. With stringed
instruments. According to *sheminith.* [a]
A psalm of David.

[1] O Lord, do not rebuke me in your
anger
or discipline me in your wrath.
[2] Be merciful to me, Lord, for I am
faint;
O Lord, heal me, for my bones are
in agony.
[3] My soul is in anguish.
How long, O Lord, how long?

[4] Turn, O Lord, and deliver me;
save me because of your unfailing
love.
[5] No one remembers you when he is
dead.
Who praises you from the grave[b]?

[6] I am worn out from groaning;
all night long I flood my bed with
weeping
and drench my couch with tears.
[7] My eyes grow weak with sorrow;
they fail because of all my foes.

[8] Away from me, all you who do evil,
for the Lord has heard my weeping.
[9] The Lord has heard my cry for mercy;
the Lord accepts my prayer.
[10] All my enemies will be ashamed and
dismayed;
they will turn back in sudden
disgrace.

Psalm 7

A *shiggaion* [c] of David, which he sang to
the Lord concerning Cush, a Benjamite.

[1] O Lord my God, I take refuge in you;
save and deliver me from all who
pursue me,
[2] or they will tear me like a lion
and rip me to pieces with no one to
rescue me.

[3] O Lord my God, if I have done this
and there is guilt on my hands—
[4] if I have done evil to him who is at
peace with me
or without cause have robbed my
foe—
[5] then let my enemy pursue and
overtake me;
let him trample my life to the
ground

a Title: Probably a musical term   *b* 5 Hebrew *Sheol*   *c* Title: Probably a literary or musical term and make me sleep in the dust.

Selah

⁶Arise, O LORD, in your anger;
   rise up against the rage of my
      enemies.
  Awake, my God; decree justice.
⁷Let the assembled peoples gather
   around you.
  Rule over them from on high;
⁸ let the LORD judge the peoples.
  Judge me, O LORD, according to my
      righteousness,
   according to my integrity, O Most
      High.
⁹O righteous God,
  who searches minds and hearts,
  bring to an end the violence of the
      wicked
  and make the righteous secure.

¹⁰My shield[a] is God Most High,
  who saves the upright in heart.
¹¹God is a righteous judge,
  a God who expresses his wrath
      every day.
¹²If he does not relent,
  he[b] will sharpen his sword;
  he will bend and string his bow.
¹³He has prepared his deadly weapons;
  he makes ready his flaming arrows.

¹⁴He who is pregnant with evil
  and conceives trouble gives birth to
      disillusionment.
¹⁵He who digs a hole and scoops it out
  falls into the pit he has made.
¹⁶The trouble he causes recoils on
      himself;
  his violence comes down on his
      own head.

¹⁷I will give thanks to the LORD because
  of his righteousness
  and will sing praise to the name of
      the LORD Most High.

Psalm 8

For the director of music. According to
gittith.[c] A psalm of David.

¹O LORD, our Lord,
  how majestic is your name in all
      the earth!

You have set your glory
  above the heavens.

²From the lips of children and infants
  you have ordained praise[d]
because of your enemies,
  to silence the foe and the avenger.

³When I consider your heavens,
  the work of your fingers,
the moon and the stars,
  which you have set in place,
⁴what is man that you are mindful of
      him,
  the son of man that you care for
      him?
⁵You made him a little lower than the
      heavenly beings[e]
  and crowned him with glory and
      honor.

⁶You made him ruler over the works of
      your hands;
  you put everything under his feet:
⁷all flocks and herds,
  and the beasts of the field,
⁸the birds of the air,
  and the fish of the sea,
  all that swim the paths of the seas.

⁹O LORD, our Lord,
  how majestic is your name in all
      the earth!

Psalm 9[f]

For the director of music. To the tune
of, "The Death of the Son." A psalm
of David.

¹I will praise you, O LORD, with all my
      heart;
  I will tell of all your wonders.
²I will be glad and rejoice in you;
  I will sing praise to your name,
      O Most High.

³My enemies turn back;
  they stumble and perish before you.
⁴For you have upheld my right and my
      cause;
  you have sat on your throne,
      judging righteously.
⁵You have rebuked the nations and
      destroyed the wicked;
  you have blotted out their name for
      ever and ever.
⁶Endless ruin has overtaken the
      enemy,

---

^a10 Or *sovereign*   ^b12 Or *If a man does not repent, / God*   ^cTitle: Probably a musical term   ^d2 Or
strength   ^e5 Or *than God*   ^fPsalms 9 and 10 may have been originally a single acrostic poem, the
stanzas of which begin with the successive letters of the Hebrew alphabet. In the Septuagint they
constitute one psalm.

VERSE FOR THE DAY:
Psalm 8:1

AUTHOR:
Debbie Smith

PASSAGE FOR THE DAY:
Psalm 8:1–9

How Majestic Is Your Name

MICHAEL and I fell in love and into marriage almost before we knew what happened! We both considered ourselves rational, logical twenty-three-year-olds; but within three weeks of laying eyes on each other, we were engaged. Five months later, after many hours of prayer and counsel, we made our life commitment—to get to know each other!

Part of getting acquainted included writing songs together. God had planned that in advance, because it had never crossed my mind that I would marry a musician, much less write songs with him! Early in our marriage, we spent some of our favorite moments in the evenings at the piano, a kerosene lamp flickering and the Bible opened to the Psalms.

One evening we turned to Psalm 8. What an expression of joy from a man who understood the majesty of creation . . . and that God had entrusted man to rule over it! Furthermore, the psalmist David affirms our worth in this psalm. No room for poor self-image here!

Michael began searching for a tune to the Scriptural line:

> O LORD, our Lord,
>   how majestic is your name in all the earth!
>   (Psalm 8:1).

Fingers busy on the keyboard, he stopped, midmelody. Turning to me, he pointed to a large, framed poster hanging in our den. It lists all the names of Jesus found in the Bible. Reading down the list, my husband chose a few that fit the tune, and the song "How Majestic Is Your Name" was born!

> O Lord our Lord, how majestic is your name
>   in all the earth.
> O Lord our Lord, how majestic is your name
>   in all the earth.
> O Lord, we praise your name.
> O Lord, we magnify your name . . .
> Prince of Peace, Mighty God, O Lord God
> Almighty!*

Michael and I discovered that not only did our musical collaboration bring us closer together, it also brought us closer to our majestic God.

Additional Scripture Readings:
Ephesians 5:19–20; Philippians 2:9–11

Go to page 562 for your next devotional reading.

you have uprooted their cities;
even the memory of them has
    perished.

7The LORD reigns forever;
he has established his throne for
    judgment.
8He will judge the world in
    righteousness;
he will govern the peoples with
    justice.
9The LORD is a refuge for the
    oppressed,
a stronghold in times of trouble.
10Those who know your name will trust
    in you,
for you, LORD, have never forsaken
    those who seek you.

11Sing praises to the LORD, enthroned in
    Zion;
proclaim among the nations what
    he has done.
12For he who avenges blood remembers;
he does not ignore the cry of the
    afflicted.

13O LORD, see how my enemies
    persecute me!
Have mercy and lift me up from the
    gates of death,
14that I may declare your praises
in the gates of the Daughter of
    Zion
and there rejoice in your salvation.
15The nations have fallen into the pit
    they have dug;
their feet are caught in the net they
    have hidden.
16The LORD is known by his justice;
the wicked are ensnared by the
    work of their hands. *Higgaion.* a
                                    Selah

17The wicked return to the grave, b
all the nations that forget
    God.
18But the needy will not always be
    forgotten,
nor the hope of the afflicted ever
    perish.

19Arise, O LORD, let not man triumph;
let the nations be judged in your
    presence.
20Strike them with terror, O LORD;
let the nations know they are but
    men.   *Selah*

Psalm 10 c

1Why, O LORD, do you stand far off?
Why do you hide yourself in times
    of trouble?

2In his arrogance the wicked man
    hunts down the weak,
who are caught in the schemes he
    devises.
3He boasts of the cravings of his heart;
he blesses the greedy and reviles
    the LORD.
4In his pride the wicked does not seek
    him;
in all his thoughts there is no room
    for God.
5His ways are always prosperous;
he is haughty and your laws are far
    from him;
he sneers at all his enemies.
6He says to himself, "Nothing will
    shake me;
I'll always be happy and never have
    trouble."
7His mouth is full of curses and lies
    and threats;
trouble and evil are under his
    tongue.
8He lies in wait near the villages;
from ambush he murders the
    innocent,
watching in secret for his victims.
9He lies in wait like a lion in cover;
he lies in wait to catch the
    helpless;
he catches the helpless and drags
    them off in his net.
10His victims are crushed, they
    collapse;
they fall under his strength.
11He says to himself, "God has
    forgotten;
he covers his face and never sees."

12Arise, LORD! Lift up your hand, O God.
Do not forget the helpless.
13Why does the wicked man revile
    God?
Why does he say to himself,
    "He won't call me to account"?
14But you, O God, do see trouble and
    grief;
you consider it to take it in hand.
The victim commits himself to you;
you are the helper of the fatherless.

---

a16 Or *Meditation*; possibly a musical notation   b17 Hebrew *Sheol*   cPsalms 9 and 10 may have
been originally a single acrostic poem, the stanzas of which begin with the successive letters of the
Hebrew alphabet. In the Septuagint they constitute one psalm.

¹⁵Break the arm of the wicked and evil
man;
call him to account for his
wickedness
that would not be found out.

¹⁶The Lord is King for ever and ever;
the nations will perish from his
land.
¹⁷You hear, O Lord, the desire of the
afflicted;
you encourage them, and you listen
to their cry,
¹⁸defending the fatherless and the
oppressed,
in order that man, who is of the
earth, may terrify no more.

Psalm 11

For the director of music. Of David.

¹In the Lord I take refuge.
How then can you say to me:
"Flee like a bird to your mountain.
²For look, the wicked bend their bows;
they set their arrows against the
strings
to shoot from the shadows
at the upright in heart.
³When the foundations are being
destroyed,
what can the righteous doᵃ?"

⁴The Lord is in his holy temple;
the Lord is on his heavenly throne.
He observes the sons of men;
his eyes examine them.
⁵The Lord examines the righteous,
but the wickedᵇ and those who
love violence
his soul hates.
⁶On the wicked he will rain
fiery coals and burning sulfur;
a scorching wind will be their
lot.

⁷For the Lord is righteous,
he loves justice;
upright men will see his face.

Psalm 12

For the director of music. According to
sheminith.ᶜ A psalm of David.

¹Help, Lord, for the godly are no more;
the faithful have vanished from
among men.

²Everyone lies to his neighbor;
their flattering lips speak with
deception.
³May the Lord cut off all flattering lips
and every boastful tongue
⁴that says, "We will triumph with our
tongues;
we own our lipsᵈ—who is our
master?"

⁵"Because of the oppression of the
weak
and the groaning of the needy,
I will now arise," says the Lord.
"I will protect them from those who
malign them."
⁶And the words of the Lord are
flawless,
like silver refined in a furnace of
clay,
purified seven times.

⁷O Lord, you will keep us safe
and protect us from such people
forever.
⁸The wicked freely strut about
when what is vile is honored among
men.

Psalm 13

For the director of music. A psalm
of David.

¹How long, O Lord? Will you forget me
forever?
How long will you hide your face
from me?
²How long must I wrestle with my
thoughts
and every day have sorrow in my
heart?
How long will my enemy triumph
over me?

³Look on me and answer, O Lord my
God.
Give light to my eyes, or I will
sleep in death;
⁴my enemy will say, "I have overcome
him,"
and my foes will rejoice when
I fall.

⁵But I trust in your unfailing love;
my heart rejoices in your salvation.
⁶I will sing to the Lord,
for he has been good to me.

ᵃ3 Or what is the Righteous One doing   ᵇ5 Or The Lord, the Righteous One, examines the wicked, /
ᶜTitle: Probably a musical term   ᵈ4 Or / our lips are our plowshares

Psalm 14

For the director of music. Of David.

[1]The fool[a] says in his heart,
　"There is no God."
They are corrupt, their deeds are vile;
　there is no one who does good.

[2]The LORD looks down from heaven
　on the sons of men
to see if there are any who
　understand,
any who seek God.
[3]All have turned aside,
　they have together become corrupt;
there is no one who does good,
　not even one.

[4]Will evildoers never learn—
　those who devour my people as
　　men eat bread
and who do not call on the LORD?
[5]There they are, overwhelmed with
　dread,

for God is present in the company
　of the righteous.
[6]You evildoers frustrate the plans of
　the poor,
but the LORD is their refuge.

[7]Oh, that salvation for Israel would
　come out of Zion!
When the LORD restores the
　fortunes of his people,
let Jacob rejoice and Israel be glad!

Psalm 15

A psalm of David.

[1]LORD, who may dwell in your
　sanctuary?
Who may live on your holy hill?

[2]He whose walk is blameless
　and who does what is righteous,
who speaks the truth from his heart
[3]　and has no slander on his tongue,
who does his neighbor no wrong

---

[a]1 The Hebrew words rendered *fool* in Psalms denote one who is morally deficient.

| TUESDAY |

VERSE FOR THE DAY:
Psalm 14:1

AUTHOR:
Ruth Bell Graham

PASSAGE FOR THE DAY:
Psalm 14:1–7

The Fools

"THE fool says in his heart, 'There is no God.'" This designation goes for those who doubt God's sovereignty as well as those who deny Him. Either He is sovereign, or He is not God. Therefore, when we become so preoccupied with and dismayed by circumstances and certain people that we doubt God's ability to handle things in His own way, and in His own time, then we, too, are fools.

Additional Scripture Readings:
1 Kings 19:1–18; Luke 24:17–25

*Go to page 567 for your next
devotional reading.*

and casts no slur on his fellowman,
⁴who despises a vile man
  but honors those who fear the LORD,
who keeps his oath
  even when it hurts,
⁵who lends his money without usury
  and does not accept a bribe against
    the innocent.

He who does these things
  will never be shaken.

Psalm 16

*A miktam*ᵃ *of David.*

¹Keep me safe, O God,
  for in you I take refuge.

²I said to the LORD, "You are my Lord;
  apart from you I have no good
    thing."
³As for the saints who are in the land,
  they are the glorious ones in whom
    is all my delight.ᵇ
⁴The sorrows of those will increase
  who run after other gods.
I will not pour out their libations of
    blood
  or take up their names on my lips.

⁵LORD, you have assigned me my
    portion and my cup;
  you have made my lot secure.
⁶The boundary lines have fallen for me
    in pleasant places;
  surely I have a delightful
    inheritance.

⁷I will praise the LORD, who counsels
    me;
  even at night my heart instructs
    me.
⁸I have set the LORD always before me.
  Because he is at my right hand,
  I will not be shaken.

⁹Therefore my heart is glad and my
    tongue rejoices;
  my body also will rest secure,
¹⁰because you will not abandon me to
    the grave,ᶜ
  nor will you let your Holy Oneᵈ see
    decay.
¹¹You have madeᵉ known to me the
    path of life;
  you will fill me with joy in your
    presence,

with eternal pleasures at your right
  hand.

Psalm 17

A prayer of David.

¹Hear, O LORD, my righteous plea;
  listen to my cry.
Give ear to my prayer—
  it does not rise from deceitful lips.
²May my vindication come from you;
  may your eyes see what is right.

³Though you probe my heart and
    examine me at night,
  though you test me, you will find
    nothing;
I have resolved that my mouth will
    not sin.
⁴As for the deeds of men—
  by the word of your lips
I have kept myself
  from the ways of the violent.
⁵My steps have held to your paths;
  my feet have not slipped.

⁶I call on you, O God, for you will
    answer me;
  give ear to me and hear my prayer.
⁷Show the wonder of your great love,
  you who save by your right hand
those who take refuge in you from
    their foes.
⁸Keep me as the apple of your eye;
  hide me in the shadow of your
    wings
⁹from the wicked who assail me,
  from my mortal enemies who
    surround me.

¹⁰They close up their callous hearts,
  and their mouths speak with
    arrogance.
¹¹They have tracked me down, they
    now surround me,
  with eyes alert, to throw me to the
    ground.
¹²They are like a lion hungry for prey,
  like a great lion crouching in cover.
¹³Rise up, O LORD, confront them, bring
    them down;
  rescue me from the wicked by your
    sword.
¹⁴O LORD, by your hand save me from
    such men,

ᵃTitle: Probably a literary or musical term   ᵇ3 Or *As for the pagan priests who are in the land / and the
nobles in whom all delight, I said:*   ᶜ10 Hebrew *Sheol*   ᵈ10 Or *your faithful one*   ᵉ11 Or *You will
make*

from men of this world whose
reward is in this life.

You still the hunger of those you
cherish;
their sons have plenty,
and they store up wealth for their
children.
15And I—in righteousness I will see
your face;
when I awake, I will be satisfied
with seeing your likeness.

Psalm 18

For the director of music. Of David the
servant of the LORD. He sang to the LORD
the words of this song when the LORD
delivered him from the hand of all
his enemies and from the hand
of Saul. He said:

1I love you, O LORD, my strength.

2The LORD is my rock, my fortress and
my deliverer;
my God is my rock, in whom I take
refuge.
He is my shield and the horn*a* of
my salvation, my stronghold.
3I call to the LORD, who is worthy of
praise,
and I am saved from my enemies.

4The cords of death entangled me;
the torrents of destruction
overwhelmed me.
5The cords of the grave*b* coiled around
me;
the snares of death confronted me.
6In my distress I called to the LORD;
I cried to my God for help.
From his temple he heard my voice;
my cry came before him, into his
ears.

7The earth trembled and quaked,
and the foundations of the
mountains shook;
they trembled because he was
angry.
8Smoke rose from his nostrils;
consuming fire came from his
mouth,
burning coals blazed out of it.
9He parted the heavens and came
down;
dark clouds were under his feet.
10He mounted the cherubim and flew;

he soared on the wings of the wind.
11He made darkness his covering, his
canopy around him—
the dark rain clouds of the sky.
12Out of the brightness of his presence
clouds advanced,
with hailstones and bolts of
lightning.
13The LORD thundered from heaven;
the voice of the Most High
resounded.*c*
14He shot his arrows and scattered the
enemies,
great bolts of lightning and routed
them.
15The valleys of the sea were exposed
and the foundations of the earth
laid bare
at your rebuke, O LORD,
at the blast of breath from your
nostrils.

16He reached down from on high and
took hold of me;
he drew me out of deep waters.
17He rescued me from my powerful
enemy,
from my foes, who were too strong
for me.
18They confronted me in the day of my
disaster,
but the LORD was my support.
19He brought me out into a spacious
place;
he rescued me because he
delighted in me.

20The LORD has dealt with me according
to my righteousness;
according to the cleanness of my
hands he has rewarded me.
21For I have kept the ways of the LORD;
I have not done evil by turning
from my God.
22All his laws are before me;
I have not turned away from his
decrees.
23I have been blameless before him
and have kept myself from sin.
24The LORD has rewarded me according
to my righteousness,
according to the cleanness of my
hands in his sight.

25To the faithful you show yourself
faithful,
to the blameless you show yourself
blameless,

a2 Horn here symbolizes strength.   *b5* Hebrew *Sheol*   *c13* Some Hebrew manuscripts and
Septuagint (see also 2 Samuel 22:14); most Hebrew manuscripts *resounded, / amid hailstones and bolts of
lightning*

²⁶to the pure you show yourself pure,
but to the crooked you show
yourself shrewd.
²⁷You save the humble
but bring low those whose eyes are
haughty.
²⁸You, O LORD, keep my lamp burning;
my God turns my darkness into
light.
²⁹With your help I can advance against
a troop^a;
with my God I can scale a wall.

³⁰As for God, his way is perfect;
the word of the LORD is flawless.
He is a shield
for all who take refuge in him.
³¹For who is God besides the LORD?
And who is the Rock except our
God?
³²It is God who arms me with strength
and makes my way perfect.
³³He makes my feet like the feet of a
deer;
he enables me to stand on the
heights.
³⁴He trains my hands for battle;
my arms can bend a bow of bronze.
³⁵You give me your shield of victory,
and your right hand sustains me;
you stoop down to make me great.
³⁶You broaden the path beneath me,
so that my ankles do not turn.

³⁷I pursued my enemies and overtook
them;
I did not turn back till they were
destroyed.
³⁸I crushed them so that they could not
rise;
they fell beneath my feet.
³⁹You armed me with strength for
battle;
you made my adversaries bow at my
feet.
⁴⁰You made my enemies turn their
backs in flight,
and I destroyed my foes.
⁴¹They cried for help, but there was no
one to save them—
to the LORD, but he did not answer.
⁴²I beat them as fine as dust borne on
the wind;
I poured them out like mud in the
streets.

⁴³You have delivered me from the
attacks of the people;

you have made me the head of
nations;
people I did not know are subject
to me.
⁴⁴As soon as they hear me, they obey
me;
foreigners cringe before me.
⁴⁵They all lose heart;
they come trembling from their
strongholds.

⁴⁶The LORD lives! Praise be to my Rock!
Exalted be God my Savior!
⁴⁷He is the God who avenges me,
who subdues nations under me,
⁴⁸   who saves me from my enemies.
You exalted me above my foes;
from violent men you rescued me.
⁴⁹Therefore I will praise you among the
nations, O LORD;
I will sing praises to your name.
⁵⁰He gives his king great victories;
he shows unfailing kindness to his
anointed,
to David and his descendants
forever.

Psalm 19

For the director of music. A psalm
of David.

¹The heavens declare the glory of God;
the skies proclaim the work of his
hands.
²Day after day they pour forth speech;
night after night they display
knowledge.
³There is no speech or language
where their voice is not heard.^b
⁴Their voice^c goes out into all the
earth,
their words to the ends of the
world.

In the heavens he has pitched a tent
for the sun,
⁵   which is like a bridegroom coming
forth from his pavilion,
like a champion rejoicing to run his
course.
⁶It rises at one end of the heavens
and makes its circuit to the other;
nothing is hidden from its heat.

⁷The law of the LORD is perfect,
reviving the soul.
The statutes of the LORD are
trustworthy,

^a29 Or can run through a barricade   ^b3 Or They have no speech, there are no words; / no sound is heard
from them   ^c4 Septuagint, Jerome and Syriac; Hebrew line

making wise the simple.
8The precepts of the LORD are right,
　giving joy to the heart.
The commands of the LORD are
　radiant,
　giving light to the eyes.
9The fear of the LORD is pure,
　enduring forever.
The ordinances of the LORD are sure
　and altogether righteous.
10They are more precious than gold,
　than much pure gold;
they are sweeter than honey,
　than honey from the comb.
11By them is your servant warned;
　in keeping them there is great
　　reward.

12Who can discern his errors?
　Forgive my hidden faults.
13Keep your servant also from willful
　　sins;
　may they not rule over me.
Then will I be blameless,
　innocent of great transgression.

14May the words of my mouth and the
　　meditation of my heart
be pleasing in your sight,
O LORD, my Rock and my
　　Redeemer.

Psalm 20

For the director of music. A psalm
of David.

1May the LORD answer you when you
　are in distress;
　may the name of the God of Jacob
　　protect you.
2May he send you help from the
　sanctuary
and grant you support from Zion.
3May he remember all your sacrifices
　and accept your burnt offerings.
　　　　　　　　　　　　Selah
4May he give you the desire of your
　heart
and make all your plans succeed.
5We will shout for joy when you are
　victorious
and will lift up our banners in the
　name of our God.
May the LORD grant all your requests.

6Now I know that the LORD saves his
　anointed;
he answers him from his holy
　heaven

with the saving power of his right
　hand.
7Some trust in chariots and some in
　horses,
but we trust in the name of the
　LORD our God.
8They are brought to their knees and
　fall,
but we rise up and stand firm.

9O LORD, save the king!
Answer[a] us when we call!

Psalm 21

For the director of music. A psalm
of David.

1O LORD, the king rejoices in your
　strength.
How great is his joy in the victories
　you give!
2You have granted him the desire of
　his heart
and have not withheld the request
　of his lips.　　　　　Selah
3You welcomed him with rich blessings
and placed a crown of pure gold on
　his head.
4He asked you for life, and you gave it
　to him—
length of days, for ever and ever.
5Through the victories you gave, his
　glory is great;
you have bestowed on him splendor
　and majesty.
6Surely you have granted him eternal
　blessings
and made him glad with the joy of
　your presence.
7For the king trusts in the LORD;
through the unfailing love of the
　Most High
he will not be shaken.

8Your hand will lay hold on all your
　enemies;
your right hand will seize your foes.
9At the time of your appearing
you will make them like a fiery
　furnace.
In his wrath the LORD will swallow
　them up,
and his fire will consume them.
10You will destroy their descendants
　from the earth,
their posterity from mankind.
11Though they plot evil against you

a9 Or save! / O King, answer

VERSE FOR THE DAY:
Psalm 19:1

AUTHOR:
Gloria Gaither

PASSAGE FOR THE DAY:
Psalm 19:1–14

I Declare

IT was the sun pouring through the kitchen window at 7:00 A.M., for the first time after the long winter, that made me turn to Psalm 19 instead of the chapter in Colossians we had been reading that week to the kids at the breakfast table. I was reading it for the kids, right? So they would focus on the glorious, first sunny morning of early spring.

But as I read, I became overwhelmed with the way this fellow-poet had reached from the circumstances of his life into mine. The psalm opened with the familiar verse:

> The heavens declare the glory of God;
> the skies proclaim the work of his hands.

The psalmist then moves on to list the all-encompassing, beautiful declarations of God's law. These declarations so powerfully bring into focus what life should be about, so speak to our human frailties, so heal our broken dreams, so reassure our lost confidences, so pinpoint our areas of weakness, that the psalmist literally falls to his knees in repentance.

His error and hidden faults, his smallness and willful sins are all exposed. And more than that, he begins to ask himself, "If we are supposed to be the most articulate of all God's creatures, what are our lives saying? What are we making as the declaration of our days?"

Shamed by the articulate heavens, we hear our own voices praying aloud with the psalmist in repentance and supplication:

> May the words of my mouth and the meditation
> of my heart
> be pleasing in your sight,
> O LORD, my Rock and my Redeemer
> (Psalm 19:14).

The children were very silent as I, overwhelmed by what I had read, sobbed through these final words of the psalm. Then together we prayed, "Jesus, this day let our actions and attitudes be in sync with all creation. May we articulate praise with the moments we are given today. Amen."

(As a result of this experience, Gloria wrote: "Praise You; I Will Praise You," "Anthem," "What Are the Words?" "I'd Say 'I Love You' in a Thousand Ways," and "Hallelu—Hallelujah!")

Additional Scripture Readings:
Proverbs 4:23–27; Matthew 5:14–16

Go to page 569 for your next devotional reading.

and devise wicked schemes, they
cannot succeed;
¹²for you will make them turn their
backs
when you aim at them with drawn
bow.

¹³Be exalted, O LORD, in your strength;
we will sing and praise your might.

Psalm 22

For the director of music. To the tune
of, "The Doe of the Morning." A psalm
of David.

¹My God, my God, why have you
forsaken me?
Why are you so far from saving me,
so far from the words of my
groaning?
²O my God, I cry out by day, but you
do not answer,
by night, and am not silent.

³Yet you are enthroned as the Holy
One;
you are the praise of Israel. ᵃ
⁴In you our fathers put their trust;
they trusted and you delivered
them.
⁵They cried to you and were saved;
in you they trusted and were not
disappointed.

⁶But I am a worm and not a man,
scorned by men and despised by
the people.
⁷All who see me mock me;
they hurl insults, shaking their
heads:
⁸"He trusts in the LORD;
let the LORD rescue him.
Let him deliver him,
since he delights in him."

⁹Yet you brought me out of the womb;
you made me trust in you
even at my mother's breast.
¹⁰From birth I was cast upon you;
from my mother's womb you have
been my God.
¹¹Do not be far from me,
for trouble is near
and there is no one to help.

¹²Many bulls surround me;
strong bulls of Bashan encircle me.
¹³Roaring lions tearing their prey

open their mouths wide against me.
¹⁴I am poured out like water,
and all my bones are out of joint.
My heart has turned to wax;
it has melted away within me.
¹⁵My strength is dried up like a
potsherd,
and my tongue sticks to the roof of
my mouth;
you lay me ᵇ in the dust of death.
¹⁶Dogs have surrounded me;
a band of evil men has encircled
me,
they have pierced ᶜ my hands and
my feet.
¹⁷I can count all my bones;
people stare and gloat over me.
¹⁸They divide my garments among them
and cast lots for my clothing.

¹⁹But you, O LORD, be not far off;
O my Strength, come quickly to
help me.
²⁰Deliver my life from the sword,
my precious life from the power of
the dogs.
²¹Rescue me from the mouth of the
lions;
save ᵈ me from the horns of the
wild oxen.

²²I will declare your name to my
brothers;
in the congregation I will praise
you.
²³You who fear the LORD, praise him!
All you descendants of Jacob,
honor him!
Revere him, all you descendants of
Israel!
²⁴For he has not despised or disdained
the suffering of the afflicted one;
he has not hidden his face from him
but has listened to his cry for help.

²⁵From you comes the theme of my
praise in the great assembly;
before those who fear you ᵉ will I
fulfill my vows.
²⁶The poor will eat and be satisfied;
they who seek the LORD will praise
him—
may your hearts live forever!
²⁷All the ends of the earth
will remember and turn to the
LORD,
and all the families of the nations
will bow down before him,

ᵃ3 Or Yet you are holy, / enthroned on the praises of Israel   ᵇ15 Or / I am laid   ᶜ16 Some Hebrew
manuscripts, Septuagint and Syriac; most Hebrew manuscripts / like the lion,   ᵈ21 Or / you have heard
ᵉ25 Hebrew him

VERSE FOR THE DAY:
Psalm 22:11

AUTHOR:
Susan L. Lenzkes

PASSAGE FOR THE DAY:
Psalm 22:1–24

Teen Trouble

SOME days should never be recorded, repeated or remembered.

Take today, for instance. After a morning of upheaval with my daughter, she confided in me that she was in the absolute pits of a mood (she could have saved the trouble of making the announcement). Then she needed my complete attention for the next hour to gripe about everything and anything that has ever touched her nineteen-year-old world. She said she didn't know what's the matter with her lately, and I have a permanent crease across my tongue from resisting the urge to tell her!

She finally left for work, and my number-one son must have thought I'd be lonely for disaster, so he proceeded to erupt. He became incensed over some infraction to his personal sense of justice and shoved a bike at his brother, nearly wiping out his ability to father succeeding generations.

After tending to the offended, I tried to deal with the offender and got a verbal volley that could knock any mother off her Nikes. An impartial jury surely would have labeled it "mother abuse" and given him a few years in solitary.

So in the middle of this—I mean in the very middle of this scene, not knowing whether to laugh or to cry because this five-foot-ten-inch kid is exhibiting every characteristic of the "terrible twos" in outsized triplicate—a man called and asked if he had reached the Lenzkes' residence . . . the Susan L. Lenzkes' residence.

It seems he had discovered my book *When the Handwriting on the Wall Is in Brown Crayon* in, of all places, a doctor's waiting room, and he and his wife were so taken by it that they had headed straight for a bookstore and bought one.

At the bookstore they found out where I live. Then they found my phone number in the directory and called to tell me what a blessing my life was to them! (The Lord's timing is most humbling!)

But, I know that our Lord is faithful. He promised we could pick up snakes with our bare hands and drink deadly poison, and live with teenagers (well, that last addition seems to fit nicely here) and not be hurt at all!

Additional Scripture Readings:
Mark 16:14–18; Philippians 2:1–4

Go to page 574 for your next devotional reading.

²⁸for dominion belongs to the LORD
and he rules over the nations.

²⁹All the rich of the earth will feast and
worship;
all who go down to the dust will
kneel before him—
those who cannot keep themselves
alive.
³⁰Posterity will serve him;
future generations will be told
about the Lord.
³¹They will proclaim his righteousness
to a people yet unborn—
for he has done it.

Psalm 23

A psalm of David.

¹The LORD is my shepherd, I shall not
be in want.
²   He makes me lie down in green
pastures,
he leads me beside quiet waters,
³   he restores my soul.
He guides me in paths of
righteousness
for his name's sake.
⁴Even though I walk
through the valley of the shadow of
death,ᵃ
I will fear no evil,
for you are with me;
your rod and your staff,
they comfort me.

⁵You prepare a table before me
in the presence of my enemies.
You anoint my head with oil;
my cup overflows.
⁶Surely goodness and love will follow
me
all the days of my life,
and I will dwell in the house of the
LORD
forever.

Psalm 24

Of David. A psalm.

¹The earth is the LORD's, and
everything in it,
the world, and all who live in it;
²for he founded it upon the seas
and established it upon the waters.

³Who may ascend the hill of the LORD?
Who may stand in his holy place?
⁴He who has clean hands and a pure
heart,
who does not lift up his soul to an
idol
or swear by what is false.ᵇ
⁵He will receive blessing from the LORD
and vindication from God his
Savior.
⁶Such is the generation of those who
seek him,
who seek your face, O God of
Jacob.ᶜ   Selah

⁷Lift up your heads, O you gates;
be lifted up, you ancient doors,
that the King of glory may come in.
⁸Who is this King of glory?
The LORD strong and mighty,
the LORD mighty in battle.
⁹Lift up your heads, O you gates;
lift them up, you ancient doors,
that the King of glory may come in.
¹⁰Who is he, this King of glory?
The LORD Almighty—
he is the King of glory.   Selah

Psalm 25ᵈ

Of David.

¹To you, O LORD, I lift up my soul;
²   in you I trust, O my God.
Do not let me be put to shame,
nor let my enemies triumph over
me.
³No one whose hope is in you
will ever be put to shame,
but they will be put to shame
who are treacherous without
excuse.

⁴Show me your ways, O LORD,
teach me your paths;
⁵guide me in your truth and teach me,
for you are God my Savior,
and my hope is in you all day long.
⁶Remember, O LORD, your great mercy
and love,
for they are from of old.
⁷Remember not the sins of my youth
and my rebellious ways;
according to your love remember me,
for you are good, O LORD.

⁸Good and upright is the LORD;

ᵃ4 Or *through the darkest valley*   ᵇ4 Or *swear falsely*
also Septuagint); most Hebrew manuscripts *face, Jacob*
which begin with the successive letters of the Hebrew alphabet.   ᶜ6 Two Hebrew manuscripts and Syriac (see
ᵈThis psalm is an acrostic poem, the verses of

therefore he instructs sinners in his ways.

⁹He guides the humble in what is right
　and teaches them his way.
¹⁰All the ways of the LORD are loving
　　and faithful
　for those who keep the demands of
　　his covenant.
¹¹For the sake of your name, O LORD,
　forgive my iniquity, though it is
　　great.
¹²Who, then, is the man that fears the
　　LORD?
　He will instruct him in the way
　　chosen for him.
¹³He will spend his days in prosperity,
　and his descendants will inherit the
　　land.
¹⁴The LORD confides in those who fear
　　him;
　he makes his covenant known to
　　them.
¹⁵My eyes are ever on the LORD,
　for only he will release my feet
　　from the snare.

¹⁶Turn to me and be gracious to me,
　for I am lonely and afflicted.
¹⁷The troubles of my heart have
　　multiplied;
　free me from my anguish.
¹⁸Look upon my affliction and my
　　distress
　and take away all my sins.
¹⁹See how my enemies have increased
　and how fiercely they hate me!
²⁰Guard my life and rescue me;
　let me not be put to shame,
　for I take refuge in you.
²¹May integrity and uprightness protect
　　me,
　because my hope is in you.

²²Redeem Israel, O God,
　from all their troubles!

Psalm 26

Of David.

¹Vindicate me, O LORD,
　for I have led a blameless life;
I have trusted in the LORD
　without wavering.
²Test me, O LORD, and try me,
　examine my heart and my mind;
³for your love is ever before me,
　and I walk continually in your
　　truth.

⁴I do not sit with deceitful men,
　nor do I consort with hypocrites;
⁵I abhor the assembly of evildoers
　and refuse to sit with the wicked.
⁶I wash my hands in innocence,
　and go about your altar, O LORD,
⁷proclaiming aloud your praise
　and telling of all your wonderful
　　deeds.
⁸I love the house where you live,
　　O LORD,
　the place where your glory dwells.

⁹Do not take away my soul along with
　　sinners,
　my life with bloodthirsty men,
¹⁰in whose hands are wicked schemes,
　whose right hands are full of bribes.
¹¹But I lead a blameless life;
　redeem me and be merciful to me.

¹²My feet stand on level ground;
　in the great assembly I will praise
　　the LORD.

Psalm 27

Of David.

¹The LORD is my light and my
　　salvation—
　whom shall I fear?
The LORD is the stronghold of my
　　life—
　of whom shall I be afraid?
²When evil men advance against me
　to devour my flesh,ᵃ
when my enemies and my foes attack
　　me,
　they will stumble and fall.
³Though an army besiege me,
　my heart will not fear;
though war break out against me,
　even then will I be confident.

⁴One thing I ask of the LORD,
　this is what I seek:
that I may dwell in the house of the
　　LORD
　all the days of my life,
to gaze upon the beauty of the LORD
　and to seek him in his temple.
⁵For in the day of trouble
　he will keep me safe in his
　　dwelling;
he will hide me in the shelter of his
　　tabernacle
　and set me high upon a rock.
⁶Then my head will be exalted

ᵃ2 Or to slander me

above the enemies who surround
  me;
at his tabernacle will I sacrifice with
  shouts of joy;
I will sing and make music to the
  LORD.

⁷Hear my voice when I call, O LORD;
  be merciful to me and answer me.
⁸My heart says of you, "Seek his*ᵃ*
  face!"
  Your face, LORD, I will seek.
⁹Do not hide your face from me,
  do not turn your servant away in
    anger;
  you have been my helper.
Do not reject me or forsake me,
  O God my Savior.
¹⁰Though my father and mother forsake
  me,
  the LORD will receive me.
¹¹Teach me your way, O LORD;
  lead me in a straight path
  because of my oppressors.
¹²Do not turn me over to the desire of
  my foes,
  for false witnesses rise up against
    me,
  breathing out violence.

¹³I am still confident of this:
  I will see the goodness of the LORD
  in the land of the living.
¹⁴Wait for the LORD;
  be strong and take heart
  and wait for the LORD.

Psalm 28

Of David.

¹To you I call, O LORD my Rock;
  do not turn a deaf ear to me.
For if you remain silent,
  I will be like those who have gone
    down to the pit.
²Hear my cry for mercy
  as I call to you for help,
as I lift up my hands
  toward your Most Holy Place.

³Do not drag me away with the
  wicked,
  with those who do evil,
who speak cordially with their
  neighbors
  but harbor malice in their hearts.
⁴Repay them for their deeds
  and for their evil work;

repay them for what their hands have
  done
  and bring back upon them what
    they deserve.
⁵Since they show no regard for the
  works of the LORD
  and what his hands have done,
he will tear them down
  and never build them up again.

⁶Praise be to the LORD,
  for he has heard my cry for mercy.
⁷The LORD is my strength and my
  shield;
  my heart trusts in him, and I am
    helped.
My heart leaps for joy
  and I will give thanks to him in
    song.

⁸The LORD is the strength of his
  people,
  a fortress of salvation for his
    anointed one.
⁹Save your people and bless your
  inheritance;
  be their shepherd and carry them
    forever.

Psalm 29

A psalm of David.

¹Ascribe to the LORD, O mighty ones,
  ascribe to the LORD glory and
    strength.
²Ascribe to the LORD the glory due his
  name;
  worship the LORD in the splendor of
    his*ᵇ* holiness.

³The voice of the LORD is over the
  waters;
  the God of glory thunders,
  the LORD thunders over the mighty
    waters.
⁴The voice of the LORD is powerful;
  the voice of the LORD is majestic.
⁵The voice of the LORD breaks the
  cedars;
  the LORD breaks in pieces the
    cedars of Lebanon.
⁶He makes Lebanon skip like a calf,
  Sirion*ᶜ* like a young wild ox.
⁷The voice of the LORD strikes
  with flashes of lightning.
⁸The voice of the LORD shakes the
  desert;

ᵃ8 Or To you, O my heart, he has said, "Seek my
Mount Hermon   *ᵇ2 Or LORD with the splendor of*   *ᶜ6 That is,*

the Lord shakes the Desert of
Kadesh.
⁹The voice of the Lord twists the
oaks*ᵃ*
and strips the forests bare.
And in his temple all cry, "Glory!"

¹⁰The Lord sits*ᵇ* enthroned over the
flood;
the Lord is enthroned as King
forever.
¹¹The Lord gives strength to his people;
the Lord blesses his people with
peace.

Psalm 30

A psalm. A song. For the dedication of
the temple.*ᶜ* Of David.

¹I will exalt you, O Lord,
for you lifted me out of the depths
and did not let my enemies gloat
over me.
²O Lord my God, I called to you for
help
and you healed me.
³O Lord, you brought me up from the
grave*ᵈ*;
you spared me from going down
into the pit.

⁴Sing to the Lord, you saints of his;
praise his holy name.
⁵For his anger lasts only a moment,
but his favor lasts a lifetime;
weeping may remain for a night,
but rejoicing comes in the morning.

⁶When I felt secure, I said,
"I will never be shaken."
⁷O Lord, when you favored me,
you made my mountain*ᵉ* stand
firm;
but when you hid your face,
I was dismayed.

⁸To you, O Lord, I called;
to the Lord I cried for mercy:
⁹"What gain is there in my
destruction,*ᶠ*
in my going down into the pit?
Will the dust praise you?
Will it proclaim your faithfulness?
¹⁰Hear, O Lord, and be merciful to me;
O Lord, be my help."

¹¹You turned my wailing into dancing;
you removed my sackcloth and
clothed me with joy,

¹²that my heart may sing to you and
not be silent.
O Lord my God, I will give you
thanks forever.

Psalm 31

For the director of music. A psalm
of David.

¹In you, O Lord, I have taken refuge;
let me never be put to shame;
deliver me in your righteousness.
²Turn your ear to me,
come quickly to my rescue;
be my rock of refuge,
a strong fortress to save me.
³Since you are my rock and my
fortress,
for the sake of your name lead and
guide me.
⁴Free me from the trap that is set for
me,
for you are my refuge.
⁵Into your hands I commit my spirit;
redeem me, O Lord, the God of
truth.

⁶I hate those who cling to worthless
idols;
I trust in the Lord.
⁷I will be glad and rejoice in your
love,
for you saw my affliction
and knew the anguish of my soul.
⁸You have not handed me over to the
enemy
but have set my feet in a spacious
place.

⁹Be merciful to me, O Lord, for I am
in distress;
my eyes grow weak with sorrow,
my soul and my body with grief.
¹⁰My life is consumed by anguish
and my years by groaning;
my strength fails because of my
affliction,*ᵍ*
and my bones grow weak.
¹¹Because of all my enemies,
I am the utter contempt of my
neighbors;
I am a dread to my friends—
those who see me on the street flee
from me.
¹²I am forgotten by them as though I
were dead;
I have become like broken pottery.

ᵃ9 Or Lord makes the deer give birth   *ᵇ10* Or sat   *ᶜTitle:* Or palace   *ᵈ3* Hebrew Sheol   *ᵉ7* Or
hill country   *ᶠ9* Or there if I am silenced   *ᵍ10* Or guilt

¹³For I hear the slander of many;
　　there is terror on every side;
they conspire against me
　　and plot to take my life.

¹⁴But I trust in you, O LORD;
　　I say, "You are my God."
¹⁵My times are in your hands;
　　deliver me from my enemies

and from those who pursue me.
¹⁶Let your face shine on your servant;
　　save me in your unfailing love.
¹⁷Let me not be put to shame, O LORD,
　　for I have cried out to you;
but let the wicked be put to shame
　　and lie silent in the grave.[a]
¹⁸Let their lying lips be silenced,
　　for with pride and contempt

[a]17 Hebrew *Sheol*

FRIDAY

VERSE FOR THE DAY:　　**AUTHOR:**　　**PASSAGE FOR THE DAY:**
Psalm 30:5　　Mary Jane Worden　　Psalm 30:1–12

Night Weeping

AS I walked past the kitchen bulletin board I glanced, as usual, at our family picture. I was surprised by the sudden intense pain, the almost doubling-over kind from those first days of grief, after my husband Jim's death. Somehow there aren't enough words (in my vocabulary at least) to describe the great varieties of pain. Today it was the stomach-turning kind, producing that urge to bolt, to run or somehow try to squirm away from the source of pain. Impossible—like trying to crawl out from under the labor contractions of childbirth. Agonizing, but necessary I guess, and (sometimes to my disappointment) survivable. Just there, and unavoidable, at least for this moment. Do I need to learn to work with it, sort of "riding" it rather than fighting it, as they taught us in childbirth classes? Sometimes the evil behind death peers through, and it seems such a horror. It makes me wish I were a screamer. Instead the silent tears slip down my cheeks. Tonight the pain and sadness are specific and profound, not just the vague weeping of fatigue.

As I read back in my journals I find myself almost relieved to see the variety of feelings. One big component of the pain is fear—a fear that this experience of pain may not be momentary but might settle down on me as a permanent condition, an incurable disease, an overwhelming and unmoving cloud cover. This time it's got me and it may never let me go. I need to keep reminding myself, in the midst of the pain, that I can acknowledge it and give in to it because it isn't a life sentence.

Weeping may remain for a night,
but rejoicing comes in the morning
(Psalm 30:5).

Additional Scripture Readings:
Matthew 5:4; Revelation 21:3–4

*Go to page 576 for your next
devotional reading.*

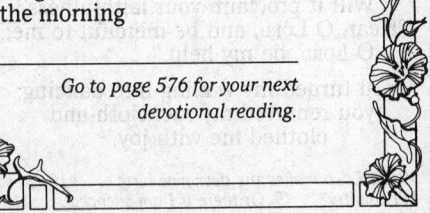

they speak arrogantly against the
righteous.

[19]How great is your goodness,
which you have stored up for those
who fear you,
which you bestow in the sight of men
on those who take refuge in you.
[20]In the shelter of your presence you
hide them
from the intrigues of men;
in your dwelling you keep them safe
from accusing tongues.

[21]Praise be to the LORD,
for he showed his wonderful love to
me
when I was in a besieged city.
[22]In my alarm I said,
"I am cut off from your sight!"
Yet you heard my cry for mercy
when I called to you for help.

[23]Love the LORD, all his saints!
The LORD preserves the faithful,
but the proud he pays back in full.
[24]Be strong and take heart,
all you who hope in the LORD.

Psalm 32

Of David. A maskil. [a]

[1]Blessed is he
whose transgressions are forgiven,
whose sins are covered.
[2]Blessed is the man
whose sin the LORD does not count
against him
and in whose spirit is no deceit.

[3]When I kept silent,
my bones wasted away
through my groaning all day long.
[4]For day and night
your hand was heavy upon me;
my strength was sapped
as in the heat of summer.   *Selah*
[5]Then I acknowledged my sin to you
and did not cover up my iniquity.
I said, "I will confess
my transgressions to the LORD"—
and you forgave
the guilt of my sin.   *Selah*

[6]Therefore let everyone who is godly
pray to you
while you may be found;
surely when the mighty waters rise,
they will not reach him.
[7]You are my hiding place;

you will protect me from trouble
and surround me with songs of
deliverance.   *Selah*

[8]I will instruct you and teach you in
the way you should go;
I will counsel you and watch over
you.
[9]Do not be like the horse or the mule,
which have no understanding
but must be controlled by bit and
bridle
or they will not come to you.
[10]Many are the woes of the wicked,
but the LORD's unfailing love
surrounds the man who trusts in
him.

[11]Rejoice in the LORD and be glad, you
righteous;
sing, all you who are upright in
heart!

Psalm 33

[1]Sing joyfully to the LORD, you
righteous;
it is fitting for the upright to praise
him.
[2]Praise the LORD with the harp;
make music to him on the
ten-stringed lyre.
[3]Sing to him a new song;
play skillfully, and shout for joy.

[4]For the word of the LORD is right and
true;
he is faithful in all he does.
[5]The LORD loves righteousness and
justice;
the earth is full of his unfailing
love.

[6]By the word of the LORD were the
heavens made,
their starry host by the breath of
his mouth.
[7]He gathers the waters of the sea into
jars[b];
he puts the deep into storehouses.
[8]Let all the earth fear the LORD;
let all the people of the world
revere him.
[9]For he spoke, and it came to be;
he commanded, and it stood firm.
[10]The LORD foils the plans of the
nations;
he thwarts the purposes of the
peoples.

[a]Title: Probably a literary or musical term   [b]7 Or *sea as into a heap*

WEEKENDING

RELATE

In the late 1800's Mrs. Louisa M.R. Stead watched as her husband died while trying to save a drowning boy. This familiar hymn was written as a response to her struggle with the "why?" questions she asked God during that difficult time.

RESPOND

'Tis so sweet to trust in Jesus,
Just to take Him at His word,
Just to rest upon His promise,
Just to know, "Thus saith the Lord."

I'm so glad I learned to trust Thee,
Precious Jesus, Savior, Friend;
And I know that Thou art with me,
Wilt be with me to the end.

Jesus, Jesus, how I trust Him!
How I've proved Him o'er and o'er!
Jesus, Jesus, precious Jesus!
O for grace to trust Him more!

– Louisa M.R. Stead

REVIVE

Saturday: Psalm 125:1–5
Sunday: John 14:1–4

Go to page 578 for your next devotional reading.

[11]But the plans of the LORD stand firm
forever,
the purposes of his heart through
all generations.

[12]Blessed is the nation whose God is
the LORD,
the people he chose for his
inheritance.
[13]From heaven the LORD looks down
and sees all mankind;
[14]from his dwelling place he watches
all who live on earth—
[15]he who forms the hearts of all,
who considers everything they do.
[16]No king is saved by the size of his
army;
no warrior escapes by his great
strength.
[17]A horse is a vain hope for deliverance;
despite all its great strength it
cannot save.
[18]But the eyes of the LORD are on those
who fear him,
on those whose hope is in his
unfailing love,
[19]to deliver them from death
and keep them alive in famine.

[20]We wait in hope for the LORD;
he is our help and our shield.
[21]In him our hearts rejoice,
for we trust in his holy name.
[22]May your unfailing love rest upon us,
O LORD,
even as we put our hope in you.

Psalm 34[a]

Of David. When he pretended to be
insane before Abimelech, who drove
him away, and he left.

[1]I will extol the LORD at all times;
his praise will always be on my lips.
[2]My soul will boast in the LORD;
let the afflicted hear and rejoice.
[3]Glorify the LORD with me;
let us exalt his name together.

[4]I sought the LORD, and he answered
me;
he delivered me from all my fears.
[5]Those who look to him are radiant;
their faces are never covered with
shame.
[6]This poor man called, and the LORD
heard him;

he saved him out of all his
troubles.
[7]The angel of the LORD encamps
around those who fear him,
and he delivers them.

[8]Taste and see that the LORD is good;
blessed is the man who takes
refuge in him.
[9]Fear the LORD, you his saints,
for those who fear him lack
nothing.
[10]The lions may grow weak and hungry,
but those who seek the LORD lack
no good thing.

[11]Come, my children, listen to me;
I will teach you the fear of the
LORD.
[12]Whoever of you loves life
and desires to see many good days,
[13]keep your tongue from evil
and your lips from speaking lies.
[14]Turn from evil and do good;
seek peace and pursue it.

[15]The eyes of the LORD are on the
righteous
and his ears are attentive to their
cry;
[16]the face of the LORD is against those
who do evil,
to cut off the memory of them from
the earth.

[17]The righteous cry out, and the LORD
hears them;
he delivers them from all their
troubles.
[18]The LORD is close to the
brokenhearted
and saves those who are crushed in
spirit.

[19]A righteous man may have many
troubles,
but the LORD delivers him from
them all;
[20]he protects all his bones,
not one of them will be broken.

[21]Evil will slay the wicked;
the foes of the righteous will be
condemned.
[22]The LORD redeems his servants;
no one will be condemned who
takes refuge in him.

[a]This psalm is an acrostic poem, the verses of which begin with the successive letters of the Hebrew
alphabet.

Psalm 35

Of David.

[1]Contend, O LORD, with those who
    contend with me;
fight against those who fight
    against me.
[2]Take up shield and buckler;

a3 Or and block the way

arise and come to my aid.
[3]Brandish spear and javelin[a]
    against those who pursue me.
Say to my soul,
    "I am your salvation."

[4]May those who seek my life
    be disgraced and put to shame;
may those who plot my ruin

VERSE FOR THE DAY: AUTHOR: PASSAGE FOR THE DAY:
Psalm 34:6   Wanda K. Jones   Psalm 34:1–22

The Lord Hears

PSALM 34 has been a source of strength and encouragement
ever since I drank from the "living waters" of eternal salvation in
Jesus Christ. Praising, glorifying and honoring the Lord as David
did has proven to be a great blessing even in extremely difficult
circumstances.

As a young Christian in college I was often on my knees asking
the Lord to help with college fees and even incidentals—stock-
ings, underwear, notebook paper and a warm scarf. The wonderful thing was that when I sought him in prayer, he answered!

The main building on our college campus was perched on a
hill overlooking the Hudson River. The setting was beautiful.
Maneuvering was more difficult. It was easy going when we
walked down into the town but coming back was the struggle.
Groups of students often stopped along the way to rest.

I learned and quoted Psalm 34 on those walks up the hillside.
I had no problem with verse 6:

> This poor man called, and the LORD heard him;
>   he saved him out of all his troubles.

I knew then, as I know now, that anyone—man, woman,
young, old, rich, poor, black or white—can call on the Lord, and
he will answer and meet the need.

If you have been going through a difficult period in your life, if
you have been crushed by some unkind deed, or if you have lost
a loved one and are feeling the pangs of loneliness, remember:
the psalmist said that "the LORD is close to the brokenhearted"
(Psalm 34:18).

Why not take refuge in him?

Additional Scripture Readings: *Go to page 581 for your next*
Isaiah 41:17–20; 2 Thessalonians 2:11–12   *devotional reading.*

be turned back in dismay.
⁵May they be like chaff before the
    wind,
    with the angel of the LORD driving
        them away;
⁶may their path be dark and slippery,
    with the angel of the LORD pursuing
        them.
⁷Since they hid their net for me
        without cause
    and without cause dug a pit for me,
⁸may ruin overtake them by surprise—
    may the net they hid entangle
        them,
    may they fall into the pit, to their
        ruin.
⁹Then my soul will rejoice in the LORD
    and delight in his salvation.
¹⁰My whole being will exclaim,
    "Who is like you, O LORD?
    You rescue the poor from those too
        strong for them,
        the poor and needy from those who
            rob them."

¹¹Ruthless witnesses come forward;
    they question me on things I know
        nothing about.
¹²They repay me evil for good
    and leave my soul forlorn.
¹³Yet when they were ill, I put on
        sackcloth
    and humbled myself with fasting.
    When my prayers returned to me
        unanswered,
¹⁴   I went about mourning
        as though for my friend or brother.
    I bowed my head in grief
        as though weeping for my mother.
¹⁵But when I stumbled, they gathered
        in glee;
    attackers gathered against me when
        I was unaware.
    They slandered me without ceasing.
¹⁶Like the ungodly they maliciously
        mockedᵃ;
    they gnashed their teeth at me.
¹⁷O Lord, how long will you look on?
    Rescue my life from their ravages,
    my precious life from these lions.
¹⁸I will give you thanks in the great
        assembly;
    among throngs of people I will
        praise you.

¹⁹Let not those gloat over me
    who are my enemies without
        cause;

let not those who hate me without
        reason
    maliciously wink the eye.
²⁰They do not speak peaceably,
    but devise false accusations
    against those who live quietly in
        the land.
²¹They gape at me and say, "Aha! Aha!
    With our own eyes we have seen
        it."

²²O LORD, you have seen this; be not
        silent.
    Do not be far from me, O Lord.
²³Awake, and rise to my defense!
    Contend for me, my God and Lord.
²⁴Vindicate me in your righteousness,
    O LORD my God;
    do not let them gloat over me.
²⁵Do not let them think, "Aha, just
        what we wanted!"
    or say, "We have swallowed him
        up."

²⁶May all who gloat over my distress
    be put to shame and confusion;
    may all who exalt themselves over me
    be clothed with shame and
        disgrace.
²⁷May those who delight in my
        vindication
    shout for joy and gladness;
    may they always say, "The LORD be
        exalted,
    who delights in the well-being of
        his servant."
²⁸My tongue will speak of your
        righteousness
    and of your praises all day long.

Psalm 36

For the director of music. Of David the
    servant of the LORD.

¹An oracle is within my heart
    concerning the sinfulness of the
        wicked:ᵇ
    There is no fear of God
        before his eyes.
²For in his own eyes he flatters
        himself
    too much to detect or hate his sin.
³The words of his mouth are wicked
        and deceitful;
    he has ceased to be wise and to do
        good.
⁴Even on his bed he plots evil;

ᵃ16 Septuagint; Hebrew may mean *ungodly circle of mockers.*   ᵇ1 Or *heart: / Sin proceeds from the
wicked.*

he commits himself to a sinful
course
and does not reject what is wrong.

5Your love, O LORD, reaches to the
heavens,
your faithfulness to the skies.
6Your righteousness is like the mighty
mountains,
your justice like the great deep.
O LORD, you preserve both man and
beast.
7 How priceless is your unfailing love!
Both high and low among men
find*a* refuge in the shadow of your
wings.
8They feast on the abundance of your
house;
you give them drink from your river
of delights.
9For with you is the fountain of life;
in your light we see light.

10Continue your love to those who
know you,
your righteousness to the upright in
heart.
11May the foot of the proud not come
against me,
nor the hand of the wicked drive
me away.
12See how the evildoers lie fallen —
thrown down, not able to rise!

Psalm 37*b*

Of David.

1Do not fret because of evil men
or be envious of those who do
wrong;
2for like the grass they will soon
wither,
like green plants they will soon die
away.

3Trust in the LORD and do good;
dwell in the land and enjoy safe
pasture.
4Delight yourself in the LORD
and he will give you the desires of
your heart.

5Commit your way to the LORD;
trust in him and he will do this:
6He will make your righteousness
shine like the dawn,
the justice of your cause like the
noonday sun.

7Be still before the LORD and wait
patiently for him;
do not fret when men succeed in
their ways,
when they carry out their wicked
schemes.

8Refrain from anger and turn from
wrath;
do not fret — it leads only to evil.
9For evil men will be cut off,
but those who hope in the LORD
will inherit the land.

10A little while, and the wicked will be
no more;
though you look for them, they will
not be found.
11But the meek will inherit the land
and enjoy great peace.

12The wicked plot against the righteous
and gnash their teeth at them;
13but the Lord laughs at the wicked,
for he knows their day is coming.

14The wicked draw the sword
and bend the bow
to bring down the poor and needy,
to slay those whose ways are
upright.
15But their swords will pierce their own
hearts,
and their bows will be broken.

16Better the little that the righteous
have
than the wealth of many wicked;
17for the power of the wicked will be
broken,
but the LORD upholds the righteous.

18The days of the blameless are known
to the LORD,
and their inheritance will endure
forever.
19In times of disaster they will not
wither;
in days of famine they will enjoy
plenty.

20But the wicked will perish:
The LORD's enemies will be like the
beauty of the fields,
they will vanish — vanish like
smoke.

21The wicked borrow and do not repay,
but the righteous give generously;
22those the LORD blesses will inherit the
land,

---

*a*7 Or *love, O God! / Men find*; or *love! / Both heavenly beings and men / find*   *b*This psalm is an acrostic
poem, the stanzas of which begin with the successive letters of the Hebrew alphabet.

TUESDAY

Commit to God

THE Amplified Bible pictures us committing our load to God by rolling it onto Him. It is helpful to note that we can roll something that is too heavy to carry or to cast.

What are we to commit—to trust—to God?

Ourselves. Psalm 22:8:

> He trusts in the LORD;
>> let the LORD rescue him.
> Let him deliver him, since he delights in him.

Our Burden. Psalm 55:22:

> Cast your cares on the LORD
>> and he will sustain you;
>> he will never let the righteous fall.

Our Souls. 1 Peter 4:19:

So then, those who suffer according to God's will should commit themselves to their faithful Creator and continue to do good.

Our Way. Psalm 37:5:

> Commit your way to the LORD;
>> trust in him.

Our Cause. 1 Peter 2:23:

When they hurled their insults at him, he did not retaliate; when he suffered, he made no threats. Instead, he entrusted himself to him who judges justly.

Our Works. Proverbs 16:3:

> Commit to the LORD whatever you do,
>> and your plans will succeed.

Additional Scripture Readings:
1 Samuel 7:2–4; Acts 14:23–26

Go to page 582 for your next devotional reading.

but those he curses will be cut
off.

²³If the LORD delights in a man's
way,
he makes his steps firm;
²⁴though he stumble, he will not fall,
for the LORD upholds him with his
hand.

²⁵I was young and now I am old,
yet I have never seen the righteous
forsaken
or their children begging bread.
²⁶They are always generous and lend
freely;
their children will be blessed.

²⁷Turn from evil and do good;
then you will dwell in the land
forever.
²⁸For the LORD loves the just
and will not forsake his faithful
ones.

They will be protected forever,
but the offspring of the wicked will
be cut off;

²⁹the righteous will inherit the land
and dwell in it forever.

³⁰The mouth of the righteous man
utters wisdom,
and his tongue speaks what is just.
³¹The law of his God is in his heart;
his feet do not slip.

³²The wicked lie in wait for the
righteous,
seeking their very lives;
³³but the LORD will not leave them in
their power
or let them be condemned when
brought to trial.

³⁴Wait for the LORD
and keep his way.
He will exalt you to inherit the land;
when the wicked are cut off, you
will see it.

³⁵I have seen a wicked and ruthless
man
flourishing like a green tree in its
native soil,

WEDNESDAY

VERSE FOR THE DAY:	AUTHOR:	PASSAGE FOR THE DAY:
Psalm 37:12–13	Ruth Bell Graham	Psalm 37:10–17

Don't Fret

WHEN "the wicked plot . . . the LORD laughs" (also see Psalm
2:4).
When he prospers, don't fret (Psalm 39:6–7).
When he persecutes:

> Rejoice and be glad (Matthew 5:12).
> Love your enemies (Matthew 5:44).
> Bless them (Romans 12:14).
> Do good to them (Luke 6:27).
> Pray for them (Matthew 5:44).

Additional Scripture Readings:
Genesis 50:15–20; Psalm 73:2,21–24

*Go to page 588 for your next
devotional reading.*

36but he soon passed away and was no
more;
though I looked for him, he could
not be found.

37Consider the blameless, observe the
upright;
there is a future[a] for the man of
peace.
38But all sinners will be destroyed;
the future[b] of the wicked will be
cut off.

39The salvation of the righteous comes
from the LORD;
he is their stronghold in time of
trouble.
40The LORD helps them and delivers
them;
he delivers them from the wicked
and saves them,
because they take refuge in him.

Psalm 38

A psalm of David. A petition.

1O LORD, do not rebuke me in your
anger
or discipline me in your wrath.
2For your arrows have pierced me,
and your hand has come down
upon me.
3Because of your wrath there is no
health in my body;
my bones have no soundness
because of my sin.
4My guilt has overwhelmed me
like a burden too heavy to bear.

5My wounds fester and are loathsome
because of my sinful folly.
6I am bowed down and brought very
low;
all day long I go about mourning.
7My back is filled with searing pain;
there is no health in my body.
8I am feeble and utterly crushed;
I groan in anguish of heart.

9All my longings lie open before you,
O Lord;
my sighing is not hidden from you.
10My heart pounds, my strength fails
me;
even the light has gone from my
eyes.
11My friends and companions avoid me
because of my wounds;
my neighbors stay far away.

12Those who seek my life set their
traps,
those who would harm me talk of
my ruin;
all day long they plot deception.

13I am like a deaf man, who cannot
hear,
like a mute, who cannot open his
mouth;
14I have become like a man who does
not hear,
whose mouth can offer no reply.
15I wait for you, O LORD;
you will answer, O Lord my God.
16For I said, "Do not let them gloat
or exalt themselves over me when
my foot slips."

17For I am about to fall,
and my pain is ever with me.
18I confess my iniquity;
I am troubled by my sin.
19Many are those who are my vigorous
enemies;
those who hate me without reason
are numerous.
20Those who repay my good with evil
slander me when I pursue what is
good.

21O LORD, do not forsake me;
be not far from me, O my God.
22Come quickly to help me,
O Lord my Savior.

Psalm 39

For the director of music. For Jeduthun.
A psalm of David.

1I said, "I will watch my ways
and keep my tongue from sin;
I will put a muzzle on my mouth
as long as the wicked are in my
presence."
2But when I was silent and still,
not even saying anything good,
my anguish increased.
3My heart grew hot within me,
and as I meditated, the fire burned;
then I spoke with my tongue:

4"Show me, O LORD, my life's end
and the number of my days;
let me know how fleeting is my life.
5You have made my days a mere
handbreadth;
the span of my years is as nothing
before you.

---

a37 Or *there will be posterity*   *b38* Or *posterity*

Each man's life is but a breath.
              Selah
6Man is a mere phantom as he goes to
    and fro:
He bustles about, but only in vain;
    he heaps up wealth, not knowing
      who will get it.

7"But now, Lord, what do I look for?
    My hope is in you.
8Save me from all my transgressions;
    do not make me the scorn of fools.
9I was silent; I would not open my
      mouth,
for you are the one who has done
      this.
10Remove your scourge from me;
    I am overcome by the blow of your
      hand.
11You rebuke and discipline men for
      their sin;
you consume their wealth like a
      moth—
each man is but a breath.   *Selah*

12"Hear my prayer, O Lord,
    listen to my cry for help;
    be not deaf to my weeping.
For I dwell with you as an alien,
    a stranger, as all my fathers were.
13Look away from me, that I may
      rejoice again
before I depart and am no more."

Psalm 40

For the director of music. Of David.
A psalm.

1I waited patiently for the Lord;
    he turned to me and heard my cry.
2He lifted me out of the slimy pit,
    out of the mud and mire;
he set my feet on a rock
    and gave me a firm place to stand.
3He put a new song in my mouth,
    a hymn of praise to our God.
Many will see and fear
    and put their trust in the Lord.

4Blessed is the man
    who makes the Lord his trust,
who does not look to the proud,
    to those who turn aside to false
      gods.*a*
5Many, O Lord my God,
    are the wonders you have done.
The things you planned for us
    no one can recount to you;

were I to speak and tell of them,
    they would be too many to declare.

6Sacrifice and offering you did not
      desire,
but my ears you have pierced*b, c*;
burnt offerings and sin offerings
    you did not require.
7Then I said, "Here I am, I have
      come—
it is written about me in the
      scroll.*d*
8I desire to do your will, O my God;
    your law is within my heart."

9I proclaim righteousness in the great
      assembly;
I do not seal my lips,
    as you know, O Lord.
10I do not hide your righteousness in
      my heart;
I speak of your faithfulness and
      salvation.
I do not conceal your love and your
      truth
from the great assembly.

11Do not withhold your mercy from me,
    O Lord;
may your love and your truth
    always protect me.
12For troubles without number
      surround me;
my sins have overtaken me, and I
      cannot see.
They are more than the hairs of my
      head,
and my heart fails within me.

13Be pleased, O Lord, to save me;
    O Lord, come quickly to help me.
14May all who seek to take my life
    be put to shame and confusion;
may all who desire my ruin
    be turned back in disgrace.
15May those who say to me, "Aha!
      Aha!"
be appalled at their own shame.
16But may all who seek you
    rejoice and be glad in you;
may those who love your salvation
    always say,
    "The Lord be exalted!"

17Yet I am poor and needy;
    may the Lord think of me.
You are my help and my deliverer;
    O my God, do not delay.

---

*a*4 Or *to falsehood*   *b*6 Hebrew; Septuagint *but a body you have prepared for me* (see also Symmachus and Theodotion)   *c*6 Or *opened*   *d*7 Or *come / with the scroll written for me*

Psalm 41

For the director of music. A psalm
of David.

¹Blessed is he who has regard for the
weak;
the LORD delivers him in times of
trouble.
²The LORD will protect him and
preserve his life;
he will bless him in the land
and not surrender him to the desire
of his foes.
³The LORD will sustain him on his
sickbed
and restore him from his bed of
illness.

⁴I said, "O LORD, have mercy on me;
heal me, for I have sinned against
you."
⁵My enemies say of me in malice,
"When will he die and his name
perish?"
⁶Whenever one comes to see me,
he speaks falsely, while his heart
gathers slander;
then he goes out and spreads it
abroad.

⁷All my enemies whisper together
against me;
they imagine the worst for me,
saying,
⁸"A vile disease has beset him;
he will never get up from the place
where he lies."
⁹Even my close friend, whom I trusted,
he who shared my bread,
has lifted up his heel against me.

¹⁰But you, O LORD, have mercy on
me;
raise me up, that I may repay
them.
¹¹I know that you are pleased with
me,
for my enemy does not triumph
over me.
¹²In my integrity you uphold me
and set me in your presence
forever.

¹³Praise be to the LORD, the God of
Israel,
from everlasting to everlasting.
Amen and Amen.

BOOK II

Psalms 42–72

Psalm 42 ᵃ

For the director of music. A *maskil* ᵇ of
the Sons of Korah.

¹As the deer pants for streams of
water,
so my soul pants for you, O God.
²My soul thirsts for God, for the living
God.
When can I go and meet with God?
³My tears have been my food
day and night,
while men say to me all day long,
"Where is your God?"
⁴These things I remember
as I pour out my soul:
how I used to go with the multitude,
leading the procession to the house
of God,
with shouts of joy and thanksgiving
among the festive throng.

⁵Why are you downcast, O my soul?
Why so disturbed within me?
Put your hope in God,
for I will yet praise him,
my Savior and ⁶my God.

Myᶜ soul is downcast within me;
therefore I will remember you
from the land of the Jordan,
the heights of Hermon—from
Mount Mizar.
⁷Deep calls to deep
in the roar of your waterfalls;
all your waves and breakers
have swept over me.

⁸By day the LORD directs his love,
at night his song is with me—
a prayer to the God of my life.

⁹I say to God my Rock,
"Why have you forgotten me?
Why must I go about mourning,
oppressed by the enemy?"
¹⁰My bones suffer mortal agony
as my foes taunt me,
saying to me all day long,
"Where is your God?"

¹¹Why are you downcast, O my soul?
Why so disturbed within me?
Put your hope in God,

ᵃIn many Hebrew manuscripts Psalms 42 and 43 constitute one psalm.   ᵇTitle: Probably a literary or
musical term   ᶜ5,6 A few Hebrew manuscripts, Septuagint and Syriac; most Hebrew manuscripts *praise
him for his saving help.* / ⁶O my God, my

for I will yet praise him,
my Savior and my God.

Psalm 43[a]

[1]Vindicate me, O God,
and plead my cause against an
ungodly nation;
rescue me from deceitful and
wicked men.
[2]You are God my stronghold.
Why have you rejected me?
Why must I go about mourning,
oppressed by the enemy?
[3]Send forth your light and your truth,
let them guide me;
let them bring me to your holy
mountain,
to the place where you dwell.
[4]Then will I go to the altar of God,
to God, my joy and my delight.
I will praise you with the harp,
O God, my God.

[5]Why are you downcast, O my soul?
Why so disturbed within me?
Put your hope in God,
for I will yet praise him,
my Savior and my God.

Psalm 44

For the director of music. Of the Sons
of Korah. A *maskil*.[b]

[1]We have heard with our ears, O God;
our fathers have told us
what you did in their days,
in days long ago.
[2]With your hand you drove out the
nations
and planted our fathers;
you crushed the peoples
and made our fathers flourish.
[3]It was not by their sword that they
won the land,
nor did their arm bring them
victory;
it was your right hand, your arm,
and the light of your face, for you
loved them.

[4]You are my King and my God,
who decrees[c] victories for Jacob.
[5]Through you we push back our
enemies;
through your name we trample our
foes.
[6]I do not trust in my bow,

my sword does not bring me
victory;
[7]but you give us victory over our
enemies,
you put our adversaries to shame.
[8]In God we make our boast all day
long,
and we will praise your name
forever. *Selah*

[9]But now you have rejected and
humbled us;
you no longer go out with our
armies.
[10]You made us retreat before the
enemy,
and our adversaries have plundered
us.
[11]You gave us up to be devoured like
sheep
and have scattered us among the
nations.
[12]You sold your people for a pittance,
gaining nothing from their sale.

[13]You have made us a reproach to our
neighbors,
the scorn and derision of those
around us.
[14]You have made us a byword among
the nations;
the peoples shake their heads at us.
[15]My disgrace is before me all day long,
and my face is covered with shame
[16]at the taunts of those who reproach
and revile me,
because of the enemy, who is bent
on revenge.

[17]All this happened to us,
though we had not forgotten you
or been false to your covenant.
[18]Our hearts had not turned back;
our feet had not strayed from your
path.
[19]But you crushed us and made us a
haunt for jackals
and covered us over with deep
darkness.

[20]If we had forgotten the name of our
God
or spread out our hands to a
foreign god,
[21]would not God have discovered it,
since he knows the secrets of the
heart?
[22]Yet for your sake we face death all
day long;

we are considered as sheep to be
slaughtered.

²³Awake, O Lord! Why do you sleep?
Rouse yourself! Do not reject us
forever.
²⁴Why do you hide your face
and forget our misery and
oppression?

²⁵We are brought down to the dust;
our bodies cling to the ground.
²⁶Rise up and help us;
redeem us because of your
unfailing love.

Psalm 45

For the director of music. To the tune
of, "Lilies." Of the Sons of Korah. A
maskil.[a] A wedding song.

¹My heart is stirred by a noble theme
as I recite my verses for the king;
my tongue is the pen of a skillful
writer.

²You are the most excellent of men
and your lips have been anointed
with grace,
since God has blessed you forever.
³Gird your sword upon your side,
O mighty one;
clothe yourself with splendor and
majesty.
⁴In your majesty ride forth victoriously
in behalf of truth, humility and
righteousness;
let your right hand display awesome
deeds.
⁵Let your sharp arrows pierce the
hearts of the king's enemies;
let the nations fall beneath your
feet.
⁶Your throne, O God, will last for ever
and ever;
a scepter of justice will be the
scepter of your kingdom.
⁷You love righteousness and hate
wickedness;
therefore God, your God, has set
you above your companions
by anointing you with the oil of joy.
⁸All your robes are fragrant with myrrh
and aloes and cassia;
from palaces adorned with ivory
the music of the strings makes you
glad.

⁹Daughters of kings are among your
honored women;
at your right hand is the royal bride
in gold of Ophir.

¹⁰Listen, O daughter, consider and give
ear:
Forget your people and your
father's house.
¹¹The king is enthralled by your beauty;
honor him, for he is your lord.
¹²The Daughter of Tyre will come with
a gift,[b]
men of wealth will seek your favor.

¹³All glorious is the princess within her
chamber;
her gown is interwoven with gold.
¹⁴In embroidered garments she is led to
the king;
her virgin companions follow her
and are brought to you.
¹⁵They are led in with joy and gladness;
they enter the palace of the king.

¹⁶Your sons will take the place of your
fathers;
you will make them princes
throughout the land.
¹⁷I will perpetuate your memory
through all generations;
therefore the nations will praise you
for ever and ever.

Psalm 46

For the director of music. Of the Sons
of Korah. According to *alamoth.*[c]
A song.

¹God is our refuge and strength,
an ever-present help in trouble.
²Therefore we will not fear, though the
earth give way
and the mountains fall into the
heart of the sea,
³though its waters roar and foam
and the mountains quake with their
surging. *Selah*

⁴There is a river whose streams make
glad the city of God,
the holy place where the Most High
dwells.
⁵God is within her, she will not fall;
God will help her at break of day.
⁶Nations are in uproar, kingdoms fall;
he lifts his voice, the earth melts.

⁷The Lord Almighty is with us;

---

*a*Title: Probably a literary or musical term   *b12* Or *A Tyrian robe is among the gifts*   *c*Title: Probably
a musical term

the God of Jacob is our fortress.
Selah

8Come and see the works of the LORD,
the desolations he has brought on
the earth.
9He makes wars cease to the ends of
the earth;
he breaks the bow and shatters the
spear,
he burns the shields*a* with fire.
10"Be still, and know that I am God;
I will be exalted among the nations,
I will be exalted in the earth."

11The LORD Almighty is with us;
the God of Jacob is our fortress.
Selah

a9 Or *chariots*

Psalm 47

For the director of music. Of the Sons
of Korah. A psalm.

1Clap your hands, all you nations;
shout to God with cries of joy.
2How awesome is the LORD Most High,
the great King over all the earth!
3He subdued nations under us,
peoples under our feet.
4He chose our inheritance for us,
the pride of Jacob, whom he loved.
Selah

5God has ascended amid shouts of joy,
the LORD amid the sounding of
trumpets.

THURSDAY

VERSE FOR THE DAY:
Psalm 46:10

AUTHOR:
Hannah Whitall Smith

PASSAGE FOR THE DAY:
Psalm 46:1–11

Resting, Not Worrying

AMONG the peaks of the Sierra Nevada mountains, not far from
the busy whirl of San Francisco, lies Lake Tahoe. It is twenty-
three miles long, ten miles wide, and so deep that a line
dropped nineteen hundred feet does not touch bottom; and it
lies five thousand feet above the neighboring ocean. Storms
come and go in waters that are lower down the mountains, but
this lake is so still and clear that the eye can penetrate, it is said,
a hundred feet into its depths. Around its mild verdant sides are
the mountains, ever crowned with snow. The sky above is as
calm as the motionless water. Nature loses scarcely anything of
its clear outline as it is reflected there. Here the soul may learn
something of what rest is, as day after day one opens one's heart
to let the sweet influence of nature's sabbath enter and reign.
This is but a faint type of what we may find in Christ.

In the pressure of the greatest responsibilities, in the worry of
the smallest cares, in the perplexities of life's moments of crisis,
we may have the Lake Tahoe rest in the security of God's will.
Learn to live in this rest. In the calmness of spirit it will give,
your soul will reflect, as in a mirror, the beauty of the Lord; and
the tumult of men's lives will be calmed in your presence, as
your tumults have been calmed in his presence.

Additional Scripture Readings:
Psalm 131:1–3; Philippians 4:4–7

*Go to page 592 for your next
devotional reading.*

6Sing praises to God, sing praises;
  sing praises to our King, sing
    praises.
7For God is the King of all the earth;
  sing to him a psalm[a] of praise.
8God reigns over the nations;
  God is seated on his holy throne.
9The nobles of the nations assemble
  as the people of the God of
    Abraham,
for the kings[b] of the earth belong to
  God;
he is greatly exalted.

Psalm 48

A song. A psalm of the Sons of Korah.

1Great is the LORD, and most worthy of
    praise,
  in the city of our God, his holy
    mountain.
2It is beautiful in its loftiness,
  the joy of the whole earth.
Like the utmost heights of Zaphon[c]
  is Mount Zion,
  the[d] city of the Great King.
3God is in her citadels;
  he has shown himself to be her
    fortress.

4When the kings joined forces,
  when they advanced together,
5they saw her, and were astounded;
  they fled in terror.
6Trembling seized them there,
  pain like that of a woman in labor.
7You destroyed them like ships of
    Tarshish
  shattered by an east wind.

8As we have heard,
  so have we seen
in the city of the LORD Almighty,
  in the city of our God:
God makes her secure forever.
                                          Selah

9Within your temple, O God,
  we meditate on your unfailing love.
10Like your name, O God,
  your praise reaches to the ends of
    the earth;
  your right hand is filled with
    righteousness.
11Mount Zion rejoices,
  the villages of Judah are glad

because of your judgments.
12Walk about Zion, go around her,
  count her towers,
13consider well her ramparts,
  view her citadels,
  that you may tell of them to the
    next generation.
14For this God is our God for ever and
    ever;
  he will be our guide even to the
    end.

Psalm 49

For the director of music. Of the Sons
of Korah. A psalm.

1Hear this, all you peoples;
  listen, all who live in this world,
2both low and high,
  rich and poor alike:
3My mouth will speak words of
    wisdom;
  the utterance from my heart will
    give understanding.
4I will turn my ear to a proverb;
  with the harp I will expound my
    riddle:

5Why should I fear when evil days
    come,
  when wicked deceivers surround
    me—
6those who trust in their wealth
  and boast of their great riches?
7No man can redeem the life of
    another
  or give to God a ransom for him—
8the ransom for a life is costly,
  no payment is ever enough—
9that he should live on forever
  and not see decay.

10For all can see that wise men die;
  the foolish and the senseless alike
    perish
  and leave their wealth to others.
11Their tombs will remain their houses[e]
    forever,
  their dwellings for endless
    generations,
  though they had[f] named lands
    after themselves.

12But man, despite his riches, does not
    endure;
  he is[g] like the beasts that perish.

---

[a]7 Or a maskil (probably a literary or musical term)   [b]9 Or shields   [c]2 Zaphon can refer to a sacred
mountain or the direction north.   [d]2 Or earth, / Mount Zion, on the northern side / of the
[e]11 Septuagint and Syriac; Hebrew In their thoughts their houses will remain   [f]11 Or / for they have
[g]12 Hebrew; Septuagint and Syriac read verse 12 the same as verse 20.

¹³This is the fate of those who trust in
    themselves,
and of their followers, who approve
    their sayings.   *Selah*
¹⁴Like sheep they are destined for the
    grave,ᵃ
and death will feed on them.
  The upright will rule over them in the
    morning;
their forms will decay in the
    grave,ᵃ
far from their princely mansions.
¹⁵But God will redeem my lifeᵇ from
    the grave;
he will surely take me to himself.
    Selah

¹⁶Do not be overawed when a man
    grows rich,
when the splendor of his house
    increases;
¹⁷for he will take nothing with him
    when he dies,
his splendor will not descend with
    him.
¹⁸Though while he lived he counted
    himself blessed—
and men praise you when you
    prosper—
¹⁹he will join the generation of his
    fathers,
who will never see the light ₍of life₎.

²⁰A man who has riches without
    understanding
is like the beasts that perish.

Psalm 50

A psalm of Asaph.

¹The Mighty One, God, the LORD,
  speaks and summons the earth
  from the rising of the sun to the
    place where it sets.
²From Zion, perfect in beauty,
  God shines forth.
³Our God comes and will not be silent;
  a fire devours before him,
  and around him a tempest rages.
⁴He summons the heavens above,
  and the earth, that he may judge
    his people:
⁵"Gather to me my consecrated ones,
  who made a covenant with me by
    sacrifice."
⁶And the heavens proclaim his
    righteousness,
for God himself is judge.   *Selah*

⁷"Hear, O my people, and I will speak,
  O Israel, and I will testify against
    you:
  I am God, your God.
⁸I do not rebuke you for your sacrifices
  or your burnt offerings, which are
    ever before me.
⁹I have no need of a bull from your
    stall
  or of goats from your pens,
¹⁰for every animal of the forest is mine,
  and the cattle on a thousand hills.
¹¹I know every bird in the mountains,
  and the creatures of the field are
    mine.
¹²If I were hungry I would not tell
    you,
  for the world is mine, and all that
    is in it.
¹³Do I eat the flesh of bulls
  or drink the blood of goats?
¹⁴Sacrifice thank offerings to God,
  fulfill your vows to the Most High,
¹⁵and call upon me in the day of
    trouble;
  I will deliver you, and you will
    honor me."

¹⁶But to the wicked, God says:

"What right have you to recite my
    laws
  or take my covenant on your
    lips?
¹⁷You hate my instruction
  and cast my words behind you.
¹⁸When you see a thief, you join with
    him;
  you throw in your lot with
    adulterers.
¹⁹You use your mouth for evil
  and harness your tongue to deceit.
²⁰You speak continually against your
    brother
  and slander your own mother's
    son.
²¹These things you have done and I
    kept silent;
  you thought I was altogetherᶜ like
    you.
But I will rebuke you
  and accuse you to your face.

²²"Consider this, you who forget God,
  or I will tear you to pieces, with
    none to rescue:
²³He who sacrifices thank offerings
    honors me,
  and he prepares the way

ᵃ*14* Hebrew *Sheol*; also in verse 15   ᵇ*15* Or *soul*   ᶜ*21* Or *thought the 'I AM' was*

so that I may show him*a* the
salvation of God."

Psalm 51

For the director of music. A psalm of
David. When the prophet Nathan came
to him after David had committed
adultery with Bathsheba.

¹Have mercy on me, O God,
    according to your unfailing love;
according to your great compassion
    blot out my transgressions.
²Wash away all my iniquity
    and cleanse me from my sin.

³For I know my transgressions,
    and my sin is always before me.
⁴Against you, you only, have I sinned
    and done what is evil in your sight,
so that you are proved right when you
    speak
    and justified when you judge.
⁵Surely I was sinful at birth,
    sinful from the time my mother
    conceived me.
⁶Surely you desire truth in the inner
    parts*b*;
    you teach*c* me wisdom in the
    inmost place.

⁷Cleanse me with hyssop, and I will be
    clean;
    wash me, and I will be whiter than
    snow.
⁸Let me hear joy and gladness;
    let the bones you have crushed
    rejoice.
⁹Hide your face from my sins
    and blot out all my iniquity.

¹⁰Create in me a pure heart, O God,
    and renew a steadfast spirit within
    me.
¹¹Do not cast me from your presence
    or take your Holy Spirit from me.
¹²Restore to me the joy of your
    salvation
    and grant me a willing spirit, to
    sustain me.

¹³Then I will teach transgressors your
    ways,
    and sinners will turn back to you.
¹⁴Save me from bloodguilt, O God,
    the God who saves me,
    and my tongue will sing of your
    righteousness.

¹⁵O Lord, open my lips,
    and my mouth will declare your
    praise.
¹⁶You do not delight in sacrifice, or I
    would bring it;
    you do not take pleasure in burnt
    offerings.
¹⁷The sacrifices of God are*d* a broken
    spirit;
    a broken and contrite heart,
    O God, you will not despise.

¹⁸In your good pleasure make Zion
    prosper;
    build up the walls of Jerusalem.
¹⁹Then there will be righteous
    sacrifices,
    whole burnt offerings to delight
    you;
    then bulls will be offered on your
    altar.

Psalm 52

For the director of music. A *maskil*[e]
of David. When Doeg the Edomite had
gone to Saul and told him: "David has
gone to the house of Ahimelech."

¹Why do you boast of evil, you mighty
    man?
Why do you boast all day long,
    you who are a disgrace in the eyes
    of God?
²Your tongue plots destruction;
    it is like a sharpened razor,
    you who practice deceit.
³You love evil rather than good,
    falsehood rather than speaking the
    truth.   *Selah*
⁴You love every harmful word,
    O you deceitful tongue!

⁵Surely God will bring you down to
    everlasting ruin:
He will snatch you up and tear you
    from your tent;
    he will uproot you from the land of
    the living.   *Selah*
⁶The righteous will see and fear;
    they will laugh at him, saying,
⁷"Here now is the man
    who did not make God his
    stronghold
but trusted in his great wealth
    and grew strong by destroying
    others!"

---

*a*23 Or *and to him who considers his way / I will show*
is uncertain.   *c*6 Or *you desired . . . ; / you taught*
Probably a literary or musical term

*b*6 The meaning of the Hebrew for this phrase
*d*17 Or *My sacrifice, O God, is*   *e*Title:

VERSE FOR THE DAY:
Psalm 51:3–4

AUTHOR:
Gini Andrews

PASSAGE FOR THE DAY:
Psalm 51:1–19

Losing the Way

FROM top to bottom, our society is success oriented, however one may define that in terms of one's own goals. Christians are not immune; "Everything comes out okay for Christians," "The King's kids are always winners" are misleading slogans to live by. We develop unrealistic expectations of the Christian life and of ourselves; and then when our wings get broken, we think failure ends our usefulness.

For those of us who know too well the salt taste of failure, it helps to remember that even the great ones of the faith failed, yet God continued to use them, often in a deeper way *after* their fall.

Some of David's greatest psalms came after his greatest mistakes. God called him "a man after his own heart" (1 Samuel 13:14). Abraham lied, perhaps to save his skin, yet he is the towering example of faith for three major religions and is called "God's friend" (James 2:23).

It is those who have plumbed the depths of failure to whom God invariably gives the call to shepherd others. This is not a call given only to the gifted, the highly trained, or the polished as such. Without a bitter experience of their own inadequacy and poverty, they are quite unfitted to bear the burden of spiritual ministry. It takes a person who has discovered something of the measure of his own weakness to be patient with the foibles of others.

Too often we live in a quid-pro-quo relationship with God: "I've been faithful to you, I've worked hard, so please give me this or that." Or, "I've failed again; I can't expect any blessing." We forget that the whole of our life is grace.

Too many sincere Christians, facing their failures, berate themselves unmercifully and keep asking God for forgiveness. Each of us should memorize, hang on the mirror, and make forever our own the ringing truth: "There is now no [repeat *no*] condemnation for those who are in Christ Jesus" (Romans 8:1).

Not only does he not condemn us; he even brings blessings from the ashes of our failures.

Additional Scripture Readings:
John 18:15–27; 21:15–17; Acts 9:1–6,15–16

Go to page 595 for your next devotional reading.

8But I am like an olive tree
  flourishing in the house of God;
I trust in God's unfailing love
  for ever and ever.
9I will praise you forever for what you
    have done;
  in your name I will hope, for your
    name is good.
  I will praise you in the presence of
    your saints.

Psalm 53

For the director of music. According to
mahalath.[a] A maskil[b] of David.

1The fool says in his heart,
  "There is no God."
They are corrupt, and their ways are
    vile;
  there is no one who does good.

2God looks down from heaven
    on the sons of men
to see if there are any who
    understand,
  any who seek God.
3Everyone has turned away,
  they have together become corrupt;
there is no one who does good,
  not even one.

4Will the evildoers never learn—
  those who devour my people as
    men eat bread
  and who do not call on God?
5There they were, overwhelmed with
    dread,
  where there was nothing to dread.
God scattered the bones of those who
    attacked you;
  you put them to shame, for God
    despised them.

6Oh, that salvation for Israel would
    come out of Zion!
  When God restores the fortunes of
    his people,
  let Jacob rejoice and Israel be glad!

Psalm 54

For the director of music. With stringed
instruments. A maskil[b] of David. When
the Ziphites had gone to Saul and said,
"Is not David hiding among us?"

1Save me, O God, by your name;
  vindicate me by your might.

2Hear my prayer, O God;
  listen to the words of my mouth.

3Strangers are attacking me;
  ruthless men seek my life—
  men without regard for God. *Selah*

4Surely God is my help;
  the Lord is the one who sustains
    me.

5Let evil recoil on those who slander
    me;
  in your faithfulness destroy them.

6I will sacrifice a freewill offering to
    you;
  I will praise your name, O LORD,
  for it is good.
7For he has delivered me from all my
    troubles,
  and my eyes have looked in
    triumph on my foes.

Psalm 55

For the director of music. With stringed
instruments. A maskil[b] of David.

1Listen to my prayer, O God,
  do not ignore my plea;
2 hear me and answer me.
My thoughts trouble me and I am
    distraught
3 at the voice of the enemy,
  at the stares of the wicked;
for they bring down suffering upon
    me
  and revile me in their anger.

4My heart is in anguish within me;
  the terrors of death assail me.
5Fear and trembling have beset me;
  horror has overwhelmed me.
6I said, "Oh, that I had the wings of a
    dove!
  I would fly away and be at rest—
7I would flee far away
  and stay in the desert; *Selah*
8I would hurry to my place of shelter,
  far from the tempest and storm."

9Confuse the wicked, O Lord,
  confound their speech,
  for I see violence and strife in the
    city.
10Day and night they prowl about on its
    walls;
  malice and abuse are within it.

aTitle: Probably a musical term   bTitle: Probably a literary or musical term

¹¹Destructive forces are at work in the
      city;
      threats and lies never leave its
           streets.

¹²If an enemy were insulting me,
      I could endure it;
      if a foe were raising himself against
           me,
      I could hide from him.
¹³But it is you, a man like myself,
      my companion, my close friend,
¹⁴with whom I once enjoyed sweet
           fellowship
      as we walked with the throng at the
           house of God.

¹⁵Let death take my enemies by
           surprise;
      let them go down alive to the
           grave,^a
      for evil finds lodging among
           them.

¹⁶But I call to God,
      and the LORD saves me.
¹⁷Evening, morning and noon
      I cry out in distress,
      and he hears my voice.
¹⁸He ransoms me unharmed
      from the battle waged against me,
      even though many oppose me.
¹⁹God, who is enthroned forever,
      will hear them and afflict them—
                     Selah

      men who never change their ways
      and have no fear of God.

²⁰My companion attacks his friends;
      he violates his covenant.
²¹His speech is smooth as butter,
      yet war is in his heart;
      his words are more soothing than
           oil,
      yet they are drawn swords.

²²Cast your cares on the LORD
      and he will sustain you;
      he will never let the righteous
           fall.
²³But you, O God, will bring down
           the wicked
      into the pit of corruption;
      bloodthirsty and deceitful men
      will not live out half their
           days.

But as for me, I trust in you.

Psalm 56

For the director of music. To the tune
of, "A Dove on Distant Oaks." Of David.
A *miktam.*^b When the Philistines had
seized him in Gath.

¹Be merciful to me, O God, for men
           hotly pursue me;
      all day long they press their attack.
²My slanderers pursue me all day long;
      many are attacking me in their
           pride.

³When I am afraid,
      I will trust in you.
⁴In God, whose word I praise,
      in God I trust; I will not be afraid.
      What can mortal man do to me?

⁵All day long they twist my words;
      they are always plotting to harm
           me.
⁶They conspire, they lurk,
      they watch my steps,
      eager to take my life.

⁷On no account let them escape;
      in your anger, O God, bring down
           the nations.
⁸Record my lament;
      list my tears on your scroll^c—
      are they not in your record?

⁹Then my enemies will turn back
      when I call for help.
      By this I will know that God is for
           me.
¹⁰In God, whose word I praise,
      in the LORD, whose word I praise—
¹¹in God I trust; I will not be afraid.
      What can man do to me?

¹²I am under vows to you, O God;
      I will present my thank offerings to
           you.
¹³For you have delivered me^d from
           death
      and my feet from stumbling,
that I may walk before God
      in the light of life.^e

Psalm 57

For the director of music. To the tune
of, "Do Not Destroy." Of David. A
miktam.^b When he had fled from Saul
into the cave.

¹Have mercy on me, O God, have
           mercy on me,

---

^a15 Hebrew *Sheol*   ^bTitle: Probably a literary or musical term   ^c8 Or *I put my tears in your wineskin*
^d13 Or *my soul*   ^e13 Or *the land of the living*

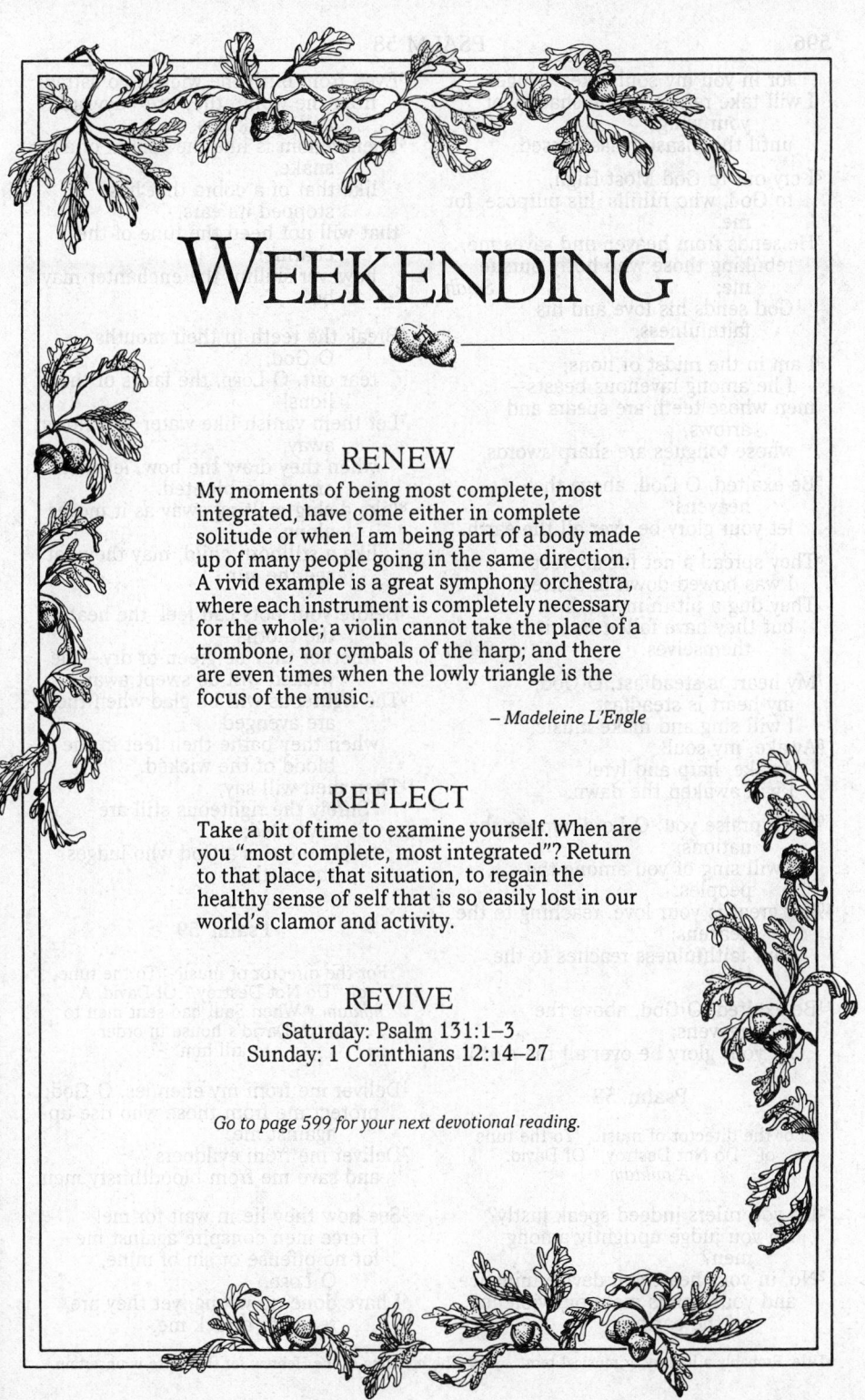

WEEKENDING

RENEW

My moments of being most complete, most
integrated, have come either in complete
solitude or when I am being part of a body made
up of many people going in the same direction.
A vivid example is a great symphony orchestra,
where each instrument is completely necessary
for the whole; a violin cannot take the place of a
trombone, nor cymbals of the harp; and there
are even times when the lowly triangle is the
focus of the music.

– *Madeleine L'Engle*

REFLECT

Take a bit of time to examine yourself. When are
you "most complete, most integrated"? Return
to that place, that situation, to regain the
healthy sense of self that is so easily lost in our
world's clamor and activity.

REVIVE

Saturday: Psalm 131:1–3
Sunday: 1 Corinthians 12:14–27

Go to page 599 for your next devotional reading.

for in you my soul takes refuge.
I will take refuge in the shadow of
    your wings
until the disaster has passed.

²I cry out to God Most High,
    to God, who fulfills his purpose, for
        me.
³He sends from heaven and saves me,
    rebuking those who hotly pursue
        me;   *Selah*
    God sends his love and his
        faithfulness.

⁴I am in the midst of lions;
    I lie among ravenous beasts—
men whose teeth are spears and
    arrows,
    whose tongues are sharp swords.

⁵Be exalted, O God, above the
    heavens;
    let your glory be over all the earth.

⁶They spread a net for my feet—
    I was bowed down in distress.
They dug a pit in my path—
    but they have fallen into it
        themselves.   *Selah*

⁷My heart is steadfast, O God,
    my heart is steadfast;
    I will sing and make music.
⁸Awake, my soul!
    Awake, harp and lyre!
    I will awaken the dawn.

⁹I will praise you, O Lord, among the
    nations;
    I will sing of you among the
        peoples.
¹⁰For great is your love, reaching to the
    heavens;
    your faithfulness reaches to the
        skies.

¹¹Be exalted, O God, above the
    heavens;
    let your glory be over all the earth.

Psalm 58

For the director of music. To the tune
of, "Do Not Destroy." Of David.
A *miktam.* ᵃ

¹Do you rulers indeed speak justly?
    Do you judge uprightly among
        men?
²No, in your heart you devise injustice,
    and your hands mete out violence
        on the earth.

³Even from birth the wicked go astray;
    from the womb they are wayward
        and speak lies.
⁴Their venom is like the venom of a
    snake,
    like that of a cobra that has
        stopped its ears,
⁵that will not heed the tune of the
    charmer,
    however skillful the enchanter may
        be.

⁶Break the teeth in their mouths,
    O God;
    tear out, O LORD, the fangs of the
        lions!
⁷Let them vanish like water that flows
    away;
    when they draw the bow, let their
        arrows be blunted.
⁸Like a slug melting away as it moves
    along,
    like a stillborn child, may they not
        see the sun.

⁹Before your pots can feel the heat of
    the thorns—
    whether they be green or dry—the
        wicked will be swept away.ᵇ
¹⁰The righteous will be glad when they
    are avenged,
    when they bathe their feet in the
        blood of the wicked.
¹¹Then men will say,
    "Surely the righteous still are
        rewarded;
    surely there is a God who judges
        the earth."

Psalm 59

For the director of music. To the tune
of, "Do Not Destroy." Of David. A
miktam. ᵃ When Saul had sent men to
    watch David's house in order
    to kill him.

¹Deliver me from my enemies, O God;
    protect me from those who rise up
        against me.
²Deliver me from evildoers
    and save me from bloodthirsty men.

³See how they lie in wait for me!
    Fierce men conspire against me
for no offense or sin of mine,
    O LORD.
⁴I have done no wrong, yet they are
    ready to attack me.

ᵃTitle: Probably a literary or musical term   ᵇ9 The meaning of the Hebrew for this verse is uncertain.

Arise to help me; look on my
plight!
5O LORD God Almighty, the God of
Israel,
rouse yourself to punish all the
nations;
show no mercy to wicked traitors.
Selah

6They return at evening,
snarling like dogs,
and prowl about the city.
7See what they spew from their
mouths—
they spew out swords from their
lips,
and they say, "Who can hear us?"
8But you, O LORD, laugh at them;
you scoff at all those nations.

9O my Strength, I watch for you;
you, O God, are my fortress, 10my
loving God.

God will go before me
and will let me gloat over those
who slander me.
11But do not kill them, O Lord our
shield,*a*
or my people will forget.
In your might make them wander
about,
and bring them down.
12For the sins of their mouths,
for the words of their lips,
let them be caught in their pride.
For the curses and lies they utter,
13 consume them in wrath,
consume them till they are no
more.
Then it will be known to the ends of
the earth
that God rules over Jacob.   *Selah*

14They return at evening,
snarling like dogs,
and prowl about the city.
15They wander about for food
and howl if not satisfied.
16But I will sing of your strength,
in the morning I will sing of your
love;
for you are my fortress,
my refuge in times of trouble.

17O my Strength, I sing praise to you;
you, O God, are my fortress, my
loving God.

Psalm 60

*For the director of music. To the tune
of, "The Lily of the Covenant." A
miktam b of David. For teaching. When
he fought Aram Naharaim c and Aram
Zobah, d and when Joab returned and
struck down twelve thousand Edomites
in the Valley of Salt.*

1You have rejected us, O God, and
burst forth upon us;
you have been angry—now restore
us!
2You have shaken the land and torn it
open;
mend its fractures, for it is
quaking.
3You have shown your people
desperate times;
you have given us wine that makes
us stagger.

4But for those who fear you, you have
raised a banner
to be unfurled against the bow.
Selah

5Save us and help us with your right
hand,
that those you love may be
delivered.
6God has spoken from his sanctuary:
"In triumph I will parcel out
Shechem
and measure off the Valley of
Succoth.
7Gilead is mine, and Manasseh is
mine;
Ephraim is my helmet,
Judah my scepter.
8Moab is my washbasin,
upon Edom I toss my sandal;
over Philistia I shout in
triumph."

9Who will bring me to the fortified
city?
Who will lead me to Edom?
10Is it not you, O God, you who have
rejected us
and no longer go out with our
armies?
11Give us aid against the enemy,
for the help of man is worthless.
12With God we will gain the
victory,
and he will trample down our
enemies.

---

a11 Or sovereign   *bTitle: Probably a literary or musical term*   *cTitle: That is, Arameans of Northwest*
Mesopotamia   *dTitle: That is, Arameans of central Syria*

Psalm 61

For the director of music. With stringed
　　instruments. Of David.

1Hear my cry, O God;
　　listen to my prayer.

2From the ends of the earth I call to
　　you,
　　I call as my heart grows faint;
　　lead me to the rock that is higher
　　　　than I.
3For you have been my refuge,
　　a strong tower against the foe.

4I long to dwell in your tent forever
　　and take refuge in the shelter of
　　　　your wings.　　　　　　Selah
5For you have heard my vows, O God;
　　you have given me the heritage of
　　　　those who fear your name.

6Increase the days of the king's life,
　　his years for many generations.
7May he be enthroned in God's
　　　　presence forever;
　　appoint your love and faithfulness
　　　　to protect him.

8Then will I ever sing praise to your
　　　　name
　　and fulfill my vows day after day.

Psalm 62

For the director of music. For Jeduthun.
　　A psalm of David.

1My soul finds rest in God alone;
　　my salvation comes from him.
2He alone is my rock and my salvation;
　　he is my fortress, I will never be
　　　　shaken.

3How long will you assault a man?
　　Would all of you throw him down—
　　this leaning wall, this tottering
　　　　fence?
4They fully intend to topple him
　　from his lofty place;
　　they take delight in lies.
With their mouths they bless,
　　but in their hearts they curse. Selah

5Find rest, O my soul, in God alone;
　　my hope comes from him.
6He alone is my rock and my salvation;
　　he is my fortress, I will not be
　　　　shaken.
7My salvation and my honor depend
　　　　on God a;

he is my mighty rock, my refuge.
8Trust in him at all times, O people;
　　pour out your hearts to him,
　　for God is our refuge.　　Selah

9Lowborn men are but a breath,
　　the highborn are but a lie;
if weighed on a balance, they are
　　　　nothing;
　　together they are only a breath.
10Do not trust in extortion
　　or take pride in stolen goods;
though your riches increase,
　　do not set your heart on them.

11One thing God has spoken,
　　two things have I heard:
that you, O God, are strong,
12　　and that you, O Lord, are loving.
Surely you will reward each person
　　according to what he has done.

Psalm 63

A psalm of David. When he was in the
　　Desert of Judah.

1O God, you are my God,
　　earnestly I seek you;
my soul thirsts for you,
　　my body longs for you,
in a dry and weary land
　　where there is no water.

2I have seen you in the sanctuary
　　and beheld your power and your
　　　　glory.
3Because your love is better than life,
　　my lips will glorify you.
4I will praise you as long as I live,
　　and in your name I will lift up my
　　　　hands.
5My soul will be satisfied as with the
　　　　richest of foods;
　　with singing lips my mouth will
　　　　praise you.

6On my bed I remember you;
　　I think of you through the watches
　　　　of the night.
7Because you are my help,
　　I sing in the shadow of your wings.
8My soul clings to you;
　　your right hand upholds me.

9They who seek my life will be
　　　　destroyed;
　　they will go down to the depths of
　　　　the earth.
10They will be given over to the sword
　　and become food for jackals.

a7 Or / God Most High is my salvation and my honor

VERSE FOR THE DAY:
Psalm 63:1

AUTHOR:
Rosalind Rinker

PASSAGE FOR THE DAY:
Psalm 63:1–11

A Spring of Living Water

O GOD, you are my God,
  earnestly I seek you;
my soul thirsts for you . . .
  in a dry and weary land
    where there is no water (Psalm 63:1).

The book of Psalms is a book of prayer that embraces every experience possible to human beings. As we read Psalm 63, we see that David was a fugitive in the desert of Judah. He was greatly distressed. He thirsted after God.

We can identify with David's great thirst, but that may be where the parallel ends. Unlike David, who fought on the side of God, often our enemies are the result of our personal failures.

The thirst that we have in common with David is worth looking into. We thirst for different things at different times: recognition, friends, a life-mate, a home, children, a home church, an education, a job and money, and gifts to serve our Lord (wisdom, insight, courage). But most of all we thirst to love and be loved.

In John 4, Jesus used earthly water to introduce living water, which alone can quench our thirsty hearts, no matter who we are. When Jesus asked for a drink from the Samaritan woman, he did so even though the request broke all Jewish religious, racial, and sexual laws. These laws and customs, however, were not as important to Jesus as his desire to offer the woman living water.

Today the invitation still stands: "Everyone who drinks this water will be thirsty again, but whoever drinks the water I give him will never thirst. Indeed, the water I give him will become in him a spring of water welling up to eternal life" (John 4:13–14).

Psalm 63 joyfully proclaims the blessings David received when he cried out to God; they can be yours also: to see the glory of God, to know God's love is better than life, to praise him with singing lips, to meditate on him when sleepless, and to stay close to him because his right hand upholds you.

We serve a risen Savior who has given us his Holy Spirit (John 7:37–39) as "living water," which becomes like an artesian well within us. He invites us: If anyone thirsts, let her ask, "for everyone who asks receives" (Matthew 7:7–9).

Additional Scripture Readings:
Isaiah 55:1–3; Matthew 5:6

*Go to page 605 for your next
devotional reading.*

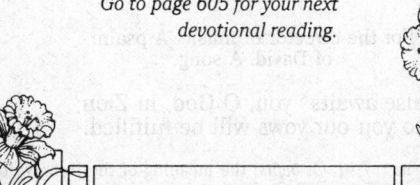

11But the king will rejoice in God;
all who swear by God's name will
praise him,
while the mouths of liars will be
silenced.

Psalm 64

For the director of music. A psalm
of David.

1Hear me, O God, as I voice my
complaint;
protect my life from the threat of
the enemy.
2Hide me from the conspiracy of the
wicked,
from that noisy crowd of evildoers.
3They sharpen their tongues like
swords
and aim their words like deadly
arrows.
4They shoot from ambush at the
innocent man;
they shoot at him suddenly,
without fear.
5They encourage each other in evil
plans,
they talk about hiding their snares;
they say, "Who will see them*a*?"
6They plot injustice and say,
"We have devised a perfect plan!"
Surely the mind and heart of man
are cunning.
7But God will shoot them with arrows;
suddenly they will be struck down.
8He will turn their own tongues
against them
and bring them to ruin;
all who see them will shake their
heads in scorn.
9All mankind will fear;
they will proclaim the works of God
and ponder what he has done.
10Let the righteous rejoice in the LORD
and take refuge in him;
let all the upright in heart praise
him!

Psalm 65

For the director of music. A psalm
of David. A song.

1Praise awaits*b* you, O God, in Zion;
to you our vows will be fulfilled.

2O you who hear prayer,
to you all men will come.
3When we were overwhelmed by sins,
you forgave*c* our transgressions.
4Blessed are those you choose
and bring near to live in your
courts!
We are filled with the good things of
your house,
of your holy temple.
5You answer us with awesome deeds of
righteousness,
O God our Savior,
the hope of all the ends of the earth
and of the farthest seas,
6who formed the mountains by your
power,
having armed yourself with
strength,
7who stilled the roaring of the seas,
the roaring of their waves,
and the turmoil of the nations.
8Those living far away fear your
wonders;
where morning dawns and evening
fades
you call forth songs of joy.

9You care for the land and water it;
you enrich it abundantly.
The streams of God are filled with
water
to provide the people with grain,
for so you have ordained it.*d*
10You drench its furrows
and level its ridges;
you soften it with showers
and bless its crops.
11You crown the year with your bounty,
and your carts overflow with
abundance.
12The grasslands of the desert overflow;
the hills are clothed with gladness.
13The meadows are covered with flocks
and the valleys are mantled with
grain;
they shout for joy and sing.

Psalm 66

For the director of music. A song.
A psalm.

1Shout with joy to God, all the earth!
2 Sing the glory of his name;
make his praise glorious!

*a5 Or us   b1 Or befits; the meaning of the Hebrew for this word is uncertain.   c3 Or made
atonement for   d9 Or for that is how you prepare the land*

³Say to God, "How awesome are your deeds!
So great is your power
that your enemies cringe before you.
⁴All the earth bows down to you;
they sing praise to you,
they sing praise to your name." *Selah*

⁵Come and see what God has done,
how awesome his works in man's behalf!
⁶He turned the sea into dry land,
they passed through the waters on foot—
come, let us rejoice in him.
⁷He rules forever by his power,
his eyes watch the nations—
let not the rebellious rise up against him. *Selah*

⁸Praise our God, O peoples,
let the sound of his praise be heard;
⁹he has preserved our lives
and kept our feet from slipping.
¹⁰For you, O God, tested us;
you refined us like silver.
¹¹You brought us into prison
and laid burdens on our backs.
¹²You let men ride over our heads;
we went through fire and water,
but you brought us to a place of abundance.

¹³I will come to your temple with burnt offerings
and fulfill my vows to you—
¹⁴vows my lips promised and my mouth spoke
when I was in trouble.
¹⁵I will sacrifice fat animals to you
and an offering of rams;
I will offer bulls and goats. *Selah*

¹⁶Come and listen, all you who fear God;
let me tell you what he has done for me.
¹⁷I cried out to him with my mouth;
his praise was on my tongue.
¹⁸If I had cherished sin in my heart,
the Lord would not have listened;
¹⁹but God has surely listened
and heard my voice in prayer.
²⁰Praise be to God,
who has not rejected my prayer
or withheld his love from me!

Psalm 67

For the director of music. With stringed instruments. A psalm. A song.

¹May God be gracious to us and bless us
and make his face shine upon us, *Selah*
²that your ways may be known on earth,
your salvation among all nations.

³May the peoples praise you, O God;
may all the peoples praise you.
⁴May the nations be glad and sing for joy,
for you rule the peoples justly
and guide the nations of the earth. *Selah*
⁵May the peoples praise you, O God;
may all the peoples praise you.

⁶Then the land will yield its harvest,
and God, our God, will bless us.
⁷God will bless us,
and all the ends of the earth will fear him.

Psalm 68

For the director of music. Of David. A psalm. A song.

¹May God arise, may his enemies be scattered;
may his foes flee before him.
²As smoke is blown away by the wind,
may you blow them away;
as wax melts before the fire,
may the wicked perish before God.
³But may the righteous be glad
and rejoice before God;
may they be happy and joyful.

⁴Sing to God, sing praise to his name,
extol him who rides on the clouds*ᵃ*—
his name is the LORD—
and rejoice before him.
⁵A father to the fatherless, a defender of widows,
is God in his holy dwelling.
⁶God sets the lonely in families,*ᵇ*
he leads forth the prisoners with singing;
but the rebellious live in a sun-scorched land.

⁷When you went out before your people, O God,

ᵃ4 Or *I prepare the way for him who rides through the deserts*   *ᵇ6* Or *the desolate in a homeland*

when you marched through the
   wasteland,   *Selah*
[8]the earth shook,
   the heavens poured down rain,
before God, the One of Sinai,
   before God, the God of Israel.
[9]You gave abundant showers, O God;
   you refreshed your weary
    inheritance.
[10]Your people settled in it,
   and from your bounty, O God, you
    provided for the poor.

[11]The Lord announced the word,
   and great was the company of those
    who proclaimed it:
[12]"Kings and armies flee in haste;
   in the camps men divide the
    plunder.
[13]Even while you sleep among the
    campfires,[a]
the wings of .my, dove are sheathed
   with silver,
   its feathers with shining gold."
[14]When the Almighty[b] scattered the
    kings in the land,
   it was like snow fallen on Zalmon.

[15]The mountains of Bashan are
    majestic mountains;
   rugged are the mountains of Bashan.
[16]Why gaze in envy, O rugged
    mountains,
at the mountain where God chooses
   to reign,
where the LORD himself will dwell
   forever?
[17]The chariots of God are tens of
    thousands
and thousands of thousands;
   the Lord .has come, from Sinai into
    his sanctuary.
[18]When you ascended on high,
   you led captives in your train;
   you received gifts from men,
even from[c] the rebellious—
   that you,[d] O LORD God, might dwell
    there.

[19]Praise be to the Lord, to God our
    Savior,
who daily bears our burdens.   *Selah*
[20]Our God is a God who saves;
   from the Sovereign LORD comes
    escape from death.
[21]Surely God will crush the heads of his
    enemies,

the hairy crowns of those who go
   on in their sins.
[22]The Lord says, "I will bring them
   from Bashan;
I will bring them from the depths of
   the sea,
[23]that you may plunge your feet in the
   blood of your foes,
while the tongues of your dogs have
   their share."

[24]Your procession has come into view,
   O God,
the procession of my God and King
   into the sanctuary.
[25]In front are the singers, after them
   the musicians;
with them are the maidens playing
   tambourines.
[26]Praise God in the great congregation;
   praise the LORD in the assembly of
    Israel.
[27]There is the little tribe of Benjamin,
   leading them,
there the great throng of Judah's
   princes,
and there the princes of Zebulun
   and of Naphtali.

[28]Summon your power, O God[e];
   show us your strength, O God, as
    you have done before.
[29]Because of your temple at Jerusalem
   kings will bring you gifts.
[30]Rebuke the beast among the reeds,
   the herd of bulls among the calves
    of the nations.
Humbled, may it bring bars of silver.
   Scatter the nations who delight in
    war.
[31]Envoys will come from Egypt;
   Cush[f] will submit herself to God.

[32]Sing to God, O kingdoms of the earth,
   sing praise to the Lord,   *Selah*
[33]to him who rides the ancient skies
    above,
who thunders with mighty voice.
[34]Proclaim the power of God,
   whose majesty is over Israel,
   whose power is in the skies.
[35]You are awesome, O God, in your
    sanctuary;
the God of Israel gives power and
   strength to his people.
Praise be to God!

---

[a]13 Or *saddlebags*   [b]14 Hebrew *Shaddai*   [c]18 Or *gifts for men, / even*   [d]18 Or *they*   [e]28 Many
Hebrew manuscripts, Septuagint and Syriac; most Hebrew manuscripts *Your God has summoned power for
you*   [f]31 That is, the upper Nile region

Psalm 69

For the director of music. To ˌthe tune
of, "Lilies." Of David.

¹Save me, O God,
  for the waters have come up to my
  neck.
²I sink in the miry depths,
  where there is no foothold.
I have come into the deep waters;
  the floods engulf me.
³I am worn out calling for help;
  my throat is parched.
My eyes fail,
  looking for my God.
⁴Those who hate me without reason
  outnumber the hairs of my head;
many are my enemies without cause,
  those who seek to destroy me.
I am forced to restore
  what I did not steal.

⁵You know my folly, O God;
  my guilt is not hidden from you.

⁶May those who hope in you
  not be disgraced because of me,
  O Lord, the LORD Almighty;
may those who seek you
  not be put to shame because of me,
  O God of Israel.
⁷For I endure scorn for your sake,
  and shame covers my face.
⁸I am a stranger to my brothers,
  an alien to my own mother's sons;
⁹for zeal for your house consumes me,
  and the insults of those who insult
  you fall on me.
¹⁰When I weep and fast,
  I must endure scorn;
¹¹when I put on sackcloth,
  people make sport of me.
¹²Those who sit at the gate mock me,
  and I am the song of the drunkards.

¹³But I pray to you, O LORD,
  in the time of your favor;
in your great love, O God,
  answer me with your sure salvation.
¹⁴Rescue me from the mire,
  do not let me sink;
deliver me from those who hate me,
  from the deep waters.
¹⁵Do not let the floodwaters engulf
  me
or the depths swallow me up
or the pit close its mouth over
  me.

¹⁶Answer me, O LORD, out of the
  goodness of your love;
in your great mercy turn to me.
¹⁷Do not hide your face from your
  servant;
answer me quickly, for I am in
  trouble.
¹⁸Come near and rescue me;
  redeem me because of my foes.

¹⁹You know how I am scorned,
  disgraced and shamed;
all my enemies are before you.
²⁰Scorn has broken my heart
  and has left me helpless;
I looked for sympathy, but there was
  none,
  for comforters, but I found none.
²¹They put gall in my food
  and gave me vinegar for my thirst.

²²May the table set before them
  become a snare;
may it become retribution andª a
  trap.
²³May their eyes be darkened so they
  cannot see,
  and their backs be bent forever.
²⁴Pour out your wrath on them;
  let your fierce anger overtake them.
²⁵May their place be deserted;
  let there be no one to dwell in their
  tents.
²⁶For they persecute those you wound
  and talk about the pain of those
  you hurt.
²⁷Charge them with crime upon crime;
  do not let them share in your
  salvation.
²⁸May they be blotted out of the book
  of life
  and not be listed with the
  righteous.

²⁹I am in pain and distress;
  may your salvation, O God, protect
  me.
³⁰I will praise God's name in song
  and glorify him with thanksgiving.
³¹This will please the LORD more than
  an ox,
  more than a bull with its horns and
  hoofs.
³²The poor will see and be glad—
  you who seek God, may your hearts
  live!
³³The LORD hears the needy
  and does not despise his captive
  people.

ª22 Or snare / and their fellowship become

³⁴Let heaven and earth praise him,
  the seas and all that move in them,
³⁵for God will save Zion
  and rebuild the cities of Judah.
Then people will settle there and
    possess it;
³⁶ the children of his servants will
    inherit it,
  and those who love his name will
    dwell there.

Psalm 70

For the director of music. Of David.
A petition.

¹Hasten, O God, to save me;
  O LORD, come quickly to help me.
²May those who seek my life
  be put to shame and confusion;
may all who desire my ruin
  be turned back in disgrace.
³May those who say to me, "Aha!
    Aha!"
  turn back because of their shame.
⁴But may all who seek you
  rejoice and be glad in you;
may those who love your salvation
    always say,
  "Let God be exalted!"

⁵Yet I am poor and needy;
  come quickly to me, O God.
You are my help and my deliverer;
  O LORD, do not delay.

Psalm 71

¹In you, O LORD, I have taken refuge;
  let me never be put to shame.
²Rescue me and deliver me in your
    righteousness;
  turn your ear to me and save me.
³Be my rock of refuge,
  to which I can always go;
give the command to save me,
  for you are my rock and my
    fortress.
⁴Deliver me, O my God, from the hand
    of the wicked,
  from the grasp of evil and cruel
    men.

⁵For you have been my hope,
  O Sovereign LORD,
my confidence since my youth.
⁶From birth I have relied on you;
  you brought me forth from my
    mother's womb.
I will ever praise you.
⁷I have become like a portent to many,
  but you are my strong refuge.
⁸My mouth is filled with your praise,
  declaring your splendor all day
    long.

⁹Do not cast me away when I am old;
  do not forsake me when my
    strength is gone.
¹⁰For my enemies speak against me;
  those who wait to kill me conspire
    together.
¹¹They say, "God has forsaken him;
  pursue him and seize him,
  for no one will rescue him."
¹²Be not far from me, O God;
  come quickly, O my God, to help
    me.
¹³May my accusers perish in shame;
  may those who want to harm me
  be covered with scorn and disgrace.

¹⁴But as for me, I will always have
    hope;
  I will praise you more and more.
¹⁵My mouth will tell of your
    righteousness,
  of your salvation all day long,
  though I know not its measure.
¹⁶I will come and proclaim your mighty
    acts, O Sovereign LORD;
  I will proclaim your righteousness,
    yours alone.
¹⁷Since my youth, O God, you have
    taught me,
  and to this day I declare your
    marvelous deeds.
¹⁸Even when I am old and gray,
  do not forsake me, O God,
till I declare your power to the next
    generation,
  your might to all who are to come.

¹⁹Your righteousness reaches to the
    skies, O God,
  you who have done great things.
  Who, O God, is like you?
²⁰Though you have made me see
    troubles, many and bitter,
  you will restore my life again;
from the depths of the earth
  you will again bring me up.
²¹You will increase my honor
  and comfort me once again.

²²I will praise you with the harp
  for your faithfulness, O my God;
I will sing praise to you with the lyre,
  O Holy One of Israel.
²³My lips will shout for joy
  when I sing praise to you—
  I, whom you have redeemed.

TUESDAY

VERSE FOR THE DAY:
Psalm 71:3

AUTHOR:
Gloria Gaither

PASSAGE FOR THE DAY:
Psalm 71:1–24

The Cleft

SO that is what a "cleft of the rock" looks like! I thought of the Fanny Crosby hymn "He Hideth My Soul" as I looked at this place "overshadowed" by a desert mountain, which is nothing more than a "towering" rock. I've heard all these words and phrases in hymns and ancient poetry. Yet, having grown up in Michigan, I more easily related to "the ageless billows roll," or having sins buried in "the depths" never to be remembered again. I could easily visualize the Master warning the man "who puts his hand to the plow and looks back" (Luke 9:62). Or Jesus taking in his hand a mustard seed, planting it in the moist black soil, then pointing to a matured plant so big "that the birds of the air come and perch in its branches" (Matthew 13:32).

I could relate to "shifting sand," for I've seen the "waves" of the sand dunes, or the "shelter from the storm," for I've been caught in the fury of a Midwestern thunderstorm. I've experienced the eye of a tornado, the area that is peaceful and quiet while the circle around it rages and destroys.

But clefts. I'd never really thought much of hiding in the cleft of a rock. Yet, here above me is exactly that: a "cleft of the rock." All around this indentation made eons ago are rugged surfaces exposed constantly to the fury and heat of the desert climate. Yet, inside this cleft the rock is its original pink color, unspoiled and protected. I realize that if the "storm in fury beat around me" I'd want to be in the solid rock, halfway up the mountain, hiding in the fortress made by nature itself, in the cleft of the rock. Perhaps it was about such a place that Fanny Crosby wrote:

A wonderful Savior is Jesus My Lord,
  A wonderful Savior to me;
He hideth my soul in the cleft of the rock,
  Where rivers of pleasure I see.

He hideth my soul in the cleft of the rock
  That shadows a dry, thirsty land;
He hideth my life in the depths of His love,
  And covers me there with His hand,
  And covers me there with His hand.

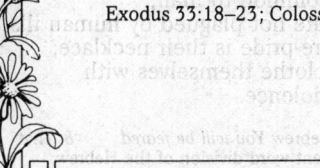

Additional Scripture Readings:
Exodus 33:18–23; Colossians 3:1–3

Go to page 615 for your next devotional reading.

²⁴My tongue will tell of your righteous
acts
all day long,
for those who wanted to harm me
have been put to shame and
confusion.

Psalm 72

Of Solomon.

¹Endow the king with your justice,
O God,
the royal son with your
righteousness.
²He will*ᵃ* judge your people in
righteousness,
your afflicted ones with justice.
³The mountains will bring prosperity
to the people,
the hills the fruit of righteousness.
⁴He will defend the afflicted among
the people
and save the children of the needy;
he will crush the oppressor.

⁵He will endure*ᵇ* as long as the sun,
as long as the moon, through all
generations.
⁶He will be like rain falling on a mown
field,
like showers watering the earth.
⁷In his days the righteous will flourish;
prosperity will abound till the moon
is no more.

⁸He will rule from sea to sea
and from the River*ᶜ* to the ends of
the earth.*ᵈ*
⁹The desert tribes will bow before him
and his enemies will lick the dust.
¹⁰The kings of Tarshish and of distant
shores
will bring tribute to him;
the kings of Sheba and Seba
will present him gifts.
¹¹All kings will bow down to him
and all nations will serve him.

¹²For he will deliver the needy who cry
out,
the afflicted who have no one to
help.
¹³He will take pity on the weak and the
needy
and save the needy from death.
¹⁴He will rescue them from oppression
and violence,

for precious is their blood in his
sight.

¹⁵Long may he live!
May gold from Sheba be given him.
May people ever pray for him
and bless him all day long.
¹⁶Let grain abound throughout the
land;
on the tops of the hills may it sway.
Let its fruit flourish like Lebanon;
let it thrive like the grass of the
field.
¹⁷May his name endure forever;
may it continue as long as the sun.

All nations will be blessed through
him,
and they will call him blessed.

¹⁸Praise be to the Lᴏʀᴅ God, the God of
Israel,
who alone does marvelous deeds.
¹⁹Praise be to his glorious name forever;
may the whole earth be filled with
his glory.
Amen and Amen.

²⁰This concludes the prayers of David
son of Jesse.

BOOK III

Psalms 73–89

Psalm 73

A psalm of Asaph.

¹Surely God is good to Israel,
to those who are pure in heart.

²But as for me, my feet had almost
slipped;
I had nearly lost my foothold.
³For I envied the arrogant
when I saw the prosperity of the
wicked.

⁴They have no struggles;
their bodies are healthy and
strong.*ᵉ*
⁵They are free from the burdens
common to man;
they are not plagued by human ills.
⁶Therefore pride is their necklace;
they clothe themselves with
violence.

ᵃ2 Or *May he*; similarly in verses 3-11 and 17   *ᵇ5* Septuagint; Hebrew *You will be feared*   *ᶜ8* That
is, the Euphrates   *ᵈ8* Or *the end of the land*   *ᵉ4* With a different word division of the Hebrew;
Masoretic Text *struggles at their death; / their bodies are healthy*

7From their callous hearts comes
    iniquity[a];
  the evil conceits of their minds
    know no limits.
8They scoff, and speak with malice;
  in their arrogance they threaten
    oppression.
9Their mouths lay claim to heaven,
  and their tongues take possession
    of the earth.
10Therefore their people turn to them
  and drink up waters in
    abundance.[b]
11They say, "How can God know?
  Does the Most High have
    knowledge?"

12This is what the wicked are like—
  always carefree, they increase in
    wealth.

13Surely in vain have I kept my heart
    pure;
  in vain have I washed my hands in
    innocence.
14All day long I have been plagued;
  I have been punished every
    morning.

15If I had said, "I will speak thus,"
  I would have betrayed your
    children.
16When I tried to understand all this,
  it was oppressive to me
17till I entered the sanctuary of God;
  then I understood their final
    destiny.

18Surely you place them on slippery
    ground;
  you cast them down to ruin.
19How suddenly are they destroyed,
  completely swept away by terrors!
20As a dream when one awakes,
  so when you arise, O Lord,
  you will despise them as fantasies.

21When my heart was grieved
  and my spirit embittered,
22I was senseless and ignorant;
  I was a brute beast before you.

23Yet I am always with you;
  you hold me by my right hand.
24You guide me with your counsel,
  and afterward you will take me into
    glory.
25Whom have I in heaven but you?
  And earth has nothing I desire
    besides you.

26My flesh and my heart may fail,
  but God is the strength of my heart
    and my portion forever.
27Those who are far from you will
    perish;
  you destroy all who are unfaithful
    to you.
28But as for me, it is good to be near
    God.
  I have made the Sovereign Lord my
    refuge;
  I will tell of all your deeds.

Psalm 74

A maskil[c] of Asaph.

1Why have you rejected us forever,
    O God?
  Why does your anger smolder
    against the sheep of your
    pasture?
2Remember the people you purchased
    of old,
  the tribe of your inheritance, whom
    you redeemed—
  Mount Zion, where you dwelt.
3Turn your steps toward these
    everlasting ruins,
  all this destruction the enemy has
    brought on the sanctuary.

4Your foes roared in the place where
    you met with us;
  they set up their standards as signs.
5They behaved like men wielding axes
  to cut through a thicket of trees.
6They smashed all the carved paneling
  with their axes and hatchets.
7They burned your sanctuary to the
    ground;
  they defiled the dwelling place of
    your Name.
8They said in their hearts, "We will
    crush them completely!"
  They burned every place where God
    was worshiped in the land.

9We are given no miraculous signs;
  no prophets are left,
  and none of us knows how long
    this will be.
10How long will the enemy mock you,
    O God?
  Will the foe revile your name
    forever?
11Why do you hold back your hand,
  your right hand?

---

a7 Syriac (see also Septuagint); Hebrew Their eyes bulge with fat   b10 The meaning of the Hebrew for
this verse is uncertain.   cTitle: Probably a literary or musical term

Take it from the folds of your
garment and destroy them!
¹²But you, O God, are my king from of
old;
you bring salvation upon the earth.
¹³It was you who split open the sea by
your power;
you broke the heads of the monster
in the waters.
¹⁴It was you who crushed the heads of
Leviathan
and gave him as food to the
creatures of the desert.
¹⁵It was you who opened up springs
and streams;
you dried up the ever flowing rivers.
¹⁶The day is yours, and yours also the
night;
you established the sun and moon.
¹⁷It was you who set all the boundaries
of the earth;
you made both summer and winter.
¹⁸Remember how the enemy has
mocked you, O LORD,
how foolish people have reviled
your name.
¹⁹Do not hand over the life of your dove
to wild beasts;
do not forget the lives of your
afflicted people forever.
²⁰Have regard for your covenant,
because haunts of violence fill the
dark places of the land.
²¹Do not let the oppressed retreat in
disgrace;
may the poor and needy praise your
name.
²²Rise up, O God, and defend your
cause;
remember how fools mock you all
day long.
²³Do not ignore the clamor of your
adversaries,
the uproar of your enemies, which
rises continually.

Psalm 75

For the director of music. To the tune
of, "Do Not Destroy." A psalm of Asaph.
A song.

¹We give thanks to you, O God,
we give thanks, for your Name is
near;
men tell of your wonderful deeds.

²You say, "I choose the appointed
time;

it is I who judge uprightly.
³When the earth and all its people
quake,
it is I who hold its pillars firm.
Selah
⁴To the arrogant I say, 'Boast no
more,'
and to the wicked, 'Do not lift up
your horns.
⁵Do not lift your horns against heaven;
do not speak with outstretched
neck.' "

⁶No one from the east or the west
or from the desert can exalt a man.
⁷But it is God who judges:
He brings one down, he exalts
another.
⁸In the hand of the LORD is a cup
full of foaming wine mixed with
spices;
he pours it out, and all the wicked of
the earth
drink it down to its very dregs.

⁹As for me, I will declare this forever;
I will sing praise to the God of
Jacob.
¹⁰I will cut off the horns of all the
wicked,
but the horns of the righteous will
be lifted up.

Psalm 76

For the director of music. With stringed
instruments. A psalm of Asaph. A song.

¹In Judah God is known;
his name is great in Israel.
²His tent is in Salem,
his dwelling place in Zion.
³There he broke the flashing arrows,
the shields and the swords, the
weapons of war. *Selah*

⁴You are resplendent with light,
more majestic than mountains rich
with game.
⁵Valiant men lie plundered,
they sleep their last sleep;
not one of the warriors
can lift his hands.
⁶At your rebuke, O God of Jacob,
both horse and chariot lie still.
⁷You alone are to be feared.
Who can stand before you when
you are angry?
⁸From heaven you pronounced
judgment,

and the land feared and was
    quiet—
⁹when you, O God, rose up to judge,
    to save all the afflicted of the land.
                                    Selah
¹⁰Surely your wrath against men brings
        you praise,
    and the survivors of your wrath are
        restrained.ᵃ
¹¹Make vows to the Lᴏʀᴅ your God and
        fulfill them;
    let all the neighboring lands
        bring gifts to the One to be feared.
¹²He breaks the spirit of rulers;
    he is feared by the kings of the
        earth.

Psalm 77

For the director of music. For Jeduthun.
    Of Asaph. A psalm.

¹I cried out to God for help;
    I cried out to God to hear me.
²When I was in distress, I sought the
        Lord;
    at night I stretched out untiring
        hands
    and my soul refused to be
        comforted.

³I remembered you, O God, and I
        groaned;
    I mused, and my spirit grew faint.
                                    Selah
⁴You kept my eyes from closing;
    I was too troubled to speak.
⁵I thought about the former days,
    the years of long ago;
⁶I remembered my songs in the night.
    My heart mused and my spirit
        inquired:

⁷"Will the Lord reject forever?
    Will he never show his favor again?
⁸Has his unfailing love vanished
        forever?
    Has his promise failed for all time?
⁹Has God forgotten to be merciful?
    Has he in anger withheld his
        compassion?"   *Selah*

¹⁰Then I thought, "To this I will appeal:
    the years of the right hand of the
        Most High."
¹¹I will remember the deeds of the
        Lᴏʀᴅ;

yes, I will remember your miracles
        of long ago.
¹²I will meditate on all your works
    and consider all your mighty deeds.

¹³Your ways, O God, are holy.
    What god is so great as our God?
¹⁴You are the God who performs
        miracles;
    you display your power among the
        peoples.
¹⁵With your mighty arm you redeemed
        your people,
    the descendants of Jacob and
        Joseph.   *Selah*

¹⁶The waters saw you, O God,
    the waters saw you and writhed;
    the very depths were convulsed.
¹⁷The clouds poured down water,
    the skies resounded with thunder;
    your arrows flashed back and forth.
¹⁸Your thunder was heard in the
        whirlwind,
    your lightning lit up the world;
    the earth trembled and quaked.
¹⁹Your path led through the sea,
    your way through the mighty
        waters,
    though your footprints were not
        seen.

²⁰You led your people like a flock
    by the hand of Moses and Aaron.

Psalm 78

A *maskil*ᵇ of Asaph.

¹O my people, hear my teaching;
    listen to the words of my mouth.
²I will open my mouth in parables,
    I will utter hidden things, things
        from of old—
³what we have heard and known,
    what our fathers have told us.
⁴We will not hide them from their
        children;
    we will tell the next generation
    the praiseworthy deeds of the Lᴏʀᴅ,
        his power, and the wonders he has
        done.
⁵He decreed statutes for Jacob
    and established the law in Israel,
    which he commanded our forefathers
        to teach their children,
⁶so the next generation would know
        them,
    even the children yet to be born,

ᵃ10 Or *Surely the wrath of men brings you praise, / and with the remainder of wrath you arm yourself*
ᵇTitle: Probably a literary or musical term

and they in turn would tell their
   children.
⁷Then they would put their trust in
   God
and would not forget his deeds
   but would keep his commands.
⁸They would not be like their
   forefathers—
a stubborn and rebellious
   generation,
whose hearts were not loyal to God,
   whose spirits were not faithful to
   him.

⁹The men of Ephraim, though armed
   with bows,
turned back on the day of battle;
¹⁰they did not keep God's covenant
   and refused to live by his law.
¹¹They forgot what he had done,
   the wonders he had shown them.
¹²He did miracles in the sight of their
   fathers
in the land of Egypt, in the region
   of Zoan.
¹³He divided the sea and led them
   through;
he made the water stand firm like a
   wall.
¹⁴He guided them with the cloud by
   day
and with light from the fire all
   night.
¹⁵He split the rocks in the desert
   and gave them water as abundant
   as the seas;
¹⁶he brought streams out of a rocky
   crag
and made water flow down like
   rivers.

¹⁷But they continued to sin against
   him,
rebelling in the desert against the
   Most High.
¹⁸They willfully put God to the test
   by demanding the food they craved.
¹⁹They spoke against God, saying,
   "Can God spread a table in the
   desert?
²⁰When he struck the rock, water
   gushed out,
and streams flowed abundantly.
But can he also give us food?
   Can he supply meat for his
   people?"
²¹When the LORD heard them, he was
   very angry;
his fire broke out against Jacob,
   and his wrath rose against Israel,
²²for they did not believe in God

or trust in his deliverance.
²³Yet he gave a command to the skies
   above
and opened the doors of the
   heavens;
²⁴he rained down manna for the people
   to eat,
he gave them the grain of heaven.
²⁵Men ate the bread of angels;
   he sent them all the food they
   could eat.
²⁶He let loose the east wind from the
   heavens
and led forth the south wind by his
   power.
²⁷He rained meat down on them like
   dust,
flying birds like sand on the
   seashore.
²⁸He made them come down inside
   their camp,
all around their tents.
²⁹They ate till they had more than
   enough,
for he had given them what they
   craved.
³⁰But before they turned from the food
   they craved,
even while it was still in their
   mouths,
³¹God's anger rose against them;
   he put to death the sturdiest
   among them,
cutting down the young men of
   Israel.

³²In spite of all this, they kept on
   sinning;
in spite of his wonders, they did
   not believe.
³³So he ended their days in futility
   and their years in terror.
³⁴Whenever God slew them, they would
   seek him;
they eagerly turned to him again.
³⁵They remembered that God was their
   Rock,
that God Most High was their
   Redeemer.
³⁶But then they would flatter him with
   their mouths,
lying to him with their tongues;
³⁷their hearts were not loyal to him,
   they were not faithful to his
   covenant.
³⁸Yet he was merciful;
   he forgave their iniquities
   and did not destroy them.
Time after time he restrained his
   anger

and did not stir up his full wrath.
³⁹He remembered that they were but
flesh,
a passing breeze that does not
return.

⁴⁰How often they rebelled against him
in the desert
and grieved him in the wasteland!
⁴¹Again and again they put God to the
test;
they vexed the Holy One of Israel.
⁴²They did not remember his power—
the day he redeemed them from the
oppressor,
⁴³the day he displayed his miraculous
signs in Egypt,
his wonders in the region of Zoan.
⁴⁴He turned their rivers to blood;
they could not drink from their
streams.
⁴⁵He sent swarms of flies that devoured
them,
and frogs that devastated them.
⁴⁶He gave their crops to the
grasshopper,
their produce to the locust.
⁴⁷He destroyed their vines with hail
and their sycamore-figs with sleet.
⁴⁸He gave over their cattle to the hail,
their livestock to bolts of lightning.
⁴⁹He unleashed against them his hot
anger,
his wrath, indignation and
hostility—
a band of destroying angels.
⁵⁰He prepared a path for his anger;
he did not spare them from death
but gave them over to the plague.
⁵¹He struck down all the firstborn of
Egypt,
the firstfruits of manhood in the
tents of Ham.
⁵²But he brought his people out like a
flock;
he led them like sheep through the
desert.
⁵³He guided them safely, so they were
unafraid;
but the sea engulfed their enemies.
⁵⁴Thus he brought them to the border
of his holy land,
to the hill country his right hand
had taken.
⁵⁵He drove out nations before them
and allotted their lands to them as
an inheritance;
he settled the tribes of Israel in
their homes.

⁵⁶But they put God to the test

and rebelled against the Most High;
they did not keep his statutes.
⁵⁷Like their fathers they were disloyal
and faithless,
as unreliable as a faulty bow.
⁵⁸They angered him with their high
places;
they aroused his jealousy with their
idols.
⁵⁹When God heard them, he was very
angry;
he rejected Israel completely.
⁶⁰He abandoned the tabernacle of
Shiloh,
the tent he had set up among men.
⁶¹He sent the ark of his might into
captivity,
his splendor into the hands of the
enemy.
⁶²He gave his people over to the sword;
he was very angry with his
inheritance.
⁶³Fire consumed their young men,
and their maidens had no wedding
songs;
⁶⁴their priests were put to the sword,
and their widows could not weep.

⁶⁵Then the Lord awoke as from sleep,
as a man wakes from the stupor of
wine.
⁶⁶He beat back his enemies;
he put them to everlasting shame.
⁶⁷Then he rejected the tents of Joseph,
he did not choose the tribe of
Ephraim;
⁶⁸but he chose the tribe of Judah,
Mount Zion, which he loved.
⁶⁹He built his sanctuary like the
heights,
like the earth that he established
forever.
⁷⁰He chose David his servant
and took him from the sheep pens;
⁷¹from tending the sheep he brought
him
to be the shepherd of his people
Jacob,
of Israel his inheritance.
⁷²And David shepherded them with
integrity of heart;
with skillful hands he led them.

Psalm 79

A psalm of Asaph.

¹O God, the nations have invaded your
inheritance;
they have defiled your holy temple,

they have reduced Jerusalem to
rubble.
2They have given the dead bodies of
your servants
as food to the birds of the air,
the flesh of your saints to the
beasts of the earth.
3They have poured out blood like
water
all around Jerusalem,
and there is no one to bury the
dead.
4We are objects of reproach to our
neighbors,
of scorn and derision to those
around us.

5How long, O LORD? Will you be angry
forever?
How long will your jealousy burn
like fire?
6Pour out your wrath on the
nations
that do not acknowledge you,
on the kingdoms
that do not call on your name;
7for they have devoured Jacob
and destroyed his homeland.
8Do not hold against us the sins of the
fathers;
may your mercy come quickly to
meet us,
for we are in desperate need.

9Help us, O God our Savior,
for the glory of your name;
deliver us and forgive our sins
for your name's sake.
10Why should the nations say,
"Where is their God?"
Before our eyes, make known among
the nations
that you avenge the outpoured
blood of your servants.
11May the groans of the prisoners come
before you;
by the strength of your arm
preserve those condemned to
die.

12Pay back into the laps of our
neighbors seven times
the reproach they have hurled at
you, O Lord.
13Then we your people, the sheep of
your pasture,
will praise you forever;
from generation to generation
we will recount your praise.

Psalm 80

For the director of music. To the tune
of, "The Lilies of the Covenant."
Of Asaph. A psalm.

1Hear us, O Shepherd of Israel,
you who lead Joseph like a flock;
you who sit enthroned between the
cherubim, shine forth
2 before Ephraim, Benjamin and
Manasseh.
Awaken your might;
come and save us.

3Restore us, O God;
make your face shine upon us,
that we may be saved.

4O LORD God Almighty,
how long will your anger smolder
against the prayers of your people?
5You have fed them with the bread of
tears;
you have made them drink tears by
the bowlful.
6You have made us a source of
contention to our neighbors,
and our enemies mock us.

7Restore us, O God Almighty;
make your face shine upon us,
that we may be saved.

8You brought a vine out of Egypt;
you drove out the nations and
planted it.
9You cleared the ground for it,
and it took root and filled the land.
10The mountains were covered with its
shade,
the mighty cedars with its
branches.
11It sent out its boughs to the Sea,[a]
its shoots as far as the River.[b]

12Why have you broken down its walls
so that all who pass by pick its
grapes?
13Boars from the forest ravage it
and the creatures of the field feed
on it.
14Return to us, O God Almighty!
Look down from heaven and see!
Watch over this vine,
15 the root your right hand has
planted,
the son[c] you have raised up for
yourself.

a11 Probably the Mediterranean   b11 That is, the Euphrates   c15 Or branch

16Your vine is cut down, it is burned
with fire;
at your rebuke your people perish.
17Let your hand rest on the man at
your right hand,
the son of man you have raised up
for yourself.
18Then we will not turn away from you;
revive us, and we will call on your
name.

19Restore us, O Lord God Almighty;
make your face shine upon us,
that we may be saved.

Psalm 81

For the director of music. According to
gittith. a Of Asaph.

1Sing for joy to God our strength;
shout aloud to the God of Jacob!
2Begin the music, strike the
tambourine,
play the melodious harp and lyre.

3Sound the ram's horn at the New
Moon,
and when the moon is full, on the
day of our Feast;
4this is a decree for Israel,
an ordinance of the God of Jacob.
5He established it as a statute for
Joseph
when he went out against Egypt,
where we heard a language we did
not understand. b

6He says, "I removed the burden from
their shoulders;
their hands were set free from the
basket.
7In your distress you called and I
rescued you,
I answered you out of a
thundercloud;
I tested you at the waters of
Meribah.   *Selah*

8"Hear, O my people, and I will warn
you—
if you would but listen to me,
O Israel!
9You shall have no foreign god among
you;
you shall not bow down to an alien
god.
10I am the Lord your God,
who brought you up out of Egypt.

Open wide your mouth and I will
fill it.

11"But my people would not listen to
me;
Israel would not submit to me.
12So I gave them over to their stubborn
hearts
to follow their own devices.

13"If my people would but listen to me,
if Israel would follow my ways,
14how quickly would I subdue their
enemies
and turn my hand against their
foes!
15Those who hate the Lord would
cringe before him,
and their punishment would last
forever.
16But you would be fed with the finest
of wheat;
with honey from the rock I would
satisfy you."

Psalm 82

A psalm of Asaph.

1God presides in the great assembly;
he gives judgment among the
"gods":

2"How long will youc defend the
unjust
and show partiality to the wicked?
Selah
3Defend the cause of the weak and
fatherless;
maintain the rights of the poor and
oppressed.
4Rescue the weak and needy;
deliver them from the hand of the
wicked.

5"They know nothing, they understand
nothing.
They walk about in darkness;
all the foundations of the earth are
shaken.

6"I said, 'You are "gods";
you are all sons of the Most High.'
7But you will die like mere men;
you will fall like every other ruler."

8Rise up, O God, judge the earth,
for all the nations are your
inheritance.

---

aTitle: Probably a musical term   b5 Or / and we heard a voice we had not known   c2 The Hebrew is
plural.

Psalm 83

A song. A psalm of Asaph.

¹O God, do not keep silent;
　be not quiet, O God, be not
　　still.
²See how your enemies are astir,
　how your foes rear their heads.
³With cunning they conspire against
　your people;
　they plot against those you cherish.
⁴"Come," they say, "let us destroy
　　them as a nation,
　that the name of Israel be
　remembered no more."

⁵With one mind they plot together;
　they form an alliance against
　　you—
⁶the tents of Edom and the
　　Ishmaelites,
　of Moab and the Hagrites,
⁷Gebal,ᵃ Ammon and Amalek,
　Philistia, with the people of Tyre.
⁸Even Assyria has joined them
　to lend strength to the descendants
　　of Lot.　　　*Selah*

⁹Do to them as you did to Midian,
　as you did to Sisera and Jabin at
　　the river Kishon,
¹⁰who perished at Endor
　and became like refuse on the
　　ground.
¹¹Make their nobles like Oreb and
　　Zeeb,
　all their princes like Zebah and
　　Zalmunna,
¹²who said, "Let us take possession
　of the pasturelands of God."

¹³Make them like tumbleweed, O my
　　God,
　like chaff before the wind.
¹⁴As fire consumes the forest
　or a flame sets the mountains
　　ablaze,
¹⁵so pursue them with your tempest
　and terrify them with your storm.
¹⁶Cover their faces with shame
　so that men will seek your name,
　　O LORD.

¹⁷May they ever be ashamed and
　　dismayed;
　may they perish in disgrace.
¹⁸Let them know that you, whose name
　is the LORD—

that you alone are the Most High
　over all the earth.

Psalm 84

*For the director of music. According to
gittith.ᵇ Of the Sons of Korah. A psalm.*

¹How lovely is your dwelling place,
　O LORD Almighty!
²My soul yearns, even faints,
　for the courts of the LORD;
my heart and my flesh cry out
　for the living God.

³Even the sparrow has found a home,
　and the swallow a nest for herself,
　where she may have her young—
a place near your altar,
　O LORD Almighty, my King and my
　　God.
⁴Blessed are those who dwell in your
　　house;
　they are ever praising you.　*Selah*

⁵Blessed are those whose strength is in
　　you,
　who have set their hearts on
　　pilgrimage.
⁶As they pass through the Valley of
　　Baca,
　they make it a place of springs;
　the autumn rains also cover it with
　　pools.ᶜ
⁷They go from strength to strength,
　till each appears before God in
　　Zion.

⁸Hear my prayer, O LORD God
　　Almighty;
　listen to me, O God of Jacob.　*Selah*
⁹Look upon our shield,ᵈ O God;
　look with favor on your anointed
　　one.

¹⁰Better is one day in your courts
　than a thousand elsewhere;
I would rather be a doorkeeper in the
　house of my God
　than dwell in the tents of the
　　wicked.
¹¹For the LORD God is a sun and shield;
　the LORD bestows favor and honor;
no good thing does he withhold
　from those whose walk is
　　blameless.

¹²O LORD Almighty,
　blessed is the man who trusts in
　　you.

ᵃ7 That is, Byblos　　ᵇTitle: Probably a musical term　　ᶜ6 Or *blessings*　　ᵈ9 Or *sovereign*

VERSE FOR THE DAY:
Psalm 84:3

AUTHOR:
Debby Boone

PASSAGE FOR THE DAY:
Psalm 84:1–12

I Will Meet All Their Needs

I READ Psalm 84:3 one morning while on an airplane flying across the country, after I'd left my family for a few days to sing in different churches. As I read the verse, I knew that the Lord wanted to use this Scripture to teach me something about raising children. I took out my journal to record some thoughts about this "nest" where I could lay down my own young: 1. A nest is a place of security, rest and provision. 2. It is a place to lay my children on God's altar daily. 3. It will take a sacrifice of time to seek knowledge and wisdom for my young.

I closed my journal, feeling a sense of accomplishment and great motivation to begin building the perfect nest for my four children.

The next morning I was on another plane headed for one more concert when I read the psalm again. This time the second verse jumped out at me:

> My soul yearns, even faints,
> for the courts of the LORD;
> my heart and my flesh cry out
> for the living God.

I was overwhelmed by this expression of great love and desire to be with the Lord. Yet it did not match the uneasy feeling in my own heart. My feeling of impending failure. The feeling that, sure, I can make a great list of how to raise my kids, but can I live up to it? Instead of seeking God's presence, I wanted to hide from him and avoid facing my own discouragement and his disappointment.

Then I felt the Lord speak gently to my heart: "Debby, this nest is not made up of *your* sacrifices. It is made up of *mine.* I have made every sacrifice necessary to provide a place for your family to dwell. There I will meet all their needs. Come to my courts and be reminded of my love for you and all that that love has made available to you."

Joseph Scriven's hymn "What a Friend We Have in Jesus" came to my heart as the plane started to descend. I now knew that I could trust. Not in the nest I could build, but in the Lord's altar.

Additional Scripture Readings:
Psalm 23:5–6; John 14:1–4

Go to page 621 for your next devotional reading.

Psalm 85

For the director of music. Of the Sons of Korah. A psalm.

[1]You showed favor to your land, O LORD;
  you restored the fortunes of Jacob.
[2]You forgave the iniquity of your people
  and covered all their sins.   *Selah*
[3]You set aside all your wrath
  and turned from your fierce anger.

[4]Restore us again, O God our Savior,
  and put away your displeasure toward us.
[5]Will you be angry with us forever?
  Will you prolong your anger through all generations?
[6]Will you not revive us again,
  that your people may rejoice in you?
[7]Show us your unfailing love, O LORD,
  and grant us your salvation.

[8]I will listen to what God the LORD will say;
  he promises peace to his people, his saints —
  but let them not return to folly.
[9]Surely his salvation is near those who fear him,
  that his glory may dwell in our land.

[10]Love and faithfulness meet together;
  righteousness and peace kiss each other.
[11]Faithfulness springs forth from the earth,
  and righteousness looks down from heaven.
[12]The LORD will indeed give what is good,
  and our land will yield its harvest.
[13]Righteousness goes before him
  and prepares the way for his steps.

Psalm 86

A prayer of David.

[1]Hear, O LORD, and answer me,
  for I am poor and needy.
[2]Guard my life, for I am devoted to you.
  You are my God; save your servant who trusts in you.

[3]Have mercy on me, O Lord,
  for I call to you all day long.
[4]Bring joy to your servant,
  for to you, O Lord,
  I lift up my soul.

[5]You are forgiving and good, O Lord,
  abounding in love to all who call to you.
[6]Hear my prayer, O LORD;
  listen to my cry for mercy.
[7]In the day of my trouble I will call to you,
  for you will answer me.

[8]Among the gods there is none like you, O Lord;
  no deeds can compare with yours.
[9]All the nations you have made
  will come and worship before you, O Lord;
  they will bring glory to your name.
[10]For you are great and do marvelous deeds;
  you alone are God.

[11]Teach me your way, O LORD,
  and I will walk in your truth;
  give me an undivided heart,
  that I may fear your name.
[12]I will praise you, O Lord my God,
  with all my heart;
  I will glorify your name forever.
[13]For great is your love toward me;
  you have delivered me from the depths of the grave.[a]

[14]The arrogant are attacking me, O God;
  a band of ruthless men seeks my life —
  men without regard for you.
[15]But you, O Lord, are a compassionate and gracious God,
  slow to anger, abounding in love and faithfulness.
[16]Turn to me and have mercy on me;
  grant your strength to your servant
  and save the son of your maidservant.[b]
[17]Give me a sign of your goodness,
  that my enemies may see it and be put to shame,
  for you, O LORD, have helped me and comforted me.

---

[a]13 Hebrew *Sheol*   [b]16 Or *save your faithful son*

Psalm 87

Of the Sons of Korah. A psalm. A song.

[1]He has set his foundation on the holy
     mountain;
[2] the Lord loves the gates of Zion
     more than all the dwellings of
     Jacob.
[3]Glorious things are said of you,
     O city of God: *Selah*
[4]"I will record Rahab[a] and Babylon
     among those who acknowledge
     me—
Philistia too, and Tyre, along with
     Cush[b]—
     and will say, 'This[c] one was born
     in Zion.' "

[5]Indeed, of Zion it will be said,
     "This one and that one were born
     in her,
     and the Most High himself will
     establish her."
[6]The Lord will write in the register of
     the peoples:
     "This one was born in Zion." *Selah*
[7]As they make music they will sing,
     "All my fountains are in you."

Psalm 88

A song. A psalm of the Sons of Korah.
For the director of music. According to
mahalath leannoth.[d] A *maskil*[e] of
Heman the Ezrahite.

[1]O Lord, the God who saves me,
     day and night I cry out before you.
[2]May my prayer come before you;
     turn your ear to my cry.

[3]For my soul is full of trouble
     and my life draws near the grave.[f]
[4]I am counted among those who go
          down to the pit;
     I am like a man without strength.
[5]I am set apart with the dead,
     like the slain who lie in the grave,
whom you remember no more,
     who are cut off from your care.

[6]You have put me in the lowest pit,
     in the darkest depths.
[7]Your wrath lies heavily upon me;
     you have overwhelmed me with all
          your waves.   *Selah*

[8]You have taken from me my closest
          friends
     and have made me repulsive to
          them.
I am confined and cannot escape;
[9] my eyes are dim with grief.

I call to you, O Lord, every day;
     I spread out my hands to you.
[10]Do you show your wonders to the
          dead?
     Do those who are dead rise up and
          praise you?   *Selah*
[11]Is your love declared in the grave,
     your faithfulness in Destruction[g]?
[12]Are your wonders known in the place
          of darkness,
     or your righteous deeds in the land
          of oblivion?

[13]But I cry to you for help, O Lord;
     in the morning my prayer comes
          before you.
[14]Why, O Lord, do you reject me
     and hide your face from me?

[15]From my youth I have been afflicted
          and close to death;
     I have suffered your terrors and am
          in despair.
[16]Your wrath has swept over me;
     your terrors have destroyed me.
[17]All day long they surround me like a
          flood;
     they have completely engulfed me.
[18]You have taken my companions and
          loved ones from me;
     the darkness is my closest friend.

Psalm 89

A *maskil*[e] of Ethan the Ezrahite.

[1]I will sing of the Lord's great love
          forever;
     with my mouth I will make your
          faithfulness known through all
          generations.
[2]I will declare that your love stands
          firm forever,
     that you established your
          faithfulness in heaven itself.

[3]You said, "I have made a covenant
          with my chosen one,
     I have sworn to David my servant,
[4]'I will establish your line forever

---

a4 A poetic name for Egypt   *b4* That is, the upper Nile region   *c4* Or "O Rahab and Babylon, /
Philistia, Tyre and Cush, / I will record concerning those who acknowledge me: / 'This   *d*Title: Possibly a
tune, "The Suffering of Affliction"   *e*Title: Probably a literary or musical term   *f3* Hebrew *Sheol*
g11 Hebrew *Abaddon*

and make your throne firm through
all generations.' "   *Selah*

⁵The heavens praise your wonders,
O LORD,
your faithfulness too, in the
assembly of the holy ones.
⁶For who in the skies above can
compare with the LORD?
Who is like the LORD among the
heavenly beings?
⁷In the council of the holy ones God is
greatly feared;
he is more awesome than all who
surround him.
⁸O LORD God Almighty, who is like
you?
You are mighty, O LORD, and your
faithfulness surrounds you.

⁹You rule over the surging sea;
when its waves mount up, you still
them.
¹⁰You crushed Rahab like one of the
slain;
with your strong arm you scattered
your enemies.
¹¹The heavens are yours, and yours also
the earth;
you founded the world and all that
is in it.
¹²You created the north and the south;
Tabor and Hermon sing for joy at
your name.
¹³Your arm is endued with power;
your hand is strong, your right hand
exalted.

¹⁴Righteousness and justice are the
foundation of your throne;
love and faithfulness go before you.
¹⁵Blessed are those who have learned to
acclaim you,
who walk in the light of your
presence, O LORD.
¹⁶They rejoice in your name all day
long;
they exult in your righteousness.
¹⁷For you are their glory and strength,
and by your favor you exalt our
horn.ᵃ
¹⁸Indeed, our shieldᵇ belongs to the
LORD,
our king to the Holy One of Israel.

¹⁹Once you spoke in a vision,
to your faithful people you said:
"I have bestowed strength on a
warrior;

I have exalted a young man from
among the people.
²⁰I have found David my servant;
with my sacred oil I have anointed
him.
²¹My hand will sustain him;
surely my arm will strengthen him.
²²No enemy will subject him to tribute;
no wicked man will oppress him.
²³I will crush his foes before him
and strike down his adversaries.
²⁴My faithful love will be with him,
and through my name his hornᶜ
will be exalted.
²⁵I will set his hand over the sea,
his right hand over the rivers.
²⁶He will call out to me, 'You are my
Father,
my God, the Rock my Savior.'
²⁷I will also appoint him my firstborn,
the most exalted of the kings of the
earth.
²⁸I will maintain my love to him
forever,
and my covenant with him will
never fail.
²⁹I will establish his line forever,
his throne as long as the heavens
endure.

³⁰"If his sons forsake my law
and do not follow my statutes,
³¹if they violate my decrees
and fail to keep my commands,
³²I will punish their sin with the rod,
their iniquity with flogging;
³³but I will not take my love from him,
nor will I ever betray my
faithfulness.
³⁴I will not violate my covenant
or alter what my lips have uttered.
³⁵Once for all, I have sworn by my
holiness—
and I will not lie to David—
³⁶that his line will continue forever
and his throne endure before me
like the sun;
³⁷it will be established forever like the
moon,
the faithful witness in the sky."
Selah

³⁸But you have rejected, you have
spurned,
you have been very angry with your
anointed one.
³⁹You have renounced the covenant
with your servant

ᵃ17 *Horn* here symbolizes strong one.   ᵇ18 Or *sovereign*   ᶜ24 *Horn* here symbolizes strength.

and have defiled his crown in the
    dust.
40You have broken through all his walls
    and reduced his strongholds to
        ruins.
41All who pass by have plundered him;
    he has become the scorn of his
        neighbors.
42You have exalted the right hand of his
        foes;
    you have made all his enemies
        rejoice.
43You have turned back the edge of his
        sword
    and have not supported him in
        battle.
44You have put an end to his splendor
    and cast his throne to the ground.
45You have cut short the days of his
        youth;
    you have covered him with a
        mantle of shame.   *Selah*

46How long, O Lord? Will you hide
        yourself forever?
    How long will your wrath burn like
        fire?
47Remember how fleeting is my life.
    For what futility you have created
        all men!
48What man can live and not see death,
    or save himself from the power of
        the grave*a*?   *Selah*
49O Lord, where is your former great
        love,
    which in your faithfulness you
        swore to David?
50Remember, Lord, how your servant
        has*b* been mocked,
    how I bear in my heart the taunts
        of all the nations,
51the taunts with which your enemies
        have mocked, O Lord,
    with which they have mocked every
        step of your anointed one.

52Praise be to the Lord forever!
    Amen and Amen.

BOOK IV

Psalms 90–106

Psalm 90

A prayer of Moses the man of God.

1Lord, you have been our dwelling
        place

throughout all generations.
2Before the mountains were born
    or you brought forth the earth and
        the world,
    from everlasting to everlasting you
        are God.

3You turn men back to dust,
    saying, "Return to dust, O sons of
        men."
4For a thousand years in your sight
    are like a day that has just gone by,
    or like a watch in the night.
5You sweep men away in the sleep of
        death;
    they are like the new grass of the
        morning—
6though in the morning it springs up
        new,
    by evening it is dry and withered.

7We are consumed by your anger
    and terrified by your indignation.
8You have set our iniquities before
        you,
    our secret sins in the light of your
        presence.
9All our days pass away under your
        wrath;
    we finish our years with a moan.
10The length of our days is seventy
        years—
    or eighty, if we have the strength;
    yet their span*c* is but trouble and
        sorrow,
    for they quickly pass, and we fly
        away.

11Who knows the power of your anger?
    For your wrath is as great as the
        fear that is due you.
12Teach us to number our days aright,
    that we may gain a heart of
        wisdom.

13Relent, O Lord! How long will it be?
    Have compassion on your servants.
14Satisfy us in the morning with your
        unfailing love,
    that we may sing for joy and be
        glad all our days.
15Make us glad for as many days as you
        have afflicted us,
    for as many years as we have seen
        trouble.
16May your deeds be shown to your
        servants,
    your splendor to their children.

---

a48 Hebrew *Sheol*   *b50* Or *your servants have*   *c10* Or *yet the best of them*

17May the favor[a] of the Lord our God
   rest upon us;
   establish the work of our hands for
   us—
   yes, establish the work of our
   hands.

Psalm 91

1He who dwells in the shelter of the
   Most High
   will rest in the shadow of the
   Almighty.[b]
2I will say[c] of the LORD, "He is my
   refuge and my fortress,
   my God, in whom I trust."

3Surely he will save you from the
   fowler's snare
   and from the deadly pestilence.
4He will cover you with his feathers,
   and under his wings you will find
   refuge;
   his faithfulness will be your shield
   and rampart.
5You will not fear the terror of night,
   nor the arrow that flies by day,
6nor the pestilence that stalks in the
   darkness,
   nor the plague that destroys at
   midday.
7A thousand may fall at your side,
   ten thousand at your right hand,
   but it will not come near you.
8You will only observe with your eyes
   and see the punishment of the
   wicked.

9If you make the Most High your
   dwelling—
   even the LORD, who is my refuge—
10then no harm will befall you,
   no disaster will come near your
   tent.
11For he will command his angels
   concerning you
   to guard you in all your ways;
12they will lift you up in their hands,
   so that you will not strike your foot
   against a stone.
13You will tread upon the lion and the
   cobra;
   you will trample the great lion and
   the serpent.

14"Because he loves me," says the LORD,
   "I will rescue him;
   I will protect him, for he
   acknowledges my name.

15He will call upon me, and I will
   answer him;
   I will be with him in trouble,
   I will deliver him and honor him.
16With long life will I satisfy him
   and show him my salvation."

Psalm 92

A psalm. A song. For the Sabbath day.

1It is good to praise the LORD
   and make music to your name,
   O Most High,
2to proclaim your love in the morning
   and your faithfulness at night,
3to the music of the ten-stringed lyre
   and the melody of the harp.

4For you make me glad by your deeds,
   O LORD;
   I sing for joy at the works of your
   hands.
5How great are your works, O LORD,
   how profound your thoughts!
6The senseless man does not know,
   fools do not understand,
7that though the wicked spring up like
   grass
   and all evildoers flourish,
   they will be forever destroyed.

8But you, O LORD, are exalted forever.

9For surely your enemies, O LORD,
   surely your enemies will perish;
   all evildoers will be scattered.
10You have exalted my horn[d] like that
   of a wild ox;
   fine oils have been poured upon
   me.
11My eyes have seen the defeat of my
   adversaries;
   my ears have heard the rout of my
   wicked foes.

12The righteous will flourish like a palm
   tree,
   they will grow like a cedar of
   Lebanon;
13planted in the house of the LORD,
   they will flourish in the courts of
   our God.
14They will still bear fruit in old age,
   they will stay fresh and green,
15proclaiming, "The LORD is upright;
   he is my Rock, and there is no
   wickedness in him."

a17 Or beauty   b1 Hebrew Shaddai   c2 Or He says   d10 Horn here symbolizes strength.

VERSE FOR THE DAY:	AUTHOR:	PASSAGE FOR THE DAY:
Psalm 91:2	Hope MacDonald	Psalm 91:1–16

Our Dwelling Place

THE other night I took care of my grandchildren. Six-year-old Shane woke up crying. He had been dreaming of goblins and other childhood terrors. After he quieted down, he showed me the well-worn Bible his grandfather had given him. Shane always keeps it under his pillow. As I left the room, he said, "You know, Grandma, when you sleep with your Bible, it's almost like sleeping with Jesus!" And he lay down like a little lamb and went to sleep. He was resting in the shadow of the Almighty. Later I found myself asking, "Is this where I'm resting today?"

Try reading Psalm 91 every day for the next month. Your life will be changed, as mine was, because this is a triumphant song of faith. In it we learn that God is our dwelling place. It's under his wings that we find refuge, even in the midst of the universal evil that surrounds us.

We all face dangers and heartaches in life because we live in a lost and fallen world. But in the midst of these difficulties we can be absolutely confident that we are not left alone to deal with them. God's faithfulness is our constant shield. We are covered by the shadow of the Almighty! Oh, the security that is ours in God's promise that he will be with us in trouble (Psalm 91:15)!

These unchanging promises are for those who choose, by an act of their will, to put themselves under the care and protection of the living God. These promises are for those who dwell within the shelter of the Most High, who make their home with Jesus.

Why is this a psalm of irrepressible beauty? Because in it we are given a fresh glimpse into all that is ours through Jesus Christ our Lord. We come away from this psalm with an overwhelming sense of awe and wonder at God's continual provision for us.

Additional Scripture Readings:
Psalm 121:1–8; Lamentations 3:19–26

Go to page 627 for your next devotional reading.

Psalm 93

¹The Lord reigns, he is robed in
      majesty;
   the Lord is robed in majesty
   and is armed with strength.
   The world is firmly established;
   it cannot be moved.
²Your throne was established long
      ago;
   you are from all eternity.

³The seas have lifted up, O Lord,
   the seas have lifted up their voice;
   the seas have lifted up their
      pounding waves.
⁴Mightier than the thunder of the great
      waters,
   mightier than the breakers of the
      sea—
   the Lord on high is mighty.

⁵Your statutes stand firm;
   holiness adorns your house
   for endless days, O Lord.

Psalm 94

¹O Lord, the God who avenges,
   O God who avenges, shine forth.
²Rise up, O Judge of the earth;
   pay back to the proud what they
      deserve.
³How long will the wicked, O Lord,
   how long will the wicked be
      jubilant?

⁴They pour out arrogant words;
   all the evildoers are full of boasting.
⁵They crush your people, O Lord;
   they oppress your inheritance.
⁶They slay the widow and the alien;
   they murder the fatherless.
⁷They say, "The Lord does not see;
   the God of Jacob pays no heed."

⁸Take heed, you senseless ones among
      the people;
   you fools, when will you become
      wise?
⁹Does he who implanted the ear not
      hear?
   Does he who formed the eye not
      see?
¹⁰Does he who disciplines nations not
      punish?
   Does he who teaches man lack
      knowledge?
¹¹The Lord knows the thoughts of man;
   he knows that they are futile.

¹²Blessed is the man you discipline,
   O Lord,

the man you teach from your law;
¹³you grant him relief from days of
      trouble,
   till a pit is dug for the wicked.
¹⁴For the Lord will not reject his
      people;
   he will never forsake his
      inheritance.
¹⁵Judgment will again be founded on
      righteousness,
   and all the upright in heart will
      follow it.

¹⁶Who will rise up for me against the
      wicked?
   Who will take a stand for me
      against evildoers?
¹⁷Unless the Lord had given me help,
   I would soon have dwelt in the
      silence of death.
¹⁸When I said, "My foot is slipping,"
   your love, O Lord, supported me.
¹⁹When anxiety was great within me,
   your consolation brought joy to my
      soul.

²⁰Can a corrupt throne be allied with
      you—
   one that brings on misery by its
      decrees?
²¹They band together against the
      righteous
   and condemn the innocent to
      death.
²²But the Lord has become my fortress,
   and my God the rock in whom I
      take refuge.
²³He will repay them for their sins
   and destroy them for their
      wickedness;
   the Lord our God will destroy them.

Psalm 95

¹Come, let us sing for joy to the Lord;
   let us shout aloud to the Rock of
      our salvation.
²Let us come before him with
      thanksgiving
   and extol him with music and song.

³For the Lord is the great God,
   the great King above all gods.
⁴In his hand are the depths of the
      earth,
   and the mountain peaks belong to
      him.
⁵The sea is his, for he made it,
   and his hands formed the dry land.

⁶Come, let us bow down in worship,

let us kneel before the Lord our
Maker;
⁷for he is our God
and we are the people of his
pasture,
the flock under his care.

Today, if you hear his voice,
⁸   do not harden your hearts as you
did at Meribah,ᵃ
as you did that day at Massahᵇ in
the desert,
⁹where your fathers tested and tried
me,
though they had seen what I did.
¹⁰For forty years I was angry with that
generation;
I said, "They are a people whose
hearts go astray,
and they have not known my ways."
¹¹So I declared on oath in my anger,
"They shall never enter my rest."

Psalm 96

¹Sing to the Lord a new song;
sing to the Lord, all the earth.
²Sing to the Lord, praise his name;
proclaim his salvation day after day.
³Declare his glory among the nations,
his marvelous deeds among all
peoples.

⁴For great is the Lord and most worthy
of praise;
he is to be feared above all gods.
⁵For all the gods of the nations are
idols,
but the Lord made the heavens.
⁶Splendor and majesty are before him;
strength and glory are in his
sanctuary.

⁷Ascribe to the Lord, O families of
nations,
ascribe to the Lord glory and
strength.
⁸Ascribe to the Lord the glory due his
name;
bring an offering and come into his
courts.
⁹Worship the Lord in the splendor of
hisᶜ holiness;
tremble before him, all the earth.

¹⁰Say among the nations, "The Lord
reigns."
The world is firmly established, it
cannot be moved;

he will judge the peoples with
equity.
¹¹Let the heavens rejoice, let the earth
be glad;
let the sea resound, and all that is
in it;
¹²   let the fields be jubilant, and
everything in them.
Then all the trees of the forest will
sing for joy;
¹³   they will sing before the Lord, for
he comes,
he comes to judge the earth.
He will judge the world in
righteousness
and the peoples in his truth.

Psalm 97

¹The Lord reigns, let the earth be glad;
let the distant shores rejoice.

²Clouds and thick darkness surround
him;
righteousness and justice are the
foundation of his throne.
³Fire goes before him
and consumes his foes on every
side.
⁴His lightning lights up the world;
the earth sees and trembles.
⁵The mountains melt like wax before
the Lord,
before the Lord of all the earth.
⁶The heavens proclaim his
righteousness,
and all the peoples see his glory.

⁷All who worship images are put to
shame,
those who boast in idols—
worship him, all you gods!

⁸Zion hears and rejoices
and the villages of Judah are glad
because of your judgments, O Lord.
⁹For you, O Lord, are the Most High
over all the earth;
you are exalted far above all gods.

¹⁰Let those who love the Lord hate evil,
for he guards the lives of his
faithful ones
and delivers them from the hand of
the wicked.
¹¹Light is shed upon the righteous
and joy on the upright in heart.
¹²Rejoice in the Lord, you who are
righteous,
and praise his holy name.

ᵃ8 Meribah means quarreling.   ᵇ8 Massah means testing.   ᶜ9 Or Lord with the splendor of

Psalm 98

A psalm.

¹Sing to the LORD a new song,
  for he has done marvelous things;
his right hand and his holy arm
  have worked salvation for him.
²The LORD has made his salvation
    known
  and revealed his righteousness to
    the nations.
³He has remembered his love
  and his faithfulness to the house of
    Israel;
all the ends of the earth have seen
  the salvation of our God.

⁴Shout for joy to the LORD, all the
    earth,
  burst into jubilant song with music;
⁵make music to the LORD with the
    harp,
  with the harp and the sound of
    singing,
⁶with trumpets and the blast of the
    ram's horn—
  shout for joy before the LORD, the
    King.

⁷Let the sea resound, and everything
    in it,
  the world, and all who live in it.
⁸Let the rivers clap their hands,
  let the mountains sing together for
    joy;
⁹let them sing before the LORD,
  for he comes to judge the earth.
He will judge the world in
    righteousness
  and the peoples with equity.

Psalm 99

¹The LORD reigns,
  let the nations tremble;
he sits enthroned between the
    cherubim,
  let the earth shake.
²Great is the LORD in Zion;
  he is exalted over all the nations.
³Let them praise your great and
    awesome name—
  he is holy.

⁴The King is mighty, he loves justice—
  you have established equity;
in Jacob you have done
  what is just and right.
⁵Exalt the LORD our God

and worship at his footstool;
  he is holy.

⁶Moses and Aaron were among his
    priests,
  Samuel was among those who
    called on his name;
they called on the LORD
  and he answered them.
⁷He spoke to them from the pillar of
    cloud;
  they kept his statutes and the
    decrees he gave them.

⁸O LORD our God,
  you answered them;
you were to Israelᵃ a forgiving God,
  though you punished their
    misdeeds.ᵇ
⁹Exalt the LORD our God
  and worship at his holy mountain,
for the LORD our God is holy.

Psalm 100

A psalm. For giving thanks.

¹Shout for joy to the LORD, all the
    earth.
² Worship the LORD with gladness;
  come before him with joyful songs.
³Know that the LORD is God.
  It is he who made us, and we are
    hisᶜ;
  we are his people, the sheep of his
    pasture.

⁴Enter his gates with thanksgiving
  and his courts with praise;
give thanks to him and praise his
    name.
⁵For the LORD is good and his love
  endures forever;
his faithfulness continues through
    all generations.

Psalm 101

Of David. A psalm.

¹I will sing of your love and justice;
  to you, O LORD, I will sing praise.
²I will be careful to lead a blameless
    life—
  when will you come to me?

I will walk in my house
  with blameless heart.
³I will set before my eyes
  no vile thing.

ᵃ8 Hebrew *them*   ᵇ8 Or *I an avenger of the wrongs done to them*   ᶜ3 Or *and not we ourselves*

The deeds of faithless men I hate;
  they will not cling to me.
⁴Men of perverse heart shall be far
    from me;
  I will have nothing to do with evil.

⁵Whoever slanders his neighbor in
    secret,
  him will I put to silence;
whoever has haughty eyes and a
    proud heart,
  him will I not endure.

⁶My eyes will be on the faithful in the
    land,
  that they may dwell with me;
he whose walk is blameless
  will minister to me.

⁷No one who practices deceit
  will dwell in my house;
no one who speaks falsely
  will stand in my presence.

⁸Every morning I will put to silence
  all the wicked in the land;
I will cut off every evildoer
  from the city of the LORD.

Psalm 102

*A prayer of an afflicted man. When he is
faint and pours out his lament before
the LORD.*

¹Hear my prayer, O LORD;
  let my cry for help come to you.
²Do not hide your face from me
  when I am in distress.
Turn your ear to me;
  when I call, answer me quickly.

³For my days vanish like smoke;
  my bones burn like glowing embers.
⁴My heart is blighted and withered like
    grass;
  I forget to eat my food.
⁵Because of my loud groaning
  I am reduced to skin and bones.
⁶I am like a desert owl,
  like an owl among the ruins.
⁷I lie awake; I have become
  like a bird alone on a roof.
⁸All day long my enemies taunt me;
  those who rail against me use my
    name as a curse.
⁹For I eat ashes as my food
  and mingle my drink with tears
¹⁰because of your great wrath,
  for you have taken me up and
    thrown me aside.

¹¹My days are like the evening shadow;
  I wither away like grass.

¹²But you, O LORD, sit enthroned
    forever;
  your renown endures through all
    generations.
¹³You will arise and have compassion
    on Zion,
  for it is time to show favor to her;
  the appointed time has come.
¹⁴For her stones are dear to your
    servants;
  her very dust moves them to pity.
¹⁵The nations will fear the name of the
    LORD,
  all the kings of the earth will revere
    your glory.
¹⁶For the LORD will rebuild Zion
  and appear in his glory.
¹⁷He will respond to the prayer of the
    destitute;
  he will not despise their plea.

¹⁸Let this be written for a future
    generation,
  that a people not yet created may
    praise the LORD:
¹⁹"The LORD looked down from his
    sanctuary on high,
  from heaven he viewed the earth,
²⁰to hear the groans of the prisoners
  and release those condemned to
    death."
²¹So the name of the LORD will be
    declared in Zion
  and his praise in Jerusalem
²²when the peoples and the kingdoms
    assemble to worship the LORD.

²³In the course of my life*ᵃ* he broke my
    strength;
  he cut short my days.
²⁴So I said:
  "Do not take me away, O my God,
    in the midst of my days;
  your years go on through all
    generations.
²⁵In the beginning you laid the
    foundations of the earth,
  and the heavens are the work of
    your hands.
²⁶They will perish, but you remain;
  they will all wear out like a
    garment.
Like clothing you will change them
  and they will be discarded.
²⁷But you remain the same,
  and your years will never end.

ᵃ23 Or By his power

²⁸The children of your servants will live
in your presence;
their descendants will be
established before you."

Psalm 103

Of David.

¹Praise the LORD, O my soul;
all my inmost being, praise his holy
name.
²Praise the LORD, O my soul,
and forget not all his benefits—
³who forgives all your sins
and heals all your diseases,
⁴who redeems your life from the pit
and crowns you with love and
compassion,
⁵who satisfies your desires with good
things
so that your youth is renewed like
the eagle's.

⁶The LORD works righteousness
and justice for all the oppressed.

⁷He made known his ways to Moses,
his deeds to the people of Israel:
⁸The LORD is compassionate and
gracious,
slow to anger, abounding in love.
⁹He will not always accuse,
nor will he harbor his anger forever;
¹⁰he does not treat us as our sins
deserve
or repay us according to our
iniquities.
¹¹For as high as the heavens are above
the earth,
so great is his love for those who
fear him;
¹²as far as the east is from the west,
so far has he removed our
transgressions from us.
¹³As a father has compassion on his
children,
so the LORD has compassion on
those who fear him;
¹⁴for he knows how we are formed,
he remembers that we are dust.
¹⁵As for man, his days are like grass,
he flourishes like a flower of the
field;
¹⁶the wind blows over it and it is gone,
and its place remembers it no
more.
¹⁷But from everlasting to everlasting

the LORD's love is with those who
fear him,
and his righteousness with their
children's children—
¹⁸with those who keep his covenant
and remember to obey his precepts.

¹⁹The LORD has established his throne
in heaven,
and his kingdom rules over all.

²⁰Praise the LORD, you his angels,
you mighty ones who do his
bidding,
who obey his word.
²¹Praise the LORD, all his heavenly
hosts,
you his servants who do his will.
²²Praise the LORD, all his works
everywhere in his dominion.

Praise the LORD, O my soul.

Psalm 104

¹Praise the LORD, O my soul.

O LORD my God, you are very great;
you are clothed with splendor and
majesty.
²He wraps himself in light as with a
garment;
he stretches out the heavens like a
tent
³ and lays the beams of his upper
chambers on their waters.
He makes the clouds his chariot
and rides on the wings of the wind.
⁴He makes winds his messengers,ª
flames of fire his servants.

⁵He set the earth on its foundations;
it can never be moved.
⁶You covered it with the deep as with
a garment;
the waters stood above the
mountains.
⁷But at your rebuke the waters fled,
at the sound of your thunder they
took to flight;
⁸they flowed over the mountains,
they went down into the valleys,
to the place you assigned for them.
⁹You set a boundary they cannot cross;
never again will they cover the
earth.

¹⁰He makes springs pour water into the
ravines;
it flows between the mountains.

ª4 Or angels

VERSE FOR THE DAY: Psalm 103:3	*AUTHOR:* Janice Kempe	*PASSAGE FOR THE DAY:* Psalm 103:1–22

Time With Daddy

KEVIN and I walked Krista to kindergarten today. Her school is up and over a large hill and through a woods, so we noticed each flower and green leaf that told us spring was near and listened to the birds that had returned after a long, cold winter.

After the good-by kisses Kevin and I began our walk back up and over the big hill. He was fascinated by the selection of rocks and sticks and immediately began gathering a collection. Our progress was slow because we had to stop every few steps to retrieve dropped treasures. The capacity of his two hands just wasn't enough to accommodate the desires of his curious little mind! He had no more time for noticing birds and flowers. With grim determination, he tended to the safe passage of his wonderful new collection.

I couldn't understand why each stone was so special, nor why he needed so many sticks, but he guarded them with great care and knew instantly if he had dropped one.

Upon reaching our front door, Kevin and I were both exhausted!

He struggled up the front steps through the front door. But suddenly he let go of his precious treasures, and they fell to the front hall floor. His determined scowl melted into a wide grin. He ran off as if the things he had struggled to bring home had lost their value. Kevin had seen something far more important, and immediately his focus had changed to a new center of attention—Daddy!

I long to keep in mind that picture of my little boy dropping his burdensome treasures to run to his father. I too get burdened down by my treasures. My house, my belongings, my responsibilities, and all the things I've spent so much time and energy acquiring seem to take me over sometimes. I find myself attending to their care with an overwhelming single-mindedness. Sometimes I need to see God and do more than just acknowledge his presence. I need to drop everything else and run to him. I need to forsake the housework, the shopping, and the thousand other things that occupy my time, and go to him for a time of togetherness.

Additional Scripture Readings:
Luke 10:38–42; John 21:4–7

*Go to page 632 for your next
devotional reading.*

11They give water to all the beasts of
the field;
the wild donkeys quench their
thirst.
12The birds of the air nest by the
waters;
they sing among the branches.
13He waters the mountains from his
upper chambers;
the earth is satisfied by the fruit of
his work.
14He makes grass grow for the cattle,
and plants for man to cultivate—
bringing forth food from the earth:
15wine that gladdens the heart of man,
oil to make his face shine,
and bread that sustains his heart.
16The trees of the LORD are well
watered,
the cedars of Lebanon that he
planted.
17There the birds make their nests;
the stork has its home in the pine
trees.
18The high mountains belong to the
wild goats;
the crags are a refuge for the
coneys.a

19The moon marks off the seasons,
and the sun knows when to go
down.
20You bring darkness, it becomes night,
and all the beasts of the forest
prowl.
21The lions roar for their prey
and seek their food from God.
22The sun rises, and they steal away;
they return and lie down in their
dens.
23Then man goes out to his work,
to his labor until evening.

24How many are your works, O LORD!
In wisdom you made them all;
the earth is full of your creatures.
25There is the sea, vast and spacious,
teeming with creatures beyond
number—
living things both large and small.
26There the ships go to and fro,
and the leviathan, which you
formed to frolic there.

27These all look to you
to give them their food at the
proper time.
28When you give it to them,

they gather it up;
when you open your hand,
they are satisfied with good things.
29When you hide your face,
they are terrified;
when you take away their breath,
they die and return to the dust.
30When you send your Spirit,
they are created,
and you renew the face of the
earth.

31May the glory of the LORD endure
forever;
may the LORD rejoice in his works—
32he who looks at the earth, and it
trembles,
who touches the mountains, and
they smoke.

33I will sing to the LORD all my life;
I will sing praise to my God as long
as I live.
34May my meditation be pleasing to
him,
as I rejoice in the LORD.
35But may sinners vanish from the earth
and the wicked be no more.

Praise the LORD, O my soul.

Praise the LORD.b

Psalm 105

1Give thanks to the LORD, call on his
name;
make known among the nations
what he has done.
2Sing to him, sing praise to him;
tell of all his wonderful acts.
3Glory in his holy name;
let the hearts of those who seek the
LORD rejoice.
4Look to the LORD and his strength;
seek his face always.

5Remember the wonders he has done,
his miracles, and the judgments he
pronounced,
6O descendants of Abraham his
servant,
O sons of Jacob, his chosen ones.
7He is the LORD our God;
his judgments are in all the earth.

8He remembers his covenant forever,
the word he commanded, for a
thousand generations,
9the covenant he made with Abraham,

a18 That is, the hyrax or rock badger   b35 Hebrew Hallelu Yah; in the Septuagint this line stands at
the beginning of Psalm 105.

the oath he swore to Isaac.
¹⁰He confirmed it to Jacob as a decree,
　to Israel as an everlasting covenant:
¹¹"To you I will give the land of Canaan
　as the portion you will inherit."

¹²When they were but few in number,
　few indeed, and strangers in it,
¹³they wandered from nation to nation,
　from one kingdom to another.
¹⁴He allowed no one to oppress them;
　for their sake he rebuked kings:
¹⁵"Do not touch my anointed ones;
　do my prophets no harm."

¹⁶He called down famine on the land
　and destroyed all their supplies of
　　food;
¹⁷and he sent a man before them—
　Joseph, sold as a slave.
¹⁸They bruised his feet with shackles,
　his neck was put in irons,
¹⁹till what he foretold came to pass,
　till the word of the Lord proved
　　him true.
²⁰The king sent and released him,
　the ruler of peoples set him free.
²¹He made him master of his
　　household,
　ruler over all he possessed,
²²to instruct his princes as he pleased
　and teach his elders wisdom.

²³Then Israel entered Egypt;
　Jacob lived as an alien in the land
　　of Ham.
²⁴The Lord made his people very
　　fruitful;
　he made them too numerous for
　　their foes,
²⁵whose hearts he turned to hate his
　　people,
　to conspire against his servants.
²⁶He sent Moses his servant,
　and Aaron, whom he had chosen.
²⁷They performed his miraculous signs
　　among them,
　his wonders in the land of Ham.
²⁸He sent darkness and made the land
　　dark—
　for had they not rebelled against
　　his words?
²⁹He turned their waters into blood,
　causing their fish to die.
³⁰Their land teemed with frogs,
　which went up into the bedrooms
　　of their rulers.
³¹He spoke, and there came swarms of
　　flies,

and gnats throughout their country.
³²He turned their rain into hail,
　with lightning throughout their
　　land;
³³he struck down their vines and fig
　　trees
　and shattered the trees of their
　　country.
³⁴He spoke, and the locusts came,
　grasshoppers without number;
³⁵they ate up every green thing in their
　　land,
　ate up the produce of their soil.
³⁶Then he struck down all the firstborn
　　in their land,
　the firstfruits of all their manhood.

³⁷He brought out Israel, laden with
　　silver and gold,
　and from among their tribes no one
　　faltered.
³⁸Egypt was glad when they left,
　because dread of Israel had fallen
　　on them.
³⁹He spread out a cloud as a covering,
　and a fire to give light at night.
⁴⁰They asked, and he brought them
　　quail
　and satisfied them with the bread
　　of heaven.
⁴¹He opened the rock, and water
　　gushed out;
　like a river it flowed in the desert.

⁴²For he remembered his holy promise
　given to his servant Abraham.
⁴³He brought out his people with
　　rejoicing,
　his chosen ones with shouts of joy;
⁴⁴he gave them the lands of the
　　nations,
　and they fell heir to what others
　　had toiled for—
⁴⁵that they might keep his precepts
　and observe his laws.

Praise the Lord.ᵃ

Psalm 106

¹Praise the Lord.ᵇ

Give thanks to the Lord, for he is
　　good;
　his love endures forever.
²Who can proclaim the mighty acts of
　　the Lord
　or fully declare his praise?
³Blessed are they who maintain
　　justice,

ᵃ45 Hebrew Hallelu Yah   ᵇ1 Hebrew Hallelu Yah; also in verse 48

who constantly do what is right.
⁴Remember me, O LORD, when you
show favor to your people,
come to my aid when you save
them,
⁵that I may enjoy the prosperity of
your chosen ones,
that I may share in the joy of your
nation
and join your inheritance in giving
praise.

⁶We have sinned, even as our fathers
did;
we have done wrong and acted
wickedly.
⁷When our fathers were in Egypt,
they gave no thought to your
miracles;
they did not remember your many
kindnesses,
and they rebelled by the sea, the
Red Sea.ᵃ
⁸Yet he saved them for his name's
sake,
to make his mighty power known.
⁹He rebuked the Red Sea, and it dried
up;
he led them through the depths as
through a desert.
¹⁰He saved them from the hand of the
foe;
from the hand of the enemy he
redeemed them.
¹¹The waters covered their adversaries;
not one of them survived.
¹²Then they believed his promises
and sang his praise.

¹³But they soon forgot what he had
done
and did not wait for his counsel.
¹⁴In the desert they gave in to their
craving;
in the wasteland they put God to
the test.
¹⁵So he gave them what they asked for,
but sent a wasting disease upon
them.

¹⁶In the camp they grew envious of
Moses
and of Aaron, who was consecrated
to the LORD.
¹⁷The earth opened up and swallowed
Dathan;
it buried the company of Abiram.
¹⁸Fire blazed among their followers;

a flame consumed the wicked.

¹⁹At Horeb they made a calf
and worshiped an idol cast from
metal.
²⁰They exchanged their Glory
for an image of a bull, which eats
grass.
²¹They forgot the God who saved them,
who had done great things in
Egypt,
²²miracles in the land of Ham
and awesome deeds by the Red
Sea.
²³So he said he would destroy them—
had not Moses, his chosen one,
stood in the breach before him
to keep his wrath from destroying
them.

²⁴Then they despised the pleasant land;
they did not believe his promise.
²⁵They grumbled in their tents
and did not obey the LORD.
²⁶So he swore to them with uplifted
hand
that he would make them fall in
the desert,
²⁷make their descendants fall among
the nations
and scatter them throughout the
lands.

²⁸They yoked themselves to the Baal of
Peor
and ate sacrifices offered to lifeless
gods;
²⁹they provoked the LORD to anger by
their wicked deeds,
and a plague broke out among
them.
³⁰But Phinehas stood up and
intervened,
and the plague was checked.
³¹This was credited to him as
righteousness
for endless generations to come.

³²By the waters of Meribah they
angered the LORD,
and trouble came to Moses because
of them;
³³for they rebelled against the Spirit of
God,
and rash words came from Moses'
lips.ᵇ

³⁴They did not destroy the peoples
as the LORD had commanded them,

ᵃ7 Hebrew *Yam Suph*; that is, Sea of Reeds; also in verses 9 and 22   ᵇ33 Or *against his spirit, / and rash words came from his lips*

³⁵but they mingled with the nations
  and adopted their customs.
³⁶They worshiped their idols,
  which became a snare to them.
³⁷They sacrificed their sons
  and their daughters to demons.
³⁸They shed innocent blood,
  the blood of their sons and
    daughters,
  whom they sacrificed to the idols of
    Canaan,
  and the land was desecrated by
    their blood.
³⁹They defiled themselves by what they
    did;
  by their deeds they prostituted
    themselves.

⁴⁰Therefore the LORD was angry with his
    people
  and abhorred his inheritance.
⁴¹He handed them over to the nations,
  and their foes ruled over them.
⁴²Their enemies oppressed them
  and subjected them to their power.
⁴³Many times he delivered them,
  but they were bent on rebellion
  and they wasted away in their sin.

⁴⁴But he took note of their distress
  when he heard their cry;
⁴⁵for their sake he remembered his
    covenant
  and out of his great love he
    relented.
⁴⁶He caused them to be pitied
  by all who held them captive.

⁴⁷Save us, O LORD our God,
  and gather us from the nations,
  that we may give thanks to your holy
    name
  and glory in your praise.

⁴⁸Praise be to the LORD, the God of
    Israel,
  from everlasting to everlasting.
Let all the people say, "Amen!"

Praise the LORD.

BOOK V

Psalms 107–150

Psalm 107

¹Give thanks to the LORD, for he is
    good;
  his love endures forever.

²Let the redeemed of the LORD say
    this—
  those he redeemed from the hand
    of the foe,
³those he gathered from the lands,
  from east and west, from north and
    south. ᵃ

⁴Some wandered in desert wastelands,
  finding no way to a city where they
    could settle.
⁵They were hungry and thirsty,
  and their lives ebbed away.
⁶Then they cried out to the LORD in
    their trouble,
  and he delivered them from their
    distress.
⁷He led them by a straight way
  to a city where they could settle.
⁸Let them give thanks to the LORD for
    his unfailing love
  and his wonderful deeds for men,
⁹for he satisfies the thirsty
  and fills the hungry with good
    things.

¹⁰Some sat in darkness and the deepest
    gloom,
  prisoners suffering in iron chains,
¹¹for they had rebelled against the
    words of God
  and despised the counsel of the
    Most High.
¹²So he subjected them to bitter labor;
  they stumbled, and there was no
    one to help.
¹³Then they cried to the LORD in their
    trouble,
  and he saved them from their
    distress.
¹⁴He brought them out of darkness and
    the deepest gloom
  and broke away their chains.
¹⁵Let them give thanks to the LORD for
    his unfailing love
  and his wonderful deeds for men,
¹⁶for he breaks down gates of bronze
  and cuts through bars of iron.

¹⁷Some became fools through their
    rebellious ways
  and suffered affliction because of
    their iniquities.
¹⁸They loathed all food
  and drew near the gates of death.
¹⁹Then they cried to the LORD in their
    trouble,
  and he saved them from their
    distress.

ᵃ3 *Hebrew* north and the sea

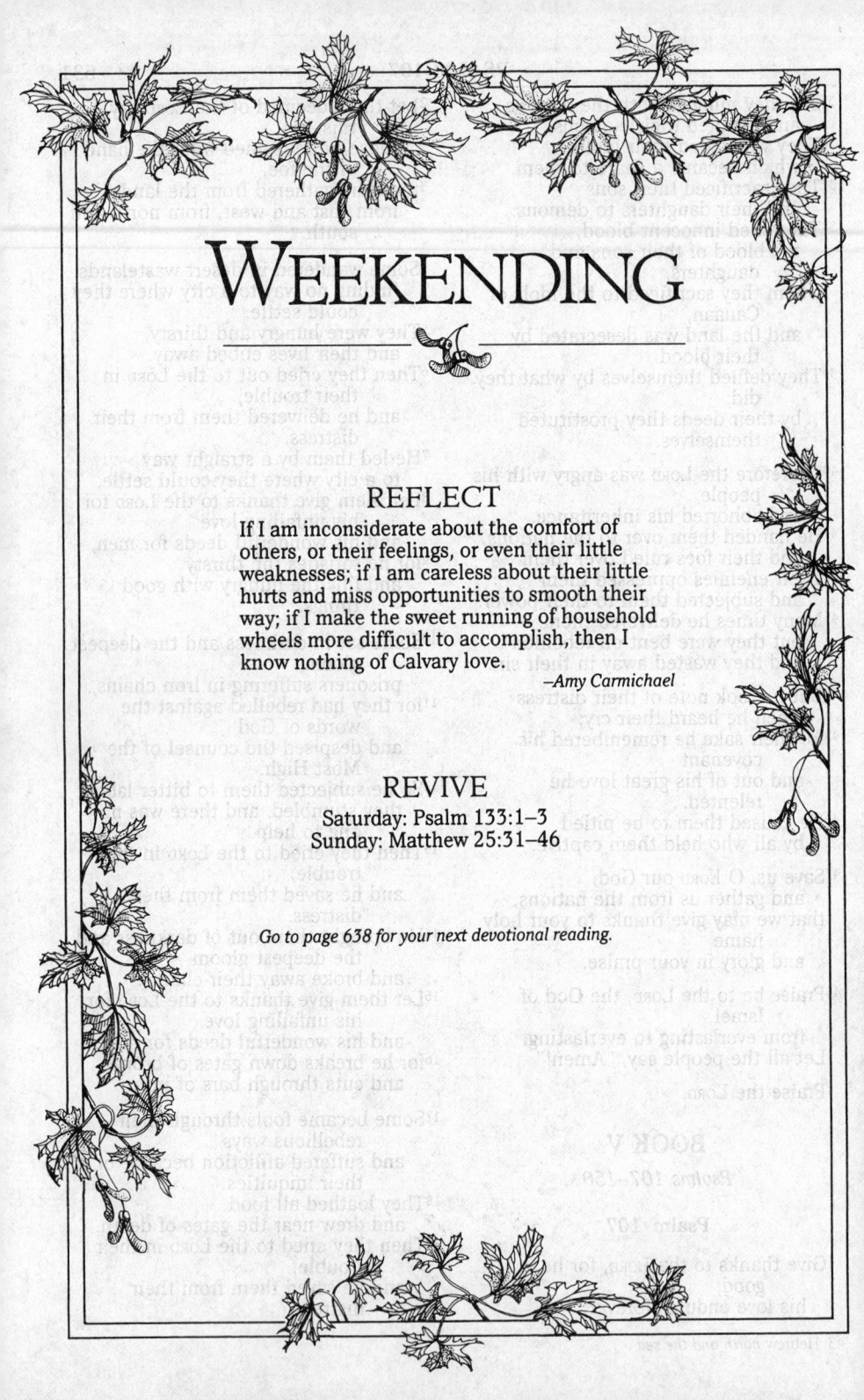

WEEKENDING

REFLECT

If I am inconsiderate about the comfort of
others, or their feelings, or even their little
weaknesses; if I am careless about their little
hurts and miss opportunities to smooth their
way; if I make the sweet running of household
wheels more difficult to accomplish, then I
know nothing of Calvary love.

—Amy Carmichael

REVIVE

Saturday: Psalm 133:1–3
Sunday: Matthew 25:31–46

Go to page 638 for your next devotional reading.

²⁰He sent forth his word and healed
     them;
   he rescued them from the grave.
²¹Let them give thanks to the LORD for
     his unfailing love
   and his wonderful deeds for men.
²²Let them sacrifice thank offerings
   and tell of his works with songs of
     joy.

²³Others went out on the sea in ships;
   they were merchants on the mighty
     waters.
²⁴They saw the works of the LORD,
   his wonderful deeds in the deep.
²⁵For he spoke and stirred up a tempest
   that lifted high the waves.
²⁶They mounted up to the heavens and
     went down to the depths;
   in their peril their courage melted
     away.
²⁷They reeled and staggered like
     drunken men;
   they were at their wits' end.
²⁸Then they cried out to the LORD in
     their trouble,
   and he brought them out of their
     distress.
²⁹He stilled the storm to a whisper;
   the waves of the sea were hushed.
³⁰They were glad when it grew calm,
   and he guided them to their desired
     haven.
³¹Let them give thanks to the LORD for
     his unfailing love
   and his wonderful deeds for men.
³²Let them exalt him in the assembly
     of the people
   and praise him in the council of
     the elders.

³³He turned rivers into a desert,
   flowing springs into thirsty ground,
³⁴and fruitful land into a salt waste,
   because of the wickedness of those
     who lived there.
³⁵He turned the desert into pools of
     water
   and the parched ground into
     flowing springs;
³⁶there he brought the hungry to live,
   and they founded a city where they
     could settle.
³⁷They sowed fields and planted
     vineyards
   that yielded a fruitful harvest;
³⁸he blessed them, and their numbers
     greatly increased,
   and he did not let their herds
     diminish.

³⁹Then their numbers decreased, and
     they were humbled
   by oppression, calamity and sorrow;
⁴⁰he who pours contempt on nobles
   made them wander in a trackless
     waste.
⁴¹But he lifted the needy out of their
     affliction
   and increased their families like
     flocks.
⁴²The upright see and rejoice,
   but all the wicked shut their
     mouths.

⁴³Whoever is wise, let him heed these
     things
   and consider the great love of the
     LORD.

Psalm 108

A song. A psalm of David.

¹My heart is steadfast, O God;
   I will sing and make music with all
     my soul.
²Awake, harp and lyre!
   I will awaken the dawn.
³I will praise you, O LORD, among the
     nations;
   I will sing of you among the
     peoples.
⁴For great is your love, higher than the
     heavens;
   your faithfulness reaches to the
     skies.
⁵Be exalted, O God, above the
     heavens,
   and let your glory be over all the
     earth.

⁶Save us and help us with your right
     hand,
   that those you love may be
     delivered.
⁷God has spoken from his sanctuary:
   "In triumph I will parcel out
     Shechem
   and measure off the Valley of
     Succoth.
⁸Gilead is mine, Manasseh is mine;
   Ephraim is my helmet,
   Judah my scepter.
⁹Moab is my washbasin,
   upon Edom I toss my sandal;
   over Philistia I shout in triumph."

¹⁰Who will bring me to the fortified
     city?
   Who will lead me to Edom?

[11]Is it not you, O God, you who have
   rejected us
   and no longer go out with our
      armies?
[12]Give us aid against the enemy,
   for the help of man is worthless.
[13]With God we will gain the victory,
   and he will trample down our
      enemies.

Psalm 109

For the director of music. Of David.
A psalm.

[1]O God, whom I praise,
   do not remain silent,
[2]for wicked and deceitful men
   have opened their mouths against
      me;
   they have spoken against me with
      lying tongues.
[3]With words of hatred they surround
      me;
   they attack me without cause.
[4]In return for my friendship they
      accuse me,
   but I am a man of prayer.
[5]They repay me evil for good,
   and hatred for my friendship.

[6]Appoint[a] an evil man[b] to oppose
      him;
   let an accuser[c] stand at his right
      hand.
[7]When he is tried, let him be found
      guilty,
   and may his prayers condemn him.
[8]May his days be few;
   may another take his place of
      leadership.
[9]May his children be fatherless
   and his wife a widow.
[10]May his children be wandering
      beggars;
   may they be driven[d] from their
      ruined homes.
[11]May a creditor seize all he has;
   may strangers plunder the fruits of
      his labor.
[12]May no one extend kindness to him
   or take pity on his fatherless
      children.
[13]May his descendants be cut off,
   their names blotted out from the
      next generation.
[14]May the iniquity of his fathers be
   remembered before the LORD;

may the sin of his mother never be
   blotted out.
[15]May their sins always remain before
      the LORD,
   that he may cut off the memory of
      them from the earth.

[16]For he never thought of doing a
      kindness,
   but hounded to death the poor
   and the needy and the
      brokenhearted.
[17]He loved to pronounce a curse —
   may it[e] come on him;
   he found no pleasure in blessing —
   may it be[f] far from him.
[18]He wore cursing as his garment;
   it entered into his body like water,
   into his bones like oil.
[19]May it be like a cloak wrapped about
      him,
   like a belt tied forever around him.
[20]May this be the LORD's payment to my
      accusers,
   to those who speak evil of me.

[21]But you, O Sovereign LORD,
   deal well with me for your name's
      sake;
   out of the goodness of your love,
      deliver me.
[22]For I am poor and needy,
   and my heart is wounded within
      me.
[23]I fade away like an evening shadow;
   I am shaken off like a locust.
[24]My knees give way from fasting;
   my body is thin and gaunt.
[25]I am an object of scorn to my
      accusers;
   when they see me, they shake their
      heads.

[26]Help me, O LORD my God;
   save me in accordance with your
      love.
[27]Let them know that it is your hand,
   that you, O LORD, have done it.
[28]They may curse, but you will bless;
   when they attack they will be put
      to shame,
   but your servant will rejoice.
[29]My accusers will be clothed with
      disgrace
   and wrapped in shame as in a
      cloak.

[30]With my mouth I will greatly extol
   the LORD;

a6 Or They say:, "Appoint (with quotation marks at the end of verse 19)   b6 Or the Evil One   c6 Or
let Satan   d10 Septuagint; Hebrew sought   e17 Or curse, / and it has   f17 Or blessing, / and it is

in the great throng I will praise
    him.
³¹For he stands at the right hand of the
    needy one,
    to save his life from those who
    condemn him.

Psalm 110

Of David. A psalm.

¹The LORD says to my Lord:
    "Sit at my right hand
until I make your enemies
    a footstool for your feet."

²The LORD will extend your mighty
    scepter from Zion;
    you will rule in the midst of your
    enemies.
³Your troops will be willing
    on your day of battle.
Arrayed in holy majesty,
    from the womb of the dawn
    you will receive the dew of your
    youth.ᵃ

⁴The LORD has sworn
    and will not change his mind:
"You are a priest forever,
    in the order of Melchizedek."

⁵The Lord is at your right hand;
    he will crush kings on the day of
    his wrath.
⁶He will judge the nations, heaping up
    the dead
    and crushing the rulers of the
    whole earth.
⁷He will drink from a brook beside the
    wayᵇ;
    therefore he will lift up his head.

Psalm 111ᶜ

¹Praise the LORD.ᵈ

I will extol the LORD with all my heart
    in the council of the upright and in
    the assembly.

²Great are the works of the LORD;
    they are pondered by all who
    delight in them.
³Glorious and majestic are his deeds,
    and his righteousness endures
    forever.

⁴He has caused his wonders to be
    remembered;
    the LORD is gracious and
    compassionate.
⁵He provides food for those who fear
    him;
    he remembers his covenant forever.
⁶He has shown his people the power of
    his works,
    giving them the lands of other
    nations.
⁷The works of his hands are faithful
    and just;
    all his precepts are trustworthy.
⁸They are steadfast for ever and ever,
    done in faithfulness and
    uprightness.
⁹He provided redemption for his
    people;
    he ordained his covenant forever—
    holy and awesome is his name.
¹⁰The fear of the LORD is the beginning
    of wisdom;
    all who follow his precepts have
    good understanding.
    To him belongs eternal praise.

Psalm 112ᶜ

¹Praise the LORD.ᵈ

Blessed is the man who fears the
    LORD,
    who finds great delight in his
    commands.

²His children will be mighty in the
    land;
    the generation of the upright will
    be blessed.
³Wealth and riches are in his house,
    and his righteousness endures
    forever.
⁴Even in darkness light dawns for the
    upright,
    for the gracious and compassionate
    and righteous man.ᵉ
⁵Good will come to him who is
    generous and lends freely,
    who conducts his affairs with
    justice.
⁶Surely he will never be shaken;
    a righteous man will be
    remembered forever.
⁷He will have no fear of bad news;

ᵃ3 Or / your young men will come to you like the dew
him in authority   ᶜThis psalm is an acrostic poem,
of the Hebrew alphabet.   ᵈ1 Hebrew Hallelu Yah
compassionate and righteous

ᵇ7 Or / The One who grants succession will set
the lines of which begin with the successive letters
ᵉ4 Or / for the LORD, is gracious and

his heart is steadfast, trusting in
  the LORD.
8His heart is secure, he will have no
    fear;
  in the end he will look in triumph
    on his foes.
9He has scattered abroad his gifts to
    the poor,
  his righteousness endures forever;
  his horn*a* will be lifted high in
    honor.

10The wicked man will see and be
    vexed,
  he will gnash his teeth and waste
    away;
  the longings of the wicked will
    come to nothing.

Psalm 113

1Praise the LORD.*b*

Praise, O servants of the LORD,
  praise the name of the LORD.
2Let the name of the LORD be praised,
  both now and forevermore.
3From the rising of the sun to the
    place where it sets,
  the name of the LORD is to be
    praised.

4The LORD is exalted over all the
    nations,
  his glory above the heavens.
5Who is like the LORD our God,
  the One who sits enthroned on
    high,
6who stoops down to look
  on the heavens and the earth?

7He raises the poor from the dust
  and lifts the needy from the ash
    heap;
8he seats them with princes,
  with the princes of their people.
9He settles the barren woman in her
    home
  as a happy mother of children.

Praise the LORD.

Psalm 114

1When Israel came out of Egypt,
  the house of Jacob from a people
    of foreign tongue,
2Judah became God's sanctuary,
  Israel his dominion.

3The sea looked and fled,

the Jordan turned back;
4the mountains skipped like rams,
  the hills like lambs.

5Why was it, O sea, that you fled,
  O Jordan, that you turned back,
6you mountains, that you skipped like
    rams,
  you hills, like lambs?

7Tremble, O earth, at the presence of
    the Lord,
  at the presence of the God of
    Jacob,
8who turned the rock into a pool,
  the hard rock into springs of water.

Psalm 115

1Not to us, O LORD, not to us
  but to your name be the glory,
  because of your love and
    faithfulness.

2Why do the nations say,
  "Where is their God?"
3Our God is in heaven;
  he does whatever pleases him.
4But their idols are silver and gold,
  made by the hands of men.
5They have mouths, but cannot speak,
  eyes, but they cannot see;
6they have ears, but cannot hear,
  noses, but they cannot smell;
7they have hands, but cannot feel,
  feet, but they cannot walk;
  nor can they utter a sound with
    their throats.
8Those who make them will be like
    them,
  and so will all who trust in them.

9O house of Israel, trust in the LORD—
  he is their help and shield.
10O house of Aaron, trust in the LORD—
  he is their help and shield.
11You who fear him, trust in the LORD—
  he is their help and shield.

12The LORD remembers us and will bless
    us:
  He will bless the house of Israel,
  he will bless the house of Aaron,
13he will bless those who fear the
    LORD—
  small and great alike.

14May the LORD make you increase,
  both you and your children.
15May you be blessed by the LORD,
  the Maker of heaven and earth.

---

a9 Horn here symbolizes dignity.   *b1* Hebrew *Hallelu Yah*; also in verse 9

¹⁶The highest heavens belong to the
    LORD,
  but the earth he has given to man.
¹⁷It is not the dead who praise the
    LORD,
  those who go down to silence;
¹⁸it is we who extol the LORD,
  both now and forevermore.

Praise the LORD.ᵃ

Psalm 116

¹I love the LORD, for he heard my
    voice;
  he heard my cry for mercy.
²Because he turned his ear to me,
  I will call on him as long as I live.

³The cords of death entangled me,
  the anguish of the graveᵇ came
    upon me;
  I was overcome by trouble and
    sorrow.
⁴Then I called on the name of the
    LORD:
  "O LORD, save me!"

⁵The LORD is gracious and righteous;
  our God is full of compassion.
⁶The LORD protects the simplehearted;
  when I was in great need, he saved
    me.

⁷Be at rest once more, O my soul,
  for the LORD has been good to you.

⁸For you, O LORD, have delivered my
    soul from death,
  my eyes from tears,
  my feet from stumbling,
⁹that I may walk before the LORD
  in the land of the living.
¹⁰I believed; thereforeᶜ I said,
  "I am greatly afflicted."
¹¹And in my dismay I said,
  "All men are liars."

¹²How can I repay the LORD
  for all his goodness to me?
¹³I will lift up the cup of salvation
  and call on the name of the LORD.
¹⁴I will fulfill my vows to the LORD
  in the presence of all his people.

¹⁵Precious in the sight of the LORD
  is the death of his saints.
¹⁶O LORD, truly I am your servant;
  I am your servant, the son of your
    maidservantᵈ;
  you have freed me from my chains.

¹⁷I will sacrifice a thank offering to you
  and call on the name of the LORD.
¹⁸I will fulfill my vows to the LORD
  in the presence of all his people,
¹⁹in the courts of the house of the
    LORD—
  in your midst, O Jerusalem.

Praise the LORD.ᵃ

Psalm 117

¹Praise the LORD, all you nations;
  extol him, all you peoples.
²For great is his love toward us,
  and the faithfulness of the LORD
    endures forever.

Praise the LORD.ᵃ

Psalm 118

¹Give thanks to the LORD, for he is
    good;
  his love endures forever.

²Let Israel say:
  "His love endures forever."
³Let the house of Aaron say:
  "His love endures forever."
⁴Let those who fear the LORD say:
  "His love endures forever."

⁵In my anguish I cried to the LORD,
  and he answered by setting me free.
⁶The LORD is with me; I will not be
    afraid.
  What can man do to me?
⁷The LORD is with me; he is my helper.
  I will look in triumph on my
    enemies.

⁸It is better to take refuge in the LORD
  than to trust in man.
⁹It is better to take refuge in the LORD
  than to trust in princes.

¹⁰All the nations surrounded me,
  but in the name of the LORD I cut
    them off.
¹¹They surrounded me on every side,
  but in the name of the LORD I cut
    them off.
¹²They swarmed around me like bees,
  but they died out as quickly as
    burning thorns;
  in the name of the LORD I cut them
    off.
¹³I was pushed back and about to fall,
  but the LORD helped me.

ᵃ18,19,2 Hebrew *Hallelu Yah*   ᵇ3 Hebrew *Sheol*   ᶜ10 Or *believed even when*   ᵈ16 Or *servant, your
faithful son*

VERSE FOR THE DAY:
Psalm 116:3

AUTHOR:
Carol L. Baldwin

PASSAGE FOR THE DAY:
Psalm 116:1–19

Comfort in Bereavement

"I FEEL like I could cry forever. I miss him so much that I actually hurt inside. Will my life ever be the same?"

Have you felt the deep sorrow of the mourning widow? If you have lost a child, parent, close relative or friend, perhaps you have also felt comfortless. Is there anyone who can minister to you when you feel overwhelmed with grief?

The psalmist shows that he identifies with the pain of the bereaved:

> The cords of death entangled me,
> the anguish of the grave came upon me;
> I was overcome by trouble and sorrow
> (Psalm 116:3).

Enveloped by emptiness, loneliness and stress, who does the psalmist turn to?

> I called on the name of the LORD:
> "O LORD, save me!' (Psalm 116:4).

He turns to the only one who will dry all of our tears (Isaiah 25:8); the one who carries all of our sorrows (Isaiah 53:4); the man acquainted with grief (Isaiah 53:3).

Likewise, we must turn to God and his Word for comfort in our times of sorrow. Without denying our pain, Scripture gives us a proper perspective, something we can easily lose in times of emotional trauma and crisis.

God's Word gives hope when we feel utterly alone and hopeless. We can take comfort in knowing that God does not allow a trial in our lives that is too great for us to bear (1 Corinthians 10:13). We can also be assured that death does not conquer those who die in Christ (1 Corinthians 15:22,53-56).

God is in charge of all things. Even the terrible destruction and the traumatic aftermath of death for those who mourn are under his lordship. God's Word and Spirit can comfort our grieving hearts so that we will be able to say with the psalmist:

> I may walk before the LORD
> in the land of the living . . .
> I am [his] servant. . . .
> Praise the LORD (Psalm 116:9,16,19).

Additional Scripture Readings:
2 Corinthians 1:3–4; 1 Thessalonians 4:13–18

Go to page 646 for your next devotional reading.

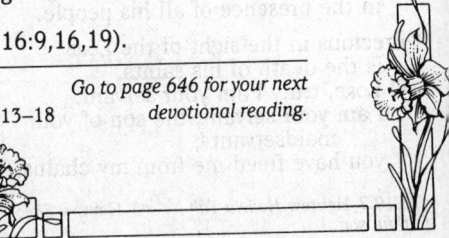

¹⁴The LORD is my strength and my song;
  he has become my salvation.

¹⁵Shouts of joy and victory
  resound in the tents of the
    righteous:
  "The LORD's right hand has done
    mighty things!
¹⁶ The LORD's right hand is lifted high;
  the LORD's right hand has done
    mighty things!"

¹⁷I will not die but live,
  and will proclaim what the LORD
    has done.
¹⁸The LORD has chastened me severely,
  but he has not given me over to
    death.

¹⁹Open for me the gates of
    righteousness;
  I will enter and give thanks to the
    LORD.
²⁰This is the gate of the LORD
  through which the righteous may
    enter.
²¹I will give you thanks, for you
    answered me;
  you have become my salvation.

²²The stone the builders rejected
  has become the capstone;
²³the LORD has done this,
  and it is marvelous in our eyes.
²⁴This is the day the LORD has made;
  let us rejoice and be glad in it.

²⁵O LORD, save us;
  O LORD, grant us success.
²⁶Blessed is he who comes in the name
    of the LORD.
  From the house of the LORD we
    bless you. ^a
²⁷The LORD is God,
  and he has made his light shine
    upon us.
  With boughs in hand, join in the
    festal procession
  up^b to the horns of the altar.

²⁸You are my God, and I will give you
    thanks;
  you are my God, and I will exalt
    you.

²⁹Give thanks to the LORD, for he is
    good;
  his love endures forever.

Psalm 119^c

א Aleph

¹Blessed are they whose ways are
    blameless,
  who walk according to the law of
    the LORD.
²Blessed are they who keep his
    statutes
  and seek him with all their heart.
³They do nothing wrong;
  they walk in his ways.
⁴You have laid down precepts
  that are to be fully obeyed.
⁵Oh, that my ways were steadfast
  in obeying your decrees!
⁶Then I would not be put to shame
  when I consider all your
    commands.
⁷I will praise you with an upright heart
  as I learn your righteous laws.
⁸I will obey your decrees;
  do not utterly forsake me.

ב Beth

⁹How can a young man keep his way
    pure?
  By living according to your word.
¹⁰I seek you with all my heart;
  do not let me stray from your
    commands.
¹¹I have hidden your word in my heart
  that I might not sin against you.
¹²Praise be to you, O LORD;
  teach me your decrees.
¹³With my lips I recount
  all the laws that come from your
    mouth.
¹⁴I rejoice in following your statutes
  as one rejoices in great riches.
¹⁵I meditate on your precepts
  and consider your ways.
¹⁶I delight in your decrees;
  I will not neglect your word.

ג Gimel

¹⁷Do good to your servant, and I will
    live;
  I will obey your word.
¹⁸Open my eyes that I may see
  wonderful things in your law.
¹⁹I am a stranger on earth;
  do not hide your commands from
    me.
²⁰My soul is consumed with longing
  for your laws at all times.

^a26 The Hebrew is plural.   ^b27 Or *Bind the festal sacrifice with ropes / and take it*   ^cThis psalm is
an acrostic poem; the verses of each stanza begin with the same letter of the Hebrew alphabet.

²¹You rebuke the arrogant, who are
    cursed
  and who stray from your
    commands.
²²Remove from me scorn and contempt,
  for I keep your statutes.
²³Though rulers sit together and slander
    me,
  your servant will meditate on your
    decrees.
²⁴Your statutes are my delight;
  they are my counselors.

ד   Daleth

²⁵I am laid low in the dust;
  preserve my life according to your
    word.
²⁶I recounted my ways and you
    answered me;
  teach me your decrees.
²⁷Let me understand the teaching of
    your precepts;
  then I will meditate on your
    wonders.
²⁸My soul is weary with sorrow;
  strengthen me according to your
    word.
²⁹Keep me from deceitful ways;
  be gracious to me through your law.
³⁰I have chosen the way of truth;
  I have set my heart on your laws.
³¹I hold fast to your statutes, O Lord;
  do not let me be put to shame.
³²I run in the path of your commands,
  for you have set my heart free.

ה   He

³³Teach me, O Lord, to follow your
    decrees;
  then I will keep them to the end.
³⁴Give me understanding, and I will
    keep your law
  and obey it with all my heart.
³⁵Direct me in the path of your
    commands,
  for there I find delight.
³⁶Turn my heart toward your statutes
  and not toward selfish gain.
³⁷Turn my eyes away from worthless
    things;
  preserve my life according to your
    word.ᵃ
³⁸Fulfill your promise to your servant,
  so that you may be feared.
³⁹Take away the disgrace I dread,
  for your laws are good.
⁴⁰How I long for your precepts!

Preserve my life in your
  righteousness.

ו   Waw

⁴¹May your unfailing love come to me,
    O Lord,
  your salvation according to your
    promise;
⁴²then I will answer the one who taunts
    me,
  for I trust in your word.
⁴³Do not snatch the word of truth from
    my mouth,
  for I have put my hope in your
    laws.
⁴⁴I will always obey your law,
  for ever and ever.
⁴⁵I will walk about in freedom,
  for I have sought out your precepts.
⁴⁶I will speak of your statutes before
    kings
  and will not be put to shame,
⁴⁷for I delight in your commands
  because I love them.
⁴⁸I lift up my hands toᵇ your
    commands, which I love,
  and I meditate on your decrees.

ז   Zayin

⁴⁹Remember your word to your servant,
  for you have given me hope.
⁵⁰My comfort in my suffering is this:
  Your promise preserves my life.
⁵¹The arrogant mock me without
    restraint,
  but I do not turn from your law.
⁵²I remember your ancient laws,
    O Lord,
  and I find comfort in them.
⁵³Indignation grips me because of the
    wicked,
  who have forsaken your law.
⁵⁴Your decrees are the theme of my
    song
  wherever I lodge.
⁵⁵In the night I remember your name,
    O Lord,
  and I will keep your law.
⁵⁶This has been my practice:
  I obey your precepts.

ח   Heth

⁵⁷You are my portion, O Lord;
  I have promised to obey your
    words.
⁵⁸I have sought your face with all my
    heart;

ᵃ37 Two manuscripts of the Masoretic Text and Dead Sea Scrolls; most manuscripts of the Masoretic
Text *life in your way*   ᵇ48 Or *for*

be gracious to me according to your
promise.
⁵⁹I have considered my ways
and have turned my steps to your
statutes.
⁶⁰I will hasten and not delay
to obey your commands.
⁶¹Though the wicked bind me with
ropes,
I will not forget your law.
⁶²At midnight I rise to give you thanks
for your righteous laws.
⁶³I am a friend to all who fear you,
to all who follow your precepts.
⁶⁴The earth is filled with your love,
O LORD;
teach me your decrees.

ט Teth

⁶⁵Do good to your servant
according to your word, O LORD.
⁶⁶Teach me knowledge and good
judgment,
for I believe in your commands.
⁶⁷Before I was afflicted I went astray,
but now I obey your word.
⁶⁸You are good, and what you do is
good;
teach me your decrees.
⁶⁹Though the arrogant have smeared
me with lies,
I keep your precepts with all my
heart.
⁷⁰Their hearts are callous and
unfeeling,
but I delight in your law.
⁷¹It was good for me to be afflicted
so that I might learn your decrees.
⁷²The law from your mouth is more
precious to me
than thousands of pieces of silver
and gold.

י Yodh

⁷³Your hands made me and formed me;
give me understanding to learn your
commands.
⁷⁴May those who fear you rejoice when
they see me,
for I have put my hope in your
word.
⁷⁵I know, O LORD, that your laws are
righteous,
and in faithfulness you have
afflicted me.
⁷⁶May your unfailing love be my
comfort,
according to your promise to your
servant.

⁷⁷Let your compassion come to me that
I may live,
for your law is my delight.
⁷⁸May the arrogant be put to shame for
wronging me without cause;
but I will meditate on your
precepts.
⁷⁹May those who fear you turn to me,
those who understand your
statutes.
⁸⁰May my heart be blameless toward
your decrees,
that I may not be put to shame.

כ Kaph

⁸¹My soul faints with longing for your
salvation,
but I have put my hope in your
word.
⁸²My eyes fail, looking for your promise;
I say, "When will you comfort me?"
⁸³Though I am like a wineskin in the
smoke,
I do not forget your decrees.
⁸⁴How long must your servant wait?
When will you punish my
persecutors?
⁸⁵The arrogant dig pitfalls for me,
contrary to your law.
⁸⁶All your commands are trustworthy;
help me, for men persecute me
without cause.
⁸⁷They almost wiped me from the earth,
but I have not forsaken your
precepts.
⁸⁸Preserve my life according to your
love,
and I will obey the statutes of your
mouth.

ל Lamedh

⁸⁹Your word, O LORD, is eternal;
it stands firm in the heavens.
⁹⁰Your faithfulness continues through
all generations;
you established the earth, and it
endures.
⁹¹Your laws endure to this day,
for all things serve you.
⁹²If your law had not been my delight,
I would have perished in my
affliction.
⁹³I will never forget your precepts,
for by them you have preserved my
life.
⁹⁴Save me, for I am yours;
I have sought out your precepts.
⁹⁵The wicked are waiting to destroy me,
but I will ponder your statutes.
⁹⁶To all perfection I see a limit;

but your commands are boundless.

מ Mem

97Oh, how I love your law!
   I meditate on it all day long.
98Your commands make me wiser than
      my enemies,
   for they are ever with me.
99I have more insight than all my
      teachers,
   for I meditate on your statutes.
100I have more understanding than the
      elders,
   for I obey your precepts.
101I have kept my feet from every evil
      path
   so that I might obey your word.
102I have not departed from your laws,
   for you yourself have taught me.
103How sweet are your words to my
      taste,
   sweeter than honey to my mouth!
104I gain understanding from your
      precepts;
   therefore I hate every wrong path.

נ Nun

105Your word is a lamp to my feet
   and a light for my path.
106I have taken an oath and confirmed
      it,
   that I will follow your righteous
      laws.
107I have suffered much;
   preserve my life, O Lord, according
      to your word.
108Accept, O Lord, the willing praise of
      my mouth,
   and teach me your laws.
109Though I constantly take my life in
      my hands,
   I will not forget your law.
110The wicked have set a snare for me,
   but I have not strayed from your
      precepts.
111Your statutes are my heritage forever;
   they are the joy of my heart.
112My heart is set on keeping your
      decrees
   to the very end.

ס Samekh

113I hate double-minded men,
   but I love your law.
114You are my refuge and my shield;
   I have put my hope in your word.
115Away from me, you evildoers,
   that I may keep the commands of
      my God!

116Sustain me according to your
      promise, and I will live;
   do not let my hopes be dashed.
117Uphold me, and I will be delivered;
   I will always have regard for your
      decrees.
118You reject all who stray from your
      decrees,
   for their deceitfulness is in vain.
119All the wicked of the earth you
      discard like dross;
   therefore I love your statutes.
120My flesh trembles in fear of you;
   I stand in awe of your laws.

ע Ayin

121I have done what is righteous and
      just;
   do not leave me to my oppressors.
122Ensure your servant's well-being;
   let not the arrogant oppress me.
123My eyes fail, looking for your
      salvation,
   looking for your righteous promise.
124Deal with your servant according to
      your love
   and teach me your decrees.
125I am your servant; give me
      discernment
   that I may understand your
      statutes.
126It is time for you to act, O Lord;
   your law is being broken.
127Because I love your commands
   more than gold, more than pure
      gold,
128and because I consider all your
      precepts right,
   I hate every wrong path.

פ Pe

129Your statutes are wonderful;
   therefore I obey them.
130The unfolding of your words gives
      light;
   it gives understanding to the
      simple.
131I open my mouth and pant,
   longing for your commands.
132Turn to me and have mercy on me,
   as you always do to those who love
      your name.
133Direct my footsteps according to
      your word;
   let no sin rule over me.
134Redeem me from the oppression of
      men,
   that I may obey your precepts.
135Make your face shine upon your
      servant

and teach me your decrees.
¹³⁶Streams of tears flow from my eyes,
for your law is not obeyed.

צ Tsadhe

¹³⁷Righteous are you, O LORD,
and your laws are right.
¹³⁸The statutes you have laid down are
righteous;
they are fully trustworthy.
¹³⁹My zeal wears me out,
for my enemies ignore your words.
¹⁴⁰Your promises have been thoroughly
tested,
and your servant loves them.
¹⁴¹Though I am lowly and despised,
I do not forget your precepts.
¹⁴²Your righteousness is everlasting
and your law is true.
¹⁴³Trouble and distress have come upon
me,
but your commands are my delight.
¹⁴⁴Your statutes are forever right;
give me understanding that I may
live.

ק Qoph

¹⁴⁵I call with all my heart; answer me,
O LORD,
and I will obey your decrees.
¹⁴⁶I call out to you; save me
and I will keep your statutes.
¹⁴⁷I rise before dawn and cry for help;
I have put my hope in your word.
¹⁴⁸My eyes stay open through the
watches of the night,
that I may meditate on your
promises.
¹⁴⁹Hear my voice in accordance with
your love;
preserve my life, O LORD, according
to your laws.
¹⁵⁰Those who devise wicked schemes
are near,
but they are far from your law.
¹⁵¹Yet you are near, O LORD,
and all your commands are true.
¹⁵²Long ago I learned from your
statutes
that you established them to last
forever.

ר Resh

¹⁵³Look upon my suffering and deliver
me,
for I have not forgotten your law.
¹⁵⁴Defend my cause and redeem me;
preserve my life according to your
promise.
¹⁵⁵Salvation is far from the wicked,
for they do not seek out your
decrees.
¹⁵⁶Your compassion is great, O LORD;
preserve my life according to your
laws.
¹⁵⁷Many are the foes who persecute me,
but I have not turned from your
statutes.
¹⁵⁸I look on the faithless with loathing,
for they do not obey your word.
¹⁵⁹See how I love your precepts;
preserve my life, O LORD, according
to your love.
¹⁶⁰All your words are true;
all your righteous laws are eternal.

ש Sin and Shin

¹⁶¹Rulers persecute me without cause,
but my heart trembles at your word.
¹⁶²I rejoice in your promise
like one who finds great spoil.
¹⁶³I hate and abhor falsehood
but I love your law.
¹⁶⁴Seven times a day I praise you
for your righteous laws.
¹⁶⁵Great peace have they who love your
law,
and nothing can make them
stumble.
¹⁶⁶I wait for your salvation, O LORD,
and I follow your commands.
¹⁶⁷I obey your statutes,
for I love them greatly.
¹⁶⁸I obey your precepts and your
statutes,
for all my ways are known to you.

ת Taw

¹⁶⁹May my cry come before you,
O LORD;
give me understanding according to
your word.
¹⁷⁰May my supplication come before
you;
deliver me according to your
promise.
¹⁷¹May my lips overflow with praise,
for you teach me your decrees.
¹⁷²May my tongue sing of your word,
for all your commands are
righteous.
¹⁷³May your hand be ready to help me,
for I have chosen your precepts.
¹⁷⁴I long for your salvation, O LORD,
and your law is my delight.
¹⁷⁵Let me live that I may praise you,
and may your laws sustain me.
¹⁷⁶I have strayed like a lost sheep.
Seek your servant,

for I have not forgotten your
    commands.

Psalm 120

A song of ascents.

¹I call on the LORD in my distress,
    and he answers me.
²Save me, O LORD, from lying lips
    and from deceitful tongues.

³What will he do to you,
    and what more besides, O deceitful
      tongue?
⁴He will punish you with a warrior's
      sharp arrows,
    with burning coals of the broom
      tree.

⁵Woe to me that I dwell in Meshech,
    that I live among the tents of
      Kedar!
⁶Too long have I lived
    among those who hate peace.
⁷I am a man of peace;
    but when I speak, they are for war.

Psalm 121

A song of ascents.

¹I lift up my eyes to the hills—
    where does my help come from?
²My help comes from the LORD,
    the Maker of heaven and earth.

³He will not let your foot slip—
    he who watches over you will not
      slumber;
⁴indeed, he who watches over Israel
    will neither slumber nor sleep.

⁵The LORD watches over you—
    the LORD is your shade at your right
      hand;
⁶the sun will not harm you by day,
    nor the moon by night.

⁷The LORD will keep you from all
      harm—
    he will watch over your life;
⁸the LORD will watch over your coming
      and going
    both now and forevermore.

Psalm 122

A song of ascents. Of David.

¹I rejoiced with those who said to me,
    "Let us go to the house of the
      LORD."
²Our feet are standing
    in your gates, O Jerusalem.

³Jerusalem is built like a city
    that is closely compacted together.
⁴That is where the tribes go up,
    the tribes of the LORD,
to praise the name of the LORD
    according to the statute given to
      Israel.
⁵There the thrones for judgment stand,
    the thrones of the house of David.

⁶Pray for the peace of Jerusalem:
    "May those who love you be secure.
⁷May there be peace within your walls
    and security within your citadels."
⁸For the sake of my brothers and
      friends,
    I will say, "Peace be within you."
⁹For the sake of the house of the LORD
      our God,
    I will seek your prosperity.

Psalm 123

A song of ascents.

¹I lift up my eyes to you,
    to you whose throne is in heaven.
²As the eyes of slaves look to the hand
    of their master,
    as the eyes of a maid look to the
      hand of her mistress,
so our eyes look to the LORD our God,
    till he shows us his mercy.

³Have mercy on us, O LORD, have
      mercy on us,
    for we have endured much
      contempt.
⁴We have endured much ridicule from
      the proud,
    much contempt from the arrogant.

Psalm 124

A song of ascents. Of David.

¹If the LORD had not been on our
      side—
    let Israel say—
²if the LORD had not been on our side
    when men attacked us,
³when their anger flared against us,
    they would have swallowed us alive;
⁴the flood would have engulfed us,
    the torrent would have swept over
      us,
⁵the raging waters
    would have swept us away.

⁶Praise be to the LORD,
  who has not let us be torn by their
    teeth.
⁷We have escaped like a bird
  out of the fowler's snare;
the snare has been broken,
  and we have escaped.
⁸Our help is in the name of the LORD,
  the Maker of heaven and earth.

Psalm 125

A song of ascents.

¹Those who trust in the LORD are like
    Mount Zion,
  which cannot be shaken but
    endures forever.
²As the mountains surround
    Jerusalem,
  so the LORD surrounds his people
    both now and forevermore.

³The scepter of the wicked will not
    remain
  over the land allotted to the
    righteous,
for then the righteous might use
  their hands to do evil.

⁴Do good, O LORD, to those who are
    good,
  to those who are upright in heart.
⁵But those who turn to crooked ways
  the LORD will banish with the
    evildoers.

Peace be upon Israel.

Psalm 126

A song of ascents.

¹When the LORD brought back the
    captives toᵃ Zion,
  we were like men who dreamed.ᵇ
²Our mouths were filled with laughter,
  our tongues with songs of joy.
Then it was said among the nations,
  "The LORD has done great things for
    them."
³The LORD has done great things for us,
  and we are filled with joy.

⁴Restore our fortunes,ᶜ O LORD,
  like streams in the Negev.
⁵Those who sow in tears
  will reap with songs of joy.
⁶He who goes out weeping,
  carrying seed to sow,

will return with songs of joy,
  carrying sheaves with him.

Psalm 127

A song of ascents. Of Solomon.

¹Unless the LORD builds the house,
  its builders labor in vain.
Unless the LORD watches over the city,
  the watchmen stand guard in vain.
²In vain you rise early
  and stay up late,
toiling for food to eat—
  for he grants sleep toᵈ those he
    loves.

³Sons are a heritage from the LORD,
  children a reward from him.
⁴Like arrows in the hands of a warrior
  are sons born in one's youth.
⁵Blessed is the man
  whose quiver is full of them.
They will not be put to shame
  when they contend with their
    enemies in the gate.

Psalm 128

A song of ascents.

¹Blessed are all who fear the LORD,
  who walk in his ways.
²You will eat the fruit of your labor;
  blessings and prosperity will be
    yours.
³Your wife will be like a fruitful vine
  within your house;
your sons will be like olive shoots
  around your table.
⁴Thus is the man blessed
  who fears the LORD.

⁵May the LORD bless you from Zion
  all the days of your life;
may you see the prosperity of
    Jerusalem,
⁶ and may you live to see your
    children's children.

Peace be upon Israel.

Psalm 129

A song of ascents.

¹They have greatly oppressed me from
    my youth—
  let Israel say—

ᵃ1 Or LORD *restored the fortunes of*   ᵇ1 Or *men restored to health*   ᶜ4 Or *Bring back our captives*
ᵈ2 Or *eat— / for while they sleep he provides for*

VERSE FOR THE DAY:
Psalm 126:5

AUTHOR:
Ruth A. Tucker

PASSAGE FOR THE DAY:
Psalm 126:1–6

Sowing in Tears

SO often it is assumed that someone who is going through difficult times is incapable of effectively ministering to someone else. Indeed, as we are counseling those who are depressed and struggling with personal problems, it never seems to occur to us to encourage them to reach out to minister to others rather than focus exclusively on themselves. How insightful the psalmist was in writing:

> He who goes out weeping,
>   carrying seed to sow,
> will return with songs of joy,
>   carrying sheaves with him (Psalm 126:6).

It was during a very stressful period in my own life a few years ago that I was thrust suddenly into a care-giving situation. I had promised a friend that I would be a "daughter" to her mother while she and her husband fulfilled a two-year mission commitment in Africa. I might have had second thoughts about my new role had I realized that the day after my friend would leave, her mother would enter the hospital where her condition would utterly bewilder the doctors until she died several weeks later.

I was in no condition to minister to someone else—so I thought. But as I began making those daily hospital visits to Clara, I discovered that instead of adding to my stress, my time with her was rejuvenating. As I identified with her needs, my own problems paled into insignificance. And as I served her and focused on her well-being, I felt better about myself. Clara certainly was not passive in the care-giving process. She responded to my love and gave back to me far more than I gave her. She helped me make it through a very tough time in my life, and I will always have the sweet memories of being close to her during her final days, when I went out weeping and returned with songs of joy.

Additional Scripture Readings:
Isaiah 61:1–3; 2 Timothy 1:6–12

*Go to page 648 for your next
devotional reading.*

²they have greatly oppressed me from
　　my youth,
　　but they have not gained the victory
　　　over me.
³Plowmen have plowed my back
　　and made their furrows long.
⁴But the LORD is righteous;
　　he has cut me free from the cords
　　　of the wicked.

⁵May all who hate Zion
　　be turned back in shame.
⁶May they be like grass on the roof,
　　which withers before it can grow;
⁷with it the reaper cannot fill his
　　hands,
　　nor the one who gathers fill his
　　　arms.
⁸May those who pass by not say,
　　"The blessing of the LORD be upon
　　　you;
　　we bless you in the name of the
　　　LORD."

Psalm 130

A song of ascents.

¹Out of the depths I cry to you,
　　O LORD;
²　O Lord, hear my voice.
Let your ears be attentive
　　to my cry for mercy.

³If you, O LORD, kept a record of sins,
　　O Lord, who could stand?
⁴But with you there is forgiveness;
　　therefore you are feared.

⁵I wait for the LORD, my soul waits,
　　and in his word I put my hope.
⁶My soul waits for the Lord
　　more than watchmen wait for the
　　　morning,
　　more than watchmen wait for the
　　　morning.

⁷O Israel, put your hope in the LORD,
　　for with the LORD is unfailing love
　　and with him is full redemption.
⁸He himself will redeem Israel
　　from all their sins.

Psalm 131

A song of ascents. Of David.

¹My heart is not proud, O LORD,
　　my eyes are not haughty;

I do not concern myself with great
　　matters
　　or things too wonderful for me.
²But I have stilled and quieted my
　　soul;
　　like a weaned child with its mother,
　　like a weaned child is my soul
　　　within me.

³O Israel, put your hope in the LORD
　　both now and forevermore.

Psalm 132

A song of ascents.

¹O LORD, remember David
　　and all the hardships he endured.

²He swore an oath to the LORD
　　and made a vow to the Mighty One
　　　of Jacob:
³"I will not enter my house
　　or go to my bed—
⁴I will allow no sleep to my eyes,
　　no slumber to my eyelids,
⁵till I find a place for the LORD,
　　a dwelling for the Mighty One of
　　　Jacob."

⁶We heard it in Ephrathah,
　　we came upon it in the fields of
　　　Jaar^{a:}^{b}
⁷"Let us go to his dwelling place;
　　let us worship at his footstool—
⁸arise, O LORD, and come to your
　　resting place,
　　you and the ark of your might.
⁹May your priests be clothed with
　　righteousness;
　　may your saints sing for joy."

¹⁰For the sake of David your servant,
　　do not reject your anointed one.

¹¹The LORD swore an oath to David,
　　a sure oath that he will not revoke:
"One of your own descendants
　　I will place on your throne—
¹²if your sons keep my covenant
　　and the statutes I teach them,
　　then their sons will sit
　　on your throne for ever and ever."

¹³For the LORD has chosen Zion,
　　he has desired it for his dwelling:
¹⁴"This is my resting place for ever and
　　ever;
　　here I will sit enthroned, for I have
　　　desired it—

a6 That is, Kiriath Jearim　　b6 Or heard of it in Ephrathah, / we found it in the fields of Jaar. (And no
quotes around verses 7-9)

VERSE FOR THE DAY:	AUTHOR:	PASSAGE FOR THE DAY:
Psalm 130:1–2	*Janice Kempe*	*Psalm 130:1–8*

Out of the Depths

I'LL bet I've washed that dish a million times! My kitchen sink seems like a hole that I keep falling into and can't escape from. I wonder how many spoons and forks I've washed in the last ten years? And the laundry basket. It's perpetually full! I'll bet I could go to the dryer any time, day or night, and find at least ten ragged towels, six wrinkled shirts, and twenty-three socks, five of which have no mate. Who cares?

> Out of the depths I cry to you, O LORD;
> O LORD, hear my voice.
> Let your ears be attentive
> to my cry for mercy (Psalm 130:1–2)

Am I in the depths? Is this utter despair? I don't think so, but it is definitely uncomfortable. I'm having the blahs.

"Out of my blahs I cry to you, O Lord. Lord, hear my voice; Let your ears be attentive to my cry for mercy" (Kempe 1983).

That's my translation! Sometimes I have trouble relating to the trials and tragedies that drove God's people of the Old Testament to cry to him for deliverance. They make my own trial seem unimportant in comparison. But today I think God is telling me to stop comparing and to realize that the depressions and setbacks I experience are just as important to him as the conflicts and moral dilemmas faced by people in Bible times. They were his children, and he heard their voices and led them out of the depths. I also am his child, and he hears my voice and will lead me out of my depths. God is as eager to hear my pleas as he was to hear theirs.

My Lord cares! He cares when I feel like a failure. He cares when I feel as if all my education and training have led me to nothing but a sinkful of dishes. I think he smiles when I mop up spilled milk at each meal. I think he smiles when he hears a resounding "Yuck" in response to a new recipe I tried. He smiles and gives me gentle words of encouragement.

Additional Scripture Readings:
Numbers 11:10–23; Hebrews 4:14–16

Go to page 652 for your next devotional reading.

¹⁵I will bless her with abundant
provisions;
her poor will I satisfy with food.
¹⁶I will clothe her priests with
salvation,
and her saints will ever sing for joy.

¹⁷"Here I will make a horn[a] grow for
David
and set up a lamp for my anointed
one.
¹⁸I will clothe his enemies with shame,
but the crown on his head will be
resplendent."

Psalm 133

A song of ascents. Of David.

¹How good and pleasant it is
when brothers live together in
unity!
²It is like precious oil poured on the
head,
running down on the beard,
running down on Aaron's beard,
down upon the collar of his robes.
³It is as if the dew of Hermon
were falling on Mount Zion.
For there the LORD bestows his
blessing,
even life forevermore.

Psalm 134

A song of ascents.

¹Praise the LORD, all you servants of
the LORD
who minister by night in the house
of the LORD.
²Lift up your hands in the sanctuary
and praise the LORD.

³May the LORD, the Maker of heaven
and earth,
bless you from Zion.

Psalm 135

¹Praise the LORD.[b]

Praise the name of the LORD;
praise him, you servants of the
LORD,
²you who minister in the house of the
LORD,
in the courts of the house of our
God.

³Praise the LORD, for the LORD is good;

sing praise to his name, for that is
pleasant.
⁴For the LORD has chosen Jacob to be
his own,
Israel to be his treasured
possession.

⁵I know that the LORD is great,
that our Lord is greater than all
gods.
⁶The LORD does whatever pleases him,
in the heavens and on the earth,
in the seas and all their depths.
⁷He makes clouds rise from the ends
of the earth;
he sends lightning with the rain
and brings out the wind from his
storehouses.

⁸He struck down the firstborn of
Egypt,
the firstborn of men and animals.
⁹He sent his signs and wonders into
your midst, O Egypt,
against Pharaoh and all his
servants.
¹⁰He struck down many nations
and killed mighty kings—
¹¹Sihon king of the Amorites,
Og king of Bashan
and all the kings of Canaan—
¹²and he gave their land as an
inheritance,
an inheritance to his people Israel.

¹³Your name, O LORD, endures forever,
your renown, O LORD, through all
generations.
¹⁴For the LORD will vindicate his people
and have compassion on his
servants.

¹⁵The idols of the nations are silver and
gold,
made by the hands of men.
¹⁶They have mouths, but cannot speak,
eyes, but they cannot see;
¹⁷they have ears, but cannot hear,
nor is there breath in their mouths.
¹⁸Those who make them will be like
them,
and so will all who trust in them.

¹⁹O house of Israel, praise the LORD;
O house of Aaron, praise the LORD;
²⁰O house of Levi, praise the LORD;
you who fear him, praise the LORD.
²¹Praise be to the LORD from Zion,
to him who dwells in Jerusalem.

Praise the LORD.

---

a17 Horn here symbolizes strong one, that is, king.   *b1* Hebrew *Hallelu Yah*; also in verses 3 and 21

Psalm 136

[1]Give thanks to the Lord, for he is
    good.
          His love endures forever.
[2]Give thanks to the God of gods.
          His love endures forever.
[3]Give thanks to the Lord of lords:
          His love endures forever.

[4]to him who alone does great wonders,
          His love endures forever.
[5]who by his understanding made the
    heavens,
          His love endures forever.
[6]who spread out the earth upon the
    waters,
          His love endures forever.
[7]who made the great lights—
          His love endures forever.
[8]the sun to govern the day,
          His love endures forever.
[9]the moon and stars to govern the
    night;
          His love endures forever.

[10]to him who struck down the firstborn
    of Egypt
          His love endures forever.
[11]and brought Israel out from among
    them
          His love endures forever.
[12]with a mighty hand and outstretched
    arm;
          His love endures forever.

[13]to him who divided the Red Sea[a]
    asunder
          His love endures forever.
[14]and brought Israel through the midst
    of it,
          His love endures forever.
[15]but swept Pharaoh and his army into
    the Red Sea;
          His love endures forever.

[16]to him who led his people through
    the desert,
          His love endures forever.
[17]who struck down great kings,
          His love endures forever.
[18]and killed mighty kings—
          His love endures forever.
[19]Sihon king of the Amorites
          His love endures forever.
[20]and Og king of Bashan—
          His love endures forever.
[21]and gave their land as an inheritance,
          His love endures forever.

[22]an inheritance to his servant Israel;
          His love endures forever.
[23]to the One who remembered us in
    our low estate
          His love endures forever.
[24]and freed us from our enemies,
          His love endures forever.
[25]and who gives food to every creature.
          His love endures forever.

[26]Give thanks to the God of heaven.
          His love endures forever.

Psalm 137

[1]By the rivers of Babylon we sat and
    wept
  when we remembered Zion.
[2]There on the poplars
  we hung our harps,
[3]for there our captors asked us for
    songs,
  our tormentors demanded songs of
    joy;
  they said, "Sing us one of the songs
    of Zion!"

[4]How can we sing the songs of the
    Lord
  while in a foreign land?
[5]If I forget you, O Jerusalem,
  may my right hand forget ⸢its skill⸣.
[6]May my tongue cling to the roof of
    my mouth
  if I do not remember you,
  if I do not consider Jerusalem
  my highest joy.

[7]Remember, O Lord, what the
    Edomites did
  on the day Jerusalem fell.
  "Tear it down," they cried,
  "tear it down to its foundations!"

[8]O Daughter of Babylon, doomed to
    destruction,
  happy is he who repays you
  for what you have done to us—
[9]he who seizes your infants
  and dashes them against the rocks.

Psalm 138

Of David.

[1]I will praise you, O Lord, with all my
    heart;
  before the "gods" I will sing your
    praise.

---

a13 Hebrew *Yam Suph*; that is, Sea of Reeds; also in verse 15

²I will bow down toward your holy
    temple
and will praise your name
for your love and your faithfulness,
for you have exalted above all things
    your name and your word.
³When I called, you answered me;
    you made me bold and
        stouthearted.

⁴May all the kings of the earth praise
        you, O LORD,
    when they hear the words of your
        mouth.
⁵May they sing of the ways of the
        LORD,
    for the glory of the LORD is great.

⁶Though the LORD is on high, he looks
        upon the lowly,
    but the proud he knows from afar.
⁷Though I walk in the midst of
        trouble,
    you preserve my life;
you stretch out your hand against the
        anger of my foes,
    with your right hand you save me.
⁸The LORD will fulfill his purpose for
        me;
    your love, O LORD, endures
        forever—
    do not abandon the works of your
        hands.

Psalm 139

For the director of music. Of David.
    A psalm.

¹O LORD, you have searched me
    and you know me.
²You know when I sit and when I rise;
    you perceive my thoughts from afar.
³You discern my going out and my
        lying down;
    you are familiar with all my ways.
⁴Before a word is on my tongue
    you know it completely, O LORD.

⁵You hem me in—behind and before;
    you have laid your hand upon me.
⁶Such knowledge is too wonderful for
        me,
    too lofty for me to attain.

⁷Where can I go from your Spirit?
    Where can I flee from your
        presence?
⁸If I go up to the heavens, you are
        there;

if I make my bed in the depths,ᵃ
    you are there.
⁹If I rise on the wings of the dawn,
    if I settle on the far side of the sea,
¹⁰even there your hand will guide me,
    your right hand will hold me fast.

¹¹If I say, "Surely the darkness will hide
        me
    and the light become night around
        me,"
¹²even the darkness will not be dark to
        you;
    the night will shine like the day,
    for darkness is as light to you.

¹³For you created my inmost being;
    you knit me together in my
        mother's womb.
¹⁴I praise you because I am fearfully
        and wonderfully made;
    your works are wonderful,
    I know that full well.
¹⁵My frame was not hidden from you
    when I was made in the secret
        place.
When I was woven together in the
        depths of the earth,
¹⁶   your eyes saw my unformed body.
All the days ordained for me
    were written in your book
    before one of them came to be.

¹⁷How precious toᵇ me are your
        thoughts, O God!
    How vast is the sum of them!
¹⁸Were I to count them,
    they would outnumber the grains of
        sand.
When I awake,
    I am still with you.

¹⁹If only you would slay the wicked,
        O God!
    Away from me, you bloodthirsty
        men!
²⁰They speak of you with evil intent;
    your adversaries misuse your name.
²¹Do I not hate those who hate you,
        O LORD,
    and abhor those who rise up
        against you?
²²I have nothing but hatred for them;
    I count them my enemies.

²³Search me, O God, and know my
        heart;
    test me and know my anxious
        thoughts.

ᵃ8 Hebrew *Sheol*   ᵇ17 Or *concerning*

VERSE FOR THE DAY:	*AUTHOR:*	*PASSAGE FOR THE DAY:*
Psalm 139:1	Hope MacDonald	Psalm 139:1–24

God's Active Presence

"OH! If only I could take this big tummy and set it on a chair for just one hour," sighed my eight-month-pregnant daughter. But we both knew that she couldn't. That little life went with her wherever she went, day or night.

I thought about that as I read this psalm today. I believe it is one of the most personal passages in all of Scripture. It is a psalm about God's continual, active presence with me wherever I go, day or night.

Christ in me means that God knows everything about me. He knows when I sit down and when I stand up (Psalm 139:2). He knows my name (Isaiah 43:1). He knows how many hairs I have on my head (Luke 12:7)! He knows my words completely, even before they are spoken (Psalm 139:4)! In fact, he saw me when I was being formed in my mother's womb. He was there, knitting me together (Psalm 139:13–16)! Indeed, such knowledge is too wonderful, too lofty for any of us to fully comprehend (Psalm 139:6).

Not only do we learn about God's eternal presence *with* us every moment, but we also get a tiny glimpse into the absolute holiness of God and his unconditional love for us. We are reminded that God knows and understands us better than anyone else ever will. His love for us is everlasting and personal. St. Augustine said, "God loves each one of us as though there were only one of us to love." What a treasure this truth is. Because of it, we can live in the certainty that his grace is sufficient for us today, regardless of our circumstances.

Just as my daughter could not set aside that little life she was carrying, not even for an hour, neither can we, who have received Jesus as Savior, ever be without him. We are bonded together in love. His Spirit is at work within us, making us more like Jesus with each passing day. We are each an everlasting child of God.

Additional Scripture Readings:
Jeremiah 1:4–8; Ephesians 1:17–21

Go to page 655 for your next devotional reading.

24See if there is any offensive way in
me,
and lead me in the way everlasting.

Psalm 140

For the director of music. A psalm
of David.

1Rescue me, O Lord, from evil men;
protect me from men of violence,
2who devise evil plans in their hearts
and stir up war every day.
3They make their tongues as sharp as
a serpent's;
the poison of vipers is on their lips.
Selah

4Keep me, O Lord, from the hands of
the wicked;
protect me from men of violence
who plan to trip my feet.
5Proud men have hidden a snare for
me;
they have spread out the cords of
their net
and have set traps for me along my
path. *Selah*

6O Lord, I say to you, "You are my
God."
Hear, O Lord, my cry for mercy.
7O Sovereign Lord, my strong deliverer,
who shields my head in the day of
battle —
8do not grant the wicked their desires,
O Lord;
do not let their plans succeed,
or they will become proud. *Selah*

9Let the heads of those who surround
me
be covered with the trouble their
lips have caused.
10Let burning coals fall upon them;
may they be thrown into the fire,
into miry pits, never to rise.
11Let slanderers not be established in
the land;
may disaster hunt down men of
violence.

12I know that the Lord secures justice
for the poor
and upholds the cause of the
needy.
13Surely the righteous will praise your
name
and the upright will live before you.

Psalm 141

A psalm of David.

1O Lord, I call to you; come quickly to
me.
Hear my voice when I call to you.
2May my prayer be set before you like
incense;
may the lifting up of my hands be
like the evening sacrifice.

3Set a guard over my mouth, O Lord;
keep watch over the door of my
lips.
4Let not my heart be drawn to what is
evil,
to take part in wicked deeds
with men who are evildoers;
let me not eat of their delicacies.

5Let a righteous man*a* strike me — it is
a kindness;
let him rebuke me — it is oil on my
head.
My head will not refuse it.

Yet my prayer is ever against the
deeds of evildoers;
6   their rulers will be thrown down
from the cliffs,
and the wicked will learn that my
words were well spoken.
7They will say, "As one plows and
breaks up the earth,
so our bones have been scattered at
the mouth of the grave.*b*"

8But my eyes are fixed on you,
O Sovereign Lord;
in you I take refuge — do not give
me over to death.
9Keep me from the snares they have
laid for me,
from the traps set by evildoers.
10Let the wicked fall into their own
nets,
while I pass by in safety.

Psalm 142

A *maskil*c of David. When he was in the
cave. A prayer.

1I cry aloud to the Lord;
I lift up my voice to the Lord for
mercy.
2I pour out my complaint before him;
before him I tell my trouble.

3When my spirit grows faint within me,

*a*5 Or *Let the Righteous One*   *b*7 Hebrew *Sheol*   *c*Title: Probably a literary or musical term

it is you who know my way.
In the path where I walk
men have hidden a snare for me.
⁴Look to my right and see;
no one is concerned for me.
I have no refuge;
no one cares for my life.

⁵I cry to you, O LORD;
I say, "You are my refuge,
my portion in the land of the
living."
⁶Listen to my cry,
for I am in desperate need;
rescue me from those who pursue me,
for they are too strong for me.
⁷Set me free from my prison,
that I may praise your name.

Then the righteous will gather about
me
because of your goodness to me.

Psalm 143

A psalm of David.

¹O LORD, hear my prayer,
listen to my cry for mercy;
in your faithfulness and righteousness
come to my relief.
²Do not bring your servant into
judgment,
for no one living is righteous before
you.

³The enemy pursues me,
he crushes me to the ground;
he makes me dwell in darkness
like those long dead.
⁴So my spirit grows faint within me;
my heart within me is dismayed.

⁵I remember the days of long ago;
I meditate on all your works
and consider what your hands have
done.
⁶I spread out my hands to you;
my soul thirsts for you like a
parched land.   *Selah*

⁷Answer me quickly, O LORD;
my spirit fails.
Do not hide your face from me
or I will be like those who go down
to the pit.
⁸Let the morning bring me word of
your unfailing love,
for I have put my trust in you.
Show me the way I should go,

for to you I lift up my soul.
⁹Rescue me from my enemies, O LORD,
for I hide myself in you.
¹⁰Teach me to do your will,
for you are my God;
may your good Spirit
lead me on level ground.

¹¹For your name's sake, O LORD,
preserve my life;
in your righteousness, bring me out
of trouble.
¹²In your unfailing love, silence my
enemies;
destroy all my foes,
for I am your servant.

Psalm 144

Of David.

¹Praise be to the LORD my Rock,
who trains my hands for war,
my fingers for battle.
²He is my loving God and my fortress,
my stronghold and my deliverer,
my shield, in whom I take refuge,
who subdues peoples[a] under me.

³O LORD, what is man that you care for
him,
the son of man that you think of
him?
⁴Man is like a breath;
his days are like a fleeting shadow.

⁵Part your heavens, O LORD, and come
down;
touch the mountains, so that they
smoke.
⁶Send forth lightning and scatter the
enemies;
shoot your arrows and rout them.
⁷Reach down your hand from on high;
deliver me and rescue me
from the mighty waters,
from the hands of foreigners
⁸whose mouths are full of lies,
whose right hands are deceitful.

⁹I will sing a new song to you, O God;
on the ten-stringed lyre I will make
music to you,
¹⁰to the One who gives victory to kings,
who delivers his servant David from
the deadly sword.

¹¹Deliver me and rescue me
from the hands of foreigners
whose mouths are full of lies,

---

*a2 Many manuscripts of the Masoretic Text, Dead Sea Scrolls, Aquila, Jerome and Syriac; most
manuscripts of the Masoretic Text subdues my people*

VERSE FOR THE DAY:	AUTHOR:	PASSAGE FOR THE DAY:
Psalm 145:18	Debbie Smith	Psalm 145:1–21

The Lord Is Faithful

"CAROL has gone into labor. She's at the hospital now . . . but they think the baby is dead!"

How could Carol, a friend who had suffered through three miscarriages, be asked to endure this tragedy? I hung up the phone, only to pick it up again to dial friends and family with a plea for prayer. God in his power could save that child!

The afternoon stretched on, and I remember praying almost constantly. "The LORD is near to all who call on him" (Psalm 145:18). I felt his presence, knowing that Carol and Bill surely felt it too.

Responding to a nudge to go to the hospital, I left the children with a sitter and set out on the thirty-minute drive, both desiring to "be there" for my friends and dreading what I might have to face.

By the time I reached the hospital the baby had been born, dead. Our pastor emerged from the room, assuring those of us waiting outside that Carol and Bill were taking their loss well, resting on faith. I wept with my friends, then listened as they spoke of the faith and comfort that God was providing. They recognized that God was in control, and they insisted that the prayers of believers had eased the pain. His peace was on their faces and in their words.

I left, numbed by the ordeal, yet strangely consoled. Driving home, I thanked my "gracious and compassionate" Lord (Psalm 145:8) for guiding my steps to that hospital room. The experience seemed an answer to many prayers for courage—for myself. For years I had struggled to believe that "the LORD watches over all who love him" (Psalm 145:20)—that he would be enough in any crisis I might have to face. My doubts were put to rest in five minutes inside that room.

The song Michael and I had written years before became vibrant again for me:

Great is the Lord, he is holy and just;
By his power we trust in his love.*

Yes. God is sufficient.

Additional Scripture Readings:
1 Corinthians 1:4–9; 1 Peter 1:3–9

Go to page 657 for your next devotional reading.

whose right hands are deceitful.

¹²Then our sons in their youth
will be like well-nurtured plants,
and our daughters will be like pillars
carved to adorn a palace.
¹³Our barns will be filled
with every kind of provision.
Our sheep will increase by thousands,
by tens of thousands in our fields;
¹⁴ our oxen will draw heavy loads.ᵃ
There will be no breaching of walls,
no going into captivity,
no cry of distress in our streets.

¹⁵Blessed are the people of whom this
is true;
blessed are the people whose God
is the LORD.

Psalm 145ᵇ

A psalm of praise. Of David.

¹I will exalt you, my God the King;
I will praise your name for ever and
ever.
²Every day I will praise you
and extol your name for ever and
ever.

³Great is the LORD and most worthy of
praise;
his greatness no one can fathom.
⁴One generation will commend your
works to another;
they will tell of your mighty acts.
⁵They will speak of the glorious
splendor of your majesty,
and I will meditate on your
wonderful works.ᶜ
⁶They will tell of the power of your
awesome works,
and I will proclaim your great
deeds.
⁷They will celebrate your abundant
goodness
and joyfully sing of your
righteousness.

⁸The LORD is gracious and
compassionate,
slow to anger and rich in love.
⁹The LORD is good to all;
he has compassion on all he has
made.

¹⁰All you have made will praise you,
O LORD;
your saints will extol you.
¹¹They will tell of the glory of your
kingdom
and speak of your might,
¹²so that all men may know of your
mighty acts
and the glorious splendor of your
kingdom.
¹³Your kingdom is an everlasting
kingdom,
and your dominion endures through
all generations.

The LORD is faithful to all his
promises
and loving toward all he has
made.ᵈ
¹⁴The LORD upholds all those who fall
and lifts up all who are bowed
down.
¹⁵The eyes of all look to you,
and you give them their food at the
proper time.
¹⁶You open your hand
and satisfy the desires of every
living thing.

¹⁷The LORD is righteous in all his ways
and loving toward all he has made.
¹⁸The LORD is near to all who call on
him,
to all who call on him in truth.
¹⁹He fulfills the desires of those who
fear him;
he hears their cry and saves them.
²⁰The LORD watches over all who love
him,
but all the wicked he will destroy.

²¹My mouth will speak in praise of the
LORD.
Let every creature praise his holy
name
for ever and ever.

Psalm 146

¹Praise the LORD.ᵉ

Praise the LORD, O my soul.
² I will praise the LORD all my life;
I will sing praise to my God as long
as I live.

ᵃ14 Or our chieftains will be firmly established   ᵇThis psalm is an acrostic poem, the verses of which
(including verse 13b) begin with the successive letters of the Hebrew alphabet.   ᶜ5 Dead Sea Scrolls
and Syriac (see also Septuagint); Masoretic Text On the glorious splendor of your majesty / and on your
wonderful works I will meditate   ᵈ13 One manuscript of the Masoretic Text, Dead Sea Scrolls and
Syriac (see also Septuagint); most manuscripts of the Masoretic Text do not have the last two lines of
verse 13.   ᵉ1 Hebrew Hallelu Yah; also in verse 10

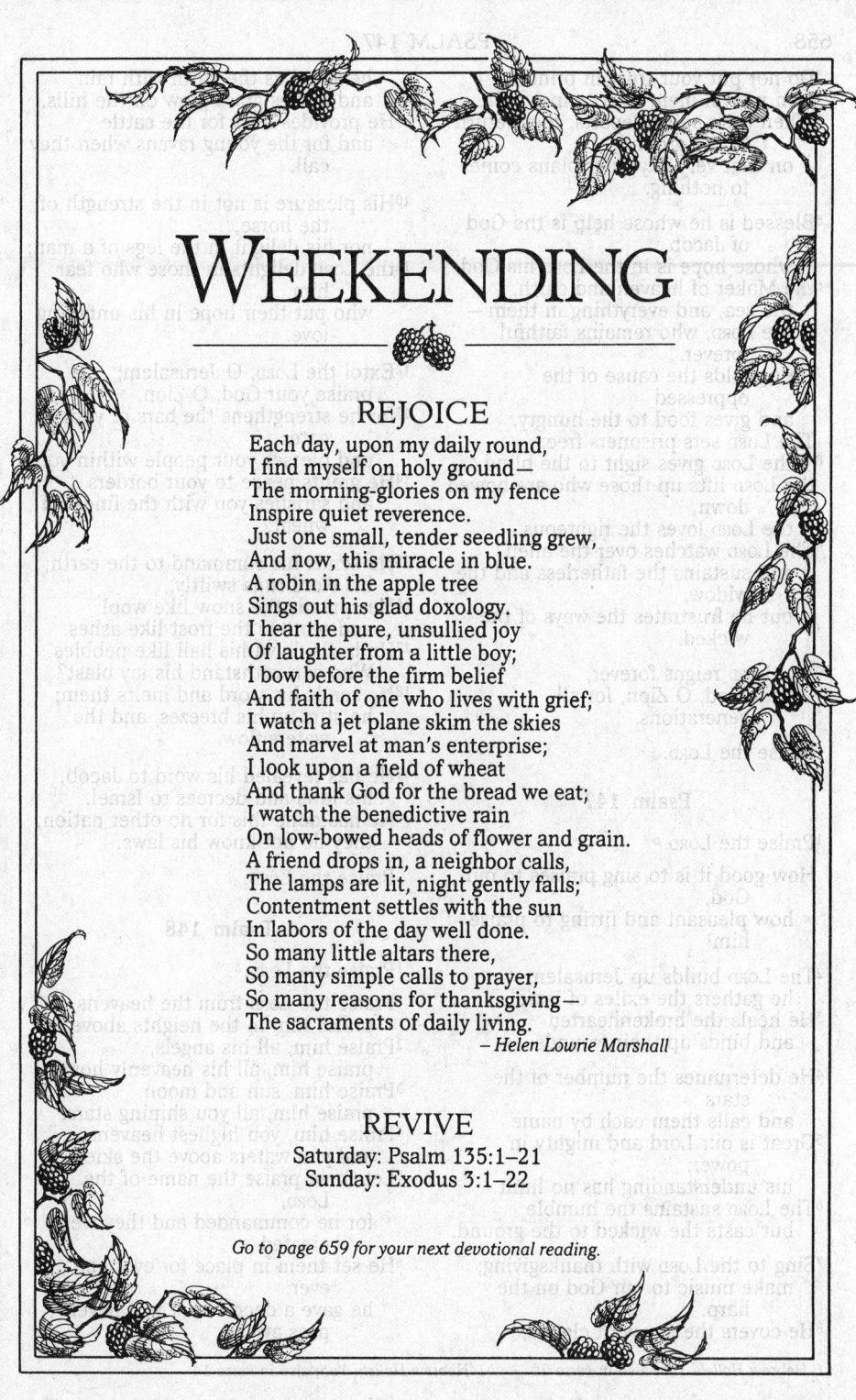

WEEKENDING

REJOICE

Each day, upon my daily round,
I find myself on holy ground—
The morning-glories on my fence
Inspire quiet reverence.
Just one small, tender seedling grew,
And now, this miracle in blue.
A robin in the apple tree
Sings out his glad doxology.
I hear the pure, unsullied joy
Of laughter from a little boy;
I bow before the firm belief
And faith of one who lives with grief;
I watch a jet plane skim the skies
And marvel at man's enterprise;
I look upon a field of wheat
And thank God for the bread we eat;
I watch the benedictive rain
On low-bowed heads of flower and grain.
A friend drops in, a neighbor calls,
The lamps are lit, night gently falls;
Contentment settles with the sun
In labors of the day well done.
So many little altars there,
So many simple calls to prayer,
So many reasons for thanksgiving—
The sacraments of daily living.

– Helen Lowrie Marshall

REVIVE

Saturday: Psalm 135:1–21
Sunday: Exodus 3:1–22

Go to page 659 for your next devotional reading.

³Do not put your trust in princes,
   in mortal men, who cannot save.
⁴When their spirit departs, they return
      to the ground;
   on that very day their plans come
      to nothing.

⁵Blessed is he whose help is the God
      of Jacob,
   whose hope is in the LORD his God,
⁶the Maker of heaven and earth,
   the sea, and everything in them—
   the LORD, who remains faithful
      forever.
⁷He upholds the cause of the
      oppressed
   and gives food to the hungry.
   The LORD sets prisoners free,
⁸   the LORD gives sight to the blind,
   the LORD lifts up those who are bowed
      down,
   the LORD loves the righteous.
⁹The LORD watches over the alien
   and sustains the fatherless and the
      widow,
   but he frustrates the ways of the
      wicked.

¹⁰The LORD reigns forever,
   your God, O Zion, for all
      generations.

Praise the LORD.

Psalm 147

¹Praise the LORD. ᵃ

How good it is to sing praises to our
      God,
   how pleasant and fitting to praise
      him!

²The LORD builds up Jerusalem;
   he gathers the exiles of Israel.
³He heals the brokenhearted
   and binds up their wounds.
⁴He determines the number of the
      stars
   and calls them each by name.
⁵Great is our Lord and mighty in
      power;
   his understanding has no limit.
⁶The LORD sustains the humble
   but casts the wicked to the ground.

⁷Sing to the LORD with thanksgiving;
   make music to our God on the
      harp.
⁸He covers the sky with clouds;

he supplies the earth with rain
   and makes grass grow on the hills.
⁹He provides food for the cattle
   and for the young ravens when they
      call.

¹⁰His pleasure is not in the strength of
      the horse,
   nor his delight in the legs of a man;
¹¹the LORD delights in those who fear
      him,
   who put their hope in his unfailing
      love.

¹²Extol the LORD, O Jerusalem;
   praise your God, O Zion,
¹³for he strengthens the bars of your
      gates
   and blesses your people within you.
¹⁴He grants peace to your borders
   and satisfies you with the finest of
      wheat.

¹⁵He sends his command to the earth;
   his word runs swiftly.
¹⁶He spreads the snow like wool
   and scatters the frost like ashes.
¹⁷He hurls down his hail like pebbles.
   Who can withstand his icy blast?
¹⁸He sends his word and melts them;
   he stirs up his breezes, and the
      waters flow.

¹⁹He has revealed his word to Jacob,
   his laws and decrees to Israel.
²⁰He has done this for no other nation;
   they do not know his laws.

Praise the LORD.

Psalm 148

¹Praise the LORD. ᵇ

Praise the LORD from the heavens,
   praise him in the heights above.
²Praise him, all his angels,
   praise him, all his heavenly hosts.
³Praise him, sun and moon,
   praise him, all you shining stars.
⁴Praise him, you highest heavens
   and you waters above the skies.
⁵Let them praise the name of the
      LORD,
   for he commanded and they were
      created.
⁶He set them in place for ever and
      ever;
   he gave a decree that will never
      pass away.

ᵃ1 Hebrew *Hallelu Yah*; also in verse 20   ᵇ1 Hebrew *Hallelu Yah*; also in verse 14

VERSE FOR THE DAY:
Psalm 147:10

AUTHOR:
Debbie Smith

PASSAGE FOR THE DAY:
Psalm 147:7–11

Delight Only in Him

I AM convinced that there is no insignificant verse in the Bible. Surely the Holy Spirit has used them all to convict, correct, encourage and edify. When I recall a very difficult time in my life, I also remember how he showed me an important, though unlikely, verse in his Word:

> His pleasure is not in the strength of the horse,
> *nor his delight in the legs of a man* (Psalm
> 147:10, italics mine).

I was struggling with anorexia nervosa when that verse jumped out of the page and hit my heart. I had been obsessed with the size of legs, arms, waist—with *everything* about my physical appearance. Here, God tells me that the condition of my heart is important to him, much more important than the condition of my body. David goes on to say:

> The LORD delights in those who fear him,
> who put their hope in his unfailing love
> (Psalm 147:11).

I realized that I had feared the opinions of others; I had feared that I would not measure up. I had placed my hope, not in God's unconditional love, but in controlling my weight.

What began in the eighth grade as a week-long diet with a friend became seven years of starvation for me. For some deep psychological, emotional and spiritual reasons, I kept losing weight. By my senior year of high school, I was five feet, three inches tall and all of seventy-nine pounds.

When I sank below eighty pounds, my internal battle intensified. I was a Christian, desiring to serve God, yet enslaved to food. I was miserable. Night after night I sobbed into my pillow, pleading that God would make me normal.

He answered those prayers slowly and gently. First, he showed me my sin and forgave me. He gave me caring friends to talk to, reassurance from his Word, and a wonderful husband. Michael loves *me*, not my dress size!

And, as confirmation that my healing is complete, God has given us three beautiful children—our three miracles, we call them, since I was told I would never be able to bear children as a result of my anorexia.

Now I desire only to fear God and put my hope in his love . . . and through his strength, I will delight only in him!

Additional Scripture Readings:
Jeremiah 17:5–8; 1 Peter 3:3–4

Go to page 664 for your next devotional reading.

⁷Praise the LORD from the earth,
  you great sea creatures and all
    ocean depths,
⁸lightning and hail, snow and clouds,
  stormy winds that do his bidding,
⁹you mountains and all hills,
  fruit trees and all cedars,
¹⁰wild animals and all cattle,
  small creatures and flying birds,
¹¹kings of the earth and all nations,
  you princes and all rulers on earth,
¹²young men and maidens,
  old men and children.

¹³Let them praise the name of the
  LORD,
  for his name alone is exalted;
  his splendor is above the earth and
    the heavens.
¹⁴He has raised up for his people a
  horn,ᵃ
  the praise of all his saints,
  of Israel, the people close to his
    heart.

Praise the LORD.

Psalm 149

¹Praise the LORD.ᵇ

Sing to the LORD a new song,
  his praise in the assembly of the
    saints.

²Let Israel rejoice in their Maker;
  let the people of Zion be glad in
    their King.
³Let them praise his name with
  dancing
  and make music to him with
    tambourine and harp.
⁴For the LORD takes delight in his
  people;

he crowns the humble with
  salvation.
⁵Let the saints rejoice in this honor
  and sing for joy on their beds.

⁶May the praise of God be in their
  mouths
  and a double-edged sword in their
    hands,
⁷to inflict vengeance on the nations
  and punishment on the peoples,
⁸to bind their kings with fetters,
  their nobles with shackles of iron,
⁹to carry out the sentence written
  against them.
  This is the glory of all his saints.

Praise the LORD.

Psalm 150

¹Praise the LORD.ᶜ

Praise God in his sanctuary;
  praise him in his mighty heavens.
²Praise him for his acts of power;
  praise him for his surpassing
    greatness.
³Praise him with the sounding of the
  trumpet,
  praise him with the harp and lyre,
⁴praise him with tambourine and
  dancing,
  praise him with the strings and
    flute,
⁵praise him with the clash of cymbals,
  praise him with resounding
    cymbals.

⁶Let everything that has breath praise
  the LORD.

Praise the LORD.

ᵃ14 *Horn* here symbolizes strong one, that is, king.   ᵇ1 Hebrew *Hallelu Yah*; also in verse 9
ᶜ1 Hebrew *Hallelu Yah*; also in verse 6

*S*OLOMON *"spoke three thousand proverbs" (1 Kings 4:32), many of which are collected in this book. These wise sayings describe patterns that operate in everyday life, offering us advice on how to conduct ourselves in various situations. Solomon's fundamental instruction is to fear and trust the Lord. As you read this book, remember that God has something to say about every aspect of your life; seek his wisdom in the decisions you must make each day.*

PROVERBS

Prologue: Purpose and Theme

1 The proverbs of Solomon son of David, king of Israel:

² for attaining wisdom and discipline;
  for understanding words of insight;
³ for acquiring a disciplined and prudent life,
  doing what is right and just and fair;
⁴ for giving prudence to the simple,
  knowledge and discretion to the young—

⁵ let the wise listen and add to their learning,
  and let the discerning get guidance—
⁶ for understanding proverbs and parables,
  the sayings and riddles of the wise.

⁷ The fear of the LORD is the beginning of knowledge,
  but fools*ᵃ* despise wisdom and discipline.

ᵃ7 The Hebrew words rendered fool in Proverbs, and often elsewhere in the Old Testament, denote one who is morally deficient.

Exhortations to Embrace Wisdom

Warning Against Enticement

⁸Listen, my son, to your father's
  instruction
  and do not forsake your mother's
  teaching.
⁹They will be a garland to grace your
  head
  and a chain to adorn your neck.

¹⁰My son, if sinners entice you,
  do not give in to them.
¹¹If they say, "Come along with us;
  let's lie in wait for someone's
  blood,
  let's waylay some harmless soul;
¹²let's swallow them alive, like the
  grave,ᵃ
  and whole, like those who go down
  to the pit;
¹³we will get all sorts of valuable things
  and fill our houses with plunder;
¹⁴throw in your lot with us,
  and we will share a common
  purse"—
¹⁵my son, do not go along with them,
  do not set foot on their paths;
¹⁶for their feet rush into sin,
  they are swift to shed blood.
¹⁷How useless to spread a net
  in full view of all the birds!
¹⁸These men lie in wait for their own
  blood;
  they waylay only themselves!
¹⁹Such is the end of all who go after
  ill-gotten gain;
  it takes away the lives of those who
  get it.

Warning Against Rejecting Wisdom

²⁰Wisdom calls aloud in the street,
  she raises her voice in the public
  squares;
²¹at the head of the noisy streetsᵇ she
  cries out,
  in the gateways of the city she
  makes her speech:

²²"How long will you simple onesᶜ love
  your simple ways?
  How long will mockers delight in
  mockery
  and fools hate knowledge?
²³If you had responded to my rebuke,
  I would have poured out my heart
  to you

and made my thoughts known to
  you.
²⁴But since you rejected me when I
  called
  and no one gave heed when I
  stretched out my hand,
²⁵since you ignored all my advice
  and would not accept my rebuke,
²⁶I in turn will laugh at your disaster;
  I will mock when calamity
  overtakes you—
²⁷when calamity overtakes you like a
  storm,
  when disaster sweeps over you like
  a whirlwind,
  when distress and trouble
  overwhelm you.

²⁸"Then they will call to me but I will
  not answer;
  they will look for me but will not
  find me.
²⁹Since they hated knowledge
  and did not choose to fear the
  LORD,
³⁰since they would not accept my
  advice
  and spurned my rebuke,
³¹they will eat the fruit of their ways
  and be filled with the fruit of their
  schemes.
³²For the waywardness of the simple
  will kill them,
  and the complacency of fools will
  destroy them;
³³but whoever listens to me will live in
  safety
  and be at ease, without fear of
  harm."

Moral Benefits of Wisdom

2 My son, if you accept my words
  and store up my commands within
  you,
²turning your ear to wisdom
  and applying your heart to
  understanding,
³and if you call out for insight
  and cry aloud for understanding,
⁴and if you look for it as for silver
  and search for it as for hidden
  treasure,
⁵then you will understand the fear of
  the LORD
  and find the knowledge of God.
⁶For the LORD gives wisdom,

ᵃ12 Hebrew *Sheol*   ᵇ21 Hebrew; Septuagint / *on the tops of the walls*   ᶜ22 The Hebrew word
rendered *simple* in Proverbs generally denotes one without moral direction and inclined to evil.

and from his mouth come
  knowledge and understanding.
7He holds victory in store for the
  upright,
  he is a shield to those whose walk
  is blameless,
8for he guards the course of the just
  and protects the way of his faithful
  ones.

9Then you will understand what is
  right and just
  and fair—every good path.
10For wisdom will enter your heart,
  and knowledge will be pleasant to
  your soul.
11Discretion will protect you,
  and understanding will guard you.

12Wisdom will save you from the ways
  of wicked men,
  from men whose words are
  perverse,
13who leave the straight paths
  to walk in dark ways,
14who delight in doing wrong
  and rejoice in the perverseness of
  evil,
15whose paths are crooked
  and who are devious in their ways.

16It will save you also from the
  adulteress,
  from the wayward wife with her
  seductive words,
17who has left the partner of her youth
  and ignored the covenant she made
  before God. a
18For her house leads down to death
  and her paths to the spirits of the
  dead.
19None who go to her return
  or attain the paths of life.

20Thus you will walk in the ways of
  good men
  and keep to the paths of the
  righteous.
21For the upright will live in the land,
  and the blameless will remain in it;
22but the wicked will be cut off from
  the land,
  and the unfaithful will be torn from
  it.

Further Benefits of Wisdom

3 My son, do not forget my teaching,
  but keep my commands in your
  heart,

2for they will prolong your life many
  years
  and bring you prosperity.

3Let love and faithfulness never leave
  you;
  bind them around your neck,
  write them on the tablet of your
  heart.
4Then you will win favor and a good
  name
  in the sight of God and man.

5Trust in the LORD with all your heart
  and lean not on your own
  understanding;
6in all your ways acknowledge him,
  and he will make your paths
  straight. b

7Do not be wise in your own eyes;
  fear the LORD and shun evil.
8This will bring health to your body
  and nourishment to your bones.

9Honor the LORD with your wealth,
  with the firstfruits of all your crops;
10then your barns will be filled to
  overflowing,
  and your vats will brim over with
  new wine.

11My son, do not despise the LORD's
  discipline
  and do not resent his rebuke,
12because the LORD disciplines those he
  loves,
  as a father c the son he delights in.

13Blessed is the man who finds wisdom,
  the man who gains understanding,
14for she is more profitable than silver
  and yields better returns than gold.
15She is more precious than rubies;
  nothing you desire can compare
  with her.
16Long life is in her right hand;
  in her left hand are riches and
  honor.
17Her ways are pleasant ways,
  and all her paths are peace.
18She is a tree of life to those who
  embrace her;
  those who lay hold of her will be
  blessed.

19By wisdom the LORD laid the earth's
  foundations,
  by understanding he set the
  heavens in place;

a17 Or covenant of her God   b6 Or will direct your paths   c12 Hebrew; Septuagint / and he punishes

VERSE FOR THE DAY:
Proverbs 3:5–6

AUTHOR:
ann kiemel anderson

PASSAGE FOR THE DAY:
Proverbs 3:1–8

trust

THIS is another verse with a command: "TRUST . . . LEAN NOT on your own understanding"; and a promise: "he WILL make your paths straight" (caps mine).

trust is such a lovely word in a world thoroughly self-indulged and complicated. it is quiet. simple. it represents freedom. rest. letting go.

a favorite, old hymn my father would often sing was, "tis so sweet to trust in Jesus, just to take him at his word . . . just to REST upon his promise. . . . " most of us are too busy and noisy to hear the "still, small voice." to identify it. to trust in its power above our human strivings.

friends of ours, who had been down the battered road of infertility, longed for another baby. a perfect situation came about. a young birth mother who felt the only answer for her baby was adoption.

a precious baby girl was born. i loved the birth mother and knew that this was a very painful decision. the adoptive couple came from another city to meet the birth mother and to take their new baby home. it was thanksgiving week. relatives had flown in for a family celebration. the birth mother signed the papers, releasing the baby from the hospital. but in the courtroom, days later, she broke down. she just couldn't give up her baby. she drove hundreds of miles on thanksgiving day to take back her baby.

the couple's celebration turned to heartbreak. immediately, they began to trust. not to figure it all out, or judge the birth mother. they waited quietly. in a year, twin girls were born and theirs was the chosen family. they lost one, and God gave them back two.

there are very many unknowns in life. a husband's job. our children's struggles. a tentative move. critical talk behind our backs. a search for our own identity. bills to pay. aged parents to look after.

let go completely. trust. live with it all in an open hand before God. Jesus promises he WILL work it all out. i do believe for you, always . . . a new sunrise.

Additional Scripture Readings:
Isaiah 26:3–14; Romans 15:13

Go to page 673 for your next devotional reading.

²⁰by his knowledge the deeps were
    divided,
  and the clouds let drop the dew.

²¹My son, preserve sound judgment and
    discernment,
  do not let them out of your sight;
²²they will be life for you,
  an ornament to grace your neck.
²³Then you will go on your way in
    safety,
  and your foot will not stumble;
²⁴when you lie down, you will not be
    afraid;
  when you lie down, your sleep will
    be sweet.
²⁵Have no fear of sudden disaster
  or of the ruin that overtakes the
    wicked,
²⁶for the LORD will be your confidence
  and will keep your foot from being
    snared.

²⁷Do not withhold good from those who
    deserve it,
  when it is in your power to act.
²⁸Do not say to your neighbor,
  "Come back later; I'll give it
    tomorrow"—
  when you now have it with you.

²⁹Do not plot harm against your
    neighbor,
  who lives trustfully near you.
³⁰Do not accuse a man for no reason—
  when he has done you no harm.

³¹Do not envy a violent man
  or choose any of his ways,
³²for the LORD detests a perverse man
  but takes the upright into his
    confidence.

³³The LORD's curse is on the house of
    the wicked,
  but he blesses the home of the
    righteous.
³⁴He mocks proud mockers
  but gives grace to the humble.
³⁵The wise inherit honor,
  but fools he holds up to shame.

Wisdom Is Supreme

4 Listen, my sons, to a father's
    instruction;
  pay attention and gain
    understanding.
²I give you sound learning,
  so do not forsake my teaching.

³When I was a boy in my father's
    house,
  still tender, and an only child of my
    mother,
⁴he taught me and said,
  "Lay hold of my words with all your
    heart;
  keep my commands and you will
    live.
⁵Get wisdom, get understanding;
  do not forget my words or swerve
    from them.
⁶Do not forsake wisdom, and she will
    protect you;
  love her, and she will watch over
    you.
⁷Wisdom is supreme; therefore get
    wisdom.
  Though it cost all you have,ᵃ get
    understanding.
⁸Esteem her, and she will exalt you;
  embrace her, and she will honor
    you.
⁹She will set a garland of grace on
    your head
  and present you with a crown of
    splendor."

¹⁰Listen, my son, accept what I say,
  and the years of your life will be
    many.
¹¹I guide you in the way of wisdom
  and lead you along straight paths.
¹²When you walk, your steps will not be
    hampered;
  when you run, you will not
    stumble.
¹³Hold on to instruction, do not let it
    go;
  guard it well, for it is your life.
¹⁴Do not set foot on the path of the
    wicked
  or walk in the way of evil men.
¹⁵Avoid it, do not travel on it;
  turn from it and go on your way.
¹⁶For they cannot sleep till they do evil;
  they are robbed of slumber till they
    make someone fall.
¹⁷They eat the bread of wickedness
  and drink the wine of violence.

¹⁸The path of the righteous is like the
    first gleam of dawn,
  shining ever brighter till the full
    light of day.
¹⁹But the way of the wicked is like
    deep darkness;
  they do not know what makes them
    stumble.

ᵃ7 Or *Whatever else you get*

20My son, pay attention to what I say;
  listen closely to my words.
21Do not let them out of your sight,
  keep them within your heart;
22for they are life to those who find
    them
  and health to a man's whole body.
23Above all else, guard your heart,
  for it is the wellspring of life.
24Put away perversity from your mouth;
  keep corrupt talk far from your lips.
25Let your eyes look straight ahead,
  fix your gaze directly before you.
26Make level*a* paths for your feet
  and take only ways that are firm.
27Do not swerve to the right or the left;
  keep your foot from evil.

Warning Against Adultery

5 My son, pay attention to my
    wisdom,
  listen well to my words of insight,
2that you may maintain discretion
  and your lips may preserve
    knowledge.
3For the lips of an adulteress drip
    honey,
  and her speech is smoother than
    oil;
4but in the end she is bitter as gall,
  sharp as a double-edged sword.
5Her feet go down to death;
  her steps lead straight to the
    grave.*b*
6She gives no thought to the way of
    life;
  her paths are crooked, but she
    knows it not.

7Now then, my sons, listen to me;
  do not turn aside from what I say.
8Keep to a path far from her,
  do not go near the door of her
    house,
9lest you give your best strength to
    others
  and your years to one who is cruel,
10lest strangers feast on your wealth
  and your toil enrich another man's
    house.
11At the end of your life you will groan,
  when your flesh and body are
    spent.
12You will say, "How I hated discipline!
  How my heart spurned correction!
13I would not obey my teachers
  or listen to my instructors.
14I have come to the brink of utter ruin

in the midst of the whole
    assembly."

15Drink water from your own cistern,
  running water from your own well.
16Should your springs overflow in the
    streets,
  your streams of water in the public
    squares?
17Let them be yours alone,
  never to be shared with strangers.
18May your fountain be blessed,
  and may you rejoice in the wife of
    your youth.
19A loving doe, a graceful deer—
  may her breasts satisfy you always,
  may you ever be captivated by her
    love.
20Why be captivated, my son, by an
    adulteress?
  Why embrace the bosom of another
    man's wife?
21For a man's ways are in full view of
    the LORD,
  and he examines all his paths.
22The evil deeds of a wicked man
    ensnare him;
  the cords of his sin hold him fast.
23He will die for lack of discipline,
  led astray by his own great folly.

Warnings Against Folly

6 My son, if you have put up security
    for your neighbor,
  if you have struck hands in pledge
    for another,
2if you have been trapped by what you
    said,
  ensnared by the words of your
    mouth,
3then do this, my son, to free yourself,
  since you have fallen into your
    neighbor's hands:
  Go and humble yourself;
  press your plea with your neighbor!
4Allow no sleep to your eyes,
  no slumber to your eyelids.
5Free yourself, like a gazelle from the
    hand of the hunter,
  like a bird from the snare of the
    fowler.

6Go to the ant, you sluggard;
  consider its ways and be wise!
7It has no commander,
  no overseer or ruler,
8yet it stores its provisions in summer
  and gathers its food at harvest.

a26 Or Consider the   b5 Hebrew Sheol

⁹How long will you lie there, you
   sluggard?
When will you get up from your
   sleep?
¹⁰A little sleep, a little slumber,
   a little folding of the hands to
      rest—
¹¹and poverty will come on you like a
      bandit
   and scarcity like an armed man.ᵃ

¹²A scoundrel and villain,
   who goes about with a corrupt
      mouth,
¹³ who winks with his eye,
   signals with his feet
   and motions with his fingers,
¹⁴ who plots evil with deceit in his
      heart—
   he always stirs up dissension.
¹⁵Therefore disaster will overtake him
      in an instant;
   he will suddenly be
      destroyed—without remedy.

¹⁶There are six things the LORD hates,
   seven that are detestable to him:
¹⁷   haughty eyes,
   a lying tongue,
   hands that shed innocent blood,
¹⁸   a heart that devises wicked
         schemes,
   feet that are quick to rush into
      evil,
¹⁹   a false witness who pours out lies
   and a man who stirs up
      dissension among brothers.

Warning Against Adultery

²⁰My son, keep your father's commands
   and do not forsake your mother's
      teaching.
²¹Bind them upon your heart forever;
   fasten them around your neck.
²²When you walk, they will guide you;
   when you sleep, they will watch
      over you;
   when you awake, they will speak to
      you.
²³For these commands are a lamp,
   this teaching is a light,
   and the corrections of discipline
      are the way to life,
²⁴keeping you from the immoral
      woman,
   from the smooth tongue of the
      wayward wife.
²⁵Do not lust in your heart after her
      beauty

or let her captivate you with her
   eyes,
²⁶for the prostitute reduces you to a
      loaf of bread,
   and the adulteress preys upon your
      very life.
²⁷Can a man scoop fire into his lap
   without his clothes being burned?
²⁸Can a man walk on hot coals
   without his feet being scorched?
²⁹So is he who sleeps with another
      man's wife;
   no one who touches her will go
      unpunished.

³⁰Men do not despise a thief if he
      steals
   to satisfy his hunger when he is
      starving.
³¹Yet if he is caught, he must pay
      sevenfold,
   though it costs him all the wealth
      of his house.
³²But a man who commits adultery
      lacks judgment;
   whoever does so destroys himself.
³³Blows and disgrace are his lot,
   and his shame will never be wiped
      away;
³⁴for jealousy arouses a husband's fury,
   and he will show no mercy when he
      takes revenge.
³⁵He will not accept any compensation;
   he will refuse the bribe, however
      great it is.

Warning Against the Adulteress

7 My son, keep my words
   and store up my commands within
      you.
²Keep my commands and you will live;
   guard my teachings as the apple of
      your eye.
³Bind them on your fingers;
   write them on the tablet of your
      heart.
⁴Say to wisdom, "You are my sister,"
   and call understanding your
      kinsman;
⁵they will keep you from the
      adulteress,
   from the wayward wife with her
      seductive words.

⁶At the window of my house
   I looked out through the lattice.
⁷I saw among the simple,
   I noticed among the young men,
   a youth who lacked judgment.

ᵃ11 Or like a vagrant / and scarcity like a beggar

⁸He was going down the street near
      her corner,
   walking along in the direction of
      her house
⁹at twilight, as the day was fading,
   as the dark of night set in.

¹⁰Then out came a woman to meet
      him,
   dressed like a prostitute and with
      crafty intent.
¹¹(She is loud and defiant,
   her feet never stay at home;
¹²now in the street, now in the squares,
   at every corner she lurks.)
¹³She took hold of him and kissed him
   and with a brazen face she said:

¹⁴"I have fellowship offerings ᵃ at home;
   today I fulfilled my vows.
¹⁵So I came out to meet you;
   I looked for you and have found
      you!
¹⁶I have covered my bed
   with colored linens from Egypt.
¹⁷I have perfumed my bed
   with myrrh, aloes and cinnamon.
¹⁸Come, let's drink deep of love till
      morning;
   let's enjoy ourselves with love!
¹⁹My husband is not at home;
   he has gone on a long journey.
²⁰He took his purse filled with money
   and will not be home till full
      moon."

²¹With persuasive words she led him
      astray;
   she seduced him with her smooth
      talk.
²²All at once he followed her
   like an ox going to the slaughter,
   like a deer ᵇ stepping into a noose ᶜ
²³   till an arrow pierces his liver,
   like a bird darting into a snare,
   little knowing it will cost him his
      life.

²⁴Now then, my sons, listen to me;
   pay attention to what I say.
²⁵Do not let your heart turn to her ways
   or stray into her paths.
²⁶Many are the victims she has brought
      down;
   her slain are a mighty throng.
²⁷Her house is a highway to the grave, ᵈ
   leading down to the chambers of
      death.

Wisdom's Call

8 Does not wisdom call out?
   Does not understanding raise her
      voice?
²On the heights along the way,
   where the paths meet, she takes
      her stand;
³beside the gates leading into the city,
   at the entrances, she cries aloud:
⁴"To you, O men, I call out;
   I raise my voice to all mankind.
⁵You who are simple, gain prudence;
   you who are foolish, gain
      understanding.
⁶Listen, for I have worthy things to
      say;
   I open my lips to speak what is
      right.
⁷My mouth speaks what is true,
   for my lips detest wickedness.
⁸All the words of my mouth are just;
   none of them is crooked or
      perverse.
⁹To the discerning all of them are
      right;
   they are faultless to those who have
      knowledge.
¹⁰Choose my instruction instead of
      silver,
   knowledge rather than choice gold,
¹¹for wisdom is more precious than
      rubies,
   and nothing you desire can
      compare with her.

¹²"I, wisdom, dwell together with
      prudence;
   I possess knowledge and discretion.
¹³To fear the LORD is to hate evil;
   I hate pride and arrogance,
   evil behavior and perverse speech.
¹⁴Counsel and sound judgment are
      mine;
   I have understanding and power.
¹⁵By me kings reign
   and rulers make laws that are just;
¹⁶by me princes govern,
   and all nobles who rule on earth. ᵉ
¹⁷I love those who love me,
   and those who seek me find me.
¹⁸With me are riches and honor,
   enduring wealth and prosperity.
¹⁹My fruit is better than fine gold;
   what I yield surpasses choice silver.
²⁰I walk in the way of righteousness,
   along the paths of justice,

ᵃ14 Traditionally *peace offerings*   ᵇ22 Syriac (see also Septuagint); Hebrew *fool*   ᶜ22 The meaning
of the Hebrew for this line is uncertain.   ᵈ27 Hebrew *Sheol*   ᵉ16 Many Hebrew manuscripts and
Septuagint; most Hebrew manuscripts *and nobles—all righteous rulers*

²¹bestowing wealth on those who love
me
and making their treasuries full.

²²"The Lord brought me forth as the
first of his works,ᵃ, ᵇ
before his deeds of old;
²³I was appointedᶜ from eternity,
from the beginning, before the
world began.
²⁴When there were no oceans, I was
given birth,
when there were no springs
abounding with water;
²⁵before the mountains were settled in
place,
before the hills, I was given birth,
²⁶before he made the earth or its fields
or any of the dust of the world.
²⁷I was there when he set the heavens
in place,
when he marked out the horizon on
the face of the deep,
²⁸when he established the clouds above
and fixed securely the fountains of
the deep,
²⁹when he gave the sea its boundary
so the waters would not overstep
his command,
and when he marked out the
foundations of the earth.
³⁰ Then I was the craftsman at his
side.
I was filled with delight day after day,
rejoicing always in his presence,
³¹rejoicing in his whole world
and delighting in mankind.

³²"Now then, my sons, listen to me;
blessed are those who keep my
ways.
³³Listen to my instruction and be wise;
do not ignore it.
³⁴Blessed is the man who listens to me,
watching daily at my doors,
waiting at my doorway.
³⁵For whoever finds me finds life
and receives favor from the Lord.
³⁶But whoever fails to find me harms
himself;
all who hate me love death."

Invitations of Wisdom and of Folly

9 Wisdom has built her house;
she has hewn out its seven pillars.
²She has prepared her meat and mixed
her wine;
she has also set her table.

³She has sent out her maids, and she
calls
from the highest point of the
city.
⁴"Let all who are simple come in
here!"
she says to those who lack
judgment.
⁵"Come, eat my food
and drink the wine I have mixed.
⁶Leave your simple ways and you will
live;
walk in the way of understanding.

⁷"Whoever corrects a mocker invites
insult;
whoever rebukes a wicked man
incurs abuse.
⁸Do not rebuke a mocker or he will
hate you;
rebuke a wise man and he will love
you.
⁹Instruct a wise man and he will be
wiser still;
teach a righteous man and he will
add to his learning.

¹⁰"The fear of the Lord is the beginning
of wisdom,
and knowledge of the Holy One is
understanding.
¹¹For through me your days will be
many,
and years will be added to your
life.
¹²If you are wise, your wisdom will
reward you;
if you are a mocker, you alone will
suffer."

¹³The woman Folly is loud;
she is undisciplined and without
knowledge.
¹⁴She sits at the door of her house,
on a seat at the highest point of
the city,
¹⁵calling out to those who pass by,
who go straight on their way.
¹⁶"Let all who are simple come in
here!"
she says to those who lack
judgment.
¹⁷"Stolen water is sweet;
food eaten in secret is delicious!"
¹⁸But little do they know that the dead
are there,
that her guests are in the depths of
the grave.ᵈ

ᵃ22 Or way; or dominion   ᵇ22 Or The Lord possessed me at the beginning of his work; or The Lord
brought me forth at the beginning of his work   ᶜ23 Or fashioned   ᵈ18 Hebrew Sheol

Proverbs of Solomon

10 The proverbs of Solomon:

A wise son brings joy to his
father,
but a foolish son grief to his
mother.

2Ill-gotten treasures are of no value,
but righteousness delivers from
death.

3The LORD does not let the righteous
go hungry
but he thwarts the craving of the
wicked.

4Lazy hands make a man poor,
but diligent hands bring wealth.

5He who gathers crops in summer is a
wise son,
but he who sleeps during harvest is
a disgraceful son.

6Blessings crown the head of the
righteous,
but violence overwhelms the mouth
of the wicked. *a*

7The memory of the righteous will be a
blessing,
but the name of the wicked will
rot.

8The wise in heart accept commands,
but a chattering fool comes to ruin.

9The man of integrity walks securely,
but he who takes crooked paths
will be found out.

10He who winks maliciously causes
grief,
and a chattering fool comes to ruin.

11The mouth of the righteous is a
fountain of life,
but violence overwhelms the mouth
of the wicked.

12Hatred stirs up dissension,
but love covers over all wrongs.

13Wisdom is found on the lips of the
discerning,
but a rod is for the back of him
who lacks judgment.

14Wise men store up knowledge,
but the mouth of a fool invites
ruin.

15The wealth of the rich is their
fortified city,

but poverty is the ruin of the poor.

16The wages of the righteous bring
them life,
but the income of the wicked
brings them punishment.

17He who heeds discipline shows the
way to life,
but whoever ignores correction
leads others astray.

18He who conceals his hatred has lying
lips,
and whoever spreads slander is a
fool.

19When words are many, sin is not
absent,
but he who holds his tongue is
wise.

20The tongue of the righteous is choice
silver,
but the heart of the wicked is of
little value.

21The lips of the righteous nourish
many,
but fools die for lack of judgment.

22The blessing of the LORD brings
wealth,
and he adds no trouble to it.

23A fool finds pleasure in evil conduct,
but a man of understanding
delights in wisdom.

24What the wicked dreads will overtake
him;
what the righteous desire will be
granted.

25When the storm has swept by, the
wicked are gone,
but the righteous stand firm
forever.

26As vinegar to the teeth and smoke to
the eyes,
so is a sluggard to those who send
him.

27The fear of the LORD adds length to
life,
but the years of the wicked are cut
short.

28The prospect of the righteous is joy,
but the hopes of the wicked come
to nothing.

29The way of the LORD is a refuge for
the righteous,

---

a6 Or but the mouth of the wicked conceals violence; also in verse 11 but it is the ruin of those who do evil.

30The righteous will never be uprooted,
but the wicked will not remain in the land.

31The mouth of the righteous brings forth wisdom,
but a perverse tongue will be cut out.

32The lips of the righteous know what is fitting,
but the mouth of the wicked only what is perverse.

11 The Lord abhors dishonest scales,
but accurate weights are his delight.

2When pride comes, then comes disgrace,
but with humility comes wisdom.

3The integrity of the upright guides them,
but the unfaithful are destroyed by their duplicity.

4Wealth is worthless in the day of wrath,
but righteousness delivers from death.

5The righteousness of the blameless makes a straight way for them,
but the wicked are brought down by their own wickedness.

6The righteousness of the upright delivers them,
but the unfaithful are trapped by evil desires.

7When a wicked man dies, his hope perishes;
all he expected from his power comes to nothing.

8The righteous man is rescued from trouble,
and it comes on the wicked instead.

9With his mouth the godless destroys his neighbor,
but through knowledge the righteous escape.

10When the righteous prosper, the city rejoices;
when the wicked perish, there are shouts of joy.

11Through the blessing of the upright a city is exalted,
but by the mouth of the wicked it is destroyed.

12A man who lacks judgment derides his neighbor,
but a man of understanding holds his tongue.

13A gossip betrays a confidence,
but a trustworthy man keeps a secret.

14For lack of guidance a nation falls,
but many advisers make victory sure.

15He who puts up security for another will surely suffer,
but whoever refuses to strike hands in pledge is safe.

16A kindhearted woman gains respect,
but ruthless men gain only wealth.

17A kind man benefits himself,
but a cruel man brings trouble on himself.

18The wicked man earns deceptive wages,
but he who sows righteousness reaps a sure reward.

19The truly righteous man attains life,
but he who pursues evil goes to his death.

20The Lord detests men of perverse heart
but he delights in those whose ways are blameless.

21Be sure of this: The wicked will not go unpunished,
but those who are righteous will go free.

22Like a gold ring in a pig's snout
is a beautiful woman who shows no discretion.

23The desire of the righteous ends only in good,
but the hope of the wicked only in wrath.

24One man gives freely, yet gains even more;
another withholds unduly, but comes to poverty.

25A generous man will prosper;
he who refreshes others will himself be refreshed.

²⁶People curse the man who hoards
grain,
but blessing crowns him who is
willing to sell.

²⁷He who seeks good finds goodwill,
but evil comes to him who searches
for it.

²⁸Whoever trusts in his riches will fall,
but the righteous will thrive like a
green leaf.

²⁹He who brings trouble on his family
will inherit only wind,
and the fool will be servant to the
wise.

³⁰The fruit of the righteous is a tree of
life,
and he who wins souls is wise.

³¹If the righteous receive their due on
earth,
how much more the ungodly and
the sinner!

12 Whoever loves discipline loves
knowledge,
but he who hates correction is
stupid.

²A good man obtains favor from the
LORD,
but the LORD condemns a crafty
man.

³A man cannot be established through
wickedness,
but the righteous cannot be
uprooted.

⁴A wife of noble character is her
husband's crown,
but a disgraceful wife is like decay
in his bones.

⁵The plans of the righteous are just,
but the advice of the wicked is
deceitful.

⁶The words of the wicked lie in wait
for blood,
but the speech of the upright
rescues them.

⁷Wicked men are overthrown and are
no more,
but the house of the righteous
stands firm.

⁸A man is praised according to his
wisdom,
but men with warped minds are
despised.

⁹Better to be a nobody and yet have a
servant
than pretend to be somebody and
have no food.

¹⁰A righteous man cares for the needs
of his animal,
but the kindest acts of the wicked
are cruel.

¹¹He who works his land will have
abundant food,
but he who chases fantasies lacks
judgment.

¹²The wicked desire the plunder of evil
men,
but the root of the righteous
flourishes.

¹³An evil man is trapped by his sinful
talk,
but a righteous man escapes
trouble.

¹⁴From the fruit of his lips a man is
filled with good things
as surely as the work of his hands
rewards him.

¹⁵The way of a fool seems right to him,
but a wise man listens to advice.

¹⁶A fool shows his annoyance at once,
but a prudent man overlooks an
insult.

¹⁷A truthful witness gives honest
testimony,
but a false witness tells lies.

¹⁸Reckless words pierce like a sword,
but the tongue of the wise brings
healing.

¹⁹Truthful lips endure forever,
but a lying tongue lasts only a
moment.

²⁰There is deceit in the hearts of those
who plot evil,
but joy for those who promote
peace.

²¹No harm befalls the righteous,
but the wicked have their fill of
trouble.

²²The LORD detests lying lips,
but he delights in men who are
truthful.

²³A prudent man keeps his knowledge
to himself,
but the heart of fools blurts out
folly.

24Diligent hands will rule,
   but laziness ends in slave labor.

25An anxious heart weighs a man down,
   but a kind word cheers him up.

26A righteous man is cautious in
      friendship,a
   but the way of the wicked leads
      them astray.

27The lazy man does not roastb his
      game,
   but the diligent man prizes his
      possessions.

28In the way of righteousness there is
      life;
   along that path is immortality.

13 A wise son heeds his father's
         instruction,

but a mocker does not listen to
   rebuke.

2From the fruit of his lips a man
   enjoys good things,
   but the unfaithful have a craving
   for violence.

3He who guards his lips guards his life,
   but he who speaks rashly will come
   to ruin.

4The sluggard craves and gets nothing,
   but the desires of the diligent are
   fully satisfied.

5The righteous hate what is false,
   but the wicked bring shame and
   disgrace.

6Righteousness guards the man of
   integrity,

a26 Or *man is a guide to his neighbor*   b27 The meaning of the Hebrew for this word is uncertain.

VERSE FOR THE DAY: *AUTHOR:*   *PASSAGE FOR THE DAY:*
Proverbs 12:16   Pamela Reeve   Proverbs 12:14–28

Relationships: Why Bother

THE other morning I was studying the section of Proverbs that
says:

> A fool shows his annoyance at once,
>   but a prudent man overlooks an insult
>   (Proverbs 12:16).

I said to the Lord, "You know, that's great, that's tremendous!
That's where I want to be, Lord. That's for me today." Within
two hours after I arrived at my office, I did not ignore what I saw
as an insult. I showed my annoyance immediately!

All of the good spiritual input that we receive and enjoy is put
to the test as we relate to other people. My real growth that
morning did not take place as I was reading the Bible verse and
thinking, "Isn't that marvelous?" The real growth came from
blowing it and realizing I had really blown it. "Lord, forgive me.
Wrong way. No good. Bring me another test and help me respond properly." That is growth.

Additional Scripture Readings: *Go to page 675 for your next*
James 1:22–25; 1 John 2:1–6   *devotional reading.*

but wickedness overthrows the
sinner.

7One man pretends to be rich, yet has
nothing;
another pretends to be poor, yet
has great wealth.

8A man's riches may ransom his life,
but a poor man hears no threat.

9The light of the righteous shines
brightly,
but the lamp of the wicked is
snuffed out.

10Pride only breeds quarrels,
but wisdom is found in those who
take advice.

11Dishonest money dwindles away,
but he who gathers money little by
little makes it grow.

12Hope deferred makes the heart sick,
but a longing fulfilled is a tree of
life.

13He who scorns instruction will pay for
it,
but he who respects a command is
rewarded.

14The teaching of the wise is a fountain
of life,
turning a man from the snares of
death.

15Good understanding wins favor,
but the way of the unfaithful is
hard.a

16Every prudent man acts out of
knowledge,
but a fool exposes his folly.

17A wicked messenger falls into trouble,
but a trustworthy envoy brings
healing.

18He who ignores discipline comes to
poverty and shame,
but whoever heeds correction is
honored.

19A longing fulfilled is sweet to the
soul,
but fools detest turning from evil.

20He who walks with the wise grows
wise,
but a companion of fools suffers
harm.

21Misfortune pursues the sinner,

but prosperity is the reward of the
righteous.

22A good man leaves an inheritance for
his children's children,
but a sinner's wealth is stored up
for the righteous.

23A poor man's field may produce
abundant food,
but injustice sweeps it away.

24He who spares the rod hates his son,
but he who loves him is careful to
discipline him.

25The righteous eat to their hearts'
content,
but the stomach of the wicked goes
hungry.

14 The wise woman builds her
house,
but with her own hands the foolish
one tears hers down.

2He whose walk is upright fears the
LORD,
but he whose ways are devious
despises him.

3A fool's talk brings a rod to his back,
but the lips of the wise protect
them.

4Where there are no oxen, the manger
is empty,
but from the strength of an ox
comes an abundant harvest.

5A truthful witness does not deceive,
but a false witness pours out lies.

6The mocker seeks wisdom and finds
none,
but knowledge comes easily to the
discerning.

7Stay away from a foolish man,
for you will not find knowledge on
his lips.

8The wisdom of the prudent is to give
thought to their ways,
but the folly of fools is deception.

9Fools mock at making amends for sin,
but goodwill is found among the
upright.

10Each heart knows its own bitterness,
and no one else can share its joy.

11The house of the wicked will be
destroyed,

a15 Or unfaithful does not endure

VERSE FOR THE DAY:
Proverbs 13:3

AUTHOR:
Susan L. Lenzkes

PASSAGE FOR THE DAY:
Proverbs 13:1–5

That's a Mouthful!

DON'T look now, Lord!
I don't want You
to see me
standing here with
my big foot
crammed in my mouth.

Don't worry, child.
If I didn't love you
just as much with your
foot in your mouth,
I'd hardly ever get a
chance to love you.

Mothers are often forced to utter things other people wouldn't even think. One day I actually heard myself yelling in my hands-on-hips tone of voice, "All right! Who put the fire truck in the toilet?"

A lot of motherly queries seem to be preceded by the weary word, "Who put the . . . ," and end with a scramble of objects so strange they could be a mad Parker Brothers' game of chance.

Over the years, anyone who happened to be in the wrong place at the right time could have heard me asking who put: the cereal behind the couch? (the ants found it first); the pine cones in my purse? (I discovered them during church); the lemon pudding mix in the wading pool? (it was gelling in the corners); the toothpaste on the wall? (it looked like a fluoridated Picasso); the toy dish in the oven? (the flames were leaping out the vent).

Actually, parents should be taught not to ask questions, because either no one did it, or the other guy did it. And if you ever do manage to pin the culprit, you tend to ask why. "Why did you put the rock in the refrigerator?" And then you get an answer: "Because I wanted a cold rock."

It's obvious that parenthood requires carloads of patience. And I could feel reasonably righteous about boisterously losing that patience when the going gets rough, if it weren't for the fact that God has to lavish so much of it on me.

Occasionally, after I've lost my temper at the children, I've heard my heavenly Father patiently asking, "Who put the foot in the mouth?"

Additional Scripture Readings:
Ephesians 5:29; James 1:19–21

Go to page 677 for your next devotional reading.

but the tent of the upright will
flourish.

¹²There is a way that seems right to a
man,
but in the end it leads to death.

¹³Even in laughter the heart may ache,
and joy may end in grief.

¹⁴The faithless will be fully repaid for
their ways,
and the good man rewarded for his.

¹⁵A simple man believes anything,
but a prudent man gives thought to
his steps.

¹⁶A wise man fears the LORD and shuns
evil,
but a fool is hotheaded and
reckless.

¹⁷A quick-tempered man does foolish
things,
and a crafty man is hated.

¹⁸The simple inherit folly,
but the prudent are crowned with
knowledge.

¹⁹Evil men will bow down in the
presence of the good,
and the wicked at the gates of the
righteous.

²⁰The poor are shunned even by their
neighbors,
but the rich have many friends.

²¹He who despises his neighbor sins,
but blessed is he who is kind to the
needy.

²²Do not those who plot evil go astray?
But those who plan what is good
find*ᵃ* love and faithfulness.

²³All hard work brings a profit,
but mere talk leads only to poverty.

²⁴The wealth of the wise is their crown,
but the folly of fools yields folly.

²⁵A truthful witness saves lives,
but a false witness is deceitful.

²⁶He who fears the LORD has a secure
fortress,
and for his children it will be a
refuge.

²⁷The fear of the LORD is a fountain of
life,
turning a man from the snares of
death.

²⁸A large population is a king's glory,
but without subjects a prince is
ruined.

²⁹A patient man has great
understanding,
but a quick-tempered man displays
folly.

³⁰A heart at peace gives life to the
body,
but envy rots the bones.

³¹He who oppresses the poor shows
contempt for their Maker,
but whoever is kind to the needy
honors God.

³²When calamity comes, the wicked are
brought down,
but even in death the righteous
have a refuge.

³³Wisdom reposes in the heart of the
discerning
and even among fools she lets
herself be known.*ᵇ*

³⁴Righteousness exalts a nation,
but sin is a disgrace to any people.

³⁵A king delights in a wise servant,
but a shameful servant incurs his
wrath.

15 A gentle answer turns away
wrath,
but a harsh word stirs up anger.

²The tongue of the wise commends
knowledge,
but the mouth of the fool gushes
folly.

³The eyes of the LORD are everywhere,
keeping watch on the wicked and
the good.

⁴The tongue that brings healing is a
tree of life,
but a deceitful tongue crushes the
spirit.

⁵A fool spurns his father's discipline,
but whoever heeds correction shows
prudence.

⁶The house of the righteous contains
great treasure,
but the income of the wicked
brings them trouble.

⁷The lips of the wise spread
knowledge;

ᵃ22 Or *show*   *ᵇ33* Hebrew; Septuagint and Syriac / *but in the heart of fools she is not known* not so the hearts of fools.

8The LORD detests the sacrifice of the
    wicked,
but the prayer of the upright
    pleases him.

9The LORD detests the way of the
    wicked
but he loves those who pursue
    righteousness.

10Stern discipline awaits him who
    leaves the path;
he who hates correction will die.

11Death and Destruction[a] lie open
    before the LORD—
how much more the hearts of men!

12A mocker resents correction;
    he will not consult the wise.

13A happy heart makes the face
    cheerful,
but heartache crushes the spirit.

14The discerning heart seeks
    knowledge,
but the mouth of a fool feeds on
    folly.

15All the days of the oppressed are
    wretched,
but the cheerful heart has a
    continual feast.

16Better a little with the fear of the
    LORD

a 11 Hebrew *Sheol and Abaddon*

FRIDAY

VERSE FOR THE DAY:
Proverbs 15:13,15,30

AUTHOR:
Marjorie Holmes

PASSAGE FOR THE DAY:
Proverbs 15:13–33

It's Been a Good Day

IT'S been a good day, Lord. Yes, a very good day.

I didn't realize it while it was happening. There were many frustrations. I was very discouraged when the letter I was praying for didn't come. Then the telephone rang, bringing good news.

When a child was carried home from the playground hurt and we rushed him to the hospital, you knew my awful fears. But to learn that it wasn't really serious brought a sense of heightened joy. (Sheer relief can generate sheer bliss.)

So now the child is asleep, with the bandage slipped rather comically from his head. My husband stands in the yard, leaning on his rake as he visits with a neighbor.

Other children come spilling across the yard. The sun is a golden glory behind the trees. I can smell the pot roast mingling with the tangy fragrance of burning leaves.

I look back on this day with its usual ups and downs. Its moments of anguish, its moments of gratefulness and joy. And now that it's ending, an aching awareness fills me. I realize that it's been a good day, Lord. A very good day.

For it's been filled with life. The life you have given me to cope with, and to contribute to. And I wouldn't want to have missed it, not a single moment of it.

Thank you, God, for this good day.

Additional Scripture Readings:
Psalm 118:24; Matthew 6:33–34

*Go to page 680 for your next
devotional reading.*

than great wealth with turmoil.

¹⁷Better a meal of vegetables where
there is love
than a fattened calf with hatred.

¹⁸A hot-tempered man stirs up
dissension,
but a patient man calms a quarrel.

¹⁹The way of the sluggard is blocked
with thorns,
but the path of the upright is a
highway.

²⁰A wise son brings joy to his father,
but a foolish man despises his
mother.

²¹Folly delights a man who lacks
judgment,
but a man of understanding keeps a
straight course.

²²Plans fail for lack of counsel,
but with many advisers they
succeed.

²³A man finds joy in giving an apt
reply—
and how good is a timely word!

²⁴The path of life leads upward for the
wise
to keep him from going down to
the grave.ᵃ

²⁵The Lord tears down the proud man's
house
but he keeps the widow's
boundaries intact.

²⁶The Lord detests the thoughts of the
wicked,
but those of the pure are pleasing
to him.

²⁷A greedy man brings trouble to his
family,
but he who hates bribes will live.

²⁸The heart of the righteous weighs its
answers,
but the mouth of the wicked
gushes evil.

²⁹The Lord is far from the wicked
but he hears the prayer of the
righteous.

³⁰A cheerful look brings joy to the
heart,
and good news gives health to the
bones.

³¹He who listens to a life-giving rebuke
will be at home among the wise.

³²He who ignores discipline despises
himself,
but whoever heeds correction gains
understanding.

³³The fear of the Lord teaches a man
wisdom,ᵇ
and humility comes before honor.

16 To man belong the plans of the
heart,
but from the Lord comes the reply
of the tongue.

²All a man's ways seem innocent to
him,
but motives are weighed by the
Lord.

³Commit to the Lord whatever you do,
and your plans will succeed.

⁴The Lord works out everything for his
own ends—
even the wicked for a day of
disaster.

⁵The Lord detests all the proud of
heart.
Be sure of this: They will not go
unpunished.

⁶Through love and faithfulness sin is
atoned for;
through the fear of the Lord a man
avoids evil.

⁷When a man's ways are pleasing to
the Lord,
he makes even his enemies live at
peace with him.

⁸Better a little with righteousness
than much gain with injustice.

⁹In his heart a man plans his course,
but the Lord determines his steps.

¹⁰The lips of a king speak as an oracle,
and his mouth should not betray
justice.

¹¹Honest scales and balances are from
the Lord;
all the weights in the bag are of his
making.

¹²Kings detest wrongdoing,
for a throne is established through
righteousness.

¹³Kings take pleasure in honest lips;

ᵃ24 Hebrew *Sheol*   ᵇ33 Or *Wisdom teaches the fear of the Lord* they value a man who speaks the truth.

¹⁴A king's wrath is a messenger of death,
but a wise man will appease it.

¹⁵When a king's face brightens, it means life;
his favor is like a rain cloud in spring.

¹⁶How much better to get wisdom than gold,
to choose understanding rather than silver!

¹⁷The highway of the upright avoids evil;
he who guards his way guards his life.

¹⁸Pride goes before destruction,
a haughty spirit before a fall.

¹⁹Better to be lowly in spirit and among the oppressed
than to share plunder with the proud.

²⁰Whoever gives heed to instruction prospers,
and blessed is he who trusts in the LORD.

²¹The wise in heart are called discerning,
and pleasant words promote instruction.ᵃ

²²Understanding is a fountain of life to those who have it,
but folly brings punishment to fools.

²³A wise man's heart guides his mouth,
and his lips promote instruction.ᵇ

²⁴Pleasant words are a honeycomb,
sweet to the soul and healing to the bones.

²⁵There is a way that seems right to a man,
but in the end it leads to death.

²⁶The laborer's appetite works for him;
his hunger drives him on.

²⁷A scoundrel plots evil,
and his speech is like a scorching fire.

²⁸A perverse man stirs up dissension,
and a gossip separates close friends.

²⁹A violent man entices his neighbor
and leads him down a path that is not good.

³⁰He who winks with his eye is plotting perversity;
he who purses his lips is bent on evil.

³¹Gray hair is a crown of splendor;
it is attained by a righteous life.

³²Better a patient man than a warrior,
a man who controls his temper
than one who takes a city.

³³The lot is cast into the lap,
but its every decision is from the LORD.

17 Better a dry crust with peace and quiet
than a house full of feasting,ᶜ with strife.

²A wise servant will rule over a disgraceful son,
and will share the inheritance as one of the brothers.

³The crucible for silver and the furnace for gold,
but the LORD tests the heart.

⁴A wicked man listens to evil lips;
a liar pays attention to a malicious tongue.

⁵He who mocks the poor shows contempt for their Maker;
whoever gloats over disaster will not go unpunished.

⁶Children's children are a crown to the aged,
and parents are the pride of their children.

⁷Arrogantᵈ lips are unsuited to a fool—
how much worse lying lips to a ruler!

⁸A bribe is a charm to the one who gives it;
wherever he turns, he succeeds.

⁹He who covers over an offense promotes love,
but whoever repeats the matter separates close friends.

ᵃ21 Or *words make a man persuasive*   ᵇ23 Or *mouth / and makes his lips persuasive*   ᶜ1 Hebrew *sacrifices*   ᵈ7 Or *Eloquent*

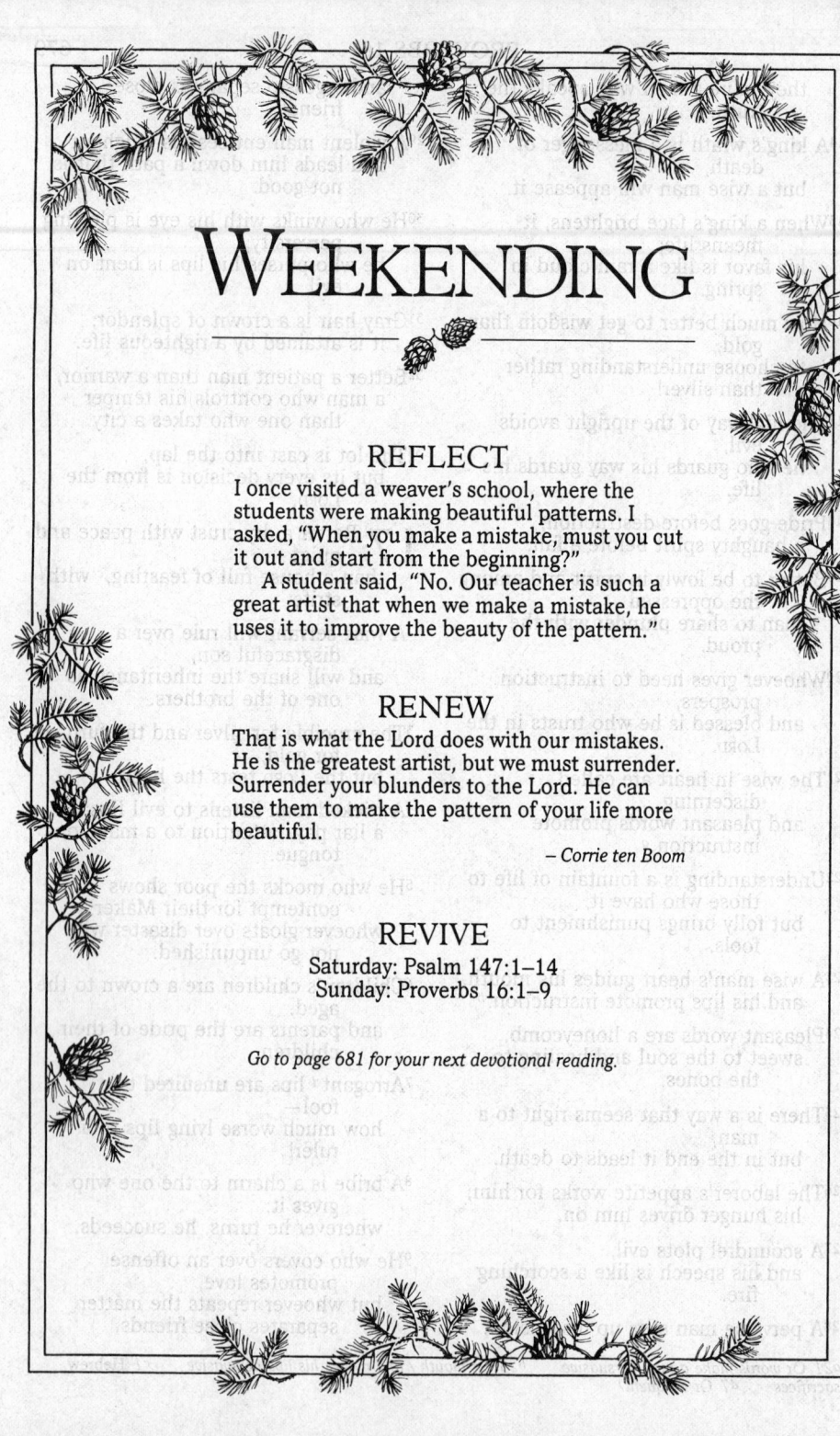

WEEKENDING

REFLECT

I once visited a weaver's school, where the students were making beautiful patterns. I asked, "When you make a mistake, must you cut it out and start from the beginning?"

A student said, "No. Our teacher is such a great artist that when we make a mistake, he uses it to improve the beauty of the pattern."

RENEW

That is what the Lord does with our mistakes. He is the greatest artist, but we must surrender. Surrender your blunders to the Lord. He can use them to make the pattern of your life more beautiful.

— *Corrie ten Boom*

REVIVE

Saturday: Psalm 147:1–14
Sunday: Proverbs 16:1–9

Go to page 681 for your next devotional reading.

10A rebuke impresses a man of
   discernment
more than a hundred lashes a fool.

11An evil man is bent only on rebellion;
   a merciless official will be sent
   against him.

12Better to meet a bear robbed of her
   cubs
than a fool in his folly.

13If a man pays back evil for good,
   evil will never leave his house.

14Starting a quarrel is like breaching a
   dam;
so drop the matter before a dispute
   breaks out.

15Acquitting the guilty and condemning
   the innocent—
the LORD detests them both.

16Of what use is money in the hand of
   a fool,
since he has no desire to get
   wisdom?

17A friend loves at all times,
   and a brother is born for adversity.

18A man lacking in judgment strikes
   hands in pledge
and puts up security for his
   neighbor.

19He who loves a quarrel loves sin;
   he who builds a high gate invites
   destruction.

20A man of perverse heart does not
   prosper;
he whose tongue is deceitful falls
   into trouble.

21To have a fool for a son brings grief;
   there is no joy for the father of a
   fool.

22A cheerful heart is good medicine,
   but a crushed spirit dries up the
   bones.

MONDAY

VERSE FOR THE DAY:
Proverbs 17:17

AUTHOR:
Susan L. Lenzkes

PASSAGE FOR THE DAY:
Proverbs 17:14–22

A Friend in Need

FRIENDSHIP gives license to show up at the door of need without asking, "When would you like me to come?" or "What would you like me to do?" Nor does friendship call out, "Just let me know if you need anything."

Practiced friendship whispers, "I'll be there" and promptly steps through the door with sensitivity, respect, and understanding.

But what about honoring the right to invite? Those who wait for parchment invitations wait long, for need rarely throws a party—rarely even has a voice.

Yet need has its own needs. It needs protection from strangers tromping in with work boots and good intentions. And it needs relief from acquaintances wearing the spiked heels of advice and pat answers.

Need waits with longing for the familiar entrance of dear ones who pad barefoot through the soul on ordinary days.

Additional Scripture Readings:
Ruth 1:11–18; Mark 2:1–5

*Go to page 684 for your next
devotional reading.*

23A wicked man accepts a bribe in
secret
to pervert the course of justice.

24A discerning man keeps wisdom in
view,
but a fool's eyes wander to the
ends of the earth.

25A foolish son brings grief to his father
and bitterness to the one who bore
him.

26It is not good to punish an innocent
man,
or to flog officials for their integrity.

27A man of knowledge uses words with
restraint,
and a man of understanding is
even-tempered.

28Even a fool is thought wise if he
keeps silent,
and discerning if he holds his
tongue.

18 An unfriendly man pursues
selfish ends;
he defies all sound judgment.

2A fool finds no pleasure in
understanding
but delights in airing his own
opinions.

3When wickedness comes, so does
contempt,
and with shame comes disgrace.

4The words of a man's mouth are deep
waters,
but the fountain of wisdom is a
bubbling brook.

5It is not good to be partial to the
wicked
or to deprive the innocent of
justice.

6A fool's lips bring him strife,
and his mouth invites a beating.

7A fool's mouth is his undoing,
and his lips are a snare to his soul.

8The words of a gossip are like choice
morsels;
they go down to a man's inmost
parts.

9One who is slack in his work
is brother to one who destroys.

10The name of the LORD is a strong
tower;
the righteous run to it and are safe.

11The wealth of the rich is their
fortified city;
they imagine it an unscalable wall.

12Before his downfall a man's heart is
proud,
but humility comes before honor.

13He who answers before listening—
that is his folly and his shame.

14A man's spirit sustains him in
sickness,
but a crushed spirit who can bear?

15The heart of the discerning acquires
knowledge;
the ears of the wise seek it out.

16A gift opens the way for the giver
and ushers him into the presence
of the great.

17The first to present his case seems
right,
till another comes forward and
questions him.

18Casting the lot settles disputes
and keeps strong opponents apart.

19An offended brother is more
unyielding than a fortified city,
and disputes are like the barred
gates of a citadel.

20From the fruit of his mouth a man's
stomach is filled;
with the harvest from his lips he is
satisfied.

21The tongue has the power of life and
death,
and those who love it will eat its
fruit.

22He who finds a wife finds what is
good
and receives favor from the LORD.

23A poor man pleads for mercy,
but a rich man answers harshly.

24A man of many companions may
come to ruin,
but there is a friend who sticks
closer than a brother.

19 Better a poor man whose walk is
blameless
than a fool whose lips are perverse.

2It is not good to have zeal without
knowledge,
nor to be hasty and miss the way.

3A man's own folly ruins his life,
yet his heart rages against the LORD.

⁴Wealth brings many friends,
but a poor man's friend deserts
him.

⁵A false witness will not go
unpunished,
and he who pours out lies will not
go free.

⁶Many curry favor with a ruler,
and everyone is the friend of a man
who gives gifts.

⁷A poor man is shunned by all his
relatives—
how much more do his friends
avoid him!
Though he pursues them with
pleading,
they are nowhere to be found.ᵃ

⁸He who gets wisdom loves his own
soul;
he who cherishes understanding
prospers.

⁹A false witness will not go
unpunished,
and he who pours out lies will
perish.

¹⁰It is not fitting for a fool to live in
luxury—
how much worse for a slave to rule
over princes!

¹¹A man's wisdom gives him patience;
it is to his glory to overlook an
offense.

¹²A king's rage is like the roar of a lion,
but his favor is like dew on the
grass.

¹³A foolish son is his father's ruin,
and a quarrelsome wife is like a
constant dripping.

¹⁴Houses and wealth are inherited from
parents,
but a prudent wife is from the
LORD.

¹⁵Laziness brings on deep sleep,
and the shiftless man goes hungry.

¹⁶He who obeys instructions guards his
life,
but he who is contemptuous of his
ways will die.

¹⁷He who is kind to the poor lends to
the LORD,

and he will reward him for what he
has done.

¹⁸Discipline your son, for in that there
is hope;
do not be a willing party to his
death.

¹⁹A hot-tempered man must pay the
penalty;
if you rescue him, you will have to
do it again.

²⁰Listen to advice and accept
instruction,
and in the end you will be wise.

²¹Many are the plans in a man's heart,
but it is the LORD's purpose that
prevails.

²²What a man desires is unfailing loveᵇ;
better to be poor than a liar.

²³The fear of the LORD leads to life:
Then one rests content, untouched
by trouble.

²⁴The sluggard buries his hand in the
dish;
he will not even bring it back to his
mouth!

²⁵Flog a mocker, and the simple will
learn prudence;
rebuke a discerning man, and he
will gain knowledge.

²⁶He who robs his father and drives out
his mother
is a son who brings shame and
disgrace.

²⁷Stop listening to instruction, my son,
and you will stray from the words
of knowledge.

²⁸A corrupt witness mocks at justice,
and the mouth of the wicked gulps
down evil.

²⁹Penalties are prepared for mockers,
and beatings for the backs of fools.

20 Wine is a mocker and beer a
brawler;
whoever is led astray by them is not
wise.

²A king's wrath is like the roar of a
lion;
he who angers him forfeits his life.

³It is to a man's honor to avoid strife,
but every fool is quick to quarrel.

ᵃ7 The meaning of the Hebrew for this sentence is uncertain.　ᵇ22 Or *A man's greed is his shame*

⁴A sluggard does not plow in season;
   so at harvest time he looks but
     finds nothing.

⁵The purposes of a man's heart are
   deep waters,
but a man of understanding draws
   them out.

⁶Many a man claims to have unfailing
   love,

but a faithful man who can
   find?

⁷The righteous man leads a blameless
   life;
blessed are his children after him.

⁸When a king sits on his throne to
   judge,
he winnows out all evil with his
   eyes.

TUESDAY

VERSE FOR THE DAY:
Proverbs 19:21

AUTHOR:
Marlene Obie

PASSAGE FOR THE DAY:
Proverbs 19:21–29

I Got It!

I CAN'T believe I got the job, Lord.

Well, I can too believe it. What's the matter with my faith anyway? No matter how often you answer my prayers, I always do a double take when I get the answer.

I asked for your guidance about whether or not to go to work and where I should work. Thank you for showing me your will.

Now I'm really in trouble. My wardrobe is straight out of the frumpville collection. Except for my combination interview-banquet-church outfit, I honestly have nothing decent to wear. I know my closet is crammed with material that resembles clothing. However half of these pieces have some permanent spot on them. And the other half doesn't match. Help me to figure something out, Lord. I can't afford to buy anything new right now. I'll have to make do.

I have a few days to try to organize our family schedules and duties, but I'm afraid my faith is weak here, too. If I couldn't get it together in the last twenty years, can I reasonably assume I'll do it in the next two days? Some people say that working outside the home forces you to be more organized. I hope that's true.

My feelings are jumbled. I'm glad I got the job and feel both confident and nervous about my competence. I wonder what my bosses and co-workers will really be like. Will they accept me? Will the job be exciting and challenging? Can I handle juggling a career with being a wife and mother?

Lord, keep me from these needless questions and worries. I know you led me to this job, and I know that you'll walk with me. Because I know this is your plan, I can face anything—even a new job.

Additional Scripture Readings:
Matthew 7:7–11; 1 John 5:14–15

*Go to page 689 for your next
devotional reading.*

⁹Who can say, "I have kept my heart
    pure;
  I am clean and without sin"?

¹⁰Differing weights and differing
    measures—
  the LORD detests them both.

¹¹Even a child is known by his actions,
  by whether his conduct is pure and
    right.

¹²Ears that hear and eyes that see—
  the LORD has made them both.

¹³Do not love sleep or you will grow
    poor;
  stay awake and you will have food
    to spare.

¹⁴"It's no good, it's no good!" says the
    buyer;
  then off he goes and boasts about
    his purchase.

¹⁵Gold there is, and rubies in
    abundance,
  but lips that speak knowledge are a
    rare jewel.

¹⁶Take the garment of one who puts up
    security for a stranger;
  hold it in pledge if he does it for a
    wayward woman.

¹⁷Food gained by fraud tastes sweet to
    a man,
  but he ends up with a mouth full of
    gravel.

¹⁸Make plans by seeking advice;
  if you wage war, obtain guidance.

¹⁹A gossip betrays a confidence;
  so avoid a man who talks too
    much.

²⁰If a man curses his father or mother,
  his lamp will be snuffed out in
    pitch darkness.

²¹An inheritance quickly gained at the
    beginning
  will not be blessed at the end.

²²Do not say, "I'll pay you back for this
    wrong!"
  Wait for the LORD, and he will
    deliver you.

²³The LORD detests differing weights,
  and dishonest scales do not please
    him.

²⁴A man's steps are directed by the
    LORD.
  How then can anyone understand
    his own way?

²⁵It is a trap for a man to dedicate
    something rashly
  and only later to consider his vows.

²⁶A wise king winnows out the wicked;
  he drives the threshing wheel over
    them.

²⁷The lamp of the LORD searches the
    spirit of a man[a];
  it searches out his inmost being.

²⁸Love and faithfulness keep a king
    safe;
  through love his throne is made
    secure.

²⁹The glory of young men is their
    strength,
  gray hair the splendor of the old.

³⁰Blows and wounds cleanse away evil,
  and beatings purge the inmost
    being.

21 The king's heart is in the hand
    of the LORD;
  he directs it like a watercourse
    wherever he pleases.

²All a man's ways seem right to him,
  but the LORD weighs the heart.

³To do what is right and just
  is more acceptable to the LORD than
    sacrifice.

⁴Haughty eyes and a proud heart,
  the lamp of the wicked, are sin!

⁵The plans of the diligent lead to
    profit
  as surely as haste leads to poverty.

⁶A fortune made by a lying tongue
  is a fleeting vapor and a deadly
    snare.[b]

⁷The violence of the wicked will drag
    them away,
  for they refuse to do what is right.

⁸The way of the guilty is devious,
  but the conduct of the innocent is
    upright.

⁹Better to live on a corner of the roof
  than share a house with a
    quarrelsome wife.

---

[a]27 Or *The spirit of man is the LORD's lamp*   [b]6 Some Hebrew manuscripts, Septuagint and Vulgate;
most Hebrew manuscripts *vapor for those who seek death*

10The wicked man craves evil;
his neighbor gets no mercy from
him.

11When a mocker is punished, the
simple gain wisdom;
when a wise man is instructed, he
gets knowledge.

12The Righteous One[a] takes note of the
house of the wicked
and brings the wicked to ruin.

13If a man shuts his ears to the cry of
the poor,
he too will cry out and not be
answered.

14A gift given in secret soothes anger,
and a bribe concealed in the cloak
pacifies great wrath.

15When justice is done, it brings joy to
the righteous
but terror to evildoers.

16A man who strays from the path of
understanding
comes to rest in the company of
the dead.

17He who loves pleasure will become
poor;
whoever loves wine and oil will
never be rich.

18The wicked become a ransom for the
righteous,
and the unfaithful for the upright.

19Better to live in a desert
than with a quarrelsome and
ill-tempered wife.

20In the house of the wise are stores of
choice food and oil,
but a foolish man devours all he
has.

21He who pursues righteousness and
love
finds life, prosperity[b] and honor.

22A wise man attacks the city of the
mighty
and pulls down the stronghold in
which they trust.

23He who guards his mouth and his
tongue
keeps himself from calamity.

24The proud and arrogant
man—"Mocker" is his name;

he behaves with overweening pride.

25The sluggard's craving will be the
death of him,
because his hands refuse to work.

26All day long he craves for more,
but the righteous give without
sparing.

27The sacrifice of the wicked is
detestable—
how much more so when brought
with evil intent!

28A false witness will perish,
and whoever listens to him will be
destroyed forever.[c]

29A wicked man puts up a bold front,
but an upright man gives thought
to his ways.

30There is no wisdom, no insight, no
plan
that can succeed against the LORD.

31The horse is made ready for the day
of battle,
but victory rests with the LORD.

22 A good name is more desirable
than great riches;
to be esteemed is better than silver
or gold.

2Rich and poor have this in common:
The LORD is the Maker of them all.

3A prudent man sees danger and takes
refuge,
but the simple keep going and
suffer for it.

4Humility and the fear of the LORD
bring wealth and honor and life.

5In the paths of the wicked lie thorns
and snares,
but he who guards his soul stays far
from them.

6Train[d] a child in the way he should
go,
and when he is old he will not turn
from it.

7The rich rule over the poor,
and the borrower is servant to the
lender.

8He who sows wickedness reaps
trouble,
and the rod of his fury will be
destroyed.

---

a12 Or *The righteous man*   b21 Or *righteousness*   c28 Or / *but the words of an obedient man will live*
on   d6 Or *Start*

⁹A generous man will himself be
    blessed,
  for he shares his food with the
    poor.

¹⁰Drive out the mocker, and out goes
    strife;
  quarrels and insults are ended.

¹¹He who loves a pure heart and whose
    speech is gracious
  will have the king for his friend.

¹²The eyes of the LORD keep watch over
    knowledge,
  but he frustrates the words of the
    unfaithful.

¹³The sluggard says, "There is a lion
    outside!"
  or, "I will be murdered in the
    streets!"

¹⁴The mouth of an adulteress is a deep
    pit;
  he who is under the LORD's wrath
    will fall into it.

¹⁵Folly is bound up in the heart of a
    child,
  but the rod of discipline will drive
    it far from him.

¹⁶He who oppresses the poor to
    increase his wealth
  and he who gives gifts to the
    rich—both come to poverty.

Sayings of the Wise

¹⁷Pay attention and listen to the
    sayings of the wise;
  apply your heart to what I teach,
¹⁸for it is pleasing when you keep them
    in your heart
  and have all of them ready on your
    lips.
¹⁹So that your trust may be in the LORD,
  I teach you today, even you.
²⁰Have I not written thirty*a* sayings for
    you,
  sayings of counsel and knowledge,
²¹teaching you true and reliable words,
  so that you can give sound answers
    to him who sent you?

²²Do not exploit the poor because they
    are poor
  and do not crush the needy in
    court,
²³for the LORD will take up their case

and will plunder those who plunder
    them.

²⁴Do not make friends with a
    hot-tempered man,
  do not associate with one easily
    angered,
²⁵or you may learn his ways
  and get yourself ensnared.

²⁶Do not be a man who strikes hands in
    pledge
  or puts up security for debts;
²⁷if you lack the means to pay,
  your very bed will be snatched from
    under you.

²⁸Do not move an ancient boundary
    stone
  set up by your forefathers.

²⁹Do you see a man skilled in his work?
  He will serve before kings;
  he will not serve before obscure
    men.

23 When you sit to dine with a
    ruler,
  note well what*b* is before you,
²and put a knife to your throat
  if you are given to gluttony.
³Do not crave his delicacies,
  for that food is deceptive.

⁴Do not wear yourself out to get rich;
  have the wisdom to show restraint.
⁵Cast but a glance at riches, and they
    are gone,
  for they will surely sprout wings
  and fly off to the sky like an eagle.

⁶Do not eat the food of a stingy man,
  do not crave his delicacies;
⁷for he is the kind of man
  who is always thinking about the
    cost.*c*
"Eat and drink," he says to you,
  but his heart is not with you.
⁸You will vomit up the little you have
    eaten
  and will have wasted your
    compliments.

⁹Do not speak to a fool,
  for he will scorn the wisdom of
    your words.

¹⁰Do not move an ancient boundary
    stone
  or encroach on the fields of the
    fatherless,

---

a20 Or *not formerly written; or not written excellent
himself, / so he is; or for as he puts on a feast, / so he is*   *b1* Or *who*   *c7* Or *for as he thinks within*

¹¹for their Defender is strong;
    he will take up their case against
      you.

¹²Apply your heart to instruction
    and your ears to words of
      knowledge.

¹³Do not withhold discipline from a
      child;
    if you punish him with the rod, he
      will not die.
¹⁴Punish him with the rod
    and save his soul from death.^a

¹⁵My son, if your heart is wise,
    then my heart will be glad;
¹⁶my inmost being will rejoice
    when your lips speak what is right.

¹⁷Do not let your heart envy sinners,
    but always be zealous for the fear
      of the LORD.
¹⁸There is surely a future hope for you,
    and your hope will not be cut off.

¹⁹Listen, my son, and be wise,
    and keep your heart on the right
      path.
²⁰Do not join those who drink too
      much wine
    or gorge themselves on meat,
²¹for drunkards and gluttons become
      poor,
    and drowsiness clothes them in
      rags.

²²Listen to your father, who gave you
      life,
    and do not despise your mother
      when she is old.
²³Buy the truth and do not sell it;
    get wisdom, discipline and
      understanding.
²⁴The father of a righteous man has
      great joy;
    he who has a wise son delights in
      him.
²⁵May your father and mother be glad;
    may she who gave you birth rejoice!

²⁶My son, give me your heart
    and let your eyes keep to my ways,
²⁷for a prostitute is a deep pit
    and a wayward wife is a narrow
      well.
²⁸Like a bandit she lies in wait,
    and multiplies the unfaithful among
      men.

²⁹Who has woe? Who has sorrow?

^a14 Hebrew *Sheol*

Who has strife? Who has
      complaints?
    Who has needless bruises? Who has
      bloodshot eyes?
³⁰Those who linger over wine,
    who go to sample bowls of mixed
      wine.
³¹Do not gaze at wine when it is red,
    when it sparkles in the cup,
    when it goes down smoothly!
³²In the end it bites like a snake
    and poisons like a viper.
³³Your eyes will see strange sights
    and your mind imagine confusing
      things.
³⁴You will be like one sleeping on the
      high seas,
    lying on top of the rigging.
³⁵"They hit me," you will say, "but I'm
      not hurt!
    They beat me, but I don't feel it!
When will I wake up
    so I can find another drink?"

24 Do not envy wicked men,
    do not desire their company;
²for their hearts plot violence,
    and their lips talk about making
      trouble.

³By wisdom a house is built,
    and through understanding it is
      established;
⁴through knowledge its rooms are
      filled
    with rare and beautiful treasures.

⁵A wise man has great power,
    and a man of knowledge increases
      strength;
⁶for waging war you need guidance,
    and for victory many advisers.

⁷Wisdom is too high for a fool;
    in the assembly at the gate he has
      nothing to say.

⁸He who plots evil
    will be known as a schemer.
⁹The schemes of folly are sin,
    and men detest a mocker.

¹⁰If you falter in times of trouble,
    how small is your strength!

¹¹Rescue those being led away to death;
    hold back those staggering toward
      slaughter.
¹²If you say, "But we knew nothing
    about this,"

does not he who weighs the heart
  perceive it?
Does not he who guards your life
  know it?
Will he not repay each person
  according to what he has done?

¹³Eat honey, my son, for it is good;
  honey from the comb is sweet to
  your taste.
¹⁴Know also that wisdom is sweet to
  your soul;

if you find it, there is a future hope
  for you,
and your hope will not be cut off.

¹⁵Do not lie in wait like an outlaw
  against a righteous man's
  house,
do not raid his dwelling place;
¹⁶for though a righteous man falls seven
  times, he rises again,
but the wicked are brought down
  by calamity.

WEDNESDAY

VERSE FOR THE DAY:	AUTHOR:	PASSAGE FOR THE DAY:
Proverbs 23:25	Shirley Dobson	Proverbs 23:17–25

Sunshine of My Life

THE gift was not one that you would expect to receive from an eight-year-old boy. He had bought me a lovely desk set. The ostrich-feathered white pen looked like an old fashioned quill that Ben Franklin might have used to sign the Declaration of Independence. The stand was padded in matching white, with a spray of pink flowers delicately painted around the edges. I was so touched that my eyes brimmed with tears as I hugged and thanked my son for such an extravagant gift. It has been five years since that day and the pen still sits on the nightstand near my bed as a reminder of Ryan's spontaneous gift of love.

There are times in our lives when the cost of parenting seems staggeringly high! No matter how you look at it, children are emotionally exhausting, time-consuming, sometimes frustrating, and always maddeningly complex. In fact, their developmental years are governed entirely by "Murphy's Law." For example, if they drop a slice of bread on the carpet, it will inevitably land buttered side down. And when they catch the flu, they never vomit in the bathroom. They turn up their noses at their oatmeal and gag at the sight of their eggs, but enthusiastically drink the dog's water and float their rubber duckies in the toilet. I'm sure you could add to this list of childhood "Murphyisms."

But in moments when you are touched by the soul of a child, as I was through Ryan's act of love, you suddenly realize the eternal significance of these precious years. Then, no other task on earth seems quite as important or meaningful as raising and training and guiding him through his developmental experiences.

Additional Scripture Readings:
2 Kings 4:1–7; Luke 2:51–52

Go to page 697 for your next devotional reading.

¹⁷Do not gloat when your enemy falls;
  when he stumbles, do not let your
    heart rejoice,
¹⁸or the LORD will see and disapprove
  and turn his wrath away from him.

¹⁹Do not fret because of evil men
  or be envious of the wicked,
²⁰for the evil man has no future hope,
  and the lamp of the wicked will be
    snuffed out.

²¹Fear the LORD and the king, my son,
  and do not join with the rebellious,
²²for those two will send sudden
    destruction upon them,
  and who knows what calamities
    they can bring?

Further Sayings of the Wise

²³These also are sayings of the wise:

To show partiality in judging is not
    good:
²⁴Whoever says to the guilty, "You are
    innocent"—
  peoples will curse him and nations
    denounce him.
²⁵But it will go well with those who
    convict the guilty,
  and rich blessing will come upon
    them.

²⁶An honest answer
  is like a kiss on the lips.

²⁷Finish your outdoor work
  and get your fields ready;
  after that, build your house.

²⁸Do not testify against your neighbor
    without cause,
  or use your lips to deceive.
²⁹Do not say, "I'll do to him as he has
    done to me;
  I'll pay that man back for what he
    did."

³⁰I went past the field of the sluggard,
  past the vineyard of the man who
    lacks judgment;
³¹thorns had come up everywhere,
  the ground was covered with weeds,
  and the stone wall was in ruins.
³²I applied my heart to what I observed
  and learned a lesson from what I
    saw:
³³A little sleep, a little slumber,
  a little folding of the hands to
    rest—

³⁴and poverty will come on you like a
    bandit
  and scarcity like an armed man.^a

More Proverbs of Solomon

25 These are more proverbs of Solomon, copied by the men of Hezekiah king of Judah:

²It is the glory of God to conceal a
    matter;
  to search out a matter is the glory
    of kings.

³As the heavens are high and the earth
    is deep,
  so the hearts of kings are
    unsearchable.

⁴Remove the dross from the silver,
  and out comes material for^b the
    silversmith;
⁵remove the wicked from the king's
    presence,
  and his throne will be established
    through righteousness.

⁶Do not exalt yourself in the king's
    presence,
  and do not claim a place among
    great men;
⁷it is better for him to say to you,
    "Come up here,"
  than for him to humiliate you
    before a nobleman.

What you have seen with your eyes
⁸ do not bring^c hastily to court,
  for what will you do in the end
  if your neighbor puts you to shame?

⁹If you argue your case with a
    neighbor,
  do not betray another man's
    confidence,
¹⁰or he who hears it may shame you
  and you will never lose your bad
    reputation.

¹¹A word aptly spoken
  is like apples of gold in settings of
    silver.

¹²Like an earring of gold or an
    ornament of fine gold
  is a wise man's rebuke to a
    listening ear.

¹³Like the coolness of snow at harvest
    time

---

^a34 Or like a vagrant / and scarcity like a beggar
whom you had set your eyes. / ⁸Do not go   ^b4 Or comes a vessel from   ^c7,8 Or nobleman / on

is a trustworthy messenger to those
  who send him;
he refreshes the spirit of his
  masters.

¹⁴Like clouds and wind without rain
  is a man who boasts of gifts he
    does not give.

¹⁵Through patience a ruler can be
  persuaded,
  and a gentle tongue can break a
    bone.

¹⁶If you find honey, eat just enough—
  too much of it, and you will vomit.

¹⁷Seldom set foot in your neighbor's
  house—
  too much of you, and he will hate
    you.

¹⁸Like a club or a sword or a sharp
  arrow
  is the man who gives false
    testimony against his neighbor.

¹⁹Like a bad tooth or a lame foot
  is reliance on the unfaithful in
    times of trouble.

²⁰Like one who takes away a garment
  on a cold day,
  or like vinegar poured on soda,
  is one who sings songs to a heavy
    heart.

²¹If your enemy is hungry, give him
  food to eat;
  if he is thirsty, give him water to
    drink.
²²In doing this, you will heap burning
  coals on his head,
  and the LORD will reward you.

²³As a north wind brings rain,
  so a sly tongue brings angry looks.

²⁴Better to live on a corner of the roof
  than share a house with a
    quarrelsome wife.

²⁵Like cold water to a weary soul
  is good news from a distant land.

²⁶Like a muddied spring or a polluted
  well
  is a righteous man who gives way to
    the wicked.

²⁷It is not good to eat too much honey,
  nor is it honorable to seek one's
    own honor.

²⁸Like a city whose walls are broken
  down
  is a man who lacks self-control.

26 Like snow in summer or rain in
  harvest,
  honor is not fitting for a fool.

²Like a fluttering sparrow or a darting
  swallow,
  an undeserved curse does not come
    to rest.

³A whip for the horse, a halter for the
  donkey,
  and a rod for the backs of fools!

⁴Do not answer a fool according to his
  folly,
  or you will be like him yourself.

⁵Answer a fool according to his folly,
  or he will be wise in his own eyes.

⁶Like cutting off one's feet or drinking
  violence
  is the sending of a message by the
    hand of a fool.

⁷Like a lame man's legs that hang
  limp
  is a proverb in the mouth of a fool.

⁸Like tying a stone in a sling
  is the giving of honor to a fool.

⁹Like a thornbush in a drunkard's
  hand
  is a proverb in the mouth of a fool.

¹⁰Like an archer who wounds at
  random
  is he who hires a fool or any
    passer-by.

¹¹As a dog returns to its vomit,
  so a fool repeats his folly.

¹²Do you see a man wise in his own
  eyes?
  There is more hope for a fool than
    for him.

¹³The sluggard says, "There is a lion in
  the road,
  a fierce lion roaming the streets!"

¹⁴As a door turns on its hinges,
  so a sluggard turns on his bed.

¹⁵The sluggard buries his hand in the
  dish;
  he is too lazy to bring it back to his
    mouth.

¹⁶The sluggard is wiser in his own eyes
  than seven men who answer
    discreetly.

¹⁷Like one who seizes a dog by the ears
  is a passer-by who meddles in a
    quarrel not his own.

¹⁸Like a madman shooting
    firebrands or deadly arrows
¹⁹is a man who deceives his neighbor
    and says, "I was only joking!"

²⁰Without wood a fire goes out;
    without gossip a quarrel dies down.

²¹As charcoal to embers and as wood to
    fire,
    so is a quarrelsome man for
        kindling strife.

²²The words of a gossip are like choice
    morsels;
    they go down to a man's inmost
        parts.

²³Like a coating of glaze[a] over
    earthenware
    are fervent lips with an evil heart.

²⁴A malicious man disguises himself
    with his lips,
    but in his heart he harbors deceit.
²⁵Though his speech is charming, do
    not believe him,
    for seven abominations fill his
        heart.
²⁶His malice may be concealed by
    deception,
    but his wickedness will be exposed
        in the assembly.

²⁷If a man digs a pit, he will fall into it;
    if a man rolls a stone, it will roll
        back on him.

²⁸A lying tongue hates those it hurts,
    and a flattering mouth works ruin.

27 Do not boast about tomorrow,
    for you do not know what a day
    may bring forth.

²Let another praise you, and not your
    own mouth;
    someone else, and not your own
        lips.

³Stone is heavy and sand a burden,
    but provocation by a fool is heavier
        than both.

⁴Anger is cruel and fury overwhelming,
    but who can stand before jealousy?

⁵Better is open rebuke
    than hidden love.

⁶Wounds from a friend can be trusted,
    but an enemy multiplies kisses.

⁷He who is full loathes honey,

but to the hungry even what is
    bitter tastes sweet.

⁸Like a bird that strays from its nest
    is a man who strays from his home.

⁹Perfume and incense bring joy to the
    heart,
    and the pleasantness of one's friend
        springs from his earnest
        counsel.

¹⁰Do not forsake your friend and the
    friend of your father,
    and do not go to your brother's
        house when disaster strikes
        you—
    better a neighbor nearby than a
        brother far away.

¹¹Be wise, my son, and bring joy to my
    heart;
    then I can answer anyone who
        treats me with contempt.

¹²The prudent see danger and take
    refuge,
    but the simple keep going and
        suffer for it.

¹³Take the garment of one who puts up
    security for a stranger;
    hold it in pledge if he does it for a
        wayward woman.

¹⁴If a man loudly blesses his neighbor
    early in the morning,
    it will be taken as a curse.

¹⁵A quarrelsome wife is like
    a constant dripping on a rainy day;
¹⁶restraining her is like restraining the
    wind
    or grasping oil with the hand.

¹⁷As iron sharpens iron,
    so one man sharpens another.

¹⁸He who tends a fig tree will eat its
    fruit,
    and he who looks after his master
        will be honored.

¹⁹As water reflects a face,
    so a man's heart reflects the man.

²⁰Death and Destruction[b] are never
    satisfied,
    and neither are the eyes of man.

²¹The crucible for silver and the furnace
    for gold,

---

[a]23 With a different word division of the Hebrew; Masoretic Text *of silver dross*   [b]20 Hebrew *Sheol and Abaddon*

but man is tested by the praise he
receives.

²²Though you grind a fool in a mortar,
grinding him like grain with a
pestle,
you will not remove his folly from
him.

²³Be sure you know the condition of
your flocks,
give careful attention to your herds;
²⁴for riches do not endure forever,
and a crown is not secure for all
generations.
²⁵When the hay is removed and new
growth appears
and the grass from the hills is
gathered in,
²⁶the lambs will provide you with
clothing,
and the goats with the price of a
field.
²⁷You will have plenty of goats' milk
to feed you and your family
and to nourish your servant girls.

28 The wicked man flees though no
one pursues,
but the righteous are as bold as a
lion.

²When a country is rebellious, it has
many rulers,
but a man of understanding and
knowledge maintains order.

³A ruler^a who oppresses the poor
is like a driving rain that leaves no
crops.

⁴Those who forsake the law praise the
wicked,
but those who keep the law resist
them.

⁵Evil men do not understand justice,
but those who seek the LORD
understand it fully.

⁶Better a poor man whose walk is
blameless
than a rich man whose ways are
perverse.

⁷He who keeps the law is a discerning
son,
but a companion of gluttons
disgraces his father.

⁸He who increases his wealth by
exorbitant interest

amasses it for another, who will be
kind to the poor.

⁹If anyone turns a deaf ear to the law,
even his prayers are detestable.

¹⁰He who leads the upright along an
evil path
will fall into his own trap,
but the blameless will receive a
good inheritance.

¹¹A rich man may be wise in his own
eyes,
but a poor man who has
discernment sees through him.

¹²When the righteous triumph, there is
great elation;
but when the wicked rise to power,
men go into hiding.

¹³He who conceals his sins does not
prosper,
but whoever confesses and
renounces them finds mercy.

¹⁴Blessed is the man who always fears
the LORD,
but he who hardens his heart falls
into trouble.

¹⁵Like a roaring lion or a charging bear
is a wicked man ruling over a
helpless people.

¹⁶A tyrannical ruler lacks judgment,
but he who hates ill-gotten gain
will enjoy a long life.

¹⁷A man tormented by the guilt of
murder
will be a fugitive till death;
let no one support him.

¹⁸He whose walk is blameless is kept
safe,
but he whose ways are perverse will
suddenly fall.

¹⁹He who works his land will have
abundant food,
but the one who chases fantasies
will have his fill of poverty.

²⁰A faithful man will be richly blessed,
but one eager to get rich will not
go unpunished.

²¹To show partiality is not good—
yet a man will do wrong for a piece
of bread.

²²A stingy man is eager to get rich

^a3 Or A poor man

and is unaware that poverty awaits
him.

²³He who rebukes a man will in the
end gain more favor
than he who has a flattering
tongue.

²⁴He who robs his father or mother
and says, "It's not wrong"—
he is partner to him who destroys.

²⁵A greedy man stirs up dissension,
but he who trusts in the LORD will
prosper.

²⁶He who trusts in himself is a fool,
but he who walks in wisdom is kept
safe.

²⁷He who gives to the poor will lack
nothing,
but he who closes his eyes to them
receives many curses.

²⁸When the wicked rise to power,
people go into hiding;
but when the wicked perish, the
righteous thrive.

29 A man who remains stiff-necked
after many rebukes
will suddenly be
destroyed—without remedy.

²When the righteous thrive, the people
rejoice;
when the wicked rule, the people
groan.

³A man who loves wisdom brings joy
to his father,
but a companion of prostitutes
squanders his wealth.

⁴By justice a king gives a country
stability,
but one who is greedy for bribes
tears it down.

⁵Whoever flatters his neighbor
is spreading a net for his feet.

⁶An evil man is snared by his own sin,
but a righteous one can sing and be
glad.

⁷The righteous care about justice for
the poor,
but the wicked have no such
concern.

⁸Mockers stir up a city,
but wise men turn away anger.

⁹If a wise man goes to court with a
fool,
the fool rages and scoffs, and there
is no peace.

¹⁰Bloodthirsty men hate a man of
integrity
and seek to kill the upright.

¹¹A fool gives full vent to his anger,
but a wise man keeps himself
under control.

¹²If a ruler listens to lies,
all his officials become wicked.

¹³The poor man and the oppressor have
this in common:
The LORD gives sight to the eyes of
both.

¹⁴If a king judges the poor with
fairness,
his throne will always be secure.

¹⁵The rod of correction imparts wisdom,
but a child left to himself disgraces
his mother.

¹⁶When the wicked thrive, so does sin,
but the righteous will see their
downfall.

¹⁷Discipline your son, and he will give
you peace;
he will bring delight to your soul.

¹⁸Where there is no revelation, the
people cast off restraint;
but blessed is he who keeps the
law.

¹⁹A servant cannot be corrected by
mere words;
though he understands, he will not
respond.

²⁰Do you see a man who speaks in
haste?
There is more hope for a fool than
for him.

²¹If a man pampers his servant from
youth,
he will bring grief[a] in the end.

²²An angry man stirs up dissension,
and a hot-tempered one commits
many sins.

²³A man's pride brings him low,
but a man of lowly spirit gains
honor.

---

a21 The meaning of the Hebrew for this word is uncertain.

²⁴The accomplice of a thief is his own
enemy;
he is put under oath and dare not
testify.

²⁵Fear of man will prove to be a snare,
but whoever trusts in the LORD is
kept safe.

²⁶Many seek an audience with a ruler,
but it is from the LORD that man
gets justice.

²⁷The righteous detest the dishonest;
the wicked detest the upright.

Sayings of Agur

30 The sayings of Agur son of
Jakeh—an oracle*ᵃ*:

This man declared to Ithiel,
to Ithiel and to Ucal:*ᵇ*

²"I am the most ignorant of men;
I do not have a man's
understanding.
³I have not learned wisdom,
nor have I knowledge of the Holy
One.
⁴Who has gone up to heaven and come
down?
Who has gathered up the wind in
the hollow of his hands?
Who has wrapped up the waters in his
cloak?
Who has established all the ends of
the earth?
What is his name, and the name of
his son?
Tell me if you know!

⁵"Every word of God is flawless;
he is a shield to those who take
refuge in him.
⁶Do not add to his words,
or he will rebuke you and prove you
a liar.

⁷"Two things I ask of you, O LORD;
do not refuse me before I die:
⁸Keep falsehood and lies far from me;
give me neither poverty nor riches,
but give me only my daily bread.
⁹Otherwise, I may have too much and
disown you
and say, 'Who is the LORD?'
Or I may become poor and steal,
and so dishonor the name of my
God.

¹⁰"Do not slander a servant to his
master,
or he will curse you, and you will
pay for it.

¹¹"There are those who curse their
fathers
and do not bless their mothers;
¹²those who are pure in their own eyes
and yet are not cleansed of their
filth;
¹³those whose eyes are ever so haughty,
whose glances are so disdainful;
¹⁴those whose teeth are swords
and whose jaws are set with knives
to devour the poor from the earth,
the needy from among mankind.

¹⁵"The leech has two daughters.
'Give! Give!' they cry.

"There are three things that are never
satisfied,
four that never say, 'Enough!':
¹⁶the grave,*ᶜ* the barren womb,
land, which is never satisfied with
water,
and fire, which never says,
'Enough!'

¹⁷"The eye that mocks a father,
that scorns obedience to a mother,
will be pecked out by the ravens of
the valley,
will be eaten by the vultures.

¹⁸"There are three things that are too
amazing for me,
four that I do not understand:
¹⁹the way of an eagle in the sky,
the way of a snake on a rock,
the way of a ship on the high seas,
and the way of a man with a
maiden.

²⁰"This is the way of an adulteress:
She eats and wipes her mouth
and says, 'I've done nothing wrong.'

²¹"Under three things the earth
trembles,
under four it cannot bear up:
²²a servant who becomes king,
a fool who is full of food,
²³an unloved woman who is married,
and a maidservant who displaces
her mistress.

²⁴"Four things on earth are small,
yet they are extremely wise:
²⁵Ants are creatures of little strength,

ᵃ1 Or *Jakeh of Massa*   *ᵇ1* Masoretic Text; with a different word division of the Hebrew *declared,* "I am
weary, O God; / I am weary, O God, and faint.   *ᶜ16* Hebrew *Sheol*

yet they store up their food in the summer;
[26]coneys[a] are creatures of little power,
yet they make their home in the crags;
[27]locusts have no king,
yet they advance together in ranks;
[28]a lizard can be caught with the hand,
yet it is found in kings' palaces.

[29]"There are three things that are stately in their stride,
four that move with stately bearing:
[30]a lion, mighty among beasts,
who retreats before nothing;
[31]a strutting rooster, a he-goat,
and a king with his army around him.[b]

[32]"If you have played the fool and exalted yourself,
or if you have planned evil,
clap your hand over your mouth!
[33]For as churning the milk produces butter,
and as twisting the nose produces blood,
so stirring up anger produces strife."

Sayings of King Lemuel

31 The sayings of King Lemuel—an oracle[c] his mother taught him:

[2]"O my son, O son of my womb,
O son of my vows,[d]
[3]do not spend your strength on women,
your vigor on those who ruin kings.

[4]"It is not for kings, O Lemuel—
not for kings to drink wine,
not for rulers to crave beer,
[5]lest they drink and forget what the law decrees,
and deprive all the oppressed of their rights.
[6]Give beer to those who are perishing,
wine to those who are in anguish;
[7]let them drink and forget their poverty
and remember their misery no more.

[8]"Speak up for those who cannot speak for themselves,
for the rights of all who are destitute.

[9]Speak up and judge fairly;
defend the rights of the poor and needy."

Epilogue: The Wife of Noble Character

[10e]A wife of noble character who can find?
She is worth far more than rubies.
[11]Her husband has full confidence in her
and lacks nothing of value.
[12]She brings him good, not harm,
all the days of her life.
[13]She selects wool and flax
and works with eager hands.
[14]She is like the merchant ships,
bringing her food from afar.
[15]She gets up while it is still dark;
she provides food for her family
and portions for her servant girls.
[16]She considers a field and buys it;
out of her earnings she plants a vineyard.
[17]She sets about her work vigorously;
her arms are strong for her tasks.
[18]She sees that her trading is profitable,
and her lamp does not go out at night.
[19]In her hand she holds the distaff
and grasps the spindle with her fingers.
[20]She opens her arms to the poor
and extends her hands to the needy.
[21]When it snows, she has no fear for her household;
for all of them are clothed in scarlet.
[22]She makes coverings for her bed;
she is clothed in fine linen and purple.
[23]Her husband is respected at the city gate,
where he takes his seat among the elders of the land.
[24]She makes linen garments and sells them,
and supplies the merchants with sashes.
[25]She is clothed with strength and dignity;
she can laugh at the days to come.
[26]She speaks with wisdom,

---

a26 That is, the hyrax or rock badger   b31 Or king secure against revolt   c1 Or of Lemuel king of Massa, which   d2 Or / the answer to my prayers   e10 Verses 10-31 are an acrostic, each verse beginning with a successive letter of the Hebrew alphabet.

THURSDAY

VERSE FOR THE DAY:
Proverbs 31:30–31

AUTHOR:
Dorothy Patterson

PASSAGE FOR THE DAY:
Proverbs 31:10–31

Strength in Wisdom

THE Sabbath service in the Jewish home unashamedly reveals the high position of women in Israel from Biblical times until the present. Sabbath is primarily a home-centered, family celebration, which makes it only natural that the mother of the home receive the honor of welcoming the Sabbath by lighting of the candles. Traditionally, the husband recites what is without doubt the most eloquent tribute to a godly woman that has ever been penned.*

Proverbs 31:10–31 presents the divine challenge for womanhood—diligent homemaker, valuable helper, nurturing mother, upright and God-fearing woman. The "wife of noble character" receives a reward for faithfulness because she is not dependent on the temporary, superficial, deceptive façade of "charm," which is a mere outward varnish easily scarred and marred by people and circumstances, and "beauty," which can depart like an unfaithful friend to make room for wrinkles and blemishes. Rather she crowns an enduring, satisfying fear of the Lord with a reverent and obedient spirit that makes her worthy of praise and honor from her family and the Creator himself (Proverbs 31:30).

Homemaking is unique in combining the most menial jobs with the most meaningful tasks: it is a challenge to accommodate others without losing one's own identity: it is a demanding pursuit, but the fringe benefits are terrific!

William Booth, the founder of the Salvation Army, gave this glowing tribute of his wife Catherine at the time of her death:

> To me she has been made of God, never-failing sympathy, reliable wisdom, and unvarnished truth—in short, all that is noble and good; and consequently a tower of strength, a mine of wealth, and an everflowing fountain of comfort and joy.†

With "undistracted devotion to the Lord" Catherine Booth was a woman to be praised because she feared the Lord.

Additional Scripture Readings:
Genesis 2:18–24; Luke 1:39–49

Go to page 701 for your next devotional reading.

*Hyman E. Goldin, *The Jewish Woman and Her Home*, New York: Hebrew Publishing Company, 1941, pp. 124-131.
† T. Stead, *Catherine Booth,* Oakville, Canada: Triumph Press, pp. 119, 120-121.

and faithful instruction is on her
  tongue.
27She watches over the affairs of her
    household
  and does not eat the bread of
    idleness.
28Her children arise and call her
    blessed;
  her husband also, and he praises
    her:

29"Many women do noble things,
  but you surpass them all."
30Charm is deceptive, and beauty is
    fleeting;
  but a woman who fears the LORD is
    to be praised.
31Give her the reward she has
    earned,
  and let her works bring her praise
    at the city gate.

THE Teacher, a king in Jerusalem, searches in this book for a purpose to his life. After various pursuits, frustrated by not finding satisfactory answers, he discovers that happiness is in the Lord and in obeying his word (Ecclesiastes 12:11–14). As you read this book, think about how life without God has no meaning but how life regulated by God and his word is wonderful indeed. Be sure to dedicate your life to the Lord when you are young (Ecclesiastes 12:1).

ECCLESIASTES

Everything Is Meaningless

1 The words of the Teacher,ᵃ son of David, king in Jerusalem:

²"Meaningless! Meaningless!"
　　says the Teacher.
"Utterly meaningless!
　　Everything is meaningless."

³What does man gain from all his labor
　　at which he toils under the sun?
⁴Generations come and generations go,
　　but the earth remains forever.

⁵The sun rises and the sun sets,
　　and hurries back to where it rises.
⁶The wind blows to the south
　　and turns to the north;
round and round it goes,
　　ever returning on its course.
⁷All streams flow into the sea,
　　yet the sea is never full.
To the place the streams come from,
　　there they return again.
⁸All things are wearisome,
　　more than one can say.
The eye never has enough of seeing,
　　nor the ear its fill of hearing.

ᵃ1 Or leader of the assembly; also in verses 2 and 12

⁹What has been will be again,
   what has been done will be done
      again;
   there is nothing new under the sun.
¹⁰Is there anything of which one can
     say,
   "Look! This is something new"?
It was here already, long ago;
   it was here before our time.
¹¹There is no remembrance of men of
     old,
   and even those who are yet to
     come
will not be remembered
   by those who follow.

Wisdom Is Meaningless

¹²I, the Teacher, was king over Israel in Jerusalem. ¹³I devoted myself to study and to explore by wisdom all that is done under heaven. What a heavy burden God has laid on men! ¹⁴I have seen all the things that are done under the sun; all of them are meaningless, a chasing after the wind.

¹⁵What is twisted cannot be
     straightened;
   what is lacking cannot be counted.

¹⁶I thought to myself, "Look, I have grown and increased in wisdom more than anyone who has ruled over Jerusalem before me; I have experienced much of wisdom and knowledge." ¹⁷Then I applied myself to the understanding of wisdom, and also of madness and folly, but I learned that this, too, is a chasing after the wind.

¹⁸For with much wisdom comes much
     sorrow;
   the more knowledge, the more
     grief.

Pleasures Are Meaningless

2 I thought in my heart, "Come now, I will test you with pleasure to find out what is good." But that also proved to be meaningless. ²"Laughter," I said, "is foolish. And what does pleasure accomplish?" ³I tried cheering myself with wine, and embracing folly—my mind still guiding me with wisdom. I wanted to see what was worthwhile for men to do under heaven during the few days of their lives.

⁴I undertook great projects: I built houses for myself and planted vineyards. ⁵I made gardens and parks and planted all

kinds of fruit trees in them. ⁶I made reservoirs to water groves of flourishing trees. ⁷I bought male and female slaves and had other slaves who were born in my house. I also owned more herds and flocks than anyone in Jerusalem before me. ⁸I amassed silver and gold for myself, and the treasure of kings and provinces. I acquired men and women singers, and a harem*ᵃ* as well—the delights of the heart of man. ⁹I became greater by far than anyone in Jerusalem before me. In all this my wisdom stayed with me.

¹⁰I denied myself nothing my eyes
     desired;
   I refused my heart no pleasure.
My heart took delight in all my work,
   and this was the reward for all my
     labor.
¹¹Yet when I surveyed all that my hands
     had done
   and what I had toiled to achieve,
everything was meaningless, a chasing
     after the wind;
   nothing was gained under the sun.

Wisdom and Folly Are Meaningless

¹²Then I turned my thoughts to
     consider wisdom,
   and also madness and folly.
What more can the king's successor
     do
   than what has already been done?
¹³I saw that wisdom is better than folly,
   just as light is better than darkness.
¹⁴The wise man has eyes in his head,
   while the fool walks in the
     darkness;
but I came to realize
   that the same fate overtakes them
     both.

¹⁵Then I thought in my heart,

"The fate of the fool will overtake me
     also.
   What then do I gain by being
     wise?"
I said in my heart,
   "This too is meaningless."
¹⁶For the wise man, like the fool, will
     not be long remembered;
   in days to come both will be
     forgotten.
Like the fool, the wise man too must
     die!

ᵃ8 The meaning of the Hebrew for this phrase is uncertain.

Toil Is Meaningless

¹⁷So I hated life, because the work that is done under the sun was grievous to me. All of it is meaningless, a chasing after the wind. ¹⁸I hated all the things I had toiled for under the sun, because I must leave them to the one who comes after me. ¹⁹And who knows whether he will be a wise man or a fool? Yet he will have control over all the work into which I have poured my effort and skill under the sun. This too is meaningless. ²⁰So my heart began to despair over all my toilsome labor under the sun. ²¹For a man may do his work with wisdom, knowledge and skill, and then he must leave all he owns to someone who has not worked for it. This too is meaningless and a great misfortune. ²²What does a man get for all the toil and anxious striving with which he labors under the sun? ²³All his days his work is pain and grief; even at night his mind does not rest. This too is meaningless.

²⁴A man can do nothing better than to eat and drink and find satisfaction in his work. This too, I see, is from the hand of

FRIDAY

VERSE FOR THE DAY:
Ecclesiastes 2:24

AUTHOR:
Marlene Obie

PASSAGE FOR THE DAY:
Ecclesiastes 2:17–26

With No Apologies

SHOULD I apologize for liking my career, Lord?

I've had inklings that I'm expected to dislike working. Some women pity me because my house and yard resemble a junk shop and I can't attend the neighborhood coffees and luncheons. They shake their heads at my time-clock schedule. They think I couldn't possibly enjoy such an existence.

Sure, I have days when everything goes wrong and I question whether this is a calling or a sentence in a forced labor camp. However, when the boss is grumpy, customers are unreasonable and auditors are looking over my shoulder, I remember comparable days when I worked solely at home. Those days were not without disasters, interruptions and stresses.

Thank you for showing me the joys of each of the different businesses I've worked in. I especially appreciate the way I'm treated by my peers. (My family would be surprised to know that I'm respected at the office.) Requests for my assistance are made politely and are addressed to my given name. I feel like a member of a team and not a quarterback without anyone to pass to.

No, I won't apologize for liking my careers. I feel my work as a wife, a mother, a homemaker, a writer, and a secretary are all important.

Lord, thank you for giving me gifts to use in these various capacities. What I have I must use, and no matter what anyone else thinks, I won't apologize. I like who I am and what I do at least ninety percent of the time.

Additional Scripture Readings:
Judges 4:4–10; 1 Thessalonians 4:11–12

Go to page 702 for your next devotional reading.

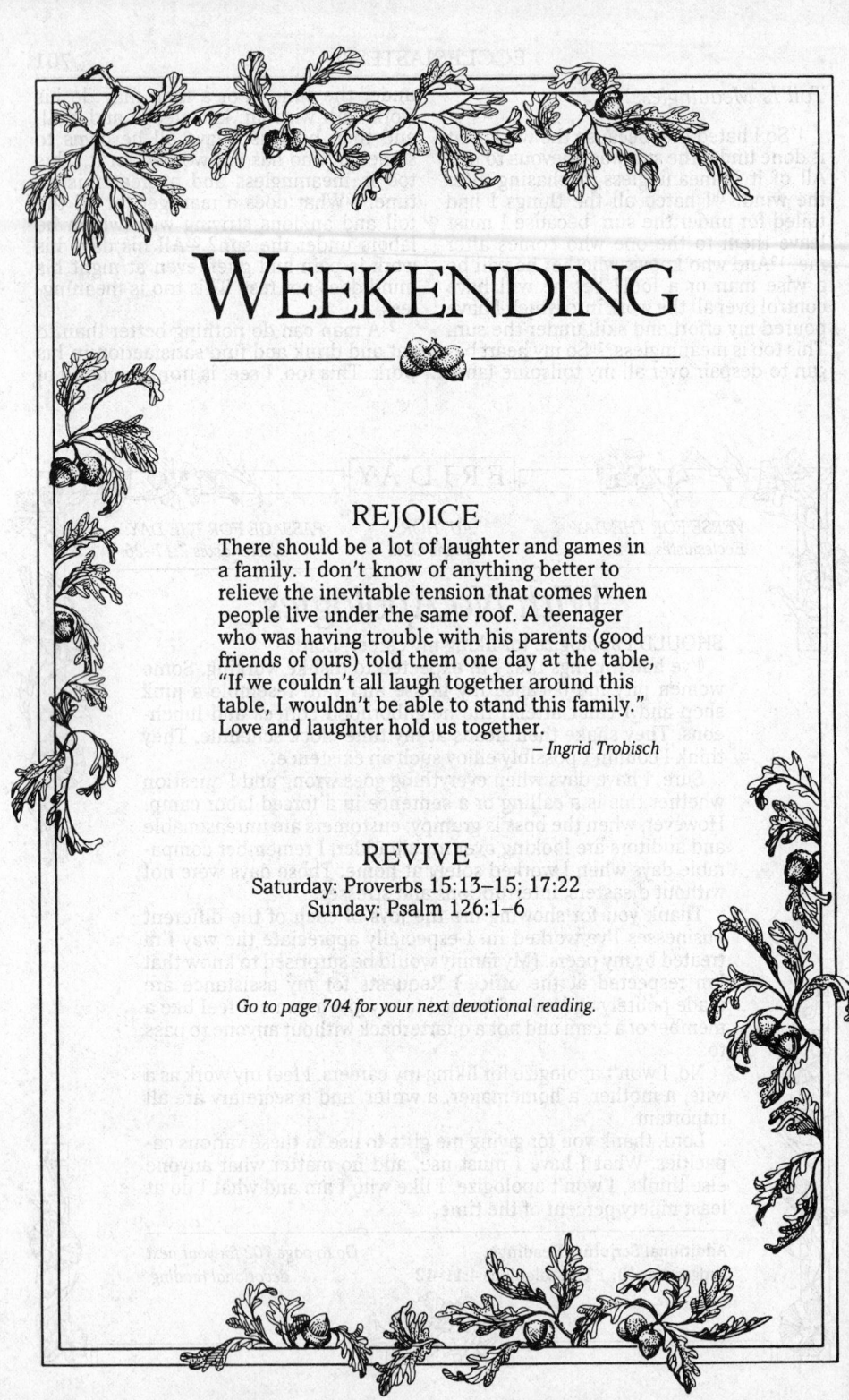

WEEKENDING

REJOICE

There should be a lot of laughter and games in a family. I don't know of anything better to relieve the inevitable tension that comes when people live under the same roof. A teenager who was having trouble with his parents (good friends of ours) told them one day at the table, "If we couldn't all laugh together around this table, I wouldn't be able to stand this family." Love and laughter hold us together.

— *Ingrid Trobisch*

REVIVE

Saturday: Proverbs 15:13–15; 17:22
Sunday: Psalm 126:1–6

Go to page 704 for your next devotional reading.

God, [25]for without him, who can eat or find enjoyment? [26]To the man who pleases him, God gives wisdom, knowledge and happiness, but to the sinner he gives the task of gathering and storing up wealth to hand it over to the one who pleases God. This too is meaningless, a chasing after the wind.

A Time for Everything

3 There is a time for everything,
and a season for every activity
under heaven:

[2] a time to be born and a time to
die,
a time to plant and a time to
uproot,
[3] a time to kill and a time to heal,
a time to tear down and a time to
build,
[4] a time to weep and a time to laugh,
a time to mourn and a time to
dance,
[5] a time to scatter stones and a time
to gather them,
a time to embrace and a time to
refrain,
[6] a time to search and a time to give
up,
a time to keep and a time to throw
away,
[7] a time to tear and a time to mend,
a time to be silent and a time to
speak,
[8] a time to love and a time to hate,
a time for war and a time for peace.

[9]What does the worker gain from his toil? [10]I have seen the burden God has laid on men. [11]He has made everything beautiful in its time. He has also set eternity in the hearts of men; yet they cannot fathom what God has done from beginning to end. [12]I know that there is nothing better for men than to be happy and do good while they live. [13]That everyone may eat and drink, and find satisfaction in all his toil—this is the gift of God. [14]I know that everything God does will endure forever; nothing can be added to it and nothing taken from it. God does it so that men will revere him.

[15]Whatever is has already been,
and what will be has been before;
and God will call the past to
account.[a]

[16]And I saw something else under the sun:

In the place of judgment—wickedness
was there,
in the place of justice—wickedness
was there.

[17]I thought in my heart,

"God will bring to judgment
both the righteous and the wicked,
for there will be a time for every
activity,
a time for every deed."

[18]I also thought, "As for men, God tests them so that they may see that they are like the animals. [19]Man's fate is like that of the animals; the same fate awaits them both: As one dies, so dies the other. All have the same breath[b]; man has no advantage over the animal. Everything is meaningless. [20]All go to the same place; all come from dust, and to dust all return. [21]Who knows if the spirit of man rises upward and if the spirit of the animal[c] goes down into the earth?"

[22]So I saw that there is nothing better for a man than to enjoy his work, because that is his lot. For who can bring him to see what will happen after him?

Oppression, Toil, Friendlessness

4 Again I looked and saw all the oppression that was taking place under the sun:

I saw the tears of the oppressed—
and they have no comforter;
power was on the side of their
oppressors—
and they have no comforter.
[2]And I declared that the dead,
who had already died,
are happier than the living,
who are still alive.
[3]But better than both
is he who has not yet been,
who has not seen the evil
that is done under the sun.

[4]And I saw that all labor and all achievement spring from man's envy of his neighbor. This too is meaningless, a chasing after the wind.

[5]The fool folds his hands
and ruins himself.

---

[a]15 Or *God calls back the past*   [b]19 Or *spirit upward, or the spirit of the animal, which*   [c]21 Or *Who knows the spirit of man, which rises*

VERSE FOR THE DAY:
Ecclesiastes 3:13

AUTHOR:
Luci Swindoll

PASSAGE FOR THE DAY:
Ecclesiastes 3:9–14

The Beauty and Burden of Work

IN music there is a wonderful thing called phrasing where the performer punctuates or caresses the flow of sound according to the mood and emotion she wants to convey. The rising and falling, the peaks and valleys are what make music interesting. This is what allows the artist to achieve both unity and variety—to hold our attention and move our spirits. Without unity, there would be chaos; without variety, we'd be bored. Phrasing distinguishes the supreme artist from one of lesser inspiration.

I am reminded of God's phrasing over my life as the unity of Solomon's thought develops here on the beauty and the burden of work. God's gift to us through work is a sense of satisfaction because he knows the value of honest labor. His design through the phrasing of our lives, the sometimes unpleasant labor, is to perfect us in himself. From his first thought of us at the beginning of creation, he saw us as complete and finished in Christ.

Solomon uses contrasting thoughts: work and toil coupled with beauty and satisfaction; the beginning of God's plan as opposed to the end; the eternal viewpoint versus the temporal; human inability to fathom reflected against God's total understanding.

As the melody of our lives unfolds on a daily basis, the high point lies in the fact that God is never going to make a mistake with the motif that he's specifically designed for us. Whatever he does will endure forever. He brings out the beauty of harmony and richness as he directs every facet of our lives. This fact guarantees that all crises already have been met and overcome in him. As we live, work, and bear our burdens, be assured that the melody of our lives is controlled by the eternal God of the universe who knows us from beginning to end. Let there be no question of what our song is all about.

Additional Scripture Readings:
Philippians 1:6; 2 Thessalonians 3:6–13

Go to page 706 for your next devotional reading.

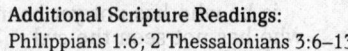

6Better one handful with tranquillity
    than two handfuls with toil
    and chasing after the wind.

7Again I saw something meaningless
under the sun:

8There was a man all alone;
    he had neither son nor brother.
There was no end to his toil,
    yet his eyes were not content with
      his wealth.
"For whom am I toiling," he asked,
    "and why am I depriving myself of
      enjoyment?"
This too is meaningless—
    a miserable business!

9Two are better than one,
    because they have a good return for
      their work:
10If one falls down,
    his friend can help him up.
But pity the man who falls
    and has no one to help him up!
11Also, if two lie down together, they
    will keep warm.
But how can one keep warm alone?
12Though one may be overpowered,
    two can defend themselves.
A cord of three strands is not quickly
    broken.

Advancement Is Meaningless

13Better a poor but wise youth than an
old but foolish king who no longer knows
how to take warning. 14The youth may
have come from prison to the kingship, or
he may have been born in poverty within
his kingdom. 15I saw that all who lived
and walked under the sun followed the
youth, the king's successor. 16There was
no end to all the people who were before
them. But those who came later were not
pleased with the successor. This too is
meaningless, a chasing after the wind.

Stand in Awe of God

5 Guard your steps when you go to the
house of God. Go near to listen rather
than to offer the sacrifice of fools, who do
not know that they do wrong.

2Do not be quick with your mouth,
    do not be hasty in your heart
    to utter anything before God.
God is in heaven
    and you are on earth,
    so let your words be few.
3As a dream comes when there are
    many cares,

so the speech of a fool when there
    are many words.
4When you make a vow to God, do not
delay in fulfilling it. He has no pleasure in
fools; fulfill your vow. 5It is better not to
vow than to make a vow and not fulfill it.
6Do not let your mouth lead you into sin.
And do not protest to the temple messenger, "My vow was a mistake." Why
should God be angry at what you say and
destroy the work of your hands? 7Much
dreaming and many words are meaningless. Therefore stand in awe of God.

Riches Are Meaningless

8If you see the poor oppressed in a district, and justice and rights denied, do not
be surprised at such things; for one official is eyed by a higher one, and over
them both are others higher still. 9The increase from the land is taken by all; the
king himself profits from the fields.

10Whoever loves money never has
    money enough;
whoever loves wealth is never
    satisfied with his income.
This too is meaningless.

11As goods increase,
    so do those who consume them.
And what benefit are they to the
    owner
except to feast his eyes on them?

12The sleep of a laborer is sweet,
    whether he eats little or much,
but the abundance of a rich man
    permits him no sleep.

13I have seen a grievous evil under the
sun:

wealth hoarded to the harm of its
    owner,
14 or wealth lost through some
    misfortune,
so that when he has a son
    there is nothing left for him.
15Naked a man comes from his
    mother's womb,
and as he comes, so he departs.
He takes nothing from his labor
    that he can carry in his hand.

16This too is a grievous evil:

As a man comes, so he departs,
    and what does he gain,
    since he toils for the wind?
17All his days he eats in darkness,
    with great frustration, affliction and
      anger.

VERSE FOR THE DAY:	AUTHOR:	PASSAGE FOR THE DAY:
Ecclesiastes 5:19	Jean Shaw	Ecclesiastes 5:18–20

Enjoying Riches

ISN'T it great to know that God isn't against rich people! Here we see that God actually makes some people rich and then tops this off by enabling them to enjoy it! They are so busy using their money for the glory of God, they don't think about getting old.

On the other hand, there are those who work and sweat, worrying about how they are going to get the pleasure that God offers as a gift. All they have to do is seek it in the manner that he has chosen to give it. "How much more will your Father in heaven give good gifts to those who ask him!" Jesus said, immediately relating the promise to the summary of the Law and the Prophets. "In everything, do to others what you would have them do to you" (Matthew 7:11–12).

Doing kind things without money makes our hearts glad. We have all experienced the excitement of giving someone a gift—seeing her face light up, hearing her cry of delight. Or perhaps she was overwhelmed and cried. Yet we are probably not so aware of the fact that kindness keeps us busy. There are so many needs to be met, we can never be bored. One of the cures for depression is helping another person; we simply don't have time to think about ourselves. And there is the physical activity involved that tires us so we fall asleep as soon as our head hits the pillow.

A retired schoolteacher who volunteered in a city mission was asked how she could go on day after day. "I don't ever have time to think about it," she replied. She had accepted her lot: God wanted her in the mission. She was happy in her work; it was exhilarating to see children learn. Her wealth and possessions, though not monumental, were quite adequate. They did not have to supply all of life's satisfactions. These she found in her work, and she was grateful.

Additional Scripture Readings:
Acts 4:32–35; 2 Corinthians 9:6–11

Go to page 710 for your next devotional reading.

[18]Then I realized that it is good and proper for a man to eat and drink, and to find satisfaction in his toilsome labor under the sun during the few days of life God has given him—for this is his lot. [19]Moreover, when God gives any man wealth and possessions, and enables him to enjoy them, to accept his lot and be happy in his work—this is a gift of God. [20]He seldom reflects on the days of his life, because God keeps him occupied with gladness of heart.

6 I have seen another evil under the sun, and it weighs heavily on men: [2]God gives a man wealth, possessions and honor, so that he lacks nothing his heart desires, but God does not enable him to enjoy them, and a stranger enjoys them instead. This is meaningless, a grievous evil.

[3]A man may have a hundred children and live many years; yet no matter how long he lives, if he cannot enjoy his prosperity and does not receive proper burial, I say that a stillborn child is better off than he. [4]It comes without meaning, it departs in darkness, and in darkness its name is shrouded. [5]Though it never saw the sun or knew anything, it has more rest than does that man— [6]even if he lives a thousand years twice over but fails to enjoy his prosperity. Do not all go to the same place?

[7]All man's efforts are for his mouth,
  yet his appetite is never satisfied.
[8]What advantage has a wise man
  over a fool?
What does a poor man gain
  by knowing how to conduct himself
    before others?
[9]Better what the eye sees
  than the roving of the appetite.
This too is meaningless,
  a chasing after the wind.

[10]Whatever exists has already been
    named,
  and what man is has been known;
no man can contend
  with one who is stronger than he.
[11]The more the words,
  the less the meaning,
  and how does that profit anyone?

[12]For who knows what is good for a man in life, during the few and meaningless days he passes through like a shadow? Who can tell him what will happen under the sun after he is gone?

Wisdom

7 A good name is better than fine
    perfume,
  and the day of death better than
    the day of birth.
[2]It is better to go to a house of
    mourning
  than to go to a house of feasting,
for death is the destiny of every man;
  the living should take this to heart.
[3]Sorrow is better than laughter,
  because a sad face is good for the
    heart.
[4]The heart of the wise is in the house
    of mourning,
  but the heart of fools is in the
    house of pleasure.
[5]It is better to heed a wise man's
    rebuke
  than to listen to the song of fools.
[6]Like the crackling of thorns under the
    pot,
  so is the laughter of fools.
  This too is meaningless.

[7]Extortion turns a wise man into a
    fool,
  and a bribe corrupts the heart.

[8]The end of a matter is better than its
    beginning,
  and patience is better than pride.
[9]Do not be quickly provoked in your
    spirit,
  for anger resides in the lap of fools.

[10]Do not say, "Why were the old days
    better than these?"
  For it is not wise to ask such
    questions.

[11]Wisdom, like an inheritance, is a
    good thing
  and benefits those who see the sun.
[12]Wisdom is a shelter
  as money is a shelter,
but the advantage of knowledge is
    this:
  that wisdom preserves the life of its
    possessor.

[13]Consider what God has done:

Who can straighten
  what he has made crooked?
[14]When times are good, be happy;
  but when times are bad, consider:
God has made the one
  as well as the other.
Therefore, a man cannot discover
  anything about his future.

15In this meaningless life of mine I have
seen both of these:

a righteous man perishing in his
righteousness,
and a wicked man living long in his
wickedness.
16Do not be overrighteous,
neither be overwise—
why destroy yourself?
17Do not be overwicked,
and do not be a fool—
why die before your time?
18It is good to grasp the one
and not let go of the other.
The man who fears God will avoid
all extremes.a

19Wisdom makes one wise man more
powerful
than ten rulers in a city.

20There is not a righteous man on earth
who does what is right and never
sins.

21Do not pay attention to every word
people say,
or you may hear your servant
cursing you—
22for you know in your heart
that many times you yourself have
cursed others.

23All this I tested by wisdom and I said,

"I am determined to be wise"—
but this was beyond me.
24Whatever wisdom may be,
it is far off and most profound—
who can discover it?
25So I turned my mind to understand,
to investigate and to search out
wisdom and the scheme of
things
and to understand the stupidity of
wickedness
and the madness of folly.

26I find more bitter than death
the woman who is a snare,
whose heart is a trap
and whose hands are chains.
The man who pleases God will escape
her,
but the sinner she will ensnare.

27"Look," says the Teacher,b "this is
what I have discovered:

"Adding one thing to another to

discover the scheme of
things—
28   while I was still searching
but not finding—
I found one upright man among a
thousand,
but not one upright woman among
them all.
29This only have I found:
God made mankind upright,
but men have gone in search of
many schemes."

8 Who is like the wise man?
Who knows the explanation of
things?
Wisdom brightens a man's face
and changes its hard appearance.

Obey the King

2Obey the king's command, I say, because you took an oath before God. 3Do
not be in a hurry to leave the king's presence. Do not stand up for a bad cause, for
he will do whatever he pleases. 4Since a
king's word is supreme, who can say to
him, "What are you doing?"

5Whoever obeys his command will
come to no harm,
and the wise heart will know the
proper time and procedure.
6For there is a proper time and
procedure for every matter,
though a man's misery weighs
heavily upon him.

7Since no man knows the future,
who can tell him what is to come?
8No man has power over the wind to
contain itc;
so no one has power over the day
of his death.
As no one is discharged in time of
war,
so wickedness will not release
those who practice it.

9All this I saw, as I applied my mind to
everything done under the sun. There is a
time when a man lords it over others to
his ownd hurt. 10Then too, I saw the wicked buried—those who used to come and
go from the holy place and receive
praisee in the city where they did this.
This too is meaningless.
11When the sentence for a crime is not
quickly carried out, the hearts of the peo-

---

a18 Or will follow them both   b27 Or leader of the assembly   c8 Or over his spirit to retain it
d9 Or to their   e10 Some Hebrew manuscripts and Septuagint (Aquila); most Hebrew manuscripts and
are forgotten

ple are filled with schemes to do wrong. [12]Although a wicked man commits a hundred crimes and still lives a long time, I know that it will go better with God-fearing men, who are reverent before God. [13]Yet because the wicked do not fear God, it will not go well with them, and their days will not lengthen like a shadow.

[14]There is something else meaningless that occurs on earth: righteous men who get what the wicked deserve, and wicked men who get what the righteous deserve. This too, I say, is meaningless. [15]So I commend the enjoyment of life, because nothing is better for a man under the sun than to eat and drink and be glad. Then joy will accompany him in his work all the days of the life God has given him under the sun.

[16]When I applied my mind to know wisdom and to observe man's labor on earth —his eyes not seeing sleep day or night— [17]then I saw all that God has done. No one can comprehend what goes on under the sun. Despite all his efforts to search it out, man cannot discover its meaning. Even if a wise man claims he knows, he cannot really comprehend it.

A Common Destiny for All

9 So I reflected on all this and concluded that the righteous and the wise and what they do are in God's hands, but no man knows whether love or hate awaits him. [2]All share a common destiny —the righteous and the wicked, the good and the bad,[a] the clean and the unclean, those who offer sacrifices and those who do not.

As it is with the good man,
  so with the sinner;
as it is with those who take oaths,
  so with those who are afraid to take
    them.

[3]This is the evil in everything that happens under the sun: The same destiny overtakes all. The hearts of men, moreover, are full of evil and there is madness in their hearts while they live, and afterward they join the dead. [4]Anyone who is among the living has hope[b]—even a live dog is better off than a dead lion!

[5]For the living know that they will die,
  but the dead know nothing;
they have no further reward,

and even the memory of them is
    forgotten.
[6]Their love, their hate
and their jealousy have long since
    vanished;
never again will they have a part
  in anything that happens under the
    sun.

[7]Go, eat your food with gladness, and drink your wine with a joyful heart, for it is now that God favors what you do. [8]Always be clothed in white, and always anoint your head with oil. [9]Enjoy life with your wife, whom you love, all the days of this meaningless life that God has given you under the sun— all your meaningless days. For this is your lot in life and in your toilsome labor under the sun. [10]Whatever your hand finds to do, do it with all your might, for in the grave,[c] where you are going, there is neither working nor planning nor knowledge nor wisdom.

[11]I have seen something else under the sun:

The race is not to the swift
  or the battle to the strong,
nor does food come to the wise
  or wealth to the brilliant
  or favor to the learned;
but time and chance happen to them
    all.

[12]Moreover, no man knows when his hour will come:

As fish are caught in a cruel net,
  or birds are taken in a snare,
so men are trapped by evil times
  that fall unexpectedly upon them.

Wisdom Better Than Folly

[13]I also saw under the sun this example of wisdom that greatly impressed me: [14]There was once a small city with only a few people in it. And a powerful king came against it, surrounded it and built huge siegeworks against it. [15]Now there lived in that city a man poor but wise, and he saved the city by his wisdom. But nobody remembered that poor man. [16]So I said, "Wisdom is better than strength." But the poor man's wisdom is despised, and his words are no longer heeded.

[17]The quiet words of the wise are more
    to be heeded
  than the shouts of a ruler of fools.

[a]2 Septuagint (Aquila), Vulgate and Syriac; Hebrew does not have *and the bad.*   [b]4 Or *What then is to be chosen? With all who live, there is hope*   [c]10 Hebrew *Sheol*

VERSE FOR THE DAY:	AUTHOR:	PASSAGE FOR THE DAY:
Ecclesiastes 9:8	Alma Barkman	Ecclesiastes 9:7–10

Full Loads, Empty Pockets

EVERY time I do the laundry, I think back to the days when we had to melt snow for washday. The copper boiler on top of the old wood stove sputtered and rocked in protest as Mother stoked up the fire. Those old kitchens were not too warm to begin with, and all those tubs full of snow certainly did nothing to raise the temperature of the room.

It seemed to me that I would have just nicely thawed out when it was time to bring in a line full of frozen wash. Fleece-lined suits of underwear had a habit of freezing into grotesque shapes, and we kids used to have great fun matching them up to local personalities. Draped over the wooden clotheshorse, they gradually assumed their conventional shape, a chilling rebuke to our active imaginations.

Despite modern conveniences, some aspects of laundry day never change. You still need a clothespin on your nose when you peel apart the teenager's socks. And kids still leave all sorts of junk in their pockets, to be claimed long after the trinkets have disintegrated in the wash and the papers have plugged the lint trap.

And in their work pants, husbands still carry nails and the wing nut from last year's lawn mower as well as springs and sprockets from various machines—all sorts of mechanical equipment they never use but are loath to part with. "I might need it sometime. Be sure you keep it!" I have a collection down there that fills a three-pound pail.

I am also expert at patching pockets. As I mend the holes and reinforce the seams, I am reminded of all the worries, fears, anxieties and doubts we carry around from week to week without really noticing them. Suddenly the accumulated weight becomes too much, and we break under the strain.

We need to develop the habit of emptying our pockets, so to speak. We must spread out our feelings before the Lord, prayerfully sort things through, and ask him to dispose of the trash. In so doing we will discover that we have exchanged our "spirit of despair" for a "garment of praise" (Isaiah 61:3).

Additional Scripture Readings:
Psalm 55:12–18; 2 Peter 1:5–8

Go to page 712 for your next devotional reading.

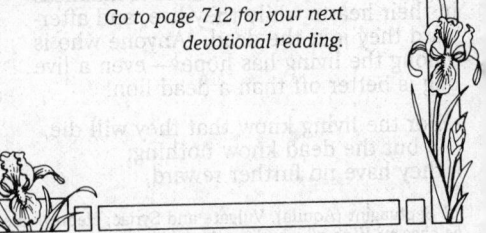

¹⁸Wisdom is better than weapons of
war,
  but one sinner destroys much good.

10 As dead flies give perfume a bad
smell,
  so a little folly outweighs wisdom
  and honor.
²The heart of the wise inclines to the
right,
  but the heart of the fool to the left.
³Even as he walks along the road,
  the fool lacks sense
  and shows everyone how stupid he
  is.
⁴If a ruler's anger rises against you,
  do not leave your post;
  calmness can lay great errors to
  rest.

⁵There is an evil I have seen under the
sun,
  the sort of error that arises from a
  ruler:
⁶Fools are put in many high positions,
  while the rich occupy the low ones.
⁷I have seen slaves on horseback,
  while princes go on foot like slaves.

⁸Whoever digs a pit may fall into it;
  whoever breaks through a wall may
  be bitten by a snake.
⁹Whoever quarries stones may be
  injured by them;
  whoever splits logs may be
  endangered by them.

¹⁰If the ax is dull
  and its edge unsharpened,
  more strength is needed
  but skill will bring success.

¹¹If a snake bites before it is charmed,
  there is no profit for the charmer.

¹²Words from a wise man's mouth are
gracious,
  but a fool is consumed by his own
  lips.
¹³At the beginning his words are folly;
  at the end they are wicked
  madness—
¹⁴ and the fool multiplies words.

No one knows what is coming—
  who can tell him what will happen
  after him?

¹⁵A fool's work wearies him;
  he does not know the way to town.

¹⁶Woe to you, O land whose king was a
servant[a]
  and whose princes feast in the
  morning.
¹⁷Blessed are you, O land whose king is
of noble birth
  and whose princes eat at a proper
  time—
  for strength and not for
  drunkenness.

¹⁸If a man is lazy, the rafters sag;
  if his hands are idle, the house
  leaks.

¹⁹A feast is made for laughter,
  and wine makes life merry,
  but money is the answer for
  everything.

²⁰Do not revile the king even in your
thoughts,
  or curse the rich in your bedroom,
  because a bird of the air may carry
  your words,
  and a bird on the wing may report
  what you say.

Bread Upon the Waters

11 Cast your bread upon the waters,
for after many days you will find
it again.
²Give portions to seven, yes to eight,
  for you do not know what disaster
  may come upon the land.

³If clouds are full of water,
  they pour rain upon the earth.
Whether a tree falls to the south or to
  the north,
  in the place where it falls, there
  will it lie.
⁴Whoever watches the wind will not
plant;
  whoever looks at the clouds will
  not reap.

⁵As you do not know the path of the
wind,
  or how the body is formed[b] in a
  mother's womb,
  so you cannot understand the work of
  God,
  the Maker of all things.

⁶Sow your seed in the morning,
  and at evening let not your hands
  be idle,
  for you do not know which will
  succeed,
  whether this or that,

---

a16 Or king is a child   b5 Or know how life (or the spirit) / enters the body being formed

or whether both will do equally
well.

Remember Your Creator While Young

7Light is sweet,
  and it pleases the eyes to see the
    sun.
8However many years a man may live,
  let him enjoy them all.
But let him remember the days of
    darkness,
  for they will be many.
  Everything to come is meaningless.

9Be happy, young man, while you are
    young,
  and let your heart give you joy in
    the days of your youth.
Follow the ways of your heart
  and whatever your eyes see,
but know that for all these things
  God will bring you to judgment.
10So then, banish anxiety from your
    heart
  and cast off the troubles of your
    body,
  for youth and vigor are
    meaningless.

THURSDAY

VERSE FOR THE DAY:
Ecclesiastes 12:1

AUTHOR:
Jean Shaw

PASSAGE FOR THE DAY:
Ecclesiastes 12:1–8

Never Too Old

OUR writer uses poetic imagery to describe old age. Our sensitivity grows dull. Legs and arms aren't steady. Our teeth fall out. Our eyes require stronger and stronger glasses, perhaps an operation for cataracts. All the marvels of geriatric medicine cannot forestall the effects of time.

We are told to remember our Creator before this happens. According to recent research, these physical effects will not be experienced by most people until they are past seventy-five. Some people won't feel them until they are around ninety. If you are sixty as you read this, you have at least fifteen years to remember your Creator. Think what you can do in fifteen years!

In his letter to the Colossian church, Paul says to "make the most of every opportunity" (Colossians 4:5). Paul gives specific instruction for how this can be done: "Devote yourselves to prayer. . . . Be wise in the way you act toward outsiders. . . . Let your conversation be always full of grace, seasoned with salt, so that you may know how to answer everyone" (Colossians 4:2,5–6).

Isn't it reassuring—yes, exciting!—to know that we can follow every one of these instructions even though we have poor eyes, trembling hands and false teeth? Truly we are never too old to serve God!

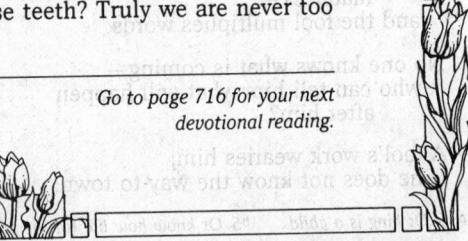

Additional Scripture Readings:
Psalm 92:14–15; Joel 2:28–29

*Go to page 716 for your next
devotional reading.*

12 Remember your Creator
in the days of your youth,
before the days of trouble come
and the years approach when you
will say,
"I find no pleasure in them"—
[2]before the sun and the light
and the moon and the stars grow
dark,
and the clouds return after the rain;
[3]when the keepers of the house
tremble,
and the strong men stoop,
when the grinders cease because they
are few,
and those looking through the
windows grow dim;
[4]when the doors to the street are
closed
and the sound of grinding fades;
when men rise up at the sound of
birds,
but all their songs grow faint;
[5]when men are afraid of heights
and of dangers in the streets;
when the almond tree blossoms
and the grasshopper drags himself
along
and desire no longer is stirred.
Then man goes to his eternal home
and mourners go about the streets.

[6]Remember him—before the silver
cord is severed,
or the golden bowl is broken;
before the pitcher is shattered at the
spring,

or the wheel broken at the well,
[7]and the dust returns to the ground it
came from,
and the spirit returns to God who
gave it.

[8]"Meaningless! Meaningless!" says the
Teacher.[a]
"Everything is meaningless!"

The Conclusion of the Matter

[9]Not only was the Teacher wise, but
also he imparted knowledge to the people. He pondered and searched out and
set in order many proverbs. [10]The Teacher
searched to find just the right words, and
what he wrote was upright and true.
[11]The words of the wise are like goads,
their collected sayings like firmly embed-
ded nails—given by one Shepherd. [12]Be
warned, my son, of anything in addition
to them.
Of making many books there is no end,
and much study wearies the body.

[13]Now all has been heard;
here is the conclusion of the
matter:
Fear God and keep his
commandments,
for this is the whole ˌduty, of man.
[14]For God will bring every deed into
judgment,
including every hidden thing,
whether it is good or evil.

---

[a]8 Or the leader of the assembly; also in verses 9 and 10

*S*OLOMON'S *"songs numbered a thousand and five" (1 Kings 4:32), of which this is one. It focuses on the spontaneous and exclusive love between a lover and his beloved, demonstrating at the same time the sort of love Christ has for his beloved bride, the church. As you read this book, rejoice not only in the love that can exist between a man and woman, but also bask in the warmth of a personal love relationship with Christ.*

SONG OF SONGS

1 Solomon's Song of Songs.

Beloved[a]

2Let him kiss me with the kisses of his
    mouth—
  for your love is more delightful than
    wine.
3Pleasing is the fragrance of your
    perfumes;
  your name is like perfume poured
    out.
  No wonder the maidens love you!

4Take me away with you—let us hurry!
  Let the king bring me into his
    chambers.

Friends

  We rejoice and delight in you[b];
  we will praise your love more than
    wine.

Beloved

  How right they are to adore you!

5Dark am I, yet lovely,

---

[a]Primarily on the basis of the gender of the Hebrew pronouns used, male and female speakers are indicated in the margins by the captions *Lover* and *Beloved* respectively. The words of others are marked *Friends.* In some instances the divisions and their captions are debatable.   [b]*4* The Hebrew is masculine singular.

O daughters of Jerusalem,
  dark like the tents of Kedar,
  like the tent curtains of Solomon. *a*
⁶Do not stare at me because I am
    dark,
  because I am darkened by the sun.
My mother's sons were angry with me
  and made me take care of the
    vineyards;
  my own vineyard I have neglected.
⁷Tell me, you whom I love, where you
    graze your flock
  and where you rest your sheep at
    midday.
Why should I be like a veiled woman
  beside the flocks of your friends?

Friends

⁸If you do not know, most beautiful of
    women,
  follow the tracks of the sheep
and graze your young goats
  by the tents of the shepherds.

Lover

⁹I liken you, my darling, to a mare
  harnessed to one of the chariots of
    Pharaoh.
¹⁰Your cheeks are beautiful with
    earrings,
  your neck with strings of jewels.
¹¹We will make you earrings of gold,
  studded with silver.

Beloved

¹²While the king was at his table,
  my perfume spread its fragrance.
¹³My lover is to me a sachet of myrrh
  resting between my breasts.
¹⁴My lover is to me a cluster of henna
    blossoms
  from the vineyards of En Gedi.

Lover

¹⁵How beautiful you are, my darling!
  Oh, how beautiful!
  Your eyes are doves.

Beloved

¹⁶How handsome you are, my lover!
  Oh, how charming!
  And our bed is verdant.

Lover

¹⁷The beams of our house are cedars;
  our rafters are firs.

Beloved *b*

2 I am a rose *c* of Sharon,
  a lily of the valleys.

Lover

²Like a lily among thorns
  is my darling among the maidens.

Beloved

³Like an apple tree among the trees of
    the forest
  is my lover among the young men.
I delight to sit in his shade,
  and his fruit is sweet to my taste.
⁴He has taken me to the banquet hall,
  and his banner over me is love.
⁵Strengthen me with raisins,
  refresh me with apples,
  for I am faint with love.
⁶His left arm is under my head,
  and his right arm embraces me.
⁷Daughters of Jerusalem, I charge you
  by the gazelles and by the does of
    the field:
Do not arouse or awaken love
  until it so desires.

⁸Listen! My lover!
  Look! Here he comes,
leaping across the mountains,
  bounding over the hills.
⁹My lover is like a gazelle or a young
    stag.
Look! There he stands behind our
    wall,
gazing through the windows,
  peering through the lattice.
¹⁰My lover spoke and said to me,
  "Arise, my darling,
  my beautiful one, and come with
    me.
¹¹See! The winter is past;
  the rains are over and gone.
¹²Flowers appear on the earth;
  the season of singing has come,
the cooing of doves
  is heard in our land.
¹³The fig tree forms its early fruit;
  the blossoming vines spread their
    fragrance.
Arise, come, my darling;
  my beautiful one, come with me."

Lover

¹⁴My dove in the clefts of the rock,
  in the hiding places on the
    mountainside,

---

*a*5 Or *Salma*   *b*1 Or *Lover*   *c*1 Possibly a member of the crocus family

VERSE FOR THE DAY:	AUTHOR:	PASSAGE FOR THE DAY:
Song of Songs 2:7	Dorothy Patterson	Song of Songs 2:2–7

A Treasure to Protect

THE Jewish people held Song of Songs in high esteem and considered it among their holiest books. This book honors conjugal love, including its most romantic expression. One finds there a theology of sexuality, which, as designed by God, offers unfailing beauty and incomparable worth. The Creator designed this most intimate union to reveal knowledge on the ultimate level (Genesis 4:1), to demonstrate the most absolute unity (Genesis 2:24), to unleash the deepest comfort (Genesis 24:67; 2 Samuel 12:24), to continue the generations through procreation (Genesis 1:28), to guard against temptation (1 Corinthians 7:2–5), and even to provide relaxation and play (Song of Songs 2:8–17; 4:1–16). If used in the proper place and time (one man and one woman, within the God-blessed union of marriage), sexual intimacy is good, powerful, life-giving and unifying in a unique and meaningful way. For a woman it is the key to her unique task—conceiving and nurturing in the womb new life, producing hand-in-hand with the Creator God the next generation.

Outside of marriage, sex is a counterfeit relationship in which abiding satisfaction is exchanged for immediate gratification and something of great value is forfeited for a transient pleasure. The beauty and lasting worth of a God-designed intimacy is sacrificed for an unseemly and fleeting encounter that perverts the perfect plan of God.

The phrase "Do not arouse or awaken love until it so desires" (Song of Songs 2:7) may be interpreted as a warning against the arousal of sexual passion before marriage. The young bride is pleading with the women of the court not to be promiscuous—not to deny them earthly sexual pleasure but to protect for them the divinely designed treasure of sexual intimacy within marriage.

The mutual love beween Solomon and the Shulammite is a beautiful example of marital bliss in physical intimacy. Nowhere else in Scripture is the physical beauty of womanhood more effectively portrayed. Yet in the midst of the pleasure and beauty found in sexual intimacy is always the duty to follow the designer's plan for reciprocity as each partner seeks to meet the needs of the other and for exclusivity as each protects the treasured "one flesh" relationship (Genesis 2:24–25). This intimacy may then be fully enjoyed and the purpose of the Creator fulfilled. We dare not prostitute through our own selfishness and unbridled desires the unique intimacy that is God's glorious seal of unity on the marriage.

Additional Scripture Readings:
Ephesians 5:25–33; Hebrews 13:4

Go to page 721 for your next devotional reading.

show me your face,
let me hear your voice;
for your voice is sweet,
and your face is lovely.
¹⁵Catch for us the foxes,
the little foxes
that ruin the vineyards,
our vineyards that are in bloom.

Beloved

¹⁶My lover is mine and I am his;
he browses among the lilies.
¹⁷Until the day breaks
and the shadows flee,
turn, my lover,
and be like a gazelle
or like a young stag
on the rugged hills. *a*

3 All night long on my bed
I looked for the one my heart loves;
I looked for him but did not find
him.
²I will get up now and go about the
city,
through its streets and squares;
I will search for the one my heart
loves.
So I looked for him but did not find
him.
³The watchmen found me
as they made their rounds in the
city.
"Have you seen the one my heart
loves?"
⁴Scarcely had I passed them
when I found the one my heart
loves.
I held him and would not let him go
till I had brought him to my
mother's house,
to the room of the one who
conceived me.
⁵Daughters of Jerusalem, I charge you
by the gazelles and by the does of
the field:
Do not arouse or awaken love
until it so desires.

⁶Who is this coming up from the
desert
like a column of smoke,
perfumed with myrrh and incense
made from all the spices of the
merchant?
⁷Look! It is Solomon's carriage,
escorted by sixty warriors,
the noblest of Israel,

⁸all of them wearing the sword,
all experienced in battle,
each with his sword at his side,
prepared for the terrors of the
night.
⁹King Solomon made for himself the
carriage;
he made it of wood from Lebanon.
¹⁰Its posts he made of silver,
its base of gold.
Its seat was upholstered with purple,
its interior lovingly inlaid
by*b* the daughters of Jerusalem.
¹¹Come out, you daughters of Zion,
and look at King Solomon wearing
the crown,
the crown with which his mother
crowned him
on the day of his wedding,
the day his heart rejoiced.

Lover

4 How beautiful you are, my darling!
Oh, how beautiful!
Your eyes behind your veil are
doves.
Your hair is like a flock of goats
descending from Mount Gilead.
²Your teeth are like a flock of sheep
just shorn,
coming up from the washing.
Each has its twin;
not one of them is alone.
³Your lips are like a scarlet ribbon;
your mouth is lovely.
Your temples behind your veil
are like the halves of a
pomegranate.
⁴Your neck is like the tower of David,
built with elegance*c*;
on it hang a thousand shields,
all of them shields of warriors.
⁵Your two breasts are like two fawns,
like twin fawns of a gazelle
that browse among the lilies.
⁶Until the day breaks
and the shadows flee,
I will go to the mountain of myrrh
and to the hill of incense.
⁷All beautiful you are, my darling;
there is no flaw in you.

⁸Come with me from Lebanon, my
bride,
come with me from Lebanon.
Descend from the crest of Amana,

---

a17 Or *the hills of Bether* *b10* Or *its inlaid interior a gift of love / from* *c4* The meaning of the
Hebrew for this word is uncertain.

from the top of Senir, the summit
    of Hermon,
from the lions' dens
    and the mountain haunts of the
        leopards.
9You have stolen my heart, my sister,
    my bride;
you have stolen my heart
with one glance of your eyes,
    with one jewel of your necklace.
10How delightful is your love, my sister,
    my bride!
How much more pleasing is your
    love than wine,
    and the fragrance of your perfume
        than any spice!
11Your lips drop sweetness as the
    honeycomb, my bride;
    milk and honey are under your
        tongue.
The fragrance of your garments is
    like that of Lebanon.
12You are a garden locked up, my sister,
    my bride;
    you are a spring enclosed, a sealed
        fountain.
13Your plants are an orchard of
    pomegranates
    with choice fruits,
    with henna and nard,
14   nard and saffron,
    calamus and cinnamon,
    with every kind of incense tree,
    with myrrh and aloes
    and all the finest spices.
15You are a a garden fountain,
    a well of flowing water
    streaming down from Lebanon.

Beloved

16Awake, north wind,
    and come, south wind!
Blow on my garden,
    that its fragrance may spread
        abroad.
Let my lover come into his garden
    and taste its choice fruits.

Lover

5   I have come into my garden, my
        sister, my bride;
    I have gathered my myrrh with my
        spice.
    I have eaten my honeycomb and my
        honey;
    I have drunk my wine and my milk.

Friends

Eat, O friends, and drink;
    drink your fill, O lovers.

Beloved

2I slept but my heart was awake.
    Listen! My lover is knocking:
"Open to me, my sister, my darling,
    my dove, my flawless one.
My head is drenched with dew,
    my hair with the dampness of the
        night."
3I have taken off my robe—
    must I put it on again?
I have washed my feet—
    must I soil them again?
4My lover thrust his hand through the
    latch-opening;
    my heart began to pound for him.
5I arose to open for my lover,
    and my hands dripped with myrrh,
    my fingers with flowing myrrh,
    on the handles of the lock.
6I opened for my lover,
    but my lover had left; he was gone.
    My heart sank at his departure.b
I looked for him but did not find him.
    I called him but he did not answer.
7The watchmen found me
    as they made their rounds in the
        city.
They beat me, they bruised me;
    they took away my cloak,
    those watchmen of the walls!
8O daughters of Jerusalem, I charge
    you—
    if you find my lover,
what will you tell him?
    Tell him I am faint with love.

Friends

9How is your beloved better than
    others,
    most beautiful of women?
How is your beloved better than
    others,
    that you charge us so?

Beloved

10My lover is radiant and ruddy,
    outstanding among ten thousand.
11His head is purest gold;
    his hair is wavy
    and black as a raven.
12His eyes are like doves
    by the water streams,

a15 Or *I am* (spoken by the *Beloved*)   b6 Or *heart had gone out to him when he spoke*

washed in milk,
  mounted like jewels.
¹³His cheeks are like beds of spice
    yielding perfume.
His lips are like lilies
    dripping with myrrh.
¹⁴His arms are rods of gold
    set with chrysolite.
His body is like polished ivory
    decorated with sapphires. ᵃ
¹⁵His legs are pillars of marble
    set on bases of pure gold.
His appearance is like Lebanon,
    choice as its cedars.
¹⁶His mouth is sweetness itself;
    he is altogether lovely.
This is my lover, this my friend,
    O daughters of Jerusalem.

Friends

6 Where has your lover gone,
    most beautiful of women?
Which way did your lover turn,
    that we may look for him with you?

Beloved

²My lover has gone down to his
    garden,
  to the beds of spices,
to browse in the gardens
    and to gather lilies.
³I am my lover's and my lover is mine;
    he browses among the lilies.

Lover

⁴You are beautiful, my darling, as
    Tirzah,
  lovely as Jerusalem,
  majestic as troops with banners.
⁵Turn your eyes from me;
    they overwhelm me.
Your hair is like a flock of goats
    descending from Gilead.
⁶Your teeth are like a flock of sheep
    coming up from the washing.
Each has its twin,
    not one of them is alone.
⁷Your temples behind your veil
    are like the halves of a
      pomegranate.
⁸Sixty queens there may be,
    and eighty concubines,
    and virgins beyond number;
⁹but my dove, my perfect one, is
    unique,
  the only daughter of her mother,

the favorite of the one who bore
    her.
The maidens saw her and called her
    blessed;
the queens and concubines praised
    her.

Friends

¹⁰Who is this that appears like the
    dawn,
  fair as the moon, bright as the sun,
  majestic as the stars in procession?

Lover

¹¹I went down to the grove of nut trees
    to look at the new growth in the
      valley,
  to see if the vines had budded
    or the pomegranates were in bloom.
¹²Before I realized it,
    my desire set me among the royal
      chariots of my people. ᵇ

Friends

¹³Come back, come back,
    O Shulammite;
  come back, come back, that we
    may gaze on you!

Lover

Why would you gaze on the
    Shulammite
  as on the dance of Mahanaim?

7 How beautiful your sandaled feet,
    O prince's daughter!
Your graceful legs are like jewels,
    the work of a craftsman's hands.
²Your navel is a rounded goblet
    that never lacks blended wine.
Your waist is a mound of wheat
    encircled by lilies.
³Your breasts are like two fawns,
    twins of a gazelle.
⁴Your neck is like an ivory tower.
Your eyes are the pools of Heshbon
    by the gate of Bath Rabbim.
Your nose is like the tower of
    Lebanon
  looking toward Damascus.
⁵Your head crowns you like Mount
    Carmel.
Your hair is like royal tapestry;
    the king is held captive by its
      tresses.

ᵃ14 Or *lapis lazuli*   ᵇ12 Or *among the chariots of Amminadab; or among the chariots of the people of the
prince*

⁶How beautiful you are and how
        pleasing,
    O love, with your delights!
⁷Your stature is like that of the
        palm,
    and your breasts like clusters of
        fruit.
⁸I said, "I will climb the palm tree;
    I will take hold of its fruit."
May your breasts be like the clusters
        of the vine,
    the fragrance of your breath like
        apples,
⁹   and your mouth like the best wine.

Beloved

May the wine go straight to my lover,
    flowing gently over lips and teeth.ᵃ
¹⁰I belong to my lover,
    and his desire is for me.
¹¹Come, my lover, let us go to the
        countryside,
    let us spend the night in the
        villages.ᵇ
¹²Let us go early to the vineyards
    to see if the vines have budded,
if their blossoms have opened,
    and if the pomegranates are in
        bloom—
    there I will give you my love.
¹³The mandrakes send out their
        fragrance,
    and at our door is every delicacy,
both new and old,
    that I have stored up for you, my
        lover.

8 If only you were to me like a
        brother,
    who was nursed at my mother's
        breasts!
Then, if I found you outside,
    I would kiss you,
    and no one would despise me.
²I would lead you
    and bring you to my mother's
        house—
    she who has taught me.
I would give you spiced wine to drink,
    the nectar of my pomegranates.
³His left arm is under my head
    and his right arm embraces me.
⁴Daughters of Jerusalem, I charge you:
    Do not arouse or awaken love
        until it so desires.

Friends

⁵Who is this coming up from the
        desert
    leaning on her lover?

Beloved

Under the apple tree I roused you;
    there your mother conceived
        you,
    there she who was in labor gave
        you birth.
⁶Place me like a seal over your heart,
    like a seal on your arm;
for love is as strong as death,
    its jealousyᶜ unyielding as the
        grave.ᵈ
It burns like blazing fire,
    like a mighty flame.ᵉ
⁷Many waters cannot quench love;
    rivers cannot wash it away.
If one were to give
    all the wealth of his house for love,
    itᶠ would be utterly scorned.

Friends

⁸We have a young sister,
    and her breasts are not yet
        grown.
What shall we do for our sister
    for the day she is spoken for?
⁹If she is a wall,
    we will build towers of silver on
        her.
If she is a door,
    we will enclose her with panels of
        cedar.

Beloved

¹⁰I am a wall,
    and my breasts are like towers.
Thus I have become in his eyes
    like one bringing contentment.
¹¹Solomon had a vineyard in Baal
        Hamon;
    he let out his vineyard to tenants.
Each was to bring for its fruit
    a thousand shekelsᵍ of silver.
¹²But my own vineyard is mine to
        give;
    the thousand shekels are for you,
        O Solomon,
    and two hundredʰ are for those
        who tend its fruit.

ᵃ9 Septuagint, Aquila, Vulgate and Syriac; Hebrew *lips of sleepers*   ᵇ11 Or *henna bushes*   ᶜ6 Or
ardor   ᵈ6 Hebrew *Sheol*   ᵉ6 Or / *like the very flame of the LORD*   ᶠ7 Or *he*   ᵍ11 That is, about
25 pounds (about 11.5 kilograms); also in verse 12   ʰ12 That is, about 5 pounds (about 2.3 kilograms)

WEEKENDING

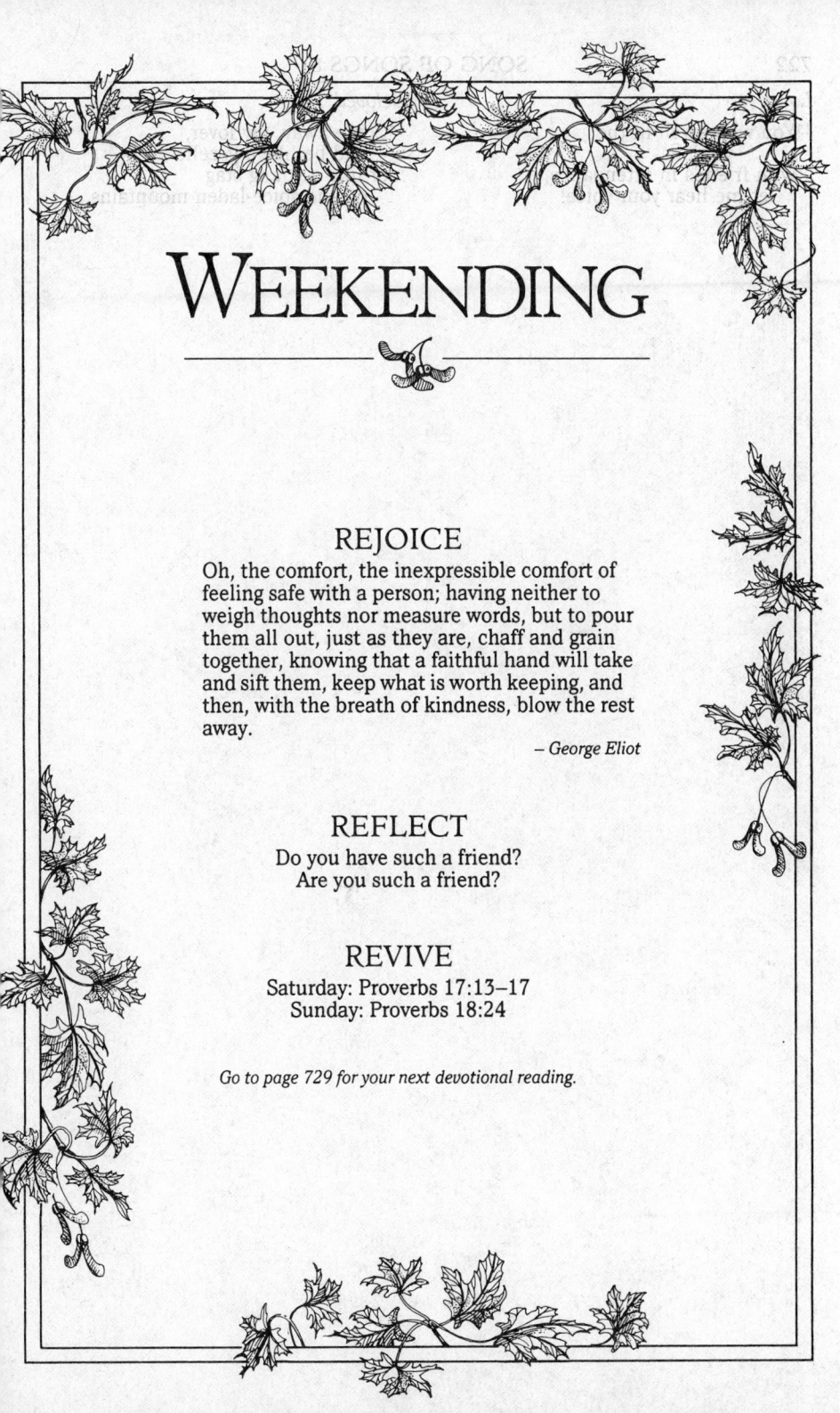

REJOICE

Oh, the comfort, the inexpressible comfort of
feeling safe with a person; having neither to
weigh thoughts nor measure words, but to pour
them all out, just as they are, chaff and grain
together, knowing that a faithful hand will take
and sift them, keep what is worth keeping, and
then, with the breath of kindness, blow the rest
away.

– George Eliot

REFLECT

Do you have such a friend?
Are you such a friend?

REVIVE

Saturday: Proverbs 17:13–17
Sunday: Proverbs 18:24

Go to page 729 for your next devotional reading.

Lover

¹³You who dwell in the
　　gardens
with friends in attendance,
　let me hear your voice!

Beloved

¹⁴Come away, my lover,
　and be like a gazelle
or like a young stag
　on the spice-laden mountains.

*I*SAIAH ministers during the events
recorded in 2 Chronicles 26–32. He
portrays graphically the sins of the
kingdom of Judah (idolatry, hypocrisy,
materialism, and oppression of the
poor) and prophesies that severe judgment is coming. At the same time, he
extends to God's people the promise of
redemption, offering hope for a glorious
future, particularly when the Messiah
comes. As you read this book, listen to
God's offer to redeem you through
Jesus, the Messiah; express your own
Christian joy by singing one of Isaiah's
songs of thanksgiving.

ISAIAH

1 The vision concerning Judah and Jerusalem that Isaiah son of Amoz saw
during the reigns of Uzziah, Jotham, Ahaz
and Hezekiah, kings of Judah.

A Rebellious Nation

²Hear, O heavens! Listen, O earth!
  For the LORD has spoken:
"I reared children and brought them
    up,
  but they have rebelled against me.
³The ox knows his master,
  the donkey his owner's manger,

but Israel does not know,
  my people do not understand."

⁴Ah, sinful nation,
  a people loaded with guilt,
a brood of evildoers,
  children given to corruption!
They have forsaken the LORD;
  they have spurned the Holy One of
    Israel
  and turned their backs on him.

⁵Why should you be beaten anymore?

Why do you persist in rebellion?
Your whole head is injured,
    your whole heart afflicted.
⁶From the sole of your foot to the top
        of your head
    there is no soundness—
only wounds and welts
        and open sores,
not cleansed or bandaged
    or soothed with oil.

⁷Your country is desolate,
    your cities burned with fire;
your fields are being stripped by
        foreigners
    right before you,
    laid waste as when overthrown by
        strangers.
⁸The Daughter of Zion is left
    like a shelter in a vineyard,
like a hut in a field of melons,
    like a city under siege.
⁹Unless the LORD Almighty
    had left us some survivors,
we would have become like Sodom,
    we would have been like Gomorrah.

¹⁰Hear the word of the LORD,
    you rulers of Sodom;
listen to the law of our God,
    you people of Gomorrah!
¹¹"The multitude of your sacrifices—
    what are they to me?" says the
        LORD.
"I have more than enough of burnt
        offerings,
    of rams and the fat of fattened
        animals;
I have no pleasure
    in the blood of bulls and lambs and
        goats.
¹²When you come to appear before me,
    who has asked this of you,
    this trampling of my courts?
¹³Stop bringing meaningless offerings!
    Your incense is detestable to me.
New Moons, Sabbaths and
        convocations—
    I cannot bear your evil assemblies.
¹⁴Your New Moon festivals and your
        appointed feasts
    my soul hates.
They have become a burden to me;
    I am weary of bearing them.
¹⁵When you spread out your hands in
        prayer,
    I will hide my eyes from you;
even if you offer many prayers,
    I will not listen.

Your hands are full of blood;
¹⁶   wash and make yourselves clean.
Take your evil deeds
    out of my sight!
Stop doing wrong,
¹⁷   learn to do right!
Seek justice,
    encourage the oppressed.ᵃ
Defend the cause of the fatherless,
    plead the case of the widow.

¹⁸"Come now, let us reason together,"
    says the LORD.
"Though your sins are like scarlet,
    they shall be as white as snow;
though they are red as crimson,
    they shall be like wool.
¹⁹If you are willing and obedient,
    you will eat the best from the land;
²⁰but if you resist and rebel,
    you will be devoured by the sword."
        For the mouth of the LORD
            has spoken.

²¹See how the faithful city
    has become a harlot!
She once was full of justice;
    righteousness used to dwell in
        her—
    but now murderers!
²²Your silver has become dross,
    your choice wine is diluted with
        water.
²³Your rulers are rebels,
    companions of thieves;
they all love bribes
    and chase after gifts.
They do not defend the cause of the
        fatherless;
    the widow's case does not come
        before them.
²⁴Therefore the Lord, the LORD
        Almighty,
    the Mighty One of Israel, declares:
"Ah, I will get relief from my foes
    and avenge myself on my enemies.
²⁵I will turn my hand against you;
    I will thoroughly purge away your
        dross
    and remove all your impurities.
²⁶I will restore your judges as in days of
        old,
    your counselors as at the beginning.
Afterward you will be called
    the City of Righteousness,
    the Faithful City."

²⁷Zion will be redeemed with justice,

her penitent ones with
righteousness.
28But rebels and sinners will both be
broken,
and those who forsake the LORD will
perish.

29"You will be ashamed because of the
sacred oaks
in which you have delighted;
you will be disgraced because of the
gardens
that you have chosen.
30You will be like an oak with fading
leaves,
like a garden without water.
31The mighty man will become tinder
and his work a spark;
both will burn together,
with no one to quench the fire."

The Mountain of the LORD

2 This is what Isaiah son of Amoz saw
concerning Judah and Jerusalem:

2In the last days

the mountain of the LORD's temple
will be established
as chief among the mountains;
it will be raised above the hills,
and all nations will stream to it.

3Many peoples will come and say,

"Come, let us go up to the mountain
of the LORD,
to the house of the God of Jacob.
He will teach us his ways,
so that we may walk in his paths."
The law will go out from Zion,
the word of the LORD from
Jerusalem.
4He will judge between the nations
and will settle disputes for many
peoples.
They will beat their swords into
plowshares
and their spears into pruning
hooks.
Nation will not take up sword against
nation,
nor will they train for war anymore.

5Come, O house of Jacob,
let us walk in the light of the LORD.

The Day of the LORD

6You have abandoned your people,
the house of Jacob.

They are full of superstitions from the
East;
they practice divination like the
Philistines
and clasp hands with pagans.
7Their land is full of silver and gold;
there is no end to their treasures.
Their land is full of horses;
there is no end to their chariots.
8Their land is full of idols;
they bow down to the work of their
hands,
to what their fingers have made.
9So man will be brought low
and mankind humbled—
do not forgive them. a

10Go into the rocks,
hide in the ground
from dread of the LORD
and the splendor of his majesty!
11The eyes of the arrogant man will be
humbled
and the pride of men brought low;
the LORD alone will be exalted in that
day.

12The LORD Almighty has a day in store
for all the proud and lofty,
for all that is exalted
(and they will be humbled),
13for all the cedars of Lebanon, tall and
lofty,
and all the oaks of Bashan,
14for all the towering mountains
and all the high hills,
15for every lofty tower
and every fortified wall,
16for every trading shipb
and every stately vessel.
17The arrogance of man will be brought
low
and the pride of men humbled;
the LORD alone will be exalted in that
day,
18 and the idols will totally disappear.

19Men will flee to caves in the rocks
and to holes in the ground
from dread of the LORD
and the splendor of his majesty,
when he rises to shake the earth.
20In that day men will throw away
to the rodents and bats
their idols of silver and idols of gold,
which they made to worship.
21They will flee to caverns in the rocks
and to the overhanging crags
from dread of the LORD

a9 Or not raise them up   b16 Hebrew every ship of Tarshish

and the splendor of his majesty,
when he rises to shake the earth.

²²Stop trusting in man,
who has but a breath in his
nostrils.
Of what account is he?

Judgment on Jerusalem and Judah

3 See now, the Lord,
the LORD Almighty,
is about to take from Jerusalem and
Judah
both supply and support:
all supplies of food and all supplies of
water,
² the hero and warrior,
the judge and prophet,
the soothsayer and elder,
³the captain of fifty and man of rank,
the counselor, skilled craftsman
and clever enchanter.

⁴I will make boys their officials;
mere children will govern them.
⁵People will oppress each other—
man against man, neighbor against
neighbor.
The young will rise up against the
old,
the base against the honorable.

⁶A man will seize one of his brothers
at his father's home, and say,
"You have a cloak, you be our leader;
take charge of this heap of ruins!"
⁷But in that day he will cry out,
"I have no remedy.
I have no food or clothing in my
house;
do not make me the leader of the
people."

⁸Jerusalem staggers,
Judah is falling;
their words and deeds are against the
LORD,
defying his glorious presence.
⁹The look on their faces testifies
against them;
they parade their sin like Sodom;
they do not hide it.
Woe to them!
They have brought disaster upon
themselves.

¹⁰Tell the righteous it will be well with
them,
for they will enjoy the fruit of their
deeds.
¹¹Woe to the wicked! Disaster is upon
them!

They will be paid back for what their
hands have done.

¹²Youths oppress my people,
women rule over them.
O my people, your guides lead you
astray;
they turn you from the path.

¹³The LORD takes his place in court;
he rises to judge the people.
¹⁴The LORD enters into judgment
against the elders and leaders of his
people:
"It is you who have ruined my
vineyard;
the plunder from the poor is in
your houses.
¹⁵What do you mean by crushing my
people
and grinding the faces of the poor?"
declares the Lord,
the LORD Almighty.

¹⁶The LORD says,
"The women of Zion are haughty,
walking along with outstretched
necks,
flirting with their eyes,
tripping along with mincing steps,
with ornaments jingling on their
ankles.
¹⁷Therefore the Lord will bring sores on
the heads of the women of
Zion;
the LORD will make their scalps
bald."

¹⁸In that day the Lord will snatch away
their finery: the bangles and headbands
and crescent necklaces, ¹⁹the earrings
and bracelets and veils, ²⁰the headdresses
and ankle chains and sashes, the perfume
bottles and charms, ²¹the signet rings and
nose rings, ²²the fine robes and the capes
and cloaks, the purses ²³and mirrors, and
the linen garments and tiaras and shawls.

²⁴Instead of fragrance there will be a
stench;
instead of a sash, a rope;
instead of well-dressed hair, baldness;
instead of fine clothing, sackcloth;
instead of beauty, branding.
²⁵Your men will fall by the sword,
your warriors in battle.
²⁶The gates of Zion will lament and
mourn;
destitute, she will sit on the
ground.

4 In that day seven women
will take hold of one man

and say, "We will eat our own food
and provide our own clothes;
only let us be called by your name.
Take away our disgrace!"

The Branch of the LORD

2In that day the Branch of the LORD will
be beautiful and glorious, and the fruit of
the land will be the pride and glory of the
survivors in Israel. 3Those who are left in
Zion, who remain in Jerusalem, will be
called holy, all who are recorded among
the living in Jerusalem. 4The Lord will
wash away the filth of the women of Zion;
he will cleanse the bloodstains from Jerusalem by a spirit*a* of judgment and a spirit*a* of fire. 5Then the LORD will create over
all of Mount Zion and over those who assemble there a cloud of smoke by day and
a glow of flaming fire by night; over all the
glory will be a canopy. 6It will be a shelter
and shade from the heat of the day, and
a refuge and hiding place from the storm
and rain.

The Song of the Vineyard

5 I will sing for the one I love
a song about his vineyard:
My loved one had a vineyard
on a fertile hillside.
2He dug it up and cleared it of stones
and planted it with the choicest
vines.
He built a watchtower in it
and cut out a winepress as well.
Then he looked for a crop of good
grapes,
but it yielded only bad fruit.

3"Now you dwellers in Jerusalem and
men of Judah,
judge between me and my vineyard.
4What more could have been done for
my vineyard
than I have done for it?
When I looked for good grapes,
why did it yield only bad?
5Now I will tell you
what I am going to do to my
vineyard:
I will take away its hedge,
and it will be destroyed;
I will break down its wall,
and it will be trampled.
6I will make it a wasteland,
neither pruned nor cultivated,

and briers and thorns will grow
there.
I will command the clouds
not to rain on it."

7The vineyard of the LORD Almighty
is the house of Israel,
and the men of Judah
are the garden of his delight.
And he looked for justice, but saw
bloodshed;
for righteousness, but heard cries of
distress.

Woes and Judgments

8Woe to you who add house to house
and join field to field
till no space is left
and you live alone in the land.

9The LORD Almighty has declared in my
hearing:

"Surely the great houses will become
desolate,
the fine mansions left without
occupants.
10A ten-acre*b* vineyard will produce
only a bath*c* of wine,
a homer*d* of seed only an ephah*e*
of grain."

11Woe to those who rise early in the
morning
to run after their drinks,
who stay up late at night
till they are inflamed with wine.
12They have harps and lyres at their
banquets,
tambourines and flutes and wine,
but they have no regard for the deeds
of the LORD,
no respect for the work of his
hands.
13Therefore my people will go into exile
for lack of understanding;
their men of rank will die of hunger
and their masses will be parched
with thirst.
14Therefore the grave*f* enlarges its
appetite
and opens its mouth without limit;
into it will descend their nobles and
masses
with all their brawlers and revelers.
15So man will be brought low
and mankind humbled,
the eyes of the arrogant humbled.

---

a4 Or *the Spirit*   *b10* Hebrew *ten-yoke*, that is, the land plowed by 10 yoke of oxen in one day
c10 That is, probably about 6 gallons (about 22 liters)   *d10* That is, probably about 6 bushels (about
220 liters)   *e10* That is, probably about 3/5 bushel (about 22 liters)   *f14* Hebrew *Sheol*

¹⁶But the Lᴏʀᴅ Almighty will be exalted
by his justice,
and the holy God will show himself
holy by his righteousness.
¹⁷Then sheep will graze as in their own
pasture;
lambs will feed*ᵃ* among the ruins
of the rich.

¹⁸Woe to those who draw sin along with
cords of deceit,
and wickedness as with cart ropes,
¹⁹to those who say, "Let God hurry,
let him hasten his work
so we may see it.
Let it approach,
let the plan of the Holy One of
Israel come,
so we may know it."

²⁰Woe to those who call evil good
and good evil,
who put darkness for light
and light for darkness,
who put bitter for sweet
and sweet for bitter.

²¹Woe to those who are wise in their
own eyes
and clever in their own sight.

²²Woe to those who are heroes at
drinking wine
and champions at mixing drinks,
²³who acquit the guilty for a bribe,
but deny justice to the innocent.
²⁴Therefore, as tongues of fire lick up
straw
and as dry grass sinks down in the
flames,
so their roots will decay
and their flowers blow away like
dust;
for they have rejected the law of the
Lᴏʀᴅ Almighty
and spurned the word of the Holy
One of Israel.
²⁵Therefore the Lᴏʀᴅ's anger burns
against his people;
his hand is raised and he strikes
them down.
The mountains shake,
and the dead bodies are like refuse
in the streets.

Yet for all this, his anger is not
turned away,
his hand is still upraised.

²⁶He lifts up a banner for the distant
nations,

he whistles for those at the ends of
the earth.
Here they come,
swiftly and speedily!
²⁷Not one of them grows tired or
stumbles,
not one slumbers or sleeps;
not a belt is loosened at the waist,
not a sandal thong is broken.
²⁸Their arrows are sharp,
all their bows are strung;
their horses' hoofs seem like flint,
their chariot wheels like a
whirlwind.
²⁹Their roar is like that of the lion,
they roar like young lions;
they growl as they seize their prey
and carry it off with no one to
rescue.
³⁰In that day they will roar over it
like the roaring of the sea.
And if one looks at the land,
he will see darkness and distress;
even the light will be darkened by
the clouds.

Isaiah's Commission

6 In the year that King Uzziah died, I
saw the Lord seated on a throne, high
and exalted, and the train of his robe
filled the temple. ²Above him were seraphs, each with six wings: With two wings
they covered their faces, with two they
covered their feet, and with two they were
flying. ³And they were calling to one another:

"Holy, holy, holy is the Lᴏʀᴅ
Almighty;
the whole earth is full of his glory."

⁴At the sound of their voices the doorposts and thresholds shook and the temple was filled with smoke.
⁵"Woe to me!" I cried. "I am ruined! For
I am a man of unclean lips, and I live
among a people of unclean lips, and my
eyes have seen the King, the Lᴏʀᴅ Almighty."
⁶Then one of the seraphs flew to me
with a live coal in his hand, which he had
taken with tongs from the altar. ⁷With it
he touched my mouth and said, "See, this
has touched your lips; your guilt is taken
away and your sin atoned for."
⁸Then I heard the voice of the Lord saying, "Whom shall I send? And who will go
for us?"
And I said, "Here am I. Send me!"

Send Me

WHAT a majestic and breathtaking view the prophet Isaiah has as the sixth chapter opens. He was entranced by the awe-inspiring glimpse of the eternal God on his throne, with the seraphs flying about and calling to each other:

> Holy, holy, holy is the LORD Almighty;
> the whole earth is full of his glory (Isaiah 6:3).

Isaiah was never the same after he gazed on the triune God and heard the glorious sounds of heaven. His response was, "Woe to me! . . . I am ruined! For I am a man of unclean lips" (Isaiah 6:5). Here we see a man distraught before the king of heaven. Isaiah saw himself as he was—a sinner. His reaction was much like our response when we come face to face with God as revealed in Jesus Christ. Each of us cries out for cleansing.

After Isaiah received the cleansing, he heard the voice of the Lord speak those challenging and gripping words, "Whom shall I send? And who will go for us?" (Isaiah 6:8). The prophet immediately responded, "Here am I. Send me!"

Just like Isaiah, we are living in a world full of people who not only have unclean lips but whose lives are being destroyed by immorality, drugs and now AIDS. The Lord wants us to serve him by reaching others. Perhaps he may send you to witness to a loved one, to a neighbor, or even to a country where many have not heard of Jesus and his love.

I remember clearly that after I accepted Jesus as my Lord and Savior, I had a great desire to tell others what Jesus had just done in my life. Little did I realize that one day that desire would lead me to ministry as a pastor's wife and to involvement in a gospel radio broadcasting station in Monrovia, Liberia.

Perhaps the Lord will send you to witness of your faith to someone who needs to hear of Jesus' love. Will you respond as Isaiah did? "Here am I. Send me!"

Additional Scripture Readings:
1 Kings 19:9–19; 2 Corinthians 5:17–20

Go to page 731 for your next devotional reading.

[9]He said, "Go and tell this people:

" 'Be ever hearing, but never
　　understanding;
be ever seeing, but never
　　perceiving.'
[10]Make the heart of this people
　　calloused;
make their ears dull
　　and close their eyes.[a]
Otherwise they might see with their
　　eyes,
hear with their ears,
understand with their hearts,
and turn and be healed."

[11]Then I said, "For how long, O Lord?"
And he answered:

"Until the cities lie ruined
　　and without inhabitant,
until the houses are left deserted
　　and the fields ruined and ravaged,
[12]until the LORD has sent everyone far
　　away
and the land is utterly forsaken.
[13]And though a tenth remains in the
　　land,
it will again be laid waste.
But as the terebinth and oak
　　leave stumps when they are cut
　　down,
so the holy seed will be the stump
　　in the land."

The Sign of Immanuel

7 When Ahaz son of Jotham, the son of
　　Uzziah, was king of Judah, King Rezin
of Aram and Pekah son of Remaliah king
of Israel marched up to fight against Jerusalem, but they could not overpower it.
[2]Now the house of David was told,
"Aram has allied itself with[b] Ephraim";
so the hearts of Ahaz and his people were
shaken, as the trees of the forest are shak-
en by the wind.

[3]Then the LORD said to Isaiah, "Go out,
you and your son Shear-Jashub,[c] to meet
Ahaz at the end of the aqueduct of the
Upper Pool, on the road to the Washerman's Field. [4]Say to him, 'Be careful,
keep calm and don't be afraid. Do not
lose heart because of these two smoldering stubs of firewood—because of the
fierce anger of Rezin and Aram and of the
son of Remaliah. [5]Aram, Ephraim and

Remaliah's son have plotted your ruin,
saying, [6]"Let us invade Judah; let us tear
it apart and divide it among ourselves,
and make the son of Tabeel king over it."
[7]Yet this is what the Sovereign LORD says:

" 'It will not take place,
　　it will not happen,
[8]for the head of Aram is Damascus,
　　and the head of Damascus is only
　　Rezin.
Within sixty-five years
　　Ephraim will be too shattered to be
　　a people.
[9]The head of Ephraim is Samaria,
　　and the head of Samaria is only
　　Remaliah's son.
If you do not stand firm in your faith,
　　you will not stand at all.' "

[10]Again the LORD spoke to Ahaz, [11]"Ask
the LORD your God for a sign, whether in
the deepest depths or in the highest
heights."

[12]But Ahaz said, "I will not ask; I will
not put the LORD to the test."

[13]Then Isaiah said, "Hear now, you
house of David! Is it not enough to try the
patience of men? Will you try the patience of my God also? [14]Therefore the
Lord himself will give you[d] a sign: The
virgin will be with child and will give birth
to a son, and[e] will call him Immanuel.[f]
[15]He will eat curds and honey when he
knows enough to reject the wrong and
choose the right. [16]But before the boy
knows enough to reject the wrong and
choose the right, the land of the two kings
you dread will be laid waste. [17]The LORD
will bring on you and on your people and
on the house of your father a time unlike
any since Ephraim broke away from Judah—he will bring the king of Assyria."

[18]In that day the LORD will whistle for
flies from the distant streams of Egypt
and for bees from the land of Assyria.
[19]They will all come and settle in the
steep ravines and in the crevices in the
rocks, on all the thornbushes and at all
the water holes. [20]In that day the Lord
will use a razor hired from beyond the
River[g]—the king of Assyria—to shave
your head and the hair of your legs, and
to take off your beards also. [21]In that day,
a man will keep alive a young cow and

---

[a]9,10 Hebrew; Septuagint *You will be ever hearing, but never understanding; / you will be ever seeing, but
never perceiving.' / [10]This people's heart has become calloused; / they hardly hear with their ears, / and they
have closed their eyes* 　[b]2 Or *has set up camp in* 　[c]3 *Shear-Jashub* means *a remnant will return.*
[d]14 The Hebrew is plural. 　[e]14 Masoretic Text; Dead Sea Scrolls *and he* or *and they* 　[f]14 *Immanuel*
means *God with us.* 　[g]20 That is, the Euphrates

VERSE FOR THE DAY:
Isaiah 7:15

AUTHOR:
June Masters Bacher

PASSAGE FOR THE DAY:
Isaiah 7:13–17

In the Midst of a Sinister Garden

THE graceful collection of lantana, bird-of-paradise, and wisteria (the list goes on) on a local hospital's grounds looks deceptively innocent. Until you read the signs!

Every plant in this "sinister garden" bears a warning: "Toxic, entire plant" or "Toxic, fruit and seeds."

The message is clear: *Do Not Eat!* And yet the guide tells guests, "An alarming number scoff at warnings, saying that everything here is *natural,* therefore harmless. Natural, yes, but it's possible to die a 'natural death' by sampling!"

I gasped. "Surely nobody would dare," I whispered to my friend Millie as we shepherded the children back to school after a study trip. Millie looked at me darkly. "I'd have said the same about Adam and Eve," she replied.

I winced—feeling somewhat like I was aboard a plane zooming down the runway when a wing fell off. I was so confident—but now?

Well, I might as well face it. I had given voice to what I wanted to believe. Too, I was denying a little voice inside me the right to a hearing. But the voice would not go away: "Aren't you a little guilty, too? Not overindulging, mind you, just nibbling a bit here and there? A berry to garnish the gossip you heard? A leaf of criticism . . . a seed of self-pity. . . ."

Maybe I learned more than the children that day. We don't sin a little and get by with it, do we? It poisons us. And it harms others as well. I guess claiming that it is "natural" is the greatest evil of all. Only with God's help can we avoid that "sinister garden." We need something called self-denial (not denying the self, but denying the self to indulge in wrongdoing).

To think and pray about: Choose the good and live. Be long on self-denial in other ways, too.

Additional Scripture Readings:
Deuteronomy 30:11–19; James 4:1–8

Go to page 737 for your next devotional reading.

two goats. 22And because of the abundance of the milk they give, he will have curds to eat. All who remain in the land will eat curds and honey. 23In that day, in every place where there were a thousand vines worth a thousand silver shekels,a there will be only briers and thorns. 24Men will go there with bow and arrow, for the land will be covered with briers and thorns. 25As for all the hills once cultivated by the hoe, you will no longer go there for fear of the briers and thorns; they will become places where cattle are turned loose and where sheep run.

Assyria, the LORD's Instrument

8 The LORD said to me, "Take a large scroll and write on it with an ordinary pen: Maher-Shalal-Hash-Baz.b 2And I will call in Uriah the priest and Zechariah son of Jeberekiah as reliable witnesses for me."

3Then I went to the prophetess, and she conceived and gave birth to a son. And the LORD said to me, "Name him Maher-Shalal-Hash-Baz. 4Before the boy knows how to say 'My father' or 'My mother,' the wealth of Damascus and the plunder of Samaria will be carried off by the king of Assyria."

5The LORD spoke to me again:

6"Because this people has rejected
    the gently flowing waters of Shiloah
and rejoices over Rezin
    and the son of Remaliah,
7therefore the Lord is about to bring against them
    the mighty floodwaters of the River c—
    the king of Assyria with all his pomp.
It will overflow all its channels,
    run over all its banks
8and sweep on into Judah, swirling over it,
    passing through it and reaching up to the neck.
Its outspread wings will cover the breadth of your land,
    O Immanueld!"

9Raise the war cry,e you nations, and be shattered!
    Listen, all you distant lands.
Prepare for battle, and be shattered!
    Prepare for battle, and be shattered!
10Devise your strategy, but it will be thwarted;
    propose your plan, but it will not stand,
    for God is with us.f

Fear God

11The LORD spoke to me with his strong hand upon me, warning me not to follow the way of this people. He said:

12"Do not call conspiracy
    everything that these people call conspiracyg;
do not fear what they fear,
    and do not dread it.
13The LORD Almighty is the one you are to regard as holy,
    he is the one you are to fear,
    he is the one you are to dread,
14and he will be a sanctuary;
    but for both houses of Israel he will be
a stone that causes men to stumble
    and a rock that makes them fall.
And for the people of Jerusalem he will be
    a trap and a snare.
15Many of them will stumble;
    they will fall and be broken,
    they will be snared and captured."

16Bind up the testimony
    and seal up the law among my disciples.
17I will wait for the LORD,
    who is hiding his face from the house of Jacob.
I will put my trust in him.

18Here am I, and the children the LORD has given me. We are signs and symbols in Israel from the LORD Almighty, who dwells on Mount Zion.

19When men tell you to consult mediums and spiritists, who whisper and mutter, should not a people inquire of their God? Why consult the dead on behalf of the living? 20To the law and to the testimony! If they do not speak according to this word, they have no light of dawn. 21Distressed and hungry, they will roam through the land; when they are famished, they will become enraged and, looking upward, will curse their king and their God. 22Then they will look toward

---

a23 That is, about 25 pounds (about 11.5 kilograms) plunder, swift to the spoil; also in verse 3.   c7 That is, the Euphrates   d8 Immanuel means God with us.   e9 Or Do your worst   f10 Hebrew Immanuel people call for a treaty

b1 Maher-Shalal-Hash-Baz means quick to the   d8 Immanuel means God with   g12 Or Do not call for a treaty / every time these the earth and see only distress and darkness and fearful gloom, and they will be thrust into utter darkness.

To Us a Child Is Born

9 Nevertheless, there will be no more gloom for those who were in distress. In the past he humbled the land of Zebulun and the land of Naphtali, but in the future he will honor Galilee of the Gentiles, by the way of the sea, along the Jordan—

²The people walking in darkness
  have seen a great light;
on those living in the land of the
    shadow of death*a*
  a light has dawned.
³You have enlarged the nation
  and increased their joy;
they rejoice before you
  as people rejoice at the harvest,
as men rejoice
  when dividing the plunder.
⁴For as in the day of Midian's defeat,
  you have shattered
the yoke that burdens them,
  the bar across their shoulders,
  the rod of their oppressor.
⁵Every warrior's boot used in battle
  and every garment rolled in blood
will be destined for burning,
  will be fuel for the fire.
⁶For to us a child is born,
  to us a son is given,
  and the government will be on his
    shoulders.
And he will be called
  Wonderful Counselor,*b* Mighty God,
  Everlasting Father, Prince of Peace.
⁷Of the increase of his government and
    peace
  there will be no end.
He will reign on David's throne
  and over his kingdom,
establishing and upholding it
  with justice and righteousness
  from that time on and forever.
The zeal of the Lord Almighty
  will accomplish this.

The Lord's Anger Against Israel

⁸The Lord has sent a message against
    Jacob;
  it will fall on Israel.
⁹All the people will know it—
  Ephraim and the inhabitants of
    Samaria—

who say with pride
  and arrogance of heart,
¹⁰"The bricks have fallen down,
  but we will rebuild with dressed
    stone;
the fig trees have been felled,
  but we will replace them with
    cedars."
¹¹But the Lord has strengthened Rezin's
    foes against them
  and has spurred their enemies on.
¹²Arameans from the east and
    Philistines from the west
have devoured Israel with open
    mouth.

Yet for all this, his anger is not
    turned away,
  his hand is still upraised.

¹³But the people have not returned to
    him who struck them,
  nor have they sought the Lord
    Almighty.
¹⁴So the Lord will cut off from Israel
    both head and tail,
  both palm branch and reed in a
    single day;
¹⁵the elders and prominent men are the
    head,
  the prophets who teach lies are the
    tail.
¹⁶Those who guide this people mislead
    them,
  and those who are guided are led
    astray.
¹⁷Therefore the Lord will take no
    pleasure in the young men,
  nor will he pity the fatherless and
    widows,
for everyone is ungodly and wicked,
  every mouth speaks vileness.

Yet for all this, his anger is not
    turned away,
  his hand is still upraised.

¹⁸Surely wickedness burns like a fire;
  it consumes briers and thorns,
it sets the forest thickets ablaze,
  so that it rolls upward in a column
    of smoke.
¹⁹By the wrath of the Lord Almighty
  the land will be scorched
and the people will be fuel for the
    fire;
  no one will spare his brother.
²⁰On the right they will devour,
  but still be hungry;
on the left they will eat,

---

a2 Or land of darkness   b6 Or Wonderful, Counselor

but not be satisfied.
Each will feed on the flesh of his own
    offspring*ª*:
21 Manasseh will feed on Ephraim,
    and Ephraim on Manasseh;
together they will turn against
    Judah.

Yet for all this, his anger is not
    turned away,
his hand is still upraised.

10 Woe to those who make unjust
    laws,
to those who issue oppressive
    decrees,
²to deprive the poor of their rights
    and withhold justice from the
    oppressed of my people,
making widows their prey
    and robbing the fatherless.
³What will you do on the day of
    reckoning,
when disaster comes from afar?
To whom will you run for help?
    Where will you leave your riches?
⁴Nothing will remain but to cringe
    among the captives
or fall among the slain.

Yet for all this, his anger is not
    turned away,
his hand is still upraised.

God's Judgment on Assyria

⁵"Woe to the Assyrian, the rod of my
    anger,
in whose hand is the club of my
    wrath!
⁶I send him against a godless nation,
    I dispatch him against a people
    who anger me,
to seize loot and snatch plunder,
    and to trample them down like
    mud in the streets.
⁷But this is not what he intends,
    this is not what he has in mind;
his purpose is to destroy,
    to put an end to many nations.
⁸'Are not my commanders all kings?'
    he says.
9 'Has not Calno fared like
    Carchemish?
Is not Hamath like Arpad,
    and Samaria like Damascus?
¹⁰As my hand seized the kingdoms of
    the idols,
kingdoms whose images excelled

those of Jerusalem and
    Samaria—
¹¹shall I not deal with Jerusalem and
    her images
as I dealt with Samaria and her
    idols?' "

¹²When the Lord has finished all his
work against Mount Zion and Jerusalem,
he will say, "I will punish the king of Assyria for the willful pride of his heart and
the haughty look in his eyes. ¹³For he
says:

" 'By the strength of my hand I have
    done this,
and by my wisdom, because I have
    understanding.
I removed the boundaries of nations,
    I plundered their treasures;
like a mighty one I subdued*ᵇ* their
    kings.
¹⁴As one reaches into a nest,
    so my hand reached for the wealth
    of the nations;
as men gather abandoned eggs,
    so I gathered all the countries;
not one flapped a wing,
    or opened its mouth to chirp.' "

¹⁵Does the ax raise itself above him
    who swings it,
or the saw boast against him who
    uses it?
As if a rod were to wield him who
    lifts it up,
or a club brandish him who is not
    wood!
¹⁶Therefore, the Lord, the LORD
    Almighty,
will send a wasting disease upon
    his sturdy warriors;
under his pomp a fire will be kindled
    like a blazing flame.
¹⁷The Light of Israel will become a fire,
    their Holy One a flame;
in a single day it will burn and
    consume
his thorns and his briers.
¹⁸The splendor of his forests and fertile
    fields
it will completely destroy,
    as when a sick man wastes away.
¹⁹And the remaining trees of his forests
    will be so few
that a child could write them down.

The Remnant of Israel

²⁰In that day the remnant of Israel,

ª20 Or arm   *ᵇ13 Or / I subdued the mighty,*

the survivors of the house of Jacob,
will no longer rely on him
who struck them down
but will truly rely on the Lord,
the Holy One of Israel.
²¹A remnant will return,ᵃ a remnant of
Jacob
will return to the Mighty God.
²²Though your people, O Israel, be like
the sand by the sea,
only a remnant will return.
Destruction has been decreed,
overwhelming and righteous.
²³The Lord, the Lord Almighty, will
carry out
the destruction decreed upon the
whole land.

²⁴Therefore, this is what the Lord, the
Lord Almighty, says:

"O my people who live in Zion,
do not be afraid of the Assyrians,
who beat you with a rod
and lift up a club against you, as
Egypt did.
²⁵Very soon my anger against you will
end
and my wrath will be directed to
their destruction."

²⁶The Lord Almighty will lash them
with a whip,
as when he struck down Midian at
the rock of Oreb;
and he will raise his staff over the
waters,
as he did in Egypt.
²⁷In that day their burden will be lifted
from your shoulders,
their yoke from your neck;
the yoke will be broken
because you have grown so fat.ᵇ

²⁸They enter Aiath;
they pass through Migron;
they store supplies at Micmash.
²⁹They go over the pass, and say,
"We will camp overnight at
Geba."
Ramah trembles;
Gibeah of Saul flees.
³⁰Cry out, O Daughter of Gallim!
Listen, O Laishah!
Poor Anathoth!
³¹Madmenah is in flight;
the people of Gebim take cover.
³²This day they will halt at Nob;
they will shake their fist

at the mount of the Daughter of Zion,
at the hill of Jerusalem.

³³See, the Lord, the Lord Almighty,
will lop off the boughs with great
power.
The lofty trees will be felled,
the tall ones will be brought low.
³⁴He will cut down the forest thickets
with an ax;
Lebanon will fall before the Mighty
One.

The Branch From Jesse

11

A shoot will come up from the
stump of Jesse;
from his roots a Branch will bear
fruit.
²The Spirit of the Lord will rest on
him—
the Spirit of wisdom and of
understanding,
the Spirit of counsel and of power,
the Spirit of knowledge and of the
fear of the Lord—
³and he will delight in the fear of the
Lord.

He will not judge by what he sees
with his eyes,
or decide by what he hears with his
ears;
⁴but with righteousness he will judge
the needy,
with justice he will give decisions
for the poor of the earth.
He will strike the earth with the rod
of his mouth;
with the breath of his lips he will
slay the wicked.
⁵Righteousness will be his belt
and faithfulness the sash around
his waist.

⁶The wolf will live with the lamb,
the leopard will lie down with the
goat,
the calf and the lion and the
yearlingᶜ together;
and a little child will lead them.
⁷The cow will feed with the bear,
their young will lie down together,
and the lion will eat straw like the
ox.
⁸The infant will play near the hole of
the cobra,
and the young child put his hand
into the viper's nest.

ᵃ21 Hebrew shear-jashub; also in verse 22   ᵇ27 Hebrew; Septuagint broken / from your shoulders
ᶜ6 Hebrew; Septuagint lion will feed

9They will neither harm nor destroy
    on all my holy mountain,
for the earth will be full of the
        knowledge of the Lord
    as the waters cover the sea.

10In that day the Root of Jesse will
stand as a banner for the peoples; the nations will rally to him, and his place of
rest will be glorious. 11In that day the
Lord will reach out his hand a second
time to reclaim the remnant that is left
of his people from Assyria, from Lower
Egypt, from Upper Egypt,a from Cush,b
from Elam, from Babylonia,c from Hamath and from the islands of the sea.

12He will raise a banner for the nations
    and gather the exiles of Israel;
he will assemble the scattered people
        of Judah
    from the four quarters of the earth.
13Ephraim's jealousy will vanish,
    and Judah's enemiesd will be cut
        off;
Ephraim will not be jealous of Judah,
    nor Judah hostile toward Ephraim.
14They will swoop down on the slopes
        of Philistia to the west;
    together they will plunder the
        people to the east.
They will lay hands on Edom and
        Moab,
    and the Ammonites will be subject
        to them.
15The Lord will dry up
    the gulf of the Egyptian sea;
with a scorching wind he will sweep
        his hand
    over the Euphrates River.e
He will break it up into seven streams
    so that men can cross over in
        sandals.
16There will be a highway for the
        remnant of his people
    that is left from Assyria,
as there was for Israel
    when they came up from Egypt.

Songs of Praise

12 In that day you will say:
    "I will praise you, O Lord.
    Although you were angry with me,
    your anger has turned away
        and you have comforted me.
2Surely God is my salvation;

I will trust and not be afraid.
The Lord, the Lord, is my strength
        and my song;
    he has become my salvation."
3With joy you will draw water
    from the wells of salvation.

4In that day you will say:

"Give thanks to the Lord, call on his
        name;
    make known among the nations
        what he has done,
    and proclaim that his name is
        exalted.
5Sing to the Lord, for he has done
        glorious things;
    let this be known to all the world.
6Shout aloud and sing for joy, people
        of Zion,
    for great is the Holy One of Israel
        among you."

A Prophecy Against Babylon

13 An oracle concerning Babylon that
Isaiah son of Amoz saw:

2Raise a banner on a bare hilltop,
        shout to them;
beckon to them
    to enter the gates of the nobles.
3I have commanded my holy ones;
    I have summoned my warriors to
        carry out my wrath—
    those who rejoice in my triumph.

4Listen, a noise on the mountains,
    like that of a great multitude!
Listen, an uproar among the
        kingdoms,
    like nations massing together!
The Lord Almighty is mustering
    an army for war.
5They come from faraway lands,
    from the ends of the heavens—
the Lord and the weapons of his
        wrath—
    to destroy the whole country.

6Wail, for the day of the Lord is near;
    it will come like destruction from
        the Almighty.f
7Because of this, all hands will go
        limp,
    every man's heart will melt.
8Terror will seize them,
    pain and anguish will grip them;
    they will writhe like a woman in
        labor.

a11 Hebrew from Pathros   b11 That is, the upper Nile region   c11 Hebrew Shinar   d13 Or
hostility   e15 Hebrew the River   f6 Hebrew Shaddai

VERSE FOR THE DAY:
Isaiah 12:2

AUTHOR:
Gini Andrews

PASSAGE FOR THE DAY:
Isaiah 12:1–6

Change and Trust

LIFE for most of us is not a steady-paced stroll through time, with a beginning, a middle, and an end, like a well-constructed play. It's filled with change. We change schools, careers, homes, relationships, and "images" almost as casually as our great-grandparents changed horses.

Not that all change is by choice. Tragedy strikes and our lives change forever. A marriage dissolves, and a woman, linked to her husband by a thousand threads, finds those threads snapped and wonders who she is. Cherished friendships change in character or another person's choice cuts directly across our own, bringing us where we never wanted to be.

A career change, voluntary or involuntary, may disrupt our lives, leaving us searching for the chain that holds the beads of our lives together. Financial losses sweep away our props. Even geographic change can be disorienting.

And always there is the unchangeable, the irreversible. We long to go back and begin again, to undo our mistakes. Impossible, of course. When we pull out the nails of our failures, the ugly holes remain.

For the believer, then, the question is vital: Is our God the Lord of change? Will he be with us *in* change, especially when it strains our trust to its limit? Ironically, while we trust him with our eternal fate, we may find it difficult to trust him for next month's car payment, a new relationship, or an unexpected turn in our lives. The assumption that the Almighty is unacquainted with the complex people he has made keeps us hanging onto bits and pieces of our lives, deceived by Satan's ancient lie that God does not want the best for us.

In a threatened world, in the kaleidoscopic whirl of our life patterns, it can be enormously reassuring to remind ourselves that God is unchanging: "I the LORD do not change" (Malachi 3:6). "Jesus Christ is the same yesterday and today and forever" (Hebrews 13:8).

Additional Scripture Readings:
Psalm 102:25–28; Hebrews 6:10–19

Go to page 749 for your next devotional reading.

They will look aghast at each other,
  their faces aflame.

⁹See, the day of the LORD is coming
  —a cruel day, with wrath and fierce
    anger—
to make the land desolate
  and destroy the sinners within it.
¹⁰The stars of heaven and their
    constellations
  will not show their light.
The rising sun will be darkened
  and the moon will not give its light.
¹¹I will punish the world for its evil,
  the wicked for their sins.
I will put an end to the arrogance of
    the haughty
  and will humble the pride of the
    ruthless.
¹²I will make man scarcer than pure
    gold,
  more rare than the gold of Ophir.
¹³Therefore I will make the heavens
    tremble;
  and the earth will shake from its
    place
at the wrath of the LORD Almighty,
  in the day of his burning anger.

¹⁴Like a hunted gazelle,
  like sheep without a shepherd,
each will return to his own people,
  each will flee to his native land.
¹⁵Whoever is captured will be thrust
    through;
  all who are caught will fall by the
    sword.
¹⁶Their infants will be dashed to pieces
    before their eyes;
  their houses will be looted and
    their wives ravished.

¹⁷See, I will stir up against them the
    Medes,
who do not care for silver
  and have no delight in gold.
¹⁸Their bows will strike down the young
    men;
they will have no mercy on infants
  nor will they look with compassion
    on children.
¹⁹Babylon, the jewel of kingdoms,
  the glory of the Babylonians'ᵃ pride,
will be overthrown by God
  like Sodom and Gomorrah.
²⁰She will never be inhabited
  or lived in through all generations;
no Arab will pitch his tent there,

no shepherd will rest his flocks
    there.
²¹But desert creatures will lie there,
  jackals will fill her houses;
there the owls will dwell,
  and there the wild goats will leap
    about.
²²Hyenas will howl in her strongholds,
  jackals in her luxurious palaces.
Her time is at hand,
  and her days will not be prolonged.

14 The LORD will have compassion
  on Jacob;
once again he will choose Israel
  and will settle them in their own
    land.
Aliens will join them
  and unite with the house of Jacob.
²Nations will take them
  and bring them to their own place.
And the house of Israel will possess
    the nations
  as menservants and maidservants in
    the LORD's land.
They will make captives of their
    captors
  and rule over their oppressors.

³On the day the LORD gives you relief
from suffering and turmoil and cruel
bondage, ⁴you will take up this taunt
against the king of Babylon:

How the oppressor has come to an
    end!
  How his furyᵇ has ended!
⁵The LORD has broken the rod of the
    wicked,
  the scepter of the rulers,
⁶which in anger struck down peoples
  with unceasing blows,
and in fury subdued nations
  with relentless aggression.
⁷All the lands are at rest and at peace;
  they break into singing.
⁸Even the pine trees and the cedars of
    Lebanon
exult over you and say,
"Now that you have been laid low,
  no woodsman comes to cut us
    down."

⁹The graveᶜ below is all astir
  to meet you at your coming;
it rouses the spirits of the departed to
    greet you—

ᵃ19 Or Chaldeans'   ᵇ4 Dead Sea Scrolls, Septuagint and Syriac; the meaning of the word in the
Masoretic Text is uncertain.   ᶜ9 Hebrew Sheol; also in verses 11 and 15

all those who were leaders in the
world;
it makes them rise from their
thrones—
all those who were kings over the
nations.
¹⁰They will all respond,
they will say to you,
"You also have become weak, as we
are;
you have become like us."
¹¹All your pomp has been brought down
to the grave,
along with the noise of your harps;
maggots are spread out beneath you
and worms cover you.

¹²How you have fallen from heaven,
O morning star, son of the dawn!
You have been cast down to the
earth,
you who once laid low the nations!
¹³You said in your heart,
"I will ascend to heaven;
I will raise my throne
above the stars of God;
I will sit enthroned on the mount of
assembly,
on the utmost heights of the sacred
mountain.^a
¹⁴I will ascend above the tops of the
clouds;
I will make myself like the Most
High."
¹⁵But you are brought down to the
grave,
to the depths of the pit.

¹⁶Those who see you stare at you,
they ponder your fate:
"Is this the man who shook the earth
and made kingdoms tremble,
¹⁷the man who made the world a
desert,
who overthrew its cities
and would not let his captives go
home?"

¹⁸All the kings of the nations lie in
state,
each in his own tomb.
¹⁹But you are cast out of your tomb
like a rejected branch;
you are covered with the slain,
with those pierced by the sword,
those who descend to the stones of
the pit.
Like a corpse trampled underfoot,
²⁰ you will not join them in burial,

for you have destroyed your land
and killed your people.

The offspring of the wicked
will never be mentioned again.
²¹Prepare a place to slaughter his sons
for the sins of their forefathers;
they are not to rise to inherit the land
and cover the earth with their
cities.

²²"I will rise up against them,"
declares the LORD Almighty.
"I will cut off from Babylon her name
and survivors,
her offspring and descendants,"
declares the LORD.
²³"I will turn her into a place for owls
and into swampland;
I will sweep her with the broom of
destruction,"
declares the LORD Almighty.

A Prophecy Against Assyria

²⁴The LORD Almighty has sworn,

"Surely, as I have planned, so it will
be,
and as I have purposed, so it will
stand.
²⁵I will crush the Assyrian in my land;
on my mountains I will trample
him down.
His yoke will be taken from my
people,
and his burden removed from their
shoulders."

²⁶This is the plan determined for the
whole world;
this is the hand stretched out over
all nations.
²⁷For the LORD Almighty has purposed,
and who can thwart him?
His hand is stretched out, and who
can turn it back?

A Prophecy Against the Philistines

²⁸This oracle came in the year King
Ahaz died:

²⁹Do not rejoice, all you Philistines,
that the rod that struck you is
broken;
from the root of that snake will spring
up a viper,
its fruit will be a darting, venomous
serpent.
³⁰The poorest of the poor will find
pasture,

^a13 Or the north; Hebrew Zaphon

and the needy will lie down in
  safety.
But your root I will destroy by famine;
  it will slay your survivors.

31Wail, O gate! Howl, O city!
  Melt away, all you Philistines!
A cloud of smoke comes from the
    north,
  and there is not a straggler in its
    ranks.
32What answer shall be given
  to the envoys of that nation?
"The LORD has established Zion,
  and in her his afflicted people will
    find refuge."

A Prophecy Against Moab

15 An oracle concerning Moab:

Ar in Moab is ruined,
  destroyed in a night!
Kir in Moab is ruined,
  destroyed in a night!
2Dibon goes up to its temple,
  to its high places to weep;
Moab wails over Nebo and Medeba.
Every head is shaved
  and every beard cut off.
3In the streets they wear sackcloth;
  on the roofs and in the public
    squares
they all wail,
  prostrate with weeping.
4Heshbon and Elealeh cry out,
  their voices are heard all the way to
    Jahaz.
Therefore the armed men of Moab cry
    out,
  and their hearts are faint.

5My heart cries out over Moab;
  her fugitives flee as far as Zoar,
  as far as Eglath Shelishiyah.
They go up the way to Luhith,
  weeping as they go;
on the road to Horonaim
  they lament their destruction.
6The waters of Nimrim are dried up
  and the grass is withered;
the vegetation is gone
  and nothing green is left.
7So the wealth they have acquired and
    stored up
  they carry away over the Ravine of
    the Poplars.
8Their outcry echoes along the border
  of Moab;

their wailing reaches as far as
    Eglaim,
  their lamentation as far as Beer
    Elim.
9Dimon'sª waters are full of blood,
  but I will bring still more upon
    Dimonª—
a lion upon the fugitives of Moab
  and upon those who remain in the
    land.

16 Send lambs as tribute
  to the ruler of the land,
from Sela, across the desert,
  to the mount of the Daughter of
    Zion.
2Like fluttering birds
  pushed from the nest,
so are the women of Moab
  at the fords of the Arnon.

3"Give us counsel,
  render a decision.
Make your shadow like night—
  at high noon.
Hide the fugitives,
  do not betray the refugees.
4Let the Moabite fugitives stay with
    you;
  be their shelter from the destroyer."

The oppressor will come to an end,
  and destruction will cease;
  the aggressor will vanish from the
    land.
5In love a throne will be established;
  in faithfulness a man will sit on
    it—
  one from the houseᵇ of David—
one who in judging seeks justice
  and speeds the cause of
    righteousness.

6We have heard of Moab's pride—
  her overweening pride and conceit,
  her pride and her insolence—
  but her boasts are empty.
7Therefore the Moabites wail,
  they wail together for Moab.
Lament and grieve
  for the menᶜ of Kir Hareseth.
8The fields of Heshbon wither,
  the vines of Sibmah also.
The rulers of the nations
  have trampled down the choicest
    vines,
which once reached Jazer
  and spread toward the desert.

ª9 Masoretic Text; Dead Sea Scrolls, some Septuagint manuscripts and Vulgate *Dibon*   ᵇ5 Hebrew *tent*
ᶜ7 Or "*raisin cakes,*" a wordplay

Their shoots spread out
　　and went as far as the sea.
⁹So I weep, as Jazer weeps,
　　for the vines of Sibmah.
O Heshbon, O Elealeh,
　　I drench you with tears!
The shouts of joy over your ripened
　　fruit
　　and over your harvests have been
　　　stilled.
¹⁰Joy and gladness are taken away from
　　the orchards;
　　no one sings or shouts in the
　　　vineyards;
　　no one treads out wine at the presses,
　　for I have put an end to the
　　　shouting.
¹¹My heart laments for Moab like a
　　harp,
　　my inmost being for Kir Hareseth.
¹²When Moab appears at her high
　　place,
　　she only wears herself out;
　　when she goes to her shrine to pray,
　　　it is to no avail.

¹³This is the word the Lord has already
spoken concerning Moab. ¹⁴But now the
Lord says: "Within three years, as a servant bound by contract would count
them, Moab's splendor and all her many
people will be despised, and her survivors
will be very few and feeble."

An Oracle Against Damascus

17 An oracle concerning Damascus:

"See, Damascus will no longer
　　be a city
　　but will become a heap of ruins.
²The cities of Aroer will be deserted
　　and left to flocks, which will lie
　　　down,
　　with no one to make them afraid.
³The fortified city will disappear from
　　Ephraim,
　　and royal power from Damascus;
　　the remnant of Aram will be
　　like the glory of the Israelites,"
　　　declares the Lord Almighty.

⁴"In that day the glory of Jacob will
　　fade;
　　the fat of his body will waste away.
⁵It will be as when a reaper gathers
　　the standing grain
　　and harvests the grain with his
　　　arm—
　　as when a man gleans heads of grain

in the Valley of Rephaim.
⁶Yet some gleanings will remain,
　　as when an olive tree is beaten,
leaving two or three olives on the
　　topmost branches,
　　four or five on the fruitful boughs,"
　　　declares the Lord,
　　　　the God of Israel.

⁷In that day men will look to their
　　Maker
　　and turn their eyes to the Holy One
　　　of Israel.
⁸They will not look to the altars,
　　the work of their hands,
　　and they will have no regard for the
　　　Asherah poles ᵃ
　　and the incense altars their fingers
　　have made.

⁹In that day their strong cities, which
they left because of the Israelites, will be
like places abandoned to thickets and un-
dergrowth. And all will be desolation.

¹⁰You have forgotten God your Savior;
　　you have not remembered the
　　　Rock, your fortress.
Therefore, though you set out the
　　finest plants
　　and plant imported vines,
¹¹though on the day you set them out,
　　you make them grow,
　　and on the morning when you plant
　　　them, you bring them to bud,
yet the harvest will be as nothing
　　in the day of disease and incurable
　　　pain.

¹²Oh, the raging of many nations—
　　they rage like the raging sea!
Oh, the uproar of the peoples—
　　they roar like the roaring of great
　　　waters!
¹³Although the peoples roar like the
　　roar of surging waters,
　　when he rebukes them they flee far
　　　away,
　　driven before the wind like chaff on
　　　the hills,
　　like tumbleweed before a gale.
¹⁴In the evening, sudden terror!
Before the morning, they are gone!
This is the portion of those who loot
　　us,
　　the lot of those who plunder us.

A Prophecy Against Cush

18 Woe to the land of whirring
　　wings ᵇ

ᵃ8 That is, symbols of the goddess Asherah　　ᵇ1 Or of locusts

along the rivers of Cush,*a*
²which sends envoys by sea
  in papyrus boats over the water.

Go, swift messengers,
to a people tall and smooth-skinned,
  to a people feared far and wide,
an aggressive nation of strange
    speech,
  whose land is divided by rivers.

³All you people of the world,
  you who live on the earth,
when a banner is raised on the
    mountains,
  you will see it,
and when a trumpet sounds,
  you will hear it.
⁴This is what the Lord says to me:
  "I will remain quiet and will look
    on from my dwelling place,
like shimmering heat in the sunshine,
  like a cloud of dew in the heat of
    harvest."
⁵For, before the harvest, when the
    blossom is gone
  and the flower becomes a ripening
    grape,
he will cut off the shoots with
    pruning knives,
  and cut down and take away the
    spreading branches.
⁶They will all be left to the mountain
    birds of prey
  and to the wild animals;
the birds will feed on them all
    summer,
  the wild animals all winter.

⁷At that time gifts will be brought to
the Lord Almighty

from a people tall and
    smooth-skinned,
  from a people feared far and wide,
an aggressive nation of strange
    speech,
  whose land is divided by rivers—

the gifts will be brought to Mount Zion,
the place of the Name of the Lord Almighty.

A Prophecy About Egypt

19 An oracle concerning Egypt:

See, the Lord rides on a swift
    cloud
and is coming to Egypt.
The idols of Egypt tremble before
    him,

*a*1 That is, the upper Nile region

and the hearts of the Egyptians
  melt within them.

²"I will stir up Egyptian against
    Egyptian—
brother will fight against brother,
  neighbor against neighbor,
  city against city,
  kingdom against kingdom.
³The Egyptians will lose heart,
  and I will bring their plans to
    nothing;
they will consult the idols and the
    spirits of the dead,
  the mediums and the spiritists.
⁴I will hand the Egyptians over
  to the power of a cruel master,
and a fierce king will rule over them,"
  declares the Lord, the Lord
    Almighty.

⁵The waters of the river will dry up,
  and the riverbed will be parched
    and dry.
⁶The canals will stink;
  the streams of Egypt will dwindle
    and dry up.
The reeds and rushes will wither,
⁷ also the plants along the Nile,
  at the mouth of the river.
Every sown field along the Nile
  will become parched, will blow
    away and be no more.
⁸The fishermen will groan and lament,
  all who cast hooks into the Nile;
those who throw nets on the water
  will pine away.
⁹Those who work with combed flax
    will despair,
  the weavers of fine linen will lose
    hope.
¹⁰The workers in cloth will be dejected,
  and all the wage earners will be
    sick at heart.

¹¹The officials of Zoan are nothing but
    fools;
  the wise counselors of Pharaoh give
    senseless advice.
How can you say to Pharaoh,
  "I am one of the wise men,
  a disciple of the ancient kings"?

¹²Where are your wise men now?
  Let them show you and make
    known
what the Lord Almighty
  has planned against Egypt.
¹³The officials of Zoan have become
    fools,

the leaders of Memphis*a* are
deceived;
the cornerstones of her peoples
have led Egypt astray.
¹⁴The LORD has poured into them
a spirit of dizziness;
they make Egypt stagger in all that
she does,
as a drunkard staggers around in
his vomit.
¹⁵There is nothing Egypt can do—
head or tail, palm branch or reed.

¹⁶In that day the Egyptians will be like
women. They will shudder with fear at
the uplifted hand that the LORD Almighty
raises against them. ¹⁷And the land of Judah will bring terror to the Egyptians; everyone to whom Judah is mentioned will
be terrified, because of what the LORD Almighty is planning against them.
¹⁸In that day five cities in Egypt will
speak the language of Canaan and swear
allegiance to the LORD Almighty. One of
them will be called the City of Destruction.*b*
¹⁹In that day there will be an altar to
the LORD in the heart of Egypt, and a monument to the LORD at its border. ²⁰It will
be a sign and witness to the LORD Almighty in the land of Egypt. When they
cry out to the LORD because of their oppressors, he will send them a savior and
defender, and he will rescue them. ²¹So
the LORD will make himself known to the
Egyptians, and in that day they will acknowledge the LORD. They will worship
with sacrifices and grain offerings; they
will make vows to the LORD and keep
them. ²²The LORD will strike Egypt with a
plague; he will strike them and heal
them. They will turn to the LORD, and he
will respond to their pleas and heal them.
²³In that day there will be a highway
from Egypt to Assyria. The Assyrians will
go to Egypt and the Egyptians to Assyria.
The Egyptians and Assyrians will worship
together. ²⁴In that day Israel will be the
third, along with Egypt and Assyria, a
blessing on the earth. ²⁵The LORD Almighty will bless them, saying, "Blessed
be Egypt my people, Assyria my handiwork, and Israel my inheritance."

A Prophecy Against Egypt and Cush

20 In the year that the supreme commander, sent by Sargon king of As-

syria, came to Ashdod and attacked and
captured it— ²at that time the LORD
spoke through Isaiah son of Amoz. He
said to him, "Take off the sackcloth from
your body and the sandals from your
feet." And he did so, going around
stripped and barefoot.
³Then the LORD said, "Just as my servant Isaiah has gone stripped and barefoot for three years, as a sign and portent
against Egypt and Cush,*c* ⁴so the king of
Assyria will lead away stripped and barefoot the Egyptian captives and Cushite
exiles, young and old, with buttocks
bared—to Egypt's shame. ⁵Those who
trusted in Cush and boasted in Egypt will
be afraid and put to shame. ⁶In that day
the people who live on this coast will say,
'See what has happened to those we relied on, those we fled to for help and deliverance from the king of Assyria! How
then can we escape?' "

A Prophecy Against Babylon

21 An oracle concerning the Desert
by the Sea:

Like whirlwinds sweeping through the
southland,
an invader comes from the desert,
from a land of terror.

²A dire vision has been shown to me:
The traitor betrays, the looter takes
loot.
Elam, attack! Media, lay siege!
I will bring to an end all the
groaning she caused.

³At this my body is racked with pain,
pangs seize me, like those of a
woman in labor;
I am staggered by what I hear,
I am bewildered by what I see.
⁴My heart falters,
fear makes me tremble;
the twilight I longed for
has become a horror to me.

⁵They set the tables,
they spread the rugs,
they eat, they drink!
Get up, you officers,
oil the shields!

⁶This is what the Lord says to me:

"Go, post a lookout
and have him report what he sees.

---

a13 Hebrew *Noph*   *b18* Most manuscripts of the Masoretic Text; some manuscripts of the Masoretic
Text, Dead Sea Scrolls and Vulgate *City of the Sun* (that is, Heliopolis)   *c3* That is, the upper Nile
region; also in verse 5

7When he sees chariots
      with teams of horses,
riders on donkeys
      or riders on camels,
let him be alert,
      fully alert."

8And the lookout[a] shouted,

"Day after day, my lord, I stand on
      the watchtower;
every night I stay at my post.
9Look, here comes a man in a chariot
      with a team of horses.
And he gives back the answer:
      'Babylon has fallen, has fallen!
All the images of its gods
      lie shattered on the ground!'"

10O my people, crushed on the
      threshing floor,
I tell you what I have heard
from the LORD Almighty,
      from the God of Israel.

A Prophecy Against Edom

11An oracle concerning Dumah[b]:

Someone calls to me from Seir,
      "Watchman, what is left of the
      night?
Watchman, what is left of the
      night?"
12The watchman replies,
      "Morning is coming, but also the
      night.
If you would ask, then ask;
      and come back yet again."

A Prophecy Against Arabia

13An oracle concerning Arabia:

You caravans of Dedanites,
      who camp in the thickets of Arabia,
14   bring water for the thirsty;
you who live in Tema,
      bring food for the fugitives.
15They flee from the sword,
      from the drawn sword,
from the bent bow
      and from the heat of battle.

16This is what the Lord says to me:
"Within one year, as a servant bound by
contract would count it, all the pomp of
Kedar will come to an end. 17The survivors of the bowmen, the warriors of Kedar, will be few." The LORD, the God of
Israel, has spoken.

A Prophecy About Jerusalem

22 An oracle concerning the Valley of
Vision:

What troubles you now,
      that you have all gone up on the
      roofs,
2O town full of commotion,
      O city of tumult and revelry?
Your slain were not killed by the
      sword,
      nor did they die in battle.
3All your leaders have fled together;
      they have been captured without
      using the bow.
All you who were caught were taken
      prisoner together,
having fled while the enemy was
      still far away.
4Therefore I said, "Turn away from me;
      let me weep bitterly.
Do not try to console me
      over the destruction of my people."

5The Lord, the LORD Almighty, has a
      day
      of tumult and trampling and terror
      in the Valley of Vision,
a day of battering down walls
      and of crying out to the mountains.
6Elam takes up the quiver,
      with her charioteers and horses;
      Kir uncovers the shield.
7Your choicest valleys are full of
      chariots,
      and horsemen are posted at the city
      gates;
8   the defenses of Judah are stripped
      away.

And you looked in that day
      to the weapons in the Palace of the
      Forest;
9you saw that the City of David
      had many breaches in its defenses;
you stored up water
      in the Lower Pool.
10You counted the buildings in
      Jerusalem
      and tore down houses to strengthen
      the wall.
11You built a reservoir between the two
      walls
      for the water of the Old Pool,
but you did not look to the One who
      made it,
      or have regard for the One who
      planned it long ago.

a8 Dead Sea Scrolls and Syriac; Masoretic Text *A lion*
wordplay on *Edom*.   b11 *Dumah* means *silence* or *stillness*, a

¹²The Lord, the LORD Almighty,
  called you on that day
to weep and to wail,
  to tear out your hair and put on
    sackcloth.
¹³But see, there is joy and revelry,
  slaughtering of cattle and killing of
    sheep,
  eating of meat and drinking of
    wine!
"Let us eat and drink," you say,
  "for tomorrow we die!"

¹⁴The LORD Almighty has revealed this
in my hearing: "Till your dying day this
sin will not be atoned for," says the Lord,
the LORD Almighty.

¹⁵This is what the Lord, the LORD Almighty, says:

"Go, say to this steward,
  to Shebna, who is in charge of the
    palace:
¹⁶What are you doing here and who
    gave you permission
  to cut out a grave for yourself here,
hewing your grave on the height
  and chiseling your resting place in
    the rock?

¹⁷"Beware, the LORD is about to take
    firm hold of you
  and hurl you away, O you mighty
    man.
¹⁸He will roll you up tightly like a ball
  and throw you into a large country.
There you will die
  and there your splendid chariots
    will remain—
you disgrace to your master's
    house!
¹⁹I will depose you from your office,
  and you will be ousted from your
    position.

²⁰"In that day I will summon my servant, Eliakim son of Hilkiah. ²¹I will
clothe him with your robe and fasten your
sash around him and hand your authority
over to him. He will be a father to those
who live in Jerusalem and to the house of
Judah. ²²I will place on his shoulder the
key to the house of David; what he opens
no one can shut, and what he shuts no
one can open. ²³I will drive him like a peg
into a firm place; he will be a seat[a] of
honor for the house of his father. ²⁴All the
glory of his family will hang on him: its

offspring and offshoots—all its lesser vessels, from the bowls to all the jars.

²⁵"In that day," declares the LORD Almighty, "the peg driven into the firm
place will give way; it will be sheared off
and will fall, and the load hanging on it
will be cut down." The LORD has spoken.

A Prophecy About Tyre

23 An oracle concerning Tyre:

Wail, O ships of Tarshish!
  For Tyre is destroyed
  and left without house or harbor.
From the land of Cyprus[b]
  word has come to them.

²Be silent, you people of the island
  and you merchants of Sidon,
  whom the seafarers have enriched.
³On the great waters
  came the grain of the Shihor;
the harvest of the Nile[c] was the
    revenue of Tyre,
  and she became the marketplace of
    the nations.

⁴Be ashamed, O Sidon, and you,
    O fortress of the sea,
  for the sea has spoken:
"I have neither been in labor nor
    given birth;
  I have neither reared sons nor
    brought up daughters."
⁵When word comes to Egypt,
  they will be in anguish at the report
    from Tyre.

⁶Cross over to Tarshish;
  wail, you people of the island.
⁷Is this your city of revelry,
  the old, old city,
whose feet have taken her
  to settle in far-off lands?
⁸Who planned this against Tyre,
  the bestower of crowns,
whose merchants are princes,
  whose traders are renowned in the
    earth?
⁹The LORD Almighty planned it,
  to bring low the pride of all glory
  and to humble all who are
    renowned on the earth.

¹⁰Till[d] your land as along the Nile,
    O Daughter of Tarshish,
  for you no longer have a harbor.

---

a23 Or *throne*   *b1* Hebrew *Kittim*   *c2,3* Masoretic Text; one Dead Sea Scroll *Sidon, / who cross
over the sea; / your envoys* ³*are on the great waters. / The grain of the Shihor, / the harvest of the Nile,*
d10 Dead Sea Scrolls and some Septuagint manuscripts; Masoretic Text *Go through*

¹¹The LORD has stretched out his hand
    over the sea
and made its kingdoms tremble.
He has given an order concerning
    Phoenicia*a*
    that her fortresses be destroyed.
¹²He said, "No more of your reveling,
    O Virgin Daughter of Sidon, now
        crushed!

"Up, cross over to Cyprus*b*;
    even there you will find no rest."
¹³Look at the land of the Babylonians,*c*
    this people that is now of no
        account!
The Assyrians have made it
    a place for desert creatures;
they raised up their siege towers,
    they stripped its fortresses bare
    and turned it into a ruin.

¹⁴Wail, you ships of Tarshish;
    your fortress is destroyed!

¹⁵At that time Tyre will be forgotten for
seventy years, the span of a king's life.
But at the end of these seventy years, it
will happen to Tyre as in the song of the
prostitute:

¹⁶"Take up a harp, walk through the
        city,
    O prostitute forgotten;
play the harp well, sing many a song,
    so that you will be remembered."

¹⁷At the end of seventy years, the LORD
will deal with Tyre. She will return to her
hire as a prostitute and will ply her trade
with all the kingdoms on the face of the
earth. ¹⁸Yet her profit and her earnings
will be set apart for the LORD; they will not
be stored up or hoarded. Her profits will
go to those who live before the LORD, for
abundant food and fine clothes.

The LORD's Devastation of the Earth

24 See, the LORD is going to lay
        waste the earth
    and devastate it;
he will ruin its face
    and scatter its inhabitants—
²it will be the same
    for priest as for people,
    for master as for servant,
    for mistress as for maid,
    for seller as for buyer,
    for borrower as for lender,
    for debtor as for creditor.

³The earth will be completely laid
        waste
    and totally plundered.
    The LORD has spoken this word.

⁴The earth dries up and withers,
    the world languishes and withers,
    the exalted of the earth languish.
⁵The earth is defiled by its people;
    they have disobeyed the laws,
violated the statutes
    and broken the everlasting
        covenant.
⁶Therefore a curse consumes the earth;
    its people must bear their guilt.
Therefore earth's inhabitants are
        burned up,
    and very few are left.
⁷The new wine dries up and the vine
        withers;
    all the merrymakers groan.
⁸The gaiety of the tambourines is
        stilled,
    the noise of the revelers has
        stopped,
    the joyful harp is silent.
⁹No longer do they drink wine with a
        song;
    the beer is bitter to its drinkers.
¹⁰The ruined city lies desolate;
    the entrance to every house is
        barred.
¹¹In the streets they cry out for wine;
    all joy turns to gloom,
    all gaiety is banished from the
        earth.
¹²The city is left in ruins,
    its gate is battered to pieces.
¹³So will it be on the earth
    and among the nations,
as when an olive tree is beaten,
    or as when gleanings are left after
        the grape harvest.

¹⁴They raise their voices, they shout for
        joy;
    from the west they acclaim the
        LORD's majesty.
¹⁵Therefore in the east give glory to the
        LORD;
    exalt the name of the LORD, the
        God of Israel,
    in the islands of the sea.
¹⁶From the ends of the earth we hear
        singing:
    "Glory to the Righteous One."

But I said, "I waste away, I waste
        away!

a11 Hebrew Canaan   b12 Hebrew Kittim   c13 Or Chaldeans

Woe to me!
The treacherous betray!
 With treachery the treacherous
  betray!"
[17]Terror and pit and snare await you,
 O people of the earth.
[18]Whoever flees at the sound of terror
 will fall into a pit;
whoever climbs out of the pit
 will be caught in a snare.

The floodgates of the heavens are
  opened,
 the foundations of the earth shake.
[19]The earth is broken up,
 the earth is split asunder,
 the earth is thoroughly shaken.
[20]The earth reels like a drunkard,
 it sways like a hut in the wind;
so heavy upon it is the guilt of its
  rebellion
 that it falls—never to rise again.

[21]In that day the LORD will punish
 the powers in the heavens above
 and the kings on the earth below.
[22]They will be herded together
 like prisoners bound in a dungeon;
they will be shut up in prison
 and be punished[a] after many days.
[23]The moon will be abashed, the sun
  ashamed;
 for the LORD Almighty will reign
on Mount Zion and in Jerusalem,
 and before its elders, gloriously.

Praise to the LORD

25 O LORD, you are my God;
 I will exalt you and praise your
  name,
for in perfect faithfulness
 you have done marvelous things,
 things planned long ago.
[2]You have made the city a heap of
  rubble,
 the fortified town a ruin,
 the foreigners' stronghold a city no
  more;
 it will never be rebuilt.
[3]Therefore strong peoples will honor
  you;
 cities of ruthless nations will revere
  you.
[4]You have been a refuge for the poor,
 a refuge for the needy in his
  distress,
a shelter from the storm
 and a shade from the heat.
For the breath of the ruthless

is like a storm driving against a
  wall
 [5] and like the heat of the desert.
You silence the uproar of foreigners;
 as heat is reduced by the shadow of
  a cloud,
 so the song of the ruthless is
  stilled.

[6]On this mountain the LORD Almighty
  will prepare
 a feast of rich food for all peoples,
a banquet of aged wine—
 the best of meats and the finest of
  wines.
[7]On this mountain he will destroy
 the shroud that enfolds all peoples,
 the sheet that covers all nations;
 [8] he will swallow up death forever.
The Sovereign LORD will wipe away
  the tears
 from all faces;
he will remove the disgrace of his
  people
 from all the earth.
           The LORD has spoken.

[9]In that day they will say,

"Surely this is our God;
 we trusted in him, and he saved us.
This is the LORD, we trusted in him;
 let us rejoice and be glad in his
  salvation."

[10]The hand of the LORD will rest on this
  mountain;
 but Moab will be trampled under
  him
 as straw is trampled down in the
  manure.
[11]They will spread out their hands in it,
 as a swimmer spreads out his hands
  to swim.
God will bring down their pride
 despite the cleverness[b] of their
  hands.
[12]He will bring down your high fortified
  walls
 and lay them low;
he will bring them down to the
  ground,
 to the very dust.

A Song of Praise

26 In that day this song will be sung
 in the land of Judah:

We have a strong city;
 God makes salvation

---

[a]22 Or *released*   [b]11 The meaning of the Hebrew for this word is uncertain.

its walls and ramparts.
²Open the gates
  that the righteous nation may
    enter,
  the nation that keeps faith.
³You will keep in perfect peace
  him whose mind is steadfast,
  because he trusts in you.
⁴Trust in the LORD forever,
  for the LORD, the LORD, is the Rock
    eternal.
⁵He humbles those who dwell on high,
  he lays the lofty city low;
  he levels it to the ground
  and casts it down to the dust.
⁶Feet trample it down—
  the feet of the oppressed,
  the footsteps of the poor.

⁷The path of the righteous is level;
  O upright One, you make the way
    of the righteous smooth.
⁸Yes, LORD, walking in the way of your
    laws,ᵃ
  we wait for you;
  your name and renown
  are the desire of our hearts.
⁹My soul yearns for you in the night;
  in the morning my spirit longs for
    you.
  When your judgments come upon the
    earth,
  the people of the world learn
    righteousness.
¹⁰Though grace is shown to the wicked,
  they do not learn righteousness;
  even in a land of uprightness they go
    on doing evil
  and regard not the majesty of the
    LORD.
¹¹O LORD, your hand is lifted high,
  but they do not see it.
  Let them see your zeal for your
    people and be put to shame;
  let the fire reserved for your
    enemies consume them.

¹²LORD, you establish peace for us;
  all that we have accomplished you
    have done for us.
¹³O LORD, our God, other lords besides
    you have ruled over us,
  but your name alone do we honor.
¹⁴They are now dead, they live no more;
  those departed spirits do not rise.
  You punished them and brought them
    to ruin;
  you wiped out all memory of them.
¹⁵You have enlarged the nation, O LORD;

you have enlarged the nation.
  You have gained glory for yourself;
  you have extended all the borders
    of the land.

¹⁶LORD, they came to you in their
    distress;
  when you disciplined them,
  they could barely whisper a
    prayer.ᵇ
¹⁷As a woman with child and about to
    give birth
  writhes and cries out in her pain,
  so were we in your presence,
    O LORD.
¹⁸We were with child, we writhed in
    pain,
  but we gave birth to wind.
  We have not brought salvation to the
    earth;
  we have not given birth to people
    of the world.

¹⁹But your dead will live;
  their bodies will rise.
  You who dwell in the dust,
  wake up and shout for joy.
  Your dew is like the dew of the
    morning;
  the earth will give birth to her
    dead.

²⁰Go, my people, enter your rooms
  and shut the doors behind you;
  hide yourselves for a little while
  until his wrath has passed by.
²¹See, the LORD is coming out of his
    dwelling
  to punish the people of the earth
    for their sins.
  The earth will disclose the blood shed
    upon her;
  she will conceal her slain no longer.

Deliverance of Israel

27 In that day,
  the LORD will punish with his
    sword,
  his fierce, great and powerful
    sword,
  Leviathan the gliding serpent,
  Leviathan the coiling serpent;
  he will slay the monster of the sea.

²In that day—

  "Sing about a fruitful vineyard:
³   I, the LORD, watch over it;
  I water it continually.
  I guard it day and night

ᵃ8 Or judgments   ᵇ16 The meaning of the Hebrew for this clause is uncertain.

so that no one may harm it.
4 I am not angry.
 If only there were briers and thorns
    confronting me!
 I would march against them in
    battle;
 I would set them all on fire.
5Or else let them come to me for
    refuge;
 let them make peace with me,
 yes, let them make peace with me."

6In days to come Jacob will take root,
 Israel will bud and blossom
 and fill all the world with fruit.

7Has the LORD struck her
    as he struck down those who struck
    her?
 Has she been killed
    as those were killed who killed her?
8By warfare[a] and exile you contend
    with her—
 with his fierce blast he drives her
    out,
    as on a day the east wind blows.
9By this, then, will Jacob's guilt be
    atoned for,
 and this will be the full fruitage of
    the removal of his sin:
 When he makes all the altar stones

[a]8 See Septuagint; the meaning of the Hebrew for this word is uncertain.

THURSDAY

VERSE FOR THE DAY:
Isaiah 26:9

AUTHOR:
Karen Burton Mains

PASSAGE FOR THE DAY:
Isaiah 26:1–12

Greeting the Day

MOST of us have forgotten how to greet the day. The knowledge is all but lost to us that a new day is sacred: a gift from God, a rare and precious gift. A new day brings with it another opportunity to start all over, to raise one's head from the pillow with a glad heart, to watch the clouds roll across the dark sky now diffusing pink, and to breathe that child prayer of gratitude, "Oh, God, life again. Again, one more day of life."

We must relearn how to stand in awe, how to face for a moment the eastern sky with praise and thanksgiving and allow our hearts to be filled with a corresponding inner daybreak of adoration.

We must learn to not ever take for granted—no matter how pain-filled our life—that we are alive and the earth still turns on its axis, that evil has not wobbled the world off its course while we slept; and we must understand this sacramental symbol, this reenactment of life which comes resurrecting every twenty-four hours.

Celebrating each new day helps us develop the ability to be grateful for all new moments and for the God who is in each one. The discipline of celebrating each new day influences our attitude toward all of life.

A new day signifies: The Lord of mornings is still sovereign over the world.

Additional Scripture Readings:
Psalm 3:3–6; Lamentations 3:22–23

Go to page 754 for your next
devotional reading.

to be like chalk stones crushed to
  pieces,
no Asherah poles^a or incense altars
  will be left standing.
¹⁰The fortified city stands desolate,
  an abandoned settlement, forsaken
    like the desert;
  there the calves graze,
    there they lie down;
  they strip its branches bare.
¹¹When its twigs are dry, they are
    broken off
  and women come and make fires
    with them.

For this is a people without
    understanding;
  so their Maker has no compassion
    on them,
  and their Creator shows them no
    favor.

¹²In that day the LORD will thresh from
the flowing Euphrates^b to the Wadi of
Egypt, and you, O Israelites, will be gathered up one by one. ¹³And in that day a
great trumpet will sound. Those who were
perishing in Assyria and those who were
exiled in Egypt will come and worship the
LORD on the holy mountain in Jerusalem.

Woe to Ephraim

28 Woe to that wreath, the pride of
      Ephraim's drunkards,
  to the fading flower, his glorious
    beauty,
set on the head of a fertile valley—
  to that city, the pride of those laid
    low by wine!
²See, the Lord has one who is
    powerful and strong.
  Like a hailstorm and a destructive
    wind,
  like a driving rain and a flooding
    downpour,
  he will throw it forcefully to the
    ground.
³That wreath, the pride of Ephraim's
    drunkards,
  will be trampled underfoot.
⁴That fading flower, his glorious
    beauty,
  set on the head of a fertile valley,
will be like a fig ripe before harvest—
  as soon as someone sees it and
    takes it in his hand,
  he swallows it.

⁵In that day the LORD Almighty
  will be a glorious crown,
  a beautiful wreath
    for the remnant of his people.
⁶He will be a spirit of justice
  to him who sits in judgment,
  a source of strength
    to those who turn back the battle
      at the gate.

⁷And these also stagger from wine
  and reel from beer:
Priests and prophets stagger from
    beer
  and are befuddled with wine;
they reel from beer,
  they stagger when seeing visions,
  they stumble when rendering
    decisions.
⁸All the tables are covered with vomit
  and there is not a spot without
    filth.

⁹"Who is it he is trying to teach?
  To whom is he explaining his
    message?
To children weaned from their milk,
  to those just taken from the breast?
¹⁰For it is:
  Do and do, do and do,
  rule on rule, rule on rule^c;
  a little here, a little there."

¹¹Very well then, with foreign lips and
    strange tongues
  God will speak to this people,
¹²to whom he said,
  "This is the resting place, let the
    weary rest";
and, "This is the place of repose"—
  but they would not listen.
¹³So then, the word of the LORD to
    them will become:
  Do and do, do and do,
  rule on rule, rule on rule;
  a little here, a little there—
so that they will go and fall backward,
  be injured and snared and
    captured.

¹⁴Therefore hear the word of the LORD,
    you scoffers
  who rule this people in Jerusalem.
¹⁵You boast, "We have entered into a
    covenant with death,
  with the grave^d we have made an
    agreement.

---

^a9 That is, symbols of the goddess Asherah   ^b12 Hebrew *River*   ^c10 Hebrew / *sav lasav sav lasav* /
kav lakav kav lakav (possibly meaningless sounds; perhaps a mimicking of the prophet's words); also in
verse 13   ^d15 Hebrew *Sheol*; also in verse 18

When an overwhelming scourge
    sweeps by,
    it cannot touch us,
for we have made a lie our refuge
    and falsehood*a* our hiding place."

¹⁶So this is what the Sovereign Lᴏʀᴅ
says:

"See, I lay a stone in Zion,
    a tested stone,
a precious cornerstone for a sure
        foundation;
    the one who trusts will never be
        dismayed.
¹⁷I will make justice the measuring line
    and righteousness the plumb line;
hail will sweep away your refuge, the
        lie,
    and water will overflow your hiding
        place.
¹⁸Your covenant with death will be
        annulled;
    your agreement with the grave will
        not stand.
When the overwhelming scourge
        sweeps by,
    you will be beaten down by it.
¹⁹As often as it comes it will carry you
        away;
    morning after morning, by day and
        by night,
    it will sweep through."

The understanding of this message
    will bring sheer terror.
²⁰The bed is too short to stretch out
        on,
    the blanket too narrow to wrap
        around you.
²¹The Lᴏʀᴅ will rise up as he did at
        Mount Perazim,
    he will rouse himself as in the
        Valley of Gibeon—
to do his work, his strange work,
    and perform his task, his alien task.
²²Now stop your mocking,
    or your chains will become heavier;
the Lord, the Lᴏʀᴅ Almighty, has told
        me
    of the destruction decreed against
        the whole land.

²³Listen and hear my voice;
    pay attention and hear what I say.
²⁴When a farmer plows for planting,
    does he plow continually?
Does he keep on breaking up and
    harrowing the soil?

²⁵When he has leveled the surface,
    does he not sow caraway and
        scatter cummin?
Does he not plant wheat in its
        place,*b*
    barley in its plot,*b*
    and spelt in its field?
²⁶His God instructs him
    and teaches him the right way.

²⁷Caraway is not threshed with a
        sledge,
    nor is a cartwheel rolled over
        cummin;
caraway is beaten out with a rod,
    and cummin with a stick.
²⁸Grain must be ground to make bread;
    so one does not go on threshing it
        forever.
Though he drives the wheels of his
        threshing cart over it,
    his horses do not grind it.
²⁹All this also comes from the Lᴏʀᴅ
        Almighty,
    wonderful in counsel and
        magnificent in wisdom.

Woe to David's City

29 Woe to you, Ariel, Ariel,
    the city where David settled!
Add year to year
    and let your cycle of festivals go on.
²Yet I will besiege Ariel;
    she will mourn and lament,
    she will be to me like an altar
        hearth.*c*
³I will encamp against you all around;
    I will encircle you with towers
    and set up my siege works against
        you.
⁴Brought low, you will speak from the
        ground;
    your speech will mumble out of the
        dust.
Your voice will come ghostlike from
        the earth;
    out of the dust your speech will
        whisper.

⁵But your many enemies will become
        like fine dust,
    the ruthless hordes like blown
        chaff.
Suddenly, in an instant,
⁶ the Lᴏʀᴅ Almighty will come
with thunder and earthquake and
        great noise,

---

a15 Or *false gods*   *b25* The meaning of the Hebrew for this word is uncertain.   *c2* The Hebrew for
altar hearth sounds like the Hebrew for *Ariel.*

with windstorm and tempest and
flames of a devouring fire.
⁷Then the hordes of all the nations
that fight against Ariel,
that attack her and her fortress and
besiege her,
will be as it is with a dream,
with a vision in the night—
⁸as when a hungry man dreams that he
is eating,
but he awakens, and his hunger
remains;
as when a thirsty man dreams that he
is drinking,
but he awakens faint, with his
thirst unquenched.
So will it be with the hordes of all the
nations
that fight against Mount Zion.

⁹Be stunned and amazed,
blind yourselves and be sightless;
be drunk, but not from wine,
stagger, but not from beer.
¹⁰The Lᴏʀᴅ has brought over you a deep
sleep:
He has sealed your eyes (the
prophets);
he has covered your heads (the
seers).

¹¹For you this whole vision is nothing
but words sealed in a scroll. And if you
give the scroll to someone who can read,
and say to him, "Read this, please," he
will answer, "I can't; it is sealed." ¹²Or if
you give the scroll to someone who cannot read, and say, "Read this, please," he
will answer, "I don't know how to read."

¹³The Lord says:

"These people come near to me with
their mouth
and honor me with their lips,
but their hearts are far from me.
Their worship of me
is made up only of rules taught by
men.ᵃ
¹⁴Therefore once more I will astound
these people
with wonder upon wonder;
the wisdom of the wise will perish,
the intelligence of the intelligent
will vanish."
¹⁵Woe to those who go to great depths
to hide their plans from the Lᴏʀᴅ,
who do their work in darkness and
think,
"Who sees us? Who will know?"

¹⁶You turn things upside down,
as if the potter were thought to be
like the clay!
Shall what is formed say to him who
formed it,
"He did not make me"?
Can the pot say of the potter,
"He knows nothing"?

¹⁷In a very short time, will not Lebanon
be turned into a fertile field
and the fertile field seem like a
forest?
¹⁸In that day the deaf will hear the
words of the scroll,
and out of gloom and darkness
the eyes of the blind will see.
¹⁹Once more the humble will rejoice in
the Lᴏʀᴅ;
the needy will rejoice in the Holy
One of Israel.
²⁰The ruthless will vanish,
the mockers will disappear,
and all who have an eye for evil
will be cut down—
²¹those who with a word make a man
out to be guilty,
who ensnare the defender in court
and with false testimony deprive
the innocent of justice.

²²Therefore this is what the Lᴏʀᴅ, who
redeemed Abraham, says to the house of
Jacob:

"No longer will Jacob be ashamed;
no longer will their faces grow pale.
²³When they see among them their
children,
the work of my hands,
they will keep my name holy;
they will acknowledge the holiness
of the Holy One of Jacob,
and will stand in awe of the God of
Israel.
²⁴Those who are wayward in spirit will
gain understanding;
those who complain will accept
instruction."

Woe to the Obstinate Nation

30 "Woe to the obstinate children,"
declares the Lᴏʀᴅ,
"to those who carry out plans that are
not mine,
forming an alliance, but not by my
Spirit,
heaping sin upon sin;
²who go down to Egypt

ᵃ13 Hebrew; Septuagint *They worship me in vain; / their teachings are but rules taught by men*

without consulting me;
who look for help to Pharaoh's
protection,
to Egypt's shade for refuge.
³But Pharaoh's protection will be to
your shame,
Egypt's shade will bring you
disgrace.
⁴Though they have officials in Zoan
and their envoys have arrived in
Hanes,
⁵everyone will be put to shame
because of a people useless to
them,
who bring neither help nor advantage,
but only shame and disgrace."

⁶An oracle concerning the animals of
the Negev:

Through a land of hardship and
distress,
of lions and lionesses,
of adders and darting snakes,
the envoys carry their riches on
donkeys' backs,
their treasures on the humps of
camels,
to that unprofitable nation,
⁷ to Egypt, whose help is utterly
useless.
Therefore I call her
Rahab the Do-Nothing.

⁸Go now, write it on a tablet for them,
inscribe it on a scroll,
that for the days to come
it may be an everlasting witness.
⁹These are rebellious people, deceitful
children,
children unwilling to listen to the
LORD's instruction.
¹⁰They say to the seers,
"See no more visions!"
and to the prophets,
"Give us no more visions of what is
right!
Tell us pleasant things,
prophesy illusions.
¹¹Leave this way,
get off this path,
and stop confronting us
with the Holy One of Israel!"

¹²Therefore, this is what the Holy One
of Israel says:

"Because you have rejected this
message,
relied on oppression
and depended on deceit,
¹³this sin will become for you

like a high wall, cracked and
bulging,
that collapses suddenly, in an
instant.
¹⁴It will break in pieces like pottery,
shattered so mercilessly
that among its pieces not a fragment
will be found
for taking coals from a hearth
or scooping water out of a cistern."

¹⁵This is what the Sovereign LORD, the
Holy One of Israel, says:

"In repentance and rest is your
salvation,
in quietness and trust is your
strength,
but you would have none of it.
¹⁶You said, 'No, we will flee on horses.'
Therefore you will flee!
You said, 'We will ride off on swift
horses.'
Therefore your pursuers will be
swift!
¹⁷A thousand will flee
at the threat of one;
at the threat of five
you will all flee away,
till you are left
like a flagstaff on a mountaintop,
like a banner on a hill."

¹⁸Yet the LORD longs to be gracious to
you;
he rises to show you compassion.
For the LORD is a God of justice.
Blessed are all who wait for him!

¹⁹O people of Zion, who live in Jerusalem, you will weep no more. How gracious he will be when you cry for help! As
soon as he hears, he will answer you. ²⁰Al-
though the Lord gives you the bread
of adversity and the water of affliction,
your teachers will be hidden no more;
with your own eyes you will see them.
²¹Whether you turn to the right or to the
left, your ears will hear a voice behind
you, saying, "This is the way; walk in it."
²²Then you will defile your idols overlaid
with silver and your images covered with
gold; you will throw them away like a
menstrual cloth and say to them, "Away
with you!"

²³He will also send you rain for the seed
you sow in the ground, and the food that
comes from the land will be rich and
plentiful. In that day your cattle will graze
in broad meadows. ²⁴The oxen and don-

keys that work the soil will eat fodder and mash, spread out with fork and shovel. ²⁵In the day of great slaughter, when the towers fall, streams of water will flow on every high mountain and every lofty hill. ²⁶The moon will shine like the sun, and the sunlight will be seven times brighter, like the light of seven full days, when the LORD binds up the bruises of his people and heals the wounds he inflicted.

²⁷See, the Name of the LORD comes
from afar,
with burning anger and dense
clouds of smoke;
his lips are full of wrath,

and his tongue is a consuming fire.
²⁸His breath is like a rushing torrent,
rising up to the neck.
He shakes the nations in the sieve of
destruction;
he places in the jaws of the peoples
a bit that leads them astray.
²⁹And you will sing
as on the night you celebrate a holy
festival;
your hearts will rejoice
as when people go up with flutes
to the mountain of the LORD,
to the Rock of Israel.
³⁰The LORD will cause men to hear his
majestic voice

FRIDAY

VERSE FOR THE DAY:
Isaiah 30:15

AUTHOR:
Eugenia Price

PASSAGE FOR THE DAY:
Isaiah 30:15-18

The Problem of Busyness

MOST people are just too busy. This is a point for quick agreement, but the subtle danger involved in our busyness is that most of us never stop to realize that in most cases we can do something about it! We tend to look wildly and unrealistically in every other direction for the cause of our trouble. Most of us feel like helpless victims where our work and activity schedules are concerned. For five or six years, this was entirely true of me.

Then one day, when I had actually fallen asleep on someone's sofa in the middle of a conversation, I began to take stock.

What was actually important? How much of this activity was God actually instigating? How much of it was the consequence of my own bad judgment, and how much was guided by the Holy Spirit within me? What was really gained that evening I fell asleep during what to me was no longer "sweet fellowship"?

A woman's ego often pushes her into a whirlwind life of busyness, too. If you are capable, and if the ladies adore you and heap compliments on your pretty head every time you teach the class or preside at the circle meeting, just be wary. It is easy to mistake the voice of flattery for the voice of God. Especially if you've been busy for so long, there hasn't been a really quiet time to hear God speak.

The voice of God is always speaking to us, and always trying to get our attention. But his voice is a "still, small voice," and we must at least slow down in order to listen.

Additional Scripture Readings:
Mark 6:30-31; Revelation 3:20

Go to page 760 for your next
devotional reading.

and will make them see his arm
coming down
with raging anger and consuming fire,
with cloudburst, thunderstorm and
hail.
³¹The voice of the LORD will shatter
Assyria;
with his scepter he will strike them
down.
³²Every stroke the LORD lays on them
with his punishing rod
will be to the music of tambourines
and harps,
as he fights them in battle with the
blows of his arm.
³³Topheth has long been prepared;
it has been made ready for the
king.
Its fire pit has been made deep and
wide,
with an abundance of fire and
wood;
the breath of the LORD,
like a stream of burning sulfur,
sets it ablaze.

Woe to Those Who Rely on Egypt

31 Woe to those who go down to
Egypt for help,
who rely on horses,
who trust in the multitude of their
chariots
and in the great strength of their
horsemen,
but do not look to the Holy One of
Israel,
or seek help from the LORD.
²Yet he too is wise and can bring
disaster;
he does not take back his words.
He will rise up against the house of
the wicked,
against those who help evildoers.
³But the Egyptians are men and not
God;
their horses are flesh and not spirit.
When the LORD stretches out his
hand,
he who helps will stumble,
he who is helped will fall;
both will perish together.

⁴This is what the LORD says to me:

"As a lion growls,
a great lion over his prey—
and though a whole band of
shepherds
is called together against him,
he is not frightened by their shouts

or disturbed by their clamor—
so the LORD Almighty will come down
to do battle on Mount Zion and on
its heights.
⁵Like birds hovering overhead,
the LORD Almighty will shield
Jerusalem;
he will shield it and deliver it,
he will 'pass over' it and will rescue
it."

⁶Return to him you have so greatly revolted against, O Israelites. ⁷For in that
day every one of you will reject the idols
of silver and gold your sinful hands have
made.

⁸"Assyria will fall by a sword that is
not of man;
a sword, not of mortals, will devour
them.
They will flee before the sword
and their young men will be put to
forced labor.
⁹Their stronghold will fall because of
terror;
at sight of the battle standard their
commanders will panic,"
declares the LORD,
whose fire is in Zion,
whose furnace is in Jerusalem.

The Kingdom of Righteousness

32 See, a king will reign in
righteousness
and rulers will rule with justice.
²Each man will be like a shelter from
the wind
and a refuge from the storm,
like streams of water in the desert
and the shadow of a great rock in a
thirsty land.

³Then the eyes of those who see will
no longer be closed,
and the ears of those who hear will
listen.
⁴The mind of the rash will know and
understand,
and the stammering tongue will be
fluent and clear.
⁵No longer will the fool be called
noble
nor the scoundrel be highly
respected.
⁶For the fool speaks folly,
his mind is busy with evil:
He practices ungodliness
and spreads error concerning the
LORD;
the hungry he leaves empty

and from the thirsty he withholds
    water.
7The scoundrel's methods are wicked,
    he makes up evil schemes
to destroy the poor with lies,
    even when the plea of the needy is
      just.
8But the noble man makes noble
    plans,
and by noble deeds he stands.

The Women of Jerusalem

9You women who are so complacent,
    rise up and listen to me;
you daughters who feel secure,
    hear what I have to say!
10In little more than a year
    you who feel secure will tremble;
the grape harvest will fail,
    and the harvest of fruit will not
      come.
11Tremble, you complacent women;
    shudder, you daughters who feel
      secure!
Strip off your clothes,
    put sackcloth around your waists.
12Beat your breasts for the pleasant
    fields,
for the fruitful vines
13and for the land of my people,
    a land overgrown with thorns and
      briers—
yes, mourn for all houses of
    merriment
and for this city of revelry.
14The fortress will be abandoned,
    the noisy city deserted;
citadel and watchtower will become a
    wasteland forever,
the delight of donkeys, a pasture
    for flocks,
15till the Spirit is poured upon us from
    on high,
and the desert becomes a fertile
    field,
and the fertile field seems like a
    forest.
16Justice will dwell in the desert
    and righteousness live in the fertile
    field.
17The fruit of righteousness will be
    peace;
the effect of righteousness will be
    quietness and confidence
    forever.
18My people will live in peaceful
    dwelling places,
in secure homes,

in undisturbed places of rest.
19Though hail flattens the forest
    and the city is leveled completely,
20how blessed you will be,
    sowing your seed by every stream,
and letting your cattle and donkeys
    range free.

Distress and Help

33 Woe to you, O destroyer,
    you who have not been
      destroyed!
Woe to you, O traitor,
    you who have not been betrayed!
When you stop destroying,
    you will be destroyed;
when you stop betraying,
    you will be betrayed.

2O LORD, be gracious to us;
    we long for you.
Be our strength every morning,
    our salvation in time of distress.
3At the thunder of your voice, the
    peoples flee;
when you rise up, the nations
    scatter.
4Your plunder, O nations, is harvested
    as by young locusts;
like a swarm of locusts men pounce
    on it.

5The LORD is exalted, for he dwells on
    high;
he will fill Zion with justice and
    righteousness.
6He will be the sure foundation for
    your times,
a rich store of salvation and
    wisdom and knowledge;
the fear of the LORD is the key to
    this treasure.[a]

7Look, their brave men cry aloud in
    the streets;
the envoys of peace weep bitterly.
8The highways are deserted,
    no travelers are on the roads.
The treaty is broken,
    its witnesses[b] are despised,
no one is respected.
9The land mourns[c] and wastes away,
    Lebanon is ashamed and withers;
Sharon is like the Arabah,
    and Bashan and Carmel drop their
    leaves.

10"Now will I arise," says the LORD.
    "Now will I be exalted;
now will I be lifted up.

---

a6 Or *is a treasure from him*   b8 Dead Sea Scrolls; Masoretic Text / *the cities*   c9 Or *dries up*

¹¹You conceive chaff,
  you give birth to straw;
  your breath is a fire that consumes
    you.
¹²The peoples will be burned as if to
    lime;
  like cut thornbushes they will be
    set ablaze."

¹³You who are far away, hear what I
    have done;
  you who are near, acknowledge my
    power!
¹⁴The sinners in Zion are terrified;
  trembling grips the godless:
  "Who of us can dwell with the
    consuming fire?
  Who of us can dwell with
    everlasting burning?"
¹⁵He who walks righteously
  and speaks what is right,
who rejects gain from extortion
  and keeps his hand from accepting
    bribes,
who stops his ears against plots of
    murder
  and shuts his eyes against
    contemplating evil—
¹⁶this is the man who will dwell on the
    heights,
  whose refuge will be the mountain
    fortress.
His bread will be supplied,
  and water will not fail him.

¹⁷Your eyes will see the king in his
    beauty
  and view a land that stretches afar.
¹⁸In your thoughts you will ponder the
    former terror:
  "Where is that chief officer?
  Where is the one who took the
    revenue?
  Where is the officer in charge of
    the towers?"
¹⁹You will see those arrogant people no
    more,
  those people of an obscure speech,
  with their strange,
    incomprehensible tongue.

²⁰Look upon Zion, the city of our
    festivals;
  your eyes will see Jerusalem,
  a peaceful abode, a tent that will
    not be moved;
its stakes will never be pulled up,
  nor any of its ropes broken.

²¹There the Lord will be our Mighty
    One.
  It will be like a place of broad
    rivers and streams.
No galley with oars will ride them,
  no mighty ship will sail them.
²²For the Lord is our judge,
  the Lord is our lawgiver,
  the Lord is our king;
  it is he who will save us.

²³Your rigging hangs loose:
  The mast is not held secure,
  the sail is not spread.
Then an abundance of spoils will be
    divided
  and even the lame will carry off
    plunder.
²⁴No one living in Zion will say, "I am
    ill";
  and the sins of those who dwell
    there will be forgiven.

Judgment Against the Nations

34 Come near, you nations, and
    listen;
  pay attention, you peoples!
Let the earth hear, and all that is in
    it,
  the world, and all that comes out of
    it!
²The Lord is angry with all nations;
  his wrath is upon all their armies.
He will totally destroy[a] them,
  he will give them over to slaughter.
³Their slain will be thrown out,
  their dead bodies will send up a
    stench;
  the mountains will be soaked with
    their blood.
⁴All the stars of the heavens will be
    dissolved
  and the sky rolled up like a scroll;
all the starry host will fall
  like withered leaves from the vine,
  like shriveled figs from the fig tree.

⁵My sword has drunk its fill in the
    heavens;
  see, it descends in judgment on
    Edom,
  the people I have totally destroyed.
⁶The sword of the Lord is bathed in
    blood,
  it is covered with fat—
the blood of lambs and goats,
  fat from the kidneys of rams.
For the Lord has a sacrifice in Bozrah

---

a2 The Hebrew term refers to the irrevocable giving over of things or persons to the Lord, often by totally destroying them; also in verse 5.

and a great slaughter in Edom.
⁷And the wild oxen will fall with them,
  the bull calves and the great bulls.
Their land will be drenched with
    blood,
  and the dust will be soaked with
    fat.

⁸For the LORD has a day of vengeance,
  a year of retribution, to uphold
    Zion's cause.
⁹Edom's streams will be turned into
    pitch,
  her dust into burning sulfur;
  her land will become blazing pitch!
¹⁰It will not be quenched night and
    day;
  its smoke will rise forever.
From generation to generation it will
    lie desolate;
  no one will ever pass through it
    again.
¹¹The desert owl*a* and screech owl*a*
    will possess it;
  the great owl*a* and the raven will
    nest there.
God will stretch out over Edom
  the measuring line of chaos
  and the plumb line of desolation.
¹²Her nobles will have nothing there to
    be called a kingdom,
  all her princes will vanish away.
¹³Thorns will overrun her citadels,
  nettles and brambles her
    strongholds.
She will become a haunt for jackals,
  a home for owls.
¹⁴Desert creatures will meet with
    hyenas,
  and wild goats will bleat to each
    other;
there the night creatures will also
    repose
  and find for themselves places of
    rest.
¹⁵The owl will nest there and lay eggs,
  she will hatch them, and care for
    her young under the shadow of
    her wings;
there also the falcons will gather,
  each with its mate.

¹⁶Look in the scroll of the LORD and
read:

None of these will be missing,
  not one will lack her mate.
For it is his mouth that has given the
    order,

and his Spirit will gather them
    together.
¹⁷He allots their portions;
  his hand distributes them by
    measure.
They will possess it forever
  and dwell there from generation to
    generation.

Joy of the Redeemed

35 The desert and the parched land
    will be glad;
  the wilderness will rejoice and
    blossom.
Like the crocus, ²it will burst into
    bloom;
  it will rejoice greatly and shout for
    joy.
The glory of Lebanon will be given to
    it,
  the splendor of Carmel and Sharon;
they will see the glory of the LORD,
  the splendor of our God.

³Strengthen the feeble hands,
  steady the knees that give way;
⁴say to those with fearful hearts,
  "Be strong, do not fear;
your God will come,
  he will come with vengeance;
with divine retribution
  he will come to save you."

⁵Then will the eyes of the blind be
    opened
  and the ears of the deaf unstopped.
⁶Then will the lame leap like a deer,
  and the mute tongue shout for joy.
Water will gush forth in the
    wilderness
  and streams in the desert.
⁷The burning sand will become a pool,
  the thirsty ground bubbling springs.
In the haunts where jackals once lay,
  grass and reeds and papyrus will
    grow.

⁸And a highway will be there;
  it will be called the Way of
    Holiness.
The unclean will not journey on it;
  it will be for those who walk in that
    Way;
  wicked fools will not go about on
    it.*b*
⁹No lion will be there,
  nor will any ferocious beast get up
    on it;
  they will not be found there.

---

a11 The precise identification of these birds is uncertain. *b8* Or / *the simple will not stray from it*

But only the redeemed will walk
there,
10 and the ransomed of the LORD will
return.
They will enter Zion with singing;
everlasting joy will crown their
heads.
Gladness and joy will overtake them,
and sorrow and sighing will flee
away.

Sennacherib Threatens Jerusalem

36 In the fourteenth year of King Hezekiah's reign, Sennacherib king of Assyria attacked all the fortified cities of Judah and captured them. ²Then the king of Assyria sent his field commander with a large army from Lachish to King Hezekiah at Jerusalem. When the commander stopped at the aqueduct of the Upper Pool, on the road to the Washerman's Field, ³Eliakim son of Hilkiah the palace administrator, Shebna the secretary, and Joah son of Asaph the recorder went out to him.

⁴The field commander said to them, "Tell Hezekiah,

" 'This is what the great king, the king of Assyria, says: On what are you basing this confidence of yours? ⁵You say you have strategy and military strength—but you speak only empty words. On whom are you depending, that you rebel against me? ⁶Look now, you are depending on Egypt, that splintered reed of a staff, which pierces a man's hand and wounds him if he leans on it! Such is Pharaoh king of Egypt to all who depend on him. ⁷And if you say to me, "We are depending on the LORD our God"—isn't he the one whose high places and altars Hezekiah removed, saying to Judah and Jerusalem, "You must worship before this altar"?

⁸" 'Come now, make a bargain with my master, the king of Assyria: I will give you two thousand horses—if you can put riders on them! ⁹How then can you repulse one officer of the least of my master's officials, even though you are depending on Egypt for chariots and horsemen? ¹⁰Furthermore, have I come to attack and destroy this land without the LORD? The LORD himself told me to march against this country and destroy it.' "

¹¹Then Eliakim, Shebna and Joah said to the field commander, "Please speak to your servants in Aramaic, since we understand it. Don't speak to us in Hebrew in the hearing of the people on the wall."

¹²But the commander replied, "Was it only to your master and you that my master sent me to say these things, and not to the men sitting on the wall—who, like you, will have to eat their own filth and drink their own urine?"

¹³Then the commander stood and called out in Hebrew, "Hear the words of the great king, the king of Assyria! ¹⁴This is what the king says: Do not let Hezekiah deceive you. He cannot deliver you! ¹⁵Do not let Hezekiah persuade you to trust in the LORD when he says, 'The LORD will surely deliver us; this city will not be given into the hand of the king of Assyria.'

¹⁶"Do not listen to Hezekiah. This is what the king of Assyria says: Make peace with me and come out to me. Then every one of you will eat from his own vine and fig tree and drink water from his own cistern, ¹⁷until I come and take you to a land like your own—a land of grain and new wine, a land of bread and vineyards.

¹⁸"Do not let Hezekiah mislead you when he says, 'The LORD will deliver us.' Has the god of any nation ever delivered his land from the hand of the king of Assyria? ¹⁹Where are the gods of Hamath and Arpad? Where are the gods of Sepharvaim? Have they rescued Samaria from my hand? ²⁰Who of all the gods of these countries has been able to save his land from me? How then can the LORD deliver Jerusalem from my hand?"

²¹But the people remained silent and said nothing in reply, because the king had commanded, "Do not answer him."

²²Then Eliakim son of Hilkiah the palace administrator, Shebna the secretary, and Joah son of Asaph the recorder went to Hezekiah, with their clothes torn, and told him what the field commander had said.

Jerusalem's Deliverance Foretold

37 When King Hezekiah heard this, he tore his clothes and put on sackcloth and went into the temple of the LORD. ²He sent Eliakim the palace administrator, Shebna the secretary, and the leading priests, all wearing sackcloth, to the prophet Isaiah son of Amoz. ³They told him, "This is what Hezekiah says: This day is a day of distress and rebuke and disgrace, as when children come to the point of birth and there is no strength

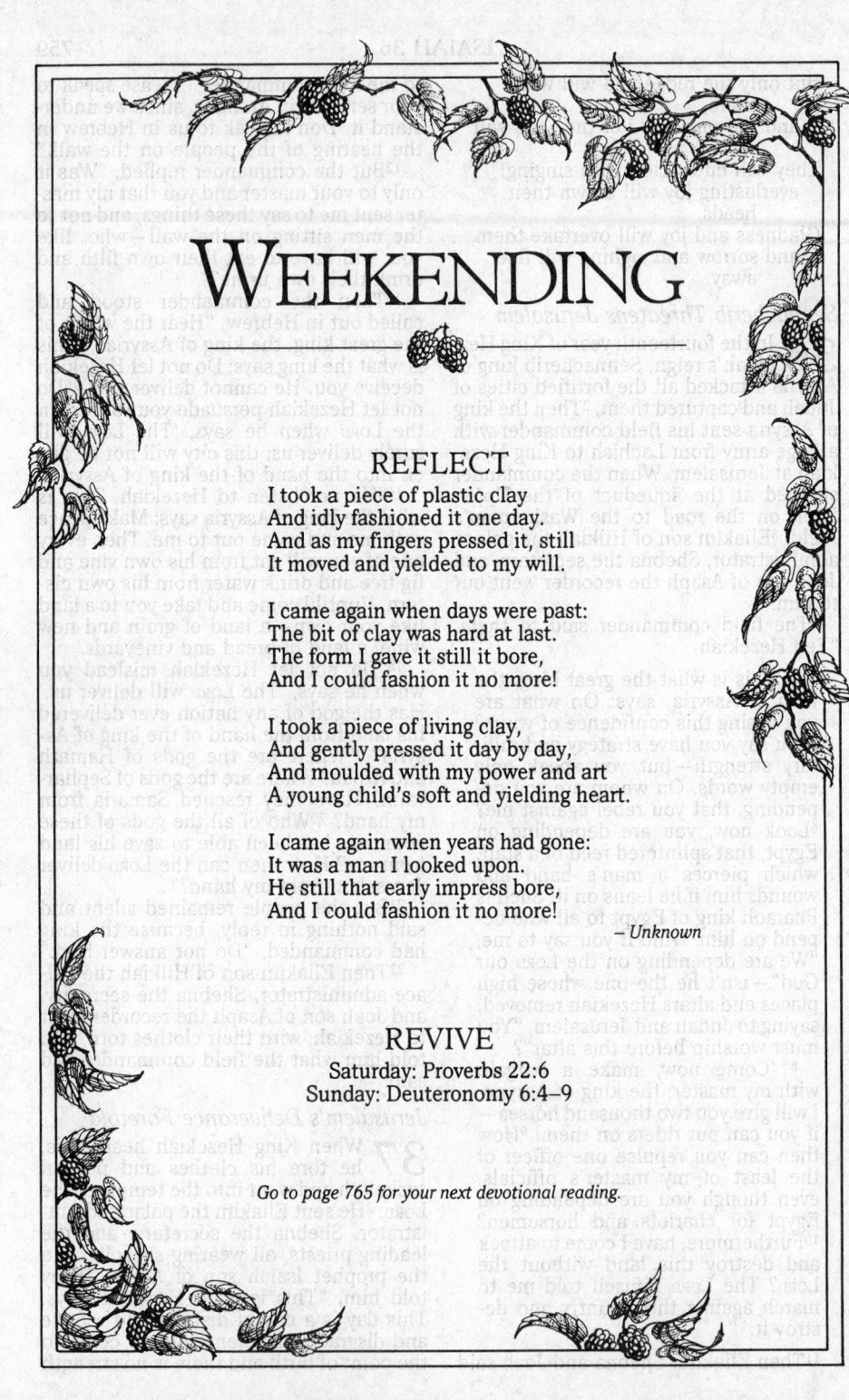

WEEKENDING

REFLECT

I took a piece of plastic clay
And idly fashioned it one day.
And as my fingers pressed it, still
It moved and yielded to my will.

I came again when days were past:
The bit of clay was hard at last.
The form I gave it still it bore,
And I could fashion it no more!

I took a piece of living clay,
And gently pressed it day by day,
And moulded with my power and art
A young child's soft and yielding heart.

I came again when years had gone:
It was a man I looked upon.
He still that early impress bore,
And I could fashion it no more!

– Unknown

REVIVE

Saturday: Proverbs 22:6
Sunday: Deuteronomy 6:4–9

Go to page 765 for your next devotional reading.

to deliver them. ⁴It may be that the LORD your God will hear the words of the field commander, whom his master, the king of Assyria, has sent to ridicule the living God, and that he will rebuke him for the words the LORD your God has heard. Therefore pray for the remnant that still survives."

⁵When King Hezekiah's officials came to Isaiah, ⁶Isaiah said to them, "Tell your master, 'This is what the LORD says: Do not be afraid of what you have heard—those words with which the underlings of the king of Assyria have blasphemed me. ⁷Listen! I am going to put a spirit in him so that when he hears a certain report, he will return to his own country, and there I will have him cut down with the sword.' "

⁸When the field commander heard that the king of Assyria had left Lachish, he withdrew and found the king fighting against Libnah.

⁹Now Sennacherib received a report that Tirhakah, the Cushiteᵃ king of Egypt, was marching out to fight against him. When he heard it, he sent messengers to Hezekiah with this word: ¹⁰"Say to Hezekiah king of Judah: Do not let the god you depend on deceive you when he says, 'Jerusalem will not be handed over to the king of Assyria.' ¹¹Surely you have heard what the kings of Assyria have done to all the countries, destroying them completely. And will you be delivered? ¹²Did the gods of the nations that were destroyed by my forefathers deliver them—the gods of Gozan, Haran, Rezeph and the people of Eden who were in Tel Assar? ¹³Where is the king of Hamath, the king of Arpad, the king of the city of Sepharvaim, or of Hena or Ivvah?"

Hezekiah's Prayer

¹⁴Hezekiah received the letter from the messengers and read it. Then he went up to the temple of the LORD and spread it out before the LORD. ¹⁵And Hezekiah prayed to the LORD: ¹⁶"O LORD Almighty, God of Israel, enthroned between the cherubim, you alone are God over all the kingdoms of the earth. You have made heaven and earth. ¹⁷Give ear, O LORD, and hear; open your eyes, O LORD, and see; listen to all the words Sennacherib has sent to insult the living God.

¹⁸"It is true, O LORD, that the Assyrian kings have laid waste all these peoples and their lands. ¹⁹They have thrown their gods into the fire and destroyed them, for they were not gods but only wood and stone, fashioned by human hands. ²⁰Now, O LORD our God, deliver us from his hand, so that all kingdoms on earth may know that you alone, O LORD, are God.ᵇ"

Sennacherib's Fall

²¹Then Isaiah son of Amoz sent a message to Hezekiah: "This is what the LORD, the God of Israel, says: Because you have prayed to me concerning Sennacherib king of Assyria, ²²this is the word the LORD has spoken against him:

"The Virgin Daughter of Zion
  despises and mocks you.
The Daughter of Jerusalem
  tosses her head as you flee.
²³Who is it you have insulted and
  blasphemed?
  Against whom have you raised your
    voice
and lifted your eyes in pride?
  Against the Holy One of Israel!
²⁴By your messengers
  you have heaped insults on the
    Lord.
And you have said,
  'With my many chariots
I have ascended the heights of the
    mountains,
  the utmost heights of Lebanon.
I have cut down its tallest cedars,
  the choicest of its pines.
I have reached its remotest heights,
  the finest of its forests.
²⁵I have dug wells in foreign landsᶜ
  and drunk the water there.
With the soles of my feet
  I have dried up all the streams of
    Egypt.'

²⁶"Have you not heard?
  Long ago I ordained it.
In days of old I planned it;
  now I have brought it to pass,
that you have turned fortified cities
  into piles of stone.
²⁷Their people, drained of power,
  are dismayed and put to shame.
They are like plants in the field,
  like tender green shoots,

ᵃ9 That is, from the upper Nile region   ᵇ20 Dead Sea Scrolls (see also 2 Kings 19:19); Masoretic Text *alone are the LORD*   ᶜ25 Dead Sea Scrolls (see also 2 Kings 19:24); Masoretic Text does not have *in foreign lands.*

like grass sprouting on the roof,
   scorched[a] before it grows up.
28"But I know where you stay
   and when you come and go
   and how you rage against me.
29Because you rage against me
   and because your insolence has
      reached my ears,
I will put my hook in your nose
   and my bit in your mouth,
and I will make you return
   by the way you came.

30"This will be the sign for you, O Hezekiah:

"This year you will eat what grows by
      itself,
   and the second year what springs
      from that.
But in the third year sow and reap,
   plant vineyards and eat their fruit.
31Once more a remnant of the house of
      Judah
   will take root below and bear fruit
      above.
32For out of Jerusalem will come a
      remnant,
   and out of Mount Zion a band of
      survivors.
The zeal of the LORD Almighty
   will accomplish this.

33"Therefore this is what the LORD says
concerning the king of Assyria:

"He will not enter this city
   or shoot an arrow here.
He will not come before it with shield
   or build a siege ramp against it.
34By the way that he came he will
      return;
   he will not enter this city,"
                  declares the LORD.
35"I will defend this city and save it,
   for my sake and for the sake of
      David my servant!"

36Then the angel of the LORD went out
and put to death a hundred and eighty-
five thousand men in the Assyrian camp.
When the people got up the next morning
—there were all the dead bodies! 37So
Sennacherib king of Assyria broke camp
and withdrew. He returned to Nineveh
and stayed there.
38One day, while he was worshiping
in the temple of his god Nisroch, his

sons Adrammelech and Sharezer cut him
down with the sword, and they escaped to
the land of Ararat. And Esarhaddon his
son succeeded him as king.

Hezekiah's Illness

38 In those days Hezekiah became ill
and was at the point of death. The
prophet Isaiah son of Amoz went to him
and said, "This is what the LORD says: Put
your house in order, because you are going to die; you will not recover."
2Hezekiah turned his face to the wall
and prayed to the LORD, 3"Remember, O
LORD, how I have walked before you faithfully and with wholehearted devotion and
have done what is good in your eyes." And
Hezekiah wept bitterly.
4Then the word of the LORD came to Isaiah: 5"Go and tell Hezekiah, 'This is what
the LORD, the God of your father David,
says: I have heard your prayer and seen
your tears; I will add fifteen years to your
life. 6And I will deliver you and this city
from the hand of the king of Assyria. I will
defend this city.
7" 'This is the LORD's sign to you that
the LORD will do what he has promised: 8I
will make the shadow cast by the sun go
back the ten steps it has gone down on
the stairway of Ahaz.' " So the sunlight
went back the ten steps it had gone down.

9A writing of Hezekiah king of Judah
after his illness and recovery:

10I said, "In the prime of my life
   must I go through the gates of
      death[b]
   and be robbed of the rest of my
      years?"
11I said, "I will not again see the LORD,
   the LORD, in the land of the living;
no longer will I look on mankind,
   or be with those who now dwell in
      this world.[c]
12Like a shepherd's tent my house
   has been pulled down and taken
      from me.
Like a weaver I have rolled up my life,
   and he has cut me off from the
      loom;
   day and night you made an end of
      me.
13I waited patiently till dawn,
   but like a lion he broke all my
      bones;

a27 Some manuscripts of the Masoretic Text, Dead Sea Scrolls and some Septuagint manuscripts (see
also 2 Kings 19:26); most manuscripts of the Masoretic Text roof / and terraced fields   b10 Hebrew
Sheol   c11 A few Hebrew manuscripts; most Hebrew manuscripts in the place of cessation

day and night you made an end of
   me.
14I cried like a swift or thrush,
   I moaned like a mourning dove.
My eyes grew weak as I looked to the
   heavens.
   I am troubled; O Lord, come to my
   aid!"

15But what can I say?
   He has spoken to me, and he
      himself has done this.
I will walk humbly all my years
   because of this anguish of my soul.
16Lord, by such things men live;
   and my spirit finds life in them too.
You restored me to health
   and let me live.
17Surely it was for my benefit
   that I suffered such anguish.
In your love you kept me
   from the pit of destruction;
you have put all my sins
   behind your back.
18For the grave a cannot praise you,
   death cannot sing your praise;
those who go down to the pit
   cannot hope for your faithfulness.
19The living, the living—they praise
      you,
   as I am doing today;
fathers tell their children
   about your faithfulness.

20The Lord will save me,
   and we will sing with stringed
      instruments
all the days of our lives
   in the temple of the Lord.

21Isaiah had said, "Prepare a poultice
of figs and apply it to the boil, and he will
recover."

22Hezekiah had asked, "What will be
the sign that I will go up to the temple of
the Lord?"

Envoys From Babylon

39 At that time Merodach-Baladan
son of Baladan king of Babylon
sent Hezekiah letters and a gift, because
he had heard of his illness and recovery.
2Hezekiah received the envoys gladly and
showed them what was in his storehouses
—the silver, the gold, the spices, the fine
oil, his entire armory and everything
found among his treasures. There was

nothing in his palace or in all his kingdom
that Hezekiah did not show them.

3Then Isaiah the prophet went to King
Hezekiah and asked, "What did those
men say, and where did they come from?"

"From a distant land," Hezekiah replied. "They came to me from Babylon."

4The prophet asked, "What did they see
in your palace?"

"They saw everything in my palace,"
Hezekiah said. "There is nothing among
my treasures that I did not show them."

5Then Isaiah said to Hezekiah, "Hear
the word of the Lord Almighty: 6The time
will surely come when everything in your
palace, and all that your fathers have
stored up until this day, will be carried off
to Babylon. Nothing will be left, says the
Lord. 7And some of your descendants,
your own flesh and blood who will be
born to you, will be taken away, and they
will become eunuchs in the palace of the
king of Babylon."

8"The word of the Lord you have spoken is good," Hezekiah replied. For he
thought, "There will be peace and security in my lifetime."

Comfort for God's People

40 Comfort, comfort my people,
says your God.
2Speak tenderly to Jerusalem,
   and proclaim to her
that her hard service has been
      completed,
   that her sin has been paid for,
that she has received from the Lord's
      hand
   double for all her sins.

3A voice of one calling:
"In the desert prepare
   the way for the Lord b;
make straight in the wilderness
   a highway for our God. c
4Every valley shall be raised up,
   every mountain and hill made low;
the rough ground shall become level,
   the rugged places a plain.
5And the glory of the Lord will be
      revealed,
   and all mankind together will see
      it.
      For the mouth of the Lord
            has spoken."

6A voice says, "Cry out."
   And I said, "What shall I cry?"

a18 Hebrew *Sheol*   b3 Or *A voice of one calling in the desert: / "Prepare the way for the Lord*
c3 Hebrew; Septuagint *make straight the paths of our God*

"All men are like grass,
and all their glory is like the
flowers of the field.
⁷The grass withers and the flowers fall,
because the breath of the LORD
blows on them.
Surely the people are grass.
⁸The grass withers and the flowers fall,
but the word of our God stands
forever."

⁹You who bring good tidings to Zion,
go up on a high mountain.
You who bring good tidings to
Jerusalem,ᵃ
lift up your voice with a shout,
lift it up, do not be afraid;
say to the towns of Judah,
"Here is your God!"
¹⁰See, the Sovereign LORD comes with
power,
and his arm rules for him.
See, his reward is with him,
and his recompense accompanies
him.
¹¹He tends his flock like a shepherd:
He gathers the lambs in his arms
and carries them close to his heart;
he gently leads those that have
young.

¹²Who has measured the waters in the
hollow of his hand,
or with the breadth of his hand
marked off the heavens?
Who has held the dust of the earth in
a basket,
or weighed the mountains on the
scales
and the hills in a balance?
¹³Who has understood the mindᵇ of the
LORD,
or instructed him as his counselor?
¹⁴Whom did the LORD consult to
enlighten him,
and who taught him the right way?
Who was it that taught him
knowledge
or showed him the path of
understanding?

¹⁵Surely the nations are like a drop in a
bucket;
they are regarded as dust on the
scales;
he weighs the islands as though
they were fine dust.

¹⁶Lebanon is not sufficient for altar
fires,
nor its animals enough for burnt
offerings.
¹⁷Before him all the nations are as
nothing;
they are regarded by him as
worthless
and less than nothing.

¹⁸To whom, then, will you compare
God?
What image will you compare him
to?
¹⁹As for an idol, a craftsman casts it,
and a goldsmith overlays it with
gold
and fashions silver chains for it.
²⁰A man too poor to present such an
offering
selects wood that will not rot.
He looks for a skilled craftsman
to set up an idol that will not
topple.

²¹Do you not know?
Have you not heard?
Has it not been told you from the
beginning?
Have you not understood since the
earth was founded?
²²He sits enthroned above the circle of
the earth,
and its people are like
grasshoppers.
He stretches out the heavens like a
canopy,
and spreads them out like a tent to
live in.
²³He brings princes to naught
and reduces the rulers of this world
to nothing.
²⁴No sooner are they planted,
no sooner are they sown,
no sooner do they take root in the
ground,
than he blows on them and they
wither,
and a whirlwind sweeps them away
like chaff.

²⁵"To whom will you compare me?
Or who is my equal?" says the Holy
One.
²⁶Lift your eyes and look to the
heavens:
Who created all these?

ᵃ9 Or *O Zion, bringer of good tidings, / go up on a high mountain. / O Jerusalem, bringer of good tidings*
ᵇ13 Or *Spirit*; or *spirit*

VERSE FOR THE DAY:
Isaiah 40:11

AUTHOR:
Shirley Dobson

PASSAGE FOR THE DAY:
Isaiah 40:1–11

Shirley's Story

I SEE a little girl skipping home from school in the late afternoon sun. Her dress is a hand-me-down, her shoes are unpolished and her socks no longer have elastic around the top. She walks across a barren yard toward a small house. It is badly in need of paint and repair.

How tenderly I feel for this little child of poverty. It is almost as though she were my own daughter, and I ache to hold her in my arms . . . to buy her a pretty new dress . . . to give her a shiny new bicycle. But that is impossible—for we are separated by three decades of time. I can neither talk to her nor meet her needs. For that little girl, you see, is the memory of my own childhood. I walked in her shoes. I lived in that small unpainted house. And I can still feel the indescribable yearning of a child who knew that something vital was missing from her life.

I was the daughter of a confirmed alcoholic. Only those who have lived through this nightmare will understand the full implication of this experience.

It was only through the wisdom and devotion of my mother that I survived the emotional pressures of those years. She is a strong woman, and she marshaled all of her resources to hold our little family together.

Most important, Mom convinced my brother and me that she loved us. And because of that love, she constantly sought ways to get us through those difficult years. She had the wisdom to know that she needed help in raising two rambunctious kids, and she turned for assistance to a local evangelical church.

It was in that little neighborhood church that I was introduced to Jesus Christ, and invited him into my heart and life. He became my special friend, and I've never been the same since that moment.

As I look back on the painful experience of my childhood, I am overwhelmed with gratitude to God for answering my early prayers. He heard the desperate cries of a ten-year-old girl who could offer him nothing in return. I had no status, no special abilities, no money to contribute. I was totally without dignity or social influence. Yet the Creator of the universe entered my little room and communed with me about the difficulties I was experiencing. It was awesome to realize that he loved me just as I was, and my pain became his pain. What a magnificent God we serve!

Additional Scripture Readings:
Psalm 145:14–20; 1 Corinthians 1:26–31

Go to page 767 for your next devotional reading.

He who brings out the starry host one
by one,
and calls them each by name.
Because of his great power and
mighty strength,
not one of them is missing.

27Why do you say, O Jacob,
and complain, O Israel,
"My way is hidden from the LORD;
my cause is disregarded by my
God"?
28Do you not know?
Have you not heard?
The LORD is the everlasting God,
the Creator of the ends of the
earth.
He will not grow tired or weary,
and his understanding no one can
fathom.
29He gives strength to the weary
and increases the power of the
weak.
30Even youths grow tired and weary,
and young men stumble and fall;
31but those who hope in the LORD
will renew their strength.
They will soar on wings like eagles;
they will run and not grow weary,
they will walk and not be faint.

The Helper of Israel

41 "Be silent before me, you
islands!
Let the nations renew their
strength!
Let them come forward and speak;
let us meet together at the place of
judgment.

2"Who has stirred up one from the
east,
calling him in righteousness to his
service*a*?
He hands nations over to him
and subdues kings before him.
He turns them to dust with his sword,
to windblown chaff with his bow.
3He pursues them and moves on
unscathed,
by a path his feet have not traveled
before.
4Who has done this and carried it
through,
calling forth the generations from
the beginning?
I, the LORD—with the first of them
and with the last—I am he."

5The islands have seen it and fear;
the ends of the earth tremble.
They approach and come forward;
6   each helps the other
and says to his brother, "Be
strong!"
7The craftsman encourages the
goldsmith,
and he who smooths with the
hammer
spurs on him who strikes the anvil.
He says of the welding, "It is good."
He nails down the idol so it will
not topple.

8"But you, O Israel, my servant,
Jacob, whom I have chosen,
you descendants of Abraham my
friend,
9I took you from the ends of the earth,
from its farthest corners I called
you.
I said, 'You are my servant';
I have chosen you and have not
rejected you.
10So do not fear, for I am with you;
do not be dismayed, for I am your
God.
I will strengthen you and help you;
I will uphold you with my righteous
right hand.

11"All who rage against you
will surely be ashamed and
disgraced;
those who oppose you
will be as nothing and perish.
12Though you search for your enemies,
you will not find them.
Those who wage war against you
will be as nothing at all.
13For I am the LORD, your God,
who takes hold of your right hand
and says to you, Do not fear;
I will help you.
14Do not be afraid, O worm Jacob,
O little Israel,
for I myself will help you," declares
the LORD,
your Redeemer, the Holy One of
Israel.
15"See, I will make you into a threshing
sledge,
new and sharp, with many teeth.
You will thresh the mountains and
crush them,
and reduce the hills to chaff.
16You will winnow them, the wind will
pick them up,

---

*a*2 Or / whom victory meets at every step

VERSE FOR THE DAY:
Isaiah 40:31

AUTHOR:
Beverly LaHaye

PASSAGE FOR THE DAY:
Isaiah 40:27–31

Waiting and Hoping

FOR several years God had placed on my heart a growing concern for Latin women living in the United States. The more Concerned Women for America reached out to them, however, the less we succeeded. We were building prayer chapters across the nation, and we wanted Latin women to be a part of this through their churches. Finally I decided to just wait and hope in the Lord because we were pushing too hard. After all, we were willing, but nothing was happening. Meanwhile, C.W.A. continued to awaken other women to the need for "protecting their families through prayer and action." Prayer Action Chapters were springing up across the nation.

During this time of waiting and hoping, God began leading us in a new direction that was difficult to understand. Doors began to open to establish a humanitarian aid division of C.W.A. for Nicaraguan people who had fled communism in their country and were now refugees in Costa Rica. Although I had many reasons not to get involved, God would not take no for an answer. So, in 1986 we finally gave in to the Lord's leading.

We have helped the refugees in a variety of ways. Thousands have been given food and clothing, we have helped many by conducting medical clinics, and a host of children have received a Christian education in the school we started near the Nicaraguan border. It was, and still is, a ministry of love and obedience to the Scriptural teaching that we are to help the poor and needy.

As the situation worsened in Nicaragua, many desperate people sought political asylum in the United States. Thousands settled in Miami. Once again God moved in a miraculous way as he led us to assist in an outreach to help the refugees living in Dade County, Florida. People donated over forty-five tons of clothing and commodities to C.W.A. for these needy people. It was as though we, rising "on wings like eagles," were beginning to soar over the difficulties.

Latin churches in the Miami area began to take note that C.W.A. was helping the refugees. Doors began to open to the Latin churches. The very thing I had tried to force a few years earlier was now beginning to happen. By giving physical assistance, we could now be trusted to build prayer chapters and help spiritually. God's timing does not always coincide with our immediate plans. Sometimes his timing requires that we wait and hope.

Additional Scripture Readings:
Romans 4:18–22; 2 Peter 3:8–9

Go to page 771 for your next
devotional reading.

and a gale will blow them away.
But you will rejoice in the LORD
and glory in the Holy One of Israel.

17"The poor and needy search for water,
but there is none;
their tongues are parched with
thirst.
But I the LORD will answer them;
I, the God of Israel, will not forsake
them.
18I will make rivers flow on barren
heights,
and springs within the valleys.
I will turn the desert into pools of
water,
and the parched ground into
springs.
19I will put in the desert
the cedar and the acacia, the
myrtle and the olive.
I will set pines in the wasteland,
the fir and the cypress together,
20so that people may see and know,
may consider and understand,
that the hand of the LORD has done
this,
that the Holy One of Israel has
created it.

21"Present your case," says the LORD.
"Set forth your arguments," says
Jacob's King.
22"Bring in your idols, to tell us
what is going to happen.
Tell us what the former things were,
so that we may consider them
and know their final outcome.
Or declare to us the things to come,
23   tell us what the future holds,
so we may know that you are gods.
Do something, whether good or bad,
so that we will be dismayed and
filled with fear.
24But you are less than nothing
and your works are utterly
worthless;
he who chooses you is detestable.

25"I have stirred up one from the north,
and he comes—
one from the rising sun who calls
on my name.
He treads on rulers as if they were
mortar,
as if he were a potter treading the
clay.
26Who told of this from the beginning,
so we could know,
or beforehand, so we could say, 'He
was right'?

No one told of this,
no one foretold it,
no one heard any words from you.
27I was the first to tell Zion, 'Look, here
they are!'
I gave to Jerusalem a messenger of
good tidings.
28I look but there is no one—
no one among them to give
counsel,
no one to give answer when I ask
them.
29See, they are all false!
Their deeds amount to nothing;
their images are but wind and
confusion.

The Servant of the LORD

42 "Here is my servant, whom I
uphold,
my chosen one in whom I delight;
I will put my Spirit on him
and he will bring justice to the
nations.
2He will not shout or cry out,
or raise his voice in the streets.
3A bruised reed he will not break,
and a smoldering wick he will not
snuff out.
In faithfulness he will bring forth
justice;
4   he will not falter or be discouraged
till he establishes justice on earth.
In his law the islands will put their
hope."

5This is what God the LORD says—
he who created the heavens and
stretched them out,
who spread out the earth and all
that comes out of it,
who gives breath to its people,
and life to those who walk on it:
6"I, the LORD, have called you in
righteousness;
I will take hold of your hand.
I will keep you and will make you
to be a covenant for the people
and a light for the Gentiles,
7to open eyes that are blind,
to free captives from prison
and to release from the dungeon
those who sit in darkness.

8"I am the LORD; that is my name!
I will not give my glory to another
or my praise to idols.
9See, the former things have taken
place,
and new things I declare;

before they spring into being
I announce them to you."

Song of Praise to the LORD

¹⁰Sing to the LORD a new song,
his praise from the ends of the
earth,
you who go down to the sea, and all
that is in it,
you islands, and all who live in
them.
¹¹Let the desert and its towns raise
their voices;
let the settlements where Kedar
lives rejoice.
Let the people of Sela sing for joy;
let them shout from the
mountaintops.
¹²Let them give glory to the LORD
and proclaim his praise in the
islands.
¹³The LORD will march out like a mighty
man,
like a warrior he will stir up his
zeal;
with a shout he will raise the battle
cry
and will triumph over his enemies.

¹⁴"For a long time I have kept silent,
I have been quiet and held myself
back.
But now, like a woman in childbirth,
I cry out, I gasp and pant.
¹⁵I will lay waste the mountains and
hills
and dry up all their vegetation;
I will turn rivers into islands
and dry up the pools.
¹⁶I will lead the blind by ways they
have not known,
along unfamiliar paths I will guide
them;
I will turn the darkness into light
before them
and make the rough places smooth.
These are the things I will do;
I will not forsake them.
¹⁷But those who trust in idols,
who say to images, 'You are our
gods,'
will be turned back in utter shame.

Israel Blind and Deaf

¹⁸"Hear, you deaf;
look, you blind, and see!
¹⁹Who is blind but my servant,
and deaf like the messenger I send?

Who is blind like the one committed
to me,
blind like the servant of the LORD?
²⁰You have seen many things, but have
paid no attention;
your ears are open, but you hear
nothing."
²¹It pleased the LORD
for the sake of his righteousness
to make his law great and glorious.
²²But this is a people plundered and
looted,
all of them trapped in pits
or hidden away in prisons.
They have become plunder,
with no one to rescue them;
they have been made loot,
with no one to say, "Send them
back."

²³Which of you will listen to this
or pay close attention in time to
come?
²⁴Who handed Jacob over to become
loot,
and Israel to the plunderers?
Was it not the LORD,
against whom we have sinned?
For they would not follow his ways;
they did not obey his law.
²⁵So he poured out on them his
burning anger,
the violence of war.
It enveloped them in flames, yet they
did not understand;
it consumed them, but they did not
take it to heart.

Israel's Only Savior

43 But now, this is what the LORD
says—
he who created you, O Jacob,
he who formed you, O Israel:
"Fear not, for I have redeemed you;
I have summoned you by name; you
are mine.
²When you pass through the waters,
I will be with you;
and when you pass through the rivers,
they will not sweep over you.
When you walk through the fire,
you will not be burned;
the flames will not set you ablaze.
³For I am the LORD, your God,
the Holy One of Israel, your Savior;
I give Egypt for your ransom,
Cushᵃ and Seba in your stead.

ᵃ3 That is, the upper Nile region

⁴Since you are precious and honored
in my sight,
and because I love you,
I will give men in exchange for you,
and people in exchange for your
life.
⁵Do not be afraid, for I am with you;
I will bring your children from the
east
and gather you from the west.
⁶I will say to the north, 'Give them
up!'
and to the south, 'Do not hold
them back.'
Bring my sons from afar
and my daughters from the ends of
the earth—
⁷everyone who is called by my name,
whom I created for my glory,
whom I formed and made."

⁸Lead out those who have eyes but are
blind,
who have ears but are deaf.
⁹All the nations gather together
and the peoples assemble.
Which of them foretold this
and proclaimed to us the former
things?
Let them bring in their witnesses to
prove they were right,
so that others may hear and say, "It
is true."
¹⁰"You are my witnesses," declares the
LORD,
"and my servant whom I have
chosen,
so that you may know and believe me
and understand that I am he.
Before me no god was formed,
nor will there be one after me.
¹¹I, even I, am the LORD,
and apart from me there is no
savior.
¹²I have revealed and saved and
proclaimed—
I, and not some foreign god among
you.
You are my witnesses," declares the
LORD, "that I am God.
¹³ Yes, and from ancient days I am he.
No one can deliver out of my hand.
When I act, who can reverse it?"

God's Mercy and Israel's Unfaithfulness

¹⁴This is what the LORD says—

your Redeemer, the Holy One of
Israel:
"For your sake I will send to Babylon
and bring down as fugitives all the
Babylonians,ᵃ
in the ships in which they took
pride.
¹⁵I am the LORD, your Holy One,
Israel's Creator, your King."

¹⁶This is what the LORD says—
he who made a way through the
sea,
a path through the mighty waters,
¹⁷who drew out the chariots and horses,
the army and reinforcements
together,
and they lay there, never to rise
again,
extinguished, snuffed out like a
wick:
¹⁸"Forget the former things;
do not dwell on the past.
¹⁹See, I am doing a new thing!
Now it springs up; do you not
perceive it?
I am making a way in the desert
and streams in the wasteland.
²⁰The wild animals honor me,
the jackals and the owls,
because I provide water in the desert
and streams in the wasteland,
to give drink to my people, my
chosen,
²¹ the people I formed for myself
that they may proclaim my praise.

²²"Yet you have not called upon me,
O Jacob,
you have not wearied yourselves for
me, O Israel.
²³You have not brought me sheep for
burnt offerings,
nor honored me with your
sacrifices.
I have not burdened you with grain
offerings
nor wearied you with demands for
incense.
²⁴You have not bought any fragrant
calamus for me,
or lavished on me the fat of your
sacrifices.
But you have burdened me with your
sins
and wearied me with your offenses.

²⁵"I, even I, am he who blots out

ᵃ14 Or Chaldeans

VERSE FOR THE DAY:
Isaiah 43:1–3

AUTHOR:
Elisabeth Elliot

PASSAGE FOR THE DAY:
Isaiah 43:1–13

Big Enough to Worship

I HAVE summoned you by name; you are mine.
When you pass through the waters,
  I will be with you;
and when you pass through the rivers,
  they will not sweep over you.
When you walk through the fire,
  you will not be burned . . . .
For I am the LORD your God (Isaiah 43:1–3).

Thirty years ago I was standing beside a shortwave radio in a house on the Atun Yacu, one of the principal headwaters of the Amazon, when I learned that my husband, Jim Elliot, was one of the five missionaries missing. They had gone into the territory of the Auca Indians, a people who had never heard even the name of Jesus Christ. What did I do? I suppose I said out loud, "O Lord!"

And he answered me. Not with an audible voice (I've never heard him speak that way in my life). But God brought to mind this ancient promise from the book of Isaiah.

I am the Lord your God. Think of it! The One who engineered this incredible universe with such exquisite precision that astronomers can predict exactly where and when Halley's comet will appear—this God is my Lord.

Evelyn Underhill said, "If God were small enough to be understood, he would not be big enough to be worshiped."

Can we imagine that God, who is concerned with so many stupendous things, can possibly be concerned about us? We do imagine it. We hope he is. That is why we turn to him in desperation and cry out, as I did, "O Lord!" Where else can we possibly turn when we have come to the end of our resources?

Does God love us? Karl Barth, the great theologian, was once asked if he could condense all the theology he had ever written into one simple sentence.

"Yes," he said. "I can. 'Jesus loves me, this I know, for the Bible tells me so.' "

Additional Scripture Readings:
Romans 8:26–28; Ephesians 3:16–19

*Go to page 776 for your next
devotional reading.*

your transgressions, for my own
sake,
and remembers your sins no more.
²⁶Review the past for me,
let us argue the matter together;
state the case for your innocence.
²⁷Your first father sinned;
your spokesmen rebelled against
me.
²⁸So I will disgrace the dignitaries of
your temple,
and I will consign Jacob to
destruction^a
and Israel to scorn.

Israel the Chosen

44 "But now listen, O Jacob, my
servant,
Israel, whom I have chosen.
²This is what the LORD says—
he who made you, who formed you
in the womb,
and who will help you:
Do not be afraid, O Jacob, my
servant,
Jeshurun, whom I have chosen.
³For I will pour water on the thirsty
land,
and streams on the dry ground;
I will pour out my Spirit on your
offspring,
and my blessing on your
descendants.
⁴They will spring up like grass in a
meadow,
like poplar trees by flowing streams.
⁵One will say, 'I belong to the LORD';
another will call himself by the
name of Jacob;
still another will write on his hand,
'The LORD's,'
and will take the name Israel.

The LORD, Not Idols

⁶"This is what the LORD says—
Israel's King and Redeemer, the
LORD Almighty:
I am the first and I am the last;
apart from me there is no God
⁷Who then is like me? Let him
proclaim it.
Let him declare and lay out before
me
what has happened since I
established my ancient people,
and what is yet to come—
yes, let him foretell what will come.

⁸Do not tremble, do not be afraid.
Did I not proclaim this and foretell
it long ago?
You are my witnesses. Is there any
God besides me?
No, there is no other Rock; I know
not one."

⁹All who make idols are nothing,
and the things they treasure are
worthless.
Those who would speak up for them
are blind;
they are ignorant, to their own
shame.
¹⁰Who shapes a god and casts an idol,
which can profit him nothing?
¹¹He and his kind will be put to shame;
craftsmen are nothing but men.
Let them all come together and take
their stand;
they will be brought down to terror
and infamy.
¹²The blacksmith takes a tool
and works with it in the coals;
he shapes an idol with hammers,
he forges it with the might of his
arm.
He gets hungry and loses his strength;
he drinks no water and grows faint.
¹³The carpenter measures with a line
and makes an outline with a
marker;
he roughs it out with chisels
and marks it with compasses.
He shapes it in the form of man,
of man in all his glory,
that it may dwell in a shrine.
¹⁴He cut down cedars,
or perhaps took a cypress or oak.
He let it grow among the trees of the
forest,
or planted a pine, and the rain
made it grow.
¹⁵It is man's fuel for burning;
some of it he takes and warms
himself,
he kindles a fire and bakes bread.
But he also fashions a god and
worships it;
he makes an idol and bows down to
it.
¹⁶Half of the wood he burns in the fire;
over it he prepares his meal,
he roasts his meat and eats his fill.
He also warms himself and says,
"Ah! I am warm; I see the fire."

^a28 The Hebrew term refers to the irrevocable giving over of things or persons to the LORD, often by
totally destroying them.

¹⁷From the rest he makes a god, his
idol;
he bows down to it and worships.
He prays to it and says,
"Save me; you are my god."
¹⁸They know nothing, they understand
nothing;
their eyes are plastered over so they
cannot see,
and their minds closed so they
cannot understand.
¹⁹No one stops to think,
no one has the knowledge or
understanding to say,
"Half of it I used for fuel;
I even baked bread over its coals,
I roasted meat and I ate.
Shall I make a detestable thing from
what is left?
Shall I bow down to a block of
wood?"
²⁰He feeds on ashes, a deluded heart
misleads him;
he cannot save himself, or say,
"Is not this thing in my right hand
a lie?"

²¹"Remember these things, O Jacob,
for you are my servant, O Israel.
I have made you, you are my servant;
O Israel, I will not forget you.
²²I have swept away your offenses like a
cloud,
your sins like the morning mist.
Return to me,
for I have redeemed you."

²³Sing for joy, O heavens, for the LORD
has done this;
shout aloud, O earth beneath.
Burst into song, you mountains,
you forests and all your trees,
for the LORD has redeemed Jacob,
he displays his glory in Israel.

Jerusalem to Be Inhabited

²⁴"This is what the LORD says—
your Redeemer, who formed you in
the womb:

I am the LORD,
who has made all things,
who alone stretched out the heavens,
who spread out the earth by myself,

²⁵who foils the signs of false prophets
and makes fools of diviners,
who overthrows the learning of the
wise
and turns it into nonsense,

²⁶who carries out the words of his
servants
and fulfills the predictions of his
messengers,

who says of Jerusalem, 'It shall be
inhabited,'
of the towns of Judah, 'They shall
be built,'
and of their ruins, 'I will restore
them,'
²⁷who says to the watery deep, 'Be dry,
and I will dry up your streams,'
²⁸who says of Cyrus, 'He is my
shepherd
and will accomplish all that I
please;
he will say of Jerusalem, "Let it be
rebuilt,"
and of the temple, "Let its
foundations be laid." '

45 "This is what the LORD says to
his anointed,
to Cyrus, whose right hand I take
hold of
to subdue nations before him
and to strip kings of their armor,
to open doors before him
so that gates will not be shut:
²I will go before you
and will level the mountains ᵃ;
I will break down gates of bronze
and cut through bars of iron.
³I will give you the treasures of
darkness,
riches stored in secret places,
so that you may know that I am the
LORD,
the God of Israel, who summons
you by name.
⁴For the sake of Jacob my servant,
of Israel my chosen,
I summon you by name
and bestow on you a title of honor,
though you do not acknowledge
me.
⁵I am the LORD, and there is no other;
apart from me there is no God.
I will strengthen you,
though you have not acknowledged
me,
⁶so that from the rising of the sun
to the place of its setting
men may know there is none besides
me.
I am the LORD, and there is no
other.

ᵃ2 Dead Sea Scrolls and Septuagint; the meaning of the word in the Masoretic Text is uncertain.

⁷I form the light and create darkness,
I bring prosperity and create
disaster;
I, the LORD, do all these things.

⁸"You heavens above, rain down
righteousness;
let the clouds shower it down.
Let the earth open wide,
let salvation spring up,
let righteousness grow with it;
I, the LORD, have created it.

⁹"Woe to him who quarrels with his
Maker,
to him who is but a potsherd
among the potsherds on the
ground.
Does the clay say to the potter,
'What are you making?'
Does your work say,
'He has no hands'?
¹⁰Woe to him who says to his father,
'What have you begotten?'
or to his mother,
'What have you brought to birth?'

¹¹"This is what the LORD says—
the Holy One of Israel, and its
Maker:
Concerning things to come,
do you question me about my
children,
or give me orders about the work of
my hands?
¹²It is I who made the earth
and created mankind upon it.
My own hands stretched out the
heavens;
I marshaled their starry hosts.
¹³I will raise up Cyrus*ᵃ* in my
righteousness:
I will make all his ways straight.
He will rebuild my city
and set my exiles free,
but not for a price or reward,
says the LORD Almighty."

¹⁴This is what the LORD says:

"The products of Egypt and the
merchandise of Cush,ᵇ
and those tall Sabeans—
they will come over to you
and will be yours;
they will trudge behind you,
coming over to you in chains.
They will bow down before you
and plead with you, saying,

'Surely God is with you, and there is
no other;
there is no other god.' "

¹⁵Truly you are a God who hides
himself,
O God and Savior of Israel.
¹⁶All the makers of idols will be put to
shame and disgraced;
they will go off into disgrace
together.
¹⁷But Israel will be saved by the LORD
with an everlasting salvation;
you will never be put to shame or
disgraced,
to ages everlasting.

¹⁸For this is what the LORD says—
he who created the heavens,
he is God;
he who fashioned and made the
earth,
he founded it;
he did not create it to be empty,
but formed it to be inhabited—
he says:
"I am the LORD,
and there is no other.
¹⁹I have not spoken in secret,
from somewhere in a land of
darkness;
I have not said to Jacob's
descendants,
'Seek me in vain.'
I, the LORD, speak the truth;
I declare what is right.

²⁰"Gather together and come;
assemble, you fugitives from the
nations.
Ignorant are those who carry about
idols of wood,
who pray to gods that cannot save.
²¹Declare what is to be, present it—
let them take counsel together.
Who foretold this long ago,
who declared it from the distant
past?
Was it not I, the LORD?
And there is no God apart from me,
a righteous God and a Savior;
there is none but me.

²²"Turn to me and be saved,
all you ends of the earth;
for I am God, and there is no other.
²³By myself I have sworn,
my mouth has uttered in all
integrity
a word that will not be revoked:

ᵃ13 Hebrew *him*   ᵇ14 That is, the upper Nile region

Before me every knee will bow;
    by me every tongue will swear.
24They will say of me, 'In the LORD
        alone
    are righteousness and strength.' "
All who have raged against him
    will come to him and be put to
        shame.
25But in the LORD all the descendants of
        Israel
    will be found righteous and will
        exult.

Gods of Babylon

46 Bel bows down, Nebo stoops
        low;
    their idols are borne by beasts of
        burden.a
The images that are carried about are
        burdensome,
    a burden for the weary.
2They stoop and bow down together;
    unable to rescue the burden,
    they themselves go off into
        captivity.

3"Listen to me, O house of Jacob,
    all you who remain of the house of
        Israel,
you whom I have upheld since you
        were conceived,
    and have carried since your birth.
4Even to your old age and gray hairs
    I am he, I am he who will sustain
        you.
I have made you and I will carry you;
    I will sustain you and I will rescue
        you.

5"To whom will you compare me or
        count me equal?
    To whom will you liken me that we
        may be compared?
6Some pour out gold from their bags
    and weigh out silver on the scales;
    they hire a goldsmith to make it into
        a god,
    and they bow down and worship it.
7They lift it to their shoulders and
        carry it;
    they set it up in its place, and there
        it stands.
    From that spot it cannot move.
Though one cries out to it, it does
        not answer;
    it cannot save him from his
        troubles.

8"Remember this, fix it in mind,
    take it to heart, you rebels.
9Remember the former things, those of
        long ago;
    I am God, and there is no other;
    I am God, and there is none like
        me.
10I make known the end from the
        beginning,
    from ancient times, what is still to
        come.
I say: My purpose will stand,
    and I will do all that I please.
11From the east I summon a bird of
        prey;
    from a far-off land, a man to fulfill
        my purpose.
What I have said, that will I bring
        about;
    what I have planned, that will I do.
12Listen to me, you stubborn-hearted,
    you who are far from righteousness.
13I am bringing my righteousness near,
    it is not far away;
    and my salvation will not be
        delayed.
I will grant salvation to Zion,
    my splendor to Israel.

The Fall of Babylon

47 "Go down, sit in the dust,
        Virgin Daughter of Babylon;
sit on the ground without a throne,
    Daughter of the Babylonians.b
No more will you be called
    tender or delicate.
2Take millstones and grind flour;
    take off your veil.
Lift up your skirts, bare your legs,
    and wade through the streams.
3Your nakedness will be exposed
    and your shame uncovered.
I will take vengeance;
    I will spare no one."

4Our Redeemer—the LORD Almighty is
        his name—
    is the Holy One of Israel.

5"Sit in silence, go into darkness,
        Daughter of the Babylonians;
no more will you be called
    queen of kingdoms.
6I was angry with my people
    and desecrated my inheritance;
I gave them into your hand,
    and you showed them no mercy.
Even on the aged
    you laid a very heavy yoke.
7You said, 'I will continue forever—

---

a1 Or are but beasts and cattle   b1 Or Chaldeans; also in verse 5

VERSE FOR THE DAY:
Isaiah 46:3–4

AUTHOR:
Elisabeth Elliot

PASSAGE FOR THE DAY:
Isaiah 46:1–13

I Won't Bother With a Face-lift

BECAUSE tomorrow I will begin the last of threescore years, and because my mother is now closer to ninety than to eighty, I do a lot of thinking about old age.

I don't mind getting old. Before the day began this morning I was looking out at starlight on a still, wintry sea. A little song we used to sing at camp came to mind—"Just One Day Nearer Home." That idea thrills me. I can understand why people who have nothing much to look forward to try frantically and futilely to hang on to the past—youth and all that. Get a face-lift, plaster the makeup on ever more thickly (but Estee Lauder says false eyelashes can add ten years to your looks), wear running shoes and sweatsuits, dye your hair—anything to create the illusion you're young. (The illusion is yours, of course, nobody else's.)

Let's be honest. Old age entails suffering. I'm acutely aware of this now as I watch my mother, once so alive and alert and quick, now so quiet and confused and slow. She suffers. We who love her suffer. We see the "preview of coming attractions," ourselves in her shoes, and ponder what this interval means in terms of the glory of God in an old woman.

It would be terrifying if it weren't for something that ought to make the Christian's attitude toward aging utterly distinct from the rest. *We know it is not for nothing.*

> And he made known to us the mystery of his will according to his good pleasure, which he purposed in Christ, to be put into effect when the times have reached their fulfillment (Ephesians 1:9–10).

In the meantime, we look at what's happening—limitations of hearing, seeing, moving, digesting, remembering; distortions of countenance, figure, and perspective. If that's all we could see, we'd certainly want a face-lift or something.

But we're on a pilgrim road. It's rough and steep, and it winds uphill to the very end. We can lift up our eyes and see the unseen: a celestial city, a light, a welcome and an ineffable face. We shall behold him. We shall be like him. And that makes a difference in how we go about aging.

Additional Scripture Readings:
Luke 2:36–38; 2 Corinthians 4:16–18

Go to page 779 for your next devotional reading.

the eternal queen!'
But you did not consider these things
or reflect on what might happen.

8"Now then, listen, you wanton
creature,
lounging in your security
and saying to yourself,
'I am, and there is none besides
me.
I will never be a widow
or suffer the loss of children.'
9Both of these will overtake you
in a moment, on a single day:
loss of children and widowhood.
They will come upon you in full
measure,
in spite of your many sorceries
and all your potent spells.
10You have trusted in your wickedness
and have said, 'No one sees me.'
Your wisdom and knowledge mislead
you
when you say to yourself,
'I am, and there is none besides
me.'
11Disaster will come upon you,
and you will not know how to
conjure it away.
A calamity will fall upon you
that you cannot ward off with a
ransom;
a catastrophe you cannot foresee
will suddenly come upon you.

12"Keep on, then, with your magic
spells
and with your many sorceries,
which you have labored at since
childhood.
Perhaps you will succeed,
perhaps you will cause terror.
13All the counsel you have received has
only worn you out!
Let your astrologers come forward,
those stargazers who make
predictions month by month,
let them save you from what is
coming upon you.
14Surely they are like stubble;
the fire will burn them up.
They cannot even save themselves
from the power of the flame.
Here are no coals to warm anyone;
here is no fire to sit by.
15That is all they can do for you—
these you have labored with
and trafficked with since childhood.
Each of them goes on in his error;
there is not one that can save you.

Stubborn Israel

48 "Listen to this, O house of
Jacob,
you who are called by the name of
Israel
and come from the line of Judah,
you who take oaths in the name of
the LORD
and invoke the God of Israel—
but not in truth or righteousness—
2you who call yourselves citizens of the
holy city
and rely on the God of Israel—
the LORD Almighty is his name:
3I foretold the former things long ago,
my mouth announced them and I
made them known;
then suddenly I acted, and they
came to pass.
4For I knew how stubborn you were;
the sinews of your neck were iron,
your forehead was bronze.
5Therefore I told you these things long
ago;
before they happened I announced
them to you
so that you could not say,
'My idols did them;
my wooden image and metal god
ordained them.'
6You have heard these things; look at
them all.
Will you not admit them?

"From now on I will tell you of new
things,
of hidden things unknown to you.
7They are created now, and not long
ago;
you have not heard of them before
today.
So you cannot say,
'Yes, I knew of them.'
8You have neither heard nor
understood;
from of old your ear has not been
open.
Well do I know how treacherous you
are;
you were called a rebel from birth.
9For my own name's sake I delay my
wrath;
for the sake of my praise I hold it
back from you,
so as not to cut you off.
10See, I have refined you, though not as
silver;
I have tested you in the furnace of
affliction.

¹¹For my own sake, for my own sake, I
do this.
How can I let myself be defamed?
I will not yield my glory to another.

Israel Freed

¹²"Listen to me, O Jacob,
Israel, whom I have called:
I am he;
I am the first and I am the last.
¹³My own hand laid the foundations of
the earth,
and my right hand spread out the
heavens;
when I summon them,
they all stand up together.

¹⁴"Come together, all of you, and listen:
Which of the idols has foretold
these things?
The LORD's chosen ally
will carry out his purpose against
Babylon;
his arm will be against the
Babylonians.ᵃ
¹⁵I, even I, have spoken;
yes, I have called him.
I will bring him,
and he will succeed in his mission.

¹⁶"Come near me and listen to this:

"From the first announcement I have
not spoken in secret;
at the time it happens, I am there."

And now the Sovereign LORD has sent
me,
with his Spirit.

¹⁷This is what the LORD says—
your Redeemer, the Holy One of
Israel:
"I am the LORD your God,
who teaches you what is best for
you,
who directs you in the way you
should go.
¹⁸If only you had paid attention to my
commands,
your peace would have been like a
river,
your righteousness like the waves of
the sea.
¹⁹Your descendants would have been
like the sand,
your children like its numberless
grains;
their name would never be cut off
nor destroyed from before me."

²⁰Leave Babylon,
flee from the Babylonians!
Announce this with shouts of joy
and proclaim it.
Send it out to the ends of the earth;
say, "The LORD has redeemed his
servant Jacob."
²¹They did not thirst when he led them
through the deserts;
he made water flow for them from
the rock;
he split the rock
and water gushed out.

²²"There is no peace," says the LORD,
"for the wicked."

The Servant of the LORD

49 Listen to me, you islands;
hear this, you distant nations:
Before I was born the LORD called me;
from my birth he has made
mention of my name.
²He made my mouth like a sharpened
sword,
in the shadow of his hand he hid
me;
he made me into a polished arrow
and concealed me in his quiver.
³He said to me, "You are my servant,
Israel, in whom I will display my
splendor."
⁴But I said, "I have labored to no
purpose;
I have spent my strength in vain
and for nothing.
Yet what is due me is in the LORD's
hand,
and my reward is with my God."

⁵And now the LORD says—
he who formed me in the womb to
be his servant
to bring Jacob back to him
and gather Israel to himself,
for I am honored in the eyes of the
LORD
and my God has been my
strength—
⁶he says:
"It is too small a thing for you to be
my servant
to restore the tribes of Jacob
and bring back those of Israel I
have kept.
I will also make you a light for the
Gentiles,
that you may bring my salvation to
the ends of the earth."

ᵃ14 Or *Chaldeans*; also in verse 20

VERSE FOR THE DAY:
Isaiah 48:17

AUTHOR:
Marjorie Holmes

PASSAGE FOR THE DAY:
Isaiah 48:12–19

For Showing Me Purpose

I AM grateful, God, that I have finally come to realize your purpose for me.

Just when or how this came about I can't say. It wasn't sudden and dramatic, the way it happened to Paul on the road to Damascus, or Peter Marshall with his experience on the Scottish moors.

There have been no visions, no voices, no letters written in fire upon a wall saying: "Do this." "Do that." "This is your reason for being."

No, my search for you and for the meaning you had for my life has been uncertain, groping, erratic, filled with accidents, false goals. Sometimes I seemed to sense that purpose, clearly see it; but it vanished like a mirage in the harried, often cruel business of everyday.

Yet somehow you keep track of your floundering creatures.

Maybe because life is so filled with defeat and heartbreak, we find ourselves turning to you, yielding ourselves to your will, fighting less furiously for selfish, often empty goals. And when this happens we find that you have turned our sufferings and our failures into little stepping-stones.

Looking back, we see them. These rocks which gradually, all unknown to us, you have been shaping to lead us toward our purpose . . . And we have been following! However blindly, however zigzag the course, yet we have been moving toward it.

And looking about, we see there are results. There are signals, heartening little affirmations, unexpected proofs.

However humble our circumstances or undramatic our talents, our true purpose has been revealed. We were meant to be this person at this time and place. Not only for ourselves, but for you and other people—we were meant to make this particular contribution to the world.

And so we must do it well. Do it with faith and patience, with all our strength and passion. And in so doing discover who we really are.

Additional Scripture Readings:
Ephesians 2:8–10; Philippians 2:12–13

Go to page 787 for your next devotional reading.

7This is what the LORD says—
    the Redeemer and Holy One of
        Israel—
to him who was despised and
    abhorred by the nation,
to the servant of rulers:
"Kings will see you and rise up,
    princes will see and bow down,
because of the LORD, who is faithful,
    the Holy One of Israel, who has
        chosen you."

Restoration of Israel

8This is what the LORD says:

"In the time of my favor I will answer
    you,
    and in the day of salvation I will
        help you;
I will keep you and will make you
    to be a covenant for the people,
to restore the land
    and to reassign its desolate
        inheritances,
9to say to the captives, 'Come out,'
    and to those in darkness, 'Be
        free!'

"They will feed beside the roads
    and find pasture on every barren
        hill.
10They will neither hunger nor thirst,
    nor will the desert heat or the sun
        beat upon them.
He who has compassion on them will
    guide them
and lead them beside springs of
    water.
11I will turn all my mountains into
    roads,
and my highways will be raised up.
12See, they will come from afar—
    some from the north, some from
        the west,
some from the region of Aswan.*a*"

13Shout for joy, O heavens;
    rejoice, O earth;
    burst into song, O mountains!
For the LORD comforts his people
    and will have compassion on his
        afflicted ones.

14But Zion said, "The LORD has forsaken
    me,
    the Lord has forgotten me."

15"Can a mother forget the baby at her
    breast

and have no compassion on the
    child she has borne?
Though she may forget,
    I will not forget you!
16See, I have engraved you on the
    palms of my hands;
    your walls are ever before me.
17Your sons hasten back,
    and those who laid you waste
        depart from you.
18Lift up your eyes and look around;
    all your sons gather and come to
        you.
As surely as I live," declares the LORD,
    "you will wear them all as
        ornaments;
    you will put them on, like a bride.

19"Though you were ruined and made
    desolate
    and your land laid waste,
now you will be too small for your
    people,
and those who devoured you will be
    far away.
20The children born during your
    bereavement
    will yet say in your hearing,
'This place is too small for us;
    give us more space to live in.'
21Then you will say in your heart,
    'Who bore me these?
I was bereaved and barren;
    I was exiled and rejected.
Who brought these up?
I was left all alone,
    but these—where have they come
        from?' "

22This is what the Sovereign LORD says:

"See, I will beckon to the Gentiles,
    I will lift up my banner to the
        peoples;
they will bring your sons in their arms
    and carry your daughters on their
        shoulders.
23Kings will be your foster fathers,
    and their queens your nursing
        mothers.
They will bow down before you with
    their faces to the ground;
    they will lick the dust at your feet.
Then you will know that I am the
    LORD;
    those who hope in me will not be
        disappointed."

24Can plunder be taken from warriors,

---

a12 Dead Sea Scrolls; Masoretic Text Sinim

or captives rescued from the
fierce*a*?

25But this is what the LORD says:

"Yes, captives will be taken from
warriors,
and plunder retrieved from the
fierce;
I will contend with those who
contend with you,
and your children I will save.
26I will make your oppressors eat their
own flesh;
they will be drunk on their own
blood, as with wine.
Then all mankind will know
that I, the LORD, am your Savior,
your Redeemer, the Mighty One of
Jacob."

Israel's Sin and the Servant's Obedience

50 This is what the LORD says:

"Where is your mother's
certificate of divorce
with which I sent her away?
Or to which of my creditors
did I sell you?
Because of your sins you were sold;
because of your transgressions your
mother was sent away.
2When I came, why was there no one?
When I called, why was there no
one to answer?
Was my arm too short to ransom you?
Do I lack the strength to rescue
you?
By a mere rebuke I dry up the sea,
I turn rivers into a desert;
their fish rot for lack of water
and die of thirst.
3I clothe the sky with darkness
and make sackcloth its covering."

4The Sovereign LORD has given me an
instructed tongue,
to know the word that sustains the
weary.
He wakens me morning by morning,
wakens my ear to listen like one
being taught.
5The Sovereign LORD has opened my
ears,
and I have not been rebellious;
I have not drawn back.
6I offered my back to those who beat
me,

my cheeks to those who pulled out
my beard;
I did not hide my face
from mocking and spitting.
7Because the Sovereign LORD helps me,
I will not be disgraced.
Therefore have I set my face like flint,
and I know I will not be put to
shame.
8He who vindicates me is near.
Who then will bring charges against
me?
Let us face each other!
Who is my accuser?
Let him confront me!
9It is the Sovereign LORD who helps
me.
Who is he that will condemn me?
They will all wear out like a garment;
the moths will eat them up.

10Who among you fears the LORD
and obeys the word of his servant?
Let him who walks in the dark,
who has no light,
trust in the name of the LORD
and rely on his God.
11But now, all you who light fires
and provide yourselves with flaming
torches,
go, walk in the light of your fires
and of the torches you have set
ablaze.
This is what you shall receive from
my hand:
You will lie down in torment.

Everlasting Salvation for Zion

51 "Listen to me, you who pursue
righteousness
and who seek the LORD:
Look to the rock from which you were
cut
and to the quarry from which you
were hewn;
2look to Abraham, your father,
and to Sarah, who gave you birth.
When I called him he was but one,
and I blessed him and made him
many.
3The LORD will surely comfort Zion
and will look with compassion on
all her ruins;
he will make her deserts like Eden,
her wastelands like the garden of
the LORD.
Joy and gladness will be found in her,

*a*24 Dead Sea Scrolls, Vulgate and Syriac (see also Septuagint and verse 25); Masoretic Text *righteous*

thanksgiving and the sound of
singing.

4"Listen to me, my people;
hear me, my nation:
The law will go out from me;
my justice will become a light to
the nations.
5My righteousness draws near speedily,
my salvation is on the way,
and my arm will bring justice to the
nations.
The islands will look to me
and wait in hope for my arm.
6Lift up your eyes to the heavens,
look at the earth beneath;
the heavens will vanish like smoke,
the earth will wear out like a
garment
and its inhabitants die like flies.
But my salvation will last forever,
my righteousness will never fail.

7"Hear me, you who know what is
right,
you people who have my law in
your hearts:
Do not fear the reproach of men
or be terrified by their insults.
8For the moth will eat them up like a
garment;
the worm will devour them like
wool.
But my righteousness will last forever,
my salvation through all
generations."

9Awake, awake! Clothe yourself with
strength,
O arm of the LORD;
awake, as in days gone by,
as in generations of old.
Was it not you who cut Rahab to
pieces,
who pierced that monster through?
10Was it not you who dried up the sea,
the waters of the great deep,
who made a road in the depths of the
sea
so that the redeemed might cross
over?
11The ransomed of the LORD will return.
They will enter Zion with singing;
everlasting joy will crown their
heads.
Gladness and joy will overtake them,
and sorrow and sighing will flee
away.

12"I, even I, am he who comforts you.

Who are you that you fear mortal
men,
the sons of men, who are but grass,
13that you forget the LORD your Maker,
who stretched out the heavens
and laid the foundations of the
earth,
that you live in constant terror every
day
because of the wrath of the
oppressor,
who is bent on destruction?
For where is the wrath of the
oppressor?
14 The cowering prisoners will soon be
set free;
they will not die in their dungeon,
nor will they lack bread.
15For I am the LORD your God,
who churns up the sea so that its
waves roar—
the LORD Almighty is his name.
16I have put my words in your mouth
and covered you with the shadow of
my hand—
I who set the heavens in place,
who laid the foundations of the
earth,
and who say to Zion, 'You are my
people.' "

The Cup of the LORD's Wrath

17Awake, awake!
Rise up, O Jerusalem,
you who have drunk from the hand of
the LORD
the cup of his wrath,
you who have drained to its dregs
the goblet that makes men stagger.
18Of all the sons she bore
there was none to guide her;
of all the sons she reared
there was none to take her by the
hand.
19These double calamities have come
upon you—
who can comfort you?—
ruin and destruction, famine and
sword—
who cana console you?
20Your sons have fainted;
they lie at the head of every street,
like antelope caught in a net.
They are filled with the wrath of the
LORD
and the rebuke of your God.

21Therefore hear this, you afflicted one,

a19 Dead Sea Scrolls, Septuagint, Vulgate and Syriac; Masoretic Text / how can I

made drunk, but not with wine.
22This is what your Sovereign LORD says,
   your God, who defends his people:
"See, I have taken out of your hand
   the cup that made you stagger;
from that cup, the goblet of my
     wrath,
   you will never drink again.
23I will put it into the hands of your
     tormentors,
   who said to you,
   'Fall prostrate that we may walk
     over you.'
And you made your back like the
     ground,
   like a street to be walked over."

52 Awake, awake, O Zion,
   clothe yourself with strength.
Put on your garments of splendor,
   O Jerusalem, the holy city.
The uncircumcised and defiled
   will not enter you again.
2Shake off your dust;
   rise up, sit enthroned, O Jerusalem.
Free yourself from the chains on your
     neck,
   O captive Daughter of Zion.

3For this is what the LORD says:

"You were sold for nothing,
   and without money you will be
     redeemed."

4For this is what the Sovereign LORD
says:

"At first my people went down to
   Egypt to live;
lately, Assyria has oppressed them.

5"And now what do I have here?" declares the LORD.

"For my people have been taken away
   for nothing,
   and those who rule them mock,*a"*
           declares the LORD.
"And all day long
   my name is constantly blasphemed.
6Therefore my people will know my
     name;
   therefore in that day they will know
that it is I who foretold it.
   Yes, it is I."

7How beautiful on the mountains
   are the feet of those who bring
     good news,

who proclaim peace,
   who bring good tidings,
   who proclaim salvation,
who say to Zion,
   "Your God reigns!"
8Listen! Your watchmen lift up their
     voices;
   together they shout for joy.
When the LORD returns to Zion,
   they will see it with their own eyes.
9Burst into songs of joy together,
   you ruins of Jerusalem,
for the LORD has comforted his
     people,
   he has redeemed Jerusalem.
10The LORD will lay bare his holy arm
   in the sight of all the nations,
and all the ends of the earth will see
   the salvation of our God.

11Depart, depart, go out from there!
   Touch no unclean thing!
Come out from it and be pure,
   you who carry the vessels of the
     LORD.
12But you will not leave in haste
   or go in flight;
for the LORD will go before you,
   the God of Israel will be your rear
     guard.

The Suffering and Glory of the Servant

13See, my servant will act wisely*b*;
   he will be raised and lifted up and
     highly exalted.
14Just as there were many who were
     appalled at him*c*—
   his appearance was so disfigured
     beyond that of any man
   and his form marred beyond human
     likeness—
15so will he sprinkle many nations,*d*
   and kings will shut their mouths
     because of him.
For what they were not told, they will
     see,
   and what they have not heard, they
     will understand.

53 Who has believed our message
   and to whom has the arm of the
     LORD been revealed?
2He grew up before him like a tender
     shoot,
   and like a root out of dry ground.
He had no beauty or majesty to
     attract us to him,

a5 Dead Sea Scrolls and Vulgate; Masoretic Text *wail*   *b13* Or *will prosper*   *c14* Hebrew *you*
d15 Hebrew; Septuagint *so will many nations marvel at him*

nothing in his appearance that we
  should desire him.
³He was despised and rejected by men,
  a man of sorrows, and familiar with
  suffering.
Like one from whom men hide their
  faces
  he was despised, and we esteemed
  him not.

⁴Surely he took up our infirmities
  and carried our sorrows,
yet we considered him stricken by
  God,
  smitten by him, and afflicted.
⁵But he was pierced for our
  transgressions,
  he was crushed for our iniquities;
the punishment that brought us peace
  was upon him,
  and by his wounds we are healed.
⁶We all, like sheep, have gone astray,
  each of us has turned to his own
  way;
and the LORD has laid on him
  the iniquity of us all.

⁷He was oppressed and afflicted,
  yet he did not open his mouth;
he was led like a lamb to the
  slaughter,
  and as a sheep before her shearers
  is silent,
  so he did not open his mouth.
⁸By oppression ᵃ and judgment he was
  taken away.
  And who can speak of his
  descendants?
For he was cut off from the land of
  the living;
  for the transgression of my people
  he was stricken. ᵇ
⁹He was assigned a grave with the
  wicked,
  and with the rich in his death,
though he had done no violence,
  nor was any deceit in his mouth.

¹⁰Yet it was the LORD's will to crush
  him and cause him to suffer,
  and though the LORD makesᶜ his
  life a guilt offering,
he will see his offspring and prolong
  his days,
  and the will of the LORD will
  prosper in his hand.

¹¹After the suffering of his soul,
  he will see the light ‚of life, ᵈ and be
  satisfiedᵉ;
by his knowledgeᶠ my righteous
  servant will justify many,
  and he will bear their iniquities.
¹²Therefore I will give him a portion
  among the great,ᵍ
  and he will divide the spoils with
  the strong,ʰ
because he poured out his life unto
  death,
  and was numbered with the
  transgressors.
For he bore the sin of many,
  and made intercession for the
  transgressors.

The Future Glory of Zion

54 "Sing, O barren woman,
  you who never bore a child;
burst into song, shout for joy,
  you who were never in labor;
because more are the children of the
  desolate woman
than of her who has a husband,"
                            says the LORD.
²"Enlarge the place of your tent,
  stretch your tent curtains wide,
  do not hold back;
lengthen your cords,
  strengthen your stakes.
³For you will spread out to the right
  and to the left;
  your descendants will dispossess
  nations
  and settle in their desolate cities.

⁴"Do not be afraid; you will not suffer
  shame.
  Do not fear disgrace; you will not
  be humiliated.
You will forget the shame of your
  youth
  and remember no more the
  reproach of your widowhood.
⁵For your Maker is your husband—
  the LORD Almighty is his name—
the Holy One of Israel is your
  Redeemer;
  he is called the God of all the
  earth.
⁶The LORD will call you back
  as if you were a wife deserted and
  distressed in spirit—

ᵃ8 Or From arrest   ᵇ8 Or away. / Yet who of his generation considered / that he was cut off from the
land of the living / for the transgression of my people, / to whom the blow was due?   ᶜ10 Hebrew though
you make   ᵈ11 Dead Sea Scrolls (see also Septuagint); Masoretic Text does not have the light ‚of life‚.
ᵉ11 Or (with Masoretic Text) ¹¹He will see the result of the suffering of his soul / and be satisfied
ᶠ11 Or by knowledge of him   ᵍ12 Or many   ʰ12 Or numerous

a wife who married young,
only to be rejected," says your God.
⁷"For a brief moment I abandoned
you,
but with deep compassion I will
bring you back.
⁸In a surge of anger
I hid my face from you for a
moment,
but with everlasting kindness
I will have compassion on you,"
says the LORD your Redeemer.

⁹"To me this is like the days of Noah,
when I swore that the waters of
Noah would never again cover
the earth.
So now I have sworn not to be angry
with you,
never to rebuke you again.
¹⁰Though the mountains be shaken
and the hills be removed,
yet my unfailing love for you will not
be shaken
nor my covenant of peace be
removed,"
says the LORD, who has compassion
on you.

¹¹"O afflicted city, lashed by storms
and not comforted,
I will build you with stones of
turquoise,ᵃ
your foundations with sapphires.ᵇ
¹²I will make your battlements of
rubies,
your gates of sparkling jewels,
and all your walls of precious
stones.
¹³All your sons will be taught by the
LORD,
and great will be your children's
peace.
¹⁴In righteousness you will be
established:
Tyranny will be far from you;
you will have nothing to fear.
Terror will be far removed;
it will not come near you.
¹⁵If anyone does attack you, it will not
be my doing;
whoever attacks you will surrender
to you.

¹⁶"See, it is I who created the
blacksmith
who fans the coals into flame
and forges a weapon fit for its work.

And it is I who have created the
destroyer to work havoc;
¹⁷ no weapon forged against you will
prevail,
and you will refute every tongue
that accuses you.
This is the heritage of the servants of
the LORD,
and this is their vindication from
me,"
declares the LORD.

Invitation to the Thirsty

55 "Come, all you who are thirsty,
come to the waters;
and you who have no money,
come, buy and eat!
Come, buy wine and milk
without money and without cost.
²Why spend money on what is not
bread,
and your labor on what does not
satisfy?
Listen, listen to me, and eat what is
good,
and your soul will delight in the
richest of fare.
³Give ear and come to me;
hear me, that your soul may live.
I will make an everlasting covenant
with you,
my faithful love promised to David.
⁴See, I have made him a witness to the
peoples,
a leader and commander of the
peoples.
⁵Surely you will summon nations you
know not,
and nations that do not know you
will hasten to you,
because of the LORD your God,
the Holy One of Israel,
for he has endowed you with
splendor."

⁶Seek the LORD while he may be found;
call on him while he is near.
⁷Let the wicked forsake his way
and the evil man his thoughts.
Let him turn to the LORD, and he will
have mercy on him,
and to our God, for he will freely
pardon.

⁸"For my thoughts are not your
thoughts,
neither are your ways my ways,"
declares the LORD.

ᵃ11 The meaning of the Hebrew for this word is uncertain.   ᵇ11 Or *lapis lazuli*

9"As the heavens are higher than the
earth,
so are my ways higher than your
ways
and my thoughts than your
thoughts.
10As the rain and the snow
come down from heaven,
and do not return to it
without watering the earth
and making it bud and flourish,
so that it yields seed for the sower
and bread for the eater,
11so is my word that goes out from my
mouth:
It will not return to me empty,
but will accomplish what I desire
and achieve the purpose for which I
sent it.
12You will go out in joy
and be led forth in peace;
the mountains and hills
will burst into song before you,
and all the trees of the field
will clap their hands.
13Instead of the thornbush will grow
the pine tree,
and instead of briers the myrtle will
grow.
This will be for the LORD's renown,
for an everlasting sign,
which will not be destroyed."

Salvation for Others

56 This is what the LORD says:
"Maintain justice
and do what is right,
for my salvation is close at hand
and my righteousness will soon be
revealed.
2Blessed is the man who does this,
the man who holds it fast,
who keeps the Sabbath without
desecrating it,
and keeps his hand from doing any
evil."

3Let no foreigner who has bound
himself to the LORD say,
"The LORD will surely exclude me
from his people."
And let not any eunuch complain,
"I am only a dry tree."

4For this is what the LORD says:

"To the eunuchs who keep my
Sabbaths,
who choose what pleases me
and hold fast to my covenant—

5to them I will give within my temple
and its walls
a memorial and a name
better than sons and daughters;
I will give them an everlasting name
that will not be cut off.
6And foreigners who bind themselves
to the LORD
to serve him,
to love the name of the LORD,
and to worship him,
all who keep the Sabbath without
desecrating it
and who hold fast to my
covenant—
7these I will bring to my holy
mountain
and give them joy in my house of
prayer.
Their burnt offerings and sacrifices
will be accepted on my altar;
for my house will be called
a house of prayer for all nations."
8The Sovereign LORD declares—
he who gathers the exiles of Israel:
"I will gather still others to them
besides those already gathered."

God's Accusation Against the Wicked

9Come, all you beasts of the field,
come and devour, all you beasts of
the forest!
10Israel's watchmen are blind,
they all lack knowledge;
they are all mute dogs,
they cannot bark;
they lie around and dream,
they love to sleep.
11They are dogs with mighty appetites;
they never have enough.
They are shepherds who lack
understanding;
they all turn to their own way,
each seeks his own gain.
12"Come," each one cries, "let me get
wine!
Let us drink our fill of beer!
And tomorrow will be like today,
or even far better."

57 The righteous perish,
and no one ponders it in his
heart;
devout men are taken away,
and no one understands
that the righteous are taken away
to be spared from evil.
2Those who walk uprightly

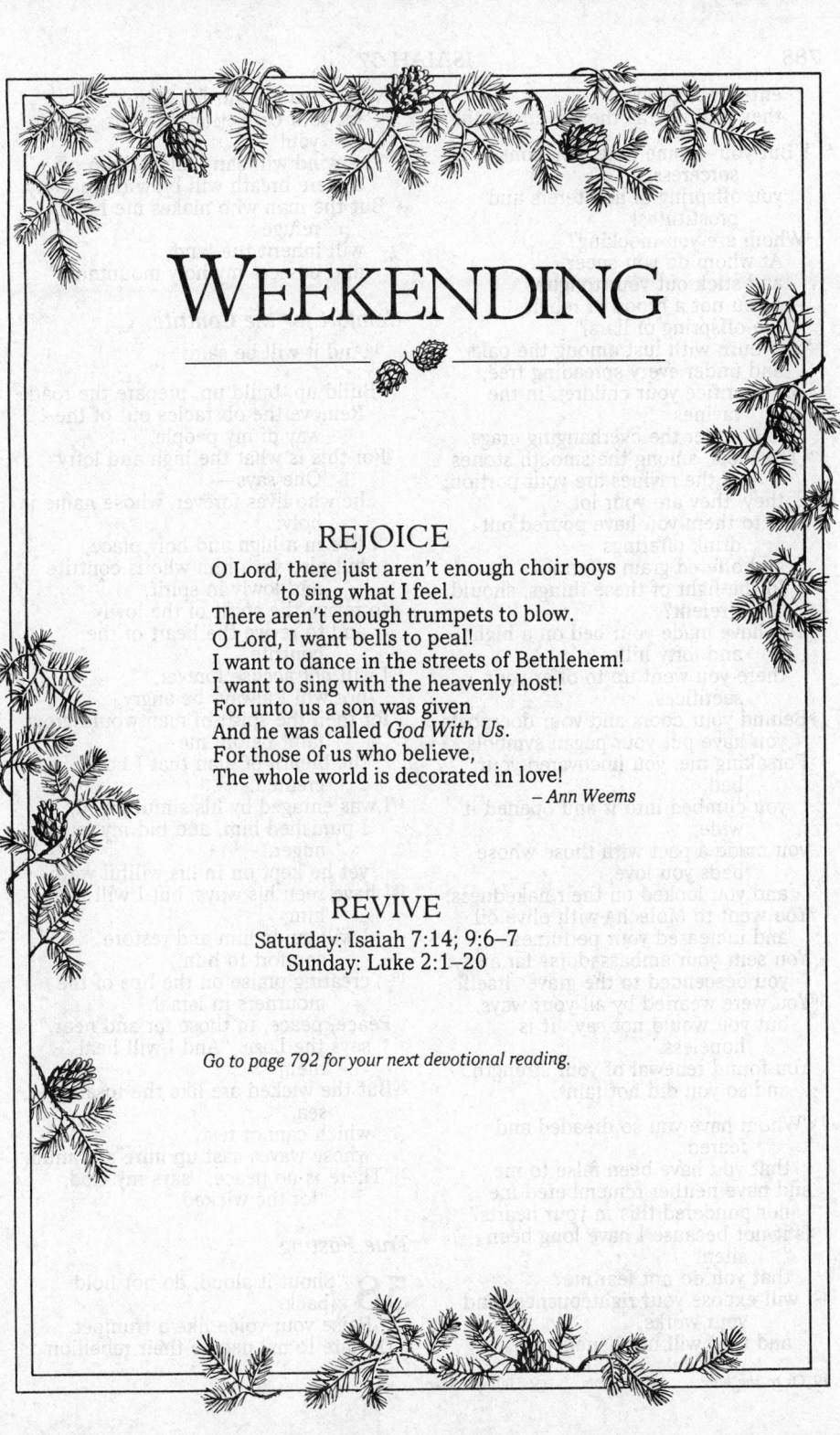

WEEKENDING

REJOICE

O Lord, there just aren't enough choir boys
    to sing what I feel.
There aren't enough trumpets to blow.
O Lord, I want bells to peal!
I want to dance in the streets of Bethlehem!
I want to sing with the heavenly host!
For unto us a son was given
And he was called *God With Us*.
For those of us who believe,
The whole world is decorated in love!

– *Ann Weems*

REVIVE

Saturday: Isaiah 7:14; 9:6–7
Sunday: Luke 2:1–20

Go to page 792 for your next devotional reading.

enter into peace;
they find rest as they lie in death.

3"But you—come here, you sons of a
    sorceress,
you offspring of adulterers and
    prostitutes!
4Whom are you mocking?
At whom do you sneer
    and stick out your tongue?
Are you not a brood of rebels,
    the offspring of liars?
5You burn with lust among the oaks
    and under every spreading tree;
you sacrifice your children in the
    ravines
    and under the overhanging crags.
6The idols, among the smooth stones
    of the ravines are your portion;
they, they are your lot.
Yes, to them you have poured out
    drink offerings
    and offered grain offerings.
In the light of these things, should
    I relent?
7You have made your bed on a high
    and lofty hill;
there you went up to offer your
    sacrifices.
8Behind your doors and your doorposts
    you have put your pagan symbols.
Forsaking me, you uncovered your
    bed,
you climbed into it and opened it
    wide;
you made a pact with those whose
    beds you love,
    and you looked on their nakedness.
9You went to Molech[a] with olive oil
    and increased your perfumes.
You sent your ambassadors[b] far away;
    you descended to the grave[c] itself!
10You were wearied by all your ways,
    but you would not say, 'It is
    hopeless.'
You found renewal of your strength,
    and so you did not faint.

11"Whom have you so dreaded and
    feared
that you have been false to me,
and have neither remembered me
    nor pondered this in your hearts?
Is it not because I have long been
    silent
    that you do not fear me?
12I will expose your righteousness and
    your works,
    and they will not benefit you.

13When you cry out for help,
    let your collection of idols save
    you!
The wind will carry all of them off,
    a mere breath will blow them away.
But the man who makes me his
    refuge
will inherit the land
    and possess my holy mountain."

Comfort for the Contrite

14And it will be said:

"Build up, build up, prepare the road!
    Remove the obstacles out of the
    way of my people."
15For this is what the high and lofty
    One says—
he who lives forever, whose name is
    holy:
"I live in a high and holy place,
    but also with him who is contrite
    and lowly in spirit,
to revive the spirit of the lowly
    and to revive the heart of the
    contrite.
16I will not accuse forever,
    nor will I always be angry,
for then the spirit of man would grow
    faint before me—
    the breath of man that I have
    created.
17I was enraged by his sinful greed;
    I punished him, and hid my face in
    anger,
    yet he kept on in his willful ways.
18I have seen his ways, but I will heal
    him;
I will guide him and restore
    comfort to him,
19   creating praise on the lips of the
    mourners in Israel.
Peace, peace, to those far and near,"
    says the Lord. "And I will heal
    them."
20But the wicked are like the tossing
    sea,
    which cannot rest,
    whose waves cast up mire and mud.
21"There is no peace," says my God,
    "for the wicked."

True Fasting

58 "Shout it aloud, do not hold
    back.
Raise your voice like a trumpet.
Declare to my people their rebellion

---

a9 Or to the king   b9 Or idols   c9 Hebrew Sheol

and to the house of Jacob their
      sins.
²For day after day they seek me out;
      they seem eager to know my ways,
as if they were a nation that does
            what is right
      and has not forsaken the
            commands of its God.
They ask me for just decisions
      and seem eager for God to come
            near them.
³'Why have we fasted,' they say,
      'and you have not seen it?
Why have we humbled ourselves,
      and you have not noticed?'

"Yet on the day of your fasting, you
            do as you please
      and exploit all your workers.
⁴Your fasting ends in quarreling and
            strife,
      and in striking each other with
            wicked fists.
You cannot fast as you do today
      and expect your voice to be heard
            on high.
⁵Is this the kind of fast I have chosen,
      only a day for a man to humble
            himself?
Is it only for bowing one's head like a
            reed
      and for lying on sackcloth and
            ashes?
Is that what you call a fast,
      a day acceptable to the LORD?

⁶"Is not this the kind of fasting I have
            chosen:
      to loose the chains of injustice
      and untie the cords of the yoke,
to set the oppressed free
      and break every yoke?
⁷Is it not to share your food with the
            hungry
      and to provide the poor wanderer
            with shelter—
when you see the naked, to clothe
            him,
      and not to turn away from your
            own flesh and blood?
⁸Then your light will break forth like
            the dawn,
      and your healing will quickly
            appear;
then your righteousness*a* will go
            before you,
      and the glory of the LORD will be
            your rear guard.

⁹Then you will call, and the LORD will
            answer;
      you will cry for help, and he will
            say: Here am I.

"If you do away with the yoke of
            oppression,
      with the pointing finger and
            malicious talk,
¹⁰and if you spend yourselves in behalf
            of the hungry
      and satisfy the needs of the
            oppressed,
then your light will rise in the
            darkness,
      and your night will become like the
            noonday.
¹¹The LORD will guide you always;
      he will satisfy your needs in a
            sun-scorched land
      and will strengthen your frame.
You will be like a well-watered
            garden,
      like a spring whose waters never
            fail.
¹²Your people will rebuild the ancient
            ruins
      and will raise up the age-old
            foundations;
you will be called Repairer of Broken
            Walls,
      Restorer of Streets with Dwellings.

¹³"If you keep your feet from breaking
            the Sabbath
      and from doing as you please on
            my holy day,
if you call the Sabbath a delight
      and the LORD's holy day honorable,
and if you honor it by not going your
            own way
      and not doing as you please or
            speaking idle words,
¹⁴then you will find your joy in the
            LORD,
      and I will cause you to ride on the
            heights of the land
      and to feast on the inheritance of
            your father Jacob."
                  The mouth of the LORD
                              has spoken.

Sin, Confession and Redemption

59 Surely the arm of the LORD is not
            too short to save,
      nor his ear too dull to hear.
²But your iniquities have separated
      you from your God;

---

a8 Or your righteous One

your sins have hidden his face from
   you,
   so that he will not hear.
³For your hands are stained with
   blood,
   your fingers with guilt.
Your lips have spoken lies,
   and your tongue mutters wicked
      things.
⁴No one calls for justice;
   no one pleads his case with
      integrity.
They rely on empty arguments and
      speak lies;
   they conceive trouble and give birth
      to evil.
⁵They hatch the eggs of vipers
   and spin a spider's web.
Whoever eats their eggs will die,
   and when one is broken, an adder
      is hatched.
⁶Their cobwebs are useless for
      clothing;
   they cannot cover themselves with
      what they make.
Their deeds are evil deeds,
   and acts of violence are in their
      hands.
⁷Their feet rush into sin;
   they are swift to shed innocent
      blood.
Their thoughts are evil thoughts;
   ruin and destruction mark their
      ways.
⁸The way of peace they do not know;
   there is no justice in their paths.
They have turned them into crooked
      roads;
   no one who walks in them will
      know peace.

⁹So justice is far from us,
   and righteousness does not reach
      us.
We look for light, but all is darkness;
   for brightness, but we walk in deep
      shadows.
¹⁰Like the blind we grope along the
      wall,
   feeling our way like men without
      eyes.
At midday we stumble as if it were
      twilight;
   among the strong, we are like the
      dead.
¹¹We all growl like bears;
   we moan mournfully like doves.
We look for justice, but find none;

for deliverance, but it is far away.
¹²For our offenses are many in your
      sight,
   and our sins testify against us.
Our offenses are ever with us,
   and we acknowledge our iniquities:
¹³rebellion and treachery against the
      LORD,
   turning our backs on our God,
fomenting oppression and revolt,
   uttering lies our hearts have
      conceived.
¹⁴So justice is driven back,
   and righteousness stands at a
      distance;
truth has stumbled in the streets,
   honesty cannot enter.
¹⁵Truth is nowhere to be found,
   and whoever shuns evil becomes a
      prey.

The LORD looked and was displeased
   that there was no justice.
¹⁶He saw that there was no one,
   he was appalled that there was no
      one to intervene;
so his own arm worked salvation for
      him,
   and his own righteousness
      sustained him.
¹⁷He put on righteousness as his
      breastplate,
   and the helmet of salvation on his
      head;
he put on the garments of vengeance
   and wrapped himself in zeal as in a
      cloak.
¹⁸According to what they have done,
   so will he repay
wrath to his enemies
   and retribution to his foes;
   he will repay the islands their due.
¹⁹From the west, men will fear the
      name of the LORD,
   and from the rising of the sun, they
      will revere his glory.
For he will come like a pent-up flood
   that the breath of the LORD drives
      along.ᵃ

²⁰"The Redeemer will come to Zion,
   to those in Jacob who repent of
      their sins,"
                    declares the LORD.

²¹"As for me, this is my covenant with
them," says the LORD. "My Spirit, who is
on you, and my words that I have put in
your mouth will not depart from your

ᵃ19 Or When the enemy comes in like a flood, / the Spirit of the LORD will put him to flight mouth, or from the mouths of your children, or from the mouths of their descendants from this time on and forever," says the LORD.

The Glory of Zion

60 "Arise, shine, for your light has come,
and the glory of the LORD rises upon you.
²See, darkness covers the earth
and thick darkness is over the peoples,
but the LORD rises upon you
and his glory appears over you.
³Nations will come to your light,
and kings to the brightness of your dawn.

⁴"Lift up your eyes and look about you:
All assemble and come to you;
your sons come from afar,
and your daughters are carried on the arm.
⁵Then you will look and be radiant,
your heart will throb and swell with joy;
the wealth on the seas will be brought to you,
to you the riches of the nations will come.
⁶Herds of camels will cover your land,
young camels of Midian and Ephah.
And all from Sheba will come,
bearing gold and incense
and proclaiming the praise of the LORD.
⁷All Kedar's flocks will be gathered to you,
the rams of Nebaioth will serve you;
they will be accepted as offerings on my altar,
and I will adorn my glorious temple.

⁸"Who are these that fly along like clouds,
like doves to their nests?
⁹Surely the islands look to me;
in the lead are the ships of Tarshish,ᵃ
bringing your sons from afar,
with their silver and gold,
to the honor of the LORD your God,
the Holy One of Israel,
for he has endowed you with splendor.

¹⁰"Foreigners will rebuild your walls,
and their kings will serve you.
Though in anger I struck you,
in favor I will show you compassion.
¹¹Your gates will always stand open,
they will never be shut, day or night,
so that men may bring you the wealth of the nations—
their kings led in triumphal procession.
¹²For the nation or kingdom that will not serve you will perish;
it will be utterly ruined.

¹³"The glory of Lebanon will come to you,
the pine, the fir and the cypress together,
to adorn the place of my sanctuary;
and I will glorify the place of my feet.
¹⁴The sons of your oppressors will come bowing before you;
all who despise you will bow down at your feet
and will call you the City of the LORD,
Zion of the Holy One of Israel.

¹⁵"Although you have been forsaken and hated,
with no one traveling through,
I will make you the everlasting pride
and the joy of all generations.
¹⁶You will drink the milk of nations
and be nursed at royal breasts.
Then you will know that I, the LORD,
am your Savior,
your Redeemer, the Mighty One of Jacob.
¹⁷Instead of bronze I will bring you gold,
and silver in place of iron.
Instead of wood I will bring you bronze,
and iron in place of stones.
I will make peace your governor
and righteousness your ruler.
¹⁸No longer will violence be heard in your land,
nor ruin or destruction within your borders,
but you will call your walls Salvation
and your gates Praise.
¹⁹The sun will no more be your light by day,
nor will the brightness of the moon shine on you,

ᵃ9 Or the trading ships

VERSE FOR THE DAY:
Isaiah 60:1–3

AUTHOR:
Debby Boone

PASSAGE FOR THE DAY:
Isaiah 60:1–9

The Presence of Light

EVERY school morning for the past two years, precisely at 7:00 A.M., I have taken a deep breath, climbed up the stairs, and opened the door to my eight-year-old son Jordan's bedroom. Each time I've steeled myself for the coming battle required to wrench his eyelids apart to start a new day. Most of the time I would leave his room convinced that he was well on his way to being dressed and would be downstairs ready to eat breakfast within ten minutes, only to climb those same stairs at 7:30 A.M., push back the door, and find him sound asleep.

A couple of weeks ago, all this changed. And I had nothing to do with it. Jordan started leaving his window shutters wide open when he would go to sleep. The morning light would gently filter in and quite naturally and quickly awaken him. I now walk into his room and find him sitting at his small desk, completely dressed in his school uniform, wondering when breakfast will be ready.

Jordan and I no longer have struggles in the morning. The presence of light has solved the problem completely. As I read the beginning verses of Isaiah 60, my mornings with Jordan came to mind. I asked the Lord to show me how to allow his light to awaken places in my heart that I have been content to leave sleeping in the darkness and comfort of my soul. It's hard to wake up when you are surrounded by darkness. And we can't transform ourselves into what we should or want to be any more than Jordan could wake himself up just because he knows he should be up.

Exposing ourselves to the light and presence of the Lord's love not only will uncover the dark places of our hearts but also will fill them with light so that "the glory of the LORD rises upon you" (Isaiah 60:1).

But how do we expose ourselves to his light? That's the easy part . . . just by leaving the shutters of our hearts open. Come to God with an honest expression of willingness to allow him to change us—by his wonderful and brilliant light.

Additional Scripture Readings:
John 12:44–46; 1 John 1:5–7

Go to page 794 for your next devotional reading.

for the Lord will be your everlasting
   light,
   and your God will be your glory.
20Your sun will never set again,
   and your moon will wane no more;
the Lord will be your everlasting light,
   and your days of sorrow will end.
21Then will all your people be righteous
   and they will possess the land
      forever.
They are the shoot I have planted,
   the work of my hands,
   for the display of my splendor.
22The least of you will become a
      thousand,
   the smallest a mighty nation.
I am the Lord;
   in its time I will do this swiftly."

The Year of the Lord's Favor

61 The Spirit of the Sovereign Lord
         is on me,
   because the Lord has anointed me
to preach good news to the poor.
He has sent me to bind up the
      brokenhearted,
   to proclaim freedom for the
      captives
   and release from darkness for the
      prisoners,[a]
2to proclaim the year of the Lord's
      favor
   and the day of vengeance of our
      God,
to comfort all who mourn,
3 and provide for those who grieve in
      Zion—
to bestow on them a crown of beauty
   instead of ashes,
the oil of gladness
   instead of mourning,
and a garment of praise
   instead of a spirit of despair.
They will be called oaks of
      righteousness,
   a planting of the Lord
   for the display of his splendor.

4They will rebuild the ancient ruins
   and restore the places long
      devastated;
they will renew the ruined cities
   that have been devastated for
      generations.
5Aliens will shepherd your flocks;
   foreigners will work your fields and
      vineyards.

6And you will be called priests of the
      Lord,
   you will be named ministers of our
      God.
You will feed on the wealth of
      nations,
   and in their riches you will boast.

7Instead of their shame
   my people will receive a double
      portion,
and instead of disgrace
   they will rejoice in their
      inheritance;
and so they will inherit a double
      portion in their land,
   and everlasting joy will be theirs.

8"For I, the Lord, love justice;
   I hate robbery and iniquity.
In my faithfulness I will reward them
   and make an everlasting covenant
      with them.
9Their descendants will be known
      among the nations
   and their offspring among the
      peoples.
All who see them will acknowledge
   that they are a people the Lord has
      blessed."

10I delight greatly in the Lord;
   my soul rejoices in my God.
For he has clothed me with garments
      of salvation
   and arrayed me in a robe of
      righteousness,
as a bridegroom adorns his head like
      a priest,
   and as a bride adorns herself with
      her jewels.
11For as the soil makes the sprout
      come up
   and a garden causes seeds to grow,
so the Sovereign Lord will make
      righteousness and praise
   spring up before all nations.

Zion's New Name

62 For Zion's sake I will not keep
         silent,
   for Jerusalem's sake I will not
      remain quiet,
till her righteousness shines out like
      the dawn,
   her salvation like a blazing torch.
2The nations will see your
      righteousness,
   and all kings your glory;

[a]1 Hebrew; Septuagint the blind

VERSE FOR THE DAY:
Isaiah 61:3

AUTHOR:
Mary Jane Worden

PASSAGE FOR THE DAY:
Isaiah 61:1–6

Grief Work

I DISCOVERED after the death of my husband Jim that grieving is work: exhausting and regressive. I found it didn't progress in neat and predictable stages but was frustratingly erratic and repetitive. As I stepped aside periodically to evaluate, I saw improvement overall: a gradual lessening of the pain and fear, a growing confidence in my ability to handle life's everydayness. But setbacks were sudden and frequent those first months. I would often find terrain which I thought I had traversed and left behind me was maddeningly underfoot again. I tried to learn to evaluate life in bigger chunks. Looking back over a month's progress can be more encouraging than too-frequent scrutiny.

Six months after Jim's death I wrote in a letter to friends:

> I am still occasionally swept by an unexpected wave of pain and hurt, the staggering awareness that Jim is not, and never will be, with us here again. But I'm learning that the best way to get to the other side is to go through it, to face it and to name it, to accept the pain and deal with it as directly as I can. I'm also finding, to my surprise, that there are frequent stretches of days without tears, and any feelings of despair have been only fleeting.

In looking back over that first year of deliberate grief work, I began to see patterns in my choices and a new principle about life began to take shape in my mind. The principle is this: beauty can help to bring healing—rainbows, mountains, woolly lambs, fresh strawberries on homemade ice cream, the crisp clean feel of sun-dried sheets. These places and things were somehow soothing to my soul.

I am convinced that God has built into all of us, in varying degrees, the capacity for an appreciation of beauty, and has even allowed us the privilege of participating in the creation of beautiful things and beautiful places. I think it may be one way God brings healing to our brokenness, and a way that we can contribute toward bringing wholeness to our fallen world.

Additional Scripture Readings:
Psalm 103:1–5; Jeremiah 31:12–13

Go to page 809 for your next devotional reading.

you will be called by a new name
   that the mouth of the LORD will
     bestow.
³You will be a crown of splendor in
   the LORD's hand,
   a royal diadem in the hand of your
     God.
⁴No longer will they call you Deserted,
   or name your land Desolate.
But you will be called Hephzibah,ᵃ
   and your land Beulahᵇ;
for the LORD will take delight in you,
   and your land will be married.
⁵As a young man marries a maiden,
   so will your sonsᶜ marry you;
as a bridegroom rejoices over his
     bride,
   so will your God rejoice over you.

⁶I have posted watchmen on your
     walls, O Jerusalem;
they will never be silent day or
     night.
You who call on the LORD,
   give yourselves no rest,
⁷and give him no rest till he
     establishes Jerusalem
and makes her the praise of the
     earth.

⁸The LORD has sworn by his right hand
   and by his mighty arm:
"Never again will I give your grain
   as food for your enemies,
and never again will foreigners drink
     the new wine
   for which you have toiled;
⁹but those who harvest it will eat it
   and praise the LORD,
and those who gather the grapes will
     drink it
   in the courts of my sanctuary."

¹⁰Pass through, pass through the gates!
   Prepare the way for the people.
Build up, build up the highway!
   Remove the stones.
Raise a banner for the nations.

¹¹The LORD has made proclamation
   to the ends of the earth:
"Say to the Daughter of Zion,
   'See, your Savior comes!
See, his reward is with him,
   and his recompense accompanies
     him.' "
¹²They will be called the Holy People,
   the Redeemed of the LORD;
and you will be called Sought After,
   the City No Longer Deserted.

God's Day of Vengeance and Redemption

63 Who is this coming from Edom,
     from Bozrah, with his garments
     stained crimson?
Who is this, robed in splendor,
   striding forward in the greatness of
     his strength?

"It is I, speaking in righteousness,
   mighty to save."

²Why are your garments red,
   like those of one treading the
     winepress?

³"I have trodden the winepress alone;
   from the nations no one was with
     me.
I trampled them in my anger
   and trod them down in my wrath;
their blood spattered my garments,
   and I stained all my clothing.
⁴For the day of vengeance was in my
     heart,
   and the year of my redemption has
     come.
⁵I looked, but there was no one to
     help,
I was appalled that no one gave
     support;
so my own arm worked salvation for
     me,
   and my own wrath sustained me.
⁶I trampled the nations in my anger;
   in my wrath I made them drunk
   and poured their blood on the
     ground."

Praise and Prayer

⁷I will tell of the kindnesses of the
     LORD,
   the deeds for which he is to be
     praised,
   according to all the LORD has done
     for us—
yes, the many good things he has
     done
   for the house of Israel,
   according to his compassion and
     many kindnesses.
⁸He said, "Surely they are my people,
   sons who will not be false to me";
   and so he became their Savior.
⁹In all their distress he too was
     distressed,
   and the angel of his presence saved
     them.

ᵃ4 *Hephzibah* means *my delight is in her.*   ᵇ4 *Beulah* means *married.*   ᶜ5 Or *Builder*

In his love and mercy he redeemed
　　them;
　he lifted them up and carried them
　　all the days of old.
[10]Yet they rebelled
　　and grieved his Holy Spirit.
So he turned and became their enemy
　and he himself fought against
　　them.

[11]Then his people recalled[a] the days of
　　old,
　the days of Moses and his people—
where is he who brought them
　　through the sea,
　with the shepherd of his flock?
Where is he who set
　　his Holy Spirit among them,
[12]who sent his glorious arm of power
　　to be at Moses' right hand,
who divided the waters before them,
　to gain for himself everlasting
　　renown,
[13]who led them through the depths?
Like a horse in open country,
　　they did not stumble;
[14]like cattle that go down to the plain,
　they were given rest by the Spirit of
　　the LORD.
This is how you guided your people
　to make for yourself a glorious
　　name.

[15]Look down from heaven and see
　from your lofty throne, holy and
　　glorious.
Where are your zeal and your might?
　Your tenderness and compassion
　　are withheld from us.
[16]But you are our Father,
　though Abraham does not know us
　　or Israel acknowledge us;
you, O LORD, are our Father,
　our Redeemer from of old is your
　　name.
[17]Why, O LORD, do you make us wander
　　from your ways
　and harden our hearts so we do not
　　revere you?
Return for the sake of your servants,
　the tribes that are your inheritance.
[18]For a little while your people
　　possessed your holy place,
　but now our enemies have trampled
　　down your sanctuary.
[19]We are yours from of old;
　but you have not ruled over them,

they have not been called by your
　　name.[b]

64

Oh, that you would rend the
heavens and come down,
that the mountains would tremble
　before you!
[2]As when fire sets twigs ablaze
　and causes water to boil,
come down to make your name
　　known to your enemies
and cause the nations to quake
　before you!
[3]For when you did awesome things
　　that we did not expect,
　you came down, and the mountains
　　trembled before you.
[4]Since ancient times no one has heard,
　no ear has perceived,
no eye has seen any God besides you,
　who acts on behalf of those who
　　wait for him.
[5]You come to the help of those who
　　gladly do right,
　who remember your ways.
But when we continued to sin against
　　them,
　you were angry.
　How then can we be saved?
[6]All of us have become like one who is
　　unclean,
　and all our righteous acts are like
　　filthy rags;
we all shrivel up like a leaf,
　and like the wind our sins sweep us
　　away.
[7]No one calls on your name
　or strives to lay hold of you;
for you have hidden your face from us
　and made us waste away because of
　　our sins.

[8]Yet, O LORD, you are our Father.
　We are the clay, you are the potter;
　we are all the work of your hand.
[9]Do not be angry beyond measure,
　　O LORD;
　do not remember our sins forever.
Oh, look upon us, we pray,
　for we are all your people.
[10]Your sacred cities have become a
　　desert;
　even Zion is a desert, Jerusalem a
　　desolation.
[11]Our holy and glorious temple, where
　　our fathers praised you,
　has been burned with fire,

---

a11 Or But may he recall　　*b19 Or We are like those you have never ruled, / like those never called by your name*

and all that we treasured lies in
    ruins.
¹²After all this, O LORD, will you hold
    yourself back?
Will you keep silent and punish us
    beyond measure?

Judgment and Salvation

65 "I revealed myself to those who
    did not ask for me;
I was found by those who did not
    seek me.
To a nation that did not call on my
    name,
I said, 'Here am I, here am I.'
²All day long I have held out my hands
    to an obstinate people,
who walk in ways not good,
    pursuing their own imaginations—
³a people who continually provoke me
    to my very face,
offering sacrifices in gardens
    and burning incense on altars of
    brick;
⁴who sit among the graves
    and spend their nights keeping
    secret vigil;
who eat the flesh of pigs,
    and whose pots hold broth of
    unclean meat;
⁵who say, 'Keep away; don't come near
    me,
    for I am too sacred for you!'
Such people are smoke in my nostrils,
    a fire that keeps burning all day.

⁶"See, it stands written before me:
    I will not keep silent but will pay
    back in full;
I will pay it back into their laps—
⁷both your sins and the sins of your
    fathers,"
    says the LORD.
"Because they burned sacrifices on
    the mountains
and defied me on the hills,
I will measure into their laps
    the full payment for their former
    deeds."

⁸This is what the LORD says:

"As when juice is still found in a
    cluster of grapes
and men say, 'Don't destroy it,
    there is yet some good in it,'
so will I do in behalf of my servants;
    I will not destroy them all.
⁹I will bring forth descendants from
    Jacob,

and from Judah those who will
    possess my mountains;
my chosen people will inherit them,
    and there will my servants live.
¹⁰Sharon will become a pasture for
    flocks,
and the Valley of Achor a resting
    place for herds,
for my people who seek me.

¹¹"But as for you who forsake the LORD
    and forget my holy mountain,
who spread a table for Fortune
    and fill bowls of mixed wine for
    Destiny,
¹²I will destine you for the sword,
    and you will all bend down for the
    slaughter;
for I called but you did not answer,
    I spoke but you did not listen.
You did evil in my sight
    and chose what displeases me."

¹³Therefore this is what the Sovereign
LORD says:

"My servants will eat,
    but you will go hungry;
my servants will drink,
    but you will go thirsty;
my servants will rejoice,
    but you will be put to shame.
¹⁴My servants will sing
    out of the joy of their hearts,
but you will cry out
    from anguish of heart
    and wail in brokenness of spirit.
¹⁵You will leave your name
    to my chosen ones as a curse;
the Sovereign LORD will put you to
    death,
but to his servants he will give
    another name.
¹⁶Whoever invokes a blessing in the
    land
will do so by the God of truth;
he who takes an oath in the land
    will swear by the God of truth.
For the past troubles will be forgotten
    and hidden from my eyes.

New Heavens and a New Earth

¹⁷"Behold, I will create
    new heavens and a new earth.
The former things will not be
    remembered,
    nor will they come to mind.
¹⁸But be glad and rejoice forever
    in what I will create,
for I will create Jerusalem to be a
    delight

and its people a joy.
¹⁹I will rejoice over Jerusalem
and take delight in my people;
the sound of weeping and of crying
will be heard in it no more.

²⁰"Never again will there be in it
an infant who lives but a few
days,
or an old man who does not live
out his years;
he who dies at a hundred
will be thought a mere youth;
he who fails to reach^a a hundred
will be considered accursed.
²¹They will build houses and dwell in
them;
they will plant vineyards and eat
their fruit.
²²No longer will they build houses and
others live in them,
or plant and others eat.
For as the days of a tree,
so will be the days of my people;
my chosen ones will long enjoy
the works of their hands.
²³They will not toil in vain
or bear children doomed to
misfortune;
for they will be a people blessed by
the Lord,
they and their descendants with
them.
²⁴Before they call I will answer;
while they are still speaking I will
hear.
²⁵The wolf and the lamb will feed
together,
and the lion will eat straw like the
ox,
but dust will be the serpent's food.
They will neither harm nor destroy
on all my holy mountain,"
says the Lord.

Judgment and Hope

66 This is what the Lord says:
"Heaven is my throne,
and the earth is my footstool.
Where is the house you will build for
me?
Where will my resting place be?
²Has not my hand made all these
things,
and so they came into being?"
declares the Lord.

"This is the one I esteem:
he who is humble and contrite in
spirit,
and trembles at my word.
³But whoever sacrifices a bull
is like one who kills a man,
and whoever offers a lamb,
like one who breaks a dog's neck;
whoever makes a grain offering
is like one who presents pig's
blood,
and whoever burns memorial incense,
like one who worships an idol.
They have chosen their own ways,
and their souls delight in their
abominations;
⁴so I also will choose harsh treatment
for them
and will bring upon them what they
dread.
For when I called, no one answered,
when I spoke, no one listened.
They did evil in my sight
and chose what displeases me."

⁵Hear the word of the Lord,
you who tremble at his word:
"Your brothers who hate you,
and exclude you because of my
name, have said,
'Let the Lord be glorified,
that we may see your joy!'
Yet they will be put to shame.
⁶Hear that uproar from the city,
hear that noise from the temple!
It is the sound of the Lord
repaying his enemies all they
deserve.

⁷"Before she goes into labor,
she gives birth;
before the pains come upon her,
she delivers a son.
⁸Who has ever heard of such a thing?
Who has ever seen such things?
Can a country be born in a day
or a nation be brought forth in a
moment?
Yet no sooner is Zion in labor
than she gives birth to her children.
⁹Do I bring to the moment of birth
and not give delivery?" says the
Lord.
"Do I close up the womb
when I bring to delivery?" says your
God.
¹⁰"Rejoice with Jerusalem and be glad
for her,
all you who love her;

^a20 Or / the sinner who reaches

rejoice greatly with her,
   all you who mourn over her.
¹¹For you will nurse and be satisfied
   at her comforting breasts;
you will drink deeply
   and delight in her overflowing
      abundance."

¹²For this is what the LORD says:

"I will extend peace to her like a
   river,
   and the wealth of nations like a
      flooding stream;
you will nurse and be carried on her
   arm
   and dandled on her knees.
¹³As a mother comforts her child,
   so will I comfort you;
   and you will be comforted over
      Jerusalem."

¹⁴When you see this, your heart will
   rejoice
   and you will flourish like grass;
the hand of the LORD will be made
   known to his servants,
   but his fury will be shown to his
      foes.
¹⁵See, the LORD is coming with fire,
   and his chariots are like a
      whirlwind;
he will bring down his anger with
   fury,
   and his rebuke with flames of
      fire.
¹⁶For with fire and with his sword
   the LORD will execute judgment
      upon all men,
   and many will be those slain by the
      LORD.

¹⁷"Those who consecrate and purify themselves to go into the gardens, following the one in the midst of[a] those who eat the flesh of pigs and rats and other abominable things—they will meet their end together," declares the LORD.

¹⁸"And I, because of their actions and their imaginations, am about to come[b] and gather all nations and tongues, and they will come and see my glory.

¹⁹"I will set a sign among them, and I will send some of those who survive to the nations—to Tarshish, to the Libyans[c] and Lydians (famous as archers), to Tubal and Greece, and to the distant islands that have not heard of my fame or seen my glory. They will proclaim my glory among the nations. ²⁰And they will bring all your brothers, from all the nations, to my holy mountain in Jerusalem as an offering to the LORD—on horses, in chariots and wagons, and on mules and camels," says the LORD. "They will bring them, as the Israelites bring their grain offerings, to the temple of the LORD in ceremonially clean vessels. ²¹And I will select some of them also to be priests and Levites," says the LORD.

²²"As the new heavens and the new earth that I make will endure before me," declares the LORD, "so will your name and descendants endure. ²³From one New Moon to another and from one Sabbath to another, all mankind will come and bow down before me," says the LORD. ²⁴"And they will go out and look upon the dead bodies of those who rebelled against me; their worm will not die, nor will their fire be quenched, and they will be loathsome to all mankind."

---

*J*EREMIAH prophesies in the kingdom of Judah as Jerusalem is being
destroyed and God's people are being
carried away into Babylon because of
their sins (see 2 Chronicles 36). It is a
time of judgment and of suffering for
all the people and for Jeremiah personally. But Jeremiah also cites God's
promise of restoration after seventy
years, assuring the people of a coming
new covenant. As you read this book,
remember that sin has its consequences
but also that through Jesus, your mediator, God's last word is forgiveness and
eternal life.

JEREMIAH

1 The words of Jeremiah son of Hilkiah, one of the priests at Anathoth in
the territory of Benjamin. ²The word of
the LORD came to him in the thirteenth
year of the reign of Josiah son of Amon
king of Judah, ³and through the reign of
Jehoiakim son of Josiah king of Judah,
down to the fifth month of the eleventh
year of Zedekiah son of Josiah king of Judah, when the people of Jerusalem went
into exile.

The Call of Jeremiah

⁴The word of the LORD came to me, saying,

⁵"Before I formed you in the womb I
    knew*ᵃ* you,
  before you were born I set you
    apart;
  I appointed you as a prophet to the
    nations."

ᵃ5 Or chose

6"Ah, Sovereign Lord," I said, "I do not know how to speak; I am only a child."

7But the Lord said to me, "Do not say, 'I am only a child.' You must go to everyone I send you to and say whatever I command you. 8Do not be afraid of them, for I am with you and will rescue you," declares the Lord.

9Then the Lord reached out his hand and touched my mouth and said to me, "Now, I have put my words in your mouth. 10See, today I appoint you over nations and kingdoms to uproot and tear down, to destroy and overthrow, to build and to plant."

11The word of the Lord came to me: "What do you see, Jeremiah?"

"I see the branch of an almond tree," I replied.

12The Lord said to me, "You have seen correctly, for I am watching*a* to see that my word is fulfilled."

13The word of the Lord came to me again: "What do you see?"

"I see a boiling pot, tilting away from the north," I answered.

14The Lord said to me, "From the north disaster will be poured out on all who live in the land. 15I am about to summon all the peoples of the northern kingdoms," declares the Lord.

"Their kings will come and set up
    their thrones
  in the entrance of the gates of
      Jerusalem;
they will come against all her
      surrounding walls
  and against all the towns of Judah.
16I will pronounce my judgments on my
      people
  because of their wickedness in
      forsaking me,
in burning incense to other gods
  and in worshiping what their hands
      have made.

17"Get yourself ready! Stand up and say to them whatever I command you. Do not be terrified by them, or I will terrify you before them. 18Today I have made you a fortified city, an iron pillar and a bronze wall to stand against the whole land—against the kings of Judah, its officials, its priests and the people of the land. 19They will fight against you but will not over-come you, for I am with you and will rescue you," declares the Lord.

Israel Forsakes God

2 The word of the Lord came to me: 2"Go and proclaim in the hearing of Jerusalem:

" 'I remember the devotion of your
      youth,
  how as a bride you loved me
and followed me through the desert,
  through a land not sown.
3Israel was holy to the Lord,
  the firstfruits of his harvest;
all who devoured her were held guilty,
  and disaster overtook them,' "
                    declares the Lord.

4Hear the word of the Lord, O house
      of Jacob,
  all you clans of the house of Israel.

5This is what the Lord says:

"What fault did your fathers find in
      me,
  that they strayed so far from me?
They followed worthless idols
  and became worthless themselves.
6They did not ask, 'Where is the Lord,
  who brought us up out of Egypt
and led us through the barren
      wilderness,
  through a land of deserts and rifts,
a land of drought and darkness,*b*
  a land where no one travels and no
      one lives?'
7I brought you into a fertile land
  to eat its fruit and rich produce.
But you came and defiled my land
  and made my inheritance
      detestable.
8The priests did not ask,
  'Where is the Lord?'
Those who deal with the law did not
      know me;
  the leaders rebelled against me.
The prophets prophesied by Baal,
  following worthless idols.

9"Therefore I bring charges against you
      again,"
                    declares the Lord.
"And I will bring charges against
  your children's children.
10Cross over to the coasts of Kittim*c*
      and look,
  send to Kedar*d* and observe closely;

---

a12 The Hebrew for *watching* sounds like the Hebrew for *almond tree*.   *b6* Or *and the shadow of death*
c10 That is, Cyprus and western coastlands   *d10* The home of Bedouin tribes in the Syro-Arabian desert

see if there has ever been anything
like this:

¹¹Has a nation ever changed its gods?
(Yet they are not gods at all.)
But my people have exchanged their*a*
Glory
for worthless idols.
¹²Be appalled at this, O heavens,
and shudder with great horror,"
declares the LORD.
¹³"My people have committed two sins:
They have forsaken me,
the spring of living water,
and have dug their own cisterns,
broken cisterns that cannot hold
water.
¹⁴Is Israel a servant, a slave by birth?
Why then has he become plunder?
¹⁵Lions have roared;
they have growled at him.
They have laid waste his land;
his towns are burned and deserted.
¹⁶Also, the men of Memphis*b* and
Tahpanhes
have shaved the crown of your
head.*c*
¹⁷Have you not brought this on
yourselves
by forsaking the LORD your God
when he led you in the way?
¹⁸Now why go to Egypt
to drink water from the Shihor*d*?
And why go to Assyria
to drink water from the River*e*?
¹⁹Your wickedness will punish you;
your backsliding will rebuke you.
Consider then and realize
how evil and bitter it is for you
when you forsake the LORD your God
and have no awe of me,"
declares the Lord,
the LORD Almighty.

²⁰"Long ago you broke off your yoke
and tore off your bonds;
you said, 'I will not serve you!'
Indeed, on every high hill
and under every spreading tree
you lay down as a prostitute.
²¹I had planted you like a choice vine
of sound and reliable stock.
How then did you turn against me
into a corrupt, wild vine?
²²Although you wash yourself with soda
and use an abundance of soap,
the stain of your guilt is still before
me,"
declares the Sovereign LORD.

²³"How can you say, 'I am not defiled;
I have not run after the Baals'?
See how you behaved in the valley;
consider what you have done.
You are a swift she-camel
running here and there,
²⁴a wild donkey accustomed to the
desert,
sniffing the wind in her craving—
in her heat who can restrain her?
Any males that pursue her need not
tire themselves;
at mating time they will find
her.
²⁵Do not run until your feet are bare
and your throat is dry.
But you said, 'It's no use!
I love foreign gods,
and I must go after them.'

²⁶"As a thief is disgraced when he is
caught,
so the house of Israel is
disgraced—
they, their kings and their officials,
their priests and their prophets.
²⁷They say to wood, 'You are my
father,'
and to stone, 'You gave me birth.'
They have turned their backs to me
and not their faces;
yet when they are in trouble, they
say,
'Come and save us!'
²⁸Where then are the gods you made for
yourselves?
Let them come if they can save you
when you are in trouble!
For you have as many gods
as you have towns, O Judah.

²⁹"Why do you bring charges against
me?
You have all rebelled against me,"
declares the LORD.
³⁰"In vain I punished your people;
they did not respond to correction.
Your sword has devoured your
prophets
like a ravening lion.

³¹"You of this generation, consider the
word of the LORD:

"Have I been a desert to Israel
or a land of great darkness?
Why do my people say, 'We are free
to roam;
we will come to you no more'?

---

*a*11 Masoretic Text; an ancient Hebrew scribal tradition *my
cracked your skull*   *d*18 That is, a branch of the Nile   *b*16 Hebrew *Noph*   *c*16 Or *have*
*e*18 That is, the Euphrates

³²Does a maiden forget her jewelry,
    a bride her wedding ornaments?
Yet my people have forgotten me,
    days without number.
³³How skilled you are at pursuing love!
    Even the worst of women can learn
        from your ways.
³⁴On your clothes men find
    the lifeblood of the innocent
        poor,
    though you did not catch them
        breaking in.
Yet in spite of all this
³⁵   you say, 'I am innocent;
    he is not angry with me.'
But I will pass judgment on you
    because you say, 'I have not
        sinned.'
³⁶Why do you go about so much,
    changing your ways?
You will be disappointed by Egypt
    as you were by Assyria.
³⁷You will also leave that place
    with your hands on your head,
for the LORD has rejected those you
        trust;
    you will not be helped by them.

3 "If a man divorces his wife
    and she leaves him and marries
        another man,
should he return to her again?
    Would not the land be completely
        defiled?
But you have lived as a prostitute
    with many lovers—
would you now return to me?"
                    declares the LORD.
²"Look up to the barren heights and
        see.
    Is there any place where you have
        not been ravished?
By the roadside you sat waiting for
        lovers,
    sat like a nomad*a* in the desert.
You have defiled the land
    with your prostitution and
        wickedness.
³Therefore the showers have been
        withheld,
    and no spring rains have fallen.
Yet you have the brazen look of a
        prostitute;
    you refuse to blush with shame.
⁴Have you not just called to me:
    'My Father, my friend from my
        youth,
⁵will you always be angry?

a2 Or an Arab

Will your wrath continue forever?'
This is how you talk,
    but you do all the evil you can."

Unfaithful Israel

⁶During the reign of King Josiah, the
LORD said to me, "Have you seen what
faithless Israel has done? She has gone up
on every high hill and under every spreading tree and has committed adultery
there. ⁷I thought that after she had done
all this she would return to me but she
did not, and her unfaithful sister Judah
saw it. ⁸I gave faithless Israel her certificate of divorce and sent her away because
of all her adulteries. Yet I saw that her
unfaithful sister Judah had no fear; she
also went out and committed adultery.
⁹Because Israel's immorality mattered so
little to her, she defiled the land and
committed adultery with stone and wood.
¹⁰In spite of all this, her unfaithful sister
Judah did not return to me with all her
heart, but only in pretense," declares the
LORD.
¹¹The LORD said to me, "Faithless Israel
is more righteous than unfaithful Judah.
¹²Go, proclaim this message toward the
north:

" 'Return, faithless Israel,' declares
        the LORD,
    'I will frown on you no longer,
for I am merciful,' declares the LORD,
    'I will not be angry forever.
¹³Only acknowledge your guilt—
    you have rebelled against the LORD
        your God,
you have scattered your favors to
        foreign gods
    under every spreading tree,
    and have not obeyed me,' "
                    declares the LORD.

¹⁴"Return, faithless people," declares
the LORD, "for I am your husband. I will
choose you—one from a town and two
from a clan—and bring you to Zion.
¹⁵Then I will give you shepherds after my
own heart, who will lead you with knowledge and understanding. ¹⁶In those days,
when your numbers have increased greatly in the land," declares the LORD, "men
will no longer say, 'The ark of the covenant of the LORD.' It will never enter their
minds or be remembered; it will not be
missed, nor will another one be made.
¹⁷At that time they will call Jerusalem
The Throne of the LORD, and all nations

will gather in Jerusalem to honor the name of the LORD. No longer will they follow the stubbornness of their evil hearts. ¹⁸In those days the house of Judah will join the house of Israel, and together they will come from a northern land to the land I gave your forefathers as an inheritance.

¹⁹"I myself said,

" 'How gladly would I treat you like sons
and give you a desirable land,
the most beautiful inheritance of any nation.'
I thought you would call me 'Father'
and not turn away from following me.
²⁰But like a woman unfaithful to her husband,
so you have been unfaithful to me,
O house of Israel,"
declares the LORD.

²¹A cry is heard on the barren heights,
the weeping and pleading of the people of Israel,
because they have perverted their ways
and have forgotten the LORD their God.

²²"Return, faithless people;
I will cure you of backsliding."

"Yes, we will come to you,
for you are the LORD our God.
²³Surely the idolatrous commotion on the hills
and mountains is a deception;
surely in the LORD our God
is the salvation of Israel.
²⁴From our youth shameful gods have consumed
the fruits of our fathers' labor—
their flocks and herds,
their sons and daughters.
²⁵Let us lie down in our shame,
and let our disgrace cover us.
We have sinned against the LORD our God,
both we and our fathers;
from our youth till this day
we have not obeyed the LORD our God."

4 "If you will return, O Israel,
return to me,"
declares the LORD.
"If you put your detestable idols out of my sight
and no longer go astray,

²and if in a truthful, just and righteous way
you swear, 'As surely as the LORD lives,'
then the nations will be blessed by him
and in him they will glory."

³This is what the LORD says to the men of Judah and to Jerusalem:

"Break up your unplowed ground
and do not sow among thorns.
⁴Circumcise yourselves to the LORD,
circumcise your hearts,
you men of Judah and people of Jerusalem,
or my wrath will break out and burn like fire
because of the evil you have done—
burn with no one to quench it.

Disaster From the North

⁵"Announce in Judah and proclaim in Jerusalem and say:
'Sound the trumpet throughout the land!'
Cry aloud and say:
'Gather together!
Let us flee to the fortified cities!'
⁶Raise the signal to go to Zion!
Flee for safety without delay!
For I am bringing disaster from the north,
even terrible destruction."

⁷A lion has come out of his lair;
a destroyer of nations has set out.
He has left his place
to lay waste your land.
Your towns will lie in ruins
without inhabitant.
⁸So put on sackcloth,
lament and wail,
for the fierce anger of the LORD
has not turned away from us.

⁹"In that day," declares the LORD,
"the king and the officials will lose heart,
the priests will be horrified,
and the prophets will be appalled."

¹⁰Then I said, "Ah, Sovereign LORD, how completely you have deceived this people and Jerusalem by saying, 'You will have peace,' when the sword is at our throats."

¹¹At that time this people and Jerusalem will be told, "A scorching wind from the barren heights in the desert blows toward my people, but not to winnow or

cleanse; [12]a wind too strong for that comes from me.[a] Now I pronounce my judgments against them."

[13]Look! He advances like the clouds,
    his chariots come like a whirlwind,
his horses are swifter than eagles.
    Woe to us! We are ruined!
[14]O Jerusalem, wash the evil from your
       heart and be saved.
    How long will you harbor wicked
       thoughts?
[15]A voice is announcing from Dan,
    proclaiming disaster from the hills
       of Ephraim.
[16]"Tell this to the nations,
    proclaim it to Jerusalem:
'A besieging army is coming from a
       distant land,
raising a war cry against the cities
       of Judah.
[17]They surround her like men guarding
       a field,
    because she has rebelled against
       me,'"
                       declares the LORD.
[18]"Your own conduct and actions
    have brought this upon you.
This is your punishment.
    How bitter it is!
    How it pierces to the heart!"

[19]Oh, my anguish, my anguish!
    I writhe in pain.
Oh, the agony of my heart!
    My heart pounds within me,
    I cannot keep silent.
For I have heard the sound of the
       trumpet;
    I have heard the battle cry.
[20]Disaster follows disaster;
    the whole land lies in ruins.
In an instant my tents are destroyed,
    my shelter in a moment.
[21]How long must I see the battle
       standard
    and hear the sound of the trumpet?

[22]"My people are fools;
    they do not know me.
They are senseless children;
    they have no understanding.
They are skilled in doing evil;
    they know not how to do good."

[23]I looked at the earth,
    and it was formless and empty;
and at the heavens,
    and their light was gone.
[24]I looked at the mountains,

and they were quaking;
    all the hills were swaying.
[25]I looked, and there were no people;
    every bird in the sky had flown
       away.
[26]I looked, and the fruitful land was a
       desert;
    all its towns lay in ruins
    before the LORD, before his fierce
       anger.

[27]This is what the LORD says:

"The whole land will be ruined,
    though I will not destroy it
       completely.
[28]Therefore the earth will mourn
    and the heavens above grow dark,
because I have spoken and will not
       relent,
    I have decided and will not turn
       back."

[29]At the sound of horsemen and archers
    every town takes to flight.
Some go into the thickets;
    some climb up among the rocks.
All the towns are deserted;
    no one lives in them.

[30]What are you doing, O devastated
       one?
    Why dress yourself in scarlet
    and put on jewels of gold?
Why shade your eyes with paint?
    You adorn yourself in vain.
Your lovers despise you;
    they seek your life.

[31]I hear a cry as of a woman in labor,
    a groan as of one bearing her first
       child—
the cry of the Daughter of Zion
    gasping for breath,
    stretching out her hands and
       saying,
"Alas! I am fainting;
    my life is given over to murderers."

Not One Is Upright

5 "Go up and down the streets of
       Jerusalem,
    look around and consider,
    search through her squares.
If you can find but one person
    who deals honestly and seeks the
       truth,
    I will forgive this city.
[2]Although they say, 'As surely as the
       LORD lives,'

---

[a]12 Or comes at my command

still they are swearing falsely."

³O LORD, do not your eyes look for
   truth?
You struck them, but they felt no
   pain;
you crushed them, but they refused
   correction.
They made their faces harder than
      stone
and refused to repent.
⁴I thought, "These are only the poor;
   they are foolish,
for they do not know the way of the
   LORD,
   the requirements of their God.
⁵So I will go to the leaders
   and speak to them;
surely they know the way of the LORD,
   the requirements of their God."
But with one accord they too had
   broken off the yoke
and torn off the bonds.
⁶Therefore a lion from the forest will
   attack them,
a wolf from the desert will ravage
   them,
a leopard will lie in wait near their
   towns
to tear to pieces any who venture
   out,
for their rebellion is great
   and their backslidings many.

⁷"Why should I forgive you?
Your children have forsaken me
   and sworn by gods that are not
      gods.
I supplied all their needs,
   yet they committed adultery
   and thronged to the houses of
      prostitutes.
⁸They are well-fed, lusty stallions,
   each neighing for another man's
      wife.
⁹Should I not punish them for this?"
   declares the LORD.
"Should I not avenge myself
   on such a nation as this?

¹⁰"Go through her vineyards and ravage
   them,
   but do not destroy them
      completely.
Strip off her branches,
   for these people do not belong to
      the LORD.
¹¹The house of Israel and the house of
      Judah
   have been utterly unfaithful to me,"
      declares the LORD.

¹²They have lied about the LORD;
   they said, "He will do nothing!
No harm will come to us;
   we will never see sword or famine.
¹³The prophets are but wind
   and the word is not in them;
   so let what they say be done to
      them."

¹⁴Therefore this is what the LORD God
Almighty says:

"Because the people have spoken
      these words,
   I will make my words in your
      mouth a fire
   and these people the wood it
      consumes.
¹⁵O house of Israel," declares the LORD,
"I am bringing a distant nation
      against you—
an ancient and enduring nation,
   a people whose language you do
      not know,
   whose speech you do not
      understand.
¹⁶Their quivers are like an open grave;
   all of them are mighty warriors.
¹⁷They will devour your harvests and
      food,
   devour your sons and daughters;
   they will devour your flocks and
      herds,
   devour your vines and fig trees.
With the sword they will destroy
   the fortified cities in which you
      trust.

¹⁸"Yet even in those days," declares the
LORD, "I will not destroy you completely.
¹⁹And when the people ask, 'Why has the
LORD our God done all this to us?' you will
tell them, 'As you have forsaken me and
served foreign gods in your own land, so
now you will serve foreigners in a land not
your own.'

²⁰"Announce this to the house of Jacob
   and proclaim it in Judah:
²¹Hear this, you foolish and senseless
      people,
   who have eyes but do not see,
   who have ears but do not hear:
²²Should you not fear me?" declares the
      LORD.
"Should you not tremble in my
      presence?
I made the sand a boundary for the
      sea,
   an everlasting barrier it cannot
      cross.

The waves may roll, but they cannot
    prevail;
  they may roar, but they cannot
    cross it.
23But these people have stubborn and
    rebellious hearts;
  they have turned aside and gone
    away.
24They do not say to themselves,
  'Let us fear the LORD our God,
who gives autumn and spring rains in
    season,
  who assures us of the regular weeks
    of harvest.'
25Your wrongdoings have kept these
    away;
  your sins have deprived you of
    good.

26"Among my people are wicked men
  who lie in wait like men who snare
    birds
  and like those who set traps to
    catch men.
27Like cages full of birds,
  their houses are full of deceit;
they have become rich and powerful
28 and have grown fat and sleek.
  Their evil deeds have no limit;
  they do not plead the case of the
    fatherless to win it,
  they do not defend the rights of the
    poor.
29Should I not punish them for this?"
    declares the LORD.
  "Should I not avenge myself
    on such a nation as this?

30"A horrible and shocking thing
  has happened in the land:
31The prophets prophesy lies,
  the priests rule by their own
    authority,
and my people love it this way.
  But what will you do in the end?

Jerusalem Under Siege

6 "Flee for safety, people of
    Benjamin!
  Flee from Jerusalem!
Sound the trumpet in Tekoa!
  Raise the signal over Beth
    Hakkerem!
For disaster looms out of the north,
  even terrible destruction.
2I will destroy the Daughter of Zion,
  so beautiful and delicate.
3Shepherds with their flocks will come
    against her;

they will pitch their tents around
    her,
  each tending his own portion."

4"Prepare for battle against her!
  Arise, let us attack at noon!
But, alas, the daylight is fading,
  and the shadows of evening grow
    long.
5So arise, let us attack at night
  and destroy her fortresses!"

6This is what the LORD Almighty says:

"Cut down the trees
  and build siege ramps against
    Jerusalem.
This city must be punished;
  it is filled with oppression.
7As a well pours out its water,
  so she pours out her wickedness.
Violence and destruction resound in
    her;
  her sickness and wounds are ever
    before me.
8Take warning, O Jerusalem,
  or I will turn away from you
and make your land desolate
  so no one can live in it."

9This is what the LORD Almighty says:

"Let them glean the remnant of Israel
  as thoroughly as a vine;
pass your hand over the branches
    again,
  like one gathering grapes."

10To whom can I speak and give
    warning?
  Who will listen to me?
Their ears are closed[a]
  so they cannot hear.
The word of the LORD is offensive to
    them;
  they find no pleasure in it.
11But I am full of the wrath of the
    LORD,
  and I cannot hold it in.

"Pour it out on the children in the
    street
  and on the young men gathered
    together;
both husband and wife will be caught
    in it,
  and the old, those weighed down
    with years.
12Their houses will be turned over to
    others,

_____
a10 Hebrew *uncircumcised*

together with their fields and their wives,
when I stretch out my hand
against those who live in the land,"
declares the LORD.
¹³"From the least to the greatest,
all are greedy for gain;
prophets and priests alike,
all practice deceit.
¹⁴They dress the wound of my people
as though it were not serious.
'Peace, peace,' they say,
when there is no peace.
¹⁵Are they ashamed of their loathsome conduct?
No, they have no shame at all;
they do not even know how to blush.
So they will fall among the fallen;
they will be brought down when I punish them,"
says the LORD.

¹⁶This is what the LORD says:

"Stand at the crossroads and look;
ask for the ancient paths,
ask where the good way is, and walk in it,
and you will find rest for your souls.
But you said, 'We will not walk in it.'
¹⁷I appointed watchmen over you and said,
'Listen to the sound of the trumpet!'
But you said, 'We will not listen.'
¹⁸Therefore hear, O nations;
observe, O witnesses,
what will happen to them.
¹⁹Hear, O earth:
I am bringing disaster on this people,
the fruit of their schemes,
because they have not listened to my words
and have rejected my law.
²⁰What do I care about incense from Sheba
or sweet calamus from a distant land?
Your burnt offerings are not acceptable;
your sacrifices do not please me."

²¹Therefore this is what the LORD says:

"I will put obstacles before this people.
Fathers and sons alike will stumble over them;
neighbors and friends will perish."

²²This is what the LORD says:

"Look, an army is coming
from the land of the north;
a great nation is being stirred up
from the ends of the earth.
²³They are armed with bow and spear;
they are cruel and show no mercy.
They sound like the roaring sea
as they ride on their horses;
they come like men in battle formation
to attack you, O Daughter of Zion."

²⁴We have heard reports about them,
and our hands hang limp.
Anguish has gripped us,
pain like that of a woman in labor.
²⁵Do not go out to the fields
or walk on the roads,
for the enemy has a sword,
and there is terror on every side.
²⁶O my people, put on sackcloth
and roll in ashes;
mourn with bitter wailing
as for an only son,
for suddenly the destroyer
will come upon us.

²⁷"I have made you a tester of metals
and my people the ore,
that you may observe
and test their ways.
²⁸They are all hardened rebels,
going about to slander.
They are bronze and iron;
they all act corruptly.
²⁹The bellows blow fiercely
to burn away the lead with fire,
but the refining goes on in vain;
the wicked are not purged out.
³⁰They are called rejected silver,
because the LORD has rejected them."

False Religion Worthless

7 This is the word that came to Jeremiah from the LORD: ²"Stand at the gate of the LORD's house and there proclaim this message:

" 'Hear the word of the LORD, all you people of Judah who come through these gates to worship the LORD. ³This is what the LORD Almighty, the God of Israel, says: Reform your ways and your actions, and I will let you live in this place. ⁴Do not trust in deceptive words and say, "This is the temple of the LORD, the temple of the LORD, the temple of the LORD!" ⁵If you really change your ways and your actions and deal with each other justly, ⁶if you do not oppress the alien, the fatherless or the widow and do not shed innocent blood in this place, and if you do not follow other gods to your own harm, [7]then I will let you live in this place, in the land I gave your forefathers for ever and ever. [8]But look, you are trusting in deceptive words that are worthless.

[9]" 'Will you steal and murder, commit adultery and perjury,[a] burn incense to Baal and follow other gods you have not known, [10]and then come and stand before me in this house, which bears my Name, and say, "We are safe"—safe to do all these detestable things? [11]Has this house, which bears my Name, become a den of robbers to you? But I have been watching! declares the LORD.

[12]" 'Go now to the place in Shiloh where I first made a dwelling for my Name, and see what I did to it because of the wickedness of my people Israel. [13]While you were doing all these things, declares the LORD, I spoke to you again and again, but you did not listen; I called you, but you did not answer. [14]Therefore, what I did to Shiloh I will now do to the house that bears my Name, the temple you trust in, the place I gave to you and your fathers. [15]I will thrust you from my presence, just as I did all your brothers, the people of Ephraim.'

[a]9 Or *and swear by false gods*

WEDNESDAY

VERSE FOR THE DAY:	*AUTHOR:*	*PASSAGE FOR THE DAY:*
Jeremiah 6:16	Gigi Graham Tchividjian	Jeremiah 6:9–20

Wearily, Wearily I Say Unto You

ON a day when I was feeling particularly tired, I decided to look up the word *weariness* in *Webster's Dictionary*. The definition read: "Worn out in strength, endurance, vigor or freshness. Having one's patience, tolerance, or pleasure exhausted."

It almost sounds as if Webster were describing a busy mother, doesn't it? And with a large family and all that goes with such a lifestyle, it is not unusual for me to find myself in this state. But weariness is not always limited to the physical. I often find that my emotions and my spirit suffer as well.

The world is full of weary people. Many are beaten down by worry, disappointment and despair. Some find so little meaning in their lives that they wonder why they are existing. Others are simply bored to death. Still others are frustrated spiritually because of moral defeats, weary of struggling with their heavy burden of guilt.

Christians are not immune to weariness, either external or internal. But the difference is that we know to whom to go (Jesus Christ) and where to go (his Word) for much-needed rest and refreshment.

Long ago Jesus said, "Come with me by yourselves to a quiet place and get some rest" (Mark 6:31). The rest that Christ gives is real and can be yours and mine.

Additional Scripture Readings:
Isaiah 40:28–31; Matthew 11:28–30

Go to page 813 for your next devotional reading.

16"So do not pray for this people nor offer any plea or petition for them; do not plead with me, for I will not listen to you. 17Do you not see what they are doing in the towns of Judah and in the streets of Jerusalem? 18The children gather wood, the fathers light the fire, and the women knead the dough and make cakes of bread for the Queen of Heaven. They pour out drink offerings to other gods to provoke me to anger. 19But am I the one they are provoking? declares the LORD. Are they not rather harming themselves, to their own shame?

20" 'Therefore this is what the Sovereign LORD says: My anger and my wrath will be poured out on this place, on man and beast, on the trees of the field and on the fruit of the ground, and it will burn and not be quenched.

21" 'This is what the LORD Almighty, the God of Israel, says: Go ahead, add your burnt offerings to your other sacrifices and eat the meat yourselves! 22For when I brought your forefathers out of Egypt and spoke to them, I did not just give them commands about burnt offerings and sacrifices, 23but I gave them this command: Obey me, and I will be your God and you will be my people. Walk in all the ways I command you, that it may go well with you. 24But they did not listen or pay attention; instead, they followed the stubborn inclinations of their evil hearts. They went backward and not forward. 25From the time your forefathers left Egypt until now, day after day, again and again I sent you my servants the prophets. 26But they did not listen to me or pay attention. They were stiff-necked and did more evil than their forefathers.'

27"When you tell them all this, they will not listen to you; when you call to them, they will not answer. 28Therefore say to them, 'This is the nation that has not obeyed the LORD its God or responded to correction. Truth has perished; it has vanished from their lips. 29Cut off your hair and throw it away; take up a lament on the barren heights, for the LORD has rejected and abandoned this generation that is under his wrath.

The Valley of Slaughter

30" 'The people of Judah have done evil in my eyes, declares the LORD. They have set up their detestable idols in the house that bears my Name and have defiled it. 31They have built the high places of Topheth in the Valley of Ben Hinnom to burn their sons and daughters in the fire —something I did not command, nor did it enter my mind. 32So beware, the days are coming, declares the LORD, when people will no longer call it Topheth or the Valley of Ben Hinnom, but the Valley of Slaughter, for they will bury the dead in Topheth until there is no more room. 33Then the carcasses of this people will become food for the birds of the air and the beasts of the earth, and there will be no one to frighten them away. 34I will bring an end to the sounds of joy and gladness and to the voices of bride and bridegroom in the towns of Judah and the streets of Jerusalem, for the land will become desolate.

8 " 'At that time, declares the LORD, the bones of the kings and officials of Judah, the bones of the priests and prophets, and the bones of the people of Jerusalem will be removed from their graves. 2They will be exposed to the sun and the moon and all the stars of the heavens, which they have loved and served and which they have followed and consulted and worshiped. They will not be gathered up or buried, but will be like refuse lying on the ground. 3Wherever I banish them, all the survivors of this evil nation will prefer death to life, declares the LORD Almighty.'

Sin and Punishment

4"Say to them, 'This is what the LORD says:

" 'When men fall down, do they not
  get up?
When a man turns away, does he
  not return?
5Why then have these people turned
  away?
Why does Jerusalem always turn
  away?
They cling to deceit;
  they refuse to return.
6I have listened attentively,
  but they do not say what is right.
No one repents of his wickedness,
  saying, "What have I done?"
Each pursues his own course
  like a horse charging into battle.
7Even the stork in the sky
  knows her appointed seasons,
and the dove, the swift and the
  thrush
  observe the time of their migration.
But my people do not know
  the requirements of the LORD.

8" 'How can you say, "We are wise,
  for we have the law of the LORD,"
when actually the lying pen of the
    scribes
  has handled it falsely?
9The wise will be put to shame;
  they will be dismayed and trapped.
Since they have rejected the word of
    the LORD,
  what kind of wisdom do they have?
10Therefore I will give their wives to
    other men
  and their fields to new owners.
From the least to the greatest,
  all are greedy for gain;
prophets and priests alike,
  all practice deceit.
11They dress the wound of my people
  as though it were not serious.
"Peace, peace," they say,
  when there is no peace.
12Are they ashamed of their loathsome
    conduct?
No, they have no shame at all;
  they do not even know how to
    blush.
So they will fall among the fallen;
  they will be brought down when
    they are punished,
                    says the LORD.

13" 'I will take away their harvest,
                  declares the LORD.
There will be no grapes on the vine.
There will be no figs on the tree,
  and their leaves will wither.
What I have given them
  will be taken from them.a' "

14"Why are we sitting here?
  Gather together!
Let us flee to the fortified cities
  and perish there!
For the LORD our God has doomed us
    to perish
  and given us poisoned water to
    drink,
  because we have sinned against
    him.
15We hoped for peace
  but no good has come,
for a time of healing
  but there was only terror.
16The snorting of the enemy's horses
  is heard from Dan;
at the neighing of their stallions
  the whole land trembles.
They have come to devour

the land and everything in it,
  the city and all who live there."

17"See, I will send venomous snakes
    among you,
  vipers that cannot be charmed,
  and they will bite you,"
                  declares the LORD.

18O my Comforterb in sorrow,
  my heart is faint within me.
19Listen to the cry of my people
  from a land far away:
"Is the LORD not in Zion?
  Is her King no longer there?"

"Why have they provoked me to anger
    with their images,
  with their worthless foreign idols?"

20"The harvest is past,
  the summer has ended,
  and we are not saved."

21Since my people are crushed, I am
    crushed;
  I mourn, and horror grips me.
22Is there no balm in Gilead?
  Is there no physician there?
Why then is there no healing
  for the wound of my people?

9 1Oh, that my head were a spring of
    water
  and my eyes a fountain of tears!
I would weep day and night
  for the slain of my people.
2Oh, that I had in the desert
  a lodging place for travelers,
so that I might leave my people
  and go away from them;
for they are all adulterers,
  a crowd of unfaithful people.

3"They make ready their tongue
  like a bow, to shoot lies;
it is not by truth
  that they triumphc in the land.
They go from one sin to another;
  they do not acknowledge me,"
                  declares the LORD.
4"Beware of your friends;
  do not trust your brothers.
For every brother is a deceiver,d
  and every friend a slanderer.
5Friend deceives friend,
  and no one speaks the truth.
They have taught their tongues to lie;
  they weary themselves with sinning.

a13 The meaning of the Hebrew for this sentence is uncertain.   b18 The meaning of the Hebrew for
this word is uncertain.   c3 Or lies; / they are not valiant for truth   d4 Or a deceiving Jacob

⁶You*a* live in the midst of deception;
  in their deceit they refuse to
    acknowledge me,"
              declares the LORD.

⁷Therefore this is what the LORD Almighty says:

"See, I will refine and test them,
  for what else can I do
  because of the sin of my people?
⁸Their tongue is a deadly arrow;
  it speaks with deceit.
With his mouth each speaks cordially
    to his neighbor,
  but in his heart he sets a trap for
    him.
⁹Should I not punish them for this?"
  declares the LORD.
"Should I not avenge myself
  on such a nation as this?"

¹⁰I will weep and wail for the
    mountains
  and take up a lament concerning
    the desert pastures.
They are desolate and untraveled,
  and the lowing of cattle is not
    heard.
The birds of the air have fled
  and the animals are gone.

¹¹"I will make Jerusalem a heap of
    ruins,
  a haunt of jackals;
and I will lay waste the towns of
    Judah
  so no one can live there."

¹²What man is wise enough to understand this? Who has been instructed by the LORD and can explain it? Why has the land been ruined and laid waste like a desert that no one can cross?

¹³The LORD said, "It is because they have forsaken my law, which I set before them; they have not obeyed me or followed my law. ¹⁴Instead, they have followed the stubbornness of their hearts; they have followed the Baals, as their fathers taught them." ¹⁵Therefore, this is what the LORD Almighty, the God of Israel, says: "See, I will make this people eat bitter food and drink poisoned water. ¹⁶I will scatter them among nations that neither they nor their fathers have known, and I will pursue them with the sword until I have destroyed them."

¹⁷This is what the LORD Almighty says:

"Consider now! Call for the wailing
    women to come;
  send for the most skillful of them.
¹⁸Let them come quickly
  and wail over us
till our eyes overflow with tears
  and water streams from our eyelids.
¹⁹The sound of wailing is heard from
    Zion:
'How ruined we are!
  How great is our shame!
We must leave our land
  because our houses are in ruins.'"

²⁰Now, O women, hear the word of the
    LORD;
  open your ears to the words of his
    mouth.
Teach your daughters how to wail;
  teach one another a lament.
²¹Death has climbed in through our
    windows
  and has entered our fortresses;
it has cut off the children from the
    streets
  and the young men from the public
    squares.

²²Say, "This is what the LORD declares:

"'The dead bodies of men will lie
  like refuse on the open field,
like cut grain behind the reaper,
  with no one to gather them.'"

²³This is what the LORD says:

"Let not the wise man boast of his
    wisdom
  or the strong man boast of his
    strength
  or the rich man boast of his riches,
²⁴but let him who boasts boast about
    this:
  that he understands and knows me,
that I am the LORD, who exercises
    kindness,
  justice and righteousness on earth,
  for in these I delight,"
              declares the LORD.

²⁵"The days are coming," declares the LORD, "when I will punish all who are circumcised only in the flesh— ²⁶Egypt, Judah, Edom, Ammon, Moab and all who live in the desert in distant places.*b* For all these nations are really uncircumcised, and even the whole house of Israel is uncircumcised in heart."

a6 That is, Jeremiah (the Hebrew is singular)   *b26* Or *desert and who clip the hair by their foreheads*

God and Idols

10 Hear what the LORD says to you, O house of Israel. ²This is what the LORD says:

"Do not learn the ways of the nations
  or be terrified by signs in the sky,
  though the nations are terrified by
  them.
³For the customs of the peoples are
  worthless;
  they cut a tree out of the forest,
and a craftsman shapes it with his
  chisel.
⁴They adorn it with silver and gold;
  they fasten it with hammer and
  nails
so it will not totter.
⁵Like a scarecrow in a melon patch,
  their idols cannot speak;
they must be carried
  because they cannot walk.
Do not fear them;
  they can do no harm
  nor can they do any good."

THURSDAY

VERSE FOR THE DAY:
Jeremiah 9:24

AUTHOR:
Debby Boone

PASSAGE FOR THE DAY:
Jeremiah 9:23–24

Boast of This

I AM sure that a single day does not go by that I am not intimidated by another person's beauty, intelligence, talent or accomplishments. It usually surfaces as a strong tendency for me to be critical—an attitude that temporarily but effectively anesthetizes the gnawing pang of inadequacy. The only trouble is that my faultfinding does little except perpetuate my own insecurities, because I am convinced that I am the subject of similar ruthless comments by others.

This in turn leads to elaborate schemes for self-improvement—the latest diet plans, new and more complicated exercise routines, classes to nurture untapped talents, and lists of books to buy. And like trying to use one of those large inflatable pool toys, if I'm not too discouraged just at the thought of having to blow the thing up, I am certainly too tired to enjoy it after I'm done.

What an oppressive existence to live our lives trying to please one another! Then, as I read and reread Jeremiah 9:23–24, the Lord's gentle voice reminds me that what is important is not what I am or can attain, but who I know him to be in and through me. A light goes on in my little brain, priorities take shape, and the weight of this backward world is lifted off my shoulders.

We need to understand the Lord as our most worthy pursuit. Let's thank him for transforming us into his beautiful likeness and for delivering us from a stubborn struggle to align ourselves to a fading culture.

Additional Scripture Readings:
Romans 12:1–3; 2 Corinthians 12:6–10

Go to page 822 for your next devotional reading.

⁶No one is like you, O LORD;
  you are great,
  and your name is mighty in power.
⁷Who should not revere you,
  O King of the nations?
  This is your due.
Among all the wise men of the
    nations
  and in all their kingdoms,
  there is no one like you.
⁸They are all senseless and foolish;
  they are taught by worthless
    wooden idols.
⁹Hammered silver is brought from
    Tarshish
  and gold from Uphaz.
What the craftsman and goldsmith
    have made
  is then dressed in blue and
    purple—
  all made by skilled workers.
¹⁰But the LORD is the true God;
  he is the living God, the eternal
    King.
When he is angry, the earth trembles;
  the nations cannot endure his
    wrath.

¹¹"Tell them this: 'These gods, who did
not make the heavens and the earth, will
perish from the earth and from under the
heavens.' "ᵃ

¹²But God made the earth by his power;
  he founded the world by his
    wisdom
  and stretched out the heavens by
    his understanding.
¹³When he thunders, the waters in the
    heavens roar;
  he makes clouds rise from the ends
    of the earth.
He sends lightning with the rain
  and brings out the wind from his
    storehouses.
¹⁴Everyone is senseless and without
    knowledge;
  every goldsmith is shamed by his
    idols.
His images are a fraud;
  they have no breath in them.
¹⁵They are worthless, the objects of
    mockery;
  when their judgment comes, they
    will perish.
¹⁶He who is the Portion of Jacob is not
    like these,
  for he is the Maker of all things,

including Israel, the tribe of his
    inheritance—
  the LORD Almighty is his name.

Coming Destruction

¹⁷Gather up your belongings to leave
    the land,
  you who live under siege.
¹⁸For this is what the LORD says:
  "At this time I will hurl out
    those who live in this land;
  I will bring distress on them
    so that they may be captured."

¹⁹Woe to me because of my injury!
  My wound is incurable!
Yet I said to myself,
  "This is my sickness, and I must
    endure it."
²⁰My tent is destroyed;
  all its ropes are snapped.
My sons are gone from me and are no
    more;
  no one is left now to pitch my tent
  or to set up my shelter.
²¹The shepherds are senseless
  and do not inquire of the LORD;
so they do not prosper
  and all their flock is scattered.
²²Listen! The report is coming—
  a great commotion from the land of
    the north!
It will make the towns of Judah
    desolate,
  a haunt of jackals.

Jeremiah's Prayer

²³I know, O LORD, that a man's life is
    not his own;
  it is not for man to direct his steps.
²⁴Correct me, LORD, but only with
    justice—
  not in your anger,
    lest you reduce me to nothing.
²⁵Pour out your wrath on the nations
    that do not acknowledge you,
  on the peoples who do not call on
    your name.
For they have devoured Jacob;
  they have devoured him completely
  and destroyed his homeland.

The Covenant Is Broken

11 This is the word that came to Jeremiah from the LORD: ²"Listen to the terms of this covenant and tell them to the people of Judah and to those who live in Jerusalem. ³Tell them that this is

ᵃ11 The text of this verse is in Aramaic.

what the LORD, the God of Israel, says: 'Cursed is the man who does not obey the terms of this covenant— ⁴the terms I commanded your forefathers when I brought them out of Egypt, out of the iron-smelting furnace.' I said, 'Obey me and do everything I command you, and you will be my people, and I will be your God. ⁵Then I will fulfill the oath I swore to your forefathers, to give them a land flowing with milk and honey'—the land you possess today."

I answered, "Amen, LORD."

⁶The LORD said to me, "Proclaim all these words in the towns of Judah and in the streets of Jerusalem: 'Listen to the terms of this covenant and follow them. ⁷From the time I brought your forefathers up from Egypt until today, I warned them again and again, saying, "Obey me." ⁸But they did not listen or pay attention; instead, they followed the stubbornness of their evil hearts. So I brought on them all the curses of the covenant I had commanded them to follow but that they did not keep.' "

⁹Then the LORD said to me, "There is a conspiracy among the people of Judah and those who live in Jerusalem. ¹⁰They have returned to the sins of their forefathers, who refused to listen to my words. They have followed other gods to serve them. Both the house of Israel and the house of Judah have broken the covenant I made with their forefathers. ¹¹Therefore this is what the LORD says: 'I will bring on them a disaster they cannot escape. Although they cry out to me, I will not listen to them. ¹²The towns of Judah and the people of Jerusalem will go and cry out to the gods to whom they burn incense, but they will not help them at all when disaster strikes. ¹³You have as many gods as you have towns, O Judah; and the altars you have set up to burn incense to that shameful god Baal are as many as the streets of Jerusalem.'

¹⁴"Do not pray for this people nor offer any plea or petition for them, because I will not listen when they call to me in the time of their distress.

¹⁵"What is my beloved doing in my temple
as she works out her evil schemes with many?
Can consecrated meat avert ˪your punishment˺?

When you engage in your wickedness,
then you rejoice.ᵃ "
¹⁶The LORD called you a thriving olive tree
with fruit beautiful in form.
But with the roar of a mighty storm
he will set it on fire,
and its branches will be broken.

¹⁷The LORD Almighty, who planted you, has decreed disaster for you, because the house of Israel and the house of Judah have done evil and provoked me to anger by burning incense to Baal.

Plot Against Jeremiah

¹⁸Because the LORD revealed their plot to me, I knew it, for at that time he showed me what they were doing. ¹⁹I had been like a gentle lamb led to the slaughter; I did not realize that they had plotted against me, saying,

"Let us destroy the tree and its fruit;
let us cut him off from the land of the living,
that his name be remembered no more."
²⁰But, O LORD Almighty, you who judge righteously
and test the heart and mind,
let me see your vengeance upon them,
for to you I have committed my cause.

²¹"Therefore this is what the LORD says about the men of Anathoth who are seeking your life and saying, 'Do not prophesy in the name of the LORD or you will die by our hands'— ²²therefore this is what the LORD Almighty says: 'I will punish them. Their young men will die by the sword, their sons and daughters by famine. ²³Not even a remnant will be left to them, because I will bring disaster on the men of Anathoth in the year of their punishment.' "

Jeremiah's Complaint

12 You are always righteous,
O LORD,
when I bring a case before you.
Yet I would speak with you about your justice:
Why does the way of the wicked prosper?
Why do all the faithless live at ease?

ᵃ15 Or *Could consecrated meat avert your punishment? / Then you would rejoice*

²You have planted them, and they
  have taken root;
they grow and bear fruit.
You are always on their lips
  but far from their hearts.
³Yet you know me, O LORD;
  you see me and test my thoughts
    about you.
Drag them off like sheep to be
  butchered!
Set them apart for the day of
  slaughter!
⁴How long will the land lie parched*ᵃ*
  and the grass in every field be
    withered?
Because those who live in it are
  wicked,
  the animals and birds have
    perished.
Moreover, the people are saying,
  "He will not see what happens to
    us."

God's Answer

⁵"If you have raced with men on foot
  and they have worn you out,
  how can you compete with horses?
If you stumble in safe country,*ᵇ*
  how will you manage in the
    thickets by*ᶜ* the Jordan?
⁶Your brothers, your own family—
  even they have betrayed you;
  they have raised a loud cry against
    you.
Do not trust them,
  though they speak well of you.

⁷"I will forsake my house,
  abandon my inheritance;
I will give the one I love
  into the hands of her enemies.
⁸My inheritance has become to me
  like a lion in the forest.
She roars at me;
  therefore I hate her.
⁹Has not my inheritance become to
  me
  like a speckled bird of prey
  that other birds of prey surround
    and attack?
Go and gather all the wild beasts;
  bring them to devour.
¹⁰Many shepherds will ruin my vineyard
  and trample down my field;
they will turn my pleasant field
  into a desolate wasteland.
¹¹It will be made a wasteland,
  parched and desolate before me;

the whole land will be laid waste
  because there is no one who cares.
¹²Over all the barren heights in the
  desert
  destroyers will swarm,
for the sword of the LORD will devour
  from one end of the land to the
    other;
  no one will be safe.
¹³They will sow wheat but reap thorns;
  they will wear themselves out but
    gain nothing.
So bear the shame of your harvest
  because of the LORD's fierce anger."

¹⁴This is what the LORD says: "As for all
my wicked neighbors who seize the inheritance I gave my people Israel, I will uproot them from their lands and I will uproot the house of Judah from among
them. ¹⁵But after I uproot them, I will
again have compassion and will bring
each of them back to his own inheritance
and his own country. ¹⁶And if they learn
well the ways of my people and swear by
my name, saying, 'As surely as the LORD
lives'—even as they once taught my people to swear by Baal—then they will be
established among my people. ¹⁷But if
any nation does not listen, I will completely uproot and destroy it," declares
the LORD.

A Linen Belt

13 This is what the LORD said to me:
"Go and buy a linen belt and put it
around your waist, but do not let it touch
water." ²So I bought a belt, as the LORD
directed, and put it around my waist.

³Then the word of the LORD came to me
a second time: ⁴"Take the belt you
bought and are wearing around your
waist, and go now to Perath*ᵈ* and hide it
there in a crevice in the rocks." ⁵So I went
and hid it at Perath, as the LORD told me.

⁶Many days later the LORD said to me,
"Go now to Perath and get the belt I told
you to hide there." ⁷So I went to Perath
and dug up the belt and took it from the
place where I had hidden it, but now it
was ruined and completely useless.

⁸Then the word of the LORD came to me:
⁹"This is what the LORD says: 'In the same
way I will ruin the pride of Judah and the
great pride of Jerusalem. ¹⁰These wicked
people, who refuse to listen to my words,
who follow the stubbornness of their

ᵃ4 Or *land mourn*   *ᵇ5* Or *If you put your trust in a land of safety*   *ᶜ5* Or *the flooding of*   *ᵈ4* Or
possibly *the Euphrates*; also in verses 5-7

hearts and go after other gods to serve and worship them, will be like this belt—completely useless! ¹¹For as a belt is bound around a man's waist, so I bound the whole house of Israel and the whole house of Judah to me,' declares the LORD, 'to be my people for my renown and praise and honor. But they have not listened.'

Wineskins

¹²"Say to them: 'This is what the LORD, the God of Israel, says: Every wineskin should be filled with wine.' And if they say to you, 'Don't we know that every wineskin should be filled with wine?' ¹³then tell them, 'This is what the LORD says: I am going to fill with drunkenness all who live in this land, including the kings who sit on David's throne, the priests, the prophets and all those living in Jerusalem. ¹⁴I will smash them one against the other, fathers and sons alike, declares the LORD. I will allow no pity or mercy or compassion to keep me from destroying them.' "

Threat of Captivity

¹⁵Hear and pay attention,
    do not be arrogant,
    for the LORD has spoken.
¹⁶Give glory to the LORD your God
    before he brings the darkness,
before your feet stumble
    on the darkening hills.
You hope for light,
    but he will turn it to thick darkness
    and change it to deep gloom.
¹⁷But if you do not listen,
    I will weep in secret
    because of your pride;
my eyes will weep bitterly,
    overflowing with tears,
    because the LORD's flock will be
        taken captive.

¹⁸Say to the king and to the queen
        mother,
    "Come down from your thrones,
for your glorious crowns
    will fall from your heads."
¹⁹The cities in the Negev will be shut
        up,
    and there will be no one to open
        them.
All Judah will be carried into exile,
    carried completely away.

²⁰Lift up your eyes and see
    those who are coming from the
        north.
Where is the flock that was entrusted
        to you,
    the sheep of which you boasted?
²¹What will you say when ‚the LORD‚ sets
        over you
    those you cultivated as your special
        allies?
Will not pain grip you
    like that of a woman in labor?
²²And if you ask yourself,
    "Why has this happened to me?"—
it is because of your many sins
    that your skirts have been torn off
    and your body mistreated.
²³Can the Ethiopian*ᵃ* change his skin
    or the leopard its spots?
Neither can you do good
    who are accustomed to doing evil.

²⁴"I will scatter you like chaff
    driven by the desert wind.
²⁵This is your lot,
    the portion I have decreed for you,"
                declares the LORD,
"because you have forgotten me
    and trusted in false gods.
²⁶I will pull up your skirts over your
        face
    that your shame may be seen—
²⁷your adulteries and lustful neighings,
    your shameless prostitution!
I have seen your detestable acts
    on the hills and in the fields.
Woe to you, O Jerusalem!
    How long will you be unclean?"

Drought, Famine, Sword

14 This is the word of the LORD to Jeremiah concerning the drought:

²"Judah mourns,
    her cities languish;
they wail for the land,
    and a cry goes up from Jerusalem.
³The nobles send their servants for
        water;
    they go to the cisterns
    but find no water.
They return with their jars unfilled;
    dismayed and despairing,
    they cover their heads.
⁴The ground is cracked
    because there is no rain in the
        land;
    the farmers are dismayed
    and cover their heads.
⁵Even the doe in the field

ᵃ23 Hebrew *Cushite* (probably a person from the upper Nile region)

deserts her newborn fawn
because there is no grass.
⁶Wild donkeys stand on the barren
heights
and pant like jackals;
their eyesight fails
for lack of pasture."

⁷Although our sins testify against us,
O LORD, do something for the sake
of your name.
For our backsliding is great;
we have sinned against you.
⁸O Hope of Israel,
its Savior in times of distress,
why are you like a stranger in the
land,
like a traveler who stays only a
night?
⁹Why are you like a man taken by
surprise,
like a warrior powerless to save?
You are among us, O LORD,
and we bear your name;
do not forsake us!

¹⁰This is what the LORD says about this
people:

"They greatly love to wander;
they do not restrain their feet.
So the LORD does not accept them;
he will now remember their
wickedness
and punish them for their sins."

¹¹Then the LORD said to me, "Do not
pray for the well-being of this people.
¹²Although they fast, I will not listen to
their cry; though they offer burnt offerings and grain offerings, I will not accept
them. Instead, I will destroy them with
the sword, famine and plague."

¹³But I said, "Ah, Sovereign LORD, the
prophets keep telling them, 'You will not
see the sword or suffer famine. Indeed, I
will give you lasting peace in this place.' "

¹⁴Then the LORD said to me, "The
prophets are prophesying lies in my
name. I have not sent them or appointed
them or spoken to them. They are prophesying to you false visions, divinations,
idolatries*a* and the delusions of their own
minds. ¹⁵Therefore, this is what the LORD
says about the prophets who are prophesying in my name: I did not send them,
yet they are saying, 'No sword or famine
will touch this land.' Those same prophets will perish by sword and famine.
¹⁶And the people they are prophesying to

will be thrown out into the streets of Jerusalem because of the famine and sword.
There will be no one to bury them or their
wives, their sons or their daughters. I will
pour out on them the calamity they deserve.

¹⁷"Speak this word to them:

" 'Let my eyes overflow with tears
night and day without ceasing;
for my virgin daughter—my people—
has suffered a grievous wound,
a crushing blow.
¹⁸If I go into the country,
I see those slain by the sword;
if I go into the city,
I see the ravages of famine.
Both prophet and priest
have gone to a land they know
not.' "

¹⁹Have you rejected Judah completely?
Do you despise Zion?
Why have you afflicted us
so that we cannot be healed?
We hoped for peace
but no good has come,
for a time of healing
but there is only terror.
²⁰O LORD, we acknowledge our
wickedness
and the guilt of our fathers;
we have indeed sinned against you.
²¹For the sake of your name do not
despise us;
do not dishonor your glorious
throne.
Remember your covenant with us
and do not break it.
²²Do any of the worthless idols of the
nations bring rain?
Do the skies themselves send down
showers?
No, it is you, O LORD our God.
Therefore our hope is in you,
for you are the one who does all this.

15 Then the LORD said to me: "Even if
Moses and Samuel were to stand
before me, my heart would not go out to
this people. Send them away from my
presence! Let them go! ²And if they ask
you, 'Where shall we go?' tell them, 'This
is what the LORD says:

" 'Those destined for death, to death;
those for the sword, to the sword;
those for starvation, to starvation;
those for captivity, to captivity.'

---

a14 Or *visions, worthless divinations*

³"I will send four kinds of destroyers against them," declares the LORD, "the sword to kill and the dogs to drag away and the birds of the air and the beasts of the earth to devour and destroy. ⁴I will make them abhorrent to all the kingdoms of the earth because of what Manasseh son of Hezekiah king of Judah did in Jerusalem.

⁵"Who will have pity on you,
    O Jerusalem?
Who will mourn for you?
Who will stop to ask how you are?
⁶You have rejected me," declares the
    LORD.
"You keep on backsliding.
So I will lay hands on you and destroy
    you;
I can no longer show compassion.
⁷I will winnow them with a winnowing
    fork
    at the city gates of the land.
I will bring bereavement and
    destruction on my people,
    for they have not changed their
    ways.
⁸I will make their widows more
    numerous
    than the sand of the sea.
At midday I will bring a destroyer
    against the mothers of their young
    men;
suddenly I will bring down on them
    anguish and terror.
⁹The mother of seven will grow faint
    and breathe her last.
Her sun will set while it is still day;
    she will be disgraced and
    humiliated.
I will put the survivors to the sword
    before their enemies,"
                    declares the LORD.

¹⁰Alas, my mother, that you gave me
    birth,
    a man with whom the whole land
    strives and contends!
I have neither lent nor borrowed,
    yet everyone curses me.

¹¹The LORD said,

"Surely I will deliver you for a good
    purpose;
    surely I will make your enemies
    plead with you

in times of disaster and times of
    distress.

¹²"Can a man break iron—
    iron from the north—or bronze?

¹³Your wealth and your treasures
    I will give as plunder, without
    charge,
because of all your sins
    throughout your country.
¹⁴I will enslave you to your enemies
    inᵃ a land you do not know,
for my anger will kindle a fire
    that will burn against you."

¹⁵You understand, O LORD;
    remember me and care for me.
    Avenge me on my persecutors.
You are long-suffering—do not take
    me away;
    think of how I suffer reproach for
    your sake.
¹⁶When your words came, I ate them;
    they were my joy and my heart's
    delight,
for I bear your name,
    O LORD God Almighty.
¹⁷I never sat in the company of revelers,
    never made merry with them;
I sat alone because your hand was on
    me
    and you had filled me with
    indignation.
¹⁸Why is my pain unending
    and my wound grievous and
    incurable?
Will you be to me like a deceptive
    brook,
    like a spring that fails?

¹⁹Therefore this is what the LORD says:

"If you repent, I will restore you
    that you may serve me;
if you utter worthy, not worthless,
    words,
    you will be my spokesman.
Let this people turn to you,
    but you must not turn to them.
²⁰I will make you a wall to this people,
    a fortified wall of bronze;
they will fight against you
    but will not overcome you,
for I am with you
    to rescue and save you,"
                    declares the LORD.
²¹"I will save you from the hands of the
    wicked

ᵃ14 Some Hebrew manuscripts, Septuagint and Syriac (see also Jer. 17:4); most Hebrew manuscripts *I will cause your enemies to bring you / into*

and redeem you from the grasp of
the cruel."

Day of Disaster

16 Then the word of the Lord came to
me: ²"You must not marry and
have sons or daughters in this place."
³For this is what the Lord says about the
sons and daughters born in this land and
about the women who are their mothers
and the men who are their fathers: ⁴"They
will die of deadly diseases. They will not
be mourned or buried but will be like refuse lying on the ground. They will perish
by sword and famine, and their dead bodies will become food for the birds of the
air and the beasts of the earth."

⁵For this is what the Lord says: "Do not
enter a house where there is a funeral
meal; do not go to mourn or show sympathy, because I have withdrawn my blessing, my love and my pity from this people," declares the Lord. ⁶"Both high and
low will die in this land. They will not be
buried or mourned, and no one will cut
himself or shave his head for them. ⁷No
one will offer food to comfort those who
mourn for the dead—not even for a father
or a mother—nor will anyone give them a
drink to console them.

⁸"And do not enter a house where there
is feasting and sit down to eat and drink.
⁹For this is what the Lord Almighty, the
God of Israel, says: Before your eyes and
in your days I will bring an end to the
sounds of joy and gladness and to the
voices of bride and bridegroom in this
place.

¹⁰"When you tell these people all this
and they ask you, 'Why has the Lord decreed such a great disaster against us?
What wrong have we done? What sin have
we committed against the Lord our God?'
¹¹then say to them, 'It is because your fathers forsook me,' declares the Lord, 'and
followed other gods and served and worshiped them. They forsook me and did
not keep my law. ¹²But you have behaved
more wickedly than your fathers. See how
each of you is following the stubbornness
of his evil heart instead of obeying me.
¹³So I will throw you out of this land into
a land neither you nor your fathers have
known, and there you will serve other
gods day and night, for I will show you no
favor.'

¹⁴"However, the days are coming," declares the Lord, "when men will no longer
say, 'As surely as the Lord lives, who
brought the Israelites up out of Egypt,'
¹⁵but they will say, 'As surely as the Lord
lives, who brought the Israelites up out of
the land of the north and out of all the
countries where he had banished them.'
For I will restore them to the land I gave
their forefathers.

¹⁶"But now I will send for many fishermen," declares the Lord, "and they will
catch them. After that I will send for
many hunters, and they will hunt them
down on every mountain and hill and
from the crevices of the rocks. ¹⁷My eyes
are on all their ways; they are not hidden
from me, nor is their sin concealed from
my eyes. ¹⁸I will repay them double for
their wickedness and their sin, because
they have defiled my land with the lifeless
forms of their vile images and have filled
my inheritance with their detestable
idols."

¹⁹O Lord, my strength and my fortress,
　　my refuge in time of distress,
to you the nations will come
　　from the ends of the earth and say,
"Our fathers possessed nothing but
　　　false gods,
　　worthless idols that did them no
　　　good.
²⁰Do men make their own gods?
　　Yes, but they are not gods!"

²¹"Therefore I will teach them—
　　this time I will teach them
　　my power and might.
Then they will know
　　that my name is the Lord.

17 "Judah's sin is engraved with an
iron tool,
　　inscribed with a flint point,
on the tablets of their hearts
　　and on the horns of their altars.
²Even their children remember
　　their altars and Asherah poles ᵃ
beside the spreading trees
　　and on the high hills.
³My mountain in the land
　　and your ᵇ wealth and all your
　　　treasures
I will give away as plunder,
　　together with your high places,
　　because of sin throughout your
　　　country.
⁴Through your own fault you will lose
　　the inheritance I gave you.
I will enslave you to your enemies

ᵃ2 That is, symbols of the goddess Asherah　　ᵇ2,3 Or hills / ³and the mountains of the land. / Your

in a land you do not know,
for you have kindled my anger,
　　and it will burn forever."

⁵This is what the LORD says:

"Cursed is the one who trusts in man,
　　who depends on flesh for his
　　　strength
　　and whose heart turns away from
　　　the LORD.
⁶He will be like a bush in the
　　wastelands;
　　he will not see prosperity when it
　　　comes.
He will dwell in the parched places of
　　the desert,
　　in a salt land where no one lives.

⁷"But blessed is the man who trusts in
　　the LORD,
　　whose confidence is in him.
⁸He will be like a tree planted by the
　　water
　　that sends out its roots by the
　　　stream.
It does not fear when heat comes;
　　its leaves are always green.
It has no worries in a year of drought
　　and never fails to bear fruit."

⁹The heart is deceitful above all things
　　and beyond cure.
　　Who can understand it?

¹⁰"I the LORD search the heart
　　and examine the mind,
to reward a man according to his
　　conduct,
　　according to what his deeds
　　　deserve."

¹¹Like a partridge that hatches eggs it
　　did not lay
　　is the man who gains riches by
　　　unjust means.
When his life is half gone, they will
　　desert him,
　　and in the end he will prove to be a
　　　fool.

¹²A glorious throne, exalted from the
　　beginning,
　　is the place of our sanctuary.
¹³O LORD, the hope of Israel,
　　all who forsake you will be put to
　　　shame.
Those who turn away from you will be
　　written in the dust
because they have forsaken the
　　LORD,
　　the spring of living water.

¹⁴Heal me, O LORD, and I will be
　　healed;
save me and I will be saved,
　　for you are the one I praise.
¹⁵They keep saying to me,
　　"Where is the word of the LORD?
　　Let it now be fulfilled!"
¹⁶I have not run away from being your
　　shepherd;
you know I have not desired the
　　day of despair.
What passes my lips is open before
　　you.
¹⁷Do not be a terror to me;
　　you are my refuge in the day of
　　　disaster.
¹⁸Let my persecutors be put to shame,
　　but keep me from shame;
let them be terrified,
　　but keep me from terror.
Bring on them the day of disaster;
　　destroy them with double
　　　destruction.

Keeping the Sabbath Holy

¹⁹This is what the LORD said to me: "Go
and stand at the gate of the people,
through which the kings of Judah go in
and out; stand also at all the other gates
of Jerusalem. ²⁰Say to them, 'Hear the
word of the LORD, O kings of Judah and all
people of Judah and everyone living in
Jerusalem who come through these gates.
²¹This is what the LORD says: Be careful
not to carry a load on the Sabbath day or
bring it through the gates of Jerusalem.
²²Do not bring a load out of your houses
or do any work on the Sabbath, but keep
the Sabbath day holy, as I commanded
your forefathers. ²³Yet they did not listen
or pay attention; they were stiff-necked
and would not listen or respond to discipline. ²⁴But if you are careful to obey me,
declares the LORD, and bring no load
through the gates of this city on the Sabbath, but keep the Sabbath day holy by
not doing any work on it, ²⁵then kings
who sit on David's throne will come
through the gates of this city with their
officials. They and their officials will
come riding in chariots and on horses, accompanied by the men of Judah and
those living in Jerusalem, and this city
will be inhabited forever. ²⁶People will
come from the towns of Judah and the
villages around Jerusalem, from the territory of Benjamin and the western foothills, from the hill country and the Negev,
bringing burnt offerings and sacrifices,
grain offerings, incense and thank offer-

VERSE FOR THE DAY:
Jeremiah 17:7

AUTHOR:
Susan L. Lenzkes

PASSAGE FOR THE DAY:
Jeremiah 17:1–10

Trust

STOOP-shouldered,
foot-dragging,
sighing
resignation
is not trust.

Real trust
bounces on eager toes of
anticipation—
laughs with pure delight
of knowing
in whom it believes—
rests easy
knowing
on whom it waits.

Lord,
so wrap me in the
knowledge of You
that my trust is no longer
in You, but
is You.

Children are cutest when no one's watching—or they think
no one is.

I had just stepped into the kitchen with an armload of wash
when the sight of our boys standing together on the back step
caught my eye. Their backs were turned, so they didn't see me
looking as the little one wrapped his arm around his brother's
knees and tilted his blond head back, gazing up. He barely
reached his brother's belt loops.

In a tiny voice he said, "Bend your ear down a minute—I want
to tell you a secret."

Then, very quietly, he whispered something that delighted
them both.

You know, Jesus, I can't help thinking as I watch them . . . after all these years of walking with you, I still don't even stretch
to your knees. Bend your ear down a minute, I want to tell you a
secret. I think you're wonderful. And I really do trust you. When
I grow up I want to be just like you.

Additional Scripture Readings:
Psalm 52:8–9; Romans 8:15–17

*Go to page 828 for your next
devotional reading.*

ings to the house of the Lord. 27But if you do not obey me to keep the Sabbath day holy by not carrying any load as you come through the gates of Jerusalem on the Sabbath day, then I will kindle an unquenchable fire in the gates of Jerusalem that will consume her fortresses.' "

At the Potter's House

18 This is the word that came to Jeremiah from the Lord: 2"Go down to the potter's house, and there I will give you my message." 3So I went down to the potter's house, and I saw him working at the wheel. 4But the pot he was shaping from the clay was marred in his hands; so the potter formed it into another pot, shaping it as seemed best to him.

5Then the word of the Lord came to me: 6"O house of Israel, can I not do with you as this potter does?" declares the Lord. "Like clay in the hand of the potter, so are you in my hand, O house of Israel. 7If at any time I announce that a nation or kingdom is to be uprooted, torn down and destroyed, 8and if that nation I warned repents of its evil, then I will relent and not inflict on it the disaster I had planned. 9And if at another time I announce that a nation or kingdom is to be built up and planted, 10and if it does evil in my sight and does not obey me, then I will reconsider the good I had intended to do for it.

11"Now therefore say to the people of Judah and those living in Jerusalem, 'This is what the Lord says: Look! I am preparing a disaster for you and devising a plan against you. So turn from your evil ways, each one of you, and reform your ways and your actions.' 12But they will reply, 'It's no use. We will continue with our own plans; each of us will follow the stubbornness of his evil heart.' "

13Therefore this is what the Lord says:

"Inquire among the nations:
    Who has ever heard anything like
        this?
A most horrible thing has been done
    by Virgin Israel.
14Does the snow of Lebanon
    ever vanish from its rocky slopes?
Do its cool waters from distant
        sources
    ever cease to flow?*a*
15Yet my people have forgotten me;

they burn incense to worthless
    idols,
which made them stumble in their
    ways
    and in the ancient paths.
They made them walk in bypaths
    and on roads not built up.
16Their land will be laid waste,
    an object of lasting scorn;
all who pass by will be appalled
    and will shake their heads.
17Like a wind from the east,
    I will scatter them before their
        enemies;
I will show them my back and not my
        face
    in the day of their disaster."

18They said, "Come, let's make plans against Jeremiah; for the teaching of the law by the priest will not be lost, nor will counsel from the wise, nor the word from the prophets. So come, let's attack him with our tongues and pay no attention to anything he says."

19Listen to me, O Lord;
    hear what my accusers are saying!
20Should good be repaid with evil?
    Yet they have dug a pit for me.
Remember that I stood before you
    and spoke in their behalf
    to turn your wrath away from them.
21So give their children over to famine;
    hand them over to the power of the
        sword.
Let their wives be made childless and
        widows;
    let their men be put to death,
    their young men slain by the sword
        in battle.
22Let a cry be heard from their houses
    when you suddenly bring invaders
        against them,
for they have dug a pit to capture me
    and have hidden snares for my feet.
23But you know, O Lord,
    all their plots to kill me.
Do not forgive their crimes
    or blot out their sins from your
        sight.
Let them be overthrown before you;
    deal with them in the time of your
        anger.

19 This is what the Lord says: "Go and buy a clay jar from a potter. Take along some of the elders of the people and of the priests 2and go out to the

---

*a14 The meaning of the Hebrew for this sentence is uncertain.

Valley of Ben Hinnom, near the entrance of the Potsherd Gate. There proclaim the words I tell you, ³and say, 'Hear the word of the LORD, O kings of Judah and people of Jerusalem. This is what the LORD Almighty, the God of Israel, says: Listen! I am going to bring a disaster on this place that will make the ears of everyone who hears of it tingle. ⁴For they have forsaken me and made this a place of foreign gods; they have burned sacrifices in it to gods that neither they nor their fathers nor the kings of Judah ever knew, and they have filled this place with the blood of the innocent. ⁵They have built the high places of Baal to burn their sons in the fire as offerings to Baal—something I did not command or mention, nor did it enter my mind. ⁶So beware, the days are coming, declares the LORD, when people will no longer call this place Topheth or the Valley of Ben Hinnom, but the Valley of Slaughter.

⁷" 'In this place I will ruin*a* the plans of Judah and Jerusalem. I will make them fall by the sword before their enemies, at the hands of those who seek their lives, and I will give their carcasses as food to the birds of the air and the beasts of the earth. ⁸I will devastate this city and make it an object of scorn; all who pass by will be appalled and will scoff because of all its wounds. ⁹I will make them eat the flesh of their sons and daughters, and they will eat one another's flesh during the stress of the siege imposed on them by the enemies who seek their lives.'

¹⁰"Then break the jar while those who go with you are watching, ¹¹and say to them, 'This is what the LORD Almighty says: I will smash this nation and this city just as this potter's jar is smashed and cannot be repaired. They will bury the dead in Topheth until there is no more room. ¹²This is what I will do to this place and to those who live here, declares the LORD. I will make this city like Topheth. ¹³The houses in Jerusalem and those of the kings of Judah will be defiled like this place, Topheth—all the houses where they burned incense on the roofs to all the starry hosts and poured out drink offerings to other gods.' "

¹⁴Jeremiah then returned from Topheth, where the LORD had sent him to prophesy, and stood in the court of the LORD's temple and said to all the people,

¹⁵"This is what the LORD Almighty, the God of Israel, says: 'Listen! I am going to bring on this city and the villages around it every disaster I pronounced against them, because they were stiff-necked and would not listen to my words.' "

Jeremiah and Pashhur

20 When the priest Pashhur son of Immer, the chief officer in the temple of the LORD, heard Jeremiah prophesying these things, ²he had Jeremiah the prophet beaten and put in the stocks at the Upper Gate of Benjamin at the LORD's temple. ³The next day, when Pashhur released him from the stocks, Jeremiah said to him, "The LORD's name for you is not Pashhur, but Magor-Missabib.*b* ⁴For this is what the LORD says: 'I will make you a terror to yourself and to all your friends; with your own eyes you will see them fall by the sword of their enemies. I will hand all Judah over to the king of Babylon, who will carry them away to Babylon or put them to the sword. ⁵I will hand over to their enemies all the wealth of this city—all its products, all its valuables and all the treasures of the kings of Judah. They will take it away as plunder and carry it off to Babylon. ⁶And you, Pashhur, and all who live in your house will go into exile to Babylon. There you will die and be buried, you and all your friends to whom you have prophesied lies.' "

Jeremiah's Complaint

⁷O LORD, you deceived*c* me, and I was
    deceived*c*;
  you overpowered me and prevailed.
I am ridiculed all day long;
    everyone mocks me.
⁸Whenever I speak, I cry out
    proclaiming violence and
        destruction.
So the word of the LORD has brought
        me
    insult and reproach all day long.
⁹But if I say, "I will not mention him
    or speak any more in his name,"
his word is in my heart like a fire,
    a fire shut up in my bones.
I am weary of holding it in;
    indeed, I cannot.
¹⁰I hear many whispering,
    "Terror on every side!
    Report him! Let's report him!"

---

a7 The Hebrew for *ruin* sounds like the Hebrew for *jar* (see verses 1 and 10).   *b3* *Magor-Missabib* means *terror on every side.*   *c7* Or *persuaded*

All my friends
    are waiting for me to slip, saying,
"Perhaps he will be deceived;
    then we will prevail over him
    and take our revenge on him."

¹¹But the LORD is with me like a mighty
    warrior;
    so my persecutors will stumble and
      not prevail.
They will fail and be thoroughly
    disgraced;
    their dishonor will never be
      forgotten.
¹²O LORD Almighty, you who examine
    the righteous
    and probe the heart and mind,
let me see your vengeance upon
    them,
    for to you I have committed my
      cause.

¹³Sing to the LORD!
    Give praise to the LORD!
He rescues the life of the needy
    from the hands of the wicked.

¹⁴Cursed be the day I was born!
    May the day my mother bore me
      not be blessed!
¹⁵Cursed be the man who brought my
    father the news,
    who made him very glad, saying,
    "A child is born to you—a son!"
¹⁶May that man be like the towns
    the LORD overthrew without pity.
May he hear wailing in the morning,
    a battle cry at noon.
¹⁷For he did not kill me in the womb,
    with my mother as my grave,
    her womb enlarged forever.
¹⁸Why did I ever come out of the womb
    to see trouble and sorrow
    and to end my days in shame?

God Rejects Zedekiah's Request

21 The word came to Jeremiah from
the LORD when King Zedekiah sent
to him Pashhur son of Malkijah and the
priest Zephaniah son of Maaseiah. They
said: ²"Inquire now of the LORD for us because Nebuchadnezzar*ᵃ* king of Babylon
is attacking us. Perhaps the LORD will perform wonders for us as in times past so
that he will withdraw from us."

³But Jeremiah answered them, "Tell
Zedekiah, ⁴'This is what the LORD, the
God of Israel, says: I am about to turn

against you the weapons of war that are in
your hands, which you are using to fight
the king of Babylon and the Babylonians*ᵇ* who are outside the wall besieging
you. And I will gather them inside this
city. ⁵I myself will fight against you with
an outstretched hand and a mighty arm in
anger and fury and great wrath. ⁶I will
strike down those who live in this city—
both men and animals—and they will die
of a terrible plague. ⁷After that, declares
the LORD, I will hand over Zedekiah king
of Judah, his officials and the people in
this city who survive the plague, sword
and famine, to Nebuchadnezzar king of
Babylon and to their enemies who seek
their lives. He will put them to the sword;
he will show them no mercy or pity or
compassion.'

⁸"Furthermore, tell the people, 'This is
what the LORD says: See, I am setting before you the way of life and the way of
death. ⁹Whoever stays in this city will die
by the sword, famine or plague. But whoever goes out and surrenders to the Babylonians who are besieging you will live;
he will escape with his life. ¹⁰I have determined to do this city harm and not good,
declares the LORD. It will be given into the
hands of the king of Babylon, and he will
destroy it with fire.'

¹¹"Moreover, say to the royal house of
Judah, 'Hear the word of the LORD; ¹²O
house of David, this is what the LORD says:

" 'Administer justice every morning;
    rescue from the hand of his
      oppressor
    the one who has been robbed,
or my wrath will break out and burn
    like fire
because of the evil you have
    done—
    burn with no one to quench it.
¹³I am against you, Jerusalem,
    you who live above this valley
    on the rocky plateau,
          declares the LORD—
you who say, "Who can come against
    us?
    Who can enter our refuge?"
¹⁴I will punish you as your deeds
    deserve,
          declares the LORD.
I will kindle a fire in your forests
    that will consume everything
      around you.' "

ᵃ2 Hebrew *Nebuchadrezzar,* of which *Nebuchadnezzar* is a variant; here and often in Jeremiah and Ezekiel
ᵇ4 Or *Chaldeans;* also in verse 9

Judgment Against Evil Kings

22 This is what the LORD says: "Go down to the palace of the king of Judah and proclaim this message there: ²'Hear the word of the LORD, O king of Judah, you who sit on David's throne—you, your officials and your people who come through these gates. ³This is what the LORD says: Do what is just and right. Rescue from the hand of his oppressor the one who has been robbed. Do no wrong or violence to the alien, the fatherless or the widow, and do not shed innocent blood in this place. ⁴For if you are careful to carry out these commands, then kings who sit on David's throne will come through the gates of this palace, riding in chariots and on horses, accompanied by their officials and their people. ⁵But if you do not obey these commands, declares the LORD, I swear by myself that this palace will become a ruin.'"

⁶For this is what the LORD says about the palace of the king of Judah:

"Though you are like Gilead to me,
    like the summit of Lebanon,
I will surely make you like a desert,
    like towns not inhabited.
⁷I will send destroyers against you,
    each man with his weapons,
and they will cut up your fine cedar
        beams
    and throw them into the fire.

⁸"People from many nations will pass by this city and will ask one another, 'Why has the LORD done such a thing to this great city?' ⁹And the answer will be: 'Because they have forsaken the covenant of the LORD their God and have worshiped and served other gods.'"

¹⁰Do not weep for the dead king, or
        mourn his loss;
    rather, weep bitterly for him who is
        exiled,
because he will never return
    nor see his native land again.

¹¹For this is what the LORD says about Shallum[a] son of Josiah, who succeeded his father as king of Judah but has gone from this place: "He will never return. ¹²He will die in the place where they have led him captive; he will not see this land again."

¹³"Woe to him who builds his palace by
        unrighteousness,

his upper rooms by injustice,
making his countrymen work for
        nothing,
    not paying them for their
        labor.
¹⁴He says, 'I will build myself a great
        palace
    with spacious upper rooms.'
So he makes large windows in it,
    panels it with cedar
    and decorates it in red.

¹⁵"Does it make you a king
    to have more and more cedar?
Did not your father have food and
        drink?
    He did what was right and
        just,
    so all went well with him.
¹⁶He defended the cause of the poor
        and needy,
    and so all went well.
Is that not what it means to know
        me?"
    declares the LORD.
¹⁷"But your eyes and your heart
    are set only on dishonest gain,
on shedding innocent blood
    and on oppression and extortion."

¹⁸Therefore this is what the LORD says about Jehoiakim son of Josiah king of Judah:

"They will not mourn for him:
    'Alas, my brother! Alas, my sister!'
They will not mourn for him:
    'Alas, my master! Alas, his
        splendor!'
¹⁹He will have the burial of a donkey—
    dragged away and thrown
    outside the gates of Jerusalem."

²⁰"Go up to Lebanon and cry out,
    let your voice be heard in Bashan,
cry out from Abarim,
    for all your allies are crushed.
²¹I warned you when you felt secure,
    but you said, 'I will not listen!'
This has been your way from your
        youth;
    you have not obeyed me.
²²The wind will drive all your shepherds
        away,
    and your allies will go into exile.
Then you will be ashamed and
        disgraced
    because of all your wickedness.
²³You who live in 'Lebanon,'[b]
    who are nestled in cedar buildings,

ᵃ11 Also called *Jehoahaz*   ᵇ23 That is, the palace in Jerusalem (see 1 Kings 7:2)

how you will groan when pangs come
upon you,
pain like that of a woman in labor!

²⁴"As surely as I live," declares the
Lord, "even if you, Jehoiachin*ᵃ* son of Jehoiakim king of Judah, were a signet ring
on my right hand, I would still pull you
off. ²⁵I will hand you over to those who
seek your life, those you fear—to Nebuchadnezzar king of Babylon and to the
Babylonians.*ᵇ* ²⁶I will hurl you and the
mother who gave you birth into another
country, where neither of you was born,
and there you both will die. ²⁷You will
never come back to the land you long to
return to."

²⁸Is this man Jehoiachin a despised,
broken pot,
an object no one wants?
Why will he and his children be
hurled out,
cast into a land they do not know?
²⁹O land, land, land,
hear the word of the Lord!
³⁰This is what the Lord says:
"Record this man as if childless,
a man who will not prosper in his
lifetime,
for none of his offspring will prosper,
none will sit on the throne of David
or rule anymore in Judah."

The Righteous Branch

23 "Woe to the shepherds who are destroying and scattering the sheep
of my pasture!" declares the Lord. ²Therefore this is what the Lord, the God of Israel, says to the shepherds who tend my
people: "Because you have scattered my
flock and driven them away and have not
bestowed care on them, I will bestow
punishment on you for the evil you have
done," declares the Lord. ³"I myself will
gather the remnant of my flock out of all
the countries where I have driven them
and will bring them back to their pasture,
where they will be fruitful and increase in
number. ⁴I will place shepherds over
them who will tend them, and they will
no longer be afraid or terrified, nor will
any be missing," declares the Lord.

⁵"The days are coming," declares the
Lord,
"when I will raise up to David*ᶜ* a
righteous Branch,

a King who will reign wisely
and do what is just and right in the
land.
⁶In his days Judah will be saved
and Israel will live in safety.
This is the name by which he will be
called:
The Lord Our Righteousness.

⁷"So then, the days are coming," declares
the Lord, "when people will no longer
say, 'As surely as the Lord lives, who
brought the Israelites up out of Egypt,'
⁸but they will say, 'As surely as the Lord
lives, who brought the descendants of Israel up out of the land of the north and
out of all the countries where he had banished them.' Then they will live in their
own land."

Lying Prophets

⁹Concerning the prophets:

My heart is broken within me;
all my bones tremble.
I am like a drunken man,
like a man overcome by wine,
because of the Lord
and his holy words.
¹⁰The land is full of adulterers;
because of the curse*ᵈ* the land lies
parched*ᵉ*
and the pastures in the desert are
withered.
The prophets follow an evil course
and use their power unjustly.

¹¹"Both prophet and priest are godless;
even in my temple I find their
wickedness,"
declares the Lord.
¹²"Therefore their path will become
slippery;
they will be banished to darkness
and there they will fall.
I will bring disaster on them
in the year they are punished,"
declares the Lord.

¹³"Among the prophets of Samaria
I saw this repulsive thing:
They prophesied by Baal
and led my people Israel astray.
¹⁴And among the prophets of Jerusalem
I have seen something horrible:
They commit adultery and live a
lie.
They strengthen the hands of
evildoers,

ᵃ24 Hebrew *Coniah,* a variant of *Jehoiachin;* also in verse 28   *ᵇ25* Or *Chaldeans*   *ᶜ5* Or *up from
David's line*   *ᵈ10* Or *because of these things*   *ᵉ10* Or *land mourns*

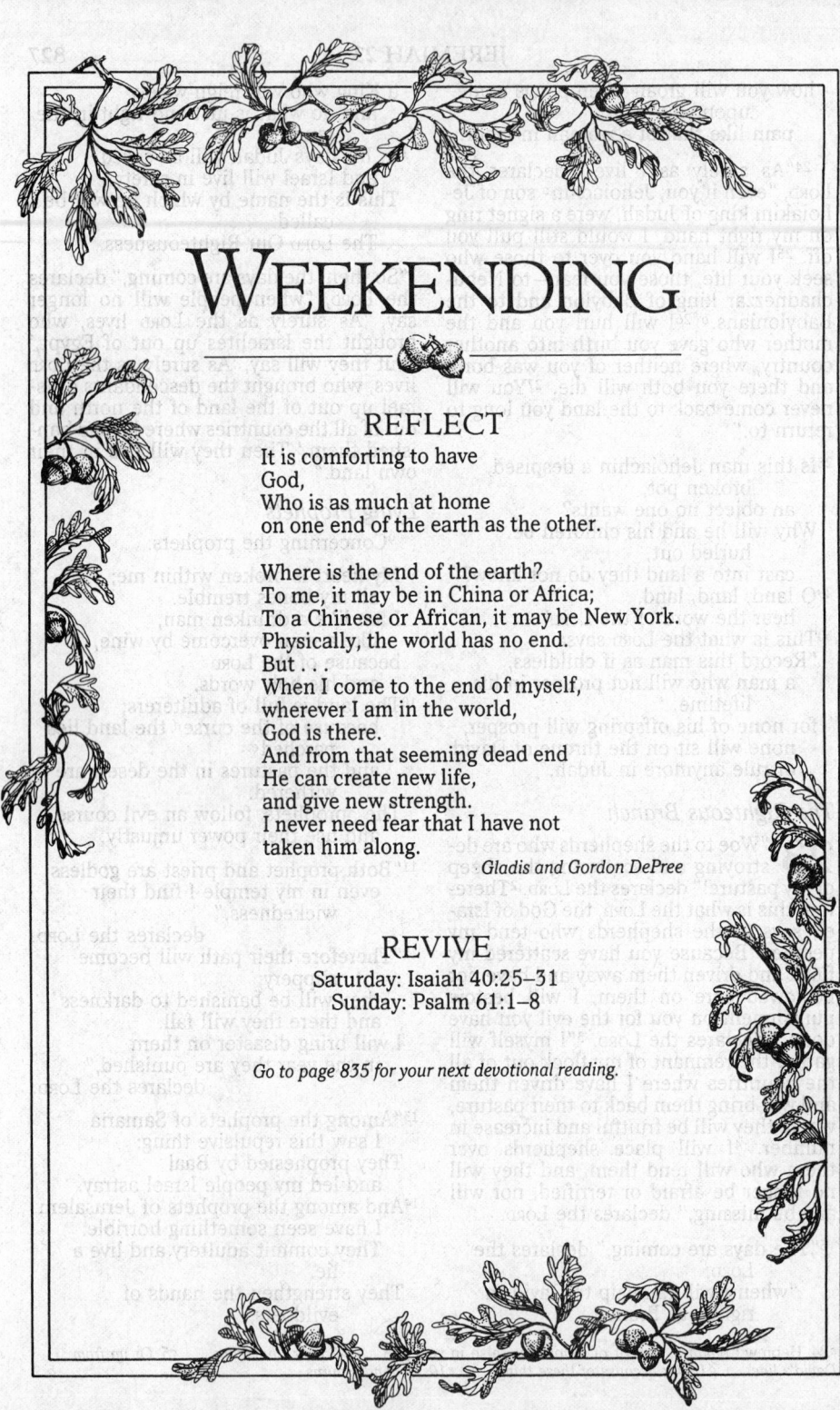

WEEKENDING

REFLECT

It is comforting to have
God,
Who is as much at home
on one end of the earth as the other.

Where is the end of the earth?
To me, it may be in China or Africa;
To a Chinese or African, it may be New York.
Physically, the world has no end.
But . . .
When I come to the end of myself,
wherever I am in the world,
God is there.
And from that seeming dead end
He can create new life,
and give new strength.
I never need fear that I have not
taken him along.

Gladis and Gordon DePree

REVIVE

Saturday: Isaiah 40:25–31
Sunday: Psalm 61:1–8

Go to page 835 for your next devotional reading.

so that no one turns from his
wickedness.
They are all like Sodom to me;
the people of Jerusalem are like
Gomorrah."

¹⁵Therefore, this is what the Lord Almighty says concerning the prophets:

"I will make them eat bitter food
and drink poisoned water,
because from the prophets of
Jerusalem
ungodliness has spread throughout
the land."

¹⁶This is what the Lord Almighty says:

"Do not listen to what the prophets
are prophesying to you;
they fill you with false hopes.
They speak visions from their own
minds,
not from the mouth of the Lord.
¹⁷They keep saying to those who
despise me,
'The Lord says: You will have
peace.'
And to all who follow the
stubbornness of their hearts
they say, 'No harm will come to
you.'
¹⁸But which of them has stood in the
council of the Lord
to see or to hear his word?
Who has listened and heard his
word?
¹⁹See, the storm of the Lord
will burst out in wrath,
a whirlwind swirling down
on the heads of the wicked.
²⁰The anger of the Lord will not turn
back
until he fully accomplishes
the purposes of his heart.
In days to come
you will understand it clearly.
²¹I did not send these prophets,
yet they have run with their
message;
I did not speak to them,
yet they have prophesied.
²²But if they had stood in my council,
they would have proclaimed my
words to my people
and would have turned them from
their evil ways
and from their evil deeds.

²³"Am I only a God nearby,"
declares the Lord,
"and not a God far away?
²⁴Can anyone hide in secret places
so that I cannot see him?"
declares the Lord.
"Do not I fill heaven and earth?"
declares the Lord.

²⁵"I have heard what the prophets say
who prophesy lies in my name. They say,
'I had a dream! I had a dream!' ²⁶How
long will this continue in the hearts of
these lying prophets, who prophesy the
delusions of their own minds? ²⁷They
think the dreams they tell one another
will make my people forget my name, just
as their fathers forgot my name through
Baal worship. ²⁸Let the prophet who has
a dream tell his dream, but let the one
who has my word speak it faithfully. For
what has straw to do with grain?" declares the Lord. ²⁹"Is not my word like
fire," declares the Lord, "and like a hammer that breaks a rock in pieces?

³⁰"Therefore," declares the Lord, "I am
against the prophets who steal from one
another words supposedly from me.
³¹Yes," declares the Lord, "I am against
the prophets who wag their own tongues
and yet declare, 'The Lord declares.' ³²In-
deed, I am against those who prophesy
false dreams," declares the Lord. "They
tell them and lead my people astray with
their reckless lies, yet I did not send or
appoint them. They do not benefit these
people in the least," declares the Lord.

False Oracles and False Prophets

³³"When these people, or a prophet or
a priest, ask you, 'What is the oracle*a* of
the Lord?' say to them, 'What oracle?*b* I
will forsake you, declares the Lord.' ³⁴If a
prophet or a priest or anyone else claims,
'This is the oracle of the Lord,' I will punish that man and his household. ³⁵This is
what each of you keeps on saying to his
friend or relative: 'What is the Lord's answer?' or 'What has the Lord spoken?'
³⁶But you must not mention 'the oracle of
the Lord' again, because every man's own
word becomes his oracle and so you distort the words of the living God, the Lord
Almighty, our God. ³⁷This is what you
keep saying to a prophet: 'What is the
Lord's answer to you?' or 'What has
the Lord spoken?' ³⁸Although you claim,

---

a33 Or *burden* (see Septuagint and Vulgate)   *b33* Hebrew; Septuagint and Vulgate *'You are the burden.*
(The Hebrew for *oracle* and *burden* is the same.)

'This is the oracle of the LORD,' this is what the LORD says: You used the words, 'This is the oracle of the LORD,' even though I told you that you must not claim, 'This is the oracle of the LORD.' ³⁹Therefore, I will surely forget you and cast you out of my presence along with the city I gave to you and your fathers. ⁴⁰I will bring upon you everlasting disgrace —everlasting shame that will not be forgotten."

Two Baskets of Figs

24 After Jehoiachin*a* son of Jehoiakim king of Judah and the officials, the craftsmen and the artisans of Judah were carried into exile from Jerusalem to Babylon by Nebuchadnezzar king of Babylon, the LORD showed me two baskets of figs placed in front of the temple of the LORD. ²One basket had very good figs, like those that ripen early; the other basket had very poor figs, so bad they could not be eaten.

³Then the LORD asked me, "What do you see, Jeremiah?"

"Figs," I answered. "The good ones are very good, but the poor ones are so bad they cannot be eaten."

⁴Then the word of the LORD came to me: ⁵"This is what the LORD, the God of Israel, says: 'Like these good figs, I regard as good the exiles from Judah, whom I sent away from this place to the land of the Babylonians.*b* ⁶My eyes will watch over them for their good, and I will bring them back to this land. I will build them up and not tear them down; I will plant them and not uproot them. ⁷I will give them a heart to know me, that I am the LORD. They will be my people, and I will be their God, for they will return to me with all their heart.

⁸" 'But like the poor figs, which are so bad they cannot be eaten,' says the LORD, 'so will I deal with Zedekiah king of Judah, his officials and the survivors from Jerusalem, whether they remain in this land or live in Egypt. ⁹I will make them abhorrent and an offense to all the kingdoms of the earth, a reproach and a byword, an object of ridicule and cursing, wherever I banish them. ¹⁰I will send the sword, famine and plague against them until they are destroyed from the land I gave to them and their fathers.' "

Seventy Years of Captivity

25 The word came to Jeremiah concerning all the people of Judah in the fourth year of Jehoiakim son of Josiah king of Judah, which was the first year of Nebuchadnezzar king of Babylon. ²So Jeremiah the prophet said to all the people of Judah and to all those living in Jerusalem: ³For twenty-three years—from the thirteenth year of Josiah son of Amon king of Judah until this very day—the word of the LORD has come to me and I have spoken to you again and again, but you have not listened.

⁴And though the LORD has sent all his servants the prophets to you again and again, you have not listened or paid any attention. ⁵They said, "Turn now, each of you, from your evil ways and your evil practices, and you can stay in the land the LORD gave to you and your fathers for ever and ever. ⁶Do not follow other gods to serve and worship them; do not provoke me to anger with what your hands have made. Then I will not harm you."

⁷"But you did not listen to me," declares the LORD, "and you have provoked me with what your hands have made, and you have brought harm to yourselves."

⁸Therefore the LORD Almighty says this: "Because you have not listened to my words, ⁹I will summon all the peoples of the north and my servant Nebuchadnezzar king of Babylon," declares the LORD, "and I will bring them against this land and its inhabitants and against all the surrounding nations. I will completely destroy*c* them and make them an object of horror and scorn, and an everlasting ruin. ¹⁰I will banish from them the sounds of joy and gladness, the voices of bride and bridegroom, the sound of millstones and the light of the lamp. ¹¹This whole country will become a desolate wasteland, and these nations will serve the king of Babylon seventy years.

¹²"But when the seventy years are fulfilled, I will punish the king of Babylon and his nation, the land of the Babylonians,*b* for their guilt," declares the LORD, "and will make it desolate forever. ¹³I will bring upon that land all the things I have spoken against it, all that are written in this book and prophesied by Jeremiah against all the nations. ¹⁴They themselves will be enslaved by many nations and

---

a1 Hebrew *Jeconiah*, a variant of *Jehoiachin*   *b5,12* Or *Chaldeans*   *c9* The Hebrew term refers to the irrevocable giving over of things or persons to the LORD, often by totally destroying them.

great kings; I will repay them according to their deeds and the work of their hands."

The Cup of God's Wrath

¹⁵This is what the LORD, the God of Israel, said to me: "Take from my hand this cup filled with the wine of my wrath and make all the nations to whom I send you drink it. ¹⁶When they drink it, they will stagger and go mad because of the sword I will send among them."

¹⁷So I took the cup from the LORD's hand and made all the nations to whom he sent me drink it: ¹⁸Jerusalem and the towns of Judah, its kings and officials, to make them a ruin and an object of horror and scorn and cursing, as they are today; ¹⁹Pharaoh king of Egypt, his attendants, his officials and all his people, ²⁰and all the foreign people there; all the kings of Uz; all the kings of the Philistines (those of Ashkelon, Gaza, Ekron, and the people left at Ashdod); ²¹Edom, Moab and Ammon; ²²all the kings of Tyre and Sidon; the kings of the coastlands across the sea; ²³Dedan, Tema, Buz and all who are in distant places*a*; ²⁴all the kings of Arabia and all the kings of the foreign people who live in the desert; ²⁵all the kings of Zimri, Elam and Media; ²⁶and all the kings of the north, near and far, one after the other—all the kingdoms on the face of the earth. And after all of them, the king of Sheshach*b* will drink it too.

²⁷"Then tell them, 'This is what the LORD Almighty, the God of Israel, says: Drink, get drunk and vomit, and fall to rise no more because of the sword I will send among you.' ²⁸But if they refuse to take the cup from your hand and drink, tell them, 'This is what the LORD Almighty says: You must drink it! ²⁹See, I am beginning to bring disaster on the city that bears my Name, and will you indeed go unpunished? You will not go unpunished, for I am calling down a sword upon all who live on the earth, declares the LORD Almighty.'

³⁰"Now prophesy all these words against them and say to them:

" 'The LORD will roar from on high;
    he will thunder from his holy
        dwelling
    and roar mightily against his land.
He will shout like those who tread
    the grapes,

shout against all who live on the
        earth.
³¹The tumult will resound to the ends
        of the earth,
    for the LORD will bring charges
        against the nations;
    he will bring judgment on all
        mankind
    and put the wicked to the sword,' "
                        declares the LORD.

³²This is what the LORD Almighty says:

"Look! Disaster is spreading
    from nation to nation;
a mighty storm is rising
    from the ends of the earth."

³³At that time those slain by the LORD will be everywhere—from one end of the earth to the other. They will not be mourned or gathered up or buried, but will be like refuse lying on the ground.

³⁴Weep and wail, you shepherds;
    roll in the dust, you leaders of the
        flock.
For your time to be slaughtered has
        come;
    you will fall and be shattered like
        fine pottery.
³⁵The shepherds will have nowhere to
        flee,
    the leaders of the flock no place to
        escape.
³⁶Hear the cry of the shepherds,
    the wailing of the leaders of the
        flock,
    for the LORD is destroying their
        pasture.
³⁷The peaceful meadows will be laid
        waste
    because of the fierce anger of the
        LORD.
³⁸Like a lion he will leave his lair,
    and their land will become desolate
because of the sword*c* of the
        oppressor
    and because of the LORD's fierce
        anger.

Jeremiah Threatened With Death

26 Early in the reign of Jehoiakim son of Josiah king of Judah, this word came from the LORD: ²"This is what the LORD says: Stand in the courtyard of the LORD's house and speak to all the people of the towns of Judah who come to worship in the house of the LORD. Tell them

---

a23 Or *who clip the hair by their foreheads*   *b26 Sheshach* is a cryptogram for Babylon.   *c38* Some Hebrew manuscripts and Septuagint (see also Jer. 46:16 and 50:16); most Hebrew manuscripts *anger* everything I command you; do not omit a word. ³Perhaps they will listen and each will turn from his evil way. Then I will relent and not bring on them the disaster I was planning because of the evil they have done. ⁴Say to them, 'This is what the LORD says: If you do not listen to me and follow my law, which I have set before you, ⁵and if you do not listen to the words of my servants the prophets, whom I have sent to you again and again (though you have not listened), ⁶then I will make this house like Shiloh and this city an object of cursing among all the nations of the earth.'"

⁷The priests, the prophets and all the people heard Jeremiah speak these words in the house of the LORD. ⁸But as soon as Jeremiah finished telling all the people everything the LORD had commanded him to say, the priests, the prophets and all the people seized him and said, "You must die! ⁹Why do you prophesy in the LORD's name that this house will be like Shiloh and this city will be desolate and deserted?" And all the people crowded around Jeremiah in the house of the LORD.

¹⁰When the officials of Judah heard about these things, they went up from the royal palace to the house of the LORD and took their places at the entrance of the New Gate of the LORD's house. ¹¹Then the priests and the prophets said to the officials and all the people, "This man should be sentenced to death because he has prophesied against this city. You have heard it with your own ears!"

¹²Then Jeremiah said to all the officials and all the people: "The LORD sent me to prophesy against this house and this city all the things you have heard. ¹³Now reform your ways and your actions and obey the LORD your God. Then the LORD will relent and not bring the disaster he has pronounced against you. ¹⁴As for me, I am in your hands; do with me whatever you think is good and right. ¹⁵Be assured, however, that if you put me to death, you will bring the guilt of innocent blood on yourselves and on this city and on those who live in it, for in truth the LORD has sent me to you to speak all these words in your hearing."

¹⁶Then the officials and all the people said to the priests and the prophets, "This man should not be sentenced to death!

He has spoken to us in the name of the LORD our God."

¹⁷Some of the elders of the land stepped forward and said to the entire assembly of people, ¹⁸"Micah of Moresheth prophesied in the days of Hezekiah king of Judah. He told all the people of Judah, 'This is what the LORD Almighty says:

" 'Zion will be plowed like a field,
    Jerusalem will become a heap of
        rubble,
    the temple hill a mound overgrown
        with thickets.'ᵃ

¹⁹"Did Hezekiah king of Judah or anyone else in Judah put him to death? Did not Hezekiah fear the LORD and seek his favor? And did not the LORD relent, so that he did not bring the disaster he pronounced against them? We are about to bring a terrible disaster on ourselves!"

²⁰(Now Uriah son of Shemaiah from Kiriath Jearim was another man who prophesied in the name of the LORD; he prophesied the same things against this city and this land as Jeremiah did. ²¹When King Jehoiakim and all his officers and officials heard his words, the king sought to put him to death. But Uriah heard of it and fled in fear to Egypt. ²²King Jehoiakim, however, sent Elnathan son of Acbor to Egypt, along with some other men. ²³They brought Uriah out of Egypt and took him to King Jehoiakim, who had him struck down with a sword and his body thrown into the burial place of the common people.)

²⁴Furthermore, Ahikam son of Shaphan supported Jeremiah, and so he was not handed over to the people to be put to death.

Judah to Serve Nebuchadnezzar

27 Early in the reign of Zedekiahᵇ son of Josiah king of Judah, this word came to Jeremiah from the LORD: ²This is what the LORD said to me: "Make a yoke out of straps and crossbars and put it on your neck. ³Then send word to the kings of Edom, Moab, Ammon, Tyre and Sidon through the envoys who have come to Jerusalem to Zedekiah king of Judah. ⁴Give them a message for their masters and say, 'This is what the LORD Almighty, the God of Israel, says: "Tell this to your masters: ⁵With my great power and outstretched arm I made the earth and its

---

ᵃ18 Micah 3:12   ᵇ1 A few Hebrew manuscripts and Syriac (see also Jer. 27:3, 12 and 28:1); most Hebrew manuscripts *Jehoiakim* (Most Septuagint manuscripts do not have this verse.)

people and the animals that are on it, and I give it to anyone I please. 6Now I will hand all your countries over to my servant Nebuchadnezzar king of Babylon; I will make even the wild animals subject to him. 7All nations will serve him and his son and his grandson until the time for his land comes; then many nations and great kings will subjugate him.

8" ' "If, however, any nation or kingdom will not serve Nebuchadnezzar king of Babylon or bow its neck under his yoke, I will punish that nation with the sword, famine and plague, declares the LORD, until I destroy it by his hand. 9So do not listen to your prophets, your diviners, your interpreters of dreams, your mediums or your sorcerers who tell you, 'You will not serve the king of Babylon.' 10They prophesy lies to you that will only serve to remove you far from your lands; I will banish you and you will perish. 11But if any nation will bow its neck under the yoke of the king of Babylon and serve him, I will let that nation remain in its own land to till it and to live there, declares the LORD." ' "

12I gave the same message to Zedekiah king of Judah. I said, "Bow your neck under the yoke of the king of Babylon; serve him and his people, and you will live. 13Why will you and your people die by the sword, famine and plague with which the LORD has threatened any nation that will not serve the king of Babylon? 14Do not listen to the words of the prophets who say to you, 'You will not serve the king of Babylon,' for they are prophesying lies to you. 15'I have not sent them,' declares the LORD. 'They are prophesying lies in my name. Therefore, I will banish you and you will perish, both you and the prophets who prophesy to you.' "

16Then I said to the priests and all these people, "This is what the LORD says: Do not listen to the prophets who say, 'Very soon now the articles from the LORD's house will be brought back from Babylon.' They are prophesying lies to you. 17Do not listen to them. Serve the king of Babylon, and you will live. Why should this city become a ruin? 18If they are prophets and have the word of the LORD, let them plead with the LORD Almighty that the furnishings remaining in the house of the LORD and in the palace of the king of Judah and in Jerusalem not be taken to Babylon. 19For this is what the

LORD Almighty says about the pillars, the Sea, the movable stands and the other furnishings that are left in this city, 20which Nebuchadnezzar king of Babylon did not take away when he carried Jehoiachin*a* son of Jehoiakim king of Judah into exile from Jerusalem to Babylon, along with all the nobles of Judah and Jerusalem— 21yes, this is what the LORD Almighty, the God of Israel, says about the things that are left in the house of the LORD and in the palace of the king of Judah and in Jerusalem: 22'They will be taken to Babylon and there they will remain until the day I come for them,' declares the LORD. 'Then I will bring them back and restore them to this place.' "

The False Prophet Hananiah

28 In the fifth month of that same year, the fourth year, early in the reign of Zedekiah king of Judah, the prophet Hananiah son of Azzur, who was from Gibeon, said to me in the house of the LORD in the presence of the priests and all the people: 2"This is what the LORD Almighty, the God of Israel, says: 'I will break the yoke of the king of Babylon. 3Within two years I will bring back to this place all the articles of the LORD's house that Nebuchadnezzar king of Babylon removed from here and took to Babylon. 4I will also bring back to this place Jehoiachin*a* son of Jehoiakim king of Judah and all the other exiles from Judah who went to Babylon,' declares the LORD, 'for I will break the yoke of the king of Babylon.' "

5Then the prophet Jeremiah replied to the prophet Hananiah before the priests and all the people who were standing in the house of the LORD. 6He said, "Amen! May the LORD do so! May the LORD fulfill the words you have prophesied by bringing the articles of the LORD's house and all the exiles back to this place from Babylon. 7Nevertheless, listen to what I have to say in your hearing and in the hearing of all the people: 8From early times the prophets who preceded you and me have prophesied war, disaster and plague against many countries and great kingdoms. 9But the prophet who prophesies peace will be recognized as one truly sent by the LORD only if his prediction comes true."

10Then the prophet Hananiah took the yoke off the neck of the prophet Jeremiah and broke it, 11and he said before all the

*a20,4 Hebrew *Jeconiah,* a variant of *Jehoiachin*

people, "This is what the LORD says: 'In the same way will I break the yoke of Nebuchadnezzar king of Babylon off the neck of all the nations within two years.' " At this, the prophet Jeremiah went on his way.

[12]Shortly after the prophet Hananiah had broken the yoke off the neck of the prophet Jeremiah, the word of the LORD came to Jeremiah: [13]"Go and tell Hananiah, 'This is what the LORD says: You have broken a wooden yoke, but in its place you will get a yoke of iron. [14]This is what the LORD Almighty, the God of Israel, says: I will put an iron yoke on the necks of all these nations to make them serve Nebuchadnezzar king of Babylon, and they will serve him. I will even give him control over the wild animals.' "

[15]Then the prophet Jeremiah said to Hananiah the prophet, "Listen, Hananiah! The LORD has not sent you, yet you have persuaded this nation to trust in lies. [16]Therefore, this is what the LORD says: 'I am about to remove you from the face of the earth. This very year you are going to die, because you have preached rebellion against the LORD.' "

[17]In the seventh month of that same year, Hananiah the prophet died.

A Letter to the Exiles

29 This is the text of the letter that the prophet Jeremiah sent from Jerusalem to the surviving elders among the exiles and to the priests, the prophets and all the other people Nebuchadnezzar had carried into exile from Jerusalem to Babylon. [2](This was after King Jehoiachin[a] and the queen mother, the court officials and the leaders of Judah and Jerusalem, the craftsmen and the artisans had gone into exile from Jerusalem.) [3]He entrusted the letter to Elasah son of Shaphan and to Gemariah son of Hilkiah, whom Zedekiah king of Judah sent to King Nebuchadnezzar in Babylon. It said:

[4]This is what the LORD Almighty, the God of Israel, says to all those I carried into exile from Jerusalem to Babylon: [5]"Build houses and settle down; plant gardens and eat what they produce. [6]Marry and have sons and daughters; find wives for your sons and give your daughters in marriage, so that they too may have sons and daughters. Increase in number

there; do not decrease. [7]Also, seek the peace and prosperity of the city to which I have carried you into exile. Pray to the LORD for it, because if it prospers, you too will prosper." [8]Yes, this is what the LORD Almighty, the God of Israel, says: "Do not let the prophets and diviners among you deceive you. Do not listen to the dreams you encourage them to have. [9]They are prophesying lies to you in my name. I have not sent them," declares the LORD.

[10]This is what the LORD says: "When seventy years are completed for Babylon, I will come to you and fulfill my gracious promise to bring you back to this place. [11]For I know the plans I have for you," declares the LORD, "plans to prosper you and not to harm you, plans to give you hope and a future. [12]Then you will call upon me and come and pray to me, and I will listen to you. [13]You will seek me and find me when you seek me with all your heart. [14]I will be found by you," declares the LORD, "and will bring you back from captivity.[b] I will gather you from all the nations and places where I have banished you," declares the LORD, "and will bring you back to the place from which I carried you into exile."

[15]You may say, "The LORD has raised up prophets for us in Babylon," [16]but this is what the LORD says about the king who sits on David's throne and all the people who remain in this city, your countrymen who did not go with you into exile— [17]yes, this is what the LORD Almighty says: "I will send the sword, famine and plague against them and I will make them like poor figs that are so bad they cannot be eaten. [18]I will pursue them with the sword, famine and plague and will make them abhorrent to all the kingdoms of the earth and an object of cursing and horror, of scorn and reproach, among all the nations where I drive them. [19]For they have not listened to my words," declares the LORD, "words that I sent to them again and again by my servants the prophets. And you exiles have not listened either," declares the LORD.

[20]Therefore, hear the word of the

VERSE FOR THE DAY:
Jeremiah 29:11

AUTHOR:
Sue Richards

PASSAGE FOR THE DAY:
Jeremiah 29:4–14

Plans

FOR eight years I had the opportunity to be home as a full-time mommy, until both Matthew and Sarah were ready to attend school full-time. As I began to look ahead to the time when Sarah would also be gone all day, I had an increasing feeling that I should be doing something new. Each day I seemed to grow more and more restless, wondering what in the world I wanted to do. I submitted paperwork to Tallahassee in order to obtain a Florida teaching certificate, but I had only taught summer school previously, and I didn't know if I would be able to get a job. And I wasn't even sure I wanted to teach.

Finally, my husband asked me if I had asked God what I should do. He reminded me of Jeremiah 29:11–14:

> "For I know the plans I have for you," declares the
> LORD, "plans to prosper you and not to harm you,
> plans to give you hope and a future. Then you will
> call upon me and come and pray to me, and I will
> listen to you. You will seek me and find me when
> you seek me with all your heart. I will be found by
> you," declares the LORD, "and will bring you
> back . . . to the place from which I carried you into
> exile."

I began to seek the Lord with all my heart, asking him what he had in mind for my life. I found peace quickly as I sought the Lord's plan for my life. As I explored possibilities, I found I had peace as some teaching interviews began. Instead of asking for a special job, I asked the Lord to place me where I would fit in and where I was needed. I have just finished my fourth year in a public secondary school. My job brings me fulfillment. There is no doubt that I am where I belong and doing what he would have me do. I pray for my one hundred teenagers daily, and I pray for grace to model a loving and caring attitude. I appreciate sometimes even being able to share a little of my faith. I occasionally tell my students how I appreciate their position in life, as I'm not sure of what I want to be when I grow up either. Right now the only career goal I have is to be living the plans God has for me, to be seeking him with all my heart.

Thank you, Father, for having plans for my life. Not just when things are going great, but especially for having plans when life calls for a change, and you are there showing me the path you have chosen just for me. Amen.

Additional Scripture Readings:
Proverbs 19:20–21; Ephesians 1:11–12

*Go to page 838 for your next
devotional reading.*

LORD, all you exiles whom I have sent away from Jerusalem to Babylon. [21]This is what the LORD Almighty, the God of Israel, says about Ahab son of Kolaiah and Zedekiah son of Maaseiah, who are prophesying lies to you in my name: "I will hand them over to Nebuchadnezzar king of Babylon, and he will put them to death before your very eyes. [22]Because of them, all the exiles from Judah who are in Babylon will use this curse: 'The LORD treat you like Zedekiah and Ahab, whom the king of Babylon burned in the fire.' [23]For they have done outrageous things in Israel; they have committed adultery with their neighbors' wives and in my name have spoken lies, which I did not tell them to do. I know it and am a witness to it," declares the LORD.

Message to Shemaiah

[24]Tell Shemaiah the Nehelamite, [25]"This is what the LORD Almighty, the God of Israel, says: You sent letters in your own name to all the people in Jerusalem, to Zephaniah son of Maaseiah the priest, and to all the other priests. You said to Zephaniah, [26]'The LORD has appointed you priest in place of Jehoiada to be in charge of the house of the LORD; you should put any madman who acts like a prophet into the stocks and neck-irons. [27]So why have you not reprimanded Jeremiah from Anathoth, who poses as a prophet among you? [28]He has sent this message to us in Babylon: It will be a long time. Therefore build houses and settle down; plant gardens and eat what they produce.' "

[29]Zephaniah the priest, however, read the letter to Jeremiah the prophet. [30]Then the word of the LORD came to Jeremiah: [31]"Send this message to all the exiles: 'This is what the LORD says about Shemaiah the Nehelamite: Because Shemaiah has prophesied to you, even though I did not send him, and has led you to believe a lie, [32]this is what the LORD says: I will surely punish Shemaiah the Nehelamite and his descendants. He will have no one left among this people, nor will he see the good things I will do for my people, declares the LORD, because he has preached rebellion against me.' "

Restoration of Israel

30 This is the word that came to Jeremiah from the LORD: [2]"This is what the LORD, the God of Israel, says: 'Write in a book all the words I have spoken to you. [3]The days are coming,' declares the LORD, 'when I will bring my people Israel and Judah back from captivity[a] and restore them to the land I gave their forefathers to possess,' says the LORD."

[4]These are the words the LORD spoke concerning Israel and Judah: [5]"This is what the LORD says:

" 'Cries of fear are heard—
   terror, not peace.
[6]Ask and see:
   Can a man bear children?
Then why do I see every strong man
   with his hands on his stomach like
     a woman in labor,
every face turned deathly pale?
[7]How awful that day will be!
   None will be like it.
It will be a time of trouble for Jacob,
   but he will be saved out of it.

[8]" 'In that day,' declares the LORD
    Almighty,
'I will break the yoke off their
   necks
and will tear off their bonds;
   no longer will foreigners enslave
    them.
[9]Instead, they will serve the LORD their
   God
and David their king,
   whom I will raise up for them.

[10]" 'So do not fear, O Jacob my servant;
   do not be dismayed, O Israel,'
             declares the LORD.
'I will surely save you out of a distant
   place,
your descendants from the land of
   their exile.
Jacob will again have peace and
   security,
   and no one will make him afraid.
[11]I am with you and will save you,'
   declares the LORD.
'Though I completely destroy all the
   nations
among which I scatter you,
   I will not completely destroy you.
I will discipline you but only with
   justice;
   I will not let you go entirely
    unpunished.'

---

a3 Or will restore the fortunes of my people Israel and Judah

¹²"This is what the Lord says:

" 'Your wound is incurable,
your injury beyond healing.
¹³There is no one to plead your cause,
no remedy for your sore,
no healing for you.
¹⁴All your allies have forgotten you;
they care nothing for you.
I have struck you as an enemy would
and punished you as would the
cruel,
because your guilt is so great
and your sins so many.
¹⁵Why do you cry out over your wound,
your pain that has no cure?
Because of your great guilt and many
sins
I have done these things to you.

¹⁶" 'But all who devour you will be
devoured;
all your enemies will go into exile.
Those who plunder you will be
plundered;
all who make spoil of you I will
despoil.
¹⁷But I will restore you to health
and heal your wounds,
declares the Lord,
'because you are called an outcast,
Zion for whom no one cares.'

¹⁸"This is what the Lord says:

" 'I will restore the fortunes of Jacob's
tents
and have compassion on his
dwellings;
the city will be rebuilt on her ruins,
and the palace will stand in its
proper place.
¹⁹From them will come songs of
thanksgiving
and the sound of rejoicing.
I will add to their numbers,
and they will not be decreased;
I will bring them honor,
and they will not be disdained.
²⁰Their children will be as in days of
old,
and their community will be
established before me;
I will punish all who oppress them.
²¹Their leader will be one of their own;
their ruler will arise from among
them.
I will bring him near and he will
come close to me,

for who is he who will devote
himself
to be close to me?'
declares the Lord.
²²" 'So you will be my people,
and I will be your God.' "

²³See, the storm of the Lord
will burst out in wrath,
a driving wind swirling down
on the heads of the wicked.
²⁴The fierce anger of the Lord will not
turn back
until he fully accomplishes
the purposes of his heart.
In days to come
you will understand this.

31 "At that time," declares the Lord,
"I will be the God of all the clans
of Israel, and they will be my people."

²This is what the Lord says:

"The people who survive the sword
will find favor in the desert;
I will come to give rest to Israel."

³The Lord appeared to us in the past,^a
saying:

"I have loved you with an everlasting
love;
I have drawn you with
loving-kindness.
⁴I will build you up again
and you will be rebuilt, O Virgin
Israel.
Again you will take up your
tambourines
and go out to dance with the joyful.
⁵Again you will plant vineyards
on the hills of Samaria;
the farmers will plant them
and enjoy their fruit.
⁶There will be a day when watchmen
cry out
on the hills of Ephraim,
'Come, let us go up to Zion,
to the Lord our God.' "

⁷This is what the Lord says:

"Sing with joy for Jacob;
shout for the foremost of the
nations.
Make your praises heard, and say,
'O Lord, save your people,
the remnant of Israel.'
⁸See, I will bring them from the land
of the north

---

^a3 Or Lord has appeared to us from afar

VERSE FOR THE DAY:
Jeremiah 31:3

AUTHOR:
Marie Chapian

PASSAGE FOR THE DAY:
Jeremiah 31:3–6

An Everlasting Love

IN church school I learned that Jesus loved us. I've believed it all my life. As an adult I became the teacher who taught God's love in church school classes, Bible studies, churches, and conferences around the world. I thought I really understood how much God cares for us. But then tragedy hit. I was forced to reach into the spiritual well within me, and I came up lacking. I asked the Lord why good people suffer. Night and day I prayed, pleading with God to either perform a tangible miracle or change my heart and remove the pain. I felt abandoned.

Then I decided I simply *must* discover the magnitude of God's love and learn to know him on a deeper spiritual level. I couldn't depend on circumstances for proof of his love and approval. Even though I had been through trials before, I still needed to learn that his love transcends both good and bad circumstances.

That is when he spoke clearly to me through Jeremiah 31:3:

> I have loved you with an everlasting love;
> I have drawn you with loving-kindness.

The words struck me hard, like bolts of lightning. I was stunned, overwhelmed. It was as though God personally put his loving arms around me and said, "Marie, I don't promise that my children will never suffer in this life, but I assure you that through every experience I'll love you with love that is everlasting. I'll constantly draw you to myself with my loving-kindness in spite of anything you're experiencing."

The magnitude of his love—even through sorrow and tragedy—revolutionized my life. Jeremiah 31:3 became my life verse. I labeled myself a "Loved Person," and I've continued to believe it. Though I've lived through other hardships since that time, I've never lost my awareness of his love for me.

God wants us to participate in this love relationship because it is the foundation of life. This love is everlasting. Unchanging. Forever. We can each consider ourselves a Loved Person, not because of our circumstances or situations but simply because God loves us perfectly, totally and eternally.

Additional Scripture Readings:
John 16:20–23; Colossians 3:12–14

Go to page 842 for your next devotional reading.

and gather them from the ends of
the earth.
Among them will be the blind and
the lame,
expectant mothers and women in
labor;
a great throng will return.
⁹They will come with weeping;
they will pray as I bring them back.
I will lead them beside streams of
water
on a level path where they will not
stumble,
because I am Israel's father,
and Ephraim is my firstborn son.

¹⁰"Hear the word of the Lord,
O nations;
proclaim it in distant coastlands:
'He who scattered Israel will gather
them
and will watch over his flock like a
shepherd.'
¹¹For the Lord will ransom Jacob
and redeem them from the hand of
those stronger than they.
¹²They will come and shout for joy on
the heights of Zion;
they will rejoice in the bounty of
the Lord—
the grain, the new wine and the oil,
the young of the flocks and herds.
They will be like a well-watered
garden,
and they will sorrow no more.
¹³Then maidens will dance and be glad,
young men and old as well.
I will turn their mourning into
gladness;
I will give them comfort and joy
instead of sorrow.
¹⁴I will satisfy the priests with
abundance,
and my people will be filled with
my bounty,"
declares the Lord.

¹⁵This is what the Lord says:

"A voice is heard in Ramah,
mourning and great weeping,
Rachel weeping for her children
and refusing to be comforted,
because her children are no more."

¹⁶This is what the Lord says:

"Restrain your voice from weeping
and your eyes from tears,

for your work will be rewarded,"
declares the Lord.
"They will return from the land of
the enemy.
¹⁷So there is hope for your future,"
declares the Lord.
"Your children will return to their
own land.

¹⁸"I have surely heard Ephraim's
moaning:
'You disciplined me like an unruly
calf,
and I have been disciplined.
Restore me, and I will return,
because you are the Lord my God.
¹⁹After I strayed,
I repented;
after I came to understand,
I beat my breast.
I was ashamed and humiliated
because I bore the disgrace of my
youth.'
²⁰Is not Ephraim my dear son,
the child in whom I delight?
Though I often speak against him,
I still remember him.
Therefore my heart yearns for him;
I have great compassion for him,"
declares the Lord.

²¹"Set up road signs;
put up guideposts.
Take note of the highway,
the road that you take.
Return, O Virgin Israel,
return to your towns.
²²How long will you wander,
O unfaithful daughter?
The Lord will create a new thing on
earth—
a woman will surround ᵃ a man."

²³This is what the Lord Almighty, the
God of Israel, says: "When I bring them
back from captivity, ᵇ the people in the
land of Judah and in its towns will once
again use these words: 'The Lord bless
you, O righteous dwelling, O sacred
mountain.' ²⁴People will live together in
Judah and all its towns—farmers and
those who move about with their flocks.
²⁵I will refresh the weary and satisfy the
faint."

²⁶At this I awoke and looked around.
My sleep had been pleasant to me.

²⁷"The days are coming," declares the
Lord, "when I will plant the house of Israel and the house of Judah with the off-

---

ᵃ22 Or will go about ˌseeking.ˌ; or will protect   ᵇ23 Or I restore their fortunes spring of men and of animals. ²⁸Just as I watched over them to uproot and tear down, and to overthrow, destroy and bring disaster, so I will watch over them to build and to plant," declares the LORD. ²⁹"In those days people will no longer say,

'The fathers have eaten sour grapes,
and the children's teeth are set on
edge.'

³⁰Instead, everyone will die for his own sin; whoever eats sour grapes—his own teeth will be set on edge.

³¹"The time is coming," declares the
LORD,
"when I will make a new covenant
with the house of Israel
and with the house of Judah.
³²It will not be like the covenant
I made with their forefathers
when I took them by the hand
to lead them out of Egypt,
because they broke my covenant,
though I was a husband to^a
them,^b"
declares the LORD.
³³"This is the covenant I will make with
the house of Israel
after that time," declares the LORD.
"I will put my law in their minds
and write it on their hearts.
I will be their God,
and they will be my people.
³⁴No longer will a man teach his
neighbor,
or a man his brother, saying, 'Know
the LORD,'
because they will all know me,
from the least of them to the
greatest,"
declares the LORD.
"For I will forgive their wickedness
and will remember their sins no
more."

³⁵This is what the LORD says,

he who appoints the sun
to shine by day,
who decrees the moon and stars
to shine by night,
who stirs up the sea
so that its waves roar—
the LORD Almighty is his name:
³⁶"Only if these decrees vanish from my
sight,"
declares the LORD,

"will the descendants of Israel ever
cease
to be a nation before me."

³⁷This is what the LORD says:

"Only if the heavens above can be
measured
and the foundations of the earth
below be searched out
will I reject all the descendants of
Israel
because of all they have done,"
declares the LORD.

³⁸"The days are coming," declares the LORD, "when this city will be rebuilt for me from the Tower of Hananel to the Corner Gate. ³⁹The measuring line will stretch from there straight to the hill of Gareb and then turn to Goah. ⁴⁰The whole valley where dead bodies and ashes are thrown, and all the terraces out to the Kidron Valley on the east as far as the corner of the Horse Gate, will be holy to the LORD. The city will never again be uprooted or demolished."

Jeremiah Buys a Field

32 This is the word that came to Jeremiah from the LORD in the tenth year of Zedekiah king of Judah, which was the eighteenth year of Nebuchadnezzar. ²The army of the king of Babylon was then besieging Jerusalem, and Jeremiah the prophet was confined in the courtyard of the guard in the royal palace of Judah.

³Now Zedekiah king of Judah had imprisoned him there, saying, "Why do you prophesy as you do? You say, 'This is what the LORD says: I am about to hand this city over to the king of Babylon, and he will capture it. ⁴Zedekiah king of Judah will not escape out of the hands of the Babylonians^c but will certainly be handed over to the king of Babylon, and will speak with him face to face and see him with his own eyes. ⁵He will take Zedekiah to Babylon, where he will remain until I deal with him, declares the LORD. If you fight against the Babylonians, you will not succeed.' "

⁶Jeremiah said, "The word of the LORD came to me: ⁷Hanamel son of Shallum your uncle is going to come to you and say, 'Buy my field at Anathoth, because as nearest relative it is your right and duty to buy it.'

a32 Hebrew; Septuagint and Syriac / *and I turned away from*
Chaldeans; also in verses 5, 24, 25, 28, 29 and 43   *b32* Or *was their master*   *c4* Or

8"Then, just as the LORD had said, my cousin Hanamel came to me in the courtyard of the guard and said, 'Buy my field at Anathoth in the territory of Benjamin. Since it is your right to redeem it and possess it, buy it for yourself.'

"I knew that this was the word of the LORD; 9so I bought the field at Anathoth from my cousin Hanamel and weighed out for him seventeen shekels[a] of silver. 10I signed and sealed the deed, had it witnessed, and weighed out the silver on the scales. 11I took the deed of purchase—the sealed copy containing the terms and conditions, as well as the unsealed copy — 12and I gave this deed to Baruch son of Neriah, the son of Mahseiah, in the presence of my cousin Hanamel and of the witnesses who had signed the deed and of all the Jews sitting in the courtyard of the guard.

13"In their presence I gave Baruch these instructions: 14'This is what the LORD Almighty, the God of Israel, says: Take these documents, both the sealed and unsealed copies of the deed of purchase, and put them in a clay jar so they will last a long time. 15For this is what the LORD Almighty, the God of Israel, says: Houses, fields and vineyards will again be bought in this land.'

16"After I had given the deed of purchase to Baruch son of Neriah, I prayed to the LORD:

17"Ah, Sovereign LORD, you have made the heavens and the earth by your great power and outstretched arm. Nothing is too hard for you. 18You show love to thousands but bring the punishment for the fathers' sins into the laps of their children after them. O great and powerful God, whose name is the LORD Almighty, 19great are your purposes and mighty are your deeds. Your eyes are open to all the ways of men; you reward everyone according to his conduct and as his deeds deserve. 20You performed miraculous signs and wonders in Egypt and have continued them to this day, both in Israel and among all mankind, and have gained the renown that is still yours. 21You brought your people Israel out of Egypt with signs and wonders, by a mighty hand and an outstretched

arm and with great terror. 22You gave them this land you had sworn to give their forefathers, a land flowing with milk and honey. 23They came in and took possession of it, but they did not obey you or follow your law; they did not do what you commanded them to do. So you brought all this disaster upon them.

24"See how the siege ramps are built up to take the city. Because of the sword, famine and plague, the city will be handed over to the Babylonians who are attacking it. What you said has happened, as you now see. 25And though the city will be handed over to the Babylonians, you, O Sovereign LORD, say to me, 'Buy the field with silver and have the transaction witnessed.' "

26Then the word of the LORD came to Jeremiah: 27"I am the LORD, the God of all mankind. Is anything too hard for me? 28Therefore, this is what the LORD says: I am about to hand this city over to the Babylonians and to Nebuchadnezzar king of Babylon, who will capture it. 29The Babylonians who are attacking this city will come in and set it on fire; they will burn it down, along with the houses where the people provoked me to anger by burning incense on the roofs to Baal and by pouring out drink offerings to other gods.

30"The people of Israel and Judah have done nothing but evil in my sight from their youth; indeed, the people of Israel have done nothing but provoke me with what their hands have made, declares the LORD. 31From the day it was built until now, this city has so aroused my anger and wrath that I must remove it from my sight. 32The people of Israel and Judah have provoked me by all the evil they have done—they, their kings and officials, their priests and prophets, the men of Judah and the people of Jerusalem. 33They turned their backs to me and not their faces; though I taught them again and again, they would not listen or respond to discipline. 34They set up their abominable idols in the house that bears my Name and defiled it. 35They built high places for Baal in the Valley of Ben Hinnom to sacrifice their sons and daughters[b] to Molech, though I never com-

---

[a]9 That is, about 7 ounces (about 200 grams)
[b]35 Or to make their sons and daughters pass through the fire

VERSE FOR THE DAY:
Jeremiah 32:17,27

AUTHOR:
Diane Head

PASSAGE FOR THE DAY:
Jeremiah 32:16–29

His Power

WHEN we consider creation we can't help but wonder about the omnipotence of the God who brought it into being. All we see and know of his creation was called into existence by his word. He created substance from *nothing*.

Our God hasn't changed. The God of creation is the same yesterday, today, and forever. His power hasn't diminished.

It blesses my heart to know I belong to a God such as this! But because I'm human . . . and busy . . . and have a mind occupied with four dozen other things at any given moment—I forget about his power.

I forget what he can do for *me*. I forget he has the power to change those areas in my life that desperately need his touch.

Sometimes I think my life is like my linen closet—constantly in need of cleaning, discarding, rearranging and straightening.

There are always a few undesirables that need to be discarded—gossip, yelling, gluttony, complaining, bitterness, fretting, jealousy, worry, pride, uncommitted struggles, impatience—all jammed way back into the corners (*shudder*).

Unfortunately, linen closets never straighten or clean themselves. Likewise, we can't—*by our own power*—change our lives. To bring about a permanent change of heart we need more power than our tired, human selves can muster.

When we open the door and allow God's life-changing power to enter in . . . step by step, moment by moment . . . he begins a good work in us. Deadwood is cut out. Discipline is applied. Priorities rearranged. In some areas he works quickly. In others, painfully slow. But his timing is perfect.

Let's swing wide open those "closet doors" to our hearts and let *El-Shaddai* exert his resurrection power, tenderly cleaning and straightening our lives.

Additional Scripture Readings:
Titus 2:11–14; 2 Peter 1:3–9

*Go to page 857 for your next
devotional reading.*

manded, nor did it enter my mind, that they should do such a detestable thing and so make Judah sin.

³⁶"You are saying about this city, 'By the sword, famine and plague it will be handed over to the king of Babylon'; but this is what the LORD, the God of Israel, says: ³⁷I will surely gather them from all the lands where I banish them in my furious anger and great wrath; I will bring them back to this place and let them live in safety. ³⁸They will be my people, and I will be their God. ³⁹I will give them singleness of heart and action, so that they will always fear me for their own good and the good of their children after them. ⁴⁰I will make an everlasting covenant with them: I will never stop doing good to them, and I will inspire them to fear me, so that they will never turn away from me. ⁴¹I will rejoice in doing them good and will assuredly plant them in this land with all my heart and soul.

⁴²"This is what the LORD says: As I have brought all this great calamity on this people, so I will give them all the prosperity I have promised them. ⁴³Once more fields will be bought in this land of which you say, 'It is a desolate waste, without men or animals, for it has been handed over to the Babylonians.' ⁴⁴Fields will be bought for silver, and deeds will be signed, sealed and witnessed in the territory of Benjamin, in the villages around Jerusalem, in the towns of Judah and in the towns of the hill country, of the western foothills and of the Negev, because I will restore their fortunes,ᵃ declares the LORD."

Promise of Restoration

33 While Jeremiah was still confined in the courtyard of the guard, the word of the LORD came to him a second time: ²"This is what the LORD says, he who made the earth, the LORD who formed it and established it—the LORD is his name: ³'Call to me and I will answer you and tell you great and unsearchable things you do not know.' ⁴For this is what the LORD, the God of Israel, says about the houses in this city and the royal palaces of Judah that have been torn down to be used against the siege ramps and the sword ⁵in the fight with the Babyloniansᵇ: 'They will be filled with the dead bodies of the men I will slay in my anger and wrath. I

will hide my face from this city because of all its wickedness.

⁶" 'Nevertheless, I will bring health and healing to it; I will heal my people and will let them enjoy abundant peace and security. ⁷I will bring Judah and Israel back from captivityᶜ and will rebuild them as they were before. ⁸I will cleanse them from all the sin they have committed against me and will forgive all their sins of rebellion against me. ⁹Then this city will bring me renown, joy, praise and honor before all nations on earth that hear of all the good things I do for it; and they will be in awe and will tremble at the abundant prosperity and peace I provide for it.'

¹⁰"This is what the LORD says: 'You say about this place, "It is a desolate waste, without men or animals." Yet in the towns of Judah and the streets of Jerusalem that are deserted, inhabited by neither men nor animals, there will be heard once more ¹¹the sounds of joy and gladness, the voices of bride and bridegroom, and the voices of those who bring thank offerings to the house of the LORD, saying,

"Give thanks to the LORD Almighty,
  for the LORD is good;
  his love endures forever."

For I will restore the fortunes of the land as they were before,' says the LORD.

¹²"This is what the LORD Almighty says: 'In this place, desolate and without men or animals—in all its towns there will again be pastures for shepherds to rest their flocks. ¹³In the towns of the hill country, of the western foothills and of the Negev, in the territory of Benjamin, in the villages around Jerusalem and in the towns of Judah, flocks will again pass under the hand of the one who counts them,' says the LORD.

¹⁴" 'The days are coming,' declares the LORD, 'when I will fulfill the gracious promise I made to the house of Israel and to the house of Judah.

¹⁵" 'In those days and at that time
  I will make a righteous Branch
    sprout from David's line;
  he will do what is just and right in
    the land.
¹⁶In those days Judah will be saved
  and Jerusalem will live in safety.

ᵃ44 Or will bring them back from captivity   ᵇ5 Or Chaldeans   ᶜ7 Or will restore the fortunes of Judah
and Israel

This is the name by which it*a* will be called:
    The LORD Our Righteousness.'

17For this is what the LORD says: 'David will never fail to have a man to sit on the throne of the house of Israel, 18nor will the priests, who are Levites, ever fail to have a man to stand before me continually to offer burnt offerings, to burn grain offerings and to present sacrifices.' "

19The word of the LORD came to Jeremiah: 20"This is what the LORD says: 'If you can break my covenant with the day and my covenant with the night, so that day and night no longer come at their appointed time, 21then my covenant with David my servant—and my covenant with the Levites who are priests ministering before me—can be broken and David will no longer have a descendant to reign on his throne. 22I will make the descendants of David my servant and the Levites who minister before me as countless as the stars of the sky and as measureless as the sand on the seashore.' "

23The word of the LORD came to Jeremiah: 24"Have you not noticed that these people are saying, 'The LORD has rejected the two kingdoms*b* he chose'? So they despise my people and no longer regard them as a nation. 25This is what the LORD says: 'If I have not established my covenant with day and night and the fixed laws of heaven and earth, 26then I will reject the descendants of Jacob and David my servant and will not choose one of his sons to rule over the descendants of Abraham, Isaac and Jacob. For I will restore their fortunes*c* and have compassion on them.' "

Warning to Zedekiah

34 While Nebuchadnezzar king of Babylon and all his army and all the kingdoms and peoples in the empire he ruled were fighting against Jerusalem and all its surrounding towns, this word came to Jeremiah from the LORD: 2"This is what the LORD, the God of Israel, says: Go to Zedekiah king of Judah and tell him, 'This is what the LORD says: I am about to hand this city over to the king of Babylon, and he will burn it down. 3You will not escape from his grasp but will surely be captured and handed over to him. You will see the king of Babylon with your

own eyes, and he will speak with you face to face. And you will go to Babylon.

4" 'Yet hear the promise of the LORD, O Zedekiah king of Judah. This is what the LORD says concerning you: You will not die by the sword; 5you will die peacefully. As people made a funeral fire in honor of your fathers, the former kings who preceded you, so they will make a fire in your honor and lament, "Alas, O master!" I myself make this promise, declares the LORD.' "

6Then Jeremiah the prophet told all this to Zedekiah king of Judah, in Jerusalem, 7while the army of the king of Babylon was fighting against Jerusalem and the other cities of Judah that were still holding out—Lachish and Azekah. These were the only fortified cities left in Judah.

Freedom for Slaves

8The word came to Jeremiah from the LORD after King Zedekiah had made a covenant with all the people in Jerusalem to proclaim freedom for the slaves. 9Everyone was to free his Hebrew slaves, both male and female; no one was to hold a fellow Jew in bondage. 10So all the officials and people who entered into this covenant agreed that they would free their male and female slaves and no longer hold them in bondage. They agreed, and set them free. 11But afterward they changed their minds and took back the slaves they had freed and enslaved them again.

12Then the word of the LORD came to Jeremiah: 13"This is what the LORD, the God of Israel, says: I made a covenant with your forefathers when I brought them out of Egypt, out of the land of slavery. I said, 14'Every seventh year each of you must free any fellow Hebrew who has sold himself to you. After he has served you six years, you must let him go free.'*d* Your fathers, however, did not listen to me or pay attention to me. 15Recently you repented and did what is right in my sight: Each of you proclaimed freedom to his countrymen. You even made a covenant before me in the house that bears my Name. 16But now you have turned around and profaned my name; each of you has taken back the male and female slaves you had set free to go where they wished. You have forced them to become your slaves again.

17"Therefore, this is what the LORD says:

---

a16 Or he   b24 Or families   c26 Or will bring them back from captivity   d14 Deut. 15:12

You have not obeyed me; you have not proclaimed freedom for your fellow countrymen. So I now proclaim 'freedom' for you, declares the LORD — 'freedom' to fall by the sword, plague and famine. I will make you abhorrent to all the kingdoms of the earth. 18The men who have violated my covenant and have not fulfilled the terms of the covenant they made before me, I will treat like the calf they cut in two and then walked between its pieces. 19The leaders of Judah and Jerusalem, the court officials, the priests and all the people of the land who walked between the pieces of the calf, 20I will hand over to their enemies who seek their lives. Their dead bodies will become food for the birds of the air and the beasts of the earth.

21"I will hand Zedekiah king of Judah and his officials over to their enemies who seek their lives, to the army of the king of Babylon, which has withdrawn from you. 22I am going to give the order, declares the LORD, and I will bring them back to this city. They will fight against it, take it and burn it down. And I will lay waste the towns of Judah so no one can live there."

The Recabites

35 This is the word that came to Jeremiah from the LORD during the reign of Jehoiakim son of Josiah king of Judah: 2"Go to the Recabite family and invite them to come to one of the side rooms of the house of the LORD and give them wine to drink."

3So I went to get Jaazaniah son of Jeremiah, the son of Habazziniah, and his brothers and all his sons — the whole family of the Recabites. 4I brought them into the house of the LORD, into the room of the sons of Hanan son of Igdaliah the man of God. It was next to the room of the officials, which was over that of Maaseiah son of Shallum the doorkeeper. 5Then I set bowls full of wine and some cups before the men of the Recabite family and said to them, "Drink some wine."

6But they replied, "We do not drink wine, because our forefather Jonadab son of Recab gave us this command: 'Neither you nor your descendants must ever drink wine. 7Also you must never build houses, sow seed or plant vineyards; you must never have any of these things, but must always live in tents. Then you will live a

long time in the land where you are nomads.' 8We have obeyed everything our forefather Jonadab son of Recab commanded us. Neither we nor our wives nor our sons and daughters have ever drunk wine 9or built houses to live in or had vineyards, fields or crops. 10We have lived in tents and have fully obeyed everything our forefather Jonadab commanded us. 11But when Nebuchadnezzar king of Babylon invaded this land, we said, 'Come, we must go to Jerusalem to escape the Babylonian*a* and Aramean armies.' So we have remained in Jerusalem."

12Then the word of the LORD came to Jeremiah, saying: 13"This is what the LORD Almighty, the God of Israel, says: Go and tell the men of Judah and the people of Jerusalem, 'Will you not learn a lesson and obey my words?' declares the LORD. 14'Jonadab son of Recab ordered his sons not to drink wine and this command has been kept. To this day they do not drink wine, because they obey their forefather's command. But I have spoken to you again and again, yet you have not obeyed me. 15Again and again I sent all my servants the prophets to you. They said, "Each of you must turn from your wicked ways and reform your actions; do not follow other gods to serve them. Then you will live in the land I have given to you and your fathers." But you have not paid attention or listened to me. 16The descendants of Jonadab son of Recab have carried out the command their forefather gave them, but these people have not obeyed me.'

17"Therefore, this is what the LORD God Almighty, the God of Israel, says: 'Listen! I am going to bring on Judah and on everyone living in Jerusalem every disaster I pronounced against them. I spoke to them, but they did not listen; I called to them, but they did not answer.' "

18Then Jeremiah said to the family of the Recabites, "This is what the LORD Almighty, the God of Israel, says: 'You have obeyed the command of your forefather Jonadab and have followed all his instructions and have done everything he ordered.' 19Therefore, this is what the LORD Almighty, the God of Israel, says: 'Jonadab son of Recab will never fail to have a man to serve me.' "

Jehoiakim Burns Jeremiah's Scroll

36 In the fourth year of Jehoiakim son of Josiah king of Judah, this

a11 Or Chaldean

word came to Jeremiah from the LORD: 2"Take a scroll and write on it all the words I have spoken to you concerning Israel, Judah and all the other nations from the time I began speaking to you in the reign of Josiah till now. 3Perhaps when the people of Judah hear about every disaster I plan to inflict on them, each of them will turn from his wicked way; then I will forgive their wickedness and their sin."

4So Jeremiah called Baruch son of Neriah, and while Jeremiah dictated all the words the LORD had spoken to him, Baruch wrote them on the scroll. 5Then Jeremiah told Baruch, "I am restricted; I cannot go to the LORD's temple. 6So you go to the house of the LORD on a day of fasting and read to the people from the scroll the words of the LORD that you wrote as I dictated. Read them to all the people of Judah who come in from their towns. 7Perhaps they will bring their petition before the LORD, and each will turn from his wicked ways, for the anger and wrath pronounced against this people by the LORD are great."

8Baruch son of Neriah did everything Jeremiah the prophet told him to do; at the LORD's temple he read the words of the LORD from the scroll. 9In the ninth month of the fifth year of Jehoiakim son of Josiah king of Judah, a time of fasting before the LORD was proclaimed for all the people in Jerusalem and those who had come from the towns of Judah. 10From the room of Gemariah son of Shaphan the secretary, which was in the upper courtyard at the entrance of the New Gate of the temple, Baruch read to all the people at the LORD's temple the words of Jeremiah from the scroll.

11When Micaiah son of Gemariah, the son of Shaphan, heard all the words of the LORD from the scroll, 12he went down to the secretary's room in the royal palace, where all the officials were sitting: Elishama the secretary, Delaiah son of Shemaiah, Elnathan son of Acbor, Gemariah son of Shaphan, Zedekiah son of Hananiah, and all the other officials. 13After Micaiah told them everything he had heard Baruch read to the people from the scroll, 14all the officials sent Jehudi son of Nethaniah, the son of Shelemiah, the son of Cushi, to say to Baruch, "Bring the scroll from which you have read to the people and come." So Baruch son of Neriah went to them with the scroll in his hand.

15They said to him, "Sit down, please, and read it to us."

So Baruch read it to them. 16When they heard all these words, they looked at each other in fear and said to Baruch, "We must report all these words to the king." 17Then they asked Baruch, "Tell us, how did you come to write all this? Did Jeremiah dictate it?"

18"Yes," Baruch replied, "he dictated all these words to me, and I wrote them in ink on the scroll."

19Then the officials said to Baruch, "You and Jeremiah, go and hide. Don't let anyone know where you are."

20After they put the scroll in the room of Elishama the secretary, they went to the king in the courtyard and reported everything to him. 21The king sent Jehudi to get the scroll, and Jehudi brought it from the room of Elishama the secretary and read it to the king and all the officials standing beside him. 22It was the ninth month and the king was sitting in the winter apartment, with a fire burning in the firepot in front of him. 23Whenever Jehudi had read three or four columns of the scroll, the king cut them off with a scribe's knife and threw them into the firepot, until the entire scroll was burned in the fire. 24The king and all his attendants who heard all these words showed no fear, nor did they tear their clothes. 25Even though Elnathan, Delaiah and Gemariah urged the king not to burn the scroll, he would not listen to them. 26Instead, the king commanded Jerahmeel, a son of the king, Seraiah son of Azriel and Shelemiah son of Abdeel to arrest Baruch the scribe and Jeremiah the prophet. But the LORD had hidden them.

27After the king burned the scroll containing the words that Baruch had written at Jeremiah's dictation, the word of the LORD came to Jeremiah: 28"Take another scroll and write on it all the words that were on the first scroll, which Jehoiakim king of Judah burned up. 29Also tell Jehoiakim king of Judah, 'This is what the LORD says: You burned that scroll and said, "Why did you write on it that the king of Babylon would certainly come and destroy this land and cut off both men and animals from it?" 30Therefore, this is what the LORD says about Jehoiakim king of Judah: He will have no one to sit on the throne of David; his body will be thrown out and exposed to the heat by day and the frost by night. 31I will punish him and his children and his attendants for their wickedness; I will bring on them and those living in Jerusalem and the people of Judah every disaster I pronounced against them, because they have not listened.' "

³²So Jeremiah took another scroll and gave it to the scribe Baruch son of Neriah, and as Jeremiah dictated, Baruch wrote on it all the words of the scroll that Jehoiakim king of Judah had burned in the fire. And many similar words were added to them.

Jeremiah in Prison

37 Zedekiah son of Josiah was made king of Judah by Nebuchadnezzar king of Babylon; he reigned in place of Jehoiachin^a son of Jehoiakim. ²Neither he nor his attendants nor the people of the land paid any attention to the words the LORD had spoken through Jeremiah the prophet.

³King Zedekiah, however, sent Jehucal son of Shelemiah with the priest Zephaniah son of Maaseiah to Jeremiah the prophet with this message: "Please pray to the LORD our God for us."

⁴Now Jeremiah was free to come and go among the people, for he had not yet been put in prison. ⁵Pharaoh's army had marched out of Egypt, and when the Babylonians^b who were besieging Jerusalem heard the report about them, they withdrew from Jerusalem.

⁶Then the word of the LORD came to Jeremiah the prophet: ⁷"This is what the LORD, the God of Israel, says: Tell the king of Judah, who sent you to inquire of me, 'Pharaoh's army, which has marched out to support you, will go back to its own land, to Egypt. ⁸Then the Babylonians will return and attack this city; they will capture it and burn it down.'

⁹"This is what the LORD says: Do not deceive yourselves, thinking, 'The Babylonians will surely leave us.' They will not! ¹⁰Even if you were to defeat the entire Babylonian^c army that is attacking you and only wounded men were left in their tents, they would come out and burn this city down."

¹¹After the Babylonian army had withdrawn from Jerusalem because of Pharaoh's army, ¹²Jeremiah started to leave the city to go to the territory of Benjamin to get his share of the property among the people there. ¹³But when he reached the Benjamin Gate, the captain of the guard, whose name was Irijah son of Shelemiah, the son of Hananiah, arrested him and said, "You are deserting to the Babylonians!"

¹⁴"That's not true!" Jeremiah said. "I am not deserting to the Babylonians." But Irijah would not listen to him; instead, he arrested Jeremiah and brought him to the officials. ¹⁵They were angry with Jeremiah and had him beaten and imprisoned in the house of Jonathan the secretary, which they had made into a prison.

¹⁶Jeremiah was put into a vaulted cell in a dungeon, where he remained a long time. ¹⁷Then King Zedekiah sent for him and had him brought to the palace, where he asked him privately, "Is there any word from the LORD?"

"Yes," Jeremiah replied, "you will be handed over to the king of Babylon."

¹⁸Then Jeremiah said to King Zedekiah, "What crime have I committed against you or your officials or this people, that you have put me in prison? ¹⁹Where are your prophets who prophesied to you, 'The king of Babylon will not attack you or this land'? ²⁰But now, my lord the king, please listen. Let me bring my petition before you: Do not send me back to the house of Jonathan the secretary, or I will die there."

²¹King Zedekiah then gave orders for Jeremiah to be placed in the courtyard of the guard and given bread from the street of the bakers each day until all the bread in the city was gone. So Jeremiah remained in the courtyard of the guard.

Jeremiah Thrown Into a Cistern

38 Shephatiah son of Mattan, Gedaliah son of Pashhur, Jehucal^d son of Shelemiah, and Pashhur son of Malkijah heard what Jeremiah was telling all the people when he said, ²"This is what the LORD says: 'Whoever stays in this city will die by the sword, famine or plague, but whoever goes over to the Babylonians^e will live. He will escape with his life; he will live.' ³And this is what the LORD says: 'This city will certainly be handed over to the army of the king of Babylon, who will capture it.' "

⁴Then the officials said to the king,

"This man should be put to death. He is discouraging the soldiers who are left in this city, as well as all the people, by the things he is saying to them. This man is not seeking the good of these people but their ruin."

⁵"He is in your hands," King Zedekiah answered. "The king can do nothing to oppose you."

⁶So they took Jeremiah and put him into the cistern of Malkijah, the king's son, which was in the courtyard of the guard. They lowered Jeremiah by ropes into the cistern; it had no water in it, only mud, and Jeremiah sank down into the mud.

⁷But Ebed-Melech, a Cushite,ᵃ an official ᵇ in the royal palace, heard that they had put Jeremiah into the cistern. While the king was sitting in the Benjamin Gate, ⁸Ebed-Melech went out of the palace and said to him, ⁹"My lord the king, these men have acted wickedly in all they have done to Jeremiah the prophet. They have thrown him into a cistern, where he will starve to death when there is no longer any bread in the city."

¹⁰Then the king commanded Ebed-Melech the Cushite, "Take thirty men from here with you and lift Jeremiah the prophet out of the cistern before he dies."

¹¹So Ebed-Melech took the men with him and went to a room under the treasury in the palace. He took some old rags and worn-out clothes from there and let them down with ropes to Jeremiah in the cistern. ¹²Ebed-Melech the Cushite said to Jeremiah, "Put these old rags and worn-out clothes under your arms to pad the ropes." Jeremiah did so, ¹³and they pulled him up with the ropes and lifted him out of the cistern. And Jeremiah remained in the courtyard of the guard.

Zedekiah Questions Jeremiah Again

¹⁴Then King Zedekiah sent for Jeremiah the prophet and had him brought to the third entrance to the temple of the Lord. "I am going to ask you something," the king said to Jeremiah. "Do not hide anything from me."

¹⁵Jeremiah said to Zedekiah, "If I give you an answer, will you not kill me? Even if I did give you counsel, you would not listen to me."

¹⁶But King Zedekiah swore this oath secretly to Jeremiah: "As surely as the Lord lives, who has given us breath, I will nei-

ther kill you nor hand you over to those who are seeking your life."

¹⁷Then Jeremiah said to Zedekiah, "This is what the Lord God Almighty, the God of Israel, says: 'If you surrender to the officers of the king of Babylon, your life will be spared and this city will not be burned down; you and your family will live. ¹⁸But if you will not surrender to the officers of the king of Babylon, this city will be handed over to the Babylonians and they will burn it down; you yourself will not escape from their hands.'"

¹⁹King Zedekiah said to Jeremiah, "I am afraid of the Jews who have gone over to the Babylonians, for the Babylonians may hand me over to them and they will mistreat me."

²⁰"They will not hand you over," Jeremiah replied. "Obey the Lord by doing what I tell you. Then it will go well with you, and your life will be spared. ²¹But if you refuse to surrender, this is what the Lord has revealed to me: ²²All the women left in the palace of the king of Judah will be brought out to the officials of the king of Babylon. Those women will say to you:

" 'They misled you and overcame
        you —
  those trusted friends of yours.
Your feet are sunk in the mud;
  your friends have deserted you.'

²³"All your wives and children will be brought out to the Babylonians. You yourself will not escape from their hands but will be captured by the king of Babylon; and this city willᶜ be burned down."

²⁴Then Zedekiah said to Jeremiah, "Do not let anyone know about this conversation, or you may die. ²⁵If the officials hear that I talked with you, and they come to you and say, 'Tell us what you said to the king and what the king said to you; do not hide it from us or we will kill you,' ²⁶then tell them, 'I was pleading with the king not to send me back to Jonathan's house to die there.'"

²⁷All the officials did come to Jeremiah and question him, and he told them everything the king had ordered him to say. So they said no more to him, for no one had heard his conversation with the king.

²⁸And Jeremiah remained in the courtyard of the guard until the day Jerusalem was captured.

ᵃ7 Probably from the upper Nile region   ᵇ7 Or a eunuch   ᶜ23 Or and you will cause this city to

The Fall of Jerusalem

39 This is how Jerusalem was taken: ¹In the ninth year of Zedekiah king of Judah, in the tenth month, Nebuchadnezzar king of Babylon marched against Jerusalem with his whole army and laid siege to it. ²And on the ninth day of the fourth month of Zedekiah's eleventh year, the city wall was broken through. ³Then all the officials of the king of Babylon came and took seats in the Middle Gate: Nergal-Sharezer of Samgar, Nebo-Sarsekim*a* a chief officer, Nergal-Sharezer a high official and all the other officials of the king of Babylon. ⁴When Zedekiah king of Judah and all the soldiers saw them, they fled; they left the city at night by way of the king's garden, through the gate between the two walls, and headed toward the Arabah.*b*

⁵But the Babylonian*c* army pursued them and overtook Zedekiah in the plains of Jericho. They captured him and took him to Nebuchadnezzar king of Babylon at Riblah in the land of Hamath, where he pronounced sentence on him. ⁶There at Riblah the king of Babylon slaughtered the sons of Zedekiah before his eyes and also killed all the nobles of Judah. ⁷Then he put out Zedekiah's eyes and bound him with bronze shackles to take him to Babylon.

⁸The Babylonians*d* set fire to the royal palace and the houses of the people and broke down the walls of Jerusalem. ⁹Nebuzaradan commander of the imperial guard carried into exile to Babylon the people who remained in the city, along with those who had gone over to him, and the rest of the people. ¹⁰But Nebuzaradan the commander of the guard left behind in the land of Judah some of the poor people, who owned nothing; and at that time he gave them vineyards and fields.

¹¹Now Nebuchadnezzar king of Babylon had given these orders about Jeremiah through Nebuzaradan commander of the imperial guard: ¹²"Take him and look after him; don't harm him but do for him whatever he asks." ¹³So Nebuzaradan the commander of the guard, Nebushazban a chief officer, Nergal-Sharezer a high official and all the other officers of the king of Babylon ¹⁴sent and had Jeremiah taken out of the courtyard of the guard. They turned him over to Gedaliah son of Ahikam, the son of Shaphan, to take him

back to his home. So he remained among his own people.

¹⁵While Jeremiah had been confined in the courtyard of the guard, the word of the LORD came to him: ¹⁶"Go and tell Ebed-Melech the Cushite, 'This is what the LORD Almighty, the God of Israel, says: I am about to fulfill my words against this city through disaster, not prosperity. At that time they will be fulfilled before your eyes. ¹⁷But I will rescue you on that day, declares the LORD; you will not be handed over to those you fear. ¹⁸I will save you; you will not fall by the sword but will escape with your life, because you trust in me, declares the LORD.' "

Jeremiah Freed

40 The word came to Jeremiah from the LORD after Nebuzaradan commander of the imperial guard had released him at Ramah. He had found Jeremiah bound in chains among all the captives from Jerusalem and Judah who were being carried into exile to Babylon. ²When the commander of the guard found Jeremiah, he said to him, "The LORD your God decreed this disaster for this place. ³And now the LORD has brought it about; he has done just as he said he would. All this happened because you people sinned against the LORD and did not obey him. ⁴But today I am freeing you from the chains on your wrists. Come with me to Babylon, if you like, and I will look after you; but if you do not want to, then don't come. Look, the whole country lies before you; go wherever you please." ⁵However, before Jeremiah turned to go,*e* Nebuzaradan added, "Go back to Gedaliah son of Ahikam, the son of Shaphan, whom the king of Babylon has appointed over the towns of Judah, and live with him among the people, or go anywhere else you please."

Then the commander gave him provisions and a present and let him go. ⁶So Jeremiah went to Gedaliah son of Ahikam at Mizpah and stayed with him among the people who were left behind in the land.

Gedaliah Assassinated

⁷When all the army officers and their men who were still in the open country heard that the king of Babylon had appointed Gedaliah son of Ahikam as gover-

---

a3 Or *Nergal-Sharezer, Samgar-Nebo, Sarsekim*   *b4* Or *the Jordan Valley*   *c5* Or *Chaldean*   *d8* Or *Chaldeans*   *e5* Or *Jeremiah answered* nor over the land and had put him in charge of the men, women and children who were the poorest in the land and who had not been carried into exile to Babylon, ⁸they came to Gedaliah at Mizpah — Ishmael son of Nethaniah, Johanan and Jonathan the sons of Kareah, Seraiah son of Tanhumeth, the sons of Ephai the Netophathite, and Jaazaniah ᵃ the son of the Maacathite, and their men. ⁹Gedaliah son of Ahikam, the son of Shaphan, took an oath to reassure them and their men. "Do not be afraid to serve the Babylonians, ᵇ" he said. "Settle down in the land and serve the king of Babylon, and it will go well with you. ¹⁰I myself will stay at Mizpah to represent you before the Babylonians who come to us, but you are to harvest the wine, summer fruit and oil, and put them in your storage jars, and live in the towns you have taken over."

¹¹When all the Jews in Moab, Ammon, Edom and all the other countries heard that the king of Babylon had left a remnant in Judah and had appointed Gedaliah son of Ahikam, the son of Shaphan, as governor over them, ¹²they all came back to the land of Judah, to Gedaliah at Mizpah, from all the countries where they had been scattered. And they harvested an abundance of wine and summer fruit.

¹³Johanan son of Kareah and all the army officers still in the open country came to Gedaliah at Mizpah ¹⁴and said to him, "Don't you know that Baalis king of the Ammonites has sent Ishmael son of Nethaniah to take your life?" But Gedaliah son of Ahikam did not believe them.

¹⁵Then Johanan son of Kareah said privately to Gedaliah in Mizpah, "Let me go and kill Ishmael son of Nethaniah, and no one will know it. Why should he take your life and cause all the Jews who are gathered around you to be scattered and the remnant of Judah to perish?"

¹⁶But Gedaliah son of Ahikam said to Johanan son of Kareah, "Don't do such a thing! What you are saying about Ishmael is not true."

41 In the seventh month Ishmael son of Nethaniah, the son of Elishama, who was of the king's blood and had been one of the king's officers, came with ten men to Gedaliah son of Ahikam at Mizpah. While they were eating together there, ²Ishmael son of Nethaniah and the ten men who were with him got up and struck down Gedaliah son of Ahikam, the son of

Shaphan, with the sword, killing the one whom the king of Babylon had appointed as governor over the land. ³Ishmael also killed all the Jews who were with Gedaliah at Mizpah, as well as the Babylonian ᶜ soldiers who were there.

⁴The day after Gedaliah's assassination, before anyone knew about it, ⁵eighty men who had shaved off their beards, torn their clothes and cut themselves came from Shechem, Shiloh and Samaria, bringing grain offerings and incense with them to the house of the LORD. ⁶Ishmael son of Nethaniah went out from Mizpah to meet them, weeping as he went. When he met them, he said, "Come to Gedaliah son of Ahikam." ⁷When they went into the city, Ishmael son of Nethaniah and the men who were with him slaughtered them and threw them into a cistern. ⁸But ten of them said to Ishmael, "Don't kill us! We have wheat and barley, oil and honey, hidden in a field." So he let them alone and did not kill them with the others. ⁹Now the cistern where he threw all the bodies of the men he had killed along with Gedaliah was the one King Asa had made as part of his defense against Baasha king of Israel. Ishmael son of Nethaniah filled it with the dead.

¹⁰Ishmael made captives of all the rest of the people who were in Mizpah — the king's daughters along with all the others who were left there, over whom Nebuzaradan commander of the imperial guard had appointed Gedaliah son of Ahikam. Ishmael son of Nethaniah took them captive and set out to cross over to the Ammonites.

¹¹When Johanan son of Kareah and all the army officers who were with him heard about all the crimes Ishmael son of Nethaniah had committed, ¹²they took all their men and went to fight Ishmael son of Nethaniah. They caught up with him near the great pool in Gibeon. ¹³When all the people Ishmael had with him saw Johanan son of Kareah and the army officers who were with him, they were glad. ¹⁴All the people Ishmael had taken captive at Mizpah turned and went over to Johanan son of Kareah. ¹⁵But Ishmael son of Nethaniah and eight of his men escaped from Johanan and fled to the Ammonites.

Flight to Egypt

¹⁶Then Johanan son of Kareah and all

the army officers who were with him led away all the survivors from Mizpah whom he had recovered from Ishmael son of Nethaniah after he had assassinated Gedaliah son of Ahikam: the soldiers, women, children and court officials he had brought from Gibeon. ¹⁷And they went on, stopping at Geruth Kimham near Bethlehem on their way to Egypt ¹⁸to escape the Babylonians.ᵃ They were afraid of them because Ishmael son of Nethaniah had killed Gedaliah son of Ahikam, whom the king of Babylon had appointed as governor over the land.

42 Then all the army officers, including Johanan son of Kareah and Jezaniahᵇ son of Hoshaiah, and all the people from the least to the greatest approached ²Jeremiah the prophet and said to him, "Please hear our petition and pray to the LORD your God for this entire remnant. For as you now see, though we were once many, now only a few are left. ³Pray that the LORD your God will tell us where we should go and what we should do."

⁴"I have heard you," replied Jeremiah the prophet. "I will certainly pray to the LORD your God as you have requested; I will tell you everything the LORD says and will keep nothing back from you."

⁵Then they said to Jeremiah, "May the LORD be a true and faithful witness against us if we do not act in accordance with everything the LORD your God sends you to tell us. ⁶Whether it is favorable or unfavorable, we will obey the LORD our God, to whom we are sending you, so that it will go well with us, for we will obey the LORD our God."

⁷Ten days later the word of the LORD came to Jeremiah. ⁸So he called together Johanan son of Kareah and all the army officers who were with him and all the people from the least to the greatest. ⁹He said to them, "This is what the LORD, the God of Israel, to whom you sent me to present your petition, says: ¹⁰'If you stay in this land, I will build you up and not tear you down; I will plant you and not uproot you, for I am grieved over the disaster I have inflicted on you. ¹¹Do not be afraid of the king of Babylon, whom you now fear. Do not be afraid of him, declares the LORD, for I am with you and will save you and deliver you from his hands. ¹²I will show you compassion so that he will have compassion on you and restore you to your land.'

¹³"However, if you say, 'We will not stay in this land,' and so disobey the LORD your God, ¹⁴and if you say, 'No, we will go and live in Egypt, where we will not see war or hear the trumpet or be hungry for bread,' ¹⁵then hear the word of the LORD, O remnant of Judah. This is what the LORD Almighty, the God of Israel, says: 'If you are determined to go to Egypt and you do go to settle there, ¹⁶then the sword you fear will overtake you there, and the famine you dread will follow you into Egypt, and there you will die. ¹⁷Indeed, all who are determined to go to Egypt to settle there will die by the sword, famine and plague; not one of them will survive or escape the disaster I will bring on them.' ¹⁸This is what the LORD Almighty, the God of Israel, says: 'As my anger and wrath have been poured out on those who lived in Jerusalem, so will my wrath be poured out on you when you go to Egypt. You will be an object of cursing and horror, of condemnation and reproach; you will never see this place again.'

¹⁹"O remnant of Judah, the LORD has told you, 'Do not go to Egypt.' Be sure of this: I warn you today ²⁰that you made a fatal mistakeᶜ when you sent me to the LORD your God and said, 'Pray to the LORD our God for us; tell us everything he says and we will do it.' ²¹I have told you today, but you still have not obeyed the LORD your God in all he sent me to tell you. ²²So now, be sure of this: You will die by the sword, famine and plague in the place where you want to go to settle."

43 When Jeremiah finished telling the people all the words of the LORD their God—everything the LORD had sent him to tell them— ²Azariah son of Hoshaiah and Johanan son of Kareah and all the arrogant men said to Jeremiah, "You are lying! The LORD our God has not sent you to say, 'You must not go to Egypt to settle there.' ³But Baruch son of Neriah is inciting you against us to hand us over to the Babylonians,ᵃ so they may kill us or carry us into exile to Babylon."

⁴So Johanan son of Kareah and all the army officers and all the people disobeyed the LORD's command to stay in the land of Judah. ⁵Instead, Johanan son of Kareah and all the army officers led away all the remnant of Judah who had come back to live in the land of Judah from all the nations where they had been scattered. ⁶They also led away all the men,

---

ᵃ18,3 Or *Chaldeans*   ᵇ1 Hebrew; Septuagint (see also 43:2) *Azariah*   ᶜ20 Or *you erred in your hearts* women and children and the king's daughters whom Nebuzaradan commander of the imperial guard had left with Gedaliah son of Ahikam, the son of Shaphan, and Jeremiah the prophet and Baruch son of Neriah. [7]So they entered Egypt in disobedience to the Lord and went as far as Tahpanhes.

[8]In Tahpanhes the word of the Lord came to Jeremiah: [9]"While the Jews are watching, take some large stones with you and bury them in clay in the brick pavement at the entrance to Pharaoh's palace in Tahpanhes. [10]Then say to them, 'This is what the Lord Almighty, the God of Israel, says: I will send for my servant Nebuchadnezzar king of Babylon, and I will set his throne over these stones I have buried here; he will spread his royal canopy above them. [11]He will come and attack Egypt, bringing death to those destined for death, captivity to those destined for captivity, and the sword to those destined for the sword. [12]He[a] will set fire to the temples of the gods of Egypt; he will burn their temples and take their gods captive. As a shepherd wraps his garment around him, so will he wrap Egypt around himself and depart from there unscathed. [13]There in the temple of the sun[b] in Egypt he will demolish the sacred pillars and will burn down the temples of the gods of Egypt.' "

Disaster Because of Idolatry

44 This word came to Jeremiah concerning all the Jews living in Lower Egypt—in Migdol, Tahpanhes and Memphis[c]—and in Upper Egypt[d]: [2]"This is what the Lord Almighty, the God of Israel, says: You saw the great disaster I brought on Jerusalem and on all the towns of Judah. Today they lie deserted and in ruins [3]because of the evil they have done. They provoked me to anger by burning incense and by worshiping other gods that neither they nor you nor your fathers ever knew. [4]Again and again I sent my servants the prophets, who said, 'Do not do this detestable thing that I hate!' [5]But they did not listen or pay attention; they did not turn from their wickedness or stop burning incense to other gods. [6]Therefore, my fierce anger was poured out; it raged against the towns of Judah and the streets of Jerusalem and made them the desolate ruins they are today.

[7]"Now this is what the Lord God Almighty, the God of Israel, says: Why bring such great disaster on yourselves by cutting off from Judah the men and women, the children and infants, and so leave yourselves without a remnant? [8]Why provoke me to anger with what your hands have made, burning incense to other gods in Egypt, where you have come to live? You will destroy yourselves and make yourselves an object of cursing and reproach among all the nations on earth. [9]Have you forgotten the wickedness committed by your fathers and by the kings and queens of Judah and the wickedness committed by you and your wives in the land of Judah and the streets of Jerusalem? [10]To this day they have not humbled themselves or shown reverence, nor have they followed my law and the decrees I set before you and your fathers.

[11]"Therefore, this is what the Lord Almighty, the God of Israel, says: I am determined to bring disaster on you and to destroy all Judah. [12]I will take away the remnant of Judah who were determined to go to Egypt to settle there. They will all perish in Egypt; they will fall by the sword or die from famine. From the least to the greatest, they will die by sword or famine. They will become an object of cursing and horror, of condemnation and reproach. [13]I will punish those who live in Egypt with the sword, famine and plague, as I punished Jerusalem. [14]None of the remnant of Judah who have gone to live in Egypt will escape or survive to return to the land of Judah, to which they long to return and live; none will return except a few fugitives."

[15]Then all the men who knew that their wives were burning incense to other gods, along with all the women who were present—a large assembly—and all the people living in Lower and Upper Egypt,[e] said to Jeremiah, [16]"We will not listen to the message you have spoken to us in the name of the Lord! [17]We will certainly do everything we said we would: We will burn incense to the Queen of Heaven and will pour out drink offerings to her just as we and our fathers, our kings and our officials did in the towns of Judah and in the streets of Jerusalem. At that time we had plenty of food and were well off and suffered no harm. [18]But ever since we stopped burning incense to the Queen of

---

[a]12 Or I
and Pathros　　　[b]13 Or in Heliopolis　　　[c]1 Hebrew Noph　　　[d]1 Hebrew in Pathros　　　[e]15 Hebrew in Egypt

Heaven and pouring out drink offerings to her, we have had nothing and have been perishing by sword and famine."

¹⁹The women added, "When we burned incense to the Queen of Heaven and poured out drink offerings to her, did not our husbands know that we were making cakes like her image and pouring out drink offerings to her?"

²⁰Then Jeremiah said to all the people, both men and women, who were answering him, ²¹"Did not the LORD remember and think about the incense burned in the towns of Judah and the streets of Jerusalem by you and your fathers, your kings and your officials and the people of the land? ²²When the LORD could no longer endure your wicked actions and the detestable things you did, your land became an object of cursing and a desolate waste without inhabitants, as it is today. ²³Because you have burned incense and have sinned against the LORD and have not obeyed him or followed his law or his decrees or his stipulations, this disaster has come upon you, as you now see."

²⁴Then Jeremiah said to all the people, including the women, "Hear the word of the LORD, all you people of Judah in Egypt. ²⁵This is what the LORD Almighty, the God of Israel, says: You and your wives have shown by your actions what you promised when you said, 'We will certainly carry out the vows we made to burn incense and pour out drink offerings to the Queen of Heaven.'

"Go ahead then, do what you promised! Keep your vows! ²⁶But hear the word of the LORD, all Jews living in Egypt: 'I swear by my great name,' says the LORD, 'that no one from Judah living anywhere in Egypt will ever again invoke my name or swear, "As surely as the Sovereign LORD lives." ²⁷For I am watching over them for harm, not for good; the Jews in Egypt will perish by sword and famine until they are all destroyed. ²⁸Those who escape the sword and return to the land of Judah from Egypt will be very few. Then the whole remnant of Judah who came to live in Egypt will know whose word will stand—mine or theirs.

²⁹" 'This will be the sign to you that I will punish you in this place,' declares the LORD, 'so that you will know that my threats of harm against you will surely stand.' ³⁰This is what the LORD says: 'I am going to hand Pharaoh Hophra king of Egypt over to his enemies who seek his life, just as I handed Zedekiah king of Ju-

dah over to Nebuchadnezzar king of Babylon, the enemy who was seeking his life.' "

A Message to Baruch

45 This is what Jeremiah the prophet told Baruch son of Neriah in the fourth year of Jehoiakim son of Josiah king of Judah, after Baruch had written on a scroll the words Jeremiah was then dictating: ²"This is what the LORD, the God of Israel, says to you, Baruch: ³You said, 'Woe to me! The LORD has added sorrow to my pain; I am worn out with groaning and find no rest.' "

⁴The LORD said, "Say this to him: 'This is what the LORD says: I will overthrow what I have built and uproot what I have planted, throughout the land. ⁵Should you then seek great things for yourself? Seek them not. For I will bring disaster on all people, declares the LORD, but wherever you go I will let you escape with your life.' "

A Message About Egypt

46 This is the word of the LORD that came to Jeremiah the prophet concerning the nations:

²Concerning Egypt:

This is the message against the army of Pharaoh Neco king of Egypt, which was defeated at Carchemish on the Euphrates River by Nebuchadnezzar king of Babylon in the fourth year of Jehoiakim son of Josiah king of Judah:

³"Prepare your shields, both large and
small,
and march out for battle!
⁴Harness the horses,
mount the steeds!
Take your positions
with helmets on!
Polish your spears,
put on your armor!
⁵What do I see?
They are terrified,
they are retreating,
their warriors are defeated.
They flee in haste
without looking back,
and there is terror on every side,"
declares the LORD.
⁶"The swift cannot flee
nor the strong escape.
In the north by the River Euphrates
they stumble and fall.

7"Who is this that rises like the Nile,
  like rivers of surging waters?
8Egypt rises like the Nile,
  like rivers of surging waters.
She says, 'I will rise and cover the
    earth;
  I will destroy cities and their
    people.'
9Charge, O horses!
  Drive furiously, O charioteers!
March on, O warriors—
  men of Cush[a] and Put who carry
    shields,
  men of Lydia who draw the bow.
10But that day belongs to the Lord, the
    LORD Almighty—
  a day of vengeance, for vengeance
    on his foes.
The sword will devour till it is
    satisfied,
  till it has quenched its thirst with
    blood.
For the Lord, the LORD Almighty, will
    offer sacrifice
  in the land of the north by the
    River Euphrates.

11"Go up to Gilead and get balm,
  O Virgin Daughter of Egypt.
But you multiply remedies in vain;
  there is no healing for you.
12The nations will hear of your shame;
  your cries will fill the earth.
One warrior will stumble over
    another;
  both will fall down together."

13This is the message the LORD spoke to
Jeremiah the prophet about the coming
of Nebuchadnezzar king of Babylon to attack Egypt:

14"Announce this in Egypt, and
    proclaim it in Migdol;
  proclaim it also in Memphis[b] and
    Tahpanhes:
'Take your positions and get ready,
  for the sword devours those around
    you.'
15Why will your warriors be laid low?
  They cannot stand, for the LORD will
    push them down.
16They will stumble repeatedly;
  they will fall over each other.
They will say, 'Get up, let us go back
  to our own people and our native
    lands,
  away from the sword of the
    oppressor.'

17There they will exclaim,
  'Pharaoh king of Egypt is only a
    loud noise;
  he has missed his opportunity.'

18"As surely as I live," declares the
    King,
  whose name is the LORD Almighty,
"one will come who is like Tabor
    among the mountains,
  like Carmel by the sea.
19Pack your belongings for exile,
  you who live in Egypt,
for Memphis will be laid waste
  and lie in ruins without inhabitant.

20"Egypt is a beautiful heifer,
  but a gadfly is coming
    against her from the north.
21The mercenaries in her ranks
  are like fattened calves.
They too will turn and flee together,
  they will not stand their ground,
for the day of disaster is coming upon
    them,
  the time for them to be punished.
22Egypt will hiss like a fleeing serpent
  as the enemy advances in force;
they will come against her with axes,
  like men who cut down trees.
23They will chop down her forest,"
                    declares the LORD,
  "dense though it be.
They are more numerous than
    locusts,
  they cannot be counted.
24The Daughter of Egypt will be put to
    shame,
  handed over to the people of the
    north."

25The LORD Almighty, the God of Israel,
says: "I am about to bring punishment
on Amon god of Thebes,[c] on Pharaoh, on
Egypt and her gods and her kings, and on
those who rely on Pharaoh. 26I will hand
them over to those who seek their lives, to
Nebuchadnezzar king of Babylon and his
officers. Later, however, Egypt will be inhabited as in times past," declares the
LORD.

27"Do not fear, O Jacob my servant;
  do not be dismayed, O Israel.
I will surely save you out of a distant
    place,
  your descendants from the land of
    their exile.
Jacob will again have peace and
    security,

a9 That is, the upper Nile region   b14 Hebrew Noph; also in verse 19   c25 Hebrew No

and no one will make him afraid.
²⁸Do not fear, O Jacob my servant,
for I am with you," declares the
Lord.
"Though I completely destroy all the
nations
among which I scatter you,
I will not completely destroy you.
I will discipline you but only with
justice;
I will not let you go entirely
unpunished.'"

A Message About the Philistines

47 This is the word of the Lord that
came to Jeremiah the prophet
concerning the Philistines before Pharaoh attacked Gaza:

²This is what the Lord says:

"See how the waters are rising in the
north;
they will become an overflowing
torrent.
They will overflow the land and
everything in it,
the towns and those who live in
them.
The people will cry out;
all who dwell in the land will wail
³at the sound of the hoofs of galloping
steeds,
at the noise of enemy chariots
and the rumble of their wheels.
Fathers will not turn to help their
children;
their hands will hang limp.
⁴For the day has come
to destroy all the Philistines
and to cut off all survivors
who could help Tyre and Sidon.
The Lord is about to destroy the
Philistines,
the remnant from the coasts of
Caphtor.^a
⁵Gaza will shave her head in
mourning;
Ashkelon will be silenced.
O remnant on the plain,
how long will you cut yourselves?

⁶" 'Ah, sword of the Lord,' you cry,
'how long till you rest?
Return to your scabbard;
cease and be still.'
⁷But how can it rest
when the Lord has commanded it,

when he has ordered it
to attack Ashkelon and the coast?"

A Message About Moab

48 Concerning Moab:

This is what the Lord Almighty,
the God of Israel, says:

"Woe to Nebo, for it will be ruined.
Kiriathaim will be disgraced and
captured;
the stronghold^b will be disgraced
and shattered.
²Moab will be praised no more;
in Heshbon^c men will plot her
downfall:
'Come, let us put an end to that
nation.'
You too, O Madmen,^d will be
silenced;
the sword will pursue you.
³Listen to the cries from Horonaim,
cries of great havoc and
destruction.
⁴Moab will be broken;
her little ones will cry out.^e
⁵They go up the way to Luhith,
weeping bitterly as they go;
on the road down to Horonaim
anguished cries over the destruction
are heard.
⁶Flee! Run for your lives;
become like a bush^f in the desert.
⁷Since you trust in your deeds and
riches,
you too will be taken captive,
and Chemosh will go into exile,
together with his priests and
officials.
⁸The destroyer will come against every
town,
and not a town will escape.
The valley will be ruined
and the plateau destroyed,
because the Lord has spoken.
⁹Put salt on Moab,
for she will be laid waste^g;
her towns will become desolate,
with no one to live in them.

¹⁰"A curse on him who is lax in doing
the Lord's work!
A curse on him who keeps his
sword from bloodshed!

¹¹"Moab has been at rest from youth,
like wine left on its dregs,

---

^a4 That is, Crete   ^b1 Or / Misgab   ^c2 The Hebrew for *Heshbon* sounds like the Hebrew for *plot.*
^d2 The name of the Moabite town Madmen sounds like the Hebrew for *be silenced.*   ^e4 Hebrew;
Septuagint / *proclaim it to Zoar*   ^f6 Or *like Aroer*   ^g9 Or *Give wings to Moab, / for she will fly away*

not poured from one jar to another—
she has not gone into exile.
So she tastes as she did,
and her aroma is unchanged.
¹²But days are coming,"
declares the LORD,
"when I will send men who pour from
jars,
and they will pour her out;
they will empty her jars
and smash her jugs.
¹³Then Moab will be ashamed of
Chemosh,
as the house of Israel was ashamed
when they trusted in Bethel.

¹⁴"How can you say, 'We are warriors,
men valiant in battle'?
¹⁵Moab will be destroyed and her towns
invaded;
her finest young men will go down
in the slaughter,"
declares the King, whose name is
the LORD Almighty.
¹⁶"The fall of Moab is at hand;
her calamity will come quickly.
¹⁷Mourn for her, all who live around
her,
all who know her fame;
say, 'How broken is the mighty
scepter,
how broken the glorious staff!'

¹⁸"Come down from your glory
and sit on the parched ground,
O inhabitants of the Daughter of
Dibon,
for he who destroys Moab
will come up against you
and ruin your fortified cities.
¹⁹Stand by the road and watch,
you who live in Aroer.
Ask the man fleeing and the woman
escaping,
ask them, 'What has happened?'
²⁰Moab is disgraced, for she is
shattered.
Wail and cry out!
Announce by the Arnon
that Moab is destroyed.
²¹Judgment has come to the plateau—
to Holon, Jahzah and Mephaath,
²² to Dibon, Nebo and Beth
Diblathaim,
²³ to Kiriathaim, Beth Gamul and
Beth Meon,
²⁴ to Kerioth and Bozrah—
to all the towns of Moab, far and
near.

²⁵Moab's horn[a] is cut off;
her arm is broken,"
declares the LORD.

²⁶"Make her drunk,
for she has defied the LORD.
Let Moab wallow in her vomit;
let her be an object of ridicule.
²⁷Was not Israel the object of your
ridicule?
Was she caught among thieves,
that you shake your head in scorn
whenever you speak of her?
²⁸Abandon your towns and dwell among
the rocks,
you who live in Moab.
Be like a dove that makes its nest
at the mouth of a cave.

²⁹"We have heard of Moab's pride—
her overweening pride and conceit,
her pride and arrogance
and the haughtiness of her heart.
³⁰I know her insolence but it is futile,"
declares the LORD,
"and her boasts accomplish
nothing.
³¹Therefore I wail over Moab,
for all Moab I cry out,
I moan for the men of Kir
Hareseth.
³²I weep for you, as Jazer weeps,
O vines of Sibmah.
Your branches spread as far as the
sea;
they reached as far as the sea of
Jazer.
The destroyer has fallen
on your ripened fruit and grapes.
³³Joy and gladness are gone
from the orchards and fields of
Moab.
I have stopped the flow of wine from
the presses;
no one treads them with shouts of
joy.
Although there are shouts,
they are not shouts of joy.

³⁴"The sound of their cry rises
from Heshbon to Elealeh and
Jahaz,
from Zoar as far as Horonaim and
Eglath Shelishiyah,
for even the waters of Nimrim are
dried up.
³⁵In Moab I will put an end
to those who make offerings on the
high places

---

a25 Horn here symbolizes strength.

VERSE FOR THE DAY:
Jeremiah 48:31,33

AUTHOR:
Maureen Rank

PASSAGE FOR THE DAY:
Jeremiah 48:29–38

The Validity of Mourning

I CAUGHT just enough of the radio speaker's thoughts on grieving to come away with this particular gem: "A trembling lower lip may be more the sign of a true Christian than a stiff upper lip." And I realize now how much that man understood of a godly perspective on grieving.

The Old Testament reveals a grieving God. "I wail over Moab," he says, "for all Moab I cry out" (Jeremiah 48:31). And in the New Testament, God the Son bares his heartbreak at the loss of those he loves: "O Jerusalem, Jerusalem, you who kill the prophets and stone those sent to you, how often I have longed to gather your children together, as a hen gathers her chicks under her wings, but you were not willing!" (Luke 13:34). He mourned the children he loved. He expects you will mourn the loss of yours.

I don't want to romanticize grieving. Real mourning is ugly and deep and wrenching, no matter how flowery and tasteful sympathy cards try to make it out to be. But trying to sidestep grief represents a proud and silly effort to avoid the unavoidable. When Jesus promised that those who mourn would be comforted, he laid down an inescapable prerequisite for receiving the deep, rich wonder of God's healing (Matthew 5:4). To become a candidate for his comfort, you first must open yourself up to the pain of mourning.

Paul admonished the Christians at Thessalonica, "Brothers, we do not want you to . . . grieve like the rest of men, who have no hope" (1 Thessalonians 4:13). Paul told his fellow believers not to grieve hopelessly, but he did not challenge them to forego grieving.

Grief is different for a follower of Christ. Even in the depths of sorrow, hope breathes. Hope that you will see your loved one again in heaven. Hope in God's capacity to infuse suffering with purpose. And hope that because of his healing power, your sorrow will not go on forever.

Additional Scripture Readings:
Psalm 42:1–8; Lamentations 3:31–33

Go to page 873 for your next
devotional reading.

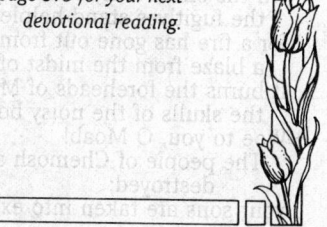

and burn incense to their gods,"
                    declares the LORD.
36"So my heart laments for Moab like a
    flute;
  it laments like a flute for the men
    of Kir Hareseth.
  The wealth they acquired is gone.
37Every head is shaved
    and every beard cut off;
  every hand is slashed
    and every waist is covered with
      sackcloth.
38On all the roofs in Moab
    and in the public squares
  there is nothing but mourning,
    for I have broken Moab
  like a jar that no one wants,"
                    declares the LORD.
39"How shattered she is! How they wail!
  How Moab turns her back in
    shame!
  Moab has become an object of
    ridicule,
  an object of horror to all those
    around her."

40This is what the LORD says:

"Look! An eagle is swooping down,
  spreading its wings over Moab.
41Kerioth*a* will be captured
  and the strongholds taken.
In that day the hearts of Moab's
    warriors
  will be like the heart of a woman in
    labor.
42Moab will be destroyed as a nation
  because she defied the LORD.
43Terror and pit and snare await you,
  O people of Moab,"
                    declares the LORD.
44"Whoever flees from the terror
  will fall into a pit,
whoever climbs out of the pit
  will be caught in a snare;
for I will bring upon Moab
  the year of her punishment,"
                    declares the LORD.

45"In the shadow of Heshbon
  the fugitives stand helpless,
for a fire has gone out from Heshbon,
  a blaze from the midst of Sihon;
it burns the foreheads of Moab,
  the skulls of the noisy boasters.
46Woe to you, O Moab!
  The people of Chemosh are
    destroyed;
  your sons are taken into exile

and your daughters into captivity.
47"Yet I will restore the fortunes of
    Moab
  in days to come,"
                    declares the LORD.

Here ends the judgment on Moab.

A Message About Ammon

49 Concerning the Ammonites:

  This is what the LORD says:

"Has Israel no sons?
  Has she no heirs?
Why then has Molech*b* taken
    possession of Gad?
  Why do his people live in its towns?
2But the days are coming,"
                    declares the LORD,
"when I will sound the battle cry
    against Rabbah of the Ammonites;
it will become a mound of ruins,
  and its surrounding villages will be
    set on fire.
Then Israel will drive out
  those who drove her out,"
                    says the LORD.
3"Wail, O Heshbon, for Ai is destroyed!
  Cry out, O inhabitants of Rabbah!
Put on sackcloth and mourn;
  rush here and there inside the
    walls,
for Molech will go into exile,
  together with his priests and
    officials.
4Why do you boast of your valleys,
  boast of your valleys so fruitful?
O unfaithful daughter,
  you trust in your riches and say,
  'Who will attack me?'
5I will bring terror on you
  from all those around you,"
                    declares the Lord,
                    the LORD Almighty.
"Every one of you will be driven away,
  and no one will gather the fugitives.

6"Yet afterward, I will restore the
    fortunes of the Ammonites,"
                    declares the LORD.

A Message About Edom

7Concerning Edom:

This is what the LORD Almighty says:

"Is there no longer wisdom in Teman?
  Has counsel perished from the
    prudent?

---

*a*41 Or *The cities*   *b*1 Or *their king*; Hebrew *malcam*; also in verse 3

Has their wisdom decayed?
[8]Turn and flee, hide in deep caves,
  you who live in Dedan,
for I will bring disaster on Esau
  at the time I punish him.
[9]If grape pickers came to you,
  would they not leave a few grapes?
If thieves came during the night,
  would they not steal only as much
    as they wanted?
[10]But I will strip Esau bare;
  I will uncover his hiding places,
  so that he cannot conceal himself.
His children, relatives and neighbors
    will perish,
  and he will be no more.
[11]Leave your orphans; I will protect
    their lives.
  Your widows too can trust in
    me."

[12]This is what the LORD says: "If those
who do not deserve to drink the cup must
drink it, why should you go unpunished?
You will not go unpunished, but must
drink it. [13]I swear by myself," declares the
LORD, "that Bozrah will become a ruin and
an object of horror, of reproach and of
cursing; and all its towns will be in ruins
forever."

[14]I have heard a message from the
  LORD:
An envoy was sent to the nations to
    say,
"Assemble yourselves to attack it!
  Rise up for battle!"

[15]"Now I will make you small among
    the nations,
  despised among men.
[16]The terror you inspire
  and the pride of your heart have
    deceived you,
you who live in the clefts of the
    rocks,
  who occupy the heights of the hill.
Though you build your nest as high as
    the eagle's,
  from there I will bring you down,"
    declares the LORD.
[17]"Edom will become an object of
    horror;
  all who pass by will be appalled
  and will scoff
  because of all its wounds.
[18]As Sodom and Gomorrah were
    overthrown,

along with their neighboring
    towns,"
    says the LORD,
"so no one will live there;
  no man will dwell in it.

[19]"Like a lion coming up from Jordan's
    thickets
  to a rich pastureland,
I will chase Edom from its land in an
    instant.
Who is the chosen one I will
    appoint for this?
Who is like me and who can
    challenge me?
And what shepherd can stand
    against me?"
[20]Therefore, hear what the LORD has
    planned against Edom,
  what he has purposed against those
    who live in Teman:
The young of the flock will be
    dragged away;
  he will completely destroy their
    pasture because of them.
[21]At the sound of their fall the earth
    will tremble;
  their cry will resound to the Red
    Sea.[a]
[22]Look! An eagle will soar and swoop
    down,
  spreading its wings over Bozrah.
In that day the hearts of Edom's
    warriors
  will be like the heart of a woman in
    labor.

A Message About Damascus

[23]Concerning Damascus:

"Hamath and Arpad are dismayed,
  for they have heard bad news.
They are disheartened,
  troubled like[b] the restless sea.
[24]Damascus has become feeble,
  she has turned to flee
  and panic has gripped her;
anguish and pain have seized her,
  pain like that of a woman in labor.
[25]Why has the city of renown not been
    abandoned,
  the town in which I delight?
[26]Surely, her young men will fall in the
    streets;
  all her soldiers will be silenced in
    that day,"
    declares the LORD Almighty.
[27]"I will set fire to the walls of
    Damascus;

---

[a]21 Hebrew *Yam Suph*; that is, Sea of Reeds   [b]23 Hebrew *on* or *by*

it will consume the fortresses of
Ben-Hadad."

A Message About Kedar and Hazor

²⁸Concerning Kedar and the kingdoms
of Hazor, which Nebuchadnezzar king of
Babylon attacked:

This is what the LORD says:

"Arise, and attack Kedar
  and destroy the people of the East.
²⁹Their tents and their flocks will be
    taken;
  their shelters will be carried off
  with all their goods and camels.
Men will shout to them,
  'Terror on every side!'

³⁰"Flee quickly away!
  Stay in deep caves, you who live in
    Hazor,"
                    declares the LORD.
"Nebuchadnezzar king of Babylon has
    plotted against you;
  he has devised a plan against you.

³¹"Arise and attack a nation at ease,
  which lives in confidence,"
                    declares the LORD,
"a nation that has neither gates nor
    bars;
  its people live alone.
³²Their camels will become plunder,
  and their large herds will be booty.
I will scatter to the winds those who
    are in distant places^a
  and will bring disaster on them
    from every side,"
                    declares the LORD.
³³"Hazor will become a haunt of
    jackals,
  a desolate place forever.
No one will live there;
  no man will dwell in it."

A Message About Elam

³⁴This is the word of the LORD that came
to Jeremiah the prophet concerning
Elam, early in the reign of Zedekiah king
of Judah:

³⁵This is what the LORD Almighty says:

"See, I will break the bow of Elam,
  the mainstay of their might.
³⁶I will bring against Elam the four
    winds
  from the four quarters of the
    heavens;
I will scatter them to the four winds,

and there will not be a nation
  where Elam's exiles do not go.
³⁷I will shatter Elam before their foes,
  before those who seek their lives;
I will bring disaster upon them,
  even my fierce anger,"
                    declares the LORD.
"I will pursue them with the sword
  until I have made an end of them.
³⁸I will set my throne in Elam
  and destroy her king and officials,"
                    declares the LORD.

³⁹"Yet I will restore the fortunes of
    Elam
  in days to come,"
                    declares the LORD.

A Message About Babylon

50 This is the word the LORD spoke
through Jeremiah the prophet
concerning Babylon and the land of the
Babylonians^b:

²"Announce and proclaim among the
    nations,
  lift up a banner and proclaim it;
  keep nothing back, but say,
'Babylon will be captured;
  Bel will be put to shame,
  Marduk filled with terror.
Her images will be put to shame
  and her idols filled with terror.'
³A nation from the north will attack
    her
  and lay waste her land.
No one will live in it;
  both men and animals will flee
    away.

⁴"In those days, at that time,"
                    declares the LORD,
"the people of Israel and the people
    of Judah together
  will go in tears to seek the LORD
    their God.
⁵They will ask the way to Zion
  and turn their faces toward it.
They will come and bind themselves
    to the LORD
  in an everlasting covenant
  that will not be forgotten.

⁶"My people have been lost sheep;
  their shepherds have led them
    astray
  and caused them to roam on the
    mountains.
They wandered over mountain and
    hill

---

^a32 Or who clip the hair by their foreheads   ^b1 Or Chaldeans; also in verses 8, 25, 35 and 45

and forgot their own resting place.
⁷Whoever found them devoured them;
their enemies said, 'We are not
guilty,
for they sinned against the LORD, their
true pasture,
the LORD, the hope of their fathers.'

⁸"Flee out of Babylon;
leave the land of the Babylonians,
and be like the goats that lead the
flock.
⁹For I will stir up and bring against
Babylon
an alliance of great nations from
the land of the north.
They will take up their positions
against her,
and from the north she will be
captured.
Their arrows will be like skilled
warriors
who do not return empty-handed.
¹⁰So Babylonia*ᵃ* will be plundered;
all who plunder her will have their
fill,"
          declares the LORD.

¹¹"Because you rejoice and are glad,
you who pillage my inheritance,
because you frolic like a heifer
threshing grain
and neigh like stallions,
¹²your mother will be greatly ashamed;
she who gave you birth will be
disgraced.
She will be the least of the nations —
a wilderness, a dry land, a desert.
¹³Because of the LORD's anger she will
not be inhabited
but will be completely desolate.
All who pass Babylon will be horrified
and scoff
because of all her wounds.

¹⁴"Take up your positions around
Babylon,
all you who draw the bow.
Shoot at her! Spare no arrows,
for she has sinned against the LORD.
¹⁵Shout against her on every side!
She surrenders, her towers fall,
her walls are torn down.
Since this is the vengeance of the
LORD,
take vengeance on her;
do to her as she has done to others.
¹⁶Cut off from Babylon the sower,

and the reaper with his sickle at
harvest.
Because of the sword of the oppressor
let everyone return to his own
people,
let everyone flee to his own land.

¹⁷"Israel is a scattered flock
that lions have chased away.
The first to devour him
was the king of Assyria;
the last to crush his bones
was Nebuchadnezzar king of
Babylon."

¹⁸Therefore this is what the LORD Almighty, the God of Israel, says:

"I will punish the king of Babylon and
his land
as I punished the king of Assyria.
¹⁹But I will bring Israel back to his own
pasture
and he will graze on Carmel and
Bashan;
his appetite will be satisfied
on the hills of Ephraim and Gilead.
²⁰In those days, at that time,"
declares the LORD,
"search will be made for Israel's guilt,
but there will be none,
and for the sins of Judah,
but none will be found,
for I will forgive the remnant I
spare.

²¹"Attack the land of Merathaim
and those who live in Pekod.
Pursue, kill and completely destroyᵇ
them,"
          declares the LORD.
"Do everything I have commanded
you.
²²The noise of battle is in the land,
the noise of great destruction!
²³How broken and shattered
is the hammer of the whole earth!
How desolate is Babylon
among the nations!
²⁴I set a trap for you, O Babylon,
and you were caught before you
knew it;
you were found and captured
because you opposed the LORD.
²⁵The LORD has opened his arsenal
and brought out the weapons of his
wrath,
for the Sovereign LORD Almighty has
work to do

ᵃ10 Or *Chaldea*   *ᵇ21* The Hebrew term refers to the irrevocable giving over of things or persons to the
LORD, often by totally destroying them; also in verse 26.

in the land of the Babylonians.
26Come against her from afar.
Break open her granaries;
pile her up like heaps of grain.
Completely destroy her
and leave her no remnant.
27Kill all her young bulls;
let them go down to the slaughter!
Woe to them! For their day has come,
the time for them to be punished.
28Listen to the fugitives and refugees
from Babylon
declaring in Zion
how the LORD our God has taken
vengeance,
vengeance for his temple.

29"Summon archers against Babylon,
all those who draw the bow.
Encamp all around her;
let no one escape.
Repay her for her deeds;
do to her as she has done.
For she has defied the LORD,
the Holy One of Israel.
30Therefore, her young men will fall in
the streets;
all her soldiers will be silenced in
that day,"
declares the LORD.
31"See, I am against you, O arrogant
one,"
declares the Lord, the LORD
Almighty,
"for your day has come,
the time for you to be punished.
32The arrogant one will stumble and
fall
and no one will help her up;
I will kindle a fire in her towns
that will consume all who are
around her."

33This is what the LORD Almighty says:

"The people of Israel are oppressed,
and the people of Judah as well.
All their captors hold them fast,
refusing to let them go.
34Yet their Redeemer is strong;
the LORD Almighty is his name.
He will vigorously defend their cause
so that he may bring rest to their
land,
but unrest to those who live in
Babylon.

35"A sword against the Babylonians!"
declares the LORD —
"against those who live in Babylon

and against her officials and wise
men!
36A sword against her false prophets!
They will become fools.
A sword against her warriors!
They will be filled with terror.
37A sword against her horses and
chariots
and all the foreigners in her ranks!
They will become women.
A sword against her treasures!
They will be plundered.
38A drought on[a] her waters!
They will dry up.
For it is a land of idols,
idols that will go mad with terror.

39"So desert creatures and hyenas will
live there,
and there the owl will dwell.
It will never again be inhabited
or lived in from generation to
generation.
40As God overthrew Sodom and
Gomorrah
along with their neighboring
towns,"
declares the LORD,
"so no one will live there;
no man will dwell in it.

41"Look! An army is coming from the
north;
a great nation and many kings
are being stirred up from the ends
of the earth.
42They are armed with bows and spears;
they are cruel and without mercy.
They sound like the roaring sea
as they ride on their horses;
they come like men in battle
formation
to attack you, O Daughter of
Babylon.
43The king of Babylon has heard reports
about them,
and his hands hang limp.
Anguish has gripped him,
pain like that of a woman in labor.
44Like a lion coming up from Jordan's
thickets
to a rich pastureland,
I will chase Babylon from its land in
an instant.
Who is the chosen one I will
appoint for this?
Who is like me and who can
challenge me?

a38 Or A sword against

And what shepherd can stand
  against me?"
[45]Therefore, hear what the LORD has
    planned against Babylon,
  what he has purposed against the
    land of the Babylonians:
The young of the flock will be
    dragged away;
  he will completely destroy their
    pasture because of them.
[46]At the sound of Babylon's capture the
    earth will tremble;
  its cry will resound among the
    nations.

51

This is what the LORD says:
  "See, I will stir up the spirit of a
    destroyer
  against Babylon and the people of
    Leb Kamai.[a]
[2]I will send foreigners to Babylon
  to winnow her and to devastate her
    land;
  they will oppose her on every side
    in the day of her disaster.
[3]Let not the archer string his bow,
    nor let him put on his armor.
  Do not spare her young men;
    completely destroy[b] her army.
[4]They will fall down slain in Babylon,[c]
    fatally wounded in her streets.
[5]For Israel and Judah have not been
    forsaken
  by their God, the LORD Almighty,
  though their land[d] is full of guilt
    before the Holy One of Israel.

[6]"Flee from Babylon!
    Run for your lives!
  Do not be destroyed because of her
    sins.
  It is time for the LORD's vengeance;
    he will pay her what she deserves.
[7]Babylon was a gold cup in the LORD's
    hand;
  she made the whole earth drunk.
  The nations drank her wine;
    therefore they have now gone mad.
[8]Babylon will suddenly fall and be
    broken.
    Wail over her!
  Get balm for her pain;
    perhaps she can be healed.

[9]" 'We would have healed Babylon,
    but she cannot be healed;

let us leave her and each go to his
    own land,
  for her judgment reaches to the
    skies,
  it rises as high as the clouds.'

[10]" 'The LORD has vindicated us;
    come, let us tell in Zion
  what the LORD our God has done.'

[11]"Sharpen the arrows,
    take up the shields!
  The LORD has stirred up the kings of
    the Medes,
  because his purpose is to destroy
    Babylon.
  The LORD will take vengeance,
    vengeance for his temple.
[12]Lift up a banner against the walls of
    Babylon!
  Reinforce the guard,
  station the watchmen,
    prepare an ambush!
  The LORD will carry out his purpose,
    his decree against the people of
      Babylon.
[13]You who live by many waters
    and are rich in treasures,
  your end has come,
    the time for you to be cut off.
[14]The LORD Almighty has sworn by
    himself:
  I will surely fill you with men, as
    with a swarm of locusts,
  and they will shout in triumph over
    you.

[15]"He made the earth by his power;
  he founded the world by his
    wisdom
  and stretched out the heavens by
    his understanding.
[16]When he thunders, the waters in the
    heavens roar;
  he makes clouds rise from the ends
    of the earth.
  He sends lightning with the rain
    and brings out the wind from his
      storehouses.

[17]"Every man is senseless and without
    knowledge;
  every goldsmith is shamed by his
    idols.
  His images are a fraud;
    they have no breath in them.
[18]They are worthless, the objects of
    mockery;

---

[a]1 *Leb Kamai* is a cryptogram for Chaldea, that is, Babylonia.   [b]3 The Hebrew term refers to the
irrevocable giving over of things or persons to the LORD, often by totally destroying them.   [c]4 Or
Chaldea   [d]5 Or / *and the land of the Babylonians,*

when their judgment comes, they
 will perish.
¹⁹He who is the Portion of Jacob is not
 like these,
 for he is the Maker of all things,
 including the tribe of his
 inheritance—
 the LORD Almighty is his name.

²⁰"You are my war club,
 my weapon for battle—
with you I shatter nations,
 with you I destroy kingdoms,
²¹with you I shatter horse and rider,
 with you I shatter chariot and
 driver,
²²with you I shatter man and woman,
 with you I shatter old man and
 youth,
 with you I shatter young man and
 maiden,
²³with you I shatter shepherd and flock,
 with you I shatter farmer and oxen,
 with you I shatter governors and
 officials.

²⁴"Before your eyes I will repay Babylon
and all who live in Babylonia*a* for all the
wrong they have done in Zion," declares
the LORD.

²⁵"I am against you, O destroying
 mountain,
 you who destroy the whole earth,"
 declares the LORD.
 "I will stretch out my hand against
 you,
 roll you off the cliffs,
 and make you a burned-out
 mountain.
²⁶No rock will be taken from you for a
 cornerstone,
 nor any stone for a foundation,
 for you will be desolate forever,"
 declares the LORD.

²⁷"Lift up a banner in the land!
 Blow the trumpet among the
 nations!
Prepare the nations for battle against
 her;
 summon against her these
 kingdoms:
 Ararat, Minni and Ashkenaz.
Appoint a commander against her;
 send up horses like a swarm of
 locusts.
²⁸Prepare the nations for battle against
 her—
 the kings of the Medes,

their governors and all their officials,
 and all the countries they rule.
²⁹The land trembles and writhes,
 for the LORD's purposes against
 Babylon stand—
 to lay waste the land of Babylon
 so that no one will live there.
³⁰Babylon's warriors have stopped
 fighting;
 they remain in their strongholds.
Their strength is exhausted;
 they have become like women.
Her dwellings are set on fire;
 the bars of her gates are broken.
³¹One courier follows another
 and messenger follows messenger
to announce to the king of Babylon
 that his entire city is captured,
³²the river crossings seized,
 the marshes set on fire,
 and the soldiers terrified."

³³This is what the LORD Almighty, the
God of Israel, says:

"The Daughter of Babylon is like a
 threshing floor
 at the time it is trampled;
 the time to harvest her will soon
 come."

³⁴"Nebuchadnezzar king of Babylon has
 devoured us,
 he has thrown us into confusion,
 he has made us an empty jar.
Like a serpent he has swallowed us
 and filled his stomach with our
 delicacies,
 and then has spewed us out.
³⁵May the violence done to our flesh*b*
 be upon Babylon,"
 say the inhabitants of Zion.
"May our blood be on those who live
 in Babylonia,"
 says Jerusalem.

³⁶Therefore, this is what the LORD says:

"See, I will defend your cause
 and avenge you;
I will dry up her sea
 and make her springs dry.
³⁷Babylon will be a heap of ruins,
 a haunt of jackals,
 an object of horror and scorn,
 a place where no one lives.
³⁸Her people all roar like young lions,
 they growl like lion cubs.
³⁹But while they are aroused,
 I will set out a feast for them

---

a24 Or *Chaldea;* also in verse 35   *b35* Or *done to us and to our children*

and make them drunk,
so that they shout with laughter—
then sleep forever and not awake,"
        declares the Lord.

40"I will bring them down
    like lambs to the slaughter,
    like rams and goats.

41"How Sheshach[a] will be captured,
    the boast of the whole earth
        seized!
What a horror Babylon will be
    among the nations!
42The sea will rise over Babylon;
    its roaring waves will cover her.
43Her towns will be desolate,
    a dry and desert land,
    a land where no one lives,
        through which no man travels.
44I will punish Bel in Babylon
    and make him spew out what he
        has swallowed.
The nations will no longer stream to
    him.
And the wall of Babylon will fall.

45"Come out of her, my people!
    Run for your lives!
    Run from the fierce anger of the
        Lord.
46Do not lose heart or be afraid
    when rumors are heard in the
        land;
    one rumor comes this year, another
        the next,
    rumors of violence in the land
    and of ruler against ruler.
47For the time will surely come
    when I will punish the idols of
        Babylon;
    her whole land will be disgraced
    and her slain will all lie fallen
        within her.
48Then heaven and earth and all that is
    in them
    will shout for joy over Babylon,
for out of the north
    destroyers will attack her,"
        declares the Lord.

49"Babylon must fall because of Israel's
    slain,
    just as the slain in all the earth
    have fallen because of Babylon.
50You who have escaped the sword,
    leave and do not linger!
Remember the Lord in a distant
    land,
    and think on Jerusalem."

51"We are disgraced,
    for we have been insulted
    and shame covers our faces,
    because foreigners have entered
    the holy places of the Lord's
        house."

52"But days are coming," declares the
    Lord,
    "when I will punish her idols,
and throughout her land
    the wounded will groan.
53Even if Babylon reaches the sky
    and fortifies her lofty stronghold,
    I will send destroyers against her,"
        declares the Lord.

54"The sound of a cry comes from
    Babylon,
    the sound of great destruction
    from the land of the Babylonians.[b]
55The Lord will destroy Babylon;
    he will silence her noisy din.
Waves of enemies will rage like great
    waters;
    the roar of their voices will
        resound.
56A destroyer will come against
    Babylon;
    her warriors will be captured,
    and their bows will be broken.
For the Lord is a God of retribution;
    he will repay in full.
57I will make her officials and wise men
    drunk,
    her governors, officers and warriors
        as well;
they will sleep forever and not
    awake,"
    declares the King, whose name is
        the Lord Almighty.

58This is what the Lord Almighty says:

"Babylon's thick wall will be
    leveled
    and her high gates set on fire;
the peoples exhaust themselves for
    nothing,
    the nations' labor is only fuel for
        the flames."

59This is the message Jeremiah gave to
the staff officer Seraiah son of Neriah, the
son of Mahseiah, when he went to Babylon with Zedekiah king of Judah in the
fourth year of his reign. 60Jeremiah had
written on a scroll about all the disasters
that would come upon Babylon—all that

had been recorded concerning Babylon. [61]He said to Seraiah, "When you get to Babylon, see that you read all these words aloud. [62]Then say, 'O LORD, you have said you will destroy this place, so that neither man nor animal will live in it; it will be desolate forever.' [63]When you finish reading this scroll, tie a stone to it and throw it into the Euphrates. [64]Then say, 'So will Babylon sink to rise no more because of the disaster I will bring upon her. And her people will fall.' "

The words of Jeremiah end here.

The Fall of Jerusalem

52 Zedekiah was twenty-one years old when he became king, and he reigned in Jerusalem eleven years. His mother's name was Hamutal daughter of Jeremiah; she was from Libnah. [2]He did evil in the eyes of the LORD, just as Jehoiakim had done. [3]It was because of the LORD's anger that all this happened to Jerusalem and Judah, and in the end he thrust them from his presence.

Now Zedekiah rebelled against the king of Babylon.

[4]So in the ninth year of Zedekiah's reign, on the tenth day of the tenth month, Nebuchadnezzar king of Babylon marched against Jerusalem with his whole army. They camped outside the city and built siege works all around it. [5]The city was kept under siege until the eleventh year of King Zedekiah.

[6]By the ninth day of the fourth month the famine in the city had become so severe that there was no food for the people to eat. [7]Then the city wall was broken through, and the whole army fled. They left the city at night through the gate between the two walls near the king's garden, though the Babylonians[a] were surrounding the city. They fled toward the Arabah,[b] [8]but the Babylonian[c] army pursued King Zedekiah and overtook him in the plains of Jericho. All his soldiers were separated from him and scattered, [9]and he was captured.

He was taken to the king of Babylon at Riblah in the land of Hamath, where he pronounced sentence on him. [10]There at Riblah the king of Babylon slaughtered the sons of Zedekiah before his eyes; he also killed all the officials of Judah.

[11]Then he put out Zedekiah's eyes, bound him with bronze shackles and took him to Babylon, where he put him in prison till the day of his death.

[12]On the tenth day of the fifth month, in the nineteenth year of Nebuchadnezzar king of Babylon, Nebuzaradan commander of the imperial guard, who served the king of Babylon, came to Jerusalem. [13]He set fire to the temple of the LORD, the royal palace and all the houses of Jerusalem. Every important building he burned down. [14]The whole Babylonian army under the commander of the imperial guard broke down all the walls around Jerusalem. [15]Nebuzaradan the commander of the guard carried into exile some of the poorest people and those who remained in the city, along with the rest of the craftsmen[d] and those who had gone over to the king of Babylon. [16]But Nebuzaradan left behind the rest of the poorest people of the land to work the vineyards and fields.

[17]The Babylonians broke up the bronze pillars, the movable stands and the bronze Sea that were at the temple of the LORD and they carried all the bronze to Babylon. [18]They also took away the pots, shovels, wick trimmers, sprinkling bowls, dishes and all the bronze articles used in the temple service. [19]The commander of the imperial guard took away the basins, censers, sprinkling bowls, pots, lampstands, dishes and bowls used for drink offerings—all that were made of pure gold or silver.

[20]The bronze from the two pillars, the Sea and the twelve bronze bulls under it, and the movable stands, which King Solomon had made for the temple of the LORD, was more than could be weighed. [21]Each of the pillars was eighteen cubits high and twelve cubits in circumference[e]; each was four fingers thick, and hollow. [22]The bronze capital on top of the one pillar was five cubits[f] high and was decorated with a network and pomegranates of bronze all around. The other pillar, with its pomegranates, was similar. [23]There were ninety-six pomegranates on the sides; the total number of pomegranates above the surrounding network was a hundred.

[24]The commander of the guard took as

---

a7 Or *Chaldeans*; also in verse 17   *b7* Or *the Jordan Valley*   *c8* Or *Chaldean*; also in verse 14   *d15* Or *populace*   *e21* That is, about 27 feet (about 8.1 meters) high and 18 feet (about 5.4 meters) in circumference   *f22* That is, about 7 1/2 feet (about 2.3 meters) prisoners Seraiah the chief priest, Zephaniah the priest next in rank and the three doorkeepers. ²⁵Of those still in the city, he took the officer in charge of the fighting men, and seven royal advisers. He also took the secretary who was chief officer in charge of conscripting the people of the land and sixty of his men who were found in the city. ²⁶Nebuzaradan the commander took them all and brought them to the king of Babylon at Riblah. ²⁷There at Riblah, in the land of Hamath, the king had them executed.

So Judah went into captivity, away from her land. ²⁸This is the number of the people Nebuchadnezzar carried into exile:

in the seventh year, 3,023 Jews;
²⁹in Nebuchadnezzar's eighteenth year,
832 people from Jerusalem;

³⁰in his twenty-third year,
745 Jews taken into exile by Nebuzaradan the commander of the imperial guard.
There were 4,600 people in all.

Jehoiachin Released

³¹In the thirty-seventh year of the exile of Jehoiachin king of Judah, in the year Evil-Merodach*a* became king of Babylon, he released Jehoiachin king of Judah and freed him from prison on the twenty-fifth day of the twelfth month. ³²He spoke kindly to him and gave him a seat of honor higher than those of the other kings who were with him in Babylon. ³³So Jehoiachin put aside his prison clothes and for the rest of his life ate regularly at the king's table. ³⁴Day by day the king of Babylon gave Jehoiachin a regular allowance as long as he lived, till the day of his death.

a31 Also called *Amel-Marduk*

JEREMIAH writes these laments as he watches the intense suffering of God's people and the utter devastation of Jerusalem and the temple. He does not question God's justice in sending this suffering; instead, in the middle of the suffering, he celebrates God's faithfulness and unfailing love (Lamentations 3:22–32). As you read this book, think about what Jesus suffered to pay the penalty for your sins and rejoice in the incredible love of the God who offers you salvation.

LAMENTATIONS

1[a] How deserted lies the city,
   once so full of people!
How like a widow is she,
   who once was great among the
      nations!
She who was queen among the
      provinces
   has now become a slave.

[2]Bitterly she weeps at night,
   tears are upon her cheeks.
Among all her lovers
   there is none to comfort her.
All her friends have betrayed her;

they have become her enemies.

[3]After affliction and harsh labor,
   Judah has gone into exile.
She dwells among the nations;
   she finds no resting place.
All who pursue her have overtaken
      her
   in the midst of her distress.

[4]The roads to Zion mourn,
   for no one comes to her appointed
      feasts.
All her gateways are desolate,

[a]This chapter is an acrostic poem, the verses of which begin with the successive letters of the Hebrew alphabet.

her priests groan,
her maidens grieve,
and she is in bitter anguish.

⁵Her foes have become her masters;
her enemies are at ease.
The LORD has brought her grief
because of her many sins.
Her children have gone into exile
captive before the foe.

⁶All the splendor has departed
from the Daughter of Zion.
Her princes are like deer
that find no pasture;
in weakness they have fled
before the pursuer.

⁷In the days of her affliction and
wandering
Jerusalem remembers all the
treasures
that were hers in days of old.
When her people fell into enemy
hands,
there was no one to help her.
Her enemies looked at her
and laughed at her destruction.

⁸Jerusalem has sinned greatly
and so has become unclean.
All who honored her despise her,
for they have seen her nakedness;
she herself groans
and turns away.

⁹Her filthiness clung to her skirts;
she did not consider her future.
Her fall was astounding;
there was none to comfort her.
"Look, O LORD, on my affliction,
for the enemy has triumphed."

¹⁰The enemy laid hands
on all her treasures;
she saw pagan nations
enter her sanctuary—
those you had forbidden
to enter your assembly.

¹¹All her people groan
as they search for bread;
they barter their treasures for food
to keep themselves alive.
"Look, O LORD, and consider,
for I am despised."

¹²"Is it nothing to you, all you who pass
by?
Look around and see.
Is any suffering like my suffering

that was inflicted on me,
that the LORD brought on me
in the day of his fierce anger?

¹³"From on high he sent fire,
sent it down into my bones.
He spread a net for my feet
and turned me back.
He made me desolate,
faint all the day long.

¹⁴"My sins have been bound into a
yoke *a*;
by his hands they were woven
together.
They have come upon my neck
and the Lord has sapped my
strength.
He has handed me over
to those I cannot withstand.

¹⁵"The Lord has rejected
all the warriors in my midst;
he has summoned an army against
me
to *b* crush my young men.
In his winepress the Lord has
trampled
the Virgin Daughter of Judah.

¹⁶"This is why I weep
and my eyes overflow with tears.
No one is near to comfort me,
no one to restore my spirit.
My children are destitute
because the enemy has prevailed."

¹⁷Zion stretches out her hands,
but there is no one to comfort her.
The LORD has decreed for Jacob
that his neighbors become his foes;
Jerusalem has become
an unclean thing among them.

¹⁸"The LORD is righteous,
yet I rebelled against his command.
Listen, all you peoples;
look upon my suffering.
My young men and maidens
have gone into exile.

¹⁹"I called to my allies
but they betrayed me.
My priests and my elders
perished in the city
while they searched for food
to keep themselves alive.

²⁰"See, O LORD, how distressed I am!
I am in torment within,
and in my heart I am disturbed,

---

a14 Most Hebrew manuscripts; Septuagint *He kept watch over my sins*   *b15* Or *has set a time for me /*
when he will

for I have been most rebellious.
Outside, the sword bereaves;
inside, there is only death.

21"People have heard my groaning,
    but there is no one to comfort me.
All my enemies have heard of my
    distress;
they rejoice at what you have done.
May you bring the day you have
    announced
so they may become like me.

22"Let all their wickedness come before
    you;
    deal with them
as you have dealt with me
    because of all my sins.
My groans are many
    and my heart is faint."

2 *a* How the Lord has covered the
    Daughter of Zion
    with the cloud of his anger*b*!
He has hurled down the splendor of
    Israel
    from heaven to earth;
he has not remembered his footstool
    in the day of his anger.

2Without pity the Lord has swallowed
    up
    all the dwellings of Jacob;
in his wrath he has torn down
    the strongholds of the Daughter of
    Judah.
He has brought her kingdom and its
    princes
    down to the ground in dishonor.

3In fierce anger he has cut off
    every horn*c* of Israel.
He has withdrawn his right hand
    at the approach of the enemy.
He has burned in Jacob like a flaming
    fire
    that consumes everything around it.

4Like an enemy he has strung his bow;
    his right hand is ready.
Like a foe he has slain
    all who were pleasing to the eye;
he has poured out his wrath like fire
    on the tent of the Daughter of Zion.

5The Lord is like an enemy;
    he has swallowed up Israel.
He has swallowed up all her palaces
    and destroyed her strongholds.

He has multiplied mourning and
    lamentation
    for the Daughter of Judah.

6He has laid waste his dwelling like a
    garden;
    he has destroyed his place of
    meeting.
The LORD has made Zion forget
    her appointed feasts and her
    Sabbaths;
in his fierce anger he has spurned
    both king and priest.

7The Lord has rejected his altar
    and abandoned his sanctuary.
He has handed over to the enemy
    the walls of her palaces;
they have raised a shout in the house
    of the LORD
    as on the day of an appointed feast.

8The LORD determined to tear down
    the wall around the Daughter of
    Zion.
He stretched out a measuring line
    and did not withhold his hand from
    destroying.
He made ramparts and walls lament;
    together they wasted away.

9Her gates have sunk into the ground;
    their bars he has broken and
    destroyed.
Her king and her princes are exiled
    among the nations,
    the law is no more,
and her prophets no longer find
    visions from the LORD.

10The elders of the Daughter of Zion
    sit on the ground in silence;
they have sprinkled dust on their
    heads
    and put on sackcloth.
The young women of Jerusalem
    have bowed their heads to the
    ground.

11My eyes fail from weeping,
    I am in torment within,
my heart is poured out on the ground
    because my people are destroyed,
because children and infants faint
    in the streets of the city.

12They say to their mothers,
    "Where is bread and wine?"
as they faint like wounded men
    in the streets of the city,

---

*a*This chapter is an acrostic poem, the verses of which begin with the successive letters of the Hebrew
alphabet.   *b1* Or *How the Lord in his anger / has treated the Daughter of Zion with contempt*   *c3* Or /
all the strength; or *every king*; *horn* here symbolizes strength.

as their lives ebb away
　in their mothers' arms.

¹³What can I say for you?
　With what can I compare you,
　　O Daughter of Jerusalem?
To what can I liken you,
　that I may comfort you,
　　O Virgin Daughter of Zion?
Your wound is as deep as the sea.
　Who can heal you?

¹⁴The visions of your prophets
　were false and worthless;
they did not expose your sin
　to ward off your captivity.
The oracles they gave you
　were false and misleading.

¹⁵All who pass your way
　clap their hands at you;
they scoff and shake their heads
　at the Daughter of Jerusalem:
"Is this the city that was called
　the perfection of beauty,
　the joy of the whole earth?"

¹⁶All your enemies open their mouths
　wide against you;
they scoff and gnash their teeth
　and say, "We have swallowed her
　　up.
This is the day we have waited for;
　we have lived to see it."

¹⁷The LORD has done what he planned;
　he has fulfilled his word,
　which he decreed long ago.
He has overthrown you without pity,
　he has let the enemy gloat over
　　you,
　he has exalted the horn*a* of your
　　foes.

¹⁸The hearts of the people
　cry out to the Lord.
O wall of the Daughter of Zion,
　let your tears flow like a river
　　day and night;
give yourself no relief,
　your eyes no rest.

¹⁹Arise, cry out in the night,
　as the watches of the night begin;
pour out your heart like water
　in the presence of the Lord.
Lift up your hands to him
　for the lives of your children,
who faint from hunger
　at the head of every street.

²⁰"Look, O LORD, and consider:
　Whom have you ever treated like
　　this?
Should women eat their offspring,
　the children they have cared for?
Should priest and prophet be killed
　in the sanctuary of the Lord?

²¹"Young and old lie together
　in the dust of the streets;
my young men and maidens
　have fallen by the sword.
You have slain them in the day of
　your anger;
　you have slaughtered them without
　　pity.

²²"As you summon to a feast day,
　so you summoned against me
　　terrors on every side.
In the day of the LORD's anger
　no one escaped or survived;
those I cared for and reared,
　my enemy has destroyed."

3 *b*I am the man who has seen
　　affliction
　by the rod of his wrath.
²He has driven me away and made me
　　walk
　in darkness rather than light;
³indeed, he has turned his hand
　　against me
　again and again, all day long.

⁴He has made my skin and my flesh
　　grow old
　and has broken my bones.
⁵He has besieged me and surrounded
　　me
　with bitterness and hardship.
⁶He has made me dwell in darkness
　like those long dead.

⁷He has walled me in so I cannot
　　escape;
　he has weighed me down with
　　chains.
⁸Even when I call out or cry for help,
　he shuts out my prayer.
⁹He has barred my way with blocks of
　　stone;
　he has made my paths crooked.

¹⁰Like a bear lying in wait,
　like a lion in hiding,
¹¹he dragged me from the path and
　　mangled me
　and left me without help.

---

*a*17 *Horn* here symbolizes strength.　　　*b*This chapter is an acrostic poem; the verses of each stanza begin
with the successive letters of the Hebrew alphabet, and the verses within each stanza begin with the same
letter.

¹²He drew his bow
　　and made me the target for his
　　　arrows.
¹³He pierced my heart
　　with arrows from his quiver.
¹⁴I became the laughingstock of all my
　　　people;
　　they mock me in song all day long.
¹⁵He has filled me with bitter herbs
　　and sated me with gall.
¹⁶He has broken my teeth with gravel;
　　he has trampled me in the dust.
¹⁷I have been deprived of peace;
　　I have forgotten what prosperity is.
¹⁸So I say, "My splendor is gone
　　and all that I had hoped from the
　　　LORD."

¹⁹I remember my affliction and my
　　　wandering,
　　the bitterness and the gall.
²⁰I well remember them,
　　and my soul is downcast within me.
²¹Yet this I call to mind
　　and therefore I have hope:

²²Because of the LORD's great love we
　　　are not consumed,
　　for his compassions never fail.
²³They are new every morning;
　　great is your faithfulness.
²⁴I say to myself, "The LORD is my
　　　portion;
　　therefore I will wait for him."

²⁵The LORD is good to those whose hope
　　　is in him,
　　to the one who seeks him;
²⁶it is good to wait quietly
　　for the salvation of the LORD.
²⁷It is good for a man to bear the yoke
　　while he is young.

²⁸Let him sit alone in silence,
　　for the LORD has laid it on him.
²⁹Let him bury his face in the dust—
　　there may yet be hope.
³⁰Let him offer his cheek to one who
　　　would strike him,
　　and let him be filled with disgrace.

³¹For men are not cast off
　　by the Lord forever.
³²Though he brings grief, he will show
　　　compassion,
　　so great is his unfailing love.
³³For he does not willingly bring
　　　affliction
　　or grief to the children of men.

³⁴To crush underfoot
　　all prisoners in the land,
³⁵to deny a man his rights
　　before the Most High,
³⁶to deprive a man of justice—
　　would not the Lord see such
　　　things?

³⁷Who can speak and have it happen
　　if the Lord has not decreed it?
³⁸Is it not from the mouth of the Most
　　　High
　　that both calamities and good
　　　things come?
³⁹Why should any living man complain
　　when punished for his sins?

⁴⁰Let us examine our ways and test
　　　them,
　　and let us return to the LORD.
⁴¹Let us lift up our hearts and our
　　　hands
　　to God in heaven, and say:
⁴²"We have sinned and rebelled
　　and you have not forgiven.

⁴³"You have covered yourself with anger
　　　and pursued us;
　　you have slain without pity.
⁴⁴You have covered yourself with a
　　　cloud
　　so that no prayer can get through.
⁴⁵You have made us scum and refuse
　　among the nations.

⁴⁶"All our enemies have opened their
　　　mouths
　　wide against us.
⁴⁷We have suffered terror and pitfalls,
　　ruin and destruction."
⁴⁸Streams of tears flow from my eyes
　　because my people are destroyed.

⁴⁹My eyes will flow unceasingly,
　　without relief,
⁵⁰until the LORD looks down
　　from heaven and sees.
⁵¹What I see brings grief to my soul
　　because of all the women of my
　　　city.

⁵²Those who were my enemies without
　　　cause
　　hunted me like a bird.
⁵³They tried to end my life in a pit
　　and threw stones at me;
⁵⁴the waters closed over my head,
　　and I thought I was about to be cut
　　　off.

⁵⁵I called on your name, O LORD,
　　from the depths of the pit.
⁵⁶You heard my plea: "Do not close
　　　your ears
　　to my cry for relief."

VERSE FOR THE DAY:	AUTHOR:	PASSAGE FOR THE DAY:
Lamentations 3:22–23	Marie Chapian	Lamentations 3:22–33

We Are Not Consumed

WORRY wastes time. Worry cannot produce good fruit—the only fruit we reap from it is more worry. It can become a way of life. We worry whether someone will like us, if we will do a job well, if we can pay our bills each month, if our health will fail us. We worry about war. Prices. Traffic. Germs. We worry if we gain or lose a pound. We become consumed.

Thousands of people have lost weight on the *Free to Be Thin* (Bethany House, 1979) program. As coauthor of the books, I receive many letters. One woman who lost seventy pounds wrote, "I have a new life. I no longer have to hide, lie or cheat. I eat healthy foods. I have more energy than ever and I feel better than I've ever felt in my life." But then she added, "One worry consumes me. Will I gain back the weight?"

I see worry everywhere. Each time it reminds me of Lamentations 3:22–23:

> Because of the LORD's great love we are not
> consumed,
>   for his compassions never fail.
> They are new every morning;
>   great is your faithfulness.

Worry could consume us like fire—like a pile of smoldering embers that quietly destroys everything around it. Because we worry, we work hard to get ahead, do well and avoid pain. But our efforts may fail. Only the compassion of the Lord will never fail. His faithfulness is monumental, majestic, true and permanently dependable.

The woman who feared gaining weight needed to trust in Lamentations 3:22–23. When she fully grasped that she was not alone in her desire to be healthy and strong—that the Lord was blessing her to that end—she began to trust his faithfulness. Each morning she dedicated her whole self to the glory of God, and each morning she discovered his compassions to be new and fresh.

Now, five years later, she still has not gained weight and she has learned some valuable spiritual lessons. This woman can sing, along with all of us who offer up our whole selves to God, "Great is your faithfulness!"

Additional Scripture Readings:
Psalm 56:3–4; Proverbs 12:25

Go to page 880 for your next devotional reading.

57You came near when I called you,
and you said, "Do not fear."

58O Lord, you took up my case;
you redeemed my life.
59You have seen, O Lord, the wrong
done to me.
Uphold my cause!
60You have seen the depth of their
vengeance,
all their plots against me.

61O Lord, you have heard their insults,
all their plots against me—
62what my enemies whisper and mutter
against me all day long.
63Look at them! Sitting or standing,
they mock me in their songs.

64Pay them back what they deserve,
O Lord,
for what their hands have done.
65Put a veil over their hearts,
and may your curse be on them!
66Pursue them in anger and destroy
them
from under the heavens of the
Lord.

4 aHow the gold has lost its luster,
the fine gold become dull!
The sacred gems are scattered
at the head of every street.

2How the precious sons of Zion,
once worth their weight in gold,
are now considered as pots of clay,
the work of a potter's hands!

3Even jackals offer their breasts
to nurse their young,
but my people have become heartless
like ostriches in the desert.

4Because of thirst the infant's tongue
sticks to the roof of its mouth;
the children beg for bread,
but no one gives it to them.

5Those who once ate delicacies
are destitute in the streets.
Those nurtured in purple
now lie on ash heaps.

6The punishment of my people
is greater than that of Sodom,
which was overthrown in a moment
without a hand turned to help her.

7Their princes were brighter than snow
and whiter than milk,

their bodies more ruddy than rubies,
their appearance like sapphires.b

8But now they are blacker than soot;
they are not recognized in the
streets.
Their skin has shriveled on their
bones;
it has become as dry as a stick.

9Those killed by the sword are better
off
than those who die of famine;
racked with hunger, they waste away
for lack of food from the field.

10With their own hands compassionate
women
have cooked their own children,
who became their food
when my people were destroyed.

11The Lord has given full vent to his
wrath;
he has poured out his fierce anger.
He kindled a fire in Zion
that consumed her foundations.

12The kings of the earth did not
believe,
nor did any of the world's people,
that enemies and foes could enter
the gates of Jerusalem.

13But it happened because of the sins
of her prophets
and the iniquities of her priests,
who shed within her
the blood of the righteous.

14Now they grope through the streets
like men who are blind.
They are so defiled with blood
that no one dares to touch their
garments.

15"Go away! You are unclean!" men cry
to them.
"Away! Away! Don't touch us!"
When they flee and wander about,
people among the nations say,
"They can stay here no longer."

16The Lord himself has scattered them;
he no longer watches over them.
The priests are shown no honor,
the elders no favor.

17Moreover, our eyes failed,
looking in vain for help;
from our towers we watched
for a nation that could not save us.

---

aThis chapter is an acrostic poem, the verses of which begin with the successive letters of the Hebrew alphabet.   b7 Or lapis lazuli

¹⁸Men stalked us at every step,
    so we could not walk in our streets.
Our end was near, our days were
        numbered,
    for our end had come.

¹⁹Our pursuers were swifter
        than eagles in the sky;
    they chased us over the mountains
        and lay in wait for us in the desert.

²⁰The Lord's anointed, our very life
        breath,
    was caught in their traps.
We thought that under his shadow
    we would live among the nations.

²¹Rejoice and be glad, O Daughter of
        Edom,
    you who live in the land of Uz.
But to you also the cup will be
        passed;
    you will be drunk and stripped
        naked.

²²O Daughter of Zion, your punishment
        will end;
    he will not prolong your exile.
But, O Daughter of Edom, he will
        punish your sin
    and expose your wickedness.

5 Remember, O Lord, what has
        happened to us;
    look, and see our disgrace.
²Our inheritance has been turned over
        to aliens,
    our homes to foreigners.
³We have become orphans and
        fatherless,
    our mothers like widows.
⁴We must buy the water we drink;
    our wood can be had only at a
        price.
⁵Those who pursue us are at our heels;
    we are weary and find no rest.

⁶We submitted to Egypt and Assyria
    to get enough bread.
⁷Our fathers sinned and are no more,
    and we bear their punishment.
⁸Slaves rule over us,
    and there is none to free us from
        their hands.
⁹We get our bread at the risk of our
        lives
    because of the sword in the desert.
¹⁰Our skin is hot as an oven,
    feverish from hunger.
¹¹Women have been ravished in Zion,
    and virgins in the towns of Judah.
¹²Princes have been hung up by their
        hands;
    elders are shown no respect.
¹³Young men toil at the millstones;
    boys stagger under loads of wood.
¹⁴The elders are gone from the city
        gate;
    the young men have stopped their
        music.
¹⁵Joy is gone from our hearts;
    our dancing has turned to
        mourning.
¹⁶The crown has fallen from our head.
    Woe to us, for we have sinned!
¹⁷Because of this our hearts are faint,
    because of these things our eyes
        grow dim
¹⁸for Mount Zion, which lies desolate,
    with jackals prowling over it.

¹⁹You, O Lord, reign forever;
    your throne endures from
        generation to generation.
²⁰Why do you always forget us?
    Why do you forsake us so long?
²¹Restore us to yourself, O Lord, that
        we may return;
    renew our days as of old
²²unless you have utterly rejected us
    and are angry with us beyond
        measure.

EZEKIEL, living among the exiles in Babylon, wants the people to know that God is everywhere. He reminds them that worshiping false gods has brought about this catastrophe, he emphasizes the need for a new personal relationship with God, and he assures them that God wants a new covenant of peace with them. As you read this book, think of the Prince of Peace who has come to give you eternal life in his name. Be sure to make your own personal commitment to Jesus Christ.

EZEKIEL

The Living Creatures and the Glory of the LORD

1 In the[a] thirtieth year, in the fourth month on the fifth day, while I was among the exiles by the Kebar River, the heavens were opened and I saw visions of God.

²On the fifth of the month—it was the fifth year of the exile of King Jehoiachin — ³the word of the LORD came to Ezekiel the priest, the son of Buzi,[b] by the Kebar River in the land of the Babylonians.[c] There the hand of the LORD was upon him.

⁴I looked, and I saw a windstorm coming out of the north—an immense cloud with flashing lightning and surrounded by brilliant light. The center of the fire looked like glowing metal, ⁵and in the fire was what looked like four living creatures. In appearance their form was that of a man, ⁶but each of them had four faces and four wings. ⁷Their legs were straight; their feet were like those of a calf and gleamed like burnished bronze. ⁸Under their wings on their four sides they had the hands of a man. All four of them had faces and wings, ⁹and their wings

---

a1 Or *my,*   b3 Or *Ezekiel son of Buzi the priest*   c3 Or *Chaldeans* touched one another. Each one went straight ahead; they did not turn as they moved.

[10]Their faces looked like this: Each of the four had the face of a man, and on the right side each had the face of a lion, and on the left the face of an ox; each also had the face of an eagle. [11]Such were their faces. Their wings were spread out upward; each had two wings, one touching the wing of another creature on either side, and two wings covering its body. [12]Each one went straight ahead. Wherever the spirit would go, they would go, without turning as they went. [13]The appearance of the living creatures was like burning coals of fire or like torches. Fire moved back and forth among the creatures; it was bright, and lightning flashed out of it. [14]The creatures sped back and forth like flashes of lightning.

[15]As I looked at the living creatures, I saw a wheel on the ground beside each creature with its four faces. [16]This was the appearance and structure of the wheels: They sparkled like chrysolite, and all four looked alike. Each appeared to be made like a wheel intersecting a wheel. [17]As they moved, they would go in any one of the four directions the creatures faced; the wheels did not turn about[a] as the creatures went. [18]Their rims were high and awesome, and all four rims were full of eyes all around.

[19]When the living creatures moved, the wheels beside them moved; and when the living creatures rose from the ground, the wheels also rose. [20]Wherever the spirit would go, they would go, and the wheels would rise along with them, because the spirit of the living creatures was in the wheels. [21]When the creatures moved, they also moved; when the creatures stood still, they also stood still; and when the creatures rose from the ground, the wheels rose along with them, because the spirit of the living creatures was in the wheels.

[22]Spread out above the heads of the living creatures was what looked like an expanse, sparkling like ice, and awesome. [23]Under the expanse their wings were stretched out one toward the other, and each had two wings covering its body. [24]When the creatures moved, I heard the sound of their wings, like the roar of rushing waters, like the voice of the Almighty,[b] like the tumult of an army.

When they stood still, they lowered their wings.

[25]Then there came a voice from above the expanse over their heads as they stood with lowered wings. [26]Above the expanse over their heads was what looked like a throne of sapphire,[c] and high above on the throne was a figure like that of a man. [27]I saw that from what appeared to be his waist up he looked like glowing metal, as if full of fire, and that from there down he looked like fire; and brilliant light surrounded him. [28]Like the appearance of a rainbow in the clouds on a rainy day, so was the radiance around him.

This was the appearance of the likeness of the glory of the LORD. When I saw it, I fell facedown, and I heard the voice of one speaking.

Ezekiel's Call

2 He said to me, "Son of man, stand up on your feet and I will speak to you." [2]As he spoke, the Spirit came into me and raised me to my feet, and I heard him speaking to me.

[3]He said: "Son of man, I am sending you to the Israelites, to a rebellious nation that has rebelled against me; they and their fathers have been in revolt against me to this very day. [4]The people to whom I am sending you are obstinate and stubborn. Say to them, 'This is what the Sovereign LORD says.' [5]And whether they listen or fail to listen—for they are a rebellious house—they will know that a prophet has been among them. [6]And you, son of man, do not be afraid of them or their words. Do not be afraid, though briers and thorns are all around you and you live among scorpions. Do not be afraid of what they say or terrified by them, though they are a rebellious house. [7]You must speak my words to them, whether they listen or fail to listen, for they are rebellious. [8]But you, son of man, listen to what I say to you. Do not rebel like that rebellious house; open your mouth and eat what I give you."

[9]Then I looked, and I saw a hand stretched out to me. In it was a scroll, [10]which he unrolled before me. On both sides of it were written words of lament and mourning and woe.

3 And he said to me, "Son of man, eat what is before you, eat this scroll; then go and speak to the house of Israel."

a17 Or aside   b24 Hebrew Shaddai   c26 Or lapis lazuli

²So I opened my mouth, and he gave me the scroll to eat.

³Then he said to me, "Son of man, eat this scroll I am giving you and fill your stomach with it." So I ate it, and it tasted as sweet as honey in my mouth.

⁴He then said to me: "Son of man, go now to the house of Israel and speak my words to them. ⁵You are not being sent to a people of obscure speech and difficult language, but to the house of Israel— ⁶not to many peoples of obscure speech and difficult language, whose words you cannot understand. Surely if I had sent you to them, they would have listened to you. ⁷But the house of Israel is not willing to listen to you because they are not willing to listen to me, for the whole house of Israel is hardened and obstinate. ⁸But I will make you as unyielding and hardened as they are. ⁹I will make your forehead like the hardest stone, harder than flint. Do not be afraid of them or terrified by them, though they are a rebellious house."

¹⁰And he said to me, "Son of man, listen carefully and take to heart all the words I speak to you. ¹¹Go now to your countrymen in exile and speak to them. Say to them, 'This is what the Sovereign LORD says,' whether they listen or fail to listen."

¹²Then the Spirit lifted me up, and I heard behind me a loud rumbling sound —May the glory of the LORD be praised in his dwelling place!— ¹³the sound of the wings of the living creatures brushing against each other and the sound of the wheels beside them, a loud rumbling sound. ¹⁴The Spirit then lifted me up and took me away, and I went in bitterness and in the anger of my spirit, with the strong hand of the LORD upon me. ¹⁵I came to the exiles who lived at Tel Abib near the Kebar River. And there, where they were living, I sat among them for seven days—overwhelmed.

Warning to Israel

¹⁶At the end of seven days the word of the LORD came to me: ¹⁷"Son of man, I have made you a watchman for the house of Israel; so hear the word I speak and give them warning from me. ¹⁸When I say to a wicked man, 'You will surely die,' and you do not warn him or speak out to dissuade him from his evil ways in order to save his life, that wicked man will die

forᵃ his sin, and I will hold you accountable for his blood. ¹⁹But if you do warn the wicked man and he does not turn from his wickedness or from his evil ways, he will die for his sin; but you will have saved yourself.

²⁰"Again, when a righteous man turns from his righteousness and does evil, and I put a stumbling block before him, he will die. Since you did not warn him, he will die for his sin. The righteous things he did will not be remembered, and I will hold you accountable for his blood. ²¹But if you do warn the righteous man not to sin and he does not sin, he will surely live because he took warning, and you will have saved yourself."

²²The hand of the LORD was upon me there, and he said to me, "Get up and go out to the plain, and there I will speak to you." ²³So I got up and went out to the plain. And the glory of the LORD was standing there, like the glory I had seen by the Kebar River, and I fell facedown. ²⁴Then the Spirit came into me and raised me to my feet. He spoke to me and said: "Go, shut yourself inside your house. ²⁵And you, son of man, they will tie with ropes; you will be bound so that you cannot go out among the people. ²⁶I will make your tongue stick to the roof of your mouth so that you will be silent and unable to rebuke them, though they are a rebellious house. ²⁷But when I speak to you, I will open your mouth and you shall say to them, 'This is what the Sovereign LORD says.' Whoever will listen let him listen, and whoever will refuse let him refuse; for they are a rebellious house.

Siege of Jerusalem Symbolized

4 "Now, son of man, take a clay tablet, put it in front of you and draw the city of Jerusalem on it. ²Then lay siege to it: Erect siege works against it, build a ramp up to it, set up camps against it and put battering rams around it. ³Then take an iron pan, place it as an iron wall between you and the city and turn your face toward it. It will be under siege, and you shall besiege it. This will be a sign to the house of Israel.

⁴"Then lie on your left side and put the sin of the house of Israel upon yourself.ᵇ You are to bear their sin for the number of days you lie on your side. ⁵I have assigned you the same number of days as the years of their sin. So for 390 days you

ᵃ18 Or in; also in verses 19 and 20   ᵇ4 Or your side

will bear the sin of the house of Israel.

⁶"After you have finished this, lie down again, this time on your right side, and bear the sin of the house of Judah. I have assigned you 40 days, a day for each year. ⁷Turn your face toward the siege of Jerusalem and with bared arm prophesy against her. ⁸I will tie you up with ropes so that you cannot turn from one side to the other until you have finished the days of your siege.

⁹"Take wheat and barley, beans and lentils, millet and spelt; put them in a storage jar and use them to make bread for yourself. You are to eat it during the 390 days you lie on your side. ¹⁰Weigh out twenty shekels *ª* of food to eat each day and eat it at set times. ¹¹Also measure out a sixth of a hin *ᵇ* of water and drink it at set times. ¹²Eat the food as you would a barley cake; bake it in the sight of the people, using human excrement for fuel."

¹³The LORD said, "In this way the people of Israel will eat defiled food among the nations where I will drive them."

¹⁴Then I said, "Not so, Sovereign LORD! I have never defiled myself. From my youth until now I have never eaten anything found dead or torn by wild animals. No unclean meat has ever entered my mouth."

¹⁵"Very well," he said, "I will let you bake your bread over cow manure instead of human excrement."

¹⁶He then said to me: "Son of man, I will cut off the supply of food in Jerusalem. The people will eat rationed food in anxiety and drink rationed water in despair, ¹⁷for food and water will be scarce. They will be appalled at the sight of each other and will waste away because of *ᶜ* their sin.

5 "Now, son of man, take a sharp sword and use it as a barber's razor to shave your head and your beard. Then take a set of scales and divide up the hair. ²When the days of your siege come to an end, burn a third of the hair with fire inside the city. Take a third and strike it with the sword all around the city. And scatter a third to the wind. For I will pursue them with drawn sword. ³But take a few strands of hair and tuck them away in the folds of your garment. ⁴Again, take a few of these and throw them into the fire and burn them up. A fire will spread from there to the whole house of Israel.

⁵"This is what the Sovereign LORD says: This is Jerusalem, which I have set in the center of the nations, with countries all around her. ⁶Yet in her wickedness she has rebelled against my laws and decrees more than the nations and countries around her. She has rejected my laws and has not followed my decrees.

⁷"Therefore this is what the Sovereign LORD says: You have been more unruly than the nations around you and have not followed my decrees or kept my laws. You have not even *ᵈ* conformed to the standards of the nations around you.

⁸"Therefore this is what the Sovereign LORD says: I myself am against you, Jerusalem, and I will inflict punishment on you in the sight of the nations. ⁹Because of all your detestable idols, I will do to you what I have never done before and will never do again. ¹⁰Therefore in your midst fathers will eat their children, and children will eat their fathers. I will inflict punishment on you and will scatter all your survivors to the winds. ¹¹Therefore as surely as I live, declares the Sovereign LORD, because you have defiled my sanctuary with all your vile images and detestable practices, I myself will withdraw my favor; I will not look on you with pity or spare you. ¹²A third of your people will die of the plague or perish by famine inside you; a third will fall by the sword outside your walls; and a third I will scatter to the winds and pursue with drawn sword.

¹³"Then my anger will cease and my wrath against them will subside, and I will be avenged. And when I have spent my wrath upon them, they will know that I the LORD have spoken in my zeal.

¹⁴"I will make you a ruin and a reproach among the nations around you, in the sight of all who pass by. ¹⁵You will be a reproach and a taunt, a warning and an object of horror to the nations around you when I inflict punishment on you in anger and in wrath and with stinging rebuke. I the LORD have spoken. ¹⁶When I shoot at you with my deadly and destructive arrows of famine, I will shoot to destroy you. I will bring more and more famine upon you and cut off your supply of food. ¹⁷I will send famine and wild beasts against you, and they will leave you childless. Plague and bloodshed will sweep through you, and I will bring the sword against you. I the LORD have spoken."

ª10 That is, about 8 ounces (about 0.2 kilogram)   *ᵇ11* That is, about 2/3 quart (about 0.6 liter)   *ᶜ17* Or *away in*   *ᵈ7* Most Hebrew manuscripts; some Hebrew manuscripts and Syriac *You have*

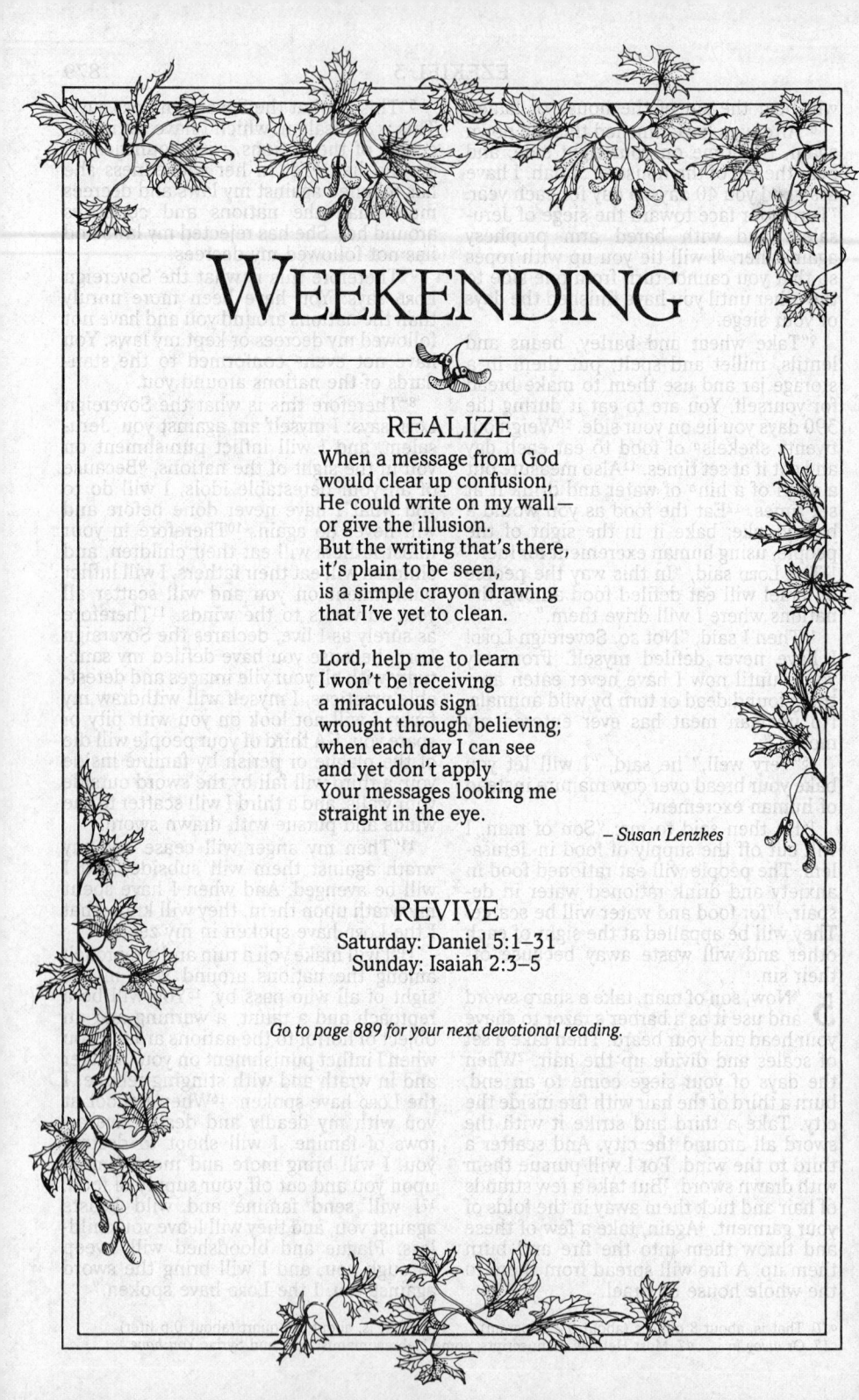

WEEKENDING

REALIZE

When a message from God
would clear up confusion,
He could write on my wall—
or give the illusion.
But the writing that's there,
it's plain to be seen,
is a simple crayon drawing
that I've yet to clean.

Lord, help me to learn
I won't be receiving
a miraculous sign
wrought through believing;
when each day I can see
and yet don't apply
Your messages looking me
straight in the eye.

— *Susan Lenzkes*

REVIVE

Saturday: Daniel 5:1–31
Sunday: Isaiah 2:3–5

Go to page 889 for your next devotional reading.

A Prophecy Against the Mountains of Israel

6 The word of the Lord came to me: 2"Son of man, set your face against the mountains of Israel; prophesy against them 3and say: 'O mountains of Israel, hear the word of the Sovereign Lord. This is what the Sovereign Lord says to the mountains and hills, to the ravines and valleys: I am about to bring a sword against you, and I will destroy your high places. 4Your altars will be demolished and your incense altars will be smashed; and I will slay your people in front of your idols. 5I will lay the dead bodies of the Israelites in front of their idols, and I will scatter your bones around your altars. 6Wherever you live, the towns will be laid waste and the high places demolished, so that your altars will be laid waste and devastated, your idols smashed and ruined, your incense altars broken down, and what you have made wiped out. 7Your people will fall slain among you, and you will know that I am the Lord.

8" 'But I will spare some, for some of you will escape the sword when you are scattered among the lands and nations. 9Then in the nations where they have been carried captive, those who escape will remember me — how I have been grieved by their adulterous hearts, which have turned away from me, and by their eyes, which have lusted after their idols. They will loathe themselves for the evil they have done and for all their detestable practices. 10And they will know that I am the Lord; I did not threaten in vain to bring this calamity on them.

11" 'This is what the Sovereign Lord says: Strike your hands together and stamp your feet and cry out "Alas!" because of all the wicked and detestable practices of the house of Israel, for they will fall by the sword, famine and plague. 12He that is far away will die of the plague, and he that is near will fall by the sword, and he that survives and is spared will die of famine. So will I spend my wrath upon them. 13And they will know that I am the Lord, when their people lie slain among their idols around their altars, on every high hill and on all the mountaintops, under every spreading tree and every leafy oak — places where they offered fragrant incense to all their idols.

14And I will stretch out my hand against them and make the land a desolate waste from the desert to Diblah[a] — wherever they live. Then they will know that I am the Lord.' "

The End Has Come

7 The word of the Lord came to me: 2"Son of man, this is what the Sovereign Lord says to the land of Israel: The end! The end has come upon the four corners of the land. 3The end is now upon you and I will unleash my anger against you. I will judge you according to your conduct and repay you for all your detestable practices. 4I will not look on you with pity or spare you; I will surely repay you for your conduct and the detestable practices among you. Then you will know that I am the Lord.

5"This is what the Sovereign Lord says: Disaster! An unheard-of[b] disaster is coming. 6The end has come! The end has come! It has roused itself against you. It has come! 7Doom has come upon you — you who dwell in the land. The time has come, the day is near; there is panic, not joy, upon the mountains. 8I am about to pour out my wrath on you and spend my anger against you; I will judge you according to your conduct and repay you for all your detestable practices. 9I will not look on you with pity or spare you; I will repay you in accordance with your conduct and the detestable practices among you. Then you will know that it is I the Lord who strikes the blow.

10"The day is here! It has come! Doom has burst forth, the rod has budded, arrogance has blossomed! 11Violence has grown into[c] a rod to punish wickedness; none of the people will be left, none of that crowd — no wealth, nothing of value. 12The time has come, the day has arrived. Let not the buyer rejoice nor the seller grieve, for wrath is upon the whole crowd. 13The seller will not recover the land he has sold as long as both of them live, for the vision concerning the whole crowd will not be reversed. Because of their sins, not one of them will preserve his life. 14Though they blow the trumpet and get everything ready, no one will go into battle, for my wrath is upon the whole crowd.

15"Outside is the sword, inside are plague and famine; those in the country will die by the sword, and those in the city

---

a14 Most Hebrew manuscripts; a few Hebrew manuscripts *Riblah*   *b5* Most Hebrew manuscripts; some Hebrew manuscripts and Syriac *Disaster after*   *c11* Or *The violent one has become* will be devoured by famine and plague. [16]All who survive and escape will be in the mountains, moaning like doves of the valleys, each because of his sins. [17]Every hand will go limp, and every knee will become as weak as water. [18]They will put on sackcloth and be clothed with terror. Their faces will be covered with shame and their heads will be shaved. [19]They will throw their silver into the streets, and their gold will be an unclean thing. Their silver and gold will not be able to save them in the day of the Lord's wrath. They will not satisfy their hunger or fill their stomachs with it, for it has made them stumble into sin. [20]They were proud of their beautiful jewelry and used it to make their detestable idols and vile images. Therefore I will turn these into an unclean thing for them. [21]I will hand it all over as plunder to foreigners and as loot to the wicked of the earth, and they will defile it. [22]I will turn my face away from them, and they will desecrate my treasured place; robbers will enter it and desecrate it.

[23]"Prepare chains, because the land is full of bloodshed and the city is full of violence. [24]I will bring the most wicked of the nations to take possession of their houses; I will put an end to the pride of the mighty, and their sanctuaries will be desecrated. [25]When terror comes, they will seek peace, but there will be none. [26]Calamity upon calamity will come, and rumor upon rumor. They will try to get a vision from the prophet; the teaching of the law by the priest will be lost, as will the counsel of the elders. [27]The king will mourn, the prince will be clothed with despair, and the hands of the people of the land will tremble. I will deal with them according to their conduct, and by their own standards I will judge them. Then they will know that I am the Lord."

Idolatry in the Temple

8 In the sixth year, in the sixth month on the fifth day, while I was sitting in my house and the elders of Judah were sitting before me, the hand of the Sovereign Lord came upon me there. [2]I looked, and I saw a figure like that of a man.*a* From what appeared to be his waist down he was like fire, and from there up his appearance was as bright as glowing metal. [3]He stretched out what looked like a hand and took me by the hair of my head.

The Spirit lifted me up between earth and heaven and in visions of God he took me to Jerusalem, to the entrance to the north gate of the inner court, where the idol that provokes to jealousy stood. [4]And there before me was the glory of the God of Israel, as in the vision I had seen in the plain.

[5]Then he said to me, "Son of man, look toward the north." So I looked, and in the entrance north of the gate of the altar I saw this idol of jealousy.

[6]And he said to me, "Son of man, do you see what they are doing—the utterly detestable things the house of Israel is doing here, things that will drive me far from my sanctuary? But you will see things that are even more detestable."

[7]Then he brought me to the entrance to the court. I looked, and I saw a hole in the wall. [8]He said to me, "Son of man, now dig into the wall." So I dug into the wall and saw a doorway there.

[9]And he said to me, "Go in and see the wicked and detestable things they are doing here." [10]So I went in and looked, and I saw portrayed all over the walls all kinds of crawling things and detestable animals and all the idols of the house of Israel. [11]In front of them stood seventy elders of the house of Israel, and Jaazaniah son of Shaphan was standing among them. Each had a censer in his hand, and a fragrant cloud of incense was rising.

[12]He said to me, "Son of man, have you seen what the elders of the house of Israel are doing in the darkness, each at the shrine of his own idol? They say, 'The Lord does not see us; the Lord has forsaken the land.'" [13]Again, he said, "You will see them doing things that are even more detestable."

[14]Then he brought me to the entrance to the north gate of the house of the Lord, and I saw women sitting there, mourning for Tammuz. [15]He said to me, "Do you see this, son of man? You will see things that are even more detestable than this."

[16]He then brought me into the inner court of the house of the Lord, and there at the entrance to the temple, between the portico and the altar, were about twenty-five men. With their backs toward the temple of the Lord and their faces toward the east, they were bowing down to the sun in the east.

[17]He said to me, "Have you seen this, son of man? Is it a trivial matter for the house of Judah to do the detestable

a2 Or saw a fiery figure

things they are doing here? Must they also fill the land with violence and continually provoke me to anger? Look at them putting the branch to their nose! ¹⁸Therefore I will deal with them in anger; I will not look on them with pity or spare them. Although they shout in my ears, I will not listen to them."

Idolaters Killed

9 Then I heard him call out in a loud voice, "Bring the guards of the city here, each with a weapon in his hand." ²And I saw six men coming from the direction of the upper gate, which faces north, each with a deadly weapon in his hand. With them was a man clothed in linen who had a writing kit at his side. They came in and stood beside the bronze altar.

³Now the glory of the God of Israel went up from above the cherubim, where it had been, and moved to the threshold of the temple. Then the Lord called to the man clothed in linen who had the writing kit at his side ⁴and said to him, "Go throughout the city of Jerusalem and put a mark on the foreheads of those who grieve and lament over all the detestable things that are done in it."

⁵As I listened, he said to the others, "Follow him through the city and kill, without showing pity or compassion. ⁶Slaughter old men, young men and maidens, women and children, but do not touch anyone who has the mark. Begin at my sanctuary." So they began with the elders who were in front of the temple.

⁷Then he said to them, "Defile the temple and fill the courts with the slain. Go!" So they went out and began killing throughout the city. ⁸While they were killing and I was left alone, I fell facedown, crying out, "Ah, Sovereign Lord! Are you going to destroy the entire remnant of Israel in this outpouring of your wrath on Jerusalem?"

⁹He answered me, "The sin of the house of Israel and Judah is exceedingly great; the land is full of bloodshed and the city is full of injustice. They say, 'The Lord has forsaken the land; the Lord does not see.' ¹⁰So I will not look on them with pity or spare them, but I will bring down on their own heads what they have done."

¹¹Then the man in linen with the writing kit at his side brought back word, saying, "I have done as you commanded."

The Glory Departs From the Temple

10 I looked, and I saw the likeness of a throne of sapphire[a] above the expanse that was over the heads of the cherubim. ²The Lord said to the man clothed in linen, "Go in among the wheels beneath the cherubim. Fill your hands with burning coals from among the cherubim and scatter them over the city." And as I watched, he went in.

³Now the cherubim were standing on the south side of the temple when the man went in, and a cloud filled the inner court. ⁴Then the glory of the Lord rose from above the cherubim and moved to the threshold of the temple. The cloud filled the temple, and the court was full of the radiance of the glory of the Lord. ⁵The sound of the wings of the cherubim could be heard as far away as the outer court, like the voice of God Almighty[b] when he speaks.

⁶When the Lord commanded the man in linen, "Take fire from among the wheels, from among the cherubim," the man went in and stood beside a wheel. ⁷Then one of the cherubim reached out his hand to the fire that was among them. He took up some of it and put it into the hands of the man in linen, who took it and went out. ⁸(Under the wings of the cherubim could be seen what looked like the hands of a man.)

⁹I looked, and I saw beside the cherubim four wheels, one beside each of the cherubim; the wheels sparkled like chrysolite. ¹⁰As for their appearance, the four of them looked alike; each was like a wheel intersecting a wheel. ¹¹As they moved, they would go in any one of the four directions the cherubim faced; the wheels did not turn about[c] as the cherubim went. The cherubim went in whatever direction the head faced, without turning as they went. ¹²Their entire bodies, including their backs, their hands and their wings, were completely full of eyes, as were their four wheels. ¹³I heard the wheels being called "the whirling wheels." ¹⁴Each of the cherubim had four faces: One face was that of a cherub, the second the face of a man, the third the face of a lion, and the fourth the face of an eagle.

¹⁵Then the cherubim rose upward. These were the living creatures I had seen

---

a1 Or lapis lazuli   *b5 Hebrew El-Shaddai*   *c11 Or aside* by the Kebar River. [16]When the cherubim moved, the wheels beside them moved; and when the cherubim spread their wings to rise from the ground, the wheels did not leave their side. [17]When the cherubim stood still, they also stood still; and when the cherubim rose, they rose with them, because the spirit of the living creatures was in them.

[18]Then the glory of the Lord departed from over the threshold of the temple and stopped above the cherubim. [19]While I watched, the cherubim spread their wings and rose from the ground, and as they went, the wheels went with them. They stopped at the entrance to the east gate of the Lord's house, and the glory of the God of Israel was above them.

[20]These were the living creatures I had seen beneath the God of Israel by the Kebar River, and I realized that they were cherubim. [21]Each had four faces and four wings, and under their wings was what looked like the hands of a man. [22]Their faces had the same appearance as those I had seen by the Kebar River. Each one went straight ahead.

Judgment on Israel's Leaders

11 Then the Spirit lifted me up and brought me to the gate of the house of the Lord that faces east. There at the entrance to the gate were twenty-five men, and I saw among them Jaazaniah son of Azzur and Pelatiah son of Benaiah, leaders of the people. [2]The Lord said to me, "Son of man, these are the men who are plotting evil and giving wicked advice in this city. [3]They say, 'Will it not soon be time to build houses?[a] This city is a cooking pot, and we are the meat.' [4]Therefore prophesy against them; prophesy, son of man."

[5]Then the Spirit of the Lord came upon me, and he told me to say: "This is what the Lord says: That is what you are saying, O house of Israel, but I know what is going through your mind. [6]You have killed many people in this city and filled its streets with the dead.

[7]"Therefore this is what the Sovereign Lord says: The bodies you have thrown there are the meat and this city is the pot, but I will drive you out of it. [8]You fear the sword, and the sword is what I will bring against you, declares the Sovereign Lord. [9]I will drive you out of the city and hand you over to foreigners and inflict punishment on you. [10]You will fall by the sword, and I will execute judgment on you at the borders of Israel. Then you will know that I am the Lord. [11]This city will not be a pot for you, nor will you be the meat in it; I will execute judgment on you at the borders of Israel. [12]And you will know that I am the Lord, for you have not followed my decrees or kept my laws but have conformed to the standards of the nations around you."

[13]Now as I was prophesying, Pelatiah son of Benaiah died. Then I fell facedown and cried out in a loud voice, "Ah, Sovereign Lord! Will you completely destroy the remnant of Israel?"

[14]The word of the Lord came to me: [15]"Son of man, your brothers—your brothers who are your blood relatives[b] and the whole house of Israel—are those of whom the people of Jerusalem have said, 'They are[c] far away from the Lord; this land was given to us as our possession.'

Promised Return of Israel

[16]"Therefore say: 'This is what the Sovereign Lord says: Although I sent them far away among the nations and scattered them among the countries, yet for a little while I have been a sanctuary for them in the countries where they have gone.'

[17]"Therefore say: 'This is what the Sovereign Lord says: I will gather you from the nations and bring you back from the countries where you have been scattered, and I will give you back the land of Israel again.'

[18]"They will return to it and remove all its vile images and detestable idols. [19]I will give them an undivided heart and put a new spirit in them; I will remove from them their heart of stone and give them a heart of flesh. [20]Then they will follow my decrees and be careful to keep my laws. They will be my people, and I will be their God. [21]But as for those whose hearts are devoted to their vile images and detestable idols, I will bring down on their own heads what they have done, declares the Sovereign Lord."

[22]Then the cherubim, with the wheels beside them, spread their wings, and the glory of the God of Israel was above them. [23]The glory of the Lord went up from within the city and stopped above the

---

[a]3 Or This is not the time to build houses.   [b]15 Or are in exile with you (see Septuagint and Syriac)
[c]15 Or those to whom the people of Jerusalem have said, 'Stay

mountain east of it. ²⁴The Spirit lifted me up and brought me to the exiles in Babylonia*a* in the vision given by the Spirit of God.

Then the vision I had seen went up from me, ²⁵and I told the exiles everything the LORD had shown me.

The Exile Symbolized

12 The word of the LORD came to me: ²"Son of man, you are living among a rebellious people. They have eyes to see but do not see and ears to hear but do not hear, for they are a rebellious people.

³"Therefore, son of man, pack your belongings for exile and in the daytime, as they watch, set out and go from where you are to another place. Perhaps they will understand, though they are a rebellious house. ⁴During the daytime, while they watch, bring out your belongings packed for exile. Then in the evening, while they are watching, go out like those who go into exile. ⁵While they watch, dig through the wall and take your belongings out through it. ⁶Put them on your shoulder as they are watching and carry them out at dusk. Cover your face so that you cannot see the land, for I have made you a sign to the house of Israel."

⁷So I did as I was commanded. During the day I brought out my things packed for exile. Then in the evening I dug through the wall with my hands. I took my belongings out at dusk, carrying them on my shoulders while they watched.

⁸In the morning the word of the LORD came to me: ⁹"Son of man, did not that rebellious house of Israel ask you, 'What are you doing?'

¹⁰"Say to them, 'This is what the Sovereign LORD says: This oracle concerns the prince in Jerusalem and the whole house of Israel who are there.' ¹¹Say to them, 'I am a sign to you.'

"As I have done, so it will be done to them. They will go into exile as captives.

¹²"The prince among them will put his things on his shoulder at dusk and leave, and a hole will be dug in the wall for him to go through. He will cover his face so that he cannot see the land. ¹³I will spread my net for him, and he will be caught in my snare; I will bring him to Babylonia, the land of the Chaldeans, but he will not see it, and there he will die. ¹⁴I will scatter to the winds all those around

him—his staff and all his troops—and I will pursue them with drawn sword.

¹⁵"They will know that I am the LORD, when I disperse them among the nations and scatter them through the countries. ¹⁶But I will spare a few of them from the sword, famine and plague, so that in the nations where they go they may acknowledge all their detestable practices. Then they will know that I am the LORD."

¹⁷The word of the LORD came to me: ¹⁸"Son of man, tremble as you eat your food, and shudder in fear as you drink your water. ¹⁹Say to the people of the land: 'This is what the Sovereign LORD says about those living in Jerusalem and in the land of Israel: They will eat their food in anxiety and drink their water in despair, for their land will be stripped of everything in it because of the violence of all who live there. ²⁰The inhabited towns will be laid waste and the land will be desolate. Then you will know that I am the LORD.'"

²¹The word of the LORD came to me: ²²"Son of man, what is this proverb you have in the land of Israel: 'The days go by and every vision comes to nothing'? ²³Say to them, 'This is what the Sovereign LORD says: I am going to put an end to this proverb, and they will no longer quote it in Israel.' Say to them, 'The days are near when every vision will be fulfilled. ²⁴For there will be no more false visions or flattering divinations among the people of Israel. ²⁵But I the LORD will speak what I will, and it shall be fulfilled without delay. For in your days, you rebellious house, I will fulfill whatever I say, declares the Sovereign LORD.'"

²⁶The word of the LORD came to me: ²⁷"Son of man, the house of Israel is saying, 'The vision he sees is for many years from now, and he prophesies about the distant future.'

²⁸"Therefore say to them, 'This is what the Sovereign LORD says: None of my words will be delayed any longer; whatever I say will be fulfilled, declares the Sovereign LORD.'"

False Prophets Condemned

13 The word of the LORD came to me: ²"Son of man, prophesy against the prophets of Israel who are now prophesying. Say to those who prophesy out of their own imagination: 'Hear the word of the LORD! ³This is what the Sovereign LORD

---

a24 Or Chaldea

says: Woe to the foolish[a] prophets who follow their own spirit and have seen nothing! [4]Your prophets, O Israel, are like jackals among ruins. [5]You have not gone up to the breaks in the wall to repair it for the house of Israel so that it will stand firm in the battle on the day of the LORD. [6]Their visions are false and their divinations a lie. They say, "The LORD declares," when the LORD has not sent them; yet they expect their words to be fulfilled. [7]Have you not seen false visions and uttered lying divinations when you say, "The LORD declares," though I have not spoken?

[8]" 'Therefore this is what the Sovereign LORD says: Because of your false words and lying visions, I am against you, declares the Sovereign LORD. [9]My hand will be against the prophets who see false visions and utter lying divinations. They will not belong to the council of my people or be listed in the records of the house of Israel, nor will they enter the land of Israel. Then you will know that I am the Sovereign LORD.

[10]" 'Because they lead my people astray, saying, "Peace," when there is no peace, and because, when a flimsy wall is built, they cover it with whitewash, [11]therefore tell those who cover it with whitewash that it is going to fall. Rain will come in torrents, and I will send hailstones hurtling down, and violent winds will burst forth. [12]When the wall collapses, will people not ask you, "Where is the whitewash you covered it with?"

[13]" 'Therefore this is what the Sovereign LORD says: In my wrath I will unleash a violent wind, and in my anger hailstones and torrents of rain will fall with destructive fury. [14]I will tear down the wall you have covered with whitewash and will level it to the ground so that its foundation will be laid bare. When it[b] falls, you will be destroyed in it; and you will know that I am the LORD. [15]So I will spend my wrath against the wall and against those who covered it with whitewash. I will say to you, "The wall is gone and so are those who whitewashed it, [16]those prophets of Israel who prophesied to Jerusalem and saw visions of peace for her when there was no peace, declares the Sovereign LORD." '

[17]"Now, son of man, set your face against the daughters of your people who prophesy out of their own imagination.

Prophesy against them [18]and say, 'This is what the Sovereign LORD says: Woe to the women who sew magic charms on all their wrists and make veils of various lengths for their heads in order to ensnare people. Will you ensnare the lives of my people but preserve your own? [19]You have profaned me among my people for a few handfuls of barley and scraps of bread. By lying to my people, who listen to lies, you have killed those who should not have died and have spared those who should not live.

[20]" 'Therefore this is what the Sovereign LORD says: I am against your magic charms with which you ensnare people like birds and I will tear them from your arms; I will set free the people that you ensnare like birds. [21]I will tear off your veils and save my people from your hands, and they will no longer fall prey to your power. Then you will know that I am the LORD. [22]Because you disheartened the righteous with your lies, when I had brought them no grief, and because you encouraged the wicked not to turn from their evil ways and so save their lives, [23]therefore you will no longer see false visions or practice divination. I will save my people from your hands. And then you will know that I am the LORD.' "

Idolaters Condemned

14 Some of the elders of Israel came to me and sat down in front of me. [2]Then the word of the LORD came to me: [3]"Son of man, these men have set up idols in their hearts and put wicked stumbling blocks before their faces. Should I let them inquire of me at all? [4]Therefore speak to them and tell them, 'This is what the Sovereign LORD says: When any Israelite sets up idols in his heart and puts a wicked stumbling block before his face and then goes to a prophet, I the LORD will answer him myself in keeping with his great idolatry. [5]I will do this to recapture the hearts of the people of Israel, who have all deserted me for their idols.'

[6]"Therefore say to the house of Israel, 'This is what the Sovereign LORD says: Repent! Turn from your idols and renounce all your detestable practices!

[7]" 'When any Israelite or any alien living in Israel separates himself from me and sets up idols in his heart and puts a wicked stumbling block before his face and then goes to a prophet to inquire of

---

[a]3 Or wicked   [b]14 Or the city

me, I the LORD will answer him myself. [8]I will set my face against that man and make him an example and a byword. I will cut him off from my people. Then you will know that I am the LORD.

[9]" 'And if the prophet is enticed to utter a prophecy, I the LORD have enticed that prophet, and I will stretch out my hand against him and destroy him from among my people Israel. [10]They will bear their guilt—the prophet will be as guilty as the one who consults him. [11]Then the people of Israel will no longer stray from me, nor will they defile themselves anymore with all their sins. They will be my people, and I will be their God, declares the Sovereign LORD.' "

Judgment Inescapable

[12]The word of the LORD came to me: [13]"Son of man, if a country sins against me by being unfaithful and I stretch out my hand against it to cut off its food supply and send famine upon it and kill its men and their animals, [14]even if these three men—Noah, Daniel[a] and Job—were in it, they could save only themselves by their righteousness, declares the Sovereign LORD.

[15]"Or if I send wild beasts through that country and they leave it childless and it becomes desolate so that no one can pass through it because of the beasts, [16]as surely as I live, declares the Sovereign LORD, even if these three men were in it, they could not save their own sons or daughters. They alone would be saved, but the land would be desolate.

[17]"Or if I bring a sword against that country and say, 'Let the sword pass throughout the land,' and I kill its men and their animals, [18]as surely as I live, declares the Sovereign LORD, even if these three men were in it, they could not save their own sons or daughters. They alone would be saved.

[19]"Or if I send a plague into that land and pour out my wrath upon it through bloodshed, killing its men and their animals, [20]as surely as I live, declares the Sovereign LORD, even if Noah, Daniel and Job were in it, they could save neither son nor daughter. They would save only themselves by their righteousness.

[21]"For this is what the Sovereign LORD says: How much worse will it be when I send against Jerusalem my four dreadful judgments—sword and famine and wild beasts and plague—to kill its men and their animals! [22]Yet there will be some survivors—sons and daughters who will be brought out of it. They will come to you, and when you see their conduct and their actions, you will be consoled regarding the disaster I have brought upon Jerusalem—every disaster I have brought upon it. [23]You will be consoled when you see their conduct and their actions, for you will know that I have done nothing in it without cause, declares the Sovereign LORD."

Jerusalem, A Useless Vine

15 The word of the LORD came to me: [2]"Son of man, how is the wood of a vine better than that of a branch on any of the trees in the forest? [3]Is wood ever taken from it to make anything useful? Do they make pegs from it to hang things on? [4]And after it is thrown on the fire as fuel and the fire burns both ends and chars the middle, is it then useful for anything? [5]If it was not useful for anything when it was whole, how much less can it be made into something useful when the fire has burned it and it is charred?

[6]"Therefore this is what the Sovereign LORD says: As I have given the wood of the vine among the trees of the forest as fuel for the fire, so will I treat the people living in Jerusalem. [7]I will set my face against them. Although they have come out of the fire, the fire will yet consume them. And when I set my face against them, you will know that I am the LORD. [8]I will make the land desolate because they have been unfaithful, declares the Sovereign LORD."

An Allegory of Unfaithful Jerusalem

16 The word of the LORD came to me: [2]"Son of man, confront Jerusalem with her detestable practices [3]and say, 'This is what the Sovereign LORD says to Jerusalem: Your ancestry and birth were in the land of the Canaanites; your father was an Amorite and your mother a Hittite. [4]On the day you were born your cord was not cut, nor were you washed with water to make you clean, nor were you rubbed with salt or wrapped in cloths. [5]No one looked on you with pity or had compassion enough to do any of these things for you. Rather, you were thrown out into the open field, for on the day you were born you were despised.

---

[a]14 Or *Danel*; the Hebrew spelling may suggest a person other than the prophet Daniel; also in verse 20.

6" 'Then I passed by and saw you kicking about in your blood, and as you lay there in your blood I said to you, "Live!"[a] 7I made you grow like a plant of the field. You grew up and developed and became the most beautiful of jewels.[b] Your breasts were formed and your hair grew, you who were naked and bare.

8" 'Later I passed by, and when I looked at you and saw that you were old enough for love, I spread the corner of my garment over you and covered your nakedness. I gave you my solemn oath and entered into a covenant with you, declares the Sovereign LORD, and you became mine.

9" 'I bathed[c] you with water and washed the blood from you and put ointments on you. 10I clothed you with an embroidered dress and put leather sandals on you. I dressed you in fine linen and covered you with costly garments. 11I adorned you with jewelry: I put bracelets on your arms and a necklace around your neck, 12and I put a ring on your nose, earrings on your ears and a beautiful crown on your head. 13So you were adorned with gold and silver; your clothes were of fine linen and costly fabric and embroidered cloth. Your food was fine flour, honey and olive oil. You became very beautiful and rose to be a queen. 14And your fame spread among the nations on account of your beauty, because the splendor I had given you made your beauty perfect, declares the Sovereign LORD.

15" 'But you trusted in your beauty and used your fame to become a prostitute. You lavished your favors on anyone who passed by and your beauty became his.[d] 16You took some of your garments to make gaudy high places, where you carried on your prostitution. Such things should not happen, nor should they ever occur. 17You also took the fine jewelry I gave you, the jewelry made of my gold and silver, and you made for yourself male idols and engaged in prostitution with them. 18And you took your embroidered clothes to put on them, and you offered my oil and incense before them. 19Also the food I provided for you—the fine flour, olive oil and honey I gave you to eat—you offered as fragrant incense before them. That is what happened, declares the Sovereign LORD.

20" 'And you took your sons and daughters whom you bore to me and sacrificed them as food to the idols. Was your prostitution not enough? 21You slaughtered my children and sacrificed them[e] to the idols. 22In all your detestable practices and your prostitution you did not remember the days of your youth, when you were naked and bare, kicking about in your blood.

23" 'Woe! Woe to you, declares the Sovereign LORD. In addition to all your other wickedness, 24you built a mound for yourself and made a lofty shrine in every public square. 25At the head of every street you built your lofty shrines and degraded your beauty, offering your body with increasing promiscuity to anyone who passed by. 26You engaged in prostitution with the Egyptians, your lustful neighbors, and provoked me to anger with your increasing promiscuity. 27So I stretched out my hand against you and reduced your territory; I gave you over to the greed of your enemies, the daughters of the Philistines, who were shocked by your lewd conduct. 28You engaged in prostitution with the Assyrians too, because you were insatiable; and even after that, you still were not satisfied. 29Then you increased your promiscuity to include Babylonia,[f] a land of merchants, but even with this you were not satisfied.

30" 'How weak-willed you are, declares the Sovereign LORD, when you do all these things, acting like a brazen prostitute! 31When you built your mounds at the head of every street and made your lofty shrines in every public square, you were unlike a prostitute, because you scorned payment.

32" 'You adulterous wife! You prefer strangers to your own husband! 33Every prostitute receives a fee, but you give gifts to all your lovers, bribing them to come to you from everywhere for your illicit favors. 34So in your prostitution you are the opposite of others; no one runs after you for your favors. You are the very opposite, for you give payment and none is given to you.

35" 'Therefore, you prostitute, hear the word of the LORD! 36This is what the Sovereign LORD says: Because you poured out your wealth[g] and exposed your naked-

---

a6 A few Hebrew manuscripts, Septuagint and Syriac; most Hebrew manuscripts "Live!" And as you lay there in your blood I said to you, "Live!"   b7 Or became mature   c9 Or I had bathed   d15 Most Hebrew manuscripts; one Hebrew manuscript (see some Septuagint manuscripts) by. Such a thing should not happen   e21 Or and made them pass through the fire,   f29 Or Chaldea   g36 Or lust

VERSE FOR THE DAY:
Ezekiel 16:20–21

AUTHOR:
Dorothy Patterson

PASSAGE FOR THE DAY:
Ezekiel 16:20–22

Sacrificing the Children

EZEKIEL, an aristocratic priest of Jerusalem, was among those carried captive to Babylon. His message to the people of Israel was that before they could ever hope to return to their beloved Jerusalem, they must return to the Lord.

No pagan practice was more deplorable than human sacrifice, especially when involving a helpless child. In adopting this practice, the Israelites had forgotten that children are a blessing from God (Psalm 127:3). While looking on such barbarity with disdain, many of us are unmoved by couples who express longing for a child and then promptly ignore all parental responsibility for nurturing and rearing the child. As women, we have a particular vulnerability here because God has given to us the biological assignment for the physical nurture of children during their growth in the womb and the awesome spiritual task of teaching children in the early years (2 Timothy 1:5).

Parenting requires undergirding our children with prayer, enveloping them with love, and overshadowing them with consistent spiritual nurture. It requires training through lifestyle and faithful instruction as we " . . . sit at home . . . walk along the road . . . lie down and . . . get up" (Deuteronomy 6:7).

A leading Russian theorist expressed deep concern for the ill effects on those children whose mothers spend less than thirty minutes weekly rearing them and pleaded with Soviet mothers to make their children their prime mission. We, too, have been warned that for the first time a generation has spent most of its waking hours in an institution. These children have received their primary guidance and teaching during the formative years from caregivers other than their parents.

After completing our graduate work, my husband and I decided that I should give my full energies and creativity to keeping our home and rearing our children. With unbounded joy and enthusiastic effort I have poured my life into home and family, putting aside professional pursuits and personal ambitions. Nothing has challenged my body and mind any more or showered more rewards on my heart and soul than investing my education, skills and energies in the people I love most and want most to succeed.

Additional Scripture Readings:
Proverbs 22:6; 2 Timothy 3:14–15

Go to page 898 for your next devotional reading.

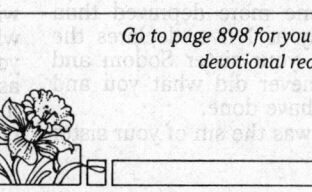

ness in your promiscuity with your lovers, and because of all your detestable idols, and because you gave them your children's blood, ³⁷therefore I am going to gather all your lovers, with whom you found pleasure, those you loved as well as those you hated. I will gather them against you from all around and will strip you in front of them, and they will see all your nakedness. ³⁸I will sentence you to the punishment of women who commit adultery and who shed blood; I will bring upon you the blood vengeance of my wrath and jealous anger. ³⁹Then I will hand you over to your lovers, and they will tear down your mounds and destroy your lofty shrines. They will strip you of your clothes and take your fine jewelry and leave you naked and bare. ⁴⁰They will bring a mob against you, who will stone you and hack you to pieces with their swords. ⁴¹They will burn down your houses and inflict punishment on you in the sight of many women. I will put a stop to your prostitution, and you will no longer pay your lovers. ⁴²Then my wrath against you will subside and my jealous anger will turn away from you; I will be calm and no longer angry.

⁴³" 'Because you did not remember the days of your youth but enraged me with all these things, I will surely bring down on your head what you have done, declares the Sovereign LORD. Did you not add lewdness to all your other detestable practices?

⁴⁴" 'Everyone who quotes proverbs will quote this proverb about you: "Like mother, like daughter." ⁴⁵You are a true daughter of your mother, who despised her husband and her children; and you are a true sister of your sisters, who despised their husbands and their children. Your mother was a Hittite and your father an Amorite. ⁴⁶Your older sister was Samaria, who lived to the north of you with her daughters; and your younger sister, who lived to the south of you with her daughters, was Sodom. ⁴⁷You not only walked in their ways and copied their detestable practices, but in all your ways you soon became more depraved than they. ⁴⁸As surely as I live, declares the Sovereign LORD, your sister Sodom and her daughters never did what you and your daughters have done.

⁴⁹" 'Now this was the sin of your sister Sodom: She and her daughters were arrogant, overfed and unconcerned; they did not help the poor and needy. ⁵⁰They were haughty and did detestable things before me. Therefore I did away with them as you have seen. ⁵¹Samaria did not commit half the sins you did. You have done more detestable things than they, and have made your sisters seem righteous by all these things you have done. ⁵²Bear your disgrace, for you have furnished some justification for your sisters. Because your sins were more vile than theirs, they appear more righteous than you. So then, be ashamed and bear your disgrace, for you have made your sisters appear righteous.

⁵³" 'However, I will restore the fortunes of Sodom and her daughters and of Samaria and her daughters, and your fortunes along with them, ⁵⁴so that you may bear your disgrace and be ashamed of all you have done in giving them comfort. ⁵⁵And your sisters, Sodom with her daughters and Samaria with her daughters, will return to what they were before; and you and your daughters will return to what you were before. ⁵⁶You would not even mention your sister Sodom in the day of your pride, ⁵⁷before your wickedness was uncovered. Even so, you are now scorned by the daughters of Edom^a and all her neighbors and the daughters of the Philistines—all those around you who despise you. ⁵⁸You will bear the consequences of your lewdness and your detestable practices, declares the LORD.

⁵⁹" 'This is what the Sovereign LORD says: I will deal with you as you deserve, because you have despised my oath by breaking the covenant. ⁶⁰Yet I will remember the covenant I made with you in the days of your youth, and I will establish an everlasting covenant with you. ⁶¹Then you will remember your ways and be ashamed when you receive your sisters, both those who are older than you and those who are younger. I will give them to you as daughters, but not on the basis of my covenant with you. ⁶²So I will establish my covenant with you, and you will know that I am the LORD. ⁶³Then, when I make atonement for you for all you have done, you will remember and be ashamed and never again open your mouth because of your humiliation, declares the Sovereign LORD.' "

---

^a57 Many Hebrew manuscripts and Syriac; most Hebrew manuscripts, Septuagint and Vulgate *Aram*

Two Eagles and a Vine

17 The word of the LORD came to me: 2"Son of man, set forth an allegory and tell the house of Israel a parable. 3Say to them, 'This is what the Sovereign LORD says: A great eagle with powerful wings, long feathers and full plumage of varied colors came to Lebanon. Taking hold of the top of a cedar, 4he broke off its topmost shoot and carried it away to a land of merchants, where he planted it in a city of traders.

5" 'He took some of the seed of your land and put it in fertile soil. He planted it like a willow by abundant water, 6and it sprouted and became a low, spreading vine. Its branches turned toward him, but its roots remained under it. So it became a vine and produced branches and put out leafy boughs.

7" 'But there was another great eagle with powerful wings and full plumage. The vine now sent out its roots toward him from the plot where it was planted and stretched out its branches to him for water. 8It had been planted in good soil by abundant water so that it would produce branches, bear fruit and become a splendid vine.'

9"Say to them, 'This is what the Sovereign LORD says: Will it thrive? Will it not be uprooted and stripped of its fruit so that it withers? All its new growth will wither. It will not take a strong arm or many people to pull it up by the roots. 10Even if it is transplanted, will it thrive? Will it not wither completely when the east wind strikes it—wither away in the plot where it grew?' "

11Then the word of the LORD came to me: 12"Say to this rebellious house, 'Do you not know what these things mean?' Say to them: 'The king of Babylon went to Jerusalem and carried off her king and her nobles, bringing them back with him to Babylon. 13Then he took a member of the royal family and made a treaty with him, putting him under oath. He also carried away the leading men of the land, 14so that the kingdom would be brought low, unable to rise again, surviving only by keeping his treaty. 15But the king rebelled against him by sending his envoys to Egypt to get horses and a large army. Will he succeed? Will he who does such things escape? Will he break the treaty and yet escape?

16" 'As surely as I live, declares the Sovereign LORD, he shall die in Babylon, in the land of the king who put him on the throne, whose oath he despised and whose treaty he broke. 17Pharaoh with his mighty army and great horde will be of no help to him in war, when ramps are built and siege works erected to destroy many lives. 18He despised the oath by breaking the covenant. Because he had given his hand in pledge and yet did all these things, he shall not escape.

19" 'Therefore this is what the Sovereign LORD says: As surely as I live, I will bring down on his head my oath that he despised and my covenant that he broke. 20I will spread my net for him, and he will be caught in my snare. I will bring him to Babylon and execute judgment upon him there because he was unfaithful to me. 21All his fleeing troops will fall by the sword, and the survivors will be scattered to the winds. Then you will know that I the LORD have spoken.

22" 'This is what the Sovereign LORD says: I myself will take a shoot from the very top of a cedar and plant it; I will break off a tender sprig from its topmost shoots and plant it on a high and lofty mountain. 23On the mountain heights of Israel I will plant it; it will produce branches and bear fruit and become a splendid cedar. Birds of every kind will nest in it; they will find shelter in the shade of its branches. 24All the trees of the field will know that I the LORD bring down the tall tree and make the low tree grow tall. I dry up the green tree and make the dry tree flourish.

" 'I the LORD have spoken, and I will do it.' "

The Soul Who Sins Will Die

18 The word of the LORD came to me: 2"What do you people mean by quoting this proverb about the land of Israel:

" 'The fathers eat sour grapes,
    and the children's teeth are set on
        edge'?

3"As surely as I live, declares the Sovereign LORD, you will no longer quote this proverb in Israel. 4For every living soul belongs to me, the father as well as the son—both alike belong to me. The soul who sins is the one who will die.

5"Suppose there is a righteous man
    who does what is just and right.
6He does not eat at the mountain
    shrines

or look to the idols of the house of
Israel.
He does not defile his neighbor's wife
or lie with a woman during her
period.
7He does not oppress anyone,
but returns what he took in pledge
for a loan.
He does not commit robbery
but gives his food to the hungry
and provides clothing for the naked.
8He does not lend at usury
or take excessive interest.ᵃ
He withholds his hand from doing
wrong
and judges fairly between man and
man.
9He follows my decrees
and faithfully keeps my laws.
That man is righteous;
he will surely live,
declares the Sovereign LORD.

10"Suppose he has a violent son, who
sheds blood or does any of these other
thingsᵇ 11(though the father has done
none of them):

"He eats at the mountain shrines.
He defiles his neighbor's wife.
12He oppresses the poor and needy.
He commits robbery.
He does not return what he took in
pledge.
He looks to the idols.
He does detestable things.
13He lends at usury and takes excessive
interest.

Will such a man live? He will not! Because he has done all these detestable
things, he will surely be put to death and
his blood will be on his own head.

14"But suppose this son has a son who
sees all the sins his father commits, and
though he sees them, he does not do such
things:

15"He does not eat at the mountain
shrines
or look to the idols of the house of
Israel.
He does not defile his neighbor's
wife.
16He does not oppress anyone
or require a pledge for a loan.
He does not commit robbery
but gives his food to the hungry
and provides clothing for the naked.

17He withholds his hand from sinᶜ
and takes no usury or excessive
interest.
He keeps my laws and follows my
decrees.

He will not die for his father's sin; he will
surely live. 18But his father will die for his
own sin, because he practiced extortion,
robbed his brother and did what was
wrong among his people.

19"Yet you ask, 'Why does the son not
share the guilt of his father?' Since the
son has done what is just and right and
has been careful to keep all my decrees,
he will surely live. 20The soul who sins is
the one who will die. The son will not
share the guilt of the father, nor will the
father share the guilt of the son. The
righteousness of the righteous man will
be credited to him, and the wickedness
of the wicked will be charged against
him.
21"But if a wicked man turns away from
all the sins he has committed and keeps
all my decrees and does what is just and
right, he will surely live; he will not die.
22None of the offenses he has committed
will be remembered against him. Because
of the righteous things he has done, he
will live. 23Do I take any pleasure in the
death of the wicked? declares the Sovereign LORD. Rather, am I not pleased when
they turn from their ways and live?
24"But if a righteous man turns from his
righteousness and commits sin and does
the same detestable things the wicked
man does, will he live? None of the righteous things he has done will be remembered. Because of the unfaithfulness he is
guilty of and because of the sins he has
committed, he will die.
25"Yet you say, 'The way of the Lord is
not just.' Hear, O house of Israel: Is my
way unjust? Is it not your ways that are
unjust? 26If a righteous man turns from
his righteousness and commits sin, he
will die for it; because of the sin he has
committed he will die. 27But if a wicked
man turns away from the wickedness he
has committed and does what is just and
right, he will save his life. 28Because he
considers all the offenses he has committed and turns away from them, he will
surely live; he will not die. 29Yet the
house of Israel says, 'The way of the Lord
is not just.' Are my ways unjust, O house

ᵃ8 Or take interest; similarly in verses 13 and 17
also verse 8); Hebrew from the poor   ᵇ10 Or things to a brother   ᶜ17 Septuagint (see

of Israel? Is it not your ways that are unjust?

30"Therefore, O house of Israel, I will judge you, each one according to his ways, declares the Sovereign LORD. Repent! Turn away from all your offenses; then sin will not be your downfall. 31Rid yourselves of all the offenses you have committed, and get a new heart and a new spirit. Why will you die, O house of Israel? 32For I take no pleasure in the death of anyone, declares the Sovereign LORD. Repent and live!

A Lament for Israel's Princes

19 "Take up a lament concerning the princes of Israel 2and say:

" 'What a lioness was your mother
    among the lions!
She lay down among the young lions
    and reared her cubs.
3She brought up one of her cubs,
    and he became a strong lion.
He learned to tear the prey
    and he devoured men.
4The nations heard about him,
    and he was trapped in their pit.
They led him with hooks
    to the land of Egypt.

5" 'When she saw her hope unfulfilled,
    her expectation gone,
she took another of her cubs
    and made him a strong lion.
6He prowled among the lions,
    for he was now a strong lion.
He learned to tear the prey
    and he devoured men.
7He broke down a their strongholds
    and devastated their towns.
The land and all who were in it
    were terrified by his roaring.
8Then the nations came against him,
    those from regions round about.
They spread their net for him,
    and he was trapped in their pit.
9With hooks they pulled him into a
        cage
    and brought him to the king of
        Babylon.
They put him in prison,
    so his roar was heard no longer
    on the mountains of Israel.

10" 'Your mother was like a vine in your
        vineyard b
    planted by the water;

it was fruitful and full of branches
    because of abundant water.
11Its branches were strong,
    fit for a ruler's scepter.
It towered high
    above the thick foliage,
conspicuous for its height
    and for its many branches.
12But it was uprooted in fury
    and thrown to the ground.
The east wind made it shrivel,
    it was stripped of its fruit;
its strong branches withered
    and fire consumed them.
13Now it is planted in the desert,
    in a dry and thirsty land.
14Fire spread from one of its main c
        branches
    and consumed its fruit.
No strong branch is left on it
    fit for a ruler's scepter.'

This is a lament and is to be used as a lament."

Rebellious Israel

20 In the seventh year, in the fifth month on the tenth day, some of the elders of Israel came to inquire of the LORD, and they sat down in front of me. 2Then the word of the LORD came to me: 3"Son of man, speak to the elders of Israel and say to them, 'This is what the Sovereign LORD says: Have you come to inquire of me? As surely as I live, I will not let you inquire of me, declares the Sovereign LORD.'

4"Will you judge them? Will you judge them, son of man? Then confront them with the detestable practices of their fathers 5and say to them: 'This is what the Sovereign LORD says: On the day I chose Israel, I swore with uplifted hand to the descendants of the house of Jacob and revealed myself to them in Egypt. With uplifted hand I said to them, "I am the LORD your God." 6On that day I swore to them that I would bring them out of Egypt into a land I had searched out for them, a land flowing with milk and honey, the most beautiful of all lands. 7And I said to them, "Each of you, get rid of the vile images you have set your eyes on, and do not defile yourselves with the idols of Egypt. I am the LORD your God."

8" 'But they rebelled against me and would not listen to me; they did not get

---

a7 Targum (see Septuagint); Hebrew He knew   b10 Two Hebrew manuscripts; most Hebrew
manuscripts your blood   c14 Or from under its

rid of the vile images they had set their eyes on, nor did they forsake the idols of Egypt. So I said I would pour out my wrath on them and spend my anger against them in Egypt. ⁹But for the sake of my name I did what would keep it from being profaned in the eyes of the nations they lived among and in whose sight I had revealed myself to the Israelites by bringing them out of Egypt. ¹⁰Therefore I led them out of Egypt and brought them into the desert. ¹¹I gave them my decrees and made known to them my laws, for the man who obeys them will live by them. ¹²Also I gave them my Sabbaths as a sign between us, so they would know that I the LORD made them holy.

¹³" 'Yet the people of Israel rebelled against me in the desert. They did not follow my decrees but rejected my laws — although the man who obeys them will live by them — and they utterly desecrated my Sabbaths. So I said I would pour out my wrath on them and destroy them in the desert. ¹⁴But for the sake of my name I did what would keep it from being profaned in the eyes of the nations in whose sight I had brought them out. ¹⁵Also with uplifted hand I swore to them in the desert that I would not bring them into the land I had given them — a land flowing with milk and honey, most beautiful of all lands — ¹⁶because they rejected my laws and did not follow my decrees and desecrated my Sabbaths. For their hearts were devoted to their idols. ¹⁷Yet I looked on them with pity and did not destroy them or put an end to them in the desert. ¹⁸I said to their children in the desert, "Do not follow the statutes of your fathers or keep their laws or defile yourselves with their idols. ¹⁹I am the LORD your God; follow my decrees and be careful to keep my laws. ²⁰Keep my Sabbaths holy, that they may be a sign between us. Then you will know that I am the LORD your God."

²¹" 'But the children rebelled against me: They did not follow my decrees, they were not careful to keep my laws — although the man who obeys them will live by them — and they desecrated my Sabbaths. So I said I would pour out my wrath on them and spend my anger against them in the desert. ²²But I withheld my hand, and for the sake of my name I did what would keep it from being profaned in the eyes of the nations in whose sight I had brought them out. ²³Also with uplifted hand I swore to them in the desert that I would disperse them among the nations and scatter them through the countries, ²⁴because they had not obeyed my laws but had rejected my decrees and desecrated my Sabbaths, and their eyes lusted after their fathers' idols. ²⁵I also gave them over to statutes that were not good and laws they could not live by; ²⁶I let them become defiled through their gifts — the sacrifice of every firstborn ᵃ — that I might fill them with horror so they would know that I am the LORD.'

²⁷"Therefore, son of man, speak to the people of Israel and say to them, 'This is what the Sovereign LORD says: In this also your fathers blasphemed me by forsaking me: ²⁸When I brought them into the land I had sworn to give them and they saw any high hill or any leafy tree, there they offered their sacrifices, made offerings that provoked me to anger, presented their fragrant incense and poured out their drink offerings. ²⁹Then I said to them: What is this high place you go to?' " (It is called Bamah ᵇ to this day.)

Judgment and Restoration

³⁰"Therefore say to the house of Israel: 'This is what the Sovereign LORD says: Will you defile yourselves the way your fathers did and lust after their vile images? ³¹When you offer your gifts — the sacrifice of your sons in ᶜ the fire — you continue to defile yourselves with all your idols to this day. Am I to let you inquire of me, O house of Israel? As surely as I live, declares the Sovereign LORD, I will not let you inquire of me.

³²" 'You say, "We want to be like the nations, like the peoples of the world, who serve wood and stone." But what you have in mind will never happen. ³³As surely as I live, declares the Sovereign LORD, I will rule over you with a mighty hand and an outstretched arm and with outpoured wrath. ³⁴I will bring you from the nations and gather you from the countries where you have been scattered — with a mighty hand and an outstretched arm and with outpoured wrath. ³⁵I will bring you into the desert of the nations and there, face to face, I will execute judgment upon you. ³⁶As I judged your fathers in the desert of the land of

---

ᵃ26 Or —making every firstborn pass through the fire, —making your sons pass through   ᵇ29 Bamah means high place.   ᶜ31 Or

Egypt, so I will judge you, declares the Sovereign LORD. ³⁷I will take note of you as you pass under my rod, and I will bring you into the bond of the covenant. ³⁸I will purge you of those who revolt and rebel against me. Although I will bring them out of the land where they are living, yet they will not enter the land of Israel. Then you will know that I am the LORD.

³⁹" 'As for you, O house of Israel, this is what the Sovereign LORD says: Go and serve your idols, every one of you! But afterward you will surely listen to me and no longer profane my holy name with your gifts and idols. ⁴⁰For on my holy mountain, the high mountain of Israel, declares the Sovereign LORD, there in the land the entire house of Israel will serve me, and there I will accept them. There I will require your offerings and your choice gifts,^a along with all your holy sacrifices. ⁴¹I will accept you as fragrant incense when I bring you out from the nations and gather you from the countries where you have been scattered, and I will show myself holy among you in the sight of the nations. ⁴²Then you will know that I am the LORD, when I bring you into the land of Israel, the land I had sworn with uplifted hand to give to your fathers. ⁴³There you will remember your conduct and all the actions by which you have defiled yourselves, and you will loathe yourselves for all the evil you have done. ⁴⁴You will know that I am the LORD, when I deal with you for my name's sake and not according to your evil ways and your corrupt practices, O house of Israel, declares the Sovereign LORD.' "

Prophecy Against the South

⁴⁵The word of the LORD came to me: ⁴⁶"Son of man, set your face toward the south; preach against the south and prophesy against the forest of the southland. ⁴⁷Say to the southern forest: 'Hear the word of the LORD. This is what the Sovereign LORD says: I am about to set fire to you, and it will consume all your trees, both green and dry. The blazing flame will not be quenched, and every face from south to north will be scorched by it. ⁴⁸Everyone will see that I the LORD have kindled it; it will not be quenched.' "

⁴⁹Then I said, "Ah, Sovereign LORD! They are saying of me, 'Isn't he just telling parables?' "

Babylon, God's Sword of Judgment

21 The word of the LORD came to me: ²"Son of man, set your face against Jerusalem and preach against the sanctuary. Prophesy against the land of Israel ³and say to her: 'This is what the LORD says: I am against you. I will draw my sword from its scabbard and cut off from you both the righteous and the wicked. ⁴Because I am going to cut off the righteous and the wicked, my sword will be unsheathed against everyone from south to north. ⁵Then all people will know that I the LORD have drawn my sword from its scabbard; it will not return again.'

⁶"Therefore groan, son of man! Groan before them with broken heart and bitter grief. ⁷And when they ask you, 'Why are you groaning?' you shall say, 'Because of the news that is coming. Every heart will melt and every hand go limp; every spirit will become faint and every knee become as weak as water.' It is coming! It will surely take place, declares the Sovereign LORD."

⁸The word of the LORD came to me: ⁹"Son of man, prophesy and say, 'This is what the Lord says:

" 'A sword, a sword,
    sharpened and polished—
¹⁰sharpened for the slaughter,
    polished to flash like lightning!

" 'Shall we rejoice in the scepter of my son ˌJudahˌ? The sword despises every such stick.

¹¹" 'The sword is appointed to be
        polished,
    to be grasped with the hand;
it is sharpened and polished,
    made ready for the hand of the
        slayer.
¹²Cry out and wail, son of man,
    for it is against my people;
    it is against all the princes of Israel.
They are thrown to the sword
    along with my people.
Therefore beat your breast.

¹³" 'Testing will surely come. And what if the scepter ˌof Judahˌ, which the sword despises, does not continue? declares the Sovereign LORD.'

¹⁴"So then, son of man, prophesy
    and strike your hands together.
Let the sword strike twice,
    even three times.

^a40 Or and the gifts of your firstfruits

It is a sword for slaughter—
  a sword for great slaughter,
    closing in on them from every side.
¹⁵So that hearts may melt
  and the fallen be many,
I have stationed the sword for
    slaughter*a*
  at all their gates.
Oh! It is made to flash like lightning,
  it is grasped for slaughter.
¹⁶O sword, slash to the right,
  then to the left,
    wherever your blade is turned.
¹⁷I too will strike my hands together,
  and my wrath will subside.
I the LORD have spoken."

¹⁸The word of the LORD came to me:
¹⁹"Son of man, mark out two roads for the
sword of the king of Babylon to take, both
starting from the same country. Make a
signpost where the road branches off to
the city. ²⁰Mark out one road for the
sword to come against Rabbah of the Ammonites and another against Judah and
fortified Jerusalem. ²¹For the king of Babylon will stop at the fork in the road, at
the junction of the two roads, to seek an
omen: He will cast lots with arrows, he
will consult his idols, he will examine the
liver. ²²Into his right hand will come the
lot for Jerusalem, where he is to set up
battering rams, to give the command to
slaughter, to sound the battle cry, to set
battering rams against the gates, to build
a ramp and to erect siege works. ²³It will
seem like a false omen to those who have
sworn allegiance to him, but he will remind them of their guilt and take them
captive.

²⁴"Therefore this is what the Sovereign
LORD says: 'Because you people have
brought to mind your guilt by your open
rebellion, revealing your sins in all that
you do—because you have done this, you
will be taken captive.

²⁵" 'O profane and wicked prince of Is-
rael, whose day has come, whose time of
punishment has reached its climax, ²⁶this
is what the Sovereign LORD says: Take off
the turban, remove the crown. It will not
be as it was: The lowly will be exalted and
the exalted will be brought low. ²⁷A ruin!
A ruin! I will make it a ruin! It will not be
restored until he comes to whom it rightfully belongs; to him I will give it.'

²⁸"And you, son of man, prophesy and
say, 'This is what the Sovereign LORD says

about the Ammonites and their insults:

" 'A sword, a sword,
  drawn for the slaughter,
polished to consume
  and to flash like lightning!
²⁹Despite false visions concerning you
  and lying divinations about you,
it will be laid on the necks
  of the wicked who are to be slain,
whose day has come,
  whose time of punishment has
    reached its climax.
³⁰Return the sword to its scabbard.
  In the place where you were
    created,
in the land of your ancestry,
  I will judge you.
³¹I will pour out my wrath upon you
  and breathe out my fiery anger
    against you;
I will hand you over to brutal men,
  men skilled in destruction.
³²You will be fuel for the fire,
  your blood will be shed in your
    land,
you will be remembered no more;
  for I the LORD have spoken.' "

Jerusalem's Sins

22 The word of the LORD came to me:
²"Son of man, will you judge her?
Will you judge this city of bloodshed?
Then confront her with all her detestable
practices ³and say: 'This is what the Sovereign LORD says: O city that brings on
herself doom by shedding blood in her
midst and defiles herself by making idols,
⁴you have become guilty because of the
blood you have shed and have become
defiled by the idols you have made. You
have brought your days to a close, and the
end of your years has come. Therefore I
will make you an object of scorn to the
nations and a laughingstock to all the
countries. ⁵Those who are near and those
who are far away will mock you, O infa-
mous city, full of turmoil.

⁶" 'See how each of the princes of Israel
who are in you uses his power to shed
blood. ⁷In you they have treated father
and mother with contempt; in you they
have oppressed the alien and mistreated
the fatherless and the widow. ⁸You have
despised my holy things and desecrated
my Sabbaths. ⁹In you are slanderous men
bent on shedding blood; in you are those
who eat at the mountain shrines and

---

a15 Septuagint; the meaning of the Hebrew for this word is uncertain.

commit lewd acts. ¹⁰In you are those who dishonor their fathers' bed; in you are those who violate women during their period, when they are ceremonially unclean. ¹¹In you one man commits a detestable offense with his neighbor's wife, another shamefully defiles his daughter-in-law, and another violates his sister, his own father's daughter. ¹²In you men accept bribes to shed blood; you take usury and excessive interest*a* and make unjust gain from your neighbors by extortion. And you have forgotten me, declares the Sovereign LORD.

¹³" 'I will surely strike my hands together at the unjust gain you have made and at the blood you have shed in your midst. ¹⁴Will your courage endure or your hands be strong in the day I deal with you? I the LORD have spoken, and I will do it. ¹⁵I will disperse you among the nations and scatter you through the countries; and I will put an end to your uncleanness. ¹⁶When you have been defiled*b* in the eyes of the nations, you will know that I am the LORD.' "

¹⁷Then the word of the LORD came to me: ¹⁸"Son of man, the house of Israel has become dross to me; all of them are the copper, tin, iron and lead left inside a furnace. They are but the dross of silver. ¹⁹Therefore this is what the Sovereign LORD says: 'Because you have all become dross, I will gather you into Jerusalem. ²⁰As men gather silver, copper, iron, lead and tin into a furnace to melt it with a fiery blast, so will I gather you in my anger and my wrath and put you inside the city and melt you. ²¹I will gather you and I will blow on you with my fiery wrath, and you will be melted inside her. ²²As silver is melted in a furnace, so you will be melted inside her, and you will know that I the LORD have poured out my wrath upon you.' "

²³Again the word of the LORD came to me: ²⁴"Son of man, say to the land, 'You are a land that has had no rain or showers*c* in the day of wrath.' ²⁵There is a conspiracy of her princes*d* within her like a roaring lion tearing its prey; they devour people, take treasures and precious things and make many widows within her. ²⁶Her priests do violence to my law and profane my holy things; they do not distinguish between the holy and the common; they teach that there is no difference between the unclean and the clean; and they shut their eyes to the keeping of my Sabbaths, so that I am profaned among them. ²⁷Her officials within her are like wolves tearing their prey; they shed blood and kill people to make unjust gain. ²⁸Her prophets whitewash these deeds for them by false visions and lying divinations. They say, 'This is what the Sovereign LORD says'—when the LORD has not spoken. ²⁹The people of the land practice extortion and commit robbery; they oppress the poor and needy and mistreat the alien, denying them justice.

³⁰"I looked for a man among them who would build up the wall and stand before me in the gap on behalf of the land so I would not have to destroy it, but I found none. ³¹So I will pour out my wrath on them and consume them with my fiery anger, bringing down on their own heads all they have done, declares the Sovereign LORD."

Two Adulterous Sisters

23 The word of the LORD came to me: ²"Son of man, there were two women, daughters of the same mother. ³They became prostitutes in Egypt, engaging in prostitution from their youth. In that land their breasts were fondled and their virgin bosoms caressed. ⁴The older was named Oholah, and her sister was Oholibah. They were mine and gave birth to sons and daughters. Oholah is Samaria, and Oholibah is Jerusalem.

⁵"Oholah engaged in prostitution while she was still mine; and she lusted after her lovers, the Assyrians—warriors ⁶clothed in blue, governors and commanders, all of them handsome young men, and mounted horsemen. ⁷She gave herself as a prostitute to all the elite of the Assyrians and defiled herself with all the idols of everyone she lusted after. ⁸She did not give up the prostitution she began in Egypt, when during her youth men slept with her, caressed her virgin bosom and poured out their lust upon her.

⁹"Therefore I handed her over to her lovers, the Assyrians, for whom she lusted. ¹⁰They stripped her naked, took away her sons and daughters and killed her with the sword. She became a byword among women, and punishment was inflicted on her.

---

a12 Or *usury and interest*   *b16* Or *When I have allotted you your inheritance*   *c24* Septuagint; Hebrew *has not been cleansed or rained on*   *d25* Septuagint; Hebrew *prophets*

¹¹"Her sister Oholibah saw this, yet in her lust and prostitution she was more depraved than her sister. ¹²She too lusted after the Assyrians—governors and commanders, warriors in full dress, mounted horsemen, all handsome young men. ¹³I saw that she too defiled herself; both of them went the same way.

¹⁴"But she carried her prostitution still further. She saw men portrayed on a wall, figures of Chaldeans[a] portrayed in red, ¹⁵with belts around their waists and flowing turbans on their heads; all of them looked like Babylonian chariot officers, natives of Chaldea.[b] ¹⁶As soon as she saw them, she lusted after them and sent messengers to them in Chaldea. ¹⁷Then the Babylonians came to her, to the bed of love, and in their lust they defiled her. After she had been defiled by them, she turned away from them in disgust. ¹⁸When she carried on her prostitution openly and exposed her nakedness, I turned away from her in disgust, just as I had turned away from her sister. ¹⁹Yet she became more and more promiscuous as

---

[a]14 Or *Babylonians*   [b]15 Or *Babylonia*; also in verse 16

TUESDAY

VERSE FOR THE DAY:
Ezekiel 22:30

AUTHOR:
Kathi Mills

PASSAGE FOR THE DAY:
Ezekiel 22:23–31

Standing in the Gap

LOOKING back on my life prior to my conversion in 1974, I realize now there were many intercessors on my behalf. In addition to my own dear family who prayed for me faithfully, I remember one instance in particular when God burdened the heart of a woman I hardly knew to pray for me.

I was in a hospital, far from home and family, drifting in and out of consciousness. Several times I became aware of a woman's voice praying for my salvation, as well as for my physical healing. At one point I heard a doctor describing my condition as critical, warning that I might not survive.

It was then that I recognized the voice of my intercessor once again as she spoke out in faith, "Doctor, I respect what you say, but I cannot accept it. I've been praying for Kathi and I believe she will not only recover, she will walk out of here and live for God someday!"

Before long, I did walk out of that hospital, returned to work, and learned that it was my boss's wife (I had only met her twice) who had "stood in the gap" for me. When I tried to thank her, she responded with a confident smile, "Don't thank me—thank God! He has great plans for your life."

Soon after that I moved away, never to see her again; but five years later when I gave my life to Christ, I remembered her—this faithful woman of God who never saw the results of her prayers for my salvation, but who believed God to answer those prayers in his time.

Additional Scripture Readings:
Exodus 32:7–14; James 5:13–20

Go to page 913 for your next devotional reading.

she recalled the days of her youth, when she was a prostitute in Egypt. [20]There she lusted after her lovers, whose genitals were like those of donkeys and whose emission was like that of horses. [21]So you longed for the lewdness of your youth, when in Egypt your bosom was caressed and your young breasts fondled. [a]

[22]"Therefore, Oholibah, this is what the Sovereign Lord says: I will stir up your lovers against you, those you turned away from in disgust, and I will bring them against you from every side— [23]the Babylonians and all the Chaldeans, the men of Pekod and Shoa and Koa, and all the Assyrians with them, handsome young men, all of them governors and commanders, chariot officers and men of high rank, all mounted on horses. [24]They will come against you with weapons, [b] chariots and wagons and with a throng of people; they will take up positions against you on every side with large and small shields and with helmets. I will turn you over to them for punishment, and they will punish you according to their standards. [25]I will direct my jealous anger against you, and they will deal with you in fury. They will cut off your noses and your ears, and those of you who are left will fall by the sword. They will take away your sons and daughters, and those of you who are left will be consumed by fire. [26]They will also strip you of your clothes and take your fine jewelry. [27]So I will put a stop to the lewdness and prostitution you began in Egypt. You will not look on these things with longing or remember Egypt anymore.

[28]"For this is what the Sovereign Lord says: I am about to hand you over to those you hate, to those you turned away from in disgust. [29]They will deal with you in hatred and take away everything you have worked for. They will leave you naked and bare, and the shame of your prostitution will be exposed. Your lewdness and promiscuity [30]have brought this upon you, because you lusted after the nations and defiled yourself with their idols. [31]You have gone the way of your sister; so I will put her cup into your hand.

[32]"This is what the Sovereign Lord says:

"You will drink your sister's cup,
    a cup large and deep;
it will bring scorn and derision,

for it holds so much.
[33]You will be filled with drunkenness
    and sorrow,
    the cup of ruin and desolation,
    the cup of your sister Samaria.
[34]You will drink it and drain it dry;
    you will dash it to pieces
    and tear your breasts.

I have spoken, declares the Sovereign Lord.

[35]"Therefore this is what the Sovereign Lord says: Since you have forgotten me and thrust me behind your back, you must bear the consequences of your lewdness and prostitution."

[36]The Lord said to me: "Son of man, will you judge Oholah and Oholibah? Then confront them with their detestable practices, [37]for they have committed adultery and blood is on their hands. They committed adultery with their idols; they even sacrificed their children, whom they bore to me, [c] as food for them. [38]They have also done this to me: At that same time they defiled my sanctuary and desecrated my Sabbaths. [39]On the very day they sacrificed their children to their idols, they entered my sanctuary and desecrated it. That is what they did in my house.

[40]"They even sent messengers for men who came from far away, and when they arrived you bathed yourself for them, painted your eyes and put on your jewelry. [41]You sat on an elegant couch, with a table spread before it on which you had placed the incense and oil that belonged to me.

[42]"The noise of a carefree crowd was around her; Sabeans [d] were brought from the desert along with men from the rabble, and they put bracelets on the arms of the woman and her sister and beautiful crowns on their heads. [43]Then I said about the one worn out by adultery, 'Now let them use her as a prostitute, for that is all she is.' [44]And they slept with her. As men sleep with a prostitute, so they slept with those lewd women, Oholah and Oholibah. [45]But righteous men will sentence them to the punishment of women who commit adultery and shed blood, because they are adulterous and blood is on their hands.

[46]"This is what the Sovereign Lord says:

---

[a]21 Syriac (see also verse 3); Hebrew *caressed because of your young breasts*   [b]24 The meaning of the Hebrew for this word is uncertain.   [c]37 Or *even made the children they bore to me pass through ,the fire,*   [d]42 Or *drunkards*

Bring a mob against them and give them over to terror and plunder. 47The mob will stone them and cut them down with their swords; they will kill their sons and daughters and burn down their houses.

48"So I will put an end to lewdness in the land, that all women may take warning and not imitate you. 49You will suffer the penalty for your lewdness and bear the consequences of your sins of idolatry. Then you will know that I am the Sovereign LORD."

The Cooking Pot

24 In the ninth year, in the tenth month on the tenth day, the word of the LORD came to me: 2"Son of man, record this date, this very date, because the king of Babylon has laid siege to Jerusalem this very day. 3Tell this rebellious house a parable and say to them: 'This is what the Sovereign LORD says:

" 'Put on the cooking pot; put it on
and pour water into it.
4Put into it the pieces of meat,
all the choice pieces—the leg and
the shoulder.
Fill it with the best of these bones;
5 take the pick of the flock.
Pile wood beneath it for the bones;
bring it to a boil
and cook the bones in it.

6" 'For this is what the Sovereign LORD says:

" 'Woe to the city of bloodshed,
to the pot now encrusted,
whose deposit will not go away!
Empty it piece by piece
without casting lots for them.

7" 'For the blood she shed is in her
midst:
She poured it on the bare rock;
she did not pour it on the ground,
where the dust would cover it.
8To stir up wrath and take revenge
I put her blood on the bare rock,
so that it would not be covered.

9" 'Therefore this is what the Sovereign LORD says:

" 'Woe to the city of bloodshed!
I, too, will pile the wood high.
10So heap on the wood
and kindle the fire.
Cook the meat well,
mixing in the spices;

and let the bones be charred.
11Then set the empty pot on the coals
till it becomes hot and its copper
glows
so its impurities may be melted
and its deposit burned away.
12It has frustrated all efforts;
its heavy deposit has not been
removed,
not even by fire.

13" 'Now your impurity is lewdness. Because I tried to cleanse you but you would not be cleansed from your impurity, you will not be clean again until my wrath against you has subsided.

14" 'I the LORD have spoken. The time has come for me to act. I will not hold back; I will not have pity, nor will I relent. You will be judged according to your conduct and your actions, declares the Sovereign LORD.' "

Ezekiel's Wife Dies

15The word of the LORD came to me: 16"Son of man, with one blow I am about to take away from you the delight of your eyes. Yet do not lament or weep or shed any tears. 17Groan quietly; do not mourn for the dead. Keep your turban fastened and your sandals on your feet; do not cover the lower part of your face or eat the customary food of mourners."

18So I spoke to the people in the morning, and in the evening my wife died. The next morning I did as I had been commanded.

19Then the people asked me, "Won't you tell us what these things have to do with us?"

20So I said to them, "The word of the LORD came to me: 21Say to the house of Israel, 'This is what the Sovereign LORD says: I am about to desecrate my sanctuary—the stronghold in which you take pride, the delight of your eyes, the object of your affection. The sons and daughters you left behind will fall by the sword. 22And you will do as I have done. You will not cover the lower part of your face or eat the customary food of mourners. 23You will keep your turbans on your heads and your sandals on your feet. You will not mourn or weep but will waste away because of[a] your sins and groan among yourselves. 24Ezekiel will be a sign to you; you will do just as he has done. When this

a23 Or away in

happens, you will know that I am the Sovereign LORD.'

25"And you, son of man, on the day I take away their stronghold, their joy and glory, the delight of their eyes, their heart's desire, and their sons and daughters as well — 26on that day a fugitive will come to tell you the news. 27At that time your mouth will be opened; you will speak with him and will no longer be silent. So you will be a sign to them, and they will know that I am the LORD."

A Prophecy Against Ammon

25 The word of the LORD came to me: 2"Son of man, set your face against the Ammonites and prophesy against them. 3Say to them, 'Hear the word of the Sovereign LORD. This is what the Sovereign LORD says: Because you said "Aha!" over my sanctuary when it was desecrated and over the land of Israel when it was laid waste and over the people of Judah when they went into exile, 4therefore I am going to give you to the people of the East as a possession. They will set up their camps and pitch their tents among you; they will eat your fruit and drink your milk. 5I will turn Rabbah into a pasture for camels and Ammon into a resting place for sheep. Then you will know that I am the LORD. 6For this is what the Sovereign LORD says: Because you have clapped your hands and stamped your feet, rejoicing with all the malice of your heart against the land of Israel, 7therefore I will stretch out my hand against you and give you as plunder to the nations. I will cut you off from the nations and exterminate you from the countries. I will destroy you, and you will know that I am the LORD.' "

A Prophecy Against Moab

8"This is what the Sovereign LORD says: 'Because Moab and Seir said, "Look, the house of Judah has become like all the other nations," 9therefore I will expose the flank of Moab, beginning at its frontier towns — Beth Jeshimoth, Baal Meon and Kiriathaim — the glory of that land. 10I will give Moab along with the Ammonites to the people of the East as a possession, so that the Ammonites will not be remembered among the nations; 11and I will inflict punishment on Moab. Then they will know that I am the LORD.' "

A Prophecy Against Edom

12"This is what the Sovereign LORD says: 'Because Edom took revenge on the house of Judah and became very guilty by doing so, 13therefore this is what the Sovereign LORD says: I will stretch out my hand against Edom and kill its men and their animals. I will lay it waste, and from Teman to Dedan they will fall by the sword. 14I will take vengeance on Edom by the hand of my people Israel, and they will deal with Edom in accordance with my anger and my wrath; they will know my vengeance, declares the Sovereign LORD.' "

A Prophecy Against Philistia

15"This is what the Sovereign LORD says: 'Because the Philistines acted in vengeance and took revenge with malice in their hearts, and with ancient hostility sought to destroy Judah, 16therefore this is what the Sovereign LORD says: I am about to stretch out my hand against the Philistines, and I will cut off the Kerethites and destroy those remaining along the coast. 17I will carry out great vengeance on them and punish them in my wrath. Then they will know that I am the LORD, when I take vengeance on them.' "

A Prophecy Against Tyre

26 In the eleventh year, on the first day of the month, the word of the LORD came to me: 2"Son of man, because Tyre has said of Jerusalem, 'Aha! The gate to the nations is broken, and its doors have swung open to me; now that she lies in ruins I will prosper,' 3therefore this is what the Sovereign LORD says: I am against you, O Tyre, and I will bring many nations against you, like the sea casting up its waves. 4They will destroy the walls of Tyre and pull down her towers; I will scrape away her rubble and make her a bare rock. 5Out in the sea she will become a place to spread fishnets, for I have spoken, declares the Sovereign LORD. She will become plunder for the nations, 6and her settlements on the mainland will be ravaged by the sword. Then they will know that I am the LORD.

7"For this is what the Sovereign LORD says: From the north I am going to bring against Tyre Nebuchadnezzar[a] king of Babylon, king of kings, with horses and chariots, with horsemen and a great

a7 Hebrew *Nebuchadrezzar*, of which *Nebuchadnezzar* is a variant; here and often in Ezekiel and Jeremiah army. [8]He will ravage your settlements on the mainland with the sword; he will set up siege works against you, build a ramp up to your walls and raise his shields against you. [9]He will direct the blows of his battering rams against your walls and demolish your towers with his weapons. [10]His horses will be so many that they will cover you with dust. Your walls will tremble at the noise of the war horses, wagons and chariots when he enters your gates as men enter a city whose walls have been broken through. [11]The hoofs of his horses will trample all your streets; he will kill your people with the sword, and your strong pillars will fall to the ground. [12]They will plunder your wealth and loot your merchandise; they will break down your walls and demolish your fine houses and throw your stones, timber and rubble into the sea. [13]I will put an end to your noisy songs, and the music of your harps will be heard no more. [14]I will make you a bare rock, and you will become a place to spread fishnets. You will never be rebuilt, for I the LORD have spoken, declares the Sovereign LORD.

[15]"This is what the Sovereign LORD says to Tyre: Will not the coastlands tremble at the sound of your fall, when the wounded groan and the slaughter takes place in you? [16]Then all the princes of the coast will step down from their thrones and lay aside their robes and take off their embroidered garments. Clothed with terror, they will sit on the ground, trembling every moment, appalled at you. [17]Then they will take up a lament concerning you and say to you:

" 'How you are destroyed, O city of renown,
    peopled by men of the sea!
You were a power on the seas,
    you and your citizens;
you put your terror
    on all who lived there.
[18]Now the coastlands tremble
    on the day of your fall;
the islands in the sea
    are terrified at your collapse.'

[19]"This is what the Sovereign LORD says: When I make you a desolate city, like cities no longer inhabited, and when I bring the ocean depths over you and its vast waters cover you, [20]then I will bring you down with those who go down to the pit,

to the people of long ago. I will make you dwell in the earth below, as in ancient ruins, with those who go down to the pit, and you will not return or take your place[a] in the land of the living. [21]I will bring you to a horrible end and you will be no more. You will be sought, but you will never again be found, declares the Sovereign LORD."

A Lament for Tyre

27 The word of the LORD came to me: [2]"Son of man, take up a lament concerning Tyre. [3]Say to Tyre, situated at the gateway to the sea, merchant of peoples on many coasts, 'This is what the Sovereign LORD says:

" 'You say, O Tyre,
    "I am perfect in beauty."
[4]Your domain was on the high seas;
    your builders brought your beauty
        to perfection.
[5]They made all your timbers
    of pine trees from Senir[b];
they took a cedar from Lebanon
    to make a mast for you.
[6]Of oaks from Bashan
    they made your oars;
of cypress wood[c] from the coasts of
        Cyprus[d]
    they made your deck, inlaid with
        ivory.
[7]Fine embroidered linen from Egypt
        was your sail
    and served as your banner;
your awnings were of blue and purple
    from the coasts of Elishah.
[8]Men of Sidon and Arvad were your
        oarsmen;
    your skilled men, O Tyre, were
        aboard as your seamen.
[9]Veteran craftsmen of Gebal[e] were on
        board
    as shipwrights to caulk your seams.
All the ships of the sea and their
        sailors
    came alongside to trade for your
        wares.

[10]" 'Men of Persia, Lydia and Put
    served as soldiers in your army.
They hung their shields and helmets
        on your walls,
    bringing you splendor.
[11]Men of Arvad and Helech
    manned your walls on every side;
    men of Gammad

---

[a]20 Septuagint; Hebrew *return, and I will give glory*; Text has a different division of the consonants.   [b]5 That is, Hermon   [c]6 Targum; the Masoretic   [d]6 Hebrew *Kittim*   [e]9 That is, Byblos

were in your towers.
They hung their shields around your
walls;
they brought your beauty to
perfection.

12" 'Tarshish did business with you because of your great wealth of goods; they
exchanged silver, iron, tin and lead for
your merchandise.

13" 'Greece, Tubal and Meshech traded
with you; they exchanged slaves and articles of bronze for your wares.

14" 'Men of Beth Togarmah exchanged
work horses, war horses and mules for
your merchandise.

15" 'The men of Rhodes*a* traded with
you, and many coastlands were your customers; they paid you with ivory tusks
and ebony.

16" 'Aram*b* did business with you because of your many products; they exchanged turquoise, purple fabric, embroidered work, fine linen, coral and rubies
for your merchandise.

17" 'Judah and Israel traded with you;
they exchanged wheat from Minnith and
confections,*c* honey, oil and balm for
your wares.

18" 'Damascus, because of your many
products and great wealth of goods, did
business with you in wine from Helbon
and wool from Zahar.

19" 'Danites and Greeks from Uzal
bought your merchandise; they exchanged wrought iron, cassia and calamus for your wares.

20" 'Dedan traded in saddle blankets
with you.

21" 'Arabia and all the princes of Kedar
were your customers; they did business
with you in lambs, rams and goats.

22" 'The merchants of Sheba and Raamah traded with you; for your merchandise they exchanged the finest of all kinds
of spices and precious stones, and gold.

23" 'Haran, Canneh and Eden and merchants of Sheba, Asshur and Kilmad traded with you. 24In your marketplace they
traded with you beautiful garments, blue
fabric, embroidered work and multicol-
ored rugs with cords twisted and tightly
knotted.

25" 'The ships of Tarshish serve
as carriers for your wares.
You are filled with heavy cargo
in the heart of the sea.

26Your oarsmen take you
out to the high seas.
But the east wind will break you to
pieces
in the heart of the sea.
27Your wealth, merchandise and wares,
your mariners, seamen and
shipwrights,
your merchants and all your soldiers,
and everyone else on board
will sink into the heart of the sea
on the day of your shipwreck.
28The shorelands will quake
when your seamen cry out.
29All who handle the oars
will abandon their ships;
the mariners and all the seamen
will stand on the shore.
30They will raise their voice
and cry bitterly over you;
they will sprinkle dust on their heads
and roll in ashes.
31They will shave their heads because
of you
and will put on sackcloth.
They will weep over you with anguish
of soul
and with bitter mourning.
32As they wail and mourn over you,
they will take up a lament
concerning you:
"Who was ever silenced like Tyre,
surrounded by the sea?"
33When your merchandise went out on
the seas,
you satisfied many nations;
with your great wealth and your wares
you enriched the kings of the earth.
34Now you are shattered by the sea
in the depths of the waters;
your wares and all your company
have gone down with you.
35All who live in the coastlands
are appalled at you;
their kings shudder with horror
and their faces are distorted with
fear.
36The merchants among the nations
hiss at you;
you have come to a horrible end
and will be no more.' "

A Prophecy Against the King of Tyre

28 The word of the LORD came to me:
2"Son of man, say to the ruler of
Tyre, 'This is what the Sovereign LORD
says:

---

a15 Septuagint; Hebrew *Dedan*   *b16* Most Hebrew manuscripts; some Hebrew manuscripts and Syriac
Edom   *c17* The meaning of the Hebrew for this word is uncertain.

" 'In the pride of your heart
  you say, "I am a god;
I sit on the throne of a god
  in the heart of the seas."
But you are a man and not a god,
  though you think you are as wise as
    a god.
³Are you wiser than Daniel*?*
  Is no secret hidden from you?
⁴By your wisdom and understanding
  you have gained wealth for yourself
and amassed gold and silver
  in your treasuries.
⁵By your great skill in trading
  you have increased your wealth,
and because of your wealth
  your heart has grown proud.

⁶" 'Therefore this is what the Sovereign
Lᴏʀᴅ says:

" 'Because you think you are wise,
  as wise as a god,
⁷I am going to bring foreigners against
    you,
  the most ruthless of nations;
they will draw their swords against
    your beauty and wisdom
  and pierce your shining splendor.
⁸They will bring you down to the pit,
  and you will die a violent death
    in the heart of the seas.
⁹Will you then say, "I am a god,"
  in the presence of those who kill
    you?
You will be but a man, not a god,
  in the hands of those who slay you.
¹⁰You will die the death of the
    uncircumcised
  at the hands of foreigners.

I have spoken, declares the Sovereign
Lᴏʀᴅ.' "

¹¹The word of the Lᴏʀᴅ came to me:
¹²"Son of man, take up a lament concerning the king of Tyre and say to him: 'This
is what the Sovereign Lᴏʀᴅ says:

" 'You were the model of perfection,
  full of wisdom and perfect in
    beauty.
¹³You were in Eden,
  the garden of God;
every precious stone adorned you:
  ruby, topaz and emerald,
  chrysolite, onyx and jasper,
  sapphire,ᵇ turquoise and beryl.ᶜ

Your settings and mountingsᵈ were
  made of gold;
on the day you were created they
  were prepared.
¹⁴You were anointed as a guardian
    cherub,
  for so I ordained you.
You were on the holy mount of God;
  you walked among the fiery stones.
¹⁵You were blameless in your ways
  from the day you were created
till wickedness was found in you.
¹⁶Through your widespread trade
  you were filled with violence,
    and you sinned.
So I drove you in disgrace from the
    mount of God,
  and I expelled you, O guardian
    cherub,
from among the fiery stones.
¹⁷Your heart became proud
  on account of your beauty,
and you corrupted your wisdom
  because of your splendor.
So I threw you to the earth;
  I made a spectacle of you before
    kings.
¹⁸By your many sins and dishonest
    trade
  you have desecrated your
    sanctuaries.
So I made a fire come out from you,
  and it consumed you,
and I reduced you to ashes on the
    ground
  in the sight of all who were
    watching.
¹⁹All the nations who knew you
  are appalled at you;
you have come to a horrible end
  and will be no more.' "

A Prophecy Against Sidon

²⁰The word of the Lᴏʀᴅ came to me:
²¹"Son of man, set your face against Sidon; prophesy against her ²²and say: 'This
is what the Sovereign Lᴏʀᴅ says:

" 'I am against you, O Sidon,
  and I will gain glory within you.
They will know that I am the Lᴏʀᴅ,
  when I inflict punishment on her
and show myself holy within her.
²³I will send a plague upon her
  and make blood flow in her streets.
The slain will fall within her,

ᵃ3 Or *Danel;* the Hebrew spelling may suggest a person other than the prophet Daniel.   *ᵇ13* Or *lapis lazuli*   *ᶜ13* The precise identification of some of these precious stones is uncertain.   *ᵈ13* The meaning of the Hebrew for this phrase is uncertain.

with the sword against her on every
side.
Then they will know that I am the
Lord.

24" 'No longer will the people of Israel
have malicious neighbors who are painful
briers and sharp thorns. Then they will
know that I am the Sovereign Lord.

25" 'This is what the Sovereign Lord
says: When I gather the people of Israel
from the nations where they have been
scattered, I will show myself holy among
them in the sight of the nations. Then
they will live in their own land, which I
gave to my servant Jacob. 26They will live
there in safety and will build houses and
plant vineyards; they will live in safety
when I inflict punishment on all their
neighbors who maligned them. Then they
will know that I am the Lord their God.' "

A Prophecy Against Egypt

29 In the tenth year, in the tenth
month on the twelfth day, the
word of the Lord came to me: 2"Son of
man, set your face against Pharaoh king
of Egypt and prophesy against him and
against all Egypt. 3Speak to him and say:
'This is what the Sovereign Lord says:

" 'I am against you, Pharaoh king of
      Egypt,
   you great monster lying among your
      streams.
You say, "The Nile is mine;
   I made it for myself."
4But I will put hooks in your jaws
   and make the fish of your streams
      stick to your scales.
I will pull you out from among your
      streams,
   with all the fish sticking to your
      scales.
5I will leave you in the desert,
   you and all the fish of your
      streams.
You will fall on the open field
   and not be gathered or picked up.
I will give you as food
   to the beasts of the earth and the
      birds of the air.

6Then all who live in Egypt will know that
I am the Lord.

" 'You have been a staff of reed for the
house of Israel. 7When they grasped you
with their hands, you splintered and you

tore open their shoulders; when they
leaned on you, you broke and their backs
were wrenched. a

8" 'Therefore this is what the Sovereign
Lord says: I will bring a sword against you
and kill your men and their animals.
9Egypt will become a desolate wasteland.
Then they will know that I am the Lord.

" 'Because you said, "The Nile is mine;
I made it," 10therefore I am against you
and against your streams, and I will make
the land of Egypt a ruin and a desolate
waste from Migdol to Aswan, as far as the
border of Cush. b 11No foot of man or animal will pass through it; no one will live
there for forty years. 12I will make the
land of Egypt desolate among devastated
lands, and her cities will lie desolate forty
years among ruined cities. And I will disperse the Egyptians among the nations
and scatter them through the countries.

13" 'Yet this is what the Sovereign Lord
says: At the end of forty years I will gather
the Egyptians from the nations where
they were scattered. 14I will bring them
back from captivity and return them to
Upper Egypt, c the land of their ancestry.
There they will be a lowly kingdom. 15It
will be the lowliest of kingdoms and will
never again exalt itself above the other
nations. I will make it so weak that it will
never again rule over the nations. 16Egypt
will no longer be a source of confidence
for the people of Israel but will be a reminder of their sin in turning to her for
help. Then they will know that I am the
Sovereign Lord.' "

17In the twenty-seventh year, in the
first month on the first day, the word of
the Lord came to me: 18"Son of man,
Nebuchadnezzar king of Babylon drove
his army in a hard campaign against Tyre;
every head was rubbed bare and every
shoulder made raw. Yet he and his army
got no reward from the campaign he led
against Tyre. 19Therefore this is what the
Sovereign Lord says: I am going to give
Egypt to Nebuchadnezzar king of Babylon, and he will carry off its wealth. He
will loot and plunder the land as pay for
his army. 20I have given him Egypt as a
reward for his efforts because he and his
army did it for me, declares the Sovereign
Lord.

21"On that day I will make a horn d
grow for the house of Israel, and I will

---

a7 Syriac (see also Septuagint and Vulgate); Hebrew and you caused their backs to stand   b10 That is,
the upper Nile region   c14 Hebrew to Pathros   d21 Horn here symbolizes strength.

open your mouth among them. Then they will know that I am the LORD."

A Lament for Egypt

30 The word of the LORD came to me: ²"Son of man, prophesy and say: 'This is what the Sovereign LORD says:

" 'Wail and say,
   "Alas for that day!"
³For the day is near,
   the day of the LORD is near—
a day of clouds,
   a time of doom for the nations.
⁴A sword will come against Egypt,
   and anguish will come upon Cush.ᵃ
When the slain fall in Egypt,
   her wealth will be carried away
   and her foundations torn down.

⁵Cush and Put, Lydia and all Arabia, Libyaᵇ and the people of the covenant land will fall by the sword along with Egypt.

⁶" 'This is what the LORD says:

" 'The allies of Egypt will fall
   and her proud strength will fail.
From Migdol to Aswan
   they will fall by the sword within
      her,
         declares the Sovereign LORD.
⁷" 'They will be desolate
   among desolate lands,
and their cities will lie
   among ruined cities.
⁸Then they will know that I am the
      LORD,
   when I set fire to Egypt
   and all her helpers are crushed.

⁹" 'On that day messengers will go out from me in ships to frighten Cush out of her complacency. Anguish will take hold of them on the day of Egypt's doom, for it is sure to come.

¹⁰" 'This is what the Sovereign LORD says:

" 'I will put an end to the hordes of
      Egypt
   by the hand of Nebuchadnezzar
      king of Babylon.
¹¹He and his army—the most ruthless
      of nations—
   will be brought in to destroy the
      land.
They will draw their swords against
      Egypt

and fill the land with the slain.
¹²I will dry up the streams of the Nile
   and sell the land to evil men;
by the hand of foreigners
   I will lay waste the land and
      everything in it.

I the LORD have spoken.

¹³" 'This is what the Sovereign LORD says:

" 'I will destroy the idols
   and put an end to the images in
      Memphis.ᶜ
No longer will there be a prince in
      Egypt,
   and I will spread fear throughout
      the land.
¹⁴I will lay waste Upper Egypt,ᵈ
   set fire to Zoan
   and inflict punishment on Thebes.ᵉ
¹⁵I will pour out my wrath on
      Pelusium,ᶠ
   the stronghold of Egypt,
   and cut off the hordes of Thebes.
¹⁶I will set fire to Egypt;
   Pelusium will writhe in agony.
Thebes will be taken by storm;
   Memphis will be in constant
      distress.
¹⁷The young men of Heliopolisᵍ and
      Bubastisʰ
   will fall by the sword,
   and the cities themselves will go
      into captivity.
¹⁸Dark will be the day at Tahpanhes
   when I break the yoke of Egypt;
   there her proud strength will come
      to an end.
She will be covered with clouds,
   and her villages will go into
      captivity.
¹⁹So I will inflict punishment on Egypt,
   and they will know that I am the
      LORD.' "

²⁰In the eleventh year, in the first month on the seventh day, the word of the LORD came to me: ²¹"Son of man, I have broken the arm of Pharaoh king of Egypt. It has not been bound up for healing or put in a splint so as to become strong enough to hold a sword. ²²Therefore this is what the Sovereign LORD says: I am against Pharaoh king of Egypt. I will break both his arms, the good arm as well as the broken one, and make the sword

---

ᵃ4 That is, the upper Nile region; also in verses 5 and 9   ᵇ5 Hebrew *Cub*   ᶜ13 Hebrew *Noph*; also in verse 16   ᵈ14 Hebrew *waste Pathros*   ᵉ14 Hebrew *No*; also in verses 15 and 16   ᶠ15 Hebrew *Sin*; also in verse 16   ᵍ17 Hebrew *Awen* (or *On*)   ʰ17 Hebrew *Pi Beseth* fall from his hand. 23I will disperse the Egyptians among the nations and scatter them through the countries. 24I will strengthen the arms of the king of Babylon and put my sword in his hand, but I will break the arms of Pharaoh, and he will groan before him like a mortally wounded man. 25I will strengthen the arms of the king of Babylon, but the arms of Pharaoh will fall limp. Then they will know that I am the LORD, when I put my sword into the hand of the king of Babylon and he brandishes it against Egypt. 26I will disperse the Egyptians among the nations and scatter them through the countries. Then they will know that I am the LORD."

A Cedar in Lebanon

31 In the eleventh year, in the third month on the first day, the word of the LORD came to me: 2"Son of man, say to Pharaoh king of Egypt and to his hordes:

" 'Who can be compared with you in
   majesty?
3Consider Assyria, once a cedar in
   Lebanon,
  with beautiful branches
    overshadowing the forest;
  it towered on high,
    its top above the thick foliage.
4The waters nourished it,
   deep springs made it grow tall;
  their streams flowed
    all around its base
  and sent their channels
    to all the trees of the field.
5So it towered higher
   than all the trees of the field;
  its boughs increased
    and its branches grew long,
  spreading because of abundant
    waters.
6All the birds of the air
   nested in its boughs,
  all the beasts of the field
    gave birth under its branches;
  all the great nations
    lived in its shade.
7It was majestic in beauty,
   with its spreading boughs,
  for its roots went down
    to abundant waters.
8The cedars in the garden of God
   could not rival it,

nor could the pine trees
   equal its boughs,
nor could the plane trees
   compare with its branches—
no tree in the garden of God
   could match its beauty.
9I made it beautiful
   with abundant branches,
the envy of all the trees of Eden
   in the garden of God.

10" 'Therefore this is what the Sovereign LORD says: Because it towered on high, lifting its top above the thick foliage, and because it was proud of its height, 11I handed it over to the ruler of the nations, for him to deal with according to its wickedness. I cast it aside, 12and the most ruthless of foreign nations cut it down and left it. Its boughs fell on the mountains and in all the valleys; its branches lay broken in all the ravines of the land. All the nations of the earth came out from under its shade and left it. 13All the birds of the air settled on the fallen tree, and all the beasts of the field were among its branches. 14Therefore no other trees by the waters are ever to tower proudly on high, lifting their tops above the thick foliage. No other trees so well-watered are ever to reach such a height; they are all destined for death, for the earth below, among mortal men, with those who go down to the pit.

15" 'This is what the Sovereign LORD says: On the day it was brought down to the grave*a* I covered the deep springs with mourning for it; I held back its streams, and its abundant waters were restrained. Because of it I clothed Lebanon with gloom, and all the trees of the field withered away. 16I made the nations tremble at the sound of its fall when I brought it down to the grave with those who go down to the pit. Then all the trees of Eden, the choicest and best of Lebanon, all the trees that were well-watered, were consoled in the earth below. 17Those who lived in its shade, its allies among the nations, had also gone down to the grave with it, joining those killed by the sword.

18" 'Which of the trees of Eden can be compared with you in splendor and majesty? Yet you, too, will be brought down with the trees of Eden to the earth below; you will lie among the uncircumcised, with those killed by the sword.

a15 Hebrew Sheol; also in verses 16 and 17

" 'This is Pharaoh and all his hordes, declares the Sovereign LORD.' "

A Lament for Pharaoh

32 In the twelfth year, in the twelfth month on the first day, the word of the LORD came to me: 2"Son of man, take up a lament concerning Pharaoh king of Egypt and say to him:

" 'You are like a lion among the
  nations;
you are like a monster in the seas
thrashing about in your streams,
  churning the water with your feet
  and muddying the streams.

3" 'This is what the Sovereign LORD says:

" 'With a great throng of people
  I will cast my net over you,
  and they will haul you up in my
  net.
4I will throw you on the land
  and hurl you on the open field.
I will let all the birds of the air settle
  on you
  and all the beasts of the earth
  gorge themselves on you.
5I will spread your flesh on the
  mountains
  and fill the valleys with your
  remains.
6I will drench the land with your
  flowing blood
all the way to the mountains,
  and the ravines will be filled with
  your flesh.
7When I snuff you out, I will cover the
  heavens
  and darken their stars;
I will cover the sun with a cloud,
  and the moon will not give its light.
8All the shining lights in the heavens
  I will darken over you;
I will bring darkness over your land,
  declares the Sovereign LORD.
9I will trouble the hearts of many
  peoples
  when I bring about your destruction
  among the nations,
  among*a* lands you have not known.
10I will cause many peoples to be
  appalled at you,
  and their kings will shudder with
  horror because of you

when I brandish my sword before
  them.
On the day of your downfall
  each of them will tremble
  every moment for his life.

11" 'For this is what the Sovereign LORD says:

" 'The sword of the king of Babylon
  will come against you.
12I will cause your hordes to fall
  by the swords of mighty men—
  the most ruthless of all nations.
They will shatter the pride of Egypt,
  and all her hordes will be
  overthrown.
13I will destroy all her cattle
  from beside abundant waters
no longer to be stirred by the foot of
  man
  or muddied by the hoofs of cattle.
14Then I will let her waters settle
  and make her streams flow like oil,
    declares the Sovereign LORD.
15When I make Egypt desolate
  and strip the land of everything in
  it,
when I strike down all who live there,
  then they will know that I am the
  LORD.'

16"This is the lament they will chant for her. The daughters of the nations will chant it; for Egypt and all her hordes they will chant it, declares the Sovereign LORD."

17In the twelfth year, on the fifteenth day of the month, the word of the LORD came to me: 18"Son of man, wail for the hordes of Egypt and consign to the earth below both her and the daughters of mighty nations, with those who go down to the pit. 19Say to them, 'Are you more favored than others? Go down and be laid among the uncircumcised.' 20They will fall among those killed by the sword. The sword is drawn; let her be dragged off with all her hordes. 21From within the grave*b* the mighty leaders will say of Egypt and her allies, 'They have come down and they lie with the uncircumcised, with those killed by the sword.'

22"Assyria is there with her whole army; she is surrounded by the graves of all her slain, all who have fallen by the sword. 23Their graves are in the depths of the pit and her army lies around her grave. All who had spread terror in the land of

a9 Hebrew; Septuagint *bring you into captivity among the nations, / to*   *b21* Hebrew *Sheol*; also in verse 27 the living are slain, fallen by the sword.

²⁴"Elam is there, with all her hordes around her grave. All of them are slain, fallen by the sword. All who had spread terror in the land of the living went down uncircumcised to the earth below. They bear their shame with those who go down to the pit. ²⁵A bed is made for her among the slain, with all her hordes around her grave. All of them are uncircumcised, killed by the sword. Because their terror had spread in the land of the living, they bear their shame with those who go down to the pit; they are laid among the slain.

²⁶"Meshech and Tubal are there, with all their hordes around their graves. All of them are uncircumcised, killed by the sword because they spread their terror in the land of the living. ²⁷Do they not lie with the other uncircumcised warriors who have fallen, who went down to the grave with their weapons of war, whose swords were placed under their heads? The punishment for their sins rested on their bones, though the terror of these warriors had stalked through the land of the living.

²⁸"You too, O Pharaoh, will be broken and will lie among the uncircumcised, with those killed by the sword.

²⁹"Edom is there, her kings and all her princes; despite their power, they are laid with those killed by the sword. They lie with the uncircumcised, with those who go down to the pit.

³⁰"All the princes of the north and all the Sidonians are there; they went down with the slain in disgrace despite the terror caused by their power. They lie uncircumcised with those killed by the sword and bear their shame with those who go down to the pit.

³¹"Pharaoh—he and all his army—will see them and he will be consoled for all his hordes that were killed by the sword, declares the Sovereign LORD. ³²Although I had him spread terror in the land of the living, Pharaoh and all his hordes will be laid among the uncircumcised, with those killed by the sword, declares the Sovereign LORD."

Ezekiel a Watchman

33 The word of the LORD came to me: ²"Son of man, speak to your countrymen and say to them: 'When I bring the sword against a land, and the people of the land choose one of their men and make him their watchman, ³and he sees the sword coming against the land and blows the trumpet to warn the people, ⁴then if anyone hears the trumpet but does not take warning and the sword comes and takes his life, his blood will be on his own head. ⁵Since he heard the sound of the trumpet but did not take warning, his blood will be on his own head. If he had taken warning, he would have saved himself. ⁶But if the watchman sees the sword coming and does not blow the trumpet to warn the people and the sword comes and takes the life of one of them, that man will be taken away because of his sin, but I will hold the watchman accountable for his blood.'

⁷"Son of man, I have made you a watchman for the house of Israel; so hear the word I speak and give them warning from me. ⁸When I say to the wicked, 'O wicked man, you will surely die,' and you do not speak out to dissuade him from his ways, that wicked man will die for*ᵃ* his sin, and I will hold you accountable for his blood. ⁹But if you do warn the wicked man to turn from his ways and he does not do so, he will die for his sin, but you will have saved yourself.

¹⁰"Son of man, say to the house of Israel, 'This is what you are saying: "Our offenses and sins weigh us down, and we are wasting away because of*ᵇ* them. How then can we live?" ' ¹¹Say to them, 'As surely as I live, declares the Sovereign LORD, I take no pleasure in the death of the wicked, but rather that they turn from their ways and live. Turn! Turn from your evil ways! Why will you die, O house of Israel?'

¹²"Therefore, son of man, say to your countrymen, 'The righteousness of the righteous man will not save him when he disobeys, and the wickedness of the wicked man will not cause him to fall when he turns from it. The righteous man, if he sins, will not be allowed to live because of his former righteousness.' ¹³If I tell the righteous man that he will surely live, but then he trusts in his righteousness and does evil, none of the righteous things he has done will be remembered; he will die for the evil he has done. ¹⁴And if I say to the wicked man, 'You will surely die,' but he then turns away from his sin and does what is just and right— ¹⁵if he gives back what he took in pledge for a loan, returns what he has stolen, follows the decrees

---

ᵃ8 Or in; also in verse 9   ᵇ10 Or away in

that give life, and does no evil, he will surely live; he will not die. [16]None of the sins he has committed will be remembered against him. He has done what is just and right; he will surely live.

[17]"Yet your countrymen say, 'The way of the Lord is not just.' But it is their way that is not just. [18]If a righteous man turns from his righteousness and does evil, he will die for it. [19]And if a wicked man turns away from his wickedness and does what is just and right, he will live by doing so. [20]Yet, O house of Israel, you say, 'The way of the Lord is not just.' But I will judge each of you according to his own ways."

Jerusalem's Fall Explained

[21]In the twelfth year of our exile, in the tenth month on the fifth day, a man who had escaped from Jerusalem came to me and said, "The city has fallen!" [22]Now the evening before the man arrived, the hand of the Lord was upon me, and he opened my mouth before the man came to me in the morning. So my mouth was opened and I was no longer silent.

[23]Then the word of the Lord came to me: [24]"Son of man, the people living in those ruins in the land of Israel are saying, 'Abraham was only one man, yet he possessed the land. But we are many; surely the land has been given to us as our possession.' [25]Therefore say to them, 'This is what the Sovereign Lord says: Since you eat meat with the blood still in it and look to your idols and shed blood, should you then possess the land? [26]You rely on your sword, you do detestable things, and each of you defiles his neighbor's wife. Should you then possess the land?'

[27]"Say this to them: 'This is what the Sovereign Lord says: As surely as I live, those who are left in the ruins will fall by the sword, those out in the country I will give to the wild animals to be devoured, and those in strongholds and caves will die of a plague. [28]I will make the land a desolate waste, and her proud strength will come to an end, and the mountains of Israel will become desolate so that no one will cross them. [29]Then they will know that I am the Lord, when I have made the land a desolate waste because of all the detestable things they have done.'

[30]"As for you, son of man, your countrymen are talking together about you by the walls and at the doors of the houses, saying to each other, 'Come and hear the message that has come from the Lord.' [31]My people come to you, as they usually do, and sit before you to listen to your words, but they do not put them into practice. With their mouths they express devotion, but their hearts are greedy for unjust gain. [32]Indeed, to them you are nothing more than one who sings love songs with a beautiful voice and plays an instrument well, for they hear your words but do not put them into practice.

[33]"When all this comes true—and it surely will—then they will know that a prophet has been among them."

Shepherds and Sheep

34 The word of the Lord came to me: [2]"Son of man, prophesy against the shepherds of Israel; prophesy and say to them: 'This is what the Sovereign Lord says: Woe to the shepherds of Israel who only take care of themselves! Should not shepherds take care of the flock? [3]You eat the curds, clothe yourselves with the wool and slaughter the choice animals, but you do not take care of the flock. [4]You have not strengthened the weak or healed the sick or bound up the injured. You have not brought back the strays or searched for the lost. You have ruled them harshly and brutally. [5]So they were scattered because there was no shepherd, and when they were scattered they became food for all the wild animals. [6]My sheep wandered over all the mountains and on every high hill. They were scattered over the whole earth, and no one searched or looked for them.

[7]" 'Therefore, you shepherds, hear the word of the Lord: [8]As surely as I live, declares the Sovereign Lord, because my flock lacks a shepherd and so has been plundered and has become food for all the wild animals, and because my shepherds did not search for my flock but cared for themselves rather than for my flock, [9]therefore, O shepherds, hear the word of the Lord: [10]This is what the Sovereign Lord says: I am against the shepherds and will hold them accountable for my flock. I will remove them from tending the flock so that the shepherds can no longer feed themselves. I will rescue my flock from their mouths, and it will no longer be food for them.

[11]" 'For this is what the Sovereign Lord says: I myself will search for my sheep and look after them. [12]As a shepherd looks after his scattered flock when he is with them, so will I look after my sheep.

I will rescue them from all the places where they were scattered on a day of clouds and darkness. ¹³I will bring them out from the nations and gather them from the countries, and I will bring them into their own land. I will pasture them on the mountains of Israel, in the ravines and in all the settlements in the land. ¹⁴I will tend them in a good pasture, and the mountain heights of Israel will be their grazing land. There they will lie down in good grazing land, and there they will feed in a rich pasture on the mountains of Israel. ¹⁵I myself will tend my sheep and have them lie down, declares the Sovereign LORD. ¹⁶I will search for the lost and bring back the strays. I will bind up the injured and strengthen the weak, but the sleek and the strong I will destroy. I will shepherd the flock with justice.

¹⁷" 'As for you, my flock, this is what the Sovereign LORD says: I will judge between one sheep and another, and between rams and goats. ¹⁸Is it not enough for you to feed on the good pasture? Must you also trample the rest of your pasture with your feet? Is it not enough for you to drink clear water? Must you also muddy the rest with your feet? ¹⁹Must my flock feed on what you have trampled and drink what you have muddied with your feet?

²⁰" 'Therefore this is what the Sovereign LORD says to them: See, I myself will judge between the fat sheep and the lean sheep. ²¹Because you shove with flank and shoulder, butting all the weak sheep with your horns until you have driven them away, ²²I will save my flock, and they will no longer be plundered. I will judge between one sheep and another. ²³I will place over them one shepherd, my servant David, and he will tend them; he will tend them and be their shepherd. ²⁴I the LORD will be their God, and my servant David will be prince among them. I the LORD have spoken.

²⁵" 'I will make a covenant of peace with them and rid the land of wild beasts so that they may live in the desert and sleep in the forests in safety. ²⁶I will bless them and the places surrounding my hill.ᵃ I will send down showers in season; there will be showers of blessing. ²⁷The trees of the field will yield their fruit and the ground will yield its crops; the people will be secure in their land. They will

know that I am the LORD, when I break the bars of their yoke and rescue them from the hands of those who enslaved them. ²⁸They will no longer be plundered by the nations, nor will wild animals devour them. They will live in safety, and no one will make them afraid. ²⁹I will provide for them a land renowned for its crops, and they will no longer be victims of famine in the land or bear the scorn of the nations. ³⁰Then they will know that I, the LORD their God, am with them and that they, the house of Israel, are my people, declares the Sovereign LORD. ³¹You my sheep, the sheep of my pasture, are people, and I am your God, declares the Sovereign LORD.' "

A Prophecy Against Edom

35 The word of the LORD came to me: ²"Son of man, set your face against Mount Seir; prophesy against it ³and say: 'This is what the Sovereign LORD says: I am against you, Mount Seir, and I will stretch out my hand against you and make you a desolate waste. ⁴I will turn your towns into ruins and you will be desolate. Then you will know that I am the LORD.

⁵" 'Because you harbored an ancient hostility and delivered the Israelites over to the sword at the time of their calamity, the time their punishment reached its climax, ⁶therefore as surely as I live, declares the Sovereign LORD, I will give you over to bloodshed and it will pursue you. Since you did not hate bloodshed, bloodshed will pursue you. ⁷I will make Mount Seir a desolate waste and cut off from it all who come and go. ⁸I will fill your mountains with the slain; those killed by the sword will fall on your hills and in your valleys and in all your ravines. ⁹I will make you desolate forever; your towns will not be inhabited. Then you will know that I am the LORD.

¹⁰" 'Because you have said, "These two nations and countries will be ours and we will take possession of them," even though I the LORD was there, ¹¹therefore as surely as I live, declares the Sovereign LORD, I will treat you in accordance with the anger and jealousy you showed in your hatred of them and I will make myself known among them when I judge you. ¹²Then you will know that I the LORD have heard all the contemptible things you have said against the mountains of

---

ᵃ26 Or I will make them and the places surrounding my hill a blessing

Israel. You said, "They have been laid waste and have been given over to us to devour." ¹³You boasted against me and spoke against me without restraint, and I heard it. ¹⁴This is what the Sovereign LORD says: While the whole earth rejoices, I will make you desolate. ¹⁵Because you rejoiced when the inheritance of the house of Israel became desolate, that is how I will treat you. You will be desolate, O Mount Seir, you and all of Edom. Then they will know that I am the LORD.' "

A Prophecy to the Mountains of Israel

36 "Son of man, prophesy to the mountains of Israel and say, 'O mountains of Israel, hear the word of the LORD. ²This is what the Sovereign LORD says: The enemy said of you, "Aha! The ancient heights have become our possession." ' ³Therefore prophesy and say, 'This is what the Sovereign LORD says: Because they ravaged and hounded you from every side so that you became the possession of the rest of the nations and the object of people's malicious talk and slander, ⁴therefore, O mountains of Israel, hear the word of the Sovereign LORD: This is what the Sovereign LORD says to the mountains and hills, to the ravines and valleys, to the desolate ruins and the deserted towns that have been plundered and ridiculed by the rest of the nations around you— ⁵this is what the Sovereign LORD says: In my burning zeal I have spoken against the rest of the nations, and against all Edom, for with glee and with malice in their hearts they made my land their own possession so that they might plunder its pastureland.' ⁶Therefore prophesy concerning the land of Israel and say to the mountains and hills, to the ravines and valleys: 'This is what the Sovereign LORD says: I speak in my jealous wrath because you have suffered the scorn of the nations. ⁷Therefore this is what the Sovereign LORD says: I swear with uplifted hand that the nations around you will also suffer scorn.

⁸" 'But you, O mountains of Israel, will produce branches and fruit for my people Israel, for they will soon come home. ⁹I am concerned for you and will look on you with favor; you will be plowed and sown, ¹⁰and I will multiply the number of people upon you, even the whole house of Israel. The towns will be inhabited and the ruins rebuilt. ¹¹I will increase the number of men and animals upon you, and they will be fruitful and become numerous. I will settle people on you as in the past and will make you prosper more than before. Then you will know that I am the LORD. ¹²I will cause people, my people Israel, to walk upon you. They will possess you, and you will be their inheritance; you will never again deprive them of their children.

¹³" 'This is what the Sovereign LORD says: Because people say to you, "You devour men and deprive your nation of its children," ¹⁴therefore you will no longer devour men or make your nation childless, declares the Sovereign LORD. ¹⁵No longer will I make you hear the taunts of the nations, and no longer will you suffer the scorn of the peoples or cause your nation to fall, declares the Sovereign LORD.' "

¹⁶Again the word of the LORD came to me: ¹⁷"Son of man, when the people of Israel were living in their own land, they defiled it by their conduct and their actions. Their conduct was like a woman's monthly uncleanness in my sight. ¹⁸So I poured out my wrath on them because they had shed blood in the land and because they had defiled it with their idols. ¹⁹I dispersed them among the nations, and they were scattered through the countries; I judged them according to their conduct and their actions. ²⁰And wherever they went among the nations they profaned my holy name, for it was said of them, 'These are the LORD's people, and yet they had to leave his land.' ²¹I had concern for my holy name, which the house of Israel profaned among the nations where they had gone.

²²"Therefore say to the house of Israel, 'This is what the Sovereign LORD says: It is not for your sake, O house of Israel, that I am going to do these things, but for the sake of my holy name, which you have profaned among the nations where you have gone. ²³I will show the holiness of my great name, which has been profaned among the nations, the name you have profaned among them. Then the nations will know that I am the LORD, declares the Sovereign LORD, when I show myself holy through you before their eyes.

²⁴" 'For I will take you out of the nations; I will gather you from all the countries and bring you back into your own land. ²⁵I will sprinkle clean water on you, and you will be clean; I will cleanse you from all your impurities and from all your

VERSE FOR THE DAY:
Ezekiel 36:26

AUTHOR:
June Hunt

PASSAGE FOR THE DAY:
Ezekiel 36:13–32

A New Heart

MANY years ago, a friend brought me a cuckoo clock from Switzerland. It was clever, but not very useful—it didn't keep the right time! The little bird would peek out and chirp when it wasn't supposed to! Because I loved the clock, I took it to be repaired. The clocksmith examined the inside and said it needed a new mainspring. Laughingly, he told me, "Your clock needs a new heart!"

This is true for more than clocks. Every *person* needs a new heart. Just look around you. How many parents have intentionally trained their children to lie or encouraged them to steal from another child? Or to yell at another or hit another? Very few, if any. Yet, how many children have lied, stolen, yelled at and hit others? All have. Why? Because their hearts started out self-seeking and self-centered.

According to the Word of God, you were born with a sinful nature. Psalm 51:5 says,

> Surely I was sinful at birth,
> sinful from the time my mother
> conceived me.

And Jeremiah 17:9 adds,

> The heart is deceitful above all things
> and beyond cure.

But the good news is that God said, "I will give you a *new heart* and put a new spirit in you" (Ezekiel 36:26, my emphasis). Your need is very similar to the need of someone who has a diseased heart and whose only hope for life is a heart transplant. In a spiritual sense, God takes your "diseased" heart and replaces it with a new one.

Slowly, after this divine transplant, healing begins; and as promised, your new heart becomes capable of perfect love. Your self-centeredness is now Christ-centeredness. Once you have a changed heart, you have a changed life. You can love the unlovable, be kind to the unkind, and forgive the unforgivable. All this because you have a new heart—you have God's heart!

Additional Scripture Readings:
Romans 5:5; 2 Corinthians 1:21–22

Go to page 929 for your next devotional reading.

idols. [26]I will give you a new heart and put a new spirit in you; I will remove from you your heart of stone and give you a heart of flesh. [27]And I will put my Spirit in you and move you to follow my decrees and be careful to keep my laws. [28]You will live in the land I gave your forefathers; you will be my people, and I will be your God. [29]I will save you from all your uncleanness. I will call for the grain and make it plentiful and will not bring famine upon you. [30]I will increase the fruit of the trees and the crops of the field, so that you will no longer suffer disgrace among the nations because of famine. [31]Then you will remember your evil ways and wicked deeds, and you will loathe yourselves for your sins and detestable practices. [32]I want you to know that I am not doing this for your sake, declares the Sovereign Lord. Be ashamed and disgraced for your conduct, O house of Israel!

[33]" 'This is what the Sovereign Lord says: On the day I cleanse you from all your sins, I will resettle your towns, and the ruins will be rebuilt. [34]The desolate land will be cultivated instead of lying desolate in the sight of all who pass through it. [35]They will say, "This land that was laid waste has become like the garden of Eden; the cities that were lying in ruins, desolate and destroyed, are now fortified and inhabited." [36]Then the nations around you that remain will know that I the Lord have rebuilt what was destroyed and have replanted what was desolate. I the Lord have spoken, and I will do it.'

[37]"This is what the Sovereign Lord says: Once again I will yield to the plea of the house of Israel and do this for them: I will make their people as numerous as sheep, [38]as numerous as the flocks for offerings at Jerusalem during her appointed feasts. So will the ruined cities be filled with flocks of people. Then they will know that I am the Lord."

The Valley of Dry Bones

37 The hand of the Lord was upon me, and he brought me out by the Spirit of the Lord and set me in the middle of a valley; it was full of bones. [2]He led me back and forth among them, and I saw a great many bones on the floor of the valley, bones that were very dry. [3]He asked me, "Son of man, can these bones live?"

I said, "O Sovereign Lord, you alone know."

[4]Then he said to me, "Prophesy to these bones and say to them, 'Dry bones, hear the word of the Lord! [5]This is what the Sovereign Lord says to these bones: I will make breath[a] enter you, and you will come to life. [6]I will attach tendons to you and make flesh come upon you and cover you with skin; I will put breath in you, and you will come to life. Then you will know that I am the Lord.' "

[7]So I prophesied as I was commanded. And as I was prophesying, there was a noise, a rattling sound, and the bones came together, bone to bone. [8]I looked, and tendons and flesh appeared on them and skin covered them, but there was no breath in them.

[9]Then he said to me, "Prophesy to the breath; prophesy, son of man, and say to it, 'This is what the Sovereign Lord says: Come from the four winds, O breath, and breathe into these slain, that they may live.' " [10]So I prophesied as he commanded me, and breath entered them; they came to life and stood up on their feet—a vast army.

[11]Then he said to me: "Son of man, these bones are the whole house of Israel. They say, 'Our bones are dried up and our hope is gone; we are cut off.' [12]Therefore prophesy and say to them: 'This is what the Sovereign Lord says: O my people, I am going to open your graves and bring you up from them; I will bring you back to the land of Israel. [13]Then you, my people, will know that I am the Lord, when I open your graves and bring you up from them. [14]I will put my Spirit in you and you will live, and I will settle you in your own land. Then you will know that I the Lord have spoken, and I have done it, declares the Lord.' "

One Nation Under One King

[15]The word of the Lord came to me: [16]"Son of man, take a stick of wood and write on it, 'Belonging to Judah and the Israelites associated with him.' Then take another stick of wood, and write on it, 'Ephraim's stick, belonging to Joseph and all the house of Israel associated with him.' [17]Join them together into one stick so that they will become one in your hand.

[18]"When your countrymen ask you, 'Won't you tell us what you mean by

---

[a]5 The Hebrew for this word can also mean *wind* or *spirit* (see verses 6-14).

this?' ¹⁹say to them, 'This is what the Sovereign LORD says: I am going to take the stick of Joseph—which is in Ephraim's hand—and of the Israelite tribes associated with him, and join it to Judah's stick, making them a single stick of wood, and they will become one in my hand.' ²⁰Hold before their eyes the sticks you have written on ²¹and say to them, 'This is what the Sovereign LORD says: I will take the Israelites out of the nations where they have gone. I will gather them from all around and bring them back into their own land. ²²I will make them one nation in the land, on the mountains of Israel. There will be one king over all of them and they will never again be two nations or be divided into two kingdoms. ²³They will no longer defile themselves with their idols and vile images or with any of their offenses, for I will save them from all their sinful backsliding,ᵃ and I will cleanse them. They will be my people, and I will be their God.

²⁴" 'My servant David will be king over them, and they will all have one shepherd. They will follow my laws and be careful to keep my decrees. ²⁵They will live in the land I gave to my servant Jacob, the land where your fathers lived. They and their children and their children's children will live there forever, and David my servant will be their prince forever. ²⁶I will make a covenant of peace with them; it will be an everlasting covenant. I will establish them and increase their numbers, and I will put my sanctuary among them forever. ²⁷My dwelling place will be with them; I will be their God, and they will be my people. ²⁸Then the nations will know that I the LORD make Israel holy, when my sanctuary is among them forever.' "

A Prophecy Against Gog

38 The word of the LORD came to me: ²"Son of man, set your face against Gog, of the land of Magog, the chief prince ofᵇ Meshech and Tubal; prophesy against him ³and say: 'This is what the Sovereign LORD says: I am against you, O Gog, chief prince ofᶜ Meshech and Tubal. ⁴I will turn you around, put hooks in your jaws and bring you out with your whole army—your horses, your horsemen fully armed, and a great horde with large

and small shields, all of them brandishing their swords. ⁵Persia, Cushᵈ and Put will be with them, all with shields and helmets, ⁶also Gomer with all its troops, and Beth Togarmah from the far north with all its troops—the many nations with you.

⁷" 'Get ready; be prepared, you and all the hordes gathered about you, and take command of them. ⁸After many days you will be called to arms. In future years you will invade a land that has recovered from war, whose people were gathered from many nations to the mountains of Israel, which had long been desolate. They had been brought out from the nations, and now all of them live in safety. ⁹You and all your troops and the many nations with you will go up, advancing like a storm; you will be like a cloud covering the land.

¹⁰" 'This is what the Sovereign LORD says: On that day thoughts will come into your mind and you will devise an evil scheme. ¹¹You will say, "I will invade a land of unwalled villages; I will attack a peaceful and unsuspecting people—all of them living without walls and without gates and bars. ¹²I will plunder and loot and turn my hand against the resettled ruins and the people gathered from the nations, rich in livestock and goods, living at the center of the land." ¹³Sheba and Dedan and the merchants of Tarshish and all her villagesᵉ will say to you, "Have you come to plunder? Have you gathered your hordes to loot, to carry off silver and gold, to take away livestock and goods and to seize much plunder?" '

¹⁴"Therefore, son of man, prophesy and say to Gog: 'This is what the Sovereign LORD says: In that day, when my people Israel are living in safety, will you not take notice of it? ¹⁵You will come from your place in the far north, you and many nations with you, all of them riding on horses, a great horde, a mighty army. ¹⁶You will advance against my people Israel like a cloud that covers the land. In days to come, O Gog, I will bring you against my land, so that the nations may know me when I show myself holy through you before their eyes.

¹⁷" 'This is what the Sovereign LORD says: Are you not the one I spoke of in former days by my servants the prophets of Israel? At that time they prophesied for years that I would bring you against them.

ᵃ23 Many Hebrew manuscripts (see also Septuagint); most Hebrew manuscripts *all their dwelling places where they sinned*   ᵇ2 Or *the prince of Rosh,*   ᶜ3 Or *Gog, prince of Rosh,*   ᵈ5 That is, the upper Nile region   ᵉ13 Or *her strong lions*

18This is what will happen in that day: When Gog attacks the land of Israel, my hot anger will be aroused, declares the Sovereign LORD. 19In my zeal and fiery wrath I declare that at that time there shall be a great earthquake in the land of Israel. 20The fish of the sea, the birds of the air, the beasts of the field, every creature that moves along the ground, and all the people on the face of the earth will tremble at my presence. The mountains will be overturned, the cliffs will crumble and every wall will fall to the ground. 21I will summon a sword against Gog on all my mountains, declares the Sovereign LORD. Every man's sword will be against his brother. 22I will execute judgment upon him with plague and bloodshed; I will pour down torrents of rain, hailstones and burning sulfur on him and on his troops and on the many nations with him. 23And so I will show my greatness and my holiness, and I will make myself known in the sight of many nations. Then they will know that I am the LORD.'

39 "Son of man, prophesy against Gog and say: 'This is what the Sovereign LORD says: I am against you, O Gog, chief prince of*a* Meshech and Tubal. 2I will turn you around and drag you along. I will bring you from the far north and send you against the mountains of Israel. 3Then I will strike your bow from your left hand and make your arrows drop from your right hand. 4On the mountains of Israel you will fall, you and all your troops and the nations with you. I will give you as food to all kinds of carrion birds and to the wild animals. 5You will fall in the open field, for I have spoken, declares the Sovereign LORD. 6I will send fire on Magog and on those who live in safety in the coastlands, and they will know that I am the LORD.

7" 'I will make known my holy name among my people Israel. I will no longer let my holy name be profaned, and the nations will know that I the LORD am the Holy One in Israel. 8It is coming! It will surely take place, declares the Sovereign LORD. This is the day I have spoken of.

9" 'Then those who live in the towns of Israel will go out and use the weapons for fuel and burn them up—the small and large shields, the bows and arrows, the war clubs and spears. For seven years they will use them for fuel. 10They will not

need to gather wood from the fields or cut it from the forests, because they will use the weapons for fuel. And they will plunder those who plundered them and loot those who looted them, declares the Sovereign LORD.

11" 'On that day I will give Gog a burial place in Israel, in the valley of those who travel east toward*b* the Sea.*c* It will block the way of travelers, because Gog and all his hordes will be buried there. So it will be called the Valley of Hamon Gog.*d*

12" 'For seven months the house of Israel will be burying them in order to cleanse the land. 13All the people of the land will bury them, and the day I am glorified will be a memorable day for them, declares the Sovereign LORD.

14" 'Men will be regularly employed to cleanse the land. Some will go throughout the land and, in addition to them, others will bury those that remain on the ground. At the end of the seven months they will begin their search. 15As they go through the land and one of them sees a human bone, he will set up a marker beside it until the gravediggers have buried it in the Valley of Hamon Gog. 16(Also a town called Hamonah*e* will be there.) And so they will cleanse the land.'

17"Son of man, this is what the Sovereign LORD says: Call out to every kind of bird and all the wild animals: 'Assemble and come together from all around to the sacrifice I am preparing for you, the great sacrifice on the mountains of Israel. There you will eat flesh and drink blood. 18You will eat the flesh of mighty men and drink the blood of the princes of the earth as if they were rams and lambs, goats and bulls—all of them fattened animals from Bashan. 19At the sacrifice I am preparing for you, you will eat fat till you are glutted and drink blood till you are drunk. 20At my table you will eat your fill of horses and riders, mighty men and soldiers of every kind,' declares the Sovereign LORD.

21"I will display my glory among the nations, and all the nations will see the punishment I inflict and the hand I lay upon them. 22From that day forward the house of Israel will know that I am the LORD their God. 23And the nations will know that the people of Israel went into exile for their sin, because they were unfaithful to me. So I hid my face from them and handed them over to their enemies, and

---

a1 Or *Gog, prince of Rosh,* *b11* Or of *c11* That is, the Dead Sea *d11* *Hamon Gog* means *hordes of Gog.* *e16* *Hamonah* means *horde.*

they all fell by the sword. 24I dealt with them according to their uncleanness and their offenses, and I hid my face from them.

25"Therefore this is what the Sovereign LORD says: I will now bring Jacob back from captivity*a* and will have compassion on all the people of Israel, and I will be zealous for my holy name. 26They will forget their shame and all the unfaithfulness they showed toward me when they lived in safety in their land with no one to make them afraid. 27When I have brought them back from the nations and have gathered them from the countries of their enemies, I will show myself holy through them in the sight of many nations. 28Then they will know that I am the LORD their God, for though I sent them into exile among the nations, I will gather them to their own land, not leaving any behind. 29I will no longer hide my face from them, for I will pour out my Spirit on the house of Israel, declares the Sovereign LORD."

The New Temple Area

40 In the twenty-fifth year of our exile, at the beginning of the year, on the tenth of the month, in the fourteenth year after the fall of the city—on that very day the hand of the LORD was upon me and he took me there. 2In visions of God he took me to the land of Israel and set me on a very high mountain, on whose south side were some buildings that looked like a city. 3He took me there, and I saw a man whose appearance was like bronze; he was standing in the gateway with a linen cord and a measuring rod in his hand. 4The man said to me, "Son of man, look with your eyes and hear with your ears and pay attention to everything I am going to show you, for that is why you have been brought here. Tell the house of Israel everything you see."

The East Gate to the Outer Court

5I saw a wall completely surrounding the temple area. The length of the measuring rod in the man's hand was six long cubits, each of which was a cubit*b* and a handbreadth.*c* He measured the wall; it was one measuring rod thick and one rod high.

6Then he went to the gate facing east. He climbed its steps and measured the threshold of the gate; it was one rod deep.*d* 7The alcoves for the guards were one rod long and one rod wide, and the projecting walls between the alcoves were five cubits thick. And the threshold of the gate next to the portico facing the temple was one rod deep.

8Then he measured the portico of the gateway; 9it*e* was eight cubits deep and its jambs were two cubits thick. The portico of the gateway faced the temple.

10Inside the east gate were three alcoves on each side; the three had the same measurements, and the faces of the projecting walls on each side had the same measurements. 11Then he measured the width of the entrance to the gateway; it was ten cubits and its length was thirteen cubits. 12In front of each alcove was a wall one cubit high, and the alcoves were six cubits square. 13Then he measured the gateway from the top of the rear wall of one alcove to the top of the opposite one; the distance was twenty-five cubits from one parapet opening to the opposite one. 14He measured along the faces of the projecting walls all around the inside of the gateway—sixty cubits. The measurement was up to the portico*f* facing the courtyard.*g* 15The distance from the entrance of the gateway to the far end of its portico was fifty cubits. 16The alcoves and the projecting walls inside the gateway were surmounted by narrow parapet openings all around, as was the portico; the openings all around faced inward. The faces of the projecting walls were decorated with palm trees.

The Outer Court

17Then he brought me into the outer court. There I saw some rooms and a pavement that had been constructed all around the court; there were thirty rooms along the pavement. 18It abutted the sides of the gateways and was as wide as they were long; this was the lower pavement. 19Then he measured the distance from the inside of the lower gateway to the outside of the inner court; it was a hundred cubits on the east side as well as on the north.

a25 Or *now restore the fortunes of Jacob*   *b5* The common cubit was about 1 1/2 feet (about 0.5 meter).   *c5* That is, about 3 inches (about 8 centimeters)   *d6* Septuagint; Hebrew *deep, the first threshold, one rod deep*   *e8,9* Many Hebrew manuscripts, Septuagint, Vulgate and Syriac; most Hebrew manuscripts *gateway facing the temple; it was one rod deep.* *9Then he measured the portico of the gateway; it*   *f14* Septuagint; Hebrew *projecting wall*   *g14* The meaning of the Hebrew for this verse is uncertain.

The North Gate

²⁰Then he measured the length and width of the gate facing north, leading into the outer court. ²¹Its alcoves—three on each side—its projecting walls and its portico had the same measurements as those of the first gateway. It was fifty cubits long and twenty-five cubits wide. ²²Its openings, its portico and its palm tree decorations had the same measurements as those of the gate facing east. Seven steps led up to it, with its portico opposite them. ²³There was a gate to the inner court facing the north gate, just as there was on the east. He measured from one gate to the opposite one; it was a hundred cubits.

The South Gate

²⁴Then he led me to the south side and I saw a gate facing south. He measured its jambs and its portico, and they had the same measurements as the others. ²⁵The gateway and its portico had narrow openings all around, like the openings of the others. It was fifty cubits long and twenty-five cubits wide. ²⁶Seven steps led up to it, with its portico opposite them; it had palm tree decorations on the faces of the projecting walls on each side. ²⁷The inner court also had a gate facing south, and he measured from this gate to the outer gate on the south side; it was a hundred cubits.

Gates to the Inner Court

²⁸Then he brought me into the inner court through the south gate, and he measured the south gate; it had the same measurements as the others. ²⁹Its alcoves, its projecting walls and its portico had the same measurements as the others. The gateway and its portico had openings all around. It was fifty cubits long and twenty-five cubits wide. ³⁰(The porticoes of the gateways around the inner court were twenty-five cubits wide and five cubits deep.) ³¹Its portico faced the outer court; palm trees decorated its jambs, and eight steps led up to it. ³²Then he brought me to the inner court on the east side, and he measured the gateway; it had the same measurements as the others. ³³Its alcoves, its projecting walls and its portico had the same measurements as the others. The gateway and its portico had openings all around. It

was fifty cubits long and twenty-five cubits wide. ³⁴Its portico faced the outer court; palm trees decorated the jambs on either side, and eight steps led up to it.

³⁵Then he brought me to the north gate and measured it. It had the same measurements as the others, ³⁶as did its alcoves, its projecting walls and its portico, and it had openings all around. It was fifty cubits long and twenty-five cubits wide. ³⁷Its portico*ᵃ* faced the outer court; palm trees decorated the jambs on either side, and eight steps led up to it.

The Rooms for Preparing Sacrifices

³⁸A room with a doorway was by the portico in each of the inner gateways, where the burnt offerings were washed. ³⁹In the portico of the gateway were two tables on each side, on which the burnt offerings, sin offerings and guilt offerings were slaughtered. ⁴⁰By the outside wall of the portico of the gateway, near the steps at the entrance to the north gateway were two tables, and on the other side of the steps were two tables. ⁴¹So there were four tables on one side of the gateway and four on the other—eight tables in all—on which the sacrifices were slaughtered. ⁴²There were also four tables of dressed stone for the burnt offerings, each a cubit and a half long, a cubit and a half wide and a cubit high. On them were placed the utensils for slaughtering the burnt offerings and the other sacrifices. ⁴³And double-pronged hooks, each a handbreadth long, were attached to the wall all around. The tables were for the flesh of the offerings.

Rooms for the Priests

⁴⁴Outside the inner gate, within the inner court, were two rooms, oneᵇ at the side of the north gate and facing south, and another at the side of the southᶜ gate and facing north. ⁴⁵He said to me, "The room facing south is for the priests who have charge of the temple, ⁴⁶and the room facing north is for the priests who have charge of the altar. These are the sons of Zadok, who are the only Levites who may draw near to the Lᴏʀᴅ to minister before him."

⁴⁷Then he measured the court: It was square—a hundred cubits long and a hundred cubits wide. And the altar was in front of the temple.

ᵃ37 Septuagint (see also verses 31 and 34); Hebrew *jambs singers, which were*   ᶜ44 Septuagint; Hebrew *east*   ᵇ44 Septuagint; Hebrew *were rooms for*

The Temple

48He brought me to the portico of the temple and measured the jambs of the portico; they were five cubits wide on either side. The width of the entrance was fourteen cubits and its projecting walls were[a] three cubits wide on either side. 49The portico was twenty cubits wide, and twelve[b] cubits from front to back. It was reached by a flight of stairs,[c] and there were pillars on each side of the jambs.

41 Then the man brought me to the outer sanctuary and measured the jambs; the width of the jambs was six cubits[d] on each side.[e] 2The entrance was ten cubits wide, and the projecting walls on each side of it were five cubits wide. He also measured the outer sanctuary; it was forty cubits long and twenty cubits wide.

3Then he went into the inner sanctuary and measured the jambs of the entrance; each was two cubits wide. The entrance was six cubits wide, and the projecting walls on each side of it were seven cubits wide. 4And he measured the length of the inner sanctuary; it was twenty cubits, and its width was twenty cubits across the end of the outer sanctuary. He said to me, "This is the Most Holy Place."

5Then he measured the wall of the temple; it was six cubits thick, and each side room around the temple was four cubits wide. 6The side rooms were on three levels, one above another, thirty on each level. There were ledges all around the wall of the temple to serve as supports for the side rooms, so that the supports were not inserted into the wall of the temple. 7The side rooms all around the temple were wider at each successive level. The structure surrounding the temple was built in ascending stages, so that the rooms widened as one went upward. A stairway went up from the lowest floor to the top floor through the middle floor.

8I saw that the temple had a raised base all around it, forming the foundation of the side rooms. It was the length of the rod, six long cubits. 9The outer wall of the side rooms was five cubits thick. The open area between the side rooms of the temple 10and the priests', rooms was twenty cubits wide all around the temple. 11There were entrances to the side rooms from the open area, one on the north and another on the south; and the base adjoining the open area was five cubits wide all around.

12The building facing the temple courtyard on the west side was seventy cubits wide. The wall of the building was five cubits thick all around, and its length was ninety cubits.

13Then he measured the temple; it was a hundred cubits long, and the temple courtyard and the building with its walls were also a hundred cubits long. 14The width of the temple courtyard on the east, including the front of the temple, was a hundred cubits.

15Then he measured the length of the building facing the courtyard at the rear of the temple, including its galleries on each side; it was a hundred cubits.

The outer sanctuary, the inner sanctuary and the portico facing the court, 16as well as the thresholds and the narrow windows and galleries around the three of them—everything beyond and including the threshold was covered with wood. The floor, the wall up to the windows, and the windows were covered. 17In the space above the outside of the entrance to the inner sanctuary and on the walls at regular intervals all around the inner and outer sanctuary 18were carved cherubim and palm trees. Palm trees alternated with cherubim. Each cherub had two faces: 19the face of a man toward the palm tree on one side and the face of a lion toward the palm tree on the other. They were carved all around the whole temple. 20From the floor to the area above the entrance, cherubim and palm trees were carved on the wall of the outer sanctuary.

21The outer sanctuary had a rectangular doorframe, and the one at the front of the Most Holy Place was similar. 22There was a wooden altar three cubits high and two cubits square[f]; its corners, its base[g] and its sides were of wood. The man said to me, "This is the table that is before the LORD." 23Both the outer sanctuary and the Most Holy Place had double doors. 24Each door had two leaves—two hinged leaves for each door. 25And on the doors of the outer sanctuary were carved cherubim and palm trees like those carved on the walls, and there was a wooden over-

---

a48 Septuagint; Hebrew entrance was   b49 Septuagint; Hebrew eleven   c49 Hebrew; Septuagint Ten steps led up to it   d1 The common cubit was about 1 1/2 feet (about 0.5 meter).   e1 One Hebrew manuscript and Septuagint; most Hebrew manuscripts side, the width of the tent   f22 Septuagint; Hebrew long   g22 Septuagint; Hebrew length hang on the front of the portico. 26On the sidewalls of the portico were narrow windows with palm trees carved on each side. The side rooms of the temple also had overhangs.

Rooms for the Priests

42 Then the man led me northward into the outer court and brought me to the rooms opposite the temple courtyard and opposite the outer wall on the north side. 2The building whose door faced north was a hundred cubits*a* long and fifty cubits wide. 3Both in the section twenty cubits from the inner court and in the section opposite the pavement of the outer court, gallery faced gallery at the three levels. 4In front of the rooms was an inner passageway ten cubits wide and a hundred cubits*b* long. Their doors were on the north. 5Now the upper rooms were narrower, for the galleries took more space from them than from the rooms on the lower and middle floors of the building. 6The rooms on the third floor had no pillars, as the courts had; so they were smaller in floor space than those on the lower and middle floors. 7There was an outer wall parallel to the rooms and the outer court; it extended in front of the rooms for fifty cubits. 8While the row of rooms on the side next to the outer court was fifty cubits long, the row on the side nearest the sanctuary was a hundred cubits long. 9The lower rooms had an entrance on the east side as one enters them from the outer court.

10On the south side*c* along the length of the wall of the outer court, adjoining the temple courtyard and opposite the outer wall, were rooms 11with a passageway in front of them. These were like the rooms on the north; they had the same length and width, with similar exits and dimensions. Similar to the doorways on the north 12were the doorways of the rooms on the south. There was a doorway at the beginning of the passageway that was parallel to the corresponding wall extending eastward, by which one enters the rooms.

13Then he said to me, "The north and south rooms facing the temple courtyard are the priests' rooms, where the priests who approach the LORD will eat the most holy offerings. There they will put the most holy offerings — the grain offerings, the sin offerings and the guilt offerings — for the place is holy. 14Once the priests enter the holy precincts, they are not to go into the outer court until they leave behind the garments in which they minister, for these are holy. They are to put on other clothes before they go near the places that are for the people."

15When he had finished measuring what was inside the temple area, he led me out by the east gate and measured the area all around: 16He measured the east side with the measuring rod; it was five hundred cubits.*d* 17He measured the north side; it was five hundred cubits*e* by the measuring rod. 18He measured the south side; it was five hundred cubits by the measuring rod. 19Then he turned to the west side and measured; it was five hundred cubits by the measuring rod. 20So he measured the area on all four sides. It had a wall around it, five hundred cubits long and five hundred cubits wide, to separate the holy from the common.

The Glory Returns to the Temple

43 Then the man brought me to the gate facing east, 2and I saw the glory of the God of Israel coming from the east. His voice was like the roar of rushing waters, and the land was radiant with his glory. 3The vision I saw was like the vision I had seen when he*f* came to destroy the city and like the visions I had seen by the Kebar River, and I fell facedown. 4The glory of the LORD entered the temple through the gate facing east. 5Then the Spirit lifted me up and brought me into the inner court, and the glory of the LORD filled the temple.

6While the man was standing beside me, I heard someone speaking to me from inside the temple. 7He said: "Son of man, this is the place of my throne and the place for the soles of my feet. This is where I will live among the Israelites forever. The house of Israel will never again defile my holy name — neither they nor their kings — by their prostitution*g* and the lifeless idols*h* of their kings at their high places. 8When they placed their

---

*a2 The common cubit was about 1 1/2 feet (about 0.5 meter). *b4 Septuagint and Syriac; Hebrew *and one cubit* *c10 Septuagint; Hebrew *Eastward* *d16 See Septuagint of verse 17; Hebrew *rods*; also in verses 18 and 19. *e17 Septuagint; Hebrew *rods* *f3 Some Hebrew manuscripts and Vulgate; most Hebrew manuscripts *I* *g7 Or *their spiritual adultery*; also in verse 9 *h7 Or *the corpses*; also in verse 9 threshold next to my threshold and their doorposts beside my doorposts, with only a wall between me and them, they defiled my holy name by their detestable practices. So I destroyed them in my anger. ⁹Now let them put away from me their prostitution and the lifeless idols of their kings, and I will live among them forever.

¹⁰"Son of man, describe the temple to the people of Israel, that they may be ashamed of their sins. Let them consider the plan, ¹¹and if they are ashamed of all they have done, make known to them the design of the temple—its arrangement, its exits and entrances—its whole design and all its regulations*a* and laws. Write these down before them so that they may be faithful to its design and follow all its regulations.

¹²"This is the law of the temple: All the surrounding area on top of the mountain will be most holy. Such is the law of the temple.

The Altar

¹³"These are the measurements of the altar in long cubits, that cubit being a cubit*b* and a handbreadth*c*: Its gutter is a cubit deep and a cubit wide, with a rim of one span*d* around the edge. And this is the height of the altar: ¹⁴From the gutter on the ground up to the lower ledge it is two cubits high and a cubit wide, and from the smaller ledge up to the larger ledge it is four cubits high and a cubit wide. ¹⁵The altar hearth is four cubits high, and four horns project upward from the hearth. ¹⁶The altar hearth is square, twelve cubits long and twelve cubits wide. ¹⁷The upper ledge also is square, fourteen cubits long and fourteen cubits wide, with a rim of half a cubit and a gutter of a cubit all around. The steps of the altar face east."

¹⁸Then he said to me, "Son of man, this is what the Sovereign LORD says: These will be the regulations for sacrificing burnt offerings and sprinkling blood upon the altar when it is built: ¹⁹You are to give a young bull as a sin offering to the priests, who are Levites, of the family of Zadok, who come near to minister before me, declares the Sovereign LORD. ²⁰You are to take some of its blood and put it on the four horns of the altar and on the four corners of the upper ledge and all around

the rim, and so purify the altar and make atonement for it. ²¹You are to take the bull for the sin offering and burn it in the designated part of the temple area outside the sanctuary.

²²"On the second day you are to offer a male goat without defect for a sin offering, and the altar is to be purified as it was purified with the bull. ²³When you have finished purifying it, you are to offer a young bull and a ram from the flock, both without defect. ²⁴You are to offer them before the LORD, and the priests are to sprinkle salt on them and sacrifice them as a burnt offering to the LORD.

²⁵"For seven days you are to provide a male goat daily for a sin offering; you are also to provide a young bull and a ram from the flock, both without defect. ²⁶For seven days they are to make atonement for the altar and cleanse it; thus they will dedicate it. ²⁷At the end of these days, from the eighth day on, the priests are to present your burnt offerings and fellowship offerings*e* on the altar. Then I will accept you, declares the Sovereign LORD."

The Prince, the Levites, the Priests

44 Then the man brought me back to the outer gate of the sanctuary, the one facing east, and it was shut. ²The LORD said to me, "This gate is to remain shut. It must not be opened; no one may enter through it. It is to remain shut because the LORD, the God of Israel, has entered through it. ³The prince himself is the only one who may sit inside the gateway to eat in the presence of the LORD. He is to enter by way of the portico of the gateway and go out the same way."

⁴Then the man brought me by way of the north gate to the front of the temple. I looked and saw the glory of the LORD filling the temple of the LORD, and I fell facedown.

⁵The LORD said to me, "Son of man, look carefully, listen closely and give attention to everything I tell you concerning all the regulations regarding the temple of the LORD. Give attention to the entrance of the temple and all the exits of the sanctuary. ⁶Say to the rebellious house of Israel, 'This is what the Sovereign LORD says: Enough of your detestable practices, O house of Israel! ⁷In addition to all your other detestable practices, you

---

a11 Some Hebrew manuscripts and Septuagint; most Hebrew manuscripts *regulations and its whole design*
b13 The common cubit was about 1 1/2 feet (about 0.5 meter). *c13* That is, about 3 inches (about 8 centimeters) *d13* That is, about 9 inches (about 22 centimeters) *e27* Traditionally *peace offerings*

brought foreigners uncircumcised in heart and flesh into my sanctuary, desecrating my temple while you offered me food, fat and blood, and you broke my covenant. [8]Instead of carrying out your duty in regard to my holy things, you put others in charge of my sanctuary. [9]This is what the Sovereign LORD says: No foreigner uncircumcised in heart and flesh is to enter my sanctuary, not even the foreigners who live among the Israelites.

[10]" 'The Levites who went far from me when Israel went astray and who wandered from me after their idols must bear the consequences of their sin. [11]They may serve in my sanctuary, having charge of the gates of the temple and serving in it; they may slaughter the burnt offerings and sacrifices for the people and stand before the people and serve them. [12]But because they served them in the presence of their idols and made the house of Israel fall into sin, therefore I have sworn with uplifted hand that they must bear the consequences of their sin, declares the Sovereign LORD. [13]They are not to come near to serve me as priests or come near any of my holy things or my most holy offerings; they must bear the shame of their detestable practices. [14]Yet I will put them in charge of the duties of the temple and all the work that is to be done in it.

[15]" 'But the priests, who are Levites and descendants of Zadok and who faithfully carried out the duties of my sanctuary when the Israelites went astray from me, are to come near to minister before me; they are to stand before me to offer sacrifices of fat and blood, declares the Sovereign LORD. [16]They alone are to enter my sanctuary; they alone are to come near my table to minister before me and perform my service.

[17]" 'When they enter the gates of the inner court, they are to wear linen clothes; they must not wear any woolen garment while ministering at the gates of the inner court or inside the temple. [18]They are to wear linen turbans on their heads and linen undergarments around their waists. They must not wear anything that makes them perspire. [19]When they go out into the outer court where the people are, they are to take off the clothes they have been ministering in and are to leave them in the sacred rooms, and put

on other clothes, so that they do not consecrate the people by means of their garments.

[20]" 'They must not shave their heads or let their hair grow long, but they are to keep the hair of their heads trimmed. [21]No priest is to drink wine when he enters the inner court. [22]They must not marry widows or divorced women; they may marry only virgins of Israelite descent or widows of priests. [23]They are to teach my people the difference between the holy and the common and show them how to distinguish between the unclean and the clean.

[24]" 'In any dispute, the priests are to serve as judges and decide it according to my ordinances. They are to keep my laws and my decrees for all my appointed feasts, and they are to keep my Sabbaths holy.

[25]" 'A priest must not defile himself by going near a dead person; however, if the dead person was his father or mother, son or daughter, brother or unmarried sister, then he may defile himself. [26]After he is cleansed, he must wait seven days. [27]On the day he goes into the inner court of the sanctuary to minister in the sanctuary, he is to offer a sin offering for himself, declares the Sovereign LORD.

[28]" 'I am to be the only inheritance the priests have. You are to give them no possession in Israel; I will be their possession. [29]They will eat the grain offerings, the sin offerings and the guilt offerings; and everything in Israel devoted[a] to the LORD will belong to them. [30]The best of all the firstfruits and of all your special gifts will belong to the priests. You are to give them the first portion of your ground meal so that a blessing may rest on your household. [31]The priests must not eat anything, bird or animal, found dead or torn by wild animals.

Division of the Land

45 " 'When you allot the land as an inheritance, you are to present to the LORD a portion of the land as a sacred district, 25,000 cubits long and 20,000[b] cubits wide; the entire area will be holy. [2]Of this, a section 500 cubits square is to be for the sanctuary, with 50 cubits around it for open land. [3]In the sacred district, measure off a section 25,000 cu-

---

[a]29 The Hebrew term refers to the irrevocable giving over of things or persons to the LORD.
[b]1 Septuagint (see also verses 3 and 5 and 48:9); Hebrew *10,000*

bits*a* long and 10,000 cubits*b* wide. In it will be the sanctuary, the Most Holy Place. ⁴It will be the sacred portion of the land for the priests, who minister in the sanctuary and who draw near to minister before the LORD. It will be a place for their houses as well as a holy place for the sanctuary. ⁵An area 25,000 cubits long and 10,000 cubits wide will belong to the Levites, who serve in the temple, as their possession for towns to live in.*c*

⁶" 'You are to give the city as its property an area 5,000 cubits wide and 25,000 cubits long, adjoining the sacred portion; it will belong to the whole house of Israel.

⁷" 'The prince will have the land bordering each side of the area formed by the sacred district and the property of the city. It will extend westward from the west side and eastward from the east side, running lengthwise from the western to the eastern border parallel to one of the tribal portions. ⁸This land will be his possession in Israel. And my princes will no longer oppress my people but will allow the house of Israel to possess the land according to their tribes.

⁹" 'This is what the Sovereign LORD says: You have gone far enough, O princes of Israel! Give up your violence and oppression and do what is just and right. Stop dispossessing my people, declares the Sovereign LORD. ¹⁰You are to use accurate scales, an accurate ephah*d* and an accurate bath.*e* ¹¹The ephah and the bath are to be the same size, the bath containing a tenth of a homer*f* and the ephah a tenth of a homer; the homer is to be the standard measure for both. ¹²The shekel*g* is to consist of twenty gerahs. Twenty shekels plus twenty-five shekels plus fifteen shekels equal one mina.*h*

Offerings and Holy Days

¹³" 'This is the special gift you are to offer: a sixth of an ephah from each homer of wheat and a sixth of an ephah from each homer of barley. ¹⁴The prescribed portion of oil, measured by the bath, is a tenth of a bath from each cor (which consists of ten baths or one homer, for ten baths are equivalent to a homer). ¹⁵Also one sheep is to be taken from every flock of two hundred from the well-watered

pastures of Israel. These will be used for the grain offerings, burnt offerings and fellowship offerings*i* to make atonement for the people, declares the Sovereign LORD. ¹⁶All the people of the land will participate in this special gift for the use of the prince in Israel. ¹⁷It will be the duty of the prince to provide the burnt offerings, grain offerings and drink offerings at the festivals, the New Moons and the Sabbaths—at all the appointed feasts of the house of Israel. He will provide the sin offerings, grain offerings, burnt offerings and fellowship offerings to make atonement for the house of Israel.

¹⁸" 'This is what the Sovereign LORD says: In the first month on the first day you are to take a young bull without defect and purify the sanctuary. ¹⁹The priest is to take some of the blood of the sin offering and put it on the doorposts of the temple, on the four corners of the upper ledge of the altar and on the gateposts of the inner court. ²⁰You are to do the same on the seventh day of the month for anyone who sins unintentionally or through ignorance; so you are to make atonement for the temple.

²¹" 'In the first month on the fourteenth day you are to observe the Passover, a feast lasting seven days, during which you shall eat bread made without yeast. ²²On that day the prince is to provide a bull as a sin offering for himself and for all the people of the land. ²³Every day during the seven days of the Feast he is to provide seven bulls and seven rams without defect as a burnt offering to the LORD, and a male goat for a sin offering. ²⁴He is to provide as a grain offering an ephah for each bull and an ephah for each ram, along with a hin*j* of oil for each ephah.

²⁵" 'During the seven days of the Feast, which begins in the seventh month on the fifteenth day, he is to make the same provision for sin offerings, burnt offerings, grain offerings and oil.

46 " 'This is what the Sovereign LORD says: The gate of the inner court facing east is to be shut on the six working days, but on the Sabbath day and on the day of the New Moon it is to be opened. ²The prince is to enter from the

---

a3 That is, about 7 miles (about 12 kilometers)   *b3* That is, about 3 miles (about 5 kilometers)
c5 Septuagint; Hebrew *temple; they will have as their possession 20 rooms*   *d10* An ephah was a dry
measure.   *e10* A bath was a liquid measure.   *f11* A homer was a dry measure.   *g12* A shekel
weighed about 2/5 ounce (about 11.5 grams).   *h12* That is, 60 shekels; the common mina was 50
shekels.   *i15* Traditionally *peace offerings*; also in verse 17   *j24* That is, probably about 4 quarts
(about 4 liters)

outside through the portico of the gateway and stand by the gatepost. The priests are to sacrifice his burnt offering and his fellowship offerings.*a* He is to worship at the threshold of the gateway and then go out, but the gate will not be shut until evening. 3On the Sabbaths and New Moons the people of the land are to worship in the presence of the LORD at the entrance to that gateway. 4The burnt offering the prince brings to the LORD on the Sabbath day is to be six male lambs and a ram, all without defect. 5The grain offering given with the ram is to be an ephah,*b* and the grain offering with the lambs is to be as much as he pleases, along with a hin*c* of oil for each ephah. 6On the day of the New Moon he is to offer a young bull, six lambs and a ram, all without defect. 7He is to provide as a grain offering one ephah with the bull, one ephah with the ram, and with the lambs as much as he wants to give, along with a hin of oil with each ephah. 8When the prince enters, he is to go in through the portico of the gateway, and he is to come out the same way.

9" 'When the people of the land come before the LORD at the appointed feasts, whoever enters by the north gate to worship is to go out the south gate; and whoever enters by the south gate is to go out the north gate. No one is to return through the gate by which he entered, but each is to go out the opposite gate. 10The prince is to be among them, going in when they go in and going out when they go out.

11" 'At the festivals and the appointed feasts, the grain offering is to be an ephah with a bull, an ephah with a ram, and with the lambs as much as one pleases, along with a hin of oil for each ephah. 12When the prince provides a freewill offering to the LORD—whether a burnt offering or fellowship offerings—the gate facing east is to be opened for him. He shall offer his burnt offering or his fellowship offerings as he does on the Sabbath day. Then he shall go out, and after he has gone out, the gate will be shut.

13" 'Every day you are to provide a year-old lamb without defect for a burnt offering to the LORD; morning by morning you shall provide it. 14You are also to provide with it morning by morning a grain offering, consisting of a sixth of an ephah with

a third of a hin of oil to moisten the flour. The presenting of this grain offering to the LORD is a lasting ordinance. 15So the lamb and the grain offering and the oil shall be provided morning by morning for a regular burnt offering.

16" 'This is what the Sovereign LORD says: If the prince makes a gift from his inheritance to one of his sons, it will also belong to his descendants; it is to be their property by inheritance. 17If, however, he makes a gift from his inheritance to one of his servants, the servant may keep it until the year of freedom; then it will revert to the prince. His inheritance belongs to his sons only; it is theirs. 18The prince must not take any of the inheritance of the people, driving them off their property. He is to give his sons their inheritance out of his own property, so that none of my people will be separated from his property.' "

19Then the man brought me through the entrance at the side of the gate to the sacred rooms facing north, which belonged to the priests, and showed me a place at the western end. 20He said to me, "This is the place where the priests will cook the guilt offering and the sin offering and bake the grain offering, to avoid bringing them into the outer court and consecrating the people."

21He then brought me to the outer court and led me around to its four corners, and I saw in each corner another court. 22In the four corners of the outer court were enclosed*d* courts, forty cubits long and thirty cubits wide; each of the courts in the four corners was the same size. 23Around the inside of each of the four courts was a ledge of stone, with places for fire built all around under the ledge. 24He said to me, "These are the kitchens where those who minister at the temple will cook the sacrifices of the people."

The River From the Temple

47 The man brought me back to the entrance of the temple, and I saw water coming out from under the threshold of the temple toward the east (for the temple faced east). The water was coming down from under the south side of the temple, south of the altar. 2He then brought me out through the north gate

and led me around the outside to the outer gate facing east, and the water was flowing from the south side.

³As the man went eastward with a measuring line in his hand, he measured off a thousand cubits[a] and then led me through water that was ankle-deep. ⁴He measured off another thousand cubits and led me through water that was knee-deep. He measured off another thousand and led me through water that was up to the waist. ⁵He measured off another thousand, but now it was a river that I could not cross, because the water had risen and was deep enough to swim in—a river that no one could cross. ⁶He asked me, "Son of man, do you see this?"

Then he led me back to the bank of the river. ⁷When I arrived there, I saw a great number of trees on each side of the river. ⁸He said to me, "This water flows toward the eastern region and goes down into the Arabah,[b] where it enters the Sea.[c] When it empties into the Sea,[c] the water there becomes fresh. ⁹Swarms of living creatures will live wherever the river flows. There will be large numbers of fish, because this water flows there and makes the salt water fresh; so where the river flows everything will live. ¹⁰Fishermen will stand along the shore; from En Gedi to En Eglaim there will be places for spreading nets. The fish will be of many kinds—like the fish of the Great Sea.[d] ¹¹But the swamps and marshes will not become fresh; they will be left for salt. ¹²Fruit trees of all kinds will grow on both banks of the river. Their leaves will not wither, nor will their fruit fail. Every month they will bear, because the water from the sanctuary flows to them. Their fruit will serve for food and their leaves for healing."

The Boundaries of the Land

¹³This is what the Sovereign LORD says: "These are the boundaries by which you are to divide the land for an inheritance among the twelve tribes of Israel, with two portions for Joseph. ¹⁴You are to divide it equally among them. Because I swore with uplifted hand to give it to your forefathers, this land will become your inheritance.

¹⁵"This is to be the boundary of the land:

"On the north side it will run from the Great Sea by the Hethlon road past Lebo[e] Hamath to Zedad, ¹⁶Berothah[f] and Sibraim (which lies on the border between Damascus and Hamath), as far as Hazer Hatticon, which is on the border of Hauran. ¹⁷The boundary will extend from the sea to Hazar Enan,[g] along the northern border of Damascus, with the border of Hamath to the north. This will be the north boundary.

¹⁸"On the east side the boundary will run between Hauran and Damascus, along the Jordan between Gilead and the land of Israel, to the eastern sea and as far as Tamar.[h] This will be the east boundary.

¹⁹"On the south side it will run from Tamar as far as the waters of Meribah Kadesh, then along the Wadi of Egypt, to the Great Sea. This will be the south boundary.

²⁰"On the west side, the Great Sea will be the boundary to a point opposite Lebo[i] Hamath. This will be the west boundary.

²¹"You are to distribute this land among yourselves according to the tribes of Israel. ²²You are to allot it as an inheritance for yourselves and for the aliens who have settled among you and who have children. You are to consider them as native-born Israelites; along with you they are to be allotted an inheritance among the tribes of Israel. ²³In whatever tribe the alien settles, there you are to give him his inheritance," declares the Sovereign LORD.

The Division of the Land

48 "These are the tribes, listed by name: At the northern frontier, Dan will have one portion; it will follow the Hethlon road to Lebo[j] Hamath; Hazar Enan and the northern border of Damascus next to Hamath will be part of its border from the east side to the west side.

²"Asher will have one portion; it will border the territory of Dan from east to west.

---

[a]3 That is, about 1,500 feet (about 450 meters)   [b]8 Or the Jordan Valley   [c]8 That is, the Dead Sea
[d]10 That is, the Mediterranean; also in verses 15, 19 and 20   [e]15 Or past the entrance to
[f]15,16 See Septuagint and Ezekiel 48:1; Hebrew road to go into Zedad, ¹⁶Hamath, Berothah
[g]17 Hebrew Enon, a variant of Enan   [h]18 Septuagint and Syriac; Hebrew Israel. You will measure to the
eastern sea   [i]20 Or opposite the entrance to   [j]1 Or to the entrance to

3"Naphtali will have one portion; it will border the territory of Asher from east to west.

4"Manasseh will have one portion; it will border the territory of Naphtali from east to west.

5"Ephraim will have one portion; it will border the territory of Manasseh from east to west.

6"Reuben will have one portion; it will border the territory of Ephraim from east to west.

7"Judah will have one portion; it will border the territory of Reuben from east to west.

8"Bordering the territory of Judah from east to west will be the portion you are to present as a special gift. It will be 25,000 cubits*a* wide, and its length from east to west will equal one of the tribal portions; the sanctuary will be in the center of it.

9"The special portion you are to offer to the LORD will be 25,000 cubits long and 10,000 cubits*b* wide. 10This will be the sacred portion for the priests. It will be 25,000 cubits long on the north side, 10,000 cubits wide on the west side, 10,000 cubits wide on the east side and 25,000 cubits long on the south side. In the center of it will be the sanctuary of the LORD. 11This will be for the consecrated priests, the Zadokites, who were faithful in serving me and did not go astray as the Levites did when the Israelites went astray. 12It will be a special gift to them from the sacred portion of the land, a most holy portion, bordering the territory of the Levites.

13"Alongside the territory of the priests, the Levites will have an allotment 25,000 cubits long and 10,000 cubits wide. Its total length will be 25,000 cubits and its width 10,000 cubits. 14They must not sell or exchange any of it. This is the best of the land and must not pass into other hands, because it is holy to the LORD.

15"The remaining area, 5,000 cubits wide and 25,000 cubits long, will be for the common use of the city, for houses and for pastureland. The city will be in the center of it 16and will have these measurements: the north side 4,500 cubits, the south side 4,500 cubits, the east side 4,500 cubits, and the west side 4,500 cubits. 17The pastureland for the city will be 250 cubits on the north,

250 cubits on the south, 250 cubits on the east, and 250 cubits on the west. 18What remains of the area, bordering on the sacred portion and running the length of it, will be 10,000 cubits on the east side and 10,000 cubits on the west side. Its produce will supply food for the workers of the city. 19The workers from the city who farm it will come from all the tribes of Israel. 20The entire portion will be a square, 25,000 cubits on each side. As a special gift you will set aside the sacred portion, along with the property of the city.

21"What remains on both sides of the area formed by the sacred portion and the city property will belong to the prince. It will extend eastward from the 25,000 cubits of the sacred portion to the eastern border, and westward from the 25,000 cubits to the western border. Both these areas running the length of the tribal portions will belong to the prince, and the sacred portion with the temple sanctuary will be in the center of them. 22So the property of the Levites and the property of the city will lie in the center of the area that belongs to the prince. The area belonging to the prince will lie between the border of Judah and the border of Benjamin.

23"As for the rest of the tribes: Benjamin will have one portion; it will extend from the east side to the west side.

24"Simeon will have one portion; it will border the territory of Benjamin from east to west.

25"Issachar will have one portion; it will border the territory of Simeon from east to west.

26"Zebulun will have one portion; it will border the territory of Issachar from east to west.

27"Gad will have one portion; it will border the territory of Zebulun from east to west.

28"The southern boundary of Gad will run south from Tamar to the waters of Meribah Kadesh, then along the Wadi ,of Egypt, to the Great Sea.*c*

29"This is the land you are to allot as an inheritance to the tribes of Israel, and these will be their portions," declares the Sovereign LORD.

The Gates of the City

30"These will be the exits of the city:

a8 That is, about 7 miles (about 12 kilometers)   *b9* That is, about 3 miles (about 5 kilometers)
c28 That is, the Mediterranean

Beginning on the north side, which is 4,500 cubits long, ³¹the gates of the city will be named after the tribes of Israel. The three gates on the north side will be the gate of Reuben, the gate of Judah and the gate of Levi.

³²"On the east side, which is 4,500 cubits long, will be three gates: the gate of Joseph, the gate of Benjamin and the gate of Dan.

³³"On the south side, which measures 4,500 cubits, will be three gates:

the gate of Simeon, the gate of Issachar and the gate of Zebulun.

³⁴"On the west side, which is 4,500 cubits long, will be three gates: the gate of Gad, the gate of Asher and the gate of Naphtali.

³⁵"The distance all around will be 18,000 cubits.

"And the name of the city from that time on will be:

THE LORD IS THERE."

DANIEL, writing from Babylon during the time of the exile, wants us to know that God controls everything and that the victory always belongs to the Lord and to those who do his will. Even the pagan kings in Babylon must admit this truth. As you read this book, think about how God controls your life and how you will win out over the forces of evil because you obey the Lord.

DANIEL

Daniel's Training in Babylon

1 In the third year of the reign of Jehoiakim king of Judah, Nebuchadnezzar king of Babylon came to Jerusalem and besieged it. ²And the Lord delivered Jehoiakim king of Judah into his hand, along with some of the articles from the temple of God. These he carried off to the temple of his god in Babylonia*ᵃ* and put in the treasure house of his god.

³Then the king ordered Ashpenaz, chief of his court officials, to bring in some of the Israelites from the royal family and the nobility— ⁴young men without any physical defect, handsome, showing aptitude for every kind of learning, well informed, quick to understand, and qualified to serve in the king's palace. He was to teach them the language and literature of the Babylonians.*ᵇ* ⁵The king assigned them a daily amount of food and wine from the king's table. They were to be trained for three years, and after that they were to enter the king's service.

⁶Among these were some from Judah: Daniel, Hananiah, Mishael and Azariah. ⁷The chief official gave them new names: to Daniel, the name Belteshazzar; to Hananiah, Shadrach; to Mishael, Meshach; and to Azariah, Abednego.

⁸But Daniel resolved not to defile himself with the royal food and wine, and he asked the chief official for permission not

---

ᵃ2 Hebrew *Shinar*   *ᵇ4* Or *Chaldeans*

to defile himself this way. ⁹Now God had caused the official to show favor and sympathy to Daniel, ¹⁰but the official told Daniel, "I am afraid of my lord the king, who has assigned your*ᵃ* food and drink. Why should he see you looking worse than the other young men your age? The king would then have my head because of you."

¹¹Daniel then said to the guard whom the chief official had appointed over Daniel, Hananiah, Mishael and Azariah, ¹²"Please test your servants for ten days: Give us nothing but vegetables to eat and water to drink. ¹³Then compare our appearance with that of the young men who eat the royal food, and treat your servants in accordance with what you see." ¹⁴So he

ᵃ10 The Hebrew for *your* and *you* in this verse is plural.

THURSDAY

VERSE FOR THE DAY:
Daniel 1:8

AUTHOR:
Doris Rikkers

PASSAGE FOR THE DAY:
Daniel 1:1–21

A Son to Make a Mother Proud

THERE he stood. Someone's tall, handsome, intelligent son who addressed his superiors with respect. He was polite yet firm in his convictions. He hung on to all his years of upbringing. He chose only healthy foods—not the rich, artery-clogging king's meat and sensory-numbing wines. He was young and he loved his God. He would make any mother proud to say, "That's my boy."

Daniel didn't just grow like a bean stalk in someone's garden. He was born to an Israelite mother who did a wonderful, caring job of raising a son who, in even the gravest of circumstances (captivity in a hostile land), held on to all he believed.

Never before had I thought about Daniel's mother. Who was she? What happened to her when the Israelites were taken captive? But now that I have two sons of my own, I couldn't help but think about Daniel's mother. We will never know who she was, but she certainly raised an outstanding young man.

Maybe she never heard of his exemplary behavior. Maybe she never realized what a great job she had done in nurturing and educating this young Israelite.

She may have prayed for him daily when he was a young child. She may have continued to pray for him during the exile. Whether or not she knew what he had achieved, she had done her job—to raise a child who as an adult would follow the leading of his God.

I don't know the potential of my sons. Maybe, like Daniel's mother, I will never know what they will become or achieve as young men. But, like Daniel's mother, I must believe and continue as best I know how to raise and prepare my sons for God's calling—whatever and wherever that may be.

Additional Scripture Readings:
Luke 2:41–52; Hebrews 11:23–28

Go to page 937 for your next devotional reading.

agreed to this and tested them for ten days.

¹⁵At the end of the ten days they looked healthier and better nourished than any of the young men who ate the royal food. ¹⁶So the guard took away their choice food and the wine they were to drink and gave them vegetables instead.

¹⁷To these four young men God gave knowledge and understanding of all kinds of literature and learning. And Daniel could understand visions and dreams of all kinds.

¹⁸At the end of the time set by the king to bring them in, the chief official presented them to Nebuchadnezzar. ¹⁹The king talked with them, and he found none equal to Daniel, Hananiah, Mishael and Azariah; so they entered the king's service. ²⁰In every matter of wisdom and understanding about which the king questioned them, he found them ten times better than all the magicians and enchanters in his whole kingdom.

²¹And Daniel remained there until the first year of King Cyrus.

Nebuchadnezzar's Dream

2 In the second year of his reign, Nebuchadnezzar had dreams; his mind was troubled and he could not sleep. ²So the king summoned the magicians, enchanters, sorcerers and astrologers*a* to tell him what he had dreamed. When they came in and stood before the king, ³he said to them, "I have had a dream that troubles me and I want to know what it means.*b*"

⁴Then the astrologers answered the king in Aramaic,*c* "O king, live forever! Tell your servants the dream, and we will interpret it."

⁵The king replied to the astrologers, "This is what I have firmly decided: If you do not tell me what my dream was and interpret it, I will have you cut into pieces and your houses turned into piles of rubble. ⁶But if you tell me the dream and explain it, you will receive from me gifts and rewards and great honor. So tell me the dream and interpret it for me."

⁷Once more they replied, "Let the king tell his servants the dream, and we will interpret it."

⁸Then the king answered, "I am certain that you are trying to gain time, because you realize that this is what I have firmly decided: ⁹If you do not tell me the dream, there is just one penalty for you. You have conspired to tell me misleading and wicked things, hoping the situation will change. So then, tell me the dream, and I will know that you can interpret it for me."

¹⁰The astrologers answered the king, "There is not a man on earth who can do what the king asks! No king, however great and mighty, has ever asked such a thing of any magician or enchanter or astrologer. ¹¹What the king asks is too difficult. No one can reveal it to the king except the gods, and they do not live among men."

¹²This made the king so angry and furious that he ordered the execution of all the wise men of Babylon. ¹³So the decree was issued to put the wise men to death, and men were sent to look for Daniel and his friends to put them to death.

¹⁴When Arioch, the commander of the king's guard, had gone out to put to death the wise men of Babylon, Daniel spoke to him with wisdom and tact. ¹⁵He asked the king's officer, "Why did the king issue such a harsh decree?" Arioch then explained the matter to Daniel. ¹⁶At this, Daniel went in to the king and asked for time, so that he might interpret the dream for him.

¹⁷Then Daniel returned to his house and explained the matter to his friends Hananiah, Mishael and Azariah. ¹⁸He urged them to plead for mercy from the God of heaven concerning this mystery, so that he and his friends might not be executed with the rest of the wise men of Babylon. ¹⁹During the night the mystery was revealed to Daniel in a vision. Then Daniel praised the God of heaven ²⁰and said:

"Praise be to the name of God for
        ever and ever;
    wisdom and power are his.
²¹He changes times and seasons;
    he sets up kings and deposes them.
He gives wisdom to the wise
    and knowledge to the discerning.
²²He reveals deep and hidden things;
    he knows what lies in darkness,
    and light dwells with him.
²³I thank and praise you, O God of my
        fathers:

---

*a*2 Or *Chaldeans*; also in verses 4, 5 and 10   *b*3 Or *was*   *c*4 The text from here through chapter 7 is in Aramaic.

You have given me wisdom and
power,
you have made known to me what we
asked of you,
you have made known to us the
dream of the king."

Daniel Interprets the Dream

²⁴Then Daniel went to Arioch, whom
the king had appointed to execute the
wise men of Babylon, and said to him,
"Do not execute the wise men of Babylon. Take me to the king, and I will interpret his dream for him."

²⁵Arioch took Daniel to the king at
once and said, "I have found a man
among the exiles from Judah who can tell
the king what his dream means."

²⁶The king asked Daniel (also called
Belteshazzar), "Are you able to tell me
what I saw in my dream and interpret it?"

²⁷Daniel replied, "No wise man, enchanter, magician or diviner can explain
to the king the mystery he has asked
about, ²⁸but there is a God in heaven who
reveals mysteries. He has shown King
Nebuchadnezzar what will happen in
days to come. Your dream and the visions
that passed through your mind as you lay
on your bed are these:

²⁹"As you were lying there, O king, your
mind turned to things to come, and the
revealer of mysteries showed you what is
going to happen. ³⁰As for me, this mystery
has been revealed to me, not because
I have greater wisdom than other living men, but so that you, O king, may
know the interpretation and that you
may understand what went through
your mind.

³¹"You looked, O king, and there before
you stood a large statue—an enormous,
dazzling statue, awesome in appearance.
³²The head of the statue was made of
pure gold, its chest and arms of silver, its
belly and thighs of bronze, ³³its legs of
iron, its feet partly of iron and partly of
baked clay. ³⁴While you were watching, a
rock was cut out, but not by human
hands. It struck the statue on its feet of
iron and clay and smashed them. ³⁵Then
the iron, the clay, the bronze, the silver
and the gold were broken to pieces at the
same time and became like chaff on a
threshing floor in the summer. The wind
swept them away without leaving a trace.
But the rock that struck the statue became a huge mountain and filled the
whole earth.

³⁶"This was the dream, and now we will

interpret it to the king. ³⁷You, O king, are
the king of kings. The God of heaven has
given you dominion and power and might
and glory; ³⁸in your hands he has placed
mankind and the beasts of the field and
the birds of the air. Wherever they live, he
has made you ruler over them all. You are
that head of gold.

³⁹"After you, another kingdom will rise,
inferior to yours. Next, a third kingdom,
one of bronze, will rule over the whole
earth. ⁴⁰Finally, there will be a fourth
kingdom, strong as iron—for iron breaks
and smashes everything—and as iron
breaks things to pieces, so it will crush
and break all the others. ⁴¹Just as you saw
that the feet and toes were partly of
baked clay and partly of iron, so this will
be a divided kingdom; yet it will have
some of the strength of iron in it, even as
you saw iron mixed with clay. ⁴²As the
toes were partly iron and partly clay, so
this kingdom will be partly strong and
partly brittle. ⁴³And just as you saw the
iron mixed with baked clay, so the people
will be a mixture and will not remain
united, any more than iron mixes with
clay.

⁴⁴"In the time of those kings, the God
of heaven will set up a kingdom that will
never be destroyed, nor will it be left to
another people. It will crush all those
kingdoms and bring them to an end, but
it will itself endure forever. ⁴⁵This is the
meaning of the vision of the rock cut out
of a mountain, but not by human hands
—a rock that broke the iron, the bronze,
the clay, the silver and the gold to pieces.

"The great God has shown the king
what will take place in the future. The
dream is true and the interpretation is
trustworthy."

⁴⁶Then King Nebuchadnezzar fell prostrate before Daniel and paid him honor
and ordered that an offering and incense
be presented to him. ⁴⁷The king said to
Daniel, "Surely your God is the God of
gods and the Lord of kings and a revealer
of mysteries, for you were able to reveal
this mystery."

⁴⁸Then the king placed Daniel in a high
position and lavished many gifts on him.
He made him ruler over the entire province of Babylon and placed him in charge
of all its wise men. ⁴⁹Moreover, at Daniel's request the king appointed Shadrach, Meshach and Abednego administrators over the province of Babylon,
while Daniel himself remained at the royal court.

The Image of Gold and the Fiery Furnace

3 King Nebuchadnezzar made an image of gold, ninety feet high and nine feet[a] wide, and set it up on the plain of Dura in the province of Babylon. ²He then summoned the satraps, prefects, governors, advisers, treasurers, judges, magistrates and all the other provincial officials to come to the dedication of the image he had set up. ³So the satraps, prefects, governors, advisers, treasurers, judges, magistrates and all the other provincial officials assembled for the dedication of the image that King Nebuchadnezzar had set up, and they stood before it.

⁴Then the herald loudly proclaimed, "This is what you are commanded to do, O peoples, nations and men of every language: ⁵As soon as you hear the sound of the horn, flute, zither, lyre, harp, pipes and all kinds of music, you must fall down and worship the image of gold that King Nebuchadnezzar has set up. ⁶Whoever does not fall down and worship will immediately be thrown into a blazing furnace."

⁷Therefore, as soon as they heard the sound of the horn, flute, zither, lyre, harp and all kinds of music, all the peoples, nations and men of every language fell down and worshiped the image of gold that King Nebuchadnezzar had set up.

⁸At this time some astrologers[b] came forward and denounced the Jews. ⁹They said to King Nebuchadnezzar, "O king, live forever! ¹⁰You have issued a decree, O king, that everyone who hears the sound of the horn, flute, zither, lyre, harp, pipes and all kinds of music must fall down and worship the image of gold, ¹¹and that whoever does not fall down and worship will be thrown into a blazing furnace. ¹²But there are some Jews whom you have set over the affairs of the province of Babylon—Shadrach, Meshach and Abednego—who pay no attention to you, O king. They neither serve your gods nor worship the image of gold you have set up."

¹³Furious with rage, Nebuchadnezzar summoned Shadrach, Meshach and Abednego. So these men were brought before the king, ¹⁴and Nebuchadnezzar said to them, "Is it true, Shadrach, Meshach and Abednego, that you do not

serve my gods or worship the image of gold I have set up? ¹⁵Now when you hear the sound of the horn, flute, zither, lyre, harp, pipes and all kinds of music, if you are ready to fall down and worship the image I made, very good. But if you do not worship it, you will be thrown immediately into a blazing furnace. Then what god will be able to rescue you from my hand?"

¹⁶Shadrach, Meshach and Abednego replied to the king, "O Nebuchadnezzar, we do not need to defend ourselves before you in this matter. ¹⁷If we are thrown into the blazing furnace, the God we serve is able to save us from it, and he will rescue us from your hand, O king. ¹⁸But even if he does not, we want you to know, O king, that we will not serve your gods or worship the image of gold you have set up."

¹⁹Then Nebuchadnezzar was furious with Shadrach, Meshach and Abednego, and his attitude toward them changed. He ordered the furnace heated seven times hotter than usual ²⁰and commanded some of the strongest soldiers in his army to tie up Shadrach, Meshach and Abednego and throw them into the blazing furnace. ²¹So these men, wearing their robes, trousers, turbans and other clothes, were bound and thrown into the blazing furnace. ²²The king's command was so urgent and the furnace so hot that the flames of the fire killed the soldiers who took up Shadrach, Meshach and Abednego, ²³and these three men, firmly tied, fell into the blazing furnace.

²⁴Then King Nebuchadnezzar leaped to his feet in amazement and asked his advisers, "Weren't there three men that we tied up and threw into the fire?"

They replied, "Certainly, O king."

²⁵He said, "Look! I see four men walking around in the fire, unbound and unharmed, and the fourth looks like a son of the gods."

²⁶Nebuchadnezzar then approached the opening of the blazing furnace and shouted, "Shadrach, Meshach and Abednego, servants of the Most High God, come out! Come here!"

So Shadrach, Meshach and Abednego came out of the fire, ²⁷and the satraps, prefects, governors and royal advisers crowded around them. They saw that the fire had not harmed their bodies, nor was a hair of their heads singed; their robes

ᵃ1 Aramaic sixty cubits high and six cubits wide (about 27 meters high and 2.7 meters wide)   ᵇ8 Or Chaldeans were not scorched, and there was no smell of fire on them.

²⁸Then Nebuchadnezzar said, "Praise be to the God of Shadrach, Meshach and Abednego, who has sent his angel and rescued his servants! They trusted in him and defied the king's command and were willing to give up their lives rather than serve or worship any god except their own God. ²⁹Therefore I decree that the people of any nation or language who say anything against the God of Shadrach, Meshach and Abednego be cut into pieces and their houses be turned into piles of rubble, for no other god can save in this way."

³⁰Then the king promoted Shadrach, Meshach and Abednego in the province of Babylon.

Nebuchadnezzar's Dream of a Tree

4 King Nebuchadnezzar,

To the peoples, nations and men of every language, who live in all the world:

May you prosper greatly!

²It is my pleasure to tell you about the miraculous signs and wonders that the Most High God has performed for me.

³How great are his signs,
    how mighty his wonders!
His kingdom is an eternal
        kingdom;
his dominion endures from
        generation to generation.

⁴I, Nebuchadnezzar, was at home in my palace, contented and prosperous. ⁵I had a dream that made me afraid. As I was lying in my bed, the images and visions that passed through my mind terrified me. ⁶So I commanded that all the wise men of Babylon be brought before me to interpret the dream for me. ⁷When the magicians, enchanters, astrologers*ᵃ* and diviners came, I told them the dream, but they could not interpret it for me. ⁸Finally, Daniel came into my presence and I told him the dream. (He is called Belteshazzar, after the name of my god, and the spirit of the holy gods is in him.)

⁹I said, "Belteshazzar, chief of the magicians, I know that the spirit of the holy gods is in you, and no mystery is too difficult for you. Here is my dream; interpret it for me. ¹⁰These are the visions I saw while lying in my bed: I looked, and there before me stood a tree in the middle of the land. Its height was enormous. ¹¹The tree grew large and strong and its top touched the sky; it was visible to the ends of the earth. ¹²Its leaves were beautiful, its fruit abundant, and on it was food for all. Under it the beasts of the field found shelter, and the birds of the air lived in its branches; from it every creature was fed.

¹³"In the visions I saw while lying in my bed, I looked, and there before me was a messenger,*ᵇ* a holy one, coming down from heaven. ¹⁴He called in a loud voice: 'Cut down the tree and trim off its branches; strip off its leaves and scatter its fruit. Let the animals flee from under it and the birds from its branches. ¹⁵But let the stump and its roots, bound with iron and bronze, remain in the ground, in the grass of the field.

" 'Let him be drenched with the dew of heaven, and let him live with the animals among the plants of the earth. ¹⁶Let his mind be changed from that of a man and let him be given the mind of an animal, till seven times*ᶜ* pass by for him.

¹⁷" 'The decision is announced by messengers, the holy ones declare the verdict, so that the living may know that the Most High is sovereign over the kingdoms of men and gives them to anyone he wishes and sets over them the lowliest of men.'

¹⁸"This is the dream that I, King Nebuchadnezzar, had. Now, Belteshazzar, tell me what it means, for none of the wise men in my kingdom can interpret it for me. But you can, because the spirit of the holy gods is in you."

Daniel Interprets the Dream

¹⁹Then Daniel (also called Belteshazzar) was greatly perplexed for a time, and his thoughts terrified him. So the king said, "Belteshazzar, do

---

ᵃ7 Or *Chaldeans*   *ᵇ13* Or *watchman*; also in verses 17 and 23   *ᶜ16* Or *years*; also in verses 23, 25 and 32 not let the dream or its meaning alarm you."

Belteshazzar answered, "My lord, if only the dream applied to your enemies and its meaning to your adversaries! 20The tree you saw, which grew large and strong, with its top touching the sky, visible to the whole earth, 21with beautiful leaves and abundant fruit, providing food for all, giving shelter to the beasts of the field, and having nesting places in its branches for the birds of the air— 22you, O king, are that tree! You have become great and strong; your greatness has grown until it reaches the sky, and your dominion extends to distant parts of the earth.

23"You, O king, saw a messenger, a holy one, coming down from heaven and saying, 'Cut down the tree and destroy it, but leave the stump, bound with iron and bronze, in the grass of the field, while its roots remain in the ground. Let him be drenched with the dew of heaven; let him live like the wild animals, until seven times pass by for him.'

24"This is the interpretation, O king, and this is the decree the Most High has issued against my lord the king: 25You will be driven away from people and will live with the wild animals; you will eat grass like cattle and be drenched with the dew of heaven. Seven times will pass by for you until you acknowledge that the Most High is sovereign over the kingdoms of men and gives them to anyone he wishes. 26The command to leave the stump of the tree with its roots means that your kingdom will be restored to you when you acknowledge that Heaven rules. 27Therefore, O king, be pleased to accept my advice: Renounce your sins by doing what is right, and your wickedness by being kind to the oppressed. It may be that then your prosperity will continue."

The Dream Is Fulfilled

28All this happened to King Nebuchadnezzar. 29Twelve months later, as the king was walking on the roof of the royal palace of Babylon, 30he said, "Is not this the great Babylon I have built as the royal residence, by my mighty power and for the glory of my majesty?"

31The words were still on his lips when a voice came from heaven, "This is what is decreed for you, King Nebuchadnezzar: Your royal authority has been taken from you. 32You will be driven away from people and will live with the wild animals; you will eat grass like cattle. Seven times will pass by for you until you acknowledge that the Most High is sovereign over the kingdoms of men and gives them to anyone he wishes."

33Immediately what had been said about Nebuchadnezzar was fulfilled. He was driven away from people and ate grass like cattle. His body was drenched with the dew of heaven until his hair grew like the feathers of an eagle and his nails like the claws of a bird.

34At the end of that time, I, Nebuchadnezzar, raised my eyes toward heaven, and my sanity was restored. Then I praised the Most High; I honored and glorified him who lives forever.

His dominion is an eternal dominion;
  his kingdom endures from
    generation to generation.
35All the peoples of the earth
  are regarded as nothing.
He does as he pleases
  with the powers of heaven
  and the peoples of the earth.
No one can hold back his hand
  or say to him: "What have you
    done?"

36At the same time that my sanity was restored, my honor and splendor were returned to me for the glory of my kingdom. My advisers and nobles sought me out, and I was restored to my throne and became even greater than before. 37Now I, Nebuchadnezzar, praise and exalt and glorify the King of heaven, because everything he does is right and all his ways are just. And those who walk in pride he is able to humble.

The Writing on the Wall

5 King Belshazzar gave a great banquet for a thousand of his nobles and drank wine with them. 2While Belshazzar was drinking his wine, he gave orders to bring in the gold and silver goblets that

Nebuchadnezzar his father[a] had taken from the temple in Jerusalem, so that the king and his nobles, his wives and his concubines might drink from them. [3]So they brought in the gold goblets that had been taken from the temple of God in Jerusalem, and the king and his nobles, his wives and his concubines drank from them. [4]As they drank the wine, they praised the gods of gold and silver, of bronze, iron, wood and stone.

[5]Suddenly the fingers of a human hand appeared and wrote on the plaster of the wall, near the lampstand in the royal palace. The king watched the hand as it wrote. [6]His face turned pale and he was so frightened that his knees knocked together and his legs gave way.

[7]The king called out for the enchanters, astrologers[b] and diviners to be brought and said to these wise men of Babylon, "Whoever reads this writing and tells me what it means will be clothed in purple and have a gold chain placed around his neck, and he will be made the third highest ruler in the kingdom."

[8]Then all the king's wise men came in, but they could not read the writing or tell the king what it meant. [9]So King Belshazzar became even more terrified and his face grew more pale. His nobles were baffled.

[10]The queen,[c] hearing the voices of the king and his nobles, came into the banquet hall. "O king, live forever!" she said. "Don't be alarmed! Don't look so pale! [11]There is a man in your kingdom who has the spirit of the holy gods in him. In the time of your father he was found to have insight and intelligence and wisdom like that of the gods. King Nebuchadnezzar your father—your father the king, I say—appointed him chief of the magicians, enchanters, astrologers and diviners. [12]This man Daniel, whom the king called Belteshazzar, was found to have a keen mind and knowledge and understanding, and also the ability to interpret dreams, explain riddles and solve difficult problems. Call for Daniel, and he will tell you what the writing means."

[13]So Daniel was brought before the king, and the king said to him, "Are you Daniel, one of the exiles my father the king brought from Judah? [14]I have heard that the spirit of the gods is in you and

that you have insight, intelligence and outstanding wisdom. [15]The wise men and enchanters were brought before me to read this writing and tell me what it means, but they could not explain it. [16]Now I have heard that you are able to give interpretations and to solve difficult problems. If you can read this writing and tell me what it means, you will be clothed in purple and have a gold chain placed around your neck, and you will be made the third highest ruler in the kingdom."

[17]Then Daniel answered the king, "You may keep your gifts for yourself and give your rewards to someone else. Nevertheless, I will read the writing for the king and tell him what it means.

[18]"O king, the Most High God gave your father Nebuchadnezzar sovereignty and greatness and glory and splendor. [19]Because of the high position he gave him, all the peoples and nations and men of every language dreaded and feared him. Those the king wanted to put to death, he put to death; those he wanted to spare, he spared; those he wanted to promote, he promoted; and those he wanted to humble, he humbled. [20]But when his heart became arrogant and hardened with pride, he was deposed from his royal throne and stripped of his glory. [21]He was driven away from people and given the mind of an animal; he lived with the wild donkeys and ate grass like cattle; and his body was drenched with the dew of heaven, until he acknowledged that the Most High God is sovereign over the kingdoms of men and sets over them anyone he wishes.

[22]"But you his son,[d] O Belshazzar, have not humbled yourself, though you knew all this. [23]Instead, you have set yourself up against the Lord of heaven. You had the goblets from his temple brought to you, and you and your nobles, your wives and your concubines drank wine from them. You praised the gods of silver and gold, of bronze, iron, wood and stone, which cannot see or hear or understand. But you did not honor the God who holds in his hand your life and all your ways. [24]Therefore he sent the hand that wrote the inscription.

[25]"This is the inscription that was written:

MENE, MENE, TEKEL, PARSIN[e]

---

a2 Or ancestor; or predecessor; also in verses 11, 13 and 18
c10 Or queen mother   d22 Or descendant; or successor
PARSIN)

b7 Or Chaldeans; also in verse 11
e25 Aramaic UPARSIN (that is, AND

26"This is what these words mean:

> Mene*a*: God has numbered the
> days of your reign and
> brought it to an end.
>
> 27Tekel*b*: You have been weighed
> on the scales and found
> wanting.
>
> 28Peres*c*: Your kingdom is divided
> and given to the Medes and
> Persians."

29Then at Belshazzar's command, Daniel was clothed in purple, a gold chain was placed around his neck, and he was proclaimed the third highest ruler in the kingdom.

30That very night Belshazzar, king of the Babylonians,*d* was slain, 31and Darius the Mede took over the kingdom, at the age of sixty-two.

Daniel in the Den of Lions

6 It pleased Darius to appoint 120 satraps to rule throughout the kingdom, 2with three administrators over them, one of whom was Daniel. The satraps were made accountable to them so that the king might not suffer loss. 3Now Daniel so distinguished himself among the administrators and the satraps by his exceptional qualities that the king planned to set him over the whole kingdom. 4At this, the administrators and the satraps tried to find grounds for charges against Daniel in his conduct of government affairs, but they were unable to do so. They could find no corruption in him, because he was trustworthy and neither corrupt nor negligent. 5Finally these men said, "We will never find any basis for charges against this man Daniel unless it has something to do with the law of his God."

6So the administrators and the satraps went as a group to the king and said: "O King Darius, live forever! 7The royal administrators, prefects, satraps, advisers and governors have all agreed that the king should issue an edict and enforce the decree that anyone who prays to any god or man during the next thirty days, except to you, O king, shall be thrown into the lions' den. 8Now, O king, issue the decree and put it in writing so that it cannot be altered—in accordance with the laws of the Medes and Persians,

which cannot be repealed." 9So King Darius put the decree in writing.

10Now when Daniel learned that the decree had been published, he went home to his upstairs room where the windows opened toward Jerusalem. Three times a day he got down on his knees and prayed, giving thanks to his God, just as he had done before. 11Then these men went as a group and found Daniel praying and asking God for help. 12So they went to the king and spoke to him about his royal decree: "Did you not publish a decree that during the next thirty days anyone who prays to any god or man except to you, O king, would be thrown into the lions' den?"

The king answered, "The decree stands —in accordance with the laws of the Medes and Persians, which cannot be repealed."

13Then they said to the king, "Daniel, who is one of the exiles from Judah, pays no attention to you, O king, or to the decree you put in writing. He still prays three times a day." 14When the king heard this, he was greatly distressed; he was determined to rescue Daniel and made every effort until sundown to save him.

15Then the men went as a group to the king and said to him, "Remember, O king, that according to the law of the Medes and Persians no decree or edict that the king issues can be changed."

16So the king gave the order, and they brought Daniel and threw him into the lions' den. The king said to Daniel, "May your God, whom you serve continually, rescue you!"

17A stone was brought and placed over the mouth of the den, and the king sealed it with his own signet ring and with the rings of his nobles, so that Daniel's situation might not be changed. 18Then the king returned to his palace and spent the night without eating and without any entertainment being brought to him. And he could not sleep.

19At the first light of dawn, the king got up and hurried to the lions' den. 20When he came near the den, he called to Daniel in an anguished voice, "Daniel, servant of the living God, has your God, whom you serve continually, been able to rescue you from the lions?"

21Daniel answered, "O king, live forev-

---

a26 Mene can mean *numbered* or *mina* (a unit of money).   *b27 Tekel* can mean *weighed* or *shekel*.   *c28 Peres* (the singular of *Parsin*) can mean *divided* or *Persia* or *a half mina* or *a half shekel*.   *d30* Or *Chaldeans* er! [22]My God sent his angel, and he shut the mouths of the lions. They have not hurt me, because I was found innocent in his sight. Nor have I ever done any wrong before you, O king."

[23]The king was overjoyed and gave orders to lift Daniel out of the den. And when Daniel was lifted from the den, no wound was found on him, because he had trusted in his God.

[24]At the king's command, the men who had falsely accused Daniel were brought in and thrown into the lions' den, along with their wives and children. And before they reached the floor of the den, the lions overpowered them and crushed all their bones.

[25]Then King Darius wrote to all the peoples, nations and men of every language throughout the land:

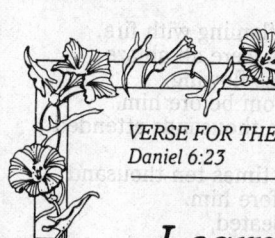

FRIDAY

VERSE FOR THE DAY:
Daniel 6:23

AUTHOR:
Sue Monk Kidd

PASSAGE FOR THE DAY:
Daniel 6:1–23

Learning to Wait on God: Trust

DANIEL worked for a king in a pagan land where it was against the law to pray to God for help. One day Daniel was discovered breaking the law and was cast into a den of lions. A stone was rolled over the entrance, locking him in. There he waited through the long night for deliverance . . . trusting God.

My husband Sandy and I once spent a year in Africa. One afternoon while driving in a game preserve, our car broke down. We knew absolutely nothing about mechanics, and going for help was out of the question when you could easily round a tree and meet a hungry lion. In fact, we had passed a pride of lions a few miles back.

I looked at my watch. The park closed at dark, and given our remote location I figured no one would find us till the next day. So there we were, waiting in our own "den" of lions. Sandy peered under the hood, then climbed back in the car with a shrug. As the sun sank, we grew more and more anxious.

At last I blurted out, "Lord, I'm trusting that you will somehow get us out of this." With that tangible act of trust I actually started to believe God would deliver us. While I watched for our rescue, Sandy looked again at the baffling maze of engine parts. "Well, how did I miss this before? Here's a loose wire," he said. "Just pray I attach it to the right thing!" I prayed, and with the last traces of daylight slipping away, he turned the key and the car sputtered to life.

I've thought about that experience lots of times, those anxious hours we spent waiting for deliverance. But only when we began to nurture the wait with trust did deliverance come. If, like Daniel, you're waiting in some den of helplessness, won't you spend the time as he did—trusting God?

Additional Scripture Readings:
Exodus 14:13–15; 2 Timothy 4:17–18

*Go to page 941 for your next
devotional reading.*

"May you prosper greatly!

26"I issue a decree that in every part of my kingdom people must fear and reverence the God of Daniel.

"For he is the living God
    and he endures forever;
his kingdom will not be destroyed,
    his dominion will never end.
27He rescues and he saves;
    he performs signs and wonders
in the heavens and on the earth.
He has rescued Daniel
    from the power of the lions."

28So Daniel prospered during the reign of Darius and the reign of Cyrus*a* the Persian.

Daniel's Dream of Four Beasts

7 In the first year of Belshazzar king of Babylon, Daniel had a dream, and visions passed through his mind as he was lying on his bed. He wrote down the substance of his dream.

2Daniel said: "In my vision at night I looked, and there before me were the four winds of heaven churning up the great sea. 3Four great beasts, each different from the others, came up out of the sea.

4"The first was like a lion, and it had the wings of an eagle. I watched until its wings were torn off and it was lifted from the ground so that it stood on two feet like a man, and the heart of a man was given to it.

5"And there before me was a second beast, which looked like a bear. It was raised up on one of its sides, and it had three ribs in its mouth between its teeth. It was told, 'Get up and eat your fill of flesh!'

6"After that, I looked, and there before me was another beast, one that looked like a leopard. And on its back it had four wings like those of a bird. This beast had four heads, and it was given authority to rule.

7"After that, in my vision at night I looked, and there before me was a fourth beast—terrifying and frightening and very powerful. It had large iron teeth; it crushed and devoured its victims and trampled underfoot whatever was left. It was different from all the former beasts, and it had ten horns.

8"While I was thinking about the horns, there before me was another horn, a little one, which came up among them; and three of the first horns were uprooted before it. This horn had eyes like the eyes of a man and a mouth that spoke boastfully.

9"As I looked,

"thrones were set in place,
    and the Ancient of Days took his
        seat.
His clothing was as white as snow;
    the hair of his head was white like
        wool.
His throne was flaming with fire,
    and its wheels were all ablaze.
10A river of fire was flowing,
    coming out from before him.
Thousands upon thousands attended
        him;
    ten thousand times ten thousand
        stood before him.
The court was seated,
    and the books were opened.

11"Then I continued to watch because of the boastful words the horn was speaking. I kept looking until the beast was slain and its body destroyed and thrown into the blazing fire. 12(The other beasts had been stripped of their authority, but were allowed to live for a period of time.)

13"In my vision at night I looked, and there before me was one like a son of man, coming with the clouds of heaven. He approached the Ancient of Days and was led into his presence. 14He was given authority, glory and sovereign power; all peoples, nations and men of every language worshiped him. His dominion is an everlasting dominion that will not pass away, and his kingdom is one that will never be destroyed.

The Interpretation of the Dream

15"I, Daniel, was troubled in spirit, and the visions that passed through my mind disturbed me. 16I approached one of those standing there and asked him the true meaning of all this.

"So he told me and gave me the interpretation of these things: 17'The four great beasts are four kingdoms that will rise from the earth. 18But the saints of the Most High will receive the kingdom and will possess it forever—yes, for ever and ever.'

19"Then I wanted to know the true meaning of the fourth beast, which was different from all the others and most terrifying, with its iron teeth and bronze

a28 Or Darius, that is, the reign of Cyrus

claws—the beast that crushed and devoured its victims and trampled underfoot whatever was left. [20]I also wanted to know about the ten horns on its head and about the other horn that came up, before which three of them fell—the horn that looked more imposing than the others and that had eyes and a mouth that spoke boastfully. [21]As I watched, this horn was waging war against the saints and defeating them, [22]until the Ancient of Days came and pronounced judgment in favor of the saints of the Most High, and the time came when they possessed the kingdom.

[23]"He gave me this explanation: 'The fourth beast is a fourth kingdom that will appear on earth. It will be different from all the other kingdoms and will devour the whole earth, trampling it down and crushing it. [24]The ten horns are ten kings who will come from this kingdom. After them another king will arise, different from the earlier ones; he will subdue three kings. [25]He will speak against the Most High and oppress his saints and try to change the set times and the laws. The saints will be handed over to him for a time, times and half a time. [a]

[26]" 'But the court will sit, and his power will be taken away and completely destroyed forever. [27]Then the sovereignty, power and greatness of the kingdoms under the whole heaven will be handed over to the saints, the people of the Most High. His kingdom will be an everlasting kingdom, and all rulers will worship and obey him.'

[28]"This is the end of the matter. I, Daniel, was deeply troubled by my thoughts, and my face turned pale, but I kept the matter to myself."

Daniel's Vision of a Ram and a Goat

8 In the third year of King Belshazzar's reign, I, Daniel, had a vision, after the one that had already appeared to me. [2]In my vision I saw myself in the citadel of Susa in the province of Elam; in the vision I was beside the Ulai Canal. [3]I looked up, and there before me was a ram with two horns, standing beside the canal, and the horns were long. One of the horns was longer than the other but grew up later. [4]I watched the ram as he charged toward the west and the north and the south. No animal could stand against him, and none could rescue from his power. He did as he pleased and became great.

[5]As I was thinking about this, suddenly a goat with a prominent horn between his eyes came from the west, crossing the whole earth without touching the ground. [6]He came toward the two-horned ram I had seen standing beside the canal and charged at him in great rage. [7]I saw him attack the ram furiously, striking the ram and shattering his two horns. The ram was powerless to stand against him; the goat knocked him to the ground and trampled on him, and none could rescue the ram from his power. [8]The goat became very great, but at the height of his power his large horn was broken off, and in its place four prominent horns grew up toward the four winds of heaven.

[9]Out of one of them came another horn, which started small but grew in power to the south and to the east and toward the Beautiful Land. [10]It grew until it reached the host of the heavens, and it threw some of the starry host down to the earth and trampled on them. [11]It set itself up to be as great as the Prince of the host; it took away the daily sacrifice from him, and the place of his sanctuary was brought low. [12]Because of rebellion, the host of the saints [b] and the daily sacrifice were given over to it. It prospered in everything it did, and truth was thrown to the ground.

[13]Then I heard a holy one speaking, and another holy one said to him, "How long will it take for the vision to be fulfilled—the vision concerning the daily sacrifice, the rebellion that causes desolation, and the surrender of the sanctuary and of the host that will be trampled underfoot?"

[14]He said to me, "It will take 2,300 evenings and mornings; then the sanctuary will be reconsecrated."

The Interpretation of the Vision

[15]While I, Daniel, was watching the vision and trying to understand it, there before me stood one who looked like a man. [16]And I heard a man's voice from the Ulai calling, "Gabriel, tell this man the meaning of the vision."

[17]As he came near the place where I was standing, I was terrified and fell prostrate. "Son of man," he said to me, "understand that the vision concerns the time of the end."

[18]While he was speaking to me, I was in

---

[a]25 Or *for a year, two years and half a year*   [b]12 Or *rebellion, the armies*

a deep sleep, with my face to the ground. Then he touched me and raised me to my feet.

¹⁹He said: "I am going to tell you what will happen later in the time of wrath, because the vision concerns the appointed time of the end.ᵃ ²⁰The two-horned ram that you saw represents the kings of Media and Persia. ²¹The shaggy goat is the king of Greece, and the large horn between his eyes is the first king. ²²The four horns that replaced the one that was broken off represent four kingdoms that will emerge from his nation but will not have the same power.

²³"In the latter part of their reign, when rebels have become completely wicked, a stern-faced king, a master of intrigue, will arise. ²⁴He will become very strong, but not by his own power. He will cause astounding devastation and will succeed in whatever he does. He will destroy the mighty men and the holy people. ²⁵He will cause deceit to prosper, and he will consider himself superior. When they feel secure, he will destroy many and take his stand against the Prince of princes. Yet he will be destroyed, but not by human power.

²⁶"The vision of the evenings and mornings that has been given you is true, but seal up the vision, for it concerns the distant future."

²⁷I, Daniel, was exhausted and lay ill for several days. Then I got up and went about the king's business. I was appalled by the vision; it was beyond understanding.

Daniel's Prayer

9 In the first year of Darius son of Xerxesᵇ (a Mede by descent), who was made ruler over the Babylonianᶜ kingdom— ²in the first year of his reign, I, Daniel, understood from the Scriptures, according to the word of the LORD given to Jeremiah the prophet, that the desolation of Jerusalem would last seventy years. ³So I turned to the Lord God and pleaded with him in prayer and petition, in fasting, and in sackcloth and ashes.

⁴I prayed to the LORD my God and confessed:

"O Lord, the great and awesome God, who keeps his covenant of love with all who love him and obey his commands, ⁵we have sinned and done wrong. We have been wicked and have rebelled; we have turned away from your commands and laws. ⁶We have not listened to your servants the prophets, who spoke in your name to our kings, our princes and our fathers, and to all the people of the land.

⁷"Lord, you are righteous, but this day we are covered with shame—the men of Judah and people of Jerusalem and all Israel, both near and far, in all the countries where you have scattered us because of our unfaithfulness to you. ⁸O LORD, we and our kings, our princes and our fathers are covered with shame because we have sinned against you. ⁹The Lord our God is merciful and forgiving, even though we have rebelled against him; ¹⁰we have not obeyed the LORD our God or kept the laws he gave us through his servants the prophets. ¹¹All Israel has transgressed your law and turned away, refusing to obey you.

"Therefore the curses and sworn judgments written in the Law of Moses, the servant of God, have been poured out on us, because we have sinned against you. ¹²You have fulfilled the words spoken against us and against our rulers by bringing upon us great disaster. Under the whole heaven nothing has ever been done like what has been done to Jerusalem. ¹³Just as it is written in the Law of Moses, all this disaster has come upon us, yet we have not sought the favor of the LORD our God by turning from our sins and giving attention to your truth. ¹⁴The LORD did not hesitate to bring the disaster upon us, for the LORD our God is righteous in everything he does; yet we have not obeyed him.

¹⁵"Now, O Lord our God, who brought your people out of Egypt with a mighty hand and who made for yourself a name that endures to this day, we have sinned, we have done wrong. ¹⁶O Lord, in keeping with all your righteous acts, turn away your anger and your wrath from Jerusalem, your city, your holy hill. Our sins and the iniquities of our fathers have made Jerusalem and your

---

ᵃ19 Or *because the end will be at the appointed time*   ᵇ1 Hebrew *Ahasuerus*   ᶜ1 Or *Chaldean*

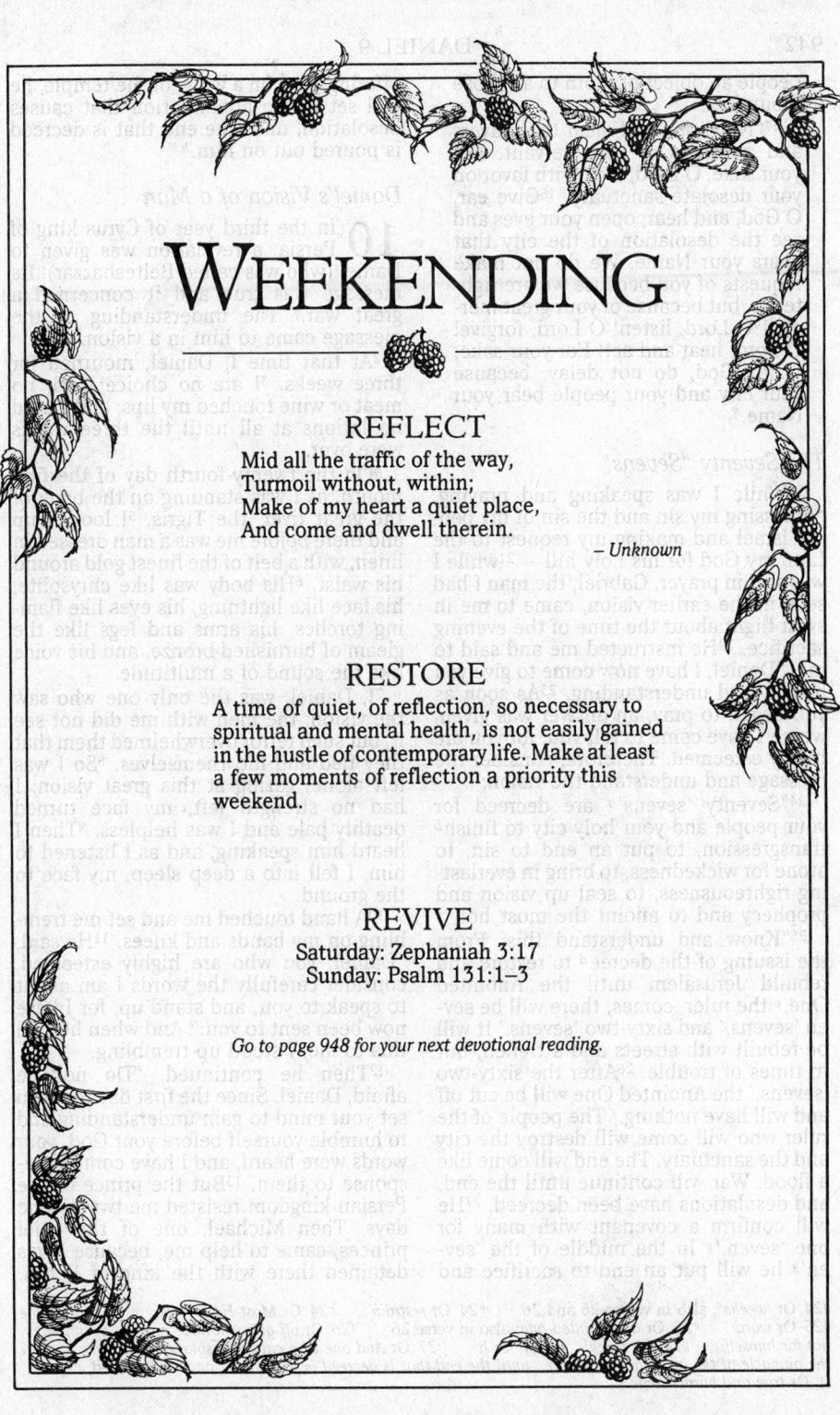

WEEKENDING

REFLECT

Mid all the traffic of the way,
Turmoil without, within;
Make of my heart a quiet place,
And come and dwell therein.

— *Unknown*

RESTORE

A time of quiet, of reflection, so necessary to
spiritual and mental health, is not easily gained
in the hustle of contemporary life. Make at least
a few moments of reflection a priority this
weekend.

REVIVE

Saturday: Zephaniah 3:17
Sunday: Psalm 131:1–3

Go to page 948 for your next devotional reading.

people an object of scorn to all those around us.

¹⁷"Now, our God, hear the prayers and petitions of your servant. For your sake, O Lord, look with favor on your desolate sanctuary. ¹⁸Give ear, O God, and hear; open your eyes and see the desolation of the city that bears your Name. We do not make requests of you because we are righteous, but because of your great mercy. ¹⁹O Lord, listen! O Lord, forgive! O Lord, hear and act! For your sake, O my God, do not delay, because your city and your people bear your Name."

The Seventy "Sevens"

²⁰While I was speaking and praying, confessing my sin and the sin of my people Israel and making my request to the Lord my God for his holy hill— ²¹while I was still in prayer, Gabriel, the man I had seen in the earlier vision, came to me in swift flight about the time of the evening sacrifice. ²²He instructed me and said to me, "Daniel, I have now come to give you insight and understanding. ²³As soon as you began to pray, an answer was given, which I have come to tell you, for you are highly esteemed. Therefore, consider the message and understand the vision:

²⁴"Seventy 'sevens'^a are decreed for your people and your holy city to finish^b transgression, to put an end to sin, to atone for wickedness, to bring in everlasting righteousness, to seal up vision and prophecy and to anoint the most holy.^c

²⁵"Know and understand this: From the issuing of the decree^d to restore and rebuild Jerusalem until the Anointed One,^e the ruler, comes, there will be seven 'sevens,' and sixty-two 'sevens.' It will be rebuilt with streets and a trench, but in times of trouble. ²⁶After the sixty-two 'sevens,' the Anointed One will be cut off and will have nothing.^f The people of the ruler who will come will destroy the city and the sanctuary. The end will come like a flood: War will continue until the end, and desolations have been decreed. ²⁷He will confirm a covenant with many for one 'seven.'^g In the middle of the 'seven'^g he will put an end to sacrifice and

offering. And on a wing ,of the temple, he will set up an abomination that causes desolation, until the end that is decreed is poured out on him.^h"ⁱ

Daniel's Vision of a Man

10 In the third year of Cyrus king of Persia, a revelation was given to Daniel (who was called Belteshazzar). Its message was true and it concerned a great war.^j The understanding of the message came to him in a vision.

²At that time I, Daniel, mourned for three weeks. ³I ate no choice food; no meat or wine touched my lips; and I used no lotions at all until the three weeks were over.

⁴On the twenty-fourth day of the first month, as I was standing on the bank of the great river, the Tigris, ⁵I looked up and there before me was a man dressed in linen, with a belt of the finest gold around his waist. ⁶His body was like chrysolite, his face like lightning, his eyes like flaming torches, his arms and legs like the gleam of burnished bronze, and his voice like the sound of a multitude.

⁷I, Daniel, was the only one who saw the vision; the men with me did not see it, but such terror overwhelmed them that they fled and hid themselves. ⁸So I was left alone, gazing at this great vision; I had no strength left, my face turned deathly pale and I was helpless. ⁹Then I heard him speaking, and as I listened to him, I fell into a deep sleep, my face to the ground.

¹⁰A hand touched me and set me trembling on my hands and knees. ¹¹He said, "Daniel, you who are highly esteemed, consider carefully the words I am about to speak to you, and stand up, for I have now been sent to you." And when he said this to me, I stood up trembling.

¹²Then he continued, "Do not be afraid, Daniel. Since the first day that you set your mind to gain understanding and to humble yourself before your God, your words were heard, and I have come in response to them. ¹³But the prince of the Persian kingdom resisted me twenty-one days. Then Michael, one of the chief princes, came to help me, because I was detained there with the king of Persia.

---

^a24 Or 'weeks'; also in verses 25 and 26   ^b24 Or restrain   ^c24 Or Most Holy Place; or most holy One ^d25 Or word   ^e25 Or an anointed one; also in verse 26   ^f26 Or off and will have no one; or off, but not for himself   ^g27 Or 'week'   ^h27 Or it   ⁱ27 Or And one who causes desolation will come upon the pinnacle of the abominable ,temple,, until the end that is decreed is poured out on the desolated ,city, ^j1 Or true and burdensome

¹⁴Now I have come to explain to you what will happen to your people in the future, for the vision concerns a time yet to come."

¹⁵While he was saying this to me, I bowed with my face toward the ground and was speechless. ¹⁶Then one who looked like a manᵃ touched my lips, and I opened my mouth and began to speak. I said to the one standing before me, "I am overcome with anguish because of the vision, my lord, and I am helpless. ¹⁷How can I, your servant, talk with you, my lord? My strength is gone and I can hardly breathe."

¹⁸Again the one who looked like a man touched me and gave me strength. ¹⁹"Do not be afraid, O man highly esteemed," he said. "Peace! Be strong now; be strong."

When he spoke to me, I was strengthened and said, "Speak, my lord, since you have given me strength."

²⁰So he said, "Do you know why I have come to you? Soon I will return to fight against the prince of Persia, and when I go, the prince of Greece will come; ²¹but first I will tell you what is written in the Book of Truth. (No one supports me against them except Michael, your

11 prince. ¹And in the first year of Darius the Mede, I took my stand to support and protect him.)

The Kings of the South and the North

²"Now then, I tell you the truth: Three more kings will appear in Persia, and then a fourth, who will be far richer than all the others. When he has gained power by his wealth, he will stir up everyone against the kingdom of Greece. ³Then a mighty king will appear, who will rule with great power and do as he pleases. ⁴After he has appeared, his empire will be broken up and parceled out toward the four winds of heaven. It will not go to his descendants, nor will it have the power he exercised, because his empire will be uprooted and given to others.

⁵"The king of the South will become strong, but one of his commanders will become even stronger than he and will rule his own kingdom with great power. ⁶After some years, they will become allies. The daughter of the king of the

South will go to the king of the North to make an alliance, but she will not retain her power, and he and his powerᵇ will not last. In those days she will be handed over, together with her royal escort and her fatherᶜ and the one who supported her.

⁷"One from her family line will arise to take her place. He will attack the forces of the king of the North and enter his fortress; he will fight against them and be victorious. ⁸He will also seize their gods, their metal images and their valuable articles of silver and gold and carry them off to Egypt. For some years he will leave the king of the North alone. ⁹Then the king of the North will invade the realm of the king of the South but will retreat to his own country. ¹⁰His sons will prepare for war and assemble a great army, which will sweep on like an irresistible flood and carry the battle as far as his fortress.

¹¹"Then the king of the South will march out in a rage and fight against the king of the North, who will raise a large army, but it will be defeated. ¹²When the army is carried off, the king of the South will be filled with pride and will slaughter many thousands, yet he will not remain triumphant. ¹³For the king of the North will muster another army, larger than the first; and after several years, he will advance with a huge army fully equipped.

¹⁴"In those times many will rise against the king of the South. The violent men among your own people will rebel in fulfillment of the vision, but without success. ¹⁵Then the king of the North will come and build up siege ramps and will capture a fortified city. The forces of the South will be powerless to resist; even their best troops will not have the strength to stand. ¹⁶The invader will do as he pleases; no one will be able to stand against him. He will establish himself in the Beautiful Land and will have the power to destroy it. ¹⁷He will determine to come with the might of his entire kingdom and will make an alliance with the king of the South. And he will give him a daughter in marriage in order to overthrow the kingdom, but his plansᵈ will not succeed or help him. ¹⁸Then he will turn his attention to the coastlands and will take many of them, but a commander will put an end to his insolence and will

---

ᵃ16 Most manuscripts of the Masoretic Text; one manuscript of the Masoretic Text, Dead Sea Scrolls and Septuagint *Then something that looked like a man's hand*   ᵇ6 Or *offspring*   ᶜ6 Or *child* (see Vulgate and Syriac)   ᵈ17 Or *but she* turn his insolence back upon him. ¹⁹After this, he will turn back toward the fortresses of his own country but will stumble and fall, to be seen no more.

²⁰"His successor will send out a tax collector to maintain the royal splendor. In a few years, however, he will be destroyed, yet not in anger or in battle.

²¹"He will be succeeded by a contemptible person who has not been given the honor of royalty. He will invade the kingdom when its people feel secure, and he will seize it through intrigue. ²²Then an overwhelming army will be swept away before him; both it and a prince of the covenant will be destroyed. ²³After coming to an agreement with him, he will act deceitfully, and with only a few people he will rise to power. ²⁴When the richest provinces feel secure, he will invade them and will achieve what neither his fathers nor his forefathers did. He will distribute plunder, loot and wealth among his followers. He will plot the overthrow of fortresses—but only for a time.

²⁵"With a large army he will stir up his strength and courage against the king of the South. The king of the South will wage war with a large and very powerful army, but he will not be able to stand because of the plots devised against him. ²⁶Those who eat from the king's provisions will try to destroy him; his army will be swept away, and many will fall in battle. ²⁷The two kings, with their hearts bent on evil, will sit at the same table and lie to each other, but to no avail, because an end will still come at the appointed time. ²⁸The king of the North will return to his own country with great wealth, but his heart will be set against the holy covenant. He will take action against it and then return to his own country.

²⁹"At the appointed time he will invade the South again, but this time the outcome will be different from what it was before. ³⁰Ships of the western coastlands[a] will oppose him, and he will lose heart. Then he will turn back and vent his fury against the holy covenant. He will return and show favor to those who forsake the holy covenant.

³¹"His armed forces will rise up to desecrate the temple fortress and will abolish the daily sacrifice. Then they will set up the abomination that causes desolation. ³²With flattery he will corrupt those who

have violated the covenant, but the people who know their God will firmly resist him.

³³"Those who are wise will instruct many, though for a time they will fall by the sword or be burned or captured or plundered. ³⁴When they fall, they will receive a little help, and many who are not sincere will join them. ³⁵Some of the wise will stumble, so that they may be refined, purified and made spotless until the time of the end, for it will still come at the appointed time.

The King Who Exalts Himself

³⁶"The king will do as he pleases. He will exalt and magnify himself above every god and will say unheard-of things against the God of gods. He will be successful until the time of wrath is completed, for what has been determined must take place. ³⁷He will show no regard for the gods of his fathers or for the one desired by women, nor will he regard any god, but will exalt himself above them all. ³⁸Instead of them, he will honor a god of fortresses; a god unknown to his fathers he will honor with gold and silver, with precious stones and costly gifts. ³⁹He will attack the mightiest fortresses with the help of a foreign god and will greatly honor those who acknowledge him. He will make them rulers over many people and will distribute the land at a price.[b]

⁴⁰"At the time of the end the king of the South will engage him in battle, and the king of the North will storm out against him with chariots and cavalry and a great fleet of ships. He will invade many countries and sweep through them like a flood. ⁴¹He will also invade the Beautiful Land. Many countries will fall, but Edom, Moab and the leaders of Ammon will be delivered from his hand. ⁴²He will extend his power over many countries; Egypt will not escape. ⁴³He will gain control of the treasures of gold and silver and all the riches of Egypt, with the Libyans and Nubians in submission. ⁴⁴But reports from the east and the north will alarm him, and he will set out in a great rage to destroy and annihilate many. ⁴⁵He will pitch his royal tents between the seas at[c] the beautiful holy mountain. Yet he will come to his end, and no one will help him.

---

[a]30 Hebrew of Kittim   [b]39 Or land for a reward   [c]45 Or the sea and

The End Times

12 "At that time Michael, the great prince who protects your people, will arise. There will be a time of distress such as has not happened from the beginning of nations until then. But at that time your people—everyone whose name is found written in the book—will be delivered. ²Multitudes who sleep in the dust of the earth will awake: some to everlasting life, others to shame and everlasting contempt. ³Those who are wise*a* will shine like the brightness of the heavens, and those who lead many to righteousness, like the stars for ever and ever. ⁴But you, Daniel, close up and seal the words of the scroll until the time of the end. Many will go here and there to increase knowledge."

⁵Then I, Daniel, looked, and there before me stood two others, one on this bank of the river and one on the opposite bank. ⁶One of them said to the man clothed in linen, who was above the waters of the river, "How long will it be before these astonishing things are fulfilled?"

⁷The man clothed in linen, who was above the waters of the river, lifted his right hand and his left hand toward heaven, and I heard him swear by him who lives forever, saying, "It will be for a time, times and half a time.*b* When the power of the holy people has been finally broken, all these things will be completed."

⁸I heard, but I did not understand. So I asked, "My lord, what will the outcome of all this be?"

⁹He replied, "Go your way, Daniel, because the words are closed up and sealed until the time of the end. ¹⁰Many will be purified, made spotless and refined, but the wicked will continue to be wicked. None of the wicked will understand, but those who are wise will understand.

¹¹"From the time that the daily sacrifice is abolished and the abomination that causes desolation is set up, there will be 1,290 days. ¹²Blessed is the one who waits for and reaches the end of the 1,335 days.

¹³"As for you, go your way till the end. You will rest, and then at the end of the days you will rise to receive your allotted inheritance."

---

a3 Or *who impart wisdom*   *b7* Or *a year, two years and half a year*

*HOSEA prophesies during the last
days of Israel (see 2 Kings
14:23–17:41), focusing on her sin of
spiritual adultery (that is, idolatry).
He warns them that God will punish
them unless they change their ways.
But he also reminds them of God's incredible love, pleading with them to
repent. As you read this book, think of
God's love in sending his Son Jesus to
die for you, in spite of your sins. Repent
of your unfaithfulness to the Lord and
turn to him.*

HOSEA

1 The word of the LORD that came to
Hosea son of Beeri during the reigns
of Uzziah, Jotham, Ahaz and Hezekiah,
kings of Judah, and during the reign of
Jeroboam son of Jehoash[a] king of Israel:

Hosea's Wife and Children

2When the LORD began to speak
through Hosea, the LORD said to him, "Go,
take to yourself an adulterous wife and
children of unfaithfulness, because the
land is guilty of the vilest adultery in de-
parting from the LORD." 3So he married
Gomer daughter of Diblaim, and she conceived and bore him a son.

4Then the LORD said to Hosea, "Call
him Jezreel, because I will soon punish
the house of Jehu for the massacre at Jezreel, and I will put an end to the kingdom
of Israel. 5In that day I will break Israel's
bow in the Valley of Jezreel."

6Gomer conceived again and gave birth
to a daughter. Then the LORD said to Hosea, "Call her Lo-Ruhamah,[b] for I will no
longer show love to the house of Israel,
that I should at all forgive them. 7Yet I
will show love to the house of Judah; and

---

a1 Hebrew *Joash*, a variant of *Jehoash*   b6 *Lo-Ruhamah* means *not loved.*

I will save them—not by bow, sword or battle, or by horses and horsemen, but by the LORD their God."

⁸After she had weaned Lo-Ruhamah, Gomer had another son. ⁹Then the LORD said, "Call him Lo-Ammi,ᵃ for you are not my people, and I am not your God.

¹⁰Yet the Israelites will be like the sand on the seashore, which cannot be measured or counted. In the place where it was said to them, 'You are not my people,' they will be called 'sons of the living God.' ¹¹The people of Judah and the people of Israel will be reunited, and they will appoint one leader and will come up out of the land, for great will be the day of Jezreel.

2 "Say of your brothers, 'My people,' and of your sisters, 'My loved one.'

Israel Punished and Restored

²"Rebuke your mother, rebuke her,
    for she is not my wife,
    and I am not her husband.
Let her remove the adulterous look
        from her face
    and the unfaithfulness from
        between her breasts.
³Otherwise I will strip her naked
    and make her as bare as on the day
        she was born;
I will make her like a desert,
    turn her into a parched land,
    and slay her with thirst.
⁴I will not show my love to her
        children,
    because they are the children of
        adultery.
⁵Their mother has been unfaithful
    and has conceived them in
        disgrace.
She said, 'I will go after my lovers,
    who give me my food and my
        water,
    my wool and my linen, my oil and
        my drink.'
⁶Therefore I will block her path with
        thornbushes;
    I will wall her in so that she cannot
        find her way.
⁷She will chase after her lovers but not
        catch them;
    she will look for them but not find
        them.
Then she will say,
    'I will go back to my husband as at
        first,
    for then I was better off than now.'

⁸She has not acknowledged that I was
        the one
    who gave her the grain, the new
        wine and oil,
    who lavished on her the silver and
        gold—
    which they used for Baal.

⁹"Therefore I will take away my grain
        when it ripens,
    and my new wine when it is ready.
I will take back my wool and my
        linen,
    intended to cover her nakedness.
¹⁰So now I will expose her lewdness
    before the eyes of her lovers;
    no one will take her out of my
        hands.
¹¹I will stop all her celebrations:
    her yearly festivals, her New Moons,
    her Sabbath days—all her
        appointed feasts.
¹²I will ruin her vines and her fig trees,
    which she said were her pay from
        her lovers;
I will make them a thicket,
    and wild animals will devour them.
¹³I will punish her for the days
    she burned incense to the Baals;
    she decked herself with rings and
        jewelry,
    and went after her lovers,
    but me she forgot,"
                            declares the LORD.

¹⁴"Therefore I am now going to allure
        her;
    I will lead her into the desert
    and speak tenderly to her.
¹⁵There I will give her back her
        vineyards,
    and will make the Valley of Achorᵇ
        a door of hope.
There she will singᶜ as in the days of
        her youth,
    as in the day she came up out of
        Egypt.

¹⁶"In that day," declares the LORD,
    "you will call me 'my husband';
    you will no longer call me 'my
        master.'ᵈ'
¹⁷I will remove the names of the Baals
        from her lips;
    no longer will their names be
        invoked.
¹⁸In that day I will make a covenant for
        them

ᵃ9 Lo-Ammi means not my people.   ᵇ15 Achor means trouble.   ᶜ15 Or respond   ᵈ16 Hebrew baal

VERSE FOR THE DAY:
Hosea 2:16

AUTHOR:
Hannah Whitall Smith

PASSAGE FOR THE DAY:
Hosea 2:14–23

Serving by Loving

PAUL entreats us: "Stand firm, then, and do not let yourselves be burdened again by a yoke of slavery" (Galatians 5:1).

Our freedom from bondage to sin can be illustrated this way. It is as if a woman had a male employer; she is paid for her work in weekly wages and is under the rules of her employer, whom she had tried to please but toward whom her service had been one of obligation only. Finally, however, the employer falls in love with her, and she becomes his bride and shares all his fortunes. At once the whole spirit of her service is changed. She may perhaps continue to do the same things that she did before, but she does them now from a different motive. The old sense of duty is lost in the new sense of love. The cold word "employer" is transformed into the loving word "husband."

> "In that day," declares the LORD,
> "You will call me 'my husband';
> you will no longer call me 'my master' "
> (Hosea 2:16).

But imagine this bride beginning after a while to look back on her low estate and to be so overwhelmed by the retrospect as to feel unworthy of union with her husband, and consequently to lose the inward sense of this union. Who can doubt that very soon the old sense of working for wages would drive out the new sense of working for love, and in spirit the old name, "my employer," would take the place of the new name, "my husband"?

We exclaim at the folly of such a course. But isn't this just what happens to many Christians!

We are not slaves but the children of God and therefore his heirs; and our possessions come to us not by working for them but by inheritance from our Father.

Additional Scripture Readings:
Romans 8:12–17; Colossians 1:10–13

Go to page 955 for your next devotional reading.

with the beasts of the field and the
    birds of the air
and the creatures that move along
    the ground.
Bow and sword and battle
    I will abolish from the land,
    so that all may lie down in safety.
¹⁹I will betroth you to me forever;
    I will betroth you in ᵃ righteousness
        and justice,
    in ᵇ love and compassion.
²⁰I will betroth you in faithfulness,
    and you will acknowledge the LORD.

²¹"In that day I will respond,"
    declares the LORD—
    "I will respond to the skies,
        and they will respond to the earth;
²²and the earth will respond to the
        grain,
    the new wine and oil,
        and they will respond to Jezreel. ᶜ
²³I will plant her for myself in the land;
    I will show my love to the one I
        called 'Not my loved one.ᵈ'
    I will say to those called 'Not my
        people,ᵉ' 'You are my people';
    and they will say, 'You are my
        God.' "

Hosea's Reconciliation With His Wife

3 The LORD said to me, "Go, show your
love to your wife again, though she is
loved by another and is an adulteress.
Love her as the LORD loves the Israelites,
though they turn to other gods and love
the sacred raisin cakes."

²So I bought her for fifteen shekelsᶠ of
silver and about a homer and a lethekᵍ of
barley. ³Then I told her, "You are to live
withʰ me many days; you must not be a
prostitute or be intimate with any man,
and I will live withʰ you."

⁴For the Israelites will live many days
without king or prince, without sacrifice
or sacred stones, without ephod or idol.
⁵Afterward the Israelites will return and
seek the LORD their God and David their
king. They will come trembling to the
LORD and to his blessings in the last days.

The Charge Against Israel

4 Hear the word of the LORD, you
Israelites,

because the LORD has a charge to
    bring
against you who live in the land:
    "There is no faithfulness, no love,
    no acknowledgment of God in the
        land.
²There is only cursing,ⁱ lying and
        murder,
    stealing and adultery;
they break all bounds,
    and bloodshed follows bloodshed.
³Because of this the land mourns,ʲ
    and all who live in it waste away;
the beasts of the field and the birds
        of the air
    and the fish of the sea are dying.

⁴"But let no man bring a charge,
    let no man accuse another,
for your people are like those
    who bring charges against a priest.
⁵You stumble day and night,
    and the prophets stumble with you.
So I will destroy your mother—
⁶   my people are destroyed from lack
        of knowledge.

"Because you have rejected
        knowledge,
    I also reject you as my priests;
because you have ignored the law of
        your God,
    I also will ignore your children.
⁷The more the priests increased,
    the more they sinned against me;
    they exchangedᵏ theirˡ Glory for
        something disgraceful.
⁸They feed on the sins of my people
    and relish their wickedness.
⁹And it will be: Like people, like
        priests.
    I will punish both of them for their
        ways
    and repay them for their deeds.

¹⁰"They will eat but not have enough;
    they will engage in prostitution but
        not increase,
because they have deserted the LORD
    to give themselves ¹¹to prostitution,
to old wine and new,
    which take away the understanding
¹²of my people.
They consult a wooden idol
    and are answered by a stick of
        wood.

ᵃ19 Or with; also in verse 20   ᵇ19 Or with   ᶜ22 Jezreel means God plants.   ᵈ23 Hebrew
Lo-Ruhamah   ᵉ23 Hebrew Lo-Ammi   ᶠ2 That is, about 6 ounces (about 170 grams)   ᵍ2 That is,
probably about 10 bushels (about 330 liters)   ʰ3 Or wait for   ⁱ2 That is, to pronounce a curse upon
ʲ3 Or dries up   ᵏ7 Syriac and an ancient Hebrew scribal tradition; Masoretic Text I will exchange
ˡ7 Masoretic Text; an ancient Hebrew scribal tradition my

A spirit of prostitution leads them
  astray;
  they are unfaithful to their God.
¹³They sacrifice on the mountaintops
  and burn offerings on the hills,
under oak, poplar and terebinth,
  where the shade is pleasant.
Therefore your daughters turn to
  prostitution
and your daughters-in-law to
  adultery.

¹⁴"I will not punish your daughters
  when they turn to prostitution,
nor your daughters-in-law
  when they commit adultery,
because the men themselves consort
  with harlots
and sacrifice with shrine
  prostitutes—
a people without understanding will
  come to ruin!

¹⁵"Though you commit adultery,
  O Israel,
  let not Judah become guilty.

"Do not go to Gilgal;
  do not go up to Beth Aven.ᵃ
  And do not swear, 'As surely as the
  LORD lives!'
¹⁶The Israelites are stubborn,
  like a stubborn heifer.
How then can the LORD pasture them
  like lambs in a meadow?
¹⁷Ephraim is joined to idols;
  leave him alone!
¹⁸Even when their drinks are gone,
  they continue their prostitution;
  their rulers dearly love shameful
  ways.
¹⁹A whirlwind will sweep them away,
  and their sacrifices will bring them
  shame.

Judgment Against Israel

5 "Hear this, you priests!
  Pay attention, you Israelites!
Listen, O royal house!
  This judgment is against you:
You have been a snare at Mizpah,
  a net spread out on Tabor.
²The rebels are deep in slaughter.
  I will discipline all of them.
³I know all about Ephraim;
  Israel is not hidden from me.
Ephraim, you have now turned to
  prostitution;
  Israel is corrupt.

⁴"Their deeds do not permit them
  to return to their God.
A spirit of prostitution is in their
  heart;
  they do not acknowledge the LORD.
⁵Israel's arrogance testifies against
  them;
  the Israelites, even Ephraim,
  stumble in their sin;
  Judah also stumbles with them.
⁶When they go with their flocks and
  herds
  to seek the LORD,
  they will not find him;
  he has withdrawn himself from
  them.
⁷They are unfaithful to the LORD;
  they give birth to illegitimate
  children.
Now their New Moon festivals
  will devour them and their
  fields.

⁸"Sound the trumpet in Gibeah,
  the horn in Ramah.
Raise the battle cry in Beth Avenᵃ;
  lead on, O Benjamin.
⁹Ephraim will be laid waste
  on the day of reckoning.
Among the tribes of Israel
  I proclaim what is certain.
¹⁰Judah's leaders are like those
  who move boundary stones.
I will pour out my wrath on them
  like a flood of water.
¹¹Ephraim is oppressed,
  trampled in judgment,
  intent on pursuing idols.ᵇ
¹²I am like a moth to Ephraim,
  like rot to the people of Judah.

¹³"When Ephraim saw his sickness,
  and Judah his sores,
then Ephraim turned to Assyria,
  and sent to the great king for
  help.
But he is not able to cure you,
  not able to heal your sores.
¹⁴For I will be like a lion to Ephraim,
  like a great lion to Judah.
I will tear them to pieces and go
  away;
  I will carry them off, with no one to
  rescue them.
¹⁵Then I will go back to my place
  until they admit their guilt.
And they will seek my face;

ᵃ15,8 Beth Aven means house of wickedness (a name for Bethel, which means house of God).   ᵇ11 The
meaning of the Hebrew for this word is uncertain.

in their misery they will earnestly
  seek me."

Israel Unrepentant

6 "Come, let us return to the LORD.
He has torn us to pieces
  but he will heal us;
he has injured us
  but he will bind up our wounds.
²After two days he will revive us;
  on the third day he will restore us,
  that we may live in his presence.
³Let us acknowledge the LORD;
  let us press on to acknowledge him.
As surely as the sun rises,
  he will appear;
he will come to us like the winter
    rains,
  like the spring rains that water the
    earth."

⁴"What can I do with you, Ephraim?
  What can I do with you, Judah?
Your love is like the morning mist,
  like the early dew that disappears.
⁵Therefore I cut you in pieces with my
    prophets,
  I killed you with the words of my
    mouth;
  my judgments flashed like lightning
    upon you.
⁶For I desire mercy, not sacrifice,
  and acknowledgment of God rather
    than burnt offerings.
⁷Like Adam,ᵃ they have broken the
    covenant—
  they were unfaithful to me there.
⁸Gilead is a city of wicked men,
  stained with footprints of blood.
⁹As marauders lie in ambush for a
    man,
  so do bands of priests;
they murder on the road to Shechem,
  committing shameful crimes.
¹⁰I have seen a horrible thing
  in the house of Israel.
There Ephraim is given to prostitution
  and Israel is defiled.

¹¹"Also for you, Judah,
  a harvest is appointed.

"Whenever I would restore the
    fortunes of my people,
7 ¹whenever I would heal Israel,
  the sins of Ephraim are exposed
  and the crimes of Samaria revealed.
They practice deceit,
  thieves break into houses,

bandits rob in the streets;
²but they do not realize
  that I remember all their evil deeds.
Their sins engulf them;
  they are always before me.

³"They delight the king with their
    wickedness,
  the princes with their lies.
⁴They are all adulterers,
  burning like an oven
whose fire the baker need not stir
  from the kneading of the dough till
    it rises.
⁵On the day of the festival of our king
  the princes become inflamed with
    wine,
  and he joins hands with the
    mockers.
⁶Their hearts are like an oven;
  they approach him with intrigue.
Their passion smolders all night;
  in the morning it blazes like a
    flaming fire.
⁷All of them are hot as an oven;
  they devour their rulers.
All their kings fall,
  and none of them calls on me.

⁸"Ephraim mixes with the nations;
  Ephraim is a flat cake not turned
    over.
⁹Foreigners sap his strength,
  but he does not realize it.
His hair is sprinkled with gray,
  but he does not notice.
¹⁰Israel's arrogance testifies against
    him,
  but despite all this
he does not return to the LORD his
    God
  or search for him.

¹¹"Ephraim is like a dove,
  easily deceived and senseless—
now calling to Egypt,
  now turning to Assyria.
¹²When they go, I will throw my net
    over them;
  I will pull them down like birds of
    the air.
When I hear them flocking together,
  I will catch them.
¹³Woe to them,
  because they have strayed from me!
Destruction to them,
  because they have rebelled against
    me!
I long to redeem them

ᵃ7 Or *As at Adam*; or *Like men*

but they speak lies against me.
¹⁴They do not cry out to me from their
hearts
but wail upon their beds.
They gather together*a* for grain and
new wine
but turn away from me.
¹⁵I trained them and strengthened
them,
but they plot evil against me.
¹⁶They do not turn to the Most High;
they are like a faulty bow.
Their leaders will fall by the sword
because of their insolent words.
For this they will be ridiculed
in the land of Egypt.

Israel to Reap the Whirlwind

8 "Put the trumpet to your lips!
An eagle is over the house of the
LORD
because the people have broken my
covenant
and rebelled against my law.
²Israel cries out to me,
'O our God, we acknowledge you!'
³But Israel has rejected what is good;
an enemy will pursue him.
⁴They set up kings without my
consent;
they choose princes without my
approval.
With their silver and gold
they make idols for themselves
to their own destruction.
⁵Throw out your calf-idol, O Samaria!
My anger burns against them.
How long will they be incapable of
purity?
6 They are from Israel!
This calf—a craftsman has made it;
it is not God.
It will be broken in pieces,
that calf of Samaria.

⁷"They sow the wind
and reap the whirlwind.
The stalk has no head;
it will produce no flour.
Were it to yield grain,
foreigners would swallow it up.
⁸Israel is swallowed up;
now she is among the nations
like a worthless thing.
⁹For they have gone up to Assyria
like a wild donkey wandering alone.
Ephraim has sold herself to lovers.

¹⁰Although they have sold themselves
among the nations,
I will now gather them together.
They will begin to waste away
under the oppression of the mighty
king.
¹¹"Though Ephraim built many altars
for sin offerings,
these have become altars for
sinning.
¹²I wrote for them the many things of
my law,
but they regarded them as
something alien.
¹³They offer sacrifices given to me
and they eat the meat,
but the LORD is not pleased with
them.
Now he will remember their
wickedness
and punish their sins:
They will return to Egypt.
¹⁴Israel has forgotten his Maker
and built palaces;
Judah has fortified many towns.
But I will send fire upon their cities
that will consume their fortresses."

Punishment for Israel

9 Do not rejoice, O Israel;
do not be jubilant like the other
nations.
For you have been unfaithful to your
God;
you love the wages of a prostitute
at every threshing floor.
²Threshing floors and winepresses will
not feed the people;
the new wine will fail them.
³They will not remain in the LORD's
land;
Ephraim will return to Egypt
and eat unclean*b* food in Assyria.
⁴They will not pour out wine offerings
to the LORD,
nor will their sacrifices please him.
Such sacrifices will be to them like
the bread of mourners;
all who eat them will be unclean.
This food will be for themselves;
it will not come into the temple of
the LORD.

⁵What will you do on the day of your
appointed feasts,
on the festival days of the LORD?
⁶Even if they escape from destruction,

---

a14 Most Hebrew manuscripts; some Hebrew manuscripts and Septuagint *They slash themselves*
b3 That is, ceremonially unclean

Egypt will gather them,
and Memphis will bury them.
Their treasures of silver will be taken
over by briers,
and thorns will overrun their tents.
⁷The days of punishment are coming,
the days of reckoning are at hand.
Let Israel know this.
Because your sins are so many
and your hostility so great,
the prophet is considered a fool,
the inspired man a maniac.
⁸The prophet, along with my God,
is the watchman over Ephraim,ᵃ
yet snares await him on all his paths,
and hostility in the house of his
God.
⁹They have sunk deep into corruption,
as in the days of Gibeah.
God will remember their wickedness
and punish them for their sins.

¹⁰"When I found Israel,
it was like finding grapes in the
desert;
when I saw your fathers,
it was like seeing the early fruit on
the fig tree.
But when they came to Baal Peor,
they consecrated themselves to that
shameful idol
and became as vile as the thing
they loved.
¹¹Ephraim's glory will fly away like a
bird—
no birth, no pregnancy, no
conception.
¹²Even if they rear children,
I will bereave them of every one.
Woe to them
when I turn away from them!
¹³I have seen Ephraim, like Tyre,
planted in a pleasant place.
But Ephraim will bring out
their children to the slayer."
¹⁴Give them, O Lord—
what will you give them?
Give them wombs that miscarry
and breasts that are dry.

¹⁵"Because of all their wickedness in
Gilgal,
I hated them there.
Because of their sinful deeds,
I will drive them out of my house.
I will no longer love them;
all their leaders are rebellious.

¹⁶Ephraim is blighted,
their root is withered,
they yield no fruit.
Even if they bear children,
I will slay their cherished
offspring."

¹⁷My God will reject them
because they have not obeyed him;
they will be wanderers among the
nations.

10 Israel was a spreading vine;
he brought forth fruit for
himself.
As his fruit increased,
he built more altars;
as his land prospered,
he adorned his sacred stones.
²Their heart is deceitful,
and now they must bear their guilt.
The Lord will demolish their altars
and destroy their sacred stones.

³Then they will say, "We have no king
because we did not revere the Lord.
But even if we had a king,
what could he do for us?"
⁴They make many promises,
take false oaths
and make agreements;
therefore lawsuits spring up
like poisonous weeds in a plowed
field.
⁵The people who live in Samaria fear
for the calf-idol of Beth Aven.ᵇ
Its people will mourn over it,
and so will its idolatrous priests,
those who had rejoiced over its
splendor,
because it is taken from them into
exile.
⁶It will be carried to Assyria
as tribute for the great king.
Ephraim will be disgraced;
Israel will be ashamed of its
wooden idols.ᶜ
⁷Samaria and its king will float away
like a twig on the surface of the
waters.
⁸The high places of wickednessᵈ will
be destroyed—
it is the sin of Israel.
Thorns and thistles will grow up
and cover their altars.
Then they will say to the mountains,
"Cover us!"
and to the hills, "Fall on us!"

ᵃ8 Or *The prophet is the watchman over Ephraim, / the people of my God* ᵇ5 *Beth Aven* means *house of wickedness* (a name for Bethel, which means *house of God*). ᶜ6 Or *its counsel* ᵈ8 Hebrew *aven*, a reference to Beth Aven (a derogatory name for Bethel)

9"Since the days of Gibeah, you have
    sinned, O Israel,
and there you have remained. *a*
Did not war overtake
    the evildoers in Gibeah?
10When I please, I will punish them;
    nations will be gathered against
      them
to put them in bonds for their
    double sin.
11Ephraim is a trained heifer
    that loves to thresh;
so I will put a yoke
    on her fair neck.
I will drive Ephraim,
    Judah must plow,
    and Jacob must break up the
      ground.
12Sow for yourselves righteousness,
    reap the fruit of unfailing love,
and break up your unplowed ground;
    for it is time to seek the LORD,
until he comes
    and showers righteousness on you.
13But you have planted wickedness,
    you have reaped evil,
    you have eaten the fruit of
      deception.
Because you have depended on your
    own strength
and on your many warriors,
14the roar of battle will rise against
    your people,
so that all your fortresses will be
    devastated—
as Shalman devastated Beth Arbel on
    the day of battle,
when mothers were dashed to the
    ground with their children.
15Thus will it happen to you, O Bethel,
    because your wickedness is great.
When that day dawns,
    the king of Israel will be completely
      destroyed.

God's Love for Israel

11 "When Israel was a child, I loved
    him,
and out of Egypt I called my son.
2But the more I *b* called Israel,
    the further they went from me. *c*
They sacrificed to the Baals
    and they burned incense to images.
3It was I who taught Ephraim to walk,
    taking them by the arms;
but they did not realize

it was I who healed them.
4I led them with cords of human
    kindness,
    with ties of love;
I lifted the yoke from their neck
    and bent down to feed them.

5"Will they not return to Egypt
    and will not Assyria rule over them
    because they refuse to repent?
6Swords will flash in their cities,
    will destroy the bars of their gates
    and put an end to their plans.
7My people are determined to turn
    from me.
Even if they call to the Most High,
    he will by no means exalt them.

8"How can I give you up, Ephraim?
    How can I hand you over, Israel?
How can I treat you like Admah?
    How can I make you like Zeboiim?
My heart is changed within me;
    all my compassion is aroused.
9I will not carry out my fierce anger,
    nor will I turn and devastate
      Ephraim.
For I am God, and not man—
    the Holy One among you.
I will not come in wrath. *d*
10They will follow the LORD;
    he will roar like a lion.
When he roars,
    his children will come trembling
      from the west.
11They will come trembling
    like birds from Egypt,
    like doves from Assyria.
I will settle them in their homes,"
    declares the LORD.

Israel's Sin

12Ephraim has surrounded me with lies,
    the house of Israel with deceit.
And Judah is unruly against God,
    even against the faithful Holy One.

12 1Ephraim feeds on the wind;
    he pursues the east wind all day
    and multiplies lies and violence.
He makes a treaty with Assyria
    and sends olive oil to Egypt.
2The LORD has a charge to bring
    against Judah;
he will punish Jacob *e* according to
    his ways
and repay him according to his
    deeds.

---

a9 Or *there a stand was taken*   *b2* Some Septuagint manuscripts; Hebrew *they*   *c2* Septuagint;
Hebrew *them*   *d9* Or *come against any city*   *e2 Jacob* means *he grasps the heel* (figuratively, *he
deceives*).

³In the womb he grasped his brother's
heel;
  as a man he struggled with God.
⁴He struggled with the angel and
overcame him;
  he wept and begged for his favor.
He found him at Bethel
  and talked with him there—
⁵the LORD God Almighty,
  the LORD is his name of renown!
⁶But you must return to your God;
  maintain love and justice,
  and wait for your God always.

⁷The merchant uses dishonest scales;
  he loves to defraud.
⁸Ephraim boasts,
  "I am very rich; I have become
wealthy.
With all my wealth they will not find
in me
  any iniquity or sin."
⁹"I am the LORD your God,
  ,who brought you, out of ᵃ Egypt;
I will make you live in tents again,
  as in the days of your appointed
feasts.

ᵃ9 Or God / ever since you were in

TUESDAY

VERSE FOR THE DAY:
Hosea 11:8

AUTHOR:
Barbara Bush

PASSAGE FOR THE DAY:
Hosea 11:1–11

Compassion Is Active

CHRISTIANS are sometimes accused of being so heavenly-minded that they are no earthly good. We get caught up in choir rehearsals, studies of the end times or other church activities, and ignore needs around us. When problems are brought to our attention, we content ourselves with feeling sorry about them while doing nothing. But sympathetic thoughts or kindly musings are not true compassion.

With the divine power he possessed, Jesus could have met the multitude's needs merely by forming a thought or speaking a command. He could even have done it from heaven without coming to earth. But his compassion caused him not only to come and live and die among us, but also to touch lepers (Mark 1:40–41) and blind men (Matthew 20:34), and to take little children in his arms (Mark 10:13–16). True compassion is personal, active involvement that expresses God's merciful heart in words and deeds.

God's chosen people are to "clothe" themselves with compassion (Colossians 3:12). We are to meet others' needs, not to continually satisfy our selfish desires. As God showers us with comfort through his Word and through other believers, we in turn are to redirect the stream of his mercy to others. We are not to hoard God's love, but to overflow with the good news of his compassion to all.

Additional Scripture Readings:
2 Corinthians 1:3–4; 1 John 3:16–18

Go to page 957 for your next
devotional reading.

¹⁰I spoke to the prophets,
    gave them many visions
    and told parables through them."

¹¹Is Gilead wicked?
    Its people are worthless!
Do they sacrifice bulls in Gilgal?
    Their altars will be like piles of
        stones
    on a plowed field.
¹²Jacob fled to the country of Aram*a*;
    Israel served to get a wife,
    and to pay for her he tended sheep.
¹³The LORD used a prophet to bring
        Israel up from Egypt,
    by a prophet he cared for him.
¹⁴But Ephraim has bitterly provoked
        him to anger;
    his Lord will leave upon him the
        guilt of his bloodshed
    and will repay him for his
        contempt.

The LORD's Anger Against Israel

13 When Ephraim spoke, men
        trembled;
    he was exalted in Israel.
    But he became guilty of Baal
        worship and died.
²Now they sin more and more;
    they make idols for themselves
        from their silver,
    cleverly fashioned images,
    all of them the work of craftsmen.
It is said of these people,
    "They offer human sacrifice
    and kiss*b* the calf-idols."
³Therefore they will be like the
        morning mist,
    like the early dew that disappears,
    like chaff swirling from a threshing
        floor,
    like smoke escaping through a
        window.

⁴"But I am the LORD your God,
    who brought you out of*c* Egypt.
You shall acknowledge no God but
        me,
    no Savior except me.
⁵I cared for you in the desert,
    in the land of burning heat.
⁶When I fed them, they were satisfied;
    when they were satisfied, they
        became proud;
    then they forgot me.
⁷So I will come upon them like a lion,

like a leopard I will lurk by the
        path.
⁸Like a bear robbed of her cubs,
    I will attack them and rip them
        open.
Like a lion I will devour them;
    a wild animal will tear them apart.

⁹"You are destroyed, O Israel,
    because you are against me, against
        your helper.
¹⁰Where is your king, that he may save
        you?
    Where are your rulers in all your
        towns,
    of whom you said,
    'Give me a king and princes'?
¹¹So in my anger I gave you a king,
    and in my wrath I took him away.
¹²The guilt of Ephraim is stored up,
    his sins are kept on record.
¹³Pains as of a woman in childbirth
        come to him,
    but he is a child without wisdom;
    when the time arrives,
    he does not come to the opening of
        the womb.

¹⁴"I will ransom them from the power
        of the grave*d*;
    I will redeem them from death.
Where, O death, are your plagues?
    Where, O grave,*d* is your
        destruction?

"I will have no compassion,
¹⁵   even though he thrives among his
        brothers.
An east wind from the LORD will
        come,
    blowing in from the desert;
    his spring will fail
    and his well dry up.
His storehouse will be plundered
    of all its treasures.
¹⁶The people of Samaria must bear
        their guilt,
    because they have rebelled against
        their God.
They will fall by the sword;
    their little ones will be dashed to
        the ground,
    their pregnant women ripped
        open."

Repentance to Bring Blessing

14 Return, O Israel, to the LORD
        your God.

---

a12 That is, Northwest Mesopotamia   *b2* Or *"Men who sacrifice / kiss*   *c4* Or *God / ever since you*
were in   *d14* Hebrew *Sheol*

Your sins have been your
downfall!
²Take words with you
and return to the Lord.
Say to him:
"Forgive all our sins
and receive us graciously,
that we may offer the fruit of our
lips. *ᵃ*
³Assyria cannot save us;
we will not mount war-horses.
We will never again say 'Our gods'

to what our own hands have made,
for in you the fatherless find
compassion."
⁴"I will heal their waywardness
and love them freely,
for my anger has turned away from
them.
⁵I will be like the dew to Israel;
he will blossom like a lily.
Like a cedar of Lebanon
he will send down his roots;
6   his young shoots will grow.

ᵃ2 Or offer our lips as sacrifices of bulls

WEDNESDAY

VERSE FOR THE DAY:
Hosea 14:3

AUTHOR:
Rita Schweitz

PASSAGE FOR THE DAY:
Hosea 14:1–9

A Father to the Fatherless

THERE are scattered moments in every person's life that dramatically change the rest of their life. When I was twelve, I faced a moment of crisis. My father was killed in a car accident.

I was especially close to my dad, and I took his death very hard. In my loneliness, I searched for answers to those painful questions: Why did God let the person I loved most die? Where was God when the accident occurred—why didn't God prevent it?

I looked in the Bible for answers. Starting with page one, as any young girl would, I read through to the back cover. One phrase stuck with me—God is "a father to the fatherless" (Psalm 68:5).

I remember feeling a keen awareness that I had to make a choice. I could turn from God, blaming him for my father's death; or I could turn to God, accepting his offer to love and comfort me. I prayed simply, "If you will be my Father, God, I will be your child."

Over the years, God has been faithful to his word, protecting me and providing for me at every turn. I've never regretted my decision to trust God.

My experience underscores the importance of those few profound moments in each person's life, where a significant choice is to be made. Moments when the choice to walk with God, or to go our own way, will have consequences for the rest of our lives. It is at such times that our compassionate Father draws closest, whispering love and hope in our hearts.

Additional Scripture Readings:
Psalm 10:14–18; John 10:27–29

*Go to page 962 for your next
devotional reading.*

His splendor will be like an olive tree,
  his fragrance like a cedar of
    Lebanon.
7Men will dwell again in his shade.
  He will flourish like the grain.
He will blossom like a vine,
  and his fame will be like the wine
    from Lebanon.
8O Ephraim, what more have I[a] to do
  with idols?
  I will answer him and care for him.

I am like a green pine tree;
  your fruitfulness comes from me."

9Who is wise? He will realize these
  things.
  Who is discerning? He will
    understand them.
The ways of the LORD are right;
  the righteous walk in them,
  but the rebellious stumble in
    them.

---

a8 Or What more has Ephraim

*J*OEL uses a famine (due to a devastating plague of locusts) to picture the coming day of the Lord. He calls on God's people to repent and turn to the Lord, promising that everyone who does so will be saved and will receive God's Spirit. As you read this book, listen to God's call to repent of your sins, so that you may be saved and be filled with the Holy Spirit.

JOEL

1 The word of the LORD that came to Joel son of Pethuel.

An Invasion of Locusts

²Hear this, you elders;
    listen, all who live in the land.
Has anything like this ever happened
        in your days
    or in the days of your forefathers?
³Tell it to your children,
    and let your children tell it to their
        children,
    and their children to the next
        generation.
⁴What the locust swarm has left
    the great locusts have eaten;
what the great locusts have left

the young locusts have eaten;
    what the young locusts have left
        other locusts^a have eaten.

⁵Wake up, you drunkards, and weep!
    Wail, all you drinkers of wine;
wail because of the new wine,
    for it has been snatched from your
        lips.
⁶A nation has invaded my land,
    powerful and without number;
it has the teeth of a lion,
    the fangs of a lioness.
⁷It has laid waste my vines
    and ruined my fig trees.
It has stripped off their bark
    and thrown it away,
    leaving their branches white.

---

^a4 The precise meaning of the four Hebrew words used here for locusts is uncertain.

⁸Mourn like a virgin^a in sackcloth
　grieving for the husband^b of her
　　youth.
⁹Grain offerings and drink offerings
　are cut off from the house of the
　　LORD.
The priests are in mourning,
　those who minister before the LORD.
¹⁰The fields are ruined,
　the ground is dried up^c;
the grain is destroyed,
　the new wine is dried up,
　　the oil fails.
¹¹Despair, you farmers,
　wail, you vine growers;
grieve for the wheat and the barley,
　because the harvest of the field is
　　destroyed.
¹²The vine is dried up
　and the fig tree is withered;
the pomegranate, the palm and the
　　apple tree—
　all the trees of the field—are dried
　　up.
Surely the joy of mankind
　is withered away.

A Call to Repentance

¹³Put on sackcloth, O priests, and
　　mourn;
　wail, you who minister before the
　　altar.
Come, spend the night in sackcloth,
　you who minister before my God;
for the grain offerings and drink
　　offerings
　are withheld from the house of your
　　God.
¹⁴Declare a holy fast;
　call a sacred assembly.
Summon the elders
　and all who live in the land
to the house of the LORD your God,
　and cry out to the LORD.

¹⁵Alas for that day!
　For the day of the LORD is near;
　it will come like destruction from
　　the Almighty.^d

¹⁶Has not the food been cut off
　before our very eyes—
joy and gladness
　from the house of our God?
¹⁷The seeds are shriveled
　beneath the clods.^e
The storehouses are in ruins,

the granaries have been broken
　　down,
　for the grain has dried up.
¹⁸How the cattle moan!
　The herds mill about
because they have no pasture;
　even the flocks of sheep are
　　suffering.

¹⁹To you, O LORD, I call,
　for fire has devoured the open
　　pastures
　and flames have burned up all the
　　trees of the field.
²⁰Even the wild animals pant for you;
　the streams of water have dried up
　and fire has devoured the open
　　pastures.

An Army of Locusts

2 Blow the trumpet in Zion;
　sound the alarm on my holy hill.
Let all who live in the land tremble,
　for the day of the LORD is coming.
It is close at hand—
²　a day of darkness and gloom,
　a day of clouds and blackness.
Like dawn spreading across the
　　mountains
　a large and mighty army comes,
such as never was of old
　nor ever will be in ages to come.

³Before them fire devours,
　behind them a flame blazes.
Before them the land is like the
　　garden of Eden,
　behind them, a desert waste—
　nothing escapes them.
⁴They have the appearance of horses;
　they gallop along like cavalry.
⁵With a noise like that of chariots
　they leap over the mountaintops,
like a crackling fire consuming
　　stubble,
like a mighty army drawn up for
　　battle.

⁶At the sight of them, nations are in
　　anguish;
　every face turns pale.
⁷They charge like warriors;
　they scale walls like soldiers.
They all march in line,
　not swerving from their course.
⁸They do not jostle each other;
　each marches straight ahead.
They plunge through defenses

^a8 Or young woman　^b8 Or betrothed　^c10 Or ground mourns　^d15 Hebrew Shaddai　^e17 The
meaning of the Hebrew for this word is uncertain.

without breaking ranks.
⁹They rush upon the city;
   they run along the wall.
They climb into the houses;
   like thieves they enter through the
      windows.

¹⁰Before them the earth shakes,
   the sky trembles,
the sun and moon are darkened,
   and the stars no longer shine.
¹¹The LORD thunders
   at the head of his army;
his forces are beyond number,
   and mighty are those who obey his
      command.
The day of the LORD is great;
   it is dreadful.
Who can endure it?

Rend Your Heart

¹²"Even now," declares the LORD,
   "return to me with all your heart,
with fasting and weeping and
   mourning."

¹³Rend your heart
   and not your garments.
Return to the LORD your God,
   for he is gracious and
      compassionate,
slow to anger and abounding in love,
   and he relents from sending
      calamity.
¹⁴Who knows? He may turn and have
      pity
   and leave behind a blessing—
grain offerings and drink offerings
   for the LORD your God.

¹⁵Blow the trumpet in Zion,
   declare a holy fast,
   call a sacred assembly.
¹⁶Gather the people,
   consecrate the assembly;
bring together the elders,
   gather the children,
   those nursing at the breast.
Let the bridegroom leave his room
   and the bride her chamber.
¹⁷Let the priests, who minister before
      the LORD,
weep between the temple porch
   and the altar.
Let them say, "Spare your people,
   O LORD.

Do not make your inheritance an
      object of scorn,
   a byword among the nations.
Why should they say among the
      peoples,
   'Where is their God?' "

The LORD's Answer

¹⁸Then the LORD will be jealous for his
      land
   and take pity on his people.

¹⁹The LORD will reply^a to them:

"I am sending you grain, new wine
      and oil,
   enough to satisfy you fully;
never again will I make you
   an object of scorn to the nations.

²⁰"I will drive the northern army far
      from you,
   pushing it into a parched and
      barren land,
with its front columns going into the
      eastern sea,^{b}
and those in the rear into the
      western sea.^{c}
And its stench will go up;
   its smell will rise."

Surely he has done great things.^{d}
21   Be not afraid, O land;
   be glad and rejoice.
Surely the LORD has done great things.
22   Be not afraid, O wild animals,
   for the open pastures are becoming
      green.
The trees are bearing their fruit;
   the fig tree and the vine yield their
      riches.
²³Be glad, O people of Zion,
   rejoice in the LORD your God,
for he has given you
   the autumn rains in righteousness.^{e}
He sends you abundant showers,
   both autumn and spring rains, as
      before.
²⁴The threshing floors will be filled with
      grain;
   the vats will overflow with new
      wine and oil.

²⁵"I will repay you for the years the
      locusts have eaten—
   the great locust and the young
      locust,

^{a}18,19 Or LORD was jealous . . . / and took pity . . . / ¹⁹The LORD replied ^{b}20 That is, the Dead Sea
^{c}20 That is, the Mediterranean ^{d}20 Or rise. / Surely it has done great things." ^{e}23 Or / the teacher
for righteousness:

the other locusts and the locust
swarm[a] —
my great army that I sent among you.
²⁶You will have plenty to eat, until you
are full,
and you will praise the name of the
LORD your God,
who has worked wonders for you;
never again will my people be
shamed.
²⁷Then you will know that I am in
Israel,
that I am the LORD your God,
and that there is no other;
never again will my people be
shamed.

The Day of the LORD

²⁸"And afterward,

I will pour out my Spirit on all
people.
Your sons and daughters will
prophesy,
your old men will dream dreams,
your young men will see visions.
²⁹Even on my servants, both men and
women,
I will pour out my Spirit in those
days.
³⁰I will show wonders in the heavens
and on the earth,
blood and fire and billows of
smoke.
³¹The sun will be turned to darkness
and the moon to blood
before the coming of the great and
dreadful day of the LORD.
³²And everyone who calls

---

a25 The precise meaning of the four Hebrew words used here for locusts is uncertain.

THURSDAY

VERSE FOR THE DAY:	AUTHOR:	PASSAGE FOR THE DAY:
Joel 2:25	Corrie ten Boom	Joel 2:18–27

Our "If Onlies"

MISSED opportunities!
If only . . .

It is good to regret missed opportunities, but quite wrong to
be miserable about them. You cannot look back across your past
life without seeing things to regret. That is as it should be. But
we have to draw a subtle distinction between a legitimate regret
and a wrong condition of heart. Give God your "if onlies."

Think of those laborers in the vineyard in the parable which
Jesus told in Matthew 20:1–16. They all received the same
wages, although some had worked the whole day and some had
worked for only an hour. Compare that to a person's life. Some
people enter the kingdom right at the end of their lives. They
may regret all those years when they were not serving Christ. But
the important thing is that they are in the kingdom. The thing
that matters first of all, if you are a Christian, is not what you
once were but what you are now.

Lord Jesus, I give my "if onlies" to you. Make me a faithful laborer here and now.

Additional Scripture Readings:
Genesis 50:15–21; 2 Corinthians 7:9–10

*Go to page 967 for your next
devotional reading.*

on the name of the LORD will be
saved;
for on Mount Zion and in Jerusalem
there will be deliverance,
as the LORD has said,
among the survivors
whom the LORD calls.

The Nations Judged

3 "In those days and at that time,
when I restore the fortunes of
Judah and Jerusalem,
²I will gather all nations
and bring them down to the Valley
of Jehoshaphat.ᵃ
There I will enter into judgment
against them
concerning my inheritance, my
people Israel,
for they scattered my people among
the nations
and divided up my land.
³They cast lots for my people
and traded boys for prostitutes;
they sold girls for wine
that they might drink.

⁴"Now what have you against me, O
Tyre and Sidon and all you regions of Philistia? Are you repaying me for something
I have done? If you are paying me back, I
will swiftly and speedily return on your
own heads what you have done. ⁵For you
took my silver and my gold and carried off
my finest treasures to your temples. ⁶You
sold the people of Judah and Jerusalem
to the Greeks, that you might send them
far from their homeland.

⁷"See, I am going to rouse them out of
the places to which you sold them, and I
will return on your own heads what you
have done. ⁸I will sell your sons and
daughters to the people of Judah, and
they will sell them to the Sabeans, a nation far away." The LORD has spoken.

⁹Proclaim this among the nations:
Prepare for war!
Rouse the warriors!
Let all the fighting men draw near
and attack.
¹⁰Beat your plowshares into swords
and your pruning hooks into spears.
Let the weakling say,
"I am strong!"
¹¹Come quickly, all you nations from
every side,
and assemble there.

Bring down your warriors, O LORD!

¹²"Let the nations be roused;
let them advance into the Valley of
Jehoshaphat,
for there I will sit
to judge all the nations on every
side.
¹³Swing the sickle,
for the harvest is ripe.
Come, trample the grapes,
for the winepress is full
and the vats overflow—
so great is their wickedness!"

¹⁴Multitudes, multitudes
in the valley of decision!
For the day of the LORD is near
in the valley of decision.
¹⁵The sun and moon will be darkened,
and the stars no longer shine.
¹⁶The LORD will roar from Zion
and thunder from Jerusalem;
the earth and the sky will tremble.
But the LORD will be a refuge for his
people,
a stronghold for the people of
Israel.

Blessings for God's People

¹⁷"Then you will know that I, the LORD
your God,
dwell in Zion, my holy hill.
Jerusalem will be holy;
never again will foreigners invade
her.

¹⁸"In that day the mountains will drip
new wine,
and the hills will flow with milk;
all the ravines of Judah will run
with water.
A fountain will flow out of the LORD's
house
and will water the valley of
acacias.ᵇ
¹⁹But Egypt will be desolate,
Edom a desert waste,
because of violence done to the
people of Judah,
in whose land they shed innocent
blood.
²⁰Judah will be inhabited forever
and Jerusalem through all
generations.
²¹Their bloodguilt, which I have not
pardoned,
I will pardon."

The LORD dwells in Zion!

ᵃ2 *Jehoshaphat* means *the LORD judges;* also in verse 12.   ᵇ18 Or *Valley of Shittim*

AMOS prophesies during the time of Jeroboam II (2 Kings 14:23–29), a time of prosperity for some but extreme poverty for many others. He reprimands those who oppress the poor and make them suffer even more. As you read this book, think about how angry God becomes when you show more interest in your wealth than in obeying him. Remember, though, that God will forgive you, if you confess your sins and seek to do his will.

AMOS

1 The words of Amos, one of the shepherds of Tekoa—what he saw concerning Israel two years before the earthquake, when Uzziah was king of Judah and Jeroboam son of Jehoash[a] was king of Israel.

²He said:

"The Lord roars from Zion
    and thunders from Jerusalem;
the pastures of the shepherds dry
        up,[b]
    and the top of Carmel withers."

Judgment on Israel's Neighbors

³This is what the Lord says:

"For three sins of Damascus,
    even for four, I will not turn back
        my wrath,.
Because she threshed Gilead
    with sledges having iron teeth,
⁴I will send fire upon the house of
        Hazael
    that will consume the fortresses of
        Ben-Hadad.
⁵I will break down the gate of
        Damascus;

---

a1 Hebrew *Joash*, a variant of *Jehoash*   b2 Or *shepherds mourn*

I will destroy the king who is in*a*
the Valley of Aven*b*
and the one who holds the scepter in
Beth Eden.
The people of Aram will go into
exile to Kir,"
says the LORD.

6This is what the LORD says:

"For three sins of Gaza,
even for four, I will not turn back
my wrath.
Because she took captive whole
communities
and sold them to Edom,
7I will send fire upon the walls of Gaza
that will consume her fortresses.
8I will destroy the king*c* of Ashdod
and the one who holds the scepter
in Ashkelon.
I will turn my hand against Ekron,
till the last of the Philistines is
dead,"
says the Sovereign LORD.

9This is what the LORD says:

"For three sins of Tyre,
even for four, I will not turn back
my wrath.
Because she sold whole communities
of captives to Edom,
disregarding a treaty of
brotherhood,
10I will send fire upon the walls of Tyre
that will consume her fortresses."

11This is what the LORD says:

"For three sins of Edom,
even for four, I will not turn back
my wrath.
Because he pursued his brother with
a sword,
stifling all compassion,*d*
because his anger raged continually
and his fury flamed unchecked,
12I will send fire upon Teman
that will consume the fortresses of
Bozrah."

13This is what the LORD says:

"For three sins of Ammon,
even for four, I will not turn back
my wrath.
Because he ripped open the pregnant
women of Gilead
in order to extend his borders,

14I will set fire to the walls of Rabbah
that will consume her fortresses
amid war cries on the day of battle,
amid violent winds on a stormy
day.
15Her king*e* will go into exile,
he and his officials together,"
says the LORD.

2 This is what the LORD says:

"For three sins of Moab,
even for four, I will not turn back
my wrath.
Because he burned, as if to lime,
the bones of Edom's king,
2I will send fire upon Moab
that will consume the fortresses of
Kerioth.*f*
Moab will go down in great tumult
amid war cries and the blast of the
trumpet.
3I will destroy her ruler
and kill all her officials with him,"
says the LORD.

4This is what the LORD says:

"For three sins of Judah,
even for four, I will not turn back
my wrath.
Because they have rejected the law of
the LORD
and have not kept his decrees,
because they have been led astray by
false gods,*g*
the gods*h* their ancestors followed,
5I will send fire upon Judah
that will consume the fortresses of
Jerusalem."

Judgment on Israel

6This is what the LORD says:

"For three sins of Israel,
even for four, I will not turn back
my wrath.
They sell the righteous for silver,
and the needy for a pair of sandals.
7They trample on the heads of the
poor
as upon the dust of the ground
and deny justice to the oppressed.
Father and son use the same girl
and so profane my holy name.
8They lie down beside every altar
on garments taken in pledge.
In the house of their god
they drink wine taken as fines.

---

*a*5 Or *the inhabitants of*   *b*5 *Aven* means *wickedness.*
destroyed his allies   *e*15 Or / *Molech*; Hebrew *malcam*
lies   *c*8 Or *inhabitants*   *d*11 Or *sword / and*
*f*2 Or *of her cities*   *g*4 Or *by lies*   *h*4 Or

9"I destroyed the Amorite before them,
 though he was tall as the cedars
 and strong as the oaks.
 I destroyed his fruit above
 and his roots below.

10"I brought you up out of Egypt,
 and I led you forty years in the
 desert
 to give you the land of the
 Amorites.
11I also raised up prophets from among
 your sons
 and Nazirites from among your
 young men.
 Is this not true, people of Israel?"
 declares the LORD.

12"But you made the Nazirites drink
 wine
 and commanded the prophets not
 to prophesy.

13"Now then, I will crush you
 as a cart crushes when loaded with
 grain.
14The swift will not escape,
 the strong will not muster their
 strength,
 and the warrior will not save his
 life.
15The archer will not stand his ground,
 the fleet-footed soldier will not get
 away,
 and the horseman will not save his
 life.
16Even the bravest warriors
 will flee naked on that day,"
 declares the LORD.

Witnesses Summoned Against Israel

3 Hear this word the LORD has spoken
 against you, O people of Israel—
against the whole family I brought up out
of Egypt:

2"You only have I chosen
 of all the families of the earth;
 therefore I will punish you
 for all your sins."

3Do two walk together
 unless they have agreed to do so?
4Does a lion roar in the thicket
 when he has no prey?
 Does he growl in his den
 when he has caught nothing?
5Does a bird fall into a trap on the
 ground
 where no snare has been set?

Does a trap spring up from the earth
 when there is nothing to catch?
6When a trumpet sounds in a city,
 do not the people tremble?
 When disaster comes to a city,
 has not the LORD caused it?

7Surely the Sovereign LORD does
 nothing
 without revealing his plan
 to his servants the prophets.

8The lion has roared—
 who will not fear?
 The Sovereign LORD has spoken—
 who can but prophesy?

9Proclaim to the fortresses of Ashdod
 and to the fortresses of Egypt:
 "Assemble yourselves on the
 mountains of Samaria;
 see the great unrest within her
 and the oppression among her
 people."

10"They do not know how to do right,"
 declares the LORD,
 "who hoard plunder and loot in
 their fortresses."

11Therefore this is what the Sovereign
LORD says:

"An enemy will overrun the land;
 he will pull down your strongholds
 and plunder your fortresses."

12This is what the LORD says:

"As a shepherd saves from the lion's
 mouth
 only two leg bones or a piece of an
 ear,
 so will the Israelites be saved,
those who sit in Samaria
 on the edge of their beds
 and in Damascus on their
 couches.a"

13"Hear this and testify against the
house of Jacob," declares the Lord, the
LORD God Almighty.

14"On the day I punish Israel for her
 sins,
 I will destroy the altars of Bethel;
 the horns of the altar will be cut off
 and fall to the ground.
15I will tear down the winter house
 along with the summer house;
 the houses adorned with ivory will be
 destroyed

---

a12 The meaning of the Hebrew for this line is uncertain.

and the mansions will be
demolished,"

    declares the LORD.

Israel Has Not Returned to God

4 Hear this word, you cows of Bashan
   on Mount Samaria,
you women who oppress the poor
   and crush the needy
and say to your husbands, "Bring us
   some drinks!"

[2]The Sovereign LORD has sworn by his
   holiness:
"The time will surely come
when you will be taken away with
   hooks,
   the last of you with fishhooks.
[3]You will each go straight out
   through breaks in the wall,
   and you will be cast out toward
     Harmon, *a* "

    declares the LORD.

[4]"Go to Bethel and sin;
   go to Gilgal and sin yet more.

---

a 3 Masoretic Text; with a different word division of the Hebrew (see Septuagint) *out, O mountain of oppression*

FRIDAY

VERSE FOR THE DAY: AUTHOR: PASSAGE FOR THE DAY:
Amos 4:1   Jean E. Syswerda   Amos 4:1–5

Those Cows of Bashan

"YOU cows of Bashan," Amos called the privileged women of his day.

Cows! I don't know about you, but I would definitely rather not be called a cow. What an insult.

Bashan, in northern Canaan, was cattle-raising country. The cows raised there were pampered and indulged and were thought to be the best Canaan offered. Amos was comparing Bashan's pampered cows to the pampered women of his day. They not only enjoyed being spoiled . . . they expected it . . . they looked on it as their due. They cared nothing for those around them and were only worried about getting their own needs and desires indulged.

Now, don't get me wrong. I enjoy being pampered now and then. But I have to be careful not to think my husband and children and friends owe it to me.

Will I be judged as harshly as these women of Israel if I give in to my self-centered nature? If I say to my husband, "Bring me a cup of coffee!" (Amos 4:1)? If I say to my children (by word or action or facial expression), "You owe it to me after all I've given up for you." If I say to my friends, "If you love me, you'll . . . ."

I'm certainly a privileged woman in today's American society. I'm often pampered and indulged. And I usually enjoy it. But may I never become selfish or self-centered enough to expect it or think it my due. May I never resemble those "cows of Bashan"!

Additional Scripture Readings:
Mark 10:41–45; John 13:12–15

Go to page 972 for your next devotional reading.

Bring your sacrifices every morning
  your tithes every three years.[a]
[5]Burn leavened bread as a thank
    offering
  and brag about your freewill
    offerings—
boast about them, you Israelites,
  for this is what you love to do,"
    declares the Sovereign LORD.

[6]"I gave you empty stomachs[b] in every
    city
  and lack of bread in every town,
  yet you have not returned to me,"
    declares the LORD.

[7]"I also withheld rain from you
  when the harvest was still three
    months away.
I sent rain on one town,
  but withheld it from another.
One field had rain;
  another had none and dried up.
[8]People staggered from town to town
    for water
  but did not get enough to drink,
  yet you have not returned to me,"
    declares the LORD.

[9]"Many times I struck your gardens
    and vineyards,
  I struck them with blight and
    mildew.
Locusts devoured your fig and olive
    trees,
  yet you have not returned to me,"
    declares the LORD.

[10]"I sent plagues among you
    as I did to Egypt.
I killed your young men with the
    sword,
  along with your captured horses.
I filled your nostrils with the stench
    of your camps,
  yet you have not returned to me,"
    declares the LORD.

[11]"I overthrew some of you
  as I[c] overthrew Sodom and
    Gomorrah.
You were like a burning stick
    snatched from the fire,
  yet you have not returned to me,"
    declares the LORD.

[12]"Therefore this is what I will do to
    you, Israel,
  and because I will do this to you,

prepare to meet your God,
  O Israel."

[13]He who forms the mountains,
  creates the wind,
  and reveals his thoughts to man,
he who turns dawn to darkness,
  and treads the high places of the
    earth—
  the LORD God Almighty is his name.

A Lament and Call to Repentance

5 Hear this word, O house of Israel, this
  lament I take up concerning you:

[2]"Fallen is Virgin Israel,
    never to rise again,
  deserted in her own land,
    with no one to lift her up."

[3]This is what the Sovereign LORD says:

"The city that marches out a
    thousand strong for Israel
  will have only a hundred left;
  the town that marches out a hundred
    strong
  will have only ten left."

[4]This is what the LORD says to the house
of Israel:

"Seek me and live;
[5] do not seek Bethel,
  do not go to Gilgal,
  do not journey to Beersheba.
For Gilgal will surely go into exile,
  and Bethel will be reduced to
    nothing.[d]"
[6]Seek the LORD and live,
  or he will sweep through the house
    of Joseph like a fire;
it will devour,
  and Bethel will have no one to
    quench it.

[7]You who turn justice into bitterness
  and cast righteousness to the
    ground
[8](he who made the Pleiades and
    Orion,
  who turns blackness into dawn
  and darkens day into night,
who calls for the waters of the sea
  and pours them out over the face of
    the land—
  the LORD is his name—
[9]he flashes destruction on the
    stronghold
  and brings the fortified city to
    ruin),

[a]4 Or tithes on the third day   [b]6 Hebrew you cleanness of teeth   [c]11 Hebrew God
[d]5 Or grief; or wickedness; Hebrew aven, a reference to Beth Aven (a derogatory name for Bethel)

[10]you hate the one who reproves in
court
and despise him who tells the
truth.
[11]You trample on the poor
and force him to give you grain.
Therefore, though you have built
stone mansions,
you will not live in them;
though you have planted lush
vineyards,
you will not drink their wine.
[12]For I know how many are your
offenses
and how great your sins.

You oppress the righteous and take
bribes
and you deprive the poor of justice
in the courts.
[13]Therefore the prudent man keeps
quiet in such times,
for the times are evil.

[14]Seek good, not evil,
that you may live.
Then the LORD God Almighty will be
with you,
just as you say he is.
[15]Hate evil, love good;
maintain justice in the courts.
Perhaps the LORD God Almighty will
have mercy
on the remnant of Joseph.

[16]Therefore this is what the Lord, the
LORD God Almighty, says:

"There will be wailing in all the
streets
and cries of anguish in every public
square.
The farmers will be summoned to
weep
and the mourners to wail.
[17]There will be wailing in all the
vineyards,
for I will pass through your midst,"
says the LORD.

The Day of the LORD

[18]Woe to you who long
for the day of the LORD!
Why do you long for the day of the
LORD?
That day will be darkness, not light.
[19]It will be as though a man fled from a
lion

only to meet a bear,
as though he entered his house
and rested his hand on the wall
only to have a snake bite him.
[20]Will not the day of the LORD be
darkness, not light—
pitch-dark, without a ray of
brightness?

[21]"I hate, I despise your religious feasts;
I cannot stand your assemblies.
[22]Even though you bring me burnt
offerings and grain offerings,
I will not accept them.
Though you bring choice fellowship
offerings,[a]
I will have no regard for them.
[23]Away with the noise of your songs!
I will not listen to the music of
your harps.
[24]But let justice roll on like a river,
righteousness like a never-failing
stream!

[25]"Did you bring me sacrifices and
offerings
forty years in the desert, O house of
Israel?
[26]You have lifted up the shrine of your
king,
the pedestal of your idols,
the star of your god[b]—
which you made for yourselves.
[27]Therefore I will send you into exile
beyond Damascus,"
says the LORD, whose name is God
Almighty.

Woe to the Complacent

6 Woe to you who are complacent in
Zion,
and to you who feel secure on
Mount Samaria,
you notable men of the foremost
nation,
to whom the people of Israel come!
[2]Go to Calneh and look at it;
go from there to great Hamath,
and then go down to Gath in
Philistia.
Are they better off than your two
kingdoms?
Is their land larger than yours?
[3]You put off the evil day
and bring near a reign of terror.
[4]You lie on beds inlaid with ivory
and lounge on your couches.
You dine on choice lambs

and fattened calves.
⁵You strum away on your harps like David
and improvise on musical instruments.
⁶You drink wine by the bowlful
and use the finest lotions,
but you do not grieve over the ruin of Joseph.
⁷Therefore you will be among the first to go into exile;
your feasting and lounging will end.

The LORD Abhors the Pride of Israel

⁸The Sovereign LORD has sworn by himself—the LORD God Almighty declares:

"I abhor the pride of Jacob
and detest his fortresses;
I will deliver up the city
and everything in it."

⁹If ten men are left in one house, they too will die. ¹⁰And if a relative who is to burn the bodies comes to carry them out of the house and asks anyone still hiding there, "Is anyone with you?" and he says, "No," then he will say, "Hush! We must not mention the name of the LORD."

¹¹For the LORD has given the command,
and he will smash the great house into pieces
and the small house into bits.

¹²Do horses run on the rocky crags?
Does one plow there with oxen?
But you have turned justice into poison
and the fruit of righteousness into bitterness—
¹³you who rejoice in the conquest of Lo Debar*
and say, "Did we not take Karnaim* by our own strength?"

¹⁴For the LORD God Almighty declares,
"I will stir up a nation against you,
O house of Israel,
that will oppress you all the way
from Lebo* Hamath to the valley of the Arabah."

Locusts, Fire and a Plumb Line

7 This is what the Sovereign LORD showed me: He was preparing swarms of locusts after the king's share had been harvested and just as the second crop was coming up. ²When they had stripped the land clean, I cried out, "Sovereign LORD, forgive! How can Jacob survive? He is so small!"

³So the LORD relented.

"This will not happen," the LORD said.

⁴This is what the Sovereign LORD showed me: The Sovereign LORD was calling for judgment by fire; it dried up the great deep and devoured the land. ⁵Then I cried out, "Sovereign LORD, I beg you, stop! How can Jacob survive? He is so small!"

⁶So the LORD relented.

"This will not happen either," the Sovereign LORD said.

⁷This is what he showed me: The Lord was standing by a wall that had been built true to plumb, with a plumb line in his hand. ⁸And the LORD asked me, "What do you see, Amos?"

"A plumb line," I replied.

Then the Lord said, "Look, I am setting a plumb line among my people Israel; I will spare them no longer.

⁹"The high places of Isaac will be destroyed
and the sanctuaries of Israel will be ruined;
with my sword I will rise against the house of Jeroboam."

Amos and Amaziah

¹⁰Then Amaziah the priest of Bethel sent a message to Jeroboam king of Israel: "Amos is raising a conspiracy against you in the very heart of Israel. The land cannot bear all his words. ¹¹For this is what Amos is saying:

" 'Jeroboam will die by the sword,
and Israel will surely go into exile,
away from their native land.' "

¹²Then Amaziah said to Amos, "Get out, you seer! Go back to the land of Judah. Earn your bread there and do your prophesying there. ¹³Don't prophesy anymore at Bethel, because this is the king's sanctuary and the temple of the kingdom."

¹⁴Amos answered Amaziah, "I was neither a prophet nor a prophet's son, but I was a shepherd, and I also took care of sycamore-fig trees. ¹⁵But the LORD took me from tending the flock and said to me, 'Go, prophesy to my people Israel.' ¹⁶Now

---

*13 Lo Debar means nothing. *13 Karnaim means horns; horn here symbolizes strength. *14 Or from the entrance to then, hear the word of the LORD. You say,

" 'Do not prophesy against Israel,
    and stop preaching against the
        house of Isaac.'

17"Therefore this is what the LORD says:

" 'Your wife will become a prostitute
    in the city,
and your sons and daughters will
    fall by the sword.
Your land will be measured and
    divided up,
and you yourself will die in a
    pagan*a* country.
And Israel will certainly go into exile,
    away from their native land.' "

A Basket of Ripe Fruit

8 This is what the Sovereign LORD
showed me: a basket of ripe fruit.
2"What do you see, Amos?" he asked.

"A basket of ripe fruit," I answered.

Then the LORD said to me, "The time is
ripe for my people Israel; I will spare
them no longer.

3"In that day," declares the Sovereign
LORD, "the songs in the temple will turn to
wailing.*b* Many, many bodies—flung everywhere! Silence!"

4Hear this, you who trample the needy
    and do away with the poor of the
        land,

5saying,

"When will the New Moon be over
    that we may sell grain,
and the Sabbath be ended
    that we may market wheat?"—
skimping the measure,
    boosting the price
    and cheating with dishonest scales,
6buying the poor with silver
    and the needy for a pair of sandals,
    selling even the sweepings with the
        wheat.

7The LORD has sworn by the Pride of
Jacob: "I will never forget anything they
have done.

8"Will not the land tremble for this,
    and all who live in it mourn?
The whole land will rise like the Nile;
    it will be stirred up and then sink
    like the river of Egypt.

9"In that day," declares the Sovereign
LORD,

"I will make the sun go down at noon
    and darken the earth in broad
        daylight.
10I will turn your religious feasts into
    mourning
    and all your singing into weeping.
I will make all of you wear sackcloth
    and shave your heads.
I will make that time like mourning
    for an only son
    and the end of it like a bitter day.

11"The days are coming," declares the
    Sovereign LORD,
"when I will send a famine through
    the land—
not a famine of food or a thirst for
    water,
but a famine of hearing the words
    of the LORD.
12Men will stagger from sea to sea
    and wander from north to east,
searching for the word of the LORD,
    but they will not find it.

13"In that day

"the lovely young women and strong
    young men
    will faint because of thirst.
14They who swear by the shame*c* of
    Samaria,
or say, 'As surely as your god lives,
    O Dan,'
or, 'As surely as the god*d* of
    Beersheba lives'—
they will fall,
    never to rise again."

Israel to Be Destroyed

9 I saw the Lord standing by the altar,
and he said:

"Strike the tops of the pillars
    so that the thresholds shake.
Bring them down on the heads of all
    the people;
    those who are left I will kill with
        the sword.
Not one will get away,
    none will escape.
2Though they dig down to the depths
    of the grave,*e*
    from there my hand will take them.
Though they climb up to the heavens,
    from there I will bring them down.

---

a17 Hebrew *an unclean*   *b3* Or *"the temple singers will wail*   *c14* Or *by Ashima; or by the idol*
d14 Or *power*   *e2* Hebrew *to Sheol*

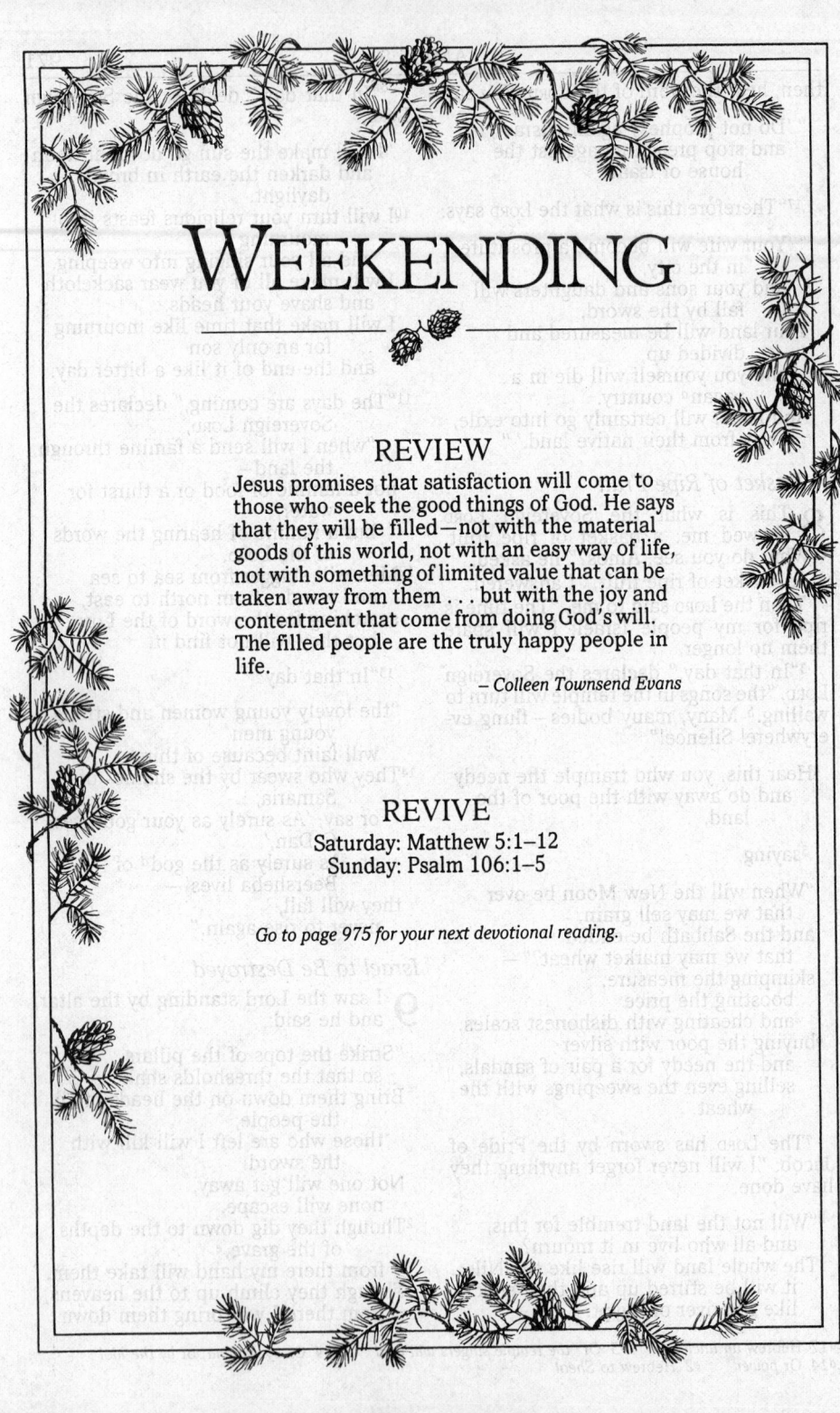

WEEKENDING

REVIEW

Jesus promises that satisfaction will come to those who seek the good things of God. He says that they will be filled—not with the material goods of this world, not with an easy way of life, not with something of limited value that can be taken away from them . . . but with the joy and contentment that come from doing God's will. The filled people are the truly happy people in life.

— Colleen Townsend Evans

REVIVE

Saturday: Matthew 5:1–12
Sunday: Psalm 106:1–5

Go to page 975 for your next devotional reading.

³Though they hide themselves on the
    top of Carmel,
  there I will hunt them down and
    seize them.
Though they hide from me at the
    bottom of the sea,
  there I will command the serpent
    to bite them.
⁴Though they are driven into exile by
    their enemies,
  there I will command the sword to
    slay them.
I will fix my eyes upon them
  for evil and not for good."

⁵The Lord, the LORD Almighty,
  he who touches the earth and it
    melts,
  and all who live in it mourn—
the whole land rises like the Nile,
  then sinks like the river of Egypt—
⁶he who builds his lofty palace*a* in the
    heavens
  and sets its foundation*b* on the
    earth,
who calls for the waters of the sea
  and pours them out over the face of
    the land—
  the LORD is his name.

⁷"Are not you Israelites
  the same to me as the Cushites*c*?"
                declares the LORD.
"Did I not bring Israel up from Egypt,
  the Philistines from Caphtor*d*
  and the Arameans from Kir?

⁸"Surely the eyes of the Sovereign LORD
  are on the sinful kingdom.
I will destroy it
  from the face of the earth—
yet I will not totally destroy
  the house of Jacob,"
                declares the LORD.
⁹"For I will give the command,
  and I will shake the house of Israel

among all the nations
as grain is shaken in a sieve,
  and not a pebble will reach the
    ground.
¹⁰All the sinners among my people
  will die by the sword,
all those who say,
  'Disaster will not overtake or meet
    us.'

Israel's Restoration

¹¹"In that day I will restore
  David's fallen tent.
I will repair its broken places,
  restore its ruins,
  and build it as it used to be,
¹²so that they may possess the remnant
    of Edom
  and all the nations that bear my
    name,*e*"
                declares the LORD, who will do
                    these things.

¹³"The days are coming," declares the
LORD,

"when the reaper will be overtaken by
    the plowman
  and the planter by the one treading
    grapes.
New wine will drip from the
    mountains
  and flow from all the hills.
¹⁴I will bring back my exiled*f* people
    Israel;
  they will rebuild the ruined cities
    and live in them.
They will plant vineyards and drink
    their wine;
  they will make gardens and eat
    their fruit.
¹⁵I will plant Israel in their own land,
  never again to be uprooted
  from the land I have given them,"
                says the LORD your God.

---

a6 The meaning of the Hebrew for this phrase is uncertain.   *b6* The meaning of the Hebrew for this
word is uncertain.   *c7* That is, people from the upper Nile region   *d7* That is, Crete
e12 Hebrew; Septuagint *so that the remnant of men / and all the nations that bear my name may seek the
Lord,*   *f14* Or *will restore the fortunes of my*

*O*BADIAH *prophesies judgment against Edom for her violence against Israel, promising that God will restore his people. As you read this book, remember that no one can fight against God's people and hope to win in the end. The final victory belongs to Christ and his church.*

OBADIAH

¹The vision of Obadiah.

This is what the Sovereign Lord says about Edom—

We have heard a message from the
   Lord:
   An envoy was sent to the nations to
      say,
   "Rise, and let us go against her for
      battle"—

²"See, I will make you small among
      the nations;
   you will be utterly despised.
³The pride of your heart has deceived
      you,
   you who live in the clefts of the
      rocks*ᵃ*
   and make your home on the
      heights,

you who say to yourself,
   'Who can bring me down to the
      ground?'
⁴Though you soar like the eagle
   and make your nest among the
      stars,
   from there I will bring you down,"
                     declares the Lord.
⁵"If thieves came to you,
   if robbers in the night—
   Oh, what a disaster awaits you—
   would they not steal only as much
      as they wanted?
   If grape pickers came to you,
   would they not leave a few grapes?
⁶But how Esau will be ransacked,
   his hidden treasures pillaged!
⁷All your allies will force you to the
      border;
   your friends will deceive and
      overpower you;

those who eat your bread will set a
trap for you,[a]
but you will not detect it.

8"In that day," declares the LORD,
"will I not destroy the wise men of
Edom,
men of understanding in the
mountains of Esau?
9Your warriors, O Teman, will be
terrified,
and everyone in Esau's mountains
will be cut down in the slaughter.
10Because of the violence against your
brother Jacob,

you will be covered with shame;
you will be destroyed forever.
11On the day you stood aloof
while strangers carried off his
wealth
and foreigners entered his gates
and cast lots for Jerusalem,
you were like one of them.
12You should not look down on your
brother
in the day of his misfortune,
nor rejoice over the people of Judah
in the day of their destruction,
nor boast so much
in the day of their trouble.

[a]7 The meaning of the Hebrew for this clause is uncertain.

MONDAY

VERSE FOR THE DAY:
Obadiah 3–4

AUTHOR:
Doris Rikkers

PASSAGE FOR THE DAY:
Obadiah 1–21

Reading Obadiah

HOW many times have you read the book of Obadiah? Never, you say? Well, don't feel too bad. I'm sure there are millions of Christians who would return a blank stare to the question, "What's Obadiah all about?"

But Obadiah has a message. Historically, it's a warning to the country of Edom—the country founded by Jacob's brother Esau (Genesis 25:30; 36:1). But for today it reiterates the proverb:

Pride goes before destruction,
a haughty spirit before a fall (Proverbs
16:18).

And it reminds us that God is in control. We may think that we are in control, that we have prestige or power or success. We have a status title at work or a gorgeous "home on the heights" (Obadiah 3) with a spectacular view. We may hobnob with people who are "someone" and soar through life feeling high enough and good enough to touch the stars (Obadiah 4). But Obadiah reminds us that we're not in control—God is. And if our pride gets in the way, God's warning is to us as it was to Edom: "I will bring you down."

Take some time. Read Obadiah once, twice, maybe three times. It's a short book; most think it a strange book. But like every book of the Bible, it has a message for us today.

Additional Scripture Readings:
Isaiah 31:1–3; Luke 12:16–21

Go to page 979 for your next
devotional reading.

¹³You should not march through the
    gates of my people
      in the day of their disaster,
    nor look down on them in their
      calamity
      in the day of their disaster,
    nor seize their wealth
      in the day of their disaster.
¹⁴You should not wait at the crossroads
      to cut down their fugitives,
    nor hand over their survivors
      in the day of their trouble.
¹⁵"The day of the LORD is near
      for all nations.
    As you have done, it will be done to
      you;
    your deeds will return upon your
      own head.
¹⁶Just as you drank on my holy hill,
    so all the nations will drink
      continually;
    they will drink and drink
      and be as if they had never been.
¹⁷But on Mount Zion will be
      deliverance;
    it will be holy,
    and the house of Jacob
      will possess its inheritance.
¹⁸The house of Jacob will be a fire

and the house of Joseph a flame;
    the house of Esau will be stubble,
      and they will set it on fire and
      consume it.
There will be no survivors
    from the house of Esau."
              The LORD has spoken.

¹⁹People from the Negev will occupy
    the mountains of Esau,
    and people from the foothills will
      possess
    the land of the Philistines.
They will occupy the fields of
    Ephraim and Samaria,
    and Benjamin will possess Gilead.
²⁰This company of Israelite exiles who
    are in Canaan
    will possess the land as far as
      Zarephath;
    the exiles from Jerusalem who are in
      Sepharad
    will possess the towns of the
      Negev.
²¹Deliverers will go up onᵃ Mount
    Zion
    to govern the mountains of Esau.
    And the kingdom will be the
      LORD's.

*J*ONAH *is sent by God to Nineveh, the city of the enemy of God's people during the time of Jeroboam II (2 Kings 14:23–29). After he tries to run away, God gives him a second chance to prophesy, for the Lord wants the whole world to hear the message of his grace. As you read this book, think about how many times God gives you a second opportunity. Don't forget to tell others about your Lord.*

JONAH

Jonah Flees From the LORD

1 The word of the LORD came to Jonah son of Amittai: ²"Go to the great city of Nineveh and preach against it, because its wickedness has come up before me."

³But Jonah ran away from the LORD and headed for Tarshish. He went down to Joppa, where he found a ship bound for that port. After paying the fare, he went aboard and sailed for Tarshish to flee from the LORD.

⁴Then the LORD sent a great wind on the sea, and such a violent storm arose that the ship threatened to break up. ⁵All the sailors were afraid and each cried out to his own god. And they threw the cargo into the sea to lighten the ship.

But Jonah had gone below deck, where he lay down and fell into a deep sleep. ⁶The captain went to him and said, "How can you sleep? Get up and call on your god! Maybe he will take notice of us, and we will not perish."

⁷Then the sailors said to each other, "Come, let us cast lots to find out who is responsible for this calamity." They cast lots and the lot fell on Jonah.

⁸So they asked him, "Tell us, who is responsible for making all this trouble for us? What do you do? Where do you come from? What is your country? From what people are you?"

⁹He answered, "I am a Hebrew and I worship the LORD, the God of heaven, who made the sea and the land."

¹⁰This terrified them and they asked, "What have you done?" (They knew he was running away from the LORD, because he had already told them so.)

¹¹The sea was getting rougher and rougher. So they asked him, "What should we do to you to make the sea calm down for us?"

¹²"Pick me up and throw me into the sea," he replied, "and it will become calm. I know that it is my fault that this great storm has come upon you."

¹³Instead, the men did their best to row back to land. But they could not, for the sea grew even wilder than before. ¹⁴Then they cried to the LORD, "O LORD, please do not let us die for taking this man's life. Do not hold us accountable for killing an innocent man, for you, O LORD, have done as you pleased." ¹⁵Then they took Jonah and threw him overboard, and the raging sea grew calm. ¹⁶At this the men greatly feared the LORD, and they offered a sacrifice to the LORD and made vows to him.

¹⁷But the LORD provided a great fish to swallow Jonah, and Jonah was inside the fish three days and three nights.

Jonah's Prayer

2 From inside the fish Jonah prayed to the LORD his God. ²He said:

"In my distress I called to the LORD,
    and he answered me.
From the depths of the grave*a* I
        called for help,
    and you listened to my cry.
³You hurled me into the deep,
        into the very heart of the seas,
    and the currents swirled about me;
all your waves and breakers
    swept over me.
⁴I said, 'I have been banished
        from your sight;
    yet I will look again
        toward your holy temple.'
⁵The engulfing waters threatened me,*b*
        the deep surrounded me;
    seaweed was wrapped around my
        head.
⁶To the roots of the mountains I sank
        down;
    the earth beneath barred me in
        forever.
But you brought my life up from the
        pit,
    O LORD my God.

⁷"When my life was ebbing away,
    I remembered you, LORD,
and my prayer rose to you,
    to your holy temple.

⁸"Those who cling to worthless idols
    forfeit the grace that could be
        theirs.
⁹But I, with a song of thanksgiving,
    will sacrifice to you.
What I have vowed I will make good.
    Salvation comes from the LORD."

¹⁰And the LORD commanded the fish, and it vomited Jonah onto dry land.

Jonah Goes to Nineveh

3 Then the word of the LORD came to Jonah a second time: ²"Go to the great city of Nineveh and proclaim to it the message I give you."

³Jonah obeyed the word of the LORD and went to Nineveh. Now Nineveh was a very important city—a visit required three days. ⁴On the first day, Jonah started into the city. He proclaimed: "Forty more days and Nineveh will be overturned." ⁵The Ninevites believed God. They declared a fast, and all of them, from the greatest to the least, put on sackcloth.

⁶When the news reached the king of Nineveh, he rose from his throne, took off his royal robes, covered himself with sackcloth and sat down in the dust. ⁷Then he issued a proclamation in Nineveh:

"By the decree of the king and his nobles:

Do not let any man or beast, herd or flock, taste anything; do not let them eat or drink. ⁸But let man and beast be covered with sackcloth. Let everyone call urgently on God. Let them give up their evil ways and their violence. ⁹Who knows? God may yet relent and with compassion turn from his fierce anger so that we will not perish."

¹⁰When God saw what they did and how they turned from their evil ways, he had compassion and did not bring upon them the destruction he had threatened.

Jonah's Anger at the LORD's Compassion

4 But Jonah was greatly displeased and became angry. ²He prayed to the LORD, "O LORD, is this not what I said when I was still at home? That is why I was so quick to flee to Tarshish. I knew that you are a gracious and compassionate God, slow to anger and abounding in love, a God who relents from sending calamity. ³Now, O Lord, take away my life, for it is better for me to die than to live."

⁴But the Lord replied, "Have you any right to be angry?"

⁵Jonah went out and sat down at a place east of the city. There he made himself a shelter, sat in its shade and waited to see what would happen to the city. ⁶Then the Lord God provided a vine and made it grow up over Jonah to give shade for his head to ease his discomfort, and Jonah was very happy about the vine. ⁷But at dawn the next day God provided a worm, which chewed the vine so that it withered. ⁸When the sun rose, God provided a scorching east wind, and the sun blazed on Jonah's head so that he grew

TUESDAY

VERSE FOR THE DAY:
Jonah 4:3–4

AUTHOR:
Doris Rikkers

PASSAGE FOR THE DAY:
Jonah 4:1–11

It's Not Fair!

"THAT'S not fair!"

How many times have I heard that from one of my kids when someone's eaten the last piece of peach pie or stayed up ten minutes longer than the other or been given a little bit more attention when they were sick?

And how often have I replied in all my motherly wisdom, the stock reply on every mother's tongue (isn't it written in the mother's handbook?): "Life's not fair."

Too bad Jonah didn't have his mother around to remind him that life's not fair. Jonah thought that God should punish those bad old Ninevites, just like moms or teachers or somebody are supposed to punish the bullies on the playground or the kid who chews gum in the classroom.

But surprise, surprise, Jonah! God didn't want it that way with Nineveh. He wanted to save the city. Yet Jonah wanted it his way—the righteous and God-fearing people, like Jonah, were to get all the blessing. And the wicked people, like the Ninevites, were to be destroyed. When things didn't go Jonah's way he sat down and pouted and could easily have muttered, "It's not fair!"

Life isn't always the way we want it to be; it doesn't always seem fair, in our eyes or from our perspective, that is. But all is fair and just in God's eyes. And we must resist the urge to doubt or judge like Jonah. Our part is to have faith and believe that God is just and all is in his control, whether or not we think, "It's just not fair."

Additional Scripture Readings:
Matthew 20:1–15; Romans 9:10–21

Go to page 986 for your next devotional reading.

faint. He wanted to die, and said, "It would be better for me to die than to live."

⁹But God said to Jonah, "Do you have a right to be angry about the vine?"

"I do," he said. "I am angry enough to die."

¹⁰But the LORD said, "You have been concerned about this vine, though you did not tend it or make it grow. It sprang up overnight and died overnight. ¹¹But Nineveh has more than a hundred and twenty thousand people who cannot tell their right hand from their left, and many cattle as well. Should I not be concerned about that great city?"

MICAH prophesies during the time of Jotham and Ahaz (2 Chronicles 27–28) against the numerous sins of the kingdom of Judah, insisting that God wants justice in society. He inspires hope by speaking of the coming Messiah and his kingdom of peace. As you read this book, promise the Lord that your lifestyle will be one of justice, mercy and peace in his Son Jesus Christ.

MICAH

1 The word of the LORD that came to Micah of Moresheth during the reigns of Jotham, Ahaz and Hezekiah, kings of Judah—the vision he saw concerning Samaria and Jerusalem.

²Hear, O peoples, all of you,
　listen, O earth and all who are in
　　it,
　that the Sovereign LORD may witness
　　against you,
　the Lord from his holy temple.

Judgment Against Samaria and Jerusalem

³Look! The LORD is coming from his
　dwelling place;
　he comes down and treads the high
　　places of the earth.
⁴The mountains melt beneath him
　and the valleys split apart,
　like wax before the fire,
　like water rushing down a slope.
⁵All this is because of Jacob's
　　transgression,
　because of the sins of the house of
　　Israel.
What is Jacob's transgression?
　Is it not Samaria?
What is Judah's high place?
　Is it not Jerusalem?

⁶"Therefore I will make Samaria a
　　heap of rubble,
　a place for planting vineyards.
I will pour her stones into the valley
　and lay bare her foundations.
⁷All her idols will be broken to
　　pieces;

all her temple gifts will be burned
with fire;
I will destroy all her images.
Since she gathered her gifts from the
wages of prostitutes,
as the wages of prostitutes they will
again be used."

Weeping and Mourning

⁸Because of this I will weep and wail;
I will go about barefoot and naked.
I will howl like a jackal
and moan like an owl.
⁹For her wound is incurable;
it has come to Judah.
It*a* has reached the very gate of my
people,
even to Jerusalem itself.
¹⁰Tell it not in Gath*b*;
weep not at all.*c*
In Beth Ophrah*d*
roll in the dust.
¹¹Pass on in nakedness and shame,
you who live in Shaphir.*e*
Those who live in Zaanan*f*
will not come out.
Beth Ezel is in mourning;
its protection is taken from you.
¹²Those who live in Maroth*g* writhe in
pain,
waiting for relief,
because disaster has come from the
LORD,
even to the gate of Jerusalem.
¹³You who live in Lachish,*h*
harness the team to the chariot.
You were the beginning of sin
to the Daughter of Zion,
for the transgressions of Israel
were found in you.
¹⁴Therefore you will give parting gifts
to Moresheth Gath.
The town of Aczib*i* will prove
deceptive
to the kings of Israel.
¹⁵I will bring a conqueror against you
who live in Mareshah.*j*
He who is the glory of Israel
will come to Adullam.
¹⁶Shave your heads in mourning
for the children in whom you
delight;
make yourselves as bald as the vulture,
for they will go from you into exile.

Man's Plans and God's

2 Woe to those who plan iniquity,
to those who plot evil on their
beds!
At morning's light they carry it out
because it is in their power to
do it.
²They covet fields and seize them,
and houses, and take them.
They defraud a man of his home,
a fellowman of his inheritance.

³Therefore, the LORD says:

"I am planning disaster against this
people,
from which you cannot save
yourselves.
You will no longer walk proudly,
for it will be a time of calamity.
⁴In that day men will ridicule you;
they will taunt you with this
mournful song:
'We are utterly ruined;
my people's possession is divided
up.
He takes it from me!
He assigns our fields to traitors.' "

⁵Therefore you will have no one in the
assembly of the LORD
to divide the land by lot.

False Prophets

⁶"Do not prophesy," their prophets
say.
"Do not prophesy about these
things;
disgrace will not overtake us."
⁷Should it be said, O house of Jacob:
"Is the Spirit of the LORD angry?
Does he do such things?"

"Do not my words do good
to him whose ways are upright?
⁸Lately my people have risen up
like an enemy.
You strip off the rich robe
from those who pass by without a
care,
like men returning from battle.
⁹You drive the women of my people
from their pleasant homes.
You take away my blessing
from their children forever.

---

a9 Or *He*   *b10 Gath* sounds like the Hebrew for *tell.*   *c10* Hebrew; Septuagint may suggest *not in
Acco.* The Hebrew for *in Acco* sounds like the Hebrew for *weep.*   *d10 Beth Ophrah* means *house of
dust.*   *e11 Shaphir* means *pleasant.*   *f11 Zaanan* sounds like the Hebrew for *come out.*
g12 Maroth sounds like the Hebrew for *bitter.*   *h13 Lachish* sounds like the Hebrew for *team.*
i14 Aczib means *deception.*   *j15 Mareshah* sounds like the Hebrew for *conqueror.*

¹⁰Get up, go away!
For this is not your resting place,
because it is defiled,
it is ruined, beyond all remedy.
¹¹If a liar and deceiver comes and says,
'I will prophesy for you plenty of
wine and beer,'
he would be just the prophet for
this people!

Deliverance Promised

¹²"I will surely gather all of you,
O Jacob;
I will surely bring together the
remnant of Israel.
I will bring them together like sheep
in a pen,
like a flock in its pasture;
the place will throng with people.
¹³One who breaks open the way will go
up before them;
they will break through the gate
and go out.
Their king will pass through before
them,
the LORD at their head."

Leaders and Prophets Rebuked

3 Then I said,

"Listen, you leaders of Jacob,
you rulers of the house of Israel.
Should you not know justice,
²   you who hate good and love evil;
who tear the skin from my people
and the flesh from their bones;
³who eat my people's flesh,
strip off their skin
and break their bones in pieces;
who chop them up like meat for the
pan,
like flesh for the pot?"

⁴Then they will cry out to the LORD,
but he will not answer them.
At that time he will hide his face
from them
because of the evil they have done.

⁵This is what the LORD says:

"As for the prophets
who lead my people astray,
if one feeds them,
they proclaim 'peace';
if he does not,
they prepare to wage war against
him.
⁶Therefore night will come over you,
without visions,
and darkness, without divination.
The sun will set for the prophets,
and the day will go dark for them.
⁷The seers will be ashamed
and the diviners disgraced.
They will all cover their faces
because there is no answer from
God."

⁸But as for me, I am filled with power,
with the Spirit of the LORD,
and with justice and might,
to declare to Jacob his transgression,
to Israel his sin.
⁹Hear this, you leaders of the house of
Jacob,
you rulers of the house of Israel,
who despise justice
and distort all that is right;
¹⁰who build Zion with bloodshed,
and Jerusalem with wickedness.
¹¹Her leaders judge for a bribe,
her priests teach for a price,
and her prophets tell fortunes for
money.
Yet they lean upon the LORD and say,
"Is not the LORD among us?
No disaster will come upon us."
¹²Therefore because of you,
Zion will be plowed like a field,
Jerusalem will become a heap of
rubble,
the temple hill a mound overgrown
with thickets.

The Mountain of the LORD

4 In the last days

the mountain of the LORD's temple
will be established
as chief among the mountains;
it will be raised above the hills,
and peoples will stream to it.

²Many nations will come and say,

"Come, let us go up to the mountain
of the LORD,
to the house of the God of Jacob.
He will teach us his ways,
so that we may walk in his paths."
The law will go out from Zion,
the word of the LORD from
Jerusalem.
³He will judge between many peoples
and will settle disputes for strong
nations far and wide.
They will beat their swords into
plowshares
and their spears into pruning
hooks.
Nation will not take up sword against
nation,

nor will they train for war anymore.
⁴Every man will sit under his own vine
and under his own fig tree,
and no one will make them afraid,
for the LORD Almighty has spoken.
⁵All the nations may walk
in the name of their gods;
we will walk in the name of the LORD
our God for ever and ever.

The LORD's Plan

⁶"In that day," declares the LORD,

"I will gather the lame;
I will assemble the exiles
and those I have brought to grief.
⁷I will make the lame a remnant,
those driven away a strong nation.
The LORD will rule over them in
Mount Zion
from that day and forever.
⁸As for you, O watchtower of the flock,
O stronghold*ᵃ* of the Daughter of
Zion,
the former dominion will be restored
to you;
kingship will come to the Daughter
of Jerusalem."

⁹Why do you now cry aloud—
have you no king?
Has your counselor perished,
that pain seizes you like that of a
woman in labor?
¹⁰Writhe in agony, O Daughter of Zion,
like a woman in labor,
for now you must leave the city
to camp in the open field.
You will go to Babylon;
there you will be rescued.
There the LORD will redeem you
out of the hand of your enemies.

¹¹But now many nations
are gathered against you.
They say, "Let her be defiled,
let our eyes gloat over Zion!"
¹²But they do not know
the thoughts of the LORD;
they do not understand his plan,
he who gathers them like sheaves
to the threshing floor.

¹³"Rise and thresh, O Daughter of Zion,
for I will give you horns of iron;
I will give you hoofs of bronze
and you will break to pieces many
nations."

You will devote their ill-gotten gains
to the LORD,
their wealth to the Lord of all the
earth.

A Promised Ruler From Bethlehem

5 Marshal your troops, O city of
troops,*ᵇ*
for a siege is laid against us.
They will strike Israel's ruler
on the cheek with a rod.

²"But you, Bethlehem Ephrathah,
though you are small among the
clans*ᶜ* of Judah,
out of you will come for me
one who will be ruler over Israel,
whose origins*ᵈ* are from of old,
from ancient times.*ᵉ*"

³Therefore Israel will be abandoned
until the time when she who is in
labor gives birth
and the rest of his brothers return
to join the Israelites.

⁴He will stand and shepherd his flock
in the strength of the LORD,
in the majesty of the name of the
LORD his God.
And they will live securely, for then
his greatness
will reach to the ends of the earth.
⁵ And he will be their peace.

Deliverance and Destruction

When the Assyrian invades our land
and marches through our fortresses,
we will raise against him seven
shepherds,
even eight leaders of men.
⁶They will rule*ᶠ* the land of Assyria
with the sword,
the land of Nimrod with drawn
sword.*ᵍ*
He will deliver us from the Assyrian
when he invades our land
and marches into our borders.

⁷The remnant of Jacob will be
in the midst of many peoples
like dew from the LORD,
like showers on the grass,
which do not wait for man
or linger for mankind.
⁸The remnant of Jacob will be among
the nations,
in the midst of many peoples,

ᵃ8 Or hill   ᵇ1 Or Strengthen your walls, O walled city   ᶜ2 Or rulers   ᵈ2 Hebrew goings out
ᵉ2 Or from days of eternity   ᶠ6 Or crush   ᵍ6 Or Nimrod in its gates

like a lion among the beasts of the
  forest,
  like a young lion among flocks of
  sheep,
which mauls and mangles as it goes,
  and no one can rescue.
⁹Your hand will be lifted up in triumph
  over your enemies,
  and all your foes will be destroyed.

¹⁰"In that day," declares the LORD,

"I will destroy your horses from
  among you
  and demolish your chariots.
¹¹I will destroy the cities of your land
  and tear down all your strongholds.
¹²I will destroy your witchcraft
  and you will no longer cast spells.
¹³I will destroy your carved images
  and your sacred stones from among
  you;
  you will no longer bow down
  to the work of your hands.
¹⁴I will uproot from among you your
  Asherah poles*a*
  and demolish your cities.
¹⁵I will take vengeance in anger and
  wrath
  upon the nations that have not
  obeyed me."

The LORD's Case Against Israel

6 Listen to what the LORD says:

"Stand up, plead your case before
  the mountains;
  let the hills hear what you have to
  say.
²Hear, O mountains, the LORD's
  accusation;
  listen, you everlasting foundations
  of the earth.
For the LORD has a case against his
  people;
  he is lodging a charge against
  Israel.

³"My people, what have I done to you?
  How have I burdened you? Answer
  me.
⁴I brought you up out of Egypt
  and redeemed you from the land of
  slavery.
I sent Moses to lead you,
  also Aaron and Miriam.
⁵My people, remember
  what Balak king of Moab counseled

and what Balaam son of Beor
  answered.
Remember ⌊your journey⌋ from
  Shittim to Gilgal,
  that you may know the righteous
  acts of the LORD."

⁶With what shall I come before the
  LORD
  and bow down before the exalted
  God?
Shall I come before him with burnt
  offerings,
  with calves a year old?
⁷Will the LORD be pleased with
  thousands of rams,
  with ten thousand rivers of oil?
Shall I offer my firstborn for my
  transgression,
  the fruit of my body for the sin of
  my soul?
⁸He has showed you, O man, what is
  good.
  And what does the LORD require of
  you?
To act justly and to love mercy
  and to walk humbly with your God.

Israel's Guilt and Punishment

⁹Listen! The LORD is calling to the
  city—
  and to fear your name is wisdom—
  "Heed the rod and the One who
  appointed it.*b*
¹⁰Am I still to forget, O wicked house,
  your ill-gotten treasures
  and the short ephah,*c* which is
  accursed?
¹¹Shall I acquit a man with dishonest
  scales,
  with a bag of false weights?
¹²Her rich men are violent;
  her people are liars
  and their tongues speak deceitfully.
¹³Therefore, I have begun to destroy
  you,
  to ruin you because of your sins.
¹⁴You will eat but not be satisfied;
  your stomach will still be empty.*d*
You will store up but save nothing,
  because what you save I will give to
  the sword.
¹⁵You will plant but not harvest;
  you will press olives but not use
  the oil on yourselves,
  you will crush grapes but not drink
  the wine.

---

a14 That is, symbols of the goddess Asherah   *b9* The meaning of the Hebrew for this line is uncertain.
c10 An ephah was a dry measure.   *d14* The meaning of the Hebrew for this word is uncertain.

VERSE FOR THE DAY:
Micah 6:8

AUTHOR:
Debby Boone

PASSAGE FOR THE DAY:
Micah 6:1–8

Simplicity of Truth

IN all my running around, in all my crowded life, as I try to find more things and more activities that will make God pleased with me, Micah 6:8 creeps in and defuses all my noble but erroneous intentions. The prophet has put it very simply, very eloquently. Look at this verse . . . what do you think I could bring before the Lord of the universe? What? With what could I hope to impress him? And what will be the teachings and heritage that I leave with my children? What will be their overall impression of how God would have us walk in this world? I think this is the beauty of the passage: No great theology. No ten-point sermon. No list of self-improvement plans. Just the simplicity of truth. Three things. Three things that cover the Ten Commandments, the Golden Rule, the Sermon on the Mount:

> What does the LORD require of you?
> To act justly and to love mercy
> and to walk humbly with your God
> (Micah 6:8).

Every child in kindergarten knows what justice means. (We share our blocks. If one person gets juice, we all do.) Every toddler knows how to love kindness and mercy. (That's right, kiss the baby gently . . . aww, that's good.) And children also happen to be quite good at walking humbly with God. Maybe it's because they haven't done anything "great" yet for God. Or maybe it's because in their young lives they haven't offended God so badly that they feel the need to make up for it. Whatever the reason, children have a wonderful ability to accept the gifts of God at face value, without feeling pride or embarrassment.

We as "mature" adults struggle with it. But the more we can walk humbly with God—accepting his wonderful goodness to us, his tender graciousness toward us, his unfailing mercies that are new every morning—the more we can turn to others and love mercy . . . and do justice. And encourage our children to do the same.

Additional Scripture Readings:
Zechariah 7:8–10; Titus 3:4–8

*Go to page 988 for your next
devotional reading.*

16You have observed the statutes of
Omri
and all the practices of Ahab's
house,
and you have followed their
traditions.
Therefore I will give you over to ruin
and your people to derision;
you will bear the scorn of the
nations.ᵃ"

Israel's Misery

7 What misery is mine!
I am like one who gathers summer
fruit
at the gleaning of the vineyard;
there is no cluster of grapes to eat,
none of the early figs that I crave.
2The godly have been swept from the
land;
not one upright man remains.
All men lie in wait to shed blood;
each hunts his brother with a net.
3Both hands are skilled in doing evil;
the ruler demands gifts,
the judge accepts bribes,
the powerful dictate what they
desire —
they all conspire together.
4The best of them is like a brier,
the most upright worse than a
thorn hedge.
The day of your watchmen has come,
the day God visits you.
Now is the time of their confusion.
5Do not trust a neighbor;
put no confidence in a friend.
Even with her who lies in your
embrace
be careful of your words.
6For a son dishonors his father,
a daughter rises up against her
mother,
a daughter-in-law against her
mother-in-law —
a man's enemies are the members
of his own household.

7But as for me, I watch in hope for the
LORD,
I wait for God my Savior;
my God will hear me.

Israel Will Rise

8Do not gloat over me, my enemy!
Though I have fallen, I will rise.
Though I sit in darkness,
the LORD will be my light.

9Because I have sinned against him,
I will bear the LORD's wrath,
until he pleads my case
and establishes my right.
He will bring me out into the light;
I will see his righteousness.
10Then my enemy will see it
and will be covered with shame,
she who said to me,
"Where is the LORD your God?"
My eyes will see her downfall;
even now she will be trampled
underfoot
like mire in the streets.
11The day for building your walls will
come,
the day for extending your
boundaries.
12In that day people will come to
you
from Assyria and the cities of
Egypt,
even from Egypt to the Euphrates
and from sea to sea
and from mountain to mountain.
13The earth will become desolate
because of its inhabitants,
as the result of their deeds.

Prayer and Praise

14Shepherd your people with your
staff,
the flock of your inheritance,
which lives by itself in a forest,
in fertile pasturelands.ᵇ
Let them feed in Bashan and Gilead
as in days long ago.

15"As in the days when you came out of
Egypt,
I will show them my wonders."

16Nations will see and be ashamed,
deprived of all their power.
They will lay their hands on their
mouths
and their ears will become deaf.
17They will lick dust like a snake,
like creatures that crawl on the
ground.
They will come trembling out of their
dens;
they will turn in fear to the LORD
our God
and will be afraid of you.
18Who is a God like you,
who pardons sin and forgives the
transgression

ᵃ16 Septuagint; Hebrew scorn due my people   ᵇ14 Or in the middle of Carmel

VERSE FOR THE DAY:
Micah 7:8

AUTHOR:
Diane Head

PASSAGE FOR THE DAY:
Micah 7:1–9

His Light

THERE are some days in a mother's life when the sun just doesn't seem to rise. We may have been disappointed by someone. Or maybe we're not feeling good about ourselves or about our relationships with others. Maybe we're just lonely. Whatever the reason, a cloud settles in . . . .

Usually this cloud of gloom brings with it a refusal to be cheered up. In fact, if anyone tries to cheer or uplift us we grudgingly summon a ghostly smile and slide back into our pit of despair.

This mood can almost be enjoyable. After all, our very lives are dedicated to the welfare of our husbands and children. Isn't it fun to let them know it—along with how wronged we've been—regardless of whether or not it's their fault? Poor us.

Does this sound familiar? I confess I am to some degee an authority on this subject. Alas, it comes from firsthand experience.

We are all affected by different circumstances. For some of us, something as simple as a cloudy day may touch off the blues. Fatigue often precedes them. Sometimes our depression is caused by someone who has spoken critically of us or a family member. The list is endless. The funny thing is that even when most of the reasons are legitimate, the resulting dejection isn't.

It would be depressing enough if we were the only ones affected by our dark days. But like it or not, we are the hubs of emotional stability in our families. If our outlook is sunny, it is reflected in every member of our household. If, however, clouds of self-pity, gloom and despair hover over us, they also rain down on all who come near.

The trouble with darkness is that it seems to be stronger . . . denser . . . and deeper . . . than light. We are almost fooled into believing that it is just as it seems.

But just as one small candle can dispel the darkness in an arena, so can the entrance of light into our souls dispel the bleak and dreary darkness lurking there. And how much greater that light—the light of the Lord—than one little candle . . . .

Additional Scripture Readings:
2 Samuel 22:29–30; Isaiah 59:9–10; 60:1–3

Go to page 991 for your next devotional reading.

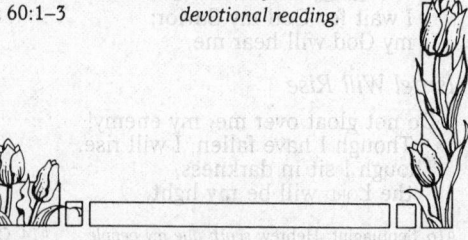

of the remnant of his inheritance?
You do not stay angry forever
but delight to show mercy.
[19]You will again have compassion on
us;
you will tread our sins underfoot

and hurl all our iniquities into the
depths of the sea.
[20]You will be true to Jacob,
and show mercy to Abraham,
as you pledged on oath to our fathers
in days long ago.

of the remnant of his inheritance?
You do not stay angry forever
but delight to show mercy.
¹⁹You will again have compassion on
us;
you will tread our sins underfoot

*N*AHUM *prophesies against the wicked and cruel nation of Assyria, probably during the time of Josiah (2 Kings 22–23). In so doing he testifies that God, as the judge of the nations, is in control of all that happens. As you read this book, be comforted (Nahum means "comfort") by the thought that God is Lord of history.*

NAHUM

1 An oracle concerning Nineveh. The book of the vision of Nahum the Elkoshite.

The LORD's Anger Against Nineveh

²The LORD is a jealous and avenging God;
  the LORD takes vengeance and is filled with wrath.
The LORD takes vengeance on his foes
  and maintains his wrath against his enemies.
³The LORD is slow to anger and great in power;
  the LORD will not leave the guilty unpunished.
His way is in the whirlwind and the storm,
  and clouds are the dust of his feet.
⁴He rebukes the sea and dries it up;
  he makes all the rivers run dry.
Bashan and Carmel wither
  and the blossoms of Lebanon fade.
⁵The mountains quake before him
  and the hills melt away.
The earth trembles at his presence,
  the world and all who live in it.
⁶Who can withstand his indignation?
  Who can endure his fierce anger?
His wrath is poured out like fire;
  the rocks are shattered before him.

⁷The LORD is good,
  a refuge in times of trouble.
He cares for those who trust in him,
⁸ but with an overwhelming flood
he will make an end of Nineveh;
  he will pursue his foes into darkness.

⁹Whatever they plot against the LORD

VERSE FOR THE DAY:
Nahum 1:3

AUTHOR:
Gigi Graham Tchividjian

PASSAGE FOR THE DAY:
Nahum 1:2–8

The Storm

I LAY on the soft white sand while the children played happily in the surf nearby. Suddenly a shadow fell across my face. I looked up just in time to see the sun disappearing behind a big thunderhead. I turned my gaze to the ocean, which only moments before had been a bright mirror reflecting the blue sky. Now the whitecaps danced restlessly, and the gray waves angrily pounded the shore. Before I could collect the children and run for shelter, the heavens opened and the rain poured down. I was amazed how quickly the storm had gathered.

As we huddled in the shelter, my mind wandered back to another storm:

Jesus had had a busy day. Helping, healing, and teaching, he was surrounded constantly by people. Now it was evening. As Jesus gazed out over the peaceful blue of Lake Galilee, he said to his disciples, "Let us go over to the other side" (Mark 4:35). They set out in a small boat and soon Jesus fell asleep.

While he was resting, a powerful storm arose. The waves beat against the sides of the ship, filling it with water. The disciples were afraid and cried out to him, saying, "Teacher, don't you care if we drown?" Jesus got up and looked out over the sea. He saw the waves and felt the wind and said, "Quiet! Be still!" And all was calm again. Then he turned to his disciples, "Why do you have so little faith?" (Mark 4:35–41, author's paraphrase).

Storms arise in our lives, too. A telephone call brings sudden jolting news. A letter brings disappointment. A child has an accident. A small pain develops into a serious illness. Death . . . divorce . . . financial reverses. Or maybe the source of distress is just the everyday pressures and tensions that build and build until the thunderhead erupts into a storm.

I, too, have had my share of storms. Some have been brief afternoon showers. Others have been caused by tensions that have built up, threatening my serenity and peace. Still others have burst upon my life suddenly, hitting hard and leaving in their wake damage and debris. Like the disciples I have been afraid and have cried out, "Lord, don't you care?" And later, when all is calm again, I hear him say, "Gigi, why do you have so little faith?"

He has never promised a life free from storms, but he has promised to be with us in the midst of them and to bring us safely to the other side if we believe in him and rely on him.

Additional Scripture Readings:
Isaiah 25:4–5; 2 Corinthians 1:8–10

*Go to page 993 for your next
devotional reading.*

he[a] will bring to an end;
trouble will not come a second
time.
10They will be entangled among thorns
and drunk from their wine;
they will be consumed like dry
stubble.[b]
11From you, O Nineveh, has one come
forth
who plots evil against the LORD
and counsels wickedness.

12This is what the LORD says:

"Although they have allies and are
numerous,
they will be cut off and pass away.
Although I have afflicted you,
O Judah,
I will afflict you no more.
13Now I will break their yoke from your
neck
and tear your shackles away."

14The LORD has given a command
concerning you, Nineveh:
"You will have no descendants to
bear your name.
I will destroy the carved images and
cast idols
that are in the temple of your gods.
I will prepare your grave,
for you are vile."

15Look, there on the mountains,
the feet of one who brings good
news,
who proclaims peace!
Celebrate your festivals, O Judah,
and fulfill your vows.
No more will the wicked invade you;
they will be completely destroyed.

Nineveh to Fall

2 An attacker advances against you,
Nineveh.
Guard the fortress,
watch the road,
brace yourselves,
marshal all your strength!

2The LORD will restore the splendor of
Jacob
like the splendor of Israel,
though destroyers have laid them
waste
and have ruined their vines.

3The shields of his soldiers are red;
the warriors are clad in scarlet.
The metal on the chariots flashes
on the day they are made ready;
the spears of pine are brandished.[c]
4The chariots storm through the
streets,
rushing back and forth through the
squares.
They look like flaming torches;
they dart about like lightning.

5He summons his picked troops,
yet they stumble on their way.
They dash to the city wall;
the protective shield is put in
place.
6The river gates are thrown open
and the palace collapses.
7It is decreed[d] that the city,
be exiled and carried away.
Its slave girls moan like doves
and beat upon their breasts.
8Nineveh is like a pool,
and its water is draining away.
"Stop! Stop!" they cry,
but no one turns back.
9Plunder the silver!
Plunder the gold!
The supply is endless,
the wealth from all its treasures!
10She is pillaged, plundered, stripped!
Hearts melt, knees give way,
bodies tremble, every face grows
pale.
11Where now is the lions' den,
the place where they fed their
young,
where the lion and lioness went,
and the cubs, with nothing to fear?
12The lion killed enough for his cubs
and strangled the prey for his mate,
filling his lairs with the kill
and his dens with the prey.

13"I am against you,"
declares the LORD Almighty.
"I will burn up your chariots in
smoke,
and the sword will devour your
young lions.
I will leave you no prey on the
earth.
The voices of your messengers
will no longer be heard."

---

a9 Or What do you foes plot against the LORD? / He
uncertain.   c3 Hebrew; Septuagint and Syriac / the horsemen rush to and fro   d7 The meaning of the
Hebrew for this word is uncertain.   b10 The meaning of the Hebrew for this verse is

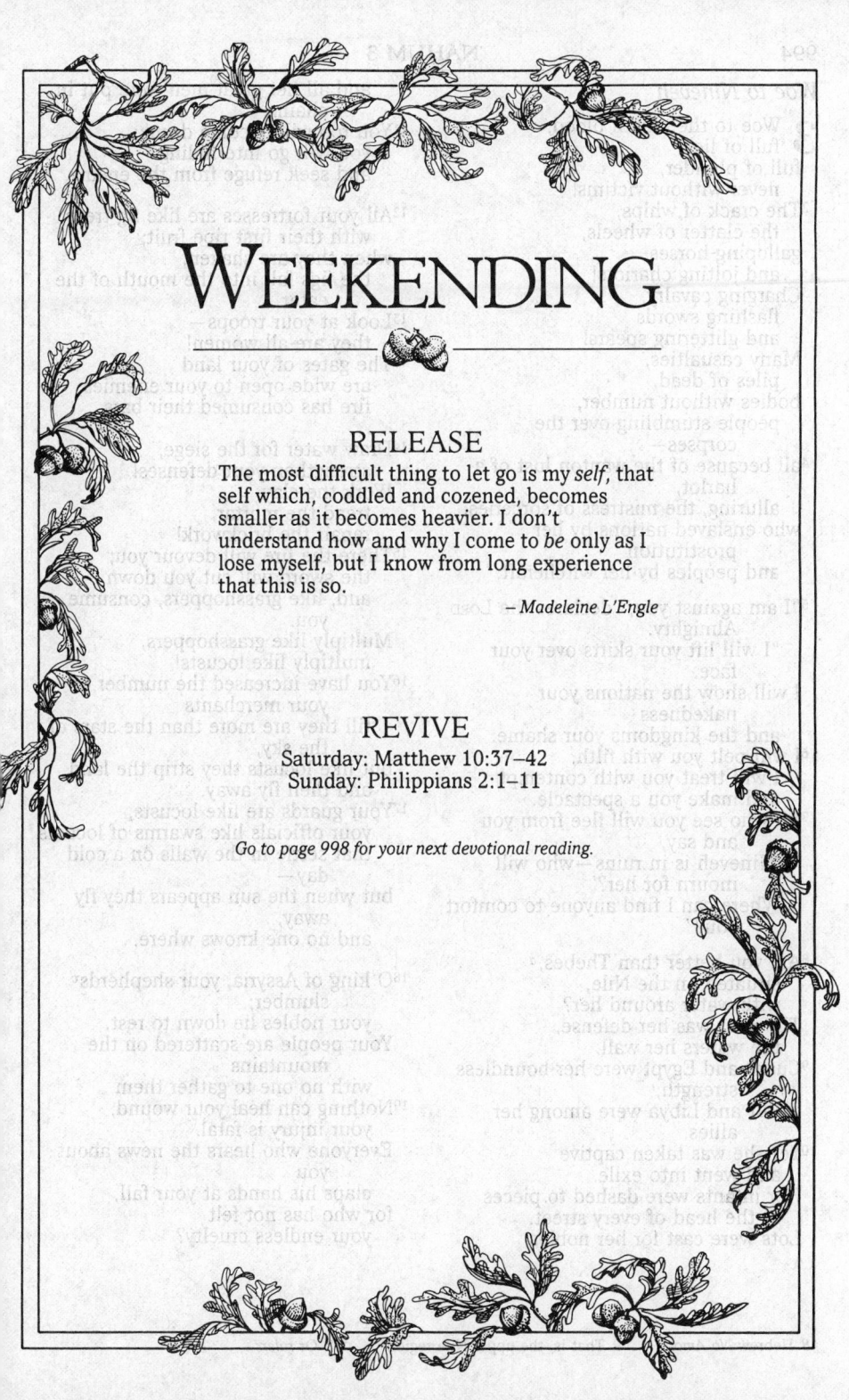

WEEKENDING

RELEASE

The most difficult thing to let go is my *self*, that self which, coddled and cozened, becomes smaller as it becomes heavier. I don't understand how and why I come to *be* only as I lose myself, but I know from long experience that this is so.

– *Madeleine L'Engle*

REVIVE

Saturday: Matthew 10:37–42
Sunday: Philippians 2:1–11

Go to page 998 for your next devotional reading.

Woe to Nineveh

3 Woe to the city of blood,
full of lies,
full of plunder,
never without victims!
²The crack of whips,
the clatter of wheels,
galloping horses
and jolting chariots!
³Charging cavalry,
flashing swords
and glittering spears!
Many casualties,
piles of dead,
bodies without number,
people stumbling over the
corpses—
⁴all because of the wanton lust of a
harlot,
alluring, the mistress of sorceries,
who enslaved nations by her
prostitution
and peoples by her witchcraft.

⁵"I am against you," declares the LORD
Almighty.
"I will lift your skirts over your
face.
I will show the nations your
nakedness
and the kingdoms your shame.
⁶I will pelt you with filth,
I will treat you with contempt
and make you a spectacle.
⁷All who see you will flee from you
and say,
'Nineveh is in ruins—who will
mourn for her?'
Where can I find anyone to comfort
you?"

⁸Are you better than Thebes,ᵃ
situated on the Nile,
with water around her?
The river was her defense,
the waters her wall.
⁹Cushᵇ and Egypt were her boundless
strength;
Put and Libya were among her
allies.
¹⁰Yet she was taken captive
and went into exile.
Her infants were dashed to pieces
at the head of every street.
Lots were cast for her nobles,
and all her great men were put in
chains.
¹¹You too will become drunk;
you will go into hiding
and seek refuge from the enemy.

¹²All your fortresses are like fig trees
with their first ripe fruit;
when they are shaken,
the figs fall into the mouth of the
eater.
¹³Look at your troops—
they are all women!
The gates of your land
are wide open to your enemies;
fire has consumed their bars.

¹⁴Draw water for the siege,
strengthen your defenses!
Work the clay,
tread the mortar,
repair the brickwork!
¹⁵There the fire will devour you;
the sword will cut you down
and, like grasshoppers, consume
you.
Multiply like grasshoppers,
multiply like locusts!
¹⁶You have increased the number of
your merchants
till they are more than the stars of
the sky,
but like locusts they strip the land
and then fly away.
¹⁷Your guards are like locusts,
your officials like swarms of locusts
that settle in the walls on a cold
day—
but when the sun appears they fly
away,
and no one knows where.

¹⁸O king of Assyria, your shepherdsᶜ
slumber;
your nobles lie down to rest.
Your people are scattered on the
mountains
with no one to gather them.
¹⁹Nothing can heal your wound;
your injury is fatal.
Everyone who hears the news about
you
claps his hands at your fall,
for who has not felt
your endless cruelty?

ᵃ8 Hebrew *No Amon*   ᵇ9 That is, the upper Nile region   ᶜ18 Or *rulers*

*H*ABAKKUK *prophesies in Judah when the power of Babylon is growing (2 Chronicles 35:20–36:8). When he questions God's justice in allowing evil to go unchecked, he receives the answer that God knows what he is doing, leading to a concluding celebration of God's glory and power. As you read this book, remember that the majestic God is in control of your life, no matter what happens to you.*

HABAKKUK

1

The oracle that Habakkuk the prophet received.

Habakkuk's Complaint

²How long, O Lᴏʀᴅ, must I call for
help,
but you do not listen?
Or cry out to you, "Violence!"
but you do not save?
³Why do you make me look at
injustice?
Why do you tolerate wrong?
Destruction and violence are before
me;
there is strife, and conflict
abounds.
⁴Therefore the law is paralyzed,

and justice never prevails.
The wicked hem in the righteous,
so that justice is perverted.

The Lᴏʀᴅ's Answer

⁵"Look at the nations and watch—
and be utterly amazed.
For I am going to do something in
your days
that you would not believe,
even if you were told.
⁶I am raising up the Babylonians,ᵃ
that ruthless and impetuous people,
who sweep across the whole earth
to seize dwelling places not their
own.
⁷They are a feared and dreaded people;

ᵃ6 Or *Chaldeans*

they are a law to themselves
and promote their own honor.
8Their horses are swifter than leopards,
fiercer than wolves at dusk.
Their cavalry gallops headlong;
their horsemen come from afar.
They fly like a vulture swooping to
devour;
9   they all come bent on violence.
Their hordes*a* advance like a desert
wind
and gather prisoners like sand.
10They deride kings
and scoff at rulers.
They laugh at all fortified cities;
they build earthen ramps and
capture them.
11Then they sweep past like the wind
and go on —
guilty men, whose own strength is
their god."

Habakkuk's Second Complaint

12O LORD, are you not from everlasting?
My God, my Holy One, we will not
die.
O LORD, you have appointed them to
execute judgment;
O Rock, you have ordained them to
punish.
13Your eyes are too pure to look on evil;
you cannot tolerate wrong.
Why then do you tolerate the
treacherous?
Why are you silent while the
wicked
swallow up those more righteous
than themselves?
14You have made men like fish in the
sea,
like sea creatures that have no
ruler.
15The wicked foe pulls all of them up
with hooks,
he catches them in his net,
he gathers them up in his dragnet;
and so he rejoices and is glad.
16Therefore he sacrifices to his net
and burns incense to his dragnet,
for by his net he lives in luxury
and enjoys the choicest food.
17Is he to keep on emptying his net,
destroying nations without mercy?

2 I will stand at my watch
and station myself on the ramparts;

I will look to see what he will say to
me,
and what answer I am to give to
this complaint.*b*

The LORD's Answer

2Then the LORD replied:

"Write down the revelation
and make it plain on tablets
so that a herald*c* may run with it.
3For the revelation awaits an
appointed time;
it speaks of the end
and will not prove false.
Though it linger, wait for it;
it*d* will certainly come and will not
delay.

4"See, he is puffed up;
his desires are not upright —
but the righteous will live by his
faith*e* —
5indeed, wine betrays him;
he is arrogant and never at rest.
Because he is as greedy as the grave*f*
and like death is never satisfied,
he gathers to himself all the nations
and takes captive all the peoples.

6"Will not all of them taunt him with
ridicule and scorn, saying,

" 'Woe to him who piles up stolen
goods
and makes himself wealthy by
extortion!
How long must this go on?'
7Will not your debtors*g* suddenly
arise?
Will they not wake up and make
you tremble?
Then you will become their victim.
8Because you have plundered many
nations,
the peoples who are left will
plunder you.
For you have shed man's blood;
you have destroyed lands and cities
and everyone in them.

9"Woe to him who builds his realm by
unjust gain
to set his nest on high,
to escape the clutches of ruin!
10You have plotted the ruin of many
peoples,

---

a9 The meaning of the Hebrew for this word is uncertain.   *b1* Or *and what to answer when I am*
rebuked   *c2* Or *so that whoever reads it*   *d3* Or *Though he linger, wait for him; / he*   *e4* Or
faithfulness   *f5* Hebrew *Sheol*   *g7* Or *creditors*

shaming your own house and
forfeiting your life.
[11]The stones of the wall will cry out,
and the beams of the woodwork
will echo it.

[12]"Woe to him who builds a city with
bloodshed
and establishes a town by
crime!
[13]Has not the LORD Almighty
determined
that the people's labor is only fuel
for the fire,
that the nations exhaust themselves
for nothing?
[14]For the earth will be filled with the
knowledge of the glory of the
LORD,
as the waters cover the sea.

[15]"Woe to him who gives drink to his
neighbors,
pouring it from the wineskin till
they are drunk,
so that he can gaze on their naked
bodies.
[16]You will be filled with shame instead
of glory.
Now it is your turn! Drink and be
exposed[a]!
The cup from the LORD's right hand is
coming around to you,
and disgrace will cover your glory.
[17]The violence you have done to
Lebanon will overwhelm you,
and your destruction of animals will
terrify you.
For you have shed man's blood;
you have destroyed lands and cities
and everyone in them.

[18]"Of what value is an idol, since a
man has carved it?
Or an image that teaches lies?
For he who makes it trusts in his own
creation;
he makes idols that cannot speak.
[19]Woe to him who says to wood, 'Come
to life!'
Or to lifeless stone, 'Wake up!'
Can it give guidance?
It is covered with gold and silver;
there is no breath in it.
[20]But the LORD is in his holy temple;
let all the earth be silent before
him."

Habakkuk's Prayer

3 A prayer of Habakkuk the prophet.
On *shigionoth*.[b]

[2]LORD, I have heard of your fame;
I stand in awe of your deeds,
O LORD.
Renew them in our day,
in our time make them known;
in wrath remember mercy.

[3]God came from Teman,
the Holy One from Mount Paran.
Selah[c]

His glory covered the heavens
and his praise filled the earth.
[4]His splendor was like the sunrise;
rays flashed from his hand,
where his power was hidden.
[5]Plague went before him;
pestilence followed his steps.
[6]He stood, and shook the earth;
he looked, and made the nations
tremble.
The ancient mountains crumbled
and the age-old hills collapsed.
His ways are eternal.
[7]I saw the tents of Cushan in distress,
the dwellings of Midian in anguish.

[8]Were you angry with the rivers,
O LORD?
Was your wrath against the
streams?
Did you rage against the sea
when you rode with your horses
and your victorious chariots?
[9]You uncovered your bow,
you called for many arrows.   *Selah*
You split the earth with rivers;
10 the mountains saw you and
writhed.
Torrents of water swept by;
the deep roared
and lifted its waves on high.
[11]Sun and moon stood still in the
heavens
at the glint of your flying arrows,
at the lightning of your flashing
spear.
[12]In wrath you strode through the earth
and in anger you threshed the
nations.
[13]You came out to deliver your people,
to save your anointed one.
You crushed the leader of the land of
wickedness,

---

[a]16 Masoretic Text; Dead Sea Scrolls, Aquila, Vulgate and Syriac (see also Septuagint) *and stagger*
[b]1 Probably a literary or musical term   [c]3 A word of uncertain meaning; possibly a musical term; also
in verses 9 and 13

VERSE FOR THE DAY:
Habakkuk 3:17–18

AUTHOR:
Martha Manikas-Foster

PASSAGE FOR THE DAY:
Habakkuk 3:1–19

Yet I Will Rejoice

ABOUT two years ago my network of Christian friends began unraveling. One couple who had ministered to me announced plans to divorce. A longtime friend who had been enthusiastic for God declared that she now considered him irrelevant and was going to live on her own terms. Family members who had looked to God as their source of guidance and joy became bitter in the face of misfortune.

How could God allow the evil one to lead my believing friends away from him? How could he permit disillusionment and unclear thinking to conquer the faithful?

> The wicked foe pulls all of them up with hooks,
>   he catches them in his net,
> he gathers them up in his dragnet;
>   and so he rejoices and is glad
>   (Habakkuk 1:15).

For several months each new week brought a disheartening letter or phone call: another friend had relinquished her faith or "adjusted" his Christian commitment. Each bit of news crushed me.

The prophet Habakkuk asks such questions of God in the unprecedented dialogue recorded in the book bearing his name. How can God allow justice to be perverted? How can he ignore the plight of the faithful in Judah? But upon hearing God's reply, the prophet comes to peace on the issue. He is willing to wait on God's timing. In chapter 3, in fact, his prayer is so brimming with faith that it was later used as a psalm in temple worship:

> Though the olive crop fails
>   and the fields produce no food,
> though there are no sheep in the pen
>   and no cattle in the stalls,
> yet I will rejoice in the LORD,
> I will be joyful in God my Savior
>   (Habakkuk 3:17–18).

I needed to learn to rest in God's sufficiency. I will probably never know God's specific plans for my friends. But even though I see no outward indications that the Lord is working in their lives, I know that he has not neglected them. For that "I will be joyful in God my Savior."

Additional Scripture Readings:
Psalm 27:13–14; Hebrews 10:35–11:1

*Go to page 1003 for your next
devotional reading.*

you stripped him from head to foot.
Selah

¹⁴With his own spear you pierced his
head
when his warriors stormed out to
scatter us,
gloating as though about to devour
the wretched who were in hiding.
¹⁵You trampled the sea with your
horses,
churning the great waters.

¹⁶I heard and my heart pounded,
my lips quivered at the sound;
decay crept into my bones,
and my legs trembled.
Yet I will wait patiently for the day of
calamity

to come on the nation invading us.
¹⁷Though the fig tree does not bud
and there are no grapes on the
vines,
though the olive crop fails
and the fields produce no food,
though there are no sheep in the pen
and no cattle in the stalls,
¹⁸yet I will rejoice in the LORD,
I will be joyful in God my Savior.

¹⁹The Sovereign LORD is my strength;
he makes my feet like the feet of a
deer,
he enables me to go on the heights.

For the director of music. On my
stringed instruments.

ZEPHANIAH, early in Josiah's reign and before his reforms (2 Chronicles 34:1–13), prophesies about a coming devastating day of the Lord. But he promises a wonderful future to those who humble themselves, seek the Lord, and live righteously. As you read this book, remember that a day of judgment is coming but that you can escape by turning to the Lord Jesus Christ.

ZEPHANIAH

1 The word of the LORD that came to Zephaniah son of Cushi, the son of Gedaliah, the son of Amariah, the son of Hezekiah, during the reign of Josiah son of Amon king of Judah:

Warning of Coming Destruction

²"I will sweep away everything
　from the face of the earth,"
　　　　　declares the LORD.
³"I will sweep away both men and
　　animals;
　I will sweep away the birds of the
　　air
　and the fish of the sea.
　The wicked will have only heaps of
　　rubble*ᵃ*

when I cut off man from the face of
　the earth,"
　　　　　declares the LORD.

Against Judah

⁴"I will stretch out my hand against
　　Judah
　and against all who live in
　　Jerusalem.
　I will cut off from this place every
　　remnant of Baal,
　the names of the pagan and the
　　idolatrous priests—
⁵those who bow down on the roofs
　to worship the starry host,
　those who bow down and swear by
　　the LORD
　and who also swear by Molech,*ᵇ*

ᵃ3 The meaning of the Hebrew for this line is uncertain.　　*ᵇ5* Hebrew *Malcam*, that is, Milcom

⁶those who turn back from following
    the LORD
and neither seek the LORD nor
    inquire of him.
⁷Be silent before the Sovereign LORD,
    for the day of the LORD is near.
The LORD has prepared a sacrifice;
    he has consecrated those he has
    invited.
⁸On the day of the LORD's sacrifice
    I will punish the princes
    and the king's sons
and all those clad
    in foreign clothes.
⁹On that day I will punish
    all who avoid stepping on the
    threshold,ᵃ
who fill the temple of their gods
    with violence and deceit.

¹⁰"On that day," declares the LORD,
    "a cry will go up from the Fish
    Gate,
wailing from the New Quarter,
    and a loud crash from the hills.
¹¹Wail, you who live in the market
    districtᵇ;
all your merchants will be wiped
    out,
all who trade withᶜ silver will be
    ruined.
¹²At that time I will search Jerusalem
    with lamps
and punish those who are
    complacent,
who are like wine left on its dregs,
who think, 'The LORD will do nothing,
    either good or bad.'
¹³Their wealth will be plundered,
    their houses demolished.
They will build houses
    but not live in them;
they will plant vineyards
    but not drink the wine.

The Great Day of the LORD

¹⁴"The great day of the LORD is near—
    near and coming quickly.
Listen! The cry on the day of the LORD
    will be bitter,
    the shouting of the warrior there.
¹⁵That day will be a day of wrath,
    a day of distress and anguish,
    a day of trouble and ruin,
    a day of darkness and gloom,
    a day of clouds and blackness,
¹⁶a day of trumpet and battle cry

against the fortified cities
    and against the corner towers.
¹⁷I will bring distress on the people
    and they will walk like blind men,
because they have sinned against
    the LORD.
Their blood will be poured out like
    dust
    and their entrails like filth.
¹⁸Neither their silver nor their gold
    will be able to save them
    on the day of the LORD's wrath.
In the fire of his jealousy
    the whole world will be consumed,
for he will make a sudden end
    of all who live in the earth."

2 Gather together, gather together,
    O shameful nation,
²before the appointed time arrives
    and that day sweeps on like chaff,
before the fierce anger of the LORD
    comes upon you,
before the day of the LORD's wrath
    comes upon you.
³Seek the LORD, all you humble of the
    land,
    you who do what he commands.
Seek righteousness, seek humility;
    perhaps you will be sheltered
    on the day of the LORD's anger.

Against Philistia

⁴Gaza will be abandoned
    and Ashkelon left in ruins.
At midday Ashdod will be emptied
    and Ekron uprooted.
⁵Woe to you who live by the sea,
    O Kerethite people;
the word of the LORD is against you,
    O Canaan, land of the Philistines.

"I will destroy you,
    and none will be left."
⁶The land by the sea, where the
    Kerethitesᵈ dwell,
will be a place for shepherds and
    sheep pens.
⁷It will belong to the remnant of the
    house of Judah;
    there they will find pasture.
In the evening they will lie down
    in the houses of Ashkelon.
The LORD their God will care for
    them;
    he will restore their fortunes.ᵉ

ᵃ9 See 1 Samuel 5:5.   ᵇ11 Or the Mortar   ᶜ11 Or in   ᵈ6 The meaning of the Hebrew for this
word is uncertain.   ᵉ7 Or will bring back their captives

Against Moab and Ammon

8"I have heard the insults of Moab
  and the taunts of the Ammonites,
who insulted my people
  and made threats against their
    land.
9Therefore, as surely as I live,"
  declares the LORD Almighty, the
    God of Israel,
"surely Moab will become like
    Sodom,
  the Ammonites like Gomorrah—
a place of weeds and salt pits,
  a wasteland forever.
The remnant of my people will
    plunder them;
  the survivors of my nation will
    inherit their land."

10This is what they will get in return for
    their pride,
  for insulting and mocking the
    people of the LORD Almighty.
11The LORD will be awesome to them
  when he destroys all the gods of
    the land.
The nations on every shore will
    worship him,
  every one in its own land.

Against Cush

12"You too, O Cushites,[a]
  will be slain by my sword."

Against Assyria

13He will stretch out his hand against
    the north
  and destroy Assyria,
leaving Nineveh utterly desolate
  and dry as the desert.
14Flocks and herds will lie down there,
  creatures of every kind.
The desert owl and the screech owl
  will roost on her columns.
Their calls will echo through the
    windows,
  rubble will be in the doorways,
  the beams of cedar will be exposed.
15This is the carefree city
  that lived in safety.
She said to herself,
  "I am, and there is none besides
    me."
What a ruin she has become,
  a lair for wild beasts!

All who pass by her scoff
  and shake their fists.

The Future of Jerusalem

3 Woe to the city of oppressors,
  rebellious and defiled!
2She obeys no one,
  she accepts no correction.
She does not trust in the LORD,
  she does not draw near to her God.
3Her officials are roaring lions,
  her rulers are evening wolves,
  who leave nothing for the morning.
4Her prophets are arrogant;
  they are treacherous men.
Her priests profane the sanctuary
  and do violence to the law.
5The LORD within her is righteous;
  he does no wrong.
Morning by morning he dispenses his
    justice,
  and every new day he does not fail,
  yet the unrighteous know no
    shame.

6"I have cut off nations;
  their strongholds are demolished.
I have left their streets deserted,
  with no one passing through.
Their cities are destroyed;
  no one will be left—no one at all.
7I said to the city,
  'Surely you will fear me
  and accept correction!'
Then her dwelling would not be cut off,
  nor all my punishments come upon
    her.
But they were still eager
  to act corruptly in all they did.
8Therefore wait for me," declares the
    LORD,
  "for the day I will stand up to
    testify.[b]
I have decided to assemble the
    nations,
  to gather the kingdoms
and to pour out my wrath on them—
  all my fierce anger.
The whole world will be consumed
  by the fire of my jealous anger.

9"Then will I purify the lips of the
    peoples,
  that all of them may call on the
    name of the LORD
  and serve him shoulder to shoulder.
10From beyond the rivers of Cush[c]

---

[a]12 That is, people from the upper Nile region
plunder   [c]10 That is, the upper Nile region
[b]8 Septuagint and Syriac; Hebrew *will rise up to*

my worshipers, my scattered
people,
will bring me offerings.
¹¹On that day you will not be put to
shame
for all the wrongs you have done to
me,
because I will remove from this
city
those who rejoice in their pride.
Never again will you be haughty
on my holy hill.
¹²But I will leave within you
the meek and humble,
who trust in the name of the Lᴏʀᴅ.

¹³The remnant of Israel will do no
wrong;
they will speak no lies,
nor will deceit be found in their
mouths.
They will eat and lie down
and no one will make them afraid."

¹⁴Sing, O Daughter of Zion;
shout aloud, O Israel!
Be glad and rejoice with all your
heart,
O Daughter of Jerusalem!
¹⁵The Lᴏʀᴅ has taken away your
punishment,

TUESDAY

VERSE FOR THE DAY: AUTHOR: PASSAGE FOR THE DAY:
Zephaniah 3:20   *Ingrid Trobisch*   *Zephaniah 3:14–20*

Finding the Way Home

SOME of our hidden strength comes from knowing where our
home is. Recently I returned from a six-week trip to five Euro-
pean countries, including East Germany. During that time, I seldom spent more than two nights in the same bed. I lived out of
my suitcase. For a few weeks, my Bible, my copy of the Moravian
Daily Texts with the pictures of my family pasted on its blank
pages, my journal and my notebook became my "home." Could
I have made it without knowing that after six weeks of such living I would return to my "place" in Springfield, my *Haus
Geborgenheit* (my house of steadfast shelter)? I don't know. The
day I safely returned, my heart was filled with praise to my heavenly Father for providing me with this home base. I think I felt
what the Israelites felt when they went back to Jerusalem after
being in exile:

We were like men who dreamed.
Our mouths were filled with laughter,
Our tongues with songs of joy (Psalm 126:1–2).

If there is such joy when we return to our earthly homes,
imagine the joy of our reaching our heavenly home!
My oldest son Daniel and his wife Betty work with troubled
youth in Austria. One day I turned to my son and asked, "What
is your goal in your ministry?"
"To show people the way home," was his quiet answer.

Additional Scripture Readings: *Go to page 1006 for your next*
John 14:23; 1 Peter 2:25   *devotional reading.*

he has turned back your enemy.
The LORD, the King of Israel, is with
    you;
never again will you fear any harm.
¹⁶On that day they will say to
        Jerusalem,
    "Do not fear, O Zion;
    do not let your hands hang limp.
¹⁷The LORD your God is with you,
    he is mighty to save.
He will take great delight in you,
    he will quiet you with his love,
    he will rejoice over you with
        singing."

¹⁸"The sorrows for the appointed feasts
    I will remove from you;

they are a burden and a reproach to
    you.ᵃ
¹⁹At that time I will deal
    with all who oppressed you;
I will rescue the lame
    and gather those who have been
        scattered.
I will give them praise and honor
    in every land where they were put
        to shame.
²⁰At that time I will gather you;
    at that time I will bring you home.
I will give you honor and praise
    among all the peoples of the earth
    when I restore your fortunesᵇ
    before your very eyes,"
                        says the LORD.

ᵃ18 Or "I will gather you who mourn for the appointed feasts; / your reproach is a burden to you   ᵇ20 Or
I bring back your captives

HAGGAI encourages the returning exiles (Ezra 4:24–5:2) to set proper priorities by rebuilding the temple of the Lord before they rebuild their own houses. He goes on to envision a time when all nations will come to the temple. As you read this book, decide to seek God's kingdom first, and rejoice in his promise of a new world when people everywhere will worship the Lord together.

HAGGAI

A Call to Build the House of the LORD

1 In the second year of King Darius, on the first day of the sixth month, the word of the LORD came through the prophet Haggai to Zerubbabel son of Shealtiel, governor of Judah, and to Joshua*a* son of Jehozadak, the high priest:

²This is what the LORD Almighty says: "These people say, 'The time has not yet come for the LORD's house to be built.' "

³Then the word of the LORD came through the prophet Haggai: ⁴"Is it a time for you yourselves to be living in your paneled houses, while this house remains a ruin?"

⁵Now this is what the LORD Almighty says: "Give careful thought to your ways. ⁶You have planted much, but have harvested little. You eat, but never have enough. You drink, but never have your fill. You put on clothes, but are not warm. You earn wages, only to put them in a purse with holes in it."

⁷This is what the LORD Almighty says: "Give careful thought to your ways. ⁸Go up into the mountains and bring down timber and build the house, so that I may take pleasure in it and be honored," says the LORD. ⁹"You expected much, but see, it turned out to be little. What you brought home, I blew away. Why?" de-

a1 A variant of *Jeshua*; here and elsewhere in Haggai

clares the LORD Almighty. "Because of my house, which remains a ruin, while each of you is busy with his own house. [10]Therefore, because of you the heavens have withheld their dew and the earth its crops. [11]I called for a drought on the fields and the mountains, on the grain, the new wine, the oil and whatever the ground produces, on men and cattle, and on the labor of your hands."

[12]Then Zerubbabel son of Shealtiel, Joshua son of Jehozadak, the high priest, and the whole remnant of the people obeyed the voice of the LORD their God and the message of the prophet Haggai, because the LORD their God had sent him. And the people feared the LORD.

[13]Then Haggai, the LORD's messenger, gave this message of the LORD to the people: "I am with you," declares the LORD.

WEDNESDAY

VERSE FOR THE DAY:
Haggai 2:5

AUTHOR:
Doris Rikkers

PASSAGE FOR THE DAY:
Haggai 2:1–9

You Promised

I COULD hear my son say it even before he opened his mouth. "But you promised!" And I knew my reply. I knew I had promised, but somehow I forgot—work got hectic, I had to run off to a meeting, my father was in the hospital—and my promise to take my eight-year-old to the tennis courts no longer had the same priority as it had had a few days ago.

Another broken promise. We break promises all the time because . . . well, because we're human, I suppose. God, however, always keeps his promises. Just look at this verse: "This is what I covenanted with you when you came out of Egypt. And my Spirit remains among you. Do not fear" (Haggai 2:5). Now that's keeping a promise!

God kept this promise for almost a thousand years. Many generations had passed in between the exodus from Egypt and the return from captivity. If God had forgotten that promise, nobody would have been around to remember. Probably nobody would have noticed.

Our God is still in the business of keeping promises. The promise of this verse is true for you today just as it was true for those exiled Jews in captivity. Read it again: "My Spirit remains among you. Do not fear."

Additional Scripture Readings:
1 Kings 8:56–61; Romans 4:20–21

Go to page 1011 for your next
devotional reading.

[14]So the LORD stirred up the spirit of Zerubbabel son of Shealtiel, governor of Judah, and the spirit of Joshua son of Jehozadak, the high priest, and the spirit of the whole remnant of the people. They came and began to work on the house of the LORD Almighty, their God, [15]on the twenty-fourth day of the sixth month in the second year of King Darius.

The Promised Glory of the New House

2 On the twenty-first day of the seventh month, the word of the LORD came through the prophet Haggai: [2]"Speak to Zerubbabel son of Shealtiel, governor of Judah, to Joshua son of Jehozadak, the high priest, and to the remnant of the people. Ask them, [3]'Who of you is left who saw this house in its former glory? How does it look to you now? Does it not seem to you like nothing? [4]But now be strong, O Zerubbabel,' declares the LORD. 'Be strong, O Joshua son of Jehozadak, the high priest. Be strong, all you people of the land,' declares the LORD, 'and work. For I am with you,' declares the LORD Almighty. [5]'This is what I covenanted with you when you came out of Egypt. And my Spirit remains among you. Do not fear.'

[6]"This is what the LORD Almighty says: 'In a little while I will once more shake the heavens and the earth, the sea and the dry land. [7]I will shake all nations, and the desired of all nations will come, and I will fill this house with glory,' says the LORD Almighty. [8]'The silver is mine and the gold is mine,' declares the LORD Almighty. [9]'The glory of this present house will be greater than the glory of the former house,' says the LORD Almighty. 'And in this place I will grant peace,' declares the LORD Almighty.'"

Blessings for a Defiled People

[10]On the twenty-fourth day of the ninth month, in the second year of Darius, the word of the LORD came to the prophet Haggai: [11]"This is what the LORD Almighty says: 'Ask the priests what the law says: [12]If a person carries consecrated meat in the fold of his garment, and that fold touches some bread or stew, some wine, oil or other food, does it become consecrated?' "

The priests answered, "No."

[13]Then Haggai said, "If a person defiled by contact with a dead body touches one of these things, does it become defiled?"

"Yes," the priests replied, "it becomes defiled."

[14]Then Haggai said, " 'So it is with this people and this nation in my sight,' declares the LORD. 'Whatever they do and whatever they offer there is defiled.

[15]" 'Now give careful thought to this from this day on[a]—consider how things were before one stone was laid on another in the LORD's temple. [16]When anyone came to a heap of twenty measures, there were only ten. When anyone went to a wine vat to draw fifty measures, there were only twenty. [17]I struck all the work of your hands with blight, mildew and hail, yet you did not turn to me,' declares the LORD. [18]'From this day on, from this twenty-fourth day of the ninth month, give careful thought to the day when the foundation of the LORD's temple was laid. Give careful thought: [19]Is there yet any seed left in the barn? Until now, the vine and the fig tree, the pomegranate and the olive tree have not borne fruit.

" 'From this day on I will bless you.' "

Zerubbabel the LORD's Signet Ring

[20]The word of the LORD came to Haggai a second time on the twenty-fourth day of the month: [21]"Tell Zerubbabel governor of Judah that I will shake the heavens and the earth. [22]I will overturn royal thrones and shatter the power of the foreign kingdoms. I will overthrow chariots and their drivers; horses and their riders will fall, each by the sword of his brother.

[23]" 'On that day,' declares the LORD Almighty, 'I will take you, my servant Zerubbabel son of Shealtiel,' declares the LORD, 'and I will make you like my signet ring, for I have chosen you,' declares the LORD Almighty."

---

[a]15 Or to the days past

ZECHARIAH *writes to inspire the returning exiles to turn to the Lord and continue rebuilding the temple in Jerusalem (Ezra 4:24–5:2). He encourages them with his visions that show God's control over everything and the coming new kingdom of the Messiah. As you read this book, be sure you have turned to the Lord and let these visions of hope inspire you to continue serving the Lord.*

ZECHARIAH

A Call to Return to the LORD

1 In the eighth month of the second year of Darius, the word of the LORD came to the prophet Zechariah son of Berekiah, the son of Iddo:

²"The LORD was very angry with your forefathers. ³Therefore tell the people: This is what the LORD Almighty says: 'Return to me,' declares the LORD Almighty, 'and I will return to you,' says the LORD Almighty. ⁴Do not be like your forefathers, to whom the earlier prophets proclaimed: This is what the LORD Almighty says: 'Turn from your evil ways and your evil practices.' But they would not listen or pay attention to me, declares the LORD. ⁵Where are your forefathers now? And the prophets, do they live forever? ⁶But did not my words and my decrees, which I commanded my servants the prophets, overtake your forefathers?

"Then they repented and said, 'The LORD Almighty has done to us what our ways and practices deserve, just as he determined to do.' "

The Man Among the Myrtle Trees

⁷On the twenty-fourth day of the eleventh month, the month of Shebat, in the second year of Darius, the word of the LORD came to the prophet Zechariah son of Berekiah, the son of Iddo.

⁸During the night I had a vision—and there before me was a man riding a red horse! He was standing among the myrtle trees in a ravine. Behind him were red, brown and white horses.

⁹I asked, "What are these, my lord?"

The angel who was talking with me answered, "I will show you what they are."

¹⁰Then the man standing among the myrtle trees explained, "They are the ones the LORD has sent to go throughout the earth."

¹¹And they reported to the angel of the LORD, who was standing among the myrtle trees, "We have gone throughout the earth and found the whole world at rest and in peace."

¹²Then the angel of the LORD said, "LORD Almighty, how long will you withhold mercy from Jerusalem and from the towns of Judah, which you have been angry with these seventy years?" ¹³So the LORD spoke kind and comforting words to the angel who talked with me.

¹⁴Then the angel who was speaking to me said, "Proclaim this word: This is what the LORD Almighty says: 'I am very jealous for Jerusalem and Zion, ¹⁵but I am very angry with the nations that feel secure. I was only a little angry, but they added to the calamity.'

¹⁶"Therefore, this is what the LORD says: 'I will return to Jerusalem with mercy, and there my house will be rebuilt. And the measuring line will be stretched out over Jerusalem,' declares the LORD Almighty.

¹⁷"Proclaim further: This is what the LORD Almighty says: 'My towns will again overflow with prosperity, and the LORD will again comfort Zion and choose Jerusalem.' "

Four Horns and Four Craftsmen

¹⁸Then I looked up—and there before me were four horns! ¹⁹I asked the angel who was speaking to me, "What are these?"

He answered me, "These are the horns that scattered Judah, Israel and Jerusalem."

²⁰Then the LORD showed me four craftsmen. ²¹I asked, "What are these coming to do?"

He answered, "These are the horns that scattered Judah so that no one could raise his head, but the craftsmen have come to terrify them and throw down these horns of the nations who lifted up their horns against the land of Judah to scatter its people."

A Man With a Measuring Line

2 Then I looked up—and there before me was a man with a measuring line in his hand! ²I asked, "Where are you going?"

He answered me, "To measure Jerusalem, to find out how wide and how long it is."

³Then the angel who was speaking to me left, and another angel came to meet him ⁴and said to him: "Run, tell that young man, 'Jerusalem will be a city without walls because of the great number of men and livestock in it. ⁵And I myself will be a wall of fire around it,' declares the LORD, 'and I will be its glory within.'

⁶"Come! Come! Flee from the land of the north," declares the LORD, "for I have scattered you to the four winds of heaven," declares the LORD.

⁷"Come, O Zion! Escape, you who live in the Daughter of Babylon!" ⁸For this is what the LORD Almighty says: "After he has honored me and has sent me against the nations that have plundered you—for whoever touches you touches the apple of his eye— ⁹I will surely raise my hand against them so that their slaves will plunder them.ᵃ Then you will know that the LORD Almighty has sent me.

¹⁰"Shout and be glad, O Daughter of Zion. For I am coming, and I will live among you," declares the LORD. ¹¹"Many nations will be joined with the LORD in that day and will become my people. I will live among you and you will know that the LORD Almighty has sent me to you. ¹²The LORD will inherit Judah as his portion in the holy land and will again choose Jerusalem. ¹³Be still before the LORD, all mankind, because he has roused himself from his holy dwelling."

Clean Garments for the High Priest

3 Then he showed me Joshuaᵇ the high priest standing before the angel of the LORD, and Satanᶜ standing at his right side to accuse him. ²The LORD said to Satan, "The LORD rebuke you, Satan! The LORD, who has chosen Jerusalem, rebuke you! Is not this man a burning stick snatched from the fire?"

³Now Joshua was dressed in filthy clothes as he stood before the angel. ⁴The angel said to those who were standing before him, "Take off his filthy clothes."

Then he said to Joshua, "See, I have

ᵃ8,9 Or says after . . . eye: ⁹"I . . . plunder them."
Zechariah   ᶜ1 Satan means accuser.   ᵇ1 A variant of Jeshua; here and elsewhere in

taken away your sin, and I will put rich garments on you."

5Then I said, "Put a clean turban on his head." So they put a clean turban on his head and clothed him, while the angel of the LORD stood by.

6The angel of the LORD gave this charge to Joshua: 7"This is what the LORD Almighty says: 'If you will walk in my ways and keep my requirements, then you will govern my house and have charge of my courts, and I will give you a place among these standing here.

8" 'Listen, O high priest Joshua and your associates seated before you, who are men symbolic of things to come: I am going to bring my servant, the Branch. 9See, the stone I have set in front of Joshua! There are seven eyes*a* on that one stone, and I will engrave an inscription on it,' says the LORD Almighty, 'and I will remove the sin of this land in a single day.

10" 'In that day each of you will invite his neighbor to sit under his vine and fig tree,' declares the LORD Almighty."

The Gold Lampstand and the Two Olive Trees

4 Then the angel who talked with me returned and wakened me, as a man is wakened from his sleep. 2He asked me, "What do you see?"

I answered, "I see a solid gold lampstand with a bowl at the top and seven lights on it, with seven channels to the lights. 3Also there are two olive trees by it, one on the right of the bowl and the other on its left."

4I asked the angel who talked with me, "What are these, my lord?"

5He answered, "Do you not know what these are?"

"No, my lord," I replied.

6So he said to me, "This is the word of the LORD to Zerubbabel: 'Not by might nor by power, but by my Spirit,' says the LORD Almighty.

7"What*b* are you, O mighty mountain? Before Zerubbabel you will become level ground. Then he will bring out the capstone to shouts of 'God bless it! God bless it!' "

8Then the word of the LORD came to me: 9"The hands of Zerubbabel have laid the foundation of this temple; his hands will also complete it. Then you will know that

the LORD Almighty has sent me to you.

10"Who despises the day of small things? Men will rejoice when they see the plumb line in the hand of Zerubbabel.

"(These seven are the eyes of the LORD, which range throughout the earth.)"

11Then I asked the angel, "What are these two olive trees on the right and the left of the lampstand?"

12Again I asked him, "What are these two olive branches beside the two gold pipes that pour out golden oil?"

13He replied, "Do you not know what these are?"

"No, my lord," I said.

14So he said, "These are the two who are anointed to*c* serve the Lord of all the earth."

The Flying Scroll

5 I looked again—and there before me was a flying scroll!

2He asked me, "What do you see?"

I answered, "I see a flying scroll, thirty feet long and fifteen feet wide.*d* "

3And he said to me, "This is the curse that is going out over the whole land; for according to what it says on one side, every thief will be banished, and according to what it says on the other, everyone who swears falsely will be banished. 4The LORD Almighty declares, 'I will send it out, and it will enter the house of the thief and the house of him who swears falsely by my name. It will remain in his house and destroy it, both its timbers and its stones.' "

The Woman in a Basket

5Then the angel who was speaking to me came forward and said to me, "Look up and see what this is that is appearing."

6I asked, "What is it?"

He replied, "It is a measuring basket.*e*" And he added, "This is the iniquity*f* of the people throughout the land."

7Then the cover of lead was raised, and there in the basket sat a woman! 8He said, "This is wickedness," and he pushed her back into the basket and pushed the lead cover down over its mouth.

9Then I looked up—and there before me were two women, with the wind in their wings! They had wings like those of a stork, and they lifted up the basket between heaven and earth.

---

*a*9 Or *facets*   *b*7 Or *Who*   *c*14 Or *two who bring oil and cubits wide* (about 9 meters long and 4.5 meters wide)   *d*2 Hebrew *twenty cubits long and ten*   *e*6 Hebrew *an ephah*; also in verses 7-11   *f*6 Or *appearance*

¹⁰"Where are they taking the basket?" I asked the angel who was speaking to me.

¹¹He replied, "To the country of Babylonia[a] to build a house for it. When it is ready, the basket will be set there in its place."

Four Chariots

6 I looked up again—and there before me were four chariots coming out from between two mountains—mountains of bronze! ²The first chariot had red horses, the second black, ³the third white, and the fourth dappled—all of them powerful. ⁴I asked the angel who

was speaking to me, "What are these, my lord?"

⁵The angel answered me, "These are the four spirits[b] of heaven, going out from standing in the presence of the Lord of the whole world. ⁶The one with the black horses is going toward the north country, the one with the white horses toward the west,[c] and the one with the dappled horses toward the south."

⁷When the powerful horses went out, they were straining to go throughout the earth. And he said, "Go throughout the earth!" So they went throughout the earth.

---

[a]11 Hebrew *Shinar*   [b]5 Or *winds*   [c]6 Or *horses after them*

THURSDAY

VERSE FOR THE DAY:
Zechariah 4:6

AUTHOR:
Nicole Hill

PASSAGE FOR THE DAY:
Zechariah 4:1–7

One-Woman Juggler

LIKE most women today, I lead an active life. Often, I feel like a one-woman juggling act. Sometimes, it gets out of control—or, rather, I get out of control.

Recently, I found myself waking up in the morning, dreading to face the new day and my seemingly endless chores and duties. My prayer time was suffering because I felt so overwhelmed with pressures and responsibilities. Yet, I kept taking on more and more.

Then, one morning, I glanced down at a note pad a friend had given me for Christmas. It said, *One day at a time.* Seeking God's guidance, I sat down and made a list of the things I truly needed to accomplish that day. I didn't worry about what I had failed to do yesterday, or what I hoped to do tomorrow. I just concentrated on today.

As the day progressed (beginning with a renewed and refreshed prayer time), I found time to straighten my home, attend a friend's funeral, visit with a neighbor, do my marketing, work in the garden, and even spend a little time on my writing. As I climbed into bed that night, I looked at my list and smiled. I was right on schedule.

Lord, help me to remember it's not by my power, nor by my might, but by your Spirit that we accomplish anything worthwhile. Amen.

Additional Scripture Readings:
Ecclesiastes 2:17–26; Philippians 3:12–14

Go to page 1019 for your next devotional reading.

⁸Then he called to me, "Look, those going toward the north country have given my Spirit*a* rest in the land of the north."

A Crown for Joshua

⁹The word of the LORD came to me: ¹⁰"Take silver and gold from the exiles Heldai, Tobijah and Jedaiah, who have arrived from Babylon. Go the same day to the house of Josiah son of Zephaniah. ¹¹Take the silver and gold and make a crown, and set it on the head of the high priest, Joshua son of Jehozadak. ¹²Tell him this is what the LORD Almighty says: 'Here is the man whose name is the Branch, and he will branch out from his place and build the temple of the LORD. ¹³It is he who will build the temple of the LORD, and he will be clothed with majesty and will sit and rule on his throne. And he will be a priest on his throne. And there will be harmony between the two.' ¹⁴The crown will be given to Heldai,*b* Tobijah, Jedaiah and Hen*c* son of Zephaniah as a memorial in the temple of the LORD. ¹⁵Those who are far away will come and help to build the temple of the LORD, and you will know that the LORD Almighty has sent me to you. This will happen if you diligently obey the LORD your God."

Justice and Mercy, Not Fasting

7 In the fourth year of King Darius, the word of the LORD came to Zechariah on the fourth day of the ninth month, the month of Kislev. ²The people of Bethel had sent Sharezer and Regem-Melech, together with their men, to entreat the LORD ³by asking the priests of the house of the LORD Almighty and the prophets, "Should I mourn and fast in the fifth month, as I have done for so many years?"

⁴Then the word of the LORD Almighty came to me: ⁵"Ask all the people of the land and the priests, 'When you fasted and mourned in the fifth and seventh months for the past seventy years, was it really for me that you fasted? ⁶And when you were eating and drinking, were you not just feasting for yourselves? ⁷Are these not the words the LORD proclaimed through the earlier prophets when Jerusalem and its surrounding towns were at rest and prosperous, and the Negev and the western foothills were settled?' "

⁸And the word of the LORD came again to Zechariah: ⁹"This is what the LORD Almighty says: 'Administer true justice; show mercy and compassion to one another. ¹⁰Do not oppress the widow or the fatherless, the alien or the poor. In your hearts do not think evil of each other.'

¹¹"But they refused to pay attention; stubbornly they turned their backs and stopped up their ears. ¹²They made their hearts as hard as flint and would not listen to the law or to the words that the LORD Almighty had sent by his Spirit through the earlier prophets. So the LORD Almighty was very angry.

¹³" 'When I called, they did not listen; so when they called, I would not listen,' says the LORD Almighty. ¹⁴'I scattered them with a whirlwind among all the nations, where they were strangers. The land was left so desolate behind them that no one could come or go. This is how they made the pleasant land desolate.' "

The LORD Promises to Bless Jerusalem

8 Again the word of the LORD Almighty came to me. ²This is what the LORD Almighty says: "I am very jealous for Zion; I am burning with jealousy for her."

³This is what the LORD says: "I will return to Zion and dwell in Jerusalem. Then Jerusalem will be called the City of Truth, and the mountain of the LORD Almighty will be called the Holy Mountain."

⁴This is what the LORD Almighty says: "Once again men and women of ripe old age will sit in the streets of Jerusalem, each with cane in hand because of his age. ⁵The city streets will be filled with boys and girls playing there."

⁶This is what the LORD Almighty says: "It may seem marvelous to the remnant of this people at that time, but will it seem marvelous to me?" declares the LORD Almighty.

⁷This is what the LORD Almighty says: "I will save my people from the countries of the east and the west. ⁸I will bring them back to live in Jerusalem; they will be my people, and I will be faithful and righteous to them as their God."

⁹This is what the LORD Almighty says: "You who now hear these words spoken by the prophets who were there when the foundation was laid for the house of the LORD Almighty, let your hands be strong so that the temple may be built. ¹⁰Before that time there were no wages for man or beast. No one could go about his business safely because of his enemy, for I had

---

a8 Or *spirit*   *b14* Syriac; Hebrew *Helem*   *c14* Or *and the gracious one, the* turned every man against his neighbor. ¹¹But now I will not deal with the remnant of this people as I did in the past," declares the LORD Almighty.

¹²"The seed will grow well, the vine will yield its fruit, the ground will produce its crops, and the heavens will drop their dew. I will give all these things as an inheritance to the remnant of this people. ¹³As you have been an object of cursing among the nations, O Judah and Israel, so will I save you, and you will be a blessing. Do not be afraid, but let your hands be strong."

¹⁴This is what the LORD Almighty says: "Just as I had determined to bring disaster upon you and showed no pity when your fathers angered me," says the LORD Almighty, ¹⁵"so now I have determined to do good again to Jerusalem and Judah. Do not be afraid. ¹⁶These are the things you are to do: Speak the truth to each other, and render true and sound judgment in your courts; ¹⁷do not plot evil against your neighbor, and do not love to swear falsely. I hate all this," declares the LORD.

¹⁸Again the word of the LORD Almighty came to me. ¹⁹This is what the LORD Almighty says: "The fasts of the fourth, fifth, seventh and tenth months will become joyful and glad occasions and happy festivals for Judah. Therefore love truth and peace."

²⁰This is what the LORD Almighty says: "Many peoples and the inhabitants of many cities will yet come, ²¹and the inhabitants of one city will go to another and say, 'Let us go at once to entreat the LORD and seek the LORD Almighty. I myself am going.' ²²And many peoples and powerful nations will come to Jerusalem to seek the LORD Almighty and to entreat him."

²³This is what the LORD Almighty says: "In those days ten men from all languages and nations will take firm hold of one Jew by the hem of his robe and say, 'Let us go with you, because we have heard that God is with you.'"

Judgment on Israel's Enemies

An Oracle

9 The word of the LORD is against the land of Hadrach
and will rest upon Damascus —

for the eyes of men and all the tribes of Israel
are on the LORD — ᵃ
²and upon Hamath too, which borders on it,
and upon Tyre and Sidon, though they are very skillful.
³Tyre has built herself a stronghold;
she has heaped up silver like dust,
and gold like the dirt of the streets.
⁴But the Lord will take away her possessions
and destroy her power on the sea,
and she will be consumed by fire.
⁵Ashkelon will see it and fear;
Gaza will writhe in agony,
and Ekron too, for her hope will wither.
Gaza will lose her king
and Ashkelon will be deserted.
⁶Foreigners will occupy Ashdod,
and I will cut off the pride of the Philistines.
⁷I will take the blood from their mouths,
the forbidden food from between their teeth.
Those who are left will belong to our God
and become leaders in Judah,
and Ekron will be like the Jebusites.
⁸But I will defend my house
against marauding forces.
Never again will an oppressor overrun my people,
for now I am keeping watch.

The Coming of Zion's King

⁹Rejoice greatly, O Daughter of Zion!
Shout, Daughter of Jerusalem!
See, your kingᵇ comes to you,
righteous and having salvation,
gentle and riding on a donkey,
on a colt, the foal of a donkey.
¹⁰I will take away the chariots from Ephraim
and the war-horses from Jerusalem,
and the battle bow will be broken.
He will proclaim peace to the nations.
His rule will extend from sea to sea
and from the Riverᶜ to the ends of the earth.ᵈ
¹¹As for you, because of the blood of my covenant with you,
I will free your prisoners from the waterless pit.

ᵃ1 Or Damascus. / For the eye of the LORD is on all mankind, / as well as on the tribes of Israel,
ᵇ9 Or King   ᶜ10 That is, the Euphrates   ᵈ10 Or the end of the land

¹²Return to your fortress, O prisoners of
hope;
even now I announce that I will
restore twice as much to you.
¹³I will bend Judah as I bend my bow
and fill it with Ephraim.
I will rouse your sons, O Zion,
against your sons, O Greece,
and make you like a warrior's
sword.

The LORD Will Appear

¹⁴Then the LORD will appear over them;
his arrow will flash like lightning.
The Sovereign LORD will sound the
trumpet;
he will march in the storms of the
south,
15   and the LORD Almighty will shield
them.
They will destroy
and overcome with slingstones.
They will drink and roar as with wine;
they will be full like a bowl
used for sprinkling*ᵃ* the corners of
the altar.
¹⁶The LORD their God will save them on
that day
as the flock of his people.
They will sparkle in his land
like jewels in a crown.
¹⁷How attractive and beautiful they will
be!
Grain will make the young men
thrive,
and new wine the young women.

The LORD Will Care for Judah

10 Ask the LORD for rain in the
springtime;
it is the LORD who makes the storm
clouds.
He gives showers of rain to men,
and plants of the field to everyone.
²The idols speak deceit,
diviners see visions that lie;
they tell dreams that are false,
they give comfort in vain.
Therefore the people wander like
sheep
oppressed for lack of a shepherd.

³"My anger burns against the
shepherds,
and I will punish the leaders;
for the LORD Almighty will care

for his flock, the house of Judah,
and make them like a proud horse
in battle.
⁴From Judah will come the
cornerstone,
from him the tent peg,
from him the battle bow,
from him every ruler.
⁵Together they*ᵇ* will be like mighty
men
trampling the muddy streets in
battle.
Because the LORD is with them,
they will fight and overthrow the
horsemen.

⁶"I will strengthen the house of Judah
and save the house of Joseph.
I will restore them
because I have compassion on
them.
They will be as though
I had not rejected them,
for I am the LORD their God
and I will answer them.
⁷The Ephraimites will become like
mighty men,
and their hearts will be glad as with
wine.
Their children will see it and be
joyful;
their hearts will rejoice in the LORD.
⁸I will signal for them
and gather them in.
Surely I will redeem them;
they will be as numerous as before.
⁹Though I scatter them among the
peoples,
yet in distant lands they will
remember me.
They and their children will survive,
and they will return.
¹⁰I will bring them back from Egypt
and gather them from Assyria.
I will bring them to Gilead and
Lebanon,
and there will not be room enough
for them.
¹¹They will pass through the sea of
trouble;
the surging sea will be subdued
and all the depths of the Nile will
dry up.
Assyria's pride will be brought down
and Egypt's scepter will pass away.
¹²I will strengthen them in the LORD
and in his name they will walk,"
declares the LORD.

ᵃ15 Or *bowl, / like*   *ᵇ4,5* Or *ruler, all of them together. / ⁵They*

11 Open your doors, O Lebanon,
so that fire may devour your
cedars!
²Wail, O pine tree, for the cedar has
fallen;
the stately trees are ruined!
Wail, oaks of Bashan;
the dense forest has been cut
down!
³Listen to the wail of the shepherds;
their rich pastures are destroyed!
Listen to the roar of the lions;
the lush thicket of the Jordan is
ruined!

Two Shepherds

⁴This is what the LORD my God says:
"Pasture the flock marked for slaughter.
⁵Their buyers slaughter them and go
unpunished. Those who sell them
say, 'Praise the LORD, I am rich!' Their
own shepherds do not spare them. ⁶For
I will no longer have pity on the people of the land," declares the LORD. "I
will hand everyone over to his neighbor
and his king. They will oppress the land,
and I will not rescue them from their
hands."

⁷So I pastured the flock marked for
slaughter, particularly the oppressed of
the flock. Then I took two staffs and
called one Favor and the other Union,
and I pastured the flock. ⁸In one month I
got rid of the three shepherds.

The flock detested me, and I grew weary of them ⁹and said, "I will not be your
shepherd. Let the dying die, and the perishing perish. Let those who are left eat
one another's flesh."

¹⁰Then I took my staff called Favor and
broke it, revoking the covenant I had
made with all the nations. ¹¹It was revoked on that day, and so the afflicted of
the flock who were watching me knew it
was the word of the LORD.

¹²I told them, "If you think it best, give
me my pay; but if not, keep it." So they
paid me thirty pieces of silver.

¹³And the LORD said to me, "Throw it to
the potter"—the handsome price at
which they priced me! So I took the thirty
pieces of silver and threw them into the
house of the LORD to the potter.

¹⁴Then I broke my second staff called
Union, breaking the brotherhood between Judah and Israel.

¹⁵Then the LORD said to me, "Take
again the equipment of a foolish shepherd. ¹⁶For I am going to raise up a shepherd over the land who will not care for
the lost, or seek the young, or heal the
injured, or feed the healthy, but will eat
the meat of the choice sheep, tearing off
their hoofs.

¹⁷"Woe to the worthless shepherd,
who deserts the flock!
May the sword strike his arm and his
right eye!
May his arm be completely
withered,
his right eye totally blinded!"

Jerusalem's Enemies to Be Destroyed

An Oracle

12 This is the word of the LORD concerning Israel. The LORD, who
stretches out the heavens, who lays the
foundation of the earth, and who forms
the spirit of man within him, declares: ²"I
am going to make Jerusalem a cup that
sends all the surrounding peoples reeling.
Judah will be besieged as well as Jerusalem. ³On that day, when all the nations of
the earth are gathered against her, I will
make Jerusalem an immovable rock for
all the nations. All who try to move it will
injure themselves. ⁴On that day I will
strike every horse with panic and its rider
with madness," declares the LORD. "I will
keep a watchful eye over the house of Judah, but I will blind all the horses of the
nations. ⁵Then the leaders of Judah will
say in their hearts, 'The people of Jerusalem are strong, because the LORD Almighty is their God.'

⁶"On that day I will make the leaders of
Judah like a firepot in a woodpile, like a
flaming torch among sheaves. They will
consume right and left all the surrounding peoples, but Jerusalem will remain
intact in her place.

⁷"The LORD will save the dwellings of
Judah first, so that the honor of the house
of David and of Jerusalem's inhabitants may not be greater than that of Judah. ⁸On that day the LORD will shield
those who live in Jerusalem, so that the
feeblest among them will be like David,
and the house of David will be like
God, like the Angel of the LORD going
before them. ⁹On that day I will set out
to destroy all the nations that attack
Jerusalem.

Mourning for the One They Pierced

¹⁰"And I will pour out on the house of
David and the inhabitants of Jerusalem a

spirit*a* of grace and supplication. They will look on*b* me, the one they have pierced, and they will mourn for him as one mourns for an only child, and grieve bitterly for him as one grieves for a first-born son. [11]On that day the weeping in Jerusalem will be great, like the weeping of Hadad Rimmon in the plain of Megiddo. [12]The land will mourn, each clan by itself, with their wives by themselves: the clan of the house of David and their wives, the clan of the house of Nathan and their wives, [13]the clan of the house of Levi and their wives, the clan of Shimei and their wives, [14]and all the rest of the clans and their wives.

Cleansing From Sin

13 "On that day a fountain will be opened to the house of David and the inhabitants of Jerusalem, to cleanse them from sin and impurity.

[2]"On that day, I will banish the names of the idols from the land, and they will be remembered no more," declares the LORD Almighty. "I will remove both the prophets and the spirit of impurity from the land. [3]And if anyone still prophesies, his father and mother, to whom he was born, will say to him, 'You must die, because you have told lies in the LORD's name.' When he prophesies, his own parents will stab him.

[4]"On that day every prophet will be ashamed of his prophetic vision. He will not put on a prophet's garment of hair in order to deceive. [5]He will say, 'I am not a prophet. I am a farmer; the land has been my livelihood since my youth.*c*' [6]If someone asks him, 'What are these wounds on your body*d*?' he will answer, 'The wounds I was given at the house of my friends.'

The Shepherd Struck, the Sheep Scattered

[7]"Awake, O sword, against my
    shepherd,
    against the man who is close to
    me!"
    declares the LORD Almighty.
"Strike the shepherd,
    and the sheep will be scattered,
    and I will turn my hand against the
    little ones.
[8]In the whole land," declares the LORD,

"two-thirds will be struck down and
    perish;
    yet one-third will be left in it.
[9]This third I will bring into the fire;
    I will refine them like silver
    and test them like gold.
They will call on my name
    and I will answer them;
I will say, 'They are my people,'
    and they will say, 'The LORD is our
    God.'"

The LORD Comes and Reigns

14 A day of the LORD is coming when your plunder will be divided among you.

[2]I will gather all the nations to Jerusalem to fight against it; the city will be captured, the houses ransacked, and the women raped. Half of the city will go into exile, but the rest of the people will not be taken from the city. [3]Then the LORD will go out and fight against those nations, as he fights in the day of battle. [4]On that day his feet will stand on the Mount of Olives, east of Jerusalem, and the Mount of Olives will be split in two from east to west, forming a great valley, with half of the mountain moving north and half moving south. [5]You will flee by my mountain valley, for it will extend to Azel. You will flee as you fled from the earthquake*e* in the days of Uzziah king of Judah. Then the LORD my God will come, and all the holy ones with him.

[6]On that day there will be no light, no cold or frost. [7]It will be a unique day, without daytime or nighttime—a day known to the LORD. When evening comes, there will be light.

[8]On that day living water will flow out from Jerusalem, half to the eastern sea*f* and half to the western sea,*g* in summer and in winter.

[9]The LORD will be king over the whole earth. On that day there will be one LORD, and his name the only name.

[10]The whole land, from Geba to Rimmon, south of Jerusalem, will become like the Arabah. But Jerusalem will be raised up and remain in its place, from the Benjamin Gate to the site of the First Gate, to the Corner Gate, and from the Tower of Hananel to the royal winepresses. [11]It will be inhabited; never again

---

a10 Or the Spirit   b10 Or to   c5 Or farmer; a man sold me in my youth   d6 Or wounds between your hands   e5 Or 5My mountain valley will be blocked and will extend to Azel. It will be blocked as it was blocked because of the earthquake   f8 That is, the Dead Sea   g8 That is, the Mediterranean will it be destroyed. Jerusalem will be secure.

¹²This is the plague with which the LORD will strike all the nations that fought against Jerusalem: Their flesh will rot while they are still standing on their feet, their eyes will rot in their sockets, and their tongues will rot in their mouths. ¹³On that day men will be stricken by the LORD with great panic. Each man will seize the hand of another, and they will attack each other. ¹⁴Judah too will fight at Jerusalem. The wealth of all the surrounding nations will be collected—great quantities of gold and silver and clothing. ¹⁵A similar plague will strike the horses and mules, the camels and donkeys, and all the animals in those camps.

¹⁶Then the survivors from all the nations that have attacked Jerusalem will go up year after year to worship the King, the LORD Almighty, and to celebrate the Feast of Tabernacles. ¹⁷If any of the peoples of the earth do not go up to Jerusalem to worship the King, the LORD Almighty, they will have no rain. ¹⁸If the Egyptian people do not go up and take part, they will have no rain. The LORD*a* will bring on them the plague he inflicts on the nations that do not go up to celebrate the Feast of Tabernacles. ¹⁹This will be the punishment of Egypt and the punishment of all the nations that do not go up to celebrate the Feast of Tabernacles.

²⁰On that day HOLY TO THE LORD will be inscribed on the bells of the horses, and the cooking pots in the LORD's house will be like the sacred bowls in front of the altar. ²¹Every pot in Jerusalem and Judah will be holy to the LORD Almighty, and all who come to sacrifice will take some of the pots and cook in them. And on that day there will no longer be a Canaanite*b* in the house of the LORD Almighty.

---

a18 Or part, then the LORD   b21 Or merchant

*M*ALACHI *prophesies during the deplorable conditions described in Nehemiah 13. He calls those complacent in their spiritual life to a renewed relationship with God, promising them God's blessing if they do. As you read this book, promise the Lord that you will not be complacent in your faith but will put his will before your own concerns.*

MALACHI

1 An oracle: The word of the LORD to Israel through Malachi.*ᵃ*

Jacob Loved, Esau Hated

²"I have loved you," says the LORD.

"But you ask, 'How have you loved us?'

"Was not Esau Jacob's brother?" the LORD says. "Yet I have loved Jacob, ³but Esau I have hated, and I have turned his mountains into a wasteland and left his inheritance to the desert jackals."

⁴Edom may say, "Though we have been crushed, we will rebuild the ruins."

But this is what the LORD Almighty says: "They may build, but I will demolish. They will be called the Wicked Land, a people always under the wrath of the LORD. ⁵You will see it with your own eyes and say, 'Great is the LORD—even beyond the borders of Israel!'

Blemished Sacrifices

⁶"A son honors his father, and a servant his master. If I am a father, where is the honor due me? If I am a master, where is the respect due me?" says the LORD Almighty. "It is you, O priests, who show contempt for my name.

"But you ask, 'How have we shown contempt for your name?'

⁷"You place defiled food on my altar.

"But you ask, 'How have we defiled you?'

"By saying that the LORD's table is contemptible. ⁸When you bring blind animals for sacrifice, is that not wrong? When you sacrifice crippled or diseased animals, is

ᵃ1 Malachi means my messenger.

FRIDAY

VERSE FOR THE DAY:
Malachi 3:8

AUTHOR:
Martha Manikas-Foster

PASSAGE FOR THE DAY:
Malachi 1:6–14; 3:6–10

Honoring God

MY husband found the church talent survey still on the desk, forgotten, when he recently cleaned the study. It was a simple form requiring only a list of basic skills and interests. Yet each time I'd put pen to paper, I'd gotten no further than writing my name at the top of the page.

To my shame, I discovered that I was not having difficulty identifying my skills—only volunteering them. I can paint, I can clean, and I can teach and organize games. But did I want to sacrifice time with my husband and daughter in order to cook for a church supper or help care for the homebound? I wondered whether God really wanted me to fill up my few free evenings—my positive mental health time—by assisting with post-funeral receptions.

Then I reread Malachi. Here the prophet addresses people not unlike me, who gladly receive God's good gifts . . . and then hoard them. This is not just impoliteness—it is robbery (Malachi 3:8). With that in mind, I began to assess my priorities. If I attacked my job with the enthusiasm I give God, would my employer be impressed? If I attended to my daughter the way I attend to the body of Christ, would she feel neglected? God has given me my family and my job, but was I focusing on them during those times when God wanted me to be focusing on him?

Convinced I was in error, I turned back to Malachi for direction. Here I found the example of Levi, a priest who pleased God because he revered God and "stood in awe" of his name (Malachi 2:5). The prophet Malachi also guided me by recording God's instruction that I stop robbing him and instead bring him "the whole tithe" (Malachi 3:10).

I have no doubt that spending time with my family—and some time alone—are appropriate priorities. But I must remember that if in the process of meeting personal and family needs I hide my talents from the church, I am disobedient to God and I rob the body of Christ. God wants and deserves the honor and reverence we give him when we offer him the best of ourselves.

Additional Scripture Readings:
Romans 12:3–8; 2 Corinthians 9:6–11

Go to page 1021 for your next devotional reading.

that not wrong? Try offering them to your governor! Would he be pleased with you? Would he accept you?" says the LORD Almighty.

9"Now implore God to be gracious to us. With such offerings from your hands, will he accept you?"—says the LORD Almighty.

10"Oh, that one of you would shut the temple doors, so that you would not light useless fires on my altar! I am not pleased with you," says the LORD Almighty, "and I will accept no offering from your hands. 11My name will be great among the nations, from the rising to the setting of the sun. In every place incense and pure offerings will be brought to my name, because my name will be great among the nations," says the LORD Almighty.

12"But you profane it by saying of the Lord's table, 'It is defiled,' and of its food, 'It is contemptible.' 13And you say, 'What a burden!' and you sniff at it contemptuously," says the LORD Almighty.

"When you bring injured, crippled or diseased animals and offer them as sacrifices, should I accept them from your hands?" says the LORD. 14"Cursed is the cheat who has an acceptable male in his flock and vows to give it, but then sacrifices a blemished animal to the Lord. For I am a great king," says the LORD Almighty, "and my name is to be feared among the nations.

Admonition for the Priests

2 "And now this admonition is for you, O priests. 2If you do not listen, and if you do not set your heart to honor my name," says the LORD Almighty, "I will send a curse upon you, and I will curse your blessings. Yes, I have already cursed them, because you have not set your heart to honor me.

3"Because of you I will rebuke[a] your descendants[b]; I will spread on your faces the offal from your festival sacrifices, and you will be carried off with it. 4And you will know that I have sent you this admonition so that my covenant with Levi may continue," says the LORD Almighty. 5"My covenant was with him, a covenant of life and peace, and I gave them to him; this called for reverence and he revered me

and stood in awe of my name. 6True instruction was in his mouth and nothing false was found on his lips. He walked with me in peace and uprightness, and turned many from sin.

7"For the lips of a priest ought to preserve knowledge, and from his mouth men should seek instruction—because he is the messenger of the LORD Almighty. 8But you have turned from the way and by your teaching have caused many to stumble; you have violated the covenant with Levi," says the LORD Almighty. 9"So I have caused you to be despised and humiliated before all the people, because you have not followed my ways but have shown partiality in matters of the law."

Judah Unfaithful

10Have we not all one Father[c]? Did not one God create us? Why do we profane the covenant of our fathers by breaking faith with one another?

11Judah has broken faith. A detestable thing has been committed in Israel and in Jerusalem: Judah has desecrated the sanctuary the LORD loves, by marrying the daughter of a foreign god. 12As for the man who does this, whoever he may be, may the LORD cut him off from the tents of Jacob[d]—even though he brings offerings to the LORD Almighty.

13Another thing you do: You flood the LORD's altar with tears. You weep and wail because he no longer pays attention to your offerings or accepts them with pleasure from your hands. 14You ask, "Why?" It is because the LORD is acting as the witness between you and the wife of your youth, because you have broken faith with her, though she is your partner, the wife of your marriage covenant.

15Has not .the LORD, made them one? In flesh and spirit they are his. And why one? Because he was seeking godly offspring.[e] So guard yourself in your spirit, and do not break faith with the wife of your youth.

16"I hate divorce," says the LORD God of Israel, "and I hate a man's covering himself[f] with violence as well as with his garment," says the LORD Almighty.

So guard yourself in your spirit, and do not break faith.

---

a3 Or cut off (see Septuagint)   b3 Or will blight your grain   c10 Or father   d12 Or 12May the LORD cut off from the tents of Jacob anyone who gives testimony in behalf of the man who does this   e15 Or 15But the one ,who is our father, did not do this, not as long as life remained in him. And what was he seeking? An offspring from God   f16 Or his wife

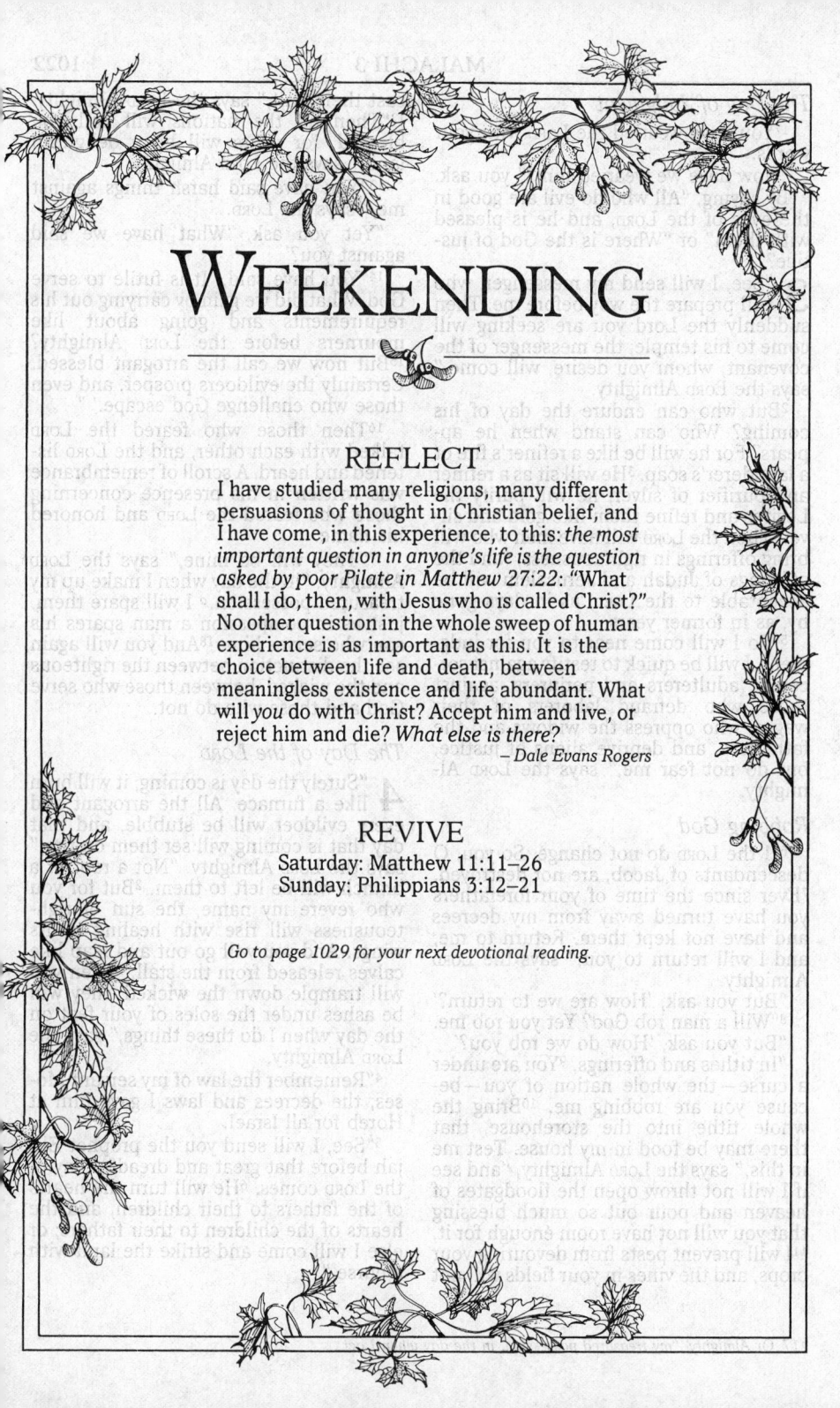

WEEKENDING

REFLECT

I have studied many religions, many different persuasions of thought in Christian belief, and I have come, in this experience, to this: *the most important question in anyone's life is the question asked by poor Pilate in Matthew 27:22*: "What shall I do, then, with Jesus who is called Christ?" No other question in the whole sweep of human experience is as important as this. It is the choice between life and death, between meaningless existence and life abundant. What will *you* do with Christ? Accept him and live, or reject him and die? *What else is there?*

— *Dale Evans Rogers*

REVIVE

Saturday: Matthew 11:11–26
Sunday: Philippians 3:12–21

Go to page 1029 for your next devotional reading.

The Day of Judgment

17You have wearied the LORD with your words.

"How have we wearied him?" you ask.

By saying, "All who do evil are good in the eyes of the LORD, and he is pleased with them" or "Where is the God of justice?"

3 "See, I will send my messenger, who will prepare the way before me. Then suddenly the Lord you are seeking will come to his temple; the messenger of the covenant, whom you desire, will come," says the LORD Almighty.

2But who can endure the day of his coming? Who can stand when he appears? For he will be like a refiner's fire or a launderer's soap. 3He will sit as a refiner and purifier of silver; he will purify the Levites and refine them like gold and silver. Then the LORD will have men who will bring offerings in righteousness, 4and the offerings of Judah and Jerusalem will be acceptable to the LORD, as in days gone by, as in former years.

5"So I will come near to you for judgment. I will be quick to testify against sorcerers, adulterers and perjurers, against those who defraud laborers of their wages, who oppress the widows and the fatherless, and deprive aliens of justice, but do not fear me," says the LORD Almighty.

Robbing God

6"I the LORD do not change. So you, O descendants of Jacob, are not destroyed. 7Ever since the time of your forefathers you have turned away from my decrees and have not kept them. Return to me, and I will return to you," says the LORD Almighty.

"But you ask, 'How are we to return?'

8"Will a man rob God? Yet you rob me.

"But you ask, 'How do we rob you?'

"In tithes and offerings. 9You are under a curse—the whole nation of you—because you are robbing me. 10Bring the whole tithe into the storehouse, that there may be food in my house. Test me in this," says the LORD Almighty, "and see if I will not throw open the floodgates of heaven and pour out so much blessing that you will not have room enough for it. 11I will prevent pests from devouring your crops, and the vines in your fields will not

cast their fruit," says the LORD Almighty. 12"Then all the nations will call you blessed, for yours will be a delightful land," says the LORD Almighty.

13"You have said harsh things against me," says the LORD.

"Yet you ask, 'What have we said against you?'

14"You have said, 'It is futile to serve God. What did we gain by carrying out his requirements and going about like mourners before the LORD Almighty? 15But now we call the arrogant blessed. Certainly the evildoers prosper, and even those who challenge God escape.' "

16Then those who feared the LORD talked with each other, and the LORD listened and heard. A scroll of remembrance was written in his presence concerning those who feared the LORD and honored his name.

17"They will be mine," says the LORD Almighty, "in the day when I make up my treasured possession.*a* I will spare them, just as in compassion a man spares his son who serves him. 18And you will again see the distinction between the righteous and the wicked, between those who serve God and those who do not.

The Day of the LORD

4 "Surely the day is coming; it will burn like a furnace. All the arrogant and every evildoer will be stubble, and that day that is coming will set them on fire," says the LORD Almighty. "Not a root or a branch will be left to them. 2But for you who revere my name, the sun of righteousness will rise with healing in its wings. And you will go out and leap like calves released from the stall. 3Then you will trample down the wicked; they will be ashes under the soles of your feet on the day when I do these things," says the LORD Almighty.

4"Remember the law of my servant Moses, the decrees and laws I gave him at Horeb for all Israel.

5"See, I will send you the prophet Elijah before that great and dreadful day of the LORD comes. 6He will turn the hearts of the fathers to their children, and the hearts of the children to their fathers; or else I will come and strike the land with a curse."

---

a17 Or Almighty, "my treasured possession, in the day when I act

NEW TESTAMENT

NEW TESTAMENT

*M*ATTHEW *writes this gospel to emphasize how Jesus fulfills God's promises from the Old Testament. He includes numerous sayings of Jesus about living as one of his disciples and as a member of the church, concluding with the command of Jesus to make disciples of all nations. As you read this book, ask yourself whether you are living as a disciple of Jesus, as well as how you can tell others the story of Jesus.*

MATTHEW

The Genealogy of Jesus

1 A record of the genealogy of Jesus Christ the son of David, the son of Abraham:

2Abraham was the father of Isaac,
   Isaac the father of Jacob,
   Jacob the father of Judah and his brothers,
3Judah the father of Perez and Zerah, whose mother was Tamar,
   Perez the father of Hezron,
   Hezron the father of Ram,
4Ram the father of Amminadab,
   Amminadab the father of Nahshon,
   Nahshon the father of Salmon,

5Salmon the father of Boaz, whose mother was Rahab,
   Boaz the father of Obed, whose mother was Ruth,
   Obed the father of Jesse,
6and Jesse the father of King David.

David was the father of Solomon, whose mother had been Uriah's wife,
7Solomon the father of Rehoboam,
   Rehoboam the father of Abijah,
   Abijah the father of Asa,
8Asa the father of Jehoshaphat,
   Jehoshaphat the father of Jehoram,
   Jehoram the father of Uzziah,
9Uzziah the father of Jotham,

Jotham the father of Ahaz,
Ahaz the father of Hezekiah,
¹⁰Hezekiah the father of Manasseh,
Manasseh the father of Amon,
Amon the father of Josiah,
¹¹and Josiah the father of Jeconiah*a*
and his brothers at the time of
the exile to Babylon.

¹²After the exile to Babylon:
Jeconiah was the father of Sheal-
tiel,
Shealtiel the father of Zerubbabel,
¹³Zerubbabel the father of Abiud,
Abiud the father of Eliakim,
Eliakim the father of Azor,
¹⁴Azor the father of Zadok,
Zadok the father of Akim,
Akim the father of Eliud,
¹⁵Eliud the father of Eleazar,
Eleazar the father of Matthan,
Matthan the father of Jacob,
¹⁶and Jacob the father of Joseph,
the husband of Mary, of whom
was born Jesus, who is called
Christ.

¹⁷Thus there were fourteen generations
in all from Abraham to David, fourteen
from David to the exile to Babylon, and
fourteen from the exile to the Christ.*b*

The Birth of Jesus Christ

¹⁸This is how the birth of Jesus Christ
came about: His mother Mary was
pledged to be married to Joseph, but before they came together, she was found to
be with child through the Holy Spirit.
¹⁹Because Joseph her husband was a righteous man and did not want to expose her
to public disgrace, he had in mind to divorce her quietly.

²⁰But after he had considered this, an
angel of the Lord appeared to him in a
dream and said, "Joseph son of David, do
not be afraid to take Mary home as your
wife, because what is conceived in her is
from the Holy Spirit. ²¹She will give birth
to a son, and you are to give him the name
Jesus,*c* because he will save his people
from their sins."

²²All this took place to fulfill what the
Lord had said through the prophet:
²³"The virgin will be with child and will
give birth to a son, and they will call him

Immanuel"*d*—which means, "God with
us."

²⁴When Joseph woke up, he did what
the angel of the Lord had commanded
him and took Mary home as his wife.
²⁵But he had no union with her until she
gave birth to a son. And he gave him the
name Jesus.

The Visit of the Magi

2 After Jesus was born in Bethlehem in
Judea, during the time of King Herod,
Magi*e* from the east came to Jerusalem
²and asked, "Where is the one who has
been born king of the Jews? We saw his
star in the east*f* and have come to worship him."

³When King Herod heard this he was
disturbed, and all Jerusalem with him.
⁴When he had called together all the people's chief priests and teachers of the law,
he asked them where the Christ*g* was to
be born. ⁵"In Bethlehem in Judea," they
replied, "for this is what the prophet has
written:

⁶" 'But you, Bethlehem, in the land of
Judah,
are by no means least among the
rulers of Judah;
for out of you will come a ruler
who will be the shepherd of my
people Israel.'*h*"

⁷Then Herod called the Magi secretly
and found out from them the exact time
the star had appeared. ⁸He sent them to
Bethlehem and said, "Go and make a
careful search for the child. As soon as
you find him, report to me, so that I too
may go and worship him."

⁹After they had heard the king, they
went on their way, and the star they had
seen in the east*i* went ahead of them until it stopped over the place where the
child was. ¹⁰When they saw the star, they
were overjoyed. ¹¹On coming to the
house, they saw the child with his mother
Mary, and they bowed down and worshiped him. Then they opened their treasures and presented him with gifts of gold
and of incense and of myrrh. ¹²And having
been warned in a dream not to go back to
Herod, they returned to their country by
another route.

---

*a*11 That is, Jehoiachin; also in verse 12   *b*17 Or *Messiah.* "The Christ" (Greek) and "the Messiah"
(Hebrew) both mean "the Anointed One."   *c*21 *Jesus* is the Greek form of *Joshua,* which means *the*
Lord saves.   *d*23 Isaiah 7:14   *e*1 Traditionally *Wise Men*   *f*2 Or *star when it rose*   *g*4 Or
Messiah   *h*6 Micah 5:2   *i*9 Or *seen when it rose*

The Escape to Egypt

¹³When they had gone, an angel of the Lord appeared to Joseph in a dream. "Get up," he said, "take the child and his mother and escape to Egypt. Stay there until I tell you, for Herod is going to search for the child to kill him."

¹⁴So he got up, took the child and his mother during the night and left for Egypt, ¹⁵where he stayed until the death of Herod. And so was fulfilled what the Lord had said through the prophet: "Out of Egypt I called my son."ᵃ

¹⁶When Herod realized that he had been outwitted by the Magi, he was furious, and he gave orders to kill all the boys in Bethlehem and its vicinity who were two years old and under, in accordance with the time he had learned from the Magi. ¹⁷Then what was said through the prophet Jeremiah was fulfilled:

¹⁸"A voice is heard in Ramah,
    weeping and great mourning,
Rachel weeping for her children
    and refusing to be comforted,
because they are no more."ᵇ

The Return to Nazareth

¹⁹After Herod died, an angel of the Lord appeared in a dream to Joseph in Egypt ²⁰and said, "Get up, take the child and his mother and go to the land of Israel, for those who were trying to take the child's life are dead."

²¹So he got up, took the child and his mother and went to the land of Israel. ²²But when he heard that Archelaus was reigning in Judea in place of his father Herod, he was afraid to go there. Having been warned in a dream, he withdrew to the district of Galilee, ²³and he went and lived in a town called Nazareth. So was fulfilled what was said through the prophets: "He will be called a Nazarene."

John the Baptist Prepares the Way

3 In those days John the Baptist came, preaching in the Desert of Judea ²and saying, "Repent, for the kingdom of heaven is near." ³This is he who was spoken of through the prophet Isaiah:

"A voice of one calling in the desert,
'Prepare the way for the Lord,
    make straight paths for him.' "ᶜ

⁴John's clothes were made of camel's hair, and he had a leather belt around his waist. His food was locusts and wild honey. ⁵People went out to him from Jerusalem and all Judea and the whole region of the Jordan. ⁶Confessing their sins, they were baptized by him in the Jordan River.

⁷But when he saw many of the Pharisees and Sadducees coming to where he was baptizing, he said to them: "You brood of vipers! Who warned you to flee from the coming wrath? ⁸Produce fruit in keeping with repentance. ⁹And do not think you can say to yourselves, 'We have Abraham as our father.' I tell you that out of these stones God can raise up children for Abraham. ¹⁰The ax is already at the root of the trees, and every tree that does not produce good fruit will be cut down and thrown into the fire.

¹¹"I baptize you withᵈ water for repentance. But after me will come one who is more powerful than I, whose sandals I am not fit to carry. He will baptize you with the Holy Spirit and with fire. ¹²His winnowing fork is in his hand, and he will clear his threshing floor, gathering his wheat into the barn and burning up the chaff with unquenchable fire."

The Baptism of Jesus

¹³Then Jesus came from Galilee to the Jordan to be baptized by John. ¹⁴But John tried to deter him, saying, "I need to be baptized by you, and do you come to me?"

¹⁵Jesus replied, "Let it be so now; it is proper for us to do this to fulfill all righteousness." Then John consented.

¹⁶As soon as Jesus was baptized, he went up out of the water. At that moment heaven was opened, and he saw the Spirit of God descending like a dove and lighting on him. ¹⁷And a voice from heaven said, "This is my Son, whom I love; with him I am well pleased."

The Temptation of Jesus

4 Then Jesus was led by the Spirit into the desert to be tempted by the devil. ²After fasting forty days and forty nights, he was hungry. ³The tempter came to him and said, "If you are the Son of God, tell these stones to become bread."

⁴Jesus answered, "It is written: 'Man does not live on bread alone, but on every word that comes from the mouth of God.'ᵉ"

⁵Then the devil took him to the holy city and had him stand on the highest

---

ᵃ15 Hosea 11:1   ᵇ18 Jer. 31:15   ᶜ3 Isaiah 40:3   ᵈ11 Or *in*   ᵉ4 Deut. 8:3

point of the temple. 6"If you are the Son of God," he said, "throw yourself down. For it is written:

> " 'He will command his angels
> concerning you,
> and they will lift you up in their
> hands,
> so that you will not strike your foot
> against a stone.'ᵃ "

7Jesus answered him, "It is also written: 'Do not put the Lord your God to the test.'ᵇ "

8Again, the devil took him to a very high mountain and showed him all the kingdoms of the world and their splendor. 9"All this I will give you," he said, "if you will bow down and worship me."

10Jesus said to him, "Away from me, Satan! For it is written: 'Worship the Lord your God, and serve him only.'ᶜ "

11Then the devil left him, and angels came and attended him.

Jesus Begins to Preach

12When Jesus heard that John had been put in prison, he returned to Galilee. 13Leaving Nazareth, he went and lived in Capernaum, which was by the lake in the area of Zebulun and Naphtali — 14to fulfill what was said through the prophet Isaiah:

> 15"Land of Zebulun and land of
> Naphtali,
> the way to the sea, along the
> Jordan,
> Galilee of the Gentiles—
> 16the people living in darkness
> have seen a great light;
> on those living in the land of the
> shadow of death
> a light has dawned."ᵈ

17From that time on Jesus began to preach, "Repent, for the kingdom of heaven is near."

The Calling of the First Disciples

18As Jesus was walking beside the Sea of Galilee, he saw two brothers, Simon called Peter and his brother Andrew. They were casting a net into the lake, for they were fishermen. 19"Come, follow me," Jesus said, "and I will make you fishers of men." 20At once they left their nets and followed him.

21Going on from there, he saw two other brothers, James son of Zebedee and his brother John. They were in a boat with their father Zebedee, preparing their nets. Jesus called them, 22and immediately they left the boat and their father and followed him.

Jesus Heals the Sick

23Jesus went throughout Galilee, teaching in their synagogues, preaching the good news of the kingdom, and healing every disease and sickness among the people. 24News about him spread all over Syria, and people brought to him all who were ill with various diseases, those suffering severe pain, the demon-possessed, those having seizures, and the paralyzed, and he healed them. 25Large crowds from Galilee, the Decapolis,ᵉ Jerusalem, Judea and the region across the Jordan followed him.

The Beatitudes

5 Now when he saw the crowds, he went up on a mountainside and sat down. His disciples came to him, 2and he began to teach them, saying:

> 3"Blessed are the poor in spirit,
> for theirs is the kingdom of heaven.
> 4Blessed are those who mourn,
> for they will be comforted.
> 5Blessed are the meek,
> for they will inherit the earth.
> 6Blessed are those who hunger and
> thirst for righteousness,
> for they will be filled.
> 7Blessed are the merciful,
> for they will be shown mercy.
> 8Blessed are the pure in heart,
> for they will see God.
> 9Blessed are the peacemakers,
> for they will be called sons of God.
> 10Blessed are those who are persecuted
> because of righteousness,
> for theirs is the kingdom of heaven.

11"Blessed are you when people insult you, persecute you and falsely say all kinds of evil against you because of me. 12Rejoice and be glad, because great is your reward in heaven, for in the same way they persecuted the prophets who were before you.

Salt and Light

13"You are the salt of the earth. But if the salt loses its saltiness, how can it be

---

ᵃ6 Psalm 91:11,12   ᵇ7 Deut. 6:16   ᶜ10 Deut. 6:13   ᵈ16 Isaiah 9:1,2   ᵉ25 That is, the Ten Cities made salty again? It is no longer good for anything, except to be thrown out and trampled by men.

¹⁴"You are the light of the world. A city on a hill cannot be hidden. ¹⁵Neither do people light a lamp and put it under a bowl. Instead they put it on its stand, and it gives light to everyone in the house. ¹⁶In the same way, let your light shine before men, that they may see your good deeds and praise your Father in heaven.

The Fulfillment of the Law

¹⁷"Do not think that I have come to abolish the Law or the Prophets; I have not come to abolish them but to fulfill them. ¹⁸I tell you the truth, until heaven

and earth disappear, not the smallest letter, not the least stroke of a pen, will by any means disappear from the Law until everything is accomplished. ¹⁹Anyone who breaks one of the least of these commandments and teaches others to do the same will be called least in the kingdom of heaven, but whoever practices and teaches these commands will be called great in the kingdom of heaven. ²⁰For I tell you that unless your righteousness surpasses that of the Pharisees and the teachers of the law, you will certainly not enter the kingdom of heaven.

Murder

²¹"You have heard that it was said to

MONDAY

VERSE FOR THE DAY:	AUTHOR:	PASSAGE FOR THE DAY:
Matthew 5:16	Charlotte Stemple	Matthew 5:13–16

Keep Shining

THIS verse was dramatically illustrated when we were missionaries in Vietnam during the war. While our husbands were away from home, a missionary friend and I were invited by a Korean general to an important military ceremony. The only women amidst thousands of Korean, Vietnamese and American troops, we sat on the reviewing stand with the three-nation generals to watch the elaborate ceremonies and observe the presentation of medals to individuals and units. Later, after hors d'oeuvres, we were among the guests selected to receive lovely gifts.

Still thoroughly mystified as to why we had been invited, we were conducted to the general's mess where we ate a sumptuous meal on crested china and gold-plated flatware.

Finally, at the end of the meal, the Korean general called for his interpreter and, after polite opening conversation on both sides, said to me, "I am sure you are wondering why I invited you here today!" He continued with this remarkable comment: "When I was a small boy in Korea, an American lady missionary led me to Jesus Christ, and I never had an opportunity to thank her. So wherever I go, I look up the missionaries and honor them!"

There are no doubt many who have illuminated our paths through this life. As we are obedient to his command there will be those whose lives we may brighten. Let your light so shine!

Additional Scripture Readings:
Philippians 2:12–16; 1 Thessalonians 1:6–9

Go to page 1032 for your next devotional reading.

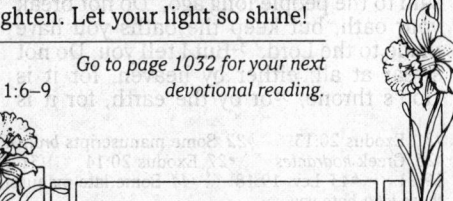

the people long ago, 'Do not murder,*a* and anyone who murders will be subject to judgment.' 22But I tell you that anyone who is angry with his brother*b* will be subject to judgment. Again, anyone who says to his brother, 'Raca,*c*' is answerable to the Sanhedrin. But anyone who says, 'You fool!' will be in danger of the fire of hell.

23"Therefore, if you are offering your gift at the altar and there remember that your brother has something against you, 24leave your gift there in front of the altar. First go and be reconciled to your brother; then come and offer your gift.

25"Settle matters quickly with your adversary who is taking you to court. Do it while you are still with him on the way, or he may hand you over to the judge, and the judge may hand you over to the officer, and you may be thrown into prison. 26I tell you the truth, you will not get out until you have paid the last penny.*d*

Adultery

27"You have heard that it was said, 'Do not commit adultery.'*e* 28But I tell you that anyone who looks at a woman lustfully has already committed adultery with her in his heart. 29If your right eye causes you to sin, gouge it out and throw it away. It is better for you to lose one part of your body than for your whole body to be thrown into hell. 30And if your right hand causes you to sin, cut it off and throw it away. It is better for you to lose one part of your body than for your whole body to go into hell.

Divorce

31"It has been said, 'Anyone who divorces his wife must give her a certificate of divorce.'*f* 32But I tell you that anyone who divorces his wife, except for marital unfaithfulness, causes her to become an adulteress, and anyone who marries the divorced woman commits adultery.

Oaths

33"Again, you have heard that it was said to the people long ago, 'Do not break your oath, but keep the oaths you have made to the Lord.' 34But I tell you, Do not swear at all: either by heaven, for it is God's throne; 35or by the earth, for it is

his footstool; or by Jerusalem, for it is the city of the Great King. 36And do not swear by your head, for you cannot make even one hair white or black. 37Simply let your 'Yes' be 'Yes,' and your 'No,' 'No'; anything beyond this comes from the evil one.

An Eye for an Eye

38"You have heard that it was said, 'Eye for eye, and tooth for tooth.'*g* 39But I tell you, Do not resist an evil person. If someone strikes you on the right cheek, turn to him the other also. 40And if someone wants to sue you and take your tunic, let him have your cloak as well. 41If someone forces you to go one mile, go with him two miles. 42Give to the one who asks you, and do not turn away from the one who wants to borrow from you.

Love for Enemies

43"You have heard that it was said, 'Love your neighbor*h* and hate your enemy.' 44But I tell you: Love your enemies*i* and pray for those who persecute you, 45that you may be sons of your Father in heaven. He causes his sun to rise on the evil and the good, and sends rain on the righteous and the unrighteous. 46If you love those who love you, what reward will you get? Are not even the tax collectors doing that? 47And if you greet only your brothers, what are you doing more than others? Do not even pagans do that? 48Be perfect, therefore, as your heavenly Father is perfect.

Giving to the Needy

6 "Be careful not to do your 'acts of righteousness' before men, to be seen by them. If you do, you will have no reward from your Father in heaven.

2"So when you give to the needy, do not announce it with trumpets, as the hypocrites do in the synagogues and on the streets, to be honored by men. I tell you the truth, they have received their reward in full. 3But when you give to the needy, do not let your left hand know what your right hand is doing, 4so that your giving may be in secret. Then your Father, who sees what is done in secret, will reward you.

---

a21 Exodus 20:13   *b22* Some manuscripts *brother without cause*   *c22* An Aramaic term of contempt   *d26* Greek *kodrantes*   *e27* Exodus 20:14   *f31* Deut. 24:1   *g38* Exodus 21:24; Lev. 24:20; Deut. 19:21   *h43* Lev. 19:18   *i44* Some late manuscripts *enemies, bless those who curse you, do good to those who hate you*

Prayer

⁵"And when you pray, do not be like the hypocrites, for they love to pray standing in the synagogues and on the street corners to be seen by men. I tell you the truth, they have received their reward in full. ⁶But when you pray, go into your room, close the door and pray to your Father, who is unseen. Then your Father, who sees what is done in secret, will reward you. ⁷And when you pray, do not keep on babbling like pagans, for they think they will be heard because of their many words. ⁸Do not be like them, for your Father knows what you need before you ask him.

⁹"This, then, is how you should pray:

" 'Our Father in heaven,
    hallowed be your name,
¹⁰your kingdom come,
    your will be done
        on earth as it is in heaven.
¹¹Give us today our daily bread.
¹²Forgive us our debts,
    as we also have forgiven our
        debtors.
¹³And lead us not into temptation,
    but deliver us from the evil one.ᵃ'

¹⁴For if you forgive men when they sin against you, your heavenly Father will also forgive you. ¹⁵But if you do not forgive men their sins, your Father will not forgive your sins.

Fasting

¹⁶"When you fast, do not look somber as the hypocrites do, for they disfigure their faces to show men they are fasting. I tell you the truth, they have received their reward in full. ¹⁷But when you fast, put oil on your head and wash your face, ¹⁸so that it will not be obvious to men that you are fasting, but only to your Father, who is unseen; and your Father, who sees what is done in secret, will reward you.

Treasures in Heaven

¹⁹"Do not store up for yourselves treasures on earth, where moth and rust destroy, and where thieves break in and steal. ²⁰But store up for yourselves treasures in heaven, where moth and rust do not destroy, and where thieves do not break in and steal. ²¹For where your treasure is, there your heart will be also.

²²"The eye is the lamp of the body. If your eyes are good, your whole body will be full of light. ²³But if your eyes are bad, your whole body will be full of darkness. If then the light within you is darkness, how great is that darkness!

²⁴"No one can serve two masters. Either he will hate the one and love the other, or he will be devoted to the one and despise the other. You cannot serve both God and Money.

Do Not Worry

²⁵"Therefore I tell you, do not worry about your life, what you will eat or drink; or about your body, what you will wear. Is not life more important than food, and the body more important than clothes? ²⁶Look at the birds of the air; they do not sow or reap or store away in barns, and yet your heavenly Father feeds them. Are you not much more valuable than they? ²⁷Who of you by worrying can add a single hour to his lifeᵇ?

²⁸"And why do you worry about clothes? See how the lilies of the field grow. They do not labor or spin. ²⁹Yet I tell you that not even Solomon in all his splendor was dressed like one of these. ³⁰If that is how God clothes the grass of the field, which is here today and tomorrow is thrown into the fire, will he not much more clothe you, O you of little faith? ³¹So do not worry, saying, 'What shall we eat?' or 'What shall we drink?' or 'What shall we wear?' ³²For the pagans run after all these things, and your heavenly Father knows that you need them. ³³But seek first his kingdom and his righteousness, and all these things will be given to you as well. ³⁴Therefore do not worry about tomorrow, for tomorrow will worry about itself. Each day has enough trouble of its own.

Judging Others

7 "Do not judge, or you too will be judged. ²For in the same way you judge others, you will be judged, and with the measure you use, it will be measured to you.

³"Why do you look at the speck of sawdust in your brother's eye and pay no attention to the plank in your own eye? ⁴How can you say to your brother, 'Let me take the speck out of your eye,' when all the time there is a plank in your own eye?

ᵃ13 Or *from evil*; some late manuscripts *one, / for yours is the kingdom and the power and the glory forever. Amen.*   ᵇ27 Or *single cubit to his height*

⁵You hypocrite, first take the plank out of your own eye, and then you will see clearly to remove the speck from your brother's eye.

⁶"Do not give dogs what is sacred; do not throw your pearls to pigs. If you do, they may trample them under their feet, and then turn and tear you to pieces.

Ask, Seek, Knock

⁷"Ask and it will be given to you; seek and you will find; knock and the door will be opened to you. ⁸For everyone who asks receives; he who seeks finds; and to him who knocks, the door will be opened.

⁹"Which of you, if his son asks for bread, will give him a stone? ¹⁰Or if he asks for a fish, will give him a snake? ¹¹If you, then, though you are evil, know how to give good gifts to your children, how much more will your Father in heaven give good gifts to those who ask him! ¹²So in everything, do to others what you

TUESDAY

VERSE FOR THE DAY:
Matthew 6:27

AUTHOR:
Beth Donigan Seversen

PASSAGE FOR THE DAY:
Matthew 6:25–34

Those Baby Monitors!

WORRY and exhaustion were creeping up on me. My daughter Kate was ten days old and asleep in her crib on the second floor of our small Cape Cod home. I had neglected to ask my husband to instruct me in the use of our new baby monitor and was certain it was quite beyond me. "What did mothers do before the invention of baby monitors?" I asked myself as I ironed in the basement.

The doctor had given me strict instructions due to the trauma of Kate's birth: "One trip up and down the stairs a day, for two weeks!" Yet, there I was, running up two flights of stairs in between each garment I ironed, leaning breathlessly over the crib rail to assure myself that my helpless little babe was still breathing. On the trip back to the basement I would scold myself harshly for being this silly. But, once again, while I was bending over the ironing board, fearful thoughts relentlessly teased, "What if crib death steals my baby away or what if she chokes and I'm not there?" So, back up the stairs I tread.

After one of those completed round trips, the question I'd asked earlier interrupted my fretting. What did mothers do before baby monitors? The still small voice residing in my heart replied, "They trusted in the Lord far more, worried far less, and got a lot more accomplished!" My thoughts were drawn next to Matthew 6:25,27: "Therefore I tell you, do not worry about your life . . . . Who of you by worrying can add a single hour to his life?" I knew then it was time to pause and confess: "Thank you, Father, that little Kate is of great value to you and that she is under your constant watch. I am ashamed of my worries. Please forgive me and help me to trust her life to you. Amen."

Additional Scripture Readings:
Ezra 8:21–23; Psalm 94:17–19

Go to page 1036 for your next devotional reading.

would have them do to you, for this sums up the Law and the Prophets.

The Narrow and Wide Gates

13"Enter through the narrow gate. For wide is the gate and broad is the road that leads to destruction, and many enter through it. 14But small is the gate and narrow the road that leads to life, and only a few find it.

A Tree and Its Fruit

15"Watch out for false prophets. They come to you in sheep's clothing, but inwardly they are ferocious wolves. 16By their fruit you will recognize them. Do people pick grapes from thornbushes, or figs from thistles? 17Likewise every good tree bears good fruit, but a bad tree bears bad fruit. 18A good tree cannot bear bad fruit, and a bad tree cannot bear good fruit. 19Every tree that does not bear good fruit is cut down and thrown into the fire. 20Thus, by their fruit you will recognize them.

21"Not everyone who says to me, 'Lord, Lord,' will enter the kingdom of heaven, but only he who does the will of my Father who is in heaven. 22Many will say to me on that day, 'Lord, Lord, did we not prophesy in your name, and in your name drive out demons and perform many miracles?' 23Then I will tell them plainly, 'I never knew you. Away from me, you evildoers!'

The Wise and Foolish Builders

24"Therefore everyone who hears these words of mine and puts them into practice is like a wise man who built his house on the rock. 25The rain came down, the streams rose, and the winds blew and beat against that house; yet it did not fall, because it had its foundation on the rock. 26But everyone who hears these words of mine and does not put them into practice is like a foolish man who built his house on sand. 27The rain came down, the streams rose, and the winds blew and beat against that house, and it fell with a great crash."

28When Jesus had finished saying these things, the crowds were amazed at his teaching, 29because he taught as one who had authority, and not as their teachers of the law.

The Man With Leprosy

8 When he came down from the mountainside, large crowds followed him. 2A man with leprosy*a* came and knelt before him and said, "Lord, if you are willing, you can make me clean."

3Jesus reached out his hand and touched the man. "I am willing," he said. "Be clean!" Immediately he was cured*b* of his leprosy. 4Then Jesus said to him, "See that you don't tell anyone. But go, show yourself to the priest and offer the gift Moses commanded, as a testimony to them."

The Faith of the Centurion

5When Jesus had entered Capernaum, a centurion came to him, asking for help. 6"Lord," he said, "my servant lies at home paralyzed and in terrible suffering."

7Jesus said to him, "I will go and heal him."

8The centurion replied, "Lord, I do not deserve to have you come under my roof. But just say the word, and my servant will be healed. 9For I myself am a man under authority, with soldiers under me. I tell this one, 'Go,' and he goes; and that one, 'Come,' and he comes. I say to my servant, 'Do this,' and he does it."

10When Jesus heard this, he was astonished and said to those following him, "I tell you the truth, I have not found anyone in Israel with such great faith. 11I say to you that many will come from the east and the west, and will take their places at the feast with Abraham, Isaac and Jacob in the kingdom of heaven. 12But the subjects of the kingdom will be thrown outside, into the darkness, where there will be weeping and gnashing of teeth."

13Then Jesus said to the centurion, "Go! It will be done just as you believed it would." And his servant was healed at that very hour.

Jesus Heals Many

14When Jesus came into Peter's house, he saw Peter's mother-in-law lying in bed with a fever. 15He touched her hand and the fever left her, and she got up and began to wait on him.

16When evening came, many who were demon-possessed were brought to him,

---

a2 The Greek word was used for various diseases affecting the skin—not necessarily leprosy.   *b3* Greek *made clean* and he drove out the spirits with a word and healed all the sick. [17]This was to fulfill what was spoken through the prophet Isaiah:

"He took up our infirmities
and carried our diseases."[a]

The Cost of Following Jesus

[18]When Jesus saw the crowd around him, he gave orders to cross to the other side of the lake. [19]Then a teacher of the law came to him and said, "Teacher, I will follow you wherever you go."

[20]Jesus replied, "Foxes have holes and birds of the air have nests, but the Son of Man has no place to lay his head."

[21]Another disciple said to him, "Lord, first let me go and bury my father."

[22]But Jesus told him, "Follow me, and let the dead bury their own dead."

Jesus Calms the Storm

[23]Then he got into the boat and his disciples followed him. [24]Without warning, a furious storm came up on the lake, so that the waves swept over the boat. But Jesus was sleeping. [25]The disciples went and woke him, saying, "Lord, save us! We're going to drown!"

[26]He replied, "You of little faith, why are you so afraid?" Then he got up and rebuked the winds and the waves, and it was completely calm.

[27]The men were amazed and asked, "What kind of man is this? Even the winds and the waves obey him!"

The Healing of Two Demon-possessed Men

[28]When he arrived at the other side in the region of the Gadarenes,[b] two demon-possessed men coming from the tombs met him. They were so violent that no one could pass that way. [29]"What do you want with us, Son of God?" they shouted. "Have you come here to torture us before the appointed time?"

[30]Some distance from them a large herd of pigs was feeding. [31]The demons begged Jesus, "If you drive us out, send us into the herd of pigs."

[32]He said to them, "Go!" So they came out and went into the pigs, and the whole herd rushed down the steep bank into the lake and died in the water. [33]Those tending the pigs ran off, went into the town and reported all this, including what had happened to the demon-possessed men. [34]Then the whole town went out to meet Jesus. And when they saw him, they pleaded with him to leave their region.

Jesus Heals a Paralytic

9 Jesus stepped into a boat, crossed over and came to his own town. [2]Some men brought to him a paralytic, lying on a mat. When Jesus saw their faith, he said to the paralytic, "Take heart, son; your sins are forgiven."

[3]At this, some of the teachers of the law said to themselves, "This fellow is blaspheming!"

[4]Knowing their thoughts, Jesus said, "Why do you entertain evil thoughts in your hearts? [5]Which is easier: to say, 'Your sins are forgiven,' or to say, 'Get up and walk'? [6]But so that you may know that the Son of Man has authority on earth to forgive sins. . . ." Then he said to the paralytic, "Get up, take your mat and go home." [7]And the man got up and went home. [8]When the crowd saw this, they were filled with awe; and they praised God, who had given such authority to men.

The Calling of Matthew

[9]As Jesus went on from there, he saw a man named Matthew sitting at the tax collector's booth. "Follow me," he told him, and Matthew got up and followed him.

[10]While Jesus was having dinner at Matthew's house, many tax collectors and "sinners" came and ate with him and his disciples. [11]When the Pharisees saw this, they asked his disciples, "Why does your teacher eat with tax collectors and 'sinners'?"

[12]On hearing this, Jesus said, "It is not the healthy who need a doctor, but the sick. [13]But go and learn what this means: 'I desire mercy, not sacrifice.'[c] For I have not come to call the righteous, but sinners."

Jesus Questioned About Fasting

[14]Then John's disciples came and asked him, "How is it that we and the Pharisees fast, but your disciples do not fast?"

[15]Jesus answered, "How can the guests of the bridegroom mourn while he is with them? The time will come when the

---

[a]17 Isaiah 53:4   [b]28 Some manuscripts Gergesenes; others Gerasenes   [c]13 Hosea 6:6

bridegroom will be taken from them; then they will fast.

16"No one sews a patch of unshrunk cloth on an old garment, for the patch will pull away from the garment, making the tear worse. 17Neither do men pour new wine into old wineskins. If they do, the skins will burst, the wine will run out and the wineskins will be ruined. No, they pour new wine into new wineskins, and both are preserved."

A Dead Girl and a Sick Woman

18While he was saying this, a ruler came and knelt before him and said, "My daughter has just died. But come and put your hand on her, and she will live." 19Jesus got up and went with him, and so did his disciples.

20Just then a woman who had been subject to bleeding for twelve years came up behind him and touched the edge of his cloak. 21She said to herself, "If I only touch his cloak, I will be healed."

22Jesus turned and saw her. "Take heart, daughter," he said, "your faith has healed you." And the woman was healed from that moment.

23When Jesus entered the ruler's house and saw the flute players and the noisy crowd, 24he said, "Go away. The girl is not dead but asleep." But they laughed at him. 25After the crowd had been put outside, he went in and took the girl by the hand, and she got up. 26News of this spread through all that region.

Jesus Heals the Blind and Mute

27As Jesus went on from there, two blind men followed him, calling out, "Have mercy on us, Son of David!"

28When he had gone indoors, the blind men came to him, and he asked them, "Do you believe that I am able to do this?"

"Yes, Lord," they replied.

29Then he touched their eyes and said, "According to your faith will it be done to you"; 30and their sight was restored. Jesus warned them sternly, "See that no one knows about this." 31But they went out and spread the news about him all over that region.

32While they were going out, a man who was demon-possessed and could not talk was brought to Jesus. 33And when the demon was driven out, the man who had

been mute spoke. The crowd was amazed and said, "Nothing like this has ever been seen in Israel."

34But the Pharisees said, "It is by the prince of demons that he drives out demons."

The Workers Are Few

35Jesus went through all the towns and villages, teaching in their synagogues, preaching the good news of the kingdom and healing every disease and sickness. 36When he saw the crowds, he had compassion on them, because they were harassed and helpless, like sheep without a shepherd. 37Then he said to his disciples, "The harvest is plentiful but the workers are few. 38Ask the Lord of the harvest, therefore, to send out workers into his harvest field."

Jesus Sends Out the Twelve

10 He called his twelve disciples to him and gave them authority to drive out evil*a* spirits and to heal every disease and sickness.

2These are the names of the twelve apostles: first, Simon (who is called Peter) and his brother Andrew; James son of Zebedee, and his brother John; 3Philip and Bartholomew; Thomas and Matthew the tax collector; James son of Alphaeus, and Thaddaeus; 4Simon the Zealot and Judas Iscariot, who betrayed him.

5These twelve Jesus sent out with the following instructions: "Do not go among the Gentiles or enter any town of the Samaritans. 6Go rather to the lost sheep of Israel. 7As you go, preach this message: 'The kingdom of heaven is near.' 8Heal the sick, raise the dead, cleanse those who have leprosy,*b* drive out demons. Freely you have received, freely give. 9Do not take along any gold or silver or copper in your belts; 10take no bag for the journey, or extra tunic, or sandals or a staff; for the worker is worth his keep.

11"Whatever town or village you enter, search for some worthy person there and stay at his house until you leave. 12As you enter the home, give it your greeting. 13If the home is deserving, let your peace rest on it; if it is not, let your peace return to you. 14If anyone will not welcome you or listen to your words, shake the dust off your feet when you leave that home or town. 15I tell you the truth, it will be more

---

*a*1 Greek *unclean*   *b*8 The Greek word was used for various diseases affecting the skin—not necessarily leprosy.

bearable for Sodom and Gomorrah on the day of judgment than for that town. ¹⁶I am sending you out like sheep among wolves. Therefore be as shrewd as snakes and as innocent as doves.

¹⁷"Be on your guard against men; they will hand you over to the local councils and flog you in their synagogues. ¹⁸On my account you will be brought before governors and kings as witnesses to them and to the Gentiles. ¹⁹But when they arrest you, do not worry about what to say or how to say it. At that time you will be given what to say, ²⁰for it will not be you speaking, but the Spirit of your Father speaking through you.

²¹"Brother will betray brother to death,

ᵃ25 Greek *Beezeboul* or *Beelzeboul*

and a father his child; children will rebel against their parents and have them put to death. ²²All men will hate you because of me, but he who stands firm to the end will be saved. ²³When you are persecuted in one place, flee to another. I tell you the truth, you will not finish going through the cities of Israel before the Son of Man comes.

²⁴"A student is not above his teacher, nor a servant above his master. ²⁵It is enough for the student to be like his teacher, and the servant like his master. If the head of the house has been called Beelzebub,ᵃ how much more the members of his household!

²⁶"So do not be afraid of them. There is

WEDNESDAY

VERSE FOR THE DAY:	AUTHOR:	PASSAGE FOR THE DAY:
Matthew 10:8	Phyllis Hobe	Matthew 10:1–16

The Gift of Understanding

SOMETIMES, when we love someone, we feel we just can't give them enough. We may even do without things we need ourselves. I think most parents feel that way about their children. Love makes us generous.

But generosity is more than giving.

If anyone could have showered gifts on those he loved, it was Jesus Christ. But he didn't. He provided for their basic needs; he saw to it that they had shelter and enough to eat. He watched them counting coins when he could have filled their laps with riches.

Jesus gave something more precious and more lasting than gifts. He gave understanding. He knew how hard it is to live in this world. He felt what others felt and couldn't put into words. And out of his understanding he gave what people truly need, such as forgiveness for Zacchaeus's guilt, hope for the cynical woman at the well, recovery for a dying child.

The next time you want to give a gift to someone you love, don't worry about how much you can afford to spend or how big the present ought to be. Consider, instead, what generosity really means: *understanding*. That's something each of us can afford to give—all the time.

Additional Scripture Readings:
Proverbs 20:5–6; John 4:10–14

Go to page 1038 for your next devotional reading.

nothing concealed that will not be disclosed, or hidden that will not be made known. ²⁷What I tell you in the dark, speak in the daylight; what is whispered in your ear, proclaim from the roofs. ²⁸Do not be afraid of those who kill the body but cannot kill the soul. Rather, be afraid of the One who can destroy both soul and body in hell. ²⁹Are not two sparrows sold for a penny*a*? Yet not one of them will fall to the ground apart from the will of your Father. ³⁰And even the very hairs of your head are all numbered. ³¹So don't be afraid; you are worth more than many sparrows.

³²"Whoever acknowledges me before men, I will also acknowledge him before my Father in heaven. ³³But whoever disowns me before men, I will disown him before my Father in heaven.

³⁴"Do not suppose that I have come to bring peace to the earth. I did not come to bring peace, but a sword. ³⁵For I have come to turn

" 'a man against his father,
    a daughter against her mother,
a daughter-in-law against her
        mother-in-law—
³⁶   a man's enemies will be the
        members of his own
        household.'*b*

³⁷"Anyone who loves his father or mother more than me is not worthy of me; anyone who loves his son or daughter more than me is not worthy of me; ³⁸and anyone who does not take his cross and follow me is not worthy of me. ³⁹Whoever finds his life will lose it, and whoever loses his life for my sake will find it.

⁴⁰"He who receives you receives me, and he who receives me receives the one who sent me. ⁴¹Anyone who receives a prophet because he is a prophet will receive a prophet's reward, and anyone who receives a righteous man because he is a righteous man will receive a righteous man's reward. ⁴²And if anyone gives even a cup of cold water to one of these little ones because he is my disciple, I tell you the truth, he will certainly not lose his reward."

Jesus and John the Baptist

11 After Jesus had finished instructing his twelve disciples, he went on from there to teach and preach in the towns of Galilee.*c*

²When John heard in prison what Christ was doing, he sent his disciples ³to ask him, "Are you the one who was to come, or should we expect someone else?"

⁴Jesus replied, "Go back and report to John what you hear and see: ⁵The blind receive sight, the lame walk, those who have leprosy*d* are cured, the deaf hear, the dead are raised, and the good news is preached to the poor. ⁶Blessed is the man who does not fall away on account of me."

⁷As John's disciples were leaving, Jesus began to speak to the crowd about John: "What did you go out into the desert to see? A reed swayed by the wind? ⁸If not, what did you go out to see? A man dressed in fine clothes? No, those who wear fine clothes are in kings' palaces. ⁹Then what did you go out to see? A prophet? Yes, I tell you, and more than a prophet. ¹⁰This is the one about whom it is written:

" 'I will send my messenger ahead of
        you,
    who will prepare your way before
        you.'*e*

¹¹I tell you the truth: Among those born of women there has not risen anyone greater than John the Baptist; yet he who is least in the kingdom of heaven is greater than he. ¹²From the days of John the Baptist until now, the kingdom of heaven has been forcefully advancing, and forceful men lay hold of it. ¹³For all the Prophets and the Law prophesied until John. ¹⁴And if you are willing to accept it, he is the Elijah who was to come. ¹⁵He who has ears, let him hear.

¹⁶"To what can I compare this generation? They are like children sitting in the marketplaces and calling out to others:

¹⁷" 'We played the flute for you,
        and you did not dance;
    we sang a dirge,
        and you did not mourn.'

¹⁸For John came neither eating nor drinking, and they say, 'He has a demon.' ¹⁹The Son of Man came eating and drinking, and they say, 'Here is a glutton and a

---

a29 Greek *an assarion*   *b36* Micah 7:6   *c1* Greek *in their towns*   *d5* The Greek word was used for various diseases affecting the skin—not necessarily leprosy.   *e10* Mal. 3:1

drunkard, a friend of tax collectors and "sinners." ' But wisdom is proved right by her actions."

Woe on Unrepentant Cities

20Then Jesus began to denounce the cities in which most of his miracles had been performed, because they did not repent. 21"Woe to you, Korazin! Woe to you, Bethsaida! If the miracles that were performed in you had been performed in Tyre and Sidon, they would have repented long ago in sackcloth and ashes. 22But

*a*23 Greek *Hades*

I tell you, it will be more bearable for Tyre and Sidon on the day of judgment than for you. 23And you, Capernaum, will you be lifted up to the skies? No, you will go down to the depths. *a* If the miracles that were performed in you had been performed in Sodom, it would have remained to this day. 24But I tell you that it will be more bearable for Sodom on the day of judgment than for you."

Rest for the Weary

25At that time Jesus said, "I praise you,

THURSDAY

| VERSE FOR THE DAY: | AUTHOR: | PASSAGE FOR THE DAY: |
| Matthew 10:34 | Jill Briscoe | Matthew 10:32–42 |

The Hate Principle

JESUS cared about the family. But he knew that ministry would bring its own strains. One day he was talking to his people and he said, "If anyone comes to me and does not hate his father and mother, his wife and children, his brothers and sisters—yes, even his own life—he cannot be my disciple" (Luke 14:26). This has been called the "hate" principle. Jesus obviously did not mean we are to hate those people in our families who are closest to us. He had already told us to love God with all our hearts and our neighbors as ourselves.

Terms used to define the emotions and affections were frequently comparative. Jesus was saying that "natural affection is to be, as compared with the Christian's devotedness to Christ, as if it were hate" (*Oxford NIV Scofield Study Bible*, p. 1074). Christ illustrated this principle in his own person when talking of the new relationships of the kingdom: "Pointing to his disciples, he said, 'Here are my mother and my brothers. For whoever does the will of my Father in heaven is my brother and sister and mother'" (Matthew 12:49–50).

Jesus knew the coming of the gospel would bring division within families—it brought it in his own. But this did not mean that Jesus was not firmly in favor of "family." He cared for his mother from his cross, appeared to his oldest brother James after the resurrection, and united his family in ministry in Jerusalem. The gospel will bring reactions and responses—even from within our families. Disciples must be ready for them.

Additional Scripture Readings:
Mark 7:9–13; John 19:25–27

Go to page 1040 for your next devotional reading.

Father, Lord of heaven and earth, because you have hidden these things from the wise and learned, and revealed them to little children. ²⁶Yes, Father, for this was your good pleasure.

²⁷"All things have been committed to me by my Father. No one knows the Son except the Father, and no one knows the Father except the Son and those to whom the Son chooses to reveal him.

²⁸"Come to me, all you who are weary and burdened, and I will give you rest. ²⁹Take my yoke upon you and learn from me, for I am gentle and humble in heart, and you will find rest for your souls. ³⁰For my yoke is easy and my burden is light."

Lord of the Sabbath

12 At that time Jesus went through the grainfields on the Sabbath. His disciples were hungry and began to pick some heads of grain and eat them. ²When the Pharisees saw this, they said to him, "Look! Your disciples are doing what is unlawful on the Sabbath."

³He answered, "Haven't you read what David did when he and his companions were hungry? ⁴He entered the house of God, and he and his companions ate the consecrated bread—which was not lawful for them to do, but only for the priests. ⁵Or haven't you read in the Law that on the Sabbath the priests in the temple desecrate the day and yet are innocent? ⁶I tell you that one*ᵃ* greater than the temple is here. ⁷If you had known what these words mean, 'I desire mercy, not sacrifice,'*ᵇ* you would not have condemned the innocent. ⁸For the Son of Man is Lord of the Sabbath."

⁹Going on from that place, he went into their synagogue, ¹⁰and a man with a shriveled hand was there. Looking for a reason to accuse Jesus, they asked him, "Is it lawful to heal on the Sabbath?"

¹¹He said to them, "If any of you has a sheep and it falls into a pit on the Sabbath, will you not take hold of it and lift it out? ¹²How much more valuable is a man than a sheep! Therefore it is lawful to do good on the Sabbath."

¹³Then he said to the man, "Stretch out your hand." So he stretched it out and it was completely restored, just as sound as the other. ¹⁴But the Pharisees went out and plotted how they might kill Jesus.

God's Chosen Servant

¹⁵Aware of this, Jesus withdrew from that place. Many followed him, and he healed all their sick, ¹⁶warning them not to tell who he was. ¹⁷This was to fulfill what was spoken through the prophet Isaiah:

¹⁸"Here is my servant whom I have
  chosen,
  the one I love, in whom I delight;
I will put my Spirit on him,
  and he will proclaim justice to the
    nations.
¹⁹He will not quarrel or cry out;
  no one will hear his voice in the
    streets.
²⁰A bruised reed he will not break,
  and a smoldering wick he will not
    snuff out,
  till he leads justice to victory.
²¹   In his name the nations will put
    their hope."*ᶜ*

Jesus and Beelzebub

²²Then they brought him a demon-possessed man who was blind and mute, and Jesus healed him, so that he could both talk and see. ²³All the people were astonished and said, "Could this be the Son of David?"

²⁴But when the Pharisees heard this, they said, "It is only by Beelzebub,*ᵈ* the prince of demons, that this fellow drives out demons."

²⁵Jesus knew their thoughts and said to them, "Every kingdom divided against itself will be ruined, and every city or household divided against itself will not stand. ²⁶If Satan drives out Satan, he is divided against himself. How then can his kingdom stand? ²⁷And if I drive out demons by Beelzebub, by whom do your people drive them out? So then, they will be your judges. ²⁸But if I drive out demons by the Spirit of God, then the kingdom of God has come upon you.

²⁹"Or again, how can anyone enter a strong man's house and carry off his possessions unless he first ties up the strong man? Then he can rob his house.

³⁰"He who is not with me is against me, and he who does not gather with me scatters. ³¹And so I tell you, every sin and blasphemy will be forgiven men, but the blasphemy against the Spirit will not be forgiven. ³²Anyone who speaks a word

---

ᵃ6 Or something; also in verses 41 and 42   ᵇ7 Hosea 6:6   ᶜ21 Isaiah 42:1-4   ᵈ24 Greek Beezeboul or Beelzeboul; also in verse 27

VERSE FOR THE DAY:
Matthew 11:28

AUTHOR:
Diane Head

PASSAGE FOR THE DAY:
Matthew 11:25–30

His Rest

DO you ever feel as though you have nothing to give? That so many demands are made of you that you've become depleted . . . empty . . . exhausted?

Do you have an automatic signal when your posterior hits the bottom of a chair—immediately a voice from the farthest room in the house calls "MOTHER . . ." as if the house were on fire?

If you answered a hearty "amen" to the above, congratulations. You're a bonafide member of twentieth-century motherhood. One of the conditions of membership is that you exchange your calm and orderly life for upheaval, busyness and whirlwind activity.

We entered motherhood so eagerly—babes in our arms and stars in our eyes. So cuddly and cute, these wee ones took hold of our hearts and lives. We didn't know the gentle thump, thump, thump of their hearts was the ticking of a time bomb, ready to explode with the energy of an atomic bomb at any minute. As parents, we are the managers and harnessers of this energy, so we fill our days with clever schemes and fancy plans to keep our children occupied. Soon we find ourselves caught in the great car pool of life. We pick up and drop off miniballerinas, soccer players, piano virtuosos and future NFL champions until life is little more than a blur.

If ever anyone needed rest, it's today's mother. And I have great news. There is rest for us—a rest more rejuvenating than a long and leisurely nap, and more soothing to frayed nerves than a Brahms concert. This rest reaches into the depths of our souls and claims us from within.

This special promise of rest comes from Jesus' words in Matthew 11:29: "Take my yoke upon you and learn from me . . . and you will find rest." The yoke spoken of in this passage is fashioned of discipline and discipleship; its lining is love. Rather than bringing restriction, it brings refreshment. Through this yoke he calls us to learn of himself and find quietness and blessed rest.

Rest for the soul is the most desirable rest. It affects not only our spiritual health, but our emotional and physical health as well. The only way to receive this rest is to sit at Christ's feet and hear his word, to take the time to learn more about who he is and what he is like.

Additional Scripture Readings:
Exodus 33:12–14; Mark 6:30–31

Go to page 1044 for your next devotional reading.

against the Son of Man will be forgiven, but anyone who speaks against the Holy Spirit will not be forgiven, either in this age or in the age to come.

33"Make a tree good and its fruit will be good, or make a tree bad and its fruit will be bad, for a tree is recognized by its fruit. 34You brood of vipers, how can you who are evil say anything good? For out of the overflow of the heart the mouth speaks. 35The good man brings good things out of the good stored up in him, and the evil man brings evil things out of the evil stored up in him. 36But I tell you that men will have to give account on the day of judgment for every careless word they have spoken. 37For by your words you will be acquitted, and by your words you will be condemned."

The Sign of Jonah

38Then some of the Pharisees and teachers of the law said to him, "Teacher, we want to see a miraculous sign from you."

39He answered, "A wicked and adulterous generation asks for a miraculous sign! But none will be given it except the sign of the prophet Jonah. 40For as Jonah was three days and three nights in the belly of a huge fish, so the Son of Man will be three days and three nights in the heart of the earth. 41The men of Nineveh will stand up at the judgment with this generation and condemn it; for they repented at the preaching of Jonah, and now one*a* greater than Jonah is here. 42The Queen of the South will rise at the judgment with this generation and condemn it; for she came from the ends of the earth to listen to Solomon's wisdom, and now one greater than Solomon is here.

43"When an evil*b* spirit comes out of a man, it goes through arid places seeking rest and does not find it. 44Then it says, 'I will return to the house I left.' When it arrives, it finds the house unoccupied, swept clean and put in order. 45Then it goes and takes with it seven other spirits more wicked than itself, and they go in and live there. And the final condition of that man is worse than the first. That is how it will be with this wicked generation."

Jesus' Mother and Brothers

46While Jesus was still talking to the crowd, his mother and brothers stood outside, wanting to speak to him. 47Someone told him, "Your mother and brothers are standing outside, wanting to speak to you."*c*

48He replied to him, "Who is my mother, and who are my brothers?" 49Pointing to his disciples, he said, "Here are my mother and my brothers. 50For whoever does the will of my Father in heaven is my brother and sister and mother."

The Parable of the Sower

13 That same day Jesus went out of the house and sat by the lake. 2Such large crowds gathered around him that he got into a boat and sat in it, while all the people stood on the shore. 3Then he told them many things in parables, saying: "A farmer went out to sow his seed. 4As he was scattering the seed, some fell along the path, and the birds came and ate it up. 5Some fell on rocky places, where it did not have much soil. It sprang up quickly, because the soil was shallow. 6But when the sun came up, the plants were scorched, and they withered because they had no root. 7Other seed fell among thorns, which grew up and choked the plants. 8Still other seed fell on good soil, where it produced a crop—a hundred, sixty or thirty times what was sown. 9He who has ears, let him hear."

10The disciples came to him and asked, "Why do you speak to the people in parables?"

11He replied, "The knowledge of the secrets of the kingdom of heaven has been given to you, but not to them. 12Whoever has will be given more, and he will have an abundance. Whoever does not have, even what he has will be taken from him. 13This is why I speak to them in parables:

"Though seeing, they do not see;
   though hearing, they do not hear or
     understand.

14In them is fulfilled the prophecy of Isaiah:

" 'You will be ever hearing but never
     understanding;
   you will be ever seeing but never
     perceiving.
15For this people's heart has become
     calloused;
   they hardly hear with their ears,

---

*a*41 Or *something*; also in verse 42   *b*43 Greek *unclean*   *c*47 Some manuscripts do not have verse 47.

and they have closed their eyes.
Otherwise they might see with their eyes,
hear with their ears,
understand with their hearts
and turn, and I would heal them.'ᵃ

16But blessed are your eyes because they see, and your ears because they hear. 17For I tell you the truth, many prophets and righteous men longed to see what you see but did not see it, and to hear what you hear but did not hear it.

18"Listen then to what the parable of the sower means: 19When anyone hears the message about the kingdom and does not understand it, the evil one comes and snatches away what was sown in his heart. This is the seed sown along the path. 20The one who received the seed that fell on rocky places is the man who hears the word and at once receives it with joy. 21But since he has no root, he lasts only a short time. When trouble or persecution comes because of the word, he quickly falls away. 22The one who received the seed that fell among the thorns is the man who hears the word, but the worries of this life and the deceitfulness of wealth choke it, making it unfruitful. 23But the one who received the seed that fell on good soil is the man who hears the word and understands it. He produces a crop, yielding a hundred, sixty or thirty times what was sown."

The Parable of the Weeds

24Jesus told them another parable: "The kingdom of heaven is like a man who sowed good seed in his field. 25But while everyone was sleeping, his enemy came and sowed weeds among the wheat, and went away. 26When the wheat sprouted and formed heads, then the weeds also appeared.

27"The owner's servants came to him and said, 'Sir, didn't you sow good seed in your field? Where then did the weeds come from?'

28" 'An enemy did this,' he replied.

"The servants asked him, 'Do you want us to go and pull them up?'

29" 'No,' he answered, 'because while you are pulling the weeds, you may root up the wheat with them. 30Let both grow together until the harvest. At that time I will tell the harvesters: First collect the weeds and tie them in bundles to be burned; then gather the wheat and bring it into my barn.' "

The Parables of the Mustard Seed and the Yeast

31He told them another parable: "The kingdom of heaven is like a mustard seed, which a man took and planted in his field. 32Though it is the smallest of all your seeds, yet when it grows, it is the largest of garden plants and becomes a tree, so that the birds of the air come and perch in its branches."

33He told them still another parable: "The kingdom of heaven is like yeast that a woman took and mixed into a large amountᵇ of flour until it worked all through the dough."

34Jesus spoke all these things to the crowd in parables; he did not say anything to them without using a parable. 35So was fulfilled what was spoken through the prophet:

"I will open my mouth in parables,
I will utter things hidden since the creation of the world."ᶜ

The Parable of the Weeds Explained

36Then he left the crowd and went into the house. His disciples came to him and said, "Explain to us the parable of the weeds in the field."

37He answered, "The one who sowed the good seed is the Son of Man. 38The field is the world, and the good seed stands for the sons of the kingdom. The weeds are the sons of the evil one, 39and the enemy who sows them is the devil. The harvest is the end of the age, and the harvesters are angels.

40"As the weeds are pulled up and burned in the fire, so it will be at the end of the age. 41The Son of Man will send out his angels, and they will weed out of his kingdom everything that causes sin and all who do evil. 42They will throw them into the fiery furnace, where there will be weeping and gnashing of teeth. 43Then the righteous will shine like the sun in the kingdom of their Father. He who has ears, let him hear.

The Parables of the Hidden Treasure and the Pearl

44"The kingdom of heaven is like treasure hidden in a field. When a man found it, he hid it again, and then in his joy went

ᵃ15 Isaiah 6:9,10   ᵇ33 Greek three satas (probably about 1/2 bushel or 22 liters)   ᶜ35 Psalm 78:2

and sold all he had and bought that field.

45"Again, the kingdom of heaven is like a merchant looking for fine pearls. 46When he found one of great value, he went away and sold everything he had and bought it.

The Parable of the Net

47"Once again, the kingdom of heaven is like a net that was let down into the lake and caught all kinds of fish. 48When it was full, the fishermen pulled it up on the shore. Then they sat down and collected the good fish in baskets, but threw the bad away. 49This is how it will be at the end of the age. The angels will come and separate the wicked from the righteous 50and throw them into the fiery furnace, where there will be weeping and gnashing of teeth.

51"Have you understood all these things?" Jesus asked.

"Yes," they replied.

52He said to them, "Therefore every teacher of the law who has been instructed about the kingdom of heaven is like the owner of a house who brings out of his storeroom new treasures as well as old."

A Prophet Without Honor

53When Jesus had finished these parables, he moved on from there. 54Coming to his hometown, he began teaching the people in their synagogue, and they were amazed. "Where did this man get this wisdom and these miraculous powers?" they asked. 55"Isn't this the carpenter's son? Isn't his mother's name Mary, and aren't his brothers James, Joseph, Simon and Judas? 56Aren't all his sisters with us? Where then did this man get all these things?" 57And they took offense at him.

But Jesus said to them, "Only in his hometown and in his own house is a prophet without honor."

58And he did not do many miracles there because of their lack of faith.

John the Baptist Beheaded

14 At that time Herod the tetrarch heard the reports about Jesus, 2and he said to his attendants, "This is John the Baptist; he has risen from the dead! That is why miraculous powers are at work in him."

3Now Herod had arrested John and bound him and put him in prison because of Herodias, his brother Philip's wife, 4for John had been saying to him: "It is not lawful for you to have her." 5Herod wanted to kill John, but he was afraid of the people, because they considered him a prophet.

6On Herod's birthday the daughter of Herodias danced for them and pleased Herod so much 7that he promised with an oath to give her whatever she asked. 8Prompted by her mother, she said, "Give me here on a platter the head of John the Baptist." 9The king was distressed, but because of his oaths and his dinner guests, he ordered that her request be granted 10and had John beheaded in the prison. 11His head was brought in on a platter and given to the girl, who carried it to her mother. 12John's disciples came and took his body and buried it. Then they went and told Jesus.

Jesus Feeds the Five Thousand

13When Jesus heard what had happened, he withdrew by boat privately to a solitary place. Hearing of this, the crowds followed him on foot from the towns. 14When Jesus landed and saw a large crowd, he had compassion on them and healed their sick.

15As evening approached, the disciples came to him and said, "This is a remote place, and it's already getting late. Send the crowds away, so they can go to the villages and buy themselves some food."

16Jesus replied, "They do not need to go away. You give them something to eat."

17"We have here only five loaves of bread and two fish," they answered.

18"Bring them here to me," he said. 19And he directed the people to sit down on the grass. Taking the five loaves and the two fish and looking up to heaven, he gave thanks and broke the loaves. Then he gave them to the disciples, and the disciples gave them to the people. 20They all ate and were satisfied, and the disciples picked up twelve basketfuls of broken pieces that were left over. 21The number of those who ate was about five thousand men, besides women and children.

Jesus Walks on the Water

22Immediately Jesus made the disciples get into the boat and go on ahead of him to the other side, while he dismissed the crowd. 23After he had dismissed them, he went up on a mountainside by himself to pray. When evening came, he was there alone, 24but the boat was

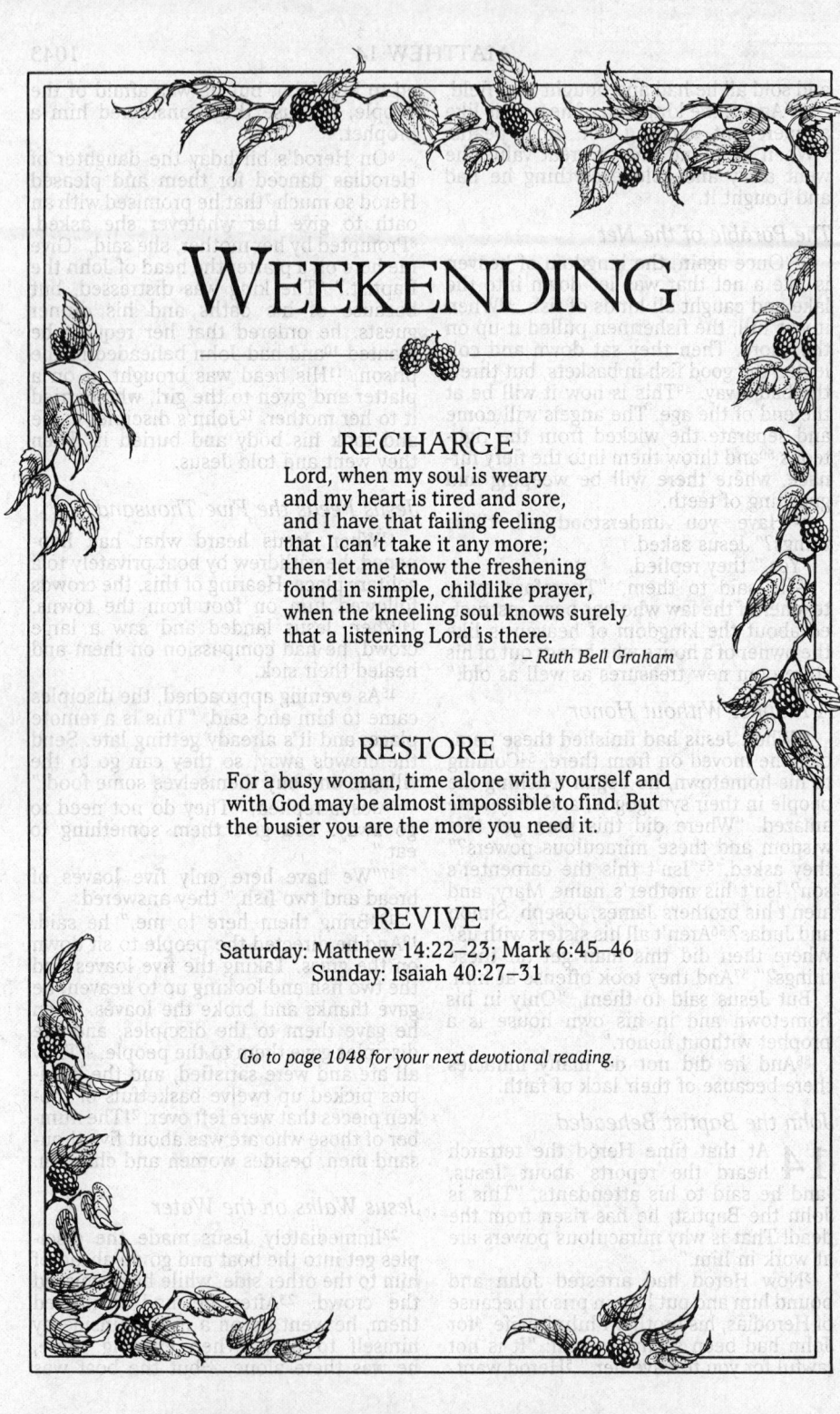

WEEKENDING

RECHARGE

Lord, when my soul is weary
and my heart is tired and sore,
and I have that failing feeling
that I can't take it any more;
then let me know the freshening
found in simple, childlike prayer,
when the kneeling soul knows surely
that a listening Lord is there.

— Ruth Bell Graham

RESTORE

For a busy woman, time alone with yourself and
with God may be almost impossible to find. But
the busier you are the more you need it.

REVIVE

Saturday: Matthew 14:22–23; Mark 6:45–46
Sunday: Isaiah 40:27–31

Go to page 1048 for your next devotional reading.

already a considerable distance[a] from land, buffeted by the waves because the wind was against it.

25During the fourth watch of the night Jesus went out to them, walking on the lake. 26When the disciples saw him walking on the lake, they were terrified. "It's a ghost," they said, and cried out in fear.

27But Jesus immediately said to them: "Take courage! It is I. Don't be afraid."

28"Lord, if it's you," Peter replied, "tell me to come to you on the water."

29"Come," he said.

Then Peter got down out of the boat, walked on the water and came toward Jesus. 30But when he saw the wind, he was afraid and, beginning to sink, cried out, "Lord, save me!"

31Immediately Jesus reached out his hand and caught him. "You of little faith," he said, "why did you doubt?"

32And when they climbed into the boat, the wind died down. 33Then those who were in the boat worshiped him, saying, "Truly you are the Son of God."

34When they had crossed over, they landed at Gennesaret. 35And when the men of that place recognized Jesus, they sent word to all the surrounding country. People brought all their sick to him 36and begged him to let the sick just touch the edge of his cloak, and all who touched him were healed.

Clean and Unclean

15 Then some Pharisees and teachers of the law came to Jesus from Jerusalem and asked, 2"Why do your disciples break the tradition of the elders? They don't wash their hands before they eat!"

3Jesus replied, "And why do you break the command of God for the sake of your tradition? 4For God said, 'Honor your father and mother'[b] and 'Anyone who curses his father or mother must be put to death.'[c] 5But you say that if a man says to his father or mother, 'Whatever help you might otherwise have received from me is a gift devoted to God,' 6he is not to 'honor his father[d]' with it. Thus you nullify the word of God for the sake of your tradition. 7You hypocrites! Isaiah was right when he prophesied about you:

8" 'These people honor me with their lips,

but their hearts are far from me.
9They worship me in vain;
    their teachings are but rules taught
        by men.'[e]"

10Jesus called the crowd to him and said, "Listen and understand. 11What goes into a man's mouth does not make him 'unclean,' but what comes out of his mouth, that is what makes him 'unclean.'"

12Then the disciples came to him and asked, "Do you know that the Pharisees were offended when they heard this?"

13He replied, "Every plant that my heavenly Father has not planted will be pulled up by the roots. 14Leave them; they are blind guides.[f] If a blind man leads a blind man, both will fall into a pit."

15Peter said, "Explain the parable to us."

16"Are you still so dull?" Jesus asked them. 17"Don't you see that whatever enters the mouth goes into the stomach and then out of the body? 18But the things that come out of the mouth come from the heart, and these make a man 'unclean.' 19For out of the heart come evil thoughts, murder, adultery, sexual immorality, theft, false testimony, slander. 20These are what make a man 'unclean'; but eating with unwashed hands does not make him 'unclean.'"

The Faith of the Canaanite Woman

21Leaving that place, Jesus withdrew to the region of Tyre and Sidon. 22A Canaanite woman from that vicinity came to him, crying out, "Lord, Son of David, have mercy on me! My daughter is suffering terribly from demon-possession."

23Jesus did not answer a word. So his disciples came to him and urged him, "Send her away, for she keeps crying out after us."

24He answered, "I was sent only to the lost sheep of Israel."

25The woman came and knelt before him. "Lord, help me!" she said.

26He replied, "It is not right to take the children's bread and toss it to their dogs."

27"Yes, Lord," she said, "but even the dogs eat the crumbs that fall from their masters' table."

28Then Jesus answered, "Woman, you have great faith! Your request is granted."

---

[a]24 Greek many stadia   [b]4 Exodus 20:12; Deut. 5:16   [c]4 Exodus 21:17; Lev. 20:9   [d]6 Some manuscripts father or his mother   [e]9 Isaiah 29:13   [f]14 Some manuscripts guides of the blind

And her daughter was healed from that very hour.

Jesus Feeds the Four Thousand

29Jesus left there and went along the Sea of Galilee. Then he went up on a mountainside and sat down. 30Great crowds came to him, bringing the lame, the blind, the crippled, the mute and many others, and laid them at his feet; and he healed them. 31The people were amazed when they saw the mute speaking, the crippled made well, the lame walking and the blind seeing. And they praised the God of Israel.

32Jesus called his disciples to him and said, "I have compassion for these people; they have already been with me three days and have nothing to eat. I do not want to send them away hungry, or they may collapse on the way."

33His disciples answered, "Where could we get enough bread in this remote place to feed such a crowd?"

34"How many loaves do you have?" Jesus asked.

"Seven," they replied, "and a few small fish."

35He told the crowd to sit down on the ground. 36Then he took the seven loaves and the fish, and when he had given thanks, he broke them and gave them to the disciples, and they in turn to the people. 37They all ate and were satisfied. Afterward the disciples picked up seven basketfuls of broken pieces that were left over. 38The number of those who ate was four thousand, besides women and children. 39After Jesus had sent the crowd away, he got into the boat and went to the vicinity of Magadan.

The Demand for a Sign

16 The Pharisees and Sadducees came to Jesus and tested him by asking him to show them a sign from heaven.

2He replied,[a] "When evening comes, you say, 'It will be fair weather, for the sky is red,' 3and in the morning, 'Today it will be stormy, for the sky is red and overcast.' You know how to interpret the appearance of the sky, but you cannot interpret the signs of the times. 4A wicked and adulterous generation looks for a miraculous sign, but none will be given it except the sign of Jonah." Jesus then left them and went away.

The Yeast of the Pharisees and Sadducees

5When they went across the lake, the disciples forgot to take bread. 6"Be careful," Jesus said to them. "Be on your guard against the yeast of the Pharisees and Sadducees."

7They discussed this among themselves and said, "It is because we didn't bring any bread."

8Aware of their discussion, Jesus asked, "You of little faith, why are you talking among yourselves about having no bread? 9Do you still not understand? Don't you remember the five loaves for the five thousand, and how many basketfuls you gathered? 10Or the seven loaves for the four thousand, and how many basketfuls you gathered? 11How is it you don't understand that I was not talking to you about bread? But be on your guard against the yeast of the Pharisees and Sadducees." 12Then they understood that he was not telling them to guard against the yeast used in bread, but against the teaching of the Pharisees and Sadducees.

Peter's Confession of Christ

13When Jesus came to the region of Caesarea Philippi, he asked his disciples, "Who do people say the Son of Man is?"

14They replied, "Some say John the Baptist; others say Elijah; and still others, Jeremiah or one of the prophets."

15"But what about you?" he asked. "Who do you say I am?"

16Simon Peter answered, "You are the Christ,[b] the Son of the living God."

17Jesus replied, "Blessed are you, Simon son of Jonah, for this was not revealed to you by man, but by my Father in heaven. 18And I tell you that you are Peter,[c] and on this rock I will build my church, and the gates of Hades[d] will not overcome it.[e] 19I will give you the keys of the kingdom of heaven; whatever you bind on earth will be[f] bound in heaven, and whatever you loose on earth will be[f] loosed in heaven." 20Then he warned his disciples not to tell anyone that he was the Christ.

---

a2 Some early manuscripts do not have the rest of verse 2 and all of verse 3.   b16 Or *Messiah*; also in verse 20   c18 *Peter* means *rock*.   d18 Or *hell*   e18 Or *not prove stronger than it*   f19 Or *have been*

Jesus Predicts His Death

21From that time on Jesus began to explain to his disciples that he must go to Jerusalem and suffer many things at the hands of the elders, chief priests and teachers of the law, and that he must be killed and on the third day be raised to life.

22Peter took him aside and began to rebuke him. "Never, Lord!" he said. "This shall never happen to you!"

23Jesus turned and said to Peter, "Get behind me, Satan! You are a stumbling block to me; you do not have in mind the things of God, but the things of men."

24Then Jesus said to his disciples, "If anyone would come after me, he must deny himself and take up his cross and follow me. 25For whoever wants to save his life *a* will lose it, but whoever loses his life for me will find it. 26What good will it be for a man if he gains the whole world, yet forfeits his soul? Or what can a man give in exchange for his soul? 27For the Son of Man is going to come in his Father's glory with his angels, and then he will reward each person according to what he has done. 28I tell you the truth, some who are standing here will not taste death before they see the Son of Man coming in his kingdom."

The Transfiguration

17 After six days Jesus took with him Peter, James and John the brother of James, and led them up a high mountain by themselves. 2There he was transfigured before them. His face shone like the sun, and his clothes became as white as the light. 3Just then there appeared before them Moses and Elijah, talking with Jesus.

4Peter said to Jesus, "Lord, it is good for us to be here. If you wish, I will put up three shelters—one for you, one for Moses and one for Elijah."

5While he was still speaking, a bright cloud enveloped them, and a voice from the cloud said, "This is my Son, whom I love; with him I am well pleased. Listen to him!"

6When the disciples heard this, they fell facedown to the ground, terrified. 7But Jesus came and touched them. "Get up," he said. "Don't be afraid." 8When they looked up, they saw no one except Jesus.

9As they were coming down the mountain, Jesus instructed them, "Don't tell anyone what you have seen, until the Son of Man has been raised from the dead."

10The disciples asked him, "Why then do the teachers of the law say that Elijah must come first?"

11Jesus replied, "To be sure, Elijah comes and will restore all things. 12But I tell you, Elijah has already come, and they did not recognize him, but have done to him everything they wished. In the same way the Son of Man is going to suffer at their hands." 13Then the disciples understood that he was talking to them about John the Baptist.

The Healing of a Boy With a Demon

14When they came to the crowd, a man approached Jesus and knelt before him. 15"Lord, have mercy on my son," he said. "He has seizures and is suffering greatly. He often falls into the fire or into the water. 16I brought him to your disciples, but they could not heal him."

17"O unbelieving and perverse generation," Jesus replied, "how long shall I stay with you? How long shall I put up with you? Bring the boy here to me." 18Jesus rebuked the demon, and it came out of the boy, and he was healed from that moment.

19Then the disciples came to Jesus in private and asked, "Why couldn't we drive it out?"

20He replied, "Because you have so little faith. I tell you the truth, if you have faith as small as a mustard seed, you can say to this mountain, 'Move from here to there' and it will move. Nothing will be impossible for you. *b* "

22When they came together in Galilee, he said to them, "The Son of Man is going to be betrayed into the hands of men. 23They will kill him, and on the third day he will be raised to life." And the disciples were filled with grief.

The Temple Tax

24After Jesus and his disciples arrived in Capernaum, the collectors of the two-drachma tax came to Peter and asked, "Doesn't your teacher pay the temple tax *c*?"

25"Yes, he does," he replied.

When Peter came into the house, Je-

a25 The Greek word means either *life* or *soul*; also in verse 26.   *b20* Some manuscripts *you. 21But this kind does not go out except by prayer and fasting.*   *c24* Greek *the two drachmas* sus was the first to speak. "What do you think, Simon?" he asked. "From whom do the kings of the earth collect duty and taxes—from their own sons or from others?"

26"From others," Peter answered.

"Then the sons are exempt," Jesus said to him. 27"But so that we may not offend them, go to the lake and throw out your line. Take the first fish you catch; open its mouth and you will find a four-drachma

coin. Take it and give it to them for my tax and yours."

The Greatest in the Kingdom of Heaven

18 At that time the disciples came to Jesus and asked, "Who is the greatest in the kingdom of heaven?" 2He called a little child and had him stand among them. 3And he said:

MONDAY

VERSE FOR THE DAY:	AUTHOR:	PASSAGE FOR THE DAY:
Matthew 16:24–25	Catherine Marshall	Matthew 16:21–28

Happiness Is . . .

AS I've been pondering the subject of happiness this morning—an elusive and seemingly unattainable state for so many—I am led to these words of Jesus:

> If anyone would come after me, he must deny himself and take up his cross and follow me. For whoever wants to save his life will lose it, but whoever loses his life for me will find it (Matthew 16:24–25).

I believe the secret of happiness lies imbedded in those words, painful though they appear to be. How else explain radiant people like the young man who sat in our living room and described how his six-year-old boy had died in his arms from leukemia. Today this man finds fulfillment in giving himself totally to helping college students. Or the woman I visited recently whose husband had turned out to be a homosexual and demanded a divorce. Some years later, this woman also lost her eyesight. Yet she is a cheerful, loving person, fully self-supporting.

You might say that such people almost have a right to be unhappy. That they are not, lies in the way they spend themselves for others.

I have observed that when any of us embarks on the pursuit of happiness for ourselves, it eludes us. Often I've asked myself why. It must be because happiness comes to us only as a dividend. When we become absorbed in something demanding and worthwhile above and beyond ourselves, happiness seems to be there as a by-product of the self-giving.

Additional Scripture Readings:
Luke 10:30–37; Acts 2:42–47

Go to page 1050 for your next devotional reading.

you the truth, unless you change and become like little children, you will never enter the kingdom of heaven. [4]Therefore, whoever humbles himself like this child is the greatest in the kingdom of heaven.

[5]"And whoever welcomes a little child like this in my name welcomes me. [6]But if anyone causes one of these little ones who believe in me to sin, it would be better for him to have a large millstone hung around his neck and to be drowned in the depths of the sea.

[7]"Woe to the world because of the things that cause people to sin! Such things must come, but woe to the man through whom they come! [8]If your hand or your foot causes you to sin, cut it off and throw it away. It is better for you to enter life maimed or crippled than to have two hands or two feet and be thrown into eternal fire. [9]And if your eye causes you to sin, gouge it out and throw it away. It is better for you to enter life with one eye than to have two eyes and be thrown into the fire of hell.

The Parable of the Lost Sheep

[10]"See that you do not look down on one of these little ones. For I tell you that their angels in heaven always see the face of my Father in heaven.[a]

[12]"What do you think? If a man owns a hundred sheep, and one of them wanders away, will he not leave the ninety-nine on the hills and go to look for the one that wandered off? [13]And if he finds it, I tell you the truth, he is happier about that one sheep than about the ninety-nine that did not wander off. [14]In the same way your Father in heaven is not willing that any of these little ones should be lost.

A Brother Who Sins Against You

[15]"If your brother sins against you,[b] go and show him his fault, just between the two of you. If he listens to you, you have won your brother over. [16]But if he will not listen, take one or two others along, so that 'every matter may be established by the testimony of two or three witnesses.'[c] [17]If he refuses to listen to them, tell it to the church; and if he refuses to listen even to the church, treat him as you would a pagan or a tax collector.

[18]"I tell you the truth, whatever you bind on earth will be[d] bound in heaven, and whatever you loose on earth will be[d] loosed in heaven.

[19]"Again, I tell you that if two of you on earth agree about anything you ask for, it will be done for you by my Father in heaven. [20]For where two or three come together in my name, there am I with them."

The Parable of the Unmerciful Servant

[21]Then Peter came to Jesus and asked, "Lord, how many times shall I forgive my brother when he sins against me? Up to seven times?"

[22]Jesus answered, "I tell you, not seven times, but seventy-seven times.[e]

[23]"Therefore, the kingdom of heaven is like a king who wanted to settle accounts with his servants. [24]As he began the settlement, a man who owed him ten thousand talents[f] was brought to him. [25]Since he was not able to pay, the master ordered that he and his wife and his children and all that he had be sold to repay the debt.

[26]"The servant fell on his knees before him. 'Be patient with me,' he begged, 'and I will pay back everything.' [27]The servant's master took pity on him, canceled the debt and let him go.

[28]"But when that servant went out, he found one of his fellow servants who owed him a hundred denarii.[g] He grabbed him and began to choke him. 'Pay back what you owe me!' he demanded.

[29]"His fellow servant fell to his knees and begged him, 'Be patient with me, and I will pay you back.'

[30]"But he refused. Instead, he went off and had the man thrown into prison until he could pay the debt. [31]When the other servants saw what had happened, they were greatly distressed and went and told their master everything that had happened.

[32]"Then the master called the servant in. 'You wicked servant,' he said, 'I canceled all that debt of yours because you begged me to. [33]Shouldn't you have had mercy on your fellow servant just as I had on you?' [34]In anger his master turned him over to the jailers to be tortured, until he should pay back all he owed.

[35]"This is how my heavenly Father will

---

[a]10 Some manuscripts *heaven.* [11]*The Son of Man came to save what was lost.*   [b]15 Some manuscripts do not have *against you.*   [c]16 Deut. 19:15   [d]18 Or *have been*   [e]22 Or *seventy times seven*
[f]24 That is, millions of dollars   [g]28 That is, a few dollars

VERSE FOR THE DAY:
Matthew 18:19

AUTHOR:
Rosalind Rinker

PASSAGE FOR THE DAY:
Matthew 18:18–20

The Secret of Power

JESUS teaches us to pray together in dialogue prayer in order to release God's power to bind evil and release good. Dialogue prayer is simply conversational prayer, two people praying back and forth. The audible words are necessary for agreement and for giving love. This prayer-power requires the presence of our risen Lord and our cooperation in audible prayer. This changes us and the situations for which we pray.

We abandon clichés and use short childlike sentences that are honest, specific and personal. In a nutshell: pray to Jesus, our risen Lord, from the child in your heart. This enables the child we each keep silent in our hearts to pray with others and together find love, freedom and joy.

Here are four subjects to guide you: 1. *Jesus is here* (worship). 2. *Thank you, Lord* (for gifts given: spiritual, physical, material, for people, and for the good earth). 3. *Forgive me, Lord* (confession, using "I" not "we"). 4. *Help my sister/brother* (intercession).

Experience has taught us that first worship, and then thanksgiving, open our hearts and mouths. Confession, the third point, is necessary because without it, we do not easily receive the Spirit's guidance for intercession.

Here's an example of confession: "Lord, help us to love others more than we do." But when urged to be personal, honest and specific, the woman's confession becomes: "Lord, help me to love that person I work with."

This then leads into the prayer partner's intercession, when she can pray, "Lord, you promised forgiveness when we confess (1 John 1:9). Now show her what next she should do in her life," or similar comforting words blended with thanksgiving.

In this way we share one another's joys and burdens and become living members of our risen Lord, who teaches us to love one another as he loves us.

Additional Scripture Readings:
Colossians 4:2–4; James 5:13–16

Go to page 1059 for your next devotional reading.

treat each of you unless you forgive your brother from your heart."

Divorce

19 When Jesus had finished saying these things, he left Galilee and went into the region of Judea to the other side of the Jordan. ²Large crowds followed him, and he healed them there.

³Some Pharisees came to him to test him. They asked, "Is it lawful for a man to divorce his wife for any and every reason?"

⁴"Haven't you read," he replied, "that at the beginning the Creator 'made them male and female,'ᵃ ⁵and said, 'For this reason a man will leave his father and mother and be united to his wife, and the two will become one flesh'ᵇ? ⁶So they are no longer two, but one. Therefore what God has joined together, let man not separate."

⁷"Why then," they asked, "did Moses command that a man give his wife a certificate of divorce and send her away?"

⁸Jesus replied, "Moses permitted you to divorce your wives because your hearts were hard. But it was not this way from the beginning. ⁹I tell you that anyone who divorces his wife, except for marital unfaithfulness, and marries another woman commits adultery."

¹⁰The disciples said to him, "If this is the situation between a husband and wife, it is better not to marry."

¹¹Jesus replied, "Not everyone can accept this word, but only those to whom it has been given. ¹²For some are eunuchs because they were born that way; others were made that way by men; and others have renounced marriageᶜ because of the kingdom of heaven. The one who can accept this should accept it."

The Little Children and Jesus

¹³Then little children were brought to Jesus for him to place his hands on them and pray for them. But the disciples rebuked those who brought them.

¹⁴Jesus said, "Let the little children come to me, and do not hinder them, for the kingdom of heaven belongs to such as these." ¹⁵When he had placed his hands on them, he went on from there.

The Rich Young Man

¹⁶Now a man came up to Jesus and asked, "Teacher, what good thing must I do to get eternal life?"

¹⁷"Why do you ask me about what is good?" Jesus replied. "There is only One who is good. If you want to enter life, obey the commandments."

¹⁸"Which ones?" the man inquired.

Jesus replied, " 'Do not murder, do not commit adultery, do not steal, do not give false testimony, ¹⁹honor your father and mother,'ᵈ and 'love your neighbor as yourself.'ᵉ "

²⁰"All these I have kept," the young man said. "What do I still lack?"

²¹Jesus answered, "If you want to be perfect, go, sell your possessions and give to the poor, and you will have treasure in heaven. Then come, follow me."

²²When the young man heard this, he went away sad, because he had great wealth.

²³Then Jesus said to his disciples, "I tell you the truth, it is hard for a rich man to enter the kingdom of heaven. ²⁴Again I tell you, it is easier for a camel to go through the eye of a needle than for a rich man to enter the kingdom of God."

²⁵When the disciples heard this, they were greatly astonished and asked, "Who then can be saved?"

²⁶Jesus looked at them and said, "With man this is impossible, but with God all things are possible."

²⁷Peter answered him, "We have left everything to follow you! What then will there be for us?"

²⁸Jesus said to them, "I tell you the truth, at the renewal of all things, when the Son of Man sits on his glorious throne, you who have followed me will also sit on twelve thrones, judging the twelve tribes of Israel. ²⁹And everyone who has left houses or brothers or sisters or father or motherᶠ or children or fields for my sake will receive a hundred times as much and will inherit eternal life. ³⁰But many who are first will be last, and many who are last will be first.

The Parable of the Workers in the Vineyard

20 "For the kingdom of heaven is like a landowner who went out early in the morning to hire men to work in his vineyard. ²He agreed to pay them a denarius for the day and sent them into his vineyard.

ᵃ4 Gen. 1:27   ᵇ5 Gen. 2:24   ᶜ12 Or *have made themselves eunuchs*   ᵈ19 Exodus 20:12-16; Deut. 5:16-20   ᵉ19 Lev. 19:18   ᶠ29 Some manuscripts *mother or wife*

³"About the third hour he went out and saw others standing in the marketplace doing nothing. ⁴He told them, 'You also go and work in my vineyard, and I will pay you whatever is right.' ⁵So they went.

"He went out again about the sixth hour and the ninth hour and did the same thing. ⁶About the eleventh hour he went out and found still others standing around. He asked them, 'Why have you been standing here all day long doing nothing?'

⁷"'Because no one has hired us,' they answered.

"He said to them, 'You also go and work in my vineyard.'

⁸"When evening came, the owner of the vineyard said to his foreman, 'Call the workers and pay them their wages, beginning with the last ones hired and going on to the first.'

⁹"The workers who were hired about the eleventh hour came and each received a denarius. ¹⁰So when those came who were hired first, they expected to receive more. But each one of them also received a denarius. ¹¹When they received it, they began to grumble against the landowner. ¹²'These men who were hired last worked only one hour,' they said, 'and you have made them equal to us who have borne the burden of the work and the heat of the day.'

¹³"But he answered one of them, 'Friend, I am not being unfair to you. Didn't you agree to work for a denarius? ¹⁴Take your pay and go. I want to give the man who was hired last the same as I gave you. ¹⁵Don't I have the right to do what I want with my own money? Or are you envious because I am generous?'

¹⁶"So the last will be first, and the first will be last."

Jesus Again Predicts His Death

¹⁷Now as Jesus was going up to Jerusalem, he took the twelve disciples aside and said to them, ¹⁸"We are going up to Jerusalem, and the Son of Man will be betrayed to the chief priests and the teachers of the law. They will condemn him to death ¹⁹and will turn him over to the Gentiles to be mocked and flogged and crucified. On the third day he will be raised to life!"

A Mother's Request

²⁰Then the mother of Zebedee's sons came to Jesus with her sons and, kneeling down, asked a favor of him.

²¹"What is it you want?" he asked.

She said, "Grant that one of these two sons of mine may sit at your right and the other at your left in your kingdom."

²²"You don't know what you are asking," Jesus said to them. "Can you drink the cup I am going to drink?"

"We can," they answered.

²³Jesus said to them, "You will indeed drink from my cup, but to sit at my right or left is not for me to grant. These places belong to those for whom they have been prepared by my Father."

²⁴When the ten heard about this, they were indignant with the two brothers. ²⁵Jesus called them together and said, "You know that the rulers of the Gentiles lord it over them, and their high officials exercise authority over them. ²⁶Not so with you. Instead, whoever wants to become great among you must be your servant, ²⁷and whoever wants to be first must be your slave— ²⁸just as the Son of Man did not come to be served, but to serve, and to give his life as a ransom for many."

Two Blind Men Receive Sight

²⁹As Jesus and his disciples were leaving Jericho, a large crowd followed him. ³⁰Two blind men were sitting by the roadside, and when they heard that Jesus was going by, they shouted, "Lord, Son of David, have mercy on us!"

³¹The crowd rebuked them and told them to be quiet, but they shouted all the louder, "Lord, Son of David, have mercy on us!"

³²Jesus stopped and called them. "What do you want me to do for you?" he asked.

³³"Lord," they answered, "we want our sight."

³⁴Jesus had compassion on them and touched their eyes. Immediately they received their sight and followed him.

The Triumphal Entry

21 As they approached Jerusalem and came to Bethphage on the Mount of Olives, Jesus sent two disciples, ²saying to them, "Go to the village ahead of you, and at once you will find a donkey tied there, with her colt by her. Untie them and bring them to me. ³If anyone says anything to you, tell him that the Lord needs them, and he will send them right away."

⁴This took place to fulfill what was spoken through the prophet:

5"Say to the Daughter of Zion,
'See, your king comes to you,
gentle and riding on a donkey,
on a colt, the foal of a donkey.' "[a]

6The disciples went and did as Jesus had instructed them. 7They brought the donkey and the colt, placed their cloaks on them, and Jesus sat on them. 8A very large crowd spread their cloaks on the road, while others cut branches from the trees and spread them on the road. 9The crowds that went ahead of him and those that followed shouted,

"Hosanna[b] to the Son of David!"

"Blessed is he who comes in the
name of the Lord!"[c]

"Hosanna[b] in the highest!"

10When Jesus entered Jerusalem, the whole city was stirred and asked, "Who is this?"

11The crowds answered, "This is Jesus, the prophet from Nazareth in Galilee."

Jesus at the Temple

12Jesus entered the temple area and drove out all who were buying and selling there. He overturned the tables of the money changers and the benches of those selling doves. 13"It is written," he said to them, " 'My house will be called a house of prayer,'[d] but you are making it a 'den of robbers.'[e]"

14The blind and the lame came to him at the temple, and he healed them. 15But when the chief priests and the teachers of the law saw the wonderful things he did and the children shouting in the temple area, "Hosanna to the Son of David," they were indignant.

16"Do you hear what these children are saying?" they asked him.

"Yes," replied Jesus, "have you never read,

" 'From the lips of children and
infants
you have ordained praise'[f]?"

17And he left them and went out of the city to Bethany, where he spent the night.

The Fig Tree Withers

18Early in the morning, as he was on his way back to the city, he was hungry. 19Seeing a fig tree by the road, he went up

to it but found nothing on it except leaves. Then he said to it, "May you never bear fruit again!" Immediately the tree withered.

20When the disciples saw this, they were amazed. "How did the fig tree wither so quickly?" they asked.

21Jesus replied, "I tell you the truth, if you have faith and do not doubt, not only can you do what was done to the fig tree, but also you can say to this mountain, 'Go, throw yourself into the sea,' and it will be done. 22If you believe, you will receive whatever you ask for in prayer."

The Authority of Jesus Questioned

23Jesus entered the temple courts, and, while he was teaching, the chief priests and the elders of the people came to him. "By what authority are you doing these things?" they asked. "And who gave you this authority?"

24Jesus replied, "I will also ask you one question. If you answer me, I will tell you by what authority I am doing these things. 25John's baptism—where did it come from? Was it from heaven, or from men?"

They discussed it among themselves and said, "If we say, 'From heaven,' he will ask, 'Then why didn't you believe him?' 26But if we say, 'From men'—we are afraid of the people, for they all hold that John was a prophet."

27So they answered Jesus, "We don't know."

Then he said, "Neither will I tell you by what authority I am doing these things.

The Parable of the Two Sons

28"What do you think? There was a man who had two sons. He went to the first and said, 'Son, go and work today in the vineyard.'

29" 'I will not,' he answered, but later he changed his mind and went.

30"Then the father went to the other son and said the same thing. He answered, 'I will, sir,' but he did not go.

31"Which of the two did what his father wanted?"

"The first," they answered.

Jesus said to them, "I tell you the truth, the tax collectors and the prostitutes are entering the kingdom of God ahead of you. 32For John came to you to show you the way of righteousness, and you did not

---

a5 Zech. 9:9   b9 A Hebrew expression meaning "Save!" which became an exclamation of praise; also in verse 15   c9 Psalm 118:26   d13 Isaiah 56:7   e13 Jer. 7:11   f16 Psalm 8:2

believe him, but the tax collectors and the prostitutes did. And even after you saw this, you did not repent and believe him.

The Parable of the Tenants

33"Listen to another parable: There was a landowner who planted a vineyard. He put a wall around it, dug a winepress in it and built a watchtower. Then he rented the vineyard to some farmers and went away on a journey. 34When the harvest time approached, he sent his servants to the tenants to collect his fruit.

35"The tenants seized his servants; they beat one, killed another, and stoned a third. 36Then he sent other servants to them, more than the first time, and the tenants treated them the same way. 37Last of all, he sent his son to them. 'They will respect my son,' he said.

38"But when the tenants saw the son, they said to each other, 'This is the heir. Come, let's kill him and take his inheritance.' 39So they took him and threw him out of the vineyard and killed him.

40"Therefore, when the owner of the vineyard comes, what will he do to those tenants?"

41"He will bring those wretches to a wretched end," they replied, "and he will rent the vineyard to other tenants, who will give him his share of the crop at harvest time."

42Jesus said to them, "Have you never read in the Scriptures:

" 'The stone the builders rejected
　　has become the capstone[a];
the Lord has done this,
　　and it is marvelous in our eyes'[b]?

43"Therefore I tell you that the kingdom of God will be taken away from you and given to a people who will produce its fruit. 44He who falls on this stone will be broken to pieces, but he on whom it falls will be crushed."[c]

45When the chief priests and the Pharisees heard Jesus' parables, they knew he was talking about them. 46They looked for a way to arrest him, but they were afraid of the crowd because the people held that he was a prophet.

The Parable of the Wedding Banquet

22 Jesus spoke to them again in parables, saying: 2"The kingdom of heaven is like a king who prepared a wedding banquet for his son. 3He sent his servants to those who had been invited to the banquet to tell them to come, but they refused to come.

4"Then he sent some more servants and said, 'Tell those who have been invited that I have prepared my dinner: My oxen and fattened cattle have been butchered, and everything is ready. Come to the wedding banquet.'

5"But they paid no attention and went off—one to his field, another to his business. 6The rest seized his servants, mistreated them and killed them. 7The king was enraged. He sent his army and destroyed those murderers and burned their city.

8"Then he said to his servants, 'The wedding banquet is ready, but those I invited did not deserve to come. 9Go to the street corners and invite to the banquet anyone you find.' 10So the servants went out into the streets and gathered all the people they could find, both good and bad, and the wedding hall was filled with guests.

11"But when the king came in to see the guests, he noticed a man there who was not wearing wedding clothes. 12'Friend,' he asked, 'how did you get in here without wedding clothes?' The man was speechless.

13"Then the king told the attendants, 'Tie him hand and foot, and throw him outside, into the darkness, where there will be weeping and gnashing of teeth.'

14"For many are invited, but few are chosen."

Paying Taxes to Caesar

15Then the Pharisees went out and laid plans to trap him in his words. 16They sent their disciples to him along with the Herodians. "Teacher," they said, "we know you are a man of integrity and that you teach the way of God in accordance with the truth. You aren't swayed by men, because you pay no attention to who they are. 17Tell us then, what is your opinion? Is it right to pay taxes to Caesar or not?"

18But Jesus, knowing their evil intent, said, "You hypocrites, why are you trying to trap me? 19Show me the coin used for paying the tax." They brought him a denarius, 20and he asked them, "Whose portrait is this? And whose inscription?"

21"Caesar's," they replied.

Then he said to them, "Give to Caesar

---

a42 Or *cornerstone*　　*b42* Psalm 118:22,23　　*c44* Some manuscripts do not have verse 44.

what is Caesar's, and to God what is God's."

²²When they heard this, they were amazed. So they left him and went away.

Marriage at the Resurrection

²³That same day the Sadducees, who say there is no resurrection, came to him with a question. ²⁴"Teacher," they said, "Moses told us that if a man dies without having children, his brother must marry the widow and have children for him. ²⁵Now there were seven brothers among us. The first one married and died, and since he had no children, he left his wife to his brother. ²⁶The same thing happened to the second and third brother, right on down to the seventh. ²⁷Finally, the woman died. ²⁸Now then, at the resurrection, whose wife will she be of the seven, since all of them were married to her?"

²⁹Jesus replied, "You are in error because you do not know the Scriptures or the power of God. ³⁰At the resurrection people will neither marry nor be given in marriage; they will be like the angels in heaven. ³¹But about the resurrection of the dead—have you not read what God said to you, ³²'I am the God of Abraham, the God of Isaac, and the God of Jacob'ᵃ? He is not the God of the dead but of the living."

³³When the crowds heard this, they were astonished at his teaching.

The Greatest Commandment

³⁴Hearing that Jesus had silenced the Sadducees, the Pharisees got together. ³⁵One of them, an expert in the law, tested him with this question: ³⁶"Teacher, which is the greatest commandment in the Law?"

³⁷Jesus replied: " 'Love the Lord your God with all your heart and with all your soul and with all your mind.'ᵇ ³⁸This is the first and greatest commandment. ³⁹And the second is like it: 'Love your neighbor as yourself.'ᶜ ⁴⁰All the Law and the Prophets hang on these two commandments."

Whose Son Is the Christ?

⁴¹While the Pharisees were gathered together, Jesus asked them, ⁴²"What do you think about the Christᵈ? Whose son is he?"

"The son of David," they replied.

⁴³He said to them, "How is it then that David, speaking by the Spirit, calls him 'Lord'? For he says,

⁴⁴" 'The Lord said to my Lord:
  "Sit at my right hand
  until I put your enemies
    under your feet." 'ᵉ

⁴⁵If then David calls him 'Lord,' how can he be his son?" ⁴⁶No one could say a word in reply, and from that day on no one dared to ask him any more questions.

Seven Woes

23 Then Jesus said to the crowds and to his disciples: ²"The teachers of the law and the Pharisees sit in Moses' seat. ³So you must obey them and do everything they tell you. But do not do what they do, for they do not practice what they preach. ⁴They tie up heavy loads and put them on men's shoulders, but they themselves are not willing to lift a finger to move them.

⁵"Everything they do is done for men to see: They make their phylacteriesᶠ wide and the tassels on their garments long; ⁶they love the place of honor at banquets and the most important seats in the synagogues; ⁷they love to be greeted in the marketplaces and to have men call them 'Rabbi.'

⁸"But you are not to be called 'Rabbi,' for you have only one Master and you are all brothers. ⁹And do not call anyone on earth 'father,' for you have one Father, and he is in heaven. ¹⁰Nor are you to be called 'teacher,' for you have one Teacher, the Christ.ᵈ ¹¹The greatest among you will be your servant. ¹²For whoever exalts himself will be humbled, and whoever humbles himself will be exalted.

¹³"Woe to you, teachers of the law and Pharisees, you hypocrites! You shut the kingdom of heaven in men's faces. You yourselves do not enter, nor will you let those enter who are trying to.ᵍ

¹⁵"Woe to you, teachers of the law and Pharisees, you hypocrites! You travel over land and sea to win a single convert, and when he becomes one, you make him twice as much a son of hell as you are.

ᵃ32 Exodus 3:6   ᵇ37 Deut. 6:5   ᶜ39 Lev. 19:18   ᵈ42,10 Or Messiah   ᵉ44 Psalm 110:1
ᶠ5 That is, boxes containing Scripture verses, worn on forehead and arm   ᵍ13 Some manuscripts to.
¹⁴Woe to you, teachers of the law and Pharisees, you hypocrites! You devour widows' houses and for a show make lengthy prayers. Therefore you will be punished more severely.

16"Woe to you, blind guides! You say, 'If anyone swears by the temple, it means nothing; but if anyone swears by the gold of the temple, he is bound by his oath.' 17You blind fools! Which is greater: the gold, or the temple that makes the gold sacred? 18You also say, 'If anyone swears by the altar, it means nothing; but if anyone swears by the gift on it, he is bound by his oath.' 19You blind men! Which is greater: the gift, or the altar that makes the gift sacred? 20Therefore, he who swears by the altar swears by it and by everything on it. 21And he who swears by the temple swears by it and by the one who dwells in it. 22And he who swears by heaven swears by God's throne and by the one who sits on it.

23"Woe to you, teachers of the law and Pharisees, you hypocrites! You give a tenth of your spices—mint, dill and cummin. But you have neglected the more important matters of the law—justice, mercy and faithfulness. You should have practiced the latter, without neglecting the former. 24You blind guides! You strain out a gnat but swallow a camel.

25"Woe to you, teachers of the law and Pharisees, you hypocrites! You clean the outside of the cup and dish, but inside they are full of greed and self-indulgence. 26Blind Pharisee! First clean the inside of the cup and dish, and then the outside also will be clean.

27"Woe to you, teachers of the law and Pharisees, you hypocrites! You are like whitewashed tombs, which look beautiful on the outside but on the inside are full of dead men's bones and everything unclean. 28In the same way, on the outside you appear to people as righteous but on the inside you are full of hypocrisy and wickedness.

29"Woe to you, teachers of the law and Pharisees, you hypocrites! You build tombs for the prophets and decorate the graves of the righteous. 30And you say, 'If we had lived in the days of our forefathers, we would not have taken part with them in shedding the blood of the prophets.' 31So you testify against yourselves that you are the descendants of those who murdered the prophets. 32Fill up, then, the measure of the sin of your forefathers!

33"You snakes! You brood of vipers! How will you escape being condemned to hell? 34Therefore I am sending you proph-

ets and wise men and teachers. Some of them you will kill and crucify; others you will flog in your synagogues and pursue from town to town. 35And so upon you will come all the righteous blood that has been shed on earth, from the blood of righteous Abel to the blood of Zechariah son of Berekiah, whom you murdered between the temple and the altar. 36I tell you the truth, all this will come upon this generation.

37"O Jerusalem, Jerusalem, you who kill the prophets and stone those sent to you, how often I have longed to gather your children together, as a hen gathers her chicks under her wings, but you were not willing. 38Look, your house is left to you desolate. 39For I tell you, you will not see me again until you say, 'Blessed is he who comes in the name of the Lord.'*a*"

Signs of the End of the Age

24 Jesus left the temple and was walking away when his disciples came up to him to call his attention to its buildings. 2"Do you see all these things?" he asked. "I tell you the truth, not one stone here will be left on another; every one will be thrown down."

3As Jesus was sitting on the Mount of Olives, the disciples came to him privately. "Tell us," they said, "when will this happen, and what will be the sign of your coming and of the end of the age?"

4Jesus answered: "Watch out that no one deceives you. 5For many will come in my name, claiming, 'I am the Christ,*b*' and will deceive many. 6You will hear of wars and rumors of wars, but see to it that you are not alarmed. Such things must happen, but the end is still to come. 7Nation will rise against nation, and kingdom against kingdom. There will be famines and earthquakes in various places. 8All these are the beginning of birth pains.

9"Then you will be handed over to be persecuted and put to death, and you will be hated by all nations because of me. 10At that time many will turn away from the faith and will betray and hate each other, 11and many false prophets will appear and deceive many people. 12Because of the increase of wickedness, the love of most will grow cold, 13but he who stands firm to the end will be saved. 14And this gospel of the kingdom will be preached in the whole world as a testimony to all nations, and then the end will come.

a39 Psalm 118:26   *b5* Or *Messiah*; also in verse 23

15"So when you see standing in the holy place 'the abomination that causes desolation,'[a] spoken of through the prophet Daniel—let the reader understand—16then let those who are in Judea flee to the mountains. 17Let no one on the roof of his house go down to take anything out of the house. 18Let no one in the field go back to get his cloak. 19How dreadful it will be in those days for pregnant women and nursing mothers! 20Pray that your flight will not take place in winter or on the Sabbath. 21For then there will be great distress, unequaled from the beginning of the world until now—and never to be equaled again. 22If those days had not been cut short, no one would survive, but for the sake of the elect those days will be shortened. 23At that time if anyone says to you, 'Look, here is the Christ!' or, 'There he is!' do not believe it. 24For false Christs and false prophets will appear and perform great signs and miracles to deceive even the elect—if that were possible. 25See, I have told you ahead of time.

26"So if anyone tells you, 'There he is, out in the desert,' do not go out; or, 'Here he is, in the inner rooms,' do not believe it. 27For as lightning that comes from the east is visible even in the west, so will be the coming of the Son of Man. 28Wherever there is a carcass, there the vultures will gather.

29"Immediately after the distress of those days

" 'the sun will be darkened,
    and the moon will not give its light;
the stars will fall from the sky,
    and the heavenly bodies will be
        shaken.'[b]

30"At that time the sign of the Son of Man will appear in the sky, and all the nations of the earth will mourn. They will see the Son of Man coming on the clouds of the sky, with power and great glory. 31And he will send his angels with a loud trumpet call, and they will gather his elect from the four winds, from one end of the heavens to the other.

32"Now learn this lesson from the fig tree: As soon as its twigs get tender and its leaves come out, you know that summer is near. 33Even so, when you see all these things, you know that it[c] is near, right at the door. 34I tell you the truth, this generation[d] will certainly not pass

away until all these things have happened. 35Heaven and earth will pass away, but my words will never pass away.

The Day and Hour Unknown

36"No one knows about that day or hour, not even the angels in heaven, nor the Son,[e] but only the Father. 37As it was in the days of Noah, so it will be at the coming of the Son of Man. 38For in the days before the flood, people were eating and drinking, marrying and giving in marriage, up to the day Noah entered the ark; 39and they knew nothing about what would happen until the flood came and took them all away. That is how it will be at the coming of the Son of Man. 40Two men will be in the field; one will be taken and the other left. 41Two women will be grinding with a hand mill; one will be taken and the other left.

42"Therefore keep watch, because you do not know on what day your Lord will come. 43But understand this: If the owner of the house had known at what time of night the thief was coming, he would have kept watch and would not have let his house be broken into. 44So you also must be ready, because the Son of Man will come at an hour when you do not expect him.

45"Who then is the faithful and wise servant, whom the master has put in charge of the servants in his household to give them their food at the proper time? 46It will be good for that servant whose master finds him doing so when he returns. 47I tell you the truth, he will put him in charge of all his possessions. 48But suppose that servant is wicked and says to himself, 'My master is staying away a long time,' 49and he then begins to beat his fellow servants and to eat and drink with drunkards. 50The master of that servant will come on a day when he does not expect him and at an hour he is not aware of. 51He will cut him to pieces and assign him a place with the hypocrites, where there will be weeping and gnashing of teeth.

The Parable of the Ten Virgins

25 "At that time the kingdom of heaven will be like ten virgins who took their lamps and went out to meet the bridegroom. 2Five of them were foolish and five were wise. 3The foolish ones took

---

[a]15 Daniel 9:27; 11:31; 12:11   [b]29 Isaiah 13:10; 34:4   [c]33 Or he   [d]34 Or race   [e]36 Some manuscripts do not have nor the Son.

their lamps but did not take any oil with them. ⁴The wise, however, took oil in jars along with their lamps. ⁵The bridegroom was a long time in coming, and they all became drowsy and fell asleep.

⁶"At midnight the cry rang out: 'Here's the bridegroom! Come out to meet him!'

⁷"Then all the virgins woke up and trimmed their lamps. ⁸The foolish ones said to the wise, 'Give us some of your oil; our lamps are going out.'

⁹" 'No,' they replied, 'there may not be enough for both us and you. Instead, go to those who sell oil and buy some for yourselves.'

¹⁰"But while they were on their way to buy the oil, the bridegroom arrived. The virgins who were ready went in with him to the wedding banquet. And the door was shut.

¹¹"Later the others also came. 'Sir! Sir!' they said. 'Open the door for us!'

¹²"But he replied, 'I tell you the truth, I don't know you.'

¹³"Therefore keep watch, because you do not know the day or the hour.

The Parable of the Talents

¹⁴"Again, it will be like a man going on a journey, who called his servants and entrusted his property to them. ¹⁵To one he gave five talents*ᵃ* of money, to another two talents, and to another one talent, each according to his ability. Then he went on his journey. ¹⁶The man who had received the five talents went at once and put his money to work and gained five more. ¹⁷So also, the one with the two talents gained two more. ¹⁸But the man who had received the one talent went off, dug a hole in the ground and hid his master's money.

¹⁹"After a long time the master of those servants returned and settled accounts with them. ²⁰The man who had received the five talents brought the other five. 'Master,' he said, 'you entrusted me with five talents. See, I have gained five more.'

²¹"His master replied, 'Well done, good and faithful servant! You have been faithful with a few things; I will put you in charge of many things. Come and share your master's happiness!'

²²"The man with the two talents also came. 'Master,' he said, 'you entrusted me with two talents; see, I have gained two more.'

²³"His master replied, 'Well done, good

and faithful servant! You have been faithful with a few things; I will put you in charge of many things. Come and share your master's happiness!'

²⁴"Then the man who had received the one talent came. 'Master,' he said, 'I knew that you are a hard man, harvesting where you have not sown and gathering where you have not scattered seed. ²⁵So I was afraid and went out and hid your talent in the ground. See, here is what belongs to you.'

²⁶"His master replied, 'You wicked, lazy servant! So you knew that I harvest where I have not sown and gather where I have not scattered seed? ²⁷Well then, you should have put my money on deposit with the bankers, so that when I returned I would have received it back with interest.

²⁸" 'Take the talent from him and give it to the one who has the ten talents. ²⁹For everyone who has will be given more, and he will have an abundance. Whoever does not have, even what he has will be taken from him. ³⁰And throw that worthless servant outside, into the darkness, where there will be weeping and gnashing of teeth.'

The Sheep and the Goats

³¹"When the Son of Man comes in his glory, and all the angels with him, he will sit on his throne in heavenly glory. ³²All the nations will be gathered before him, and he will separate the people one from another as a shepherd separates the sheep from the goats. ³³He will put the sheep on his right and the goats on his left.

³⁴"Then the King will say to those on his right, 'Come, you who are blessed by my Father; take your inheritance, the kingdom prepared for you since the creation of the world. ³⁵For I was hungry and you gave me something to eat, I was thirsty and you gave me something to drink, I was a stranger and you invited me in, ³⁶I needed clothes and you clothed me, I was sick and you looked after me, I was in prison and you came to visit me.'

³⁷"Then the righteous will answer him, 'Lord, when did we see you hungry and feed you, or thirsty and give you something to drink? ³⁸When did we see you a stranger and invite you in, or needing clothes and clothe you? ³⁹When did we

---

ᵃ15 A talent was worth more than a thousand dollars.

VERSE FOR THE DAY:
Matthew 25:24–25

AUTHOR:
Hope MacDonald

PASSAGE FOR THE DAY:
Matthew 25:14–30

Burying Our Talents

THIS is a parable of God's call for faithfulness in the use of our talents. It is also a parable of warning and promise.

Not long ago, I was sitting in a small group. The discussion centered around evangelism. One of the members breathed a sigh of relief and said, "Well, that's just not my gift." With that statement he buried his God-given talent to share the love of Jesus with others. How many of us have buried our talents in search of that "special" gift?

Today we often expect our talents to come completely developed, neatly labeled, and tied with a shining red ribbon. If they don't, then we proclaim, they aren't "my gifts." The result is that we limit God—he is put in a box—and we restrict our potential for service. I wonder how many neglected opportunities slip by because of this kind of thinking? Gordon Fee refers to these self-imposed limitations as "hardening of the categories"!

We forget in this day of instant satisfaction that none of our talents come full-grown. It's only as we cultivate them that they begin to mature and multiply. The more we use them, the more others are blessed through them. Soon we discover that God has given us a multitude of gifts and equipped us with endless resources.

God is calling each of us to a life of adventure. Remember, an adventure is not an adventure unless there is some risk involved. Are we willing to take risks in our walk with Jesus? Are we willing to look a little foolish from time to time as we seek to develop new talents? If we are, God will continue to bring us new opportunities of service.

The warning of this parable is this: God holds us responsible for our lives and what we do with them.

The joyful reward is this: One day we will stand before our great God and hear him say, "Well done, good and faithful servant!" (Matthew 25:21).

Additional Scripture Readings:
Exodus 4:10–12; Ephesians 3:14–21

Go to page 1061 for your next devotional reading.

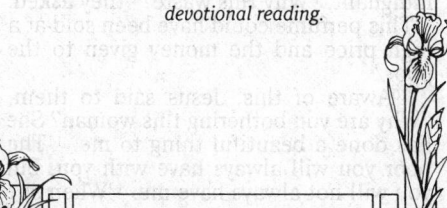

see you sick or in prison and go to visit you?'

⁴⁰"The King will reply, 'I tell you the truth, whatever you did for one of the least of these brothers of mine, you did for me.'

⁴¹"Then he will say to those on his left, 'Depart from me, you who are cursed, into the eternal fire prepared for the devil and his angels. ⁴²For I was hungry and you gave me nothing to eat, I was thirsty and you gave me nothing to drink, ⁴³I was a stranger and you did not invite me in, I needed clothes and you did not clothe me, I was sick and in prison and you did not look after me.'

⁴⁴"They also will answer, 'Lord, when did we see you hungry or thirsty or a stranger or needing clothes or sick or in prison, and did not help you?'

⁴⁵"He will reply, 'I tell you the truth, whatever you did not do for one of the least of these, you did not do for me.'

⁴⁶"Then they will go away to eternal punishment, but the righteous to eternal life."

The Plot Against Jesus

26 When Jesus had finished saying all these things, he said to his disciples, ²"As you know, the Passover is two days away—and the Son of Man will be handed over to be crucified."

³Then the chief priests and the elders of the people assembled in the palace of the high priest, whose name was Caiaphas, ⁴and they plotted to arrest Jesus in some sly way and kill him. ⁵"But not during the Feast," they said, "or there may be a riot among the people."

Jesus Anointed at Bethany

⁶While Jesus was in Bethany in the home of a man known as Simon the Leper, ⁷a woman came to him with an alabaster jar of very expensive perfume, which she poured on his head as he was reclining at the table.

⁸When the disciples saw this, they were indignant. "Why this waste?" they asked. ⁹"This perfume could have been sold at a high price and the money given to the poor."

¹⁰Aware of this, Jesus said to them, "Why are you bothering this woman? She has done a beautiful thing to me. ¹¹The poor you will always have with you, but you will not always have me. ¹²When she

poured this perfume on my body, she did it to prepare me for burial. ¹³I tell you the truth, wherever this gospel is preached throughout the world, what she has done will also be told, in memory of her."

Judas Agrees to Betray Jesus

¹⁴Then one of the Twelve—the one called Judas Iscariot—went to the chief priests ¹⁵and asked, "What are you willing to give me if I hand him over to you?" So they counted out for him thirty silver coins. ¹⁶From then on Judas watched for an opportunity to hand him over.

The Lord's Supper

¹⁷On the first day of the Feast of Unleavened Bread, the disciples came to Jesus and asked, "Where do you want us to make preparations for you to eat the Passover?"

¹⁸He replied, "Go into the city to a certain man and tell him, 'The Teacher says: My appointed time is near. I am going to celebrate the Passover with my disciples at your house.' " ¹⁹So the disciples did as Jesus had directed them and prepared the Passover.

²⁰When evening came, Jesus was reclining at the table with the Twelve. ²¹And while they were eating, he said, "I tell you the truth, one of you will betray me."

²²They were very sad and began to say to him one after the other, "Surely not I, Lord?"

²³Jesus replied, "The one who has dipped his hand into the bowl with me will betray me. ²⁴The Son of Man will go just as it is written about him. But woe to that man who betrays the Son of Man! It would be better for him if he had not been born."

²⁵Then Judas, the one who would betray him, said, "Surely not I, Rabbi?"

Jesus answered, "Yes, it is you."ᵃ

²⁶While they were eating, Jesus took bread, gave thanks and broke it, and gave it to his disciples, saying, "Take and eat; this is my body."

²⁷Then he took the cup, gave thanks and offered it to them, saying, "Drink from it, all of you. ²⁸This is my blood of theᵇ covenant, which is poured out for many for the forgiveness of sins. ²⁹I tell you, I will not drink of this fruit of the vine from now on until that day when I

ᵃ25 Or "You yourself have said it"   ᵇ28 Some manuscripts the new drink it anew with you in my Father's kingdom."

30When they had sung a hymn, they went out to the Mount of Olives.

Jesus Predicts Peter's Denial

31Then Jesus told them, "This very night you will all fall away on account of me, for it is written:

a31 Zech. 13:7

" 'I will strike the shepherd,
 and the sheep of the flock will be
 scattered.'*a*

32But after I have risen, I will go ahead of you into Galilee."

33Peter replied, "Even if all fall away on account of you, I never will."

34"I tell you the truth," Jesus answered,

THURSDAY

VERSE FOR THE DAY:	AUTHOR:	PASSAGE FOR THE DAY:
Matthew 26:12	Sue Richards	Matthew 26:6–13

A Gift

SHE came bearing a gift of love, probably without invitation, and certainly without forewarning. We are told that while Christ was reclining at table at the home of Simon the Leper, she came and poured a very expensive perfume on his head. The disciples, Christ's specially chosen men, became indignant when they saw her anoint the Lord in this manner. " 'Why this waste?' they asked. 'This perfume could have been sold at a high price and the money given to the poor.' " But Christ said to them, "Why are you bothering this woman? She has done a beautiful thing to me . . . . When she poured this perfume on my body, she did it to prepare me for burial" (Matthew 26:8–9).

She was obviously a very sensitive woman, wanting to give something special to the Lord before he was taken away. She had a great deal of spiritual discernment as well. She had heard of Christ's coming execution, and believed it. Even so, her gift and her basis for giving it were not understood even by these special men, the leaders of the early church. But Jesus understood. He appreciated her outpouring of love and made a promise like no other in Scripture. Christ said, "Wherever this gospel is preached throughout the world, what she has done will also be told, in memory of her" (Matthew 26:13).

Just as this woman's gift was misunderstood by the leaders of the early church, many churches today criticize women for trying to share their special gifts. It's comforting to know that our gifts are acceptable, accepted and appreciated by the Lord when given in love. He understands our motivations; he accepts what we bring.

Father, help us to give cheerfully and to accept graciously.

Additional Scripture Readings:
Luke 21:1–4; Romans 14:6–8

Go to page 1063 for your next devotional reading.

"this very night, before the rooster crows, you will disown me three times."

35But Peter declared, "Even if I have to die with you, I will never disown you." And all the other disciples said the same.

Gethsemane

36Then Jesus went with his disciples to a place called Gethsemane, and he said to them, "Sit here while I go over there and pray." 37He took Peter and the two sons of Zebedee along with him, and he began to be sorrowful and troubled. 38Then he said to them, "My soul is overwhelmed with sorrow to the point of death. Stay here and keep watch with me."

39Going a little farther, he fell with his face to the ground and prayed, "My Father, if it is possible, may this cup be taken from me. Yet not as I will, but as you will."

40Then he returned to his disciples and found them sleeping. "Could you men not keep watch with me for one hour?" he asked Peter. 41"Watch and pray so that you will not fall into temptation. The spirit is willing, but the body is weak."

42He went away a second time and prayed, "My Father, if it is not possible for this cup to be taken away unless I drink it, may your will be done."

43When he came back, he again found them sleeping, because their eyes were heavy. 44So he left them and went away once more and prayed the third time, saying the same thing.

45Then he returned to the disciples and said to them, "Are you still sleeping and resting? Look, the hour is near, and the Son of Man is betrayed into the hands of sinners. 46Rise, let us go! Here comes my betrayer!"

Jesus Arrested

47While he was still speaking, Judas, one of the Twelve, arrived. With him was a large crowd armed with swords and clubs, sent from the chief priests and the elders of the people. 48Now the betrayer had arranged a signal with them: "The one I kiss is the man; arrest him." 49Going at once to Jesus, Judas said, "Greetings, Rabbi!" and kissed him.

50Jesus replied, "Friend, do what you came for."a

Then the men stepped forward, seized Jesus and arrested him. 51With that, one of Jesus' companions reached for his sword, drew it out and struck the servant of the high priest, cutting off his ear.

52"Put your sword back in its place," Jesus said to him, "for all who draw the sword will die by the sword. 53Do you think I cannot call on my Father, and he will at once put at my disposal more than twelve legions of angels? 54But how then would the Scriptures be fulfilled that say it must happen in this way?"

55At that time Jesus said to the crowd, "Am I leading a rebellion, that you have come out with swords and clubs to capture me? Every day I sat in the temple courts teaching, and you did not arrest me. 56But this has all taken place that the writings of the prophets might be fulfilled." Then all the disciples deserted him and fled.

Before the Sanhedrin

57Those who had arrested Jesus took him to Caiaphas, the high priest, where the teachers of the law and the elders had assembled. 58But Peter followed him at a distance, right up to the courtyard of the high priest. He entered and sat down with the guards to see the outcome.

59The chief priests and the whole Sanhedrin were looking for false evidence against Jesus so that they could put him to death. 60But they did not find any, though many false witnesses came forward.

Finally two came forward 61and declared, "This fellow said, 'I am able to destroy the temple of God and rebuild it in three days.' "

62Then the high priest stood up and said to Jesus, "Are you not going to answer? What is this testimony that these men are bringing against you?" 63But Jesus remained silent.

The high priest said to him, "I charge you under oath by the living God: Tell us if you are the Christ,b the Son of God."

64"Yes, it is as you say," Jesus replied. "But I say to all of you: In the future you will see the Son of Man sitting at the right hand of the Mighty One and coming on the clouds of heaven."

65Then the high priest tore his clothes and said, "He has spoken blasphemy! Why do we need any more witnesses? Look, now you have heard the blasphemy. 66What do you think?"

"He is worthy of death," they answered.

---

a50 Or "Friend, why have you come?"   b63 Or Messiah; also in verse 68

⁶⁷Then they spit in his face and struck him with their fists. Others slapped him ⁶⁸and said, "Prophesy to us, Christ. Who hit you?"

Peter Disowns Jesus

⁶⁹Now Peter was sitting out in the courtyard, and a servant girl came to him. "You also were with Jesus of Galilee," she said.

⁷⁰But he denied it before them all. "I don't know what you're talking about," he said.

⁷¹Then he went out to the gateway, where another girl saw him and said to the people there, "This fellow was with Jesus of Nazareth."

⁷²He denied it again, with an oath: "I don't know the man!"

⁷³After a little while, those standing there went up to Peter and said, "Surely

---

FRIDAY

VERSE FOR THE DAY:	AUTHOR:	PASSAGE FOR THE DAY:
Matthew 26:39	Carol L. Baldwin	Matthew 26:36–46

Trust and Confidence

PICTURE Jesus. Alone in the Garden of Gethsemane, deserted by even his closest disciples, he is preparing to face the painful death of crucifixion. Not only will he die an innocent man; he will experience a bitter separation from his heavenly Father and the agony of bearing the punishment for the sins of his people.

How does our Lord respond at this moment of tremendous trial and testing?

His simple yet powerful response pricks our consciences as he speaks the ultimate prayer of trust and confidence: "My Father, if it is possible, may this cup be taken from me. Yet not as I will, but as you will" (Matthew 26:39). Can there be a more graphic demonstration of trust in God? Can there ever be a better example of submission to our heavenly Father's will?

Jesus' actions and attitude provide a model to all believers of how we are to face the difficult tasks, and the emotional, spiritual or physical struggles that God ordains for us.

Scripture reminds us that we are not to be surprised when suffering and trials come into our lives (1 Peter 1:6–7; 4:12–13); rather we are to rejoice that God is refining in us the precious jewel of faith, which is of far greater worth than gold.

Every problem with our children, each disagreement with our husbands, each stressful assignment at our jobs provides an opportunity to call on God to strengthen our faith, to develop our perseverance, to build our character and to ground our hope deeper in him (Romans 5:3–4).

May God grant us an increase in our trust in him, even as Jesus displayed. May he build in us precious Christian character, refined in the furnace of his discipline and love.

Additional Scripture Readings:
Daniel 3:13–19; James 1:2–4

Go to page 1065 for your next devotional reading.

you are one of them, for your accent gives you away."

74Then he began to call down curses on himself and he swore to them, "I don't know the man!"

Immediately a rooster crowed. 75Then Peter remembered the word Jesus had spoken: "Before the rooster crows, you will disown me three times." And he went outside and wept bitterly.

Judas Hangs Himself

27 Early in the morning, all the chief priests and the elders of the people came to the decision to put Jesus to death. 2They bound him, led him away and handed him over to Pilate, the governor.

3When Judas, who had betrayed him, saw that Jesus was condemned, he was seized with remorse and returned the thirty silver coins to the chief priests and the elders. 4"I have sinned," he said, "for I have betrayed innocent blood."

"What is that to us?" they replied. "That's your responsibility."

5So Judas threw the money into the temple and left. Then he went away and hanged himself.

6The chief priests picked up the coins and said, "It is against the law to put this into the treasury, since it is blood money." 7So they decided to use the money to buy the potter's field as a burial place for foreigners. 8That is why it has been called the Field of Blood to this day. 9Then what was spoken by Jeremiah the prophet was fulfilled: "They took the thirty silver coins, the price set on him by the people of Israel, 10and they used them to buy the potter's field, as the Lord commanded me."a

Jesus Before Pilate

11Meanwhile Jesus stood before the governor, and the governor asked him, "Are you the king of the Jews?"

"Yes, it is as you say," Jesus replied. 12When he was accused by the chief priests and the elders, he gave no answer. 13Then Pilate asked him, "Don't you hear the testimony they are bringing against you?" 14But Jesus made no reply, not even to a single charge—to the great amazement of the governor.

15Now it was the governor's custom at the Feast to release a prisoner chosen by the crowd. 16At that time they had a no-

torious prisoner, called Barabbas. 17So when the crowd had gathered, Pilate asked them, "Which one do you want me to release to you: Barabbas, or Jesus who is called Christ?" 18For he knew it was out of envy that they had handed Jesus over to him.

19While Pilate was sitting on the judge's seat, his wife sent him this message: "Don't have anything to do with that innocent man, for I have suffered a great deal today in a dream because of him."

20But the chief priests and the elders persuaded the crowd to ask for Barabbas and to have Jesus executed.

21"Which of the two do you want me to release to you?" asked the governor.

"Barabbas," they answered.

22"What shall I do, then, with Jesus who is called Christ?" Pilate asked.

They all answered, "Crucify him!"

23"Why? What crime has he committed?" asked Pilate.

But they shouted all the louder, "Crucify him!"

24When Pilate saw that he was getting nowhere, but that instead an uproar was starting, he took water and washed his hands in front of the crowd. "I am innocent of this man's blood," he said. "It is your responsibility!"

25All the people answered, "Let his blood be on us and on our children!"

26Then he released Barabbas to them. But he had Jesus flogged, and handed him over to be crucified.

The Soldiers Mock Jesus

27Then the governor's soldiers took Jesus into the Praetorium and gathered the whole company of soldiers around him. 28They stripped him and put a scarlet robe on him, 29and then twisted together a crown of thorns and set it on his head. They put a staff in his right hand and knelt in front of him and mocked him. "Hail, king of the Jews!" they said. 30They spit on him, and took the staff and struck him on the head again and again. 31After they had mocked him, they took off the robe and put his own clothes on him. Then they led him away to crucify him.

The Crucifixion

32As they were going out, they met a man from Cyrene, named Simon, and

a10 See Zech. 11:12,13; Jer. 19:1-13; 32:6-9.

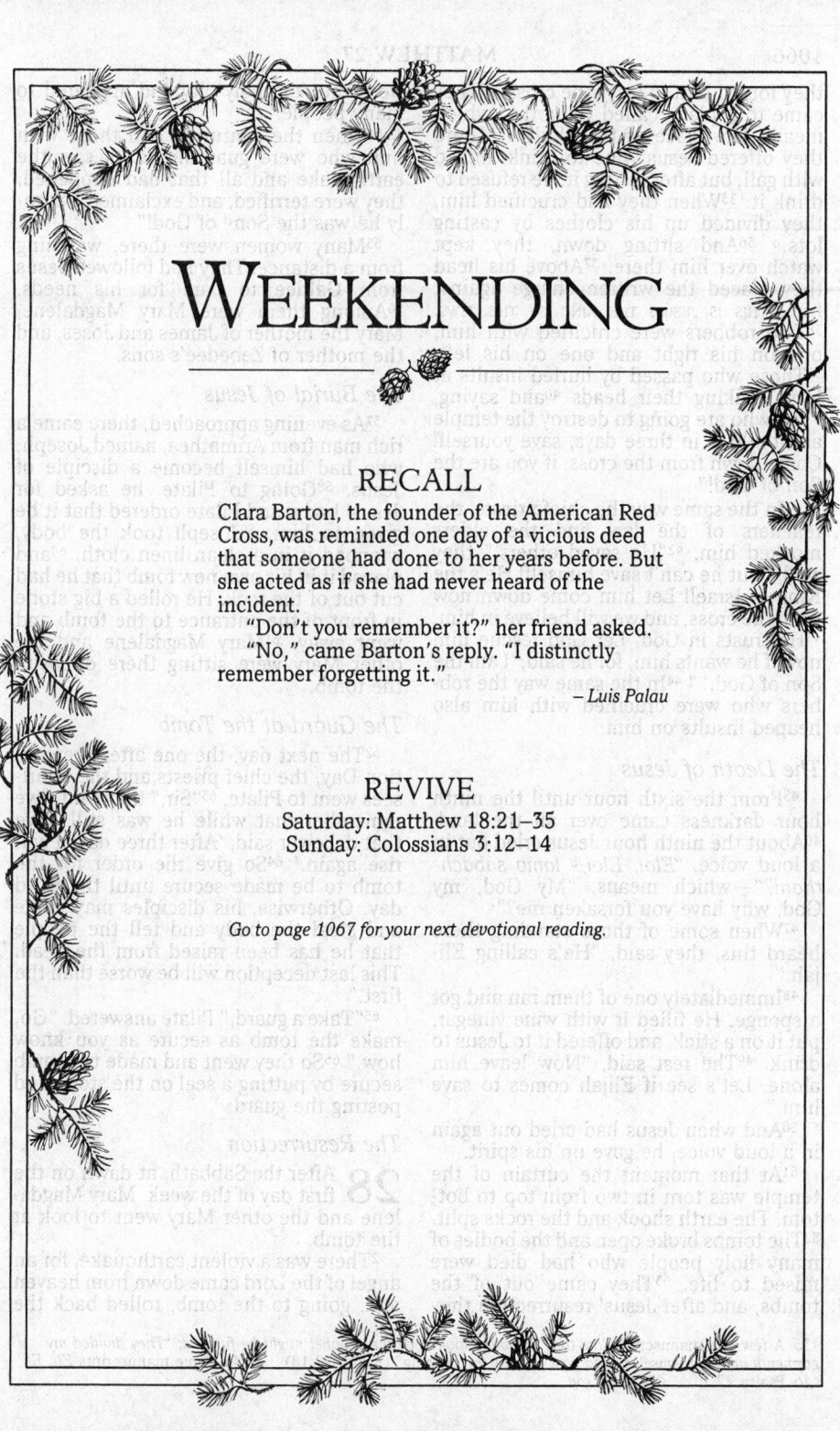

WEEKENDING

RECALL

Clara Barton, the founder of the American Red Cross, was reminded one day of a vicious deed that someone had done to her years before. But she acted as if she had never heard of the incident.

"Don't you remember it?" her friend asked.

"No," came Barton's reply. "I distinctly remember forgetting it."

– *Luis Palau*

REVIVE

Saturday: Matthew 18:21–35
Sunday: Colossians 3:12–14

Go to page 1067 for your next devotional reading.

they forced him to carry the cross. ³³They came to a place called Golgotha (which means The Place of the Skull). ³⁴There they offered Jesus wine to drink, mixed with gall; but after tasting it, he refused to drink it. ³⁵When they had crucified him, they divided up his clothes by casting lots.ᵃ ³⁶And sitting down, they kept watch over him there. ³⁷Above his head they placed the written charge against him: THIS IS JESUS, THE KING OF THE JEWS. ³⁸Two robbers were crucified with him, one on his right and one on his left. ³⁹Those who passed by hurled insults at him, shaking their heads ⁴⁰and saying, "You who are going to destroy the temple and build it in three days, save yourself! Come down from the cross, if you are the Son of God!"

⁴¹In the same way the chief priests, the teachers of the law and the elders mocked him. ⁴²"He saved others," they said, "but he can't save himself! He's the King of Israel! Let him come down now from the cross, and we will believe in him. ⁴³He trusts in God. Let God rescue him now if he wants him, for he said, 'I am the Son of God.' " ⁴⁴In the same way the robbers who were crucified with him also heaped insults on him.

The Death of Jesus

⁴⁵From the sixth hour until the ninth hour darkness came over all the land. ⁴⁶About the ninth hour Jesus cried out in a loud voice, *"Eloi, Eloi,*ᵇ *lama sabachthani?"* —which means, "My God, my God, why have you forsaken me?"ᶜ ⁴⁷When some of those standing there heard this, they said, "He's calling Elijah." ⁴⁸Immediately one of them ran and got a sponge. He filled it with wine vinegar, put it on a stick, and offered it to Jesus to drink. ⁴⁹The rest said, "Now leave him alone. Let's see if Elijah comes to save him."

⁵⁰And when Jesus had cried out again in a loud voice, he gave up his spirit. ⁵¹At that moment the curtain of the temple was torn in two from top to bottom. The earth shook and the rocks split. ⁵²The tombs broke open and the bodies of many holy people who had died were raised to life. ⁵³They came out of the tombs, and after Jesus' resurrection they went into the holy city and appeared to many people.

⁵⁴When the centurion and those with him who were guarding Jesus saw the earthquake and all that had happened, they were terrified, and exclaimed, "Surely he was the Sonᵈ of God!"

⁵⁵Many women were there, watching from a distance. They had followed Jesus from Galilee to care for his needs. ⁵⁶Among them were Mary Magdalene, Mary the mother of James and Joses, and the mother of Zebedee's sons.

The Burial of Jesus

⁵⁷As evening approached, there came a rich man from Arimathea, named Joseph, who had himself become a disciple of Jesus. ⁵⁸Going to Pilate, he asked for Jesus' body, and Pilate ordered that it be given to him. ⁵⁹Joseph took the body, wrapped it in a clean linen cloth, ⁶⁰and placed it in his own new tomb that he had cut out of the rock. He rolled a big stone in front of the entrance to the tomb and went away. ⁶¹Mary Magdalene and the other Mary were sitting there opposite the tomb.

The Guard at the Tomb

⁶²The next day, the one after Preparation Day, the chief priests and the Pharisees went to Pilate. ⁶³"Sir," they said, "we remember that while he was still alive that deceiver said, 'After three days I will rise again.' ⁶⁴So give the order for the tomb to be made secure until the third day. Otherwise, his disciples may come and steal the body and tell the people that he has been raised from the dead. This last deception will be worse than the first."

⁶⁵"Take a guard," Pilate answered. "Go, make the tomb as secure as you know how." ⁶⁶So they went and made the tomb secure by putting a seal on the stone and posting the guard.

The Resurrection

28 After the Sabbath, at dawn on the first day of the week, Mary Magdalene and the other Mary went to look at the tomb.

²There was a violent earthquake, for an angel of the Lord came down from heaven and, going to the tomb, rolled back the

---

ᵃ35 A few late manuscripts *lots that the word spoken by the prophet might be fulfilled: "They divided my garments among themselves and cast lots for my clothing"* (Psalm 22:18)   ᵇ46 Some manuscripts *Eli, Eli*   ᶜ46 Psalm 22:1   ᵈ54 Or *a son* stone and sat on it. ³His appearance was like lightning, and his clothes were white as snow. ⁴The guards were so afraid of him that they shook and became like dead men.

⁵The angel said to the women, "Do not be afraid, for I know that you are looking for Jesus, who was crucified. ⁶He is not here; he has risen, just as he said. Come and see the place where he lay. ⁷Then go

quickly and tell his disciples: 'He has risen from the dead and is going ahead of you into Galilee. There you will see him.' Now I have told you."

⁸So the women hurried away from the tomb, afraid yet filled with joy, and ran to tell his disciples. ⁹Suddenly Jesus met them. "Greetings," he said. They came to him, clasped his feet and worshiped him. ¹⁰Then Jesus said to them, "Do not be

MONDAY

VERSE FOR THE DAY:
Matthew 28:19

AUTHOR:
Janice Kempe

PASSAGE FOR THE DAY:
Matthew 28:16–20

Dandelions

DANDELIONS! No matter how carefully I try to pull one up, I never get the whole thing. The root stays deep in the ground, threatening to grow up and blossom again.

But despite their bad reputation, dandelions are pretty little flowers with their yellow strands all tucked neatly into the center. And truly they are the most beautiful of all flowers when presented clutched in a child's dirty little hand. No one gets yelled at for picking them. Perhaps they grow only to be used and enjoyed by children.

Dandelions are ignored or attacked, never nurtured or cared for, and yet they always bloom profusely. They demand no pampering or special attention to yield their bright blossoms; they pop up in fields, in lawns, and between cracks in the sidewalk, even in the best neighborhoods. Can you imagine trying to grow them in a garden? They'd sneak through the boundaries and pop their sunny yellow faces up in the surrounding lawn. They would never stay put!

Christians should be more like dandelions. Our sunny yellow faces should be a reminder that simple faith has deep roots that are impossible to dislodge. Our vast number would show the world that even though we are not fancy or pampered we are evident everywhere, even in the best neighborhoods.

We should be as easily accessible as a dandelion. Jesus was. We need to get out of our gardens and jump across the boundaries that keep us where people expect to find us. We need to show our sunny yellow faces in all the spots that need a little brightening up—the crack in the sidewalk or the lawn of a country club.

Additional Scripture Readings:
Acts 8:1–4; Colossians 2:6–7

Go to page 1071 for your next devotional reading.

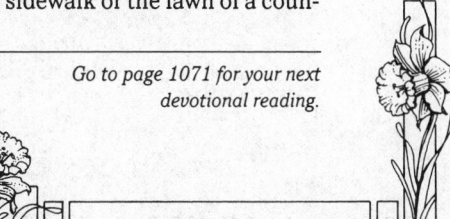

afraid. Go and tell my brothers to go to Galilee; there they will see me."

The Guards' Report

11While the women were on their way, some of the guards went into the city and reported to the chief priests everything that had happened. 12When the chief priests had met with the elders and devised a plan, they gave the soldiers a large sum of money, 13telling them, "You are to say, 'His disciples came during the night and stole him away while we were asleep.' 14If this report gets to the governor, we will satisfy him and keep you out of trouble." 15So the soldiers took the money and did as they were instructed.

And this story has been widely circulated among the Jews to this very day.

The Great Commission

16Then the eleven disciples went to Galilee, to the mountain where Jesus had told them to go. 17When they saw him, they worshiped him; but some doubted. 18Then Jesus came to them and said, "All authority in heaven and on earth has been given to me. 19Therefore go and make disciples of all nations, baptizing them in*a* the name of the Father and of the Son and of the Holy Spirit, 20and teaching them to obey everything I have commanded you. And surely I am with you always, to the very end of the age."

a19 Or into; see Acts 8:16; 19:5; Romans 6:3; 1 Cor. 1:13; 10:2 and Gal. 3:27.

*M*ARK *writes this gospel to tell the basic story about Jesus. He recounts miracles, parables and other sayings of Jesus. Almost half of his book deals with the final week of Jesus' life, ending with his death on the cross and his resurrection from the dead. As you read this book, notice how full of life and emotion Jesus is and how caring he is. Note too why he came into the world—to give his life for you (Mark 10:45). God wants you to accept his Son Jesus as your own personal Savior and Lord.*

MARK

John the Baptist Prepares the Way

1 The beginning of the gospel about Jesus Christ, the Son of God.*a*

²It is written in Isaiah the prophet:

"I will send my messenger ahead of
        you,
    who will prepare your way"*b*—
³"a voice of one calling in the desert,
    'Prepare the way for the Lord,
    make straight paths for him.' "*c*

⁴And so John came, baptizing in the desert region and preaching a baptism of repentance for the forgiveness of sins. ⁵The whole Judean countryside and all the people of Jerusalem went out to him. Confessing their sins, they were baptized by him in the Jordan River. ⁶John wore clothing made of camel's hair, with a leather belt around his waist, and he ate locusts and wild honey. ⁷And this was his message: "After me will come one more powerful than I, the thongs of whose sandals I am not worthy to stoop down and

---

a1 Some manuscripts do not have *the Son of God.*   *b2* Mal. 3:1   *c3* Isaiah 40:3

untie. 8I baptize you with*a* water, but he will baptize you with the Holy Spirit."

The Baptism and Temptation of Jesus

9At that time Jesus came from Nazareth in Galilee and was baptized by John in the Jordan. 10As Jesus was coming up out of the water, he saw heaven being torn open and the Spirit descending on him like a dove. 11And a voice came from heaven: "You are my Son, whom I love; with you I am well pleased."

12At once the Spirit sent him out into the desert, 13and he was in the desert forty days, being tempted by Satan. He was with the wild animals, and angels attended him.

The Calling of the First Disciples

14After John was put in prison, Jesus went into Galilee, proclaiming the good news of God. 15"The time has come," he said. "The kingdom of God is near. Repent and believe the good news!"

16As Jesus walked beside the Sea of Galilee, he saw Simon and his brother Andrew casting a net into the lake, for they were fishermen. 17"Come, follow me," Jesus said, "and I will make you fishers of men." 18At once they left their nets and followed him.

19When he had gone a little farther, he saw James son of Zebedee and his brother John in a boat, preparing their nets. 20Without delay he called them, and they left their father Zebedee in the boat with the hired men and followed him.

Jesus Drives Out an Evil Spirit

21They went to Capernaum, and when the Sabbath came, Jesus went into the synagogue and began to teach. 22The people were amazed at his teaching, because he taught them as one who had authority, not as the teachers of the law. 23Just then a man in their synagogue who was possessed by an evil*b* spirit cried out, 24"What do you want with us, Jesus of Nazareth? Have you come to destroy us? I know who you are—the Holy One of God!"

25"Be quiet!" said Jesus sternly. "Come out of him!" 26The evil spirit shook the man violently and came out of him with a shriek.

27The people were all so amazed that they asked each other, "What is this? A new teaching—and with authority! He even gives orders to evil spirits and they obey him." 28News about him spread quickly over the whole region of Galilee.

Jesus Heals Many

29As soon as they left the synagogue, they went with James and John to the home of Simon and Andrew. 30Simon's mother-in-law was in bed with a fever, and they told Jesus about her. 31So he went to her, took her hand and helped her up. The fever left her and she began to wait on them.

32That evening after sunset the people brought to Jesus all the sick and demon-possessed. 33The whole town gathered at the door, 34and Jesus healed many who had various diseases. He also drove out many demons, but he would not let the demons speak because they knew who he was.

Jesus Prays in a Solitary Place

35Very early in the morning, while it was still dark, Jesus got up, left the house and went off to a solitary place, where he prayed. 36Simon and his companions went to look for him, 37and when they found him, they exclaimed: "Everyone is looking for you!"

38Jesus replied, "Let us go somewhere else—to the nearby villages—so I can preach there also. That is why I have come." 39So he traveled throughout Galilee, preaching in their synagogues and driving out demons.

A Man With Leprosy

40A man with leprosy*c* came to him and begged him on his knees, "If you are willing, you can make me clean."

41Filled with compassion, Jesus reached out his hand and touched the man. "I am willing," he said. "Be clean!" 42Immediately the leprosy left him and he was cured.

43Jesus sent him away at once with a strong warning: 44"See that you don't tell this to anyone. But go, show yourself to the priest and offer the sacrifices that Moses commanded for your cleansing, as a testimony to them." 45Instead he went out and began to talk freely, spreading the news. As a result, Jesus could no

---

a8 Or *in*   *b23* Greek *unclean*; also in verses 26 and 27 diseases affecting the skin—not necessarily leprosy.   *c40* The Greek word was used for various longer enter a town openly but stayed outside in lonely places. Yet the people still came to him from everywhere.

Jesus Heals a Paralytic

2 A few days later, when Jesus again entered Capernaum, the people heard that he had come home. ²So many gathered that there was no room left, not even outside the door, and he preached the word to them. ³Some men came, bringing to him a paralytic, carried by four of them. ⁴Since they could not get him to Jesus because of the crowd, they made an opening in the roof above Jesus and, after digging through it, lowered the mat the paralyzed man was lying on.

⁵When Jesus saw their faith, he said to the paralytic, "Son, your sins are forgiven."

⁶Now some teachers of the law were sitting there, thinking to themselves, ⁷"Why does this fellow talk like that? He's blaspheming! Who can forgive sins but God alone?"

⁸Immediately Jesus knew in his spirit that this was what they were thinking in their hearts, and he said to them, "Why are you thinking these things? ⁹Which is easier: to say to the paralytic, 'Your sins are forgiven,' or to say, 'Get up, take your mat and walk'? ¹⁰But that you may know that the Son of Man has authority on earth to forgive sins . . . ." He said to the

TUESDAY

VERSE FOR THE DAY:	AUTHOR:	PASSAGE FOR THE DAY:
Mark 1:31	Jill Briscoe	Mark 1:29–34

A Must, Not a Maybe

WHEN you have a heart for God you have a heart for ministry. The two go hand in hand. When Jesus captured a life, healed a sick body or soul or mind, the recipient of those blessings invariably began to minister. Only on two occasions did Jesus have to tell them to do so. When Jairus's daughter was brought back from the dead, Jesus told her parents to "give her something to eat" (Mark 5:43), and when the Lord appeared first to Mary Magdalene after his resurrection, he told her to go tell the disciples that she had seen the Lord (John 20:17–18).

When you meet the Master, ministry naturally follows. Jesus forgave a sinful woman "her many sins," and she began to love him much (Luke 7:47). Having been forgiven much you begin to love much, and ministry is the natural outcome.

Martha and Mary, greatly loved by Jesus, loved him back by serving him, each in her own way. The mother of the disciple James, along with others, served the Lord by preparing his body for burial (Luke 24:10), while Joanna supported Jesus out of her own means (Luke 8:3). Even the woman at the well, having met Jesus, began at once to share her discovery with the people in her town (John 4:28–29).

You do not need to twist arms once you have had a personal encounter with the Christ of Galilee. Ministry is not then a maybe—it's a must.

Additional Scripture Readings:
Mark 2:14–15; John 1:43–46

Go to page 1076 for your next devotional reading.

paralytic, ¹¹"I tell you, get up, take your mat and go home." ¹²He got up, took his mat and walked out in full view of them all. This amazed everyone and they praised God, saying, "We have never seen anything like this!"

The Calling of Levi

¹³Once again Jesus went out beside the lake. A large crowd came to him, and he began to teach them. ¹⁴As he walked along, he saw Levi son of Alphaeus sitting at the tax collector's booth. "Follow me," Jesus told him, and Levi got up and followed him.

¹⁵While Jesus was having dinner at Levi's house, many tax collectors and "sinners" were eating with him and his disciples, for there were many who followed him. ¹⁶When the teachers of the law who were Pharisees saw him eating with the "sinners" and tax collectors, they asked his disciples: "Why does he eat with tax collectors and 'sinners'?"

¹⁷On hearing this, Jesus said to them, "It is not the healthy who need a doctor, but the sick. I have not come to call the righteous, but sinners."

Jesus Questioned About Fasting

¹⁸Now John's disciples and the Pharisees were fasting. Some people came and asked Jesus, "How is it that John's disciples and the disciples of the Pharisees are fasting, but yours are not?"

¹⁹Jesus answered, "How can the guests of the bridegroom fast while he is with them? They cannot, so long as they have him with them. ²⁰But the time will come when the bridegroom will be taken from them, and on that day they will fast.

²¹"No one sews a patch of unshrunk cloth on an old garment. If he does, the new piece will pull away from the old, making the tear worse. ²²And no one pours new wine into old wineskins. If he does, the wine will burst the skins, and both the wine and the wineskins will be ruined. No, he pours new wine into new wineskins."

Lord of the Sabbath

²³One Sabbath Jesus was going through the grainfields, and as his disciples walked along, they began to pick some heads of grain. ²⁴The Pharisees said to him, "Look, why are they doing what is unlawful on the Sabbath?"

²⁵He answered, "Have you never read what David did when he and his companions were hungry and in need? ²⁶In the days of Abiathar the high priest, he entered the house of God and ate the consecrated bread, which is lawful only for priests to eat. And he also gave some to his companions."

²⁷Then he said to them, "The Sabbath was made for man, not man for the Sabbath. ²⁸So the Son of Man is Lord even of the Sabbath."

3 Another time he went into the synagogue, and a man with a shriveled hand was there. ²Some of them were looking for a reason to accuse Jesus, so they watched him closely to see if he would heal him on the Sabbath. ³Jesus said to the man with the shriveled hand, "Stand up in front of everyone."

⁴Then Jesus asked them, "Which is lawful on the Sabbath: to do good or to do evil, to save life or to kill?" But they remained silent.

⁵He looked around at them in anger and, deeply distressed at their stubborn hearts, said to the man, "Stretch out your hand." He stretched it out, and his hand was completely restored. ⁶Then the Pharisees went out and began to plot with the Herodians how they might kill Jesus.

Crowds Follow Jesus

⁷Jesus withdrew with his disciples to the lake, and a large crowd from Galilee followed. ⁸When they heard all he was doing, many people came to him from Judea, Jerusalem, Idumea, and the regions across the Jordan and around Tyre and Sidon. ⁹Because of the crowd he told his disciples to have a small boat ready for him, to keep the people from crowding him. ¹⁰For he had healed many, so that those with diseases were pushing forward to touch him. ¹¹Whenever the evil*ᵃ* spirits saw him, they fell down before him and cried out, "You are the Son of God." ¹²But he gave them strict orders not to tell who he was.

The Appointing of the Twelve Apostles

¹³Jesus went up on a mountainside and called to him those he wanted, and they came to him. ¹⁴He appointed twelve—designating them apostles*ᵇ*—that they might be with him and that he might send them out to preach ¹⁵and to have authori-

---

ᵃ11 Greek *unclean*; also in verse 30   *ᵇ14* Some manuscripts do not have *designating them apostles.*

ty to drive out demons. ¹⁶These are the twelve he appointed: Simon (to whom he gave the name Peter); ¹⁷James son of Zebedee and his brother John (to them he gave the name Boanerges, which means Sons of Thunder); ¹⁸Andrew, Philip, Bartholomew, Matthew, Thomas, James son of Alphaeus, Thaddaeus, Simon the Zealot ¹⁹and Judas Iscariot, who betrayed him.

Jesus and Beelzebub

²⁰Then Jesus entered a house, and again a crowd gathered, so that he and his disciples were not even able to eat. ²¹When his family heard about this, they went to take charge of him, for they said, "He is out of his mind."

²²And the teachers of the law who came down from Jerusalem said, "He is possessed by Beelzebub*a*! By the prince of demons he is driving out demons."

²³So Jesus called them and spoke to them in parables: "How can Satan drive out Satan? ²⁴If a kingdom is divided against itself, that kingdom cannot stand. ²⁵If a house is divided against itself, that house cannot stand. ²⁶And if Satan opposes himself and is divided, he cannot stand; his end has come. ²⁷In fact, no one can enter a strong man's house and carry off his possessions unless he first ties up the strong man. Then he can rob his house. ²⁸I tell you the truth, all the sins and blasphemies of men will be forgiven them. ²⁹But whoever blasphemes against the Holy Spirit will never be forgiven; he is guilty of an eternal sin."

³⁰He said this because they were saying, "He has an evil spirit."

Jesus' Mother and Brothers

³¹Then Jesus' mother and brothers arrived. Standing outside, they sent someone in to call him. ³²A crowd was sitting around him, and they told him, "Your mother and brothers are outside looking for you."

³³"Who are my mother and my brothers?" he asked.

³⁴Then he looked at those seated in a circle around him and said, "Here are my mother and my brothers! ³⁵Whoever does God's will is my brother and sister and mother."

The Parable of the Sower

4 Again Jesus began to teach by the lake. The crowd that gathered around him was so large that he got into a boat and sat in it out on the lake, while all the people were along the shore at the water's edge. ²He taught them many things by parables, and in his teaching said: ³"Listen! A farmer went out to sow his seed. ⁴As he was scattering the seed, some fell along the path, and the birds came and ate it up. ⁵Some fell on rocky places, where it did not have much soil. It sprang up quickly, because the soil was shallow. ⁶But when the sun came up, the plants were scorched, and they withered because they had no root. ⁷Other seed fell among thorns, which grew up and choked the plants, so that they did not bear grain. ⁸Still other seed fell on good soil. It came up, grew and produced a crop, multiplying thirty, sixty, or even a hundred times."

⁹Then Jesus said, "He who has ears to hear, let him hear."

¹⁰When he was alone, the Twelve and the others around him asked him about the parables. ¹¹He told them, "The secret of the kingdom of God has been given to you. But to those on the outside everything is said in parables ¹²so that,

" 'they may be ever seeing but never
        perceiving,
    and ever hearing but never
        understanding;
  otherwise they might turn and be
        forgiven!'*b*"

¹³Then Jesus said to them, "Don't you understand this parable? How then will you understand any parable? ¹⁴The farmer sows the word. ¹⁵Some people are like seed along the path, where the word is sown. As soon as they hear it, Satan comes and takes away the word that was sown in them. ¹⁶Others, like seed sown on rocky places, hear the word and at once receive it with joy. ¹⁷But since they have no root, they last only a short time. When trouble or persecution comes because of the word, they quickly fall away. ¹⁸Still others, like seed sown among thorns, hear the word; ¹⁹but the worries of this life, the deceitfulness of wealth and the desires for other things come in and choke the word, making it unfruitful. ²⁰Others, like seed sown on good soil,

---

a22 Greek *Beezeboul* or *Beelzeboul*   *b12* Isaiah 6:9,10 hear the word, accept it, and produce a crop—thirty, sixty or even a hundred times what was sown."

A Lamp on a Stand

²¹He said to them, "Do you bring in a lamp to put it under a bowl or a bed? Instead, don't you put it on its stand? ²²For whatever is hidden is meant to be disclosed, and whatever is concealed is meant to be brought out into the open. ²³If anyone has ears to hear, let him hear."

²⁴"Consider carefully what you hear," he continued. "With the measure you use, it will be measured to you—and even more. ²⁵Whoever has will be given more; whoever does not have, even what he has will be taken from him."

The Parable of the Growing Seed

²⁶He also said, "This is what the kingdom of God is like. A man scatters seed on the ground. ²⁷Night and day, whether he sleeps or gets up, the seed sprouts and grows, though he does not know how. ²⁸All by itself the soil produces grain—first the stalk, then the head, then the full kernel in the head. ²⁹As soon as the grain is ripe, he puts the sickle to it, because the harvest has come."

The Parable of the Mustard Seed

³⁰Again he said, "What shall we say the kingdom of God is like, or what parable shall we use to describe it? ³¹It is like a mustard seed, which is the smallest seed you plant in the ground. ³²Yet when planted, it grows and becomes the largest of all garden plants, with such big branches that the birds of the air can perch in its shade."

³³With many similar parables Jesus spoke the word to them, as much as they could understand. ³⁴He did not say anything to them without using a parable. But when he was alone with his own disciples, he explained everything.

Jesus Calms the Storm

³⁵That day when evening came, he said to his disciples, "Let us go over to the other side." ³⁶Leaving the crowd behind, they took him along, just as he was, in the boat. There were also other boats with him. ³⁷A furious squall came up, and the waves broke over the boat, so that it was nearly swamped. ³⁸Jesus was in the stern, sleeping on a cushion. The disciples woke him and said to him, "Teacher, don't you care if we drown?"

³⁹He got up, rebuked the wind and said to the waves, "Quiet! Be still!" Then the wind died down and it was completely calm.

⁴⁰He said to his disciples, "Why are you so afraid? Do you still have no faith?"

⁴¹They were terrified and asked each other, "Who is this? Even the wind and the waves obey him!"

The Healing of a Demon-possessed Man

5 They went across the lake to the region of the Gerasenes.ᵃ ²When Jesus got out of the boat, a man with an evilᵇ spirit came from the tombs to meet him. ³This man lived in the tombs, and no one could bind him any more, not even with a chain. ⁴For he had often been chained hand and foot, but he tore the chains apart and broke the irons on his feet. No one was strong enough to subdue him. ⁵Night and day among the tombs and in the hills he would cry out and cut himself with stones.

⁶When he saw Jesus from a distance, he ran and fell on his knees in front of him. ⁷He shouted at the top of his voice, "What do you want with me, Jesus, Son of the Most High God? Swear to God that you won't torture me!" ⁸For Jesus had said to him, "Come out of this man, you evil spirit!"

⁹Then Jesus asked him, "What is your name?"

"My name is Legion," he replied, "for we are many." ¹⁰And he begged Jesus again and again not to send them out of the area.

¹¹A large herd of pigs was feeding on the nearby hillside. ¹²The demons begged Jesus, "Send us among the pigs; allow us to go into them." ¹³He gave them permission, and the evil spirits came out and went into the pigs. The herd, about two thousand in number, rushed down the steep bank into the lake and were drowned.

¹⁴Those tending the pigs ran off and reported this in the town and countryside, and the people went out to see what had happened. ¹⁵When they came to Jesus, they saw the man who had been pos-

---

ᵃ1 Some manuscripts *Gadarenes*; other manuscripts *Gergesenes* and 13　　　ᵇ2 Greek *unclean*; also in verses 8 sessed by the legion of demons, sitting there, dressed and in his right mind; and they were afraid. 16Those who had seen it told the people what had happened to the demon-possessed man—and told about the pigs as well. 17Then the people began to plead with Jesus to leave their region.

18As Jesus was getting into the boat, the man who had been demon-possessed begged to go with him. 19Jesus did not let him, but said, "Go home to your family and tell them how much the Lord has done for you, and how he has had mercy on you." 20So the man went away and began to tell in the Decapolis*a* how much Jesus had done for him. And all the people were amazed.

A Dead Girl and a Sick Woman

21When Jesus had again crossed over by boat to the other side of the lake, a large crowd gathered around him while he was by the lake. 22Then one of the synagogue rulers, named Jairus, came there. Seeing Jesus, he fell at his feet 23and pleaded earnestly with him, "My little daughter is dying. Please come and put your hands on her so that she will be healed and live." 24So Jesus went with him.

A large crowd followed and pressed around him. 25And a woman was there who had been subject to bleeding for twelve years. 26She had suffered a great deal under the care of many doctors and had spent all she had, yet instead of getting better she grew worse. 27When she heard about Jesus, she came up behind him in the crowd and touched his cloak, 28because she thought, "If I just touch his clothes, I will be healed." 29Immediately her bleeding stopped and she felt in her body that she was freed from her suffering.

30At once Jesus realized that power had gone out from him. He turned around in the crowd and asked, "Who touched my clothes?"

31"You see the people crowding against you," his disciples answered, "and yet you can ask, 'Who touched me?'"

32But Jesus kept looking around to see who had done it. 33Then the woman, knowing what had happened to her, came and fell at his feet and, trembling with fear, told him the whole truth. 34He said to her, "Daughter, your faith has healed you. Go in peace and be freed from your suffering."

35While Jesus was still speaking, some men came from the house of Jairus, the synagogue ruler. "Your daughter is dead," they said. "Why bother the teacher any more?"

36Ignoring what they said, Jesus told the synagogue ruler, "Don't be afraid; just believe."

37He did not let anyone follow him except Peter, James and John the brother of James. 38When they came to the home of the synagogue ruler, Jesus saw a commotion, with people crying and wailing loudly. 39He went in and said to them, "Why all this commotion and wailing? The child is not dead but asleep." 40But they laughed at him.

After he put them all out, he took the child's father and mother and the disciples who were with him, and went in where the child was. 41He took her by the hand and said to her, "Talitha koum!" (which means, "Little girl, I say to you, get up!"). 42Immediately the girl stood up and walked around (she was twelve years old). At this they were completely astonished. 43He gave strict orders not to let anyone know about this, and told them to give her something to eat.

A Prophet Without Honor

6 Jesus left there and went to his hometown, accompanied by his disciples. 2When the Sabbath came, he began to teach in the synagogue, and many who heard him were amazed.

"Where did this man get these things?" they asked. "What's this wisdom that has been given him, that he even does miracles! 3Isn't this the carpenter? Isn't this Mary's son and the brother of James, Joseph,*b* Judas and Simon? Aren't his sisters here with us?" And they took offense at him.

4Jesus said to them, "Only in his hometown, among his relatives and in his own house is a prophet without honor." 5He could not do any miracles there, except lay his hands on a few sick people and heal them. 6And he was amazed at their lack of faith.

Jesus Sends Out the Twelve

Then Jesus went around teaching from village to village. 7Calling the Twelve to him, he sent them out two by two and gave them authority over evil*c* spirits.

8These were his instructions: "Take

a20 That is, the Ten Cities   b3 Greek Joses, a variant of Joseph   c7 Greek unclean

VERSE FOR THE DAY:
Mark 5:34

AUTHOR:
Wanda K. Jones

PASSAGE FOR THE DAY:
Mark 5:25–34

Touch the Lord

MARK 5:25–34 speaks of a woman who had been bleeding for twelve years. She had seen many doctors but none were able to make her well. And while she spent all her money seeking a cure, her condition only grew worse.

Then she heard about Jesus and believed that if she could get to him and just touch him she would be healed. What a testimony to her persistence!

Imagine the scene: "A large crowd followed and pressed around him" (Mark 5:24). Some were blind, some deaf, some were mothers carrying children. And no doubt the day was hot and the road dusty. But this particular woman determined that in spite of the crowd she was going to touch Jesus and be healed. And she was!

Jesus responded to faith's touch by asking, "Who touched my clothes?" (Mark 5:30). The woman fell at his feet and told him her problem. How characteristic of the Master to respond in a comforting voice when he said, "Daughter, your faith has healed you. Go in peace and be freed from your suffering" (Mark 5:34).

Jesus is just as interested in your need as he was in this woman's need many years ago. Whatever your situation, whatever your problem, he stands ready to help you.

About two years ago I had the opportunity to witness about my faith to a woman who was near death. At the same time I had the privilege to hear her reaffirm her faith in Jesus Christ. She sang many of the hymns she had loved as a young girl, including "Blessed Assurance" and "What a Friend We Have in Jesus." We prayed together, and the next day she went to heaven with a smile on her face. She had touched the Lord on earth, and now she would be with him in heaven.

You may be looking for answers because you're in a faltering marriage. Or you may be hurting because you have been abused or neglected. Remember the woman of Mark 5. She sought Jesus and was determined to find him. When she did, he met her needs. He will meet yours. Ask him.

Additional Scripture Readings:
John 20:24–29; Hebrews 4:14–16

Go to page 1079 for your next devotional reading.

nothing for the journey except a staff—no bread, no bag, no money in your belts. 9Wear sandals but not an extra tunic. 10Whenever you enter a house, stay there until you leave that town. 11And if any place will not welcome you or listen to you, shake the dust off your feet when you leave, as a testimony against them."

12They went out and preached that people should repent. 13They drove out many demons and anointed many sick people with oil and healed them.

John the Baptist Beheaded

14King Herod heard about this, for Jesus' name had become well known. Some were saying,*a* "John the Baptist has been raised from the dead, and that is why miraculous powers are at work in him."

15Others said, "He is Elijah."

And still others claimed, "He is a prophet, like one of the prophets of long ago."

16But when Herod heard this, he said, "John, the man I beheaded, has been raised from the dead!"

17For Herod himself had given orders to have John arrested, and he had him bound and put in prison. He did this because of Herodias, his brother Philip's wife, whom he had married. 18For John had been saying to Herod, "It is not lawful for you to have your brother's wife." 19So Herodias nursed a grudge against John and wanted to kill him. But she was not able to, 20because Herod feared John and protected him, knowing him to be a righteous and holy man. When Herod heard John, he was greatly puzzled*b*; yet he liked to listen to him.

21Finally the opportune time came. On his birthday Herod gave a banquet for his high officials and military commanders and the leading men of Galilee. 22When the daughter of Herodias came in and danced, she pleased Herod and his dinner guests.

The king said to the girl, "Ask me for anything you want, and I'll give it to you." 23And he promised her with an oath, "Whatever you ask I will give you, up to half my kingdom."

24She went out and said to her mother, "What shall I ask for?"

"The head of John the Baptist," she answered.

25At once the girl hurried in to the king with the request: "I want you to give me right now the head of John the Baptist on a platter."

26The king was greatly distressed, but because of his oaths and his dinner guests, he did not want to refuse her. 27So he immediately sent an executioner with orders to bring John's head. The man went, beheaded John in the prison, 28and brought back his head on a platter. He presented it to the girl, and she gave it to her mother. 29On hearing of this, John's disciples came and took his body and laid it in a tomb.

Jesus Feeds the Five Thousand

30The apostles gathered around Jesus and reported to him all they had done and taught. 31Then, because so many people were coming and going that they did not even have a chance to eat, he said to them, "Come with me by yourselves to a quiet place and get some rest."

32So they went away by themselves in a boat to a solitary place. 33But many who saw them leaving recognized them and ran on foot from all the towns and got there ahead of them. 34When Jesus landed and saw a large crowd, he had compassion on them, because they were like sheep without a shepherd. So he began teaching them many things.

35By this time it was late in the day, so his disciples came to him. "This is a remote place," they said, "and it's already very late. 36Send the people away so they can go to the surrounding countryside and villages and buy themselves something to eat."

37But he answered, "You give them something to eat."

They said to him, "That would take eight months of a man's wages*c*! Are we to go and spend that much on bread and give it to them to eat?"

38"How many loaves do you have?" he asked. "Go and see."

When they found out, they said, "Five—and two fish."

39Then Jesus directed them to have all the people sit down in groups on the green grass. 40So they sat down in groups of hundreds and fifties. 41Taking the five loaves and the two fish and looking up to heaven, he gave thanks and broke the loaves. Then he gave them to his disciples to set before the people. He also divided the two fish among them all. ⁴²They all ate and were satisfied, ⁴³and the disciples picked up twelve basketfuls of broken pieces of bread and fish. ⁴⁴The number of the men who had eaten was five thousand.

Jesus Walks on the Water

⁴⁵Immediately Jesus made his disciples get into the boat and go on ahead of him to Bethsaida, while he dismissed the crowd. ⁴⁶After leaving them, he went up on a mountainside to pray.

⁴⁷When evening came, the boat was in the middle of the lake, and he was alone on land. ⁴⁸He saw the disciples straining at the oars, because the wind was against them. About the fourth watch of the night he went out to them, walking on the lake. He was about to pass by them, ⁴⁹but when they saw him walking on the lake, they thought he was a ghost. They cried out, ⁵⁰because they all saw him and were terrified.

Immediately he spoke to them and said, "Take courage! It is I. Don't be afraid." ⁵¹Then he climbed into the boat with them, and the wind died down. They were completely amazed, ⁵²for they had not understood about the loaves; their hearts were hardened.

⁵³When they had crossed over, they landed at Gennesaret and anchored there. ⁵⁴As soon as they got out of the boat, people recognized Jesus. ⁵⁵They ran throughout that whole region and carried the sick on mats to wherever they heard he was. ⁵⁶And wherever he went—into villages, towns or countryside—they placed the sick in the marketplaces. They begged him to let them touch even the edge of his cloak, and all who touched him were healed.

Clean and Unclean

7 The Pharisees and some of the teachers of the law who had come from Jerusalem gathered around Jesus and ²saw some of his disciples eating food with hands that were "unclean," that is, unwashed. ³(The Pharisees and all the Jews do not eat unless they give their hands a ceremonial washing, holding to the tradition of the elders. ⁴When they come from

the marketplace they do not eat unless they wash. And they observe many other traditions, such as the washing of cups, pitchers and kettles.ᵃ)

⁵So the Pharisees and teachers of the law asked Jesus, "Why don't your disciples live according to the tradition of the elders instead of eating their food with 'unclean' hands?"

⁶He replied, "Isaiah was right when he prophesied about you hypocrites; as it is written:

" 'These people honor me with their
        lips,
    but their hearts are far from me.
⁷They worship me in vain;
    their teachings are but rules taught
        by men.'ᵇ

⁸You have let go of the commands of God and are holding on to the traditions of men."

⁹And he said to them: "You have a fine way of setting aside the commands of God in order to observeᶜ your own traditions! ¹⁰For Moses said, 'Honor your father and your mother,'ᵈ and, 'Anyone who curses his father or mother must be put to death.'ᵉ ¹¹But you say that if a man says to his father or mother: 'Whatever help you might otherwise have received from me is Corban' (that is, a gift devoted to God), ¹²then you no longer let him do anything for his father or mother. ¹³Thus you nullify the word of God by your tradition that you have handed down. And you do many things like that."

¹⁴Again Jesus called the crowd to him and said, "Listen to me, everyone, and understand this. ¹⁵Nothing outside a man can make him 'unclean' by going into him. Rather, it is what comes out of a man that makes him 'unclean.'ᶠ"

¹⁷After he had left the crowd and entered the house, his disciples asked him about this parable. ¹⁸"Are you so dull?" he asked. "Don't you see that nothing that enters a man from the outside can make him 'unclean'? ¹⁹For it doesn't go into his heart but into his stomach, and then out of his body." (In saying this, Jesus declared all foods "clean.")

²⁰He went on: "What comes out of a man is what makes him 'unclean.' ²¹For from within, out of men's hearts, come

---

ᵃ4 Some early manuscripts *pitchers, kettles and dining couches*   ᵇ6,7 Isaiah 29:13   ᶜ9 Some manuscripts *set up*   ᵈ10 Exodus 20:12; Deut. 5:16   ᵉ10 Exodus 21:17; Lev. 20:9   ᶠ15 Some early manuscripts *'unclean.'* ¹⁶*If anyone has ears to hear, let him hear.*

VERSE FOR THE DAY:
Mark 6:46

AUTHOR:
Elisabeth Elliot

PASSAGE FOR THE DAY:
Mark 6:45–52

Meeting God Alone

A VERY tall man, wrapped in a steamer rug, kneeling alone by a chair. When I think of my father, who died in 1963, this is often the first image that comes to mind. It was the habit of his life to rise early in the morning—usually between 4:30 and 5:00 A. M. to study his Bible and to pray. We did not often see him during that solitary hour (he purposed to make it solitary), but we were used to seeing him on his knees.

My father, an honest and humble disciple of the Lord Jesus, wanted to follow his example: "Very early in the morning . . . Jesus got up, left the house and went off to a solitary place, where he prayed" (Mark 1:35).

Christians may (and ought to) pray anytime and anywhere, but we cannot well do without a special time and place to be alone with God. Most of us find that early morning is not an easy time to pray. I wonder if there is an *easy* time.

The simple fact is that early morning is probably the *only* time when we can be fairly sure of not being interrupted. Where can we go? We may need to find a literal closet or a bathroom or a parked car. We may walk outdoors and pray. But we must *arrange* to pray, to be alone with God sometime every day.

The Bible is God's message to everybody. We deceive ourselves if we claim to want to hear his voice but neglect the primary channel through which it comes. We must read his Word. We must obey it.

When we have heard God speak, what then shall we say to God? In an emergency or when we suddenly need help, the words come easily: "Oh, God!" or "Lord, help me!" During our quiet time however, it is a good thing to remember that we are here not to pester God but to adore him.

All creation praises him all the time—the winds, the tides, the oceans, the rivers, move in obedience; the song sparrow, the molecules in their cells, the stars in their courses, and the burning seraphim do, without protest of slovenliness, exactly what their Maker intended, and thus praise him.

We read that our heavenly Father actually looks for people who will worship him in spirit and in reality. Imagine! God is looking for worshipers. Will he always have to go to a church to find them, or might there be one here and there in an ordinary house, kneeling alone by a chair?

Additional Scripture Readings:
Isaiah 55:6–11; John 4:23–24

Go to page 1082 for your next devotional reading.

evil thoughts, sexual immorality, theft, murder, adultery, [22]greed, malice, deceit, lewdness, envy, slander, arrogance and folly. [23]All these evils come from inside and make a man 'unclean.' "

The Faith of a Syrophoenician Woman

[24]Jesus left that place and went to the vicinity of Tyre.[a] He entered a house and did not want anyone to know it; yet he could not keep his presence secret. [25]In fact, as soon as she heard about him, a woman whose little daughter was possessed by an evil[b] spirit came and fell at his feet. [26]The woman was a Greek, born in Syrian Phoenicia. She begged Jesus to drive the demon out of her daughter.

[27]"First let the children eat all they want," he told her, "for it is not right to take the children's bread and toss it to their dogs."

[28]"Yes, Lord," she replied, "but even the dogs under the table eat the children's crumbs."

[29]Then he told her, "For such a reply, you may go; the demon has left your daughter."

[30]She went home and found her child lying on the bed, and the demon gone.

The Healing of a Deaf and Mute Man

[31]Then Jesus left the vicinity of Tyre and went through Sidon, down to the Sea of Galilee and into the region of the Decapolis.[c] [32]There some people brought to him a man who was deaf and could hardly talk, and they begged him to place his hand on the man.

[33]After he took him aside, away from the crowd, Jesus put his fingers into the man's ears. Then he spit and touched the man's tongue. [34]He looked up to heaven and with a deep sigh said to him, *"Ephphatha!"* (which means, "Be opened!"). [35]At this, the man's ears were opened, his tongue was loosened and he began to speak plainly.

[36]Jesus commanded them not to tell anyone. But the more he did so, the more they kept talking about it. [37]People were overwhelmed with amazement. "He has done everything well," they said. "He even makes the deaf hear and the mute speak."

Jesus Feeds the Four Thousand

8 During those days another large crowd gathered. Since they had nothing to eat, Jesus called his disciples to him and said, [2]"I have compassion for these people; they have already been with me three days and have nothing to eat. [3]If I send them home hungry, they will collapse on the way, because some of them have come a long distance."

[4]His disciples answered, "But where in this remote place can anyone get enough bread to feed them?"

[5]"How many loaves do you have?" Jesus asked.

"Seven," they replied.

[6]He told the crowd to sit down on the ground. When he had taken the seven loaves and given thanks, he broke them and gave them to his disciples to set before the people, and they did so. [7]They had a few small fish as well; he gave thanks for them also and told the disciples to distribute them. [8]The people ate and were satisfied. Afterward the disciples picked up seven basketfuls of broken pieces that were left over. [9]About four thousand men were present. And having sent them away, [10]he got into the boat with his disciples and went to the region of Dalmanutha.

[11]The Pharisees came and began to question Jesus. To test him, they asked him for a sign from heaven. [12]He sighed deeply and said, "Why does this generation ask for a miraculous sign? I tell you the truth, no sign will be given to it." [13]Then he left them, got back into the boat and crossed to the other side.

The Yeast of the Pharisees and Herod

[14]The disciples had forgotten to bring bread, except for one loaf they had with them in the boat. [15]"Be careful," Jesus warned them. "Watch out for the yeast of the Pharisees and that of Herod."

[16]They discussed this with one another and said, "It is because we have no bread."

[17]Aware of their discussion, Jesus asked them: "Why are you talking about having no bread? Do you still not see or understand? Are your hearts hardened? [18]Do you have eyes but fail to see, and ears but fail to hear? And don't you remember? [19]When I broke the five loaves

---

a24 Many early manuscripts *Tyre and Sidon*   *b25* Greek *unclean*   *c31* That is, the Ten Cities for the five thousand, how many basketfuls of pieces did you pick up?"

"Twelve," they replied.

20"And when I broke the seven loaves for the four thousand, how many basketfuls of pieces did you pick up?"

They answered, "Seven."

21He said to them, "Do you still not understand?"

The Healing of a Blind Man at Bethsaida

22They came to Bethsaida, and some people brought a blind man and begged Jesus to touch him. 23He took the blind man by the hand and led him outside the village. When he had spit on the man's eyes and put his hands on him, Jesus asked, "Do you see anything?"

24He looked up and said, "I see people; they look like trees walking around."

25Once more Jesus put his hands on the man's eyes. Then his eyes were opened, his sight was restored, and he saw everything clearly. 26Jesus sent him home, saying, "Don't go into the village.*a* "

Peter's Confession of Christ

27Jesus and his disciples went on to the villages around Caesarea Philippi. On the way he asked them, "Who do people say I am?"

28They replied, "Some say John the Baptist; others say Elijah; and still others, one of the prophets."

29"But what about you?" he asked. "Who do you say I am?"

Peter answered, "You are the Christ.*b* "

30Jesus warned them not to tell anyone about him.

Jesus Predicts His Death

31He then began to teach them that the Son of Man must suffer many things and be rejected by the elders, chief priests and teachers of the law, and that he must be killed and after three days rise again. 32He spoke plainly about this, and Peter took him aside and began to rebuke him.

33But when Jesus turned and looked at his disciples, he rebuked Peter. "Get behind me, Satan!" he said. "You do not have in mind the things of God, but the things of men."

34Then he called the crowd to him along with his disciples and said: "If anyone would come after me, he must deny himself and take up his cross and follow me. 35For whoever wants to save his life*c* will lose it, but whoever loses his life for me and for the gospel will save it. 36What good is it for a man to gain the whole world, yet forfeit his soul? 37Or what can a man give in exchange for his soul? 38If anyone is ashamed of me and my words in this adulterous and sinful generation, the Son of Man will be ashamed of him when he comes in his Father's glory with the holy angels."

9 And he said to them, "I tell you the truth, some who are standing here will not taste death before they see the kingdom of God come with power."

The Transfiguration

2After six days Jesus took Peter, James and John with him and led them up a high mountain, where they were all alone. There he was transfigured before them. 3His clothes became dazzling white, whiter than anyone in the world could bleach them. 4And there appeared before them Elijah and Moses, who were talking with Jesus.

5Peter said to Jesus, "Rabbi, it is good for us to be here. Let us put up three shelters—one for you, one for Moses and one for Elijah." 6(He did not know what to say, they were so frightened.)

7Then a cloud appeared and enveloped them, and a voice came from the cloud: "This is my Son, whom I love. Listen to him!"

8Suddenly, when they looked around, they no longer saw anyone with them except Jesus.

9As they were coming down the mountain, Jesus gave them orders not to tell anyone what they had seen until the Son of Man had risen from the dead. 10They kept the matter to themselves, discussing what "rising from the dead" meant.

11And they asked him, "Why do the teachers of the law say that Elijah must come first?"

12Jesus replied, "To be sure, Elijah does come first, and restores all things. Why then is it written that the Son of Man must suffer much and be rejected? 13But I tell you, Elijah has come, and they have

---

a26 Some manuscripts Don't go and tell anyone in the village and "the Messiah" (Hebrew) both mean "the Anointed One." *soul*; also in verse 36.

b29 Or Messiah. "The Christ" (Greek)
c35 The Greek word means either life or

VERSE FOR THE DAY:
Mark 9:23

AUTHOR:
Mrs. Charles E. Cowman

PASSAGE FOR THE DAY:
Mark 9:14–32

Training in the Faith Life

THE "everything" in this verse does not always come simply for the asking. God is ever seeking to teach us the way of faith, and in our training in the faith life there must be room for the trial of faith, the discipline of faith, the patience of faith, the courage of faith, and often many stages are passed before we really realize what is the end of faith, namely, the victory of faith.

Real moral fiber is developed through discipline of faith. You have made your request of God, but the answer does not come. What are you to do?

Keep on believing God's Word; never be moved away from it by what you see or feel, and thus as you stand steady, enlarged power and experience is being developed. The fact of looking at the apparent contradiction as to God's Word and being unmoved from your position of faith make you stronger on every other line.

Often God delays purposely, and the delay is just as much an answer to your prayer as is the fulfillment when it comes.

In the lives of all the great Bible characters, God worked thus. Abraham, Moses and Elijah were not great in the beginning, but were made great through the discipline of their faith, and only thus were they fitted for the positions to which God had called them.

For example, in the case of Joseph whom the Lord was training for the throne of Egypt, it was not the prison life with its hard beds or poor food that tried him, but it was the word God had spoken into his heart in the early years concerning elevation and honor which were greater than his brethren were to receive; it was this which was ever before him, when every step in his career made it seem more and more impossible of fulfillment. These were hours that tried his soul, but hours of spiritual growth and development.

No amount of persecution tries like such experiences as these. When God has spoken of his purpose to do, and yet the days go on and he does not do it, that is truly hard; but it is a discipline of faith that will bring us into a knowledge of God which would otherwise be impossible.

Additional Scripture Readings:
James 5:10–11; 1 Peter 5:8–10

Go to page 1084 for your next devotional reading.

done to him everything they wished, just as it is written about him."

The Healing of a Boy With an Evil Spirit

[14]When they came to the other disciples, they saw a large crowd around them and the teachers of the law arguing with them. [15]As soon as all the people saw Jesus, they were overwhelmed with wonder and ran to greet him.

[16]"What are you arguing with them about?" he asked.

[17]A man in the crowd answered, "Teacher, I brought you my son, who is possessed by a spirit that has robbed him of speech. [18]Whenever it seizes him, it throws him to the ground. He foams at the mouth, gnashes his teeth and becomes rigid. I asked your disciples to drive out the spirit, but they could not."

[19]"O unbelieving generation," Jesus replied, "how long shall I stay with you? How long shall I put up with you? Bring the boy to me."

[20]So they brought him. When the spirit saw Jesus, it immediately threw the boy into a convulsion. He fell to the ground and rolled around, foaming at the mouth.

[21]Jesus asked the boy's father, "How long has he been like this?"

"From childhood," he answered. [22]"It has often thrown him into fire or water to kill him. But if you can do anything, take pity on us and help us."

[23]"'If you can'?" said Jesus. "Everything is possible for him who believes."

[24]Immediately the boy's father exclaimed, "I do believe; help me overcome my unbelief!"

[25]When Jesus saw that a crowd was running to the scene, he rebuked the evil[a] spirit. "You deaf and mute spirit," he said, "I command you, come out of him and never enter him again."

[26]The spirit shrieked, convulsed him violently and came out. The boy looked so much like a corpse that many said, "He's dead." [27]But Jesus took him by the hand and lifted him to his feet, and he stood up.

[28]After Jesus had gone indoors, his disciples asked him privately, "Why couldn't we drive it out?"

[29]He replied, "This kind can come out only by prayer.[b]"

[30]They left that place and passed through Galilee. Jesus did not want anyone to know where they were, [31]because he was teaching his disciples. He said to them, "The Son of Man is going to be betrayed into the hands of men. They will kill him, and after three days he will rise." [32]But they did not understand what he meant and were afraid to ask him about it.

Who Is the Greatest?

[33]They came to Capernaum. When he was in the house, he asked them, "What were you arguing about on the road?" [34]But they kept quiet because on the way they had argued about who was the greatest.

[35]Sitting down, Jesus called the Twelve and said, "If anyone wants to be first, he must be the very last, and the servant of all."

[36]He took a little child and had him stand among them. Taking him in his arms, he said to them, [37]"Whoever welcomes one of these little children in my name welcomes me; and whoever welcomes me does not welcome me but the one who sent me."

Whoever Is Not Against Us Is for Us

[38]"Teacher," said John, "we saw a man driving out demons in your name and we told him to stop, because he was not one of us."

[39]"Do not stop him," Jesus said. "No one who does a miracle in my name can in the next moment say anything bad about me, [40]for whoever is not against us is for us. [41]I tell you the truth, anyone who gives you a cup of water in my name because you belong to Christ will certainly not lose his reward.

Causing to Sin

[42]"And if anyone causes one of these little ones who believe in me to sin, it would be better for him to be thrown into the sea with a large millstone tied around his neck. [43]If your hand causes you to sin, cut it off. It is better for you to enter life maimed than with two hands to go into hell, where the fire never goes out.[c] [45]And if your foot causes you to sin, cut it off. It is better for you to enter life crippled than to have two feet and be thrown

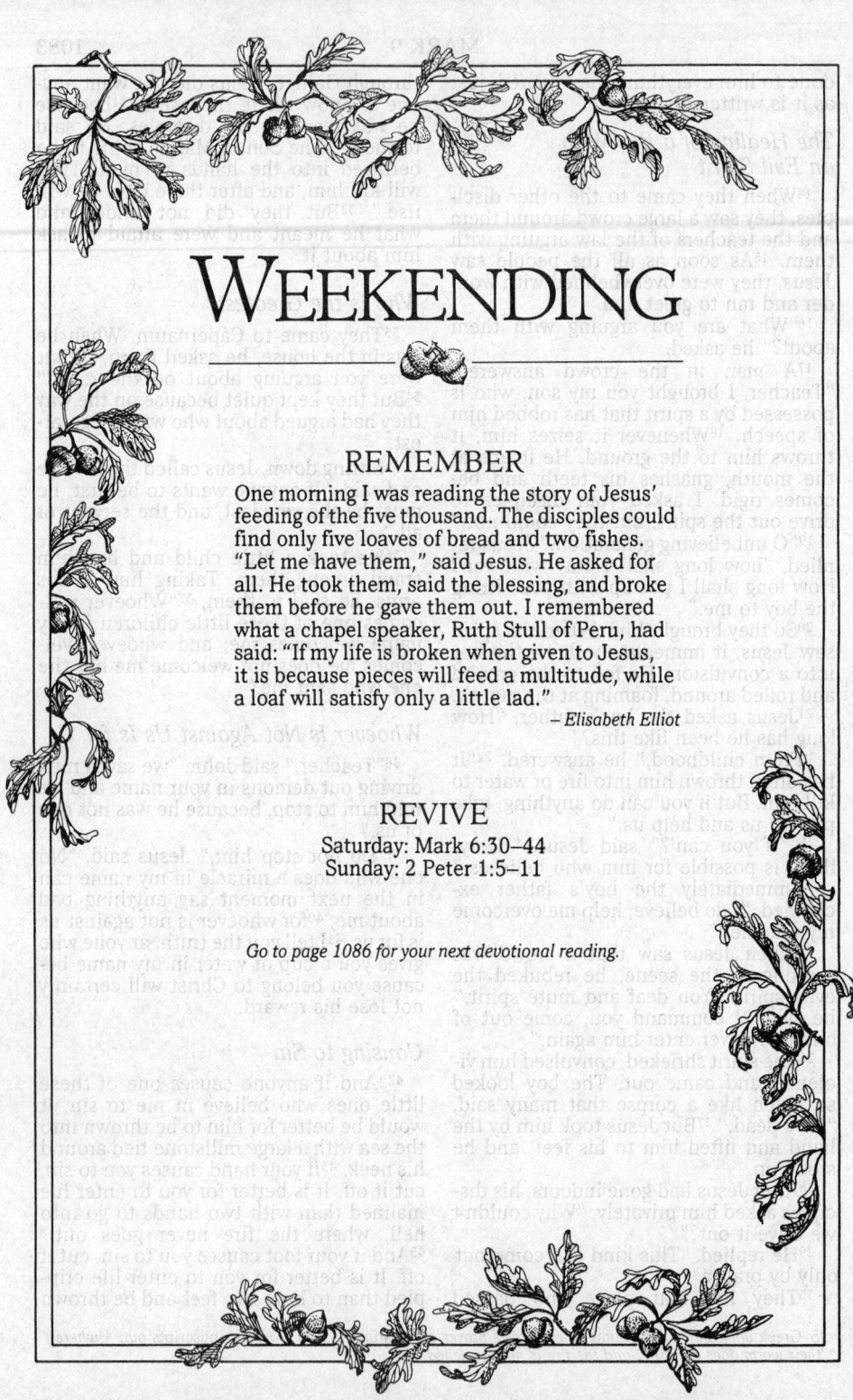

WEEKENDING

REMEMBER

One morning I was reading the story of Jesus'
feeding of the five thousand. The disciples could
find only five loaves of bread and two fishes.
"Let me have them," said Jesus. He asked for
all. He took them, said the blessing, and broke
them before he gave them out. I remembered
what a chapel speaker, Ruth Stull of Peru, had
said: "If my life is broken when given to Jesus,
it is because pieces will feed a multitude, while
a loaf will satisfy only a little lad."

— *Elisabeth Elliot*

REVIVE

Saturday: Mark 6:30–44
Sunday: 2 Peter 1:5–11

Go to page 1086 for your next devotional reading.

into hell.[a] [47]And if your eye causes you to sin, pluck it out. It is better for you to enter the kingdom of God with one eye than to have two eyes and be thrown into hell, [48]where

" 'their worm does not die,
and the fire is not quenched.'[b]

[49]Everyone will be salted with fire.

[50]"Salt is good, but if it loses its saltiness, how can you make it salty again? Have salt in yourselves, and be at peace with each other."

Divorce

10 Jesus then left that place and went into the region of Judea and across the Jordan. Again crowds of people came to him, and as was his custom, he taught them.

[2]Some Pharisees came and tested him by asking, "Is it lawful for a man to divorce his wife?"

[3]"What did Moses command you?" he replied.

[4]They said, "Moses permitted a man to write a certificate of divorce and send her away."

[5]"It was because your hearts were hard that Moses wrote you this law," Jesus replied. [6]"But at the beginning of creation God 'made them male and female.'[c] [7]For this reason a man will leave his father and mother and be united to his wife,[d] [8]and the two will become one flesh.'[e] So they are no longer two, but one. [9]Therefore what God has joined together, let man not separate."

[10]When they were in the house again, the disciples asked Jesus about this. [11]He answered, "Anyone who divorces his wife and marries another woman commits adultery against her. [12]And if she divorces her husband and marries another man, she commits adultery."

The Little Children and Jesus

[13]People were bringing little children to Jesus to have him touch them, but the disciples rebuked them. [14]When Jesus saw this, he was indignant. He said to them, "Let the little children come to me, and do not hinder them, for the kingdom of God belongs to such as these. [15]I tell you the truth, anyone who will not receive the kingdom of God like a little child will never enter it." [16]And he took the children in his arms, put his hands on them and blessed them.

The Rich Young Man

[17]As Jesus started on his way, a man ran up to him and fell on his knees before him. "Good teacher," he asked, "what must I do to inherit eternal life?"

[18]"Why do you call me good?" Jesus answered. "No one is good—except God alone. [19]You know the commandments: 'Do not murder, do not commit adultery, do not steal, do not give false testimony, do not defraud, honor your father and mother.'[f]"

[20]"Teacher," he declared, "all these I have kept since I was a boy."

[21]Jesus looked at him and loved him. "One thing you lack," he said. "Go, sell everything you have and give to the poor, and you will have treasure in heaven. Then come, follow me."

[22]At this the man's face fell. He went away sad, because he had great wealth.

[23]Jesus looked around and said to his disciples, "How hard it is for the rich to enter the kingdom of God!"

[24]The disciples were amazed at his words. But Jesus said again, "Children, how hard it is[g] to enter the kingdom of God! [25]It is easier for a camel to go through the eye of a needle than for a rich man to enter the kingdom of God."

[26]The disciples were even more amazed, and said to each other, "Who then can be saved?"

[27]Jesus looked at them and said, "With man this is impossible, but not with God; all things are possible with God."

[28]Peter said to him, "We have left everything to follow you!"

[29]"I tell you the truth," Jesus replied, "no one who has left home or brothers or sisters or mother or father or children or fields for me and the gospel [30]will fail to receive a hundred times as much in this present age (homes, brothers, sisters, mothers, children and fields—and with them, persecutions) and in the age to come, eternal life. [31]But many who are first will be last, and the last first."

---

[a]45 Some manuscripts *hell,* [46]*where* / " 'their worm does not die, / and the fire is not quenched.'*
[b]48 Isaiah 66:24   [c]6 Gen. 1:27   [d]7 Some early manuscripts do not have *and be united to his wife.*
[e]8 Gen. 2:24   [f]19 Exodus 20:12-16; Deut. 5:16-20   [g]24 Some manuscripts *is for those who trust in riches*

| VERSE FOR THE DAY: | AUTHOR: | PASSAGE FOR THE DAY: |
| Mark 10:14 | Rosalind Rinker | Mark 10:13–16 |

Jesus and Little Children

AS you read Mark 10:13–16, picture yourself in the time of Christ, the sun warm on your hair and your sandals dusty as you watch Jesus surrounded by numerous people. In your imagination stand in one of the following roles:

> As a parent bringing your children to Jesus,
> As one of the crowd waiting to see Jesus,
> As a child yourself, needing Jesus.

Hear the indignation in Jesus' voice when the disciples tried to shield him. Hear the loving care and concern in his voice as he held out his arms inviting the children to come.

As a parent: Picture yourself bringing your child (or children). Watch other parents push a shy child forward, or an ailing child. The children love Jesus, and they touch him; one little girl lays her head on his shoulder. Jesus takes time for each one . . . blessing, touching, loving, and sending each back to his or her parents with joy. Who can ever be the same after having been touched by Jesus!

Are your children grown? Yet in your mind they are still your little ones, so bring those grown men or women to Jesus as the children you know them to be. Jesus will touch them and bless them. Do it now and do it often.

As a single person: There are children you love among your neighbors or relatives, whom you can bring to Jesus in your prayers as, in your imagination, you watch Jesus hold and bless them.

You, yourself: Right now be a child in the arms of Jesus, whatever your age. Let him hold you. No matter what age, deep in our hearts we are all children who desire to rest in those strong arms. My dear mother, at age eighty-three, reflected some of that when she said, "I am still a little girl of twelve running around my father's farm in Minnesota."

Close your eyes and see yourself as a child in the arms of Jesus. In reassuring words he speaks to you:

> "My child, I care about you. I love you unconditionally. Trust me. I love you."

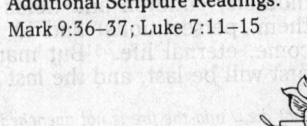

Additional Scripture Readings:
Mark 9:36–37; Luke 7:11–15

Go to page 1088 for your next devotional reading.

Jesus Again Predicts His Death

³²They were on their way up to Jerusalem, with Jesus leading the way, and the disciples were astonished, while those who followed were afraid. Again he took the Twelve aside and told them what was going to happen to him. ³³"We are going up to Jerusalem," he said, "and the Son of Man will be betrayed to the chief priests and teachers of the law. They will condemn him to death and will hand him over to the Gentiles, ³⁴who will mock him and spit on him, flog him and kill him. Three days later he will rise."

The Request of James and John

³⁵Then James and John, the sons of Zebedee, came to him. "Teacher," they said, "we want you to do for us whatever we ask."

³⁶"What do you want me to do for you?" he asked.

³⁷They replied, "Let one of us sit at your right and the other at your left in your glory."

³⁸"You don't know what you are asking," Jesus said. "Can you drink the cup I drink or be baptized with the baptism I am baptized with?"

³⁹"We can," they answered.

Jesus said to them, "You will drink the cup I drink and be baptized with the baptism I am baptized with, ⁴⁰but to sit at my right or left is not for me to grant. These places belong to those for whom they have been prepared."

⁴¹When the ten heard about this, they became indignant with James and John. ⁴²Jesus called them together and said, "You know that those who are regarded as rulers of the Gentiles lord it over them, and their high officials exercise authority over them. ⁴³Not so with you. Instead, whoever wants to become great among you must be your servant, ⁴⁴and whoever wants to be first must be slave of all. ⁴⁵For even the Son of Man did not come to be served, but to serve, and to give his life as a ransom for many."

Blind Bartimaeus Receives His Sight

⁴⁶Then they came to Jericho. As Jesus and his disciples, together with a large crowd, were leaving the city, a blind man, Bartimaeus (that is, the Son of Timaeus), was sitting by the roadside begging. ⁴⁷When he heard that it was Jesus of Nazareth, he began to shout, "Jesus, Son of David, have mercy on me!"

⁴⁸Many rebuked him and told him to be quiet, but he shouted all the more, "Son of David, have mercy on me!"

⁴⁹Jesus stopped and said, "Call him."

So they called to the blind man, "Cheer up! On your feet! He's calling you." ⁵⁰Throwing his cloak aside, he jumped to his feet and came to Jesus.

⁵¹"What do you want me to do for you?" Jesus asked him.

The blind man said, "Rabbi, I want to see."

⁵²"Go," said Jesus, "your faith has healed you." Immediately he received his sight and followed Jesus along the road.

The Triumphal Entry

11 As they approached Jerusalem and came to Bethphage and Bethany at the Mount of Olives, Jesus sent two of his disciples, ²saying to them, "Go to the village ahead of you, and just as you enter it, you will find a colt tied there, which no one has ever ridden. Untie it and bring it here. ³If anyone asks you, 'Why are you doing this?' tell him, 'The Lord needs it and will send it back here shortly.' "

⁴They went and found a colt outside in the street, tied at a doorway. As they untied it, ⁵some people standing there asked, "What are you doing, untying that colt?" ⁶They answered as Jesus had told them to, and the people let them go. ⁷When they brought the colt to Jesus and threw their cloaks over it, he sat on it. ⁸Many people spread their cloaks on the road, while others spread branches they had cut in the fields. ⁹Those who went ahead and those who followed shouted,

"Hosanna!ᵃ"

"Blessed is he who comes in the
name of the Lord!"ᵇ

¹⁰"Blessed is the coming kingdom of
our father David!"

"Hosanna in the highest!"

¹¹Jesus entered Jerusalem and went to the temple. He looked around at everything, but since it was already late, he went out to Bethany with the Twelve.

Jesus Clears the Temple

¹²The next day as they were leaving

ᵃ9 A Hebrew expression meaning "Save!" which became an exclamation of praise; also in verse 10
ᵇ9 Psalm 118:25,26

Bethany, Jesus was hungry. ¹³Seeing in the distance a fig tree in leaf, he went to find out if it had any fruit. When he reached it, he found nothing but leaves, because it was not the season for figs. ¹⁴Then he said to the tree, "May no one ever eat fruit from you again." And his disciples heard him say it.

¹⁵On reaching Jerusalem, Jesus en-tered the temple area and began driving out those who were buying and selling there. He overturned the tables of the money changers and the benches of those selling doves, ¹⁶and would not al-low anyone to carry merchandise through the temple courts. ¹⁷And as he taught them, he said, "Is it not writ-ten:

TUESDAY

VERSE FOR THE DAY:
Mark 10:37

AUTHOR:
Ruth A. Tucker

PASSAGE FOR THE DAY:
Mark 10:35–45

The Sin of Self-Promotion

AS Americans, competition and rivalry seem to be in our blood. We are taught from early childhood that we must be better than others. We strive for recognition and prestige and tend to focus solely on ourselves. James and John would have fit well into our society. They sought the ultimate recognition—to sit at the right and left hand of Jesus in the kingdom.

Jesus had a pointed response for them that should give us all pause for reflection. While the rulers of the Gentiles lord it over those under them, such behavior is not befitting one who fol-lows Christ. "Instead, whoever wants to become great among you must be your servant" (Mark 10:43).

That spirit of servanthood, which often is lacking in American culture, is much more visible among Africans—at least among African students at Moffat College of Bible in Kenya, where I have taught for several summers. Instead of the dog-eat-dog competition that is evident among my American students, I have noted a genuine concern for one another, especially in re-gard to grades at testing times. My African students appear most pleased, not when they alone perform well, but when the others perform well also. Indeed, if they were all to receive A's, there would be jubilation. Not so with my American students, whose real satisfaction comes only from being on top.

I have had to do some soul-searching myself on this issue. The competition for grades and the struggle for recognition in athletics that characterized my own student days have been subtly replaced by other forms of competition that are more be-fitting teachers and writers. But such a spirit is not becoming for a follower of Jesus. The Lord's words were direct, and he offered no excuses for those "handicapped" by their cultural heritage.

Additional Scripture Readings:
1 Samuel 24:1–13; Philippians 2:3–5

Go to page 1090 for your next devotional reading.

" 'My house will be called
    a house of prayer for all nations'*a*?

But you have made it 'a den of robbers.'*b*"

¹⁸The chief priests and the teachers of the law heard this and began looking for a way to kill him, for they feared him, because the whole crowd was amazed at his teaching.

¹⁹When evening came, they*c* went out of the city.

The Withered Fig Tree

²⁰In the morning, as they went along, they saw the fig tree withered from the roots. ²¹Peter remembered and said to Jesus, "Rabbi, look! The fig tree you cursed has withered!"

²²"Have*d* faith in God," Jesus answered. ²³"I tell you the truth, if anyone says to this mountain, 'Go, throw yourself into the sea,' and does not doubt in his heart but believes that what he says will happen, it will be done for him. ²⁴Therefore I tell you, whatever you ask for in prayer, believe that you have received it, and it will be yours. ²⁵And when you stand praying, if you hold anything against anyone, forgive him, so that your Father in heaven may forgive you your sins.*e* "

The Authority of Jesus Questioned

²⁷They arrived again in Jerusalem, and while Jesus was walking in the temple courts, the chief priests, the teachers of the law and the elders came to him. ²⁸"By what authority are you doing these things?" they asked. "And who gave you authority to do this?"

²⁹Jesus replied, "I will ask you one question. Answer me, and I will tell you by what authority I am doing these things. ³⁰John's baptism—was it from heaven, or from men? Tell me!"

³¹They discussed it among themselves and said, "If we say, 'From heaven,' he will ask, 'Then why didn't you believe him?' ³²But if we say, 'From men' . . . ." (They feared the people, for everyone held that John really was a prophet.)

³³So they answered Jesus "We don't know."

Jesus said, "Neither will I tell you by what authority I am doing these things."

The Parable of the Tenants

12 He then began to speak to them in parables: "A man planted a vineyard. He put a wall around it, dug a pit for the winepress and built a watchtower. Then he rented the vineyard to some farmers and went away on a journey. ²At harvest time he sent a servant to the tenants to collect from them some of the fruit of the vineyard. ³But they seized him, beat him and sent him away empty-handed. ⁴Then he sent another servant to them; they struck this man on the head and treated him shamefully. ⁵He sent still another, and that one they killed. He sent many others; some of them they beat, others they killed.

⁶"He had one left to send, a son, whom he loved. He sent him last of all, saying, 'They will respect my son.'

⁷"But the tenants said to one another, 'This is the heir. Come, let's kill him, and the inheritance will be ours.' ⁸So they took him and killed him, and threw him out of the vineyard.

⁹"What then will the owner of the vineyard do? He will come and kill those tenants and give the vineyard to others. ¹⁰Haven't you read this scripture:

" 'The stone the builders rejected
    has become the capstone*f*;
¹¹the Lord has done this,
    and it is marvelous in our eyes'*g*?"

¹²Then they looked for a way to arrest him because they knew he had spoken the parable against them. But they were afraid of the crowd; so they left him and went away.

Paying Taxes to Caesar

¹³Later they sent some of the Pharisees and Herodians to Jesus to catch him in his words. ¹⁴They came to him and said, "Teacher, we know you are a man of integrity. You aren't swayed by men, because you pay no attention to who they are; but you teach the way of God in accordance with the truth. Is it right to pay taxes to Caesar or not? ¹⁵Should we pay or shouldn't we?"

But Jesus knew their hypocrisy. "Why are you trying to trap me?" he asked. "Bring me a denarius and let me look at it." ¹⁶They brought the coin, and he asked

---

a17 Isaiah 56:7   *b17* Jer. 7:11   *c19* Some early manuscripts *he*   *d22* Some early manuscripts *If you have*   *e25* Some manuscripts *sins. 26But if you do not forgive, neither will your Father who is in heaven forgive your sins.*   *f10* Or *cornerstone*   *g11* Psalm 118:22,23

VERSE FOR THE DAY:
Mark 11:24

AUTHOR:
Hope MacDonald

PASSAGE FOR THE DAY:
Mark 11:22–25

Our Great Helper

WHILE searching for a book I wanted to buy recently, I heard a pleasant voice ask, "May I help you?" Once I described the book, we soon found it. I left the store with my requested treasure happily tucked under my arm, and I thought, "I wonder how often God asks me this same question, but I'm too busy to hear?"

Maybe he's asking if there are any mountains in our lives that we need help in moving today—mountains of disappointment, heartache or fear. Sometimes these mountains can loom so large before us that we are no longer able to see Jesus. Yet it's here, while sitting in the shadow of our dark, cold mountain, that we can turn to Mark 11 and read what Jesus said. He gives us his pattern for prayer and sums up all we will ever need to know about it. The pattern is this: pray, ask, believe, forgive.

To pray is a supernatural way of getting to know a supernatural God. When we pray, God makes us his partners! He chooses us to become part of his ministry here on earth.

When Jesus inquires, "May I help you?" he wants us to respond in childlike trust. He wants us to ask. Sometimes he answers in a miraculous way, but most of the time he simply opens our spiritual eyes and shows us what *we* can do to bring about the answer. Then he gives us the ability to do it.

To believe is to give God the right to answer our prayer in the way he sees best. Remember, Jesus never gave a sermon on unanswered prayer because, from his viewpoint, all prayers are answered. When we learn to believe God, we find our attention is no longer on our mountain. It becomes focused instead on Jesus, who alone is worthy of our trust.

When we forgive, we open a channel to God. Jesus asks us to forgive others "so that your Father in heaven may forgive you your sins" (Mark 11:25).

God longs for us to live in the joy of walking by faith—praying, asking, believing, forgiving. When we do, we find we're no longer sitting alone in the shadow of the mountain.

Additional Scripture Readings:
Matthew 6:5–15; Philippians 4:6–7

Go to page 1096 for your next
devotional reading.

them, "Whose portrait is this? And whose inscription?"

"Caesar's," they replied.

[17]Then Jesus said to them, "Give to Caesar what is Caesar's and to God what is God's."

And they were amazed at him.

Marriage at the Resurrection

[18]Then the Sadducees, who say there is no resurrection, came to him with a question. [19]"Teacher," they said, "Moses wrote for us that if a man's brother dies and leaves a wife but no children, the man must marry the widow and have children for his brother. [20]Now there were seven brothers. The first one married and died without leaving any children. [21]The second one married the widow, but he also died, leaving no child. It was the same with the third. [22]In fact, none of the seven left any children. Last of all, the woman died too. [23]At the resurrection[a] whose wife will she be, since the seven were married to her?"

[24]Jesus replied, "Are you not in error because you do not know the Scriptures or the power of God? [25]When the dead rise, they will neither marry nor be given in marriage; they will be like the angels in heaven. [26]Now about the dead rising— have you not read in the book of Moses, in the account of the bush, how God said to him, 'I am the God of Abraham, the God of Isaac, and the God of Jacob'[b]? [27]He is not the God of the dead, but of the living. You are badly mistaken!"

The Greatest Commandment

[28]One of the teachers of the law came and heard them debating. Noticing that Jesus had given them a good answer, he asked him, "Of all the commandments, which is the most important?"

[29]"The most important one," answered Jesus, "is this: 'Hear, O Israel, the Lord our God, the Lord is one.[c] [30]Love the Lord your God with all your heart and with all your soul and with all your mind and with all your strength.'[d] [31]The second is this: 'Love your neighbor as yourself.'[e] There is no commandment greater than these."

[32]"Well said, teacher," the man replied. "You are right in saying that God is one and there is no other but him. [33]To love

him with all your heart, with all your understanding and with all your strength, and to love your neighbor as yourself is more important than all burnt offerings and sacrifices."

[34]When Jesus saw that he had answered wisely, he said to him, "You are not far from the kingdom of God." And from then on no one dared ask him any more questions.

Whose Son Is the Christ?

[35]While Jesus was teaching in the temple courts, he asked, "How is it that the teachers of the law say that the Christ[f] is the son of David? [36]David himself, speaking by the Holy Spirit, declared:

" 'The Lord said to my Lord:
"Sit at my right hand
until I put your enemies
    under your feet." '[g]

[37]David himself calls him 'Lord.' How then can he be his son?"

The large crowd listened to him with delight.

[38]As he taught, Jesus said, "Watch out for the teachers of the law. They like to walk around in flowing robes and be greeted in the marketplaces, [39]and have the most important seats in the synagogues and the places of honor at banquets. [40]They devour widows' houses and for a show make lengthy prayers. Such men will be punished most severely."

The Widow's Offering

[41]Jesus sat down opposite the place where the offerings were put and watched the crowd putting their money into the temple treasury. Many rich people threw in large amounts. [42]But a poor widow came and put in two very small copper coins,[h] worth only a fraction of a penny.[i]

[43]Calling his disciples to him, Jesus said, "I tell you the truth, this poor widow has put more into the treasury than all the others. [44]They all gave out of their wealth; but she, out of her poverty, put in everything—all she had to live on."

Signs of the End of the Age

13 As he was leaving the temple, one of his disciples said to him, "Look, Teacher! What massive stones! What magnificent buildings!"

---

[a]23 Some manuscripts *resurrection, when men rise from the dead,*   [b]26 Exodus 3:6   [c]29 Or *the Lord our God is one Lord*   [d]30 Deut. 6:4,5   [e]31 Lev. 19:18   [f]35 Or *Messiah*   [g]36 Psalm 110:1   [h]42 Greek *two lepta*   [i]42 Greek *kodrantes*

2"Do you see all these great buildings?" replied Jesus. "Not one stone here will be left on another; every one will be thrown down."

3As Jesus was sitting on the Mount of Olives opposite the temple, Peter, James, John and Andrew asked him privately, 4"Tell us, when will these things happen? And what will be the sign that they are all about to be fulfilled?"

5Jesus said to them: "Watch out that no one deceives you. 6Many will come in my name, claiming, 'I am he,' and will deceive many. 7When you hear of wars and rumors of wars, do not be alarmed. Such things must happen, but the end is still to come. 8Nation will rise against nation, and kingdom against kingdom. There will be earthquakes in various places, and famines. These are the beginning of birth pains.

9"You must be on your guard. You will be handed over to the local councils and flogged in the synagogues. On account of me you will stand before governors and kings as witnesses to them. 10And the gospel must first be preached to all nations. 11Whenever you are arrested and brought to trial, do not worry beforehand about what to say. Just say whatever is given you at the time, for it is not you speaking, but the Holy Spirit.

12"Brother will betray brother to death, and a father his child. Children will rebel against their parents and have them put to death. 13All men will hate you because of me, but he who stands firm to the end will be saved.

14"When you see 'the abomination that causes desolation'ᵃ standing where itᵇ does not belong—let the reader understand—then let those who are in Judea flee to the mountains. 15Let no one on the roof of his house go down or enter the house to take anything out. 16Let no one in the field go back to get his cloak. 17How dreadful it will be in those days for pregnant women and nursing mothers! 18Pray that this will not take place in winter, 19because those will be days of distress unequaled from the beginning, when God created the world, until now— and never to be equaled again. 20If the Lord had not cut short those days, no one would survive. But for the sake of the elect, whom he has chosen, he has shortened them. 21At that time if anyone says

to you, 'Look, here is the Christᶜ!' or, 'Look, there he is!' do not believe it. 22For false Christs and false prophets will appear and perform signs and miracles to deceive the elect—if that were possible. 23So be on your guard; I have told you everything ahead of time.

24"But in those days, following that distress,

" 'the sun will be darkened,
    and the moon will not give its light;
25the stars will fall from the sky,
    and the heavenly bodies will be
        shaken.'ᵈ

26"At that time men will see the Son of Man coming in clouds with great power and glory. 27And he will send his angels and gather his elect from the four winds, from the ends of the earth to the ends of the heavens.

28"Now learn this lesson from the fig tree: As soon as its twigs get tender and its leaves come out, you know that summer is near. 29Even so, when you see these things happening, you know that it is near, right at the door. 30I tell you the truth, this generationᵉ will certainly not pass away until all these things have happened. 31Heaven and earth will pass away, but my words will never pass away.

The Day and Hour Unknown

32"No one knows about that day or hour, not even the angels in heaven, nor the Son, but only the Father. 33Be on guard! Be alert!ᶠ You do not know when that time will come. 34It's like a man going away: He leaves his house and puts his servants in charge, each with his assigned task, and tells the one at the door to keep watch.

35"Therefore keep watch because you do not know when the owner of the house will come back—whether in the evening, or at midnight, or when the rooster crows, or at dawn. 36If he comes suddenly, do not let him find you sleeping. 37What I say to you, I say to everyone: 'Watch!' "

Jesus Anointed at Bethany

14 Now the Passover and the Feast of Unleavened Bread were only two days away, and the chief priests and the teachers of the law were looking for some sly way to arrest Jesus and kill him. 2"But

---

ᵃ14 Daniel 9:27; 11:31; 12:11   ᵇ14 Or he; also in verse 29   ᶜ21 Or Messiah   ᵈ25 Isaiah 13:10; 34:4   ᵉ30 Or race   ᶠ33 Some manuscripts alert and pray not during the Feast," they said, "or the people may riot."

3While he was in Bethany, reclining at the table in the home of a man known as Simon the Leper, a woman came with an alabaster jar of very expensive perfume, made of pure nard. She broke the jar and poured the perfume on his head.

4Some of those present were saying indignantly to one another, "Why this waste of perfume? 5It could have been sold for more than a year's wages *a* and the money given to the poor." And they rebuked her harshly.

6"Leave her alone," said Jesus. "Why are you bothering her? She has done a beautiful thing to me. 7The poor you will always have with you, and you can help them any time you want. But you will not always have me. 8She did what she could. She poured perfume on my body beforehand to prepare for my burial. 9I tell you the truth, wherever the gospel is preached throughout the world, what she has done will also be told, in memory of her."

10Then Judas Iscariot, one of the Twelve, went to the chief priests to betray Jesus to them. 11They were delighted to hear this and promised to give him money. So he watched for an opportunity to hand him over.

The Lord's Supper

12On the first day of the Feast of Unleavened Bread, when it was customary to sacrifice the Passover lamb, Jesus' disciples asked him, "Where do you want us to go and make preparations for you to eat the Passover?"

13So he sent two of his disciples, telling them, "Go into the city, and a man carrying a jar of water will meet you. Follow him. 14Say to the owner of the house he enters, 'The Teacher asks: Where is my guest room, where I may eat the Passover with my disciples?' 15He will show you a large upper room, furnished and ready. Make preparations for us there."

16The disciples left, went into the city and found things just as Jesus had told them. So they prepared the Passover.

17When evening came, Jesus arrived with the Twelve. 18While they were reclining at the table eating, he said, "I tell you the truth, one of you will betray me—one who is eating with me."

19They were saddened, and one by one they said to him, "Surely not I?"

20"It is one of the Twelve," he replied, "one who dips bread into the bowl with me. 21The Son of Man will go just as it is written about him. But woe to that man who betrays the Son of Man! It would be better for him if he had not been born."

22While they were eating, Jesus took bread, gave thanks and broke it, and gave it to his disciples, saying, "Take it; this is my body."

23Then he took the cup, gave thanks and offered it to them, and they all drank from it.

24"This is my blood of the *b* covenant, which is poured out for many," he said to them. 25"I tell you the truth, I will not drink again of the fruit of the vine until that day when I drink it anew in the kingdom of God."

26When they had sung a hymn, they went out to the Mount of Olives.

Jesus Predicts Peter's Denial

27"You will all fall away," Jesus told them, "for it is written:

" 'I will strike the shepherd,
    and the sheep will be scattered.' *c*

28But after I have risen, I will go ahead of you into Galilee."

29Peter declared, "Even if all fall away, I will not."

30"I tell you the truth," Jesus answered, "today—yes, tonight—before the rooster crows twice *d* you yourself will disown me three times."

31But Peter insisted emphatically, "Even if I have to die with you, I will never disown you." And all the others said the same.

Gethsemane

32They went to a place called Gethsemane, and Jesus said to his disciples, "Sit here while I pray." 33He took Peter, James and John along with him, and he began to be deeply distressed and troubled. 34"My soul is overwhelmed with sorrow to the point of death," he said to them. "Stay here and keep watch."

35Going a little farther, he fell to the ground and prayed that if possible the hour might pass from him. 36"Abba, *e* Father," he said, "everything is possible for

a5 Greek *than three hundred denarii*   *b24* Some manuscripts *the new*   *c27* Zech. 13:7   *d30* Some early manuscripts do not have *twice.*   *e36* Aramaic for *Father* you. Take this cup from me. Yet not what I will, but what you will."

37Then he returned to his disciples and found them sleeping. "Simon," he said to Peter, "are you asleep? Could you not keep watch for one hour? 38Watch and pray so that you will not fall into temptation. The spirit is willing, but the body is weak."

39Once more he went away and prayed the same thing. 40When he came back, he again found them sleeping, because their eyes were heavy. They did not know what to say to him.

41Returning the third time, he said to them, "Are you still sleeping and resting? Enough! The hour has come. Look, the Son of Man is betrayed into the hands of sinners. 42Rise! Let us go! Here comes my betrayer!"

Jesus Arrested

43Just as he was speaking, Judas, one of the Twelve, appeared. With him was a crowd armed with swords and clubs, sent from the chief priests, the teachers of the law, and the elders.

44Now the betrayer had arranged a signal with them: "The one I kiss is the man; arrest him and lead him away under guard." 45Going at once to Jesus, Judas said, "Rabbi!" and kissed him. 46The men seized Jesus and arrested him. 47Then one of those standing near drew his sword and struck the servant of the high priest, cutting off his ear.

48"Am I leading a rebellion," said Jesus, "that you have come out with swords and clubs to capture me? 49Every day I was with you, teaching in the temple courts, and you did not arrest me. But the Scriptures must be fulfilled." 50Then everyone deserted him and fled.

51A young man, wearing nothing but a linen garment, was following Jesus. When they seized him, 52he fled naked, leaving his garment behind.

Before the Sanhedrin

53They took Jesus to the high priest, and all the chief priests, elders and teachers of the law came together. 54Peter followed him at a distance, right into the courtyard of the high priest. There he sat with the guards and warmed himself at the fire.

55The chief priests and the whole San-hedrin were looking for evidence against Jesus so that they could put him to death, but they did not find any. 56Many testified falsely against him, but their statements did not agree.

57Then some stood up and gave this false testimony against him: 58"We heard him say, 'I will destroy this man-made temple and in three days will build another, not made by man.' " 59Yet even then their testimony did not agree.

60Then the high priest stood up before them and asked Jesus, "Are you not going to answer? What is this testimony that these men are bringing against you?" 61But Jesus remained silent and gave no answer.

Again the high priest asked him, "Are you the Christ,a the Son of the Blessed One?"

62"I am," said Jesus. "And you will see the Son of Man sitting at the right hand of the Mighty One and coming on the clouds of heaven."

63The high priest tore his clothes. "Why do we need any more witnesses?" he asked. 64"You have heard the blasphemy. What do you think?"

They all condemned him as worthy of death. 65Then some began to spit at him; they blindfolded him, struck him with their fists, and said, "Prophesy!" And the guards took him and beat him.

Peter Disowns Jesus

66While Peter was below in the courtyard, one of the servant girls of the high priest came by. 67When she saw Peter warming himself, she looked closely at him.

"You also were with that Nazarene, Jesus," she said.

68But he denied it. "I don't know or understand what you're talking about," he said, and went out into the entryway.b

69When the servant girl saw him there, she said again to those standing around, "This fellow is one of them." 70Again he denied it.

After a little while, those standing near said to Peter, "Surely you are one of them, for you are a Galilean."

71He began to call down curses on himself, and he swore to them, "I don't know this man you're talking about."

72Immediately the rooster crowed the second time.c Then Peter remembered

---

a61 Or Messiah   b68 Some early manuscripts entryway and the rooster crowed   c72 Some early manuscripts do not have the second time.

the word Jesus had spoken to him: "Before the rooster crows twice[a] you will disown me three times." And he broke down and wept.

Jesus Before Pilate

15 Very early in the morning, the chief priests, with the elders, the teachers of the law and the whole Sanhedrin, reached a decision. They bound Jesus, led him away and handed him over to Pilate.

[2]"Are you the king of the Jews?" asked Pilate.

"Yes, it is as you say," Jesus replied.

[3]The chief priests accused him of many things. [4]So again Pilate asked him, "Aren't you going to answer? See how many things they are accusing you of."

[5]But Jesus still made no reply, and Pilate was amazed.

[6]Now it was the custom at the Feast to release a prisoner whom the people requested. [7]A man called Barabbas was in prison with the insurrectionists who had committed murder in the uprising. [8]The crowd came up and asked Pilate to do for them what he usually did.

[9]"Do you want me to release to you the king of the Jews?" asked Pilate, [10]knowing it was out of envy that the chief priests had handed Jesus over to him. [11]But the chief priests stirred up the crowd to have Pilate release Barabbas instead.

[12]"What shall I do, then, with the one you call the king of the Jews?" Pilate asked them.

[13]"Crucify him!" they shouted.

[14]"Why? What crime has he committed?" asked Pilate.

But they shouted all the louder, "Crucify him!"

[15]Wanting to satisfy the crowd, Pilate released Barabbas to them. He had Jesus flogged, and handed him over to be crucified.

The Soldiers Mock Jesus

[16]The soldiers led Jesus away into the palace (that is, the Praetorium) and called together the whole company of soldiers. [17]They put a purple robe on him, then twisted together a crown of thorns and set it on him. [18]And they began to call out to him, "Hail, king of the Jews!"

[19]Again and again they struck him on the head with a staff and spit on him. Falling on their knees, they paid homage to him. [20]And when they had mocked him, they took off the purple robe and put his own clothes on him. Then they led him out to crucify him.

The Crucifixion

[21]A certain man from Cyrene, Simon, the father of Alexander and Rufus, was passing by on his way in from the country, and they forced him to carry the cross. [22]They brought Jesus to the place called Golgotha (which means The Place of the Skull). [23]Then they offered him wine mixed with myrrh, but he did not take it. [24]And they crucified him. Dividing up his clothes, they cast lots to see what each would get.

[25]It was the third hour when they crucified him. [26]The written notice of the charge against him read: THE KING OF THE JEWS. [27]They crucified two robbers with him, one on his right and one on his left.[b] [29]Those who passed by hurled insults at him, shaking their heads and saying, "So! You who are going to destroy the temple and build it in three days, [30]come down from the cross and save yourself!"

[31]In the same way the chief priests and the teachers of the law mocked him among themselves. "He saved others," they said, "but he can't save himself! [32]Let this Christ,[c] this King of Israel, come down now from the cross, that we may see and believe." Those crucified with him also heaped insults on him.

The Death of Jesus

[33]At the sixth hour darkness came over the whole land until the ninth hour. [34]And at the ninth hour Jesus cried out in a loud voice, *"Eloi, Eloi, lama sabachthani?"*—which means, "My God, my God, why have you forsaken me?"[d]

[35]When some of those standing near heard this, they said, "Listen, he's calling Elijah."

[36]One man ran, filled a sponge with wine vinegar, put it on a stick, and offered it to Jesus to drink. "Now leave him alone. Let's see if Elijah comes to take him down," he said.

[37]With a loud cry, Jesus breathed his last.

---

a72 Some early manuscripts do not have twice.   b27 Some manuscripts left, 28and the scripture was fulfilled which says, "He was counted with the lawless ones" (Isaiah 53:12)   c32 Or Messiah   d34 Psalm 22:1

³⁸The curtain of the temple was torn in two from top to bottom. ³⁹And when the centurion, who stood there in front of Jesus, heard his cry and^a saw how he died, he said, "Surely this man was the Son^b of God!"

⁴⁰Some women were watching from a distance. Among them were Mary Magdalene, Mary the mother of James the younger and of Joses, and Salome. ⁴¹In Galilee these women had followed him and cared for his needs. Many other women who had come up with him to Jerusalem were also there.

The Burial of Jesus

⁴²It was Preparation Day (that is, the day before the Sabbath). So as evening approached, ⁴³Joseph of Arimathea, a prominent member of the Council, who was himself waiting for the kingdom of God, went boldly to Pilate and asked for Jesus' body. ⁴⁴Pilate was surprised to hear that he was already dead. Summoning the centurion, he asked him if Jesus had already died. ⁴⁵When he learned from the centurion that it was so, he gave the body to Joseph. ⁴⁶So Joseph bought some linen cloth, took down the body, wrapped it in the linen, and placed it in a tomb cut out of rock. Then he rolled a stone against the entrance of the tomb. ⁴⁷Mary Magdalene and Mary the mother of Joses saw where he was laid.

The Resurrection

16 When the Sabbath was over, Mary Magdalene, Mary the mother of James, and Salome bought spices so that they might go to anoint Jesus' body. ²Very early on the first day of the week, just after sunrise, they were on their way to the tomb ³and they asked each other,

---

^a39 Some manuscripts do not have *heard his cry and*   ^b39 Or *a son*

THURSDAY

VERSE FOR THE DAY:
Mark 15:18

AUTHOR:
Anne Ortlund

PASSAGE FOR THE DAY:
Mark 15:16–37

Ponderings of the Praetorium

O CHRIST, the crown of death was on Thy brow,
And in Thine eyes deep mystery and pain;
The Kingdom seemed forgotten then—but now,
    Lord, take Thy crown and reign!

O Christ, with what derision did they bow
And mock Thee, stripped of robings and of throne;
And hatred seemed to win the day—but now,
    Lord, reign, and reign alone!

O Jesus, when I think of Peter's vow,
I wonder: might I curse Thee and depart?
Hold fast my consecration here and now;
    Lord, reign within my heart!

Additional Scripture Readings:
Philippians 2:8–11; Hebrews 12:2–3

Go to page 1100 for your next devotional reading.

"Who will roll the stone away from the entrance of the tomb?"

⁴But when they looked up, they saw that the stone, which was very large, had been rolled away. ⁵As they entered the tomb, they saw a young man dressed in a white robe sitting on the right side, and they were alarmed.

⁶"Don't be alarmed," he said. "You are looking for Jesus the Nazarene, who was crucified. He has risen! He is not here. See the place where they laid him. ⁷But go, tell his disciples and Peter, 'He is going ahead of you into Galilee. There you will see him, just as he told you.' "

⁸Trembling and bewildered, the women went out and fled from the tomb. They said nothing to anyone, because they were afraid.

[The earliest manuscripts and some other ancient witnesses do not have Mark 16:9–20.]

⁹When Jesus rose early on the first day of the week, he appeared first to Mary Magdalene, out of whom he had driven seven demons. ¹⁰She went and told those who had been with him and who were mourning and weeping. ¹¹When they heard that Jesus was alive and that she had seen him, they did not believe it.

¹²Afterward Jesus appeared in a different form to two of them while they were walking in the country. ¹³These returned and reported it to the rest; but they did not believe them either.

¹⁴Later Jesus appeared to the Eleven as they were eating; he rebuked them for their lack of faith and their stubborn refusal to believe those who had seen him after he had risen.

¹⁵He said to them, "Go into all the world and preach the good news to all creation. ¹⁶Whoever believes and is baptized will be saved, but whoever does not believe will be condemned. ¹⁷And these signs will accompany those who believe: In my name they will drive out demons; they will speak in new tongues; ¹⁸they will pick up snakes with their hands; and when they drink deadly poison, it will not hurt them at all; they will place their hands on sick people, and they will get well."

¹⁹After the Lord Jesus had spoken to them, he was taken up into heaven and he sat at the right hand of God. ²⁰Then the disciples went out and preached everywhere, and the Lord worked with them and confirmed his word by the signs that accompanied it.

*L*UKE writes this gospel to present Jesus as a Savior for the whole human race. The stories emphasize how kind and loving Jesus is to those despised by society (such as tax collectors, Samaritans, the poor, and women). He stresses the importance of prayer in Jesus' life. As you read this book, be sure that you have repented of your sins and have claimed Jesus as your own personal Savior. Ask yourself whether you show the same sort of compassion to others that Jesus showed.

LUKE

Introduction

1 Many have undertaken to draw up an account of the things that have been fulfilled*ᵃ* among us, ²just as they were handed down to us by those who from the first were eyewitnesses and servants of the word. ³Therefore, since I myself have carefully investigated everything from the beginning, it seemed good also to me to write an orderly account for you, most excellent Theophilus, ⁴so that you may know the certainty of the things you have been taught.

The Birth of John the Baptist Foretold

⁵In the time of Herod king of Judea there was a priest named Zechariah, who belonged to the priestly division of Abijah; his wife Elizabeth was also a descendant of Aaron. ⁶Both of them were upright in the sight of God, observing all the Lord's commandments and regulations blamelessly. ⁷But they had no children, because Elizabeth was barren; and they were both well along in years.

⁸Once when Zechariah's division was

on duty and he was serving as priest before God, ⁹he was chosen by lot, according to the custom of the priesthood, to go into the temple of the Lord and burn incense. ¹⁰And when the time for the burning of incense came, all the assembled worshipers were praying outside.

¹¹Then an angel of the Lord appeared to him, standing at the right side of the altar of incense. ¹²When Zechariah saw him, he was startled and was gripped with fear. ¹³But the angel said to him: "Do not be afraid, Zechariah; your prayer has been heard. Your wife Elizabeth will bear you a son, and you are to give him the name John. ¹⁴He will be a joy and delight to you, and many will rejoice because of his birth, ¹⁵for he will be great in the sight of the Lord. He is never to take wine or other fermented drink, and he will be filled with the Holy Spirit even from birth.^a ¹⁶Many of the people of Israel will he bring back to the Lord their God. ¹⁷And he will go on before the Lord, in the spirit and power of Elijah, to turn the hearts of the fathers to their children and the disobedient to the wisdom of the righteous —to make ready a people prepared for the Lord."

¹⁸Zechariah asked the angel, "How can I be sure of this? I am an old man and my wife is well along in years."

¹⁹The angel answered, "I am Gabriel. I stand in the presence of God, and I have been sent to speak to you and to tell you this good news. ²⁰And now you will be silent and not able to speak until the day this happens, because you did not believe my words, which will come true at their proper time."

²¹Meanwhile, the people were waiting for Zechariah and wondering why he stayed so long in the temple. ²²When he came out, he could not speak to them. They realized he had seen a vision in the temple, for he kept making signs to them but remained unable to speak.

²³When his time of service was completed, he returned home. ²⁴After this his wife Elizabeth became pregnant and for five months remained in seclusion. ²⁵"The Lord has done this for me," she said. "In these days he has shown his favor and taken away my disgrace among the people."

The Birth of Jesus Foretold

²⁶In the sixth month, God sent the angel Gabriel to Nazareth, a town in Galilee, ²⁷to a virgin pledged to be married to a man named Joseph, a descendant of David. The virgin's name was Mary. ²⁸The angel went to her and said, "Greetings, you who are highly favored! The Lord is with you."

²⁹Mary was greatly troubled at his words and wondered what kind of greeting this might be. ³⁰But the angel said to her, "Do not be afraid, Mary, you have found favor with God. ³¹You will be with child and give birth to a son, and you are to give him the name Jesus. ³²He will be great and will be called the Son of the Most High. The Lord God will give him the throne of his father David, ³³and he will reign over the house of Jacob forever; his kingdom will never end."

³⁴"How will this be," Mary asked the angel, "since I am a virgin?"

³⁵The angel answered, "The Holy Spirit will come upon you, and the power of the Most High will overshadow you. So the holy one to be born will be called^b the Son of God. ³⁶Even Elizabeth your relative is going to have a child in her old age, and she who was said to be barren is in her sixth month. ³⁷For nothing is impossible with God."

³⁸"I am the Lord's servant," Mary answered. "May it be to me as you have said." Then the angel left her.

Mary Visits Elizabeth

³⁹At that time Mary got ready and hurried to a town in the hill country of Judea, ⁴⁰where she entered Zechariah's home and greeted Elizabeth. ⁴¹When Elizabeth heard Mary's greeting, the baby leaped in her womb, and Elizabeth was filled with the Holy Spirit. ⁴²In a loud voice she exclaimed: "Blessed are you among women, and blessed is the child you will bear! ⁴³But why am I so favored, that the mother of my Lord should come to me? ⁴⁴As soon as the sound of your greeting reached my ears, the baby in my womb leaped for joy. ⁴⁵Blessed is she who has believed that what the Lord has said to her will be accomplished!"

Mary's Song

⁴⁶And Mary said:

"My soul glorifies the Lord
⁴⁷ and my spirit rejoices in God my
      Savior,

---

^a15 Or *from his mother's womb*   ^b35 Or *So the child to be born will be called holy,*

VERSE FOR THE DAY:
Luke 1:46–47

AUTHOR:
Anne Ortlund

PASSAGE FOR THE DAY:
Luke 1:26–38

Incarnation

"THE Lord is in His holy house"—
Oh, grace beyond describing,
That Christ in me should please to dwell—
Immanuel residing!
"My soul doth magnify the Lord,"
I sing with lowly Mary,
That God should choose to enter in
This
humble sanctuary!

Not now in little Bethlehem,
As in the tender story;
Not now upon a mercy seat,
The bright *Shekinah* glory,
But in the body of His saint
He maketh His residing,
Both He in me and I in Him
In
fellowship abiding.

Within my heart a burning bush,
Within, a mountain smoking;
This flesh of mine a temple veil,
The wondrous Presence cloaking;
Within this broken earthenware
A high and holy treasure:
Oh, mystery of mysteries!
Oh, grace
beyond all measure!

"The Lord is in His Holy house"—
Mysterious habitation!
I feel His presence here within
And offer my oblation.
Keep burning, incense of my soul,
Keep cleansing me, O Laver!
I want to serve and praise my God
Forever
and forever!

Additional Scripture Readings:
John 14:23–27; 2 Corinthians 1:21–22

*Go to page 1102 for your next
devotional reading.*

48for he has been mindful
of the humble state of his servant.
From now on all generations will call
me blessed,
49 for the Mighty One has done great
things for me—
holy is his name.
50His mercy extends to those who fear
him,
from generation to generation.
51He has performed mighty deeds with
his arm;
he has scattered those who are
proud in their inmost thoughts.
52He has brought down rulers from
their thrones
but has lifted up the humble.
53He has filled the hungry with good
things
but has sent the rich away empty.
54He has helped his servant Israel,
remembering to be merciful
55to Abraham and his descendants
forever,
even as he said to our fathers."

56Mary stayed with Elizabeth for about
three months and then returned home.

The Birth of John the Baptist

57When it was time for Elizabeth to
have her baby, she gave birth to a son.
58Her neighbors and relatives heard that
the Lord had shown her great mercy, and
they shared her joy.

59On the eighth day they came to circumcise the child, and they were going to
name him after his father Zechariah,
60but his mother spoke up and said, "No!
He is to be called John."

61They said to her, "There is no one
among your relatives who has that
name."

62Then they made signs to his father, to
find out what he would like to name the
child. 63He asked for a writing tablet, and
to everyone's astonishment he wrote,
"His name is John." 64Immediately his
mouth was opened and his tongue was
loosed, and he began to speak, praising
God. 65The neighbors were all filled with
awe, and throughout the hill country of
Judea people were talking about all these
things. 66Everyone who heard this wondered about it, asking, "What then is this
child going to be?" For the Lord's hand
was with him.

Zechariah's Song

67His father Zechariah was filled with
the Holy Spirit and prophesied:

68"Praise be to the Lord, the God of
Israel,
because he has come and has
redeemed his people.
69He has raised up a horn[a] of salvation
for us
in the house of his servant David
70(as he said through his holy prophets
of long ago),
71salvation from our enemies
and from the hand of all who hate
us—
72to show mercy to our fathers
and to remember his holy covenant,
73 the oath he swore to our father
Abraham:
74to rescue us from the hand of our
enemies,
and to enable us to serve him
without fear
75 in holiness and righteousness
before him all our days.

76And you, my child, will be called a
prophet of the Most High;
for you will go on before the Lord
to prepare the way for him,
77to give his people the knowledge of
salvation
through the forgiveness of their
sins,
78because of the tender mercy of our
God,
by which the rising sun will come
to us from heaven
79to shine on those living in darkness
and in the shadow of death,
to guide our feet into the path of
peace."

80And the child grew and became
strong in spirit; and he lived in the desert
until he appeared publicly to Israel.

The Birth of Jesus

2 In those days Caesar Augustus issued
a decree that a census should be tak-
en of the entire Roman world. 2(This was
the first census that took place while Qui-
rinius was governor of Syria.) 3And everyone went to his own town to register.

4So Joseph also went up from the town
of Nazareth in Galilee to Judea, to Bethlehem the town of David, because he be-

---

a69 Horn here symbolizes strength.

WEEKENDING

REFLECT

The hard thing to understand is that faith is the
one area in our lives where growing up means
we must grow to be more like a child, trusting
simply in the goodness and complete knowledge
of a Father who has our best interests at heart.

— *Colleen Townsend Evans*

REVIVE

Saturday: Mark 10:13–16
Sunday: Hebrews 11:5–6

Go to page 1105 for your next devotional reading.

longed to the house and line of David. ⁵He went there to register with Mary, who was pledged to be married to him and was expecting a child. ⁶While they were there, the time came for the baby to be born, ⁷and she gave birth to her firstborn, a son. She wrapped him in cloths and placed him in a manger, because there was no room for them in the inn.

The Shepherds and the Angels

⁸And there were shepherds living out in the fields nearby, keeping watch over their flocks at night. ⁹An angel of the Lord appeared to them, and the glory of the Lord shone around them, and they were terrified. ¹⁰But the angel said to them, "Do not be afraid. I bring you good news of great joy that will be for all the people. ¹¹Today in the town of David a Savior has been born to you; he is Christ[a] the Lord. ¹²This will be a sign to you: You will find a baby wrapped in cloths and lying in a manger."

¹³Suddenly a great company of the heavenly host appeared with the angel, praising God and saying,

¹⁴"Glory to God in the highest,
and on earth peace to men on
    whom his favor rests."

¹⁵When the angels had left them and gone into heaven, the shepherds said to one another, "Let's go to Bethlehem and see this thing that has happened, which the Lord has told us about."

¹⁶So they hurried off and found Mary and Joseph, and the baby, who was lying in the manger. ¹⁷When they had seen him, they spread the word concerning what had been told them about this child, ¹⁸and all who heard it were amazed at what the shepherds said to them. ¹⁹But Mary treasured up all these things and pondered them in her heart. ²⁰The shepherds returned, glorifying and praising God for all the things they had heard and seen, which were just as they had been told.

Jesus Presented in the Temple

²¹On the eighth day, when it was time to circumcise him, he was named Jesus, the name the angel had given him before he had been conceived.

²²When the time of their purification according to the Law of Moses had been completed, Joseph and Mary took him to Jerusalem to present him to the Lord ²³(as it is written in the Law of the Lord, "Every firstborn male is to be consecrated to the Lord"[b]), ²⁴and to offer a sacrifice in keeping with what is said in the Law of the Lord: "a pair of doves or two young pigeons."[c]

²⁵Now there was a man in Jerusalem called Simeon, who was righteous and devout. He was waiting for the consolation of Israel, and the Holy Spirit was upon him. ²⁶It had been revealed to him by the Holy Spirit that he would not die before he had seen the Lord's Christ. ²⁷Moved by the Spirit, he went into the temple courts. When the parents brought in the child Jesus to do for him what the custom of the Law required, ²⁸Simeon took him in his arms and praised God, saying:

²⁹"Sovereign Lord, as you have
    promised,
you now dismiss[d] your servant in
    peace.
³⁰For my eyes have seen your salvation,
³¹ which you have prepared in the
    sight of all people,
³²a light for revelation to the Gentiles
    and for glory to your people Israel."

³³The child's father and mother marveled at what was said about him. ³⁴Then Simeon blessed them and said to Mary, his mother: "This child is destined to cause the falling and rising of many in Israel, and to be a sign that will be spoken against, ³⁵so that the thoughts of many hearts will be revealed. And a sword will pierce your own soul too."

³⁶There was also a prophetess, Anna, the daughter of Phanuel, of the tribe of Asher. She was very old; she had lived with her husband seven years after her marriage, ³⁷and then was a widow until she was eighty-four.[e] She never left the temple but worshiped night and day, fasting and praying. ³⁸Coming up to them at that very moment, she gave thanks to God and spoke about the child to all who were looking forward to the redemption of Jerusalem.

³⁹When Joseph and Mary had done everything required by the Law of the Lord, they returned to Galilee to their own town of Nazareth. ⁴⁰And the child grew

---

a11 Or Messiah. "The Christ" (Greek) and "the Messiah" (Hebrew) both mean "the Anointed One"; also in verse 26.   b23 Exodus 13:2,12   c24 Lev. 12:8   d29 Or promised, / now dismiss   e37 Or widow for eighty-four years and became strong; he was filled with wisdom, and the grace of God was upon him.

The Boy Jesus at the Temple

⁴¹Every year his parents went to Jerusalem for the Feast of the Passover. ⁴²When he was twelve years old, they went up to the Feast, according to the custom. ⁴³After the Feast was over, while his parents were returning home, the boy Jesus stayed behind in Jerusalem, but they were unaware of it. ⁴⁴Thinking he was in their company, they traveled on for a day. Then they began looking for him among their relatives and friends. ⁴⁵When they did not find him, they went back to Jerusalem to look for him. ⁴⁶After three days they found him in the temple courts, sitting among the teachers, listening to them and asking them questions. ⁴⁷Everyone who heard him was amazed at his understanding and his answers. ⁴⁸When his parents saw him, they were astonished. His mother said to him, "Son, why have you treated us like this? Your father and I have been anxiously searching for you."

⁴⁹"Why were you searching for me?" he asked. "Didn't you know I had to be in my Father's house?" ⁵⁰But they did not understand what he was saying to them.

⁵¹Then he went down to Nazareth with them and was obedient to them. But his mother treasured all these things in her heart. ⁵²And Jesus grew in wisdom and stature, and in favor with God and men.

John the Baptist Prepares the Way

3 In the fifteenth year of the reign of Tiberius Caesar—when Pontius Pilate was governor of Judea, Herod tetrarch of Galilee, his brother Philip tetrarch of Iturea and Traconitis, and Lysanias tetrarch of Abilene— ²during the high priesthood of Annas and Caiaphas, the word of God came to John son of Zechariah in the desert. ³He went into all the country around the Jordan, preaching a baptism of repentance for the forgiveness of sins. ⁴As is written in the book of the words of Isaiah the prophet:

"A voice of one calling in the desert,
'Prepare the way for the Lord,
    make straight paths for him.
⁵Every valley shall be filled in,
    every mountain and hill made low.

The crooked roads shall become
    straight,
    the rough ways smooth.
⁶And all mankind will see God's
    salvation.' "ᵃ

⁷John said to the crowds coming out to be baptized by him, "You brood of vipers! Who warned you to flee from the coming wrath? ⁸Produce fruit in keeping with repentance. And do not begin to say to yourselves, 'We have Abraham as our father.' For I tell you that out of these stones God can raise up children for Abraham. ⁹The ax is already at the root of the trees, and every tree that does not produce good fruit will be cut down and thrown into the fire."

¹⁰"What should we do then?" the crowd asked.

¹¹John answered, "The man with two tunics should share with him who has none, and the one who has food should do the same."

¹²Tax collectors also came to be baptized. "Teacher," they asked, "what should we do?"

¹³"Don't collect any more than you are required to," he told them.

¹⁴Then some soldiers asked him, "And what should we do?"

He replied, "Don't extort money and don't accuse people falsely—be content with your pay."

¹⁵The people were waiting expectantly and were all wondering in their hearts if John might possibly be the Christ.ᵇ ¹⁶John answered them all, "I baptize you withᶜ water. But one more powerful than I will come, the thongs of whose sandals I am not worthy to untie. He will baptize you with the Holy Spirit and with fire. ¹⁷His winnowing fork is in his hand to clear his threshing floor and to gather the wheat into his barn, but he will burn up the chaff with unquenchable fire." ¹⁸And with many other words John exhorted the people and preached the good news to them.

¹⁹But when John rebuked Herod the tetrarch because of Herodias, his brother's wife, and all the other evil things he had done, ²⁰Herod added this to them all: He locked John up in prison.

The Baptism and Genealogy of Jesus

²¹When all the people were being baptized, Jesus was baptized too. And as he

ᵃ6 Isaiah 40:3-5   ᵇ15 Or Messiah   ᶜ16 Or in

VERSE FOR THE DAY:
Luke 2:52

AUTHOR:
Rosemary Jensen

PASSAGE FOR THE DAY:
Luke 2:41–52

Growing in Wisdom

IN Luke 2:52 we learn that "Jesus grew in wisdom and stature, and in favor with God and men." It is not difficult to understand how Jesus grew in stature—he just got taller! But how could the Son of God grow in wisdom? Did he not already have all wisdom? Did he lack anything? Was he not perfect? Yes, he was filled with wisdom—as much wisdom as a child without life experience can have.

It may help to remember that a few ounces of milk can fill an infant boy, but it would take a few quarts to fill a teenage boy. The difference is that the teenager has increased his capacity for milk. As Jesus grew physically, he also grew in his capacity for wisdom as he learned from his experiences. What is our individual capacity for wisdom? Could we increase that capacity?

Wisdom comes when we examine the experiences God gives us and discern what we have (or should have) learned from them. Nothing that has happened to us should be wasted (Romans 8:28). Because it is sometimes painful, often we do not take the time or effort to discover the reason for the "gift" of our personal experiences. When we do not learn as we should, we stop growing until we learn those same lessons through another experience tailor-made by God to make us mature (James 1:2–4). Most often we gain insight into our experiences only after earnest, persistent prayer. Psalm 43 is a wonderful model of persistent prayer; it opens up to us a person searching to know what God wants to reveal about a specific experience.

Perhaps we should try writing out what we have learned about God, ourselves and life during and then after an important experience. As we learn these lessons, I think we'll find that we will not need to learn them again in exactly the same way! This increases our individual capacity to learn greater lessons and gain deeper wisdom (Matthew 13:12).

Additional Scripture Readings:
1 Corinthians 13:11–12; James 1:22–25

Go to page 1109 for your next devotional reading.

was praying, heaven was opened 22and the Holy Spirit descended on him in bodily form like a dove. And a voice came from heaven: "You are my Son, whom I love; with you I am well pleased."

23Now Jesus himself was about thirty years old when he began his ministry. He was the son, so it was thought, of Joseph,

the son of Heli, 24the son of Matthat,
the son of Levi, the son of Melki,
the son of Jannai, the son of Joseph,
25the son of Mattathias, the son of Amos,
the son of Nahum, the son of Esli,
the son of Naggai, 26the son of Maath,
the son of Mattathias, the son of Semein,
the son of Josech, the son of Joda,
27the son of Joanan, the son of Rhesa,
the son of Zerubbabel, the son of Shealtiel,
the son of Neri, 28the son of Melki,
the son of Addi, the son of Cosam,
the son of Elmadam, the son of Er,
29the son of Joshua, the son of Eliezer,
the son of Jorim, the son of Matthat,
the son of Levi, 30the son of Simeon,
the son of Judah, the son of Joseph,
the son of Jonam, the son of Eliakim,
31the son of Melea, the son of Menna,
the son of Mattatha, the son of Nathan,
the son of David, 32the son of Jesse,
the son of Obed, the son of Boaz,
the son of Salmon,ᵃ the son of Nahshon,
33the son of Amminadab, the son of Ram,ᵇ
the son of Hezron, the son of Perez,
the son of Judah, 34the son of Jacob,
the son of Isaac, the son of Abraham,
the son of Terah, the son of Nahor,
35the son of Serug, the son of Reu,
the son of Peleg, the son of Eber,
the son of Shelah, 36the son of Cainan,
the son of Arphaxad, the son of Shem,
the son of Noah, the son of Lamech,
37the son of Methuselah, the son of Enoch,
the son of Jared, the son of Mahalalel,
the son of Kenan, 38the son of Enosh,

the son of Seth, the son of Adam,
the son of God.

The Temptation of Jesus

4 Jesus, full of the Holy Spirit, returned from the Jordan and was led by the Spirit in the desert, 2where for forty days he was tempted by the devil. He ate nothing during those days, and at the end of them he was hungry.

3The devil said to him, "If you are the Son of God, tell this stone to become bread."

4Jesus answered, "It is written: 'Man does not live on bread alone.'ᶜ"

5The devil led him up to a high place and showed him in an instant all the kingdoms of the world. 6And he said to him, "I will give you all their authority and splendor, for it has been given to me, and I can give it to anyone I want to. 7So if you worship me, it will all be yours."

8Jesus answered, "It is written: 'Worship the Lord your God and serve him only.'ᵈ"

9The devil led him to Jerusalem and had him stand on the highest point of the temple. "If you are the Son of God," he said, "throw yourself down from here. 10For it is written:

" 'He will command his angels
   concerning you
to guard you carefully;
11they will lift you up in their hands,
   so that you will not strike your foot
   against a stone.'ᵉ"

12Jesus answered, "It says: 'Do not put the Lord your God to the test.'ᶠ"

13When the devil had finished all this tempting, he left him until an opportune time.

Jesus Rejected at Nazareth

14Jesus returned to Galilee in the power of the Spirit, and news about him spread through the whole countryside. 15He taught in their synagogues, and everyone praised him.

16He went to Nazareth, where he had been brought up, and on the Sabbath day he went into the synagogue, as was his custom. And he stood up to read. 17The scroll of the prophet Isaiah was handed to him. Unrolling it, he found the place where it is written:

18"The Spirit of the Lord is on me,

ᵃ32 Some early manuscripts *Sala*   ᵇ33 Some manuscripts *Amminadab, the son of Admin, the son of Arni*; other manuscripts vary widely.   ᶜ4 Deut. 8:3   ᵈ8 Deut. 6:13   ᵉ11 Psalm 91:11,12   ᶠ12 Deut. 6:16

because he has anointed me
   to preach good news to the poor.
He has sent me to proclaim freedom
   for the prisoners
and recovery of sight for the blind,
   to release the oppressed,
¹⁹   to proclaim the year of the Lord's
      favor."ᵃ

²⁰Then he rolled up the scroll, gave it back to the attendant and sat down. The eyes of everyone in the synagogue were fastened on him, ²¹and he began by saying to them, "Today this scripture is fulfilled in your hearing."

²²All spoke well of him and were amazed at the gracious words that came from his lips. "Isn't this Joseph's son?" they asked.

²³Jesus said to them, "Surely you will quote this proverb to me: 'Physician, heal yourself! Do here in your hometown what we have heard that you did in Capernaum.'"

²⁴"I tell you the truth," he continued, "no prophet is accepted in his hometown. ²⁵I assure you that there were many widows in Israel in Elijah's time, when the sky was shut for three and a half years and there was a severe famine throughout the land. ²⁶Yet Elijah was not sent to any of them, but to a widow in Zarephath in the region of Sidon. ²⁷And there were many in Israel with leprosyᵇ in the time of Elisha the prophet, yet not one of them was cleansed—only Naaman the Syrian."

²⁸All the people in the synagogue were furious when they heard this. ²⁹They got up, drove him out of the town, and took him to the brow of the hill on which the town was built, in order to throw him down the cliff. ³⁰But he walked right through the crowd and went on his way.

Jesus Drives Out an Evil Spirit

³¹Then he went down to Capernaum, a town in Galilee, and on the Sabbath began to teach the people. ³²They were amazed at his teaching, because his message had authority.

³³In the synagogue there was a man possessed by a demon, an evilᶜ spirit. He cried out at the top of his voice, ³⁴"Ha! What do you want with us, Jesus of Nazareth? Have you come to destroy us? I know who you are—the Holy One of God!"

³⁵"Be quiet!" Jesus said sternly. "Come out of him!" Then the demon threw the man down before them all and came out without injuring him.

³⁶All the people were amazed and said to each other, "What is this teaching? With authority and power he gives orders to evil spirits and they come out!" ³⁷And the news about him spread throughout the surrounding area.

Jesus Heals Many

³⁸Jesus left the synagogue and went to the home of Simon. Now Simon's mother-in-law was suffering from a high fever, and they asked Jesus to help her. ³⁹So he bent over her and rebuked the fever, and it left her. She got up at once and began to wait on them.

⁴⁰When the sun was setting, the people brought to Jesus all who had various kinds of sickness, and laying his hands on each one, he healed them. ⁴¹Moreover, demons came out of many people, shouting, "You are the Son of God!" But he rebuked them and would not allow them to speak, because they knew he was the Christ.ᵈ

⁴²At daybreak Jesus went out to a solitary place. The people were looking for him and when they came to where he was, they tried to keep him from leaving them. ⁴³But he said, I must preach the good news of the kingdom of God to the other towns also, because that is why I was sent." ⁴⁴And he kept on preaching in the synagogues of Judea.ᵉ

The Calling of the First Disciples

5 One day as Jesus was standing by the Lake of Gennesaret,ᶠ with the people crowding around him and listening to the word of God, ²he saw at the water's edge two boats, left there by the fishermen, who were washing their nets. ³He got into one of the boats, the one belonging to Simon, and asked him to put out a little from shore. Then he sat down and taught the people from the boat.

⁴When he had finished speaking, he said to Simon, "Put out into deep water, and let downᵍ the nets for a catch."

⁵Simon answered, "Master, we've worked hard all night and haven't caught anything. But because you say so, I will let down the nets."

ᵃ19 Isaiah 61:1,2   ᵇ27 The Greek word was used for various diseases affecting the skin—not necessarily leprosy.   ᶜ33 Greek *unclean*; also in verse 36   ᵈ41 Or *Messiah*   ᵉ44 Or *the land of the Jews*; some manuscripts *Galilee*   ᶠ1 That is, Sea of Galilee   ᵍ4 The Greek verb is plural.

6When they had done so, they caught such a large number of fish that their nets began to break. 7So they signaled their partners in the other boat to come and help them, and they came and filled both boats so full that they began to sink.

8When Simon Peter saw this, he fell at Jesus' knees and said, "Go away from me, Lord; I am a sinful man!" 9For he and all his companions were astonished at the catch of fish they had taken, 10and so were James and John, the sons of Zebedee, Simon's partners.

Then Jesus said to Simon, "Don't be afraid; from now on you will catch men." 11So they pulled their boats up on shore, left everything and followed him.

The Man With Leprosy

12While Jesus was in one of the towns, a man came along who was covered with leprosy.a When he saw Jesus, he fell with his face to the ground and begged him, "Lord, if you are willing, you can make me clean."

13Jesus reached out his hand and touched the man. "I am willing," he said. "Be clean!" And immediately the leprosy left him.

14Then Jesus ordered him, "Don't tell anyone, but go, show yourself to the priest and offer the sacrifices that Moses commanded for your cleansing, as a testimony to them."

15Yet the news about him spread all the more, so that crowds of people came to hear him and to be healed of their sicknesses. 16But Jesus often withdrew to lonely places and prayed.

Jesus Heals a Paralytic

17One day as he was teaching, Pharisees and teachers of the law, who had come from every village of Galilee and from Judea and Jerusalem, were sitting there. And the power of the Lord was present for him to heal the sick. 18Some men came carrying a paralytic on a mat and tried to take him into the house to lay him before Jesus. 19When they could not find a way to do this because of the crowd, they went up on the roof and lowered him on his mat through the tiles into the middle of the crowd, right in front of Jesus.

20When Jesus saw their faith, he said, "Friend, your sins are forgiven."

21The Pharisees and the teachers of the law began thinking to themselves, "Who is this fellow who speaks blasphemy? Who can forgive sins but God alone?"

22Jesus knew what they were thinking and asked, "Why are you thinking these things in your hearts? 23Which is easier: to say, 'Your sins are forgiven,' or to say, 'Get up and walk'? 24But that you may know that the Son of Man has authority on earth to forgive sins. . . ." He said to the paralyzed man, "I tell you, get up, take your mat and go home." 25Immediately he stood up in front of them, took what he had been lying on and went home praising God. 26Everyone was amazed and gave praise to God. They were filled with awe and said, "We have seen remarkable things today."

The Calling of Levi

27After this, Jesus went out and saw a tax collector by the name of Levi sitting at his tax booth. "Follow me," Jesus said to him, 28and Levi got up, left everything and followed him.

29Then Levi held a great banquet for Jesus at his house, and a large crowd of tax collectors and others were eating with them. 30But the Pharisees and the teachers of the law who belonged to their sect complained to his disciples, "Why do you eat and drink with tax collectors and 'sinners'?"

31Jesus answered them, "It is not the healthy who need a doctor, but the sick. 32I have not come to call the righteous, but sinners to repentance."

Jesus Questioned About Fasting

33They said to him, "John's disciples often fast and pray, and so do the disciples of the Pharisees, but yours go on eating and drinking."

34Jesus answered, "Can you make the guests of the bridegroom fast while he is with them? 35But the time will come when the bridegroom will be taken from them; in those days they will fast."

36He told them this parable: "No one tears a patch from a new garment and sews it on an old one. If he does, he will have torn the new garment, and the patch from the new will not match the old. 37And no one pours new wine into old wineskins. If he does, the new wine will burst the skins, the wine will run out and the wineskins will be ruined. 38No, new wine must be poured into new wineskins.

---

a12 The Greek word was used for various diseases affecting the skin—not necessarily leprosy.

VERSE FOR THE DAY:	AUTHOR:	PASSAGE FOR THE DAY:
Luke 5:16	*Gini Andrews*	*Luke 5:12–16*

Loneliness

LIKE fatigue, like hunger, loneliness is part of being human. Fatigue is cured by sleep and hunger by eating, but how do we handle loneliness? It's our very nature to seek an alter ego, a heart that responds to our human ache for understanding.

Our favorite women of the Bible were no strangers to periods of aloneness, which, interestingly, often presaged important events: Mary, during her pregnancy; Ruth, bereaved in Moab; Esther, in a pagan harem; Hannah, childless for years in a culture where barrenness was a disgrace.

In his crowded adult life, there were times when Jesus chose to be alone, deliberately making himself unavailable so that he might nourish his soul in communion with his Father. He experienced both isolation and alienation. His query to his disciples when the fawning crowds drifted off, "Will you also go away?" and his Gethsemane "Watch with me"—these are lonely words.

Yet even Jesus did not use his relationship with God as a substitute for human companionship. He found sustenance with his three closest disciples—Peter, James and John—and in the home of Mary, Martha and Lazarus.

But even the most congenial marriage, the closest friendship, the most satisfying child-parent relationship is both transient and unpredictable. Although some 1,500 years have passed since St. Augustine remarked that our hearts will never be at rest away from the One who made them, it's still true.

Just because he has created us as unique individuals, our Father knows the best way to fill each one's empty places. It is only God who can fill our deepest longings, who never has an appointment elsewhere, who never replaces us with someone he likes better, who promises never to leave us totally alone. He is the only one who wants to be and always can be the unfailing companion on our journey.

Additional Scripture Readings:
1 Kings 19:1–10; Psalm 27:7–10

Go to page 1117 for your next devotional reading.

³⁹And no one after drinking old wine wants the new, for he says, 'The old is better.' "

Lord of the Sabbath

6 One Sabbath Jesus was going through the grainfields, and his disciples began to pick some heads of grain, rub them in their hands and eat the kernels. ²Some of the Pharisees asked, "Why are you doing what is unlawful on the Sabbath?"

³Jesus answered them, "Have you never read what David did when he and his companions were hungry? ⁴He entered the house of God, and taking the consecrated bread, he ate what is lawful only for priests to eat. And he also gave some to his companions." ⁵Then Jesus said to them, "The Son of Man is Lord of the Sabbath."

⁶On another Sabbath he went into the synagogue and was teaching, and a man was there whose right hand was shriveled. ⁷The Pharisees and the teachers of the law were looking for a reason to accuse Jesus, so they watched him closely to see if he would heal on the Sabbath. ⁸But Jesus knew what they were thinking and said to the man with the shriveled hand, "Get up and stand in front of everyone." So he got up and stood there.

⁹Then Jesus said to them, "I ask you, which is lawful on the Sabbath: to do good or to do evil, to save life or to destroy it?"

¹⁰He looked around at them all, and then said to the man, "Stretch out your hand." He did so, and his hand was completely restored. ¹¹But they were furious and began to discuss with one another what they might do to Jesus.

The Twelve Apostles

¹²One of those days Jesus went out to a mountainside to pray, and spent the night praying to God. ¹³When morning came, he called his disciples to him and chose twelve of them, whom he also designated apostles: ¹⁴Simon (whom he named Peter), his brother Andrew, James, John, Philip, Bartholomew, ¹⁵Matthew, Thomas, James son of Alphaeus, Simon who was called the Zealot, ¹⁶Judas son of James, and Judas Iscariot, who became a traitor.

Blessings and Woes

¹⁷He went down with them and stood on a level place. A large crowd of his disciples was there and a great number of people from all over Judea, from Jerusalem, and from the coast of Tyre and Sidon, ¹⁸who had come to hear him and to be healed of their diseases. Those troubled by evil*ᵃ* spirits were cured, ¹⁹and the people all tried to touch him, because power was coming from him and healing them all.

²⁰Looking at his disciples, he said:

"Blessed are you who are poor,
   for yours is the kingdom of God.
²¹Blessed are you who hunger now,
   for you will be satisfied.
Blessed are you who weep now,
   for you will laugh.
²²Blessed are you when men hate you,
   when they exclude you and insult
     you
   and reject your name as evil,
     because of the Son of Man.

²³"Rejoice in that day and leap for joy, because great is your reward in heaven. For that is how their fathers treated the prophets.

²⁴"But woe to you who are rich,
   for you have already received your
     comfort.
²⁵Woe to you who are well fed now,
   for you will go hungry.
Woe to you who laugh now,
   for you will mourn and weep.
²⁶Woe to you when all men speak well
     of you,
   for that is how their fathers treated
     the false prophets.

Love for Enemies

²⁷"But I tell you who hear me: Love your enemies, do good to those who hate you, ²⁸bless those who curse you, pray for those who mistreat you. ²⁹If someone strikes you on one cheek, turn to him the other also. If someone takes your cloak, do not stop him from taking your tunic. ³⁰Give to everyone who asks you, and if anyone takes what belongs to you, do not demand it back. ³¹Do to others as you would have them do to you.

³²"If you love those who love you, what credit is that to you? Even 'sinners' love those who love them. ³³And if you do good to those who are good to you, what

credit is that to you? Even 'sinners' do that. ³⁴And if you lend to those from whom you expect repayment, what credit is that to you? Even 'sinners' lend to 'sinners,' expecting to be repaid in full. ³⁵But love your enemies, do good to them, and lend to them without expecting to get anything back. Then your reward will be great, and you will be sons of the Most High, because he is kind to the ungrateful and wicked. ³⁶Be merciful, just as your Father is merciful.

Judging Others

³⁷"Do not judge, and you will not be judged. Do not condemn, and you will not be condemned. Forgive, and you will be forgiven. ³⁸Give, and it will be given to you. A good measure, pressed down, shaken together and running over, will be poured into your lap. For with the measure you use, it will be measured to you."

³⁹He also told them this parable: "Can a blind man lead a blind man? Will they not both fall into a pit? ⁴⁰A student is not above his teacher, but everyone who is fully trained will be like his teacher.

⁴¹"Why do you look at the speck of sawdust in your brother's eye and pay no attention to the plank in your own eye? ⁴²How can you say to your brother, 'Brother, let me take the speck out of your eye,' when you yourself fail to see the plank in your own eye? You hypocrite, first take the plank out of your eye, and then you will see clearly to remove the speck from your brother's eye.

A Tree and Its Fruit

⁴³"No good tree bears bad fruit, nor does a bad tree bear good fruit. ⁴⁴Each tree is recognized by its own fruit. People do not pick figs from thornbushes, or grapes from briers. ⁴⁵The good man brings good things out of the good stored up in his heart, and the evil man brings evil things out of the evil stored up in his heart. For out of the overflow of his heart his mouth speaks.

The Wise and Foolish Builders

⁴⁶"Why do you call me, 'Lord, Lord,' and do not do what I say? ⁴⁷I will show you what he is like who comes to me and hears my words and puts them into practice. ⁴⁸He is like a man building a house, who dug down deep and laid the foundation on rock. When a flood came, the torrent struck that house but could not shake it, because it was well built. ⁴⁹But

the one who hears my words and does not put them into practice is like a man who built a house on the ground without a foundation. The moment the torrent struck that house, it collapsed and its destruction was complete."

The Faith of the Centurion

7 When Jesus had finished saying all this in the hearing of the people, he entered Capernaum. ²There a centurion's servant, whom his master valued highly, was sick and about to die. ³The centurion heard of Jesus and sent some elders of the Jews to him, asking him to come and heal his servant. ⁴When they came to Jesus, they pleaded earnestly with him, "This man deserves to have you do this, ⁵because he loves our nation and has built our synagogue." ⁶So Jesus went with them.

He was not far from the house when the centurion sent friends to say to him: "Lord, don't trouble yourself, for I do not deserve to have you come under my roof. ⁷That is why I did not even consider myself worthy to come to you. But say the word, and my servant will be healed. ⁸For I myself am a man under authority, with soldiers under me. I tell this one, 'Go,' and he goes; and that one, 'Come,' and he comes. I say to my servant, 'Do this,' and he does it."

⁹When Jesus heard this, he was amazed at him, and turning to the crowd following him, he said, "I tell you, I have not found such great faith even in Israel." ¹⁰Then the men who had been sent returned to the house and found the servant well.

Jesus Raises a Widow's Son

¹¹Soon afterward, Jesus went to a town called Nain, and his disciples and a large crowd went along with him. ¹²As he approached the town gate, a dead person was being carried out—the only son of his mother, and she was a widow. And a large crowd from the town was with her. ¹³When the Lord saw her, his heart went out to her and he said, "Don't cry."

¹⁴Then he went up and touched the coffin, and those carrying it stood still. He said, "Young man, I say to you, get up!" ¹⁵The dead man sat up and began to talk, and Jesus gave him back to his mother.

¹⁶They were all filled with awe and praised God. "A great prophet has appeared among us," they said. "God has come to help his people." ¹⁷This news

about Jesus spread throughout Judea[a] and the surrounding country.

Jesus and John the Baptist

[18]John's disciples told him about all these things. Calling two of them, [19]he sent them to the Lord to ask, "Are you the one who was to come, or should we expect someone else?"

[20]When the men came to Jesus, they said, "John the Baptist sent us to you to ask, 'Are you the one who was to come, or should we expect someone else?' "

[21]At that very time Jesus cured many who had diseases, sicknesses and evil spirits, and gave sight to many who were blind. [22]So he replied to the messengers, "Go back and report to John what you have seen and heard: The blind receive sight, the lame walk, those who have leprosy[b] are cured, the deaf hear, the dead are raised, and the good news is preached to the poor. [23]Blessed is the man who does not fall away on account of me."

[24]After John's messengers left, Jesus began to speak to the crowd about John: "What did you go out into the desert to see? A reed swayed by the wind? [25]If not, what did you go out to see? A man dressed in fine clothes? No, those who wear expensive clothes and indulge in luxury are in palaces. [26]But what did you go out to see? A prophet? Yes, I tell you, and more than a prophet. [27]This is the one about whom it is written:

" 'I will send my messenger ahead of
    you,
who will prepare your way before
    you.'[c]

[28]I tell you, among those born of women there is no one greater than John; yet the one who is least in the kingdom of God is greater than he."

[29](All the people, even the tax collectors, when they heard Jesus' words, acknowledged that God's way was right, because they had been baptized by John. [30]But the Pharisees and experts in the law rejected God's purpose for themselves, because they had not been baptized by John.)

[31]"To what, then, can I compare the people of this generation? What are they like? [32]They are like children sitting in the marketplace and calling out to each other:

" 'We played the flute for you,
    and you did not dance;
we sang a dirge,
    and you did not cry.'

[33]For John the Baptist came neither eating bread nor drinking wine, and you say, 'He has a demon.' [34]The Son of Man came eating and drinking, and you say, 'Here is a glutton and a drunkard, a friend of tax collectors and "sinners." ' [35]But wisdom is proved right by all her children."

Jesus Anointed by a Sinful Woman

[36]Now one of the Pharisees invited Jesus to have dinner with him, so he went to the Pharisee's house and reclined at the table. [37]When a woman who had lived a sinful life in that town learned that Jesus was eating at the Pharisee's house, she brought an alabaster jar of perfume, [38]and as she stood behind him at his feet weeping, she began to wet his feet with her tears. Then she wiped them with her hair, kissed them and poured perfume on them.

[39]When the Pharisee who had invited him saw this, he said to himself, "If this man were a prophet, he would know who is touching him and what kind of woman she is—that she is a sinner."

[40]Jesus answered him, "Simon, I have something to tell you."

"Tell me, teacher," he said.

[41]"Two men owed money to a certain moneylender. One owed him five hundred denarii,[d] and the other fifty. [42]Neither of them had the money to pay him back, so he canceled the debts of both. Now which of them will love him more?"

[43]Simon replied, "I suppose the one who had the bigger debt canceled."

"You have judged correctly," Jesus said.

[44]Then he turned toward the woman and said to Simon, "Do you see this woman? I came into your house. You did not give me any water for my feet, but she wet my feet with her tears and wiped them with her hair. [45]You did not give me a kiss, but this woman, from the time I entered, has not stopped kissing my feet. [46]You did not put oil on my head, but she has poured perfume on my feet. [47]Therefore, I tell you, her many sins have been forgiven—for she loved much. But he who has been forgiven little loves little."

---

[a]17 Or *the land of the Jews*   [b]22 The Greek word was used for various diseases affecting the skin—not necessarily leprosy.   [c]27 Mal. 3:1   [d]41 A denarius was a coin worth about a day's wages.

⁴⁸Then Jesus said to her, "Your sins are forgiven."

⁴⁹The other guests began to say among themselves, "Who is this who even forgives sins?"

⁵⁰Jesus said to the woman, "Your faith has saved you; go in peace."

The Parable of the Sower

8 After this, Jesus traveled about from one town and village to another, proclaiming the good news of the kingdom of God. The Twelve were with him, ²and also some women who had been cured of evil spirits and diseases: Mary (called Magdalene) from whom seven demons had come out; ³Joanna the wife of Cuza, the manager of Herod's household; Susanna; and many others. These women were helping to support them out of their own means.

⁴While a large crowd was gathering and people were coming to Jesus from town after town, he told this parable: ⁵"A farmer went out to sow his seed. As he was scattering the seed, some fell along the path; it was trampled on, and the birds of the air ate it up. ⁶Some fell on rock, and when it came up, the plants withered because they had no moisture. ⁷Other seed fell among thorns, which grew up with it and choked the plants. ⁸Still other seed fell on good soil. It came up and yielded a crop, a hundred times more than was sown."

When he said this, he called out, "He who has ears to hear, let him hear."

⁹His disciples asked him what this parable meant. ¹⁰He said, "The knowledge of the secrets of the kingdom of God has been given to you, but to others I speak in parables, so that,

" 'though seeing, they may not see;
    though hearing, they may not
        understand.' ᵃ

¹¹"This is the meaning of the parable: The seed is the word of God. ¹²Those along the path are the ones who hear, and then the devil comes and takes away the word from their hearts, so that they may not believe and be saved. ¹³Those on the rock are the ones who receive the word with joy when they hear it, but they have no root. They believe for a while, but in the time of testing they fall away. ¹⁴The seed that fell among thorns stands for those who hear, but as they go on their way they are choked by life's worries, riches and pleasures, and they do not mature. ¹⁵But the seed on good soil stands for those with a noble and good heart, who hear the word, retain it, and by persevering produce a crop.

A Lamp on a Stand

¹⁶"No one lights a lamp and hides it in a jar or puts it under a bed. Instead, he puts it on a stand, so that those who come in can see the light. ¹⁷For there is nothing hidden that will not be disclosed, and nothing concealed that will not be known or brought out into the open. ¹⁸Therefore consider carefully how you listen. Whoever has will be given more; whoever does not have, even what he thinks he has will be taken from him."

Jesus' Mother and Brothers

¹⁹Now Jesus' mother and brothers came to see him, but they were not able to get near him because of the crowd. ²⁰Someone told him, "Your mother and brothers are standing outside, wanting to see you."

²¹He replied, "My mother and brothers are those who hear God's word and put it into practice."

Jesus Calms the Storm

²²One day Jesus said to his disciples, "Let's go over to the other side of the lake." So they got into a boat and set out. ²³As they sailed, he fell asleep. A squall came down on the lake, so that the boat was being swamped, and they were in great danger.

²⁴The disciples went and woke him, saying, "Master, Master, we're going to drown!"

He got up and rebuked the wind and the raging waters; the storm subsided, and all was calm. ²⁵"Where is your faith?" he asked his disciples.

In fear and amazement they asked one another, "Who is this? He commands even the winds and the water, and they obey him."

The Healing of a Demon-possessed Man

²⁶They sailed to the region of the Gerasenes,ᵇ which is across the lake from Galilee. ²⁷When Jesus stepped ashore, he was met by a demon-possessed man from the town. For a long time this man had

ᵃ10 Isaiah 6:9   ᵇ26 Some manuscripts *Gadarenes*; other manuscripts *Gergesenes*; also in verse 37 not worn clothes or lived in a house, but had lived in the tombs. 28When he saw Jesus, he cried out and fell at his feet, shouting at the top of his voice, "What do you want with me, Jesus, Son of the Most High God? I beg you, don't torture me!" 29For Jesus had commanded the evil[a] spirit to come out of the man. Many times it had seized him, and though he was chained hand and foot and kept under guard, he had broken his chains and had been driven by the demon into solitary places.

30Jesus asked him, "What is your name?"

"Legion," he replied, because many demons had gone into him. 31And they begged him repeatedly not to order them to go into the Abyss.

32A large herd of pigs was feeding there on the hillside. The demons begged Jesus to let them go into them, and he gave them permission. 33When the demons came out of the man, they went into the pigs, and the herd rushed down the steep bank into the lake and was drowned.

34When those tending the pigs saw what had happened, they ran off and reported this in the town and countryside, 35and the people went out to see what had happened. When they came to Jesus, they found the man from whom the demons had gone out, sitting at Jesus' feet, dressed and in his right mind; and they were afraid. 36Those who had seen it told the people how the demon-possessed man had been cured. 37Then all the people of the region of the Gerasenes asked Jesus to leave them, because they were overcome with fear. So he got into the boat and left.

38The man from whom the demons had gone out begged to go with him, but Jesus sent him away, saying, 39"Return home and tell how much God has done for you." So the man went away and told all over town how much Jesus had done for him.

A Dead Girl and a Sick Woman

40Now when Jesus returned, a crowd welcomed him, for they were all expecting him. 41Then a man named Jairus, a ruler of the synagogue, came and fell at Jesus' feet, pleading with him to come to his house 42because his only daughter, a girl of about twelve, was dying.

As Jesus was on his way, the crowds almost crushed him. 43And a woman was there who had been subject to bleeding for twelve years,[b] but no one could heal her. 44She came up behind him and touched the edge of his cloak, and immediately her bleeding stopped.

45"Who touched me?" Jesus asked.

When they all denied it, Peter said, "Master, the people are crowding and pressing against you."

46But Jesus said, "Someone touched me; I know that power has gone out from me."

47Then the woman, seeing that she could not go unnoticed, came trembling and fell at his feet. In the presence of all the people, she told why she had touched him and how she had been instantly healed. 48Then he said to her, "Daughter, your faith has healed you. Go in peace."

49While Jesus was still speaking, someone came from the house of Jairus, the synagogue ruler. "Your daughter is dead," he said. "Don't bother the teacher any more."

50Hearing this, Jesus said to Jairus, "Don't be afraid; just believe, and she will be healed."

51When he arrived at the house of Jairus, he did not let anyone go in with him except Peter, John and James, and the child's father and mother. 52Meanwhile, all the people were wailing and mourning for her. "Stop wailing," Jesus said. "She is not dead but asleep."

53They laughed at him, knowing that she was dead. 54But he took her by the hand and said, "My child, get up!" 55Her spirit returned, and at once she stood up. Then Jesus told them to give her something to eat. 56Her parents were astonished, but he ordered them not to tell anyone what had happened.

Jesus Sends Out the Twelve

9 When Jesus had called the Twelve together, he gave them power and authority to drive out all demons and to cure diseases, 2and he sent them out to preach the kingdom of God and to heal the sick. 3He told them: "Take nothing for the journey—no staff, no bag, no bread, no money, no extra tunic. 4Whatever house you enter, stay there until you leave that town. 5If people do not welcome you, shake the dust off your feet when you leave their town, as a testimony against them." 6So they set out and went

a29 Greek *unclean*   *b43* Many manuscripts *years, and she had spent all she had on doctors* from village to village, preaching the gospel and healing people everywhere.

⁷Now Herod the tetrarch heard about all that was going on. And he was perplexed, because some were saying that John had been raised from the dead, ⁸others that Elijah had appeared, and still others that one of the prophets of long ago had come back to life. ⁹But Herod said, "I beheaded John. Who, then, is this I hear such things about?" And he tried to see him.

Jesus Feeds the Five Thousand

¹⁰When the apostles returned, they reported to Jesus what they had done. Then he took them with him and they withdrew by themselves to a town called Bethsaida, ¹¹but the crowds learned about it and followed him. He welcomed them and spoke to them about the kingdom of God, and healed those who needed healing.

¹²Late in the afternoon the Twelve came to him and said, "Send the crowd away so they can go to the surrounding villages and countryside and find food and lodging, because we are in a remote place here."

¹³He replied, "You give them something to eat."

They answered, "We have only five loaves of bread and two fish—unless we go and buy food for all this crowd." ¹⁴(About five thousand men were there.)

But he said to his disciples, "Have them sit down in groups of about fifty each." ¹⁵The disciples did so, and everybody sat down. ¹⁶Taking the five loaves and the two fish and looking up to heaven, he gave thanks and broke them. Then he gave them to the disciples to set before the people. ¹⁷They all ate and were satisfied, and the disciples picked up twelve basketfuls of broken pieces that were left over.

Peter's Confession of Christ

¹⁸Once when Jesus was praying in private and his disciples were with him, he asked them, "Who do the crowds say I am?"

¹⁹They replied, "Some say John the Baptist; others say Elijah; and still others, that one of the prophets of long ago has come back to life."

²⁰"But what about you?" he asked. "Who do you say I am?"

Peter answered, "The Christ*a* of God."

a20 Or Messiah

²¹Jesus strictly warned them not to tell this to anyone. ²²And he said, "The Son of Man must suffer many things and be rejected by the elders, chief priests and teachers of the law, and he must be killed and on the third day be raised to life."

²³Then he said to them all: "If anyone would come after me, he must deny himself and take up his cross daily and follow me. ²⁴For whoever wants to save his life will lose it, but whoever loses his life for me will save it. ²⁵What good is it for a man to gain the whole world, and yet lose or forfeit his very self? ²⁶If anyone is ashamed of me and my words, the Son of Man will be ashamed of him when he comes in his glory and in the glory of the Father and of the holy angels. ²⁷I tell you the truth, some who are standing here will not taste death before they see the kingdom of God."

The Transfiguration

²⁸About eight days after Jesus said this, he took Peter, John and James with him and went up onto a mountain to pray. ²⁹As he was praying, the appearance of his face changed, and his clothes became as bright as a flash of lightning. ³⁰Two men, Moses and Elijah, ³¹appeared in glorious splendor, talking with Jesus. They spoke about his departure, which he was about to bring to fulfillment at Jerusalem. ³²Peter and his companions were very sleepy, but when they became fully awake, they saw his glory and the two men standing with him. ³³As the men were leaving Jesus, Peter said to him, "Master, it is good for us to be here. Let us put up three shelters—one for you, one for Moses and one for Elijah." (He did not know what he was saying.)

³⁴While he was speaking, a cloud appeared and enveloped them, and they were afraid as they entered the cloud. ³⁵A voice came from the cloud, saying, "This is my Son, whom I have chosen; listen to him." ³⁶When the voice had spoken, they found that Jesus was alone. The disciples kept this to themselves, and told no one at that time what they had seen.

The Healing of a Boy With an Evil Spirit

³⁷The next day, when they came down from the mountain, a large crowd met him. ³⁸A man in the crowd called out, "Teacher, I beg you to look at my son, for

he is my only child. ³⁹A spirit seizes him and he suddenly screams; it throws him into convulsions so that he foams at the mouth. It scarcely ever leaves him and is destroying him. ⁴⁰I begged your disciples to drive it out, but they could not."

⁴¹"O unbelieving and perverse generation," Jesus replied, "how long shall I stay with you and put up with you? Bring your son here."

⁴²Even while the boy was coming, the demon threw him to the ground in a convulsion. But Jesus rebuked the evilᵃ spirit, healed the boy and gave him back to his father. ⁴³And they were all amazed at the greatness of God.

While everyone was marveling at all that Jesus did, he said to his disciples, ⁴⁴"Listen carefully to what I am about to tell you: The Son of Man is going to be betrayed into the hands of men." ⁴⁵But they did not understand what this meant. It was hidden from them, so that they did not grasp it, and they were afraid to ask him about it.

Who Will Be the Greatest?

⁴⁶An argument started among the disciples as to which of them would be the greatest. ⁴⁷Jesus, knowing their thoughts, took a little child and had him stand beside him. ⁴⁸Then he said to them, "Whoever welcomes this little child in my name welcomes me; and whoever welcomes me welcomes the one who sent me. For he who is least among you all— he is the greatest."

⁴⁹"Master," said John, "we saw a man driving out demons in your name and we tried to stop him, because he is not one of us."

⁵⁰"Do not stop him," Jesus said, "for whoever is not against you is for you."

Samaritan Opposition

⁵¹As the time approached for him to be taken up to heaven, Jesus resolutely set out for Jerusalem. ⁵²And he sent messengers on ahead, who went into a Samaritan village to get things ready for him; ⁵³but the people there did not welcome him, because he was heading for Jerusalem. ⁵⁴When the disciples James and John saw this, they asked, "Lord, do you want us to call fire down from heaven to destroy themᵇ?" ⁵⁵But Jesus turned and rebuked

them, ⁵⁶andᶜ they went to another village.

The Cost of Following Jesus

⁵⁷As they were walking along the road, a man said to him, "I will follow you wherever you go."

⁵⁸Jesus replied, "Foxes have holes and birds of the air have nests, but the Son of Man has no place to lay his head."

⁵⁹He said to another man, "Follow me."

But the man replied, "Lord, first let me go and bury my father."

⁶⁰Jesus said to him, "Let the dead bury their own dead, but you go and proclaim the kingdom of God."

⁶¹Still another said, "I will follow you, Lord; but first let me go back and say good-by to my family."

⁶²Jesus replied, "No one who puts his hand to the plow and looks back is fit for service in the kingdom of God."

Jesus Sends Out the Seventy-two

10 After this the Lord appointed seventy-twoᵈ others and sent them two by two ahead of him to every town and place where he was about to go. ²He told them, "The harvest is plentiful, but the workers are few. Ask the Lord of the harvest, therefore, to send out workers into his harvest field. ³Go! I am sending you out like lambs among wolves. ⁴Do not take a purse or bag or sandals; and do not greet anyone on the road.

⁵"When you enter a house, first say, 'Peace to this house.' ⁶If a man of peace is there, your peace will rest on him; if not, it will return to you. ⁷Stay in that house, eating and drinking whatever they give you, for the worker deserves his wages. Do not move around from house to house.

⁸"When you enter a town and are welcomed, eat what is set before you. ⁹Heal the sick who are there and tell them, 'The kingdom of God is near you.' ¹⁰But when you enter a town and are not welcomed, go into its streets and say, ¹¹'Even the dust of your town that sticks to our feet we wipe off against you. Yet be sure of this: The kingdom of God is near.' ¹²I tell you, it will be more bearable on that day for Sodom than for that town.

¹³"Woe to you, Korazin! Woe to you,

ᵃ42 Greek *unclean* ᵇ54 Some manuscripts *them, even as Elijah did* ᶜ55,56 Some manuscripts *them. And he said, "You do not know what kind of spirit you are of, for the Son of Man did not come to destroy men's lives, but to save them." 56And* ᵈ1 Some manuscripts *seventy*; also in verse 17

VERSE FOR THE DAY:	*AUTHOR:*	*PASSAGE FOR THE DAY:*
Luke 10:33	Alma Barkman	Luke 10:25–37

First Aid

ALTHOUGH not a registered professional, I do get my share of nursing experience, particularly while substituting for the school secretary. The minute I set foot inside the door, casualties start gravitating toward the office—scraped elbows, skinned knees, old wounds, fresh nosebleeds, raised toenails, broken blisters, upset stomachs.

I have learned that a school secretary opens a well-stocked first-aid kit long before sharpening any pencils. By midafternoon the office is apt to resemble a hospital ward.

Not only that, but old Florence Nightingale is not accorded any degree of privacy. The casualty victims from school are beginning to spill over into my house. Yesterday the doorbell rang, and a terrified young fellow hopping up and down on my doorstep tried to tell me that his pal was bleeding to death on the road—massive hemorrhage.

I ran to the site of the accident, where the victim was just untangling himself from the wreckage of his bicycle. Judging from his groans, I thought he had amputated his leg.

Somehow I managed to get him into my bathroom and wash off his wounds. An accurate diagnosis confirmed my suspicions: he had simply scraped the scab from a previous injury. I solemnly conjured up an impressive-looking bandage, and he was back on the road in no time at all, completely cured.

The therapeutic value of Band-Aids may well be disputed, but this is one "lady of the lamp" who keeps her medicine chest well stocked.

Whether it is a tiny sliver in a chubby finger, or cancer clawing at a ravaged frame, pain demands priority. Why then am I so hesitant in dispensing consolation? Do I wait until an emergency demands it before investing in a "first-aid" kit? Must I first suffer physically, mentally, emotionally, or spiritually before I learn the healing value of a soothing hand, a mutual tear, a sympathizing heart, an understanding word?

Surely I do well to keep my medicine chest well stocked with love and compassion as well as with bandages, for I never know when I will be called upon to deal with tragedy, or when tragedy may call to deal with me.

Additional Scripture Readings:
Acts 3:1–10; James 2:14–17

Go to page 1119 for your next devotional reading.

Bethsaida! For if the miracles that were performed in you had been performed in Tyre and Sidon, they would have repented long ago, sitting in sackcloth and ashes. ¹⁴But it will be more bearable for Tyre and Sidon at the judgment than for you. ¹⁵And you, Capernaum, will you be lifted up to the skies? No, you will go down to the depths.ᵃ

¹⁶"He who listens to you listens to me; he who rejects you rejects me; but he who rejects me rejects him who sent me."

¹⁷The seventy-two returned with joy and said, "Lord, even the demons submit to us in your name."

¹⁸He replied, "I saw Satan fall like lightning from heaven. ¹⁹I have given you authority to trample on snakes and scorpions and to overcome all the power of the enemy; nothing will harm you. ²⁰However, do not rejoice that the spirits submit to you, but rejoice that your names are written in heaven."

²¹At that time Jesus, full of joy through the Holy Spirit, said, "I praise you, Father, Lord of heaven and earth, because you have hidden these things from the wise and learned, and revealed them to little children. Yes, Father, for this was your good pleasure.

²²"All things have been committed to me by my Father. No one knows who the Son is except the Father, and no one knows who the Father is except the Son and those to whom the Son chooses to reveal him."

²³Then he turned to his disciples and said privately, "Blessed are the eyes that see what you see. ²⁴For I tell you that many prophets and kings wanted to see what you see but did not see it, and to hear what you hear but did not hear it."

The Parable of the Good Samaritan

²⁵On one occasion an expert in the law stood up to test Jesus. "Teacher," he asked, "what must I do to inherit eternal life?"

²⁶"What is written in the Law?" he replied. "How do you read it?"

²⁷He answered: " 'Love the Lord your God with all your heart and with all your soul and with all your strength and with all your mind'ᵇ; and, 'Love your neighbor as yourself.'ᶜ "

²⁸"You have answered correctly," Jesus replied. "Do this and you will live."

²⁹But he wanted to justify himself, so he asked Jesus, "And who is my neighbor?"

³⁰In reply Jesus said: "A man was going down from Jerusalem to Jericho, when he fell into the hands of robbers. They stripped him of his clothes, beat him and went away, leaving him half dead. ³¹A priest happened to be going down the same road, and when he saw the man, he passed by on the other side. ³²So too, a Levite, when he came to the place and saw him, passed by on the other side. ³³But a Samaritan, as he traveled, came where the man was; and when he saw him, he took pity on him. ³⁴He went to him and bandaged his wounds, pouring on oil and wine. Then he put the man on his own donkey, took him to an inn and took care of him. ³⁵The next day he took out two silver coinsᵈ and gave them to the innkeeper. 'Look after him,' he said, 'and when I return, I will reimburse you for any extra expense you may have.'

³⁶"Which of these three do you think was a neighbor to the man who fell into the hands of robbers?"

³⁷The expert in the law replied, "The one who had mercy on him."

Jesus told him, "Go and do likewise."

At the Home of Martha and Mary

³⁸As Jesus and his disciples were on their way, he came to a village where a woman named Martha opened her home to him. ³⁹She had a sister called Mary, who sat at the Lord's feet listening to what he said. ⁴⁰But Martha was distracted by all the preparations that had to be made. She came to him and asked, "Lord, don't you care that my sister has left me to do the work by myself? Tell her to help me!"

⁴¹"Martha, Martha," the Lord answered, "you are worried and upset about many things, ⁴²but only one thing is needed.ᵉ Mary has chosen what is better, and it will not be taken away from her."

Jesus' Teaching on Prayer

11 One day Jesus was praying in a certain place. When he finished, one of his disciples said to him, "Lord, teach us to pray, just as John taught his disciples."

²He said to them, "When you pray, say:

ᵃ15 Greek *Hades*   ᵇ27 Deut. 6:5   ᶜ27 Lev. 19:18   ᵈ35 Greek *two denarii*   ᵉ42 Some manuscripts *but few things are needed—or only one*

" 'Father,[a]
hallowed be your name,
your kingdom come.[b]
[3]Give us each day our daily bread.
[4]Forgive us our sins,
  for we also forgive everyone who
    sins against us.[c]
And lead us not into temptation.[d]' "

[5]Then he said to them, "Suppose one of

you has a friend, and he goes to him at midnight and says, 'Friend, lend me three loaves of bread, [6]because a friend of mine on a journey has come to me, and I have nothing to set before him.'

[7]"Then the one inside answers, 'Don't bother me. The door is already locked, and my children are with me in bed. I can't get up and give you anything.' [8]I tell you, though he will not get up and give him the bread because he is his friend,

---

[a]2 Some manuscripts *Our Father in heaven*   [b]2 Some manuscripts *come. May your will be done on earth as it is in heaven.*   [c]4 Greek *everyone who is indebted to us*   [d]4 Some manuscripts *temptation but deliver us from the evil one*

THURSDAY

VERSE FOR THE DAY:
Luke 10:40

AUTHOR:
Jill Briscoe

PASSAGE FOR THE DAY:
Luke 10:38–42

First Things First

I LOVE the way Jesus solved problems. He tackled them head on! He was a master at confronting people in such a way that it did not hinder his relationship with them afterward. Think of Martha, for instance. Jesus visited the home of Martha, Mary and Lazarus. Mary, Martha's sister, sat at Jesus' feet and listened to his words while Martha got mad about it! She got mad at Mary and she got mad at Jesus! There was a meal to prepare and nobody would help! I'm sure she got mad at Martha too, because you can't be happy with yourself when you're griping at other people!

It wasn't that Martha didn't know what it was to enjoy the Master's company, because we understand that Martha also sat at Jesus' feet. It was just a question of priorities. Martha was busy getting a banquet ready when soup and sandwiches would have been quite adequate. Jesus gently reminded her that she was worried and troubled about many "dishes" but Mary had chosen the best "dish"!

When Jesus saw women who were "distracted" by their serving—he did not fail to remind them that "man does not live on bread alone" (Matthew 4:4). First things need to come first! "First the Master, then the meat," he reminded Martha.

It isn't that the *doing* doesn't need doing, it's that the *being* must come first, and then we will find that the necessary part of the doing will get done! Later in Jesus' ministry we read that Martha served, and this time there was no complaining and no rebuke—first things *were* first (John 12:2).

Additional Scripture Readings:
Luke 9:57–62; John 12:1–3

*Go to page 1121 for your next
devotional reading.*

yet because of the man's boldness[a] he will get up and give him as much as he needs.

9"So I say to you: Ask and it will be given to you; seek and you will find; knock and the door will be opened to you. 10For everyone who asks receives; he who seeks finds; and to him who knocks, the door will be opened.

11"Which of you fathers, if your son asks for[b] a fish, will give him a snake instead? 12Or if he asks for an egg, will give him a scorpion? 13If you then, though you are evil, know how to give good gifts to your children, how much more will your Father in heaven give the Holy Spirit to those who ask him!"

Jesus and Beelzebub

14Jesus was driving out a demon that was mute. When the demon left, the man who had been mute spoke, and the crowd was amazed. 15But some of them said, "By Beelzebub,[c] the prince of demons, he is driving out demons." 16Others tested him by asking for a sign from heaven.

17Jesus knew their thoughts and said to them: "Any kingdom divided against itself will be ruined, and a house divided against itself will fall. 18If Satan is divided against himself, how can his kingdom stand? I say this because you claim that I drive out demons by Beelzebub. 19Now if I drive out demons by Beelzebub, by whom do your followers drive them out? So then, they will be your judges. 20But if I drive out demons by the finger of God, then the kingdom of God has come to you.

21"When a strong man, fully armed, guards his own house, his possessions are safe. 22But when someone stronger attacks and overpowers him, he takes away the armor in which the man trusted and divides up the spoils.

23"He who is not with me is against me, and he who does not gather with me, scatters.

24"When an evil[d] spirit comes out of a man, it goes through arid places seeking rest and does not find it. Then it says, 'I will return to the house I left.' 25When it arrives, it finds the house swept clean and put in order. 26Then it goes and takes seven other spirits more wicked than itself, and they go in and live there. And the final condition of that man is worse than the first."

27As Jesus was saying these things, a woman in the crowd called out, "Blessed is the mother who gave you birth and nursed you."

28He replied, "Blessed rather are those who hear the word of God and obey it."

The Sign of Jonah

29As the crowds increased, Jesus said, "This is a wicked generation. It asks for a miraculous sign, but none will be given it except the sign of Jonah. 30For as Jonah was a sign to the Ninevites, so also will the Son of Man be to this generation. 31The Queen of the South will rise at the judgment with the men of this generation and condemn them; for she came from the ends of the earth to listen to Solomon's wisdom, and now one[e] greater than Solomon is here. 32The men of Nineveh will stand up at the judgment with this generation and condemn it; for they repented at the preaching of Jonah, and now one greater than Jonah is here.

The Lamp of the Body

33"No one lights a lamp and puts it in a place where it will be hidden, or under a bowl. Instead he puts it on its stand, so that those who come in may see the light. 34Your eye is the lamp of your body. When your eyes are good, your whole body also is full of light. But when they are bad, your body also is full of darkness. 35See to it, then, that the light within you is not darkness. 36Therefore, if your whole body is full of light, and no part of it dark, it will be completely lighted, as when the light of a lamp shines on you."

Six Woes

37When Jesus had finished speaking, a Pharisee invited him to eat with him; so he went in and reclined at the table. 38But the Pharisee, noticing that Jesus did not first wash before the meal, was surprised. 39Then the Lord said to him, "Now then, you Pharisees clean the outside of the cup and dish, but inside you are full of greed and wickedness. 40You foolish people! Did not the one who made the outside make the inside also? 41But give what is inside the dish,[f] to the poor, and everything will be clean for you.

---

a8 Or persistence   b11 Some manuscripts for bread, will give him a stone; or if he asks for
c15 Greek Beezeboul or Beelzeboul; also in verses 18 and 19   d24 Greek unclean   e31 Or something; also in verse 32   f41 Or what you have

VERSE FOR THE DAY:
Luke 11:33

AUTHOR:
June Masters Bacher

PASSAGE FOR THE DAY:
Luke 11:33–36

Where Are the Lamps?

IN a certain mountain village in Europe several centuries ago (so the story goes), a nobleman wondered what legacy to leave his townspeople. At last he decided to build them a church.

Nobody saw the complete plans until the church was finished. When the people gathered, they marveled at its beauty. But one noticed an incompleteness. "Where are the lamps?" he asked. "How will the church be lighted?"

The nobleman smiled. Then he gave each family a lamp. "Each time you are here, the area in which you sit will be lighted. But when you are not here, some part of God's house will be dark."

Today we live in a world of darkness, a darkness in which even our secular problem-solvers are beginning to stumble. In spite of our "social conscience," all around us is evidence of ignorance, illiteracy, and dark imaginings. Romans 2:19 tells us that we, as Christians, are "a light for those who are in the dark."

But the world is so big. And our lamp is so small. Yes, but we can light some small part each day. Look to the star-struck heavens. How small each star looks in the distance. Yet, put together, those tiny jewels can light the darkest night. Not one of those little lamps of heaven is ever missing—else the heavens would be less bright. Each of us is a star (or a lamp, if you will). And yes, we can make this world a brighter place. It all begins with the desire expressed in Michelangelo's prayer: "God, grant me the desire always to desire to be more that I can ever accomplish."

To think and pray about: Light your lamps. Let God send you in a new direction today. Meet someone at the crossroads of his or her life. Put on a bright face whether you feel like it or not. Gladness will come.

Additional Scripture Readings:
Matthew 5:14–16; 1 John 1:5–7

*Go to page 1124 for your next
devotional reading.*

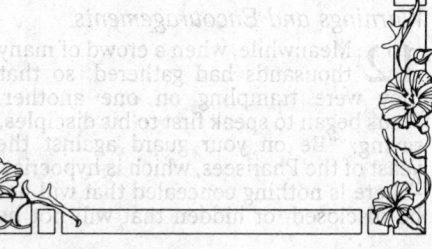

42"Woe to you Pharisees, because you give God a tenth of your mint, rue and all other kinds of garden herbs, but you neglect justice and the love of God. You should have practiced the latter without leaving the former undone.

43"Woe to you Pharisees, because you love the most important seats in the synagogues and greetings in the marketplaces.

44"Woe to you, because you are like unmarked graves, which men walk over without knowing it."

45One of the experts in the law answered him, "Teacher, when you say these things, you insult us also."

46Jesus replied, "And you experts in the law, woe to you, because you load people down with burdens they can hardly carry, and you yourselves will not lift one finger to help them.

47"Woe to you, because you build tombs for the prophets, and it was your forefathers who killed them. 48So you testify that you approve of what your forefathers did; they killed the prophets, and you build their tombs. 49Because of this, God in his wisdom said, 'I will send them prophets and apostles, some of whom they will kill and others they will persecute.' 50Therefore this generation will be held responsible for the blood of all the prophets that has been shed since the beginning of the world, 51from the blood of Abel to the blood of Zechariah, who was killed between the altar and the sanctuary. Yes, I tell you, this generation will be held responsible for it all.

52"Woe to you experts in the law, because you have taken away the key to knowledge. You yourselves have not entered, and you have hindered those who were entering."

53When Jesus left there, the Pharisees and the teachers of the law began to oppose him fiercely and to besiege him with questions, 54waiting to catch him in something he might say.

Warnings and Encouragements

12 Meanwhile, when a crowd of many thousands had gathered, so that they were trampling on one another, Jesus began to speak first to his disciples, saying: "Be on your guard against the yeast of the Pharisees, which is hypocrisy. 2There is nothing concealed that will not be disclosed, or hidden that will not be

made known. 3What you have said in the dark will be heard in the daylight, and what you have whispered in the ear in the inner rooms will be proclaimed from the roofs.

4"I tell you, my friends, do not be afraid of those who kill the body and after that can do no more. 5But I will show you whom you should fear: Fear him who, after the killing of the body, has power to throw you into hell. Yes, I tell you, fear him. 6Are not five sparrows sold for two penniesª? Yet not one of them is forgotten by God. 7Indeed, the very hairs of your head are all numbered. Don't be afraid; you are worth more than many sparrows.

8"I tell you, whoever acknowledges me before men, the Son of Man will also acknowledge him before the angels of God. 9But he who disowns me before men will be disowned before the angels of God. 10And everyone who speaks a word against the Son of Man will be forgiven, but anyone who blasphemes against the Holy Spirit will not be forgiven.

11"When you are brought before synagogues, rulers and authorities, do not worry about how you will defend yourselves or what you will say, 12for the Holy Spirit will teach you at that time what you should say."

The Parable of the Rich Fool

13Someone in the crowd said to him, "Teacher, tell my brother to divide the inheritance with me."

14Jesus replied, "Man, who appointed me a judge or an arbiter between you?" 15Then he said to them, "Watch out! Be on your guard against all kinds of greed; a man's life does not consist in the abundance of his possessions."

16And he told them this parable: "The ground of a certain rich man produced a good crop. 17He thought to himself, 'What shall I do? I have no place to store my crops.'

18"Then he said, 'This is what I'll do. I will tear down my barns and build bigger ones, and there I will store all my grain and my goods. 19And I'll say to myself, "You have plenty of good things laid up for many years. Take life easy; eat, drink and be merry." '

20"But God said to him, 'You fool! This very night your life will be demanded from you. Then who will get what you have prepared for yourself?'

ª6 Greek two assaria

²¹"This is how it will be with anyone who stores up things for himself but is not rich toward God."

Do Not Worry

²²Then Jesus said to his disciples: "Therefore I tell you, do not worry about your life, what you will eat; or about your body, what you will wear. ²³Life is more than food, and the body more than clothes. ²⁴Consider the ravens: They do not sow or reap, they have no storeroom or barn; yet God feeds them. And how much more valuable you are than birds! ²⁵Who of you by worrying can add a single hour to his life*? ²⁶Since you cannot do this very little thing, why do you worry about the rest?

²⁷"Consider how the lilies grow. They do not labor or spin. Yet I tell you, not even Solomon in all his splendor was dressed like one of these. ²⁸If that is how God clothes the grass of the field, which is here today, and tomorrow is thrown into the fire, how much more will he clothe you, O you of little faith! ²⁹And do not set your heart on what you will eat or drink; do not worry about it. ³⁰For the pagan world runs after all such things, and your Father knows that you need them. ³¹But seek his kingdom, and these things will be given to you as well.

³²"Do not be afraid, little flock, for your Father has been pleased to give you the kingdom. ³³Sell your possessions and give to the poor. Provide purses for yourselves that will not wear out, a treasure in heaven that will not be exhausted, where no thief comes near and no moth destroys. ³⁴For where your treasure is, there your heart will be also.

Watchfulness

³⁵"Be dressed ready for service and keep your lamps burning, ³⁶like men waiting for their master to return from a wedding banquet, so that when he comes and knocks they can immediately open the door for him. ³⁷It will be good for those servants whose master finds them watching when he comes. I tell you the truth, he will dress himself to serve, will have them recline at the table and will come and wait on them. ³⁸It will be good for those servants whose master finds them ready, even if he comes in the second or third watch of the night. ³⁹But understand this: If the owner of the house

had known at what hour the thief was coming, he would not have let his house be broken into. ⁴⁰You also must be ready, because the Son of Man will come at an hour when you do not expect him."

⁴¹Peter asked, "Lord, are you telling this parable to us, or to everyone?"

⁴²The Lord answered, "Who then is the faithful and wise manager, whom the master puts in charge of his servants to give them their food allowance at the proper time? ⁴³It will be good for that servant whom the master finds doing so when he returns. ⁴⁴I tell you the truth, he will put him in charge of all his possessions. ⁴⁵But suppose the servant says to himself, 'My master is taking a long time in coming,' and he then begins to beat the menservants and maidservants and to eat and drink and get drunk. ⁴⁶The master of that servant will come on a day when he does not expect him and at an hour he is not aware of. He will cut him to pieces and assign him a place with the unbelievers.

⁴⁷"That servant who knows his master's will and does not get ready or does not do what his master wants will be beaten with many blows. ⁴⁸But the one who does not know and does things deserving punishment will be beaten with few blows. From everyone who has been given much, much will be demanded; and from the one who has been entrusted with much, much more will be asked.

Not Peace but Division

⁴⁹"I have come to bring fire on the earth, and how I wish it were already kindled! ⁵⁰But I have a baptism to undergo, and how distressed I am until it is completed! ⁵¹Do you think I came to bring peace on earth? No, I tell you, but division. ⁵²From now on there will be five in one family divided against each other, three against two and two against three. ⁵³They will be divided, father against son and son against father, mother against daughter and daughter against mother, mother-in-law against daughter-in-law and daughter-in-law against mother-in-law."

Interpreting the Times

⁵⁴He said to the crowd: "When you see a cloud rising in the west, immediately you say, 'It's going to rain,' and it does. ⁵⁵And when the south wind blows, you

*25 Or single cubit to his height

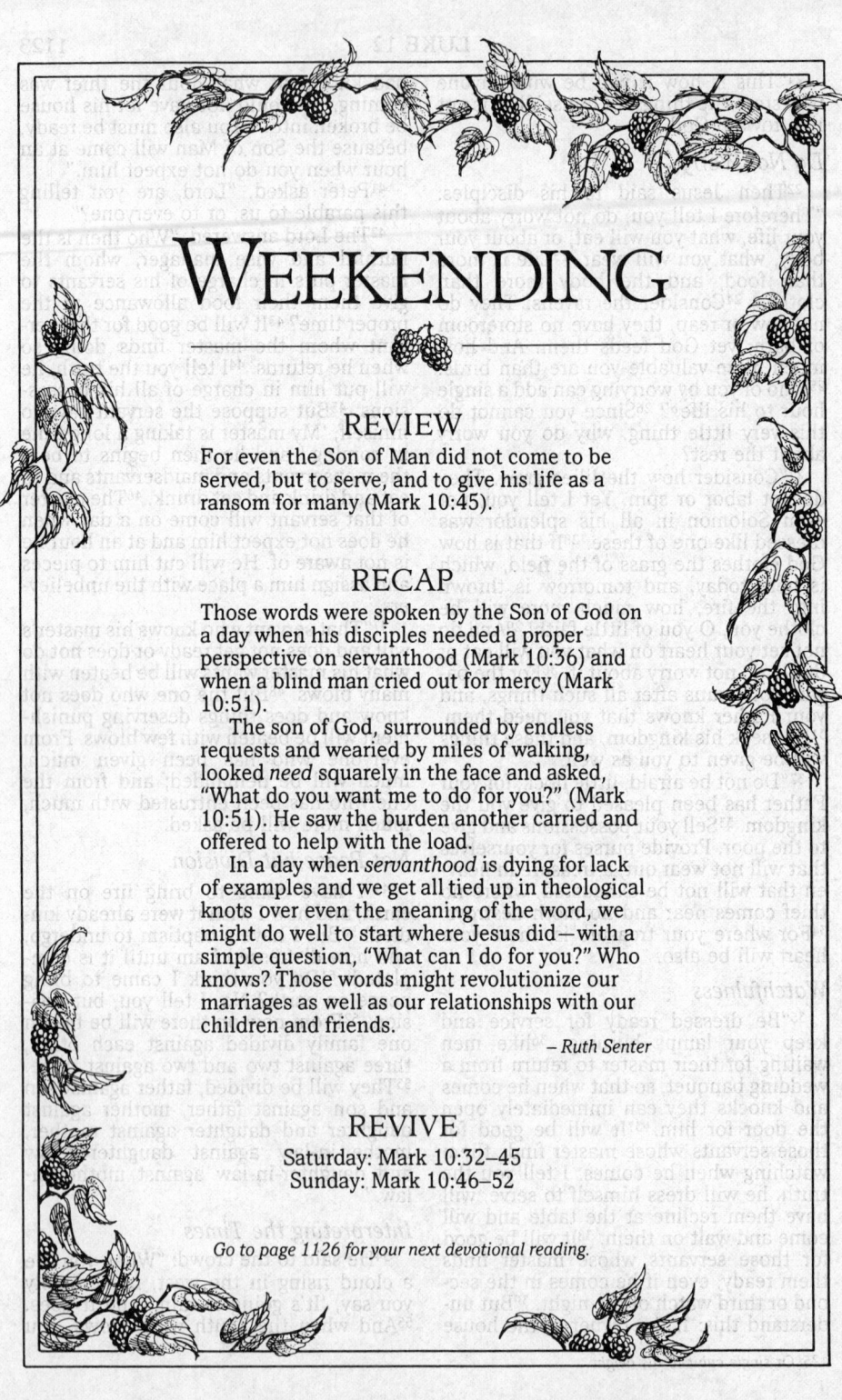

WEEKENDING

REVIEW

For even the Son of Man did not come to be
served, but to serve, and to give his life as a
ransom for many (Mark 10:45).

RECAP

Those words were spoken by the Son of God on
a day when his disciples needed a proper
perspective on servanthood (Mark 10:36) and
when a blind man cried out for mercy (Mark
10:51).

The son of God, surrounded by endless
requests and wearied by miles of walking,
looked *need* squarely in the face and asked,
"What do you want me to do for you?" (Mark
10:51). He saw the burden another carried and
offered to help with the load.

In a day when *servanthood* is dying for lack
of examples and we get all tied up in theological
knots over even the meaning of the word, we
might do well to start where Jesus did—with a
simple question, "What can I do for you?" Who
knows? Those words might revolutionize our
marriages as well as our relationships with our
children and friends.

— Ruth Senter

REVIVE

Saturday: Mark 10:32–45
Sunday: Mark 10:46–52

Go to page 1126 for your next devotional reading.

say, 'It's going to be hot,' and it is. 56Hypocrites! You know how to interpret the appearance of the earth and the sky. How is it that you don't know how to interpret this present time?

57"Why don't you judge for yourselves what is right? 58As you are going with your adversary to the magistrate, try hard to be reconciled to him on the way, or he may drag you off to the judge, and the judge turn you over to the officer, and the officer throw you into prison. 59I tell you, you will not get out until you have paid the last penny.*"

Repent or Perish

13 Now there were some present at that time who told Jesus about the Galileans whose blood Pilate had mixed with their sacrifices. 2Jesus answered, "Do you think that these Galileans were worse sinners than all the other Galileans because they suffered this way? 3I tell you, no! But unless you repent, you too will all perish. 4Or those eighteen who died when the tower in Siloam fell on them—do you think they were more guilty than all the others living in Jerusalem? 5I tell you, no! But unless you repent, you too will all perish."

6Then he told this parable: "A man had a fig tree, planted in his vineyard, and he went to look for fruit on it, but did not find any. 7So he said to the man who took care of the vineyard, 'For three years now I've been coming to look for fruit on this fig tree and haven't found any. Cut it down! Why should it use up the soil?'

8" 'Sir,' the man replied, 'leave it alone for one more year, and I'll dig around it and fertilize it. 9If it bears fruit next year, fine! If not, then cut it down.' "

A Crippled Woman Healed on the Sabbath

10On a Sabbath Jesus was teaching in one of the synagogues, 11and a woman was there who had been crippled by a spirit for eighteen years. She was bent over and could not straighten up at all. 12When Jesus saw her, he called her forward and said to her, "Woman, you are set free from your infirmity." 13Then he put his hands on her, and immediately she straightened up and praised God.

14Indignant because Jesus had healed on the Sabbath, the synagogue ruler said to the people, "There are six days for work. So come and be healed on those days, not on the Sabbath."

15The Lord answered him, "You hypocrites! Doesn't each of you on the Sabbath untie his ox or donkey from the stall and lead it out to give it water? 16Then should not this woman, a daughter of Abraham, whom Satan has kept bound for eighteen long years, be set free on the Sabbath day from what bound her?"

17When he said this, all his opponents were humiliated, but the people were delighted with all the wonderful things he was doing.

The Parables of the Mustard Seed and the Yeast

18Then Jesus asked, "What is the kingdom of God like? What shall I compare it to? 19It is like a mustard seed, which a man took and planted in his garden. It grew and became a tree, and the birds of the air perched in its branches."

20Again he asked, "What shall I compare the kingdom of God to? 21It is like yeast that a woman took and mixed into a large amount*b* of flour until it worked all through the dough."

The Narrow Door

22Then Jesus went through the towns and villages, teaching as he made his way to Jerusalem. 23Someone asked him, "Lord, are only a few people going to be saved?"

He said to them, 24"Make every effort to enter through the narrow door, because many, I tell you, will try to enter and will not be able to. 25Once the owner of the house gets up and closes the door, you will stand outside knocking and pleading, 'Sir, open the door for us.'

"But he will answer, 'I don't know you or where you come from.'

26"Then you will say, 'We ate and drank with you, and you taught in our streets.'

27"But he will reply, 'I don't know you or where you come from. Away from me, all you evildoers!'

28"There will be weeping there, and gnashing of teeth, when you see Abraham, Isaac and Jacob and all the prophets in the kingdom of God, but you yourselves thrown out. 29People will come from east and west and north and south, and will take their places at the feast in

---

a59 Greek *lepton*   *b21* Greek *three satas* (probably about 1/2 bushel or 22 liters) the kingdom of God. ³⁰Indeed there are those who are last who will be first, and first who will be last."

Jesus' Sorrow for Jerusalem

³¹At that time some Pharisees came to Jesus and said to him, "Leave this place and go somewhere else. Herod wants to kill you."

³²He replied, "Go tell that fox, 'I will drive out demons and heal people today and tomorrow, and on the third day I will reach my goal.' ³³In any case, I must keep going today and tomorrow and the next day—for surely no prophet can die outside Jerusalem!

³⁴"O Jerusalem, Jerusalem, you who kill the prophets and stone those sent to you, how often I have longed to gather your children together, as a hen gathers her chicks under her wings, but you were not willing! ³⁵Look, your house is left to you desolate. I tell you, you will not see me again until you say, 'Blessed is he who comes in the name of the Lord.'ᵃ"

ᵃ35 Psalm 118:26

VERSE FOR THE DAY:	AUTHOR:	PASSAGE FOR THE DAY:
Luke 13:16	Jill Briscoe	Luke 13:10–17

The Language of Love

JESUS understood us. Yes, he did! You can tell it by his language. It was the language of love. Paul says that love has good manners (1 Corinthians 13:5), and if you care to read the way the Lord Jesus addressed the women he met, you can actually hear love talking. He said "daughter," "little girl," and even "daughter of Abraham," as in this passage. What courtesy and comfort, for women in Jesus' day were treated like dirt. When the priggish Pharisees dragged a woman in front of him who was "caught in adultery," Jesus saved her from possible stoning and then dealt firmly with her (John 8:3–11). He was not rude or rough, but polite while firm.

It's awfully important how you talk to people. Jesus always seemed to say the right thing the right way! When I was a young youth worker I was given a lot of responsibility suddenly. It went to my head. Being a strong sort of character, it was not long before I was busy bossing everyone about. "Jill," my fellow worker sweetly said to me one day, "I would like to be asked—not told." I needed that! Jesus didn't boss women around. He understood us; he knew we liked to be asked, not told. He used the language of love, and so must we if we would follow in his steps and if we would see anything accomplished. Let's try a few good manners. It's amazing how many people will respond. Try saying "please" and "thank you" and "do you mind"—this is the language of love.

Additional Scripture Readings:
John 4:7–27; Colossians 4:6

Go to page 1128 for your next
devotional reading.

Jesus at a Pharisee's House

14 One Sabbath, when Jesus went to eat in the house of a prominent Pharisee, he was being carefully watched. [2]There in front of him was a man suffering from dropsy. [3]Jesus asked the Pharisees and experts in the law, "Is it lawful to heal on the Sabbath or not?" [4]But they remained silent. So taking hold of the man, he healed him and sent him away.

[5]Then he asked them, "If one of you has a son[a] or an ox that falls into a well on the Sabbath day, will you not immediately pull him out?" [6]And they had nothing to say.

[7]When he noticed how the guests picked the places of honor at the table, he told them this parable: [8]"When someone invites you to a wedding feast, do not take the place of honor, for a person more distinguished than you may have been invited. [9]If so, the host who invited both of you will come and say to you, 'Give this man your seat.' Then, humiliated, you will have to take the least important place. [10]But when you are invited, take the lowest place, so that when your host comes, he will say to you, 'Friend, move up to a better place.' Then you will be honored in the presence of all your fellow guests. [11]For everyone who exalts himself will be humbled, and he who humbles himself will be exalted."

[12]Then Jesus said to his host, "When you give a luncheon or dinner, do not invite your friends, your brothers or relatives, or your rich neighbors; if you do, they may invite you back and so you will be repaid. [13]But when you give a banquet, invite the poor, the crippled, the lame, the blind, [14]and you will be blessed. Although they cannot repay you, you will be repaid at the resurrection of the righteous."

The Parable of the Great Banquet

[15]When one of those at the table with him heard this, he said to Jesus, "Blessed is the man who will eat at the feast in the kingdom of God."

[16]Jesus replied: "A certain man was preparing a great banquet and invited many guests. [17]At the time of the banquet he sent his servant to tell those who had been invited, 'Come, for everything is now ready.'

[18]"But they all alike began to make excuses. The first said, 'I have just bought a field, and I must go and see it. Please excuse me.'

[19]"Another said, 'I have just bought five yoke of oxen, and I'm on my way to try them out. Please excuse me.'

[20]"Still another said, 'I just got married, so I can't come.'

[21]"The servant came back and reported this to his master. Then the owner of the house became angry and ordered his servant, 'Go out quickly into the streets and alleys of the town and bring in the poor, the crippled, the blind and the lame.'

[22]"'Sir,' the servant said, 'what you ordered has been done, but there is still room.'

[23]"Then the master told his servant, 'Go out to the roads and country lanes and make them come in, so that my house will be full. [24]I tell you, not one of those men who were invited will get a taste of my banquet.' "

The Cost of Being a Disciple

[25]Large crowds were traveling with Jesus, and turning to them he said: [26]"If anyone comes to me and does not hate his father and mother, his wife and children, his brothers and sisters—yes, even his own life—he cannot be my disciple. [27]And anyone who does not carry his cross and follow me cannot be my disciple.

[28]"Suppose one of you wants to build a tower. Will he not first sit down and estimate the cost to see if he has enough money to complete it? [29]For if he lays the foundation and is not able to finish it, everyone who sees it will ridicule him, [30]saying, 'This fellow began to build and was not able to finish.'

[31]"Or suppose a king is about to go to war against another king. Will he not first sit down and consider whether he is able with ten thousand men to oppose the one coming against him with twenty thousand? [32]If he is not able, he will send a delegation while the other is still a long way off and will ask for terms of peace. [33]In the same way, any of you who does not give up everything he has cannot be my disciple.

[34]"Salt is good, but if it loses its saltiness, how can it be made salty again? [35]It is fit neither for the soil nor for the manure pile; it is thrown out.

[a]5 Some manuscripts donkey

VERSE FOR THE DAY:
Luke 14:12

AUTHOR:
Joni Eareckson Tada

PASSAGE FOR THE DAY:
Luke 14:1–35

Changing the Subject

IMAGINE the scene in Luke 14:1–24. Jesus was invited to dinner at a Pharisee's home in the rich suburbs of Jerusalem. He noticed the wealthy people grabbing the best seats around the table. At that point, Jesus launched into a story about the sorts of dinner parties people ought to give—feasts for the forgotten, the homeless, the poor and the disabled.

The Lord added that although these poor people would not be able to repay them, the hosts would, nevertheless, be repaid at the resurrection (Luke 14:14).

You can imagine what happened next. Jesus probably sat down, put his napkin on his lap, and quietly picked up an hors d'oeuvre. Dead silence hung over the table as the wealthy people shot nervous glances at each other. Jesus had put a damper on the party spirit.

Finally, one of the dinner guests cleared his throat and spoke up. "Blessed is the man who will eat at the feast in the kingdom of God" (Luke 14:15). What an odd thing to say! It's as if he was thinking:

> *Jesus, I can't say that I follow your strange ideas about dining with cripples, but I do agree with what you said about heaven—it's so comforting to know that everything will turn out perfectly in the end.* *

The man, in other words, was trying his best to change the spiritual subject.

Sound familiar? I can't tell you how many times I have either consciously or unconsciously tried to change the spiritual subject with God when I sensed he was laying heavy, convicting things on my heart. But just as the Lord did not allow those dinner guests to change the subject (read Luke 14:15–24), we will find it just as difficult to divert God's attention from those issues that need to be addressed in our lives.

Additional Scripture Readings:
Luke 11:27–28; James 2:1–7

Go to page 1130 for your next
devotional reading.

*Robert Farrar Capon, *The Parables of Grace* (Grand Rapids: William B. Eerdmans Publishing Company. 1988), 130-131.

"He who has ears to hear, let him hear."

The Parable of the Lost Sheep

15 Now the tax collectors and "sinners" were all gathering around to hear him. ²But the Pharisees and the teachers of the law muttered, "This man welcomes sinners and eats with them."

³Then Jesus told them this parable: ⁴"Suppose one of you has a hundred sheep and loses one of them. Does he not leave the ninety-nine in the open country and go after the lost sheep until he finds it? ⁵And when he finds it, he joyfully puts it on his shoulders ⁶and goes home. Then he calls his friends and neighbors together and says, 'Rejoice with me; I have found my lost sheep.' ⁷I tell you that in the same way there will be more rejoicing in heaven over one sinner who repents than over ninety-nine righteous persons who do not need to repent.

The Parable of the Lost Coin

⁸"Or suppose a woman has ten silver coins*ᵃ* and loses one. Does she not light a lamp, sweep the house and search carefully until she finds it? ⁹And when she finds it, she calls her friends and neighbors together and says, 'Rejoice with me; I have found my lost coin.' ¹⁰In the same way, I tell you, there is rejoicing in the presence of the angels of God over one sinner who repents."

The Parable of the Lost Son

¹¹Jesus continued: "There was a man who had two sons. ¹²The younger one said to his father, 'Father, give me my share of the estate.' So he divided his property between them.

¹³"Not long after that, the younger son got together all he had, set off for a distant country and there squandered his wealth in wild living. ¹⁴After he had spent everything, there was a severe famine in that whole country, and he began to be in need. ¹⁵So he went and hired himself out to a citizen of that country, who sent him to his fields to feed pigs. ¹⁶He longed to fill his stomach with the pods that the pigs were eating, but no one gave him anything.

¹⁷"When he came to his senses, he said, 'How many of my father's hired men have food to spare, and here I am starving to

death! ¹⁸I will set out and go back to my father and say to him: Father, I have sinned against heaven and against you. ¹⁹I am no longer worthy to be called your son; make me like one of your hired men.' ²⁰So he got up and went to his father.

"But while he was still a long way off, his father saw him and was filled with compassion for him; he ran to his son, threw his arms around him and kissed him.

²¹"The son said to him, 'Father, I have sinned against heaven and against you. I am no longer worthy to be called your son.*ᵇ*' ²²"But the father said to his servants, 'Quick! Bring the best robe and put it on him. Put a ring on his finger and sandals on his feet. ²³Bring the fattened calf and kill it. Let's have a feast and celebrate. ²⁴For this son of mine was dead and is alive again; he was lost and is found.' So they began to celebrate.

²⁵"Meanwhile, the older son was in the field. When he came near the house, he heard music and dancing. ²⁶So he called one of the servants and asked him what was going on. ²⁷'Your brother has come,' he replied, 'and your father has killed the fattened calf because he has him back safe and sound.'

²⁸"The older brother became angry and refused to go in. So his father went out and pleaded with him. ²⁹But he answered his father, 'Look! All these years I've been slaving for you and never disobeyed your orders. Yet you never gave me even a young goat so I could celebrate with my friends. ³⁰But when this son of yours who has squandered your property with prostitutes comes home, you kill the fattened calf for him!'

³¹" 'My son,' the father said, 'you are always with me, and everything I have is yours. ³²But we had to celebrate and be glad, because this brother of yours was dead and is alive again; he was lost and is found.' "

The Parable of the Shrewd Manager

16 Jesus told his disciples: "There was a rich man whose manager was accused of wasting his possessions. ²So he called him in and asked him, 'What is this I hear about you? Give an account of your management, because you cannot be manager any longer.'

ᵃ8 Greek *ten drachmas,* each worth about a day's wages *like one of your hired men.*
ᵇ21 Some early manuscripts *son. Make me*

VERSE FOR THE DAY:
Luke 15:6

AUTHOR:
Rosalind Rinker

PASSAGE FOR THE DAY:
Luke 15:1–7

The Parable of the Lost Sheep

JESUS told the parable of the lost sheep to self-righteous leaders who criticized him because he welcomed sinners and even ate with them. His love and mercy are still reaching out to us today, for we are his sheep who have (with or without our consent) wandered into forbidden paths that seemed very innocent. We often shrink from calling anything "sin," but we do admit that sometimes we find ourselves alone, lost, and away from our Shepherd.

For a few moments, imagine you are that little lost one. How did you get lost?

* * * *

There you are, with the rest of the flock, on a hilltop chosen for its tender green grass. Suddenly something tastes better than grass. You don't know that it is tender young thistles but you do know you want more. Searching here and there, you are unaware that you are going downhill to find that delicious stuff. Then, your tummy full, you tuck your legs under your belly and fall right to sleep.

In the meantime, your Good Shepherd takes his flock back to the shelter. Only ninety-nine! Where is that missing little one? Leaving his faithful dog to guard the flock, he retraces his steps to the hilltop, searching, calling, praying.

And what about you? After a good nap you awaken, and . . . oh-oh . . . where are you? It is pitch-dark. Where are the other sheep? Where is your Shepherd? Strange noises frighten you and you say to yourself, "How did I ever get into this mess? How can I ever get out of it?"

With all your strength you cry out, "Maaa . . . maaa . . . Jesus, here I am!" The Good Shepherd hears that cry, and soon you are in his arms. His strong, tender hands are holding you. Feeling the beating of your little heart, he reassures you of his love, and your fears quiet down as you nestle in his arms.

> "My little one, you belong to me. I know what led you astray, but I found you. I'll always be there when you need me. My love is unconditional and eternal."

Additional Scripture Readings:
Psalm 23:1–4; John 10:11–16

*Go to page 1134 for your next
devotional reading.*

³"The manager said to himself, 'What shall I do now? My master is taking away my job. I'm not strong enough to dig, and I'm ashamed to beg— ⁴I know what I'll do so that, when I lose my job here, people will welcome me into their houses.'

⁵"So he called in each one of his master's debtors. He asked the first, 'How much do you owe my master?'

⁶" 'Eight hundred gallons*a* of olive oil,' he replied.

"The manager told him, 'Take your bill, sit down quickly, and make it four hundred.'

⁷"Then he asked the second, 'And how much do you owe?'

" 'A thousand bushels*b* of wheat,' he replied.

"He told him, 'Take your bill and make it eight hundred.'

⁸"The master commended the dishonest manager because he had acted shrewdly. For the people of this world are more shrewd in dealing with their own kind than are the people of the light. ⁹I tell you, use worldly wealth to gain friends for yourselves, so that when it is gone, you will be welcomed into eternal dwellings.

¹⁰"Whoever can be trusted with very little can also be trusted with much, and whoever is dishonest with very little will also be dishonest with much. ¹¹So if you have not been trustworthy in handling worldly wealth, who will trust you with true riches? ¹²And if you have not been trustworthy with someone else's property, who will give you property of your own?

¹³"No servant can serve two masters. Either he will hate the one and love the other, or he will be devoted to the one and despise the other. You cannot serve both God and Money."

¹⁴The Pharisees, who loved money, heard all this and were sneering at Jesus. ¹⁵He said to them, "You are the ones who justify yourselves in the eyes of men, but God knows your hearts. What is highly valued among men is detestable in God's sight.

Additional Teachings

¹⁶"The Law and the Prophets were proclaimed until John. Since that time, the good news of the kingdom of God is being preached, and everyone is forcing his way

into it. ¹⁷It is easier for heaven and earth to disappear than for the least stroke of a pen to drop out of the Law.

¹⁸"Anyone who divorces his wife and marries another woman commits adultery, and the man who marries a divorced woman commits adultery.

The Rich Man and Lazarus

¹⁹"There was a rich man who was dressed in purple and fine linen and lived in luxury every day. ²⁰At his gate was laid a beggar named Lazarus, covered with sores ²¹and longing to eat what fell from the rich man's table. Even the dogs came and licked his sores.

²²"The time came when the beggar died and the angels carried him to Abraham's side. The rich man also died and was buried. ²³In hell,*c* where he was in torment, he looked up and saw Abraham far away, with Lazarus by his side. ²⁴So he called to him, 'Father Abraham, have pity on me and send Lazarus to dip the tip of his finger in water and cool my tongue, because I am in agony in this fire.'

²⁵"But Abraham replied, 'Son, remember that in your lifetime you received your good things, while Lazarus received bad things, but now he is comforted here and you are in agony. ²⁶And besides all this, between us and you a great chasm has been fixed, so that those who want to go from here to you cannot, nor can anyone cross over from there to us.'

²⁷"He answered, 'Then I beg you, father, send Lazarus to my father's house, ²⁸for I have five brothers. Let him warn them, so that they will not also come to this place of torment.'

²⁹"Abraham replied, 'They have Moses and the Prophets; let them listen to them.'

³⁰" 'No, father Abraham,' he said, 'but if someone from the dead goes to them, they will repent.'

³¹"He said to him, 'If they do not listen to Moses and the Prophets, they will not be convinced even if someone rises from the dead.' "

Sin, Faith, Duty

17 Jesus said to his disciples: "Things that cause people to sin are bound to come, but woe to that person through whom they come. ²It would be better for him to be thrown into the sea with a mill-

---

a6 Greek one hundred batous (probably about 3 kiloliters)   *b7 Greek one hundred korous (probably about 35 kiloliters)*   *c23 Greek Hades* stone tied around his neck than for him to cause one of these little ones to sin. ³So watch yourselves.

"If your brother sins, rebuke him, and if he repents, forgive him. ⁴If he sins against you seven times in a day, and seven times comes back to you and says, 'I repent,' forgive him."

⁵The apostles said to the Lord, "Increase our faith!"

⁶He replied, "If you have faith as small as a mustard seed, you can say to this mulberry tree, 'Be uprooted and planted in the sea,' and it will obey you.

⁷"Suppose one of you had a servant plowing or looking after the sheep. Would he say to the servant when he comes in from the field, 'Come along now and sit down to eat'? ⁸Would he not rather say, 'Prepare my supper, get yourself ready and wait on me while I eat and drink; after that you may eat and drink'? ⁹Would he thank the servant because he did what he was told to do? ¹⁰So you also, when you have done everything you were told to do, should say, 'We are unworthy servants; we have only done our duty.' "

Ten Healed of Leprosy

¹¹Now on his way to Jerusalem, Jesus traveled along the border between Samaria and Galilee. ¹²As he was going into a village, ten men who had leprosy[a] met him. They stood at a distance ¹³and called out in a loud voice, "Jesus, Master, have pity on us!"

¹⁴When he saw them, he said, "Go, show yourselves to the priests." And as they went, they were cleansed.

¹⁵One of them, when he saw he was healed, came back, praising God in a loud voice. ¹⁶He threw himself at Jesus' feet and thanked him—and he was a Samaritan.

¹⁷Jesus asked, "Were not all ten cleansed? Where are the other nine? ¹⁸Was no one found to return and give praise to God except this foreigner?" ¹⁹Then he said to him, "Rise and go; your faith has made you well."

The Coming of the Kingdom of God

²⁰Once, having been asked by the Pharisees when the kingdom of God would come, Jesus replied, "The kingdom of God does not come with your careful observation, ²¹nor will people say, 'Here it is,' or 'There it is,' because the kingdom of God is within[b] you."

²²Then he said to his disciples, "The time is coming when you will long to see one of the days of the Son of Man, but you will not see it. ²³Men will tell you, 'There he is!' or 'Here he is!' Do not go running off after them. ²⁴For the Son of Man in his day[c] will be like the lightning, which flashes and lights up the sky from one end to the other. ²⁵But first he must suffer many things and be rejected by this generation.

²⁶"Just as it was in the days of Noah, so also will it be in the days of the Son of Man. ²⁷People were eating, drinking, marrying and being given in marriage up to the day Noah entered the ark. Then the flood came and destroyed them all.

²⁸"It was the same in the days of Lot. People were eating and drinking, buying and selling, planting and building. ²⁹But the day Lot left Sodom, fire and sulfur rained down from heaven and destroyed them all.

³⁰"It will be just like this on the day the Son of Man is revealed. ³¹On that day no one who is on the roof of his house, with his goods inside, should go down to get them. Likewise, no one in the field should go back for anything. ³²Remember Lot's wife! ³³Whoever tries to keep his life will lose it, and whoever loses his life will preserve it. ³⁴I tell you, on that night two people will be in one bed; one will be taken and the other left. ³⁵Two women will be grinding grain together; one will be taken and the other left.[d] "

³⁷"Where, Lord?" they asked.

He replied, "Where there is a dead body, there the vultures will gather."

The Parable of the Persistent Widow

18 Then Jesus told his disciples a parable to show them that they should always pray and not give up. ²He said: "In a certain town there was a judge who neither feared God nor cared about men. ³And there was a widow in that town who kept coming to him with the plea, 'Grant me justice against my adversary.'

⁴"For some time he refused. But finally he said to himself, 'Even though I don't fear God or care about men, ⁵yet because this widow keeps bothering me, I will see

---

[a]12 The Greek word was used for various diseases affecting the skin—not necessarily leprosy.   [b]21 Or among   [c]24 Some manuscripts do not have in his day.   [d]35 Some manuscripts left. 36Two men will be in the field; one will be taken and the other left.

that she gets justice, so that she won't eventually wear me out with her coming!'."

⁶And the Lord said, "Listen to what the unjust judge says. ⁷And will not God bring about justice for his chosen ones, who cry out to him day and night? Will he keep putting them off? ⁸I tell you, he will see that they get justice, and quickly. However, when the Son of Man comes, will he find faith on the earth?"

The Parable of the Pharisee and the Tax Collector

⁹To some who were confident of their own righteousness and looked down on everybody else, Jesus told this parable: ¹⁰"Two men went up to the temple to pray, one a Pharisee and the other a tax collector. ¹¹The Pharisee stood up and prayed about ᵃ himself: 'God, I thank you that I am not like other men—robbers, evildoers, adulterers—or even like this tax collector. ¹²I fast twice a week and give a tenth of all I get.'

¹³"But the tax collector stood at a distance. He would not even look up to heaven, but beat his breast and said, 'God, have mercy on me, a sinner.'

¹⁴"I tell you that this man, rather than the other, went home justified before God. For everyone who exalts himself will be humbled, and he who humbles himself will be exalted."

The Little Children and Jesus

¹⁵People were also bringing babies to Jesus to have him touch them. When the disciples saw this, they rebuked them. ¹⁶But Jesus called the children to him and said, "Let the little children come to me, and do not hinder them, for the kingdom of God belongs to such as these. ¹⁷I tell you the truth, anyone who will not receive the kingdom of God like a little child will never enter it."

The Rich Ruler

¹⁸A certain ruler asked him, "Good teacher, what must I do to inherit eternal life?"

¹⁹"Why do you call me good?" Jesus answered. "No one is good—except God alone. ²⁰You know the commandments: 'Do not commit adultery, do not murder, do not steal, do not give false testimony, honor your father and mother.'ᵇ"

²¹"All these I have kept since I was a boy," he said.

²²When Jesus heard this, he said to him, 'You still lack one thing. Sell everything you have and give to the poor, and you will have treasure in heaven. Then come, follow me."

²³When he heard this, he became very sad, because he was a man of great wealth. ²⁴Jesus looked at him and said, "How hard it is for the rich to enter the kingdom of God! ²⁵Indeed, it is easier for a camel to go through the eye of a needle than for a rich man to enter the kingdom of God."

²⁶Those who heard this asked, "Who then can be saved?"

²⁷Jesus replied, "What is impossible with men is possible with God."

²⁸Peter said to him, "We have left all we had to follow you!"

²⁹"I tell you the truth," Jesus said to them, "no one who has left home or wife or brothers or parents or children for the sake of the kingdom of God ³⁰will fail to receive many times as much in this age and, in the age to come, eternal life."

Jesus Again Predicts His Death

³¹Jesus took the Twelve aside and told them, "We are going up to Jerusalem, and everything that is written by the prophets about the Son of Man will be fulfilled. ³²He will be handed over to the Gentiles. They will mock him, insult him, spit on him, flog him and kill him. ³³On the third day he will rise again."

³⁴The disciples did not understand any of this. Its meaning was hidden from them, and they did not know what he was talking about.

A Blind Beggar Receives His Sight

³⁵As Jesus approached Jericho, a blind man was sitting by the roadside begging. ³⁶When he heard the crowd going by, he asked what was happening. ³⁷They told him, "Jesus of Nazareth is passing by."

³⁸He called out, "Jesus, Son of David, have mercy on me!"

³⁹Those who led the way rebuked him and told him to be quiet, but he shouted all the more, "Son of David, have mercy on me!"

⁴⁰Jesus stopped and ordered the man to be brought to him. When he came near, Jesus asked him, ⁴¹"What do you want me to do for you?"

ᵃ11 Or to   ᵇ20 Exodus 20:12-16; Deut. 5:16-20

"Lord, I want to see," he replied.
42Jesus said to him, "Receive your sight; your faith has healed you." 43Immediately he received his sight and followed Jesus, praising God. When all the people saw it, they also praised God.

Zacchaeus the Tax Collector

19 Jesus entered Jericho and was passing through. 2A man was there by the name of Zacchaeus; he was a chief tax collector and was wealthy. 3He wanted to see who Jesus was, but being a short man he could not, because of the crowd. 4So he ran ahead and climbed a sycamore-fig tree to see him, since Jesus was coming that way.

5When Jesus reached the spot, he looked up and said to him, "Zacchaeus, come down immediately. I must stay at your house today." 6So he came down at once and welcomed him gladly.

7All the people saw this and began to mutter, "He has gone to be the guest of a 'sinner.' "

8But Zacchaeus stood up and said to the Lord, "Look, Lord! Here and now I give half of my possessions to the poor, and if I have cheated anybody out of anything, I will pay back four times the amount."

9Jesus said to him, "Today salvation has come to this house, because this man, too, is a son of Abraham. 10For the Son of Man came to seek and to save what was lost."

The Parable of the Ten Minas

11While they were listening to this, he went on to tell them a parable, because he was near Jerusalem and the people

THURSDAY

VERSE FOR THE DAY:	AUTHOR:	PASSAGE FOR THE DAY:
Luke 18:29–30	Corrie ten Boom	Luke 18:18–30

Sisters

BETSIE'S sleeping place beside me in prison was empty. She had just died. I motioned to a newly arrived Russian prisoner who was looking for a place to sleep, and she gratefully joined me.

We were sharing the same pillow, and with our faces so close, I wanted to speak. But I did not know her language.

"Jezus Christus?" I asked softly.

"Oh!" she exclaimed. Quickly making the sign of the cross, she threw her arms around me.

She who had been my sister for fifty-two years had left me. A Russian woman now claimed my love. And there would be others, too, who would be my sisters and brothers in Christ all around the world.

> "I tell you the truth," Jesus said to them, "no one who has left home or wife or brothers or parents or children for the sake of the kingdom of God will fail to receive many times as much in this age and, in the age to come, eternal life" (Luke 18:29–30).

Additional Scripture Readings:
Galatians 6:9–10; Philemon 10–16

Go to page 1137 for your next devotional reading.

thought that the kingdom of God was going to appear at once. ¹²He said: "A man of noble birth went to a distant country to have himself appointed king and then to return. ¹³So he called ten of his servants and gave them ten minas.ᵃ 'Put this money to work,' he said, 'until I come back.'

¹⁴"But his subjects hated him and sent a delegation after him to say, 'We don't want this man to be our king.'

¹⁵"He was made king, however, and returned home. Then he sent for the servants to whom he had given the money, in order to find out what they had gained with it.

¹⁶"The first one came and said, 'Sir, your mina has earned ten more.'

¹⁷" 'Well done, my good servant!' his master replied. 'Because you have been trustworthy in a very small matter, take charge of ten cities.'

¹⁸"The second came and said, 'Sir, your mina has earned five more.'

¹⁹"His master answered, 'You take charge of five cities.'

²⁰"Then another servant came and said, 'Sir, here is your mina; I have kept it laid away in a piece of cloth. ²¹I was afraid of you, because you are a hard man. You take out what you did not put in and reap what you did not sow.'

²²"His master replied, 'I will judge you by your own words, you wicked servant! You knew, did you, that I am a hard man, taking out what I did not put in, and reaping what I did not sow? ²³Why then didn't you put my money on deposit, so that when I came back, I could have collected it with interest?'

²⁴"Then he said to those standing by, 'Take his mina away from him and give it to the one who has ten minas.'

²⁵" 'Sir,' they said, 'he already has ten!'

²⁶"He replied, 'I tell you that to everyone who has, more will be given, but as for the one who has nothing, even what he has will be taken away. ²⁷But those enemies of mine who did not want me to be king over them—bring them here and kill them in front of me.' "

The Triumphal Entry

²⁸After Jesus had said this, he went on ahead, going up to Jerusalem. ²⁹As he approached Bethphage and Bethany at the hill called the Mount of Olives, he sent two of his disciples, saying to them, ³⁰"Go to the village ahead of you, and as you enter it, you will find a colt tied there, which no one has ever ridden. Untie it and bring it here. ³¹If anyone asks you, 'Why are you untying it?' tell him, 'The Lord needs it.' "

³²Those who were sent ahead went and found it just as he had told them. ³³As they were untying the colt, its owners asked them, "Why are you untying the colt?"

³⁴They replied, "The Lord needs it."

³⁵They brought it to Jesus, threw their cloaks on the colt and put Jesus on it. ³⁶As he went along, people spread their cloaks on the road.

³⁷When he came near the place where the road goes down the Mount of Olives, the whole crowd of disciples began joyfully to praise God in loud voices for all the miracles they had seen:

³⁸"Blessed is the king who comes in the name of the Lord!"ᵇ

"Peace in heaven and glory in the highest!"

³⁹Some of the Pharisees in the crowd said to Jesus, "Teacher, rebuke your disciples!"

⁴⁰"I tell you," he replied, "if they keep quiet, the stones will cry out."

⁴¹As he approached Jerusalem and saw the city, he wept over it ⁴²and said, "If you, even you, had only known on this day what would bring you peace—but now it is hidden from your eyes. ⁴³The days will come upon you when your enemies will build an embankment against you and encircle you and hem you in on every side. ⁴⁴They will dash you to the ground, you and the children within your walls. They will not leave one stone on another, because you did not recognize the time of God's coming to you."

Jesus at the Temple

⁴⁵Then he entered the temple area and began driving out those who were selling. ⁴⁶"It is written," he said to them, " 'My house will be a house of prayer'ᶜ; but you have made it 'a den of robbers.'ᵈ"

⁴⁷Every day he was teaching at the temple. But the chief priests, the teachers of the law and the leaders among the people were trying to kill him. ⁴⁸Yet they could not find any way to do it, because all the people hung on his words.

ᵃ13 A mina was about three months' wages.   ᵇ38 Psalm 118:26   ᶜ46 Isaiah 56:7   ᵈ46 Jer. 7:11

The Authority of Jesus Questioned

20 One day as he was teaching the people in the temple courts and preaching the gospel, the chief priests and the teachers of the law, together with the elders, came up to him. ²"Tell us by what authority you are doing these things," they said. "Who gave you this authority?"

³He replied, "I will also ask you a question. Tell me, ⁴John's baptism—was it from heaven, or from men?"

⁵They discussed it among themselves and said, "If we say, 'From heaven,' he will ask, 'Why didn't you believe him?' ⁶But if we say, 'From men,' all the people will stone us, because they are persuaded that John was a prophet."

⁷So they answered, "We don't know where it was from."

⁸Jesus said, "Neither will I tell you by what authority I am doing these things."

The Parable of the Tenants

⁹He went on to tell the people this parable: A man planted a vineyard, rented it to some farmers and went away for a long time. ¹⁰At harvest time he sent a servant to the tenants so they would give him some of the fruit of the vineyard. But the tenants beat him and sent him away empty-handed. ¹¹He sent another servant, but that one also they beat and treated shamefully and sent away empty-handed. ¹²He sent still a third, and they wounded him and threw him out.

¹³"Then the owner of the vineyard said, 'What shall I do? I will send my son, whom I love; perhaps they will respect him.'

¹⁴"But when the tenants saw him, they talked the matter over. 'This is the heir,' they said. 'Let's kill him, and the inheritance will be ours.' ¹⁵So they threw him out of the vineyard and killed him.

"What then will the owner of the vineyard do to them? ¹⁶He will come and kill those tenants and give the vineyard to others."

When the people heard this, they said, "May this never be!"

¹⁷Jesus looked directly at them and asked, "Then what is the meaning of that which is written:

" 'The stone the builders rejected
    has become the capstone*ᵃᵇ*?

¹⁸Everyone who falls on that stone will be broken to pieces, but he on whom it falls will be crushed."

¹⁹The teachers of the law and the chief priests looked for a way to arrest him immediately, because they knew he had spoken this parable against them. But they were afraid of the people.

Paying Taxes to Caesar

²⁰Keeping a close watch on him, they sent spies, who pretended to be honest. They hoped to catch Jesus in something he said so that they might hand him over to the power and authority of the governor. ²¹So the spies questioned him: "Teacher, we know that you speak and teach what is right, and that you do not show partiality but teach the way of God in accordance with the truth. ²²Is it right for us to pay taxes to Caesar or not?"

²³He saw through their duplicity and said to them, ²⁴"Show me a denarius. Whose portrait and inscription are on it?"

²⁵"Caesar's," they replied.

He said to them, "Then give to Caesar what is Caesar's, and to God what is God's."

²⁶They were unable to trap him in what he had said there in public. And astonished by his answer, they became silent.

The Resurrection and Marriage

²⁷Some of the Sadducees, who say there is no resurrection, came to Jesus with a question. ²⁸"Teacher," they said, "Moses wrote for us that if a man's brother dies and leaves a wife but no children, the man must marry the widow and have children for his brother. ²⁹Now there were seven brothers. The first one married a woman and died childless. ³⁰The second ³¹and then the third married her, and in the same way the seven died, leaving no children. ³²Finally, the woman died too. ³³Now then, at the resurrection whose wife will she be, since the seven were married to her?"

³⁴Jesus replied, "The people of this age marry and are given in marriage. ³⁵But those who are considered worthy of taking part in that age and in the resurrection from the dead will neither marry nor be given in marriage, ³⁶and they can no longer die; for they are like the angels. They are God's children, since they are children of the resurrection. ³⁷But in the account of the bush, even Moses showed

ᵃ17 Or cornerstone   ᵇ17 Psalm 118:22

that the dead rise, for he calls the Lord 'the God of Abraham, and the God of Isaac, and the God of Jacob.'[a] [38]He is not the God of the dead, but of the living, for to him all are alive."

[39]Some of the teachers of the law responded, "Well said, teacher!" [40]And no one dared to ask him any more questions.

Whose Son Is the Christ?

[41]Then Jesus said to them, "How is it that they say the Christ[b] is the Son of David? [42]David himself declares in the Book of Psalms:

" 'The Lord said to my Lord:
"Sit at my right hand
[43]until I make your enemies
a footstool for your feet." '[c]

[44]David calls him 'Lord.' How then can he be his son?"

[45]While all the people were listening, Jesus said to his disciples, [46]"Beware of the teachers of the law. They like to walk around in flowing robes and love to be greeted in the marketplaces and have the most important seats in the synagogues and the places of honor at banquets.

---

[a]37 Exodus 3:6   [b]41 Or *Messiah*   [c]43 Psalm 110:1

FRIDAY

VERSE FOR THE DAY:
Luke 21:2

AUTHOR:
Jill Briscoe

PASSAGE FOR THE DAY:
Luke 21:1–4

When God Says Thank You

JESUS always notices women who throw everything they've got into the Lord's work! Sitting near the treasury at the temple, Jesus drew his disciples' attention to a poor widow. She was, I'm sure, unaware that Jesus was watching. She didn't have to be watched as she gave God everything she had. Her two small copper coins would have bought her a morsel of bread or five sparrows to eat (Luke 12:6–7), but she decided to go hungry and give her money to God instead. Two small coins weren't much. They weren't noticed, they weren't appreciated by other people until Jesus came along and saw what she did and made sure the twelve apostles saw it. He made sure that Luke and Mark recorded it and that the whole world read about it! Solomon's temple would stand without the help of the widow's coins, but Jesus knew that that sort of giving was the stuff of which the kingdom was made.

Jesus always notices the small offerings. Even if the widow herself didn't think her offering was worth the notice, Jesus disagreed and affirmed her in her service. Have you cast in all you can? Are you married to a man who will not allow you to serve God as you wish? Does financial strain limit you to giving little when you desire to give much? If you've indeed cast in all you possibly can of your money, time and service, God understands. He affirms you in it. He says thank you.

Additional Scripture Readings:
Acts 10:1–4; 2 Corinthians 9:6–7

Go to page 1139 for your next devotional reading.

47They devour widows' houses and for a show make lengthy prayers. Such men will be punished most severely."

The Widow's Offering

21 As he looked up, Jesus saw the rich putting their gifts into the temple treasury. 2He also saw a poor widow put in two very small copper coins.*a* 3"I tell you the truth," he said, "this poor widow has put in more than all the others. 4All these people gave their gifts out of their wealth; but she out of her poverty put in all she had to live on."

Signs of the End of the Age

5Some of his disciples were remarking about how the temple was adorned with beautiful stones and with gifts dedicated to God. But Jesus said, 6"As for what you see here, the time will come when not one stone will be left on another; every one of them will be thrown down."

7"Teacher," they asked, "when will these things happen? And what will be the sign that they are about to take place?"

8He replied: "Watch out that you are not deceived. For many will come in my name, claiming, 'I am he,' and, 'The time is near.' Do not follow them. 9When you hear of wars and revolutions, do not be frightened. These things must happen first, but the end will not come right away."

10Then he said to them: "Nation will rise against nation, and kingdom against kingdom. 11There will be great earthquakes, famines and pestilences in various places, and fearful events and great signs from heaven.

12"But before all this, they will lay hands on you and persecute you. They will deliver you to synagogues and prisons, and you will be brought before kings and governors, and all on account of my name. 13This will result in your being witnesses to them. 14But make up your mind not to worry beforehand how you will defend yourselves. 15For I will give you words and wisdom that none of your adversaries will be able to resist or contradict. 16You will be betrayed even by parents, brothers, relatives and friends, and they will put some of you to death. 17All men will hate you because of me. 18But

not a hair of your head will perish. 19By standing firm you will gain life.

20"When you see Jerusalem being surrounded by armies, you will know that its desolation is near. 21Then let those who are in Judea flee to the mountains, let those in the city get out, and let those in the country not enter the city. 22For this is the time of punishment in fulfillment of all that has been written. 23How dreadful it will be in those days for pregnant women and nursing mothers! There will be great distress in the land and wrath against this people. 24They will fall by the sword and will be taken as prisoners to all the nations. Jerusalem will be trampled on by the Gentiles until the times of the Gentiles are fulfilled.

25"There will be signs in the sun, moon and stars. On the earth, nations will be in anguish and perplexity at the roaring and tossing of the sea. 26Men will faint from terror, apprehensive of what is coming on the world, for the heavenly bodies will be shaken. 27At that time they will see the Son of Man coming in a cloud with power and great glory. 28When these things begin to take place, stand up and lift up your heads, because your redemption is drawing near."

29He told them this parable: "Look at the fig tree and all the trees. 30When they sprout leaves, you can see for yourselves and know that summer is near. 31Even so, when you see these things happening, you know that the kingdom of God is near.

32"I tell you the truth, this generation*b* will certainly not pass away until all these things have happened. 33Heaven and earth will pass away, but my words will never pass away.

34"Be careful, or your hearts will be weighed down with dissipation, drunkenness and the anxieties of life, and that day will close on you unexpectedly like a trap. 35For it will come upon all those who live on the face of the whole earth. 36Be always on the watch, and pray that you may be able to escape all that is about to happen, and that you may be able to stand before the Son of Man."

37Each day Jesus was teaching at the temple, and each evening he went out to spend the night on the hill called the Mount of Olives, 38and all the people came early in the morning to hear him at the temple.

---

a2 Greek *two lepta*   *b32* Or *race*

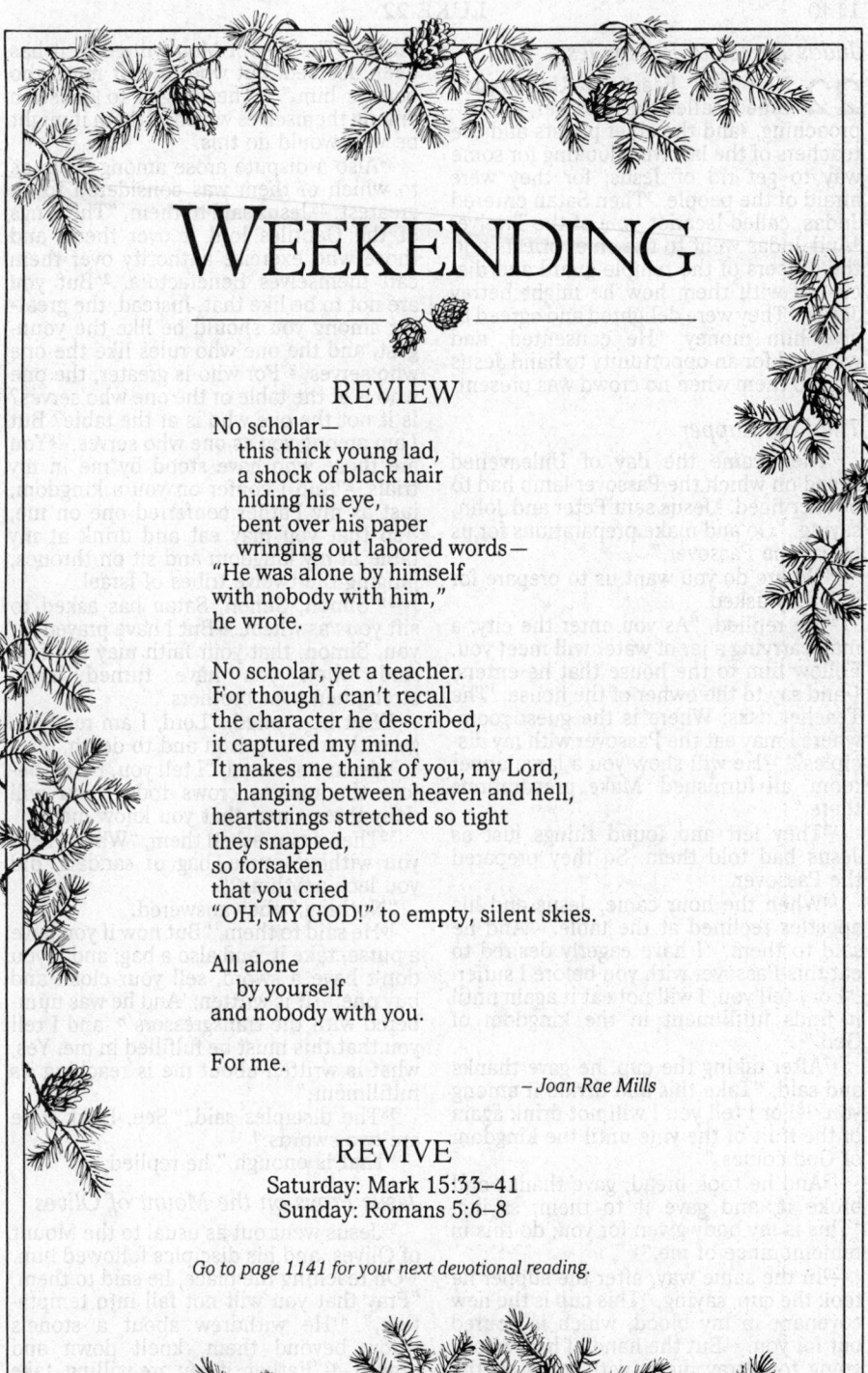

WEEKENDING

REVIEW

No scholar—
   this thick young lad,
   a shock of black hair
   hiding his eye,
   bent over his paper
   wringing out labored words—
"He was alone by himself
with nobody with him,"
he wrote.

No scholar, yet a teacher.
For though I can't recall
the character he described,
it captured my mind.
It makes me think of you, my Lord,
   hanging between heaven and hell,
heartstrings stretched so tight
they snapped,
so forsaken
that you cried
"OH, MY GOD!" to empty, silent skies.

All alone
   by yourself
and nobody with you.

For me.

                              – Joan Rae Mills

REVIVE

Saturday: Mark 15:33–41
Sunday: Romans 5:6–8

Go to page 1141 for your next devotional reading.

Judas Agrees to Betray Jesus

22 Now the Feast of Unleavened Bread, called the Passover, was approaching, ²and the chief priests and the teachers of the law were looking for some way to get rid of Jesus, for they were afraid of the people. ³Then Satan entered Judas, called Iscariot, one of the Twelve. ⁴And Judas went to the chief priests and the officers of the temple guard and discussed with them how he might betray Jesus. ⁵They were delighted and agreed to give him money. ⁶He consented, and watched for an opportunity to hand Jesus over to them when no crowd was present.

The Last Supper

⁷Then came the day of Unleavened Bread on which the Passover lamb had to be sacrificed. ⁸Jesus sent Peter and John, saying, "Go and make preparations for us to eat the Passover."

⁹"Where do you want us to prepare for it?" they asked.

¹⁰He replied, "As you enter the city, a man carrying a jar of water will meet you. Follow him to the house that he enters, ¹¹and say to the owner of the house, 'The Teacher asks: Where is the guest room, where I may eat the Passover with my disciples?' ¹²He will show you a large upper room, all furnished. Make preparations there."

¹³They left and found things just as Jesus had told them. So they prepared the Passover.

¹⁴When the hour came, Jesus and his apostles reclined at the table. ¹⁵And he said to them, "I have eagerly desired to eat this Passover with you before I suffer. ¹⁶For I tell you, I will not eat it again until it finds fulfillment in the kingdom of God."

¹⁷After taking the cup, he gave thanks and said, "Take this and divide it among you. ¹⁸For I tell you I will not drink again of the fruit of the vine until the kingdom of God comes."

¹⁹And he took bread, gave thanks and broke it, and gave it to them, saying, "This is my body given for you; do this in remembrance of me."

²⁰In the same way, after the supper he took the cup, saying, "This cup is the new covenant in my blood, which is poured out for you. ²¹But the hand of him who is going to betray me is with mine on the table. ²²The Son of Man will go as it has been decreed, but woe to that man who betrays him." ²³They began to question among themselves which of them it might be who would do this.

²⁴Also a dispute arose among them as to which of them was considered to be greatest. ²⁵Jesus said to them, "The kings of the Gentiles lord it over them; and those who exercise authority over them call themselves Benefactors. ²⁶But you are not to be like that. Instead, the greatest among you should be like the youngest, and the one who rules like the one who serves. ²⁷For who is greater, the one who is at the table or the one who serves? Is it not the one who is at the table? But I am among you as one who serves. ²⁸You are those who have stood by me in my trials. ²⁹And I confer on you a kingdom, just as my Father conferred one on me, ³⁰so that you may eat and drink at my table in my kingdom and sit on thrones, judging the twelve tribes of Israel.

³¹"Simon, Simon, Satan has asked to sift you[a] as wheat. ³²But I have prayed for you, Simon, that your faith may not fail. And when you have turned back, strengthen your brothers."

³³But he replied, "Lord, I am ready to go with you to prison and to death."

³⁴Jesus answered, "I tell you, Peter, before the rooster crows today, you will deny three times that you know me."

³⁵Then Jesus asked them, "When I sent you without purse, bag or sandals, did you lack anything?"

"Nothing," they answered.

³⁶He said to them, "But now if you have a purse, take it, and also a bag; and if you don't have a sword, sell your cloak and buy one. ³⁷It is written: 'And he was numbered with the transgressors'[b]; and I tell you that this must be fulfilled in me. Yes, what is written about me is reaching its fulfillment."

³⁸The disciples said, "See, Lord, here are two swords."

"That is enough," he replied.

Jesus Prays on the Mount of Olives

³⁹Jesus went out as usual to the Mount of Olives, and his disciples followed him. ⁴⁰On reaching the place, he said to them, "Pray that you will not fall into temptation." ⁴¹He withdrew about a stone's throw beyond them, knelt down and prayed, ⁴²"Father, if you are willing, take

---

a31 The Greek is plural.　　*b37* Isaiah 53:12

this cup from me; yet not my will, but yours be done." 43An angel from heaven appeared to him and strengthened him. 44And being in anguish, he prayed more earnestly, and his sweat was like drops of blood falling to the ground. *a*

45When he rose from prayer and went back to the disciples, he found them asleep, exhausted from sorrow. 46"Why are you sleeping?" he asked them. "Get up and pray so that you will not fall into temptation."

Jesus Arrested

47While he was still speaking a crowd came up, and the man who was called Judas, one of the Twelve, was leading them. He approached Jesus to kiss him, 48but Jesus asked him, "Judas, are you betraying the Son of Man with a kiss?"

49When Jesus' followers saw what was going to happen, they said, "Lord, should we strike with our swords?" 50And one of them struck the servant of the high priest, cutting off his right ear.

51But Jesus answered, "No more of this!" And he touched the man's ear and healed him.

52Then Jesus said to the chief priests, the officers of the temple guard, and the elders, who had come for him, "Am I leading a rebellion, that you have come with swords and clubs? 53Every day I was with you in the temple courts, and you did not lay a hand on me. But this is your hour—when darkness reigns."

Peter Disowns Jesus

54Then seizing him, they led him away and took him into the house of the high

a44 Some early manuscripts do not have verses 43 and 44.

MONDAY

VERSE FOR THE DAY:	AUTHOR:	PASSAGE FOR THE DAY:
Luke 22:27	Karen Burton Mains	Luke 22:24–30

Servanting

BEING a servant is one of the most important lessons for Christians to learn; but unfortunately, we often have to work through gross misconceptions. We have fears about entrusting ourselves to any boss, but we must learn in our spiritual journey that this Master is unlike any other. He will not abuse us or misuse us. He has our greatest interest at heart. He encourages us through our servanting to be all that we can be and then gives us his own Holy Spirit to empower us to become so. This Master is one who even laid down his life for those who were his servants.

He is a Master unlike any other. Not to be feared, he is worthy of our service.

Many of us think servanting means losing ourselves in such a way that we become people without personality, people without original thinking ability, people without giftedness. But when one serves this Master, the opposite is true: He makes us full, complete human beings filled with his own image, with his own amazing mentality. Paradoxically, while teaching us to be more like him, we become more of whom he created us to be.

Additional Scripture Readings:
John 13:12–17; 1 Peter 4:8–11

Go to page 1143 for your next devotional reading.

priest. Peter followed at a distance. ⁵⁵But when they had kindled a fire in the middle of the courtyard and had sat down together, Peter sat down with them. ⁵⁶A servant girl saw him seated there in the firelight. She looked closely at him and said, "This man was with him."

⁵⁷But he denied it. "Woman, I don't know him," he said.

⁵⁸A little later someone else saw him and said, "You also are one of them."

"Man, I am not!" Peter replied.

⁵⁹About an hour later another asserted, "Certainly this fellow was with him, for he is a Galilean."

⁶⁰Peter replied, "Man, I don't know what you're talking about!" Just as he was speaking, the rooster crowed. ⁶¹The Lord turned and looked straight at Peter. Then Peter remembered the word the Lord had spoken to him: "Before the rooster crows today, you will disown me three times." ⁶²And he went outside and wept bitterly.

The Guards Mock Jesus

⁶³The men who were guarding Jesus began mocking and beating him. ⁶⁴They blindfolded him and demanded, "Prophesy! Who hit you?" ⁶⁵And they said many other insulting things to him.

Jesus Before Pilate and Herod

⁶⁶At daybreak the council of the elders of the people, both the chief priests and teachers of the law, met together, and Jesus was led before them. ⁶⁷"If you are the Christ,ᵃ" they said, "tell us."

Jesus answered, "If I tell you, you will not believe me, ⁶⁸and if I asked you, you would not answer. ⁶⁹But from now on, the Son of Man will be seated at the right hand of the mighty God."

⁷⁰They all asked, "Are you then the Son of God?"

He replied, "You are right in saying I am."

⁷¹Then they said, "Why do we need any more testimony? We have heard it from his own lips."

23 Then the whole assembly rose and led him off to Pilate. ²And they began to accuse him, saying, "We have found this man subverting our nation. He opposes payment of taxes to Caesar and claims to be Christ,ᵇ a king."

³So Pilate asked Jesus, "Are you the king of the Jews?"

"Yes, it is as you say," Jesus replied.

⁴Then Pilate announced to the chief priests and the crowd, "I find no basis for a charge against this man."

⁵But they insisted, "He stirs up the people all over Judeaᶜ by his teaching. He started in Galilee and has come all the way here."

⁶On hearing this, Pilate asked if the man was a Galilean. ⁷When he learned that Jesus was under Herod's jurisdiction, he sent him to Herod, who was also in Jerusalem at that time.

⁸When Herod saw Jesus, he was greatly pleased, because for a long time he had been wanting to see him. From what he had heard about him, he hoped to see him perform some miracle. ⁹He plied him with many questions, but Jesus gave him no answer. ¹⁰The chief priests and the teachers of the law were standing there, vehemently accusing him. ¹¹Then Herod and his soldiers ridiculed and mocked him. Dressing him in an elegant robe, they sent him back to Pilate. ¹²That day Herod and Pilate became friends — before this they had been enemies.

¹³Pilate called together the chief priests, the rulers and the people, ¹⁴and said to them, "You brought me this man as one who was inciting the people to rebellion. I have examined him in your presence and have found no basis for your charges against him. ¹⁵Neither has Herod, for he sent him back to us; as you can see, he has done nothing to deserve death. ¹⁶Therefore, I will punish him and then release him.ᵈ"

¹⁸With one voice they cried out, "Away with this man! Release Barabbas to us!" ¹⁹(Barabbas had been thrown into prison for an insurrection in the city, and for murder.)

²⁰Wanting to release Jesus, Pilate appealed to them again. ²¹But they kept shouting, "Crucify him! Crucify him!"

²²For the third time he spoke to them: "Why? What crime has this man committed? I have found in him no grounds for the death penalty. Therefore I will have him punished and then release him."

²³But with loud shouts they insistently demanded that he be crucified, and their shouts prevailed. ²⁴So Pilate decided to grant their demand. ²⁵He released the man who had been thrown into prison for insurrection and murder,

---

ᵃ67 Or Messiah   ᵇ2 Or Messiah; also in verses 35 and 39   ᶜ5 Or over the land of the Jews
ᵈ16 Some manuscripts him." ¹⁷Now he was obliged to release one man to them at the Feast.

the one they asked for, and surrendered Jesus to their will.

The Crucifixion

26As they led him away, they seized Simon from Cyrene, who was on his way in from the country, and put the cross on him and made him carry it behind Jesus. 27A large number of people followed him, including women who mourned and wailed for him. 28Jesus turned and said to them, "Daughters of Jerusalem, do not weep for me; weep for yourselves and for your children. 29For the time will come when you will say, 'Blessed are the barren women, the wombs that never bore and the breasts that never nursed!' 30Then

" 'they will say to the mountains,
    "Fall on us!"
    and to the hills, "Cover us!" ' *a*

31For if men do these things when the tree is green, what will happen when it is dry?"

32Two other men, both criminals, were also led out with him to be executed. 33When they came to the place called the Skull, there they crucified him, along with the criminals—one on his right, the other on his left. 34Jesus said, "Father, forgive them, for they do not know what they are doing." *b* And they divided up his clothes by casting lots.

35The people stood watching, and the rulers even sneered at him. They said,

a30 Hosea 10:8   *b34* Some early manuscripts do not have this sentence.

TUESDAY

| VERSE FOR THE DAY: | AUTHOR: | PASSAGE FOR THE DAY: |
| Luke 23:34 | Eugenia Price | Luke 23:26–43 |

Redemptive Love

FOR three days they thought they had made it. His quiet, unbroken strength (almighty meekness) fanned their fury as they stood watching the heavy nails pierce his hands and feet, when the Roman soldiers secured him to his cross. He was taking into his heart the very sin that motivated this. Their hearts and minds were blinded by that sin. The same dark, inner drive which prodded the first man and woman toward the forbidden tree to satisfy their desire to know as much as God knew. In the heart of each man who plotted his death, there twisted the tormentor whom God hated. He did not hate these murderers, he hated the disease that had made them murderers. As the God-Man hung above them, praying for them, he loved them with the kind of love that could have healed them on the spot!

"Father, forgive them, for they do not know what they are doing" (Luke 23:34).

Down from his cross poured redemptive love in quantity enough for the whole human race. Enough for you. Enough for me. Far from decreasing because of our behavior against him, it seemed rather to increase. The same situation still exists today and will exist as long as the earth stands.

Additional Scripture Readings:
Matthew 23:37; Romans 5:8–11

Go to page 1148 for your next devotional reading.

"He saved others; let him save himself if he is the Christ of God, the Chosen One."

³⁶The soldiers also came up and mocked him. They offered him wine vinegar ³⁷and said, "If you are the king of the Jews, save yourself."

³⁸There was a written notice above him, which read: THIS IS THE KING OF THE JEWS.

³⁹One of the criminals who hung there hurled insults at him: "Aren't you the Christ? Save yourself and us!"

⁴⁰But the other criminal rebuked him. "Don't you fear God," he said, "since you are under the same sentence? ⁴¹We are punished justly, for we are getting what our deeds deserve. But this man has done nothing wrong."

⁴²Then he said, "Jesus, remember me when you come into your kingdom.ᵃ"

⁴³Jesus answered him, "I tell you the truth, today you will be with me in paradise."

Jesus' Death

⁴⁴It was now about the sixth hour, and darkness came over the whole land until the ninth hour, ⁴⁵for the sun stopped shining. And the curtain of the temple was torn in two. ⁴⁶Jesus called out with a loud voice, "Father, into your hands I commit my spirit." When he had said this, he breathed his last.

⁴⁷The centurion, seeing what had happened, praised God and said, "Surely this was a righteous man." ⁴⁸When all the people who had gathered to witness this sight saw what took place, they beat their breasts and went away. ⁴⁹But all those who knew him, including the women who had followed him from Galilee, stood at a distance, watching these things.

Jesus' Burial

⁵⁰Now there was a man named Joseph, a member of the Council, a good and upright man, ⁵¹who had not consented to their decision and action. He came from the Judean town of Arimathea and he was waiting for the kingdom of God. ⁵²Going to Pilate, he asked for Jesus' body. ⁵³Then he took it down, wrapped it in linen cloth and placed it in a tomb cut in the rock, one in which no one had yet been laid. ⁵⁴It was Preparation Day, and the Sabbath was about to begin.

⁵⁵The women who had come with Jesus from Galilee followed Joseph and saw the tomb and how his body was laid in it. ⁵⁶Then they went home and prepared spices and perfumes. But they rested on the Sabbath in obedience to the commandment.

The Resurrection

24 On the first day of the week, very early in the morning, the women took the spices they had prepared and went to the tomb. ²They found the stone rolled away from the tomb, ³but when they entered, they did not find the body of the Lord Jesus. ⁴While they were wondering about this, suddenly two men in clothes that gleamed like lightning stood beside them. ⁵In their fright the women bowed down with their faces to the ground, but the men said to them, "Why do you look for the living among the dead? ⁶He is not here; he has risen! Remember how he told you, while he was still with you in Galilee: ⁷'The Son of Man must be delivered into the hands of sinful men, be crucified and on the third day be raised again.' " ⁸Then they remembered his words.

⁹When they came back from the tomb, they told all these things to the Eleven and to all the others. ¹⁰It was Mary Magdalene, Joanna, Mary the mother of James, and the others with them who told this to the apostles. ¹¹But they did not believe the women, because their words seemed to them like nonsense. ¹²Peter, however, got up and ran to the tomb. Bending over, he saw the strips of linen lying by themselves, and he went away, wondering to himself what had happened.

On the Road to Emmaus

¹³Now that same day two of them were going to a village called Emmaus, about seven milesᵇ from Jerusalem. ¹⁴They were talking with each other about everything that had happened. ¹⁵As they talked and discussed these things with each other, Jesus himself came up and walked along with them; ¹⁶but they were kept from recognizing him.

¹⁷He asked them, "What are you discussing together as you walk along?"

They stood still, their faces downcast. ¹⁸One of them, named Cleopas, asked him, "Are you only a visitor to Jerusalem and do not know the things that have happened there in these days?"

ᵃ42 Some manuscripts *come with your kingly power*   ᵇ13 Greek *sixty stadia* (about 11 kilometers)

19"What things?" he asked.

"About Jesus of Nazareth," they replied. "He was a prophet, powerful in word and deed before God and all the people. 20The chief priests and our rulers handed him over to be sentenced to death, and they crucified him; 21but we had hoped that he was the one who was going to redeem Israel. And what is more, it is the third day since all this took place. 22In addition, some of our women amazed us. They went to the tomb early this morning 23but didn't find his body. They came and told us that they had seen a vision of angels, who said he was alive. 24Then some of our companions went to the tomb and found it just as the women had said, but him they did not see."

25He said to them, "How foolish you are, and how slow of heart to believe all that the prophets have spoken! 26Did not the Christ*a* have to suffer these things and then enter his glory?" 27And beginning with Moses and all the Prophets, he explained to them what was said in all the Scriptures concerning himself.

28As they approached the village to which they were going, Jesus acted as if he were going farther. 29But they urged him strongly, "Stay with us, for it is nearly evening; the day is almost over." So he went in to stay with them.

30When he was at the table with them, he took bread, gave thanks, broke it and began to give it to them. 31Then their eyes were opened and they recognized him, and he disappeared from their sight. 32They asked each other, "Were not our hearts burning within us while he talked with us on the road and opened the Scriptures to us?"

33They got up and returned at once to Jerusalem. There they found the Eleven and those with them, assembled together 34and saying, "It is true! The Lord has risen and has appeared to Simon." 35Then the two told what had happened on the way, and how Jesus was recognized by them when he broke the bread.

Jesus Appears to the Disciples

36While they were still talking about this, Jesus himself stood among them and said to them, "Peace be with you."

37They were startled and frightened, thinking they saw a ghost. 38He said to them, "Why are you troubled, and why do doubts rise in your minds? 39Look at my hands and my feet. It is I myself! Touch me and see; a ghost does not have flesh and bones, as you see I have."

40When he had said this, he showed them his hands and feet. 41And while they still did not believe it because of joy and amazement, he asked them, "Do you have anything here to eat?" 42They gave him a piece of broiled fish, 43and he took it and ate it in their presence.

44He said to them, "This is what I told you while I was still with you: Everything must be fulfilled that is written about me in the Law of Moses, the Prophets and the Psalms."

45Then he opened their minds so they could understand the Scriptures. 46He told them, "This is what is written: The Christ will suffer and rise from the dead on the third day, 47and repentance and forgiveness of sins will be preached in his name to all nations, beginning at Jerusalem. 48You are witnesses of these things. 49I am going to send you what my Father has promised; but stay in the city until you have been clothed with power from on high."

The Ascension

50When he had led them out to the vicinity of Bethany, he lifted up his hands and blessed them. 51While he was blessing them, he left them and was taken up into heaven. 52Then they worshiped him and returned to Jerusalem with great joy. 53And they stayed continually at the temple, praising God.

a26 Or Messiah; also in verse 46

JOHN writes this gospel to present Jesus, the powerful Son of God, who comes in human flesh, gives his life on the cross, and then returns to the Father—all with a view that we may believe in him and receive eternal life. His coming shows us how much the Father and the Son love us, and his parting command is that we should show the same sacrificial love to one another. As you read this book, be sure that you believe that Jesus is the Christ, the Son of God, and promise him that you will love others as he loves you.

JOHN

The Word Became Flesh

1 In the beginning was the Word, and the Word was with God, and the Word was God. ²He was with God in the beginning. ³Through him all things were made; without him nothing was made that has been made. ⁴In him was life, and that life was the light of men. ⁵The light shines in the darkness, but the darkness has not understood*ᵃ* it.

⁶There came a man who was sent from God; his name was John. ⁷He came as a witness to testify concerning that light, so that through him all men might believe. ⁸He himself was not the light; he came only as a witness to the light. ⁹The true light that gives light to every man was coming into the world.*ᵇ*

¹⁰He was in the world, and though the world was made through him, the world did not recognize him. ¹¹He came to that which was his own, but his own did not

---

ᵃ5 Or darkness, and the darkness has not overcome every man who comes into the world *ᵇ9 Or This was the true light that gives light to* receive him. ¹²Yet to all who received him, to those who believed in his name, he gave the right to become children of God— ¹³children born not of natural descent,ᵃ nor of human decision or a husband's will, but born of God.

¹⁴The Word became flesh and made his dwelling among us. We have seen his glory, the glory of the One and Only,ᵇ who came from the Father, full of grace and truth.

¹⁵John testifies concerning him. He cries out, saying, "This was he of whom I said, 'He who comes after me has surpassed me because he was before me.'" ¹⁶From the fullness of his grace we have all received one blessing after another. ¹⁷For the law was given through Moses; grace and truth came through Jesus Christ. ¹⁸No one has ever seen God, but God the One and Only,ᵇ,ᶜ who is at the Father's side, has made him known.

John the Baptist Denies Being the Christ

¹⁹Now this was John's testimony when the Jews of Jerusalem sent priests and Levites to ask him who he was. ²⁰He did not fail to confess, but confessed freely, "I am not the Christ.ᵈ"

²¹They asked him, "Then who are you? Are you Elijah?"

He said, "I am not."

"Are you the Prophet?"

He answered, "No."

²²Finally they said, "Who are you? Give us an answer to take back to those who sent us. What do you say about yourself?"

²³John replied in the words of Isaiah the prophet, "I am the voice of one calling in the desert, 'Make straight the way for the Lord.'"ᵉ

²⁴Now some Pharisees who had been sent ²⁵questioned him, "Why then do you baptize if you are not the Christ, nor Elijah, nor the Prophet?"

²⁶"I baptize withᶠ water," John replied, "but among you stands one you do not know. ²⁷He is the one who comes after me, the thongs of whose sandals I am not worthy to untie."

²⁸This all happened at Bethany on the other side of the Jordan, where John was baptizing.

Jesus the Lamb of God

²⁹The next day John saw Jesus coming toward him and said, "Look, the Lamb of God, who takes away the sin of the world! ³⁰This is the one I meant when I said, 'A man who comes after me has surpassed me because he was before me.' ³¹I myself did not know him, but the reason I came baptizing with water was that he might be revealed to Israel."

³²Then John gave this testimony: "I saw the Spirit come down from heaven as a dove and remain on him. ³³I would not have known him, except that the one who sent me to baptize with water told me, 'The man on whom you see the Spirit come down and remain is he who will baptize with the Holy Spirit.' ³⁴I have seen and I testify that this is the Son of God."

Jesus' First Disciples

³⁵The next day John was there again with two of his disciples. ³⁶When he saw Jesus passing by, he said, "Look, the Lamb of God!"

³⁷When the two disciples heard him say this, they followed Jesus. ³⁸Turning around, Jesus saw them following and asked, "What do you want?"

They said, "Rabbi" (which means Teacher), "where are you staying?"

³⁹"Come," he replied, "and you will see."

So they went and saw where he was staying, and spent that day with him. It was about the tenth hour.

⁴⁰Andrew, Simon Peter's brother, was one of the two who heard what John had said and who had followed Jesus. ⁴¹The first thing Andrew did was to find his brother Simon and tell him, "We have found the Messiah" (that is, the Christ). ⁴²And he brought him to Jesus.

Jesus looked at him and said, "You are Simon son of John. You will be called Cephas" (which, when translated, is Peterᵍ).

Jesus Calls Philip and Nathanael

⁴³The next day Jesus decided to leave for Galilee. Finding Philip, he said to him, "Follow me."

⁴⁴Philip, like Andrew and Peter, was from the town of Bethsaida. ⁴⁵Philip

ᵃ13 Greek of bloods   ᵇ14,18 Or the Only Begotten begotten) Son   ᵈ20 Or Messiah. "The Christ" (Greek) and "the Messiah" (Hebrew) both mean "the Anointed One"; also in verse 25.   ᵉ23 Isaiah 40:3   ᶜ18 Some manuscripts but the only (or only   ᶠ26 Or in; also in verses 31 and 33   ᵍ42 Both Cephas (Aramaic) and Peter (Greek) mean rock.

VERSE FOR THE DAY:
John 1:14

AUTHOR:
Rosemary Jensen

PASSAGE FOR THE DAY:
John 1:1–18

The Word Became Flesh

THAT the Word, Jesus Christ, became a man is the wonder of wonders expressed simply in the phrase, "The Word became flesh" (John 1:14). Jesus had a human body just like you and I have. The *extraordinary* embraced the *ordinary* and produced a living person, fully God and fully human. The Holy Spirit extraordinarily impregnated an egg within the ordinary body of a woman. How could it happen? This is a mystery too profound to understand, but the written Word clearly says it is true.

And the Word "made his dwelling among us." He lived, breathed, ate, drank, slept, worked, laughed and spoke among us. He was real to the eye, real to the touch, real to the ear. He was here—in human flesh—living with men and women and little children.

You have probably wished that Jesus lived today in human flesh and that his house was in your neighborhood. Have you ever thought how wonderful it would be to knock on his door and say, "Jesus, would you show me what the Father is like?" Or, "Jesus, could you give me a hand building a desk for my child?" Or, "Jesus, I'm miserable, please tell me what I should do to patch it up with my husband."

As children of God we have the privilege of "fleshing out" Jesus Christ to others who also would like him as a neighbor. We, as Christians, have received the written Word into our hearts as a seed, miraculously affecting our whole person so that the very life of Christ is produced in us. We each live next door to people who can knock on our doors and say, "Will you please show me what God the Father is like?" And you and I can show them, because we have become somewhat like him as we have studied, worshiped and obeyed him. When someone says, "Could you please help me?" we can lend a helping hand because we have given our bodies over to be used in service to others. When a friend says, "Please help me with a broken relationship," we can give loving counsel because we have contemplated the Lord Jesus Christ in his Word and are able to tackle the problems that the people around us face.

As Christ became flesh and made his dwelling in us, will we become Christ in flesh to our neighbors?

Additional Scripture Readings:
John 14:11–14; Hebrews 2:14–18

Go to page 1151 for your next devotional reading.

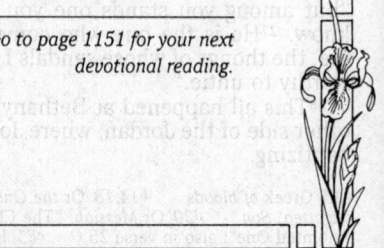

found Nathanael and told him, "We have found the one Moses wrote about in the Law, and about whom the prophets also wrote—Jesus of Nazareth, the son of Joseph."

46"Nazareth! Can anything good come from there?" Nathanael asked.

"Come and see," said Philip.

47When Jesus saw Nathanael approaching, he said of him, "Here is a true Israelite, in whom there is nothing false."

48"How do you know me?" Nathanael asked.

Jesus answered, "I saw you while you were still under the fig tree before Philip called you."

49Then Nathanael declared, "Rabbi, you are the Son of God; you are the King of Israel."

50Jesus said, "You believe*a* because I told you I saw you under the fig tree. You shall see greater things than that." 51He then added, "I tell you*b* the truth, you*b* shall see heaven open, and the angels of God ascending and descending on the Son of Man."

Jesus Changes Water to Wine

2 On the third day a wedding took place at Cana in Galilee. Jesus' mother was there, 2and Jesus and his disciples had also been invited to the wedding. 3When the wine was gone, Jesus' mother said to him, "They have no more wine."

4"Dear woman, why do you involve me?" Jesus replied. "My time has not yet come."

5His mother said to the servants, "Do whatever he tells you."

6Nearby stood six stone water jars, the kind used by the Jews for ceremonial washing, each holding from twenty to thirty gallons.*c*

7Jesus said to the servants, "Fill the jars with water"; so they filled them to the brim.

8Then he told them, "Now draw some out and take it to the master of the banquet."

They did so, 9and the master of the banquet tasted the water that had been turned into wine. He did not realize where it had come from, though the servants who had drawn the water knew. Then he called the bridegroom aside 10and said, "Everyone brings out the choice wine first and then the cheaper wine after the guests have had too much to drink; but you have saved the best till now."

11This, the first of his miraculous signs, Jesus performed at Cana in Galilee. He thus revealed his glory, and his disciples put their faith in him.

Jesus Clears the Temple

12After this he went down to Capernaum with his mother and brothers and his disciples. There they stayed for a few days.

13When it was almost time for the Jewish Passover, Jesus went up to Jerusalem. 14In the temple courts he found men selling cattle, sheep and doves, and others sitting at tables exchanging money. 15So he made a whip out of cords, and drove all from the temple area, both sheep and cattle; he scattered the coins of the money changers and overturned their tables. 16To those who sold doves he said, "Get these out of here! How dare you turn my Father's house into a market!"

17His disciples remembered that it is written: "Zeal for your house will consume me."*d*

18Then the Jews demanded of him, "What miraculous sign can you show us to prove your authority to do all this?"

19Jesus answered them, "Destroy this temple, and I will raise it again in three days."

20The Jews replied, "It has taken forty-six years to build this temple, and you are going to raise it in three days?" 21But the temple he had spoken of was his body. 22After he was raised from the dead, his disciples recalled what he had said. Then they believed the Scripture and the words that Jesus had spoken.

23Now while he was in Jerusalem at the Passover Feast, many people saw the miraculous signs he was doing and believed in his name.*e* 24But Jesus would not entrust himself to them, for he knew all men. 25He did not need man's testimony about man, for he knew what was in a man.

Jesus Teaches Nicodemus

3 Now there was a man of the Pharisees named Nicodemus, a member of the Jewish ruling council. 2He came to Jesus at night and said, "Rabbi, we know you are a teacher who has come from God.

a50 Or *Do you believe . . . ?*   *b51* The Greek is plural.   *c6* Greek *two to three metretes* (probably about 75 to 115 liters)   *d17* Psalm 69:9   *e23* Or *and believed in him*

For no one could perform the miraculous signs you are doing if God were not with him."

[3]In reply Jesus declared, "I tell you the truth, no one can see the kingdom of God unless he is born again.[a]"

[4]"How can a man be born when he is old?" Nicodemus asked. "Surely he cannot enter a second time into his mother's womb to be born!"

[5]Jesus answered, "I tell you the truth, no one can enter the kingdom of God unless he is born of water and the Spirit. [6]Flesh gives birth to flesh, but the Spirit[b] gives birth to spirit. [7]You should not be surprised at my saying, 'You[c] must be born again.' [8]The wind blows wherever it pleases. You hear its sound, but you cannot tell where it comes from or where it is going. So it is with everyone born of the Spirit."

[9]"How can this be?" Nicodemus asked.

[10]"You are Israel's teacher," said Jesus, "and do you not understand these things? [11]I tell you the truth, we speak of what we know, and we testify to what we have seen, but still you people do not accept our testimony. [12]I have spoken to you of earthly things and you do not believe; how then will you believe if I speak of heavenly things? [13]No one has ever gone into heaven except the one who came from heaven—the Son of Man.[d] [14]Just as Moses lifted up the snake in the desert, so the Son of Man must be lifted up, [15]that everyone who believes in him may have eternal life.[e]

[16]"For God so loved the world that he gave his one and only Son,[f] that whoever believes in him shall not perish but have eternal life. [17]For God did not send his Son into the world to condemn the world, but to save the world through him. [18]Whoever believes in him is not condemned, but whoever does not believe stands condemned already because he has not believed in the name of God's one and only Son.[g] [19]This is the verdict: Light has come into the world, but men loved darkness instead of light because their deeds were evil. [20]Everyone who does evil hates the light, and will not come into the light for fear that his deeds will be exposed. [21]But whoever lives by the truth comes into the light, so that it may be seen plainly that what he has done has been done through God."[h]

John the Baptist's Testimony About Jesus

[22]After this, Jesus and his disciples went out into the Judean countryside, where he spent some time with them, and baptized. [23]Now John also was baptizing at Aenon near Salim, because there was plenty of water, and people were constantly coming to be baptized. [24](This was before John was put in prison.) [25]An argument developed between some of John's disciples and a certain Jew[i] over the matter of ceremonial washing. [26]They came to John and said to him, "Rabbi, that man who was with you on the other side of the Jordan—the one you testified about—well, he is baptizing, and everyone is going to him."

[27]To this John replied, "A man can receive only what is given him from heaven. [28]You yourselves can testify that I said, 'I am not the Christ[j] but am sent ahead of him.' [29]The bride belongs to the bridegroom. The friend who attends the bridegroom waits and listens for him, and is full of joy when he hears the bridegroom's voice. That joy is mine, and it is now complete. [30]He must become greater; I must become less.

[31]"The one who comes from above is above all; the one who is from the earth belongs to the earth, and speaks as one from the earth. The one who comes from heaven is above all. [32]He testifies to what he has seen and heard, but no one accepts his testimony. [33]The man who has accepted it has certified that God is truthful. [34]For the one whom God has sent speaks the words of God, for God[k] gives the Spirit without limit. [35]The Father loves the Son and has placed everything in his hands. [36]Whoever believes in the Son has eternal life, but whoever rejects the Son will not see life, for God's wrath remains on him."[l]

Jesus Talks With a Samaritan Woman

4 The Pharisees heard that Jesus was gaining and baptizing more disciples

---

[a]3 Or born from above; also in verse 7   [b]6 Or but spirit   [c]7 The Greek is plural.   [d]13 Some manuscripts Man, who is in heaven   [e]15 Or believes may have eternal life in him   [f]16 Or his only begotten Son   [g]18 Or God's only begotten Son   [h]21 Some interpreters end the quotation after verse 15.   [i]25 Some manuscripts and certain Jews   [j]28 Or Messiah   [k]34 Greek he   [l]36 Some interpreters end the quotation after verse 30.

than John, ²although in fact it was not Jesus who baptized, but his disciples. ³When the Lord learned of this, he left Judea and went back once more to Galilee.

⁴Now he had to go through Samaria. ⁵So he came to a town in Samaria called Sychar, near the plot of ground Jacob had given to his son Joseph. ⁶Jacob's well was there, and Jesus, tired as he was from the journey, sat down by the well. It was about the sixth hour.

⁷When a Samaritan woman came to draw water, Jesus said to her, "Will you give me a drink?" ⁸(His disciples had gone into the town to buy food.)

⁹The Samaritan woman said to him,

"You are a Jew and I am a Samaritan woman. How can you ask me for a drink?" (For Jews do not associate with Samaritans.ᵃ)

¹⁰Jesus answered her, "If you knew the gift of God and who it is that asks you for a drink, you would have asked him and he would have given you living water."

¹¹"Sir," the woman said, "you have nothing to draw with and the well is deep. Where can you get this living water? ¹²Are you greater than our father Jacob, who gave us the well and drank from it himself, as did also his sons and his flocks and herds?"

¹³Jesus answered, "Everyone who drinks this water will be thirsty again,

ᵃ9 Or do not use dishes Samaritans have used

THURSDAY

VERSE FOR THE DAY:
John 3:16

AUTHOR:
Kathryn Hillen

PASSAGE FOR THE DAY:
John 3:1–21

Chosen

IT was the day before Mother's Day, and our daughter Linda wanted to go shopping even though she was so little that her head was hardly visible over the store counter. Asking me to stay at the front, she headed for the back of Woolworth's, clutching her dollar bill. As I watched, she chose a relish dish and stood by the cash register, where she was overlooked by the busy clerks. She waited, dish in hand, jostled by other customers and ignored by the salespeople but firm in her resolve to buy a gift of her own choosing for her mother. She finally returned to me with her package and a smile of triumph.

That inexpensive dish is one of my most prized possessions, for it cost someone I love all that she had. It was bought with real sacrifice by one who went alone with no other aim than to please me. I cherish it, display it with my crystal and china, and use it proudly.

God's beloved Son, Jesus, came to the dime store of earth and chose to sacrifice his all for our redemption. As the Father watched, his love for his Son must have deepened. And how does God feel about those he purchased through death on the cross? Does God love us even more because of what his Son did for us? After all, that's what gives us worth.

Additional Scripture Readings:
2 Thessalonians 2:13–14; 1 Peter 2:9–10

Go to page 1153 for your next devotional reading.

14but whoever drinks the water I give him will never thirst. Indeed, the water I give him will become in him a spring of water welling up to eternal life."

15The woman said to him, "Sir, give me this water so that I won't get thirsty and have to keep coming here to draw water."

16He told her, "Go, call your husband and come back."

17"I have no husband," she replied.

Jesus said to her, "You are right when you say you have no husband. 18The fact is, you have had five husbands, and the man you now have is not your husband. What you have just said is quite true."

19"Sir," the woman said, "I can see that you are a prophet. 20Our fathers worshiped on this mountain, but you Jews claim that the place where we must worship is in Jerusalem."

21Jesus declared, "Believe me, woman, a time is coming when you will worship the Father neither on this mountain nor in Jerusalem. 22You Samaritans worship what you do not know; we worship what we do know, for salvation is from the Jews. 23Yet a time is coming and has now come when the true worshipers will worship the Father in spirit and truth, for they are the kind of worshipers the Father seeks. 24God is spirit, and his worshipers must worship in spirit and in truth."

25The woman said, "I know that Messiah" (called Christ) "is coming. When he comes, he will explain everything to us."

26Then Jesus declared, "I who speak to you am he."

The Disciples Rejoin Jesus

27Just then his disciples returned and were surprised to find him talking with a woman. But no one asked, "What do you want?" or "Why are you talking with her?"

28Then, leaving her water jar, the woman went back to the town and said to the people, 29"Come, see a man who told me everything I ever did. Could this be the Christ*a*?" 30They came out of the town and made their way toward him.

31Meanwhile his disciples urged him, "Rabbi, eat something."

32But he said to them, "I have food to eat that you know nothing about."

33Then his disciples said to each other, "Could someone have brought him food?"

34"My food," said Jesus, "is to do the will of him who sent me and to finish his work. 35Do you not say, 'Four months more and then the harvest'? I tell you, open your eyes and look at the fields! They are ripe for harvest. 36Even now the reaper draws his wages, even now he harvests the crop for eternal life, so that the sower and the reaper may be glad together. 37Thus the saying 'One sows and another reaps' is true. 38I sent you to reap what you have not worked for. Others have done the hard work, and you have reaped the benefits of their labor."

Many Samaritans Believe

39Many of the Samaritans from that town believed in him because of the woman's testimony, "He told me everything I ever did." 40So when the Samaritans came to him, they urged him to stay with them, and he stayed two days. 41And because of his words many more became believers.

42They said to the woman, "We no longer believe just because of what you said; now we have heard for ourselves, and we know that this man really is the Savior of the world."

Jesus Heals the Official's Son

43After the two days he left for Galilee. 44(Now Jesus himself had pointed out that a prophet has no honor in his own country.) 45When he arrived in Galilee, the Galileans welcomed him. They had seen all that he had done in Jerusalem at the Passover Feast, for they also had been there.

46Once more he visited Cana in Galilee, where he had turned the water into wine. And there was a certain royal official whose son lay sick at Capernaum. 47When this man heard that Jesus had arrived in Galilee from Judea, he went to him and begged him to come and heal his son, who was close to death.

48"Unless you people see miraculous signs and wonders," Jesus told him, "you will never believe."

49The royal official said, "Sir, come down before my child dies."

50Jesus replied, "You may go. Your son will live."

The man took Jesus at his word and departed. 51While he was still on the way, his servants met him with the news that

---

*a29 Or Messiah

his boy was living. [52]When he inquired as to the time when his son got better, they said to him, "The fever left him yesterday at the seventh hour."

[53]Then the father realized that this was the exact time at which Jesus had said to him, "Your son will live." So he and all his household believed.

[54]This was the second miraculous sign that Jesus performed, having come from Judea to Galilee.

The Healing at the Pool

5 Some time later, Jesus went up to Jerusalem for a feast of the Jews. [2]Now there is in Jerusalem near the Sheep Gate a pool, which in Aramaic is called Bethesda[a] and which is surrounded by five covered colonnades. [3]Here a great number of disabled people used to lie—the blind, the lame, the paralyzed.[b] [5]One who was there had been an invalid for thirty-eight

[a]2 Some manuscripts *Bethzatha*; other manuscripts *Bethsaida*   [b]3 Some less important manuscripts *paralyzed—and they waited for the moving of the waters.* [4]*From time to time an angel of the Lord would come down and stir up the waters. The first one into the pool after each such disturbance would be cured of whatever disease he had.*

FRIDAY

VERSE FOR THE DAY:
John 4:34

AUTHOR:
Jill Briscoe

PASSAGE FOR THE DAY:
John 4:27–38

More Important Than Lunch

JESUS had a heart for God. He had a sense of urgency that meant that some things were even more important than his lunch. I suspect some of us would rather die before we missed our lunch in order to do something for God! Jesus had a sense of purpose. He knew what he was supposed to be doing. He was on earth to talk to men and women about himself. That was why he took time out—even when he was tired and hungry—to explain the things of God to a rather disreputable lady. By the time the disciples came back after buying food, they found Jesus sitting by the well where they had left him; he was tired but triumphant. There is nothing that lifts the spirits as much as seeing someone respond to the gospel. As he watched the woman bringing back the men of her village to "see a man who told me everything I ever did," Jesus was satisfied!

There is nothing quite so fulfilling as completing an assignment for God. You said what was needed, you prayed with a child, you organized the study, you cooked for the homeless, and you finished it! You stuck to it till the job was done. The joy comes, of course, when you are doing *his* work. I will lose heart if I consider the work mine. Stuart caught me talking about "my women in my Bible study" one day, and he rightly rebuked me. They were not "my" women at all—they were Jesus' women! When I have a heart for God he will give me a heart for women, and ministry with them will always be more important than my lunch!

Additional Scripture Readings:
Mark 3:20; Hebrews 6:10–12

Go to page 1155 for your next devotional reading.

years. 6When Jesus saw him lying there and learned that he had been in this condition for a long time, he asked him, "Do you want to get well?"

7"Sir," the invalid replied, "I have no one to help me into the pool when the water is stirred. While I am trying to get in, someone else goes down ahead of me."

8Then Jesus said to him, "Get up! Pick up your mat and walk." 9At once the man was cured; he picked up his mat and walked.

The day on which this took place was a Sabbath, 10and so the Jews said to the man who had been healed, "It is the Sabbath; the law forbids you to carry your mat."

11But he replied, "The man who made me well said to me, 'Pick up your mat and walk.'

12So they asked him, "Who is this fellow who told you to pick it up and walk?"

13The man who was healed had no idea who it was, for Jesus had slipped away into the crowd that was there.

14Later Jesus found him at the temple and said to him, "See, you are well again. Stop sinning or something worse may happen to you." 15The man went away and told the Jews that it was Jesus who had made him well.

Life Through the Son

16So, because Jesus was doing these things on the Sabbath, the Jews persecuted him. 17Jesus said to them, "My Father is always at his work to this very day, and I, too, am working." 18For this reason the Jews tried all the harder to kill him; not only was he breaking the Sabbath, but he was even calling God his own Father, making himself equal with God.

19Jesus gave them this answer: "I tell you the truth, the Son can do nothing by himself; he can do only what he sees his Father doing, because whatever the Father does the Son also does. 20For the Father loves the Son and shows him all he does. Yes, to your amazement he will show him even greater things than these. 21For just as the Father raises the dead and gives them life, even so the Son gives life to whom he is pleased to give it. 22Moreover, the Father judges no one, but has entrusted all judgment to the Son, 23that all may honor the Son just as they honor the Father. He who does not honor

the Son does not honor the Father, who sent him.

24"I tell you the truth, whoever hears my word and believes him who sent me has eternal life and will not be condemned; he has crossed over from death to life. 25I tell you the truth, a time is coming and has now come when the dead will hear the voice of the Son of God and those who hear will live. 26For as the Father has life in himself, so he has granted the Son to have life in himself. 27And he has given him authority to judge because he is the Son of Man.

28"Do not be amazed at this, for a time is coming when all who are in their graves will hear his voice 29and come out—those who have done good will rise to live, and those who have done evil will rise to be condemned. 30By myself I can do nothing; I judge only as I hear, and my judgment is just, for I seek not to please myself but him who sent me.

Testimonies About Jesus

31"If I testify about myself, my testimony is not valid. 32There is another who testifies in my favor, and I know that his testimony about me is valid.

33"You have sent to John and he has testified to the truth. 34Not that I accept human testimony; but I mention it that you may be saved. 35John was a lamp that burned and gave light, and you chose for a time to enjoy his light.

36"I have testimony weightier than that of John. For the very work that the Father has given me to finish, and which I am doing, testifies that the Father has sent me. 37And the Father who sent me has himself testified concerning me. You have never heard his voice nor seen his form, 38nor does his word dwell in you, for you do not believe the one he sent. 39You diligently study*a* the Scriptures because you think that by them you possess eternal life. These are the Scriptures that testify about me, 40yet you refuse to come to me to have life.

41"I do not accept praise from men, 42but I know you. I know that you do not have the love of God in your hearts. 43I have come in my Father's name, and you do not accept me; but if someone else comes in his own name, you will accept him. 44How can you believe if you accept praise from one another, yet make no ef-

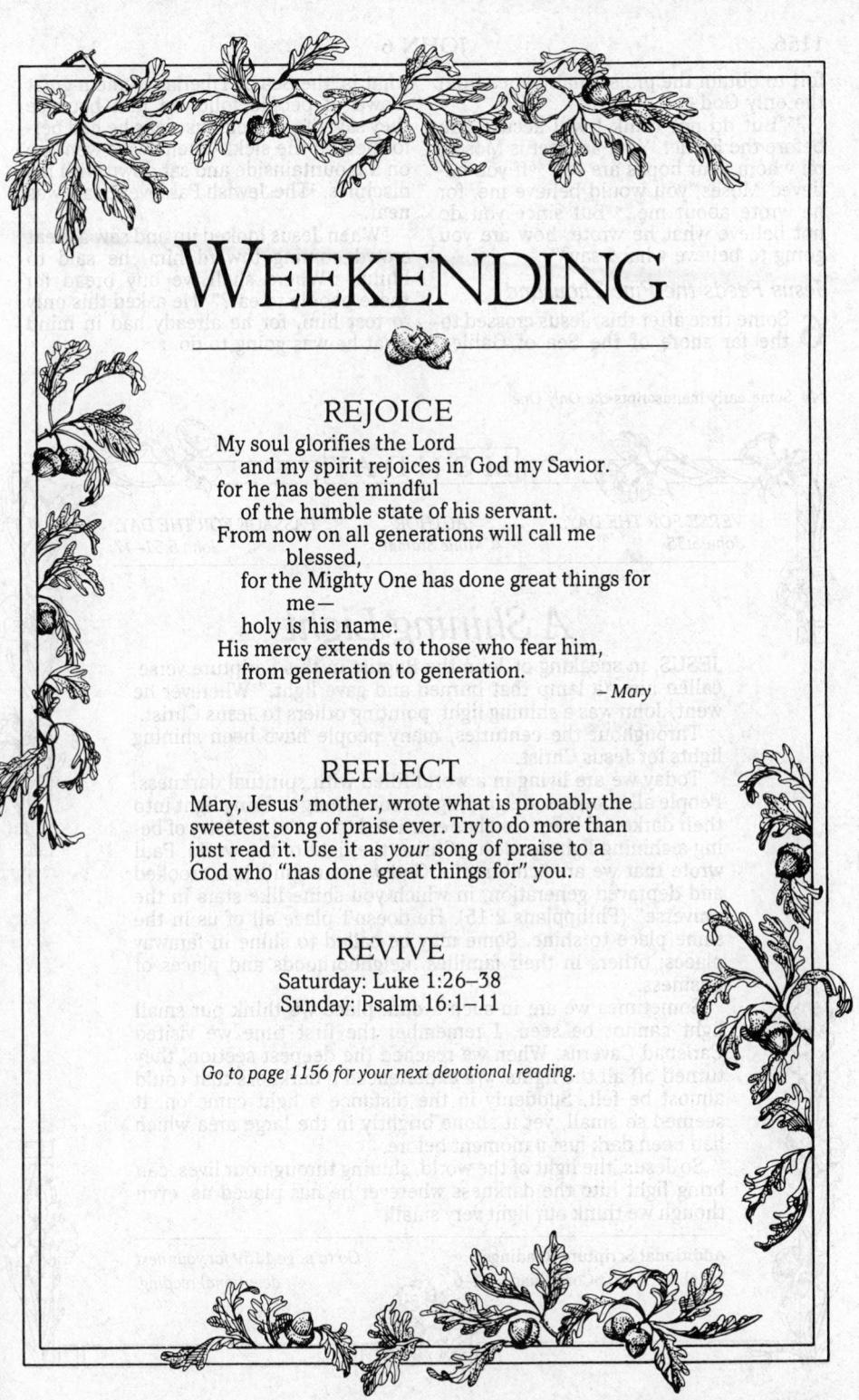

WEEKENDING

REJOICE

My soul glorifies the Lord
    and my spirit rejoices in God my Savior.
for he has been mindful
    of the humble state of his servant.
From now on all generations will call me
       blessed,
    for the Mighty One has done great things for
       me—
    holy is his name.
His mercy extends to those who fear him,
    from generation to generation.

– Mary

REFLECT

Mary, Jesus' mother, wrote what is probably the
sweetest song of praise ever. Try to do more than
just read it. Use it as *your* song of praise to a
God who "has done great things for" you.

REVIVE

Saturday: Luke 1:26–38
Sunday: Psalm 16:1–11

Go to page 1156 for your next devotional reading.

fort to obtain the praise that comes from the only God[a]?

45"But do not think I will accuse you before the Father. Your accuser is Moses, on whom your hopes are set. 46If you believed Moses, you would believe me, for he wrote about me. 47But since you do not believe what he wrote, how are you going to believe what I say?"

Jesus Feeds the Five Thousand

6 Some time after this, Jesus crossed to the far shore of the Sea of Galilee (that is, the Sea of Tiberias), 2and a great crowd of people followed him because they saw the miraculous signs he had performed on the sick. 3Then Jesus went up on a mountainside and sat down with his disciples. 4The Jewish Passover Feast was near.

5When Jesus looked up and saw a great crowd coming toward him, he said to Philip, "Where shall we buy bread for these people to eat?" 6He asked this only to test him, for he already had in mind what he was going to do.

[a]44 Some early manuscripts the Only One

VERSE FOR THE DAY:	AUTHOR:	PASSAGE FOR THE DAY:
John 5:35	Millie Stamm	John 5:31–47

A Shining Light

JESUS, in speaking of John the Baptist in this Scripture verse, called him "a lamp that burned and gave light." Wherever he went, John was a shining light, pointing others to Jesus Christ.

Throughout the centuries, many people have been shining lights for Jesus Christ.

Today we are living in a world filled with spiritual darkness. People all about us are groping for something to bring light into their darkened lives. God has entrusted to us the ministry of being a shining light for Jesus Christ, the light of the world. Paul wrote that we are "children of God without fault in a crooked and depraved generation, in which you shine like stars in the universe" (Philippians 2:15). He doesn't place all of us in the same place to shine. Some may be called to shine in faraway places; others in their families, neighborhoods and places of business.

Sometimes we are in such a dark place we think our small light cannot be seen. I remember the first time we visited Carlsbad Caverns. When we reached the deepest section, they turned off all the lights. We experienced a darkness that could almost be felt. Suddenly in the distance a light came on. It seemed so small, yet it shone brightly in the large area which had been dark just a moment before.

So Jesus, the light of the world, shining through our lives, can bring light into the darkness wherever he has placed us, even though we think our light very small.

Additional Scripture Readings:
Isaiah 49:5–6; 2 Corinthians 4:4–6

Go to page 1159 for your next devotional reading.

[7]Philip answered him, "Eight months' wages[a] would not buy enough bread for each one to have a bite!"

[8]Another of his disciples, Andrew, Simon Peter's brother, spoke up, [9]"Here is a boy with five small barley loaves and two small fish, but how far will they go among so many?"

[10]Jesus said, "Have the people sit down." There was plenty of grass in that place, and the men sat down, about five thousand of them. [11]Jesus then took the loaves, gave thanks, and distributed to those who were seated as much as they wanted. He did the same with the fish.

[12]When they had all had enough to eat, he said to his disciples, "Gather the pieces that are left over. Let nothing be wasted." [13]So they gathered them and filled twelve baskets with the pieces of the five barley loaves left over by those who had eaten.

[14]After the people saw the miraculous sign that Jesus did, they began to say, "Surely this is the Prophet who is to come into the world." [15]Jesus, knowing that they intended to come and make him king by force, withdrew again to a mountain by himself.

Jesus Walks on the Water

[16]When evening came, his disciples went down to the lake, [17]where they got into a boat and set off across the lake for Capernaum. By now it was dark, and Jesus had not yet joined them. [18]A strong wind was blowing and the waters grew rough. [19]When they had rowed three or three and a half miles,[b] they saw Jesus approaching the boat, walking on the water; and they were terrified. [20]But he said to them, "It is I; don't be afraid." [21]Then they were willing to take him into the boat, and immediately the boat reached the shore where they were heading.

[22]The next day the crowd that had stayed on the opposite shore of the lake realized that only one boat had been there, and that Jesus had not entered it with his disciples, but that they had gone away alone. [23]Then some boats from Tiberias landed near the place where the people had eaten the bread after the Lord had given thanks. [24]Once the crowd realized that neither Jesus nor his disciples were there, they got into the boats and went to Capernaum in search of Jesus.

Jesus the Bread of Life

[25]When they found him on the other side of the lake, they asked him, "Rabbi, when did you get here?"

[26]Jesus answered, "I tell you the truth, you are looking for me, not because you saw miraculous signs but because you ate the loaves and had your fill. [27]Do not work for food that spoils, but for food that endures to eternal life, which the Son of Man will give you. On him God the Father has placed his seal of approval."

[28]Then they asked him, "What must we do to do the works God requires?"

[29]Jesus answered, "The work of God is this: to believe in the one he has sent."

[30]So they asked him, "What miraculous sign then will you give that we may see it and believe you? What will you do? [31]Our forefathers ate the manna in the desert; as it is written: 'He gave them bread from heaven to eat.'[c]"

[32]Jesus said to them, "I tell you the truth, it is not Moses who has given you the bread from heaven, but it is my Father who gives you the true bread from heaven. [33]For the bread of God is he who comes down from heaven and gives life to the world."

[34]"Sir," they said, "from now on give us this bread."

[35]Then Jesus declared, "I am the bread of life. He who comes to me will never go hungry, and he who believes in me will never be thirsty. [36]But as I told you, you have seen me and still you do not believe. [37]All that the Father gives me will come to me, and whoever comes to me I will never drive away. [38]For I have come down from heaven not to do my will but to do the will of him who sent me. [39]And this is the will of him who sent me, that I shall lose none of all that he has given me, but raise them up at the last day. [40]For my Father's will is that everyone who looks to the Son and believes in him shall have eternal life, and I will raise him up at the last day."

[41]At this the Jews began to grumble about him because he said, "I am the bread that came down from heaven." [42]They said, "Is this not Jesus, the son of Joseph, whose father and mother we know? How can he now say, 'I came down from heaven'?"

[43]"Stop grumbling among yourselves," Jesus answered. [44]"No one can come to

---

[a]7 Greek *two hundred denarii*   [b]19 Greek *rowed twenty-five or thirty stadia* (about 5 or 6 kilometers)
[c]31 Exodus 16:4; Neh. 9:15; Psalm 78:24,25

me unless the Father who sent me draws him, and I will raise him up at the last day. ⁴⁵It is written in the Prophets: 'They will all be taught by God.'ᵃ Everyone who listens to the Father and learns from him comes to me. ⁴⁶No one has seen the Father except the one who is from God; only he has seen the Father. ⁴⁷I tell you the truth, he who believes has everlasting life. ⁴⁸I am the bread of life. ⁴⁹Your forefathers ate the manna in the desert, yet they died. ⁵⁰But here is the bread that comes down from heaven, which a man may eat and not die. ⁵¹I am the living bread that came down from heaven. If anyone eats of this bread, he will live forever. This bread is my flesh, which I will give for the life of the world."

⁵²Then the Jews began to argue sharply among themselves, "How can this man give us his flesh to eat?"

⁵³Jesus said to them, "I tell you the truth, unless you eat the flesh of the Son of Man and drink his blood, you have no life in you. ⁵⁴Whoever eats my flesh and drinks my blood has eternal life, and I will raise him up at the last day. ⁵⁵For my flesh is real food and my blood is real drink. ⁵⁶Whoever eats my flesh and drinks my blood remains in me, and I in him. ⁵⁷Just as the living Father sent me and I live because of the Father, so the one who feeds on me will live because of me. ⁵⁸This is the bread that came down from heaven. Your forefathers ate manna and died, but he who feeds on this bread will live forever." ⁵⁹He said this while teaching in the synagogue in Capernaum.

Many Disciples Desert Jesus

⁶⁰On hearing it, many of his disciples said, "This is a hard teaching. Who can accept it?"

⁶¹Aware that his disciples were grumbling about this, Jesus said to them, "Does this offend you? ⁶²What if you see the Son of Man ascend to where he was before! ⁶³The Spirit gives life; the flesh counts for nothing. The words I have spoken to you are spiritᵇ and they are life. ⁶⁴Yet there are some of you who do not believe." For Jesus had known from the beginning which of them did not believe and who would betray him. ⁶⁵He went on to say, "This is why I told you that no one can come to me unless the Father has enabled him."

⁶⁶From this time many of his disciples turned back and no longer followed him.

⁶⁷"You do not want to leave too, do you?" Jesus asked the Twelve.

⁶⁸Simon Peter answered him, "Lord, to whom shall we go? You have the words of eternal life. ⁶⁹We believe and know that you are the Holy One of God."

⁷⁰Then Jesus replied, "Have I not chosen you, the Twelve? Yet one of you is a devil!" ⁷¹(He meant Judas, the son of Simon Iscariot, who, though one of the Twelve, was later to betray him.)

Jesus Goes to the Feast of Tabernacles

7 After this, Jesus went around in Galilee, purposely staying away from Judea because the Jews there were waiting to take his life. ²But when the Jewish Feast of Tabernacles was near, ³Jesus' brothers said to him, "You ought to leave here and go to Judea, so that your disciples may see the miracles you do. ⁴No one who wants to become a public figure acts in secret. Since you are doing these things, show yourself to the world." ⁵For even his own brothers did not believe in him.

⁶Therefore Jesus told them, "The right time for me has not yet come; for you any time is right. ⁷The world cannot hate you, but it hates me because I testify that what it does is evil. ⁸You go to the Feast. I am not yetᶜ going up to this Feast, because for me the right time has not yet come." ⁹Having said this, he stayed in Galilee.

¹⁰However, after his brothers had left for the Feast, he went also, not publicly, but in secret. ¹¹Now at the Feast the Jews were watching for him and asking, "Where is that man?"

¹²Among the crowds there was widespread whispering about him. Some said, "He is a good man."

Others replied, "No, he deceives the people." ¹³But no one would say anything publicly about him for fear of the Jews.

Jesus Teaches at the Feast

¹⁴Not until halfway through the Feast did Jesus go up to the temple courts and begin to teach. ¹⁵The Jews were amazed and asked, "How did this man get such learning without having studied?"

¹⁶Jesus answered, "My teaching is not my own. It comes from him who sent me.

ᵃ45 Isaiah 54:13   ᵇ63 Or *Spirit*   ᶜ8 Some early manuscripts do not have *yet.*

VERSE FOR THE DAY:	AUTHOR:	PASSAGE FOR THE DAY:
John 6:35	Rosalind Rinker	John 6:1–71

I Am the Living Bread

JOHN 6 is another miracle chapter. Here we see one more instance when Jesus taught spiritual truth through everyday things, as he had with water, seeds, a candle, a lamp, and a pearl.

This time, Jesus fed more than five thousand people when he broke five small barley loaves and distributed two small fish. Bread and water can sustain physical life indefinitely, yet Jesus said, "Man does not live on bread alone, but on every word that comes from the mouth of God" (Matthew 4:4).

Bread must be given, broken, and taken before it sustains life. The little boy gave his lunch, but Jesus gave his life. This relates directly to the central truth of the John 6 miracle because it concerns the person of our Lord. "I am the living bread that came down from heaven. If anyone eats of this bread, he will live forever. This bread is my flesh, which I will give for the life of the world" (John 6:51). Much as the barley loaves were broken, so too was Christ's *body* broken so that we could be takers of "living bread."

Jesus is capable of being the living bread because he is the Son of God. Just by observing Jesus in John 6 we can see how he deals with the crowd from an other-worldly perspective: 1. He knew what he was going to do (John 6:6). 2. He knew the superficial curiosity of the crowd (John 6:2). 3. He had compassion because of their physical and spiritual hunger (John 6:5,36–37). 4. He wanted cooperation (the boy, the disciples) before he would feed the crowd (John 6:8–9). 5. He had a sense of order and frugality (John 6:10,12–13). 6. He had a deep sense of mission, and the courage to tell of it in a language the crowd could understand and remember (John 6:35–40). 7. He predicted the Eucharist (Holy Communion) (John 6:56–57). 8. He was able to make a little count for a lot (John 6:10–11).

Dear ones, let us be takers and feed on the words of Jesus, the Son of God, our living bread. His words lead us directly back to him, the Redeemer and Savior of the world.

> I am the bread of life. He who comes to me will never go hungry, and he who believes in me will never be thirsty (John 6:35).

Additional Scripture Readings:
Psalm 119:103–104; Matthew 26:26

Go to page 1169 for your next devotional reading.

¹⁷If anyone chooses to do God's will, he will find out whether my teaching comes from God or whether I speak on my own. ¹⁸He who speaks on his own does so to gain honor for himself, but he who works for the honor of the one who sent him is a man of truth; there is nothing false about him. ¹⁹Has not Moses given you the law? Yet not one of you keeps the law. Why are you trying to kill me?"

²⁰"You are demon-possessed," the crowd answered. "Who is trying to kill you?"

²¹Jesus said to them, "I did one miracle, and you are all astonished. ²²Yet, because Moses gave you circumcision (though actually it did not come from Moses, but from the patriarchs), you circumcise a child on the Sabbath. ²³Now if a child can be circumcised on the Sabbath so that the law of Moses may not be broken, why are you angry with me for healing the whole man on the Sabbath? ²⁴Stop judging by mere appearances, and make a right judgment."

Is Jesus the Christ?

²⁵At that point some of the people of Jerusalem began to ask, "Isn't this the man they are trying to kill? ²⁶Here he is, speaking publicly, and they are not saying a word to him. Have the authorities really concluded that he is the Christ*ᵃ*? ²⁷But we know where this man is from; when the Christ comes, no one will know where he is from."

²⁸Then Jesus, still teaching in the temple courts, cried out, "Yes, you know me, and you know where I am from. I am not here on my own, but he who sent me is true. You do not know him, ²⁹but I know him because I am from him and he sent me."

³⁰At this they tried to seize him, but no one laid a hand on him, because his time had not yet come. ³¹Still, many in the crowd put their faith in him. They said, "When the Christ comes, will he do more miraculous signs than this man?"

³²The Pharisees heard the crowd whispering such things about him. Then the chief priests and the Pharisees sent temple guards to arrest him.

³³Jesus said, "I am with you for only a short time, and then I go to the one who sent me. ³⁴You will look for me, but you will not find me; and where I am, you cannot come."

³⁵The Jews said to one another, "Where does this man intend to go that we cannot find him? Will he go where our people live scattered among the Greeks, and teach the Greeks? ³⁶What did he mean when he said, 'You will look for me, but you will not find me,' and 'Where I am, you cannot come'?"

³⁷On the last and greatest day of the Feast, Jesus stood and said in a loud voice, "If anyone is thirsty, let him come to me and drink. ³⁸Whoever believes in me, as*ᵇ* the Scripture has said, streams of living water will flow from within him." ³⁹By this he meant the Spirit, whom those who believed in him were later to receive. Up to that time the Spirit had not been given, since Jesus had not yet been glorified.

⁴⁰On hearing his words, some of the people said, "Surely this man is the Prophet."

⁴¹Others said, "He is the Christ."

Still others asked, "How can the Christ come from Galilee? ⁴²Does not the Scripture say that the Christ will come from David's family*ᶜ* and from Bethlehem, the town where David lived?" ⁴³Thus the people were divided because of Jesus. ⁴⁴Some wanted to seize him, but no one laid a hand on him.

Unbelief of the Jewish Leaders

⁴⁵Finally the temple guards went back to the chief priests and Pharisees, who asked them, "Why didn't you bring him in?"

⁴⁶"No one ever spoke the way this man does," the guards declared.

⁴⁷"You mean he has deceived you also?" the Pharisees retorted. ⁴⁸"Has any of the rulers or of the Pharisees believed in him? ⁴⁹No! But this mob that knows nothing of the law—there is a curse on them."

⁵⁰Nicodemus, who had gone to Jesus earlier and who was one of their own number, asked, ⁵¹"Does our law condemn anyone without first hearing him to find out what he is doing?"

⁵²They replied, "Are you from Galilee, too? Look into it, and you will find that a prophet*ᵈ* does not come out of Galilee."

ᵃ26 Or *Messiah*; also in verses 27, 31, 41 and 42   *ᵇ37,38* Or / *If anyone is thirsty, let him come to me. / And let him drink,* *³⁸who believes in me. / As*   *ᶜ42* Greek *seed*   *ᵈ52* Two early manuscripts *the Prophet*

53Then each went to his own home.

8 But Jesus went to the Mount of Olives. 2At dawn he appeared again in the temple courts, where all the people gathered around him, and he sat down to teach them. 3The teachers of the law and the Pharisees brought in a woman caught in adultery. They made her stand before the group 4and said to Jesus, "Teacher, this woman was caught in the act of adultery. 5In the Law Moses commanded us to stone such women. Now what do you say?" 6They were using this question as a trap, in order to have a basis for accusing him.

But Jesus bent down and started to write on the ground with his finger. 7When they kept on questioning him, he straightened up and said to them, "If any one of you is without sin, let him be the first to throw a stone at her." 8Again he stooped down and wrote on the ground.

9At this, those who heard began to go away one at a time, the older ones first, until only Jesus was left, with the woman still standing there. 10Jesus straightened up and asked her, "Woman, where are they? Has no one condemned you?"

11"No one, sir," she said.

"Then neither do I condemn you," Jesus declared. "Go now and leave your life of sin."

The Validity of Jesus' Testimony

12When Jesus spoke again to the people, he said, "I am the light of the world. Whoever follows me will never walk in darkness, but will have the light of life." 13The Pharisees challenged him, "Here you are, appearing as your own witness; your testimony is not valid."

14Jesus answered, "Even if I testify on my own behalf, my testimony is valid, for I know where I came from and where I am going. But you have no idea where I come from or where I am going. 15You judge by human standards; I pass judgment on no one. 16But if I do judge, my decisions are right, because I am not alone. I stand with the Father, who sent me. 17In your own Law it is written that the testimony of two

men is valid. 18I am one who testifies for myself; my other witness is the Father, who sent me."

19Then they asked him, "Where is your father?"

"You do not know me or my Father," Jesus replied. "If you knew me, you would know my Father also." 20He spoke these words while teaching in the temple area near the place where the offerings were put. Yet no one seized him, because his time had not yet come.

21Once more Jesus said to them, "I am going away, and you will look for me, and you will die in your sin. Where I go, you cannot come."

22This made the Jews ask, "Will he kill himself? Is that why he says, 'Where I go, you cannot come'?"

23But he continued, "You are from below; I am from above. You are of this world; I am not of this world. 24I told you that you would die in your sins; if you do not believe that I am the one I claim to be,*a* you will indeed die in your sins."

25"Who are you?" they asked.

"Just what I have been claiming all along," Jesus replied. 26"I have much to say in judgment of you. But he who sent me is reliable, and what I have heard from him I tell the world."

27They did not understand that he was telling them about his Father. 28So Jesus said, "When you have lifted up the Son of Man, then you will know that I am the one I claim to be, and that I do nothing on my own but speak just what the Father has taught me. 29The one who sent me is with me; he has not left me alone, for I always do what pleases him."

The Children of Abraham

31To the Jews who had believed him, Jesus said, "If you hold to my teaching, you are really my disciples. 32Then you will know the truth, and the truth will set you free."

33They answered him, "We are Abraham's descendants*b* and have never been slaves of anyone. How can you say that we shall be set free?"

34Jesus replied, "I tell you the truth, everyone who sins is a slave to sin. 35Now a slave has no permanent place in the family, but a son belongs to it forever. 36So if the Son sets you free, you will be free indeed. 37I know you are Abraham's

a24 Or I am he; also in verse 28   b33 Greek seed; also in verse 37 descendants. Yet you are ready to kill me, because you have no room for my word. [38]I am telling you what I have seen in the Father's presence, and you do what you have heard from your father.[a]"

[39]"Abraham is our father," they answered.

"If you were Abraham's children," said Jesus, "then you would[b] do the things Abraham did. [40]As it is, you are determined to kill me, a man who has told you the truth that I heard from God. Abraham did not do such things. [41]You are doing the things your own father does."

"We are not illegitimate children," they protested. "The only Father we have is God himself."

The Children of the Devil

[42]Jesus said to them, "If God were your Father, you would love me, for I came from God and now am here. I have not come on my own; but he sent me. [43]Why is my language not clear to you? Because you are unable to hear what I say. [44]You belong to your father, the devil, and you want to carry out your father's desire. He was a murderer from the beginning, not holding to the truth, for there is no truth in him. When he lies, he speaks his native language, for he is a liar and the father of lies. [45]Yet because I tell the truth, you do not believe me! [46]Can any of you prove me guilty of sin? If I am telling the truth, why don't you believe me? [47]He who belongs to God hears what God says. The reason you do not hear is that you do not belong to God."

The Claims of Jesus About Himself

[48]The Jews answered him, "Aren't we right in saying that you are a Samaritan and demon-possessed?"

[49]"I am not possessed by a demon," said Jesus, "but I honor my Father and you dishonor me. [50]I am not seeking glory for myself; but there is one who seeks it, and he is the judge. [51]I tell you the truth, if anyone keeps my word, he will never see death."

[52]At this the Jews exclaimed, "Now we know that you are demon-possessed! Abraham died and so did the prophets, yet you say that if anyone keeps your word, he will never taste death. [53]Are you greater than our father Abraham? He

died, and so did the prophets. Who do you think you are?"

[54]Jesus replied, "If I glorify myself, my glory means nothing. My Father, whom you claim as your God, is the one who glorifies me. [55]Though you do not know him, I know him. If I said I did not, I would be a liar like you, but I do know him and keep his word. [56]Your father Abraham rejoiced at the thought of seeing my day; he saw it and was glad."

[57]"You are not yet fifty years old," the Jews said to him, "and you have seen Abraham!"

[58]"I tell you the truth," Jesus answered, "before Abraham was born, I am!" [59]At this, they picked up stones to stone him, but Jesus hid himself, slipping away from the temple grounds.

Jesus Heals a Man Born Blind

9 As he went along, he saw a man blind from birth. [2]His disciples asked him, "Rabbi, who sinned, this man or his parents, that he was born blind?"

[3]"Neither this man nor his parents sinned," said Jesus, "but this happened so that the work of God might be displayed in his life. [4]As long as it is day, we must do the work of him who sent me. Night is coming, when no one can work. [5]While I am in the world, I am the light of the world."

[6]Having said this, he spit on the ground, made some mud with the saliva, and put it on the man's eyes. [7]"Go," he told him, "wash in the Pool of Siloam" (this word means Sent). So the man went and washed, and came home seeing.

[8]His neighbors and those who had formerly seen him begging asked, "Isn't this the same man who used to sit and beg?" [9]Some claimed that he was.

Others said, "No, he only looks like him."

But he himself insisted, "I am the man."

[10]"How then were your eyes opened?" they demanded.

[11]He replied, "The man they call Jesus made some mud and put it on my eyes. He told me to go to Siloam and wash. So I went and washed, and then I could see."

[12]"Where is this man?" they asked him.

"I don't know," he said.

---

[a]38 Or presence. Therefore do what you have heard from the Father. [b]39 Some early manuscripts "If you are Abraham's children," said Jesus, "then

The Pharisees Investigate the Healing

13They brought to the Pharisees the man who had been blind. 14Now the day on which Jesus had made the mud and opened the man's eyes was a Sabbath. 15Therefore the Pharisees also asked him how he had received his sight. "He put mud on my eyes," the man replied, "and I washed, and now I see."

16Some of the Pharisees said, "This man is not from God, for he does not keep the Sabbath."

But others asked, "How can a sinner do such miraculous signs?" So they were divided.

17Finally they turned again to the blind man, "What have you to say about him? It was your eyes he opened."

The man replied, "He is a prophet."

18The Jews still did not believe that he had been blind and had received his sight until they sent for the man's parents. 19"Is this your son?" they asked. "Is this the one you say was born blind? How is it that now he can see?"

20"We know he is our son," the parents answered, "and we know he was born blind. 21But how he can see now, or who opened his eyes, we don't know. Ask him. He is of age; he will speak for himself." 22His parents said this because they were afraid of the Jews, for already the Jews had decided that anyone who acknowledged that Jesus was the Christ*a* would be put out of the synagogue. 23That was why his parents said, "He is of age; ask him."

24A second time they summoned the man who had been blind. "Give glory to God,*b*" they said. "We know this man is a sinner."

25He replied, "Whether he is a sinner or not, I don't know. One thing I do know. I was blind but now I see!"

26Then they asked him, "What did he do to you? How did he open your eyes?"

27He answered, "I have told you already and you did not listen. Why do you want to hear it again? Do you want to become his disciples, too?"

28Then they hurled insults at him and said, "You are this fellow's disciple! We are disciples of Moses! 29We know that God spoke to Moses, but as for this fellow, we don't even know where he comes from."

30The man answered, "Now that is remarkable! You don't know where he comes from, yet he opened my eyes. 31We know that God does not listen to sinners. He listens to the godly man who does his will. 32Nobody has ever heard of opening the eyes of a man born blind. 33If this man were not from God, he could do nothing."

34To this they replied, "You were steeped in sin at birth; how dare you lecture us!" And they threw him out.

Spiritual Blindness

35Jesus heard that they had thrown him out, and when he found him, he said, "Do you believe in the Son of Man?"

36"Who is he, sir?" the man asked. "Tell me so that I may believe in him."

37Jesus said, "You have now seen him; in fact, he is the one speaking with you."

38Then the man said, "Lord, I believe," and he worshiped him.

39Jesus said, "For judgment I have come into this world, so that the blind will see and those who see will become blind."

40Some Pharisees who were with him heard him say this and asked, "What? Are we blind too?"

41Jesus said, "If you were blind, you would not be guilty of sin; but now that you claim you can see, your guilt remains.

The Shepherd and His Flock

10 "I tell you the truth, the man who does not enter the sheep pen by the gate, but climbs in by some other way, is a thief and a robber. 2The man who enters by the gate is the shepherd of his sheep. 3The watchman opens the gate for him, and the sheep listen to his voice. He calls his own sheep by name and leads them out. 4When he has brought out all his own, he goes on ahead of them, and his sheep follow him because they know his voice. 5But they will never follow a stranger; in fact, they will run away from him because they do not recognize a stranger's voice." 6Jesus used this figure of speech, but they did not understand what he was telling them.

7Therefore Jesus said again, "I tell you the truth, I am the gate for the sheep. 8All who ever came before me were thieves and robbers, but the sheep did not listen to them. 9I am the gate; whoever enters through me will be saved.*c* He will come in and go out, and find pasture. 10The thief comes only to steal and kill and destroy; I have come that they may have life, and have it to the full.

[11]"I am the good shepherd. The good shepherd lays down his life for the sheep. [12]The hired hand is not the shepherd who owns the sheep. So when he sees the wolf coming, he abandons the sheep and runs away. Then the wolf attacks the flock and scatters it. [13]The man runs away because he is a hired hand and cares nothing for the sheep.

[14]"I am the good shepherd; I know my sheep and my sheep know me— [15]just as the Father knows me and I know the Father—and I lay down my life for the sheep. [16]I have other sheep that are not of this sheep pen. I must bring them also. They too will listen to my voice, and there shall be one flock and one shepherd. [17]The reason my Father loves me is that I lay down my life—only to take it up again. [18]No one takes it from me, but I lay it down of my own accord. I have authority to lay it down and authority to take it up again. This command I received from my Father."

[19]At these words the Jews were again divided. [20]Many of them said, "He is demon-possessed and raving mad. Why listen to him?"

[21]But others said, "These are not the sayings of a man possessed by a demon. Can a demon open the eyes of the blind?"

The Unbelief of the Jews

[22]Then came the Feast of Dedication[a] at Jerusalem. It was winter, [23]and Jesus was in the temple area walking in Solomon's Colonnade. [24]The Jews gathered around him, saying, "How long will you keep us in suspense? If you are the Christ,[b] tell us plainly."

[25]Jesus answered, "I did tell you, but you do not believe. The miracles I do in my Father's name speak for me, [26]but you do not believe because you are not my sheep. [27]My sheep listen to my voice; I know them, and they follow me. [28]I give them eternal life, and they shall never perish; no one can snatch them out of my hand. [29]My Father, who has given them to me, is greater than all[c]; no one can snatch them out of my Father's hand. [30]I and the Father are one."

[31]Again the Jews picked up stones to stone him, [32]but Jesus said to them, "I

have shown you many great miracles from the Father. For which of these do you stone me?"

[33]"We are not stoning you for any of these," replied the Jews, "but for blasphemy, because you, a mere man, claim to be God."

[34]Jesus answered them, "Is it not written in your Law, 'I have said you are gods'[d]? [35]If he called them 'gods,' to whom the word of God came—and the Scripture cannot be broken— [36]what about the one whom the Father set apart as his very own and sent into the world? Why then do you accuse me of blasphemy because I said, 'I am God's Son'? [37]Do not believe me unless I do what my Father does. [38]But if I do it, even though you do not believe me, believe the miracles, that you may know and understand that the Father is in me, and I in the Father." [39]Again they tried to seize him, but he escaped their grasp.

[40]Then Jesus went back across the Jordan to the place where John had been baptizing in the early days. Here he stayed [41]and many people came to him. They said, "Though John never performed a miraculous sign, all that John said about this man was true." [42]And in that place many believed in Jesus.

The Death of Lazarus

11 Now a man named Lazarus was sick. He was from Bethany, the village of Mary and her sister Martha. [2]This Mary, whose brother Lazarus now lay sick, was the same one who poured perfume on the Lord and wiped his feet with her hair. [3]So the sisters sent word to Jesus, "Lord, the one you love is sick."

[4]When he heard this, Jesus said, "This sickness will not end in death. No, it is for God's glory so that God's Son may be glorified through it." [5]Jesus loved Martha and her sister and Lazarus. [6]Yet when he heard that Lazarus was sick, he stayed where he was two more days.

[7]Then he said to his disciples, "Let us go back to Judea."

[8]"But Rabbi," they said, "a short while ago the Jews tried to stone you, and yet you are going back there?"

[9]Jesus answered, "Are there not twelve hours of daylight? A man who walks by day will not stumble, for he sees by this world's light. [10]It is when he walks by

---

night that he stumbles, for he has no light."

¹¹After he had said this, he went on to tell them, "Our friend Lazarus has fallen asleep; but I am going there to wake him up."

¹²His disciples replied, "Lord, if he sleeps, he will get better." ¹³Jesus had been speaking of his death, but his disciples thought he meant natural sleep.

¹⁴So then he told them plainly, "Lazarus is dead, ¹⁵and for your sake I am glad I was not there, so that you may believe. But let us go to him."

¹⁶Then Thomas (called Didymus) said to the rest of the disciples, "Let us also go, that we may die with him."

Jesus Comforts the Sisters

¹⁷On his arrival, Jesus found that Lazarus had already been in the tomb for four days. ¹⁸Bethany was less than two miles^a from Jerusalem, ¹⁹and many Jews had come to Martha and Mary to comfort them in the loss of their brother. ²⁰When Martha heard that Jesus was coming, she went out to meet him, but Mary stayed at home.

²¹"Lord," Martha said to Jesus, "if you had been here, my brother would not have died. ²²But I know that even now God will give you whatever you ask."

²³Jesus said to her, "Your brother will rise again."

²⁴Martha answered, "I know he will rise again in the resurrection at the last day."

²⁵Jesus said to her, "I am the resurrection and the life. He who believes in me will live, even though he dies; ²⁶and whoever lives and believes in me will never die. Do you believe this?"

²⁷"Yes, Lord," she told him, "I believe that you are the Christ,^b the Son of God, who was to come into the world."

²⁸And after she had said this, she went back and called her sister Mary aside. "The Teacher is here," she said, "and is asking for you." ²⁹When Mary heard this, she got up quickly and went to him. ³⁰Now Jesus had not yet entered the village, but was still at the place where Martha had met him. ³¹When the Jews who had been with Mary in the house, comforting her, noticed how quickly she got up and went out, they followed her, supposing she was going to the tomb to mourn there.

³²When Mary reached the place where Jesus was and saw him, she fell at his feet and said, "Lord, if you had been here, my brother would not have died."

³³When Jesus saw her weeping, and the Jews who had come along with her also weeping, he was deeply moved in spirit and troubled. ³⁴"Where have you laid him?" he asked.

"Come and see, Lord," they replied.

³⁵Jesus wept.

³⁶Then the Jews said, "See how he loved him!"

³⁷But some of them said, "Could not he who opened the eyes of the blind man have kept this man from dying?"

Jesus Raises Lazarus From the Dead

³⁸Jesus, once more deeply moved, came to the tomb. It was a cave with a stone laid across the entrance. ³⁹"Take away the stone," he said.

"But, Lord," said Martha, the sister of the dead man, "by this time there is a bad odor, for he has been there four days."

⁴⁰Then Jesus said, "Did I not tell you that if you believed, you would see the glory of God?"

⁴¹So they took away the stone. Then Jesus looked up and said, "Father, I thank you that you have heard me. ⁴²I knew that you always hear me, but I said this for the benefit of the people standing here, that they may believe that you sent me."

⁴³When he had said this, Jesus called in a loud voice, "Lazarus, come out!" ⁴⁴The dead man came out, his hands and feet wrapped with strips of linen, and a cloth around his face.

Jesus said to them, "Take off the grave clothes and let him go."

The Plot to Kill Jesus

⁴⁵Therefore many of the Jews who had come to visit Mary, and had seen what Jesus did, put their faith in him. ⁴⁶But some of them went to the Pharisees and told them what Jesus had done. ⁴⁷Then the chief priests and the Pharisees called a meeting of the Sanhedrin.

"What are we accomplishing?" they asked. "Here is this man performing many miraculous signs. ⁴⁸If we let him go on like this, everyone will believe in him, and then the Romans will come and take away both our place^c and our nation."

⁴⁹Then one of them, named Caiaphas, who was high priest that year, spoke up,

---

^a18 Greek *fifteen stadia* (about 3 kilometers)   ^b27 Or *Messiah*   ^c48 Or *temple*

"You know nothing at all! ⁵⁰You do not realize that it is better for you that one man die for the people than that the whole nation perish."

⁵¹He did not say this on his own, but as high priest that year he prophesied that Jesus would die for the Jewish nation, ⁵²and not only for that nation but also for the scattered children of God, to bring them together and make them one. ⁵³So from that day on they plotted to take his life.

⁵⁴Therefore Jesus no longer moved about publicly among the Jews. Instead he withdrew to a region near the desert, to a village called Ephraim, where he stayed with his disciples.

⁵⁵When it was almost time for the Jewish Passover, many went up from the country to Jerusalem for their ceremonial cleansing before the Passover. ⁵⁶They kept looking for Jesus, and as they stood in the temple area they asked one another, "What do you think? Isn't he coming to the Feast at all?" ⁵⁷But the chief priests and Pharisees had given orders that if anyone found out where Jesus was, he should report it so that they might arrest him.

Jesus Anointed at Bethany

12 Six days before the Passover, Jesus arrived at Bethany, where Lazarus lived, whom Jesus had raised from the dead. ²Here a dinner was given in Jesus' honor. Martha served, while Lazarus was among those reclining at the table with him. ³Then Mary took about a pint*a* of pure nard, an expensive perfume; she poured it on Jesus' feet and wiped his feet with her hair. And the house was filled with the fragrance of the perfume.

⁴But one of his disciples, Judas Iscariot, who was later to betray him, objected, ⁵"Why wasn't this perfume sold and the money given to the poor? It was worth a year's wages.*b*" ⁶He did not say this because he cared about the poor but because he was a thief; as keeper of the money bag, he used to help himself to what was put into it.

⁷"Leave her alone," Jesus replied. "It was intended that she should save this perfume for the day of my burial. ⁸You will always have the poor among you, but you will not always have me."

⁹Meanwhile a large crowd of Jews found out that Jesus was there and came, not only because of him but also to see Lazarus, whom he had raised from the dead. ¹⁰So the chief priests made plans to kill Lazarus as well, ¹¹for on account of him many of the Jews were going over to Jesus and putting their faith in him.

The Triumphal Entry

¹²The next day the great crowd that had come for the Feast heard that Jesus was on his way to Jerusalem. ¹³They took palm branches and went out to meet him, shouting,

"Hosanna!*c*"

"Blessed is he who comes in the
  name of the Lord!"*d*

"Blessed is the King of Israel!"

¹⁴Jesus found a young donkey and sat upon it, as it is written,

¹⁵"Do not be afraid, O Daughter of
  Zion;
  see, your king is coming,
  seated on a donkey's colt."*e*

¹⁶At first his disciples did not understand all this. Only after Jesus was glorified did they realize that these things had been written about him and that they had done these things to him.

¹⁷Now the crowd that was with him when he called Lazarus from the tomb and raised him from the dead continued to spread the word. ¹⁸Many people, because they had heard that he had given this miraculous sign, went out to meet him. ¹⁹So the Pharisees said to one another, "See, this is getting us nowhere. Look how the whole world has gone after him!"

Jesus Predicts His Death

²⁰Now there were some Greeks among those who went up to worship at the Feast. ²¹They came to Philip, who was from Bethsaida in Galilee, with a request. "Sir," they said, "we would like to see Jesus." ²²Philip went to tell Andrew; Andrew and Philip in turn told Jesus.

²³Jesus replied, "The hour has come for the Son of Man to be glorified. ²⁴I tell you the truth, unless a kernel of wheat falls to the ground and dies, it remains only a single seed. But if it dies, it produces many

a3 Greek *a litra* (probably about 0.5 liter)   *b5* Greek *three hundred denarii*   *c13* A Hebrew expression meaning "Save!" which became an exclamation of praise   *d13* Psalm 118:25, 26   *e15* Zech. 9:9

seeds. 25The man who loves his life will lose it, while the man who hates his life in this world will keep it for eternal life. 26Whoever serves me must follow me; and where I am, my servant also will be. My Father will honor the one who serves me.

27"Now my heart is troubled, and what shall I say? 'Father, save me from this hour'? No, it was for this very reason I came to this hour. 28Father, glorify your name!"

Then a voice came from heaven, "I have glorified it, and will glorify it again." 29The crowd that was there and heard it said it had thundered; others said an angel had spoken to him.

30Jesus said, "This voice was for your benefit, not mine. 31Now is the time for judgment on this world; now the prince of this world will be driven out. 32But I, when I am lifted up from the earth, will draw all men to myself." 33He said this to show the kind of death he was going to die.

34The crowd spoke up, "We have heard from the Law that the Christ*a* will remain forever, so how can you say, 'The Son of Man must be lifted up'? Who is this 'Son of Man'?"

35Then Jesus told them, "You are going to have the light just a little while longer. Walk while you have the light, before darkness overtakes you. The man who walks in the dark does not know where he is going. 36Put your trust in the light while you have it, so that you may become sons of light." When he had finished speaking, Jesus left and hid himself from them.

The Jews Continue in Their Unbelief

37Even after Jesus had done all these miraculous signs in their presence, they still would not believe in him. 38This was to fulfill the word of Isaiah the prophet:

"Lord, who has believed our message
    and to whom has the arm of the
        Lord been revealed?"*b*

39For this reason they could not believe, because, as Isaiah says elsewhere:

40"He has blinded their eyes
    and deadened their hearts,
so they can neither see with their
        eyes,
    nor understand with their hearts,
    nor turn—and I would heal
        them."*c*

41Isaiah said this because he saw Jesus' glory and spoke about him.

42Yet at the same time many even among the leaders believed in him. But because of the Pharisees they would not confess their faith for fear they would be put out of the synagogue; 43for they loved praise from men more than praise from God.

44Then Jesus cried out, "When a man believes in me, he does not believe in me only, but in the one who sent me. 45When he looks at me, he sees the one who sent me. 46I have come into the world as a light, so that no one who believes in me should stay in darkness.

47"As for the person who hears my words but does not keep them, I do not judge him. For I did not come to judge the world, but to save it. 48There is a judge for the one who rejects me and does not accept my words; that very word which I spoke will condemn him at the last day. 49For I did not speak of my own accord, but the Father who sent me commanded me what to say and how to say it. 50I know that his command leads to eternal life. So whatever I say is just what the Father has told me to say."

Jesus Washes His Disciples' Feet

13 It was just before the Passover Feast. Jesus knew that the time had come for him to leave this world and go to the Father. Having loved his own who were in the world, he now showed them the full extent of his love.*d*

2The evening meal was being served, and the devil had already prompted Judas Iscariot, son of Simon, to betray Jesus. 3Jesus knew that the Father had put all things under his power, and that he had come from God and was returning to God; 4so he got up from the meal, took off his outer clothing, and wrapped a towel around his waist. 5After that, he poured water into a basin and began to wash his disciples' feet, drying them with the towel that was wrapped around him.

6He came to Simon Peter, who said to him, "Lord, are you going to wash my feet?"

7Jesus replied, "You do not realize now what I am doing, but later you will understand."

8"No," said Peter, "you shall never wash my feet."

a34 Or Messiah   b38 Isaiah 53:1   c40 Isaiah 6:10   d1 Or he loved them to the last

Jesus answered, "Unless I wash you, you have no part with me."

9"Then, Lord," Simon Peter replied, "not just my feet but my hands and my head as well!"

10Jesus answered, "A person who has had a bath needs only to wash his feet; his whole body is clean. And you are clean, though not every one of you." 11For he knew who was going to betray him, and that was why he said not every one was clean.

12When he had finished washing their feet, he put on his clothes and returned to his place. "Do you understand what I have done for you?" he asked them. 13"You call me 'Teacher' and 'Lord,' and rightly so, for that is what I am. 14Now that I, your Lord and Teacher, have washed your feet, you also should wash one another's feet. 15I have set you an example that you should do as I have done for you. 16I tell you the truth, no servant is greater than his master, nor is a messenger greater than the one who sent him. 17Now that you know these things, you will be blessed if you do them.

Jesus Predicts His Betrayal

18"I am not referring to all of you; I know those I have chosen. But this is to fulfill the scripture: 'He who shares my bread has lifted up his heel against me.'a

19"I am telling you now before it happens, so that when it does happen you will believe that I am He. 20I tell you the truth, whoever accepts anyone I send accepts me; and whoever accepts me accepts the one who sent me."

21After he had said this, Jesus was troubled in spirit and testified, "I tell you the truth, one of you is going to betray me."

22His disciples stared at one another, at a loss to know which of them he meant. 23One of them, the disciple whom Jesus loved, was reclining next to him. 24Simon Peter motioned to this disciple and said, "Ask him which one he means."

25Leaning back against Jesus, he asked him, "Lord, who is it?"

26Jesus answered, "It is the one to whom I will give this piece of bread when I have dipped it in the dish." Then, dipping the piece of bread, he gave it to Judas Iscariot, son of Simon. 27As soon as Judas took the bread, Satan entered into him.

"What you are about to do, do quickly," Jesus told him, 28but no one at the meal understood why Jesus said this to him. 29Since Judas had charge of the money, some thought Jesus was telling him to buy what was needed for the Feast, or to give something to the poor. 30As soon as Judas had taken the bread, he went out. And it was night.

Jesus Predicts Peter's Denial

31When he was gone, Jesus said, "Now is the Son of Man glorified and God is glorified in him. 32If God is glorified in him,b God will glorify the Son in himself, and will glorify him at once. 33"My children, I will be with you only a little longer. You will look for me, and just as I told the Jews, so I tell you now: Where I am going, you cannot come.

34"A new command I give you: Love one another. As I have loved you, so you must love one another. 35By this all men will know that you are my disciples, if you love one another."

36Simon Peter asked him, "Lord, where are you going?"

Jesus replied, "Where I am going, you cannot follow now, but you will follow later."

37Peter asked, "Lord, why can't I follow you now? I will lay down my life for you."

38Then Jesus answered, "Will you really lay down your life for me? I tell you the truth, before the rooster crows, you will disown me three times!

Jesus Comforts His Disciples

14 "Do not let your hearts be troubled. Trust in Godc; trust also in me. 2In my Father's house are many rooms; if it were not so, I would have told you. I am going there to prepare a place for you. 3And if I go and prepare a place for you, I will come back and take you to be with me that you also may be where I am. 4You know the way to the place where I am going."

Jesus the Way to the Father

5Thomas said to him, "Lord, we don't know where you are going, so how can we know the way?"

6Jesus answered, "I am the way and the truth and the life. No one comes to the Father except through me. 7If you really knew me, you would knowd my Father as

a18 Psalm 41:9   b32 Many early manuscripts do not have If God is glorified in him.   c1 Or You trust in God   d7 Some early manuscripts If you really have known me, you will know

VERSE FOR THE DAY:
John 14:1

AUTHOR:
Gloria Gaither

PASSAGE FOR THE DAY:
John 13:1–14:31

On Saying Good-by

TRAVELING has been a part of our lives from the very early days of our marriage. When our children were little, our singing took us away nearly every weekend and occasionally for longer periods of time. Although leaving was common, it was never easy. Suzanne said to us when she was three, "I know you have to go, but don't go without saying good-by." She knew that the leave-taking was very important to everyone's security and sense of purpose.

Even when the children were young, before we left they always insisted on knowing the answers to five very important questions: Where are you going? How long will you be gone? Can we come with you? Who will stay with us? When will you be back?

Over and over we would answer those questions with specific information. Then we would give advice like, "Don't argue. Take care of the dogs, and always love each other. Remember that whatever you do or wherever you go, you represent our family."

When Jesus was leaving his disciples to return to his Father, he, too, knew that leave-taking was very important. He didn't leave them without saying good-by. And the questions his children asked were the same ones our children used to ask. With specific clarity Jesus gave them answers, although they could not fully comprehend the dimensions of what he was telling them.

"I go to my Father," he said. "You can't come with me yet, but don't worry, I won't leave you alone. The Holy Spirit will be your constant companion, and I must go so that he can come. While I'm gone he will teach you everything you need to know. I will be gone, by my time, only a little while, though it may seem long to you. When I come again, it will be to take you where I have been all this time fixing up a special place for all of us to be together . . . forever. After that, we won't have to say good-by again."

Then Jesus gave some special parental instructions. "Love and take care of each other. The way you treat each other will tell the world about our family, so remember whose child you are. Some problems may come up, but whatever you need, you can ask for it using my name. All I have is at your disposal, and the Holy Spirit will see that you have it. When you feel lonely or afraid, rely on my promise that I have insulated you in prayer, and you belong to me."

Additional Scripture Readings:
Acts 1:6–11; 20:17–38

Go to page 1171 for your next
devotional reading.

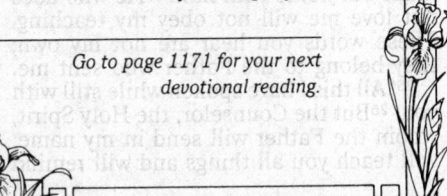

well. From now on, you do know him and have seen him."

⁸Philip said, "Lord, show us the Father and that will be enough for us."

⁹Jesus answered: "Don't you know me, Philip, even after I have been among you such a long time? Anyone who has seen me has seen the Father. How can you say, 'Show us the Father'? ¹⁰Don't you believe that I am in the Father, and that the Father is in me? The words I say to you are not just my own. Rather, it is the Father, living in me, who is doing his work. ¹¹Believe me when I say that I am in the Father and the Father is in me; or at least believe on the evidence of the miracles themselves. ¹²I tell you the truth, anyone who has faith in me will do what I have been doing. He will do even greater things than these, because I am going to the Father. ¹³And I will do whatever you ask in my name, so that the Son may bring glory to the Father. ¹⁴You may ask me for anything in my name, and I will do it.

Jesus Promises the Holy Spirit

¹⁵"If you love me, you will obey what I command. ¹⁶And I will ask the Father, and he will give you another Counselor to be with you forever— ¹⁷the Spirit of truth. The world cannot accept him, because it neither sees him nor knows him. But you know him, for he lives with you and will be[a] in you. ¹⁸I will not leave you as orphans; I will come to you. ¹⁹Before long, the world will not see me anymore, but you will see me. Because I live, you also will live. ²⁰On that day you will realize that I am in my Father, and you are in me, and I am in you. ²¹Whoever has my commands and obeys them, he is the one who loves me. He who loves me will be loved by my Father, and I too will love him and show myself to him."

²²Then Judas (not Judas Iscariot) said, "But, Lord, why do you intend to show yourself to us and not to the world?"

²³Jesus replied, "If anyone loves me, he will obey my teaching. My Father will love him, and we will come to him and make our home with him. ²⁴He who does not love me will not obey my teaching. These words you hear are not my own; they belong to the Father who sent me.

²⁵"All this I have spoken while still with you. ²⁶But the Counselor, the Holy Spirit, whom the Father will send in my name, will teach you all things and will remind you of everything I have said to you. ²⁷Peace I leave with you; my peace I give you. I do not give to you as the world gives. Do not let your hearts be troubled and do not be afraid.

²⁸"You heard me say, 'I am going away and I am coming back to you.' If you loved me, you would be glad that I am going to the Father, for the Father is greater than I. ²⁹I have told you now before it happens, so that when it does happen you will believe. ³⁰I will not speak with you much longer, for the prince of this world is coming. He has no hold on me, ³¹but the world must learn that I love the Father and that I do exactly what my Father has commanded me.

"Come now; let us leave.

The Vine and the Branches

15 "I am the true vine, and my Father is the gardener. ²He cuts off every branch in me that bears no fruit, while every branch that does bear fruit he prunes[b] so that it will be even more fruitful. ³You are already clean because of the word I have spoken to you. ⁴Remain in me, and I will remain in you. No branch can bear fruit by itself; it must remain in the vine. Neither can you bear fruit unless you remain in me.

⁵"I am the vine; you are the branches. If a man remains in me and I in him, he will bear much fruit; apart from me you can do nothing. ⁶If anyone does not remain in me, he is like a branch that is thrown away and withers; such branches are picked up, thrown into the fire and burned. ⁷If you remain in me and my words remain in you, ask whatever you wish, and it will be given you. ⁸This is to my Father's glory, that you bear much fruit, showing yourselves to be my disciples.

⁹"As the Father has loved me, so have I loved you. Now remain in my love. ¹⁰If you obey my commands, you will remain in my love, just as I have obeyed my Father's commands and remain in his love. ¹¹I have told you this so that my joy may be in you and that your joy may be complete. ¹²My command is this: Love each other as I have loved you. ¹³Greater love has no one than this, that he lay down his life for his friends. ¹⁴You are my friends if you do what I command. ¹⁵I no longer call you servants, because a servant does not know his master's business. Instead, I

---

a17 Some early manuscripts and is   *b2 The Greek for prunes also means cleans.*

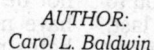
VERSE FOR THE DAY:
John 15:2

AUTHOR:
Carol L. Baldwin

PASSAGE FOR THE DAY:
John 15:1–6

Divine Pruning

WHAT would you think if your best friend told you that she thought you needed to endure a long, intense and difficult trial so that God could prune away some of the sin in your life? You would probably think she was crazy! What if she persisted and said that you would perform your job as a mother, wife, teacher or saleswoman better after your trial was over? Which of us would willingly submit to those pruning shears, and which of us would turn, run and hide?

Jesus himself is the one who says that we need pruning:

> "I am the true vine, and my Father is the gardener.
> He cuts off every branch in me that bears no fruit,
> while every branch that does bear fruit he prunes
> so that it will be even more fruitful. . . . Neither can
> you bear fruit unless you remain in me" (John
> 15:1–2,4).

Here Jesus has issued warnings to all who profess to be believers. Unfruitful branches are those who confess Christ but never bear fruit because they don't genuinely remain in him—they will be cut away. Fruitful branches, those who truly remain in Christ, will be pruned in order to bear more fruit for his glory.

When was the last time you felt "pruned"? Perhaps it was when your invalid mother came to live with you and suddenly your responsibilities and work load at home increased dramatically. Or maybe it was when your employer passed you over for a promotion because he thought you weren't working hard enough.

Pruning is painful but profitable. James tells us that trials are occasions for joy because they will test our faith and develop in us perseverance and maturity (James 1:2–4).

We need God's help even to *desire* to yield ourselves to his pruning. May God bring people and events into our lives that will sanctify us so that we might bear true spiritual fruit for his glory and his kingdom's sake.

Additional Scripture Readings:
Matthew 7:16–20; Luke 13:6–9

Go to page 1172 for your next devotional reading.

have called you friends, for everything that I learned from my Father I have made known to you. 16You did not choose me, but I chose you and appointed you to go and bear fruit—fruit that will last. Then the Father will give you whatever you ask in my name. 17This is my command: Love each other.

The World Hates the Disciples

18"If the world hates you, keep in mind that it hated me first. 19If you belonged to the world, it would love you as its own. As it is, you do not belong to the world, but I have chosen you out of the world. That is why the world hates you. 20Remember the words I spoke to you: 'No servant is greater than his master.'*a* If they persecuted me, they will persecute you also. If they obeyed my teaching, they will obey yours also. 21They will treat you this way

because of my name, for they do not know the One who sent me. 22If I had not come and spoken to them, they would not be guilty of sin. Now, however, they have no excuse for their sin. 23He who hates me hates my Father as well. 24If I had not done among them what no one else did, they would not be guilty of sin. But now they have seen these miracles, and yet they have hated both me and my Father. 25But this is to fulfill what is written in their Law: 'They hated me without reason.'*b*

26"When the Counselor comes, whom I will send to you from the Father, the Spirit of truth who goes out from the Father, he will testify about me. 27And you also must testify, for you have been with me from the beginning.

16 "All this I have told you so that you will not go astray. 2They will put

---

a20 John 13:16   *b25* Psalms 35:19; 69:4

FRIDAY

VERSE FOR THE DAY: AUTHOR: PASSAGE FOR THE DAY:
John 15:12–13   Kathy Narramore   John 15:9–17
                           Alice Hill

Velvet and Sandpaper

WE all have known family or friends who bring out the worst in us instead of the best, rubbing us at just the wrong spots, uncovering our weaknesses rather than our strengths. They're like sandpaper. It is good to remember that Jesus encountered these sandpaper experiences at times even from within his inner circle. It is also good to remember that one of his close friends was one he knew would never understand him and would even betray him. He was a constant sandpaper to Jesus, yet Jesus loved him daily as he did the others. Even in this way he was laying down his life. Since we are also loved sacrificially we are to lay down our lives for each other (1 John 3:16).

But the Lord gives us others who are like velvet, whose words are comforting and supportive, and who really understand us. They are the soft cushions we need when we are scraped with the "sandpapers" and can listen to us as we explore the weaknesses and needs they bring out in us. They tangibly reveal God's perspective—just when we most need it.

Additional Scripture Readings: *Go to page 1173 for your next*
John 13:18–30; Acts 9:23–28; 11:22–26   *devotional reading.*

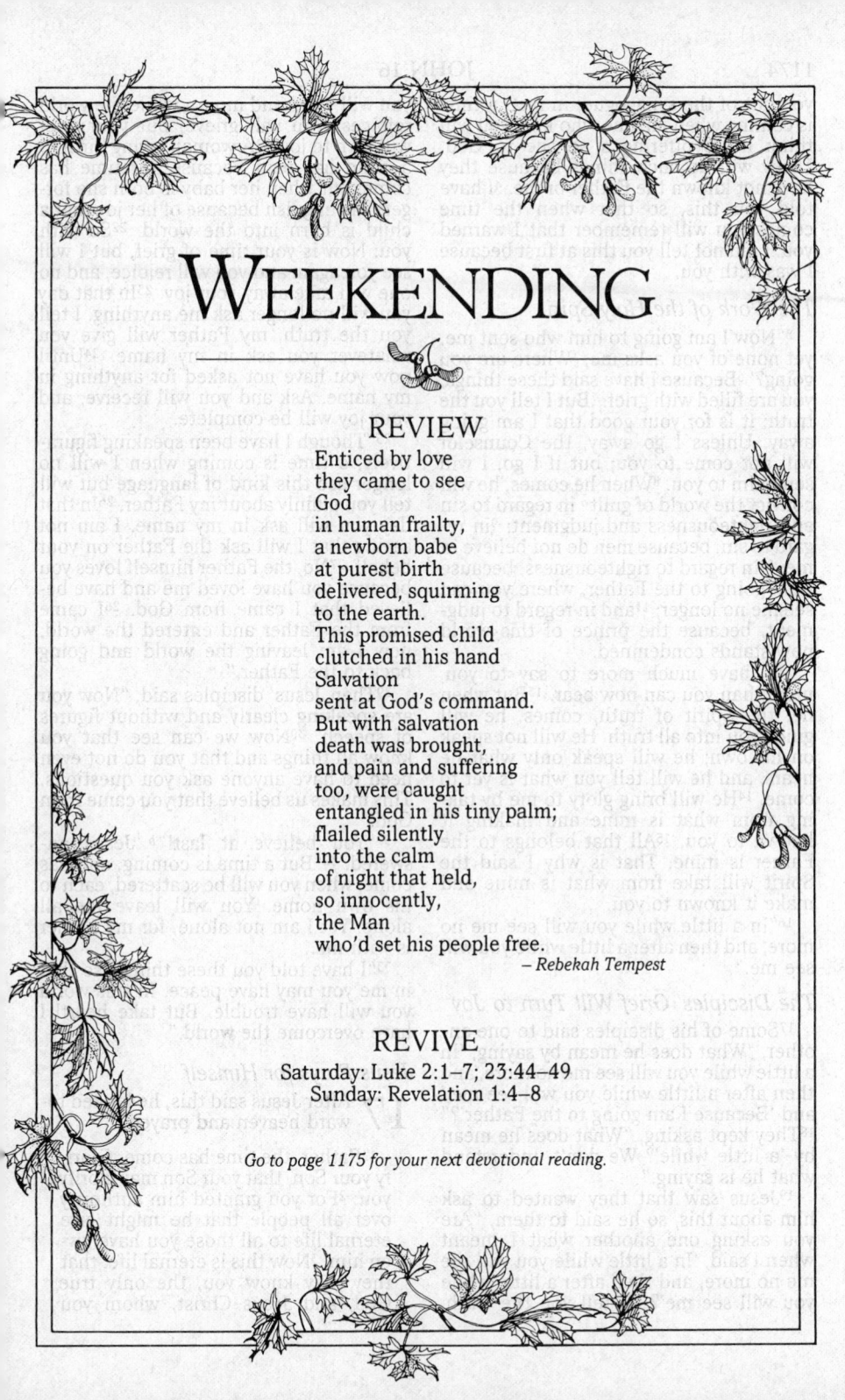

WEEKENDING

REVIEW

Enticed by love
they came to see
God
in human frailty,
a newborn babe
at purest birth
delivered, squirming
to the earth.
This promised child
clutched in his hand
Salvation
sent at God's command.
But with salvation
death was brought,
and pain and suffering
too, were caught
entangled in his tiny palm;
flailed silently
into the calm
of night that held,
so innocently,
the Man
who'd set his people free.

– Rebekah Tempest

REVIVE

Saturday: Luke 2:1–7; 23:44–49
Sunday: Revelation 1:4–8

Go to page 1175 for your next devotional reading.

you out of the synagogue; in fact, a time is coming when anyone who kills you will think he is offering a service to God. ³They will do such things because they have not known the Father or me. ⁴I have told you this, so that when the time comes you will remember that I warned you. I did not tell you this at first because I was with you.

The Work of the Holy Spirit

⁵"Now I am going to him who sent me, yet none of you asks me, 'Where are you going?' ⁶Because I have said these things, you are filled with grief. ⁷But I tell you the truth: It is for your good that I am going away. Unless I go away, the Counselor will not come to you; but if I go, I will send him to you. ⁸When he comes, he will convict the world of guilt ª in regard to sin and righteousness and judgment: ⁹in regard to sin, because men do not believe in me; ¹⁰in regard to righteousness, because I am going to the Father, where you can see me no longer; ¹¹and in regard to judgment, because the prince of this world now stands condemned.

¹²"I have much more to say to you, more than you can now bear. ¹³But when he, the Spirit of truth, comes, he will guide you into all truth. He will not speak on his own; he will speak only what he hears, and he will tell you what is yet to come. ¹⁴He will bring glory to me by taking from what is mine and making it known to you. ¹⁵All that belongs to the Father is mine. That is why I said the Spirit will take from what is mine and make it known to you.

¹⁶"In a little while you will see me no more, and then after a little while you will see me."

The Disciples' Grief Will Turn to Joy

¹⁷Some of his disciples said to one another, "What does he mean by saying, 'In a little while you will see me no more, and then after a little while you will see me,' and 'Because I am going to the Father'?" ¹⁸They kept asking, "What does he mean by 'a little while'? We don't understand what he is saying."

¹⁹Jesus saw that they wanted to ask him about this, so he said to them, "Are you asking one another what I meant when I said, 'In a little while you will see me no more, and then after a little while you will see me'? ²⁰I tell you the truth, you will weep and mourn while the world rejoices. You will grieve, but your grief will turn to joy. ²¹A woman giving birth to a child has pain because her time has come; but when her baby is born she forgets the anguish because of her joy that a child is born into the world. ²²So with you: Now is your time of grief, but I will see you again and you will rejoice, and no one will take away your joy. ²³In that day you will no longer ask me anything. I tell you the truth, my Father will give you whatever you ask in my name. ²⁴Until now you have not asked for anything in my name. Ask and you will receive, and your joy will be complete.

²⁵"Though I have been speaking figuratively, a time is coming when I will no longer use this kind of language but will tell you plainly about my Father. ²⁶In that day you will ask in my name. I am not saying that I will ask the Father on your behalf. ²⁷No, the Father himself loves you because you have loved me and have believed that I came from God. ²⁸I came from the Father and entered the world; now I am leaving the world and going back to the Father."

²⁹Then Jesus' disciples said, "Now you are speaking clearly and without figures of speech. ³⁰Now we can see that you know all things and that you do not even need to have anyone ask you questions. This makes us believe that you came from God."

³¹"You believe at last!" ᵇ Jesus answered. ³²"But a time is coming, and has come, when you will be scattered, each to his own home. You will leave me all alone. Yet I am not alone, for my Father is with me.

³³"I have told you these things, so that in me you may have peace. In this world you will have trouble. But take heart! I have overcome the world."

Jesus Prays for Himself

17 After Jesus said this, he looked toward heaven and prayed:

"Father, the time has come. Glorify your Son, that your Son may glorify you. ²For you granted him authority over all people that he might give eternal life to all those you have given him. ³Now this is eternal life: that they may know you, the only true God, and Jesus Christ, whom you

VERSE FOR THE DAY:
John 16:20,22

AUTHOR:
Sue Richards

PASSAGE FOR THE DAY:
John 16:17–24

Coming Joy

AS much as two years after becoming single, I frequently found myself in tears at suppertime. My toddlers seemed to be tired by then, scrapping with each other, whining, hanging on me, and incessantly tattling on the crimes they committed against each other.

This is when Daddy is supposed to appear at the door, and both children run to their hero. Dad's arrival gives Mom a few minutes of peace while she prepares the evening meal, and later she has someone to share and commiserate with.

But no one comes while I'm preparing supper. And all I have to look forward to in the hours that lie ahead is refereeing my young wrecking crew, doing dishes, giving baths, reading stories, ending the nightly bedtime battle, and then my own lonely bed.

The thought that I'll always be a single parent is enough to start me sobbing at suppertime.

After a year of grieving for the loss of mate, companion, and father of my children, I knew I had to do something to survive the suppertime slump. I remembered some promises about joy that I'd cut out and stuck in a drawer years before. Though yellowed, wrinkled, and stained with an ancient cake batter, my promises were more precious than gold!

"Restore to me the joy of your salvation" (Psalm 51:12).

"You will grieve, but your grief will turn to joy . . . . and no one will take away your joy" (John 16:20,22).

> "He who goes out weeping,
>   carrying seed to sow,
> will return with songs of joy,
>   carrying sheaves with him" (Psalm 126:6).

Those words don't always start me dancing around the house. But they give me the courage to continue.

Thank you, Father, that joy will follow my sorrows.

Additional Scripture Readings:
Psalm 51:11–12; Isaiah 35:3–10

Go to page 1177 for your next devotional reading.

have sent. ⁴I have brought you glory on earth by completing the work you gave me to do. ⁵And now, Father, glorify me in your presence with the glory I had with you before the world began.

Jesus Prays for His Disciples

⁶"I have revealed you*a* to those whom you gave me out of the world. They were yours; you gave them to me and they have obeyed your word. ⁷Now they know that everything you have given me comes from you. ⁸For I gave them the words you gave me and they accepted them. They knew with certainty that I came from you, and they believed that you sent me. ⁹I pray for them. I am not praying for the world, but for those you have given me, for they are yours. ¹⁰All I have is yours, and all you have is mine. And glory has come to me through them. ¹¹I will remain in the world no longer, but they are still in the world, and I am coming to you. Holy Father, protect them by the power of your name—the name you gave me—so that they may be one as we are one. ¹²While I was with them, I protected them and kept them safe by that name you gave me. None has been lost except the one doomed to destruction so that Scripture would be fulfilled.

¹³"I am coming to you now, but I say these things while I am still in the world, so that they may have the full measure of my joy within them. ¹⁴I have given them your word and the world has hated them, for they are not of the world any more than I am of the world. ¹⁵My prayer is not that you take them out of the world but that you protect them from the evil one. ¹⁶They are not of the world, even as I am not of it. ¹⁷Sanctify*b* them by the truth; your word is truth. ¹⁸As you sent me into the world, I have sent them into the world. ¹⁹For them I sanctify myself, that they too may be truly sanctified.

Jesus Prays for All Believers

²⁰"My prayer is not for them alone. I pray also for those who will believe in me through their message, ²¹that

all of them may be one, Father, just as you are in me and I am in you. May they also be in us so that the world may believe that you have sent me. ²²I have given them the glory that you gave me, that they may be one as we are one: ²³I in them and you in me. May they be brought to complete unity to let the world know that you sent me and have loved them even as you have loved me.

²⁴"Father, I want those you have given me to be with me where I am, and to see my glory, the glory you have given me because you loved me before the creation of the world.

²⁵"Righteous Father, though the world does not know you, I know you, and they know that you have sent me. ²⁶I have made you known to them, and will continue to make you known in order that the love you have for me may be in them and that I myself may be in them."

Jesus Arrested

18 When he had finished praying, Jesus left with his disciples and crossed the Kidron Valley. On the other side there was an olive grove, and he and his disciples went into it.

²Now Judas, who betrayed him, knew the place, because Jesus had often met there with his disciples. ³So Judas came to the grove, guiding a detachment of soldiers and some officials from the chief priests and Pharisees. They were carrying torches, lanterns and weapons.

⁴Jesus, knowing all that was going to happen to him, went out and asked them, "Who is it you want?"

⁵"Jesus of Nazareth," they replied.

"I am he," Jesus said. (And Judas the traitor was standing there with them.) ⁶When Jesus said, "I am he," they drew back and fell to the ground.

⁷Again he asked them, "Who is it you want?"

And they said, "Jesus of Nazareth."

⁸"I told you that I am he," Jesus answered. "If you are looking for me, then let these men go." ⁹This happened so that the words he had spoken would be fulfilled: "I have not lost one of those you gave me."*c*

¹⁰Then Simon Peter, who had a sword, drew it and struck the high priest's ser-

---

*a*6 Greek *your name*; also in verse 26　　　*b*17 Greek *hagiazo (set apart for sacred use* or *make holy)*; also in verse 19　　　*c*9 John 6:39

TUESDAY

VERSE FOR THE DAY:
John 17:26

AUTHOR:
Anne Ortlund

PASSAGE FOR THE DAY:
John 17:1–26

Holy Ground

IT'S time to take off your shoes. You're about to move onto holy ground.

In all the literature written by human beings on this planet, John 17 is the only lengthy conversation ever recorded between God and God! You have quickies: "Let us make man in our image" (Genesis 1:26). "I praise you, Father . . . because you have hidden these things from the wise and learned, and revealed them to little children" (Matthew 11:25).

But here's a long discussion by God the Son with God the Father. (How self-revealing God is!) And when God talks with God, what are his godly, all-encompassing concerns? There are basically three:

1. John 17:1–5: the glory of the Father and the glory of the Son.

2. John 17:6–19: the well-being of believers—their protection, their unity, their joy, their sanctification . . . How he loves us!

3. John 17:20–26: the salvation of the world—that others will believe, that they will know. God yearns for them!

Do you want to move into the heart of God? Do you want to be "in sync" with him, sharing his own priorities? In John 15, just before Jesus went to the cross, he communicated these same three priorities among his final commands to his eleven disciples. And they're for you and me as well:

1. Make your chief concern the glory of the Father and the glory of the Son, through the power of the Spirit. Be zealous above all to put him first, first, first! Move away from all competition with his firstness; settle into him. As he said, "Remain in me" (John 15:1–11). That's your first priority.

2. Share his concern for the well-being of your fellow believers—their protection, their unity, their joy, their sanctification. Give your time, your gifts, yourself! As Jesus said, "Love each other" (John 15:12–17). That's your second priority.

3. Share his concern for this needy world; reach out! As he said, "You also must testify, for you have been with me from the beginning" (John 15:18–27). That's your third priority, your third area of concern.

So, here in John 17, take off your shoes. You're on holy ground. Sit at Jesus' feet. Learn his thinking. And give all you are to share his concerns, love his loves, accomplish his purposes.

Additional Scripture Readings:
Exodus 3:1–10; Mark 4:13–20

Go to page 1181 for your next
devotional reading.

vant, cutting off his right ear. (The servant's name was Malchus.)

11Jesus commanded Peter, "Put your sword away! Shall I not drink the cup the Father has given me?"

Jesus Taken to Annas

12Then the detachment of soldiers with its commander and the Jewish officials arrested Jesus. They bound him 13and brought him first to Annas, who was the father-in-law of Caiaphas, the high priest that year. 14Caiaphas was the one who had advised the Jews that it would be good if one man died for the people.

Peter's First Denial

15Simon Peter and another disciple were following Jesus. Because this disciple was known to the high priest, he went with Jesus into the high priest's courtyard, 16but Peter had to wait outside at the door. The other disciple, who was known to the high priest, came back, spoke to the girl on duty there and brought Peter in.

17"You are not one of his disciples, are you?" the girl at the door asked Peter.

He replied, "I am not."

18It was cold, and the servants and officials stood around a fire they had made to keep warm. Peter also was standing with them, warming himself.

The High Priest Questions Jesus

19Meanwhile, the high priest questioned Jesus about his disciples and his teaching.

20"I have spoken openly to the world," Jesus replied. "I always taught in synagogues or at the temple, where all the Jews come together. I said nothing in secret. 21Why question me? Ask those who heard me. Surely they know what I said."

22When Jesus said this, one of the officials nearby struck him in the face. "Is this the way you answer the high priest?" he demanded.

23"If I said something wrong," Jesus replied, "testify as to what is wrong. But if I spoke the truth, why did you strike me?" 24Then Annas sent him, still bound, to Caiaphas the high priest.*a*

Peter's Second and Third Denials

25As Simon Peter stood warming himself, he was asked, "You are not one of his disciples, are you?"

He denied it, saying, "I am not."

26One of the high priest's servants, a relative of the man whose ear Peter had cut off, challenged him, "Didn't I see you with him in the olive grove?" 27Again Peter denied it, and at that moment a rooster began to crow.

Jesus Before Pilate

28Then the Jews led Jesus from Caiaphas to the palace of the Roman governor. By now it was early morning, and to avoid ceremonial uncleanness the Jews did not enter the palace; they wanted to be able to eat the Passover. 29So Pilate came out to them and asked, "What charges are you bringing against this man?"

30"If he were not a criminal," they replied, "we would not have handed him over to you."

31Pilate said, "Take him yourselves and judge him by your own law."

"But we have no right to execute anyone," the Jews objected. 32This happened so that the words Jesus had spoken indicating the kind of death he was going to die would be fulfilled.

33Pilate then went back inside the palace, summoned Jesus and asked him, "Are you the king of the Jews?"

34"Is that your own idea," Jesus asked, "or did others talk to you about me?"

35"Am I a Jew?" Pilate replied. "It was your people and your chief priests who handed you over to me. What is it you have done?"

36Jesus said, "My kingdom is not of this world. If it were, my servants would fight to prevent my arrest by the Jews. But now my kingdom is from another place."

37"You are a king, then!" said Pilate.

Jesus answered, "You are right in saying I am a king. In fact, for this reason I was born, and for this I came into the world, to testify to the truth. Everyone on the side of truth listens to me."

38"What is truth?" Pilate asked. With this he went out again to the Jews and said, "I find no basis for a charge against him. 39But it is your custom for me to release to you one prisoner at the time of the Passover. Do you want me to release 'the king of the Jews'?"

40They shouted back, "No, not him! Give us Barabbas!" Now Barabbas had taken part in a rebellion.

---

a24 Or (Now Annas had sent him, still bound, to Caiaphas the high priest.)

Jesus Sentenced to be Crucified

19 Then Pilate took Jesus and had him flogged. [2]The soldiers twisted together a crown of thorns and put it on his head. They clothed him in a purple robe [3]and went up to him again and again, saying, "Hail, king of the Jews!" And they struck him in the face.

[4]Once more Pilate came out and said to the Jews, "Look, I am bringing him out to you to let you know that I find no basis for a charge against him." [5]When Jesus came out wearing the crown of thorns and the purple robe, Pilate said to them, "Here is the man!"

[6]As soon as the chief priests and their officials saw him, they shouted, "Crucify! Crucify!"

But Pilate answered, "You take him and crucify him. As for me, I find no basis for a charge against him."

[7]The Jews insisted, "We have a law, and according to that law he must die, because he claimed to be the Son of God."

[8]When Pilate heard this, he was even more afraid, [9]and he went back inside the palace. "Where do you come from?" he asked Jesus, but Jesus gave him no answer. [10]"Do you refuse to speak to me?" Pilate said. "Don't you realize I have power either to free you or to crucify you?"

[11]Jesus answered, "You would have no power over me if it were not given to you from above. Therefore the one who handed me over to you is guilty of a greater sin."

[12]From then on, Pilate tried to set Jesus free, but the Jews kept shouting, "If you let this man go, you are no friend of Caesar. Anyone who claims to be a king opposes Caesar."

[13]When Pilate heard this, he brought Jesus out and sat down on the judge's seat at a place known as the Stone Pavement (which in Aramaic is Gabbatha). [14]It was the day of Preparation of Passover Week, about the sixth hour.

"Here is your king," Pilate said to the Jews.

[15]But they shouted, "Take him away! Take him away! Crucify him!"

"Shall I crucify your king?" Pilate asked.

"We have no king but Caesar," the chief priests answered.

[16]Finally Pilate handed him over to them to be crucified.

The Crucifixion

So the soldiers took charge of Jesus. [17]Carrying his own cross, he went out to the place of the Skull (which in Aramaic is called Golgotha). [18]Here they crucified him, and with him two others—one on each side and Jesus in the middle.

[19]Pilate had a notice prepared and fastened to the cross. It read: JESUS OF NAZARETH, THE KING OF THE JEWS. [20]Many of the Jews read this sign, for the place where Jesus was crucified was near the city, and the sign was written in Aramaic, Latin and Greek. [21]The chief priests of the Jews protested to Pilate, "Do not write 'The King of the Jews,' but that this man claimed to be king of the Jews."

[22]Pilate answered, "What I have written, I have written."

[23]When the soldiers crucified Jesus, they took his clothes, dividing them into four shares, one for each of them, with the undergarment remaining. This garment was seamless, woven in one piece from top to bottom.

[24]"Let's not tear it," they said to one another. "Let's decide by lot who will get it."

This happened that the scripture might be fulfilled which said,

"They divided my garments among them
and cast lots for my clothing."[a]

So this is what the soldiers did.

[25]Near the cross of Jesus stood his mother, his mother's sister, Mary the wife of Clopas, and Mary Magdalene. [26]When Jesus saw his mother there, and the disciple whom he loved standing nearby, he said to his mother, "Dear woman, here is your son," [27]and to the disciple, "Here is your mother." From that time on, this disciple took her into his home.

The Death of Jesus

[28]Later, knowing that all was now completed, and so that the Scripture would be fulfilled, Jesus said, "I am thirsty." [29]A jar of wine vinegar was there, so they soaked a sponge in it, put the sponge on a stalk of the hyssop plant, and lifted it to Jesus' lips. [30]When he had received the drink, Jesus said, "It is finished." With that, he bowed his head and gave up his spirit.

a24 Psalm 22:18

31Now it was the day of Preparation, and the next day was to be a special Sabbath. Because the Jews did not want the bodies left on the crosses during the Sabbath, they asked Pilate to have the legs broken and the bodies taken down. 32The soldiers therefore came and broke the legs of the first man who had been crucified with Jesus, and then those of the other. 33But when they came to Jesus and found that he was already dead, they did not break his legs. 34Instead, one of the soldiers pierced Jesus' side with a spear, bringing a sudden flow of blood and water. 35The man who saw it has given testimony, and his testimony is true. He knows that he tells the truth, and he testifies so that you also may believe. 36These things happened so that the scripture would be fulfilled: "Not one of his bones will be broken,"a 37and, as another scripture says, "They will look on the one they have pierced."b

The Burial of Jesus

38Later, Joseph of Arimathea asked Pilate for the body of Jesus. Now Joseph was a disciple of Jesus, but secretly because he feared the Jews. With Pilate's permission, he came and took the body away. 39He was accompanied by Nicodemus, the man who earlier had visited Jesus at night. Nicodemus brought a mixture of myrrh and aloes, about seventy-five pounds.c 40Taking Jesus' body, the two of them wrapped it, with the spices, in strips of linen. This was in accordance with Jewish burial customs. 41At the place where Jesus was crucified, there was a garden, and in the garden a new tomb, in which no one had ever been laid. 42Because it was the Jewish day of Preparation and since the tomb was nearby, they laid Jesus there.

The Empty Tomb

20 Early on the first day of the week, while it was still dark, Mary Magdalene went to the tomb and saw that the stone had been removed from the entrance. 2So she came running to Simon Peter and the other disciple, the one Jesus loved, and said, "They have taken the Lord out of the tomb, and we don't know where they have put him!"

3So Peter and the other disciple started for the tomb. 4Both were running, but the other disciple outran Peter and reached the tomb first. 5He bent over and looked in at the strips of linen lying there but did not go in. 6Then Simon Peter, who was behind him, arrived and went into the tomb. He saw the strips of linen lying there, 7as well as the burial cloth that had been around Jesus' head. The cloth was folded up by itself, separate from the linen. 8Finally the other disciple, who had reached the tomb first, also went inside. He saw and believed. 9(They still did not understand from Scripture that Jesus had to rise from the dead.)

Jesus Appears to Mary Magdalene

10Then the disciples went back to their homes, 11but Mary stood outside the tomb crying. As she wept, she bent over to look into the tomb 12and saw two angels in white, seated where Jesus' body had been, one at the head and the other at the foot.

13They asked her, "Woman, why are you crying?"

"They have taken my Lord away," she said, "and I don't know where they have put him." 14At this, she turned around and saw Jesus standing there, but she did not realize that it was Jesus.

15"Woman," he said, "why are you crying? Who is it you are looking for?"

Thinking he was the gardener, she said, "Sir, if you have carried him away, tell me where you have put him, and I will get him."

16Jesus said to her, "Mary."

She turned toward him and cried out in Aramaic, "Rabboni!" (which means Teacher).

17Jesus said, "Do not hold on to me, for I have not yet returned to the Father. Go instead to my brothers and tell them, 'I am returning to my Father and your Father, to my God and your God.' "

18Mary Magdalene went to the disciples with the news: "I have seen the Lord!" And she told them that he had said these things to her.

Jesus Appears to His Disciples

19On the evening of that first day of the week, when the disciples were together, with the doors locked for fear of the Jews, Jesus came and stood among them and said, "Peace be with you!" 20After he said this, he showed them his hands and side.

a36 Exodus 12:46; Num. 9:12; Psalm 34:20   b37 Zech. 12:10   c39 Greek *a hundred litrai* (about 34 kilograms)

VERSE FOR THE DAY:
John 20:25

AUTHOR:
Ruth A. Tucker

PASSAGE FOR THE DAY:
John 20:24–31

Doubting Believers

IT is not the faithful women (who told the doubting disciples of their risen Lord) with whom I identify most in the cast of characters who surround Jesus in the days before and after his death and resurrection. No, as I examine myself and my struggle with faith *and* doubt, I find that it is Thomas with whom I most identify.

Thomas was more than simply one doubting disciple who held out for proof of the resurrection—a skeptic who will be remembered forever for his lack of faith. No, Thomas stood in for all the rest of the followers of Jesus who, through the ages, have been afflicted with a disposition toward doubt. Like him, we are disciples, but disciples who are cynical at times, who often need more time to assimilate and test the facts.

Thomas merits no praise for his unbelieving mindset. But he and the other disciples, who initially doubted, offer skeptics through the ages assurance because they did not take for granted anything involving the Easter events. Indeed, the most powerful evidence for the resurrection of Jesus is the very fact that the disciples doubted. They were not like some people who are ready to latch on to any rumor or report that comes along—particularly if it bolsters their position. No, they demanded proof, and in doing so benefited the Christian church for all time.

For Jesus, however, the disciples' lack of faith was a deep disappointment, and I know that my own lack of faith at times surely must grieve the heart of my Lord. Yet, I know he understands my struggle, and I know he understands my prayer that reiterates the plea of another who struggled with unbelief when he cried out, "I do believe; help me overcome my unbelief!" (Mark 9:24).

Additional Scripture Readings:
Matthew 14:28–31; 1 John 1:1–3

Go to page 1185 for your next
devotional reading.

The disciples were overjoyed when they saw the Lord.

21Again Jesus said, "Peace be with you! As the Father has sent me, I am sending you." 22And with that he breathed on them and said, "Receive the Holy Spirit. 23If you forgive anyone his sins, they are forgiven; if you do not forgive them, they are not forgiven."

Jesus Appears to Thomas

24Now Thomas (called Didymus), one of the Twelve, was not with the disciples when Jesus came. 25So the other disciples told him, "We have seen the Lord!"

But he said to them, "Unless I see the nail marks in his hands and put my finger where the nails were, and put my hand into his side, I will not believe it."

26A week later his disciples were in the house again, and Thomas was with them. Though the doors were locked, Jesus came and stood among them and said, "Peace be with you!" 27Then he said to Thomas, "Put your finger here; see my hands. Reach out your hand and put it into my side. Stop doubting and believe."

28Thomas said to him, "My Lord and my God!"

29Then Jesus told him, "Because you have seen me, you have believed; blessed are those who have not seen and yet have believed."

30Jesus did many other miraculous signs in the presence of his disciples, which are not recorded in this book. 31But these are written that you may*a* believe that Jesus is the Christ, the Son of God, and that by believing you may have life in his name.

Jesus and the Miraculous Catch of Fish

21 Afterward Jesus appeared again to his disciples, by the Sea of Tiberias.*b* It happened this way: 2Simon Peter, Thomas (called Didymus), Nathanael from Cana in Galilee, the sons of Zebedee, and two other disciples were together. 3"I'm going out to fish," Simon Peter told them, and they said, "We'll go with you." So they went out and got into the boat, but that night they caught nothing.

4Early in the morning, Jesus stood on the shore, but the disciples did not realize that it was Jesus.

5He called out to them, "Friends, haven't you any fish?"

"No," they answered.

6He said, "Throw your net on the right side of the boat and you will find some." When they did, they were unable to haul the net in because of the large number of fish.

7Then the disciple whom Jesus loved said to Peter, "It is the Lord!" As soon as Simon Peter heard him say, "It is the Lord," he wrapped his outer garment around him (for he had taken it off) and jumped into the water. 8The other disciples followed in the boat, towing the net full of fish, for they were not far from shore, about a hundred yards.*c* 9When they landed, they saw a fire of burning coals there with fish on it, and some bread.

10Jesus said to them, "Bring some of the fish you have just caught."

11Simon Peter climbed aboard and dragged the net ashore. It was full of large fish, 153, but even with so many the net was not torn. 12Jesus said to them, "Come and have breakfast." None of the disciples dared ask him, "Who are you?" They knew it was the Lord. 13Jesus came, took the bread and gave it to them, and did the same with the fish. 14This was now the third time Jesus appeared to his disciples after he was raised from the dead.

Jesus Reinstates Peter

15When they had finished eating, Jesus said to Simon Peter, "Simon son of John, do you truly love me more than these?"

"Yes, Lord," he said, "you know that I love you."

Jesus said, "Feed my lambs."

16Again Jesus said, "Simon son of John, do you truly love me?"

He answered, "Yes, Lord, you know that I love you."

Jesus said, "Take care of my sheep."

17The third time he said to him, "Simon son of John, do you love me?"

Peter was hurt because Jesus asked him the third time, "Do you love me?" He said, "Lord, you know all things; you know that I love you."

Jesus said, "Feed my sheep. 18I tell you the truth, when you were younger you dressed yourself and went where you wanted; but when you are old you will stretch out your hands, and someone else

---

a31 Some manuscripts *may continue to cubits* (about 90 meters)   *b1* That is, Sea of Galilee   *c8* Greek *about two hundred* will dress you and lead you where you do not want to go." [19]Jesus said this to indicate the kind of death by which Peter would glorify God. Then he said to him, "Follow me!"

[20]Peter turned and saw that the disciple whom Jesus loved was following them. (This was the one who had leaned back against Jesus at the supper and had said, "Lord, who is going to betray you?") [21]When Peter saw him, he asked, "Lord, what about him?"

[22]Jesus answered, "If I want him to remain alive until I return, what is that to you? You must follow me." [23]Because of this, the rumor spread among the brothers that this disciple would not die. But Jesus did not say that he would not die; he only said, "If I want him to remain alive until I return, what is that to you?"

[24]This is the disciple who testifies to these things and who wrote them down. We know that his testimony is true.

[25]Jesus did many other things as well. If every one of them were written down, I suppose that even the whole world would not have room for the books that would be written.

LUKE begins the second volume of his history of Christianity (Acts 1:1–3) by telling how Jesus pours out the Holy Spirit on the apostles. The Spirit in turn inspires them to spread the message of salvation from Jerusalem to Rome. In his story Luke stresses how unity and love prevail in the church and how God protects the missionaries from their enemies. As you read this book, think about how powerful the Holy Spirit still is in the church and in your own life and how God protects you against the forces of evil.

ACTS

Jesus Taken Up Into Heaven

1 In my former book, Theophilus, I wrote about all that Jesus began to do and to teach ²until the day he was taken up to heaven, after giving instructions through the Holy Spirit to the apostles he had chosen. ³After his suffering, he showed himself to these men and gave many convincing proofs that he was alive. He appeared to them over a period of forty days and spoke about the kingdom of God. ⁴On one occasion, while he was eating with them, he gave them this command: "Do not leave Jerusalem, but wait for the gift my Father promised, which you have heard me speak about. ⁵For John baptized with*ᵃ* water, but in a few days you will be baptized with the Holy Spirit."

⁶So when they met together, they asked him, "Lord, are you at this time going to restore the kingdom to Israel?"

⁷He said to them: "It is not for you to know the times or dates the Father has

ᵃ5 Or in

set by his own authority. ⁸But you will receive power when the Holy Spirit comes on you; and you will be my witnesses in Jerusalem, and in all Judea and Samaria, and to the ends of the earth."

⁹After he said this, he was taken up before their very eyes, and a cloud hid him from their sight.

¹⁰They were looking intently up into the sky as he was going, when suddenly two men dressed in white stood beside

them. ¹¹"Men of Galilee," they said, "why do you stand here looking into the sky? This same Jesus, who has been taken from you into heaven, will come back in the same way you have seen him go into heaven."

Matthias Chosen to Replace Judas

¹²Then they returned to Jerusalem from the hill called the Mount of Olives, a Sabbath day's walkᵃ from the city.

ᵃ12 That is, about 3/4 mile (about 1,100 meters)

THURSDAY

VERSE FOR THE DAY:	AUTHOR:	PASSAGE FOR THE DAY:
Acts 1:8	Rebecca Manley Pippert	Acts 1:1–11

Jesus the Evangelist

JESUS told us that as the Father sent him into the world, so he is sending us (John 17:18; Acts 1:8). How then did the Father send him? Essentially he became one of us. "The Word became flesh" (John 1:14). God didn't send a telegram or shower evangelistic Bible study books from heaven or drop a million bumper stickers from the sky saying, "Smile, Jesus loves you." He sent a man, his Son, to communicate the message. His strategy hasn't changed. He still sends men and women—before he sends tracts and techniques—to change the world. You may think his strategy is risky, but that is God's problem, not yours.

In Jesus, then, we have our model for how to relate to the world, and it is a model of openness and identification. Jesus was a remarkably open man. He didn't think it was unspiritual for him (fully realizing he was the Son of God) to share his physical needs (John 4:7). He didn't fear losing his testimony by revealing to his disciples the depths of his emotional stress in the Garden of Gethsemane (Mark 14:32–52). Here is our model for genuine godliness. We see him asking for support and desiring others to minister to him. We must learn then to relate transparently and genuinely to others because that is God's style of relating to us. Jesus commands us to go and then preach, not to preach and then leave. We are not to shout the gospel from a safe and respectable distance, and remain detached. We must open our lives enough to let people see that we too laugh and hurt and cry. If Jesus left all of heaven and glory to become one of us, shouldn't we at least be willing to leave our dorm room or Bible study circle to reach out to a friend?

Additional Scripture Readings:
John 11:33–44; 1 Corinthians 2:1–5

Go to page 1189 for your next devotional reading.

13When they arrived, they went upstairs to the room where they were staying. Those present were Peter, John, James and Andrew; Philip and Thomas, Bartholomew and Matthew; James son of Alphaeus and Simon the Zealot, and Judas son of James. 14They all joined together constantly in prayer, along with the women and Mary the mother of Jesus, and with his brothers.

15In those days Peter stood up among the believers*a* (a group numbering about a hundred and twenty) 16and said, "Brothers, the Scripture had to be fulfilled which the Holy Spirit spoke long ago through the mouth of David concerning Judas, who served as guide for those who arrested Jesus— 17he was one of our number and shared in this ministry."

18(With the reward he got for his wickedness, Judas bought a field; there he fell headlong, his body burst open and all his intestines spilled out. 19Everyone in Jerusalem heard about this, so they called that field in their language Akeldama, that is, Field of Blood.)

20"For," said Peter, "it is written in the book of Psalms,

" 'May his place be deserted;
    let there be no one to dwell in it,'*b*

and,

" 'May another take his place of
    leadership.'*c*

21Therefore it is necessary to choose one of the men who have been with us the whole time the Lord Jesus went in and out among us, 22beginning from John's baptism to the time when Jesus was taken up from us. For one of these must become a witness with us of his resurrection."

23So they proposed two men: Joseph called Barsabbas (also known as Justus) and Matthias. 24Then they prayed, "Lord, you know everyone's heart. Show us which of these two you have chosen 25to take over this apostolic ministry, which Judas left to go where he belongs." 26Then they cast lots, and the lot fell to Matthias; so he was added to the eleven apostles.

The Holy Spirit Comes at Pentecost

2 When the day of Pentecost came, they were all together in one place.

2Suddenly a sound like the blowing of a violent wind came from heaven and filled the whole house where they were sitting. 3They saw what seemed to be tongues of fire that separated and came to rest on each of them. 4All of them were filled with the Holy Spirit and began to speak in other tongues*d* as the Spirit enabled them.

5Now there were staying in Jerusalem God-fearing Jews from every nation under heaven. 6When they heard this sound, a crowd came together in bewilderment, because each one heard them speaking in his own language. 7Utterly amazed, they asked: "Are not all these men who are speaking Galileans? 8Then how is it that each of us hears them in his own native language? 9Parthians, Medes and Elamites; residents of Mesopotamia, Judea and Cappadocia, Pontus and Asia, 10Phrygia and Pamphylia, Egypt and the parts of Libya near Cyrene; visitors from Rome 11(both Jews and converts to Judaism); Cretans and Arabs—we hear them declaring the wonders of God in our own tongues!" 12Amazed and perplexed, they asked one another, "What does this mean?"

13Some, however, made fun of them and said, "They have had too much wine.*e*"

Peter Addresses the Crowd

14Then Peter stood up with the Eleven, raised his voice and addressed the crowd: "Fellow Jews and all of you who live in Jerusalem, let me explain this to you; listen carefully to what I say. 15These men are not drunk, as you suppose. It's only nine in the morning! 16No, this is what was spoken by the prophet Joel:

17" 'In the last days, God says,
    I will pour out my Spirit on all
        people.
Your sons and daughters will
        prophesy,
    your young men will see visions,
    your old men will dream dreams.
18Even on my servants, both men and
        women,
    I will pour out my Spirit in those
        days,
    and they will prophesy.
19I will show wonders in the heaven
        above

a15 Greek *brothers*   *b20* Psalm 69:25   *c20* Psalm 109:8   *d4* Or *languages*; also in verse 11
e13 Or *sweet wine*

and signs on the earth below,
blood and fire and billows of
smoke.
20The sun will be turned to darkness
and the moon to blood
before the coming of the great and
glorious day of the Lord.
21And everyone who calls
on the name of the Lord will be
saved.'*a*

22"Men of Israel, listen to this: Jesus of
Nazareth was a man accredited by God
to you by miracles, wonders and signs,
which God did among you through him,
as you yourselves know. 23This man was
handed over to you by God's set purpose
and foreknowledge; and you, with the
help of wicked men,*b* put him to death by
nailing him to the cross. 24But God raised
him from the dead, freeing him from the
agony of death, because it was impossible
for death to keep its hold on him. 25David
said about him:

" 'I saw the Lord always before me.
Because he is at my right hand,
I will not be shaken.
26Therefore my heart is glad and my
tongue rejoices;
my body also will live in hope,
27because you will not abandon me to
the grave,
nor will you let your Holy One see
decay.
28You have made known to me the
paths of life;
you will fill me with joy in your
presence.'*c*

29"Brothers, I can tell you confidently
that the patriarch David died and was buried, and his tomb is here to this day.
30But he was a prophet and knew that
God had promised him on oath that he
would place one of his descendants on
his throne. 31Seeing what was ahead, he
spoke of the resurrection of the Christ,*d*
that he was not abandoned to the grave,
nor did his body see decay. 32God has
raised this Jesus to life, and we are all
witnesses of the fact. 33Exalted to the
right hand of God, he has received from
the Father the promised Holy Spirit and
has poured out what you now see and
hear. 34For David did not ascend to heav-
en, and yet he said,

" 'The Lord said to my Lord:
"Sit at my right hand
35until I make your enemies
a footstool for your feet." '*e*

36"Therefore let all Israel be assured of
this: God has made this Jesus, whom you
crucified, both Lord and Christ."

37When the people heard this, they
were cut to the heart and said to Peter
and the other apostles, "Brothers, what
shall we do?"

38Peter replied, "Repent and be baptized, every one of you, in the name of
Jesus Christ for the forgiveness of your
sins. And you will receive the gift of the
Holy Spirit. 39The promise is for you and
your children and for all who are far off—
for all whom the Lord our God will call."

40With many other words he warned
them; and he pleaded with them, "Save
yourselves from this corrupt generation."
41Those who accepted his message were
baptized, and about three thousand were
added to their number that day.

The Fellowship of the Believers

42They devoted themselves to the apostles' teaching and to the fellowship, to
the breaking of bread and to prayer. 43Ev-
eryone was filled with awe, and many
wonders and miraculous signs were done
by the apostles. 44All the believers were
together and had everything in common.
45Selling their possessions and goods,
they gave to anyone as he had need. 46Ev-
ery day they continued to meet together
in the temple courts. They broke bread in
their homes and ate together with glad
and sincere hearts, 47praising God and
enjoying the favor of all the people. And
the Lord added to their number daily
those who were being saved.

Peter Heals the Crippled Beggar

3 One day Peter and John were going
up to the temple at the time of prayer
—at three in the afternoon. 2Now a man
crippled from birth was being carried to
the temple gate called Beautiful, where
he was put every day to beg from those
going into the temple courts. 3When he
saw Peter and John about to enter, he
asked them for money. 4Peter looked
straight at him, as did John. Then Peter
said, "Look at us!" 5So the man gave them

a21 Joel 2:28-32   *b23* Or *of those not having the law* (that is, Gentiles)   *c28* Psalm 16:8-11
d31 Or *Messiah.* "The Christ" (Greek) and "the Messiah" (Hebrew) both mean "the Anointed One"; also
in verse 36.   *e35* Psalm 110:1

his attention, expecting to get something from them.

⁶Then Peter said, "Silver or gold I do not have, but what I have I give you. In the name of Jesus Christ of Nazareth, walk." ⁷Taking him by the right hand, he helped him up, and instantly the man's feet and ankles became strong. ⁸He jumped to his feet and began to walk. Then he went with them into the temple courts, walking and jumping, and praising God. ⁹When all the people saw him walking and praising God, ¹⁰they recognized him as the same man who used to sit begging at the temple gate called Beautiful, and they were filled with wonder and amazement at what had happened to him.

Peter Speaks to the Onlookers

¹¹While the beggar held on to Peter and John, all the people were astonished and came running to them in the place called Solomon's Colonnade. ¹²When Peter saw this, he said to them: "Men of Israel, why does this surprise you? Why do you stare at us as if by our own power or godliness we had made this man walk? ¹³The God of Abraham, Isaac and Jacob, the God of our fathers, has glorified his servant Jesus. You handed him over to be killed, and you disowned him before Pilate, though he had decided to let him go. ¹⁴You disowned the Holy and Righteous One and asked that a murderer be released to you. ¹⁵You killed the author of life, but God raised him from the dead. We are witnesses of this. ¹⁶By faith in the name of Jesus, this man whom you see and know was made strong. It is Jesus' name and the faith that comes through him that has given this complete healing to him, as you can all see.

¹⁷"Now, brothers, I know that you acted in ignorance, as did your leaders. ¹⁸But this is how God fulfilled what he had foretold through all the prophets, saying that his Christ[a] would suffer. ¹⁹Repent, then, and turn to God, so that your sins may be wiped out, that times of refreshing may come from the Lord, ²⁰and that he may send the Christ, who has been appointed for you—even Jesus. ²¹He must remain in heaven until the time comes for God to restore everything, as he promised long ago through his holy prophets. ²²For Moses said, 'The Lord your God will raise up for you a prophet like me from among

your own people; you must listen to everything he tells you. ²³Anyone who does not listen to him will be completely cut off from among his people.'[b]

²⁴"Indeed, all the prophets from Samuel on, as many as have spoken, have foretold these days. ²⁵And you are heirs of the prophets and of the covenant God made with your fathers. He said to Abraham, 'Through your offspring all peoples on earth will be blessed.'[c] ²⁶When God raised up his servant, he sent him first to you to bless you by turning each of you from your wicked ways."

Peter and John Before the Sanhedrin

4 The priests and the captain of the temple guard and the Sadducees came up to Peter and John while they were speaking to the people. ²They were greatly disturbed because the apostles were teaching the people and proclaiming in Jesus the resurrection of the dead. ³They seized Peter and John, and because it was evening, they put them in jail until the next day. ⁴But many who heard the message believed, and the number of men grew to about five thousand.

⁵The next day the rulers, elders and teachers of the law met in Jerusalem. ⁶Annas the high priest was there, and so were Caiaphas, John, Alexander and the other men of the high priest's family. ⁷They had Peter and John brought before them and began to question them: "By what power or what name did you do this?"

⁸Then Peter, filled with the Holy Spirit, said to them: "Rulers and elders of the people! ⁹If we are being called to account today for an act of kindness shown to a cripple and are asked how he was healed, ¹⁰then know this, you and all the people of Israel: It is by the name of Jesus Christ of Nazareth, whom you crucified but whom God raised from the dead, that this man stands before you healed. ¹¹He is

" 'the stone you builders rejected,
    which has become the capstone.[d][e]

¹²Salvation is found in no one else, for there is no other name under heaven given to men by which we must be saved."

¹³When they saw the courage of Peter and John and realized that they were unschooled, ordinary men, they were astonished and they took note that these men

---

a18 Or *Messiah*; also in verse 20   b23 Deut. 18:15,18,19   c25 Gen. 22:18; 26:4   d11 Or *cornerstone*   e11 Psalm 118:22

had been with Jesus. ¹⁴But since they could see the man who had been healed standing there with them, there was nothing they could say. ¹⁵So they ordered them to withdraw from the Sanhedrin and then conferred together. ¹⁶"What are we going to do with these men?" they asked. "Everybody living in Jerusalem knows they have done an outstanding miracle, and we cannot deny it. ¹⁷But to stop this thing from spreading any further among the people, we must warn these men to speak no longer to anyone in this name."

¹⁸Then they called them in again and commanded them not to speak or teach at all in the name of Jesus. ¹⁹But Peter and John replied, "Judge for yourselves whether it is right in God's sight to obey you rather than God. ²⁰For we cannot help speaking about what we have seen and heard."

²¹After further threats they let them go. They could not decide how to punish

---

FRIDAY

VERSE FOR THE DAY: Acts 4:32	*AUTHOR:* Linda Ching Sledge	*PASSAGE FOR THE DAY:* Acts 4:23–35

No East or West

MY hometown church is on a winding street on the outskirts of old Honolulu. It was built in the 1880s by Boston missionaries who served the earliest Christian immigrants to Hawaii from Canton, China. After a century, the descendants of those first Cantonese Christians still worship there. It's a proud heritage. But for a youngster growing up in that church, it was sometimes confusing.

There were two sermons, one in English and one in Cantonese for the "old folks" who couldn't speak the language of their adopted homeland. As a child, I found the Chinese sermon long and boring. I could understand only a few words of Chinese so the words made no sense. Oh, how the long minutes dragged by!

Then one Sunday, at the closing hymn, I heard strange sounds from the pew behind me. It was an old Chinese grandfather singing at the top of his lungs . . . in Chinese!

It was so funny to hear two sets of words sung to the same tune at the same time. I couldn't resist peeking. The old man's head was thrown back, his eyes closed, and he was singing as if the words were pulled from his heart.

And suddenly, though I didn't know his words, I understood their meaning. And I began to sing too, straight from the heart:

> In Christ there is no East or West,
> In Him no South or North;
> But one great fellowship of love
> Throughout the whole wide earth.

Additional Scripture Readings:
Ephesians 2:12–20; Revelation 7:9–10

Go to page 1191 for your next devotional reading.

them, because all the people were praising God for what had happened. 22For the man who was miraculously healed was over forty years old.

The Believers' Prayer

23On their release, Peter and John went back to their own people and reported all that the chief priests and elders had said to them. 24When they heard this, they raised their voices together in prayer to God. "Sovereign Lord," they said, "you made the heaven and the earth and the sea, and everything in them. 25You spoke by the Holy Spirit through the mouth of your servant, our father David:

" 'Why do the nations rage
    and the peoples plot in vain?
26The kings of the earth take their stand
    and the rulers gather together
        against the Lord
    and against his Anointed One.ᵃ'ᵇ

27Indeed Herod and Pontius Pilate met together with the Gentiles and the peopleᶜ of Israel in this city to conspire against your holy servant Jesus, whom you anointed. 28They did what your power and will had decided beforehand should happen. 29Now, Lord, consider their threats and enable your servants to speak your word with great boldness. 30Stretch out your hand to heal and perform miraculous signs and wonders through the name of your holy servant Jesus." 31After they prayed, the place where they were meeting was shaken. And they were all filled with the Holy Spirit and spoke the word of God boldly.

The Believers Share Their Possessions

32All the believers were one in heart and mind. No one claimed that any of his possessions was his own, but they shared everything they had. 33With great power the apostles continued to testify to the resurrection of the Lord Jesus, and much grace was upon them all. 34There were no needy persons among them. For from time to time those who owned lands or houses sold them, brought the money from the sales 35and put it at the apostles' feet, and it was distributed to anyone as he had need.

36Joseph, a Levite from Cyprus, whom the apostles called Barnabas (which means Son of Encouragement), 37sold a

field he owned and brought the money and put it at the apostles' feet.

Ananias and Sapphira

5 Now a man named Ananias, together with his wife Sapphira, also sold a piece of property. 2With his wife's full knowledge he kept back part of the money for himself, but brought the rest and put it at the apostles' feet.

3Then Peter said, "Ananias, how is it that Satan has so filled your heart that you have lied to the Holy Spirit and have kept for yourself some of the money you received for the land? 4Didn't it belong to you before it was sold? And after it was sold, wasn't the money at your disposal? What made you think of doing such a thing? You have not lied to men but to God."

5When Ananias heard this, he fell down and died. And great fear seized all who heard what had happened. 6Then the young men came forward, wrapped up his body, and carried him out and buried him.

7About three hours later his wife came in, not knowing what had happened. 8Peter asked her, "Tell me, is this the price you and Ananias got for the land?"

"Yes," she said, "that is the price."

9Peter said to her, "How could you agree to test the Spirit of the Lord? Look! The feet of the men who buried your husband are at the door, and they will carry you out also."

10At that moment she fell down at his feet and died. Then the young men came in and, finding her dead, carried her out and buried her beside her husband. 11Great fear seized the whole church and all who heard about these events.

The Apostles Heal Many

12The apostles performed many miraculous signs and wonders among the people. And all the believers used to meet together in Solomon's Colonnade. 13No one else dared join them, even though they were highly regarded by the people. 14Nevertheless, more and more men and women believed in the Lord and were added to their number. 15As a result, people brought the sick into the streets and laid them on beds and mats so that at least Peter's shadow might fall on some of them as he passed by. 16Crowds gathered

---

ᵃ26 That is, Christ or Messiah   ᵇ26 Psalm 2:1,2   ᶜ27 The Greek is plural.

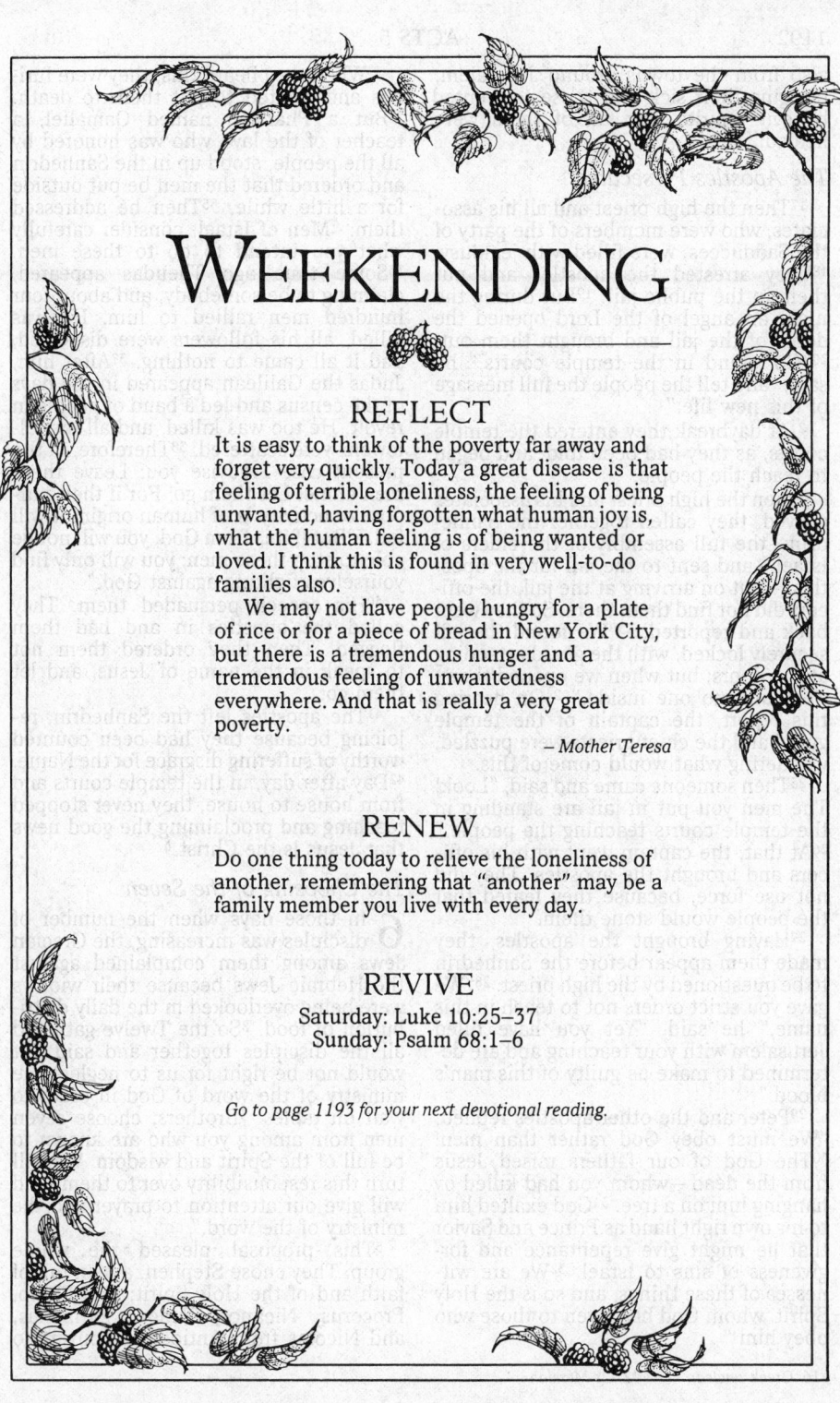

WEEKENDING

REFLECT

It is easy to think of the poverty far away and forget very quickly. Today a great disease is that feeling of terrible loneliness, the feeling of being unwanted, having forgotten what human joy is, what the human feeling is of being wanted or loved. I think this is found in very well-to-do families also.

We may not have people hungry for a plate of rice or for a piece of bread in New York City, but there is a tremendous hunger and a tremendous feeling of unwantedness everywhere. And that is really a very great poverty.

— Mother Teresa

RENEW

Do one thing today to relieve the loneliness of another, remembering that "another" may be a family member you live with every day.

REVIVE

Saturday: Luke 10:25–37
Sunday: Psalm 68:1–6

Go to page 1193 for your next devotional reading.

also from the towns around Jerusalem, bringing their sick and those tormented by evil*a* spirits, and all of them were healed.

The Apostles Persecuted

17Then the high priest and all his associates, who were members of the party of the Sadducees, were filled with jealousy. 18They arrested the apostles and put them in the public jail. 19But during the night an angel of the Lord opened the doors of the jail and brought them out. 20"Go, stand in the temple courts," he said, "and tell the people the full message of this new life."

21At daybreak they entered the temple courts, as they had been told, and began to teach the people.

When the high priest and his associates arrived, they called together the Sanhedrin—the full assembly of the elders of Israel—and sent to the jail for the apostles. 22But on arriving at the jail, the officers did not find them there. So they went back and reported, 23"We found the jail securely locked, with the guards standing at the doors; but when we opened them, we found no one inside." 24On hearing this report, the captain of the temple guard and the chief priests were puzzled, wondering what would come of this.

25Then someone came and said, "Look! The men you put in jail are standing in the temple courts teaching the people." 26At that, the captain went with his officers and brought the apostles. They did not use force, because they feared that the people would stone them.

27Having brought the apostles, they made them appear before the Sanhedrin to be questioned by the high priest. 28"We gave you strict orders not to teach in this name," he said. "Yet you have filled Jerusalem with your teaching and are determined to make us guilty of this man's blood."

29Peter and the other apostles replied: "We must obey God rather than men! 30The God of our fathers raised Jesus from the dead—whom you had killed by hanging him on a tree. 31God exalted him to his own right hand as Prince and Savior that he might give repentance and forgiveness of sins to Israel. 32We are witnesses of these things, and so is the Holy Spirit, whom God has given to those who obey him."

33When they heard this, they were furious and wanted to put them to death. 34But a Pharisee named Gamaliel, a teacher of the law, who was honored by all the people, stood up in the Sanhedrin and ordered that the men be put outside for a little while. 35Then he addressed them: "Men of Israel, consider carefully what you intend to do to these men. 36Some time ago Theudas appeared, claiming to be somebody, and about four hundred men rallied to him. He was killed, all his followers were dispersed, and it all came to nothing. 37After him, Judas the Galilean appeared in the days of the census and led a band of people in revolt. He too was killed, and all his followers were scattered. 38Therefore, in the present case I advise you: Leave these men alone! Let them go! For if their purpose or activity is of human origin, it will fail. 39But if it is from God, you will not be able to stop these men; you will only find yourselves fighting against God."

40His speech persuaded them. They called the apostles in and had them flogged. Then they ordered them not to speak in the name of Jesus, and let them go.

41The apostles left the Sanhedrin, rejoicing because they had been counted worthy of suffering disgrace for the Name. 42Day after day, in the temple courts and from house to house, they never stopped teaching and proclaiming the good news that Jesus is the Christ.*b*

The Choosing of the Seven

6 In those days when the number of disciples was increasing, the Grecian Jews among them complained against the Hebraic Jews because their widows were being overlooked in the daily distribution of food. 2So the Twelve gathered all the disciples together and said, "It would not be right for us to neglect the ministry of the word of God in order to wait on tables. 3Brothers, choose seven men from among you who are known to be full of the Spirit and wisdom. We will turn this responsibility over to them 4and will give our attention to prayer and the ministry of the word."

5This proposal pleased the whole group. They chose Stephen, a man full of faith and of the Holy Spirit; also Philip, Procorus, Nicanor, Timon, Parmenas, and Nicolas from Antioch, a convert to

a16 Greek *unclean*   *b42* Or *Messiah*

VERSE FOR THE DAY:
Acts 5:9

AUTHOR:
June Gunden

PASSAGE FOR THE DAY:
Acts 5:1–11

Giving to Receive Praise

GIVING generously to the needy is one sure way of impressing other Christians. If it becomes known that a certain family has given a lot of money or service to the church, other people respect and admire them for it.

This must have been especially true in a day when "from time to time those who owned lands or houses sold them, brought the money from the sales and put it at the apostles' feet, and it was distributed to anyone as he had need" (Acts 4:34–35). When someone sold property it would have been common knowledge what it was worth, and therefore other people would know how much had been given to the apostles.

In light of such widespread generosity, people of that day may have felt a little chagrined for it to be known that they had sold some property but had not shared the profits. Their "spiritual" reputation may have become tarnished, and they may never have been as highly thought of as those who were willing to give it all.

Accordingly, Ananias and Sapphira probably convinced themselves that by keeping some of the money for themselves they wouldn't be hurting anyone else (and they wouldn't be hurting their own reputation either). They opted to let others think they had given more than they really had. This hypocrisy, and the love of money and praise that motivated it, cost them their lives.

Jesus taught very clearly that giving to the needy must not be done for praise (Matthew 6:1–4). "When you give to the needy," he said, give "in secret" and "your Father . . . will reward you."

What if no one ever finds out that I've made a large contribution to the church? Does it matter? What if no one notices the hours I've spent helping someone else? Do I care? What if my efforts for the kingdom are largely unappreciated? Do I become discouraged?

If I am happy to serve when no one is there to give me credit, I am truly working for the Lord.

Additional Scripture Readings:
Matthew 23:5–12; Ephesians 6:7–8

Go to page 1198 for your next devotional reading.

Judaism. ⁶They presented these men to the apostles, who prayed and laid their hands on them.

⁷So the word of God spread. The number of disciples in Jerusalem increased rapidly, and a large number of priests became obedient to the faith.

Stephen Seized

⁸Now Stephen, a man full of God's grace and power, did great wonders and miraculous signs among the people. ⁹Opposition arose, however, from members of the Synagogue of the Freedmen (as it was called)—Jews of Cyrene and Alexandria as well as the provinces of Cilicia and Asia. These men began to argue with Stephen, ¹⁰but they could not stand up against his wisdom or the Spirit by whom he spoke.

¹¹Then they secretly persuaded some men to say, "We have heard Stephen speak words of blasphemy against Moses and against God."

¹²So they stirred up the people and the elders and the teachers of the law. They seized Stephen and brought him before the Sanhedrin. ¹³They produced false witnesses, who testified, "This fellow never stops speaking against this holy place and against the law. ¹⁴For we have heard him say that this Jesus of Nazareth will destroy this place and change the customs Moses handed down to us."

¹⁵All who were sitting in the Sanhedrin looked intently at Stephen, and they saw that his face was like the face of an angel.

Stephen's Speech to the Sanhedrin

7 Then the high priest asked him, "Are these charges true?"

²To this he replied: "Brothers and fathers, listen to me! The God of glory appeared to our father Abraham while he was still in Mesopotamia, before he lived in Haran. ³'Leave your country and your people,' God said, 'and go to the land I will show you.'ᵃ

⁴"So he left the land of the Chaldeans and settled in Haran. After the death of his father, God sent him to this land where you are now living. ⁵He gave him no inheritance here, not even a foot of ground. But God promised him that he and his descendants after him would possess the land, even though at that time Abraham had no child. ⁶God spoke to him in this way: 'Your descendants will be strangers in a country not their own, and they will be enslaved and mistreated four hundred years. ⁷But I will punish the nation they serve as slaves,' God said, 'and afterward they will come out of that country and worship me in this place.'ᵇ ⁸Then he gave Abraham the covenant of circumcision. And Abraham became the father of Isaac and circumcised him eight days after his birth. Later Isaac became the father of Jacob, and Jacob became the father of the twelve patriarchs.

⁹"Because the patriarchs were jealous of Joseph, they sold him as a slave into Egypt. But God was with him ¹⁰and rescued him from all his troubles. He gave Joseph wisdom and enabled him to gain the goodwill of Pharaoh king of Egypt; so he made him ruler over Egypt and all his palace.

¹¹"Then a famine struck all Egypt and Canaan, bringing great suffering, and our fathers could not find food. ¹²When Jacob heard that there was grain in Egypt, he sent our fathers on their first visit. ¹³On their second visit, Joseph told his brothers who he was, and Pharaoh learned about Joseph's family. ¹⁴After this, Joseph sent for his father Jacob and his whole family, seventy-five in all. ¹⁵Then Jacob went down to Egypt, where he and our fathers died. ¹⁶Their bodies were brought back to Shechem and placed in the tomb that Abraham had bought from the sons of Hamor at Shechem for a certain sum of money.

¹⁷"As the time drew near for God to fulfill his promise to Abraham, the number of our people in Egypt greatly increased. ¹⁸Then another king, who knew nothing about Joseph, became ruler of Egypt. ¹⁹He dealt treacherously with our people and oppressed our forefathers by forcing them to throw out their newborn babies so that they would die.

²⁰"At that time Moses was born, and he was no ordinary child.ᶜ For three months he was cared for in his father's house. ²¹When he was placed outside, Pharaoh's daughter took him and brought him up as her own son. ²²Moses was educated in all the wisdom of the Egyptians and was powerful in speech and action.

²³"When Moses was forty years old, he decided to visit his fellow Israelites. ²⁴He saw one of them being mistreated by an Egyptian, so he went to his defense and avenged him by killing the Egyptian.

ᵃ3 Gen. 12:1   ᵇ7 Gen. 15:13,14   ᶜ20 Or was fair in the sight of God

25Moses thought that his own people would realize that God was using him to rescue them, but they did not. 26The next day Moses came upon two Israelites who were fighting. He tried to reconcile them by saying, 'Men, you are brothers; why do you want to hurt each other?'

27"But the man who was mistreating the other pushed Moses aside and said, 'Who made you ruler and judge over us? 28Do you want to kill me as you killed the Egyptian yesterday?'*a* 29When Moses heard this, he fled to Midian, where he settled as a foreigner and had two sons.

30"After forty years had passed, an angel appeared to Moses in the flames of a burning bush in the desert near Mount Sinai. 31When he saw this, he was amazed at the sight. As he went over to look more closely, he heard the Lord's voice: 32'I am the God of your fathers, the God of Abraham, Isaac and Jacob.'*b* Moses trembled with fear and did not dare to look.

33"Then the Lord said to him, 'Take off your sandals; the place where you are standing is holy ground. 34I have indeed seen the oppression of my people in Egypt. I have heard their groaning and have come down to set them free. Now come, I will send you back to Egypt.'*c*

35"This is the same Moses whom they had rejected with the words, 'Who made you ruler and judge?' He was sent to be their ruler and deliverer by God himself, through the angel who appeared to him in the bush. 36He led them out of Egypt and did wonders and miraculous signs in Egypt, at the Red Sea*d* and for forty years in the desert.

37"This is that Moses who told the Israelites, 'God will send you a prophet like me from your own people.'*e* 38He was in the assembly in the desert, with the angel who spoke to him on Mount Sinai, and with our fathers; and he received living words to pass on to us.

39"But our fathers refused to obey him. Instead, they rejected him and in their hearts turned back to Egypt. 40They told Aaron, 'Make us gods who will go before us. As for this fellow Moses who led us out of Egypt—we don't know what has happened to him!'*f* 41That was the time they made an idol in the form of a calf. They brought sacrifices to it and held a celebration in honor of what their hands had made. 42But God turned away and gave them over to the worship of the heavenly bodies. This agrees with what is written in the book of the prophets:

" 'Did you bring me sacrifices and
    offerings
  forty years in the desert, O house of
    Israel?
43You have lifted up the shrine of
    Molech
  and the star of your god Rephan,
    the idols you made to worship.
Therefore I will send you into exile'*g*
    beyond Babylon.

44"Our forefathers had the tabernacle of the Testimony with them in the desert. It had been made as God directed Moses, according to the pattern he had seen. 45Having received the tabernacle, our fathers under Joshua brought it with them when they took the land from the nations God drove out before them. It remained in the land until the time of David, 46who enjoyed God's favor and asked that he might provide a dwelling place for the God of Jacob.*h* 47But it was Solomon who built the house for him.

48"However, the Most High does not live in houses made by men. As the prophet says:

49" 'Heaven is my throne,
    and the earth is my footstool.
  What kind of house will you build for
    me?
                           says the Lord.
  Or where will my resting place be?
50Has not my hand made all these
    things?'*i*

51"You stiff-necked people, with uncircumcised hearts and ears! You are just like your fathers: You always resist the Holy Spirit! 52Was there ever a prophet your fathers did not persecute? They even killed those who predicted the coming of the Righteous One. And now you have betrayed and murdered him— 53you who have received the law that was put into effect through angels but have not obeyed it."

The Stoning of Stephen

54When they heard this, they were furious and gnashed their teeth at him. 55But

---

a28 Exodus 2:14   *b32* Exodus 3:6   *c34* Exodus 3:5,7,8,10   *d36* That is, Sea of Reeds
e37 Deut. 18:15   *f40* Exodus 32:1   *g43* Amos 5:25-27   *h46* Some early manuscripts *the house of*
Jacob   *i50* Isaiah 66:1,2

Stephen, full of the Holy Spirit, looked up to heaven and saw the glory of God, and Jesus standing at the right hand of God. 56"Look," he said, "I see heaven open and the Son of Man standing at the right hand of God."

57At this they covered their ears and, yelling at the top of their voices, they all rushed at him, 58dragged him out of the city and began to stone him. Meanwhile, the witnesses laid their clothes at the feet of a young man named Saul.

59While they were stoning him, Stephen prayed, "Lord Jesus, receive my spirit." 60Then he fell on his knees and cried out, "Lord, do not hold this sin against them." When he had said this, he fell asleep.

8 And Saul was there, giving approval to his death.

The Church Persecuted and Scattered

On that day a great persecution broke out against the church at Jerusalem, and all except the apostles were scattered throughout Judea and Samaria. 2Godly men buried Stephen and mourned deeply for him. 3But Saul began to destroy the church. Going from house to house, he dragged off men and women and put them in prison.

Philip in Samaria

4Those who had been scattered preached the word wherever they went. 5Philip went down to a city in Samaria and proclaimed the Christ*a* there. 6When the crowds heard Philip and saw the miraculous signs he did, they all paid close attention to what he said. 7With shrieks, evil*b* spirits came out of many, and many paralytics and cripples were healed. 8So there was great joy in that city.

Simon the Sorcerer

9Now for some time a man named Simon had practiced sorcery in the city and amazed all the people of Samaria. He boasted that he was someone great, 10and all the people, both high and low, gave him their attention and exclaimed, "This man is the divine power known as the Great Power." 11They followed him because he had amazed them for a long time with his magic. 12But when they be-

lieved Philip as he preached the good news of the kingdom of God and the name of Jesus Christ, they were baptized, both men and women. 13Simon himself believed and was baptized. And he followed Philip everywhere, astonished by the great signs and miracles he saw.

14When the apostles in Jerusalem heard that Samaria had accepted the word of God, they sent Peter and John to them. 15When they arrived, they prayed for them that they might receive the Holy Spirit, 16because the Holy Spirit had not yet come upon any of them; they had simply been baptized into*c* the name of the Lord Jesus. 17Then Peter and John placed their hands on them, and they received the Holy Spirit.

18When Simon saw that the Spirit was given at the laying on of the apostles' hands, he offered them money 19and said, "Give me also this ability so that everyone on whom I lay my hands may receive the Holy Spirit."

20Peter answered: "May your money perish with you, because you thought you could buy the gift of God with money! 21You have no part or share in this ministry, because your heart is not right before God. 22Repent of this wickedness and pray to the Lord. Perhaps he will forgive you for having such a thought in your heart. 23For I see that you are full of bitterness and captive to sin."

24Then Simon answered, "Pray to the Lord for me so that nothing you have said may happen to me."

25When they had testified and proclaimed the word of the Lord, Peter and John returned to Jerusalem, preaching the gospel in many Samaritan villages.

Philip and the Ethiopian

26Now an angel of the Lord said to Philip, "Go south to the road—the desert road—that goes down from Jerusalem to Gaza." 27So he started out, and on his way he met an Ethiopian*d* eunuch, an important official in charge of all the treasury of Candace, queen of the Ethiopians. This man had gone to Jerusalem to worship, 28and on his way home was sitting in his chariot reading the book of Isaiah the prophet. 29The Spirit told Philip, "Go to that chariot and stay near it."

30Then Philip ran up to the chariot and heard the man reading Isaiah the pro-

a5 Or *Messiah*   *b7* Greek *unclean*   *c16* Or *in*   *d27* That is, from the upper Nile region phet. "Do you understand what you are reading?" Philip asked.

³¹"How can I," he said, "unless someone explains it to me?" So he invited Philip to come up and sit with him.

³²The eunuch was reading this passage of Scripture:

"He was led like a sheep to the
    slaughter,
and as a lamb before the shearer is
    silent,
so he did not open his mouth.
³³In his humiliation he was deprived of
    justice.
Who can speak of his descendants?
For his life was taken from the
    earth."ᵃ

³⁴The eunuch asked Philip, "Tell me, please, who is the prophet talking about, himself or someone else?" ³⁵Then Philip began with that very passage of Scripture and told him the good news about Jesus.

³⁶As they traveled along the road, they came to some water and the eunuch said, "Look, here is water. Why shouldn't I be baptized?"ᵇ ³⁸And he gave orders to stop the chariot. Then both Philip and the eunuch went down into the water and Philip baptized him. ³⁹When they came up out of the water, the Spirit of the Lord suddenly took Philip away, and the eunuch did not see him again, but went on his way rejoicing. ⁴⁰Philip, however, appeared at Azotus and traveled about, preaching the gospel in all the towns until he reached Caesarea.

Saul's Conversion

9 Meanwhile, Saul was still breathing out murderous threats against the Lord's disciples. He went to the high priest ²and asked him for letters to the synagogues in Damascus, so that if he found any there who belonged to the Way, whether men or women, he might take them as prisoners to Jerusalem. ³As he neared Damascus on his journey, suddenly a light from heaven flashed around him. ⁴He fell to the ground and heard a voice say to him, "Saul, Saul, why do you persecute me?"

⁵"Who are you, Lord?" Saul asked.

"I am Jesus, whom you are persecuting," he replied. ⁶"Now get up and go into the city, and you will be told what you must do."

⁷The men traveling with Saul stood there speechless; they heard the sound but did not see anyone. ⁸Saul got up from the ground, but when he opened his eyes he could see nothing. So they led him by the hand into Damascus. ⁹For three days he was blind, and did not eat or drink anything.

¹⁰In Damascus there was a disciple named Ananias. The Lord called to him in a vision, "Ananias!"

"Yes, Lord," he answered.

¹¹The Lord told him, "Go to the house of Judas on Straight Street and ask for a man from Tarsus named Saul, for he is praying. ¹²In a vision he has seen a man named Ananias come and place his hands on him to restore his sight."

¹³"Lord," Ananias answered, "I have heard many reports about this man and all the harm he has done to your saints in Jerusalem. ¹⁴And he has come here with authority from the chief priests to arrest all who call on your name."

¹⁵But the Lord said to Ananias, "Go! This man is my chosen instrument to carry my name before the Gentiles and their kings and before the people of Israel. ¹⁶I will show him how much he must suffer for my name."

¹⁷Then Ananias went to the house and entered it. Placing his hands on Saul, he said, "Brother Saul, the Lord—Jesus, who appeared to you on the road as you were coming here—has sent me so that you may see again and be filled with the Holy Spirit." ¹⁸Immediately, something like scales fell from Saul's eyes, and he could see again. He got up and was baptized, ¹⁹and after taking some food, he regained his strength.

Saul in Damascus and Jerusalem

Saul spent several days with the disciples in Damascus. ²⁰At once he began to preach in the synagogues that Jesus is the Son of God. ²¹All those who heard him were astonished and asked, "Isn't he the man who raised havoc in Jerusalem among those who call on this name? And hasn't he come here to take them as prisoners to the chief priests?" ²²Yet Saul grew more and more powerful and baffled the Jews living in Damascus by proving that Jesus is the Christ.ᶜ

²³After many days had gone by, the Jews conspired to kill him, ²⁴but Saul

---

ᵃ33 Isaiah 53:7,8   ᵇ36 Some late manuscripts baptized?" ³⁷Philip said, "If you believe with all your heart, you may." The eunuch answered, "I believe that Jesus Christ is the Son of God."   ᶜ22 Or Messiah

VERSE FOR THE DAY:
Acts 9:3–4

AUTHOR:
Jean Syswerda

PASSAGE FOR THE DAY:
Acts 9:1–19

My Walk

SAUL was about as opposed to Christ and Christianity as one could get. He stood at Stephen's stoning, "giving approval to his death" (Acts 8:1). He was the one who was "breathing out murderous threats against the Lord's disciples" (Acts 9:1). Doesn't sound like someone I'd like to know on a personal basis.

Then, Christ appeared to Saul. A flashy conversion experience, with Christ speaking from the heaven to which he had returned. And Saul became Paul, the most effective Christian missionary the world has ever known.

It's hard for me to relate to that sort of experience. You see, I can't recall a time when I didn't love the Lord and want to serve him. I don't say that to sound pious or self-righteous . . . it's just the truth. I rebelled as a teenager against parental strictures and traditional structures, but I never rebelled against God.

There have been times when I thought I was lacking something because I had no dazzling experience to relate. But over the years I've come to realize the value of my quiet sort of experience.

And even though there haven't been blinding visions or bright lights, there have been times of definite comfort and guidance from God. Like when he spoke to me from Isaiah as a teenager, reassuring me that I wasn't a nobody:

> Fear not, for I have redeemed you;
> I have summoned you by name; you are mine
> (Isaiah 43:1).

Or when, as a young single adult, he promised to always stay with the project of making me all I should be in him: "Being confident of this, that he who began a good work in you will carry it on to completion until the day of Christ Jesus" (Philippians 1:6).

Your walk with God may not resemble Saul's (or Connie's or Mary's or Cheryl's), but it's *your* walk with a God who loves you and relates to you where you are.

Additional Scripture Readings:
Romans 8:30–39; 2 Peter 1:3–11

Go to page 1201 for your next devotional reading.

learned of their plan. Day and night they kept close watch on the city gates in order to kill him. 25But his followers took him by night and lowered him in a basket through an opening in the wall.

26When he came to Jerusalem, he tried to join the disciples, but they were all afraid of him, not believing that he really was a disciple. 27But Barnabas took him and brought him to the apostles. He told them how Saul on his journey had seen the Lord and that the Lord had spoken to him, and how in Damascus he had preached fearlessly in the name of Jesus. 28So Saul stayed with them and moved about freely in Jerusalem, speaking boldly in the name of the Lord. 29He talked and debated with the Grecian Jews, but they tried to kill him. 30When the brothers learned of this, they took him down to Caesarea and sent him off to Tarsus.

31Then the church throughout Judea, Galilee and Samaria enjoyed a time of peace. It was strengthened; and encouraged by the Holy Spirit, it grew in numbers, living in the fear of the Lord.

Aeneas and Dorcas

32As Peter traveled about the country, he went to visit the saints in Lydda. 33There he found a man named Aeneas, a paralytic who had been bedridden for eight years. 34"Aeneas," Peter said to him, "Jesus Christ heals you. Get up and take care of your mat." Immediately Aeneas got up. 35All those who lived in Lydda and Sharon saw him and turned to the Lord.

36In Joppa there was a disciple named Tabitha (which, when translated, is Dorcas*a*), who was always doing good and helping the poor. 37About that time she became sick and died, and her body was washed and placed in an upstairs room. 38Lydda was near Joppa; so when the disciples heard that Peter was in Lydda, they sent two men to him and urged him, "Please come at once!"

39Peter went with them, and when he arrived he was taken upstairs to the room. All the widows stood around him, crying and showing him the robes and other clothing that Dorcas had made while she was still with them.

40Peter sent them all out of the room; then he got down on his knees and prayed. Turning toward the dead woman, he said, "Tabitha, get up." She opened her eyes, and seeing Peter she sat up.

41He took her by the hand and helped her to her feet. Then he called the believers and the widows and presented her to them alive. 42This became known all over Joppa, and many people believed in the Lord. 43Peter stayed in Joppa for some time with a tanner named Simon.

Cornelius Calls for Peter

10 At Caesarea there was a man named Cornelius, a centurion in what was known as the Italian Regiment. 2He and all his family were devout and God-fearing; he gave generously to those in need and prayed to God regularly. 3One day at about three in the afternoon he had a vision. He distinctly saw an angel of God, who came to him and said, "Cornelius!"

4Cornelius stared at him in fear. "What is it, Lord?" he asked.

The angel answered, "Your prayers and gifts to the poor have come up as a memorial offering before God. 5Now send men to Joppa to bring back a man named Simon who is called Peter. 6He is staying with Simon the tanner, whose house is by the sea."

7When the angel who spoke to him had gone, Cornelius called two of his servants and a devout soldier who was one of his attendants. 8He told them everything that had happened and sent them to Joppa.

Peter's Vision

9About noon the following day as they were on their journey and approaching the city, Peter went up on the roof to pray. 10He became hungry and wanted something to eat, and while the meal was being prepared, he fell into a trance. 11He saw heaven opened and something like a large sheet being let down to earth by its four corners. 12It contained all kinds of four-footed animals, as well as reptiles of the earth and birds of the air. 13Then a voice told him, "Get up, Peter. Kill and eat."

14"Surely not, Lord!" Peter replied. "I have never eaten anything impure or unclean."

15The voice spoke to him a second time, "Do not call anything impure that God has made clean."

16This happened three times, and immediately the sheet was taken back to heaven.

17While Peter was wondering about the

---

a36 Both *Tabitha* (Aramaic) and *Dorcas* (Greek) mean *gazelle*.

meaning of the vision, the men sent by Cornelius found out where Simon's house was and stopped at the gate. [18]They called out, asking if Simon who was known as Peter was staying there.

[19]While Peter was still thinking about the vision, the Spirit said to him, "Simon, three[a] men are looking for you. [20]So get up and go downstairs. Do not hesitate to go with them, for I have sent them."

[21]Peter went down and said to the men, "I'm the one you're looking for. Why have you come?"

[22]The men replied, "We have come from Cornelius the centurion. He is a righteous and God-fearing man, who is respected by all the Jewish people. A holy angel told him to have you come to his house so that he could hear what you have to say." [23]Then Peter invited the men into the house to be his guests.

Peter at Cornelius' House

The next day Peter started out with them, and some of the brothers from Joppa went along. [24]The following day he arrived in Caesarea. Cornelius was expecting them and had called together his relatives and close friends. [25]As Peter entered the house, Cornelius met him and fell at his feet in reverence. [26]But Peter made him get up. "Stand up," he said, "I am only a man myself."

[27]Talking with him, Peter went inside and found a large gathering of people. [28]He said to them: "You are well aware that it is against our law for a Jew to associate with a Gentile or visit him. But God has shown me that I should not call any man impure or unclean. [29]So when I was sent for, I came without raising any objection. May I ask why you sent for me?"

[30]Cornelius answered: "Four days ago I was in my house praying at this hour, at three in the afternoon. Suddenly a man in shining clothes stood before me [31]and said, 'Cornelius, God has heard your prayer and remembered your gifts to the poor. [32]Send to Joppa for Simon who is called Peter. He is a guest in the home of Simon the tanner, who lives by the sea.' [33]So I sent for you immediately, and it was good of you to come. Now we are all here in the presence of God to listen to everything the Lord has commanded you to tell us."

[34]Then Peter began to speak: "I now realize how true it is that God does not show favoritism [35]but accepts men from every nation who fear him and do what is right. [36]You know the message God sent to the people of Israel, telling the good news of peace through Jesus Christ, who is Lord of all. [37]You know what has happened throughout Judea, beginning in Galilee after the baptism that John preached— [38]how God anointed Jesus of Nazareth with the Holy Spirit and power, and how he went around doing good and healing all who were under the power of the devil, because God was with him.

[39]"We are witnesses of everything he did in the country of the Jews and in Jerusalem. They killed him by hanging him on a tree, [40]but God raised him from the dead on the third day and caused him to be seen. [41]He was not seen by all the people, but by witnesses whom God had already chosen—by us who ate and drank with him after he rose from the dead. [42]He commanded us to preach to the people and to testify that he is the one whom God appointed as judge of the living and the dead. [43]All the prophets testify about him that everyone who believes in him receives forgiveness of sins through his name."

[44]While Peter was still speaking these words, the Holy Spirit came on all who heard the message. [45]The circumcised believers who had come with Peter were astonished that the gift of the Holy Spirit had been poured out even on the Gentiles. [46]For they heard them speaking in tongues[b] and praising God.

Then Peter said, [47]"Can anyone keep these people from being baptized with water? They have received the Holy Spirit just as we have." [48]So he ordered that they be baptized in the name of Jesus Christ. Then they asked Peter to stay with them for a few days.

Peter Explains His Actions

11 The apostles and the brothers throughout Judea heard that the Gentiles also had received the word of God. [2]So when Peter went up to Jerusalem, the circumcised believers criticized him [3]and said, "You went into the house of uncircumcised men and ate with them."

[4]Peter began and explained everything to them precisely as it had happened: [5]"I was in the city of Joppa praying, and in a trance I saw a vision. I saw something like

---

[a]19 One early manuscript *two*; other manuscripts do not have the number.   [b]46 Or *other languages*

VERSE FOR THE DAY:
Acts 10:34

AUTHOR:
Mary Beckwith

PASSAGE FOR THE DAY:
Acts 10:34–38

When Did Prejudice Creep In?

"IT must be a gentlemanbug," I thought I heard my little boy say.

"What did you say?" I asked him.

He said it again. "It must be a gentlemanbug."

Rob, then Robbie, gently pushed the ladybug onto his pudgy little hand. He had been playing with it for at least ten minutes. I was impressed that, at four years old, he knew the opposite for lady was gentleman and was able to label his new little friend accordingly.

But then I asked, "Why do you think it's a gentlemanbug?"

"Because he's smart!" was his ready reply.

Needless to say, I was in shock for a moment. Where had he gotten the idea that, in order to be smart, you had to be a man? And at the age of four, at that!

I quickly tried to recall if, in the last few days, I had said something that would have implied men were smarter than women. I couldn't remember anything. Maybe his father had made that implication somehow. I'd have to ask him.

I do recall at times when the kids asked me questions I didn't have the answers to I'd say, "We'll ask Daddy when he gets home." Maybe I'd done it enough to give the impression that dads are smarter than moms.

Anyway, this little episode made me question, How do prejudice and bias enter our lives? What causes us to judge others because of gender or color or whatever? It also taught me that when we show partiality and prejudice, we are setting examples for our children.

I am so thankful we have a heavenly Father who is no respecter of persons. He loves each one of us the same. And he desires that we in turn love one another with the same kind of love.

When I'm reminded of his unconditional, steadfast love, it helps me fight against the prejudice that tries to creep in, distort my conception of others, and tempts me to look at myself more highly than I should.

Additional Scripture Readings:
Romans 12:3–5; Galatians 3:26–28

Go to page 1206 for your next devotional reading.

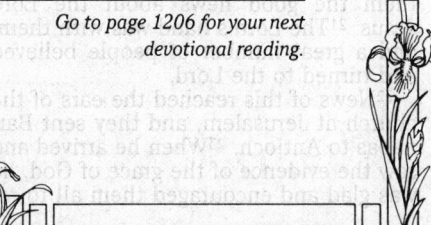

a large sheet being let down from heaven by its four corners, and it came down to where I was. ⁶I looked into it and saw four-footed animals of the earth, wild beasts, reptiles, and birds of the air. ⁷Then I heard a voice telling me, 'Get up, Peter. Kill and eat.'

⁸"I replied, 'Surely not, Lord! Nothing impure or unclean has ever entered my mouth.'

⁹"The voice spoke from heaven a second time, 'Do not call anything impure that God has made clean.' ¹⁰This happened three times, and then it was all pulled up to heaven again.

¹¹"Right then three men who had been sent to me from Caesarea stopped at the house where I was staying. ¹²The Spirit told me to have no hesitation about going with them. These six brothers also went with me, and we entered the man's house. ¹³He told us how he had seen an angel appear in his house and say, 'Send to Joppa for Simon who is called Peter. ¹⁴He will bring you a message through which you and all your household will be saved.'

¹⁵"As I began to speak, the Holy Spirit came on them as he had come on us at the beginning. ¹⁶Then I remembered what the Lord had said: 'John baptized with*a* water, but you will be baptized with the Holy Spirit.' ¹⁷So if God gave them the same gift as he gave us, who believed in the Lord Jesus Christ, who was I to think that I could oppose God?"

¹⁸When they heard this, they had no further objections and praised God, saying, "So then, God has granted even the Gentiles repentance unto life."

The Church in Antioch

¹⁹Now those who had been scattered by the persecution in connection with Stephen traveled as far as Phoenicia, Cyprus and Antioch, telling the message only to Jews. ²⁰Some of them, however, men from Cyprus and Cyrene, went to Antioch and began to speak to Greeks also, telling them the good news about the Lord Jesus. ²¹The Lord's hand was with them, and a great number of people believed and turned to the Lord.

²²News of this reached the ears of the church at Jerusalem, and they sent Barnabas to Antioch. ²³When he arrived and saw the evidence of the grace of God, he was glad and encouraged them all to remain true to the Lord with all their hearts. ²⁴He was a good man, full of the Holy Spirit and faith, and a great number of people were brought to the Lord.

²⁵Then Barnabas went to Tarsus to look for Saul, ²⁶and when he found him, he brought him to Antioch. So for a whole year Barnabas and Saul met with the church and taught great numbers of people. The disciples were called Christians first at Antioch.

²⁷During this time some prophets came down from Jerusalem to Antioch. ²⁸One of them, named Agabus, stood up and through the Spirit predicted that a severe famine would spread over the entire Roman world. (This happened during the reign of Claudius.) ²⁹The disciples, each according to his ability, decided to provide help for the brothers living in Judea. ³⁰This they did, sending their gift to the elders by Barnabas and Saul.

Peter's Miraculous Escape From Prison

12 It was about this time that King Herod arrested some who belonged to the church, intending to persecute them. ²He had James, the brother of John, put to death with the sword. ³When he saw that this pleased the Jews, he proceeded to seize Peter also. This happened during the Feast of Unleavened Bread. ⁴After arresting him, he put him in prison, handing him over to be guarded by four squads of four soldiers each. Herod intended to bring him out for public trial after the Passover.

⁵So Peter was kept in prison, but the church was earnestly praying to God for him.

⁶The night before Herod was to bring him to trial, Peter was sleeping between two soldiers, bound with two chains, and sentries stood guard at the entrance. ⁷Suddenly an angel of the Lord appeared and a light shone in the cell. He struck Peter on the side and woke him up. "Quick, get up!" he said, and the chains fell off Peter's wrists.

⁸Then the angel said to him, "Put on your clothes and sandals." And Peter did so. "Wrap your cloak around you and follow me," the angel told him. ⁹Peter followed him out of the prison, but he had no idea that what the angel was doing was really happening; he thought he was seeing a vision. ¹⁰They passed the first and

a16 Or in

second guards and came to the iron gate leading to the city. It opened for them by itself, and they went through it. When they had walked the length of one street, suddenly the angel left him.

[11]Then Peter came to himself and said, "Now I know without a doubt that the Lord sent his angel and rescued me from Herod's clutches and from everything the Jewish people were anticipating."

[12]When this had dawned on him, he went to the house of Mary the mother of John, also called Mark, where many people had gathered and were praying. [13]Peter knocked at the outer entrance, and a servant girl named Rhoda came to answer the door. [14]When she recognized Peter's voice, she was so overjoyed she ran back without opening it and exclaimed, "Peter is at the door!"

[15]"You're out of your mind," they told her. When she kept insisting that it was so, they said, "It must be his angel."

[16]But Peter kept on knocking, and when they opened the door and saw him, they were astonished. [17]Peter motioned with his hand for them to be quiet and described how the Lord had brought him out of prison. "Tell James and the brothers about this," he said, and then he left for another place.

[18]In the morning, there was no small commotion among the soldiers as to what had become of Peter. [19]After Herod had a thorough search made for him and did not find him, he cross-examined the guards and ordered that they be executed.

Herod's Death

Then Herod went from Judea to Caesarea and stayed there a while. [20]He had been quarreling with the people of Tyre and Sidon; they now joined together and sought an audience with him. Having secured the support of Blastus, a trusted personal servant of the king, they asked for peace, because they depended on the king's country for their food supply.

[21]On the appointed day Herod, wearing his royal robes, sat on his throne and delivered a public address to the people. [22]They shouted, "This is the voice of a god, not of a man." [23]Immediately, because Herod did not give praise to God, an angel of the Lord struck him down, and he was eaten by worms and died.

[24]But the word of God continued to increase and spread.

[25]When Barnabas and Saul had finished their mission, they returned from[a] Jerusalem, taking with them John, also called Mark.

Barnabas and Saul Sent Off

13 In the church at Antioch there were prophets and teachers: Barnabas, Simeon called Niger, Lucius of Cyrene, Manaen (who had been brought up with Herod the tetrarch) and Saul. [2]While they were worshiping the Lord and fasting, the Holy Spirit said, "Set apart for me Barnabas and Saul for the work to which I have called them." [3]So after they had fasted and prayed, they placed their hands on them and sent them off.

On Cyprus

[4]The two of them, sent on their way by the Holy Spirit, went down to Seleucia and sailed from there to Cyprus. [5]When they arrived at Salamis, they proclaimed the word of God in the Jewish synagogues. John was with them as their helper.

[6]They traveled through the whole island until they came to Paphos. There they met a Jewish sorcerer and false prophet named Bar-Jesus, [7]who was an attendant of the proconsul, Sergius Paulus. The proconsul, an intelligent man, sent for Barnabas and Saul because he wanted to hear the word of God. [8]But Elymas the sorcerer (for that is what his name means) opposed them and tried to turn the proconsul from the faith. [9]Then Saul, who was also called Paul, filled with the Holy Spirit, looked straight at Elymas and said, [10]"You are a child of the devil and an enemy of everything that is right! You are full of all kinds of deceit and trickery. Will you never stop perverting the right ways of the Lord? [11]Now the hand of the Lord is against you. You are going to be blind, and for a time you will be unable to see the light of the sun."

Immediately mist and darkness came over him, and he groped about, seeking someone to lead him by the hand. [12]When the proconsul saw what had happened, he believed, for he was amazed at the teaching about the Lord.

In Pisidian Antioch

[13]From Paphos, Paul and his compan-

ions sailed to Perga in Pamphylia, where John left them to return to Jerusalem. [14]From Perga they went on to Pisidian Antioch. On the Sabbath they entered the synagogue and sat down. [15]After the reading from the Law and the Prophets, the synagogue rulers sent word to them, saying, "Brothers, if you have a message of encouragement for the people, please speak."

[16]Standing up, Paul motioned with his hand and said: "Men of Israel and you Gentiles who worship God, listen to me! [17]The God of the people of Israel chose our fathers; he made the people prosper during their stay in Egypt, with mighty power he led them out of that country, [18]he endured their conduct[a] for about forty years in the desert, [19]he overthrew seven nations in Canaan and gave their land to his people as their inheritance. [20]All this took about 450 years.

"After this, God gave them judges until the time of Samuel the prophet. [21]Then the people asked for a king, and he gave them Saul son of Kish, of the tribe of Benjamin, who ruled forty years. [22]After removing Saul, he made David their king. He testified concerning him: 'I have found David son of Jesse a man after my own heart; he will do everything I want him to do.'

[23]"From this man's descendants God has brought to Israel the Savior Jesus, as he promised. [24]Before the coming of Jesus, John preached repentance and baptism to all the people of Israel. [25]As John was completing his work, he said: 'Who do you think I am? I am not that one. No, but he is coming after me, whose sandals I am not worthy to untie.'

[26]"Brothers, children of Abraham, and you God-fearing Gentiles, it is to us that this message of salvation has been sent. [27]The people of Jerusalem and their rulers did not recognize Jesus, yet in condemning him they fulfilled the words of the prophets that are read every Sabbath. [28]Though they found no proper ground for a death sentence, they asked Pilate to have him executed. [29]When they had carried out all that was written about him, they took him down from the tree and laid him in a tomb. [30]But God raised him from the dead, [31]and for many days he was seen by those who had traveled with

him from Galilee to Jerusalem. They are now his witnesses to our people.

[32]"We tell you the good news: What God promised our fathers [33]he has fulfilled for us, their children, by raising up Jesus. As it is written in the second Psalm:

" 'You are my Son;
    today I have become your
        Father.'[b][c]

[34]The fact that God raised him from the dead, never to decay, is stated in these words:

" 'I will give you the holy and sure
        blessings promised to David.'[d]

[35]So it is stated elsewhere:

" 'You will not let your Holy One see
        decay.'[e]

[36]"For when David had served God's purpose in his own generation, he fell asleep; he was buried with his fathers and his body decayed. [37]But the one whom God raised from the dead did not see decay.

[38]"Therefore, my brothers, I want you to know that through Jesus the forgiveness of sins is proclaimed to you. [39]Through him everyone who believes is justified from everything you could not be justified from by the law of Moses. [40]Take care that what the prophets have said does not happen to you:

[41]" 'Look, you scoffers,
    wonder and perish,
for I am going to do something in
        your days
    that you would never believe,
    even if someone told you.'[f]"

[42]As Paul and Barnabas were leaving the synagogue, the people invited them to speak further about these things on the next Sabbath. [43]When the congregation was dismissed, many of the Jews and devout converts to Judaism followed Paul and Barnabas, who talked with them and urged them to continue in the grace of God.

[44]On the next Sabbath almost the whole city gathered to hear the word of the Lord. [45]When the Jews saw the crowds, they were filled with jealousy and talked abusively against what Paul was saying.

---

[a]18 Some manuscripts *and cared for them* 55:3   [b]33 Or *have begotten you*   [c]33 Psalm 2:7   [d]34 Isaiah   [e]35 Psalm 16:10   [f]41 Hab. 1:5

[46]Then Paul and Barnabas answered them boldly: "We had to speak the word of God to you first. Since you reject it and do not consider yourselves worthy of eternal life, we now turn to the Gentiles. [47]For this is what the Lord has commanded us:

" 'I have made you[a] a light for the
    Gentiles,
  that you[a] may bring salvation to
    the ends of the earth.'[b] "

[48]When the Gentiles heard this, they were glad and honored the word of the Lord; and all who were appointed for eternal life believed.

[49]The word of the Lord spread through the whole region. [50]But the Jews incited the God-fearing women of high standing and the leading men of the city. They stirred up persecution against Paul and Barnabas, and expelled them from their region. [51]So they shook the dust from their feet in protest against them and went to Iconium. [52]And the disciples were filled with joy and with the Holy Spirit.

In Iconium

14 At Iconium Paul and Barnabas went as usual into the Jewish synagogue. There they spoke so effectively that a great number of Jews and Gentiles believed. [2]But the Jews who refused to believe stirred up the Gentiles and poisoned their minds against the brothers. [3]So Paul and Barnabas spent considerable time there, speaking boldly for the Lord, who confirmed the message of his grace by enabling them to do miraculous signs and wonders. [4]The people of the city were divided; some sided with the Jews, others with the apostles. [5]There was a plot afoot among the Gentiles and Jews, together with their leaders, to mistreat them and stone them. [6]But they found out about it and fled to the Lycaonian cities of Lystra and Derbe and to the surrounding country, [7]where they continued to preach the good news.

In Lystra and Derbe

[8]In Lystra there sat a man crippled in his feet, who was lame from birth and had never walked. [9]He listened to Paul as he was speaking. Paul looked directly at him, saw that he had faith to be healed [10]and called out, "Stand up on your feet!"

At that, the man jumped up and began to walk.

[11]When the crowd saw what Paul had done, they shouted in the Lycaonian language, "The gods have come down to us in human form!" [12]Barnabas they called Zeus, and Paul they called Hermes because he was the chief speaker. [13]The priest of Zeus, whose temple was just outside the city, brought bulls and wreaths to the city gates because he and the crowd wanted to offer sacrifices to them.

[14]But when the apostles Barnabas and Paul heard of this, they tore their clothes and rushed out into the crowd, shouting: [15]"Men, why are you doing this? We too are only men, human like you. We are bringing you good news, telling you to turn from these worthless things to the living God, who made heaven and earth and sea and everything in them. [16]In the past, he let all nations go their own way. [17]Yet he has not left himself without testimony: He has shown kindness by giving you rain from heaven and crops in their seasons; he provides you with plenty of food and fills your hearts with joy." [18]Even with these words, they had difficulty keeping the crowd from sacrificing to them.

[19]Then some Jews came from Antioch and Iconium and won the crowd over. They stoned Paul and dragged him outside the city, thinking he was dead. [20]But after the disciples had gathered around him, he got up and went back into the city. The next day he and Barnabas left for Derbe.

The Return to Antioch in Syria

[21]They preached the good news in that city and won a large number of disciples. Then they returned to Lystra, Iconium and Antioch, [22]strengthening the disciples and encouraging them to remain true to the faith. "We must go through many hardships to enter the kingdom of God," they said. [23]Paul and Barnabas appointed elders[c] for them in each church and, with prayer and fasting, committed them to the Lord, in whom they had put their trust. [24]After going through Pisidia, they came into Pamphylia, [25]and when they had preached the word in Perga, they went down to Attalia.

[26]From Attalia they sailed back to Antioch, where they had been committed to

---

a47 The Greek is singular.   *b47* Isaiah 49:6   *c23* Or *Barnabas ordained elders*; or *Barnabas had elders elected*

VERSE FOR THE DAY:
Acts 14:17

AUTHOR:
June Masters Bacher

PASSAGE FOR THE DAY:
Acts 14:14–18

After the Storm

I WONDER how agnostics or atheists deal with mornings like this. But then, I (a believer!) had had trouble dealing with yesterday.

Following days of drenching rain, killer floods and general chaos, there came a freak downpour. Without warning, a black curtain of rain simply swallowed our city. I waded a lake that came to the hem of my skirt trying to find my car in the teachers' parking lot. Paperwork for the day was a total loss. My freshly done hair was soaked. I dripped in the front door to hear three children screaming like banshees (one mine, two somebody else's); a cold-nosed dog demanding dinner; and a husband who announced cheerfully that the roof was leaking in five places and the septic tank was overflowing.

"Let me in the door, *please!* " So began our evening. When my husband and I crept into bed, exhausted (at midnight), the boys were still giggling. The roof was still leaking (into pans and buckets). The rain was still raining. And the septic tank would have to be dealt with tomorrow.

I awoke with a start, wondering if once again the power had failed and our electric clock had stopped. It was full daylight, surely seven o'clock on a March day, and far too late to hope to get everybody off on a weekday morning. The clock appeared to be working, but how could it be so light at 4:30 A.M.?

I ran barefoot to the window and there hung the most breathtaking moon I've ever seen, suspended in a sky so clear that it appeared blue even in the pre-dawn. I watched in prayerful wonder until it was time to get the day on its feet. Only God could create such a day from yesterday's chaos—and put my heart back together!

To think and pray about: Do you think this kind of beauty follows chaos by accident? In what other ways does God, through nature, cleanse the world, the spirit? We walk through storms that strip us bare or cleanse us so we can grow again—according to our faith. God assures us that he's in charge. We can cope through prayer.

Additional Scripture Readings:
Genesis 9:12–16; Jonah 2:3–3:3

Go to page 1209 for your next devotional reading.

the grace of God for the work they had now completed. 27On arriving there, they gathered the church together and reported all that God had done through them and how he had opened the door of faith to the Gentiles. 28And they stayed there a long time with the disciples.

The Council at Jerusalem

15 Some men came down from Judea to Antioch and were teaching the brothers: "Unless you are circumcised, according to the custom taught by Moses, you cannot be saved." 2This brought Paul and Barnabas into sharp dispute and debate with them. So Paul and Barnabas were appointed, along with some other believers, to go up to Jerusalem to see the apostles and elders about this question. 3The church sent them on their way, and as they traveled through Phoenicia and Samaria, they told how the Gentiles had been converted. This news made all the brothers very glad. 4When they came to Jerusalem, they were welcomed by the church and the apostles and elders, to whom they reported everything God had done through them.

5Then some of the believers who belonged to the party of the Pharisees stood up and said, "The Gentiles must be circumcised and required to obey the law of Moses."

6The apostles and elders met to consider this question. 7After much discussion, Peter got up and addressed them: "Brothers, you know that some time ago God made a choice among you that the Gentiles might hear from my lips the message of the gospel and believe. 8God, who knows the heart, showed that he accepted them by giving the Holy Spirit to them, just as he did to us. 9He made no distinction between us and them, for he purified their hearts by faith. 10Now then, why do you try to test God by putting on the necks of the disciples a yoke that neither we nor our fathers have been able to bear? 11No! We believe it is through the grace of our Lord Jesus that we are saved, just as they are."

12The whole assembly became silent as they listened to Barnabas and Paul telling about the miraculous signs and wonders God had done among the Gentiles through them. 13When they finished, James spoke up: "Brothers, listen to me.

14Simon*a* has described to us how God at first showed his concern by taking from the Gentiles a people for himself. 15The words of the prophets are in agreement with this, as it is written:

16" 'After this I will return
    and rebuild David's fallen tent.
  Its ruins I will rebuild,
    and I will restore it,
17that the remnant of men may seek
      the Lord,
    and all the Gentiles who bear my
      name,
  says the Lord, who does these
      things'*b*
18   that have been known for ages.*c*

19"It is my judgment, therefore, that we should not make it difficult for the Gentiles who are turning to God. 20Instead we should write to them, telling them to abstain from food polluted by idols, from sexual immorality, from the meat of strangled animals and from blood. 21For Moses has been preached in every city from the earliest times and is read in the synagogues on every Sabbath."

The Council's Letter to Gentile Believers

22Then the apostles and elders, with the whole church, decided to choose some of their own men and send them to Antioch with Paul and Barnabas. They chose Judas (called Barsabbas) and Silas, two men who were leaders among the brothers. 23With them they sent the following letter:

The apostles and elders, your brothers,

To the Gentile believers in Antioch, Syria and Cilicia:

Greetings.

24We have heard that some went out from us without our authorization and disturbed you, troubling your minds by what they said. 25So we all agreed to choose some men and send them to you with our dear friends Barnabas and Paul— 26men who have risked their lives for the name of our Lord Jesus Christ. 27Therefore we are sending Judas and Silas to confirm by word of

---

a14 Greek *Simeon*, a variant of *Simon*; that is, Peter   *b17* Amos 9:11,12   *c17,18* Some manuscripts
things'— / 18known to the Lord for ages is his work

mouth what we are writing. ²⁸It seemed good to the Holy Spirit and to us not to burden you with anything beyond the following requirements: ²⁹You are to abstain from food sacrificed to idols, from blood, from the meat of strangled animals and from sexual immorality. You will do well to avoid these things.

Farewell.

³⁰The men were sent off and went down to Antioch, where they gathered the church together and delivered the letter. ³¹The people read it and were glad for its encouraging message. ³²Judas and Silas, who themselves were prophets, said much to encourage and strengthen the brothers. ³³After spending some time there, they were sent off by the brothers with the blessing of peace to return to those who had sent them.ᵃ ³⁵But Paul and Barnabas remained in Antioch, where they and many others taught and preached the word of the Lord.

Disagreement Between Paul and Barnabas

³⁶Some time later Paul said to Barnabas, "Let us go back and visit the brothers in all the towns where we preached the word of the Lord and see how they are doing." ³⁷Barnabas wanted to take John, also called Mark, with them, ³⁸but Paul did not think it wise to take him, because he had deserted them in Pamphylia and had not continued with them in the work. ³⁹They had such a sharp disagreement that they parted company. Barnabas took Mark and sailed for Cyprus, ⁴⁰but Paul chose Silas and left, commended by the brothers to the grace of the Lord. ⁴¹He went through Syria and Cilicia, strengthening the churches.

Timothy Joins Paul and Silas

16 He came to Derbe and then to Lystra, where a disciple named Timothy lived, whose mother was a Jewess and a believer, but whose father was a Greek. ²The brothers at Lystra and Iconium spoke well of him. ³Paul wanted to take him along on the journey, so he circumcised him because of the Jews who lived in that area, for they all knew that his father was a Greek. ⁴As they traveled from town to town, they delivered the decisions reached by the apostles and elders in Jerusalem for the people to obey. ⁵So the churches were strengthened in the faith and grew daily in numbers.

Paul's Vision of the Man of Macedonia

⁶Paul and his companions traveled throughout the region of Phrygia and Galatia, having been kept by the Holy Spirit from preaching the word in the province of Asia. ⁷When they came to the border of Mysia, they tried to enter Bithynia, but the Spirit of Jesus would not allow them to. ⁸So they passed by Mysia and went down to Troas. ⁹During the night Paul had a vision of a man of Macedonia standing and begging him, "Come over to Macedonia and help us." ¹⁰After Paul had seen the vision, we got ready at once to leave for Macedonia, concluding that God had called us to preach the gospel to them.

Lydia's Conversion in Philippi

¹¹From Troas we put out to sea and sailed straight for Samothrace, and the next day on to Neapolis. ¹²From there we traveled to Philippi, a Roman colony and the leading city of that district of Macedonia. And we stayed there several days. ¹³On the Sabbath we went outside the city gate to the river, where we expected to find a place of prayer. We sat down and began to speak to the women who had gathered there. ¹⁴One of those listening was a woman named Lydia, a dealer in purple cloth from the city of Thyatira, who was a worshiper of God. The Lord opened her heart to respond to Paul's message. ¹⁵When she and the members of her household were baptized, she invited us to her home. "If you consider me a believer in the Lord," she said, "come and stay at my house." And she persuaded us.

Paul and Silas in Prison

¹⁶Once when we were going to the place of prayer, we were met by a slave girl who had a spirit by which she predicted the future. She earned a great deal of money for her owners by fortune-telling. ¹⁷This girl followed Paul and the rest of us, shouting, "These men are servants of the Most High God, who are telling you the way to be saved." ¹⁸She kept this up for many days. Finally Paul became so troubled that he turned around and said to the spirit, "In the name of Jesus Christ

---

ᵃ33 Some manuscripts *them,* ³⁴*but Silas decided to remain there*

I command you to come out of her!" At that moment the spirit left her.

¹⁹When the owners of the slave girl realized that their hope of making money was gone, they seized Paul and Silas and dragged them into the marketplace to face the authorities. ²⁰They brought them before the magistrates and said, "These men are Jews, and are throwing our city into an uproar ²¹by advocating customs unlawful for us Romans to accept or practice."

²²The crowd joined in the attack against Paul and Silas, and the magis-

trates ordered them to be stripped and beaten. ²³After they had been severely flogged, they were thrown into prison, and the jailer was commanded to guard them carefully. ²⁴Upon receiving such orders, he put them in the inner cell and fastened their feet in the stocks.

²⁵About midnight Paul and Silas were praying and singing hymns to God, and the other prisoners were listening to them. ²⁶Suddenly there was such a violent earthquake that the foundations of the prison were shaken. At once all the prison doors flew open, and everybody's

FRIDAY

VERSE FOR THE DAY:
Act 16:30

AUTHOR:
June Masters Bacher

PASSAGE FOR THE DAY:
Acts 16:25–40

What Can I Do?

"WHAT must I do to be saved?" asked the Philippian jailer. "Believe in the Lord Jesus " was the apostle Paul's answer. This single question and answer neatly summarize the teachings of the New Testament.

"What can I do?" ask our ministers and our doctors. "What can I do?" ask men caught in financial straits. Parents ask the question of teachers regarding their children's behavior or academic problems. A survey might show that this is one of the most common questions around. It became such a common rainy-day question in our home, I made a list of activities for our son to engage in so that he began looking forward to a storm! I made a list of stories, collected craft ideas, added suggestions for poems and Scripture passages to memorize and ended with "Look for a rainbow." The result was a happy day.

Jesus tells us that he came to earth that we might have life and have it more abundantly. How do we achieve an abundant Christian life? First, we believe with a faith so strong that the storms of life can threaten, but they cannot destroy. The abundant life begins for us here on earth and leads in natural transition into eternity. A wonderful thing, faith; a positive thing.

The positive attitude of Christian living communicates to those around us. "I am convinced," said my retiring principal after having spent over forty years in education (and an equal number of years teaching church school class), "that most folks are just about as happy as they set out to be!" He had the happiest faculty I have ever worked with.

Additional Scripture Readings:
John 10:9–10; Philippians 4:11–13

Go to page 1210 for your next devotional reading.

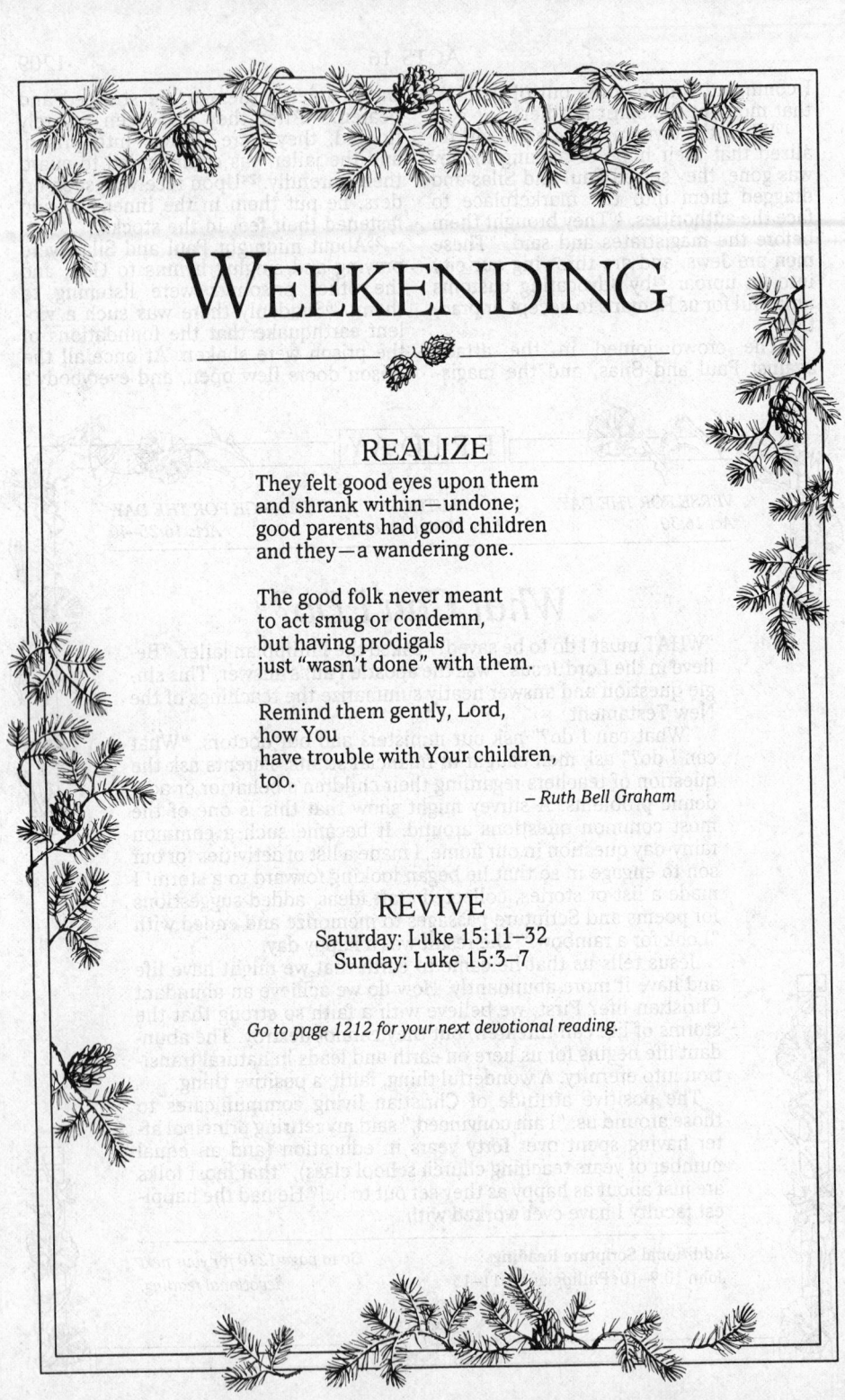

WEEKENDING

REALIZE

They felt good eyes upon them
and shrank within—undone;
good parents had good children
and they—a wandering one.

The good folk never meant
to act smug or condemn,
but having prodigals
just "wasn't done" with them.

Remind them gently, Lord,
how You
have trouble with Your children,
too.

– Ruth Bell Graham

REVIVE

Saturday: Luke 15:11–32
Sunday: Luke 15:3–7

Go to page 1212 for your next devotional reading.

chains came loose. ²⁷The jailer woke up, and when he saw the prison doors open, he drew his sword and was about to kill himself because he thought the prisoners had escaped. ²⁸But Paul shouted, "Don't harm yourself! We are all here!"

²⁹The jailer called for lights, rushed in and fell trembling before Paul and Silas. ³⁰He then brought them out and asked, "Sirs, what must I do to be saved?"

³¹They replied, "Believe in the Lord Jesus, and you will be saved—you and your household." ³²Then they spoke the word of the Lord to him and to all the others in his house. ³³At that hour of the night the jailer took them and washed their wounds; then immediately he and all his family were baptized. ³⁴The jailer brought them into his house and set a meal before them; he was filled with joy because he had come to believe in God— he and his whole family.

³⁵When it was daylight, the magistrates sent their officers to the jailer with the order: "Release those men." ³⁶The jailer told Paul, "The magistrates have ordered that you and Silas be released. Now you can leave. Go in peace."

³⁷But Paul said to the officers: "They beat us publicly without a trial, even though we are Roman citizens, and threw us into prison. And now do they want to get rid of us quietly? No! Let them come themselves and escort us out."

³⁸The officers reported this to the magistrates, and when they heard that Paul and Silas were Roman citizens, they were alarmed. ³⁹They came to appease them and escorted them from the prison, requesting them to leave the city. ⁴⁰After Paul and Silas came out of the prison, they went to Lydia's house, where they met with the brothers and encouraged them. Then they left.

In Thessalonica

17 When they had passed through Amphipolis and Apollonia, they came to Thessalonica, where there was a Jewish synagogue. ²As his custom was, Paul went into the synagogue, and on three Sabbath days he reasoned with them from the Scriptures, ³explaining and proving that the Christ[a] had to suffer and rise from the dead. "This Jesus I am proclaiming to you is the Christ,[a] " he said. ⁴Some of the Jews were persuaded and joined Paul and Silas, as did a large

number of God-fearing Greeks and not a few prominent women.

⁵But the Jews were jealous; so they rounded up some bad characters from the marketplace, formed a mob and started a riot in the city. They rushed to Jason's house in search of Paul and Silas in order to bring them out to the crowd.[b] ⁶But when they did not find them, they dragged Jason and some other brothers before the city officials, shouting: "These men who have caused trouble all over the world have now come here, ⁷and Jason has welcomed them into his house. They are all defying Caesar's decrees, saying that there is another king, one called Jesus." ⁸When they heard this, the crowd and the city officials were thrown into turmoil. ⁹Then they made Jason and the others post bond and let them go.

In Berea

¹⁰As soon as it was night, the brothers sent Paul and Silas away to Berea. On arriving there, they went to the Jewish synagogue. ¹¹Now the Bereans were of more noble character than the Thessalonians, for they received the message with great eagerness and examined the Scriptures every day to see if what Paul said was true. ¹²Many of the Jews believed, as did also a number of prominent Greek women and many Greek men.

¹³When the Jews in Thessalonica learned that Paul was preaching the word of God at Berea, they went there too, agitating the crowds and stirring them up. ¹⁴The brothers immediately sent Paul to the coast, but Silas and Timothy stayed at Berea. ¹⁵The men who escorted Paul brought him to Athens and then left with instructions for Silas and Timothy to join him as soon as possible.

In Athens

¹⁶While Paul was waiting for them in Athens, he was greatly distressed to see that the city was full of idols. ¹⁷So he reasoned in the synagogue with the Jews and the God-fearing Greeks, as well as in the marketplace day by day with those who happened to be there. ¹⁸A group of Epicurean and Stoic philosophers began to dispute with him. Some of them asked, "What is this babbler trying to say?" Others remarked, "He seems to be advocating foreign gods." They said this because

---

a3 Or Messiah   *b5 Or the assembly of the people*

VERSE FOR THE DAY:	*AUTHOR:*	*PASSAGE FOR THE DAY:*
Acts 17:11	Elizabeth Larson	Acts 17:10–15

Counting the Cost

WE have many Bibles in our home, but one in particular is my sentimental favorite. It belonged to my husband before I adopted it, which makes it all the more dear to me. It has all his favorite passages underlined, his many little notes in the margins (I've read each one), and innumerable creases, smudges and torn spots, which are inevitable when a book is subjected to prolonged, loving abuse.

I must confess, I have added some features of my own: a few scribbles, various folds to mark my spot when I stop reading, the footprints of my preschooler who trampled the poor old book when I threw it behind the front seat of my car. But, worst of all, the cover is now threatening to fall off, due to the fact that I literally drop everything when my attention is caught by something else.

My favorite Bible. Its worth to me is great, but it wasn't until a few months ago that I realized the true cost of that book—a cost paid by others that I might freely possess my beloved book.

I was studying a history book when I came across a paragraph noting the words of a fifteenth-century bishop of England who wrote scornfully of certain women "which make themselves so wise by the Bible." It was the opinion of this bishop that women should have no right to study the Word of God. As I continued to read, I learned that some of the women so ridiculed by this bishop were wives and mothers who eventually died at the stake for refusing to accept any beliefs as God's truth "save what they can find expressly in the Bible."

I turned to my old favorite then, seeing it afresh. This book, which I handle with such careless, casual ease and freedom, would not be mine if it were not for those women (and men) who boldly claimed their right to have the Word of God—a right they paid for with their own blood.

Additional Scripture Readings:
Psalm 119:129–131; 2 Peter 1:15–21

Go to page 1217 for your next devotional reading.

Paul was preaching the good news about Jesus and the resurrection. ¹⁹Then they took him and brought him to a meeting of the Areopagus, where they said to him, "May we know what this new teaching is that you are presenting? ²⁰You are bringing some strange ideas to our ears, and we want to know what they mean." ²¹(All the Athenians and the foreigners who lived there spent their time doing nothing but talking about and listening to the latest ideas.)

²²Paul then stood up in the meeting of the Areopagus and said: "Men of Athens! I see that in every way you are very religious. ²³For as I walked around and looked carefully at your objects of worship, I even found an altar with this inscription: TO AN UNKNOWN GOD. Now what you worship as something unknown I am going to proclaim to you.

²⁴"The God who made the world and everything in it is the Lord of heaven and earth and does not live in temples built by hands. ²⁵And he is not served by human hands, as if he needed anything, because he himself gives all men life and breath and everything else. ²⁶From one man he made every nation of men, that they should inhabit the whole earth; and he determined the times set for them and the exact places where they should live. ²⁷God did this so that men would seek him and perhaps reach out for him and find him, though he is not far from each one of us. ²⁸'For in him we live and move and have our being.' As some of your own poets have said, 'We are his offspring.'

²⁹"Therefore since we are God's offspring, we should not think that the divine being is like gold or silver or stone — an image made by man's design and skill. ³⁰In the past God overlooked such ignorance, but now he commands all people everywhere to repent. ³¹For he has set a day when he will judge the world with justice by the man he has appointed. He has given proof of this to all men by raising him from the dead."

³²When they heard about the resurrection of the dead, some of them sneered, but others said, "We want to hear you again on this subject." ³³At that, Paul left the Council. ³⁴A few men became followers of Paul and believed. Among them was Dionysius, a member of the Areopagus, also a woman named Damaris, and a number of others.

In Corinth

18 After this, Paul left Athens and went to Corinth. ²There he met a Jew named Aquila, a native of Pontus, who had recently come from Italy with his wife Priscilla, because Claudius had ordered all the Jews to leave Rome. Paul went to see them, ³and because he was a tentmaker as they were, he stayed and worked with them. ⁴Every Sabbath he reasoned in the synagogue, trying to persuade Jews and Greeks.

⁵When Silas and Timothy came from Macedonia, Paul devoted himself exclusively to preaching, testifying to the Jews that Jesus was the Christ.ᵃ ⁶But when the Jews opposed Paul and became abusive, he shook out his clothes in protest and said to them, "Your blood be on your own heads! I am clear of my responsibility. From now on I will go to the Gentiles."

⁷Then Paul left the synagogue and went next door to the house of Titius Justus, a worshiper of God. ⁸Crispus, the synagogue ruler, and his entire household believed in the Lord; and many of the Corinthians who heard him believed and were baptized.

⁹One night the Lord spoke to Paul in a vision: "Do not be afraid; keep on speaking, do not be silent. ¹⁰For I am with you, and no one is going to attack and harm you, because I have many people in this city." ¹¹So Paul stayed for a year and a half, teaching them the word of God.

¹²While Gallio was proconsul of Achaia, the Jews made a united attack on Paul and brought him into court. ¹³"This man," they charged, "is persuading the people to worship God in ways contrary to the law."

¹⁴Just as Paul was about to speak, Gallio said to the Jews, "If you Jews were making a complaint about some misdemeanor or serious crime, it would be reasonable for me to listen to you. ¹⁵But since it involves questions about words and names and your own law — settle the matter yourselves. I will not be a judge of such things." ¹⁶So he had them ejected from the court. ¹⁷Then they all turned on Sosthenes the synagogue ruler and beat him in front of the court. But Gallio showed no concern whatever.

Priscilla, Aquila and Apollos

¹⁸Paul stayed on in Corinth for some

ᵃ5 Or *Messiah;* also in verse 28

time. Then he left the brothers and sailed for Syria, accompanied by Priscilla and Aquila. Before he sailed, he had his hair cut off at Cenchrea because of a vow he had taken. ¹⁹They arrived at Ephesus, where Paul left Priscilla and Aquila. He himself went into the synagogue and reasoned with the Jews. ²⁰When they asked him to spend more time with them, he declined. ²¹But as he left, he promised, "I will come back if it is God's will." Then he set sail from Ephesus. ²²When he landed at Caesarea, he went up and greeted the church and then went down to Antioch.

²³After spending some time in Antioch, Paul set out from there and traveled from place to place throughout the region of Galatia and Phrygia, strengthening all the disciples.

²⁴Meanwhile a Jew named Apollos, a native of Alexandria, came to Ephesus. He was a learned man, with a thorough knowledge of the Scriptures. ²⁵He had been instructed in the way of the Lord, and he spoke with great fervor[a] and taught about Jesus accurately, though he knew only the baptism of John. ²⁶He began to speak boldly in the synagogue. When Priscilla and Aquila heard him, they invited him to their home and explained to him the way of God more adequately.

²⁷When Apollos wanted to go to Achaia, the brothers encouraged him and wrote to the disciples there to welcome him. On arriving, he was a great help to those who by grace had believed. ²⁸For he vigorously refuted the Jews in public debate, proving from the Scriptures that Jesus was the Christ.

Paul in Ephesus

19 While Apollos was at Corinth, Paul took the road through the interior and arrived at Ephesus. There he found some disciples ²and asked them, "Did you receive the Holy Spirit when[b] you believed?"

They answered, "No, we have not even heard that there is a Holy Spirit."

³So Paul asked, "Then what baptism did you receive?"

"John's baptism," they replied.

⁴Paul said, "John's baptism was a baptism of repentance. He told the people to believe in the one coming after him, that is, in Jesus." ⁵On hearing this, they were baptized into[c] the name of the Lord Jesus. ⁶When Paul placed his hands on them, the Holy Spirit came on them, and they spoke in tongues[d] and prophesied. ⁷There were about twelve men in all.

⁸Paul entered the synagogue and spoke boldly there for three months, arguing persuasively about the kingdom of God. ⁹But some of them became obstinate; they refused to believe and publicly maligned the Way. So Paul left them. He took the disciples with him and had discussions daily in the lecture hall of Tyrannus. ¹⁰This went on for two years, so that all the Jews and Greeks who lived in the province of Asia heard the word of the Lord.

¹¹God did extraordinary miracles through Paul, ¹²so that even handkerchiefs and aprons that had touched him were taken to the sick, and their illnesses were cured and the evil spirits left them.

¹³Some Jews who went around driving out evil spirits tried to invoke the name of the Lord Jesus over those who were demon-possessed. They would say, "In the name of Jesus, whom Paul preaches, I command you to come out." ¹⁴Seven sons of Sceva, a Jewish chief priest, were doing this. ¹⁵One day, the evil spirit answered them, "Jesus I know, and I know about Paul, but who are you?" ¹⁶Then the man who had the evil spirit jumped on them and overpowered them all. He gave them such a beating that they ran out of the house naked and bleeding.

¹⁷When this became known to the Jews and Greeks living in Ephesus, they were all seized with fear, and the name of the Lord Jesus was held in high honor. ¹⁸Many of those who believed now came and openly confessed their evil deeds. ¹⁹A number who had practiced sorcery brought their scrolls together and burned them publicly. When they calculated the value of the scrolls, the total came to fifty thousand drachmas.[e] ²⁰In this way the word of the Lord spread widely and grew in power.

²¹After all this had happened, Paul decided to go to Jerusalem, passing through Macedonia and Achaia. "After I have been there," he said, "I must visit Rome also." ²²He sent two of his helpers, Timothy and Erastus, to Macedonia, while

---

a25 Or with fervor in the Spirit　　b2 Or after　　c5 Or in　　d6 Or other languages　　e19 A drachma was a silver coin worth about a day's wages.

he stayed in the province of Asia a little longer.

The Riot in Ephesus

23About that time there arose a great disturbance about the Way. 24A silversmith named Demetrius, who made silver shrines of Artemis, brought in no little business for the craftsmen. 25He called them together, along with the workmen in related trades, and said: "Men, you know we receive a good income from this business. 26And you see and hear how this fellow Paul has convinced and led astray large numbers of people here in Ephesus and in practically the whole province of Asia. He says that man-made gods are no gods at all. 27There is danger not only that our trade will lose its good name, but also that the temple of the great goddess Artemis will be discredited, and the goddess herself, who is worshiped throughout the province of Asia and the world, will be robbed of her divine majesty."

28When they heard this, they were furious and began shouting: "Great is Artemis of the Ephesians!" 29Soon the whole city was in an uproar. The people seized Gaius and Aristarchus, Paul's traveling companions from Macedonia, and rushed as one man into the theater. 30Paul wanted to appear before the crowd, but the disciples would not let him. 31Even some of the officials of the province, friends of Paul, sent him a message begging him not to venture into the theater.

32The assembly was in confusion: Some were shouting one thing, some another. Most of the people did not even know why they were there. 33The Jews pushed Alexander to the front, and some of the crowd shouted instructions to him. He motioned for silence in order to make a defense before the people. 34But when they realized he was a Jew, they all shouted in unison for about two hours: "Great is Artemis of the Ephesians!"

35The city clerk quieted the crowd and said: "Men of Ephesus, doesn't all the world know that the city of Ephesus is the guardian of the temple of the great Artemis and of her image, which fell from heaven? 36Therefore, since these facts are undeniable, you ought to be quiet and not do anything rash. 37You have brought these men here, though they have neither robbed temples nor blasphemed our goddess. 38If, then, Demetrius and his fellow craftsmen have a grievance against any-

body, the courts are open and there are proconsuls. They can press charges. 39If there is anything further you want to bring up, it must be settled in a legal assembly. 40As it is, we are in danger of being charged with rioting because of today's events. In that case we would not be able to account for this commotion, since there is no reason for it." 41After he had said this, he dismissed the assembly.

Through Macedonia and Greece

20 When the uproar had ended, Paul sent for the disciples and, after encouraging them, said good-by and set out for Macedonia. 2He traveled through that area, speaking many words of encouragement to the people, and finally arrived in Greece, 3where he stayed three months. Because the Jews made a plot against him just as he was about to sail for Syria, he decided to go back through Macedonia. 4He was accompanied by Sopater son of Pyrrhus from Berea, Aristarchus and Secundus from Thessalonica, Gaius from Derbe, Timothy also, and Tychicus and Trophimus from the province of Asia. 5These men went on ahead and waited for us at Troas. 6But we sailed from Philippi after the Feast of Unleavened Bread, and five days later joined the others at Troas, where we stayed seven days.

Eutychus Raised From the Dead at Troas

7On the first day of the week we came together to break bread. Paul spoke to the people and, because he intended to leave the next day, kept on talking until midnight. 8There were many lamps in the upstairs room where we were meeting. 9Seated in a window was a young man named Eutychus, who was sinking into a deep sleep as Paul talked on and on. When he was sound asleep, he fell to the ground from the third story and was picked up dead. 10Paul went down, threw himself on the young man and put his arms around him. "Don't be alarmed," he said. "He's alive!" 11Then he went upstairs again and broke bread and ate. After talking until daylight, he left. 12The people took the young man home alive and were greatly comforted.

Paul's Farewell to the Ephesian Elders

13We went on ahead to the ship and sailed for Assos, where we were going to take Paul aboard. He had made this arrangement because he was going there on foot. [14]When he met us at Assos, we took him aboard and went on to Mitylene. [15]The next day we set sail from there and arrived off Kios. The day after that we crossed over to Samos, and on the following day arrived at Miletus. [16]Paul had decided to sail past Ephesus to avoid spending time in the province of Asia, for he was in a hurry to reach Jerusalem, if possible, by the day of Pentecost.

[17]From Miletus, Paul sent to Ephesus for the elders of the church. [18]When they arrived, he said to them: "You know how I lived the whole time I was with you, from the first day I came into the province of Asia. [19]I served the Lord with great humility and with tears, although I was severely tested by the plots of the Jews. [20]You know that I have not hesitated to preach anything that would be helpful to you but have taught you publicly and from house to house. [21]I have declared to both Jews and Greeks that they must turn to God in repentance and have faith in our Lord Jesus.

[22]"And now, compelled by the Spirit, I am going to Jerusalem, not knowing what will happen to me there. [23]I only know that in every city the Holy Spirit warns me that prison and hardships are facing me. [24]However, I consider my life worth nothing to me, if only I may finish the race and complete the task the Lord Jesus has given me—the task of testifying to the gospel of God's grace.

[25]"Now I know that none of you among whom I have gone about preaching the kingdom will ever see me again. [26]Therefore, I declare to you today that I am innocent of the blood of all men. [27]For I have not hesitated to proclaim to you the whole will of God. [28]Keep watch over yourselves and all the flock of which the Holy Spirit has made you overseers.[a] Be shepherds of the church of God,[b] which he bought with his own blood. [29]I know that after I leave, savage wolves will come in among you and will not spare the flock. [30]Even from your own number men will arise and distort the truth in order to draw away disciples after them. [31]So be on your guard! Remember that for three years I never stopped warning each of you night and day with tears.

[32]"Now I commit you to God and to the word of his grace, which can build you up

and give you an inheritance among all those who are sanctified. [33]I have not coveted anyone's silver or gold or clothing. [34]You yourselves know that these hands of mine have supplied my own needs and the needs of my companions. [35]In everything I did, I showed you that by this kind of hard work we must help the weak, remembering the words the Lord Jesus himself said: 'It is more blessed to give than to receive.' "

[36]When he had said this, he knelt down with all of them and prayed. [37]They all wept as they embraced him and kissed him. [38]What grieved them most was his statement that they would never see his face again. Then they accompanied him to the ship.

On to Jerusalem

21 After we had torn ourselves away from them, we put out to sea and sailed straight to Cos. The next day we went to Rhodes and from there to Patara. [2]We found a ship crossing over to Phoenicia, went on board and set sail. [3]After sighting Cyprus and passing to the south of it, we sailed on to Syria. We landed at Tyre, where our ship was to unload its cargo. [4]Finding the disciples there, we stayed with them seven days. Through the Spirit they urged Paul not to go on to Jerusalem. [5]But when our time was up, we left and continued on our way. All the disciples and their wives and children accompanied us out of the city, and there on the beach we knelt to pray. [6]After saying good-by to each other, we went aboard the ship, and they returned home.

[7]We continued our voyage from Tyre and landed at Ptolemais, where we greeted the brothers and stayed with them for a day. [8]Leaving the next day, we reached Caesarea and stayed at the house of Philip the evangelist, one of the Seven. [9]He had four unmarried daughters who prophesied.

[10]After we had been there a number of days, a prophet named Agabus came down from Judea. [11]Coming over to us, he took Paul's belt, tied his own hands and feet with it and said, "The Holy Spirit says, 'In this way the Jews of Jerusalem will bind the owner of this belt and will hand him over to the Gentiles.' "

[12]When we heard this, we and the people there pleaded with Paul not to go up to Jerusalem. [13]Then Paul answered,

---

a28 Traditionally *bishops*   *b28* Many manuscripts *of the Lord*

"Why are you weeping and breaking my heart? I am ready not only to be bound, but also to die in Jerusalem for the name of the Lord Jesus." [14]When he would not be dissuaded, we gave up and said, "The Lord's will be done."

[15]After this, we got ready and went up to Jerusalem. [16]Some of the disciples from Caesarea accompanied us and brought us to the home of Mnason, where we were to stay. He was a man from Cyprus and one of the early disciples.

Paul's Arrival at Jerusalem

[17]When we arrived at Jerusalem, the brothers received us warmly. [18]The next day Paul and the rest of us went to see James, and all the elders were present. [19]Paul greeted them and reported in detail what God had done among the Gentiles through his ministry.

[20]When they heard this, they praised God. Then they said to Paul: "You see, brother, how many thousands of Jews have believed, and all of them are zealous for the law. [21]They have been informed that you teach all the Jews who live among the Gentiles to turn away from Moses, telling them not to circumcise their children or live according to our customs. [22]What shall we do? They will certainly hear that you have come, [23]so do

TUESDAY

VERSE FOR THE DAY:
Acts 20:35

AUTHOR:
Sue Monk Kidd

PASSAGE FOR THE DAY:
Acts 20:13–38

On Giving

I have always been fascinated with Brother Roger of Taize, France, the founder of a Christian community where persons from twenty different countries and many Christian denominations live, work and pray together. One of the remarkable things about Taize is that so many young people have flocked there.

In an interview Brother Roger was asked why the young were so attracted to Taize. He responded by telling a story about his life. When he was young, children were made to keep their distance from their elders, he said. More that anything he longed for someone to give him an ear, to listen and understand what was in his heart of hearts. But it never happened. Finally Brother Roger made the resolution that became the motivation of his entire life. He determined to give to others the very thing he yearned for himself. He committed himself to listen to and understand every human being, especially the young. So at Taize he sat and listened to the young, asking himself: What are they suffering? What lies beneath their hearts? What are their gifts?

By attempting to give the very understanding he was seeking, Brother Roger found it in even greater measure. This principle never fails. If you seek to be understood, then dedicate your life to understanding others. If you seek to be comforted, then dedicate yourself to giving comfort. If you seek a greater faith, then commit yourself to planting it in others.

Additional Scripture Readings:
Luke 6:32–38; 1 John 4:10–12

Go to page 1228 for your next devotional reading.

what we tell you. There are four men with us who have made a vow. ²⁴Take these men, join in their purification rites and pay their expenses, so that they can have their heads shaved. Then everybody will know there is no truth in these reports about you, but that you yourself are living in obedience to the law. ²⁵As for the Gentile believers, we have written to them our decision that they should abstain from food sacrificed to idols, from blood, from the meat of strangled animals and from sexual immorality."

²⁶The next day Paul took the men and purified himself along with them. Then he went to the temple to give notice of the date when the days of purification would end and the offering would be made for each of them.

Paul Arrested

²⁷When the seven days were nearly over, some Jews from the province of Asia saw Paul at the temple. They stirred up the whole crowd and seized him, ²⁸shouting, "Men of Israel, help us! This is the man who teaches all men everywhere against our people and our law and this place. And besides, he has brought Greeks into the temple area and defiled this holy place." ²⁹(They had previously seen Trophimus the Ephesian in the city with Paul and assumed that Paul had brought him into the temple area.)

³⁰The whole city was aroused, and the people came running from all directions. Seizing Paul, they dragged him from the temple, and immediately the gates were shut. ³¹While they were trying to kill him, news reached the commander of the Roman troops that the whole city of Jerusalem was in an uproar. ³²He at once took some officers and soldiers and ran down to the crowd. When the rioters saw the commander and his soldiers, they stopped beating Paul.

³³The commander came up and arrested him and ordered him to be bound with two chains. Then he asked who he was and what he had done. ³⁴Some in the crowd shouted one thing and some another, and since the commander could not get at the truth because of the uproar, he ordered that Paul be taken into the barracks. ³⁵When Paul reached the steps, the violence of the mob was so great he had to be carried by the soldiers. ³⁶The crowd that followed kept shouting, "Away with him!"

Paul Speaks to the Crowd

³⁷As the soldiers were about to take Paul into the barracks, he asked the commander, "May I say something to you?"

"Do you speak Greek?" he replied. ³⁸"Aren't you the Egyptian who started a revolt and led four thousand terrorists out into the desert some time ago?"

³⁹Paul answered, "I am a Jew, from Tarsus in Cilicia, a citizen of no ordinary city. Please let me speak to the people."

⁴⁰Having received the commander's permission, Paul stood on the steps and motioned to the crowd. When they were all silent, he said to them in Aramaic^a:

22 ¹"Brothers and fathers, listen now to my defense."

²When they heard him speak to them in Aramaic, they became very quiet.

Then Paul said: ³"I am a Jew, born in Tarsus of Cilicia, but brought up in this city. Under Gamaliel I was thoroughly trained in the law of our fathers and was just as zealous for God as any of you are today. ⁴I persecuted the followers of this Way to their death, arresting both men and women and throwing them into prison, ⁵as also the high priest and all the Council can testify. I even obtained letters from them to their brothers in Damascus, and went there to bring these people as prisoners to Jerusalem to be punished.

⁶"About noon as I came near Damascus, suddenly a bright light from heaven flashed around me. ⁷I fell to the ground and heard a voice say to me. 'Saul! Saul! Why do you persecute me?'

⁸" 'Who are you, Lord?' I asked.

" 'I am Jesus of Nazareth, whom you are persecuting,' he replied. ⁹My companions saw the light, but they did not understand the voice of him who was speaking to me.

¹⁰" 'What shall I do, Lord?' I asked.

" 'Get up,' the Lord said, Damascus. There you will be told all that you have been assigned to do.' ¹¹My companions led me by the hand into Damascus, because the brilliance of the light had blinded me.

¹²"A man named Ananias came to see me. He was a devout observer of the law and highly respected by all the Jews living there. ¹³He stood beside me and said,

^a40 Or possibly *Hebrew*; also in 22:2

'Brother Saul, receive your sight!' And at that very moment I was able to see him.

14"Then he said: 'The God of our fathers has chosen you to know his will and to see the Righteous One and to hear words from his mouth. 15You will be his witness to all men of what you have seen and heard. 16And now what are you waiting for? Get up, be baptized and wash your sins away, calling on his name.'

17"When I returned to Jerusalem and was praying at the temple, I fell into a trance 18and saw the Lord speaking. 'Quick!' he said to me. 'Leave Jerusalem immediately, because they will not accept your testimony about me.'

19" 'Lord,' I replied, 'these men know that I went from one synagogue to another to imprison and beat those who believe in you. 20And when the blood of your martyr[a] Stephen was shed, I stood there giving my approval and guarding the clothes of those who were killing him.'

21"Then the Lord said to me, 'Go; I will send you far away to the Gentiles.' "

Paul the Roman Citizen

22The crowd listened to Paul until he said this. Then they raised their voices and shouted, "Rid the earth of him! He's not fit to live!"

23As they were shouting and throwing off their cloaks and flinging dust into the air, 24the commander ordered Paul to be taken into the barracks. He directed that he be flogged and questioned in order to find out why the people were shouting at him like this. 25As they stretched him out to flog him, Paul said to the centurion standing there, "Is it legal for you to flog a Roman citizen who hasn't even been found guilty?"

26When the centurion heard this, he went to the commander and reported it. "What are you going to do?" he asked. "This man is a Roman citizen."

27The commander went to Paul and asked, "Tell me, are you a Roman citizen?"

"Yes, I am," he answered.

28Then the commander said, "I had to pay a big price for my citizenship."

"But I was born a citizen," Paul replied.

29Those who were about to question him withdrew immediately. The commander himself was alarmed when he realized that he had put Paul, a Roman citizen, in chains.

Before the Sanhedrin

30The next day, since the commander wanted to find out exactly why Paul was being accused by the Jews, he released him and ordered the chief priests and all the Sanhedrin to assemble. Then he brought Paul and had him stand before them.

23 Paul looked straight at the Sanhedrin and said, "My brothers, I have fulfilled my duty to God in all good conscience to this day." 2At this the high priest Ananias ordered those standing near Paul to strike him on the mouth. 3Then Paul said to him, "God will strike you, you whitewashed wall! You sit there to judge me according to the law, yet you yourself violate the law by commanding that I be struck!"

4Those who were standing near Paul said, "You dare to insult God's high priest?"

5Paul replied, "Brothers, I did not realize that he was the high priest; for it is written: 'Do not speak evil about the ruler of your people.'[b]"

6Then Paul, knowing that some of them were Sadducees and the others Pharisees, called out in the Sanhedrin, "My brothers, I am a Pharisee, the son of a Pharisee. I stand on trial because of my hope in the resurrection of the dead." 7When he said this, a dispute broke out between the Pharisees and the Sadducees, and the assembly was divided. 8(The Sadducees say that there is no resurrection, and that there are neither angels nor spirits, but the Pharisees acknowledge them all.)

9There was a great uproar, and some of the teachers of the law who were Pharisees stood up and argued vigorously. "We find nothing wrong with this man," they said. "What if a spirit or an angel has spoken to him?" 10The dispute became so violent that the commander was afraid Paul would be torn to pieces by them. He ordered the troops to go down and take him away from them by force and bring him into the barracks.

11The following night the Lord stood near Paul and said, "Take courage! As you have testified about me in Jerusalem, so you must also testify in Rome."

The Plot to Kill Paul

12The next morning the Jews formed a

a20 Or witness   b5 Exodus 22:28

conspiracy and bound themselves with an oath not to eat or drink until they had killed Paul. [13]More than forty men were involved in this plot. [14]They went to the chief priests and elders and said, "We have taken a solemn oath not to eat anything until we have killed Paul. [15]Now then, you and the Sanhedrin petition the commander to bring him before you on the pretext of wanting more accurate information about his case. We are ready to kill him before he gets here."

[16]But when the son of Paul's sister heard of this plot, he went into the barracks and told Paul.

[17]Then Paul called one of the centurions and said, "Take this young man to the commander; he has something to tell him." [18]So he took him to the commander.

The centurion said, "Paul, the prisoner, sent for me and asked me to bring this young man to you because he has something to tell you."

[19]The commander took the young man by the hand, drew him aside and asked, "What is it you want to tell me?"

[20]He said: "The Jews have agreed to ask you to bring Paul before the Sanhedrin tomorrow on the pretext of wanting more accurate information about him. [21]Don't give in to them, because more than forty of them are waiting in ambush for him. They have taken an oath not to eat or drink until they have killed him. They are ready now, waiting for your consent to their request."

[22]The commander dismissed the young man and cautioned him, "Don't tell anyone that you have reported this to me."

Paul Transferred to Caesarea

[23]Then he called two of his centurions and ordered them, "Get ready a detachment of two hundred soldiers, seventy horsemen and two hundred spearmen[a] to go to Caesarea at nine tonight. [24]Provide mounts for Paul so that he may be taken safely to Governor Felix."

[25]He wrote a letter as follows:

[26]Claudius Lysias,

To His Excellency, Governor Felix:

Greetings.

[27]This man was seized by the Jews and they were about to kill him, but I came with my troops and rescued him, for I had learned that he is a Roman citizen. [28]I wanted to know why they were accusing him, so I brought him to their Sanhedrin. [29]I found that the accusation had to do with questions about their law, but there was no charge against him that deserved death or imprisonment. [30]When I was informed of a plot to be carried out against the man, I sent him to you at once. I also ordered his accusers to present to you their case against him.

[31]So the soldiers, carrying out their orders, took Paul with them during the night and brought him as far as Antipatris. [32]The next day they let the cavalry go on with him, while they returned to the barracks. [33]When the cavalry arrived in Caesarea, they delivered the letter to the governor and handed Paul over to him. [34]The governor read the letter and asked what province he was from. Learning that he was from Cilicia, [35]he said, "I will hear your case when your accusers get here." Then he ordered that Paul be kept under guard in Herod's palace.

The Trial Before Felix

24 Five days later the high priest Ananias went down to Caesarea with some of the elders and a lawyer named Tertullus, and they brought their charges against Paul before the governor. [2]When Paul was called in, Tertullus presented his case before Felix: "We have enjoyed a long period of peace under you, and your foresight has brought about reforms in this nation. [3]Everywhere and in every way, most excellent Felix, we acknowledge this with profound gratitude. [4]But in order not to weary you further, I would request that you be kind enough to hear us briefly.

[5]"We have found this man to be a troublemaker, stirring up riots among the Jews all over the world. He is a ringleader of the Nazarene sect [6]and even tried to desecrate the temple; so we seized him. [8]By[b] examining him yourself you will be able to learn the truth about all these charges we are bringing against him."

---

[a]23 The meaning of the Greek for this word is uncertain.   [b]6-8 Some manuscripts him and wanted to judge him according to our law. [7]But the commander, Lysias, came and with the use of much force snatched him from our hands [8]and ordered his accusers to come before you. By

9The Jews joined in the accusation, asserting that these things were true.

10When the governor motioned for him to speak, Paul replied: "I know that for a number of years you have been a judge over this nation; so I gladly make my defense. 11You can easily verify that no more than twelve days ago I went up to Jerusalem to worship. 12My accusers did not find me arguing with anyone at the temple, or stirring up a crowd in the synagogues or anywhere else in the city. 13And they cannot prove to you the charges they are now making against me. 14However, I admit that I worship the God of our fathers as a follower of the Way, which they call a sect. I believe everything that agrees with the Law and that is written in the Prophets, 15and I have the same hope in God as these men, that there will be a resurrection of both the righteous and the wicked. 16So I strive always to keep my conscience clear before God and man.

17"After an absence of several years, I came to Jerusalem to bring my people gifts for the poor and to present offerings. 18I was ceremonially clean when they found me in the temple courts doing this. There was no crowd with me, nor was I involved in any disturbance. 19But there are some Jews from the province of Asia, who ought to be here before you and bring charges if they have anything against me. 20Or these who are here should state what crime they found in me when I stood before the Sanhedrin— 21unless it was this one thing I shouted as I stood in their presence: 'It is concerning the resurrection of the dead that I am on trial before you today.'"

22Then Felix, who was well acquainted with the Way, adjourned the proceedings. "When Lysias the commander comes," he said, "I will decide your case." 23He ordered the centurion to keep Paul under guard but to give him some freedom and permit his friends to take care of his needs.

24Several days later Felix came with his wife Drusilla, who was a Jewess. He sent for Paul and listened to him as he spoke about faith in Christ Jesus. 25As Paul discoursed on righteousness, self-control and the judgment to come, Felix was afraid and said, "That's enough for now! You may leave. When I find it convenient, I will send for you." 26At the same time he was hoping that Paul would offer him a bribe, so he sent for him frequently and talked with him.

27When two years had passed, Felix was succeeded by Porcius Festus, but because Felix wanted to grant a favor to the Jews, he left Paul in prison.

The Trial Before Festus

25 Three days after arriving in the province, Festus went up from Caesarea to Jerusalem, 2where the chief priests and Jewish leaders appeared before him and presented the charges against Paul. 3They urgently requested Festus, as a favor to them, to have Paul transferred to Jerusalem, for they were preparing an ambush to kill him along the way. 4Festus answered, "Paul is being held at Caesarea, and I myself am going there soon. 5Let some of your leaders come with me and press charges against the man there, if he has done anything wrong."

6After spending eight or ten days with them, he went down to Caesarea, and the next day he convened the court and ordered that Paul be brought before him. 7When Paul appeared, the Jews who had come down from Jerusalem stood around him, bringing many serious charges against him, which they could not prove.

8Then Paul made his defense: "I have done nothing wrong against the law of the Jews or against the temple or against Caesar."

9Festus, wishing to do the Jews a favor, said to Paul, "Are you willing to go up to Jerusalem and stand trial before me there on these charges?"

10Paul answered: "I am now standing before Caesar's court, where I ought to be tried. I have not done any wrong to the Jews, as you yourself know very well. 11If, however, I am guilty of doing anything deserving death, I do not refuse to die. But if the charges brought against me by these Jews are not true, no one has the right to hand me over to them. I appeal to Caesar!"

12After Festus had conferred with his council, he declared: "You have appealed to Caesar. To Caesar you will go!"

Festus Consults King Agrippa

13A few days later King Agrippa and Bernice arrived at Caesarea to pay their respects to Festus. 14Since they were spending many days there, Festus discussed Paul's case with the king. He said: "There is a man here whom Felix left as a prisoner. 15When I went to Jerusalem, the chief priests and elders of the Jews brought charges against him and asked that he be condemned.

16"I told them that it is not the Roman custom to hand over any man before he has faced his accusers and has had an opportunity to defend himself against their charges. 17When they came here with me, I did not delay the case, but convened the court the next day and ordered the man to be brought in. 18When his accusers got up to speak, they did not charge him with any of the crimes I had expected. 19Instead, they had some points of dispute with him about their own religion and about a dead man named Jesus who Paul claimed was alive. 20I was at a loss how to investigate such matters; so I asked if he would be willing to go to Jerusalem and stand trial there on these charges. 21When Paul made his appeal to be held over for the Emperor's decision, I ordered him held until I could send him to Caesar."

22Then Agrippa said to Festus, "I would like to hear this man myself."

He replied, "Tomorrow you will hear him."

Paul Before Agrippa

23The next day Agrippa and Bernice came with great pomp and entered the audience room with the high ranking officers and the leading men of the city. At the command of Festus, Paul was brought in. 24Festus said: "King Agrippa, and all who are present with us, you see this man! The whole Jewish community has petitioned me about him in Jerusalem and here in Caesarea, shouting that he ought not to live any longer. 25I found he had done nothing deserving of death, but because he made his appeal to the Emperor I decided to send him to Rome. 26But I have nothing definite to write to His Majesty about him. Therefore I have brought him before all of you, and especially before you, King Agrippa, so that as a result of this investigation I may have something to write. 27For I think it is unreasonable to send on a prisoner without specifying the charges against him."

26 Then Agrippa said to Paul, "You have permission to speak for yourself."

So Paul motioned with his hand and began his defense: 2"King Agrippa, I consider myself fortunate to stand before you today as I make my defense against all the accusations of the Jews, 3and especially so because you are well acquainted with all the Jewish customs and controversies. Therefore, I beg you to listen to me patiently.

4"The Jews all know the way I have lived ever since I was a child, from the beginning of my life in my own country, and also in Jerusalem. 5They have known me for a long time and can testify, if they are willing, that according to the strictest sect of our religion, I lived as a Pharisee. 6And now it is because of my hope in what God has promised our fathers that I am on trial today. 7This is the promise our twelve tribes are hoping to see fulfilled as they earnestly serve God day and night. O king, it is because of this hope that the Jews are accusing me. 8Why should any of you consider it incredible that God raises the dead?

9"I too was convinced that I ought to do all that was possible to oppose the name of Jesus of Nazareth. 10And that is just what I did in Jerusalem. On the authority of the chief priests I put many of the saints in prison, and when they were put to death, I cast my vote against them. 11Many a time I went from one synagogue to another to have them punished, and I tried to force them to blaspheme. In my obsession against them, I even went to foreign cities to persecute them.

12"On one of these journeys I was going to Damascus with the authority and commission of the chief priests. 13About noon, O king, as I was on the road, I saw a light from heaven, brighter than the sun, blazing around me and my companions. 14We all fell to the ground, and I heard a voice saying to me in Aramaic,ᵃ 'Saul, Saul, why do you persecute me? It is hard for you to kick against the goads.'

15"Then I asked, 'Who are you, Lord?'

" 'I am Jesus, whom you are persecuting,' the Lord replied. 16'Now get up and stand on your feet. I have appeared to you to appoint you as a servant and as a witness of what you have seen of me and what I will show you. 17I will rescue you from your own people and from the Gentiles. I am sending you to them 18to open their eyes and turn them from darkness to light, and from the power of Satan to God, so that they may receive forgiveness of sins and a place among those who are sanctified by faith in me.'

19"So then, King Agrippa, I was not

disobedient to the vision from heaven. [20]First to those in Damascus, then to those in Jerusalem and in all Judea, and to the Gentiles also, I preached that they should repent and turn to God and prove their repentance by their deeds. [21]That is why the Jews seized me in the temple courts and tried to kill me. [22]But I have had God's help to this very day, and so I stand here and testify to small and great alike. I am saying nothing beyond what the prophets and Moses said would happen— [23]that the Christ[a] would suffer and, as the first to rise from the dead, would proclaim light to his own people and to the Gentiles."

[24]At this point Festus interrupted Paul's defense. "You are out of your mind, Paul!" he shouted. "Your great learning is driving you insane."

[25]"I am not insane, most excellent Festus," Paul replied. "What I am saying is true and reasonable. [26]The king is familiar with these things, and I can speak freely to him. I am convinced that none of this has escaped his notice, because it was not done in a corner. [27]King Agrippa, do you believe the prophets? I know you do."

[28]Then Agrippa said to Paul, "Do you think that in such a short time you can persuade me to be a Christian?"

[29]Paul replied, "Short time or long—I pray God that not only you but all who are listening to me today may become what I am, except for these chains."

[30]The king rose, and with him the governor and Bernice and those sitting with them. [31]They left the room, and while talking with one another, they said, "This man is not doing anything that deserves death or imprisonment."

[32]Agrippa said to Festus, "This man could have been set free if he had not appealed to Caesar."

Paul Sails for Rome

27 When it was decided that we would sail for Italy, Paul and some other prisoners were handed over to a centurion named Julius, who belonged to the Imperial Regiment. [2]We boarded a ship from Adramyttium about to sail for ports along the coast of the province of Asia, and we put out to sea. Aristarchus, a Macedonian from Thessalonica, was with us.

[3]The next day we landed at Sidon; and Julius, in kindness to Paul, allowed him to go to his friends so they might provide for his needs. [4]From there we put out to sea again and passed to the lee of Cyprus because the winds were against us. [5]When we had sailed across the open sea off the coast of Cilicia and Pamphylia, we landed at Myra in Lycia. [6]There the centurion found an Alexandrian ship sailing for Italy and put us on board. [7]We made slow headway for many days and had difficulty arriving off Cnidus. When the wind did not allow us to hold our course, we sailed to the lee of Crete, opposite Salmone. [8]We moved along the coast with difficulty and came to a place called Fair Havens, near the town of Lasea.

[9]Much time had been lost, and sailing had already become dangerous because by now it was after the Fast.[b] So Paul warned them, [10]"Men, I can see that our voyage is going to be disastrous and bring great loss to ship and cargo, and to our own lives also." [11]But the centurion, instead of listening to what Paul said, followed the advice of the pilot and of the owner of the ship. [12]Since the harbor was unsuitable to winter in, the majority decided that we should sail on, hoping to reach Phoenix and winter there. This was a harbor in Crete, facing both southwest and northwest.

The Storm

[13]When a gentle south wind began to blow, they thought they had obtained what they wanted; so they weighed anchor and sailed along the shore of Crete. [14]Before very long, a wind of hurricane force, called the "northeaster," swept down from the island. [15]The ship was caught by the storm and could not head into the wind; so we gave way to it and were driven along. [16]As we passed to the lee of a small island called Cauda, we were hardly able to make the lifeboat secure. [17]When the men had hoisted it aboard, they passed ropes under the ship itself to hold it together. Fearing that they would run aground on the sandbars of Syrtis, they lowered the sea anchor and let the ship be driven along. [18]We took such a violent battering from the storm that the next day they began to throw the cargo overboard. [19]On the third day, they threw the ship's tackle overboard with their own hands. [20]When neither sun nor stars appeared for many days and the

storm continued raging, we finally gave up all hope of being saved.

²¹After the men had gone a long time without food, Paul stood up before them and said: "Men, you should have taken my advice not to sail from Crete; then you would have spared yourselves this damage and loss. ²²But now I urge you to keep up your courage, because not one of you will be lost; only the ship will be destroyed. ²³Last night an angel of the God whose I am and whom I serve stood beside me ²⁴and said, 'Do not be afraid, Paul. You must stand trial before Caesar; and God has graciously given you the lives of all who sail with you.' ²⁵So keep up your courage, men, for I have faith in God that it will happen just as he told me. ²⁶Nevertheless, we must run aground on some island."

The Shipwreck

²⁷On the fourteenth night we were still being driven across the Adriatic[a] Sea, when about midnight the sailors sensed they were approaching land. ²⁸They took soundings and found that the water was a hundred and twenty feet[b] deep. A short time later they took soundings again and found it was ninety feet[c] deep. ²⁹Fearing that we would be dashed against the rocks, they dropped four anchors from the stern and prayed for daylight. ³⁰In an attempt to escape from the ship, the sailors let the lifeboat down into the sea, pretending they were going to lower some anchors from the bow. ³¹Then Paul said to the centurion and the soldiers, "Unless these men stay with the ship, you cannot be saved." ³²So the soldiers cut the ropes that held the lifeboat and let it fall away.

³³Just before dawn Paul urged them all to eat. "For the last fourteen days," he said, "you have been in constant suspense and have gone without food — you haven't eaten anything. ³⁴Now I urge you to take some food. You need it to survive. Not one of you will lose a single hair from his head." ³⁵After he said this, he took some bread and gave thanks to God in front of them all. Then he broke it and began to eat. ³⁶They were all encouraged and ate some food themselves. ³⁷Altogether there were 276 of us on board. ³⁸When they had eaten as much as they wanted, they lightened the ship by throwing the grain into the sea.

³⁹When daylight came, they did not recognize the land, but they saw a bay with a sandy beach, where they decided to run the ship aground if they could. ⁴⁰Cutting loose the anchors, they left them in the sea and at the same time untied the ropes that held the rudders. Then they hoisted the foresail to the wind and made for the beach. ⁴¹But the ship struck a sandbar and ran aground. The bow stuck fast and would not move, and the stern was broken to pieces by the pounding of the surf.

⁴²The soldiers planned to kill the prisoners to prevent any of them from swimming away and escaping. ⁴³But the centurion wanted to spare Paul's life and kept them from carrying out their plan. He ordered those who could swim to jump overboard first and get to land. ⁴⁴The rest were to get there on planks or on pieces of the ship. In this way everyone reached land in safety.

Ashore on Malta

28 Once safely on shore, we found out that the island was called Malta. ²The islanders showed us unusual kindness. They built a fire and welcomed us all because it was raining and cold. ³Paul gathered a pile of brushwood and, as he put it on the fire, a viper, driven out by the heat, fastened itself on his hand. ⁴When the islanders saw the snake hanging from his hand, they said to each other, "This man must be a murderer; for though he escaped from the sea, Justice has not allowed him to live." ⁵But Paul shook the snake off into the fire and suffered no ill effects. ⁶The people expected him to swell up or suddenly fall dead, but after waiting a long time and seeing nothing unusual happen to him, they changed their minds and said he was a god.

⁷There was an estate nearby that belonged to Publius, the chief official of the island. He welcomed us to his home and for three days entertained us hospitably. ⁸His father was sick in bed, suffering from fever and dysentery. Paul went in to see him and, after prayer, placed his hands on him and healed him. ⁹When this had happened, the rest of the sick on the island came and were cured. ¹⁰They honored us in many ways and when we were ready to sail, they furnished us with the supplies we needed.

---

a27 In ancient times the name referred to an area extending well south of Italy.   *b28* Greek *twenty orguias* (about 37 meters)   *c28* Greek *fifteen orguias* (about 27 meters)

Arrival at Rome

[11]After three months we put out to sea in a ship that had wintered in the island. It was an Alexandrian ship with the figurehead of the twin gods Castor and Pollux. [12]We put in at Syracuse and stayed there three days. [13]From there we set sail and arrived at Rhegium. The next day the south wind came up, and on the following day we reached Puteoli. [14]There we found some brothers who invited us to spend a week with them. And so we came to Rome. [15]The brothers there had heard that we were coming, and they traveled as far as the Forum of Appius and the Three Taverns to meet us. At the sight of these men Paul thanked God and was encouraged. [16]When we got to Rome, Paul was allowed to live by himself, with a soldier to guard him.

Paul Preaches at Rome Under Guard

[17]Three days later he called together the leaders of the Jews. When they had assembled, Paul said to them: "My brothers, although I have done nothing against our people or against the customs of our ancestors, I was arrested in Jerusalem and handed over to the Romans. [18]They examined me and wanted to release me, because I was not guilty of any crime deserving death. [19]But when the Jews objected, I was compelled to appeal to Caesar—not that I had any charge to bring against my own people. [20]For this reason I have asked to see you and talk with you. It is because of the hope of Israel that I am bound with this chain."

[21]They replied, "We have not received any letters from Judea concerning you, and none of the brothers who have come from there has reported or said anything

bad about you. [22]But we want to hear what your views are, for we know that people everywhere are talking against this sect."

[23]They arranged to meet Paul on a certain day, and came in even larger numbers to the place where he was staying. From morning till evening he explained and declared to them the kingdom of God and tried to convince them about Jesus from the Law of Moses and from the Prophets. [24]Some were convinced by what he said, but others would not believe. [25]They disagreed among themselves and began to leave after Paul had made this final statement: "The Holy Spirit spoke the truth to your forefathers when he said through Isaiah the prophet:

[26]" 'Go to this people and say,
"You will be ever hearing but never understanding;
   you will be ever seeing but never perceiving."
[27]For this people's heart has become calloused;
   they hardly hear with their ears,
   and they have closed their eyes.
Otherwise they might see with their eyes,
   hear with their ears,
   understand with their hearts
and turn, and I would heal them.'[a]

[28]"Therefore I want you to know that God's salvation has been sent to the Gentiles, and they will listen!"[b]

[30]For two whole years Paul stayed there in his own rented house and welcomed all who came to see him. [31]Boldly and without hindrance he preached the kingdom of God and taught about the Lord Jesus Christ.

---

[a]27 Isaiah 6:9,10   [b]28 Some manuscripts listen!" [29]After he said this, the Jews left, arguing vigorously among themselves.

PAUL, planning a mission trip to Spain (Romans 15:23–29), writes this letter to introduce himself to the church at Rome. In it he summarizes what he has been preaching about sin, Christ, and the way of salvation. Everything you need to know about God's great plan for redemption lies in these sixteen chapters. As you read the book, think about how much God loves you in sending his Son Jesus and how you can say thank you to him by the life you live.

ROMANS

1 Paul, a servant of Christ Jesus, called to be an apostle and set apart for the gospel of God— ²the gospel he promised beforehand through his prophets in the Holy Scriptures ³regarding his Son, who as to his human nature was a descendant of David, ⁴and who through the Spirit*ᵃ* of holiness was declared with power to be the Son of God*ᵇ* by his resurrection from the dead: Jesus Christ our Lord. ⁵Through him and for his name's sake, we received grace and apostleship to call people from among all the Gentiles to the obedience that comes from faith. ⁶And you also are among those who are called to belong to Jesus Christ.

⁷To all in Rome who are loved by God and called to be saints:

Grace and peace to you from God our Father and from the Lord Jesus Christ.

Paul's Longing to Visit Rome

⁸First, I thank my God through Jesus Christ for all of you, because your faith is being reported all over the world. ⁹God, whom I serve with my whole heart in preaching the gospel of his Son, is my witness how constantly I remember you ¹⁰in my prayers at all times; and I pray that

ᵃ4 Or who as to his spirit   *ᵇ4 Or was appointed to be the Son of God with power* now at last by God's will the way may be opened for me to come to you.

[11]I long to see you so that I may impart to you some spiritual gift to make you strong— [12]that is, that you and I may be mutually encouraged by each other's faith. [13]I do not want you to be unaware, brothers, that I planned many times to come to you (but have been prevented from doing so until now) in order that I might have a harvest among you, just as I have had among the other Gentiles.

[14]I am obligated both to Greeks and non-Greeks, both to the wise and the foolish. [15]That is why I am so eager to preach the gospel also to you who are at Rome.

[16]I am not ashamed of the gospel, because it is the power of God for the salvation of everyone who believes: first for the Jew, then for the Gentile. [17]For in the gospel a righteousness from God is revealed, a righteousness that is by faith from first to last,[a] just as it is written: "The righteous will live by faith."[b]

God's Wrath Against Mankind

[18]The wrath of God is being revealed from heaven against all the godlessness and wickedness of men who suppress the truth by their wickedness, [19]since what may be known about God is plain to them, because God has made it plain to them. [20]For since the creation of the world God's invisible qualities—his eternal power and divine nature—have been clearly seen, being understood from what has been made, so that men are without excuse.

[21]For although they knew God, they neither glorified him as God nor gave thanks to him, but their thinking became futile and their foolish hearts were darkened. [22]Although they claimed to be wise, they became fools [23]and exchanged the glory of the immortal God for images made to look like mortal man and birds and animals and reptiles.

[24]Therefore God gave them over in the sinful desires of their hearts to sexual impurity for the degrading of their bodies with one another. [25]They exchanged the truth of God for a lie, and worshiped and served created things rather than the Creator—who is forever praised. Amen.

[26]Because of this, God gave them over to shameful lusts. Even their women exchanged natural relations for unnatural ones. [27]In the same way the men also abandoned natural relations with women and were inflamed with lust for one another. Men committed indecent acts with other men, and received in themselves the due penalty for their perversion.

[28]Furthermore, since they did not think it worthwhile to retain the knowledge of God, he gave them over to a depraved mind, to do what ought not to be done. [29]They have become filled with every kind of wickedness, evil, greed and depravity. They are full of envy, murder, strife, deceit and malice. They are gossips, [30]slanderers, God-haters, insolent, arrogant and boastful; they invent ways of doing evil; they disobey their parents; [31]they are senseless, faithless, heartless, ruthless. [32]Although they know God's righteous decree that those who do such things deserve death, they not only continue to do these very things but also approve of those who practice them.

God's Righteous Judgment

2 You, therefore, have no excuse, you who pass judgment on someone else, for at whatever point you judge the other, you are condemning yourself, because you who pass judgment do the same things. [2]Now we know that God's judgment against those who do such things is based on truth. [3]So when you, a mere man, pass judgment on them and yet do the same things, do you think you will escape God's judgment? [4]Or do you show contempt for the riches of his kindness, tolerance and patience, not realizing that God's kindness leads you toward repentance?

[5]But because of your stubbornness and your unrepentant heart, you are storing up wrath against yourself for the day of God's wrath, when his righteous judgment will be revealed. [6]God "will give to each person according to what he has done."[c] [7]To those who by persistence in doing good seek glory, honor and immortality, he will give eternal life. [8]But for those who are self-seeking and who reject the truth and follow evil, there will be wrath and anger. [9]There will be trouble and distress for every human being who does evil: first for the Jew, then for the Gentile; [10]but glory, honor and peace for

[a]17 Or is from faith to faith   [b]17 Hab. 2:4   [c]6 Psalm 62:12; Prov. 24:12

VERSE FOR THE DAY:
Romans 1:25

AUTHOR:
Carol L. Baldwin

PASSAGE FOR THE DAY:
Romans 1:18–25

From the Created to the Creator

WHICH one of us hasn't looked on a newborn baby with amazement and wondered at the exquisite delicacy of each limb, facial feature, fingernail or eyelash? Especially if that baby is our own, there is always the temptation to think this child is the perfect example of human conception—in spite of the fact that he or she may have no hair, be bright red or be shaped like a little potato!

Even the psalmist agrees that every baby has been "fearfully and wonderfully made" (Psalm 139:14).

From the first moment of awe when we gaze at our newborn children, and then during the hours, days and years that go into caring for them, it is tempting for us to allow these children to become the center of our lives—almost to become objects of our *worship*.

How can we keep ourselves from revolving our whole lives around these precious gifts from the Lord?

The answer is to look up from the intricacy and delicacy of these *creations* to see the one behind the magnificent way they have been knit together—their *Creator*.

Isn't this a part of Paul's warning to us in Romans 1:25? We must avoid the sin of the unbeliever, who sees God's eternal power and divine nature in all of creation, but neither glorifies him nor gives thanks to him (Romans 1:20–21). Unlike unbelievers, we Christians have been given by God new hearts and minds, enabling us to look at the product and praise the Master Craftsman.

It is our responsibility and joy to look at those babies and delight in their perfectly formed tiny hands and feet—and then worship the one who created those parts with infinite wisdom, care and direction.

Additional Scripture Readings:
Psalm 104:24–31; Acts 17:24–27

*Go to page 1231 for your next
devotional reading.*

everyone who does good: first for the Jew, then for the Gentile. [11]For God does not show favoritism.

[12]All who sin apart from the law will also perish apart from the law, and all who sin under the law will be judged by the law. [13]For it is not those who hear the law who are righteous in God's sight, but it is those who obey the law who will be declared righteous. [14](Indeed, when Gentiles, who do not have the law, do by nature things required by the law, they are a law for themselves, even though they do not have the law, [15]since they show that the requirements of the law are written on their hearts, their consciences also bearing witness, and their thoughts now accusing, now even defending them.) [16]This will take place on the day when God will judge men's secrets through Jesus Christ, as my gospel declares.

The Jews and the Law

[17]Now you, if you call yourself a Jew; if you rely on the law and brag about your relationship to God; [18]if you know his will and approve of what is superior because you are instructed by the law; [19]if you are convinced that you are a guide for the blind, a light for those who are in the dark, [20]an instructor of the foolish, a teacher of infants, because you have in the law the embodiment of knowledge and truth— [21]you, then, who teach others, do you not teach yourself? You who preach against stealing, do you steal? [22]You who say that people should not commit adultery, do you commit adultery? You who abhor idols, do you rob temples? [23]You who brag about the law, do you dishonor God by breaking the law? [24]As it is written: "God's name is blasphemed among the Gentiles because of you."[a]

[25]Circumcision has value if you observe the law, but if you break the law, you have become as though you had not been circumcised. [26]If those who are not circumcised keep the law's requirements, will they not be regarded as though they were circumcised? [27]The one who is not circumcised physically and yet obeys the law will condemn you who, even though you have the[b] written code and circumcision, are a lawbreaker.

[28]A man is not a Jew if he is only one outwardly, nor is circumcision merely outward and physical. [29]No, a man is a Jew if he is one inwardly; and circumcision is circumcision of the heart, by the Spirit, not by the written code. Such a man's praise is not from men, but from God.

God's Faithfulness

3 What advantage, then, is there in being a Jew, or what value is there in circumcision? [2]Much in every way! First of all, they have been entrusted with the very words of God.

[3]What if some did not have faith? Will their lack of faith nullify God's faithfulness? [4]Not at all! Let God be true, and every man a liar. As it is written:

"So that you may be proved right
    when you speak
and prevail when you judge."[c]

[5]But if our unrighteousness brings out God's righteousness more clearly, what shall we say? That God is unjust in bringing his wrath on us? (I am using a human argument.) [6]Certainly not! If that were so, how could God judge the world? [7]Someone might argue, "If my falsehood enhances God's truthfulness and so increases his glory, why am I still condemned as a sinner?" [8]Why not say—as we are being slanderously reported as saying and as some claim that we say— "Let us do evil that good may result"? Their condemnation is deserved.

No One Is Righteous

[9]What shall we conclude then? Are we any better[d]? Not at all! We have already made the charge that Jews and Gentiles alike are all under sin. [10]As it is written:

"There is no one righteous, not even
    one;
[11] there is no one who understands,
    no one who seeks God.
[12]All have turned away,
    they have together become
        worthless;
there is no one who does good,
    not even one."[e]
[13]"Their throats are open graves;
    their tongues practice deceit."[f]
"The poison of vipers is on their
    lips."[g]
[14] "Their mouths are full of cursing
    and bitterness."[h]

a24 Isaiah 52:5; Ezek. 36:22   b27 Or who, by means of a   c4 Psalm 51:4   d9 Or worse
e12 Psalms 14:1-3; 53:1-3; Eccles. 7:20   f13 Psalm 5:9   g13 Psalm 140:3   h14 Psalm 10:7

15"Their feet are swift to shed blood;
16 ruin and misery mark their ways,
17and the way of peace they do not
      know."*a*
18 "There is no fear of God before
      their eyes."*b*

19Now we know that whatever the law
says, it says to those who are under the
law, so that every mouth may be silenced
and the whole world held accountable to
God. 20Therefore no one will be declared
righteous in his sight by observing the
law; rather, through the law we become
conscious of sin.

Righteousness Through Faith

21But now a righteousness from God,
apart from law, has been made known, to
which the Law and the Prophets testify.
22This righteousness from God comes
through faith in Jesus Christ to all who
believe. There is no difference, 23for all
have sinned and fall short of the glory of
God, 24and are justified freely by his grace
through the redemption that came by
Christ Jesus. 25God presented him as a
sacrifice of atonement,*c* through faith in
his blood. He did this to demonstrate his
justice, because in his forbearance he had
left the sins committed beforehand unpunished— 26he did it to demonstrate his
justice at the present time, so as to be
just and the one who justifies those who
have faith in Jesus.

27Where, then, is boasting? It is excluded. On what principle? On that of observing the law? No, but on that of faith. 28For
we maintain that a man is justified by
faith apart from observing the law. 29Is
God the God of Jews only? Is he not the
God of Gentiles too? Yes, of Gentiles too,
30since there is only one God, who will
justify the circumcised by faith and the
uncircumcised through that same faith.
31Do we, then, nullify the law by this
faith? Not at all! Rather, we uphold the
law.

Abraham Justified by Faith

4 What then shall we say that Abraham,
   our forefather, discovered in this matter? 2If, in fact, Abraham was justified by
works, he had something to boast about
—but not before God. 3What does the

Scripture say? "Abraham believed God,
and it was credited to him as righteousness."*d*

4Now when a man works, his wages are
not credited to him as a gift, but as an
obligation. 5However, to the man who
does not work but trusts God who justifies the wicked, his faith is credited as
righteousness. 6David says the same thing
when he speaks of the blessedness of the
man to whom God credits righteousness
apart from works:

7"Blessed are they
      whose transgressions are forgiven,
      whose sins are covered.
8Blessed is the man
      whose sin the Lord will never count
      against him."*e*

9Is this blessedness only for the circumcised, or also for the uncircumcised?
We have been saying that Abraham's faith
was credited to him as righteousness.
10Under what circumstances was it credited? Was it after he was circumcised, or
before? It was not after, but before! 11And
he received the sign of circumcision, a
seal of the righteousness that he had by
faith while he was still uncircumcised. So
then, he is the father of all who believe
but have not been circumcised, in order
that righteousness might be credited to
them. 12And he is also the father of the
circumcised who not only are circumcised but who also walk in the footsteps
of the faith that our father Abraham had
before he was circumcised.

13It was not through law that Abraham
and his offspring received the promise
that he would be heir of the world, but
through the righteousness that comes by
faith. 14For if those who live by law are
heirs, faith has no value and the promise
is worthless, 15because law brings wrath.
And where there is no law there is no
transgression.

16Therefore, the promise comes by
faith, so that it may be by grace and may
be guaranteed to all Abraham's offspring
—not only to those who are of the law but
also to those who are of the faith of
Abraham. He is the father of us all. 17As
it is written: "I have made you a father of
many nations."*f* He is our father in the
sight of God, in whom he believed—the
God who gives life to the dead and calls

a17 Isaiah 59:7,8   *b18* Psalm 36:1   *c25* Or *as the one who would turn aside his wrath, taking away
sin*   *d3* Gen. 15:6; also in verse 22   *e8* Psalm 32:1,2   *f17* Gen. 17:5

VERSE FOR THE DAY:	*AUTHOR:*	*PASSAGE FOR THE DAY:*
Romans 3:22	Gladys M. Hunt	Romans 3:9–27

Changed to Fit the Standard

THESE verses tell it like it is. No one is good enough for God. You can't pile up Brownie points and hope they make you acceptable in his sight. The only people who think they can make it on their own are people who have cut God down to their size. The problem is that God is *who he is* and he is perfect holiness. That's the bad news and it's the good news.

How can people like you or me be made right with God? Where do we get the righteousness we need? The good news is that God's kind of righteousness has been made available to us (Romans 3:21) as a free gift (Romans 3:24). It's for anyone who has faith in Jesus Christ (Romans 3:22), which simply means you don't get the gift unless you take it.

God can't pretend sin doesn't exist. He doesn't look at us and make excuses for us. He had to do something about sin to break its power over us. So he sent Jesus and we have been rescued—redeemed—by him (Romans 3:24). Jesus died as a sacrifice to pay sin's penalty (Romans 3:25), and to those who believe and receive his offer, he does a wonderful thing: he justifies us (Romans 3:24).

If you need to be justified, it means something is wrong. You don't match the standard. In justifying us, God takes care of our sin—and then does something even greater—he gives us the righteousness of Jesus Christ. It's like receiving new clothes that fit us and are appropriate for going into the presence of the king. What do we lack? Righteousness. What does Jesus give us? His righteousness. He doesn't change his standard in order to include us. He changes us to fit the standard.

We must take a good look at ourselves. Do we deserve this? No, it is God's grace (Romans 3:24) that brings about this marvelous change in our lives. How should a person respond to such a gift? Receive it thankfully. Remember who you are and whose clothes you are wearing. Remember how you came to belong to Jesus Christ. Share the Good News.

Additional Scripture Readings:
Matthew 22:8–13; Titus 3:3–7

Go to page 1233 for your next devotional reading.

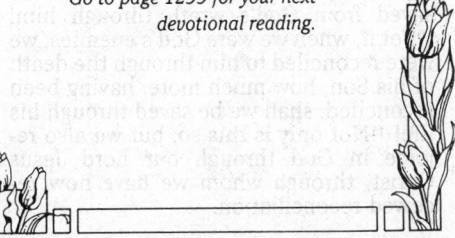

things that are not as though they were.
¹⁸Against all hope, Abraham in hope believed and so became the father of many nations, just as it had been said to him, "So shall your offspring be."ᵃ ¹⁹Without weakening in his faith, he faced the fact that his body was as good as dead—since he was about a hundred years old—and that Sarah's womb was also dead. ²⁰Yet he did not waver through unbelief regarding the promise of God, but was strengthened in his faith and gave glory to God, ²¹being fully persuaded that God had power to do what he had promised. ²²This is why "it was credited to him as righteousness." ²³The words "it was credited to him" were written not for him alone, ²⁴but also for us, to whom God will credit righteousness—for us who believe in him who raised Jesus our Lord from the dead. ²⁵He was delivered over to death for our sins and was raised to life for our justification.

Peace and Joy

5 Therefore, since we have been justified through faith, weᵇ have peace with God through our Lord Jesus Christ, ²through whom we have gained access by faith into this grace in which we now stand. And weᵇ rejoice in the hope of the glory of God. ³Not only so, but weᵇ also rejoice in our sufferings, because we know that suffering produces perseverance; ⁴perseverance, character; and character, hope. ⁵And hope does not disappoint us, because God has poured out his love into our hearts by the Holy Spirit, whom he has given us.

⁶You see, at just the right time, when we were still powerless, Christ died for the ungodly. ⁷Very rarely will anyone die for a righteous man, though for a good man someone might possibly dare to die. ⁸But God demonstrates his own love for us in this: While we were still sinners, Christ died for us.

⁹Since we have now been justified by his blood, how much more shall we be saved from God's wrath through him! ¹⁰For if, when we were God's enemies, we were reconciled to him through the death of his Son, how much more, having been reconciled, shall we be saved through his life! ¹¹Not only is this so, but we also rejoice in God through our Lord Jesus Christ, through whom we have now received reconciliation.

Death Through Adam, Life Through Christ

¹²Therefore, just as sin entered the world through one man, and death through sin, and in this way death came to all men, because all sinned— ¹³for before the law was given, sin was in the world. But sin is not taken into account when there is no law. ¹⁴Nevertheless, death reigned from the time of Adam to the time of Moses, even over those who did not sin by breaking a command, as did Adam, who was a pattern of the one to come.

¹⁵But the gift is not like the trespass. For if the many died by the trespass of the one man, how much more did God's grace and the gift that came by the grace of the one man, Jesus Christ, overflow to the many! ¹⁶Again, the gift of God is not like the result of the one man's sin: The judgment followed one sin and brought condemnation, but the gift followed many trespasses and brought justification. ¹⁷For if, by the trespass of the one man, death reigned through that one man, how much more will those who receive God's abundant provision of grace and of the gift of righteousness reign in life through the one man, Jesus Christ.

¹⁸Consequently, just as the result of one trespass was condemnation for all men, so also the result of one act of righteousness was justification that brings life for all men. ¹⁹For just as through the disobedience of the one man the many were made sinners, so also through the obedience of the one man the many will be made righteous.

²⁰The law was added so that the trespass might increase. But where sin increased, grace increased all the more, ²¹so that, just as sin reigned in death, so also grace might reign through righteousness to bring eternal life through Jesus Christ our Lord.

Dead to Sin, Alive in Christ

6 What shall we say, then? Shall we go on sinning so that grace may increase? ²By no means! We died to sin; how can we live in it any longer? ³Or don't you know that all of us who were baptized into Christ Jesus were baptized into his death? ⁴We were therefore buried with him through baptism into death in order that, just as Christ was raised from the

---

ᵃ18 Gen. 15:5   ᵇ1,2,3 Or let us

VERSE FOR THE DAY:
Romans 5:1

AUTHOR:
Gladys M. Hunt

PASSAGE FOR THE DAY:
Romans 5:1–5

Access to God

BECOMING a Christian has enormous consequences. Relationships are changed; we are given privileges; we look at life differently; our resources are inexhaustible. How do we receive all of this? Paul makes it clear: *through our Lord Jesus Christ* (Romans 5:1).

Our relationships are changed: we have peace *with* God (Romans 5:1). When we are at odds with God, inner peace eludes us. Becoming a Christian necessitates being made right with God, and what a difference it makes! *Peace with God* is enough to sing about.

We are given privileges: we have access by faith into God's very presence (Romans 5:2). Once we knew only hostility; now we are invited into the King's presence. Once we were outside; now we are welcome inside. Access. What are you doing with the privilege of coming into God's presence?

We look at life differently: we can be joyful even when facing the hard things that come into our lives (Romans 5:3). We know life isn't purposeless. God is taking the stuff of our lives and making something good out of it. We are on our way somewhere. God wants to get us ready for heaven. Our joy is real because we know we will one day share the glory of God.

Our resources are inexhaustible: God keeps pouring his love into our hearts (Romans 5:5). He not only makes us feel very loved, but he is so generous in his supply that we have an overflow of love for other people. He gives us the Holy Spirit, who not only transforms our thinking, but makes God's love real to us.

Our trouble begins when we forget these great realities and concentrate on our inadequacies, our fears, and all the other manifestations of our smallness. The proof of God's love is that Jesus Christ died for us. We are no longer shivering outside in the cold with no credentials to come before the King. Jesus has invited us into his very presence and has given us all we need and more besides. This passage in Romans 5 is a renewed invitation to take advantage of your privileges as a daughter of the King.

Additional Scripture Readings:
John 14:6–14; Hebrews 4:14–16

Go to page 1235 for your next devotional reading.

dead through the glory of the Father, we too may live a new life.

5If we have been united with him like this in his death, we will certainly also be united with him in his resurrection. 6For we know that our old self was crucified with him so that the body of sin might be done away with,a that we should no longer be slaves to sin— 7because anyone who has died has been freed from sin.

8Now if we died with Christ, we believe that we will also live with him. 9For we know that since Christ was raised from the dead, he cannot die again; death no longer has mastery over him. 10The death he died, he died to sin once for all; but the life he lives, he lives to God.

11In the same way, count yourselves dead to sin but alive to God in Christ Jesus. 12Therefore do not let sin reign in your mortal body so that you obey its evil desires. 13Do not offer the parts of your body to sin, as instruments of wickedness, but rather offer yourselves to God, as those who have been brought from death to life; and offer the parts of your body to him as instruments of righteousness. 14For sin shall not be your master, because you are not under law, but under grace.

Slaves to Righteousness

15What then? Shall we sin because we are not under law but under grace? By no means! 16Don't you know that when you offer yourselves to someone to obey him as slaves, you are slaves to the one whom you obey—whether you are slaves to sin, which leads to death, or to obedience, which leads to righteousness? 17But thanks be to God that, though you used to be slaves to sin, you wholeheartedly obeyed the form of teaching to which you were entrusted. 18You have been set free from sin and have become slaves to righteousness.

19I put this in human terms because you are weak in your natural selves. Just as you used to offer the parts of your body in slavery to impurity and to ever-increasing wickedness, so now offer them in slavery to righteousness leading to holiness. 20When you were slaves to sin, you were free from the control of righteousness. 21What benefit did you reap at that time from the things you are now ashamed of? Those things result in death! 22But now

that you have been set free from sin and have become slaves to God, the benefit you reap leads to holiness, and the result is eternal life. 23For the wages of sin is death, but the gift of God is eternal life inb Christ Jesus our Lord.

An Illustration From Marriage

7 Do you not know, brothers—for I am speaking to men who know the law— that the law has authority over a man only as long as he lives? 2For example, by law a married woman is bound to her husband as long as he is alive, but if her husband dies, she is released from the law of marriage. 3So then, if she marries another man while her husband is still alive, she is called an adulteress. But if her husband dies, she is released from that law and is not an adulteress, even though she marries another man.

4So, my brothers, you also died to the law through the body of Christ, that you might belong to another, to him who was raised from the dead, in order that we might bear fruit to God. 5For when we were controlled by the sinful nature,c the sinful passions aroused by the law were at work in our bodies, so that we bore fruit for death. 6But now, by dying to what once bound us, we have been released from the law so that we serve in the new way of the Spirit, and not in the old way of the written code.

Struggling With Sin

7What shall we say, then? Is the law sin? Certainly not! Indeed I would not have known what sin was except through the law. For I would not have known what coveting really was if the law had not said, "Do not covet."d 8But sin, seizing the opportunity afforded by the commandment, produced in me every kind of covetous desire. For apart from law, sin is dead. 9Once I was alive apart from law; but when the commandment came, sin sprang to life and I died. 10I found that the very commandment that was intended to bring life actually brought death. 11For sin, seizing the opportunity afforded by the commandment, deceived me, and through the commandment put me to death. 12So then, the law is holy, and the commandment is holy, righteous and good.

---

a6 Or be rendered powerless   b23 Or through   c5 Or the flesh; also in verse 25   d7 Exodus 20:17; Deut. 5:21

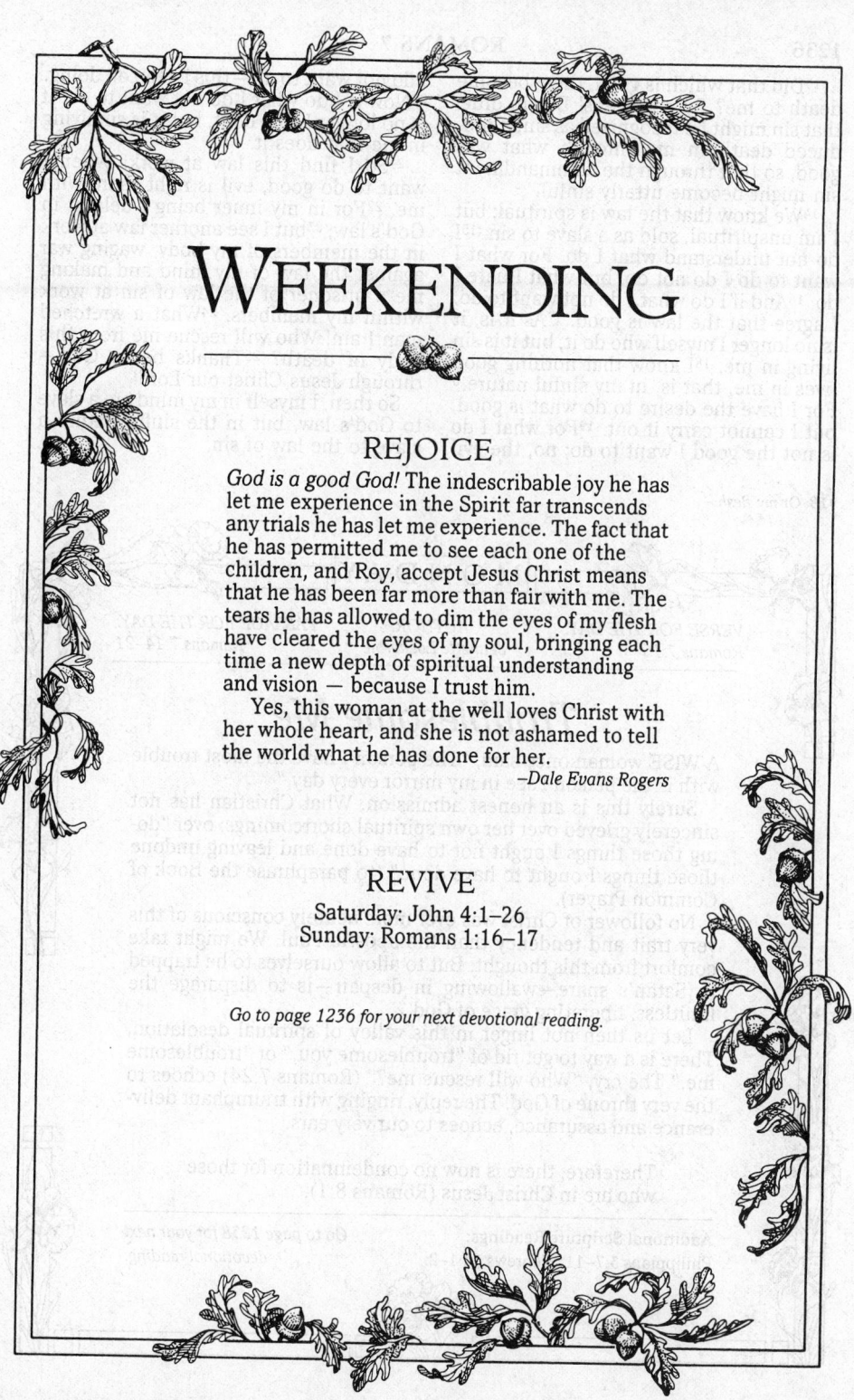

WEEKENDING

REJOICE

God is a good God! The indescribable joy he has
let me experience in the Spirit far transcends
any trials he has let me experience. The fact that
he has permitted me to see each one of the
children, and Roy, accept Jesus Christ means
that he has been far more than fair with me. The
tears he has allowed to dim the eyes of my flesh
have cleared the eyes of my soul, bringing each
time a new depth of spiritual understanding
and vision — because I trust him.

Yes, this woman at the well loves Christ with
her whole heart, and she is not ashamed to tell
the world what he has done for her.

–Dale Evans Rogers

REVIVE

Saturday: John 4:1–26
Sunday: Romans 1:16–17

Go to page 1236 for your next devotional reading.

¹³Did that which is good, then, become death to me? By no means! But in order that sin might be recognized as sin, it produced death in me through what was good, so that through the commandment sin might become utterly sinful.

¹⁴We know that the law is spiritual; but I am unspiritual, sold as a slave to sin. ¹⁵I do not understand what I do. For what I want to do I do not do, but what I hate I do. ¹⁶And if I do what I do not want to do, I agree that the law is good. ¹⁷As it is, it is no longer I myself who do it, but it is sin living in me. ¹⁸I know that nothing good lives in me, that is, in my sinful nature.ᵃ For I have the desire to do what is good, but I cannot carry it out. ¹⁹For what I do is not the good I want to do; no, the evil I do not want to do—this I keep on doing. ²⁰Now if I do what I do not want to do, it is no longer I who do it, but it is sin living in me that does it.

²¹So I find this law at work: When I want to do good, evil is right there with me. ²²For in my inner being I delight in God's law; ²³but I see another law at work in the members of my body, waging war against the law of my mind and making me a prisoner of the law of sin at work within my members. ²⁴What a wretched man I am! Who will rescue me from this body of death? ²⁵Thanks be to God— through Jesus Christ our Lord!

So then, I myself in my mind am a slave to God's law, but in the sinful nature a slave to the law of sin.

ᵃ18 Or *my flesh*

MONDAY

VERSE FOR THE DAY:
Romans 7:15

AUTHOR:
Jeanette Lockerbie

PASSAGE FOR THE DAY:
Romans 7:14–21

Troublesome Me

A WISE woman once said, "The person I have the most trouble with is the person I see in my mirror every day."

Surely this is an honest admission. What Christian has not sincerely grieved over her own spiritual shortcomings: over "doing those things I ought not to have done and leaving undone those things I ought to have done" (to paraphrase the Book of Common Prayer).

No follower of Christ was ever more acutely conscious of this very trait and tendency than the apostle Paul. We might take comfort from this thought. But to allow ourselves to be trapped in Satan's snare—wallowing in despair—is to disparage the limitless, liberating grace of God.

Let us then not linger in this valley of spiritual desolation. There is a way to get rid of "troublesome you," or "troublesome me." The cry, "Who will rescue me?" (Romans 7:24) echoes to the very throne of God. The reply, ringing with triumphant deliverance and assurance, echoes to our very ears.

Therefore, there is now no condemnation for those who are in Christ Jesus (Romans 8:1).

Additional Scripture Readings:
Philippians 3:7–11; Hebrews 12:1–2

Go to page 1238 for your next devotional reading.

Life Through the Spirit

8 Therefore, there is now no condemnation for those who are in Christ Jesus,^{a} ²because through Christ Jesus the law of the Spirit of life set me free from the law of sin and death. ³For what the law was powerless to do in that it was weakened by the sinful nature,^{b} God did by sending his own Son in the likeness of sinful man to be a sin offering.^{c} And so he condemned sin in sinful man,^{d} ⁴in order that the righteous requirements of the law might be fully met in us, who do not live according to the sinful nature but according to the Spirit.

⁵Those who live according to the sinful nature have their minds set on what that nature desires; but those who live in accordance with the Spirit have their minds set on what the Spirit desires. ⁶The mind of sinful man^e is death, but the mind controlled by the Spirit is life and peace; ⁷the sinful mind^f is hostile to God. It does not submit to God's law, nor can it do so. ⁸Those controlled by the sinful nature cannot please God.

⁹You, however, are controlled not by the sinful nature but by the Spirit, if the Spirit of God lives in you. And if anyone does not have the Spirit of Christ, he does not belong to Christ. ¹⁰But if Christ is in you, your body is dead because of sin, yet your spirit is alive because of righteousness. ¹¹And if the Spirit of him who raised Jesus from the dead is living in you, he who raised Christ from the dead will also give life to your mortal bodies through his Spirit, who lives in you.

¹²Therefore, brothers, we have an obligation—but it is not to the sinful nature, to live according to it. ¹³For if you live according to the sinful nature, you will die; but if by the Spirit you put to death the misdeeds of the body, you will live, ¹⁴because those who are led by the Spirit of God are sons of God. ¹⁵For you did not receive a spirit that makes you a slave again to fear, but you received the Spirit of sonship.^{g} And by him we cry, *"Abba,^{h} Father."* ¹⁶The Spirit himself testifies with our spirit that we are God's children. ¹⁷Now if we are children, then we are heirs—heirs of God and co-heirs with Christ, if indeed we share in his sufferings in order that we may also share in his glory.

Future Glory

¹⁸I consider that our present sufferings are not worth comparing with the glory that will be revealed in us. ¹⁹The creation waits in eager expectation for the sons of God to be revealed. ²⁰For the creation was subjected to frustration, not by its own choice, but by the will of the one who subjected it, in hope ²¹that^i the creation itself will be liberated from its bondage to decay and brought into the glorious freedom of the children of God.

²²We know that the whole creation has been groaning as in the pains of childbirth right up to the present time. ²³Not only so, but we ourselves, who have the firstfruits of the Spirit, groan inwardly as we wait eagerly for our adoption as sons, the redemption of our bodies. ²⁴For in this hope we were saved. But hope that is seen is no hope at all. Who hopes for what he already has? ²⁵But if we hope for what we do not yet have, we wait for it patiently.

²⁶In the same way, the Spirit helps us in our weakness. We do not know what we ought to pray for, but the Spirit himself intercedes for us with groans that words cannot express. ²⁷And he who searches our hearts knows the mind of the Spirit, because the Spirit intercedes for the saints in accordance with God's will.

More Than Conquerors

²⁸And we know that in all things God works for the good of those who love him,^{j} who^k have been called according to his purpose. ²⁹For those God foreknew he also predestined to be conformed to the likeness of his Son, that he might be the firstborn among many brothers. ³⁰And those he predestined, he also called; those he called, he also justified; those he justified, he also glorified.

³¹What, then, shall we say in response to this? If God is for us, who can be against us? ³²He who did not spare his own Son, but gave him up for us all—how will he not also, along with him, graciously give us all things? ³³Who will bring any

---

$^a1$ Some later manuscripts *Jesus, who do not live according to the sinful nature but according to the Spirit,*
$^b3$ Or *the flesh*; also in verses 4, 5, 8, 9, 12 and 13 $^c3$ Or *man, for sin* $^d3$ Or *in the flesh* $^e6$ Or *mind set on the flesh* $^f7$ Or *the mind set on the flesh* $^g15$ Or *adoption* $^h15$ Aramaic for *Father*
$^i20,21$ Or *subjected it in hope.* ^{21}*For* $^j28$ Some manuscripts *And we know that all things work together for good to those who love God* $^k28$ Or *works together with those who love him to bring about what is good—with those who*

VERSE FOR THE DAY:
Romans 8:26–27

AUTHOR:
Sue Richards

PASSAGE FOR THE DAY:
Romans 8:18–27

When It Hurts So Much . . .

THERE are times in the lives of all God's children when we are called on to suffer. We read in Romans 5:3–4 that "suffering produces perseverance; perseverance, character; and character, hope." For me suffering has also produced times of physical and emotional weakness. After the death of my first child, as I lay near death myself, I tried to pray, but I was in shock and heavily medicated. No words would come into my mind or to my lips. I wish I had known Romans 8:26–27 then. Yet, although I could not speak, I felt in close communication with the Lord. I just didn't understand how this was possible.

While believers are sustained in their suffering by hope, we also are sustained in our weakness in the most special way of all:

> The Spirit helps us in our weakness. We do not know what we ought to pray for, but the Spirit himself intercedes for us with groans that words cannot express. And he who searches our hearts knows the mind of the Spirit, because the Spirit intercedes for the saints in accordance with God's will (Romans 8:26–27).

God himself, who dwells within us in the person of the Holy Spirit, intercedes for us in our weakness. Not with flowery or powerful words, but with groans that words cannot express. How empowering in our weakest moments, when we don't know how to express our own overwhelming needs, to cling to the words of God.

"The Spirit himself intercedes for us with groans that words cannot express." And all of this intercession on our behalf is done "in accordance with God's will" for us personally. When Christ gave us the Holy Spirit, he left us much more than an inner spiritual discernment. Our triune God lives within and intercedes for each of us when we are in our weakest moments.

Abba, Father, your love and concern for me when I am at my most vulnerable times in life is beyond my understanding. I thank you for the gracious gift of your Holy Spirit. Amen.

Additional Scripture Readings:
John 14:26–27; Ephesians 6:17–18

Go to page 1240 for your next devotional reading.

charge against those whom God has chosen? It is God who justifies. ³⁴Who is he that condemns? Christ Jesus, who died—more than that, who was raised to life—is at the right hand of God and is also interceding for us. ³⁵Who shall separate us from the love of Christ? Shall trouble or hardship or persecution or famine or nakedness or danger or sword? ³⁶As it is written:

"For your sake we face death all day
　　long;
　we are considered as sheep to be
　　slaughtered."ᵃ

³⁷No, in all these things we are more than conquerors through him who loved us. ³⁸For I am convinced that neither death nor life, neither angels nor demons,ᵇ neither the present nor the future, nor any powers, ³⁹neither height nor depth, nor anything else in all creation, will be able to separate us from the love of God that is in Christ Jesus our Lord.

God's Sovereign Choice

9 I speak the truth in Christ—I am not lying, my conscience confirms it in the Holy Spirit— ²I have great sorrow and unceasing anguish in my heart. ³For I could wish that I myself were cursed and cut off from Christ for the sake of my brothers, those of my own race, ⁴the people of Israel. Theirs is the adoption as sons; theirs the divine glory, the covenants, the receiving of the law, the temple worship and the promises. ⁵Theirs are the patriarchs, and from them is traced the human ancestry of Christ, who is God over all, forever praised!ᶜ Amen.

⁶It is not as though God's word had failed. For not all who are descended from Israel are Israel. ⁷Nor because they are his descendants are they all Abraham's children. On the contrary, "It is through Isaac that your offspring will be reckoned."ᵈ ⁸In other words, it is not the natural children who are God's children, but it is the children of the promise who are regarded as Abraham's offspring. ⁹For this was how the promise was stated: "At the appointed time I will return, and Sarah will have a son."ᵉ

¹⁰Not only that, but Rebekah's children had one and the same father, our father Isaac. ¹¹Yet, before the twins were born or had done anything good or bad—in order that God's purpose in election might stand: ¹²not by works but by him who calls—she was told, "The older will serve the younger."ᶠ ¹³Just as it is written: "Jacob I loved, but Esau I hated."ᵍ

¹⁴What then shall we say? Is God unjust? Not at all! ¹⁵For he says to Moses,

"I will have mercy on whom I have
　　mercy,
　and I will have compassion on
　　whom I have compassion."ʰ

¹⁶It does not, therefore, depend on man's desire or effort, but on God's mercy. ¹⁷For the Scripture says to Pharaoh: "I raised you up for this very purpose, that I might display my power in you and that my name might be proclaimed in all the earth."ⁱ ¹⁸Therefore God has mercy on whom he wants to have mercy, and he hardens whom he wants to harden.

¹⁹One of you will say to me: "Then why does God still blame us? For who resists his will?" ²⁰But who are you, O man, to talk back to God? "Shall what is formed say to him who formed it, 'Why did you make me like this?'"ʲ ²¹Does not the potter have the right to make out of the same lump of clay some pottery for noble purposes and some for common use?

²²What if God, choosing to show his wrath and make his power known, bore with great patience the objects of his wrath—prepared for destruction? ²³What if he did this to make the riches of his glory known to the objects of his mercy, whom he prepared in advance for glory— ²⁴even us, whom he also called, not only from the Jews but also from the Gentiles? ²⁵As he says in Hosea:

"I will call them 'my people' who are
　　not my people;
　and I will call her 'my loved one'
　　who is not my loved one,"ᵏ

²⁶and,

"It will happen that in the very place
　　where it was said to them,
　'You are not my people,'
　they will be called 'sons of the living
　　God.'"ˡ

²⁷Isaiah cries out concerning Israel:

ᵃ36 Psalm 44:22　　ᵇ38 Or nor heavenly rulers　　ᶜ5 Or Christ, who is over all. God be forever praised!
Or Christ. God who is over all be forever praised!　　ᵈ7 Gen. 21:12　　ᵉ9 Gen. 18:10,14
ᶠ12 Gen. 25:23　　ᵍ13 Mal. 1:2,3　　ʰ15 Exodus 33:19　　ⁱ17 Exodus 9:16　　ʲ20 Isaiah 29:16; 45:9
ᵏ25 Hosea 2:23　　ˡ26 Hosea 1:10

"Though the number of the Israelites
   be like the sand by the sea,
only the remnant will be saved.
[28] For the Lord will carry out
   his sentence on earth with speed
   and finality."[a]

[29] It is just as Isaiah said previously:

"Unless the Lord Almighty
   had left us descendants,

[a] 28 Isaiah 10:22,23   [b] 29 Isaiah 1:9

we would have become like Sodom,
   we would have been like
   Gomorrah."[b]

Israel's Unbelief

[30] What then shall we say? That the
Gentiles, who did not pursue righteousness, have obtained it, a righteousness
that is by faith; [31] but Israel, who pursued
a law of righteousness, has not attained

VERSE FOR THE DAY:
Romans 8:28

AUTHOR:
ann kiemel anderson

PASSAGE FOR THE DAY:
Romans 8:28–39

all things . . .

ROMANS 8:28 is engraved in my wedding band. it was the
theme at my house as a child. my father, a preacher, clung to
these words because they were a PROMISE from a Sovereign
God with a PERFECT track record.

"in ALL things God works for the good" (caps mine). the rejection in one's childhood. alcoholic parents. the birth of a
handicapped child. a husband leaving home for another
woman. illness. no matter what life may have in store . . . absolutely ANYTHING . . . will turn into blessing if we love God.

i was 35 and will 38 when we married. both for the first time.
we decided to try for a baby our first year. but i found i had a tendency to miscarry. to work with singleminded concentration to
get pregnant and then be disappointed over and over. without
romans 8:28 becoming my best friend, i would have been
sucked under. i had been taught to UTTERLY trust God's Word.
this verse had been stamped across my forehead and my heart.

it means God never takes away except to give us back something better. it means we must be brave enough and determined
enough to wait . . . because it often takes God time to turn a
painful situation to good. it means we can embrace our pain and
not resent it because a blessing is coming!

today will and i stand in awe over four little boys . . . age four
and under . . . God gave us through adoption. and we would be
so shallow and careless with our love had we not traveled that
black, seemingly hopeless, journey.

i love you. i run this glorious, hard race beside you. because of
Jesus, everything . . . anything . . . will work for good as you love
God.

Additional Scripture Readings:
Proverbs 19:21; Isaiah 55:8–11

*Go to page 1243 for your next
devotional reading.*

it. ³²Why not? Because they pursued it not by faith but as if it were by works. They stumbled over the "stumbling stone." ³³As it is written:

"See, I lay in Zion a stone that causes
    men to stumble
and a rock that makes them fall,
and the one who trusts in him will
    never be put to shame."ᵃ

10 Brothers, my heart's desire and prayer to God for the Israelites is that they may be saved. ²For I can testify about them that they are zealous for God, but their zeal is not based on knowledge. ³Since they did not know the righteousness that comes from God and sought to establish their own, they did not submit to God's righteousness. ⁴Christ is the end of the law so that there may be righteousness for everyone who believes.

⁵Moses describes in this way the righteousness that is by the law: "The man who does these things will live by them."ᵇ ⁶But the righteousness that is by faith says: "Do not say in your heart, 'Who will ascend into heaven?'ᶜ" (that is, to bring Christ down) ⁷"or 'Who will descend into the deep?'ᵈ" (that is, to bring Christ up from the dead). ⁸But what does it say? "The word is near you; it is in your mouth and in your heart,"ᵉ that is, the word of faith we are proclaiming: ⁹That if you confess with your mouth, "Jesus is Lord," and believe in your heart that God raised him from the dead, you will be saved. ¹⁰For it is with your heart that you believe and are justified, and it is with your mouth that you confess and are saved. ¹¹As the Scripture says, "Anyone who trusts in him will never be put to shame."ᶠ ¹²For there is no difference between Jew and Gentile—the same Lord is Lord of all and richly blesses all who call on him, ¹³for, "Everyone who calls on the name of the Lord will be saved."ᵍ

¹⁴How, then, can they call on the one they have not believed in? And how can they believe in the one of whom they have not heard? And how can they hear without someone preaching to them? ¹⁵And how can they preach unless they are sent? As it is written, "How beautiful are the feet of those who bring good news!"ʰ

¹⁶But not all the Israelites accepted the good news. For Isaiah says, "Lord, who has believed our message?"ⁱ ¹⁷Consequently, faith comes from hearing the message, and the message is heard through the word of Christ. ¹⁸But I ask: Did they not hear? Of course they did:

"Their voice has gone out into all the
    earth,
    their words to the ends of the
    world."ʲ

¹⁹Again I ask: Did Israel not understand? First, Moses says,

"I will make you envious by those
    who are not a nation;
I will make you angry by a nation
    that has no understanding."ᵏ

²⁰And Isaiah boldly says,

"I was found by those who did not
    seek me;
I revealed myself to those who did
    not ask for me."ˡ

²¹But concerning Israel he says,

"All day long I have held out my
    hands
to a disobedient and obstinate
    people."ᵐ

The Remnant of Israel

11 I ask then: Did God reject his people? By no means! I am an Israelite myself, a descendant of Abraham, from the tribe of Benjamin. ²God did not reject his people, whom he foreknew. Don't you know what the Scripture says in the passage about Elijah—how he appealed to God against Israel: ³"Lord, they have killed your prophets and torn down your altars; I am the only one left, and they are trying to kill me"ⁿ? ⁴And what was God's answer to him? "I have reserved for myself seven thousand who have not bowed the knee to Baal."ᵒ ⁵So too, at the present time there is a remnant chosen by grace. ⁶And if by grace, then it is no longer by works; if it were, grace would no longer be grace.ᵖ

⁷What then? What Israel sought so earnestly it did not obtain, but the elect did. The others were hardened, ⁸as it is written:

ᵃ33 Isaiah 8:14; 28:16   ᵇ5 Lev. 18:5   ᶜ6 Deut. 30:12   ᵈ7 Deut. 30:13   ᵉ8 Deut. 30:14
ᶠ11 Isaiah 28:16   ᵍ13 Joel 2:32   ʰ15 Isaiah 52:7   ⁱ16 Isaiah 53:1   ʲ18 Psalm 19:4
ᵏ19 Deut. 32:21   ˡ20 Isaiah 65:1   ᵐ21 Isaiah 65:2   ⁿ3 1 Kings 19:10,14   ᵒ4 1 Kings 19:18
ᵖ6 Some manuscripts by grace. But if by works, then it is no longer grace; if it were, work would no longer be work.

"God gave them a spirit of stupor,
eyes so that they could not see
and ears so that they could not
hear,
to this very day."[a]

⁹And David says:

"May their table become a snare and
a trap,
a stumbling block and a retribution
for them.
¹⁰May their eyes be darkened so they
cannot see,
and their backs be bent forever."[b]

Ingrafted Branches

¹¹Again I ask: Did they stumble so as to fall beyond recovery? Not at all! Rather, because of their transgression, salvation has come to the Gentiles to make Israel envious. ¹²But if their transgression means riches for the world, and their loss means riches for the Gentiles, how much greater riches will their fullness bring!

¹³I am talking to you Gentiles. Inasmuch as I am the apostle to the Gentiles, I make much of my ministry ¹⁴in the hope that I may somehow arouse my own people to envy and save some of them. ¹⁵For if their rejection is the reconciliation of the world, what will their acceptance be but life from the dead? ¹⁶If the part of the dough offered as firstfruits is holy, then the whole batch is holy; if the root is holy, so are the branches.

¹⁷If some of the branches have been broken off, and you, though a wild olive shoot, have been grafted in among the others and now share in the nourishing sap from the olive root, ¹⁸do not boast over those branches. If you do, consider this: You do not support the root, but the root supports you. ¹⁹You will say then, "Branches were broken off so that I could be grafted in." ²⁰Granted. But they were broken off because of unbelief, and you stand by faith. Do not be arrogant, but be afraid. ²¹For if God did not spare the natural branches, he will not spare you either.

²²Consider therefore the kindness and sternness of God: sternness to those who fell, but kindness to you, provided that you continue in his kindness. Otherwise, you also will be cut off. ²³And if they do not persist in unbelief, they will be graft-

ed in, for God is able to graft them in again. ²⁴After all, if you were cut out of an olive tree that is wild by nature, and contrary to nature were grafted into a cultivated olive tree, how much more readily will these, the natural branches, be grafted into their own olive tree!

All Israel Will Be Saved

²⁵I do not want you to be ignorant of this mystery, brothers, so that you may not be conceited: Israel has experienced a hardening in part until the full number of the Gentiles has come in. ²⁶And so all Israel will be saved, as it is written:

"The deliverer will come from Zion;
he will turn godlessness away from
Jacob.
²⁷And this is[c] my covenant with them
when I take away their sins."[d]

²⁸As far as the gospel is concerned, they are enemies on your account; but as far as election is concerned, they are loved on account of the patriarchs, ²⁹for God's gifts and his call are irrevocable. ³⁰Just as you who were at one time disobedient to God have now received mercy as a result of their disobedience, ³¹so they too have now become disobedient in order that they too may now[e] receive mercy as a result of God's mercy to you. ³²For God has bound all men over to disobedience so that he may have mercy on them all.

Doxology

³³Oh, the depth of the riches of the
wisdom and[f] knowledge of
God!
How unsearchable his judgments,
and his paths beyond tracing out!
³⁴"Who has known the mind of the
Lord?
Or who has been his counselor?"[g]
³⁵"Who has ever given to God,
that God should repay him?"[h]
³⁶For from him and through him and to
him are all things.
To him be the glory forever! Amen.

Living Sacrifices

12 Therefore, I urge you, brothers, in view of God's mercy, to offer your bodies as living sacrifices, holy and pleasing to God—this is your spiritual[i] act of worship. ²Do not conform any longer to

---

[a]8 Deut. 29:4; Isaiah 29:10   [b]10 Psalm 69:22,23   [c]27 Or will be   [d]27 Isaiah 59:20,21; 27:9;
Jer. 31:33,34   [e]31 Some manuscripts do not have now.   [f]33 Or riches and the wisdom and the
[g]34 Isaiah 40:13   [h]35 Job 41:11   [i]1 Or reasonable

VERSE FOR THE DAY:
Romans 12:1–2

AUTHOR:
Marie Chapian

PASSAGE FOR THE DAY:
Romans 12:1–8

Living Sacrifices

IT is a challenge to live our lives as sacrifices to God. When we do, we aren't the masters of our bodies and minds—God is. All that we do or think must conform to the Word of God. Such a high calling is impossible without the Holy Spirit's guidance and help. We cannot make spiritual progress without the Holy Spirit, and that is why in Romans 12:1 the Lord tells us to offer our bodies to him as living sacrifices. If we try to grow and change spiritually without the supernatural empowering of the Holy Spirit, we are conforming to the pattern of the world. The Lord tells us to avoid this by becoming transformed by the renewing of our minds (Romans 12:1–2).

As a sacrificial act of worship, God expects us to be holy and pleasing to him. When I was sharing Romans 12 with a group of young people, one fifteen-year-old girl asked, "Does that mean that everything I do every day—at school, at home, in sports, in art and with friends—all these should be an act of worship to God?"

Another student replied, "How can I stay on my knees that long?"

We chuckled, knowing that we worship not only on our knees but also as we live our lives. Our everyday lives are important to God, important enough that he sent his Son to die on the cross so that Jesus could live in us through each day—including the ordinary ones.

We can now say: "I'm going to school to worship God." "I'm going to paint a picture to worship God." "I'm going to clean the kitchen to worship God." "I'm going to my job to worship God," as well as "I'm going to church to worship God."

When we conform to the world's patterns and methods, we do not please God, no matter how good we feel about ourselves or how much other people approve of us. But we do please God when our minds are renewed. Then we are able to test and approve God's perfect will (Romans 12:2).

Additional Scripture Readings:
Ephesians 4:22–24; 1 Peter 1:13–16

Go to page 1245 for your next devotional reading.

the pattern of this world, but be transformed by the renewing of your mind. Then you will be able to test and approve what God's will is—his good, pleasing and perfect will.

³For by the grace given me I say to every one of you: Do not think of yourself more highly than you ought, but rather think of yourself with sober judgment, in accordance with the measure of faith God has given you. ⁴Just as each of us has one body with many members, and these members do not all have the same function, ⁵so in Christ we who are many form one body, and each member belongs to all the others. ⁶We have different gifts, according to the grace given us. If a man's gift is prophesying, let him use it in proportion to his*a* faith. ⁷If it is serving, let him serve; if it is teaching, let him teach; ⁸if it is encouraging, let him encourage; if it is contributing to the needs of others, let him give generously; if it is leadership, let him govern diligently; if it is showing mercy, let him do it cheerfully.

Love

⁹Love must be sincere. Hate what is evil; cling to what is good. ¹⁰Be devoted to one another in brotherly love. Honor one another above yourselves. ¹¹Never be lacking in zeal, but keep your spiritual fervor, serving the Lord. ¹²Be joyful in hope, patient in affliction, faithful in prayer. ¹³Share with God's people who are in need. Practice hospitality.

¹⁴Bless those who persecute you; bless and do not curse. ¹⁵Rejoice with those who rejoice; mourn with those who mourn. ¹⁶Live in harmony with one another. Do not be proud, but be willing to associate with people of low position.*b* Do not be conceited.

¹⁷Do not repay anyone evil for evil. Be careful to do what is right in the eyes of everybody. ¹⁸If it is possible, as far as it depends on you, live at peace with everyone. ¹⁹Do not take revenge, my friends, but leave room for God's wrath, for it is written: "It is mine to avenge; I will repay,"*c* says the Lord. ²⁰On the contrary:

"If your enemy is hungry, feed him;
    if he is thirsty, give him something
        to drink.
In doing this, you will heap burning
    coals on his head."*d*

²¹Do not be overcome by evil, but overcome evil with good.

Submission to the Authorities

13 Everyone must submit himself to the governing authorities, for there is no authority except that which God has established. The authorities that exist have been established by God. ²Consequently, he who rebels against the authority is rebelling against what God has instituted, and those who do so will bring judgment on themselves. ³For rulers hold no terror for those who do right, but for those who do wrong. Do you want to be free from fear of the one in authority? Then do what is right and he will commend you. ⁴For he is God's servant to do you good. But if you do wrong, be afraid, for he does not bear the sword for nothing. He is God's servant, an agent of wrath to bring punishment on the wrongdoer. ⁵Therefore, it is necessary to submit to the authorities, not only because of possible punishment but also because of conscience.

⁶This is also why you pay taxes, for the authorities are God's servants, who give their full time to governing. ⁷Give everyone what you owe him: If you owe taxes, pay taxes; if revenue, then revenue; if respect, then respect; if honor, then honor.

Love, for the Day Is Near

⁸Let no debt remain outstanding, except the continuing debt to love one another, for he who loves his fellowman has fulfilled the law. ⁹The commandments, "Do not commit adultery," "Do not murder," "Do not steal," "Do not covet,"*e* and whatever other commandment there may be, are summed up in this one rule: "Love your neighbor as yourself."*f* ¹⁰Love does no harm to its neighbor. Therefore love is the fulfillment of the law.

¹¹And do this, understanding the present time. The hour has come for you to wake up from your slumber, because our salvation is nearer now than when we first believed. ¹²The night is nearly over; the day is almost here. So let us put aside the deeds of darkness and put on the armor of light. ¹³Let us behave decently, as in the daytime, not in orgies and drunkenness, not in sexual immorality and debauchery, not in dissension and jealousy. ¹⁴Rather,

a6 Or in agreement with the   b16 Or willing to do menial work   c19 Deut. 32:35   d20 Prov. 25:21,22   e9 Exodus 20:13-15,17; Deut. 5:17-19,21   f9 Lev. 19:18

FRIDAY

VERSE FOR THE DAY:
Romans 12:11,16

AUTHOR:
Gigi Graham Tchividjian

PASSAGE FOR THE DAY:
Romans 12:9–21

Even This?

THOUGH early morning is not my best time of day, after a couple of cups of coffee, I managed to fix breakfast, wash the dishes, and usher six children out the door to school before heading for the laundry room.

I stopped abruptly at the door and stood gazing in disbelief at the mountain of dirty clothes. Hadn't I just washed three loads yesterday? Sudden tears of frustration stung my eyes. I quickly brushed them away, a bit ashamed of myself, and put the first load in the washer.

Then I continued to tidy up, picking up the morning newspaper and various cups and glasses left from snacks the night before. Soon I found myself in my son's bathroom, scrubbing the tub. Once again the tears insisted on imposing themselves against my will. This time they found little resistance. I was frustrated and discouraged, and my self-esteem was about as low as it could get.

It was still morning, but I was tired—tired of the same mess day after day—of washing clothes that only yesterday I had folded and returned to their proper places; of doing the dishes, only to get them out a short time later to reset the table. I was sick of spending hours cooking a meal that was consumed in minutes.

Sitting in the middle of the bathroom floor, sponge and cleanser in hand and tears streaming down my cheeks, I found myself fussing, crying and praying all at the same time.

God in his loving-kindness came to meet me: "I tell you the truth, whatever you did for one of the least of these brothers of mine, you did for me" (Matthew 25:40).

"Lord, even this?" I asked.

"Especially this," he replied. "Who else is going to do it for me? In all these small ways, you are serving me."

Lovingly reassured and encouraged, I dried my tears and continued to scrub the tub.

Additional Scripture Readings:
Matthew 11:28–30; Philippians 2:1–8

Go to page 1247 for your next devotional reading.

clothe yourselves with the Lord Jesus Christ, and do not think about how to gratify the desires of the sinful nature.*

The Weak and the Strong

14 Accept him whose faith is weak, without passing judgment on disputable matters. ²One man's faith allows him to eat everything, but another man, whose faith is weak, eats only vegetables. ³The man who eats everything must not look down on him who does not, and the man who does not eat everything must not condemn the man who does, for God has accepted him. ⁴Who are you to judge someone else's servant? To his own master he stands or falls. And he will stand, for the Lord is able to make him stand.

⁵One man considers one day more sacred than another; another man considers every day alike. Each one should be fully convinced in his own mind. ⁶He who regards one day as special, does so to the Lord. He who eats meat, eats to the Lord, for he gives thanks to God; and he who abstains, does so to the Lord and gives thanks to God. ⁷For none of us lives to himself alone and none of us dies to himself alone. ⁸If we live, we live to the Lord; and if we die, we die to the Lord. So, whether we live or die, we belong to the Lord.

⁹For this very reason, Christ died and returned to life so that he might be the Lord of both the dead and the living. ¹⁰You, then, why do you judge your brother? Or why do you look down on your brother? For we will all stand before God's judgment seat. ¹¹It is written:

" 'As surely as I live,' says the Lord,
'every knee will bow before me;
   every tongue will confess to
      God.' "*b*

¹²So then, each of us will give an account of himself to God.

¹³Therefore let us stop passing judgment on one another. Instead, make up your mind not to put any stumbling block or obstacle in your brother's way. ¹⁴As one who is in the Lord Jesus, I am fully convinced that no food*c* is unclean in itself. But if anyone regards something as unclean, then for him it is unclean. ¹⁵If your brother is distressed because of what you eat, you are no longer acting in love. Do not by your eating destroy your broth-

er for whom Christ died. ¹⁶Do not allow what you consider good to be spoken of as evil. ¹⁷For the kingdom of God is not a matter of eating and drinking, but of righteousness, peace and joy in the Holy Spirit, ¹⁸because anyone who serves Christ in this way is pleasing to God and approved by men.

¹⁹Let us therefore make every effort to do what leads to peace and to mutual edification. ²⁰Do not destroy the work of God for the sake of food. All food is clean, but it is wrong for a man to eat anything that causes someone else to stumble. ²¹It is better not to eat meat or drink wine or to do anything else that will cause your brother to fall.

²²So whatever you believe about these things keep between yourself and God. Blessed is the man who does not condemn himself by what he approves. ²³But the man who has doubts is condemned if he eats, because his eating is not from faith; and everything that does not come from faith is sin.

15 We who are strong ought to bear with the failings of the weak and not to please ourselves. ²Each of us should please his neighbor for his good, to build him up. ³For even Christ did not please himself but, as it is written: "The insults of those who insult you have fallen on me."*d* ⁴For everything that was written in the past was written to teach us, so that through endurance and the encouragement of the Scriptures we might have hope.

⁵May the God who gives endurance and encouragement give you a spirit of unity among yourselves as you follow Christ Jesus, ⁶so that with one heart and mouth you may glorify the God and Father of our Lord Jesus Christ.

⁷Accept one another, then, just as Christ accepted you, in order to bring praise to God. ⁸For I tell you that Christ has become a servant of the Jews*e* on behalf of God's truth, to confirm the promises made to the patriarchs ⁹so that the Gentiles may glorify God for his mercy, as it is written:

"Therefore I will praise you among
      the Gentiles;
   I will sing hymns to your name."*f*

¹⁰Again, it says,

---

a14 Or *the flesh*   *b11* Isaiah 45:23   *c14* Or *that nothing*   *d3* Psalm 69:9   *e8* Greek *circumcision*   *f9* 2 Samuel 22:50; Psalm 18:49

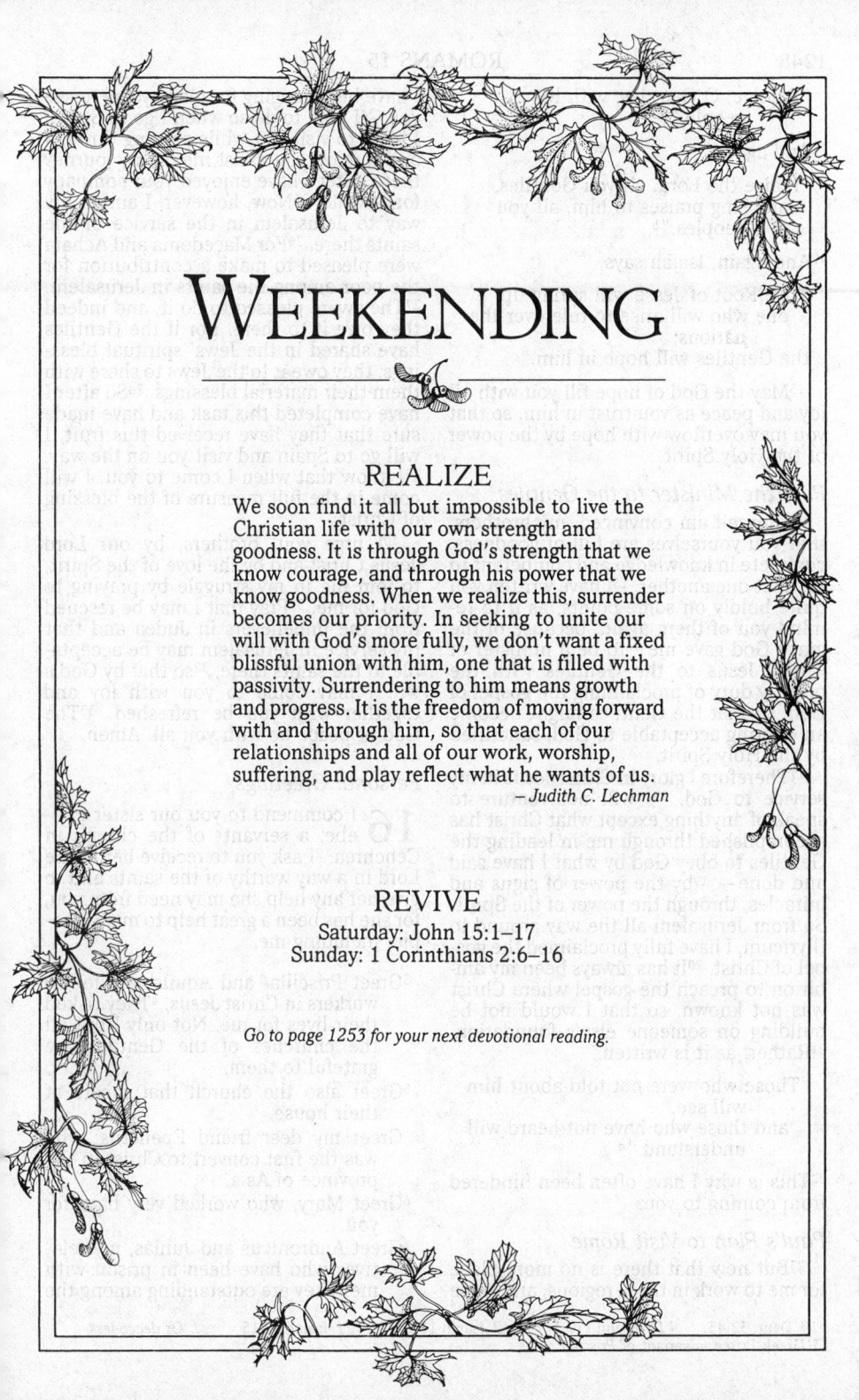

WEEKENDING

REALIZE

We soon find it all but impossible to live the
Christian life with our own strength and
goodness. It is through God's strength that we
know courage, and through his power that we
know goodness. When we realize this, surrender
becomes our priority. In seeking to unite our
will with God's more fully, we don't want a fixed
blissful union with him, one that is filled with
passivity. Surrendering to him means growth
and progress. It is the freedom of moving forward
with and through him, so that each of our
relationships and all of our work, worship,
suffering, and play reflect what he wants of us.

— *Judith C. Lechman*

REVIVE

Saturday: John 15:1–17
Sunday: 1 Corinthians 2:6–16

Go to page 1253 for your next devotional reading.

"Rejoice, O Gentiles, with his
    people."ᵃ

¹¹And again,

"Praise the Lord, all you Gentiles,
    and sing praises to him, all you
    peoples."ᵇ

¹²And again, Isaiah says,

"The Root of Jesse will spring up,
    one who will arise to rule over the
    nations;
the Gentiles will hope in him."ᶜ

¹³May the God of hope fill you with all
joy and peace as you trust in him, so that
you may overflow with hope by the power
of the Holy Spirit.

Paul the Minister to the Gentiles

¹⁴I myself am convinced, my brothers,
that you yourselves are full of goodness,
complete in knowledge and competent to
instruct one another. ¹⁵I have written you
quite boldly on some points, as if to remind you of them again, because of the
grace God gave me ¹⁶to be a minister of
Christ Jesus to the Gentiles with the
priestly duty of proclaiming the gospel of
God, so that the Gentiles might become
an offering acceptable to God, sanctified
by the Holy Spirit.

¹⁷Therefore I glory in Christ Jesus in my
service to God. ¹⁸I will not venture to
speak of anything except what Christ has
accomplished through me in leading the
Gentiles to obey God by what I have said
and done— ¹⁹by the power of signs and
miracles, through the power of the Spirit.
So from Jerusalem all the way around to
Illyricum, I have fully proclaimed the gospel of Christ. ²⁰It has always been my ambition to preach the gospel where Christ
was not known, so that I would not be
building on someone else's foundation.
²¹Rather, as it is written:

"Those who were not told about him
    will see,
and those who have not heard will
    understand."ᵈ

²²This is why I have often been hindered
from coming to you.

Paul's Plan to Visit Rome

²³But now that there is no more place
for me to work in these regions, and since

I have been longing for many years to see
you, ²⁴I plan to do so when I go to Spain.
I hope to visit you while passing through
and to have you assist me on my journey
there, after I have enjoyed your company
for a while. ²⁵Now, however, I am on my
way to Jerusalem in the service of the
saints there. ²⁶For Macedonia and Achaia
were pleased to make a contribution for
the poor among the saints in Jerusalem.
²⁷They were pleased to do it, and indeed
they owe it to them. For if the Gentiles
have shared in the Jews' spiritual blessings, they owe it to the Jews to share with
them their material blessings. ²⁸So after I
have completed this task and have made
sure that they have received this fruit, I
will go to Spain and visit you on the way.
²⁹I know that when I come to you, I will
come in the full measure of the blessing
of Christ.

³⁰I urge you, brothers, by our Lord
Jesus Christ and by the love of the Spirit,
to join me in my struggle by praying to
God for me. ³¹Pray that I may be rescued
from the unbelievers in Judea and that
my service in Jerusalem may be acceptable to the saints there, ³²so that by God's
will I may come to you with joy and
together with you be refreshed. ³³The
God of peace be with you all. Amen.

Personal Greetings

16 I commend to you our sister Pho-
ebe, a servantᵉ of the church in
Cenchrea. ²I ask you to receive her in the
Lord in a way worthy of the saints and to
give her any help she may need from you,
for she has been a great help to many people, including me.

³Greet Priscillaᶠ and Aquila, my fellow
    workers in Christ Jesus. ⁴They risked
    their lives for me. Not only I but all
    the churches of the Gentiles are
    grateful to them.
⁵Greet also the church that meets at
    their house.
Greet my dear friend Epenetus, who
    was the first convert to Christ in the
    province of Asia.
⁶Greet Mary, who worked very hard for
    you.
⁷Greet Andronicus and Junias, my rela-
    tives who have been in prison with
    me. They are outstanding among the

ᵃ10 Deut. 32:43   ᵇ11 Psalm 117:1   ᶜ12 Isaiah 11:10   ᵈ21 Isaiah 52:15   ᵉ1 Or deaconess
ᶠ3 Greek Prisca, a variant of Priscilla

apostles, and they were in Christ before I was.

[8]Greet Ampliatus, whom I love in the Lord.

[9]Greet Urbanus, our fellow worker in Christ, and my dear friend Stachys.

[10]Greet Apelles, tested and approved in Christ.

Greet those who belong to the household of Aristobulus.

[11]Greet Herodion, my relative.

Greet those in the household of Narcissus who are in the Lord.

[12]Greet Tryphena and Tryphosa, those women who work hard in the Lord.

Greet my dear friend Persis, another woman who has worked very hard in the Lord.

[13]Greet Rufus, chosen in the Lord, and his mother, who has been a mother to me, too.

[14]Greet Asyncritus, Phlegon, Hermes, Patrobas, Hermas and the brothers with them.

[15]Greet Philologus, Julia, Nereus and his sister, and Olympas and all the saints with them.

[16]Greet one another with a holy kiss.

All the churches of Christ send greetings.

[17]I urge you, brothers, to watch out for those who cause divisions and put obstacles in your way that are contrary to the teaching you have learned. Keep away from them. [18]For such people are not serving our Lord Christ, but their own appetites. By smooth talk and flattery they deceive the minds of naive people. [19]Everyone has heard about your obedience, so I am full of joy over you; but I want you to be wise about what is good, and innocent about what is evil.

[20]The God of peace will soon crush Satan under your feet.

The grace of our Lord Jesus be with you.

[21]Timothy, my fellow worker, sends his greetings to you, as do Lucius, Jason and Sosipater, my relatives.

[22]I, Tertius, who wrote down this letter, greet you in the Lord.

[23]Gaius, whose hospitality I and the whole church here enjoy, sends you his greetings.

Erastus, who is the city's director of public works, and our brother Quartus send you their greetings.[a]

[25]Now to him who is able to establish you by my gospel and the proclamation of Jesus Christ, according to the revelation of the mystery hidden for long ages past, [26]but now revealed and made known through the prophetic writings by the command of the eternal God, so that all nations might believe and obey him— [27]to the only wise God be glory forever through Jesus Christ! Amen.

---

a23 Some manuscripts *their greetings.* *24May the grace of our Lord Jesus Christ be with all of you. Amen.*

PAUL, while staying in Ephesus (Acts 19), writes this letter to the church he started in Corinth (Acts 18:1–17). He addresses various problems he has heard about and answers questions they have asked of him in a letter (see 1 Corinthians 7:1). He places a high priority on being obedient to Christ and on striving for unity, humility and love in the church. As you read this book, make a decision to seek the Lord's will in everything you do and to work hard to be humble, to love others, and to become one in spirit with your fellow believers.

1 CORINTHIANS

1 Paul, called to be an apostle of Christ Jesus by the will of God, and our brother Sosthenes,

²To the church of God in Corinth, to those sanctified in Christ Jesus and called to be holy, together with all those everywhere who call on the name of our Lord Jesus Christ—their Lord and ours:

³Grace and peace to you from God our Father and the Lord Jesus Christ.

Thanksgiving

⁴I always thank God for you because of his grace given you in Christ Jesus. ⁵For in him you have been enriched in every way—in all your speaking and in all your knowledge— ⁶because our testimony about Christ was confirmed in you. ⁷Therefore you do not lack any spiritual gift as you eagerly wait for our Lord Jesus Christ to be revealed. ⁸He will keep you strong to the end, so that you will be blameless on the day of our Lord Jesus

Christ. 9God, who has called you into fellowship with his Son Jesus Christ our Lord, is faithful.

Divisions in the Church

10I appeal to you, brothers, in the name of our Lord Jesus Christ, that all of you agree with one another so that there may be no divisions among you and that you may be perfectly united in mind and thought. 11My brothers, some from Chloe's household have informed me that there are quarrels among you. 12What I mean is this: One of you says, "I follow Paul"; another, "I follow Apollos"; another, "I follow Cephas*a*"; still another, "I follow Christ."

13Is Christ divided? Was Paul crucified for you? Were you baptized into*b* the name of Paul? 14I am thankful that I did not baptize any of you except Crispus and Gaius, 15so no one can say that you were baptized into my name. 16(Yes, I also baptized the household of Stephanas; beyond that, I don't remember if I baptized anyone else.) 17For Christ did not send me to baptize, but to preach the gospel—not with words of human wisdom, lest the cross of Christ be emptied of its power.

Christ the Wisdom and Power of God

18For the message of the cross is foolishness to those who are perishing, but to us who are being saved it is the power of God. 19For it is written:

"I will destroy the wisdom of the
    wise;
the intelligence of the intelligent I
    will frustrate."*c*

20Where is the wise man? Where is the scholar? Where is the philosopher of this age? Has not God made foolish the wisdom of the world? 21For since in the wisdom of God the world through its wisdom did not know him, God was pleased through the foolishness of what was preached to save those who believe. 22Jews demand miraculous signs and Greeks look for wisdom, 23but we preach Christ crucified: a stumbling block to Jews and foolishness to Gentiles, 24but to those whom God has called, both Jews and Greeks, Christ the power of God and the wisdom of God. 25For the foolishness of God is wiser than man's wisdom, and

the weakness of God is stronger than man's strength.

26Brothers, think of what you were when you were called. Not many of you were wise by human standards; not many were influential; not many were of noble birth. 27But God chose the foolish things of the world to shame the wise; God chose the weak things of the world to shame the strong. 28He chose the lowly things of this world and the despised things—and the things that are not—to nullify the things that are, 29so that no one may boast before him. 30It is because of him that you are in Christ Jesus, who has become for us wisdom from God—that is, our righteousness, holiness and redemption. 31Therefore, as it is written: "Let him who boasts boast in the Lord."*d*

2 When I came to you, brothers, I did not come with eloquence or superior wisdom as I proclaimed to you the testimony about God.*e* 2For I resolved to know nothing while I was with you except Jesus Christ and him crucified. 3I came to you in weakness and fear, and with much trembling. 4My message and my preaching were not with wise and persuasive words, but with a demonstration of the Spirit's power, 5so that your faith might not rest on men's wisdom, but on God's power.

Wisdom From the Spirit

6We do, however, speak a message of wisdom among the mature, but not the wisdom of this age or of the rulers of this age, who are coming to nothing. 7No, we speak of God's secret wisdom, a wisdom that has been hidden and that God destined for our glory before time began. 8None of the rulers of this age understood it, for if they had, they would not have crucified the Lord of glory. 9However, as it is written:

"No eye has seen,
    no ear has heard,
    no mind has conceived
what God has prepared for those
    who love him"*f*—

10but God has revealed it to us by his Spirit.

The Spirit searches all things, even the deep things of God. 11For who among men knows the thoughts of a man except the man's spirit within him? In the same

---

a12 That is, Peter   *b13* Or *in;* also in verse 15 manuscripts *as I proclaimed to you God's mystery*   *c19* Isaiah 29:14   *d31* Jer. 9:24   *e1* Some   *f9* Isaiah 64:4

way no one knows the thoughts of God except the Spirit of God. [12]We have not received the spirit of the world but the Spirit who is from God, that we may understand what God has freely given us. [13]This is what we speak, not in words taught us by human wisdom but in words taught by the Spirit, expressing spiritual truths in spiritual words.[a] [14]The man without the Spirit does not accept the things that come from the Spirit of God, for they are foolishness to him, and he cannot understand them, because they are spiritually discerned. [15]The spiritual man makes judgments about all things, but he himself is not subject to any man's judgment:

[16]"For who has known the mind of the Lord
   that he may instruct him?"[b]

But we have the mind of Christ.

On Divisions in the Church

3 Brothers, I could not address you as spiritual but as worldly—mere infants in Christ. [2]I gave you milk, not solid food, for you were not yet ready for it. Indeed, you are still not ready. [3]You are still worldly. For since there is jealousy and quarreling among you, are you not worldly? Are you not acting like mere men? [4]For when one says, "I follow Paul," and another, "I follow Apollos," are you not mere men?

[5]What, after all, is Apollos? And what is Paul? Only servants, through whom you came to believe—as the Lord has assigned to each his task. [6]I planted the seed, Apollos watered it, but God made it grow. [7]So neither he who plants nor he who waters is anything, but only God, who makes things grow. [8]The man who plants and the man who waters have one purpose, and each will be rewarded according to his own labor. [9]For we are God's fellow workers; you are God's field, God's building.

[10]By the grace God has given me, I laid a foundation as an expert builder, and someone else is building on it. But each one should be careful how he builds. [11]For no one can lay any foundation other than the one already laid, which is Jesus Christ. [12]If any man builds on this foundation using gold, silver, costly stones, wood, hay or straw, [13]his work will be

shown for what it is, because the Day will bring it to light. It will be revealed with fire, and the fire will test the quality of each man's work. [14]If what he has built survives, he will receive his reward. [15]If it is burned up, he will suffer loss; he himself will be saved, but only as one escaping through the flames.

[16]Don't you know that you yourselves are God's temple and that God's Spirit lives in you? [17]If anyone destroys God's temple, God will destroy him; for God's temple is sacred, and you are that temple.

[18]Do not deceive yourselves. If any one of you thinks he is wise by the standards of this age, he should become a "fool" so that he may become wise. [19]For the wisdom of this world is foolishness in God's sight. As it is written: "He catches the wise in their craftiness"[c]; [20]and again, "The Lord knows that the thoughts of the wise are futile."[d] [21]So then, no more boasting about men! All things are yours, [22]whether Paul or Apollos or Cephas[e] or the world or life or death or the present or the future—all are yours, [23]and you are of Christ, and Christ is of God.

Apostles of Christ

4 So then, men ought to regard us as servants of Christ and as those entrusted with the secret things of God. [2]Now it is required that those who have been given a trust must prove faithful. [3]I care very little if I am judged by you or by any human court; indeed, I do not even judge myself. [4]My conscience is clear, but that does not make me innocent. It is the Lord who judges me. [5]Therefore judge nothing before the appointed time; wait till the Lord comes. He will bring to light what is hidden in darkness and will expose the motives of men's hearts. At that time each will receive his praise from God.

[6]Now, brothers, I have applied these things to myself and Apollos for your benefit, so that you may learn from us the meaning of the saying, "Do not go beyond what is written." Then you will not take pride in one man over against another. [7]For who makes you different from anyone else? What do you have that you did not receive? And if you did receive it, why do you boast as though you did not?

[8]Already you have all you want! Already you have become rich! You have become

---

a13 Or *Spirit, interpreting spiritual truths to spiritual men*   *b16* Isaiah 40:13   *c19* Job 5:13
d20 Psalm 94:11   *e22* That is, Peter

VERSE FOR THE DAY:
1 Corinthians 2:12

AUTHOR:
June Hunt

PASSAGE FOR THE DAY:
1 Corinthians 2:11–16

The Holy Spirit

THE blackout took my neighborhood by surprise. Suddenly in total darkness, I inched my way to the bedside table and fumbled for the flashlight. What frustration . . . it didn't work. How useless—a flashlight that didn't function.

Just as useless is the person unable to function according to God's divine plan. Why? Because God originally designed the human spirit to contain the Holy Spirit. In the garden, Adam and Eve had perfect oneness with God. The Holy Spirit lived in their human spirits and enlightened every aspect of their lives. Once they pronounced their "declaration of independence" from God, however, sin came in and the Spirit went out. The pair were like a flashlight without batteries; with no power on the inside, there was no light on the outside. They spiraled downward into spiritual darkness.

Yet God did not give up on all those who were to be born into that same darkness. "The lamp of the LORD searches the spirit of a man" (Proverbs 20:27). God desired to reunite the Holy Spirit with the human spirit so that they could again be one.

When you feel the frustration of wandering in the dark, know that the Lord has already provided the perfect guide for your life. For "when he, the Spirit of truth, comes, he will guide you into all truth" (John 16:13). Your own personal Counselor, Conscience, Convictor and Comforter fills your soul—your mind, will and emotions—with perfect truth. He teaches your mind, directs your will and guides your emotions. As a result, those who are joined to the Spirit better understand spiritual things (1 Corinthians 2:14).

Like the flashlight, you were designed to shine; but you can never shine with your own power. The Holy Spirit provides the power to produce the light. And once you shine as you were intended to shine, you will never be useless!

Additional Scripture Readings:
Ephesians 5:8–14; 2 Timothy 1:8–14

Go to page 1255 for your next devotional reading.

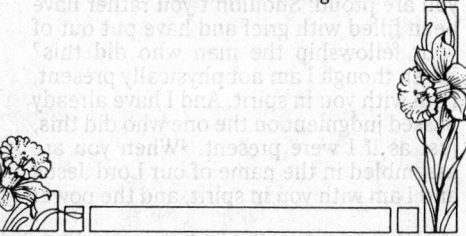

kings—and that without us! How I wish that you really had become kings so that we might be kings with you! 9For it seems to me that God has put us apostles on display at the end of the procession, like men condemned to die in the arena. We have been made a spectacle to the whole universe, to angels as well as to men. 10We are fools for Christ, but you are so wise in Christ! We are weak, but you are strong! You are honored, we are dishonored! 11To this very hour we go hungry and thirsty, we are in rags, we are brutally treated, we are homeless. 12We work hard with our own hands. When we are cursed, we bless; when we are persecuted, we endure it; 13when we are slandered, we answer kindly. Up to this moment we have become the scum of the earth, the refuse of the world.

14I am not writing this to shame you, but to warn you, as my dear children. 15Even though you have ten thousand guardians in Christ, you do not have many fathers, for in Christ Jesus I became your father through the gospel. 16Therefore I urge you to imitate me. 17For this reason I am sending to you Timothy, my son whom I love, who is faithful in the Lord. He will remind you of my way of life in Christ Jesus, which agrees with what I teach everywhere in every church.

18Some of you have become arrogant, as if I were not coming to you. 19But I will come to you very soon, if the Lord is willing, and then I will find out not only how these arrogant people are talking, but what power they have. 20For the kingdom of God is not a matter of talk but of power. 21What do you prefer? Shall I come to you with a whip, or in love and with a gentle spirit?

Expel the Immoral Brother!

5 It is actually reported that there is sexual immorality among you, and of a kind that does not occur even among pagans: A man has his father's wife. 2And you are proud! Shouldn't you rather have been filled with grief and have put out of your fellowship the man who did this? 3Even though I am not physically present, I am with you in spirit. And I have already passed judgment on the one who did this, just as if I were present. 4When you are assembled in the name of our Lord Jesus and I am with you in spirit, and the power

of our Lord Jesus is present, 5hand this man over to Satan, so that the sinful nature*a* may be destroyed and his spirit saved on the day of the Lord.

6Your boasting is not good. Don't you know that a little yeast works through the whole batch of dough? 7Get rid of the old yeast that you may be a new batch without yeast—as you really are. For Christ, our Passover lamb, has been sacrificed. 8Therefore let us keep the Festival, not with the old yeast, the yeast of malice and wickedness, but with bread without yeast, the bread of sincerity and truth.

9I have written you in my letter not to associate with sexually immoral people— 10not at all meaning the people of this world who are immoral, or the greedy and swindlers, or idolaters. In that case you would have to leave this world. 11But now I am writing you that you must not associate with anyone who calls himself a brother but is sexually immoral or greedy, an idolater or a slanderer, a drunkard or a swindler. With such a man do not even eat.

12What business is it of mine to judge those outside the church? Are you not to judge those inside? 13God will judge those outside. "Expel the wicked man from among you."*b*

Lawsuits Among Believers

6 If any of you has a dispute with another, dare he take it before the ungodly for judgment instead of before the saints? 2Do you not know that the saints will judge the world? And if you are to judge the world, are you not competent to judge trivial cases? 3Do you not know that we will judge angels? How much more the things of this life! 4Therefore, if you have disputes about such matters, appoint as judges even men of little account in the church!*c* 5I say this to shame you. Is it possible that there is nobody among you wise enough to judge a dispute between believers? 6But instead, one brother goes to law against another— and this in front of unbelievers!

7The very fact that you have lawsuits among you means you have been completely defeated already. Why not rather be wronged? Why not rather be cheated? 8Instead, you yourselves cheat and do wrong, and you do this to your brothers. 9Do you not know that the wicked will

---

*a*5 Or *that his body;* or *that the flesh*   *b*13 Deut. 17:7; 19:19; 21:21; 22:21,24; 24:7   *c*4 Or *matters, do you appoint as judges men of little account in the church?*

VERSE FOR THE DAY:	AUTHOR:	PASSAGE FOR THE DAY:
1 Corinthians 4:21	Rebecca Manley Pippert	1 Corinthians 4:14–21

With Love and Gentleness

WHEN I first came to Portland, Oregon, I met a student on one of the campuses where I worked. He was brilliant and looked like he was always pondering the esoteric. His hair was always mussy, and in the entire time I knew him, I never once saw him wear a pair of shoes. Rain, sleet or snow, Bill was always barefoot. While he was attending college he had become a Christian. At this time a well-dressed, middle-class church across the street from the campus wanted to develop more of a ministry to the students. They were not sure how to go about it, but they tried to make them feel welcome. One day Bill decided to worship there. He walked into this church, wearing his blue jeans, tee shirt and of course no shoes. People looked a bit uncomfortable, but no one said anything. So Bill began walking down the aisle looking for a seat. The church was quite crowded that Sunday, so as he got down to the front pew and realized that there were no seats, he just squatted on the carpet—perfectly acceptable behavior at a college fellowship, but perhaps unnerving for a church.

Suddenly an elderly man began walking down the aisle toward the boy. Was he going to scold Bill? My friends who saw him approaching said they thought, "You can't blame him. He'd never guess Bill is a Christian. And his world is too distant from Bill's to understand. You can't blame him for what he's going to do."

As the man kept walking slowly down the aisle, the church became utterly silent, all eyes were focused on him, you could not hear anyone breathe. When the man reached Bill, with some difficulty he lowered himself and sat down next to him on the carpet. He and Bill worshiped together on the floor that Sunday. I was told there was not a dry eye in the congregation.

The irony is that probably the only one who failed to see how great the giving had been that Sunday was Bill. But grace is always that way. It gives without the receiver realizing how great the gift really is. As this man walked alongside his brother and loved him with all that he had received from Christ's love, so must we.

Additional Scripture Readings:
1 Samuel 16:7; James 2:1–5

Go to page 1256 for your next devotional reading.

not inherit the kingdom of God? Do not be deceived: Neither the sexually immoral nor idolaters nor adulterers nor male prostitutes nor homosexual offenders [10]nor thieves nor the greedy nor drunkards nor slanderers nor swindlers will inherit the kingdom of God. [11]And that is what some of you were. But you were washed, you were sanctified, you were justified in the name of the Lord Jesus Christ and by the Spirit of our God.

Sexual Immorality

[12]"Everything is permissible for me" — but not everything is beneficial. "Everything is permissible for me" — but I will not be mastered by anything. [13]"Food for the stomach and the stomach for food" — but God will destroy them both. The body is not meant for sexual immorality, but for the Lord, and the Lord for the body. [14]By his power God raised the Lord from the dead, and he will raise us also. [15]Do you not know that your bodies are members of Christ himself? Shall I then take the members of Christ and unite them with a prostitute? Never! [16]Do you not know that he who unites himself with a prostitute is one with her in body? For it is said, "The two will become one

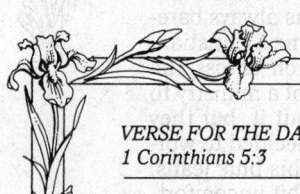

WEDNESDAY

VERSE FOR THE DAY:
1 Corinthians 5:3

AUTHOR:
Susan L. Lenzkes

PASSAGE FOR THE DAY:
1 Corinthians 5:1–5

Saying Good-by

ONE of the most heartrending moments of life comes when close friends say good-by, knowing that many miles will separate them from their countless shared experiences. Distance takes on the menacing look of an enemy when it dares to stand between such friends!

Soon they will find themselves building protective shields around the ache of separation. They will feel themselves both courting and resisting the urge to clip those threads that bind their hearts in love. And they will argue repeatedly with a voice that warns, "Don't build new friendships — life has a demolition crew around every corner!"

But discovery lies ahead. Real friendship is resilient. The very cords that make it strong — commitment, creativity, caring and sharing — are elastic, and friends can remain committed and even more creative in their long-distance sharing.

Now cards and letters — stackable memories to be relived over a cup of coffee — will communicate love in indelible ink. Now calls — where the value of every word, enhanced by the coming bill — will set precious priorities and release sentiment from the soul. Anticipated visits will be far richer for their infrequency. Thoughts and feelings long saved and protected will be unlocked and shared.

Best of all, a discovery will be made that hearts in harmony can just as easily carry a tune long-distance.

Additional Scripture Readings:
1 Samuel 20:41–42; Philippians 2:25–30

Go to page 1260 for your next devotional reading.

flesh."*a* [17]But he who unites himself with the Lord is one with him in spirit.

[18]Flee from sexual immorality. All other sins a man commits are outside his body, but he who sins sexually sins against his own body. [19]Do you not know that your body is a temple of the Holy Spirit, who is in you, whom you have received from God? You are not your own; [20]you were bought at a price. Therefore honor God with your body.

Marriage

7 Now for the matters you wrote about: It is good for a man not to marry.*b* [2]But since there is so much immorality, each man should have his own wife, and each woman her own husband. [3]The husband should fulfill his marital duty to his wife, and likewise the wife to her husband. [4]The wife's body does not belong to her alone but also to her husband. In the same way, the husband's body does not belong to him alone but also to his wife. [5]Do not deprive each other except by mutual consent and for a time, so that you may devote yourselves to prayer. Then come together again so that Satan will not tempt you because of your lack of self-control. [6]I say this as a concession, not as a command. [7]I wish that all men were as I am. But each man has his own gift from God; one has this gift, another has that.

[8]Now to the unmarried and the widows I say: It is good for them to stay unmarried, as I am. [9]But if they cannot control themselves, they should marry, for it is better to marry than to burn with passion. [10]To the married I give this command (not I, but the Lord): A wife must not separate from her husband. [11]But if she does, she must remain unmarried or else be reconciled to her husband. And a husband must not divorce his wife.

[12]To the rest I say this (I, not the Lord): If any brother has a wife who is not a believer and she is willing to live with him, he must not divorce her. [13]And if a woman has a husband who is not a believer and he is willing to live with her, she must not divorce him. [14]For the unbelieving husband has been sanctified through his wife, and the unbelieving wife has been sanctified through her believing husband. Otherwise your children would be unclean, but as it is, they are holy.

[15]But if the unbeliever leaves, let him do so. A believing man or woman is not bound in such circumstances; God has called us to live in peace. [16]How do you know, wife, whether you will save your husband? Or, how do you know, husband, whether you will save your wife?

[17]Nevertheless, each one should retain the place in life that the Lord assigned to him and to which God has called him. This is the rule I lay down in all the churches. [18]Was a man already circumcised when he was called? He should not become uncircumcised. Was a man uncircumcised when he was called? He should not be circumcised. [19]Circumcision is nothing and uncircumcision is nothing. Keeping God's commands is what counts. [20]Each one should remain in the situation which he was in when God called him. [21]Were you a slave when you were called? Don't let it trouble you—although if you can gain your freedom, do so. [22]For he who was a slave when he was called by the Lord is the Lord's freedman; similarly, he who was a free man when he was called is Christ's slave. [23]You were bought at a price; do not become slaves of men. [24]Brothers, each man, as responsible to God, should remain in the situation God called him to.

[25]Now about virgins: I have no command from the Lord, but I give a judgment as one who by the Lord's mercy is trustworthy. [26]Because of the present crisis, I think that it is good for you to remain as you are. [27]Are you married? Do not seek a divorce. Are you unmarried? Do not look for a wife. [28]But if you do marry, you have not sinned; and if a virgin marries, she has not sinned. But those who marry will face many troubles in this life, and I want to spare you this.

[29]What I mean, brothers, is that the time is short. From now on those who have wives should live as if they had none; [30]those who mourn, as if they did not; those who are happy, as if they were not; those who buy something, as if it were not theirs to keep; [31]those who use the things of the world, as if not engrossed in them. For this world in its present form is passing away.

[32]I would like you to be free from concern. An unmarried man is concerned about the Lord's affairs—how he can please the Lord. [33]But a married man is concerned about the affairs of this world —how he can please his wife— [34]and his

---

a16 Gen. 2:24　　*b1* Or *"It is good for a man not to have sexual relations with a woman."*

interests are divided. An unmarried woman or virgin is concerned about the Lord's affairs: Her aim is to be devoted to the Lord in both body and spirit. But a married woman is concerned about the affairs of this world—how she can please her husband. [35]I am saying this for your own good, not to restrict you, but that you may live in a right way in undivided devotion to the Lord.

[36]If anyone thinks he is acting improperly toward the virgin he is engaged to, and if she is getting along in years and he feels he ought to marry, he should do as he wants. He is not sinning. They should get married. [37]But the man who has settled the matter in his own mind, who is under no compulsion but has control over his own will, and who has made up his mind not to marry the virgin—this man also does the right thing. [38]So then, he who marries the virgin does right, but he who does not marry her does even better.[a]

[39]A woman is bound to her husband as long as he lives. But if her husband dies, she is free to marry anyone she wishes, but he must belong to the Lord. [40]In my judgment, she is happier if she stays as she is—and I think that I too have the Spirit of God.

Food Sacrificed to Idols

8 Now about food sacrificed to idols: We know that we all possess knowledge.[b] Knowledge puffs up, but love builds up. [2]The man who thinks he knows something does not yet know as he ought to know. [3]But the man who loves God is known by God.

[4]So then, about eating food sacrificed to idols: We know that an idol is nothing at all in the world and that there is no God but one. [5]For even if there are so-called gods, whether in heaven or on earth (as indeed there are many "gods" and many "lords"), [6]yet for us there is but one God, the Father, from whom all things came and for whom we live; and there is but one Lord, Jesus Christ, through whom all things came and through whom we live.

[7]But not everyone knows this. Some people are still so accustomed to idols that when they eat such food they think of it as having been sacrificed to an idol, and since their conscience is weak, it is defiled. [8]But food does not bring us near to God; we are no worse if we do not eat, and no better if we do.

[9]Be careful, however, that the exercise of your freedom does not become a stumbling block to the weak. [10]For if anyone with a weak conscience sees you who have this knowledge eating in an idol's temple, won't he be emboldened to eat what has been sacrificed to idols? [11]So this weak brother, for whom Christ died, is destroyed by your knowledge. [12]When you sin against your brothers in this way and wound their weak conscience, you sin against Christ. [13]Therefore, if what I eat causes my brother to fall into sin, I will never eat meat again, so that I will not cause him to fall.

The Rights of an Apostle

9 Am I not free? Am I not an apostle? Have I not seen Jesus our Lord? Are you not the result of my work in the Lord? [2]Even though I may not be an apostle to others, surely I am to you! For you are the seal of my apostleship in the Lord.

[3]This is my defense to those who sit in judgment on me. [4]Don't we have the right to food and drink? [5]Don't we have the right to take a believing wife along with us, as do the other apostles and the Lord's brothers and Cephas[c]? [6]Or is it only I and Barnabas who must work for a living?

[7]Who serves as a soldier at his own expense? Who plants a vineyard and does not eat of its grapes? Who tends a flock and does not drink of the milk? [8]Do I say this merely from a human point of view? Doesn't the Law say the same thing? [9]For it is written in the Law of Moses: "Do not muzzle an ox while it is treading out the grain."[d] Is it about oxen that God is concerned? [10]Surely he says this for us, doesn't he? Yes, this was written for us, because when the plowman plows and the thresher threshes, they ought to do so in the hope of sharing in the harvest. [11]If we have sown spiritual seed among you, is it

---

[a]36-38 Or [36]If anyone thinks he is not treating his daughter properly, and if she is getting along in years, and he feels she ought to marry, he should do as he wants. He is not sinning. He should let her get married. [37]But the man who has settled the matter in his own mind, who is under no compulsion but has control over his own will, and who has made up his mind to keep the virgin unmarried—this man also does the right thing. [38]So then, he who gives his virgin in marriage does right, but he who does not give her in marriage does even better.   [b]1 Or "We all possess knowledge," as you say   [c]5 That is, Peter   [d]9 Deut. 25:4

too much if we reap a material harvest from you? 12If others have this right of support from you, shouldn't we have it all the more?

But we did not use this right. On the contrary, we put up with anything rather than hinder the gospel of Christ. 13Don't you know that those who work in the temple get their food from the temple, and those who serve at the altar share in what is offered on the altar? 14In the same way, the Lord has commanded that those who preach the gospel should receive their living from the gospel.

15But I have not used any of these rights. And I am not writing this in the hope that you will do such things for me. I would rather die than have anyone deprive me of this boast. 16Yet when I preach the gospel, I cannot boast, for I am compelled to preach. Woe to me if I do not preach the gospel! 17If I preach voluntarily, I have a reward; if not voluntarily, I am simply discharging the trust committed to me. 18What then is my reward? Just this: that in preaching the gospel I may offer it free of charge, and so not make use of my rights in preaching it.

19Though I am free and belong to no man, I make myself a slave to everyone, to win as many as possible. 20To the Jews I became like a Jew, to win the Jews. To those under the law I became like one under the law (though I myself am not under the law), so as to win those under the law. 21To those not having the law I became like one not having the law (though I am not free from God's law but am under Christ's law), so as to win those not having the law. 22To the weak I became weak, to win the weak. I have become all things to all men so that by all possible means I might save some. 23I do all this for the sake of the gospel, that I may share in its blessings.

24Do you not know that in a race all the runners run, but only one gets the prize? Run in such a way as to get the prize. 25Everyone who competes in the games goes into strict training. They do it to get a crown that will not last; but we do it to get a crown that will last forever. 26Therefore I do not run like a man running aimlessly; I do not fight like a man beating the air. 27No, I beat my body and make it my slave so that after I have preached to others, I myself will not be disqualified for the prize.

Warnings From Israel's History

10 For I do not want you to be ignorant of the fact, brothers, that our forefathers were all under the cloud and that they all passed through the sea. 2They were all baptized into Moses in the cloud and in the sea. 3They all ate the same spiritual food 4and drank the same spiritual drink; for they drank from the spiritual rock that accompanied them, and that rock was Christ. 5Nevertheless, God was not pleased with most of them; their bodies were scattered over the desert.

6Now these things occurred as examples*a* to keep us from setting our hearts on evil things as they did. 7Do not be idolaters, as some of them were; as it is written: "The people sat down to eat and drink and got up to indulge in pagan revelry."*b* 8We should not commit sexual immorality, as some of them did—and in one day twenty-three thousand of them died. 9We should not test the Lord, as some of them did—and were killed by snakes. 10And do not grumble, as some of them did—and were killed by the destroying angel.

11These things happened to them as examples and were written down as warnings for us, on whom the fulfillment of the ages has come. 12So, if you think you are standing firm, be careful that you don't fall! 13No temptation has seized you except what is common to man. And God is faithful; he will not let you be tempted beyond what you can bear. But when you are tempted, he will also provide a way out so that you can stand up under it.

Idol Feasts and the Lord's Supper

14Therefore, my dear friends, flee from idolatry. 15I speak to sensible people; judge for yourselves what I say. 16Is not the cup of thanksgiving for which we give thanks a participation in the blood of Christ? And is not the bread that we break a participation in the body of Christ? 17Because there is one loaf, we, who are many, are one body, for we all partake of the one loaf.

18Consider the people of Israel: Do not those who eat the sacrifices participate in the altar? 19Do I mean then that a sacrifice offered to an idol is anything, or that an idol is anything? 20No, but the sacrifices of pagans are offered to demons, not

a6 Or types; also in verse 11   *b7 Exodus 32:6*

VERSE FOR THE DAY:
1 Corinthians 10:13

AUTHOR:
June Hunt

PASSAGE FOR THE DAY:
1 Corinthians 10:1–13

God Gives Me Strength

FOR thousands of years a popular club has been offering memberships throughout the world. It's a prolific club. It's the "I Can't" club.

Under the bylaws, club members are required to make "I can't" statements with conviction: "I can't help but hate after what he's done to me." "I can't quit this sin." "I can't forgive again!" Because of the fervor of these statements, it sounds as if each is an unchangeable, universal law.

Everyone is subject to one law of science, the law of gravity—the force that pulls every object to the center of the earth. In a similar way, members of the "I Can't" club are prisoners to the downward pull of defeat—they are not only ground-bound, but sin-bound.

Do you feel bound to a specific sin? Does quitting the "I Can't" club seem impossible? The Father refuses to let "can't" be the universal password of his children. At your salvation he gave you the Spirit of God so that you would have the *strength* of God. He made it possible for you to overcome any sin. How? By replacing one law with another:

> The law of the Spirit of life set me free from the law
> of sin and death (Romans 8:2).

Let's think about the law of gravity again. Can you imagine a 190-ton mass of metal rising against gravity's pull? Impossible? It can't be done! Oh, yes it can . . . by using a "higher law." When you, in faith, give yourself over to the principle of aerodynamics, you can enter an airplane with full confidence that it will fly you from one city to another. You are no longer ground-bound.

Similarly, when you, in faith, give yourself over to the Spirit's control, the "I can't" statements will no longer bind you. When God fills your spirit with his Spirit and infuses you with his strength, you are no longer captive to any temptation. Every *can't* becomes a *can.*

Additional Scripture Readings:
2 Corinthians 12:7–10; 1 Peter 5:6–11

*Go to page 1262 for your next
devotional reading.*

to God, and I do not want you to be participants with demons. 21You cannot drink the cup of the Lord and the cup of demons too; you cannot have a part in both the Lord's table and the table of demons. 22Are we trying to arouse the Lord's jealousy? Are we stronger than he?

The Believer's Freedom

23"Everything is permissible"—but not everything is beneficial. "Everything is permissible"—but not everything is constructive. 24Nobody should seek his own good, but the good of others.

25Eat anything sold in the meat market without raising questions of conscience, 26for, "The earth is the Lord's, and everything in it."a

27If some unbeliever invites you to a meal and you want to go, eat whatever is put before you without raising questions of conscience. 28But if anyone says to you, "This has been offered in sacrifice," then do not eat it, both for the sake of the man who told you and for conscience' sakeb— 29the other man's conscience, I mean, not yours. For why should my freedom be judged by another's conscience? 30If I take part in the meal with thankfulness, why am I denounced because of something I thank God for?

31So whether you eat or drink or whatever you do, do it all for the glory of God. 32Do not cause anyone to stumble, whether Jews, Greeks or the church of God— 33even as I try to please everybody in every way. For I am not seeking my own good but the good of many, so that they **11** may be saved. 1Follow my example, as I follow the example of Christ.

Propriety in Worship

2I praise you for remembering me in everything and for holding to the teachings,c just as I passed them on to you. 3Now I want you to realize that the head of every man is Christ, and the head of the woman is man, and the head of Christ is God. 4Every man who prays or prophesies with his head covered dishonors his head. 5And every woman who

prays or prophesies with her head uncovered dishonors her head—it is just as though her head were shaved. 6If a woman does not cover her head, she should have her hair cut off; and if it is a disgrace for a woman to have her hair cut or shaved off, she should cover her head. 7A man ought not to cover his head,d since he is the image and glory of God; but the woman is the glory of man. 8For man did not come from woman, but woman from man; 9neither was man created for woman, but woman for man. 10For this reason, and because of the angels, the woman ought to have a sign of authority on her head.

11In the Lord, however, woman is not independent of man, nor is man independent of woman. 12For as woman came from man, so also man is born of woman. But everything comes from God. 13Judge for yourselves: Is it proper for a woman to pray to God with her head uncovered? 14Does not the very nature of things teach you that if a man has long hair, it is a disgrace to him, 15but that if a woman has long hair, it is her glory? For long hair is given to her as a covering. 16If anyone wants to be contentious about this, we have no other practice—nor do the churches of God.

The Lord's Supper

17In the following directives I have no praise for you, for your meetings do more harm than good. 18In the first place, I hear that when you come together as a church, there are divisions among you, and to some extent I believe it. 19No doubt there have to be differences among you to show which of you have God's approval. 20When you come together, it is not the Lord's Supper you eat, 21for as you eat, each of you goes ahead without waiting for anybody else. One remains hungry, another gets drunk. 22Don't you have homes to eat and drink in? Or do you despise the church of God and humiliate those who have nothing? What shall I say to you? Shall I praise you for this? Certainly not!

23For I received from the Lord what I also passed on to you: The Lord Jesus, on

---

a26 Psalm 24:1   b28 Some manuscripts conscience' sake, for "the earth is the Lord's and everything in it"   c2 Or traditions   d4-7 Or 4Every man who prays or prophesies with long hair dishonors his 5Head. And every woman who prays or prophesies with no covering of hair, on her head dishonors her head— she is just like one of the "shorn women." 6If a woman has no covering, let her be for now with short hair, but since it is a disgrace for a woman to have her hair shorn or shaved, she should grow it again. 7A man ought not to have long hair

VERSE FOR THE DAY:
1 Corinthians 11:2

AUTHOR:
Alma Barkman

PASSAGE FOR THE DAY:
1 Corinthians 11:2–16

Pass It On

BACK in the days of our courtship, friend Hubby suggested I get the recipe for Jam Gem cookies from his mother. I duly inquired as to the ingredients, mixed up a batch and proudly served them to him the next time he came to call.

"They are quite good," he remarked as he reached for seconds.

"Quite good" was not good enough. I tried again. And again. I could never solicit the kind of praise I hoped to hear.

It wasn't until long after we were married that he very sheepishly divulged the reason for his reserved comments. "Those cookies have to be a certain shape to taste best."

"And what shape is that, pray tell?"

"Oval and about so big."

I went on a wild goose chase the likes of which uncovered every conceivable cookie cutter ever invented, but not one was "oval and about so big."

Months later I decided to confide in his mother. "Do you know," I whispered, "that your son insists that a genuine Jam Gem cookie has to be oval and about so big?"

She chuckled. "I suppose that's because I always made them that shape. Would you like my cookie cutter?"

I literally pounced on the offer. Wiping her hands on her apron, she pulled open a drawer and produced the elusive cookie cutter. It was the lid of a talcum powder can.

I have it still. Most people would consider it just another piece of junk, but my teenage daughter already has claimed it as an heirloom.

I suppose every family has little traditions that are handed down from one generation to the next. The family of God is no exception. Those spiritual values that have shaped our lives are cherished and retained for the benefit of our children. Sometimes, like Grandma's cookie cutter, they are temporarily forgotten, tossed aside in the clutter of daily living.

But eventually a growing emptiness creates a hunger for the Christian principles that once guided us, the fellowship that church involvement provided us, the family devotions that once united us. I believe the Holy Spirit uses our childhood memories to whet our appetite for the things of God. As we obediently search out his will and obey it, we in turn are establishing a Christian tradition for our children.

Additional Scripture Readings:
Psalm 78:4–7; 2 Timothy 3:14–15

*Go to page 1264 for your next
devotional reading.*

the night he was betrayed, took bread, ²⁴and when he had given thanks, he broke it and said, "This is my body, which is for you; do this in remembrance of me." ²⁵In the same way, after supper he took the cup, saying, "This cup is the new covenant in my blood; do this, whenever you drink it, in remembrance of me." ²⁶For whenever you eat this bread and drink this cup, you proclaim the Lord's death until he comes.

²⁷Therefore, whoever eats the bread or drinks the cup of the Lord in an unworthy manner will be guilty of sinning against the body and blood of the Lord. ²⁸A man ought to examine himself before he eats of the bread and drinks of the cup. ²⁹For anyone who eats and drinks without recognizing the body of the Lord eats and drinks judgment on himself. ³⁰That is why many among you are weak and sick, and a number of you have fallen asleep. ³¹But if we judged ourselves, we would not come under judgment. ³²When we are judged by the Lord, we are being disciplined so that we will not be condemned with the world.

³³So then, my brothers, when you come together to eat, wait for each other. ³⁴If anyone is hungry, he should eat at home, so that when you meet together it may not result in judgment.

And when I come I will give further directions.

Spiritual Gifts

12 Now about spiritual gifts, brothers, I do not want you to be ignorant. ²You know that when you were pagans, somehow or other you were influenced and led astray to mute idols. ³Therefore I tell you that no one who is speaking by the Spirit of God says, "Jesus be cursed," and no one can say, "Jesus is Lord," except by the Holy Spirit.

⁴There are different kinds of gifts, but the same Spirit. ⁵There are different kinds of service, but the same Lord. ⁶There are different kinds of working, but the same God works all of them in all men.

⁷Now to each one the manifestation of the Spirit is given for the common good. ⁸To one there is given through the Spirit the message of wisdom, to another the message of knowledge by means of the same Spirit, ⁹to another faith by the same Spirit, to another gifts of healing by that one Spirit, ¹⁰to another miraculous powers, to another prophecy, to another distinguishing between spirits, to another speaking in different kinds of tongues,[a] and to still another the interpretation of tongues.[a] ¹¹All these are the work of one and the same Spirit, and he gives them to each one, just as he determines.

One Body, Many Parts

¹²The body is a unit, though it is made up of many parts; and though all its parts are many, they form one body. So it is with Christ. ¹³For we were all baptized by[b] one Spirit into one body—whether Jews or Greeks, slave or free—and we were all given the one Spirit to drink.

¹⁴Now the body is not made up of one part but of many. ¹⁵If the foot should say, "Because I am not a hand, I do not belong to the body," it would not for that reason cease to be part of the body. ¹⁶And if the ear should say, "Because I am not an eye, I do not belong to the body," it would not for that reason cease to be part of the body. ¹⁷If the whole body were an eye, where would the sense of hearing be? If the whole body were an ear, where would the sense of smell be? ¹⁸But in fact God has arranged the parts in the body, every one of them, just as he wanted them to be. ¹⁹If they were all one part, where would the body be? ²⁰As it is, there are many parts, but one body.

²¹The eye cannot say to the hand, "I don't need you!" And the head cannot say to the feet, "I don't need you!" ²²On the contrary, those parts of the body that seem to be weaker are indispensable, ²³and the parts that we think are less honorable we treat with special honor. And the parts that are unpresentable are treated with special modesty, ²⁴while our presentable parts need no special treatment. But God has combined the members of the body and has given greater honor to the parts that lacked it, ²⁵so that there should be no division in the body, but that its parts should have equal concern for each other. ²⁶If one part suffers, every part suffers with it; if one part is honored, every part rejoices with it.

²⁷Now you are the body of Christ, and each one of you is a part of it. ²⁸And in the church God has appointed first of all apostles, second prophets, third teachers,

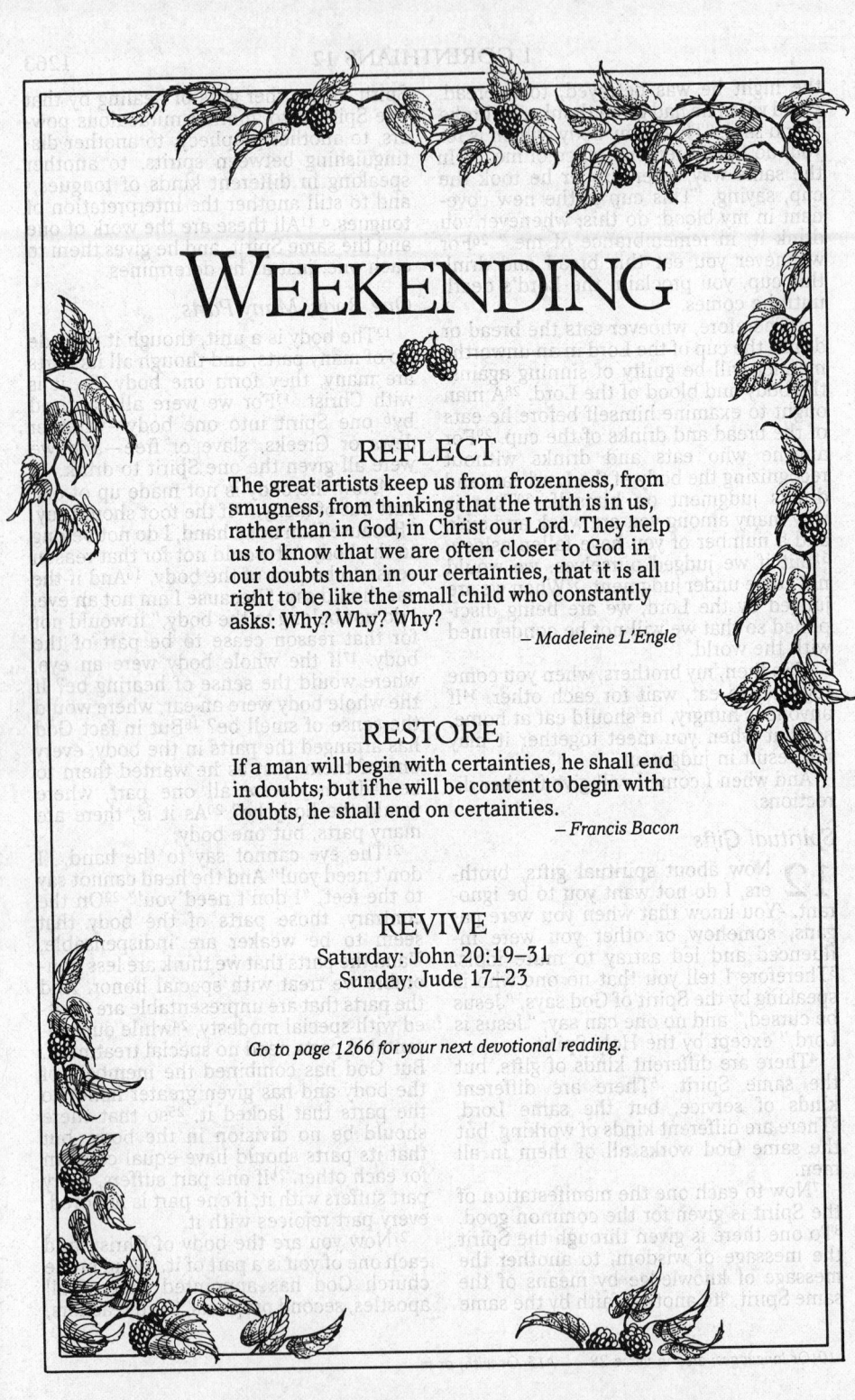

WEEKENDING

REFLECT

The great artists keep us from frozenness, from smugness, from thinking that the truth is in us, rather than in God, in Christ our Lord. They help us to know that we are often closer to God in our doubts than in our certainties, that it is all right to be like the small child who constantly asks: Why? Why? Why?

— *Madeleine L'Engle*

RESTORE

If a man will begin with certainties, he shall end in doubts; but if he will be content to begin with doubts, he shall end on certainties.

— *Francis Bacon*

REVIVE

Saturday: John 20:19–31
Sunday: Jude 17–23

Go to page 1266 for your next devotional reading.

then workers of miracles, also those having gifts of healing, those able to help others, those with gifts of administration, and those speaking in different kinds of tongues. ²⁹Are all apostles? Are all prophets? Are all teachers? Do all work miracles? ³⁰Do all have gifts of healing? Do all speak in tongues^a? Do all interpret? ³¹But eagerly desire^b the greater gifts.

Love

And now I will show you the most excellent way.

13 If I speak in the tongues^c of men and of angels, but have not love, I am only a resounding gong or a clanging cymbal. ²If I have the gift of prophecy and can fathom all mysteries and all knowledge, and if I have a faith that can move mountains, but have not love, I am nothing. ³If I give all I possess to the poor and surrender my body to the flames,^d but have not love, I gain nothing.

⁴Love is patient, love is kind. It does not envy, it does not boast, it is not proud. ⁵It is not rude, it is not self-seeking, it is not easily angered, it keeps no record of wrongs. ⁶Love does not delight in evil but rejoices with the truth. ⁷It always protects, always trusts, always hopes, always perseveres.

⁸Love never fails. But where there are prophecies, they will cease; where there are tongues, they will be stilled; where there is knowledge, it will pass away. ⁹For we know in part and we prophesy in part, ¹⁰but when perfection comes, the imperfect disappears. ¹¹When I was a child, I talked like a child, I thought like a child, I reasoned like a child. When I became a man, I put childish ways behind me. ¹²Now we see but a poor reflection as in a mirror; then we shall see face to face. Now I know in part; then I shall know fully, even as I am fully known.

¹³And now these three remain: faith, hope and love. But the greatest of these is love.

Gifts of Prophecy and Tongues

14 Follow the way of love and eagerly desire spiritual gifts, especially the gift of prophecy. ²For anyone who speaks in a tongue^e does not speak to men but to God. Indeed, no one understands him; he utters mysteries with his spirit.^f ³But everyone who prophesies speaks to men for their strengthening, encouragement and comfort. ⁴He who speaks in a tongue edifies himself, but he who prophesies edifies the church. ⁵I would like every one of you to speak in tongues,^g but I would rather have you prophesy. He who prophesies is greater than one who speaks in tongues,^g unless he interprets, so that the church may be edified.

⁶Now, brothers, if I come to you and speak in tongues, what good will I be to you, unless I bring you some revelation or knowledge or prophecy or word of instruction? ⁷Even in the case of lifeless things that make sounds, such as the flute or harp, how will anyone know what tune is being played unless there is a distinction in the notes? ⁸Again, if the trumpet does not sound a clear call, who will get ready for battle? ⁹So it is with you. Unless you speak intelligible words with your tongue, how will anyone know what you are saying? You will just be speaking into the air. ¹⁰Undoubtedly there are all sorts of languages in the world, yet none of them is without meaning. ¹¹If then I do not grasp the meaning of what someone is saying, I am a foreigner to the speaker, and he is a foreigner to me. ¹²So it is with you. Since you are eager to have spiritual gifts, try to excel in gifts that build up the church.

¹³For this reason anyone who speaks in a tongue should pray that he may interpret what he says. ¹⁴For if I pray in a tongue, my spirit prays, but my mind is unfruitful. ¹⁵So what shall I do? I will pray with my spirit, but I will also pray with my mind; I will sing with my spirit, but I will also sing with my mind. ¹⁶If you are praising God with your spirit, how can one who finds himself among those who do not understand^h say "Amen" to your thanksgiving, since he does not know what you are saying? ¹⁷You may be giving thanks well enough, but the other man is not edified.

¹⁸I thank God that I speak in tongues more than all of you. ¹⁹But in the church

---

^a30 Or other languages   ^b31 Or But you are eagerly desiring   ^c1 Or languages   ^d3 Some early manuscripts body that I may boast   ^e2 Or another language; also in verses 4, 13, 14, 19, 26 and 27   ^f2 Or by the Spirit   ^g5 Or other languages; also in verses 6, 18, 22, 23 and 39   ^h16 Or among the inquirers

I would rather speak five intelligible words to instruct others than ten thousand words in a tongue.

[20]Brothers, stop thinking like children. In regard to evil be infants, but in your thinking be adults. [21]In the Law it is written:

"Through men of strange tongues
    and through the lips of foreigners
I will speak to this people,
    but even then they will not listen
        to me,"[a]
says the Lord.

[22]Tongues, then, are a sign, not for believers but for unbelievers; prophecy, however, is for believers, not for unbelievers. [23]So if the whole church comes together and everyone speaks in tongues, and some who do not understand[b] or some unbelievers come in, will they not say that you are out of your mind? [24]But if an unbeliever or someone who does not understand[c] comes in while everybody is prophesying, he will be convinced by all that he is a sinner and will be judged by all, [25]and the secrets of his heart will be laid bare. So he will fall down and worship God, exclaiming, "God is really among you!"

Orderly Worship

[26]What then shall we say, brothers? When you come together, everyone has a hymn, or a word of instruction, a revelation, a tongue or an interpretation. All of these must be done for the strengthening of the church. [27]If anyone speaks in a

[a]21 Isaiah 28:11,12   [b]23 Or some inquirers   [c]24 Or or some inquirer

MONDAY

VERSE FOR THE DAY:	AUTHOR:	PASSAGE FOR THE DAY:
1 Corinthians 13:5	Shirley Pope Waite	1 Corinthians 13:1–13

Love Is Not "Rudeness"

WE have a Japanese "daughter," whom we first met when we hosted her and a classmate during a student exchange program. Later we were able to visit Sayuri and her family in Kamakura, Japan.

Our guidebook had told us that the Japanese are a very correct, proper people and offense is easily taken. So we were a little surprised when the family said good-by with such emotion. Sayuri shed tears and pointed to her watch, which she kept set at Walla Walla time.

Our surprise continued when we received the next letter from Sayuri. She ended with these words, "Can I write 'love'! Is it rudeness? But, I love you."

Yes, Sayuri, you may write love any time you want. Love is never rudeness. In fact 1 Corinthians 13 states, "Love . . . is not rude." Love transcends all cultures, races, nationalities and social status.

We love you too, dear Sayuri, our Japanese "daughter"!

Additional Scripture Readings:
John 13:34–35; 1 John 4:19–21

Go to page 1267 for your next devotional reading.

tongue, two—or at the most three—should speak, one at a time, and someone must interpret. [28]If there is no interpreter, the speaker should keep quiet in the church and speak to himself and God.

[29]Two or three prophets should speak, and the others should weigh carefully what is said. [30]And if a revelation comes to someone who is sitting down, the first speaker should stop. [31]For you can all prophesy in turn so that everyone may be instructed and encouraged. [32]The spirits of prophets are subject to the control of prophets. [33]For God is not a God of disorder but of peace.

As in all the congregations of the saints, [34]women should remain silent in the churches. They are not allowed to speak, but must be in submission, as the Law says. [35]If they want to inquire about something, they should ask their own husbands at home; for it is disgraceful for a woman to speak in the church.

[36]Did the word of God originate with you? Or are you the only people it has reached? [37]If anybody thinks he is a prophet or spiritually gifted, let him acknowledge that what I am writing to you is the Lord's command. [38]If he ignores this, he himself will be ignored. [a]

[39]Therefore, my brothers, be eager to prophesy, and do not forbid speaking in tongues. [40]But everything should be done in a fitting and orderly way.

[a]38 Some manuscripts *If he is ignorant of this, let him be ignorant*

TUESDAY

VERSE FOR THE DAY:
1 Corinthians 14:7–8

AUTHOR:
Delores Taylor

PASSAGE FOR THE DAY:
1 Corinthians 14:6–12

Sounds of Distinction

PAUL says that it is better to speak five words that people can understand than to speak volumes that they cannot comprehend. What good is a flute, harp or trumpet unless they play the notes written on the score? But when each player plays the notes written for her instrument, the result is beautiful harmony.

Paul adds that if the trumpet does not give a clear sound, men will not know to prepare for battle. How interesting that Paul mentions both types of instruments. The flute and harp are soft, melodic instruments. Some people are like that—so gentle, kind, comforting and calming. But there is also a need in God's musical ensemble for a trumpeter to warn us of his approach.

When the "notes" are sounding clear, the unbeliever who comes into our Christian gatherings will be convicted of his sin, and his heart will be laid open to the Word of God. Another lost one will have joined God's family.

May he help us to live according to the notes in the "Book."

Additional Scripture Readings:
Judges 7:17–22; Ezekiel 33:1–9

Go to page 1272 for your next devotional reading.

The Resurrection of Christ

15 Now, brothers, I want to remind you of the gospel I preached to you, which you received and on which you have taken your stand. [2]By this gospel you are saved, if you hold firmly to the word I preached to you. Otherwise, you have believed in vain.

[3]For what I received I passed on to you as of first importance[a]: that Christ died for our sins according to the Scriptures, [4]that he was buried, that he was raised on the third day according to the Scriptures, [5]and that he appeared to Peter,[b] and then to the Twelve. [6]After that, he appeared to more than five hundred of the brothers at the same time, most of whom are still living, though some have fallen asleep. [7]Then he appeared to James, then to all the apostles, [8]and last of all he appeared to me also, as to one abnormally born.

[9]For I am the least of the apostles and do not even deserve to be called an apostle, because I persecuted the church of God. [10]But by the grace of God I am what I am, and his grace to me was not without effect. No, I worked harder than all of them—yet not I, but the grace of God that was with me. [11]Whether, then, it was I or they, this is what we preach, and this is what you believed.

The Resurrection of the Dead

[12]But if it is preached that Christ has been raised from the dead, how can some of you say that there is no resurrection of the dead? [13]If there is no resurrection of the dead, then not even Christ has been raised. [14]And if Christ has not been raised, our preaching is useless and so is your faith. [15]More than that, we are then found to be false witnesses about God, for we have testified about God that he raised Christ from the dead. But he did not raise him if in fact the dead are not raised. [16]For if the dead are not raised, then Christ has not been raised either. [17]And if Christ has not been raised, your faith is futile; you are still in your sins. [18]Then those also who have fallen asleep in Christ are lost. [19]If only for this life we have hope in Christ, we are to be pitied more than all men.

[20]But Christ has indeed been raised from the dead, the firstfruits of those who have fallen asleep. [21]For since death came through a man, the resurrection of the dead comes also through a man. [22]For as in Adam all die, so in Christ all will be made alive. [23]But each in his own turn: Christ, the firstfruits; then, when he comes, those who belong to him. [24]Then the end will come, when he hands over the kingdom to God the Father after he has destroyed all dominion, authority and power. [25]For he must reign until he has put all his enemies under his feet. [26]The last enemy to be destroyed is death. [27]For he "has put everything under his feet."[c] Now when it says that "everything" has been put under him, it is clear that this does not include God himself, who put everything under Christ. [28]When he has done this, then the Son himself will be made subject to him who put everything under him, so that God may be all in all.

[29]Now if there is no resurrection, what will those who are baptized for the dead? If the dead are not raised at all, why are people baptized for them? [30]And as for us, why do we endanger ourselves every hour? [31]I die every day—I mean that, brothers—just as surely as I glory over you in Christ Jesus our Lord. [32]If I fought wild beasts in Ephesus for merely human reasons, what have I gained? If the dead are not raised,

"Let us eat and drink,
    for tomorrow we die."[d]

[33]Do not be misled: "Bad company corrupts good character." [34]Come back to your senses as you ought, and stop sinning; for there are some who are ignorant of God—I say this to your shame.

The Resurrection Body

[35]But someone may ask, "How are the dead raised? With what kind of body will they come?" [36]How foolish! What you sow does not come to life unless it dies. [37]When you sow, you do not plant the body that will be, but just a seed, perhaps of wheat or of something else. [38]But God gives it a body as he has determined, and to each kind of seed he gives its own body. [39]All flesh is not the same: Men have one kind of flesh, animals have another, birds another and fish another. [40]There are also heavenly bodies and

---

a3 Or *you at the first*   *b5* Greek *Cephas*   *c27* Psalm 8:6   *d32* Isaiah 22:13

there are earthly bodies; but the splendor of the heavenly bodies is one kind, and the splendor of the earthly bodies is another. ⁴¹The sun has one kind of splendor, the moon another and the stars another; and star differs from star in splendor.

⁴²So will it be with the resurrection of the dead. The body that is sown is perishable, it is raised imperishable; ⁴³it is sown in dishonor, it is raised in glory; it is sown in weakness, it is raised in power; ⁴⁴it is sown a natural body, it is raised a spiritual body.

If there is a natural body, there is also a spiritual body. ⁴⁵So it is written: "The first man Adam became a living being"ᵃ; the last Adam, a life-giving spirit. ⁴⁶The spiritual did not come first, but the natural, and after that the spiritual. ⁴⁷The first man was of the dust of the earth, the second man from heaven. ⁴⁸As was the earthly man, so are those who are of the earth; and as is the man from heaven, so also are those who are of heaven. ⁴⁹And just as we have borne the likeness of the earthly man, so shall weᵇ bear the likeness of the man from heaven.

⁵⁰I declare to you, brothers, that flesh and blood cannot inherit the kingdom of God, nor does the perishable inherit the imperishable. ⁵¹Listen, I tell you a mystery: We will not all sleep, but we will all be changed— ⁵²in a flash, in the twinkling of an eye, at the last trumpet. For the trumpet will sound, the dead will be raised imperishable, and we will be changed. ⁵³For the perishable must clothe itself with the imperishable, and the mortal with immortality. ⁵⁴When the perishable has been clothed with the imperishable, and the mortal with immortality, then the saying that is written will come true: "Death has been swallowed up in victory."ᶜ

⁵⁵"Where, O death, is your victory?
Where, O death, is your sting?"ᵈ

⁵⁶The sting of death is sin, and the power of sin is the law. ⁵⁷But thanks be to God! He gives us the victory through our Lord Jesus Christ.

⁵⁸Therefore, my dear brothers, stand firm. Let nothing move you. Always give yourselves fully to the work of the Lord, because you know that your labor in the Lord is not in vain.

The Collection for God's People

16 Now about the collection for God's people: Do what I told the Galatian churches to do. ²On the first day of every week, each one of you should set aside a sum of money in keeping with his income, saving it up, so that when I come no collections will have to be made. ³Then, when I arrive, I will give letters of introduction to the men you approve and send them with your gift to Jerusalem. ⁴If it seems advisable for me to go also, they will accompany me.

Personal Requests

⁵After I go through Macedonia, I will come to you—for I will be going through Macedonia. ⁶Perhaps I will stay with you awhile, or even spend the winter, so that you can help me on my journey, wherever I go. ⁷I do not want to see you now and make only a passing visit; I hope to spend some time with you, if the Lord permits. ⁸But I will stay on at Ephesus until Pentecost, ⁹because a great door for effective work has opened to me, and there are many who oppose me.

¹⁰If Timothy comes, see to it that he has nothing to fear while he is with you, for he is carrying on the work of the Lord, just as I am. ¹¹No one, then, should refuse to accept him. Send him on his way in peace so that he may return to me. I am expecting him along with the brothers.

¹²Now about our brother Apollos: I strongly urged him to go to you with the brothers. He was quite unwilling to go now, but he will go when he has the opportunity.

¹³Be on your guard; stand firm in the faith; be men of courage; be strong. ¹⁴Do everything in love.

¹⁵You know that the household of Stephanas were the first converts in Achaia, and they have devoted themselves to the service of the saints. I urge you, brothers, ¹⁶to submit to such as these and to everyone who joins in the work, and labors at it. ¹⁷I was glad when Stephanas, Fortunatus and Achaicus arrived, because they have supplied what was lacking from you. ¹⁸For they refreshed my spirit and yours also. Such men deserve recognition.

ᵃ45 Gen. 2:7   ᵇ49 Some early manuscripts *so let us*   ᶜ54 Isaiah 25:8   ᵈ55 Hosea 13:14

Final Greetings

[19]The churches in the province of Asia send you greetings. Aquila and Priscilla[a] greet you warmly in the Lord, and so does the church that meets at their house. [20]All the brothers here send you greetings. Greet one another with a holy kiss.

[21]I, Paul, write this greeting in my own hand.

[22]If anyone does not love the Lord—a curse be on him. Come, O Lord[b]!

[23]The grace of the Lord Jesus be with you.

[24]My love to all of you in Christ Jesus. Amen.[c]

---

[a]19 Greek *Prisca*, a variant of *Priscilla*   [b]22 In Aramaic the expression *Come, O Lord* is *Marana tha.*
[c]24 Some manuscripts do not have *Amen.*

PAUL writes this second letter to the church in Corinth from Macedonia (Acts 20:1; 2 Corinthians 7:5), while on his way to Corinth (2 Corinthians 13:1). As the most personal of all his letters, he expresses both how exciting and how painful his life as a missionary has been. He also finds it necessary to defend himself against those who are criticizing him. As you read this letter, think about how exciting it can be to serve the Lord, but realize too that being a Christian can sometimes lead to ain and suffering.

2 CORINTHIANS

1 Paul, an apostle of Christ Jesus by the will of God, and Timothy our brother,

To the church of God in Corinth, together with all the saints throughout Achaia:

²Grace and peace to you from God our Father and the Lord Jesus Christ.

The God of All Comfort

³Praise be to the God and Father of our Lord Jesus Christ, the Father of compassion and the God of all comfort, ⁴who comforts us in all our troubles, so that we can comfort those in any trouble with the comfort we ourselves have received from God. ⁵For just as the sufferings of Christ flow over into our lives, so also through Christ our comfort overflows. ⁶If we are distressed, it is for your comfort and salvation; if we are comforted, it is for your comfort, which produces in you patient endurance of the same sufferings we suffer. ⁷And our hope for you is firm, because we know that just as you share in our sufferings, so also you share in our comfort.

⁸We do not want you to be uninformed, brothers, about the hardships we suffered in the province of Asia. We were under great pressure, far beyond our ability to endure, so that we despaired even of life. ⁹Indeed, in our hearts we felt the sentence of death. But this happened that we might not rely on ourselves but on God, who raises the dead. ¹⁰He has delivered us from such a deadly peril, and he will deliver us. On him we have set our hope that he will continue to deliver us, ¹¹as you help us by your prayers. Then many will give thanks on our*a* behalf for the gracious favor granted us in answer to the prayers of many.

a11 Many manuscripts your

Paul's Change of Plans

¹²Now this is our boast: Our conscience testifies that we have conducted ourselves in the world, and especially in our relations with you, in the holiness and sincerity that are from God. We have done so not according to worldly wisdom but according to God's grace. ¹³For we do not write you anything you cannot read or understand. And I hope that, ¹⁴as you have understood us in part, you will come to understand fully that you can boast of us just as we will boast of you in the day of the Lord Jesus.

¹⁵Because I was confident of this, I planned to visit you first so that you

WEDNESDAY

VERSE FOR THE DAY:	AUTHOR:	PASSAGE FOR THE DAY:
2 Corinthians 1:6	Barbara Bush	2 Corinthians 1:3–11

Contented Heart, Patient Heart

IT is common to hear women bemoaning their lack of patience as if it were the most difficult gift to pry from God's hand. In fact impatience stems almost solely from our exaggerated notions of what is due us. If we could but lower our estimation of the importance of *our* time, *our* plans and *our* feelings, we would find ourselves almost automatically more patient.

If we are impatient about the same things that anger God—repeated sin, inattention to his Word, social injustice—we cannot really be called impatient (as long as our opinions are expressed in love). Neither can we expect a woman to remain totally unperturbed if someone smashes into her new car. Certainly "learning patience" is not an acceptable reason for failure to discipline a rebellious child. Patience is not the same thing as resignation or the cynical attitude that always expects the worst possible outcome.

Patience is a more positive trait. It is the ability to bear affliction, delay and interruption with calmness, perseverance and confidence in the goodness of God (Colossians 1:11–12). It is inward peace as well as outward control. It is the submission of our schedules, our viewpoints, our dreams to the greater plan of God, with the conviction that he has a good reason for every delay he allows to come our way.

Additional Scripture Readings:
Romans 2:1–8; Colossians 1:10–12

Go to page 1274 for your next devotional reading.

might benefit twice. 16I planned to visit you on my way to Macedonia and to come back to you from Macedonia, and then to have you send me on my way to Judea. 17When I planned this, did I do it lightly? Or do I make my plans in a worldly manner so that in the same breath I say, "Yes, yes" and "No, no"?

18But as surely as God is faithful, our message to you is not "Yes" and "No." 19For the Son of God, Jesus Christ, who was preached among you by me and Silas[a] and Timothy, was not "Yes" and "No," but in him it has always been "Yes." 20For no matter how many promises God has made, they are "Yes" in Christ. And so through him the "Amen" is spoken by us to the glory of God. 21Now it is God who makes both us and you stand firm in Christ. He anointed us, 22set his seal of ownership on us, and put his Spirit in our hearts as a deposit, guaranteeing what is to come.

23I call God as my witness that it was in order to spare you that I did not return to Corinth. 24Not that we lord it over your faith, but we work with you for your joy, because it is by faith you stand firm.

2 1So I made up my mind that I would not make another painful visit to you. 2For if I grieve you, who is left to make me glad but you whom I have grieved? 3I wrote as I did so that when I came I should not be distressed by those who ought to make me rejoice. I had confidence in all of you, that you would all share my joy. 4For I wrote you out of great distress and anguish of heart and with many tears, not to grieve you but to let you know the depth of my love for you.

Forgiveness for the Sinner

5If anyone has caused grief, he has not so much grieved me as he has grieved all of you, to some extent—not to put it too severely. 6The punishment inflicted on him by the majority is sufficient for him. 7Now instead, you ought to forgive and comfort him, so that he will not be overwhelmed by excessive sorrow. 8I urge you, therefore, to reaffirm your love for him. 9The reason I wrote you was to see if you would stand the test and be obedient in everything. 10If you forgive anyone, I also forgive him. And what I have forgiven—if there was anything to forgive—I have forgiven in the sight of Christ for your sake,

11in order that Satan might not outwit us. For we are not unaware of his schemes.

Ministers of the New Covenant

12Now when I went to Troas to preach the gospel of Christ and found that the Lord had opened a door for me, 13I still had no peace of mind, because I did not find my brother Titus there. So I said good-by to them and went on to Macedonia.

14But thanks be to God, who always leads us in triumphal procession in Christ and through us spreads everywhere the fragrance of the knowledge of him. 15For we are to God the aroma of Christ among those who are being saved and those who are perishing. 16To the one we are the smell of death; to the other, the fragrance of life. And who is equal to such a task? 17Unlike so many, we do not peddle the word of God for profit. On the contrary, in Christ we speak before God with sincerity, like men sent from God.

3 Are we beginning to commend ourselves again? Or do we need, like some people, letters of recommendation to you or from you? 2You yourselves are our letter, written on our hearts, known and read by everybody. 3You show that you are a letter from Christ, the result of our ministry, written not with ink but with the Spirit of the living God, not on tablets of stone but on tablets of human hearts.

4Such confidence as this is ours through Christ before God. 5Not that we are competent in ourselves to claim anything for ourselves, but our competence comes from God. 6He has made us competent as ministers of a new covenant—not of the letter but of the Spirit; for the letter kills, but the Spirit gives life.

The Glory of the New Covenant

7Now if the ministry that brought death, which was engraved in letters on stone, came with glory, so that the Israelites could not look steadily at the face of Moses because of its glory, fading though it was, 8will not the ministry of the Spirit be even more glorious? 9If the ministry that condemns men is glorious, how much more glorious is the ministry that brings righteousness! 10For what was glorious has no glory now in comparison with the surpassing glory. 11And if what

a19 Greek Silvanus, a variant of Silas

VERSE FOR THE DAY:	*AUTHOR:*	*PASSAGE FOR THE DAY:*
2 Corinthians 3:3	Beth Donigan Seversen	2 Corinthians 3:3–5

A Lost Letter

The Screwtape Letters, by C. S. Lewis, is a fictitious diary of scolding letters from a mature demon (Screwtape) to his young nephew (Wormwood). It is Wormwood's job to keep a recent convert to Christianity from being productive for Christ (the Enemy). Screwtape's letters point out where Wormwood has failed or missed an opportunity. I have often mused that there must be a missing appendix to these letters somewhere that reads like this . . .

My dear Wormwood,

The following instructions shall help you proceed in handicapping your convert's effectiveness in the Enemy's kingdom. One of our great allies at present is her perception of herself. It is your task, therefore, to feed her poor self-esteem. Already she wastes time primping in front of the mirror and worrying about her looks.

You must continue to encourage her to compare herself with so-called "spiritual giants" whom she admires. This will eventually immobilize her. When she feels inadequate she will no longer attempt anything for the Enemy's kingdom because of her fear of failure. Her warped self-image will lead to unhealthy relationships and hinder her ability to love others. The more often she tells herself that she is a bad person—that she's not competent—the more easily she will feel threatened by others. This will turn others off to the Enemy and his loathsome Christianity.

Ultimately, her relationship with the Enemy himself will be adversely affected. Since she is not satisfied with how the Enemy has created her, her intimacy with him will be destroyed and she will find it difficult to trust the Enemy, pray to him or read that detestable Book.

Finally, emphasize her weaknesses so repeatedly that she begins to believe that she is unimportant to the Enemy. This will push her to compulsive striving to please him through her own accomplishments. Her works will no longer be motivated by faith, but by a dislike for herself. Confuse her so that she never feels forgiven. If you successfully convince her that the Enemy is never pleased with her, she will grow weary and give up altogether. But, more of this in my next letter.

Your affectionate uncle,
Screwtape

Additional Scripture Readings:
Jeremiah 17:7–8; Galatians 6:2–10

Go to page 1276 for your next devotional reading.

was fading away came with glory, how much greater is the glory of that which lasts!

¹²Therefore, since we have such a hope, we are very bold. ¹³We are not like Moses, who would put a veil over his face to keep the Israelites from gazing at it while the radiance was fading away. ¹⁴But their minds were made dull, for to this day the same veil remains when the old covenant is read. It has not been removed, because only in Christ is it taken away. ¹⁵Even to this day when Moses is read, a veil covers their hearts. ¹⁶But whenever anyone turns to the Lord, the veil is taken away. ¹⁷Now the Lord is the Spirit, and where the Spirit of the Lord is, there is freedom. ¹⁸And we, who with unveiled faces all reflect*a* the Lord's glory, are being transformed into his likeness with ever-increasing glory, which comes from the Lord, who is the Spirit.

Treasures in Jars of Clay

4 Therefore, since through God's mercy we have this ministry, we do not lose heart. ²Rather, we have renounced secret and shameful ways; we do not use deception, nor do we distort the word of God. On the contrary, by setting forth the truth plainly we commend ourselves to every man's conscience in the sight of God. ³And even if our gospel is veiled, it is veiled to those who are perishing. ⁴The god of this age has blinded the minds of unbelievers, so that they cannot see the light of the gospel of the glory of Christ, who is the image of God. ⁵For we do not preach ourselves, but Jesus Christ as Lord, and ourselves as your servants for Jesus' sake. ⁶For God, who said, "Let light shine out of darkness,"*b* made his light shine in our hearts to give us the light of the knowledge of the glory of God in the face of Christ.

⁷But we have this treasure in jars of clay to show that this all-surpassing power is from God and not from us. ⁸We are hard pressed on every side, but not crushed; perplexed, but not in despair; ⁹persecuted, but not abandoned; struck down, but not destroyed. ¹⁰We always carry around in our body the death of Jesus, so that the life of Jesus may also be revealed in our body. ¹¹For we who are alive are always being given over to death for Jesus' sake, so that his life may be revealed in our mortal body. ¹²So then,

death is at work in us, but life is at work in you.

¹³It is written: "I believed; therefore I have spoken."*c* With that same spirit of faith we also believe and therefore speak, ¹⁴because we know that the one who raised the Lord Jesus from the dead will also raise us with Jesus and present us with you in his presence. ¹⁵All this is for your benefit, so that the grace that is reaching more and more people may cause thanksgiving to overflow to the glory of God.

¹⁶Therefore we do not lose heart. Though outwardly we are wasting away, yet inwardly we are being renewed day by day. ¹⁷For our light and momentary troubles are achieving for us an eternal glory that far outweighs them all. ¹⁸So we fix our eyes not on what is seen, but on what is unseen. For what is seen is temporary, but what is unseen is eternal.

Our Heavenly Dwelling

5 Now we know that if the earthly tent we live in is destroyed, we have a building from God, an eternal house in heaven, not built by human hands. ²Meanwhile we groan, longing to be clothed with our heavenly dwelling, ³because when we are clothed, we will not be found naked. ⁴For while we are in this tent, we groan and are burdened, because we do not wish to be unclothed but to be clothed with our heavenly dwelling, so that what is mortal may be swallowed up by life. ⁵Now it is God who has made us for this very purpose and has given us the Spirit as a deposit, guaranteeing what is to come.

⁶Therefore we are always confident and know that as long as we are at home in the body we are away from the Lord. ⁷We live by faith, not by sight. ⁸We are confident, I say, and would prefer to be away from the body and at home with the Lord. ⁹So we make it our goal to please him, whether we are at home in the body or away from it. ¹⁰For we must all appear before the judgment seat of Christ, that each one may receive what is due him for the things done while in the body, whether good or bad.

The Ministry of Reconciliation

¹¹Since, then, we know what it is to fear the Lord, we try to persuade men. What we are is plain to God, and I hope it is also

a18 Or *contemplate*   *b6* Gen. 1:3   *c13* Psalm 116:10

VERSE FOR THE DAY:
2 Corinthians 4:16

AUTHOR:
Karen Burton Mains

PASSAGE FOR THE DAY:
2 Corinthians 4:1–18

Keepin' Talkin'

FOR years, February days when I was housebound with small children were the hardest times of all. I longed for the sun to shine two days in a row. I yearned for spring, knowing all too well that madding March with its melted layers of accreted winter's filth barred my isolated heart from the rioting green blooms of April. It was during these shadowy days, dragging with plodding prisoner's feet, that I learned how important it is to "keepin' talkin' " (a phrase coined by my son David when he was two) with God.

A major part of the mature Christian journey is learning how to handle those times when the heavens are locked, when our lives are weighted with the winter garments of despair, pain, worry and loss. We try desperately to convince ourselves that we don't serve a God who has absented himself from the listening post, who has hung up a "Shop's Closed" sign and taken off to vacation somewhere in the balmy south.

The Psalms are a prayer journal, an ongoing record of one man's conversations with God. Many of these poem-songs are about times when David hit a roadblock to intimate dialogue with God:

> O LORD, how many are my foes!
>   How many rise up against me!
> Many are saying of me,
>   "God will not deliver him" (Psalm 3:1).
>
> Give ear to my words, O LORD,
>   consider my sighing.
> Listen to my cry for help,
>   my King and my God (Psalm 5:1–2).
>
> O LORD, do not rebuke me in your anger
>   or discipline me in your wrath.
> Be merciful to me, LORD, for I am faint;
>   O LORD, heal me, for my bones are in agony
>   (Psalm 6:1–2).

David's words reiterate the old truth I began to learn while sitting at the dining table, tutored by my own small child: When your soul feels like a gray February day, and all seems to be rain, fog and chill drizzle, the overcast can be lifted if you will learn to just "keepin' talkin' " with God.

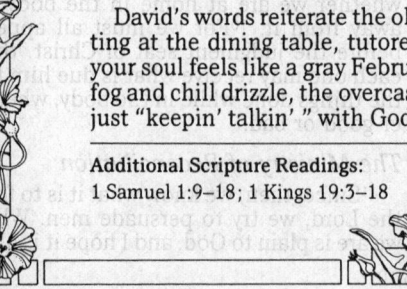

Additional Scripture Readings:
1 Samuel 1:9–18; 1 Kings 19:3–18

Go to page 1278 for your next devotional reading.

plain to your conscience. [12]We are not trying to commend ourselves to you again, but are giving you an opportunity to take pride in us, so that you can answer those who take pride in what is seen rather than in what is in the heart. [13]If we are out of our mind, it is for the sake of God; if we are in our right mind, it is for you. [14]For Christ's love compels us, because we are convinced that one died for all, and therefore all died. [15]And he died for all, that those who live should no longer live for themselves but for him who died for them and was raised again.

[16]So from now on we regard no one from a worldly point of view. Though we once regarded Christ in this way, we do so no longer. [17]Therefore, if anyone is in Christ, he is a new creation; the old has gone, the new has come! [18]All this is from God, who reconciled us to himself through Christ and gave us the ministry of reconciliation: [19]that God was reconciling the world to himself in Christ, not counting men's sins against them. And he has committed to us the message of reconciliation. [20]We are therefore Christ's ambassadors, as though God were making his appeal through us. We implore you on Christ's behalf: Be reconciled to God. [21]God made him who had no sin to be sin[a] for us, so that in him we might become the righteousness of God.

6 As God's fellow workers we urge you not to receive God's grace in vain. [2]For he says,

"In the time of my favor I heard you,
    and in the day of salvation I helped
        you."[b]

I tell you, now is the time of God's favor, now is the day of salvation.

Paul's Hardships

[3]We put no stumbling block in anyone's path, so that our ministry will not be discredited. [4]Rather, as servants of God we commend ourselves in every way: in great endurance; in troubles, hardships and distresses; [5]in beatings, imprisonments and riots; in hard work, sleepless nights and hunger; [6]in purity, understanding, patience and kindness; in the Holy Spirit and in sincere love; [7]in truthful speech and in the power of God; with weapons of righteousness in the right hand and in the left; [8]through glory and dishonor, bad report and good report; genuine, yet regarded as impostors; [9]known, yet regarded as unknown; dying, and yet we live on; beaten, and yet not killed; [10]sorrowful, yet always rejoicing; poor, yet making many rich; having nothing, and yet possessing everything.

[11]We have spoken freely to you, Corinthians, and opened wide our hearts to you. [12]We are not withholding our affection from you, but you are withholding yours from us. [13]As a fair exchange—I speak as to my children—open wide your hearts also.

Do Not Be Yoked With Unbelievers

[14]Do not be yoked together with unbelievers. For what do righteousness and wickedness have in common? Or what fellowship can light have with darkness? [15]What harmony is there between Christ and Belial[c]? What does a believer have in common with an unbeliever? [16]What agreement is there between the temple of God and idols? For we are the temple of the living God. As God has said: "I will live with them and walk among them, and I will be their God, and they will be my people."[d]

[17]"Therefore come out from them
    and be separate,
                    says the Lord.
Touch no unclean thing,
    and I will receive you."[e]
[18]"I will be a Father to you,
    and you will be my sons and
        daughters,
                says the Lord Almighty."[f]

7 Since we have these promises, dear friends, let us purify ourselves from everything that contaminates body and spirit, perfecting holiness out of reverence for God.

Paul's Joy

[2]Make room for us in your hearts. We have wronged no one, we have corrupted no one, we have exploited no one. [3]I do not say this to condemn you; I have said before that you have such a place in our hearts that we would live or die with you. [4]I have great confidence in you; I take great pride in you. I am greatly encouraged; in all our troubles my joy knows no bounds.

[5]For when we came into Macedonia,

---

[a]21 Or *be a sin offering*   [b]2 Isaiah 49:8   [c]15 Greek *Beliar*, a variant of *Belial*   [d]16 Lev. 26:12; Jer. 32:38; Ezek. 37:27   [e]17 Isaiah 52:11; Ezek. 20:34,41   [f]18 2 Samuel 7:14; 7:8

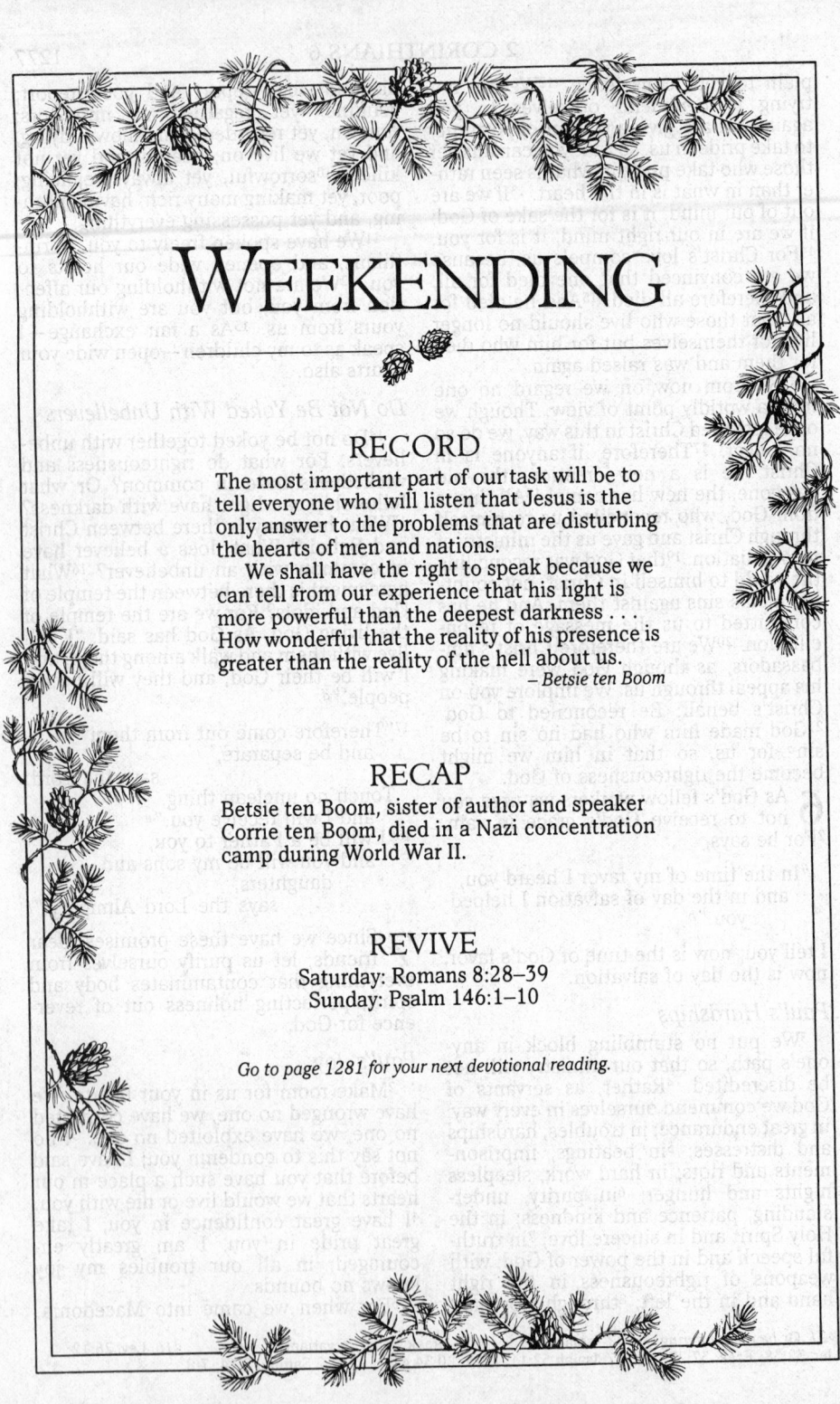

WEEKENDING

RECORD

The most important part of our task will be to tell everyone who will listen that Jesus is the only answer to the problems that are disturbing the hearts of men and nations.

We shall have the right to speak because we can tell from our experience that his light is more powerful than the deepest darkness . . . How wonderful that the reality of his presence is greater than the reality of the hell about us.

– Betsie ten Boom

RECAP

Betsie ten Boom, sister of author and speaker Corrie ten Boom, died in a Nazi concentration camp during World War II.

REVIVE

Saturday: Romans 8:28–39
Sunday: Psalm 146:1–10

Go to page 1281 for your next devotional reading.

this body of ours had no rest, but we were harassed at every turn—conflicts on the outside, fears within. [6]But God, who comforts the downcast, comforted us by the coming of Titus, [7]and not only by his coming but also by the comfort you had given him. He told us about your longing for me, your deep sorrow, your ardent concern for me, so that my joy was greater than ever.

[8]Even if I caused you sorrow by my letter, I do not regret it. Though I did regret it—I see that my letter hurt you, but only for a little while— [9]yet now I am happy, not because you were made sorry, but because your sorrow led you to repentance. For you became sorrowful as God intended and so were not harmed in any way by us. [10]Godly sorrow brings repentance that leads to salvation and leaves no regret, but worldly sorrow brings death. [11]See what this godly sorrow has produced in you: what earnestness, what eagerness to clear yourselves, what indignation, what alarm, what longing, what concern, what readiness to see justice done. At every point you have proved yourselves to be innocent in this matter. [12]So even though I wrote to you, it was not on account of the one who did the wrong or of the injured party, but rather that before God you could see for yourselves how devoted to us you are. [13]By all this we are encouraged.

In addition to our own encouragement, we were especially delighted to see how happy Titus was, because his spirit has been refreshed by all of you. [14]I had boasted to him about you, and you have not embarrassed me. But just as everything we said to you was true, so our boasting about you to Titus has proved to be true as well. [15]And his affection for you is all the greater when he remembers that you were all obedient, receiving him with fear and trembling. [16]I am glad I can have complete confidence in you.

Generosity Encouraged

8 And now, brothers, we want you to know about the grace that God has given the Macedonian churches. [2]Out of the most severe trial, their overflowing joy and their extreme poverty welled up in rich generosity. [3]For I testify that they gave as much as they were able, and even beyond their ability. Entirely on their own, [4]they urgently pleaded with us for the privilege of sharing in this service to the saints. [5]And they did not do as we expected, but they gave themselves first to the Lord and then to us in keeping with God's will. [6]So we urged Titus, since he had earlier made a beginning, to bring also to completion this act of grace on your part. [7]But just as you excel in everything—in faith, in speech, in knowledge, in complete earnestness and in your love for us[a]—see that you also excel in this grace of giving.

[8]I am not commanding you, but I want to test the sincerity of your love by comparing it with the earnestness of others. [9]For you know the grace of our Lord Jesus Christ, that though he was rich, yet for your sakes he became poor, so that you through his poverty might become rich.

[10]And here is my advice about what is best for you in this matter: Last year you were the first not only to give but also to have the desire to do so. [11]Now finish the work, so that your eager willingness to do it may be matched by your completion of it, according to your means. [12]For if the willingness is there, the gift is acceptable according to what one has, not according to what he does not have.

[13]Our desire is not that others might be relieved while you are hard pressed, but that there might be equality. [14]At the present time your plenty will supply what they need, so that in turn their plenty will supply what you need. Then there will be equality, [15]as it is written: "He who gathered much did not have too much, and he who gathered little did not have too little."[b]

Titus Sent to Corinth

[16]I thank God, who put into the heart of Titus the same concern I have for you. [17]For Titus not only welcomed our appeal, but he is coming to you with much enthusiasm and on his own initiative. [18]And we are sending along with him the brother who is praised by all the churches for his service to the gospel. [19]What is more, he was chosen by the churches to accompany us as we carry the offering, which we administer in order to honor the Lord himself and to show our eagerness to help. [20]We want to avoid any criticism of the way we administer this liberal gift. [21]For we are taking pains to do what is right, not only in the eyes of the Lord but also in the eyes of men.

---

[a]7 Some manuscripts *in our love for you*   [b]15 Exodus 16:18

²²In addition, we are sending with them our brother who has often proved to us in many ways that he is zealous, and now even more so because of his great confidence in you. ²³As for Titus, he is my partner and fellow worker among you; as for our brothers, they are representatives of the churches and an honor to Christ. ²⁴Therefore show these men the proof of your love and the reason for our pride in you, so that the churches can see it.

9 There is no need for me to write to you about this service to the saints. ²For I know your eagerness to help, and I have been boasting about it to the Macedonians, telling them that since last year you in Achaia were ready to give; and your enthusiasm has stirred most of them to action. ³But I am sending the brothers in order that our boasting about you in this matter should not prove hollow, but that you may be ready, as I said you would be. ⁴For if any Macedonians come with me and find you unprepared, we—not to say anything about you—would be ashamed of having been so confident. ⁵So I thought it necessary to urge the brothers to visit you in advance and finish the arrangements for the generous gift you had promised. Then it will be ready as a generous gift, not as one grudgingly given.

Sowing Generously

⁶Remember this: Whoever sows sparingly will also reap sparingly, and whoever sows generously will also reap generously. ⁷Each man should give what he has decided in his heart to give, not reluctantly or under compulsion, for God loves a cheerful giver. ⁸And God is able to make all grace abound to you, so that in all things at all times, having all that you need, you will abound in every good work. ⁹As it is written:

> "He has scattered abroad his gifts to the poor;
> his righteousness endures forever."ᵃ

¹⁰Now he who supplies seed to the sower and bread for food will also supply and increase your store of seed and will enlarge the harvest of your righteousness. ¹¹You will be made rich in every way so that you can be generous on every occasion, and through us your generosity will result in thanksgiving to God.

¹²This service that you perform is not only supplying the needs of God's people but is also overflowing in many expressions of thanks to God. ¹³Because of the service by which you have proved yourselves, men will praise God for the obedience that accompanies your confession of the gospel of Christ, and for your generosity in sharing with them and with everyone else. ¹⁴And in their prayers for you their hearts will go out to you, because of the surpassing grace God has given you. ¹⁵Thanks be to God for his indescribable gift!

Paul's Defense of His Ministry

10 By the meekness and gentleness of Christ, I appeal to you—I, Paul, who am "timid" when face to face with you, but "bold" when away! ²I beg you that when I come I may not have to be as bold as I expect to be toward some people who think that we live by the standards of this world. ³For though we live in the world, we do not wage war as the world does. ⁴The weapons we fight with are not the weapons of the world. On the contrary, they have divine power to demolish strongholds. ⁵We demolish arguments and every pretension that sets itself up against the knowledge of God, and we take captive every thought to make it obedient to Christ. ⁶And we will be ready to punish every act of disobedience, once your obedience is complete.

⁷You are looking only on the surface of things.ᵇ If anyone is confident that he belongs to Christ, he should consider again that we belong to Christ just as much as he. ⁸For even if I boast somewhat freely about the authority the Lord gave us for building you up rather than pulling you down, I will not be ashamed of it. ⁹I do not want to seem to be trying to frighten you with my letters. ¹⁰For some say, "His letters are weighty and forceful, but in person he is unimpressive and his speaking amounts to nothing." ¹¹Such people should realize that what we are in our letters when we are absent, we will be in our actions when we are present.

¹²We do not dare to classify or compare ourselves with some who commend themselves. When they measure themselves by themselves and compare themselves with themselves, they are not wise. ¹³We, however, will not boast beyond

proper limits, but will confine our boasting to the field God has assigned to us, a field that reaches even to you. [14]We are not going too far in our boasting, as would be the case if we had not come to you, for we did get as far as you with the gospel of Christ. [15]Neither do we go beyond our limits by boasting of work done by others.[a] Our hope is that, as your faith continues to grow, our area of activity among you will greatly expand, [16]so that we can preach the gospel in the regions beyond you. For we do not want to boast about work already done in another man's territory. [17]But, "Let him who boasts boast in the Lord."[b] [18]For it is not the one who commends himself who is approved, but the one whom the Lord commends.

[a]13-15 Or [13]We, however, will not boast about things that cannot be measured, but we will boast according to the standard of measurement that the God of measure has assigned us—a measurement that relates even to you. [14] . . . . [15]Neither do we boast about things that cannot be measured in regard to the work done by others.　[b]17 Jer. 9:24

MONDAY

VERSE FOR THE DAY:	AUTHOR:	PASSAGE FOR THE DAY:
2 Corinthians 9:8	Wanda K. Jones	2 Corinthians 9:6–11

God Is Able

I NEEDED assurance from God that he would be with me when I was about to graduate from college, get married six weeks later and then leave with my minister husband to work in Harlem, New York. He gave me that assurance in 2 Corinthians 9:8.

The Lord proved to me over and over that his grace and favor are plentiful. He gave me wisdom and love as I sought to help young people handle the problems of daily living in the midst of poverty. As a result, many found that God is able to help them "abound in every good work." I found that God was able to give our family strength and courage during the time my husband was caught in a coup d'etat just as his evangelistic meetings had ended in Ghana. And God was able to bring my husband back to us.

I found that God was able to quiet fear when I visited one of my retarded students who was very ill in the hospital. She was apprehensive because she was not able to be at home or at school with the rest of her friends. But I prayed with her and said softly when I left, "Mary, don't be afraid. Jesus is in this very room. He is able to keep you from being afraid. He is here even though you can't see him." With that assurance of God's ability to care for her, Mary quietly smiled.

Perhaps as you read the "all's" of God in 2 Corinthians 9:8, you might think of some circumstances in your life that seem insurmountable. It's true that sometimes simple, everyday things can loom so large that you feel caught up in a maze with no exit.

In times like these, remember: God is able!

Additional Scripture Readings:
Ephesians 1:18–21; Jude 20–25

Go to page 1282 for your next devotional reading.

Paul and the False Apostles

11 I hope you will put up with a little of my foolishness; but you are already doing that. ²I am jealous for you with a godly jealousy. I promised you to one husband, to Christ, so that I might present you as a pure virgin to him. ³But I am afraid that just as Eve was deceived by the serpent's cunning, your minds may somehow be led astray from your sincere and pure devotion to Christ. ⁴For if someone comes to you and preaches a Jesus other than the Jesus we preached, or if you receive a different spirit from the one you received, or a different gospel from the one you accepted, you put up with it easily enough. ⁵But I do not think I am in the least inferior to those "super-apostles." ⁶I may not be a trained speaker, but I do have knowledge. We have made this perfectly clear to you in every way.

⁷Was it a sin for me to lower myself in order to elevate you by preaching the gospel of God to you free of charge? ⁸I robbed other churches by receiving support from them so as to serve you. ⁹And when I was with you and needed something, I was

TUESDAY

VERSE FOR THE DAY:
2 Corinthians 10:14

AUTHOR:
Linda Ching Sledge

PASSAGE FOR THE DAY:
2 Corinthians 10:12–18

Just Right!

"HEY, it fits good!" said five-year-old Geoffrey from inside the floppy tent of his older brother's sweatshirt.

When he heard me laugh, Geoffrey poked his head out like a turtle and said, "I'm NOT too little!" Then he stormed upstairs and slammed his door.

Later, I peeked in to find both boys sprawled on the bed.

"You're big enough," Tim was saying. "Bigger than the babies next door. You're just right for five years old."

I was struck by Tim's answer: You're just right . . . . For the last year, I had tried to model myself after a woman I admired: a well-known Christian churchwoman, mother and wife. How did she integrate God so effortlessly into her busy life? With a simple phrase, she turned ordinary events into unforgettable celebrations of God's love. I, on the other hand, was always scrambling to pull together a church school lesson a half hour before church.

It took me some time to see it, but gradually it dawned on me that growing spiritually is not climbing to perfection; it's doing what you do with genuine devotion. Looking back, I hadn't even come close to emulating the woman I admired. I wasn't her size! Nevertheless I had grown in simple and essential areas: reading the Bible regularly, enjoying teaching at church, praying often and walking closer to him.

Sometimes the desire to grow makes us feel "too little," when in reality we are just the right size for now—and always good enough in God's eyes.

Additional Scripture Readings:
Ephesians 2:8–10; 2 Thessalonians 1:3–4

Go to page 1284 for your next devotional reading.

not a burden to anyone, for the brothers who came from Macedonia supplied what I needed. I have kept myself from being a burden to you in any way, and will continue to do so. 10As surely as the truth of Christ is in me, nobody in the regions of Achaia will stop this boasting of mine. 11Why? Because I do not love you? God knows I do! 12And I will keep on doing what I am doing in order to cut the ground from under those who want an opportunity to be considered equal with us in the things they boast about.

13For such men are false apostles, deceitful workmen, masquerading as apostles of Christ. 14And no wonder, for Satan himself masquerades as an angel of light. 15It is not surprising, then, if his servants masquerade as servants of righteousness. Their end will be what their actions deserve.

Paul Boasts About His Sufferings

16I repeat: Let no one take me for a fool. But if you do, then receive me just as you would a fool, so that I may do a little boasting. 17In this self-confident boasting I am not talking as the Lord would, but as a fool. 18Since many are boasting in the way the world does, I too will boast. 19You gladly put up with fools since you are so wise! 20In fact, you even put up with anyone who enslaves you or exploits you or takes advantage of you or pushes himself forward or slaps you in the face. 21To my shame I admit that we were too weak for that!

What anyone else dares to boast about —I am speaking as a fool—I also dare to boast about. 22Are they Hebrews? So am I. Are they Israelites? So am I. Are they Abraham's descendants? So am I. 23Are they servants of Christ? (I am out of my mind to talk like this.) I am more. I have worked much harder, been in prison more frequently, been flogged more severely, and been exposed to death again and again. 24Five times I received from the Jews the forty lashes minus one. 25Three times I was beaten with rods, once I was stoned, three times I was shipwrecked, I spent a night and a day in the open sea, 26I have been constantly on the move. I have been in danger from rivers, in danger from bandits, in danger from my own countrymen, in danger from Gentiles; in danger in the city, in danger in the country, in danger at sea; and in danger from false brothers. 27I have labored and toiled and have often gone without sleep; I have

known hunger and thirst and have often gone without food; I have been cold and naked. 28Besides everything else, I face daily the pressure of my concern for all the churches. 29Who is weak, and I do not feel weak? Who is led into sin, and I do not inwardly burn?

30If I must boast, I will boast of the things that show my weakness. 31The God and Father of the Lord Jesus, who is to be praised forever, knows that I am not lying. 32In Damascus the governor under King Aretas had the city of the Damascenes guarded in order to arrest me. 33But I was lowered in a basket from a window in the wall and slipped through his hands.

Paul's Vision and His Thorn

12 I must go on boasting. Although there is nothing to be gained, I will go on to visions and revelations from the Lord. 2I know a man in Christ who fourteen years ago was caught up to the third heaven. Whether it was in the body or out of the body I do not know—God knows. 3And I know that this man—whether in the body or apart from the body I do not know, but God knows— 4was caught up to paradise. He heard inexpressible things, things that man is not permitted to tell. 5I will boast about a man like that, but I will not boast about myself, except about my weaknesses. 6Even if I should choose to boast, I would not be a fool, because I would be speaking the truth. But I refrain, so no one will think more of me than is warranted by what I do or say.

7To keep me from becoming conceited because of these surpassingly great revelations, there was given me a thorn in my flesh, a messenger of Satan, to torment me. 8Three times I pleaded with the Lord to take it away from me. 9But he said to me, "My grace is sufficient for you, for my power is made perfect in weakness." Therefore I will boast all the more gladly about my weaknesses, so that Christ's power may rest on me. 10That is why, for Christ's sake, I delight in weaknesses, in insults, in hardships, in persecutions, in difficulties. For when I am weak, then I am strong.

Paul's Concern for the Corinthians

11I have made a fool of myself, but you drove me to it. I ought to have been commended by you, for I am not in the least inferior to the "super-apostles," even though I am nothing. 12The things that mark an apostle—signs, wonders and

VERSE FOR THE DAY:
2 Corinthians 12:9

AUTHOR:
Marie Chapian

PASSAGE FOR THE DAY:
2 Corinthians 12:1–10

His Power Made Perfect

WHILE in Europe researching my book *Of Whom the World Was Not Worthy* (Bethany House, 1979), I traveled through Yugoslavia from Slovenia to Macedonia. I interviewed factory workers, peasants, gypsies, doctors and laborers, as well as former Communist party officials. I wanted to know how Christians sustained their faith through the devastation of two world wars. I heard story after story of courage in the face of seemingly insurmountable obstacles.

I talked to those who had been imprisoned and whose future seemed hopeless; people who had been sick and wasted physically; frail women who fought in the Partisan army against the Fascists with only sticks for weapons; people who were starving, who ate scraps out of garbage cans. These were brave people—weak, defenseless people—but those for whom the grace of the Lord was sufficient. In their weakness, his power was made perfect.

I looked at my own life and asked myself if my weaknesses were an opportunity for God's power to be made perfect in me. Did I really accept his grace as sufficient in every situation? The apostle Paul suffered a thorn in the flesh that he begged the Lord to remove. The Lord responded not by removing the agonizing source of pain but by giving the apostle the strength to bear it (2 Corinthians 12:7–9). This is how God often works. He does not spare us from suffering but enables us to conquer it.

I've seen shy people become great leaders, and I've seen physically ill people become charged with spiritual energy and touch other lives with the power of the gospel of Christ. I've seen suffering people become shining examples of strength and power. And through this I've learned that nothing can break or destroy us when we allow our weaknesses to make us strong.

There is sublime joy in holy boasting of the power of God in a life that is totally dependent on him. There is sublime peace in accepting the sufficiency of God's grace by allowing him to be strong in us where we are weak.

Additional Scripture Readings:
Romans 8:26–27; 1 Corinthians 1:25–31

Go to page 1287 for your next devotional reading.

miracles—were done among you with great perseverance. [13]How were you inferior to the other churches, except that I was never a burden to you? Forgive me this wrong!

[14]Now I am ready to visit you for the third time, and I will not be a burden to you, because what I want is not your possessions but you. After all, children should not have to save up for their parents, but parents for their children. [15]So I will very gladly spend for you everything I have and expend myself as well. If I love you more, will you love me less? [16]Be that as it may, I have not been a burden to you. Yet, crafty fellow that I am, I caught you by trickery! [17]Did I exploit you through any of the men I sent you? [18]I urged Titus to go to you and I sent our brother with him. Titus did not exploit you, did he? Did we not act in the same spirit and follow the same course?

[19]Have you been thinking all along that we have been defending ourselves to you? We have been speaking in the sight of God as those in Christ; and everything we do, dear friends, is for your strengthening. [20]For I am afraid that when I come I may not find you as I want you to be, and you may not find me as you want me to be. I fear that there may be quarreling, jealousy, outbursts of anger, factions, slander, gossip, arrogance and disorder. [21]I am afraid that when I come again my God will humble me before you, and I will be grieved over many who have sinned earlier and have not repented of the impurity, sexual sin and debauchery in which they have indulged.

Final Warnings

13 This will be my third visit to you. "Every matter must be established by the testimony of two or three witnesses."[a] [2]I already gave you a warning when I was with you the second time. I now repeat it while absent: On my return I will not spare those who sinned earlier or any of the others, [3]since you are demanding proof that Christ is speaking through me. He is not weak in dealing with you, but is powerful among you. [4]For to be sure, he was crucified in weakness, yet he lives by God's power. Likewise, we are weak in him, yet by God's power we will live with him to serve you.

[5]Examine yourselves to see whether you are in the faith; test yourselves. Do you not realize that Christ Jesus is in you —unless, of course, you fail the test? [6]And I trust that you will discover that we have not failed the test. [7]Now we pray to God that you will not do anything wrong. Not that people will see that we have stood the test but that you will do what is right even though we may seem to have failed. [8]For we cannot do anything against the truth, but only for the truth. [9]We are glad whenever we are weak but you are strong; and our prayer is for your perfection. [10]This is why I write these things when I am absent, that when I come I may not have to be harsh in my use of authority—the authority the Lord gave me for building you up, not for tearing you down.

Final Greetings

[11]Finally, brothers, good-by. Aim for perfection, listen to my appeal, be of one mind, live in peace. And the God of love and peace will be with you.

[12]Greet one another with a holy kiss. [13]All the saints send their greetings.

[14]May the grace of the Lord Jesus Christ, and the love of God, and the fellowship of the Holy Spirit be with you all.

*P*AUL writes this letter to the churches
he founded in Galatia (Acts
13:13–14:28), warning them against
certain false teachers. He reminds them
of the simple message of salvation by
faith alone, which he and other church
leaders teach, and concludes with advice on how to live a Spirit-filled life.
As you read this book, be sure that you
are saved by a personal faith in Jesus,
and ask God's Spirit to help you walk
in Christian love and peace.

GALATIANS

1 Paul, an apostle—sent not from men
nor by man, but by Jesus Christ and
God the Father, who raised him from
the dead— ²and all the brothers with
me,

To the churches in Galatia:

³Grace and peace to you from God our
Father and the Lord Jesus Christ, ⁴who
gave himself for our sins to rescue us from
the present evil age, according to the will
of our God and Father, ⁵to whom be glory
for ever and ever. Amen.

No Other Gospel

⁶I am astonished that you are so quickly deserting the one who called you by the
grace of Christ and are turning to a different gospel— ⁷which is really no gospel at
all. Evidently some people are throwing
you into confusion and are trying to pervert the gospel of Christ. ⁸But even if we
or an angel from heaven should preach a
gospel other than the one we preached to
you, let him be eternally condemned! ⁹As
we have already said, so now I say again:
If anybody is preaching to you a gospel
other than what you accepted, let him be
eternally condemned!

¹⁰Am I now trying to win the approval
of men, or of God? Or am I trying to
please men? If I were still trying to please
men, I would not be a servant of Christ.

Paul Called by God

¹¹I want you to know, brothers, that the gospel I preached is not something that man made up. ¹²I did not receive it from any man, nor was I taught it; rather, I received it by revelation from Jesus Christ.

¹³For you have heard of my previous way of life in Judaism, how intensely I persecuted the church of God and tried to destroy it. ¹⁴I was advancing in Judaism beyond many Jews of my own age and was extremely zealous for the traditions of my fathers. ¹⁵But when God, who set me apart from birth*ᵃ* and called me by his grace, was pleased ¹⁶to reveal his Son in me so that I might preach him among the Gentiles, I did not consult any man, ¹⁷nor did I go up to Jerusalem to see those who were apostles before I was, but I went immediately into Arabia and later returned to Damascus.

¹⁸Then after three years, I went up to Jerusalem to get acquainted with Peter*ᵇ*

ᵃ15 Or from my mother's womb   ᵇ18 Greek Cephas

THURSDAY

VERSE FOR THE DAY:
Galatians 2:20

AUTHOR:
Rebecca Manley Pippert

PASSAGE FOR THE DAY:
Galatians 2:15–21

More Myself

CHRISTIANITY isn't a narcotic that dulls you into obedience. It involves battle—it's excruciating to give up control. But that is why we must not feel despair if we are struggling. To struggle does not mean we are incorrigible. It means we are *alive*!

A disciple says, "I hear you, Lord. It's the nuttiest thing I ever heard of. It's risky. I'll look like a fool, but I'll do it. Because my life is no longer committed to doing my thing but your thing." Heaven will not be filled with innocent people, running around saying, "Oh, was there another way? I guess I never noticed." Rather they will say, "You bet there were other options that begged to control me. By God's grace and my struggle, Jesus is my Lord."

Is Jesus' desire to be the Lord of our lives some little fetish of his? Why is it so important to him? Why should we want him to have control of our lives? Besides the fact that he deserves it because of who he is, he knows he is the only one in the universe who can control us without destroying us. No one will ever love you like Jesus. No one will ever know you better, care more for your wholeness. The last breath Jesus breathed on this planet was for you. Jesus will meet you wherever you are and he will help you. He is not intimidated by past failures, broken promises or wounds. He will make sense out of your brokenness. But he can only begin to be the Lord of your life today, not next Monday or next month, but now.

And the great and joyful paradox is that while he totally transforms us he makes us more ourselves than ever before.

Additional Scripture Readings:
Luke 9:23–25; Philippians 3:20–21

Go to page 1289 for your next devotional reading.

and stayed with him fifteen days. ¹⁹I saw none of the other apostles—only James, the Lord's brother. ²⁰I assure you before God that what I am writing you is no lie. ²¹Later I went to Syria and Cilicia. ²²I was personally unknown to the churches of Judea that are in Christ. ²³They only heard the report: "The man who formerly persecuted us is now preaching the faith he once tried to destroy." ²⁴And they praised God because of me.

Paul Accepted by the Apostles

2 Fourteen years later I went up again to Jerusalem, this time with Barnabas. I took Titus along also. ²I went in response to a revelation and set before them the gospel that I preach among the Gentiles. But I did this privately to those who seemed to be leaders, for fear that I was running or had run my race in vain. ³Yet not even Titus, who was with me, was compelled to be circumcised, even though he was a Greek. ⁴This matter arose, because some false brothers had infiltrated our ranks to spy on the freedom we have in Christ Jesus and to make us slaves. ⁵We did not give in to them for a moment, so that the truth of the gospel might remain with you.

⁶As for those who seemed to be important—whatever they were makes no difference to me; God does not judge by external appearance—those men added nothing to my message. ⁷On the contrary, they saw that I had been entrusted with the task of preaching the gospel to the Gentiles,ᵃ just as Peter had been to the Jews.ᵇ ⁸For God, who was at work in the ministry of Peter as an apostle to the Jews, was also at work in my ministry as an apostle to the Gentiles. ⁹James, Peterᶜ and John, those reputed to be pillars, gave me and Barnabas the right hand of fellowship when they recognized the grace given to me. They agreed that we should go to the Gentiles, and they to the Jews. ¹⁰All they asked was that we should continue to remember the poor, the very thing I was eager to do.

Paul Opposes Peter

¹¹When Peter came to Antioch, I opposed him to his face, because he was clearly in the wrong. ¹²Before certain men came from James, he used to eat with the Gentiles. But when they arrived, he began to draw back and separate himself from the Gentiles because he was afraid of those who belonged to the circumcision group. ¹³The other Jews joined him in his hypocrisy, so that by their hypocrisy even Barnabas was led astray.

¹⁴When I saw that they were not acting in line with the truth of the gospel, I said to Peter in front of them all, "You are a Jew, yet you live like a Gentile and not like a Jew. How is it, then, that you force Gentiles to follow Jewish customs?

¹⁵"We who are Jews by birth and not 'Gentile sinners' ¹⁶know that a man is not justified by observing the law, but by faith in Jesus Christ. So we, too, have put our faith in Christ Jesus that we may be justified by faith in Christ and not by observing the law, because by observing the law no one will be justified.

¹⁷"If, while we seek to be justified in Christ, it becomes evident that we ourselves are sinners, does that mean that Christ promotes sin? Absolutely not! ¹⁸If I rebuild what I destroyed, I prove that I am a lawbreaker. ¹⁹For through the law I died to the law so that I might live for God. ²⁰I have been crucified with Christ and I no longer live, but Christ lives in me. The life I live in the body, I live by faith in the Son of God, who loved me and gave himself for me. ²¹I do not set aside the grace of God, for if righteousness could be gained through the law, Christ died for nothing!"ᵈ

Faith or Observance of the Law

3 You foolish Galatians! Who has bewitched you? Before your very eyes Jesus Christ was clearly portrayed as crucified. ²I would like to learn just one thing from you: Did you receive the Spirit by observing the law, or by believing what you heard? ³Are you so foolish? After beginning with the Spirit, are you now trying to attain your goal by human effort? ⁴Have you suffered so much for nothing— if it really was for nothing? ⁵Does God give you his Spirit and work miracles among you because you observe the law, or because you believe what you heard?

⁶Consider Abraham: "He believed God, and it was credited to him as righteousness."ᵉ ⁷Understand, then, that those who believe are children of Abraham. ⁸The Scripture foresaw that God would justify the Gentiles by faith, and an-

---

ᵃ7 Greek uncircumcised   ᵇ7 Greek circumcised; also in verses 8 and 9   ᶜ9 Greek Cephas; also in verses 11 and 14   ᵈ21 Some interpreters end the quotation after verse 14.   ᵉ6 Gen. 15:6

Righteousness and Authority

YOU'RE at the beach . . . you're famished . . . you find a restaurant . . . you rush in . . . you spot a sign:

> No Shirt
> No Shoes
> No Service

This message is clear. To be accepted, you must be clothed according to the restaurant's standard.

God also has a standard. But he makes it possible for you to be acceptable to him at all times when he gives you "righteousness as [your] clothing" (Job 29:14). The word *righteous*, in its simplest form, means "right" and "just." The word also means "acquitted, vindicated." Your faith in Christ enables God to regard you as righteous. He doesn't see your sin any longer, but he sees you as clothed with the righteousness of Christ. As such you are acceptable and properly dressed to "come and dine."

If you have struggled with feeling too unworthy to be called "the righteousness of God" (2 Corinthians 5:21), realize that this "clothing" you are given is like a uniform that, because it represents righteousness, also carries authority.

Have you ever seen a gigantic eighteen-wheel semitrailer truck groaning to a stop just because a police officer walks in front of the traffic and holds up his or her hand? What gives this person the right to command such respect? Certainly not parentage, social status, education, personality or even church affiliation. The officer stands confidently in front of this awesome "king of the road" because of the *right clothing*—the uniform has undeniable authority.

At the moment of conversion you were issued a righteous uniform. The Lord not only covered your past but also gave you authority over your future. With the "breastplate of righteousness" (Ephesians 6:14), God gave you power over sin.

As a child of God, you have the righteousness of God. You have the power that backs the badge.

Additional Scripture Readings: *Go to page 1290 for your next*
Isaiah 61:10; Revelation 3:4–5   *devotional reading.*

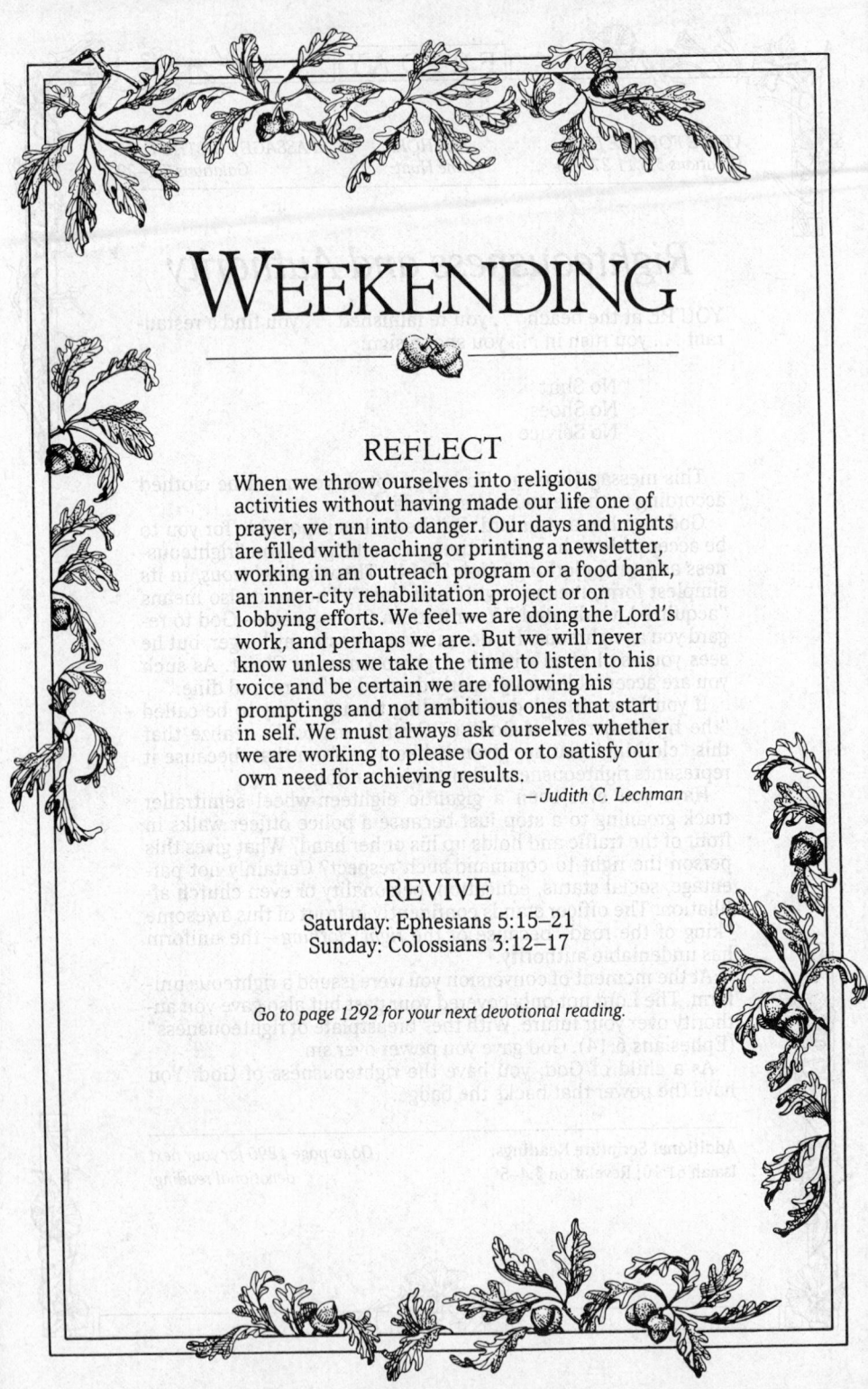

WEEKENDING

REFLECT

When we throw ourselves into religious activities without having made our life one of prayer, we run into danger. Our days and nights are filled with teaching or printing a newsletter, working in an outreach program or a food bank, an inner-city rehabilitation project or on lobbying efforts. We feel we are doing the Lord's work, and perhaps we are. But we will never know unless we take the time to listen to his voice and be certain we are following his promptings and not ambitious ones that start in self. We must always ask ourselves whether we are working to please God or to satisfy our own need for achieving results.

— *Judith C. Lechman*

REVIVE

Saturday: Ephesians 5:15–21
Sunday: Colossians 3:12–17

Go to page 1292 for your next devotional reading.

nounced the gospel in advance to Abraham: "All nations will be blessed through you."*a* ⁹So those who have faith are blessed along with Abraham, the man of faith.

¹⁰All who rely on observing the law are under a curse, for it is written: "Cursed is everyone who does not continue to do everything written in the Book of the Law."*b* ¹¹Clearly no one is justified before God by the law, because, "The righteous will live by faith."*c* ¹²The law is not based on faith; on the contrary, "The man who does these things will live by them."*d* ¹³Christ redeemed us from the curse of the law by becoming a curse for us, for it is written: "Cursed is everyone who is hung on a tree."*e* ¹⁴He redeemed us in order that the blessing given to Abraham might come to the Gentiles through Christ Jesus, so that by faith we might receive the promise of the Spirit.

The Law and the Promise

¹⁵Brothers, let me take an example from everyday life. Just as no one can set aside or add to a human covenant that has been duly established, so it is in this case. ¹⁶The promises were spoken to Abraham and to his seed. The Scripture does not say "and to seeds," meaning many people, but "and to your seed,"*f* meaning one person, who is Christ. ¹⁷What I mean is this: The law, introduced 430 years later, does not set aside the covenant previously established by God and thus do away with the promise. ¹⁸For if the inheritance depends on the law, then it no longer depends on a promise; but God in his grace gave it to Abraham through a promise.

¹⁹What, then, was the purpose of the law? It was added because of transgressions until the Seed to whom the promise referred had come. The law was put into effect through angels by a mediator. ²⁰A mediator, however, does not represent just one party; but God is one.

²¹Is the law, therefore, opposed to the promises of God? Absolutely not! For if a law had been given that could impart life, then righteousness would certainly have come by the law. ²²But the Scripture declares that the whole world is a prisoner of sin, so that what was promised, being given through faith in Jesus Christ, might be given to those who believe.

²³Before this faith came, we were held prisoners by the law, locked up until faith should be revealed. ²⁴So the law was put in charge to lead us to Christ*g* that we might be justified by faith. ²⁵Now that faith has come, we are no longer under the supervision of the law.

Sons of God

²⁶You are all sons of God through faith in Christ Jesus, ²⁷for all of you who were baptized into Christ have clothed yourselves with Christ. ²⁸There is neither Jew nor Greek, slave nor free, male nor female, for you are all one in Christ Jesus. ²⁹If you belong to Christ, then you are Abraham's seed, and heirs according to the promise.

4 What I am saying is that as long as the heir is a child, he is no different from a slave, although he owns the whole estate. ²He is subject to guardians and trustees until the time set by his father. ³So also, when we were children, we were in slavery under the basic principles of the world. ⁴But when the time had fully come, God sent his Son, born of a woman, born under law, ⁵to redeem those under law, that we might receive the full rights of sons. ⁶Because you are sons, God sent the Spirit of his Son into our hearts, the Spirit who calls out, *"Abba,*h* Father."* ⁷So you are no longer a slave, but a son; and since you are a son, God has made you also an heir.

Paul's Concern for the Galatians

⁸Formerly, when you did not know God, you were slaves to those who by nature are not gods. ⁹But now that you know God—or rather are known by God—how is it that you are turning back to those weak and miserable principles? Do you wish to be enslaved by them all over again? ¹⁰You are observing special days and months and seasons and years! ¹¹I fear for you, that somehow I have wasted my efforts on you.

¹²I plead with you, brothers, become like me, for I became like you. You have done me no wrong. ¹³As you know, it was because of an illness that I first preached the gospel to you. ¹⁴Even though my illness was a trial to you, you did not treat me with contempt or scorn. Instead, you welcomed me as if I were an angel of God, as if I were Christ Jesus himself. ¹⁵What

---

*a*8 Gen. 12:3; 18:18; 22:18   *b*10 Deut. 27:26   *c*11 Hab. 2:4   *d*12 Lev. 18:5   *e*13 Deut. 21:23
*f*16 Gen. 12:7; 13:15; 24:7   *g*24 Or *charge until Christ came*   *h*6 Aramaic for *Father*

VERSE FOR THE DAY:
Galatians 5:13

AUTHOR:
Kathy Narramore
Alice Hill

PASSAGE FOR THE DAY:
Galatians 5:13–15

Serving as a Friend

AS friends we need to be two people discovering Christ together, standing at eye level equally in need of the Lord's redemption and grace, seeing each other as both gifted and needy. This Biblical perspective of each other creates a safe emotional climate in which we "serve one another" (Galatians 5:13) and "submit to one another" (Ephesians 5:21).

Serving each other is another way of expressing God's love. It means freely undertaking any task or commitment necessary or helpful to another's spiritual, emotional or physical welfare. It may even be menial such as Jesus offered when he bathed the sore and dirty feet of his followers, or it may be offering empathy, bearing a burden, comforting. But however we do serve in his spirit, we make his love tangible.

We also make his love real to each other as we submit to each other. We are to be adaptable to each other in working out decisions, solutions to problems, and in accepting instruction. Keep in mind that this is quite different from obedience, which is something that can be demanded or coerced. Submission in this Biblical sense must be freely and voluntarily given. It is self-imposed out of humility and desire to serve. The motives to be submissive can only be healthy when the choice is coming from a strong sense of worth and identity in Christ. Then it will not be submission out of fear and a slavish desire to please. It will reflect that characteristic of Christ so contrary to human nature, "Who, being in very nature God, did not consider equality with God something to be grasped, but made himself nothing, taking the very nature of a servant, being made in human likeness" (Philippians 2:6–7).

You may not encounter any of the barriers we have faced as friends, but you can be sure Satan will put some roadblocks in the path of godly friendships. He would love to have you limp along as a Christian lone ranger or as a person with many nice acquaintances but no one who really knows you well.

Additional Scripture Readings:
Ephesians 4:22–32; Philippians 2:1–4

Go to page 1294 for your next devotional reading.

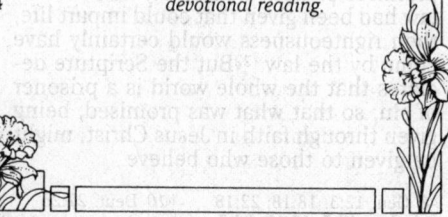

has happened to all your joy? I can testify that, if you could have done so, you would have torn out your eyes and given them to me. [16]Have I now become your enemy by telling you the truth?

[17]Those people are zealous to win you over, but for no good. What they want is to alienate you from us, so that you may be zealous for them. [18]It is fine to be zealous, provided the purpose is good, and to be so always and not just when I am with you. [19]My dear children, for whom I am again in the pains of childbirth until Christ is formed in you, [20]how I wish I could be with you now and change my tone, because I am perplexed about you!

Hagar and Sarah

[21]Tell me, you who want to be under the law, are you not aware of what the law says? [22]For it is written that Abraham had two sons, one by the slave woman and the other by the free woman. [23]His son by the slave woman was born in the ordinary way; but his son by the free woman was born as the result of a promise.

[24]These things may be taken figuratively, for the women represent two covenants. One covenant is from Mount Sinai and bears children who are to be slaves: This is Hagar. [25]Now Hagar stands for Mount Sinai in Arabia and corresponds to the present city of Jerusalem, because she is in slavery with her children. [26]But the Jerusalem that is above is free, and she is our mother. [27]For it is written:

"Be glad, O barren woman,
    who bears no children;
break forth and cry aloud,
    you who have no labor pains;
because more are the children of the
    desolate woman
than of her who has a husband."[a]

[28]Now you, brothers, like Isaac, are children of promise. [29]At that time the son born in the ordinary way persecuted the son born by the power of the Spirit. It is the same now. [30]But what does the Scripture say? "Get rid of the slave woman and her son, for the slave woman's son will never share in the inheritance with the free woman's son."[b] [31]Therefore, brothers, we are not children of the slave woman, but of the free woman.

Freedom in Christ

5 It is for freedom that Christ has set us free. Stand firm, then, and do not let yourselves be burdened again by a yoke of slavery.

[2]Mark my words! I, Paul, tell you that if you let yourselves be circumcised, Christ will be of no value to you at all. [3]Again I declare to every man who lets himself be circumcised that he is obligated to obey the whole law. [4]You who are trying to be justified by law have been alienated from Christ; you have fallen away from grace. [5]But by faith we eagerly await through the Spirit the righteousness for which we hope. [6]For in Christ Jesus neither circumcision nor uncircumcision has any value. The only thing that counts is faith expressing itself through love.

[7]You were running a good race. Who cut in on you and kept you from obeying the truth? [8]That kind of persuasion does not come from the one who calls you. [9]"A little yeast works through the whole batch of dough." [10]I am confident in the Lord that you will take no other view. The one who is throwing you into confusion will pay the penalty, whoever he may be. [11]Brothers, if I am still preaching circumcision, why am I still being persecuted? In that case the offense of the cross has been abolished. [12]As for those agitators, I wish they would go the whole way and emasculate themselves!

[13]You, my brothers, were called to be free. But do not use your freedom to indulge the sinful nature[c]; rather, serve one another in love. [14]The entire law is summed up in a single command: "Love your neighbor as yourself."[d] [15]If you keep on biting and devouring each other, watch out or you will be destroyed by each other.

Life by the Spirit

[16]So I say, live by the Spirit, and you will not gratify the desires of the sinful nature. [17]For the sinful nature desires what is contrary to the Spirit, and the Spirit what is contrary to the sinful nature. They are in conflict with each other, so that you do not do what you want. [18]But if you are led by the Spirit, you are not under law.

[19]The acts of the sinful nature are obvious: sexual immorality, impurity and debauchery; [20]idolatry and witchcraft; ha-

a27 Isaiah 54:1   *b30* Gen. 21:10   *c13* Or *the flesh*; also in verses 16, 17, 19 and 24   *d14* Lev. 19:18

tred, discord, jealousy, fits of rage, selfish ambition, dissensions, factions ²¹and envy; drunkenness, orgies, and the like. I warn you, as I did before, that those who live like this will not inherit the kingdom of God.

²²But the fruit of the Spirit is love, joy, peace, patience, kindness, goodness, faithfulness, ²³gentleness and self-control. Against such things there is no law. ²⁴Those who belong to Christ Jesus have crucified the sinful nature with its pas-

TUESDAY

VERSE FOR THE DAY:
Galatians 6:4

AUTHOR:
June Masters Bacher

PASSAGE FOR THE DAY:
Galatians 6:1–10

Starting Anew at 65

MY mother's friend had a thing about birthdays. She overcame it at 65.

It rained on Jo's birthday. "That figures," she said. "Gray month. Gray hair. Gray mood." She inspected herself from all angles looking for a bigger bulge or a new liver spot. Always bad, this one was the worst of all—a time (she said) when husbands became interesting "older men" and wives became dull "elderly women."

"Wanting to punish myself," she remembers, "I looked in my scrapbook at the list of advantages of being 21. A glorious day!"

She could vote, date, marry, seek a career, choose her own clothes, travel, live where she wished, read what she chose, forget school routine for a time and *enjoy her freedom!* So?

"That one did it," Jo admitted. "When had I ever been as free as *now?* " And that was when the dear lady began her list of advantages of turning 65.

Ah yes, she could draw Social Security, ride the city bus free, visit city parks without paying for admission, take adult ed courses free, collect Medicare, serve as the sage whose ideas were considered wise and whose services were valuable. There was nothing, in fact, in the first list Jo was unable to do or had not done already. There were countless things she could do now but not then. "Why, I'm a liberated woman!" she cried in discovery.

To think and pray about: It is good to pause and count our blessings at every birthday. They pile up with the years. God is changeless. He has work for us here and each milestone shows that he chose to have us remain to give him a hand. Resolve this year to enjoy your new freedom. Ask God how you can make it count.

Additional Scripture Readings:
Genesis 12:1–4; Hebrews 6:9–12

Go to page 1297 for your next devotional reading.

sions and desires. 25Since we live by the Spirit, let us keep in step with the Spirit. 26Let us not become conceited, provoking and envying each other.

Doing Good to All

6 Brothers, if someone is caught in a sin, you who are spiritual should restore him gently. But watch yourself, or you also may be tempted. 2Carry each other's burdens, and in this way you will fulfill the law of Christ. 3If anyone thinks he is something when he is nothing, he deceives himself. 4Each one should test his own actions. Then he can take pride in himself, without comparing himself to somebody else, 5for each one should carry his own load.

6Anyone who receives instruction in the word must share all good things with his instructor.

7Do not be deceived: God cannot be mocked. A man reaps what he sows. 8The one who sows to please his sinful nature, from that nature*a* will reap destruction; the one who sows to please the Spirit, from the Spirit will reap eternal life. 9Let us not become weary in doing good, for at the proper time we will reap a harvest if we do not give up. 10Therefore, as we have opportunity, let us do good to all people, especially to those who belong to the family of believers.

Not Circumcision but a New Creation

11See what large letters I use as I write to you with my own hand!

12Those who want to make a good impression outwardly are trying to compel you to be circumcised. The only reason they do this is to avoid being persecuted for the cross of Christ. 13Not even those who are circumcised obey the law, yet they want you to be circumcised that they may boast about your flesh. 14May I never boast except in the cross of our Lord Jesus Christ, through which*b* the world has been crucified to me, and I to the world. 15Neither circumcision nor uncircumcision means anything; what counts is a new creation. 16Peace and mercy to all who follow this rule, even to the Israel of God.

17Finally, let no one cause me trouble, for I bear on my body the marks of Jesus.

18The grace of our Lord Jesus Christ be with your spirit, brothers. Amen.

a8 Or his flesh, from the flesh   *b14 Or whom*

PAUL writes this letter from prison (Ephesians 4:1; probably in Rome, see Acts 28:30–31) to the church he started in Ephesus (Acts 19). In the first half he explains God's great plan to redeem the world through Christ, showing what this means for individual Christians and for the whole church. In the second half he gives practical advice on how to live the Christian life. As you read this book, first examine yourself to be sure that you are saved. Then move on to fight against Satan and show your love to your family, your church and your community.

EPHESIANS

1 Paul, an apostle of Christ Jesus by the will of God,

To the saints in Ephesus,[a] the faithful[b] in Christ Jesus:

[2]Grace and peace to you from God our Father and the Lord Jesus Christ.

Spiritual Blessings in Christ

[3]Praise be to the God and Father of our Lord Jesus Christ, who has blessed us in the heavenly realms with every spiritual blessing in Christ. [4]For he chose us in him before the creation of the world to be holy and blameless in his sight. In love [5]he[c] predestined us to be adopted as his sons through Jesus Christ, in accordance with his pleasure and will — [6]to the praise of his glorious grace, which he has freely given us in the One he loves. [7]In him we

---

[a]1 Some early manuscripts do not have *in Ephesus.*   [b]1 Or *believers who are*   [c]4,5 Or *sight in love.* [5]*He*

VERSE FOR THE DAY:
Ephesians 1:17–23

AUTHOR:
Debby Boone

PASSAGE FOR THE DAY:
Ephesians 1:3–23

Resurrection Power

JAMES talks about the prayer of a righteous man being "powerful and effective" (James 5:16). I think Paul's prayer for the people of Ephesus here in Ephesians 1:17–23 is a model for one of the most essential and important prayers we could ever pray for ourselves or one another. This prayer has taken hold of my heart so firmly that I have committed it to memory (quite a feat in itself) and pray it for family members, friends who are struggling, and for the body of Christ in general. Frequently, I pray it aloud over the people at my concerts.

Of course, there are other ways one should pray for people's needs, but this one prayer seems to cover the most basic and fundamental needs of every believer. It addresses our core desire that God will enlighten our hearts with the truth about himself and the hope to which he has called each of us.

The way we see God—the positive or negative way we view him as a father and provider—will shape the way we live our lives as believers in a dark and weary world. All of us, to some extent, no matter how long or fervently we have walked with the Lord, have shades and colorations of falseness about what God is like or how we are to relate to him. Only as he reveals himself in truth can we be set free to walk with an understanding of the hope of the riches of the inheritance he has set before us.

The question that naturally evolves from this is: "Yes, that would be great, but can God really do that for me? I am so weak." That's exactly why Paul spends the rest of Ephesians 1 talking about the greatness of God's power and the strength of his might . . . the same power he used when he raised Jesus from the dead. That's the power that God has committed to use while working in my life. Resurrection power! And the areas of my life that I feel are barren . . . useless . . . dead . . . burnt-out . . . those are the areas that he will fill with nothing less than himself so that I too can be "the fullness of him who fills everything in every way" (Ephesians 1:23). Hallelujah!

Additional Scripture Readings:
Romans 6:8–14; 1 Corinthians 15:56–58

*Go to page 1299 for your next
devotional reading.*

have redemption through his blood, the forgiveness of sins, in accordance with the riches of God's grace [8]that he lavished on us with all wisdom and understanding. [9]And he[a] made known to us the mystery of his will according to his good pleasure, which he purposed in Christ, [10]to be put into effect when the times will have reached their fulfillment—to bring all things in heaven and on earth together under one head, even Christ.

[11]In him we were also chosen,[b] having been predestined according to the plan of him who works out everything in conformity with the purpose of his will, [12]in order that we, who were the first to hope in Christ, might be for the praise of his glory. [13]And you also were included in Christ when you heard the word of truth, the gospel of your salvation. Having believed, you were marked in him with a seal, the promised Holy Spirit, [14]who is a deposit guaranteeing our inheritance until the redemption of those who are God's possession—to the praise of his glory.

Thanksgiving and Prayer

[15]For this reason, ever since I heard about your faith in the Lord Jesus and your love for all the saints, [16]I have not stopped giving thanks for you, remembering you in my prayers. [17]I keep asking that the God of our Lord Jesus Christ, the glorious Father, may give you the Spirit[c] of wisdom and revelation, so that you may know him better. [18]I pray also that the eyes of your heart may be enlightened in order that you may know the hope to which he has called you, the riches of his glorious inheritance in the saints, [19]and his incomparably great power for us who believe. That power is like the working of his mighty strength, [20]which he exerted in Christ when he raised him from the dead and seated him at his right hand in the heavenly realms, [21]far above all rule and authority, power and dominion, and every title that can be given, not only in the present age but also in the one to come. [22]And God placed all things under his feet and appointed him to be head over everything for the church, [23]which is his body, the fullness of him who fills everything in every way.

Made Alive in Christ

2 As for you, you were dead in your transgressions and sins, [2]in which you used to live when you followed the ways of this world and of the ruler of the kingdom of the air, the spirit who is now at work in those who are disobedient. [3]All of us also lived among them at one time, gratifying the cravings of our sinful nature[d] and following its desires and thoughts. Like the rest, we were by nature objects of wrath. [4]But because of his great love for us, God, who is rich in mercy, [5]made us alive with Christ even when we were dead in transgressions—it is by grace you have been saved. [6]And God raised us up with Christ and seated us with him in the heavenly realms in Christ Jesus, [7]in order that in the coming ages he might show the incomparable riches of his grace, expressed in his kindness to us in Christ Jesus. [8]For it is by grace you have been saved, through faith—and this not from yourselves, it is the gift of God— [9]not by works, so that no one can boast. [10]For we are God's workmanship, created in Christ Jesus to do good works, which God prepared in advance for us to do.

One in Christ

[11]Therefore, remember that formerly you who are Gentiles by birth and called "uncircumcised" by those who call themselves "the circumcision" (that done in the body by the hands of men)— [12]remember that at that time you were separate from Christ, excluded from citizenship in Israel and foreigners to the covenants of the promise, without hope and without God in the world. [13]But now in Christ Jesus you who once were far away have been brought near through the blood of Christ.

[14]For he himself is our peace, who has made the two one and has destroyed the barrier, the dividing wall of hostility, [15]by abolishing in his flesh the law with its commandments and regulations. His purpose was to create in himself one new man out of the two, thus making peace, [16]and in this one body to reconcile both of them to God through the cross, by which he put to death their hostility. [17]He came and preached peace to you who were far away and peace to those who were near. [18]For through him we both

---

[a]8,9 Or us. With all wisdom and understanding, [9]he   [b]11 Or were made heirs   [c]17 Or a spirit
[d]3 Or our flesh

have access to the Father by one Spirit.

¹⁹Consequently, you are no longer foreigners and aliens, but fellow citizens with God's people and members of God's household, ²⁰built on the foundation of the apostles and prophets, with Christ Jesus himself as the chief cornerstone. ²¹In him the whole building is joined together and rises to become a holy temple in the Lord. ²²And in him you too are being built together to become a dwelling in which God lives by his Spirit.

Paul the Preacher to the Gentiles

3 For this reason I, Paul, the prisoner of Christ Jesus for the sake of you Gentiles—

²Surely you have heard about the administration of God's grace that was given to me for you, ³that is, the mystery made known to me by revelation, as I have already written briefly. ⁴In reading this, then, you will be able to understand my insight into the mystery of Christ, ⁵which was not made known to men in

THURSDAY

VERSE FOR THE DAY:	AUTHOR:	PASSAGE FOR THE DAY:
Ephesians 3:16	Gloria Gaither	Ephesians 3:16–20

I Wish You

IT was Suzanne's college graduation party. Family friends and relatives, schoolmates and former teachers all sipped punch and ate raspberry cake under the willow trees beside the gazebo at the creek. She had played there as a child, fishing for catfish and catching turtles and garter snakes. Memories raced across the green hillside and peeped out from behind the apple tree in the orchard.

I listened as our friends wished her success as a writer, fame as a lyricist, fortune in her chosen work, and honor in grad school. What would we wish her, Bill and I later asked ourselves, as we sat in the yard swing apart from the others. It wouldn't be wealth, we decided, or notability. And success would be hard to define. What we would wish her would be some sunshine and some rain. We would wish her growth . . . and vision . . . and the ability to feel what those who are hurt or left out or lonely feel.

As we had done very often before, we found ourselves drawn that night to the passage of Scripture that had been read probably more often in our home than any other, for it stated very well what we wished then for Suzanne and for all our children as they faced life's shifts and changes . . . "that out of his glorious riches he may strengthen you with power through his Spirit in your inner being, so that Christ may dwell in your hearts through faith. And I pray that you, being rooted and established in love, may have power, together with all the saints, to grasp how wide and long and high and deep is the love of Christ, and to know this love that surpasses knowledge—that you may be filled to the measure of all the fullness of God" (Ephesians 3:16–19).

Additional Scripture Readings:
Philippians 1:9–11; Colossians 2:2–7

Go to page 1300 for your next devotional reading.

VERSE FOR THE DAY:	AUTHOR:	PASSAGE FOR THE DAY:
Ephesians 5:8	Luci Swindoll	Ephesians 5:8–10

We Are Light

A FRIEND of mine was caught in an elevator in New York City during a power failure. He just happened to have a tiny flashlight in his pocket . . . the type of guy who always was prepared for emergencies. There were seven people, all strangers, on the elevator; and at first, in that pitch-black darkness, there was momentary panic as everybody talked at once. When he remembered the flashlight in his pocket and turned it on, the fear dissipated. During the forty-five minutes they were stuck shoulder-to-shoulder in that small space, they became pretty good friends, laughing, telling jokes, and even singing. The way he presented the story to me, it sounded more fun than fearsome.

Ephesians 5:8 says we are that flashlight. Note, it doesn't say we are like light, it says we *are* light. Just as the flashlight draws power from its batteries, we draw power from the Son of God. As light, we dissipate fear, bring relief and lift spirits. We don't even have to be big to be effective. We just have to be "on."

The last two lines of T.S. Eliot's poem, "The Rock," read:

> And we thank Thee that the darkness reminds us
> of light.
> O Light Invisible, we give Thee Thanks for Thy
> great glory!

As we grope in darkness, what do we want most? Light! We want direction, illumination. Darkness reminds us of our oppressive, burdensome need. It "feels" heavy even though it's intangible. Only light, which also is intangible, pushes that feeling away. It provides relief.

Today, let's pursue that which is good, right and truthful by shining through darkened circumstances. Don't keep the switch off or hold back as though our batteries have run down. Our source is the glorious "Light Invisible." Being switched on pleases the Lord. Stay on. Stay bright.

Additional Scripture Readings:
Proverbs 4:18–19; Matthew 6:14–16

Go to page 1302 for your next devotional reading.

other generations as it has now been revealed by the Spirit to God's holy apostles and prophets. 6This mystery is that through the gospel the Gentiles are heirs together with Israel, members together of one body, and sharers together in the promise in Christ Jesus.

7I became a servant of this gospel by the gift of God's grace given me through the working of his power. 8Although I am less than the least of all God's people, this grace was given me: to preach to the Gentiles the unsearchable riches of Christ, 9and to make plain to everyone the administration of this mystery, which for ages past was kept hidden in God, who created all things. 10His intent was that now, through the church, the manifold wisdom of God should be made known to the rulers and authorities in the heavenly realms, 11according to his eternal purpose which he accomplished in Christ Jesus our Lord. 12In him and through faith in him we may approach God with freedom and confidence. 13I ask you, therefore, not to be discouraged because of my sufferings for you, which are your glory.

A Prayer for the Ephesians

14For this reason I kneel before the Father, 15from whom his whole family*a* in heaven and on earth derives its name. 16I pray that out of his glorious riches he may strengthen you with power through his Spirit in your inner being, 17so that Christ may dwell in your hearts through faith. And I pray that you, being rooted and established in love, 18may have power, together with all the saints, to grasp how wide and long and high and deep is the love of Christ, 19and to know this love that surpasses knowledge—that you may be filled to the measure of all the fullness of God.

20Now to him who is able to do immeasurably more than all we ask or imagine, according to his power that is at work within us, 21to him be glory in the church and in Christ Jesus throughout all generations, for ever and ever! Amen.

Unity in the Body of Christ

4 As a prisoner for the Lord, then, I urge you to live a life worthy of the calling you have received. 2Be completely humble and gentle; be patient, bearing with one another in love. 3Make every effort to keep the unity of the Spirit through the

bond of peace. 4There is one body and one Spirit— just as you were called to one hope when you were called— 5one Lord, one faith, one baptism; 6one God and Father of all, who is over all and through all and in all.

7But to each one of us grace has been given as Christ apportioned it. 8This is why it*b* says:

"When he ascended on high,
  he led captives in his train
  and gave gifts to men."*c*

9(What does "he ascended" mean except that he also descended to the lower, earthly regions*d*? 10He who descended is the very one who ascended higher than all the heavens, in order to fill the whole universe.) 11It was he who gave some to be apostles, some to be prophets, some to be evangelists, and some to be pastors and teachers, 12to prepare God's people for works of service, so that the body of Christ may be built up 13until we all reach unity in the faith and in the knowledge of the Son of God and become mature, attaining to the whole measure of the fullness of Christ.

14Then we will no longer be infants, tossed back and forth by the waves, and blown here and there by every wind of teaching and by the cunning and craftiness of men in their deceitful scheming. 15Instead, speaking the truth in love, we will in all things grow up into him who is the Head, that is, Christ. 16From him the whole body, joined and held together by every supporting ligament, grows and builds itself up in love, as each part does its work.

Living as Children of Light

17So I tell you this, and insist on it in the Lord, that you must no longer live as the Gentiles do, in the futility of their thinking. 18They are darkened in their understanding and separated from the life of God because of the ignorance that is in them due to the hardening of their hearts. 19Having lost all sensitivity, they have given themselves over to sensuality so as to indulge in every kind of impurity, with a continual lust for more.

20You, however, did not come to know Christ that way. 21Surely you heard of him and were taught in him in accordance with the truth that is in Jesus. 22You were taught, with regard to your former way of

*a*15 Or *whom all fatherhood*   *b*8 Or *God*   *c*8 Psalm 68:18   *d*9 Or *the depths of the earth*

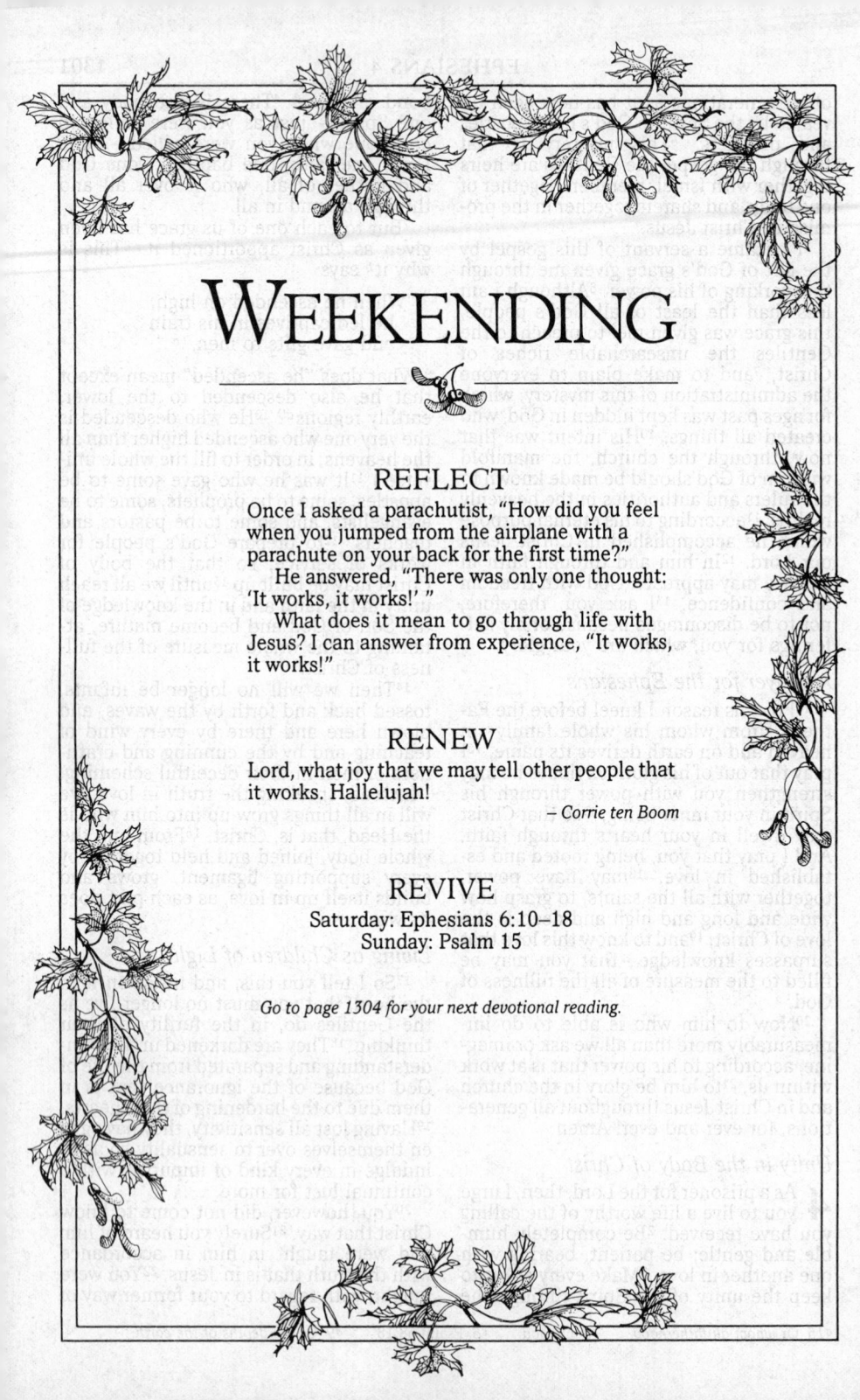

WEEKENDING

REFLECT

Once I asked a parachutist, "How did you feel
when you jumped from the airplane with a
parachute on your back for the first time?"

He answered, "There was only one thought:
'It works, it works!'"

What does it mean to go through life with
Jesus? I can answer from experience, "It works,
it works!"

RENEW

Lord, what joy that we may tell other people that
it works. Hallelujah!

– Corrie ten Boom

REVIVE

Saturday: Ephesians 6:10–18
Sunday: Psalm 15

Go to page 1304 for your next devotional reading.

life, to put off your old self, which is being corrupted by its deceitful desires; 23to be made new in the attitude of your minds; 24and to put on the new self, created to be like God in true righteousness and holiness.

25Therefore each of you must put off falsehood and speak truthfully to his neighbor, for we are all members of one body. 26"In your anger do not sin"*a*: Do not let the sun go down while you are still angry, 27and do not give the devil a foothold. 28He who has been stealing must steal no longer, but must work, doing something useful with his own hands, that he may have something to share with those in need.

29Do not let any unwholesome talk come out of your mouths, but only what is helpful for building others up according to their needs, that it may benefit those who listen. 30And do not grieve the Holy Spirit of God, with whom you were sealed for the day of redemption. 31Get rid of all bitterness, rage and anger, brawling and slander, along with every form of malice. 32Be kind and compassionate to one another, forgiving each other, just as in Christ God forgave you.

5 Be imitators of God, therefore, as dearly loved children 2and live a life of love, just as Christ loved us and gave himself up for us as a fragrant offering and sacrifice to God.

3But among you there must not be even a hint of sexual immorality, or of any kind of impurity, or of greed, because these are improper for God's holy people. 4Nor should there be obscenity, foolish talk or coarse joking, which are out of place, but rather thanksgiving. 5For of this you can be sure: No immoral, impure or greedy person—such a man is an idolater—has any inheritance in the kingdom of Christ and of God.*b* 6Let no one deceive you with empty words, for because of such things God's wrath comes on those who are disobedient. 7Therefore do not be partners with them.

8For you were once darkness, but now you are light in the Lord. Live as children of light 9(for the fruit of the light consists in all goodness, righteousness and truth) 10and find out what pleases the Lord. 11Have nothing to do with the fruitless deeds of darkness, but rather expose them. 12For it is shameful even to mention what the disobedient do in secret.

13But everything exposed by the light becomes visible, 14for it is light that makes everything visible. This is why it is said:

"Wake up, O sleeper,
    rise from the dead,
and Christ will shine on you."

15Be very careful, then, how you live—not as unwise but as wise, 16making the most of every opportunity, because the days are evil. 17Therefore do not be foolish, but understand what the Lord's will is. 18Do not get drunk on wine, which leads to debauchery. Instead, be filled with the Spirit. 19Speak to one another with psalms, hymns and spiritual songs. Sing and make music in your heart to the Lord, 20always giving thanks to God the Father for everything, in the name of our Lord Jesus Christ.

21Submit to one another out of reverence for Christ.

Wives and Husbands

22Wives, submit to your husbands as to the Lord. 23For the husband is the head of the wife as Christ is the head of the church, his body, of which he is the Savior. 24Now as the church submits to Christ, so also wives should submit to their husbands in everything.

25Husbands, love your wives, just as Christ loved the church and gave himself up for her 26to make her holy, cleansing*c* her by the washing with water through the word, 27and to present her to himself as a radiant church, without stain or wrinkle or any other blemish, but holy and blameless. 28In this same way, husbands ought to love their wives as their own bodies. He who loves his wife loves himself. 29After all, no one ever hated his own body, but he feeds and cares for it, just as Christ does the church— 30for we are members of his body. 31"For this reason a man will leave his father and mother and be united to his wife, and the two will become one flesh."*d* 32This is a profound mystery—but I am talking about Christ and the church. 33However, each one of you also must love his wife as he loves himself, and the wife must respect her husband.

Children and Parents

6 Children, obey your parents in the Lord, for this is right. 2"Honor your father and mother"—which is the first

---

a26 Psalm 4:4   *b5* Or *kingdom of the Christ and God*   *c26* Or *having cleansed*   *d31* Gen. 2:24

VERSE FOR THE DAY:
Ephesians 6:13

AUTHOR:
Beverly LaHaye

PASSAGE FOR THE DAY:
Ephesians 6:10–18

Worth Defending in Battle

WHEN you read Ephesians 6:10–18, you begin to realize that these verses prepare us for warfare. One of those battles is to fight against those things that keep us from having strong marriages and families. The last half of chapter five discusses husband-wife relationships within marriage. The first half of chapter six teaches children to obey, and then discusses the responsibilities of the father. Then verse ten says, "Finally, be strong in the Lord. . . ." These instructions help us clearly see that there *is* a way to keep marriages and families strong.

In this time when the divorce rate has skyrocketed, marriages *can* be strong in the Lord. Even now when family life is rapidly deteriorating, families *can* be strong.

The promises of Ephesians are an encouragement to young couples who wonder if they should marry in light of the high divorce rate. Other couples question if they should have children because the world is such an evil place in which to raise them. Ephesians 6:11 and 13 encourage us to know that we can stand against the schemes of the devil and that we can withstand in the evil day by taking the whole armor of God as our defense—the armor made up of truth, righteousness, the gospel of peace, faith, salvation, and the sword of the Spirit. A lasting marriage is of great value, but you have to be prepared for warfare to preserve it. The same is true with the family. It will be necessary to stand against the schemes of the devil to keep a family strong.

These verses have been a source of great strength to us in raising our family. There were times when all would have been lost were it not for the wisdom and strength we derived from the Word of God.

My husband and I have been teaching Family Life Seminars for many years. Most of the books we have written are based on some phase of family life. We have come across almost every problem possible in marriage and family relationships, and we still believe that it is possible to have a strong family life and marriage relationship if the Word of God is used as the armor to withstand every trial. We must use the Word of God as our basis for sorting out right from wrong, the basis for making decisions or resolving conflicts.

Marriage and the family are institutions founded by God. They are considered his highest priority for individuals next to personal salvation. They are worth defending in battle.

Additional Scripture Readings:
Malachi 2:13–16; Matthew 19:3–14

Go to page 1307 for your next devotional reading.

commandment with a promise— [3]"that it may go well with you and that you may enjoy long life on the earth."[a]

[4]Fathers, do not exasperate your children; instead, bring them up in the training and instruction of the Lord.

Slaves and Masters

[5]Slaves, obey your earthly masters with respect and fear, and with sincerity of heart, just as you would obey Christ. [6]Obey them not only to win their favor when their eye is on you, but like slaves of Christ, doing the will of God from your heart. [7]Serve wholeheartedly, as if you were serving the Lord, not men, [8]because you know that the Lord will reward everyone for whatever good he does, whether he is slave or free.

[9]And masters, treat your slaves in the same way. Do not threaten them, since you know that he who is both their Master and yours is in heaven, and there is no favoritism with him.

The Armor of God

[10]Finally, be strong in the Lord and in his mighty power. [11]Put on the full armor of God so that you can take your stand against the devil's schemes. [12]For our struggle is not against flesh and blood, but against the rulers, against the authorities, against the powers of this dark world and against the spiritual forces of evil in the heavenly realms. [13]Therefore put on the full armor of God, so that when the day of evil comes, you may be able to stand your ground, and after you have done everything, to stand. [14]Stand firm then, with the belt of truth buckled around your waist, with the breastplate of righteousness in place, [15]and with your feet fitted with the readiness that comes from the gospel of peace. [16]In addition to all this, take up the shield of faith, with which you can extinguish all the flaming arrows of the evil one. [17]Take the helmet of salvation and the sword of the Spirit, which is the word of God. [18]And pray in the Spirit on all occasions with all kinds of prayers and requests. With this in mind, be alert and always keep on praying for all the saints.

[19]Pray also for me, that whenever I open my mouth, words may be given me so that I will fearlessly make known the mystery of the gospel, [20]for which I am an ambassador in chains. Pray that I may declare it fearlessly, as I should.

Final Greetings

[21]Tychicus, the dear brother and faithful servant in the Lord, will tell you everything, so that you also may know how I am and what I am doing. [22]I am sending him to you for this very purpose, that you may know how we are, and that he may encourage you.

[23]Peace to the brothers, and love with faith from God the Father and the Lord Jesus Christ. [24]Grace to all who love our Lord Jesus Christ with an undying love.

---

[a]3 Deut. 5:16

PAUL writes this letter to the church he started in Philippi (Acts 16:11–40). Even though he is in prison, he feels happy when he thinks of what Christ means to him and of what the Philippians are doing for him. He gives some very practical advice on how to live the Christian life. As you read this book, remember always to rejoice in the Lord and to be content, whatever the circumstances.

PHILIPPIANS

1 Paul and Timothy, servants of Christ Jesus,

To all the saints in Christ Jesus at Philippi, together with the overseers*a* and deacons:

²Grace and peace to you from God our Father and the Lord Jesus Christ.

Thanksgiving and Prayer

³I thank my God every time I remember you. ⁴In all my prayers for all of you, I always pray with joy ⁵because of your partnership in the gospel from the first day until now, ⁶being confident of this, that he who began a good work in you will carry it on to completion until the day of Christ Jesus.

⁷It is right for me to feel this way about all of you, since I have you in my heart; for whether I am in chains or defending and confirming the gospel, all of you share in God's grace with me. ⁸God can testify how I long for all of you with the affection of Christ Jesus.

⁹And this is my prayer: that your love may abound more and more in knowledge and depth of insight, ¹⁰so that you may be able to discern what is best and may be pure and blameless until the day of Christ, ¹¹filled with the fruit of righteousness that comes through Jesus Christ — to the glory and praise of God.

a1 Traditionally *bishops*

VERSE FOR THE DAY:	AUTHOR:	PASSAGE FOR THE DAY:
Philippians 2:5	Gigi Graham Tchividjian	Philippians 2:1–5

The Problem

I STOOD in the upstairs hallway, looking down over the bannister and waiting for the younger children to come in for their baths. My oldest daughter, taking a piano lesson, was in the living room directly below, and the repetitive melody she was playing echoed through my mind.

Suddenly the little ones bounded through the door. They bounced up to their rooms, cheeks flushed and eyes bright from their play.

I noticed, however, that one of my young sons was trudging slowly up the stairs, his head bowed, grubby hands covering his small, dirt-streaked face. When he reached the top, I asked him what was wrong.

"Aw, nothing," he replied.

"Then why are you holding your face in your hands?" I persisted.

"Oh, I was just praying."

Quite curious now, I asked what he was praying about.

"I can't tell you," he insisted, "because if I do, you'll be mad."

After much persuasion I convinced him that he could confide in me and that, whatever he told me, I would not get mad. So he explained that he was praying about a problem he had with his mind.

"A problem with your mind?" I asked, now more curious than ever, wondering what kind of problem a child of six could have with his mind. "What kind of problem?"

"Well," he said, "You see, every time I pass by the living room, I see my piano teacher, and my tongue sticks out."

Needless to say, it was hard to keep a straight face, but I took his problem seriously and assured him that God could, indeed, help him with it.

Later, on my knees beside the bathtub as I bathed this little fellow, I thought how I still struggle with the problem of controlling my mind and my tongue. That afternoon as I knelt to scrub that sturdy little body, the tub became my altar; the bathroom, my temple. I bowed my head, covered my face, and acknowledged that I, like my son, had a problem with my mind and tongue. I asked the Lord to forgive me and to give me more and more the mind and heart and attitude of Christ.

Additional Scripture Readings:
Psalm 39:1–2; James 1:26; 3:3–8

Go to page 1309 for your next devotional reading.

Paul's Chains Advance the Gospel

12Now I want you to know, brothers, that what has happened to me has really served to advance the gospel. 13As a result, it has become clear throughout the whole palace guard*a* and to everyone else that I am in chains for Christ. 14Because of my chains, most of the brothers in the Lord have been encouraged to speak the word of God more courageously and fearlessly.

15It is true that some preach Christ out of envy and rivalry, but others out of goodwill. 16The latter do so in love, knowing that I am put here for the defense of the gospel. 17The former preach Christ out of selfish ambition, not sincerely, supposing that they can stir up trouble for me while I am in chains.*b* 18But what does it matter? The important thing is that in every way, whether from false motives or true, Christ is preached. And because of this I rejoice.

Yes, and I will continue to rejoice, 19for I know that through your prayers and the help given by the Spirit of Jesus Christ, what has happened to me will turn out for my deliverance.*c* 20I eagerly expect and hope that I will in no way be ashamed, but will have sufficient courage so that now as always Christ will be exalted in my body, whether by life or by death. 21For to me, to live is Christ and to die is gain. 22If I am to go on living in the body, this will mean fruitful labor for me. Yet what shall I choose? I do not know! 23I am torn between the two: I desire to depart and be with Christ, which is better by far; 24but it is more necessary for you that I remain in the body. 25Convinced of this, I know that I will remain, and I will continue with all of you for your progress and joy in the faith, 26so that through my being with you again your joy in Christ Jesus will overflow on account of me.

27Whatever happens, conduct yourselves in a manner worthy of the gospel of Christ. Then, whether I come and see you or only hear about you in my absence, I will know that you stand firm in one spirit, contending as one man for the faith of the gospel 28without being frightened in any way by those who oppose you. This is a sign to them that they will be destroyed, but that you will be saved—and that by God. 29For it has been granted to you on behalf of Christ not only to believe in him, but also to suffer for him, 30since you are going through the same struggle you saw I had, and now hear that I still have.

Imitating Christ's Humility

2 If you have any encouragement from being united with Christ, if any comfort from his love, if any fellowship with the Spirit, if any tenderness and compassion, 2then make my joy complete by being like-minded, having the same love, being one in spirit and purpose. 3Do nothing out of selfish ambition or vain conceit, but in humility consider others better than yourselves. 4Each of you should look not only to your own interests, but also to the interests of others.

5Your attitude should be the same as that of Christ Jesus:

6Who, being in very nature*d* God,
　did not consider equality with God
　　something to be grasped,
7but made himself nothing,
　taking the very nature*e* of a
　　servant,
　being made in human likeness.
8And being found in appearance as a
　　man,
　he humbled himself
　and became obedient to death—
　　even death on a cross!
9Therefore God exalted him to the
　　highest place
　and gave him the name that is
　　above every name,
10that at the name of Jesus every knee
　　should bow,
　in heaven and on earth and under
　　the earth,
11and every tongue confess that Jesus
　　Christ is Lord,
　to the glory of God the Father.

Shining as Stars

12Therefore, my dear friends, as you have always obeyed—not only in my presence, but now much more in my absence—continue to work out your salvation with fear and trembling, 13for it is God who works in you to will and to act according to his good purpose.

14Do everything without complaining or arguing, 15so that you may become blameless and pure, children of God without fault in a crooked and depraved

a13 Or *whole palace*　　*b16,17* Some late manuscripts have verses 16 and 17 in reverse order.
c19 Or *salvation*　　*d6* Or *in the form of*　　*e7* Or *the form*

VERSE FOR THE DAY:
Philippians 3:13

AUTHOR:
Anne Ortlund

PASSAGE FOR THE DAY:
Philippians 3:12–14

"One-Thing" People

"NOT that I've already arrived!" says the apostle Paul as he begins these comments. Well, whew! That makes us all identify with him!

Then we'd better pay attention to the rest of what he says—that even with all his imperfections and weaknesses Paul has in mind only *one thing:*

> Forgetting what is behind and straining toward
> what is ahead, I press on toward the goal to win the
> prize for which God has called me heavenward in
> Christ Jesus (Philippians 3:13–14).

"Forgetting what is behind"! We're little amateur psychologists these days, trying to remember all our pasts—bringing up why our mothers did this and our fathers did that—to explain all our idiosyncrasies and quirks.

The Bible doesn't so deal with us. It pronounces us sinners and then says to *get on with it,* to look up and forward! All the great people of faith in Hebrews 11 *looked forward* (Hebrews 11:10,14–16,20–22,26,39–40). So did Jesus: he endured the cross "for the joy set before him" (Hebrews 12:2).

Then, with Paul, we must strain toward what's ahead and fix our attention on that: all God's promises, all our inheritance, and the goal, the prize—Jesus himself!

"One thing I do," says Paul. It's "one-thing" believers who shed the clutter and baggage and *get there.* They "eliminate and concentrate," and they *make it.*

Take David, for instance:

> *One thing* I ask of the LORD,
>   this is what I seek:
> that I may dwell in the house of the LORD
>   all the days of my life,
> to gaze upon the beauty of the LORD
>   and to seek him in his temple (Psalm 27:4,
>   italics mine).

Or take Mary. She sat at the feet of Jesus. And he said to her bustling sister Martha, "Only *one thing* is needed. Mary has chosen what is better, and it will not be taken away from her" (Luke 10:42, italics mine).

Be a "one-thing" Christian! Focus! Concentrate! Press on —and up!

Additional Scripture Readings:
Colossians 3:1–2; Hebrews 12:1–2

*Go to page 1311 for your next
devotional reading.*

generation, in which you shine like stars in the universe [16]as you hold out[a] the word of life—in order that I may boast on the day of Christ that I did not run or labor for nothing. [17]But even if I am being poured out like a drink offering on the sacrifice and service coming from your faith, I am glad and rejoice with all of you. [18]So you too should be glad and rejoice with me.

Timothy and Epaphroditus

[19]I hope in the Lord Jesus to send Timothy to you soon, that I also may be cheered when I receive news about you. [20]I have no one else like him, who takes a genuine interest in your welfare. [21]For everyone looks out for his own interests, not those of Jesus Christ. [22]But you know that Timothy has proved himself, because as a son with his father he has served with me in the work of the gospel. [23]I hope, therefore, to send him as soon as I see how things go with me. [24]And I am confident in the Lord that I myself will come soon.

[25]But I think it is necessary to send back to you Epaphroditus, my brother, fellow worker and fellow soldier, who is also your messenger, whom you sent to take care of my needs. [26]For he longs for all of you and is distressed because you heard he was ill. [27]Indeed he was ill, and almost died. But God had mercy on him, and not on him only but also on me, to spare me sorrow upon sorrow. [28]Therefore I am all the more eager to send him, so that when you see him again you may be glad and I may have less anxiety. [29]Welcome him in the Lord with great joy, and honor men like him, [30]because he almost died for the work of Christ, risking his life to make up for the help you could not give me.

No Confidence in the Flesh

3 Finally, my brothers, rejoice in the Lord! It is no trouble for me to write the same things to you again, and it is a safeguard for you.

[2]Watch out for those dogs, those men who do evil, those mutilators of the flesh. [3]For it is we who are the circumcision, we who worship by the Spirit of God, who glory in Christ Jesus, and who put no confidence in the flesh— [4]though I myself have reasons for such confidence.

If anyone else thinks he has reasons to put confidence in the flesh, I have more: [5]circumcised on the eighth day, of the people of Israel, of the tribe of Benjamin, a Hebrew of Hebrews; in regard to the law, a Pharisee; [6]as for zeal, persecuting the church; as for legalistic righteousness, faultless.

[7]But whatever was to my profit I now consider loss for the sake of Christ. [8]What is more, I consider everything a loss compared to the surpassing greatness of knowing Christ Jesus my Lord, for whose sake I have lost all things. I consider them rubbish, that I may gain Christ [9]and be found in him, not having a righteousness of my own that comes from the law, but that which is through faith in Christ—the righteousness that comes from God and is by faith. [10]I want to know Christ and the power of his resurrection and the fellowship of sharing in his sufferings, becoming like him in his death, [11]and so, somehow, to attain to the resurrection from the dead.

Pressing on Toward the Goal

[12]Not that I have already obtained all this, or have already been made perfect, but I press on to take hold of that for which Christ Jesus took hold of me. [13]Brothers, I do not consider myself yet to have taken hold of it. But one thing I do: Forgetting what is behind and straining toward what is ahead, [14]I press on toward the goal to win the prize for which God has called me heavenward in Christ Jesus.

[15]All of us who are mature should take such a view of things. And if on some point you think differently, that too God will make clear to you. [16]Only let us live up to what we have already attained.

[17]Join with others in following my example, brothers, and take note of those who live according to the pattern we gave you. [18]For, as I have often told you before and now say again even with tears, many live as enemies of the cross of Christ. [19]Their destiny is destruction, their god is their stomach, and their glory is in their shame. Their mind is on earthly things. [20]But our citizenship is in heaven. And we eagerly await a Savior from there, the Lord Jesus Christ, [21]who, by the power that enables him to bring everything under his control, will transform our lowly bodies so that they will be like his glorious body.

[a]16 Or hold on to

VERSE FOR THE DAY:	*AUTHOR:*	*PASSAGE FOR THE DAY:*
Philippians 4:6	*Hope MacDonald*	*Philippians 4:4–9*

The Lord Is Near

THIS passage was very significant to me today. My life seemed filled with worries and anxieties. It was the kind of day when I just wanted to pull the covers back over my head and forget everything. Have you ever felt that way?

While reading these verses, I was reminded of the profound truth that prayer isn't something I *had* to do, rather, prayer is something I *get* to do. I *get* to bring to God every worry and concern that is on my heart today. In fact, I discovered when worry and anxiety knock on the door of life, if the door is opened by prayer, no one is there! God's cure for worry is always the same—prayer—not pulling the covers back over my head. His way is always action. That action begins with making everything known to him.

Why do we get to pray this way? Because "the Lord is near" (Philippians 4:5). This is the key to this entire magnificent passage. Because he is near, we need not be anxious for anything. Because he is near, we have peace within. A deep, abiding peace that passes all understanding. Because the Lord is near, a wellspring of joy fills every part of our lives. And because the Lord is near, our hearts and minds are renewed and restored in Christ Jesus. With this restoration we become, once again, fresh, vibrant and alive Christians.

Then we can understand the importance of taking our eyes off ourselves and thinking instead about whatever is true and noble, right, pure, admirable and lovely. We can see clearly again that a great deal that surrounds us is excellent and praiseworthy (Philippians 4:8). This doesn't come naturally to us, does it? But then, God never called us to a natural lifestyle.

This is the encouragement and comfort I received this morning as I set out to face another day under the care and direction of the Holy Spirit.

"Thank you, Jesus, for your power in every part of my life today—renewing me physically, mentally and spiritually."

Additional Scripture Readings:
Psalm 73:23–26; 2 Corinthians 4:16–18

Go to page 1314 for your next devotional reading.

4 Therefore, my brothers, you whom I love and long for, my joy and crown, that is how you should stand firm in the Lord, dear friends!

Exhortations

²I plead with Euodia and I plead with Syntyche to agree with each other in the Lord. ³Yes, and I ask you, loyal yokefellow,ᵃ help these women who have contended at my side in the cause of the gospel, along with Clement and the rest of my fellow workers, whose names are in the book of life.

⁴Rejoice in the Lord always. I will say it again: Rejoice! ⁵Let your gentleness be evident to all. The Lord is near. ⁶Do not be anxious about anything, but in everything, by prayer and petition, with thanksgiving, present your requests to God. ⁷And the peace of God, which transcends all understanding, will guard your hearts and your minds in Christ Jesus.

⁸Finally, brothers, whatever is true, whatever is noble, whatever is right, whatever is pure, whatever is lovely, whatever is admirable—if anything is excellent or praiseworthy—think about such things. ⁹Whatever you have learned or received or heard from me, or seen in me—put it into practice. And the God of peace will be with you.

Thanks for Their Gifts

¹⁰I rejoice greatly in the Lord that at last you have renewed your concern for me. Indeed, you have been concerned, but you had no opportunity to show it. ¹¹I am not saying this because I am in need,

for I have learned to be content whatever the circumstances. ¹²I know what it is to be in need, and I know what it is to have plenty. I have learned the secret of being content in any and every situation, whether well fed or hungry, whether living in plenty or in want. ¹³I can do everything through him who gives me strength.

¹⁴Yet it was good of you to share in my troubles. ¹⁵Moreover, as you Philippians know, in the early days of your acquaintance with the gospel, when I set out from Macedonia, not one church shared with me in the matter of giving and receiving, except you only; ¹⁶for even when I was in Thessalonica, you sent me aid again and again when I was in need. ¹⁷Not that I am looking for a gift, but I am looking for what may be credited to your account. ¹⁸I have received full payment and even more; I am amply supplied, now that I have received from Epaphroditus the gifts you sent. They are a fragrant offering, an acceptable sacrifice, pleasing to God. ¹⁹And my God will meet all your needs according to his glorious riches in Christ Jesus.

²⁰To our God and Father be glory for ever and ever. Amen.

Final Greetings

²¹Greet all the saints in Christ Jesus. The brothers who are with me send greetings. ²²All the saints send you greetings, especially those who belong to Caesar's household.

²³The grace of the Lord Jesus Christ be with your spirit. Amen.ᵇ

ᵃ3 Or loyal Syzygus   ᵇ23 Some manuscripts do not have Amen.

PAUL writes this letter to the church in Colosse at about the same time as he writes Ephesians. False teachers are deceiving some of those to whom he writes (Colossians 2:4). Therefore, Paul stresses the power and glory of Christ and instructs his readers on how to live as Christians. As you read this book, put your faith in this glorious Savior who died for you, and promise him that you will show Christian love and compassion to others.

COLOSSIANS

1 Paul, an apostle of Christ Jesus by the will of God, and Timothy our brother,

[2]To the holy and faithful[a] brothers in Christ at Colosse:

Grace and peace to you from God our Father.[b]

Thanksgiving and Prayer

[3]We always thank God, the Father of our Lord Jesus Christ, when we pray for you, [4]because we have heard of your faith in Christ Jesus and of the love you have for all the saints— [5]the faith and love that spring from the hope that is stored up for you in heaven and that you have already heard about in the word of truth, the gospel [6]that has come to you. All over the world this gospel is bearing fruit and growing, just as it has been doing among you since the day you heard it and understood God's grace in all its truth. [7]You learned it from Epaphras, our dear fellow servant, who is a faithful minister of Christ on our[c] behalf, [8]and who also told us of your love in the Spirit.

[9]For this reason, since the day we heard about you, we have not stopped praying for you and asking God to fill you with the knowledge of his will through

---

[a]2 Or *believing*   [b]2 Some manuscripts *Father and the Lord Jesus Christ*   [c]7 Some manuscripts *your*

all spiritual wisdom and understanding. [10]And we pray this in order that you may live a life worthy of the Lord and may please him in every way: bearing fruit in every good work, growing in the knowledge of God, [11]being strengthened with all power according to his glorious might so that you may have great endurance and patience, and joyfully [12]giving thanks to the Father, who has qualified you[a] to share in the inheritance of the saints in the kingdom of light. [13]For he has rescued us from the dominion of darkness and brought us into the kingdom of the Son he loves, [14]in whom we have redemption,[b] the forgiveness of sins.

The Supremacy of Christ

[15]He is the image of the invisible God, the firstborn over all creation. [16]For by

a12 Some manuscripts us   b14 A few late manuscripts redemption through his blood

FRIDAY

VERSE FOR THE DAY:
Colossians 1:9

AUTHOR:
Debbie Smith

PASSAGE FOR THE DAY:
Colossians 1:3–14

Friends Forever

TIME has a way of defining true friends. I have discovered that passing years and growing distance are ineffective obstacles to the mutual love between my friends and me. Perhaps it is because of our common walk with the Lord that we can just pick up where we left off whenever we are together. And these are the dear ones I will spend eternity loving!

Of course, prayer is an important part of continuing that bond. Colossians 1:3–14 is an eloquent description of a Christian's prayer for her friends. Even though Paul had not even visited the Christians at Colosse (Colossians 1:7), his love for them through Christ was strong and ardent.

One Sunday afternoon soon after our wedding, Michael and I were getting ready for the weekly Bible study that would meet in our living room that night. It would be the final study led by Bill Jackson before he moved away. On a sudden whim, we decided to write a song for Bill. Michael went to take a shower; I sat down with the Bible and a pen. In less than an hour Michael had found a melody on the piano for the lyrics to "friends." We were happy to have something special for Bill, though it never occurred to us that anyone else would find this simple song meaningful.

God had different plans! He has used "Friends" for graduations, funerals, weddings and gatherings of all kinds. Michael and I continue to be blessed by letters from people who identify with this song and find comfort in its message. Both the Colossians passage and the song are a call to prayer for those we love—and a reminder that God's love unites people as friends forever!

Additional Scripture Readings:
Ephesians 3:14–19; Philemon 4–7

Go to page 1315 for your next devotional reading.

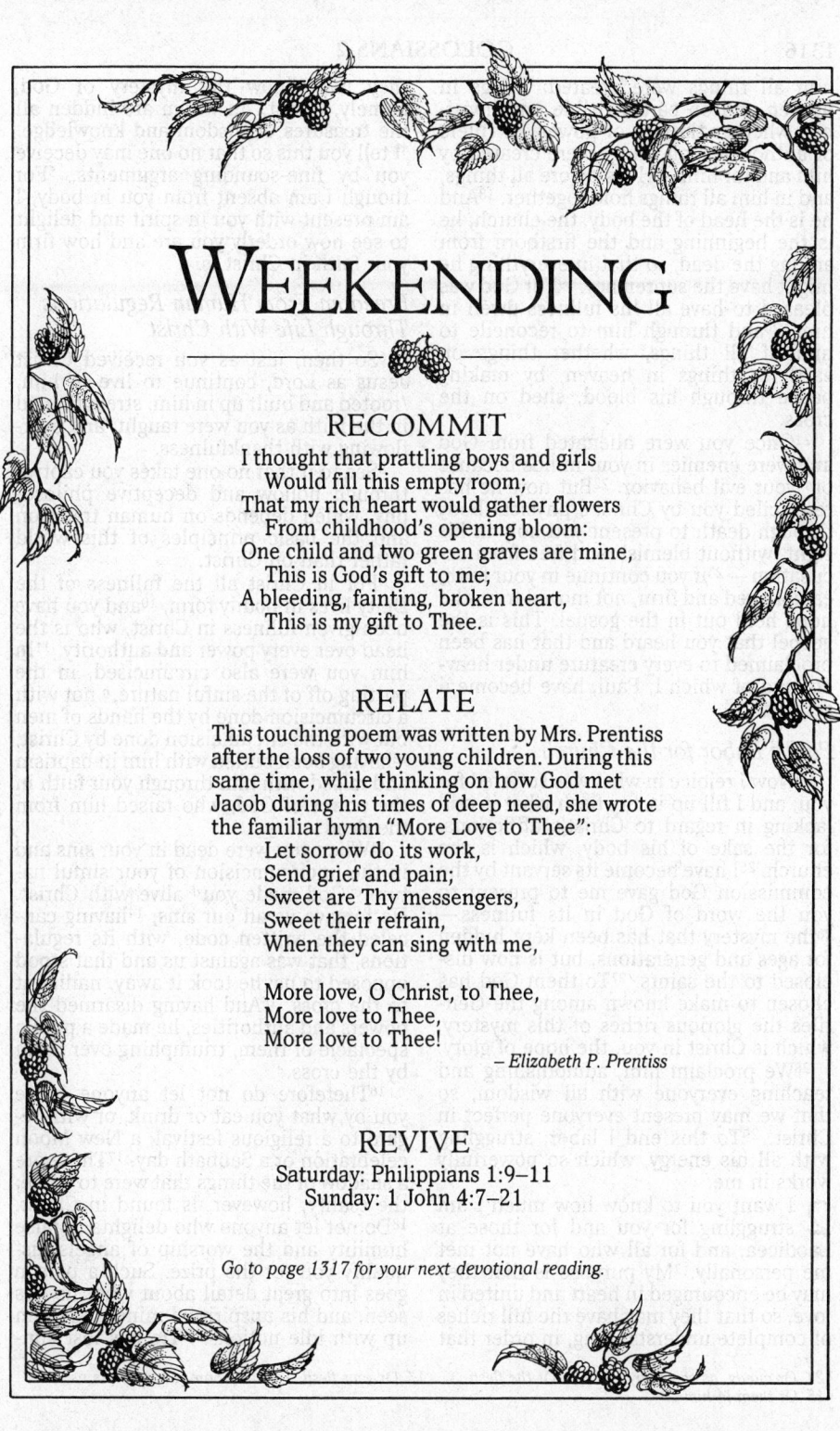

WEEKENDING

RECOMMIT

I thought that prattling boys and girls
    Would fill this empty room;
That my rich heart would gather flowers
    From childhood's opening bloom:
One child and two green graves are mine,
    This is God's gift to me;
A bleeding, fainting, broken heart,
    This is my gift to Thee.

RELATE

This touching poem was written by Mrs. Prentiss
after the loss of two young children. During this
same time, while thinking on how God met
Jacob during his times of deep need, she wrote
the familiar hymn "More Love to Thee":

    Let sorrow do its work,
    Send grief and pain;
    Sweet are Thy messengers,
    Sweet their refrain,
    When they can sing with me,

    More love, O Christ, to Thee,
    More love to Thee,
    More love to Thee!

        — Elizabeth P. Prentiss

REVIVE

Saturday: Philippians 1:9–11
Sunday: 1 John 4:7–21

Go to page 1317 for your next devotional reading.

him all things were created: things in heaven and on earth, visible and invisible, whether thrones or powers or rulers or authorities; all things were created by him and for him. 17He is before all things, and in him all things hold together. 18And he is the head of the body, the church; he is the beginning and the firstborn from among the dead, so that in everything he might have the supremacy. 19For God was pleased to have all his fullness dwell in him, 20and through him to reconcile to himself all things, whether things on earth or things in heaven, by making peace through his blood, shed on the cross.

21Once you were alienated from God and were enemies in your minds because of*a* your evil behavior. 22But now he has reconciled you by Christ's physical body through death to present you holy in his sight, without blemish and free from accusation— 23if you continue in your faith, established and firm, not moved from the hope held out in the gospel. This is the gospel that you heard and that has been proclaimed to every creature under heaven, and of which I, Paul, have become a servant.

Paul's Labor for the Church

24Now I rejoice in what was suffered for you, and I fill up in my flesh what is still lacking in regard to Christ's afflictions, for the sake of his body, which is the church. 25I have become its servant by the commission God gave me to present to you the word of God in its fullness— 26the mystery that has been kept hidden for ages and generations, but is now disclosed to the saints. 27To them God has chosen to make known among the Gentiles the glorious riches of this mystery, which is Christ in you, the hope of glory.

28We proclaim him, admonishing and teaching everyone with all wisdom, so that we may present everyone perfect in Christ. 29To this end I labor, struggling with all his energy, which so powerfully works in me.

2 I want you to know how much I am struggling for you and for those at Laodicea, and for all who have not met me personally. 2My purpose is that they may be encouraged in heart and united in love, so that they may have the full riches of complete understanding, in order that

they may know the mystery of God, namely, Christ, 3in whom are hidden all the treasures of wisdom and knowledge. 4I tell you this so that no one may deceive you by fine-sounding arguments. 5For though I am absent from you in body, I am present with you in spirit and delight to see how orderly you are and how firm your faith in Christ is.

Freedom From Human Regulations Through Life With Christ

6So then, just as you received Christ Jesus as Lord, continue to live in him, 7rooted and built up in him, strengthened in the faith as you were taught, and overflowing with thankfulness.

8See to it that no one takes you captive through hollow and deceptive philosophy, which depends on human tradition and the basic principles of this world rather than on Christ.

9For in Christ all the fullness of the Deity lives in bodily form, 10and you have been given fullness in Christ, who is the head over every power and authority. 11In him you were also circumcised, in the putting off of the sinful nature,*b* not with a circumcision done by the hands of men but with the circumcision done by Christ, 12having been buried with him in baptism and raised with him through your faith in the power of God, who raised him from the dead.

13When you were dead in your sins and in the uncircumcision of your sinful nature,*c* God made you*d* alive with Christ. He forgave us all our sins, 14having canceled the written code, with its regulations, that was against us and that stood opposed to us; he took it away, nailing it to the cross. 15And having disarmed the powers and authorities, he made a public spectacle of them, triumphing over them by the cross.*e*

16Therefore do not let anyone judge you by what you eat or drink, or with regard to a religious festival, a New Moon celebration or a Sabbath day. 17These are a shadow of the things that were to come; the reality, however, is found in Christ. 18Do not let anyone who delights in false humility and the worship of angels disqualify you for the prize. Such a person goes into great detail about what he has seen, and his unspiritual mind puffs him up with idle notions. 19He has lost con-

---

*a*21 Or *minds, as shown by*   *b*11 Or *the flesh*   *c*13 Or *your flesh*   *d*13 Some manuscripts *us*
*e*15 Or *them in him*

VERSE FOR THE DAY:
Colossians 2:10

AUTHOR:
Marie Chapian

PASSAGE FOR THE DAY:
Colossians 2:6–12

Fullness in Christ

EVERY time somebody asks me what my astrological sign is, I tell them, "Jesus is my sign. I'm a Christian." Often the person will continue, "Yes, but what month were you born in?" Still I persist, "I'm a Christian. I'm born again."

For centuries people have believed that their destiny is controlled by the month of their birth. They are slaves to the stars. Thank goodness that for those who believe in Jesus Christ there is freedom from such bondage.

Colossians 2:10 tells us we are complete in Christ—not in anything else. He is the head over every power in the universe. We need never be threatened by the forces of darkness that may surround us. Christ reigns above those forces. The stars can't control our destinies—Jesus created the stars! He is our authority.

It is a wonderful thing to be made whole and full. This means we can stop searching for identity and self-worth in the elemental and base philosophies of the world. Our future is sure in Christ because no longer are we incomplete creatures, helpless in the face of an unseen destiny.

Nonetheless, we must guard against seductive philosophies and false religions, just as we must look inward at our own personal, unbridled needs. I have counseled countless people who are insecure, fearful, moody, and desperately dependent on the approval of other people. These things can imprison us just as miserably as the deceptive philosophy of astrology.

Jesus Christ is the head over every power and authority, and he is more powerful than sorrow, gloom, fear, insecurity and the need for approval. It is important that we tell ourselves daily, "I find my personhood in the Lord Jesus and not in other people, not in success, relationships, ideal circumstances or the stars." Then tell the Lord triumphantly, "Thank you for giving me fullness in you."

Additional Scripture Readings:
Isaiah 47:8–15; Ephesians 6:11–18

Go to page 1319 for your next devotional reading.

nection with the Head, from whom the whole body, supported and held together by its ligaments and sinews, grows as God causes it to grow.

20Since you died with Christ to the basic principles of this world, why, as though you still belonged to it, do you submit to its rules: 21"Do not handle! Do not taste! Do not touch!"? 22These are all destined to perish with use, because they are based on human commands and teachings. 23Such regulations indeed have an appearance of wisdom, with their self-imposed worship, their false humility and their harsh treatment of the body, but they lack any value in restraining sensual indulgence.

Rules for Holy Living

3 Since, then, you have been raised with Christ, set your hearts on things above, where Christ is seated at the right hand of God. 2Set your minds on things above, not on earthly things. 3For you died, and your life is now hidden with Christ in God. 4When Christ, who is your*a* life, appears, then you also will appear with him in glory.

5Put to death, therefore, whatever belongs to your earthly nature: sexual immorality, impurity, lust, evil desires and greed, which is idolatry. 6Because of these, the wrath of God is coming.*b* 7You used to walk in these ways, in the life you once lived. 8But now you must rid yourselves of all such things as these: anger, rage, malice, slander, and filthy language from your lips. 9Do not lie to each other, since you have taken off your old self with its practices 10and have put on the new self, which is being renewed in knowledge in the image of its Creator. 11Here there is no Greek or Jew, circumcised or uncircumcised, barbarian, Scythian, slave or free, but Christ is all, and is in all.

12Therefore, as God's chosen people, holy and dearly loved, clothe yourselves with compassion, kindness, humility, gentleness and patience. 13Bear with each other and forgive whatever grievances you may have against one another. Forgive as the Lord forgave you. 14And over all these virtues put on love, which binds them all together in perfect unity.

15Let the peace of Christ rule in your hearts, since as members of one body you were called to peace. And be thankful.

16Let the word of Christ dwell in you richly as you teach and admonish one another with all wisdom, and as you sing psalms, hymns and spiritual songs with gratitude in your hearts to God. 17And whatever you do, whether in word or deed, do it all in the name of the Lord Jesus, giving thanks to God the Father through him.

Rules for Christian Households

18Wives, submit to your husbands, as is fitting in the Lord.

19Husbands, love your wives and do not be harsh with them.

20Children, obey your parents in everything, for this pleases the Lord.

21Fathers, do not embitter your children, or they will become discouraged.

22Slaves, obey your earthly masters in everything; and do it, not only when their eye is on you and to win their favor, but with sincerity of heart and reverence for the Lord. 23Whatever you do, work at it with all your heart, as working for the Lord, not for men, 24since you know that you will receive an inheritance from the Lord as a reward. It is the Lord Christ you are serving. 25Anyone who does wrong will be repaid for his wrong, and there is no favoritism.

4 Masters, provide your slaves with what is right and fair, because you know that you also have a Master in heaven.

Further Instructions

2Devote yourselves to prayer, being watchful and thankful. 3And pray for us, too, that God may open a door for our message, so that we may proclaim the mystery of Christ, for which I am in chains. 4Pray that I may proclaim it clearly, as I should. 5Be wise in the way you act toward outsiders; make the most of every opportunity. 6Let your conversation be always full of grace, seasoned with salt, so that you may know how to answer everyone.

Final Greetings

7Tychicus will tell you all the news about me. He is a dear brother, a faithful minister and fellow servant in the Lord. 8I am sending him to you for the express purpose that you may know about our*c* circumstances and that he may encour-

---

a4 Some manuscripts *our*   *b6* Some early manuscripts *coming on those who are disobedient*
c8 Some manuscripts *that he may know about your*

VERSE FOR THE DAY:
Colossians 3:15–17

AUTHOR:
Martha Manikas-Foster

PASSAGE FOR THE DAY:
Colossians 3:1–17

The Peace of Christ

IT was a working holiday for my husband. It turned into two weeks of baby-tending isolation for me. The chill of the northern Michigan spring was too much for my three-month-old daughter. So we spent much of our time in the small bedroom of a cottage bordering Lake Huron.

I was held captive. I was trapped only a few feet from my favorite piece of wilderness. I had spent times very close to God here, skiing among these trees and walking within range of the sound of the waves. But that was before.

This visit, I resigned myself to spending two weeks in closed quarters, and I unpacked the pens and editing supplies from my briefcase. I determined not to yearn for the birch trees, the sandy cove and the bay outside my window.

Several days into our stay, Connie's nap extended beyond its usual, frustratingly short fifteen-minute duration. I seized the opportunity and, grabbing the portable baby monitor, dashed out the door. I wanted to appreciate God's spellbinding creation. But my electronic tether kept me close to the cabin.

With the zeal of an eager girl scout, I began cutting tall grass and reed from along the bay and laying the bundles on a picnic table in the sun. I watched the sea gulls, sang favorite hymns, and from the pile on the table began to weave the still-damp materials into something of a basket. It wasn't much of a basket, but my efforts were sincere and my spirit exuberant.

I was at peace. It shouldn't have surprised me that enjoying God as revealed through his creation would bring peace. But it did. And once peaceful, it was easier to see my circumstances as opportunities to worship God through all I did. Thus, when my daughter woke up and called me to return, I went with renewed compassion and patience.

Since that time, when I have felt confined or frustrated, I have reached again to touch a part of God's creation. God's character is revealed, in part, through his excellent work in the details—his attention to the minuscule fibers of each tulip, each pine needle, each crab apple blossom. It is only by focusing on the One whose creation surrounds us and brings us peace that we can do "all in the name of the Lord Jesus, giving thanks to God the Father through him" (Colossians 3:17).

Additional Scripture Readings:
Psalm 104:24–34; Isaiah 55:12–13

Go to page 1323 for your next devotional reading.

age your hearts. ⁹He is coming with Onesimus, our faithful and dear brother, who is one of you. They will tell you everything that is happening here.

¹⁰My fellow prisoner Aristarchus sends you his greetings, as does Mark, the cousin of Barnabas. (You have received instructions about him; if he comes to you, welcome him.) ¹¹Jesus, who is called Justus, also sends greetings. These are the only Jews among my fellow workers for the kingdom of God, and they have proved a comfort to me. ¹²Epaphras, who is one of you and a servant of Christ Jesus, sends greetings. He is always wrestling in prayer for you, that you may stand firm in all the will of God, mature and

fully assured. ¹³I vouch for him that he is working hard for you and for those at Laodicea and Hierapolis. ¹⁴Our dear friend Luke, the doctor, and Demas send greetings. ¹⁵Give my greetings to the brothers at Laodicea, and to Nympha and the church in her house.

¹⁶After this letter has been read to you, see that it is also read in the church of the Laodiceans and that you in turn read the letter from Laodicea.

¹⁷Tell Archippus: "See to it that you complete the work you have received in the Lord."

¹⁸I, Paul, write this greeting in my own hand. Remember my chains. Grace be with you.

PAUL writes this letter to the church he began in Thessalonica (Acts 17:1–9), shortly after leaving them and being unable to return (1 Thessalonians 2:17–18). He is excited about their Christian faith, reminds them of his intense love for them, and answers questions about what death means for a Christian. As you read this book, find comfort as a believer that when you die you will still be under God's care and will "be with the Lord forever" (1 Thessalonians 4:17).

1 THESSALONIANS

1 Paul, Silas[a] and Timothy,

To the church of the Thessalonians in God the Father and the Lord Jesus Christ:

Grace and peace to you.[b]

Thanksgiving for the Thessalonians' Faith

[2] We always thank God for all of you, mentioning you in our prayers. [3] We continually remember before our God and Father your work produced by faith, your labor prompted by love, and your endurance inspired by hope in our Lord Jesus Christ.

[4] For we know, brothers loved by God, that he has chosen you, [5] because our gospel came to you not simply with words, but also with power, with the Holy Spirit and with deep conviction. You know how we lived among you for your sake. [6] You became imitators of us and of the Lord; in spite of severe suffering, you welcomed the message with the joy given by the Holy Spirit. [7] And so you became a model to all the believers in Macedonia and

Achaia. ⁸The Lord's message rang out from you not only in Macedonia and Achaia—your faith in God has become known everywhere. Therefore we do not need to say anything about it, ⁹for they themselves report what kind of reception you gave us. They tell how you turned to God from idols to serve the living and true God, ¹⁰and to wait for his Son from heaven, whom he raised from the dead—Jesus, who rescues us from the coming wrath.

Paul's Ministry in Thessalonica

2 You know, brothers, that our visit to you was not a failure. ²We had previously suffered and been insulted in Philippi, as you know, but with the help of our God we dared to tell you his gospel in spite of strong opposition. ³For the appeal we make does not spring from error or impure motives, nor are we trying to trick you. ⁴On the contrary, we speak as men approved by God to be entrusted with the gospel. We are not trying to please men but God, who tests our hearts. ⁵You know we never used flattery, nor did we put on a mask to cover up greed—God is our witness. ⁶We were not looking for praise from men, not from you or anyone else.

As apostles of Christ we could have been a burden to you, ⁷but we were gentle among you, like a mother caring for her little children. ⁸We loved you so much that we were delighted to share with you not only the gospel of God but our lives as well, because you had become so dear to us. ⁹Surely you remember, brothers, our toil and hardship; we worked night and day in order not to be a burden to anyone while we preached the gospel of God to you.

¹⁰You are witnesses, and so is God, of how holy, righteous and blameless we were among you who believed. ¹¹For you know that we dealt with each of you as a father deals with his own children, ¹²encouraging, comforting and urging you to live lives worthy of God, who calls you into his kingdom and glory.

¹³And we also thank God continually because, when you received the word of God, which you heard from us, you accepted it not as the word of men, but as it actually is, the word of God, which is at work in you who believe. ¹⁴For you, brothers, became imitators of God's churches in Judea, which are in Christ Jesus: You suffered from your own countrymen the same things those churches suffered from the Jews, ¹⁵who killed the Lord Jesus and the prophets and also drove us out. They displease God and are hostile to all men ¹⁶in their effort to keep us from speaking to the Gentiles so that they may be saved. In this way they always heap up their sins to the limit. The wrath of God has come upon them at last.ᵃ

Paul's Longing to See the Thessalonians

¹⁷But, brothers, when we were torn away from you for a short time (in person, not in thought), out of our intense longing we made every effort to see you. ¹⁸For we wanted to come to you—certainly I, Paul, did, again and again—but Satan stopped us. ¹⁹For what is our hope, our joy, or the crown in which we will glory in the presence of our Lord Jesus when he comes? Is it not you? ²⁰Indeed, you are our glory and joy.

3 So when we could stand it no longer, we thought it best to be left by ourselves in Athens. ²We sent Timothy, who is our brother and God's fellow workerᵇ in spreading the gospel of Christ, to strengthen and encourage you in your faith, ³so that no one would be unsettled by these trials. You know quite well that we were destined for them. ⁴In fact, when we were with you, we kept telling you that we would be persecuted. And it turned out that way, as you well know. ⁵For this reason, when I could stand it no longer, I sent to find out about your faith. I was afraid that in some way the tempter might have tempted you and our efforts might have been useless.

Timothy's Encouraging Report

⁶But Timothy has just now come to us from you and has brought good news about your faith and love. He has told us that you always have pleasant memories of us and that you long to see us, just as we also long to see you. ⁷Therefore, brothers, in all our distress and persecution we were encouraged about you because of your faith. ⁸For now we really live, since you are standing firm in the Lord. ⁹How can we thank God enough for you in return for all the joy we have in the

ᵃ16 Or them fully   ᵇ2 Some manuscripts brother and fellow worker; other manuscripts brother and God's servant

VERSE FOR THE DAY:
1 Thessalonians 4:14

AUTHOR:
Martha Manikas-Foster

PASSAGE FOR THE DAY:
1 Thessalonians 4:13–15

Because of the Resurrection

WHEN I was in high school, a Campus Life leader commented that before our group graduated, quite likely one of our class-mates would die. Death is that near, he said. Even young people die.

His prediction was wrong. None of my high school classmates died. But a few years later, on one day, in the instant it takes for a car and truck to collide, six college classmates died.

These weren't anonymous men and women; I knew each of them. When they died I was hundreds of miles away taking classes at another university. After the phone call, I was over-whelmed by my powerlessness. Alone, I had no one to share my grief, to hold me when I sobbed. To grieve for one would have been torture enough. Grieving for six tore me apart.

Loving sets us up for sorrow, that's true. But it also encour-ages us to hope. Although I didn't understand it immediately, I grew to realize that the affection I had for these classmates had grown from a foundation of common faith. On such a founda-tion my hope began to flourish. What we had most in common was the very thing that assured me of their well-being. Because of the resurrection, the horror of death melted away. I would see them again because:

> We believe that Jesus died and rose again and so we believe that God will bring with Jesus those who have fallen asleep in him. According to the Lord's own word, we tell you that we who are still alive, who are left till the coming of the Lord, will certainly not precede those who have fallen asleep. . . . And so we will be with the Lord forever. Therefore encourage each other with these words (1 Thessalonians 4:14–15,17–18).

I can't help but grow sad when I look at some of the photo-graphs in my college yearbooks. But I have hope because I know that "death has been swallowed up in victory" (1 Corinthians 15:54). Jesus Christ is the victor! He "has destroyed death and has brought life and immortality to light through the gospel" (2 Timothy 1:10).

Additional Scripture Readings:
John 11:21–27; 1 Corinthians 15:20–23

Go to page 1325 for your next devotional reading.

presence of our God because of you? [10]Night and day we pray most earnestly that we may see you again and supply what is lacking in your faith.

[11]Now may our God and Father himself and our Lord Jesus clear the way for us to come to you. [12]May the Lord make your love increase and overflow for each other and for everyone else, just as ours does for you. [13]May he strengthen your hearts so that you will be blameless and holy in the presence of our God and Father when our Lord Jesus comes with all his holy ones.

Living to Please God

4 Finally, brothers, we instructed you how to live in order to please God, as in fact you are living. Now we ask you and urge you in the Lord Jesus to do this more and more. [2]For you know what instructions we gave you by the authority of the Lord Jesus.

[3]It is God's will that you should be sanctified: that you should avoid sexual immorality; [4]that each of you should learn to control his own body[a] in a way that is holy and honorable, [5]not in passionate lust like the heathen, who do not know God; [6]and that in this matter no one should wrong his brother or take advantage of him. The Lord will punish men for all such sins, as we have already told you and warned you. [7]For God did not call us to be impure, but to live a holy life. [8]Therefore, he who rejects this instruction does not reject man but God, who gives you his Holy Spirit.

[9]Now about brotherly love we do not need to write to you, for you yourselves have been taught by God to love each other. [10]And in fact, you do love all the brothers throughout Macedonia. Yet we urge you, brothers, to do so more and more. [11]Make it your ambition to lead a quiet life, to mind your own business and to work with your hands, just as we told you, [12]so that your daily life may win the respect of outsiders and so that you will not be dependent on anybody.

The Coming of the Lord

[13]Brothers, we do not want you to be ignorant about those who fall asleep, or to grieve like the rest of men, who have no hope. [14]We believe that Jesus died and rose again and so we believe that God will bring with Jesus those who have fallen asleep in him. [15]According to the Lord's own word, we tell you that we who are still alive, who are left till the coming of the Lord, will certainly not precede those who have fallen asleep. [16]For the Lord himself will come down from heaven, with a loud command, with the voice of the archangel and with the trumpet call of God, and the dead in Christ will rise first. [17]After that, we who are still alive and are left will be caught up together with them in the clouds to meet the Lord in the air. And so we will be with the Lord forever. [18]Therefore encourage each other with these words.

5 Now, brothers, about times and dates we do not need to write to you, [2]for you know very well that the day of the Lord will come like a thief in the night. [3]While people are saying, "Peace and safety," destruction will come on them suddenly, as labor pains on a pregnant woman, and they will not escape.

[4]But you, brothers, are not in darkness so that this day should surprise you like a thief. [5]You are all sons of the light and sons of the day. We do not belong to the night or to the darkness. [6]So then, let us not be like others, who are asleep, but let us be alert and self-controlled. [7]For those who sleep, sleep at night, and those who get drunk, get drunk at night. [8]But since we belong to the day, let us be self-controlled, putting on faith and love as a breastplate, and the hope of salvation as a helmet. [9]For God did not appoint us to suffer wrath but to receive salvation through our Lord Jesus Christ. [10]He died for us so that, whether we are awake or asleep, we may live together with him. [11]Therefore encourage one another and build each other up, just as in fact you are doing.

Final Instructions

[12]Now we ask you, brothers, to respect those who work hard among you, who are over you in the Lord and who admonish you. [13]Hold them in the highest regard in love because of their work. Live in peace with each other. [14]And we urge you, brothers, warn those who are idle, encourage the timid, help the weak, be patient with everyone. [15]Make sure that nobody pays back wrong for wrong, but always try to be kind to each other and to everyone else.

[16]Be joyful always; [17]pray continually; [18]give thanks in all circumstances, for

a4 Or learn to live with his own wife; or learn to acquire a wife

VERSE FOR THE DAY:
1 Thessalonians 5:18

AUTHOR:
Carol L. Baldwin

PASSAGE FOR THE DAY:
1 Thessalonians 5:16–22

Thanksgiving for All Things

"LORD, how can I thank you when I am single and want to be married?"

"Dear God, how can I ever be happy in this dead-end job?"

"God, how can I thank you for broken plumbing in our bathroom when we don't have the money to make repairs?"

How can we have thankful, contented hearts when the circumstances in our lives are not what we had planned and when they lie outside our control or our power to change?

Let's look at our alternatives. If we are not thankful, we become bitter and angry with God: he is not providing what we "rightfully" deserve. If we are not content, we become rebellious and complaining: after all, he gives our friends everything they pray for—why does he refuse us?

Underlying these complaints and questions lie two errors in our thinking: that God is not trustworthy and that he does not desire our good. When we compare these conclusions with Scripture, we discover how wrong we are! God's Word instructs us that God is sovereignly in control, providing for and working out *all* the circumstances in the lives of those who love him and whom he has called (Romans 8:28; 1 Corinthians 10:13a; Philippians 4:6–7). He is intimately involved with us; he works out his purposes through the events in our lives so that we may be conformed to the image of his Son.

We have further reason to praise him. The same God who formed the world in six days knows every hair on our heads. The same God who chose a people for himself before we were born sent his Son to die on the cross to redeem us from our sins.

God's love for his people is not determined by the circumstances in our lives. His love is steadfast. Our marital status, career or finances might fluctuate or totally break apart. In spite of that, however, we can and must give him thanks for his love toward us. We must serve him with unhesitating hearts.

Additional Scripture Readings:
Philippians 1:12–19; Colossians 2:6–7

Go to page 1329 for your next devotional reading.

this is God's will for you in Christ Jesus.

¹⁹Do not put out the Spirit's fire; ²⁰do not treat prophecies with contempt. ²¹Test everything. Hold on to the good. ²²Avoid every kind of evil.

²³May God himself, the God of peace, sanctify you through and through. May your whole spirit, soul and body be kept blameless at the coming of our Lord Jesus Christ. ²⁴The one who calls you is faithful and he will do it.

²⁵Brothers, pray for us. ²⁶Greet all the brothers with a holy kiss. ²⁷I charge you before the Lord to have this letter read to all the brothers.

²⁸The grace of our Lord Jesus Christ be with you.

*PAUL writes this letter shortly after
1 Thessalonians to clarify some things
that the church failed to understand in
his first letter. He tells them that the
antichrist is coming, but they must continue with their regular schedules until
Jesus returns. As you read this book,
remember that God wants you to look
forward to Christ's return as well as to
continue doing your daily work.*

2 THESSALONIANS

1 Paul, Silas^a and Timothy,

To the church of the Thessalonians in God our Father and the Lord Jesus Christ:

²Grace and peace to you from God the Father and the Lord Jesus Christ.

Thanksgiving and Prayer

³We ought always to thank God for you, brothers, and rightly so, because your faith is growing more and more, and the love every one of you has for each other is increasing. ⁴Therefore, among God's churches we boast about your persever-ance and faith in all the persecutions and trials you are enduring.

⁵All this is evidence that God's judg-ment is right, and as a result you will be counted worthy of the kingdom of God,

for which you are suffering. ⁶God is just: He will pay back trouble to those who trouble you ⁷and give relief to you who are troubled, and to us as well. This will hap-pen when the Lord Jesus is revealed from heaven in blazing fire with his powerful angels. ⁸He will punish those who do not know God and do not obey the gospel of our Lord Jesus. ⁹They will be punished with everlasting destruction and shut out from the presence of the Lord and from the majesty of his power ¹⁰on the day he comes to be glorified in his holy people and to be marveled at among all those who have believed. This includes you, be-cause you believed our testimony to you.

¹¹With this in mind, we constantly pray for you, that our God may count you worthy of his calling, and that by his pow-

^a1 Greek *Silvanus*, a variant of *Silas*

er he may fulfill every good purpose of yours and every act prompted by your faith. [12]We pray this so that the name of our Lord Jesus may be glorified in you, and you in him, according to the grace of our God and the Lord Jesus Christ. [a]

The Man of Lawlessness

2 Concerning the coming of our Lord Jesus Christ and our being gathered to him, we ask you, brothers, [2]not to become easily unsettled or alarmed by some prophecy, report or letter supposed to have come from us, saying that the day of the Lord has already come. [3]Don't let anyone deceive you in any way, for that day will not come, until the rebellion occurs and the man of lawlessness[b] is revealed, the man doomed to destruction. [4]He will oppose and will exalt himself over everything that is called God or is worshiped, so that he sets himself up in God's temple, proclaiming himself to be God.

[5]Don't you remember that when I was with you I used to tell you these things? [6]And now you know what is holding him back, so that he may be revealed at the proper time. [7]For the secret power of lawlessness is already at work; but the one who now holds it back will continue to do so till he is taken out of the way. [8]And then the lawless one will be revealed, whom the Lord Jesus will overthrow with the breath of his mouth and destroy by the splendor of his coming. [9]The coming of the lawless one will be in accordance with the work of Satan displayed in all kinds of counterfeit miracles, signs and wonders, [10]and in every sort of evil that deceives those who are perishing. They perish because they refused to love the truth and so be saved. [11]For this reason God sends them a powerful delusion so that they will believe the lie [12]and so that all will be condemned who have not believed the truth but have delighted in wickedness.

Stand Firm

[13]But we ought always to thank God for you, brothers loved by the Lord, because from the beginning God chose you[c] to be saved through the sanctifying work of the Spirit and through belief in the truth.

[14]He called you to this through our gospel, that you might share in the glory of our Lord Jesus Christ. [15]So then, brothers, stand firm and hold to the teachings[d] we passed on to you, whether by word of mouth or by letter.

[16]May our Lord Jesus Christ himself and God our Father, who loved us and by his grace gave us eternal encouragement and good hope, [17]encourage your hearts and strengthen you in every good deed and word.

Request for Prayer

3 Finally, brothers, pray for us that the message of the Lord may spread rapidly and be honored, just as it was with you. [2]And pray that we may be delivered from wicked and evil men, for not everyone has faith. [3]But the Lord is faithful, and he will strengthen and protect you from the evil one. [4]We have confidence in the Lord that you are doing and will continue to do the things we command. [5]May the Lord direct your hearts into God's love and Christ's perseverance.

Warning Against Idleness

[6]In the name of the Lord Jesus Christ, we command you, brothers, to keep away from every brother who is idle and does not live according to the teaching[e] you received from us. [7]For you yourselves know how you ought to follow our example. We were not idle when we were with you, [8]nor did we eat anyone's food without paying for it. On the contrary, we worked night and day, laboring and toiling so that we would not be a burden to any of you. [9]We did this, not because we do not have the right to such help, but in order to make ourselves a model for you to follow. [10]For even when we were with you, we gave you this rule: "If a man will not work, he shall not eat."

[11]We hear that some among you are idle. They are not busy; they are busybodies. [12]Such people we command and urge in the Lord Jesus Christ to settle down and earn the bread they eat. [13]And as for you, brothers, never tire of doing what is right.

[14]If anyone does not obey our instruction in this letter, take special note of him. Do not associate with him, in order

---

[a]12 Or God and Lord, Jesus Christ　　[b]3 Some manuscripts sin　　[c]13 Some manuscripts because God chose you as his firstfruits　　[d]15 Or traditions　　[e]6 Or tradition

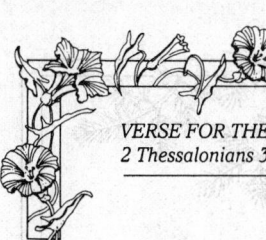

VERSE FOR THE DAY:
2 Thessalonians 3:5,16

AUTHOR:
Gien Karssen

PASSAGE FOR THE DAY:
2 Thessalonians 3:1–18

Practicing Peace

EACH of Paul's letters begins with a greeting of peace. Some, like this one to the Christians in the Greek city of Thessalonica, end the same way. These words were full of meaning. Paul was reminding the Thessalonians that the Lord, the author of peace, would give his peace always, in every way and under all circumstances. The Thessalonians needed this encouragement badly. They were people who suffered from oppression and persecution, who were confronted with the problem of immorality, who were full of sorrow because of loved ones who had died, who lived among difficult and pagan people, and who were confronted by false religious teachers and people with warped minds.

Paul's words referred back to the reality of the night in which Christ was born. The Lord who gives peace, because he himself is peace, was born to command peace. It is the same peace of which the Lord later would say to his disciples, "Peace I leave with you; my peace I give you" (John 14:27). "I have told you these things, so that in me you may have peace. In this world you will have trouble. But take heart! I have overcome the world" (John 16:33).

The Thessalonians claimed this peace, and proved it to be applicable and sufficient in their varied situations. This peace lifted them above their problems. In spite of pressure and adversity, their faith grew so that they became examples to others.

Even today we can draw comfort from the experiences of those who have gone before us. We can try to follow their good example, learn not to lose heart, and nurture hope.

Circumstances in the eighties are far from rosy. The world finds itself in chaos. Many a family is in a crisis. The church is often at a loss for the right answers. Small wonder that our hearts lack peace and are full of uncertainty. But in spite of this we can experience the Lord's peace continually, and in every way.

Peace must be practical and practiced! We best begin each new day with God, reading his Word and praying. Then we can think back to this quiet time throughout the day to claim his peace when unrest and discord are knocking at our door. We must remind ourselves that no situation we find ourselves in is beyond the range of God's interest in us.

Additional Scripture Readings:
Isaiah 26:3–4; James 3:17–18

Go to page 1330 for your next devotional reading.

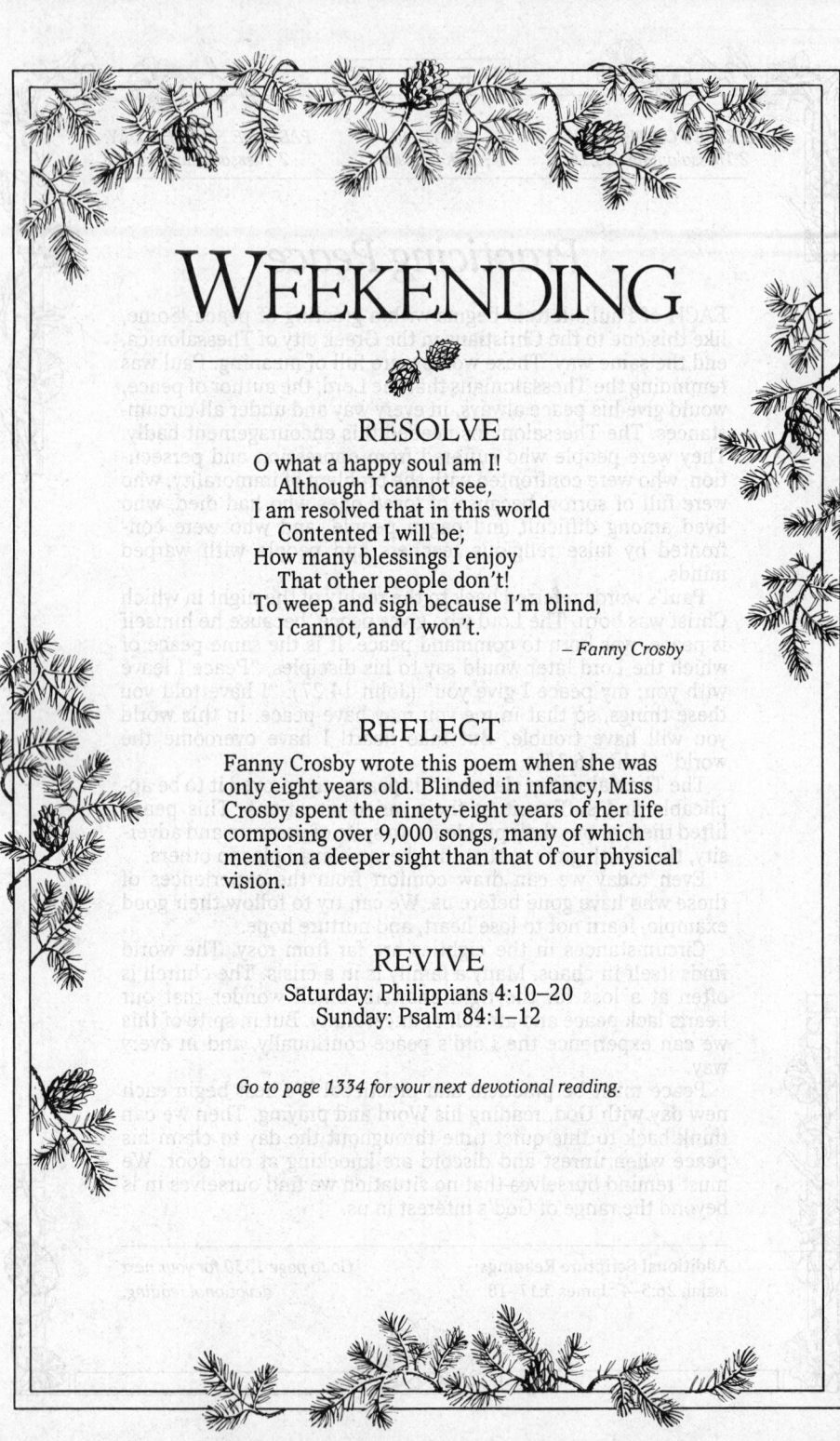

WEEKENDING

RESOLVE

O what a happy soul am I!
Although I cannot see,
I am resolved that in this world
Contented I will be;
How many blessings I enjoy
That other people don't!
To weep and sigh because I'm blind,
I cannot, and I won't.

– Fanny Crosby

REFLECT

Fanny Crosby wrote this poem when she was
only eight years old. Blinded in infancy, Miss
Crosby spent the ninety-eight years of her life
composing over 9,000 songs, many of which
mention a deeper sight than that of our physical
vision.

REVIVE

Saturday: Philippians 4:10–20
Sunday: Psalm 84:1–12

Go to page 1334 for your next devotional reading.

that he may feel ashamed. 15Yet do not regard him as an enemy, but warn him as a brother.

Final Greetings

16Now may the Lord of peace himself give you peace at all times and in every way. The Lord be with all of you.

17I, Paul, write this greeting in my own hand, which is the distinguishing mark in all my letters. This is how I write. 18The grace of our Lord Jesus Christ be with you all.

PAUL writes this letter to young Timothy, who is serving as a pastor in Ephesus. He instructs him how to organize and run the church and how to deal with false teachers and refute what they say. As you read this book, promise God that you will not stray from true faith.

1 TIMOTHY

1 Paul, an apostle of Christ Jesus by the command of God our Savior and of Christ Jesus our hope,

²To Timothy my true son in the faith:

Grace, mercy and peace from God the Father and Christ Jesus our Lord.

Warning Against False Teachers of the Law

³As I urged you when I went into Macedonia, stay there in Ephesus so that you may command certain men not to teach false doctrines any longer ⁴nor to devote themselves to myths and endless genealogies. These promote controversies rather than God's work—which is by faith. ⁵The goal of this command is love, which comes from a pure heart and a good conscience and a sincere faith. ⁶Some have wandered away from these and turned to meaningless talk. ⁷They want to be teachers of the law, but they do not know what they are talking about or what they so confidently affirm.

⁸We know that the law is good if one uses it properly. ⁹We also know that law*a* is made not for the righteous but for lawbreakers and rebels, the ungodly and sinful, the unholy and irreligious; for those who kill their fathers or mothers, for murderers, ¹⁰for adulterers and perverts, for slave traders and liars and perjurers—and for whatever else is contrary to the sound doctrine ¹¹that conforms to the glorious gospel of the blessed God, which he entrusted to me.

The Lord's Grace to Paul

¹²I thank Christ Jesus our Lord, who has given me strength, that he considered me faithful, appointing me to his service. ¹³Even though I was once a blasphemer and a persecutor and a violent man, I was

a9 Or that the law

shown mercy because I acted in ignorance and unbelief. [14]The grace of our Lord was poured out on me abundantly, along with the faith and love that are in Christ Jesus.

[15]Here is a trustworthy saying that deserves full acceptance: Christ Jesus came into the world to save sinners — of whom I am the worst. [16]But for that very reason I was shown mercy so that in me, the worst of sinners, Christ Jesus might display his unlimited patience as an example for those who would believe on him and receive eternal life. [17]Now to the King eternal, immortal, invisible, the only God, be honor and glory for ever and ever. Amen.

[18]Timothy, my son, I give you this instruction in keeping with the prophecies once made about you, so that by following them you may fight the good fight, [19]holding on to faith and a good conscience. Some have rejected these and so have shipwrecked their faith. [20]Among them are Hymenaeus and Alexander, whom I have handed over to Satan to be taught not to blaspheme.

Instructions on Worship

2 I urge, then, first of all, that requests, prayers, intercession and thanksgiving be made for everyone — [2]for kings and all those in authority, that we may live peaceful and quiet lives in all godliness and holiness. [3]This is good, and pleases God our Savior, [4]who wants all men to be saved and to come to a knowledge of the truth. [5]For there is one God and one mediator between God and men, the man Christ Jesus, [6]who gave himself as a ransom for all men — the testimony given in its proper time. [7]And for this purpose I was appointed a herald and an apostle — I am telling the truth, I am not lying — and a teacher of the true faith to the Gentiles.

[8]I want men everywhere to lift up holy hands in prayer, without anger or disputing.

[9]I also want women to dress modestly, with decency and propriety, not with braided hair or gold or pearls or expensive clothes, [10]but with good deeds, appropriate for women who profess to worship God.

[11]A woman should learn in quietness and full submission. [12]I do not permit a woman to teach or to have authority over a man; she must be silent. [13]For Adam was formed first, then Eve. [14]And Adam was not the one deceived; it was the woman who was deceived and became a sinner. [15]But women[a] will be saved[b] through childbearing — if they continue in faith, love and holiness with propriety.

Overseers and Deacons

3 Here is a trustworthy saying: If anyone sets his heart on being an overseer,[c] he desires a noble task. [2]Now the overseer must be above reproach, the husband of but one wife, temperate, self-controlled, respectable, hospitable, able to teach, [3]not given to drunkenness, not violent but gentle, not quarrelsome, not a lover of money. [4]He must manage his own family well and see that his children obey him with proper respect. [5](If anyone does not know how to manage his own family, how can he take care of God's church?) [6]He must not be a recent convert, or he may become conceited and fall under the same judgment as the devil. [7]He must also have a good reputation with outsiders, so that he will not fall into disgrace and into the devil's trap.

[8]Deacons, likewise, are to be men worthy of respect, sincere, not indulging in much wine, and not pursuing dishonest gain. [9]They must keep hold of the deep truths of the faith with a clear conscience. [10]They must first be tested; and then if there is nothing against them, let them serve as deacons.

[11]In the same way, their wives[d] are to be women worthy of respect, not malicious talkers but temperate and trustworthy in everything.

[12]A deacon must be the husband of but one wife and must manage his children and his household well. [13]Those who have served well gain an excellent standing and great assurance in their faith in Christ Jesus.

[14]Although I hope to come to you soon, I am writing you these instructions so that, [15]if I am delayed, you will know how people ought to conduct themselves in God's household, which is the church of the living God, the pillar and foundation of the truth. [16]Beyond all question, the mystery of godliness is great:

He[e] appeared in a body,[f]
    was vindicated by the Spirit,

[a]15 Greek she   [b]15 Or restored   [c]1 Traditionally bishop; also in verse 2   [d]11 Or way,
deaconesses   [e]16 Some manuscripts God   [f]16 Or in the flesh

was seen by angels,
was preached among the nations,
was believed on in the world,
was taken up in glory.

Instructions to Timothy

4 The Spirit clearly says that in later times some will abandon the faith and follow deceiving spirits and things taught by demons. ²Such teachings come through hypocritical liars, whose consciences have been seared as with a hot iron. ³They forbid people to marry and order them to abstain from certain foods, which God created to be received with thanksgiving by those who believe and who know the truth. ⁴For everything God created is good, and nothing is to be rejected if it is received with thanksgiving, ⁵because it is consecrated by the word of God and prayer.

⁶If you point these things out to the brothers, you will be a good minister of Christ Jesus, brought up in the truths of the faith and of the good teaching that you have followed. ⁷Have nothing to do with godless myths and old wives' tales; rather, train yourself to be godly. ⁸For physical training is of some value, but godliness has value for all things, holding promise for both the present life and the life to come.

⁹This is a trustworthy saying that deserves full acceptance ¹⁰(and for this we labor and strive), that we have put our hope in the living God, who is the Savior of all men, and especially of those who believe.

¹¹Command and teach these things. ¹²Don't let anyone look down on you because you are young, but set an example for the believers in speech, in life, in love, in faith and in purity. ¹³Until I come, devote yourself to the public reading of

MONDAY

VERSE FOR THE DAY:
1 Timothy 2:1

AUTHOR:
Corrie ten Boom

PASSAGE FOR THE DAY:
1 Timothy 2:1–8

An Important Power

PRAYER is such an important power. In the concentration camp, seven hundred of us lived in a room built for two hundred people. We were all dirty, nervous and tense. One day a horrible fight broke out amongst the prisoners. Betsie began to pray aloud. It was as if a storm laid down, until at last all was quiet. Then Betsie said, "Thank you, Father." A tired old woman was used by the Lord to save the situation for seven hundred fellow prisoners through her prayers.

I urge, then, first of all, that requests, prayers, intercession and thanksgiving be made for everyone
(1 Timothy 2:1).

There may be days of darkness and distress,
When sin has power to tempt, and care to press.
Yet in the darkest day I will not fear,
For 'midst the shadows, You will still be near.
Thank You, Lord Jesus.

Additional Scripture Readings:
Colossians 4:2–5; James 5:13–18

Go to page 1335 for your next devotional reading.

Scripture, to preaching and to teaching. ¹⁴Do not neglect your gift, which was given you through a prophetic message when the body of elders laid their hands on you.

¹⁵Be diligent in these matters; give yourself wholly to them, so that everyone may see your progress. ¹⁶Watch your life and doctrine closely. Persevere in them, because if you do, you will save both yourself and your hearers.

Advice About Widows, Elders and Slaves

5 Do not rebuke an older man harshly, but exhort him as if he were your father. Treat younger men as brothers, ²older women as mothers, and younger women as sisters, with absolute purity.

³Give proper recognition to those widows who are really in need. ⁴But if a widow has children or grandchildren, these

ᵃ9 Or has had but one husband

should learn first of all to put their religion into practice by caring for their own family and so repaying their parents and grandparents, for this is pleasing to God. ⁵The widow who is really in need and left all alone puts her hope in God and continues night and day to pray and to ask God for help. ⁶But the widow who lives for pleasure is dead even while she lives. ⁷Give the people these instructions, too, so that no one may be open to blame. ⁸If anyone does not provide for his relatives, and especially for his immediate family, he has denied the faith and is worse than an unbeliever.

⁹No widow may be put on the list of widows unless she is over sixty, has been faithful to her husband,ᵃ ¹⁰and is well known for her good deeds, such as bringing up children, showing hospitality, washing the feet of the saints, helping those in trouble and devoting herself to all kinds of good deeds.

¹¹As for younger widows, do not put

VERSE FOR THE DAY: 1 Timothy 4:16	**AUTHOR:** Florence Littauer	**PASSAGE FOR THE DAY:** 1 Timothy 4:9–16

Cramming for Finals

A NINETY-six-year-old lady was a faithful attendant at my women's club Bible studies. She came with her lessons prepared and knew all the answers. One day a tactless member asked her, "Why do you work so hard on these lessons when you're so old and it doesn't matter?"

Little Bess Elkins looked up and said confidently, "I'm cramming for my finals."

It's never too late to get ready for our finals. Narrow is the way which leads to life and few there be that find it. It takes so little to be above average, but it does take a desire to learn and it does take preparation so when the great target appears we'll be able to hit the bull's-eye.

Additional Scripture Readings:
Psalm 119:33–37; Philippians 3:12–14

Go to page 1337 for your next devotional reading.

them on such a list. For when their sensual desires overcome their dedication to Christ, they want to marry. [12]Thus they bring judgment on themselves, because they have broken their first pledge. [13]Besides, they get into the habit of being idle and going about from house to house. And not only do they become idlers, but also gossips and busybodies, saying things they ought not to. [14]So I counsel younger widows to marry, to have children, to manage their homes and to give the enemy no opportunity for slander. [15]Some have in fact already turned away to follow Satan.

[16]If any woman who is a believer has widows in her family, she should help them and not let the church be burdened with them, so that the church can help those widows who are really in need.

[17]The elders who direct the affairs of the church well are worthy of double honor, especially those whose work is preaching and teaching. [18]For the Scripture says, "Do not muzzle the ox while it is treading out the grain,"[a] and "The worker deserves his wages."[b] [19]Do not entertain an accusation against an elder unless it is brought by two or three witnesses. [20]Those who sin are to be rebuked publicly, so that the others may take warning.

[21]I charge you, in the sight of God and Christ Jesus and the elect angels, to keep these instructions without partiality, and to do nothing out of favoritism.

[22]Do not be hasty in the laying on of hands, and do not share in the sins of others. Keep yourself pure.

[23]Stop drinking only water, and use a little wine because of your stomach and your frequent illnesses.

[24]The sins of some men are obvious, reaching the place of judgment ahead of them; the sins of others trail behind them. [25]In the same way, good deeds are obvious, and even those that are not cannot be hidden.

6 All who are under the yoke of slavery should consider their masters worthy of full respect, so that God's name and our teaching may not be slandered. [2]Those who have believing masters are not to show less respect for them because they are brothers. Instead, they are to serve them even better, because those who benefit from their service are believers, and dear to them. These are the things you are to teach and urge on them.

Love of Money

[3]If anyone teaches false doctrines and does not agree to the sound instruction of our Lord Jesus Christ and to godly teaching, [4]he is conceited and understands nothing. He has an unhealthy interest in controversies and quarrels about words that result in envy, strife, malicious talk, evil suspicions [5]and constant friction between men of corrupt mind, who have been robbed of the truth and who think that godliness is a means to financial gain.

[6]But godliness with contentment is great gain. [7]For we brought nothing into the world, and we can take nothing out of it. [8]But if we have food and clothing, we will be content with that. [9]People who want to get rich fall into temptation and a trap and into many foolish and harmful desires that plunge men into ruin and destruction. [10]For the love of money is a root of all kinds of evil. Some people, eager for money, have wandered from the faith and pierced themselves with many griefs.

Paul's Charge to Timothy

[11]But you, man of God, flee from all this, and pursue righteousness, godliness, faith, love, endurance and gentleness. [12]Fight the good fight of the faith. Take hold of the eternal life to which you were called when you made your good confession in the presence of many witnesses. [13]In the sight of God, who gives life to everything, and of Christ Jesus, who while testifying before Pontius Pilate made the good confession, I charge you [14]to keep this command without spot or blame until the appearing of our Lord Jesus Christ, [15]which God will bring about in his own time—God, the blessed and only Ruler, the King of kings and Lord of lords, [16]who alone is immortal and who lives in unapproachable light, whom no one has seen or can see. To him be honor and might forever. Amen.

[17]Command those who are rich in this present world not to be arrogant nor to put their hope in wealth, which is so uncertain, but to put their hope in God, who richly provides us with everything for our enjoyment. [18]Command them to do good, to be rich in good deeds, and to be gen-

a18 Deut. 25:4　　b18 Luke 10:7

VERSE FOR THE DAY:
1 Timothy 6:9–10

AUTHOR:
Martha Manikas-Foster

PASSAGE FOR THE DAY:
1 Timothy 6:1–21

True Success

I RECLINED on my hospital bed with my two-day-old daughter cuddled on my chest. As she slept I caressed her tiny fingers and wondered how she would use them as she grew up. Would they tap formulas and technical data into a now unimagined computer? Would they intricately stitch wounded human tissue? Or perhaps sculpt or paint using vibrant textures and colors? Although I randomly pictured professions at which she might excel, I focused my prayers then as I focus them now, not on *what* she might be, but on *who* she could be.

I know that one day, probably before she puts away her dolls and crayons, she'll learn that some people measure excellence and success solely by "the bottom line"—the money they take home. Some "put their hope in wealth" (1 Timothy 6:17) and build their lives to accommodate its pursuit.

I trust that by that time we'll have taught her to value many things above money. Scripture teaches not that riches themselves are evil but that the value we place on them can lead to our undoing.

> People who want to get rich fall into temptation
> and a trap and into many foolish and harmful de-
> sires that plunge men into ruin and destruction
> (1 Timothy 6:9).

On the other hand, "godliness with contentment is great gain" (1 Timothy 6:6). The apostle Paul's charge to young Timothy in 1 Timothy 6:11–16 is to flee from the pursuit of riches and instead pursue godliness. Paul further instructs Timothy to:

> Command those who are rich . . . to put their hope
> in God . . . . Command them to do good, to be rich
> in good deeds, and to be generous and willing to
> share (1 Timothy 6:17–18).

When Connie reaches elementary school and her teachers ask her what she wants to be when she grows up, I expect that she will list "teacher," "firefighter," and perhaps "doctor" among her choices. But my prayer will continue to be that no matter what profession she chooses, at the core she will truly succeed by being a righteous and godly woman, full of "faith, love, endurance and gentleness" (1 Timothy 6:11).

Additional Scripture Readings:
Proverbs 22:1–2; Mark 10:17–25

*Go to page 1340 for your next
devotional reading.*

erous and willing to share. [19]In this way they will lay up treasure for themselves as a firm foundation for the coming age, so that they may take hold of the life that is truly life.

[20]Timothy, guard what has been entrusted to your care. Turn away from godless chatter and the opposing ideas of what is falsely called knowledge, [21]which some have professed and in so doing have wandered from the faith.

Grace be with you.

THIS second letter to Timothy is written by Paul shortly before Paul dies (2 Timothy 4:6–8). Times are difficult, both morally and spiritually, and Paul wants to encourage Timothy to persevere in his Christian faith and life. As you read this book, be sure to find your daily strength in Jesus Christ and in God's inspired word.

2 TIMOTHY

1 Paul, an apostle of Christ Jesus by the will of God, according to the promise of life that is in Christ Jesus,

[2] To Timothy, my dear son:

Grace, mercy and peace from God the Father and Christ Jesus our Lord.

Encouragement to Be Faithful

[3] I thank God, whom I serve, as my forefathers did, with a clear conscience, as night and day I constantly remember you in my prayers. [4] Recalling your tears, I long to see you, so that I may be filled with joy. [5] I have been reminded of your sincere faith, which first lived in your grandmother Lois and in your mother Eunice and, I am persuaded, now lives in you also. [6] For this reason I remind you to fan into flame the gift of God, which is in you through the laying on of my hands. [7] For God did not give us a spirit of timidi-

ty, but a spirit of power, of love and of self-discipline.

[8] So do not be ashamed to testify about our Lord, or ashamed of me his prisoner. But join with me in suffering for the gospel, by the power of God, [9] who has saved us and called us to a holy life—not because of anything we have done but because of his own purpose and grace. This grace was given us in Christ Jesus before the beginning of time, [10] but it has now been revealed through the appearing of our Savior, Christ Jesus, who has destroyed death and has brought life and immortality to light through the gospel. [11] And of this gospel I was appointed a herald and an apostle and a teacher. [12] That is why I am suffering as I am. Yet I am not ashamed, because I know whom I have believed, and am convinced that he is able to guard what I have entrusted to him for that day.

VERSE FOR THE DAY:	AUTHOR:	PASSAGE FOR THE DAY:
2 Timothy 1:7	Beverly LaHaye	2 Timothy 1:3–7

Living With Fear

WHEN I was a young minister's wife and new mother, I suffered from a serious case of low self-image and overcautiousness. Perhaps, more accurately, I could have been called fearful and anxious. It was very difficult for me to speak to a group of more than seven or eight ladies. When asked to speak, I would often hide behind my husband's ministerial cloak and say that he was the speaker and I was his "helpmeet." Mainly because I was fearful that I would make a mistake and not be accepted by my listeners, I would refuse an invitation to speak to adults. I was only comfortable working with children in church school and in the music department of our church.

In my heart I admired those who were poised in public and could speak articulately, and often I longed to be able to do so myself. But the more I thought about it, the greater my fear. This anxiety affected other areas of my life as well. I knew that sooner or later I would have to face this fear head-on.

After seventeen years as a minister's wife I came to realize that I did not have to continue like this. Living with fear was a choice I was making.

While attending a church school conference at beautiful Forest Home Christian Camp in California, God used Dr. Henry Brandt, a Christian psychologist, to minister his truth to me. Dr. Brandt used 2 Timothy 1:7 as his text; and that day, for the first time, I began to realize that my fears and anxieties were self-imposed. God's choice for me was to have power, love and self-discipline. God did not give me a spirit of fear! My poor self-image, my anxieties, my fears were all my own doing and my sin because I lacked faith to receive the power, love and self-discipline that God really wanted me to have.

As God began to help me with my fearfulness, my own self-image began to improve. Over a period of weeks, and then months, it began to be obvious that God was changing me.

Now, many years later, I can say "Thank you, Lord" for what he has done in me. I would not want to go back to the former Beverly for anything in the world—and the greatest thing is that God is not finished with me yet!

Additional Scripture Readings:
Psalm 34:4–10; Jeremiah 1:4–8

Go to page 1341 for your next devotional reading.

¹³What you heard from me, keep as the pattern of sound teaching, with faith and love in Christ Jesus. ¹⁴Guard the good deposit that was entrusted to you — guard it with the help of the Holy Spirit who lives in us.

¹⁵You know that everyone in the province of Asia has deserted me, including Phygelus and Hermogenes.

¹⁶May the Lord show mercy to the household of Onesiphorus, because he often refreshed me and was not ashamed of my chains. ¹⁷On the contrary, when he was in Rome, he searched hard for me until he found me. ¹⁸May the Lord grant that he will find mercy from the Lord on that day! You know very well in how many ways he helped me in Ephesus.

2 You then, my son, be strong in the grace that is in Christ Jesus. ²And the things you have heard me say in the presence of many witnesses entrust to relia-

ble men who will also be qualified to teach others. ³Endure hardship with us like a good soldier of Christ Jesus. ⁴No one serving as a soldier gets involved in civilian affairs — he wants to please his commanding officer. ⁵Similarly, if anyone competes as an athlete, he does not receive the victor's crown unless he competes according to the rules. ⁶The hardworking farmer should be the first to receive a share of the crops. ⁷Reflect on what I am saying, for the Lord will give you insight into all this.

⁸Remember Jesus Christ, raised from the dead, descended from David. This is my gospel, ⁹for which I am suffering even to the point of being chained like a criminal. But God's word is not chained. ¹⁰Therefore I endure everything for the sake of the elect, that they too may obtain the salvation that is in Christ Jesus, with eternal glory.

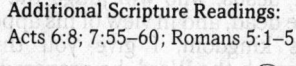

FRIDAY

VERSE FOR THE DAY:
2 Timothy 2:1

AUTHOR:
Doris Haase

PASSAGE FOR THE DAY:
2 Timothy 2:1–13

Be Strong in God's Grace

AFTER a long and terrifying captivity, Iranian hostage Gary Lee was home. It was a Sunday morning in February 1981, and I joined with others in his father's church to welcome him. Celebration filled the air as joyful voices sang "Amazing Grace." From my seat I noticed the bearded young man smile and shake his head as though in wonder at the miracle of his safe return.

Months earlier, however, he had experienced another miracle. Shortly after his capture he was allowed to have a Bible and one day he read Isaiah 43:5: "Do not be afraid, for I am with you; I will bring your children from the east and gather you from the west."

"When I read those words," he told his father later, "I felt God was making me a promise. Somehow I knew I would reach home safely. The whole experience became a lot easier after that."

How much lighter trials become when we realize God's grace is twofold. It is not only the happy ending. It is also the peace we can feel during a painful journey, when we trust in God — all the way.

Additional Scripture Readings:
Acts 6:8; 7:55–60; Romans 5:1–5

Go to page 1343 for your next devotional reading.

11Here is a trustworthy saying:

If we died with him,
　　we will also live with him;
12if we endure,
　　we will also reign with him.
If we disown him,
　　he will also disown us;
13if we are faithless,
　　he will remain faithful,
　　for he cannot disown himself.

A Workman Approved by God

14Keep reminding them of these things. Warn them before God against quarreling about words; it is of no value, and only ruins those who listen. 15Do your best to present yourself to God as one approved, a workman who does not need to be ashamed and who correctly handles the word of truth. 16Avoid godless chatter, because those who indulge in it will become more and more ungodly. 17Their teaching will spread like gangrene. Among them are Hymenaeus and Philetus, 18who have wandered away from the truth. They say that the resurrection has already taken place, and they destroy the faith of some. 19Nevertheless, God's solid foundation stands firm, sealed with this inscription: "The Lord knows those who are his,"ᵃ and, "Everyone who confesses the name of the Lord must turn away from wickedness."

20In a large house there are articles not only of gold and silver, but also of wood and clay; some are for noble purposes and some for ignoble. 21If a man cleanses himself from the latter, he will be an instrument for noble purposes, made holy, useful to the Master and prepared to do any good work.

22Flee the evil desires of youth, and pursue righteousness, faith, love and peace, along with those who call on the Lord out of a pure heart. 23Don't have anything to do with foolish and stupid arguments, because you know they produce quarrels. 24And the Lord's servant must not quarrel; instead, he must be kind to everyone, able to teach, not resentful. 25Those who oppose him he must gently instruct, in the hope that God will grant them repentance leading them to a knowledge of the truth, 26and that they will come to their senses and escape from the trap of the devil, who has taken them captive to do his will.

Godlessness in the Last Days

3 But mark this: There will be terrible times in the last days. 2People will be lovers of themselves, lovers of money, boastful, proud, abusive, disobedient to their parents, ungrateful, unholy, 3without love, unforgiving, slanderous, without self-control, brutal, not lovers of the good, 4treacherous, rash, conceited, lovers of pleasure rather than lovers of God — 5having a form of godliness but denying its power. Have nothing to do with them.

6They are the kind who worm their way into homes and gain control over weak-willed women, who are loaded down with sins and are swayed by all kinds of evil desires, 7always learning but never able to acknowledge the truth. 8Just as Jannes and Jambres opposed Moses, so also these men oppose the truth—men of depraved minds, who, as far as the faith is concerned, are rejected. 9But they will not get very far because, as in the case of those men, their folly will be clear to everyone.

Paul's Charge to Timothy

10You, however, know all about my teaching, my way of life, my purpose, faith, patience, love, endurance, 11persecutions, sufferings—what kinds of things happened to me in Antioch, Iconium and Lystra, the persecutions I endured. Yet the Lord rescued me from all of them. 12In fact, everyone who wants to live a godly life in Christ Jesus will be persecuted, 13while evil men and impostors will go from bad to worse, deceiving and being deceived. 14But as for you, continue in what you have learned and have become convinced of, because you know those from whom you learned it, 15and how from infancy you have known the holy Scriptures, which are able to make you wise for salvation through faith in Christ Jesus. 16All Scripture is God-breathed and is useful for teaching, rebuking, correcting and training in righteousness, 17so that the man of God may be thoroughly equipped for every good work.

4 In the presence of God and of Christ Jesus, who will judge the living and the dead, and in view of his appearing and his kingdom, I give you this charge: 2Preach the Word; be prepared in season

---

ᵃ19 Num. 16:5 (see Septuagint)

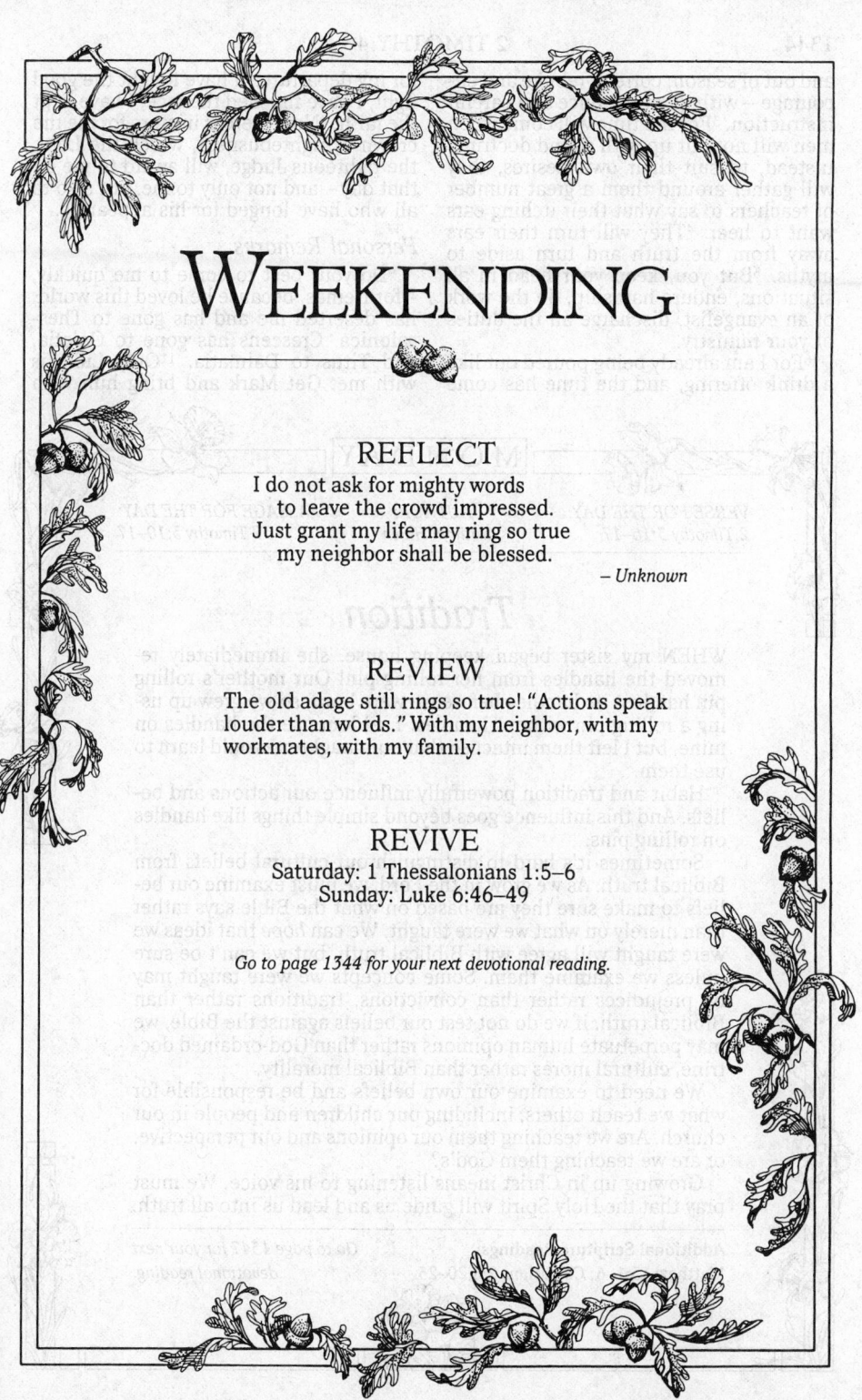

WEEKENDING

REFLECT

I do not ask for mighty words
to leave the crowd impressed.
Just grant my life may ring so true
my neighbor shall be blessed.

– Unknown

REVIEW

The old adage still rings so true! "Actions speak louder than words." With my neighbor, with my workmates, with my family.

REVIVE

Saturday: 1 Thessalonians 1:5–6
Sunday: Luke 6:46–49

Go to page 1344 for your next devotional reading.

and out of season; correct, rebuke and encourage—with great patience and careful instruction. ³For the time will come when men will not put up with sound doctrine. Instead, to suit their own desires, they will gather around them a great number of teachers to say what their itching ears want to hear. ⁴They will turn their ears away from the truth and turn aside to myths. ⁵But you, keep your head in all situations, endure hardship, do the work of an evangelist, discharge all the duties of your ministry.

⁶For I am already being poured out like a drink offering, and the time has come for my departure. ⁷I have fought the good fight, I have finished the race, I have kept the faith. ⁸Now there is in store for me the crown of righteousness, which the Lord, the righteous Judge, will award to me on that day—and not only to me, but also to all who have longed for his appearing.

Personal Remarks

⁹Do your best to come to me quickly, ¹⁰for Demas, because he loved this world, has deserted me and has gone to Thessalonica. Crescens has gone to Galatia, and Titus to Dalmatia. ¹¹Only Luke is with me. Get Mark and bring him with

MONDAY

VERSE FOR THE DAY:	AUTHOR:	PASSAGE FOR THE DAY:
2 Timothy 3:16–17	Kathryn Hillen	2 Timothy 3:10–17

Tradition

WHEN my sister began keeping house, she immediately removed the handles from her rolling pin! Our mother's rolling pin had lost its handles before we were born, so we grew up using a rolling pin without handles. I seldom use the handles on mine, but I left them intact so that our daughters would learn to use them.

Habit and tradition powerfully influence our actions and beliefs. And this influence goes beyond simple things like handles on rolling pins.

Sometimes it's hard to distinguish our cultural beliefs from Biblical truth. As we grow in the Lord, we must examine our beliefs to make sure they are based on what the Bible says rather than merely on what we were taught. We can *hope* that ideas we were taught will agree with Biblical truth, but we can't be sure unless we examine them. Some concepts we were taught may be prejudices rather than convictions, traditions rather than Biblical truth. If we do not test our beliefs against the Bible, we may perpetuate human opinions rather than God-ordained doctrine, cultural mores rather than Biblical morality.

We need to examine our own beliefs and be responsible for what we teach others, including our children and people in our church. Are we teaching them our opinions and our perspective, or are we teaching them God's?

Growing up in Christ means listening to his voice. We must pray that the Holy Spirit will guide us and lead us into all truth.

Additional Scripture Readings:
Matthew 15:1–6; Colossians 2:8,20–23

Go to page 1347 for your next devotional reading.

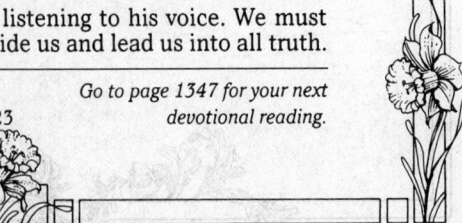

you, because he is helpful to me in my ministry. ¹²I sent Tychicus to Ephesus. ¹³When you come, bring the cloak that I left with Carpus at Troas, and my scrolls, especially the parchments.

¹⁴Alexander the metalworker did me a great deal of harm. The Lord will repay him for what he has done. ¹⁵You too should be on your guard against him, because he strongly opposed our message.

¹⁶At my first defense, no one came to my support, but everyone deserted me. May it not be held against them. ¹⁷But the Lord stood at my side and gave me strength, so that through me the message might be fully proclaimed and all the Gentiles might hear it. And I was delivered from the lion's mouth. ¹⁸The Lord will rescue me from every evil attack and will bring me safely to his heavenly kingdom. To him be glory for ever and ever. Amen.

Final Greetings

¹⁹Greet Priscilla[a] and Aquila and the household of Onesiphorus. ²⁰Erastus stayed in Corinth, and I left Trophimus sick in Miletus. ²¹Do your best to get here before winter. Eubulus greets you, and so do Pudens, Linus, Claudia and all the brothers.

²²The Lord be with your spirit. Grace be with you.

---

[a]19 Greek *Prisca*, a variant of *Priscilla*

*P*AUL *writes to Titus, a pastor serving in Crete, to advise him both on what to teach the churches and on how to organize them, especially with false teachers around. As you read this book, note God's concern for proper order in the church and for true teaching about Christ.*

TITUS

1 Paul, a servant of God and an apostle of Jesus Christ for the faith of God's elect and the knowledge of the truth that leads to godliness— [2]a faith and knowledge resting on the hope of eternal life, which God, who does not lie, promised before the beginning of time, [3]and at his appointed season he brought his word to light through the preaching entrusted to me by the command of God our Savior,

[4]To Titus, my true son in our common faith:

Grace and peace from God the Father and Christ Jesus our Savior.

Titus' Task on Crete

[5]The reason I left you in Crete was that you might straighten out what was left unfinished and appoint[a] elders in every town, as I directed you. [6]An elder must be blameless, the husband of but one wife, a man whose children believe and are not open to the charge of being wild and disobedient. [7]Since an overseer[b] is entrusted with God's work, he must be blameless—not overbearing, not quick-tempered, not given to drunkenness, not violent, not pursuing dishonest gain. [8]Rather he must be hospitable, one who loves what is good, who is self-controlled, upright, holy and disciplined. [9]He must hold firmly to the trustworthy message as it has been taught, so that he can encourage others by sound doctrine and refute those who oppose it.

[10]For there are many rebellious people, mere talkers and deceivers, especially those of the circumcision group. [11]They must be silenced, because they are ruining whole households by teaching things they ought not to teach—and that for the sake of dishonest gain. [12]Even one of their own prophets has said, "Cretans

a5 Or *ordain*   *b7* Traditionally *bishop*

are always liars, evil brutes, lazy gluttons." [13]This testimony is true. Therefore,
rebuke them sharply, so that they will be
sound in the faith [14]and will pay no attention to Jewish myths or to the commands
of those who reject the truth. [15]To the
pure, all things are pure, but to those who
are corrupted and do not believe, nothing
is pure. In fact, both their minds and consciences are corrupted. [16]They claim to
know God, but by their actions they deny
him. They are detestable, disobedient
and unfit for doing anything good.

What Must Be Taught to Various Groups

2 You must teach what is in accord
with sound doctrine. [2]Teach the older
men to be temperate, worthy of respect,
self-controlled, and sound in faith, in love
and in endurance.

[3]Likewise, teach the older women to be
reverent in the way they live, not to be
slanderers or addicted to much wine, but
to teach what is good. [4]Then they can
train the younger women to love their
husbands and children, [5]to be self-controlled and pure, to be busy at home, to
be kind, and to be subject to their husbands, so that no one will malign the
word of God.

[6]Similarly, encourage the young men to
be self-controlled. [7]In everything set
them an example by doing what is good.
In your teaching show integrity, serious-
ness [8]and soundness of speech that cannot be condemned, so that those who oppose you may be ashamed because they
have nothing bad to say about us.

[9]Teach slaves to be subject to their
masters in everything, to try to please
them, not to talk back to them, [10]and not

TUESDAY

VERSE FOR THE DAY: *AUTHOR:*   *PASSAGE FOR THE DAY:*
Titus 1:13   Doris Haase   Titus 1:5–16

Walk Upright!

ONCE upon a time, in the early days of our country, a weary
traveler arrived at the banks of the Mississippi. There was no
bridge. It was winter and the water was covered by a layer of ice.
Was it strong enough to hold his weight, he wondered? Still, he
had to get across before nightfall, and so, terrified, he crept
slowly on hands and knees across the frozen surface, certain he
would never live to see the other side.

Suddenly he heard the clop, clop of a horse-drawn wagon. As
it rattled past, he could hear the driver singing merrily. Unlike
himself, the man, obviously familiar with these conditions, had
no doubt at all that their glacial road was strong.

I sympathize with that traveler, for I too, am a creeper. I know
God has promised no harm will befall me (Psalm 91:10) and
that I should cast my cares upon him and he will sustain me
(Psalm 55:22). So why do I so often forget that God is one who
keeps his promises? He really can bear the weight of my every
problem.

Today I resolve to follow the example of that long-ago
wagoner. I will believe, walk upright and sing!

Additional Scripture Readings: *Go to page 1348 for your next*
Deuteronomy 10:12–22; Psalm 23:4   *devotional reading.*

to steal from them, but to show that they can be fully trusted, so that in every way they will make the teaching about God our Savior attractive.

¹¹For the grace of God that brings salvation has appeared to all men. ¹²It teaches us to say "No" to ungodliness and worldly passions, and to live self-controlled, upright and godly lives in this present age, ¹³while we wait for the

WEDNESDAY

VERSE FOR THE DAY:	*AUTHOR:*	*PASSAGE FOR THE DAY:*
Titus 2:4–5	Debbie Smith	Titus 2:1–8

Pleasing to God and Family

MY older son at preschool and the baby downstairs with the sitter, I settled into bed with my three-year-old daughter for a delicious afternoon nap. We giggled quietly, nose-to-nose, covers up to our chins. It was a precious mother-daughter moment that required no words . . . until Whitney spoke up.

"I like this kind of mommy!"

At times like these, I feel like I must be doing something right. Of course, the other side of the coin is obvious: sometimes I am *not* the "kind of mommy" she likes—or deserves!

That thought reminds me that loving children (and husbands) is a learning process. Titus 2:4 confirms that young mothers should be trained by the older women to love their husbands and children.

Interestingly, two Greek words for love are used in the original text. The word for love for husbands connotes nurturing as a friend: "fond of man." The word used here for love for children means maternal love: literally, "fond of one's children."

I am grateful that God addresses on the practical level the daily grind of living as women. Here he makes it clear that he expects holiness in our lives, whatever our ages. The older women are to be exemplary in speech and conduct so that "they can train the younger women" to be the same. Titus 2:5 sets the agenda for young mothers: learn to love family, learn self-control, tend to the home, and be kind and submissive to one's husband.

Running a home, Titus 2:5 implies, requires being a servant. And "if anyone serves, he should do it with the strength God provides, so that in all things God may be praised through Jesus Christ" (1 Peter 4:11).

Such a mommy is pleasing to the Lord . . . and to her children!

Additional Scripture Readings:
Proverbs 31:26–30; 1 Thessalonians 2:7–12

Go to page 1351 for your next devotional reading.

blessed hope—the glorious appearing of our great God and Savior, Jesus Christ, [14]who gave himself for us to redeem us from all wickedness and to purify for himself a people that are his very own, eager to do what is good.

[15]These, then, are the things you should teach. Encourage and rebuke with all authority. Do not let anyone despise you.

Doing What Is Good

3 Remind the people to be subject to rulers and authorities, to be obedient, to be ready to do whatever is good, [2]to slander no one, to be peaceable and considerate, and to show true humility toward all men.

[3]At one time we too were foolish, disobedient, deceived and enslaved by all kinds of passions and pleasures. We lived in malice and envy, being hated and hating one another. [4]But when the kindness and love of God our Savior appeared, [5]he saved us, not because of righteous things we had done, but because of his mercy. He saved us through the washing of rebirth and renewal by the Holy Spirit, [6]whom he poured out on us generously through Jesus Christ our Savior, [7]so that, having been justified by his grace, we might become heirs having the hope of eternal life. [8]This is a trustworthy saying. And I want you to stress these things, so that those who have trusted in God may be careful to devote themselves to doing what is good. These things are excellent and profitable for everyone.

[9]But avoid foolish controversies and genealogies and arguments and quarrels about the law, because these are unprofitable and useless. [10]Warn a divisive person once, and then warn him a second time. After that, have nothing to do with him. [11]You may be sure that such a man is warped and sinful; he is self-condemned.

Final Remarks

[12]As soon as I send Artemas or Tychicus to you, do your best to come to me at Nicopolis, because I have decided to winter there. [13]Do everything you can to help Zenas the lawyer and Apollos on their way and see that they have everything they need. [14]Our people must learn to devote themselves to doing what is good, in order that they may provide for daily necessities and not live unproductive lives.

[15]Everyone with me sends you greetings. Greet those who love us in the faith.

Grace be with you all.

*P*AUL *writes this brief letter to ask Philemon, a Christian brother living (probably) in Colosse, to forgive and take back Onesimus, a runaway slave who has become a Christian and is helping Paul in prison. As you read this book, be willing to forgive others, no matter what they do to you.*

PHILEMON

¹Paul, a prisoner of Christ Jesus, and Timothy our brother,

To Philemon our dear friend and fellow worker, ²to Apphia our sister, to Archippus our fellow soldier and to the church that meets in your home:

³Grace to you and peace from God our Father and the Lord Jesus Christ.

Thanksgiving and Prayer

⁴I always thank my God as I remember you in my prayers, ⁵because I hear about your faith in the Lord Jesus and your love for all the saints. ⁶I pray that you may be active in sharing your faith, so that you will have a full understanding of every good thing we have in Christ. ⁷Your love has given me great joy and encouragement, because you, brother, have refreshed the hearts of the saints.

Paul's Plea for Onesimus

⁸Therefore, although in Christ I could be bold and order you to do what you ought to do, ⁹yet I appeal to you on the basis of love. I then, as Paul—an old man and now also a prisoner of Christ Jesus— ¹⁰I appeal to you for my son Onesimus,ᵃ who became my son while I was in chains. ¹¹Formerly he was useless to you, but now he has become useful both to you and to me.

¹²I am sending him—who is my very heart—back to you. ¹³I would have liked to keep him with me so that he could take your place in helping me while I am in chains for the gospel. ¹⁴But I did not want to do anything without your consent, so that any favor you do will be spontaneous and not forced. ¹⁵Perhaps the reason he was separated from you for a little while was that you might have him back for

---

ᵃ10 Onesimus means *useful.*

good— [16]no longer as a slave, but better than a slave, as a dear brother. He is very dear to me but even dearer to you, both as a man and as a brother in the Lord.

[17]So if you consider me a partner, welcome him as you would welcome me. [18]If he has done you any wrong or owes you anything, charge it to me. [19]I, Paul, am writing this with my own hand. I will pay it back—not to mention that you owe me your very self. [20]I do wish, brother, that I may have some benefit from you in the Lord; refresh my heart in Christ. [21]Confi-

dent of your obedience, I write to you, knowing that you will do even more than I ask.

[22]And one thing more: Prepare a guest room for me, because I hope to be restored to you in answer to your prayers.

[23]Epaphras, my fellow prisoner in Christ Jesus, sends you greetings. [24]And so do Mark, Aristarchus, Demas and Luke, my fellow workers.

[25]The grace of the Lord Jesus Christ be with your spirit.

THURSDAY

VERSE FOR THE DAY:
Philemon 6–7

AUTHOR:
Kathryn Hillen

PASSAGE FOR THE DAY:
Philemon 1–25

Sweetheart

"LET Me Call You Sweetheart—I Can't Remember Your Name."

The pin, almost as big as a saucer, was worn by a middle-aged woman—without doubt, an extrovert. We were at a state PTA convention, encountering many unfamiliar faces. The pin seemed to be her humorous way of saying, "Let's be friends for today, but I'm not even going to attempt to remember your name."

We have many temporary relationships: those beside us on the plane or in the laundromat, the people who camp next to us at a resort, and the neighbors who move in and out with such rapidity. It's up to us to decide if these contacts will be meaningless or significant.

Ask God, "What would you like to say to this person through me?" You may be surprised. He may ask you to speak words of appreciation and encouragement, to witness about Christ, or only to be friendly. When we look a person in the eye and ask about their lives, we show that they are valuable. And even if we never do learn the person's name, we have been a channel through which God can reach him or her. That is both exciting and humbling.

Additional Scripture Readings:
2 Corinthians 5:18–20; Colossians 4:2–6

Go to page 1353 for your next devotional reading.

*T*HE author of this letter encourages Christians who are being persecuted for their faith by pointing them to the greatness of the Son of God who became man. Christ is the full expression of God's revelation, better than anything in the Old Testament; the author warns his readers to depend on Christ alone. As you read this book, commit yourself firmly to Jesus your Intercessor, and be sure to persevere and grow daily in your Christian faith and life.

HEBREWS

The Son Superior to Angels

1 In the past God spoke to our forefathers through the prophets at many times and in various ways, ²but in these last days he has spoken to us by his Son, whom he appointed heir of all things, and through whom he made the universe. ³The Son is the radiance of God's glory and the exact representation of his being, sustaining all things by his powerful word. After he had provided purification for sins, he sat down at the right hand of the Majesty in heaven. ⁴So he became as much superior to the angels as the name he has inherited is superior to theirs.

⁵For to which of the angels did God ever say,

"You are my Son;
    today I have become your
        Father*ᵃ*"*ᵇ*?

Or again,

"I will be his Father,
    and he will be my Son"*ᶜ*?

⁶And again, when God brings his firstborn into the world, he says,

---

ᵃ5 Or have begotten you   *ᵇ5 Psalm 2:7   ᶜ5 2 Samuel 7:14; 1 Chron. 17:13*

"Let all God's angels worship him." *a*

7In speaking of the angels he says,

"He makes his angels winds,
his servants flames of fire." *b*

8But about the Son he says,

"Your throne, O God, will last for ever
and ever,
and righteousness will be the
scepter of your kingdom.
9You have loved righteousness and
hated wickedness;
therefore God, your God, has set
you above your companions

a6 Deut. 32:43 (see Dead Sea Scrolls and Septuagint)

by anointing you with the oil of
joy." *c*

10He also says,

"In the beginning, O Lord, you laid
the foundations of the earth,
and the heavens are the work of
your hands.
11They will perish, but you remain;
they will all wear out like a
garment.
12You will roll them up like a robe;
like a garment they will be
changed.

b7 Psalm 104:4   *c9* Psalm 45:6,7

FRIDAY

VERSE FOR THE DAY:
Hebrews 1:12

AUTHOR:
Janet C. Jones

PASSAGE FOR THE DAY:
Hebrews 1:1–14

Changes and Choices

RECENTLY my life has been filled with changes and choices. I guess that can be said of all of our lives. Would it not be good if we could choose a period of our lives that was enjoyable and let time stand still? But we cannot. Ecclesiastes 3:11 and 14 tell us, "he has made everything beautiful in its time," and "everything God does will endure forever."

If our childhood was a happy time, we did not want it to end. Everything was new, fresh and meaningful. We wanted our teen years to be over soon so we could be adults. In young adulthood, there were many changes and choices: college, marriage, the birth of children or the choice of a job. In middle age and even in our "golden years," there are still changes and choices.

My parents are in their golden years. Both of them have had severe physical problems. Because of this, I have had to make many choices and to endure a lot of changes. But Christ was and is precious, and his Word has been very real. When it became necessary to consider retirement housing for my mother and father, it was a difficult adjustment for all of us. But each day, as I went to God's Word, he had something just for me. For example, "Now go, lead the people to the place I spoke of, and my angel will go before you" (Exodus 32:34).

Yes, life is filled with changes and choices, but the right choice is Jesus Christ. He will take you through all the changes.

Additional Scripture Readings:
Luke 10:38–42; Hebrews 11:24–26

Go to page 1355 for your next devotional reading.

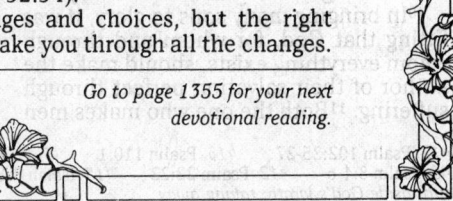

But you remain the same,
and your years will never end."ᵃ

¹³To which of the angels did God ever say,

"Sit at my right hand
until I make your enemies
a footstool for your feet"ᵇ?

¹⁴Are not all angels ministering spirits sent to serve those who will inherit salvation?

Warning to Pay Attention

2 We must pay more careful attention, therefore, to what we have heard, so that we do not drift away. ²For if the message spoken by angels was binding, and every violation and disobedience received its just punishment, ³how shall we escape if we ignore such a great salvation? This salvation, which was first announced by the Lord, was confirmed to us by those who heard him. ⁴God also testified to it by signs, wonders and various miracles, and gifts of the Holy Spirit distributed according to his will.

Jesus Made Like His Brothers

⁵It is not to angels that he has subjected the world to come, about which we are speaking. ⁶But there is a place where someone has testified:

"What is man that you are mindful of
him,
the son of man that you care for
him?
⁷You made him a littleᶜ lower than
the angels;
you crowned him with glory and
honor
⁸   and put everything under his
feet."ᵈ

In putting everything under him, God left nothing that is not subject to him. Yet at present we do not see everything subject to him. ⁹But we see Jesus, who was made a little lower than the angels, now crowned with glory and honor because he suffered death, so that by the grace of God he might taste death for everyone.

¹⁰In bringing many sons to glory, it was fitting that God, for whom and through whom everything exists, should make the author of their salvation perfect through suffering. ¹¹Both the one who makes men holy and those who are made holy are of the same family. So Jesus is not ashamed to call them brothers. ¹²He says,

"I will declare your name to my
brothers;
in the presence of the congregation
I will sing your praises."ᵉ

¹³And again,

"I will put my trust in him."ᶠ

And again he says,

"Here am I, and the children God has
given me."ᵍ

¹⁴Since the children have flesh and blood, he too shared in their humanity so that by his death he might destroy him who holds the power of death—that is, the devil— ¹⁵and free those who all their lives were held in slavery by their fear of death. ¹⁶For surely it is not angels he helps, but Abraham's descendants. ¹⁷For this reason he had to be made like his brothers in every way, in order that he might become a merciful and faithful high priest in service to God, and that he might make atonement forʰ the sins of the people. ¹⁸Because he himself suffered when he was tempted, he is able to help those who are being tempted.

Jesus Greater Than Moses

3 Therefore, holy brothers, who share in the heavenly calling, fix your thoughts on Jesus, the apostle and high priest whom we confess. ²He was faithful to the one who appointed him, just as Moses was faithful in all God's house. ³Jesus has been found worthy of greater honor than Moses, just as the builder of a house has greater honor than the house itself. ⁴For every house is built by someone, but God is the builder of everything. ⁵Moses was faithful as a servant in all God's house, testifying to what would be said in the future. ⁶But Christ is faithful as a son over God's house. And we are his house, if we hold on to our courage and the hope of which we boast.

Warning Against Unbelief

⁷So, as the Holy Spirit says:

"Today, if you hear his voice,
⁸   do not harden your hearts

ᵃ12 Psalm 102:25-27   ᵇ13 Psalm 110:1   ᶜ7 Or him for a little while; also in verse 9
ᵈ8 Psalm 8:4-6   ᵉ12 Psalm 22:22   ᶠ13 Isaiah 8:17   ᵍ13 Isaiah 8:18   ʰ17 Or and that he might turn aside God's wrath, taking away

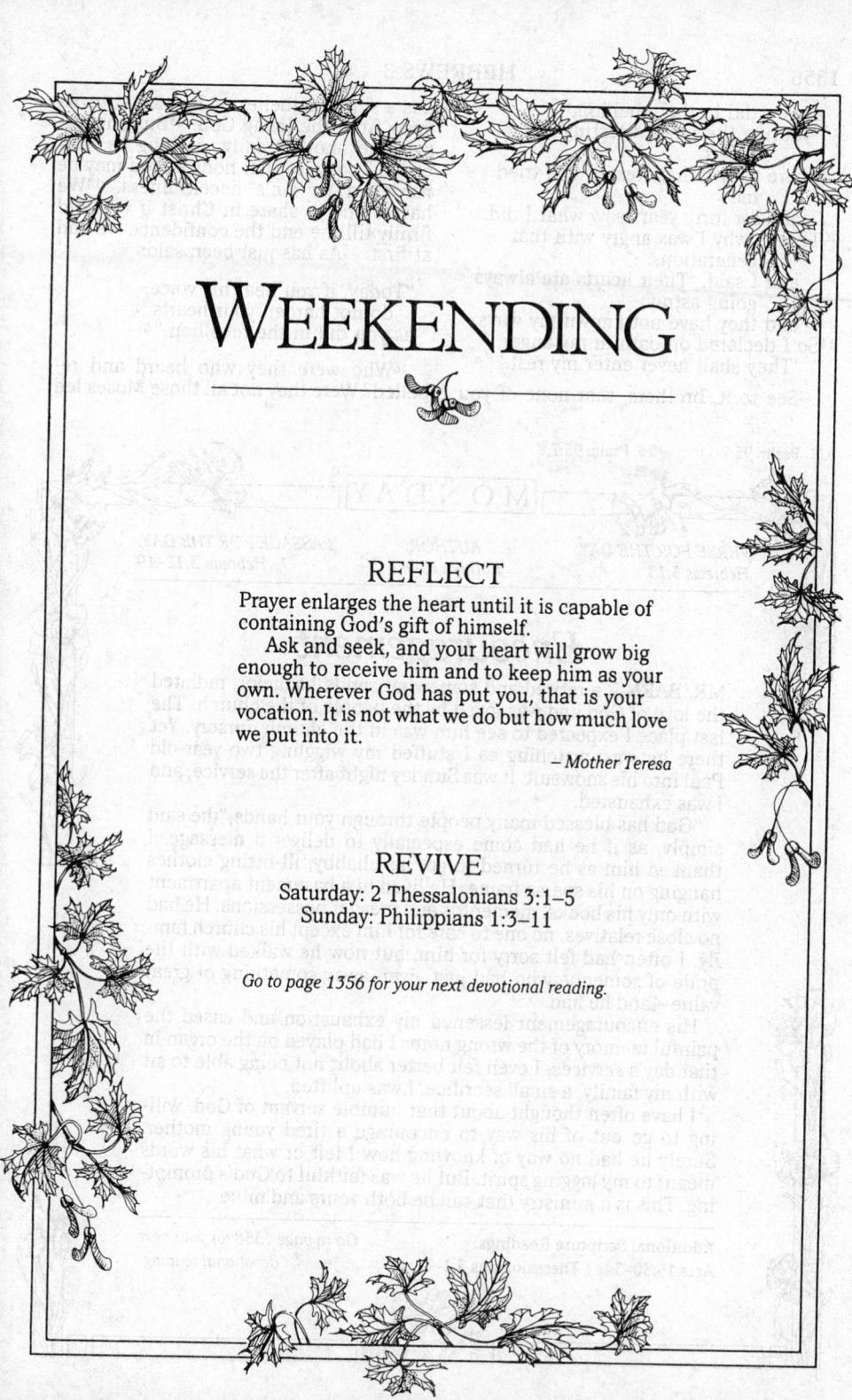

WEEKENDING

REFLECT

Prayer enlarges the heart until it is capable of containing God's gift of himself.

Ask and seek, and your heart will grow big enough to receive him and to keep him as your own. Wherever God has put you, that is your vocation. It is not what we do but how much love we put into it.

— Mother Teresa

REVIVE

Saturday: 2 Thessalonians 3:1–5
Sunday: Philippians 1:3–11

Go to page 1356 for your next devotional reading.

as you did in the rebellion,
  during the time of testing in the
    desert,
[9]where your fathers tested and tried
    me
  and for forty years saw what I did.
[10]That is why I was angry with that
    generation,
  and I said, 'Their hearts are always
    going astray,
  and they have not known my ways.'
[11]So I declared on oath in my anger,
  'They shall never enter my rest.' "[a]

[12]See to it, brothers, that none of you

has a sinful, unbelieving heart that turns away from the living God. [13]But encourage one another daily, as long as it is called Today, so that none of you may be hardened by sin's deceitfulness. [14]We have come to share in Christ if we hold firmly till the end the confidence we had at first. [15]As has just been said:

"Today, if you hear his voice,
  do not harden your hearts
  as you did in the rebellion."[b]

[16]Who were they who heard and rebelled? Were they not all those Moses led

---

[a]11 Psalm 95:7-11   [b]15 Psalm 95:7,8

MONDAY

VERSE FOR THE DAY:
Hebrews 3:13

AUTHOR:
Kathryn Hillen

PASSAGE FOR THE DAY:
Hebrews 3:12–19

Encouragement

MR. BARNS, a retired and somewhat senile bachelor, radiated the love of God and was loved by the people of the church. The last place I expected to see him was in the church nursery. Yet there he was, watching as I stuffed my wiggling two-year-old Paul into his snowsuit. It was Sunday night after the service, and I was exhausted.

"God has blessed many people through your hands," he said simply, as if he had come especially to deliver a message. I thanked him as he turned to go, his shabby, ill-fitting clothes hanging on his sparse frame. He lived in a basement apartment with only his books, mementos and meager possessions. He had no close relatives, no one to care for him except his church family. I often had felt sorry for him, but now he walked with the pride of someone who had just given away something of great value—and he had.

His encouragement lessened my exhaustion and eased the painful memory of the wrong notes I had played on the organ in that day's services. I even felt better about not being able to sit with my family, a small sacrifice. I was uplifted.

I have often thought about that humble servant of God, willing to go out of his way to encourage a tired young mother. Surely he had no way of knowing how I felt or what his words meant to my lagging spirit. But he was faithful to God's prompting. This is a ministry that can be both yours and mine.

Additional Scripture Readings:
Acts 15:30–34; 1 Thessalonians 3:1–8

Go to page 1358 for your next devotional reading.

out of Egypt? [17]And with whom was he angry for forty years? Was it not with those who sinned, whose bodies fell in the desert? [18]And to whom did God swear that they would never enter his rest if not to those who disobeyed[a]? [19]So we see that they were not able to enter, because of their unbelief.

A Sabbath-Rest for the People of God

4 Therefore, since the promise of entering his rest still stands, let us be careful that none of you be found to have fallen short of it. [2]For we also have had the gospel preached to us, just as they did; but the message they heard was of no value to them, because those who heard did not combine it with faith.[b] [3]Now we who have believed enter that rest, just as God has said,

"So I declared on oath in my anger,
    'They shall never enter my rest.' "[c]

And yet his work has been finished since the creation of the world. [4]For somewhere he has spoken about the seventh day in these words: "And on the seventh day God rested from all his work."[d] [5]And again in the passage above he says, "They shall never enter my rest."

[6]It still remains that some will enter that rest, and those who formerly had the gospel preached to them did not go in, because of their disobedience. [7]Therefore God again set a certain day, calling it Today, when a long time later he spoke through David, as was said before:

"Today, if you hear his voice,
    do not harden your hearts."[e]

[8]For if Joshua had given them rest, God would not have spoken later about another day. [9]There remains, then, a Sabbath-rest for the people of God; [10]for anyone who enters God's rest also rests from his own work, just as God did from his. [11]Let us, therefore, make every effort to enter that rest, so that no one will fall by following their example of disobedience.

[12]For the word of God is living and active. Sharper than any double-edged sword, it penetrates even to dividing soul and spirit, joints and marrow; it judges the thoughts and attitudes of the heart. [13]Nothing in all creation is hidden from God's sight. Everything is uncovered and laid bare before the eyes of him to whom we must give account.

Jesus the Great High Priest

[14]Therefore, since we have a great high priest who has gone through the heavens,[f] Jesus the Son of God, let us hold firmly to the faith we profess. [15]For we do not have a high priest who is unable to sympathize with our weaknesses, but we have one who has been tempted in every way, just as we are—yet was without sin. [16]Let us then approach the throne of grace with confidence, so that we may receive mercy and find grace to help us in our time of need.

5 Every high priest is selected from among men and is appointed to represent them in matters related to God, to offer gifts and sacrifices for sins. [2]He is able to deal gently with those who are ignorant and are going astray, since he himself is subject to weakness. [3]This is why he has to offer sacrifices for his own sins, as well as for the sins of the people.

[4]No one takes this honor upon himself; he must be called by God, just as Aaron was. [5]So Christ also did not take upon himself the glory of becoming a high priest. But God said to him,

"You are my Son;
    today I have become your
        Father.[g]"[h]

[6]And he says in another place,

"You are a priest forever,
    in the order of Melchizedek."[i]

[7]During the days of Jesus' life on earth, he offered up prayers and petitions with loud cries and tears to the one who could save him from death, and he was heard because of his reverent submission. [8]Although he was a son, he learned obedience from what he suffered [9]and, once made perfect, he became the source of eternal salvation for all who obey him [10]and was designated by God to be high priest in the order of Melchizedek.

Warning Against Falling Away

[11]We have much to say about this, but it is hard to explain because you are slow to learn. [12]In fact, though by this time you ought to be teachers, you need someone

[a]18 Or *disbelieved*   [b]2 Many manuscripts *because they did not share in the faith of those who obeyed*
[c]3 Psalm 95:11; also in verse 5   [d]4 Gen. 2:2   [e]7 Psalm 95:7,8   [f]14 Or *gone into heaven*
[g]5 Or *have begotten you*   [h]5 Psalm 2:7   [i]6 Psalm 110:4

VERSE FOR THE DAY:
Hebrews 5:14

AUTHOR:
Barbara Bush

PASSAGE FOR THE DAY:
Hebrews 5:11—6:12

The Wise Are Mature

THE writer of the letter to the Hebrews was frustrated. He had many wonderful truths he wanted to impart, but his audience did not want to expend much energy on spiritual growth. They had been Christians for some time, but they knew little more than when they first believed.

Those who feed on and digest the meat of God's Word attain maturity in their Christian lives. They gain the wisdom in speech and action that is the mark of the mature. If we are not mature, the reason is obvious: we have not been workmen but idlers in Bible study. We have not made constant use of the Scriptures to distinguish good from evil. We are still dependent on others for our knowledge, as children are, in danger of being misguided by those who sound knowledgeable but may be as ignorant as we.

This is why there are so few wise people. Those who get all their knowledge of God's Word from an hour or two on Sunday will never have a personal grasp of its content. Paul said that if we want to be wise, if we want to "correctly handle the word of truth," we must be workmen (2 Timothy 2:15). We must do the job ourselves instead of expecting a pastor or teacher to do it all for us. We must read the Bible. We must digest it, meditate on it, memorize it, understand it.

God does not want us to remain spiritually immature. He wants us to:

> . . . become mature, attaining to the whole measure of the fullness of Christ. Then we will no longer be infants, tossed back and forth by the waves, and blown here and there by every wind of teaching and by the cunning and craftiness of men in their deceitful scheming. Instead, speaking the truth in love, we will in all things grow up (Ephesians 4:13–15).

Additional Scripture Readings:
Luke 8:14–15; James 1:2–4

*Go to page 1359 for your next
devotional reading.*

to teach you the elementary truths of God's word all over again. You need milk, not solid food! [13]Anyone who lives on milk, being still an infant, is not acquainted with the teaching about righteousness. [14]But solid food is for the mature, who by constant use have trained themselves to distinguish good from evil.

6 Therefore let us leave the elementary teachings about Christ and go on to maturity, not laying again the foundation of repentance from acts that lead to death,[a] and of faith in God, [2]instruction about baptisms, the laying on of hands, the resurrection of the dead, and eternal judgment. [3]And God permitting, we will do so.

[4]It is impossible for those who have once been enlightened, who have tasted the heavenly gift, who have shared in the Holy Spirit, [5]who have tasted the goodness of the word of God and the powers of

[a]1 Or *from useless rituals*

WEDNESDAY

VERSE FOR THE DAY:
Hebrews 6:18

AUTHOR:
Neva Coyle

PASSAGE FOR THE DAY:
Hebrews 6:13–20

Keeping Promises

DID anyone ever tell you that they would do something for you that needed to be done, and then they didn't do it? Did anyone ever promise you something and then break that promise? Were you ever lied to? Did you ever count on someone for support, and then just when you needed it you found that your friend was not in a position to give that support? Did you ever read a brochure about a vacation spot, and when you got there found that the modern cabin in the photograph was the only one at the place and it was occupied? If any of these situations ring a bell with you, then you know what it is like to be disillusioned or deceived.

Deception—what a disabling, evil element. Falsehood, misrepresentation, fabrication, dishonesty, fraud—all synonymous with deception. I have used these words to illustrate what God is not. We tend to be skeptical because of past experiences. We want everything proven to us before we believe. Why? Because we may have believed something once too often, and been deceived one time too many. We are more acquainted with lies than truth.

God knows that we are more apt to be skeptical than believing. Yet we remain gullible and vulnerable. He knows that even with the intense conditioning most of us have had, we want to believe. We need to believe. We are immensely relieved when we find an honest friend whom we can trust. God can be to us that friend. Listen to his words to us from Hebrews 6:18: "It is impossible for God to lie." Think about it—impossible. When God makes a promise, you can count on him to keep it!

Additional Scripture Readings:
Psalm 103:17–18; Isaiah 40:6–8

Go to page 1362 for your next devotional reading.

the coming age, [6]if they fall away, to be brought back to repentance, because[a] to their loss they are crucifying the Son of God all over again and subjecting him to public disgrace.

[7]Land that drinks in the rain often falling on it and that produces a crop useful to those for whom it is farmed receives the blessing of God. [8]But land that produces thorns and thistles is worthless and is in danger of being cursed. In the end it will be burned.

[9]Even though we speak like this, dear friends, we are confident of better things in your case—things that accompany salvation. [10]God is not unjust; he will not forget your work and the love you have shown him as you have helped his people and continue to help them. [11]We want each of you to show this same diligence to the very end, in order to make your hope sure. [12]We do not want you to become lazy, but to imitate those who through faith and patience inherit what has been promised.

The Certainty of God's Promise

[13]When God made his promise to Abraham, since there was no one greater for him to swear by, he swore by himself, [14]saying, "I will surely bless you and give you many descendants."[b] [15]And so after waiting patiently, Abraham received what was promised.

[16]Men swear by someone greater than themselves, and the oath confirms what is said and puts an end to all argument. [17]Because God wanted to make the unchanging nature of his purpose very clear to the heirs of what was promised, he confirmed it with an oath. [18]God did this so that, by two unchangeable things in which it is impossible for God to lie, we who have fled to take hold of the hope offered to us may be greatly encouraged. [19]We have this hope as an anchor for the soul, firm and secure. It enters the inner sanctuary behind the curtain, [20]where Jesus, who went before us, has entered on our behalf. He has become a high priest forever, in the order of Melchizedek.

Melchizedek the Priest

7 This Melchizedek was king of Salem and priest of God Most High. He met Abraham returning from the defeat of the kings and blessed him, [2]and Abraham

gave him a tenth of everything. First, his name means "king of righteousness"; then also, "king of Salem" means "king of peace." [3]Without father or mother, without genealogy, without beginning of days or end of life, like the Son of God he remains a priest forever.

[4]Just think how great he was: Even the patriarch Abraham gave him a tenth of the plunder! [5]Now the law requires the descendants of Levi who become priests to collect a tenth from the people—that is, their brothers—even though their brothers are descended from Abraham. [6]This man, however, did not trace his descent from Levi, yet he collected a tenth from Abraham and blessed him who had the promises. [7]And without doubt the lesser person is blessed by the greater. [8]In the one case, the tenth is collected by men who die; but in the other case, by him who is declared to be living. [9]One might even say that Levi, who collects the tenth, paid the tenth through Abraham, [10]because when Melchizedek met Abraham, Levi was still in the body of his ancestor.

Jesus Like Melchizedek

[11]If perfection could have been attained through the Levitical priesthood (for on the basis of it the law was given to the people), why was there still need for another priest to come—one in the order of Melchizedek, not in the order of Aaron? [12]For when there is a change of the priesthood, there must also be a change of the law. [13]He of whom these things are said belonged to a different tribe, and no one from that tribe has ever served at the altar. [14]For it is clear that our Lord descended from Judah, and in regard to that tribe Moses said nothing about priests. [15]And what we have said is even more clear if another priest like Melchizedek appears, [16]one who has become a priest not on the basis of a regulation as to his ancestry but on the basis of the power of an indestructible life. [17]For it is declared:

"You are a priest forever,
　　in the order of Melchizedek."[c]

[18]The former regulation is set aside because it was weak and useless [19](for the law made nothing perfect), and a better hope is introduced, by which we draw near to God.

[20]And it was not without an oath! Oth-

ers became priests without any oath, [21]but he became a priest with an oath when God said to him:

"The Lord has sworn
and will not change his mind:
'You are a priest forever.' "[a]

[22]Because of this oath, Jesus has become the guarantee of a better covenant.

[23]Now there have been many of those priests, since death prevented them from continuing in office; [24]but because Jesus lives forever, he has a permanent priesthood. [25]Therefore he is able to save completely[b] those who come to God through him, because he always lives to intercede for them.

[26]Such a high priest meets our need— one who is holy, blameless, pure, set apart from sinners, exalted above the heavens. [27]Unlike the other high priests, he does not need to offer sacrifices day after day, first for his own sins, and then for the sins of the people. He sacrificed for their sins once for all when he offered himself. [28]For the law appoints as high priests men who are weak; but the oath, which came after the law, appointed the Son, who has been made perfect forever.

The High Priest of a New Covenant

8 The point of what we are saying is this: We do have such a high priest, who sat down at the right hand of the throne of the Majesty in heaven, [2]and who serves in the sanctuary, the true tabernacle set up by the Lord, not by man.

[3]Every high priest is appointed to offer both gifts and sacrifices, and so it was necessary for this one also to have something to offer. [4]If he were on earth, he would not be a priest, for there are already men who offer the gifts prescribed by the law. [5]They serve at a sanctuary that is a copy and shadow of what is in heaven. This is why Moses was warned when he was about to build the tabernacle: "See to it that you make everything according to the pattern shown you on the mountain."[c] [6]But the ministry Jesus has received is as superior to theirs as the covenant of which he is mediator is superior to the old one, and it is founded on better promises.

[7]For if there had been nothing wrong with that first covenant, no place would have been sought for another. [8]But God found fault with the people and said[d]:

"The time is coming, declares the Lord,
when I will make a new covenant
with the house of Israel
and with the house of Judah.
[9]It will not be like the covenant
I made with their forefathers
when I took them by the hand
to lead them out of Egypt,
because they did not remain faithful
to my covenant,
and I turned away from them,
declares the Lord.
[10]This is the covenant I will make with
the house of Israel
after that time, declares the Lord.
I will put my laws in their minds
and write them on their hearts.
I will be their God,
and they will be my people.
[11]No longer will a man teach his
neighbor,
or a man his brother, saying, 'Know
the Lord,'
because they will all know me,
from the least of them to the
greatest.
[12]For I will forgive their wickedness
and will remember their sins no
more."[e]

[13]By calling this covenant "new," he has made the first one obsolete; and what is obsolete and aging will soon disappear.

Worship in the Earthly Tabernacle

9 Now the first covenant had regulations for worship and also an earthly sanctuary. [2]A tabernacle was set up. In its first room were the lampstand, the table and the consecrated bread; this was called the Holy Place. [3]Behind the second curtain was a room called the Most Holy Place, [4]which had the golden altar of incense and the gold-covered ark of the covenant. This ark contained the gold jar of manna, Aaron's staff that had budded, and the stone tablets of the covenant. [5]Above the ark were the cherubim of the Glory, overshadowing the atonement cover.[f] But we cannot discuss these things in detail now.

[6]When everything had been arranged like this, the priests entered regularly

---

a21 Psalm 110:4   *b25* Or *forever*   *c5* Exodus 25:40   *d8* Some manuscripts may be translated *fault and said to the people.*   *e12* Jer. 31:31-34   *f5* Traditionally *the mercy seat* into the outer room to carry on their ministry. [7]But only the high priest entered the inner room, and that only once a year, and never without blood, which he offered for himself and for the sins the people had committed in ignorance. [8]The Holy Spirit was showing by this that the way into the Most Holy Place had not yet been disclosed as long as the first tabernacle was still standing. [9]This is an illustration for the present time, indicating that the gifts and sacrifices being offered were not able to clear the conscience of the worshiper. [10]They are only a matter of food and drink and various ceremonial washings — external regulations applying until the time of the new order.

The Blood of Christ

[11]When Christ came as high priest of the good things that are already here,[a] he went through the greater and more perfect tabernacle that is not man-made, that is to say, not a part of this creation. [12]He did not enter by means of the blood of goats and calves; but he entered the Most Holy Place once for all by his own blood, having obtained eternal redemption. [13]The blood of goats and bulls and

[a]11 Some early manuscripts *are to come*

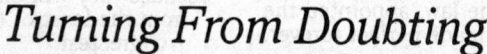

THURSDAY

VERSE FOR THE DAY:	AUTHOR:	PASSAGE FOR THE DAY:
Hebrews 10:23	Hannah Whitall Smith	Hebrews 10:19–25

Turning From Doubting

YOU cannot perhaps hinder the suggestions of doubt from coming to you any more than you can hinder someone in the street from swearing as you go by; consequently you are not sinning in the one case any more than in the other. Just as you can refuse to listen to them or join in their oaths, so can you also refuse to listen to the doubts or join in with them. They are not your doubts until you consent to them and adopt them as true. When they come to you must at once turn from them.

Give up your liberty to doubt forever. Put your will in this matter over on the Lord's side and trust him to keep you from falling. Tell him all about your weakness and your long-encouraged habits of doubt and how helpless you are before them. Then commit the whole battle to him. Tell him you will not doubt again, putting forth all your will power on his side and against his enemy and yours. Then "keep your eyes on Jesus" (Hebrews 12:2), looking away from yourself and away from your doubts, holding fast the profession of your faith without wavering, because "he who promised is faithful" (Hebrews 10:23). Rely on his faithfulness, not on your own. You have committed the keeping of your soul to him as the faithful Creator, and you must never again admit the possibility of his being unfaithful.

Cultivate a continuous habit of believing, and sooner or later all of your doubts will vanish in the glory of the absolute faithfulness of God.

Additional Scripture Readings:
Luke 1:11–20; John 20:26–29

Go to page 1364 for your next devotional reading.

the ashes of a heifer sprinkled on those who are ceremonially unclean sanctify them so that they are outwardly clean. 14How much more, then, will the blood of Christ, who through the eternal Spirit offered himself unblemished to God, cleanse our consciences from acts that lead to death,*a* so that we may serve the living God!

15For this reason Christ is the mediator of a new covenant, that those who are called may receive the promised eternal inheritance—now that he has died as a ransom to set them free from the sins committed under the first covenant.

16In the case of a will,*b* it is necessary to prove the death of the one who made it, 17because a will is in force only when somebody has died; it never takes effect while the one who made it is living. 18This is why even the first covenant was not put into effect without blood. 19When Moses had proclaimed every commandment of the law to all the people, he took the blood of calves, together with water, scarlet wool and branches of hyssop, and sprinkled the scroll and all the people. 20He said, "This is the blood of the covenant, which God has commanded you to keep."*c* 21In the same way, he sprinkled with the blood both the tabernacle and everything used in its ceremonies. 22In fact, the law requires that nearly everything be cleansed with blood, and without the shedding of blood there is no forgiveness.

23It was necessary, then, for the copies of the heavenly things to be purified with these sacrifices, but the heavenly things themselves with better sacrifices than these. 24For Christ did not enter a man-made sanctuary that was only a copy of the true one; he entered heaven itself, now to appear for us in God's presence. 25Nor did he enter heaven to offer himself again and again, the way the high priest enters the Most Holy Place every year with blood that is not his own. 26Then Christ would have had to suffer many times since the creation of the world. But now he has appeared once for all at the end of the ages to do away with sin by the sacrifice of himself. 27Just as man is destined to die once, and after that to face judgment, 28so Christ was sacrificed once to take away the sins of many people; and he will appear a second time, not to bear sin, but to bring salvation to those who are waiting for him.

Christ's Sacrifice Once for All

10 The law is only a shadow of the good things that are coming—not the realities themselves. For this reason it can never, by the same sacrifices repeated endlessly year after year, make perfect those who draw near to worship. 2If it could, would they not have stopped being offered? For the worshipers would have been cleansed once for all, and would no longer have felt guilty for their sins. 3But those sacrifices are an annual reminder of sins, 4because it is impossible for the blood of bulls and goats to take away sins.

5Therefore, when Christ came into the world, he said:

"Sacrifice and offering you did not
    desire,
    but a body you prepared for me;
6with burnt offerings and sin offerings
    you were not pleased.
7Then I said, 'Here I am—it is written
    about me in the scroll—
I have come to do your will,
    O God.' "*d*

8First he said, "Sacrifices and offerings, burnt offerings and sin offerings you did not desire, nor were you pleased with them" (although the law required them to be made). 9Then he said, "Here I am, I have come to do your will." He sets aside the first to establish the second. 10And by that will, we have been made holy through the sacrifice of the body of Jesus Christ once for all.

11Day after day every priest stands and performs his religious duties; again and again he offers the same sacrifices, which can never take away sins. 12But when this priest had offered for all time one sacrifice for sins, he sat down at the right hand of God. 13Since that time he waits for his enemies to be made his footstool, 14because by one sacrifice he has made perfect forever those who are being made holy.

15The Holy Spirit also testifies to us about this. First he says:

16"This is the covenant I will make with
    them
    after that time, says the Lord.
I will put my laws in their hearts,

*a*14 Or *from useless rituals*   *b*16 Same Greek word as *covenant*; also in verse 17   *c*20 Exodus 24:8
*d*7 Psalm 40:6-8 (see Septuagint)

VERSE FOR THE DAY:	AUTHOR:	PASSAGE FOR THE DAY:
Hebrews 11:39–40	Luci Swindoll	Hebrews 11:23–29,39–40

Moses' Choice—Your Choice

THIS inspiring chapter of Hebrews has been called the Faith Hall of Fame. These noted saints pleased God and were commended by him because, in faith, they trusted God for what they hoped for, even though they could not see the goal at the time.

The most amazing person in this whole bunch is Moses, because of a choice he made. And what did he choose? "He chose to be mistreated along with the people of God." Why would he do that? At that time, Egypt was the loftiest society of the day—rich in beauty, education, art, trade, culture—and the Hebrew people were, by comparison, nothing more than a dung heap on the outskirts of town. Moses, even though he had been reared from babyhood by the daughter of Pharaoh, chose the dung heap. Unbelievable! Instead of staying where things were nice and clean, prestigious and comfortable, he chose mistreatment. I find that thought-provoking.

Would I choose mistreatment? I wonder if I'd have that strength of character. Loving the nicer things in life, I'd have to reach down into that part of me where my values lie. What would it take to make me choose what's best rather than what's easiest? Such a decision would have to come from a sense of direction—from my faith.

By faith, Moses chose wisely and looked at the disgrace and mistreatment as a temporary burden, with his ultimate reward of greater value than what society had to offer. Faith willfully chooses even disgrace or mistreatment because it sees, through an act of trust, the eventual reward that comes from him who is invisible.

You have the same opportunity to choose either a reward that stops here or one that lies ahead in a place that cannot be seen. You have a chance to choose for your sake or for the sake of Christ. It boils down to that. How will you choose? Remember Moses.

Additional Scripture Readings:
Esther 4:6–16; Daniel 3:13–18

Go to page 1366 for your next devotional reading.

and I will write them on their minds."*a*

[17]Then he adds:

"Their sins and lawless acts
I will remember no more."*b*

[18]And where these have been forgiven, there is no longer any sacrifice for sin.

A Call to Persevere

[19]Therefore, brothers, since we have confidence to enter the Most Holy Place by the blood of Jesus, [20]by a new and living way opened for us through the curtain, that is, his body, [21]and since we have a great priest over the house of God, [22]let us draw near to God with a sincere heart in full assurance of faith, having our hearts sprinkled to cleanse us from a guilty conscience and having our bodies washed with pure water. [23]Let us hold unswervingly to the hope we profess, for he who promised is faithful. [24]And let us consider how we may spur one another on toward love and good deeds. [25]Let us not give up meeting together, as some are in the habit of doing, but let us encourage one another—and all the more as you see the Day approaching.

[26]If we deliberately keep on sinning after we have received the knowledge of the truth, no sacrifice for sins is left, [27]but only a fearful expectation of judgment and of raging fire that will consume the enemies of God. [28]Anyone who rejected the law of Moses died without mercy on the testimony of two or three witnesses. [29]How much more severely do you think a man deserves to be punished who has trampled the Son of God under foot, who has treated as an unholy thing the blood of the covenant that sanctified him, and who has insulted the Spirit of grace? [30]For we know him who said, "It is mine to avenge; I will repay,"*c* and again, "The Lord will judge his people."*d* [31]It is a dreadful thing to fall into the hands of the living God.

[32]Remember those earlier days after you had received the light, when you stood your ground in a great contest in the face of suffering. [33]Sometimes you were publicly exposed to insult and persecution; at other times you stood side by side with those who were so treated. [34]You sympathized with those in prison

and joyfully accepted the confiscation of your property, because you knew that you yourselves had better and lasting possessions.

[35]So do not throw away your confidence; it will be richly rewarded. [36]You need to persevere so that when you have done the will of God, you will receive what he has promised. [37]For in just a very little while,

"He who is coming will come and will not delay.
[38]   But my righteous one*e* will live by faith.
And if he shrinks back,
I will not be pleased with him."*f*

[39]But we are not of those who shrink back and are destroyed, but of those who believe and are saved.

By Faith

11 Now faith is being sure of what we hope for and certain of what we do not see. [2]This is what the ancients were commended for.

[3]By faith we understand that the universe was formed at God's command, so that what is seen was not made out of what was visible.

[4]By faith Abel offered God a better sacrifice than Cain did. By faith he was commended as a righteous man, when God spoke well of his offerings. And by faith he still speaks, even though he is dead. [5]By faith Enoch was taken from this life, so that he did not experience death; he could not be found, because God had taken him away. For before he was taken, he was commended as one who pleased God. [6]And without faith it is impossible to please God, because anyone who comes to him must believe that he exists and that he rewards those who earnestly seek him.

[7]By faith Noah, when warned about things not yet seen, in holy fear built an ark to save his family. By his faith he condemned the world and became heir of the righteousness that comes by faith.

[8]By faith Abraham, when called to go to a place he would later receive as his inheritance, obeyed and went, even though he did not know where he was going. [9]By faith he made his home in the promised land like a stranger in a foreign country; he lived in tents, as did Isaac and Jacob,

a16 Jer. 31:33   *b17* Jer. 31:34   *c30* Deut. 32:35   *d30* Deut. 32:36; Psalm 135:14   *e38* One early manuscript *But the righteous*   *f38* Hab. 2:3,4

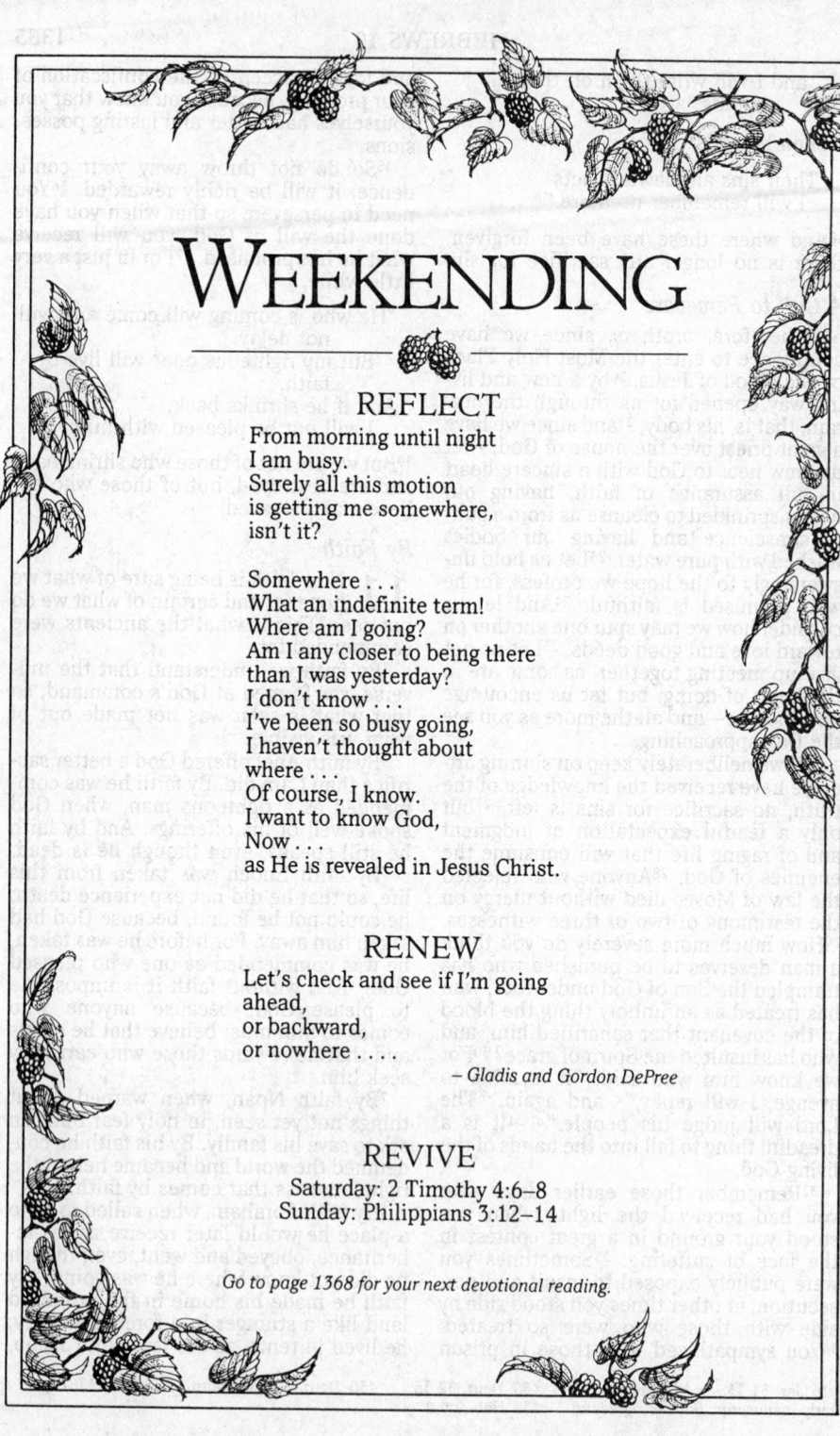

WEEKENDING

REFLECT

From morning until night
I am busy.
Surely all this motion
is getting me somewhere,
isn't it?

Somewhere . . .
What an indefinite term!
Where am I going?
Am I any closer to being there
than I was yesterday?
I don't know . . .
I've been so busy going,
I haven't thought about
where . . .
Of course, I know.
I want to know God,
Now . . .
as He is revealed in Jesus Christ.

RENEW

Let's check and see if I'm going
ahead,
or backward,
or nowhere . . . .

– Gladis and Gordon DePree

REVIVE

Saturday: 2 Timothy 4:6–8
Sunday: Philippians 3:12–14

Go to page 1368 for your next devotional reading.

who were heirs with him of the same promise. [10]For he was looking forward to the city with foundations, whose architect and builder is God.

[11]By faith Abraham, even though he was past age — and Sarah herself was barren — was enabled to become a father because he[a] considered him faithful who had made the promise. [12]And so from this one man, and he as good as dead, came descendants as numerous as the stars in the sky and as countless as the sand on the seashore.

[13]All these people were still living by faith when they died. They did not receive the things promised; they only saw them and welcomed them from a distance. And they admitted that they were aliens and strangers on earth. [14]People who say such things show that they are looking for a country of their own. [15]If they had been thinking of the country they had left, they would have had opportunity to return. [16]Instead, they were longing for a better country — a heavenly one. Therefore God is not ashamed to be called their God, for he has prepared a city for them.

[17]By faith Abraham, when God tested him, offered Isaac as a sacrifice. He who had received the promises was about to sacrifice his one and only son, [18]even though God had said to him, "It is through Isaac that your offspring[b] will be reckoned."[c] [19]Abraham reasoned that God could raise the dead, and figuratively speaking, he did receive Isaac back from death.

[20]By faith Isaac blessed Jacob and Esau in regard to their future.

[21]By faith Jacob, when he was dying, blessed each of Joseph's sons, and worshiped as he leaned on the top of his staff.

[22]By faith Joseph, when his end was near, spoke about the exodus of the Israelites from Egypt and gave instructions about his bones.

[23]By faith Moses' parents hid him for three months after he was born, because they saw he was no ordinary child, and they were not afraid of the king's edict.

[24]By faith Moses, when he had grown up, refused to be known as the son of Pharaoh's daughter. [25]He chose to be mistreated along with the people of God rather than to enjoy the pleasures of sin for a short time. [26]He regarded disgrace for the sake of Christ as of greater value than the treasures of Egypt, because he was looking ahead to his reward. [27]By faith he left Egypt, not fearing the king's anger; he persevered because he saw him who is invisible. [28]By faith he kept the Passover and the sprinkling of blood, so that the destroyer of the firstborn would not touch the firstborn of Israel.

[29]By faith the people passed through the Red Sea[d] as on dry land; but when the Egyptians tried to do so, they were drowned.

[30]By faith the walls of Jericho fell, after the people had marched around them for seven days.

[31]By faith the prostitute Rahab, because she welcomed the spies, was not killed with those who were disobedient.[e]

[32]And what more shall I say? I do not have time to tell about Gideon, Barak, Samson, Jephthah, David, Samuel and the prophets, [33]who through faith conquered kingdoms, administered justice, and gained what was promised; who shut the mouths of lions, [34]quenched the fury of the flames, and escaped the edge of the sword; whose weakness was turned to strength; and who became powerful in battle and routed foreign armies. [35]Women received back their dead, raised to life again. Others were tortured and refused to be released, so that they might gain a better resurrection. [36]Some faced jeers and flogging, while still others were chained and put in prison. [37]They were stoned[f]; they were sawed in two; they were put to death by the sword. They went about in sheepskins and goatskins, destitute, persecuted and mistreated — [38]the world was not worthy of them. They wandered in deserts and mountains, and in caves and holes in the ground.

[39]These were all commended for their faith, yet none of them received what had been promised. [40]God had planned something better for us so that only together with us would they be made perfect.

God Disciplines His Sons

12 Therefore, since we are surrounded by such a great cloud of witnesses, let us throw off everything that hinders and the sin that so easily entangles, and let us run with perseverance the

---

a11 Or By faith even Sarah, who was past age, was enabled to bear children because she   b18 Greek seed   c18 Gen. 21:12   d29 That is, Sea of Reeds   e31 Or unbelieving   f37 Some early manuscripts stoned; they were put to the test;

race marked out for us. ²Let us fix our eyes on Jesus, the author and perfecter of our faith, who for the joy set before him endured the cross, scorning its shame, and sat down at the right hand of the throne of God. ³Consider him who endured such opposition from sinful men, so that you will not grow weary and lose heart.

⁴In your struggle against sin, you have not yet resisted to the point of shedding your blood. ⁵And you have forgotten that

word of encouragement that addresses you as sons:

> "My son, do not make light of the
>   Lord's discipline,
> and do not lose heart when he
>   rebukes you,
> ⁶because the Lord disciplines those he
>   loves,
> and he punishes everyone he
>   accepts as a son."ᵃ

⁷Endure hardship as discipline; God is

ᵃ6 Prov. 3:11,12

VERSE FOR THE DAY:
Hebrews 12:10

AUTHOR:
Diane Head

PASSAGE FOR THE DAY:
Hebrews 12:1–13

His Discipline

MOST of us have had at least one week when everything seemed to go wrong. The kids knocked down the apple display at the market; the plumbing decided it was time to back up; the furnace died; the car had a flat (with the entire Brownie troop inside); and the stomach flu toppled the whole household.

These events don't always come in groups, but even one at a time they can be mildly irritating and sometimes downright exasperating.

Then there are the more serious events that enter our lives—seemingly without reason. The ones that slice at our very roots: perhaps a lost job or maybe a transfer to another city. Maybe it's the extended illness of a family member or a life-threatening accident or not enough money to go around.

Do you ever wonder about the calamities that meet us head-on in everyday life? Do you ever ask as I do, "Why me, Lord?" Are daily catastrophes just happenstance or is there a reason behind them?

God disciplines us for our good, that we may share in his holiness" (Hebrews 12:10). What a difference it makes in the atmosphere of our homes if we face those calamities with an attitude of joy. Not a fake, pasted-on joy—but a joy that comes from knowing that he is bringing us closer to a sharing in his holiness—through discipline.

So the next time those rough winds sweep through our homes—let's rejoice! It won't be long until we can lift our hearts and laugh in his sunshine . . . in his holiness.

Additional Scripture Readings:
Deuteronomy 8:1–5; Proverbs 3:11–12

Go to page 1370 for your next
devotional reading.

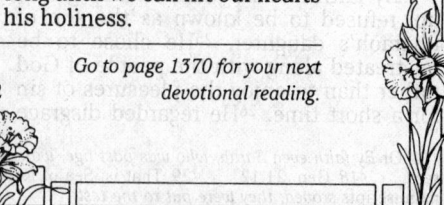

treating you as sons. For what son is not disciplined by his father? [8]If you are not disciplined (and everyone undergoes discipline), then you are illegitimate children and not true sons. [9]Moreover, we have all had human fathers who disciplined us and we respected them for it. How much more should we submit to the Father of our spirits and live! [10]Our fathers disciplined us for a little while as they thought best; but God disciplines us for our good, that we may share in his holiness. [11]No discipline seems pleasant at the time, but painful. Later on, however, it produces a harvest of righteousness and peace for those who have been trained by it.

[12]Therefore, strengthen your feeble arms and weak knees. [13]"Make level paths for your feet,"[a] so that the lame may not be disabled, but rather healed.

Warning Against Refusing God

[14]Make every effort to live in peace with all men and to be holy; without holiness no one will see the Lord. [15]See to it that no one misses the grace of God and that no bitter root grows up to cause trouble and defile many. [16]See that no one is sexually immoral, or is godless like Esau, who for a single meal sold his inheritance rights as the oldest son. [17]Afterward, as you know, when he wanted to inherit this blessing, he was rejected. He could bring about no change of mind, though he sought the blessing with tears.

[18]You have not come to a mountain that can be touched and that is burning with fire; to darkness, gloom and storm; [19]to a trumpet blast or to such a voice speaking words that those who heard it begged that no further word be spoken to them, [20]because they could not bear what was commanded: "If even an animal touches the mountain, it must be stoned."[b] [21]The sight was so terrifying that Moses said, "I am trembling with fear."[c]

[22]But you have come to Mount Zion, to the heavenly Jerusalem, the city of the living God. You have come to thousands upon thousands of angels in joyful assembly, [23]to the church of the firstborn, whose names are written in heaven. You have come to God, the judge of all men, to the spirits of righteous men made perfect, [24]to Jesus the mediator of a new covenant, and to the sprinkled blood that speaks a better word than the blood of Abel.

[25]See to it that you do not refuse him who speaks. If they did not escape when they refused him who warned them on earth, how much less will we, if we turn away from him who warns us from heaven? [26]At that time his voice shook the earth, but now he has promised, "Once more I will shake not only the earth but also the heavens."[d] [27]The words "once more" indicate the removing of what can be shaken—that is, created things—so that what cannot be shaken may remain.

[28]Therefore, since we are receiving a kingdom that cannot be shaken, let us be thankful, and so worship God acceptably with reverence and awe, [29]for our "God is a consuming fire."[e]

Concluding Exhortations

13 Keep on loving each other as brothers. [2]Do not forget to entertain strangers, for by so doing some people have entertained angels without knowing it. [3]Remember those in prison as if you were their fellow prisoners, and those who are mistreated as if you yourselves were suffering.

[4]Marriage should be honored by all, and the marriage bed kept pure, for God will judge the adulterer and all the sexually immoral. [5]Keep your lives free from the love of money and be content with what you have, because God has said,

"Never will I leave you;
    never will I forsake you."[f]

[6]So we say with confidence,

"The Lord is my helper; I will not be afraid.
    What can man do to me?"[g]

[7]Remember your leaders, who spoke the word of God to you. Consider the outcome of their way of life and imitate their faith. [8]Jesus Christ is the same yesterday and today and forever.

[9]Do not be carried away by all kinds of strange teachings. It is good for our hearts to be strengthened by grace, not by ceremonial foods, which are of no value to those who eat them. [10]We have an altar from which those who minister at the tabernacle have no right to eat. [11]The high priest carries the blood of

---

a13 Prov. 4:26   *b20* Exodus 19:12,13   *c21* Deut. 9:19   *d26* Haggai 2:6   *e29* Deut. 4:24
f5 Deut. 31:6   *g6* Psalm 118:6,7

VERSE FOR THE DAY:
Hebrews 13:5

AUTHOR:
Sue Richards

PASSAGE FOR THE DAY:
Hebrews 13:1–6

Uncoupled

MY husband of eight years left me at the beginning of my fourth month of pregnancy. I have never felt more rejected, vulnerable or unloved. I was nauseated, tired, and constantly trying to explain to my two-year-old son that Daddy wasn't coming back home because he didn't love Mommy anymore.

Michigan's howling winter winds, which seemed to seep through even brick walls, only added to my depression as I hauled groceries and toddler up three flights of stairs. We had just moved to Michigan from Virginia, and this was supposed to be our temporary apartment while our house in Virginia was being sold.

No house, no job, no husband, no church. Just an active little boy asking heartbreaking questions, a stomach that gagged at the thought of food, and an empty bed with sheets as cold as the February winds.

Yet, somewhere, there was something else too. It was deep inside my heart. It didn't feel overpowering or dramatic, but it gave me courage to get up each morning and make it through the day.

I knew that God loved me. I wish I could say I laughed in the face of all adversity, but I didn't. I sobbed into my pillow at night, then lay awake unable to breathe through my nose, wondering what would happen to me and my two babies.

I did more than wonder, though. I prayed. I prayed when I did my grocery shopping, when I bathed little Matthew, and when I strained over my ever-protruding belly to trim my toenails.

How reassuring it was for me in those lonely times to read God's words:

> Never will I leave you;
> never will I forsake you.

I held on to those words when I felt totally abandoned, totally alone. In those times, when I was willing to reach out to God and his reassuring words, he faithfully held me up.

Thank you, Lord, for granting me strength to live through the difficult times. And thank you for holding me up, especially in my most vulnerable moments.

Additional Scripture Readings:
Isaiah 40:11; 2 Corinthians 4:7–9

Go to page 1373 for your next devotional reading.

animals into the Most Holy Place as a sin offering, but the bodies are burned outside the camp. ¹²And so Jesus also suffered outside the city gate to make the people holy through his own blood. ¹³Let us, then, go to him outside the camp, bearing the disgrace he bore. ¹⁴For here we do not have an enduring city, but we are looking for the city that is to come.

¹⁵Through Jesus, therefore, let us continually offer to God a sacrifice of praise —the fruit of lips that confess his name. ¹⁶And do not forget to do good and to share with others, for with such sacrifices God is pleased.

¹⁷Obey your leaders and submit to their authority. They keep watch over you as men who must give an account. Obey them so that their work will be a joy, not a burden, for that would be of no advantage to you.

¹⁸Pray for us. We are sure that we have a clear conscience and desire to live honorably in every way. ¹⁹I particularly urge you to pray so that I may be restored to you soon.

²⁰May the God of peace, who through the blood of the eternal covenant brought back from the dead our Lord Jesus, that great Shepherd of the sheep, ²¹equip you with everything good for doing his will, and may he work in us what is pleasing to him, through Jesus Christ, to whom be glory for ever and ever. Amen.

²²Brothers, I urge you to bear with my word of exhortation, for I have written you only a short letter.

²³I want you to know that our brother Timothy has been released. If he arrives soon, I will come with him to see you.

²⁴Greet all your leaders and all God's people. Those from Italy send you their greetings.

²⁵Grace be with you all.

JAMES (a brother of Jesus) writes this letter to urge Christians to express their faith in daily living. He reminds them of what Jesus said, especially in the Sermon on the Mount (Matthew 5–7). As you read this book, ask yourself whether others can see by what you do and say that you believe in Jesus.

JAMES

1 James, a servant of God and of the Lord Jesus Christ,

To the twelve tribes scattered among the nations:

Greetings.

Trials and Temptations

²Consider it pure joy, my brothers, whenever you face trials of many kinds, ³because you know that the testing of your faith develops perseverance. ⁴Perseverance must finish its work so that you may be mature and complete, not lacking anything. ⁵If any of you lacks wisdom, he should ask God, who gives generously to all without finding fault, and it will be given to him. ⁶But when he asks, he must believe and not doubt, because he who doubts is like a wave of the sea, blown and tossed by the wind. ⁷That man should not think he will receive anything from the Lord; ⁸he is a double-minded man, unstable in all he does.

⁹The brother in humble circumstances ought to take pride in his high position. ¹⁰But the one who is rich should take pride in his low position, because he will pass away like a wild flower. ¹¹For the sun rises with scorching heat and withers the plant; its blossom falls and its beauty is destroyed. In the same way, the rich man will fade away even while he goes about his business.

¹²Blessed is the man who perseveres under trial, because when he has stood the test, he will receive the crown of life that God has promised to those who love him.

¹³When tempted, no one should say, "God is tempting me." For God cannot be tempted by evil, nor does he tempt anyone; ¹⁴but each one is tempted when, by his own evil desire, he is dragged away and enticed. ¹⁵Then, after desire has con-

ceived, it gives birth to sin; and sin, when it is full-grown, gives birth to death.

¹⁶Don't be deceived, my dear brothers. ¹⁷Every good and perfect gift is from above, coming down from the Father of the heavenly lights, who does not change like shifting shadows. ¹⁸He chose to give us birth through the word of truth, that we might be a kind of firstfruits of all he created.

Listening and Doing

¹⁹My dear brothers, take note of this: Everyone should be quick to listen, slow to speak and slow to become angry, ²⁰for man's anger does not bring about the righteous life that God desires. ²¹Therefore, get rid of all moral filth and the evil that is so prevalent and humbly accept the word planted in you, which can save you.

²²Do not merely listen to the word, and so deceive yourselves. Do what it says. ²³Anyone who listens to the word but does not do what it says is like a man who looks at his face in a mirror ²⁴and, after looking at himself, goes away and immediately forgets what he looks like. ²⁵But the man who looks intently into the perfect law that gives freedom, and continues to do this, not forgetting what he has heard, but doing it—he will be blessed in what he does.

²⁶If anyone considers himself religious and yet does not keep a tight rein on his tongue, he deceives himself and his religion is worthless. ²⁷Religion that God our Father accepts as pure and faultless is this: to look after orphans and widows in their distress and to keep oneself from being polluted by the world.

Favoritism Forbidden

2 My brothers, as believers in our glorious Lord Jesus Christ, don't show favoritism. ²Suppose a man comes into your meeting wearing a gold ring and fine clothes, and a poor man in shabby clothes also comes in. ³If you show special attention to the man wearing fine

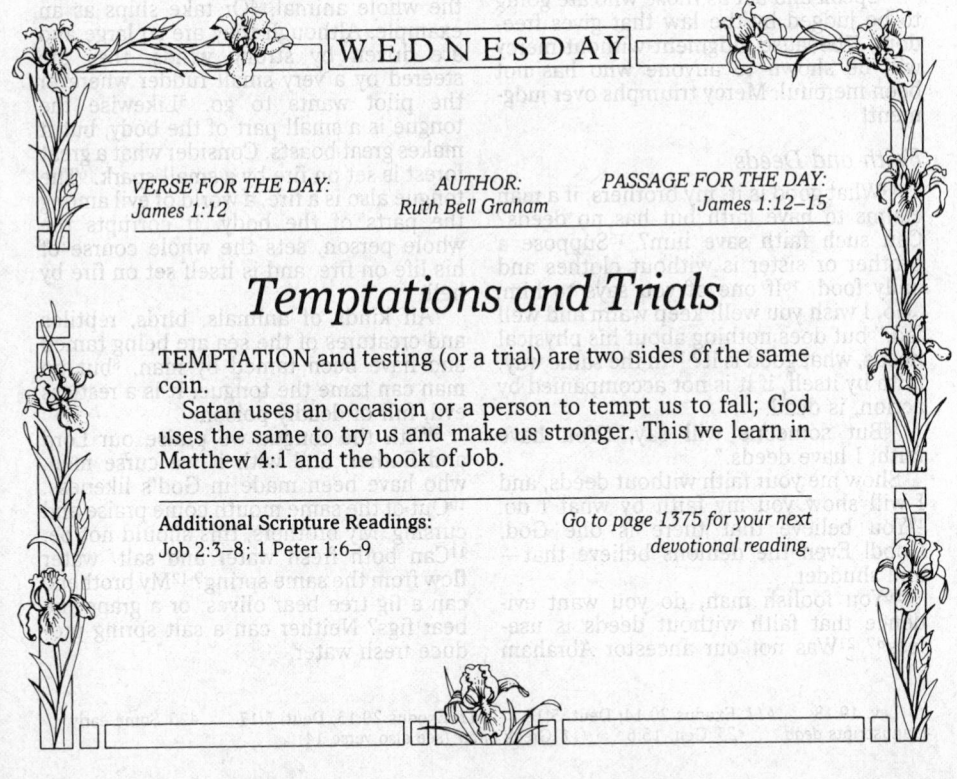

WEDNESDAY

VERSE FOR THE DAY:
James 1:12

AUTHOR:
Ruth Bell Graham

PASSAGE FOR THE DAY:
James 1:12–15

Temptations and Trials

TEMPTATION and testing (or a trial) are two sides of the same coin.

Satan uses an occasion or a person to tempt us to fall; God uses the same to try us and make us stronger. This we learn in Matthew 4:1 and the book of Job.

Additional Scripture Readings:
Job 2:3–8; 1 Peter 1:6–9

Go to page 1375 for your next devotional reading.

clothes and say, "Here's a good seat for you," but say to the poor man, "You stand there" or "Sit on the floor by my feet," ⁴have you not discriminated among yourselves and become judges with evil thoughts?

⁵Listen, my dear brothers: Has not God chosen those who are poor in the eyes of the world to be rich in faith and to inherit the kingdom he promised those who love him? ⁶But you have insulted the poor. Is it not the rich who are exploiting you? Are they not the ones who are dragging you into court? ⁷Are they not the ones who are slandering the noble name of him to whom you belong?

⁸If you really keep the royal law found in Scripture, "Love your neighbor as yourself,"ᵃ you are doing right. ⁹But if you show favoritism, you sin and are convicted by the law as lawbreakers. ¹⁰For whoever keeps the whole law and yet stumbles at just one point is guilty of breaking all of it. ¹¹For he who said, "Do not commit adultery,"ᵇ also said, "Do not murder."ᶜ If you do not commit adultery but do commit murder, you have become a lawbreaker.

¹²Speak and act as those who are going to be judged by the law that gives freedom, ¹³because judgment without mercy will be shown to anyone who has not been merciful. Mercy triumphs over judgment!

Faith and Deeds

¹⁴What good is it, my brothers, if a man claims to have faith but has no deeds? Can such faith save him? ¹⁵Suppose a brother or sister is without clothes and daily food. ¹⁶If one of you says to him, "Go, I wish you well; keep warm and well fed," but does nothing about his physical needs, what good is it? ¹⁷In the same way, faith by itself, if it is not accompanied by action, is dead.

¹⁸But someone will say, "You have faith; I have deeds."

Show me your faith without deeds, and I will show you my faith by what I do. ¹⁹You believe that there is one God. Good! Even the demons believe that—and shudder.

²⁰You foolish man, do you want evidence that faith without deeds is useless ᵈ? ²¹Was not our ancestor Abraham considered righteous for what he did when he offered his son Isaac on the altar? ²²You see that his faith and his actions were working together, and his faith was made complete by what he did. ²³And the scripture was fulfilled that says, "Abraham believed God, and it was credited to him as righteousness,"ᵉ and he was called God's friend. ²⁴You see that a person is justified by what he does and not by faith alone.

²⁵In the same way, was not even Rahab the prostitute considered righteous for what she did when she gave lodging to the spies and sent them off in a different direction? ²⁶As the body without the spirit is dead, so faith without deeds is dead.

Taming the Tongue

3 Not many of you should presume to be teachers, my brothers, because you know that we who teach will be judged more strictly. ²We all stumble in many ways. If anyone is never at fault in what he says, he is a perfect man, able to keep his whole body in check.

³When we put bits into the mouths of horses to make them obey us, we can turn the whole animal. ⁴Or take ships as an example. Although they are so large and are driven by strong winds, they are steered by a very small rudder wherever the pilot wants to go. ⁵Likewise the tongue is a small part of the body, but it makes great boasts. Consider what a great forest is set on fire by a small spark. ⁶The tongue also is a fire, a world of evil among the parts of the body. It corrupts the whole person, sets the whole course of his life on fire, and is itself set on fire by hell.

⁷All kinds of animals, birds, reptiles and creatures of the sea are being tamed and have been tamed by man, ⁸but no man can tame the tongue. It is a restless evil, full of deadly poison.

⁹With the tongue we praise our Lord and Father, and with it we curse men, who have been made in God's likeness. ¹⁰Out of the same mouth come praise and cursing. My brothers, this should not be. ¹¹Can both fresh water and saltᶠ water flow from the same spring? ¹²My brothers, can a fig tree bear olives, or a grapevine bear figs? Neither can a salt spring produce fresh water.

ᵃ8 Lev. 19:18   ᵇ11 Exodus 20:14; Deut. 5:18   ᶜ11 Exodus 20:13; Deut. 5:17   ᵈ20 Some early manuscripts *dead*   ᵉ23 Gen. 15:6   ᶠ11 Greek *bitter* (see also verse 14)

VERSE FOR THE DAY:	AUTHOR:	PASSAGE FOR THE DAY:
James 3:13	Luci Swindoll	James 3:13–18

Real Wisdom

ONCE I asked my brother Chuck if he'd rather have wisdom or youth, presupposing the two don't reside in the same person at the same time. Without hesitation he answered, "Oh, wisdom, Sis, hands down. That way I don't keep doing the same dumb things I did as a kid." Then, with a twinkle in his eye, he added, "Of course, I'd really prefer having wisdom in a young body."

Sara Teasdale informs me, in her excellent poem "Wisdom," that when I calmly look life in the eye, having grown wise from beating and flapping against its imperfections, learning to compromise, and accepting the fact that everyone and everything has its shortcomings:

> Life will have given me the truth
> And taken in exchange, my youth.

Inadvertently, one is given up for the other.

There are two kinds of wisdom, the apostle James says: worldly wisdom that is contaminated, ambitious and envious; and heavenly wisdom that is pure, content, merciful and submissive. So to be spiritually wise, a person must exhibit understanding, acceptance and peace.

James also says that the one who is understanding and wise will show it by his "good life." It's taken me over fifty years to learn that the good life is *not* attaining a college degree, succeeding in one's career, owning an expensive car, having money in the bank or vacationing in Hawaii. While that stuff is wonderful and sweet to my worldly tastes, it's not the good life.

The good life is peace—knowing that I was considerate instead of crabby, that I stood by faithfully when all the chips were down for the other guy, that I sacrificially gave to a worthy cause, that I showed impartiality when I really wanted my preference, that I was real in the midst of phonies, that I was forgiving, that I had the courage to defer reward for something better down the road.

Why couldn't I have learned this when I still had a young body?

Additional Scripture Readings:
Proverbs 4:5–7; 1 Corinthians 2:6–13

*Go to page 1377 for your next
devotional reading.*

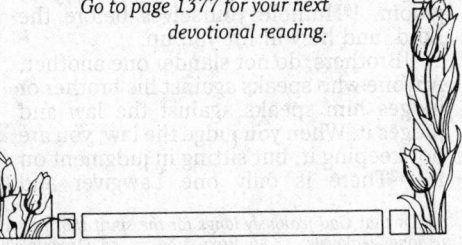

Two Kinds of Wisdom

¹³Who is wise and understanding among you? Let him show it by his good life, by deeds done in the humility that comes from wisdom. ¹⁴But if you harbor bitter envy and selfish ambition in your hearts, do not boast about it or deny the truth. ¹⁵Such "wisdom" does not come down from heaven but is earthly, unspiritual, of the devil. ¹⁶For where you have envy and selfish ambition, there you find disorder and every evil practice.

¹⁷But the wisdom that comes from heaven is first of all pure; then peace-loving, considerate, submissive, full of mercy and good fruit, impartial and sincere. ¹⁸Peacemakers who sow in peace raise a harvest of righteousness.

Submit Yourselves to God

4 What causes fights and quarrels among you? Don't they come from your desires that battle within you? ²You want something but don't get it. You kill and covet, but you cannot have what you want. You quarrel and fight. You do not have, because you do not ask God. ³When you ask, you do not receive, because you ask with wrong motives, that you may spend what you get on your pleasures.

⁴You adulterous people, don't you know that friendship with the world is hatred toward God? Anyone who chooses to be a friend of the world becomes an enemy of God. ⁵Or do you think Scripture says without reason that the spirit he caused to live in us envies intensely?[a] ⁶But he gives us more grace. That is why Scripture says:

"God opposes the proud
    but gives grace to the humble."[b]

⁷Submit yourselves, then, to God. Resist the devil, and he will flee from you. ⁸Come near to God and he will come near to you. Wash your hands, you sinners, and purify your hearts, you double-minded. ⁹Grieve, mourn and wail. Change your laughter to mourning and your joy to gloom. ¹⁰Humble yourselves before the Lord, and he will lift you up.

¹¹Brothers, do not slander one another. Anyone who speaks against his brother or judges him speaks against the law and judges it. When you judge the law, you are not keeping it, but sitting in judgment on it. ¹²There is only one Lawgiver and Judge, the one who is able to save and destroy. But you—who are you to judge your neighbor?

Boasting About Tomorrow

¹³Now listen, you who say, "Today or tomorrow we will go to this or that city, spend a year there, carry on business and make money." ¹⁴Why, you do not even know what will happen tomorrow. What is your life? You are a mist that appears for a little while and then vanishes. ¹⁵Instead, you ought to say, "If it is the Lord's will, we will live and do this or that." ¹⁶As it is, you boast and brag. All such boasting is evil. ¹⁷Anyone, then, who knows the good he ought to do and doesn't do it, sins.

Warning to Rich Oppressors

5 Now listen, you rich people, weep and wail because of the misery that is coming upon you. ²Your wealth has rotted, and moths have eaten your clothes. ³Your gold and silver are corroded. Their corrosion will testify against you and eat your flesh like fire. You have hoarded wealth in the last days. ⁴Look! The wages you failed to pay the workmen who mowed your fields are crying out against you. The cries of the harvesters have reached the ears of the Lord Almighty. ⁵You have lived on earth in luxury and self-indulgence. You have fattened yourselves in the day of slaughter.[c] ⁶You have condemned and murdered innocent men, who were not opposing you.

Patience in Suffering

⁷Be patient, then, brothers, until the Lord's coming. See how the farmer waits for the land to yield its valuable crop and how patient he is for the autumn and spring rains. ⁸You too, be patient and stand firm, because the Lord's coming is near. ⁹Don't grumble against each other, brothers, or you will be judged. The Judge is standing at the door!

¹⁰Brothers, as an example of patience in the face of suffering, take the prophets who spoke in the name of the Lord. ¹¹As you know, we consider blessed those who have persevered. You have heard of Job's perseverance and have seen what the Lord finally brought about. The Lord is full of compassion and mercy.

---

[a]5 Or that God jealously longs for the spirit that he made to live in us; or that the Spirit he caused to live in us longs jealously   [b]6 Prov. 3:34   [c]5 Or yourselves as in a day of feasting

¹²Above all, my brothers, do not swear —not by heaven or by earth or by anything else. Let your "Yes" be yes, and your "No," no, or you will be condemned.

The Prayer of Faith

¹³Is any one of you in trouble? He should pray. Is anyone happy? Let him sing songs of praise. ¹⁴Is any one of you sick? He should call the elders of the church to pray over him and anoint him with oil in the name of the Lord. ¹⁵And the prayer offered in faith will make the sick person well; the Lord will raise him up. If he has sinned, he will be forgiven. ¹⁶Therefore confess your sins to each other and pray for each other so that you may be healed. The prayer of a righteous man is powerful and effective.

¹⁷Elijah was a man just like us. He prayed earnestly that it would not rain,

FRIDAY

VERSE FOR THE DAY:
James 5:16

AUTHOR:
Karen Burton Mains

PASSAGE FOR THE DAY:
James 5:13–20

Women of Prayer

IN one year, Christianity lost three holy women of faith, Agnes Sanford, Corrie ten Boom and Catherine Marshall—as well as countless others whose names are unknown but who nevertheless did the work of God in this world. These are the women who knew what it meant to experience the presence of the unseen, who spent hours on their knees, who wept over the wounds of the world. For them, prayer was a second language. Who will take their place?

Frankly, there are very few candidates from our generation of women—those of us who have lavished hours in front of the television set, in the shopping plazas, in self-indulgence, in not developing a disciplined spiritual life.

Unless—unless, we begin to grow up spiritually. Unless we become convinced that we are the generation of Christian adults ultimately responsible for the spiritual condition of our nation. We must understand that there are increasingly few in that generation ahead of us left to pray over this world. We are coming of age. But are we coming to terms with our lack of spiritual depth and ability?

It is we who must learn the meaning of forbearing.

It is we who must develop the disciplines of spiritual perseverance, not shrinking back from growth but doing the will of God, having faith and keeping our souls.

It is we who must become women of faith and prayer and obedience and service.

It is we who must set a spiritual standard for the next generation.

It is time for us all to grow up.

Additional Scripture Readings:
Ephesians 6:18–20; Colossians 4:12–13

Go to page 1378 for your next devotional reading.

WEEKENDING

REJOICE

In heavenly love abiding,
No change my heart shall fear;
And safe is such confiding,
For nothing changes here.
The storm may roar without me,
My heart may low be laid,
But God is round about me,
And can I be dismayed?

Wherever He may guide me,
No fear shall turn me back;
My Shepherd is beside me,
And nothing shall I lack.
His wisdom ever waketh,
His sight is never dim;
He knows the way He taketh,
And I will walk with Him.

Green pastures are before me,
Which yet I have not seen;
Bright skies will soon be o'er me,
Where darkest clouds have been.
My hope I cannot measure,
My path to life is free;
My Savior is my treasure,
And he will walk with me.

– Anna L. Waring

REVIVE

Saturday: Hebrews 13:20–21
Sunday: Psalm 107:1–22

Go to page 1381 for your next devotional reading.

and it did not rain on the land for three and a half years. [18]Again he prayed, and the heavens gave rain, and the earth produced its crops.

[19]My brothers, if one of you should wander from the truth and someone should bring him back, [20]remember this: Whoever turns a sinner from the error of his way will save him from death and cover over a multitude of sins.

PETER writes this letter to a group of Christians suffering for their faith, reminding them of how much Jesus suffered. He inspires them with hope for the future and shows them how to grow in their faith. As you read this book, decide to do your best to live a holy life as you look forward to the return of Jesus and to the reward he promises to give his followers.

1 PETER

1 Peter, an apostle of Jesus Christ,

To God's elect, strangers in the world, scattered throughout Pontus, Galatia, Cappadocia, Asia and Bithynia, ²who have been chosen according to the foreknowledge of God the Father, through the sanctifying work of the Spirit, for obedience to Jesus Christ and sprinkling by his blood:

Grace and peace be yours in abundance.

Praise to God for a Living Hope

³Praise be to the God and Father of our Lord Jesus Christ! In his great mercy he has given us new birth into a living hope through the resurrection of Jesus Christ from the dead, ⁴and into an inheritance that can never perish, spoil or fade—kept in heaven for you, ⁵who through faith are shielded by God's power until the coming of the salvation that is ready to be revealed in the last time. ⁶In this you greatly rejoice, though now for a little while you may have had to suffer grief in all kinds of trials. ⁷These have come so that your faith—of greater worth than gold, which perishes even though refined by fire—may be proved genuine and may result in praise, glory and honor when Jesus Christ is revealed. ⁸Though you have not seen him, you love him; and even though you do not see him now, you believe in him and are filled with an inexpressible and glorious joy, ⁹for you are receiving the goal of your faith, the salvation of your souls.

¹⁰Concerning this salvation, the prophets, who spoke of the grace that was to

come to you, searched intently and with the greatest care, ¹¹trying to find out the time and circumstances to which the Spirit of Christ in them was pointing when he predicted the sufferings of Christ and the glories that would follow. ¹²It was revealed to them that they were not serving themselves but you, when they spoke of the things that have now been told you by those who have preached the gospel to you by the Holy Spirit sent from heav-

en. Even angels long to look into these things.

Be Holy

¹³Therefore, prepare your minds for action; be self-controlled; set your hope fully on the grace to be given you when Jesus Christ is revealed. ¹⁴As obedient children, do not conform to the evil desires you had when you lived in ignorance. ¹⁵But just as he who called you is holy, so be holy in all

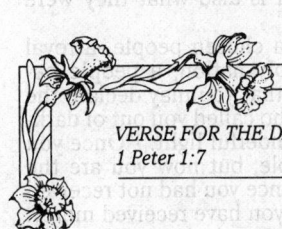

MONDAY

VERSE FOR THE DAY:
1 Peter 1:7

AUTHOR:
Mary Jane Worden

PASSAGE FOR THE DAY:
1 Peter 1:3–12

Faith and Grief

IN the early years of my marriage I had, providentially, read many books about loss and grief, always reminding God that I was willing to help others through their crisis times. But in my prayers I also shared the desire to be spared this anguish in my own life.

For whatever reason, God chose not to spare me this deep pain. After the death of my husband Jim, in those agonizing early days, I knew enough about God's character to be able to say, "Someday I will be able to look back and say even out of this God has brought good." I can't imagine what good or how that could possibly be true; it goes contrary to everything I feel right now. But I choose to believe the truth of what I've been taught all these years about God's character. Someday it will be true.

Four years later, I can see good that God has done in our lives. Had I been given the choice, I would never have chosen this. But I am grateful for the growth that I see in all of us, although I would have wished it to come in another way. What we have learned in these four years about ourselves, about our world, about God is of great value. I feel confident that Jim would like the persons we are becoming.

The Scriptures teach that God will use suffering to build character and to purify our faith (see Romans 5 and 1 Peter 1). I can't presume to know all that he is doing in our lives; that he has allowed us to see a small part of it, I'm grateful.

Those strong words in Isaiah 61:1–3 ring true for me. Change. Growth. Healing. Beauty for ashes. Gladness for mourning. Praise out of despair. But the last phrase is all-important: that it might be to his glory, "for the display of his splendor."

Additional Scripture Readings:
Isaiah 61:1–3; Romans 5:3–5

Go to page 1383 for your next devotional reading.

you do; [16]for it is written: "Be holy, because I am holy."[a]

[17]Since you call on a Father who judges each man's work impartially, live your lives as strangers here in reverent fear. [18]For you know that it was not with perishable things such as silver or gold that you were redeemed from the empty way of life handed down to you from your forefathers, [19]but with the precious blood of Christ, a lamb without blemish or defect. [20]He was chosen before the creation of the world, but was revealed in these last times for your sake. [21]Through him you believe in God, who raised him from the dead and glorified him, and so your faith and hope are in God.

[22]Now that you have purified yourselves by obeying the truth so that you have sincere love for your brothers, love one another deeply, from the heart.[b] [23]For you have been born again, not of perishable seed, but of imperishable, through the living and enduring word of God. [24]For,

"All men are like grass,
   and all their glory is like the
      flowers of the field;
the grass withers and the flowers fall,
[25] but the word of the Lord stands
      forever."[c]

And this is the word that was preached to you.

2 Therefore, rid yourselves of all malice and all deceit, hypocrisy, envy, and slander of every kind. [2]Like newborn babies, crave pure spiritual milk, so that by it you may grow up in your salvation, [3]now that you have tasted that the Lord is good.

The Living Stone and a Chosen People

[4]As you come to him, the living Stone—rejected by men but chosen by God and precious to him— [5]you also, like living stones, are being built into a spiritual house to be a holy priesthood, offering spiritual sacrifices acceptable to God through Jesus Christ. [6]For in Scripture it says:

"See, I lay a stone in Zion,
   a chosen and precious cornerstone,
and the one who trusts in him
   will never be put to shame."[d]

[7]Now to you who believe, this stone is precious. But to those who do not believe,

"The stone the builders rejected
   has become the capstone,[e]"[f]

[8]and,

"A stone that causes men to stumble
   and a rock that makes them fall."[g]

They stumble because they disobey the message—which is also what they were destined for.

[9]But you are a chosen people, a royal priesthood, a holy nation, a people belonging to God, that you may declare the praises of him who called you out of darkness into his wonderful light. [10]Once you were not a people, but now you are the people of God; once you had not received mercy, but now you have received mercy.

[11]Dear friends, I urge you, as aliens and strangers in the world, to abstain from sinful desires, which war against your soul. [12]Live such good lives among the pagans that, though they accuse you of doing wrong, they may see your good deeds and glorify God on the day he visits us.

Submission to Rulers and Masters

[13]Submit yourselves for the Lord's sake to every authority instituted among men: whether to the king, as the supreme authority, [14]or to governors, who are sent by him to punish those who do wrong and to commend those who do right. [15]For it is God's will that by doing good you should silence the ignorant talk of foolish men. [16]Live as free men, but do not use your freedom as a cover-up for evil; live as servants of God. [17]Show proper respect to everyone: Love the brotherhood of believers, fear God, honor the king.

[18]Slaves, submit yourselves to your masters with all respect, not only to those who are good and considerate, but also to those who are harsh. [19]For it is commendable if a man bears up under the pain of unjust suffering because he is conscious of God. [20]But how is it to your credit if you receive a beating for doing wrong and endure it? But if you suffer for doing good and you endure it, this is commendable before God. [21]To this you were called, because Christ suffered for you, leaving you an example, that you should follow in his steps.

---

[a]16 Lev. 11:44,45; 19:2; 20:7   [b]22 Some early manuscripts *from a pure heart*   [c]25 Isaiah 40:6-8
[d]6 Isaiah 28:16   [e]7 Or *cornerstone*   [f]7 Psalm 118:22   [g]8 Isaiah 8:14

VERSE FOR THE DAY:	AUTHOR:	PASSAGE FOR THE DAY:
1 Peter 1:16	June Hunt	1 Peter 1:13–25

Living a Holy Life

HAVE you had difficulty with this Scripture verse: "Be holy, because I am holy" (Leviticus 11:44; 1 Peter 1:16)? Since most people think being holy is synonymous with being sinless, who could possibly be holy? It's unattainable . . . unimaginable!

A friend once said to me, "I know *holy* means 'set apart,' but I don't want to be set apart. That sounds like being in quarantine for having a constant case of measles!" Some people *do* think of a holy person as one who lives a monkish existence, praying twenty-three hours a day in order to avoid sin. Holiness, however, does not bring isolation but integration. With Christ in you, his character becomes a part of you so that his nature may be expressed through you. In other words, Christlikeness will come out of you *naturally*.

When I was little, my Uncle Jimmy walked me through his watermelon patch in Idabel, Oklahoma. Holding a tiny black seed he said, "These big melons grew from seeds just like this one." That seemed impossible to me! Yet eighty miles from Idabel is Hope, Arkansas, the town where something more "impossible" became reality. Young Jason Bright gave his watermelon seed proper care and the right environment to grow. The result? A world-record 260-pound watermelon! Watermelon seeds simply do what comes naturally to them—they grow. Their seeds are set apart by God for that purpose.

When you are set apart by God, holiness becomes natural. The Father is the gardener; Christ is the seed. With Christ in you, you will grow to be like him. It is explained in 1 John 3:9:

> No one who is born of God will continue to sin, because God's seed remains in him.

It is natural for the Lord not to sin. Therefore, with God's seed in you, it becomes increasingly natural for you not to sin. What seems impossible becomes possible. You will not become instantly sinless, but you will sin less and less and less.

God calls you holy. With his presence inside you, he will produce the impossible through you. Why settle for anything less?

Additional Scripture Readings:
Colossians 3:12–17; Hebrews 12:10–14

Go to page 1385 for your next devotional reading.

22"He committed no sin,
　and no deceit was found in his
　　mouth."*a*

23When they hurled their insults at him, he did not retaliate; when he suffered, he made no threats. Instead, he entrusted himself to him who judges justly. 24He himself bore our sins in his body on the tree, so that we might die to sins and live for righteousness; by his wounds you have been healed. 25For you were like sheep going astray, but now you have returned to the Shepherd and Overseer of your souls.

Wives and Husbands

3 Wives, in the same way be submissive to your husbands so that, if any of them do not believe the word, they may be won over without words by the behavior of their wives, 2when they see the purity and reverence of your lives. 3Your beauty should not come from outward adornment, such as braided hair and the wearing of gold jewelry and fine clothes. 4Instead, it should be that of your inner self, the unfading beauty of a gentle and quiet spirit, which is of great worth in God's sight. 5For this is the way the holy women of the past who put their hope in God used to make themselves beautiful. They were submissive to their own husbands, 6like Sarah, who obeyed Abraham and called him her master. You are her daughters if you do what is right and do not give way to fear.

7Husbands, in the same way be considerate as you live with your wives, and treat them with respect as the weaker partner and as heirs with you of the gracious gift of life, so that nothing will hinder your prayers.

Suffering for Doing Good

8Finally, all of you, live in harmony with one another; be sympathetic, love as brothers, be compassionate and humble. 9Do not repay evil with evil or insult with insult, but with blessing, because to this you were called so that you may inherit a blessing. 10For,

"Whoever would love life
　and see good days
must keep his tongue from evil
　and his lips from deceitful speech.
11He must turn from evil and do good;

he must seek peace and pursue it.
12For the eyes of the Lord are on the
　righteous
and his ears are attentive to their
　prayer,
but the face of the Lord is against
　those who do evil."*b*

13Who is going to harm you if you are eager to do good? 14But even if you should suffer for what is right, you are blessed. "Do not fear what they fear*c*; do not be frightened."*d* 15But in your hearts set apart Christ as Lord. Always be prepared to give an answer to everyone who asks you to give the reason for the hope that you have. But do this with gentleness and respect, 16keeping a clear conscience, so that those who speak maliciously against your good behavior in Christ may be ashamed of their slander. 17It is better, if it is God's will, to suffer for doing good than for doing evil. 18For Christ died for sins once for all, the righteous for the unrighteous, to bring you to God. He was put to death in the body but made alive by the Spirit, 19through whom*e* also he went and preached to the spirits in prison 20who disobeyed long ago when God waited patiently in the days of Noah while the ark was being built. In it only a few people, eight in all, were saved through water, 21and this water symbolizes baptism that now saves you also—not the removal of dirt from the body but the pledge*f* of a good conscience toward God. It saves you by the resurrection of Jesus Christ, 22who has gone into heaven and is at God's right hand—with angels, authorities and powers in submission to him.

Living for God

4 Therefore, since Christ suffered in his body, arm yourselves also with the same attitude, because he who has suffered in his body is done with sin. 2As a result, he does not live the rest of his earthly life for evil human desires, but rather for the will of God. 3For you have spent enough time in the past doing what pagans choose to do—living in debauchery, lust, drunkenness, orgies, carousing and detestable idolatry. 4They think it strange that you do not plunge with them into the same flood of dissipation, and they heap abuse on you. 5But they will have to give account to him who is ready

---

a22 Isaiah 53:9　　*b12* Psalm 34:12-16　　*c14* Or *not fear their threats*　　*d14* Isaiah 8:12
e18,19 Or *alive in the spirit,* 19*through which*　　*f21* Or *response*

VERSE FOR THE DAY:
1 Peter 3:1

AUTHOR:
Beverly LaHaye

PASSAGE FOR THE DAY:
1 Peter 3:1–6

So They May Be Won Over

DURING the span of wonderful years of ministry God has given my husband and me, it has been our joy to have helped many couples during times of marital difficulty. Sometimes they were helped by reading one of our books relating to their problem, but often help came through a personal counseling meeting.

One such meeting took place several years ago when a lovely Christian woman came to us with a troubled, broken heart. She was married to a man who had professed Jesus Christ years before but who had turned away from those beliefs. Her story revealed that he was conducting himself in a manner that was disobedient to God's Word, making her miserable also.

The natural reaction for many wives caught in these circumstances is to lash back and to shut her husband out of her life. This woman quickly learned that if she took matters into her own hands there would not be much need for communication. Her heart resisted his role as head of the home.

In her attempt to separate herself from her husband—even though they remained living together—she decided to join an evening Bible study just to get out of the house.

God began to work in her heart and impress upon her that she was disobeying him by the way she lived and conducted herself. She learned through study of the Word that submission to and love for her husband was an outgrowth of spiritual development and a close relationship with the Lord.

As this woman sat before us one evening, pouring out her heart to the Lord, she longed for a close relationship with both God and her husband. We read 1 Peter 3:1–6 to her and challenged her to obey the principles taught there.

Not every wife's story ends on such a happy note, but this lovely woman found that God could change her conduct and give her a gentle and quiet spirit. As a result, her husband changed and began to walk in obedience to God.

Additional Scripture Readings:
Ephesians 5:22–33; Titus 2:3–5

*Go to page 1386 for your next
devotional reading.*

VERSE FOR THE DAY:
1 Peter 5:10

AUTHOR:
Beth Donigan Seversen

PASSAGE FOR THE DAY:
1 Peter 5:1–11

Weathering the Showers

THE *Water Garden*, by Claude Monet, is one of my favorite paintings. You will find the original in an impressionist museum, de l'Orangerie, in Paris. It is painted in the round and hangs in a circular room. When you stand in the center of the room you are completely engulfed in a luxuriant water garden!

My print, hanging over the desk in my office, is only a small representation of the delightful, full-scale original. If you study the painting, one of the surprises you will find is that the major part of the canvas is covered in dark shades of black, blue and green. These rather drab colors stand in stark contrast to the delicate pastels. Actually, they serve to highlight the beautiful florals, which appear rich and striking upon the deep, dark waters. At first glance, your eyes are drawn to the colorful petals; then you realize that Monet painted the dark tones to enhance the lighter.

Monet's painting has much to remind me about the water garden of my life, and of its Artist. First, it encourages me that there is a purpose and design to my life, and that perhaps, at times, I focus too exclusively on the darker portions of my painting.

It also reminds me that my Lord, the Artist of my life, has intentionally allowed the blue, green, and, yes, sometimes even the gray and black hues to be brushed on my canvas for a reason. God uses these shadows to make my life richer. Often, when I look back on difficulties, such as my father's death, times when I have been misunderstood by friends or my expectations have been dashed, I can see, now, his handiwork creating a brilliance of color and beauty from pain and suffering. The Artist uses a multitude of techniques in our lives to help us become the people he created us to be.

Finally, I am reminded that just like the water lilies in Monet's masterpiece, God keeps the leaves and petals afloat through the muck, wind and rain that are part of the storms of life. Water gardens survive April showers and worse, and I will too, by God's help and grace.

Additional Scripture Readings:
Matthew 7:24–27; Mark 4:35–41

Go to page 1389 for your next devotional reading.

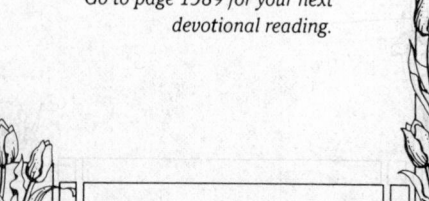

to judge the living and the dead. 6For this is the reason the gospel was preached even to those who are now dead, so that they might be judged according to men in regard to the body, but live according to God in regard to the spirit.

7The end of all things is near. Therefore be clear minded and self-controlled so that you can pray. 8Above all, love each other deeply, because love covers over a multitude of sins. 9Offer hospitality to one another without grumbling. 10Each one should use whatever gift he has received to serve others, faithfully administering God's grace in its various forms. 11If anyone speaks, he should do it as one speaking the very words of God. If anyone serves, he should do it with the strength God provides, so that in all things God may be praised through Jesus Christ. To him be the glory and the power for ever and ever. Amen.

Suffering for Being a Christian

12Dear friends, do not be surprised at the painful trial you are suffering, as though something strange were happening to you. 13But rejoice that you participate in the sufferings of Christ, so that you may be overjoyed when his glory is revealed. 14If you are insulted because of the name of Christ, you are blessed, for the Spirit of glory and of God rests on you. 15If you suffer, it should not be as a murderer or thief or any other kind of criminal, or even as a meddler. 16However, if you suffer as a Christian, do not be ashamed, but praise God that you bear that name. 17For it is time for judgment to begin with the family of God; and if it begins with us, what will the outcome be for those who do not obey the gospel of God? 18And,

"If it is hard for the righteous to be saved,
what will become of the ungodly and the sinner?"*a*

19So then, those who suffer according to God's will should commit themselves to their faithful Creator and continue to do good.

To Elders and Young Men

5 To the elders among you, I appeal as a fellow elder, a witness of Christ's sufferings and one who also will share in the glory to be revealed: 2Be shepherds of God's flock that is under your care, serving as overseers — not because you must, but because you are willing, as God wants you to be; not greedy for money, but eager to serve; 3not lording it over those entrusted to you, but being examples to the flock. 4And when the Chief Shepherd appears, you will receive the crown of glory that will never fade away.

5Young men, in the same way be submissive to those who are older. All of you, clothe yourselves with humility toward one another, because,

"God opposes the proud
    but gives grace to the humble."*b*

6Humble yourselves, therefore, under God's mighty hand, that he may lift you up in due time. 7Cast all your anxiety on him because he cares for you.

8Be self-controlled and alert. Your enemy the devil prowls around like a roaring lion looking for someone to devour. 9Resist him, standing firm in the faith, because you know that your brothers throughout the world are undergoing the same kind of sufferings.

10And the God of all grace, who called you to his eternal glory in Christ, after you have suffered a little while, will himself restore you and make you strong, firm and steadfast. 11To him be the power for ever and ever. Amen.

Final Greetings

12With the help of Silas,*c* whom I regard as a faithful brother, I have written to you briefly, encouraging you and testifying that this is the true grace of God. Stand fast in it.

13She who is in Babylon, chosen together with you, sends you her greetings, and so does my son Mark. 14Greet one another with a kiss of love.

Peace to all of you who are in Christ.

---

a18 Prov. 11:31   *b5* Prov. 3:34   *c12* Greek *Silvanus,* a variant of *Silas*

PETER writes a second letter because false teachers are troubling the church and disturbing the faith of some by their heresy, immorality and greed. He wants Christians to grow in the knowledge of the truth of God's Word. As you read this book, remember that God will eventually win the battle against false teaching, and promise the Lord that you will study to increase your knowledge of the Bible.

2 PETER

1 Simon Peter, a servant and apostle of Jesus Christ,

To those who through the righteousness of our God and Savior Jesus Christ have received a faith as precious as ours:

²Grace and peace be yours in abundance through the knowledge of God and of Jesus our Lord.

Making One's Calling and Election Sure

³His divine power has given us everything we need for life and godliness through our knowledge of him who called us by his own glory and goodness. ⁴Through these he has given us his very great and precious promises, so that through them you may participate in the divine nature and escape the corruption in the world caused by evil desires.

⁵For this very reason, make every effort to add to your faith goodness; and to goodness, knowledge; ⁶and to knowledge, self-control; and to self-control, perseverance; and to perseverance, godliness; ⁷and to godliness, brotherly kindness; and to brotherly kindness, love. ⁸For if you possess these qualities in increasing measure, they will keep you from being ineffective and unproductive in your knowledge of our Lord Jesus Christ. ⁹But if anyone does not have them, he is nearsighted and blind, and has forgotten that he has been cleansed from his past sins.

¹⁰Therefore, my brothers, be all the more eager to make your calling and elec-

tion sure. For if you do these things, you will never fall, ¹¹and you will receive a rich welcome into the eternal kingdom of our Lord and Savior Jesus Christ.

Prophecy of Scripture

¹²So I will always remind you of these things, even though you know them and are firmly established in the truth you now have. ¹³I think it is right to refresh your memory as long as I live in the tent of this body, ¹⁴because I know that I will soon put it aside, as our Lord Jesus Christ has made clear to me. ¹⁵And I will make every effort to see that after my departure you will always be able to remember these things.

¹⁶We did not follow cleverly invented stories when we told you about the power and coming of our Lord Jesus Christ, but we were eyewitnesses of his majesty. ¹⁷For he received honor and glory from God the Father when the voice came to him from the Majestic Glory, saying, "This is my Son, whom I love; with him I

FRIDAY

VERSE FOR THE DAY:	AUTHOR:	PASSAGE FOR THE DAY:
2 Peter 1:3	Jo Ann Lemon	2 Peter 1:3–11

Self-sacrifice

THERE were once two porcupines who lived in Alaska. Desiring to get warm, they drew close to each other. As they did, they needled one another. It hurt so much that they pulled apart. But when they did, they got cold again, so they drew close once more, and hurt each other as before. Their predicament—they were either cold or hurting.

All too often this is the situation even in Christian homes. Personality differences are like the quills of the porcupines. They can get tangled and cause hurt. We must work at our relationships so that we will demonstrate the Christlike qualities of love, compassion, self-sacrifice and a forgiving spirit. The motto for our homes should be: "Be completely humble and gentle; be patient, bearing with one another in love" (Ephesians 4:2).

Love demonstrates itself in action. Have we done something today to demonstrate our love for our families? Love takes pleasure in its object. Jesus' example of love and compassion teaches us that it is possible for these qualities to be part of our Christian homes.

Self-sacrifice is against our human nature, yet it should be part of our "new nature." If each of us had an attitude of self-sacrifice, what a change would come about in the atmosphere of our homes. Self-sacrifice is total unselfishness.

Loving unselfishly does not mean making the least of ourselves but making the most of someone else. We view the other person through the eyes of Jesus.

This thought can transform relationships in our homes, especially with our unsaved loved ones!

Additional Scripture Readings:
Romans 12:9–13; 1 John 3:11–18

Go to page 1391 for your next devotional reading.

am well pleased."*a* 18We ourselves heard this voice that came from heaven when we were with him on the sacred mountain.

19And we have the word of the prophets made more certain, and you will do well to pay attention to it, as to a light shining in a dark place, until the day dawns and the morning star rises in your hearts. 20Above all, you must understand that no prophecy of Scripture came about by the prophet's own interpretation. 21For prophecy never had its origin in the will of man, but men spoke from God as they were carried along by the Holy Spirit.

False Teachers and Their Destruction

2 But there were also false prophets among the people, just as there will be false teachers among you. They will secretly introduce destructive heresies, even denying the sovereign Lord who bought them — bringing swift destruction on themselves. 2Many will follow their shameful ways and will bring the way of truth into disrepute. 3In their greed these teachers will exploit you with stories they have made up. Their condemnation has long been hanging over them, and their destruction has not been sleeping.

4For if God did not spare angels when they sinned, but sent them to hell,*b* putting them into gloomy dungeons*c* to be held for judgment; 5if he did not spare the ancient world when he brought the flood on its ungodly people, but protected Noah, a preacher of righteousness, and seven others; 6if he condemned the cities of Sodom and Gomorrah by burning them to ashes, and made them an example of what is going to happen to the ungodly; 7and if he rescued Lot, a righteous man, who was distressed by the filthy lives of lawless men 8(for that righteous man, living among them day after day, was tormented in his righteous soul by the lawless deeds he saw and heard)— 9if this is so, then the Lord knows how to rescue godly men from trials and to hold the unrighteous for the day of judgment, while continuing their punishment.*d* 10This is especially true of those who follow the corrupt desire of the sinful nature*e* and despise authority.

Bold and arrogant, these men are not afraid to slander celestial beings; 11yet even angels, although they are stronger and more powerful, do not bring slanderous accusations against such beings in the presence of the Lord. 12But these men blaspheme in matters they do not understand. They are like brute beasts, creatures of instinct, born only to be caught and destroyed, and like beasts they too will perish.

13They will be paid back with harm for the harm they have done. Their idea of pleasure is to carouse in broad daylight. They are blots and blemishes, reveling in their pleasures while they feast with you.*f* 14With eyes full of adultery, they never stop sinning; they seduce the unstable; they are experts in greed — an accursed brood! 15They have left the straight way and wandered off to follow the way of Balaam son of Beor, who loved the wages of wickedness. 16But he was rebuked for his wrongdoing by a donkey — a beast without speech — who spoke with a man's voice and restrained the prophet's madness.

17These men are springs without water and mists driven by a storm. Blackest darkness is reserved for them. 18For they mouth empty, boastful words and, by appealing to the lustful desires of sinful human nature, they entice people who are just escaping from those who live in error. 19They promise them freedom, while they themselves are slaves of depravity — for a man is a slave to whatever has mastered him. 20If they have escaped the corruption of the world by knowing our Lord and Savior Jesus Christ and are again entangled in it and overcome, they are worse off at the end than they were at the beginning. 21It would have been better for them not to have known the way of righteousness, than to have known it and then to turn their backs on the sacred command that was passed on to them. 22Of them the proverbs are true: "A dog returns to its vomit,"*g* and, "A sow that is washed goes back to her wallowing in the mud."

The Day of the Lord

3 Dear friends, this is now my second letter to you. I have written both of them as reminders to stimulate you to wholesome thinking. 2I want you to recall the words spoken in the past by the holy

---

a17 Matt. 17:5; Mark 9:7; Luke 9:35   *b4* Greek *Tartarus*   *c4* Some manuscripts *into chains of darkness*   *d9* Or *unrighteous for punishment until the day of judgment*   *e10* Or *the flesh*   *f13* Some manuscripts *in their love feasts*   *g22* Prov. 26:11

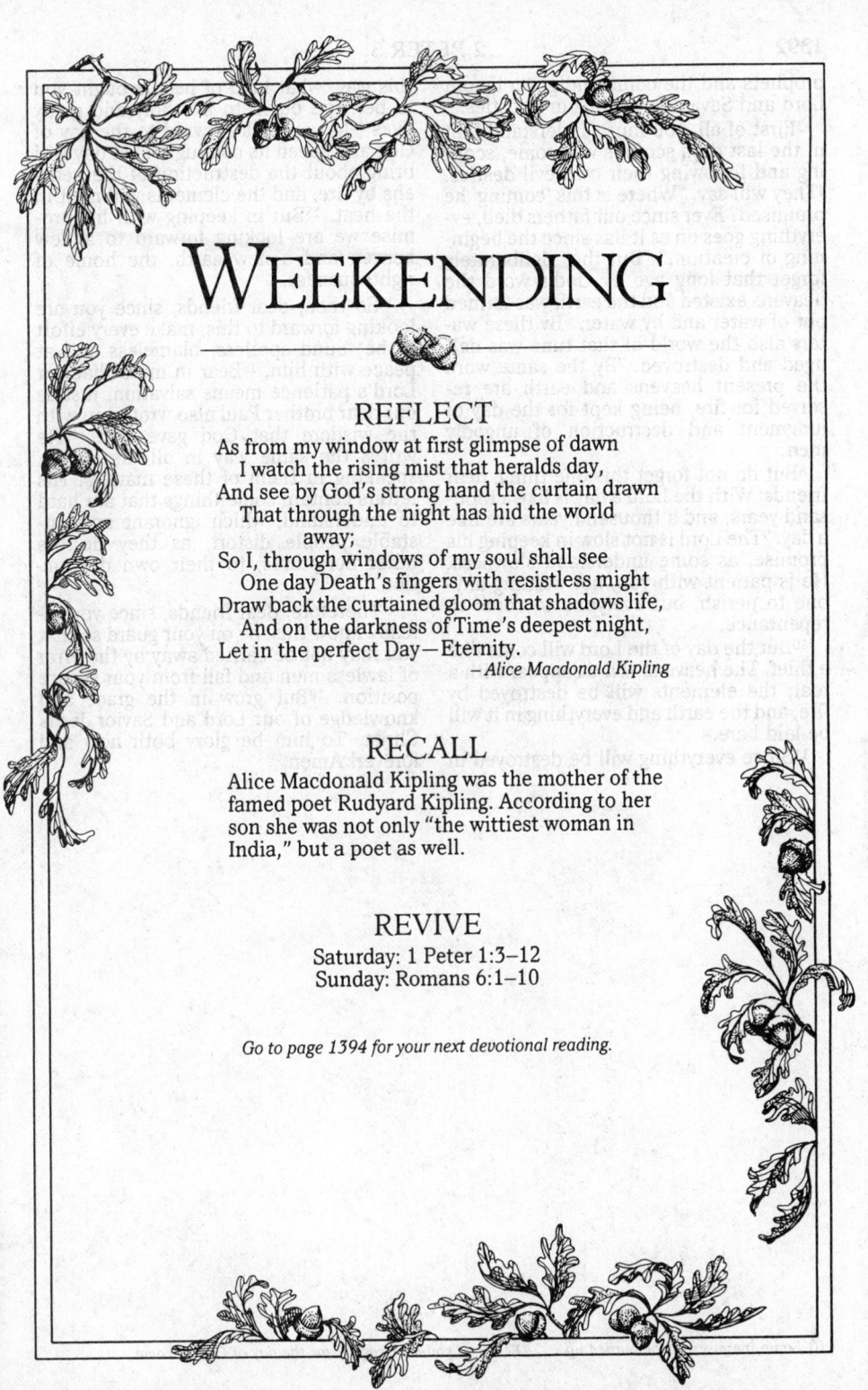

WEEKENDING

REFLECT

As from my window at first glimpse of dawn
I watch the rising mist that heralds day,
And see by God's strong hand the curtain drawn
That through the night has hid the world
away;
So I, through windows of my soul shall see
One day Death's fingers with resistless might
Draw back the curtained gloom that shadows life,
And on the darkness of Time's deepest night,
Let in the perfect Day—Eternity.

– Alice Macdonald Kipling

RECALL

Alice Macdonald Kipling was the mother of the
famed poet Rudyard Kipling. According to her
son she was not only "the wittiest woman in
India," but a poet as well.

REVIVE

Saturday: 1 Peter 1:3–12
Sunday: Romans 6:1–10

Go to page 1394 for your next devotional reading.

prophets and the command given by our Lord and Savior through your apostles.

³First of all, you must understand that in the last days scoffers will come, scoffing and following their own evil desires. ⁴They will say, "Where is this 'coming' he promised? Ever since our fathers died, everything goes on as it has since the beginning of creation." ⁵But they deliberately forget that long ago by God's word the heavens existed and the earth was formed out of water and by water. ⁶By these waters also the world of that time was deluged and destroyed. ⁷By the same word the present heavens and earth are reserved for fire, being kept for the day of judgment and destruction of ungodly men.

⁸But do not forget this one thing, dear friends: With the Lord a day is like a thousand years, and a thousand years are like a day. ⁹The Lord is not slow in keeping his promise, as some understand slowness. He is patient with you, not wanting anyone to perish, but everyone to come to repentance.

¹⁰But the day of the Lord will come like a thief. The heavens will disappear with a roar; the elements will be destroyed by fire, and the earth and everything in it will be laid bare.ᵃ

¹¹Since everything will be destroyed in this way, what kind of people ought you to be? You ought to live holy and godly lives ¹²as you look forward to the day of God and speed its coming.ᵇ That day will bring about the destruction of the heavens by fire, and the elements will melt in the heat. ¹³But in keeping with his promise we are looking forward to a new heaven and a new earth, the home of righteousness.

¹⁴So then, dear friends, since you are looking forward to this, make every effort to be found spotless, blameless and at peace with him. ¹⁵Bear in mind that our Lord's patience means salvation, just as our dear brother Paul also wrote you with the wisdom that God gave him. ¹⁶He writes the same way in all his letters, speaking in them of these matters. His letters contain some things that are hard to understand, which ignorant and unstable people distort, as they do the other Scriptures, to their own destruction.

¹⁷Therefore, dear friends, since you already know this, be on your guard so that you may not be carried away by the error of lawless men and fall from your secure position. ¹⁸But grow in the grace and knowledge of our Lord and Savior Jesus Christ. To him be glory both now and forever! Amen.

ᵃ10 Some manuscripts *be burned up*   ᵇ12 Or *as you wait eagerly for the day of God to come*

*J*OHN *writes this first letter to emphasize some of the same themes as his Gospel (such as "walking in the light," "knowing the truth," and "loving one another"). He does so because antichrists are promoting false views of the Son of God. As you read this book, realize how much God wants you to fight sin, to love others and to believe in the true Jesus for eternal life.*

1 JOHN

The Word of Life

1 That which was from the beginning, which we have heard, which we have seen with our eyes, which we have looked at and our hands have touched—this we proclaim concerning the Word of life. ²The life appeared; we have seen it and testify to it, and we proclaim to you the eternal life, which was with the Father and has appeared to us. ³We proclaim to you what we have seen and heard, so that you also may have fellowship with us. And our fellowship is with the Father and with his Son, Jesus Christ. ⁴We write this to make our*ᵃ* joy complete.

Walking in the Light

⁵This is the message we have heard from him and declare to you: God is light; in him there is no darkness at all. ⁶If we claim to have fellowship with him yet walk in the darkness, we lie and do not live by the truth. ⁷But if we walk in the light, as he is in the light, we have fellowship with one another, and the blood of Jesus, his Son, purifies us from all*ᵇ* sin.

⁸If we claim to be without sin, we deceive ourselves and the truth is not in us. ⁹If we confess our sins, he is faithful and just and will forgive us our sins and purify us from all unrighteousness. ¹⁰If we claim we have not sinned, we make him out to be a liar and his word has no place in our lives.

2 My dear children, I write this to you so that you will not sin. But if anybody does sin, we have one who speaks to

ᵃ4 Some manuscripts your   ᵇ7 Or every

VERSE FOR THE DAY:
1 John 1:3–4

AUTHOR:
Rosemary Jensen

PASSAGE FOR THE DAY:
1 John 1:1–10

Telling Brings Fellowship

IN 1 John 1:3–4 we see John eager to tell his friends and associates what he knows of Jesus—what he has "seen and heard." It seems that he could hardly wait to tell them, because by telling them what he knew of Jesus he would promote fellowship with his friends. True fellowship was what John wanted, and it is what we want too. Fellowship is not just camaraderie; it is what two or more people experience when they have the same goals and desires, when they think alike and communicate in such a way as to actually enter into the other's experience.

John wanted this kind of communication with his friends. It was as if he was saying to them, "Let me tell you what I have seen and heard of Jesus Christ *so that* we may have the same mind about him, the same desire to know him better, the same experience of him." Then he goes on to say that we will have this fellowship because we have fellowship with the same Father and the same Son, Jesus Christ. We fellowship with God (the Father and the Son), and he brings us into fellowship with each other. He is the basis for our fellowship because together we share his life.

Are you eager to declare to your family and friends what you have "seen and heard" of Jesus Christ so that you may enter into true fellowship with them? Telling them about Jesus (and also listening to them tell you!) is the most fulfilling experience you can have with other human beings. Exchanging the knowledge of Jesus Christ with others will bring you greater joy than you can imagine. At least that's what John says in 1 John 1:4: "We write this to make our [and your] joy complete." *Telling brings fellowship and fellowship brings joy.*

Talking with others about Jesus is always risky. They may label you a fanatic. You may risk turning them off. But it is worth the risk, because it will bring that complete joy you desperately desire.

Additional Scripture Readings:
Galatians 2:8–9; 3 John 3–4

Go to page 1397 for your next devotional reading.

the Father in our defense—Jesus Christ, the Righteous One. [2]He is the atoning sacrifice for our sins, and not only for ours but also for[a] the sins of the whole world.

[3]We know that we have come to know him if we obey his commands. [4]The man who says, "I know him," but does not do what he commands is a liar, and the truth is not in him. [5]But if anyone obeys his word, God's love[b] is truly made complete in him. This is how we know we are in him: [6]Whoever claims to live in him must walk as Jesus did.

[7]Dear friends, I am not writing you a new command but an old one, which you have had since the beginning. This old command is the message you have heard. [8]Yet I am writing you a new command; its truth is seen in him and you, because the darkness is passing and the true light is already shining.

[9]Anyone who claims to be in the light but hates his brother is still in the darkness. [10]Whoever loves his brother lives in the light, and there is nothing in him[c] to make him stumble. [11]But whoever hates his brother is in the darkness and walks around in the darkness; he does not know where he is going, because the darkness has blinded him.

[12]I write to you, dear children,
  because your sins have been
    forgiven on account of his
    name.
[13]I write to you, fathers,
  because you have known him who
    is from the beginning.
I write to you, young men,
  because you have overcome the evil
    one.
I write to you, dear children,
  because you have known the
    Father.
[14]I write to you, fathers,
  because you have known him who
    is from the beginning.
I write to you, young men,
  because you are strong,
  and the word of God lives in you,
  and you have overcome the evil
    one.

Do Not Love the World

[15]Do not love the world or anything in the world. If anyone loves the world, the love of the Father is not in him. [16]For ev-

erything in the world—the cravings of sinful man, the lust of his eyes and the boasting of what he has and does—comes not from the Father but from the world. [17]The world and its desires pass away, but the man who does the will of God lives forever.

Warning Against Antichrists

[18]Dear children, this is the last hour; and as you have heard that the antichrist is coming, even now many antichrists have come. This is how we know it is the last hour. [19]They went out from us, but they did not really belong to us. For if they had belonged to us, they would have remained with us; but their going showed that none of them belonged to us.

[20]But you have an anointing from the Holy One, and all of you know the truth.[d] [21]I do not write to you because you do not know the truth, but because you do know it and because no lie comes from the truth. [22]Who is the liar? It is the man who denies that Jesus is the Christ. Such a man is the antichrist—he denies the Father and the Son. [23]No one who denies the Son has the Father; whoever acknowledges the Son has the Father also.

[24]See that what you have heard from the beginning remains in you. If it does, you also will remain in the Son and in the Father. [25]And this is what he promised us—even eternal life.

[26]I am writing these things to you about those who are trying to lead you astray. [27]As for you, the anointing you received from him remains in you, and you do not need anyone to teach you. But as his anointing teaches you about all things and as that anointing is real, not counterfeit—just as it has taught you, remain in him.

Children of God

[28]And now, dear children, continue in him, so that when he appears we may be confident and unashamed before him at his coming.

[29]If you know that he is righteous, you know that everyone who does what is right has been born of him.

3 How great is the love the Father has lavished on us, that we should be called children of God! And that is what we are! The reason the world does not know us is that it did not know him. [2]Dear

---

[a]2 Or *He is the one who turns aside God's wrath, taking away our sins, and not only ours but also*
[b]5 Or *word, love for God*   [c]10 Or *it*   [d]20 Some manuscripts *and you know all things*

friends, now we are children of God, and what we will be has not yet been made known. But we know that when he appears,[a] we shall be like him, for we shall see him as he is. ³Everyone who has this hope in him purifies himself, just as he is pure.

⁴Everyone who sins breaks the law; in fact, sin is lawlessness. ⁵But you know that he appeared so that he might take away our sins. And in him is no sin. ⁶No one who lives in him keeps on sinning. No one who continues to sin has either seen him or known him.

⁷Dear children, do not let anyone lead you astray. He who does what is right is righteous, just as he is righteous. ⁸He who does what is sinful is of the devil, because the devil has been sinning from the beginning. The reason the Son of God appeared was to destroy the devil's work. ⁹No one who is born of God will continue to sin, because God's seed remains in him; he cannot go on sinning, because he has been born of God. ¹⁰This is how we know who the children of God are and who the children of the devil are: Anyone who does not do what is right is not a child of God; nor is anyone who does not love his brother.

Love One Another

¹¹This is the message you heard from the beginning: We should love one another. ¹²Do not be like Cain, who belonged to the evil one and murdered his brother. And why did he murder him? Because his own actions were evil and his brother's were righteous. ¹³Do not be surprised, my brothers, if the world hates you. ¹⁴We know that we have passed from death to life, because we love our brothers. Anyone who does not love remains in death. ¹⁵Anyone who hates his brother is a murderer, and you know that no murderer has eternal life in him.

¹⁶This is how we know what love is: Jesus Christ laid down his life for us. And we ought to lay down our lives for our brothers. ¹⁷If anyone has material possessions and sees his brother in need but has no pity on him, how can the love of God be in him? ¹⁸Dear children, let us not love with words or tongue but with actions and in truth. ¹⁹This then is how we know that we belong to the truth, and how we set our hearts at rest in his presence

²⁰whenever our hearts condemn us. For God is greater than our hearts, and he knows everything.

²¹Dear friends, if our hearts do not condemn us, we have confidence before God ²²and receive from him anything we ask, because we obey his commands and do what pleases him. ²³And this is his command: to believe in the name of his Son, Jesus Christ, and to love one another as he commanded us. ²⁴Those who obey his commands live in him, and he in them. And this is how we know that he lives in us: We know it by the Spirit he gave us.

Test the Spirits

4 Dear friends, do not believe every spirit, but test the spirits to see whether they are from God, because many false prophets have gone out into the world. ²This is how you can recognize the Spirit of God: Every spirit that acknowledges that Jesus Christ has come in the flesh is from God, ³but every spirit that does not acknowledge Jesus is not from God. This is the spirit of the antichrist, which you have heard is coming and even now is already in the world.

⁴You, dear children, are from God and have overcome them, because the one who is in you is greater than the one who is in the world. ⁵They are from the world and therefore speak from the viewpoint of the world, and the world listens to them. ⁶We are from God, and whoever knows God listens to us; but whoever is not from God does not listen to us. This is how we recognize the Spirit[b] of truth and the spirit of falsehood.

God's Love and Ours

⁷Dear friends, let us love one another, for love comes from God. Everyone who loves has been born of God and knows God. ⁸Whoever does not love does not know God, because God is love. ⁹This is how God showed his love among us: He sent his one and only Son[c] into the world that we might live through him. ¹⁰This is love: not that we loved God, but that he loved us and sent his Son as an atoning sacrifice for[d] our sins. ¹¹Dear friends, since God so loved us, we also ought to love one another. ¹²No one has ever seen God; but if we love one another, God lives in us and his love is made complete in us. ¹³We know that we live in him and he

VERSE FOR THE DAY:
1 John 5:4

AUTHOR:
Luci Swindoll

PASSAGE FOR THE DAY:
1 John 5:1–12

Real Power

THIS verse, 1 John 5:4, has been a favorite of mine for years; but only lately have I come to realize that the verse is not so much about faith as it is about power. It's not an obvious power like that displayed by bulldozing through a riverbed in a GMC truck or by the ability to lift weights. It's a quiet power, like that inherent in a seed, which causes a plant to pop out of the ground and burst into flower, or in the meaningful words that fly across the airwaves altering convictions and changing hearts for all eternity.

Power. Have you ever been so mad at a person that you wanted to walk out and never talk to her again, but decided instead to hang in there, communicate, and make it right? Or, have you felt tremendously inadequate for an assigned task, found a Scripture of encouragement, and come out a winner? Have you invested love and concern into a person who was basically unlovable and witnessed a transformation in her behavior—primarily because of your sensitivity and acceptance? That's the kind of power I'm talking about.

This verse says that we, the children of God, actually can overcome the world by faithfully believing that we have God's power to effect change. Doesn't that make you want to try it in every area of your life? It does me!

I want to quit worrying about money. I want to lose weight. I want to be a kinder, more gentle person. I want to be supportive, not envious. I want to sing more and gripe less. I want to look for the positive, not dwell on the negative. I want to reach out to those who need me, not wait for them to come to me. I want to relax and laugh. I want to live fully.

Shall I go on? You make your own list, remembering that by faith you've already overcome the world. Claim that. When God commissions, he empowers. That power is absolutely yours, by faith. Take it and head out. The victories are just beginning.

Additional Scripture Readings:
Romans 8:31–39; 1 Corinthians 15:57–58

Go to page 1400 for your next devotional reading.

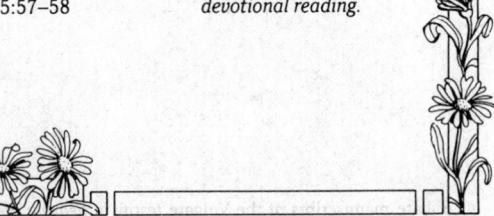

in us, because he has given us of his Spirit. ¹⁴And we have seen and testify that the Father has sent his Son to be the Savior of the world. ¹⁵If anyone acknowledges that Jesus is the Son of God, God lives in him and he in God. ¹⁶And so we know and rely on the love God has for us.

God is love. Whoever lives in love lives in God, and God in him. ¹⁷In this way, love is made complete among us so that we will have confidence on the day of judgment, because in this world we are like him. ¹⁸There is no fear in love. But perfect love drives out fear, because fear has to do with punishment. The one who fears is not made perfect in love.

¹⁹We love because he first loved us. ²⁰If anyone says, "I love God," yet hates his brother, he is a liar. For anyone who does not love his brother, whom he has seen, cannot love God, whom he has not seen. ²¹And he has given us this command: Whoever loves God must also love his brother.

Faith in the Son of God

5 Everyone who believes that Jesus is the Christ is born of God, and everyone who loves the father loves his child as well. ²This is how we know that we love the children of God: by loving God and carrying out his commands. ³This is love for God: to obey his commands. And his commands are not burdensome, ⁴for everyone born of God overcomes the world. This is the victory that has overcome the world, even our faith. ⁵Who is it that overcomes the world? Only he who believes that Jesus is the Son of God.

⁶This is the one who came by water and blood—Jesus Christ. He did not come by water only, but by water and blood. And it is the Spirit who testifies, because the Spirit is the truth. ⁷For there are three that testify: ⁸the*ᵃ* Spirit, the water and the blood; and the three are in agreement. ⁹We accept man's testimony, but God's testimony is greater because it is the testimony of God, which he has given about his Son. ¹⁰Anyone who believes in the Son of God has this testimony in his heart. Anyone who does not believe God has made him out to be a liar, because he has not believed the testimony God has given about his Son. ¹¹And this is the testimony: God has given us eternal life, and this life is in his Son. ¹²He who has the Son has life; he who does not have the Son of God does not have life.

Concluding Remarks

¹³I write these things to you who believe in the name of the Son of God so that you may know that you have eternal life. ¹⁴This is the confidence we have in approaching God: that if we ask anything according to his will, he hears us. ¹⁵And if we know that he hears us—whatever we ask—we know that we have what we asked of him.

¹⁶If anyone sees his brother commit a sin that does not lead to death, he should pray and God will give him life. I refer to those whose sin does not lead to death. There is a sin that leads to death. I am not saying that he should pray about that. ¹⁷All wrongdoing is sin, and there is sin that does not lead to death.

¹⁸We know that anyone born of God does not continue to sin; the one who was born of God keeps him safe, and the evil one cannot harm him. ¹⁹We know that we are children of God, and that the whole world is under the control of the evil one. ²⁰We know also that the Son of God has come and has given us understanding, so that we may know him who is true. And we are in him who is true—even in his Son Jesus Christ. He is the true God and eternal life.

²¹Dear children, keep yourselves from idols.

ᵃ7,8 Late manuscripts of the Vulgate *testify in heaven: the Father, the Word and the Holy Spirit, and these three are one. 8And there are three that testify on earth: the* (not found in any Greek manuscript before the sixteenth century)

JOHN writes this second letter to warn the church to stand firm against false teachers and to keep loving other Christians. As you read this book, learn how to stand up for your Lord whenever you encounter false teachers.

2 JOHN

[1]The elder,

To the chosen lady and her children, whom I love in the truth—and not I only, but also all who know the truth— [2]because of the truth, which lives in us and will be with us forever:

[3]Grace, mercy and peace from God the Father and from Jesus Christ, the Father's Son, will be with us in truth and love.

[4]It has given me great joy to find some of your children walking in the truth, just as the Father commanded us. [5]And now, dear lady, I am not writing you a new command but one we have had from the beginning. I ask that we love one another. [6]And this is love: that we walk in obedience to his commands. As you have heard from the beginning, his command is that you walk in love.

[7]Many deceivers, who do not acknowledge Jesus Christ as coming in the flesh, have gone out into the world. Any such person is the deceiver and the antichrist. [8]Watch out that you do not lose what you have worked for, but that you may be rewarded fully. [9]Anyone who runs ahead and does not continue in the teaching of Christ does not have God; whoever continues in the teaching has both the Father and the Son. [10]If anyone comes to you and does not bring this teaching, do not take him into your house or welcome him. [11]Anyone who welcomes him shares in his wicked work.

[12]I have much to write to you, but I do not want to use paper and ink. Instead, I hope to visit you and talk with you face to face, so that our joy may be complete.

[13]The children of your chosen sister send their greetings.

VERSE FOR THE DAY:	AUTHOR:	PASSAGE FOR THE DAY:
2 John 1,13	*Ruth A. Tucker*	2 John 1–13

Chosen Ladies

WHO was this "chosen lady" who merited a letter from the apostle John? Where was she from? What was her role in the ministry? How did she come to faith in Christ? How often we wish the Bible offered more details about individuals and events, and in this letter we are left to wonder about an unnamed, unidentified woman and her "chosen sister." Scholars have speculated that these two women were leaders of house churches and that the children mentioned were their spiritual children. As such they may have had an important role in the foundational growth of the early church.

In one sense, it is their lack of identity that allows them to better represent the countless "chosen ladies" from around the world who have faithfully served the Lord through the centuries—women whose names have been lost in the annals of history.

I often wonder where I would be today were it not for two "chosen ladies." Miss Salthammer and Miss Cowan moved to my rural community in northern Wisconsin several years before I was born, and out of their sacrificial church-planting ministry came the Green Grove Alliance Church.

When I was growing up in that little country church, the two women had long since packed their bags and moved on to plant other churches. I know of them through prayer requests offered on their behalf and through their occasional return visits to teach vacation Bible school. As kids, we sometimes laughed at the way they dressed, and we told jokes about how they were paid with a load of potatoes or turnips instead of money. I later learned that when Miss Cowan died she was buried in a pauper's grave.

They were very ordinary women whose span of years has ended and whose names will soon be forgotten. But their ministry lives on through the generations of their spiritual children. They were chosen ladies.

Additional Scripture Readings:
Galatians 6:7–10; Revelation 14:12–13

Go to page 1402 for your next devotional reading.

JOHN writes this third letter to commend a church leader for his hospitality and to warn against another one who is unfriendly and even cruel. As you read this book, think how you can act as a friend toward other Christians.

3 JOHN

¹The elder,

To my dear friend Gaius, whom I love in the truth.

²Dear friend, I pray that you may enjoy good health and that all may go well with you, even as your soul is getting along well. ³It gave me great joy to have some brothers come and tell about your faithfulness to the truth and how you continue to walk in the truth. ⁴I have no greater joy than to hear that my children are walking in the truth.

⁵Dear friend, you are faithful in what you are doing for the brothers, even though they are strangers to you. ⁶They have told the church about your love. You will do well to send them on their way in a manner worthy of God. ⁷It was for the sake of the Name that they went out, receiving no help from the pagans. ⁸We ought therefore to show hospitality to such men so that we may work together for the truth.

⁹I wrote to the church, but Diotrephes, who loves to be first, will have nothing to do with us. ¹⁰So if I come, I will call attention to what he is doing, gossiping maliciously about us. Not satisfied with that, he refuses to welcome the brothers. He also stops those who want to do so and puts them out of the church.

¹¹Dear friend, do not imitate what is evil but what is good. Anyone who does what is good is from God. Anyone who does what is evil has not seen God. ¹²Demetrius is well spoken of by everyone —and even by the truth itself. We also speak well of him, and you know that our testimony is true.

¹³I have much to write you, but I do not want to do so with pen and ink. ¹⁴I hope to see you soon, and we will talk face to face.

Peace to you. The friends here send their greetings. Greet the friends there by name.

VERSE FOR THE DAY:
3 John 4

AUTHOR:
Susan L. Lenzkes

PASSAGE FOR THE DAY:
3 John 1–14

My Boy

I LOOK at the shiny-shaggy hair
and round, blue-gray eyes;
the small pink tongue struggling
impatiently against tiny white teeth
to form a word,
to convey an exciting new-born thought;
the broad little boy hand
covered with dirt, reaching
to touch my cheek;
and suddenly I realize
the astounding responsibilities
that are mine before that hand
expands to a man's hand.
O God,
hold my son's hand while he crosses
the danger-filled street to manhood.

This was to be my stay-at-home-and-get-a-few-things-done day. That would be just fine, except for one thing: I have a toddler who wants to help.

I finish the washing, and he struggles the piles of clean clothes toward their dresser drawers. I suppose a hundred years from now I won't care that they started the trip neatly folded.

I sweep the floor, and he insists on helping me by emptying the dustpan. In the overall scheme of things, I suppose the fact that he dumped the dirt back onto the floor is relatively unimportant.

I begin mixing ingredients for yeast rolls, and he insists on adding the flour. If I look at the situation optimistically, unbleached white is a good color on me.

I do know he's really trying, Lord. And I know he needs practice to learn. But it would truly be so much easier to simply do it myself.

I watch, filled with apprehension, as he teeters toward me, chubby hands cupping fragile eggs, and I'm suddenly aware that you, God, have entrusted me with the fragile life of this child. Guide me as I help my little helper become your man.

Additional Scripture Readings:
Deuteronomy 6:6–7; Luke 17:1–2

*Go to page 1404 for your next
devotional reading.*

*J*UDE (a brother of Jesus and James) writes this short letter to warn Christians against false teachers in the church and to urge them to strengthen their faith and love. As you read this book, begin to grow in faith and love by depending on the Father, Son, and Holy Spirit.

JUDE

¹Jude, a servant of Jesus Christ and a brother of James,

To those who have been called, who are loved by God the Father and kept by*ᵃ* Jesus Christ:

²Mercy, peace and love be yours in abundance.

The Sin and Doom of Godless Men

³Dear friends, although I was very eager to write to you about the salvation we share, I felt I had to write and urge you to contend for the faith that was once for all entrusted to the saints. ⁴For certain men whose condemnation was written about*ᵇ* long ago have secretly slipped in among you. They are godless men, who change the grace of our God into a license for immorality and deny Jesus Christ our only Sovereign and Lord.

⁵Though you already know all this, I want to remind you that the Lord*ᶜ* delivered his people out of Egypt, but later destroyed those who did not believe. ⁶And the angels who did not keep their positions of authority but abandoned their own home—these he has kept in darkness, bound with everlasting chains for judgment on the great Day. ⁷In a similar way, Sodom and Gomorrah and the surrounding towns gave themselves up to sexual immorality and perversion. They serve as an example of those who suffer the punishment of eternal fire.

⁸In the very same way, these dreamers pollute their own bodies, reject authority and slander celestial beings. ⁹But even the archangel Michael, when he was disputing with the devil about the body of Moses, did not dare to bring a slanderous accusation against him, but said, "The

ᵃ1 Or *for; or in Jesus*   *ᵇ4* Or *men who were marked out for condemnation*   *ᶜ5* Some early manuscripts

Lord rebuke you!" ¹⁰Yet these men speak abusively against whatever they do not understand; and what things they do understand by instinct, like unreasoning animals—these are the very things that destroy them.

¹¹Woe to them! They have taken the way of Cain; they have rushed for profit into Balaam's error; they have been destroyed in Korah's rebellion.

¹²These men are blemishes at your love feasts, eating with you without the slightest qualm—shepherds who feed only themselves. They are clouds without rain, blown along by the wind; autumn trees, without fruit and uprooted—twice dead. ¹³They are wild waves of the sea, foaming up their shame; wandering stars, for whom blackest darkness has been reserved forever.

¹⁴Enoch, the seventh from Adam, prophesied about these men: "See, the Lord is coming with thousands upon thousands of his holy ones ¹⁵to judge everyone, and to convict all the ungodly of all the ungodly acts they have done in the ungodly way, and of all the harsh words ungodly sinners have spoken against him." ¹⁶These men are grumblers and faultfinders; they follow their own evil de-

FRIDAY

VERSE FOR THE DAY:
Jude 21

AUTHOR:
Ruth Senter

PASSAGE FOR THE DAY:
Jude 17–23

Obstacles and Opportunities

THE story is told of an old Scottish fisherman who was having afternoon tea with some friends in a little tearoom by the sea. As he was describing some of his fishing exploits of the day, his hand accidentally knocked over his cup of tea. An ugly, brown tea stain appeared on the freshly whitewashed wall beside him.

"Never mind about the stain," said a friend as he rose from his chair and drew from his pocket a brown crayon. There emerged from that ugly, brown tea stain a magnificent stag with antlers spread and back arched. The friend of the fisherman was one of England's most famous painters.

Life is full of ugly tea stains that splash against whitewashed walls. Reality often seems to be more obstacle than opportunity, more pain than pleasure, more chaos than calm, more hurt than happiness, more tension than tenderness. But if I interpret Romans 8:28 correctly, I must believe that as God's woman, God is using everything in my life to make me more like himself.

Together, he and I can take the tea stains in my life and make something out of them. We can take the chaos and be calm, take the tensions and be tender, take the hurts and be content, take the obstacles and build opportunities. That is what God offers me from life.

And when God says that's what he can do for me, only my unbelief keeps me from experiencing it. If the Christian life is worth living, then God is worth believing. And if I believe God, there is no end to the possibilities.

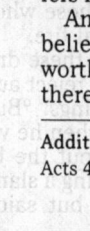

Additional Scripture Readings:
Acts 4:28–30; Philippians 1:19–21

Go to page 1405 for your next devotional reading.

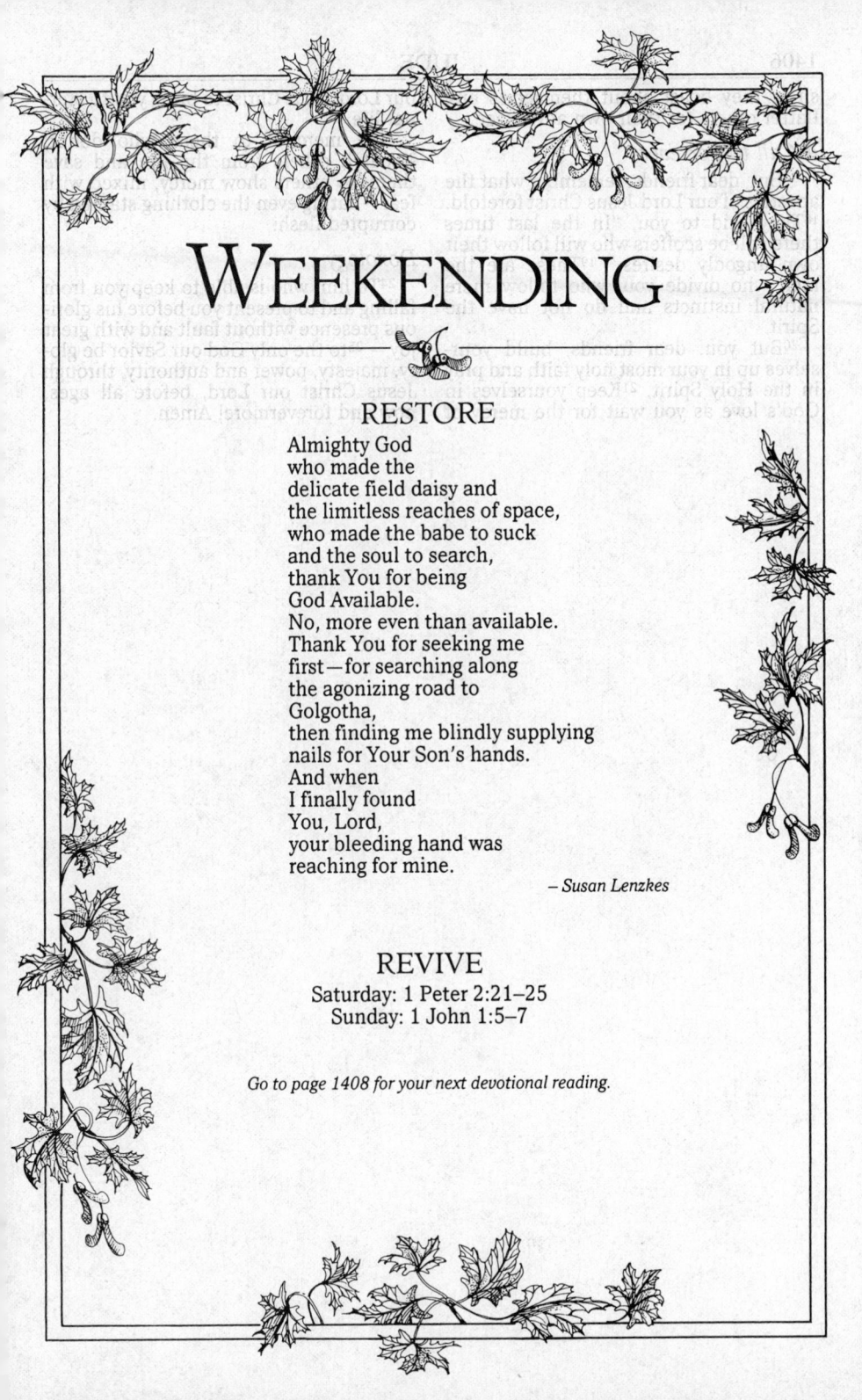

WEEKENDING

RESTORE

Almighty God
who made the
delicate field daisy and
the limitless reaches of space,
who made the babe to suck
and the soul to search,
thank You for being
God Available.
No, more even than available.
Thank You for seeking me
first—for searching along
the agonizing road to
Golgotha,
then finding me blindly supplying
nails for Your Son's hands.
And when
I finally found
You, Lord,
your bleeding hand was
reaching for mine.

— Susan Lenzkes

REVIVE

Saturday: 1 Peter 2:21–25
Sunday: 1 John 1:5–7

Go to page 1408 for your next devotional reading.

sires; they boast about themselves and flatter others for their own advantage.

A Call to Persevere

17But, dear friends, remember what the apostles of our Lord Jesus Christ foretold. 18They said to you, "In the last times there will be scoffers who will follow their own ungodly desires." 19These are the men who divide you, who follow mere natural instincts and do not have the Spirit.

20But you, dear friends, build yourselves up in your most holy faith and pray in the Holy Spirit. 21Keep yourselves in God's love as you wait for the mercy of our Lord Jesus Christ to bring you to eternal life.

22Be merciful to those who doubt; 23snatch others from the fire and save them; to others show mercy, mixed with fear—hating even the clothing stained by corrupted flesh.

Doxology

24To him who is able to keep you from falling and to present you before his glorious presence without fault and with great joy— 25to the only God our Savior be glory, majesty, power and authority, through Jesus Christ our Lord, before all ages, now and forevermore! Amen.

JOHN, *banished to the island of Patmos, writes what Christ reveals to him in order to comfort Christians suffering for their faith. Through visions of God in control of both the present and the future, he offers them hope, assuring them that in the end Christ will achieve victory over Satan, who is doomed to eternal punishment. As you read this book, rejoice in the awesome power of Christ, and remember that regardless of what happens now or in the future, nothing can ever separate you from his love.*

REVELATION

Prologue

1 The revelation of Jesus Christ, which God gave him to show his servants what must soon take place. He made it known by sending his angel to his servant John, [2]who testifies to everything he saw —that is, the word of God and the testimony of Jesus Christ. [3]Blessed is the one who reads the words of this prophecy, and blessed are those who hear it and take to heart what is written in it, because the time is near.

Greetings and Doxology

[4]John,

To the seven churches in the province of Asia:

Grace and peace to you from him who is, and who was, and who is to come, and from the seven spirits[a] before his throne, [5]and from Jesus Christ, who is the faithful witness, the firstborn from the dead, and the ruler of the kings of the earth.

To him who loves us and has freed us from our sins by his blood, [6]and has made us to be a kingdom and priests to serve his God and Father—to him be glory and power for ever and ever! Amen.

[7]Look, he is coming with the clouds,
	and every eye will see him,
	even those who pierced him;
and all the peoples of the earth will
	mourn because of him.
				So shall it be! Amen.

[8]"I am the Alpha and the Omega," says the Lord God, "who is, and who was, and who is to come, the Almighty."

One Like a Son of Man

[9]I, John, your brother and companion in the suffering and kingdom and patient endurance that are ours in Jesus, was on the island of Patmos because of the word of God and the testimony of Jesus. [10]On the Lord's Day I was in the Spirit, and I heard behind me a loud voice like a trumpet, [11]which said: "Write on a scroll what you see and send it to the seven churches:

MONDAY

VERSE FOR THE DAY:	AUTHOR:	PASSAGE FOR THE DAY:
Revelation 1:5	Marjorie Holmes	Revelation 1:4–8

God's Eraser

I'LL probably never meet Kara, now four years old. But one day she made a beautiful observation that has helped me.

"We had been standing on the hillside watching the airplane skywriting," her grandmother wrote me one day. "When the words began to disappear, she asked, 'Why, Grandma? Where do they go?'

"Then, as I groped for an answer, her little face brightened and she suddenly exclaimed, 'Maybe Jesus has an eraser!'"

I smiled as I read, but my eyes filled and suddenly I wanted to hug that little girl. For that morning I had been grieving over past mistakes. A cruel thing I had said to my mother the day I left for college. And Dad . . . if only I'd invited him to that luncheon where I was to speak—he'd have been so proud. One tender but painful memory releases others: the time I'd punished a child unfairly, humiliated my husband, let a friend down . . . .

No matter how much we mature as people, grow as Christians, try desperately to compensate, memories of our own failures rise up to haunt us, and sting—how they sting. For me, it's not the unkindnesses of others that hurt so much or last so long, it's the burden of my own. Yes, I ask God to forgive me, and try to believe that I am forgiven. But the memory won't go away. And if I can't forgive myself, how can God?

Then a little girl, in her innocence and wisdom, makes me realize: Like that writing on the sky that simply disappears, Jesus has wiped away all things I so bitterly regret. Jesus does have an eraser.

Additional Scripture Readings:
Psalm 103:11–12; Micah 7:18–19

Go to page 1412 for your next
devotional reading.

to Ephesus, Smyrna, Pergamum, Thyatira, Sardis, Philadelphia and Laodicea."

¹²I turned around to see the voice that was speaking to me. And when I turned I saw seven golden lampstands, ¹³and among the lampstands was someone "like a son of man,"ᵃ dressed in a robe reaching down to his feet and with a golden sash around his chest. ¹⁴His head and hair were white like wool, as white as snow, and his eyes were like blazing fire. ¹⁵His feet were like bronze glowing in a furnace, and his voice was like the sound of rushing waters. ¹⁶In his right hand he held seven stars, and out of his mouth came a sharp double-edged sword. His face was like the sun shining in all its brilliance.

¹⁷When I saw him, I fell at his feet as though dead. Then he placed his right hand on me and said: "Do not be afraid. I am the First and the Last. ¹⁸I am the Living One; I was dead, and behold I am alive for ever and ever! And I hold the keys of death and Hades.

¹⁹"Write, therefore, what you have seen, what is now and what will take place later. ²⁰The mystery of the seven stars that you saw in my right hand and of the seven golden lampstands is this: The seven stars are the angelsᵇ of the seven churches, and the seven lampstands are the seven churches.

To the Church in Ephesus

2 "To the angelᶜ of the church in Ephesus write:

These are the words of him who holds the seven stars in his right hand and walks among the seven golden lampstands: ²I know your deeds, your hard work and your perseverance. I know that you cannot tolerate wicked men, that you have tested those who claim to be apostles but are not, and have found them false. ³You have persevered and have endured hardships for my name, and have not grown weary.

⁴Yet I hold this against you: You have forsaken your first love. ⁵Remember the height from which you have fallen! Repent and do the things you did at first. If you do not repent, I will come to you and remove your lampstand from its place. ⁶But you have this in your fa-

vor: You hate the practices of the Nicolaitans, which I also hate.

⁷He who has an ear, let him hear what the Spirit says to the churches. To him who overcomes, I will give the right to eat from the tree of life, which is in the paradise of God.

To the Church in Smyrna

⁸"To the angel of the church in Smyrna write:

These are the words of him who is the First and the Last, who died and came to life again. ⁹I know your afflictions and your poverty—yet you are rich! I know the slander of those who say they are Jews and are not, but are a synagogue of Satan. ¹⁰Do not be afraid of what you are about to suffer. I tell you, the devil will put some of you in prison to test you, and you will suffer persecution for ten days. Be faithful, even to the point of death, and I will give you the crown of life.

¹¹He who has an ear, let him hear what the Spirit says to the churches. He who overcomes will not be hurt at all by the second death.

To the Church in Pergamum

¹²"To the angel of the church in Pergamum write:

These are the words of him who has the sharp, double-edged sword. ¹³I know where you live—where Satan has his throne. Yet you remain true to my name. You did not renounce your faith in me, even in the days of Antipas, my faithful witness, who was put to death in your city—where Satan lives.

¹⁴Nevertheless, I have a few things against you: You have people there who hold to the teaching of Balaam, who taught Balak to entice the Israelites to sin by eating food sacrificed to idols and by committing sexual immorality. ¹⁵Likewise you also have those who hold to the teaching of the Nicolaitans. ¹⁶Repent therefore! Otherwise, I will soon come to you and will fight against them with the sword of my mouth.

¹⁷He who has an ear, let him hear what the Spirit says to the churches. To him who overcomes, I will give

ᵃ13 Daniel 7:13   ᵇ20 Or *messengers*   ᶜ1 Or *messenger*; also in verses 8, 12 and 18 some of the hidden manna. I will also give him a white stone with a new name written on it, known only to him who receives it.

To the Church in Thyatira

18"To the angel of the church in Thyatira write:

These are the words of the Son of God, whose eyes are like blazing fire and whose feet are like burnished bronze. 19I know your deeds, your love and faith, your service and perseverance, and that you are now doing more than you did at first.

20Nevertheless, I have this against you: You tolerate that woman Jezebel, who calls herself a prophetess. By her teaching she misleads my servants into sexual immorality and the eating of food sacrificed to idols. 21I have given her time to repent of her immorality, but she is unwilling. 22So I will cast her on a bed of suffering, and I will make those who commit adultery with her suffer intensely, unless they repent of her ways. 23I will strike her children dead. Then all the churches will know that I am he who searches hearts and minds, and I will repay each of you according to your deeds. 24Now I say to the rest of you in Thyatira, to you who do not hold to her teaching and have not learned Satan's so-called deep secrets (I will not impose any other burden on you): 25Only hold on to what you have until I come.

26To him who overcomes and does my will to the end, I will give authority over the nations—

27'He will rule them with an iron
  scepter;
  he will dash them to pieces
    like pottery'a—

just as I have received authority from my Father. 28I will also give him the morning star. 29He who has an ear, let him hear what the Spirit says to the churches.

To the Church in Sardis

3 "To the angelb of the church in Sardis write:

These are the words of him who holds the seven spiritsc of God and the seven stars. I know your deeds; you have a reputation of being alive, but you are dead. 2Wake up! Strengthen what remains and is about to die, for I have not found your deeds complete in the sight of my God. 3Remember, therefore, what you have received and heard; obey it, and repent. But if you do not wake up, I will come like a thief, and you will not know at what time I will come to you.

4Yet you have a few people in Sardis who have not soiled their clothes. They will walk with me, dressed in white, for they are worthy. 5He who overcomes will, like them, be dressed in white. I will never blot out his name from the book of life, but will acknowledge his name before my Father and his angels. 6He who has an ear, let him hear what the Spirit says to the churches.

To the Church in Philadelphia

7"To the angel of the church in Philadelphia write:

These are the words of him who is holy and true, who holds the key of David. What he opens no one can shut, and what he shuts no one can open. 8I know your deeds. See, I have placed before you an open door that no one can shut. I know that you have little strength, yet you have kept my word and have not denied my name. 9I will make those who are of the synagogue of Satan, who claim to be Jews though they are not, but are liars—I will make them come and fall down at your feet and acknowledge that I have loved you. 10Since you have kept my command to endure patiently, I will also keep you from the hour of trial that is going to come upon the whole world to test those who live on the earth.

11I am coming soon. Hold on to what you have, so that no one will take your crown. 12Him who overcomes I will make a pillar in the temple of my God. Never again will he leave it. I will write on him the name of my God and the name of the city of my God, the new Jerusalem, which is coming down out of heaven from my God; and I will also write on

a27 Psalm 2:9   b1 Or messenger; also in verses 7 and 14   c1 Or the sevenfold Spirit him my new name. ¹³He who has an ear, let him hear what the Spirit says to the churches.

To the Church in Laodicea

¹⁴"To the angel of the church in Laodicea write:

These are the words of the Amen, the faithful and true witness, the ruler of God's creation. ¹⁵I know your deeds, that you are neither cold nor hot. I wish you were either one or the other! ¹⁶So, because you are lukewarm—neither hot nor cold—I am about to spit you out of my mouth. ¹⁷You say, 'I am rich; I have acquired wealth and do not need a thing.' But you do not realize that you are wretched, pitiful, poor, blind and naked. ¹⁸I counsel you to buy from me gold refined in the fire, so you can become rich; and white clothes to wear, so you can cover your shameful nakedness; and salve to put on your eyes, so you can see.

¹⁹Those whom I love I rebuke and discipline. So be earnest, and repent. ²⁰Here I am! I stand at the door and knock. If anyone hears my voice and opens the door, I will come in and eat with him, and he with me. ²¹To him who overcomes, I will give the right to sit with me on my throne, just as I overcame and sat down with my Father on his throne. ²²He who has an ear, let him hear what the Spirit says to the churches."

The Throne in Heaven

4 After this I looked, and there before me was a door standing open in heaven. And the voice I had first heard speaking to me like a trumpet said, "Come up here, and I will show you what must take place after this." ²At once I was in the Spirit, and there before me was a throne in heaven with someone sitting on it. ³And the one who sat there had the appearance of jasper and carnelian. A rainbow, resembling an emerald, encircled the throne. ⁴Surrounding the throne were twenty-four other thrones, and seated on them were twenty-four elders. They were dressed in white and had crowns of gold on their heads. ⁵From the throne came flashes of lightning, rumblings and peals

of thunder. Before the throne, seven lamps were blazing. These are the seven spirits*a* of God. ⁶Also before the throne there was what looked like a sea of glass, clear as crystal.

In the center, around the throne, were four living creatures, and they were covered with eyes, in front and in back. ⁷The first living creature was like a lion, the second was like an ox, the third had a face like a man, the fourth was like a flying eagle. ⁸Each of the four living creatures had six wings and was covered with eyes all around, even under his wings. Day and night they never stop saying:

"Holy, holy, holy
    is the Lord God Almighty,
    who was, and is, and is to come."

⁹Whenever the living creatures give glory, honor and thanks to him who sits on the throne and who lives for ever and ever, ¹⁰the twenty-four elders fall down before him who sits on the throne, and worship him who lives for ever and ever. They lay their crowns before the throne and say:

¹¹"You are worthy, our Lord and God,
    to receive glory and honor and
        power,
    for you created all things,
    and by your will they were created
    and have their being."

The Scroll and the Lamb

5 Then I saw in the right hand of him who sat on the throne a scroll with writing on both sides and sealed with seven seals. ²And I saw a mighty angel proclaiming in a loud voice, "Who is worthy to break the seals and open the scroll?" ³But no one in heaven or on earth or under the earth could open the scroll or even look inside it. ⁴I wept and wept because no one was found who was worthy to open the scroll or look inside. ⁵Then one of the elders said to me, "Do not weep! See, the Lion of the tribe of Judah, the Root of David, has triumphed. He is able to open the scroll and its seven seals."

⁶Then I saw a Lamb, looking as if it had been slain, standing in the center of the throne, encircled by the four living creatures and the elders. He had seven horns and seven eyes, which are the seven spirits*a* of God sent out into all the earth. ⁷He

a5,6 Or the sevenfold Spirit

TUESDAY

VERSE FOR THE DAY:
Revelation 3:15–16

AUTHOR:
Catherine Marshall

PASSAGE FOR THE DAY:
Revelation 3:14–22

Author of Creativity

I AM troubled about a quality of blandness in our nation today, a lack of creativity. It's apparent in our leaders. Most gear their lives to television ratings, are afraid to take stands on issues. Movies and stage plays focus on sex and violence, with little originality. Sex so dominates advertising and the arts that it has become commonplace, almost boring.

Jesus lashed out at the spiritless quality in the people of his time:

> I know your deeds, that you are neither cold nor hot. I wish you were either one or the other! So, because you are lukewarm—neither hot nor cold—I am about to spit you out of my mouth (Revelation 3:15–16).

One of our new neighbors is no longer trapped in a bland way of life. Yet for the first twelve years of her marriage, Cynthia felt she was losing her identity in an endless procession of social events and chauffeuring of children.

In a search for answers, Cynthia set aside an hour each day for meditation. As she did this over a period of weeks there came to her the realization that she was being met in this quiet hour, at her point of need, by something more than her own thoughts and her own psyche, by Someone who loved her and who insisted that his love must be passed on to her family and her friends.

"I realized one day that my church had little more meaning for me than did our country club," Cynthia said. "I called our pastor and asked if there was a Bible study."

That's what brought Cynthia and her husband to our house, where eight couples were already meeting twice a month to find ways to relate the Bible to some everyday problems we were all facing. Out of this experience has come a new level of shared concerns for us all and the exciting discovery of answers sought out together.

As I ponder Cynthia's story, I've concluded that we don't have to settle for blandness in life; God, who is the Author of creativity, is ready to make a dull life adventuresome the moment we allow his Holy Spirit to go to work inside us.

Additional Scripture Readings:
1 Thessalonians 5:16–23; 1 Peter 1:3–6

Go to page 1415 for your next
devotional reading.

came and took the scroll from the right hand of him who sat on the throne. [8]And when he had taken it, the four living creatures and the twenty-four elders fell down before the Lamb. Each one had a harp and they were holding golden bowls full of incense, which are the prayers of the saints. [9]And they sang a new song:

"You are worthy to take the scroll
    and to open its seals,
because you were slain,
    and with your blood you purchased
       men for God
    from every tribe and language and
       people and nation.
[10]You have made them to be a kingdom
       and priests to serve our God,
    and they will reign on the earth."

[11]Then I looked and heard the voice of many angels, numbering thousands upon thousands, and ten thousand times ten thousand. They encircled the throne and the living creatures and the elders. [12]In a loud voice they sang:

"Worthy is the Lamb, who was slain,
to receive power and wealth and
       wisdom and strength
and honor and glory and praise!"

[13]Then I heard every creature in heaven and on earth and under the earth and on the sea, and all that is in them, singing:

"To him who sits on the throne and
    to the Lamb
be praise and honor and glory and
    power,
    for ever and ever!"

[14]The four living creatures said, "Amen," and the elders fell down and worshiped.

The Seals

6 I watched as the Lamb opened the first of the seven seals. Then I heard one of the four living creatures say in a voice like thunder, "Come!" [2]I looked, and there before me was a white horse! Its rider held a bow, and he was given a crown, and he rode out as a conqueror bent on conquest.

[3]When the Lamb opened the second seal, I heard the second living creature say, "Come!" [4]Then another horse came out, a fiery red one. Its rider was given power to take peace from the earth and to make men slay each other. To him was given a large sword.

[5]When the Lamb opened the third seal, I heard the third living creature say, "Come!" I looked, and there before me was a black horse! Its rider was holding a pair of scales in his hand. [6]Then I heard what sounded like a voice among the four living creatures, saying, "A quart[a] of wheat for a day's wages,[b] and three quarts of barley for a day's wages,[b] and do not damage the oil and the wine!"

[7]When the Lamb opened the fourth seal, I heard the voice of the fourth living creature say, "Come!" [8]I looked, and there before me was a pale horse! Its rider was named Death, and Hades was following close behind him. They were given power over a fourth of the earth to kill by sword, famine and plague, and by the wild beasts of the earth.

[9]When he opened the fifth seal, I saw under the altar the souls of those who had been slain because of the word of God and the testimony they had maintained. [10]They called out in a loud voice, "How long, Sovereign Lord, holy and true, until you judge the inhabitants of the earth and avenge our blood?" [11]Then each of them was given a white robe, and they were told to wait a little longer, until the number of their fellow servants and brothers who were to be killed as they had been was completed.

[12]I watched as he opened the sixth seal. There was a great earthquake. The sun turned black like sackcloth made of goat hair, the whole moon turned blood red, [13]and the stars in the sky fell to earth, as late figs drop from a fig tree when shaken by a strong wind. [14]The sky receded like a scroll, rolling up, and every mountain and island was removed from its place.

[15]Then the kings of the earth, the princes, the generals, the rich, the mighty, and every slave and every free man hid in caves and among the rocks of the mountains. [16]They called to the mountains and the rocks, "Fall on us and hide us from the face of him who sits on the throne and from the wrath of the Lamb! [17]For the great day of their wrath has come, and who can stand?"

144,000 Sealed

7 After this I saw four angels standing at the four corners of the earth, hold-

a6 Greek a choinix (probably about a liter)   *b6 Greek a denarius* ing back the four winds of the earth to prevent any wind from blowing on the land or on the sea or on any tree. ²Then I saw another angel coming up from the east, having the seal of the living God. He called out in a loud voice to the four angels who had been given power to harm the land and the sea: ³"Do not harm the land or the sea or the trees until we put a seal on the foreheads of the servants of our God." ⁴Then I heard the number of those who were sealed: 144,000 from all the tribes of Israel.

⁵From the tribe of Judah 12,000 were sealed,
  from the tribe of Reuben 12,000,
  from the tribe of Gad 12,000,
  ⁶from the tribe of Asher 12,000,
  from the tribe of Naphtali 12,000,
  from the tribe of Manasseh 12,000,
  ⁷from the tribe of Simeon 12,000,
  from the tribe of Levi 12,000,
  from the tribe of Issachar 12,000,
  ⁸from the tribe of Zebulun 12,000,
  from the tribe of Joseph 12,000,
  from the tribe of Benjamin 12,000.

The Great Multitude in White Robes

⁹After this I looked and there before me was a great multitude that no one could count, from every nation, tribe, people and language, standing before the throne and in front of the Lamb. They were wearing white robes and were holding palm branches in their hands. ¹⁰And they cried out in a loud voice:

"Salvation belongs to our God,
  who sits on the throne,
  and to the Lamb."

¹¹All the angels were standing around the throne and around the elders and the four living creatures. They fell down on their faces before the throne and worshiped God, ¹²saying:

"Amen!
Praise and glory
and wisdom and thanks and honor
and power and strength
be to our God for ever and ever.
Amen!"

¹³Then one of the elders asked me, "These in white robes—who are they, and where did they come from?"

¹⁴I answered, "Sir, you know."

And he said, "These are they who have come out of the great tribulation; they have washed their robes and made them white in the blood of the Lamb. ¹⁵Therefore,

"they are before the throne of God
  and serve him day and night in his
    temple;
and he who sits on the throne will
  spread his tent over them.
¹⁶Never again will they hunger;
  never again will they thirst.
The sun will not beat upon them,
  nor any scorching heat.
¹⁷For the Lamb at the center of the
    throne will be their shepherd;
  he will lead them to springs of
    living water.
And God will wipe away every tear
  from their eyes."

The Seventh Seal and the Golden Censer

8 When he opened the seventh seal, there was silence in heaven for about half an hour.

²And I saw the seven angels who stand before God, and to them were given seven trumpets.

³Another angel, who had a golden censer, came and stood at the altar. He was given much incense to offer, with the prayers of all the saints, on the golden altar before the throne. ⁴The smoke of the incense, together with the prayers of the saints, went up before God from the angel's hand. ⁵Then the angel took the censer, filled it with fire from the altar, and hurled it on the earth; and there came peals of thunder, rumblings, flashes of lightning and an earthquake.

The Trumpets

⁶Then the seven angels who had the seven trumpets prepared to sound them.

⁷The first angel sounded his trumpet, and there came hail and fire mixed with blood, and it was hurled down upon the earth. A third of the earth was burned up, a third of the trees were burned up, and all the green grass was burned up.

⁸The second angel sounded his trumpet, and something like a huge mountain, all ablaze, was thrown into the sea. A third of the sea turned into blood, ⁹a third of the living creatures in the sea died, and a third of the ships were destroyed.

¹⁰The third angel sounded his trumpet, and a great star, blazing like a torch, fell from the sky on a third of the rivers and on the springs of water— ¹¹the name of

the star is Wormwood. *a* A third of the waters turned bitter, and many people died from the waters that had become bitter.

¹²The fourth angel sounded his trumpet, and a third of the sun was struck, a third of the moon, and a third of the stars, so that a third of them turned dark. A third of the day was without light, and also a third of the night.

¹³As I watched, I heard an eagle that

a11 That is, Bitterness

was flying in midair call out in a loud voice: "Woe! Woe! Woe to the inhabitants of the earth, because of the trumpet blasts about to be sounded by the other three angels!"

9 The fifth angel sounded his trumpet, and I saw a star that had fallen from the sky to the earth. The star was given the key to the shaft of the Abyss. ²When he opened the Abyss, smoke rose from it

WEDNESDAY

VERSE FOR THE DAY:
Revelation 7:9

AUTHOR:
Wanda K. Jones

PASSAGE FOR THE DAY:
Revelation 7:9–17

Among the Great Multitude

ONE of the rewards of reading the Bible in its entirety is to see that our walk with Christ ends in joy and victory! Through the eyes of the apostle John in Revelation 7, we see a God-given picture of the joyful culmination of our journey here on earth.

Over the years, as I have listened to the sermons of godly men and women and as I have sat under professors who expounded the Word of God, it was with joy and expectancy that I visualized the great multitude that will eventually gather to worship the Lord. The throng will be so great that no one will be able to count its members. People "from every nation, tribe, people and language, standing before the throne and in front of the Lamb" (Revelation 7:9). Each time I visualized this glorious band of the redeemed, I thought, "Oh, how wonderful! I'm going to be among them!" I still feel that way. What a triumphant future for every believer!

Revelation 7 tells us that we will be rewarded by serving and loving the Lord. We have many opportunities to serve. In this land, and in many other countries, people are hungry and thirsty, homeless and with no one who really cares about them. Others may be well cared for physically and financially, but they carry many burdens both day and night.

Are you included among those who carry many burdens? Or are you numbered in the throng of believers? Will the final chapter of your life close in defeat or victory? If you have not asked Jesus to take your burden of sin, ask him to "wipe away every tear" (Revelation 7:17) from your eyes, to cleanse you in his blood. Then one day you will be a member of that great multitude that no one can number!

Additional Scripture Readings:
Matthew 24:10–14; Hebrews 10:35–39

Go to page 1420 for your next devotional reading.

like the smoke from a gigantic furnace. The sun and sky were darkened by the smoke from the Abyss. ³And out of the smoke locusts came down upon the earth and were given power like that of scorpions of the earth. ⁴They were told not to harm the grass of the earth or any plant or tree, but only those people who did not have the seal of God on their foreheads. ⁵They were not given power to kill them, but only to torture them for five months. And the agony they suffered was like that of the sting of a scorpion when it strikes a man. ⁶During those days men will seek death, but will not find it; they will long to die, but death will elude them.

⁷The locusts looked like horses prepared for battle. On their heads they wore something like crowns of gold, and their faces resembled human faces. ⁸Their hair was like women's hair, and their teeth were like lions' teeth. ⁹They had breastplates like breastplates of iron, and the sound of their wings was like the thundering of many horses and chariots rushing into battle. ¹⁰They had tails and stings like scorpions, and in their tails they had power to torment people for five months. ¹¹They had as king over them the angel of the Abyss, whose name in Hebrew is Abaddon, and in Greek, Apollyon.ᵃ

¹²The first woe is past; two other woes are yet to come.

¹³The sixth angel sounded his trumpet, and I heard a voice coming from the hornsᵇ of the golden altar that is before God. ¹⁴It said to the sixth angel who had the trumpet, "Release the four angels who are bound at the great river Euphrates." ¹⁵And the four angels who had been kept ready for this very hour and day and month and year were released to kill a third of mankind. ¹⁶The number of the mounted troops was two hundred million. I heard their number.

¹⁷The horses and riders I saw in my vision looked like this: Their breastplates were fiery red, dark blue, and yellow as sulfur. The heads of the horses resembled the heads of lions, and out of their mouths came fire, smoke and sulfur. ¹⁸A third of mankind was killed by the three plagues of fire, smoke and sulfur that came out of their mouths. ¹⁹The power of the horses was in their mouths and in their tails; for their tails were like snakes, having heads with which they inflict injury.

²⁰The rest of mankind that were not killed by these plagues still did not repent of the work of their hands; they did not stop worshiping demons, and idols of gold, silver, bronze, stone and wood—idols that cannot see or hear or walk. ²¹Nor did they repent of their murders, their magic arts, their sexual immorality or their thefts.

The Angel and the Little Scroll

10 Then I saw another mighty angel coming down from heaven. He was robed in a cloud, with a rainbow above his head; his face was like the sun, and his legs were like fiery pillars. ²He was holding a little scroll, which lay open in his hand. He planted his right foot on the sea and his left foot on the land, ³and he gave a loud shout like the roar of a lion. When he shouted, the voices of the seven thunders spoke. ⁴And when the seven thunders spoke, I was about to write; but I heard a voice from heaven say, "Seal up what the seven thunders have said and do not write it down."

⁵Then the angel I had seen standing on the sea and on the land raised his right hand to heaven. ⁶And he swore by him who lives for ever and ever, who created the heavens and all that is in them, the earth and all that is in it, and the sea and all that is in it, and said, "There will be no more delay! ⁷But in the days when the seventh angel is about to sound his trumpet, the mystery of God will be accomplished, just as he announced to his servants the prophets."

⁸Then the voice that I had heard from heaven spoke to me once more: "Go, take the scroll that lies open in the hand of the angel who is standing on the sea and on the land."

⁹So I went to the angel and asked him to give me the little scroll. He said to me, "Take it and eat it. It will turn your stomach sour, but in your mouth it will be as sweet as honey." ¹⁰I took the little scroll from the angel's hand and ate it. It tasted as sweet as honey in my mouth, but when I had eaten it, my stomach turned sour. ¹¹Then I was told, "You must prophesy again about many peoples, nations, languages and kings."

The Two Witnesses

11 I was given a reed like a measuring rod and was told, "Go and meas-

---

ᵃ11 Abaddon and Apollyon mean Destroyer.   ᵇ13 That is, projections ure the temple of God and the altar, and count the worshipers there. ²But exclude the outer court; do not measure it, because it has been given to the Gentiles. They will trample on the holy city for 42 months. ³And I will give power to my two witnesses, and they will prophesy for 1,260 days, clothed in sackcloth." ⁴These are the two olive trees and the two lampstands that stand before the Lord of the earth. ⁵If anyone tries to harm them, fire comes from their mouths and devours their enemies. This is how anyone who wants to harm them must die. ⁶These men have power to shut up the sky so that it will not rain during the time they are prophesying; and they have power to turn the waters into blood and to strike the earth with every kind of plague as often as they want.

⁷Now when they have finished their testimony, the beast that comes up from the Abyss will attack them, and overpower and kill them. ⁸Their bodies will lie in the street of the great city, which is figuratively called Sodom and Egypt, where also their Lord was crucified. ⁹For three and a half days men from every people, tribe, language and nation will gaze on their bodies and refuse them burial. ¹⁰The inhabitants of the earth will gloat over them and will celebrate by sending each other gifts, because these two prophets had tormented those who live on the earth.

¹¹But after the three and a half days a breath of life from God entered them, and they stood on their feet, and terror struck those who saw them. ¹²Then they heard a loud voice from heaven saying to them, "Come up here." And they went up to heaven in a cloud, while their enemies looked on.

¹³At that very hour there was a severe earthquake and a tenth of the city collapsed. Seven thousand people were killed in the earthquake, and the survivors were terrified and gave glory to the God of heaven.

¹⁴The second woe has passed; the third woe is coming soon.

The Seventh Trumpet

¹⁵The seventh angel sounded his trumpet, and there were loud voices in heaven, which said:

"The kingdom of the world has
    become the kingdom of our
    Lord and of his Christ,

and he will reign for ever and ever."

¹⁶And the twenty-four elders, who were seated on their thrones before God, fell on their faces and worshiped God, ¹⁷saying:

"We give thanks to you, Lord God
    Almighty,
the One who is and who was,
because you have taken your great
    power
and have begun to reign.
¹⁸The nations were angry;
    and your wrath has come.
The time has come for judging the
    dead,
    and for rewarding your servants the
        prophets
and your saints and those who
        reverence your name,
    both small and great—
and for destroying those who destroy
    the earth."

¹⁹Then God's temple in heaven was opened, and within his temple was seen the ark of his covenant. And there came flashes of lightning, rumblings, peals of thunder, an earthquake and a great hailstorm.

The Woman and the Dragon

12 A great and wondrous sign appeared in heaven: a woman clothed with the sun, with the moon under her feet and a crown of twelve stars on her head. ²She was pregnant and cried out in pain as she was about to give birth. ³Then another sign appeared in heaven: an enormous red dragon with seven heads and ten horns and seven crowns on his heads. ⁴His tail swept a third of the stars out of the sky and flung them to the earth. The dragon stood in front of the woman who was about to give birth, so that he might devour her child the moment it was born. ⁵She gave birth to a son, a male child, who will rule all the nations with an iron scepter. And her child was snatched up to God and to his throne. ⁶The woman fled into the desert to a place prepared for her by God, where she might be taken care of for 1,260 days.

⁷And there was war in heaven. Michael and his angels fought against the dragon, and the dragon and his angels fought back. ⁸But he was not strong enough, and they lost their place in heaven. ⁹The great dragon was hurled down—that ancient serpent called the devil, or Satan, who

leads the whole world astray. He was hurled to the earth, and his angels with him.

¹⁰Then I heard a loud voice in heaven say:

"Now have come the salvation and
    the power and the kingdom of
    our God,
and the authority of his Christ.
For the accuser of our brothers,
    who accuses them before our God
      day and night,
    has been hurled down.
¹¹They overcame him
    by the blood of the Lamb
    and by the word of their testimony;
they did not love their lives so much
    as to shrink from death.
¹²Therefore rejoice, you heavens
    and you who dwell in them!
But woe to the earth and the sea,
    because the devil has gone down to
      you!
He is filled with fury,
    because he knows that his time is
      short."

¹³When the dragon saw that he had been hurled to the earth, he pursued the woman who had given birth to the male child. ¹⁴The woman was given the two wings of a great eagle, so that she might fly to the place prepared for her in the desert, where she would be taken care of for a time, times and half a time, out of the serpent's reach. ¹⁵Then from his mouth the serpent spewed water like a river, to overtake the woman and sweep her away with the torrent. ¹⁶But the earth helped the woman by opening its mouth and swallowing the river that the dragon had spewed out of his mouth. ¹⁷Then the dragon was enraged at the woman and went off to make war against the rest of her offspring—those who obey God's commandments and hold to the testimony of Jesus. ¹And the dragonᵃ stood on the shore of the sea.

The Beast out of the Sea

And I saw a beast coming out of the sea. He had ten horns and seven heads, with ten crowns on his horns, and on each head a blasphemous name. ²The beast I saw resembled a leopard, but had feet like those of a bear and a mouth like that of a lion. The dragon gave the beast his power and his throne and great authority. ³One of the heads of the beast seemed to have had a fatal wound, but the fatal wound had been healed. The whole world was astonished and followed the beast. ⁴Men worshiped the dragon because he had given authority to the beast, and they also worshiped the beast and asked, "Who is like the beast? Who can make war against him?"

⁵The beast was given a mouth to utter proud words and blasphemies and to exercise his authority for forty-two months. ⁶He opened his mouth to blaspheme God, and to slander his name and his dwelling place and those who live in heaven. ⁷He was given power to make war against the saints and to conquer them. And he was given authority over every tribe, people, language and nation. ⁸All inhabitants of the earth will worship the beast—all whose names have not been written in the book of life belonging to the Lamb that was slain from the creation of the world.ᵇ

⁹He who has an ear, let him hear.

¹⁰If anyone is to go into captivity,
    into captivity he will go.
If anyone is to be killedᶜ with the
      sword,
    with the sword he will be killed.

This calls for patient endurance and faithfulness on the part of the saints.

The Beast out of the Earth

¹¹Then I saw another beast, coming out of the earth. He had two horns like a lamb, but he spoke like a dragon. ¹²He exercised all the authority of the first beast on his behalf, and made the earth and its inhabitants worship the first beast, whose fatal wound had been healed. ¹³And he performed great and miraculous signs, even causing fire to come down from heaven to earth in full view of men. ¹⁴Because of the signs he was given power to do on behalf of the first beast, he deceived the inhabitants of the earth. He ordered them to set up an image in honor of the beast who was wounded by the sword and yet lived. ¹⁵He was given power to give breath to the image of the first beast, so that it could speak and cause all who refused to worship the image to be killed. ¹⁶He also forced everyone, small and great, rich and

ᵃ1 Some late manuscripts *And I*   ᵇ8 Or *written from the creation of the world in the book of life belonging to the Lamb that was slain*   ᶜ10 Some manuscripts *anyone kills* poor, free and slave, to receive a mark on his right hand or on his forehead, [17]so that no one could buy or sell unless he had the mark, which is the name of the beast or the number of his name.

[18]This calls for wisdom. If anyone has insight, let him calculate the number of the beast, for it is man's number. His number is 666.

The Lamb and the 144,000

14 Then I looked, and there before me was the Lamb, standing on Mount Zion, and with him 144,000 who had his name and his Father's name written on their foreheads. [2]And I heard a sound from heaven like the roar of rushing waters and like a loud peal of thunder. The sound I heard was like that of harpists playing their harps. [3]And they sang a new song before the throne and before the four living creatures and the elders. No one could learn the song except the 144,000 who had been redeemed from the earth. [4]These are those who did not defile themselves with women, for they kept themselves pure. They follow the Lamb wherever he goes. They were purchased from among men and offered as firstfruits to God and the Lamb. [5]No lie was found in their mouths; they are blameless.

The Three Angels

[6]Then I saw another angel flying in midair, and he had the eternal gospel to proclaim to those who live on the earth—to every nation, tribe, language and people. [7]He said in a loud voice, "Fear God and give him glory, because the hour of his judgment has come. Worship him who made the heavens, the earth, the sea and the springs of water."

[8]A second angel followed and said, "Fallen! Fallen is Babylon the Great, which made all the nations drink the maddening wine of her adulteries."

[9]A third angel followed them and said in a loud voice: "If anyone worships the beast and his image and receives his mark on the forehead or on the hand, [10]he, too, will drink of the wine of God's fury, which has been poured full strength into the cup of his wrath. He will be tormented with burning sulfur in the presence of the holy angels and of the Lamb. [11]And the smoke of their torment rises for ever and ever. There is no rest day or night for those who worship the beast and his image, or for anyone who receives the mark of his name." [12]This calls for patient endurance on the part of the saints who obey God's commandments and remain faithful to Jesus.

[13]Then I heard a voice from heaven say, "Write: Blessed are the dead who die in the Lord from now on."

"Yes," says the Spirit, "they will rest from their labor, for their deeds will follow them."

The Harvest of the Earth

[14]I looked, and there before me was a white cloud, and seated on the cloud was one "like a son of man"[a] with a crown of gold on his head and a sharp sickle in his hand. [15]Then another angel came out of the temple and called in a loud voice to him who was sitting on the cloud, "Take your sickle and reap, because the time to reap has come, for the harvest of the earth is ripe." [16]So he who was seated on the cloud swung his sickle over the earth, and the earth was harvested.

[17]Another angel came out of the temple in heaven, and he too had a sharp sickle. [18]Still another angel, who had charge of the fire, came from the altar and called in a loud voice to him who had the sharp sickle, "Take your sharp sickle and gather the clusters of grapes from the earth's vine, because its grapes are ripe." [19]The angel swung his sickle on the earth, gathered its grapes and threw them into the great winepress of God's wrath. [20]They were trampled in the winepress outside the city, and blood flowed out of the press, rising as high as the horses' bridles for a distance of 1,600 stadia.[b]

Seven Angels With Seven Plagues

15 I saw in heaven another great and marvelous sign: seven angels with the seven last plagues—last, because with them God's wrath is completed. [2]And I saw what looked like a sea of glass mixed with fire and, standing beside the sea, those who had been victorious over the beast and his image and over the number of his name. They held harps given them by God [3]and sang the song of Moses the servant of God and the song of the Lamb:

"Great and marvelous are your deeds, Lord God Almighty.

---

[a]14 Daniel 7:13   [b]20 That is, about 180 miles (about 300 kilometers)

Just and true are your ways,
   King of the ages.
⁴Who will not fear you, O Lord,
   and bring glory to your name?
For you alone are holy.
All nations will come
   and worship before you,
for your righteous acts have been
   revealed."

⁵After this I looked and in heaven the temple, that is, the tabernacle of the Testimony, was opened. ⁶Out of the temple came the seven angels with the seven plagues. They were dressed in clean,

shining linen and wore golden sashes around their chests. ⁷Then one of the four living creatures gave to the seven angels seven golden bowls filled with the wrath of God, who lives for ever and ever. ⁸And the temple was filled with smoke from the glory of God and from his power, and no one could enter the temple until the seven plagues of the seven angels were completed.

The Seven Bowls of God's Wrath

16 Then I heard a loud voice from the temple saying to the seven angels,

THURSDAY

VERSE FOR THE DAY:
Revelation 14:13

AUTHOR:
Gien Karssen

PASSAGE FOR THE DAY:
Revelation 14:6–13

Rest and Reward

THE Bible leaves no doubt that there is life after death. Humanity is created for eternity. The earthly life is but an overture, a prelude of the reality to come. Blessed—happy, to be envied—are the dead "who die in the Lord." They are people who during their earthly life believed in Jesus Christ as their Savior and Lord. When they exchange the temporal for the eternal, their work is done forever. They finally have rest. All the troubles and tensions of their earthly existence are behind them. They have arrived at their eternal destination. They are HOME!

The Scriptures paint a frightening alternative for people who do not seek God during their lifetime: "And the smoke of their torment rises for ever and ever. There is no rest day or night" (Revelation 14:11).

What a contrast!

The dead who die in the Lord not only enjoy eternally the absence of unrest, pain and sorrow, but they also are rewarded: "Their deeds will follow them."

Human beings are free to live their lives according to their own choices. But they have to keep in mind that there will be a future settling of accounts. All will—justly—be rewarded according to their deeds. The measuring staff will be administered according to their attitude toward the Lord Jesus Christ.

True rest awaits only those who during their life on earth took God seriously. Without him there is no real rest, in the present or in the future.

Additional Scripture Readings:
Matthew 25:31–46; Luke 16:19–26

*Go to page 1426 for your next
devotional reading.*

"Go, pour out the seven bowls of God's wrath on the earth."

²The first angel went and poured out his bowl on the land, and ugly and painful sores broke out on the people who had the mark of the beast and worshiped his image.

³The second angel poured out his bowl on the sea, and it turned into blood like that of a dead man, and every living thing in the sea died.

⁴The third angel poured out his bowl on the rivers and springs of water, and they became blood. ⁵Then I heard the angel in charge of the waters say:

"You are just in these judgments,
  you who are and who were, the
    Holy One,
because you have so judged;
⁶for they have shed the blood of your
    saints and prophets,
  and you have given them blood to
    drink as they deserve."

⁷And I heard the altar respond:

"Yes, Lord God Almighty,
  true and just are your judgments."

⁸The fourth angel poured out his bowl on the sun, and the sun was given power to scorch people with fire. ⁹They were seared by the intense heat and they cursed the name of God, who had control over these plagues, but they refused to repent and glorify him.

¹⁰The fifth angel poured out his bowl on the throne of the beast, and his kingdom was plunged into darkness. Men gnawed their tongues in agony ¹¹and cursed the God of heaven because of their pains and their sores, but they refused to repent of what they had done.

¹²The sixth angel poured out his bowl on the great river Euphrates, and its water was dried up to prepare the way for the kings from the East. ¹³Then I saw three evil*ᵃ* spirits that looked like frogs; they came out of the mouth of the dragon, out of the mouth of the beast and out of the mouth of the false prophet. ¹⁴They are spirits of demons performing miraculous signs, and they go out to the kings of the whole world, to gather them for the battle on the great day of God Almighty.

¹⁵"Behold, I come like a thief! Blessed is he who stays awake and keeps his clothes with him, so that he may not go naked and be shamefully exposed."

¹⁶Then they gathered the kings together to the place that in Hebrew is called Armageddon.

¹⁷The seventh angel poured out his bowl into the air, and out of the temple came a loud voice from the throne, saying, "It is done!" ¹⁸Then there came flashes of lightning, rumblings, peals of thunder and a severe earthquake. No earthquake like it has ever occurred since man has been on earth, so tremendous was the quake. ¹⁹The great city split into three parts, and the cities of the nations collapsed. God remembered Babylon the Great and gave her the cup filled with the wine of the fury of his wrath. ²⁰Every island fled away and the mountains could not be found. ²¹From the sky huge hailstones of about a hundred pounds each fell upon men. And they cursed God on account of the plague of hail, because the plague was so terrible.

The Woman on the Beast

17 One of the seven angels who had the seven bowls came and said to me, "Come, I will show you the punishment of the great prostitute, who sits on many waters. ²With her the kings of the earth committed adultery and the inhabitants of the earth were intoxicated with the wine of her adulteries."

³Then the angel carried me away in the Spirit into a desert. There I saw a woman sitting on a scarlet beast that was covered with blasphemous names and had seven heads and ten horns. ⁴The woman was dressed in purple and scarlet, and was glittering with gold, precious stones and pearls. She held a golden cup in her hand, filled with abominable things and the filth of her adulteries. ⁵This title was written on her forehead:

MYSTERY
BABYLON THE GREAT
THE MOTHER OF PROSTITUTES
AND OF THE ABOMINATIONS OF THE EARTH.

⁶I saw that the woman was drunk with the blood of the saints, the blood of those who bore testimony to Jesus.

When I saw her, I was greatly astonished. ⁷Then the angel said to me: "Why are you astonished? I will explain to you the mystery of the woman and of the beast she rides, which has the seven heads and ten horns. ⁸The beast, which you saw, once was, now is not, and will come up out of the Abyss and go to his destruction. The inhabitants of the earth whose names have not been written in the book of life from the creation of the world will be astonished when they see the beast, because he once was, now is not, and yet will come.

⁹"This calls for a mind with wisdom. The seven heads are seven hills on which the woman sits. ¹⁰They are also seven kings. Five have fallen, one is, the other has not yet come; but when he does come, he must remain for a little while. ¹¹The beast who once was, and now is not, is an eighth king. He belongs to the seven and is going to his destruction.

¹²"The ten horns you saw are ten kings who have not yet received a kingdom, but who for one hour will receive authority as kings along with the beast. ¹³They have one purpose and will give their power and authority to the beast. ¹⁴They will make war against the Lamb, but the Lamb will overcome them because he is Lord of lords and King of kings—and with him will be his called, chosen and faithful followers."

¹⁵Then the angel said to me, "The waters you saw, where the prostitute sits, are peoples, multitudes, nations and languages. ¹⁶The beast and the ten horns you saw will hate the prostitute. They will bring her to ruin and leave her naked; they will eat her flesh and burn her with fire. ¹⁷For God has put it into their hearts to accomplish his purpose by agreeing to give the beast their power to rule, until God's words are fulfilled. ¹⁸The woman you saw is the great city that rules over the kings of the earth."

The Fall of Babylon

18 After this I saw another angel coming down from heaven. He had great authority, and the earth was illuminated by his splendor. ²With a mighty voice he shouted:

"Fallen! Fallen is Babylon the Great!
    She has become a home for
        demons
and a haunt for every evil*a* spirit,
    a haunt for every unclean and
        detestable bird.
³For all the nations have drunk
    the maddening wine of her
        adulteries.

The kings of the earth committed
    adultery with her,
and the merchants of the earth
    grew rich from her excessive
    luxuries."

⁴Then I heard another voice from heaven say:

"Come out of her, my people,
    so that you will not share in her
        sins,
    so that you will not receive any of
        her plagues;
⁵for her sins are piled up to heaven,
    and God has remembered her
        crimes.
⁶Give back to her as she has given;
    pay her back double for what she
        has done.
    Mix her a double portion from her
        own cup.
⁷Give her as much torture and grief
    as the glory and luxury she gave
        herself.
In her heart she boasts,
    'I sit as queen; I am not a widow,
    and I will never mourn.'
⁸Therefore in one day her plagues will
        overtake her:
    death, mourning and famine.
She will be consumed by fire,
    for mighty is the Lord God who
        judges her.

⁹"When the kings of the earth who committed adultery with her and shared her luxury see the smoke of her burning, they will weep and mourn over her. ¹⁰Terrified at her torment, they will stand far off and cry:

" 'Woe! Woe, O great city,
    O Babylon, city of power!
In one hour your doom has come!'

¹¹"The merchants of the earth will weep and mourn over her because no one buys their cargoes any more— ¹²cargoes of gold, silver, precious stones and pearls; fine linen, purple, silk and scarlet cloth; every sort of citron wood, and articles of every kind made of ivory, costly wood, bronze, iron and marble; ¹³cargoes of cinnamon and spice, of incense, myrrh and frankincense, of wine and olive oil, of fine flour and wheat; cattle and sheep; horses and carriages; and bodies and souls of men.

¹⁴"They will say, 'The fruit you longed

---

*a*2 Greek *unclean*

for is gone from you. All your riches and splendor have vanished, never to be recovered.' ¹⁵The merchants who sold these things and gained their wealth from her will stand far off, terrified at her torment. They will weep and mourn ¹⁶and cry out:

" 'Woe! Woe, O great city,
    dressed in fine linen, purple and
        scarlet,
    and glittering with gold, precious
        stones and pearls!
¹⁷In one hour such great wealth has
        been brought to ruin!'

"Every sea captain, and all who travel by ship, the sailors, and all who earn their living from the sea, will stand far off. ¹⁸When they see the smoke of her burning, they will exclaim, 'Was there ever a city like this great city?' ¹⁹They will throw dust on their heads, and with weeping and mourning cry out:

" 'Woe! Woe, O great city,
    where all who had ships on the sea
        became rich through her wealth!
    In one hour she has been brought to
        ruin!
²⁰Rejoice over her, O heaven!
    Rejoice, saints and apostles and
        prophets!
    God has judged her for the way she
        treated you.' "

²¹Then a mighty angel picked up a boulder the size of a large millstone and threw it into the sea, and said:

"With such violence
    the great city of Babylon will be
        thrown down,
    never to be found again.
²²The music of harpists and musicians,
    flute players and trumpeters,
    will never be heard in you again.
No workman of any trade
    will ever be found in you again.
The sound of a millstone
    will never be heard in you again.
²³The light of a lamp
    will never shine in you again.
The voice of bridegroom and bride
    will never be heard in you again.
Your merchants were the world's great
    men.
    By your magic spell all the nations
        were led astray.
²⁴In her was found the blood of
    prophets and of the saints,

and of all who have been killed on
    the earth."

Hallelujah!

19 After this I heard what sounded like the roar of a great multitude in heaven shouting:

"Hallelujah!
Salvation and glory and power belong
    to our God,
² for true and just are his judgments.
He has condemned the great
    prostitute
    who corrupted the earth by her
        adulteries.
He has avenged on her the blood of
    his servants."

³And again they shouted:

"Hallelujah!
The smoke from her goes up for ever
    and ever."

⁴The twenty-four elders and the four living creatures fell down and worshiped God, who was seated on the throne. And they cried:

"Amen, Hallelujah!"

⁵Then a voice came from the throne, saying:

"Praise our God,
    all you his servants,
you who fear him,
    both small and great!"

⁶Then I heard what sounded like a great multitude, like the roar of rushing waters and like loud peals of thunder, shouting:

"Hallelujah!
    For our Lord God Almighty reigns.
⁷Let us rejoice and be glad
    and give him glory!
For the wedding of the Lamb has
    come,
    and his bride has made herself
        ready.
⁸Fine linen, bright and clean,
    was given her to wear."
(Fine linen stands for the righteous acts of the saints.)

⁹Then the angel said to me, "Write: 'Blessed are those who are invited to the wedding supper of the Lamb!' " And he added, "These are the true words of God."

¹⁰At this I fell at his feet to worship him. But he said to me, "Do not do it! I

am a fellow servant with you and with your brothers who hold to the testimony of Jesus. Worship God! For the testimony of Jesus is the spirit of prophecy."

The Rider on the White Horse

[11]I saw heaven standing open and there before me was a white horse, whose rider is called Faithful and True. With justice he judges and makes war. [12]His eyes are like blazing fire, and on his head are many crowns. He has a name written on him that no one knows but he himself. [13]He is dressed in a robe dipped in blood, and his name is the Word of God. [14]The armies of heaven were following him, riding on white horses and dressed in fine linen, white and clean. [15]Out of his mouth comes a sharp sword with which to strike down the nations. "He will rule them with an iron scepter."[a] He treads the winepress of the fury of the wrath of God Almighty. [16]On his robe and on his thigh he has this name written:

KING OF KINGS AND LORD OF LORDS.

[17]And I saw an angel standing in the sun, who cried in a loud voice to all the birds flying in midair, "Come, gather together for the great supper of God, [18]so that you may eat the flesh of kings, generals, and mighty men, of horses and their riders, and the flesh of all people, free and slave, small and great."

[19]Then I saw the beast and the kings of the earth and their armies gathered together to make war against the rider on the horse and his army. [20]But the beast was captured, and with him the false prophet who had performed the miraculous signs on his behalf. With these signs he had deluded those who had received the mark of the beast and worshiped his image. The two of them were thrown alive into the fiery lake of burning sulfur. [21]The rest of them were killed with the sword that came out of the mouth of the rider on the horse, and all the birds gorged themselves on their flesh.

The Thousand Years

20 And I saw an angel coming down out of heaven, having the key to the Abyss and holding in his hand a great chain. [2]He seized the dragon, that ancient serpent, who is the devil, or Satan, and bound him for a thousand years. [3]He threw him into the Abyss, and locked and

sealed it over him, to keep him from deceiving the nations anymore until the thousand years were ended. After that, he must be set free for a short time.

[4]I saw thrones on which were seated those who had been given authority to judge. And I saw the souls of those who had been beheaded because of their testimony for Jesus and because of the word of God. They had not worshiped the beast or his image and had not received his mark on their foreheads or their hands. They came to life and reigned with Christ a thousand years. [5](The rest of the dead did not come to life until the thousand years were ended.) This is the first resurrection. [6]Blessed and holy are those who have part in the first resurrection. The second death has no power over them, but they will be priests of God and of Christ and will reign with him for a thousand years.

Satan's Doom

[7]When the thousand years are over, Satan will be released from his prison [8]and will go out to deceive the nations in the four corners of the earth—Gog and Magog—to gather them for battle. In number they are like the sand on the seashore. [9]They marched across the breadth of the earth and surrounded the camp of God's people, the city he loves. But fire came down from heaven and devoured them. [10]And the devil, who deceived them, was thrown into the lake of burning sulfur, where the beast and the false prophet had been thrown. They will be tormented day and night for ever and ever.

The Dead Are Judged

[11]Then I saw a great white throne and him who was seated on it. Earth and sky fled from his presence, and there was no place for them. [12]And I saw the dead, great and small, standing before the throne, and books were opened. Another book was opened, which is the book of life. The dead were judged according to what they had done as recorded in the books. [13]The sea gave up the dead that were in it, and death and Hades gave up the dead that were in them, and each person was judged according to what he had done. [14]Then death and Hades were thrown into the lake of fire. The lake of fire is the second death. [15]If anyone's

name was not found written in the book of life, he was thrown into the lake of fire.

The New Jerusalem

21 Then I saw a new heaven and a new earth, for the first heaven and the first earth had passed away, and there was no longer any sea. ²I saw the Holy City, the new Jerusalem, coming down out of heaven from God, prepared as a bride beautifully dressed for her husband. ³And I heard a loud voice from the throne saying, "Now the dwelling of God is with men, and he will live with them. They will be his people, and God himself will be with them and be their God. ⁴He will wipe every tear from their eyes. There will be no more death or mourning or crying or pain, for the old order of things has passed away."

⁵He who was seated on the throne said, "I am making everything new!" Then he said, "Write this down, for these words are trustworthy and true."

⁶He said to me: "It is done. I am the Alpha and the Omega, the Beginning and the End. To him who is thirsty I will give to drink without cost from the spring of the water of life. ⁷He who overcomes will inherit all this, and I will be his God and he will be my son. ⁸But the cowardly, the unbelieving, the vile, the murderers, the sexually immoral, those who practice magic arts, the idolaters and all liars—their place will be in the fiery lake of burning sulfur. This is the second death."

⁹One of the seven angels who had the seven bowls full of the seven last plagues came and said to me, "Come, I will show you the bride, the wife of the Lamb." ¹⁰And he carried me away in the Spirit to a mountain great and high, and showed me the Holy City, Jerusalem, coming down out of heaven from God. ¹¹It shone with the glory of God, and its brilliance was like that of a very precious jewel, like a jasper, clear as crystal. ¹²It had a great, high wall with twelve gates, and with twelve angels at the gates. On the gates were written the names of the twelve tribes of Israel. ¹³There were three gates on the east, three on the north, three on the south and three on the west. ¹⁴The wall of the city had twelve foundations, and on them were the names of the twelve apostles of the Lamb.

¹⁵The angel who talked with me had a measuring rod of gold to measure the city, its gates and its walls. ¹⁶The city was laid out like a square, as long as it was wide. He measured the city with the rod and found it to be 12,000 stadia^a in length, and as wide and high as it is long. ¹⁷He measured its wall and it was 144 cubits^b thick,^{c} by man's measurement, which the angel was using. ¹⁸The wall was made of jasper, and the city of pure gold, as pure as glass. ¹⁹The foundations of the city walls were decorated with every kind of precious stone. The first foundation was jasper, the second sapphire, the third chalcedony, the fourth emerald, ²⁰the fifth sardonyx, the sixth carnelian, the seventh chrysolite, the eighth beryl, the ninth topaz, the tenth chrysoprase, the eleventh jacinth, and the twelfth amethyst.^{d} ²¹The twelve gates were twelve pearls, each gate made of a single pearl. The great street of the city was of pure gold, like transparent glass.

²²I did not see a temple in the city, because the Lord God Almighty and the Lamb are its temple. ²³The city does not need the sun or the moon to shine on it, for the glory of God gives it light, and the Lamb is its lamp. ²⁴The nations will walk by its light, and the kings of the earth will bring their splendor into it. ²⁵On no day will its gates ever be shut, for there will be no night there. ²⁶The glory and honor of the nations will be brought into it. ²⁷Nothing impure will ever enter it, nor will anyone who does what is shameful or deceitful, but only those whose names are written in the Lamb's book of life.

The River of Life

22 Then the angel showed me the river of the water of life, as clear as crystal, flowing from the throne of God and of the Lamb ²down the middle of the great street of the city. On each side of the river stood the tree of life, bearing twelve crops of fruit, yielding its fruit every month. And the leaves of the tree are for the healing of the nations. ³No longer will there be any curse. The throne of God and of the Lamb will be in the city, and his servants will serve him. ⁴They will see his face, and his name will be on their foreheads. ⁵There will be no more night. They will not need the light of a lamp or the light of the sun, for the Lord God will

---

^{a}16 That is, about 1,400 miles (about 2,200 kilometers) ^{b}17 That is, about 200 feet (about 65 meters) ^{c}17 Or high ^{d}20 The precise identification of some of these precious stones is uncertain.

give them light. And they will reign for ever and ever.

⁶The angel said to me, "These words are trustworthy and true. The Lord, the God of the spirits of the prophets, sent his angel to show his servants the things that must soon take place."

Jesus Is Coming

⁷"Behold, I am coming soon! Blessed is he who keeps the words of the prophecy in this book."

⁸I, John, am the one who heard and saw these things. And when I had heard and seen them, I fell down to worship at the feet of the angel who had been showing them to me. ⁹But he said to me, "Do not do it! I am a fellow servant with you and with your brothers the prophets and of all who keep the words of this book. Worship God!"

¹⁰Then he told me, "Do not seal up the words of the prophecy of this book, because the time is near. ¹¹Let him who does wrong continue to do wrong; let him who is vile continue to be vile; let him who does right continue to do right; and let him who is holy continue to be holy."

¹²"Behold, I am coming soon! My reward is with me, and I will give to everyone according to what he has done. ¹³I am the Alpha and the Omega, the First and the Last, the Beginning and the End.

FRIDAY

VERSE FOR THE DAY:
Revelation 22:16

AUTHOR:
Marilyn Morgan Helleberg

PASSAGE FOR THE DAY:
Revelation 22:7–16

Morning Star

"I AM . . . the bright Morning Star" (Revelation 22:16).

These words of the risen Christ correspond with a statement once made by a nineteen-year-old youth named Abe Lincoln: "I never behold the stars that I do not feel that I am looking into the face of God."

Stars! What is it about them that so kindles our sense of wonder? Scientists tell us that, when we look up at the night sky, we are seeing light that left some of those faraway stars thousands of light years ago. Tonight, if the sky is clear, you and I might actually see light rays that left some distant star on the night Jesus was born! That makes me aware that our lives touch eternity.

I need the stars. I need them because of my craving for beauty and my longing for perfection in this less-than-beautiful, imperfect world. I need them because I often buy security at the cost of my sense of enchantment, and the price is much too high. I need them to deepen my experience of awe and wonder, to remind me of the kingdom and the power and the glory of God and of his creation.

If the sky is clear tonight, let's step outside and look at the stars. Perhaps, like Abe Lincoln, we'll sense that we're looking into the face of God.

Additional Scripture Readings:
Psalm 19:1–6; Isaiah 40:25–26

Go to page 1427 for your next devotional reading.

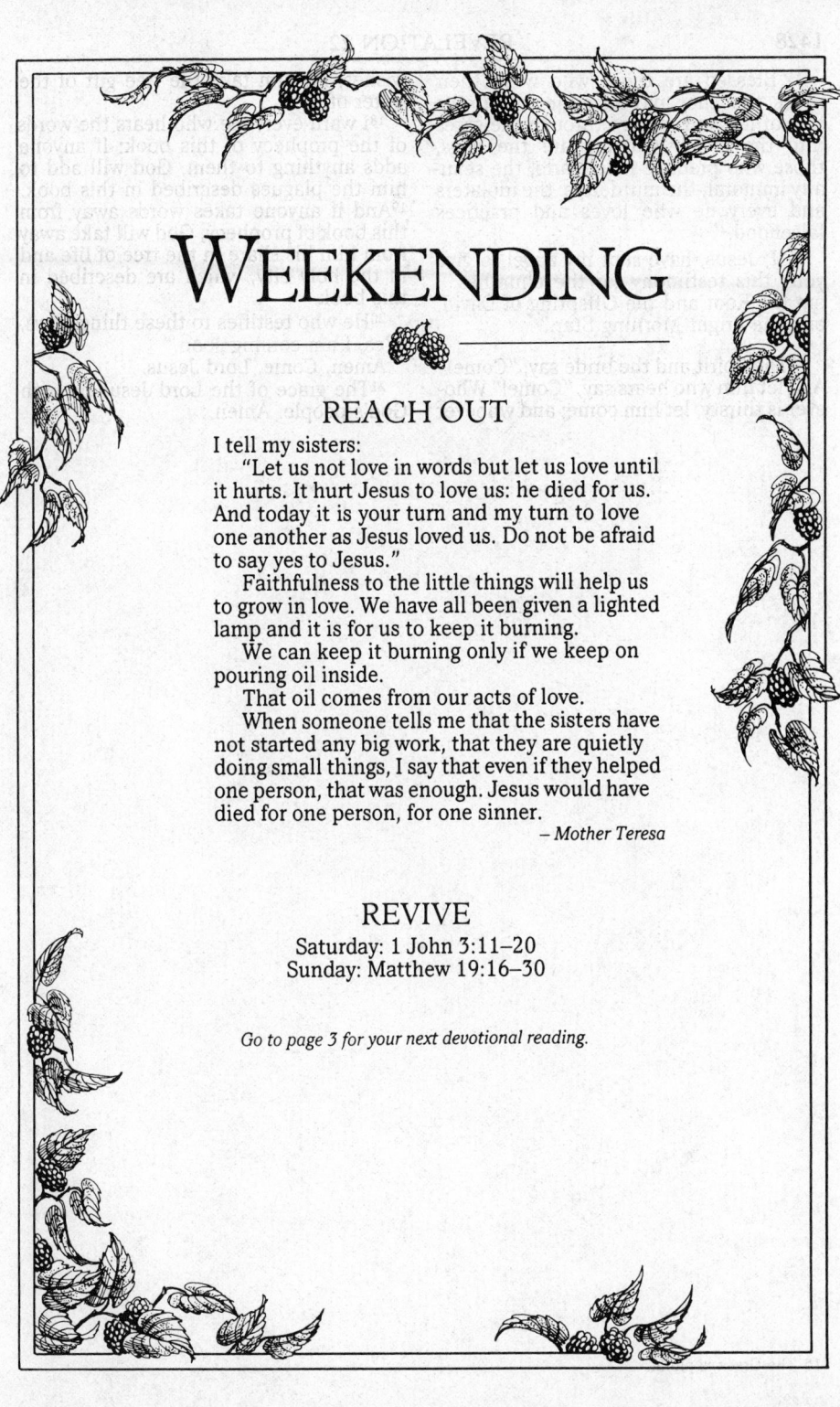

WEEKENDING

REACH OUT

I tell my sisters:

"Let us not love in words but let us love until it hurts. It hurt Jesus to love us: he died for us. And today it is your turn and my turn to love one another as Jesus loved us. Do not be afraid to say yes to Jesus."

Faithfulness to the little things will help us to grow in love. We have all been given a lighted lamp and it is for us to keep it burning.

We can keep it burning only if we keep on pouring oil inside.

That oil comes from our acts of love.

When someone tells me that the sisters have not started any big work, that they are quietly doing small things, I say that even if they helped one person, that was enough. Jesus would have died for one person, for one sinner.

— *Mother Teresa*

REVIVE

Saturday: 1 John 3:11–20
Sunday: Matthew 19:16–30

Go to page 3 for your next devotional reading.

[14]"Blessed are those who wash their robes, that they may have the right to the tree of life and may go through the gates into the city. [15]Outside are the dogs, those who practice magic arts, the sexually immoral, the murderers, the idolaters and everyone who loves and practices falsehood.

[16]"I, Jesus, have sent my angel to give you[a] this testimony for the churches. I am the Root and the Offspring of David, and the bright Morning Star."

[17]The Spirit and the bride say, "Come!" And let him who hears say, "Come!" Whoever is thirsty, let him come; and whoever wishes, let him take the free gift of the water of life.

[18]I warn everyone who hears the words of the prophecy of this book: If anyone adds anything to them, God will add to him the plagues described in this book. [19]And if anyone takes words away from this book of prophecy, God will take away from him his share in the tree of life and in the holy city, which are described in this book.

[20]He who testifies to these things says, "Yes, I am coming soon."

Amen. Come, Lord Jesus.

[21]The grace of the Lord Jesus be with God's people. Amen.

INDEXES
READING PLANS

WEIGHTS & MEASURES

The figures of the table are calculated on the basis of a shekel equaling 11.5 grams, a cubit equaling 18 inches and an ephah equaling 22 liters. The quart referred to is either a dry quart (slightly larger than a liter) or a liquid quart (slightly smaller than a liter), whichever is applicable. The ton referred to in the footnotes is the American ton of 2,000 pounds.

This table is based upon the best available information, but it is not intended to be mathematically precise; like the measurement equivalents in the footnotes, it merely gives approximate amounts and distances. Weights and measures differed somewhat at various times and places in the ancient world. There is uncertainty particularly about the ephah and the bath; further discoveries may give more light on these units of capacity.

	BIBLICAL UNIT		APPROXIMATE AMERICAN EQUIVALENT	APPROXIMATE METRIC EQUIVALENT
WEIGHTS	talent	*(60 minas)*	75 pounds	34 kilograms
	mina	*(50 shekels)*	1 1/4 pounds	0.6 kilogram
	shekel	*(2 bekas)*	2/5 ounce	11.5 grams
	pim	*(2/3 shekel)*	1/3 ounce	7.6 grams
	beka	*(10 gerahs)*	1/5 ounce	5.5 grams
	gerah		1/50 ounce	0.6 gram
LENGTH	cubit		18 inches	0.5 meter
	span		9 inches	23 centimeters
	handbreadth		3 inches	8 centimeters
CAPACITY	cor [homer]	*(10 ephahs)*	6 bushels	220 liters
Dry Measure	lethek	*(5 ephahs)*	3 bushels	110 liters
	ephah	*(10 omers)*	3/5 bushel	22 liters
	seah	*(1/3 ephah)*	7 quarts	7.3 liters
	omer	*(1/10 ephah)*	2 quarts	2 liters
	cab	*(1/18 ephah)*	1 quart	1 liter
Liquid Measure	bath	*(1 ephah)*	6 gallons	22 liters
	hin	*(1/6 bath)*	4 quarts	4 liters
	log	*(1/72 bath)*	1/3 quart	0.3 liter

ACKNOWLEDGMENTS INDEX

Page 3: By Ruth A. Tucker. Copyright © 1990 by The Zondervan Corporation.

Page 5: By Gladys M. Hunt. Copyright © 1990 by The Zondervan Corporation.

Page 7: By Ruth Bell Graham. Copyright © 1990 by Ruth Bell Graham.

Page 9: Taken from BE STILL AND KNOW by Millie Stamm. Copyright © 1978 by Millie Stamm. Used by permission of Zondervan Publishing House.

Page 11: Taken from BESIDE STILL WATERS by Gien Karssen. Copyright © 1985 by Gien Karssen. Used by permission of NavPress.

Page 14: By Ruth Bell Graham. Copyright © 1990 by Ruth Bell Graham.

Page 16: Excerpt from GROWING INTO GOD by Patricia Beall. Copyright © 1991 by Ave Maria Press, Notre Dame, IN 46556. All rights reserved. Used with permission of the publisher.

Page 20: By Gladys M. Hunt. Copyright © 1990 by The Zondervan Corporation.

Page 24: Reprinted from the Christian Herald (September 1987). Copyright © by Gloria Gaither. Used by permission.

Page 46: Taken from BE STILL AND KNOW by Millie Stamm. Copyright © 1978 by Millie Stamm. Used by permission of Zondervan Publishing House.

Page 57: By Beth Donigan Seversen. Copyright © 1990 by The Zondervan Corporation.

Page 59: Copyright © 1987, CRC Publications, A Ministry of the Christian Reformed Church. Reprinted from The Banner (May 18, 1987) with permission.

Page 63: From SALT IN MY KITCHEN by Jeannette Lockerbie. Copyright © 1967. Moody Bible Institute of Chicago. Moody Press. Used by permission.

Page 65: Copyright © 1974 by Anne Ortlund. Used by permission.

Page 67: By Joni Eareckson Tada. Copyright © 1990 by The Zondervan Corporation.

Page 77: By Joni Eareckson Tada. Copyright © 1990 by The Zondervan Corporation.

Page 79: Reprinted with permission from Daily Guideposts 1987. Copyright © 1986 by Guideposts Associates, Inc., Carmel, NY 10512.

Page 87: Take from Judges 5:2–3,10–11

Page 97: By Anne Ortlund. Copyright © 1974 by Anne Ortlund. Used by permission.

Page 123: By Joni Eareckson Tada. Copyright © 1990 by The Zondervan Corporation.

Page 127: By Joni Eareckson Tada. Copyright © 1990 by The Zondervan Corporation.

Page 147: Taken from MEDITATION MOMENTS FOR WOMEN by Mildred Stamm. Copyright © 1967 by Zondervan Publishing House. Used by permission.

Page 152: From SALT IN MY KITCHEN by Jeannette Lockerbie. Copyright © 1967. Moody Bible Institute of Chicago. Moody Press. Used by permission.

Page 158: Taken from 1 Samuel 2:1–2,8.

Page 161: Taken from MEDITATION MOMENTS FOR WOMEN by Mildred Stamm. Copyright © 1967 by Zondervan Publishing House. Used by permission.

Page 187: By Beverly LaHaye. Copyright © 1990 by The Zondervan Corporation.

Page 189: Taken from BE STILL AND KNOW by Millie Stamm. Copyright © 1978 by Millie Stamm. Used by permission of Zondervan Publishing House.

Page 192: Taken from A SILVER PEN FOR CLOUDY DAYS by Susan L. Lenzkes. Copyright © 1987 by Susan L. Lenzkes. Used by permission of Zondervan Publishing House.

Page 211: Taken from COME TO THE WATERS by Diane Head. Copyright © 1985 by Diane Head. Published by Zondervan Publishing House. Used by permission.

Page 215: "Isn't Life Glorious" from HOLD TO YOUR DREAM. Copyright © 1965 by Helen Lowrie Marshall. Used by permission.

Page 218: Taken from EARLY WIDOW by Mary Jane Worden. Copyright © 1989 by Mary Jane Worden. Used by permission of InterVarsity Press, P.O. Box 1400, Downers Grove, IL 60515.

Page 237: Taken from GOD IS ENOUGH by Hannah Whitall Smith. Published by Zondervan Publishing House.

Page 241: By Jean E. Syswerda. Copyright © 1990 by The Zondervan Corporation.

Page 247: By June Gunden. Copyright © 1990 by The Zondervan Corporation.

Page 250: Taken from AFTER EVERY WEDDING COMES A MARRIAGE by Florence Littauer. Copyright © 1981 Harvest House Publishers, Eugene, OR 97402. Used by permission.

Page 256: From the book IT'S MY TURN by Ruth Bell Graham. Copyright © 1989 by Ruth Bell Graham. Used by permission of Fleming H. Revell.

Page 260: By Jean E. Syswerda. Copyright © 1990 by The Zondervan Corporation.

Page 272: By Dorothy Patterson. Copyright © 1990 by The Zondervan Corporation.

Page 277: By Gladys M. Hunt. Copyright © 1990 by The Zondervan Corporation.

Page 283: Taken from BE STILL AND KNOW by Millie Stamm. Copyright © 1978 by Millie Stamm. Used by permission of Zondervan Publishing House.

Page 293: Taken from GOD STILL LOVES MY KITCHEN by Mab Graf Hoover. Copyright © 1981 by The Zondervan Corporation. Used by permission.

Page 304: Taken from BESIDE STILL WATERS by Gien Karssen. Copyright © 1985 by Gien Karssen. Used by permission of NavPress.

Page 318: Taken from WHAT COLOR IS MY COLLAR? by Marlene Obie. Copyright © 1985 by The Zondervan Corporation. Used by permission.

Page 321: Taken from HEART TROUBLE by Barbara Bush. Copyright © 1981 by the Zondervan Corporation. Used by permission.

Page 323: Taken from WITH HIM IN THE STRUGGLE: A WOMAN'S WORKSHOP ON II SAMUEL by Myrna Alexander. Used by permission of Zondervan Publishing House.

Page 329: Taken from WITH HIM IN THE STRUGGLE: A WOMAN'S WORKSHOP ON II SAMUEL by Myrna Alexander. Used by permission of Zondervan Publishing House.

Page 675: Taken from WHEN THE HANDWRITING ON THE WALL IS IN BROWN CRAYON by Susan L. Lenzkes. Copyright © 1981 by Susan L. Lenzkes. Used by permission of Zondervan Publishing House.

Page 677: Excerpt from WHO AM I GOD? by Marjorie Holmes. Copyright © 1970, 1971 by Marjorie Holmes Mighell. Used by permission of Doubleday, a division of Bantam, Doubleday, Dell Publishing Group, Inc.

Page 680: From the book EACH NEW DAY by Corrie ten Boom. Copyright © 1977 by Corrie ten Boom. Used by permission of Fleming H. Revell Company.

Page 681: Taken from A SILVER PEN FOR CLOUDY DAYS by Susan L. Lenzkes. Copyright © 1987 by Susan L. Lenzkes. Used by permission of Zondervan Publishing House.

Page 684: Taken from WHAT COLOR IS MY COLLAR? by Marlene Obie. Copyright © 1985 by The Zondervan Corporation. Used by permission.

Page 689: Taken from LET'S MAKE A MEMORY by Gloria Gaither and Shirley Dobson. Copyright © 1983 by Gloria Gaither, Shirley Dobson, and James Dobson, Inc. Published by Word, Inc., Dallas, Texas. Used by permission.

Page 697: By Dorothy Patterson. Copyright © 1990 by The Zondervan Corporation.

Page 701: Taken from WHAT COLOR IS MY COLLAR? by Marlene Obie. Copyright © 1985 by The Zondervan Corporation. Used by permission.

Page 702: Taken from THE HIDDEN STRENGTH by Ingrid Trobisch. Copyright © 1988 by Ingrid Trobisch. Used by permission of Here's Life Publishers.

Page 704: By Luci Swindoll. Copyright © 1990 by The Zondervan Corporation.

Page 706: Taken from THE BETTER HALF OF LIFE by Jean Shaw. Copyright © 1983 by The Zondervan Corporation. Used by permission.

Page 710: From SUNNY-SIDE UP by Alma Barkman. Copyright © 1977. Moody Bible Institute of Chicago. Moody Press. Used by permission.

Page 712: Taken from THE BETTER HALF OF LIFE by Jean Shaw. Copyright © 1983 by The Zondervan Corporation. Used by permission.

Page 716: By Dorothy Patterson. Copyright © 1990 by The Zondervan Corporation.

Page 729: By Wanda K. Jones. Copyright © 1990 by The Zondervan Corporation.

Page 731: Taken from THE QUIET HEART by June Masters Bacher. Copyright © 1988 by Harvest House Publishers, Eugene, OR 97402. Used by permission.

Page 737: Taken from A VIOLENT GRACE by Gini Andrews. Copyright © 1986 by Gini Andrews. Used by permission of Zondervan Publishing House.

Page 749: From the book WITH MY WHOLE HEART by Karen Burton Mains. Copyright © 1987 by Multnomah Press. Published by Multnomah Press, Portland, Oregon 97266. Used by permission.

Page 754: Taken from A WOMAN'S CHOICE by Eugenia Price. Copyright © 1962 by Eugenia Price. Published by Zondervan Bible Publishers. Used by permission.

Page 765: Taken from LET'S MAKE A MEMORY by Gloria Gaither and Shirley Dobson. Copyright © 1983 by Gloria Gaither, Shirley Dobson, and James Dobson, Inc. Published by Word, Inc., Dallas, Texas. Used by permission.

Page 767: By Beverly LaHaye. Copyright © 1990 by The Zondervan Corporation.

Page 771: From the book ON ASKING GOD WHY by Elisabeth Elliot. Copyright © (1989) by Fleming H. Revell. Used by permission of Fleming H. Revell Company.

Page 776: From the book ON ASKING GOD WHY by Elisabeth Elliot. Copyright © (1989) by Fleming H. Revell. Used by permission of Fleming H. Revell Company.

Page 779: Excerpt from WHO AM I GOD? by Marjorie Holmes. Copyright © 1970, 1971 by Marjorie Holmes Mighell. Used by permission of Doubleday, a division of Bantam, Doubleday, Dell Publishing Group, Inc.

Page 787: From "O Lord, You Were Born!" REACHING FOR RAINBOWS: Resources For Creative Worship by Ann Weems. Copyright © 1980 The Westminster Press. Used by permission of Westminster/John Knox Press.

Page 792: By Debby Boone. Copyright © 1990 by The Zondervan Corporation.

Page 794: Taken from EARLY WIDOW by Mary Jane Worden. Copyright © 1989 by Mary Jane Worden. Used by permission of InterVarsity Press, P.O. Box 1400, Downers Grove, IL 60515.

Page 809: Taken from SINCERELY by Gigi Graham Tchividijian. Copyright © 1984 by The Zondervan Corporation. Used by permission.

Page 813: By Debby Boone. Copyright © 1990 by The Zondervan Corporation.

Page 822: Taken from WHEN THE HANDWRITING ON THE WALL IS IN BROWN CRAYON by Susan L. Lenzkes. Copyright © 1981 by Susan L. Lenzkes. Used by permission of Zondervan Publishing House.

Page 828: Taken from A BLADE OF GRASS by Gladis and Gordon DePree. Copyright © 1967 by Gladis and Gordon DePree. Published by Zondervan Publishing House. Used by permission.

Page 835: By Sue Richards. Copyright © 1990 by The Zondervan Corporation.

Page 838: By Marie Chapian. Copyright © 1990 by The Zondervan Corporation.

Page 842: Taken from COME TO THE WATERS by Diane Head. Copyright © 1985 by Diane Head. Published by Zondervan Publishing House. Used by permission.

Page 857: Reprinted by permission from FREE TO GRIEVE by Maureen Rank, published and copyrighted 1985 by Bethany House Publishers, Minneapolis, MN 55438.

Page 873: By Marie Chapian. Copyright © 1990 by The Zondervan Corporation.

Page 880: Taken from WHEN THE HANDWRITING ON THE WALL IS IN BROWN CRAYON by Susan L. Lenzkes. Copyright © 1981 by Susan L. Lenzkes. Used by permission of Zondervan Publishing House.

Page 889: By Dorothy Patterson. Copyright © 1990 by The Zondervan Corporation.

Page 898: Taken from A MOMENT A DAY, compiled by Mary Beckwith and Kathi Mills. Copyright © 1988 by Mary Beckwith and Kathi Mills. Published by Regal Books, Ventura, CA 93006. Used by permission.

Page 913: By June Hunt. Copyright © 1990 by June Hunt.

Page 929: By Doris Rikkers. Copyright © 1990 by The Zondervan Corporation.

Page 937: Reprinted with permission from Daily Guideposts 1989. Copyright © 1988 by Guideposts Associates, Inc., Carmel, NY 10512.

Page 941: It was discovered after printing that the poem on this page was written by John Oxenham (1852-1941).

Page 948: Taken from GOD IS ENOUGH by Hannah Whitall Smith. Published by Zondervan Publishing House.

Page 955: Taken from HEART TROUBLE by Barbara Bush. Copyright © 1981 by the Zondervan Corporation. Used by permission.

Page 957: Excerpts are reprinted from MARY IN A MARTHA'S WORLD. Copyright © 1989 by Rita Schweitz. Used by permission of Augsburg Fortress.

Page 1141: From the book WITH MY WHOLE HEART by Karen Burton Mains. Copyright © 1987 by Multnomah Press. Published by Multnomah Press, Portland, Oregon 97266. Used by permission.

Page 1143: Taken from A WOMAN'S CHOICE by Eugenia Price. Copyright © 1962 by Eugenia Price. Published by Zondervan Bible Publishers. Used by permission.

Page 1148: By Rosemary Jensen. Copyright © 1990 by The Zondervan Corporation.

Page 1151: Taken from MEMORIES by Kathryn Hillen. Copyright © 1987 by Kathryn Hillen. Used by permission of Zondervan Publishing House.

Page 1153: By Jill Briscoe. Copyright © 1990 by The Zondervan Corporation.

Page 1155: Taken from Luke 1:46–50.

Page 1156: Taken from BE STILL AND KNOW by Millie Stamm. Copyright © 1978 by Millie Stamm. Used by permission of Zondervan Publishing House.

Page 1159: By Rosalind Rinker. Copyright © 1990 by The Zondervan Corporation.

Page 1169: By Gloria Gaither. Copyright © 1990 by Gloria Gaither.

Page 1171: By Carol L. Baldwin. Copyright © 1990 by The Zondervan Corporation.

Page 1172: Taken from KINDRED SPIRITS by Kathy Narramore and Alice Hill. Copyright © 1985 by The Zondervan Corporation. Used by permission.

Page 1173: Copyright © 1987, CRC Publications, a Ministry of the Christian Reformed Church. Reprinted from *The Banner* (May 18, 1987) with permission.

Page 1175: By Sue Richards. Copyright © 1990 by The Zondervan Corporation.

Page 1177: By Anne Ortlund. Copyright © 1990 by The Zondervan Corporation.

Page 1181: By Ruth A. Tucker. Copyright © 1990 by The Zondervan Corporation.

Page 1185: Taken from OUT OF THE SALTSHAKER AND INTO THE WORLD by Rebecca Manley Pippert. Copyright © 1979 by InterVarsity Christian Fellowship of the USA. Used by permission of InterVarsity Press, P.O. Box 1400, Downers Grove, IL 60515.

Page 1189: Reprinted with permission from Daily Guideposts 1987. Copyright © 1986 by Guideposts Associates, Inc., Carmel, NY 10512.

Page 1191: Taken from MY LIFE FOR THE POOR by Mother Teresa of Calcutta. Copyright © 1985 by Jose Gonzalez-Balado and Janet N. Playfoot. Published by Harper & Row, Publishers, Inc. Used by permission.

Page 1193: By June Gunden. Copyright © 1990 by The Zondervan Corporation.

Page 1198: By Jean Syswerda. Copyright © 1990 by The Zondervan Corporation.

Page 1201: Taken from A MOMENT A DAY, compiled by Mary Beckwith and Kathi Mills. Copyright © 1988 by Mary Beckwith and Kathi Mills. Published by Regal Books, Ventura, CA 93006. Used by permission.

Page 1206: Taken from THE QUIET HEART by June Masters Bacher. Copyright © 1988 by Harvest House Publishers, Eugene, OR 97402. Used by permission.

Page 1209: Taken from QUIET MOMENTS by June Masters Bacher. Copyright © 1979 by Harvest House Publishers, Eugene, OR 97402. Used by permission.

Page 1210: Taken from IT'S MY TURN by Ruth Bell Graham. Copyright © 1989 by Ruth Bell Graham. Published by Fleming H. Revell Company. Used by permission.

Page 1212: Taken from A MOMENT A DAY, compiled by Mary Beckwith and Kathi Mills. Copyright © 1988 by Mary Beckwith and Kathi Mills. Published by Regal Books, Ventura, CA 93006. Used by permission.

Page 1217: Reprinted with permission from Daily Guideposts 1987. Copyright © 1986 by Guideposts Associates, Inc., Carmel, NY 10512.

Page 1228: By Carol L. Baldwin. Copyright © 1990 by The Zondervan Corporation.

Page 1231: By Gladys M. Hunt. Copyright © 1990 by The Zondervan Corporation.

Page 1233: By Gladys M. Hunt. Copyright © 1990 by The Zondervan Corporation.

Page 1235: Taken from THE WOMAN AT THE WELL by Dale Evans Rogers. Copyright © (1970) Fleming H. Revell. Used by permission of Fleming H. Revell.

Page 1236: From SALT IN MY KITCHEN by Jeannette Lockerbie. Copyright © 1967. Moody Bible Institute of Chicago. Moody Press. Used by permission.

Page 1238: By Sue Richards. Copyright © 1990 by The Zondervan Corporation.

Page 1240: By Ann Kiemel Anderson. Copyright © 1990 by The Zondervan Corporation.

Page 1243: By Marie Chapian. Copyright © 1990 by The Zondervan Corporation.

Page 1245: Taken from SINCERELY by Gigi Graham Tchividjian. Copyright © 1984 by The Zondervan Corporation. Used by permission.

Page 1247: Taken from THE SPIRITUALITY OF GENTLENESS: GROWING TOWARD CHRISTIAN WHOLENESS by Judith C. Lechman. Copyright © 1987 by Judith C. Lechman. Published by Harper & Row Publishers, Inc. Used by permission.

Page 1253: By June Hunt. Copyright © 1990 by June Hunt.

Page 1255: Taken from OUT OF THE SALTSHAKER AND INTO THE WORLD by Rebecca Manley Pippert. Copyright © 1979 by InterVarsity Christian Fellowship of the USA. Used by permission of InterVarsity Press, P.O. Box 1400, Downers Grove, IL 60515.

Page 1256: Taken from A SILVER PEN FOR CLOUDY DAYS by Susan L. Lenzkes. Copyright © 1987 by Susan L. Lenzkes. Used by permission of Zondervan Publishing House.

Page 1260: By June Hunt. Copyright © 1990 by June Hunt.

Page 1262: Taken from RISE AND SHINE by Alma Barkman. Copyright © 1987. Moody Bible Institute of Chicago. Moody Press. Used by permission.

Page 1264: Reprinted from WALKING ON WATER: REFLECTIONS ON FAITH AND ART by Madeleine L'Engle. Copyright © 1980 by Crosswicks. Used by permission of Harold Shaw Publishers, Wheaton, IL 60189.

Page 1266: Reprinted with permission from Daily Guideposts 1988. Copyright © 1987 by Guideposts Associates, Inc., Carmel, NY 10512.

Page 1267: Taken from WOMEN IN GOD'S PRESENCE compiled by Delores Taylor. Copyright © 1988 by Christian Publications, Camphill, PA. Used by permission.

Page 1272: Taken from HEART TROUBLE by Barbara Bush. Copyright © 1981 by the Zondervan Corporation. Used by permission.

Page 1274: By Beth Donigan Seversen. Copyright © 1990 by The Zondervan Corporation.

Page 1383: By June Hunt. Copyright © 1990 by June Hunt.

Page 1385: By Beverly LaHaye. Copyright © 1990 by The Zondervan Corporation.

Page 1386: By Beth Donigan Seversen. Copyright © 1990 by The Zondervan Corporation.

Page 1389: Taken from WOMEN IN GOD'S PRESENCE compiled by Delores Taylor. Copyright © 1988 by Christian Publications, Camphill, PA. Used by permission.

Page 1394: By Rosemary Jensen. Copyright © 1990 by The Zondervan Corporation.

Page 1397: By Luci Swindoll. Copyright © 1990 by The Zondervan Corporation.

Page 1400: By Ruth A. Tucker. Copyright © 1990 by The Zondervan Corporation.

Page 1402: Taken from WHEN THE HANDWRITING ON THE WALL IS IN BROWN CRAYON by Susan L. Lenzkes. Copyright © 1981 by Susan L. Lenzkes. Used by permission of Zondervan Publishing House.

Page 1404: Taken from SO YOU'RE THE PASTOR'S WIFE by Ruth Senter. Copyright © 1990 by Victor Books. Used by permission.

Page 1405: Taken from WHEN THE HANDWRITING ON THE WALL IS IN BROWN CRAYON by Susan L. Lenzkes. Copyright © 1981 by Susan L. Lenzkes. Used by permission of Zondervan Publishing House.

Page 1408: Reprinted with permission from Daily Guideposts 1988. Copyright © 1987 by Guideposts Associates, Inc., Carmel, NY 10512.

Page 1412: Taken from A CLOSER WALK by Catherine Marshall. Copyright © 1986 by Calen, Inc. Published by Chosen Books, Fleming H. Revell Company. Used by permission.

Page 1415: By Wanda K. Jones. Copyright © 1990 by The Zondervan Corporation.

Page 1420: Taken from BESIDE STILL WATERS by Gien Karssen. Copyright © 1985 by Gien Karssen. Used by permission of NavPress.

Page 1426: Reprinted with permission from Daily Guideposts 1989. Copyright © 1988 by Guideposts Associates, Inc., Carmel, NY 10512.

Page 1427: Taken from MY LIFE FOR THE POOR by Mother Teresa of Calcutta. Copyright © 1985 by Jose Gonzalez-Balado and Janet N. Playfoot. Published by Harper & Row, Publishers, Inc. Used by permission.

Every effort has been made to give proper credit for each devotion used in this Women's Devotional Bible. If any error or inaccuracy is noted, please inform the publishers.

READING PLAN

God's Word is full of promises, encouragement and guidance for you. This reading plan gives you a simple structure for reading through the entire Bible in one year.

DATE	PASSAGE	DATE	PASSAGE
January 1	Genesis 1–4	February 17	Numbers 25–26
January 2	Genesis 5–8	February 18	Numbers 27–29
January 3	Genesis 9–12	February 19	Numbers 30–32
January 4	Genesis 13–17	February 20	Numbers 33–36
January 5	Genesis 18–20	February 21	Deuteronomy 1–2
January 6	Genesis 21–23	February 22	Deuteronomy 3–4
January 7	Genesis 24–25	February 23	Deuteronomy 5–8
January 8	Genesis 26–28	February 24	Deuteronomy 9–11
January 9	Genesis 29–31	February 25	Deuteronomy 12–15
January 10	Genesis 32–35	February 26	Deuteronomy 16–19
January 11	Genesis 36–38	February 27	Deuteronomy 20–23
January 12	Genesis 39–41	February 28	Deuteronomy 24–27
January 13	Genesis 42–43	March 1	Deuteronomy 28–29
January 14	Genesis 44–46	March 2	Deuteronomy 30–32
January 15	Genesis 47–50	March 3	Deuteronomy 33–34
January 16	Exodus 1–4	March 4	Joshua 1–4
January 17	Exodus 5–7	March 5	Joshua 5–7
January 18	Exodus 8–10	March 6	Joshua 8–10
January 19	Exodus 11–13	March 7	Joshua 11–13
January 20	Exodus 14–16	March 8	Joshua 14–17
January 21	Exodus 17–20	March 9	Joshua 18–20
January 22	Exodus 21–23	March 10	Joshua 21–22
January 23	Exodus 24–27	March 11	Joshua 23–24
January 24	Exodus 28–30	March 12	Judges 1–3
January 25	Exodus 31–34	March 13	Judges 4–5
January 26	Exodus 35–37	March 14	Judges 6–8
January 27	Exodus 38–40	March 15	Judges 9–10
January 28	Leviticus 1–4	March 16	Judges 11–13
January 29	Leviticus 5–7	March 17	Judges 14–16
January 30	Leviticus 8–10	March 18	Judges 17–19
January 31	Leviticus 11–13	March 19	Judges 20–21
February 1	Leviticus 14–15	March 20	Ruth 1–4
February 2	Leviticus 16–18	March 21	1 Samuel 1–3
February 3	Leviticus 19–21	March 22	1 Samuel 4–7
February 4	Leviticus 22–23	March 23	1 Samuel 8–12
February 5	Leviticus 24–25	March 24	1 Samuel 13–14
February 6	Leviticus 26–27	March 25	1 Samuel 15–16
February 7	Numbers 1–2	March 26	1 Samuel 17–18
February 8	Numbers 3–4	March 27	1 Samuel 19–21
February 9	Numbers 5–6	March 28	1 Samuel 22–24
February 10	Numbers 7	March 29	1 Samuel 25–27
February 11	Numbers 8–10	March 30	1 Samuel 28–31
February 12	Numbers 11–13	March 31	2 Samuel 1–3
February 13	Numbers 14–15	April 1	2 Samuel 4–7
February 14	Numbers 16–18	April 2	2 Samuel 8–11
February 15	Numbers 19–21	April 3	2 Samuel 12–13
February 16	Numbers 22–24	April 4	2 Samuel 14–16

DATE	PASSAGE	DATE	PASSAGE
April 5.	2 Samuel 17–19	June 2.	Job 21–24
April 6.	2 Samuel 20–22	June 3.	Job 25–30
April 7.	2 Samuel 23–24	June 4.	Job 31–34
April 8.	1 Kings 1–2	June 5.	Job 35–38
April 9.	1 Kings 3–5	June 6.	Job 39–42
April 10.	1 Kings 6–7	June 7.	Psalms 1–8
April 11.	1 Kings 8–9	June 8.	Psalms 9–17
April 12.	1 Kings 10–12	June 9.	Psalms 18–21
April 13.	1 Kings 13–15	June 10.	Psalms 22–27
April 14.	1 Kings 16–18	June 11.	Psalms 28–33
April 15.	1 Kings 19–20	June 12.	Psalms 34–37
April 16.	1 Kings 21–22	June 13.	Psalms 38–42
April 17.	2 Kings 1–3	June 14.	Psalms 43–49
April 18.	2 Kings 4–5	June 15.	Psalms 50–55
April 19.	2 Kings 6–8	June 16.	Psalms 56–61
April 20.	2 Kings 9–10	June 17.	Psalms 62–68
April 21.	2 Kings 11–13	June 18.	Psalms 69–72
April 22.	2 Kings 14–16	June 19.	Psalms 73–77
April 23.	2 Kings 17–18	June 20.	Psalms 78–80
April 24.	2 Kings 19–21	June 21.	Psalms 81–88
April 25.	2 Kings 22–23	June 22.	Psalms 89–94
April 26.	2 Kings 24–25	June 23.	Psalms 95–103
April 27.	1 Chronicles 1–2	June 24.	Psalms 104–106
April 28.	1 Chronicles 3–4	June 25.	Psalms 107–111
April 29.	1 Chronicles 5–6	June 26.	Psalms 112–118
April 30.	1 Chronicles 7–9	June 27.	Psalm 119
May 1.	1 Chronicles 10–12	June 28.	Psalms 120–133
May 2.	1 Chronicles 13–16	June 29.	Psalms 134–140
May 3.	1 Chronicles 17–19	June 30.	Psalms 141–150
May 4.	1 Chronicles 20–23	July 1.	Proverbs 1–3
May 5.	1 Chronicles 24–26	July 2.	Proverbs 4–7
May 6.	1 Chronicles 27–29	July 3.	Proverbs 8–11
May 7.	2 Chronicles 1–4	July 4.	Proverbs 12–14
May 8.	2 Chronicles 5–7	July 5.	Proverbs 15–17
May 9.	2 Chronicles 8–11	July 6.	Proverbs 18–20
May 10.	2 Chronicles 12–16	July 7.	Proverbs 21–23
May 11.	2 Chronicles 17–20	July 8.	Proverbs 24–26
May 12.	2 Chronicles 21–24	July 9.	Proverbs 27–29
May 13.	2 Chronicles 25–28	July 10.	Proverbs 30–31
May 14.	2 Chronicles 29–31	July 11.	Ecclesiastes 1–4
May 15.	2 Chronicles 32–34	July 12.	Ecclesiastes 5–8
May 16.	2 Chronicles 35–36	July 13.	Ecclesiastes 9–12
May 17.	Ezra 1–4	July 14.	Song of Songs 1–4
May 18.	Ezra 5–7	July 15.	Song of Songs 5–8
May 19.	Ezra 8–10	July 16.	Isaiah 1–3
May 20.	Nehemiah 1–3	July 17.	Isaiah 4–8
May 21.	Nehemiah 4–7	July 18.	Isaiah 9–11
May 22.	Nehemiah 8–9	July 19.	Isaiah 12–14
May 23.	Nehemiah 10–11	July 20.	Isaiah 15–19
May 24.	Nehemiah 12–13	July 21.	Isaiah 20–24
May 25.	Esther 1–3	July 22.	Isaiah 25–28
May 26.	Esther 4–7	July 23.	Isaiah 29–31
May 27.	Esther 8–10	July 24.	Isaiah 32–34
May 28.	Job 1–4	July 25.	Isaiah 35–37
May 29.	Job 5–8	July 26.	Isaiah 38–40
May 30.	Job 9–12	July 27.	Isaiah 41–43
May 31.	Job 13–16	July 28.	Isaiah 44–46
June 1.	Job 17–20	July 29.	Isaiah 47–49

DATE	PASSAGE	DATE	PASSAGE
July 30............ Isaiah 50–52		September 26...... Zephaniah 1–3	
July 31............ Isaiah 53–56		September 27...... Haggai	
August 1........... Isaiah 57–59		September 28...... Zechariah 1–5	
August 2........... Isaiah 60–63		September 29...... Zechariah 6–10	
August 3........... Isaiah 64–66		September 30...... Zechariah 11–14	
August 4........... Jeremiah 1–3		October 1......... Malachi 1–4	
August 5........... Jeremiah 4–5		October 2......... Matthew 1–4	
August 6........... Jeremiah 6–8		October 3......... Matthew 5–6	
August 7........... Jeremiah 9–11		October 4......... Matthew 7–9	
August 8........... Jeremiah 12–14		October 5......... Matthew 10–11	
August 9........... Jeremiah 15–17		October 6......... Matthew 12–13	
August 10......... Jeremiah 18–21		October 7......... Matthew 14–17	
August 11......... Jeremiah 22–24		October 8......... Matthew 18–20	
August 12......... Jeremiah 25–27		October 9......... Matthew 21–22	
August 13......... Jeremiah 28–30		October 10........ Matthew 23–24	
August 14......... Jeremiah 31–32		October 11........ Matthew 25–26	
August 15......... Jeremiah 33–36		October 12........ Matthew 27–28	
August 16......... Jeremiah 37–39		October 13........ Mark 1–3	
August 17......... Jeremiah 40–43		October 14........ Mark 4–5	
August 18......... Jeremiah 44–46		October 15........ Mark 6–7	
August 19......... Jeremiah 47–48		October 16........ Mark 8–9	
August 20......... Jeremiah 49		October 17........ Mark 10–11	
August 21......... Jeremiah 50		October 18........ Mark 12–13	
August 22......... Jeremiah 51–52		October 19........ Mark 14	
August 23......... Lamentations 1–2		October 20........ Mark 15–16	
August 24......... Lamentations 3–5		October 21........ Luke 1–2	
August 25......... Ezekiel 1–4		October 22........ Luke 3–4	
August 26......... Ezekiel 5–8		October 23........ Luke 5–6	
August 27......... Ezekiel 9–12		October 24........ Luke 7–8	
August 28......... Ezekiel 13–15		October 25........ Luke 9–10	
August 29......... Ezekiel 16–17		October 26........ Luke 11–12	
August 30......... Ezekiel 18–20		October 27........ Luke 13–15	
August 31......... Ezekiel 21–22		October 28........ Luke 16–18	
September 1...... Ezekiel 23–24		October 29........ Luke 19–20	
September 2...... Ezekiel 25–27		October 30........ Luke 21–22	
September 3...... Ezekiel 28–30		October 31........ Luke 23–24	
September 4...... Ezekiel 31–32		November 1....... John 1–2	
September 5...... Ezekiel 33–35		November 2....... John 3–4	
September 6...... Ezekiel 36–38		November 3....... John 5–6	
September 7...... Ezekiel 39–40		November 4....... John 7–8	
September 8...... Ezekiel 41–43		November 5....... John 9–10	
September 9...... Ezekiel 44–46		November 6....... John 11–12	
September 10..... Ezekiel 47–48		November 7....... John 13–15	
September 11..... Daniel 1–3		November 8....... John 16–17	
September 12..... Daniel 4–5		November 9....... John 18–19	
September 13..... Daniel 6–8		November 10...... John 20–21	
September 14..... Daniel 9–12		November 11...... Acts 1–3	
September 15..... Hosea 1–4		November 12...... Acts 4–5	
September 16..... Hosea 5–9		November 13...... Acts 6–7	
September 17..... Hosea 10–14		November 14...... Acts 8–9	
September 18..... Joel 1–3		November 15...... Acts 10–11	
September 19..... Amos 1–4		November 16...... Acts 12–13	
September 20..... Amos 5–9		November 17...... Acts 14–15	
September 21..... Obadiah and Jonah		November 18...... Acts 16–17	
September 22..... Micah 1–4		November 19...... Acts 18–19	
September 23..... Micah 5–7		November 20...... Acts 20–21	
September 24..... Nahum 1–3		November 21...... Acts 22–23	
September 25..... Habakkuk 1–3		November 22...... Acts 24–26	

1442 READING PLAN

AUTHOR BIOGRAPHIES

Many gifted women contributed their insights to this Women's Devotional Bible. This index gives you information about each author and tells you where her contributions can be found.

Myrna Alexander is the author of several Women's Workshop Bible study books. She has traveled extensively in the Middle East with her husband Dr. Ralph Alexander, bringing first-hand knowledge to the Bible study groups she leads. *Devotions by this author can be found on pages 323, 329, 345.*

Ann Kiemel Anderson is the author of ten books, including *I'm Out to Change My World*, and *I Love the Word Impossible*. Formerly a school teacher, a youth director and a college dean of women, she now devotes her time primarily to being a wife and the mother of four young sons. *Devotions by this author can be found on pages 664, 1240.*

Gini Andrews has written several best-selling books that reflect in a personal way her walk with God. As a single Christian woman she wrote *Your Half of the Apple*. In *A Violent Grace* she shares her failures and heartache after marriage. She also wrote *Sons of Freedom* and *Esther*. *Devotions by this author can be found on pages 592, 737, 1109.*

June Masters Bacher taught elementary school and English until her retirement several years ago. She has written several books, including *Quiet Moments for Women* and a series of pioneer romance novels. June and her husband George live in California. *Devotions by this author can be found on pages 731, 1121, 1206, 1209, 1294.*

Carol L. Baldwin is a marriage, group and individual counselor and the author of the book *Friendship Counseling*. Much of the material in her devotional readings developed from the trauma of being widowed at age twenty-seven. She is now married again and lives with her husband and their four daughters. *Devotions by this author can be found on pages 638, 1063, 1171, 1228, 1325.*

Alma Barkman is the mother of four children, living in Manitoba. As a free-lance writer she is the author of numerous articles and several books. *Devotions by this author can be found on pages 415, 710, 1117, 1262.*

Patricia Beall has traveled and ministered with the Fisherfolk, an international music and recording group. She is the author of *The Folk Arts in God's Family* and *Growing into God*. Patricia and her husband Bart Gavigan live at the South Park Community Trust in Surrey, England. *A devotion by this author can be found on page 16.*

Mary Beckwith, an editor, enjoys traveling, teaching, organizing and correspondence. She has written and conducted a variety of workshops for women, young girls and writers. She lives in California with her husband Clint and their three children. *A devotion by this author can be found on page 1201.*

Debby Boone is a popular recording artist, performer, actress and author. Debby's recording of the song "You Light Up My Life" won her the Grammy Award for the best new artist in 1977. She has since recorded ten albums and has won two additional Grammy Awards. She is the author of *Debby Boone—So Far*, and two children's books. She and her husband Gabriel have four children. *Devotions by this author can be found on pages 615, 792, 813, 986, 1297.*

Jill Briscoe is the coordinator of women's ministries at Elmbrook Church in Waukesha, Wisconsin and the director of "Telling the Truth" media ministries. She is the author of numerous books, including *There's a Snake in My Garden*, *Prime Rib and Apple*, and *Thank You for Being a Friend*. She and her husband Stuart have three children. *Devotions by this author can be found on pages 1038, 1071, 1119, 1126, 1137, 1153.*

Barbara Bush, a pastor's wife and mother of four children, has written several books including *Ask Adam* and *I Can't Stand Cindy, Lord*. She enjoys her writing as well as sewing, stitchery, music and travel. *Devotions by this author can be found on pages 321, 440, 955, 1272, 1358.*

Amy Carmichael (1867–1951) worked for many years in South India, rescuing children who had been "married to the gods" in nearby temples. Her brilliant style has made the stories of these children and the ministry of Dohnavur Fellowship known around the world. *A devotion by this author can be found on page 632.*

Marie Chapian has written twenty-four books, including the *A Heart for God* devotional series, *Mothers and Daughters*, and *Am I the Only One Here With Faded Jeans?* for which she won a Campus Life Gold Medallion award in 1988. Marie studied at Moody Bible Institute, Metropolitan State University and the University of Minnesota (where she received her Ph.D.). She is the mother of two daughters. *Devotions by this author can be found on pages 838, 873, 1243, 1284, 1317.*

Mrs. Charles E. Cowman and her husband served as pioneer missionaries in Japan and China from 1901 to 1917. Mr. Cowman's poor health forced them to return to the U.S., and Mrs. Cowman nursed him until his death six years later. Mrs. Cowman's devotional books, *Streams in the Desert*, have been popular for more than sixty years. *A devotion by this author can be found on page 1082.*

Neva Coyle was educated in Minnesota and California, where she now lives with her husband and three children. As president and founder of Overeaters Victorious, she lectures and leads her "Free to Be Thin" seminars. *A devotion by this author can be found on page 1359.*

Fanny Crosby (1820–1915) was blinded in infancy supposedly by the ministrations of a "quack" physician called in to look at her eye infection. The hymns she wrote in her lifetime, over 9,000, have influenced thousands throughout the years. *A devotion by this author can be found on page 1330.*

Gladis and Gordon DePree are the authors of several books, including *A Blade of Grass* and *Faces of God*. Gladis also wrote *Festival*, a book about life on Hong Kong Island. The DePrees live and work in the Middle East. *Devotions by this author can be found on pages 828, 1366.*

Shirley Dobson is an author, homemaker, wife, and mother of a daughter and a son. She has served as a Bible Study Fellowship leader and as director for her church's ministry to women. She and her husband Dr. James Dobson often have appeared together on radio and television. *Devotions by this author can be found on pages 689, 765.*

Elisabeth Elliot was a young missionary wife and mother when her husband and four other men were killed while attempting to reach the Auca Indians. She is the author of many books, including *Through Gates of Splendor*, *Shadow of the Almighty* and *These Strange Ashes*. *Devotions by this author can be found on pages 771, 776, 1079, 1084.*

George Eliot is a pseudonym for Mary Ann Evans (1819–1880), an English novelist and poet. *A devotion by this author can be found on page 721.*

Colleen Townsend Evans lives with her husband in the Washington, D.C., area where he pastors the National Presbyterian Church. They have four children. She is a best-selling author of many books, including *A Deeper Joy* and *Make Me Like You, Lord*. *Devotions by this author can be found on pages 972, 1102.*

Gloria Gaither is a lyricist, teacher, speaker, wife and mother. With the Bill Gaither Trio, Gloria has recorded over forty albums and is the coauthor of close to five hundred songs. Her ten books include *We Have This Moment*, and *Hands Across the Seasons*. She has won many awards, including the 1986 Dove Award for songwriter of the year. She and her husband Bill have three children. *Devotions by this author can be found on pages 24, 567, 605, 1169, 1299.*

Ruth Bell Graham is the daughter of missionaries to China, the wife of evangelist Billy Graham, the mother of five, a grandmother to eighteen, and now a great-grandmother as well. She is the author of *Our Christmas Story*, *It's My Turn*, *Legacy of a Pack Rat*, and a collection of poems titled *Sitting by My Laughing Fire*. *Devotions by this author can be found on pages 7, 14, 256, 562, 581, 582, 1044, 1210, 1373.*

June Gunden graduated from Goshen College with a degree in English. She taught that subject for several years on the junior high level. She now works as a free-lance Bible editor and proofreader. She and her husband Doug have two sons, Troy and Benjamin. *Devotions by this author can be found on pages 247, 383, 403, 428, 1193.*

Doris Haase lives in California where she is part of a support group that reaches out to troubled people. She tries daily to put into practice one of her favorite Biblical principles found in Psalm 39:1–2: "I will . . . keep my tongue from sin." *Devotions by this author can be found on pages 1341, 1347.*

Annie Hawks (1835–1918) was a busy wife, mother of three children, and writer. She composed more than 400 poems, although the only one still in use is the familiar hymn "I Need Thee Every Hour." *A devotion by this author can be found on page 446.*

Diane Head is a homemaker, free-lance writer and illustrator. She has written two books, *Come to the Waters* and *A Precious Bit of Forever*. In 1980 she was selected as an "Outstanding Young Woman of America" in recognition of her personal and professional accomplishments. She and her husband have two daughters. *Devotions by this author can be found on pages 211, 842, 988, 1040, 1368.*

Marilyn Morgan Helleberg began a lifelong career in writing when her first-grade teacher set a poem to music and taught it to the class. She has filled thirty-five notebooks over the past fifteen years and looks at them as a chronicle of her life with God. *Devotions by this author can be found on page 1426.*

Alice Hill attended Asbury College, where her friendship with Kathy Narramore began, culminating in their book *Kindred Spirits*. Alice has also written *Help!* She enjoys running and classical music. Alice and her husband Dick have two children. *Devotions by this author can be found on pages 1172, 1292.*

Nicole Hill is a former college instructor who has won awards for her poetry. She enjoys Bible study, art, music and interior decorating. She and her husband Terry have two daughters. *A devotion by this author can be found on page 1011.*

Kathryn Hillen retired several years ago from her profession as an executive secretary to pursue a degree in Biblical literature. She and her husband have four grown children. Her book credits include *There Came Unto Him . . . Women* and *Memories*. *Devotions by this author can be found on pages 381, 470, 501, 1151, 1344, 1351, 1356.*

Phyllis Hobe, a full-time writer, now makes her home in the country, after living most of her life in the city. The dog and cat who live with her are finding the free and open country lifestyle as enjoyable as she does. *A devotion by this author can be found on page 1036.*

Marjorie Holmes first gained national attention as an author for her book of prayers, *I've Got to Talk to Somebody, God*. She has also written seven novels. Now living in Pennsylvania with her husband George, their four children and their families gather at her lakefront home in Virginia every Christmas. *Devotions by this author can be found on pages 499, 677, 779, 1408.*

Mab Graff Hoover has authored numerous books, including *God Loves My Kitchen*, *In My Upstairs Room* and *In Comes Love*. Her articles have appeared in many periodicals. She has worked as a church secretary and owned and operated a Christian bookstore. *A devotion by this author can be found on page 293.*

Gladys Hunt is the author of fifteen books, including *Honey for a Child's Heart*, and *We Need Each Other: The Miracle of Relationships*. Because inductive Bible study is one of her principle interests, she is active in small group Bible studies and is the author of eight Fisherman Bible Study guides. She is an enthusiastic wife, mother and grandmother. *Devotions by this author can be found on pages 5, 20, 277, 1231, 1233.*

June Hunt is a speaker, singer, author and the host of the award-winning national radio program "Hope for the Heart." Through three music albums and her devotional book *Seeing Yourself Through God's Eyes*, she is committed to unraveling the difficult "heart" issues of life with practical help and Biblical hope. *Devotions by this author can be found on pages 913, 1253, 1260, 1289, 1383.*

Rosemary Jensen is the executive director of Bible Study Fellowship, with headquarters in San Antonio, Texas. Prior to taking the post in 1980 she served as a high school teacher, medical specialist, business woman and Bible teacher. Together with her husband, Dr. Robert T. Jensen, she served as a missionary to Tanzania, Africa, for nine years. Rosemary and her husband have three daughters and six grandchildren. *Devotions by this author can be found on pages 1105, 1148, 1394.*

Janet C. Jones was born into a Christian family and graduated from Nyack College in 1953. That same year she married Rev. George Jones. They raised three children, have cared for five foster children, and now minister to and nurture other people's children. *A devotion by this author can be found on page 1353.*

Wanda K. Jones is a popular teacher and seminar speaker and the coordinator of Christian Family Outreach, Inc. She and her husband Howard, the first black evangelist on the Billy Graham Crusade staff, have been married over forty-five years. They enjoy five children and six grandchildren. While serving as missionaries in Africa they preached, taught and became well-known personalities on radio station ELWA. *Devotions by this author can be found on pages 578, 729, 1076, 1281, 1415.*

Gien Karssen served on the Navigator's staff at The Hague in the Netherlands. She started the work of the Navigators in the Netherlands as well as Europe. Gien pursues a writing ministry and is the author of eight books. *Devotions by this author can be found on pages 11, 304, 504, 1329, 1420.*

Janice Kempe is a writer and homemaker. She and her husband are parents of two sons and one daughter. Janice has taught elementary school and has written two books, *Listening to God* and *Growing Up Together*. *Devotions by this author can be found on pages 627, 648, 1067.*

Sue Monk Kidd has written many articles for *Guideposts* magazine as well as one book *God's Joyful Surprise*. She and her husband Sandy have two teenagers, Bob and Ann. *Devotions by this author can be found on pages 79, 937, 1217.*

Alice Macdonald Kipling, who died in 1910, was the mother of famed poet Rudyard Kipling. *A devotion by this author can be found on page 1391.*

Carol Kuykendall and her husband and three children spend time as a family hiking in the nearby Rocky Mountains. Carol speaks and writes on the subject of, as parents, letting children go. *A devotion by this author can be found on page 348.*

Beverly LaHaye is the founder and president of Concerned Women for America and is an advocate, author and spokesperson on women's and family issues. She has written the books *The Restless Woman* and *Who But a Woman*, and she is the coauthor of *The Act of Marriage*. She and her husband have four children and eight grandchildren. *Devotions by this author can be found on pages 187, 767, 1304, 1340, 1385.*

Elizabeth Larsen has written one novel and enjoys reading, needlepoint, cooking and writing. She and her husband Jerry have one son. *A devotion by this author can be found on page 1212.*

Judith Lechman is a workshop leader and speaker. She has published over one hundred short stories as well as two books, *The World of Emily Howland* and *Yielding to Courage*. *Devotions by this author can be found on pages 1247, 1290.*

JoAnn Lemon and her husband Stan served as missionaries to Viet Nam from 1958–1972. In 1980 they returned overseas to serve in a church in Kowloon, Hong Kong for eight years. During these various ministries JoAnn was actively involved in women's ministries as well as music ministries. JoAnn and her husband have three children and four grandchildren. *A devotion by this author can be found on page 1389.*

Madeleine L'Engle is a graduate of Smith College and Columbia University. She has been active in theater, as a teacher, lecturer and writer. Her books for children (and those who are children at heart) have won many awards. Probably the best known is *A Wrinkle in Time*. *Devotions by this author can be found on pages 595, 993, 1264.*

Susan L. Lenzkes lives and writes in California with her three children and her husband Herb. She is the author of *A Silver Pen for Cloudy Days* and *When the Writing on the Wall Is in Brown Crayon*. Susan enjoys singing in choirs and trios and ensembles, teaching Bible studies, and arranging flowers. *Devotions by this author can be found on pages 192, 569, 675, 681, 822, 880, 1256, 1402, 1405.*

Florence Littauer graduated with honors from the University of Massachusetts and is the founder of C.L.A.S.S. (Christian Leaders and Speakers Seminars). She has authored many books, including *Hope for Hurting People* and *After Every Wedding Comes a Marriage*. She makes frequent guest appearances on radio and television and has spoken to groups all over the world. *Devotions by this author can be found on pages 250, 1335.*

Jeanette Lockerbie and her husband have retired in Florida. Before retiring she worked as an editor for *Psychology for Living*. As a free-lance writer she has published many books, including *Salt in My Kitchen* and *Time Out for Coffee*. *Devotions by this author can be found on pages 63, 152, 379, 524, 1236.*

Hope MacDonald has written articles for *Partnership*, *Today's Christian Woman* and *Faith at Work*, and is the author of *Discovering How to Pray*, *Discovering the Joy of Obedience* and *When Angels Appear*. Hope and her husband have been married forty-one years and have three children and six grandchildren. *Devotions by this author can be found on pages 621, 652, 1059, 1090, 1311.*

Karen Burton Mains lives and ministers in the Chicago area, with her husband David co-hosting and speaking on The Chapel of the Air radio program. Karen wrote the best-selling book, *Open Heart, Open Home*. Her other book credits include *Karen, Karen, Making Sunday Special* and *The Fragile Curtain*. *Devotions by this author can be found on pages 749, 1141, 1276, 1377.*

Samantha McGarrity writes and travels for *Guideposts* magazine. She enjoys having friends over and cooking for them. Other interests include gardening and fishing. *A devotion by this author can be found on page 358.*

Martha Manikas-Foster is a book editor and free-lance writer who studied at Houghton College and the University of Iowa. She worked as a newspaper reporter before entering book publishing in 1983. She has written articles for *Bookstore Journal* and *Paraplegia News*. She and her husband David have one daughter. *Devotions by this author can be found on pages 998, 1019, 1319, 1323, 1337.*

Catherine Marshall wrote many books before her death in 1983. They include: *A Man Called Peter*, *To Live Again*, and *Meeting God at Every Turn*. *Devotions by this author can be found on pages 1048, 1412.*

Helen Lowrie Marshall's (1904–1975) first book of poetry was printed and bound by hand in the home of her brother. She wrote many poems for use in Hallmark cards. A wife and mother of two sons, she was active in church and civic groups, and was in demand as a lecturer. *Devotions by this author can be found on pages 215, 657.*

Joan Rae Mills, married and the mother of two young children, is a free-lance writer and former English teacher. She enjoys restoring antiques, reading, writing and decorating. *Devotions by this author can be found on pages 59, 1139.*

Kathy Mills, an award-winning writer, is listed in *Who's Who of Writers and Authors*. She and her husband Larry are the parents of three sons. *A devotion by this author can be found on page 898.*

Kathy Narramore, a teacher and speaker, was born in Peking and lived her childhood years in several Chinese cities and the island of Taiwan. She graduated from Asbury College. Kathy and her husband Bruce live in California and are the parents of two children. *Devotions by this author can be found on pages 1172, 1292.*

Marlene Obie spends her time as a homemaker, free-lance writer, secretary, wife, and mother of three. She is the author of *What's a Mother to Do?* and *What Color Is My Collar?* Her articles have appeared in many Christian periodicals. *Devotions by this author can be found on pages 318, 684, 701.*

Anne Ortlund is an award-winning musician and the author of seven books including *Building a Great Marriage*, and *Children Are Wet Cement*, which won the Christy Award as the best marriage-family book of 1982. She and her husband Ray are the coauthors of four additional books. Anne and Ray minister together through Renewal Ministries. They have four children. *Devotions by this author can be found on pages 65, 97, 1096, 1100, 1177, 1309.*

Luis Palau's story about Clara Barton, founder of the Red Cross, appears in his book *Experiencing God's Forgiveness*. He has written several other books on the Christian walk. *A devotion by this author can be found on page 1065.*

Dorothy Patterson is a homemaker, author, conference speaker and adjunct professor of Christian Marriage and Family at the Criswell College in Dallas, Texas. She holds several degrees and is a member of the Council for Biblical Manhood and Womanhood, the Advisory Board of Concerned Women for America, and the Board of Directors for the Religious Roundtable Issue and Answers. She and her husband Dr. Paige Patterson have two children. *Devotions by this author can be found on pages 272, 514, 697, 716, 889.*

Rebecca Manley Pippert, has spoken on four continents and written several books. They include *Out of the Saltshaker*, which has been translated into more than ten languages, *Hope Has Its Reasons* and *Pizza Parlor Evangelism*. She and her husband Wesley have two children. *Devotions by this author can be found on pages 1185, 1255, 1287.*

Elizabeth Prentiss (1818–1878) early in life showed an ability for writing both prose and poetry. She taught school in Massachusetts and Virginia before marrying a minister in 1845. She wrote *Stepping Heavenward*, a popular book in her time. *A devotion by this author can be found on page 1315.*

Eugenia Price is the author of twenty-two books, which have been translated into eleven languages. She holds the Georgia Distinguished Service Award and numerous fiction awards from the Dixie Council of Authors and the Georgia Writer's Association. Her manuscripts and letters make up a special collection at Boston University's Mugar Library. *Devotions by this author can be found on pages 546, 754, 1143.*

Maureen Rank and her husband live with their children in Iowa. Maureen writes and leads seminars on various subjects. Extensive research and personal experience went into the writing of her book *Free to Grieve*. Maureen holds a degree in home economics and family relations from Iowa State University. *A devotion by this author can be found on page 857.*

Pamela Reeve graduated from New York University with a degree in architecture. After several year's work in that field, she felt God's call to build people rather than things. That change, and further education, finally led her to a position as Dean of Women for Multnomah School of the Bible. She has now retired but continues to advise, teach part-time and speak at conferences and retreats. *A devotion by this author can be found on page 673.*

Sue Richards has lived in seven states as well as West Germany. She and her two children and husband Larry now live in Florida. Sue teaches eleventh-grade English and enjoys tennis and fishing. She has written one book, *Ministry to the Divorced*. *Devotions by this author can be found on pages 835, 1061, 1175, 1238, 1370.*

Doris Rikkers has been happily married to her husband Bill for eighteen years. They have two active sons. Doris is the Director of Publications at Zondervan Bible Publishers. When not busy with work and family she enjoys reading, baking, gardening and tennis. *Devotions by this author can be found on pages 482, 929, 975, 979, 1006.*

Rosalind Rinker served for fourteen years as a missionary in China and then worked for twelve years with college students as a staff counselor with InterVarsity Christian Fellowship. She is active in a Mandarin-speaking Chinese church and teaches among Chinese churches in the Los Angeles area. For the past thirty years she has been a free-lance writer and speaker. Her fifteen books include *Prayer: Conversing With God. Devotions by this author can be found on pages 599, 1050, 1086, 1130, 1159.*

Dale Evans Rogers has traveled nationwide, appearing on radio and television as an actress, singer and speaker. She has written over a dozen books, including *Angel Unaware* and *Dearest Debbie*. She and her husband, Roy Rogers, live in California. *Devotions by this author can be found on pages 1021, 1235.*

Rita Schweitz lives with her husband and four children on a farm in rural Nebraska. A graduate of the University of Nebraska, she is a writer and has also been a teacher and coach of junior high students. *Devotions by this author can be found on pages 473, 957.*

Ruth Senter is a pastor's daughter and a pastor's wife, and therefore is uniquely capable of writing a book called *So You're the Pastor's Wife*. She has been involved in many aspects of book, periodical and curriculum publishing. She and her husband Mark have two children. *Devotions by this author can be found on pages 1124, 1404.*

Beth Donigan Seversen earned her master of divinity degree from Trinity Evangelical Divinity School and serves as the Associate pastor of Women's Ministries at Elmbrook Church, Waukesha, Wisconsin. She is also Jill Briscoe's writing assistant and in this capacity has written four inductive Bible studies. She and her husband have one daughter. *Devotions by this author can be found on pages 57, 521, 1032, 1274, 1386.*

Jean Shaw taught home economics for many years before returning to school and graduating from Covenant Theological Seminary. She has written numerous articles and books including, *Second Cup of Coffee* and *The Better Half of Life. Devotions by this author can be found on pages 706, 712.*

Linda Ching Sledge teaches at Westchester, New York, Community College. She lives there with her husband Gary and two sons. All the family enjoy trips to New York's Museum of Natural History to see the dinosaur exhibit. One of her hobbies is reading detective novels. *Devotions by this author can be found on pages 1189, 1282.*

Debbie Smith has written over one hundred songs with her husband, musician and recording artist Michael W. Smith. During her college years at Wheaton she spent six months in Haiti, where she helped establish a nutrition clinic. She now devotes most of her energies to her three children. *Devotions by this author can be found on pages 559, 655, 659, 1314, 1348.*

Hannah Whithall Smith (1832–1911) and her husband, Robert Pearsall Smith, were popular Bible conference leaders for many years. Personal tragedy led Mrs. Smith to write several books on suffering and obedience to the will of God, including *The Christian's Secret of a Happy Life* and *The God of All Comfort. Devotions by this author can be found on pages 237, 451, 538, 588, 948, 1362.*

Millie Stamm has worked for many years directing Meditation Moments, a prayer ministry to Christian women. Her concern for Christian women in all walks of life has shown itself in her writing and speaking ministry. She has published two popular devotional books, *Meditation Moments* and *Be Still and Know. Devotions by this author can be found on pages 9, 46, 147, 161, 189, 283, 1156.*

Louisa Stead (1850–1917) heard the call of God to missionary service while still a child. After the death of her first husband, Mrs. Stead and her daughter served as missionaries in South Africa. While there Mrs. Stead married a South African native and worked on the mission field there until her death. *A devotion by this author can be found on page 576.*

Charlotte Stemple and her husband spent ten years as missionaries in Viet Nam in church planting and nursing ministries. The Stemples now live in the U.S. where Charlotte is involved in women's ministries. They have two sons. *A devotion by this author can be found on page 1029.*

Luci Swindoll chose to retire early from her thirty-year career with the Mobil Oil Corporation to join Insight for Living, an international radio ministry where she is the vice president of public relations. Luci is a nationwide speaker and the author of seven books. *Devotions by this author can be found on pages 704, 1300, 1364, 1375, 1397.*

Jean E. Syswerda, an editor with Zondervan Bible Publishers, keeps busy with her work, her family, with her church's ministry to teens, and with reading, gardening and decorating with antiques. She and her husband and three children enjoy country life in West Michigan. *Devotions by this author can be found on pages 241, 260, 369, 967, 1198.*

Joni Eareckson Tada is an internationally known mouth artist and author who developed her artistic talents after a diving accident in 1967 left her paralyzed below her shoulders. Her eleven books include her autobiography *Joni* and *Choices . . . Changes*. She works for the disabled as the founder and president of Joni and Friends. She also serves on the National Council for Disability, to which she was appointed by President Reagan in 1987. *Devotions by this author can be found on pages 67, 77, 123, 127, 1128.*

Delores Taylor, a singer and songwriter, has over fifty gospel songs to her credit. She graduated from Nyack College in Nyack, New York, and spent the next fifteen years touring and singing with the Alliance Trio. Delores and her husband Roy live in Virginia, where she now operates a dress shop and is president of her church's Women's Missionary Prayer Fellowship. *A devotion by this author can be found on page 1267.*

Gigi Graham Tchividjian, daughter of Dr. Billy Graham, is first of all a wife and mother. She and her husband are the parents of seven children whose ages span twenty years. She is the author of *A Woman's Quest for Serenity* and *Sincerely, Gigi. Devotions by this author can be found on pages 809, 991, 1245, 1307.*

Rebecca Tempest works at present in a research laboratory at the University of Michigan in Ann Arbor, Michigan. She is a writer, mainly of poetry, and has had several of her poems published. *A devotion by this author can be found on page 1173.*

Betsie ten Boom, the sister of writer and speaker Corrie ten Boom, died during World War II in a Nazi concentration camp. She and her sister ministered to many during the Nazi occupation of the Netherlands, hiding Jews in their home and providing encouragement to fellow prisoners in the camps. *A devotion by this author can be found on page 1278.*

Corrie ten Boom, as a single Dutch woman, courageously hid Jews in her home during the Nazi occupation of World War II. She related her experiences in her most famous book *The Hiding Place*. After the war until her death she traveled and spoke, making people aware of the strength and contentment available in a close walk with God. *Devotions by this author can be found on pages 680, 962, 1134, 1302, 1334.*

Mother Teresa was born and raised in Albania. Her early religious training as a Sister of Loreto and her years of teaching in India were followed by the founding of her own order, the Sisters of Charity, to work with the poorest of the poor. Her work with the poor in India won her the Nobel Peace Prize. *Devotions by this author can be found on pages 1191, 1355, 1427.*

Ingrid Trobisch speaks four languages and has degrees from Augusta College and Sorbonne in Paris. She is the mother of five children. She has written several books on her own, including *The Joy of Being a Woman*, as well as numerous books with her late husband Walter Trobisch, including *I Loved a Girl*. *Devotions by this author can be found on pages 702, 1003.*

Ruth A. Tucker earned her doctorate in history from Northern Illinois University and is a visiting professor at Trinity Evangelical Divinity School and a teacher at Moffat College of Bible in Kenya. She is the author of eight books and has won Gold Medallion Awards for *First Ladies of the Parish* (1989) and *From Jerusalem to Irian Jaya* (1984). She has one son. *Devotions by this author can be found on pages 3, 646, 1088, 1181, 1400.*

Shirley Pope Waite's writing career began back in high school when a teacher encouraged her to use those abilities. She has been a free-lance writer for many years and teaches courses on writing at a nearby college. She and husband Kyle raised six children. *A devotion by this author can be found on page 1266.*

Anna L. Waring (1820–1910) was a Welsh poet. Several of her poems were set to music and became familiar and popular hymns. *A devotion by this author can be found on page 1378.*

Ann Weems has led workshop and creative worship experiences at the local as well as national church levels. She is a free-lance writer, author of *Reaching for Rainbows*. *A devotion by this author can be found on page 787.*

Clara Williams (1858–1937), a nineteenth-century hymnwriter, wrote the words to "Satisfied" in 1875 while helping with evangelistic meetings in Troy, Ohio. *A devotion by this author can be found on page 300.*

Mary Jane Worden and her husband Jim worked as staff members of Inter-Varsity Christian Fellowship until his death in a car accident in 1983. Out of those experiences came her book *Early Widow*. With her three children, Jane now lives and works in Nairobi, Kenya. *Devotions by this author can be found on pages 218, 574, 794, 1381.*

SUBJECT INDEX

The subjects covered in the devotions are many and varied. This subject index will help you locate material on just about any topic or issue of interest, or about any problem confronting you.